TOP COUNTRY SINGLES

Billboard

Chart Data Compiled From *Billboard's* Country Singles Charts, 1944-2001.

Copyright © 2002 by Joel Whitburn

Cover design by Dean Eggert Design

Portions of the *Billboard* chart material in this work were constructed by *Billboard* magazine from information provided by Broadcast Data Systems (BDS), which electronically monitors actual radio airplay, and SoundScan, Inc., which electronically collects Point of Sale information from music retail outlets.

The *Billboard* chart data used in this work is copyright © 1944-2001 by BPI Communications, Broadcast Data Systems, and SoundScan, Inc.

All Rights Reserved.

WARNING

No part of this publication may be reproduced, stored in a retrieval system, or transmitted in any form by any means, electronic, mechanical, photocopying, recording or otherwise, without the prior written permission of the author.

ISBN 0-89820-151-9

Record Research Inc.
P.O. Box 200
Menomonee Falls, Wisconsin 53052-0200   U.S.A.

Phone: (262) 251-5408
Fax: (262) 251-9452
E-Mail: books@recordresearch.com
Web site: www.recordresearch.com

CONTENTS

Dedication iv
Author's Note v
About The Author vi
Synopsis Of *Billboard's* Country Singles Charts 1944-2001 vii
Researching *Billboard's* Country Singles Charts ix
User's Guide xi
What's New With This Edition xiv

ARTIST SECTION 1
Key To Symbols 2

An alphabetical listing, by artist, of every record to chart on *Billboard's*
Country singles charts from 1944 through 2001.

SONG TITLE SECTION 411

An alphabetical listing, by song title, of every record to chart on *Billboard's*
Country singles charts from 1944 through 2001.

TOP ARTISTS
Kings & Queens Of Country (The Top 400 Artists) 544
Top 20 Artists: 1944-49 / 1950s / 1960s / 1970s / 1980s / 1990s / 2000-2001 550
Top 400 Artist Debuts 552
Top Artist Achievements: 555

Most Chart Hits	Most Consecutive #1 Hits
Most Top 40 Hits	Most Consecutive Top 10 Hits
Most Top 10 Hits	Artists With Longest Chart Careers
Most #1 Hits	Artists With Longest Span Between Chart Hits
Most Weeks At The #1 Position	Top Artists Who Never Hit #1
Most Crossover Hits	Artist's First Hit Is Their Biggest Hit
	One-Hit Wonders

CHART FACTS & FEATS
Top #1 Hits: All-Time / 1944-49 / 1950s / 1960s / 1970s / 1980s / 1990-2001 558
Singles Of Longevity: 1944-49 / 1950s / 1960s / 1970s / 1980s / 1990-2001 563
MVPs 564
Songs With Longest Titles 565
Songs With Most Charted Versions 565
Top Country Labels 565
Country Music Association Awards: 566
    Single of the Year
    Song of the Year
Country Music Hall Of Fame 567
Christmas Singles 1944-2001 568
Label Abbreviations 570

#1 HITS 571

A chronological listing, by peak date, of every title to top
Billboard's Country singles charts.

Joel dedicates Top Country Singles to...

...**Timothy White** (1952-2002), editor in chief of *Billboard* (1991-2002). I will greatly miss the inimitable wisdom and wit that flowed from his pen and the genuine warmth he extended as a treasured colleague. Timothy was a bold beacon of honesty and integrity in an industry where such can be rare. I appreciated his unabashed expression of his love of music.

The author wishes to extend a special note of thanks to:

The staff of Record Research....

Top: Joel Whitburn, Bill Hathaway, Jeanne Olynick, Kay Wagner; Middle: Frances Whitburn, Sue Hustad, Kim Bloxdorf, Paul Haney; Bottom: Brent Olynick, Nestor Vidotto

AUTHOR'S NOTE

"Ladies and Gentlemen...Please welcome The Singing Ranger and His Rainbow Ranch Boys." On my final look through this book before it hit the printing press, I was struck by the many colorful nicknames of the artists of Country music's past. Wherever these monikers came from — managers, fans, record labels, friends or family — they offered a personal connection to the artists. Prolific nicknaming to this extent is unmatched in any other music genre. This trend has nearly passed from Country music as has the naming of backing bands. Your perusal through these pages will reap other intriguing and equally fun discoveries about Country music.

In case you didn't know, the Singing Ranger and His Rainbow Ranch Boys are Hank Snow and his backing band. Test your Country trivia mettle with the match game below.

JOEL WHITBURN

Match the artist with their:

Nickname:

1. Bocephus bb
2. Cajun Valentino v
3. Cherokee Cowboy r
4. Country Caruso d
5. Gentleman Jim s
6. 'Lasses Sopper n
7. Luke The Drifter
8. Mr. Country Rock
9. Possum
10. Round Mound of Sound
11. Silver Fox
12. Smilin' Star Duster
13. Tall Texan
14. 'Tater
15. Tennessee Plowboy
16. Texas Troubadour
17. Whispering Bill
18. Young Sheriff

Royalty:

19. Father of Bluegrass
20. Father of Country Music
21. First Family of Country Music
22. First Lady of Country Music ee
23. King of Country Music a
24. King of Western Swing dd
25. Queen of Country Music z

Backing Band:

26. Buckaroos
27. Cumberland Valley Boys
28. Foggy Mountain Boys
29. Southern Gentlemen
30. Statesiders w
31. Strangers
32. Tennessee Two

Artist:

a. Roy Acuff
b. Bill Anderson
c. Eddy Arnold
d. Johnny Bush
e. The Carter Family
f. Johnny Cash
g. Billy "Crash" Craddock
h. Flatt & Scruggs
i. Red Foley
j. Merle Haggard
k. Sonny James
l. George Jones
m. Bill Monroe
n. Jim Nesbitt
o. Buck Owens
p. Bill Phillips
q. Kenny Price
r. Ray Price
s. Jim Reeves
t. Charlie Rich
u. Jimmie Rodgers
v. Jo-el Sonnier
w. Mel Tillis 30
x. Ernest Tubb
y. Billy Walker
z. Kitty Wells
aa. Slim Whitman
bb. Hank Williams, Jr.
cc. Hank Williams, Sr.
dd. Bob Wills
ee. Tammy Wynette
ff. Faron Young

For answers see bottom of page vi.

v

ABOUT THE AUTHOR

From pastime to passion to profitable enterprise, the growth of Record Research has been the outgrowth of Joel Whitburn's hobby. Joel began collecting records as a teenager in the 1950s. As his collection grew, he began to sort, categorize and file each record according to the highest position it reached on *Billboard's* Hot 100 charts. He went on to publish this information in 1970 and a business was born.

Today, Joel leads a team of researchers who delve into all of *Billboard's* music charts to an unmatched degree of depth and detail. Joel is widely recognized as the most authoritative historian on charted music. Joel's own record collection remains unrivaled the world over and includes every charted Hot 100 and pop single (back to 1920), every charted pop album (back to 1945), collections of nearly every charted Country, R&B, Bubbling Under The Hot 100 and Adult Contemporary records. Ever the consummate collector, Joel also owns one of the world's largest picture sleeve collections.

In person, this walking music encyclopedia stands 6'6" — a definite advantage when he played high school, college and semi-pro basketball. An avid sports fan, Joel actively engages in a wide variety of water, winter and motor sports. A native of Wisconsin, Joel has been married for 38 years to Fran, a native of Honduras; their daughter, Kim Bloxdorf, is part of the Record Research team, as are two of Joel's friends and key employees of 30 years, Bill Hathaway and Brent Olynick. Joel's lifelong passion for music, old and new, and his penchant for accurate detail continues into the 21st century.

Answers: 1-bb, 2-v, 3-r, 4-d, 5-s, 6-n, 7-cc, 8-g, 9-l, 10-q, 11-t, 12-aa, 13-y, 14-p, 15-c, 16-x, 17-b, 18-ff, 19-m, 20-u, 21-e, 22-ee, 23-a, 24-dd, 25-z, 26-o, 27-i, 28-h, 29-k, 30-w, 31-j, 32-f

SYNOPSIS OF BILLBOARD'S COUNTRY SINGLES CHARTS 1944-2001

JUKE BOX

Date	Positions	Chart Title
1/8/44	2-8	Most Played Juke Box Folk Records
		(9/6/47-11/1/47 shown as Most-Played Juke Box Hillbilly Records)
1/31/48	9-15	Most Played Juke Box Folk Records
6/25/49	7-15	Most Played Juke Box (Country & Western) Records
11/4/50	6-10	Most Played Juke Box Folk (Country & Western) Records
11/15/52	8-10	Most Played in Juke Boxes
6/30/56	9-10	Most Played C&W in Juke Boxes
6/17/57		final chart

BEST SELLERS

5/15/48	10-15	Best Selling Retail Folk Records
6/25/49	5-15	Best Selling Retail Folk (Country & Western) Records
11/15/52	8-10	National Best Sellers
2/20/54	9-15	Best Sellers in Stores
6/30/56	13-20	C&W Best Sellers in Stores
10/13/58		final chart

JOCKEYS

12/10/49	8-10	Country & Western Records Most Played By Folk Disk Jockeys
11/15/52	9-15	Most Played by Jockeys
6/30/56	12-15	Most Played C&W by Jockeys
10/13/58		final chart

HOT COUNTRY SINGLES

10/20/58	30	Hot C&W Sides
11/3/62	30	Hot Country Singles
1/11/64	50	Hot Country Singles
10/15/66	75	Hot Country Singles
7/14/73	100	Hot Country Singles
1/20/90*	75	Hot Country Singles
2/17/90	75	Hot Country Singles & Tracks
1/6/01	60	Hot Country Singles & Tracks

Billboard began compiling chart with information provided by Broadcast Data Systems (BDS), which electronically monitors actual radio airplay. Songs were ranked by their gross impressions, which multiplied each play by the Arbitron-estimated audience for the station at the time of the play. On December 5, 1992, *Billboard* eliminated the gross impressions method and began compiling the chart strictly on the number of detections or plays registered by each song according to BDS.

HOT COUNTRY SINGLES SALES

10/20/84	30	Hot Country Singles Sales
5/31/86	40	Hot Country Singles Sales
8/2/86	30	Hot Country Singles Sales
1/21/89–6/24/95		No chart published
7/1/95*	25	Top Country Singles Sales

*Billboard began compiling chart from a national sample of retail store and rack sales reports collected, compiled, and provided by SoundScan; this data is not a factor in the airplay only Hot Country Singles & Tracks chart.

HOT COUNTRY SINGLES AIRPLAY

10/20/84	30	Hot Country Singles Airplay
5/31/86	40	Hot Country Singles Airplay
8/2/86	30	Hot Country Singles Airplay
5/16/87		final chart

Sample of an early Country chart:

RESEARCHING BILLBOARD'S COUNTRY CHARTS

This book covers the entire history of *Billboard* magazine's Country singles charts from 1944 through 2001. Over 17,800 charted hits and over 2,200 artists are listed in all.

MULTIPLE COUNTRY SINGLES CHARTS, 1948-1958

Billboard published its first Country singles chart, *Juke Box Folk Records*, on January 8, 1944. All chart data from 1944 through May 8, 1948, refers to the Juke Box chart. On May 15, 1948, *Billboard* introduced another Country singles chart, *Best Selling Retail Folk Records*. A third Country singles chart, *Most Played by Folk Disk Jockeys,* made its debut on December 10, 1949. All of these charts were published on a weekly basis and each focused on specific areas of the music trade. The *Juke Box* chart was discontinued on June 17, 1957. On October 20, 1958, the *Best Seller* and *Disk Jockey* charts were replaced by one all-encompassing Top 30 Country singles chart titled *Hot C&W Sides*. This chart has changed in name and size over time and is known, today, as *Hot Country Singles & Tracks*. For a more detailed history of all of *Billboard's* Country singles charts, see the "Synopsis of *Billboard's* Country Singles Charts" on the previous page.

During the years of multiple charts, 1948-1958, many singles hit more than one chart. In our research, the single's debut date is taken from the chart on which it first appeared. The single's peak position is taken from the chart on which it achieved its highest ranking. Listed to the right of the title (before the listing of the B-side) is an indication of the chart(s) and peak position on which it hit. (See "Peak Position Attained On Various Country Charts" in the USER'S GUIDE for a further explanation.) The single's weeks charted and weeks at positions #1 or #2 are taken from the chart on which it achieved its highest total.

CHART METHODOLOGIES

For decades, *Billboard's* Country singles charts were compiled from playlists reported by radio stations and sales reports reported by stores. These airplay and sales reports established the weekly rankings on *Billboard's* airplay charts (*Jockeys, Hot Country Singles Airplay*) and sales charts (*Best Sellers, Hot Country Singles Sales*), and were combined for the compilation of the *Hot Country Singles* charts. On January 20, 1990, *Billboard* began basing their chart entirely on airplay with information gathered by Broadcast Data Systems (BDS). BDS is a subsidiary of *Billboard* that electronically monitors actual radio airplay. They have installed monitors throughout the country that track the airplay of songs 24 hours a day, seven days a week. These monitors can identify each song played by an encoded audio "fingerprint." *Billboard* determined weekly rankings according to gross impressions, which multiplied each play by the Arbitron-estimated audience for the station at the time of the play.

Since not all songs played on Country radio are available as singles, *Billboard* began including album tracks on the revised chart, renaming it *Hot Country Singles & Tracks* to reflect this change. In this book, all charted album tracks are identified by the words "album cut" in the "Label & Number" column; the album that the track is from is noted below the song title.

On December 5, 1992, *Billboard* began compiling the Country singles chart strictly on the number of detections or plays registered by each song according to BDS.

COUNTRY SINGLES SALES AND AIRPLAY CHARTS

Billboard began publication of the *Hot Country Singles Sales and Airplay* charts on October 20, 1984. These charts were the two ingredients that made up the *Hot Country Singles* chart. The airplay chart was discontinued in 1987; the *Hot Country Singles* chart essentially became the airplay chart after *Billboard* began compiling that chart with BDS data. The sales chart experienced a six-year hiatus beginning in 1989; however, when it returned in July of 1995, it was not figured into the compilation of the *Hot Country Singles* chart.

ISSUE DATE vs. COLLECTION DATE

All dates within *Top Country Singles* refer to the issue dates of *Billboard* magazine and not the "week ending" dates as shown on the various charts when they were originally published. The issue and week ending dates were different until January 13, 1962, when *Billboard* began using one date system for both the issue and the charts inside. *Billboard's* issue dates were all Saturdays, except from April 29, 1957 to December 25, 1961, when they changed to a Monday issue date. On January 6, 1962, *Billboard* reverted to a permanent Saturday issue date.

The *Hot Country Singles & Tracks* reports on singles activity from the seven-day period ending 12 days prior. For example, *Billboard* compiled the *Hot Country Singles & Tracks* chart dated October 27, 2001 (Saturday) on October 15 (Monday). The radio airplay reports for this chart covered a seven-day period beginning at 12:01 a.m. on October 8 (Monday) and ending at midnight on October 14 (Sunday). Delivery of the October 27 issue began on October 19 (Friday). *Billboard's* timing has changed slightly over the years.

Sample of Multiple Country Singles Charts

FEBRUARY 20, 1954 — THE BILLBOARD — MUSIC 39

The Billboard Music Popularity Charts — COUNTRY & WESTERN RECORDS

• Best Sellers in Stores
For survey week ending February 13

RECORDS are ranked in order of their current national selling importance at the retail level. Results are based on The Billboard's weekly survey among dealers throughout the country with a high volume of sales in country and western records. The reverse side of each record is also listed.

	This Week	Last Week	Weeks on Chart
1. SLOWLY—W. Pierce / You Just Can't Be True—Dec 28991—BMI		5	3
2. THERE STANDS THE GLASS—W. Pierce / I'm Walking the Dog—Dec 28834—BMI		1	18
3. BIMBO—J. Reeves / Gypsy Heart—Abbott 148—BMI		4	10
4. I REALLY DON'T WANT TO KNOW—E. Arnold / I'll Never Get Over You—Cap 20-5525—BMI		2	7
5. SECRET LOVE—S. Whitman / Why?—Imperial 8220—ASCAP		7	4
6. LET ME BE THE ONE—H. Locklin / I'm Tired of Bumming Around—Four Star 1641—BMI		5	22
7. WAKE UP, IRENE—H. Thompson / Go Cry Your Heart Out—Cap 2646—BMI		3	11
8. YOU ALL COME—A. Duff / Poor Ole Teacher—Starday 104—BMI		9	9
9. RELEASE ME—J. Heap / Just to Be With You—Cap 2518—BMI		—	5
10. DOG GONE IT, BABY, I'M IN LOVE—C. Smith / What Am I Going to Do With You?—Col 21197—BMI		8	2

• Most Played in Juke Boxes
For survey week ending February 13

RECORDS are ranked in order of the greatest number of plays in juke boxes thruout the country. Results are based on The Billboard's weekly survey among operators thruout the country using a high proportion of country and western records.

	This Week	Last Week	Weeks on Chart
1. WAKE UP, IRENE—H. Thompson / Cap 2646—BMI		2	6
1. THERE STANDS THE GLASS—W. Pierce / Dec 28834—BMI		3	16
3. LET ME BE THE ONE—H. Locklin / Four Star 1641—BMI		1	17
4. BIMBO—J. Reeves / Abbott 148—BMI		4	10
5. I REALLY DON'T WANT TO KNOW—E. Arnold / V 20-5525—BMI		8	6
6. I FORGOT MORE THAN YOU'LL EVER KNOW—Davis Sisters / V 20-5345—BMI		5	24
7. CARIBBEAN—M. Torok / Abbott 140—BMI		6	22
8. SECRET LOVE—S. Whitman / Imperial 8223—ASCAP		7	5
9. YOU ALL COME—A. Duff / Starday 104—BMI		9	5
10. RUN 'EM OFF—L. Frizzell / Col 21194—BMI		—	1

• Most Played by Jockeys
For survey week ending February 13

SIDES are ranked in order of the greatest number of plays on disk jockey radio shows thruout the country according to The Billboard's weekly survey of top disk jockey shows in all key markets.

	This Week	Last Week	Weeks on Chart
1. BIMBO—J. Reeves / Abbott 148—BMI		2	12
2. LET ME BE THE ONE—H. Locklin / Four Star 1641—BMI		3	25
3. SLOWLY—W. Pierce / Dec 28991—BMI		9	2
4. I LOVE YOU—G. Wright-J. Reeves / Fabor 101—BMI		7	7
5. CHANGING PARTNERS—P. W. King / V 20-5537—BMI		4	8
6. SECRET LOVE—S. Whitman / Imperial 8220—ASCAP		8	4
7. THERE STANDS THE GLASS—W. Pierce / Dec 28834—BMI		1	18
7. WAKE UP, IRENE—H. Thompson / Cap 2646—BMI		6	8
9. YOU BETTER NOT DO THAT—T. Collins / Cap 2701—BMI		—	1
10. DOG GONE IT, BABY, I'M IN LOVE—Carl Smith / Col 21197—BMI		—	1

USER'S GUIDE

The artist section lists each artist's charted hits in chronological order. Each of an artist's song titles is sequentially numbered. All Top 10 hits are shaded for quick identification.

EXPLANATION OF COLUMNAR HEADINGS

DEBUT: Date first charted

PEAK: Highest charted position (highlighted in bold type). All #1 singles are identified by a special #1 symbol (❶).

WKS: Total weeks charted

Gold: ● Gold single*

▲ Platinum single* (additional million units sold are indicated by a numeral following the symbol)

A-side: Song title of chart hit

B-side: Flip side of vinyl single or additional track(s) on a charted cassette or CD single

POP: Peak position achieved on *Billboard's Hot 100* or *Bubbling Under The Hot 100* Pop charts

$: Current value of near-mint commercial copy

Pic: ■ Indicates a custom picture sleeve was originally issued commercially with the record.

☐ Indicates a promotional picture sleeve was distributed to radio stations and the press.

▮ Indicates a custom picture box was originally issued commercially with the cassette single.

★ CD single

⊙ One-page insert was issued inside the record sleeve.

LABEL & NUMBER: Original record label and number of single when charted. For songs not released as singles, "album cut" is shown in the label column and the album from which the track attained its airplay is noted below the title along with its label and number.

*The primary source used to determine gold and platinum singles is the Recording Industry Association of America (RIAA), which began certifying gold singles in 1958 and platinum singles in 1976. From 1958 through 1988, RIAA required sales of one million units for a gold single and two million units for a platinum single; however, as of January 1, 1989, RIAA lowered the certification requirements for gold singles to sales of 500,000 units and for platinum to one million units. Some record labels have never requested RIAA certifications for their hits. In order to fill in the gaps, especially during the period prior to 1958, various other trade publications and reports were used to supplement RIAA's certifications.

LETTER(S) IN BRACKETS AFTER TITLES

C - Comedy
F - Foreign language
I - Instrumental
N - Novelty

R - Re-entry, reissue, remix or re-release of a previously recorded single by that artist
S - Spoken — Narrations — Recitations
X - Christmas

EXPLANATION OF SYMBOLS

★21★ — Number next to an artist name denotes an artist's ranking among the Top 400 Country Artists of All Time (see ranking on page 544).

2³ — Superior number to the right of the #1 or #2 peak position is the total weeks the single held that position — also used in POP column for #1 hits.

+ — Indicates single peaked in the year after it first charted.

/ — Divides a two-sided hit. Complete chart data (debut date, peak position, etc.) is shown for both sides if each side achieved its own peak position. If a title was shown only as the B-side, then only the weeks it was shown as a "tag along" are listed.

(v) — A 7-inch vinyl 45 rpm single is commercially available. Symbol refers only to singles from 1990 on. (See complete description under "What's New With This Edition" on page xiv.)

PEAK POSITIONS ATTAINED ON VARIOUS POP CHARTS

Prior to publishing the all-encompassing *Hot C&W Sides* chart in 1958, *Billboard* published three weekly Country singles charts: *Best Sellers In Stores*, *Most Played By Jockeys* and *Most Played In Juke Boxes*. The peak position shown in the Peak column for these charts is taken from the chart on which it achieved its highest position. The individual peak positions attained on these three charts is listed to the right of the A-side title. Also, the peak positions attained on the *Hot Country Singles Sales* and *Hot Country Singles Airplay* charts are listed to the right of the A-side titles. All of the Country singles charts consulted are listed below. The following letter designations precede the peak position attained on these charts:

A: Airplay (*Most Played By Jockeys* and *Hot Country Singles Airplay*)
S: Sales (*Best Sellers In Stores* and *Hot Country Singles Sales*)
J: *Most Played In Juke Boxes*

CONSECUTIVE TOP 3 HITS

The peak positions of an artist's string of five or more consecutive Top 3 hits are <u>shaded in a box</u>, so you can quickly spot their hot streaks. Reissues or early label affiliation releases, EP releases, B-side chart hits, recordings with other artists, or a group member's solo release that did not hit the Top 3 do not break a string nor count within a string. The peak position of a non-Top 3 B-side chart hit (of a Top 3 A-side chart hit) is shaded in a string even if it appears at the end of a string.

B-SIDES

If an A-side is recorded by a duo and its B-side is recorded by a solo artist, then the solo artist's name is shown in parentheses after the B-side.

If a B-side hit *Billboard's Hot 100* or *Bubbling Under the Hot 100* pop singles charts, its peak position is shown in parentheses to the right of the B-side.

The B-sides of cassette singles often contain one or more mixes of the A-side along with another title that may also include one or more mixes. Mixes are shown in parentheses in small letters in the B-side column — ex.: (instrumental), (live), (remix), (album version). Often an A-side and a B-side are on the same side of the cassette single. Usually cassette singles repeat the same program on both sides of the cassette.

RECORD PRICE GUIDE

This edition of *Top Country Singles* features a completely updated record price guide. The prices reflect the current estimated value of an original commercial copy in near-mint condition. You will note that the very collectable records such as rockabilly singles reflect a much higher price than most. When evaluating the more common singles, the age of the record is a major determining factor. Generally, older records are more scarce and more difficult to find in good condition and thus command a higher value.

Often, the prices within this book for near-mint copies of high- and low-charting records of the same era are very close. Although it may be easier to find a copy of a million-selling hit of the past, it is difficult to find one in near-mint condition; because popular records are usually played more, they sustain more scratching and damage. Lower-charting and less popular records are, generally, handled significantly less, thereby remaining in great condition.

PICTURES OF THE TOP 200 ARTISTS

A picture of each of the Top 200 artists is shown next to their listing in the artist section and their overall ranking is listed to the right of their name. (Ranking positions of the Top 201-400 artists appear to the left of the artist name.)

ARTIST'S TOP YEAR

The year of an artist's peak popularity (based on yearly chart performance) is listed to the right of the artist's name. The same point system used to determine an artist's overall rank (see page 542) is also used to determine their top year. The year of a record's popularity is based on its peak year and not the year it first charted. For example, an artist may chart a record with a debut date of 11/28/64+. The plus sign after the date indicates the record peaked in 1965; and therefore, the record is considered a 1965 hit.

Although the year from which an artist generates the most points is generally considered the top year, some exceptions are made. For example, if an artist had a lone major hit in one year, and a few minor hits in another year which collectively accumulated more points, the year of the major hit is considered the artist's top year.

ARTIST & TITLE NOTES

Below nearly every artist name are brief notes about the artist. Directly under some song titles are notes indicating backing vocalists, guest instrumentalists, the title of the movie in which the song was featured, the name of a famous songwriter or producer, etc. Duets and other important name variations are shown in bold capital letters. Names of artists mentioned in the artist and title notes of others, who have their own chart hits elsewhere in this book, are highlighted in bold type; a name is shown bold the first time it appears in an artist's biography. All movie, TV and album titles, and other major works, are shown in italics.

A note beneath the title shows if a Country hit was also recorded by another artist and that recording made the Pop and/or R&B charts but not the Country charts. However, if another recording of a Country hit made the Pop and/or R&B charts <u>and</u> hit the Country charts (and therefore appears in this book), we do not show a note beneath the title. If you have any questions about such hits, refer to the title section where you will see all versions of the hit including the crossover version.

As always, we gladly welcome any corrections/updates to our artist biographies or title trivia notes. Please include solid evidence.

CMA AWARDS

The Country Music Association (CMA) began giving yearly awards to Country music artists in 1967. The CMA Awards are very prestigious and we thought it was important to show the winners of the major categories listed below. The following information is shown in the artist and title notes of each winner:

    Entertainer Of The Year   Musician Of The Year
    Male and Female Vocalist Of The Year   Horizon Award (New Artist)
    Vocal Group Of The Year   Single Of The Year
    Vocal Duo Of The Year

ARTIST'S BIGGEST HITS

Listed in bold type right below the artist's biography in rank order are:
    the Top 3 hits of every artist with 10 to 19 charted hits and
    the Top 5 hits of every artist with 20 or more charted hits.

<u>Underlined</u> is the highest-charting title for an artist who charted five or more titles. The top hit is a reflection of chart performance only and may or may not relate to an artist's best seller or most popular song over the years. A tie is broken based on total weeks at the peak position, total weeks in the Top 10, total weeks in the Top 40, and finally, total weeks charted.

WHAT'S NEW WITH THIS EDITION

In our continuing efforts to improve each subsequent edition of *Top Country Singles*, we added the following to this fifth edition.

VINYL SYMBOL

All label numbers prior to 1990 refer to the vinyl single only. From 1990 on, a '(v)' is shown after the label number of all cassette and CD singles that were also released on a 45 rpm vinyl single. The label number and/or B-side title of the vinyl release is noted below the title if it is different than the cassette or CD single release. If no '(v)' is shown, then that single was released on vinyl only (as of 2002, many country singles are still available on vinyl). Album cuts later released as B-sides may also have a vinyl, cassette and/or CD availability symbol with a note in title trivia.

TOP 400 ARTIST DEBUTS

A chronological listing of the debut dates of Top 400 artists is listed in back of this book. Each artist's rank is shown in parentheses after their name. This listing was originally featured in our *Country Annual 1944-1997* book.

UPDATED & EXPANDED ARTIST BIOGRAPHIES

Many of the major artists biographies have been expanded since the last edition to provide additional insights into the lives and careers of your favorite artists.

ARTIST SECTION

Lists, alphabetically by artist name, every song in chronological sequence that charted on *Billboard's* Country Singles charts from January 1, 1944 through December 29, 2001.

KEY

Here's a quick reference guide to our symbols. Refer to *RESEARCHING BILLBOARD'S COUNTRY CHARTS* and *USER'S GUIDE* for complete descriptions. (The artist and titles below are NOT real.)

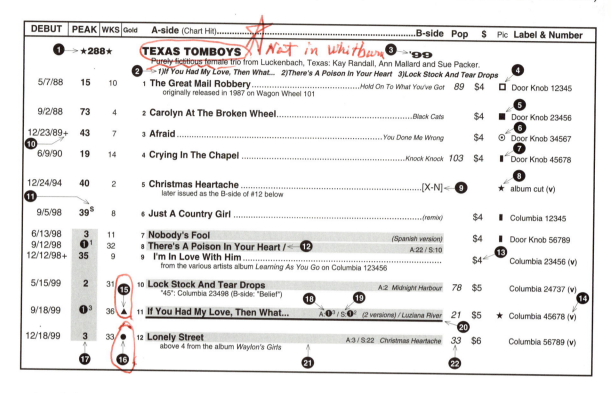

1. artist's ranking within the Top 400 artists
2. artist's top 3 or top 5 hits
3. artist's peak year of popularity
4. promotional picture sleeve (□)
5. picture sleeve (■)
6. insert (⊙) in record sleeve
7. cassette single (▮)
8. CD single (★)
9. Christmas/Novelty song [X-N]
10. peaked in the following year
11. peak position is from Sales chart (S)
12. 2-sided hit separator
13. current value of near-mint commercial single
14. 7-inch 45 rpm vinyl single ("45") availability (v)
15. platinum seller (▲)
16. gold seller (●)
17. Top 3 hit streak (shaded)
18. peak position on Airplay charts (A:)
19. peak position on Sales charts (S:)
20. artist's biggest hit (underlined)
21. Top 10 hit (shaded)
22. peak position attained on Billboard's *Hot 100* or *Bubbling Under The Hot 100* chart

DEBUT	PEAK	WKS	Gold	A-side (Chart Hit)	B-side	Pop	$	Pic	Label & Number
				A					
				ABBOTT, Jerry '78					
				Born in Dallas. Singer/songwriter.					
4/29/78	63	7		1 I Want A Little Cowboy	When It Comes To Cowgirls (I Just Can't Say "No")	—	$6		Churchill 7712
9/9/78	80	6		2 I Owe It All To You	Jack Of All Trades	—	$6		Churchill 7715
1/9/82	82	4		3 One Night Stanley	(Love Is Still) The Main Attraction	—	$6		Dallas Star 102581
				ABERNATHY, Mack '89					
				Born in Austin, Texas. Singer/songwriter.					
11/12/88	98	2		1 Slippin' Around	Pocket Rocket Ranger	—	$6		CMI 1988-8
2/18/89	80	3		2 Different Situations	Dos Hermanos Cantina	—	$6		CMI 1988-9
	★278★			**ACUFF, Roy** '44					
				Born on 9/15/03 in Maynardville, Tennessee. Died of heart failure on 11/23/92 (age 89). Joined the *Grand Ole Opry* in 1937. The Smoky Mountain Boys consisted of Pete "Bashful Brother Oswald" Kirby (dobro), Howard "Howdy" Forrester (fiddle; died on 8/1/87, age 65) and Jimmie Riddle (harmonica, piano; died on 12/10/82, age 64). Formed Acuff-Rose music publishing company in 1942 and the Hickory record label in 1953 with **Fred Rose**. Twice ran for governor of Tennessee. Elected to the Country Music Hall of Fame in 1962. Won Grammy's Lifetime Achievement Award in 1987. Known as "The King Of Country Music." Also see **Heart Of Nashville**.					
				1)I'll Forgive You But I Can't Forget 2)(Our Own) Jole Blon 3)The Prodigal Son					
				ROY ACUFF and his Smoky Mountain Boys:					
2/12/44	4	2		1 The Prodigal Son	Not A Word From Home	13	$25		Okeh 6716
11/4/44	3	8		2 I'll Forgive You But I Can't Forget /		21			
11/11/44	6	4		3 Write Me Sweetheart		—	$25		Okeh 6723
4/19/47	4	6		4 (Our Own) Jole Blon	Tennessee Central (Number 9)	—	$20		Columbia 37287
2/7/48	8	5		5 The Waltz Of The Wind	J:8 / S:13 The Songbirds Are Singing In Heaven	—	$20		Columbia 38042
6/19/48	14	2		6 Unloved And Unclaimed	S:14 I Had A Dream	—	$20		Columbia 38189
8/7/48	12	1		7 This World Can't Stand Long	S:12 It's So Hard To Smile	—	$20		Columbia 20454
11/6/48	12	1		8 Tennessee Waltz	J:12 Sweeter Than The Flowers	—	$20		Columbia 20551
12/18/48	14	1		9 A Sinner's Death	S:14 The Midnight Train	—	$20		Columbia 20475
3/31/58	8	7		10 Once More	A:8 I Don't Care (If You Don't Love Me)	—	$15		Hickory 1073
12/29/58+	16	11		11 So Many Times	They'll Never Take Her Love From Me	—	$15		Hickory 1090
6/15/59	20	3		12 Come And Knock (On The Door Of My Heart)	My Love Came Back To Me	—	$15		Hickory 1097
				ROY ACUFF:					
5/15/65	45	5		13 Freight Train Blues	All The World Is Lonely Now	—	$10		Hickory 1291
11/27/71	56	6		14 I Saw The Light	The Precious Jewel	—	$8		United Artists 50849
				NITTY GRITTY DIRT BAND with ROY ACUFF					
2/16/74	51	11		15 Back In The Country	(Our Own) Jole Blon	—	$6		Hickory/MGM 314
6/22/74	97	3		16 Old Time Sunshine Song	This World Can't Stand Long	—	$6		Hickory/MGM 319
6/17/89	87	2		17 The Precious Jewel	Buried Alive	—	$8		Hal Kat 63058
				CHARLIE LOUVIN - ROY ACUFF					
				ADAMS, Don '74					
				Born on 1/4/41 in Ross County, Ohio.					
4/1/67	64	4		1 Two Of The Usual	Wake Me 100 Years From Now	—	$10		Jack O'Diam. 1002
7/14/73	91	5		2 I'll Be Satisfied	All For The Love Of A Girl	—	$6		Atlantic 4002
				#20 Pop hit for Jackie Wilson in 1959					
11/24/73+	34	12		3 I've Already Stayed Too Long	Oh What A Future She Had	—	$6		Atlantic 4009
4/27/74	80	4		4 Baby Let Your Long Hair Down	Little Girl Blue	—	$6		Atlantic 4017
				DON ADAMS AND THE GREENFIELD EXPRESS					
8/17/74	52	9		5 That's Love	I Just Lost My Favorite Girl	—	$6		Atlantic 4027
				ADAMS, Kay '66					
				Born Princetta Kay Adams on 4/9/41 in Knox City, Texas; raised in Vernon, Texas.					
10/15/66	30	7		Little Pink Mack	That'll Be The Day	—	$15		Tower 269
				KAY ADAMS with The Cliffie Stone Group					
				ADAMS, Kaylee '86					
				Born in Navarre, Ohio. Female session/jingle singer.					
10/18/86	68	4		I Can't Help The Way I Don't Feel	Love You 'Til It Hurts	—	$4		Warner 28567
				ADAMS, Peggy Jo — see McCLINTON, O.B.					
				ADEN, Terry '82					
				Born on 8/11/52 in Poplar Bluff, Missouri. Died on 11/28/2001 (age 49). Male singer.					
10/31/81	81	3		1 What's So Good About Goodbye	I'm Here	—	$6		B&B 21
4/3/82	73	5		2 She Doesn't Belong To You	What's So Good About Goodbye	—	$6		AMI 1303
	★269★			**ADKINS, Trace** '97					
				Born on 1/13/62 in Springhill, Louisiana; raised in Sarepta, Louisiana. Male singer/songwriter/guitarist. Sang with the New Commitment gospel group while in high school. Played football for Louisiana Tech. Also see **America The Beautiful**.					
				1)(This Ain't) No Thinkin' Thing 2)I Left Something Turned On At Home 3)Every Light In The House					
4/13/96	20	20		1 There's A Girl In Texas	S:7 A Bad Way Of Saying Goodbye	—	$4	■	Capitol 58562 (v)
				"45": Capitol 19117					
8/24/96	3	21		2 Every Light In The House	S:2 If I Fall (You're Goin' With Me)	78	$4	■	Capitol 58574 (v)
				"45": Capitol 19224					
1/25/97	●1	20		3 (This Ain't) No Thinkin' Thing	634-5789	—	$4		Capitol 19524
4/26/97	2²	20		4 I Left Something Turned On At Home	I Can Only Love You Like A Man	—	$4		Capitol 19579
9/6/97	4	22		5 The Rest Of Mine	S:6 Dreamin' Out Loud	70	$4	■	Capitol 58680 (v)
				"45": Capitol 19698 (B-side: "Wayfaring Stranger")					

DEBUT	PEAK	WKS	Gold	A-side (Chart Hit)	B-side	Pop	$	Pic	Label & Number
				ADKINS, Trace — Cont'd					
1/17/98	11	20		6 Lonely Won't Leave Me Alone ....S:14 Wayfaring Stranger		112	$4	■	Capitol 58697 (v)
				"45": Capitol 19897 (B-side: "Nothin' But Taillights")					
5/9/98	27	20		7 Big Time	Snowball In El Paso	—	$4		Capitol 19976
12/26/98	64	3		8 The Christmas Song ....Wayfaring Stranger [X]		—	$4		Capitol 58744
				#3 Pop hit for Nat "King" Cole in 1946					
9/18/99+	27	20		9 Don't Lie	All Hat, No Cattle	119	$4		Capitol 58812
1/29/00	10	23		10 More	The Night He Can't Remember	65	$4		Capitol 38701
7/29/00	36	20		11 I'm Gonna Love You Anyway	I Can Dig It	—	$4		Capitol 58880
7/7/01	6	32		12 I'm Tryin'	Chrome	44	$4		Capitol 77667
				ADKINS, Wendel '77					
				Born in 1946 in Kentucky.					
2/19/77	80	4		1 I Will	Show Me The Way		$6		Hitsville 6050
4/30/77	91	3		2 Laid Back Country Picker	Texas Moon		$6		Hitsville 6055
11/26/77	98	2		3 Julieanne (Where Are You Tonight)?	She Gives Me Love		$6		MC/Curb 5002
	★354★			**AKINS, Rhett** '96					
				Born Thomas Rhett Akins on 10/13/69 in Valdosta, Georgia. Singer/songwriter/guitarist.					
				1)Don't Get Me Started 2)That Ain't My Truck 3)She Said Yes					
10/1/94	35	20		1 What They're Talkin' About	Heart To Heart	—	$4	■	Decca 54910 (v)
1/21/95	36	14		2 I Brake For Brunettes	(dance mix)	—	$4	■	Decca 54974 (v)
5/13/95	3	21		3 That Ain't My Truck ....S:15 Same Ol' Story		—	$4	■	Decca 55034 (v)
10/21/95+	17	22		4 She Said Yes	Old Dirt Road	—	$4		Decca 55085
3/30/96	❶¹	21		5 Don't Get Me Started	I Was Wrong	—	$4		Decca 55166
9/7/96	38	13		6 Love You Back	No Match (For That Old Flame)	—	$4		Decca 55223
12/7/96+	51	10		7 Every Cowboy's Dream	Carolina Line	—	$4		Decca 55291
3/22/97	69	1		8 Somebody Knew		—	$4		album cut
				from the album Somebody New on Decca 11424					
10/4/97	41	20		9 More Than Everything ....S:16 Better Than It Used To Be		121	$4	■	Decca 72022 (v)
1/24/98	47	11		10 Better Than It Used To Be	I'm Finding Out	—	$4		Decca 72036
4/18/98	56	9		11 Drivin' My Life Away ....A Man With 18 Wheels (Lee Ann Womack)		—	$4		Decca 72049
				from the movie Black Dog starring Patrick Swayze					
				ALABAMA ★15★ '85					
				Group formed as Young Country in 1969 in Fort Payne, Alabama. Changed name to Wildcountry in 1972, then to Alabama in 1977. Consisted of Randy Owen (vocals, guitar; born on 12/13/49), Jeff Cook (keyboards, fiddle, born on 8/27/49), Teddy Gentry (bass, born on 1/22/52) and Bennett Vartanian (drums). Owen, Cook and Gentry are cousins. Jackie Owen (another cousin) replaced Vartanian briefly in 1976; Rick Scott then took over as drummer later that same year. Mark Herndon (born on 5/11/55) replaced Scott as drummer in 1979. CMA Awards: 1981, 1982 & 1983 Vocal Group of the Year; 1982, 1983 & 1984 Entertainer of the Year.					
				1)Jukebox In My Mind 2)Down Home 3)I'm In A Hurry (And Don't Know Why) 4)Love In The First Degree 5)Feels So Right					
7/23/77	78	8		1 I Wanna Be With You Tonight	Lovin' You Is Killing Me	—	$15	■	GRT 129
9/29/79	33	12		2 I Wanna' Come Over	Get It While It's Hot	—	$12		MDJ 7906
				first released in 1979 on Sonny Limbo Int'l. 7906 ($40)					
2/2/80	17	13		3 My Home's In Alabama ....Some Other Time, Some Other Place / Why, Lady, Why		—	$12		MDJ 1002
				shorter version later released on RCA 12008 with a picture sleeve ($5)					
5/31/80	❶¹	17		4 Tennessee River	Can't Forget About You	—	$5		RCA 12018
9/20/80	❶¹	19		5 Why Lady Why	I Wanna Come Over	—	$5	■	RCA 12091
2/14/81	❶¹	14		6 Old Flame	I'm Stoned	103	$5		RCA 12169
5/23/81	❶²	13		7 Feels So Right	See The Embers, Feel The Flame	20	$5		RCA 12236
10/24/81	❶²	16		8 Love In The First Degree	Ride The Train	15	$5		RCA 12288
3/6/82	❶¹	18		9 Mountain Music	Never Be One	101	$5	■	RCA 13019
5/29/82	❶¹	17		10 Take Me Down	Lovin' You Is Killin' Me	18	$4		RCA 13210
8/28/82	❶¹	17		11 Close Enough To Perfect	Fantasy	65	$4		RCA 13294
12/11/82	35	7		12 Christmas In Dixie ....Christmas Is Just A Song For Us This Year [X]		—	$4		RCA 13358
				also see #63, #67 and #71 below					
2/12/83	❶¹	16		13 Dixieland Delight	Very Special Love	—	$4		RCA 13446
5/14/83	❶¹	17		14 The Closer You Get	You Turn Me On	38	$4		RCA 13524
				#103 Pop hit for Rita Coolidge in 1981					
8/20/83	❶¹	20		15 Lady Down On Love	Lovin' Man	76	$4		RCA 13590
1/21/84	❶¹	17		16 Roll On (Eighteen Wheeler)	Food On The Table	—	$4		RCA 13716
4/21/84	❶¹	19		17 When We Make Love	Carolina Mountain Dewe	72	$4		RCA 13763
8/4/84	❶¹	19		18 If You're Gonna Play In Texas (You Gotta Have A Fiddle In The Band) /	S:❶¹ / A:2	—			
		2		19 I'm Not That Way Anymore		—	$4		RCA 13840
11/10/84+	❶¹	19		20 (There's A) Fire In The Night	A:❶¹ / S:2 Rock In The Bayou	—	$4		RCA 13926
2/9/85	❶¹	21		21 There's No Way	S:❶¹ / A:❶¹ The Boy	—	$4		RCA 13992
5/18/85	❶¹	19		22 Forty Hour Week (For A Livin')	A:❶¹ / S:2 As Right Now	—	$4	■	RCA 14085
8/24/85	❶¹	22		23 Can't Keep A Good Man Down	S:❶¹ / A:❶¹ If It Ain't Dixie (It Won't Be)	—	$4		RCA 14165
1/25/86	❶¹	21		24 She And I	A:❶² / S:❶¹ The Fans	—	$4	■	RCA 14281
9/20/86	❶¹	20		25 Touch Me When We're Dancing	S:❶¹ / A:❶¹ Hanging Up My Travelin' Shoes	—	$4		RCA 5003
				#16 Pop hit for the Carpenters in 1981					
12/6/86+	10	15		26 Deep River Woman	S:❶¹ / A:10 Ballerina Girl (Richie)	71	$4	■	Motown 1873
				LIONEL RICHIE with Alabama					
1/24/87	❶¹	22		27 "You've Got" The Touch	A:❶¹ / S:3 True, True Housewife	—	$4		RCA 5081
8/22/87	7	17		28 Tar Top	S:5 If I Could Just See You Now	—	$4	□	RCA 5222

DEBUT	PEAK	WKS	Gold	A-side (Chart Hit)	B-side	Pop	$	Pic	Label & Number
				ALABAMA — Cont'd					
12/5/87+	❶¹	22		29 Face To Face K.T. Oslin (guest vocal)	S:3 Vacation	—	$4		RCA 5328
4/23/88	❶¹	17		30 Fallin' Again	S:3 I Saw The Time	—	$4		RCA 6902
11/26/88+	❶¹	19		31 Song Of The South	S:10 (I Wish It Could Always Be) '55	—	$4		RCA 8744
3/11/89	❶¹	19		32 If I Had You	I Showed Her	—	$4		RCA 8817
8/12/89	❶¹	24		33 High Cotton	"Ole" Baugh Road	—	$4		RCA 8948
12/9/89+	❶¹	26		34 Southern Star	Barefootin'	—	$4		RCA 9083
4/28/90	3	21		35 Pass It On Down	The Borderline	—	$4	■	RCA 2519
7/28/90	❶⁴	20		36 Jukebox In My Mind	Fire On Fire	—	$4		RCA 2643
11/17/90+	❶¹	20		37 Forever's As Far As I'll Go	Starting Tonight	—	$4		RCA 2706
3/2/91	❶³	20		38 Down Home	Goodbye (Kelly's Song)	—	$4		RCA 2778
6/8/91	2¹	20		39 Here We Are	Gulf Of Mexico	—	$4		RCA 2828
9/28/91	4	20		40 Then Again	Hats Off	—	$4		RCA 62059
1/11/92	2¹	20		41 Born Country	Until It Happens To You	—	$4		RCA 62168
6/6/92	2¹	20		42 Take A Little Trip	Pictures And Memories	—	$4		RCA 62253
9/26/92	❶²	20		43 I'm In A Hurry (And Don't Know Why)	Sometimes Out Of Touch	—	$4		RCA 62336
12/26/92+	3	20		44 Once Upon A Lifetime	American Pride	—	$4		RCA 62428
4/10/93	3	20		45 Hometown Honeymoon	Homesick Fever	—	$4		RCA 62495
9/11/93	❶¹	20		46 Reckless	Clear Water Blues	123	$4	■	RCA 62636 (v)
12/18/93+	7	20		47 T.L.C. A.S.A.P.	That Feeling	—	$4		RCA 62712
12/25/93	51	6		48 Angels Among Us .... S:6 Santa Claus (I Still Believe In You) [X]		122	$4	■	RCA 62643 (v)
				also see #51 below					
4/16/94	13	20		49 The Cheap Seats	This Love's On Me	—	$4		RCA 62623
9/10/94	6	20		50 We Can't Love Like This Anymore	Still Goin' Strong	—	$4	■	RCA 62897 (v)
12/31/94	28	14		51 Angels Among Us .... Santa Claus (I Still Believe In You) [X-R]		—	$4		RCA 62643 (v)
1/28/95	75	1		52 Sweet Home Alabama					album cut
				#8 Pop hit for Lynyrd Skynyrd in 1974; from the various artists album Skynyrd Frynds on MCA 11097					
2/11/95	3	20		53 Give Me One More Shot	Jukebox In My Mind	—	$4		RCA 64273
7/1/95	2¹	20		54 She Ain't Your Ordinary Girl	S:21 Heartbreak Express	—	$4	■	RCA 64346 (v)
9/30/95	4	20		55 In Pictures	S:6 Between The Two Of Them	118	$4	■	RCA 64419 (v)
1/13/96	19	20		56 It Works .... S:18 Katy Brought My Guitar Back Today		—	$4	■	RCA 64473 (v)
5/18/96	38	7		57 Say I	My Love Belongs To You	—	$4		RCA 64543
7/20/96	4	20		58 The Maker Said Take Her	Nothing Comes Close	—	$4		RCA 64588
12/28/96	72	2		59 The Blessings	[X]	—			album cut
				from the album Christmas Volume II on RCA 66927					
3/1/97	2¹	20		60 Sad Lookin' Moon	S:14 Give Me One More Shot	—	$4	■	RCA 64775 (v)
6/28/97	3	20		61 Dancin', Shaggin' On The Boulevard	Very Special Love	—	$4		RCA 64849
10/11/97	22	20		62 Of Course I'm Alright	(I Wish It Could Always Be) '55	—	$4		RCA 64965
12/27/97	47	3		63 Christmas In Dixie .... Thistlehair The Christmas Bear [X-R]		—	$4		RCA 64436
				same version as #12 above (also see #67 and #71 below)					
2/14/98	21	20		64 She's Got That Look In Her Eyes	That Feeling	—	$4		RCA 65409
8/1/98	2¹	21		65 How Do You Fall In Love/		82			
12/5/98+	14	20		66 Keepin' Up		69	$4		RCA 65561
12/19/98	40	4		67 Christmas In Dixie .... Thistlehair The Christmas Bear [X-R]		—	$4		RCA 64436
				same version as #12 above (also see #63 above and #71 below)					
12/26/98	71	1		68 Santa Claus (I Still Believe In You) [X]		—		■	album cut (v)
				from the album Christmas on RCA 7014 (first released as the B-side of #48 above)					
5/1/99	3	23		69 God Must Have Spent A Little More Time On You	S:3 Sad Lookin' Moon	29	$7	★	RCA 65759 (v)
				ALABAMA (featuring *NSYNC) #8 Pop hit for *NSYNC in 1999					
10/16/99+	24	20		70 Small Stuff .... God Must Have Spent A Little More Time On You		110	$4		RCA 65935
12/11/99	37	5		71 Christmas In Dixie .... Thistlehair The Christmas Bear [X-R]		—	$4		RCA 64436
				same version as #12 above (also see #63 and #67 above)					
12/25/99	64	3		72 Rockin' Around The Christmas Tree .... [X]		—			album cut
				from the album Christmas Volume II on RCA 66927					
1/15/00	51	3		73 Twentieth Century / S:8		—			
1/15/00	55	1		74 New Year's Eve 1999		—	$4	★	RCA 65917
				ALABAMA with Gretchen Peters					
5/20/00	63	3		75 We Made Love	Small Stuff	—	$4		RCA 60211 (v)
11/4/00+	15	20		76 When It All Goes South	Feels So Right	110	$4		RCA 69019 (v)
5/5/01	41	11		77 Will You Marry Me		—			album cut
				from the album When It All Goes South on RCA 69337					
	★267★			**ALAN, Buddy**		'68			
				Born Alvis Alan Owens on 5/23/48 in Mesa, Arizona. Singer/songwriter/guitarist. Son of **Buck Owens** and **Bonnie Owens**. 1)Let The World Keep On A Turnin' 2)Cowboy Convention 3)Big Mama's Medicine Show 4)Lodi 5)Too Old To Cut The Mustard					
7/27/68	7	15		1 Let The World Keep On A Turnin'	I'll Love You Forever And Ever	—	$10	■	Capitol 2237
				BUCK OWENS AND BUDDY ALAN AND THE BUCKAROOS					
11/23/68	54	6		2 When I Turn Twenty-One .... Adois, Farewell, Goodbye, Good Luck, So Long		—	$8	■	Capitol 2305
				written by Merle Haggard					
10/25/69	23	10		3 Lodi	I Wanna Be Wild And Free	—	$8		Capitol 2653
				#52 Pop hit for **Creedence Clearwater Revival** in 1969					
2/7/70	23	8		4 Big Mama's Medicine Show	When A Man Can't Call His Home A Home	—	$8		Capitol 2715
5/2/70	38	9		5 Down In New Orleans	I've Never Had A Dream Come True Before	—	$8		Capitol 2784

DEBUT	PEAK	WKS	Gold	A-side (Chart Hit) .... B-side	Pop	$	Pic	Label & Number
				ALAN, Buddy — Cont'd				
8/8/70	57	7		6 Santo Domingo .... That's Quite A Ride	—	$8		Capitol 2852
				#1, #5 & #6: written by **Buck Owens**				
11/7/70	19	12		7 Cowboy Convention .... We're All Gonna Get Together	—	$8		Capitol 2928
				BUDDY ALAN & DON RICH				
1/16/71	37	9		8 Lookin' Out My Back Door .... Corn Liquor	—	$8		Capitol 3010
				#2 Pop hit for **Creedence Clearwater Revival** in 1970				
3/6/71	54	5		9 I'm On The Road To Memphis .... I'll Be Swingin' Too	—	$8		Capitol 3040
				BUDDY ALAN & DON RICH				
6/5/71	48	9		10 Fishin' On The Mississippi .... If I Could Love You More	—	$8		Capitol 3110
8/21/71	46	9		11 I Will Drink Your Wine .... Doin' The Best I Can	—	$8		Capitol 3146
12/4/71+	29	10		12 Too Old To Cut The Mustard .... Wham Bam	—	$7	■	Capitol 3215
				BUCK & BUDDY				
3/4/72	68	4		13 White Line Fever .... Another By Your Side	—	$7		Capitol 3266
				written by **Merle Haggard**				
6/24/72	47	10		14 I'm In Love .... The Happiness Song	—	$7		Capitol 3346
				written by **Freddie Hart**				
9/23/72	49	7		15 Things .... One Good Woman	—	$7		Capitol 3427
				#3 Pop hit for **Bobby Darin** in 1962				
12/30/72+	60	6		16 Move It On Over .... Magic Man	—	$6		Capitol 3485
4/7/73	64	4		17 Why, Because I Love You .... She's Been On My Mind For So Long	—	$6		Capitol 3555
5/19/73	67	4		18 Caribbean .... Please, Friend, Take Me Home	—	$6		Capitol 3598
8/11/73	68	6		19 Summer Afternoons .... Maybe Things Would Be Better That Way	—	$6		Capitol 3680
11/24/73+	67	8		20 All Around Cowboy Of 1964 .... You Are My Everything	—	$6		Capitol 3749
5/4/74	70	8		21 I Never Had It So Good .... She Always Wears A Yellow Rose	—	$6		Capitol 3861
2/15/75	35	11		22 Chains .... A Whole Lot Of Somethin'	—	$6		Capitol 4019
				#17 Pop hit for **The Cookies** in 1962				
6/7/75	88	5		23 Another Saturday Night .... Nickles, Dimes And Quarters	—	$6		Capitol 4075
				#10 Pop hit for **Sam Cooke** in 1963				
				ALBERT, Urel '73				
				Born on 5/28/28 in Chicago. Died on 4/29/92 (age 63). Male comedian/impressionist.				
10/13/73	97	2		Country And Pop Music .... Just Wait [N]	—	$15		Toast 311
				"live" effects are dubbed-in				
				ALEXANDER, Daniele '89				
				Born on 12/2/54 in Fort Worth, Texas. Female singer/songwriter.				
7/22/89	19	20		1 She's There .... Goodbye Me	—	$4		Mercury 874330
11/11/89	53	8		2 Where Did The Moon Go Wrong .... First Move	—	$4		Mercury 876228
12/1/90+	56	9		3 It Wasn't You, It Wasn't Me .... Fairytale Fool (Alexander)	—	$4	■	Mercury 878256 (v)
				DANIELE ALEXANDER & BUTCH BAKER				
				ALEXANDER, Wyvon '82				
				Born on 7/2/54 in Weaverville, California. Male singer.				
2/14/81	90	2		1 Frustration .... Old Familiar Feeling	—	$6		Gervasi 633
4/18/81	86	2		2 Old Familiar Feeling	—	$6		Gervasi 644
8/15/81	74	4		3 Women /	—			
1/16/82	83	3		4 Don't Lead Me On	—	$6		Gervasi 659
8/28/82	69	6		5 Alice In Dallas (Sweet Texas) .... Hungry Man's Dream	—	$6		Gervasi 660
				co-written by **Merle Haggard**				
11/27/82	76	4		6 Midnight Cabaret .... Same Old Song	—	$6		Gervasi 661
12/10/83+	68	8		7 The Look Of A Lovin' Lady .... High Time	—	$6		Gervasi 663
				co-written by **Bill Anderson**				
				ALIBI '88				
				Vocal group from Canada.				
10/3/87	84	2		1 Roller Coaster	—	$6		Comstock 1856
5/21/88	61	6		2 Do You Have Any Doubts	—	$6		Comstock 1884
	★312★			**ALLAN, Gary** '01				
				Born Gary Herzberg on 12/5/67 in Montebello, California; raised in La Mirada, California. Singer/songwriter/guitarist.				
				1)Right Where I Need To Be 2)Her Man 3)It Would Be You				
8/24/96+	7	23		1 Her Man .... Wake Up Screaming	—	$4		Decca 55227
12/28/96	70	1		2 Please Come Home For Christmas .... [X]	—	$10	★	Decca 3864
				#18 Pop hit for the **Eagles** in 1978; available only as a promotional CD single				
1/18/97	44	11		3 Forever And A Day .... Living In A House Full Of Love	—	$4		Decca 55289
4/12/97	43	15		4 From Where I'm Sitting .... Wine Me Up	—	$4		Decca 72003
8/23/97	43	12		5 Living In A House Full Of Love .... Of All The Hearts	—	$4		Decca 72018
2/14/98	7	23		6 It Would Be You S:15 Send Back My Heart	101	$4	■	Decca 72039 (v)
8/1/98	43	11		7 No Man In His Wrong Heart .... Baby I Will	—	$4		Decca 72059
11/7/98+	47	17		8 I'll Take Today .... I've Got A Quarter In My Pocket	—	$4		Decca 72079
8/14/99+	12	29		9 Smoke Rings In The Dark .... Right Where I Need To Be	76	$4		MCA Nashville 72109
1/22/00	74	1		10 Runaway	—			album cut
				#1 Pop hit for **Del Shannon** in 1961; from the album *Smoke Rings In The Dark* on MCA Nashville 170101				
4/1/00	34	20		11 Lovin' You Against My Will .... I'm The One	—	$4		MCA Nashville 172140
4/22/00+	5	48		12 Right Where I Need To Be .... Don't Tell Mama	42	$4		MCA Nashville 172180
7/7/01	18	24		13 Man Of Me .... Sorry	107	$4		MCA Nashville 172213

DEBUT	PEAK	WKS	Gold	A-side (Chart Hit) .... B-side	Pop	$	Pic	Label & Number
	★280★			**ALLANSON, Susie** '78				
				Born on 3/17/52 in Las Vegas. Singer/actress. Performed in the musical *Hair* and both the musical and movie version of *Jesus Christ Superstar*. Formerly married to music executive Ray Ruff.				
				1)We Belong Together 2)Two Steps Forward And Three Steps Back 3)Maybe Baby				
7/9/77	23	14		1 Baby, Don't Keep Me Hangin' On .... It's Gone	—	$8		Oak 1001
				later released on Warner/Curb 8429 ($5)				
11/5/77+	20	14		2 Baby, Last Night Made My Day .... Will There Really Be A Morning	—	$5		Warner/Curb 8473
3/4/78	7	13		3 Maybe Baby .... Hide Me In Your Love	—	$5		Warner/Curb 8534
				#17 Pop hit for Buddy Holly in 1958				
6/24/78	2²	13		4 We Belong Together .... I Don't Want To Cry Anymore	—	$5		Warner/Curb 8597
10/28/78	17	11		5 Back To The Love .... I Want This Feeling To Last	—	$5		Warner/Curb 8686
2/3/79	8	11		6 Words .... We Can Make It Up To Each Other	—	$5		Elektra/Curb 46009
				#15 Pop hit for the **Bee Gees** in 1968				
4/28/79	6	12		7 Two Steps Forward And Three Steps Back .... I Will Never Leave You	—	'$5		Elektra/Curb 46036
8/18/79	79	4		8 Without You .... Heart To Heart	—	$5		Elektra/Curb 46503
				#1 Pop hit for Nilsson in 1972				
12/1/79+	38	10		9 I Must Be Crazy .... I Can't See Me Without You	—	$5		Elektra/Curb 46565
8/2/80	31	12		10 While I Was Makin' Love To You .... Michael	—	$5		United Artists 1365
11/8/80+	23	14		11 Dance The Two Step .... You Never Told Me About Goodbye	—	$5		Liberty 1383
5/30/81	53	7		12 Run To Her .... Send Me Somebody To Love	—	$5		Liberty/Curb 1408
				#2 Pop hit for Bobby Vee in 1961				
9/5/81	44	8		13 Love Is Knockin' At My Door (Here Comes Forever Again) .... Lay A Little Lovin' On Me	—	$5		Liberty/Curb 1425
12/5/81	60	7		14 Hearts (Our Hearts) .... Dreamin' Again	—	$5		Liberty/Curb 1422
4/24/82	62	6		15 Wasn't That Love .... Falling In Love For The Last Time	—	$5		Liberty/Curb 1460
12/27/86+	67	7		16 Where's The Fire	—	$6		TNP 75001
6/20/87	70	5		17 She Don't Love You	—	$6		TNP 75005
	★323★			**ALLEN, Deborah** '84				
				Born Deborah Lynn Thurmond on 9/30/53 in Memphis. Singer/songwriter. Married to songwriter Rafe Van Hoy from 1982-93. Regular on TV's *The Jim Stafford Show* in 1975.				
				1)I've Been Wrong Before 2)Baby I Lied 3)Take Me In Your Arms And Hold Me				
4/12/80	10	16		1 Take Me In Your Arms And Hold Me .... Missing Angel	—	$5		RCA 11946
				JIM REEVES/DEBORAH ALLEN				
11/22/80+	24	15		2 Nobody's Fool .... Let Me Down	—	$5		Capitol 4945
8/15/81	20	11		3 You (Make Me Wonder Why) .... Next To You	—	$5		Capitol 5014
1/9/82	33	10		4 You Look Like The One I Love .... It's Cold Inside	—	$5		Capitol 5080
5/29/82	82	3		5 After Tonight .... Don't Worry 'Bout Me Baby	—	$5		Capitol 5110
8/20/83	4	24		6 Baby I Lied .... Time Is Taking You Away From Me	26	$5	■	RCA 13600
1/28/84	2²	24		7 I've Been Wrong Before .... Fool's Paradise	—	$5		RCA 13694
5/26/84	10	20		8 I Hurt For You .... Cheat The Night	—	$5		RCA 13776
10/20/84	23	17		9 Heartache And A Half .... A:20 / S:26 It Makes Me Cry	—	$5	■	RCA 13921
12/5/92+	29	20		10 Rock Me (In The Cradle Of Love) .... Natural Tears	—	$4		Giant 18566
4/17/93	44	13		11 If You're Not Gonna Love Me .... Long Time Lovin' You	—	$4		Giant 18530
5/7/94	66	2		12 Break These Chains .... Talkin' To My Heart	—	$4	■	Giant 18199
				ALLEN, Joe '75				
				Born in Aspen, Colorado. Singer/session musician.				
1/25/75	83	5		1 Should I Come Home (Or Should I Go Crazy) .... What Kind Of A Fool	—	$5		Warner 8052
7/5/75	88	8		2 Carolyn At The Broken Wheel Inn .... Again	—	$5		Warner 8098
				ALLEN, Judy '78				
1/28/78	94	4		Sweet Little Devil .... He Was Fire	—	$5		Polydor 14440
				ALLEN, Melody '75				
2/1/75	91	6		1 Once Again I Go To Sleep With Lovin' On My Mind .... You've Got A Way With Love	—	$5		Mercury 73638
5/10/75	68	8		2 May You Rest In Peace .... When Someone Wants To Leave	—	$5		Mercury 73674
				ALLEN, Red — see OSBORNE BROTHERS				
				ALLEN, Rex '53				
				Born on 12/31/20 in Willcox, Arizona. Died after being struck by a car on 12/17/99 (age 78). Singer/guitarist/actor. Professional rodeo rider as a teenager. Acted in several western movies. Narrator for several Disney nature movies. Played "Bill Baxter" on TV's *Frontier Doctor*. Father of **Rex Allen Jr.**				
9/3/49	14	1		1 Afraid .... J:14 Cottage In The Clouds	—	$20		Mercury 6192
				REX ALLEN AND The Arizona Wranglers with Jerry Byrd				
4/21/51	10	1		2 Sparrow In The Tree Top .... J:10 Always You	28	$25		Mercury 5597-X45
				Harry Geller (orch.); Jud Conlin Singers (backing vocals)				
8/8/53	4	13		3 Crying In The Chapel .... S:4 / J:4 / A:6 I Thank The Lord	8	$20		Decca 28758
				#3 Pop hit for **Elvis Presley** in 1965				
8/14/61	21	4		4 Marines, Let's Go .... Heartaches Of A Fool	—	$12		Mercury 71844
				title song from the movie starring Tom Reese				
9/29/62	4	13		5 Don't Go Near The Indians .... Touched So Deeply	17	$12		Mercury 71997
				The Merry Melody Singers (backing vocals)				
1/11/64	44	3		6 Tear After Tear .... I'm Just Killin' Time (Till This Heartache Kills Me)	—	$10	■	Mercury 72205
6/22/68	71	5		7 Tiny Bubbles .... Jose Villa Lobo Alfredo Thomaso Vincente Lopez	—	$8		Decca 32322
				#57 Pop hit for Don Ho in 1967				

DEBUT	PEAK	WKS	Gold	A-side (Chart Hit)	B-side	Pop	$	Pic	Label & Number

ALLEN, Rex Jr. ★160★   U.S. Army   '77
Born on 8/23/47 in Chicago. Singer/songwriter/guitarist. Son of **Rex Allen**. Traveled with his father from age six. Formed the groups the Townsmen and Saturday's Children. Served in the U.S. Army from 1967-69. Hosted TNN's *Nashville On The Road* and worked as a regular performer on **The Statler Brothers** Show.

1) Two Less Lonely People 2) Lonely Street 3) No, No, No (I'd Rather Be Free) 4) Me And My Broken Heart 5) With Love

DEBUT	PEAK	WKS	#	A-side	B-side	Pop	$	Label & Number
12/29/73+	63	10	1	The Great Mail Robbery	Start Again	—	$6	Warner 7753
4/20/74	19	14	2	Goodbye	The Same Old Way	—	$6	Warner 7788
8/24/74	31	14	3	Another Goodbye Song	Yes We Have Love	—	$6	Warner 8000
12/7/74+	36	11	4	Never Coming Back Again	I Can See Clearly Now	—	$6	Warner 8046
5/31/75	70	7	5	Lying In My Arms	She Just Said Goodbye	—	$6	Warner 8095
1/24/76	34	9	6	Play Me No Sad Songs	She Just Said Goodbye	—	$6	Warner 8171
5/1/76	17	12	7	Can You Hear Those Pioneers	Streets Of Laredo	—	$6	Warner 8204
				Rex Allen and The Sons of The Pioneers (guest vocals)				
8/7/76	18	13	8	Teardrops In My Heart	Home-Made Love	—	$6	Warner 8236
12/11/76+	8	16	9	Two Less Lonely People	I Gotta Remember To Forget You	—	$6	Warner 8297
4/9/77	10	12	10	I'm Getting Good At Missing You (Solitaire)	Don't Say Goodbye	—	$6	Warner 8354
8/6/77	15	11	11	Don't Say Goodbye	There's No Use Hanging On	—	$6	Warner 8418
11/12/77+	8	15	12	Lonely Street	Don't It Make You Want To Go Home	—	$6	Warner 8482
				#5 Pop hit for Andy Williams in 1959				
3/25/78	8	15	13	No, No, No (I'd Rather Be Free)	I Got A Name	—	$6	Warner 8541
7/29/78	10	12	14	With Love	You Turned It On Again Last Night	—	$6	Warner 8608
11/25/78+	12	14	15	It's Time We Talk Things Over	Watch Me Cry	—	$6	Warner 8697
				REX ALLEN, JR. AND THE BOYS				
4/14/79	9	12	16	Me And My Broken Heart	Lovin' You Is Everything To Me	—	$6	Warner 8786
8/4/79	18	12	17	If I Fell In Love With You	Pick Up The Pieces	—	$5	Warner 49020
2/16/80	25	10	18	Yippy Cry Yi	She Has My Heart	—	$5	Warner 49168
5/24/80	14	13	19	It's Over	Why Did You Stop Lovin' Me	—	$5	Warner 49128
9/27/80	25	12	20	Drink It Down, Lady	What Was Your Name?	—	$5	Warner 49562
12/20/80+	12	14	21	Cup Of Tea	Goodbye	—	$5	Warner 49626
				REX ALLEN, JR. AND MARGO SMITH				
3/14/81	35	9	22	Just A Country Boy	Cat's In The Cradle	—	$5	Warner 49682
6/13/81	26	12	23	While The Feeling's Good	Watered Down Love	—	$5	Warner 49738
				REX ALLEN, JR. & MARGO SMITH				
3/27/82	43	10	24	Last Of The Silver Screen Cowboys	Round Up Time	—	$5	■ Warner 50035
				Rex Allen and Roy Rogers (guest vocals)				
7/10/82	44	10	25	Cowboy In A Three Piece Business Suit	Round Up Time	—	$5	Warner 29968
11/27/82	85	3	26	Ride Cowboy Ride	Three Friends Have I	—	$5	Warner 29890
10/22/83	37	15	27	The Air That I Breathe	Whiskey Cheer	—	$6	Moon Shine 3017
				#6 Pop hit for The Hollies in 1974				
3/10/84	44	9	28	Sweet Rosanna	You Sure Could Have Fooled Me	—	$6	Moon Shine 3022
7/14/84	18	16	29	Dream On Texas Ladies		—	$6	Moon Shine 3030
11/10/84+	24	19	30	Running Down Memory Lane	S:17 / A:26 Shameless Love	—	$6	Moon Shine 3034
4/20/85	62	7	31	When You Held Me In Your Arms		—	$6	Moon Shine 3036
11/14/87	59	8	32	We're Staying Together	Diamond In The Rough	—	$7	TNP 75010

ALLEN, Rosalie   Yodeler   '46
Born Julie Marlene Bedra on 6/27/24 in Old Forge, Pennsylvania. Hosted own TV show in New York City from 1949-53. Known as "The Prairie Star" and "Queen of The Yodelers."   See Wynn Stewart

DEBUT	PEAK	WKS	#	A-side	B-side	Pop	$	Label & Number
8/17/46	3	4	1	Guitar Polka (Old Monterey) /				
8/10/46	5	1	2	I Want To Be A Cowboy's Sweetheart		—	$30	RCA Victor 20-1924
2/4/50	7	4	3	Beyond The Sunset	A:7 The Game Of Broken Hearts		$30	RCA Victor 47-3105
				THE THREE SUNS with ROSALIE ALLEN and ELTON BRITT				
				78 rpm: 20-3599; #71 Pop hit for Pat Boone in 1959				
2/25/50	3	10	4	Quicksilver	A:3 / J:6 / S:9 The Yodel Blues		$30	RCA Victor 48-0168
				ELTON BRITT and ROSALIE ALLEN with The Skytoppers				
				78 rpm: 21-0157				

ALLEY, Jim   '68
Born in Hemphill, West Virginia. Singer/guitarist.

DEBUT	PEAK	WKS	#	A-side	B-side	Pop	$	Label & Number
1/20/68	73	2	1	Only Daddy That'll Walk The Line	When You Were Here	—	$15	Dot 17051
3/15/75	96	2	2	Her Memory's Gonna Kill Me	If I Didn't Have A Dime	—	$8	Avco 606

ALMOST BROTHERS, The   '86
Duo from New York City: guitarist/songwriter/producer Mike Ragogna and guitarist/pianist Steve Mosto.

DEBUT	PEAK	WKS	#	A-side	B-side	Pop	$	Label & Number
8/17/85	55	7	1	Don't Tell Me Love Is Kind	Nightime Fantasy	—	$5	MTM 72053
2/22/86	63	6	2	Birds Of A Feather	I Wanna Kiss The Bride	—	$5	MTM 72062
8/9/86	72	6	3	What's Your Name	Adventures In Love	—	$5	MTM 72072
				#7 Pop hit for Don & Juan in 1962				
11/22/86	52	8	4	I Don't Love Her Anymore	Nightime Fantasy	—	$5	MTM 72079

ALVIN & THE CHIPMUNKS — see **CHIPMUNKS, The**

AMARILLO — see **GRANT, Barry**

DEBUT	PEAK	WKS	Gold	A-side (Chart Hit)	B-side	Pop	$	Pic	Label & Number
				AMAZING RHYTHM ACES, The '76					
				Country-rock group from Memphis: **Russell Smith** (vocals, guitar), Barry "Byrd" Burton (guitar, dobro), Billy Earhart III (keyboards), James Hooker (piano), Jeff "Stick" Davis (bass) and Butch McDade (drums). Burton left in 1977; replaced by Duncan Cameron. Earhart joined **The Bama Band** in 1986. Cameron joined **Sawyer Brown** in 1991. McDade died of cancer on 11/29/98 (age 52).					
7/5/75	11	14		1 Third Rate Romance	Mystery Train	14	$6		ABC 12078
11/29/75+	9	14		2 Amazing Grace (Used To Be Her Favorite Song)	The Beautiful Lie	72	$6		ABC 12142
8/7/76	12	14		3 The End Is Not In Sight (The Cowboy Tune)	Same Ole' Me	42	$6		ABC 12202
7/15/78	100	1		4 Ashes Of Love	All That I Had Left (With You)	—	$6		ABC 12369
3/24/79	88	4		5 Lipstick Traces (On A Cigarette)	Whispering In The Night	104	$6		ABC 12454
				#48 Pop hit for The O'Jays in 1965					
11/29/80	77	6		6 I Musta Died And Gone To Texas	Give Me Flowers While I'm Living	—	$5		Warner 49600
				AMERICA THE BEAUTIFUL '01					
				All-star group: **Trace Adkins**, **Billy Dean**, **Vince Gill**, **Carolyn Dawn Johnson**, **Toby Keith**, **Brenda Lee**, **Lonestar**, **Martina McBride**, **Jamie O'Neal**, **Kenny Rogers** and **Keith Urban**.					
7/21/01	58	6		America The Beautiful	—				album cut
				available only as a computer download track					
			★	**AMES, Durelle** '87					
				Born Durelle Upchurch on 5/4/65 in Gaffney, South Carolina. Female singer. Also recorded as **De De Ames**.					
8/15/87	72	5		1 Dancin' In The Moonlight	—		$6		Advantage 175
1/16/88	75	4		2 Break Down The Walls			$6		Advantage 185
				DE DE AMES					
				AMY '79					
2/3/79	76	4		Please Be Gentle	Jump Into My Love	—	$6		Scorpion 0570
				written by Mac Davis					

				ANDERSON, Bill ★29★ '63					
				Born James William Anderson III on 11/1/37 in Columbia, South Carolina. Singer/songwriter/actor. Worked as a sportswriter in Atlanta and as a DJ in Commerce, Georgia. Joined the *Grand Ole Opry* in 1961. Appeared in such movies as *Las Vegas Hillbillies*, *Forty Acre Feud* and *Road To Nashville*. Hosted own TV show in 1966. Hosted TV game shows *The Better Sex* and *Fandango*. Host of TNN's *Opry Backstage*. Known as "Whispering Bill." Elected to the Country Music Hall of Fame in 2001.					
				1) Mama Sang A Song 2) Still 3) For Loving You 4) My Life (Throw It Away If I Want To) 5) I Get The Fever					
12/29/58+	12	17		1 That's What It's Like To Be Lonesome	Thrill Of My Life	—	$15		Decca 30773
7/6/59	13	19		2 Ninety-Nine	Back Where I Started From	—	$15		Decca 30914
12/28/59+	19	8		3 Dead Or Alive	It's Not The End Of Everything	—	$15		Decca 30993
6/20/60	7	18		4 The Tip Of My Fingers	No Man's Land	—	$12		Decca 31092
12/26/60+	9	14		5 Walk Out Backwards	The Best Of Strangers	—	$12		Decca 31168
7/10/61	9	19		6 Po' Folks	Goodbye Cruel World	—	$12		Decca 31262
4/21/62	14	10		7 Get A Little Dirt On Your Hands	Down Came The Rain	—	$12		Decca 31358
				also see #63 below					
7/28/62	❶⁷	27		8 Mama Sang A Song	On And On And On [S]	89	$10		Decca 31404
2/23/63	❶⁷	27		9 Still	You Made It Easy	8	$10		Decca 31458
8/24/63	2²	23		10 8 X 10	One Mile Over - Two Miles Back	53	$10	■	Decca 31521
1/25/64	5	18		11 Five Little Fingers /		118			
2/15/64	14	20		12 Easy Come-Easy Go		—	$10		Decca 31577
7/25/64	8	16		13 Me	Cincinnati, Ohio [S]	—	$10		Decca 31630
11/14/64+	8	18		14 Three A.M. /		—			
11/7/64	38	5		15 In Case You Ever Change Your Mind		—	$10		Decca 31681
4/3/65	12	17		16 Certain	You Can Have Her	—	$10		Decca 31743
9/4/65	11	16		17 Bright Lights And Country Music	Born	—	$10		Decca 31825
2/12/66	4	24		18 I Love You Drops /		—			
1/22/66	11	13	★	19 Golden Guitar	[S]	—	$10		Decca 31890
2/19/66	29	8		20 I Know You're Married (But I Love You Still) /		—			
3/12/66	44	1		21 Time Out		—	$10		Decca 31884
				BILL ANDERSON AND JAN HOWARD (above 2)					
8/27/66	❶¹	20		22 I Get The Fever	The First Mrs. Jones	—	$8		Decca 31999
1/14/67	5	19		23 Get While The Gettin's Good	Something To Believe In	—	$8		Decca 32077
7/1/67	10	19		24 No One's Gonna Hurt You Anymore /		—			
7/15/67	64	5		25 Papa	[S]	—	$8		Decca 32146
10/28/67	❶⁴	20		26 For Loving You	The Untouchables [S]	—	$8		Decca 32197
				BILL ANDERSON And JAN HOWARD					
11/11/67	42	9		27 Stranger On The Run	Happiness	—	$8	■	Decca 32215
3/16/68	2¹	18		28 Wild Week-End	Fun While It Lasted	—	$8		Decca 32276
8/17/68	2²	16		29 Happy State Of Mind	Time's Been Good To Me	—	$8		Decca 32360
3/1/69	❶²	19		30 My Life (Throw It Away If I Want To)	To Be Alone	—	$8		Decca 32445
7/12/69	2³	15		31 But You Know I Love You	A Picture From Life's Other Side	—	$8		Decca 32514
				#19 Pop hit for Kenny Rogers & The First Edition in 1969					
11/15/69+	2¹	15		32 If It's All The Same To You	I Thank God For You	—	$8		Decca 32511
				BILL ANDERSON And JAN HOWARD					

DEBUT	PEAK	WKS	Gold	A-side (Chart Hit)	B-side	Pop	$	Pic	Label & Number
				ANDERSON, Bill — Cont'd					
3/14/70	5	15		33 Love Is A Sometimes Thing	And I'm Still Missing You	—	$8		Decca 32643
				BILL ANDERSON And The Po' Boys					
				"live" recording					
6/20/70	4	15		34 Someday We'll Be Together	Who Is The Biggest Fool	—	$8		Decca 32689
				BILL ANDERSON And JAN HOWARD					
				#1 Pop hit for Diana Ross & The Supremes in 1969					
10/24/70	6	14		35 Where Have All Our Heroes Gone	Loving A Memory [S]	93	$8		Decca 32744
3/13/71	6	15		36 Always Remember	You Can Change My World	111	$8		Decca 32793
7/24/71	3	17		37 Quits	I'll Live For You	—	$8		Decca 32850
10/9/71	4	15		38 Dis-Satisfied	Knowing You're Mine	—	$8		Decca 32877
				BILL ANDERSON AND JAN HOWARD					
3/18/72	5	15		39 All The Lonely Women In The World	It Was Time For Me To Move On Anyway	—	$8		Decca 32930
9/9/72	2²	16		40 Don't She Look Good	I'm Just Gone	—	$8		Decca 33002
2/24/73	2¹	14		41 If You Can Live With It (I Can Live Without It)	Let's Fall Apart	—	$5		MCA 40004
7/7/73	2³	15		42 The Corner Of My Life	Home And Things	—	$5		MCA 40070
12/15/73+	❶¹	14		43 World Of Make Believe	Gonna Shine It On Again	—	$5		MCA 40164
6/1/74	24	14		44 Can I Come Home To You	I'm Happily Married (And Planning On Staying That Way)	—	$5		MCA 40243
10/5/74	7	13		45 Every Time I Turn The Radio On	You Are My Story (You Are My Song)	—	$5		MCA 40304
2/8/75	14	11		46 I Still Feel The Same About You	Talk To Me Ohio	—	$5		MCA 40351
5/10/75	36	11		47 Country D.J.	We Made Love (But Where's The Love We Made)	—	$5		MCA 40404
8/23/75	24	11		48 Thanks	Why'd The Last Time Have To Be The Best	—	$5		MCA 40443
11/29/75+	❶¹	16		49 Sometimes	Circle In A Triangle	—	$5		MCA 40488
3/27/76	7	12		50 That's What Made Me Love You	Can We Still Be Friends	—	$5		MCA 40533
				BILL ANDERSON and MARY LOU TURNER (above 2)					
8/14/76	10	14		51 Peanuts And Diamonds	Your Love Blows Me Away	—	$5		MCA 40595
12/4/76+	6	14		52 Liars One, Believers Zero	Let Me Whisper Darling One More Time	—	$5		MCA 40661
5/7/77	7	13		53 Head To Toe	Love Song For Jackie	—	$5		MCA 40713
7/16/77	18	12		54 Where Are You Going, Billy Boy	Sad Ole Shade Of Gray	—	$5		MCA 40753
				BILL ANDERSON and MARY LOU TURNER					
10/1/77	11	12		55 Still The One	This Ole Suitcase	—	$5		MCA 40794
				#5 Pop hit for Orleans in 1976					
1/28/78	25	10		56 I'm Way Ahead Of You	Just Enough To Make Me Want It All	—	$5		MCA 40852
				BILL ANDERSON & MARY LOU TURNER					
4/29/78	4	14		57 I Can't Wait Any Longer	Joanna	80	$5		MCA 40893
11/11/78	30	9		58 Double S	Married Lady [S]	—	$5		MCA 40964
2/17/79	20	13		59 This Is A Love Song	Remembering The Good	—	$5		MCA 40992
7/21/79	40	9		60 The Dream Never Dies	One More Sexy Lady	—	$5		MCA 41060
				BILL ANDERSON & THE PO' FOLKS					
				#48 Pop hit for The Cooper Brothers in 1978					
12/8/79+	51	8		61 More Than A Bedroom Thing	Love Me And I'll Be Your Best Friend	—	$5		MCA 41150
4/12/80	35	9		62 Make Mine Night Time	The Old Me And You	—	$5		MCA 41212
6/21/80	46	7		63 Get A Little Dirt On Your Hands	What Can I Do [R]	—	$5		Columbia 11277
				DAVID ALLAN COE AND BILL ANDERSON					
				new version of #7 above					
8/23/80	58	7		64 Rock 'N' Roll To Rock Of Ages	I'm Used To The Rain	—	$5		MCA 41297
11/22/80	83	3		65 I Want That Feelin' Again	She Made Me Remember	—	$5		MCA 51017
2/21/81	44	8		66 Mister Peepers	How Married Are You, Mary Ann?	—	$5		MCA 51052
8/15/81	74	4		67 Homebody	(Her Wedding Ring's A) One Man Band	—	$5		MCA 51150
				WHISPERING BILL ANDERSON					
12/26/81+	76	4		68 Whiskey Made Me Stumble (The Devil Made Me Fall)	All That Keeps Me Goin'	—	$5		MCA 51204
8/21/82	42	10		69 Southern Fried	You Turn The Light On	—	$5		Southern Tracks 1007
12/25/82+	82	5		70 Laid Off	Lovin' Tonight	—	$5		Southern Tracks 1011
3/12/83	70	6		71 Thank You Darling	Lovin' Tonight [S]	—	$5		Southern Tracks 1014
7/9/83	71	6		72 Son Of The South /		—			
		6		73 20th Century Fox		—	$5		Southern Tracks 1021
5/12/84	76	7		74 Your Eyes	I Never Get Enough Of You	—	$5		Southern Tracks 1026
2/9/85	58	7		75 Wino The Clown	Wild Weekend	—	$5		Swanee 4013
4/27/85	62	6		76 Pity Party	Don't She Look Good	—	$5		Swanee 5015
8/17/85	75	5		77 When You Leave That Way You Can Never Go Back	Quits	—	$5		Swanee 5018
12/27/86+	80	5		78 Sheet Music	Maybe Go Down	—	$5		Southern Tracks 1067
5/9/87	78	5		79 No Ordinary Memory	Sheet Music	—	$5		Southern Tracks 1077
2/9/91	60	6		80 Deck Of Cards	Thank You Darling [S]	—	$5	■	Curb 76855 (v)
				ANDERSON, Ivie '44					
				Born on 7/10/05 in Gilroy, California. Died of asthma on 12/28/49 (age 44). Female vocalist with Duke Ellington's band from 1931-42.					
4/8/44	4	2		Mexico Joe	When The Ships Come Sailing Home Again	16	$50		Exclusive 3113
				IVIE ANDERSON with CEELLE BURKE'S ORCH.					

DEBUT	PEAK	WKS	Gold	A-side (Chart Hit)	B-side	Pop	$	Pic	Label & Number

ANDERSON, John ★59★   '83

Born on 12/13/54 in Orlando, Florida; raised in Apopka, Florida. Singer/songwriter/guitarist. While a teenager led the groups the Weed Seeds and the Living End. Sang with sister Donna in the early '70s. Moved to Nashville in 1971. Worked construction on the new Grand Ole Opry building. Worked as a staff writer with Gallico Music. CMA Award: 1983 Horizon Award.

1) Wild And Blue 2) Black Sheep 3) Money In The Bank 4) Straight Tequila Night 5) Swingin'

DEBUT	PEAK	WKS	#	A-side	B-side	Pop	$	Label & Number
12/10/77+	62	8	1	I've Got A Feelin' (Somebody Stealin')	It's All The Way Together	—	$5	Warner 8480
6/24/78	69	5	2	Whine, Whistle, Whine	If There Were No Memories	—	$5	Warner 8585
11/25/78	40	9	3	The Girl At The End Of The Bar	You're Pleasin' Me	—	$5	Warner 8705
3/24/79	41	8	4	My Pledge Of Love	Why Baby Why	—	$5	Warner 8770
				#14 Pop hit for The Joe Jeffrey Group in 1969				
7/14/79	31	11	5	Low Dog Blues	Girl, For You	—	$5	Warner 8863
10/27/79+	15	16	6	Your Lying Blue Eyes	Mountain High, Valley Low	—	$5	Warner 49089
3/15/80	13	15	7	She Just Started Liking Cheatin' Songs	I Wish I Could Write You A Song	—	$5	Warner 49191
7/26/80	21	14	8	If There Were No Memories	Shoot Low Sheriff!	—	$5	Warner 49275
11/22/80+	7	17	9	1959	It Looks Like The Party Is Over	—	$5	Warner 49582
3/28/81	4	16	10	I'm Just An Old Chunk Of Coal (But I'm Gonna Be A Diamond Someday)	Havin' Hard Times	—	$5	Warner 49699
8/1/81	8	15	11	Chicken Truck /		—		
8/1/81	54	15	12	I Love You A Thousand Ways		—	$5	Warner 49772
11/21/81+	7	18	13	I Just Came Home To Count The Memories	Girl, For You	—	$5	Warner 49860
4/17/82	6	19	14	Would You Catch A Falling Star	I Danced With San Antonio Rose	—	$5	Warner 50043
9/25/82	❶²	20	15	Wild And Blue	Honky Tonk Hearts	—	$5	Warner 29917
1/15/83	❶¹	22	16	Swingin'	A Honky Tonk Saturday Night	43	$5	Warner 29788
				CMA Award: Single of the Year				
6/25/83	5	17	17	Goin' Down Hill	If A Broken Heart Could Kill	—	$5	Warner 29585
9/24/83	❶¹	21	18	Black Sheep	Call On Me	—	$5	Warner 29497
1/14/84	10	16	19	Let Somebody Else Drive	Old Mexico	—	$5	Warner 29385
5/12/84	14	17	20	I Wish I Could Write You A Song	The Sun's Gonna Shine (On Our Back Door)	—	$5	Warner 29276
8/18/84	3	25	21	She Sure Got Away With My Heart	S:3 / A:3 Lonely Is Another State	—	$5	Warner 29207
12/8/84+	20	17	22	Eye Of A Hurricane	S:18 / A:21 Chicken Truck	—	$5	Warner 29127
5/4/85	15	17	23	It's All Over Now	A:14 / S:15 Only Your Love	—	$5	Warner 29002
				#26 Pop hit for The Rolling Stones in 1964				
8/24/85	30	14	24	Tokyo, Oklahoma	A:29 / S:30 Willie's Gone	—	$5	Warner 28916
11/16/85+	12	22	25	Down In Tennessee	S:11 / A:14 I've Got Me A Woman	—	$5	Warner 28855
3/22/86	31	11	26	You Can't Keep A Good Memory Down	What's So Different About You	—	$5	Warner 28748
8/16/86	10	22	27	Honky Tonk Crowd	S:4 / A:11 If I Could Have My Way	—	$5	Warner 28639
12/6/86+	44	12	28	Countrified	Yellow Creek	—	$5	Warner 28502
3/7/87	55	8	29	What's So Different About You	Wife's Little Pleasures	—	$5	Warner 28433
9/5/87	48	8	30	When Your Yellow Brick Road Turns Blue	Lying In Her Arms	—	$4	MCA 53155
12/5/87+	23	15	31	Somewhere Between Ragged And Right	Just For You	—	$4	MCA 53226
				Waylon Jennings (guest vocal)				
4/23/88	65	4	32	It's Hard To Keep This Ship Together	There's Nothing Left For Me To Take For Granted	—	$4	MCA 53307
7/9/88	35	12	33	If It Ain't Broke Don't Fix It	Just To Hold A Little Hand	—	$4	MCA 53366
11/5/88	68	4	34	Down In The Orange Grove	The Will Of God	—	$4	MCA 53441
2/11/89	73	4	35	Lower On The Hog	The Ballad Of Zero And The Tramp	—	$4	MCA 53485
10/14/89	66	5	36	Who's Lovin' My Baby	There Was A Time When I Was Alone	—	$4	Universal 66020
9/28/91	67	3	37	Who Got Our Love	Steamy Windows	—	$4	■ BNA 62062 (v)
12/21/91+	❶¹	20	38	Straight Tequila Night	Seminole Wind	—	$4	BNA 62140
4/18/92	3	20	39	When It Comes To You	Cold Day In Hell	—	$4	■ BNA 62235 (v)
				first recorded by Dire Straits on their 1991 On Every Street album				
8/15/92	2²	20	40	Seminole Wind	Steamy Windows	—	$4	BNA 62312
11/28/92+	7	20	41	Let Go Of The Stone	Look Away	—	$4	BNA 62410
5/1/93	❶¹	20	42	Money In The Bank	Nashville Tears	—	$4	■ BNA 62443 (v)
8/28/93	13	20	43	I Fell In The Water	All Things To All Things	—	$4	BNA 62621
12/11/93+	3	20	44	I've Got It Made	Can't Get Away From You	—	$4	BNA 62709
4/23/94	4	20	45	I Wish I Could Have Been There	Solid Ground	—	$4	BNA 62795
10/1/94	35	10	46	Country 'Til I Die	Swingin'	—	$4	■ BNA 62935 (v)
12/10/94+	3	20	47	Bend It Until It Breaks	Keep Your Hands To Yourself	—	$4	BNA 64260
12/31/94	57	2	48	Christmas Time	[X]	—		album cut
				from the album Christmas Time on BNA 66411				
4/22/95	15	20	49	Mississippi Moon	It Ain't Pneumonia, It's The Blues	—	$4	BNA 64274
12/9/95+	26	20	50	Paradise	Bad Weather	—	$4	■ BNA 64465 (v)
3/9/96	51	10	51	Long Hard Lesson Learned	Paradise	—	$4	BNA 64498
6/22/96	67	4	52	My Kind Of Crazy	Long Hard Lesson Learned	—	$4	BNA 64573
7/5/97	22	20	53	Somebody Slap Me	S:11 We've Got A Good Thing Goin'	115	$4	■ Mercury 574640 (v)
9/27/97	44	11	54	Small Town	The Fall	—	$4	Mercury 574948
1/17/98	41	12	55	Takin' The Country Back	Brown Eyed Girl	—	$4	Mercury 568496
4/29/00	56	8	56	You Ain't Hurt Nothin' Yet	S:25 I Love You Again	—	$4	★ Epic 79413
9/30/00	55	9	57	Nobody's Got It All	S:14 I Ain't Afraid Of Dying	—	$4	★ Epic 79481

DEBUT	PEAK	WKS	Gold	A-side (Chart Hit)	B-side	Pop	$	Pic	Label & Number
	★292★			**ANDERSON, Liz**		'67			

Born Elizabeth Jane Haaby on 3/13/30 in Roseau, Minnesota; raised in Grand Forks, North Dakota. Singer/songwriter/guitarist. Mother of **Lynn Anderson**.

1)Mama Spank 2)The Game Of Triangles 3)Mother, May I

DEBUT	PEAK	WKS		A-side	B-side	Pop	$		Label & Number
4/2/66	23	10	1	Go Now Pay Later	The Bottle Turned Into A Blonde	—	$10		RCA Victor 8778
7/30/66	45	4	2	So Much For Me, So Much For You	Release Me	—	$10		RCA Victor 8861
10/15/66	5	17	3	The Game Of Triangles	Bye Bye, Love	—	$10		RCA Victor 8963
				BOBBY BARE, NORMA JEAN, LIZ ANDERSON					
12/3/66+	22	12	4	The Wife Of The Party	Fairytale	—	$10		RCA Victor 8999
4/22/67	5	17	5	Mama Spank	To The Landlord	—	$8		RCA Victor 9163
9/2/67	24	13	6	Tiny Tears	Grandma's House	—	$8		RCA Victor 9271
12/23/67+	40	12	7	Thanks For Tryin' Anyway	Come Walk In My Shoes	—	$8		RCA Victor 9378
2/24/68	21	12	8	Mother, May I	Better Than Life Without You	—	$8		RCA Victor 9445
				LIZ ANDERSON AND LYNN ANDERSON					
5/11/68	43	9	9	Like A Merry-Go-Round	Thanks, But No Thanks	—	$8		RCA Victor 9508
8/31/68	58	4	10	Cry, Cry Again /			—		
8/24/68	65	7	11	Me, Me, Me, Me, Me			$8		RCA Victor 9586
11/23/68	51	5	12	Love Is Ending	Blue Are The Violets	—	$8		RCA Victor 9650
2/14/70	26	8	13	Husband Hunting	All You Add Is Love	—	$8		RCA Victor 9796
8/15/70	64	6	14	All Day Sucker	Wonder If I'll Feel This Bad Tomorrow	—	$8		RCA Victor 9876
12/19/70	75	2	15	When I'm Not Lookin'	Only For Me	—	$8		RCA Victor 9924
10/23/71	69	3	16	It Don't Do No Good To Be A Good Girl	That's What Loving You Has Meant To Me	—	$6		Epic 10782
4/8/72	56	7	17	I'll Never Fall In Love Again	You Buy The Wine	—	$6		Epic 10840
				#6 Pop hit for Dionne Warwick in 1970					
8/12/72	67	4	18	Astrology	Living One Day At A Time	—	$6		Epic 10896
3/17/73	72	2	19	Time To Love Again	Wearing A Smile	—	$6		Epic 10952

ANDERSON, Lynn ★54★ '71

Born on 9/26/47 in Grand Forks, North Dakota; raised in Sacramento, California. Singer/songwriter/guitarist/actress. Daughter of **Liz Anderson**. An accomplished equestrian, she was the California Horse Show Queen in 1966. Regular on **Lawrence Welk**'s TV show from 1968. Acted in the movie *Country Gold*. Married to **Glenn Sutton** from 1968-77. CMA Award: 1971 Female Vocalist of the Year. Also see **Heart Of Nashville** and **Tomorrow's World**.

1)Rose Garden 2)How Can I Unlove You 3)You're My Man 4)Keep Me In Mind 5)What A Man, My Man Is

DEBUT	PEAK	WKS		A-side	B-side	Pop	$		Label & Number
10/29/66+	36	17	1	Ride, Ride, Ride	Tear By Tear	—	$8		Chart 1375
3/18/67	5	19	2	If I Kiss You (Will You Go Away)	Then Go	—	$8		Chart 1430
7/1/67	49	6	3	Keeping Up Appearances	You've Gotta Be The Greatest	—	$8		Chart 1425
				LYNN ANDERSON & JERRY LANE					
8/12/67	28	13	4	Too Much Of You	If This Is Love	—	$8		Chart 1475
12/2/67+	4	18	5	Promises, Promises	It Makes You Happy	—	$8		Chart 1010
2/24/68	21	12	6	Mother, May I	Better Than Life Without You	—	$8		RCA Victor 9445
				LIZ ANDERSON AND LYNN ANDERSON					
3/30/68	8	14	7	No Another Time	The Worst Is Yet To Come	—	$8		Chart 1026
8/3/68	12	14	8	Big Girls Don't Cry	I Keep Forgettin' (That I Forgot About You)	—	$8		Chart 1042
11/30/68+	11	14	9	Flattery Will Get You Everywhere	A Million Shades Of Blue	—	$8		Chart 1059
3/8/69	18	12	10	Our House Is Not A Home (If It's Never Been Loved In)	Wave Bye Bye To The Man	—	$8		Chart 5001
8/2/69	2[2]	15	11	That's A No No	If Silence Is Golden	—	$8		Chart 5021
11/22/69	15	12	12	He'd Still Love Me	All You Add Is Love	—	$8		Chart 5040
2/14/70	16	10	13	I've Been Everywhere	A Penny For Your Thoughts	—	$8		Chart 5053
3/21/70	7	16	14	Stay There 'Til I Get There	I'd Run A Mile To You	—	$6		Columbia 45101
6/6/70	17	10	15	Rocky Top	Take Me Home	—	$8		Chart 5068
8/1/70	15	12	16	No Love At All /					
				#16 Pop hit for **B.J. Thomas** in 1971					
		12	17	I Found You Just In Time		—	$6		Columbia 45190
10/31/70	20	11	18	I'm Alright	Pick Of The Week	112	$8		Chart 5098
11/7/70	❶[5]	20	19	Rose Garden	Nothing Between Us	3	$6	●	Columbia 45252
2/6/71	20	13	20	It Wasn't God Who Made Honky Tonk Angels	Be Quiet Mind	—	$8		Chart 5113
5/8/71	❶[2]	15	21	You're My Man	I'm Gonna Write A Song	63	$6		Columbia 45356
5/15/71	74	3	22	Jim Dandy	Strangers	—	$8		Chart 5125
				#17 Pop hit for **LaVern Baker** in 1957					
7/24/71	54	5	23	He Even Woke Me Up To Say Goodbye	The Pillow That Whispers	—	$8		Chart 5136
8/21/71	❶[3]	16	24	How Can I Unlove You	Don't Say Things You Don't Mean	63	$5		Columbia 45429
1/29/72	3	16	25	Cry	Simple Words	71	$5		Columbia 45529
				#1 Pop hit for **Johnnie Ray** in 1951					
6/10/72	4	13	26	Listen To A Country Song	That's What Loving You Has Meant To Me	107	$5		Columbia 45615
10/14/72	4	14	27	Fool Me	What's Made Milwaukee Famous	101	$5		Columbia 45692
				#78 Pop hit for **Joe South** in 1971					
1/13/73	❶[1]	16	28	Keep Me In Mind	Rodeo Cowboy	104	$5		Columbia 45768
6/2/73	2[1]	15	29	Top Of The World	I Wish I Was A Little Boy Again	74	$5		Columbia 45857
				#1 Pop hit for the **Carpenters** in 1973					
9/15/73	3	17	30	Sing About Love	Fickle Fortune	—	$5		Columbia 45918
3/9/74	15	13	31	Smile For Me	A Man Like Your Daddy	—	$5		Columbia 46009
6/29/74	7	14	32	Talkin' To The Wall	I Want To Be A Part Of You	—	$5		Columbia 46056
10/26/74	❶[1]	13	33	What A Man, My Man Is	Everything's Falling In Place (For Me And You)	93	$5		Columbia 10041

DEBUT	PEAK	WKS	Gold	A-side (Chart Hit)..B-side	Pop	$	Pic	Label & Number
				ANDERSON, Lynn — Cont'd				
3/8/75	13	12		34 He Turns It Into Love Again.....................Someone To Finish What You Started	—	$5		Columbia 10100
6/28/75	14	14		35 I've Never Loved Anyone More...He Worshiped Me	—	$5		Columbia 10160
11/22/75+	26	11		36 Paradise...We've Got It All Together Now	—	$5		Columbia 10240
2/7/76	20	14		37 All The King's Horses...................................If All I Have To Do Is Just Love You	—	$5		Columbia 10280
6/5/76	44	9		38 Rodeo Cowboy /	—	$5		Columbia 10337
		3		39 Dixieland, You Will Never Die	—	$5		
9/25/76	23	11		40 Sweet Talkin' Man..A Good Old Country Song	—	$5		Columbia 10401
1/22/77	12	14		41 Wrap Your Love All Around Your Man.....I Couldn't Be Lonely (Even If I Wanted To)	—	$5		Columbia 10467
5/28/77	22	10		42 I Love What Love Is Doing To Me................Will I Ever Hear Those Church Bells Ring?	—	$5		Columbia 10545
9/3/77	19	12		43 He Ain't You...It's Your Love That Keeps Me Going	—	$5		Columbia 10597
12/3/77+	26	13		44 We Got Love..Sunshine Man	—	$5		Columbia 10650
4/29/78	44	9		45 Rising Above It All....................................My World Begins And Ends With You	—	$5		Columbia 10721
9/2/78	43	8		46 Last Love Of My Life...When You Marry For Money	—	$5		Columbia 10809
3/10/79	10	13		47 Isn't It Always Love A Child With You Tonight	—	$5		Columbia 10909
6/23/79	18	12		48 I Love How You Love Me...Come As You Are	—	$5		Columbia 11006
				#5 Pop hit for The Paris Sisters in 1961				
10/13/79	33	9		49 Sea Of Heartbreak..Say You Will	—	$5		Columbia 11104
7/5/80	26	13		50 Even Cowgirls Get The Blues ....See Through Me	—	$5		Columbia 11296
10/25/80	27	13		51 Blue Baby Blue..The Lonely Hearts Cafe	—	$5		Columbia 11374
4/9/83	42	11		52 You Can't Lose What You Never Had................This Time The Heartbreak Wins	—	$5		Permian 82000
7/16/83	18	16		53 What I Learned From Loving You..Mr. Sundown	—	$5		Permian 82001
12/17/83+	9	23		54 You're Welcome To Tonight Your Kisses Lied	—	$5		Permian 82003
				LYNN ANDERSON & GARY MORRIS				
9/13/86	49	9		55 Fools For Each Other....................................S:28 Memphis Roots	—	$4		RCA 5005
				ED BRUCE with Lynn Anderson				
12/20/86+	45	9		56 Didn't We Shine..We Must Be Doing It Right	—	$4		Mercury 888209
9/19/87	38	12		57 Read Between The Lines...If This Ain't Love	—	$4		Mercury 888839
7/30/88	24	17		58 Under The Boardwalk...S:24 Turn The Page	—	$4		Mercury 870528
				#4 Pop hit for The Drifters in 1964				
12/3/88+	50	10		59 What He Does Best..It Goes Without Saying	—	$4		Mercury 872220
3/11/89	69	6		60 How Many Hearts..(long version)	—	$4		Mercury 872602
				ANDI AND THE BROWN SISTERS '89				
				Vocal trio from Albany, Oregon: Andi Brown and her sister Robin, with Darby Huffman.				
10/8/88	94	2		1 I'd Do Anything For You, Baby	—	$6		Killer 1013
2/4/89	90	2		2 This Old Feeling	—	$6		Killer 115
				ANDY & THE BROWN SISTERS (above 2)				
5/6/89	79	4		3 Labor Of Love	—	$5		Door Knob 323
7/8/89	84	3		4 Gently Hold Me	—	$5		Door Knob 329
9/30/89	90	2		5 Lighter Shade Of Blue	—	$5		Door Knob 331
11/25/89	70	6		6 Shows You What I Know Lighter Shade Of Blue	—	$5		Door Knob 337
				ANDREWS, Jessica '01				
				Born on 12/29/83 in Huntingdon, Tennessee.				
2/6/99	28	20		1 I Will Be There For You.......................................S:4 (album snippets)	108	$4	★	DreamWor. 459021 (v)
7/10/99	25	20		2 You Go First (Do You Wanna Kiss)..	117			album cut
				from the album *Heart Shaped World* on DreamWorks 450104				
12/11/99+	24	20		3 Unbreakable Heart............................S:4 (acapella version)	110	$4	★	DreamWor. 459042 (v)
6/24/00	53	8		4 I Do Now...	—			album cut
				from the album *Heart Shaped World* on DreamWorks 450104				
11/4/00+	❶³	33		5 Who I Am /	28			
6/9/01	31	19		6 Helplessly, Hopelessly..	—	$4		DreamWorks 450918
				ANDREWS, Sheila '80				
				Born in Alabama; raised in Ohio.				
12/16/78+	88	4		1 Too Fast For Rapid City..Bigger Fool Than I Am	—	$5		Ovation 1116
9/22/79	88	3		2 I Gotta Get Back The Feeling........................Diggin' And A Grindin' For His Love	—	$5		Ovation 1128
1/26/80	48	7		3 What I Had With You...I Gotta Get Back The Feeling	—	$5		Ovation 1138
				SHEILA ANDREWS with Joe Sun				
7/26/80	42	10		4 It Don't Get Better Than This.................The Softer You Touch Me The Harder I Fall	—	$5		Ovation 1146
11/29/80	58	8		5 Where Could You Take Me..Pretty Lies	—	$5		Ovation 1160
				ANDREWS SISTERS '44				
				Vocal trio from Minneapolis: sisters Patty (born on 2/26/18), Maxene (born on 1/3/16; died on 10/21/95, age 79) and LaVerne (born on 7/6/11, died on 5/8/67, age 55) Andrews. Charted 69 pop hits from 1940-51. The trio appeared in several movies.				
1/8/44	❶⁵	11	●	1 Pistol Packin' Mama...Vict'ry Polka (Pop #6)	2⁴	$20		Decca 23277
				BING CROSBY and ANDREWS SISTERS				
4/9/49	2¹	16		2 I'm Bitin' My Fingernails And Thinking Of You / J:2 / S:4	30			
				ANDREWS SISTERS and ERNEST TUBB with The Texas Troubadors				
4/16/49	6	5		3 Don't Rob Another Man's Castle.......................................J:6 / S:10	—	$20		Decca 24592
				ERNEST TUBB and ANDREWS SISTERS with The Texas Troubadors				
				ANGELLE, Lisa '99				
				Born on 12/27/65 in New Orleans. Singer/songwriter.				
4/6/85	78	4		1 Love, It's The Pits...Biloxi Blue	—	$4	■	EMI America 8258
11/16/85	96	3		2 Bring Back Love...Poor Baby	—	$4		EMI America 8294
9/25/99	19ˢ	12		3 I Wear Your Love...Midnight Rodeo	—	$4	★	DreamWor. 459031 (v)
10/30/99	75	1		4 Kiss This...	—			album cut
				from the album *Twisted* on DreamWorks 50196				
8/5/00	62	2		5 A Woman Gets Lonely...	—			album cut

DEBUT	PEAK	WKS	Gold	A-side (Chart Hit)	B-side	Pop	$	Pic	Label & Number
				ANGELLE, Lisa — Cont'd					
3/3/01	50	5		6 I Will You Love You	—				album cut
				above 2 from the album *Lisa Angelle* on DreamWorks 50116					
				ANTHONY, Rayburn		**'79**			
				Born in 1937 in Humboldt, Tennessee. Singer/songwriter/bassist.					
10/9/76	84	5		1 Crazy Again	Mother Country Music	—	$6		Polydor 14346
3/26/77	39	9		2 Lonely Eyes	Walkin'	—	$6		Polydor 14380
6/25/77	57	8		3 Hold Me	Don't Fall In Love	—	$6		Polydor 14398
10/15/77	75	5		4 She Keeps Hangin' On	Talk About A Feeling	—	$6		Polydor 14423
3/25/78	31	9		5 Maybe I Should've Been Listenin'	This Time Marie	—	$6		Polydor 14457
10/21/78	75	5		6 I Thought You Were Easy	This One's For You	—	$5		Mercury 55042
2/3/79	28	11		7 Shadows Of Love	Fire In The Night	—	$5		Mercury 55053
6/23/79	79	3		8 It Won't Go Away	Baby Take It From Me	—	$5		Mercury 55063
10/6/79	60	6		9 The Wild Side Of Life	I Don't Believe I'll Fall In Love Today	—	$5		Mercury 57006
				RAYBURN ANTHONY WITH KITTY WELLS					
				ANTHONY, Vince		**'82**			
				Born in Berwick, Louisiana.					
3/6/82	82	3		Call Me Friend	Leave Me Tonight	—	$8		Midnight Gold 160
				VINCE ANTHONY with The "Country" Blue Notes					
				ANTON, Susan — see KNOBLOCK, Fred					
				ARATA, Tony		**'85**			
				Born on 10/10/57 in Savannah, Georgia. Singer/songwriter/guitarist.					
9/22/84	76	4		1 Come On Home	Maybe I'm Over You	—	$5		Noble Vision 106
2/9/85	65	7		2 Sure Thing	Enjoy The Ride	—	$5		Noble Vision 108
				ARCHER PARK		**'94**			
				Duo of Randy Archer (b: 2/20/59 in Swainsboro, Georgia) and Johnny Park (b: 10/30/57 in Arlington, Texas).					
8/20/94	29	14		1 Where There's Smoke	'Til Something Better Comes Along	—	$4	■	Atlantic 87211 (v)
12/3/94	63	6		2 We Got A Lot In Common	I Still Wanna Jump Your Bones	—	$4	■	Atlantic 87181 (v)
				ARGO, Judy		**'79**			
				Born in Atlanta.					
4/7/79	83	6		1 Night Time Music Man	Country Hall Of Shame	—	$6		ASI 1019
8/11/79	95	3		2 He's A Good Man	Why Me	—	$5	■	MDJ 51379
9/29/79	55	7		3 Hide Me (In The Shadow Of Your Love)	Millionaire Lover	—	$5		MDJ 4633
				ARMSTRONG, Wayne		**'80**			
8/9/80	59	8		Hot Sunday Morning	I Don't Want To Be Alone	—	$5		NSD 57
				ARNOLD, Eddy ★1★		**'48**			
				Born Richard Edward Arnold on 5/15/18 in Henderson, Tennessee. Singer/songwriter/guitarist. Own radio show on WMPS in Memphis from 1934-39. Lead singer of **Pee Wee King**'s Golden West Cowboys from 1940-43. Hosted own TV show from 1952-56. Hosted TV's *Out On The Farm* in 1954. Hosted TV's *Today On The Farm* in 1960. Once known as "The Tennessee Plowboy." Elected to the Country Music Hall of Fame in 1966. CMA Award: 1967 Entertainer of the Year. Also see **Heart Of Nashville** and **Some Of Chet's Friends**.					
				1) I'll Hold You In My Heart (Till I Can Hold You In My Arms) 2) Bouquet Of Roses 3) Don't Rob Another Man's Castle 4) I Wanna Play House With You 5) There's Been A Change In Me					
				EDDY ARNOLD and his Tennessee Plowboys:					
6/30/45	5	2		1 Each Minute Seems A Million Years	The Cattle Call	—	$60		Bluebird 33-0527
7/13/46	7	1		2 All Alone In This World Without You	Can't Win, Can't Place, Can't Show	—	$30		RCA Victor 20-1855
10/12/46	2⁴	17		3 That's How Much I Love You /		—			
10/12/46	3	2		4 Chained To A Memory		—	$30		RCA Victor 20-1948
3/1/47	❶¹	22		5 What Is Life Without Love	Be Sure There's No Mistake	—	$30		RCA Victor 20-2058
5/31/47	❶⁵	38		6 It's A Sin		—			
6/21/47	4	2		7 I Couldn't Believe It Was True		—	$30		RCA Victor 20-2241
				45 rpm: 48-0198					
8/23/47	❶²¹	46		8 I'll Hold You In My Heart (Till I Can Hold In My Arms)	J:❶²¹ / S:7 Don't Bother To Cry	—	$30		RCA Victor 20-2332
				45 rpm: 48-0030					
11/8/47	2²	15		9 To My Sorrow	J:2 Easy Rocking Chair	—	$30		RCA Victor 20-2481
				45 rpm: 48-0197					
2/7/48	10	2		10 Molly Darling	J:10 / S:14 It Makes No Difference Now	—	$30		RCA Victor 20-2489
				45 rpm: 48-0017					
3/20/48	❶⁹	39		11 Anytime /	J:❶⁹ / S:❶³	17			
				#2 Pop hit for Eddie Fisher in 1952					
3/27/48	2⁵	21		12 What A Fool I Was	J:2 / S:7	29	$30		RCA Victor 20-2700
				45 rpm: 48-0002					
5/15/48	❶¹⁹	54	●	13 Bouquet Of Roses /	S:❶¹⁹ / J:❶¹⁸	13			
5/15/48	❶³	26		14 Texarkana Baby	J:❶³ / S:❶¹	18	$30		RCA Victor 20-2806
				45 rpm: 48-0001 (issued with a special "101 Best Seller's" sleeve)					
				EDDY ARNOLD, The Tennessee Plowboy and his Guitar:					
8/28/48	❶⁸	32		15 Just A Little Lovin' (Will Go A Long, Long Way) /	J:❶⁸ / S:❶⁴	13			
8/28/48	5	19		16 My Daddy Is Only A Picture	S:5 / J:6	—	$30		RCA Victor 20-3013
				45 rpm: 48-0026					
11/20/48	❶¹	21		17 A Heart Full Of Love (For A Handful Of Kisses) /	S:❶¹ / J:3	23			
11/20/48+	2¹	17		18 Then I Turned And Walked Slowly Away	J:2 / S:4	30	$30		RCA Victor 20-3174
				45 rpm: 48-0025					

DEBUT	PEAK	WKS	Gold	A-side (Chart Hit) ... B-side	Pop	$	Pic	Label & Number
				ARNOLD, Eddy — Cont'd				
2/5/49	10	1		19 Many Tears Ago J:10 Mommy Please Stay Home With Me	—	$30		RCA Victor 20-1871
				EDDY ARNOLD and his Tennessee Plowboys recorded and released in 1946				
2/19/49	❶¹²	31		20 Don't Rob Another Man's Castle / J:❶¹² / S:❶⁶	23			
2/12/49	3	10		21 There's Not A Thing (I Wouldn't Do For You) J:3 / S:7	—	$30		RCA Victor 21-0002
				45 rpm: 48-0042				
5/14/49	❶³	22		22 One Kiss Too Many / J:❶³ / S:2	23			
5/21/49	2³	19		23 The Echo Of Your Footsteps S:2 / J:3	—	$30		RCA Victor 21-0051
				45 rpm: 48-0083				
7/2/49	❶⁴	22		24 I'm Throwing Rice (At The Girl That I Love) / S:❶⁴ / J:❶³	18			
7/16/49	7	4		25 Show Me The Way Back To Your Heart S:7 / J:11	—	$30		RCA Victor 21-0083
				45 rpm: 48-0080				
12/10/49	5	4		26 Will Santy Come To Shanty Town / A:5 / J:6 / S:8 [X]				
11/19/49	7	8		27 C-H-R-I-S-T-M-A-S S:7 / A:7 / J:9 [X]	—	$30		RCA Victor 21-0124
				45 rpm: 48-0127				
12/17/49+	6	2		28 There's No Wings On My Angel J:6 / S:11 You Know How Talk Gets Around	—	$35		RCA Victor 48-0137
				from the movie Feudin' Rhythm starring Arnold; 78 rpm: 21-0134				
12/31/49+	❶¹	17		29 Take Me In Your Arms And Hold Me / J:❶¹ / A:4 / S:5				
				answer to #8 above				
1/14/50	6	7		30 Mama And Daddy Broke My Heart S:6 / J:8	—	$35		RCA Victor 48-0150
				78 rpm: 21-0146				
4/15/50	3	12		31 Little Angel With The Dirty Face / S:3 / J:7 / A:10				
4/22/50	3	13		32 Why Should I Cry? J:3 / S:5 / A:5	—	$35		RCA Victor 48-0300
7/1/50	2²	17		33 Cuddle Buggin' Baby / S:2 / J:3 / A:4				
7/1/50	6	12		34 Enclosed, One Broken Heart J:6 / S:7 / A:7	—	$35		RCA Victor 48-0342
9/30/50	2⁸	16		35 The Lovebug Itch S:2 / A:2 / J:2				
12/9/50	10	1		36 A Prison Without Walls J:10	—	$35		RCA Victor 48-0382
1/13/51	❶¹¹	23		37 There's Been A Change In Me A:❶¹¹ / S:❶⁴ / J:2 Tie Me To Your Apron Strings Again	—	$30		RCA Victor 48-0412
2/24/51	8	5		38 May The Good Lord Bless And Keep You S:8 / A:10 I'm Writing A Letter To The Lord	—	$30		RCA Victor 48-0425
4/14/51	❶³	17		39 Kentucky Waltz S:❶³ / J:❶³ / A:4 A Million Miles From Your Heart	—	$30		RCA Victor 48-0444
6/23/51	❶¹¹	24		40 I Wanna Play House With You / J:❶¹¹ / S:❶⁶ / A:2				
7/7/51	4	9		41 Something Old, Something New J:4 / S:7	—	$30		RCA Victor 48-0476
10/27/51	2¹	16		42 Somebody's Been Beatin' My Time / J:2 / A:3 / S:5				
10/27/51	5	12		43 Heart Strings S:5 / J:8	—	$25		RCA Victor 47-4273
1/26/52	4	12		44 Bundle Of Southern Sunshine S:4 / J:4 / A:5	—	$25		RCA Victor 47-4413
2/23/52	9	1		45 Call Her Your Sweetheart A:9	—	$25		RCA Victor 47-4413
4/5/52	❶¹	14		46 Easy On The Eyes S:❶¹ / A:4 / J:6 Anything That's Part Of You	—	$25		RCA Victor 47-4569
7/19/52	❶⁴	18		47 A Full Time Job A:❶⁴ / S:3 / J:3 Shepherd Of My Heart	—	$25		RCA Victor 47-4787
10/25/52	3	11		48 Older And Bolder S:3 / J:4 / A:7				
12/6/52	9	1		49 I'd Trade All Of My Tomorrows (For Just One Yesterday) J:9	—	$25		RCA Victor 47-4954
1/24/53	❶³	13		50 Eddy's Song S:❶³ / J:2 / A:5 Condemned Without Trial	—	$20		RCA Victor 5108
6/20/53	4	9		51 Free Home Demonstration / S:4 / A:5 / J:5				
7/18/53	4	10		52 How's The World Treating You A:4 / J:7	—	$20		RCA Victor 5305
10/3/53	4	10		53 Mama, Come Get Your Baby Boy A:4 / S:9 / J:9 If I Never Get To Heaven	—	$20		RCA Victor 5415
1/9/54	❶¹	37		54 I Really Don't Want To Know J:❶¹ / S:2 / A:2 I'll Never Get Over You	—	$20		RCA Victor 5525
4/10/54	7	9		55 My Everything S:7 / A:7 Second Fling	—	$20		RCA Victor 5634
8/28/54	3	23		56 This Is The Thanks I Get (For Loving You) / S:3 / A:3 / J:3	—			
8/21/54	7	14		57 Hep Cat Baby J:7 / S:9 / A:14	—	$20		RCA Victor 5805
				EDDY ARNOLD and his Guitar:				
12/18/54	12	3		58 Christmas Can't Be Far Away .... A:12 I'm Your Private Santa Claus [X]	—	$20		RCA Victor 5905
1/29/55	2⁴	25		59 I've Been Thinking / J:2 / S:3 / A:4				
2/5/55	12	7		60 Don't Forget S:12	—	$20		RCA Victor 6000
4/23/55	6	9		61 In Time / A:6 / S:7				
4/23/55	9	6		62 Two Kinds Of Love S:9 / J:9	—	$20		RCA Victor 6069
6/25/55	❶²	26		63 The Cattle Call / S:❶² / J:2 / A:4	69			
				new version of the B-side of #1 above; also see #146 below				
7/9/55	8	7		64 The Kentuckian Song J:8	—	$20		RCA Victor 6139
				from the movie The Kentuckian starring Burt Lancaster				
8/20/55	❶²	15		65 That Do Make It Nice / J:❶² / A:4 / S:11				
8/20/55	2⁷	31		66 Just Call Me Lonesome S:2 / A:2 / J:2	—	$20		RCA Victor 6198
11/26/55	6	8		67 I Walked Alone Last Night / S:6				
11/12/55	10	10		68 The Richest Man (In The World) S:10 / A:14	99			RCA Victor 6290
1/28/56	7	3		69 Trouble In Mind S:7 When You Said Goodbye	—	$20		RCA Victor 6365
				EDDY ARNOLD:				
8/25/56	15	1		70 Casey Jones (The Brave Engineer) .... A:15 You Were Mine For Awhile	—	$20		RCA Victor 6601
9/1/56	10	8		71 You Don't Know Me S:10 / A:15 The Rockin' Mockin' Bird	—	$20		RCA Victor 6502
5/27/58	12	3		72 Gonna Find Me A Bluebird .... A:12 / S:15 Little Bit	51	$20		RCA Victor 6905
3/16/59	12	9		73 Chip Off The Old Block .... I'll Hold You In My Heart	97	$15		RCA Victor 7435
6/22/59	5	19		74 Tennessee Stud What's The Good (Of All This Love)	48	$15		RCA Victor 7542
1/9/61	23	3		75 Before This Day Ends .... Just Out Of Reach	—	$15		RCA Victor 7794
5/29/61	27	1		76 (Jim) I Wore A Tie Today .... Just Call Me Lonesome	—	$15		RCA Victor 7861
10/16/61	17	10		77 One Grain Of Sand .... The Worst Night Of My Life	107	$10		RCA Victor 7926
3/17/62	7	10		78 Tears Broke Out On Me I'll Do As Much For You Someday	102	$10		RCA Victor 7984

DEBUT	PEAK	WKS	Gold	#	A-side (Chart Hit)	B-side	Pop	$	Pic	Label & Number
					ARNOLD, Eddy — Cont'd					
6/30/62	3	19		79	**A Little Heartache** /		103			
8/4/62	7	19		80	**After Loving You**		112	$10		RCA Victor 8048
12/8/62+	5	15		81	**Does He Mean That Much To You?**	Tender Touch	98	$10	■	RCA Victor 8102
4/27/63	11	10		82	**Yesterday's Memories**	Lonely Balladeer	—	$10		RCA Victor 8160
8/10/63	13	12		83	**A Million Years Or So**	Just A Ribbon	—	$10	■	RCA Victor 8207
12/7/63+	12	12		84	**Jealous Hearted Me**	I Met Her Today	—	$10		RCA Victor 8253
2/1/64	5	20		85	**Molly**	The Song Of The Coo Coo	—	$10		RCA Victor 8296
					EDDY ARNOLD and The Needmore Creek Singers					
7/18/64	26	13		86	**Sweet Adorable You**	Why	—	$10		RCA Victor 8363
11/7/64+	8	19		87	**I Thank My Lucky Stars**	I Don't Cry No More	—	$10		RCA Victor 8445
3/27/65	❶²	25		88	**What's He Doing In My World**	Laura Lee	60	$8		RCA Victor 8516
9/18/65	15	9		89	**I'm Letting You Go**	The Days Gone By	135	$8		RCA Victor 8632
10/9/65	❶³	25		90	**Make The World Go Away**	The Easy Way	6	$8	■	RCA Victor 8679
2/12/66	❶⁶	19		91	**I Want To Go With You**	You'd Better Stop Tellin' Lies (About Me)	36	$8		RCA Victor 8749
5/14/66	2¹	16		92	**The Last Word In Lonesome Is Me**	Mary Claire Melvina Rebecca Jane	40	$8		RCA Victor 8818
7/23/66	3	15		93	**The Tip Of My Fingers**	Long, Long Friendship	43	$8	■	RCA Victor 8869
10/15/66	❶⁴	19		94	**Somebody Like Me**	Taking Chances	53	$8	■	RCA Victor 8965
12/24/66+	51	8		95	**The First Word**	The Angel And The Stranger	—	$7		RCA Victor 9027
2/18/67	❶²	16		96	**Lonely Again**	Love On My Mind	87	$7		RCA Victor 9080
5/6/67	3	16		97	**Misty Blue**	Calling Mary Names	57	$7		RCA Victor 9182
					#3 Pop hit for Dorothy Moore in 1976					
8/26/67	❶¹	16		98	**Turn The World Around**	The Long Ride Home	66	$7		RCA Victor 9265
12/2/67+	2²	15		99	**Here Comes Heaven**	Baby That's Living	91	$7		RCA Victor 9368
2/17/68	4	14		100	**Here Comes The Rain, Baby**	The World I Used To Know	74	$7		RCA Victor 9437
6/1/68	4	12		101	**It's Over**	No Matter Whose Baby You Are	74	$7		RCA Victor 9525
					#37 Pop hit for Jimmie Rodgers in 1966					
8/31/68	❶²	14		102	**Then You Can Tell Me Goodbye**	Apples, Raisins And Roses	84	$7		RCA Victor 9606
					#6 Pop hit for The Casinos in 1967					
11/23/68+	10	14		103	**They Don't Make Love Like They Used To**	What A Wonderful World	99	$7		RCA Victor 9667
3/29/69	10	13		104	**Please Don't Go**	Heaven Below	129	$6		RCA Victor 0120
6/28/69	19	12		105	**But For Love**	My Lady Of Love	125	$6		RCA Victor 0175
					#69 Pop hit for Jerry Naylor in 1970					
9/27/69	69	2		106	**You Fool**	You Don't Need Me Anymore	—	$6		RCA Victor 0226
12/27/69+	73	2		107	**Since December**	Morning Of My Mind	—	$6		RCA Victor 0282
2/28/70	22	11		108	**Soul Deep**	(Today) I Started Loving You Again	—	$6		RCA Victor 9801
					#18 Pop hit for The Box Tops in 1969					
6/13/70	28	11		109	**A Man's Kind Of Woman** /		—			
		10		110	**Living Under Pressure**			$6		RCA Victor 9848
9/12/70	22	9		111	**From Heaven To Heartache**	Ten Times Forever More	—	$6		RCA Victor 9889
1/2/71	26	12		112	**Portrait Of My Woman**	I Really Don't Want To Know	—	$6		RCA Victor 9935
5/1/71	49	8		113	**A Part Of America Died**	Call Me [S]	—	$6		RCA Victor 9968
7/3/71	34	9		114	**Welcome To My World**	It Ain't No Big Thing (But It's Growing)	—	$6		RCA Victor 9993
11/13/71	55	7		115	**I Love You Dear**	Long Life, Lots Of Happiness	—	$6		RCA Victor 0559
2/26/72	38	9		116	**Lonely People**	If It's Alright With You	—	$6		RCA Victor 0641
8/5/72	62	4		117	**Lucy**	The Last Letter	—	$6		RCA Victor 0747
1/20/73	28	12		118	**So Many Ways**	Once In A While	—	$5		MGM 14478
					#6 Pop hit for Brook Benton in 1959					
5/19/73	56	9		119	**If The Whole World Stopped Lovin'**	My Son I Wish You Everything	—	$5		MGM 14535
8/18/73	29	11		120	**Oh, Oh, I'm Falling In Love Again**	Anyway You Want Me	—	$5		MGM 14600
12/8/73+	24	13		121	**She's Got Everything I Need**	I'm Glad You Happened To Me	—	$5		MGM 14672
3/30/74	56	9		122	**Just For Old Times Sake**	I Got This Thing About You	—	$5		MGM 14711
					#20 Pop hit for The McGuire Sisters in 1961					
8/3/74	19	12		123	**I Wish That I Had Loved You Better**	Let It Be Love	—	$5		MGM 14734
12/28/74+	47	9		124	**Butterfly**	If You Could Only Love Me Now	—	$5		MGM 14769
					#78 Pop hit for Danyel Gerard in 1972					
6/7/75	60	12		125	**Red Roses For A Blue Lady**	I Will	—	$5		MGM 14780
					#10 Pop hit for Vic Dana in 1965					
10/11/75	86	6		126	**Middle Of A Memory**	I Just Had You On My Mind	—	$5		MGM 14827
6/19/76	13	13		127	**Cowboy**	Don't Let The Good Times Roll Away	—	$5		RCA Victor 10701
10/23/76	43	9		128	**Put Me Back Into Your World**	Goodnight, Irene	—	$5		RCA 10794
3/5/77	22	13		129	**(I Need You) All The Time**	I've Never Loved Anyone More	—	$5		RCA 10899
7/23/77	53	7		130	**Freedom Ain't The Same As Being Free**	Till You Can Make It On Your Own	—	$5		RCA 11031
11/12/77	83	3		131	**Where Lonely People Go**	Penny Arcade	—	$5		RCA 11133
4/22/78	23	12		132	**Country Lovin'**	Feelings/Dime (Samba Soul)	—	$5		RCA 11257
8/5/78	91	2		133	**I'm The South**	You Are My Sunshine	—	$5		RCA 11319
12/9/78+	13	14		134	**If Everyone Had Someone Like You**	You're A Beautiful Place To Be	—	$5		RCA 11422
4/14/79	21	11		135	**What In Her World Did I Do**	The Love Of My Life	—	$5		RCA 11537
8/4/79	22	11		136	**Goodbye**	You're So Good At Lovin' Me	—	$5		RCA 11668
11/17/79+	28	13		137	**If I Ever Had To Say Goodbye To You**	The Love Of My Life	—	$5		RCA 11752
3/8/80	6	13		138	**Let's Get It While The Gettin's Good**	You Cared Enough (To Give Your Very Best)	—	$5		RCA 11918
6/28/80	10	15		139	**That's What I Get For Loving You**	Undivided Love	—	$5		RCA 12039
12/6/80+	11	16		140	**Don't Look Now (But We Just Fell In Love)**	There Are Women	—	$5		RCA 12136
5/16/81	32	10		141	**Bally-Hoo Days** /		—			
		5		142	**Two Hearts Beat Better Than One**		—	$4		RCA 12226
12/12/81+	30	11		143	**All I'm Missing Is You**	Don't It Break Your Heart	—	$4		RCA 13000

(?) Jerri Arnold: An Old Country Record Speaks

DEBUT	PEAK	WKS	Gold	A-side (Chart Hit)	B-side	Pop	$	Pic	Label & Number
				ARNOLD, Eddy — Cont'd					
4/24/82	73	5		144 Don't Give Up On Me..*In Love With Loving You*		—	$4		RCA 13094
3/19/83	76	6		145 The Blues Don't Care Who's Got 'Em.............................*Wooden Heart*		—	$4		RCA 13452
12/25/99	18ˢ	2		146 Cattle Call..*I Walk Alone* (Arnold) [R]		—	$4	★	Curb 73088 (v)
				EDDY ARNOLD (with LeAnn Rimes)					
				new version of #63 above					
				ARNOLD, Rick '89					
				I Must Be Crazy					
9/16/89	89	2		I Must Be Crazy...		—	$6		Lynn 51088
				ASHLEY, Leon '67					
				Born Leon Walton on 5/18/36 in Newton County, Georgia. Singer/songwriter/guitarist. Married **Margie Singleton** in 1965. Formed own Ashley record label in 1967.					
7/29/67	❶¹	18		1 Laura What's He Got That I Ain't Got *With The Help Of The Wine*		120	$10		Ashley 2003
11/11/67	54	7		2 Hangin' On..*Four O'Clock*			$10		Ashley 2015
				LEON ASHLEY & MARGIE SINGLETON					
12/2/67+	28	12		3 Anna, I'm Taking You Home ....*Curtain Of Sadness*		—	$10		Ashley 2025
3/30/68	14	14		4 Mental Journey ....*All I Can Stand*		—	$10		Ashley 2075
5/11/68	55	6		5 You'll Never Be Lonely Again...................................*Parting Of The Ways*		—	$10		Ashley 3000
				LEON ASHLEY - MARGIE SINGLETON					
7/27/68	8	15		6 Flower Of Love *Prayers Can't Reach Me*		—	$10		Ashley 4000
1/11/69	25	9		7 While Your Lover Sleeps ....*That's Alright*		—	$10		Ashley 7000
4/19/69	23	10		8 Walkin' Back To Birmingham ....*It's All Over But The Crying*		—	$10		Ashley 9000
8/16/69	55	7		9 Ain't Gonna Worry ....*Illusions Of Life*		—	$10		Ashley 22
				★**ASHTON, Susan** '99					
				Born on 7/17/67 in Houston. Christian singer/songwriter.					
1/30/99	51	9		1 Faith Of The Heart...S:25 *Spinning Like A Wheel*		—	$4	★	Capitol 58757 (v)
5/29/99	37	20		2 You're Lucky I Love You..*Think Of Me*		—	$4		Capitol 58787
	★216★			**ASHWORTH, Ernest** '63					
				Born on 12/15/28 in Huntsville, Alabama. Singer/songwriter/guitarist. Joined the *Grand Ole Opry* in 1964. Appeared in the movie *The Farmer's Other Daughter*.					
				1)Talk Back Trembling Lips 2)Everybody But Me 3)Each Moment ('Spent With You) 4)I Love To Dance With Annie 5)I Take The Chance					
5/30/60	4	16		1 Each Moment ('Spent With You) *Night Time Is Cry Time*		—	$12		Decca 31085
10/24/60	8	20		2 You Can't Pick A Rose In December *You'll Hear My Heart Break*		—	$12		Decca 31156
5/15/61	15	2		3 Forever Gone...*Life Of The Party*		—	$12		Decca 31237
6/30/62	3	20		4 Everybody But Me *(I Just Spent) Another Sleepless Night*		—	$10		Hickory 1170
12/29/62+	7	15		5 I Take The Chance *King Of The Blues*		—	$10		Hickory 1189
6/22/63	❶¹	36		6 Talk Back Trembling Lips *That's How Much I Care*		101	$10		Hickory 1214
				#7 Pop hit for **Johnny Tillotson** in 1964					
2/1/64	10	20		7 A Week In The Country *Heartbreak Avenue*		—	$10		Hickory 1237
6/20/64	4	23		8 I Love To Dance With Annie *My Heart Would Know*		—	$10		Hickory 1265
11/7/64+	11	21		9 Pushed In A Corner...*Gooder Than Good*		—	$10		Hickory 1281
5/15/65	18	13		10 Because I Cared..*Love Has Come My Way*		—	$10		Hickory 1304
8/7/65	8	20		11 The DJ Cried *Scene Of Destruction*		—	$10		Hickory 1325
				ERNIE ASHWORTH:					
1/29/66	28	11		12 I Wish ....*Crazy Me, Foolish You*		—	$10		Hickory 1358
7/16/66	13	17		13 At Ease Heart ....*The Nearest Thing To Heaven*		—	$10		Hickory 1400
12/3/66+	31	9		14 Sad Face ....*I'm From Missouri*		—	$10		Hickory 1428
4/1/67	63	4		15 Just An Empty Place ....*Just One Time*		—	$10		Hickory 1445
8/5/67	48	10		16 My Love For You (Is Like A Mountain Range)........*You're Tearing My Heart Out*		—	$10		Hickory 1466
11/25/67	48	7		17 Tender And True ....*Back On My Mind Again*		—	$10		Hickory 1484
5/25/68	39	8		18 A New Heart ....*The Next Ones (You Love)*		—	$10		Hickory 1503
3/29/69	69	4		19 Where Do You Go (When You Don't Go With Me).........*Hocus-Pocus*		—	$10		Hickory 1528
7/12/69	72	3		20 Love, I Finally Found It ....*King Of The Blues*		—	$10		Hickory 1538
7/18/70	72	3		21 That Look Of Good-Bye ....*A Woman's Touch*		—	$10		Hickory 1570
	★299★			**ASLEEP AT THE WHEEL** '75					
				Group from Paw Paw, West Virginia: **Ray Benson** (male vocals, guitar), Chris O'Connell (female vocals, guitar) Reuben "Lucky Oceans" Gosfield (steel guitar), Danny Levin (fiddle, mandolin) and Jim "Floyd Domino" Haber (piano). Numerous personnel changes with Benson the only constant. **Jann Browne** was a member from 1981-83. **Rosie Flores** joined in 1997.					
				1)The Letter That Johnny Walker Read 2)House Of Blue Lights 3)Bump Bounce Boogie 4)Nothin' Takes The Place Of You 5)Miles And Miles Of Texas					
12/21/74+	69	8		1 Choo Choo Ch'Boogie ....*Our Names Aren't Mentioned (Together Anymore)*		—	$5		Epic 50045
				#1 R&B hit for Louis Jordan in 1946					
8/9/75	10	18		2 The Letter That Johnny Walker Read *Part Two*		—	$5		Capitol 4115
12/13/75+	31	11		3 Bump Bounce Boogie..*Fat Boy Rag*		—	$5		Capitol 4187
4/3/76	35	11		4 Nothin' Takes The Place Of You.......*Tonight The Bartender Is On The Wrong Side Of The Bar*		—	$5		Capitol 4238
8/28/76	48	8		5 Route 66 ....*Shout Wa Hey*		—	$5		Capitol 4319
				#11 Pop hit for **Nat King Cole** in 1946					
11/20/76+	38	10		6 Miles And Miles Of Texas ....*Blues For Dixie*		—	$5		Capitol 4357
3/19/77	42	9		7 The Trouble With Lovin' Today ....*Ragtime Annie*		—	$5		Capitol 4393
12/2/78	75	6		8 Texas Me & You ....*One O'Clock Jump*		—	$5		Capitol 4659
2/28/87	39	14		9 Way Down Texas Way......................................S:27 *String Of Pars*		—	$4	■	Epic 06671
5/30/87	17	18		10 House Of Blue Lights ....S:10 *Big Foot Stomp*		—	$4		Epic 07125
				#9 Pop hit for Chuck Miller in 1955					

DEBUT	PEAK	WKS	Gold	A-side (Chart Hit)	B-side	Pop	$	Pic	Label & Number
				ASLEEP AT THE WHEEL — Cont'd					
10/17/87	53	7		11 Boogie Back To Texas .... Tulsa Straight Ahead		—	$4		Epic 07610
1/9/88	59	9		12 Blowin' Like A Bandit .... String Of Pars		—	$4		Epic 07659
7/23/88	55	6		13 Walk On By .... Sugarfoot Rag		—	$4		Epic 07966
10/29/88	65	11		14 Hot Rod Lincoln .... S:29 String Of Pars		—	$4		Epic 08087
				#26 Pop hit for *Johnny Bond* in 1960					
9/1/90	54	4		15 Keepin' Me Up Nights .... Pedernales Stroll		—	$4	■	Arista 2045 (v)
12/1/90+	60	14		16 That's The Way Love Is .... Beat Me Daddy (Eight To The Bar)		—	$4		Arista 2122
3/16/91	71	2		17 Dance With Who Brung You .... Quittin' Time		—	$4		Arista 2178
9/21/91	67	4		18 Four Scores And Seven Beers Ago .... Eyes		—	$4	■	Arista 12340 (v)
				RAY BENSON					
3/19/94	73	1		19 Corine, Corina		—			album cut
				ASLEEP AT THE WHEEL Featuring Brooks & Dunn					
				#9 Pop hit for Ray Peterson in 1961; from the album *Tribute To Bob Wills* on Liberty 81470					
3/25/00	65	1		20 Roly Poly		—			album cut
				ASLEEP AT THE WHEEL Featuring Dixie Chicks					
				from the album *Ride With Bob* on DreamWorks 50117					
				ATCHER, Bob '48					
				Born on 5/11/14 in Hardin County, Kentucky. Died on 10/31/93 (age 79). Singer/guitarist/fiddler. Joined the WLS *National Barn Dance* in 1948. Mayor of Schaumburg, Illinois, from 1959-75.					
7/13/46	7	1		1 I Must Have Been Wrong .... I Want To Be Wanted		—	$20		Columbia 36983
1/31/48	6	11		2 Signed, Sealed And Delivered .... Mountain Maw		—	$20		Columbia 37991
5/7/49	12	1		3 Tennessee Border .... J:12 Don't Rob Another Man's Castle		—	$20		Columbia 20557
10/8/49	9	2		4 Why Don't You Haul Off And Love Me J:9 The Warm Red Wine		—	$20		Columbia 20611
				ATKINS, Big Ben '78					
				Born in 1943 in Vernon, Alabama.					
5/13/78	72	4		We Don't Live Here, We Just Love Here .... Baby Blue Eyes		—	$5		GRT 161
				ATKINS, Chet '65					
				Born on 6/20/24 in Luttrell, Tennessee. Died of cancer on 6/30/2001 (age 77). Moved to Nashville in 1950 and became a prolific studio guitarist and producer. RCA's A&R manager in Nashville from 1960-68; RCA vice president from 1968-82. Elected to the Country Music Hall of Fame in 1973. Won Grammy's Lifetime Achievement Award in 1993. Recipient of *Billboard*'s Century Award in 1997. Inducted into the Rock and Roll Hall of Fame in 2002 (as a sideman). CMA Awards: 1967, 1968, 1969, 1981, 1982, 1983, 1984, 1985 & 1988 Musician of the Year. Also see *Some Of Chet's Friends*.					
				1) Yakety Axe 2) We Didn't See A Thing 3) Mister Sandman					
1/15/55	13	2		1 Mister Sandman .... A:13 / S:15 Set A Spell [I]		—	$20		RCA Victor 5956
				CHET ATKINS and his Gallopin' Guitar					
				#1 Pop hit for The Chordettes in 1954					
4/2/55	15	1		2 Silver Bell .... S:15 The Old Spinning Wheel [I]		—	$20		RCA Victor 5995
				HANK SNOW and CHET ATKINS					
6/26/65	4	19		3 Yakety Axe .... Letter Edged In Black [I]		98	$10		RCA Victor 8590
10/15/66	30	10		4 Prissy .... La Fiesta [I]		—	$10		RCA Victor 8927
12/1/73	75	6		5 Fiddlin' Around .... Paramaribo [I]		—	$6		RCA Victor 0146
9/20/75	77	5		6 The Night Atlanta Burned .... The Odd Folks Of Okracoke [I]		—	$6	■	RCA Victor 10346
				THE ATKINS STRING COMPANY					
6/12/76	40	12		7 Frog Kissin' .... Bill Cheatham [N]		—	$6		RCA Victor 10614
3/1/80	83	3		8 Blind Willie .... Dance With Me		—	$5		RCA 11892
				above 2 are "live" recordings					
8/23/80	83	4		9 I Can Hear Kentucky Calling Me .... Strawberry Man		—	$5		RCA 12064
12/17/83+	6	18		10 We Didn't See A Thing .... I Wish You Were Here Tonight		—	$4		Columbia 04297
				RAY CHARLES & GEORGE JONES (Featuring Chet Atkins)					
				ATKINS, Rodney '97					
				Born in Tennessee. Singer/songwriter.					
8/30/97	74	1		In A Heartbeat .... God Only Knows		—	$4		Curb 73026
				ATLANTA '84					
				Group from Atlanta: Brad Griffis and Bill Davidson (vocals), Tony Ingram (vocals, fiddle; **Spurzz**), Alan David (guitar), Allen Collay and Bill Packard (keyboards), Jeff Baker (harmonica), Dick Stevens (bass) and John Holder (drums).					
5/21/83	9	17		1 Atlanta Burned Again Last Night .... Tumblin' Tumbleweeds		—	$5		MDJ 4831
9/10/83	11	19		2 Dixie Dreaming .... Orange Blossom Special/Rocky Top		—	$5	■	MDJ 4832
2/18/84	5	23		3 Sweet Country Music .... Seven Bridges Road		—	$4		MCA 52336
6/16/84	35	12		4 Pictures .... Long Cool Woman (In A Black Dress)		—	$4		MCA 52391
9/15/84	22	16		5 Wishful Drinkin' .... S:17 / A:27 Blue Side Of The Grey		—	$4		MCA 52452
				from the movie *Ellie* starring Shelley Winters					
4/6/85	57	10		6 My Sweet-Eyed Georgia Girl .... Dancin' On The Bayou		—	$4		MCA 52552
6/22/85	58	7		7 Why Not Tonight .... Dancin' On The Bayou		—	$4		MCA 52603
1/31/87	75	6		8 We Always Agree On Love .... Close Enough For Country		—	$5		Southern Tracks 1074
1/23/88	70	5		9 Sad Cliches .... We Always Agree On Love		—	$5		Southern Tracks 1091
				ATLANTA POPS — see COLEMAN, Albert					
				ATLANTA RHYTHM SECTION '80					
				Group from Doraville, Georgia: Ronnie Hammond (vocals), Barry Bailey and J.R. Cobb (guitars), Dean Daughtry (keyboards), Paul Goddard (bass) and Robert Nix (drums; replaced by Roy Yeager in 1980). Charted 14 pop hits from 1974-81.					
7/7/79	92	3		1 Do It Or Die .... My Song		19	$5		Polydor 14568
12/6/80	75	7		2 Silver Eagle .... Strictly R & R		101	$5		Polydor 2142

DEBUT	PEAK	WKS	Gold	A-side (Chart Hit) / B-side	Pop	$	Pic	Label & Number
				AUSTIN, Bobby '66 Born on 5/5/33 in Wenatchee, Washington. Died on 1/6/2002 (age 67). Singer/songwriter/bassist.				
10/8/66	21	14		1 Apartment #9 / Gone Home To Momma	—	$15		Tally 500
4/8/67	59	6		2 Cupid's Last Arrow / Mary's Merry-Go-Round	—	$8		Capitol 5867
12/30/67+	68	5		3 This Song Is Just For You / Do-Die	—	$8		Capitol 2039
12/27/69+	65	4		4 For Your Love / (Leaning On) Your Everlasting Love #13 Pop hit for Ed Townsend in 1958	—	$8		Capitol 2681
11/11/72	39	8		5 Knoxville Station / Bitter Chill Of Lonely	—	$6		Atlantic 2913
				AUSTIN, Bryan '94 Born on 9/12/67 in Pass Christian, Mississippi. Singer/songwriter.				
5/28/94	62	9		Radio Active / Limo Driver	—	$5	■	Patriot 58176 (v)
				AUSTIN, Chris '89 Born in Boone, North Carolina. Male singer/guitarist/fiddler. Backing singer for **Reba McEntire**. Died on 3/16/91 (age 27) in the plane crash that killed seven of McEntire's band members.				
7/30/88	62	5		1 Lonesome For You / The Reason	—	$4	■	Warner 27815
12/10/88	89	6		2 I Know There's A Heart In There Somewhere / Somehow Tonight	—	$4		Warner 27661
4/1/89	54	7		3 Blues Stay Away From Me / We Will Take A Lot Of Memories When We Go	—	$4		Warner 27531
				AUSTIN, Darlene '87 Born in Salina, Kansas. Female singer.				
6/26/82	68	6		1 Sunday Go To Cheatin' Clothes / Why Baby Why	—	$6		Myrtle 1002
10/9/82	75	5		2 Take Me Tonight / Then You Can Tell Me Goodbye	—	$6		Myrtle 1003
3/12/83	79	4		3 I'm On The Outside Looking In / Heartaches By The Number #15 Pop hit for Little Anthony & The Imperials in 1964	—	$6		Myrtle 1004
7/5/86	81	4		4 Guilty Eyes / When Do We Stop Starting Over	—	$6	■	CBT 4146
9/12/87	63	6		5 I Had A Heart	—	$6		Magi 4444
				AUSTIN, Kay '80 Born on 2/3/54 in Long Beach, California. Female singer.				
5/31/80	86	3		1 The Rest Of Your Life	—	$5		e.i.o. 1122
9/13/80	75	4		2 Two Hearts Beat (Better Than One) / Like The Seasons	—	$5		e.i.o. 1127
				AUSTIN, Sherrié '99 Born on 8/28/70 in Sydney, Australia; raised in Townsville, Australia. Singer/actress. Played "Pippa McKenna" on TV's *The Facts of Life* (1987-88). Former member of pop duo Colourhaus (as Sherrié Krenn).				
5/24/97	34	20		1 Lucky In Love S:12 Put Your Heart Into It		$4	■	Arista 13083 (v)
9/13/97	41	15		2 One Solitary Tear S:19 I Want To Fall In Love (So Hard It Hurts)	—	$4	■	Arista 13099 (v)
1/31/98	34	16		3 Put Your Heart Into It S:13 That's No Way To Break A Heart	104	$4	■	Arista 13122 (v)
7/11/98	74	1		4 Innocent Man from the album *Words* on Arista 18843		$4		album cut
5/22/99	29	20		5 Never Been Kissed S:❶ Words	89	$4	★	Arista 13140 (v)
11/6/99	49	8		6 Little Bird S:4 Never Been Kissed	47	$4	★	Arista 13184 (v)
4/14/01	55	3		7 Jolene from the album *Followin' A Feelin'* on WE 1161				album cut
				AUTRY, Gene ★132★ U.S. Army '45 Born Orvon Gene Autry on 9/29/07 in Tioga, Texas. Died of respiratory failure on 10/2/98 (age 91). Singer/songwriter/guitarist/actor. Worked as a cowboy and telegraph operator for the Frisco Railroad. Played saxophone and guitar with the Fields Brothers Marvelous Medicine Show. Sang on KVOO in Tulsa in 1929 as "The Oklahoma Yodeling Cowboy." Joined the WLS National Barn Dance in 1930. Hosted own *Melody Ranch* radio series. Acted in several western movies. Starred in own TV western from 1950-56. Later owned several businesses (including the California Angels major league baseball team). Elected to the Country Music Hall of Fame in 1969. 1) At Mail Call Today 2) Rudolph, The Red-Nosed Reindeer 3) Gonna Build A Big Fence Around Texas 4) Have I Told You Lately That I Love You 5) I Wish I Had Never Met Sunshine				
1/29/44	3	9		1 I'm Thinking Tonight Of My Blue Eyes / I'll Be True While You're Gone	—	$25		Okeh 6648
4/29/44	4	1		2 I Hang My Head And Cry / You'll Be Sorry	—	$25		Okeh 6627
2/10/45	2¹	8		3 Gonna Build A Big Fence Around Texas /		$25		Okeh 6728
2/17/45	4	3		4 Don't Fence Me In from the movie *Hollywood Canteen* starring Bette Davis	—			
4/28/45	❶⁸	22		5 At Mail Call Today /		$25		Okeh 6737
4/28/45	7	2		6 I'll Be Back	—			
10/27/45	4	2		7 Don't Hang Around Me Anymore / Address Unknown	—	$20		Columbia 36840
12/29/45	4	1		8 Don't Live A Lie /	—			
12/29/45	4	1		9 I Want To Be Sure	—	$20		Columbia 36880
2/23/46	4	5		10 Silver Spurs (On The Golden Stairs) / Good Old Fashioned Hoedown	—	$20		Columbia 36904
5/25/46	3	7		11 I Wish I Had Never Met Sunshine /	—	$20		Columbia 36970
7/6/46	7	1		12 You Only Want Me When You're Lonely	—	$20		Columbia 36984
6/15/46	4	8		13 Wave To Me, My Lady / Over And Over Again	—	$20		
10/19/46	3	12		14 Have I Told You Lately That I Love You /	—	$20		Columbia 37079
10/26/46	4	3		15 Someday You'll Want Me To Want You	—			
3/8/47	3	2		16 You're Not My Darlin' Anymore / Here's To The Ladies	—	$20		Columbia 37201
12/27/47	5	1	●	17 Here Comes Santa Claus (Down Santa Claus Lane) / An Old-Fashioned Tree [X] also see #19 & #20 below	9	$20		Columbia 37942
10/9/48	6	12		18 Buttons And Bows S:6 / J:6 Can't Shake The Sands Of Texas From My Shoes from the movie *The Paleface* starring Bob Hope	17	$20		Columbia 20469
11/27/48	4	7		19 Here Comes Santa Claus (Down Santa Claus Lane) S:4 / J:7 An Old-Fashioned Tree [X-R]	8	$20		Columbia 20377

DEBUT	PEAK	WKS	Gold	A-side (Chart Hit) .... B-side	Pop	$	Pic	Label & Number
				AUTRY, Gene — Cont'd				
12/10/49	8	3		20 Here Comes Santa Claus (Down Santa Claus Lane) A:8 / S:13 An Old-Fashioned Tree [X-R]	24	$20		Columbia 20377
12/10/49	❶¹	5	●	21 Rudolph, The Red-Nosed Reindeer A:❶¹ / S:4 / J:7 If It Doesn't Snow On Christmas [X] 7" 33 1/3 rpm: 1-375; also see #22, #26 & #27 below	❶¹	$15		Columbia 38610
12/16/50	5	3		22 Rudolph, The Red-Nosed Reindeer S:5 / A:5 / J:5 If It Doesn't Snow On Christmas [X-R] GENE AUTRY and The Pinafores (above 2)	3	$15		Columbia 38610
4/8/50	3	4	●	23 Peter Cottontail S:3 / A:5 / J:7 The Funny Little Bunny (With The Powder Puff Tail) 7" 33 1/3 rpm: 1-575	5	$20		Columbia 38750
12/9/50	4	4	●	24 Frosty The Snow Man S:4 When Santa Claus Gets Your Letter [X] GENE AUTRY and The Cass County Boys 78 rpm: 38907	7	$20		Columbia 6-742
6/9/51	9	1		25 Old Soldiers Never Die A:9 God Bless America	—	$25		Columbia 4-39405
12/26/98	55	3		26 Rudolph, The Red-Nosed Reindeer .... Here Comes Santa Claus [X-R]	—	$4		Columbia 33165
12/18/99	60	2		27 Rudolph, The Red-Nosed Reindeer .... Here Comes Santa Claus [X-R]	—	$4		Columbia 33165
	★358★			**AXTON, Hoyt** '74 Born on 3/25/38 in Duncan, Oklahoma. Died of a heart attack on 10/26/99 (age 61). Singer/songwriter/guitarist/actor. Son of songwriter Mae Axton ("Heartbreak Hotel"). Started own Jeremiah label in 1978. Acted in such movies as *The Black Stallion* and *Gremlins*. 1) Boney Fingers 2) When The Morning Comes 3) A Rusty Old Halo				
3/30/74	10	15		1 When The Morning Comes Billie's Theme Linda Ronstadt (guest vocal)	54	$6		A&M 1497
8/24/74	8	16		2 Boney Fingers Life Machine Renee Armand (female vocal)	—	$6	■	A&M 1607
2/8/75	61	9		3 Nashville .... Speed Trap (Pop #105)	106	$6		A&M 1657
5/10/75	57	7		4 Lion In The Winter .... No No Song Linda Ronstadt (guest vocal)	—	$6		A&M 1683
5/15/76	18	14		5 Flash Of Fire .... Paid In Advance	—	$6		A&M 1811
4/16/77	57	7		6 You're The Hangnail In My Life .... Never Been To Spain	—	$5		MCA 40711
6/18/77	65	6		7 Little White Moon .... Funeral Of The King	—	$5		MCA 40731
5/12/79	17	15		8 Della And The Dealer .... In A Young Girls Mind	—	$5		Jeremiah 1000
10/6/79	14	14		9 A Rusty Old Halo .... Gotta Keep Rollin'	—	$5		Jeremiah 1001
1/12/80	21	12		10 Wild Bull Rider .... Torpedo	—	$5		Jeremiah 1003
4/12/80	37	12		11 Evangelina .... So Hard To Give It All Up	—	$5		Jeremiah 1005
10/11/80	80	3		12 Where Did The Money Go .... Smile As You Go By	—	$5		Jeremiah 1008
5/9/81	78	3		13 Flo's Yellow Rose .... Lion In The Winter from the TV series *Flo* starring Polly Holliday	—	$5		Elektra 47133
7/25/81	86	4		14 The Devil .... Jealous Man	—	$5		Jeremiah 1011
				AZAR, Steve '02 Born on 4/11/64 in Greenville, Mississippi. Singer/songwriter/guitarist.				
3/16/96	51	10		1 Someday .... Thunderbird	—	$4	■	River North 3008
7/6/96	50	15		2 I Never Stopped Lovin' You .... Heartbreak Town	—	$4	■	River North 3013
10/6/01+	2¹	38↑		3 I Don't Have To Be Me ('Til Monday) .... You Don't Know How It Feels	35	$4		Mercury 172230

B

				BACKROADS '83				
2/19/83	72	5		So Close .... Gonna Stay All Night	—	$5		Soundwaves 4698
				BACKTRACK '85				
4/6/85	94	3		Mexico .... I'm On The Outside BACKTRACK Featuring John Hunt	—	$6		Goldmine 11
				BADALE, Andy '80 Born Angelo Daniel Badalamenti on 3/22/37 in Brooklyn, New York. Wrote several TV and movie scores.				
1/26/80	93	4		Nashville Beer Garden .... Finger Pickin' Good [I]	—	$6		GP 577
				BAILES, Eddy '76 Born in Parkersburg, West Virginia. Singer/songwriter/guitarist.				
2/21/76	93	3		Love Isn't Love (Till You Give It Away) .... Houston	—	$6		Cin Kay 101
				BAILEY, Glen '82 Born in 1952 in Thunder Bay, Ontario, Canada.				
3/6/82	87	3		1 Stompin' On My Heart	—	$5		Yatahey 1221
6/26/82	85	3		2 Designer Jeans	—	$5	■	Yatahey 3024
				BAILEY, Johnny '83				
2/5/83	86	2		1 What's She Doing To My Mind /				
		2		2 This Country Music's Driving Me Crazy	—	$5		Soundwaves 4695
				BAILEY, Judy '81 Born on 1/6/55 in Winchester, Kentucky.				
11/29/80+	10	14		1 Following The Feeling .... Mexico Winter MOE BANDY Featuring Judy Bailey	—	$5		Columbia 11395
5/9/81	56	7		2 Slow Country Dancin' .... Anything You Can Do (I Can Do Worse)	—	$5		Columbia 02045
10/3/81	54	7		3 The Best Bedroom In Town .... I'm Guilty Of Loving You	—	$5		Columbia 02505

DEBUT	PEAK	WKS	Gold	A-side (Chart Hit) ... B-side	Pop	$	Pic	Label & Number
				BAILEY, Judy — Cont'd				
2/12/83	72	4		4 Tender Lovin' Lies ... Trying Hard Not To Be Easy	—	$5		Warner 29799
2/9/85	96	3		5 There's A Lot Of Good About Goodbye ... Comfort	—	$6		White Gold 22249
				★ **BAILEY, Lynn** '80				
				Born on 4/18/42 in Indianapolis. Female singer.				
4/5/80	94	2		Cheater Fever ... Small Talk	—	$6		Wartrace 613
				★ **BAILEY, Mary** '81				
				Born in 1945 in Toronto. Became **Shania Twain**'s first manager in the late 1980s.				
8/15/81	84	3		Too Much, Too Little, Too Late	—	$6		E & R 8101

BAILEY, Razzy ★151★   '81

Born Rasie Michael Bailey on 2/14/39 in Five Points, Alabama. Singer/songwriter/guitarist. First recorded for B&K label in 1949. Worked as a truck driver, insurance salesman and furniture salesman during the early 1960s. Formed the group Daily Bread in 1968. Formed the Aquarians in 1972. Recorded as Razzy for MGM in 1974.

1)She Left Love All Over Me   2)Friends   3)Loving Up A Storm   4)I Keep Coming Back   5)Midnight Hauler

DEBUT	PEAK	WKS	Gold	#	A-side ... B-side	Pop	$	Pic	Label & Number
10/30/76	99	2		1	Keepin' Rosie Proud Of Me ... Candy Store	—	$6		Erastus 526
8/12/78	9	15		2	What Time Do You Have To Be Back To Heaven ... That's The Way A Cowboy Rocks And Rolls	—	$5		RCA 11338
12/23/78+	6	14		3	Tonight She's Gonna Love Me (Like There Was No Tomorrow) ... Your Old Love Letters (Always Get The Better Of Me)	—	$5		RCA 11446
4/21/79	6	13		4	If Love Had A Face ... Natural Love	—	$5		RCA 11536
8/18/79	10	14		5	I Ain't Got No Business Doin' Business Today ... Conchita	—	$5		RCA 11682
12/22/79+	5	14		6	I Can't Get Enough Of You ... The North Won The War Again Last Night	—	$5		RCA 11885
4/19/80	13	14		7	Too Old To Play Cowboy ... 9,999,999 Tears	—	$5		RCA 11954
8/2/80	❶¹	15		8	Loving Up A Storm ... What's A Little Love Between Friends	—	$5	■	RCA 12062
11/22/80+	❶¹	17		9	I Keep Coming Back /				
		17		10	True Life Country Music	—	$5	■	RCA 12120
3/28/81	❶¹	16		11	Friends /				
		16		12	Anywhere There's A Jukebox	—	$5		RCA 12199
7/11/81	❶¹	18		13	Midnight Hauler /				
7/11/81	8	18		14	Scratch My Back (And Whisper In My Ear)	—	$5		RCA 12268
12/19/81+	❶¹	20		15	She Left Love All Over Me ... Blaze Of Glory	—	$5		RCA 13007
4/10/82	10	15		16	Everytime You Cross My Mind (You Break My Heart) ... Tonight She's Gonna Love Me (Like There Was No Tomorrow)	—	$5		RCA 13084
8/21/82	8	17		17	Love's Gonna Fall Here Tonight ... Singin' Other People's Songs	—	$5		RCA 13290
12/4/82+	30	14		18	Poor Boy ... What Time Do You Have To Be Back To Heaven	—	$5		RCA 13383
4/30/83	19	13		19	After The Great Depression ... Guess Who's Gonna Be A Dad	—	$5		RCA 13512
10/29/83	62	10		20	This Is Just The First Day ... Night Life	—	$5		RCA 13630
2/25/84	14	17		21	In The Midnight Hour ... Mr. Melody Man	—	$5		RCA 13718
					#21 Pop hit for Wilson Pickett in 1965				
8/4/84	29	14		22	Knock On Wood ... If You Happen To See My Baby	—	$4		MCA 52421
					#1 Pop hit for Amii Stewart in 1979				
12/8/84+	43	13		23	Touchy Situation ... Music Takes Me Past The Point	—	$4		MCA 52500
3/23/85	51	10		24	Modern Day Marriages ... New Orleans When It Rains	—	$4		MCA 52547
7/27/85	78	4		25	Fightin' Fire With Fire ... To Write A Sad Song	—	$4		MCA 52628
12/14/85+	48	9		26	Old Blue Yodeler ... To Write A Sad Song	—	$4		MCA 52701
6/28/86	63	7		27	Rockin' In The Parkin' Lot ... Baby My Baby	—	$4		MCA 52851
10/31/87	69	5		28	If Love Ever Made A Fool ...	—	$5		SOA 001
1/23/88	58	6		29	Unattended Fire ... Lover Please	—	$5		SOA 002
12/24/88+	73	6		30	Starting All Over Again	—	$5		SOA 003
					#19 Pop hit for Mel & Tim in 1972				
4/29/89	65	5		31	But You Will	—	$5		SOA 006

★308★ **BAILLIE AND THE BOYS**   '89

Trio of songwriters/session singers: Kathie Baillie (born on 2/20/51 in Morristown, New Jersey) and husband Michael Bonagura (born on 3/26/53 in Newark, New Jersey) with Alan LeBoeuf. LeBoeuf starred as **Paul McCartney** in Broadway show *Beatlemania*. Group became a duo when LeBoeuf left in January 1989.

1)(I Wish I Had A) Heart Of Stone   2)Fool Such As I   3)Long Shot

DEBUT	PEAK	WKS	#	A-side ... B-side	Pop	$	Pic	Label & Number
4/18/87	9	21	1	Oh Heart ... S:18 Waitin' Out The Storm	—	$4	□	RCA 5130
8/8/87	18	16	2	He's Letting Go ... S:29 Heartless Night	—	$4		RCA 5227
12/19/87+	9	18	3	Wilder Days ... S:23 You Fool	—	$4		RCA 5327
10/1/88+	5	27	4	Long Shot ... S:9 You Fool	—	$4		RCA 8631
2/4/89	8	21	5	She Deserves You ... The Only Lonely One	—	$4		RCA 8796
7/1/89	4	24	6	(I Wish I Had A) Heart Of Stone ... Heartache In Motion	—	$4		RCA 8944
11/4/89+	9	26	7	I Can't Turn The Tide ... The Only Lonely One	—	$4		RCA 9076
4/14/90	23	14	8	Perfect ... Lovin' By Numbers	—	$4		RCA 2500
8/11/90	5	21	9	Fool Such As I	—	$4		RCA 2641
1/5/91	18	20	10	Treat Me Like A Stranger ... I'd Love To	—	$4		RCA 2720

DEBUT	PEAK	WKS	Gold	A-side (Chart Hit) ... B-side	Pop	$	Pic	Label & Number
				BAKER, Adam '86				
				Born on 5/8/64 in Oklahoma City; raised in Edmond, Oklahoma.				
3/9/85	97	3		1 I Can See Him In Her Eyes .... —		$6		Signature 22484
2/8/86	48	10		2 In Love With Her .... They Come And They Go		$5		Avista 8610
10/18/86	46	9		3 Weren't You Listening .... Dixie Nightlife		$5		Avista 8602
2/7/87	54	7		4 You've Got A Right .... Dixie Nightlife		$5		Avista 8703
10/31/87	63	4		5 Standing Invitation .... Dixie Nightlife		$5		Avista 8704
				BAKER, Butch '86				
				Born on 10/22/58 in Sweetwater, Tennessee. Singer/songwriter/guitarist. Also see **Tomorrow's World**.				
				1) That's What Her Memory Is For 2) Don't It Make You Wanta Go Home 3) Your Loving Side				
8/4/84	80	3		1 Burn Georgia Burn (There's A Fire In Your Soul) .... Bury My Heart (In The Smoky Mountains)		$4		Mercury 880020
10/27/84	56	7		2 Thinking 'Bout Leaving .... Bury My Heart (In The Smoky Mountains)		$4		Mercury 880256
8/9/86	41	14		3 That's What Her Memory Is For .... After Losing You		$4		Mercury 884857
11/15/86	53	9		4 Your Loving Side .... After Losing You		$4		Mercury 888133
5/16/87	51	10		5 Don't It Make You Wanta Go Home .... Your Loving Side		$4		Mercury 888543
11/28/87	60	10		6 I'll Fall In Love Again .... After Losing You		$4		Mercury 888926
7/2/88	69	5		7 Party People .... After Losing You		$4		Mercury 870486
9/2/89	64	6		8 Our Little Corner .... Party People		$4		Mercury 874746
11/18/89	66	9		9 Wonderful Tonight .... Party People		$4		Mercury 876226
				#16 Pop hit for **Eric Clapton** in 1978				
12/1/90+	56	9		10 It Wasn't You, It Wasn't Me .... Fairytale Fool (Alexander)		$4	■	Mercury 878256 (v)
				DANIELE ALEXANDER & BUTCH BAKER				
				BAKER, Carroll '81				
				Born on 3/4/49 in Port Medway, Nova Scotia, Canada. Singer/songwriter. Hosted TV show *Sounds Good Country* in Canada.				
7/4/81	82	3		1 Mama What Does Cheatin' Mean .... Lover On The Shelf		$6		Excelsior 1013
7/6/85	95	1		2 It Always Hurts Like The First Time .... —		$6		Tembo 8520
				BAKER, George, Selection '76				
				Born on Johannes Bouwens on 12/9/44 in Holland. His Selection included Nelleke Brzoskowsky (female vocals), Jan Hop, Jacobus Greuter, George The and Jan Visser.				
1/10/76	33	15		Paloma Blanca .... Dreamboat	26	$5		Warner 8115
				BAKER, Two Ton — see **HOOSIER HOT SHOTS**				
				BAKER & MYERS '96				
				Songwriting team of Gary Baker and Frank Myers. Baker was a member of **The Shooters**.				
9/30/95	67	6		1 These Arms .... —			■	album cut (v)
				later released as the B-side of #2 below				
2/10/96	48	17		2 Years From Here .... These Arms		$4		Curb 76967 (v)
8/24/96	71	1		3 A Little Bit Of Honey .... —				album cut
				all of above from the album *Baker & Myers* on Curb 77806				
	★335★			**BALL, David** '94				
				Born on 7/9/53 in Rock Hill, South Carolina. Singer/songwriter/guitarist.				
				1) Riding With Private Malone 2) Thinkin' Problem 3) When The Thought Of You Catches Up With Me				
5/7/88	46	10		1 Steppin' Out .... I Wish He Was Me (And She Was You)		$4		RCA 6899
8/20/88	55	7		2 You Go, You're Gone .... I Wish He Was Me (And She Was You)		$4		RCA 8636
9/2/89	64	4		3 Gift Of Love .... I Wish He Was Me (And She Was You)		$4		RCA 8975
4/16/94	2¹	20		4 Thinkin' Problem .... Down At The Bottom Of A Broken Heart	40	$4	■	Warner 18250 (v)
9/10/94	7	20		5 When The Thought Of You Catches Up With Me .. Don't Think Twice	107	$4	■	Warner 18081 (v)
1/14/95	11	20		6 Look What Followed Me Home /		—		
5/20/95	48	10		7 What Do You Want With His Love		$4		Warner 17977 (v)
9/16/95	50	9		8 Honky Tonk Healin' .... Blowin' Smoke		$4		Warner 17785
5/4/96	49	9		9 Circle Of Friends .... S:18 No More Lonely		$4	■	Warner 17639 (v)
8/10/96	67	3		10 Hangin' In And Hangin' On .... If You'd Like Some Lovin'		$4	■	Warner 17574 (v)
5/1/99	47	10		11 Watching My Baby Not Coming Back .... Going Someplace To Forget		$4	★	Warner 16982 (v)
8/7/99	67	1		12 I Want To With You .... When I Get Lonely		$4	★	Warner 16927 (v)
9/8/01	2¹	22		13 Riding With Private Malone .... Missing Her Blues	36	$4		Dualtone 01120
			✱	**BALL, Marcia** '78				
				Born Marcia Mouton on 3/20/49 in Orange, Texas; raised in Vinton, Louisiana.				
11/18/78	91	2		I'm A Fool To Care .... 50 Words Or Less		$5		Capitol 4633
				#24 Pop hit for **Joe Barry** in 1961				
				BALLARD, Roger '93				
				Born in Kentwood, Louisiana.				
9/25/93	68	3		Two Steps In The Right Direction .... A Little Piece Of Heaven		$4	■	Atlantic 87313 (v)
				BALLEW, Michael '81				
				Born in Austin, Texas. Singer/songwriter/guitarist.				
11/7/81	67	6		1 Your Daddy Don't Live In Heaven (He's In Houston) .... Blue Water		$5		Liberty 1437
2/13/82	71	5		2 Pretending Fool .... Ain't No Future In Loving You		$5		Liberty 1447

DEBUT	PEAK	WKS	Gold	A-side (Chart Hit)	B-side	Pop	$	Pic	Label & Number

BAMA BAND, The — '83
Backing band for **Hank Williams, Jr.**: Lamar Morris (vocals, guitar), Wayne "Animal" Turner (guitar), Edward "Cowboy" Long (steel guitar), Paul Eugene "Dixie" Hatfield (keyboards), Jerry McKinney (sax), Vernon Derrick (fiddle), Ray Barrickman (bass) and William Claude Marshall (drums). Billy Earhart (of **Amazing Rhythm Aces**) replaced Hatfield in 1986.

DEBUT	PEAK	WKS		A-side	B-side	Pop	$	Pic	Label & Number
12/18/82+	54	9	1	Dallas	A Cowboy's Welcome Home	—	$6		Oasis 1
5/7/83	56	9	2	Tijuana Sunrise	It Sure Feels Like Love Tonight	—	$5		Soundwaves 4707
				first released on Oasis 2 in 1983 ($6)					
7/20/85	60	8	3	What Used To Be Crazy	White Cadillac	—	$5	■	Compleat 144
3/29/86	70	4	4	I've Changed My Mind	Stone Cold And Country	—	$5		Compleat 152
1/31/87	64	7	5	Suddenly Single	Save That Dress	—	$5		Compleat 163
8/27/88	71	5	6	Southern Accent	It's Gotta Be Love	—	$4		Mercury 870603
12/24/88+	69	6	7	Real Old-Fashioned Broken Heart	Ellen B.	—	$4		Mercury 872150
3/18/89	87	3	8	When We Get Back To The Farm		—	$4		Mercury 872650

BANDANA — '82
Group formed in Nashville: Lon Wilson (vocals), **Tim Mensy** and Joe Van Dyke (guitars), Jerry Fox (bass) and Jerry Ray Johnston (drums). In 1986 Mensy, Van Dyke and Johnston left, replaced by Michael Black and Billy Kemp (guitars) and Bob Mummert (drums). Disbanded in 1987.

1) The Killin' Kind 2) Outside Lookin' In 3) Better Our Hearts Should Bend (Than Break)

DEBUT	PEAK	WKS		A-side	B-side	Pop	$	Pic	Label & Number
1/9/82	37	12	1	Guilty Eyes	Whatta I Gotta Do?	—	$4		Warner 49872
5/1/82	61	7	2	Cheatin' State Of Mind	They Call It Love	—	$4		Warner 50045
8/21/82	17	18	3	The Killin' Kind	Whatta I Gotta Do?	—	$4		Warner 29936
12/11/82+	29	15	4	I Can't Get Over You (Getting Over Me)	Come To Me	—	$4		Warner 29831
9/3/83	18	18	5	Outside Lookin' In	Ocean Of Love	—	$4		Warner 29524
4/14/84	26	13	6	Better Our Hearts Should Bend (Than Break)	Ocean Of Love	—	$4		Warner 29315
8/18/84	52	12	7	All I Wanna Do (Is Make Love To You)	Outside Lookin' In	—	$4		Warner 29226
5/4/85	46	13	8	It's Just Another Heartache	Heat Of The Night	—	$4		Warner 29029
9/14/85	37	12	9	Lovin' Up A Storm	Good Groove	—	$4		Warner 28939
5/17/86	54	9	10	Touch Me	Heat Of The Night	—	$4		Warner 28721

BANDIT BAND, The — '87
Group from Lexington, Kentucky.

DEBUT	PEAK	WKS		A-side	B-side	Pop	$	Pic	Label & Number
4/4/87	73	4		Do You Wanna Fall In Love		—	$6		Pegasus 108

BANDIT BROTHERS — '91

DEBUT	PEAK	WKS		A-side	B-side	Pop	$	Pic	Label & Number
4/6/91	57	5		Women	(instrumental) [N]	—	$4	■	Curb 76867 (v)
				parody of "Men" by **The Forester Sisters**					

BANDY, Charlie — '84
Born in 1954 in Grundy, Virginia.

DEBUT	PEAK	WKS		A-side	B-side	Pop	$	Pic	Label & Number
7/28/84	95	2		Tenamock Georgia	All I See Is You	—	$6		RCI 2386

BANDY, Moe ★64★ — '79
Born Marion Bandy on 2/12/44 in Meridian, Mississippi; raised in San Antonio, Texas. Singer/guitarist. Played in his father's band, the Mission City Playboys, in San Antonio; also worked as a rodeo rider. Regular on the local San Antonio TV show *Country Corner* in 1973. Started his own theater in Branson, Missouri. CMA Award: 1980 Vocal Duo of the Year (with **Joe Stampley**).

1) Just Good Ol' Boys 2) I Cheated Me Right Out Of You 3) Hank Williams, You Wrote My Life
4) It's A Cheating Situation 5) She's Not Really Cheatin' (She's Just Gettin' Even)

DEBUT	PEAK	WKS		A-side	B-side	Pop	$	Pic	Label & Number
3/30/74	17	15	1	I Just Started Hatin' Cheatin' Songs Today	How Far Do You Think We Would Go	—	$6		GRC 2006
				first released on Footprint 1006 ($10)					
8/3/74	24	11	2	Honky Tonk Amnesia	Cowboys And Playboys	—	$6		GRC 2024
11/23/74+	7	14	3	It Was Always So Easy (To Find An Unhappy Woman)	I Wouldn't Cheat On Her If She Was Mine	—	$6		GRC 2036
3/22/75	13	11	4	Don't Anyone Make Love At Home Anymore	Somebody That Good	—	$6		GRC 2055
6/28/75	7	16	5	Bandy The Rodeo Clown	I'm Looking For A New Way To Love You	—	$6		GRC 2070
12/20/75+	2²	15	6	Hank Williams, You Wrote My Life	I'm The Honky-Tonk On Loser's Avenue	—	$5		Columbia 10265
4/17/76	27	10	7	The Biggest Airport In The World	I Think I've Got A Love On For You	—	$5		Columbia 10313
7/4/76	11	14	8	Here I Am Drunk Again	What Happened To Our Love	—	$5		Columbia 10361
10/30/76+	11	15	9	She Took More Than Her Share	Then You Can Let Me Go (Out Of Your Mind)	—	$5		Columbia 10428
3/5/77	9	14	10	I'm Sorry For You, My Friend	A Four Letter Fool	—	$5		Columbia 10487
				written by **Hank Williams**					
6/18/77	13	12	11	Cowboys Ain't Supposed To Cry	Till I Stop Needing You	—	$5		Columbia 10558
10/8/77	11	14	12	She Just Loved The Cheatin' Out Of Me	Up To Now I've Wanted Everything But You	—	$5		Columbia 10619
1/28/78	13	14	13	Soft Lights And Hard Country Music	There's Nobody Home On The Range Anymore	—	$5		Columbia 10671
5/20/78	11	14	14	That's What Makes The Juke Box Play	Are We Making Love Or Just Making Friends	—	$5		Columbia 10735
9/16/78	7	13	15	Two Lonely People	I Never Miss A Day (Missing You)	—	$5		Columbia 10820
1/27/79	2²	15	16	It's A Cheating Situation	Try My Love On For Size	—	$5		Columbia 10889
				Janie Fricke (backing vocal)					
6/16/79	9	14	17	Barstool Mountain	To Cheat Or Not To Cheat	—	$5		Columbia 10974
7/14/79	❶¹	16	18	Just Good Ol' Boys	Make A Little Love Each Day	—	$5		Columbia 11027
				MOE BANDY & JOE STAMPLEY					
10/6/79	❶¹	14	19	I Cheated Me Right Out Of You	Honky Tonk Merry Go Round	—	$5		Columbia 11090

DEBUT	PEAK	WKS	Gold	A-side (Chart Hit) ... B-side	Pop	$	Pic	Label & Number
				BANDY, Moe — Cont'd				
11/17/79+	7	14		20 Holding The Bag ... When It Comes To Cowgirls (We Just Can't Say No) MOE BANDY & JOE STAMPLEY	—	$5		Columbia 11147
2/2/80	13	12		21 One Of A Kind ... The Bitter With The Sweet	—	$5		Columbia 11184
4/12/80	11	15		22 Tell Ole I Ain't Here, He Better Get On Home ... Only The Names Have Been Changed MOE BANDY & JOE STAMPLEY	—	$5		Columbia 11244
4/26/80	22	12		23 The Champ ... She Took Out The Outlaw In Me	—	$5		Columbia 11255
8/2/80	10	15		24 Yesterday Once More ... I Just Can't Leave Those Honky Tonks Alone	—	$5		Columbia 11305
11/29/80+	10	14		25 Following The Feeling ... Mexico Winter MOE BANDY Featuring Judy Bailey	—	$5		Columbia 11395
3/14/81	10	15		26 Hey Joe (Hey Moe) ... Two Beers Away MOE BANDY & JOE STAMPLEY	—	$5		Columbia 60508
4/18/81	15	14		27 My Woman Loves The Devil Out Of Me ... Today I Almost Stopped Loving You	—	$5		Columbia 02039
8/1/81	12	14		28 Honky Tonk Queen ... Partners In Rhyme MOE BANDY & JOE STAMPLEY	—	$5		Columbia 02198
10/17/81+	10	17		29 Rodeo Romeo ... There's Nothing More Desperate (Than An Old Desperado)	—	$5		Columbia 02532
2/27/82	21	16		30 Someday Soon ... She's Playin' Hard To Forget	—	$5		Columbia 02735
6/19/82	4	18		31 She's Not Really Cheatin' (She's Just Gettin' Even) ... The All American Dream	—	$5		Columbia 02966
10/23/82+	12	19		32 Only If There Is Another You ... Your Memory Is Showing All Over Me	—	$5		Columbia 03309
3/5/83	19	15		33 I Still Love You In The Same Ol' Way ... Drivin' My Love Back To You	—	$5		Columbia 03625
6/25/83	10	18		34 Let's Get Over Them Together ... In Love MOE BANDY (Featuring Becky Hobbs)	—	$5		Columbia 03970
11/5/83	34	16		35 You're Gonna Lose Her Like That ... One More Port	—	$5		Columbia 04204
2/18/84	31	13		36 It Took A Lot Of Drinkin' (To Get That Woman Over Me) ... In Mexico	—	$5		Columbia 04353
6/2/84	8	16		37 Where's The Dress ... Wildlife Sanctuary [N] MOE BANDY & JOE STAMPLEY	—	$5		Columbia 04477
8/4/84	12	22		38 Woman Your Love ... A:8 / S:12 Texas Saturday Night	—	$5		Columbia 04466
10/13/84	36	10		39 The Boy's Night Out ... Alive And Well MOE BANDY and JOE STAMPLEY	—	$5	■	Columbia 04601
1/26/85	48	10		40 Daddy's Honky Tonk ... Wild And Crazy Guys MOE BANDY and JOE STAMPLEY	—	$5		Columbia 04756
4/20/85	58	8		41 Still On A Roll ... He's Back In Texas	—	$5		Columbia 04843
8/10/85	45	14		42 Barroom Roses ... That's All She Needed To Hear	—	$5		Columbia 05438
11/15/86	42	14		43 One Man Band ... Ridin' Her Memory Down	—	$4		MCA/Curb 52950
2/28/87	6	27		44 Till I'm Too Old To Die Young ... A:10 / S:11 You Can't Straddle The Fence Anymore	—	$4		MCA/Curb 53033
8/1/87	11	27		45 You Haven't Heard The Last Of Me ... S:14 I Forgot That I Don't Live Here Anymore	—	$4		MCA/Curb 53132
1/30/88	8	21		46 Americana ... S:11 What Goes Around	—	$4		Curb 10504
6/25/88	47	10		47 Ashes In The Wind ... Hittin' Close To Home	—	$4		Curb 10510
9/10/88	21	19		48 I Just Can't Say No To You ... Nobody Gets Off In This Town #42 Pop hit for Parker McGee in 1977	—	$4		Curb 10513
2/25/89	34	13		49 Many Mansions ... Yuppie Love	—	$4		Curb 10524
6/10/89	53	8		50 Brotherly Love ... Charlie	—	$4		Curb 10537
9/16/89	49	10		51 This Night Won't Last Forever ... Ain't Nothin' Gonna Slow This Train Down #19 Pop hit for Michael Johnson in 1979	—	$4		Curb 10555
	★364★			**BANNON, R.C.** '79 BORN Daniel Shipley on 5/2/45 in Dallas. Singer/songwriter/guitarist. Married to **Louise Mandrell** from 1979-91. 1)Reunited 2)Winners And Losers 3)It Doesn't Matter Anymore				
7/30/77	99	1		1 Southbound ... You Make All The Difference In The World	—	$5		Columbia 10570
10/1/77	90	4		2 Rainbows And Horseshoes ... You Make All The Difference In The World	—	$5		Columbia 10612
12/24/77+	33	12		3 It Doesn't Matter Anymore ... All Of The Best #13 Pop hit for Buddy Holly in 1959	—	$5		Columbia 10655
4/22/78	64	7		4 (The Truth Is) We're Livin' A Lie ... Love At First Sight	—	$5		Columbia 10714
11/11/78	64	5		5 Somebody's Gonna Do It Tonight ... Got That Lookin' Feelin'	—	$5		Columbia 10847
3/10/79	46	8		6 I Thought You'd Never Ask ... Yes, I Do LOUISE MANDRELL & R.C. BANNON	—	$5		Epic 50668
6/2/79	13	12		7 Reunited ... Hello There Stranger LOUISE MANDRELL & R.C. BANNON #1 Pop hit for Peaches & Herb in 1979	—	$5		Epic 50717
9/22/79	26	11		8 Winners And Losers ... Cheatin' On Him, Lovin' On Me	—	$5		Columbia 11081
11/17/79	48	8		9 We Love Each Other ... I Want To (Do Everything For You) LOUISE MANDRELL & R.C. BANNON	—	$5		Epic 50789
3/1/80	65	5		10 Lovely Lonely Lady ... I've Never Gone To Bed With An Ugly Woman	—	$5		Columbia 11210
5/24/80	61	7		11 If You're Serious About Cheatin' ... What's A Nice Girl Like You Doing (Living In A Place Like This)	—	$5		Columbia 11267
9/13/80	36	10		12 Never Be Anyone Else ... What's A Nice Girl Like You Doing (Living In A Place Like This) #6 Pop hit for Ricky Nelson in 1959	—	$5		Columbia 11346
11/28/81+	35	11		13 Where There's Smoke There's Fire ... Before You LOUISE MANDRELL AND R.C. BANNON	—	$5		RCA 12359
1/23/82	46	11		14 Til Something Better Comes Along ... You're Bring Out The Fool In Me	—	$5		RCA 13029
6/5/82	56	7		15 Our Wedding Band /	—			RCA 13095
		7		16 Just Married LOUISE MANDRELL AND R.C. BANNON (above 2)		$5		
12/11/82	35	7		17 Christmas Is Just A Song For Us This Year ... Christmas In Dixie [X] LOUISE MANDRELL/R.C. BANNON	—	$5		RCA 13358

DEBUT	PEAK	WKS	Gold	A-side (Chart Hit)	B-side	Pop	$	Pic	Label & Number
				★ **BARBER, Ava** '78 Born on 6/28/54 in Knoxville, Tennessee. Singer/pianist. Regular on **Lawrence Welk**'s TV show from 1974-82.					
2/12/77	70	8		1 Waitin' At The End Of Your Run ... Blue Eyes Crying In The Rain/Remember Me		—	$5		Ranwood 1071
6/18/77	92	2		2 Your Love Is My Refuge ... I'll Do It All Over Again		—	$5		Ranwood 1077
8/13/77	69	8		3 Don't Take My Sunshine Away ... There's More Love Where That Came From		—	$5		Ranwood 1080
2/4/78	14	14		4 Bucket To The South ... There's More Love Where That Came From		—	$5		Ranwood 1083
6/17/78	44	7		5 You're Gonna Love Love ... I'm Gonna Make It After All		—	$5		Ranwood 1085
10/28/78	75	6		6 Healin' ... I Never Will Get Over You		—	$5		Ranwood 1087
2/28/81	70	5		7 I Think I Could Love You Better Than She Did ... That's How Much I Love You		—	$5		Oak 1029
				★ **BARBER, Debra** '75 Born on 11/3/53 in Tupelo, Mississippi.					
3/29/75	97	1		1 Help Yourself To Me /		—			RCA Victor 10190
3/22/75	98	1		2 You Can't Follow Where He's Been		—	$5		
	★297★			**BARBER, Glenn** '72 Born Martin Glenn Barber on 2/2/35 in Hollis, Oklahoma; raised in Pasadena, Texas. Singer/multi-instrumentalist. 1)Unexpected Goodbye 2)Kissed By The Rain, Warmed By The Sun 3)Stronger Than Dirt 4)Love Songs Just For You 5)I'm The Man On Susie's Mind					
1/25/64	48	2		1 How Can I Forget You ... Rain Check		—	$15		Sims 148
8/29/64	27	9		2 Stronger Than Dirt /		—			
8/22/64	42	7		3 If Anyone Can Show Cause		—	$12		Starday 676
11/9/68	41	8		4 Don't Worry 'Bout The Mule (Just Load The Wagon) ... Reflex Reaction		—	$8		Hickory 1517
9/20/69	24	11		5 Kissed By The Rain, Warmed By The Sun ... My World Is Square		—	$8		Hickory 1545
1/10/70	28	11		6 She Cheats On Me ... Who's Taking The Picture		—	$8		Hickory 1557
6/20/70	72	2		7 Poison Red Berries ... Abilene		—	$8		Hickory 1568
1/16/71	75	2		8 Yes, Dear, There Is A Virginia ... I'm Only Company		—	$8		Hickory 1585
3/25/72	28	12		9 I'm The Man On Susie's Mind ... Satan's Painted Woman		—	$8		Hickory 1626
8/5/72	23	12		10 Unexpected Goodbye ... Blue Bayou		—	$8		Hickory 1645
1/6/73	67	4		11 Yes Ma'm (I Found Her In A Honky Tonk) ... Who In The World		—	$8		Hickory 1653
9/8/73	61	8		12 Country Girl (I Love You Still) ... Watching You Go		—	$7		Hickory/MGM 302
12/29/73+	45	11		13 Daddy Number Two ... We Let That Lovely Flame Die		—	$7		Hickory/MGM 311
4/13/74	65	7		14 You Only Live Once (In Awhile) ... Sweet On My Mind		—	$7		Hickory/MGM 316
11/26/77	79	6		15 (You Better Be) One Hell Of A Woman ... Is Another Man's Woman Worth Another Man's Life		—	$7		Groovy 102
1/14/78	67	6		16 Cry, Cry Darling ... Has It Been So Long		—	$7		Groovy 103
9/30/78	30	10		17 What's The Name Of That Song? ... I Can't Find A Way (To Be Free)		—	$6		Century 21 100
1/6/79	27	10		18 Love Songs Just For You ... Go Home Little Girl		—	$6		Century 21 101
4/14/79	76	2		19 Everybody Wants To Disco ... Most Wanted Man In Tennessee		—	$6		MMI 1029
6/23/79	70	4		20 Woman's Touch ... Most Wanted Man In Tennessee		—	$6		MMI 1031
8/16/80	74	2		21 First Love Feelings ... What's The Name Of That Song		—	$5		Sunbird 7551

BARE, Bobby ★47★ '74
Born on 4/7/35 in Ironton, Ohio. Singer/songwriter/guitarist. Recorded the song "The All American Boy" which hit #2 on the pop charts in 1959, credited to the song's co-writer Bill Parsons. Served in the U.S. Army from 1958-61. Acted in the movie *A Distant Trumpet*. Hosted TNN's *Bobby Bare and Friends*. His daughter Cari, heard on "Singin' In The Kitchen," died of heart failure in 1976 at age 15. Also see **Heart Of Nashville** and **Some Of Chet's Friends**.

1)Marie Laveau 2)Daddy What If 3)Four Strong Winds 4)How I Got To Memphis 5)(Margie's At) The Lincoln Park Inn

DEBUT	PEAK	WKS	A-side	B-side	Pop	$	Pic	Label & Number
9/15/62	18	8	1 Shame On Me ... Above And Beyond		23	$12		RCA Victor 8032
7/6/63	6	18	2 Detroit City ... Heart Of Ice		16	$12	■	RCA Victor 8183
10/26/63+	5	16	3 500 Miles Away From Home ... It All Depends On Linda		10	$12		RCA Victor 8238
2/8/64	4	17	4 Miller's Cave ... Jeannie's Last Kiss		33	$12		RCA Victor 8294
6/6/64	47	3	5 Have I Stayed Away Too Long ... More Than A Poor Boy Can Give #14 Pop hit for **Perry Como** in 1944		94	$12		RCA Victor 8358
11/14/64+	3	19	6 Four Strong Winds ... Take Me Home		60	$12		RCA Victor 8443
3/13/65	11	12	7 A Dear John Letter ... Too Used To Being With You **SKEETER DAVIS & BOBBY BARE** #44 Pop hit for **Pat Boone** in 1960		114	$12		RCA Victor 8496
3/27/65	30	8	8 Times Are Gettin' Hard ... One Day At A Time		—	$10		RCA Victor 8509
6/5/65	7	16	9 It's Alright ... She Picked A Perfect Day		122	$10		RCA Victor 8571
10/2/65	31	6	10 Just To Satisfy You ... Memories		—	$10		RCA Victor 8654
11/20/65+	26	12	11 Talk Me Some Sense ... Delia's Gone		—	$10		RCA Victor 8699
3/12/66	34	6	12 In The Same Old Way ... The Long Black Veil		131	$10		RCA Victor 8758
6/25/66	5	20	13 The Streets Of Baltimore ... She Took My Sunshine Away		124	$10		RCA Victor 8851
10/15/66	5	17	14 The Game Of Triangles ... Bye Bye, Love **BOBBY BARE, NORMA JEAN, LIZ ANDERSON**		—	$10		RCA Victor 8963
11/5/66	38	11	15 Homesick ... Guess I'll Move On Down The Line		—	$8		RCA Victor 8988
3/4/67	16	13	16 Charleston Railroad Tavern ... Vincennes		—	$8		RCA Victor 9098
5/20/67	14	16	17 Come Kiss Me Love ... Sandy's Crying Again		—	$8		RCA Victor 9191
10/7/67	15	13	18 The Piney Wood Hills ... They Covered Up The Old Swimmin' Hole		—	$8		RCA Victor 9314
3/2/68	15	11	19 Find Out What's Happening ... When Am I Ever Gonna Settle Down		—	$8		RCA Victor 9450
7/27/68	14	13	20 A Little Bit Later On Down The Line ... Don't Do Like I Done Son (Do Like I Say)		—	$8		RCA Victor 9568
10/26/68	16	12	21 The Town That Broke My Heart ... My Baby		—	$8		RCA Victor 9643

DEBUT	PEAK	WKS	Gold	A-side (Chart Hit) .... B-side	Pop	$	Pic	Label & Number
				BARE, Bobby — Cont'd				
3/15/69	4	17		22 (Margie's At) The Lincoln Park Inn .... Rainy Day In Richmond	—	$7		RCA Victor 0110
8/2/69	19	11		23 Which One Will It Be .... My Frame Of Mind	—	$7		RCA Victor 0202
11/15/69	16	12		24 God Bless America Again .... Baby, What Else Can I Do	—	$7		RCA Victor 0264
1/24/70	22	7		25 Your Husband, My Wife .... Before The Sunrise	—	$6		RCA Victor 9789
				BOBBY BARE AND SKEETER DAVIS				
8/8/70	3	16		26 How I Got To Memphis .... It's Freezing In El Paso	—	$6		Mercury 73097
12/26/70+	7	17		27 Come Sundown .... Woman, You Have Been A Friend To Me	122	$6		Mercury 73148
5/15/71	8	15		28 Please Don't Tell Me How The Story Ends .... Where Have All The Seasons Gone	—	$6		Mercury 73203
9/25/71	57	9		29 Short And Sweet .... A Million Miles To The City	—	$6		Mercury 73236
4/1/72	13	14		30 What Am I Gonna Do .... Love Forever	—	$6		Mercury 73279
8/26/72	12	14		31 Sylvia's Mother .... Music City U.S.A.	—	$6		Mercury 73317
				#5 Pop hit for **Dr. Hook** in 1972				
1/6/73	25	11		32 I Hate Goodbyes .... Fallin' Apart	—	$6		RCA Victor 0866
4/14/73	11	15		33 Ride Me Down Easy .... A Train That Never Runs	—	$6		RCA Victor 0918
9/8/73	30	13		34 You Know Who .... Send Tomorrow To The Moon	—	$6		RCA Victor 0063
12/22/73+	2²	16		35 Daddy What If .... A Restless Wind [N]	41	$6		RCA Victor 0197
				with 5-year-old son, Bobby, Jr.				
5/4/74	❶¹	18		36 Marie Laveau .... The Mermaid	—	$6		RCA Victor 0261
				"live" recording				
9/7/74	41	8		37 Where'd I Come From .... Scarlet Ribbons (Jeannie Bare) [N]	—	$6		RCA Victor 10037
				BOBBY BARE, JR. & MAMA (his son and wife, Jeannie)				
11/16/74+	29	13		38 Singin' In The Kitchen .... You Are [N]	—	$6		RCA Victor 10096
				BOBBY BARE AND THE FAMILY				
3/15/75	23	11		39 Back In Huntsville Again .... Warm And Free	—	$6		RCA Victor 10223
7/19/75	18	12		40 Alimony .... Daddy's Been Around The House Too Long	—	$6		RCA Victor 10318
10/25/75	29	11		41 Cowboys And Daddys .... High Plains Jamboree	—	$6		RCA Victor 10409
3/13/76	13	14		42 The Winner .... Up Against The Wall Redneck Mother	—	$6		RCA Victor 10556
7/10/76	23	11		43 Put A Little Lovin' On Me .... Those City Lights	—	$6		RCA Victor 10718
10/9/76	17	11		44 Dropkick Me, Jesus .... Baby Wants To Boogie	—	$6		RCA 10790
1/8/77	30	9		45 Vegas .... The Shelter Of Your Eyes	—	$6		RCA 10852
				BOBBY AND JEANNIE BARE				
3/12/77	21	14		46 Look Who I'm Cheating On Tonight /	—			
		14		47 If You Think I'm Crazy Now (You Should Have Seen Me When I Was A Kid)		$6		RCA 10902
7/30/77	85	3		48 Red-Neck Hippie Romance .... Bottom Dollar	—	$6		RCA 11037
4/15/78	29	11		49 Too Many Nights Alone .... Yard Full Of Rusty Cars	—	$5		Columbia 10690
10/14/78	11	12		50 Sleep Tight, Good Night Man .... Hot Afternoon (Arizona Desert)	—	$5		Columbia 10831
1/27/79	23	11		51 Healin' .... Love Is A Cold Wind	—	$5		Columbia 10891
6/9/79	42	8		52 Till I Gain Control Again .... I'll Feel A Whole Lot Better	—	$5		Columbia 10998
9/8/79	17	12		53 No Memories Hangin' Round .... This Has Happened Before	—	$5		Columbia 11045
				ROSANNE CASH with BOBBY BARE				
1/5/80	11	14		54 Numbers .... When Hippies Get Older [N]	—	$5		Columbia 11170
4/26/80	31	12		55 Tequila Sheila .... Qualudes Again	—	$5		Columbia 11259
				above 2 are "live" recordings				
10/4/80	41	8		56 Food Blues .... Used Cars	—	$5		Columbia 11365
12/20/80+	19	12		57 Willie Jones .... If That Ain't Love	—	$5		Columbia 11408
				Charlie Daniels (backing vocal)				
4/25/81	28	13		58 Learning To Live Again .... Appaloosa Rider	—	$5		Columbia 02038
8/8/81	28	11		59 Take Me As I Am (Or Let Me Go) .... White Freight Liner Blues	—	$5		Columbia 02414
11/7/81	35	11		60 Dropping Out Of Sight .... She Is Gone	—	$5		Columbia 02577
1/30/82	18	16		61 New Cut Road .... Let Him Roll	—	$5		Columbia 02690
5/29/82	31	11		62 If You Ain't Got Nothin' (You Ain't Got Nothin' To Lose) .... Golden Memories	—	$5		Columbia 02895
8/21/82	37	11		63 (I'm Not) A Candle In The Wind .... Cold Day In Hell	—	$5		Columbia 03149
11/20/82	83	3		64 Praise The Lord And Send Me The Money .... I've Been Rained On Too	—	$5		Columbia 03334
3/12/83	30	14		65 It's A Dirty Job .... Caught In The Spotlight	—	$5		Columbia 03628
				BOBBY BARE & LACY J. DALTON				
5/28/83	29	15		66 The Jogger .... Gravy Train [N]	—	$5		Columbia 03809
10/1/83	69	7		67 Diet Song .... Stacy Brown Got Two	—	$5		Columbia 04092
8/10/85	53	9		68 When I Get Home .... Party Of The First Part	—	$4		EMI America 8279
11/23/85	76	4		69 Reno And Me .... Party Of The First Part	—	$4		EMI America 8296
8/2/86	67	6		70 Real Good .... Wait Until Tomorrow	—	$4		EMI America 8333
				BAREFOOT JERRY — see **McCOY, Charlie**				
				BARKER, Aaron '92				
				Born on 4/23/68 in Texas. Singer/songwriter.				
7/18/92	73	2		The Taste Of Freedom	—			album cut
				from the album *Taste Of Freedom* on Atlantic 82354				
				BARLOW, Jack '72				
				Born Jack Butcher in Muscatine, Iowa. Singer/songwriter/guitarist. Also recorded as **Zoot Fenster**.				
10/26/68	40	4		1 Baby, Ain't That Love .... It Ain't No Big Thing	—	$8		Dot 17139
5/3/69	55	6		2 Birmingham Blues .... Papa Didn't Give Me No Love	—	$8		Dot 17212
12/13/69+	68	5		3 Nobody Wants To Hear It Like It Is .... No Time For Roses	—	$8		Dot 17317
1/23/71	59	4		4 Dayton, Ohio .... Where There Ain't No Fools (There Ain't No Fun)	—	$8		Dot 17366

DEBUT	PEAK	WKS	Gold	A-side (Chart Hit)	B-side	Pop	$	Pic	Label & Number
				BARLOW, Jack — Cont'd					
11/6/71+	26	13		5 Catch The Wind .... *Again Tonight I'm Wantin' You*		—	$8		Dot 17396
5/13/72	58	7		6 They Call The Wind Maria .... *It's A Long Way Back To Georgia*		—	$8		Dot 17414
				from the movie *Paint Your Wagon* starring **Clint Eastwood**					
8/4/73	55	9		7 Oh Woman .... *Wake Up Anna*		—	$8		Dot 17468
11/8/75	30	10		8 The Man On Page 602 .... *Vinegar In My Wine* [N]		—	$8		Antique 106
				ZOOT FENSTER					
	★255★			**BARLOW, Randy** '78					
				Born on 3/29/43 in Detroit. Singer/songwriter/guitarist.					
				1)No Sleep Tonight 2)Sweet Melinda 3)Fall In Love With Me Tonight 4)Slow And Easy 5)Love Dies Hard					
7/20/74	80	6		1 Throw Away The Pages .... *Hello Pawnshop*		—	$6		Capitol 3883
2/14/76	74	6		2 Johnny Orphan .... *We're Crazy*		—	$6		Gazelle 153
5/15/76	53	9		3 Goodnight My Love .... *Don't Worry I'm Okay*		—	$6		Gazelle 217
				#27 Pop hit for **Paul Anka** in 1969					
8/21/76	46	9		4 Lonely Eyes .... *One Night Stand*		—	$6		Gazelle 280
11/27/76+	18	14		5 Twenty-Four Hours From Tulsa .... *The Bottle Took His Mother (And My Wife)*		—	$6		Gazelle 330
				#17 Pop hit for **Gene Pitney** in 1963					
3/26/77	26	11		6 Kentucky Woman .... *I'm A Swinger*		—	$6		Gazelle 381
				#22 Pop hit for **Neil Diamond** in 1967					
6/25/77	31	9		7 California Lady .... *We're Crazy*		—	$6		Gazelle 413
10/1/77	48	8		8 Walk Away With Me .... *Johnny Orphan*		—	$6		Gazelle 427
4/1/78	10	17		9 Slow And Easy .... *Stranger I'm Married*		—	$5		Republic 017
8/12/78	10	13		10 No Sleep Tonight .... *Burning Bridges*		—	$5		Republic 024
12/9/78+	10	14		11 Fall In Love With Me Tonight .... *One More Time*		—	$5		Republic 034
4/7/79	10	12		12 Sweet Melinda .... *Heaven Here We Come*		—	$5		Republic 039
8/11/79	25	10		13 Another Easy Lovin' Night .... *Louisiana Delta*		—	$5		Republic 044
11/3/79+	13	14		14 Lay Back In The Arms Of Someone .... *Musical Hearts*		—	$5		Republic 049
10/25/80	46	8		15 Willow Run .... *Can't Believe I Fell For That Line*		—	$5		Paid 110
1/24/81	25	10		16 Dixie Man .... *Don't Give Up On Me*		—	$5		Paid 116
4/18/81	13	13		17 Love Dies Hard .... *New York City Cowboys/Deep In The Heart Of Texas*		—	$5		Paid 133
9/12/81	32	10		18 Try Me .... *Why Go Searchin' For Something More*		—	$5		Paid 144
12/19/81+	30	13		19 Love Was Born .... *Cheater's Eyes*		—	$6		Jamex 002
10/29/83	67	6		20 Don't Leave Me Lonely Loving You .... *For A Few Dollars More*		—	$5		Gazelle 001
				BARMBY, Shane '89					
				Born on 2/12/54 in Sacramento, California. Male singer. Also see **Tomorrow's World**.					
5/13/89	77	3		1 Let's Talk About Us		—	$4		Mercury 874168
11/4/89	77	3		2 A Rainbow Of Our Own		—	$4		Mercury 876020
				BARNES, Benny '56					
				Born on 1/1/36 in Beaumont, Texas. Died on 8/27/87 (age 51). Singer/guitarist.					
9/29/56	2¹	17		1 Poor Man's Riches .... J:2 / A:8 / S:15 *Those Who Know*		—	$30		Starday 262
6/12/61	22	4		2 Yearning .... *Go On, Go On*		—	$20		Mercury 71806
7/30/77	94	2		3 I've Got Some Gettin' Over You To Do .... *I'll Drink To That*		—	$8		Playboy 5808
				★ **BARNES, Kathy** '77					
				Born in Henderson, Kentucky. Female singer.					
				1)Good 'N' Country 2)Someday Soon 3)Catch The Wind					
4/26/75	64	9		1 I'm Available (For You To Hold Me Tight) .... *Come To Me*		—	$6		MGM 14797
8/30/75	94	3		2 Shhh .... *I Will*		—	$6		MGM 14822
12/6/75	92	5		3 Be Honest With Me .... *Paper Cups*		—	$6		MGM 14836
				written by **Gene Autry** and **Fred Rose**					
5/15/76	73	6		4 Sleeping With A Memory .... *I Hang My Head And Cry*		—	$5	■	Republic 223
9/11/76	39	11		5 Someday Soon .... *Your Love (Makes Our Love So Easy)*		—	$5		Republic 293
1/8/77	37	9		6 Good 'N' Country .... *One A Day Heartaches*		—	$5		Republic 338
3/26/77	92	3		7 If We Can't Do It Right		—	$5		Republic 369
				KATHY and **LARRY BARNES** (her brother)					
4/2/77	50	8		8 Catch The Wind .... *Starve A Fever*		—	$5		Republic 376
				#23 Pop hit for **Donovan** in 1965					
7/9/77	88	3		9 Tweedle-O-Twill .... *There You Go Doin' It Again*		—	$5		Republic 389
				written by **Gene Autry** and **Fred Rose**					
10/8/77	62	7		10 The Sun In Dixie .... *I Can't Make It Without You*		—	$5		Republic 005
12/24/77+	81	5		11 Something's Burning .... *Take It And Go*		—	$5		Republic 012
				#11 Pop hit for **Kenny Rogers & The First Edition** in 1970					
				BARNES, Max D. '80					
				Born Max Duane Barnes on 7/24/36 in Hardscratch, Iowa. Singer/songwriter/guitarist.					
10/22/77	97	1		1 Allegheny Lady .... *All The Way In*		—	$6		Polydor 14419
1/5/80	88	5		2 Dear Mr. President .... *Patricia* [S]		—	$5		Ovation 1139
3/8/80	79	4		3 Mean Woman Blues .... *Too Far Gone To Find*		—	$5		Ovation 1142
6/28/80	68	6		4 Cowboys Are Common As Sin .... *Only For You*		—	$5		Ovation 1149
11/22/80	88	3		5 Heaven On A Freight Train .... *Patricia*		—	$5		Ovation 1158
3/7/81	84	2		6 Don't Ever Leave Me Again .... *Singer Of Sad Songs*		—	$5		Ovation 1164
				BARNETT, Bobby '68					
				Born on 2/15/36 in Cushing, Oklahoma. Singer/songwriter.					
10/10/60	24	1		1 This Old Heart		—	$20		Razorback 306
2/22/64	47	2		2 Worst Of Luck .... *Working Man*		—	$15		Sims 159

DEBUT	PEAK	WKS	Gold	A-side (Chart Hit)..B-side	Pop	$	Pic	Label & Number
				BARNETT, Bobby — Cont'd				
5/20/67	52	12		3 Down, Down, Came The World .... Too Tough To Die	—	$10		K-Ark 741
10/14/67	74	2		4 The Losing Kind .... A Long Way To Go	—	$10		K-Ark 766
8/10/68	14	14		5 Love Me, Love Me The End Of The Lyin'	—	$7		Columbia 44589
1/4/69	44	10		6 Your Sweet Love Lifted Me .... You'll Fly Away	—	$7		Columbia 44716
6/21/69	59	8		7 Drink Canada Dry .... Image On Your Mind	—	$7		Columbia 44861
3/18/78	97	3		8 Burn Atlanta Down .... Pody And Barbara	—	$6		Cin Kay 128
			★	**BARNETT, Mandy** '96 Born on 9/28/75 in Crossville, Tennessee. Singer/actress. Portrayed **Patsy Cline** in the Nashville musical *Always Patsy Cline*.				
1/13/96	43	16		1 Now That's All Right With Me .... What's Good For You	—	$4	■	Asylum 64308 (v)
5/18/96	65	6		2 Maybe .... Wayfaring Stranger	—	$4	■	Asylum 64280 (v)
8/31/96	72	4		3 A Simple I Love You	—			album cut
				from the album *Mandy Barnett* on Asylum 61810				
				BARNHILL, Joe '89 Born on 6/13/65 in Turkey, Texas; raised in California and Tennessee. Son of Joe Bob Barnhill, leader of **Joe Bob's Nashville Sound Company**.				
7/15/89	56	7		1 Your Old Flame's Goin' Out Tonite .... For Cryin' Out Loud	—	$4		Universal 66014
12/2/89+	57	7		2 Good As Gone .... Becky Morgan (Cotton Pickin' Time)	—	$4		Universal 66032
				BARNHILL, Leslee '79				
2/25/78	92	2		1 Let's Call It A Day (And Get On With The Night) .... I Love The Way You Do What You Do	—	$5		Republic 014
5/19/79	62	6		2 Bad Day For A Breakup .... I'm Still In Love With You	—	$5		Republic 040
				BASS, Sam D. '80 Born in Oklahoma. Joined the backing bands of **Tommy Duncan**, **Tex Ritter**, **T. Texas Tyler** and **Moon Mullican**.				
7/5/80	92	2		1 How Could I Do This To Me .... Get Ready For The Blues	—	$6		3J 1003
			★	**BAUER, Kathy** '83 Born on 8/3/51 in League City, Texas.				
4/23/83	82	4		Hold Me Till The Last Waltz Is Over .... What's A Couple More	—	$5		NSD 164
				BAUGH, Phil '65 Born in 1936 in Marysville, California. Died of heart failure on 11/4/90 (age 54). Session guitarist. Member of the **Nashville Superpickers**. Former owner of the Soundwaves record label.				
6/12/65	16	15		1 Country Guitar .... Chattanooga [N]	—	$15		Longhorn 559
				Vern Stovall (vocal)				
11/6/65	27	7		2 One Man Band .... Live Wire [N]	—	$15		Longhorn 563
				BAXTER, BAXTER & BAXTER '81 Trio of brothers from Rockford, Illinois: Rick, Mark and Duncan Baxter.				
2/28/81	76	4		Take Me Back To The Country .... John	—	$5		Sun 1160
				BEACH BOYS, The '96 Surf-rock group from Hawthorne, California. Lineup in 1996: brothers Brian and Carl Wilson, their cousin Mike Love, Al Jardine and Bruce Johnston. Carl Wilson died of cancer on 2/6/98 (age 51). Group charted 59 pop hits from 1962-89. Inducted into the Rock and Roll Hall of Fame in 1988.				
8/24/96	69	1		1 Little Deuce Coupe .... (no B-side)	—	$5	■	River North 3014
				THE BEACH BOYS Featuring James House				
				#15 Pop hit for The Beach Boys in 1963				
9/7/96	73	1		2 Don't Worry Baby	—			album cut
				THE BEACH BOYS Featuring Lorrie Morgan				
				#24 Pop hit for The Beach Boys in 1964				
10/12/96	69	1		3 Long Tall Texan	—			album cut
				THE BEACH BOYS Featuring Doug Supernaw				
				#51 Pop hit for Murry Kellum in 1963; above 2 from the album *Stars And Stripes Vol. 1* on River North 1205				
				BEAN, Jim '88				
9/17/88	96	1		Lay, Lady Lay	—	$6		Hub 47
				#7 Pop hit for Bob Dylan in 1969				
				BEAR CREEK BAND '88 Group from Durand, Wisconsin. Led by Leonda Sundlin (vocals) and Dan Calllan (keyboards).				
10/22/88	99	1		Falling In Love Right & Left .... I've Had Enough (Of Romance)	—	$6		Bear Creek 103
				BEAR CREEK BAND Featuring Leonda				
				BEARDS, The '88 Brothers Randy (guitar, vocals) and Ronnie (drums, vocals) Beard from Indiana.				
5/14/88	75	4		1 Stone Cold Love .... Fearless Heart	—	$6		Beardo 001
11/26/88	71	6		2 Fearless Heart .... Stone Cold Love	—	$6		Beardo 002
			★	**BEATTY, Susi** '90 Born on 6/1/62 in Alexandria, Virginia.				
9/30/89	71	5		1 Hard Baby To Rock .... Down Home Jubilee	—	$6		Starway 1205
12/9/89+	65	6		2 Heart From A Stone .... Down Home Jubilee	—	$6		Starway 1206
				BEAVERS, Clyde '60 Born on 6/8/32 in Tennega, Georgia.				
10/24/60	13	15		1 Here I Am Drunk Again .... My Love Is Real	—	$15		Decca 31173
3/16/63	27	2		2 Still Loving You .... Happy Times	—	$12		Tempwood V 1039
8/3/63	21	1		3 Sukiyaki (I Look Up When I Walk) .... Handprints On The Window	—	$12		Tempwood V 1044
				#1 Pop hit for Kyu Sakamoto in 1963				
3/12/66	47	3		4 That's You (And What's Left Of Me) .... Old Tree	—	$10		Hickory 1346

DEBUT	PEAK	WKS	Gold	A-side (Chart Hit)	B-side	Pop	$	Pic	Label & Number
				BECKHAM, Bob '67					
				Born on 7/8/27 in Stratford, Oklahoma.					
9/2/67	73	2		Cherokee Strip	You Really Know How To Hurt A Guy	—	$10		Monument 1018
				BECKHAM, Charlie '88					
6/18/88	84	3		Think I'll Go Home		—	$6		Oak 1048
				BEE, Kathy '88					
				Born in Bloomingburg, Ohio.					
10/8/88	100	1		Let's Go Party		—	$6		Lilac 1213
				BEE, Molly '74					
				Born Molly Beachboard on 8/18/39 in Oklahoma City. Singer/actress.					
9/21/74	55	8		1 She Kept On Talkin'	Baby You Got It	—	$7		Granite 509
2/22/75	83	7		2 Right Or Left At Oak Street	I Got A Man	—	$7		Granite 515
				BEE GEES '79					
				Trio of brothers from Manchester, England: Barry and twins Robin and Maurice Gibb. Charted 43 pop hits from 1967-97. Inducted into the Rock and Roll Hall of Fame in 1997.					
11/25/78+	39	12		Rest Your Love On Me	Too Much Heaven (Pop #1)	—	$5		RSO 913
				BEESON, Marc '94					
				Born on 12/20/54 in Champaign, Illinois. Singer/songwriter/guitarist. Founding member of **Burnin' Daylight**.					
9/3/94	70	2		A Wing And A Prayer	We'll Get By	—	$4	■	BNA 62794 (v)
				BELEW, Carl '62					
				Born on 4/21/31 in Salina, Oklahoma. Died of cancer on 10/31/90 (age 59). Singer/songwriter/guitarist.					
				1)Hello Out There 2)Am I That Easy To Forget 3)Crystal Chandelier					
4/6/59	9	20		1 Am I That Easy To Forget	Such Is Life		$12		Decca 30842
				#25 Pop hit for Debbie Reynolds in 1960					
6/13/60	19	15		2 Too Much To Lose	That's What I Get For Loving You	—	$12		Decca 31086
9/29/62	8	12		3 Hello Out There	Together We Stand	120	$10		RCA Victor 8058
9/26/64	23	13		4 In The Middle Of A Memory	Cheaters Never Prosper	—	$10		RCA Victor 8406
8/7/65	12	18		5 Crystal Chandelier	Lonely Hearts Do Foolish Things	—	$10		RCA Victor 8633
2/5/66	43	4		6 Boston Jail	I Spent A Week There One Day	—	$10		RCA Victor 8744
11/26/66	64	3		7 Walking Shadow, Talking Memory	I'm Lonesome	—	$10		RCA Victor 8996
9/9/67	65	2		8 Girl Crazy	Turnabout	—	$10		RCA Victor 9272
3/16/68	68	2		9 Mary's Little Lamb	Once	—	$10		RCA Victor 9446
4/24/71	51	10		10 All I Need Is You	Funny What A Pair Of Fool Will Do	—	$8		Decca 32802
				CARL BELEW & BETTY JEAN ROBINSON					
9/14/74	56	11		11 Welcome Back To My World	Turn Out The Lights And Turn Me On	—	$6		MCA 40276
				BELL, Delia '83					
				Born Delia Nowell on 4/16/38 in Bonham, Texas; raised in Hugo, Oklahoma. Female singer.					
5/7/83	45	11		1 Flame In My Heart	Good Lord A'Mighty	—	$5		Warner 29653
8/13/83	82	3		2 Coyote Song	Lone Pilgrim	—	$5		Warner 29550
				BELL, James '68					
				Born James Mullins.					
5/4/68	51	7		He Ain't Country	A Friendly Place To Cry	—	$10		Bell 710
				BELL, Tommy '82					
				Born in 1950 in Lansing, Michigan.					
10/2/82	83	3		1 Georgiana	Untangle My Mind	—	$6	■	Gold Sound 8013
9/24/83	97	2		2 Honky Tonk Crazy		—	$6		Gold Sound 8016
				BELL, Vivian '77					
				Born in Austin, Texas.					
3/19/77	71	7		The Angel In Your Arms	What In The Name Of Love	—	$5		GRT 118
				#6 Pop hit for Hot in 1977					
				BELLAMY BROTHERS ★66★ '80					
				Duo from Darby, Florida: brothers Howard (born on 2/2/46) and David (born on 9/16/50) Bellamy. Both graduated from the University of Florida; Howard with a degree in veterinary medicine and David with a degree in psychology. David was a member of the Accidents in 1967. Both were members of Jericho from 1968-71. Moved to Los Angeles 1975. Started own Bellamy Brothers record label in 1992. Howard married **Sharon Vaughn** on 6/10/2002.					
				1)If I Said You Have A Beautiful Body Would You Hold It Against Me 2)Too Much Is Not Enough 3)Dancin' Cowboys 4)When I'm Away From You 5)Sugar Daddy					
3/13/76	21	12		1 Let Your Love Flow	Inside Of My Guitar	❶¹	$5		Warner/Curb 8169
2/18/78	86	4		2 Bird Dog	Make Me Over	—	$5		Warner/Curb 8521
4/29/78	19	12		3 Slippin' Away	Let's Give Love A Go	—	$5		Warner/Curb 8558
9/16/78	99	2		4 Wild Honey	Tumbleweed & Rosalee	—	$5		Warner/Curb 8627
11/18/78+	16	14		5 Lovin' On	My Shy Anne	—	$5		Warner/Curb 8692
3/24/79	❶³	15		6 If I Said You Have A Beautiful Body Would You Hold It Against Me	Make Me Over	39	$5		Warner/Curb 8790
8/18/79	5	13		7 You Ain't Just Whistlin' Dixie	Blue Ribbons	—	$5		Warner/Curb 49032
2/2/80	❶¹	14		8 Sugar Daddy	I Could Be Makin' Love To You	—	$5		Warner/Curb 49160
5/24/80	❶¹	17		9 Dancin' Cowboys	Dead Aim	—	$5		Warner/Curb 49241
10/11/80	3	15		10 Lovers Live Longer	Classic Case Of The Blues	—	$5		Warner/Curb 49573
1/17/81	❶¹	13		11 Do You Love As Good As You Look	Givin' Into Love Again	—	$5		Warner/Curb 49639

DEBUT	PEAK	WKS	Gold	A-side (Chart Hit) .... B-side	Pop	$	Pic	Label & Number
				BELLAMY BROTHERS — Cont'd				
6/6/81	12	13		12 They Could Put Me In Jail .... Endangered Species	—	$5		Warner/Curb 49729
10/10/81	7	17		13 You're My Favorite Star ...... It's Hard To Be A Cowboy These Days	—	$5		Warner/Curb 49815
12/19/81	62	7		14 It's So Close To Christmas (And I'm So Far From Home) .... Let Me Walk Into Your Life [X]	—	$5		Warner/Curb 49875
3/27/82	①¹	18		15 For All The Wrong Reasons .... This Time	—	$4		Elektra/Curb 47431
7/17/82	21	13		16 Get Into Reggae Cowboy ...... We're Just A Little Ole Country Band	—	$4		Elektra/Curb 69999
9/25/82	①¹	18		17 Redneck Girl .... Let Your Love Flow	—	$4		Warner/Curb 29923
1/15/83	①¹	18		18 When I'm Away From You .... Long Distance Love Affair	—	$4		Elektra/Curb 69850
5/21/83	4	17		19 I Love Her Mind .... Lazy Eyes	—	$4		Warner/Curb 29645
9/10/83	15	15		20 Strong Weakness .... Doin' It The Hard Way	—	$4		Warner/Curb 29514
6/2/84	5	18		21 Forget About Me .... We're Having Some Fun Now	—	$4		Curb/MCA 52380
9/22/84	6	21		22 World's Greatest Lover .... A:5 / S:6 Rock-A-Billy	—	$4		Curb/MCA 52446
1/19/85	①¹	20		23 I Need More Of You .... S:①¹ / A:①¹ Diesel Cafe	—	$4		Curb/MCA 52518
5/4/85	2²	20		24 Old Hippie .... S:①¹ / A:2 Wheels	—	$4		Curb/MCA 52579
9/14/85	2¹	22		25 Lie To You For Your Love .... S:2 / A:2 Season Of The Wind	—	$4		Curb/MCA 52668
2/8/86	2¹	20		26 Feelin' The Feelin' .... S:2 / A:2 The Single Man And His Wife	—	$4		Curb/MCA 52747
9/27/86	①¹	20		27 Too Much Is Not Enough .... S:①¹ / A:①¹ Restless	—	$4		Curb/MCA 52917
				THE BELLAMY BROTHERS with The Forester Sisters				
1/24/87	①¹	22		28 Kids Of The Baby Boom .... A:①¹ / S:7 Hard On A Heart	—	$4		Curb/MCA 53018
5/9/87	31	10		29 Country Rap .... S:30 One Too Many Times	—	$4		Curb/MCA 52834
8/15/87	3	24		30 Crazy From The Heart .... S:9 White Trash	—	$4		Curb/MCA 53154
1/9/88	5	21		31 Santa Fe .... S:8 White Trash	—	$4		Curb/MCA 53222
5/7/88	6	21		32 I'll Give You All My Love Tonight .... S:16 Ying Yang	—	$4		Curb/MCA 53310
9/3/88	9	19		33 Rebels Without A Clue .... S:8 A Little Naive	—	$4		Curb/MCA 53399
1/7/89	5	20		34 Big Love .... The Courthouse	—	$4		Curb/MCA 53478
5/6/89	51	7		35 Hillbilly Hell .... You're My Favorite Star	—	$4		Curb/MCA 53642
7/1/89	10	27		36 You'll Never Be Sorry .... Hillbilly Hell	—	$4		Curb/MCA 53672
11/11/89	37	12		37 The Center Of My Universe .... Hillbilly Hell	—	$4		Curb/MCA 53719
4/14/90	63	7		38 Drive South .... You Can't Have A Good Time Without Me	—	$4		Warner 19874
				THE FORESTER SISTERS with The Bellamy Brothers				
6/30/90	7	21		39 I Could Be Persuaded .... (album snippets)	—	$4	■	Curb/MCA 53824 (v)
				"45": Curb/MCA 79019 (B-side: "What's This World Coming To")				
3/23/91	46	18		40 She Don't Know That She's Perfect .... I Make Her Laugh	—	$4	■	Atlantic 87748 (v)
8/17/91	74	2		41 All In The Name Of Love .... Anyway I Can	—	$4		Atlantic 87650
6/6/92	23	20		42 Cowboy Beat	—			album cut
10/17/92	64	6		43 Can I Come On Home To You	—			album cut
3/13/93	62	7		44 Hard Way To Make An Easy Livin'	—			album cut
				above 3 from the album *The Latest And The Greatest* on Bellamy Brothers 9108				
8/7/93	66	6		45 Rip Off The Knob	—			album cut
1/15/94	71	3		46 Not	—			album cut
				above 2 from the album *Rip Off The Knob* on Bellamy Brothers 9109				
				BENEDICT, Ernie '49				
				Born on 6/20/17 in Green River, Wyoming. Died on 9/3/2000 (age 83). Accordian player/bandleader. Formed his Polkateers group in Cleveland. Hosted local *Polka Picnic* TV show.				
10/8/49	15	1		Over Three Hills .... J:15 Red Lips And Red Wine		$25		RCA Victor 20-3389
				ERNIE BENEDICT and His Polkateers				
				BENONI, Arne '89				
				Born in Norway. Male singer/songwriter/guitarist.				
6/24/89	96	1		1 Southern Lady .... Those Evening Bells	—	$6	■	Round Robin 1879
				back of picture sleeve promotes a Norwegian cruise ship				
10/7/89	88	2		2 If I Live To Be A Hundred (I'll Die Young)	—	$6		Round Robin 1881
				BENSON, Matt '89				
7/29/89	63	5		When Will The Fires End .... America	—	$4		Step One 406
				BENTLEY, Stephanie '96				
				Born on 4/29/63 in Thomasville, Georgia. Singer/songwriter. Married Brian Prout of **Diamond Rio** on 12/28/2001.				
10/14/95+	21	20		1 Heart Half Empty .... S:10 Love At 90 Miles An Hour (Herndon)	—	$4	■	Epic 78073 (v)
				TY HERNDON Featuring Stephanie Bentley				
2/3/96	32	20		2 Who's That Girl .... The Hopechest Song	—	$4	■	Epic 78234 (v)
7/27/96	60	16		3 Once I Was The Light Of Your Life .... What's Wrong With You	—	$4		Epic 78336
2/22/97	47	11		4 The Hopechest Song	—			album cut
				from the album *Hopechest* on Epic 66877				
				BENTON, Barbi '75				
				Born Barbara Klein on 1/28/50 in Sacramento, California. Singer/actress/model. Regular on TV's *Hee Haw* and *Sugar Time*.				
3/15/75	5	14		1 Brass Buckles .... Put A Little Bit On Me	—	$5		Playboy 6032
8/16/75	61	8		2 Movie Magazine, Stars In Her Eyes .... He Looks Just Like His Daddy	—	$5		Playboy 6043
10/18/75	32	9		3 Roll You Like A Wheel .... Let's Sing A Song Together	—	$5	■	Playboy 6045
				MICKEY GILLEY & BARBI BENTON				
12/27/75+	74	5		4 The Reverend Bob .... Ain't That Just The Way (That Life Goes Down)	—	$5		Playboy 6056
				BERG, Matraca '90				
				Born on 2/3/64 in Nashville. Singer/songwriter. Daughter of Nashville session singer/songwriter Icee Berg. Married to Jeff Hanna of **Nitty Gritty Dirt Band**.				
6/9/90	36	10		1 Baby, Walk On	—	$4	■	RCA 2584 (v)
9/8/90	36	15		2 The Things You Left Undone .... Dancin' On The Wire	—	$4		RCA 2644
1/12/91	43	16		3 I Got It Bad .... Calico Plains	—	$4		RCA 2710

DEBUT	PEAK	WKS	Gold	A-side (Chart Hit)..B-side	Pop	$	Pic	Label & Number
				BERG, Matraca — Cont'd				
5/25/91	55	13		4 I Must Have Been Crazy .... Alice In The Looking Glass	—	$4		RCA 2827
11/16/91	66	5		5 It's Easy To Tell .... Baby, Walk On	—	$4		RCA 62060
9/13/97	59	4		6 That Train Don't Run................................. Here You Come Raining On Me	—	$4	■	Rising Tide 56047 (v)
2/14/98	51	11		7 Back In The Saddle .... Some People Fall, Some People Fly	—	$4		Rising Tide 56055
				BERNARD, Crystal '96 Born on 9/30/61 in Houston. Singer/actress. Portrayed "Helen Chapel" on TV's **Wings**.				
11/2/96	57	15		1 Have We Forgotten What Love Is .... S:13 Eleven Roses Billy Dean (backing vocal)	—	$4	■	River North 3015
3/15/97	70	3		2 State Of Mind.. S:14 Have We Forgotten What Love Is	—	$4		River North 3016
	★231★			**BERRY, John** '95 Born on 9/14/59 in Aiken, South Carolina; raised in Atlanta. Singer/songwriter/guitarist. Began performing in 1981 in Athens, Georgia. Survived a motorcycle crash in 1981 and brain surgery in 1994. Also see **Hope**. 1) Your Love Amazes Me 2) She's Taken A Shine 3) Standing On The Edge Of Goodbye 4) I Think About It All The Time 5) You And Only You				
6/5/93	51	11		1 A Mind Of Her Own... from the album *John Berry* on Liberty 80472	—			album cut
9/25/93	22	20		2 Kiss Me In The Car.. More Than Just A Little	—	$4		Liberty 17518
2/12/94	❶¹	20		3 Your Love Amazes Me /	—			
6/25/94	5	20		4 What's In It For Me "45" issued for above 2 on Liberty 18022	120	$4	■	Liberty 58212 (v)
10/15/94+	4	20		5 You And Only You .... More Sorry Than You'll Ever Know	—	$4		Liberty 18137
3/4/95	2¹	20		6 Standing On The Edge Of Goodbye .... Ninety Miles An Hour	—	$4		Patriot 18401
7/8/95	4	20		7 I Think About It All The Time from the album *Standing On The Edge Of Goodbye* on Patriot 28495	—			album cut
10/21/95	25	20		8 If I Had Any Pride Left At All .... What Are We Fighting For	—	$4	■	Capitol 58465 (v)
12/30/95	55	2		9 O Holy Night .... O Come Emmanuel [X] also see #15 below	—	$4		Capitol 18910
2/17/96	34	11		10 Every Time My Heart Calls Your Name .... from the album *Standing On The Edge Of Goodbye* on Patriot 28495	—			album cut
7/27/96	10	20		11 Change My Mind S:5 Standing On The Edge Of Goodbye "45": Capitol 19251 (B-side: "Time To Be A Man")	103	$4	■	Capitol 58577 (v)
12/7/96+	2²	20		12 She's Taken A Shine S:10 Time To Be A Man "45": Capitol 19451	117	$4	■	Capitol 58624 (v)
4/19/97	19	20		13 I Will, If You Will .... Love Is Everything	—	$4		Capitol 19511
9/20/97	59	6		14 The Stone .... Livin' On Love	—	$4		Capitol 19724
12/27/97	63	1		15 O Holy Night .... O Come Emmanuel [X-R]	—	$4		Capitol 18910
4/25/98	62	7		16 Over My Shoulder .... I Got To Know	—	$4		Capitol 19975
8/8/98	75	1		17 Better Than A Biscuit .... Mr. Jones	—	$4		Capitol 58707
6/26/99	53	10		18 Love Is For Giving	—			album cut
9/4/99	43	17		19 Power Windows .... #35 Pop hit for Billy Falcon in 1991; above 2 from the album *Wildest Dreams* on Lyric Street 65005	—			album cut
10/2/99	70	1		20 There He Goes .... **PATSY CLINE with John Berry** from Cline's album *Duets Volume I* on Private I 417097	—			album cut
				BICKHARDT, Craig '84 Born on 9/7/54 in Haverton, Pennsylvania. Singer/songwriter. Joined **Schuyler, Knobloch & Bickhardt** in 1987.				
5/26/84	86	4		You Are What Love Means To Me .... Overnight Sensations from the movie *Tender Mercies* starring Robert Duvall	—	$4		Liberty 1518
				BIG HOUSE '97 Group from Bakersfield, California: brothers Monty (vocals) and Tanner (drums) Byrom, David Neuhauser and Chuck Seaton (guitars), Sonny California (harmonica) and Ron Mitchell (bass).				
2/8/97	30	20		1 Cold Outside .... S:21 (album snippets)	—	$4	■	MCA 55253 (v)
5/24/97	57	11		2 You Ain't Lonely Yet .... The Tables Are Turned	—	$4		MCA 72005
10/11/97	71	4		3 Love Ain't Easy .... Blue Train	—	$4		MCA 72020
5/23/98	63	6		4 Faith .... Travelin' Kind	—	$4		MCA 72052
				BILLY HILL '89 Group formed in Nashville: **Dennis Robbins** (vocals), Bob DiPiero and John Scott Sherrill (guitars), Reno Kling (bass) and Martin Parker (drums). DiPiero was formerly married to **Pam Tillis**. Also see **Tomorrow's World**.				
7/8/89	25	17		1 Too Much Month At The End Of The Money .... Rollin' Dice	—	$4		Reprise 22942
12/9/89+	58	6		2 I Can't Help Myself (Sugar Pie Honey Bunch) ... Just In Case You Want To Know #1 Pop hit for the Four Tops in 1965	—	$4		Reprise 22746
				BILLY THE KID '79				
6/16/79	50	7		What I Feel Is You .... Songpainter	—	$6		Cyclone 103
				BIRD, Vicki '88 Born on 7/9/55 in Bird's Hollow, West Virginia. Regular on TV's *Hee Haw* from 1989-91.				
10/24/87	64	6		1 I've Got Ways Of Making You Talk .... I Need A Real Good Love Real Bad	—	$4		16th Avenue 70405
4/23/88	61	6		2 A Little Bit Of Lovin' (Goes A Long Long Way)... I've Got Ways Of Making You Talk same song as "Just A Little Bit" by The Diamonds	—	$4		16th Avenue 70413
4/8/89	73	4		3 Mem'ries .... A Little Bit Of Lovin' (Goes A Long Long Way)	—	$4		16th Avenue 70421
10/14/89	87	2		4 Moanin' The Blues .... Mem'ries	—	$4		16th Avenue 70431
				BISHOP, Bob '68 Born Bishop Milton Sykes on 8/6/28 in Henry County, Tennessee. Guitarist with **Marty Robbins** and **Hank Snow**.				
11/9/68	42	6		Roses To Reno .... It's Gonna Hurt You More Than Me	—	$8		ABC 11132

DEBUT	PEAK	WKS	Gold	A-side (Chart Hit)	B-side	Pop	$	Pic	Label & Number
				BISHOP, Joni	**'87**				
8/1/87	71	4		Heart Out Of Control	Walls, Doors, Windows And Floors	—	$4		Columbia 07225
				BISHOP, Terri	**'78**				
7/22/78	97	3		One More Kiss	My Memories	—	$6		United Artists 1194
				BLACK('S), Bill, Combo	**'75**				

Born on 9/17/26 in Memphis. Died of a brain tumor on 10/21/65 (age 39). Bass guitarist. Backed Elvis Presley on most of his early records. Formed own band in 1959. Larry Rogers and Bob Tucker led group after Black's death.

DEBUT	PEAK	WKS	Gold	A-side	B-side	Pop	$	Pic	Label & Number
4/5/75	29	13		1 Boilin' Cabbage	Truck Stop [I]	—	$6		Hi 2283
9/20/75	84	5		2 Back Up And Push	Almost Persuaded [I]	—	$6		Hi 2291
1/24/76	57	8		3 Fire On The Bayou	Memphis Stroll [I]	—	$6		Hi 2301
7/24/76	100	2		4 Jump Back Joe Joe	I Can Help [I]	—	$6		Hi 2311
11/20/76	89	7		5 Redneck Rock	Yakety Sax	—	$6		Hi 2317
				"live" recording					
4/8/78	96	4		6 Cashin' In (A Tribute To Luther Perkins)	L.A. Blues [I]	—	$6		Hi 78508

BLACK, Clint ★53★   **'90**

Born on 2/4/62 in Long Branch, New Jersey; raised in Houston. Singer/songwriter/guitarist. Began singing professionally in 1981 at the Benton Springs Club in Houston. Married actress Lisa Hartman on 10/20/91. Joined the *Grand Ole Opry* in 1991. CMA Awards: 1989 Horizon Award; 1990 Male Vocalist of the Year. Also see **Same Old Train**.

1) Like The Rain   2) Nobody's Home   3) Summer's Comin'   4) When I Said I Do   5) Walkin' Away

DEBUT	PEAK	WKS	Gold	A-side	B-side	Pop	$	Pic	Label & Number
2/18/89	❶¹	24		1 A Better Man	Winding Down	—	$10		RCA 8781
7/15/89	❶¹	21		2 Killin' Time	A Better Man	—	$4		RCA 8945
11/18/89+	❶³	26		3 Nobody's Home	Winding Down	—	$4		RCA 9078
3/10/90	❶²	25		4 Walkin' Away	Straight From The Factory	—	$4		RCA 2520
7/7/90	3	21		5 Nothing's News	Live And Learn	—	$4	■	RCA 2596 (v)
10/27/90	4	20		6 Put Yourself In My Shoes	Live And Learn	—	$4		RCA 2678
2/2/91	❶²	20		7 Loving Blind	Muddy Water	—	$4		RCA 2749
4/27/91	7	20		8 One More Payment	You're Gonna Leave Me Again	—	$4		RCA 2819
7/27/91	❶²	20		9 Where Are You Now	Muddy Water	—	$4		RCA 62016
11/2/91	42	10		10 Hold On Partner	Alive And Kickin'	—	$4		RCA 62061
				ROY ROGERS & CLINT BLACK					
4/25/92	61	8		11 This Nightlife		—			album cut
				from the album *Put Yourself In My Shoes* on RCA 2372					
6/20/92	2²	20		12 We Tell Ourselves	There Never Was A Train	—	$4		RCA 62194
9/26/92	4	20		13 Burn One Down	Wake Up Yesterday	—	$4		RCA 62337
1/16/93	❶²	20		14 When My Ship Comes In	Buying Time	—	$4		RCA 62429
5/15/93	2¹	20		15 A Bad Goodbye	The Hard Way (Black)	43	$4	■	RCA 62503 (v)
				CLINT BLACK (with Wynonna)					
8/14/93	3	20		16 No Time To Kill	Happiness Alone	—	$4		RCA 62609
10/30/93	54	20		17 Desperado		—			album cut (v)
				later issued on vinyl as the B-side of #29 below; first recorded by the Eagles on their 1973 *Desperado* album; from the various artists album *Common Thread: The Songs Of The Eagles* on Giant 24531					
11/20/93+	2²	20		18 State Of Mind /		70ˢ			
2/5/94	74	1		19 Tuckered Out		—	$4	■	RCA 62700 (v)
3/5/94	❶¹	20		20 A Good Run Of Bad Luck	Half The Man	—	$4	■	RCA 62762 (v)
6/4/94	4	20		21 Half The Man	Back To Back	—	$4		RCA 62878
9/24/94	4	20		22 Untanglin' My Mind	I Can Get By	—	$4	■	RCA 62933 (v)
12/31/94+	3	20		23 Wherever You Go	You Walked By	—	$4		RCA 64267
4/8/95	❶³	20		24 Summer's Comin'	Hey Hot Rod	—	$4		RCA 64281
7/8/95	2²	20		25 One Emotion	You Made Me Feel	—	$4		RCA 64381
10/14/95	4	20		26 Life Gets Away	The Kid	—	$4		RCA 64442
12/16/95	58	4		27 Til' Santa's Gone (Milk And Cookies)	[X]	—			album cut
				also see #31, #35, #38 & #42 below					
12/30/95	71	1		28 The Kid	[X]	—			album cut
				also see #39 & #43 below; above 2 from the album *Looking For Christmas* on RCA 66593					
9/7/96	❶³	20		29 Like The Rain	Desperado	—	$4		RCA 64603
11/30/96+	6	20		30 Half Way Up	Cadillac Jack Favor	—	$4		RCA 64724
12/28/96	65	2		31 Til' Santa's Gone (Milk And Cookies)	[X-R]	—			album cut
				from the album *Looking For Christmas* on RCA 66593					
6/14/97	11	20		32 Still Holding On	(long version)	—	$4		RCA 64850
				CLINT BLACK & MARTINA McBRIDE					
8/30/97	2³	21		33 Something That We Do	S:6 (acoustic version)	76	$4	■	RCA 65336 (v)
				"45": RCA 64961 (B-side: "Bitter Side Of Sweet")					
10/18/97+	❶²	29		34 Nothin' But The Taillights	S:18 Cadillac Jack Favor	116	$4	■	RCA 65350 (v)
12/27/97	40	2		35 Til' Santa's Gone (Milk And Cookies)	[X-R]	—			album cut
				from the album *Looking For Christmas* on RCA 66593					
4/11/98	❶¹	20		36 The Shoes You're Wearing	S:20 Nothin' But The Taillights	118	$4	■	RCA 65454 (v)
8/15/98	12	20		37 Loosen Up My Strings	The Shoes You're Wearing	—	$4		RCA 65585
12/26/98	38	3		38 Til' Santa's Gone (Milk And Cookies)	[X-R]	—			album cut
12/26/98	67	1		39 The Kid	[X-R]	—			album cut
				above 2 from the album *Looking For Christmas* on RCA 66593					

DEBUT	PEAK	WKS	Gold	A-side (Chart Hit)	B-side	Pop	$	Pic	Label & Number
				BLACK, Clint — Cont'd					
1/30/99	29	15		40 You Don't Need Me Now	—				album cut (v)
				later released on vinyl as the B-side of #41 below; from the album Nothin' But The Taillights on RCA 67515					
9/4/99	●²	27		41 When I Said I Do	You Don't Need Me Now (Clint)	31	$4		RCA 65987
				CLINT BLACK (with Lisa Hartman Black)					
12/11/99	34	5		42 Til' Santa's Gone (Milk And Cookies)	[X-R]	—			album cut
12/25/99	71	1		43 The Kid	[X-R]	—			album cut
				above 2 from the album Looking For Christmas on RCA 66593					
1/15/00	5	22		44 Been There	When I Said I Do (w/Lisa Hartman Black)	44	$4		RCA 65966
				CLINT BLACK with Steve Wariner					
6/24/00	30	20		45 Love She Can't Live Without	Galaxy Song	—	$4		RCA 69005
9/22/01	27	20		46 Easy For Me To Say	—				album cut
				CLINT BLACK with Lisa Hartman Black					
				from the album Greatest Hits II on RCA 67005					
				BLACK, Jeanne '60					
				*Born Gloria Jeanne Black on 10/25/37 in Pomona, California. Regular on **Cliffie Stone**'s TV show.*					
5/2/60	6	12	●	He'll Have To Stay	Under Your Spell Again (Jeanne & Janie)	4	$12		Capitol 4368
				*answer to "He'll Have To Go" by **Jim Reeves***					
	★244★			**BLACKHAWK** '95					
				Trio of music veterans Henry Paul (member of Southern-rock bands The Outlaws and Henry Paul Band) with the songwriting team of Dave Robbins and Van Stephenson. Stephenson died of cancer on 4/8/2001 (age 47). Touring bassist Randy Threet became the third member in 2002.					
				1)I'm Not Strong Enough To Say No 2)Every Once In A While 3)Like There Ain't No Yesterday					
11/20/93+	11	20		1 Goodbye Says It All	Let 'Em Whirl	111	$4	▮	Arista 12568 (v)
4/16/94	2¹	20		2 Every Once In A While	One More Heartache	—	$4	▮	Arista 12668 (v)
8/20/94	9	20		3 I Sure Can Smell The Rain	Stone By Stone	—	$4		Arista 12718
12/17/94+	10	20		4 Down In Flames	Between Ragged And Wrong	—	$4		Arista 12769
4/15/95	7	20		5 That's Just About Right	Love Like This	—	$4		Arista 12813
7/29/95	2²	20		6 I'm Not Strong Enough To Say No	S:3 A Kiss Is Worth A Thousand Words	104	$4	▮	Arista 12857 (v)
11/11/95+	3	20		7 Like There Ain't No Yesterday	A Kiss Is Worth A Thousand Words	—	$4	▮	Arista 12897 (v)
2/24/96	11	20		8 Almost A Memory Now	Cast Iron Heart	—	$4	▮	Arista 12975 (v)
6/15/96	17	20		9 Big Guitar	S:24 Any Man With A Heartbeat	—	$4	▮	Arista 13017 (v)
10/26/96	49	9		10 King Of The World	Bad Love Gone Good	—	$4		Arista 13049
6/28/97	31	20		11 Hole In My Heart	S:13 She Dances With Her Shadow	123	$4	▮	Arista 13092 (v)
10/18/97	37	17		12 Postmarked Birmingham	It Ain't About Love Anymore	—	$4		Arista 13109
12/27/97	75	1		13 We Three Kings (Star Of Wonder)	Rudolph The Red-Nosed Reindeer (Alan Jackson) [X]	—	$4		Arista 13060
8/29/98+	4	28		14 There You Have It	S:11 When I Find It, I'll Know It	41	$4	★	Arista 13134 (v)
2/6/99	27	20		15 Your Own Little Corner Of My Heart	Nobody Knows What To Say	113	$4		Arista 13158
3/4/00	40	19		16 I Need You All The Time	—				album cut
				from the album Greatest Hits on Arista 18907					
11/3/01+	37	20		17 Days Of America	—				album cut
				from the album Spirit Dancer on Columbia 69882					
				BLACKJACK — see GRAYSON, Jack					
				BLACK TIE '91					
				*All-star trio: Jimmy Griffin (Bread; **The Remingtons**), Randy Meisner (**Eagles**; **Poco**) and Billy Swan.*					
12/15/90+	59	8		Learning The Game	—		$6		Bench 27
				written by Buddy Holly					
				BLACKWELL, Karon '77					
				Born in Ellisville, Mississippi. Female singer.					
1/22/77	93	3		Blue Skies And Roses	I Wanna Love You	—	$7		Blackland 254
				BLACKWOOD, R.W. '76					
8/7/76	32	10		1 Sunday Afternoon Boatride In The Park On The Lake	Lookin' At The World Through The Eyes Of Love	—	$6		Capitol 4302
11/13/76	91	4		2 Memory Go Round	Freedom Lives In A Country Song	—	$6		Capitol 4346
				R.W. BLACKWOOD and The Blackwood Singers (above 2)					
10/28/78	57	6		3 Dolly	Counterfeit Cowboy	—	$6		Scorpion 0561
				*tribute to **Dolly Parton***					
				BLAIR, Kenny '88					
7/2/88	84	2		Lost In Austin	—		$6		Awesome 119
				BLAKE & BRIAN '97					
				Duo of Blake Weldon (born on 9/13/66 in Lufkin, Texas) and Brian Gowen (born on 1/7/69 in Temple, Texas).					
7/19/97	45	16		1 Another Perfect Day	Straight To You	—	$4	▮	Curb 73024 (v)
11/22/97+	62	8		2 The Wish	—				album cut
				from the album Blake & Brian on Curb 77900					
4/25/98	68	1		3 Amnesia	(dance mix)	—	$4		Curb 73052
				BLAKER, Clay '88					
				Born on 6/27/50 in Houston; raised in Almeda, Texas. Singer/songwriter/guitarist.					
5/16/87	91	2		1 South Of The Border	Lonesome Rodeo Cowboy	—	$7		Texas Musik 6153
2/27/88	75	5		2 A Honky Tonk Heart (And A Hillbilly Soul)	The Only Thing I Have Left	—	$7		Rain Forest 120187
				CLAY BLAKER and The Texas Honky-Tonk Band (above 2)					

DEBUT	PEAK	WKS	Gold	A-side (Chart Hit)	B-side	Pop	$	Pic	Label & Number
				BLANCH, Arthur '78 Born in Tamworth, New South Wales, Australia. Singer/songwriter/guitarist. Father of **Jewel Blanch**.					
9/16/78	73	4		1 The Little Man's Got The Biggest Smile In Town .... Another Pretty Country Song		—	$6		MC/Curb 5015
9/1/79	82	7		2 Maybe I'll Cry Over You		—	$6		Ridgetop 00479
				BLANCH, Jewel '79 Born in Australia. Singer/actress. Daughter of **Arthur Blanch**. Played "Charlotte Sutter" in the movie *Against A Crooked Sky*.					
9/30/78	68	6		1 So Good .... Roses Ain't Red		—	$5		RCA 11329
2/10/79	33	12		2 Can I See You Tonight .... When A Love Ain't Right		—	$5		RCA 11464
	★311★			**BLANCHARD, Jack, & Misty Morgan** '70 Blanchard was born on 5/8/42 in Buffalo. Morgan was born on 5/23/45 in Buffalo. Married in 1963. 1)Tennessee Bird Walk 2)Humphrey The Camel 3)Somewhere In Virginia In The Rain					
3/1/69	59	4		1 Big Black Bird (Spirit Of Our Love) .... The Autumn Song (On a Yellow Day)		—	$7		Wayside 1028
2/7/70	❶²	19		2 Tennessee Bird Walk .... The Clock Of St. James [N]		23	$7		Wayside 010
6/20/70	5	13		3 Humphrey The Camel .... A Place In My Mind [N]		78	$7		Wayside 013
9/26/70	27	11		4 You've Got Your Troubles (I've Got Mine) .... How I Lost 31 Pounds In 17 Days #7 Pop hit for The Fortunes in 1965		—	$7		Wayside 015
7/24/71	25	13		5 There Must Be More To Life (Than Growing Old) /					
7/24/71	46	13		6 Fire Hydrant #79		—	$6		Mega 0031
11/6/71+	15	14		7 Somewhere In Virginia In The Rain .... If Eggs Had Legs		—	$6		Mega 0046
3/25/72	38	11		8 The Legendary Chicken Fairy .... The Night We Heard The Voice [N]		—	$6		Mega 0063
9/30/72	60	7		9 Second Tuesday In December .... Don't It Make You Wanta Go Home		—	$6		Mega 0089
3/10/73	65	4		10 A Handfull Of Dimes .... It Seems Like There Ain't No Going Home		—	$6		Mega 0101
12/1/73+	23	13		11 Just One More Song .... Why Did I Sleep So Long		—	$5		Epic 11058
5/11/74	53	10		12 Something On Your Mind .... Here Today And Gone Tomorrow		—	$5		Epic 11097
9/28/74	41	12		13 Down To The End Of The Wine .... You Can't Say I Didn't Try		—	$5		Epic 50023
7/26/75	74	7		14 Because We Love .... It's Me		—	$5		Epic 50122
12/27/75+	68	6		15 I'm High On You .... Let's Pretend		—	$5		Epic 50181
				BLANTON, Loy '85 Born on 7/14/45 in Victoria, Texas. Male singer.					
6/15/85	77	4		1 California Sleeping .... I Wrote The Book		—	$5		Soundwaves 4750
9/7/85	63	11		2 Sailing Home To Me .... Run For Your Life Love Affair		—	$5		Soundwaves 4760
				BLIXSETH, Tim '85					
5/4/85	91	2		It Can't Be Done .... Sometimes I Wish You Didn't Love Me TIM BLIXSETH (with Kathy Walker)		—	$5		Compleat 141
				BLOCK, Doug '84 Born on 8/13/46 in New York City. Died in January 1986 (age 39).					
1/31/81	82	3		1 Have Another Drink .... It's Only A Matter Of Time DOUGLAS first recorded by The Kinks on their 1975 *Soap Opera* album		—	$6		Door Knob 143
12/22/84	73	4		2 Have Another Drink .... It's Only A Matter Of Time [R] above 2 are the same version		—	$6		Revolver 005
				BLUE, Bobby '86 Born in Los Angeles.					
2/1/86	80	3		Once Upon A Time .... Just For You		—	$6	■	Nite 108
				BLUE BOYS, The '68 Backing band for **Jim Reeves**: Bud Logan (vocals, bass), Leo Jackson (guitar), Bunky Keels (piano) and Jimmy Orr (drums).					
7/15/67	63	3		1 My Cup Runneth Over .... Cry For The Lady #8 Pop hit for Ed Ames in 1967; from the musical *I Do! I Do!* starring Mary Martin and Robert Preston		—	$10		RCA Victor 9201
2/3/68	58	6		2 I'm Not Ready Yet .... My Heart's With You THE BLUE BOYS Featuring Bud Logan (above 2)		—	$10		RCA Victor 9418
				BLUE RIDGE RANGERS — see **FOGERTY, John**					
				BLUESTONE '80 Duo of Ray Pennington and Jerry McBee.					
2/9/80	84	3		Haven't I Loved You Somewhere Before .... A Little Thing Like A Golden Ring		—	$6		Dimension 1002
				BOARDO, Liz '87 Born on 10/22/62 in Dorchester, Massachusetts.					
2/7/87	58	6		1 There's Still Enough Of Us .... Hangin' On By A Heartache		—	$6		Master 02
6/27/87	65	5		2 I Need To Be Loved Again		—	$6		Master 03
	★200★			**BOGGUSS, Suzy** '93 Born Susan Kay Bogguss on 12/30/56 in Aledo, Illinois. Singer/songwriter/guitarist. Married to songwriter/engineer Doug Crider. CMA Award: 1992 Horizon Award. Also see **The Red Hots** and **Tomorrow's World**. 1)Drive South 2)Hey Cinderella 3)Just Like The Weather 4)Letting Go 5)Outbound Plane					
3/14/87	68	6		1 I Don't Want To Set The World On Fire .... Hopeless Romantic #1 Pop hit for Horace Hiedt & His Orchestra in 1941		—	$4		Capitol 5669
8/15/87	69	6		2 Love Will Never Slip Away .... True North		—	$4		Capitol 44045
8/13/88	77	2		3 I Want To Be A Cowboy's Sweetheart .... I Still Love You		—	$4		Capitol 44187

DEBUT	PEAK	WKS	Gold	A-side (Chart Hit)...B-side	Pop	$	Pic	Label & Number
			BOGGUSS, Suzy — Cont'd					
3/11/89	46	13		4 Somewhere Between...I'm At Home On The Range	—	$4		Capitol 44270
6/3/89	14	26		5 Cross My Broken Heart ....Hopeless Romantic	—	$4		Capitol 44399
10/14/89	38	13		6 My Sweet Love Ain't Around	—			album cut
				from the album *Somewhere Between* on Capitol 90237				
9/1/90	72	1		7 Under The Gun	—			album cut
12/15/90	72	4		8 All Things Made New Again	—			album cut
				above 2 from the album *Moment Of Truth* on Capitol 92653				
5/11/91	12	20		9 Hopelessly Yours	—			album cut
				LEE GREENWOOD with Suzy Bogguss				
				from Greenwood's album *A Perfect 10* on Capitol 95541				
9/14/91	12	20		10 Someday Soon ....Fear Of Flying	—	$4		Capitol 44772
1/4/92	9	20		11 Outbound Plane ....Yellow River Road	—	$4		Liberty 57753
4/4/92	9	20		12 Aces ....Hopelessly Yours	—	$4		Liberty 57764
8/15/92	6	20		13 Letting Go ....Music On The Wind	—	$4		Liberty 57801
12/5/92+	2¹	20		14 Drive South ....In The Day	—	$4		Liberty 56786
3/27/93	23	15		15 Heartache ....Lovin' A Hurricane	—	$4		Liberty 56972
8/7/93	5	20		16 Just Like The Weather ....No Green Eyes	—	$4		Liberty 17495
12/4/93+	5	20		17 Hey Cinderella ....You'd Be The One	—	$4		Liberty 17641
5/7/94	43	9		18 You Wouldn't Say That To A Stranger ....Something Up My Sleeve	—	$4		Liberty 17907
8/27/94	65	3		19 Souvenirs ....You'd Be The One	—	$4		Liberty 18091
6/1/96	60	6		20 Give Me Some Wheels ....Far And Away	—	$4	▍	Capitol 58564
9/14/96	53	9		21 No Way Out ....Letting Go	—	$4	▍	Capitol 58590 (v)
				"45": Capitol 19252				
3/22/97	57	9		22 She Said, He Heard ....Feeling 'Bout You	—	$4		Capitol 19508
4/11/98	33	19		23 Somebody To Love ....I Surrender	—	$4		Capitol 58699
9/19/98	63	4		24 Nobody Love, Nobody Gets Hurt ....When I Run	—	$4		Capitol 58720
11/28/98+	67	3		25 From Where I Stand ....I Wish Hearts Would Break	—	$4		Capitol 58755
8/28/99	66	5		26 Goodnight	—			album cut
				from the album *Suzy Bogguss* on Platinum 9358				
5/12/01	51	6		27 Keep Mom And Dad In Love	—			album cut
				BILLY DEAN & SUZY BOGGUSS				
			BOLT, Al	**'76**				
				Born Almos Bolt on 6/23/38 in Atlanta, Texas.				
2/28/76	85	6		1 I'm In Love With My Pet Rock ....Paint Your World Happy [N]	—	$6		Cin Kay 102
6/12/76	92	3		2 Family Man ....If Today Were A Fish	—	$6		Cin Kay 103
			BONAMY, James	**'96**				
				Born on 4/29/72 in Winter Park, Florida; raised in Daytona Beach, Florida. Singer/songwriter/guitarist.				
11/11/95	64	4		1 Dog On A Toolbox ....She's Got A Mind Of Her Own	—	$4	▍	Epic 78090 (v)
12/16/95+	26	20		2 She's Got A Mind Of Her Own ....Amy Jane	—	$4	▍	Epic 78220 (v)
5/11/96	2¹	21		3 I Don't Think I Will ....Heartbreak School	—	$4		Epic 78298
10/26/96+	27	20		4 All I Do Is Love Her ....Jimmy And Jesus	—	$4	▍	Epic 78396 (v)
4/5/97	31	20		5 The Swing ....S:22 (dance mix)	—	$4		Epic 78560
8/16/97	65	6		6 Naked To The Pain ....I Don't Think I Will	—	$4		Epic 78675
11/22/97	63	4		7 Little Blue Dot ....(remix)	—	$4	▍	Epic 78742
			BOND, Bobby	**'72**				
				Born in Grand Rapids, Michigan.				
9/30/72	66	7		You Don't Mess Around With Jim ....Looking For My Tracks	—	$8		Hickory 1649
				#8 Pop hit for **Jim Croce** in 1972				
	★330★		**BOND, Johnny**	**'47**				
				Born Cyrus Whitfield Bond on 6/1/15 in Enville, Oklahoma. Died of a heart attack on 6/12/78 (age 63). Singer/songwriter/guitarist. Regular on radio shows *Melody Ranch*, *Hollywood Barn Dance* and *Town Hall Party*. Acted in several western movies. Wrote book *The Tex Ritter Story*. Elected to the Country Music Hall of Fame in 1999.				
				1)10 Little Bottles 2)So Round, So Firm, So Fully Packed 3)The Daughter Of Jole Blon				
2/22/47	4	1		1 Divorce Me C.O.D. ....Rainbow At Midnight	—	$25		Columbia 37217
3/8/47	3	5		2 So Round, So Firm, So Fully Packed ....You Brought Sorrow To My Heart	—	$25		Columbia 37255
8/16/47	4	3		3 The Daughter Of Jole Blon ....It's A Sin	—	$25		Columbia 37566
				JOHNNY BOND and his Red River Valley Boys (above 3)				
6/12/48	9	6		4 Oklahoma Waltz ....J:9 John's Other Wife	—	$25		Columbia 38160
4/9/49	12	2		5 Till The End Of The World ....J:12 Take It Or Leave It Baby	—	$25		Columbia 20549
7/23/49	11	1		6 Tennessee Saturday Night............J:11 A Heart Full Of Love (For A Handful Of Kisses)	—	$25		Columbia 20545
4/15/50	8	2		7 Love Song In 32 Bars ....J:8 Tennessee, Kentucky And Alabam'	—	$25		Columbia 20671
				JOHNNY BOND and his Red River Valley Boys				
8/4/51	7	3		8 Sick, Sober And Sorry ....J:7 Tennessee Walking Horse	—	$30		Columbia 4-20808
11/2/63	30	1		9 Three Sheets In The Wind ....Let The Tears Begin	—	$15		Starday 649
2/6/65	2⁴	21		10 10 Little Bottles ....Let It Be Me [N]	43	$15		Starday 704
2/20/71	59	6		11 Here Come The Elephants ....Take Me Back To Tulsa [N]	—	$10		Starday 916
			BON JOVI, Jon — see LeDOUX, Chris					
			BONNERS, The Blacks	**'88**				
				Black vocal group from Cucamonga, California: Jim and wife Edith Bonner, with children Teresa, Cheryl, Kenny and Jim Jr.				
9/10/88	99	1		Way Beyond The Blue ....You Haven't Tried Me	—	$6		OL 126
			BONNIE & BUDDY — see GUITAR, Bonnie					

See Bonnie Guitar (under Guitar)

DEBUT	PEAK	WKS	Gold	A-side (Chart Hit)	B-side	Pop	$	Pic	Label & Number
				BONNIE LOU '53					
				Born Mary Kath on 10/27/24 in Towanda, Illinois. Singer/guitarist. Regular on the WLW *Midwestern Hayride*.					
5/9/53	7	5		1 Seven Lonely Days ... A:7 / S:8 / J:9 *Just Out Of Reach*		—	$40		King 1192
				#5 Pop hit for Georgia Gibbs in 1953					
9/19/53	6	9		2 Tennessee Wig Walk ... S:6 / J:6 *Hand-Me-Down Heart*		—	$40		King 1237
				BONSALL, "Cat" Joe — see **SAWYER BROWN**					
				BOOKER, Jay '87					
				Born in Pensacola, Florida. Singer/songwriter/guitarist.					
5/2/87	61	8		Hot Red Sweater ... *Mary Mandolin*		—	$4		EMI America 8379
	★327★			**BOONE, Debby** '80					
				Born on 9/22/56 in Leonia, New Jersey. Daughter of **Pat Boone** and granddaughter of **Red Foley**. Worked with the Boone Family from 1969; sang with her sisters in gospel quartet. Went solo in 1977. Won the 1977 Best New Artist Grammy Award. Married Gabriel Ferrer, the son of singer Rosemary Clooney and actor Jose Ferrer, on 9/1/79.					
				1)Are You On The Road To Lovin' Me Again 2)You Light Up My Life 3)My Heart Has A Mind Of Its Own					
10/22/77	4	14	▲	1 You Light Up My Life ... *Hasta Mañana*		❶ 10	$5		Warner/Curb 8455
				title song from the movie starring Didi Conn; first released on Warner 8446 (B-side: "He's A Rebel")					
5/20/78	22	8		2 God Knows		74			
4/29/78	33	11		3 Baby, I'm Yours		flip	$5	■	Warner/Curb 8554
11/18/78	61	4		4 In Memory Of Your Love ... *When You're Loved*		—	$5		Warner/Curb 8700
1/13/79	11	13		5 My Heart Has A Mind Of Its Own ... *I'd Rather Leave While I'm In Love*		—	$5		Warner/Curb 8739
				#1 Pop hit for **Connie Francis** in 1960					
5/26/79	25	10		6 Breakin' In A Brand New Broken Heart ... *When You're Loved*		—	$5		Warner/Curb 8814
				#7 Pop hit for **Connie Francis** in 1961					
9/1/79	41	7		7 See You In September ... *Jamie*		—	$5		Warner/Curb 49042
				#3 Pop hit for The Happenings in 1966					
11/10/79	48	6		8 Everybody's Somebody's Fool ... *I'll Never Say Goodbye*		—	$5		Warner/Curb 49107
				#1 Pop hit for **Connie Francis** in 1960					
2/16/80	❶ 1	15		9 Are You On The Road To Lovin' Me Again ... *When It's Just You And Me*		—	$5		Warner/Curb 49176
7/26/80	14	13		10 Free To Be Lonely Again ... *Love Put A Song In My Heart*		—	$5		Warner/Curb 49281
11/8/80	44	10		11 Take It Like A Woman ... *I Wish I Could Hurt That Way Again*		—	$5		Warner/Curb 49585
2/7/81	23	12		12 Perfect Fool ... *Every Day I Have To Cry*		—	$5		Warner/Curb 49652
6/27/81	46	7		13 It'll Be Him ... *Too Many Rivers*		—	$5		Warner/Curb 49720
	★353★			**BOONE, Larry** '88					
				Born on 6/7/56 in Cooper City, Florida. Singer/songwriter/guitarist.					
				1)Don't Give Candy To A Stranger 2)I Just Called To Say Goodbye Again 3)Wine Me Up					
7/26/86	64	9		1 Stranger Things Have Happened ... *Our Paths May Never Cross*			$4		Mercury 884858
10/25/86	52	9		2 She's The Trip That I've Been On ... *Honky Tonk Song*			$4		Mercury 888044
3/21/87	48	10		3 Back In The Swing Of Things Again ... *Bottom Dollar*			$4		Mercury 888427
6/6/87	52	8		4 I Talked A Lot About Leaving ... *I Don't Feel Much Like A Cowboy Tonight*			$4		Mercury 888598
12/19/87+	44	19		5 Roses In December ... *It's Too Late Now*			$4	■	Mercury 870086
4/9/88	48	10		6 Stop Me (If You've Heard This One Before) ... *Back In The Swing Of Things Again*			$4		Mercury 870267
6/18/88	10	19		7 Don't Give Candy To A Stranger ... S:18 *Back In The Swing Of Things Again*			$4		Mercury 870454
11/19/88+	16	21		8 I Just Called To Say Goodbye Again ... *A Reason For The Rain*			$4		Mercury 872046
3/25/89	19	14		9 Wine Me Up ... *Old Coyote Town*			$4		Mercury 872728
7/8/89	39	9		10 Fool's Paradise ... *Under A Lone Star Moon*			$4		Mercury 874538
3/17/90	75	1		11 Everybody Wants To Be Hank Williams ... *Lovesick Blues*			$4		Mercury 876426
3/9/91	57	8		12 I Need A Miracle ... *Rock On The Road*			$4	■	Columbia 73710 (v)
5/25/91	34	20		13 To Be With You ... *I Still Do*			$4		Columbia 73813
4/24/93	65	5		14 Get In Line ... *Watermelon Time In Georgia*			$4	■	Columbia 74913 (v)
				"live" recording					
				BOONE, Pat '76					
				Born Charles Eugene Boone on 6/1/34 in Jacksonville, Florida. Married **Red Foley**'s daughter, Shirley, in 1954. Charted 60 pop hits from 1955-69. Father of **Debby Boone**.					
4/5/75	72	7		1 Indiana Girl ... *Young Girl*		—	$6		Melodyland 6005
9/27/75	84	6		2 I'd Do It With You ... *Yester-Me, Yester-You, Yesterday* (Pat)		—	$6		Melodyland 6018
				PAT BOONE with SHIRLEY BOONE					
7/17/76	34	10		3 Texas Woman ... *It's Gone*		—	$6		Hitsville 6037
10/16/76	86	4		4 Oklahoma Sunshine ... *Won't Be Home Tonight*		—	$6		Hitsville 6042
11/15/80	60	6		5 Colorado Country Morning ... *What Ever Happened To Good Old Honky Tonk*		—	$5		Warner/Curb 49596
				BOOTH, Larry '78					
				Singer/songwriter/bassist. Brother of **Tony Booth**. Member of **Gene Watson**'s band.					
5/27/78	99	2		I See Love In Your Eyes ... *She's A Cheater Too*		—	$7		Cream 7823
	★374★			**BOOTH, Tony** '72					
				Born on 2/7/43 in Tampa, Florida. Singer/songwriter/guitarist. Brother of **Larry Booth**. Member of **Gene Watson**'s band.					
				1)The Key's In The Mailbox 2)Lonesome 7-7203 3)A Whole Lot Of Somethin'					
3/28/70	67	3		1 Irma Jackson ... *One Too Many Times*		—	$8		MGM 14112
				written by **Merle Haggard**					
12/4/71+	45	12		2 Cinderella ... *Somebody Called L.A.*		—	$7		Capitol 3214
3/25/72	15	15		3 The Key's In The Mailbox ... *The Devil Made Me Do That*		—	$7		Capitol 3269
7/8/72	18	12		4 A Whole Lot Of Somethin' ... *Nobody's Fool But Yours*		—	$7		Capitol 3356
9/30/72	16	13		5 Lonesome 7-7203 ... *Congratulations, You're Absolutely Right*		—	$7		Capitol 3441
1/27/73	32	10		6 When A Man Loves A Woman (The Way That I Love You) ... *Just A Man*		—	$6		Capitol 3515
4/28/73	41	8		7 Loving You ... *What A Liar I Am*		—	$6		Capitol 3582

DEBUT	PEAK	WKS	Gold	A-side (Chart Hit) ... B-side	Pop	$	Pic	Label & Number
				BOOTH, Tony — Cont'd				
7/7/73	49	6		8 Old Faithful .... Don't Let True Love Slip Away	—	$6		Capitol 3639
10/6/73	47	11		9 Secret Love .... Someday I'm Gonna Go To Mexico	—	$6		Capitol 3723
				#1 Pop hit for Doris Day in 1954				
12/29/73+	49	11		10 Happy Hour .... Midnight Race	—	$6		Capitol 3795
				#6-8 & 10: written by **Buck Owens**				
4/20/74	84	6		11 Lonely Street .... It Never Will Be Over For Me	—	$6		Capitol 3853
				#5 Pop hit for Andy Williams in 1959				
8/31/74	27	13		12 Workin' At The Car Wash Blues .... That Loving Feeling	—	$6		Capitol 3943
				#32 Pop hit for **Jim Croce** in 1976				
12/28/74+	72	8		13 Watch Out For Lucy .... Good As Gone	—	$6		Capitol 3994
5/21/77	95	2		14 Letting Go .... Nothing Seems To Work Anymore	—	$5		United Artists 962
	★372★			**BORCHERS, Bobby** '77				
				Born in Cincinnati; raised in Kentucky. Singer/songwriter.				
				1)Cheap Perfume And Candlelight 2)Whispers 3)What A Way To Go				
3/6/76	29	10		1 Someone's With Your Wife Tonight, Mister .... Hobo's Delight	—	$5		Playboy 6065
8/21/76	32	9		2 They Don't Make 'Em Like That Anymore .... I Can't Keep My Hands Off Of You	—	$5		Playboy 6083
12/4/76+	12	15		3 Whispers .... Just For A Minute	—	$5		Playboy 6092
5/14/77	7	14		4 Cheap Perfume And Candlelight .... Hobo's Delight	—	$5		Playboy 5803
9/3/77	18	11		5 What A Way To Go .... Lunch-Time Lovers	—	$5		Playboy 5816
12/10/77+	18	13		6 I Promised Her A Rainbow .... Brass Buckles	—	$5		Playboy 5823
4/8/78	23	10		7 I Like Ladies In Long Black Dresses .... Shawn	—	$5		Playboy 5827
8/12/78	20	11		8 Sweet Fantasy .... You Are Yesterday	—	$5		Epic 50585
1/13/79	32	8		9 Wishing I Had Listened To Your Song .... I've Had A Lovely Time	—	$5		Epic 50650
5/5/79	43	8		10 I Just Wanna Feel The Magic .... Old Emotional Me	—	$5		Epic 50687
2/21/87	80	3		11 It Was Love What It Was	—	$6		Longhorn 3002
5/2/87	86	2		12 (I Remember When I Thought) Whiskey Was A River .... It Was Love What It Was	—	$6		Longhorn 3003
				BOTTOMS, Dennis '85				
				Born on 8/28/54 in Springfield, Illinois. Singer/songwriter/banjo player.				
4/27/85	74	7		1 Did I Stay Too Long .... Pick A Little Boogie	—	$4		Warner 29035
8/3/85	80	5		2 Bring On The Sunshine .... Gone But Not Forgotten	—	$4		Warner 28944
				BOUCHER, Jessica — see MERRILL and JESSICA / STAMPLEY, Joe				
				BOWES, Margie '59				
				Born on 3/18/41 in Roxboro, North Carolina. Singer/actress. Acted in the movie *The Gold Guitar*. Once married to Doyle Wilburn of the Wilburn Brothers.				
3/23/59	10	16		1 Poor Old Heartsick Me .... Blue Dream	—	$15		Hickory 1094
8/31/59	15	14		2 My Love And Little Me .... Sweet Night Of Love	—	$15		Hickory 1102
7/24/61	21	6		3 Little Miss Belong To No One .... Bitter Sweet Kisses	—	$10		Mercury 71845
1/11/64	33	4		4 Our Things .... There's Gotta Be A Way	—	$8		Decca 31557
5/23/64	26	7		5 Understand Your Gal .... You Can Be Replaced	—	$8		Decca 31606
				answer to "Understand Your Man" by **Johnny Cash**				
				BOWLING, Roger '81				
				Born on 12/3/44 in Harlan, Kentucky. Committed suicide on 12/26/82 (age 38). Singer/songwriter/guitarist.				
6/10/78	96	5		1 Dance With Me Molly	—	$7		Louisiana Hayride 783
9/16/78	90	5		2 A Loser's Just A Learner (On His Way To Better Things) .... Lucille	—	$7		Louisiana Hayride 784
2/23/80	55	7		3 Friday Night Fool .... There'll Never Be A Love Song (As Beautiful As You)	—	$6		NSD 37
5/31/80	78	3		4 The Diplomat .... I'm Looking For A Lonely Woman	—	$6		NSD 46
8/23/80	52	8		5 Long Arm Of The Law .... I Can't Get Over You	—	$6		NSD 58
11/29/80+	30	15		6 Yellow Pages .... I Don't Feel At Home (At Home Anymore)	—	$6		NSD 71
				later released on Mercury 57042 ($5)				
4/11/81	50	8		7 A Little Bit Of Heaven .... She Can't Break It To Her Heart	—	$5		Mercury 57049
				BOWMAN, Billy Bob '72				
				Pseudonym for producer/DJ Biff Collie. Born Hiram Abiff Collie on 11/25/26 in Little Rock, Arkansas; raised in San Antonio, Texas. Died on 2/19/92 (age 65). Formerly married to **Shirley Collie**.				
11/4/72	55	5		Miss Pauline .... Showers	—	$6		United Artists 50957
				BILLY BOB BOWMAN and The Beaumont Bag & Burlap Company				
				BOWMAN, Don '64				
				Born on 8/26/37 in Lubbock, Texas. Singer/songwriter/guitarist/comedian. Discovered by **Chet Atkins**. Original host of radio's *American Country Countdown*. Also see **Some Of Chet's Friends**.				
7/25/64	14	16		1 Chit Akins, Make Me A Star .... I Never Did Finish That Song [N]	—	$8		RCA Victor 8384
6/18/66	49	2		2 Giddyup Do-Nut .... Freda On The Freeway [N]	—	$8		RCA Victor 8811
				parody of "Giddyup Go" by **Red Sovine**				
12/3/66	73	2		3 Surely Not .... Dear Sister [N]	—	$8		RCA Victor 8990
2/24/68	72	2		4 For Loving You .... Baby It's Cold Outside [N]	—	$8		RCA Victor 9415
				SKEETER DAVIS AND DON BOWMAN				
10/5/68	74	2		5 Folsom Prison Blues #2 .... House Of The Setting Sun [N]	—	$8		RCA Victor 9617
				parody of "Folsom Prison Blues" by **Johnny Cash**				
5/17/69	70	5		6 Poor Old Ugly Gladys Jones .... Boll Weevil Air Lines [N]	—	$8		RCA Victor 0133
				DON BOWMAN AND FRIENDS				
				Bobby Bare, **Waylon Jennings** and **Willie Nelson** (guest vocals)				
				BOWSER, Donnie '89				
				Born Donald Bowshier on 4/14/37 in Madison Mills, Ohio. Died of a heart attack on 2/22/2002 (age 64). Singer/guitarist.				
9/16/89	90	1		Falling For You .... You've Got My Arms To Come Back To	—	$6		Ridgewood 3002

DEBUT	PEAK	WKS	Gold	A-side (Chart Hit)	B-side	Pop	$	Pic	Label & Number
				BOXCAR WILLIE '82					
				Born Lecil Travis Martin on 9/1/31 in Sterratt, Texas. Died of leukemia on 4/12/99 (age 67). Singer/songwriter/guitarist. Adopted his on-stage hobo attire in 1976. Joined the *Grand Ole Opry* in 1981.					
				1)Bad News 2)The Man I Used To Be 3)Train Medley					
4/26/80	95	3		1 Train Medley .... *Lonesome Hobo*		—	$7		Column One 1012
				Fireball Mail/Train of Love/Walking Cane/Wreck of the Old #97/Orange Blossom Special/Wabash Cannonball/Night Train to Memphis; also see #6 below					
3/13/82	36	12		2 Bad News .... *Lefty Left Us Lonely*		—	$5		Main Street 951
7/10/82	77	5		3 We Made Memories .... *To My Baby I'm A Big Star All The Time*		—	$5		Main Street 952
				BOXCAR WILLIE and PENNY DeHAVEN					
11/13/82	70	6		4 Keep On Rollin' Down The Line /		—			
9/11/82	80	4		5 Last Train To Heaven		—	$5		Main Street 953
4/16/83	61	8		6 Train Medley / .... [R]		—			
				same version as #1 above					
2/5/83	76	6		7 Country Music Nightmare .... [N]		—	$5		Main Street 954
12/24/83+	44	12		8 The Man I Used To Be .... *No More Trains To Ride*		—	$5		Main Street 93017
5/5/84	87	3		9 Not On The Bottom Yet .... *It Ain't No Record*		—	$5		Main Street 93020
7/14/84	69	6		10 Luther .... *(long version)*		—	$5		Main Street 93021
				BOYD, Bill '45					
				Born on 9/29/10 in Fannin County, Texas. Died on 12/7/77 (age 67). Singer/guitarist. Not to be confused with William "Hopalong Cassidy" Boyd. The Cowboy Ramblers included his younger brother Jim Boyd (guitar), Ken Pitts (fiddle), Knocky Parker (piano) and Marvin "Smoky" Montgomery (banjo). Group appeared in several western movies.					
9/8/45	4	2		1 Shame On You .... *Home Coming Waltz*			$30		Bluebird 33-0530
8/24/46	5	1		2 New Steel Guitar Rag .... *New Spanish Two-Step*			$25		RCA Victor 20-1907
				BILL BOYD and his Cowboy Ramblers (above 2)					
				BOYD, Jimmy '52					
				Born on 1/9/39 in McComb, Mississippi. Played "Howard Meechim" on TV's *Bachelor Father* (1958-61).					
12/20/52	7	3	●	I Saw Mommy Kissing Santa Claus A:7 / J:7 *Thumbelina* [X-N]		❶²	$20	■	Columbia 4-39871
				BOYD, Mike '78					
				Born in Houston.					
5/22/76	98	2		1 The Leaving Was Easy .... *Time Wounds All Heels*		—	$6		Claridge 417
8/20/77	93	6		2 Stop And Think It Over .... *Whiskey*		—	$6		MBI 4816
				#8 Pop hit for Dale & Grace in 1964					
2/11/78	80	5		3 Love And Hate .... *Birds And Bees*		—	$6		Inergi 305
				BOYER TWINS, The '80					
				Twin brothers Gene and Dean Boyer.					
2/9/80	91	4		Three Little Words		—	$6		Sabre 4516
				BOY HOWDY '94					
				Group from Los Angeles: brothers Cary and Larry Parks (guitars), **Jeffrey Steele** (vocals, bass) and Hugh Wright (drums). Cary and Larry are the sons of noted bluegrass fiddler Ray Parks.					
7/4/92	43	16		1 Our Love Was Meant To Be		—	album cut		
6/19/93	12	20		2 A Cowboy's Born With A Broken Heart		—	album cut		
				above 2 from the album *Welcome To Howdywood* on Curb 77562					
11/6/93+	4	20		3 She'd Give Anything		—	album cut		
				#28 Pop hit for Gerald Levert in 1994					
4/2/94	2¹	20		4 They Don't Make 'Em Like That Anymore		—	album cut		
				above 2 from the album *She'd Give Anything* on Curb 77656					
12/10/94+	23	20		5 True To His Word .... *I'm Already Lovin' You Too Much*		—	$4	■	Curb 76934 (v)
4/8/95	57	6		6 Bigger Fish To Fry		—	album cut (v)		
				from the album *Born That Way* on Curb 77691; later issued as the B-side of #7 below					
7/1/95	48	10		7 She Can't Love You .... *Bigger Fish To Fry*		—	$4	■	Curb 76940 (v)
				BRADDOCK, Bobby '79					
				Born on 8/5/40 in Auburndale, Florida. Singer/songwriter/pianist.					
7/29/67	74	4		1 I Know How To Do It .... *Get Along*		—	$7		MGM 13737
1/11/69	62	6		2 The Girls In Country Music .... *Put Me Back Together Again*		—	$7		MGM 14017
6/2/79	58	5		3 Between The Lines .... *The Happy Hour*		—	$6		Elektra 46038
2/9/80	87	3		4 Nag, Nag, Nag .... *Rainy Florida Afternoon* [N]		—	$6		Elektra 46585
				BRADFORD, Keith '78					
				Born Arthur Guilbeault in Burrillville, Rhode Island.					
6/17/78	83	4		1 Lonely People .... *A Whole Lot Of Crying*		—	$6		Mu-Sound 421
3/17/79	86	2		2 Lonely Coming Down .... *A Whole Lot Of Crying*		—	$6		Scorpion 0572
				BRADING, Susie '84					
				Born Susan Storment in Lincoln, Illinois.					
2/4/84	94	3		Dream Lover .... *Standing On The Outside*		—	$6		Riddle 1010
				BRADLEY, Owen, Quintet '50					
				Born on 10/21/15 in Westmoreland, Tennessee. Died on 1/7/98 (age 82). Music director at WSM-Nashville from 1940-58. Nashville producer for Decca from 1947. Country A&R director for Decca from 1958-68. Vice president of MCA from 1968. Elected to the Country Music Hall of Fame in 1974.					
12/3/49+	7	4		Blues Stay Away From Me A:7 / J:8 / S:9 *Fairy Tales*		11	$20		Coral 60107
				Jack Shook and Dottie Dillard (vocals); #36 Pop hit for **Ace Cannon** in 1962					
				BRADSHAW, Carolyn '53					
8/22/53	10	1		Marriage Of Mexican Joe J:10 *Baby, Then You're Catchin' On*			$30		Abbott 141
				sequel to "Mexican Joe" by **Jim Reeves**					

DEBUT	PEAK	WKS	Gold	A-side (Chart Hit)	B-side	Pop	$	Pic	Label & Number
				BRADSHAW, Terry '76 Born on 9/2/48 in Shreveport, Louisiana. Pro football quarterback with the Pittsburgh Steelers from 1970-83. Acted in the movies *Hooper, Smokey and The Bandit II* and *Cannonball Run*.					
1/31/76	17	13		1 I'm So Lonesome I Could Cry ....Making Plans		91	$5		Mercury 73760
7/10/76	90	4		2 The Last Word In Lonesome Is Me ....Less And Less		—	$5		Mercury 73808
4/26/80	73	5		3 Until You ....Dimestore Jesus		—	$6	■	Benson 2001
				BRANDON, T.C. '89 Born in Fullerton, California. Female singer.					
9/2/89	93	1		1 You Belong To Me .... #1 Pop hit for **Jo Stafford** in 1952		—	$6	■	Bear 2006
	★392★			**BRANDT, Paul** '96 Born on 7/21/72 in Calgary, Alberta, Canada. Singer/songwriter/guitarist. 1)I Do 2)My Heart Has A History 3)It's A Beautiful Thing					
3/9/96	5	22		1 My Heart Has A History ....S:10 Calm Before The Storm		—	$4	■	Reprise 17683 (v)
6/8/96	2²	23		2 I Do ....S:3 (instrumental) "45" B-side: "One And Only Love"		63ˢ	$4	■	Reprise 17616 (v)
11/16/96+	39	20		3 I Meant To Do That ....All Over Me		—	$4		Reprise 17493
3/29/97	38	15		4 Take It From Me ....12 Step Recovery		—	$4		Reprise 17381
10/18/97	45	10		5 A Little In Love		—			album cut
1/24/98	68	3		6 What's Come Over You .... above 2 from the album *Outside The Frame* on Reprise 46635		—			album cut
4/17/99	47	20		7 That's The Truth ....Let's Live It Up		—	$4		Reprise 16985
9/18/99+	38	20		8 It's A Beautiful Thing ....S:25 Add 'Em All Up		—	$4	★	Reprise 16926 (v)
12/18/99	66	3		9 Six Tons Of Toys ....[X] from the album *A Paul Brandt Christmas - Shall I Play For You?* on Reprise 47264		—			album cut
2/5/00	68	4		10 That Hurts .... from the album *That's The Truth* on Reprise 47319		—			album cut
				BRANE, Sherry '79					
12/9/78+	56	7		1 It's My Party .... #1 Pop hit for **Lesley Gore** in 1963		—	$6		Oak 1013
5/17/80	83	2		2 Little Girls Need Daddies ....I'm Gonna Make You Love Me		—	$6		Tejas 1015
10/11/80	86	2		3 Falling In Trouble Again ....I'm Gonna Make You Love Me		—	$6		e.i.o. 1129
				BRANNON, Kippi '81 Born Kippi Brinkley in 1966 in Goodlettsville, Tennessee. Female singer.					
9/26/81	37	11		1 Slowly ....Dreamin		—	$5		MCA 51166
4/3/82	55	7		2 If I Could See You Tonight ....I'm So Afraid Of Losing You Again		—	$5		MCA 52023
9/11/82	87	4		3 He Don't Make Me Cry ....Piece Of My Heart		—	$5		MCA 52096
2/1/97	42	20		4 Daddy's Little Girl / S:6		120			
6/28/97	53	8		5 I'd Be With You		120	$4	■	Curb/Univ. 56092 (v)
				BREAKFAST BARRY — see GRANT, Barry					
				BRENNAN, Walter '62 Born on 7/25/1894 in Swampscott, Massachusetts. Died on 9/21/74 (age 80). Acted in several movies. Played "Grandpa" on TV's *The Real McCoys*.					
5/5/62	3	13		**Old Rivers** ....The Epic Ride Of John H. Glenn [S] The Johnny Mann Singers (backing vocals)		5	$10		Liberty 55436
				BRENTWOOD '84 Vocal trio formed in Nashville: Jay Kencke, Kenny Wrinn and Ron Freeman.					
10/1/83	96	1		1 Love The One You're With .... #14 Pop hit for **Stephen Stills** in 1971		—	$6	■	Hot Schatz 0051
3/17/84	80	3		2 Anything For Your Love		—	$6		Hot Schatz 0052
				BRESH, Tom '76 Born on 2/23/48 in Hollywood. Singer/songwriter/guitarist/actor. Son of **Merle Travis**. Worked as a stuntman as a child. Member of **Hank Penny**'s band. Appeared in the musicals *Finian's Rainbow, Harvey* and *The Music Man*.					
4/24/76	6	16		1 **Home Made Love** ....California Old Time Song		—	$6		Farr 004
8/14/76	17	11		2 Sad Country Love Song ....While We Make Love Together		—	$6		Farr 009
11/20/76+	33	11		3 Hey Daisy (Where Have All The Good Times Gone) ....Where Was I		—	$6		Farr 012
6/11/77	57	7		4 Until I Met You ....Wonder What It's Like		—	$5		ABC/Dot 17703
9/24/77	48	7		5 That Old Cold Shoulder ....Start All Over Again		—	$5		ABC/Dot 17720
1/28/78	78	4		6 Smoke! Smoke! Smoke! (That Cigarette) ....My Lickskillet, Indiana Home		—	$5		ABC/Dot 17738
4/29/78	74	6		7 Ways Of A Woman In Love ....Huckleberry Week-End		—	$5		ABC 12352
8/12/78	84	4		8 First Encounter Of A Close Kind ....Woman Who Will		—	$5		ABC 12389
12/11/82	77	5		9 When It Comes To Love ....Somebody Like You THOM BRESH & LANE BRODY		—	$4	■	Liberty 1487
				BR5-49 '01 Group formed in Nashville: Gary Bennett (vocals, guitar; born on 10/9/64), Chuck Mead (guitar; born on 12/22/60), Don Herron (mandolin; born on 9/23/62), Jay McDowell (bass; born on 6/11/69) and Randall Wilson (drums; born on 7/10/60). Group named after the fictional telephone number used by **Junior Samples** on TV's *Hee-Haw*.					
9/21/96	44	20		1 Cherokee Boogie ....I Ain't Never		—	$4		Arista Nashville 13039
1/18/97	68	1		2 Even If It's Wrong ....Crazy Arms		—	$4		Arista Nashville 13061
2/22/97	61	6		3 Little Ramona (Gone Hillbilly Nuts) ....Hickory Wind		—	$4		Arista Nashville 13046
6/23/01	11ˢ	22		4 Too Lazy To Work, Too Nervous To Steal ....(album snippets)		—	$4	★	Monument 79611

DEBUT	PEAK	WKS	Gold	A-side (Chart Hit)..B-side	Pop	$	Pic	Label & Number
				BRICKMAN, Jim '98 Born on 11/20/61 in Cleveland. New Age pianist.				
2/22/97	53	4		1 Valentine .... — MARTINA McBRIDE with Jim Brickman from McBride's album *Evolution* on RCA 67516				album cut (v)
1/31/98	9	16		2 Valentine .... *A Broken Wing* (McBride) [R] MARTINA McBRIDE with Jim Brickman	50	$4	■	RCA 64963 (v)
10/25/97	51	11		3 The Gift .... — COLLIN RAYE with Jim Brickman from Raye's album *Direct Hits* on Epic 67893				album cut
1/22/00	74	2		4 Your Love .... — JIM BRICKMAN featuring Michelle Wright from the album *Destiny* on Windham Hill 11396				album cut
				BRILEY, Jebry Lee '82 Featured female singer with Harry James's big band as Judy Branch.				
10/13/79	89	3		1 I Just Wonder Where He Could Be Tonight .... *(And) Robin Danced* HILKA & JEBRY	—	$6		IBC 0004
2/13/82	80	4		2 Let Your Fingers Do The Walkin' .... *Riders & Drivers*	—	$6		Paid 141
	★274★			**BRITT, Elton** *Born same day (6/27) as* '46 *Rosalie Allen* Born James Elton Baker on 6/27/13 in Zack, Arkansas. Died of a heart attack on 6/23/72 (age 58). Singer/songwriter/guitarist. Appeared in the movies *Laramie*, *The Last Doggie* and *The Prodigal Son*. 1)Someday 2)Quicksilver 3)Wave To Me, My Lady *see Pop Memories*				
1/27/45	7	1		1 I'm A Convict With Old Glory In My Heart .... *The Best Part Of Travel*	—	$30		Bluebird 33-0517
1/26/46	2⁵	18		2 Someday .... *Weep No More, My Darlin'*	—	$30		Bluebird 33-0521
3/16/46	3	9		3 Wave To Me, My Lady /	19			
4/13/46	4	1		4 Blueberry Lane		$30		Victor 20-1789
5/11/46	5	1		5 Detour .... *Make Room In Your Heart For A Friend*	—	$30		RCA Victor 20-1817
7/27/46	6	1		6 Blue Texas Moonlight .... *Thanks For The Heartaches* ELTON BRITT and The Skytoppers	—	$30		RCA Victor 20-1873
8/24/46	4	1		7 Gotta Get Together With My Gal .... *Rogue River Valley*	—	$30		RCA Victor 20-1927
10/30/48	6	6		8 Chime Bells .... S:6 / J:12 *Put My Little Shoes Away* ELTON BRITT and The Skytoppers 45 rpm: 48-0143	—	$30		RCA Victor 20-3090
3/19/49	4	12		9 Candy Kisses .... S:4 / J:12 *You'll Be Sorry From Now On* ELTON BRITT and The Skytoppers 45 rpm: 48-0218	—	$30		RCA Victor 21-0006
2/4/50	7	4		10 Beyond The Sunset .... A:7 *The Game Of Broken Hearts* THE THREE SUNS with ROSALIE ALLEN and ELTON BRITT 78 rpm: 20-3599; #71 Pop hit for Pat Boone in 1959	—	$30		RCA Victor 47-3105
2/25/50	3	10		11 Quicksilver .... A:3 / J:6 / S:9 *The Yodel Blues* ELTON BRITT and ROSALIE ALLEN with The Skytoppers 78 rpm: 21-0157	—	$30		RCA Victor 48-0168
5/4/68	26	10		12 The Jimmie Rodgers Blues .... *Singin' In The Pines*	—	$10		RCA Victor 9503
1/4/69	71	4		13 The Bitter Taste .... *My Carolina Sunshine Girl*	—	$10		RCA Victor 9658
	★397★			**BROCK, Chad** '00 Born on 7/31/63 in Ocala, Florida. Singer/songwriter/guitarist.				
8/1/98	51	16		1 Evangeline .... *'Til I Fell For You*	—	$4		Warner 17169
11/7/98+	3	29		2 Ordinary Life .... S:8 *My Memory Ain't What It Used To Be*	39	$4	★	Warner 17136 (v)
5/22/99	19	26		3 Lightning Does The Work .... S:5 *Evangeline*	86	$4	★	Warner 16984 (v)
11/20/99+	30	13		4 A Country Boy Can Survive (Y2K Version) .... S:2 *Going The Distance* CHAD BROCK (With Hank Williams, Jr. & George Jones)	75	$4	★	Warner 16895 (v)
2/19/00	❶³	36		5 Yes! .... S:3 *Tell Me Your Secret*	22	$4	★	Warner 16876 (v)
8/5/00	21	20		6 The Visit	108			album cut
				from the album *Yes!* on Warner 47659				
8/18/01	47	10		7 Tell Me How .... — from the album *III* on Warner 48008				album cut
				BROCK, Joe '76 Born in Lake Placid, Florida.				
5/29/76	98	3		Everything You'd Never Want To Be .... *That's The Way My Woman Loves Me*	—	$7		Ronnie 7601
				BRODY, Lane '84 Born Lynn Connie Voorlas on 9/24/55 in Oak Park, Illinois; raised in Racine, Wisconsin. Singer/actress. Also recorded as Lynn Nilles. 1)The Yellow Rose 2)Over You 3)He Burns Me Up				
2/12/77	93	4		1 You're Gonna Make Love To Me .... *Got A Feeling* LYNN NILLES	—	$5		GRT 100
4/24/82	60	6		2 He's Taken .... *My Side Of The Bed*	—	$4		Liberty 1457
7/17/82	61	7		3 More Nights .... *My Side Of The Bed*	—	$4		Liberty 1470
12/11/82	77	5		4 When It Comes To Love .... *Somebody Like You* THOM BRESH & LANE BRODY	—	$4	■	Liberty 1487
5/21/83	15	19		5 Over You .... *My Side Of The Bed* from the movie *Tender Mercies* starring Robert Duvall	—	$4	■	Liberty 1498
11/19/83	60	7		6 It's Another Silent Night .... *It's A Bad Night For Good Girls*	—	$4		Liberty 1509
2/4/84	❶¹	22		7 The Yellow Rose .... — JOHNNY LEE with Lane Brody same melody as "The Yellow Rose Of Texas" with new lyrics; from the TV series starring Cybill Shepherd		$4		Warner 29375
5/12/84	59	7		8 Hanging On .... *If I Were Loving You Now*	—	$4		Liberty 1519
8/25/84	81	5		9 Alibis .... *One Heart Away (From Being In Love)*	—	$4		EMI America 8218

DEBUT	PEAK	WKS	Gold	A-side (Chart Hit)	B-side	Pop	$	Pic	Label & Number
				BRODY, Lane — Cont'd					
5/18/85	29	14		10 He Burns Me Up .... S:29 / A:29	Memory Now	—	$4	■	EMI America 8266
9/7/85	51	10		11 Baby's Eyes	Anything But My Baby	—	$4		EMI America 8283
4/5/86	50	8		12 I Could Get Used To This	It Ain't The Leaving	—	$4		Warner 28747
				JOHNNY LEE & LANE BRODY					
				BROKOP, Lisa '95					
				Born on 6/6/73 in Surrey, British Columbia, Canada.					
8/20/94	52	10		1 Give Me A Ring Sometime	Let Me Live Another Day	—	$4	▌	Capitol 58191 (v)
				"45": Capitol 18094					
11/26/94+	52	20		2 Take That	Every Little Girl's Dream	—	$4	▌	Capitol 58310 (v)
4/15/95	64	5		3 One Of Those Nights	Take That	—	$4		Capitol 18585
7/29/95	60	7		4 Who Needs You	One Of Those Nights	—	$4		Capitol 58435 (v)
				"45": Capitol 18732 (B-side: "Never Did Say Goodbye")					
11/25/95+	55	12		5 She Can't Save Him	From The Heart	—	$4	▌	Capitol 58502
3/23/96	63	7		6 Before He Kissed Me	Every Little Girl's Dream	—	$4	▌	Capitol 58557
5/23/98	59	7		7 How Do I Let Go	Ain't Enough Roses	—	$4	▌	Columbia 78879
11/14/98	64	3		8 When You Get To Be You	How Do I Let Go	—	$4	▌	Columbia 79012
2/20/99	65	3		9 Ain't Enough Roses		—			album cut
				from the album *When You Get To Be You* on Columbia					

BROOKS, Garth ★28★   '93

Born Troyal Garth Brooks on 2/7/62 in Luba, Oklahoma; raised in Yukon, Oklahoma. Singer/songwriter/guitarist. His mother, Colleen Carroll, recorded with Capitol in 1954 and was a regular on **Red Foley**'s *Ozark Jubilee* TV show. Attended Oklahoma State University on a track scholarship. Played local clubs and worked as a bouncer. Joined the *Grand Ole Opry* in 1990. CMA Awards: 1990 Horizon Award; 1991, 1992, 1997 & 1998 Entertainer of the Year.

1) Friends In Low Places   2) What She's Doing Now   3) The Dance   4) Longneck Bottle   5) Unanswered Prayers

DEBUT	PEAK	WKS		A-side	B-side	Pop	$	Label & Number
3/25/89	8	26		1 Much Too Young (To Feel This Damn Old)	Alabama Clay	—	$8	Capitol 44342
9/9/89	❶¹	26		2 If Tomorrow Never Comes	Nobody Gets Off In This Town	—	$10	Capitol 44430
1/20/90	2¹	25		3 Not Counting You	Cowboy Bill	—	$6	Capitol 44492
5/5/90	❶³	21		4 The Dance	(same version)	—	$8	Capitol 44629
8/18/90	❶⁴	20		5 Friends In Low Places	Nobody Gets Off In This Town	—	$10	Capitol 44647
				CMA Award: Single of the Year				
11/3/90+	❶²	20		6 Unanswered Prayers	Alabama Clay	—	$8	Capitol 44650
2/9/91	❶¹	20		7 Two Of A Kind, Workin' On A Full House	The Dance	—	$6	Capitol 44701
5/18/91	❶²	20		8 The Thunder Rolls	Victim Of The Game	—	$8	Capitol 44727
8/17/91	3	20		9 Rodeo	New Way To Fly	—	$8	Capitol 44771
10/19/91	❶²	20		10 Shameless	Against The Grain	—	$8	Capitol 44800
				first recorded by Billy Joel on his 1989 *Storm Front* album				
1/4/92	❶⁴	20		11 What She's Doing Now	Friends In Low Places	—	$6	Liberty 57733
2/1/92	3	20		12 Papa Loved Mama	New Way To Fly	—	$6	Liberty 57734
3/21/92	66	20		13 Against The Grain		—		album cut
				from the album *Ropin' The Wind* on Capitol 96330				
5/2/92	❶¹	20		14 The River	We Bury The Hatchet	—	$6	Liberty 57765
9/12/92	12	20		15 We Shall Be Free	Night Rider's Lament	—	$6	Liberty 57994
10/17/92+	❶¹	20		16 Somewhere Other Than The Night	Mr. Right	—	$6	Liberty 56824
12/26/92	48	4		17 The Old Man's Back In Town	Santa Looked A Lot Like Daddy [X]	—	$5	Liberty 57893
				also see #54 below				
2/6/93	2¹	20		18 Learning To Live Again	Walking After Midnight	—	$5	Liberty 56973
2/13/93	73	1		19 Dixie Chicken		—		album cut (v)
				from the album *The Chase* on Liberty 98743; later issued as the B-side of #20 below				
5/8/93	❶¹	20		20 That Summer	Dixie Chicken	—	$5	Liberty 17324
8/7/93	❶²	20		21 Ain't Going Down (Til The Sun Comes Up)	Kickin' And Screamin'	—	$8	Liberty 17496
9/11/93	❶¹	20		22 American Honky-Tonk Bar Association	Everytime That It Rains	—	$6	Liberty 17639
9/18/93+	3	20		23 Standing Outside The Fire	Cold Shoulder	—	$6	Liberty 17802
9/18/93	70	5		24 Callin' Baton Rouge		—		album cut
				also see #28 below				
9/18/93	74	1		25 One Night A Day		—		album cut
				above 2 from the album *In Pieces* on Liberty 80857				
5/14/94	7	19		26 One Night A Day	Mr. Blue [R]	—	$5	Liberty 17972
7/16/94	67	11		27 Hard Luck Woman		45ᴬ		album cut
				#15 Pop hit for Kiss in 1977; from the various artists album *Kiss My Ass: Classic Kiss Regrooved* on Mercury 522123				
8/13/94	2¹	15		28 Callin' Baton Rouge	Same Old Story [R]	—	$6	Liberty 18136
11/26/94+	49	20		29 The Red Strokes	Burning Bridges	—	$5	Liberty 18554
12/31/94	70	1		30 White Christmas	God Rest Ye Merry Gentlemen [X]	—	$5	Liberty 57892
				#1 Pop hit for **Bing Crosby** in 1942; also see #69 below				
9/9/95	❶¹	20		31 She's Every Woman	The Cowboy Song	—	$6	Capitol 18842
11/25/95	23	14		32 The Fever	The Night Will Only Know	—	$6	Capitol 18948
				first recorded by Aerosmith on their 1993 *Get A Grip* album				
12/9/95	❶¹	20		33 The Beaches Of Cheyenne	Ireland	—	$6	Capitol 19022
12/9/95+	5	32		34 It's Midnight Cinderella		—		album cut
12/9/95+	19	20		35 The Change		—		album cut
12/9/95	64	1		36 The Old Stuff		—		album cut
				also see #40 below				

DEBUT	PEAK	WKS	Gold	A-side (Chart Hit)	B-side	Pop	$	Pic	Label & Number
				BROOKS, Garth — Cont'd					
12/9/95	71	1		37 Rollin'		—			album cut (v)
				later issued as the B-side of #42 below					
12/9/95	75	1		38 That Ol' Wind		—			album cut
10/5/96	4	19		39 That Ol' Wind [R]		—			album cut
2/8/97	70	3		40 The Old Stuff [R]		—			album cut
				#34-40: from the album Fresh Horses on Capitol 32080					
8/23/97	2²	20		41 In Another's Eyes	I Want To Live Again (Yearwood)	—	$4		MCA 72021
				TRISHA YEARWOOD AND GARTH BROOKS					
11/22/97	●³	20		42 Longneck Bottle	Rollin'	—	$4		Capitol 19851
12/6/97+	●¹	28		43 Two Piña Coladas		—			album cut
12/6/97+	2¹	20		44 She's Gonna Make It		—			album cut
12/6/97	41	8		45 Belleau Wood [X]		—			album cut
				also see #65 below					
12/6/97	52	2		46 Cowboy Cadillac		—			album cut
12/6/97	57	2		47 Take The Keys To My Heart		—			album cut
12/6/97	59	2		48 How You Ever Gonna Know		—			album cut
12/6/97	62	2		49 Do What You Gotta Do		—			album cut
				also see #75 below					
12/6/97	67	1		50 You Move Me		—			album cut
				also see #60 below					
12/6/97	68	1		51 A Friend To Me		—			album cut
12/6/97	70	1		52 I Don't Have To Wonder		—			album cut
				#43-52: from the album Sevens on Capitol 56599					
12/27/97	56	2		53 Santa Looked A Lot Like Daddy / [X]		—			
				first recorded by Buck Owens in 1965					
12/27/97	59	2		54 The Old Man's Back In Town [X-R]		—	$5		Liberty 57893
5/9/98	26	20		55 Burnin' The Roadhouse Down	Road Trippin' (Wariner)	—	$4		Capitol 58716
				STEVE WARINER (with Garth Brooks)					
5/16/98	●¹	20		56 To Make You Feel My Love		—			album cut
				from the movie Hope Floats starring Sandra Bullock (soundtrack on Capitol 93402)					
5/23/98	65	4		57 Uptown Down-Home Good Ol' Boy		—			album cut
5/23/98	68	1		58 Something With A Ring To It		—			album cut
				above 2 from the album Sevens on Capitol 56599					
5/30/98	69	5		59 One Heart At A Time	S:5 (same version)	56	$4	■	Atlantic 84117
				GARTH BROOKS, BILLY DEAN, FAITH HILL, OLIVIA NEWTON-JOHN, NEAL McCOY, MICHAEL McDONALD, VICTORIA SHAW, BRYAN WHITE					
8/29/98	3	19		60 You Move Me [R]		—			album cut
				from the album Sevens on Capitol 56599					
9/19/98	18	20		61 Where Your Road Leads	Bring Me All Your Lovin' (Yearwood)	—	$4		MCA Nashville 72070
				TRISHA YEARWOOD With Garth Brooks					
11/14/98	9	20		62 It's Your Song		62			album cut
12/5/98	63	1		63 Tearin' It Up (And Burnin' It Down)		—			album cut
				also see #76 below					
12/5/98	65	1		64 Wild As The Wind		—			album cut
				GARTH BROOKS (With Trisha Yearwood)					
				above 3 from the album Double Live on Capitol 97424					
12/26/98	65	2		65 Belleau Wood [X-R]		—			album cut
				from the album Sevens on Capitol 56599					
12/26/98	72	1		66 Go Tell It On The Mountain [X]		—			album cut
				from the album Beyond The Season on Liberty 98742					
8/28/99	24	15		67 It Don't Matter To The Sun /	S:●¹⁰	113			
8/7/99	62	4		68 Lost In You		5	$4	★	Capitol 58788 (v)
				GARTH BROOKS AS CHRIS GAINES (above 2)					
12/11/99	65	4		69 White Christmas	God Rest Ye Merry Gentlemen [X-R]	—	$5		Liberty 57892
12/18/99	54	4		70 Sleigh Ride [X]		—			album cut
12/18/99	62	3		71 Baby Jesus Is Born [X]		—			album cut
12/25/99	56	3		72 It's The Most Wonderful Time Of The Year [X]		—			album cut
12/25/99	63	3		73 There's No Place Like Home For The Holidays [X]		—			album cut
12/25/99	69	1		74 God Rest Ye Merry Gentlemen [X]		—			album cut (v)
				first released as the B-side of #30 above; above 5 from the album Garth Brooks & The Magic Of Christmas on Capitol 23550					
1/15/00	13	18		75 Do What You Gotta Do	A Friend To Me [R]	69	$4		Capitol 58845
1/15/00	73	1		76 Tearin' It Up (And Burnin' It Down) [R]		—			album cut
				from the album Double Live on Capitol 97424					
5/13/00	21	20		77 When You Come Back To Me Again		105	$10	★	Capitol (no #)
				from the movie Frequency starring Dennis Quaid; issued as a promo CD single only (with no number)					
6/17/00	22	20		78 Katie Wants A Fast One	I Just Do (Wariner)	109	$4		Capitol 58878
				STEVE WARINER With Garth Brooks					
11/25/00+	7	20		79 Wild Horses		50			album cut
				from the 1990 album No Fences on Capitol 93866					
10/13/01	24	20		80 Beer Run		118			album cut
				GEORGE JONES With Garth Brooks					
				from Jones's album The Rock: Stone Cold Country 2001 on Bandit 67029					
10/27/01+	5	20		81 Wrapped Up In You		46			album cut
12/1/01+	16	20		82 Squeeze Me In		102			album cut
				GARTH BROOKS with Trisha Yearwood					
12/1/01	58	1		83 Thicker Than Blood		—			album cut
				above 3 from the album Scarecrow on Capitol 31330					
12/29/01	55	2		84 Call Me Claus /	S:4 [X]	22ˢ			
12/29/01	56	1		85 'Zat You, Santa Claus? [X]		—	$4	★	Capitol 77669 (v)

DEBUT	PEAK	WKS	Gold	A-side (Chart Hit)	B-side	Pop	$	Pic	Label & Number
				BROOKS, Karen '83					
				Born on 4/29/54 in Dallas. Female singer.					
7/31/82	17	19		1 New Way Out ....Country Girl		—	$5		Warner 29958
11/20/82+	❶¹	20		2 Faking Love ....Reno And Me		—	$4		Warner/Curb 29854
				T.G. SHEPPARD AND KAREN BROOKS					
2/5/83	21	14		3 If That's What You're Thinking................................Every Beat Of My Heart		—	$5		Warner 29789
6/18/83	30	12		4 Walk On ....Every Beat Of My Heart		—	$5		Warner 29644
4/28/84	40	11		5 Born To Love You ....A Little Common Kindness		—	$5		Warner 29302
7/21/84	19	16		6 Tonight I'm Here With Someone Else ....Give It Up		—	$5		Warner 29225
1/5/85	63	8		7 A Simple I Love You ....Give It Up		—	$5		Warner 29154
7/13/85	45	9		8 I Will Dance With You ....Too Bad For Love		—	$5		Warner 28979
				KAREN BROOKS with Johnny Cash					
				BROOKS, Kix '83					
				Born Leon Eric Brooks III on 5/12/55 in Shreveport, Louisiana. Joined with **Ronnie Dunn** in 1991 in duo **Brooks & Dunn**. Also see **Tomorrow's World**.					
9/10/83	73	4		1 Baby, When Your Heart Breaks Down		—	$8		Avion 103
1/28/89	87	2		2 Sacred Ground ....Story Of My Life		—	$5		Capitol 44275
				BROOKS & DUNN ★62★ '98					
				Duo of **Kix Brooks** (born on 5/12/55 in Shreveport, Louisiana) and **Ronnie Dunn** (born on 6/1/53 in Coleman, Texas). Both sing and play guitar. CMA Awards: 1992, 1993, 1994, 1995, 1996, 1997, 1998, 1999 & 2001 Vocal Duo of the Year; 1996 Entertainer of the Year.					
				1)Ain't Nothing 'Bout You 2)Boot Scootin' Boogie 3)My Maria 4)How Long Gone 5)If You See Him/If You See Her					
6/22/91	❶²	20		1 Brand New Man ....I'm No Good		—	$4		Arista 2232
10/12/91	❶²	20		2 My Next Broken Heart ....Boot Scootin' Boogie		—	$4		Arista 12337
2/1/92	❶²	20		3 Neon Moon ....Cheating On The Blues		—	$4		Arista 12388
5/23/92	❶⁴	20		4 Boot Scootin' Boogie ....(album version)		50	$4	■	Arista 12440 (v)
				"45" B-side: "Lost And Found"					
9/19/92	6	20		5 Lost And Found ....Cool Drink Of Water		—	$4		Arista 12460
2/6/93	4	20		6 Hard Workin' Man ....Texas Women (Don't Stay Lonely Long)		—	$4		Arista 12513
5/15/93	2²	20		7 We'll Burn That Bridge ....Heartbroke Out Of My Mind		—	$4	■	Arista 12563 (v)
9/4/93	❶¹	20		8 She Used To Be Mine ....That Ain't No Way To Go		—	$4		Arista 12602
12/11/93+	2²	20		9 Rock My World (Little Country Girl) ....(club mix)		97	$4	■	Arista 12636 (v)
				"45" B-side: "Our Time Is Coming"					
3/5/94	73	4		10 Ride 'em High, Ride 'em Low		—			album cut
				from the movie *8 Seconds* starring Luke Perry; from the soundtrack on MCA 10927					
3/19/94	73	1		11 Corine, Corina		—			album cut
				ASLEEP AT THE WHEEL Featuring Brooks & Dunn					
				#9 Pop hit for Ray Peterson in 1961; from the album *Tribute To **Bob Wills*** on Liberty 81470					
4/9/94	❶¹	20		12 That Ain't No Way To Go ....I Can't Put Out This Fire		—	$4		Arista 12669
8/27/94	❶²	20		13 She's Not The Cheatin' Kind ....She's The Kind Of Trouble		—	$4		Arista 12740
11/12/94	6	20		14 I'll Never Forgive My Heart ....A Few Good Rides Away		—	$4		Arista 12779
2/18/95	❶¹	20		15 Little Miss Honky Tonk ....Silver And Gold		—	$4	■	Arista 12790 (v)
6/10/95	❶²	20		16 You're Gonna Miss Me When I'm Gone ......If That's The Way You Want It		—	$4		Arista 12831
9/23/95	5	20		17 Whiskey Under The Bridge ....My Kind Of Crazy		—	$4		Arista 12770
4/6/96	❶³	20		18 My Maria S:❶⁸ Mama Don't Get Dressed Up For Nothing		79	$4	■	Arista 12993 (v)
				#9 Pop hit for B.W. Stevenson in 1973					
4/27/96	2²	20		19 I Am That Man S:8 More Than A Margarita		—	$4	■	Arista 13018 (v)
9/14/96	13	20		20 Mama Don't Get Dressed Up For Nothing............S:15 Tequila Town		—	$4	■	Arista Nash. 13043 (v)
12/7/96+	❶¹	20		21 A Man This Lonely S:12 One Heartache At A Time		124	$4	■	Arista Nash. 13066 (v)
3/22/97	8	20		22 Why Would I Say Goodbye ....White Line Casanova		—	$4		Arista Nashville 13073
8/30/97	3	20		23 Honky Tonk Truth ....—		—		(v)	album cut
				from the album *The Greatest Hits Collection* on Arista Nashville 18852; later issued as the B-side of #24 below					
10/18/97+	2²	24		24 He's Got You ....Honky Tonk Truth		—	$4		Arista Nashville 13101
5/2/98	❶²	20		25 If You See Him/If You See Her ....(same version)		—	$4		Arista Nashville 13116
				REBA/BROOKS & DUNN					
7/4/98	❶³	21		26 How Long Gone /		—			
9/26/98	❶¹	20		27 Husbands And Wives		36	$4		Arista Nashville 13143
1/16/99	5	20		28 I Can't Get Over You ....Way Gone		51	$4		Arista Nashville 13152
5/1/99	41	10		29 South Of Santa Fe ....Your Love Don't Take A Backseat To Nothing		—	$4		Arista Nashville 13164
8/7/99	15	20		30 Missing You ....The Trouble With Angels		75	$4		Arista Nashville 13179
				#1 Pop hit for John Waite in 1984					
10/9/99+	19	20		31 Beer Thirty ....The Trouble With Angels		105	$4		Arista Nashville 13188
11/27/99+	53	13		32 Against The Wind		—			album cut
				from the animated TV series *King Of The Hill* (soundtrack on Elektra 62441); #5 Pop hit for Bob Seger in 1980					
1/22/00	60	8		33 Goin' Under Gettin' Over You		—			album cut
				from the album *Tight Rope* on Arista 18895					
3/18/00	5	29		34 You'll Always Be Loved By Me ....Don't Look Back Now		55	$4	■	Arista Nash. 13198 (v)
2/17/01	❶⁶	29		35 Ain't Nothing 'Bout You ....Husbands And Wives		20	$4		Arista Nashville 69048
6/23/01	❶¹	33		36 Only In America		33		(v)	album cut
				from the album *Steers & Stripes* on Arista Nashville 67003; later released as the B-side of #37 below					
10/27/01+	❶¹	27		37 The Long Goodbye ....Only In America		39	$4		Arista Nashville 69130

DEBUT	PEAK	WKS	Gold	A-side (Chart Hit)	B-side	Pop	$	Pic	Label & Number
				BROOKS BROTHERS BAND '85 Group from Dallas. Led by brothers Bill and Randy Brooks.					
1/12/85	81	6		Hurry On Home	—		$6		Buckboard 115
				BROTHER PHELPS '93 Duo of brothers Ricky Lee (born on 10/8/53) and Doug (born on 2/16/60) Phelps. Both formerly with **The Kentucky Headhunters**. Doug returned to Kentucky Headhunters in 1996.					
7/3/93	6	20		1 Let Go .... Everything Will Work Out Fine		—	$4	■	Asylum 64614 (v)
11/13/93+	28	18		2 Were You Really Livin' .... Playin' House		—	$4	■	Asylum 64598 (v)
3/26/94	53	9		3 Eagle Over Angel .... Let Go		—	$4	■	Asylum 64558 (v)
9/3/94	62	5		4 Ever-Changing Woman .... Watch Your Step		—	$4	■	Asylum 64517 (v)
2/18/95	54	11		5 Anyway The Wind Blows .... Lookout Mountain		—	$4	■	Asylum 64461 (v)
6/3/95	65	6		6 Not So Different After All .... Johnny		—	$4	■	Asylum 64436 (v)
				BROWN, Billy '79 Born in 1956 in Port Orange, Florida.					
12/15/79	95	3		What It Means To Be An American .... Star Spangled Banner [S]		—	$6		Bernes 101
				BROWN, Cooter '95					
12/16/95	71	1		Pure Bred Redneck .... My Apologies [N]		—	$4	■	Reprise 17711 (v)
				BROWN, Floyd '83 Born in Greenwell Springs, Louisiana.					
6/18/77	100	1		1 Let's Get Acquainted Again .... But I Do		—	$5		ABC/Dot 17702
7/9/83	79	6		2 Kiss Me Just One More Time .... Fools Like Me		—	$6		Magnum 1002
				BROWN, Jim Ed ★82★ '79 Born on 4/1/34 in Sparkman, Arkansas. Singer/songwriter/guitarist. Recorded in duo with older sister **Maxine Brown** in 1953, joined by younger sister Bonnie in 1955 (recorded as **The Browns**). Began solo recording in 1965. Hosted TNN's *You Can Be A Star* and *Going Our Way*. Joined the *Grand Ole Opry* in 1963. CMA Award: 1977 Vocal Duo of the Year (with **Helen Cornelius**). Also see **Some Of Chet's Friends**. 1) I Don't Want To Have To Marry You 2) Lying In Love With You 3) Saying Hello, Saying I Love You, Saying Goodbye 4) Pop A Top 5) Fools					
				JIM EDWARD BROWN:					
7/10/65	33	8		1 I Heard From A Memory Last Night .... Just To Satisfy You		—	$8		RCA Victor 8566
10/16/65	37	5		2 I'm Just A Country Boy .... To Be Or Not To Be		—	$8		RCA Victor 8644
4/9/66	41	4		3 Regular On My Mind .... The Mounties		—	$8		RCA Victor 8766
7/30/66	23	10		4 A Taste Of Heaven .... Paint Me The Color Of Your Wall		—	$8		RCA Victor 8867
11/19/66	57	7		5 The Last Laugh .... Party Girl		—	$8		RCA Victor 8997
2/4/67	18	11		6 You Can Have Her .... If You Were Mine, Mary #12 Pop hit for Roy Hamilton in 1961		—	$8		RCA Victor 9077
				JIM ED BROWN:					
5/20/67	3	20		7 Pop A Top .... Too Good To Be True		—	$8		RCA Victor 9192
10/14/67	13	13		8 Bottle, Bottle .... It Doesn't Know Any Better		—	$8		RCA Victor 9329
2/10/68	23	11		9 The Cajun Stripper .... You'll Never Know (The Thrill Of Loving You)		—	$8		RCA Victor 9434
5/25/68	13	12		10 The Enemy .... I Just Came From There		—	$8		RCA Victor 9518
9/28/68	49	8		11 Jack And Jill .... Honky Tonkin'		—	$8		RCA Victor 9616
12/14/68+	35	12		12 Longest Beer Of The Night .... What's A Girl Like You (Doing In A Place Like This)		—	$8		RCA Victor 9677
3/22/69	17	11		13 Man And Wife Time .... Healing Hands Of Time		—	$7		RCA Victor 0114
7/19/69	29	10		14 The Three Bells .... Beyond The Shadow new version of Jim's #1 hit with **The Browns** in 1959		—	$7		RCA Victor 0190
12/13/69+	35	9		15 Ginger Is Gentle And Waiting For Me /		—			
		7		16 Drink Boys, Drink		—	$7		RCA Victor 0274
4/4/70	71	4		17 Lift Ring, Pull Open .... Going Up The Country		—	$7		RCA Victor 9810
7/11/70	31	9		18 Baby, I Tried .... The City Cries At Night		—	$7		RCA Victor 9858
10/24/70	4	18		19 Morning .... How To Lose A Good Woman		47	$6		RCA Victor 9909
3/27/71	13	15		20 Angel's Sunday .... Every Mile Of The Way		—	$6		RCA Victor 9965
9/18/71	37	13		21 She's Leavin' (Bonnie, Please Don't Go) .... Love Is Worth The Tryin'		—	$6		RCA Victor 0509
3/4/72	55	7		22 Evening .... You Keep Right On Loving Me		—	$6		RCA Victor 0642
6/10/72	57	8		23 How I Love Them Old Songs .... "Close"		—	$6		RCA Victor 0712
9/30/72	67	6		24 All I Had To Do .... Triangle		—	$6		RCA Victor 0785
12/16/72+	29	12		25 Unbelievable Love .... If Her Blue Eyes Don't Get You		—	$6		RCA Victor 0846
4/28/73	6	15		26 Southern Loving .... How Long Does It Take A Memory To Drown		—	$6		RCA Victor 0928
9/1/73	15	14		27 Broad-Minded Man .... Helpin' Her Get Over Him		—	$6		RCA Victor 0059
12/8/73+	10	15		28 Sometime Sunshine .... Louisiana Woman		—	$6		RCA Victor 0180
5/4/74	10	17		29 It's That Time Of Night .... If Wishes Were Horses		—	$6		RCA Victor 0267
9/21/74	47	8		30 Get Up I Think I Love You .... A Nickel For The Fiddler		—	$6		RCA Victor 10047
1/11/75	63	7		31 Don Junior .... Who's Gonna Love Me		—	$6		RCA Victor 10131
3/29/75	41	9		32 Barroom Pal, Goodtime Gals .... Nearer My Love To You		—	$6		RCA Victor 10233
9/20/75	52	10		33 Fine Time To Get The Blues .... Sweetsong		—	$6		RCA Victor 10370
1/3/76	24	12		34 Another Morning .... An Old Flame Never Dies		—	$6		RCA Victor 10531
4/17/76	69	6		35 Let Me Love You Where It Hurts .... I Love You All Over Again		—	$6		RCA Victor 10619
				JIM ED BROWN/HELEN CORNELIUS:					
7/4/76	❶²	16		36 I Don't Want To Have To Marry You .... Have I Told You Lately That I Love You		—	$5		RCA Victor 10711
10/16/76	65	7		37 I've Rode With The Best .... Close The Door JIM ED BROWN		—	$5		RCA 10786

DEBUT	PEAK	WKS	Gold	A-side (Chart Hit) .... B-side	Pop	$	Pic	Label & Number
				BROWN, Jim Ed — Cont'd				
11/20/76+	2¹	17		38 Saying Hello, Saying I Love You, Saying Goodbye *My Heart Cries For You*	—	$5		RCA 10822
5/7/77	12	12		39 Born Believer ....*Here Today And Gone Tomorrow*	—	$5		RCA 10967
8/20/77	12	12		40 If It Ain't Love By Now ....*It Takes So Long*	—	$5		RCA 11044
11/12/77	66	8		41 When I Touch Her There ....*Mexican Joe*	—	$5		RCA 11134
				JIM ED BROWN				
12/24/77	91	3		42 Fall Softly Snow ....*Natividad (The Nativity)* [X]	—	$5		RCA 11162
3/11/78	11	13		43 I'll Never Be Free ....*Baby You Know How I Love You*	—	$5		RCA 11220
7/29/78	6	15		44 If The World Ran Out Of Love Tonight *Blue Ridge Mountains Turnin' Green*	—	$5		RCA 11304
11/25/78+	10	14		45 You Don't Bring Me Flowers ....*Dear Memory*	—	$5		RCA 11435
3/31/79	2²	13		46 Lying In Love With You *Let's Take The Long Way Around The World*	—	$5		RCA 11532
8/4/79	3	13		47 Fools ....*I Think About You*	—	$5		RCA 11672
10/27/79	38	11		48 You're The Part Of Me ....*Changes*	—	$5		RCA 11742
				JIM ED BROWN				
3/8/80	5	14		49 Morning Comes Too Early ....*Emotions*	—	$5		RCA 11927
7/19/80	24	12		50 The Bedroom ....*Everything Is Changing*	—	$5		RCA 12037
5/9/81	13	14		51 Don't Bother To Knock ....*Dear Memory*	—	$5		RCA 12220
				BROWN, Josie '73 Born Linda Brown in Corning, New York. Died of heart failure on 8/16/98 (age 55).				
9/15/73	44	13		1 Precious Memories Follow Me ....*After You've Had Me*	—	$5		RCA Victor 0042
2/2/74	58	8		2 Both Sides Of The Line ....*Pour A Little Water On The Flowers*	—	$5		RCA Victor 0209
5/18/74	83	7		3 Satisfy Me And I'll Satisfy You ....*Crackerbox Mansion*	—	$5		RCA Victor 0266
				BROWN, Junior '96 Born Jamieson Brown on 6/12/52 in Cottonwood, Arizona. Singer/songwriter/guitarist.				
8/26/95	73	2		1 Highway Patrol ....*Lovely Hula Hands*	—	$4	■	MCG/Curb 76953 (v)
2/17/96	68	4		2 My Wife Thinks You're Dead ....*Sugarfoot Rag*	—	$4		MCG/Curb 76983
				BROWN, Marti '73 Born in Chattanooga, Tennessee. Female singer.				
7/21/73	78	5		Let My Love Shine ....*Love Me Back To Sleep*	—	$6		Atlantic 4003
				BROWN, Marty '93 Born Dennis Marty Brown on 7/25/65 in Maceo, Kentucky. Singer/songwriter/guitarist.				
5/22/93	74	3		It Must Be The Rain ....*Honky Tonk Special*	—	$4		MCA 54612
				BROWN, Max '79				
5/19/79	91	5		1 Take Time To Smell The Flowers ....*Love Away On Me*	—	$5		Door Knob 095
8/18/79	73	8		2 Take Good Care Of My Love ....*Call Me Silly*	—	$5		Door Knob 105
				BROWN, Maxine '69 Born Ella Maxine Brown on 4/27/31 in Campti, Louisiana. Eldest member of **The Browns**.				
12/14/68+	64	11		Sugar Cane County ....*My Biggest Mistake*	—	$8		Chart 1061
				BROWN, Roy '48 Born on 9/10/25 in New Orleans. Died of a heart attack on 5/25/81 (age 55). Black singer/pianist. Charted 16 R&B hits from 1948-57.				
12/25/48	12	1		'Fore Day In The Morning ....J:12 *Rainy Weather Blues*	—	$25		DeLuxe 3198
				ROY BROWN and his Orchestra				
				BROWN, Shannon '01 Born in Spirit Lake, Iowa. Female singer.				
11/7/98	58	11		1 I Won't Lie ....*A Tour Of My Heart*	—	$4		Arista Nashville 13144
9/15/01	40	15		2 Baby I Lied ....*Untangle My Heart*	—	$4		BNA 69104
				BROWN, T. Graham ★190★ '86 Born Anthony Graham Brown on 12/30/54 in Atlanta. Singer/songwriter/actor. Former jingle singer. Acted in the movies *Greased Lightning*, *The Farm* and *Heartbreak Hotel*. Also see **Tomorrow's World**. 1)Don't Go To Strangers 2)Hell And High Water 3)Darlene 4)I Wish That I Could Hurt That Way Again 5)She Couldn't Love Me Anymore				
7/27/85	39	10		1 Drowning In Memories ....*Stop, You're Killing Me*	—	$4		Capitol 5499
10/19/85+	7	27		2 I Tell It Like It Used To Be S:7 / A:7 *Quittin' Time*	—	$4		Capitol 5524
4/26/86	3	19		3 I Wish That I Could Hurt That Way Again S:2 / A:5 *You're Trying Too Hard*	—	$4		Capitol 5571
9/6/86	0¹	23		4 Hell And High Water S:0¹ / A:0¹ *Don't Make A Liar Out Of Me*	—	$4	■	Capitol 5621
1/31/87	0¹	21		5 Don't Go To Strangers S:0² / A:0¹ *Rock It, Billy*	—	$4	■	Capitol 5664
5/30/87	9	20		6 Brilliant Conversationalist S:3 *Talkin' To It*	—	$4	■	Capitol 44008
9/12/87	4	22		7 She Couldn't Love Me Anymore S:5 *R.F.D. 30529*	—	$4	■	Capitol 44061
1/23/88	4	20		8 The Last Resort S:13 *Sittin' On The Dock Of The Bay*	—	$4		Capitol 44125
7/30/88	0¹	21		9 Darlene S:5 *Best Love I Never Had*	—	$4		Capitol 44205
12/10/88+	7	20		10 Come As You Were ....*The Time Machine*	—	$4		Capitol 44273
4/29/89	30	13		11 Never Say Never ....*I Read A Letter Today*	—	$4		Capitol 44349
4/7/90	6	21		12 If You Could Only See Me Now ....*We Tote The Note*	—	$4	■	Capitol 44534 (v)
6/23/90	6	21		13 Don't Go Out	—	$4	■	Capitol 44586 (v)
				TANYA TUCKER with T. Graham Brown				
9/15/90	18	20		14 Moonshadow Road	—			album cut

DEBUT	PEAK	WKS	Gold	A-side (Chart Hit)	B-side	Pop	$	Pic	Label & Number
				BROWN, T. Graham — Cont'd					
1/12/91	53	11		15 I'm Sending One Up For You	—				album cut
				above 2 from the album Bumper To Bumper *on Capitol 91780*					
4/20/91	31	12		16 With This Ring	—				album cut
				#14 Pop hit for The Platters in 1967; from the album You Can't Take It With You *on Capitol 93547*					
9/19/98+	44	20		17 Wine Into Water	—				album cut
2/27/99	68	6		18 Happy Ever After	—				album cut
6/5/99	63	3		19 Never In A Million Tears	—				album cut
10/23/99	73	5		20 Memphis Women & Chicken	—				album cut
				above 4 from the album Wine Into Water *on Platinum 9346*					
9/2/00	59	12		21 Now That's Awesome ....S:13 *(no B-side)* [N]			$4	★	BNA 60286
				BILL ENGVALL Featuring Tracy Byrd, Neal McCoy & T. Graham Brown					
				BROWNE, Jann '90					
				Born on 3/14/54 in Anderson, Indiana; raised in Shelbyville, Indiana. Singer with **Asleep At The Wheel** from 1981-83. Married songwriter Roger Stebner in 1985.					
7/1/89	19	21		1 You Ain't Down Home.............................I'll Never Grow Tired Of You	—		$4		Curb 10530
11/25/89+	18	26		2 Tell Me Why.......................................There Ain't No Train	—		$4		Curb 10568
9/15/90	75	1		3 Louisville...Lovebird	—		$4	■	Curb 76835 (v)
	★206★			**BROWNS, The** '59					
				Brother-and-sister trio from Sparkman, Arkansas: **Jim Ed Brown**, **Maxine Brown** and Bonnie Brown. Maxine and Jim Ed had worked as a duo from the late 1940s and Bonnie joined them in 1955. The trio worked **Red Foley**'s *Arkansas Jamboree* radio shows. Sister Norma subbed for Jim Ed while he was in the service. Joined the *Grand Ole Opry* in 1963. The trio disbanded in 1967, with Jim Ed and Maxine continuing as solo artists.					
				1)The Three Bells 2)I Take The Chance 3)I Heard The Bluebirds Sing 4)Scarlet Ribbons (For Her Hair) 5)Here Today And Gone Tomorrow					
				JIM EDWARD & MAXINE BROWN:					
6/26/54	8	15		1 Looking Back To See.....................................A:8 *Rio De Janeiro*	—		$25		Fabor 107
				JIM EDWARD, MAXINE & BONNIE BROWN:					
11/12/55	7	7		2 Here Today And Gone Tomorrow.......................A:7 *You Thought I Thought*	—		$25		Fabor 126
4/28/56	2¹	24		3 I Take The Chance...............................A:2 / S:6 / J:9 *Goo Goo Dada*	—		$20		RCA Victor 6480
9/22/56	11	2		4 Just As Long As You Love Me..................A:11 *Don't Tell Me Your Troubles*	—		$20		RCA Victor 6631
3/23/57	15	1		5 Money..A:15 *It Takes A Long Long Train With A Red Caboose*	—		$20		RCA Victor 6823
9/2/57	4	17		6 I Heard The Bluebirds Sing............................A:4 / S:15 *The Last Thing I Want*	—		$20		RCA Victor 6995
				THE BROWNS:					
10/20/58	13	2		7 Would You Care...*The Trot*	—		$15		RCA Victor 7311
2/23/59	11	12		8 Beyond The Shadow....................................*This Time I Would Know*	—		$15		RCA Victor 7427
8/3/59	❶¹⁰	19 ●		9 The Three Bells..*Heaven Fell Last Night*	❶⁴		$12		RCA Victor 7555
				#14 Pop hit for Les Compagnons De La Chanson in 1952					
11/9/59+	7	16		10 Scarlet Ribbons (For Her Hair)......................*Blue Bells Ring*	13		$12		RCA Victor 7614
				#14 Pop hit for Jo Stafford in 1950					
				THE BROWNS Featuring Jim Edward Brown:					
4/11/60	20	7		11 The Old Lamplighter...................................*Teen-Ex* (Pop #47)	5		$12	■	RCA Victor 7700
12/31/60	23	3		12 Send Me The Pillow You Dream On..................*You're So Much A Part Of Me*	56		$12		RCA Victor 7804
1/18/64	42	1		13 Oh No!..*Dear Teresa*	—		$10		RCA Victor 8242
5/16/64	12	26		14 Then I'll Stop Loving You.............................*I Know My Place*	—		$10		RCA Victor 8348
11/7/64	40	6		15 Everybody's Darlin', Plus Mine.......................*The Outskirts Of Town*	135		$10		RCA Victor 8423
2/5/66	46	4		16 Meadowgreen..*One Take Away One*	—		$10		RCA Victor 8714
				THE BROWNS:					
7/2/66	16	13		17 I'd Just Be Fool Enough..............................*Springtime*	—		$10		RCA Victor 8838
10/8/66	19	10		18 Coming Back To You.................................*Gigawackem*	—		$10		RCA Victor 8942
5/6/67	54	7		19 I Hear It Now.......................................*He Will Set Your Fields On Fire*	—		$10		RCA Victor 9153
12/16/67+	52	7		20 Big Daddy /	—				
12/30/67+	64	4		21 I Will Bring You Water	—		$10		RCA Victor 9364

BRUCE, Ed ★143★ '82

Born William Edwin Bruce, Jr. on 12/29/40 in Keiser, Arkansas; raised in Memphis. Singer/songwriter/guitarist/actor. Recorded for Sun in 1957. Moved to Nashville in 1964 and worked with the Marijohn Wilkins Singers. Did TV commercials as "The Tennessean." Played "Tom Guthrie" on TV's *Bret Maverick*. Hosted TV's *American Sports Cavalcade* and *Truckin' U.S.A.*

1)You're The Best Break This Old Heart Ever Had 2)You Turn Me On (Like A Radio) 3)Ever, Never Lovin' You 4)After All 5)Nights

DEBUT	PEAK	WKS		A-side	B-side	Pop	$	Pic	Label & Number
1/14/67	57	9		1 Walker's Woods......................................*Lonesome Is Me*	—		$10		RCA Victor 9044
4/15/67	69	5		2 Last Train To Clarksville..............................*I'm Getting Better*	—		$10		RCA Victor 9155
				#1 Pop hit for The Monkees in 1966					
7/13/68	52	5		3 Painted Girls And Wine..............................*Ninety-Seven More To Go*	—		$10		RCA Victor 9553
1/4/69	53	10		4 Song For Jenny......................................*Puzzles*	—		$8		Monument 1118
5/24/69	52	7		5 Everybody Wants To Get To Heaven..................*When A Man Becomes A Man*	—		$8		Monument 1138
12/15/73+	77	8		6 July, You're A Woman................................*The Rain In Baby's Life*	—		$6		United Artists 353
				#100 Pop hit for Pat Boone *in 1969*					
11/15/75+	15	14		7 Mammas Don't Let Your Babies Grow Up To Be Cowboys...............................*It's Not What She's Done (It's What You Didn't Do)*	—		$6		United Artists 732
3/20/76	32	10		8 The Littlest Cowboy Rides Again......................*The Feel Of Being Gone*	—		$6		United Artists 774
6/19/76	57	7		9 Sleep All Mornin'.....................................*Workingman's Prayer*	—		$6		United Artists 811

DEBUT	PEAK	WKS	Gold	A-side (Chart Hit)	B-side	Pop	$	Pic	Label & Number
				BRUCE, Ed — Cont'd					
9/25/76	36	10		10 For Love's Own Sake .... When Wide Open Spaces And Cowboys Are Gone		—	$6		United Artists 862
8/13/77	52	10		11 When I Die, Just Let Me Go To Texas .... I've Not Forgot Marie		—	$5		Epic 50424
11/19/77	54	10		12 Star-Studded Nights .... The Wedding Dress		—	$5		Epic 50475
2/11/78	57	7		13 Love Somebody To Death .... I Can't Seem To Get The Hang Of Telling Her Goodbye		—	$5		Epic 50503
5/20/78	94	3		14 Man Made Of Glass .... Never Take Candy From A Stranger		—	$5		Epic 50544
10/7/78	70	6		15 The Man That Turned My Mama On .... Give My Old Memory A Call		—	$5		Epic 50613
12/16/78+	60	9		16 Angeline .... Give My Old Memory A Call		—	$5		Epic 50645
3/8/80	21	15		17 Diane .... Blue Umbrella		—	$4		MCA 41201
7/5/80	12	15		18 The Last Cowboy Song .... The Outlaw And The Stranger		—	$4		MCA 41273
				Willie Nelson (guest vocal)					
11/8/80+	14	16		19 Girls, Women And Ladies .... The Last Thing She Said		—	$4		MCA 51018
3/28/81	24	14		20 Evil Angel .... Easy Temptations		—	$4		MCA 51076
7/25/81	14	15		21 (When You Fall In Love) Everything's A Waltz .... Thirty-Nine And Holding		—	$4		MCA 51139
11/28/81+	❶¹	21		22 You're The Best Break This Old Heart Ever Had					
				It Just Makes Me Want You More		—	$4		MCA 51210
4/24/82	13	16		23 Love's Found You And Me .... I Take The Chance		—	$4		MCA 52036
8/28/82	4	19		24 Ever, Never Lovin' You .... Theme From "Bret Maverick"		—	$4		MCA 52109
1/22/83	6	18		25 My First Taste Of Texas .... One More Shot Of "Old Back Home Again"		—	$4		MCA 52156
5/14/83	21	15		26 You're Not Leavin' Here Tonight .... I Think I'm In Love		—	$4		MCA 52210
8/6/83	19	17		27 If It Was Easy .... You've Got Her Eyes		—	$4		MCA 52251
11/12/83+	4	21		28 After All .... It Would Take A Fool		—	$4		MCA 52295
8/18/84	45	12		29 Tell 'Em I've Gone Crazy .... Birds Of Paradise		—	$4		MCA 52433
11/3/84+	3	22		30 You Turn Me On (Like A Radio) .... S:3 / A:3 If It Ain't Love		—	$4		RCA 13937
3/23/85	17	16		31 When Givin' Up Was Easy .... S:13 / A:18 Texas Girl I'm Closing In On You		—	$4		RCA 14037
8/3/85	20	16		32 If It Ain't Love .... A:18 / S:20 The Migrant		—	$4		RCA 14150
4/12/86	4	19		33 Nights .... S:4 / A:4 Fifteen To Forty-Three (Man In The Mirror)		—	$4		RCA 14305
9/13/86	49	9		34 Fools For Each Other .... S:28 Memphis Roots		—	$4		RCA 5005
				ED BRUCE with Lynn Anderson					
12/6/86+	36	14		35 Quietly Crazy .... Memphis Roots		—	$4		RCA 5077
				BRUSH ARBOR '73					
				Group from San Diego: brothers Jim (guitar), Joe (mandolin) and Wayne (banjo) Rice, Kenny Munds (vocals, guitar), Dave Rose (bass) and Dale Cooper (drums).					
11/25/72+	56	10		1 Proud Mary .... Denver Woman		—	$6		Capitol 3468
				#2 Pop hit for Creedence Clearwater Revival in 1969					
3/10/73	41	7		2 Brush Arbor Meeting .... Bear Creek Dam		—	$6		Capitol 3538
8/4/73	72	4		3 Alone Again (Naturally) .... Washington County		—	$6		Capitol 3672
				#1 Pop hit for Gilbert O'Sullivan in 1972					
11/17/73	98	2		4 Now That It's Over .... Song To Mary Anne		—	$6		Capitol 3733
12/8/73+	73	8		5 Trucker And The U.F.O. .... Song To Mary Anne		—	$6		Capitol 3774
7/31/76	90	3		6 Emmylou .... One Woman's Man		—	$5		Monument 8702
11/12/77	56	11		7 Get Down Country Music .... Don't Play That Song Again		—	$5		Monument 230
				BRYANT, Jimmy — see ORVILLE & IVY					
				BRYANT, Ronnie '89					
11/4/89	81	2		Neither One Of Us		—	$5		Evergreen 1102
				#2 Pop hit for Gladys Knight & The Pips in 1973					
	★361★			**BRYCE, Sherry** '71					
				Born in Duncanville, Alabama. Married to **Mack Sanders**; together they owned the Pilot label.					
				1)Take My Hand 2)Living And Learning 3)Don't Let Go					
6/5/71	8	15		1 Take My Hand .... Life's Little Surprises		110	$6		MGM 14255
				MEL TILLIS AND SHERRY BRYCE with The Statesiders					
10/30/71	9	14		2 Living And Learning .... Tangled Vines		—	$6		MGM 14303
				MEL TILLIS & SHERRY BRYCE					
4/8/72	38	10		3 Anything's Better Than Nothing .... Then It Will Be All Over		—	$6		MGM 14365
				MEL TILLIS & SHERRY BRYCE And The Statesiders					
8/11/73	64	10		4 Leaving's Heavy On My Mind .... Coffee & Tears		—	$6		MGM 14548
11/17/73+	26	13		5 Let's Go All The Way Tonight .... In The Vine		—	$6		MGM 14660
				MEL TILLIS & SHERRY BRYCE & The Statesiders					
2/9/74	45	11		6 Don't Stop Now .... Saving What You're Spending It For		—	$6		MGM 14695
4/13/74	11	14		7 Don't Let Go .... Why Not Do The Things (They Think We've Done)		—	$6		MGM 14714
				MEL TILLIS AND SHERRY BRYCE And The Statesiders					
				#13 Pop hit for Roy Hamilton in 1958					
6/29/74	62	9		8 Treat Me Like A Lady .... Where Love Has Died		—	$5		MGM 14726
10/5/74	70	6		9 Oh, How Happy .... Come On Down To Our House		—	$5		MGM 14747
				#12 Pop hit for Shades Of Blue in 1966					
1/4/75	14	13		10 You Are The One .... I See Heaven In You		—	$5		MGM 14776
				MEL TILLIS & SHERRY BRYCE with The Statesiders					
4/26/75	96	3		11 Love Song .... I Love Loving You		—	$5		MGM 14793
5/17/75	32	13		12 Mr. Right And Mrs. Wrong .... Just Two Strangers Passing In The Night		—	$5		MGM 14803
				MEL TILLIS AND SHERRY BRYCE And The Statesiders					
2/28/76	97	2		13 Hang On Feelin' .... This Song's For You		—	$5		MGM 14842
11/13/76	93	3		14 Everything's Coming Up Love .... Let Your Body Speak Your Mind		—	$5		MCA 40630
10/1/77	79	5		15 The Lady Ain't For Sale .... Gone, Baby Gone		—	$5		Pilot 45100

DEBUT	PEAK	WKS	Gold	A-side (Chart Hit)	B-side	Pop	$	Pic	Label & Number

BUCHANAN, Wes '68
Born in Vallejo, California. Singer/actor. Own *Hollywood Jamboree* TV series in 1967. Appeared in the movie *From Nashville With Love*.

12/7/68	72	3		Warm Red Wine .... Letting Me Down	—	$10		Columbia 44686

BUCHANAN BROTHERS '46
Duo of brothers from Trenton, Georgia: Chester and Lester Buchanan.

| 6/29/46 | 6 | 3 | | Atomic Power .... Singing An Old Hymn | — | $25 | | RCA Victor 20-1850 |

BUCK, Gary '63
Born on 3/21/40 in Thessalon, Ontario, Canada. Singer/songwriter/guitarist. Not to be confused with Gary Buck of The Four Guys.

6/29/63	11	17		1 Happy To Be Unhappy .... Savin' All My Love For You	—	$20		Petal 1011
4/11/64	37	3		2 The Wheel Song .... Suit Of Sorrow	—	$20		Petal 1500
2/13/82	93	2		3 Midnight Magic .... Kentucky Lady	—	$5		Dimension 1029

BUCKAROOS, The '68
Backing band for **Buck Owens**: Don Rich (vocals, guitar, fiddle), Tom Brumley (steel guitar), **Doyle Holly** (bass) and Jerry Wiggins (drums). Rich was killed in a motorcycle accident on 7/17/74 (age 32). Also see **Buddy Alan**.

11/25/67	69	4		1 Chicken Pickin' .... Apple Jack [I]	—	$8	■	Capitol 2010
6/8/68	38	9		2 I'm Coming Back Home To Stay .... I Can't Stop (My Loving You)	—	$8	■	Capitol 2173
9/21/68	50	8		3 I'm Goin' Back Home Where I Belong .... Too Many Chiefs (Not Enough Indians)	—	$8		Capitol 2264
				BUCK OWENS' BUCKAROOS Featuring Don Rich (above 2)				
4/19/69	63	2		4 Anywhere U.S.A. .... Gathering Dust	—	$8		Capitol 2420
				THE BUCKAROOS Featuring Don Rich				
10/25/69	43	6		5 Nobody But You .... Lay A Little Light On Me	—	$8		Capitol 2629
4/4/70	71	3		6 The Night They Drove Old Dixie Down .... One More Time	—	$8		Capitol 2750
				DON RICH And The Buckaroos (above 2)				
				#3 Pop hit for Joan Baez in 1971				

BUDDE, Rusty '86
Born in Houston. Male singer.

| 12/27/86 | 77 | 4 | | Misty Mississippi | — | $6 | | BPC 1002 |

BUFF, Beverly '63
Born in Washington, Georgia.

| 11/24/62+ | 22 | 3 | | 1 I'll Sign .... Used To Be Sweethearts | — | $15 | | Bethlehem 3027 |
| 3/30/63 | 23 | 5 | | 2 Forgive Me .... No Part Time Love | — | $15 | | Bethlehem 3065 |

BUFFALO CLUB, The '97
Trio formed by former **Restless Heart** drummer John Dittrich, with singer Ron Hemby and guitarist Charlie Kelley.

1/18/97	9	20		1 If She Don't Love You .... We Lose	—	$4		Rising Tide 56043
6/7/97	26	20		2 Nothin' Less Than Love	—			album cut
				from the album *The Buffalo Club* on Rising Tide 53044				
10/11/97	53	8		3 Heart Hold On .... We Lose	—	$4		Rising Tide 56053

BUFFETT, Jimmy ★378★ '77
Born on 12/25/46 in Pascagoula, Mississippi; raised in Mobile, Alabama. Singer/songwriter/guitarist. Earned a degree in journalism from the University of Southern Mississippi. Nashville correspondent for *Billboard* magazine from 1969-70. Settled in Key West in 1971. Owner of the Margaritaville record label and a line of tropical clothing. Authored the novels *Tales From Margaritaville* and *Where Is Joe Merchant*.
    1)Margaritaville   2)If The Phone Doesn't Ring, It's Me   3)Changes In Latitudes, Changes In Attitudes

5/12/73	58	10		1 The Great Filling Station Holdup .... Why Don't We Get Drunk	—	$6		Dunhill/ABC 4348
6/15/74	58	7		2 Come Monday .... The Wino And I Know	30	$6		Dunhill/ABC 4385
8/23/75	88	5		3 Door Number Three .... Dallas	102	$5		ABC 12113
4/30/77	13	17		4 Margaritaville .... Miss You So Badly	8	$5		ABC 12254
				also see #14 & #15 below				
10/1/77	24	10		5 Changes In Latitudes, Changes In Attitudes .... Landfall	37	$5	■	ABC 12305
8/19/78	91	3		6 Livingston Saturday Night .... Cowboy In The Jungle	52	$5		ABC 12391
9/8/84	42	13		7 When The Wild Life Betrays Me .... Ragtop Day	—	$4		MCA 52438
12/8/84+	58	13		8 Bigger Than The Both Of Us .... Come To The Moon	—	$4		MCA 52499
3/23/85	37	15		9 Who's The Blonde Stranger? .... S:24 She's Going Out Of My Mind	—	$4		MCA 52550
6/29/85	56	9		10 Gypsies In The Palace .... Jolly Mon Sing	—	$4	■	MCA 52607
9/7/85	16	19		11 If The Phone Doesn't Ring, It's Me .... A:11 / S:16 Frank And Lola	—	$4		MCA 52664
2/8/86	50	9		12 Please Bypass This Heart .... Beyond The End	—	$4		MCA 52752
8/28/93	74	1		13 Another Saturday Night .... Souvenirs	—	$4		MCA 54680
				#10 Pop hit for Sam Cooke in 1963 and #6 Pop hit for Cat Stevens in 1974				
11/6/99	63	2		14 Margaritaville	—			album cut
7/15/00	74	1		15 Margaritaville .... [R]	—			album cut
				ALAN JACKSON with Jimmy Buffett (above 2)				
				new version of #4 above; from Jackson's album *Under The Influence* on Arista 18892				

BUNZOW, John '95
Born in Portland, Oregon. Singer/songwriter.

| 4/8/95 | 69 | 4 | | Easy As One, Two, Three | — | | | album cut |
| | | | | from the album *Stories Of The Years* on Liberty 28246 | | | | |

BURBANK, Gary, with Band McNally '80
DJ at WHAS in Louisville, Kentucky, at the time of his hit.

| 7/26/80 | 91 | 2 | | Who Shot J.R.? .... Honkin' (Tennessee Valley Authority) [N] | 67 | $5 | | Ovation 1150 |
| | | | | inspired by the shooting of "J.R. Ewing" (Larry Hagman) on TV's *Dallas* | | | | |

DEBUT	PEAK	WKS	Gold	A-side (Chart Hit)	B-side	Pop	$	Pic	Label & Number

BURBANK STATION '88
Group from Fargo, North Dakota. Features female singer Bunny Davis.

| 8/6/88 | 77 | 3 | | 1 Divided .... Over Women | — | $5 | | Prairie Dust 8841 |
| 5/27/89 | 90 | 2 | | 2 Get Out Of My Way .... | — | $5 | | Prairie Dust 112 |

BURCH SISTERS, The *Sisters* '88
Sisters Cathy (born on 12/28/60), Charlene (born on 9/19/62) and Cindy (born on 8/1/63) Burch. All were born in Jacksonville, Florida. Also see **Tomorrow's World**.

5/21/88	23	18		1 Everytime You Go Outside I Hope It Rains .... S:28 *Open Arms*	—	$4		Mercury 870362
10/15/88	61	5		2 What Do Lonely People Do .... *Open Arms*	—	$4	■	Mercury 870687
12/17/88+	45	11		3 I Don't Want To Mention Any Names .... *The Only Love You Need*	—	$4		Mercury 872324
4/1/89	46	11		4 Old Flame, New Fire .... *What We Don't Know Won't Hurt Us*	—	$4		Mercury 872730
7/1/89	59	8		5 The Way I Want To Go .... *I Missed That Train Again*	—	$4		Mercury 874560

BURDICK, Kathy — see LEE, Dickey

BURGESS, Frank '89

| 11/26/88 | 88 | 3 | | 1 American Man .... | — | $6 | | True 94 |
| 5/13/89 | 81 | 3 | | 2 What It Boils Down To .... | — | $6 | | True 96 |

BURGESS, Wilma ★321★ '66
Born on 6/11/39 in Orlando, Florida. Female singer.
1) Misty Blue 2) Baby 3) Don't Touch Me

12/11/65+	7	18		1 Baby .... *Wait Till The Sun Comes Up*	—	$8		Decca 31862
5/7/66	12	17		2 Don't Touch Me .... *Turn Around Teardrops*	—	$8		Decca 31941
10/29/66	4	18		3 Misty Blue .... *Ain't Got No Man*	—	$8		Decca 32027

#3 Pop hit for Dorothy Moore in 1976

3/25/67	24	15		4 Fifteen Days .... *Two Little Rivers Of Tears*	—	$8		Decca 32105
8/26/67	16	15		5 Tear Time .... *(How Can I Write On Paper) What I Feel In My Heart*	—	$8		Decca 32178
8/17/68	59	9		6 Look At The Laughter .... *Sweet Promises*	—	$8		Decca 32359
3/22/69	68	3		7 Parting (Is Such Sweet Sorrow) .... *Shine A Little Sun On Me*	—	$8		Decca 32437
8/9/69	48	10		8 The Woman In Your Life .... *Happiness Is So Hard To Forget*	—	$8		Decca 32522
12/27/69+	48	9		9 The Sun's Gotta' Shine .... *Only Mama That'll Walk The Line*	—	$8		Decca 32593
7/11/70	63	6		10 Lonely For You .... *I Don't See My In Your Arms Anymore*	—	$8		Decca 32684
9/22/73	61	11		11 I'll Be Your Bridge (Just Lay Me Down) ...... *I'll Always Love The Days*	—	$6		Shannon 813
12/22/73+	14	17		12 Wake Me Into Love .... *Here Together*	—	$6		Shannon 816

BUD LOGAN & WILMA BURGESS

| 7/6/74 | 53 | 10 | | 13 The Best Day Of The Rest Of Our Love ...... *It Ain't Nothing But Love* | — | $6 | | Shannon 820 |

BUD LOGAN & WILMA BURGESS

| 9/14/74 | 46 | 11 | | 14 Love Is Here / .... | | | | |
| 2/8/75 | 86 | 6 | | 15 Sweet Lovin' Baby .... | — | $6 | | Shannon 821 |

BURKE, Fiddlin' Frenchie '75
Born Leon Bourke in Kaplan, Louisiana. Singer/fiddler.

| 11/23/74+ | 39 | 15 | | 1 Big Mamou .... *There'll Be Love Tonight In My House* | — | $5 | | 20th Century 2152 |

FIDDLIN' FRENCHIE BOURQUE and THE OUTLAWS

| 4/19/75 | 30 | 9 | | 2 Colinda .... *Pride, You Wouldn't Listen* | — | $5 | | 20th Century 2182 |
| 10/11/75 | 73 | 5 | | 3 The Fiddlin' Of Jacques Pierre Bordeaux ...... *Frenchie's Cotton-Eyed Joe* | — | $5 | | 20th Century 2225 |

FIDDLIN' FRENCHIE BURKE & THE OUTLAWS (above 2)

| 7/1/78 | 94 | 5 | | 4 Knock Knock Knock .... | — | $6 | | Cherry 644 |

FRENCHIE BURKE

| 3/28/81 | 93 | 3 | | 5 (Frenchie Burke's) Fire On The Mountain .... *Let's Go Get Drunk And Be Somebody* [I] | — | $6 | | Delta 11332 |

BURNETTE, Billy '85
Born on 5/8/53 in Memphis. Singer/songwriter/guitarist. Son of **Dorsey Burnette**, nephew of Johnny Burnette and cousin of Rocky Burnette. Member of Fleetwood Mac from 1987-1993. Acted in the movie *Saturday Night Special*.

11/3/79	76	5		1 What's A Little Love Between Friends .... *Precious Time*	—	$5		Polydor 2024
8/10/85	51	8		2 Ain't It Just Like Love .... *Guitar Bug*	—	$4		Curb/MCA 52626
12/28/85+	68	9		3 Try Me .... *It Ain't Over*	—	$4		Curb/MCA 52749
7/12/86	54	7		4 Soldier Of Love .... *Guitar Bug*	—	$4		Curb/MCA 52852
3/7/92	64	6		5 Nothin' To Do (And All Night To Do It) .... *Can't Get Over You*	—	$4		Warner 19042

BURNETTE, Billy Joe '90

| 1/6/90 | 90 | 1 | | Three Flags .... [S] | — | $7 | | Badger 1004 |

BURNETTE, Dorsey ★394★ '72
Born on 12/28/32 in Memphis. Died of a heart attack on 8/19/79 (age 46). Singer/songwriter/guitarist. Older brother of Johnny Burnette and father of **Billy Burnette**.
1) In The Spring (The Roses Always Turn Red) 2) Darlin' (Don't Come Back) 3) Molly (I Ain't Gettin' Any Younger)

5/13/72	21	12		1 In The Spring (The Roses Always Turn Red) ...... *The Same Old You, The Same Old Me*	—	$6		Capitol 3307
9/2/72	40	8		2 I Just Couldn't Let Her Walk Away .... *Church Bells*	—	$6		Capitol 3404
2/17/73	42	9		3 I Let Another Good One Get Away .... *Take Your Weapons, Lay 'Em Down*	—	$6		Capitol 3529
5/12/73	53	5		4 Keep Out Of My Dreams .... *Mama, Mama*	—	$6		Capitol 3588
8/11/73	26	14		5 Darlin' (Don't Come Back) .... *Sweet Lovin' Woman*	—	$6		Capitol 3678
1/12/74	85	7		6 It Happens Every Time .... *Mr. Jukebox, Sing A Lullabye*	—	$6		Capitol 3796
3/9/74	69	8		7 Bob, All The Playboys And Me .... *The Bootleggers*	—	$6		Capitol 3829

DORSEY BURNETTE with Sound Company (above 3)

6/15/74	62	8		8 Daddy Loves You Honey .... *True Love Means Forgiving*	—	$6		Capitol 3887
11/23/74	71	5		9 What Ladies Can Do (When They Want To) .... *Tangerine*	—	$6		Capitol 3963
5/31/75	28	12		10 Molly (I Ain't Gettin' Any Younger) .... *She's Feelin' Low*	—	$6		Melodyland 6007

DEBUT	PEAK	WKS	Gold	A-side (Chart Hit)	B-side	Pop	$	Pic	Label & Number
				BURNETTE, Dorsey — Cont'd					
10/18/75	97	3		11 Lyin' In Her Arms Again	Doggone The Dogs	—	$6		Melodyland 6019
4/24/76	74	5		12 Ain't No Heartbreak	I Dreamed I Saw	—	$6		Melodyland 6031
6/11/77	31	15		13 Things I Treasure	One Mornin'	—	$6		Calliope 8004
11/5/77	53	7		14 Soon As I Touched Her	Dear Hearted Children	—	$6		Calliope 8012
9/1/79	77	4		15 Here I Go Again	What Would It Profit Me	—	$5		Elektra 46513
				BURNIN' DAYLIGHT '97					
				Trio of **Marc Beeson** (vocals), Sonny Lemaire (bass; **Exile**) and Kurt Howell (keyboards; **Southern Pacific**).					
10/19/96	49	16		1 Love Worth Fighting For	—			■	album cut (v)
				later issued as the B-side of #2 below					
2/15/97	37	20		2 Say Yes	Love Worth Fighting For	—	$4	■	Curb 73005 (v)
6/21/97	58	6		3 Live To Love Again		—			album cut
				all of above from the album Burnin' Daylight on Curb 77850					
				BURNS, Brent '78					
				Born in Seminole, Oklahoma; raised in Phoenix. Singer/songwriter/guitarist.					
5/6/78	91	4		I Hear You Coming Back	Come Away With Me	—	$7		Pantheon Desert 79
				BURNS, George '80					
				Born Nathan Birnbaum on 1/20/1896 in New York City. Died on 3/9/96 (age 100). Radio, movie and TV comedian.					
1/5/80	15	14		1 I Wish I Was Eighteen Again	One Of The Mysteries Of Life	49	$5	■	Mercury 57011
5/24/80	85	4		2 The Arizona Whiz	A Real Good Cigar	—	$5		Mercury 57021
2/14/81	66	5		3 Willie, Won't You Sing A Song With Me	Just Send Me One	—	$5		Mercury 57045
				BURNS, Hughie '80					
3/8/80	95	2		The Family Inn	Tell Me A Good One	—	$6		C-S-I 002
				BURNS, Jackie '69					
				Born in Long Beach, California. Female singer.					
10/11/69	60	5		1 Something's Missing (It's You)	What's A Daddy	—	$10		Honor Brigade 5
10/21/72	71	2		2 (If Loving You Is Wrong) I Don't Want To Be Right	A World Of Lonely Men	—	$8		JMI 8
				#3 Pop hit for Luther Ingram in 1972					
				BURRITO BROTHERS '81					
				Group formed in 1968 as the **Flying Burrito Brothers** by **Chris Hillman** and Gram Parsons, ex-members of folk-rock band The Byrds. By 1980, consisted of "Sneaky" Pete Kleinow (steel guitar), Floyd "Gib" Guilbeau (fiddle; father of Ronnie Guilbeau of **Palomino Road**), Skip Battin (bass), Greg Harris (guitar) and Ed Ponder (drums). In 1981, relocated to Nashville, dropped "Flying" from band name, Harris and Ponder left and John Beland (guitar) joined. By late 1981, reduced to a duo of Guilbeau and Beland.					
				1)She Belongs To Everyone But Me 2)Does She Wish She Was Single Again 3)If Something Should Come Between Us					
3/1/80	95	2		1 White Line Fever	Big Bayou	—	$6		Regency 45001
				FLYING BURRITO BROTHERS					
				recorded "live" in Tokyo; written by Merle Haggard					
1/24/81	67	5		2 She's A Friend Of A Friend	Too Much Honky Tonkin'	—	$4		Curb 5402
4/18/81	20	13		3 Does She Wish She Was Single Again	Oh, Lonesome Me	—	$4		Curb 01011
8/8/81	16	14		4 She Belongs To Everyone But Me	Why Must The Ending Always Be So Sad	—	$4		Curb 02243
12/26/81+	27	14		5 If Something Should Come Between Us (Let It Be Love)	Damned If I'll Be Lonely Tonight	—	$4		Curb 02641
4/17/82	40	10		6 Closer To You	Coast To Coast	—	$4		Curb 02835
7/24/82	39	10		7 I'm Drinkin' Canada Dry	How'd We Ever Get This Way	—	$4		Curb 03023
11/13/82	48	10		8 Blue And Broken Hearted Me	Our Roots Are Country Music	—	$4		Curb 03314
1/28/84	49	9		9 Almost Saturday Night	Jukebox Kind Of Night	—	$4		Curb 52329
				#78 Pop hit for John Fogerty in 1975					
5/26/84	53	8		10 My Kind Of Lady	Dream Chaser	—	$4		Curb 52379
	★263★			**BUSH, Johnny** '69					
				Born John Bush Shin III on 2/17/35 in Houston. Singer/songwriter/guitarist/drummer. Worked with **Ray Price** and **Willie Nelson** in the 1960s. Known as "The Country Caruso."					
				1)You Gave Me A Mountain 2)Undo The Right 3)Whiskey River 4)Each Time 5)I'll Be There					
11/25/67	69	3		1 You Oughta Hear Me Cry	Jealously Insane	—	$10		Stop 126
3/16/68	29	13		2 What A Way To Live	I Can Feel You In His Arms	—	$10		Stop 160
8/3/68	10	16		3 Undo The Right	Conscience Turn Your Back	—	$10		Stop 193
				above 3 written by **Willie Nelson**					
12/28/68+	16	13		4 Each Time	Tonight We Steal Heaven Again	—	$10		Stop 232
3/22/69	7	15		5 You Gave Me A Mountain	Back From The Wine	—	$10		Stop 257
				#24 Pop hit for Frankie Laine in 1969					
8/16/69	26	10		6 My Cup Runneth Over	Tonight, I'm Going Home To An Angel	—	$10		Stop 310
				#8 Pop hit for Ed Ames in 1967					
1/3/70	56	8		7 Jim, Jack, And Rose /		—	$10		
			5	8 I'll Go To A Stranger		—	$10		Stop 354
5/16/70	25	11		9 Warmth Of The Wine	Daddy Lived In Houston	—	$10		Stop 371
11/7/70	44	11		10 My Joy	I'll Warm By The Flame	—	$10		Stop 380
4/10/71	53	6		11 City Lights	The Joy Of Loving You	—	$10		Stop 392
4/22/72	17	12		12 I'll Be There	I Can Feel You In His Arms	—	$8		Million 1
7/22/72	14	15		13 Whiskey River	Right Back In Your Arms Again	—	$6		RCA Victor 0745
				also see #24 below					
12/30/72+	34	9		14 There Stands The Glass	These Lips Don't Know How To Say Goodbye	—	$6		RCA Victor 0867
5/5/73	38	11		15 Here Comes The World Again	That Rain Makin' Baby Of Mine	—	$6		RCA Victor 0931
9/1/73	53	8		16 Green Snakes On The Ceiling	Drinkin' My Baby Right Out Of My Mind	—	$6		RCA Victor 0041
12/1/73+	37	10		17 We're Back In Love Again	(Wine Friend of Mine) Stand By Me	—	$6		RCA Victor 0164

DEBUT	PEAK	WKS	Gold	A-side (Chart Hit)	B-side	Pop	$	Pic	Label & Number
				BUSH, Johnny — Cont'd					
3/23/74	48	10		18 Toy Telephone /	—		$6		RCA Victor 0240
		4		19 From Tennessee To Texas	—		$6		
10/15/77	78	7		20 You'll Never Leave Me Completely /	—		$6		Gusto 165
4/29/78	99	2		21 Put Me Out Of My Memory	—		$6		Gusto 9006
9/2/78	89	3		22 She Just Made Me Love You More	Hands Can Say A Lot	—	$6		Gusto 9006
5/19/79	83	5		23 When My Conscience Hurts The Most	Drivin' Nails In My Coffin	—	$6		Whiskey River 791
2/28/81	92	2		24 Whiskey River	When My Conscience Hurts The Most [R]	—	$6		Delta 10041
				new version of #13 above					
				BUTLER, Bobby "Sofine"		'79			
				Born in El Paso, Texas. Worked as a DJ in Tucson, El Paso and Phoenix.					
12/4/76	98	2		1 Teddy Toad	Theme From Teddy Toad	—	$6		Pantheon Desert 77
5/26/79	46	6		2 Cheaper Crude Or No More Food	Bobby's (Nervous) Breakdown [N]	—	$6		IBC 0001
	★281★			**BUTLER, Carl, and Pearl**		'62			
				Carl was born on 6/2/27 in Knoxville, Tennessee. Died on 9/4/92 (age 65). Wife Pearl was born Pearl Dee Jones on 9/20/27 in Nashville. Died on 3/1/89 (age 61). Both appeared in the movie Second Fiddle To A Steel Guitar.					
				1)Don't Let Me Cross Over 2)Too Late To Try Again 3)I'm Hanging Up The Phone					
8/7/61	25	2		1 Honky Tonkitis	You Were The Orchid (She Was The Rose)	—	$15		Columbia 41997
				CARL BUTLER					
12/8/62	❶¹¹	24		2 Don't Let Me Cross Over	Wonder Drug	88	$12	▪	Columbia 42593
7/6/63	14	14		3 Loving Arms	Who'll Be Next	—	$12		Columbia 42778
1/11/64	9	8		4 Too Late To Try Again /	—		$12		Columbia 42892
1/11/64	36	1		5 My Tears Don't Show	—		$12		Columbia 42892
6/6/64	14	16		6 I'm Hanging Up The Phone	Just A Message	—	$10		Columbia 43030
9/26/64	23	10		7 Forbidden Street	When The Door Swings Shut (On Old Memories)	—	$10		Columbia 43102
3/27/65	22	13		8 Just Thought I'd Let You Know /	—		$10		Columbia 43210
2/27/65	38	10		9 We'd Destroy Each Other	—		$10		Columbia 43210
12/11/65	42	2		10 Our Ship Of Love	It's Called Cheating	—	$10		Columbia 43433
8/6/66	31	7		11 Little Pedro	Cell 29	—	$10		Columbia 43685
8/17/68	28	12		12 Punish Me Tomorrow	Goodbye Tennessee	—	$8		Columbia 44587
1/4/69	46	8		13 I Never Got Over You	I Started Loving You Again	—	$8		Columbia 44694
7/5/69	63	6		14 We'll Sweep Out The Ashes In The Morning	Your Way Of Life	—	$8		Columbia 44862
				BUZZI, Ruth		'77			
				Born on 7/24/36 in Westerley, Rhode Island. Comedienne featured on TV's Laugh-In.					
4/2/77	90	4		You Oughta Hear The Song	'57 Chevrolet	—	$5		United Artists 951
				BUZZIN' COUSINS		'92			
				Group that appeared in the movie Falling From Grace: **John Cougar Mellencamp** (director/star of the movie), **Dwight Yoakam**, **Joe Ely**, John Prine, and James McMurtry.					
2/15/92	68	5		Sweet Suzanne	—		album cut		
				from the movie Falling From Grace starring John Cougar Mellencamp (soundtrack on Mercury 512004)					
				BYERS, Brenda		'68			
				Born in Canterbury, Connecticut. Singer/banjo player.					
10/26/68	51	9		1 The Auctioneer	Rainbows And Roses	—	$8		MTA 160
10/11/69	65	6		2 Thank You For Loving Me	Night Life	—	$8		MTA 176
1/24/70	66	4		3 Homeward Bound	The Other Side Of Me	—	$8		MTA 177
				#5 Pop hit for Simon & Garfunkel in 1966					
				BYRAM, Judy		'87			
12/5/87	71	5		1 No More One More Time	—		$5		F&L 554
6/4/88	74	5		2 One Fire Between Us	—		$5		Regal 001
				BYRD, Jerry — see ALLEN, Rex / KIRK, Red					
				BYRD, Tracy ★161★		'95			
				Born on 12/17/66 in Beaumont, Texas; raised in Vidor, Texas. Male singer. Studied business at Southwest Texas State. In 1991, became a regular performer at Cutter's Nightclub in Beaumont. Signed to MCA in 1992.					
				1)Holdin' Heaven 2)The Keeper Of The Stars 3)I'm From The Country 4)Big Love 5)Don't Take Her She's All I Got					
8/22/92	71	3		1 That's The Thing About A Memory	Back In The Swing Of Things	—	$4		MCA 54426
2/13/93	42	20		2 Someone To Give My Love To	Talk To Me Texas	—	$4	▪	MCA 54497 (v)
6/19/93	❶¹	20		3 Holdin' Heaven	Edge Of A Memory	—	$4	▪	MCA 54659 (v)
10/30/93	39	15		4 Why Don't That Telephone Ring	An Out Of Control Raging Fire (w/Dawn Sears)	—	$4	▪	MCA 54735 (v)
4/30/94	4			5 Lifestyles Of The Not So Rich And Famous	You Never Know Just How Good You've Got It	115	$4	▪	MCA 54778 (v)
8/13/94	4	20		6 Watermelon Crawl	You Never Know Just How Good You've Got It	81	$4	▪	MCA 54889 (v)
11/19/94+	5	20		7 The First Step	No Ordinary Man	—	$4	▪	MCA 54945 (v)
1/21/95	2²	20		8 The Keeper Of The Stars	Pink Flamingos	68	$4	▪	MCA 54988 (v)
6/3/95	15	20		9 Walking To Jerusalem	S:3 Down On The Bottom	92	$4	▪	MCA 55049 (v)
9/9/95	9	20		10 Love Lessons	S:6 Don't Need That Heartache	119	$4	▪	MCA 55102 (v)
2/3/96	14	20		11 Heaven In My Woman's Eyes	Walkin' In	—	$4		MCA 55155
5/25/96	21	20		12 4 To 1 In Atlanta	Have A Good One	—	$4		MCA 55201

DEBUT	PEAK	WKS	Gold	A-side (Chart Hit)..B-side	Pop	$	Pic	Label & Number
				BYRD, Tracy — Cont'd				
9/21/96+	3	20		13 Big Love .... S:13 (club mix)	—	$4	■	MCA 55230 (v)
1/25/97	4	20		14 Don't Take Her She's All I Got .... I Love You, That's All	—	$4		MCA 55292
				#39 Pop hit for Freddie North in 1971				
5/17/97	17	20		15 Don't Love Make A Diamond Shine .... Tucson Too Soon	—	$4		MCA 72002
9/27/97	47	10		16 Good Ol' Fashioned Love .... Driving Me Out Of Your Mind	—	$4		MCA 72011
2/7/98	3	28		17 I'm From The Country .... S:7 For Me It's You	63	$4	■	MCA 72040 (v)
6/20/98	9	23		18 I Wanna Feel That Way Again .... Gettin' Me Over Mountains	—	$4		MCA Nashville 72058
12/19/98+	31	20		19 When Mama Ain't Happy .... Back To Texas	—	$4		MCA Nashville 72083
9/25/99+	11	25		20 Put Your Hand In Mine .... It's About Time	76	$4		RCA 65907
12/25/99	55	2		21 Merry Christmas From Texas Y'all .... (album snippets) [X]	—	$4		RCA 65913
4/1/00	44	12		22 Love, You Ain't Seen The Last Of Me .... Put Your Hand In Mine	—	$4		RCA 60210
9/2/00	43	8		23 Take Me With You When You Go .... Love, You Ain't Seen The Last Of Me	—	$4		RCA 69006
9/2/00	59	12		24 Now That's Awesome .... S:13 (no B-side) [N]	—	$4	★	BNA 60286
				BILL ENGVALL Featuring Tracy Byrd, Neal McCoy & T. Graham Brown				
3/24/01	21	20		25 A Good Way To Get On My Bad Side .... Put Your Hand In Mine (Byrd)	121	$4		RCA 69081
				TRACY BYRD (with Mark Chesnutt)				
8/25/01+	9	28		26 Just Let Me Be In Love .... Somebody's Dream	64	$4		RCA 69106

Add That's The Truth About Men WPCV

"C" Company — p. 65   **C**   "C" Company — p. 65

				CACTUS CHOIR '98				
				Group from San Francisco: Marty Atkinson (vocals), Gary Hooker (guitar), Dave Ristrim (steel guitar), Tim Hensley (banjo), Shane Hicks (keyboards), Cal Ball (bass) and Eric Nelson (drums).				
1/24/98	62	8		Step Right Up .... Hark The Herald Angels Sing	—	$4		Curb 56098
				CAGLE, Buddy '63				
				Born Walter Cagle on 2/8/36 in Concord, North Carolina; raised in Winston-Salem. Singer/guitarist.				
5/18/63	29	3		1 Your Mother's Prayer .... Once Again	—	$12		Capitol 4923
11/16/63	26	2		2 Sing A Sad Song .... Love Inside My Door	—	$12		Capitol 5043
9/25/65	37	8		3 Honky Tonkin' Again .... We The People (The Great Society)	—	$10		Mercury 72452
4/23/66	31	10		4 Tonight I'm Coming Home .... Honky Tonk College	—	$10		Imperial 66161
1/14/67	57	7		5 Apologize .... Help's On The Way	—	$10		Imperial 66218
8/12/67	75	2		6 Longtime Traveling .... Camptown Girl	—	$10		Imperial 66245
				CAGLE, Chris '02				
				Born in 1969 in Louisiana; raised in Houston. Singer/songwriter/guitarist.				
7/29/00	15	23		1 My Love Goes On And On .... S:10 Play It Loud	76	$4	★	Virgin 58867 (v)
12/2/00+	8	31		2 Laredo .... Lovin' You Lovin' Me	60	$4		Virgin 58979
9/22/01+	❶¹	36		3 I Breathe In, I Breathe Out .... Country By The Grace Of God	35	$4		Capitol 77696
				CAIN, Hunter '88				
7/16/88	82	2		1 Hollywood Heroes /	—			
5/13/89	95	1		2 She's Too Good To Be Cheated This Way	—	$6		Discovery 4587
				CALAMITY JANE Group '82				
				Female group: Pam Rose (vocals), Mary Fielder (guitar), Linda Moore (bass) and Mary Ann Kennedy (drums).				
10/17/81	61	7		1 Send Me Somebody To Love .... Don't You Leave Love Alone Too Long	—	$5		Columbia 02503
2/27/82	44	9		2 I've Just Seen A Face .... Midnight Bandit	—	$5		Columbia 02715
				first recorded by The Beatles on their 1966 Rubber Soul album				
6/19/82	60	7		3 Walkin' After Midnight .... Lover To Lover	—	$5		Columbia 02958
10/16/82	87	3		4 Love Wheel .... Pick Me Up (And Let Me Love Again)	—	$5		Columbia 03229
				CALHOUN, Linda '79				
4/28/79	85	4		I Can Feel Love .... Our Tune Of Yesterday	—	$7		Grape 2004
				CAMERON, Bart '86				
11/1/86	76	4		1 Dark Eyed Lady	—	$6		Revolver 013
5/30/87	77	3		2 Do It For The Love Of It	—	$6		Revolver 015
				CAMP, Colleen '82				
				Born on 6/7/53 in San Francisco. Singer/actress.				
1/23/82	72	4		One Day Since Yesterday .... I Would Like To See You Again	—	$7		Moon Pictures 0001
				CAMP, Shawn '93				
				Born on 8/29/66 in Little Rock, Arkansas; raised in Perryville, Arkansas. Male singer/songwriter/guitarist/fiddler.				
7/31/93	39	20		1 Fallin' Never Felt So Good .... Turn Loose Of My Pride	—	$4	■	Reprise 18465 (v)
11/20/93+	39	20		2 Confessin' My Love .... K-I-S-S-I-N-G	—	$4	■	Reprise 18331 (v)
				CAMPBELL, Archie '66				
				Born on 11/7/14 in Bulls Gap, Tennessee. Died of heart failure on 8/29/87 (age 72). Singer/songwriter/comedian. Joined the Grand Ole Opry in 1968. Chief writer and cast member of the TV series Hee Haw. Hosted TNN's Yesteryear In Nashville. Also see **Some Of Chet's Friends**.				
3/14/60	24	4		1 Trouble In The Amen Corner .... Black Is The Color Of My True Love's Hair [S]	—	$12		RCA Victor 7660
1/22/66	16	8		2 The Men In My Little Girl's Life .... Abe Lincoln Comes Home	—	$10		RCA Victor 8741
				#6 Pop hit for Mike Douglas in 1960				
3/11/67	44	10		3 The Cockfight .... Red Silk Stockings And Green Perfume [S]	—	$10		RCA Victor 9081
				ARCHIE CAMPBELL and LORENE MANN:				
1/6/68	24	15		4 The Dark End Of The Street .... The Gettin' Place	—	$8		RCA Victor 9401
6/29/68	31	10		5 Tell It Like It Is .... If That's The Only Way	—	$8		RCA Victor 9549
				#2 Pop hit for Aaron Neville in 1967				

DEBUT	PEAK	WKS	Gold	A-side (Chart Hit)	B-side	Pop	$	Pic	Label & Number
				CAMPBELL, Archie — Cont'd					
9/28/68	57	8		6 Warm And Tender Love	Pledging My Love	—	$8		RCA Victor 9615
				#17 Pop hit for Percy Sledge in 1966					
1/4/69	36	9		7 My Special Prayer	What Am I Living For	—	$8		RCA Victor 9691
12/8/73	87	4		8 Freedom Ain't The Same As Bein' Free	The House	—	$6		RCA Victor 0155
				ARCHIE CAMPBELL					
				CAMPBELL, Cecil '49					
				Born on 3/22/11 in Danbury, North Carolina. Died on 6/18/89 (age 78). Singer/songwriter/steel guitarist. Appeared in the movies *My Darling Clementine* and *Swing Your Partner*.					
5/21/49	9	1		Steel Guitar Ramble	J:9 Left All Alone With A Broken Heart		$25		RCA Victor 21-0014
				CECIL CAMPBELL'S TENNESSEE RAMBLERS					
				45 rpm: 48-0014					

CAMPBELL, Glen ★39★ '75

Born on 4/22/36 in Delight, Arkansas. Singer/songwriter/guitarist. With his uncle Dick Bills's band, 1954-58. To Los Angeles; recorded with The Champs in 1960. Became prolific studio musician; with The Hondells in 1964, **The Beach Boys** in 1965 and Sagittarius in 1967. Own TV show *The Glen Campbell Goodtime Hour*, 1968-72. Acted in the movies *True Grit*, *Norwood* and *Strange Homecoming*; voice in the animated movie *Rock-A-Doodle*. CMA Awards: 1968 Male Vocalist of the Year; 1968 Entertainer of the Year.

1) Rhinestone Cowboy   2) I Wanna Live   3) Galveston   4) Wichita Lineman   5) Southern Nights

DEBUT	PEAK	WKS		A-side	B-side	Pop	$	Pic	Label & Number
12/29/62	20	5		1 Kentucky Means Paradise	Truck Driving Man	114	$15		Capitol 4867
				THE GREEN RIVER BOYS Featuring Glen Campbell					
12/10/66+	18	13		2 Burning Bridges	Only The Lonely	—	$10		Capitol 5773
				#3 Pop hit for Jack Scott in 1960					
4/29/67	73	2		3 I Gotta Have My Baby Back	Just To Satisfy You	—	$10		Capitol 5854
7/29/67	30	12		4 Gentle On My Mind	Just Another Man	62	$8		Capitol 5939
				also see #9 below					
10/28/67+	2²	18		5 By The Time I Get To Phoenix	You've Still Got A Place In My Heart	26	$7		Capitol 2015
				also see #24 below					
2/3/68	13	12		6 Hey Little One	My Baby's Gone	54	$7	■	Capitol 2076
4/13/68	❶³	16		7 I Wanna Live	That's All That Matters	36	$7		Capitol 2146
7/6/68	3	15		8 Dreams Of The Everyday Housewife	Kelli Hoedown	32	$7		Capitol 2224
10/19/68	44	3		9 Gentle On My Mind	Just Another Man [R]	39	$8		Capitol 5939
				reissue of #4 above					
11/2/68	❶²	19	●	10 Wichita Lineman	Fate Of Man	3	$6		Capitol 2302
11/23/68	44	7		11 Less Of Me	Mornin' Glory (Pop #74)	—	$6		Capitol 2314
				BOBBIE GENTRY & GLEN CAMPBELL					
2/8/69	14	12		12 Let It Be Me	Little Green Apples	36	$6		Capitol 2387
				GLEN CAMPBELL and BOBBIE GENTRY					
3/15/69	❶³	14	●	13 Galveston	How Come Every Time I Itch I Wind Up Scratchin' You	4	$6		Capitol 2428
5/10/69	28	10		14 Where's The Playground Susie	Arkansas	26	$6		Capitol 2494
7/26/69	9	12		15 True Grit	Hava Nagila	35	$6		Capitol 2573
				from the movie starring John Wayne and Campbell					
10/25/69	2¹	13		16 Try A Little Kindness	Lonely My Lonely Friend	23	$6		Capitol 2659
1/24/70	2³	13		17 Honey Come Back	Where Do You Go	19	$6		Capitol 2718
2/21/70	6	13		18 All I Have To Do Is Dream	Less Of Me	27	$6		Capitol 2745
				BOBBIE GENTRY & GLEN CAMPBELL					
4/25/70	25	9		19 Oh Happy Day	Someone Above	40	$6		Capitol 2787
				#4 Pop hit for the Edwin Hawkins Singers in 1969					
7/18/70	5	12		20 Everything A Man Could Ever Need	Norwood (Me And My Guitar)	52	$6		Capitol 2843
				from the movie *Norwood* starring Campbell					
9/19/70	3	15		21 It's Only Make Believe	Pave Your Way Into Tomorrow	10	$6		Capitol 2905
				#1 Pop hit for Conway Twitty in 1958					
3/13/71	7	14		22 Dream Baby (How Long Must I Dream)	Here And Now	31	$6		Capitol 3062
				#4 Pop hit for Roy Orbison in 1962					
7/3/71	21	14		23 The Last Time I Saw Her	Bach Talk	61	$6		Capitol 3123
10/30/71	40	8		24 I Say A Little Prayer/By The Time I Get To Phoenix	All Through The Night	81	$6		Capitol 3200
				GLEN CAMPBELL/ANNE MURRAY					
				"I Say A Little Prayer" was a #4 Pop hit for Dionne Warwick in 1967					
1/8/72	15	12		25 Oklahoma Sunday Morning	Everybody's Got To Go There Sometime	104	$6		Capitol 3254
4/1/72	6	13		26 Manhattan Kansas	Wayfarin' Stranger	114	$6		Capitol 3305
8/26/72	45	10		27 I Will Never Pass This Way Again	We All Pull The Load	61	$6		Capitol 3411
12/16/72+	33	10		28 One Last Time	All My Tomorrows	78	$5		Capitol 3483
3/24/73	48	8		29 I Knew Jesus (Before He Was A Star)	On This Road	45	$5		Capitol 3548
7/28/73	49	9		30 Bring Back My Yesterday	Beautiful Love Song	—	$5		Capitol 3669
10/20/73	20	12		31 Wherefore And Why	Give Me Back That Old Familiar Feeling	111	$5		Capitol 3735
2/2/74	20	10		32 Houston (I'm Comin' To See You)	Honestly Love	68	$5		Capitol 3808
8/3/74	3	18		33 Bonaparte's Retreat	Too Many Mornings	—	$5		Capitol 3926
12/14/74+	16	13		34 It's A Sin When You Love Somebody	If I Were Loving You	—	$5		Capitol 3988
6/7/75	❶³	21	●	35 Rhinestone Cowboy	Lovelight	❶²	$5		Capitol 4095
11/1/75	3	15		36 Country Boy (You Got Your Feet In L.A.)	Record Collector's Dream	11	$5		Capitol 4155
4/10/76	4	12		37 Don't Pull Your Love/Then You Can Tell Me Goodbye	I Miss You Tonight	27	$5		Capitol 4245
				"Don't Pull Your Love" was a #4 Pop hit for Hamilton, Joe Frank & Reynolds in 1971; "Then You Can Tell Me Goodbye" was a #6 Pop hit for The Casinos in 1967					
7/10/76	18	11		38 See You On Sunday	Bloodline	—	$5		Capitol 4288
1/29/77	❶²	17	●	39 Southern Nights	William Tell Overture	❶¹	$5		Capitol 4376

DEBUT	PEAK	WKS	Gold	A-side (Chart Hit)	B-side	Pop	$	Pic	Label & Number
				CAMPBELL, Glen — Cont'd					
7/2/77	4	15		40 Sunflower .... *How High Did We Go* written by Neil Diamond		39	$5		Capitol 4445
12/3/77+	39	10		41 God Must Have Blessed America .... *Amazing Grace*		—	$5		Capitol 4515
6/10/78	21	12		42 Another Fine Mess .... *Can You Fool* from the movie *The End* starring Burt Reynolds		—	$5		Capitol 4584
9/23/78	16	16		43 Can You Fool .... *Let's All Sing A Song About It*		38	$5		Capitol 4638
2/17/79	13	11		44 I'm Gonna Love You .... *Love Takes You Higher*		—	$5		Capitol 4682
5/26/79	45	7		45 California .... *Never Tell You No Lies*		—	$5		Capitol 4715
9/1/79	25	10		46 Hound Dog Man .... *Tennessee Home* #58 Pop hit for Lenny LeBlanc in 1977		—	$5		Capitol 4769
11/24/79	66	6		47 My Prayer .... *Don't Lose Me In The Confusion*		—	$5		Capitol 4799
5/24/80	60	6		48 Somethin' 'Bout You Baby I Like ... *Late Night Confession* (Campbell) GLEN CAMPBELL and RITA COOLIDGE		42	$5		Capitol 4865
8/30/80	80	4		49 Hollywood Smiles .... *Hooked On Love*		—	$5		Capitol 4909
9/27/80	59	6		50 Dream Lover .... *Bronco* TANYA TUCKER AND GLEN CAMPBELL #2 Pop hit for Bobby Darin in 1959		—	$5		MCA 41323
11/22/80+	10	17		51 Any Which Way You Can ..... *Medley From "Any Which Way You Can"* from the movie starring Clint Eastwood		—	$5		Warner 49609
2/7/81	54	7		52 I Don't Want To Know Your Name .... *Daisy A Day*		65	$5		Capitol 4959
4/11/81	85	4		53 Why Don't We Just Sleep On It Tonight .... *It's Your World* GLEN CAMPBELL and TANYA TUCKER		—	$5		Capitol 4986
8/8/81	15	12		54 I Love My Truck .... *Melody's Melody* (David Shire) from the movie *The Night The Lights Went Out In Georgia* starring Kristy McNichol		94	$5		Mirage 3845
10/30/82	44	8		55 Old Home Town .... *Heartache #3*		—	$4	■	Atlantic Amer. 99967
1/15/83	17	17		56 I Love How You Love Me ..... *Hang On Baby (Ease My Mind)* #5 Pop hit for The Paris Sisters in 1961		—	$4		Atlantic Amer. 99930
6/11/83	85	3		57 On The Wings Of My Victory .... *A Few Good Men*		—	$4		Atlantic Amer. 99893
6/23/84	10	22		58 Faithless Love .... *Scene Of The Crime*		—	$4		Atlantic Amer. 99768
10/27/84	47	12		59 Slow Nights .... *Midnight Love* MEL TILLIS WITH GLEN CAMPBELL		—	$4		MCA 52474
12/1/84+	4	20		60 A Lady Like You .... A:4 / S:5 *Tennessee*		—	$4		Atlantic Amer. 99691
5/18/85	14	21		61 (Love Always) Letter To Home ... A:11 / S:18 *An American Trilogy*		—	$4		Atlantic Amer. 99647
11/16/85+	7	21		62 It's Just A Matter Of Time ... A:7 / S:7 *Gene Autry, My Hero* #3 Pop hit for Brook Benton in 1959		—	$4	■	Atlantic Amer. 99600
4/26/86	38	11		63 Cowpoke .... A:37 *Rag Doll*		—	$4		Atlantic Amer. 99559
7/26/86	52	8		64 Call Home .... *Sweet Sixteen*		—	$4		Atlantic Amer. 99525
5/30/87	6	28		65 The Hand That Rocks The Cradle ... S:11 *Arkansas* GLEN CAMPBELL with Steve Wariner		—	$4		MCA 53108
10/3/87+	5	23		66 Still Within The Sound Of My Voice ... S:20 *In My Life*		—	$4		MCA 53172
2/20/88	32	12		67 I Remember You .... *For Sure, For Certain, Forever, For Always* #5 Pop hit for Frank Ifield in 1962		—	$4		MCA 53245
5/28/88	7	23		68 I Have You .... S:28 *I'm A One Woman Man*		—	$4		MCA 53218
10/1/88	35	10		69 Light Years .... *Heart Of The Matter*		—	$4		MCA 53426
1/21/89	47	14		70 More Than Enough .... *Our Movie*		—	$4		MCA 53493
9/30/89	6	26		71 She's Gone, Gone, Gone .... *William Tell Overture*		—	$4		Universal 66024
3/17/90	61	8		72 Walkin' In The Sun .... from the album *Walkin' In The Sun* on Capitol 93884		—			album cut
1/26/91	27	16		73 Unconditional Love		—			album cut
6/1/91	70	5		74 Livin' In A House Full Of Love .... above 2 from the album *Unconditional Love* on Capitol 90992		—			album cut
1/23/93	66	9		75 Somebody Like That .... from the album *Somebody Like That* on Liberty 97962		—			album cut
				CAMPBELL, Jo Ann '62 Born on 7/20/38 in Jacksonville, Florida. Acted in the movies *Johnny Melody, Go Johnny Go* and *Hey, Let's Twist*. Married Troy Seals; recorded together as Jo Ann & Troy in 1964.					
9/22/62	24	3		(I'm The Girl On) Wolverton Mountain .... *Sloppy Joe* answer to "Wolverton Mountain" by Claude King; some pressings titled "I'm The Girl From Wolverton Mountain"		38	$25		Cameo 223
				CAMPBELL, Mike '84 Born in Odessa, Texas.					
12/26/81+	65	6		1 Barroom Games .... *All My Cloudy Days Are Gone*		—	$4		Columbia 02622
10/2/82	57	8		2 No Room To Cry .... *Just The Way I Am*		—	$4		Columbia 03154
5/14/83	76	5		3 Don't Say You Love Me (Just Love Me Again) ... *Barroom Games*		—	$4		Columbia 03838
12/17/83+	57	9		4 Sweet And Easy To Love ..... *Nothing Shines Brighter Than You*		—	$4		Columbia 04225
3/17/84	52	10		5 One Sided Love Affair .... *Sweet And Easy To Love*		—	$4		Columbia 04387
7/14/84	77	3		6 You're The Only Star (In My Blue Heaven) ... *Sweet And Easy To Love* written and recorded by Gene Autry in 1946		—	$4		Columbia 04488
				CAMPBELL, Stacy Dean '92 Born on 7/27/67 in Carlsbad, New Mexico. Male singer.					
7/4/92	54	8		1 Rosalee .... *Would You Run*		—	$4		Columbia 74357
10/17/92	65	3		2 Baby Don't You Know .... *One Little Teardrop*		—	$4		Columbia 74491
12/26/92+	55	11		3 Poor Man's Rose .... *I Won't*		—	$4		Columbia 74803
8/12/95	61	6		4 Honey I Do .... *Midnight Angel*		—	$4	■	Columbia 77942 (v)

DEBUT	PEAK	WKS	Gold	A-side (Chart Hit)	B-side	Pop	$	Pic	Label & Number
				CANADIAN SWEETHEARTS, The '64					
				Canadian husband-and-wife duo: **Bob Regan** and **Lucille Starr**. Regan was born on 3/13/31. Died on 3/5/90 (age 58). Starr was born Lucille Savoie in St. Boniface, Manitoba, Canada. Divorced in 1977.					
2/1/64	45	1		1 Hootenanny Express	Half-Breed	—	$10		A&M 727
9/30/67	72	2		2 Too Far Gone	Looking Back To See	—	$8		Epic 10205
				LUCILLE STARR					
2/10/68	51	5		3 Let's Wait A Little Longer	More Than Money Can Buy	—	$8		Epic 10258
6/8/68	63	5		4 Is It Love?	Too Lonely, Too Long	—	$8		Epic 10317
				LUCILLE STARR					
1/3/70	50	9		5 Dream Baby	South Bound Plane	—	$8		Dot 17327
				BOB REGAN and LUCILLE STARR					
				#4 Pop hit for **Roy Orbison** in 1962					
				CANNON, Ace '77					
				Born Hubert Cannon on 5/4/34 in Grenada, Mississippi. Male saxophonist. Worked with **Bill Black's Combo**. Charted 5 pop hits from 1961-64.					
2/19/77	73	4		Blue Eyes Crying In The Rain	I'll Fly Away [I]	—	$8		Hi 2313
				CANNON, Jimmi '81					
				Born in Sylacauga, Alabama. Female singer/dancer. Member of **Dean Martin**'s Golddiggers from 1971-73.					
10/24/81	63	5		1 Whole Lot Of Cheatin' Goin' On	He Just Said Goodbye	—	$4		Warner 49806
3/20/82	78	5		2 Even If It's Wrong	Stealin' Feelin'	—	$4		Warner 50024
8/28/82	81	4		3 Fool's Gold	Heartache By Heartache	—	$4		Warner 29949
				CANNONS, The '86					
				Family trio from Oklahoma: twins Karla (piano, trumpet, fiddle) and Darla (guitar, saxophone), with brother Larry (guitar, trumpet, banjo) Cannon.					
12/3/83	90	2		1 One Step Closer	Strangers Again	—	$5		Compleat 116
11/8/86	72	7		2 Do You Mind If I Step Into Your Dreams	How Can I Love Now	—	$4	■	Mercury 888048
8/1/87	73	4		3 Love'll Come Lookin' For You	I'll Save My Love For You	—	$4		Mercury 888648
				CANYON '89					
				Group from Texas: Steve Cooper (vocals, guitar), Johnny Boatright (guitar), Jay Brown (keyboards), Randy Russell Rigney (bass) and Keech Rainwater (drums). Rainwater later joined **Lonestar**.					
2/6/88	59	6		1 Overdue	In The Middle Of The Night	—	$4		16th Avenue 70410
5/28/88	54	9		2 In The Middle Of The Night	Overdue	—	$4		16th Avenue 70415
9/10/88	55	9		3 I Guess I Just Missed You	Love Wins	—	$4		16th Avenue 70419
11/26/88+	47	10		4 Love Is On The Line	Love Wins	—	$4		16th Avenue 70423
5/13/89	44	8		5 Right Track, Wrong Train	Oh, Help Me	—	$4		16th Avenue 70426
8/12/89	40	10		6 Hot Nights	Oh, Help Me	—	$4		16th Avenue 70433
11/25/89+	53	8		7 Radio Romance	Streamline	—	$4		16th Avenue 70437
5/12/90	74	1		8 Carryin' On	Streamline	—	$4		16th Avenue 70439
11/3/90	71	4		9 Dam These Tears	Carryin' On	—	$4	■	16th Avenue 70445 (v)
				CAPITALS, The '80					
				Vocal group from Columbus, Ohio: Arti Portilla, Ronnie Cochran, Terry Kaufman and Jack Crum.					
1/5/80	91	4		1 Me Touchin' You	If I Was Still Sinning	—	$5		Ridgetop 00779
9/27/80	29	11		2 A Little Ground In Texas	If I Was Still Sinnin'	—	$5		Ridgetop 01080
3/7/81	45	8		3 Bridge Over Broadway	Love Him Out Of Your Mind	—	$5		Ridgetop 01281
				CAPPS, Hank '72					
9/16/72	33	13		Bowling Green	Roll Mississippi Roll	—	$7		Capitol 3416
				#40 Pop hit for **The Everly Brothers** in 1967					
				CAPTAIN & TENNILLE, The '78					
				Husband-and-wife duo: Daryl "The Captain" Dragon (born on 8/27/42 in Los Angeles) and Toni Tennille (born on 5/8/43 in Montgomery, Alabama). Own TV show on ABC from 1976-77. Dragon is the son of noted conductor Carmen Dragon. Duo charted 14 pop hits from 1975-80.					
5/6/78	97	3		I'm On My Way	We Never Really Say Goodbye	74	$5	■	A&M 2027
				CAPTAIN STUBBY & THE BUCCANEERS '49					
				Born Thomas Fouts on 11/24/18 in Carroll County, Indiana. Played novelty instruments, such as a toilet seat with guitar strings ("gitarlet"). Worked on WLW-Cincinnati, own band from 1937. On WLS *National Barn Dance* for 10 years; made appearances on Don McNeil's *Breakfast Club*. Own *Polka-Go-Round* TV series on ABC from 1965-68. Later worked as a DJ on WLS-Chicago. The Buccaneers: Tiny Stokes (vocals, bass), Jerald Richards (tin whistle), Sonny Fleming (guitar) and Peter Kunatz (accordian).					
2/12/49	13	1		1 Lavender Blue (Dilly Dilly)	S:13 Billy Boy	16	$20		Decca 24547
				BURL IVES with Captain Stubby & The Buccaneers					
				#4 Pop hit for Sammy Kaye in 1949; #3 Pop hit for Sammy Turner in 1959					
7/16/49	12	1		2 Money, Marbles And Chalk	J:12 Tennessee Tears	—	$20		Decca 46149
				Windy Breeze (vocal)					
7/23/49	14	1		3 Come Wet Your Mustache With Me	J:14 Country Boy	—	$20		Decca 46169
				STUBBY AND THE BUCCANEERS (above 2)					
				CARDWELL, Jack '53					
				Born on 11/9/30 in Chapman, Alabama; raised in Mobile, Alabama. Singer/songwriter/guitarist.					
2/14/53	3	9		1 The Death Of Hank Williams	S:3 / A:4 / J:5 Two Arms	—	$30		King 1172
9/26/53	7	2		2 Dear Joan	S:7 You're Looking For Something	—	$25		King 1269
				answer to "A Dear John Letter" by Jean Shepard					
		★289★		**CARGILL, Henson** '68					
				Born on 2/5/41 in Oklahoma City. Studied animal husbandry at Colorado State; worked as a deputy sheriff in Oklahoma County. Appeared on the TV series *Country Hayride* in Cincinnati. Later operated a large cattle ranch in Stillwater, Oklahoma.					
				1)Skip A Rope 2)None Of My Business 3)Row Row Row					
12/9/67+	❶5	19		1 Skip A Rope	A Very Well Traveled Man	25	$8		Monument 1041
4/27/68	11	12		2 Row Row Row	Six White Horses	—	$8		Monument 1065

DEBUT	PEAK	WKS	Gold	A-side (Chart Hit) .... B-side	Pop	$	Pic	Label & Number
				CARGILL, Henson — Cont'd				
8/10/68	39	8		3 She Thinks I'm On That Train .... *It Just Don't Take Me Long To Say Goodbye*	—	$8		Monument 1084
1/25/69	8	14		4 None Of My Business .... *So Many Ways Of Saying She's Gone*	—	$8		Monument 1122
5/31/69	40	8		5 This Generation Shall Not Pass .... *Little Girls And Little Boys*	—	$8		Monument 1142
9/20/69	32	9		6 Then The Baby Came .... *Hemphill Kentucky Consolidated Coal Mine*	—	$8		Monument 1158
5/16/70	18	11		7 The Most Uncomplicated Goodbye I've Ever Heard ...... *Four Shades Of Love*	—	$8		Monument 1198
7/17/71	44	9		8 Pencil Marks On The Wall .... *Momma's Waiting*	—	$7		Mega 0030
				#107 Pop hit for Herschel Bernardi in 1971				
11/27/71	65	3		9 Naked And Crying .... *Afraid To Rock The Boat*	—	$7		Mega 0043
3/4/72	64	4		10 I Can't Face The Bed Alone .... *Daddy Don't You Walk So Fast*	—	$7		Mega 0060
10/14/72	62	7		11 Red Skies Over Georgia *1932*	—	$7		Mega 0090
10/13/73	28	13		12 Some Old California Memory .... *A Writer Of Verses And A Singer Of Songs*	—	$6		Atlantic 4007
3/2/74	78	7		13 She Still Comes To Me (To Pour The Wine) .... *But You Know I Love You*	—	$6		Atlantic 4016
5/25/74	29	13		14 Stop And Smell The Roses .... *Strawberry Roan*	—	$6		Atlantic 4021
12/22/79+	29	13		15 Silence On The Line .... *Forever In Blue Jeans*	—	$6		Copper Mountain 201
5/3/80	67	5		16 Have A Good Day	—	$6		Copper Mountain 589
				CARLETTE '85				
				Full name: Carlette Ruff. Wife of Oak Records owner Ray Ruff.				
2/9/85	60	5		1 Any Way That You Want Me .... *Oh Boy*	—	$6		Oak 1079
4/6/85	71	5		2 Showdown	—	$5		Luv 106
6/8/85	52	9		3 You Can't Measure My Love	—	$5		Luv 107
8/17/85	65	7		4 Tonight's The Night .... *You Know What I Need (When I Need It)*	—	$5		Luv 109
2/22/86	72	5		5 Two Steps From The Blues	—	$5		Luv 116
4/12/86	61	6		6 Sugar Shack .... *You Know What I Need When I Need It*	—	$5		Luv 118
				#1 Pop hit for Jimmy Gilmer & The Fireballs in 1963				
10/18/86	52	7		7 We Belong Together .... *Tennessee*	—	$5	■	Luv 125
5/2/87	63	4		8 Waltzin' With Daddy .... *Tennessee*	—	$5		Luv 137
5/30/87	57	2		9 You've Lost That Loving Feeling	—	$5		Luv 142
				#1 Pop hit for The Righteous Brothers in 1965				
				CARLILE, Tom '82				
				Born in 1943 in Miami.				
6/20/81	93	2		1 Gold Cadillac .... *Lay Down Sally*	—	$5		Door Knob 157
8/29/81	73	6		2 Get It While You Can .... *M.D. 20/20 High*	—	$5		Door Knob 162
10/17/81	49	12		3 Catch Me If You Can .... *Get It While You Can*	—	$5	■	Door Knob 167
1/30/82	84	3		4 Feel .... *Walk Around The Block, Deanna*	—	$5	■	Door Knob 172
2/20/82	70	5		5 Lover (Right Where I Want You) .... *Walk Around The Block, Deanna*	—	$5	■	Door Knob 170
5/8/82	59	9		6 Hurtin' For Your Love .... *The Man Who Loved To Drink*	—	$5	■	Door Knob 176
7/17/82	39	11		7 Back In Debbie's Arms .... *Twenty Years Ago*	—	$5	■	Door Knob 180
10/23/82	37	12		8 Green Eyes .... *No One To Tell My Heartache To*	—	$5	■	Door Knob 187
1/8/83	55	7		9 Rainin' Down In Nashville .... *(I Went To) Heaven With The Devil*	—	$5		Door Knob 191
				CARLISLE, Bob '97				
				Born on 9/29/56 in Santa Anna, California. Singer/songwriter/guitarist.				
5/24/97	45	12		Butterfly Kisses .... *(remix)*	10[A]	$5		DMG/Jive 42456
	★301★			**CARLISLES, The** '53				
				Group formed by **Bill Carlisle** (born on 12/19/08 in Wakefield, Kentucky) in 1951. Joined the *Grand Ole Opry* in 1953. From 1930-47, Bill performed with his brother **Cliff** (born on 5/6/04 in Mount Eden, Kentucky; died on 4/2/83, age 78) as the **Carlisle Brothers**.				
				1)No Help Wanted 2)Is Zat You, Myrtle 3)Knothole				
10/26/46	5	1		1 Rainbow At Midnight *Don't Tell Me Your Worries* [N]	—	$25		King 535
				CARLISLE BROTHERS				
6/19/48	14	2		2 Tramp On The Street .... S:14 / J:14 *Don't Be Ashamed Of Mother* [N]	—	$25		King 697
				BILL CARLISLE				
12/15/51+	6	8		3 Too Old To Cut The Mustard .... A:6 *My Happiness Belongs To Someone Else*	—	$20		Mercury 6348
1/10/53	●[4]	24		4 No Help Wanted .... A:●[4] / J:●[4] / S:2 *This Heart Is Not For Sale*	—	$20		Mercury 70028
4/11/53	3	13		5 Knothole .... A:3 / S:8 *Leave That Liar Alone* [N]	—	$20		Mercury 70109
7/25/53	2[1]	8		6 Is Zat You, Myrtle .... A:2 / S:9 *Something Different* [N]	—	$20		Mercury 70174
11/7/53+	5	6		7 Tain't Nice (To Talk Like That) .... A:5 / J:6 *Unpucker*	—	$20		Mercury 70232
				BILL CARLISLE & THE CARLISLES				
7/3/54	15	1		8 Shake-A-Leg .... A:15 *Let Me Hold Your Little Hand*	—	$20		Mercury 70351
10/9/54	12	5		9 Honey Love .... A:12 *Female Hercules*	—	$20		Mercury 70435
				#1 R&B hit for The Drifters in 1954				
12/11/65+	4	17		10 What Kinda Deal Is This *Shot Gun* [N]	—	$10		Hickory 1348
				BILL CARLISLE				
				CARLLILE, Kathy '80				
				Born Mary Katherine Carllile in 1963 in Nashville. Daughter of Kenneth Ray "Thumbs" Carllile (guitarist with **Jimmy Dickens** and **Roger Miller**).				
4/5/80	61	8		Stay Until The Rain Stops	—	$6	■	Frontline 705
				CARLSON, Paulette '92				
				Born on 10/11/52 in Northfield, Minnesota. Singer/songwriter/guitarist. Lead singer of **Highway 101**.				
6/25/83	65	7		1 You Gotta Get To My Heart (Before You Lay A Hand On Me) .... *With A Friend Like You (Who Needs A Lover)*	—	$4		RCA 13546
12/3/83	67	8		2 I'd Say Yes .... *Sweeter The Love*	—	$4		RCA 13599
3/10/84	72	4		3 Can You Fool .... *I Go To Pieces*	—	$4		RCA 13745

DEBUT	PEAK	WKS	Gold	A-side (Chart Hit)	B-side	Pop	$	Pic	Label & Number
				CARLSON, Paulette — Cont'd					
12/7/91+	21	20		4 I'll Start With You	—				album cut
				from the album *Love Goes On* on Capitol 97711					
5/30/92	68	1		5 Not With My Heart You Don't	It's Too Bad		$4		Liberty 57737
				CARMEN, Eric — see MANDRELL, Louise					
				CARNES, Kim '80					
				Born on 7/20/45 in Los Angeles. Singer/songwriter/pianist. Member of The New Christy Minstrels with husband/co-writer Dave Ellington and **Kenny Rogers** in the late 1960s. Also see **USA For Africa**.					
7/29/78	99	2		1 You're A Part Of Me .... Shine On (You Got To Shine On Your Light) (Cotton)		36	$5		Ariola America 7704
				GENE COTTON with Kim Carnes					
4/5/80	3	14		2 Don't Fall In Love With A Dreamer ... Goin' Home To The Rock/Gideon Tanner (Rogers)		4	$5	■	United Artists 1345
				KENNY ROGERS with Kim Carnes					
11/10/84	70	10		3 What About Me? ... The Rest Of Last Night (Rogers)		15	$4	■	RCA 13899
				KENNY ROGERS with **KIM CARNES** and **JAMES INGRAM**					
8/20/88	70	7		4 Speed Of The Sound Of Loneliness ... Blood From The Bandit		—	$4		MCA 53387
				Lyle Lovett (backing vocal)					
10/29/88	68	5		5 Crazy In Love ... Blood From The Bandit		—	$4	■	MCA 53433
				CARNES, Rick & Janis '84					
				Husband-and-wife duo: Rick (born on 6/30/50 in Fayetteville, Arkansas; guitar) and Janis (born on 5/21/47 in Shelbyville, Tennessee; keyboards) Carnes. Married in 1973; moved to Nashville in 1978.					
12/18/82+	67	6		1 Have You Heard ... Blue, Only Blue		—	$4		Elektra 69928
7/30/83	51	8		2 Poor Girl ... Am I Wastin' My Time		—	$4		Warner 29656
11/26/83+	32	16		3 Does He Ever Mention My Name ... Silver Eagle		—	$4		Warner 29448
8/18/84	74	4		4 Long Lost Causes ... Standing In The Need Of Love		—	$4		MCA 52414
				CARPENTER, Kris '81					
				Born in Amarillo, Texas. Male singer/guitarist.					
2/21/81	76	4		1 My Song Don't Sing The Same ... Cheap Wine And Watered Down Whiskey		—	$5		Door Knob 146

DEBUT	PEAK	WKS	Gold	A-side	B-side	Pop	$	Pic	Label & Number
				CARPENTER, Mary-Chapin ★149★ '94					
				Born on 2/21/58 in Princeton, New Jersey. Singer/songwriter/guitarist. Graduated from Brown University with a degree in American civilization. CMA Awards: 1992 & 1993 Female Vocalist of the Year.					
				1) Shut Up And Kiss Me 2) He Thinks He'll Keep Her 3) I Take My Chances 4) Down At The Twist And Shout 5) I Feel Lucky					
4/15/89	19	22		1 How Do ... It Don't Bring You		—	$4		Columbia 68677
9/2/89	8	26		2 Never Had It So Good ... Other Streets And Other Towns		—	$4		Columbia 69050
1/6/90	7	26		3 Quittin' Time ... Heroes And Heroines		—	$4		Columbia 73202
6/16/90	14	21		4 Something Of A Dreamer ... Slow Country Dance		—	$4	■	Columbia 73361 (v)
10/20/90+	16	20		5 You Win Again ... The Moon And St. Christopher		—	$4	■	Columbia 73567 (v)
2/16/91	15	20		6 Right Now ... What You Didn't Say		—	$4		Columbia 73699
6/8/91	2[1]	20		7 Down At The Twist And Shout ... Halley Came To Jackson		—	$4		Columbia 73838
10/26/91+	14	20		8 Going Out Tonight ... When She's Gone		—	$4		Columbia 74038
5/30/92	4	20		9 I Feel Lucky ... Middle Ground		—	$4		Columbia 74345
9/12/92	15	20		10 Not Too Much To Ask ... I Am A Town (Carpenter)		—	$4		Columbia 74485
				MARY-CHAPIN CARPENTER with Joe Diffie					
12/26/92+	4	20		11 Passionate Kisses ... Middle Ground		57	$4	■	Columbia 74795 (v)
4/17/93	11	20		12 The Hard Way ... Goodbye Again		—	$4		Columbia 74930
8/21/93	16	20		13 The Bug ... Rhythm Of The Blues		—	$4		Columbia 77134
				first recorded by Dire Straits on their 1991 *On Every Street* album					
12/18/93+	2[1]	20		14 He Thinks He'll Keep Her ... Only A Dream		—	$4		Columbia 77316
4/30/94	2[1]	20		15 I Take My Chances ... Come On Come On		—	$4		Columbia 77476
9/10/94	❶[1]	20		16 Shut Up And Kiss Me ... End Of My Pirate Days		90	$4	■	Columbia 77696 (v)
12/10/94+	6	20		17 Tender When I Want To Be ... John Doe No. 24		—	$4	■	Columbia 77780 (v)
3/25/95	21	13		18 House Of Cards ... Jubilee		—	$4	■	Columbia 77826 (v)
7/1/95	45	9		19 Why Walk When You Can Fly ... Stones In The Road		—	$4	■	Columbia 77955 (v)
10/5/96+	11	20		20 Let Me Into Your Heart ... S:18 Downtown		—	$4	■	Columbia 78453 (v)
2/1/97	35	12		21 I Want To Be Your Girlfriend ... Quittin' Time		—	$4	■	Columbia 78511 (v)
4/19/97	64	7		22 The Better To Dream Of You	—				album cut
7/19/97	58	5		23 Keeping The Faith	—				album cut
				above 2 from the album *A Place In The World* on Columbia 67501					
12/19/98	67	9		24 It's Only Love	—				album cut
				RANDY SCRUGGS (with Mary Chapin Carpenter)					
				from Scruggs's album *Crown Of Jewels* on Warner 46930					
4/10/99	22	21		25 Almost Home ... S:11 Dancing In The Dark (live)		85	$4	★	Columbia 79148
10/9/99	55	7		26 Wherever You Are	—				album cut
				from the album *Party Doll And Other Favorites* on Columbia 68571					
5/5/01	53	6		27 Simple Life ... S:8 Slave To The Beauty		—	$4	★	Columbia 79541

DEBUT	PEAK	WKS	Gold	A-side (Chart Hit)	B-side	Pop	$	Pic	Label & Number
				CARPENTERS '78					
				Brother-sister duo from New Haven, Connecticut: Richard (born on 10/15/46) and Karen (born on 3/2/50) Carpenter. Karen died of heart failure due to anorexia nervosa on 2/4/83 (age 32). Duo charted 29 pop hits from 1970-82. Won the 1970 Best New Artist Grammy Award.					
2/18/78	8	14		Sweet, Sweet Smile written by Juice Newton	I Have You	44	$5	■	A&M 2008
				CARR, Eddie Lee '89					
7/29/89	98	1		Big Bad Mama		—	$5		Evergreen 1092
				CARR, Joe "Fingers" — see **FORD, Tennessee Ernie**					
				CARR, Kenny '89					
9/10/88	96	1		1 The Writing On The Wall		—	$6		Kottage 0090
5/20/89	88	3		2 Tell Me		—	$6		Kottage 0091
				CARRINGTON, Rodney '00					
				Born in Longview, Texas. Male comedian.					
10/7/00	71	1		More Of A Man from the album *Morning Wood* on Capitol 24827	[N]				album cut
	★359★			**CARSON, Jeff** '95					
				Born Jeff Herndon on 12/16/64 in Tulsa, Oklahoma; raised in Gravette, Arkansas. Singer/songwriter/guitarist. 1)Not On Your Love 2)The Car 3)Holdin' Onto Somethin'					
3/11/95	69	4		1 Yeah Buddy	Betty's Takin' Judo	—	$4	■	MCG/Curb 76946 (v)
6/3/95	❶¹	20		2 Not On Your Love	S:5 Betty's Takin' Judo	97	$4	■	MCG/Curb 76954 (v)
10/7/95	3	20		3 The Car /	S:6	113			
3/2/96	6	20		4 Holdin' Onto Somethin'		—	$4	■	MCG/Curb 76970 (v)
12/30/95	70	1		5 Santa Got Lost In Texas available only as a promotional CD single	(no B-side) [X]		$10	★	Curb 1208
8/10/96	62	6		6 That Last Mile from the album *Jeff Carson* on MCG/Curb 77744		—			album cut
4/5/97	55	10		7 Do It Again	(remix)	—	$4		Curb 73018
6/14/97	66	7		8 Butterfly Kisses later issued as the B-side of #9 below		103		■	album cut (v)
8/16/97	64	4		9 Here's The Deal	S:6 Butterfly Kisses	101	$4	■	Curb 73023 (v)
1/24/98	52	10		10 Cheatin' On Her Heart above 4 from the album *Butterfly Kisses* on Curb 77859		—	$4		album cut
7/18/98	49	13		11 Shine On	It Wouldn't Kill Me	—	$4		Curb 73064
5/26/01	14	28		12 Real Life (I Never Was The Same Again) from the album *Real Life* on Curb 77937		103			album cut
				CARSON, Joe '64					
				Born in Brownwood, Texas. Died in a car crash on 2/28/64.					
8/3/63	27	2		1 I Gotta Get Drunk (And I Shore Do Dread It) written by Willie Nelson	Who Will Buy My Memories	—	$10		Liberty 55578
11/9/63+	19	10		2 Helpless	The Last Song (I'm Ever Gonna Sing)	—	$10		Liberty 55614
3/7/64	34	11		3 Double Life	Fort Worth Jail	—	$10		Liberty 55664
				CARSON, Wayne '83					
				Born Wayne Carson Thompson in Denver. Singer/songwriter.					
9/29/73	77	7		1 You're Gonna Love Yourself In The Morning	Laurel Canyon	—	$7		Monument 8581
12/25/76+	82	5		2 Barstool Mountain	Keep On	—	$6		Elektra 45358
6/25/77	99	2		3 Bugle Ann	Down To The River	—	$6		Elektra 45407
4/2/83	61	7		4 1 Yr 2 Mo 11 Days	The Timing's All Wrong	—	$5		EMH 0017
				CARTEE, Alan '77					
				Recorded with brother Wayne as the Cartee Brothers in 1966 on the Reprise label.					
10/8/77	98	1		Let My Fingers Do The Walking (I'm Your Telephone Man) answer to "Telephone Man" by Meri Wilson	Twenty-Five Women [N]	—	$7		Groovy 101
				CARTER, Anita '51					
				Born Ina Anita Carter on 3/31/33 in Maces Springs, Virginia. Died on 7/29/99 (age 66). Member of **The Carter Family**. Daughter of Maybelle and Ezra Carter; sister of Helen and **June Carter**.					
5/12/51	2¹	14		1 Down The Trail Of Achin' Hearts /	J:2 / S:7 / A:7	—			
4/21/51	4	11		2 Bluebird Island	S:4 / J:7		$25		RCA Victor 48-0441
				HANK SNOW (The Singing Ranger) with ANITA CARTER and the Rainbow Ranch Boys (above 2)					
9/3/66	44	3		3 I'm Gonna Leave You	You Couldn't Get My Love Back (If You Tried)	—	$10		RCA Victor 8923
10/21/67	61	3		4 Love Me Now (While I Am Living)	It's My Life (And I'll Live It)	—	$10		RCA Victor 9307
3/30/68	4	15		5 I Got You	No One's Gonna Miss Me	—	$10		RCA Victor 9480
				WAYLON JENNINGS & ANITA CARTER					
11/9/68	65	5		6 To Be A Child Again	Too Many Rivers	—	$8		United Artists 50444
4/12/69	50	7		7 The Coming Of The Roads	The Other Side Of The Coin	—	$8		United Artists 50503
				JOHNNY DARRELL & ANITA CARTER					
1/16/71	41	8		8 Tulsa County	Where Is The Start Of Lonely	—	$6		Capitol 2994
10/23/71	61	8		9 A Whole Lotta Lovin'	Loving Him Was Easier	—	$6		Capitol 3194
				CARTER, Benny, And His Orchestra '44					
				Born Bennett Lester Carter on 8/8/07 in New York City. Alto saxophonist/trumpeter/clarinetist/pianist. Played in several bands, including **Duke Ellington**, until 1935. Own band to 1946. Appeared in the movie *The Snows Of Kilimanjaro* in 1952. Won Grammy's Lifetime Achievement Award in 1987.					
2/19/44	2¹	5		Hurry, Hurry! Savannah Churchill (vocal)	Poinciana (Song of the Tree)	23	$20		Capitol 144

DEBUT	PEAK	WKS	Gold	A-side (Chart Hit)	B-side	Pop	$	Pic	Label & Number
				CARTER, Brenda — see JONES, George					
	★326★			**CARTER, Carlene**					**'90**
				Born Rebecca Carlene Smith on 9/26/55 in Madison, Tennessee. Daughter of **June Carter** and **Carl Smith**. Worked with **The Carter Family** from the late '60s into the early '70s. Went solo thereafter. Appeared in the London production of **Pump Boys And Dinettes**. Married to singer Nick Lowe from 1979-90. Later married Howie Epstein of Tom Petty & The Heartbreakers.					
				1)Every Little Thing 2)Come On Back 3)I Fell In Love					
10/27/79	42	8		1 Do It In A Heartbeat..Swap-Meat Rag		108	$5		Warner 49083
10/25/80	76	5		2 Baby Ride Easy..Too Bad About Sandy		—	$5		Warner 49572
				CARLENE CARTER with Dave Edmunds					
12/2/89+	26	18		3 Time's Up..Memphis Queen		—	$4		Warner 22714
				SOUTHERN PACIFIC and CARLENE CARTER					
7/14/90	3	21		4 I Fell In Love...Guardian Angel		—	$4	■	Reprise 19915 (v)
10/27/90+	3	20		5 Come On Back..The Leavin' Side		—	$4	■	Reprise 19564 (v)
3/16/91	25	17		6 The Sweetest Thing...Goodnight Dallas		—	$4		Reprise 19398
8/10/91	33	12		7 One Love..Easy From Now On		—	$4		Reprise 19255
5/29/93	3	20		8 Every Little Thing..Long Hard Fall		—	$4	■	Giant 18527 (v)
10/9/93	51	8		9 Unbreakable Heart...Wastin' Time With You		—	$4	■	Giant 18373 (v)
2/5/94	50	9		10 I Love You 'Cause I Want To..Nowhere Train		—	$4		Giant 18265
5/14/94	43	10		11 Something Already Gone...Amazing Grace		—	$4		Atlantic 82595
				from the movie *Maverick* starring Mel Gibson and Jodie Foster					
12/31/94	66	1		12 Rockin' Little Christmas........................The Working Elf Blues (Daron Norwood) [X]		—	$4		Giant 18006
7/22/95	70	3		13 Love Like This...One Tender Night		—	$4	■	Giant 17853 (v)
8/26/95	75	1		14 Hurricane..One Tender Night		—	$4	■	Giant 17962 (v)
	★338★			**CARTER, Deana**					**'97**
				Born on 1/4/66 in Nashville. Singer/songwriter. Daughter of **Fred Carter, Jr.**					
8/17/96	●²	20		1 Strawberry Wine.............................S:●³ Before We Ever Heard Goodbye		65	$4	■	Capitol 58585 (v)
				1997 CMA winner: Single of the Year; "45": Capitol 19223					
12/14/96+	●²	20		2 We Danced Anyway..S:●⁵ Rita Valentine		72	$4	■	Capitol 58626 (v)
				"45": Capitol 19450 (B-side: "Did I Shave My Legs For This?")					
3/29/97	5	20		3 Count Me In..Did I Shave My Legs For This?		—	$4		Capitol 19510
8/2/97	●¹	20		4 How Do I Get There...Did I Shave My Legs For This?		—	$4		Capitol 19646
11/1/97	25	17		5 Did I Shave My Legs For This?........................S:9 (live version)		85	$4	■	Capitol 58672 (v)
				"45": Capitol 19723 (B-side: hybrid version)					
9/26/98	16	20		6 Absence Of The Heart...Dickson County		83	$4		Capitol 58738
1/23/99	36	12		7 You Still Shake Me...The Train Song		—	$4		Capitol 58760
4/3/99	35	16		8 Angels Working Overtime....................................Everything's Gonna Be Alright		—	$4		Capitol 58774
				CARTER, Fred Jr.					**'67**
				Born on 12/31/33 in Winnsboro, Louisiana. Singer/guitarist. Father of **Deana Carter**.					
10/14/67	70	3		And You Wonder Why...It's A Rough Old Road		—	$8		Monument 1022
	★352★			**CARTER, June**					**'67**
				Born Valerie June Carter on 6/23/29 in Maces Springs, Virginia. Member of **The Carter Family**. Daughter of Maybelle and Ezra Carter, sister of Helen and **Anita Carter**. Married to **Carl Smith** from 1952-56; their daughter is **Carlene Carter**. Worked with **Elvis Presley**, then joined the **Johnny Cash** road show in 1961. Married Cash in 1968. CMA Award: 1969 Vocal Group of the Year (with Johnny Cash).					
				1)If I Were A Carpenter 2)Jackson 3)Long-Legged Guitar Pickin' Man					
8/27/49	9	1		1 Baby, It's Cold Outside.......................S:9 Country Girl [N]		22	$20		RCA Victor 21-0078
				HOMER and JETHRO with June Carter					
				45 rpm: 48-0075 from the movie *Neptune's Daughter* starring Esther Williams					
				JOHNNY CASH & JUNE CARTER:					
3/4/67	2¹	17		2 Jackson..Pack Up Your Sorrows		—	$8		Columbia 44011
				#14 Pop hit for **Nancy Sinatra** & Lee Hazlewood in 1967					
6/24/67	6	17		3 Long-Legged Guitar Pickin' Man...You'll Be All Right		—	$8		Columbia 44158
1/24/70	2¹	15		4 If I Were A Carpenter..'Cause I Love You		36	$8		Columbia 45064
				#8 Pop hit for **Bobby Darin** in 1966					
4/3/71	27	11		5 A Good Man..Straw Upon The Wind		—	$8		Columbia 45338
				JUNE CARTER CASH					
9/11/71	15	13		6 No Need To Worry..I'll Be Loving You		—	$8		Columbia 45431
7/15/72	29	7		7 If I Had A Hammer...I Gotta Boy (And His Name Is John)		—	$8		Columbia 45631
				#10 Pop hit for Peter, Paul & Mary in 1962					
1/20/73	27	10		8 The Loving Gift..Help Me Make It Through The Night		—	$7		Columbia 45758
9/29/73	69	10		9 Allegheny..We're For Love		—	$7		Columbia 45929
11/20/76+	26	11		10 Old Time Feeling..Far Side Banks Of Jordan		—	$6		Columbia 10436
				CARTER, Woody					**'49**
				Sittin' On The Doorstep...................................J:14 Slippin' Around		—	$50		Macy's 100
9/17/49	14	1		WOODY CARTER and his Hoedown Boys					
				CARTER FAMILY, The					**'63**
				Founded by Alvin Pleasant "A.P." Carter (born on 12/15/1893 in Maces Springs, Virginia; died on 11/7/60, age 66); with wife Sara Dougherty (born on 7/21/1899 in Flatwoods, Virginia; died on 1/8/79, age 79) and sister-in-law Maybelle Addington (born on 5/10/09 in Nickelsville, Virginia; died on 10/23/78, age 69). Joined from 1936-39 by Maybelle's daughters Helen, **Anita Carter**, and **June Carter**, and A.P.'s children Janette and Joe. Helen died on 6/2/98 (age 70). This group disbanded in 1943 and was re-formed by Maybelle and her daughters as the Carter Sisters and Mother Maybelle. Joined the *Grand Ole Opry* in 1948. Joined **Johnny Cash**'s road show in 1961. Original group entered the Country Music Hall of Fame in 1970. Known as "The First Family of Country Music." Chart hits below feature Maybelle and her daughters.					
4/6/63	13	3		1 Busted..Send A Picture Of Mother		—	$10	■	Columbia 42665
				JOHNNY CASH With The Carter Family					
				#4 Pop hit for **Ray Charles** in 1963					

DEBUT	PEAK	WKS	Gold	A-side (Chart Hit) ... B-side	Pop	$	Pic	Label & Number
				CARTER FAMILY, The — cont'd				
9/4/71	37	11		2 A Song To Mama .... One More Summer In Virginia Johnny Cash (narration and vocal backing)	—	$7		Columbia 45428
4/29/72	42	7		3 Travelin' Minstrel Band .... 2001 (Ballad To The Future)	—	$7		Columbia 45581
9/30/72	35	8		4 The World Needs A Melody .... A Bird With Broken Wings Can't Fly THE CARTER FAMILY WITH JOHNNY CASH	—	$7		Columbia 45679
8/4/73	57	7		5 Praise The Lord And Pass The Soup .... The Ballad Of Barbara JOHNNY CASH (With The Carter Family And The Oak Ridge Boys)	—	$7		Columbia 45890
11/17/73+	34	10		6 Pick The Wildwood Flower .... Diamonds In The Rough JOHNNY CASH with MOTHER MAYBELLE CARTER	—	$7		Columbia 45938
	★298★			**CARTWRIGHT, Lionel** **'91** Born on 2/10/60 in Gallipolis, Ohio; raised in Milton, West Virginia. Singer/songwriter/guitarist. 1)Leap Of Faith 2)Give Me His Last Chance 3)My Heart Is Set On You				
11/19/88+	45	13		1 You're Gonna Make Her Mine .... In My Eyes	—	$4		MCA 53444
2/18/89	14	25		2 Like Father Like Son .... A Little Lesser Blue	—	$4		MCA 53498
6/17/89	3	24		3 Give Me His Last Chance .... Let The Hard Times Roll	—	$4		MCA 53651
10/14/89+	12	21		4 In My Eyes .... That's Why They Call It Falling	—	$4		MCA 53723
3/24/90	8	23		5 I Watched It All (On My Radio) .... Hard Act To Follow	—	$4	■	MCA 53779 (v)
7/28/90	7	20		6 My Heart Is Set On You .... True Believer	—	$4	■	MCA 53849 (v)
12/1/90+	31	15		7 Say It's Not True .... In The Long Run	—	$4		MCA 53955
7/6/91	❶¹	20		8 Leap Of Faith .... Smack Dab In The Middle Of Love	—	$4		MCA 54078
11/16/91+	24	20		9 What Kind Of Fool .... I'm Your Man	—	$4		MCA 54237
4/4/92	62	4		10 Family Tree .... 30 Nothin'	—	$4		MCA 54366
8/15/92	63	11		11 Be My Angel .... Sleep Walking	—	$4		MCA 54440
10/31/92	50	15		12 Standing On The Promises .... She Will	—	$4		MCA 54514
	★217★			**CARVER, Johnny** **'73** Born on 11/24/40 in Jackson, Mississippi. Singer/songwriter/guitarist. Began singing in the family's Gospel group. Started his own band, the Capital Cowboys, while still a teenager. Moved to Los Angeles in 1965, became leader of the house band at the Palomino Club. 1)Yellow Ribbon 2)You Really Haven't Changed 3)Afternoon Delight 4)Don't Tell (That Sweet Ole Lady Of Mine) 5)Tonight Someone's Falling In Love				
12/23/67+	21	13		1 Your Lily White Hands .... What If It Happened To You	—	$10		Imperial 66268
6/1/68	48	8		2 I Still Didn't Have The Sense To Go .... Feelin' Kinda Sunday In My Thinkin'	—	$10		Imperial 66297
12/7/68+	32	11		3 Hold Me Tight .... My Heart's Been Marching #5 Pop hit for Johnny Nash in 1968	—	$10		Imperial 66341
4/5/69	26	9		4 Sweet Wine .... With Every Heartbeat	—	$10		Imperial 66361
8/2/69	41	10		5 That's Your Hang Up .... Mother-In-Law	—	$10		Imperial 66389
12/13/69+	43	9		6 Willie And The Hand Jive .... Take Sadie Out To The Country #9 Pop hit for the Johnny Otis Show in 1958	—	$10		Imperial 66423
6/20/70	68	4		7 Harvey Harrington IV .... Sybil's Rights	—	$10		Imperial 66442
12/12/70	73	2		8 If You See My Baby .... Paint Your Pretty Pictures	—	$8		United Artists 50713
8/14/71	34	15		9 If You Think That It's All Right .... This Town's Not Big Enough	—	$7		Epic 10760
12/25/71+	27	11		10 I Start Thinking About You .... Preserving Wildlife	—	$7		Epic 10813
6/24/72	35	9		11 I Want You .... I'm Talking About You Baby	—	$7		Epic 10872
4/7/73	5	17		12 Yellow Ribbon .... Since My Baby Left Me #1 Pop hit for Tony Orlando & Dawn in 1973	—	$6		ABC 11357
7/28/73	6	13		13 You Really Haven't Changed .... Treat A Lady Like A Tramp	—	$6		ABC 11374
12/8/73+	12	16		14 Tonight Someone's Falling In Love .... Frank And Don, Howard, Too, Broadway Joe And You And Me	—	$6		ABC 11403
4/13/74	27	12		15 Country Lullabye .... Pass Me By	—	$6		ABC 11425
8/24/74	10	16		16 Don't Tell (That Sweet Ole Lady Of Mine) .... 'Till We Find It All Again	—	$6		ABC 12017
1/18/75	39	11		17 January Jones .... Did We Even Try	—	$6		ABC 12052
6/7/75	64	7		18 Strings .... Double Exposure	—	$6		ABC 12097
10/4/75	74	7		19 Start All Over Again .... Love Signs	—	$5		ABC/Dot 17576
3/6/76	77	5		20 Snap, Crackle And Pop .... I Can't Go Swimming In Muddy Water	—	$5		ABC/Dot 17614
7/4/76	9	14		21 Afternoon Delight .... Double Exposure	—	$5		ABC/Dot 17640
11/6/76	47	9		22 Love Is Only Love (When Shared By Two) .... It Don't Hurt To Be A Dreamer	—	$5		ABC/Dot 17661
2/12/77	48	6		23 Sweet City Woman .... 'Till We Find It All Again #8 Pop hit for The Stampeders in 1971	—	$5		ABC/Dot 17675
3/12/77	29	10		24 Living Next Door To Alice .... Treat A Lady Like A Tramp #25 Pop hit for Smokie in 1977	—	$5		ABC/Dot 17685
6/18/77	36	9		25 Down At The Pool .... Double Exposure	—	$5		ABC/Dot 17707
11/26/77	72	6		26 Apartment .... Frank And Don, Howard, Too, Broadway Joe And You And Me	—	$5		ABC/Dot 17729
6/14/80	90	3		27 Fingertips .... Caribbean Nights	—	$6		Equity 1902
1/24/81	73	5		28 S.O.S. .... Fingertips #15 Pop hit for Abba in 1975	—	$6		Tanglewood 1905
				CASEY, Karen **'80**				
2/23/80	92	2		Leavin' On Your Mind .... Are You Lonesome Tonight?	—	$6		Western Pride 112

Hey Porter??? - on LP

CASH, Johnny ★3★ '58

Born J.R. Cash on 2/26/32 in Kingsland, Arkansas; raised in Dyess, Arkansas. In U.S. Air Force, 1950-54, where he adopted the name John Ray. Backed by The Tennessee Two: Luther Perkins (guitar) and Marshall Grant (bass). First recorded for Sun in 1955. On *Louisiana Hayride* and *Grand Ole Opry* in 1957. Own TV show for ABC from 1969-71. Worked with **June Carter** from 1961, married her in March 1968. Father of **Rosanne Cash** and stepfather of **Carlene Carter**. Brother of **Tommy Cash**. Acted on numerous TV shows. Known as "The Man In Black." CMA Awards: 1969 Vocal Group of the Year (with June Carter); 1969 Male Vocalist of the Year; 1969 Entertainer of the Year. Elected to the Country Music Hall of Fame in 1980. Won Grammy's Living Legends Award in 1990. Inducted into the Rock and Roll Hall of Fame in 1992.

1) Ballad Of A Teenage Queen 2) Guess Things Happen That Way 3) Ring Of Fire 4) I Walk The Line 5) Understand Your Man

DEBUT	PEAK	WKS	Gold	#	A-side (Chart Hit)	B-side	Pop	$	Pic	Label & Number
11/26/55	14	1		1	Cry! Cry! Cry!	S:14 Hey, Porter!	—	$40		Sun 221
2/4/56	4	23		2	So Doggone Lonesome /	J:4 / S:6 / A:6	—			
2/11/56	4	20		3	Folsom Prison Blues	A:4 / S:5 / J:5	—	$40		Sun 232
					also see #62 below					
6/9/56	●6	43		4	I Walk The Line /	J:●6 / A:●1 / S:2	17			
		9		5	Get Rhythm	S:flip / J:flip	—	$30		Sun 241
					also see #65 below					
12/22/56+	●5	28		6	There You Go /	J:●5 / S:2 / A:2	—			
12/22/56+	7	24		7	Train Of Love	A:7 / S:13	—	$30		Sun 258
5/27/57	9	15		8	Next In Line /	S:9 / A:9	99			
		9		9	Don't Make Me Go	S:flip	—	$30		Sun 266
9/16/57	3	23		10	Home Of The Blues	A:3 / S:5	88			
10/7/57	13	2		11	Give My Love To Rose	A:13	—	$30		Sun 279
1/20/58	●10	23		12	Ballad Of A Teenage Queen /	A:●10 / S:●8	14			
					also see #133 below					
2/10/58	4	14		13	Big River	A:4	flip	$25		Sun 283
					also see #72 below					
5/26/58	●8	24		14	Guess Things Happen That Way /	S:●8 / A:●3	11			
6/2/58	6	13		15	Come In Stranger	A:6	66	$25	■	Sun 295
8/25/58	2⁴	16		16	The Ways Of A Woman In Love	S:2 / A:2	24			
9/1/58	5	16		17	You're The Nearest Thing To Heaven		flip	$25		Sun 302
10/13/58	4	19		18	All Over Again		38			
10/13/58	7	15		19	What Do I Care		52	$20	■	Columbia 41251
1/19/59	●6	20		20	Don't Take Your Guns To Town	I Still Miss Someone	32	$20	■	Columbia 41313
1/19/59	30	1		21	It's Just About Time	I Just Thought You'd Like To Know	47	$25		Sun 309
3/30/59	8	13		22	Luther Played The Boogie /		—			
3/30/59	12	9		23	Thanks A Lot		57	$25		Sun 316
5/4/59	9	11		24	Frankie's Man, Johnny /		—			
5/11/59	13	11		25	You Dreamer You		—	$15		Columbia 41371
7/20/59	11	11		26	Katy Too	I Forgot To Remember To Forget	66	$20		Sun 321
8/10/59	4	20		27	I Got Stripes /		43			
8/24/59	14	9		28	Five Feet High And Rising		76	$15		Columbia 41427
11/9/59	22	5		29	Goodbye Little Darlin'	You Tell Me	—	$20		Sun 331
12/28/59	24	1		30	The Little Drummer Boy	I'll Remember You [X]	63	$15	■	Columbia 41481
					#13 Pop hit for the Harry Simeone Chorale in 1958					
2/15/60	16	10		31	Straight A's In Love /		84			
3/7/60	20	2		32	I Love You Because		—	$20		Sun 334
					JOHNNY CASH With The Gene Lowery Singers					
4/25/60	10	15		33	Seasons Of My Heart /		110			
5/9/60	13	8		34	Smiling Bill McCall	[N]	—	$15		Columbia 41618
8/22/60	15	7		35	Second Honeymoon	Honky-Tonk Girl	79	$15		Columbia 41707
12/26/60	30	1		36	Mean Eyed Cat	Port Of Lonely Hearts	—	$20		Sun 347
					JOHNNY CASH And The Tennessee Two (all of above Sun Records, except #32)					
2/6/61	13	9		37	Oh Lonesome Me	Life Goes On	93	$20		Sun 355
					JOHNNY CASH With The Gene Lowery Singers					
					all Sun records recorded from 1955-58					
6/12/61	24	2		38	The Rebel - Johnny Yuma	Forty Shades Of Green	108	$15	■	Columbia 41995
					from the TV series The Rebel *starring Nick Adams*					
12/18/61+	11	14		39	Tennessee Flat-Top Box	Tall Men	84	$12	■	Columbia 42147
3/31/62	24	3		40	The Big Battle	When I've Learned	—	$10	■	Columbia 42301
7/14/62	8	10		41	In The Jailhouse Now	A Little At A Time	—	$10	■	Columbia 42425
					#14 Pop hit for **Jimmie Rodgers** *in 1928*					
4/6/63	13	3		42	Busted	Send A Picture Of Mother	—	$10	■	Columbia 42665
					JOHNNY CASH With The Carter Family					
					#4 Pop hit for **Ray Charles** *in 1963*					
6/8/63	●7	26		43	Ring Of Fire	I'd Still Be There	17	$10	■	Columbia 42788
11/9/63	2³	16		44	The Matador	Still In Town	44	$10	■	Columbia 42880
2/22/64	●6	22		45	Understand Your Man /		35			
3/7/64	49	1		46	Dark As A Dungeon		119	$10	□	Columbia 42964
7/11/64	3	20		47	The Ballad Of Ira Hayes		—	$10		Columbia 43058
7/25/64	8	15		48	Bad News		—	$10	□	Columbia 43145
11/7/64+	4	22		49	It Ain't Me, Babe	Time And Time Again	58	$10		Columbia 43206
					June Carter (harmony vocal); #8 Pop hit for The Turtles in 1965					
2/20/65	3	16		50	Orange Blossom Special	All Of God's Children Ain't Free	80	$10		Columbia 43206
7/10/65	15	13		51	Mister Garfield	The Streets Of Laredo	—	$10		Columbia 43313
9/4/65	10	9		52	The Sons Of Katie Elder	A Certain Kinda Hurtin'	119	$10		Columbia 43342
					from the movie starring John Wayne					

DEBUT	PEAK	WKS	Gold	A-side (Chart Hit)	B-side	Pop	$	Pic	Label & Number
				CASH, Johnny — Cont'd					
11/20/65+	9	14		53 Happy To Be With You	Pickin' Time	—	$10		Columbia 43420
2/12/66	2^2	18		54 The One On The Right Is On The Left	Cotton Pickin' Hands [N]	46	$10		Columbia 43496
7/2/66	17	9		55 Everybody Loves A Nut	Austin Prison	96	$10		Columbia 43673
9/10/66	39	5		56 Boa Constrictor	Bottom Of A Mountain [N]	107	$10		Columbia 43763
12/24/66+	20	13		57 You Beat All I Ever Saw	Put The Sugar To Bed	—	$10		Columbia 43921
3/4/67	2^1	17		58 Jackson	Pack Up Your Sorrows	—	$8		Columbia 44011
				JOHNNY CASH AND JUNE CARTER					
				#14 Pop hit for **Nancy Sinatra** & Lee Hazlewood in 1967					
6/24/67	6	17		59 Long-Legged Guitar Pickin' Man	You'll Be All Right	—	$8		Columbia 44158
				JOHNNY CASH AND JUNE CARTER					
10/28/67	60	6		60 The Wind Changes		—	$8		
12/23/67+	2^2	15		61 Rosanna's Going Wild	Red Velvet	—	$8		Columbia 44288
6/1/68	●^{4}	18		62 Folsom Prison Blues	Roll Call	91	$8	■	Columbia 44373
				"live" version of #3 above; recorded at Folsom Prison	The Folk Singer	32	$8	■	Columbia 44513
12/7/68+	●^{6}	20		63 Daddy Sang Bass	He Turned The Water Into Wine	42	$8		Columbia 44689
7/26/69	●^{5}	14	●	64 A Boy Named Sue	San Quentin [N]	2^3	$8		Columbia 44944
				recorded "live" at San Quentin prison; CMA Award: Single of the Year					
10/11/69	23	12		65 Get Rhythm	Hey Porter [R]	60	$8		Sun 1103
				same version as #5 above with "live" effects dubbed-in					
11/22/69	4	13		66 Blistered /		50			
			12	67 See Ruby Fall		—	$8		Columbia 45020
1/24/70	2^1	15		68 If I Were A Carpenter	'Cause I Love You	36	$8		Columbia 45064
				JOHNNY CASH & JUNE CARTER					
				#8 Pop hit for **Bobby Darin** in 1966					
2/28/70	35	7		69 Rock Island Line	Next In Line	93	$8		Sun 1111
				#8 Pop hit for Lonnie Donegan in 1956					
4/18/70	3	14		70 What Is Truth	Sing A Traveling Song [S]	19	$8		Columbia 45134
9/5/70	●^{2}	15		71 Sunday Morning Coming Down	I'm Gonna Try To Be That Way	46	$8		Columbia 45211
				"live" recording					
12/5/70	41	8		72 Big River	Come In Stranger [R]	—	$8		Sun 1121
				same version as #13 above					
12/19/70+	●^{1}	13		73 Flesh And Blood	This Side Of The Law	54	$8		Columbia 45269
				from the movie Walk The Line starring Gregory Peck					
3/27/71	3	13		74 Man In Black	Little Bit Of Yesterday	58	$8		Columbia 45339
6/26/71	18	10		75 Singing In Viet Nam Talking Blues	You've Got A New Light Shining [S]	124	$8		Columbia 45393
9/11/71	15	13		76 No Need To Worry	I'll Be Loving You	—	$8		Columbia 45431
				JOHNNY CASH & JUNE CARTER					
10/16/71	16	11		77 Papa Was A Good Man	I Promise You	104	$8		Columbia 45460
1/29/72	2^1	16		78 A Thing Called Love	Daddy	103	$8		Columbia 45534
				JOHNNY CASH And The Evangel Temple Choir (above 2)					
5/6/72	2^3	12		79 Kate	The Miracle Man	75	$8		Columbia 45590
7/15/72	29	7		80 If I Had A Hammer	I Gotta Boy (And His Name Is John)	—	$8		Columbia 45631
				JOHNNY CASH & JUNE CARTER CASH					
				#10 Pop hit for Peter, Paul & Mary in 1962					
8/26/72	2^2	15		81 Oney	Country Trash	101	$7		Columbia 45660
9/30/72	35	8		82 The World Needs A Melody	A Bird With Broken Wings Can't Fly	—	$7		Columbia 45679
				THE CARTER FAMILY WITH JOHNNY CASH					
12/23/72+	3	15		83 Any Old Wind That Blows	Kentucky Straight	—	$7		Columbia 45740
1/20/73	27	10		84 The Loving Gift	Help Me Make It Through The Night	—	$7		Columbia 45758
				JOHNNY CASH & JUNE CARTER CASH					
4/21/73	30	9		85 Children	Last Supper	—	$7		Columbia 45786
				from the movie The Gospel Road starring Cash					
8/4/73	57	7		86 Praise The Lord And Pass The Soup	The Ballad Of Barbara	—	$7		Columbia 45890
				JOHNNY CASH (With The Carter Family And The Oak Ridge Boys)					
9/29/73	69	10		87 Allegheny	We're For Love	—	$7		Columbia 45929
				JOHNNY CASH & JUNE CARTER					
11/17/73+	34	10		88 Pick The Wildwood Flower	Diamonds In The Rough	—	$7		Columbia 45938
				JOHNNY CASH with MOTHER MAYBELLE CARTER					
2/23/74	52	8		89 Orleans Parish Prison	Jacob Green	—	$7		Columbia 45997
4/27/74	31	13		90 Ragged Old Flag	Don't Go Near The Water	—	$7		Columbia 46028
12/14/74+	14	12		91 Lady Came From Baltimore	Lonesome To The Bone	—	$6		Columbia 10066
4/12/75	42	9		92 My Old Kentucky Home (Turpentine And Dandelion Wine)	Hard Times Comin'	—	$6		Columbia 10116
7/26/75	17	12		93 Look At Them Beans	All Around Cowboy	—	$6		Columbia 10177
11/15/75+	35	12		94 Texas - 1947	I Hardly Ever Sing Beer Drinking Songs	—	$6		Columbia 10237
2/7/76	54	7		95 Strawberry Cake	I Got Stripes	—	$6		Columbia 10279
4/10/76	●^{2}	15		96 One Piece At A Time	Go On Blues [N]	29	$6		Columbia 10321
7/24/76	29	8		97 Sold Out Of Flagpoles	Mountain Lady	—	$6		Columbia 10381
10/23/76	41	8		98 It's All Over	Ridin' On The Cotton Belt	—	$6		Columbia 10424
				JOHNNY CASH & The Tennessee Three (above 3)					
11/20/76+	26	11		99 Old Time Feeling	Far Side Banks Of Jordan	—	$6		Columbia 10436
				JOHNNY CASH & JUNE CARTER CASH					
2/26/77	38	9		100 The Last Gunfighter Ballad	City Jail	—	$5		Columbia 10483
8/6/77	46	9		101 Lady	Hit The Road And Go	—	$5		Columbia 10587
10/22/77	32	12		102 After The Ball	Calilou	—	$5		Columbia 10623
2/11/78	12	13		103 I Would Like To See You Again	Lately	—	$5		Columbia 10681
5/20/78	2^2	13		104 There Ain't No Good Chain Gang /		—			
11/17/79+	22	12		105 I Wish I Was Crazy Again		—	$5		Columbia 10742
				JOHNNY CASH & WAYLON JENNINGS (above 2)					
9/9/78	44	8		106 Gone Girl	I'm Alright Now	—	$5		Columbia 10817

DEBUT	PEAK	WKS	Gold	A-side (Chart Hit)	B-side	Pop	$	Pic	Label & Number
				CASH, Johnny — Cont'd					
12/9/78	89	2		107 It'll Be Her	It Comes And Goes	—	$5		Columbia 10855
1/13/79	21	13		108 I Will Rock And Roll With You	A Song For The Life	—	$5		Columbia 10888
5/19/79	2¹	16		109 (Ghost) Riders In The Sky I'm Gonna Sit On The Porch And Pick On My Old Guitar		—	$5	■	Columbia 10961
10/20/79	42	7		110 I'll Say It's True	Cocaine Blues	—	$5		Columbia 11103
				George Jones (guest vocal)					
4/19/80	66	5		111 Bull Rider	Lonesome To The Bone	—	$5		Columbia 11237
6/7/80	54	8		112 Song Of The Patriot	She's A Go-er	—	$5		Columbia 11283
				Marty Robbins (harmony vocal)					
8/23/80	53	8		113 Cold Lonesome Morning	The Cowboy Who Started The Fight	—	$5		Columbia 11340
11/29/80	85	4		114 The Last Time	Rockabilly Blues (Texas 1955)	—	$5		Columbia 11399
1/24/81	78	5		115 Without Love	It Ain't Nothing New Babe	—	$5		Columbia 11424
3/21/81	10	15		116 The Baron	I Will Dance With You	—	$4		Columbia 60516
7/25/81	60	5		117 Mobile Bay	The Hard Way	—	$4		Columbia 02189
1/23/82	71	5		118 The Reverend Mr. Black /		—	$4		
				#8 Pop hit for The Kingston Trio in 1963					
		5		119 Chattanooga City Limit Sign		—	$4		Columbia 02669
4/17/82	26	12		120 The General Lee	Duelin' Dukes	—	$4		Scotti Brothers 02803
				from the TV series The Dukes Of Hazzard starring John Schneider and Tom Wopat					
8/7/82	55	8		121 Georgia On A Fast Train	Sing A Song	—	$4		Columbia 03058
2/26/83	84	2		122 We Must Believe In Magic	I'll Cross Over Jordan Someday	—	$4		Columbia 03524
9/24/83	75	4		123 I'm Ragged But I'm Right	Brand New Dance (w/June Carter)	—	$4		Columbia 04060
5/12/84	84	5		124 That's The Truth	Joshua Gone Barbados	—	$4		Columbia 04428
7/14/84	45	11		125 The Chicken In Black	Battle Of Nashville [N]	—	$4		Columbia 04513
5/18/85	❶¹	20		126 Highwayman S:❶¹ / A:❶¹ The Human Condition		—	$4	■	Columbia 04881
				WAYLON JENNINGS/WILLIE NELSON/JOHNNY CASH/KRIS KRISTOFFERSON					
7/13/85	45	9		127 I Will Dance With You	Too Bad For Love	—	$5		Warner 28979
				KAREN BROOKS with Johnny Cash					
9/14/85	15	18		128 Desperados Waiting For A Train S:15 / A:16 The Twentieth Century Is Almost Over		—	$4		Columbia 05594
				WAYLON JENNINGS/WILLIE NELSON/JOHNNY CASH/KRIS KRISTOFFERSON					
5/17/86	35	11		129 Even Cowgirls Get The Blues A:34 American By Birth		—	$4		Columbia 05896
				JOHNNY CASH & WAYLON JENNINGS					
3/28/87	43	11		130 The Night Hank Williams Came To Town	I'd Rather Have You	—	$4		Mercury 888459
				Waylon Jennings (guest vocal)					
12/12/87	72	5		131 W. Lee O'Daniel (And The Light Crust Dough Boys)	Letters From Home	—	$4		Mercury 870010
9/24/88	21	20		132 That Old Wheel S:17 Tennessee Flat Top Box		—	$4		Mercury 870688
				JOHNNY CASH with Hank Williams, Jr.					
2/25/89	45	9		133 Ballad Of A Teenage Queen	Get Rhythm (Cash) [R]	—	$4		Mercury 872420
				JOHNNY CASH with Rosanne Cash & The Everly Brothers					
				new version of #12 above					
3/3/90	25	14		134 Silver Stallion	American Remains	—	$4		Columbia 73233
				WAYLON JENNINGS/WILLIE NELSON/JOHNNY CASH/KRIS KRISTOFFERSON					
9/22/90	69	4		135 Goin' By The Book	Beans For Breakfast	—	$4		Mercury 878292
11/7/98	61	6		136 I Walk The Line Revisited	Stars On The Water	—	$4		Reprise 17149
				RODNEY CROWELL with Johnny Cash					

CASH, Rosanne ★126★ '88

Born on 5/24/56 in Memphis. Daughter of **Johnny Cash** and Vivian Liberto. Raised by her mother in California, then moved to Nashville after high school graduation. Worked in the Johnny Cash Road Show. Married to **Rodney Crowell** from 1979-92. Moved to New York. Married producer John Leventhal in 1995. Released short-story collection *Bodies Of Water* in 1996.

1) Never Be You   2) The Way We Make A Broken Heart   3) If You Change Your Mind   4) It's Such A Small World
5) Seven Year Ache

DEBUT	PEAK	WKS	Gold	A-side (Chart Hit)	B-side	Pop	$	Pic	Label & Number
9/8/79	17	12		1 No Memories Hangin' Round	This Has Happened Before	—	$5		Columbia 11045
				ROSANNE CASH with BOBBY BARE					
2/2/80	15	13		2 Couldn't Do Nothin' Right	Seeing's Believing	—	$5		Columbia 11188
5/31/80	25	12		3 Take Me, Take Me	Right Or Wrong	—	$5		Columbia 11268
2/21/81	❶¹	19		4 Seven Year Ache	Blue Moon With Heartache	22	$4	□	Columbia 11426
8/29/81	❶¹	16		5 My Baby Thinks He's A Train	I Can't Resist	—	$4		Columbia 02463
12/19/81+	❶¹	18		6 Blue Moon With Heartache	Only Human	104	$4		Columbia 02659
5/29/82	4	18		7 Ain't No Money	The Feelin'	—	$4		Columbia 02937
10/9/82+	8	20		8 I Wonder	Oh Yes I Can	—	$4		Columbia 03283
3/12/83	14	15		9 It Hasn't Happened Yet	Somewhere In The Stars	—	$4		Columbia 03705
6/1/85	❶¹	24		10 I Don't Know Why You Don't Want Me S:❶¹ / A:❶¹ What You Gonna Do About It		—	$4	■	Columbia 04809
10/5/85	❶¹	24		11 Never Be You S:❶¹ / A:❶¹ Closing Time		—	$4		Columbia 05621
2/15/86	5	22		12 Hold On S:5 / A:5 Never Gonna Hurt		—	$4		Columbia 05794
7/19/86	5	20		13 Second To No One A:4 / S:6 Never Alone		—	$4		Columbia 06159
6/27/87	❶¹	23		14 The Way We Make A Broken Heart S:❶¹ 707		—	$4		Columbia 07200
11/14/87+	❶¹	22		15 Tennessee Flat Top Box S:❶³ Why Don't You Quit Leaving Me Alone		—	$4		Columbia 07624
1/23/88	❶¹	23		16 It's Such A Small World S:❶³ Crazy Baby (Crowell)		—	$4		Columbia 07693
				RODNEY CROWELL & ROSANNE CASH					
4/2/88	❶¹	22		17 If You Change Your Mind S:❶² Somewhere Sometime		—	$4		Columbia 07746
8/13/88	❶¹	23		18 Runaway Train S:❶¹ Seven Year Ache		—	$4	■	Columbia 07988
2/25/89	45	9		19 Ballad Of A Teenage Queen	Get Rhythm (Cash)	—	$4		Mercury 872420
				JOHNNY CASH with Rosanne Cash & The Everly Brothers					

DEBUT	PEAK	WKS	Gold	A-side (Chart Hit) ... B-side	Pop	$	Pic	Label & Number
				CASH, Rosanne — Cont'd				
3/25/89	●¹	21		20 I Don't Want To Spoil The Party .... Look What Our Love Is Coming To	—	$4	■	Columbia 68599
				#39 Pop hit for The Beatles in 1965				
11/4/89	37	11		21 Black And White .... Never Be You	—	$4		Columbia 73054
3/3/90	63	6		22 One Step Over The Line .... Riding Alone	—	$4		MCA 53795
				THE NITTY GRITTY DIRT BAND Featuring Rosanne Cash and John Hiatt				
9/29/90	39	11		23 What We Really Want .... Portrait	—	$4	■	Columbia 73517
2/23/91	69	1		24 On The Surface .... —	—			album cut
				from the album *Interiors* on Columbia 46079				
	★272★			**CASH, Tommy** '70				
				Born on 4/5/40 in Dyess, Arkansas. Singer/songwriter/guitarist. Younger brother of **Johnny Cash**.				
				1)Six White Horses 2)Rise And Shine 3)One Song Away				
8/31/68	41	9		1 The Sounds Of Goodbye .... Easy Woman	—	$10		United Artists 50337
6/21/69	43	11		2 Your Lovin' Takes The Leavin' Out Of Me .... That Lucky Old Sun	—	$8		Epic 10469
11/22/69+	4	16		3 Six White Horses .... I Owe The World To You	79	$8		Epic 10540
3/28/70	9	14		4 Rise And Shine .... The Honest Truth	—	$8		Epic 10590
7/18/70	9	13		5 One Song Away .... The Ramblin' Kind	—	$8		Epic 10630
11/21/70	36	9		6 The Tears On Lincoln's Face .... Only Place For Me	—	$8		Epic 10673
3/13/71	20	11		7 So This Is Love .... Love Is Gone	—	$8		Epic 10700
7/10/71	28	10		8 I'm Gonna Write A Song .... I'm Nowhere Without You	—	$8		Epic 10756
12/4/71	67	2		9 Roll Truck Roll .... The Song Belongs To You	—	$8		Epic 10795
3/25/72	32	11		10 You're Everything .... Someday When All My Dreams Come True	—	$8		Epic 10838
7/15/72	22	11		11 That Certain One .... A Free Man	—	$8		Epic 10885
10/28/72	24	11		12 Listen .... Fool Maker	—	$8		Epic 10915
3/24/73	37	10		13 Workin' On A Feelin' .... Tomorrow Will Be A New Day	—	$8		Epic 10964
7/28/73	16	13		14 I Recall A Gypsy Woman .... You'll Need The Love (I Have For You One Day)	—	$8		Epic 11026
11/24/73+	21	13		15 She Met A Stranger, I Met A Train .... The Only Place For Me	—	$8		Epic 11057
3/22/75	58	9		16 The One I Sing My Love Songs To .... Goodbye Ringin' In My Ear	—	$5		Elektra 45241
1/10/76	94	4		17 Broken Bones .... The Ballad Of Jack And Lucille	—	$5		20th Century 2263
7/16/77	63	6		18 The Cowboy And The Lady .... Lady I Love You	—	$5		Monument 45222
2/11/78	98	3		19 Take My Love To Rita .... We Finally Got It Right	—	$5		Monument 45238
				CASHMAN & WEST '73				
				Duo of singer/songwriters Dennis "Terry Cashman" Minogue and Thomas "Tommy West" Picardo.				
2/10/73	69	2		Songman .... If You Were A Rainbow	59	$6		Dunhill/ABC 4333
				CASSADY, Linda '78				
				Born on 7/10/57 in Sacramento, California.				
5/22/76	83	8		1 C.B. Widow .... Do You Still Want What's Left Of Me	—	$5		Cin Kay 107
9/11/76	91	4		2 If It's Your Song You Sing It .... This Isn't Just Another Love Song	—	$5		Cin Kay 111
1/29/77	79	6		3 Little Things Mean A Lot .... Sounds Of Love	—	$5		Cin Kay 115
				#1 Pop hit for Kitty Kallen in 1954				
4/9/77	92	4		4 I Don't Hurt Anymore .... Baby There's Nothing Wrong With Me	—	$5		Cin Kay 116
2/4/78	91	3		5 Little Teardrops (Are Smarter Than You Think) .... —	—	$5		Cin Kay 127
4/29/78	87	4		6 (There's Nothing Like The Love) Between A Woman And A Man .... Finer Side Of Life	—	$5		Cin Kay 129
				LINDA CASSADY/BOBBY SPEARS				
8/5/78	76	6		7 Lonely Side Of The Bed .... That's The Way It Is	—	$5		Cin Kay 047
				CATES SISTERS, The '78				
				Duo of sisters Margie and Marcy Cates from Independence, Missouri. Both are singers and multi-instrumentalists.				
				1)I've Been Loved 2)I'll Always Love You 3)Lovin' You Off My Mind				
9/11/76	82	5		1 Mr. Guitar .... Love Is A Beautiful Thing	—	$5		Caprice 2024
1/29/77	50	8		2 Out Of My Mind .... Run Your Sweet Love By Me	—	$5		Caprice 2030
				THE CATES				
5/21/77	74	6		3 Can't Help It .... —	—	$5		Caprice 2032
8/13/77	87	5		4 Throw Out Your Loveline .... West Virginia Smile	—	$5		Caprice 2038
10/1/77	30	11		5 I'll Always Love You .... Second Chance	—	$5		Caprice 2036
12/24/77+	29	11		6 I've Been Loved .... Faded Love	—	$5		Caprice 2041
3/18/78	61	7		7 Long Gone Blues .... San Antonio Rose	—	$5		Caprice 2047
9/2/78	39	8		8 Lovin' You Off My Mind .... Amazing Grace	—	$5		Caprice 2051
				THE CATES:				
2/17/79	78	5		9 Going Down Slow .... Can I See You Tonight	—	$5		Ovation 1123
6/30/79	57	8		10 Make Love To Me .... Day After Day	—	$5	■	Ovation 1126
12/22/79+	68	7		11 Let's Go Through The Motions .... Don't Say Love	—	$5		Ovation 1134
5/24/80	72	5		12 Gonna Get Along Without You Now .... I've Been Lovin' You Too Long	—	$5		Ovation 1144
				#11 Pop hit for Patience & Prudence in 1956				
10/25/80	75	4		13 Lightnin' Strikin' .... Touch And Go	—	$5		Ovation 1155
				CATO, Connie '75				
				Born Connie Ann Cato on 3/30/55 in Carlinville, Illinois.				
				1)Hurt 2)Superskirt 3)You Better Hurry Home				
2/2/74	33	16		1 Superskirt .... Big Stick Of Dynamite	—	$5		Capitol 3788
7/13/74	73	7		2 Super Kitten .... We'd Better Stop	—	$5		Capitol 3908
10/19/74	92	6		3 Lincoln Autry .... After Midnight	—	$5		Capitol 3958
3/8/75	14	14		4 Hurt .... He'll Be Lovin' Her	—	$5		Capitol 4035
				#4 Pop hit for Timi Yuro in 1961				
7/26/75	83	6		5 Yes .... Good Hearted Woman	—	$5		Capitol 4113

DEBUT	PEAK	WKS	Gold	A-side (Chart Hit)	B-side	Pop	$	Pic	Label & Number
				CATO, Connie — Cont'd					
11/22/75+	53	10		6 Who Wants A Slightly Used Woman ...... Somewhere South Of Macon		—	$5		Capitol 4169
4/24/76	91	4		7 I Love A Beautiful Guy ...... Plastic Saddle		—	$5		Capitol 4243
8/7/76	80	5		8 Here Comes That Rainy Day Feeling Again ...... I'll Be A Lady Tomorrow		—	$5		Capitol 4303
				#15 Pop hit for The Fortunes in 1971					
11/6/76	76	6		9 I'm Sorry ...... Evil On Your Mind		—	$5		Capitol 4345
				#1 Pop hit for Brenda Lee in 1960					
2/19/77	92	3		10 Don't You Ever Get Tired (Of Hurting Me) ...... I've Been Loved By You Today		—	$5		Capitol 4379
8/16/80	49	7		11 You Better Hurry Home (Somethin's Burnin') ...... Hangin' On My Heart		—	$4		MCA 41287
				CAUDELL, Lane '87					
				Born in Asheboro, North Carolina. Male singer/actor. Played "Woody King" on TV's Days Of Our Lives.					
9/19/87	66	5		1 Souvenirs ...... The Honeymoon Is Over		—	$4		16th Avenue 70403
4/16/88	77	5		2 I Need A Good Woman Bad ...... Souvenirs		—	$4		16th Avenue 70411
				C COMPANY Featuring TERRY NELSON '71					
				Group of studio musicians led by DJ/singer Terry Nelson from Russellville, Alabama.					
5/1/71	49	3	●	Battle Hymn Of Lt. Calley ...... Routine Patrol [S]		37	$6		Plantation 73
				CEDAR CREEK '82					
				Group formed in Nashville: Dave Holcraft, Ken Harden, Don Edmunds and Ron Spearman (vocals), Sam Stricklan (guitar), Garland Craft (keyboards), Tony Perkins (bass) and Chris Golden (drums). Golden is the son of William Lee Golden and a member of The Goldens.					
11/14/81	80	4		1 Looks Like A Set-Up To Me ...... This Old Heart (Is Gonna Rise Again)		—	$5		Moon Shine 3001
2/6/82	42	10		2 Took It Like A Man, Cried Like A Baby ...... Dreamin' Thru Another Day		—	$5		Moon Shine 3003
1/22/83	83	3		3 Take A Ride On A Riverboat		—	$5		Moon Shine 3008
8/6/83	81	3		4 Lonely Heart		—	$5		Moon Shine 3013
				CERRITO '89					
				Male singer.					
4/22/89	84	3		1 Daydream		—	$5		Soundwaves 4818
				#2 Pop hit for the Lovin' Spoonful in 1966					
9/23/89	79	3		2 Bad Moon Rising ...... Born To Hurt Me		—	$5		Soundwaves 4826
				#2 Pop hit for Creedence Clearwater Revival in 1969					
				CHAIN, Michael '00					
				Born in 1955 in San Fernando, California. Singer/songwriter.					
3/18/00	67	1		Let's Go Chase Some Women		—			album cut
				from the album Let's Go Chase Some Women on Hard Ten 1062					
				CHAMBERLAIN, David '88					
				Born on 12/23/44 in Ft. Worth, Texas.					
1/30/88	72	4		I Owe, I Owe (It's Off To Work I Go) ...... Love Me Tonight		—	$6		Country Int'l. 214
				CHAMBERS, Carl '81					
				Born on 12/17/46 in Lakeland, Florida. Singer/songwriter/guitarist.					
2/28/81	91	2		Take Me Home With You		—	$6		Prairie Dust 8001
				CHANCE '85					
				Group from Texas: brothers Jeff (vocals, steel guitar) and Mick (drums) Barosh, John Buckley (guitar), Jon Mulligan (keyboards) and Billy Hafer (bass). Jeff Barosh began solo career in 1988 as Jeff Chance.					
4/20/85	35	13		1 To Be Lovers ...... Call It What You Want To (It's Still Love)		—	$4		Mercury 880555
7/27/85	45	11		2 You Could Be The One Woman ...... Free Sailin'		—	$4		Mercury 880959
10/26/85	30	15		3 She Told Me Yes A:26 / S:30 Two Hearts Are Better Than One		—	$4		Mercury 884178
3/29/86	53	7		4 I Need Some Good News Bad ...... She Needs A Man Like Me		—	$4		Mercury 884545
8/30/86	60	10		5 What Did You Do With My Heart ...... One Too Many Heartaches		—	$4		Mercury 884918
				CHANCE, Jeff '88					
				Born Jeff Barosh in El Campo, Texas. Singer/steel guitarist. Member of Chance.					
6/18/88	52	7		1 Hopelessly Falling /		—			
3/19/88	64	7		2 So Far Not So Good		—	$4		Curb 10506
11/26/88+	57	9		3 Let It Burn ...... She Loves Me		—	$4		Curb 10516
				CHANEY, Hank '86					
8/16/86	98	1		Be-Bop-A-Lula "86"		—	$7		CMI 04
				CHANTILLY '82					
				Female group: Kim Williams (lead vocals), Debbie Pierce and P.J. Allman. Pierce, daughter of Webb Pierce, was later replaced by Joci Stevens.					
5/1/82	81	4		1 Whatever Turns You On ...... Storm Of Love		—	$5		Jaroco 31082
6/26/82	43	10		2 Stumblin' In ...... Better Off Blue		—	$5		Jaroco 51282
				CHANTILLY (Featuring Kim Williams) (above 2)					
				#4 Pop hit for Suzi Quatro & Chris Norman in 1979					
10/9/82	65	6		3 Right Back Loving You Again ...... Better Off Blue		—	$5		F&L 519
12/25/82+	75	6		4 Better Off Blue ...... Right Back Loving You Again		—	$5		F&L 520
2/12/83	60	7		5 Storm Of Love ...... Right Back Loving You Again		—	$5		F&L 523
9/17/83	60	7		6 Have I Got A Heart For You ...... Reached		—	$5		F&L 527
2/11/84	72	4		7 Baby's Walkin' ...... Have I Got A Heart For You		—	$5		F&L 534
				CHAPARRAL BROTHERS '68					
				Duo of brothers John and Paul Chaparral.					
5/11/68	65	4		1 Standing In The Rain ...... Just One More Time		—	$8		Capitol 2153
2/14/70	70	2		2 Running From A Memory ...... Curly Brown		—	$8		Capitol 2708

DEBUT	PEAK	WKS	Gold	A-side (Chart Hit)..B-side	Pop	$	Pic	Label & Number
				CHAPARRO, Tammy '83 Born in 1967 in Billings, Montana.				
5/7/83	89	3		Stay With Me	—	$6		Compass 60
				CHAPMAN, Cee Cee '89 Born Melissa Carol Chapman on 12/13/58 in Portsmouth, Virginia. Female singer/songwriter/guitarist. Santa Fe is her backing band.				
11/26/88	60	8		1 Gone But Not Forgotten ....Love Is A Liar CEE CEE CHAPMAN & SANTA FE	—	$4		Curb 10518
4/8/89	51	10		2 Frontier Justice /	—			
11/4/89	64	4		3 Love Is A Liar	—	$4		Curb 10529
8/5/89	49	7		4 Twist Of Fate ....Back To Santa Fe	—	$4		Curb 10547
1/2/93	64	6		5 Two Ships That Passed In The Moonlight .... from the album *Cee Cee Chapman* on Curb/Capitol 94373	—			album cut
				CHAPMAN, Gary '88 Born on 8/19/57 in Waurika, Oklahoma; raised in DeLeon, Texas. Singer/songwriter. Married to singer Amy Grant from 1982-99. Hosted TNN's *Prime Time Country* from 1996-99.				
1/9/88	60	6		1 When We're Together ....Your Love Stays With Me	—	$4		RCA 5285
4/16/88	76	4		2 Everyday Man ....Cecil (Life Goes On)	—	$4		RCA 7601
				CHAPMAN, Marshall '77 Born on 1/7/49 in Spartanburg, South Carolina.				
3/5/77	100	2		Somewhere South Of Macon ....Sweet Carolina And Texas	—	$5		Epic 50307
				CHARLENE '82 Born Charlene D'Angelo on 6/1/50 in Hollywood. Female singer.				
4/10/82	60	8		I've Never Been To Me ....Somewhere In My Life first released on Prodigal 0636 in 1977 (hit #97 on the *Hot 100*)	3	$4		Motown 1611
				CHARLES, Kim '79 Male singer.				
2/10/79	35	9		Want To Thank You ....By Any Chance	—	$5		MCA 40987
	★329★			**CHARLES, Ray** '85 Born Ray Charles Robinson on 9/23/30 in Albany, Georgia. To Greenville, Florida, while still an infant. Partially blind at age five, completely blind at seven (glaucoma). Studied classical piano and clarinet at State School for Deaf and Blind Children, St. Augustine, Florida, 1937-45. Formed own band in 1954. Inducted into the Rock and Roll Hall of Fame in 1986. Won Grammy's Lifetime Achievement Award in 1987. Legendary performer, with many TV and movie appearances. Charted 76 pop hits from 1957-90. Also see **USA For Africa**. 1)*Seven Spanish Angels* 2)*We Didn't See A Thing* 3)*It Ain't Gonna Worry My Mind*				

11/22/80	55	10		1 Beers To You ....Cotton-Eyed Clint
				     RAY CHARLES & CLINT EASTWOOD
				     from the movie *Any Which Way You Can* starring Eastwood
					—	$5		Warner 49608

12/18/82+	20	18		2 Born To Love Me ....String Bean	—	$4		Columbia 03429
4/23/83	37	11		3 3/4 Time ....You Feel Good All Over	—	$4		Columbia 03810
9/24/83	82	3		4 Ain't Your Memory Got No Pride At All *I Don't Want No Stranger Sleepin' In My Bed*	—	$4		Columbia 04083
12/17/83+	6	18		5 We Didn't See A Thing ....I Wish You Were Here Tonight RAY CHARLES & GEORGE JONES (Featuring Chet Atkins)	—	$4		Columbia 04297
4/14/84	50	10		6 Do I Ever Cross Your Mind..They Call It Love	—	$4		Columbia 04420
8/4/84	14	18		7 Rock And Roll Shoes ....S:14 / A:21 Then I'll Be Over You RAY CHARLES (with B.J. Thomas)	—	$4		Columbia 04531
12/15/84+	❶¹	27		8 Seven Spanish Angels ....S:❶¹ / A:❶¹ Who Cares RAY CHARLES (with WILLIE NELSON)	—	$4		Columbia 04715
5/4/85	12	17		9 It Ain't Gonna Worry My Mind.............................A:11 / S:12 Crazy Old Soldier RAY CHARLES (with Mickey Gilley)	—	$4		Columbia 04860
8/31/85	14	17		10 Two Old Cats Like Us ....S:13 / A:17 Little Hotel Room RAY CHARLES (with Hank Williams, Jr.)	—	$4		Columbia 05575
7/19/86	34	13		11 The Pages Of My Mind...Slip Away	—	$4		Columbia 06172
11/1/86	66	4		12 Dixie Moon /	—			
1/31/87	76	3		13 A Little Bit Of Heaven..	—	$4		Columbia 06370
				CHARLESTON EXPRESS '85 Group from Charleston, South Carolina. Led by singer Jesse Wales.				
12/15/84+	69	7		1 Sweet Love, Don't Cry.......................................We Start Our Lives Again Today	—	$5		Soundwaves 4743
5/18/85	82	4		2 Leaving ....Take Me By Surprise CHARLESTON EXPRESS with Jesse Wales (above 2)	—	$5		Soundwaves 4749
				CHARNISSA — see **PAYCHECK, Johnny**				
				CHASE, Becky '85				
1/12/85	77	6		Until The Music Is Gone...	—	$6		Spirit Horse 102
				CHASE, Carol '80 Born Carol Schulte in Stanley, North Dakota. Singer/songwriter.				
11/10/79+	32	13		1 This Must Be My Ship.................................It Always Takes A Fool To Fool Around	—	$5		Casablanca 4501
12/15/79	92	4		2 Can't Love On Lies.. JIM WEST (with Carol Chase)	—	$6		Macho 003
2/23/80	48	7		3 Sexy Song ....Disco Devil	—	$5		Casablanca 4502
10/18/80	87	3		4 Regrets ....So Sad	—	$5		Casablanca 2301
				CHASTAIN, Dawn '79 Born in Springfield, Illinois. Female singer. Former fashion model.				
4/15/78	83	4		1 Never Knew (How Much I Loved You 'Til I Lost You)............Ain't No Doubt About It	—	$6		Prairie Dust 7623
1/6/79	72	4		2 Me Plus You Equals Love	—	$6		Oak 1018

DEBUT	PEAK	WKS	Gold	A-side (Chart Hit)	B-side	Pop	$	Pic	Label & Number
				CHASTAIN, Dawn — Cont'd					
5/5/79	91	2		3 Love Talks	—		$5		SCR 164
9/8/79	74	4		4 That's You, That's Me	—		$5		SCR 178
				CHER '79					
				Born Cherilyn Sarkisian on 5/20/46 in El Centro, California. Adopted by stepfather at age 15 and last name changed to La Piere. Singer/actress. Charted 30 pop hits from 1965-96. Starred in several movies. In 1963 formed successful recording duo Sonny & Cher with Sonny Bono, her husband from 1969-75.					
7/14/79	87	2		It's Too Late To Love Me Now...............Wasn't It Good (Pop #49)	—		$5		Casablanca 987
				CHERRY, Don '68					
				Born on 1/11/24 in Wichita Falls, Texas. Vocalist with Jan Garber's band in the late '40s. Charted 11 pop hits from 1950-56.					
10/5/68	71	2		Take A Message To Mary..................In My Youth	—		$8		Monument 1088
				#16 Pop hit for **The Everly Brothers** in 1959					

CHESNEY, Kenny ★156★   '99
Born on 3/26/68 in Knoxville; raised in Luttrell, Tennessee. Singer/songwriter/guitarist. Attended East Tennessee State University. Moved to Nashville in 1990. Worked as a staff writer at Acuff-Rose prior to his recording contract.

1)How Forever Feels 2)She's Got It All 3)Don't Happen Twice 4)You Had Me From Hello 5)Young

DEBUT	PEAK	WKS		A-side	B-side	Pop	$	Pic	Label & Number
12/18/93+	59	8		1 Whatever It Takes...............I'd Love To Change Your Name		—	$4	■	Capricorn 18323 (v)
5/14/94	70	6		2 The Tin Man...............I Finally Found Somebody		—	$4	■	Capricorn 49223
				also see #22 below					
4/1/95	6	20		3 Fall In Love...............S:14 Something About You And A Dirt Road		—	$4	■	BNA 64278 (v)
7/29/95	8	20		4 All I Need To Know...............Someone Else's Hog		—	$4	■	BNA 64347 (v)
11/11/95+	23	20		5 Grandpa Told Me So...............Whatever It Takes		—	$4	■	BNA 64352 (v)
4/6/96	41	16		6 Back In Your Arms Again...............S:22 Honey Would You Stand By Me		—	$4	■	BNA 64523 (v)
7/20/96	2¹	20		7 Me And You...............S:7 I Finally Found Somebody		112	$4	■	BNA 64589 (v)
12/21/96+	2²	21		8 When I Close My Eyes...............My Poor Old Heart		—	$4		BNA 64726
5/31/97	0³	20		9 She's Got It All...............S:8 Lonely, Needin' Lovin'		110	$4	■	BNA 64894 (v)
10/11/97+	11	22		10 A Chance...............When I Close My Eyes		—	$4		BNA 64987
3/7/98	2¹	25		11 That's Why I'm Here...............S:10 A Chance		79	$4	■	BNA 65399 (v)
8/15/98	27	20		12 I Will Stand...............S:7 She Always Said It First		101	$4	■	BNA 65570 (v)
11/28/98	64	6		13 Touchdown Tennessee...............(remix)		—	$4		BNA 65655
12/12/98+	0⁶	37		14 How Forever Feels...............S:0² You Win, I Win, We Lose		27	$4	★	BNA 65666 (v)
2/13/99	72	1		15 Team Of Destiny...............(remix)		—	$4		BNA 65704
4/17/99	0¹	32		16 You Had Me From Hello...............Everywhere We Go		34	$4		BNA 65745
6/26/99+	11	21		17 She Thinks My Tractor's Sexy...............You Had Me From Hello		74	$4		BNA 65934
12/25/99	67	1		18 Away In A Manger...............[X]		—			album cut
1/22/00	8	25		19 What I Need To Do...............She Thinks My Tractor's Sexy		56	$4		BNA 65964
8/19/00	3	25		20 I Lost It...............The Tin Man		34	$4		BNA 69007
				Pam Tillis (backing vocal)					
1/20/01	0¹	30		21 Don't Happen Twice...............I Lost It		26	$4		BNA 69035
7/28/01	19	20		22 The Tin Man...............[R]		107			album cut
				new version of #2 above; from the album *Greatest Hits* on BNA 67976					
12/29/01+	2²	25		23 Young...............For The First Time		35	$4		BNA 69131

CHESNUT, Jim   '79
Born on 12/1/44 in Midland, Texas. Singer/songwriter/pianist.

1)Let's Take The Time To Fall In Love Again 2)Bedtime Stories 3)Out Run The Sun

DEBUT	PEAK	WKS		A-side	B-side	Pop	$	Pic	Label & Number
7/23/77	99	1		1 Let Me Love You Now...............Loaf Of Bread (A Jug Of Wine)		—	$5		ABC/Hickory 54013
12/10/77+	76	8		2 The Wrong Side Of The Rainbow...............I'm So Lonely For Your Baby		—	$5		ABC/Hickory 54021
4/15/78	76	6		3 The Ninth Of September...............I Love You Babe (For All The Little Things)		—	$5		ABC/Hickory 54027
8/5/78	56	9		4 Show Me A Sign...............Whiskey Lady		—	$5		ABC/Hickory 54033
11/18/78	57	7		5 Get Back To Loving Me...............Kinder Than The Last One		—	$5		ABC/Hickory 54038
6/2/79	80	3		6 Just Let Me Make Believe...............Let Me Just Say I Love You		—	$4		MCA 41015
9/15/79	27	11		7 Let's Take The Time To Fall In Love Again A Loaf Of Bread (A Jug Of Wine)		—	$4		MCA 41106
9/13/80	46	9		8 Out Run The Sun...............Pick Up The Pieces		—	$4		United Artists 1372
6/6/81	36	10		9 Bedtime Stories...............Pick Up The Pieces		—	$4		Liberty 1405
10/24/81	70	4		10 The Rose Is For Today...............Dark Eyed Lady		—	$4		Liberty 1434

CHESNUTT, Mark ★89★   '93
Born on 9/6/63 in Beaumont, Texas. Singer/guitarist. Son of regional Texas star Bob Chesnutt. Played drums in a rock band in the early 1980s. First recorded for the Axbar label in 1984. CMA Award: 1993 Horizon Award.

1)I Don't Want To Miss A Thing 2)Brother Jukebox 3)It's A Little Too Late 4)Almost Goodbye
5)It Sure Is Monday

DEBUT	PEAK	WKS		A-side	B-side	Pop	$	Pic	Label & Number
8/4/90	3	20		1 Too Cold At Home...............Life Of A Lucky Man		—	$4	■	MCA 53856 (v)
11/24/90+	0²	20		2 Brother Jukebox...............Hey You There In The Mirror		—	$4		MCA 53965
3/30/91	5	20		3 Blame It On Texas...............Danger At My Door		—	$4		MCA 54053

DEBUT	PEAK	WKS	Gold	A-side (Chart Hit)	B-side	Pop	$	Pic	Label & Number
				CHESNUTT, Mark — Cont'd					
7/13/91	3	20		4 Your Love Is A Miracle	Too Good A Memory	—	$4		MCA 54136
10/26/91+	10	20		5 Broken Promise Land	Friends In Low Places	—	$4		MCA 54256
2/29/92	5	20		6 Old Flames Have New Names	Postpone The Pain	—	$4		MCA 54334
6/13/92	●1	20		7 I'll Think Of Something	Uptown Downtown (Misery's All The Same)	—	$4		MCA 54395
6/20/92	4	25		8 Bubba Shot The Jukebox	Blame It On Texas	121	$4	■	MCA 54471 (v)
1/2/93	4	20		9 Old Country	Talking To Hank	—	$4		MCA 54539
5/22/93	●1	20		10 It Sure Is Monday	I'm Not Getting Any Better At Goodbyes	119	$4	■	MCA 54630 (v)
9/4/93	4	20		11 Almost Goodbye	Texas Is Bigger Than It Used To Be	—	$4		MCA 54718
12/11/93+	●1	20		12 I Just Wanted You To Know	April's Fool	—	$4	■	MCA 54768 (v)
4/2/94	21	20		13 Woman, Sensuous Woman	Till A Better Memory Comes Along	—	$4	■	MCA 54822 (v)
7/23/94	6	20		14 She Dreams	What A Way To Live	—	$4		Decca 54887 (v)
10/29/94+	2²	20		15 Goin' Through The Big D	It's Almost Like You're Here	—	$4		Decca 54941 (v)
2/25/95	●1	20		16 Gonna Get A Life	Half Of Everything (And All Of My Heart)	—	$4		Decca 54978 (v)
6/17/95	23	17		17 Down In Tennessee	This Side Of The Door	—	$4		Decca 55050
9/23/95	18	20		18 Trouble	Strangers	—	$4	■	Decca 55103 (v)
12/30/95+	7	20		19 It Wouldn't Hurt To Have Wings	I May Be A Fool	—	$4		Decca 55164
5/4/96	37	20		20 Wrong Place, Wrong Time	As The Honky Tonk Turns	—	$4		Decca 55198
10/5/96+	●²	23		21 It's A Little Too Late	The King Of Broken Hearts	—	$4		Decca 55231
12/28/96	75	1		22 What Child Is This	(no B-side) [X]	—	$10	★	Decca 3863
				available only as a promotional CD single					
3/15/97	8	20		23 Let It Rain	S:16 Goin' Through The Big D	—	$4	■	Decca 55293 (v)
8/2/97	2¹	21		24 Thank God For Believers	S:16 Hello Honky Tonk	—	$4	■	Decca 72014 (v)
12/13/97+	34	13		25 It's Not Over	Useless	—	$4		Decca 72032
				MARK CHESNUTT (Featuring Vince Gill and Alison Krauss)					
3/14/98	18	20		26 I Might Even Quit Lovin' You	Numbers On The Jukebox	—	$4		Decca 72031
9/26/98	45	9		27 Wherever You Are	Goodbye Heartache	—	$4		Decca 72066
11/21/98+	●²	25		28 I Don't Want To Miss A Thing	S:●⁸ Wherever You Are	17	$4	★	Decca 72078 (v)
				#1 Pop hit for Aerosmith in 1998; from the movie Armageddon starring Bruce Willis					
4/24/99	17	21		29 This Heartache Never Sleeps	That's The Way You Make An Ex	101	$4		Decca 72090
4/22/00	52	10		30 Fallin' Never Felt So Good	Love In The Hot Afternoon	—	$4		MCA Nashville 172162
9/30/00	59	8		31 Lost In The Feeling	Tonight I'll Let My Memory Take Me Home	—	$4		MCA Nashville 172119
3/24/01	21	20		32 A Good Way To Get On My Bad Side	Put Your Hand In Mine (Byrd)	121	$4		RCA 69081
				TRACY BYRD (with Mark Chesnutt)					
				CHEVALIER, Jay, And Shelley Ford '79					
3/17/79	90	2		Disco Blues	Super Country USA	—	$6		Creole Gold 1114
				CHICK AND HIS HOT RODS — see RENO & SMILEY					
				CHILDRESS, Lisa '86					
				Born in Boliver, Missouri.					
4/26/86	51	8		1 This Time It's You	—	—	$5		A.M.I. 1941
1/17/87	55	6		2 It's Goodbye And So-Long To You	Touch My Heart	—	$5		A.M.I. 1947
5/7/88	63	6		3 (I Wanna Hear You) Say You Love Me Again	It Don't Get Better Than This	—	$5		True 89
8/20/88	73	3		4 You Didn't Have To Jump The Fence	I Never Will Outgrow My Love For You	—	$5		True 91
1/21/89	65	5		5 (Here Comes) That Old Familiar Feeling	I Should Have Known You'd Come Around	—	$5		True 95
7/15/89	83	3		6 Maybe There	I Should Have Known You'd Come Around	—	$5		True 97
				CHILDS, Andy '94					
				Born on 12/7/62 in Memphis. Singer/songwriter/guitarist.					
7/3/93	73	2		1 I Wouldn't Know	Let The Good Times Roll	—	$4		RCA 62545
10/2/93	62	6		2 Broken	Your Love Amazes Me	—	$4		RCA 62641
4/2/94	61	5		3 Simple Life	Mine All Mine	—	$4		RCA 62763
				CHINNOCK, Billy '85					
				Singer/actor. Son-in-law of Dick Curless.					
1/19/85	91	3		The Way She Makes Love	Rock N' Roll Cowboy	—	$5		Paradise 630
				CHIPMUNKS, The '92					
				Characters created by Ross Bagdasarian ("David Seville") who named Alvin, Simon and Theodore after Liberty executives Alvin Bennett, Simon Waronker and Theodore Keep. The Chipmunks starred in own prime-time animated TV show in the early 1960s and a Saturday morning cartoon series in the mid-1980s. Bagdasarian died on 1/16/72 (age 52). His son, Ross Jr., resurrected the act in 1980.					
10/31/92	71	1		Achy Breaky Heart	I Ain't No Dang Cartoon [N]	—	$4		Epic 74776
				ALVIN AND THE CHIPMUNKS					
				Billy Ray Cyrus (guest vocal)					
				CHOATES, Harry '47					
				Born on 12/26/22 in Rayne, Louisiana; raised in Port Arthur, Texas. Died while in jail on 7/17/51 (age 28) in Austin, Texas. Cajun fiddler. Label misspelled last name as Coates.					
1/4/47	4	2		Jole Blon	Dragging The Bow	—	$40		Modern Mountain 511
				HARRY COATES					
				first released in 1946 on Gold Star 1314 ($50)					
				CHRIS & LENNY '89					
				Female/male vocal duo: Chris Thompson and Lenny Grasso.					
8/5/89	93	2		When Daddy Did The Driving		—	$6	■	Happy Man 821
				CHRISTINE, Anne '71					
				Born Anne Christine Poux on 12/17/33 in Meadville, Pennsylvania.					
7/17/71	69	5		Summer Man	How Important Can It Be	—	$10		CME 4634

DEBUT	PEAK	WKS	Gold	A-side (Chart Hit)..B-side	Pop	$	Pic	Label & Number
				CHURCH, Claudia '99 Born in 1962 in Lenoir, North Carolina.				
1/16/99	41	20		1 What's The Matter With You Baby ....S:19 *Small Town Girl*	—	$4	★	Reprise 17112 (v)
6/26/99	63	3		2 Home In My Heart (North Carolina) ....*Just As Long As You Love Me*	—	$4		Reprise 16959
				CLANTON, Darrell '84 Born in Indianapolis. Singer/guitarist/banjo player.				
10/15/83+	24	19		1 Lonesome 7-7203 ....*Me-Oh-My*	—	$6		Audiograph 474
3/31/84	75	6		2 I'll Take As Much Of You As I Can Get ....*That's What Cheaters Do*	—	$6		Audiograph 479
1/19/85	56	9		3 I Forgot That I Don't Live Here Anymore ....*I Told You So*	—	$4		Warner 29185
				CLAPTON, Eric '78 Born Eric Patrick Clapp on 3/30/45 in Ripley, England. Prolific rock-blues singer/guitarist. Charted 27 pop hits from 1970-96.				
3/18/78	26	9 ●		1 Lay Down Sally ....*Next Time You See Her*	3	$5		RSO 886
10/21/78	82	7		2 Promises ....*Watch Out For Lucy* (Pop #40)	9	$5		RSO 910
				ERIC CLAPTON AND HIS BAND				
				CLARK, Guy '81 Born on 11/6/41 in Monahans, Texas; raised in Rockport, Texas. Singer/songwriter/guitarist.				
1/6/79	96	2		1 Fools For Each Other ....*Fool On The Roof*	—	$4		Warner 8714
7/11/81	38	11		2 The Partner Nobody Chose ....*Heartbroke*	—	$4		Warner 49740
7/2/83	42	13		3 Homegrown Tomatoes ....*Fool In A Mirror*	—	$4		Warner 29595
				CLARK, Jameson '01 Born in Starr, South Carolina. Singer/songwriter/guitarist.				
9/8/01	52	9		Don't Play Any Love Songs...*Still Smokin'*	—	$4		Capitol 77665
				CLARK, Jay '85 Born in 1958 in Missouri; raised in Round Rock, Texas.				
12/21/85	73	5		1 Love Gone Bad ....*Modern Day Cowboy*	—	$5		Concorde 301
4/12/86	75	4		2 Modern Day Cowboy ....*Love Gone Bad*	—	$5		Concorde 302
				CLARK, Lucky '77				
6/4/77	99	1		Everytime Two Fools Collide ....*Another Honky Tonk Tonight*	—	$6		Polydor 14393
				CLARK, Mickey '87 Born Michael Clark on 5/2/40 in Louisville, Kentucky.				
3/12/83	74	6		1 She's Gone To L.A. Again ....*The Tequila Express*	—	$5		Monument 03519
2/14/87	54	9		2 When I'm Over You (What You Gonna Do)	—	$5	■	Evergreen 1051
9/26/87	76	4		3 You Take The Leavin' Out Of Me ....*She's Gone To L.A. Again*	—	$5		Evergreen 1058
				CLARK, Petula '82 Born on 11/15/32 in Epsom, England. Singer/actress. Charted 22 pop hits from 1964-82.				
2/6/82	20	14		Natural Love...*Because I Love Him*	66	$4		Scotti Brothers 02676
				CLARK, Roy ★111★ '73 Born on 4/15/33 in Meherrin, Virginia. Singer/songwriter/guitarist/banjo player. Acted on TV's *The Beverly Hillbillies* as both "Cousin Roy" and "Big Mama Halsey." Co-host of the TV series *Hee-Haw*. Joined the *Grand Ole Opry* in 1987. CMA Awards: 1973 Entertainer of the Year; 1977, 1978 & 1980 Musician of the Year.				
				1) Come Live With Me 2) If I Had It To Do It All Over Again 3) Somewhere Between Love And Tomorrow 4) Honeymoon Feelin' 5) I Never Picked Cotton				
7/6/63	10	16		1 Tips Of My Fingers ....*Spooky Movies*	45	$10		Capitol 4956
2/8/64	31	3		2 Through The Eyes Of A Fool ....*Sweet Violets*	128	$10		Capitol 5099
				written by **Bobby Bare**				
3/20/65	37	10		3 When The Wind Blows In Chicago ....*Live Fast, Love Hard, Die Young*	—	$10		Capitol 5350
				co-written by actor Audie Murphy				
8/3/68	53	8		4 Do You Believe This Town ....*It Just Happened That Way*	—	$8		Dot 17117
1/18/69	57	6		5 Love Is Just A State Of Mind ....*Other People's Sunshine*	—	$8		Dot 17187
6/7/69	9	16		6 Yesterday, When I Was Young ....*Just Another Man*	19	$8		Dot 17246
9/27/69	40	7		7 September Song ....*For The Life Of Me*	103	$8		Dot 17299
				#51 Pop hit for Jimmy Durante in 1963				
12/6/69+	21	9		8 Right Or Left At Oak Street ....*I Need To Be Needed*	123	$8		Dot 17324
1/24/70	31	9		9 Then She's A Lover ....*Say Amen*	94	$8		Dot 17335
6/6/70	5	15		10 I Never Picked Cotton ....*Lonesome Too Long*	122	$8		Dot 17349
9/26/70	6	14		11 Thank God And Greyhound ....*Strangers*	90	$8		Dot 17355
3/27/71	74	2		12 (Where Do I Begin) Love Story ....*Theme From Love Story*	—	$8		Dot 17370
				from the movie starring Ali MacGraw and Ryan O'Neal				
4/24/71	45	9		13 A Simple Thing As Love ....*I'd Fight The World*	—	$8		Dot 17368
8/14/71	63	4		14 She Cried ....*Back In The Race*	—	$8		Dot 17386
10/30/71	39	9		15 Magnificent Sanctuary Band ....*Be Ready*	—	$8		Dot 17395
8/19/72	9	14		16 The Lawrence Welk - Hee Haw Counter-Revolution Polka *When The Wind Blows (In Chicago)* [N]	—	$8		Dot 17426
2/17/73	❶¹	16		17 Come Live With Me ....*Darby's Castle*	89	$8		Dot 17449
7/7/73	27	11		18 Riders In The Sky ....*Roy's Guitar Boogie* [I]	—	$8		Dot 17458
10/27/73+	2¹	16		19 Somewhere Between Love And Tomorrow ....*I'll Paint You A Song*	81	$8		Dot 17480
3/16/74	4	16		20 Honeymoon Feelin' ....*I Really Don't Want To Know*	—	$8		Dot 17498
8/17/74	12	17		21 The Great Divide ....*Chomp'n'*	—	$8		Dot 17518
12/21/74+	64	6		22 Dear God ....*Take Good Care Of Her*	—	$6		ABC/Dot 17530

Yodeling Slim Clark

DEBUT	PEAK	WKS	Gold	A-side (Chart Hit)	B-side	Pop	$	Pic	Label & Number
				CLARK, Roy — Cont'd					
3/29/75	35	10		23 You're Gonna Love Yourself In The Morning	Banjoy	—	$6		ABC/Dot 17545
8/9/75	16	14		24 Heart To Heart	Someone Cares For You	—	$6		ABC/Dot 17565
1/24/76	2[2]	16		25 If I Had It To Do All Over Again	It Sure Looks Good On You	—	$6		ABC/Dot 17605
6/5/76	21	11		26 Think Summer	Whatever Happened To Gauze?	—	$6		ABC/Dot 17626
12/25/76+	26	11		27 I Have A Dream, I Have A Dream /			$6		
4/9/77	80	4		28 Half A Love		—	$6		ABC/Dot 17667
8/13/77	40	10		29 We Can't Build A Fire In The Rain	I'm So Lonesome I Could Cry	—	$6		ABC/Dot 17712
2/11/78	60	6		30 Must You Throw Dirt In My Face	Lazy River	—	$5		ABC 12328
6/3/78	65	6		31 Where Have You Been All Of My Life	Near You	—	$5		ABC 12365
2/17/79	34	10		32 Shoulder To Shoulder (Arm And Arm) /			$5		
9/23/78	89	2		33 The Happy Days		—	$5		ABC 12402
12/15/79+	21	13		34 Chain Gang Of Love	Why Don't We Go Somewhere And Love	—	$5		MCA 41153
4/12/80	48	7		35 If There Were Only Time For Love	Then I'll Be Over You	—	$5		MCA 41208
8/16/80	73	5		36 For Love's Own Sake	They'll Never Take Her Love From Me	—	$5		MCA 41288
12/20/80+	60	8		37 I Ain't Got Nobody	Play Me A Little Traveling Music	—	$5		MCA 51031
4/4/81	86	2		38 She Can't Give It Away	Dig A Little Deeper In The Well	—	$5		MCA 51079
5/23/81	63	6		39 Love Takes Two	Come Sundown	—	$5		MCA 51111
9/26/81	73	4		40 The Last Word In Jesus Is Us	Shinin' Face	—	$5		Songbird 51167
5/15/82	54	9		41 Paradise Knife And Gun Club	I Don't Care	—	$5	■	Churchill 94002
9/11/82	85	3		42 Tennessee Saturday Night	Tumbling Tumbleweeds	—	$5		Churchill 94007
10/30/82	65	7		43 Here We Go Again	Early In The Morning	—	$5		Churchill 94011
				#15 Pop hit for **Ray Charles** in 1967					
2/19/83	74	5		44 I'm A Booger /			—		
		5		45 A Way Without Words		—	$5	■	Churchill 94017
8/27/83	55	9		46 Wildwood Flower	Southern Nights [I]	—	$5		Churchill 94025
10/27/84	48	11		47 Another Lonely Night With You	(instrumental)	—	$5		Churchill 52469
4/12/86	56	7		48 Tobacco Road	Black Sapphire	—	$5	■	Silver Dollar 0001
				#14 Pop hit for the **Nashville Teens** in 1964					
8/30/86	61	7		49 Juke Box Saturday Night /					
				#7 Pop hit for **Glenn Miller** in 1942					
		7		50 Night Life		—	$5		Silver Dollar 0004
3/11/89	73	4		51 What A Wonderful World	(instrumental)	—	$5		Hallmark 0001
				#32 Pop hit for **Louis Armstrong** in 1988					
10/14/89	68	5		52 But, She Loves Me		—	$5		Hallmark 0004
				CLARK, Sanford '56					
				Born in 1935 in Tulsa, Oklahoma. Singer/songwriter/guitarist.					
10/6/56	14	1		The Fool A:14	Lonesome For A Letter	7	$40		Dot 15481
				first released in 1956 on MCI 1003 ($125)					
				CLARK, Steve '84					
				Born in Big Hill, Kentucky. Singer/songwriter.					
3/10/84	68	5		That It's All Over Feeling (All Over Again)	Margarita, You're No Lady	—	$4		Mercury 818058
	★252★		★	**CLARK, Terri** '96					
				Born on 8/5/68 in Montreal; raised in Medicine Hat, Alberta, Canada. Female singer/guitarist. Also see **Hope**.					
				1)You're Easy On The Eyes 2)Now That I Found You 3)When Boy Meets Girl					
7/15/95	3	20		1 Better Things To Do S:11	Tyin' A Heart To A Tumbleweed	—	$4	■	Mercury 852046 (v)
10/28/95+	3	20		2 When Boy Meets Girl S:6	Flowers After The Fact	122	$4	■	Mercury 852388 (v)
3/9/96	8	20		3 If I Were You S:4	Something You Should've Said	113	$4	■	Mercury 852708 (v)
7/13/96	34	12		4 Suddenly Single	Catch 22	—	$4		Mercury 578280
10/12/96	5	20		5 Poor, Poor Pitiful Me S:6	Something You Should've Said	109	$4	■	Mercury 578644 (v)
1/11/97	10	20		6 Emotional Girl S:6	Something In The Water	113	$4	■	Mercury 574016 (v)
5/17/97	49	10		7 Just The Same S:23	Hold Your Horses	—	$4	■	Mercury 574456 (v)
4/4/98	2[2]	26		8 Now That I Found You S:9	Getting Even With The Blues	72	$4	■	Mercury 568746 (v)
8/29/98	❶[3]	26		9 You're Easy On The Eyes	That's Me Not Loving You	40	$4	■	Mercury 566218
2/6/99	12	20		10 Everytime I Cry	Till I Get There	69	$4		Mercury 566848
5/29/99	47	10		11 Unsung Hero	Not Getting Over You	—	$4		Mercury 172114
7/22/00	13	25		12 A Little Gasoline	Empty	75	$4		Mercury 172178
2/10/01	27	20		13 No Fear	Easy From Now On	—	$4		Mercury 172197
7/7/01	41	11		14 Getting There	Sometimes Goodbye	—	$4		Mercury 172214
				CLARK FAMILY EXPERIENCE, The '00					
				Bluegrass group from Rocky Mount, Virginia: brothers Alan (guitar), Ashley (fiddle), Austin (dobro), Adam (mandolin), Aaron (bass) and Andrew (drums) Clark.					
7/29/00	18	27		1 Meanwhile Back At The Ranch S:5	Restless	80	$4	★	Curb 73118
5/5/01	34	16		2 Standin' Still		—			album cut
10/20/01	51	12		3 To Quote Shakespeare		—			album cut
				above 2 from the album *Meanwhile Back At The Ranch* on Curb 77754					
				CLAYPOOL, Philip '95					
				Born in Memphis. Singer/songwriter/guitarist.					
6/24/95	71	5		1 Swinging On My Baby's Chain	She Kicked My Dog	—	$4	■	Curb 76952 (v)
9/2/95	60	8		2 Feel Like Makin' Love	Circus Leaving Town	—	$4	■	Curb 76966 (v)
				#10 Pop hit for **Bad Company** in 1975					
2/3/96	73	2		3 The Strength Of A Woman	Honky Tonk Nights	—	$4	■	Curb 76977
6/15/96	70	7		4 Circus Leaving Town		—		■	album cut (v)
				from the album *A Circus Leaving Town* on Curb 77755; first released as the B-side of #2 above					

Jerry Clower?

DEBUT	PEAK	WKS	Gold	A-side (Chart Hit)	B-side	Pop	$	Pic	Label & Number
				CLEMENT, Jack '78					
				Born on 4/5/32 in Memphis. Singer/songwriter/guitarist/producer. Owner of the Fernwood and JMI record labels.					
6/24/78	86	4		1 We Must Believe In Magic /		—			
		4		2 When I Dream		—	$5		Elektra 45474
9/16/78	84	4		3 All I Want To Do In Life	It'll Be Her	—	$5		Elektra 45518
				CLEMENTS, Boots '86					
				Born in Tiffin, Ohio; raised in San Diego. Male singer.					
4/19/86	96	1		Sukiyaki "My First Lonely Night"	The Other Side Of Love	—	$6		West 719
				#1 Pop hit for Kyu Sakamoto in 1963					
				CLEMENTS, Vassar '80					
				Born on 4/25/28 in Kinard, Florida; raised in Kissimmee, Florida. Singer/songwriter/fiddler. Popular session musician.					
7/12/80	70	5		1 There'll Be No Teardrops Tonight	Move	—	$6		Flying Fish 4004
				written by **Hank Williams**					
4/9/88	83	2		2 I Hear The South		—	$6		Shikata 10102
				CLIFFORD, Buzz '61					
				Born Reese Francis Clifford III on 10/8/42 in Berwyn, Illinois.					
3/20/61	28	1		Baby Sittin' Boogie	Driftwood [N]	6	$15	■	Columbia 41876
	★211★			**CLINE, Patsy** '62					
				Born Virginia Patterson Hensley on 9/8/32 in Gore, Virginia. Died in a plane crash on 3/5/63 (age 30) near Camden, Tennessee (with **Cowboy Copas** and **Hawkshaw Hawkins**). Joined the *Grand Ole Opry* in 1961. Elected to the Country Music Hall of Fame in 1973. Jessica Lange portrayed Cline in the 1985 movie biography *Sweet Dreams*. Won Grammy's Lifetime Achievement Award in 1995.					
				1) She's Got You 2) I Fall To Pieces 3) Crazy 4) Walkin' After Midnight 5) Sweet Dreams (Of You)					
3/2/57	2²	19		1 Walkin' After Midnight /	J:2 / S:3 / A:3	12			
6/10/57	14	1		2 A Poor Man's Roses (Or A Rich Man's Gold)	A:14	—	$20	■	Decca 30221
4/3/61	❶²	39		3 I Fall To Pieces	Lovin' In Vain	12	$12		Decca 31205
				also see #17 and #19 below					
11/13/61+	2²	21		4 Crazy	Who Can I Count On (Pop #99)	9	$12		Decca 31317
				written by **Willie Nelson**					
3/3/62	❶⁵	19		5 She's Got You	Strange (Pop #97)	14	$12		Decca 31354
6/2/62	10	12		6 When I Get Thru With You (You'll Love Me Too) /		53			
6/30/62	21	3		7 Imagine That		90	$12	■	Decca 31377
8/25/62	14	10		8 So Wrong	You're Stronger Than Me (Pop #107)	85	$12		Decca 31406
2/16/63	8	17		9 Leavin' On Your Mind	Tra Le La Le La Triangle	83	$12	■	Decca 31455
5/11/63	5	16		10 Sweet Dreams (Of You)	Back In Baby's Arms	44	$12		Decca 31483
9/14/63	7	13		11 Faded Love	Blue Moon Of Kentucky	96	$12		Decca 31522
1/11/64	47	3		12 When You Need A Laugh	I'll Sail My Ship Alone	—	$10		Decca 31552
10/31/64	23	12		13 He Called Me Baby	Bill Bailey, Won't You Please Come Home	—	$10		Decca 31671
1/25/69	73	2		14 Anytime	In Care Of The Blues	—	$10		Decca 25744
4/8/78	98	1		15 Life's Railway To Heaven	If I Could See The World (Through The Eyes Of A Child)	—	$8		4 Star 1033
8/30/80	18	12		16 Always	I'll Sail My Ship Alone	—	$5		MCA 41303
				#19 Pop hit for Sammy Turner in 1959					
12/20/80+	61	7		17 I Fall To Pieces	True Love [R]	—	$5		MCA 51038
				newly mixed version of #3 above (with orchestra and chorus added)					
11/7/81+	5	17		18 Have You Ever Been Lonely (Have You Ever Been Blue)	Welcome To My World	—	$5		RCA 12346
				JIM REEVES AND PATSY CLINE					
6/5/82	54	8		19 I Fall To Pieces	So Wrong [R]	—	$5		MCA 52052
				PATSY CLINE/JIM REEVES					
				new version of #3 above					
10/2/99	70	1		20 There He Goes		—			album cut
				PATSY CLINE with John Berry					
				from Cline's album *Duets Volume I* on Private I 417097					
				COCHRAN, Anita '98					
				Born on 2/6/67 in Pontiac, Michigan. Female singer/songwriter/guitarist.					
4/5/97	64	4		1 I Could Love A Man Like That	Wrong Side Of Town	—	$4	■	Warner 17486 (v)
8/9/97	69	1		2 Daddy Can You See Me		—			album cut
11/8/97+	❶¹	23		3 What If I Said	S:3 / Daddy Can You See Me (Cochran)	59	$4	■	Warner 17263 (v)
				ANITA COCHRAN with Steve Wariner					
4/4/98	69	4		4 Will You Be Here		—			album cut
				all of above from the album *Back To You* on Warner 46395					
7/31/99	58	9		5 For Crying Out Loud	What If I Said (w/**Steve Wariner**)	—	$4		Warner 16939
5/20/00	50	8		6 Good Times	Girls Like Fast Cars	—	$4		Warner 16872
8/5/00	61	7		7 You With Me		—			album cut
				from the album *Anita* on Warner 47318					
				COCHRAN, Cliff '79					
				Born in Pascagoula, Mississippi; raised in Greenville, Mississippi. Cousin of **Hank Cochran**.					
8/10/74	54	10		1 The Way I'm Needing You	Hearts Are Like That, Yes They Are	—	$6		Enterprise 9103
1/11/75	73	7		2 All The Love You'll Ever Need	I'd Do As Much For You	—	$6		Enterprise 9109
5/26/79	24	13		3 Love Me Like A Stranger	The Rose Is For Today	—	$5		RCA 11562
9/22/79	29	9		4 First Thing Each Morning (Last Thing At Night)	100% Chance Of Love Tonight	—	$5		RCA 11711
				COCHRAN, Hank '62					
				Born Garland Perry Cochran on 8/2/35 in Greenville, Mississippi. Singer/songwriter/guitarist. Cousin of **Cliff Cochran**. Formerly married to **Jeannie Seeley**.					
9/1/62	20	5		1 Sally Was A Good Old Girl ★★ *(May 31)*	The Picture Behind The Picture	—	$12		Liberty 55461
11/10/62	23	2		2 I'd Fight The World	Lucy, Let Your Lovelight Shine	—	$12		Liberty 55498

Roy Clark – Conway Twitty – Waylon Jennings (See May 31)

DEBUT	PEAK	WKS	Gold	A-side (Chart Hit)...B-side	Pop	$	Pic	Label & Number
				COCHRAN, Hank — Cont'd				
10/5/63	25	1		3 A Good Country Song..Same Old Hurt	—	$10		Gaylord 6431
4/15/67	70	2		4 All Of Me Belongs To You..................................Just Burned A Dream	—	$8		Monument 994
7/8/78	91	4		5 Willie..Uphill All The Way Merle Haggard (guest vocal)	—	$5		Capitol 4585
10/14/78	77	5		6 Ain't Life Hell..I'm Going With You This Time HANK COCHRAN & WILLIE NELSON	—	$5		Capitol 4635
11/8/80	57	9		7 A Little Bitty Tear..He's Got You Willie Nelson (harmony vocal)	—	$5		Elektra 47062
				COCHRAN, Tammy '01 Born in 1970 in Austinburg, Ohio. Singer/songwriter.				
4/8/00	41	17		1 If You Can..S:12 When Love Was Enough	68ˢ	$4	★	Epic 79415
9/9/00	51	12		2 So What..S:15 If You Can	—	$4	★	Epic 79502
3/31/01	9	32		3 Angels In Waiting	73			album cut
11/17/01+	18	28		4 I Cry	107			album cut
				all of above from the album *Tammy Cochran* on Epic 69736				
				CODY, Betty '53 Born Rita Coté on 8/17/21 in Sherbrooke, Quebec, Canada; raised in Auburn, Maine.				

12/26/53	10	1		I Found Out More Than You
				    Ever Knew ....J:10 Don't Believe Everything That You Read About Love
				    answer to "I Forgot More Than You'll Ever Know" by **The Davis Sisters**
					—	$20		RCA Victor 5462

	★222★			**COE, David Allan** '84
				    Born on 9/6/39 in Akron, Ohio. Singer/songwriter/guitarist/actor. Billed as "The Mysterious Rhinestone Cowboy" until 1978.
				    Acted in such movies as *Take This Job And Shove It*, *The Last Days Of Frank And Jesse James* and *Stagecoach*.
				      1)Mona Lisa Lost Her Smile 2)The Ride 3)You Never Even Called Me By My Name 4)She Used To Love Me A Lot
				      5)Longhaired Redneck				

11/30/74	80	6		1 (If I Could Climb) The Walls Of The Bottle...........Another Pretty Country Song	—	$5		Columbia 10024
5/10/75	91	4		2 Would You Be My Lady..Rock & Roll Holiday	—	$5		Columbia 10093
7/5/75	8	17		3 You Never Even Called Me By My Name..............Would You Lay With Me	—	$5		Columbia 10159
12/27/75+	17	11		4 Longhaired Redneck..Family Reunion	—	$5		Columbia 10254
4/24/76	60	6		5 When She's Got Me (Where She Wants Me)..............Living On The Run	—	$5		Columbia 10323
9/25/76	25	11		6 Willie, Waylon And Me.............................Please Come To Boston [N]	—	$5		Columbia 10395
2/26/77	49	8		7 Lately I've Been Thinking Too Much Lately.............Under Rachel's Wings	—	$5		Columbia 10475
8/6/77	82	5		8 Just To Prove My Love For You...............................Play Me A Sad Song	—	$5		Columbia 10583
10/29/77	92	3		9 Face To Face...Play Me A Sad Song	—	$5		Columbia 10621
3/25/78	86	3		10 Divers Do It Deeper...Million Dollar Memories	—	$5		Columbia 10701
7/22/78	85	4		11 You Can Count On Me..Bad Impressions	—	$5		Columbia 10753
9/9/78	45	8		12 If This Is Just A Game..Tomorrow's Another Day	—	$5		Columbia 10816
3/17/79	72	5		13 Jack Daniel's, If You Please..Human Emotions	—	$5		Columbia 10911
6/21/80	46	7		14 Get A Little Dirt On Your Hands..................................What Can I Do DAVID ALLAN COE AND BILL ANDERSON	—	$5		Columbia 11277
3/14/81	88	3		15 Stand By Your Man..Take This Job And Shove It	—	$4		Columbia 60501
7/4/81	77	5		16 Tennessee Whiskey..This Bottle (In My Hand)	—	$4		Columbia 02118
1/23/82	62	5		17 Now I Lay Me Down To Cheat..If I Knew	—	$4		Columbia 02678
4/10/82	58	8		18 Take Time To Know Her...................................London Homesick Blues #11 Pop hit for Percy Sledge in 1968	—	$4		Columbia 02815
3/19/83	4	19		19 The Ride...Son Of A Rebel Son	—	$4		Columbia 03778
7/23/83	45	10		20 Cheap Thrills.............................You Never Even Called Me By My Name	—	$4	■	Columbia 03997
10/22/83	85	5		21 Crazy Old Soldier...Drinkin' To Forget	—	$4		Columbia 04136
12/24/83+	48	13		22 Ride 'Em Cowboy...Yesterday's Wine	—	$4		Kat Family 04258
3/17/84	2¹	22		23 Mona Lisa Lost Her Smile..Someone Special	—	$4		Columbia 04396
8/25/84	44	11		24 It's Great To Be Single Again...Sweet Angeline	—	$4		Columbia 04553
12/8/84+	11	19		25 She Used To Love Me A Lot............................S:9 / A:19 For Lovers Only (Part IV)	—	$4		Columbia 04688
4/13/85	29	12		26 Don't Cry Darlin'.........................S:27 / A:30 You're The Only Song I Sing Today George Jones (recitation)	—	$4		Columbia 04846
11/2/85	52	8		27 I'm Gonna Hurt Her On The Radio...........He Has To Pay (For What I Get For Free)	—	$4		Columbia 05631
5/10/86	44	10		28 A Country Boy (Who Rolled The Rock Away)...............Take My Advice	—	$4		Columbia 05876
8/2/86	56	6		29 I've Already Cheated On You...................................S:29 Take My Advice DAVID ALLAN COE and WILLIE NELSON	—	$4		Columbia 06227
2/14/87	34	16		30 Need A Little Time Off For Bad Behavior.......S:22 It's A Matter Of Life And Death	—	$4		Columbia 06661
6/6/87	62	5		31 Tanya Montana..................................The Ten Commandments Of Love	—	$4		Columbia 07129
				COFFEY, Kellie '02 Born on 4/22/78 in Moore, Oklahoma. Female singer/songwriter.				
12/22/01+	10↑	28↑		When You Lie Next To Me from the album *When You Lie Next To Me* on BNA 67040	62↑			album cut
				COHN, Marc '91 Born on 7/5/59 in Cleveland. Pop singer. Won the 1991 Best New Artist Grammy Award.				
8/3/91	74	1		Walking In Memphis..Dig Down Deep	13	$3	■	Atlantic 87747 (v)
				COHRON, Phil '90 Born on 7/6/59 in Cleveland.				
1/6/90	86	2		Across The Room From You	—	$6		Air 182
				COIN, R.C. '87 Born Richard Carey Coin on 1/1/51 San Antonio, Texas.				
10/17/87	76	3		Bed Of Roses..Confidential	—	$6		BGM 82087
				COLDER, Ben — see **WOOLEY, Sheb**				

DEBUT	PEAK	WKS	Gold	A-side (Chart Hit)...B-side	Pop	$	Pic	Label & Number
				COLE, Brenda '87				
				Singer/actress.				
6/27/87	83	3		1 But I Never Do..Barefoot Lady	—	$5	■	Melody Dawn 77701
12/19/87	86	3		2 Gone, Gone, Gone	—	$5	■	Melody Dawn 77702
4/16/88	84	2		3 Boots (These Boots Are Made For Walking)..................Gone, Gone, Gone	—	$5		Melody Dawn 77703
				#1 Pop hit for **Nancy Sinatra** in 1966				
				COLE, Nat "King" '44				
				Born Nathaniel Adams Coles on 3/17/17 in Montgomery, Alabama; raised in Chicago. Died of cancer on 2/15/65 (age 47). Father of singer Natalie Cole. Won Grammy's Lifetime Achievement Award in 1990. Formed **The King Cole Trio** in 1939: Cole (vocals, piano), Oscar Moore (guitar) and Wesley Prince (bass).				
5/13/44	❶⁶	15		1 **Straighten Up And Fly Right** /	9			
5/20/44	2¹	5		2 I Can't See For Lookin'	24	$20		Capitol 154
				THE KING COLE TRIO (above 2)				
				COLE, Patsy '89				
				Born in Galesburg, Illinois; raised in Maquon, Illinois.				
4/22/89	89	2		1 I Never Had A Chance With You..Morning Train	—	$5		Tra-Star 1225
7/15/89	80	3		2 Death and Taxes (And Me Lovin' You).................................Lead Me On	—	$5		Tra-Star 1226
11/4/89	91	2		3 You And The Horse (That You Rode In On).........Lot Of Getting Over You	—	$5		Tra-Star 1227
				COLE, Sami Jo — see SAMI JO				
				COLEMAN('S), Albert, Atlanta Pops '82				
				Atlanta-based studio group conducted by Albert Coleman.				
5/29/82	42	15		1 Just Hooked On Country (Parts I & II)... [I]	—	$4		Epic 02938
9/25/82	77	4		2 Just Hooked On Country (Part III)..................Rock Around The Country [I]	—	$4		Epic 03215
				above 2 are medleys of many classic tunes				
				COLLIE, Biff — see BOWMAN, Billy Bob				
	★284★			**COLLIE, Mark** '92				
				Born George Mark Collie on 1/18/56 in Waynesboro, Tennessee. Singer/songwriter/guitarist.				
				1)Even The Man In The Moon Is Crying 2)Born To Love You 3)Hard Lovin' Woman				
2/10/90	54	11		1 Something With A Ring To It...Another Old Soldier	—	$4		MCA 53778
6/9/90	35	21		2 Looks Aren't Everything....................................Something With A Ring To It	—	$4		MCA 79023
10/6/90	59	5		3 Hardin County Line..Bound To Ramble	—	$4		MCA 79078
2/9/91	18	20		4 Let Her Go..Where There's Smoke	—	$4		MCA 53971
6/29/91	31	18		5 Calloused Hands..Johnny Was A Rebel	—	$4		MCA 54079
10/26/91+	28	20		6 She's Never Comin' Back..Lucky Dog	—	$4		MCA 54244
3/7/92	70	4		7 It Don't Take A Lot..Ballad Of Thunder Road	—	$4		MCA 54224
8/29/92	5	20		8 **Even The Man In The Moon Is Crying** Trouble's Coming Like A Train	—	$4		MCA 54448
1/30/93	6	20		9 **Born To Love You** The Heart Of The Matter	—	$4		MCA 54515
6/5/93	26	19		10 Shame Shame Shame Shame...Keep It Up	—	$4		MCA 54668
9/18/93	24	20		11 Something's Gonna Change Her Mind..................................Linda Lou	—	$4		MCA 54720
5/7/94	53	8		12 It Is No Secret..Rainy Day Woman	—	$4	■	MCA 54832 (v)
9/10/94+	13	20		13 Hard Lovin' Woman...Ring Of Fire	—	$4	■	MCA 54907 (v)
6/17/95	25	20		14 Three Words, Two Hearts, One Night................................Tunica Motel	—	$4	■	Giant 17855 (v)
11/25/95	65	2		15 Steady As She Goes...................................Memories (Still Missing Her)	—	$4	■	Giant 17762 (v)
2/24/96	72	2		16 Love To Burn..Oh King Richard	—	$4		Columbia 78236
				COLLIE, Shirley '62				
				Born Shirley Caddell on 3/16/31 in Chillicothe, Missouri. Formerly married to **Biff Collie** and **Willie Nelson**.				
6/12/61	25	5		1 Dime A Dozen...Oh Yes, Darling	—	$20		Liberty 55324
9/11/61	23	3		2 Why, Baby, Why...Why I'm Walking	—	$20		Liberty 55361
				WARREN SMITH and SHIRLEY COLLIE				
3/17/62	10	13		3 Willingly...Chain Of Love	—	$20		Liberty 55403
				WILLIE NELSON & SHIRLEY COLLIE				
				COLLINS, Brian '74				
				Born on 10/19/50 in Baltimore; raised in Texas City, Texas. Singer/songwriter/guitarist.				
				1)Statue Of A Fool 2)That's The Way Love Should Be 3)I Wish				
10/16/71	67	3		1 All I Want To Do Is Say I Love You.............................Time To Try My Wings	—	$6		Mega 0038
2/21/72	47	8		2 There's A Kind Of Hush (All Over The World)......Ain't Gonna Be Your Fool No More	—	$6		Mega 0058
				#4 Pop hit for Herman's Hermits in 1967				
7/1/72	61	6		3 Spread It Around...Let's Give It A Try	—	$6		Mega 0078
7/14/73	24	14		4 I Wish (You Had Stayed)..Hand In Hand With Love	—	$5		Dot 17466
12/8/73+	43	12		5 I Don't Plan On Losing You.......................................Lonely Too Long	—	$5		Dot 17483
5/18/74	10	15		6 **Statue Of A Fool** How Can I Tell Her (About You)	—	$5		Dot 17499
11/9/74+	23	14		7 That's The Way Love Should Be...............................Come A Little Bit Closer	—	$5		ABC/Dot 17527
4/26/75	84	5		8 I'd Still Be In Love With You......................................Sweet Memories	—	$5		ABC/Dot 17546
12/6/75	83	5		9 Queen Of Temptation...Before You Close The Door	—	$5		ABC/Dot 17593
3/6/76	65	8		10 To Show You That I Love You...............................My Heart Would Know	—	$5		ABC/Dot 17613
5/7/77	83	6		11 If You Love Me (Let Me Know).....................................Round And Round	—	$5		ABC/Dot 17694
6/24/78	86	3		12 Old Flames (Can't Hold A Candle To You)...................Falsely Accused	—	$5		RCA 11277
3/10/79	94	3		13 Hello Texas..Barefoot Angels	—	$5		RCA 11478
4/17/82	80	4		14 Before I Got To Know Her.....................................Something Very Special	—	$5		Primero 1001
7/2/83	80	4		15 Nickel's Worth Of Heaven....................................Something Very Special	—	$5		Primero 1018

DEBUT	PEAK	WKS	Gold	A-side (Chart Hit)	B-side	Pop	$	Pic	Label & Number
				COLLINS, Dugg '77					
				Born on 7/2/43 in Memphis, Texas. Singer/songwriter/DJ.					
5/21/77	92	4		1 I'm The Man	If I Don't Love You (Why Do I Miss You Now)	—	$6		SCR 143
9/17/77	99	2		2 How Do You Talk To A Baby		—	$6		SCR 147
				COLLINS, Gwen & Jerry '70					
				Husband-and-wife duo from Miami.					
1/17/70	34	9		Get Together	We're Not Bad	—	$6		Capitol 2710
				#5 Pop hit for The Youngbloods in 1969					
				COLLINS, Jim '98					
				Born in 1959 in Nacogdoches, Texas. Moved to Houston in 1975. Worked as a session musician.					
6/8/85	78	3		1 You Can Always Say Good-Bye In The Morning		—	$5		White Gold 22250
8/24/85	59	6		2 I Wanna Be A Cowboy 'Til I Die		—	$5		White Gold 22252
12/14/85	75	6		3 What A Memory You'd Think		—	$5		White Gold 22251
6/21/86	65	5		4 The Things I've Done To Me		—	$5		TKM 111216
11/1/86	59	5		5 Romance		—	$5		TKM 111217
11/22/97+	55	8		6 The Next Step	Not Me	—	$4	■	Arista 13107 (v)
3/7/98	73	4		7 My First, Last, One And Only	I Can Let Go Now	—	$4		Arista 13119
				COLLINS, Judy '84					
				Born on 5/1/39 in Seattle; raised in Denver. Female singer/songwriter. Charted 11 pop hits from 1967-79.					
9/29/84	57	9		Home Again	Dream On (Collins)	—	$4		Elektra 69697
				JUDY COLLINS with T.G. Sheppard					
	★324★			**COLLINS, Tommy** '54					
				Born Leonard Raymond Sipes on 9/28/30 in Bethany, Oklahoma. Died of emphysema on 3/14/2000 (age 69). Singer/songwriter/guitarist. Regular on the *Town Hall Party* radio series in the early 1950s. Wrote several hits for **Merle Haggard**. The song "Leonard" by Haggard is about Collins.					
				1)You Better Not Do That 2)Whatcha Gonna Do Now 3)It Tickles					
2/20/54	2⁷	21		1 You Better Not Do That	S:2 / A:2 / J:2 High On A Hilltop	—	$25		Capitol 2701
9/4/54	4	15		2 Whatcha Gonna Do Now	A:4 / S:7 You're For Me	—	$25		Capitol 2891
2/5/55	10	1		3 Untied	J:10 / S:15 Boob-I-Lak	—	$25		Capitol 3017
4/30/55	5	9		4 It Tickles	J:5 / A:9 / S:10 Let Down	—	$25		Capitol 3082
10/1/55	13	2		5 I Guess I'm Crazy /			$25		Capitol 3190
10/1/55	15	2		6 You Oughta See Pickles Now	S:13 S:15	—			
1/11/64	47	1		7 I Can Do That	You'd Better Be Nice (Tommy Collins)	—	$15		Capitol 5051
				TOMMY AND WANDA COLLINS					
2/5/66	7	13		8 If You Can't Bite, Don't Growl	Man Machine	105	$10		Columbia 43489
7/16/66	47	2		9 Shindig In The Barn	Be Serious, Ann	—	$10		Columbia 43628
3/4/67	60	5		10 Birmingham /			$10		Columbia 43972
2/11/67	62	4		11 Don't Wipe The Tears That You Cry For Him (On My Good White Shirt)		—			
9/23/67	52	6		12 Big Dummy	What-Cha Gonna Do Now?	—	$10		Columbia 44260
1/13/68	64	6		13 I Made The Prison Band	No Love Have I	—	$10		Columbia 44386
	★309★			**COLTER, Jessi** '75					
				Born Mirriam Johnson on 5/25/43 in Phoenix. Female singer/songwriter/pianist. Married to **Duane Eddy** from 1961-68. Married **Waylon Jennings** in October 1969.					
				1)I'm Not Lisa 2)Suspicious Minds 3)What's Happened To Blue Eyes					
11/14/70	25	10		1 Suspicious Minds	I Ain't The One	—	$8		RCA Victor 9920
				WAYLON JENNINGS AND JESSI COLTER					
				#1 Pop hit for Elvis Presley in 1969; also see #7 below					
6/19/71	39	8		2 Under Your Spell Again	Bridge Over Troubled Water	—	$8		RCA Victor 9992
				WAYLON JENNINGS AND JESSI COLTER					
2/15/75	●¹	18		3 I'm Not Lisa	For The First Time	4	$6		Capitol 4009
8/23/75	5	17		4 What's Happened To Blue Eyes	You Ain't Never Been Loved (Pop #64)	57	$6		Capitol 4087
1/3/76	11	13		5 It's Morning (And I Still Love You)	Would You Walk With Me (To The Lilies)	—	$6		Capitol 4200
4/17/76	50	7		6 Without You	All My Life, I've Been Your Lady	—	$6		Capitol 4252
5/1/76	2¹	14		7 Suspicious Minds	I Ain't The One [R]	—	$6		RCA Victor 10653
				WAYLON & JESSI same version as #1 above					
9/4/76	29	12		8 I Thought I Heard You Calling My Name	You Hung The Moon (Didn't You Waylon?)	—	$5		Capitol 4325
11/4/78	45	10		9 Maybe You Should've Been Listening	My Cowboy's Last Ride	—	$5		Capitol 4641
4/14/79	91	4		10 Love Me Back To Sleep	Don't You Think I Feel It Too	—	$5		Capitol 4696
2/21/81	17	12		11 Storms Never Last	I Ain't The One	—	$4		RCA 12176
				WAYLON & JESSI					
6/6/81	10	13		12 Wild Side Of Life/It Wasn't God Who Made Honky Tonk Angels	I'll Be Alright	—	$4		RCA 12245
				WAYLON & JESSI					
2/13/82	70	4		13 Holdin' On	Somewhere Along The Way	—	$4		Capitol 5073
				COMEAUX, Amie '95					
				Born on 12/4/76 in West Baton Rouge, Louisiana. Died in a car crash on 12/21/97 (age 21).					
1/14/95	64	4		Who's She To You	Written In The Stars	—	$4	■	Polydor 851208 (v)
				COMMANDER CODY And His Lost Planet Airmen '72					
				Commander Cody is George Frayne (vocals, piano). Formed His Lost Planet Airmen in San Francisco: John Tichy, Billy Farlow, Rick Higginbotham, Stan Davis, Bill Kirchen and Andy Stein.					
5/6/72	51	9		1 Hot Rod Lincoln	My Home In My Hand [N]	9	$6		Paramount 0146
7/28/73	97	2		2 Smoke! Smoke! Smoke! (That Cigarette)	Rock That Boogie [N]	94	$6	■	Paramount 0216

DEBUT	PEAK	WKS	Gold	A-side (Chart Hit)	B-side	Pop	$	Pic	Label & Number

COMO, Perry '76
Born Pierino Como on 5/18/12 in Canonsburg, Pennsylvania. Died on 5/12/2001 (age 88). Legendary singer. Charted 132 pop hits from 1943-74.

1/17/76	100	1		Just Out Of Reach	Love Put A Song In My Heart	—	$5		RCA Victor 10402
				#24 Pop hit for Solomon Burke in 1961					

COMPTON BROTHERS, The '69
Duo of brothers Bill (vocals, guitar) and Harry (vocals, guitar, drums) Compton from St. Louis. Won a Columbia Records talent contest in 1965. Operated their own publishing company, Wepedol Music.
1)Haunted House 2)Charlie Brown 3)Claudette

12/31/66+	61	5		1 Pickin' Up The Mail	Feathers To Stone	—	$8		Dot 16948
3/23/68	64	5		2 Honey	Poor Side Of Town	—	$8		Dot 17070
8/3/68	75	2		3 Two Little Hearts	Money	—	$8		Dot 17110
11/23/68	62	5		4 Everybody Needs Somebody	Loneliness Was Made By Man	—	$8		Dot 17167
9/20/69	11	12		5 Haunted House	Sound Of An Angel's Wings	—	$8		Dot 17294
				#11 Pop hit for Gene Simmons in 1964; "live" effects dubbed-in					
1/24/70	16	11		6 Charlie Brown	Just A Dream Away	—	$8		Dot 17336
				#2 Pop hit for The Coasters in 1959					
8/22/70	61	3		7 That Ain't No Stuff	I Wanna Sing A Country Song	—	$8		Dot 17352
6/12/71	65	6		8 Pine Grove	Old Memories	—	$8		Dot 17378
9/4/71	62	6		9 May Old Acquaintance Be Forgot (Before I Lose My Mind)	Learning The Hard Way	—	$8		Dot 17391
2/26/72	49	10		10 Yellow River	Sometimes You Ain't No Fun To Love	—	$8		Dot 17408
				#23 Pop hit for Christie in 1970					
8/26/72	41	9		11 Claudette	It Happens All The Time	—	$8		Dot 17427
				written by Roy Orbison					
10/6/73	65	12		12 California Blues (Blue Yodel No. 4)	Direct Distance Dialing	—	$8		Dot 17477
				written and recorded in 1929 by Jimmie Rodgers					
3/15/75	97	2		13 Cat's In The Cradle	A Bird With Broken Wings Can't Fly	—	$6		ABC/Dot 17538
				#1 Pop hit for Harry Chapin in 1974					

CONCRETE COWBOY BAND '81
Group of Nashville session musicians led by Buddy Skipper. Vocals by Donna Hazard and Nancy Walker.

7/11/81	87	2		Country Is The Closest Thing To Heaven (You Can Hear)	San Antonio Rose	—	$5		Excelsior 1011

CONFEDERATE RAILROAD ★268★ '93
Country-rock group from Marietta, Georgia: Danny Shirley (vocals; born on 8/12/56), Michael Lamb (guitar), Gates Nichols (steel guitar; born on 5/26/44), Chris McDaniel (keyboards; born on 2/4/65), Wayne Secrest (bass; born on 4/29/50) and Mark DuFresne (drums; born on 8/6/53). Jimmy Dormire (born on 3/8/60) replaced Lamb in 1995.
1)Queen Of Memphis 2)Jesus And Mama 3)Daddy Never Was The Cadillac Kind

4/4/92	37	19		1 She Took It Like A Man		—			album cut
7/4/92	4	20		2 Jesus And Mama		—		■	album cut (v)
				later released as the B-side of #3 below					
11/21/92+	2¹	20		3 Queen Of Memphis	Jesus And Mama	—	$4	■	Atlantic 87404 (v)
4/10/93	14	20		4 When You Leave That Way You Can Never Go Back		—		■	album cut (v)
				later released as the B-side of #5 below					
7/24/93	10	20		5 Trashy Women	When You Leave That Way You Can Never Go Back	113	$4	■	Atlantic 87357 (v)
12/11/93+	27	20		6 She Never Cried		—			album cut
				all of above from the album Confederate Railroad on Atlantic 82335					
3/12/94	9	20		7 Daddy Never Was The Cadillac Kind	Jesus And Mama	—	$4	■	Atlantic 87273 (v)
7/9/94	20	20		8 Elvis And Andy	Three Verses	—	$4	■	Atlantic 87229 (v)
11/5/94	55	7		9 Summer In Dixie		—			album cut
				from the album Notorious on Atlantic 82505					
5/13/95	24	20		10 When And Where /		—			
9/9/95	54	8		11 Bill's Laundromat, Bar And Grill		—	$4	■	Atlantic 87104 (v)
11/4/95	66	5		12 When He Was My Age		—			album cut
5/25/96	51	9		13 See Ya		—			album cut
				above 2 from the album When And Where on Atlantic 882774					
11/21/98	66	9		14 The Big One	I Hate Rap	—	$4		Atlantic 84441
4/3/99	70	2		15 Cowboy Cadillac	(dance mix)	—	$4		Atlantic 84464
9/2/00	71	1		16 Toss A Little Bone		—			album cut
				from the album Rockin' Country Party Pack on Atlantic 83207					
9/8/01	39	12		17 That's What Brothers Do		—			album cut
				from the album Unleashed on Audium 8137					

CONLEE, John ★91★ '84
Born on 8/11/46 in Versailles, Kentucky. Singer/songwriter/guitarist. Worked as a mortician for six years, then a newsreader in Fort Knox. Moved to WLAC-Nashville in 1971; worked as a DJ and music director. Joined the Grand Ole Opry in 1981.
1)Lady Lay Down 2)In My Eyes 3)Backside Of Thirty 4)Got My Heart Set On You 5)Common Man

5/27/78	5	20		1 Rose Colored Glasses	I'll Be Easy	—	$5		ABC 12356
11/4/78+	❶¹	16		2 Lady Lay Down	Something Special	—	$5		ABC 12420
3/3/79	❶¹	15		3 Backside Of Thirty	Hold On	—	$5		ABC 12455
8/11/79	2²	15		4 Before My Time	Forever	—	$4		MCA 41072
12/15/79+	7	14		5 Baby, You're Something	The In Crowd	—	$4		MCA 41163

DEBUT	PEAK	WKS	Gold	A-side (Chart Hit)	B-side	Pop	$	Pic	Label & Number
				CONLEE, John — Cont'd					
5/3/80	2²	16		6 Friday Night Blues	When I'm Out Of You	—	$4		MCA 41233
9/13/80	2²	17		7 She Can't Say That Anymore	Always True	—	$4		MCA 41321
1/24/81	12	14		8 What I Had With You	We Belong In Love Tonight	—	$4		MCA 51044
5/30/81	26	12		9 Could You Love Me (One More Time)	When It Hurts You Most	—	$4		MCA 51112
8/29/81	2²	20		10 Miss Emily's Picture	Love Is What You Need	—	$4		MCA 51164
2/20/82	6	18		11 Busted	I'd Rather Have What We Had	—	$4		MCA 52008
				#4 Pop hit for **Ray Charles** in 1963					
7/3/82	26	12		12 Nothing Behind You, Nothing In Sight	Shame	—	$4		MCA 52070
10/2/82+	10	22		13 I Don't Remember Loving You	Two Hearts	—	$4		MCA 52116
3/5/83	❶¹	19		14 Common Man	Rose Colored Glasses	—	$4		MCA 52178
6/25/83	❶¹	20		15 I'm Only In It For The Love	Lay Down Sally	—	$4		MCA 52231
10/15/83+	❶¹	23		16 In My Eyes	Don't Count The Rainy Days	—	$4		MCA 52282
3/10/84	❶¹	19		17 As Long As I'm Rockin' With You	An American Trilogy	—	$4		MCA 52351
6/23/84	4	19		18 Way Back	Together Alone	—	$4		MCA 52403
10/20/84+	2²	21		19 Years After You	S:❶¹ / A:2 But She Loves Me	—	$4		MCA 52470
3/2/85	7	20		20 Working Man	S:7 / A:7 Radio Lover	—	$4		MCA 52543
7/6/85	15	17		21 Blue Highway	A:14 / S:15 De Island	—	$4		MCA 52625
10/26/85+	5	21		22 Old School	S:4 / A:5 She Loves My Troubles Away	—	$4	■	MCA 52695
2/22/86	10	20		23 Harmony	S:9 / A:11 She Told Me So	—	$4		Columbia 05778
6/14/86	❶¹	22		24 Got My Heart Set On You	S:❶¹ / A:3 You've Got A Right	—	$4		Columbia 06104
10/25/86+	6	19		25 The Carpenter	S:❶¹ / A:6 I'll Be Seeing You	—	$4		Columbia 06311
2/28/87	4	24		26 Domestic Life	S:3 / A:6 I Can Sail To China	—	$4		Columbia 06707
7/18/87	11	21		27 Mama's Rockin' Chair	S:6 Faded Brown Eyes	—	$4		Columbia 07203
11/28/87	55	7		28 Living Like There's No Tomorrow (Finally Got To Me Tonight)	Slow Passin' Time	—	$4		Columbia 07643
1/21/89	43	10		29 Hit The Ground Runnin'	Hopelessly Yours	—	$4		16th Avenue 70424
4/8/89	48	9		30 Fellow Travelers	Knowin' You Were Leavin'	—	$4		16th Avenue 70427
8/19/89	67	5		31 Hopelessly Yours	I Love You	—	$4		16th Avenue 70432
12/15/90+	61	9		32 Doghouse	Love Stands Tall	—	$4	■	16th Avenue 70447 (v)

CONLEY, Earl Thomas ★68★ '83

Born on 10/17/41 in West Portsmouth, Ohio. Singer/songwriter/guitarist. Served in the U.S. Army from 1960-62. Worked in a steel mill in Huntsville, Alabama, in the early '70s. Also recorded as **The ETC Band**.

1) Fire & Smoke 2) Love Out Loud 3) What I'd Say 4) Chance Of Lovin' You 5) Once In A Blue Moon

DEBUT	PEAK	WKS	Gold	A-side (Chart Hit)	B-side	Pop	$	Pic	Label & Number
				EARL CONLEY:					
7/26/75	87	4		1 I Have Loved You Girl (But Not Like This Before)	Tryin' To Beat The Morning Home	—	$5		GRT 027
				also see #15 below					
11/22/75	87	5		2 It's The Bible Against The Bottle (In The Battle For Daddy's Soul)	I Have Loved You Girl (But Not Like This Before)	—	$5		GRT 032
3/27/76	67	6		3 High And Wild	The Weeds Outlived The Roses	—	$5		GRT 041
8/14/76	77	5		4 Queen Of New Orleans	I Have Loved You Girl (But Not Like This Before)	—	$5		GRT 064
1/6/79	32	12		5 Dreamin's All I Do	My Love	—	$5		Warner 8717
				EARL THOMAS CONLEY:					
6/23/79	41	8		6 Middle-Age Madness	When You Were Blue And I Was Green	—	$4		Warner 8798
10/6/79	26	11		7 Stranded On A Dead End Street	My Love	—	$4		Warner 49072
				THE ETC BAND					
11/15/80+	7	20		8 Silent Treatment	This Time I've Hurt Her More (Than She Loves Me)	—	$4		Sunbird 7556
4/4/81	❶¹	19		9 Fire & Smoke	I've Loved You Girl	—	$4		Sunbird 7561
10/17/81+	10	18		10 Tell Me Why	Too Much Noise (Trucker's Waltz)	—	$4		RCA 12344
2/6/82	16	13		11 After The Love Slips Away /		—			
		13		12 Smokey Mountain Memories	The Highway Home	—	$4		RCA 13053
6/12/82	8	18		13 Heavenly Bodies	The Highway Home	—	$4		RCA 13114
10/2/82	❶¹	18		14 Somewhere Between Right And Wrong	Fire And Smoke	—	$4		RCA 13320
1/15/83	2²	21		15 I Have Loved You, Girl (But Not Like This Before)	Bottled Up Blues [R]	—	$4		RCA 13414
				new version of #1 above					
5/14/83	❶¹	19		16 Your Love's On The Line	Under Control	—	$4		RCA 13525
9/10/83	❶¹	25		17 Holding Her And Loving You	Home So Fine	—	$4	■	RCA 13596
1/14/84	❶¹	18		18 Don't Make It Easy For Me	You Can't Go On (Like A Rolling Stone)	—	$4		RCA 13702
5/5/84	❶¹	21		19 Angel In Disguise	Crowd Around The Corner	—	$4	■	RCA 13758
9/8/84	❶¹	22		20 Chance Of Lovin' You	S:❶¹ / A:❶¹ Feels Like A Saturday Night	—	$4		RCA 13877
11/10/84+	8	21		21 All Tangled Up In Love	S:5 / A:8 More Or Less (Hardin)	—	$4		RCA 13938
				GUS HARDIN (with Earl Thomas Conley)					
1/5/85	❶¹	22		22 Honor Bound	S:❶¹ / A:❶¹ Too Hot To Handle	—	$4	■	RCA 13960
5/4/85	❶¹	19		23 Love Don't Care (Whose Heart It Breaks)	S:❶¹ / A:❶¹ Turn This Bus Around (Bad Bob's)	—	$4		RCA 14060
9/14/85	❶¹	22		24 Nobody Falls Like A Fool	S:❶¹ / A:❶¹ Silent Treatment	—	$4		RCA 14172
2/1/86	❶¹	22		25 Once In A Blue Moon	A:❶² / S:❶¹ I Have Loved You, Girl (But Not Like This Before)	—	$4		RCA 14282

DEBUT	PEAK	WKS	Gold	A-side (Chart Hit) ... B-side	Pop	$	Pic	Label & Number
				CONLEY, Earl Thomas — Cont'd				
8/2/86	2¹	20		26 Too Many Times　　　　S:❶¹ / A:2 Changes Of Love (Conley)	—	$4	■	RCA 14380
				EARL THOMAS CONLEY AND ANITA POINTER				
11/29/86+	❶¹	23		27 I Can't Win For Losin' You　　　A:❶¹ / S:5 Love's On The Move Again	—	$4		RCA 5064
4/4/87	❶¹	21		28 That Was A Close One　　　S:4 / A:18 Right From The Start	—	$4		RCA 5129
8/1/87	❶¹	23		29 Right From The Start　　　S:9 Attracted To Pain	—	$4		RCA 5226
3/12/88	❶¹	23		30 What She Is (Is A Woman In Love)　　　S:4 Carol	—	$4		RCA 6894
7/2/88	❶¹	21		31 We Believe In Happy Endings　　　S:3 No Chance, No Dance	—	$4		RCA 8632
				EARL THOMAS CONLEY with Emmylou Harris				
11/12/88+	❶¹	24		32 What I'd Say　　　S:13 Carol	—	$4		RCA 8717
3/18/89	❶¹	21		33 Love Out Loud　　　No Chance, No Dance	—	$4		RCA 8824
10/7/89	26	15		34 You Must Not Be Drinking Enough ... Too Far From The Heart Of It All	—	$4		RCA 8973
2/24/90	11	22		35 Bring Back Your Love To Me ... Chance Of Lovin' You	—	$4		RCA 9121
7/14/90	61	6		36 Who's Gonna Tell Her Goodbye ... Love Don't Care (Whose Heart)	—	$4		RCA 2511
6/1/91	8	20		37 Shadow Of A Doubt　　　I Wanna Be Loved Back	—	$4		RCA 2826
9/7/91	2¹	20		38 Brotherly Love　　　Backbone Job	—	$4		RCA 62037
				KEITH WHITLEY & EARL THOMAS CONLEY				
1/11/92	36	13		39 Hard Days And Honky Tonk Nights ... Borrowed Money	—	$4		RCA 62167
5/23/92	74	3		40 If Only Your Eyes Could Lie ... One Of Those Days	—	$4		RCA 62252
				CONWAY, Dave　　　　'77				
8/6/77	68	6		1 If You're Gonna Love (You Gotta Hurt) ... Too Late For Words	—	$6		True 105
				COOK, Steven Lee　　　　'80				
				Born in Shelbyville, Kentucky.				
12/22/79+	92	5		1 Please Play More Kenny Rogers .... [N]	—	$6		Grinder's Switch 1709
				STEVEN LEE COOK with The Jordanaires				
	★377★			**COOLEY, Spade**　　　　'45				
				Born Donnell Clyde Cooley on 12/17/10 in Grand, Oklahoma. Died of a heart attack on 11/23/69 (age 58). Singer/fiddler/actor. Acted in numerous movies. Hosted own TV shows from the late 1940s to 1958. Married Ella Mae Evans in 1945, murdered her on 4/3/61. Sentenced to life imprisonment at Vacaville, California. Died performing at the Oakland Deputy Sheriff's Show two months before he was to be paroled.				
3/3/45	❶⁹	31		1 Shame On You /	—			
				Tex Williams and Oakie (vocals)				
4/28/45	8	1		2 A Pair Of Broken Hearts	—	$25		Okeh 6731
10/6/45	4	1		3 I've Taken All I'm Gonna Take From You　　　Forgive Me One More Time	—	$25		Okeh 6746
3/16/46	2¹	11		4 Detour /				
				Oakie, Arkie and Tex Williams (vocals); #5 Pop hit for Patti Page in 1951				
4/20/46	3	11		5 You Can't Break My Heart	—	$20		Columbia 36935
3/8/47	4	1		6 Crazy 'Cause I Love You　　　Three Way Boogie	—	$20		Columbia 37058
				Tex Williams (vocal: #2, 3, 5 & 6)				
				COOLIDGE, Rita　　　　'80				
				Born on 5/1/44 in Nashville. Singer/songwriter/pianist. Married to Kris Kristofferson from 1973-80. Known as "The Delta Lady." Acted in the 1983 movie Club Med.				
				1)I'd Rather Leave While I'm In Love　2)Somethin' 'Bout You Baby I Like　3)The Jealous Kind				
12/22/73+	92	5		1 A Song I'd Like To Sing ... From The Bottle To The Bottom	49	$5	■	A&M 1475
				KRIS KRISTOFFERSON & RITA COOLIDGE				
3/23/74	98	2		2 Loving Arms ... I'm Down (But I Keep Falling)	86	$5		A&M 1498
				KRIS KRISTOFFERSON & RITA COOLIDGE				
8/31/74	94	5		3 Mama Lou ... Hold An Old Friend's Hand	—	$5		A&M 1545
12/28/74+	87	4		4 Rain ... What'cha Gonna Do	—	$5		Monument 8630
				KRIS KRISTOFFERSON & RITA COOLIDGE				
10/15/77	82	8	●	5 We're All Alone ... Southern Lady	7	$5	■	A&M 1965
11/25/78	63	9		6 The Jealous Kind /	—			
11/25/78	83	9		7 Love Me Again	68	$5		A&M 2090
12/22/79+	32	10		8 I'd Rather Leave While I'm In Love　　　Sweet Emotion	38	$5		A&M 2199
5/24/80	60	6		9 Somethin' 'Bout You Baby I Like ... Late Night Confession (Campbell)	42	$5		Capitol 4865
				GLEN CAMPBELL and RITA COOLIDGE				
1/31/81	72	4		10 Fool That I Am ... Can She Keep You Satisfied	46	$5		A&M 2281
				COOPER, Jerry　　　　'88				
				Born in Arlington, Virginia.				
10/3/87	88	2		1 I'll Forget You	—	$6		Bear 178
1/9/88	83	3		2 As Long As There's Women Like You	—	$6		Bear 187
				COOPER, Wilma Lee & Stoney　　　　'59				
				Husband-and-wife duo: Wilma Leigh Leary (born on 2/7/21 in Valley Head, West Virginia; vocals, guitar, banjo, piano) and Dale Troy "Stoney" Cooper (born on 10/16/18 in Harman, West Virginia; died on 3/22/77, age 58; vocals, fiddle). Joined the Grand Ole Opry in 1957. Own band, The Clinch Mountain Clan. Daughter Carolee Cooper is leader of The Carol Lee Singers.				
				WILMA LEE & STONEY COOPER and The Clinch Mountain Clan:				
9/29/56	14	1		1 Cheated Too　　　　A:14 This Crazy Crazy World	—	$20		Hickory 1051
12/15/58+	4	26		2 Come Walk With Me　　　　Is It Right	—	$15		Hickory 1085
				WILMA LEE & STONEY COOPER With Carolee and The Clinch Mountain Clan				
5/25/59	4	23		3 Big Midnight Special　　　　X Marks The Spot	—	$15		Hickory 1098
				#16 Pop hit for Paul Evans in 1960				
10/19/59	3	24		4 There's A Big Wheel　　　　Rachel's Guitar	—	$15		Hickory 1107
				written by Don Gibson				
5/16/60	17	8		5 Johnny, My Love (Grandma's Diary) ... More Love	—	$15		Hickory 1118

77

Larry Cordle: Murder On Music Row

DEBUT	PEAK	WKS	Gold	A-side (Chart Hit)	B-side	Pop	$	Pic	Label & Number
				COOPER, Wilma Lee & Stoney — Cont'd					
9/12/60	16	14		6 This Ole House .... Heartbreak Street		—	$15		Hickory 1126
				#1 Pop hit for Rosemary Clooney in 1954					
6/12/61	8	7		7 Wreck On The Highway .... Night After Night		—	$15		Hickory 1147
	★227★			**COPAS, Cowboy** '48					
				Born Lloyd Estel Copas on 7/15/13 in Blue Creek, Ohio. Died in a plane crash on 3/5/63 (age 49) near Camden, Tennessee (with **Patsy Cline** and **Hawkshaw Hawkins**). Singer/songwriter/guitarist. Replaced **Eddy Arnold** as lead singer with **Pee Wee King**'s Golden West Cowboys. Joined the *Grand Ole Opry* in 1946.					
				1)*Alabam* 2)*Signed Sealed And Delivered* 3)*Tennessee Waltz*					
8/31/46	4	1		1 Filipino Baby .... I Don't Blame You		—	$20		King 505
				COWBOY (PAPPY) COPAS					
1/3/48	2³	20		2 Signed Sealed And Delivered .... Opportunity Is Knocking At Your Door		—	$20		King 658
				also see #14 below					
5/1/48	3	17		3 Tennessee Waltz .... S:3 / J:4 How Much Do I Owe You		—	$20		King 696
7/3/48	7	9		4 Tennessee Moon .... S:7 / J:7 The Hope Of A Broken Heart		—	$20		King 714
9/18/48	12	1		5 Breeze .... J:12 Dolly Dear		—	$20		King 618
2/12/49	12	1		6 I'm Waltzing With Tears In My Eyes .... S:12 Down In Nashville, Tennessee		—	$20		King 775
2/19/49	5	13		7 Candy Kisses .... J:5 / S:7 Forever		—	$20		King 777
11/12/49	14	2		8 Hangman's Boogie .... S:14 / J:14 Blue Pacific Waltz		—	$20		King 811
				from the movie *Square Dance Jubilee*					
4/28/51	5	11		9 The Strange Little Girl .... A:5 / S:7 / J:10 You'll Never Ever See Me Cry		—	$30		King 45-951
1/19/52	8	3		10 'Tis Sweet To Be Remembered .... A:8 Because Of You		—	$30		King 45-1000
7/4/60	❶¹²	34		11 Alabam .... I Can		63	$15		Starday 501
4/24/61	9	8		12 Flat Top .... True Love (Is The Greatest Thing)		—	$15		Starday 542
7/31/61	12	10		13 Sunny Tennessee .... Dreaming		—	$15		Starday 552
9/11/61	10	8		14 Signed Sealed And Delivered .... New Filipino Baby [R]		—	$15		Starday 559
				new version of #2 above					
4/27/63	12	14		15 Goodbye Kisses .... The Gypsy Girl		—	$12		Starday 621
				CORBIN, Ray '69					
				Born in Lubbock, Texas. Died of a gunshot wound on 10/26/71 (age 35). Also known as Slim Corbin.					
1/11/69	67	2		Passin' Through .... Life Doesn't Move Me		—	$8		Monument 1102
				CORBIN/HANNER BAND, The '82					
				Duo of Bob Corbin (born on 4/9/51 in Butler, Pennsylvania) and Dave Hanner (born on 2/22/49 in Kittanning, Pennsylvania). Band included Al Snyder (keyboards), Kip Paxton (bass) and Dave Freeland (drums).					
				1)*Everyone Knows I'm Yours* 2)*Livin' The Good Life* 3)*I Will Stand By You*					
1/20/79	85	4		1 America's Sweetheart .... Like I Used To		—	$6		Lifesong 1783
				CORBIN & HANNER					
5/30/81	64	6		2 Time Has Treated You Well .... On The Wings Of My Victory		—	$5		Alfa 7001
8/8/81	46	9		3 Livin' The Good Life .... Long Gone Blues		—	$5		Alfa 7007
11/28/81+	49	10		4 Oklahoma Crude .... Too Lazy For Love		—	$5		Alfa 7010
4/10/82	46	9		5 Everyone Knows I'm Yours .... Son Of America/Let Her Go/One Fine Morning		—	$5		Alfa 7022
12/4/82	75	7		6 One Fine Morning .... Lord, I Hope This Day Is Good		—	$5		Lifesong 45120
				CORBIN/HANNER:					
8/11/90	55	8		7 Work Song .... Wild Winds		—	$4	■	Mercury 875688 (v)
3/9/91	59	4		8 Concrete Cowboy .... Wild Winds		—	$4		Mercury 878764
9/12/92	73	2		9 Just Another Hill .... Wild Winds		—	$4	■	Mercury 864146 (v)
12/12/92+	49	14		10 I Will Stand By You		—			album cut
4/24/93	71	3		11 Any Road		—			album cut
				above 2 from the album *Just Another Hill* on Mercury 512288					
	★245★			**CORNELIUS, Helen** '76					
				Born Helen Johnson on 12/6/41 in Monroe City, Missouri. Singer/songwriter. Staff writer with Screen Gems in 1970. Teamed with **Jim Ed Brown** and appeared on the *Nashville On The Road* TV series from 1976-80. CMA Award: 1977 Vocal Duo of the Year (with Jim Ed Brown).					
				1)*I Don't Want To Have To Marry You* 2)*Lying In Love With You* 3)*Saying Hello, Saying I Love You, Saying Goodbye*					
				JIM ED BROWN/HELEN CORNELIUS:					
7/4/76	❶²	16		1 I Don't Want To Have To Marry You .... Have I Told You Lately That I Love You		—	$5		RCA Victor 10711
10/30/76	91	3		2 There's Always A Goodbye .... Only Road Worth Taking		—	$5		RCA 10795
				HELEN CORNELIUS					
11/20/76+	2¹	17		3 Saying Hello, Saying I Love You, Saying Goodbye .... My Heart Cries For You		—	$5		RCA 10822
5/7/77	12	12		4 Born Believer .... Here Today And Gone Tomorrow		—	$5		RCA 10967
8/20/77	12	12		5 If It Ain't Love By Now .... It Takes So Long		—	$5		RCA 11044
12/24/77	91	3		6 Fall Softly Snow .... Natividad (The Nativity) [X]		—	$5		RCA 11162
3/11/78	11	13		7 I'll Never Be Free .... Baby You Know How I Love You		—	$5		RCA 11220
7/29/78	6	15		8 If The World Ran Out Of Love Tonight .... Blue Ridge Mountains Turnin' Green		—	$5		RCA 11304
9/30/78	30	8		9 What Cha Doin' After Midnight, Baby .... Oh What A Night For Love		—	$5		RCA 11375
				HELEN CORNELIUS					
11/25/78+	10	14		10 You Don't Bring Me Flowers .... Dear Memory		—	$5		RCA 11435
3/31/79	2²	13		11 Lying In Love With You .... Let's Take The Long Way Around The World		—	$5		RCA 11532
8/4/79	3	13		12 Fools .... I Think About You		—	$5		RCA 11672
12/1/79	68	5		13 It Started With A Smile .... I'm Changing		—	$5		RCA 11753
				HELEN CORNELIUS					
3/8/80	5	14		14 Morning Comes Too Early .... Emotions		—	$5		RCA 11927
7/19/80	24	12		15 The Bedroom .... Everything Is Changing		—	$5		RCA 12037
5/9/81	13	14		16 Don't Bother To Knock .... Dear Memory		—	$5		RCA 12220

DEBUT	PEAK	WKS	Gold	A-side (Chart Hit)	B-side	Pop	$	Pic	Label & Number
				HELEN CORNELIUS:					
12/5/81+	42	10		17 Love Never Comes Easy .... Losing You		—	$5		Elektra 47237
11/26/83	70	6		18 If Your Heart's A Rollin' Stone		—	$5		Ameri-Can 1011
				CORNOR, Randy '76					
				Born on 7/28/54 in Houston. Singer/songwriter/guitarist.					
11/1/75+	9	15		1 Sometimes I Talk In My Sleep .... Used To Be		—	$5		ABC/Dot 17592
5/15/76	33	11		2 Heart Don't Fail Me Now .... Sugar Foot Rag		—	$5		ABC/Dot 17625
10/2/76	72	6		3 I Guess You Never Loved Me Anyway .... Rocky Top		—	$5		ABC/Dot 17655
3/5/77	86	3		4 Love Doesn't Live Here Anymore .... (Play That Song Again) About The Loser		—	$5		ABC/Dot 17676
7/1/78	95	3		5 Ring Telephone Ring (Damn Telephone) ...... If You'd Love Me Like You Loved Me		—	$6		Cherry 643
12/23/78	100	2		6 Hurt As Big As Texas .... Maybe You Should've Been Listenin		—	$6		Cherry 783
				COTTON, Gene '82					
				Born on 6/30/44 in Columbus, Ohio. Singer/songwriter/guitarist.					
12/11/76+	92	7		1 You've Got Me Runnin' .... It's Over Goodbye		33	$5		ABC 12227
7/29/78	99	2		2 You're A Part Of Me .... Shine On (You Got To Shine On Your Light) (Cotton)		36	$5		Ariola America 7704
				GENE COTTON with Kim Carnes					
5/22/82	78	4		3 If I Could Get You (Into My Life) .... Rained On Before		76	$5		Knoll 5002
				COTY, Neal '01					
				Born in Maryland. Singer/songwriter/guitarist.					
11/11/00+	49	13		Legacy .... S:11 Breathin'		—	$4	★	Mercury 172183 (v)
				COUCH, Orville '63					
				Born on 2/21/35 in Ferris, Texas.					
11/24/62+	5	21		1 Hello Trouble .... Anywhere There's A Crowd		—	$20		Vee Jay 470
				first released on Custom 101 ($30)					
9/28/63	25	1		2 Did I Miss You? .... The Lonesomes		—	$20		Vee Jay 528
				COULTERS, The '83					
				Family trio from Durham, North Carolina.					
2/26/83	70	5		Caroline's Still In Georgia .... Free To Love You		—	$7	■	Dolphin 45003
				COUNTRY CAVALEERS, The '76					
				Duo of **James Marvell** and Buddy Good. Both were members of the vocal group Mercy.					
10/20/73	99	2		1 Humming Bird .... Hang On To What		—	$5		MGM 14606
8/28/76	97	2		2 Te' Quiero (I Love You In Many Ways) .... I've Got My Mind Satisfied		—	$6		Country Show. 171
				COUNTRY GENTLEMEN, The '65					
				Bluegrass group: Charlie Waller (vocals, guitar), John Duffey (mandolin; died on 12/10/96, age 62), Eddie Adcock (banjo) and Ed McGlothlin (string bass). Numerous personnel changes through the years. **Ricky Skaggs** played fiddle in the group in 1972.					
10/30/65	43	4		Bringing Mary Home .... Northbound		—	$15		Rebel 250
				COX, Don '79					
				Born in Texas. Singer/songwriter/guitarist.					
12/1/79	94	3		Smooth Southern Highway .... The Prophet And The Saint		—	$5		ARC 5902
				COX, Don '94					
				Born on 1/14/64 in Belhaven, North Carolina. Former member of the **Super Grit Cowboy Band**.					
4/9/94	53	13		All Over Town .... Chase The Moon		—	$4		Step One 474
				CRADDOCK, Billy "Crash" ★88★ '74					
				Born on 6/13/39 in Greensboro, North Carolina. Singer/songwriter/guitarist. With his brother Ronald in rock band the Four Rebels in 1957. First recorded for Colonial in 1957. Charted the pop hit "Don't Destroy Me" in 1959. Semi-retired from recording and worked outside of music in Greensboro from 1960-69. Known as "Mr. Country Rock."					
				1) Rub It In 2) Broken Down In Tiny Pieces 3) Ruby, Baby 4) Easy As Pie 5) Knock Three Times					
2/13/71	3	17		1 Knock Three Times .... The Best I Ever Had		113	$7		Cartwheel 193
				#1 Pop hit for Dawn in 1971					
6/19/71	5	14		2 Dream Lover .... I Ran Out Of Time		—	$7		Cartwheel 196
				#2 Pop hit for **Bobby Darin** in 1959					
11/6/71	10	14		3 You Better Move On .... Confidence And Common Sense		—	$7		Cartwheel 201
				#24 Pop hit for Arthur Alexander in 1962					
3/4/72	10	16		4 Ain't Nothin' Shakin' (But The Leaves On The Trees) .... She's My Angel		—	$7		Cartwheel 210
7/1/72	5	16		5 I'm Gonna Knock On Your Door .... What He Don't Know Won't Hurt Him		—	$7		Cartwheel 216
				#12 Pop hit for Eddie Hodges in 1961					
11/18/72+	22	12		6 Afraid I'll Want To Love Her One More Time .... Treat Her Right		—	$6		ABC 11342
2/24/73	33	9		7 Don't Be Angry .... White Boy		—	$6		ABC 11349
5/26/73	14	11		8 Slippin' And Slidin' .... A Living Example		—	$6		ABC 11364
				#33 Pop hit for Little Richard in 1956					
9/1/73	8	15		9 'Till The Water Stops Runnin' .... What Does A Loser Say		—	$5		ABC 11379
1/5/74	3	16		10 Sweet Magnolia Blossom .... Home Is Such A Lonely Place To Go		—	$5		ABC 11412
6/1/74	❶²	16		11 Rub It In .... It's Hard To Love A Hungry, Worried Man		16	$5		ABC 12013
11/9/74+	❶¹	14		12 Ruby, Baby .... Walk When Love Walks		33	$5		ABC 12036
				#2 Pop hit for Dion in 1963					
2/22/75	4	14		13 Still Thinkin' 'Bout You .... Stay A Little Longer In Your Bed		—	$5		ABC 12068
6/21/75	10	14		14 I Love The Blues And The Boogie Woogie .... No Deposit, No Return		—	$5		ABC 12104
10/18/75	2³	17		15 Easy As Pie .... She's Mine		54	$5		ABC/Dot 17584

DEBUT	PEAK	WKS	Gold	A-side (Chart Hit)	B-side	Pop	$	Pic	Label & Number
				CRADDOCK, Billy "Crash" — Cont'd					
4/3/76	7	13		16 Walk Softly	She's About A Mover	—	$5		ABC/Dot 17619
7/4/76	4	13		17 You Rubbed It In All Wrong	I Need Somebody To Love Me	—	$5		ABC/Dot 17635
10/23/76+	❶[1]	16		18 Broken Down In Tiny Pieces	Shake It Easy	—	$5		ABC/Dot 17659
3/12/77	28	10		19 Just A Little Thing	The First Time	—	$5		ABC/Dot 17682
6/4/77	7	15		20 A Tear Fell	Piece Of The Rock	—	$5		ABC/Dot 17701
				#5 Pop hit for Teresa Brewer in 1956					
11/12/77+	10	15		21 The First Time	Walk When Love Walks	—	$5		ABC/Dot 17725
2/4/78	4	15		22 I Cheated On A Good Woman's Love	Not A Day Goes By	—	$4		Capitol 4545
2/18/78	92	2		23 Another Woman	The Words Still Rhyme	—	$4		ABC 12335
5/6/78	50	9		24 Think I'll Go Somewhere (And Cry Myself To Sleep)	It All Came Back	—	$4		ABC 12357
5/20/78	28	10		25 I've Been Too Long Lonely Baby	Jailhouse Rock	—	$4		Capitol 4575
7/29/78	57	6		26 Don Juan	Things Are Mostly Fine	—	$4		ABC 12384
9/16/78	14	12		27 Hubba Hubba	Let's Go Back To The Beginning	—	$4		Capitol 4624
1/6/79	4	14		28 If I Could Write A Song As Beautiful As You	Never Ending	—	$4		Capitol 4672
4/28/79	28	10		29 My Mama Never Heard Me Sing	As Long As I Live	—	$4		Capitol 4707
8/4/79	16	13		30 Robinhood	We Never Made It To Chicago	—	$4		Capitol 4753
11/10/79+	24	14		31 Till I Stop Shaking	Sneak Out Of Love With You	—	$4		Capitol 4792
3/15/80	22	11		32 I Just Had You On My Mind	You Just Want To Be Mine	—	$4		Capitol 4838
6/14/80	50	8		33 Sea Cruise	She's Got Legs	—	$4		Capitol 4875
				#14 Pop hit for Frankie Ford in 1959					
10/18/80	20	13		34 A Real Cowboy (You Say You're)	One Dream Coming, One Dream Going	—	$4		Capitol 4935
2/14/81	37	10		35 It Was You	Betty Ruth	—	$4		Capitol 4972
6/20/81	11	16		36 I Just Need You For Tonight	Leave Your Love A 'Smokin'	—	$4		Capitol 5011
10/17/81	38	10		37 Now That The Feeling's Gone	She's Good To Me	—	$4		Capitol 5051
7/17/82	28	12		38 Love Busted	Darlin' Take Care Of Yourself	—	$4		Capitol 5139
11/20/82	62	5		39 The New Will Never Wear Off Of You	Hold Me Tight	—	$4		Capitol 5170
				CRASH CRADDOCK					
10/22/83	86	2		40 Tell Me When I'm Hot	When The Feeling Is Right	—	$5		Cee Cee 5400
8/5/89	68	7		41 Just Another Miserable Day (Here In Paradise)	Softly Diana	—	$4	■	Atlantic 88851
				CRAFT, Paul '74					
				Born on 8/12/38 in Memphis; raised in Richmond, Virginia. Singer/songwriter/publisher.					
10/12/74	55	10		1 It's Me Again, Margaret	For Linda (Child In The Cradle) [N]	—	$6		Truth 3205
6/11/77	98	2		2 We Know Better	Dropkick Me, Jesus	—	$5		RCA 10971
10/1/77	55	7		3 Lean On Jesus "Before He Leans On You"	Daddy Please Don't Go To Vegas	—	$5		RCA 11078
3/4/78	84	6		4 Teardrops In My Tequila	Rise Up	—	$5		RCA 11211
				CRAMER, Floyd '61					
				Born on 10/27/33 in Samti, Louisiana; raised in Huttig, Arkansas. Died of cancer on 12/31/97 (age 64). Top session pianist. Also see Some Of Chet's Friends.					
11/7/60+	11	18	●	1 Last Date	Sweetie Baby [I]	2[4]	$10		RCA Victor 7775
6/19/61	8	10		2 San Antonio Rose	I Can Just Imagine [I]	8	$10		RCA Victor 7893
				written by **Bob Wills**					
2/18/67	53	7		3 Stood Up	Good Vibrations [I]	—	$8		RCA Victor 9065
4/16/77	67	7		4 Rhythm Of The Rain	Prelude To Love [I]	—	$5		RCA 10908
				FLOYD CRAMER AND THE KEYBOARD KICK BAND					
				#3 Pop hit for The Cascades in 1963; The Keyboard Kick Band is Floyd Cramer playing eight different keyboards					
3/15/80	32	10		5 Dallas	Lover's Minuet [I]	104	$5	■	RCA 11916
				from the TV series starring Larry Hagman					
				CRAWFORD, Calvin — see HOUSTON, David					
				CRAWFORD/WEST '97					
				Duo of Rick Crawford (from Texas) and Kenny West (from Arkansas).					
6/14/97	75	1		Summertime Girls	Hard To Stop A Train	—	$4	■	Warner 17358 (v)
				CREECH, Alice '71					
				Born in Panther Branch, North Carolina.					
5/29/71	73	2		1 The Hunter	Isn't It A Shame About Jeannie	—	$8		Target 00313
11/13/71	33	11		2 The Night They Drove Old Dixie Down	When I'm Not With You	—	$8		Target 0138
				#3 Pop hit for Joan Baez in 1971					
2/12/72	34	11		3 We'll Sing In The Sunshine	I Used To Cry Over You	—	$8		Target 0144
				CREEDENCE CLEARWATER REVIVAL '82					
				Rock group from El Cerrito, California: **John Fogerty** (vocals, guitar), brother Tom Fogerty (guitar), Stu Cook (keyboards, bass) and Doug Clifford (drums). Group charted 20 pop hits from 1968-76; disbanded in 1972. Tom Fogerty died on 9/6/90 (age 48).					
12/5/81+	50	8		Cotton Fields	Lodi	—	$5		Fantasy 920
				recorded in 1969; #13 Pop hit for The Highwaymen in 1962					
				CREWS, Dwayne '90					
				Born on 5/7/56 in Dallas. Singer/songwriter/guitarist.					
1/6/90	81	2		Selfish Man		—	$7		Killer 124
				CRITTENDEN, Melodie '98					
				Born in 1969 in Moore, Oklahoma. Female singer.					
1/17/98	42	15		1 Broken Road		—			album cut
5/9/98	72	3		2 I Should've Known		—			album cut
				above 2 from the album Melodie Crittenden on Asylum 62043					

DEBUT	PEAK	WKS	Gold	A-side (Chart Hit)	B-side	Pop	$	Pic	Label & Number
				CROCE, Jim '74					
				Born on 1/10/43 in Philadelphia. Killed in a plane crash on 9/20/73 (age 30) in Natchitoches, Louisiana. Charted 10 pop hits from 1972-76.					
4/13/74	68	7		I'll Have To Say I Love You In A Song	Salon And Saloon	9	$6		ABC 11424
				CROCKETT, Howard '73					
				Born Howard Hausey on 12/25/25 in Minden, Louisiana. Died on 12/27/94 (age 69). Singer/songwriter.					
5/19/73	52	10		Last Will And Testimony (Of A Drinking Man)	House Where Momma Lived	—	$6		Dot 17457
				CROFT, Sandy '83					
				Born in 1969 in Chattanooga, Tennessee. Female singer.					
1/22/83	61	8		1 Easier	If I Was As Pretty As You	—	$6	■	Angelsong 1821
8/4/84	91	2		2 Easier	If I Was As Pretty As You [R]	—	$4		Capitol 5363
				above 2 are the same version					
6/15/85	68	6		3 Piece Of My Heart	Heart Stealer	—	$4	■	Capitol 5471
				#12 Pop hit for Big Brother and The Holding Company (Janis Joplin) in 1968					
				CROSBY, Bing '44					
				Born Harry Lillis Crosby on 5/3/03 in Tacoma, Washington. Died of a heart attack on 10/14/77 (age 74). One of the most popular entertainers of all-time. Charted 156 pop hits from 1940-65.					
1/8/44	❶⁵	11	●	1 Pistol Packin' Mama	Vict'ry Polka (Pop #6)	2⁴	$20		Decca 23277
				BING CROSBY and ANDREWS SISTERS					
8/30/52	10	1		2 Till The End Of The World	J:10 Just A Little Lovin' (Will Go A Long Way)	16	$20		Decca 9-28265
				BING CROSBY And GRADY MARTIN And His Slew Foot Five					
				CROSBY, Eddie '49					
12/10/49	7	2		Blues Stay Away From Me	A:7 / J:10 Foolish Notion	—	$20		Decca 46180
				CROSBY, Rob '91					
				Born Robert Crosby Hoar on 4/25/54 in Sumter, South Carolina. Singer/songwriter/guitarist.					
11/10/90+	12	20		1 Love Will Bring Her Around	(Nobody's Gonna) Hurt My Heart	—	$4	■	Arista 2124 (v)
4/20/91	15	20		2 She's A Natural	Somewhere Down The Line	—	$4		Arista 2180
9/28/91	20	20		3 Still Burnin' For You	Solid Ground	—	$4		Arista 12336
2/1/92	28	14		4 Working Woman	The Woman In You	—	$4		Arista 12397
7/4/92	53	9		5 She Wrote The Book	One Night Down	—	$4		Arista 12443
12/26/92+	48	12		6 In The Blood	Cold Day In Tennessee	—	$4		Arista 12481
9/30/95	64	8		7 The Trouble With Love	I've Got Just The Heart	—	$4	■	River North 3006
1/20/96	64	6		8 Lady's Man		—			album cut
				from the album Starting Now on River North 1162					
				CROSBY, STILLS & NASH '94					
				Folk-rock trio: David Crosby (guitar; from The Byrds); Stephen Stills (guitar, bass; from Buffalo Springfield) and Graham Nash (guitar; from The Hollies). Occasionally joined by Neil Young (guitar). Group charted 13 pop hits from 1969-89. Also see The Red Hots.					
8/14/82	87	4		1 Wasted On The Way	Delta	9	$4	■	Atlantic 4058
3/11/89	92	2		2 This Old House	Got It Made (Pop #69)	—	$4	■	Atlantic 88966
				CROSBY, STILLS, NASH & YOUNG					
				CROW, Alvin '77					
				Born on 9/29/50 in Oklahoma City. Leader of The Pleasant Valley Boys based in Austin, Texas.					
6/11/77	83	4		1 Yes She Do, No She Don't (I'm Satisfied With My Gal)	Retirement Run	—	$5		Polydor 14387
9/10/77	97	2		2 Crazy Little Mama (At My Front Door)	You're The One I Thought I'd Never Lose	—	$5		Polydor 14410
				ALVIN CROW And The Pleasant Valley Boys (above 2)					
				#7 Pop hit for Pat Boone in 1955					
12/17/77	94	4		3 Nyquil Blues	Fiddler's Lady	—	$5		Polydor 14437
				CROWELL, Rodney ★189★ '89					
				Born on 8/7/50 in Houston. Singer/songwriter/guitarist. Moved to Nashville in 1972 and worked as staff writer for Jerry Reed. Worked with Emmylou Harris from 1975-77. Married to Rosanne Cash from 1979-92. Cousin of Larry Willoughby.					
				1)She's Crazy For Leavin' 2)I Couldn't Leave You If I Tried 3)Above And Beyond 4)It's Such A Small World 5)After All This Time					
9/9/78	95	3		1 Elvira	Ashes By Now	—	$5		Warner 8637
5/19/79	90	3		2 (Now And Then, There's) A Fool Such As I	Voila, An American Dream	—	$5		Warner 8794
				#2 Pop hit for Elvis Presley in 1959					
5/31/80	78	6		3 Ashes By Now	Blues In The Daytime	37	$5		Warner 49224
10/10/81	30	11		4 Stars On The Water	Don't Need No Other Now	105	$5		Warner 49810
2/13/82	34	11		5 Victim Or A Fool	Only Two Hearts	—	$5		Warner 50008
11/15/86+	38	12		6 When I'm Free Again	S:29 The Best I Can	—	$4		Columbia 06415
3/21/87	71	7		7 She Loves The Jerk	Past Like A Mask	—	$4		Columbia 06584
6/20/87	59	8		8 Looking For You	Stay (Don't Be Cruel)	—	$4		Columbia 07137
1/23/88	❶¹	23		9 It's Such A Small World	S:❶³ Crazy Baby (Crowell)	—	$4		Columbia 07693
				RODNEY CROWELL & ROSANNE CASH					
6/11/88	❶¹	21		10 I Couldn't Leave You If I Tried	S:❶⁴ When The Blue Hour Comes	—	$4		Columbia 07918
10/15/88+	❶¹	19		11 She's Crazy For Leavin'	S:❶² Brand New Rag	—	$4		Columbia 08080
2/25/89	❶¹	21		12 After All This Time	Oh King Richard	—	$4		Columbia 68685
7/1/89	❶¹	20		13 Above And Beyond	She Loves The Jerk	—	$4		Columbia 68948
10/14/89+	3	26		14 Many A Long & Lonesome Highway	I Know You're Married	—	$4		Columbia 73042
3/3/90	6	26		15 If Looks Could Kill	I Didn't Know I Could Lose You	—	$4	■	Columbia 73254 (v)

DEBUT	PEAK	WKS	Gold	A-side (Chart Hit)...B-side	Pop	$	Pic	Label & Number
				CROWELL, Rodney — Cont'd				
7/14/90	22	15		16 My Past Is Present...You Been On My Mind	—	$4	■	Columbia 73423 (v)
10/20/90+	17	20		17 Now That We're Alone..............................I Guess We've Been Together For Too Long	—	$4	■	Columbia 73569 (v)
4/27/91	72	5		18 Things I Wish I'd Said...Soul Searchin'	—	$4		Columbia 73760
3/7/92	10	20		19 Lovin' All Night ....I Didn't Know I Could Lose You	—	$4		Columbia 74250
6/27/92	11	20		20 What Kind Of Love ....Nobody's Going To Tear My Playhouse Down	—	$4	■	Columbia 74360 (v)
4/2/94	60	7		21 Let The Picture Paint Itself......................................The Rose Of Memphis	—	$4	■	MCA 54821 (v)
9/17/94	75	1		22 Big Heart..The Best Years Of Our Lives	—	$4	■	MCA 54880 (v)
4/29/95	69	9		23 Please Remember Me...Give My Heart A Rest	—	$4	■	MCA 55024 (v)
11/7/98	61	6		24 I Walk The Line Revisited ....Stars On The Water	—	$4		Reprise 17149
				RODNEY CROWELL with Johnny Cash				
				CROWLEY, J.C. '89				
				Born John Crowley on 11/13/47 in Houston. Singer/songwriter/guitarist. Former member of the pop group Player ("Baby Come Back").				
9/3/88	49	7		1 Boxcar 109..Living For The Fire	—	$4		RCA 8634
10/29/88+	13	19		2 Paint The Town And Hang The Moon Tonight.....................Serenade	—	$4		RCA 8747
3/25/89	21	15		3 I Know What I've Got..Living For The Fire	—	$4		RCA 8822
7/22/89	55	9		4 Beneath The Texas Moon ....Living For The Fire	—	$4		RCA 9012
				CRUM, Simon — see HUSKY, Ferlin				
				CRYNER, Bobbie '93				
				Born on 9/13/61 in Woodland, California. Female singer.				
7/3/93	63	6		1 Daddy Laid The Blues On Me ....I'm Through Waitin' On You	—	$4	■	Epic 77044 (v)
11/20/93	68	5		2 He Feels Guilty...This Heart Speaks For Itself	—	$4	■	Epic 77195 (v)
5/14/94	72	3		3 You Could Steal Me..Leavin' Houston Blues	—	$4	■	Epic 77487 (v)
10/14/95	63	8		4 I Just Can't Stand To Be Unhappy..Nobody Leaves	—	$4	■	MCA 55099 (v)
3/2/96	56	7		5 You'd Think He'd Know Me Better ....Oh To Be The One	—	$4		MCA 55167
				CUMMINGS, Barbara '67				
12/24/66+	69	8		1 She's The Woman............................There's Something Funny Going On	—	$10		London 104
				CUMMINGS, Burton '79				
				Born on 12/31/47 in Winnipeg, Canada. Lead singer of rock group The Guess Who.				
3/3/79	33	12		1 Takes A Fool To Love A Fool ....I Will Play A Rhapsody	—	$5		Portrait 70024
				CUMMINGS, Chris '98				
				Born on 8/11/75 in Norton, New Brunswick, Canada. Male singer.				
12/20/97+	50	7		1 The Kind Of Heart That Breaks................................Almost Always	—	$4	■	Warner 17267 (v)
				CUNHA, Rick '74				
				Born in Los Angeles. Session guitarist.				
5/18/74	49	10		1 (I'm A) YoYo Man..Wild Side Of Life	61	$6		GRC 2016
				CUNNINGHAM, J.C. '84				
				Born John Collins Cunningham on 11/13/50 in Brownsville, Texas.				
7/5/80	85	2		1 The Pyramid Song ....I'm A Lover Not A Fighter [N]	104	$5		Scotti Brothers 601
4/21/84	70	6		2 Light Up..The Greatest Love	—	$5		Viva 29311
				CURB, Mike, Congregation '70				
				Born on 12/24/44 in Savannah, Georgia. Pop music mogul and politician. President of MGM Records from 1969-73. Elected lieutenant governor of California in 1978; served as governor of California in 1980. Formed own company, Sidewalk Records, in 1964; became Curb Records in 1974. Currently resides in Nashville.				
8/1/70	❶²	15		1 All For The Love Of Sunshine............................Ballad Of The Moonshine	—	$7		MGM 14152
				HANK WILLIAMS, JR. With THE MIKE CURB CONGREGATION				
				from the movie Kelly's Heroes starring Clint Eastwood				
12/19/70+	3	15		2 Rainin' In My Heart.....................................A-eee (Williams)	108	$7		MGM 14194
				HANK WILLIAMS, JR. With THE MIKE CURB CONGREGATION				
				#34 Pop hit for Slim Harpo in 1961				
12/18/71+	7	14		3 Ain't That A Shame..The End Of A Bad Day	—	$7		MGM 14317
				HANK WILLIAMS, JR. with The Mike Curb Congregation				
				#1 R&B hit for Fats Domino in 1955				
5/27/72	24	11		4 Gone (Our Endless Love).......................All I Have To Offer You Is Me	—	$7		MGM 14377
				BILLY WALKER with The Mike Curb Congregation				
	★265★			**CURLESS, Dick** '65				
				Born on 3/17/32 in Fort Fairfield, Maine. Died of cancer on 5/25/95 (age 63). Singer/guitarist. Had own radio show as "The Tumbleweed Kid" in Ware, Massachusetts, in 1948. On Armed Forces Radio Network as "The Rice-Paddy Ranger" from 1951-54. Father-in-law of Billy Chinnock.				
				1)A Tombstone Every Mile 2)Six Times A Day (The Trains Came Down) 3)Big Wheel Cannonball 4)All Of Me Belongs To You 5)Drag 'Em Off The Interstate, Sock It To 'Em, J.P. Blues				
3/13/65	5	17		1 A Tombstone Every Mile...Heart Talk	—	$15		Tower 124
				first released in 1965 on Allagash 101 ($20)				
6/19/65	12	13		2 Six Times A Day (The Trains Came Down) ....Down By The Old River	—	$15		Tower 135
11/6/65	42	3		3 'Tater Raisin' Man...The Friend Who Makes It Four	—	$15		Tower 161
1/15/66	44	3		4 Travelin' Man...Rocky Mountain Queen	—	$15		Tower 193
10/15/66	63	3		5 The Baron..A Good Job-Huntin' And Fishin'	—	$15	■	Tower 255
2/4/67	28	11		6 All Of Me Belongs To You ....My Side Of The Night	—	$15		Tower 306
7/29/67	72	1		7 House Of Memories ....(Standing) On The Outside Looking In	—	$15		Tower 335
				above 2 written by Merle Haggard				
11/4/67	70	2		8 Big Foot..Tornado Tillie	—	$15		Tower 362
3/23/68	55	7		9 Bury The Bottle With Me ....Bummin' On Track "E"	—	$15		Tower 399
6/15/68	34	9		10 I Ain't Got Nobody..Shoes	—	$15		Tower 415

DEBUT	PEAK	WKS	Gold	A-side (Chart Hit)	B-side	Pop	$	Pic	Label & Number
				CURLESS, Dick — Cont'd					
5/2/70	27	11	★	11 Big Wheel Cannonball	I Miss A Lot Of Trains	—	$8		Capitol 2780
				new "trucker" version of "Wabash Cannonball"					
8/8/70	31	10		12 Hard, Hard Traveling Man	Winter's Comin' On Again	—	$8		Capitol 2848
11/21/70	29	9		13 Drag 'Em Off The Interstate, Sock It To 'Em, J.P. Blues	Drop Some Silver In The Juke Box	—	$8		Capitol 2949
2/20/71	41	9		14 Juke Box Man	Please Buy My Flowers	—	$8		Capitol 3034
7/31/71	36	9		15 Loser's Cocktail	Hot Springs	—	$8		Capitol 3105
10/2/71	40	10		16 Snap Your Fingers	Bully Of The Town	—	$8		Capitol 3182
				#8 Pop hit for Joe Henderson in 1962					
2/26/72	34	11		17 January, April And Me	Lay Your Hands On Me (And Heal Me)	—	$8		Capitol 3267
7/1/72	31	9		18 Stonin' Around	For The Life Of Me	—	$8		Capitol 3354
11/25/72	55	7		19 She Called Me Baby	Wait A Little Longer	—	$6		Capitol 3470
3/24/73	54	7		20 Chick Inspector (That's Where My Money Goes)	Travelin' Light	—	$6		Capitol 3541
7/14/73	80	3		21 China Nights (Shina No Yoru)	Old Bob Burton	—	$6		Capitol 3630
				#58 Pop hit for Kyu Sakamoto in 1963					
9/15/73	65	7		22 The Last Blues Song	Room Full Of Roses	—	$6		Capitol 3698
				CURREY, Diana Sicily '89					
10/21/89	91	2		Longneck Lone Star (And Two Step Dancin')		—	$6		Condor 13
				CURTIS, Larry '78					
				Born in Van Nuys, California. Male singer.					
6/10/78	88	5		It Feels Like Love for the first time		—	$7		ScrimShaw 1315
				CURTIS, Mac '70					
				Born Wesley Erwin Curtis on 1/16/39 in Fort Worth, Texas; raised in Olney, Texas. Singer/songwriter.					
6/15/68	64	5		1 The Quiet Kind	Love's Been Good To Me	—	$8		Epic 10324
10/19/68	54	7		2 The Sunshine Man	It's My Way	—	$8		Epic 10385
5/24/69	63	7		3 Happiness Lives In This House	Little Old Wine Drinker	—	$8		Epic 10468
11/8/69	60	5		4 Don't Make Love	Us	—	$8		Epic 10530
2/28/70	43	9		5 Honey, Don't	Today's Teardrops	—	$8		Epic 10574
				written by Carl Perkins; recorded by The Beatles on their 1965 Beatles '65 album					
10/17/70	35	10		6 Early In The Morning	When The Hurt Moves In	—	$6		GRT 26
				#24 Pop hit for Bobby Darin in 1958					
				CURTIS, Sonny '81					
				Born on 5/9/37 in Meadow, Texas. Singer/songwriter/guitarist/fiddler. Member of Buddy Holly & The Three Tunes.					
				1)Good Ol' Girls 2)Love Is All Around 3)Married Women					
10/8/66	49	2		1 My Way Of Life	Last Call	134	$15		Viva 602
9/23/67	50	11		2 I Wanna Go Bummin' Around	I'm A Gypsy Man	—	$15		Viva 617
2/24/68	36	11		3 Atlanta Georgia Stray	Day Drinker	120	$15		Viva 626
7/20/68	45	9		4 The Straight Life	How Little Men Care	—	$15		Viva 630
11/29/75	78	5		5 Lovesick Blues	It's Only A Question Of Time	—	$6		Capitol 4158
9/15/79	77	6		6 The Cowboy Singer	Cheatin' Clouds	—	$5		Elektra 46526
1/19/80	86	3		7 Do You Remember Roll Over Beethoven	Walk Right Back	—	$5		Elektra 46568
3/29/80	38	9		8 The Real Buddy Holly Story	Ain't Nobody Honest	—	$5		Elektra 46616
7/19/80	29	10		9 Love Is All Around	The Clone Song	—	$5		Elektra 46663
				theme from TV's The Mary Tyler Moore Show					
11/8/80	70	3		10 Fifty Ways To Leave Your Lover	You Made My Life A Song	—	$5		Elektra 47048
				#1 Pop hit for Paul Simon in 1976					
4/25/81	15	16		11 Good Ol' Girls	So Used To Loving You	—	$5		Elektra 47129
8/22/81	33	10		12 Married Women	I Like Your Music	—	$5		Elektra 47176
1/25/86	69	5		13 Now I've Got A Heart Of Gold		—	$6		'Steem 110185
	★201★			**CYRUS, Billy Ray** '92					
				Born on 8/25/61 in Flatwoods, Kentucky. Singer/songwriter/guitarist/actor. Attended Kentucky's Georgetown University. Moved to Los Angeles in 1984; worked as an exotic dancer and car salesman. Formed backing band, Sly Dog, in 1986. Plays "Dr. Clint Cassidy" on the PAX-TV series Doc.					
				1)Achy Breaky Heart 2)Could've Been Me 3)Busy Man 4)In The Heart Of A Woman 5)She's Not Cryin' Anymore					
4/4/92	❶⁵	20	▲	1 Achy Breaky Heart (3 album snippets)		4	$4	■	Mercury 866522 (v)
				CMA Award: Single of the Year					
6/13/92	72	1		2 Some Gave All		—			album cut
				from the album Some Gave All on Mercury 510635; also see #6 below					
7/4/92	2¹	20		3 Could've Been Me (album version) / I'm So Miserable		72	$4	■	Mercury 866998 (v)
9/5/92+	6	20		4 She's Not Cryin' Anymore	Achy Breaky Heart (live)	70	$4	■	Mercury 864778 (v)
10/17/92	23	20		5 Wher'm I Gonna Live?	Some Gave All	—	$4		Mercury 864502
4/24/93	52	11		6 Some Gave All	Star Spangled Banner [R]	—	$4		Mercury 862094
7/3/93	3	20		7 In The Heart Of A Woman	Right Face Wrong Time	76	$4	■	Mercury 862448 (v)
10/23/93	9	20		8 Somebody New	Only Time Will Tell	104	$4	■	Mercury 862754 (v)
1/29/94	12	20		9 Words By Heart	Throwin' Stones	119	$4		Mercury 858132 (v)
6/4/94	63	2		10 Talk Some	Ain't Your Dog No More	—	$4		Mercury 858746
10/22/94	33	18		11 Storm In The Heartland	I Ain't Even Left	108	$4	■	Mercury 856260 (v)
2/4/95	66	4		12 Deja Blue	A Heart With Your Name On It	—	$4		Mercury 856482
8/19/95	75	1		13 The Fastest Horse In A One Horse Town	Cadillac Ranch (Rick Trevino)	—	$4		Columbia 77971
8/31/96	69	5		14 Trail Of Tears	Harper Valley P.T.A.	—	$4		Mercury 578304
2/8/97	65	6		15 Three Little Words		—			album cut
				from the album Trail Of Tears on Mercury 532829					
5/31/97	19	20		16 It's All The Same To Me	Achy Breaky Heart	—	$4		Mercury 574638
8/1/98	70	5		17 Time For Letting Go	Cover To Cover	—	$4		Mercury 568794

DEBUT	PEAK	WKS	Gold	A-side (Chart Hit)	B-side	Pop	$	Pic	Label & Number
				CYRUS, Billy Ray — Cont'd					
10/31/98+	3	27		18 Busy Man	Touchy Subject	46	$4		Mercury 566582
4/10/99	41	14		19 Give My Heart To You	Rock This Planet	—	$4		Mercury 870796
7/8/00	17	23		20 You Won't Be Lonely Now	S:5 Southern Rain	80	$4	★	Monument 79440 (v)
11/4/00	60	2		21 We The People	—				album cut
1/20/01	43	10		22 Burn Down The Trailer Park	—				album cut
4/21/01	58	1		23 Crazy 'Bout You Baby	—				album cut
6/9/01	45	10		24 Southern Rain	—			★	album cut (v)
				first released as the B-side of #20 above; above 4 from the album *Southern Rain* on Monument 62105					

D

DAFFAN('S), Ted, Texans '45
★347★
Born Theron Eugene Daffan on 9/21/12 in Beauregarde Parish, Louisiana; raised in Houston. Died of cancer on 10/6/96 (age 84). Singer/songwriter/guitarist. His Texans: Buddy Buller, Harry Sorensen and Freddy Courtney.

DEBUT	PEAK	WKS		A-side	B-side	Pop	$		Label & Number
1/8/44	2^3	8		1 No Letter Today /					
				Chuck Keeshan and Leon Seago (vocals)	—				
1/15/44	3	21		2 Born To Lose			$25		Okeh 6706
				#41 Pop hit for **Ray Charles** in 1962					
6/3/44	4	2		3 Look Who's Talkin'	Bluest Blues	—	$25		Okeh 6719
				Leon Seago (vocal, above 2)					
3/3/45	5	3		4 You're Breaking My Heart /					
2/24/45	6	2		5 Time Won't Heal My Broken Heart		—	$25		Okeh 6729
				Ted Daffan (vocal, above 2)					
9/1/45	2^3	13		6 Headin' Down The Wrong Highway /		—			
8/25/45	5	3		7 Shadow On My Heart		—	$25		Okeh 6744
				"Idaho" (vocal, above 2)					
10/26/46	5	3		8 Shut That Gate	Broken Vows	—	$20		Columbia 37087
				TED DAFFAN and His Texans					
				George Strange (vocal)					

DAISY, Pat '72
Born Patricia Key Deasy on 10/10/44 in Gallatin, Tennessee. Female singer.

2/19/72	20	13		1 Everybody's Reaching Out For Someone	I'll Be There	112	$6		RCA Victor 0637
7/29/72	48	7		2 Beautiful People	I Think I'm Falling	—	$6		RCA Victor 0743
				#38 Pop hit for **Kenny O'Dell** in 1967					
5/5/73	49	7		3 The Lonesomest Lonesome	I Was Meant For You And You Were Meant For Me	—	$6		RCA Victor 0932
10/13/73	53	9		4 My Love Is Deep, My Love Is Wide	You've Got Everything	—	$6		RCA Victor 0087

DALE, Kenny '79
★306★
Born Kenneth Dale Eoff on 10/3/51 in Artesia, New Mexico. Singer/songwriter/guitarist.
1) Only Love Can Break A Heart 2) Bluest Heartache Of The Year 3) Shame, Shame On Me

3/5/77	11	17		1 Bluest Heartache Of The Year	I'll Believe Every Word That You Lie	—	$5		Capitol 4389
7/30/77	11	14		2 Shame, Shame On Me (I Had Planned To Be Your Man)	Love Walked In Again	—	$5		Capitol 4457
1/21/78	17	14		3 Red Hot Memory	Love Walked In Again	—	$5		Capitol 4457
5/6/78	28	11		4 The Loser	This Is A Sad Song	—	$5		Capitol 4528
9/2/78	18	13		5 Two Hearts Tangled In Love	For Love	—	$5		Capitol 4570
4/21/79	16	11		6 Down To Earth Woman	Let's Make Love	—	$5		Capitol 4619
7/21/79	7	15		7 Only Love Can Break A Heart	Every Other Word Is You	—	$5		Capitol 4704
					Child Of The Wind		$5		Capitol 4746
				#2 Pop hit for **Gene Pitney** in 1962					
11/3/79	15	13		8 Sharing	Child Of The Wind	—	$5		Capitol 4788
2/23/80	23	10		9 Let Me In	Rainbow Man	—	$5		Capitol 4829
6/28/80	33	11		10 Thank You, Ever-Lovin'	There Are Women (Then There's My Woman)	—	$5		Capitol 4882
11/22/80+	31	13		11 When It's Just You And Me	If The World Should Ever Run Out Of Love	—	$5		Capitol 4943
3/6/82	65	6		12 Moanin The Blues	I Think I'm Losing You Again	—	$7		Funderburg 5001
1/28/84	85	6		13 Two Will Be One	One Of A Kind	—	$6		Republic 8301
9/1/84	86	3		14 Take It Slow		—	$6		Republic 8403
4/13/85	83	3		15 Look What Love Did To Me	I'm In Over My Heart	—	$6		Saba 9214
5/31/86	63	7		16 I'm Going Crazy	Macon Georgia Love	—	$6		BGM 30186

DALE, Terry '82
Male singer.

| 1/9/82 | 93 | 2 | | 1 Intimate Strangers | | — | $6 | | Lanedale 1001 |
| 3/27/82 | 73 | 4 | | 2 Loving You Is Always On My Mind | | — | $6 | | Lanedale 711 |

DALICE '90
Female singer.

| 1/6/90 | 87 | 2 | | Crazy Driver | | — | $6 | | Country Pride 0021 |

DALLAS, Johnny '67
Born on 3/6/37 in Plano, Texas.

| 12/24/66+ | 62 | 7 | | Heart Full Of Love | Gray Flannel World | — | $10 | | Little Darlin' 0013 |

DALTON, Bob '70
Born in Itman, West Virginia.

| 10/17/70 | 73 | 3 | | Mama, Call Me Home | Papa's Home | — | $6 | ■ | Mega 0003 |

DEBUT	PEAK	WKS	Gold	A-side (Chart Hit)	B-side	Pop	$	Pic	Label & Number

DALTON, Lacy J. ★176★   '81
Born Jill Byrem on 10/13/46 in Bloomsburg, Pennsylvania. Singer/songwriter/guitarist. Formed the psychedelic rock band Office in 1968. Recorded as Jill Croston in 1978.

1) Takin' It Easy   2) Everybody Makes Mistakes   3) 16th Avenue   4) Hard Times   5) Hillbilly Girl With The Blues

DEBUT	PEAK	WKS	#	A-side	B-side	Pop	$	Label & Number
10/6/79	17	13	1	Crazy Blue Eyes	Late Night Kind Of Lonesome	—	$4	Columbia 11107
2/2/80	18	12	2	Tennessee Waltz	Beer Drinkin' Song	—	$4	Columbia 11190
4/26/80	14	14	3	Losing Kind Of Love	Carolina Come-On	—	$4	Columbia 11253
8/30/80	7	14	4	Hard Times	Old Soldier	—	$4	Columbia 11343
12/13/80+	8	15	5	Hillbilly Girl With The Blues	Me 'N' You	—	$4	Columbia 11410
4/4/81	10	13	6	Whisper	China Doll	—	$4	Columbia 01036
7/18/81	2²	18	7	Takin' It Easy	Golden Memories	—	$4	Columbia 02188
12/5/81+	5	17	8	Everybody Makes Mistakes /		—		
		16	9	Wild Turkey		—	$4	Columbia 02637
5/1/82	13	15	10	Slow Down	One Of The Unsatisfied	106	$4	Columbia 02847
9/11/82	7	19	11	16th Avenue	You Can't Take The Texas Out Of Me	—	$4	Columbia 03184
3/12/83	30	14	12	It's A Dirty Job	Caught In The Spotlight	—	$5	Columbia 03628
				BOBBY BARE & LACY J. DALTON				
6/11/83	9	20	13	Dream Baby (How Long Must I Dream)	Hold Me Again	—	$4	Columbia 03926
				#4 Pop hit for Roy Orbison in 1962				
10/15/83	54	8	14	Windin' Down	Dixie Devil	—	$4	Columbia 04133
11/24/84+	15	20	15	If That Ain't Love	S:12 / A:16 Too Many Miles	—	$4	Columbia 04696
4/27/85	19	18	16	Size Seven Round (Made Of Gold)	S:17 / A:19 All I Want To Do In Life	—	$4	Epic 04876
				GEORGE JONES and LACY J. DALTON				
6/8/85	20	17	17	You Can't Run Away From Your Heart	S:19 / A:20 The Night Has A Heart Of It's Own	—	$4	Columbia 04884
10/19/85	58	8	18	The Night Has A Heart Of It's Own	Adios And Run	—	$4	Columbia 05644
1/18/86	43	16	19	Don't Fall In Love With Me	Over You	—	$4	Columbia 05759
6/14/86	16	19	20	Working Class Man	S:16 / A:16 Can't See Me Without You	—	$4	Columbia 06098
				#74 Pop hit for Jimmy Barnes in 1986				
12/6/86+	33	14	21	This Ol' Town	Up With The Wind	—	$4	Columbia 06360
1/28/89	13	16	22	The Heart	Hard Luck Ace	—	$4	Universal 53487
5/13/89	57	6	23	I'm A Survivor	Walking Wounded	—	$4	Universal 66007
7/22/89	38	10	24	Hard Luck Ace	Turn To The One	—	$4	Universal 66015
3/31/90	15	22	25	Black Coffee	I'm Right Here	—	$4	Capitol 44519

DALTON, Larry   '81
Born on 4/24/46 in Big Stone Gap, Virginia.

9/5/81	82	3		Cowboy	Too Many Nights	—	$5	Soundwaves 4645

LARRY DALTON and The Dalton Gang

DANDY   '80

4/14/79	57	6	1	Stay With Me	Come And Love Me	—	$5	Warner/Curb 8771
7/28/79	67	5	2	I Don't Want To Love You Anymore	Early Morning Love	—	$5	Warner/Curb 8880
12/1/79	71	6	3	I'm Just Your Yesterday	Number One Fan	—	$5	Warner/Curb 49111
10/18/80	54	7	4	Who Were You Thinkin' Of	Arizona Highways	49	$4	Columbia 11355

THE DOOLITTLE BAND
early pressings credit artist as: DANDY & THE DOOLITTLE BAND

DANIEL   '78
Born Daniel Willis on 11/23/53 in Washington DC.

6/25/77	91	3	1	But Tonight I'm Gonna Love You	Knight In Faded Blue Jeans	—	$7	LS 122
12/3/77	100	1	2	Stolen Moments	Knight In Faded Blue Jeans	—	$7	LS 136
7/29/78	78	5	3	I Bow My Head (When They Say Grace)	Where Does Love Go	—	$7	LS 166

DANIEL, Cooter   '80
Born on 11/9/56 in Knoxville, Tennessee. Owner of the Connection record label.

3/22/80	89	2		Where Are We Going From Here	One More Time Southern Style	—	$6	Connection 1

DANIEL, Davis   '91
Born Robert Andrykowski on 3/1/61 in Arlington Heights, Illinois; raised in Nebraska.

5/11/91	28	20	1	Picture Me	No Place To Go	—	$4	▌ Mercury 878972 (v)
8/31/91	13	20	2	For Crying Out Loud	No Place To Go	—	$4	▌ Mercury 868544 (v)
1/4/92	27	20	3	Fighting Fire With Fire	Across The Room To You	—	$4	Mercury 866132
5/9/92	48	13	4	Still Got A Crush On You	Down On My Knees	—	$4	Mercury 866822
4/30/94	74	2	5	I Miss Her Missing Me	Out Here Sits The King	—	$4	▌ Mercury 858568 (v)
9/3/94	64	6	6	William And Mary	Out Here Sits The King	—	$4	▌ Polydor 856032 (v)
1/28/95	58	9	7	Tyler	Shame On Me	—	$4	▌ Polydor 851398 (v)

DANIEL, Pebble   '80
Born on 7/28/47 in Waco, Texas. Died on 12/4/95 (age 48). Female singer.

6/21/80	86	3		Goodbye Eyes	Next To You	—	$5	Elektra 46643

DEBUT	PEAK	WKS	Gold	A-side (Chart Hit)	B-side	Pop	$	Pic	Label & Number
				DANIÉLLE, Tina '87 Born in Jena, Louisiana.					
11/15/86	75	4		1 Standing Too Close To The Moon	Treat Him Like A Dog	—	$5		Charta 202
2/14/87	71	5		2 Burned Out	Lady Blue	—	$5		Charta 204
5/9/87	73	4		3 Warmed Over Romance	Maybe Maybe	—	$5		Charta 206
				DANIELS, Charlie ★194★ '79 Born on 10/28/36 in Wilmington, North Carolina. Singer/songwriter/fiddler. His band included: Tom Crain (guitar), Joe "Taz" DiGregorio (keyboards), Charles Hayward (bass) and James W. Marshall & Fred Edwards (drums). Marshall and Edwards left in 1986; replaced by Jack Gavin. Group appeared in the movie *Urban Cowboy*. 1)The Devil Went Down To Georgia 2)Drinkin' My Baby Goodbye 3)Boogie Woogie Fiddle Country Blues 4)Simple Man 5)In America					
8/4/73	67	6		1 Uneasy Rider	Funky Junky [N]	9	$6		Kama Sutra 576
				CHARLIE DANIELS BAND:					
1/31/76	36	11		2 Texas	Everything Is Kinda Allright	91	$6		Kama Sutra 607
6/26/76	22	11		3 Wichita Jail	It's My Life	—	$5		Epic 50243
1/22/77	75	4		4 Billy The Kid	Slow Song	—	$5		Epic 50322
10/22/77	85	5		5 Heaven Can Be Anywhere (Twin Pines Theme)	Good Ole Boy	—	$5		Epic 50456
6/30/79	❶¹	14	▲	6 The Devil Went Down To Georgia	Rainbow Ride	3	$4		Epic 50700
				CMA Award: Single of the Year; also see #29 & #30 below					
10/6/79	19	11		7 Mississippi	Passing Lane	—	$4		Epic 50768
1/12/80	87	4		8 Behind Your Eyes	Blue Star	—	$4		Epic 50806
2/23/80	27	10		9 Long Haired Country Boy	Sweet Louisiana	—	$4		Epic 50845
				same version was a #56 Pop hit in 1975 on Kama Sutra 601 ($5)					
6/7/80	13	11		10 In America	Blue Star	11	$4		Epic 50888
9/6/80	80	4		11 The Legend Of Wooley Swamp	Money	31	$4		Epic 50921
12/27/80+	44	10		12 Carolina (I Remember You)	South Sea Song	—	$4		Epic 50955
7/25/81	94	2		13 Sweet Home Alabama	Falling In Love For The Night (w/Crystal Gayle)	110	$4	☐	Epic 02185
				#8 Pop hit for Lynyrd Skynyrd in 1974					
7/17/82	76	4		14 Ragin' Cajun	The Universal Hand	109	$4		Epic 02995
10/16/82	69	5		15 We Had It All One Time	Makes You Want To Go Home	—	$4		Epic 03251
8/13/83	65	6		16 Stroker's Theme	El Toreador	—	$4		Epic 03918
				from the movie *Stroker Ace* starring Burt Reynolds					
10/5/85	54	10		17 American Farmer	Runnin' With That Crowd	—	$4		Epic 05638
12/7/85+	33	17		18 Still Hurtin' Me	S:29 American Rock And Roll	—	$4	■	Epic 05699
3/22/86	8	22		19 Drinkin' My Baby Goodbye	S:7 / A:7 Ever Changing Lady	—	$4		Epic 05835
8/20/88	10	17		20 Boogie Woogie Fiddle Country Blues	S:4 Working Man You Got It All	—	$4		Epic 08002
1/21/89	36	11		21 Cowboy Hat In Dallas	Uneasy Rider '88	—	$4		Epic 68542
4/22/89	43	9		22 Midnight Train	Get Me Back To Dixie	—	$4		Epic 68738
10/14/89+	12	26		23 Simple Man	Ill Wind	—	$4		Epic 73030
2/24/90	34	18		24 Mister DJ	It's My Life	—	$4		Epic 73236
8/25/90	56	5		25 (What This World Needs Is) A Few More Rednecks	It's My Life	—	$4	■	Epic 73426 (v)
				CHARLIE DANIELS:					
4/27/91	65	7		26 Honky Tonk Life	Willie Jones	—	$4	■	Epic 73768 (v)
11/2/91	47	14		27 Little Folks	Let Freedom Ring	—	$4		Epic 74061
3/20/93	73	2		28 America, I Believe In You		—			album cut
				from the album *America, I Believe In You* on Liberty 80477					
12/25/93+	54	10		29 The Devil Comes Back To Georgia	Diggy Liggy Lo	—	$4		Warner 18342
				MARK O'CONNOR With Charlie Daniels Johnny Cash, Marty Stuart and Travis Tritt (guest vocals); sequel to #6 above					
6/20/98	60	7		30 The Devil Went Down To Georgia [R]	—				album cut
				same version as #6 above; from the album *Super Hits* on Epic 64182					
9/23/00	31	21		31 All Night Long	S:7 Merry Christmas From The Family	47ˢ	$4	★	Columbia 79515
				MONTGOMERY GENTRY Featuring Charlie Daniels					
11/10/01	33	13		32 This Ain't No Rag, It's A Flag		—			album cut
				from the album *The Live Record* on Blue Hat 8133					
				DANIELS, Clint '98 Born on 8/24/74 in Panama City, Florida. Singer/songwriter/guitarist.					
6/13/98	44	12		1 A Fool's Progress	Swing Through Dallas	—	$4		Arista 13126
10/17/98	53	9		2 When I Grow Up	Long Way Down	—	$4		Arista 13137
				DARIN, Bobby '58 Born Walden Robert Cassotto on 5/14/36 in New York City. Died of heart failure on 12/20/73 (age 37). Charted 41 pop hits from 1958-73.					
8/4/58	14	3	●	Splish Splash	S:14 Judy, Don't Be Moody	3	$25		Atco 6117
				DARLING, Helen '95 Born on 5/1/65 in Baton Rouge, Louisiana; raised in Houston.					
8/5/95	69	3		Jenny Come Back	When The Butterflies Have Flown Away	—	$4	■	Decca 55060

DEBUT	PEAK	WKS	Gold	A-side (Chart Hit)	B-side	Pop	$	Pic	Label & Number
	★294★			**DARRELL, Johnny** '68 Born on 7/23/40 in Hopewell, Alabama. Died on 10/7/97 (age 57). Singer/songwriter/guitarist. *1)With Pen In Hand 2)Ruby, Don't Take Your Love To Town 3)Why You Been Gone So Long*					
12/25/65+	30	7		1 As Long As The Wind Blows	Beggars Can't Be Choosers	—	$10		United Artists 943
6/4/66	44	3		2 Johnny Lose It All	For Old Time Sake	—	$8		United Artists 50008
11/12/66	72	4		3 She's Mighty Gone	The Baby Sitter	—	$8		United Artists 50047
				written by **Johnny Cash** and **June Carter**					
4/1/67	9	15		4 Ruby, Don't Take Your Love To Town	The Little Things I Love	—	$8		United Artists 50126
7/22/67	73	3		5 My Elusive Dreams	Pickin' White Gold	—	$8		United Artists 50183
10/7/67	37	10		6 Come See What's Left Of Your Man	Passin' Through	—	$8		United Artists 50207
12/23/67+	22	14		7 The Son Of Hickory Holler's Tramp	But That's Alright	—	$8	■	United Artists 50235
				#40 Pop hit for O.C. Smith in 1968					
4/27/68	3	18		8 With Pen In Hand	Poetry Of Love	126	$8		United Artists 50292
				#35 Pop hit for Vikki Carr in 1969					
9/21/68	27	10		9 I Ain't Buying	Little Things	—	$8		United Artists 50442
11/30/68+	20	13		10 Woman Without Love	I Fought The Law	—	$8		United Artists 50481
4/12/69	50	7		11 The Coming Of The Roads	The Other Side Of The Coin	—	$8		United Artists 50503
				JOHNNY DARRELL & ANITA CARTER					
4/26/69	17	13		12 Why You Been Gone So Long	You're Always The One	—	$8		United Artists 50518
9/13/69	23	10		13 River Bottom	Ain't That Livin'	—	$8		United Artists 50572
2/14/70	68	7		14 Mama Come'n Get Your Baby Boy	These Days	—	$8		United Artists 50629
7/11/70	75	2		15 Brother River	Bed Of Roses	—	$8		United Artists 50675
11/14/70	74	2		16 They'll Never Take Her Love From Me	One Love, Two Hearts, Three Lives	—	$8		United Artists 50716
7/28/73	66	10		17 Dakota The Dancing Bear	Just A Memory	—	$6		Monument 8579
10/12/74	63	9		18 Orange Blossom Special	Glendale, Arizona	—	$6		Capricorn 0207
				DARREN, James '78 Born James Ercolani on 10/3/36 in Philadelphia. Singer/actor. Acted in several movies. Played "Tony Newman" on TV's *The Time Tunnel* and "Jim Corrigan" on *T.J. Hooker*. Charted 10 pop hits from 1959-77.					
7/29/78	53	9		Let Me Take You In My Arms Again	California	—	$5		RCA 11316
				written by **Neil Diamond**					
	★207★			**DAVE & SUGAR** '79 Trio consisting of **Dave Rowland** (born on 1/24/42), Vicki Hackeman (born on 8/4/50) and Jackie Frantz (born on 10/8/50). Trio worked as backup singers for **Charley Pride** in 1977. Frantz was replaced by Sue Powell. Hackeman was replaced by Melissa Dean in 1979. Powell was replaced by Jamie Jaye in 1980. Rowland went solo in 1982. *1)Golden Tears 2)The Door Is Always Open 3)Tear Time 4)I'm Knee Deep In Loving You 5)I'm Gonna Love You*					
11/15/75+	25	17		1 Queen Of The Silver Dollar	Fools	—	$4		RCA Victor 10425
4/17/76	❶¹	19		2 The Door Is Always Open	Late Nite Country Lovin' Music	—	$4		RCA Victor 10625
9/11/76	3	17		3 I'm Gonna Love You	I'm Leavin' The Leavin' To You	—	$4		RCA 10768
2/12/77	5	13		4 Don't Throw It All Away	Queen Of My Heart	—	$4		RCA 10876
7/16/77	7	14		5 That's The Way Love Should Be	It's A Beautiful Morning With You	—	$4		RCA 11034
10/29/77	2⁴	16		6 I'm Knee Deep In Loving You	Livin' At The End Of The Rainbow	—	$4		RCA 11141
4/8/78	4	14		7 Gotta' Quit Lookin' At You Baby	We Are The One	—	$4		RCA 11251
8/12/78	❶¹	16		8 Tear Time	Easy To Love	—	$4	■	RCA 11322
1/20/79	❶³	14		9 Golden Tears	Feel Like A Little Love	—	$4		RCA 11427
6/30/79	6	13		10 Stay With Me	What I Feel Is You	—	$4		RCA 11654
10/20/79	4	14		11 My World Begins And Ends With You /		—	$4		RCA 11749
		14		12 Why Did You Have To Be So Good					
4/5/80	18	12		13 New York Wine And Tennessee Shine	Learnin' To Feel Love Again	—	$4		RCA 11947
8/16/80	40	8		14 A Love Song	Things To Do (Without You)	—	$4		RCA 12063
2/7/81	32	9		15 It's A Heartache	It Ain't Easy Lovin' Me	—	$4		RCA 12168
				DAVE ROWLAND & SUGAR:					
5/9/81	6	15		16 Fool By Your Side	Don't Let Our Dreams Die Young	—	$4		Elektra 47135
8/29/81	32	8		17 The Pleasure's All Mine	One Step At A Time	—	$4		Elektra 47177
				DAVE ROWLAND:					
5/15/82	77	5		18 Natalie /					
		5		19 Why Didn't I Think Of That		—	$4		Elektra 47442
7/31/82	84	3		20 Lovin' Our Lives Away	Women & Wine	—	$4		Elektra 69998
				DAVIDSON, Clay '00 Born in Saltville, Virginia. Singer/guitarist.					
1/15/00	3	31		1 Unconditional	S:7 My Best Friend And Me	49	$4	★	Virgin 38690 (v)
7/29/00	26	20		2 I Can't Lie To Me	Doghouse Rights	117	$4		Virgin 38727
1/27/01	21	20		3 Sometimes	We're All Here	112	$4		Virgin 58981
	★210★			**DAVIES, Gail** '81 Born Patricia Gail Dickerson on 6/5/48 in Broken Bow, Oklahoma. Singer/songwriter/guitarist. Did session work in Los Angeles and worked as a staff writer for Vogue Music. Moved to Nashville in the mid-1970s. Lead singer with the **Wild Choir** in 1986. *1)I'll Be There (If You Ever Want Me) 2)It's A Lovely, Lovely World 3)Blue Heartache 4)'Round The Clock Lovin' 5)Grandma's Song*					
7/8/78	26	12		1 No Love Have I	It's No Wonder I Feel Blue	—	$5		Lifesong 1771
10/21/78	27	12		2 Poison Love	Bucket To The South	—	$5		Lifesong 1777
2/10/79	11	16		3 Someone Is Looking For Someone Like You	Soft Spoken Man	—	$5		Lifesong 1784
11/17/79+	7	16		4 Blue Heartache	When I Had You In My Arms	—	$4		Warner 49108
3/22/80	21	11		5 Like Strangers	Love Is Living Around Us	—	$4		Warner 49199
				#22 Pop hit for **The Everly Brothers** in 1960					
6/28/80	21	12		6 Good Lovin' Man	Careless Love	—	$4		Warner 49263

DEBUT	PEAK	WKS	Gold	A-side (Chart Hit)..B-side	Pop	$	Pic	Label & Number
				DAVIES, Gail — Cont'd				
11/29/80+	4	16		7 I'll Be There (If You Ever Want Me) .... Farewell Song	—	$4		Warner 49592
4/4/81	5	18		8 It's A Lovely, Lovely World .... I'm Hungry, I'm Tired	—	$4		Warner 49694
8/15/81	9	15		9 Grandma's Song .... Mama's Gonna Give You Sweet Things	—	$4		Warner 49790
2/13/82	9	18		10 'Round The Clock Lovin' .... It's Amazing What A Little Love Can Do	—	$4		Warner 50004
6/26/82	17	15		11 You Turn Me On I'm A Radio .... All The Fire Is Gone	—	$4		Warner 29972
				#25 Pop hit for Joni Mitchell in 1973				
10/30/82+	24	15		12 Hold On .... Dawn	—	$4		Warner 29892
3/26/83	17	15		13 Singing The Blues .... Movin' (I Might Decide To Stay)	—	$4		Warner 29726
				#1 Pop hit for Guy Mitchell in 1956				
10/15/83	18	19		14 You're A Hard Dog (To Keep Under The Porch) ...... The Boy In You Is Showing	—	$4		Warner 29472
2/25/84	19	17		15 Boys Like You .... What Can I Say	—	$4		Warner 29374
8/4/84	55	12		16 It's You Alone .... Following You Around	—	$4		Warner 29219
10/6/84	20	25		17 Jagged Edge Of A Broken Heart .... A:18 / S:20 Lion In The Winter	—	$4	■	RCA 13912
2/23/85	37	12		18 Nothing Can Hurt Me Now .... Lovin' Me Too	—	$4		RCA 14017
6/22/85	56	8		19 Unwed Fathers .... Different Train Of Thought	—	$4		RCA 14095
9/21/85	15	25		20 Break Away .... S:12 / A:15 Not A Day Goes By	—	$4		RCA 14184
3/11/89	50	10		21 Waiting Here For You .... Meet Me Halfway	—	$4		MCA 53505
6/24/89	69	4		22 Hearts In The Wind .... I Will Rise And Shine Again	—	$4		MCA 53442
				DAVIS, Carrie **'89**				
3/4/89	84	3		Another Heart To Break The Fall .... I'm Just Looking For The Real Thing	—	$6		Fountain Hills 130
				DAVIS, Danny, & The Nashville Brass **'80**				
				Born George Nowlan on 4/29/25 in Dorchester, Massachusetts. Trumpet player/bandleader educated at the New England Conservatory of Music. Played with many swing bands including Gene Krupa, Bob Crosby, Freddy Martin, Blue Barron, and Sammy Kaye. Producer for Joy and MGM Records in the late '50s. Production assistant to **Chet Atkins** in 1965. Owner of the Wartrace record label. Formed The Nashville Brass in 1968.				
1/3/70	68	3		1 Please Help Me, I'm Falling .... Anna	—	$8		RCA Victor 0287
				HANK LOCKLIN AND DANNY DAVIS AND THE NASHVILLE BRASS				
2/14/70	63	3		2 Wabash Cannon Ball .... Sweet Dreams [I]	131	$8		RCA Victor 9785
6/27/70	56	6		3 Flying South .... Rosalita	—	$8		RCA Victor 9849
				HANK LOCKLIN AND DANNY DAVIS AND THE NASHVILLE BRASS				
7/4/70	70	2		4 Columbus Stockade Blues .... Wings Of A Dove [I]	—	$8		RCA Victor 9847
10/15/77	91	6		5 How I Love Them Old Songs .... Tara Jeanne	—	$5		RCA 11073
2/2/80	20	12		6 Night Life .... December Day	—	$5		RCA 11893
				DANNY DAVIS AND WILLIE NELSON With The Nashville Brass				
5/17/80	41	8		7 Funny How Time Slips Away .... The Local Memory	—	$5		RCA 11999
				DANNY DAVIS AND WILLIE NELSON with The Nashville Brass				
3/23/85	82	3		8 I Dropped Your Name	—	$5		Wartrace 730
				Arlene Baird (vocal)				
10/10/87	62	5		9 Green Eyes (Cryin' Those Blue Tears) .... Little Pink Cloud	—	$5		Jaroco 8742
				DANNY DAVIS AND THE NASHVILLE BRASS AND DONA MASON				
				DAVIS, Dianne **'89**				
				Born in Celina, Tennessee.				
7/29/89	75	4		Baby Don't Go	—	$4		16th Avenue 70430
				DAVIS, Gene **'76**				
11/27/76	97	4		Oh Those Texas Women .... She Says It With Love	—	$6		Maverick 301
				DAVIS, Jimmie **'45**				
				Born on 9/11/1899 in Beech Grove, Louisiana. Died on 11/5/2000 (age 101). Singer/songwriter/guitarist. Acted in the movies *Strictly In The Groove*, *Frontier Fury*, *Louisiana* and *Square Dance Katy*. Governor of Louisiana from 1944-48 and 1960-64. Elected to the Country Music Hall of Fame in 1972.				
9/2/44	3	2		1 Is It Too Late Now /				
9/30/44	4	2		2 There's A Chill On The Hill Tonight	—	$40		Decca 6100
2/17/45	●1	18		3 There's A New Moon Over My Shoulder ...... Love Please Don't Let Me Down	—	$40		Decca 6105
3/2/46	4	1		4 Grievin' My Heart Out For You .... I'm Sorry If That's The Way You Feel	—	$40		Decca 18756
1/18/47	4	2		5 Bang Bang .... I'm Gonna Write Myself A Letter	—	$30		Decca 46016
6/16/62	15	9		6 Where The Old Red River Flows .... Lonesome Whistle	—	$20		Decca 31368
				DAVIS, Joey **'78**				
				Born in Waynesboro, Virginia.				
8/12/78	99	1		1 Why Don't You Leave Me Alone	—	$6		MRC 1017
12/16/78	94	3		2 Takin' It Easy .... Got My Throttle Wide Open	—	$6		MRC 1023
		★399★		**DAVIS, Linda** **'96**				
				Born on 11/26/62 in Dodson, Texas. Former jingle singer. In duo **Skip & Linda**. Married to **Lang Scott**.				
				1)Some Things Are Meant To Be 2)I Wanna Remember This 3)A Love Story In The Making				
10/29/88	50	10		1 All The Good One's Are Taken .... Cry Baby	—	$4		Epic 08057
2/4/89	51	6		2 Back In The Swing Again .... All The Good One's Are Taken	—	$4		Epic 68544
6/10/89	67	5		3 Weak Nights .... All The Good One's Are Taken	—	$4		Epic 68919
1/12/91	61	7		4 In A Different Light /				
5/4/91	68	5		5 Some Kinda Woman	—	$4		Capitol 44684 (v)
2/26/94	43	13		6 Company Time	—	$4	■	Arista 12664 (v)
6/18/94	58	8		7 Love Didn't Do It .... How Can I Make You Love Me	—	$4	■	Arista 12701 (v)
12/2/95+	13	20		8 Some Things Are Meant To Be .... S:12 He's In Dallas / There Isn't One	—	$4	■	Arista 12896 (v)
4/13/96	33	19		9 A Love Story In The Making .... What Do I Know	—	$4	■	Arista 12991 (v)
5/16/98	20	21		10 I Wanna Remember This	—			album cut
				from the movie *Black Dog* starring Patrick Swayze (soundtrack on Decca 70027)				

DEBUT	PEAK	WKS	Gold	A-side (Chart Hit)	B-side	Pop	$	Pic	Label & Number
				DAVIS, Linda — Cont'd					
10/31/98+	38	19		11 I'm Yours	Some Things Are Meant To Be	—	$4	★	DreamWorks 59015
4/3/99	60	7		12 From The Inside Out		—			album cut
				from the album *I'm Yours* on DreamWorks 50100					
				DAVIS, Mac ★181★					'81
				Born Scott Davis on 1/21/42 in Lubbock, Texas. Singer/songwriter/guitarist. Worked as a regional rep for Vee-Jay and Liberty Records. Acted in several movies. Host of own musical variety TV series from 1974-76.					
				1) Hooked On Music 2) You're My Bestest Friend 3) Texas In My Rear View Mirror 4) Let's Keep It That Way					
				5) It's Hard To Be Humble					
4/25/70	43	13		1 Whoever Finds This, I Love You	Half And Half (Song For Sarah)	53	$6	■	Columbia 45117
8/29/70	68	4		2 I'll Paint You A Song	Closest I Ever Came	110	$6		Columbia 45192
				from the movie *Norwood* starring Glen Campbell					
8/26/72	26	11	●	3 Baby Don't Get Hooked On Me	Poem For My Little Lady	❶³	$5		Columbia 45618
2/24/73	47	8		4 Dream Me Home	Spread Your Love On Me	73	$5		Columbia 45773
5/12/73	36	11		5 Your Side Of The Bed	(Hope You Didn't) Chop No Wood	88	$5		Columbia 45839
9/1/73	29	15		6 Kiss It And Make It Better	Sunshine	105	$5		Columbia 45911
9/7/74	40	12		7 Stop And Smell The Roses	Poor Boy Boogie	9	$5		Columbia 10018
1/4/75	29	11		8 Rock N' Roll (I Gave You The Best Years Of My Life)	Emily Suzanne	15	$5		Columbia 10070
4/12/75	69	6		9 (If You Add) All The Love In The World	Smiley	54	$5		Columbia 10111
6/7/75	31	12		10 Burnin' Thing	A Special Place In Heaven	53	$5		Columbia 10148
9/27/75	81	5		11 I Still Love You (You Still Love Me)	The Hits Just Keep On Coming	—	$5		Columbia 10187
3/27/76	17	13		12 Forever Lovers	The Love Lamp	76	$5		Columbia 10304
10/9/76	34	10		13 Every Now And Then	I'm Just In Love	—	$5		Columbia 10418
5/21/77	42	9		14 Picking Up The Pieces Of My Life	Do It (With Someone You Love)	—	$5		Columbia 10535
6/10/78	92	5		15 Music In My Life	You Are	—	$5		Columbia 10745
3/22/80	10	12		16 It's Hard To Be Humble	The Greatest Gift Of All [N]	43	$4		Casablanca 2244
7/12/80	10	15		17 Let's Keep It That Way	I Know You're Out There Somewhere	—	$4		Casablanca 2286
10/11/80	9	17		18 Texas In My Rear View Mirror	Sad Songs	51	$4		Casablanca 2305
2/21/81	2²	15		19 Hooked On Music	Me And Fat Boy	102	$4		Casablanca 2327
7/18/81	47	10		20 Secrets	Remember When (Beverly's Song)	76	$4		Casablanca 2336
10/24/81+	5	18		21 You're My Bestest Friend	You Are So Lovely	106	$4		Casablanca 2341
5/29/82	37	10		22 Rodeo Clown	Dammit Girl	—	$4		Casablanca 2350
9/25/82	58	8		23 The Beer Drinkin' Song	You Are So Lovely	—	$4		Casablanca 2355
12/18/82+	62	7		24 Lying Here Lying	The Quiet Times	—	$4		Casablanca 2363
2/11/84	41	14		25 Most Of All	Springtime Down In Dixie	—	$4		Casablanca 818168
5/19/84	76	5		26 Caroline's Still In Georgia	I've Got A Dream	—	$4		Casablanca 818929
5/25/85	10	24		27 I Never Made Love (Till I Made Love With You)	S:9 / A:10 I Think I'm Gonna Rain	—	$4		MCA 52573
10/5/85	34	16		28 I Feel The Country Callin' Me	Rainy Day Lovin'	—	$4		MCA 52669
2/1/86	46	9		29 Sexy Young Girl	A Special Place In Heaven	—	$4		MCA 52765
6/7/86	65	5		30 Somewhere In America	I Need A Hug	—	$4		MCA 52826
				DAVIS, Paul					'60
				One Of Her Fools	When You Fall	—	$25		Doke 107
7/18/60	28	5							
				DAVIS, Paul					'88
				Born on 4/21/48 in Meridian, Mississippi. Singer/songwriter/producer. Charted 15 pop hits from 1970-82.					
1/11/75	47	8		1 Ride 'Em Cowboy	I'm The Only Sinner (In Salt Lake City)	23	$5		Bang 712
12/16/78+	85	4		2 Sweet Life	Bad Dream	17	$5		Bang 738
				also see #5 below					
8/30/86	❶¹	21		3 You're Still New To Me	S:❶¹ / A:❶¹ New Love	—	$4	■	Curb/Capitol 5613
				MARIE OSMOND WITH PAUL DAVIS					
11/21/87+	❶¹	24		4 I Won't Take Less Than Your Love	S:2 Heartbreaker	—	$4		Capitol 44100
				TANYA TUCKER with PAUL DAVIS & PAUL OVERSTREET					
8/20/88	47	8		5 Sweet Life	Somebody Else's Moon	—	$4		Curb/Capitol 44215
				MARIE OSMOND (with Paul Davis)					
				DAVIS, Sammy Jr.					'82
				Born on 12/8/25 in New York City. Died of throat cancer on 5/16/90 (age 64). Singer/dancer/actor. Numerous appearances on TV, Broadway and in movies. Charted 17 pop hits from 1955-72.					
12/11/82	89	2		Smoke, Smoke, Smoke (That Cigarette)	We Could Have Been The Closest Of Friends	—	$5		Applause 100

DEBUT	PEAK	WKS	Gold	A-side (Chart Hit)	B-side	Pop	$	Pic	Label & Number

A Hillbilly Singer

DAVIS, Skeeter ★116★   '63
Born Mary Frances Penick on 12/30/31 in Dry Ridge, Kentucky. Worked as **The Davis Sisters** with friend Betty Jack Davis, and later with Georgia Davis. Went solo in 1956. Joined the *Grand Ole Opry* in 1959. Married to **Ralph Emery** from 1960-64. Married to Joey Spampinato, the bassist of rock band NRBQ, from 1983-96. Also see **Some Of Chet's Friends**.

1) The End Of The World   2) (I Can't Help You) I'm Falling Too   3) What Does It Take (To Keep A Man Like You Satisfied)
4) My Last Date (With You)   5) Set Him Free

DEBUT	PEAK	WKS	#	A-side	B-side	Pop	$	Label & Number
2/24/58	15	1	1	Lost To A Geisha Girl A:15	I'm Going Steady With A Heartache	—	$15	RCA Victor 7084
				answer to "Geisha Girl" by Hank Locklin				
3/30/59	5	17	2	Set Him Free	The Devil's Doll	—	$15	RCA Victor 7471
				also see #24 below				
9/21/59	15	13	3	Homebreaker		—	$15	RCA Victor 7570
3/7/60	11	12	4	Am I That Easy To Forget?	Give Me Death	—	$15	RCA Victor 7671
8/29/60	2^3	16	5	(I Can't Help You) I'm Falling Too	No Never	39	$12	RCA Victor 7767
				answer to "Please Help Me, I'm Falling" by Hank Locklin				
12/31/60+	5	13	6	My Last Date (With You)	Someone I'd Like To Forget	26	$12	RCA Victor 7825
				answer to "Last Date" by Floyd Cramer				
4/24/61	11	11	7	The Hand You're Holding Now	Someday, Someday	—	$12	RCA Victor 7863
10/16/61	10	11	8	Optimistic	Blueberry Hill	—	$12	RCA Victor 7928
3/10/62	9	9	9	Where I Ought To Be /			—	
6/2/62	23	3	10	Something Precious		—		RCA Victor 7979
9/8/62	22	1	11	The Little Music Box	The Final Step	—	$12	RCA Victor 8055
12/15/62+	2^3	24	12	The End Of The World	Somebody Loves You	2^1	$12	RCA Victor 8098
5/25/63	9	14	13	I'm Saving My Love	Somebody Else On Your Mind	41	$12	RCA Victor 8176
10/12/63	14	10	14	I Can't Stay Mad At You	It Was Only A Heart	7	$12	RCA Victor 8219 ■
1/25/64	17	15	15	He Says The Same Things To Me	How Much Can A Lonely Heart Stand (Pop #92)	47	$12	RCA Victor 8288
5/16/64	8	14	16	Gonna Get Along Without You Now	Now You're Gone	48	$12	RCA Victor 8347
				#11 Pop hit for Patience & Prudence in 1956				
9/26/64	45	4	17	Let Me Get Close To You	The Face Of A Clown	106	$12	RCA Victor 8397
11/14/64	38	5	18	What Am I Gonna Do With You	Don't Let Me Stand In Your Way	123	$12	RCA Victor 8450
3/13/65	11	12	19	A Dear John Letter	Too Used To Being With You	114	$12	RCA Victor 8496
				SKEETER DAVIS & BOBBY BARE				
				#44 Pop hit for Pat Boone in 1960				
9/11/65	30	7	20	Sun Glasses	He Loved Me Too Little	120	$10	RCA Victor 8642
10/15/66	36	9	21	Goin' Down The Road (Feelin' Bad)	I Can't Stand The Sight Of You	—	$10	RCA Victor 8932
1/28/67	11	16	22	Fuel To The Flame	You Call This Love	—	$10	RCA Victor 9058
				co-written by Dolly Parton				
7/22/67	5	18	23	What Does It Take (To Keep A Man Like You Satisfied)	What I Go Thru (To Keep Holding On to you)	121	$10	RCA Victor 9242
12/16/67+	52	7	24	Set Him Free	Is It Worth It To You [R]	—	$10	RCA Victor 9371
				new version of #2 above				
2/24/68	72	2	25	For Loving You	Baby It's Cold Outside [N]	—	$8	RCA Victor 9415
				SKEETER DAVIS AND DON BOWMAN				
3/23/68	54	7	26	Instinct For Survival	How In The World	—	$8	RCA Victor 9459
6/22/68	16	10	27	There's A Fool Born Every Minute	I Can't See Past My Tears	—	$8	RCA Victor 9543
1/11/69	66	7	28	The Closest Thing To Love (I've Ever Seen)	Mama Your Big Girl's 'Bout To Cry	—	$8	RCA Victor 9695
12/13/69+	9	15	29	I'm A Lover (Not A Fighter)	I Didn't Cry Today	—	$8	RCA Victor 0292
1/24/70	22	7	30	Your Husband, My Wife	Before The Sunrise	—	$6	RCA Victor 9789
				BOBBY BARE AND SKEETER DAVIS				
5/9/70	65	5	31	It's Hard To Be A Woman	What A Little Girl Don't Know	—	$7	RCA Victor 9818
8/8/70	69	3	32	We Need A Lot More Of Jesus	When You Gonna Bring Our Soldiers Home	—	$7	RCA Victor 9871
9/26/70	65	2	33	Let's Get Together	Everything Is Beautiful	—	$7	RCA Victor 9893
				SKEETER DAVIS AND GEORGE HAMILTON IV				
				#5 Pop hit for The Youngbloods in 1969				
3/6/71	21	13	34	Bus Fare To Kentucky	From Her Arms Into Mine	—	$7	RCA Victor 9961
7/17/71	58	8	35	Love Takes A Lot Of My Time	Love, Love, Love	—	$7	RCA Victor 9997
1/8/72	54	7	36	One Tin Soldier	Rachel	—	$7	RCA Victor 0608
				#26 Pop hit for Coven in 1971; from the movie Billy Jack starring Tom Laughlin				
5/20/72	46	8	37	Sad Situation	All I Ever Wanted Was Love	—	$7	RCA Victor 0681
6/16/73	12	17	38	I Can't Believe That It's All Over	Try Jesus	101	$7	RCA Victor 0968
12/15/73+	44	10	39	Don't Forget To Remember	Baby, Get That Leavin' Off Your Mind	—	$7	RCA Victor 0188
				#73 Pop hit for the Bee Gees in 1969				
5/25/74	65	8	40	One More Time	Stay Awhile With Me	—	$7	RCA Victor 0277
9/18/76	60	7	41	I Love Us	It Feels So Good	—	$6		Mercury 73818

DAVIS, Stephanie   '93
Born in Montana. Singer/songwriter.

8/28/93	72	2		It's All In The Heart	Summer Nights In Dixie	—	$4	■ Asylum 64616 (v)

DAVIS SISTERS, The   *Sister roll*   '53
Vocal duo from Lexington, Kentucky. **Skeeter Davis** and Betty Jack Davis. The two were *not* related. Betty Jack was killed and Skeeter was seriously injured in a car crash on 8/2/53. Betty Jack was replaced by her sister Georgia.

8/15/53	❶[8]	26		I Forgot More Than You'll Ever Know A:❶[8] / S:❶[6] / J:❶[2] Rock-A-Bye Boogie	18	$25		RCA Victor 5345

DAWSON, Peter, Band   '00
Born in 1979 in Dallas. Singer/songwriter/guitarist.

10/21/00	72	1		Willie Nelson For President	Bad News [N]	—	$4	★ Radio 31002

→ A SUPER song.

DEBUT	PEAK	WKS	Gold	A-side (Chart Hit)..B-side	Pop	$	Pic	Label & Number
				DAY, Jennifer '00 Born on 8/22/79 in McAlpin, Florida.				
12/4/99+	31	20		1 The Fun Of Your Love...S:5 *What If It's Me*	46^S	$4	★	BNA 65939 (v)
6/3/00	67	3		2 What If It's Me...*Fearless*	—	$4		BNA 60239
				DEAL, Don '79 Born in 1939 in Iowa. Singer/songwriter/guitarist.				
6/16/79	90	2		Second Best (Is Too Far Down The Line)..*When*	—	$7		Donjim 1008

DEAN, Billy ★187★ '91
Born on 4/1/62 in Quincy, Florida. Singer/songwriter/guitarist. Attenended college in Decatur, Mississippi, on a basketball scholarship. Also see **America The Beautiful**.

1) Buy Me A Rose 2) Somewhere In My Broken Heart 3) If There Hadn't Been You 4) Only Here For A Little While
5) You Don't Count The Cost

Let 'Em Be Little

DEBUT	PEAK	WKS		A-side	B-side	Pop	$	Pic	Label & Number
12/22/90+	3	22		1 Only Here For A Little While		—			album cut
				from the album *Young Man* on Capitol 94302					
5/4/91	3	20		2 Somewhere In My Broken Heart	*Young Man*	—	$4	■	Capitol 44757
9/14/91	4	20		3 You Don't Count The Cost	*She's Taken*	—	$4		Capitol 44773
1/4/92	4	20		4 Only The Wind	*Simple Things*	—	$4		Capitol 44803
5/23/92	4	20		5 Billy The Kid	*Simple Things*	—	$4		Liberty 57745
8/29/92	3	20		6 If There Hadn't Been You	*Small Favors*	—	$4		Liberty 57884
12/12/92+	6	20		7 Tryin' To Hide A Fire In The Dark	*Steam Roller*	—	$4		Liberty 56804
4/10/93	22	20		8 I Wanna Take Care Of You /		—	$4		
8/21/93	34	13		9 I'm Not Built That Way					Liberty 56984
11/13/93+	9	20		10 We Just Disagree		—			album cut
				#12 Pop hit for Dave Mason in 1977; from the album *Fire In The Dark* on Liberty 98947					
3/5/94	53	8		11 Once In A While		—			album cut
				from the movie *8 Seconds* starring Luke Perry (soundtrack on MCA 10927)					
6/4/94	24	20		12 Cowboy Band	*Billy The Kid*	—	$4	■	Liberty 58189 (v)
				"45": Liberty 18406 (B-side: "Indian Head Penny")					
10/8/94	60	6		13 Men Will Be Boys		—			album cut
				from the album *Men'll Be Boys* on Liberty 27760					
2/3/96	5	20		14 It's What I Do	S:17 *The Mountain Moved*	—	$3	■	Capitol 58526 (v)
				"45": Capitol 19038					
6/15/96	4	20		15 That Girl's Been Spyin' On Me	S:13 *Don't Threaten Me With A Good Time*	—	$4	■	Capitol 58563 (v)
				"45": Capitol 19168					
11/2/96	45	14		16 I Wouldn't Be A Man		—			album cut
				from the album *It's What I Do* on Capitol 30525					
5/30/98	69	5		17 One Heart At A Time	S:5 *(same version)*	56	$4	■	Atlantic 84117
				GARTH BROOKS, BILLY DEAN, FAITH HILL, OLIVIA NEWTON-JOHN, NEAL McCOY, MICHAEL McDONALD, VICTORIA SHAW, BRYAN WHITE					
7/4/98	33	18		18 Real Man	*She Gets What She Wants*	—	$4		Capitol 58736
11/21/98	68	3		19 Innocent Bystander	*A Fall In Tennessee*	—	$4		Capitol 58754
10/30/99+	❶¹	37		20 Buy Me A Rose		40			album cut
				KENNY ROGERS With Alison Krauss & Billy Dean from Rogers's album *She Rides Wild Horses* on DreamCatcher 004					
5/12/01	51	6		21 Keep Mom And Dad In Love		—			album cut
				BILLY DEAN & SUZY BOGGUSS					

DEAN, Eddie '55
Born Edgar Dean Glosup on 7/9/07 in Posey, Texas. Died of emphysema on 3/4/99 (age 91). Singer/songwriter/guitarist. Regular on the WLS *National Barn Dance* and Judy Canova's radio show. Acted in several movies from 1937-48.

DEBUT	PEAK	WKS		A-side	B-side	Pop	$	Pic	Label & Number
9/25/48	11	1		1 One Has My Name (The Other Has My Heart)	S:11	—	$40		Crystal 132
				#13 Pop hit for Barry Young in 1966					
1/22/55	10	3		2 I Dreamed Of A Hill-Billy Heaven	A:10 / J:10 / S:15 *Stealing*	—	$30		Sage and Sand 180
				The Frontiersmen (instrumental backing, above 2)					

DEAN, Jimmy ★191★ '61
Born on 8/10/28 in Plainview, Texas. Singer/songwriter/guitarist. Hosted own CBS-TV series from 1957-58; ABC-TV series from 1963-66. Business interests include a line of pork sausage. Married **Donna Meade** on 10/27/91. Also see **Some Of Chet's Friends**.

1) Big Bad John 2) The First Thing Ev'ry Morning (And The Last Thing Ev'ry Night) 3) P.T. 109 4) Bumming Around
5) Dear Ivan

DEBUT	PEAK	WKS		A-side	B-side	Pop	$	Pic	Label & Number
3/7/53	5	7		1 Bumming Around	A:5 / S:9 / J:10 *Picking Sweethearts*	—	$25		4 Star 1613
				JIMMIE DEAN					
10/16/61	❶²	22	●	2 Big Bad John	*I Won't Go Huntin' With You Jake* [S]	❶⁵	$10	■	Columbia 42175
2/3/62	9	10		3 Dear Ivan	*Smoke, Smoke, Smoke That Cigarette* [S]	24	$10	■	Columbia 42259
3/10/62	15	6		4 To A Sleeping Beauty /	[S]	26			
				also see #24 below					
2/10/62	16	10		5 The Cajun Queen	[S]	22	$10	■	Columbia 42282
4/21/62	3	13		6 P.T. 109	*Walk On, Boy*	8	$10	■	Columbia 42338
				based on the sinking of John F. Kennedy's torpedo boat in 1943					

DEBUT	PEAK	WKS	Gold	A-side (Chart Hit) ... B-side	Pop	$	Pic	Label & Number
				DEAN, Jimmy — Cont'd				
9/29/62	10	11		7 Little Black Book .... Please Pass The Biscuits	29	$10	■	Columbia 42529
2/1/64	35	6		8 Mind Your Own Business .... I Really Don't Want To Know	—	$8	■	Columbia 42934
6/5/65	❶²	17		9 The First Thing Ev'ry Morning (And The Last Thing Ev'ry Night) .... Awkward Situation	91	$8		Columbia 43263
10/30/65	35	6		10 Harvest Of Sunshine .... Under The Sun	—	$8		Columbia 43382
10/22/66	10	18		11 Stand Beside Me .... A Tiny Drop Of Sadness	—	$7		RCA Victor 8971
2/18/67	16	14		12 Sweet Misery .... When Somebody Mentions Your Name	—	$7		RCA Victor 9091
7/22/67	41	9		13 Ninety Days .... In The Same Old Way	—	$7		RCA Victor 9241
11/18/67+	30	10		14 I'm A Swinger	—	$7		RCA Victor 9241
3/9/68	21	14		15 A Thing Called Love .... Your Country Boy	—	$7		RCA Victor 9350
8/10/68	52	8		16 Born To Be By Your Side .... One Last Time	—	$7		RCA Victor 9454
11/9/68	22	11		17 A Hammer And Nails .... Read 'Em And Weep	—	$7		RCA Victor 9567
4/5/69	52	7		18 A Rose Is A Rose Is A Rose .... I Taught Her Everything She Knows	—	$7		RCA Victor 9652
1/30/71	29	11		19 Slowly .... She's Mine	—	$7		RCA Victor 0122
				JIMMY DEAN AND DOTTIE WEST				
4/17/71	54	7		20 Everybody Knows .... Sweet Thang	—	$6		RCA Victor 9947
1/1/72	38	12		21 The One You Say Good Mornin' To .... Ain't Life Sweet	—	$6		RCA Victor 9966
10/6/73	90	6		22 Your Sweet Love (Keeps Me Homeward Bound) ... And I'm Still Missing You	—	$6		RCA Victor 0600
5/15/76	9	6	●	23 I.O.U. .... Let's Pick Up The Pieces (And Start Over Again) [S]	—	$5		Columbia 45922
				also see #25 & #26 below	35	$5		Casino 052
9/25/76	85	3		24 To A Sleeping Beauty .... I Didn't Have Time [S-R]	—	$5		Casino 074
				new version of #4 above				
5/14/77	90	2		25 I.O.U. .... Let's Pick Up The Pieces (And Start Over Again) [S-R]	—	$5		Casino 052
				same version as #23 above				
5/14/83	77	4		26 I.O.U. .... To A Sleeping Beauty [S-R]	—	$5	□	Churchill 94024
				new version of #23 above; picture sleeve includes a biographical promo insert				
				DEAN, Larry '89 Born in Perrytown, Texas. Singer/songwriter/guitarist. Married to actress Philece Sampler (played "Rene DuMonde" on TV's *Days Of Our Lives* from 1980-83).				
10/7/89	91	2		Outside Chance	—	$6	■	USA 620
				DEBONAIRES '85 Male vocal group from Tyler, Texas.				
4/13/85	79	6		I'm On Fire .... Loving You Is Always On My Mind	—	$6		MTM 72051
				#6 Pop hit for Bruce Springsteen in 1985				
				DEE, Duane '71 Born Duane DeRosia in Hartford, Wisconsin.				
11/11/67+	44	12		1 Before The Next Teardrop Falls .... You're Not Painting The Town	—	$10		Capitol 5986
12/21/68+	58	7		2 True Love Travels On A Gravel Road .... Have A Little Faith	—	$8		Capitol 2332
2/6/71	71	2		3 I've Got To Sing .... There Will Be An Answer	—	$6		Cartwheel 192
10/16/71	36	13		4 How Can You Mend A Broken Heart .... Georgeanna	—	$6		Cartwheel 200
				#1 Pop hit for the Bee Gees in 1971				
3/4/72	64	6		5 Sweet Apple Wine .... I Can't Get Over You	—	$6		Cartwheel 207
4/20/74	88	3		6 Morning Girl .... She's My Woman	—	$5		ABC 11417
				#17 Pop hit for Neon Philharmonic in 1969				
				DEE, Gordon '84 Born Gordon Dillingham in New Bridge, North Carolina. Singer/songwriter/guitarist.				
12/15/84	87	5		(Nothing Left Between Us) But Alabama .... Slowly Going Out Of My Mind	—	$5		Southern Tracks 1029
				DEE, Kathy '63 Born Kathleen Dearth in Moundsville, West Virginia. Died on 11/3/68.				
9/21/63	18	3		1 Unkind Words .... Only As Far As The Door	—	$10		United Artists 627
2/15/64	44	4		2 Don't Leave Me Lonely Too Long .... I Promise Not To Cry	—	$10		United Artists 687
				DEER, John '70				
10/10/70	57	7		Waxahachie Woman .... Big Train	—	$7		Royal American 21
				THE JOHN DEER COMPANY				
	★395★			**DeHAVEN, Penny** '70 Born Charlotte DeHaven on 5/17/48 in Winchester, Virginia. Singer/actress. Acted in the movies *Valley Of Blood*, *Traveling Light* and *Country Music Story*. Also recorded as **Penny Starr**. 1) Land Mark Tavern 2) Mama Lou 3) Down In The Boondocks				
1/7/67	69	3		1 A Grain Of Salt .... Thing Of Pleasure	—	$15		Band Box 372
				PENNY STARR				
8/9/69	34	11		2 Mama Lou .... That's Just The Way I Am	—	$10		Imperial 66388
11/15/69	37	10		3 Down In The Boondocks .... When The Sun Sets In Jackson	—	$10		Imperial 66421
				#9 Pop hit for Billy Joe Royal in 1965				
3/21/70	59	5		4 I Feel Fine .... Stop & Go	—	$10		Imperial 66437
				#1 Pop hit for The Beatles in 1964				
5/30/70	20	12		5 Land Mark Tavern .... So Sad	—	$7		United Artists 50669
				DEL REEVES & PENNY DeHAVEN				
9/19/70	69	2		6 Awful Lotta Lovin' .... Tomorrow Never Comes	—	$7		United Artists 50703
1/30/71	46	9		7 The First Love .... The Price I Had To Pay	—	$7		United Artists 50742
6/19/71	42	9		8 Don't Change On Me .... That's Just The Way I Am	—	$7		United Artists 50787
12/25/71+	61	9		9 Another Day Of Loving .... Mama, Have All The Good Guys Gone?	—	$7		United Artists 50854
6/24/72	54	6		10 Crying In The Rain .... Time	—	$6		United Artists 50829
				DEL REEVES & PENNY DeHAVEN				
				#6 Pop hit for The Everly Brothers in 1962				
7/14/73	96	2		11 The Lovin' Of Your Life .... When You Get Home	—	$6		Mercury 73384

DEBUT	PEAK	WKS	Gold	A-side (Chart Hit)	B-side	Pop	$	Pic	Label & Number
				DeHAVEN, Penny — Cont'd					
12/1/73+	67	8		12 I'll Be Doggone ....Love Me To Sleep #8 Pop hit for Marvin Gaye in 1965	—		$6		Mercury 73434
5/4/74	93	5		13 Play With Me ....Shine On Me	—		$6		Mercury 73468
8/7/76	83	4		14 (The Great American) Classic Cowboy ....Thank God I'm A Country Girl	—		$6	■	Starcrest 066
7/10/82	77	5		15 We Made Memories ....To My Baby I'm A Big Star All The Time BOXCAR WILLIE and PENNY DeHAVEN	—		$5		Main Street 952
11/5/83	74	5		16 Only The Names Have Been Changed ....Waltz Me Once Again	—		$5		Main Street 93015
4/14/84	78	4		17 Friendly Game Of Hearts	—		$5		Main Street 93019
				DEKLE, Mike '84 Born in Panama City, Florida; raised in Athens, Georgia. Singer/songwriter. Worked as a staff writer for **Kenny Rogers**.					
6/30/84	93	2		1 Hanky Panky ....Lady Luck (Can Be A Bitch Sometimes)	—		$5		NSD 188
11/3/84	79	4		2 The Minstrel ....April's Fool	—		$5		NSD 195
				DELICATO, Paul '75 Born in St. Louis. Pop singer/bassist.					
9/13/75	91	5		Lean On Me ....Ice Cream Sodas And Lollipops And A Red Hot Spinning Top #1 Pop hit for Bill Withers in 1972; B-side was a #7 Adult Contemporary hit in 1975	—		$5		Artists Of America 101
				DELMORE BROTHERS '50 Duo from Elkmont, Alabama: brothers Alton (born on 12/25/08; died on 6/8/64, age 55) and Rabon (born on 12/3/16; died on 12/4/52, age 36) Delmore. Both were singers/songwriters/guitarists/fiddle players. Joined the *Grand Ole Opry* in 1933. Elected to the Country Music Hall of Fame in 2001.					
12/14/46	2¹	4		1 Freight Train Boogie ....Somebody Else's Darling	—		$30		King 570
9/17/49+	❶¹	23		2 Blues Stay Away From Me ....J:❶¹ / S:2 / A:3 Goin' Back To The Blue Ridge Mountains	—		$30		King 803
2/18/50	7	1		3 Pan American Boogie ....J:7 Troubles Ain't Nothin' But The Blues	—		$30		King 826
				DELRAY, Martin '91 Born Michael Ray Martin on 9/26/49 in Texarkana, Arkansas. Also recorded as **Mike Martin**.					
3/23/85	76	3		1 Temptation ....What My Mind's Been On All Day MIKE MARTIN	—		$5		Compleat 139
2/23/91	27	20		2 Get Rhythm ....The Very Thought Of You **Johnny Cash** (guest vocal)	—		$4	■	Atlantic 87869
7/20/91	58	9		3 Lillies White Lies ....I Let Love Do My Talkin'	—		$4		Atlantic 87680
2/1/92	51	12		4 Who, What, Where, When, Why, How .... from the album *Get Rhythm* on Atlantic 82176	—				album cut
12/19/92+	61	9		5 What Kind Of Man .... from the album *What Kind Of Man* on Atlantic 82439	—				album cut
				DENNEY, Kevin '02 Born in Monticello, Kentucky. Singer/songwriter/guitarist.					
12/8/01+	16	24		That's Just Jessie ....S:2 Correct Me If I'm Right	—		$4	★	Lyric Street 64063
				DENNIS, Wesley '95 Born on 4/22/63 in Clanton, Alabama; raised in Montgomery, Alabama.					
2/25/95	46	11		1 I Don't Know (But I've Been Told) ....Borrowed Angel	—		$4	■	Mercury 856486 (v)
6/3/95	51	10		2 Don't Make Me Feel At Home ....This Hat Ain't No Act	—		$4	■	Mercury 856834 (v)
9/2/95	58	8		3 Who's Counting ....It Ain't Fair	—		$4		Mercury 852286
				DENNY, Burch '89					
3/4/89	86	2		Yesterday Is Too Far Away	—		$5		Oak 1068
				DENTON, Jack '89					
10/7/89	95	1		Anna ("Go With Him") ....Something About You #68 Pop hit for Arthur Alexander in 1962	—		$7		M.V.P. 10001

DENVER, John — ★193★ '75
Born Henry John Deutschendorf on 12/31/43 in Roswell, New Mexico. Died on 10/12/97 (age 53) at the controls of a light plane which crashed off the California coast. Singer/songwriter/guitarist. With the **Chad Mitchell Trio** from 1965-68. Starred in the 1977 movie *Oh, God*. CMA Award: 1975 Entertainer of the Year.

1) I'm Sorry 2) Thank God I'm A Country Boy 3) Back Home Again 4) Sweet Surrender 5) Dreamland Express

DEBUT	PEAK	WKS	Gold	A-side	B-side	Pop	$	Pic	Label & Number
6/26/71	50	12	●	1 Take Me Home, Country Roads ....Poems, Prayers And Promises Fat City (Bill Danoff & Taffy Nivert of **Starland Vocal Band**; backing vocals)		2¹	$6		RCA Victor 0445
12/15/73	69	7		2 Please, Daddy ....Rocky Mountain Suite (Cold Nights In Canada) [X]		69	$5		RCA Victor 0182
2/16/74	42	12	●	3 Sunshine On My Shoulders ....Around And Around		❶¹	$5		RCA Victor 0213
6/8/74	9	14	●	4 Annie's Song ....Cool An' Green An' Shady written for his wife Annie Martell (married 1967-83)		❶²	$5		RCA Victor 0295
9/28/74	❶¹	14	●	5 Back Home Again ....It's Up To You		5	$5		RCA Victor 10065
1/4/75	7	12		6 Sweet Surrender ....Summer		13	$5		RCA Victor 10148
3/29/75	❶¹	14	●	7 Thank God I'm A Country Boy ....My Sweet Lady above 2 recorded "live" at Universal City Amphitheater in California		❶¹	$5		RCA Victor 10239
8/16/75	❶¹	18	●	8 I'm Sorry ....Calypso (Pop #2)		❶¹	$5		RCA Victor 10353
12/13/75+	12	11		9 Fly Away ....Two Shots Olivia Newton-John (backing vocal)		13	$5		RCA Victor 10517
3/13/76	30	10		10 Looking For Space ....Windsong		29	$5		RCA Victor 10586
5/29/76	70	5		11 It Makes Me Giggle ....Spirit		60	$5		RCA Victor 10687
9/18/76	34	9		12 Like A Sad Song ....Pegasus		36	$4		RCA 10774

DEBUT	PEAK	WKS	Gold	A-side (Chart Hit)	B-side	Pop	$	Pic	Label & Number
				DENVER, John — Cont'd					
12/18/76+	22	11		13 Baby, You Look Good To Me Tonight.........................Wrangle Mountain Song		65	$4		RCA 10854
3/12/77	62	7		14 My Sweet Lady..............................Welcome To My Morning (Farewell Andromeda)		32	$4		RCA 10911
11/26/77+	22	13		15 How Can I Leave You Again..............................To The Wild Country		44	$4		RCA 11036
2/25/78	72	6		16 It Amazes Me			$4		RCA 11214
2/17/79	64	5		17 Downhill Stuff...Druthers		59	$4		RCA 11479
4/7/79	47	7		18 What's On Your Mind /.........................Life Is So Good		106	$4		
		7		19 Sweet Melinda		107			
3/1/80	84	5		20 Autograph			$4		RCA 11535
6/13/81	10	18		21 Some Days Are Diamonds (Some Days Are Stone)..............The Mountain Song		52	$4	■	RCA 11915
11/14/81	50	9		22 The Cowboy And The Lady.......................Country Love		36	$4		RCA 12246
7/9/83	14	19		23 Wild Montana Skies.........................Till You Opened My Eyes		66	$4		RCA 12345
				JOHN DENVER AND EMMYLOU HARRIS					
12/14/85+	9	21		24 Dreamland Express.........................I Remember Romance		—	$4		RCA 13562
8/30/86	57	9		25 Along For The Ride ('56 T-Bird).........A:7 / S:10 African Sunrise		—	$4	■	RCA 14227
10/29/88	96	2		26 Country Girl In Paris.........................Let Us Begin		—	$4		RCA 14406
5/27/89	14	23		27 And So It Goes.........................Bread And Roses		—	$5	■	Windstar 75720
				JOHN DENVER AND THE NITTY GRITTY DIRT BAND.........Amazing Grace		—	$4		Universal 66008
				DERAILERS, The '99					
				Group from Austin, Texas: Tony Villanueva (vocals, guitar), Brian Hofeldt (guitar), Ed Adkins (bass) and Mark Horn (drums).					
12/4/99	71	1		The Right Place		—			album cut
				from the album *Full Western Dress* on Sire 31062					
				DERN, Daisy '02					
				Born in 1967 in San Francisco. Distant cousin of actors Bruce and Laura Dern.					
11/3/01+	43	15		Gettin' Back To You		—			album cut
				only available as a promo single on Mercury 02147					
	★241★			**DESERT ROSE BAND, The** '88					
				Group from California. Core members: **Chris Hillman** (born on 12/4/44), John Jorgenson (born on 7/6/56) and **Herb Pedersen** (born on 4/27/44). Hillman was a founding member of The Byrds and the **Flying Burrito Brothers**. Jorgenson left in 1992. Disbanded in early 1994.					
				1)I Still Believe In You 2)He's Back And I'm Blue 3)Summer Wind					
3/21/87	26	18		1 Ashes Of Love.........................Leave This Town		—	$4		Curb/MCA 53048
7/11/87	6	21		2 Love Reunited.........................S:19 Hard Times		—	$4		Curb/MCA 53142
10/31/87+	2¹	25		3 One Step Forward.........................S:6 Glass Hearts		—	$4		Curb/MCA 53201
3/26/88	❶¹	19		4 He's Back And I'm Blue.........................S:7 One That Got Away		—	$4		Curb/MCA 53274
7/30/88	2¹	20		5 Summer Wind.........................S:8 Our Songs		—	$4		Curb/MCA 53354
11/26/88+	❶¹	20		6 I Still Believe In You.........................Livin' In The House		—	$4		Curb/MCA 53454
3/18/89	3	20		7 She Don't Love Nobody.........................Step On Out		—	$4		Curb/MCA 53616
7/8/89	11	22		8 Hello Trouble.........................Homeless		—	$4		Curb/MCA 53671
11/4/89+	6	26		9 Start All Over Again.........................Fooled Again		—	$4		Curb/MCA 53746
3/24/90	13	23		10 In Another Lifetime.........................Just A Memory		—	$4		Curb/MCA 53804
7/21/90	10	20		11 Story Of Love.........................Darkness On The Playground		—	$4		Curb/MCA 79052
2/9/91	37	12		12 Will This Be The Day.........................Our Baby's Gone		—	$4		Curb/MCA 54002
5/25/91	65	6		13 Come A Little Closer.........................Everybody's Hero		—	$4		Curb/MCA 54107
10/5/91	53	11		14 You Can Go Home.........................Glory And Power		—	$4		Curb/MCA 54188
1/25/92	67	3		15 Twilight Is Gone.........................Shades Of Blue		—	$4		Curb/MCA 54316
9/4/93	71	1		16 What About Love		—			album cut
				from the album *Life Goes On* on Curb 77627					
				DESERT WIND BAND, The — see SHAW, Ron					
				DeVAL, Buddy — see LORRIE, Myrna					
				DeWITT, Lew '85					
				Born on 3/12/38 in Roanoke, Virginia. Died on 8/15/90 (age 52). Member of **The Statler Brothers** from 1955-82.					
11/30/85	77	7		You'll Never Know.........................Wanda Glen		—	$6		Compleat 147
				#1 Pop hit for Dick Haymes in 1943					
				DEXTER, Al ★141★ '44					
				Born Clarence Albert Poindexter on 5/4/05 in Troup, Texas. Died on 1/28/84 (age 78). Singer/songwriter/guitarist/violinist. Owned his own Round-Up club in Longview, Texas. His Troopers included Aubrey Gass, Paul Sells and Holly Hollinger.					
				1)Guitar Polka 2)So Long Pal 3)I'm Losing My Mind Over You					
				AL DEXTER and his Troopers:					
1/8/44	❶³	10	●	1 Pistol Packin' Mama /		❶¹			
1/8/44	❶¹	25		2 Rosalita		22	$30		Okeh 6708
3/11/44	❶¹³	30		3 So Long Pal /					
3/11/44	❶²	30		4 Too Late To Worry		18	$30		Okeh 6718
1/20/45	❶⁷	21		5 I'm Losing My Mind Over You /		—			
1/27/45	2¹	10		6 I'll Wait For You Dear		—	$30		Okeh 6727
7/7/45	2⁵	11		7 Triflin' Gal /		—			
8/25/45	5	3		8 I'm Lost Without You		—	$30		Okeh 6740

DEBUT	PEAK	WKS	Gold	A-side (Chart Hit)	B-side	Pop	$	Pic	Label & Number
				DEXTER, Al — Cont'd					
2/2/46	①16	29		9 Guitar Polka /	[I]	16			
2/9/46	21	8		10 Honey Do You Think It's Wrong			$25		Columbia 36898
8/31/46	①5	13		11 Wine, Women And Song /			$25		Columbia 37062
9/14/46	3	5		12 It's Up To You			$25		
1/25/47	4	1		13 Kokomo Island	I Learned About Love		$25		Columbia 37200
5/10/47	4	7		14 Down At The Roadside Inn	My Love Goes With You		$25		Columbia 37303
7/3/48	14	1		15 Rock And Rye Rag	J:14 I'm Leaving My Troubles Behind [I]		$25		Columbia 20422
9/18/48	11	2		16 Calico Rag	J:11 Rose Of Mexico		$25		Columbia 20438
				DIAMOND, Neil '78					
				Born on 1/24/41 in Brooklyn, New York. Pop singer/songwriter/guitarist. Charted 56 pop hits from 1966-86.					
11/25/78	70	8 ▲		1 You Don't Bring Me Flowers	(instrumental)	①2	$4		Columbia 10840
				BARBRA & NEIL					
2/17/79	73	7		2 Forever In Blue Jeans	Remember Me	20	$4		Columbia 10897
				DIAMOND RIO ★115★ '97					
				Group formed in Nashville: Marty Roe (vocals; born on 12/28/60), Jimmy Olander (guitar; born on 8/26/61), Gene Johnson (mandolin; born on 8/10/49), Dan Truman (piano; born on 8/29/56), Dana Williams (bass; born on 5/22/61) and Brian Prout (drums; born on 12/4/55). Prout was formerly married to Nancy Given of **Wild Rose**; married Stephanie Bentley on 12/28/2001. Group joined the *Grand Ole Opry* in 1998. CMA Awards: 1992, 1993, 1994 & 1997 Vocal Group of the Year. Also see **Jed Zeppelin**.					
				1)How Your Love Makes Me Feel 2)One More Day 3)Meet In The Middle 4)Unbelievable 5)Norma Jean Riley					
3/23/91	①2	20		1 Meet In The Middle	The Ballad Of Conley And Billy (The Proof's In The Pickin')	—	$4		Arista 2182
7/20/91	3	20		2 Mirror Mirror	The Ballad Of Conley And Billy (The Proofs In The Pickin')	—	$4		Arista 2262
11/16/91+	9	20		3 Mama Don't Forget To Pray For Me	Norma Jean Riley	—	$4		Arista 2258
3/28/92	22	20		4 Norma Jean Riley	Pick Me Up	—	$4		Arista 12407
7/11/92	7	20		5 Nowhere Bound	They Don't Make Hearts (Like They Used To)	—	$4		Arista 12441
11/21/92+	22	20		6 In A Week Or Two	Close To The Edge	—	$4		Arista 12457
4/3/93	5	20		7 Oh Me, Oh My, Sweet Baby	Nothing In This World	—	$4	■	Arista 12464 (v)
7/24/93	13	20		8 This Romeo Ain't Got Julie Yet	I Was Meant To Be With You	—	$4		Arista 12580
11/27/93+	21	20		9 Sawmill Road	I Was Meant To Be With You	—	$4		Arista 12610
5/28/94	22	20		10 Love A Little Stronger	It Does Get Better Than This	—	$4	■	Arista 12696 (v)
10/22/94+	9	20		11 Night Is Fallin' In My Heart	Down By The Riverside	72S	$4		Arista 12764 (v)
2/4/95	16	20		12 Bubba Hyde	S:11 (dance mix)	71S	$4	■	Arista 12787 (v)
5/20/95	19	20		13 Finish What We Started	Appalachian Dream	—	$4		Arista 12739
12/16/95+	21	20		14 Walkin' Away	S:20 It's All In Your Head	—	$4	■	Arista 12934 (v)
5/4/96	4	20		15 That's What I Get For Lovin' You	Big	—	$4		Arista 12992
8/24/96	15	20		16 It's All In Your Head	Is That Asking Too Much	—	$4		Arista 13019
12/14/96+	4	20		17 Holdin'	She Sure Did Like To Run	—	$4		Arista Nashville 13067
6/7/97	①3	22		18 How Your Love Makes Me Feel /			$4		Arista Nashville 13091
11/1/97+	4	21		19 Imagine That		—			album cut (v)
5/30/98	4	23		20 You're Gone					
				from the album *Unbelievable* on Arista Nashville 18866; later issued as the B-side of #21 below					
10/31/98+	22	29		21 Unbelievable	You're Gone	36	$4		Arista Nashville 13138
3/27/99	33	20		22 I Know How The River Feels	What More Do You Want From Me	—	$4		Arista Nashville 13153
5/20/00	36	17		23 Stuff					album cut (v)
				from the album *One More Day* on Arista Nashville 67999; later issued as the B-side of #24 below					
11/4/00+	①2	33		24 One More Day	Stuff	29	$4		Arista Nashville 69036
5/12/01	18	20		25 Sweet Summer	I'm Already Gone	104	$4		Arista Nashville 69085
10/20/01	42	10		26 That's Just That					album cut
				from the album *One More Day* on Arista Nashville 67999					
				DIAMONDS, The '87					
				Vocal group from Canada: Bob Duncan, Gary Cech, Gary Owens and Steve Smith. The original group consisting of Dave Somerville, Ted Kowalski, Phil Leavitt and Bill Reed charted 16 pop hits from 1956-61. Duncan joined in 1978 and recruited the other three members in 1982.					
2/14/87	63	8		1 Just A Little Bit	—		$6		Churchill 94101
7/11/87	83	3		2 Two Kinds Of Woman	—		$6		Churchill 94102
				DIANA '81					
				Born Diana Murrell on 5/26/55 in Cincinnati.					
6/23/79	40	8		1 Just When I Needed You Most	Tie Me Down	—	$5		Elektra 46061
10/6/79	41	9		2 Lonely Together	This Is The Way A Woman Wants To Feel	—	$5		Elektra 46539
8/1/81	29	12		3 He's The Fire	What A Fool I Was (To Fall In Love With You)	—	$5		Sunbird 7564
12/18/82	88	3		4 Who's Been Sleeping In My Bed	—		$6	■	Adamas 103
	★254★			**DICKENS, "Little" Jimmy** '65					
				Born James Cecil Dickens on 12/19/20 in Bolt, West Virginia. Singer/songwriter/guitarist. Joined the *Grand Ole Opry* in 1948. Nicknamed "Tater." Elected to the Country Music Hall of Fame in 1982.					
				1)May The Bird Of Paradise Fly Up Your Nose 2)Hillbilly Fever 3)A-Sleeping At The Foot Of The Bed					
4/16/49	7	7		1 Take An Old Cold 'Tater (And Wait) /	S:7 / J:11 [N]	—			
9/3/49	12	1		2 Pennies For Papa	S:12		$20		Columbia 20548
				JIMMIE DICKENS (above 2)					
6/25/49	7	10		3 Country Boy	S:7 / J:8 I'm Fading Fast With The Time		$20		Columbia 20585
9/24/49	10	1		4 My Heart's Bouquet	J:10 I'll Be Back A-Sunday		$20		Columbia 20598

DEBUT	PEAK	WKS	Gold	A-side (Chart Hit)...B-side	Pop	$	Pic	Label & Number
				DICKENS, "Little" Jimmy — Cont'd				
1/14/50	6	3		5 A-Sleeping At The Foot Of The Bed .... S:6 / A:7 I'm In Love Up To My Ears	—	$20		Columbia 20644
4/22/50	3	10		6 Hillbilly Fever .... A:3 / S:5 / J:9 Then I Had To Turn Around And Get Married	—	$20		Columbia 20677
8/7/54	9	7		7 Out Behind The Barn .... A:9 Closing Time	—	$25		Columbia 21247
11/3/62	10	8		8 The Violet And A Rose .... Honky Tonk Troubles	—	$10		Columbia 42485
12/14/63	28	2		9 Another Bridge To Burn .... I Ain't Comin' Home Tonight	—	$10		Columbia 42845
4/10/65	21	18		10 He Stands Real Tall .... Life Turned Her That Way	—	$8		Columbia 43243
10/9/65	●²	19		11 May The Bird Of Paradise Fly Up Your Nose .... My Eyes Are Jealous [N]	15	$8		Columbia 43388
2/26/66	27	8		12 When The Ship Hit The Sand .... Truck Load Of Starvin' Kangaroos	103	$8		Columbia 43514
7/9/66	41	5		13 Who Licked The Red Off Your Candy .... You Don't Have Time For Me [N]	—	$8		Columbia 43701
3/11/67	23	14		14 Country Music Lover .... You've Destroyed Me [N]	—	$8		Columbia 44025
				JIMMY DICKENS:				
7/6/68	69	5		15 How To Catch An African Skeeter Alive .... Can You Build Your House [N]	—	$7		Decca 32326
1/25/69	55	8		16 When You're Seventeen .... She Never Likes Nothing For Long	—	$7		Decca 32426
5/9/70	75	2		17 (You've Been Quite A Doll) Raggedy Ann .... I'd Rather Sleep In Peace	—	$7		Decca 32644
2/13/71	70	3		18 Everyday Family Man .... One More Time	—	$6		United Artists 50730
4/15/72	61	6		19 Try It, You'll Like It .... Helpless	—	$6		United Artists 50889
				DICKEY, Dan '79				
				Born on 6/22/49 in Houston.				
6/9/79	96	2		1 Hot Mama				
10/6/79	96	2		2 Bye, Bye, Baby .... Close The Door	—	$6		Chartwheel 123
					—	$6		Chartwheel 126
				DICKINSON, Hal '66				
10/29/66	73	2		You're Cheatin' On Me Again .... Cowboy Blues	—	$12		Grass 3301

DIFFIE, Joe ★99★ '94

Born on 12/28/58 in Tulsa; raised in Duncan, Oklahoma. Singer/songwriter/guitarist. Worked in a foundry while playing local nightclubs in Oklahoma. Moved to Nashville in 1986 to work for Gibson Guitars. Signed to Epic in early 1990. Joined the *Grand Ole Opry* in 1993. Also see **Same Old Train**.

1)Pickup Man 2)Bigger Than The Beatles 3)Third Rock From The Sun 4)If The Devil Danced 5)Home

Tougher Than Nails

8/25/90	●¹	20		1 Home *Nostalgia* .... Liquid Heartache	—	$4	■	Epic 73447 (v)
12/15/90+	2²	20		2 If You Want Me To .... Home	—	$4	■	Epic 73637 (v)
4/6/91	●¹	20		3 If The Devil Danced (In Empty Pockets) .... I Ain't Leavin' 'Til She's Gone	—	$4	■	Epic 73747 (v)
8/3/91	2²	20		4 New Way (To Light Up An Old Flame) .... Coolest Fool In Town	—	$4		Epic 73935
12/7/91+	5	20		5 Is It Cold In Here .... Back To Back Heratache	—	$4		Epic 74123
4/18/92	5	20		6 Ships That Don't Come In .... Startin' Over Blues	—	$4		Epic 74285
8/15/92	16	20		7 Next Thing Smokin' .... I Just Don't Know	—	$4		Epic 74415
9/12/92	15	20		8 Not Too Much To Ask .... I Am A Town (Carpenter)	—	$4		Columbia 74485
				MARY-CHAPIN CARPENTER with Joe Diffie				
12/19/92+	41	13		9 Startin' Over Blues .... Just A Regular Joe	—	$4		Epic 74796
3/20/93	5	20		10 Honky Tonk Attitude .... Just A Regular Joe	—	$4		Epic 74911
7/24/93	3	20		11 Prop Me Up Beside The Jukebox				
				(If I Die) .... I Can Walk The Line (If It Ain't Too Straight)	122	$4	■	Epic 77071 (v)
11/13/93+	5	20		12 John Deere Green .... Somewhere Under The Rainbow	69	$4		Epic 77235 (v)
3/12/94	19	20		13 In My Own Backyard .... Here Comes That Train	—	$4		Epic 77380
7/16/94	●²	20		14 Third Rock From The Sun .... (dance mix)	84	$4	■	Epic 77577 (v)
				"45": B-side "From Here On Out"				
10/22/94	●⁴	20		15 Pickup Man .... From Here On Out	60	$4	■	Epic 77715 (v)
2/4/95	2²	20		16 So Help Me Girl .... S:8 The Cows Came Home	84	$4	■	Epic 77808 (v)
5/27/95	21	12		17 I'm In Love With A Capital "U" .... S:22 Wild Blue Yonder	—	$4	■	Epic 77902 (v)
8/12/95	40	11		18 That Road Not Taken .... The Cows Came Home	—	$4		Epic 77978
12/2/95+	●²	20		19 Bigger Than The Beatles .... S:11 Whole Lotta Gone	—	$4	■	Epic 78202 (v)
12/16/95	33	5		20 Leroy The Redneck Reindeer .... Wrap Me In Your Love [X-N]	—	$4		Epic 78201
3/2/96	23	20		21 C-O-U-N-T-R-Y .... Third Rock From The Sun	—	$4		Epic 78246
6/22/96	23	20		22 Whole Lotta Gone .... Back To The Cave	—	$4		Epic 78333
12/21/96	46	4		23 Leroy The Redneck Reindeer .... Wrap Me In Your Love [X-N-R]	—	$4		Epic 78201
3/8/97	25	17		24 This Is Your Brain	—	$4		Epic 78521
7/5/97	40	11		25 Somethin' Like This .... S:23 I Got A Feelin'	—	$4	■	Epic 78638 (v)
10/25/97	61	4		26 The Promised Land .... This Is Your Brain	—	$4		
				from the album *Twice Upon A Time* on Epic 67693	—			album cut
12/20/97	54	4		27 Leroy The Redneck Reindeer .... Wrap Me In Your Love [X-N-R]	—	$4		Epic 78201
4/4/98	4	25		28 Texas Size Heartache /				
9/12/98	43	10		29 Poor Me	—	$4		Epic 79048
11/28/98	64	10		30 Behind Closed Doors	—			
				from the various artists album *Tribute To Tradition* on Columbia 68073				album cut
3/13/99	6	29		31 A Night To Remember .... S:4 Don't Our Love Look Natural	38	$4	★	Epic 79118 (v)
9/4/99+	21	23		32 The Quittin' Kind .... S:7 Don't Our Love Look Natural	90	$4	★	Epic 79268
2/12/00	5	37		33 It's Always Somethin'	57			album cut
				from the album *A Night To Remember* on Epic 69815				
7/28/01+	10	34		34 In Another World	66			album cut
				from the album *In Another World* on Monument 85373				

DEBUT	PEAK	WKS	Gold	A-side (Chart Hit)	B-side	Pop	$	Pic	Label & Number
				DILLINGHAM, Craig '84 Born on 2/11/58 in Brownwood, Texas. Singer/songwriter/guitarist.					
12/3/83+	32	14		1 Have You Loved Your Woman Today	Every Man Should Have One	—	$4		MCA/Curb 52301
3/31/84	47	9		2 Honky Tonk Women Make Honky Tonk Men	Slow Dancin' With Fast Women	—	$4		MCA/Curb 52352
7/21/84	58	6		3 1984	Neon Light Idea	—	$4		MCA/Curb 52406
8/31/85	78	5		4 Next To You	Brand New Blues	—	$4		MCA/Curb 52647
6/14/86	80	3		5 I'll Pull You Through	Too Soon To Say It's Too Late	—	$4		MCA/Curb 52823
				TISH HINOJOSA/CRAIG DILLINGHAM					
	★317★			**DILLON, Dean** '81 Born on 3/26/55 in Lake City, Tennessee. Singer/songwriter/guitarist. 1)Nobody In His Right Mind 2)What Good Is A Heart 3)I'm Into The Bottle 4)Friday Night's Woman 5)I Go To Pieces					
12/15/79+	30	12		1 I'm Into The Bottle (To Get You Out Of My Mind)	Tonight	—	$5		RCA 11881
5/31/80	28	12		2 What Good Is A Heart	He's Number One	—	$5		RCA 12003
11/1/80+	25	15		3 Nobody In His Right Mind (Would've Left Her)	Smelling Like A Rose	—	$5		RCA 12109
5/30/81	57	6		4 They'll Never Take Me Alive	Tonight One Of Us Is Going Out Of My Mind	—	$5		RCA 12234
10/17/81	77	5		5 Jesus Let Me Slide	If You're Going Crazy	—	$5		RCA 12319
4/10/82	41	11		6 Brotherly Love	Firewater Friends	—	$4	■	RCA 13049
				GARY STEWART/DEAN DILLON					
6/19/82	74	4		7 Play This Old Working Day Away	You To Come Home To	—	$4		RCA 13208
9/18/82	65	6		8 You To Come Home To	I'm Into The Bottle (To Get You Off My Mind)	—	$4		RCA 13295
1/8/83	47	12		9 Those Were The Days	Drinkin' Thing	—	$4		RCA 13401
				GARY STEWART AND DEAN DILLON					
4/16/83	71	4		10 Smokin' In The Rockies	Hard Time For Lovers	—	$4		RCA 13472
				GARY STEWART & DEAN DILLON					
11/12/83	67	6		11 Famous Last Words Of A Fool	Ten Years And Two Babies Later	—	$4		RCA 13628
7/2/88	51	9		12 The New Never Wore Off My Sweet Baby	Appalachia Got To Have You Feelin' In My Bones	—	$4		Capitol 44179
9/17/88	39	12		13 I Go To Pieces #9 Pop hit for Peter & Gordon in 1965	Hard Time For Lovers	—	$4		Capitol 44239
12/24/88+	58	9		14 Hey Heart	Appalachia Got To Have You Feelin' In My Bones	—	$4		Capitol 44294
8/26/89	61	6		15 It's Love That Makes You Sexy	Appalachia Got To Have You Feelin' In My Bones	—	$4		Capitol 44400
11/18/89	66	5		16 Back In The Swing Of Things from the album I've Learned To Live on Capitol 92079	—				album cut
2/23/91	69	6		17 Holed Up In Some Honky Tonk	All Out Of Love	—	$4	■	Atlantic 87774 (v)
6/22/91	39	12		18 Friday Night's Woman	Her Thinkin' I'm Doing Her Wrong (Ain't Doin' Me Right)	—	$4		Atlantic 87794
9/21/91	62	12		19 Don't You Even (Think About Leavin')	She Knows What She Wants	—	$4		Atlantic 87606
5/22/93	62	5		20 Hot, Country And Single	Holding My Own	—	$4	■	Atlantic 87356 (v)
				DILLON, Lola Jean — see WHITE, L.E.					
				DIRKSEN, Senator Everett McKinley '67 Born on 1/4/1896 in Pekin, Illinois. Died on 9/7/69 (age 73). Served as a United States senator from 1950-69.					
1/7/67	58	7		Gallant Men	The New Colossus (Statue of Liberty) [S]	29	$7	■	Capitol 5805
				DIRT BAND, The — see NITTY GRITTY DIRT BAND					
				DIXIANA '92 Group from Greenville, South Carolina: Cindy Murphy (vocals), brothers Mark (bass) and Phil (guitar) Lister, Randall Griffith (keyboards) and Colonel Shuford (drums).					
2/22/92	39	20		1 Waitin' For The Deal To Go Down	It Comes And It Goes	—	$4		Epic 74221
6/27/92	40	13		2 That's What I'm Working On Tonight	If I Can't Have You	—	$4		Epic 74361
4/24/93	66	3		3 Now You're Talkin'	Love Gone Good	—	$4		Epic 74936
				DIXIE CHICKS ★183★ '98 Female trio: Natalie Maines (lead vocals), with sisters Martha "Martie" (fiddle, mandolin) and Emily (guitar, banjo) Erwin. Natalie was born on 10/14/74 in Lubbock, Texas. Daughter of Lloyd Maines (of **The Maines Brothers Band**). Married to Michael Tarabay from 1997-99; married actor Adrian Pasdar on 6/24/2000. Martie was born on 10/12/69 in York, Pennsylvania. Married to Ted Seidel (took his last name) from 1995-99; married Gareth Maguire on 8/10/2001. Emily was born on 8/16/72 in Pittsfield, Massachusetts. Married **Charlie Robison** (took his last name) on 5/1/99. Group named after the Little Feat song "Dixie Chicken." CMA Awards: 1999, 2000 Vocal Group of the Year; 2000 Entertainer of the Year. 1)Wide Open Spaces 2)Cowboy Take Me Away 3)You Were Mine					
10/25/97+	7	26		1 I Can Love You Better S:5 Give It Up Or Let Me Go		77	$4	■	Monument 78746
4/11/98	❶²	29		2 There's Your Trouble S:3 Give It Up Or Let Me Go		36	$4	■	Monument 78899 (v)
8/22/98	❶⁴	27		3 Wide Open Spaces S:5 I Can Love You Better CMA Award: Single of the Year		41	$4	★	Monument 79003 (v)
12/12/98+	❶²	25		4 You Were Mine		34			album cut
4/3/99	6	20		5 Tonight The Heartache's On Me		46			album cut
6/5/99	64	13		6 Let 'Er Rip all of above from the album Wide Open Spaces on Monument 68195		—			album cut
7/10/99	2¹	20		7 Ready To Run		39			album cut
8/14/99	60	11		8 You Can't Hurry Love #1 Pop hit for The Supremes in 1966; above 2 from the movie Runaway Bride starring Julia Roberts (soundtrack on Columbia 69923)		—			album cut
9/11/99+	❶³	41		9 Cowboy Take Me Away		27			album cut
9/11/99+	❶¹	32		10 Without You		31			album cut
9/11/99+	13	32	●	11 Goodbye Earl S:2 Stand By Your Man		19	$4	★	Monument 79352 (v)
9/11/99	65	2		12 Sin Wagon also see #14 below		—			album cut

DEBUT	PEAK	WKS	Gold	A-side (Chart Hit) .... B-side	Pop	$	Pic	Label & Number
				DIXIE CHICKS — Cont'd				
9/18/99	75	1		13 If I Fall You're Going Down With Me .... —				album cut
				also see #17 below				
3/25/00	52	18		14 Sin Wagon .... [R] —				album cut
3/25/00	65	1		15 Roly Poly .... —				album cut
				ASLEEP AT THE WHEEL Featuring Dixie Chicks				
				from the album Ride With Bob on DreamWorks 50117				
5/20/00	10	20		16 Cold Day In July	65			album cut
2/24/01	3	20		17 If I Fall You're Going Down With Me .... [R]	38			album cut
6/30/01	23	16		18 Heartbreak Town	121			album cut
9/29/01+	7	27		19 Some Days You Gotta Dance	55			album cut
				#9-14 & 16-19: from the album Fly on Monument 69678				
				DR. HOOK '77				
				Pop-rock group from New Jersey: Ray Sawyer (vocals), Dennis Locorriere (vocals, guitar), George Cummings and Rik Elswit (guitars), William Francis (keyboards), Bob Henke (bass) and John Wolters (drums). Wolters died of cancer on 6/16/97 (age 52). Group charted 21 pop hits from 1972-82.				
				1)If Not You 2)(One More Year Of) Daddy's Little Girl 3)Sharing The Night Together				
3/6/76	55	8	●	1 Only Sixteen .... Let Me Be Your Lover	6	$5		Capitol 4171
				#28 Pop hit for Sam Cooke in 1959				
6/19/76	51	12		2 A Couple More Years .... A Little Bit More (Pop #11)	—	$5		Capitol 4280
11/6/76	28	12		3 (One More Year Of) Daddy's Little Girl .... I Need The High	81	$5		Capitol 4344
				RAY SAWYER				
12/4/76+	26	13		4 If Not You .... Bad Eye Bill	55	$5		Capitol 4364
6/25/77	92	3		5 Walk Right In .... Sexy Energy	46	$5		Capitol 4423
10/7/78	50	11	●	6 Sharing The Night Together ..... You Make My Pants Want To Get Up And Dance	6	$4		Capitol 4621
2/10/79	82	4		7 All The Time In The World .... Dooley Jones	54	$4		Capitol 4677
5/19/79	68	9	●	8 When You're In Love With A Beautiful Woman .... Knowing She's There	6	$4		Capitol 4705
11/3/79	91	4		9 Better Love Next Time .... Mountain Mary	12	$4		Capitol 4785
2/16/80	80	4		10 I Don't Feel Much Like Smilin' .... Drinking Wine Alone	—	$4		Capitol 4820
				RAY SAWYER				
				DODD, Deryl '99				
				Born on 4/12/64 in Comanche, Texas; raised in Dallas. Singer/songwriter/guitarist.				
10/5/96	68	3		1 Friends Don't Drive Friends .... That's Just Me	—	$4	▌	Columbia 78437 (v)
11/9/96+	36	20		2 That's How I Got To Memphis .... (album snippets)	—	$4	▌	Columbia 78478 (v)
5/17/97	61	8		3 Movin' Out To The Country .... Friends Don't Drive Friends...	—	$4	▌	Columbia 78571
4/18/98	62	6		4 Time On My Hands .... Best I Ever Had	—	$4	▌	Columbia 78882
9/12/98+	26	23		5 A Bitter End .... S:13 Time On My Hands	88	$4	★	Columbia 79013
2/27/99	59	20		6 Sundown .... —				album cut
3/27/99	65	3		7 Good Idea Tomorrow .... —				album cut
5/29/99	64	3		8 John Roland Wood .... —				album cut
10/16/99	71	3		9 On Earth As It Is In Texas .... —				album cut
				above 4 from the album Deryl Dodd on Columbia 68793				
				DODSON, Darrell '77				
4/16/77	99	2		Love Song Sing Along .... One More Time		$7		SCR 139
				DOLAN, Madonna '88				
				Born in McLeansboro, Illinois. Female singer/multi-instrumentalist.				
9/24/88	82	3		The Home Team .... —		$6		True 92
				DOLAN, Ramblin' Jimmie '51				
				Born on 10/29/16 in Gardena, California. Died on 7/31/94 (age 77). Singer/guitarist. Known as "America's Country Troubador."				
2/3/51	7	4		Hot Rod Race .... S:7 Walkin' With The Blues [N]	—	$30		Capitol F1322
				DOLLAR, Johnny '66				
				Born on 3/8/33 in Kilgore, Texas. Died on 4/13/86 (age 53). Singer/songwriter/guitarist.				
2/12/66	49	2		1 Tear-Talk .... Big Red (The Hound)	—	$10		Columbia 43343
3/19/66	15	15		2 Stop The Start (Of Tears In My Heart) .... You Ain't Wrong	—	$10		Columbia 43537
2/25/67	65	5		3 Your Hands .... Don't Take My Future From Me	—	$8		Dot 16990
9/16/67	47	12		4 The Wheels Fell Off The Wagon Again .... Watching Me Losing You	—	$7		Date 1566
1/13/68	42	12		5 Everybody's Got To Be Somewhere .... Did You Talk To Him Today	—	$7		Date 1585
11/16/68	48	7		6 Big Rig Rollin' Man .... I've Gotta Stay High	—	$7		Chart 1057
3/15/69	65	4		7 Big Wheels Sing For Me .... Wild Cherry	—	$7		Chart 1070
2/14/70	71	3		8 Truck Driver's Lament .... Changing Her Thinking	—	$7		Chart 5049
				DOMINO, Fats '81				
				Born Antoine Domino on 2/26/28 in New Orleans. R&B singer/pianist. Charted 66 pop hits from 1955-68.				
12/20/80+	51	9		Whiskey Heaven .... Beers To You (Texas Opera Company)	—	$4		Warner 49610
				from the movie Any Which Way You Can starring Clint Eastwood				
				DONALDSON, Craig '76				
9/25/76	99	2		I Believe He's Gonna Drive That Rig To Glory .... (long version)	—	$7		Great American 281
				DON JUAN '88				
				Vocal trio from Rock Island, Illinois: Stu Stuart, Ed Allen and Toby Strause.				
3/12/88	75	4		1 We're Gonna Love Tonight .... —		$7		Maxx 821
8/20/88	78	2		2 Let It Go .... —		$7		Maxx 827
				DOOLITTLE BAND, The — see DANDY				

DEBUT	PEAK	WKS Gold	A-side (Chart Hit)	B-side	Pop	$	Pic	Label & Number
	★340★		**DOTTSY** '77					
			Born Dottsy Brodt on 4/6/54 in Seguin, Texas. Female singer.					
			1)(After Sweet Memories) Play Born To Lose Again 2)Tryin' To Satisfy You 3)I'll Be Your San Antone Rose					
5/31/75	17	17	1 Storms Never Last	Follow Me	—	$5		RCA Victor 10280
11/22/75+	12	14	2 I'll Be Your San Antone Rose	If You Say It's So	—	$5		RCA Victor 10423
5/29/76	86	4	3 The Sweetest Thing (I've Ever Known)	We Still Sing Love Songs Here In Texas	—	$5		RCA Victor 10666
9/25/76	68	6	4 Love Is A Two-Way Street	Lying In My Arms	—	$5		RCA 10766
6/4/77	10	16	5 (After Sweet Memories) Play Born To Lose Again	Send Me The Pillow You Dream On	—	$5		RCA 10982
10/29/77	22	13	6 It Should Have Been Easy	Everybody's Reaching Out For Someone	—	$5		RCA 11138
2/11/78	20	12	7 Here In Love	A Good Love Is Like A Good Song	—	$5		RCA 11203
7/8/78	21	11	8 I Just Had You On My Mind	Just Remember Who Your Friends Are	—	$5		RCA 11293
1/20/79	12	14	9 Tryin' To Satisfy You	If I Only Had The Words (To Tell You)	—	$5		RCA 11448
			Waylon Jennings (backing vocal)					
6/16/79	22	10	10 Slip Away	Love Is A Two-Way Street	—	$5		RCA 11610
11/10/79	34	10	11 When I'm Gone	Storms Never Last	—	$5		RCA 11743
6/27/81	32	12	12 Somebody's Darling, Somebody's Wife	Sing Me A Love Song	—	$6		Tanglewood 1908
9/19/81	58	8	13 Let The Little Bird Fly	Love In My Baby's Eyes	—	$6		Tanglewood 1910
			DOUGLAS — see BLOCK, Doug					
			DOUGLAS, Joe '81					
			Born in New Orleans. Singer/songwriter.					
1/20/79	84	5	1 You're Still On My Mind	Wine Flow Free		$7		D 1315
1/26/80	88	2	2 Back Street Affair	Bollweevil		$7		Foxy Cajun 1001
6/20/81	75	4	3 Leavin You Is Easier (Than Wishing You Were Gone) /		—			
		4	4 Louisiana Joe			$7		Foxy Cajun 1005
			DOUGLAS, Steve '80					
			Born on 2/17/51 in Greenville, Mississippi.					
6/7/80	67	7	1 This Is True	Saying I'm Sorry		$7		Demon 1954
8/5/89	91	2	2 To A San Antone Rose	Texas, I'm In Love With You		$7		Dorman 98915
1/13/90	80	1	3 Funny Ways Of Loving Me	Little Daughters		$7		Dorman 981101
			DOUGLAS, Tony '63					
			Born on 4/12/29 in Martins Mill, Texas.					
3/30/63	23	1	1 His And Hers	Gabby Abby		$20		Vee Jay 481
			also see #5 below					
12/30/72+	35	15	2 Thank You For Touching My Life	Walkin' Over Yonder	—	$6		Dot 17443
6/30/73	37	9	3 My Last Day	I'll Fight Every Step Of The Way	—	$6		Dot 17464
12/13/75+	72	7	4 If I Can Make It (Through The Mornin')	Honky-Tonk Man	—	$5		20th Century 2257
2/20/82	87	3	5 His 'N Hers	Shrimpin' [R]	—	$6		Cochise 118
			new version of #1 above					
			DOVE, Ronnie '75					
			Born on 9/7/35 in Herndon, Virginia; raised in Baltimore. Charted 20 pop hits from 1964-69.					
1/29/72	61	8	1 Kiss The Hurt Away	He Cries Like A Baby	—	$6		Decca 32919
2/3/73	69	5	2 Lilacs In Winter	Is It Wrong	—	$6		Decca 33038
4/12/75	75	7	3 Please Come To Nashville	Pictures On Paper	—	$5		Melodyland 6004
6/14/75	25	12	4 Things	Here We Go Again	—	$5		Melodyland 6011
			#3 Pop hit for **Bobby Darin** in 1962					
4/25/87	77	4	5 Heart		—	$5	■	Diamond 378
11/7/87	73	7	6 Rise And Shine		—	$5		Diamond 379
			DOWNEY, Sean Morton '81					
			Born on 12/9/33 in New York City. Died of cancer on 3/12/2001 (age 67). TV talk show host better known as Morton Downey, Jr.					
3/14/81	95	2	Green Eyed Girl		—	$7		ESO 932
	★380★		**DOWNING, Big Al** '79					
			Born on 1/9/40 in Centralia, Oklahoma; raised in Lenapah, Oklahoma. Black singer/songwriter/pianist.					
			1)Touch Me (I'll Be Your Fool Once More) 2)Mr. Jones 3)Bring It On Home					
12/2/78+	20	13	1 Mr. Jones	I Don't Cry (The Onion Song)	—	$5		Warner 8716
4/21/79	18	13	2 Touch Me (I'll Be Your Fool Once More)	I Ain't No Fool	—	$5		Warner 8787
9/8/79	59	5	3 Midnight Lace	Counting Highway Signs	—	$5		Warner 49034
11/17/79	73	4	4 I Ain't No Fool	Mr. Jones	—	$5		Warner 49141
2/9/80	33	8	5 The Story Behind The Story	Daddy Played The Banjo	—	$5		Warner 49161
7/12/80	20	11	6 Bring It On Home	Beer Drinking People	—	$5		Warner 49270
7/3/82	48	9	7 I'll Be Loving You	Don't Mess With An Angel	—	$5		Team 1001
10/23/82	67	7	8 Darlene	Love Was Right Here (With You All The Time)	—	$5		Team 1002
2/12/83	38	11	9 It Takes Love	If You're Leaving	—	$5		Team 1004
10/1/83	64	5	10 Let's Sing About Love	We Can Only Say Goodbye	—	$5		Team 1003
1/7/84	45	11	11 The Best Of Families	Fool Of The Year	—	$5		Team 1007
4/28/84	76	4	12 There'll Never Be A Better Night For Bein' Wrong	T.V. Women	—	$5		Team 1008
1/17/87	69	5	13 How Beautiful You Are (To Me)	The Only Thing Missing Is You	—	$6		Vine St. 103
9/12/87	67	5	14 Just One Night Won't Do	How Beautiful You Are (To Me)	—	$6		Vine St. 105
8/5/89	82	3	15 I Guess By Now		—	$5		Door Knob 328
			DOWNS, Laverne '60					
7/4/60	16	7	But You Use To	What Have I Done	—	$20		Peach 735

DEBUT	PEAK	WKS	Gold	A-side (Chart Hit)	B-side	Pop	$	Pic	Label & Number
				DRAKE, Guy '70					
				Born on 7/24/04 in Weir, Kentucky. Died on 6/17/84 (age 79). Singer/comedian.					
1/10/70	6	14		Welfare Cadilac — Keep Off My Grass [N-S]		63	$7		Royal American 1
				DRAPER, Rusty '53					
				Born Farrell Draper on 1/25/25 in Kirksville, Missouri. Male singer/songwriter/guitarist. Known as "Ol' Redhead."					
8/29/53	6	5	●	1 Gambler's Guitar — Free Home Demonstration S:6 / J:6		6	$20		Mercury 70167
7/8/67	70	3		2 My Elusive Dreams — Memory Lane		—	$8		Monument 1019
3/2/68	70	4		3 California Sunshine — The Gypsy		—	$8		Monument 1044
8/3/68	58	3		4 Buffalo Nickel — Make Believe I'm Him		—	$8		Monument 1074
4/25/70	73	2		5 Two Little Boys — It Don't Mean A Thing To Me written in 1903; #119 Pop hit for Rolf Harris in 1970		—	$8		Monument 1188
1/19/80	87	3		6 Harbor Lights — Ramblin' Man #8 Pop hit for The Platters in 1960		—	$10		KL 001
				DRESSER, Lee '83					
				Born on 5/22/41 in Washington DC; raised in Moberly, Missouri. Male singer/guitarist.					
2/11/78	78	5		1 You're All The Woman I'll Ever Need — Fallin'		—	$5		Capitol 4529
12/2/78	86	5		2 A Beautiful Song (For A Beautiful Lady) — The Man Up In The Mansion		—	$5		Capitol 4613
4/2/83	77	4		3 The Hero — All I Have To Do		—	$5		Air Int'l. 10021
9/3/83	96	1		4 Feelings Feelin Right		—	$5		Air Int'l. 10022
				DRIFTING COWBOYS, The '78					
				Former backing band for **Hank Williams**. The 1978 lineup consisted of original members Bob McNett (guitar; born on 10/16/25), Don Helms (steel guitar; born on 2/28/27) and Jerry Rivers (fiddle; born on 8/25/28; died of cancer on 10/4/96, age 68), with new members Bobby Andrews (bass) and Jimmy Heap, Jr. (drums; son of **Jimmy Heap**).					
1/28/78	97	2		1 Lovesick Blues — A Gift In The Name Of Love JIM OWEN***THE DRIFTING COWBOYS		—	$6		Epic 50498
5/6/78	90	4		2 Rag Mop — Mud Hut #1 Pop hit for the Ames Brothers in 1950		—	$6		Epic 50543
				DRIFTWOOD, Jimmie '59					
				Born James Corbett Morris on 6/20/07 in Mountain View, Arkansas. Died of heart failure on 7/12/98 (age 91). Singer/songwriter/guitarist.					
6/8/59	24	3		The Battle Of New Orleans — Damyankee Lad		—	$15		RCA Victor 7534
				DRUMM, Don '78					
				Born in Springfield, Massachusetts. Singer/guitarist/pianist.					
11/30/74+	86	7		1 In At Eight And Out At Ten — Baby's Gone		—	$6		Chart 5223
1/7/78	18	14		2 Bedroom Eyes — Stoney		—	$5		Churchill 7704
5/27/78	35	8		3 Just Another Rhinestone — If Her Love Was A Window		—	$5		Churchill 7710
10/7/78	81	3		4 Something To Believe In — Sad Songs		—	$5		Churchill 7717

DRUSKY, Roy ★98★ '65

Born on 6/22/30 in Atlanta. Singer/songwriter/guitarist. Studied veterinary medicine at Emory University. Hosted own radio show on WEAS in Decatur, Georgia. Joined the *Grand Ole Opry* in 1958. Acted in the movies *The Golden Guitar* and *Forty-Acre Feud*.

1)Yes, Mr. Peters 2)Three Hearts In A Tangle 3)Another 4)Second Hand Rose 5)Anymore

DEBUT	PEAK	WKS		A-side	B-side	Pop	$		Label & Number
1/18/60	2³	24		1 Another — The Same Corner		—	$15		Decca 31024
7/11/60	3	20		2 Anymore — I'm So Helpless		—	$15		Decca 31109
12/19/60	26	3		3 I Can't Tell My Heart That — When Do You Love Me KITTY WELLS And ROY DRUSKY		—	$15		Decca 31164
3/13/61	2⁴	27		4 Three Hearts In A Tangle /		35			Decca 31193
2/20/61	10	12		5 I'd Rather Loan You Out		—	$12		Decca 31193
9/11/61	9	20		6 I Went Out Of My Way (To Make You Happy) — I've Got Some		—	$12		Decca 31297
4/21/62	17	2		7 There's Always One (Who Loves A Lot) — Marking Time		—	$12		Decca 31366
12/22/62+	3	21		8 Second Hand Rose — It Worries Me		—	$12		Decca 31443
12/7/63+	8	19		9 Peel Me A Nanner — The Room Across The Hall		—	$10	■	Mercury 72204
5/9/64	13	16		10 Pick Of The Week — Yesterday		—	$10		Mercury 72265
12/26/64+	41	3		11 Summer, Winter, Spring And Fall — Almost Can't		—	$10		Decca 31717
1/16/65	6	21		12 (From Now On All My Friends Are Gonna Be) Strangers — Birmingham Jail		—	$8		Mercury 72376
5/29/65	❶²	23		13 Yes, Mr. Peters — More Than We Deserve ROY DRUSKY & PRISCILLA MITCHELL		—	$8		Mercury 72416
10/23/65	21	15		14 White Lightnin' Express — Lonely Thing Called Me		—	$8		Mercury 72471
12/4/65	45	2		15 Slippin' Around — Trouble On Our Line ROY DRUSKY & PRISCILLA MITCHELL		—	$8		Mercury 72497
2/26/66	20	14		16 Rainbows And Roses — A Thing Called Sadness		—	$8		Mercury 72532
6/25/66	10	16		17 The World Is Round — Unless You Make Him Set You Free		—	$8		Mercury 72586
11/19/66+	12	14		18 If The Whole World Stopped Lovin' — Too Many Footprints		—	$8		Mercury 72627
3/25/67	61	5		19 I'll Never Tell On You — Bed Of Roses ROY DRUSKY & PRISCILLA MITCHELL		—	$8		Mercury 72650
6/24/67	25	11		20 New Lips — Now		—	$8		Mercury 72689
11/11/67+	18	16		21 Weakness In A Man — I've Got A Right To The Blues		—	$8		Mercury 72742
3/30/68	28	10		22 You Better Sit Down Kids — Let's Put Our World Back Together #9 Pop hit for **Cher** in 1967		—	$8		Mercury 72784
7/20/68	24	11		23 Jody And The Kid — Your Little Deeds Of Kindness (And Your Little Words Of Love)		—	$8		Mercury 72823

DEBUT	PEAK	WKS	Gold	A-side (Chart Hit)	B-side	Pop	$	Pic	Label & Number
				DRUSKY, Roy — Cont'd					
1/25/69	10	15		24 Where The Blue And Lonely Go	I'm Gonna Get You Off My Mind	—	$7		Mercury 72886
6/7/69	14	11		25 My Grass Is Green	Alone With You	—	$7		Mercury 72928
10/4/69	7	11		26 Such A Fool	All Over My Mind	—	$7		Mercury 72964
1/17/70	11	11		27 I'll Make Amends	Our Everlasting Love Has Died	—	$7		Mercury 73007
5/9/70	5	16		28 Long Long Texas Road	Emotion - Devotion	—	$7		Mercury 73056
9/19/70	9	12		29 All My Hard Times	At Times Everybody's Blind	—	$7		Mercury 73111
3/6/71	15	12		30 I Love The Way That You've Been Lovin' Me	On And On And On	—	$7		Mercury 73178
7/3/71	37	10		31 I Can't Go On Loving You	You're Shaking The Hand	—	$7		Mercury 73212
12/11/71+	17	13		32 Red Red Wine	Without You Baby	—	$7		Mercury 73252
				written by Neil Diamond; #1 Pop hit for UB40 in 1988					
5/20/72	58	9		33 Sunshine And Rainbows /		—			
		2		34 The Night's Not Over Yet		—	$7		Mercury 73293
8/12/72	25	12		35 The Last Time I Called Somebody Darlin'	Long Way Back To Love	—	$7		Mercury 73314
1/13/73	32	10		36 I Must Be Doin' Something Right	Always You, Always Me	—	$7		Mercury 73356
5/12/73	50	7		37 That Rain Makin' Baby Of Mine	This Time Of The Year	—	$7		Mercury 73376
8/4/73	25	11		38 Satisfied Mind	I'll Take Care Of You	—	$7		Mercury 73405
4/20/74	81	6		39 Close To Home	One Day At A Time	—	$6		Capitol 3859
9/21/74	45	11		40 Dixie Lily	If I Could Paint The World	—	$6		Capitol 3942
				first recorded by Elton John on his 1974 *Caribou* album					
1/15/77	81	5		41 Night Flying	Lifetime In A Week	—	$5		Scorpion 0521
8/13/77	91	4		42 Betty's Song	Naked Truth	—	$5		Scorpion 0540
				DUCAS, George '95					
				Born on 8/1/66 in Texas City, Texas; raised in San Diego and Houston. Singer/songwriter/guitarist.					
9/10/94	38	12		1 Teardrops	Waiting And Wishing	—	$4		Liberty 18093
12/10/94+	9	20		2 Lipstick Promises	In No Time At All	—	$4		Liberty 18306
5/13/95	52	10		3 Hello Cruel World	Waiting And Wishing	—	$4		Liberty 18731
9/23/95	72	3		4 Kisses Don't Lie	In No Time At All	—	$4	■	Capitol 58464 (v)
				"45": Capitol 18845 (B-side: "My World Stopped Turning")					
6/8/96	57	12		5 Every Time She Passes By	S:22 Lipstick Promises	—	$4	■	Capitol 58565 (v)
				"45": Capitol 19169					
2/8/97	55	9		6 Long Trail Of Tears	The Invisible Man	—	$4		Capitol 19512

DUDLEY, Dave ★100★   '63

Born David Pedruska on 5/3/28 in Spencer, Wisconsin; raised in Stevens Point, Wisconsin. Singer/songwriter/guitarist. Worked as a DJ at radio stations WTWT in Wausua, Wisconsin, KBOK in Waterloo, Iowa, KCHA in Charles City, Idaho and KEVE in Minneapolis. Known as the pioneer of "truck driving" songs.

1) The Pool Shark 2) Six Days On The Road 3) Truck Drivin' Son-Of-A-Gun 4) Cowboy Boots 5) What We're Fighting For

DEBUT	PEAK	WKS		A-side	B-side	Pop	$		Label & Number
10/16/61	28	2		1 Maybe I Do	Your Only One	—	$30		Vee 7003
				reissued with a picture sleeve on Curio 7029 in 1963					
9/15/62	18	9		2 Under Cover Of The Night	Please Let Me Prove (My Love For You)	—	$20		Jubilee 5436
6/1/63	2²	21		3 Six Days On The Road	I Feel A Cry Coming On	32	$12		Golden Wing 3020
10/5/63	3	20		4 Cowboy Boots	I Think I'll Cheat (A Little Tonight)	95	$12		Golden Ring 3030
12/14/63+	7	16		5 Last Day In The Mines	Last Year's Heartaches	125	$10		Mercury 72212
10/10/64	6	17		6 Mad	Don't Be Surprised	—	$10		Mercury 72308
3/13/65	15	17		7 Two Six Packs Away	Hiding Behind The Curtain	—	$10		Mercury 72384
7/10/65	3	21		8 Truck Drivin' Son-Of-A-Gun	I Got Lost	125	$8		Mercury 72442
11/20/65+	4	16		9 What We're Fighting For	Coffee, Coffee, Coffee	—	$8		Mercury 72500
3/12/66	12	12		10 Viet Nam Blues	Then I'll Come Home Again [S]	127	$8		Mercury 72550
7/2/66	13	14		11 Lonelyville	Time And Place	—	$8		Mercury 72585
10/8/66	15	12		12 Long Time Gone	I Feel A Cry Comin' On	—	$8		Mercury 72618
2/25/67	12	15		13 My Kind Of Love	Subject To Change	—	$8		Mercury 72655
7/15/67	23	14		14 Trucker's Prayer	Don't Come Cryin' To Me	—	$8		Mercury 72697
11/4/67+	12	16		15 Anything Leaving Town Today	I'd Rather Be Forgotten	—	$7		Mercury 72741
3/2/68	10	13		16 There Ain't No Easy Run	Why I Can't Be With You (Is A Shame)	—	$7		Mercury 72779
7/13/68	14	11		17 I Keep Coming Back For More	Where Does A Little Boy Go	—	$7		Mercury 72818
11/16/68+	10	15		18 Please Let Me Prove (My Love For You)	I'll Be Moving Along	—	$7		Mercury 72856
3/29/69	12	15		19 One More Mile	Angel	—	$7		Mercury 72902
8/30/69	10	13		20 George (And The North Woods)	It's Not A Very Pleasant Day Today	—	$7		Mercury 72952
3/14/70	❶¹	16		21 The Pool Shark	The Bigger They Come, The Harder They Fall	—	$7		Mercury 73029
8/1/70	20	12		22 This Night (Ain't Fit For Nothing But Drinking)	I'm Not So Easy Anymore	—	$7		Mercury 73089
11/14/70	23	13		23 Day Drinkin'	Let's Get On With The Show	—	$7		Mercury 73139
				DAVE DUDLEY & TOM T. HALL					
12/26/70+	15	13		24 Listen Betty (I'm Singing Your Song)	I Hope My Kind Of Love	—	$7		Mercury 73138
4/17/71	8	14		25 Comin' Down	Six-O-One	—	$7		Mercury 73193
8/21/71	8	14		26 Fly Away Again	There You Are Again	—	$7		Mercury 73225
3/18/72	14	14		27 If It Feels Good Do It	Sometime In The Future	—	$7		Mercury 73274
7/22/72	12	16		28 You've Gotta Cry Girl	The Arms Of A Satisfied Woman	—	$7		Mercury 73309
12/9/72+	40	10		29 We Know It's Over	Gettin' Back Together	—	$7		Mercury 73345
				DAVE DUDLEY & KAREN O'DONNAL					

DEBUT	PEAK	WKS	Gold	A-side (Chart Hit) ... B-side	Pop	$	Pic	Label & Number
				DUDLEY, Dave — Cont'd				
3/3/73	19	12		30 Keep On Truckin' .... It Won't Hurt As Much Tomorrow picture sleeve heading shows "Mack Trucks presents Dave Dudley"	—	$7	■	Mercury 73367
8/4/73	37	9		31 It Takes Time .... I Almost Didn't Make It Through The Door	—	$7		Mercury 73404
11/3/73	47	12		32 Rollin' Rig .... Six Days On The Road	—	$8		Rice 5064
4/6/74	67	7		33 Have It Your Way .... Blue Bedroom Eyes	—	$8		Rice 5067
8/31/74	61	9		34 Counterfeit Cowboy .... That's How Cold	—	$8		Rice 5069
2/8/75	74	10		35 How Come It Took So Long (To Say Goodbye) ...... I've Lived Like A Piece Of Grass	—	$6		United Artists 585
5/3/75	21	12		36 Fireball Rolled A Seven .... Blue Bedroom Eyes	—	$6		United Artists 630
10/25/75+	12	15		37 Me And Ole C.B. .... I Can't Remember You	—	$6		United Artists 722
2/28/76	47	8		38 Sentimental Journey .... The Night You Broke The News #1 Pop hit for Les Brown in 1945	—	$6		United Artists 766
8/21/76	83	5		39 38 And Lonely .... Texas Ruby	—	$6		United Artists 836
3/4/78	95	3		40 One A.M. Alone .... If Seeing Is Believing	—	$6		Rice 5077
9/6/80	77	5		41 Rolaids, Doan's Pills And Preparation H .... Maybe I Can	—	$6		Sun 1154
				DUFF, Arlie '54 Born Arleigh Duff on 3/28/24 in Jack's Branch, Texas. Died on 7/4/96 (age 72). Male singer/DJ.				
12/5/53+	7	10		You All Come S:7 / A:7 / J:8 Poor Ole Teacher	—	$25		Starday 104
				DUGAN, Jeff '88 Born in Broussard, Louisiana. Singer/songwriter/guitarist.				
8/15/87	68	12		1 Once A Fool, Always A Fool .... Somebody Kill The Jukebox	—	$4		Warner 28376
5/28/88	52	8		2 I Wish It Was That Easy Going Home .... That Won't Ever Stop Me Loving You	—	$4		Warner 27995

DUNCAN, Johnny ★121★ '76
Born on 10/5/38 in Dublin, Texas. Singer/songwriter/guitarist. Attended Texas Christian University. Lived in Clovis, New Mexico (1959-64). Moved tro Nashville in 1964 and worked as a DJ on WAGG in Franklin, Tennessee. Related to **Brady Seals**, **Dan Seals** and **Troy Seals**.

1)Thinkin' Of A Rendezvous 2)She Can Put Her Shoes Under My Bed (Anytime) 3)It Couldn't Have Been Any Better
4)Hello Mexico (And Adios Baby To You) 5)Come A Little Bit Closer

DEBUT	PEAK	WKS		A-side ... B-side	Pop	$		Label & Number
8/12/67	54	7		1 Hard Luck Joe .... Gotta Get Back (On The Right Track)	—	$7		Columbia 44196
1/13/68	67	3		2 Baby Me Baby .... Mystery	—	$7		Columbia 44383
8/17/68	47	9		3 To My Sorrow .... I'm In This Town For Good	—	$7		Columbia 44580
10/19/68	21	8		4 Jackson Ain't A Very Big Town .... The True And Lasting Kind JOHNNY DUNCAN AND JUNE STEARNS	—	$7		Columbia 44656
2/8/69	70	4		5 I Live To Love You .... Louisville Nashville Southbound Train	—	$7		Columbia 44693
3/15/69	74	3		6 Back To Back (We're Strangers) .... If That's The Only Way JOHNNY DUNCAN AND JUNE STEARNS	—	$7		Columbia 44752
6/21/69	30	12		7 When She Touches Me .... Shreveport To L.A.	—	$7		Columbia 44864
12/13/69+	65	6		8 Window Number Five .... Day Drinker	—	$7		Columbia 45006
5/9/70	39	10		9 You're Gonna Need A Man .... Long Tall Drawn Out Day	—	$7		Columbia 45124
9/19/70	68	3		10 My Woman's Love .... (There's Still) Someone I Can't Forget	—	$7		Columbia 45201
10/31/70	27	13		11 Let Me Go (Set Me Free) .... What I Don't Know	—	$7		Columbia 45227
3/13/71	19	13		12 There's Something About A Lady .... I Don't Know Why I Keep Loving You	—	$7		Columbia 45319
7/24/71	39	9		13 One Night Of Love .... (A Whole Lot Of) Peaches In Georgia	—	$7		Columbia 45418
11/27/71+	12	13		14 Baby's Smile, Woman's Kiss .... I'd Rather Love You	—	$7		Columbia 45479
3/18/72	19	12		15 Fools .... Tiny Fingers	—	$7		Columbia 45556
9/30/72	66	5		16 Here We Go Again .... (I'll Always Love) When We Loved	—	$7		Columbia 45674
3/31/73	6	16		17 Sweet Country Woman .... The Look In Baby's Eyes	—	$6		Columbia 45818
9/8/73	18	14		18 Talkin' With My Lady .... You're My Woman	—	$6		Columbia 45917
4/6/74	47	9		19 The Pillow .... Ain't No Way That I Can Forget You	—	$6		Columbia 46018
9/21/74	66	9		20 Scarlet Water .... We're Not Fooling Our Hearts	—	$5		Columbia 10007
3/8/75	57	8		21 Charley Is My Name .... Gentle Fire	—	$5		Columbia 10085
8/23/75	26	14		22 Jo And The Cowboy .... Taking A Chance On You	—	$5		Columbia 10182
12/20/75+	86	7		23 Gentle Fire .... Good Morning Love	—	$5		Columbia 10262
3/27/76	4	20		24 Stranger Flashing, Screaming, Silent Neon Sign	—	$5		Columbia 10302
10/2/76	❶²	17		25 Thinkin' Of A Rendezvous Love Should Be Easy	—	$5		Columbia 10417
2/5/77	❶¹	15		26 It Couldn't Have Been Any Better Denver Woman	—	$5		Columbia 10474
6/4/77	5	16		27 A Song In The Night Use My Love	105	$5		Columbia 10554
10/29/77+	4	16		28 Come A Little Bit Closer Loneliness (Can Break A Good Man Down) JOHNNY DUNCAN (with Janie Fricke) #3 Pop hit for Jay & The Americans in 1964	—	$5		Columbia 10634
3/11/78	❶¹	18		29 She Can Put Her Shoes Under My Bed (Anytime) Maybe I Just Crossed Your Mind	—	$5		Columbia 10694
7/15/78	4	14		30 Hello Mexico (And Adios Baby To You) I Watched An Angel (Going Through Hell)	—	$5		Columbia 10783
2/24/79	6	14		31 Slow Dancing One Night Of Love #10 Pop hit for **Johnny Rivers** in 1977	—	$5		Columbia 10915
9/29/79	9	12		32 The Lady In The Blue Mercedes Too Far Gone	—	$5		Columbia 11097
1/5/80	17	14		33 Play Another Slow Song .... My Woman's Good To Me	—	$4		Columbia 11185
6/7/80	17	14		34 I'm Gonna Love You Tonight (In My Dreams) .... Wine Oh Wine	—	$4		Columbia 11280
7/12/80	17	14		35 He's Out Of My Life .... Loving Arms JOHNNY DUNCAN and JANIE FRICKE #10 Pop hit for Michael Jackson in 1980	—	$4		Columbia 11312
11/8/80+	16	14		36 Acapulco .... Am I That Easy To Forget	—	$4		Columbia 11385

DEBUT	PEAK	WKS	Gold	A-side (Chart Hit)	B-side	Pop	$	Pic	Label & Number
				DUNCAN, Johnny — Cont'd					
11/7/81	40	10		37 All Night Long	My Heart's Not In It	—	$4		Columbia 02570
4/12/86	69	6		38 The Look Of A Lady In Love		—	$5		Pharoah 2502
8/16/86	81	2		39 Texas Moon		—	$5		Pharoah 2503
				DUNCAN, Tommy '49					
				Born on 1/11/11 in Hillsboro, Texas. Died of a heart attack on 7/25/67 (age 56). Featured vocalist with **Bob Wills**.					
8/13/49	8	3		Gamblin' Polka Dot Blues S:8 / J:8 September		—	$25		Capitol 40178
				TOMMY DUNCAN And His Western All Stars					
				DUNN, Holly ★199★ '89					
				Born on 8/22/57 in San Antonio, Texas. Singer/songwriter/guitarist. Sister of **Chris Waters**. Former staff writer at CBS and MTM Records. Joined the *Grand Ole Opry* in 1989. Worked as a DJ at WWWW in Detroit. CMA Award: 1987 Horizon Award. Also see **Tomorrow's World**.					
				1) You Really Had Me Going 2) Are You Ever Gonna Love Me 3) Love Someone Like Me 4) Only When I Love 5) There Goes My Heart Again					
6/8/85	62	6		1 Playing For Keeps	I'm Not Through Loving You Yet	—	$4		MTM 72052
10/5/85	64	8		2 My Heart Holds On	Shot In The Dark	—	$4		MTM 72057
5/17/86	39	12		3 Two Too Many S:39 / A:39 You		—	$4		MTM 72064
8/23/86	7	25		4 Daddy's Hands S:4 / A:7 Hideaway Heart		—	$4		MTM 72075
2/7/87	4	21		5 A Face In The Crowd A:4 / S:15 You're History		—	$4		Warner 28471
				MICHAEL MARTIN MURPHEY AND HOLLY DUNN					
5/2/87	2²	25		6 Love Someone Like Me S:❶¹ Burnin' Wheel		—	$4		MTM 72082
8/29/87	4	25		7 Only When I Love S:❶¹ Little Frame House		—	$4		MTM 72091
1/16/88	7	24		8 Strangers Again S:2 Wrap Me Up		—	$4		MTM 72093
6/25/88	5	20		9 That's What Your Love Does To Me S:3 Lonesome Highway		—	$4		MTM 72108
11/5/88+	11	19		10 (It's Always Gonna Be) Someday	On The Wings Of An Angel	—	$4		MTM 72116
5/27/89	❶¹	23		11 Are You Ever Gonna Love Me	If I'd Never Loved You	—	$4		Warner 22957
9/23/89	4	26		12 There Goes My Heart Again	The Blue Rose Of Texas	—	$4		Warner 22796
2/17/90	25	13		13 Maybe	If I Knew Then What I Know Now	—	$4	■	Reprise 19972 (v)
				KENNY ROGERS (with Holly Dunn)					
6/2/90	63	4		14 My Anniversary For Being A Fool	The Light In The Window Went Out	—	$4		Warner 19847
9/1/90	❶¹	20		15 You Really Had Me Going	When No Place Is Home	—	$4	■	Warner 19756 (v)
1/5/91	19	20		16 Heart Full Of Love	Temporary Loss Of Memory	—	$4		Warner 19472
7/13/91	48	9		17 Maybe I Mean Yes	Daddy's Hands	—	$4		Warner 19266
4/25/92	67	4		18 No Love Have I	Love Someone Like Me	—	$4		Warner 18956
8/1/92	68	7		19 As Long As You Belong To Me	You Can Have Him	—	$4		Warner 18831
12/26/92+	51	10		20 Golden Years		—			album cut
				from the album *Getting It Dunn* on Warner 26949					
4/8/95	56	11		21 I Am Who I Am	Love Across The Line	—	$4	■	River North 3003
				DUNN, Ronnie '84					
				Born on 6/1/53 in Coleman, Texas. Joined with **Kix Brooks** in duo **Brooks & Dunn**.					
3/5/83	59	7		1 It's Written All Over Your Face	You Never Crossed My Mind	—	$6	■	Churchill 94018
6/23/84	59	8		2 She Put The Sad In All His Songs	Change Of Attitude	—	$6		Churchill 52083
				DURHAM, Bobby '88					
				Born in Bakersfield, California. Singer/songwriter/guitarist.					
5/21/88	92	2		1 Let's Start A Rumor Today		—	$6		Hightone 502
				DURRENCE, Sam '73					
				Worked as a DJ at WHOO in Orlando, Florida.					
9/15/73	98	3		1 Last Days Of Childhood	She Almost Believed Me	—	$7		River 3875
				DYCKE, Jerry '80					
				Born in Topeka, Kansas.					
5/3/80	93	3		1 Daddy Played Harmonica	I Never Said Goodbye	—	$6		Churchill 7757
2/28/81	94	2		2 Beethoven Was Before My Time	My Shoes Keep Walking Back To You	—	$6		Churchill 7766

E

EAGLES '75

Rock-country group formed in Los Angeles: **Don Henley** (vocals, drums; born on 7/22/47), Glenn Frey (vocals, guitar; born on 11/6/48), Randy Meisner (bass; born on 3/8/46) and Bernie Leadon (guitar; born on 7/19/47). Meisner founded **Poco**. Leadon had been in the **Flying Burrito Brothers**. Frey and Henley were with **Linda Ronstadt**. Don Felder (guitar; born on 9/21/47) added in 1975. Leadon replaced by Joe Walsh (born on 11/20/47) in 1975. Meisner replaced by Timothy B. Schmit (born on 10/30/47) in 1977. Disbanded in 1982. Henley, Frey, Felder, Walsh and Schmit reunited in 1994. Group inducted into the Rock and Roll Hall of Fame in 1998.

DEBUT	PEAK	WKS	Gold	A-side	B-side	Pop	$	Pic	Label & Number
10/11/75	8	13		1 Lyin' Eyes	Too Many Hands	2²	$5		Asylum 45279
1/8/77	43	12	●	2 New Kid In Town	Victim Of Love	❶¹	$5		Asylum 45373
1/24/81	55	7		3 Seven Bridges Road	The Long Run (live)	21	$5		Asylum 47100
				recorded "live" on 7/28/80 at the Santa Monica Civic Auditorium					
11/12/94	58	6		4 The Girl From Yesterday		—			album cut
				from the album *Hell Freezes Over* on Geffen 24725					

EAKES, Bobbie — see **RAYE, Collin**

DEBUT	PEAK	WKS	Gold	A-side (Chart Hit)	B-side	Pop	$	Pic	Label & Number
				EARL, Kenny '81					
				Singer/songwriter. Member of **The Wolfpack**.					
5/9/81	84	3		1 We Have To Start Meeting Like This... Raindrops		—	$6		Kik 904
9/19/81	73	4		2 Wasn't It Supposed To Be Me .... Raindrops		—	$6		Kari 124
				EARLE, Steve '86					
				Born on 1/17/55 in Fort Monroe, Virginia; raised in Schertz, Texas. Singer/songwriter/guitarist.					
10/1/83	70	4		1 Nothin' But You... Continental Trailways Blues		—	$5		Epic 04070
				STEVE EARLE & The Dukes					
12/8/84	76	6		2 What'll You Do About Me? .... Cry Myself To Sleep		—	$5	■	Epic 04666
3/22/86	37	13		3 Hillbilly Highway .... Down The Road		—	$4		MCA 52785
6/21/86	7	22		4 Guitar Town S:6 / A:8 Little Rock 'N' Roller		—	$4		MCA 52856
10/25/86	28	15		5 Someday.. A:28 / S:30 Hillbilly Highway		—	$4		MCA 52920
2/14/87	8	19		6 Goodbyes All We've Got Left A:8 / S:15 Good Ol' Boy (Gettin Tough)		—	$4		MCA 53011
6/13/87	20	16		7 Nowhere Road .... I Ain't Ever Satisfied		—	$4		MCA 53103
10/17/87	37	13		8 Sweet Little '66 .... Angry Young Man		—	$4		MCA 53182
1/9/88	29	13		9 Six Days On The Road .... The Week Of Living Dangerously		—	$4		Hughes/MCA 53249
				STEVE EARLE & THE DUKES (above 2)					
				from the movie *Planes, Trains & Automobiles* starring Steve Martin and John Candy					
	★276★			**EARWOOD, Mundo** '78					
				Born Raymond Earwood on 10/13/52 in Del Rio, Texas. Singer/songwriter/guitarist.					
				1)Things I'd Do For You 2)Fooled Around And Fell In Love 3)Can't Keep My Mind Off Of Her					
				4)You're In Love With The Wrong Man 5)Behind Blue Eyes					
10/21/72	57	10		1 Behind Blue Eyes .... Breaking Up Is Hard To Do		—	$7		Royal American 65
				also see #7 below					
6/29/74	59	10		2 Let's Hear It For Loneliness .... Angeline		—	$6		GRT 003
10/25/75	91	4		3 She Brings Her Lovin' Home To Me .... Life Has It's Little Ups And Downs		—	$5		Epic 50141
				MUNDO RAY					
2/7/76	86	7		4 I Can't Quit Cheatin' On You .... That's My Desire		—	$5		Epic 50185
6/26/76	70	7		5 Lonesome Is A Cowboy .... (Don't Give Your Love To Any Man) Who Buys The Wine		—	$5		Epic 50232
3/19/77	86	4		6 I Can Give You Love .... Let's Get Naked		—	$5		True 101
7/9/77	32	11		7 Behind Blue Eyes... Let's Get Naked [R]		—	$5		True 104
				same version as #1 above					
12/17/77+	69	8		8 Angelene .... Just Another One Of Those Days		—	$5		True 111
5/20/78	36	11		9 When I Get You Alone .... Let Me Down Easy		—	$5		GMC 102
9/2/78	18	13		10 Things I'd Do For You Breaking Up Is Hard To Do		—	$5		GMC 104
12/2/78+	25	13		11 Fooled Around And Fell In Love .... Love Me Now		—	$5		GMC 105
4/28/79	38	10		12 My Heart Is Not My Own .... My Weakness Is Stronger Than I Am		—	$5		GMC 106
8/4/79	34	9		13 We Got Love .... It's Magic		—	$5		GMC 107
11/24/79	67	6		14 Sometimes Love /		—			
10/13/79	73	3		15 Philodendron		—	$5		GMC 108
4/5/80	27	13		16 You're In Love With The Wrong Man .... Before We Call It Love		—	$5	■	GMC 109
				Mel Tillis (harmony vocal)					
9/27/80	26	12		17 Can't Keep My Mind Off Of Her .... Just Another One Of Those Days		—	$5		GMC 111
2/14/81	40	9		18 Blue Collar Blues .... Softer Place To Fall		—	$5		Excelsior 1005
5/16/81	32	12		19 Angela .... Pyramid Of Cans		—	$5		Excelsior 1010
10/17/81	45	8		20 I'll Still Be Loving You .... Pyramid Of Cans		—	$5		Excelsior 1019
4/17/82	58	8		21 All My Lovin .... Breaking Up Is Hard To Do		—	$6		Primero 1002
				#45 Pop hit for The Beatles in 1964					
9/4/82	68	5		22 Pyramid Of Cans.. Breaking Up Is Hard To Do		—	$6		Primero 1009
4/15/89	80	3		23 A Woman's Way .... Love Me Now		—	$5		Pegasus 110
				EAST, Lyndel '78					
				Born in Oklahoma City.					
7/29/78	97	2		Why Do You Come Around .... All She Ever Wanted		—	$6		NSD 2
				EASTON, Sheena '83					
				Born Sheena Orr on 4/27/59 in Bellshill, Scotland. Pop singer/actress. Won the 1981 Best New Artist Grammy Award. Acted on TV's *Miami Vice*.					
1/29/83	❶¹	17		1 We've Got Tonight .... You Are So Beautiful (Rogers)		6	$4	■	Liberty 1492
				KENNY ROGERS and SHEENA EASTON					
				#13 Pop hit for **Bob Seger** in 1979					
3/24/84	86	7		2 Almost Over You .... I Don't Need Your Word		25	$4		EMI America 8186
				EASTWOOD, Clint — see **CHARLES, Ray / HAGGARD, Merle**					
				EATON, Connie '75					
				Born on 3/1/50 in Nashville. Daughter of singer Bob Eaton.					
2/7/70	34	7		1 Angel Of The Morning .... One Time Too Many		—	$6		Chart 5048
				#7 Pop hit for **Merrilee Rush** in 1968					
5/23/70	44	9		2 Hit The Road Jack .... The Question		—	$6		Chart 5066
				CONNIE EATON & DAVE PEEL					
				#1 Pop hit for **Ray Charles** in 1961					
11/7/70	56	7		3 It Takes Two .... No Rest For The Wicked		—	$6		Chart 5099
				CONNIE EATON & DAVE PEEL					
				#14 Pop hit for Marvin Gaye & Kim Weston in 1967					
2/6/71	74	2		4 Sing A Happy Song .... Glad To Be Your Woman		—	$6		Chart 5110
9/11/71	56	10		5 Don't Hang No Halos On Me .... These Hills		—	$6		Chart 5138
1/25/75	23	13		6 Lonely Men, Lonely Women .... Midnight Train To Georgia		—	$5		Dunhill/ABC 15022
6/14/75	93	4		7 If I Knew Enough To Come Out Of The Rain .... Magic Mystery		—	$5		ABC 12098

DEBUT	PEAK	WKS	Gold	A-side (Chart Hit)	B-side	Pop	$	Pic	Label & Number
				EATON, Skip — see SKIP & LINDA					
				EBERLY, Bob '49					
				Born Robert Eberle on 7/24/16 in Mechanicsville, New York. Died on 11/17/81 (age 65). Vocalist with Jimmy Dorsey from 1935-43.					
1/1/49	8	1		1 **One Has My Name The Other Has My Heart** .... J:8 / S:15 *Just A Little Lovin' (Will Go A Long Way)*		—	$20		Decca 24492
				BOB EBERLY with The Sunshine Serenaders					
				#13 Pop hit for Barry Young in 1966					
				EDDY, Duane '58					
				Born on 4/26/38 in Corning, New York. Originator of the "twangy" guitar sound. Married to **Jessi Colter** from 1961-68. Charted 28 pop hits from 1958-86. Inducted into the Rock and Roll Hall of Fame in 1994.					
8/4/58	17	5		1 **Rebel-'Rouser** .... S:17 *Stalkin'* [I]		6	$30		Jamie 1104
				The Sharps (later known as The Rivingtons, rebel yells)					
5/7/77	69	6		2 **You Are My Sunshine** .... *From 8 To 7*		—	$6		Elektra 45359
				Waylon Jennings, Willie Nelson, Kin Vassy and Duane's wife, Deed Eddy (vocals); #7 Pop hit for Ray Charles in 1962; instrumental version recorded by Eddy on his 1960 album *The Twangs The Thang*					
				EDGE, Kathy '87					
				Born in Huntsville, Alabama; raised in Memphis.					
3/21/87	89	5		1 **I Take The Chance** .... *You Always Come Back To Hurting Me*		—	$5		NSD 228
				EDMUNDS, Dave — see CARTER, Carlene					
				EDWARDS, Bobby '61					
				Born Robert Moncrief on 1/18/26 in Anniston, Alabama.					
9/4/61	4	24		1 **You're The Reason** ★★★ .... *I'm A Fool For Loving You*		11	$12	★	Crest 1075
				The Four Young Men (backing vocals)					
9/14/63	23	2		2 **Don't Pretend** .... *Help Me*		—	$10		Capitol 5006
				EDWARDS, Jimmy '58					
				Born James Bullington on 2/9/33 in Senath, Missouri.					
11/11/57+	12	6		**Love Bug Crawl** .... A:12 *Honey Lovin'*		78	$30		Mercury 71209
				EDWARDS, Jonathan '89					
				Born on 7/28/46 in Aitkin, Minnesota; raised in Virginia. Singer/songwriter/guitarist.					
9/17/88	64	6		1 **We Need To Be Locked Away** .... *Back Up Grinnin'*		—	$4		MCA/Curb 53390
12/10/88+	56	14		2 **Look What We Made (When We Made Love)** .... *Fewer Threads Than These*		—	$4		MCA/Curb 53467
3/18/89	59	7		3 **It's A Natural Thing** .... *My Baby's A Country Song*		—	$4		MCA/Curb 53613
				EDWARDS, Meredith '01					
				Born on 3/15/84 in Clinton, Mississippi.					
2/3/01	37	13		1 **A Rose Is A Rose** .... S:8 *Slow Learner*		—	$4	★	Mercury 172193 (v)
5/26/01	47	9		2 **The Bird Song**		—			album cut
				from the album *Reach* on Mercury 170188					
				EDWARDS, Stoney '73					
				Born Frenchy Edwards on 12/24/29 in Seminole, Oklahoma. Died on 4/5/97 (age 67). Black singer/songwriter/guitarist.					
				1) *She's My Rock* 2) *Mississippi You're On My Mind* 3) *Hank And Lefty Raised My Country Soul*					
1/23/71	68	3		1 **A Two Dollar Toy** .... *An Old Mule's Hip*		—	$6		Capitol 3005
4/3/71	61	7		2 **Poor Folks Stick Together** .... *Mama's Love*		—	$6		Capitol 3061
8/28/71	73	2		3 **The Cute Little Waitress** .... *Please Bring A Bottle*		—	$6		Capitol 3131
11/11/72+	20	14		4 **She's My Rock** .... *I Won't Make It Through The Day*		—	$5		Capitol 3462
3/17/73	54	6		5 **You're A Believer** .... *She's Helping Me Get Over You*		—	$5		Capitol 3550
8/11/73	39	10		6 **Hank And Lefty Raised My Country Soul** .... *A Few Of The Reasons*		—	$5		Capitol 3671
12/22/73+	85	7		7 **Daddy Bluegrass** .... *It's Rainin' On My Sunny Day*		—	$5		Capitol 3766
2/8/75	77	8		8 **Clean Your Own Tables** .... *Do You Know The Man*		—	$5		Capitol 4015
4/19/75	20	12		9 **Mississippi You're On My Mind** .... *A Two Dollar Toy*		—	$5		Capitol 4051
11/29/75+	41	11		10 **Blackbird (Hold Your Head High)** .... *Pickin' Wildflowers*		—	$5		Capitol 4188
4/10/76	51	8		11 **Love Still Makes The World Go 'Round** .... *(I Want) The Real Thing*		—	$5		Capitol 4246
10/23/76	90	4		12 **Don't Give Up On Me** .... *July 12, 1939*		—	$5		Capitol 4337
11/4/78	60	7		13 **If I Had It To Do All Over Again** .... *I Feel Chained*		—	$5		JMI 47
5/24/80	53	10		14 **No Way To Drown A Memory** .... *Reverend Leroy*		—	$5		Music America 107
9/20/80	85	3		15 **One Bar At A Time** .... *Stranger In My Arms*		—	$5		Music America 109
				ELLEDGE, Jimmy '75					
				Born on 1/8/43 in Nashville. Singer/songwriter/pianist.					
5/17/75	95	4		**One By One** .... *After You*		—	$5		4 Star 1003
				ELLIOTT, Alecia '00					
				Born on 12/25/82 in Muscle Shoals, Alabama. Female singer.					
10/2/99+	50	20		1 **I'm Diggin' It** .... S:3 *(dance mix)*		—	$4	★	MCA Nash. 172121 (v)
5/13/00	70	10		2 **You Wanna What?** .... *That's The Only Way*		—	$4		MCA Nashville 172159
				ELLIS, Darryl & Don '92					
				Brothers Darryl (born on 12/1/64) and Don (born on 7/2/67) Ellis Gatlin. Both born in Norfolk, Virginia; raised in Beaver Falls, Pennsylvania.					
6/27/92	70	2		1 **Goodbye Highway** .... *I Knew You'd Come Around*		—	$4		Epic 74325
9/5/92	58	8		2 **No Sir** .... *I Knew You'd Come Around*		—	$4	▌	Epic 74454 (v)
11/21/92	73	4		3 **Something Moving In Me** .... *You Know Why*		—	$4		Epic 74758
				ELLIS, Mike '78					
				Born in San Antonio, Texas. Singer/songwriter/guitarist.					
7/29/78	89	3		**I Never Meant To Harm You** .... *West Virginian*		—	$5		Cin Kay 130

DEBUT	PEAK	WKS	Gold	A-side (Chart Hit)	B-side	Pop	$	Pic	Label & Number
				ELLWANGER, Sandy '89					
				Born on 9/10/63 in Fremont, California. Female singer/songwriter/pianist.					
7/29/89	96	2		1 I Just Came In Here (To Let A Little Hurt Out)		—	$5		Door Knob 326
11/11/89	79	2		2 What Kind Of Girl Do You Think I Am		—	$5		Door Knob 334
				ELMO & PATSY '99					
				Husband-and-wife team of Elmo Shropshire and Patsy Trigg. Divorced in 1985.					
12/31/83	92	2		1 Grandma Got Run Over By A Reindeer	Christmas [X-N]	—	$5		Soundwaves 4658
				ELMO 'N PATSY					
				originally released on Oink 2984 in 1979 ($6); first issued on Soundwaves in 1982					
12/27/97	64	2		2 Grandma Got Run Over By A Reindeer	Percy, The Puny Poinsettia [X-N-R]	—	$4	■	Epic 05479 (v)
				above 2 are different versions					
12/25/99	48	3		3 Grandma Got Run Over By A Reindeer	Percy, The Puny Poinsettia [X-N-R]	—	$4	■	Epic 05479 (v)
				ELY, Joe '77					
				Born on 2/9/47 in Amarillo, Texas; raised in Lubbock, Texas. Singer/songwriter/guitarist. Member of the **Buzzin' Cousins**.					
2/12/77	89	3		All My Love	Mardi Gras Waltz	—	$5		MCA 40666
				EME '81					
2/21/81	86	2		Every Breath I Take	Goodbye To Love	—	$7		EPI 1541
				EMERSON DRIVE '02					
				Group from Canada: Brad Mates (vocals), Danick Dupelle (guitar), Chris Hatman (keyboards), Pat Allingham (fiddle), Jeff Loberg (bass) and Mike Melancon (drums).					
11/10/01+	4	34↑		I Should Be Sleeping	S:2 (2 versions) / Hollywood Kiss	35	$4	★	DreamWor. 50362 (v)
				EMERY, Ralph '61					
				Born Walter Ralph Emery on 3/10/33 in McEwen, Tennessee. Former host of TNN's *Nashville Now*. Married to **Skeeter Davis** from 1960-64.					
8/28/61	4	15		Hello Fool	It's Not A Lot (But It's All I've Got) [S]	—	$15		Liberty 55352
				answer to "Hello Walls" by **Faron Young**					
				EMILIO '95					
				Born Emilio Navaira on 8/23/62 in San Antonio, Texas.					
8/19/95	27	20		1 It's Not The End Of The World	S:20 Life Is Good	—	$4	■	Capitol 58432 (v)
				"45": Capitol 18846 (B-side: "I Think We're On To Something")					
1/20/96	41	15		2 Even If I Tried	S:10 There'll Be No More Crying	—	$4	■	Capitol 58507
5/11/96	56	7		3 I Think We're On To Something		—		■	album cut (v)
				first issued as the "45" B-side of #1 above					
10/12/96	62	1		4 Have I Told You Lately		—			album cut
				#5 Pop hit for Rod Stewart in 1993; above 2 from the album *Life Is Good* on Capitol 32392					
2/15/97	56	9		5 I'd Love You To Love Me	S:22 Any Little Lie	—	$4	■	Capitol 58632 (v)
				"45": Capitol 19514					
6/7/97	64	3		6 She Gives	The Bottom Of Your Heart	—	$4		Capitol 19603
				ENGLAND, Ty '95					
				Born on 12/5/63 in Oklahoma City. Singer/songwriter/guitarist.					
6/10/95	3	20		1 Should've Asked Her Faster	S:11 A Swing Like That	121	$4	■	RCA 64280 (v)
10/28/95+	44	16		2 Smoke In Her Eyes	S:25 Redneck Son	—	$4		RCA 64405 (v)
2/24/96	55	7		3 Redneck Son	It's Lonesome Everywhere	—	$4		RCA 64496
8/10/96	22	20		4 Irresistible You	S:17 You'll Find Somebody New	—	$4	■	RCA 64598 (v)
12/28/96+	46	9		5 All Of The Above	Sure	—	$4		RCA 64676
2/3/01	53	9		6 I Drove Her To Dallas		—			album cut
				TYLER ENGLAND					
				from the album *Highways & Dance Halls* on Capitol 521657					
				ENGLISH, Robin '02					
				Born in 1971 in Texas. Female singer/songwriter.					
12/1/01+	10^S	31↑		Girl In Love	Tough Talkin' Cowboys	—	$4	★	Columbia 79648
				ENGVALL, Bill '97					
				Born on 7/27/57 in Galveston, Texas. Comedian/actor. Played "Bill Pelton" on TV's *The* **Jeff Foxworthy** *Show*.					
				1)*Here's Your Sign (Get The Picture)* 2)*Here's Your Sign Christmas* 3)*Warning Signs*					
1/25/97	29	20	●	1 Here's Your Sign (Get The Picture)	S:0[8] Things Have Changed [C]	43	$4	■	Warner 17491 (v)
				BILL ENGVALL with Travis Tritt					
8/16/97	56	5		2 Warning Signs	S:21 Baby Barf And The Turkey Hunt (Engvall) [C]	—	$4	■	Warner 43934
				BILL ENGVALL with John Michael Montgomery					
2/14/98	72	1		3 It's Hard To Be A Parent	[N]	—	$10	★	Warner 9165
				available only as a promotional CD single					
10/17/98	60	8		4 I'm A Cowboy	[N]	—			album cut
12/12/98	39	5		5 Here's Your Sign Christmas	[X-N]	—			album cut
4/24/99	72	1		6 Hollywood Indian Guides	[N]	—			album cut
12/11/99	46	5		7 Here's Your Sign Christmas	[X-N-R]	—			album cut
				above 4 from the album *Dorkfish* on Warner 47090					
4/15/00	63	6		8 The Blue Collar Dollar Song	[N]	—			album cut
				JEFF FOXWORTHY and BILL ENGVALL Featuring Marty Stuart					
				from Foxworthy's album *Big Funny* on DreamWorks 50200					
9/2/00	59	12		9 Now That's Awesome	S:13 (no B-side) [N]	—	$4	★	BNA 60286
				BILL ENGVALL Featuring Tracy Byrd, Neal McCoy & T. Graham Brown					
12/9/00	71	2		10 Shoulda Shut Up	[C]	—			album cut
				from the album *Now That's Awesome!* on BNA 69311					

DEBUT	PEAK	WKS	Gold	A-side (Chart Hit)	B-side	Pop	$	Pic	Label & Number
				ESMERELDY '48					
				Born Verna Sherrill on 6/1/20 in Middleton, Tennessee. Known as "The Streamlined Hillbilly." Mother of pop singer Amy Holland.					
3/20/48	10	1		**Slap Her Down Again Paw**............Red Wing [N]		—	$20		Musicraft 524
				ESMERELDY And Her Novelty Band					
				#7 Pop hit for Arthur Godfrey in 1948					
				ETC BAND, The — see CONLEY, Earl Thomas					
				ETHEL & THE SHAMELESS HUSSIES '88					
				Female trio from Huntsville, Alabama: "Ethel Beaverton" (**Gayle Zeiler**), "Blanche Hickey" (**Valerie Hunt**) and "Bunny O'Hare" (**Beki Fogle**). Name taken from a line in "The Streak" by Ray Stevens.					
5/21/88	71	5		1 **One Nite Stan**................Smokin' In Bed [N]		—	$4		MCA 53323
1/21/89	86	2		2 **It's Just The Whiskey Talkin'**................Mr. Cadillac		—	$4		MCA 53472
				EVANGELINE '94					
				Female group from Louisiana: Kathleen Stieffel (vocals, guitar), Rhonda Lohmeyer (guitar), Sharon Leger (bass) and Beth McKee (keyboards).					
1/22/94	70	4		**Let's Go Spend Your Money Honey**................On The Levee		—	$4	■	MCA 54787 (v)
				EVANS, Ashley '90					
				Female singer.					
1/6/90	76	2		**I'm So Afraid Of Losing You Again**		—	$5		Door Knob 338
				EVANS, Paul '78					
				Born on 3/5/38 in New York City. Singer/songwriter. Charted 4 pop hits from 1959-60.					
5/20/78	57	10		1 **Hello, This Is Joannie (The Telephone Answering Machine Song)**................Lullabye Tissue Paper Co.		—	$5		Spring 183
5/5/79	81	4		2 **Disneyland Daddy**................Build An Ark		—	$5		Spring 193
8/16/80	80	4		3 **One Night Led To Two**................Hangin' Out And Hangin' In		—	$5		Cinnamon 604
				EVANS, Paula Kay '77					
				Born on 11/10/57 in Garland, Texas.					
4/23/77	100	2		**Runnin' Out Again**................Hangin' Out Again		—	$6		Autumn 368
	★344★			**EVANS, Sara** '01					
				Born on 2/5/71 in Boonville, Missouri; raised in Boonesboro, Missouri.					
				1)Born To Fly 2)No Place That Far 3)I Could Not Ask For More					
3/29/97	59	6		1 **True Lies**................The Week The River Raged		—	$4	■	RCA 64784 (v)
7/12/97	44	11		2 **Three Chords And The Truth**................The Week The River Raged		—	$4		RCA 64876
12/27/97+	48	8		3 **Shame About That**................(remix)		—	$4	■	RCA 65324 (v)
6/13/98	56	10		4 **Cryin' Game**................Wait A Minute		—	$4		RCA 65517
10/3/98+	❶¹	30		5 **No Place That Far**................S:3 Cryin' Game		37	$4	★	RCA 65584 (v)
4/3/99	32	20		6 **Fool, I'm A Woman**................No Place That Far		—	$4		RCA 65744
3/25/00	22	28		7 **That's The Beat Of A Heart**................Grow Young With You (**Coley McCabe**)		—	$4		BNA 62013
				THE WARREN BROTHERS Featuring Sara Evans					
				from the movie Where The Heart Is starring Natalie Portman					
7/1/00+	❶¹	35		8 **Born To Fly**		34			
2/17/01	2³	26		9 **I Could Not Ask For More**		35	$4		RCA 69008
				#37 Pop hit for Edwin McCain in 1999					
9/15/01+	16	22		10 **Saints & Angels**................I Learned That From You		103	$4		RCA 69107
	★204★			**EVERETTE, Leon** '81					
				Born Leon Everette Baughman on 6/21/48 in Aiken, South Carolina; raised in New York City. Singer/songwriter/guitarist.					
				1)Hurricane 2)Giving Up Easy 3)I Could'a Had You 4)Just Give Me What You Think Is Fair 5)Midnight Rodeo					
12/3/77	84	5		1 **I Love That Woman (Like The Devil Loves Sin)**................Still Loving You		—	$6		True 110
				also see #6 below					
1/20/79	89	3		2 **We Let Love Fade Away**................Never Ending Crowded Circle		—	$5		Orlando 100
4/7/79	81	4		3 **Giving Up Easy**................Mama Rocked Us To Sleep (With Country Music)		—	$5		Orlando 102
				also see #9 below					
6/9/79	33	10		4 **Don't Feel Like The Lone Ranger**................We Let Love Fade Away		—	$5	■	Orlando 103
9/15/79	42	7		5 **The Sun Went Down In My World Tonight**................Cheater's Trap		—	$5		Orlando 104
12/8/79+	28	12		6 **I Love That Woman (Like The Devil Loves Sin)**................Never Ending Crowded Circle [R]		—	$5		Orlando 105
				new version of #1 above					
3/1/80	30	12		7 **I Don't Want To Lose**................Mama Rocked Us To Sleep		—	$5		Orlando 106
5/31/80	10	17		8 **Over**................Let Me Apologize		—	$5		Orlando 107
10/25/80+	5	18		9 **Giving Up Easy**................Setting Me Up [R]		—	$4		RCA 12111
				same version as #3 above					
3/7/81	11	13		10 **If I Keep On Going Crazy**................The Sun Went Down In My World Tonight		—	$4		RCA 12177
7/18/81	4	16		11 **Hurricane**................Make Me Stop Loving Her		—	$4		RCA 12270
11/14/81+	9	17		12 **Midnight Rodeo**................Don't Be Angry		—	$4		RCA 12355
3/27/82	7	18		13 **Just Give Me What You Think Is Fair**................Over		—	$4		RCA 13079
8/7/82	10	17		14 **Soul Searchin'**................Misery		—	$4		RCA 13282
11/27/82+	15	18		15 **Shadows Of My Mind**................If I Keep On Going Crazy		—	$4		RCA 13391
3/19/83	9	18		16 **My Lady Loves Me (Just As I Am)**................Somebody Killed Dewey Jones' Daughter		—	$4		RCA 13466
8/13/83	31	13		17 **The Lady, She's Right**................Knocking On Her Door		—	$4		RCA 13584
				Rex Gosdin (harmony vocal)					
2/4/84	6	20		18 **I Could'a Had You**................I Wanna Know Your Name		—	$4		RCA 13717
7/7/84	30	14		19 **Shot In The Dark**................I Want To Be In Pictures		—	$4		RCA 13834
3/30/85	47	10		20 **Too Good To Say No To**................It Never Felt Like This Before		—	$4		Mercury 880611
6/15/85	53	9		21 **A Good Love Died Tonight**................(You're Never Guilty) When Love Is Your Alibi		—	$4		Mercury 880829
10/5/85	44	9		22 **'Til A Tear Becomes A Rose**................It Never Felt Like This Before		—	$4		Mercury 884040

DEBUT	PEAK	WKS	Gold	A-side (Chart Hit) ... B-side	Pop	$	Pic	Label & Number
				EVERETTE, Leon — Cont'd				
5/24/86	46	9		23 Danger List (Give Me Someone I Can Love) .... Over	—	$5		Orlando 112
				first recorded by **John Cougar Mellencamp** *on his 1982 album* American Fool				
8/2/86	59	5		24 Sad State Of Affairs .... Danger List (Give Me Someone I Can Love)	—	$5		Orlando 114
11/15/86	56	6		25 Still In The Picture .... Danger List (Give Me Someone I Can Love)	—	$5		Orlando 115
				EVERLY, Don '76				
				Born Isaac Donald Everly on 2/1/37 in Brownie, Kentucky. One-half of **The Everly Brothers**.				
4/10/76	50	8		1 Yesterday Just Passed My Way Again .... Never Like This	—	$7		Hickory/MGM 368
2/5/77	84	4		2 Since You Broke My Heart .... Deep Water	—	$5		ABC/Hickory 54005
5/7/77	96	4		3 Brother Juke-Box .... Oh, What A Feeling	—	$5		ABC/Hickory 54012
				EVERLY, Phil '83				
				Born on 1/19/39 in Chicago. One-half of **The Everly Brothers**.				
12/27/80+	63	7		1 Dare To Dream Again .... Lonely Days, Lonely Nights	—	$5		Curb 5401
6/13/81	52	8		2 Sweet Southern Love .... In Your Eyes	—	$5		Curb 02116
2/19/83	37	12		3 Who's Gonna Keep Me Warm .... One Way Love	—	$5		Capitol 5197
	★203★			**EVERLY BROTHERS, The** '57				
				Duo of vocalists/guitarists/songwriters **Don Everly** and **Phil Everly**. Charted 38 pop hits from 1957-84. Duo split up in July 1973 and reunited in September 1983. Inducted into the Rock and Roll Hall of Fame in 1986. Elected to the Country Music Hall of Fame in 2001.				
				1) Wake Up Little Susie 2) Bye Bye Love 3) Bird Dog				
5/13/57	❶[7]	26	●	1 Bye Bye Love S:❶[7] / A:❶[7] I Wonder If I Care As Much (Pop flip)	2[4]	$25		Cadence 1315
9/30/57	❶[8]	22	●	2 Wake Up Little Susie A:❶[8] / S:❶[7] Maybe Tomorrow	❶[4]	$25	■	Cadence 1337
2/10/58	4	13		3 This Little Girl Of Mine / S:4 / A:5	26			
				#9 R&B hit for **Ray Charles** in 1955				
3/24/58	10	1		4 Should We Tell Him A:10	flip	$25		Cadence 1342
4/28/58	❶[3]	20	●	5 All I Have To Do Is Dream / S:❶[3] / A:❶[1]	❶[5]			
6/16/58	15	1		6 Claudette A:15	30	$25		Cadence 1348
				written by **Roy Orbison**				
8/18/58	❶[6]	13	●	7 Bird Dog / S:❶[6] / A:3	❶[1]			
9/1/58	7	5		8 Devoted To You A:7	10	$25		Cadence 1350
12/1/58+	17	7		9 Problems .... Love Of My Life (Pop #40)	2[1]	$25	■	Cadence 1355
8/31/59	8	12		10 ('Til) I Kissed You .... Oh, What A Feeling	4	$25		Cadence 1369
3/6/61	25	3		11 Ebony Eyes .... Walk Right Back (Pop #7)	8	$20	■	Warner 5199
9/29/84	49	12		12 On The Wings Of A Nightingale .... Asleep	50	$5		Mercury 880213
				written by **Paul McCartney**				
1/5/85	44	11		13 The First In Line .... The Story Of Me	—	$4		Mercury 880423
3/1/86	17	18		14 Born Yesterday S:12 / A:18 Don't Say Goodnight	—	$4		Mercury 884428
7/5/86	56	6		15 I Know Love /	—			
9/13/86	57	8		16 These Shoes	—	$4	■	Mercury 884694
2/25/89	45	9		17 Ballad Of A Teenage Queen .... Get Rhythm (Cash)	—	$4		Mercury 872420
				JOHNNY CASH with **Rosanne Cash** & **The Everly Brothers**				
				E.W.B. '81				
				Vocal trio: Jerrel Elliott, Richard Wesley, Gerald Bennett.				
9/12/81	96	2		1 We Could Go On Forever	—	$5		Paid 142
	★315★			**EWING, Skip** '89				
				Born Donald Ralph Ewing on 3/6/64 in Redlands, California. Singer/songwriter/guitarist.				
				1) Burnin' A Hole In My Heart 2) It's You Again 3) I Don't Have Far To Fall				
3/5/88	17	18		1 Your Memory Wins Again .... Burnin' A Hold In My Heart	—	$4	■	MCA 53271
6/25/88	8	24		2 I Don't Have Far To Fall S:17 Still Under The Weather	—	$4		MCA 53353
10/29/88+	3	22		3 Burnin' A Hole In My Heart S:21 Autumn's Not That Cold	—	$4		MCA 53435
3/4/89	10	20		4 The Gospel According To Luke .... Dad	—	$4		MCA 53481
6/24/89	15	24		5 The Coast Of Colorado .... Dad	—	$4		MCA 53663
10/7/89+	5	26		6 It's You Again .... Ain't That The Way It Always Ends	—	$4		MCA 53732
3/3/90	70	5		7 If A Man Could Live On Love Alone .... She's Makin' Plans	—	$4		MCA 53777
8/18/90	69	4		8 I'm Your Man .... The Will To Love	—	$4	■	MCA 53853 (v)
5/25/91	73	1		9 I Get The Picture	—			album cut
3/28/92	71	1		10 Naturally	—			album cut
				above 2 from the album Naturally *on Capitol 96097*				
12/30/95	68	1		11 Christmas Carol .... [X]	—			album cut
				from the album Following Yonder Star *on MCA 10068*				
4/19/97	58	12		12 Mary Go Round	—			album cut
8/23/97	66	7		13 Answer To My Prayer	—			album cut
				above 2 from the album Until I Found You *on Word 471202*				
12/27/97	60	3		14 Christmas Carol .... [X-R]	—			album cut
12/25/99	44	3		15 Christmas Carol .... [X-R]	—			album cut
				above 2 from the album Following Yonder Star *on MCA 10068*				

DEBUT	PEAK	WKS	Gold	A-side (Chart Hit)	B-side	Pop	$	Pic	Label & Number

EXILE ★147★   '84
Group from Lexington, Kentucky: **J.P. Pennington** (vocals, guitar; born on 1/22/49), **Les Taylor** (guitar; born on 12/27/48), Marlon Hargis (keyboards; born on 5/13/49), Sonny Lemaire (bass; born on 9/16/46) and Steve Goetzman (drums; born on 9/1/50). **Mark Gray** (born on 10/24/53) was a member from 1979-82. Member Bernie Faulkner formed **Hazard**. Hargis was replaced by Lee Carroll (born on 1/27/53) in 1985. Pennington was replaced by Paul Martin (born on 12/22/62) in 1989. Taylor was replaced by Mark Jones (born on 7/18/54) in 1989.

1) Give Me One More Chance 2) Hang On To Your Heart 3) It'll Be Me 4) I Don't Want To Be A Memory
5) I Can't Get Close Enough

DEBUT	PEAK	WKS	#	A-side	B-side	Pop	$	Pic	Label & Number
8/20/83	27	16	1	High Cost Of Leaving	Like A Fool's Supposed To Do	—	$4		Epic 04041
12/3/83+	❶¹	22	2	Woke Up In Love	First Things First	—	$4		Epic 04247
4/7/84	❶¹	24	3	I Don't Want To Be A Memory	After All These Years (I'm Still Chasing You)	—	$4		Epic 04421
8/11/84	❶¹	26	4	Give Me One More Chance	A:❶² / S:❶¹ Ain't That A Pity	—	$4	■	Epic 04567
12/8/84+	❶¹	23	5	Crazy For Your Love	S:❶¹ / A:❶¹ Just In Case	—	$4		Epic 04722
3/30/85	86	4	6	Stay With Me	Kiss You All Over	—	$4		Curb/MCA 52551
				recorded in 1978					
4/6/85	❶¹	22	7	She's A Miracle	S:❶¹ / A:❶¹ I've Never Seen Anything	—	$4		Epic 04864
8/17/85	❶¹	24	8	Hang On To Your Heart	S:❶¹ / A:❶¹ She Likes Her Lovin'	—	$4		Epic 05580
12/7/85+	❶¹	22	9	I Could Get Used To You	S:❶¹ / A:❶¹ Practice Makes Perfect	—	$4		Epic 05723
4/5/86	14	16	10	Super Love	A:13 / S:14 Proud To Be Her Man	—	$4		Epic 05860
7/26/86	❶¹	22	11	It'll Be Me	A:❶¹ / S:3 Music	—	$4		Epic 06229
6/6/87	❶¹	23	12	She's Too Good To Be True	S:2 Promises, Promises	—	$4		Epic 07135
10/10/87+	❶¹	22	13	I Can't Get Close Enough	S:❶² As Long As I Have Your Memory	—	$4		Epic 07597
2/20/88	60	4	14	Feel Like Foolin' Around	Showdown	—	$4		Epic 07710
4/23/88	9	18	15	Just One Kiss	S:5 As Long As I Have Your Memory	—	$4		Epic 07775
9/3/88	21	18	16	It's You Again	S:23 The Girl Can't Help It	—	$4		Epic 08020
12/16/89+	17	25	17	Keep It In The Middle Of The Road	Yet	—	$4		Arista 9911
4/14/90	2¹	21	18	Nobody's Talking	Don't Hang Up (Girl)	—	$4		Arista 2009
9/1/90	7	20	19	Yet	Show Me	—	$4	■	Arista 2075 (v)
12/15/90+	32	20	20	There You Go	I'm Still Standing	—	$4		Arista 2139
6/22/91	16	20	21	Even Now	One Too Many Times	—	$4		Arista 2228

F

★212★ FAIRCHILD, Barbara   '73
Born on 11/12/50 in Knobel, Arkansas; raised in St. Louis. Singer/songwriter/guitarist. First appeared on local St. Louis TV shows in 1963; made her first recording in 1965. Began recoding gospel music in 1990.

1) Teddy Bear Song 2) Kid Stuff 3) Baby Doll 4) Cheatin' Is 5) Standing In Your Line

DEBUT	PEAK	WKS	#	A-side	B-side	Pop	$	Pic	Label & Number
5/31/69	69	5	1	Love Is A Gentle Thing	You Can't Stop My Heart From Breaking	—	$6		Columbia 44797
8/9/69	66	6	2	A Woman's Hand	Got A Chance And I Took It	—	$6		Columbia 44925
2/14/70	26	11	3	A Girl Who'll Satisfy Her Man	Chains Of Love (Around My Neck)	—	$6		Columbia 45063
8/1/70	52	6	4	Find Out What's Happenin'	(When You Close Your Eyes) I'll Make You See	—	$6		Columbia 45173
1/2/71	33	10	5	(Loving You Is) Sunshine	What Ever Happened To Happiness	—	$6		Columbia 45272
4/10/71	62	8	6	What Do You Do	Break Away	—	$6		Columbia 45344
8/7/71	28	11	7	Love's Old Song	Back Then	—	$6		Columbia 45422
1/15/72	38	8	8	Color My World	Tell Me Again	—	$6		Columbia 45522
				#16 Pop hit for **Petula Clark** in 1967					
5/27/72	29	10	9	Thanks For The Mem'ries	Let Me Be Your Queen	—	$5		Columbia 45589
10/14/72	53	9	10	A Sweeter Love (I'll Never Know)	That's Loving You	—	$5		Columbia 45690
12/30/72+	❶²	19	11	Teddy Bear Song	(You Make Me Feel Like) Singing A Song	32	$5		Columbia 45743
7/28/73	2²	16	12	Kid Stuff	Make No Mistakes	95	$5		Columbia 45903
1/26/74	6	14	13	Baby Doll	Color Them With Love	—	$5		Columbia 45988
6/29/74	17	13	14	Standing In Your Line	You're The One I'm Living For	—	$5		Columbia 46053
11/2/74	31	10	15	Little Girl Feeling	His Green Eyes	—	$5		Columbia 10047
5/10/75	52	10	16	Let's Love While We Can	Tara	—	$5		Columbia 10128
9/6/75	41	11	17	You've Lost That Lovin' Feelin'	Singing Your Way Out Of My Life	—	$5		Columbia 10195
				#1 Pop hit for The Righteous Brothers in 1965					
12/20/75+	63	8	18	I Just Love Being A Woman	Your Good Girl's Gonna Go Bad	—	$5		Columbia 10261
4/10/76	65	7	19	Under Your Spell Again	Too Far Gone	—	$5		Columbia 10314
7/24/76	31	11	20	Mississippi	Over The Rainbow	—	$5		Columbia 10378
10/30/76	15	13	21	Cheatin' Is	Touch My Heart	—	$5		Columbia 10423
3/12/77	22	14	22	Let Me Love You Once Before You Go	You Are Always There	—	$5		Columbia 10485
				#48 Pop hit for Greg Lake in 1981					
10/1/77	49	8	23	For All The Right Reasons /		—			
5/27/78	72	6	24	The Other Side Of The Morning		—	$5		Columbia 10607
3/4/78	96	3	25	She Can't Give It Away	Painted Faces	—	$5		Columbia 10686
10/14/78	91	5	26	It's Sad To Go To The Funeral (Of A Good Love That					
				Has Died)	Good Time Days	—	$5		Columbia 10825
7/12/80	74	5	27	Let Me Be The One	If We Take Our Time	—	$5		Paid 102
				BILLY WALKER & BARBARA FAIRCHILD					
12/20/80+	70	7	28	Bye Bye Love /		—			
10/11/80	79	3	29	Love's Slipping Through Our Fingers (Leaving Time On Our Hands)		—	$5		Paid 107
				BILLY WALKER & BARBARA FAIRCHILD (above 2)					
5/17/86	84	4	30	Just Out Riding Around	You Burned Me So Bad	—	$4		Capitol 5582

DEBUT	PEAK	WKS	Gold	A-side (Chart Hit)	B-side	Pop	$	Pic	Label & Number
				FAIRGROUND ATTRACTION '89 Pop group from England: Eddi Reader (female vocals), Mark Nevin (guitar), Simon Edwards (bass) and Roy Dodds (drums).					
1/28/89	85	2		Perfect	Mythology	80	$4	■	RCA 8789
				FALLS, Ruby '77 Born Bertha Dorsey in 1946 in Jackson, Tennessee; raised in Milwaukee. Died on 6/15/86 (age 40). Black singer/songwriter.					
3/15/75	86	7		1 Sweet Country Music	Love Away The Wrong I'm About To Do	—	$5		50 States 31
7/12/75	77	8		2 He Loves Me All To Pieces	Let's Spend Summer In The Country	—	$5		50 States 33
2/7/76	81	9		3 Show Me Where	Somewhere There's A Rainbow Over Texas	—	$5		50 States 39
7/17/76	81	7		4 Beware Of The Woman (Before She Gets To Your Man)	Jump In A River Of Tears	—	$5		50 States 43
3/12/77	88	4		5 Do The Buck Dance	Too Many Hurts, Too Many Heartaches	—	$5		50 States 50
9/24/77	40	8		6 You've Got To Mend This Heartache	Loves Sweeter Than Sugar	—	$5		50 States 56
4/15/78	81	5		7 Three Nights A Week	Give Me Some Lovin'	—	$5		50 States 60
				#15 Pop hit for **Fats Domino** in 1960					
9/30/78	86	3		8 If That's Not Loving You (You Can't Say I Didn't Try)	Nobody's Baby But Mine	—	$5		50 States 63
6/9/79	56	7		9 I'm Gettin' Into Your Love	Midnight Rendezvous	—	$5		50 States 70
				FAMILY BROWN '82 Family group from Canada featuring Tracey and Barry Brown.					
7/18/81	57	8		1 It's Really Love This Time	Nothing Really Changes	—	$5		Ovation 1174
1/23/82	30	11		2 But It's Cheating	No One's Gonna Love Me (Like You Do)	—	$4		RCA 13015
8/21/82	61	7		3 Some Never Stand A Chance	Arkansas Traveler	—	$4		RCA 13285
10/22/83	67	5		4 We Really Got A Hold On Love	Mister And Misbehavin'	—	$4		RCA 13565
3/3/84	56	10		5 Repeat After Me	Everyday People	—	$4		RCA 13734
11/30/85	66	7		6 Feel The Fire	Comin' From A Blue Place	—	$4		RCA 50837
4/5/86	80	3		7 What If It's Right	Guess Who	—	$4		RCA 50851

FARGO, Donna ★107★ '72
Born Yvonne Vaughan on 11/10/45 in Mount Airy, North Carolina. Singer/songwriter. Graduated from High Point College in North Carolina; taught English at a high school in Covina, California. Married record producer Stan Silver in 1969. Hosted own syndicated TV show (1978-79). Diagnosed with multiple sclerosis in 1979.

1)The Happiest Girl In The Whole U.S.A.   2)Funny Face   3)Superman
4)You Can't Be A Beacon (If Your Light Don't Shine)   5)That Was Yesterday

DEBUT	PEAK	WKS	Gold	A-side	B-side	Pop	$	Pic	Label & Number
3/25/72	❶³	23	•	1 The Happiest Girl In The Whole U.S.A.	The Awareness Of Nothing	11	$5	■	Dot 17409
				CMA Award: Single of the Year					
9/2/72	❶³	16	•	2 Funny Face	How Close You Came (To Being Gone)	5	$5		Dot 17429
2/17/73	❶¹	14		3 Superman	Forever Is As Far As I Could Go	41	$5		Dot 17444
5/26/73	❶¹	14		4 You Were Always There	He Can Have All He Wants	93	$5		Dot 17460
9/29/73	2¹	14		5 Little Girl Gone	Just Call Me	57	$5		Dot 17476
2/23/74	6	12		6 I'll Try A Little Bit Harder	All About A Feeling	—	$5		Dot 17491
6/8/74	❶¹	15		7 You Can't Be A Beacon (If Your Light Don't Shine)	Just A Friend Of Mine	57	$5		Dot 17506
10/12/74+	9	15		8 U.S. Of A	A Woman's Prayer	86	$5	■	ABC/Dot 17523
2/15/75	7	11		9 It Do Feel Good	Only The Strong	98	$5		ABC/Dot 17541
6/7/75	14	14		10 Hello Little Bluebird	2 Sweet 2 Be 4 Gotten	—	$5		ABC/Dot 17557
10/4/75	38	11		11 Whatever I Say	Rain Song	—	$5		ABC/Dot 17579
12/20/75+	58	7		12 What Will The New Year Bring?	A Woman's Prayer	—	$5		ABC/Dot 17586
2/28/76	60	6		13 You're Not Charlie Brown (And I'm Not Raggedy Ann)	Sing, Sing, Sing	—	$5		ABC/Dot 17609
4/3/76	20	10		14 Mr. Doodles	If You Can't Love All Of Me	—	$5	■	Warner 8186
7/17/76	15	13		15 I've Loved You All Of The Way	One Of God's Children	—	$5		Warner 8227
10/23/76+	3	19		16 Don't Be Angry	You Don't Mess Around With Jim	—	$5		ABC/Dot 17660
2/12/77	9	13		17 Mockingbird Hill	Second Choice	—	$5		Warner 8305
				#2 Pop hit for **Patti Page** in 1951					
4/30/77	❶¹	14		18 That Was Yesterday	The Cricket Song	—	$5		Warner 8375
9/10/77	8	15		19 Shame On Me	Hey, Mister Music Man	—	$5		Warner 8431
1/7/78	2²	15		20 Do I Love You (Yes In Every Way)	Dee Dee	—	$5		Warner 8509
5/27/78	19	11		21 Ragamuffin Man	Everybody's Girl	—	$5		Warner 8578
8/26/78	10	13		22 Another Goodbye	Changes In My Life	—	$4		Warner 8643
1/13/79	6	15		23 Somebody Special	Changes In My Life	—	$4		Warner 8722
7/21/79	14	13		24 Daddy	For The Rest Of My Life	—	$4		Warner 8867
11/17/79	45	7		25 Preacher Berry	I Don't Know What I'd Do	—	$4		Warner 49093
3/8/80	43	7		26 Walk On By	I Wrote This Song Just For You	—	$4		Warner 49183
8/9/80	63	7		27 Land Of Cotton	I Still Believe In You	—	$4		Warner 49514
11/1/80	55	6		28 Seeing Is Believing	Look What You've Done	—	$4		Warner 49575
8/1/81	73	6		29 Lonestar Cowboy	Utah Song	—	$4	■	Warner 49757
11/21/81	72	4		30 Jacamo	Song To Celebrate Life	—	$4		Warner 49852
7/10/82	40	9		31 It's Hard To Be The Dreamer (When I Used To Be The Dream)	I Just Saw My Reflection In You	—	$4		RCA 13264
10/9/82	80	3		32 Did We Have To Go This Far (To Say Goodbye)	All I Need To Know	—	$4		RCA 13329
10/1/83	72	4		33 The Sign Of The Times	Reasons To Be	—	$4		Columbia 04097
7/7/84	80	4		34 My Heart Will Always Belong To You	Reasons To Be	—	$4		Cleveland Int'l 1
7/19/86	58	8		35 Woman Of The 80's	S:33 You Were Always There	—	$4		Mercury 884712
11/8/86+	29	17		36 Me And You	S:20 I've Laid Too Many Eggs	—	$4		Mercury 888093

DEBUT	PEAK	WKS	Gold	A-side (Chart Hit)	B-side	Pop	$	Pic	Label & Number
				FARGO, Donna — Cont'd					
6/27/87	23	15		37 Members Only ....S:21 Funny Face		—	$4		Mercury 888680
				DONNA FARGO AND BILLY JOE ROYAL					
2/16/91	71	2		38 Soldier Boy ....Stand Tall		—	$4		Cleveland Int'l 10
				#1 Pop hit for The Shirelles in 1962					
				FAUCETT, Dawnett '89					
				Born in Abilene, Texas. Female singer.					
9/30/89	74	3		Money Don't Make A Man A Lover ....Cross My Broken Heart		—	$5		Step One 407
				FAUTHEREE, Jimmy Lee — see JIMMY & JOHNNY					
				FELICIANO, José '83					
				Born on 9/8/45 in Puerto Rico; raised in New York City. Blind since birth. Singer/guitarist. Won the 1968 Best New Artist Grammy Award.					
9/3/83	64	7		Let's Find Each Other Tonight ....Cuidado		—	$4		Motown 1674
				FELL, Terry '54					
				Born on 5/13/21 in Dora, Alabama. Male singer/songwriter/guitarist.					
8/7/54	4	11		Don't Drop It J:4 / S:11 / A:12 Truck Driving Man		—	$30		"X" 0010
				TERRY FELL & The Fellers					
				FELLER, Dick '74					
				Born on 1/2/43 in Bronaugh, Missouri. Singer/songwriter/guitarist.					
11/17/73+	22	11		1 Biff, The Friendly Purple Bear ....Goodbye California [S]		101	$5		United Artists 316
6/8/74	11	14		2 Makin' The Best Of A Bad Situation ....She's Taken A Gentle Lover [N]		85	$5		Asylum 11037
9/21/74	10	15		3 The Credit Card Song Just Short Of The Line [N]		105	$5		United Artists 535
12/6/75+	49	9		4 Uncle Hiram And The Homemade Beer ....Let It Ride [N]		—	$5		Asylum 45290

				FELTS, Narvel ★148★ '75					
				Born Albert Narvel Felts on 11/11/38 near Keiser, Arkansas; raised near Bernie, Missouri. Singer/songwriter/guitarist. Known as "Narvel The Marvel." Hosted own radio show on KDEX in Dexter, Missouri. Hit the pop charts in 1960 with "Honey Love" on the Pink label. Member of **The Wolfpack**.					
				1)Reconsider Me 2)Lonely Teardrops 3)Drift Away 4)Somebody Hold Me 5)Funny How Time Slips Away					
6/16/73	8	16		1 **Drift Away** Foggy Misty Morning		—	$6		Cinnamon 763
				#5 Pop hit for **Dobie Gray** in 1973					
10/13/73	13	13		2 All In The Name Of Love ....Before You Have To Go		—	$6		Cinnamon 771
1/19/74	14	14		3 When Your Good Love Was Mine ....Fraulein		—	$6		Cinnamon 779
4/27/74	39	11		4 Until The End Of Time ....Someone To Give My Love To		—	$6		Cinnamon 793
				NARVEL FELTS and SHARON VAUGHN					
5/11/74	26	13		5 I Want To Stay ....Wrap My Arms Around The World		—	$6		Cinnamon 798
9/14/74	33	13		6 Raindrops ....Tilted Cup Of Love		—	$6		Cinnamon 809
				#2 Pop hit for **Dee Clark** in 1961					
4/5/75	2[1]	21		7 **Reconsider Me** Foggy Misty Morning		67	$6		ABC/Dot 17549
8/23/75	12	15		8 **Funny How Time Slips Away** ....No One Knows		—	$6		ABC/Dot 17569
				written by **Willie Nelson**; #13 Pop hit for **Joe Hinton** in 1964					
12/6/75+	10	16		9 Somebody Hold Me (Until She Passes By) ★★★ Away		—	$6		ABC/Dot 17598
4/3/76	5	16		10 **Lonely Teardrops** I Remember You		62	$6		ABC/Dot 17620
				#7 Pop hit for **Jackie Wilson** in 1959					
8/7/76	14	11		11 My Prayer ....If Ever Two Were One (Then Surely We Are)		—	$6		ABC/Dot 17643
				#1 Pop hit for **The Platters** in 1956					
11/13/76+	20	12		12 My Good Thing's Gone ....I'm Afraid To Be Alone		—	$6		ABC/Dot 17664
2/26/77	19	11		13 The Feeling's Right ....Another Crazy Dream		—	$6		ABC/Dot 17680
5/28/77	37	10		14 I Don't Hurt Anymore ....When We Were Together		—	$6		ABC/Dot 17700
8/20/77	22	11		15 To Love Somebody ....Remember		—	$6		ABC/Dot 17715
				#17 Pop hit for the **Bee Gees** in 1967					
12/3/77+	34	11		16 Please /		—			
		6		17 Blue Darlin'		—	$6		ABC/Dot 17731
3/18/78	30	10		18 Runaway ....Free		—	$5		ABC 12338
				#1 Pop hit for **Del Shannon** in 1961					
7/1/78	31	9		19 Just Keep It Up ....Lonely Lady		—	$5		ABC 12374
				#18 Pop hit for **Dee Clark** in 1959					
10/21/78	26	10		20 One Run For The Roses ....(Darling) Lie To Me		—	$5		ABC 12414
1/6/79	14	11		21 Everlasting Love ....Small Enough To Crawl		—	$5		ABC 12441
				#6 Pop hit for **Carl Carlton** in 1974					
4/21/79	43	8		22 Moment By Moment ....Never Again		—	$5		MCA 41011
7/7/79	33	9		23 Tower Of Strength ....You're A Heartbreaker		—	$5		MCA 41055
				#5 Pop hit for **Gene McDaniels** in 1961					
10/20/79	73	4		24 Because Of Losing You ....After You		—	$6		Collage 1001
8/22/81	67	5		25 Louisiana Lonely ....Look What Love Has Done		—	$5		GMC 114
12/12/81	84	4		26 Fire In The Night ....Look What Love Has Done		—	$5		GMC 115
2/13/82	58	8		27 I'd Love You To Want Me ....The First Time We Made Love		—	$6		Lobo 3
				Lobo (backing vocal); #2 Pop hit for **Lobo** in 1972					
6/5/82	84	3		28 Sweet Southern Moonlight ....The First Time We Made Love		—	$6		Lobo 8
7/17/82	64	6		29 Roll Over Beethoven ....I'd Love You To Want Me		—	$6		Lobo 11
				#29 Pop hit for **Chuck Berry** in 1956					

DEBUT	PEAK	WKS	Gold	A-side (Chart Hit) ..... B-side	Pop	$	Pic	Label & Number
				FELTS, Narvel — Cont'd				
12/11/82	82	4		30 You're The Reason / ..... —				
11/13/82	84	3		31 Smoke Gets In Your Eyes ..... —		$5		Compleat 101
				#1 Pop hit for The Platters in 1959				
4/2/83	52	9		32 Cry Baby ..... Now I Don't Have You To Lose	—	$5		Compleat 104
9/17/83	79	4		33 Anytime You're Ready ..... Nobody's Fool	—	$5		Evergreen 1011
12/10/83+	52	10		34 Fool ..... Anytime You're Ready	—	$5		Evergreen 1014
3/10/84	70	6		35 You Lay So Easy On My Mind ..... Nobodys Fool	—	$5		Evergreen 1017
6/30/84	53	8		36 Let's Live This Dream Together ..... Nobody's Fool	—	$5		Evergreen 1022
10/6/84	63	5		37 I'm Glad You Couldn't Sleep Last Night ..... It Amazes Me	—	$5		Evergreen 1025
1/5/85	51	10		38 Hey Lady ..... Anytime You're Ready	—	$5		Evergreen 1027
6/1/85	68	4		39 If It Was Any Better (I Couldn't Stand It) ..... Nobody's Fool	—	$5		Evergreen 1030
9/7/85	71	5		40 Out Of Sight Out Of Mind ..... It Amazes Me	—	$5		Evergreen 1034
				#23 Pop hit for The Five Keys in 1956				
6/7/86	70	5		41 Rockin' My Angel ..... Anytime You're Ready	—	$5		Evergreen 1041
5/16/87	60	7		42 When A Man Loves A Woman ..... Hey Lady	—	$5		Evergreen 1054
				#1 Pop hit for Percy Sledge in 1966				

★202★ **FENDER, Freddy** *Died 10-15-06* '75 *Ex-Marine*
Born Baldemar Huerta on 6/4/37 in San Benito, Texas. Singer/songwriter/guitarist. Acted in the movie *The Milagro Beanfield War*. Joined the Texas Tornados in 1990. Underwent a kidney transplant (donated by his daughter Marla) on 1/24/2002.
1) Wasted Days And Wasted Nights 2) Before The Next Teardrop Falls 3) Secret Love 4) You'll Lose A Good Thing 5) Living It Down

DEBUT	PEAK	WKS	Gold	#	A-side ..... B-side	Pop	$	Label & Number
1/11/75	❶²	17	●	1	Before The Next Teardrop Falls ..... Waiting For Your Love	❶¹	$6	ABC/Dot 17540
					CMA Award: Single of the Year			
6/21/75	❶²	16	●	2	Wasted Days And Wasted Nights ..... I Love My Rancho Grande	8	$6	ABC/Dot 17558
10/4/75	10	14		3	Since I Met You Baby ..... Little Mama	45	$8	GRT 031
					#12 Pop hit for Ivory Joe Hunter in 1956			
10/11/75	❶¹	16		4	Secret Love ..... Loving Cajun Style	20	$6	ABC/Dot 17585
					#1 Pop hit for Doris Day in 1954			
1/10/76	13	12		5	Wild Side Of Life ..... Go On Baby (I Can Do Without You)	—	$8	GRT 039
2/7/76	❶¹	15		6	You'll Lose A Good Thing ..... I'm To Blame	32	$6	ABC/Dot 17607
					#8 Pop hit for Barbara Lynn in 1962			
5/22/76	7	13		7	Vaya Con Dios ..... My Happiness	59	$6	ABC/Dot 17627
					#1 Pop hit for Les Paul & Mary Ford in 1953			
9/18/76	2²	14		8	Living It Down ..... Take Her A Message! I'm Lonely	72	$6	ABC/Dot 17652
3/19/77	4	15		9	The Rains Came /	—		
					#31 Pop hit for Sir Douglas Quintet in 1966			
		15		10	Sugar Coated Love		$5	ABC/Dot 17686
7/30/77	11	12		11	If You Don't Love Me (Why Don't You Just Leave Me Alone) ..... Thank You My Love	—	$5	ABC/Dot 17713
11/26/77+	18	11		12	Think About Me ..... If That's The Way You Want It (That's The Way It's Gonna Be)	—	$5	ABC/Dot 17730
3/11/78	34	9		13	If You're Looking For A Fool ..... Louisiana Woman	—	$5	ABC 12339
6/17/78	13	12		14	Talk To Me ..... Please Mr. Sandman	103	$5	ABC 12370
					#20 Pop hit for Little Willie John in 1958			
10/14/78	26	9		15	I'm Leaving It All Up To You ..... When It Rains It Really Pours	—	$5	ABC 12415
					#1 Pop hit for Dale & Grace in 1963			
2/17/79	22	12		16	Walking Piece Of Heaven ..... Sweet Summer Day	—	$5	ABC 12453
6/23/79	22	11		17	Yours ..... Rock Down In My Shoe	—	$5	Starflite 4900
10/13/79	61	5		18	Squeeze Box ..... Turn Around	—	$5	Starflite 4904
					#16 Pop hit for The Who in 1976			
1/12/80	83	3		19	My Special Prayer ..... Turn Around	—	$5	Starflite 4906
4/5/80	82	3		20	Please Talk To My Heart ..... Walk Under A Snake	—	$5	Starflite 4908
2/19/83	87	3		21	Chokin' Kind ..... I Might As Well Forget You	—	$4	Warner 29794
					#13 Pop hit for Joe Simon in 1969			

FENDERMEN, The '60
Duo of Jim Sundquist (from Niagara, Wisconsin) and Phil Humphrey (from Stoughton, Wisconsin). Both guitarists were born on 11/26/37.

| 7/11/60 | 16 | 8 | | | Mule Skinner Blues ..... Torture | 5 | $30 | Soma 1137 |

written in 1931 by **Jimmie Rodgers**; first released on Cuca 1003 in 1959 ($200)

FENSTER, Zoot — see BARLOW, Jack

FERRARI, CW '88
CW Ferrari is actually pianist Bill Ferreira.

| 3/19/88 | 76 | 4 | | | Country Highways ..... | [I] | — | $5 | Southern Sound 1001 |

FINNEY, Maury '77
Born in Humboldt, Minnesota. Saxophonist.
1) Coconut Grove 2) Lonely Wine 3) Rollin' In My Sweet Baby's Arms

1/3/76	84	9		1	Maiden's Prayer /	[F]	—		
					vocals by a female chorus				
		9		2	San Antonio Stroll	[I]	—	$5	Soundwaves 4525
4/24/76	76	7		3	Rollin' In My Sweet Baby's Arms /	[I]	—	$5	
4/24/76	78	7		4	Wild Side Of Life	[I]	—	$5	Soundwaves 4531
9/4/76	81	7		5	Waltz Across Texas /	[I]	—		
		7		6	Off And Running	[I]	—	$5	Soundwaves 4536
1/29/77	85	6		7	Everybody's Had The Blues ..... Too Pretty For Words	[I]	—	$5	Soundwaves 4541
6/25/77	72	10		8	Coconut Grove ..... It's Such A Pretty World Today	—	$5	Soundwaves 4548

vocals by a female chorus

DEBUT	PEAK	WKS	Gold	A-side (Chart Hit)	B-side	Pop	$	Pic	Label & Number
				FINNEY, Maury — Cont'd					
11/19/77	85	5		9 Poor People of Paris /	[I]	—			
				#1 Pop hit for Les Baxter in 1956					
		5		10 Almost Persuaded	[I]	—	$5		Soundwaves 4557
4/15/78	88	6		11 I Don't Wanna Cry	Happy Sax [I]	—	$5		Soundwaves 4566
8/12/78	84	7		12 Whispering	Send Me The Pillow [I]	—	$5		Soundwaves 4572
				#1 Pop hit for Paul Whiteman in 1920					
2/3/79	92	2		13 Happy Sax	Faded Love [I]	—	$5		Soundwaves 4578
6/16/79	93	2		14 Your Love Takes Me So High /	[I]	—			
		2		15 I Want To Play My Horn On The Grand Ole' Opry		—	$5		Soundwaves 4585
				vocals by Finney and a female chorus					
9/20/80	75	5		16 Lonely Wine	Misery And Gin [I]	—	$5		Soundwaves 4613
				FIRST EDITION, The — see ROGERS, Kenny					
				FISCHOFF, George '79					
				Born on 8/3/38 in South Bend, Indiana. Prolific pianist/songwriter.					
3/31/79	74	7		The Piano Picker	Love Dust [I]	—	$5		Drive 6273
				FITZGERALD, Ella '44					
				Born on 4/25/18 in Newport News, Virginia. Died of diabetes on 6/15/96 (age 78). Legendary jazz singer. Won Grammy's Lifetime Achievement Award in 1967.					
3/18/44	2¹	1		When My Sugar Walks Down The Street	Cow-Cow Boogie (Pop #10)	22	$20		Decca 18587
				ELLA FITZGERALD And Her Famous Orchestra					
				#2 Pop hit for Aileen Stanley & Gene Austin in 1925					
				5 RED CAPS '44					
				R&B vocal group from Los Angeles: Steve Gibson, Emmett Matthews, Dave Patillo, Jimmy Springs and Romaine Brown. Springs died on 10/4/87 (age 75).					
4/29/44	2¹	8		I Learned A Lesson, I'll Never Forget	Words Can't Explain	14	$25		Beacon 7120
	★240★			**FLATT & SCRUGGS** '63					
				Bluegrass duo of Lester Flatt (guitar) and Earl Scruggs (banjo). Flatt was born on 6/14/14 in Overton County, Tennessee. Died on 5/11/79 (age 64). Scruggs was born on 1/6/24 in Flintville, North Carolina. Both were members of Bill Monroe's band from 1944-48. Left Monroe to form the Foggy Mountain Boys. Joined the Grand Ole Opry in 1955. Elected to the Country Music Hall of Fame in 1985.					
				1)The Ballad Of Jed Clampett 2)Pearl Pearl Pearl 3)Cabin In The Hills 4)'Tis Sweet To Be Remembered 5)Go Home					
				LESTER FLATT, EARL SCRUGGS & The Foggy Mountain Boys:					
2/2/52	9	1		1 'Tis Sweet To Be Remembered	A:9 Earl's Breakdown	—	$20		Columbia 4-20886
6/8/59	9	30		2 Cabin In The Hills	Someone You Have Forgotten	—	$15		Columbia 41389
2/1/60	21	6		3 Crying My Heart Out Over You	Foggy Mountain Rock	—	$15		Columbia 41518
12/5/60+	12	14		4 Polka On A Banjo	Shuckin' The Corn	—	$15		Columbia 41786
10/9/61	10	16		5 Go Home	Where Will I Shelter My Sheep	—	$15		Columbia 42141
4/7/62	16	8		6 Just Ain't	Cold, Cold Loving	—	$15		Columbia 42280
6/23/62	27	1		7 The Legend Of The Johnson Boys	Hear The Whistle Blow A Hundred Miles	—	$15		Columbia 42413
12/8/62+	❶³	20		8 The Ballad Of Jed Clampett	Coal Loadin' Johnny	44	$15	■	Columbia 42606
				theme from the TV series The Beverly Hillbillies starring Buddy Ebsen (as "Jed Clampett")					
5/11/63	8	11		9 Pearl Pearl Pearl	Hard Travelin' [N]	113	$15	■	Columbia 42755
				"Cousin Pearl" (Bea Benaderet) was a featured character on TV's The Beverly Hillbillies					
9/28/63	26	3		10 New York Town	Mama Don't Allow It	—	$15		Columbia 42840
2/15/64	12	18		11 You Are My Flower /		—			
2/22/64	40	2		12 My Saro Jane		—	$15		Columbia 42954
				LESTER FLATT & EARL SCRUGGS:					
3/14/64	14	11		13 Petticoat Junction	Have You Seen My Dear Companion	—	$15		Columbia 42982
				theme from the TV series starring Edgar Buchanan					
8/15/64	21	15		14 Workin' It Out	Fireball	—	$12		Columbia 43080
3/13/65	43	10		15 I Still Miss Someone	Father's Table Grace	—	$12		Columbia 43204
4/15/67	54	5		16 Nashville Cats	Roust-A-Bout	—	$12		Columbia 44040
				#8 Pop hit for The Lovin' Spoonful in 1967					
7/29/67	20	14		17 California Up Tight Band	Last Train To Clarksville	—	$12	■	Columbia 44194
				FLATT & SCRUGGS:					
1/13/68	45	8		18 Down In The Flood		—			
4/6/68	58	6		19 Foggy Mountain Breakdown	[I]	55	$12		Columbia 44380
				from the movie Bonnie & Clyde starring Warren Beatty and Faye Dunaway; also charted on Mercury 72739 as "Theme From Bonnie & Clyde (Foggy Mountain Breakdown)"					
9/14/68	58	8		20 Like A Rolling Stone	I'd Like To Say A Word For Texas	125	$10		Columbia 44623
				#2 Pop hit for Bob Dylan in 1965					
				FLETCHER, Vicky '74					
7/20/74	92	3		1 Touching Me, Touching You	That's The Way We Fall In Love	—	$5		Columbia 46043
6/12/76	97	2		2 Ain't It Good To Be In Love Again	Countin' Charlie's Ribs	—	$6		Music Row 213
				FLORES, Rosie '87					
				Born on 9/10/56 in San Antonio, Texas; raised in San Diego. Joined Asleep At The Wheel in 1997.					
9/12/87	51	10		1 Crying Over You	Midnight To Moonlight	—	$4	■	Reprise 28250
12/26/87+	67	6		2 Somebody Loses, Somebody Wins	Heart Beats To A Different Drum	—	$4		Reprise 28134
7/9/88	74	3		3 He Cares	One-Track Mem'ry	—	$4		Reprise 27980

DEBUT	PEAK	WKS	Gold	A-side (Chart Hit)	B-side	Pop	$	Pic	Label & Number
				FLOYD, Charlie '94					
				Born in Aynor, South Carolina. Singer/songwriter/guitarist.					
10/23/93	75	1		1 I've Fallen In Love (And I Can't Get Up)	—		$4	■	Liberty 58051
1/1/94	58	7		2 Good Girls Go To Heaven	—			■	album cut
				from the album *Charlie's Nite Life* on Liberty 80475					
				FLYING BURRITO BROTHERS — see BURRITO BROTHERS					
				FOGELBERG, Dan '85					
				Born on 8/13/51 in Peoria, Illinois. Singer/songwriter/guitarist. Charted 14 pop hits from 1975-87.					
2/16/80	85	8		1 Longer	Along The Road	2^2	$4		Full Moon 50824
4/20/85	56	16		2 Go Down Easy	High Country Snows	85	$4		Full Moon 04835
8/24/85	33	13		3 Down The Road Mountain Pass	High Country Snows	—	$4		Full Moon 05446
				written by **Flatt & Scruggs**					
				FOGERTY, John '85					
				Born on 5/28/45 in Berkeley, California. Leader of **Creedence Clearwater Revival**.					
2/10/73	66	6		1 Jambalaya (On The Bayou)	Workin' On A Building	16	$6		Fantasy 689
				THE BLUE RIDGE RANGERS					
2/2/85	38	11		2 Big Train (From Memphis)	The Old Man Down The Road (Pop #10)	—	$4	■	Warner 29100
8/16/97	67	2		3 Southern Streamline	—				album cut
				from the album *Blue Moon Swamp* on Warner 45426					
				FOLEY, Betty '55					
				Born on 2/3/33 in Chicago; raised in Berea, Kentucky. Daughter of **Red Foley**.					
3/6/54	8	10		1 As Far As I'm Concerned	J:8 / A:8 / S:11 Tennessee Whistling Man	—	$20		Decca 29000
				RED FOLEY and BETTY FOLEY					
6/25/55	3	23		2 Satisfied Mind	J:3 / S:4 / A:6 How About Me	—	$20		Decca 29526
				RED FOLEY And BETTY FOLEY					
8/31/59	7	12		3 Old Moon	Magic Love	—	$25		Bandera 1304

FOLEY, Red ★31★ '50
Born Clyde Foley on 6/17/10 in Blue Lick, Kentucky. Died of a heart attack on 9/19/68 (age 58). On the WLS *National Barn Dance* from 1930-37 and the *Renfro Valley Show* from 1937-39. Member of the *Grand Ole Opry* from 1946-54. Hosted the *Ozark Jubilee* series on ABC-TV from 1954-60. Regular on TV's *Mr. Smith Goes To Washington*. **Pat Boone** married his daughter Shirley in 1953. Elected to the Country Music Hall of Fame in 1967.

1)Smoke On The Water 2)Chattanoogie Shoe Shine Boy 3)Birmingham Bounce 4)Goodnight Irene
5)New Jolie Blonde (New Pretty Blonde)

DEBUT	PEAK	WKS	A-side	B-side	Pop	$	Label & Number
8/26/44	$❶^{13}$	27	1 Smoke On The Water /		7		
9/30/44	5	1	2 There's A Blue Star Shining Bright (In A Window Tonight)	—		$20	Decca 6102
6/23/45	4	2	3 Hang Your Head In Shame /		—		
6/23/45	5	1	4 I'll Never Let You Worry My Mind		—	$20	Decca 6108
9/8/45	$❶^1$	14	5 Shame On You /		13		
11/10/45	3	2	6 At Mail Call Today		—	$20	Decca 18698
			LAWRENCE WELK AND HIS ORCHESTRA with RED FOLEY (above 2)				
5/4/46	4	1	7 Harriet	My Poor Little Heart Is Broken	—	$20	Decca 9003
11/30/46	5	1	8 Have I Told You Lately That I Love You	Atomic Power	—	$20	Decca 46014
			RED FOLEY with Roy Ross & His Ramblers (above 2)				
			from the movie *Over The Trail*; also see #65 below				
			RED FOLEY and The Cumberland Valley Boys:				
3/15/47	4	1	9 That's How Much I Love You	Rye Whiskey	—	$20	Decca 46028
4/5/47	$❶^2$	16	10 New Jolie Blonde (New Pretty Blonde)	A Pillow Of Sighs And Tears	—	$20	Decca 46034
6/21/47	5	1	11 Freight Train Boogie	Rockin' Chair Money	—	$20	Decca 46035
11/22/47	2^1	13	12 Never Trust A Woman	A Smile Will Chase Away A Tear	—	$20	Decca 46074
10/2/48+	$❶^1$	40	13 Tennessee Saturday Night /	A:$❶^1$ / S:3			
5/14/49	15	1	14 Blues In My Heart	S:15	—	$20	Decca 46136
			RED FOLEY:				
4/2/49	3	21	15 Tennessee Border /	J:3 / S:4	—		
3/26/49	4	15	16 Candy Kisses	J:4 / S:6	—	$20	Decca 46151
6/25/49	4	13	17 Tennessee Polka /	J:4 / S:6	—		
7/23/49	11	2	18 I'm Throwing Rice (At The Girl I Love)	S:11 / J:14	—	$20	Decca 46170
8/6/49	8	4	19 Two Cents, Three Eggs And A Postcard	J:8 / I Wish I Had A Nickel	—	$20	Decca 46165
12/17/49+	3	6	20 Sunday Down In Tennessee	J:3 / A:3 / S:10 Every Step Of The Way	—	$20	Decca 46197
12/31/49+	2^2	10	21 Tennessee Border No. 2	S:2 / J:2	—		
			RED FOLEY and ERNEST TUBB				
1/21/50	7	2	22 Don't Be Ashamed Of Your Age	J:7 / A:9	—	$20	Decca 46200
			ERNEST TUBB and RED FOLEY				
1/14/50	8	1	23 Careless Kisses /	J:8 / S:14	—		
1/7/50	10	1	24 I Gotta Have My Baby Back	J:10 / S:13	—	$20	Decca 46201
1/21/50	$❶^{13}$	20 •	25 Chattanoogie Shoe Shine Boy /	A:$❶^{13}$ / J:$❶^{12}$ / S:$❶^{12}$	$❶^8$		
2/18/50	4	11	26 Sugarfoot Rag	J:4 / A:8	24	$20	Decca 46205
			Hank "Sugarfoot" Garland (guitar solo)				
5/6/50	9	1	27 Steal Away /	S:9	—		
7/22/50	9	5	28 Just A Closer Walk With Thee	S:9	—	$25	Decca Faith 9-14505
			RED FOLEY With Jordanaires				

DEBUT	PEAK	WKS	Gold		A-side (Chart Hit)	B-side	Pop	$	Pic	Label & Number
					FOLEY, Red — Cont'd					
5/13/50	❶⁴	15		29	Birmingham Bounce /	S:❶⁴ / J:❶³ / A:4	14			Decca 9-46234
6/3/50	5	4		30	Choc'late Ice Cream Cone	A:5 / J:8 / S:10	—	$25		Decca 9-46234
6/3/50	❶¹	14		31	Mississippi	J:❶¹ / S:2 / A:3 Old Kentucky Fox Chase	—	$25		Decca 9-46241
					RED FOLEY with The Dixie Dons (above 2)					
8/12/50	❶³	15		32	Goodnight Irene /	J:❶³ / S:❶² / A:2	10			
					RED FOLEY-ERNEST TUBB with The Sunshine Trio					
					#1 Pop hit for Gordon Jenkins & The Weavers in 1950					
9/2/50	9	2		33	Hillbilly Fever No. 2	J:9	—	$25		Decca 9-46255
					ERNEST TUBB-RED FOLEY					
9/9/50	2¹	12		34	Cincinnati Dancing Pig	S:2 / J:3 / A:6 Somebody's Crying	7	$25		Decca 9-46261
11/4/50	8	4		35	Our Lady Of Fatima	S:8 The Rosary	16	$25		Decca Faith 9-14526
2/17/51	6	1		36	My Heart Cries For You	A:6 'Tater Pie	28	$25		Decca 9-27378
					EVELYN KNIGHT and RED FOLEY					
2/17/51	7	3		37	Hot Rod Race	S:7 / J:8 / A:10 Smoke On The Water No. 2	—	$25		Decca 9-46286
5/12/51	8	3		38	Hobo Boogie	J:8 Heska-Holka (Pretty Girl)	—	$25		Decca 9-46304
5/19/51	9	1		39	The Strange Little Girl	J:9 Kentucky Waltz	—	$25		Decca 9-46311
					RED FOLEY and ERNEST TUBB with Anita Kerr Singers					
7/7/51	5	11	●	40	There'll Be Peace In The Valley For Me	A:5 / J:5 / S:7 Old Soldiers Never Die	—	$25		Decca 9-46319
					RED FOLEY With The Sunshine Boys Quartet					
11/24/51	3	16		41	Alabama Jubilee	J:3 / S:5 / A:6 Dixie	28	$25		Decca 9-27810
					RED FOLEY with The Nashville Dixielanders					
2/2/52	5	9		42	Too Old To Cut The Mustard	S:5 / J:8 / A:10 I'm In Love With Molly	—	$25		Decca 9-46387
					ERNEST TUBB And RED FOLEY					
3/8/52	8	3		43	Milk Bucket Boogie /	J:8		$25		
3/29/52	8	2		44	Salty Dog Rag		—	$25		Decca 9-27981
11/15/52+	❶¹	11		45	Midnight	S:❶¹ / J:2 / A:5 Deep Blues	—	$20		Decca 28420
1/10/53	8	2		46	Don't Let The Stars Get In Your Eyes	S:8 Sally	—	$20		Decca 28460
					#1 Pop hit for Perry Como in 1953					
3/21/53	6	4		47	Hot Toddy	J:6 / S:10 Playin' Dominoes And Shootin' Dice	—	$20		Decca 28587
4/18/53	7	2		48	No Help Wanted #2	S:7 / J:9 You're A Real Good Friend	—	$20		Decca 28634
					ERNEST TUBB - RED FOLEY					
5/9/53	8	1		49	Slaves Of A Hopeless Love Affair	J:8 Blue Letter	—	$20		Decca 28567
10/10/53	6	4		50	Shake A Hand	S:6 / J:7 / A:10 Stranded In Deep Water	—	$20		Decca 28839
					RED FOLEY with Anita Kerr Singers					
					#1 R&B hit for Faye Adams in 1953					
3/6/54	8	10		51	As Far As I'm Concerned	J:8 / A:8 / S:11 Tennessee Whistling Man	—	$20		Decca 29000
					RED FOLEY and BETTY FOLEY					
5/8/54	7	4		52	Jilted	J:7 / S:9 Pin Ball Boogie	—	$20		Decca 29100
					KITTY WELLS AND RED FOLEY:					
5/22/54	❶¹	41		53	One By One /	J:❶¹ / S:2 / A:2	—			
7/10/54	12	1		54	I'm A Stranger In My Home	A:12 / S:15	—	$20		Decca 29065
1/8/55	4	15		55	Hearts Of Stone	A:4 / J:4 / S:6 Never	—	$20		Decca 29375
					RED FOLEY with Anita Kerr Singers					
					#1 Pop hit for The Fontane Sisters in 1955					
2/26/55	3	16		56	As Long As I Live /	J:3 / S:7 / A:8	—			
2/26/55	6	17		57	Make Believe ('Til We Can Make It Come True)	J:6 / S:7 / A:14	—	$20		Decca 29390
6/25/55	3	23		58	Satisfied Mind	J:3 / S:4 / A:6 How About Me	—	$20		Decca 29526
					RED FOLEY And BETTY FOLEY					
1/28/56	3	31		59	You And Me /	S:3 / A:3 / J:6	—			
		6		60	No One But You	S:flip / J:flip	—	$20		Decca 29740
6/29/59	29	1		61	Travelin' Man	Just This Side Of Memphis	—	$20		Decca 30882
					RED FOLEY					
5/6/67	43	11		62	Happiness Means You /		—	$10		Decca 32126
6/3/67	60	5		63	Hello Number One		—	$10		Decca 32223
12/30/67+	63	4		64	Living As Strangers	Loved And Wanted	—	$10		Decca 32223
1/18/69	74	2		65	Have I Told You Lately That I Love You?	We Need One More Chance [R]	—	$10		Decca 32427
					new version of #8 above					
					FORD, Joy '79					
					Born on 3/10/46 in Brilliant, Alabama; raised in Chicago and Poplar Bluff, Missouri.					
12/16/78+	87	4		1	Love Isn't Love (Til You Give It Away)	Another Favour	—	$5		Country Int'l. 134
10/13/79	97	4		2	Take My Love	I Love The Way You Love On Me	—	$5		Country Int'l. 142
3/26/83	97	1		3	You Are The Music In Time With My Heart	Carousel	—	$5		Country Int'l. 190
8/10/85	96	2		4	Melted Down Memories	Big City Turn Me Loose	—	$5		Country Int'l. 206
8/20/88	99	1		5	Yesterday's Rain		—	$5		Country Int'l. 216

FORD, Shelley — see CHEVALIER, Jay

DEBUT	PEAK	WKS	Gold	A-side (Chart Hit)	B-side	Pop	$	Pic	Label & Number

FORD, "Tennessee" Ernie ★128★ '51
Born on 2/13/19 in Fordtown, Tennessee. Died of liver failure on 10/17/91 (age 72). Worked as a DJ. Hosted own TV series from 1955-65. Known as "The Old Pea Picker." Elected to the Country Music Hall of Fame in 1990.

1) The Shot Gun Boogie 2) Sixteen Tons 3) Mule Train 4) The Cry Of The Wild Goose 5) I'll Never Be Free

TENNESSEE ERNIE:

DEBUT	PEAK	WKS		A-side	B-side	Pop	$	Label & Number
4/30/49	8	1	1	Tennessee Border — J:8 / S:15	I Got The Milk 'Em In The Morning Blues	—	$20	Capitol 15400
5/28/49	14	1	2	Country Junction — J:14	Philadelphia Lawyer	—	$20	Capitol 15430
9/10/49	8	4	3	Smokey Mountain Boogie — S:8 / J:13	You'll Find Her Name Written There	—	$20	Capitol 40212
11/26/49	❶⁴	10	4	Mule Train / — A:❶⁴ / J:3 / S:4		9		
				#1 Pop hit for Frankie Laine in 1949				
12/10/49	3	11	5	Anticipation Blues — A:3 / S:5 / J:8	—		$20	Capitol 40258
2/11/50	2²	10	6	The Cry Of The Wild Goose — S:2 / A:3 / J:5	The Donkey Serenade	15	$25	Capitol F40280
				#1 Pop hit for Frankie Laine in 1950				
9/16/50	2¹	16	7	I'll Never Be Free / — A:2 / J:2 / S:4		3		
8/26/50	5	6	8	Ain't Nobody's Business But My Own — A:5 / J:10		22	$25	Capitol F1124
				KAY STARR and TENNESSEE ERNIE (above 2)				
12/16/50+	❶¹⁴	25	9	The Shot Gun Boogie — J:❶¹⁴ / S:❶³ / A:❶¹	I Ain't Gonna Let It Happen No More	14	$25	Capitol F1295
3/3/51	8	2	10	Tailor Made Woman — J:8	Stack-O-Lee	—	$25	Capitol F1349
				TENNESSEE ERNIE and JOE "FINGERS" CARR				
6/16/51	2¹	7	11	Mr. And Mississippi — A:2 / S:4 / J:6	She's My Baby	18	$25	Capitol F1521
6/16/51	9	1	12	The Strange Little Girl — S:9	Kentucky Waltz	—	$25	Capitol F1470
9/20/52	6	7	13	Blackberry Boogie — J:6 / S:9 / A:9	Tennessee Local	—	$25	Capitol F2170
6/6/53	8	3	14	Hey, Mr. Cotton Picker — J:8	Three Things (A Man Must Do)	—	$20	Capitol 2443

TENNESSEE ERNIE FORD:

8/14/54	9	9	15	River Of No Return — S:9	Give Me Your Word	—	$20	Capitol 2810
				from the movie starring Robert Mitchum and Marilyn Monroe				
3/26/55	4	16	16	Ballad Of Davy Crockett — S:4 / J:5 / A:6	Farewell	5	$20	Capitol 3058
				from the ABC-TV Disneyland series starring Fess Parker as "Davy Crockett"				
7/9/55	13	2	17	His Hands — S:13	I Am A Pilgrim	—	$20	Capitol 3135
11/12/55	❶¹⁰	21	18	Sixteen Tons — S:❶¹⁰ / J:❶⁷ / A:❶³		❶⁸	$20	Capitol 3262
3/17/56	12	5	19	That's All — S:12	Bright Lights And Blonde-Haired Women	17	$20	Capitol 3343
6/26/65	9	16	20	Hicktown	Sixteen Tons	—	$15	Capitol 5425
7/26/69	54	3	21	Honey-Eyed Girl (That's You That's You)	Good Morning, Dear	—	$10	Capitol 2522
4/24/71	58	9	22	Happy Songs Of Love	Don't Let The Good Life Pass You By	—	$8	Capitol 3079
3/31/73	66	4	23	Printers Alley Stars	Baby	—	$8	Capitol 3556
7/14/73	73	5	24	Farther Down The River (Where The Fishin's Good)	You've Still Got Love All Over You	—	$8	Capitol 3631
9/22/73	70	7	25	Colorado Country Morning	Daddy Usta Say	—	$8	Capitol 3704
1/4/75	52	8	26	Come On Down	Bits And Pieces Of Life	—	$8	Capitol 3916
4/19/75	63	9	27	Baby	I'd Like To Be	—	$6	Capitol 4044
				TENNESSEE ERNIE FORD & ANDRA WILLIS				
11/22/75	96	4	28	The Devil Ain't A Lonely Woman's Friend	Smokey Taverns, Bar Room Girls	—	$6	Capitol 4160
7/31/76	95	3	29	I Been To Georgia On A Fast Train	Baby's Home	—	$6	Capitol 4285

FORESTER SISTERS, The ★173★ '86
Family vocal group from Lookout Mountain, Georgia: Kathy (born on 1/4/55), Kim (born on 11/4/60), June (born on 9/22/56) and Christy (born on 12/21/62) Forester.

1) Just In Case 2) Too Much Is Not Enough 3) You Again 4) Mama's Never Seen Those Eyes
5) I Fell In Love Again Last Night

DEBUT	PEAK	WKS		A-side	B-side	Pop	$	Pic	Label & Number
1/26/85	10	22	1	(That's What You Do) When You're In Love — S:9 / A:12	Yankee Don't Go Home	—	$4		Warner 29114
6/29/85	❶¹	22	2	I Fell In Love Again Last Night — S:❶¹ / A:❶¹	Dixie Man	—	$4		Warner 28988
11/2/85+	❶¹	20	3	Just In Case — S:❶¹ / A:❶¹	Reckless Night	—	$4		Warner 28875
3/15/86	❶¹	22	4	Mama's Never Seen Those Eyes — S:❶¹ / A:❶¹	Something Tells Me	—	$4		Warner 28795
7/5/86	2²	24	5	Lonely Alone — A:❶¹ / S:2	Heartless Night	—	$4		Warner 28687
9/27/86	❶¹	20	6	Too Much Is Not Enough — S:❶¹ / A:❶¹	Restless	—	$4		Curb/MCA 52917
				THE BELLAMY BROTHERS with The Forester Sisters					
3/7/87	5	23	7	Too Many Rivers — S:8 / A:8	If I'm Gonna Fall (I'm Gonna Fall In Love)	—	$4		Warner 28442
				#13 Pop hit for Brenda Lee in 1965					
6/27/87	❶¹	24	8	You Again — S:6	Whatever You Do, Don't	—	$4		Warner 28368
10/31/87+	5	25	9	Lyin' In His Arms Again — S:11	Wrap Me Up	—	$4		Warner 28208
6/25/88	9	24	10	Letter Home — S:23	These Lips Don't Know How To Say Goodbye	—	$4		Warner 27839
11/5/88+	8	22	11	Sincerely — S:30	On The Other Side Of The Gate	—	$4		Warner 27686
				#1 Pop hit for The McGuire Sisters in 1955					
2/18/89	7	20	12	Love Will	You Love Me	—	$4		Warner 27575
6/24/89	9	18	13	Don't You	All I Need	—	$4		Warner 22943
11/25/89+	7	26	14	Leave It Alone	I Fell In Love Again Last Night	—	$4	■	Warner 22773
4/14/90	63	7	15	Drive South	You Can't Have A Good Time Without Me	—	$4		Warner 19874
				THE FORESTER SISTERS with The Bellamy Brothers					

DEBUT	PEAK	WKS	Gold	A-side (Chart Hit)	B-side	Pop	$	Pic	Label & Number
				FORESTER SISTERS, The — Cont'd					
8/25/90	63	3		16 Nothing's Gonna Bother Me Tonight .... *Born To Give My Love To You*		—	$4	■	Warner 19744 (v)
1/26/91	8	20		17 Men .... *Just In Case*		—	$4		Warner 19450
6/29/91	62	5		18 Too Much Fun .... *The Blues Don't Stand A Chance*		—	$4		Warner 19291
3/14/92	74	3		19 What'll You Do About Me .... *Men*		—	$4		Warner 19047
7/18/92	58	6		20 I Got A Date .... *Show Me A Woman*		—	$4		Warner 18906
				FORMAN, Peggy '81					
				Born in Centerville, Louisiana. Singer/songwriter.					
8/20/77	98	4		1 The Danger Zone .... *Yours To Hurt Tomorrow*		—	$5		MCA 40757
5/24/80	89	4		2 There Ain't Nothing Like A Rainy Night .... *Sugar On Your Lies*		—	$5		Dimension 1006
8/2/80	78	5		3 Burning Up Your Memory .... *Sugar On Your Lies*		—	$5		Dimension 1008
7/4/81	70	6		4 You're More To Me (Than He's Ever Been) .... *Steppin' Aside Ain't My Style*		—	$5		Dimension 1020
10/24/81	54	6		5 I Wish You Could Have Turned My Head (And Left My Heart Alone) .... *Falling Out Of Love*		—	$5		Dimension 1023
2/27/82	71	6		6 That's What Your Lovin' Does To Me .... *Foolish Talkin'*		—	$5		Dimension 1027
				FORREST, Sylvia '89					
9/23/89	84	2		The Nights Are Never Long Enough With You		—	$5		Door Knob 319
				FOSTER, Jerry '74					
				Born on 11/19/35 in Tallapoosa, Missouri. Singer/songwriter/guitarist.					
8/18/73	98	3		1 Copperhead .... *Ain't It Sad*		—	$6		Cinnamon 764
12/8/73+	51	13		2 Looking Back .... *Hard To Handle*		—	$6		Cinnamon 774
				#5 Pop hit for **Nat King Cole** in 1958					
11/27/76	86	6		3 I Knew You When .... *One*		—	$5		Hitsville 6043
7/15/78	84	3		4 I Want To Love You .... *My Baby Left Me*		—	$5		Monument 256
				JERRY FOSTER and TENNESSEE TORNADO					
				FOSTER, Lloyd David '83					
				Born in 1952 in Wills Point, Texas. Singer/songwriter/guitarist.					
6/19/82	32	13		1 Blue Rendezvous .... *Love At First Sight*		—	$4		MCA 52061
10/23/82	65	7		2 Honky Tonk Magic .... *The First Time I Saw Her (Was The Last Time)*		—	$4		MCA 52123
2/26/83	32	12		3 Unfinished Business .... *It Takes One To Know One*		—	$4		MCA 52173
9/3/83	60	6		4 You've Got That Touch .... *Just Once*		—	$4		MCA 52248
11/24/84+	44	15		5 I'm Gonna Love You Right Out Of The Blues .... *Wishful Drinkin'*		—	$4		Columbia 04670
4/13/85	55	9		6 I Can Feel The Fire Goin' Out .... *Anywhere You Want To Go*		—	$4		Columbia 04836
10/12/85	68	6		7 I'm As Over You As I'm Ever Gonna Get .... *Anywhere You Want To Go*		—	$4		Columbia 05601
	★400★			**FOSTER, Radney** '93					
				Born on 7/20/59 in Del Rio, Texas. Half of **Foster & Lloyd** duo.					
				1)Nobody Wins 2)Just Call Me Lonesome 3)Easier Said Than Done					
8/15/92	10	20		1 Just Call Me Lonesome .... *Louisiana Blue*		—	$4		Arista 12448
1/23/93	2²	20		2 Nobody Wins .... *Don't Say Goodbye*		—	$4		Arista 12512
6/12/93	20	20		3 Easier Said Than Done .... *Don't Say Goodbye*		—	$4		Arista 12564
10/9/93	34	11		4 Hammer And Nails .... *A Fine Line*		—	$4		Arista 12608
2/26/94	59	6		5 Closing Time .... *Old Silver*		—	$4		Arista 12652
7/9/94	58	7		6 Labor Of Love .... *Jesse's Soul*		—	$4	■	Arista 12716 (v)
10/29/94	64	5		7 The Running Kind .... *Silver Wings* (**Pam Tillis**)		—	$4		Arista 12758
				written by **Merle Haggard**					
4/1/95	54	8		8 Willin' To Walk .... *Last Chance For Love*		—	$4	■	Arista 12752 (v)
9/2/95	59	5		9 If It Were Me .... *Walkin' Talkin' Woman*		—	$4	■	Arista 12861 (v)
7/3/99	74	1		10 Godspeed (Sweet Dreams)		—			album cut
				from the album *See What You Want To See* on Arista Austin 18833					
6/30/01	54	9		11 Texas In 1880		—			album cut
				RADNEY FOSTER (with Pat Green)					
				from the album *Are You Ready For The Big Show?* on Dualtone 1102					
				FOSTER, Sally — see **HOOSIER HOT SHOTS**					
	★381★			**FOSTER & LLOYD** '88					
				Duo of singers/songwriters/guitarists **Radney Foster** and **Bill Lloyd**. Foster was born on 7/20/59 in Del Rio, Texas. Lloyd was born on 12/6/55 in Bowling Green, Kentucky. Also see **Tomorrow's World**.					
7/4/87	4	21		1 Crazy Over You .... S:7 *The Part I Know By Heart*		—	$4	□	RCA 5210
11/7/87+	8	21		2 Sure Thing .... S:15 *Hart To Say No*		—	$4	■	RCA 5281
4/9/88	18	17		3 Texas In 1880 .... S:29 *Token Of Love*		—	$4		RCA 6900
8/6/88	6	23		4 What Do You Want From Me This Time .... S:17 *Don't Go Out With Him*		—	$4		RCA 8633
1/28/89	5	17		5 Fair Shake .... *After I'm Gone*		—	$4		RCA 8795
6/3/89	43	11		6 Before The Heartache Rolls In .... *Happy For A While*		—	$4		RCA 8942
8/19/89	48	8		7 Suzette .... *I'll Always Be Here Loving You*		—	$4		RCA 9028
4/7/90	43	14		8 Is It Love .... *Workin' On Me*		—	$4		RCA 2502
11/24/90+	38	12		9 Can't Have Nothin' .... *Workin' On Me*		—	$4	■	RCA 2635 (v)
				FOUR GUYS, The '82					
				Vocal group from Steubenville, Ohio: Brent Burkett (born on 7/28/39), Sam Wellington (born on 3/20/39), Gary Chadwick and Gary Buck (not to be confused with the solo singer). Buck was formerly married to **Louise Mandrell**. Buck was replaced by Laddie Cain (born on 11/22/51) in 1980. Chadwick was replaced by John Frost (born on 12/3/49) in 1981. Group joined the Grand Ole Opry in 1967.					
10/19/74	88	3		1 Too Late To Turn Back Now .... *Gatherin' Dust*		—	$5		RCA Victor 10055
12/8/79	93	4		2 Mama Rocked Us To Sleep (With Country Music) .... *Forever In Blue Jeans*		—	$6		Collage 102
3/13/82	85	4		3 Made In The U.S.A. .... *Pretty Lady*		—	$6		J&B 1001

117

curly Fox ?

DEBUT	PEAK	WKS	Gold	A-side (Chart Hit) .... B-side	Pop	$	Pic	Label & Number
				4 RUNNER '95 Vocal group: Craig Morris, Billy Crittenden, Lee Hilliard and Jim Chapman.				
3/18/95	26	20		1 Cain's Blood .... S:6 Ten Pound Hammer	118	$4	■	Polydor 851622 (v)
7/1/95	51	10		2 A Heart With 4 Wheel Drive .... Southern Wind	—	$4	■	Polydor 579450 (v)
10/14/95	65	4		3 Home Alone .... You Make The Moonlight	—	$4		Polydor 577040
1/20/96	57	9		4 Ripples .... Oh No	—	$4	■	Polydor 577730 (v)
7/6/96	54	12		5 That Was Him (This Is Now) .... Let The Good Times Roll	—	$4	■	A&M 581650 (v)
				FOWLER, Ken '86				
2/8/86	96	2		You're A Heartache To Follow .... The Way That I Remember You	—	$6	■	Deja Vu 111
				FOWLER, Wally — see TENNESSEE VALLEY BOYS				
				FOX, Dolly '78				
12/9/78	93	2		I've Got A Reason For Living .... Who's Gonna Love Me (When You're Gone)	—	$6		Artic 1025
				FOX, Kent '73 Born Walter Kent Fox on 10/16/47 in Lexington, Kentucky.				
6/2/73	73	4		New York Callin' Miami .... Have Patience ('Til I Learn To Love You)	—	$6		MCA 40038
				FOXFIRE '79 Vocal trio: Dave Hall, Russ Allison and Don Miller.				
6/9/79	30	10		1 Fell Into Love .... Head Over Heels In Love With You	—	$5		NSD 24
4/26/80	38	9		2 I Can See Forever Loving You .... Dreaming Won't Take Me That Far	—	$4		Elektra 46625
11/15/80	55	8		3 Whatever Happened To Those Drinking Songs .... Do That To Me Again	—	$4		Elektra 47070
				FOXTON, Kelly — see SNOW, Hank				
				FOXWORTHY, Jeff '95 Born on 9/6/58 in Atlanta; raised in Hapeville, Georgia. Comedian/actor. Starred in own TV sitcom, 1995-97. Began hosting own radio countdown show in April 1999. 1)Redneck 12 Days Of Christmas 2)Redneck Games 3)Party All Night				
9/10/94	67	8		1 Redneck Stomp .... S:8 Words In The South [C]	75	$4	■	Warner 18116 (v)
7/8/95	53	17		2 Party All Night .... S:5 Southern Accent (Foxworthy) [N]	101	$4	■	Warner 17806 (v)
				JEFF FOXWORTHY with Little Texas				
12/16/95	18	5		3 Redneck 12 Days Of Christmas .... 'Twas The Night After Christmas [X-N]	—	$4		Warner 17526
6/8/96	42	12		4 Redneck Games .... S:2 NASA & Alabama & Fishing Shows (Foxworthy) [C]	66	$4	■	Warner 17648 (v)
				JEFF FOXWORTHY with Alan Jackson				
12/14/96	39	5		5 Redneck 12 Days Of Christmas / .... [X-N-R]	—			
12/28/96	67	2		6 'Twas The Night After Christmas .... [X-C]	—	$4		Warner 17526
12/27/97	39	3		7 Redneck 12 Days Of Christmas .... 'Twas The Night After Christmas [X-N-R]	—	$4		Warner 17526
5/2/98	70	6		8 Totally Committed .... [N]	—			album cut
				from the album Totally Committed on Warner 46861				
12/26/98	37	2		9 Redneck 12 Days Of Christmas .... 'Twas The Night After Christmas [X-N-R]	—	$4		Warner 17526
12/25/99	35	3		10 Redneck 12 Days Of Christmas .... 'Twas The Night After Christmas [X-N-R]	—	$4		Warner 17526
4/15/00	63	6		11 The Blue Collar Dollar Song .... [N]	—			album cut
				JEFF FOXWORTHY and BILL ENGVALL Featuring Marty Stuart from the album Big Funny on DreamWorks 50200				
				FRADY, Garland '73 Born in Lexington, North Carolina. Band leader for Bob Luman and Dorsey Burnette.				
8/18/73	89	7		The Barrooms Have Found You .... Silver Moon	—	$7		Countryside 45104
				FRANCIS, Cleve '92 Born Cleveland Francis on 4/22/45 in Jennings, Louisiana. Black male singer. Worked as a cardiologist in Alexandria, Virginia.				
1/18/92	52	11		1 Love Light .... Happy	—	$4		Liberty 57728
5/2/92	47	14		2 You Do My Heart Good	—			album cut
9/19/92	74	2		3 How Can I Hold You	—			album cut
				above 2 from the album Tourist In Paradise on Liberty 96498				
5/8/93	63	8		4 Walkin'	—			album cut
				from the album Walkin' on Liberty 80033				
				FRANCIS, Connie '60 Born Concetta Rosa Maria Franconero on 12/12/38 in Newark, New Jersey. Charted 56 pop hits from 1957-69.				
7/25/60	24	3	●	1 Everybody's Somebody's Fool .... Jealous Of You (Pop #19)	❶²	$15	■	MGM 12899
3/1/69	33	10		2 The Wedding Cake .... Over Hill Underground	91	$8		MGM 14034
3/12/83	84	3		3 There's Still A Few Good Love Songs Left In Me .... Let's Make It Love Tonight	—	$5		Polydor 810087
				FRANKS, Tillman '64 Born on 9/29/20 in Stamps, Arkansas. Singer/guitarist. In the car crash which killed Johnny Horton in 1960.				
12/21/63	30	4		1 Tadpole .... Pretty Little Girls [I]	—	$15		Starday 651
				TILLMAN FRANKS and the Cedar Grove Three				
5/2/64	30	11		2 When The World's On Fire .... Uncle Eph	—	$15		Starday 670
				TILLMAN FRANKS SINGERS				
				FRAZIER, Brenda '80				
12/6/80	92	2		I've Given Up Giving In To The Blues .... Steppin' Out Tonight	—	$7		Tyro 1004
				FRAZIER, Dallas '68 Born on 10/27/39 in Spiro, Oklahoma; raised in Bakersfield, California. Singer/songwriter/guitarist.				
11/11/67+	28	11		1 Everybody Oughta Sing A Song .... Only A Fool	—	$10		Capitol 2011
4/13/68	43	8		2 The Sunshine Of My World .... Lonelier And More In Love	—	$10		Capitol 2133
9/21/68	59	5		3 I Hope I Like Mexico Blues .... I Just Thought That I Loved Her (Till I Lost You)	—	$10		Capitol 2257

DEBUT	PEAK	WKS	Gold	A-side (Chart Hit)	B-side	Pop	$	Pic	Label & Number

FRAZIER, Dallas — Cont'd

DEBUT	PEAK	WKS	A-side	B-side	Pop	$	Label & Number
3/8/69	63	9	4 The Conspiracy Of Homer Jones ... Sundown Of My Mind [N]		120	$8	Capitol 2402
			parody of "Ode To Billy Joe" by Bobbie Gentry and "Harper Valley P.T.A." by Jeannie C. Riley				
11/8/69	45	10	5 California Cotton Fields ... Sweetheart Don't Throw Yourself Away		—	$8	RCA Victor 0259
8/29/70	45	7	6 The Birthmark Henry Thompson Talks About ... If My Heart Had Windows		—	$8	RCA Victor 9881
2/27/71	43	8	7 Big Mable Murphy ... White Fences And Evergreen Trees		—	$8	RCA Victor 9950
7/29/72	42	11	8 North Carolina ... The Last Time I Called Somebody Darlin'		—	$8	RCA Victor 0748

FRAZIER RIVER '96
Group from Cincinnati: Danny Frazier, Chuck Adair, Jim Morris, Bob Wilson, Brian Braverman and Greg Amburgy.

2/10/96	57	9	1 She Got What She Deserves ... Heaven Is Smiling	—	$4	Decca 55173
6/22/96	67	8	2 Tangled Up In Texas ... Last Request	—	$4	Decca 55101

FREE, Johnny '79

4/28/79	100	1	Borrowed Time ... Call All Your Love Together (And Come On Home)	—	$7	Sabre 4509

first recorded by Olivia Newton-John on her 1979 Totally Hot album

FREEMAN, Ernie '58
Born on 8/16/22 in Cleveland. Died of a heart attack on 5/16/81 (age 58). Pianist/composer/conductor.

1/13/58	11	2	Raunchy ... S:11 Puddin' [I]	4	$25	Imperial 5474

FRICKE, Janie ★81★ '83
Born on 12/19/47 in South Whitney, Indiana. Former backing singer for RCA. Sang numerous commercial jingles. Later a regular on TNN's **The Statler Brothers** Show. Occasionally spells her name "Frickie." CMA Awards: 1982 & 1983 Female Vocalist of the Year.

1)He's A Heartache (Looking For A Place To Happen) 2)Tell Me A Lie 3)A Place To Fall Apart
4)Always Have Always Will 5)Your Heart's Not in It

DEBUT	PEAK	WKS	#	A-side	B-side	Pop	$	Pic	Label & Number
9/17/77	21	13	1	What're You Doing Tonight	We're A Love Song	—	$5		Columbia 10605
10/29/77+	4	16	2	Come A Little Bit Closer	Loneliness (Can Break A Good Man Down)	—	$5		Columbia 10634
				JOHNNY DUNCAN (with Janie Fricke)					
				#3 Pop hit for Jay & The Americans in 1964					
3/4/78	21	12	3	Baby It's You	I Loved You All The Way	—	$4		Columbia 10695
5/27/78	12	13	4	Please Help Me, I'm Falling (In Love With You)	Get Ready For My World	—	$4		Columbia 10743
10/7/78	❶¹	14	5	On My Knees	Mellow Melody	—	$4		Epic 50616
				CHARLIE RICH (with Janie Fricke)					
11/11/78+	22	12	6	Playin' Hard To Get	Let Me Love You Goodbye	—	$4		Columbia 10849
3/3/79	14	12	7	I'll Love Away Your Troubles For Awhile	River Blue	—	$4		Columbia 10910
7/7/79	28	10	8	Let's Try Again	Love Is Worth It All	—	$4		Columbia 11029
11/17/79+	26	13	9	But Love Me	One Piece At A Time	—	$4		Columbia 11139
3/22/80	22	12	10	Pass Me By (If You're Only Passing Through)	This Ain't Tennessee And He Ain't You	—	$4		Columbia 11224
7/12/80	17	14	11	He's Out Of My Life	Loving Arms	—	$4		Columbia 11312
				JOHNNY DUNCAN and JANIE FRICKE					
				#10 Pop hit for Michael Jackson in 1980					
11/1/80+	2¹	18	12	Down To My Last Broken Heart	Every Time A Teardrop Falls	—	$4		Columbia 11384
3/14/81	12	14	13	Pride	Going Through The Motions	—	$4		Columbia 60509
7/25/81	4	18	14	I'll Need Someone To Hold Me (When I Cry)	It's Raining Too	—	$4		Columbia 02197
12/12/81+	4	19	15	Do Me With Love	If You Could See Me Now	—	$4		Columbia 02644
5/8/82	❶¹	18	16	Don't Worry 'Bout Me Baby	Always	—	$4		Columbia 02859
9/18/82	❶¹	19	17	It Ain't Easy Bein' Easy	A Little More Love	—	$4		Columbia 03214
1/15/83	4	19	18	You Don't Know Love	Heart To Heart Talk	—	$4		Columbia 03498
5/21/83	❶¹	20	19	He's A Heartache (Looking For A Place To Happen)	Tryin' To Fool A Fool	—	$4		Columbia 03899
9/17/83	❶¹	20	20	Tell Me A Lie	Love Have Mercy	—	$4		Columbia 04091
1/14/84	❶¹	18	21	Let's Stop Talkin' About It	I've Had All The Love I Can Stand	—	$4		Columbia 04317
5/12/84	8	17	22	If The Fall Don't Get You	Where's The Fire	—	$4		Columbia 04454
9/1/84	❶¹	23	23	Your Heart's Not In It	S:❶¹ / A:❶¹ Take It From The Top	—	$4		Columbia 04578
10/27/84+	❶¹	22	24	A Place To Fall Apart	S:❶¹ / A:❶¹ All I Want To Do Is Sing My Song	—	$4		Epic 04663
				MERLE HAGGARD (with Janie Fricke)					
1/5/85	7	19	25	The First Word In Memory Is Me	S:6 / A:7 One Way Ticket	—	$4		Columbia 04731
5/18/85	2¹	22	26	She's Single Again	S:2 / A:2 The Only Thing You Took Away	—	$4		Columbia 04896
9/21/85	4	23	27	Somebody Else's Fire	S:4 / A:4 My Heart's Hearin' Footsteps	—	$4		Columbia 05617
2/1/86	5	22	28	Easy To Please	A:4 / S:5 Party Shoes	—	$4		Columbia 05781
				JANIE FRICKIE:					
6/28/86	❶¹	22	29	Always Have Always Will	S:❶¹ / A:2 Don't Put It Past My Heart	—	$4	■	Columbia 06144
11/8/86+	20	16	30	When A Woman Cries	S:7 / A:20 Nothing Left To Say	—	$4		Columbia 06417
3/14/87	32	11	31	Are You Satisfied	S:24 Till I Can't Take It Anymore	—	$4		Columbia 06985
				#11 Pop hit for Rusty Draper in 1956					
5/9/87	21	12	32	From Time To Time (It Feels Like Love Again)	S:18 Texas	—	$4		Columbia 07088
				LARRY GATLIN & JANIE FRICKIE (with The Gatlin Brothers)					
8/29/87	63	4	33	Baby You're Gone	I Don't Like Being Lonely	—	$4		Columbia 07353
4/16/88	54	8	34	Where Does Love Go (When It's Gone)	The Last Thing	—	$4		Columbia 07770
6/25/88	50	8	35	I'll Walk Before I'll Crawl	The Healing Hands Of Time	—	$4		Columbia 07927
			36	Heart	The Healing Hands Of Time	—	$4		Columbia 08031
5/20/89	56	7	37	Love Is One Of Those Words	No Ordinary Memory	—	$4		Columbia 68758
9/16/89	43	9	38	Give 'Em My Number	Walking On The Moon	—	$4		Columbia 69057

DEBUT	PEAK	WKS	Gold	A-side (Chart Hit)	B-side	Pop	$	Pic	Label & Number

FRIEDMAN, Kinky '73
Born Richard Friedman on 10/31/44 in Chicago; raised in Austin, Texas. Singer/songwriter/guitarist.

| 7/14/73 | 69 | 8 | | Sold American .... Western Union Wire | — | $7 | | Vanguard 35173 |

FRIZZELL, Allen '85
Singer/songwriter/guitarist. Younger brother of **Lefty Frizzell** and **David Frizzell**. Formerly married to **Shelly West**.

5/16/81	86	4		1 Beer Joint Fever .... Look What Thoughts Will Do	—	$5		Sound Factory 429
8/29/81	81	3		2 She's Livin' It Up (And I'm Drinkin' 'Em Down) .. Every Night I Take Her Memory To Bed	—	$5		Sound Factory 447
6/8/85	73	3		3 It'll Be Love By Morning .... Mystery	—	$4		Epic 04870

FRIZZELL, David ★192★ '81
Born on 9/26/41 in El Dorado, Arkansas. Singer/songwriter/guitarist. Younger brother of **Lefty Frizzell** and older brother of **Allen Frizzell**. Formed a duo with sister-in-law **Shelly West**. CMA Awards: 1981 & 1982 Vocal Duo of the Year (with Shelly West).

1) You're The Reason God Made Oklahoma 2) I'm Gonna Hire A Wino To Decorate Our Home 3) I Just Came Here To Dance 4) Lost My Baby Blues 5) Another Honky-Tonk Night On Broadway

6/20/70	67	3		1 L.A. International Airport .... Just Passing Through	—	$8		Columbia 45139
10/31/70	36	10		2 I Just Can't Help Believing .... Carmen Jones	—	$8		Columbia 45238
12/18/71	73	2		3 Goodbye				
5/19/73	63	5		#9 Pop hit for **B.J. Thomas** in 1970				
				4 Words Don't Come Easy .... It's Too Late To Keep From Losing You	—	$7		Cartwheel 202
				.... 500 Times	—	$5		Capitol 3589
8/25/73	94	4		5 Take Me One More Ride .... The Bottle, Me, And Joann	—	$5		Capitol 3684
10/2/76	100	1		6 A Case Of You .... Forever (And Always)	—	$5		RSO 856
				#67 Pop hit for Frank Stallone in 1980				
1/17/81	●1	17		7 You're The Reason God Made Oklahoma ...... That's Where Lovers Go Wrong	—	$4		Warner 49650
				DAVID FRIZZELL & SHELLY WEST				
				from the movie Any Which Way You Can starring **Clint Eastwood**				
6/20/81	9	15		8 A Texas State Of Mind .... Let's Duet	—	$4		Warner 49745
				DAVID FRIZZELL & SHELLY WEST				
9/5/81	45	9		9 Lefty .... Three Blind Hearts (w/Shelly West)	—	$4		Warner 49778
				Merle Haggard (guest vocal)				
10/10/81	16	16		10 Husbands And Wives .... Yours For The Asking	—	$4		Warner 49825
				DAVID FRIZZELL & SHELLY WEST				
2/6/82	8	18		11 Another Honky-Tonk Night On Broadway .... Three Act Play	—	$4		Warner 50007
				DAVID FRIZZELL & SHELLY WEST				
5/29/82	●1	23		12 I'm Gonna Hire A Wino To Decorate Our Home .. She's Up To All Her Old Tricks Again	—	$4		Warner 50063
7/17/82	4	18		13 I Just Came Here To Dance .... Our Day Will Come	—	$4		Warner 29980
				DAVID FRIZZELL & SHELLY WEST				
10/9/82+	5	20		14 Lost My Baby Blues .... Single And Alone	—	$4		Warner 29901
12/4/82+	43	11		15 Please Surrender .... Being A Man, Being A Woman	—	$4		Warner 29850
				DAVID FRIZZELL & SHELLY WEST				
				from the movie Honkytonk Man starring **Clint Eastwood**				
3/26/83	52	10		16 Cajun Invitation .... Yesterday's Lovers	—	$4		Warner 29756
				FRIZZELL & WEST				
5/28/83	10	16		17 Where Are You Spending Your Nights These Days .. We're Back In Love Again	—	$4		Viva 29617
9/3/83	71	4		18 Pleasure Island .... Betcha Can't Cry Just One	—	$4		Viva 29544
				FRIZZELL & WEST				
10/8/83	39	13		19 A Million Light Beers Ago .... Sweet Sweet Sin	—	$4		Viva 29498
1/14/84	64	6		20 Black And White .... All The King's Memories	—	$4		Viva 29388
2/4/84	20	17		21 Silent Partners .... Confidential	—	$4		Viva 29404
				FRIZZELL & WEST				
4/28/84	60	6		22 Who Dat .... Honest Man	—	$4		Viva 29332
7/28/84	49	9		23 When We Get Back To The Farm (That's When We Really Go To Town) .. Settin' The Night On Fire	—	$4		Viva 29232
9/15/84	13	20		24 It's A Be Together Night .... S:8 / A:16 Straight From The Heart	—	$4		Viva 29187
				FRIZZELL & WEST				
12/1/84+	49	13		25 No Way José .... Who Dat (Messin' With That Woman Of Mine)	—	$4		Viva 29158
3/2/85	63	7		26 Country Music Love Affair .... Maybe There's Love After You, After All	—	$4		Viva 29066
4/13/85	60	8		27 Do Me Right .... Easy, Soft And Slow	—	$4		Viva 29048
				FRIZZELL & WEST				
3/29/86	71	5		28 Celebrity	—	$6		Nashville Amer. 1002
5/9/87	74	7		29 Beautiful Body .... All That I Am	—	$5		Compleat 168

DEBUT	PEAK	WKS	Gold	A-side (Chart Hit)	B-side	Pop	$	Pic	Label & Number

FRIZZELL, Lefty ★83★ '51
Born William Orville Frizzell on 3/31/28 in Corsicana, Texas; raised in El Dorado, Arkansas. Died of a stroke on 7/19/75 (age 47). Singer/songwriter/guitarist. Older brother of **Allen Frizzell** and **David Frizzell**. Elected to the Country Music Hall of Fame in 1982.

1) Always Late (With Your Kisses) 2) I Want To Be With You Always 3) Saginaw, Michigan 4) I Love You A Thousand Ways
5) If You've Got The Money I've Got The Time

DEBUT	PEAK	WKS		A-side	B-side	Pop	$		Label & Number
10/28/50	❶³	22		1 If You've Got The Money I've Got The Time /	J:❶³ / S:2 / A:2	—			
11/4/50+	❶³	32		2 I Love You A Thousand Ways	A:❶³ / J:3 / S:5	—	$25		Columbia 4-20739
3/3/51	4	12		3 Look What Thoughts Will Do /	A:4 / S:9 / J:9	—			
3/10/51	7	2		4 Shine, Shave, Shower (It's Saturday)	J:7	—	$25		Columbia 4-20772
4/14/51	❶¹¹	27		5 I Want To Be With You Always A:❶¹¹ / S:❶⁶ / J:❶⁵ My Baby's Just Like Money		29	$25		Columbia 4-20799
8/4/51	❶¹²	28		6 Always Late (With Your Kisses) /	S:❶¹² / A:❶⁶ / J:❶⁶	—			
8/18/51	2⁸	29		7 Mom And Dad's Waltz	S:2 / A:2 / J:3	—	$25		Columbia 4-20837
10/13/51	6	9		8 Travellin' Blues	S:6 / J:7 / A:8 Blue Yodel No. 6	—	$25		Columbia 4-20842
12/22/51+	❶³	21		9 Give Me More, More, More (Of Your Kisses) /	A:❶³ / J:❶³ / S:3	—			
1/12/52	7	5		10 How Long Will It Take (To Stop Loving You)	A:7	—	$25		Columbia 4-20885
4/12/52	2¹	12		11 Don't Stay Away (Till Love Grows Cold)	S:2 / J:2 / A:4 You're Here, So Everything's All Right	—	$25		Columbia 4-20911
9/27/52	6	5		12 Forver (And Always)	S:6 I Know You're Lonesome While Waiting For Me	—	$25		Columbia 4-20997
12/6/52+	3	9		13 I'm An Old, Old Man (Tryin' To Live While I Can)	S:3 / J:4 You're Just Mine (Only In My Dreams)	—	$25		Columbia 21034
5/23/53	8	1		14 (Honey, Baby, Hurry!) Bring Your Sweet Self Back To Me	A:8 Time Changes Things	—	$25		Columbia 21084
2/20/54	8	2		15 Run 'Em Off	J:8 The Darkest Moment	—	$25		Columbia 21194
1/15/55	11	4		16 I Love You Mostly	S:11 / A:13 Mama!	—	$25		Columbia 21328
11/24/58+	13	11		17 Cigarettes And Coffee Blues	You're Humbuggin' Me	—	$20		Columbia 41268
				written by **Marty Robbins**					
6/8/59	6	15		18 The Long Black Veil	Knock Again, True Love	—	$15		Columbia 41384
4/27/63	23	2		19 Forbidden Lovers	A Few Steps Away	—	$12		Columbia 42676
11/9/63	30	1		20 Don't Let Her See Me Cry	James River	—	$12		Columbia 42839
1/11/64	❶⁴	26		21 Saginaw, Michigan	When It Rains The Blues	85	$12		Columbia 42924
8/8/64	28	11		22 The Nester	The Rider	—	$10		Columbia 43051
1/16/65	50	2		23 'Gator Hollow	Make That One For The Road A Cup Of Coffee	—	$10		Columbia 43169
5/1/65	12	15		24 She's Gone Gone Gone	Confused	—	$10		Columbia 43256
10/16/65	36	5		25 A Little Unfair /		—			
11/13/65	41	4		26 Love Looks Good On You		—	$10		Columbia 43364
10/15/66	51	6		27 I Just Couldn't See The Forest (For The Trees)	Everything Keeps Coming Back (But You)	—	$10		Columbia 43747
3/25/67	49	10		28 You Gotta Be Puttin' Me On	A Song From A Lonely Heart	—	$10		Columbia 44023
9/2/67	63	4		29 Get This Stranger Out Of Me	Hobo's Pride	—	$10		Columbia 44205
8/10/68	59	3		30 The Marriage Bit	When The Grass Grows Green Again	—	$10		Columbia 44563
3/22/69	64	4		31 An Article From Life	Only Way To Fly	—	$10		Columbia 44738
8/22/70	49	10		32 Watermelon Time In Georgia	Out Of You	—	$10		Columbia 45197
8/12/72	59	10		33 You, Babe	When It Rains The Blues	—	$10		Columbia 45652
9/22/73	43	13		34 I Can't Get Over You To Save My Life	Somebody's Words	—	$6		ABC 11387
2/16/74	25	12		35 I Never Go Around Mirrors	That's The Way Love Goes	—	$6		ABC 11416
6/15/74	52	9		36 Railroad Lady	If I Had Half The Sense (A Fool Was Born With)	—	$6		ABC 11442
9/21/74	21	14		37 Lucky Arms	If She Just Helps Me Get Over You	—	$6		ABC 12023
2/22/75	67	7		38 Life's Like Poetry	Sittin' And Thinkin'	—	$6		ABC 12061
7/5/75	50	11		39 Falling	I Love You A Thousand Ways	—	$6		ABC 12103

FRUSHAY, Ray '80
Born Raymond Frusha on 3/1/44 in San Diego; raised in Austin, Texas.

9/8/79	93	2		1 I Got Western Pride	Woman, Quit Walking Around In My Mind	—	$7		Western Pride 105
3/22/80	90	2		2 Pickin' Up Love	Dreamer's Room	—	$7		Western Pride 113

FUHRMAN, Micki '84
Born in Coushatta, Louisiana. Female singer/songwriter.

11/11/78	93	4		1 Leave While I'm Sleeping	Big Bright Rainbow	—	$7		Louisiana Hayride 785
7/28/79	86	3		2 Blue River Of Tears	I Need You	—	$5		MCA 41057
11/22/80	60	7		3 Hold Me, Thrill Me, Kiss Me	Holding Me	—	$5		MCA 51005
				#8 Pop hit for Mel Carter in 1965					
2/18/84	48	10		4 I Bet You Never Thought I'd Go This Far	I Don't Want To Go Too Far	—	$5		MCA 52321

FULLER, Jerry '79
Born Jerrell Lee Fuller on 11/19/38 in Fort Worth, Texas. Singer/songwriter/producer.

1/13/79	98	1		1 Salt On The Wound	No Time	—	$5		ABC 12436
6/2/79	90	4		2 Lines	Over You	—	$5		MCA 41022

DEBUT	PEAK	WKS	Gold	A-side (Chart Hit)	B-side	Pop	$	Pic	Label & Number

G

GABRIEL '81
Born Gabriel Ernest Miklos Farago in Hungary; at four months old, fled with family to Innsbruck, Austria. Emmigrated to Buffalo, New York, at age four.

DEBUT	PEAK	WKS							
1/24/81	85	3		1 I Think I Could Love You (Better Than He Did)	Til I Stop Falling In	—	$6		NSD 70
4/18/81	93	2		2 Friends Before Lovers		—	$6		Ridgetop 01381

GAINES, Chris — see BROOKS, Garth

GALLIMORE, Byron '80
Born in Puryear, Tennessee. Singer/songwriter.

6/14/80	93	2		No Ordinary Woman	Simple Ways	—	$7		Little Giant 025

GALLION, Bob '62
Born on 4/22/31 in Ashland, Kentucky. Singer/songwriter/guitarist.

11/3/58	28	1		1 That's What I Tell My Heart		—	$15		MGM 12700
5/18/59	18	9		2 You Take The Table And I'll Take The Chairs	Run Boy	—	$15		MGM 12777
11/28/60+	7	22		3 Loving You (Was Worth This Broken Heart)	Out Of A Honky Tonk		$12		Hickory 1130
6/19/61	20	4		4 One Way Street	Start All Over	—	$12		Hickory 1145
12/4/61	20	2		5 Sweethearts Again	Six Pallbearers	—	$12		Hickory 1154
11/10/62	5	15		6 Wall To Wall Love	You Don't Know (Or You Don't Care)	—	$10		Hickory 1181
8/31/63	23	2		7 Ain't Got Time For Nothin'	Happy Birthday, My Darlin'	—	$10		Hickory 1220
7/20/68	71	2		8 Pick A Little Happy Song	The Wrong Side Of Town	—	$8		United Artists 50309
9/8/73	99	2		9 Love By Appointment	Happy Anniversary	—	$7		Metromedia 0037
				PATI POWELL & BOB GALLION	If You Could Do Any Better (You'd Done Been Gone)				

GALWAY, James '83
Born on 12/8/39 in Belfast, Ireland. Classical flutist.

2/19/83	57	11		The Wayward Wind	Shenandoah	—	$4		RCA 13441
				JAMES GALWAY WITH SYLVIA					
				#1 Pop hit for Gogi Grant in 1956					

GARNER, Kristin '01
Born in Owego, New York. Female singer.

5/19/01	59	1		Let's Burn It Down		—	$10	★	Atlantic 300529
				only available as a promotional CD single					

GARNETT, Gale '64
Born on 7/17/42 in Auckland, New Zealand. Female singer/songwriter/actress.

12/5/64	43	3		We'll Sing In The Sunshine	Prism Song	4	$10		RCA Victor 8388

GARRETT, Pat '81
Born in Lebanon, Pennsylvania. Male singer/bassist.

11/12/77	98	1		1 A Little Something On The Side		—	$7		Kansa 3000
8/2/80	80	5		2 Sexy Ole Lady		—	$6		Gold Dust 101
10/18/80	89	3		3 Your Magic Touch	Humpty Dumpty	—	$6		Gold Dust 102
11/7/81	73	5		4 Everlovin' Woman	How Can I Please You	—	$6		Gold Dust 104
9/13/86	74	6		5 Rockin' My Country Heart	Daddy What Did I Do Wrong	—	$5		Compleat 157
10/3/87	82	3		6 Suck It In		—	$5		MDJ 73087

GARRISON, Al '87

9/26/87	87	2		Where Do I Go From Here		—	$6		Motion 1032

GARRISON, Glen '68
Born on 6/13/41 in Slarcy, Arkansas.

11/4/67	72	2		1 Goodbye Swingers	Hello Mama	—	$10		Imperial 66257
6/22/68	48	6		2 I'll Be Your Baby Tonight	You Know I Love You	—	$10		Imperial 66300
				first recorded by Bob Dylan on his 1968 John Wesley Harding album					

GARRON, Jess '79

3/31/79	30	11		1 Lo Que Sea (What Ever May The Future Be)	Those Good Times Are Over	—	$6		Charta 131
8/4/79	65	6		2 It's Summer Time	You Can't Love A Woman (Who Doesn't Want To Be Loved)	—	$6		Charta 136

GATLIN, Larry, & The Gatlin Brothers ★80★ '83
Trio of brothers: Larry (born on 5/2/48 in Seminole, Texas), Steve (born on 4/4/51 in Olney, Texas) and Rudy (born on 8/20/52 in Olney, Texas) Gatlin. Larry is the chief singer/songwriter with Steve (guitar) and Rudy (bass) providing the harmony vocals. Worked as a gospel trio and had their own TV series in Abilene, Texas. Joined the Grand Ole Opry in 1976.

1) Houston (Means I'm One Day Closer To You) 2) All The Gold In California 3) I Just Wish You Were Someone I Love 4) Night Time Magic 5) She Used To Be Somebody's Baby

LARRY GATLIN:

10/20/73	40	13		1 Sweet Becky Walker	You've Been Handed Down To Me		$6		Monument 8584
3/16/74	45	12		2 Bitter They Are Harder They Fall	To Make Me Wanna Stay Home		$6		Monument 8602
9/7/74	14	15		3 Delta Dirt	Those Also Love	84	$6		Monument 8622
8/23/75	71	7		4 Let's Turn The Lights On	Takin' A Chance On You		$6		Monument 8657

LARRY GATLIN with Family & Friends:

12/27/75+	5	19		5 Broken Lady	The Heart	—	$6		Monument 8680
6/12/76	43	9		6 Warm And Tender	The Heart Is Quicker Than The Eye	—	$6		Monument 8696
10/30/76+	5	16		7 Statues Without Hearts	What Will I Do Now	—	$5		Monument 201

DEBUT	PEAK	WKS	Gold	A-side (Chart Hit)	B-side	Pop	$	Pic	Label & Number
				LARRY GATLIN with Family & Friends — Cont'd					
2/26/77	12	11		8 Anything But Leavin'	Take Back 'It's Over'	—	$5		Monument 212
5/28/77	3	16		9 I Don't Wanna Cry	Mercy River	—	$5		Monument 221
9/10/77	3	14		10 Love Is Just A Game	Everytime A Plane Flies Over Our House	—	$5		Monument 226
12/10/77+	❶¹	16		11 I Just Wish You Were Someone I Love	Kiss It All Goodbye	—	$5	■	Monument 234
				LARRY GATLIN with Brothers and Friends					
				LARRY GATLIN:					
4/15/78	2²	14		12 Night Time Magic	It's Love At Last	—	$5		Monument 249
8/12/78	13	11		13 Do It Again Tonight	Cold Day In Hell	—	$5		Monument 259
11/11/78+	7	14		14 I've Done Enough Dyin' Today	Nothin' You Do	—	$5		Monument 270
				LARRY GATLIN & THE GATLIN BROTHERS BAND:					
8/25/79	❶²	15		15 All The Gold In California	How Much Is A Man Supposed To Take	—	$4		Columbia 11066
1/5/80	43	8		16 The Midnight Choir	Hold Me Closer	—	$4		Columbia 11169
3/8/80	12	12		17 Taking Somebody With Me When I Fall	Piece By Piece	108	$4		Columbia 11219
6/14/80	18	13		18 We're Number One	Can't Cry Anymore	—	$4		Columbia 11282
10/4/80	5	17		19 Take Me To Your Lovin' Place	Straight To My Heart	—	$4		Columbia 11369
2/21/81	25	11		20 It Don't Get No Better Than This	Straight To My Heart	—	$4		Columbia 11438
6/6/81	20	12		21 Wind Is Bound To Change	Help Yourself To Me	—	$4		Columbia 02123
10/3/81	4	17		22 What Are We Doin' Lonesome	You Wouldn't Know Love	—	$4		Columbia 02522
2/6/82	15	13		23 In Like With Each Other	Hard Workin' Hands	—	$4		Columbia 02698
5/29/82	19	12		24 She Used To Sing On Sunday	Can't Take It With You	—	$4		Columbia 02910
9/11/82	5	19		25 Sure Feels Like Love	Home Is Where The Healin' Is	—	$4		Columbia 03159
1/29/83	20	15		26 Almost Called Her Baby By Mistake	Somethin' Like Each Other's Arms	—	$4		Columbia 03517
5/21/83	32	11		27 Easy On The Eye	Anything But Leavin'	—	$4		Columbia 03885
9/24/83	❶²	22		28 Houston (Means I'm One Day Closer To You)	The Whole Wide World Stood Still	—	$4		Columbia 04105
3/24/84	7	18		29 Denver	A Dream That Got A Little Out Of Hand	—	$4		Columbia 04395
				LARRY GATLIN & THE GATLIN BROTHERS:					
7/21/84	3	24		30 The Lady Takes The Cowboy Everytime	S:3/A:3 It's Me	—	$4		Columbia 04533
10/12/85	43	13		31 Runaway Go Home	Nothing But Your Love Matters	—	$4		Columbia 05632
1/18/86	12	21		32 Nothing But Your Love Matters	S:12/A:13 When The Night Closes In	—	$4		Columbia 05764
				LARRY, STEVE, RUDY: THE GATLIN BROTHERS:					
8/23/86	2¹	22		33 She Used To Be Somebody's Baby	S:2/A:2 Being Alone	—	$4		Columbia 06252
12/27/86+	4	21		34 Talkin' To The Moon	S:3/A:4 Give Me A Chance	—	$4		Columbia 06592
5/9/87	21	12		35 From Time To Time (It Feels Like Love Again)	S:18 Texas	—	$4		Columbia 07088
				LARRY GATLIN & JANIE FRICKIE (with The Gatlin Brothers)					
8/15/87	16	15		36 Changin' Partners	S:15 Got A Lot Of Woman On His Hands	—	$4		Columbia 07320
3/26/88	4	21		37 Love Of A Lifetime	S:8 Don't Blame Me For Colorado	—	$4		Columbia 07747
				THE GATLIN BROS.					
8/13/88	34	13		38 Alive And Well	S:24 One On One	—	$4		Columbia 07998
				LARRY GATLIN AND THE GATLIN BROTHERS:					
2/25/89	54	7		39 When She Holds Me	Go Or Stay	—	$4		Universal 53501
5/6/89	37	10		40 I Might Be What You're Lookin' For	Rain	—	$4		Universal 66005
9/2/89	51	8		41 #1 Heartache Place	Your Door	—	$4		Universal 66021
8/4/90	65	6		42 Boogie And Beethoven	(remix)	—	$4	■	Capitol 44563
				THE GATLIN BROTHERS					

GATTIS, Keith '96
Born on 5/26/71 in Georgetown, Texas. Singer/songwriter/guitarist.

DEBUT	PEAK	WKS		A-side	B-side	Pop	$	Pic	Label & Number
3/30/96	53	9		Little Drops Of My Heart	Only Lonely Fool	—	$4	■	RCA 64488 (v)

GAULT, Lenny '79

DEBUT	PEAK	WKS		A-side	B-side	Pop	$	Pic	Label & Number
9/30/78	87	3		1 Turn On The Bright Lights	When A Woman Cries	—	$6		MRC 1020
1/6/79	78	4		2 I Just Need A Coke (To Get The Whiskey Down)	Steppin' Aside Just Ain't My Style	—	$6		MRC 1024
4/7/79	89	3		3 The Honky-Tonks Are Calling Me Again	I'm Gonna Leave	—	$6		King Coal 03

GAYLE, Crystal ★42★ '77
You have four 45s

Born Brenda Gail Webb on 1/9/51 in Paintsville, Kentucky; raised in Wabash, Indiana. Singer/songwriter. Sister of **Loretta Lynn**, **Peggy Sue** and **Jay Lee Webb**; distant cousin of **Patty Loveless**. Known for her trademark ankle-length hair. CMA Awards: 1977 & 1978 Female Vocalist of the Year.

1) Don't It Make My Brown Eyes Blue 2) Talking In Your Sleep 3) Why Have You Left The One You Left Me For 4) I'll Get Over You 5) Cry

DEBUT	PEAK	WKS		A-side	B-side	Pop	$	Pic	Label & Number
9/19/70	23	13		1 I've Cried (The Blues Right Out Of My Eyes)	Sparklin' Look Of Love	—	$8		Decca 32721
				written by Loretta Lynn; also see #14 below					
3/11/72	70	2		2 Everybody Oughta Cry	M.R.S. Degree	—	$8		Decca 32925
7/1/72	49	5		3 I Hope You're Havin' Better Luck Than Me	Too Far	—	$8		Decca 32969
5/25/74	39	12		4 Restless	Lay Back Lover	—	$5		United Artists 428
10/26/74+	6	21		5 Wrong Road Again	They Come Out At Night	—	$5		United Artists 555
3/29/75	27	11		6 Beyond You	Loving You So Long Now	—	$5		United Artists 600
7/26/75	21	15		7 This Is My Year For Mexico	When I Dream	—	$5		United Artists 680
11/29/75+	8	16		8 Somebody Loves You	Coming Closer	—	$5		United Artists 740
4/3/76	❶¹	18		9 I'll Get Over You	High Time	71	$5		United Artists 781
8/21/76	31	9		10 One More Time (Karneval)	Oh My Soul	—	$5		United Artists 838

DEBUT	PEAK	WKS	Gold	A-side (Chart Hit)	B-side	Pop	$	Pic	Label & Number
				GAYLE, Crystal — Cont'd					
11/6/76+	❶¹	16		11 You Never Miss A Real Good Thing (Till He Says Goodbye)	Forgettin' 'Bout You	—	$5		United Artists 883
3/26/77	2²	15		12 I'll Do It All Over Again	I'm Not So Far Away	—	$5		United Artists 948
7/9/77	❶⁴	18	● A	13 Don't It Make My Brown Eyes Blue	It's All Right With Me	2³	$4		United Artists 1016
12/10/77+	40	11		14 I've Cried (The Blues Right Out Of My Eyes) ... Sparklin' Look Of Love [R] same version as #1 above		—	$4		MCA 40837
2/11/78	❶¹	14		15 Ready For The Times To Get Better	Beyond You	52	$4		United Artists 1136
6/17/78	❶²	16		16 Talking In Your Sleep	Paintin' This Old Town Blue	18	$4		United Artists 1214
12/2/78+	❶²	14		17 Why Have You Left The One You Left Me For	Cry Me A River	—	$4		United Artists 1259
4/14/79	3	13		18 When I Dream	Hello I Love You	—	$4		United Artists 1288
7/21/79	7	13		19 Your Kisses Will	Time Will Prove That I'm Right	84	$4		United Artists 1306
9/1/79	2³	15		20 Half The Way	Room For One More	—	$4		Columbia 11087
12/8/79+	5	14		21 Your Old Cold Shoulder	We Should Be Together	15	$4		United Artists 1329
2/9/80	❶¹	14		22 It's Like We Never Said Goodbye	Don't Go My Love	—	$4		Columbia 11198
5/3/80	64	6		23 River Road	Come Home Daddy	63	$4		United Artists 1347
5/10/80	8	15		24 The Blue Side	Danger Zone	—	$4		Columbia 11270
7/26/80	58	7		25 Heart Mender	This Is My Year For Mexico	81	$4		United Artists 1362
9/13/80	❶¹	18		26 If You Ever Change Your Mind	I Just Can't Leave Your Love Alone	—	$4		Columbia 11359
2/7/81	17	14		27 Take It Easy	Ain't No Love In The Heart Of The City	—	$4		Columbia 11436
5/23/81	❶¹	17		28 Too Many Lovers	Help Yourselves To Each Other	—	$4		Columbia 02078
10/10/81	3	18		29 The Woman In Me	Crying In The Rain	76	$4		Columbia 02523
2/20/82	5	19		30 You Never Gave Up On Me	Tennessee	—	$4		Columbia 02718
8/7/82	9	15		31 Livin' In These Troubled Times	Ain't No Sunshine	—	$4		Columbia 03048
10/9/82	❶¹	19		32 You And I — EDDIE RABBITT with CRYSTAL GAYLE	All My Life, All My Love (Rabbitt)	7	$4		Elektra 69936
11/20/82+	❶¹	22		33 'Til I Gain Control Again	Easier Said Than Done	—	$4	■	Elektra 69893
4/2/83	❶¹	16		34 Our Love Is On The Faultline	Deeper In The Fire	—	$4		Warner 29719
7/16/83	❶¹	19		35 Baby, What About You	He Is Beautiful To Me	83	$4		Warner 29582
9/24/83	49	9		36 Keepin' Power	Half The Way	—	$4		Columbia 04093
10/29/83+	❶¹	21		37 The Sound Of Goodbye	Take Me Home	84	$4		Warner 29452
2/25/84	2²	19		38 I Don't Wanna Lose Your Love	Victim Or A Fool	—	$4		Warner 29356
7/7/84	❶¹	20		39 Turning Away	S:30 On Our Way To Love	—	$4		Warner 29254
10/27/84+	4	23		40 Me Against The Night	A:2 / S:4 You Made A Fool Of Me	—	$4		Warner 29151
3/23/85	3	21		41 Nobody Wants To Be Alone	A:3 / S:4 Coming To The Dance	—	$4		Warner 29050
8/10/85	5	18		42 A Long And Lasting Love	A:4 / S:5 Someone Like You	—	$4		Warner 28963
11/23/85+	❶¹	19		43 Makin' Up For Lost Time (The Dallas Lovers' Song) — CRYSTAL GAYLE AND GARY MORRIS from the TV series Dallas starring Larry Hagman	S:❶¹ / A:❶¹ A Few Good Men (Forester Sisters)	—	$4	■	Warner 28856
7/26/86	❶¹	19		44 Cry #1 Pop hit for Johnnie Ray in 1951	S:❶¹ / A:❶¹ Crazy In The Heart	—	$4		Warner 28689
11/22/86+	❶¹	22		45 Straight To The Heart	A:❶¹ / S:10 Do I Have To Say Goodbye	—	$4		Warner 28518
4/25/87	4	18		46 Another World — CRYSTAL GAYLE & GARY MORRIS theme from the TV serial	S:5 / A:29 Makin' Up For Lost Time	—	$4		Warner 28373
7/18/87	26	15		47 Nobody Should Have To Love This Way	A Little Bit Closer	—	$4		Warner 28409
10/24/87+	11	18		48 Only Love Can Save Me Now	Til I Gain Control Again	—	$4		Warner 28209
2/13/88	26	15		49 All Of This & More — CRYSTAL GAYLE/GARY MORRIS	Makin' Up For Lost Time	—	$4		Warner 28106
8/27/88	22	15		50 Nobody's Angel	When Love Is New	—	$4		Warner 27811
1/7/89	44	9		51 Tennessee Nights	When Love Is New	—	$4		Warner 27682
9/15/90	72	2		52 Never Ending Song Of Love #13 Pop hit for Delany & Bonnie in 1971; from the album Ain't Gonna Worry on Capitol 94301		—			album cut
				GEEZINSLAW BROTHERS, The '67 Novelty duo from Austin, Texas: Sam Allred (born on 5/5/38) and DeWayne "Son" Smith (born on 9/17/46).					
10/15/66	66	3		1 You Wouldn't Put The Shuck On Me	Snook Is The Only Town For Me [N]	—	$10		Capitol 5722
7/15/67	57	6		2 Change Of Wife	Brooklyn Bridge [N]	—	$10		Capitol 5918
10/21/67	48	8		3 Chubby (Please Take Your Love To Town) parody of "Ruby, Don't Take Your Love To Town" by Kenny Rogers	Tender-Hearted Me [N]	—	$10		Capitol 2002
8/22/92	56	13		4 Help, I'm White And I Can't Get Down — THE GEEZINSLAWS	You Belong To Me [N]	—	$5	■	Step One 442 (v)
				GENTRY, Bobbie '70 Born Roberta Streeter on 7/27/44 in Chickasaw County, Mississippi; raised in Greenwood, Mississippi. Singer/songwriter/guitarist. Formerly married to Jim Stafford. Won the 1967 Best New Artist Grammy Award.					
9/9/67	17	8	●	1 Ode To Billie Joe	Mississippi Delta	❶⁴	$6		Capitol 5950
6/1/68	72	4		2 Louisiana Man	Courtyard	100	$6		Capitol 2147
11/23/68	44	7		3 Less Of Me — BOBBIE GENTRY & GLEN CAMPBELL	Mornin' Glory (Pop #74)	—	$6		Capitol 2314
2/8/69	14	14		4 Let It Be Me — GLEN CAMPBELL and BOBBIE GENTRY	Little Green Apples	36	$6		Capitol 2387
12/13/69+	26	12		5 Fancy	Courtyard	31	$6		Capitol 2675
2/21/70	6	13		6 All I Have To Do Is Dream — BOBBIE GENTRY & GLEN CAMPBELL	Less Of Me	27	$6		Capitol 2745

DEBUT	PEAK	WKS	Gold	A-side (Chart Hit)	B-side	Pop	$	Pic	Label & Number
				GENTRY, Gary '81 Born in Athens, Texas. Singer/songwriter.					
4/25/81	84	2		1 I Sold All Of Tom T's Songs Last Night	Because Of You [N]	—	$4		Elektra 47122
12/19/81	83	4		2 (s.o.b.) Same Old Boy	The Devil Offered More	—	$4		Elektra 47238
				GENTRY, Montgomery — see MONTGOMERY GENTRY					
				GHOST TRAIN — see TAYLOR, Chip					
	★365★			**GIBBS, Terri** '81 Born on 6/15/54 in Miami; raised in Augusta, Georgia. Female singer/songwriter/pianist. Blind since birth. CMA Award: 1981 Horizon Award. 1)Somebody's Knockin' 2)Mis'ry River 3)Anybody Else's Heart But Mine					
10/11/80+	8	20		1 Somebody's Knockin'	Some Days It Rains All Night Long	13	$4		MCA 41309
6/6/81	19	12		2 Rich Man	I Won't Cry In Dallas Anymore	89	$4		MCA 51119
9/26/81	38	10		3 I Wanna Be Around #14 Pop hit for Tony Bennett in 1963	Rocky Top	—	$4		MCA 51180
12/26/81+	12	17		4 Mis'ry River	Too Long	—	$4		MCA 51225
5/1/82	19	13		5 Ashes To Ashes	Plans	—	$4		MCA 52040
8/14/82	45	8		6 Some Days It Rains All Night Long	All I Wanna Do In Life	—	$4		MCA 52088
11/13/82+	33	14		7 Baby I'm Gone	I Don't Need You (But I Want You)	—	$4		MCA 52134
8/13/83	17	17		8 Anybody Else's Heart But Mine	What A Night	—	$4		MCA 52252
12/3/83	65	8		9 Tell Mama #23 Pop hit for Etta James in 1968	Bells	—	$4		MCA 52308
3/30/85	43	12		10 A Few Good Men Kathy Mattea (guest vocal)	Ain't Nobody	—	$4		Warner 29056
7/6/85	70	5		11 Rockin' In A Brand New Cradle	You Can't Run Away From Your Heart	—	$4		Warner 28993
11/2/85	70	5		12 Someone Must Be Missing You Tonight	Here I Go Again	—	$4		Warner 28895
10/24/87	87	3		13 Turn Around		—	$4		Horizon 2963

				GIBSON, Don ★37★ '58 Born on 4/3/28 in Shelby, North Carolina. Singer/songwriter/guitarist. Worked local clubs and radio while still in high school. Moved to Knoxville in 1953 and worked on the WNOX *Barn Dance* radio series. Joined the *Grand Ole Opry* in 1958. Elected to the Country Music Hall of Fame in 2001. 1)Oh Lonesome Me 2)Blue Blue Day 3)Woman (Sensuous Woman) 4)Just One Time 5)Sea Of Heartbreak					
8/11/56	9	1		1 Sweet Dreams also see #15 below	A:9 The Road Of Life Alone	—	$30		MGM 12194
2/17/58	❶⁸	34		2 Oh Lonesome Me /	S:❶⁸ / A:❶⁸	7			
3/17/58	7	14		3 I Can't Stop Lovin' You	A:7	81	$15		RCA Victor 7133
6/9/58	❶²	24		4 Blue Blue Day	S:❶² / A:2 Too Soon To Know	20	$15		RCA Victor 7010
9/29/58	5	19		5 Give Myself A Party /		46			
10/6/58	8	9		6 Look Who's Blue	A:8	58	$15		RCA Victor 7330
2/2/59	3	16		7 Who Cares /		43			
2/23/59	27	2		8 A Stranger To Me		—	$15		RCA Victor 7437
5/11/59	11	13		9 Lonesome Old House	I Couldn't Care Less	71	$15		RCA Victor 7505
8/17/59	5	16		10 Don't Tell Me Your Troubles	Heartbreak Avenue	85	$15		RCA Victor 7566
12/7/59+	14	9		11 I'm Movin' On /		—			
1/4/60	29	1		12 Big Hearted Me		—	$15		RCA Victor 7629
3/7/60	2¹	21		13 Just One Time	I May Never Get To Heaven	29	$15		RCA Victor 7690
8/8/60	11	11		14 Far, Far Away also see #48 below	A Legend In My Time	72	$15		RCA Victor 7762
11/28/60+	6	16		15 Sweet Dreams new version of #1 above	The Same Street [R]	93	$15		RCA Victor 7805
3/13/61	22	6		16 What About Me	The World Is Waiting For The Sunrise (Pop #108)	100	$15		RCA Victor 7841
6/19/61	2¹	26		17 Sea Of Heartbreak	I Think It's Best (To Forget Me)	21	$15		RCA Victor 7890
12/18/61+	2¹	21		18 Lonesome Number One	The Same Old Trouble	59	$15		RCA Victor 7959
5/19/62	5	14		19 I Can Mend Your Broken Heart	I Let Her Get Lonely	105	$10		RCA Victor 8017
11/17/62	22	4		20 So How Come (No One Loves Me)	Baby We're Really In Love	—	$12	■	RCA Victor 8085
4/6/63	12	10		21 Head Over Heels In Love With You	It Was Worth It All	—	$12	■	RCA Victor 8144
8/31/63	22	5		22 Anything New Gets Old (Except My Love For You)	After The Heartache	—	$12	■	RCA Victor 8192
11/28/64+	23	16		23 Cause I Believe In You	A Love That Can't Be	—	$12		RCA Victor 8456
7/3/65	19	13		24 Again	You're Going Away	—	$10		RCA Victor 8589
10/9/65	10	13		25 Watch Where You're Going	There's A Big Wheel	—	$10		RCA Victor 8678
1/22/66	12	12		26 A Born Loser	All The World Is Lonely Now	—	$10		RCA Victor 8732
5/7/66	6	17		27 (Yes) I'm Hurting	My Whole World Is Hurt	—	$10		RCA Victor 8812
11/5/66+	8	17		28 Funny, Familiar, Forgotten, Feelings	Forget Me	—	$10		RCA Victor 8975
6/3/67	51	4		29 Lost Highway	Around The Town	—	$10		RCA Victor 9177
8/26/67	23	12		30 All My Love	No Doubt About It	—	$10		RCA Victor 9266
3/23/68	37	7		31 Ashes Of Love /		—			
6/1/68	71	3		32 Good Morning, Dear		—	$10		RCA Victor 9460
7/13/68	12	14		33 It's A Long, Long Way To Georgia	Low And Lonely	—	$10		RCA Victor 9563
11/23/68+	30	9		34 Ever Changing Mind	Thoughts	—	$10		RCA Victor 9663

DEBUT	PEAK	WKS	Gold	A-side (Chart Hit) ... B-side	Pop	$	Pic	Label & Number
				GIBSON, Don — Cont'd				
2/22/69	2¹	17		35 Rings Of Gold .... Final Examination	—	$8		RCA Victor 9715
				DOTTIE WEST & DON GIBSON				
5/3/69	28	9		36 Solitary .... I Just Said Goodbye To My Dreams	—	$8		RCA Victor 0143
7/12/69	32	10		37 Sweet Memories .... How's The World Treating You	—	$8		RCA Victor 0178
				DOTTIE WEST And DON GIBSON				
9/6/69	21	8		38 I Will Always .... Half As Much	—	$8		RCA Victor 0219
12/13/69+	7	13		39 There's A Story (Goin' 'Round) .... Lock, Stock, And Teardrops	—	$8		RCA Victor 0291
				DOTTIE WEST AND DON GIBSON				
3/14/70	17	12		40 Don't Take All Your Loving .... Pretending Everyday	—	$8		Hickory 1559
6/27/70	16	13		41 A Perfect Mountain .... Would You Believe Me	—	$8		Hickory 1571
7/18/70	46	10		42 Til I Can't Take It Anymore .... I Love You Because	—	$8		RCA Victor 9867
				DOTTIE WEST & DON GIBSON				
10/10/70	37	12		43 Someway .... Comfort For Your Mind	—	$8		Hickory 1579
1/23/71	19	13		44 Guess Away The Blues .... I Wanna Live	—	$8		Hickory 1588
5/22/71	29	11		45 (I Heard That) Lonesome Whistle .... Window Shopping	—	$8		Hickory 1598
				written by Hank Williams and Jimmie Davis				
8/28/71	50	8		46 The Two Of Us Together .... Oh Yes, I Love You	—	$8		Hickory 1607
				DON GIBSON & SUE THOMPSON				
10/23/71	5	17		47 Country Green .... Move It On Over	—	$8		Hickory 1614
2/19/72	12	13		48 Far, Far Away .... What's Happened To Me [R]	—	$8		Hickory 1623
				new version of #14 above				
4/22/72	71	3		49 Did You Ever Think .... Love's Garden	—	$8		Hickory 1629
				DON GIBSON & SUE THOMPSON				
6/10/72	❶¹	18		50 Woman (Sensuous Woman) .... If You Want Me To I'll Go	—	$8		Hickory 1638
8/12/72	37	11		51 I Think They Call It Love .... Over There's The Door	—	$8		Hickory 1646
				DON GIBSON AND SUE THOMPSON				
10/21/72	11	13		52 Is This The Best I'm Gonna Feel .... Watching It Go	—	$8		Hickory 1651
12/23/72	64	5		53 Cause I Love You .... My Tears Don't Show	—	$8		Hickory 1654
				DON GIBSON & SUE THOMPSON				
2/17/73	26	11		54 If You're Goin' Girl .... Lonesome Number One	—	$8		Hickory 1661
3/17/73	52	6		55 Go With Me .... The Two Of Us Together	—	$8		Hickory 1665
				DON GIBSON & SUE THOMPSON				
5/26/73	6	14		56 Touch The Morning .... Too Soon To Know	—	$8		Hickory 1671
9/15/73	53	9		57 Warm Love .... Fly The Friendly Skies With Jesus	—	$6		Hickory/MGM 303
				DON GIBSON & SUE THOMPSON				
10/6/73	30	11		58 That's What I'll Do .... Sweet Dreams	—	$6		Hickory/MGM 306
12/29/73+	12	13		59 Snap Your Fingers .... Love Is A Lonesome Thing	—	$6		Hickory/MGM 312
				#8 Pop hit for Joe Henderson in 1962				
5/4/74	8	15		60 One Day At A Time .... Rainbow Love	—	$6		Hickory/MGM 318
8/10/74	31	12		61 Good Old Fashioned Country Love .... Ages And Ages Ago	—	$6		Hickory/MGM 324
				DON GIBSON AND SUE THOMPSON				
8/31/74	9	17		62 Bring Back Your Love To Me .... Drinking Champagne	—	$6		Hickory/MGM 327
1/18/75	27	12		63 I'll Sing For You .... Pocatello	—	$6		Hickory/MGM 338
4/19/75	24	11		64 (There She Goes) I Wish Her Well .... Funny, Familiar, Forgotten Feelings	—	$6		Hickory/MGM 345
7/19/75	36	11		65 Oh, How Love Changes .... Sweet And Tender Times	—	$6		Hickory/MGM 350
				DON GIBSON AND SUE THOMPSON				
8/16/75	43	11		66 Don't Stop Loving Me .... Somebody's Words	—	$6		Hickory/MGM 353
12/6/75+	76	8		67 I Don't Think I'll Ever (Get Over You) .... It Can't Last Always	—	$6		Hickory/MGM 361
3/13/76	79	5		68 You've Got To Stop Hurting Me Darling .... Blues In My Mind	—	$6		Hickory/MGM 365
4/3/76	98	2		69 Get Ready-Here I Come .... Once More	—	$6		Hickory/MGM 367
				DON GIBSON AND SUE THOMPSON				
5/29/76	39	10		70 Doing My Time .... The World Is Waiting For The Sunrise	—	$6		Hickory/MGM 372
11/6/76	23	12		71 I'm All Wrapped Up In You .... We Live In Two Different Worlds	—	$5		ABC/Hickory 54001
3/12/77	30	10		72 Fan The Flame, Feed The Fire .... Bringin' In The Georgia Mail	—	$5		ABC/Hickory 54010
7/2/77	16	13		73 If You Ever Get To Houston (Look Me Down) .... It's All Over	—	$5		ABC/Hickory 54014
10/22/77	67	5		74 When Do We Stop Starting Over .... Love Is Not The Way (You Told Me)	—	$5		ABC/Hickory 54019
2/11/78	16	14		75 Starting All Over Again .... I'd Rather Die Young (Than Grow Old Without You)	—	$5		ABC/Hickory 54024
				#19 Pop hit for Mel & Tim in 1972				
6/3/78	22	10		76 The Fool .... Every Song I Sang Would Be Blue	—	$5		ABC/Hickory 54029
				#7 Pop hit for Sanford Clark in 1956				
10/7/78	61	7		77 Oh, Such A Stranger /	—			
		7		78 I Love You Because	—	$5		ABC/Hickory 54036
				#3 Pop hit for Al Martino in 1963				
12/23/78+	26	12		79 Any Day Now .... Baby's Not Home	—	$5		ABC/Hickory 54039
				#23 Pop hit for Chuck Jackson in 1962				
6/9/79	37	10		80 Forever One Day At A Time .... Look Who's Blue	—	$5		MCA 41031
3/29/80	42	7		81 Sweet Sensuous Sensations .... Stranger To Me	—	$4		Warner/Curb 49193
12/13/80+	80	6		82 Love Fires .... Come Back And Love Me	—	$4		Warner/Curb 49602
				GIBSON, Hal **'89**				
12/16/89	87	3		The Love She Found In Me	—	$7		Sundial 163
				GIBSON/MILLER BAND **'93**				
				Group led by singer/songwriter Dave Gibson (born on 10/1/56) and guitarist Bill "Blue" Miller (born on 7/15/52). Includes Mike Daly (steel guitar; born on 6/11/55), Bryan Grassmeyer (bass; born on 6/6/54) and Steve Grossman (drums; born on 4/3/62).				
11/14/92+	37	20		1 Big Heart .... (remix)	—	$4	■	Epic 74739 (v)
2/13/93	20	20		2 High Rollin' .... Stone Cold Country	—	$4		Epic 74856
6/12/93	22	20		3 Texas Tattoo .... Southern Man	—	$4	■	Epic 74991 (v)
9/25/93	46	11		4 Small Price .... Where There's Smoke	—	$4		Epic 77169

DEBUT	PEAK	WKS	Gold	A-side (Chart Hit)	B-side	Pop	$	Pic	Label & Number
				GIBSON/MILLER BAND — Cont'd					
1/22/94	40	13		5 Stone Cold Country .... Thank Virginia		—	$4		Epic 77355
5/28/94	49	10		6 Mammas Don't Let Your Babies Grow Up To Be Cowboys .... Right Off The Top Of My Heart		—	$4	▪	Epic 77488 (v)
				from the movie *The Cowboy Way* starring Woody Harrelson					
9/24/94	59	7		7 Red, White And Blue Collar .... Johnny Get Your Gun		—	$4	▪	Epic 77651 (v)
				GILKYSON, Terry — see WEAVERS, The					

GILL, Vince ★50★   '92

Born on 4/12/57 in Norman, Oklahoma. Singer/songwriter/guitarist. Member of **Pure Prairie League** from 1979-83. Married to Janis Oliver of **Sweethearts Of The Rodeo** from 1980-97. Married Amy Grant on 3/10/2000. Joined the *Grand Ole Opry* in 1991. CMA Awards: 1991, 1992, 1993, 1994 & 1995 Male Vocalist of the Year; 1993 & 1994 Entertainer of the Year. Also see **America The Beautiful**, **Hope** and **Tomorrow's World**.

1) Don't Let Our Love Start Slippin' Away   2) I Still Believe In You   3) The Heart Won't Lie   4) One More Last Chance
5) Tryin' To Get Over You

DEBUT	PEAK	WKS	Gold	A-side (Chart Hit)	B-side	Pop	$	Pic	Label & Number
2/11/84	40	13		1 Victim Of Life's Circumstances .... Don't Say That You Love Me		—	$4		RCA 13731
5/19/84	38	11		2 Oh Carolina .... Half A Chance		—	$4		RCA 13809
9/22/84	39	15		3 Turn Me Loose .... 'Til The Best Comes Along		—	$4		RCA 13860
3/16/85	32	17		4 True Love .... S:26 Livin' The Way I Do		—	$4		RCA 14020
7/13/85	10	18		5 If It Weren't For Him A:6 / S:10 Savannah (Do You Ever Think of Me)		—	$4		RCA 14140
				Rosanne Cash (guest vocal)					
11/23/85+	9	25		6 Oklahoma Borderline S:9 / A:9 She Don't Know		—	$4		RCA 14216
6/7/86	33	15		7 With You .... A:32 Colder Than Winter		—	$4		RCA 14371
5/2/87	5	21		8 Cinderella S:11 Something's Missing		—	$4	☐	RCA 5131
9/19/87	16	16		9 Let's Do Something .... S:25 It Doesn't Matter Anymore		—	$4		RCA 5257
1/30/88	11	17		10 Everybody's Sweetheart .... S:20 The Way Back Home		—	$4		RCA 5331
6/4/88	39	10		11 The Radio .... The Way Back Home		—	$4		RCA 8301
9/16/89	22	20		12 Never Alone .... Oh Girl (You Know Where To Find Me)		—	$4		MCA 53717
1/20/90	13	26		13 Oklahoma Swing .... We Could Have Been		—	$4		MCA 53780
				Reba McEntire (guest vocal)					
5/26/90	2²	21		14 When I Call Your Name Rita Ballou		—	$4		MCA 79011
				Patty Loveless (backing vocal); CMA Award: Single of the Year					
9/29/90	3	20		15 Never Knew Lonely Riding The Rodeo		—	$4		MCA 53892
2/16/91	7	20		16 Pocket Full Of Gold A Little Left Over		—	$4		MCA 54026
6/15/91	7	20		17 Liza Jane What's A Man To Do		—	$4		MCA 54123
9/21/91+	4	20		18 Look At Us I Quit		—	$4		MCA 54179
2/1/92	2²	20		19 Take Your Memory With You Sparkle		—	$4		MCA 54282
7/4/92	❶²	20		20 I Still Believe In You One More Last Chance		—	$4		MCA 54406
10/17/92	❶³	20		21 Don't Let Our Love Start Slippin' Away Love Never Broke Anyone's Heart		—	$4		MCA 54489
2/20/93	❶²	20		22 The Heart Won't Lie Will He Ever Go Away		—	$4		MCA 54599
				REBA McENTIRE AND VINCE GILL					
4/10/93	3	20		23 No Future In The Past Pretty Words		—	$4		MCA 54540
7/31/93	❶¹	20		24 One More Last Chance Under These Conditions		—	$4		MCA 54715
10/30/93	42	20		25 I Can't Tell You Why		—			album cut
				#8 Pop hit for the **Eagles** in 1980; from the various artists album *Common Thread: Songs Of The Eagles* on Giant 24531					
12/18/93	52	4		26 Have Yourself A Merry Little Christmas .... [X]		—			album cut
				from the album *Let There Be Peace On Earth* on MCA 10877					
1/8/94	❶¹	20		27 Tryin' To Get Over You Nothing Like A Woman		88	$4	▪	MCA 54706 (v)
4/16/94	2³	20		28 Whenever You Come Around South Side Of Dixie		72	$4	▪	MCA 54833 (v)
7/9/94	2²	20		29 What The Cowgirls Do Go Rest High On That Mountain		—	$4	▪	MCA 54879
10/15/94	3	20		30 When Love Finds You If I Had My Way		109	$4	▪	MCA 54937
12/24/94	54	3		31 Have Yourself A Merry Little Christmas .... [X-R]		—			album cut
12/31/94	74	1		32 It Won't Be The Same This Year .... [X]		—			album cut
				above 2 from the album *Let There Be Peace On Earth* on MCA 10877					
2/4/95	4	20		33 Which Bridge To Cross (Which Bridge To Burn) If There's Anything I Can Do		—	$4	▪	MCA 54976 (v)
5/13/95	2¹	20		34 You Better Think Twice A Real Lady's Man		—	$4		MCA 55035
9/2/95	14	20		35 Go Rest High On That Mountain .... Maybe Tonight		—	$4		MCA 55098
9/16/95	15	20		36 I Will Always Love You .... Speakin' Of The Devil		—	$4		Columbia 78079
				DOLLY PARTON WITH VINCE GILL					
				#1 Pop hit for Whitney Houston in 1992					
4/13/96	12	20		37 High Lonesome Sound .... (bluegrass version)		—	$4		MCA 55188
7/20/96	5	20		38 Worlds Apart Down To New Orleans		—	$4		MCA 55213
11/9/96+	2¹	20		39 Pretty Little Adriana Tell Me Lover		—	$4		MCA 55251
3/29/97	2¹	20		40 A Little More Love S:21 Jenny Dreamed Of Trains		—	$4	▪	MCA 55307 (v)
7/19/97	8	20		41 You And You Alone Given More Time		—	$4		MCA 72010
12/13/97+	34	13		42 It's Not Over .... Useless		—	$4		Decca 72032
				MARK CHESNUTT (Featuring Vince Gill and Alison Krauss)					
12/27/97	64	2		43 Have Yourself A Merry Little Christmas .... [X-R]		—			album cut
				from the album *Let There Be Peace On Earth* on MCA 10877					
5/30/98	5	20		44 If You Ever Have Forever In Mind S:6 Given More Time		60	$4	▪	MCA Nash. 72055 (v)
10/10/98	33	12		45 Kindly Keep It Country .... I Never Really Knew You		—	$4		MCA Nashville 72072
12/26/98	74	1		46 Blue Christmas .... [X]		—			album cut
				from the album *Breath Of Heaven* on MCA 70038					
1/23/99	27	19		47 Don't Come Cryin' To Me .... I'll Take Texas		115	$4		MCA Nashville 72085

127

DEBUT	PEAK	WKS	Gold	A-side (Chart Hit) .... B-side	Pop	$	Pic	Label & Number
				GILL, Vince — Cont'd				
5/29/99	27	20		48 My Kind Of Woman/My Kind Of Man .... *All Those Years* (Gill) VINCE GILL With Patty Loveless	116	$4		MCA Nashville 72107
10/23/99	62	10		49 If You Ever Leave Me .... BARBRA STREISAND / VINCE GILL from Streisand's album *A Love Like Ours* on Columbia 69601	—			album cut
1/29/00	20	20		50 Let's Make Sure We Kiss Goodbye .... *Let Her In*	—	$4		MCA Nashville 172148
5/20/00	6	32		51 Feels Like Love .... *When I Look Into Your Heart*	52	$4		MCA Nashville 172168
1/20/01	31	16		52 Shoot Straight From Your Heart .... *When I Look Into Your Heart*	—	$4		MCA Nashville 172195
				GILLETTE, Steve '80 Born in California. Singer/songwriter.				
2/23/80	76	5		Lost The Good Thing .... *Three Lines* STEVE GILLETTE (with Jennifer Warnes)	—	$5		Regency 45002

GILLEY, Mickey ★51★   '83

Born on 3/9/36 in Natchez, Mississippi; raised in Ferriday, Lousiana. Singer/songwriter/pianist. Co-owner with Sherwood Cryer of Gilleys nightclub in Pasadena, Texas, from 1971-89. Gilley and the club were featured in the movie *Urban Cowboy*. Cousin of **Jerry Lee Lewis** and Reverend Jimmy Swaggart.

1)She's Pulling Me Back Again 2)Window Up Above 3)I Overlooked An Orchid 4)Lonely Nights 5)Paradise Tonight

DEBUT	PEAK	WKS	Gold	#	A-side	B-side	Pop	$	Pic	Label & Number
10/19/68	68	6		1	Now I Can Live Again	*Without You*	—	$12		Paula 1200
4/20/74	●¹	16		2	Room Full Of Roses	*She Called Me Baby*	50	$5		Playboy 50056
					#2 Pop hit for Sammy Kaye in 1949					
8/10/74	●¹	18		3	I Overlooked An Orchid	*Swinging Doors*	—	$5		Playboy 6004
12/7/74+	●¹	12		4	City Lights	*Fraulein*	—	$5		Playboy 6015
3/15/75	●¹	15		5	Window Up Above	*I'm Moving On*	—	$5		Playboy 6031
7/5/75	11	13		6	Bouquet Of Roses	*If You Were Mine To Lose*	—	$5		Playboy 6041
10/18/75	32	9		7	Roll You Like A Wheel	*Let's Sing A Song Together*	—	$5	■	Playboy 6045
					MICKEY GILLEY & BARBI BENTON					
11/22/75+	7	13		8	Overnight Sensation	*I'll Sail My Ship Alone*	—	$5		Playboy 6055
2/21/76	●¹	16		9	Don't The Girls All Get Prettier At Closing Time	*Where Do You Go To Lose A Heartache*	—	$5		Playboy 6063
6/26/76	●¹	14		10	Bring It On Home To Me	*How's My Ex Treating You*	101	$5		Playboy 6075
					#13 Pop hit for Sam Cooke in 1962					
10/16/76	3	14		11	Lawdy Miss Clawdy	*What Is It*	—	$5		Playboy 6089
					#1 R&B hit for Lloyd Price in 1952					
2/19/77	●¹	17		12	She's Pulling Me Back Again	*Sweet Mama Goodtimes*	—	$5		Playboy 6100
6/11/77	4	14		13	Honky Tonk Memories	*Five Foot Two Eyes Of Blue (Has Anybody Seen My Girl)*	—	$5		Playboy 5807
11/5/77	9	14		14	Chains Of Love	*#1 Rock'n Roll C&W Boogie Blues Man*	—	$5		Playboy 5818
					#1 R&B hit for Joe Turner in 1951					
3/18/78	8	13		15	The Power Of Positive Drinkin'	*Playing My Old Piano*	—	$5		Playboy 5826
7/29/78	9	14		16	Here Comes The Hurt Again	*I Hate It, But I Drink It Anyway*	—	$4		Epic 50580
11/18/78+	13	15		17	The Song We Made Love To	*Memphis Memories*	—	$4		Epic 50631
3/17/79	10	14		18	Just Long Enough To Say Goodbye	*Tying One On (To Take One Off My Mind)*	—	$4		Epic 50672
7/21/79	8	14		19	My Silver Lining	*Picture Of Our Love*	—	$4		Epic 50740
11/17/79+	17	14		20	A Little Getting Used To	*Can't Nobody Love You*	—	$4		Epic 50801
5/10/80	●¹	16		21	True Love Ways	*The More I Turn The Bottle Up*	66	$4		Epic 50876
					co-written by Buddy Holly; #14 Pop hit for Peter & Gordon in 1965					
5/31/80	●¹	17		22	Stand By Me	*Cotton Eyed Joe* (The Unstrung Heroes)	22	$4	■	Full Moon 46640
					#4 Pop hit for Ben E. King in 1961; from the movie *Urban Cowboy* starring John Travolta					
10/18/80	●¹	16		23	That's All That Matters	*The Blues Don't Care Who's Got 'Em*	101	$4		Epic 50940
2/14/81	●¹	15		24	A Headache Tomorrow (Or A Heartache Tonight)	*Million Dollar Memories*	—	$4		Epic 50973
7/4/81	●¹	16		25	You Don't Know Me	*Jukebox Argument*	55	$4		Epic 02172
					#2 Pop hit for Ray Charles in 1962					
11/7/81+	●¹	18		26	Lonely Nights	*We've Watched Another Evening Waste Away*	—	$4		Epic 02578
3/20/82	3	18		27	Tears Of The Lonely	*Ladies Night*	—	$4		Epic 02774
7/31/82	●¹	16		28	Put Your Dreams Away	*If I Can't Hold Her On The Outside*	—	$4		Epic 03055
11/13/82+	●¹	18		29	Talk To Me	*Honky Tonkin' (I Guess I Done Me Some)*	106	$4		Epic 03326
					#20 Pop hit for Little Willie John in 1958					
4/2/83	●¹	18		30	Fool For Your Love	*Shakin' A Heartache*	—	$4		Epic 03783
7/16/83	●¹	22		31	Paradise Tonight	*The Four Seasons Of Love*	—	$4		Epic 04007
					CHARLY McCLAIN and MICKEY GILLEY					
9/3/83	5	21		32	Your Love Shines Through	*Wish You Were Mine Again*	—	$4		Epic 04018
1/7/84	2¹	20		33	You've Really Got A Hold On Me	*Giving Up Getting Over You*	—	$4		Epic 04269
					#8 Pop hit for The Miracles in 1963					
2/18/84	5	18		34	Candy Man	*The Phone Call*	—	$4		Epic 04368
					MICKEY GILLEY and CHARLY McCLAIN #25 Pop hit for Roy Orbison in 1961					
6/16/84	14	17		35	The Right Stuff	*We Got A Love Thing*	—	$4		Epic 04489
					CHARLY McCLAIN and MICKEY GILLEY					
9/1/84	4	22		36	Too Good To Stop Now	S:4 / A:4 *Shoulder To Cry On*	—	$4		Epic 04563
2/2/85	10	17		37	I'm The One Mama Warned You About	A:9 / S:10 *You Can Lie To Me Tonight*	—	$4		Epic 04746
5/4/85	12	17		38	It Ain't Gonna Worry My Mind	A:11 / S:12 *Crazy Old Soldier*	—	$4		Columbia 04860
					RAY CHARLES (with Mickey Gilley)					

DEBUT	PEAK	WKS	Gold	A-side (Chart Hit)	B-side	Pop	$	Pic	Label & Number
				GILLEY, Mickey — Cont'd					
8/24/85	10	22		39 You've Got Something On Your Mind .... A:9 / S:10	I Feel Good About Lovin' You	—	$4		Epic 05460
12/21/85+	5	21		40 Your Memory Ain't What It Used To Be S:2 / A:6	Lonely Nights, Lonely Heartache	—	$4		Epic 05744
7/26/86	6	19		41 Doo-Wah Days	S:6 / A:6 After She's Gone	—	$4		Epic 06184
4/4/87	16	14		42 Full Grown Fool	S:15 / A:28 To My One And Only	—	$4		Epic 07009
7/16/88	49	8		43 I'm Your Puppet .... Don't Show Me Your Memories (And I Won't Show You Mine)		—	$5		Airborne 10002
				#6 Pop hit for James & Bobby Purify in 1966					
10/29/88+	23	19		44 She Reminded Me Of You	S:28 Easy Climb	—	$5		Airborne 10008
4/15/89	62	5		45 You Still Got A Way With My Heart	It's Killing Me To Watch Love Die	—	$5		Airborne 10016
7/15/89	53	8		46 There! I've Said It Again	It's Killing Me To Watch Love Die	—	$5		Airborne 75740
				#1 Pop hit for **Bobby Vinton** in 1964					
				GILMAN, Billy '00					
				Born on 5/24/88 in Westerly, Rhode Island; raised in Hope Valley, Rhode Island.					
5/27/00	20	20		1 One Voice	S:❶⁵ 'Til I Can Make It On My Own	38	$4	★	Epic 79396 (v)
				"45": Epic 79527; B-side: "Oklahoma"					
10/14/00+	33	21		2 Oklahoma /	S:2	63			
12/9/00	50	5		3 Warm & Fuzzy	[X]	—	$4	★	Epic 79503
6/2/01	50	7		4 She's My Girl		—			album cut
9/22/01	56	2		5 Elisabeth		—			album cut
				above 2 from the album *Dare To Dream* on Epic 62087					
				GILMORE, Jimmie Dale '88					
				Born on 5/6/45 in Tulia, Texas. Singer/songwriter/guitarist.					
8/27/88	72	5		1 White Freight Liner Blues	Trying To Get To You	—	$5		Hightone 504
6/10/89	85	2		2 Honky Tonk Song		—	$5		Hightone 510
				GIMBLE, Johnny — see PRICE, Ray					
				GINO THE NEW GUY '95					
				Born Gino Ruberto on 10/14/63 in Wabasha, Minnesota; raised in Lake City, Minnesota. Morning show producer at Minneapolis radio station KEEY-FM.					
8/12/95	56	11		1 Any Gal Of Mine	[N]	—			album cut
				parody of "Any Man Of Mine" by **Shania Twain**; from his homemade album *Any Gal Of Mine* (no label or number)					
				GIRLS NEXT DOOR '86					
				Female vocal group: Doris King, Diane Williams, Cindy Nixon and Tammy Stephens. Disbanded in 1991.					
2/1/86	14	21		1 Love Will Get You Through Times With No Money .S:11 / A:16	Ruins Of Love	—	$4		MTM 72059
6/14/86	8	21		2 Slow Boat To China	S:6 / A:8 Pretty Boy's Cadillac	—	$4		MTM 72068
11/1/86	26	14		3 Baby I Want It	A:26 (sing-along version)	—	$4		MTM 72078
2/7/87	28	13		4 Walk Me In The Rain	A:28 The Fool In Me	—	$4		MTM 72084
7/4/87	43	9		5 What A Girl Next Door Could Do..............	I Think I'm Gonna Fall (In Love With You)	—	$4		MTM 72088
10/17/87	57	6		6 Easy To Find	Message From My Heart	—	$4		MTM 72095
9/10/88	73	4		7 Love And Other Fairy Tales	I Can Hear My Heart Begin To Cry	—	$4		MTM 72106
12/2/89+	54	7		8 He's Gotta Have Me	Wasn't It You	—	$4		Atlantic 88791
9/1/90	71	1		9 How 'Bout Us	Last Goodbye	—	$4	■	Atlantic 87868 (v)
				#12 Pop hit for Champaign in 1981					
				GLASER, Chuck '74					
				Born on 2/27/36 in Spalding, Nebraska. Singer/songwriter/guitarist. Member of **The Glaser Brothers**.					
1/5/74	81	7		Gypsy Queen	That's When I Love You The Most	—	$5		MGM 14663
	★253★			**GLASER, Jim** '84					
				Born on 12/16/37 in Spalding, Nebraska. Singer/songwriter/guitarist. Member of **The Glaser Brothers**.					
				1)You're Gettin' To Me Again 2)If I Could Only Dance With You 3)Let Me Down Easy 4)When You're Not A Lady 5)The Man In The Mirror					
8/31/68	32	8		1 God Help You Woman	She Was Too Good To Me	—	$6		RCA Victor 9587
1/4/69	40	10		2 Please Take Me Back	Kiss Her Once For Me	—	$6		RCA Victor 9696
5/10/69	52	7		3 I'm Not Through Loving You	Can't Keep My Mind On The Game	—	$6		RCA Victor 0142
10/11/69	53	5		4 Molly	Permanent Kind Of Lovin' (From A Temporary Man)	—	$6		RCA Victor 0231
9/1/73	67	12		5 I See His Love All Over You	It's Still A Long Way	—	$5		MGM 14590
6/15/74	68	8		6 Fool Passin' Through	If It Pleases You	—	$5		MGM 14713
12/21/74+	51	12		7 Forgettin' 'Bout You	If It Pleases You	—	$5		MGM 14758
5/31/75	88	5		8 One, Two, Three (Never Gonna Fall In Love Again)..............	One Night Man	—	$5		MGM 14798
11/15/75	43	10		9 Woman, Woman	Turn To Me	—	$5		MGM 14834
				#4 Pop hit for Gary Puckett and The Union Gap in 1968					
11/6/76	66	10		10 She's Free But She's Not Easy	Lonely Bein' Free	—	$4		MCA 40636
7/23/77	88	4		11 Chasin' My Tail	Sleeping Beauty	—	$4		MCA 40742
11/26/77	86	4		12 Don't Let My Love Stand In Your Way	Honky Tonk Lady	—	$4		MCA 40813
11/20/82+	16	22		13 When You're Not A Lady	I Don't Wanna Make Love	—	$4		Noble Vision 101
4/2/83	28	13		14 You Got Me Running	I'd Love To See You Again	—	$4		Noble Vision 102
8/27/83	17	21		15 The Man In The Mirror	Pretend	—	$4		Noble Vision 103
1/28/84	10	24		16 If I Could Only Dance With You	Woman, Woman	—	$4		Noble Vision 104
6/9/84	❶¹	24		17 You're Gettin' To Me Again	Stand By The Road	—	$4		Noble Vision 105
11/17/84+	16	19		18 Let Me Down Easy	S:15 / A:18 I'd Love To See You Again	—	$4		Noble Vision 107
6/29/85	54	8		19 I'll Be Your Fool Tonight	Tough Act To Follow	—	$4		MCA 52619
9/14/85	27	18		20 In Another Minute	A:25 / S:28 Merry-Go-Round	—	$4		MCA 52672
12/28/85+	53	9		21 If I Don't Love You	It's Not Easy	—	$4		MCA 52748
4/26/86	40	11		22 The Lights Of Albuquerque	A:37 Waltzing Through A Rock And Roll Life	—	$4		MCA 52808

DEBUT	PEAK	WKS	Gold	A-side (Chart Hit)	B-side	Pop	$	Pic	Label & Number
				GLASER, Tompall '75					
				Born Thomas Paul Glaser on 9/3/33 in Spalding, Nebraska. Singer/songwriter/guitarist. Lead singer of **The Glaser Brothers**.					
10/6/73	77	7		1 Bad, Bad, Bad Cowboy .... Let It Be Pretty		—	$6		MGM 14622
				TOMPALL GLASER Of The Glaser Brothers					
3/23/74	96	5		2 Texas Law Sez .... Pass Me On By		—	$6		MGM 14701
9/14/74	63	8		3 Musical Chairs .... Grab A Hold		—	$6		MGM 14740
5/24/75	21	19		4 Put Another Log On The Fire (Male Chauvinist					
				National Anthem) .... Mendocino [N]		103	$6		MGM 14800
				TOMPALL					
4/24/76	36	9		5 T For Texas .... Broken Down Momma		—	$5		Polydor 14314
				TOMPALL And His Outlaw Band					
				#2 Pop hit for **Jimmie Rodgers** in 1928 as "Blue Yodel"					
4/9/77	45	9		6 It'll Be Her .... Sweethearts Or Strangers/I Will Always Love You		—	$4		ABC 12261
				also see #20 under **Tompall & The Glaser Brothers**					
12/3/77	91	3		7 It Never Crossed My Mind .... Easy On My Mind		—	$4		ABC 12309
2/25/78	79	6		8 Drinking Them Beers .... Duncan And Brady		—	$4		ABC 12329
	★230★			**GLASER BROTHERS, Tompall & The** '81					
				Family trio from Spalding, Nebraska: brothers **Tompall Glaser**, **Chuck Glaser** and **Jim Glaser**. Opened own recording studio in Nashville in 1969 which was a hangout for the budding "outlaw" music movement. Trio split up in 1973. Reunited in 1979 and then split up once again in 1982. CMA Award: 1970 Vocal Group of the Year.					
				1)Lovin' Her Was Easier (Than Anything I'll Ever Do Again) 2)Rings 3)California Girl (And The Tennessee Square) 4)Ain't It All Worth Living For 5)Just One Time					
12/31/66+	24	15		1 Gone, On The Other Hand .... Streets Of Baltimore		—	$7		MGM 13611
7/22/67	27	16		2 Through The Eyes Of Love .... She Loved The Wrong Man		—	$7		MGM 13754
2/24/68	42	9		3 The Moods Of Mary .... No End Of Love		—	$7		MGM 13880
7/27/68	36	10		4 One Of These Days .... Where Has All The Love Gone		—	$7		MGM 13954
3/22/69	11	16		5 California Girl (And The Tennessee Square) .... All That Keeps Ya Goin'		92	$7		MGM 14036
7/19/69	24	11		6 Wicked California .... This Eve Of Parting		—	$7		MGM 14064
12/27/69+	30	9		7 Walk Unashamed .... Gonna Miss Me		—	$7		MGM 14096
4/11/70	33	11		8 All That Keeps Ya Goin' .... Theme From "...tick...tick...tick..."		—	$6		MGM 14113
				from the movie ...tick...tick...tick... starring George Kennedy					
10/24/70	23	11		9 Gone Girl .... I'll Say My Words		—	$6		MGM 14169
6/12/71	22	9		10 Faded Love .... Pretty Eyes		—	$6		MGM 14249
				TOMPALL AND THE GLASER BROTHERS WITH LEON McAULIFFE AND THE CIMARRON BOYS					
8/28/71	7	15		11 Rings .... That's When I Love You The Most		—	$6		MGM 14291
				#17 Pop hit for **Cymarron** in 1971					
1/15/72	23	13		12 Sweet, Love Me Good Woman .... Stand Beside Me		—	$6		MGM 14339
6/17/72	15	15		13 Ain't It All Worth Living For .... Blue Ridge Mountains		—	$6		MGM 14390
				TOMPALL & THE GLASER BROTHERS And The Nashville Studio Band					
1/20/73	46	9		14 A Girl Like You .... Delta Lost		—	$6		MGM 14462
5/12/73	47	8		15 Charlie .... Lovin' You Again		—	$6		MGM 14516
4/19/80	43	8		16 Weight Of My Chains .... The Ballad Of Lucy Jordon		—	$4		Elektra 46595
11/8/80	34	11		17 Sweet City Woman .... Tryin' To Outrun The Wind		—	$4		Elektra 47056
				#8 Pop hit for the **Stampeders** in 1971					
5/2/81	2²	16		18 **Lovin' Her Was Easier (Than Anything I'll Ever Do Again)** .... United We Fall		—	$4		Elektra 47134
				#26 Pop hit for **Kris Kristofferson** in 1971					
9/19/81	17	14		19 Just One Time .... Feelin' The Weight Of My Chains		—	$4		Elektra 47193
2/13/82	19	13		20 It'll Be Her .... A Mansion On The Hill [R]		—	$4		Elektra 47405
				new version of #6 under **Tompall Glaser**					
6/12/82	28	10		21 I Still Love You (After All These Years) .... Feelin' The Weight Of My Chains		—	$4		Elektra 47461
11/6/82	88	3		22 Maria Consuela .... I Could Never Live Alone Again		—	$4		Elektra 69947
				GLENN, Darrell '53					
				Born on 12/7/35 in Waco, Texas. Died of cancer on 4/9/90 (age 54). Son of Artie Glenn who wrote "Crying In The Chapel."					
7/25/53	4	13		Crying In The Chapel .... A:4 / J:4 / S:7 Hang Up That Telephone		6	$40		Valley 105
				#3 Pop hit for **Elvis Presley** in 1965					
				GLENN, Howdy '77					
				Black male singer.					
9/17/77	62	6		1 Touch Me .... White Line Fever		—	$5		Warner 8447
				written by **Willie Nelson**					
7/29/78	72	5		2 You Mean The World To Me .... That Lucky Old Sun		—	$5		Warner 8616
				GODFREY, Ray '60					
				Born Arnold Godfrey in Copperville, Tennessee.					
6/27/60	8	15		1 The Picture .... The Overall Song		—	$25		Savoy 3021
				first released on J&J 001 ($30)					
12/29/62+	20	6		2 Better Times A Comin' .... Ten Silver Dollars		—	$20		Sims 130
				GOLDEN, Jeff '89					
				Born in Atlanta. Singer/songwriter.					
9/10/88	91	2		1 Southern And Proud Of It		—	$5		MGA 30274
11/26/88	91	2		2 This Old World Ain't The Same		—	$5		MGA 30275
3/18/89	80	3		3 That Newsong (They're Playin)		—	$5		Soundwaves 4816
6/24/89	87	3		4 Singing The Blues		—	$5		MGA 104
				#1 Pop hit for **Guy Mitchell** in 1956					
				GOLDEN, William Lee '86					
				Born on 1/12/39 in Brewton, Alabama. Member of the **Oak Ridge Boys**. Also see **Tomorrow's World**.					
6/21/86	53	7		1 Love Is The Only Way Out .... Music For My Soul		—	$4		MCA 52819
11/1/86	72	4		2 You Can't Take It With You .... Somebody Gotta Pay		—	$4		MCA 52944

DEBUT	PEAK	WKS	Gold	A-side (Chart Hit) ... B-side	Pop	$	Pic	Label & Number
				GOLDENS, The '88				
				Duo of brothers from Brewton, Alabama: Rusty (born on 1/3/59) and Chris (born on 10/17/62) Golden. Sons of **William Lee Golden**. Chris a member of **Cedar Creek**. Rusty was a member of The Boys Band.				
3/5/88	55	6		1 Put Us Together Again ... Country Comfort	—	$4		Epic 07716
7/2/88	63	6		2 Sorry Girls ... Best Friend's Baby	—	$4		Epic 07928
5/4/91	67	3		3 Keep The Faith ...	—			album cut
				from the album *Rush For Gold* on Capitol/SBK 94395				
	★247★			**GOLDSBORO, Bobby** '68				
				Born on 1/18/41 in Marianna, Florida. Singer/songwriter/guitarist. Hosted own syndicated TV show from 1972-75.				
				1)Honey 2)Watching Scotty Grow 3)Autumn Of My Life 4)Muddy Mississippi Line 5)Goodbye Marie				
3/9/68	56	5		1 I Just Wasted The Rest ... Our Way Of Life	—	$8		United Artists 50243
				DEL REEVES & BOBBY GOLDSBORO				
3/30/68	❶³	15	●	2 Honey ... Danny	❶⁵	$7		United Artists 50283
7/13/68	15	11		3 Autumn Of My Life ... She Chased Me	19	$7	■	United Artists 50318
10/26/68	37	10		4 The Straight Life ... Tomorrow Is Forgotten	36	$7		United Artists 50461
3/15/69	49	5		5 Glad She's A Woman ... Letter To Emily	61	$7		United Artists 50497
5/3/69	22	11		6 I'm A Drifter ... Hoboes And Kings	46	$7		United Artists 50525
8/30/69	15	10		7 Muddy Mississippi Line ... Richer Man Than I	53	$7		United Artists 50565
11/1/69	31	10		8 Take A Little Good Will Home ... She Thinks I Still Care	—	$7		United Artists 50591
				BOBBY GOLDSBORO & DEL REEVES				
12/20/69+	56	7		9 Mornin Mornin ... Requiem	78	$7		United Artists 50614
5/16/70	71	2		10 Can You Feel It ... Time Good, Time Bad	75	$7		United Artists 50650
1/2/71	7	15		11 Watching Scotty Grow ... Water Color Days	11	$7		United Artists 50727
5/29/71	48	7		12 And I Love You So ... The Gentle Of A Man	83	$7		United Artists 50776
8/4/73	100	2		13 Summer (The First Time) ... Childhood — 1949	21	$6	■	United Artists 251
1/19/74	52	10		14 Marlena ... Sing Me A Smile	—	$6		United Artists 371
5/11/74	62	6		15 I Believe The South Is Gonna Rise Again ... She	—	$6		United Artists 422
				BOBBY GOLDSBORO with The TSU Chorus				
9/7/74	79	5		16 Hello Summertime ... And Then There Was Gina	—	$6		United Artists 529
5/15/76	22	14		17 A Butterfly For Bucky ... Another Night Alone	101	$6		United Artists 793
3/19/77	82	5		18 Me And The Elephants ... I Love Music	104	$5		Epic 50342
7/9/77	85	4		19 The Cowboy And The Lady ... Me And Millie	—	$5		Epic 50413
10/25/80+	17	15		20 Goodbye Marie ... Love Has Made A Woman Out Of You	—	$4		Curb 5400
3/7/81	20	12		21 Alice Doesn't Love Here Anymore ... Green Eyed Woman, Nashville, Blues	—	$4		Curb 70052
7/4/81	19	14		22 Love Ain't Never Hurt Nobody ... Wings Of An Eagle	—	$4		Curb 02117
11/14/81	31	11		23 The Round-Up Saloon ... Green Eyed Woman, Nashville, Blues	—	$4		Curb 02583
2/20/82	49	9		24 Lucy And The Stranger ... Out Run The Sun	—	$4		Curb 02726
				GOODNIGHT, Gary '82				
				Born in 1954 in Immokalee, Florida.				
11/8/80	90	3		1 I Have To Break The Chains That Bind Me ...	—	$5		Door Knob 138
1/24/81	91	2		2 Make Me Believe ... Back Door Slam	—	$5		Door Knob 141
3/21/81	90	3		3 Get Me High, Off This Low ...	—	$5		Door Knob 149
5/16/81	75	5		4 Tell Me So ... There'll Be A Blue Moon Tonight	—	$5		Door Knob 155
8/8/81	72	5		5 Let Me Fill For You A Fantasy ...	—	$5		Door Knob 159
11/28/81	90	3		6 Losin' Myself In You ... Vagabond Cowboy	—	$5		Door Knob 166
1/16/82	67	7		7 Lady, Lay Down (Lay Down On My Pillow) ...	—	$5		Door Knob 169
7/17/82	64	7		8 Bringing Out The Fool In Me ... Texas Let Me In	—	$5		Soundwaves 4675
				GOODSON, C.L. '75				
9/13/75	93	4		18 Yellow Roses ... The More She Thinks About Him	—	$7		Island 030
				#10 Pop hit for **Bobby Darin** in 1963				
				GOODSON, Lloyd '76				
12/11/76	80	6		Jesus Is The Same In California ... Wearin' Out The Patches On My Knees	—	$6		United Artists 891
				GOODSON, Mitch '80				
				Born in Dothan, Alabama.				
2/9/80	95	3		1 Draggin' Leather ... She Loves It (As Much As Me)	—	$6		Partridge 002
4/12/80	70	6		2 Do You Wanna Spend The Night ...	—	$6		Partridge 011
				GOODWIN, Bill '63				
				Born on 6/2/30 in Cumberland City, Tennessee.				
5/11/63	17	8		Shoes Of A Fool ... It Keeps Right On A-Hurtin'	—	$20		Vee Jay 501
				GORDON, Luke '59				
				Born on 4/15/32 in Quincy, Kentucky.				
12/22/58+	13	7		Dark Hollow ... You May Be Someone (Where You Come From)	—	$25		Island 0640
				GORDON, Noah '95				
				Born on 9/19/71 in Sparta, Illinois. Singer/guitarist/drummer.				
1/14/95	68	3		The Blue Pages ...	—			album cut
				from the album *I Need A Break* on Patriot 81521				
				GORDON, Robert '79				
				Born in 1947 in Washington DC. Rockabilly singer.				
3/31/79	99	1		1 It's Only Make Believe ... Rock Billy Boogie	—	$5		RCA 11471
				#1 Pop hit for **Conway Twitty** in 1958				
6/23/79	98	1		2 Walk On By ... Black Slacks	—	$5		RCA 11608

DEBUT	PEAK	WKS	Gold	A-side (Chart Hit)	B-side	Pop	$	Pic	Label & Number

GORME, Eydie '73
Born on 8/16/31 in New York City. Former big band singer. Married Steve Lawrence on 12/29/57. Charted 17 pop hits from 1956-72.

| 8/11/73 | 94 | 5 | | Take One Step .... The Garden | — | $6 | | MGM 14563 |

GOSDIN, Rex '80
Born Equen Gosdin on 5/19/38 in Woodland, Alabama. Died on 5/23/83 (age 45). Brother of **Vern Gosdin**. Member of **The Gosdin Bros.**

7/14/79	94	3		1 We're Making Up For Lost Time	—	$7		MRC 10589
5/31/80	51	10		2 Just Give Me What You Think Is Fair .... Things I Remember	—	$7		Sabre 4520
				REX GOSDIN with Tommy Jennings				
11/8/80	92	2		3 Lovin' You Is Music To My Mind .... How Can Anything That Sounds So Good	—	$7		Grape Vine 12046
6/11/83	90	3		4 That Old Time Feelin' .... Morning Noon And Night	—	$7		Sun 1178

GOSDIN, Vern ★85★ '84

Born on 8/5/34 in Woodland, Alabama. Singer/songwriter/guitarist. Joined the Gosdin Family radio show from Birmingham in the early 1950s. Moved to California in 1960 and formed The Golden State Boys with his brother **Rex Gosdin**; they later recorded together as **The Gosdin Bros.**

1) I Can Tell By The Way You Dance (You're Gonna Love Me Tonight)   2) Set 'Em Up Joe   3) I'm Still Crazy   4) Who You Gonna Blame It On This Time   5) That Just About Does It

3/5/77	9	15		1 Yesterday's Gone /		—		
10/30/76+	16	15		2 Hangin' On		—	$5	Elektra 45353
				also see The Gosdin Bros.; Emmylou Harris (harmony vocal, above 2)				
6/25/77	7	15		3 Till The End /		—		
1/21/78	23	11		4 It Started All Over Again		—	$5	Elektra 45411
10/22/77	17	13		5 Mother Country Music .... We Make Beautiful Music Together		—	$5	Elektra 45436
5/20/78	9	12		6 Never My Love .... I Sure Can Love You		—	$5	Elektra 45483
				#2 Pop hit for The Association in 1967; Janie Fricke (harmony vocal, above 2)				
10/7/78	13	11		7 Break My Mind .... Without You There's A Sadness In My Song		—	$5	Elektra 45532
3/17/79	16	13		8 You've Got Somebody, I've Got Somebody .... Till I'm Over Gettin' Over You		—	$5	Elektra 46021
7/7/79	21	14		9 All I Want And Need Forever .... Fifteen Hundred Times A Day		—	$5	Elektra 46052
11/3/79	57	6		10 Sarah's Eyes .... She's Gone		—	$5	Elektra 46550
1/24/81	28	11		11 Too Long Gone .... She's Just A Place To Fall		—	$5	Ovation 1163
5/16/81	7	17		12 Dream Of Me .... Ain't It Been Love		—	$5	Ovation 1171
1/16/82	28	15		13 Don't Ever Leave Me Again .... Love Is All We Had To Share		—	$5	AMI 1302
7/10/82	22	13		14 Your Bedroom Eyes .... Love Is All We Had To Share		—	$5	AMI 1307
10/23/82+	10	19		15 Today My World Slipped Away .... Ain't It Been Love		—	$5	AMI 1310
2/12/83	5	21		16 If You're Gonna Do Me Wrong (Do It Right) .... Favorite Fool Of All		—	$5	Compleat 102
2/12/83	49	7		17 Friday Night Feelin' .... Lovin' You Is Music To My Mind		—	$5	AMI 1312
6/4/83	5	22		18 Way Down Deep .... Today My World Slipped Away		—	$5	Compleat 108
10/1/83	10	21		19 I Wonder Where We'd Be Tonight .... I Feel Love Closin' In		—	$5	Compleat 115
3/31/84	●¹	25		20 I Can Tell By The Way You Dance (You're Gonna Love Me Tonight) .... My Heart Is In Good Hands		—	$5	Compleat 122
7/21/84	10	20		21 What Would Your Memories Do .... S:26 Love Me Right To The End		—	$5	Compleat 126
12/1/84+	10	20		22 Slow Burning Memory .... A:9 / S:10 I've Got A Heart Full Of You		—	$5	Compleat 135
5/4/85	20	17		23 Dim Lights, Thick Smoke (And Loud, Loud Music) .... S:19 / A:22 For A Minute There		—	$5	Compleat 142
8/31/85	35	13		24 I Know The Way To You By Heart .... Rainbows And Roses		—	$5	Compleat 145
3/22/86	68	8		25 It's Only Love Again .... Today My World Slipped Away		—	$5	Compleat 153
6/7/86	61	10		26 Was It Just The Wine .... Way Down Deep		—	$5	Compleat 155
9/13/86	51	8		27 Time Stood Still .... Slow Burning Memory		—	$5	Compleat 158
11/7/87+	4	23		28 Do You Believe Me Now .... S:2 Nobody Calls From Vegas Just To Say Hello		—	$4	Columbia 07627
4/9/88	●¹	22		29 Set 'Em Up Joe .... S:●² There Ain't Nothing Wrong (Just Ain't Nothing Right)		—	$4	Columbia 07762
				tribute to **Ernest Tubb**				
8/27/88	6	23	★	30 Chiseled In Stone .... S:2 Tight As Twin Fiddles		—	$4	Columbia 08003
1/7/89	2¹	22		31 Who You Gonna Blame It On This Time .... It's Not Over Yet		—	$4	Columbia 08528
5/27/89	●¹			32 I'm Still Crazy .... Paradise '83		—	$4	Columbia 68888
9/30/89+	4	26		33 That Just About Does It .... Set 'Em Up Joe		—	$4	Columbia 69084
2/3/90	10	26		34 Right In The Wrong Direction .... Tanqueray		—	$4	▪ Columbia 73221 (v)
6/23/90	75	1		35 Tanqueray .... You're Not By Yourself		—	$4	▪ Columbia 73350 (v)
9/1/90	14	20		36 This Ain't My First Rodeo .... If You're Gonna Do Me Wrong (Do It Right)		—	$4	▪ Columbia 73491 (v)
12/8/90+	10	20		37 Is It Raining At Your House .... Today My World Slipped Away		—	$4	Columbia 73632
5/25/91	64	8		38 I Knew My Day Would Come .... Love Will Keep Your Hand On The Wheel		—	$4	Columbia 73814
8/24/91	51	12		39 The Garden .... I'd Better Write It Down		—	$4	Columbia 73946
11/30/91+	54	13		40 A Month Of Sundays .... The Bridge I'm Still Building On		—	$4	Columbia 74103
4/10/93	67	5		41 Back When .... What Are We Gonna Do About Me		—	$4	Columbia 74905

GOSDIN BROS., The '67
Duo from Woodland, Alabama: **Vern Gosdin** and **Rex Gosdin**. Rex died on 5/23/83 (age 45).

| 10/7/67 | 37 | 11 | | Hangin' On .... Multiple Heartaches | | — | $15 | Bakersfield Int'l. 1002 |

DEBUT	PEAK	WKS	Gold	A-side (Chart Hit)	B-side	Pop	$	Pic	Label & Number
				GRAHAM, Tammy '97					
				Born on 2/7/68 in Little Rock, Arkansas. Singer/pianist.					
5/11/96	63	8		1 Tell Me Again...Cool Water		—	$4		Career 12953
3/22/97	37	15		2 A Dozen Red Roses..S:4 Tell Me Again		108	$4	■	Career 13075 (v)
8/2/97	59	4		3 Cool Water..More About Love		—	$4		Career 13089
				GRAMMER, Billy '59					
				Born on 8/28/25 in Benton, Illinois. Singer/songwriter/guitarist. Joined the *Grand Ole Opry* in 1959.					
1/5/59	5	13		1 Gotta Travel On...Chasing A Dream	4		$15		Monument 400
				based on 19th-century tune that originated in the British Isles					
1/19/63	18	5		2 I Wanna Go Home..The Bottom Of The Glass		—	$10		Decca 31449
				song also known as "Detroit City"					
1/11/64	43	2		3 I'll Leave The Porch Light A-Burning...Old Foolish Me		—	$10		Decca 31562
8/27/66	35	3		4 Bottles...Temporarily		—	$10		Epic 10052
12/31/66+	30	12		5 The Real Thing..Heaven Help This Heart Of Mine		—	$10		Epic 10103
9/23/67	48	11		6 Mabel (You Have Been A Friend To Me)...Papa And Mama		—	$10		Rice 5025
8/31/68	70	4		7 The Ballad Of John Dillinger..Do You Still Believe		—	$8		Mercury 72836
10/18/69	66	5		8 Jesus Is A Soul Man...Peace On Earth Begins Today		—	$8		Stop 321
				#28 Pop hit for Lawrence Reynolds in 1969					
				GRAND, Gil '99					
				Born on 1/8/68 in Sudbury, Ontario, Canada. Male singer/songwriter.					
5/16/98	73	3		1 Famous First Words..I Can't Put Your Memory To Bed		—	$4		Monument 78881
2/13/99	55	8		2 Let's Start Livin'..		—			album cut
5/22/99	70	1		3 I Already Fell...		—			album cut
				above 2 from the album *Famous First Words* on Monument					
				GRANT, Barry '81					
				Born in West Palm Beach, Florida. Also recorded as **Amarillo** and **Breakfast Barry**.					
9/29/79	95	2		1 We're In For Hard Times...Most Wanted Outlaw			$6		Countrystock 1602
				BREAKFAST BARRY					
4/26/80	89	3		2 Pretty Poison /...		—			
12/15/79	91	5		3 Out With The Boys..		—	$6		CSI 001
				AMARILLO:					
12/27/80+	82	4		4 That's The Way My Woman Loves..Pretty Poison		—	$5		NSD 72
6/13/81	70	5		5 Somehow, Someway And Someday /..		—			
3/21/81	87	3		6 How Long Has This Been Going On..		—	$5		NSD 81
10/10/81	86	4		7 A Little Bit Crazy...Out With The Boys		—	$5		NSD 104
				GRANT, Tom '79					
				Born on 8/28/50 in Milwaukee. Singer/songwriter. Member of *Trinity Lane*.					
1/27/79	40	8		1 If You Could See You Through My Eyes.......................................You're Easy To Love		—	$6		Republic 036
6/30/79	63	5		2 We've Gotta Get Away From It All..Catching Up On Love		—	$6		Republic 043
9/8/79	16	11		3 Sail On...I'll Meet You In Paradise		—	$6		Republic 045
				#4 Pop hit for the Commodores in 1979					
10/16/82	76	4		4 I'm Gonna Love You Right Out Of This World.......................................Sundown Lady		—	$5		Elektra 69961
8/10/85	63	8		5 Everyday People..		—	$7		Bermuda Dunes 110
				MARGO SMITH AND TOM GRANT					
				GRAY, Billy — see **JACKSON, Wanda**					
	★226★			**GRAY, Claude** '61					
				Born on 1/25/32 in Henderson, Texas. Singer/songwriter/guitarist. Nicknamed "The Tall Texan."					
				1)My Ears Should Burn (When Fools Are Talked About) 2)I'll Just Have A Cup Of Coffee (Then I'll Go)					
				3)I Never Had The One I Wanted 4)Family Bible 5)How Fast Them Trucks Can Go					
3/21/60	10	13		1 **Family Bible**..Crying In The Night		—	$25		D 1118
				written by **Willie Nelson**					
1/9/61	4	23		2 **I'll Just Have A Cup Of Coffee (Then I'll Go)**..........................I Just Want To Be Alone	84		$12		Mercury 71732
6/26/61	3	19		3 **My Ears Should Burn (When Fools Are Talked About)**.....................Crying In The Night		—	$12		Mercury 71826
1/13/62	26	1		4 Let's End It Before It Begins...Talk To Me Old Lonesome Heart		—	$12		Mercury 71898
10/20/62	20	5		5 Daddy Stopped In...Three Times		—	$12		Mercury 72001
2/9/63	18	6		6 Knock Again, True Love...Call Of The Wild		—	$12		Mercury 72063
3/21/64	43	12		7 Eight Years (And Two Children Later)..Lonesome		—	$12		Mercury 72236
7/30/66	22	10		8 Mean Old Woman..Then Cry You Away		—	$10		Columbia 43614
11/26/66+	9	18		9 **I Never Had The One I Wanted**......................................Effects Your Leaving Had On Me		—	$8		Decca 32039
				also see #25 below					
6/3/67	45	9		10 Because Of Him /..		—			
6/24/67	67	3		11 If I Ever Need A Lady (I'll Call You)..		—	$8		Decca 32122
				also see #24 below					
9/23/67	12	14		12 How Fast Them Trucks Can Go...Next Time You See Me		—	$8		Decca 32180
5/18/68	31	12		13 Night Life...Just Between Us Tears		—	$8		Decca 32312
11/9/68	68	2		14 The Love Of A Woman...................................The Kind You Find Tonight Forget Tomorrow		—	$8		Decca 32393
5/3/69	41	11		15 Don't Give Me A Chance..Once In Every Lifetime		—	$8		Decca 32456
10/25/69	34	10		16 Take Off Time...Sherry Ann		—	$8		Decca 32566
4/11/70	54	6		17 The Cleanest Man In Cincinnati..Crazy Arms		—	$8		Decca 32648
7/18/70	40	8		18 Everything Will Be Alright...Apartment #9		—	$8		Decca 32697
3/27/71	41	9		19 Angel...Save My Mind		—	$8		Decca 32786
9/2/72	66	7		20 What Every Woman Wants To Hear...There's You		—	$8		Million 18
1/20/73	58	8		21 Woman Ease My Mind..Don't Fight The Feeling		—	$8		Million 31

Johnny Gray? — Take It On Home To Branson

DEBUT	PEAK	WKS	Gold	A-side (Chart Hit)	B-side	Pop	$	Pic	Label & Number
				GRAY, Claude — Cont'd					
10/16/76	88	5		22 Rockin' My Memories (To Sleep)	But That's All Right	—	$7		Granny White 10001
1/22/77	92	4		23 We Fell In Love That Way	That's My Baby	—	$7		Granny White 10002
6/3/78	68	7		24 If I Ever Need A Lady	The Bar [R]	—	$7		Granny White 10006
				new version of #11 above					
1/13/79	78	6		25 I Never Had The One I Wanted	Late Cup Of Coffee [R]	—	$7		Granny White 10007
				new version of #9 above					
2/6/82	68	6		26 Let's Go All The Way	We Climbed A Mountain Last Night	—	$7		Granny White 10009
				CLAUDE GRAY and NORMA JEAN					
2/22/86	77	4		27 Sweet Caroline	Half A Mind	—	$6		Country Int'l. 208
				#4 Pop hit for Neil Diamond in 1969					
				GRAY, Damon '00					
				Born in Belen, New Mexico. Singer/songwriter/guitarist.					
2/12/00	75	1		I'm Lookin' For Trouble		—			album cut
				from the album Lookin' For Trouble on Broken Bow 7777					
				GRAY, Dobie '86					
				Born Lawrence Darrow Brown on 7/26/40 in Brookshire/Simonton, Texas. Charted 8 pop hits from 1963-79.					
3/22/86	35	13		1 That's One To Grow On	Gonna Be A Long Night	—	$4		Capitol 5562
7/12/86	42	9		2 The Dark Side Of Town	A Night In The Life Of A Country Boy	—	$4		Capitol 5596
11/15/86	67	9		3 From Where I Stand	So Far So Good	—	$4		Capitol 5647
11/21/87	82	2		4 Take It Real Easy	You Must Have Been Reading My Heart	—	$4		Capitol 44087
				GRAY, Jan '83					
				Born in Oneida, Kentucky.					
11/15/80	80	3		1 No Love At All	There's No Way We Can Go Wrong	—	$5		Paid 106
				#16 Pop hit for B.J. Thomas in 1971					
8/21/82	85	3		2 There I Go Dreamin' Again		—	$5		Jamex 006
11/6/82	89	3		3 Closer To Crazy	It's About Time	—	$5		Jamex 008
6/18/83	49	11		4 No Fair Fallin' In Love	Win Some, Lose Some, Lonesome	—	$5		Jamex 010
10/15/83	55	7		5 Before We Knew It	The Heart	—	$5		Jamex 011
1/21/84	51	9		6 Bad Night For Good Girls	Dear Me	—	$5		Jamex 012
5/10/86	64	6		7 Cross My Heart		—	$7		Cypress 8510
	★334★			**GRAY, Mark** '84					
				Born on 10/24/52 in Vicksburg, Mississippi. Singer/songwriter/pianist. Member of **Exile** from 1979-82.					
				1)Sometimes When We Touch 2)Please Be Love 3)Diamond In The Dust					
5/28/83	25	20		1 It Ain't Real (If It Ain't You)	Whatever Happened To Old Fashioned Love	—	$4		Columbia 03893
10/15/83+	18	18		2 Wounded Hearts	Til You And Your Lover Are Lovers Again	—	$4		Columbia 04137
1/28/84	10	22		3 Left Side Of The Bed	Fire From A Friend	—	$4		Columbia 04324
5/26/84	9	23		4 If All The Magic Is Gone	Til Her Heartache Is Over	—	$4		Columbia 04464
9/29/84	9	21		5 Diamond In The Dust	A:8 / S:9 I Guess You Must Have Touched Me Just Right	—	$4	■	Columbia 04610
2/23/85	6	22		6 Sometimes When We Touch	A:5 / S:6 You're Gonna Be The Last Love	—	$4		Columbia 04782
				MARK GRAY and TAMMY WYNETTE					
				#3 Pop hit for Dan Hill in 1978					
7/27/85	43	13		7 Smooth Sailing (Rock In The Road)	Dixie Girl	—	$4		Columbia 05403
11/23/85+	7	21		8 Please Be Love	S:7 / A:7 I Need You Again	—	$4		Columbia 05695
4/12/86	14	17		9 Back When Love Was Enough	S:13 / A:15 Dance With Me	—	$4		Columbia 05857
5/28/88	69	5		10 Song In My Heart		—	$6		615 1014
				MARK GRAY and BOBBI LACE					
12/17/88+	70	5		11 It's Gonna Be Love		—	$6		615 1016
				MARK GRAY and BOBBI LACE					
				GRAYGHOST '87					
				Group from Arkansas led by Bill White. Formerly known as **Razorback**.					
				RAZORBACK:					
4/11/87	70	3		1 As Long As I've Been Loving You	Out Of Control	—	$5		Compleat 166
6/13/87	61	7		2 Make A Living Out Of Loving You		—	$5		Compleat 174
11/28/87	66	7		3 This Ole House		—	$5		Compleat 184
9/17/88	70	4		4 Where Were You When I Was Blue	Something So Hot	—	$4		Mercury 870633
				GRAYGHOST:					
6/10/89	70	5		5 Let's Sleep On It		—	$4		Mercury 874194
9/23/89	69	4		6 If This Ain't Love (There Ain't No Such Thing)	Take A Little Time	—	$4		Mercury 874770
				GRAYSON, Jack '82					
				Born **Jack Lebsock** in Texas. Legally changed his name to Jack Grayson. Staff writer for ABC/Dot records in the 1970s.					
				1)When A Man Loves A Woman 2)A Loser's Night Out 3)Tonight I'm Feeling You (All Over Again)					
				JACK LEBSOCK:					
8/11/73	94	3		1 For Lovers Only	World That Cannot See	—	$6		Capitol 3665
1/5/74	76	6		2 Lovin' Comes Easy	I'll Be Damned If I Do (Damned If I Don't)	—	$6		Capitol 3751
				"BLACKJACK" JACK GRAYSON:					
4/14/79	92	3		3 I Ain't Never Been To Heaven (But I've Spent The Night With You)	Tonight I'm Feeling You (All Over Again)	—	$5		Churchill 7729
12/22/79+	65	8		4 Tonight I'm Feelin' You (All Over Again)	Free To Love	—	$5		Hitbound 4501
				also see #11 below					
6/14/80	70	6		5 The Stores Are Full Of Roses		—	$5		Hitbound 4503
8/30/80	59	7		6 The Devil Stands Only Five Foot Five	Free To Love	—	$5		Hitbound 4504

DEBUT	PEAK	WKS	Gold	A-side (Chart Hit)..B-side	Pop	$	Pic	Label & Number
				JACK GRAYSON and Blackjack:				
12/13/80+	37	14		7 A Loser's Night Out ....Devil Stands Only 5 Foot 5	—	$5		Koala 328
4/4/81	56	6		8 Magic Eyes ....The Stores Are Full Of Roses	—	$5		Koala 331
7/25/81	45	9		9 My Beginning Was You................................Hanging On By A Heartstring	—	$5		Koala 334
12/19/81+	18	17		10 When A Man Loves A Woman ....A Little Tear	—	$5		Koala 340
				#1 Pop hit for Percy Sledge in 1966				
				JACK GRAYSON:				
5/22/82	38	11		11 Tonight I'm Feeling You (All Over Again).........................Let's Hold Hands [R]	—	$5		Joe-Wes 81000
				new version of #4 above				
8/14/82+	68	6		12 I Ain't Giving Up On Her Yet ....Mama's Secret	—	$5		Joe-Wes 81006
1/14/84	77	4		13 Lean On Me	—	$5		AMI 1318
				#1 Pop hit for Bill Withers in 1972				
				GRAYSON, Kim '87				
				Born in Dallas; raised in Plano, Texas. Singer/actress.				
8/1/87	74	3		1 Love's Slippin' Up On Me	—	$5	■	Soundwaves 4787
12/5/87	62	7		2 If You Only Knew ....Love's Slippin' Up On Me	—	$5	■	Soundwaves 4795
4/16/88	65	6		3 Missin' Texas	—	$5	■	Soundwaves 4800
				GREAT DIVIDE, The '98				
				Group from Stillwater, Oklahoma: Mike McClure (vocals), Scott Lester (guitar), Kelley Green (bass) and J.J. Lester (drums).				
4/18/98	74	1		1 Never Could ....Pour Me A Vacation	—	$4		Atlantic 84102
8/15/98	59	8		2 Pour Me A Vacation ....Dodgers Were In Brooklyn	—	$4		Atlantic 84159
				GREAT PLAINS '92				
				Group of Nashville session musicians: Jack Sundrud (vocals, guitar), Russ Pahl (guitar), Denny Dadmun-Bixby (bass) and Michael Young (drums). Pahl and Young left in 1993. Lex Browning (guitar) joined in 1996.				
10/5/91	63	7		1 A Picture Of You.......................................Give It Some Time	—	$4		Columbia 73961
1/11/92	41	15		2 Faster Gun ....Oh Sweetness	—	$4		Columbia 74137
5/23/92	63	6		3 Iola ....Take Me To Topeka	—	$4		Columbia 74310
5/25/96	58	9		4 Dancin' With The Wind...Homeland	—	$4	■	Magnatone 1105
				GREEN, Bill '76				
				Born in Athens, Alabama.				
9/18/76	94	3		1 Texas On A Saturday Night ....Let's Cheat Again	—	$8		Phono 2629
12/9/78	98	1		2 Fool Such As I ....Let's Cheat Again	—	$5		NSD 11
				#2 Pop hit for Elvis Presley in 1959				
				GREEN, Jerry '77				
				Worked as a DJ at KVET-Austin, Texas.				
10/15/77	96	1		1 I Know The Feeling ....How Sweet It Is	—	$6		Concorde 152
12/10/77	96	4		2 Genuine Texas Good Guy	—	$6		Concorde 154
				GREEN, Lloyd '73				
				Born on 10/4/37 in Mobile, Alabama. Leading session steel guitarist.				
2/10/73	36	10		1 I Can See Clearly Now ....Steelin' Away [I]	—	$6		Monument 8562
				#1 Pop hit for Johnny Nash in 1972				
6/30/73	73	3		2 Here Comes The Sun..Peace [I]	—	$6		Monument 8574
				#16 Pop hit for Richie Havens in 1971				
12/25/76+	92	6		3 You And Me ....Edgewater Beach [I]	—	$6		October 1002
				GREEN, Pat '01				
				Born in 1972 in Waco, Texas. Male singer/songwriter/guitarist.				
4/7/01	60	2		1 Texas On My Mind	—			album cut
				PAT GREEN & CORY MORROW from the album Songs We Wish We'd Written on Writeon 2000				
6/30/01	54	9		2 Texas In 1880	—			album cut
				RADNEY FOSTER (with Pat Green) from the album Are You Ready For The Big Show? on Dualtone 1102				
9/15/01	35	14		3 Carry On	—			album cut
				from the album Three Days on Republic 016016				

GREENE, Jack ★118★ • '67
Born on 1/7/30 in Maryville, Tennessee. Singer/songwriter/guitarist. Drummer with **Ernest Tubb**'s group from 1962-64. Joined the Grand Ole Opry in 1967. Nicknamed the "Jolly Green Giant." CMA Award: 1967 Male Vocalist of the Year.

1)There Goes My Everything   2)All The Time   3)Statue Of A Fool   4)Until My Dreams Come True   5)You Are My Treasure

DEBUT	PEAK	WKS		A-side ....B-side	Pop	$	Pic	Label & Number
12/25/65+	37	7		1 Ever Since My Baby Went Away ....Room For One More Heartache	—	$8		Decca 31856
				written by **Marty Robbins**				
10/22/66	❶[7]	23	★	2 There Goes My Everything ....The Hardest Easy Thing	65	$8		Decca 32023
				CMA Award: Single of the Year				
4/22/67	❶[5]	20		3 All The Time /	103			
5/13/67	63	5		4 Wanting You But Never Having You...	—	$7		Decca 32123
9/30/67	2[4]	20		5 What Locks The Door ....Left Over Feelings	—	$7		Decca 32190
2/17/68	❶[1]	15		6 You Are My Treasure ....If God Can Forgive You, So Can I	—	$7		Decca 32261
7/20/68	4	16		7 Love Takes Care Of Me ....Your Favorite Fool	—	$7		Decca 32352
12/14/68+	❶[2]	17		8 Until My Dreams Come True ....We'll Try A Little Bit Harder	—	$7		Decca 32423
5/10/69	❶[2]	18		9 Statue Of A Fool ....There's More To Love	—	$7		Decca 32490

DEBUT	PEAK	WKS	Gold	A-side (Chart Hit)	B-side	Pop	$	Pic	Label & Number
				GREENE, Jack — Cont'd					
10/4/69	4	14		10 Back In The Arms Of Love /	—		$7		
10/25/69	66	2		11 The Key That Fits Her Door			$7		Decca 32558
11/15/69+	2²	16		12 Wish I Didn't Have To Miss You	My Tears Don't Show	—	$7		Decca 32580
				JACK GREENE And JEANNIE SEELY					
3/14/70	16	11		13 Lord Is That Me	Just A Little While Ago	—	$7		Decca 32631
7/18/70	14	14		14 The Whole World Comes To Me /	—				
		14		15 If This Is Love			$7		Decca 32699
11/14/70	15	12		16 Something Unseen /	—				
11/14/70	45	12		17 What's The Use			$7		Decca 32755
4/10/71	13	14		18 There's A Whole Lot About A Woman (A Man Don't Know) /	—				
		13		19 Makin' Up His Mind			$7		Decca 32823
9/4/71	26	12		20 Hanging Over Me	Birth Of Our Love	—	$7		Decca 32863
12/11/71+	15	13		21 Much Oblige	First Day	—	$7		Decca 32898
				JACK GREENE/JEANNIE SEELY					
3/25/72	31	11		22 If You Ever Need My Love	Ask Me To Stay	—	$7		Decca 32930
8/12/72	19	12		23 What In The World Has Gone Wrong With Our Love	Willingly	—	$7		Decca 32991
				JACK GREENE/JEANNIE SEELY					
12/9/72+	17	12		24 Satisfaction	From Here On Out	—	$7		Decca 33008
4/14/73	40	12		25 The Fool I've Been Today	You Left Me	—	$5		MCA 40035
8/18/73	11	16		26 I Need Somebody Bad	Joyride	—	$5		MCA 40108
2/9/74	13	13		27 It's Time To Cross That Bridge	Half That Much	—	$5		MCA 40179
7/27/74	66	9		28 Sing For The Good Times	Something Seems To Fall Apart Inside	—	$5		MCA 40263
11/22/75	88	5		29 He Little Thing'd Her Out Of My Arms	Let Me Love You Back Together Again	—	$5		MCA 40481
1/5/80	28	11		30 Yours For The Taking	Sixty Days	—	$5		Frontline 704
5/17/80	48	7		31 The Rock I'm Leaning On	I'll Do It Better The Next Time	—	$5		Frontline 706
11/1/80	63	6		32 Devil's Den	It's Not The End Of The World	—	$5		Firstline 709
3/5/83	98	2		33 The Jukebox Never Plays Home Sweet Home	I Don't Want To Be Alone Tonight	—	$5		EMH 0016
6/11/83	92	3		34 From Cotton To Satin	I'd Be Home On Christmas Day	—	$5		EMH 0019
7/14/84	93	3		35 Dying To Believe	There Goes My Everything	—	$5		EMH 0031
11/17/84	81	5		36 If It's Love (Then Bet It All)	Statue Of A Fool	—	$5		EMH 0035

GREENE, Lorne '64

Born on 2/12/14 in Ottawa, Canada. Died of heart failure on 9/11/87 (age 73). Acted in several movies. Played "Ben Cartwright" on TV's *Bonanza* and "Adama" on *Battlestar Galactica*.

12/5/64	21	10		1 Ringo	Bonanza [S]	❶¹	$8		RCA Victor 8444
8/13/66	50	2		2 Waco	All But The Remembering [S]	—	$8		RCA Victor 8901
				title song from the movie starring Howard Keel					

GREEN RIVER BOYS, The — see CAMPBELL, Glen

GREENWOOD, Lee ★90★ '85

Born Melvin Lee Greenwood on 10/27/42 in Los Angeles; raised in Sacramento. Singer/songwriter. Worked as a blackjack dealer in Las Vegas casinos from 1973-77. Married former Miss Tennessee, Kimberly Payne, on 4/11/92. CMA Awards: 1983 & 1984 Male Vocalist of the Year.

1) Dixie Road 2) Hearts Aren't Made To Break (They're Made To Love) 3) Going, Going, Gone 4) Mornin' Ride
5) I Don't Mind The Thorns (If You're The Rose)

9/19/81+	17	22		1 It Turns Me Inside Out	Thank You For Changing My Life	—	$4		MCA 51159
3/27/82	5	18		2 Ring On Her Finger, Time On Her Hands	Doncha Hear Me Callin'	—	$4		MCA 52026
8/7/82	7	17		3 She's Lying	Home Away From Home	—	$4		MCA 52087
12/11/82+	7	21		4 Ain't No Trick (It Takes Magic)	Broken Pieces Of My Heart	—	$4		MCA 52150
4/9/83	6	20		5 I.O.U.	Another You	53	$4	■	MCA 52199
8/20/83	❶¹	22		6 Somebody's Gonna Love You	You're The Woman I Love	96	$4		MCA 52257
12/17/83+	❶¹	19		7 Going, Going, Gone	Come On Back And Love Me Some More	—	$4		MCA 52322
5/26/84	7	17		8 God Bless The USA	This Old Bed	—	$4	■	MCA 52386 (v)
				also see #34 below					
7/21/84	3	20		9 To Me	S:15 / A:23 We Were Meant For Each Other	—	$4		MCA 52415
				BARBARA MANDRELL/LEE GREENWOOD					
8/18/84	3	25		10 Fool's Gold	S:2 / A:3 Worth It For The Ride	—	$4		MCA 52426
12/22/84+	9	19		11 You've Got A Good Love Comin'	A:7 / S:10 Even Love Can't Save Us Now	—	$4		MCA 52509
2/2/85	19	15		12 It Should Have Been Love By Now	A:18 / S:20 Can't Get Too Much Of A Good Thing	—	$4		MCA 52525
				BARBARA MANDRELL/LEE GREENWOOD					
4/20/85	❶¹	20		13 Dixie Road	S:❶¹ / A:❶¹ (I Found) Love In Time	—	$4	■	MCA 52564
8/31/85	❶¹	23		14 I Don't Mind The Thorns (If You're The Rose)	S:❶¹ / A:❶¹ Same Old Song	—	$4		MCA 52656
12/28/85+	❶¹	20		15 Don't Underestimate My Love For You	S:❶¹ / A:❶¹ Leave My Heart The Way You Found It	—	$4	■	MCA 52741
4/19/86	❶¹	22		16 Hearts Aren't Made To Break (They're Made To Love)	S:❶¹ / A:❶¹ The Will To Love	—	$4		MCA 52807
8/9/86	10	18		17 Didn't We	S:8 / A:10 Heartbreak Radio	—	$4		MCA 52896
11/29/86+	❶¹	24		18 Mornin' Ride	A:❶¹ / S:8 Little Red Caboose	—	$4		MCA 52984
5/9/87	5	17		19 Someone	S:7 Let's Make The Most Of Love	—	$4		MCA 53096
8/29/87	9	19		20 If There's Any Justice	S:21 We Could Have Been	—	$4		MCA 53156
12/26/87+	5	22		21 Touch And Go Crazy	S:11 Silver Dollar	—	$4		MCA 53234

DEBUT	PEAK	WKS	Gold	A-side (Chart Hit)	B-side	Pop	$	Pic	Label & Number
				GREENWOOD, Lee — Cont'd					
4/30/88	12	18		22 I Still Believe .... S:22 I'll Be Lovin' You		—	$4		MCA 53312
8/20/88	20	17		23 You Can't Fall In Love When You're Cryin' .... S:24 I'll Still Be Lovin' You		—	$4		MCA 53386
1/28/89	16	17		24 I'll Be Lovin' You .... Do That To Me One More Time		—	$4		MCA 53475
6/3/89	43	11		25 I Love The Way He Left You .... Home To Alaska		—	$4		MCA 53655
9/16/89	55	5		26 I Go Crazy .... Any Way The Law Allows		—	$4		MCA 53716
				#7 Pop hit for Paul Davis in 1978					
7/7/90	2¹	21		27 Holdin' A Good Hand /		—			
10/27/90+	14	20		28 We've Got It Made		—	$3	■	Capitol 44576
3/2/91	52	8		29 Just Like Me		—			album cut
				from the album *Holdin' A Good Hand* on Capitol 94153					
5/11/91	12	20		30 Hopelessly Yours		—			album cut
				LEE GREENWOOD with Suzy Bogguss					
				from the album *A Perfect 10* on Capitol 95541					
10/5/91	46	11		31 Between A Rock And A Heartache		—			album cut
2/8/92	58	6		32 If You'll Let This Fool Back In		—			album cut
				above 2 from the album *When You're In Love* on Capitol 95527					
8/22/92	73	2		33 Before I'm Ever Over You		—			album cut
				from the album *Love's On The Way* on Liberty 98834					
9/29/01	16	20		34 God Bless The USA .... S:❶¹⁰ Amazing Grace [R]		16	$4	★	Curb 73128 (v)
				new version of #8 above					
				GREGG, Ricky Lynn '93					
				Born on 8/22/61 in Longview, Texas. Singer/songwriter/guitarist.					
3/13/93	36	20		1 If I Had A Cheatin' Heart .... (club mix) / Can You Feel It (2 versions)		109	$4	■	Liberty 44948 (v)
				"45": Liberty 17323 (B-side: "Three Nickels And A Dime")					
7/24/93	58	9		2 Can You Feel It .... Bring On The Neon			$4		Liberty 17399
8/13/94	73	2		3 Get A Little Closer .... If I Had A Cheatin' Heart			$4	■	Liberty 18092 (v)
				GREGORY, Clinton '92					
				Born on 3/1/66 in Martinsville, Virginia. Singer/fiddle player.					
				1)Play, Ruby, Play 2)(If It Weren't For Country Music) I'd Go Crazy 3)Who Needs It					
1/5/91	64	7		1 Couldn't Love Have Picked A Better Place To Die .... You Can't Take It With You			$4		Step One 422
4/6/91	26	20		2 (If It Weren't For Country Music) I'd Go Crazy .... Darlin' Does He			$4	■	Step One 427 (v)
7/13/91	51	11		3 One Shot At A Time .... There's Never Been A Honky Tonk			$4	■	Step One 430 (v)
11/2/91	53	15		4 Satisfy Me And I'll Satisfy You .... Your Uncharted Mind			$4	■	Step One 434 (v)
2/15/92	25	20		5 Play, Ruby, Play .... She Can't Believe My Eyes			$4	■	Step One 437 (v)
7/4/92	50	13		6 She Takes The Sad Out Of Saturday Night .... Blue Country Frame Of Mind			$4		Step One 439
9/26/92	29	20		7 Who Needs It .... The Jukebox Has A 45			$4		Step One 444
3/6/93	65	5		8 Look Who's Needing Who .... I'll Never Always Love You			$4		Step One 457
6/12/93	52	7		9 Standing On The Edge Of Love .... Till This Ring Turns Green			$4	■	Step One 461 (v)
9/25/93	59	5		10 Master Of Illusion .... Watermelon Time In Georgia			$4		Step One 466
3/4/95	68	4		11 You Didn't Miss A Thing .... Hacksaw			$4	■	Polydor 851566 (v)
				GREGORY, Terry '81					
				Born Teresa Ann Gregory Burdine on 4/30/56 in Takoma Park, Maryland. Female singer.					
5/2/81	16	15		1 Just Like Me .... Love Left Over		—	$5		Handshake 70071
9/5/81	59	6		2 Cinderella .... We'd Better Talk It Over		—	$5		Handshake 02442
11/14/81+	30	13		3 I Can't Say Goodbye To You .... We Had All It Takes To Fall In Love		—	$5		Handshake 02563
3/13/82	44	11		4 I Never Knew The Devil's Eyes Were Blue .... I Need Another Lover		—	$5		Handshake 02736
6/26/82	48	7		5 I'm Takin' A Heart Break .... After You've Shopped Around		—	$5		Handshake 02959
4/21/84	75	5		6 Cowgirl In A Coupe DeVille .... The Old Songs		—	$4		Scotti Brothers 04410
2/2/85	66	7		7 Pardon Me, But This Heart's Taken .... Fallin'		—	$4		Scotti Brothers 04735
	★273★			**GRIFF, Ray** '76					
				Born John Raymond David Griff on 4/22/40 in Vancouver; raised in Winfield, Alberta, Canada. Singer/songwriter/guitarist.					
				1)If I Let Her Come In 2)The Mornin' After Baby Let Me Down 3)You Ring My Bell					
				4)That's What I Get (For Doin' My Own Thinkin') 5)Patches					
12/23/67+	49	9		1 Your Lily White Hands .... One Of The Chosen Few		—	$8		MGM 13855
4/27/68	50	7		2 The Sugar From My Candy .... Till The Right One Comes Along		—	$7		Dot 17082
10/3/70	26	9		3 Patches .... Dixie		—	$7		Royal American 19
				#4 Pop hit for Clarence Carter in 1970					
11/20/71+	14	15		4 The Mornin' After Baby Let Me Down .... I'll Love You Enough For Both Of Us		—	$7	■	Royal American 46
12/2/72	62	6		5 It Rains Just The Same In Missouri .... Somewhere Between Atlanta And Mobile		—	$6		Dot 17440
4/28/73	66	3		6 A Song For Everyone .... Another Sad Affair		—	$6		Dot 17456
11/24/73+	42	11		7 Darlin' /		—			
8/25/73	46	10		8 What Got To You (Before It Got To Me)		—	$6		Dot 17471
5/11/74	65	7		9 That Doesn't Mean (I Don't Love My God) .... Lost Love Of Mine		—	$6		Dot 17501
10/12/74	91	2		10 The Hill .... All Loved Out		—	$6		Dot 17519
3/8/75	65	9		11 If That's What It Takes .... Adam's Child		—	$6		ABC/Dot 17542
9/6/75	16	16		12 You Ring My Bell .... Dear Jesus		—	$5		Capitol 4126
1/24/76	11	15		13 If I Let Her Come In .... Runnin'		—	$5		Capitol 4208
5/22/76	40	12		14 I Love The Way That You Love Me .... Wrapped Around Your Finger		—	$5		Capitol 4266
8/28/76	24	12		15 That's What I Get (For Doin' My Own Thinkin') .... Falling		—	$5		Capitol 4320
12/18/76+	27	11		16 The Last Of The Winfield Amateurs /		—			
		6		17 You Put The Bounce Back Into My Step		—	$5		Capitol 4368
4/23/77	28	10		18 A Passing Thing .... Piano Man		—	$5		Capitol 4415
7/30/77	69	5		19 A Cold Day In July .... Rusty		—	$5		Capitol 4446
10/22/77	52	9		20 Raymond's Place .... Goodbye Baby		—	$5		Capitol 4492

See Bonnie Lou (under Bonnie Lou)

DEBUT	PEAK	WKS	Gold	A-side (Chart Hit)	B-side	Pop	$	Pic	Label & Number
				GRIFF, Ray — Cont'd					
11/7/81	87	3		21 Draw Me A Line .... Heaven		—	$5		Vision 440
7/3/82	95	2		22 Things That Songs Are Made Of .... Light As A Feather		—	$5	■	Vision 442
5/7/83	86	3		23 If Tomorrow Never Comes .... Draw Me A Line		—	$4		RCA 50722
4/19/86	71	5		24 What My Woman Does To Me		—	$4		RCA 50846
				GRIFFITH, Glenda '78					
				Born in California; raised in Wichita, Kansas.					
1/7/78	96	4		Don't Worry ('Bout Me) .... Heavenly Island		—	$5		Ariola America 7680
				GRIFFITH, Nanci '87					
				Born on 7/16/54 in Seguin, Texas; raised in Austin, Texas. Singer/songwriter/guitarist.					
6/21/86	85	3		1 Once In A Very Blue Moon		—	$5		Philo 1096
1/17/87	36	14		2 Lone Star State Of Mind ..... There's A Light Beyond These Woods (Mary Margaret)		—	$4		MCA 53008
4/25/87	57	7		3 Trouble In The Fields .... Love In A Memory		—	$4		MCA 53082
8/1/87	64	6		4 Cold Hearts/Closed Minds .... Ford Econoline		—	$4		MCA 53147
12/5/87	58	7		5 Never Mind .... From A Distance		—	$4		MCA 53184
4/9/88	37	13		6 I Knew Love .... So Long Ago		—	$4		MCA 53306
7/23/88	64	5		7 Anyone Can Be Somebody's Fool .... Love Wore A Halo (Back Before The War)		—	$4		MCA 53374
	★388★			**GRIGGS, Andy** '99					
				Born on 8/13/73 in Moore, Louisiana. Singer/songwriter/guitarist.					
12/12/98+	2²	36		1 You Won't Ever Be Lonely .... S:5 (album snippets)		28	$4	★	RCA 65646
7/17/99	10	22		2 I'll Go Crazy		65			album cut (v)
				from the album You Won't Ever Be Lonely on RCA 67596; later issued as the B-side of #3 below					
12/25/99+	2⁵	30		3 She's More .... I'll Go Crazy		37	$4		RCA 65936
3/4/00	50	10		4 Grow Young With You		—			album cut
				COLEY McCABE with Andy Griggs					
				from the movie Where The Heart Is starring Natalie Portman (soundtrack on RCA 67963)					
7/29/00	50	7		5 Waitin' On Sundown		—			album cut
9/30/00+	19	22		6 You Made Me That Way		116			album cut
				above 2 from the album You Won't Ever Be Lonely on RCA 67596					
5/19/01	22	22		7 How Cool Is That .... She's More		119	$4		RCA 69082
				GROCE, Larry '76					
				Born on 4/22/48 in Dallas. Singer/songwriter.					
1/31/76	61	8		Junk Food Junkie .... Muddy Boggy Banjo Man [N]		9	$5		Warner/Curb 8165
				recorded "live" at McCabe's guitar shop in Santa Monica					
				GROOMS, Sherry '78					
				Born in Caruthersville, Missouri; raised in West Memphis.					
10/15/77	97	1		1 The King Of Country Music Meets The Queen Of Rock & Roll .... I'm From Outer Space		—	$5		Elektra 45430
				EVEN STEVENS & SHERRY GROOMS					
9/9/78	87	4		2 Me .... Mama's Boys		—	$5		Parachute 514
				GROOVEGRASS BOYZ, The '96					
				Studio group assembled by producers Scott Rouse and Ronnie McCoury. Vocalists include **Doc Watson** and **Mac Wiseman**.					
11/23/96	70	5		Macarena (Country version) .... S:6 (2 versions)		107	$4	■	Imprint 18007
				#1 Pop hit for Los Del Rio in 1996					
				GROVES, Edgel '81					
5/9/81	42	9		Footprints In The Sand .... (instrumental) [S]		—	$6		Silver Star 20
	★291★			**GUITAR, Bonnie** '67					
				Born Bonnie Buckingham on 3/25/23 in Seattle. Singer/songwriter/guitarist. Owner of Dolphin/Dolton record labels.					
				1)A Woman In Love 2)I'm Living In Two Worlds 3)I Believe In Love					
6/10/57	14	1		1 Dark Moon .... A:14 Big Mike		6	$20		Dot 15550
11/11/57	15	1		2 Mister Fire Eyes .... A:15 There's A New Moon Over My Shoulder		71	$15		Dot 15612
3/5/66	9	16		3 I'm Living In Two Worlds .... Goodtime Charlie		99	$8		Dot 16811
7/23/66	14	9		4 Get Your Lie The Way You Want It ...... Would You Believe		—	$8		Dot 16872
10/15/66	24	10		5 The Tallest Tree .... Are You Sincere		—	$8		Dot 16919
2/25/67	64	5		6 The Kickin' Tree .... Only I		—	$8		Dot 16987
4/29/67	33	11		7 You Can Steal Me .... Ramblin' Man		—	$8		Dot 17007
8/12/67	4	16		8 A Woman In Love .... I Want My Baby		—	$8		Dot 17029
12/23/67+	13	16		9 Stop The Sun .... Wings Of A Dove		—	$8		Dot 17057
6/8/68	10	14		10 I Believe In Love .... Faded Love		—	$8		Dot 17097
9/28/68	41	10		11 Leaves Are The Tears Of Autumn ...... Almost Like Being With You		—	$7		Dot 17150
7/5/69	55	5		12 A Truer Love You'll Never Find (Than Mine) ... That's When (Our Love Will Be Over)		—	$7		Paramount 0004
				BONNIE & BUDDY (Buddy Killen)					
8/23/69	36	7		13 That See Me Later Look .... I'll Pick Up My Heart (And Go Home)		—	$7		Dot 17276
10/24/70	70	3		14 Allegheny .... Red Checkered Blazer		—	$7		Paramount 0045
8/5/72	54	7		15 Happy Everything ...... Just As Soon As I Get Over Loving You		—	$5		Columbia 45643
12/14/74+	95	6		16 From This Moment On .... Shine (And We've Got To Have It)		—	$5		MCA 40306
4/19/80	92	3		17 Honey On The Moon .... Lonely Eyes		—	$5		4 Star 1041
12/2/89	79	3		18 Still The Same .... If You Were Here		—	$5		Playback 75714
				#4 Pop hit for **Bob Seger** in 1978					
				GUNN, J.W. '82					
11/27/82	87	3		Love Me Today, Love Me Forever .... Bessie, Jane & I		—	$6		Primero 1013

DEBUT	PEAK	WKS	Gold	A-side (Chart Hit)	B-side	Pop	$	Pic	Label & Number
				GURLEY, Randy '78					
				Born Eleanor Rand Gurley on 11/29/53 in Salem, Massachusetts; raised in Burbank, California. Female singer.					
9/2/78	77	5		1 True Love Ways ... I'll Never Get Over Loving You		—	$5		ABC 12392
				co-written by Buddy Holly; #14 Pop hit for Peter & Gordon in 1965					
7/14/79	97	2		2 Don't Treat Me Like A Stranger ... Every Night		—	$4		RCA 11611
10/27/79	92	3		3 If I Ever ... How Long		—	$4		RCA 11726
				GUTHRIE, Jack, and his Oklahomans '45					
				Born Leon Guthrie on 11/13/15 in Olive, Oklahoma. Died of tuberculosis on 1/15/48 (age 32). Singer/songwriter/guitarist. Cousin of Woody Guthrie.					
7/7/45	●⁶	19		1 Oklahoma Hills /		—			
7/21/45	5	2		2 I'm A Brandin' My Darlin' With My Heart		—	$25		Capitol 201
3/1/47	3	3		3 Oakie Boogie ... The Clouds Rained Trouble Down		—	$25		Capitol 341
				GUY & RALNA '75					
				Husband-and-wife vocal duo of Guy Hovis (born on 9/24/41 in Tupelo, Mississippi) and Ralna English (born in Spur, Texas). Regulars on **Lawrence Welk**'s TV show from 1970-82. Married from 1968-84.					
7/26/75	95	3		We've Got It All Together Now ... Red River Valley		—	$5		Ranwood 1029

H

DEBUT	PEAK	WKS	Gold	A-side	B-side	Pop	$	Pic	Label & Number
				HADDOCK, Durwood '75					
				Born on 8/16/34 in Lamasco, Texas. Singer/songwriter/fiddler.					
11/23/74+	67	8		1 Angel In An Apron ... Truck Drivers Turn 'Em On		—	$6		Caprice 2004
3/12/77	98	1		2 Low Down Time ... She Gave Me Good Love		—	$5		Eagle Int'l. 1137
				also see #5 below					
6/17/78	75	9		3 The Perfect Love Song ... You Loved Me So Good (That's Why I Miss You So Bad)		—	$5		Country Int'l. 132
11/4/78	87	4		4 Everynight Sensation ... Low Down Time		—	$5		Eagle Int'l. 1148
5/12/79	96	2		5 Low Down Time ... Everynight Sensation [R]		—	$5		Country Int'l. 140
				same version as #2 above					
10/25/80	89	3		6 It Sure Looks Good On You		—	$5		Eagle Int'l. 1161
				HAGER, Charley '89					
1/14/89	88	2		Men With Broken Hearts		—	$6		Killer 114
				HAGERS, The Bros. '69					
				Identical twin brothers Jim and John Hager. Born on 8/30/46 in Chicago. Regulars on TV's *Hee Haw*.					
11/8/69	41	8		1 Gotta Get To Oklahoma ('Cause California's Gettin' To Me) ... Your Tender Loving Care		—	$6		Capitol 2647
4/4/70	74	2		2 Loneliness Without You ... Give It Time		—	$6		Capitol 2740
5/23/70	50	6		3 Goin' Home To Your Mother ... I'm Not Going Back To Jackson		—	$6		Capitol 2803
9/12/70	59	8		4 Silver Wings ... Flowers Need Sun, Too		—	$6		Capitol 2887
				written by **Merle Haggard**					
1/23/71	47	6		5 I'm Miles Away ... Loony Caboose		—	$6		Capitol 3012
				HAGGARD, Marty '88					
				Born on 6/18/58 in Bakersfield, California. Singer/songwriter/guitarist. Son of **Merle Haggard**.					
3/7/81	85	3		1 Charleston Cotton Mill ... Rain		—	$5		Dimension 1016
9/13/86	62	7		2 Talkin' Blue Eyes ... I Broke The Rules Today		—	$4		MTM 72073
3/21/87	75	6		3 Weekend Cowboys ... Forget He's Your Husband		—	$4		MTM 72085
3/26/88	57	8		4 Trains Make Me Lonesome ... By The Dawn's Early Light		—	$4		MTM 72103
6/25/88	70	5		5 Now You See 'Em, Now You Don't ... Missing California Blues		—	$4		MTM 72107
				HAGGARD, Merle ★5★ '69					
				Born on 4/6/37 in Bakersfield, California. Singer/songwriter/guitarist. Served nearly three years in San Quentin prison for burglary, from 1957-60. Granted full pardon by Governor Ronald Reagan on 3/14/72. Formed his backing band, The Strangers, in 1965. Acted in the movies *Bronco Billy*, *Huckleberry Finn*, *Killers Three* and *Doc Elliot*, and TV's *The Waltons* and *Centennial*. Formerly married to singers **Bonnie Owens** and **Leona Williams**. Father of **Marty Haggard** and **Noel Haggard**. Elected to the Country Music Hall of Fame in 1994. CMA Awards: 1970 Male Vocalist of the Year; 1970 Entertainer of the Year; 1983 Vocal Duo of the Year (with **Willie Nelson**). Also see **Same Old Train**.					
				1)Okie From Muskogee 2)Mama Tried 3)If We Make It Through December 4)Carolyn 5)The Fightin' Side Of Me					
12/28/63+	19	3		1 Sing A Sad Song ... You Don't Even Try		—	$25		Tally 155
6/6/64	45	5		2 Sam Hill ... You Don't Have Far To Go		—	$25		Tally 178
9/12/64	28	26		3 Just Between The Two Of Us ... Slowly But Surely		—	$25		Tally 181
				MERLE HAGGARD And BONNIE OWENS					
1/2/65	10	22		4 (My Friends Are Gonna Be) Strangers ... Please Mr. D.J.		—	$25		Tally 179
9/18/65	42	4		5 I'm Gonna Break Every Heart I Can ... Falling For You		—	$12		Capitol 5460
				MERLE HAGGARD And The Strangers:					
4/9/66	5	27		6 Swinging Doors ... The Girl Turned Ripe		—	$10		Capitol 5600
8/27/66	3	20		7 The Bottle Let Me Down ... The Longer You Wait		—	$10		Capitol 5704
12/17/66+	●¹	18		8 The Fugitive /		—			
12/31/66+	32	11		9 Someone Told My Story		—	$10		Capitol 5803
3/18/67	2²			10 I Threw Away The Rose ... Loneliness Is Eating Me Alive		—	$10	■	Capitol 5844
7/8/67	●¹	16		11 Branded Man ... You Don't Have Very Far To Go		—	$10		Capitol 5931
11/18/67+	●²	20		12 Sing Me Back Home ... Good Times		—	$10	■	Capitol 2017
3/9/68	●²	15		13 The Legend Of Bonnie And Clyde ... I Started Loving You Again		—	$10		Capitol 2123

DEBUT	PEAK	WKS	Gold	A-side (Chart Hit) .... B-side	Pop	$	Pic	Label & Number
				MERLE HAGGARD And The Strangers — Cont'd				
7/27/68	❶⁴	15		14 Mama Tried — You'll Never Love Me Now	—	$8	■	Capitol 2219
11/9/68+	3	16		15 I Take A Lot Of Pride In What I Am — Keep Me From Cryin' Today	—	$8	■	Capitol 2289
2/22/69	❶¹	17		16 Hungry Eyes — California Blues	—	$8	■	Capitol 2383
7/5/69	❶¹	15		17 Workin' Man Blues — Silver Wings	—	$8	■	Capitol 2503
10/11/69	❶⁴	16		18 Okie From Muskogee — If I Had Left It Up To You	41	$8	■	Capitol 2626
				CMA Award: Single of the Year				
2/7/70	❶³	14		19 The Fightin' Side Of Me — Every Fool Has A Rainbow	92	$8		Capitol 2719
4/18/70	9	13		20 Street Singer — Mexican Rose [I]	124	$8		Capitol 2778
6/13/70	3	14		21 Jesus, Take A Hold — No Reason To Quit	107	$8		Capitol 2838
10/10/70	3	17		22 I Can't Be Myself /	106			
		16		23 Sidewalks Of Chicago	flip	$8	■	Capitol 2891
2/20/71	3	13		24 Soldier's Last Letter — The Farmer's Daughter	90	$8	■	Capitol 3024
7/3/71	2²	15		25 Someday We'll Look Back — It's Great To Be Alive	119	$8		Capitol 3112
10/16/71	❶²	14		26 Daddy Frank (The Guitar Man) — My Heart Would Know	—	$8		Capitol 3198
12/4/71+	❶³	16		27 Carolyn — When The Feelin' Goes Away	58	$8		Capitol 3222
3/25/72	❶²	15		28 Grandma Harp /				
		10		29 Turnin' Off A Memory	—	$8		Capitol 3294
9/2/72	❶¹	14		30 It's Not Love (But It's Not Bad) — My Woman Keeps Lovin' Her Man	—	$8		Capitol 3419
12/9/72+	❶¹	14		31 I Wonder If They Ever Think Of Me — I Forget You Every Day	—	$7		Capitol 3488
3/10/73	3	14		32 The Emptiest Arms In The World — Radiator Man From Wasco	—	$7		Capitol 3552
6/30/73	❶²	16		33 Everybody's Had The Blues — Nobody Knows I'm Hurtin'	62	$7		Capitol 3641
10/27/73	❶⁴	17		34 If We Make It Through December — Bobby Wants A Puppy Dog For Christmas [X]	28	$7		Capitol 3746
				MERLE HAGGARD				
3/2/74	❶¹	15		35 Things Aren't Funny Anymore — Honky Tonk Night Time Man	—	$7		Capitol 3830
6/29/74	❶¹	14		36 Old Man From The Mountain — Holding Things Together	—	$7		Capitol 3900
11/9/74+	❶¹	15		37 Kentucky Gambler — I've Got A Darlin' (For A Wife)	—	$7		Capitol 3974
				written by **Dolly Parton**				
2/15/75	❶²	14		38 Always Wanting You — I've Got A Yearning	—	$7		Capitol 4027
5/24/75	❶¹	15		39 Movin' On — Here In Frisco	—	$7		Capitol 4085
				theme from the TV series starring **Claude Akins**				
10/4/75	❶¹	15		40 It's All In The Movies — Living With The Shades Pulled Down	—	$7		Capitol 4141
1/17/76	❶¹	14		41 The Roots Of My Raising — The Way It Was In '51	—	$7		Capitol 4204
5/22/76	10	11		42 Here Comes The Freedom Train — I Won't Give Up My Train	—	$7		Capitol 4267
9/11/76	❶¹	13		43 Cherokee Maiden /				
				written and recorded by **Bob Wills** in 1941				
		13		44 What Have You Got Planned Tonight Diana	—	$7		Capitol 4326
				MERLE HAGGARD:				
4/2/77	2²	14		45 If We're Not Back In Love By Monday — I Think It's Gone Forever	—	$6		MCA 40700
7/2/77	2²	14		46 Ramblin' Fever /				
		12		47 When My Blue Moon Turns To Gold Again	—	$6		MCA 40743
				#19 Pop hit for **Elvis Presley** in 1956				
9/3/77	16	13		48 A Working Man Can't Get Nowhere Today — Blues Stay Away From Me	—	$6		Capitol 4477
10/8/77	4	15		49 From Graceland To The Promised Land — Are You Lonesome Tonight	58	$6		MCA 40804
				tribute to **Elvis Presley**; The Jordanaires (backing vocals)				
1/14/78	12	12		50 Running Kind /	—			
		9		51 Making Believe	—	$5		Capitol 4525
3/18/78	2²	16		52 I'm Always On A Mountain When I Fall — Life Of A Rodeo Cowboy	—	$5		MCA 40869
8/12/78	2³	13		53 It's Been A Great Afternoon /				
		7		54 Love Me When You Can	—	$5		MCA 40936
10/28/78	8	12		55 The Bull And The Beaver — I'm Gettin' High	—	$5		MCA 40962
				MERLE HAGGARD/LEONA WILLIAMS				
10/28/78	82	4		56 The Way It Was In '51 — Moanin' The Blues	—	$5		Capitol 4636
				MERLE HAGGARD And The Strangers				
				recorded in 1975				
4/14/79	4	13		57 Red Bandana /				
		13		58 I Must Have Done Something Bad	—	$5		MCA 41007
9/15/79	4	13		59 My Own Kind Of Hat /				
		13		60 Heaven Was A Drink Of Wine	—	$5		MCA 41112
3/15/80	2²	14		61 The Way I Am — Wake Up	—	$5		MCA 41200
5/17/80	❶¹	16		62 Bar Room Buddies — The Not So Great Train Robbery	—	$5	■	Elektra 46634
				MERLE HAGGARD AND CLINT EASTWOOD				
7/5/80	3	15		63 Misery And Gin — No One To Sing For (But The Band)	—	$5	■	MCA 41255
				above 2 from the movie *Bronco Billy* starring **Clint Eastwood**				
10/25/80+	❶¹	17		64 I Think I'll Just Stay Here And Drink — Back To The Barrooms Again	—	$5		MCA 51014
2/14/81	9	14		65 Leonard — Our Paths May Never Cross	—	$5		MCA 51048
				tribute to **Tommy Collins** (real name: Leonard Sipes)				
3/28/81	41	8		66 I Can't Hold Myself In Line — Carolyn	—	$5		Epic 51012
				JOHNNY PAYCHECK AND MERLE HAGGARD				
6/6/81	4	16		67 Rainbow Stew — Blue Yodel #9 (Standin' On The Corner)	—	$5		MCA 51120
9/19/81	❶¹	17		68 My Favorite Memory — Texas Fiddle Song	—	$5		Epic 02504
1/16/82	❶¹	19		69 Big City — I Think I'm Gonna Live Forever	—	$5		Epic 02686
				Leona Williams (harmony vocal)				
4/17/82	49	10		70 Dealing With The Devil — Fiddle Breakdown	—	$5		MCA 52020

DEBUT	PEAK	WKS	Gold	A-side (Chart Hit)	B-side	Pop	$	Pic	Label & Number
				HAGGARD, Merle — Cont'd					
5/15/82	2²	18		71 Are The Good Times Really Over (I Wish A Buck Was Still Silver)	I Always Get Lucky With You	—	$5		Epic 02894
8/7/82	❶¹	15		72 Yesterday's Wine	I Haven't Found Her Yet	—	$5		Epic 03072
				MERLE HAGGARD/GEORGE JONES					
10/23/82+	❶¹	21		73 Going Where The Lonely Go	Someday You're Gonna Need Your Friends Again	—	$5		Epic 03315
12/4/82+	10	19		74 C.C. Waterback	After I Sing All My Songs	—	$5		Epic 03405
				GEORGE JONES/MERLE HAGGARD					
1/15/83	6	18		75 Reasons To Quit	Half A Man	—	$4		Epic 03494
				MERLE HAGGARD AND WILLIE NELSON					
3/12/83	❶¹	18		76 You Take Me For Granted	I Won't Give Up My Train	—	$4		Epic 03723
4/30/83	❶¹	21		77 Pancho And Lefty	Opportunity To Cry	—	$4		Epic 03842
				WILLIE NELSON AND MERLE HAGGARD					
5/28/83	42	14		78 We're Strangers Again	Sally Let Your Bangs Hang Down	—	$4		Mercury 812214
				MERLE HAGGARD & LEONA WILLIAMS					
7/16/83	3	20		79 What Am I Gonna Do (With The Rest Of My Life)	I Think I'll Stay	—	$4		Epic 04006
10/8/83	54	10		80 It's All In The Game	The New Cocaine Blues	—	$4		MCA 52276
				#1 Pop hit for Tommy Edwards in 1958					
11/19/83+	❶¹	21		81 That's The Way Love Goes	Don't Seem Like We've Been Together All Our Lives	—	$4		Epic 04226
				also see #104 below					
3/24/84	❶¹	21		82 Someday When Things Are Good	If You Hated Me	—	$4		Epic 04402
7/14/84	❶¹	18		83 Let's Chase Each Other Around The Room	You Nearly Lose Your Mind	—	$4		Epic 04512
10/27/84+	❶¹	22		84 A Place To Fall Apart	S:❶¹ / A:❶¹ All I Want To Do Is Sing My Song	—	$4		Epic 04663
				MERLE HAGGARD (with Janie Fricke)					
3/16/85	❶¹	19		85 Natural High	S:❶¹ / A:❶¹ I Never Go Home Anymore	—	$4		Epic 04830
				Janie Frickie (guest vocal)					
6/15/85	55	10		86 Make-Up And Faded Blue Jeans	Love Me When You Can	—	$4		MCA 52595
				recorded in 1980					
7/6/85	10	*17		87 Kern River	S:10 / A:10 The Old Watermill	—	$4		Epic 05426
10/5/85	36	15		88 Amber Waves Of Grain	I Wish Things Were Simple Again	—	$4		Epic 05659
12/14/85	60	11		89 American Waltz	Farmer's Daughter	—	$4		Epic 05734
1/25/86	5	20		90 I Had A Beautiful Time	S:4 / A:5 This Time I Really Do	—	$4		Epic 05782
5/31/86	9	23		91 A Friend In California	S:6 / A:7 Mama's Prayers	—	$4		Epic 06097
10/18/86	21	15		92 Out Among The Stars	S:18 / A:22 Susie	—	$4		Epic 06344
4/18/87	58	8		93 Almost Persuaded	Love Don't Hurt Everytime	—	$4		Epic 07036
9/19/87	58	5		94 If I Could Only Fly	Without You On My Side	—	$4		Epic 07400
				MERLE HAGGARD & WILLIE NELSON					
11/21/87+	❶¹	22		95 Twinkle, Twinkle Lucky Star	S:❶³ I Don't Have Any Love Around	—	$4		Epic 07631
3/19/88	9	19		96 Chill Factor	S:6 Thanking The Good Lord	—	$4		Epic 07754
7/9/88	22	18		97 We Never Touch At All	S:14 Man From Another Time	—	$4		Epic 07944
11/19/88+	23	17		98 You Babe	S:19 Thirty Again	—	$4		Epic 08111
4/8/89	18	18		99 5:01 Blues	Man From Another Time	—	$4		Epic 68598
7/22/89	4	26		100 A Better Love Next Time	Losin' In Las Vegas	—	$4		Epic 68979
12/2/89+	23	16		101 If You Want To Be My Woman	Someday We'll Know	—	$4		Epic 73076
9/1/90	60	6		102 When It Rains It Pours	Me And Crippled Soldiers	—	$4	■	Curb 76832 (v)
1/29/94	58	12		103 In My Next Life	—	—			album cut
				from the album *Merle Haggard 1994* on Curb 77636					
9/18/99	56	7		104 That's The Way Love Goes	Silver Wings [R]	—	$4		BNA 65895
				MERLE HAGGARD (with Jewel)					
				new version of #81 above					
				HAGGARD, Noel '97					
				Born on 4/4/63 in Bakersfield, California. Singer/songwriter/guitarist. Son of Merle Haggard.					
2/1/97	75	1		1 Once You Learn	—				album cut
8/9/97	75	1		2 Tell Me Something Bad About Tulsa	—				album cut
				above 2 from the album *One Lifetime* on Atlantic 82877					
				HALL, Buck '89					
				Born in Arlington, Texas. Singer/songwriter.					
9/23/89	87	2		Swinging Doors	I Like My Whiskey Chased With Women	—	$6		Track 206
				HALL, Connie '60					
				Born on 6/24/29 in Walden, Kentucky; raised in Cincinnati.					
2/15/60	21	4		1 The Bottle Or Me	After Date Rendezvous	—	$12		Mercury 71540
10/17/60	17	2		2 It's Not Wrong /		—			
				answer to "Is It Wrong (For Loving You)" by Warner Mack					
10/10/60	25	2		3 The Poison In Your Hand	—	—	$10		Decca 31130
4/24/61	20	5		4 Sleep, Baby, Sleep	Sittin' Out The Last Dance	—	$10		Decca 31208
1/20/62	23	5		5 What A Pleasure	The Key To Your World	—	$10		Decca 31310
1/5/63	14	3		6 Fool Me Once	We Don't Have Much In Common (Anymore)	—	$10		Decca 31438
				HALL, Rebecca '85					
				Born in Rustburg, Virginia.					
8/3/85	83	3		Heartbeat	Melted Down Memories	—	$4		Capitol 5486
				HALL, Sammy '84					
				Born in North Carolina. Gospel singer.					
4/28/84	88	3		Anything For Your Love	—	—	$6		Dream 300

DEBUT	PEAK	WKS	Gold	A-side (Chart Hit)...B-side	Pop	$	Pic	Label & Number

HALL, Tom T. ★65★   '74

Born Thomas Hall on 5/25/36 in Olive Hill, Kentucky. Singer/songwriter/guitarist. Worked as a DJ on WMOR-Morehead, Kentucky. Added "T." to his name when he began singing career. Hosted *Pop Goes The Country* TV series. Joined the *Grand Ole Opry* in 1980. Known as "The Storyteller."

1)The Year That Clayton Delaney Died   2)I Love   3)A Week In A Country Jail   4)Faster Horses (The Cowboy And The Poet)
5)(Old Dogs-Children And) Watermelon Wine

DEBUT	PEAK	WKS		A-side	B-side	Pop	$	Label & Number
8/5/67	30	10		1 I Washed My Face In The Morning Dew	A Picture Of Your Mother	—	$10	Mercury 72700
5/11/68	66	3		2 The World The Way I Want It	Shame On The Rain	—	$10	Mercury 72786
9/14/68	68	4		3 Ain't Got The Time	Hope	—	$10	Mercury 72835
11/16/68+	4	18		4 Ballad Of Forty Dollars	Highways	—	$8	Mercury 72863
5/10/69	40	8		5 Strawberry Farms	3	—	$8	Mercury 72913
8/23/69	5	15		6 Homecoming	Myra	—	$8	Mercury 72951
12/20/69+	❶²	15		7 A Week In A Country Jail	Flat-Footin' It	—	$8	Mercury 72998
4/4/70	8	14		8 Shoeshine Man	Kentucky In The Morning	—	$7	Mercury 73039
7/11/70	8	13		9 Salute To A Switchblade	That'll Be All Right With Me	—	$7	Mercury 73078
11/14/70	23	13		10 Day Drinkin'	Let's Get On With The Show	—	$7	Mercury 73139
				DAVE DUDLEY & TOM T. HALL				
12/26/70+	14	12		11 One Hundred Children	I Took A Memory To Lunch	—	$7	Mercury 73140
4/3/71	21	11		12 Ode To A Half A Pound Of Ground Round	Pinto The Wonder Horse Is Dead	—	$7	Mercury 73189
7/10/71	❶²	20		13 The Year That Clayton Delaney Died	Second Handed Flowers	42	$7	Mercury 73221
3/18/72	8	15		14 Me And Jesus	Coot Marseilles Blues	98	$7	Mercury 73278
				The Mt. Pisgah United Methodist Church Choir (backing vocals)				
7/8/72	11	12		15 The Monkey That Became President	She Gave Her Heart To Jethro	—	$7	Mercury 73297
10/7/72	26	9		16 More About John Henry	Windy City Anne	—	$7	Mercury 73327
12/2/72+	❶¹	15		17 (Old Dogs-Children And) Watermelon Wine	Grandma Whistled	—	$7	Mercury 73346
12/16/72+	14	12		18 Hello We're Lonely	We're Not Getting Old	—	$7	Mercury 73347
				PATTI PAGE & TOM T. HALL				
5/5/73	3	13		19 Ravishing Ruby	I Flew Over Our House Last Night	—	$7	Mercury 73377
6/30/73	16	11		20 Watergate Blues /		[N]		
		11		21 Spokane Motel Blues		—	$6	Mercury 73394
11/10/73+	❶²	18		22 I Love	Back When We Were Young	12	$6	Mercury 73436
6/1/74	2²	15		23 That Song Is Driving Me Crazy	Forget It	63	$6	Mercury 73488
9/14/74	❶¹	16		24 Country Is	God Came Through Bellville, Georgia	—	$6	Mercury 73617
12/28/74+	❶¹	15		25 I Care /				
12/21/74	69	16		26 Sneaky Snake		55	$6	Mercury 73641
5/31/75	8	15		27 Deal	It Rained In Every Town Except Paducah	—	$6	Mercury 73686
9/6/75	4	16		28 I Like Beer	From A Mansion To A Honky Tonk	—	$6	Mercury 73704
1/10/76	❶¹	16		29 Faster Horses (The Cowboy And The Poet)	No New Friends Please	—	$6	Mercury 73755
5/15/76	24	12		30 Negatory Romance	It's Got To Be Kentucky For Me	—	$6	Mercury 73795
10/16/76	9	14		31 Fox On The Run	Bluegrass Festival In The Sky	—	$6	Mercury 73850
4/9/77	4	16		32 Your Man Loves You, Honey	One Of The Mysteries Of Life	—	$6	Mercury 73899
8/6/77	12	12		33 It's All In The Game	The Little Green Flower With The Yellow On Top	—	$6	Mercury 55001
				#1 Pop hit for Tommy Edwards in 1958				
12/3/77+	13	14		34 May The Force Be With You Always	No One Feels My Hurt	—	$5	RCA 11158
				inspired by the movie *Star Wars*				
4/8/78	13	13		35 I Wish I Loved Somebody Else	Whiskey	—	$5	RCA 11253
				Bonnie and Maxine Brown (backing vocals, above 2)				
9/16/78	9	13		36 What Have You Got To Lose	The Three Sofa Story	—	$5	RCA 11376
1/20/79	14	12		37 Son Of Clayton Delaney	The Great East Broadway Onion Championship Of 1978	—	$5	RCA 11453
5/12/79	20	10		38 There Is A Miracle In You	The Saturday Morning Song	—	$5	RCA 11568
9/29/79	11	14		39 You Show Me Your Heart (And I'll Show You Mine)	Old Habits Die Hard	—	$5	RCA 11713
1/5/80	9	13		40 The Old Side Of Town /				
		13		41 Jesus On The Radio (Daddy On The Phone)		—	$5	RCA 11888
5/24/80	51	7		42 Soldier Of Fortune	The World According To Raymond	—	$5	RCA 12005
8/16/80	36	10		43 Back When Gas Was Thirty Cents A Gallon	Texas Never Fell In Love With Me	—	$5	RCA 12066
5/2/81	41	8		44 The All New Me	Poor Me (Pour Me Another Drink)	—	$5	RCA 12219
5/22/82	77	4		45 There Ain't No Country Music On This Jukebox	Don't This Road Look Rough And Rocky	—	$4	Columbia 02858
				TOM T. HALL & EARL SCRUGGS				
7/31/82	72	5		46 Song Of The South	Shackles And Chains	—	$4	Columbia 03033
				TOM T. HALL AND EARL SCRUGGS				
7/30/83	42	10		47 Everything From Jesus To Jack Daniels	Old Dogs, Children & Watermelon Wine	—	$4	Mercury 812835
7/14/84	81	3		48 Famous In Missouri	I Only Think About You When I'm Drunk	—	$4	Mercury 880030
9/8/84	8	21		49 P.S. I Love You S:8 / A:8	My Heroes Have Always Been Highways	—	$4	Mercury 880216
				#12 Pop hit for Rudy Vallee in 1934				
5/25/85	40	9		50 A Bar With No Beer	Red Sails In The Sunset	—	$4	Mercury 880690
8/31/85	42	11		51 Down In The Florida Keys	A Song In A Seashell	—	$4	Mercury 884017
7/19/86	52	8		52 Susie's Beauty Shop /				
10/4/86	79	3		53 Love Letters In The Sand		—	$4	Mercury 884850
				#1 Pop hit for Pat Boone in 1957				
12/6/86	65	7		54 Down At The Mall	We're All Through Dancing	—	$4	Mercury 888155

DEBUT	PEAK	WKS	Gold	A-side (Chart Hit)..B-side	Pop	$	Pic	Label & Number
				HALLMAN, Victoria '87				
				Singer/actress. Regular on TV's *Hee Haw* from 1980-90.				
8/22/87	92	2		Next Time I Marry..*Don't You Think It's Time*	—	$5		Evergreen 1055
				Those Hallman Girls (backing vocals)				
				HALLMARK, Roger — see THRASHER BROTHERS				
				HAMBLEN, Stuart '50				
				Born Carl Stuart Hamblen on 10/20/08 in Kellyville, Texas. Died of a brain tumor on 3/8/89 (age 80). Singer/songwriter/actor. Moved to Hollywood in the early 1930s and appeared in many western movies and on radio with own band. Ran for president on Prohibition Party ticket in 1952.				
11/12/49+	3	7		1 (I Won't Go Huntin', Jake) But I'll Go Chasin' Women J:3 / S:9 *Let's See You Fix It*	—	$20		Columbia 20625
8/5/50	2⁹	26		2 (Remember Me) I'm The One Who Loves You A:2 / S:3 / J:4 *I'll Find You*	—	$25		Columbia 4-20714
				#32 Pop hit for **Dean Martin** in 1965				
1/6/51	8	2		3 It's No Secret A:8 *Blood On Your Hands*	—	$25		Columbia 4-20724
8/21/54	2¹	30		4 This Ole House A:2 / S:3 / J:5 *When My Lord Picks Up The 'Phone*	26	$20		RCA Victor 5739
				#1 Pop hit for **Rosemary Clooney** in 1954				

HAMILTON, George IV ★117★   '63

Born on 7/19/37 in Winston-Salem, North Carolina. Singer/guitarist. Joined the *Grand Ole Opry* in 1960. Own TV series on ABC in 1959, and in Canada in the late 1970s. Father of **George Hamilton V**. Also see **Some Of Chet's Friends**.

1)Abilene 2)She's A Little Bit Country 3)Before This Day Ends 4)If You Don't Know I Ain't Gonna Tell You
5)Break My Mind

DEBUT	PEAK	WKS	Gold	#	A-side..B-side	Pop	$	Pic	Label & Number
10/10/60	4	17		1	Before This Day Ends *Loneliness All Around Me*	—	$15		ABC-Para. 10125
6/12/61	9	13		2	Three Steps To The Phone (Millions of Miles) *The Ballad Of Widder Jones*	—	$10		RCA Victor 7881
11/13/61	13	8		3	To You And Yours (From Me and Mine)..........................*I Want A Girl*	—	$10		RCA Victor 7934
6/16/62	22	2		4	China Doll *Commerce Street And Sixth Avenue North*	—	$10		RCA Victor 8001
					#38 Pop hit for the **Ames Brothers** in 1960				
8/25/62	6	14		5	If You Don't Know I Ain't Gonna Tell You *Where Nobody Knows Me*	—	$10		RCA Victor 8062
1/19/63	21	5		6	In This Very Same Room...*If You Want Me To*	—	$10		RCA Victor 8118
6/15/63	❶⁴	24		7	Abilene *Oh So Many Years*	15	$10		RCA Victor 8181
1/18/64	21	8		8	There's More Pretty Girls Than One..........*If You Don't Somebody Else Will*	116	$10		RCA Victor 8250
3/28/64	25	8		9	Linda With The Lonely Eyes /.......................................	—			
4/18/64	28	6		10	Fair And Tender Ladies..	—	$10		RCA Victor 8304
8/29/64	9	14		11	Fort Worth, Dallas Or Houston *Life's Railway To Heaven*	—	$10		RCA Victor 8392
12/5/64+	11	18		12	Truck Driving Man...*The Little Grave*	—	$10		RCA Victor 8462
7/10/65	18	16		13	Walking The Floor Over You *Driftwood On The River*	—	$8		RCA Victor 8608
					written and recorded by **Ernest Tubb** in 1941				
12/4/65+	16	12		14	Write Me A Picture *Twist Of The Wrist*	—	$8		RCA Victor 8690
4/23/66	15	17		15	Steel Rail Blues *Tobacco*	—	$8		RCA Victor 8797
9/3/66	9	16		16	Early Morning Rain *Slightly Used*	—	$8		RCA Victor 8924
					above 2 written by **Gordon Lightfoot**				
1/21/67	7	21		17	Urge For Going *Changes*	—	$8		RCA Victor 9059
					written by **Joni Mitchell**				
7/1/67	6	17		18	Break My Mind *Something Special To Me*	—	$8		RCA Victor 9239
12/23/67+	18	13		19	Little World Girl...*Song For A Winter's Night*	—	$8		RCA Victor 9385
6/1/68	50	8		20	It's My Time...*The Canadian Railroad Trilogy*	—	$8		RCA Victor 9519
10/19/68	38	10		21	Take My Hand For Awhile.............................*Wonderful World Of My Dreams*	—	$8		RCA Victor 9637
3/15/69	26	10		22	Back To Denver..*The Little Folks*	—	$7		RCA Victor 0100
6/21/69	25	13		23	Canadian Pacific *Sisters Of Mercy*	—	$7		RCA Victor 0171
11/8/69	29	9		24	Carolina In My Mind.............................*I'm Gonna Be A Country Boy Again*	—	$7		RCA Victor 0256
					#67 Pop hit for **James Taylor** in 1970				
5/2/70	3	16		25	She's A Little Bit Country *My Nova Scotia Home*	—	$7		RCA Victor 9829
8/29/70	16	12		26	Back Where It's At..*Then I Miss You*	—	$7		RCA Victor 9886
9/26/70	65	2		27	Let's Get Together *Everything Is Beautiful*	—	$7		RCA Victor 9893
					SKEETER DAVIS AND GEORGE HAMILTON IV				
					#5 Pop hit for the **Youngbloods** in 1969				
1/30/71	13	12		28	Anyway..*The Best That I Can Do*	—	$7		RCA Victor 9945
5/22/71	35	11		29	Countryfied..*My North Country Home*	—	$7		RCA Victor 0469
9/18/71	23	12		30	West Texas Highway *There's No Room In This Rat Race (For A Slowpoke Like Me)*	—	$7		RCA Victor 0531
2/5/72	33	10		31	10 Degrees & Getting Colder *Tumbleweed*	—	$7		RCA Victor 0622
5/13/72	63	8		32	Country Music In My Soul *The Child's Song*	—	$7		RCA Victor 0697
9/9/72	52	9		33	Travelin' Light...*Alberta Bound*	—	$7		RCA Victor 0776
12/23/72+	22	13		34	Blue Train (Of The Heartbreak Line)...............*Maritime Farewell*	—	$7		RCA Victor 0854
5/19/73	38	10		35	Dirty Old Man..*Abilene*	—	$7		RCA Victor 0948
9/22/73	50	7		36	Second Cup Of Coffee...*The Farmers Song*	—	$7		RCA Victor 0084
1/26/74	59	9		37	Claim On Me...*Early Morning Rain*	—	$7		RCA Victor 0203
4/9/77	81	5		38	I Wonder Who's Kissing Her Now *In The Palm Of Your Hand*	—	$6		ABC/Dot 17687
					#1 Pop hit for **Henry Burr** in 1909				
10/15/77	93	2		39	Everlasting (Everlasting Love)............................*In The Palm Of Your Hand*	—	$6		ABC/Dot 17723
4/1/78	81	4		40	Only The Best *My Ship Will Sail*	—	$6		ABC 12342

HAMILTON, George V   '88

Born on 11/11/60 in Nashville. Singer/songwriter/guitarist. Son of **George Hamilton IV**. Member of his father's touring band.

| 2/20/88 | 75 | 3 | | She Says *Grass Grows Greener* | — | $4 | | MTM 72101 |

DEBUT	PEAK	WKS	Gold	A-side (Chart Hit) ... B-side	Pop	$	Pic	Label & Number
				HAMILTON, Penny '79				
8/4/79	94	4		You Lit The Fire, Now Fan The Flame	—	$5		Door Knob 096
				HAMPTON THE HAMPSTER '00				
				Hampton is a cartoon hampster. Created by producers Robert DeBoer and Anthony Grace. Based on a real hampster owned by Deidre LeCarte.				
8/26/00	70	1		The Hampsterdance Song ...(2 versions) [I-N]	41^S	$4	★	Koch 8161
				samples "Whistle Stop" by Roger Miller				
				HANDY, Cheryl '87				
				Born in 1969 in Virginia; raised in Goodlettsville, Tennessee.				
4/14/84	83	4		1 Here I Go Again	—	$6		Audiograph 475
1/24/87	67	5		2 One Of The Boys	—	$6		RCM 00105
8/8/87	56	6		3 Will You Still Love Me Tomorrow? ...Don't Take My Heart Away	—	$6		Compleat 176
				#1 Pop hit for The Shirelles in 1961				
				HANKS, Kamryn '89				
10/21/89	85	2		Eyes Never Lie	—	$6		Country Pride 0025
				HANSON, Connie '83				
				Born in Houston. Played "Marshalene" in the movie Urban Cowboy.				
12/25/82+	64	9		There's Still A Lot Of Love In San Antone ...Muffy's Going Crazy	—	$6	■	Soundwaves 4692
				CONNIE HANSON And FRIEND				
				Darrell McCall (guest vocal)				
	★310★			**HARDEN, Arlene** '70				
				Born Ava Harden on 3/1/45 in England, Arkansas. Member of The Harden Trio.				
				1)Lovin' Man (Oh Pretty Woman) 2)Would You Walk With Me Jimmy 3)True Love Is Greater Than Friendship				
7/15/67	48	9		1 Fair Weather Love ...Don't Ask For Tomorrow	—	$7		Columbia 44133
12/9/67+	49	7		2 You're Easy To Love ...What Has The World Done To My Baby	—	$7		Columbia 44310
4/6/68	32	11		3 He's A Good Ole Boy ...When	—	$7		Columbia 44461
8/17/68	41	9		4 What Can I Say ...Like You Love Me Now	—	$7		Columbia 44581
5/3/69	45	9		5 Too Much Of A Man (To Be Tied Down) ...When True Love Walks In	—	$7		Columbia 44783
12/20/69+	63	4		6 My Friend ...Baby	—	$7		Columbia 45016
4/25/70	13	14		7 Lovin' Man (Oh Pretty Woman) ...My World Walked Away With A Blond	—	$7		Columbia 45120
				female version of the #1 Pop hit for Roy Orbison in 1964				
8/29/70	28	11		8 Crying ...It's Over	—	$7	■	Columbia 45203
				#2 Pop hit for Roy Orbison in 1961				
1/9/71	22	11		9 True Love Is Greater Than Friendship ...Funny Familiar Forgotten Feeling	—	$7		Columbia 45287
				from the movie Little Fauss And Big Halsy starring Robert Redford				
5/1/71	25	11		10 Married To A Memory ...Coming Home Soldier	—	$7		Columbia 45365
7/31/71	49	9		11 Congratulations (You Sure Made A Man Out Of Him) ...Sing Me Some Sunshine	—	$7		Columbia 45420
12/18/71+	46	9		12 Ruby Gentry's Daughter ...With Pen In Hand	—	$7		Columbia 45489
4/15/72	29	12		13 A Special Day ...What A Woman In Love Won't Do	—	$7		Columbia 45577
11/4/72	45	8		14 It Takes A Lot Of Tenderness ...It's Over	—	$7		Columbia 45708
6/30/73	21	13		15 Would You Walk With Me Jimmy ...You Can Always Have Me	—	$7		Columbia 45845
				ARLEEN HARDEN:				
7/20/74	72	8		16 Leave Me Alone (Ruby Red Dress) ...It's So Good With You	—	$6		Capitol 3911
				#3 Pop hit for Helen Reddy in 1973				
10/29/77	100	2		17 A Place Where Love Has Been ...Lady In Waiting	—	$5		Elektra 45434
4/1/78	74	4		18 You're Not Free And I'm Not Easy ...Do You Ever Dream	—	$5		Elektra 45463
				HARDEN, Bobby '75				
				Born in England, Arkansas. Member of The Harden Trio.				
3/15/75	48	8		One Step ...Holding On	—	$5		United Artists 597
				HARDEN TRIO, The '66				
				Family trio from England, Arkansas: Bobby Harden and sisters Robbie and Arlene Harden.				
2/12/66	2^1	21		1 Tippy Toeing ...Don't Remind Me	44	$7		Columbia 43463
11/5/66	28	11		2 Seven Days Of Crying (Makes One Weak) ...Husbands And Wives	—	$7		Columbia 43844
4/22/67	16	14		3 Sneaking 'Cross The Border ...Childhood Place	—	$7		Columbia 44059
2/10/68	56	4		4 He Looks A Lot Like You ...My Friend Mister Echo	—	$7		Columbia 44420
6/29/68	47	7		5 Everybody Wants To Be Somebody Else ...Diddle Diddle Dumplin'	—	$7		Columbia 44552
12/7/68+	64	6		6 Who Loves You ...This Is Where You Get Off	—	$7		Columbia 44675
				THE HARDENS ARLENE & ROBBIE				
				HARDIN, Gus '85				
				Born Carolyn Ann Blankenship on 4/9/45 in Tulsa, Oklahoma. Died on 2/18/96 (age 50). Female singer.				
				1)All Tangled Up In Love 2)After The Last Goodbye 3)If I Didn't Love You				
2/19/83	10	16		1 After The Last Goodbye ...I've Been Loving You Too Long	—	$4		RCA 13445
5/28/83	26	14		2 If I Didn't Love You ...You Can Call Me Blue	—	$4		RCA 13532
9/24/83	32	12		3 Loving You Hurts ...Since I Don't Have You	—	$4		RCA 13597
12/24/83+	41	12		4 Fallen Angel (Flyin' High Tonight) ...Not Tonight, I've Got A Heartache	—	$4		RCA 13704
3/24/84	43	11		5 I Pass ...Night Lights	—	$4	■	RCA 13751
6/23/84	52	8		6 How Are You Spending My Nights ...Night Lights	—	$4		RCA 13814
11/10/84+	8	21		7 All Tangled Up In Love S:5 / A:8 More Or Less (Hardin)	—	$4		RCA 13938
				GUS HARDIN (with Earl Thomas Conley)				
4/20/85	79	4		8 My Mind Is On You ...What About When It Rains	—	$4		RCA 14040
8/17/85	72	7		9 Just As Long As I Have You ...More Or Less	—	$4		RCA 14159
				GUS HARDIN and DAVE LOGGINS				
1/11/86	73	7		10 What We Gonna Do ...What About When It Rains	—	$4		RCA 14255

DEBUT	PEAK	WKS	Gold	A-side (Chart Hit)	B-side	Pop	$	Pic	Label & Number
				HARDING, Gayle '79					
				Born in Belmont, California.					
11/11/78	92	2		1 Sexy Eyes	Got You Back In My Mind Again	—	$6		Robchris 1008
1/27/79	84	3		2 I'm Lovin' The Lovin' Out Of You	I Fooled Around Behind You	—	$6		Robchris 1009
				HARDY, Johnny '61					
				Born in Rockmont, Georgia.					
2/13/61	17	10		In Memory Of Johnny Horton	Wasting My Time	—	$25		J&J 003
				HARGROVE, Danny '78					
				Born in Detroit. Singer/songwriter/guitarist.					
5/13/78	73	7		1 Sweet Mary	Four Strong Winds	—	$6		50 States 61
				#7 Pop hit for Wadsworth Mansion in 1971					
9/23/78	98	2		2 I Wanna Be Her #1	She Belongs To The Man At The Bar	—	$6		50 States 64
				HARGROVE, Linda '76					
				Born on 2/3/49 in Tallahassee, Florida. Singer/songwriter/pianist.					
10/19/74	98	2		1 Blue Jean Country Queen	Where Do I Begin	—	$6		Elektra 45204
12/28/74+	82	4		2 I've Never Loved Anyone More	Grandma Was The Motor	—	$6		Elektra 45215
11/8/75+	39	13		3 Love Was (Once Around The Dance Floor)	Half My Heart's In Texas	—	$5		Capitol 4153
3/6/76	86	5		4 Love, You're The Teacher	Save The Children	—	$5		Capitol 4228
7/24/76	86	4		5 Fire At First Sight	20/20 Hindsight	—	$5		Capitol 4283
4/2/77	91	3		6 Down To My Pride	Old Fashioned Love	—	$5		Capitol 4390
9/24/77	61	9		7 Mexican Love Songs	Not Even For Love	—	$5		Capitol 4447
10/14/78	93	4		8 You Are Still The One	I Forgave (But I Forgot To Forget)	—	$5		RCA 11378
				HARLESS, Ogden '88					
				Born William Harless in 1949 in Hattiesburg, Mississippi.					
9/19/87	84	2		1 Somebody Ought To Tell Him That She's Gone		—	$5		Door Knob 283
11/28/87	74	3		2 Walk On Boy		—	$5		Door Knob 287
1/16/88	64	5		3 I Wish We Were Strangers		—	$5		Door Knob 293
4/23/88	82	3		4 Down On The Bayou		—	$5		Door Knob 297
8/27/88	92	2		5 Together Alone		—	$6		MSC 188
				HARLING, Keith '98					
				Born on 5/8/63 in Greenwood, South Carolina; raised in Chattanooga, Tennessee. Singer/songwriter/guitarist.					
3/7/98	24	20		1 Papa Bear	Right In The Middle	—	$4		MCA 72042
8/1/98	39	17		2 Coming Back For You	I Never Go Around Mirrors	—	$4		MCA Nashville 72064
12/19/98+	61	6		3 Write It In Stone	There Goes The Neighborhood	—	$4		MCA Nashville 72081
2/20/99	58	4		4 There Goes The Neighborhood	I Never Go Around Mirrors	—	$4		MCA Nashville 72093
11/6/99+	52	12		5 Bring It On	Heartaches And Honky Tonks	—	$4		Giant 16900
12/25/99	60	3		6 Santa's Got A Semi	[X]	—			album cut
12/9/00	60	5		7 Santa's Got A Semi	[X-R]	—			album cut
				above 2 from the album *Bring It On* on Giant 24732					
				HARMS, Joni '89					
				Born on 11/5/59 in Canby, Oregon.					
3/11/89	34	11		1 I Need A Wife	The Only Thing Bluer Than His Eyes	—	$4		Universal 53492
6/24/89	54	8		2 The Only Thing Bluer Than His Eyes	A Woman Knows	—	$4		Universal 66012
				HARRELL & SCOTT '90					
				Vocal duo: Tony Harrell and Leland Scott.					
9/23/89	96	2		1 Weak Men Break		—	$6		Associated Artists 503
12/16/89+	75	5		2 Darkness Of The Light		—	$6		Associated Artists 505
				HARRINGTON, Carly '88					
8/6/88	64	6		Badland Preacher		—	$6		Oak 1055
				HARRIS, Donna '66					
10/1/66	45	8		He Was Almost Persuaded	I'm Sending Him Back Home To You	—	$8		ABC 10839
				answer to "Almost Persuaded" by **David Houston**					
				HARRIS, Emmylou ★61★ '76					
				Born on 4/2/47 in Birmingham, Alabama. Singer/songwriter/guitarist. Worked as a folk singer in Washington DC in the late 1960s. First recorded for Jubilee in 1969. Married to producer Brian Ahern from 1977-84. Married to British songwriter/producer Paul Kennerley from 1985-93. Joined the *Grand Ole Opry* in 1992. CMA Award: 1980 Female Vocalist of the Year. Also see **Same Old Train**.					
				1)Sweet Dreams 2)Beneath Still Waters 3)Together Again 4)We Believe In Happy Endings 5)(Lost His Love) On Our Last Dance					
4/19/75	73	8		1 Too Far Gone	Boulder To Birmingham	—	$6		Reprise 1326
				also see #13 below					
7/5/75	4	17		2 If I Could Only Win Your Love	Boulder To Birmingham	58	$6		Reprise 1332
				Herb Pedersen (harmony vocal)					
12/27/75	99	1		3 Light Of The Stable	Bluebird Wine [X]	—	$6	■	Reprise 1341
				Dolly Parton, **Linda Ronstadt** and **Neil Young** (backing vocals)					
1/3/76	12	12		4 The Sweetest Gift		—	$6		Asylum 45295
				LINDA RONSTADT AND EMMYLOU HARRIS					
3/6/76	❶¹	14		5 Together Again	Here, There And Everywhere (Pop #65)	—	$5		Reprise 1346
6/5/76	3	16		6 One Of These Days	Till I Gain Control Again	—	$5		Reprise 1353

DEBUT	PEAK	WKS	Gold	A-side (Chart Hit)	B-side	Pop	$	Pic	Label & Number
				HARRIS, Emmylou — Cont'd					
10/23/76	❶²	14		7 Sweet Dreams	Amarillo	—	$5		Reprise 1371
2/26/77	6	13		8 (You Never Can Tell) C'est La Vie	You're Supposed To Be Feeling Good	—	$5		Warner 8329
				#14 Pop hit for Chuck Berry in 1964					
5/28/77	8	14		9 Making Believe	I'll Be Your San Antone Rose	—	$5		Warner 8388
				Herb Pedersen (harmony vocal)					
12/3/77+	3	15		10 To Daddy	Tulsa Queen	102	$5		Warner 8498
				written by Dolly Parton					
4/15/78	❶¹	14		11 Two More Bottles Of Wine	I Ain't Living Long Like This	—	$5		Warner 8553
8/5/78	12	11		12 Easy From Now On	You're Supposed To Be Feeling Good	—	$5		Warner 8623
2/3/79	13	13		13 Too Far Gone	Tulsa Queen [R]	—	$5		Warner 8732
				same version as #1 above					
5/12/79	11	13		14 Play Together Again Again	He Don't Deserve You Anymore	—	$5		Warner 8830
				BUCK OWENS With Emmylou Harris					
6/2/79	4	14		15 Save The Last Dance For Me	Even Cowgirls Get The Blues	—	$5		Warner 8815
				#1 Pop hit for The Drifters in 1960					
9/8/79	91	6		16 Love Don't Care	Who's Gonna Love Me Now (Louvin)	—	$5		Little Darlin' 7922
				CHARLIE LOUVIN with Emmylou Harris					
9/22/79	6	12		17 Blue Kentucky Girl	Leaving Louisiana In The Broad Daylight	—	$5		Warner 49056
3/1/80	❶¹	14		18 Beneath Still Waters	Till I Gain Control Again	—	$5		Warner 49164
5/31/80	7	15		19 Wayfaring Stranger	Green Pastures	—	$5	■	Warner 49239
6/28/80	6	15		20 That Lovin' You Feelin' Again	Lola (Craig Hundley)	55	$5		Warner 49262
				ROY ORBISON & EMMYLOU HARRIS					
				from the movie Roadie starring Meat Loaf					
9/13/80	13	11		21 The Boxer	Precious Love	—	$4		Warner 49551
				#7 Pop hit for Simon & Garfunkel in 1969					
3/7/81	10	12		22 Mister Sandman	Fools Thin Air	37	$4		Warner 49684
				#1 Pop hit for The Chordettes in 1954					
6/13/81	44	8		23 I Don't Have To Crawl	Colors Of Your Heart	106	$4		Warner 49739
9/19/81	3	17		24 If I Needed You	Ashes By Now	—	$4		Warner 49809
				EMMYLOU HARRIS & DON WILLIAMS					
1/16/82	9	16		25 Tennessee Rose	Mama Help	—	$4		Warner 49892
5/29/82	3	17		26 Born To Run	Colors Of Your Heart	—	$4		Warner 29993
10/16/82+	❶¹	20		27 (Lost His Love) On Our Last Date	Another Pot O' Tea	—	$4		Warner 29898
3/19/83	5	17		28 I'm Movin' On	Maybe Tonight	—	$4		Warner 29729
7/2/83	28	13		29 So Sad (To Watch Good Love Go Bad)	Amarillo	—	$4		Warner 29583
				#7 Pop hit for The Everly Brothers in 1960					
7/9/83	14	19		30 Wild Montana Skies	I Remember Romance	—	$4		RCA 13562
				JOHN DENVER AND EMMYLOU HARRIS					
11/19/83+	26	13		31 Drivin' Wheel	Good News	—	$4		Warner 29443
3/24/84	9	21		32 In My Dreams	Like An Old Fashioned Waltz	—	$4		Warner 29329
8/11/84	9	22		33 Pledging My Love	S:9 / A:9 Baby, Better Start Turnin' 'Em Down	—	$4		Warner 29218
				#17 Pop hit for Johnny Ace in 1955					
11/24/84+	26	18		34 Someone Like You	S:23 Light Of The Stable	—	$4		Warner 29138
3/30/85	14	17		35 White Line	S:12 / A:14 Long Tall Sally Rose	—	$4		Warner 29041
7/20/85	44	11		36 Rhythm Guitar	Diamond In My Crown	—	$4		Warner 28952
11/30/85	55	9		37 Timberline	Sweet Chariot	—	$4		Warner 28852
3/1/86	60	6		38 I Had My Heart Set On You	Your Long Journey	—	$4		Warner 28770
5/3/86	43	13		39 Today I Started Loving You Again	When I Was Yours	—	$4		Warner 28714
				written by Merle Haggard and Bonnie Owens					
2/21/87	❶¹	19		40 To Know Him Is To Love Him	S:❶¹ / A:❶¹ Farther Along	—	$4	■	Warner 28492
				DOLLY PARTON, LINDA RONSTADT, EMMYLOU HARRIS					
				#1 Pop hit for The Teddy Bears in 1958					
5/30/87	3	18		41 Telling Me Lies	S:10 Rosewood Casket	—	$4		Warner 28371
				DOLLY PARTON, LINDA RONSTADT, EMMYLOU HARRIS					
7/11/87	60	7		42 Someday My Ship Will Sail	When He Calls	—	$4		Warner 28302
9/26/87	5	22		43 Those Memories Of You	S:10 My Dear Companion	—	$4	■	Warner 28248
				DOLLY PARTON, LINDA RONSTADT, EMMYLOU HARRIS					
12/12/87+	53	13		44 Back In Baby's Arms	I Still Dream Of You	—	$4		Hughes/MCA 53236
				from the movie Planes, Trains & Automobiles starring Steve Martin and John Candy					
3/26/88	6	18		45 Wildflowers	S:13 Hobo's Meditation	—	$4		Warner 27970
				DOLLY PARTON, LINDA RONSTADT, EMMYLOU HARRIS					
7/2/88	❶¹	21		46 We Believe In Happy Endings	S:3 No Chance, No Dance	—	$4		RCA 8632
				EARL THOMAS CONLEY with Emmylou Harris					
12/17/88+	8	22		47 Heartbreak Hill	Icy Blue Heart	—	$4		Reprise 27635
4/29/89	16	21		48 Heaven Only Knows	A River For Him	—	$4		Reprise 22999
8/26/89	51	6		49 I Still Miss Someone	No Regrets	—	$4		Reprise 22850
1/19/91	71	3		50 Wheels Of Love	Better Off Without You	—	$4		Reprise 19510
10/16/93	63	8		51 High Powered Love	Ballad Of A Runaway Horse	—	$4	■	Asylum 64610 (v)
1/29/94	65	5		52 Thanks To You	Lovin' You Again	—	$4		Asylum 64570
				HARRISON, B.J.	**'80**				
5/24/80	93	2		I Need A Little More Time		—	$7		TeleSonic 801
				HARRISON, Dixie	**'82**				
				Born on 8/17/53 in Faulkner County, Arkansas.					
10/23/82	98	2		Yes Mam (He Found Me In A Honky Tonk)	Careless Kinda Heart	—	$6		Air Int'l. 10078

DEBUT	PEAK	WKS	Gold	A-side (Chart Hit)	B-side	Pop	$	Pic	Label & Number
				HART, Clay '69 Born Henry Clay Hart III in Providence, Rhode Island. Regular on **Lawrence Welk**'s TV show from 1969-75. Married to Sally Flynn, another regular on the Welk show.					
5/31/69	30	11		1 Spring .... Child Of The Wind		—	$6		Metromedia 119
9/20/69	25	9		2 Another Day, Another Mile, Another Highway .... Penny		—	$6		Metromedia 140
1/31/70	73	3		3 Face Of A Dear Friend .... Gotta Be Free		—	$6		Metromedia 158
5/2/70	62	7		4 If I'd Only Come And Gone .... Take Your Precious Love From Me		—	$6		Metromedia 172

HART, Freddie ★75★ '72
Born Frederick Segrest on 12/21/26 in Lochapoka, Alabama. Singer/songwriter/guitarist. Served in U.S. Marines during World War II. Moved to Phoenix in 1950 and worked with **Lefty Frizzell** from 1951-52. Appeared on *Home Town Jamboree* TV series. Later operated a trucking company and school for handicapped children in Burbank, California.

1) My Hang-Up Is You   2) Easy Loving   3) Got The All Overs For You (All Over Me)   4) Bless Your Heart
5) Super Kind Of Woman

DEBUT	PEAK	WKS	Gold	A-side	B-side	Pop	$	Pic	Label & Number
4/20/59	24	4		1 The Wall .... Davy Jones		—	$12		Columbia 41345
11/16/59	17	4		2 Chain Gang .... Rock Bottom		—	$12		Columbia 41456
5/2/60	18	11		3 The Key's In The Mailbox .... Starvation Days		—	$12		Columbia 41597
1/9/61	27	2		4 Lying Again .... Do My Heart A Favor		—	$12		Columbia 41805
11/6/61	23	2		5 What A Laugh! .... Heart Attack		—	$12		Columbia 42146
10/30/65	23	12		6 Hank Williams' Guitar .... I Created A Monster		—	$10		Kapp 694
5/7/66	45	4		7 Why Should I Cry Over You .... The Key's In The Mailbox		—	$10		Kapp 743
				FREDDIE HART And The Heartbeats (above 2)					
7/8/67	63	5		8 I'll Hold You In My Heart .... Too Much Of You (Left In Me)		—	$10		Kapp 820
12/30/67+	24	15		9 Togetherness .... Portrait Of A Lonely Man		—	$10	■	Kapp 879
6/8/68	21	15		10 Born A Fool .... The Hands Of A Man		—	$10		Kapp 910
				also see #21 below					
11/23/68	70	2		11 Don't Cry Baby .... Here Lies A Heart		—	$10		Kapp 944
1/3/70	27	10		12 The Whole World Holding Hands .... Without You		—	$7		Capitol 2692
4/11/70	48	9		13 One More Mountain To Climb .... Just Another Girl		—	$7		Capitol 2768
7/4/70	41	11		14 Fingerprints .... I Can't Keep My Hands Off Of You		—	$7		Capitol 2839
11/21/70	68	4		15 California Grapevine .... What's Wrong With Your Head, Fred		—	$7		Capitol 2933
7/10/71	❶³	24	•	16 Easy Loving .... Brother Bluebird		17	$6		Capitol 3115
1/29/72	❶⁶	19		17 My Hang-Up Is You .... Big Bad Wolf		—	$6		Capitol 3261
				FREDDIE HART And The Heartbeats:					
6/24/72	❶²	14		18 Bless Your Heart .... Conscience Makes Cowards (Of Us All)		—	$6		Capitol 3353
10/14/72	❶³	17		19 Got The All Overs For You (All Over Me) .... Just Another Girl		—	$6		Capitol 3453
2/3/73	❶¹	14		20 Super Kind Of Woman .... Mother Nature Made A Believer Out Of Me		—	$6		Capitol 3524
5/19/73	41	10		21 Born A Fool .... My Anna Maria [R]		—	$6		MCA 40011
				FREDDIE HART same version as #10 above					
6/2/73	❶¹	16		22 Trip To Heaven .... Look-A Here		—	$6		Capitol 3612
10/6/73	3	16		23 If You Can't Feel It (It Ain't There) .... Skid Row Street		—	$6		Capitol 3730
2/23/74	2¹	12		24 Hang In There Girl .... You Belong To Me		—	$6		Capitol 3827
				FREDDIE HART					
6/22/74	3	14		25 The Want-To's .... Phoenix City		—	$6		Capitol 3898
11/2/74+	3	16		26 My Woman's Man .... Let's Clean Up The Country		—	$6		Capitol 3970
3/1/75	5	15		27 I'd Like To Sleep Til I Get Over You .... Nothing's Better Than That		—	$6		Capitol 4031
6/28/75	2²	12		28 The First Time .... Sexy		—	$6		Capitol 4099
10/18/75	6	15		29 Warm Side Of You .... I Love You, I Just Don't Like You		—	$6		Capitol 4152
1/31/76	11	11		30 You Are The Song (Inside Of Me) .... I Can Almost See Houston From Here		—	$6		Capitol 4210
4/10/76	12	14		31 She'll Throw Stones At You .... Love Makes It All Alright		—	$6		Capitol 4251
8/21/76	11	14		32 That Look In Her Eyes .... Try My Love For Size		—	$6		Capitol 4313
12/4/76+	8	14		33 Why Lovers Turn To Strangers .... Paper Sack Full Of Memories		—	$6		Capitol 4363
				FREDDIE HART:					
4/16/77	11	11		34 Thank God She's Mine .... Falling All Over Me		—	$5		Capitol 4409
7/16/77	13	12		35 The Pleasure's Been All Mine /		—	$5		
		10		36 It's Heaven Loving You		—	$5		Capitol 4448
11/5/77	43	10		37 The Search .... Honky Tonk Toys		—	$5		Capitol 4498
				FREDDIE Hart And The Heartbeats					
1/21/78	27	11		38 So Good, So Rare, So Fine .... There's An Angel Living There		—	$5		Capitol 4530
4/22/78	34	10		39 Only You .... I Love You, I Just Don't Like You		—	$5		Capitol 4561
				#1 Pop hit for The Platters in 1955					
8/19/78	21	12		40 Toe To Toe .... And Then Some		—	$5		Capitol 4609
2/24/79	40	8		41 My Lady .... Guilty		—	$5		Capitol 4684
5/26/79	28	12		42 Wasn't It Easy Baby .... My Lady Loves		—	$5		Capitol 4720
6/7/80	15	12		43 Sure Thing .... Makin' Love To A Memory		—	$5	■	Sunbird 7550
				also released on Sunbird 110					
9/13/80	33	10		44 Rose's Are Red .... Battle of the Sexes		—	$5		Sunbird 7553
4/18/81	31	10		45 You're Crazy Man .... Playboy's Centerfold		—	$5		Sunbird 7560
9/12/81	38	9		46 You Were There .... The Weaker Sex		—	$5		Sunbird 7565
6/29/85	81	4		47 I Don't Want To Lose You .... My Favorite Entertainer		—	$7		El Dorado 101
9/5/87	77	4		48 Best Love I Never Had .... I'm Not Going Hungry		—	$6		Fifth Street 1091

DEBUT	PEAK	WKS	Gold	A-side (Chart Hit)	B-side	Pop	$	Pic	Label & Number
				HART, J.D. '89 Born in Albemarle, North Carolina. Male singer.					
11/4/89	79	3		Come Back Brenda	Love Still Lives	—	$4		Universal 66017
				HART, Rod '77 Born in Beulah, Michigan. Acted in the movie *Junior Bonner*.					
11/27/76+	23	11		C.B. Savage	Better Off Gone [N]	67	$5	⊙	Plantation 144
				"gay" answer to "Convoy" by C.W. McCall					
				HART, Sally June '75					
9/20/75	91	3		Takin' What I Can Get	Beautiful Love Song Melodies	—	$5		Buddah 479
				HART, Tara Lyn '00 Born in Roblin, Manitoba, Canada. Singer/songwriter.					
10/16/99	67	1		1 Stuff That Matters		—		★	album cut
				later released as the B-side of #2 below					
3/18/00	65	1		2 Don't Ever Let Me Go	S:22 Stuff That Matters	—	$4	★	Columbia 79356
6/17/00	68	1		3 That's When You Came Along		—			album cut
				all of above from the album *Tara Lyn Hart* on Columbia 69602					
				HARTFORD, Chapin '78 Born Paula Hartford Foster on 5/15/44 in Boston. Female singer.					
8/26/78	91	3		I Knew The Mason	Rio Grande	—	$6		LS 165
				HARTFORD, John '67 Born on 12/30/37 in New York City; raised in St. Louis. Died of cancer on 6/4/2001 (age 63). Singer/songwriter/banjo player. Regular on TV's *The Smothers Brothers Comedy Hour*.					
5/27/67	60	7		1 Gentle On My Mind	(Good Old Electric) Washing Machine (Circa. 1943)	—	$10		RCA Victor 9175
8/18/84	81	3		2 Piece Of My Heart	No Expectations	—	$6		Flying Fish 4013
				#12 Pop hit for Big Brother & The Holding Company (Janis Joplin) in 1968					
				HARTSOOK, Jimmy '74 Born on 8/10/59 in Lenoir City, Tennessee.					
1/26/74	94	5		Anything To Prove My Love To You	Dreamin' Again	—	$6	■	RCA Victor 0202
				HARTT, Dolly '88					
2/13/88	85	3		Here Comes The Night		—	$6		Kass 1015
				HARVELL, Nate '78 Born in Alabama. Singer/songwriter.					
7/15/78	23	13		1 Three Times A Lady	Happy Ending	—	$5		Republic 025
				#1 Pop hit for the Commodores in 1978					
12/2/78	73	5		2 One In A Million	Silver Rails	—	$5		Republic 033
				HATFIELD, Vince and Dianne '82					
8/1/81	83	4		1 I Won't Last A Day Without You	Divided Love	—	$5		Soundwaves 4638
				#11 Pop hit for the Carpenters in 1974					
5/1/82	81	3		2 Back In My Baby's Arms	Travelin' Man	—	$5		Soundwaves 4668
7/2/83	90	2		3 Love Has Made A Woman Out Of You	Texas, I Dream Of You	—	$5		Soundwaves 4704
				HAUSER, Bruce '85 Born in Kansas. Singer/songwriter.					
10/24/81	90	3		1 Barely Gettin' By	Friends	—	$6		Cowboy 1045
				SAWMILL CREEK					
12/21/85	77	6		2 I Just Came Back (To Break My Heart Again)		—	$6		Cowboy 200
				BRUCE HAUSER AND THE SAWMILL CREEK BAND					
7/19/86	81	3		3 Bidding America Goodbye (The Auction)		—	$6		Cowboy 202
				BRUCE HAUSER and Sawmill Creek					
				HAVENS, Bobby '78 Born on 3/13/48 in Baird, Texas. Singer/songwriter/guitarist.					
12/9/78	100	2		Hey You	Typical Saturday Night	—	$6		Cin Kay 043
				BOBBY HAVENS and Country Company					
				HAWKINS, Brad '98 Born on 1/13/74 in Dallas. Singer/songwriter/guitarist.					
2/28/98	68	6		We Lose	Come Back To Me Blues	—	$4		Curb 56097
				HAWKINS, Debi '77 Born Deborah Kaye Hawkins in Paso Robles, California.					
3/22/75	61	9		1 Making Believe	The Man In My Life	—	$5		Warner 8076
7/26/75	80	5		2 What I Keep Sayin', Is A Lie	A Beautiful Memory Tonight	—	$5		Warner 8104
11/8/75	88	3		3 When I Stop Dreaming	I Want To Hold You In My Arms	—	$5		Warner 8140
3/27/76	97	2		4 Walnut Street Wrangler	Magic Cloud Of Love	—	$5		Warner 8188
6/18/77	57	8		5 Love Letters	Hey Mister Train	—	$5		Warner 8394
				#5 Pop hit for Ketty Lester in 1962					
				HAWKINS, Erskine, and his Orchestra '44 Born on 7/26/14 in Birmingham, Alabama. Died on 11/11/93 (age 79). Trumpeter/bandleader/composer.					
2/5/44	6	1		Don't Cry, Baby	Bear-Mash Blues	15	$20		Bluebird 30-0813
				Jimmy Mitchelle (vocal)					
	★382★			**HAWKINS, Hawkshaw** '63 Born Harold Franklin Hawkins on 12/22/21 in Huntington, West Virginia. Died in a plane crash on 3/5/63 (age 41) near Camden, Tennessee (with Patsy Cline and Cowboy Copas). Singer/songwriter/guitarist. Joined the *Grand Ole Opry* in 1955. Married Jean Shepard on 11/26/60.					
5/1/48	9	4		1 Pan American	J:9 I Suppose	—	$25		King 689
8/21/48	6	15		2 Dog House Boogie	J:6 / S:12 I Can't Tell My Broken Heart A Lie	—	$25		King 720

DEBUT	PEAK	WKS	Gold	A-side (Chart Hit) ... B-side	Pop	$	Pic	Label & Number
				HAWKINS, Hawkshaw — Cont'd				
12/24/49	15	1		3 I Wasted A Nickel .... S:15 *I'm Kissing Your Picture Counting Tears*	—	$25		King 821
3/17/51	8	1		4 I Love You A Thousand Ways .... A:8 *Teardrops From My Eyes*	—	$25		King 918
10/13/51	8	2		5 I'm Waiting Just For You .... A:8 *A Heartache To Recall*	—	$30		King 45-969
12/8/51+	7	4		6 Slow Poke .... J:7 / S:8 *Two Roads*	26	$30		King 45-998
8/10/59	15	7		7 Soldier's Joy .... *Big Red Benson*	87	$20		Columbia 41419
3/2/63	❶⁴	25		8 Lonesome 7-7203 .... *Everything Has Changed*	108	$15		King 5712
				HAWKS, Mickey '89 Born in High Point, North Carolina. Male singer.				
9/23/89	94	2		Me And My Harley-Davidson .... *The Good Old Days*	—	$10		C-Horse 589
	★264★			**HAYES, Wade** '95 Born on 4/20/69 in Bethel Acres, Oklahoma. Singer/songwriter/guitarist. 1)Old Enough To Know Better 2)On A Good Night 3)I'm Still Dancin' With You				
11/19/94+	❶²	20		1 Old Enough To Know Better .... *Family Reunion*	—	$4	■	Columbia 77739 (v)
3/18/95	4	20		2 I'm Still Dancin' With You .... S:3 *It's Gonna Take A Miracle*	113	$4		Columbia 77842 (v)
7/15/95	10	20		3 Don't Stop .... S:16 *Someone Had To Teach You*	—	$4		Columbia 77954 (v)
10/28/95+	5	20		4 What I Meant To Say .... S:6 *Kentucky Bluebird*	116	$4		Columbia 78087 (v)
5/11/96	2²	20		5 On A Good Night .... S:11 *Steady As She Goes*	—	$4		Columbia 78312 (v)
10/5/96	42	9		6 Where Do I Go To Start All Over .... *My Side Of Town*	—	$4		Columbia 78369 (v)
12/21/96+	46	11		7 It's Over My Head .... *Hurts Don't It*	—	$4		Columbia 78486
8/9/97	55	8		8 Wichita Lineman .... S:18 *On A Good Night*	—	$4	■	Columbia 78674 (v)
11/1/97+	5	25		9 The Day That She Left Tulsa (In A Chevy) .... S:8 *Wichita Lineman*	86	$4		Columbia 78745
4/11/98	50	10		10 When The Wrong One Loves You Right .... —	—	—		album cut
7/4/98	13	24		11 How Do You Sleep At Night .... —	67	—		album cut
1/16/99	57	8		12 Tore Up From The Floor Up .... —	—	—		album cut
				Above 3 from the album When The Wrong One Loves You Right *on Columbia 68037*				
2/5/00	48	12		13 Up North (Down South, Back East, Out West) .... S:11 *I'm Lonesome Too*	—	$4	★	Monument 79361
5/6/00	45	14		14 Goodbye Is The Wrong Way To Go .... S:19 *She's Actin' Single (I'm Drinkin' Doubles)*	—	$4	★	Monument 79414
				HAZARD '83 Vocal trio from Hazard, Kentucky: Wayne Davis, Bernie Faulkner and Bruce Dees. Faulkner was a member of **Exile**.				
4/2/83	69	5		Love Letters .... *Island*	—	$4		Warner 29755
				#5 Pop hit for Ketty Lester in 1962				
				HAZARD, Donna '81 Session vocalist with **The Concrete Cowboy Band**.				
1/17/81	45	9		1 My Turn .... *I Don't Want To Dance With You (No More)*	—	$5		Excelsior 1004
5/2/81	55	7		2 Go Home And Go To Pieces .... *Slow Texas Dancing*	—	$5		Excelsior 1009
7/11/81	54	8		3 Love Never Hurt So Good .... *I'm Your Lady*	—	$5		Excelsior 1016
12/26/81+	76	5		4 Slow Texas Dancing .... *Tailwinds*	—	$5		Excelsior 1020
	★282★			**HEAD, Roy** '78 Born on 9/1/41 in Three Rivers, Texas. Singer/songwriter/guitarist. Charted seven pop hits from 1965-71. 1)Come To Me 2)The Most Wanted Woman In Town 3)Now You See 'Em, Now You Don't 4)The Door I Used To Close 5)Tonight's The Night (It's Gonna Be Alright)				
10/19/74	66	9		1 Baby's Not Home .... *Do What You Can Do*	—	$6		Mega 1219
4/5/75	19	14		2 The Most Wanted Woman In Town .... *Gingers Breade Man*	—	$5		Shannon 829
8/16/75	47	10		3 Help Yourself To Me .... *To Make A Big Man Cry*	—	$5		Shannon 833
11/22/75+	55	8		4 I'll Take It .... *The One That Got Away*	—	$5		Shannon 838
2/7/76	28	11		5 The Door I Used To Close .... *Lady Luck And Mother Nature*	—	$5		ABC/Dot 17608
6/5/76	50	8		6 Bridge For Crawling Back .... *Ain't It Funny (How Times Haven't Changed)*	—	$5		ABC/Dot 17629
9/4/76	51	8		7 One Night .... *Deep Elem Blues*	—	$5		ABC/Dot 17650
				#11 R&B hit for Smiley Lewis in 1956				
12/25/76+	57	8		8 Angel With A Broken Wing .... *Just Because*	—	$5		ABC/Dot 17669
7/2/77	79	6		9 Julianne .... *Velvet Strings*	—	$5		ABC/Dot 17706
10/8/77+	16	20		10 Come To Me .... *Georgia On My Mind*	—	$5		ABC/Dot 17722
4/1/78	19	13		11 Now You See 'Em, Now You Don't .... *Smooth Whiskey*	—	$5		ABC 12346
7/22/78	28	10		12 Tonight's The Night (It's Gonna Be Alright) .... *The Lady In My Room*	—	$5		ABC 12383
				#1 Pop hit for Rod Stewart in 1976				
11/4/78	45	7		13 Love Survived .... *Dixie*	—	$5		ABC 12418
3/24/79	74	5		14 Kiss You And Make It Better .... *Do It Again*	—	$5		ABC 12462
				written by Mac Davis				
11/10/79	79	4		15 In Our Room .... *Things I Never Could Leave Behind*	—	$4		Elektra 46549
2/2/80	65	4		16 The Fire Of Two Old Flames .... *Under Suspicion*	—	$4		Elektra 46582
7/5/80	59	6		17 Long Drop .... *Gonna Save It For My Baby*	—	$4		Elektra 46653
9/27/80	70	5		18 Drinkin' Them Long Necks .... *Baby's Found Another Way To Love Me*	—	$4		Elektra 47029
10/24/81	75	5		19 After Texas .... *California Day*	—	$5		Churchill 7778
5/29/82	89	3		20 Play Another Gettin' Drunk And Take Somebody Home Song .... *Your Next One And Only*	—	$5		NSD 129
9/11/82	64	7		21 The Trouble With Hearts .... *Naughty Smile*	—	$5		NSD 146
1/8/83	85	4		22 Your Mama Don't Dance .... *Party Time*	—	$5		NSD 156
				#4 Pop hit for Loggins & Messina *in 1973*				
12/10/83	79	5		23 Where Did He Go Right .... —	—	$7		Avion 105
9/7/85	93	2		24 Break Out The Good Stuff .... *She Needs Time*	—	$7		Texas Crude 614

DEBUT	PEAK	WKS	Gold	A-side (Chart Hit)	B-side	Pop	$	Pic	Label & Number
				HEAP, Jimmy '54					
				Born on 3/3/22 in Taylor, Texas. Drowned in a boating accident on 12/4/77 (age 55). Singer/songwriter/guitarist. Leader of swing band, The Melody Masters, which featured lead singer Houston "Perk" Williams. Father of Jimmy Heap, Jr., of **The Drifting Cowboys**.					
1/9/54	5	13		Release Me S:5 / J:8 / A:10 JIMMY HEAP and The Melody Masters with PERK WILLIAMS #4 Pop hit for **Engelbert Humperdinck** in 1967	Just To Be With You	—	$25		Capitol 2518
				HEARTLAND '89					
9/24/88	79	3		1 New River	Way Down	—	$5		Tra-Star 1221
12/17/88	82	3		2 Making Love To Dixie		—	$5		Tra-Star 1222
3/18/89	61	5		3 Keep The Faith		—	$5		Tra-Star 1223
				HEART OF NASHVILLE '85					
				The Heart of Nashville Foundation was founded to benefit the nation's hungry and homeless. Some of the singers participating in this recording include **Roy Acuff**, **Lynn Anderson**, **Eddy Arnold**, **Bobby Bare**, **Sonny James**, **George Jones**, **Webb Pierce**, **Jerry Reed**, **Tanya Tucker**, **Porter Wagoner** and **Faron Young**.					
6/8/85	61	9		One Big Family written and produced by **Ronnie McDowell**	(instrumental)	—	$5	■	Compleat 679001
				HEATH, Boyd '45					
				Emcee of the NBC-TV show *Saturday Night Jamboree* in 1949.					
5/5/45	7	1		Smoke On The Water	Dreamy Rio Grande	—	$30		Bluebird 33-0522
				HEATHERLY, Eric '00					
				Born on 2/2/70 in Chattanooga, Tennessee. Singer/songwriter/guitarist.					
2/26/00	6	28		1 Flowers On The Wall S:7	Someone Else's Cadillac	50	$4	★	Mercury 172152 (v)
9/16/00	46	10		2 Swimming In Champagne	Freedom Chain	—	$4		Mercury 172176
11/4/00+	32	21		3 Wrong Five O' Clock	WhyDon'tCha	—	$4		Mercury 172191
				HEAVENER, David '82					
				Born on 12/22/53 in Louisville, Kentucky.					
11/28/81	73	4		1 Cheat On Him Tonight	Please Help Me Lord	—	$5		Brent 1017
2/20/82	70	4		2 Honky Tonk Tonight	Jesus Is Coming To Town	—	$5		Brent 1019
7/31/82	86	3		3 I Am The Fire		—	$5		Brent 1020
				HECKEL, Beverly '78					
				Born in Elkins, West Virginia. Member of **The Heckels**. Married **Johnny Russell** in 1977.					
6/11/77	88	5		1 Don't Hand Me No Hand Me Down Love	Halfway To Paradise	—	$5		RCA 10981
9/16/78	56	7		2 Bluer Than Blue	Living Without	—	$5		RCA 11360
				Wayland Holyfield (guest vocal); #12 Pop hit for **Michael Johnson** in 1978					
				HECKELS, The '76					
				Family vocal trio from Elkins, West Virginia: sisters Susie and **Beverly Heckel**, with Susie's husband Denny Franks.					
6/26/76	91	5		A Cowboy Like You	The Devil's Way Of Tempting Me	—	$5		RCA Victor 10685
	★285★			**HELMS, Bobby** '57					
				Born on 8/15/35 in Bloomington, Indiana. Died of emphysema on 6/19/97 (age 61). Singer/songwriter/guitarist. 1)Fraulein 2)My Special Angel 3)Jacqueline					
3/30/57	❶⁴	52		1 Fraulein A:❶⁴ / S:❶³ / J:9	(Got A) Heartsick Feeling	36	$25	■	Decca 30194
10/14/57	❶⁴	26	●	2 My Special Angel S:❶⁴ / A:❶¹	Standing At The End Of My World	7	$25		Decca 30423
12/23/57	13	1	●	3 Jingle Bell Rock A:13 Captain Santa Claus (And His Reindeer Space Patrol) also see #13 below		6	$20	■	Decca 30513 [X]
3/3/58	10	9		4 Just A Little Lonesome		—	$20		Decca 30557
5/12/58	5	12		5 Jacqueline S:10 / A:12 Love My Lady from the movie *The Case Against Brooklyn* starring Darren McGavin	Living In The Shadow Of The Past	63	$20		Decca 30619
3/30/59	26	3		6 New River Train	Miss Memory	—	$20		Decca 30831
10/24/60	16	4		7 Lonely River Rhine	Guess We Thought The World Would End	—	$20		Decca 31148
6/24/67	46	7		8 He Thought He'd Die Laughing	You'd Better Make Up Your Mind	—	$10		Little Darlin' 0030
12/30/67+	60	6		9 The Day You Stop Loving Me	You Can Tell The World	—	$10		Little Darlin' 0034
4/20/68	53	9		10 I Feel You, I Love You	All I Need Is You	—	$10		Little Darlin' 0041
8/2/69	43	9		11 So Long	Just Do The Best You Can	—	$10		Little Darlin' 0062
6/27/70	41	9		12 Mary Goes 'Round	Cold Winds Blow On Me	—	$10		Certron 10002
12/28/96	60	2		13 Jingle Bell Rock [X-R] same version as #3 above; from the movie *Jingle All The Way* starring Arnold Schwarzenegger (soundtrack on TVT 8070)		—			album cut
				HENDERSON, Brice '83					
				Born on 1/4/54 in Frederick, Maryland.					
1/22/83	61	7		1 Lonely Eyes	She Still Has That Hold On Me	—	$6		Union Station 1000
4/30/83	55	8		2 Lovers Again	She Still Has That Hold On Me	—	$6		Union Station 1001
9/17/83	64	5		3 Flames	Crossing The Love Line	—	$6		Union Station 1003
				HENDERSON, Mike '94					
				Born on 7/14/53 in Independence, Missouri. Singer/songwriter.					
2/5/94	69	4		Hillbilly Jitters	That Train Don't Stop Here Anymore	—	$4	■	RCA 62730 (v)
				HENHOUSE FIVE PLUS TOO — see **STEVENS, Ray**					
				HENLEY, Don '93					
				Born on 7/22/47 in Gilmer, Texas. Rock singer/songwriter/drummer. Member of the **Eagles**. Married model Sharon Summerall on 5/20/95.					
11/7/92+	2¹	20		1 Walkaway Joe You Don't Have To Move That Mountain (Yearwood) TRISHA YEARWOOD with Don Henley		—	$4		MCA 54495
10/28/00	61	6		2 For My Wedding from the album *Inside Job* on Warner 47083		—			album cut

DEBUT	PEAK	WKS	Gold	A-side (Chart Hit) / B-side	Pop	$	Pic	Label & Number
				HENLEY, Don — Cont'd				
12/1/01+	31	19		3 Inside Out .... Love Let Go (Yearwood)	—	$4		MCA Nashville 172219
				TRISHA YEARWOOD Featuring Don Henley				
				HENRY, Audie '85				
				Born in Brazil; raised in Canada. Female singer.				
1/19/85	97	3		1 You'll Never Find A Good Man (Playing In A Country Band)	—	$5		Canyon Creek 2025
4/27/85	91	2		2 Being A Fool Again	—	$5		Canyon Creek 2008
7/27/85	73	5		3 Heaven Knows .... I Knew The First Time I Saw You	—	$5		Canyon Creek 5020
10/19/85	71	5		4 Sweet Salvation .... A Step In The Right Direction	—	$5		Canyon Creek 8019
				HENSLEY, Tari '86				
				Born Tari Dean Hodges on 3/6/53 in Independence, Missouri. Female singer.				
4/9/83	86	3		1 Falling In Love .... Down To My Last Time	—	$4		Mercury 76197
9/8/84	69	4		2 Love Isn't Love ('Til You Give It Away) .... Sweet Nights	—	$4		Mercury 880054
2/9/85	61	6		3 I'm The One Who's Breaking Up .... It's The Nights That Drive Me Crazy	—	$4		Mercury 880424
7/27/85	64	6		4 Hard Baby To Rock .... Down To My Last Time	—	$4		Mercury 880801
4/5/86	57	7		5 Oh Yes I Can .... Sweet Nights	—	$4		Mercury 884484
7/26/86	52	10		6 I've Cried A Mile .... We Can't Communicate	—	$4		Mercury 884852
				HERMAN, Woody — see WISEMAN, Mac				
	★246★			**HERNDON, Ty** '98				
				Born Boyd Tyrone Herndon on 5/2/62 in Meridian, Mississippi; raised in Butler, Alabama. Singer/songwriter/guitarist.				
				1) Living In A Moment 2) It Must Be Love 3) What Mattered Most				
2/25/95	●¹	20		1 What Mattered Most .... S:4 You Don't Mess Around With Jim	—	$4	■	Epic 77843 (v)
6/10/95	7	20		2 I Want My Goodbye Back .... S:22 Heart Half Empty	—	$4		Epic 77946 (v)
10/14/95+	21	20		3 Heart Half Empty .... S:10 Love At 90 Miles An Hour (Herndon)	—	$4		Epic 78073 (v)
				TY HERNDON Featuring Stephanie Bentley				
3/30/96	63	2		4 In Your Face .... What Mattered Most	—	$4		Epic 78247
6/29/96	●¹	20		5 Living In A Moment .... S:8 Returning The Faith	—	$4	■	Epic 78364 (v)
11/2/96+	21	20		6 She Wants To Be Wanted Again .... S:20 Before There Was You	—	$4	■	Epic 78482 (v)
3/22/97	2²	20		7 Loved Too Much	—			album cut
9/20/97	17	20		8 I Have To Surrender	—			album cut
				above 2 from the album Living In A Moment on Epic 67564				
3/28/98	5	23		9 A Man Holdin' On (To A Woman Lettin' Go) .... S:11 Just Enough To Get To Memphis	81	$4	■	Epic 78904 (v)
8/15/98	●¹	26		10 It Must Be Love .... A Man Holdin' On (To A Woman Lettin' Go)	38	$4		Epic 79049
12/26/98+	5	26		11 Hands Of A Working Man	47			album cut
				from the album Big Hopes on Epic 68167				
8/21/99	18	20		12 Steam .... S:3 Lookin' For The Good Life	83	$4	★	Epic 79269 (v)
				later issued on vinyl as the B-side of #14 below				
1/15/00	72	2		13 You Can Leave Your Hat On	—			album cut
				written by Randy Newman				
1/22/00	26	20		14 No Mercy .... S:6 Tears In God's Eyes	92	$4	★	Epic 79345 (v)
				"45" B-side: "Steam"				
7/15/00	58	9		15 A Love Like That	—			album cut
				above 4 from the album Steam on Epic 79269				
12/29/01+	37	19		16 Heather's Wall	—			album cut
				from the album This Is Ty Herndon on Epic 85360				
				HERRING, Red '60				
7/4/60	27	2		Wasted Love	—	$25		Country Jubilee 533
				HESTER, Hoot '79				
				Born Hubert Hester on 8/13/51 in Louisville, Kentucky.				
4/21/79	95	3		I Still Love Her Memory .... Forever Ended Yesterday	—	$7		Little Darlin' 7911
				HEWITT, Dolph '49				
				Born Dolph Edward Hewitt on 7/15/14 in West Finley, Pennsylvania. Regular on the WLS National Barn Dance from 1946-60.				
12/17/49	8	1		I Wish I Knew .... A:8 I Would Send You Roses	—	$20		RCA Victor 21-0107
				45 rpm: 48-0107				
				HIATT, John — see NITTY GRITTY DIRT BAND				
				HICKEY, Sara "Honeybear" '83				
6/25/83	82	2		This Ain't Tennessee And He Ain't You	—	$7		PCM 203
				HICKS, Jeanette — see JONES, George				
				HICKS, Laney — see SMALLWOOD, Laney				
				HIGGINS, Bertie '82				
				Born Elbert Higgins on 12/8/44 in Tarpon Springs, Florida. Singer/songwriter.				
3/13/82	50	10	●	1 Key Largo .... White Line Fever	8	$5		Kat Family 02524
				inspired by the movie starring Humphrey Bogart and Lauren Bacall				
6/19/82	90	3		2 Just Another Day In Paradise .... She's Gone To Live On The Mountain	46	$5		Kat Family 02839
9/3/88	72	5		3 You Blossom Me .... Florida	—	$5		Southern Tracks 2000
1/21/89	75	5		4 Homeless People .... Cannonball	—	$5		Southern Tracks 2005
				HIGHFILL, George '87				
				Born in Fort Smith, Arkansas; raised in Stigler, Oklahoma. Singer/songwriter.				
7/18/87	69	4		1 Waitin' Up .... West Texas	—	$4		Warner 28312
10/31/87	72	4		2 Mad Money .... Nickels And Dimes	—	$4		Warner 28177

DEBUT	PEAK	WKS	Gold	A-side (Chart Hit)	B-side	Pop	$	Pic	Label & Number

HIGHWAY 101 ★196★   '87
Group formed in Los Angeles: **Paulette Carlson** (vocals, guitar; born on 10/11/53), Jack Daniels (guitar; born on 10/27/49), Curtis Stone (bass; born on 4/3/50) and Scott "Cactus" Moser (drums; born on 5/3/57). Stone is the son of **Cliffie Stone**. Carlson left in late 1990; replaced by Nikki Nelson (born on 1/3/69). CMA Awards: 1988 & 1989 Vocal Group of the Year. Also see **Tomorrow's World**.

1) Somewhere Tonight   2) Who's Lonely Now   3) Cry, Cry, Cry

Debut	Peak	Wks	Gold	#	A-side	B-side	Pop	$	Pic	Label & Number
1/10/87	4	24		1	The Bed You Made For Me	S:4 / A:4 I'm Gonna Run Through The Wind	—	$4		Warner 28483
5/23/87	2¹	23		2	Whiskey, If You Were A Woman	S:❶¹ I'll Take You (Heartache And All)	—	$4		Warner 28372
9/26/87	❶²	23		3	Somewhere Tonight	S:3 Are You Still Mine	—	$4		Warner 28223
2/13/88	❶¹	19		4	Cry, Cry, Cry	S:2 One Step Closer	—	$4	■	Warner 28105
6/18/88	❶¹	20		5	(Do You Love Me) Just Say Yes	S:2 I'll Be Missing You	—	$4	■	Warner 27867
10/22/88+	5	19		6	All The Reasons Why	S:6 Higher Ground	—	$4		Warner 27735
2/11/89	7	18		7	Setting Me Up — first recorded by Dire Straits on their 1979 Dire Straits album	Long Way Down	—	$4		Warner 27581
6/17/89	6	21		8	Honky Tonk Heart	Desperate Road	—	$4		Warner 22955
10/7/89+	❶¹	26		9	Who's Lonely Now	Don't It Make Your Mama Cry	—	$4		Warner 22779
2/10/90	4	26		10	Walkin', Talkin', Cryin', Barely Beatin' Broken Heart	Sweet Baby James	—	$4	■	Warner 19968 (v)
5/26/90	11	21		11	This Side Of Goodbye	If Love Had A Heart	—	$4	■	Warner 19829 (v)
9/22/90	14	20		12	Someone Else's Trouble Now	The Bed You Made For Me	—	$4	■	Warner 19593 (v)
4/13/91	14	20		13	Bing Bang Boom	Baby, I'm Missing You	—	$4	■	Warner 19346 (v)
9/14/91	31	20		14	The Blame	River Of Tears	—	$4		Warner 19203
1/11/92	22	20		15	Baby, I'm Missing You	Desperate	—	$4		Warner 19043
5/23/92	54	7		16	Honky Tonk Baby	Storm Of Love	—	$4		Warner 18878
10/2/93	67	2		17	You Baby You	You Are What You Do	—	$4		Liberty 17497

HILKA   '79
Born Hilka Maria Cornelius in Germany; raised in Salt Lake City. Female singer.

10/13/79	89	3		1	I Just Wonder Where He Could Be Tonight — HILKA & JEBRY (Jebry Lee Briley)	(And) Robin Danced	—	$6		IBC 0004
2/9/80	96	2		2	(I'm Just The) Cuddle Up Kind	Here Comes The Dawn	—	$6		IBC 0006

HILL, Billy — see BILLY

HILL, Faith   ★103★   '94
Born on 9/21/67 in Jackson, Mississippi. Adopted at less than a week old and raised as Audrey Faith Perry in Star, Mississippi. Began singing in church at age three. Moved to Nashville in 1987. Briefly married to musician Daniel Hill in the late 1980s (took his last name). Married **Tim McGraw** on 10/6/96. CMA Award: 2000 Female Vocalist of the Year. Also see **Hope**.

1) Breathe   2) It's Your Love   3) The Way You Love Me   4) Wild One   5) This Kiss

Debut	Peak	Wks	Gold	#	A-side	B-side	Pop	$	Pic	Label & Number
10/16/93+	❶⁴	20		1	Wild One	Go The Distance	—	$4	■	Warner 18411 (v)
2/12/94	❶¹	20		2	Piece Of My Heart — #12 Pop hit for Big Brother & The Holding Company (Janis Joplin) in 1968	I Would Be Stronger Than That	115	$4	■	Warner 18261 (v)
6/4/94	35	12		3	But I Will	Life's Too Short To Love Like That	—	$4	■	Warner 18179 (v)
9/24/94	2²	20		4	Take Me As I Am — #1-4 from the album Take Me As I Am on Warner 45389	—				album cut
8/5/95	5	20		5	Let's Go To Vegas	S:8 You Will Be Mine	122	$4	■	Warner 17817 (v)
11/11/95+	❶³	20		6	It Matters To Me	S:❶¹⁰ Keep Walkin' On (w/Shelby Lynne)	74	$4	■	Warner 17718 (v)
2/24/96	3	20		7	Someone Else's Dream	—				album cut
7/13/96	6	20		8	You Can't Lose Me	—				album cut
10/19/96+	8	20		9	I Can't Do That Anymore — #5-9 from the album It Matters To Me on Warner 45872	Take Me As I Am	—	$4		Warner 17531
5/10/97	❶⁶	20	▲	10	It's Your Love — TIM McGRAW with Faith Hill	S:❶¹² She Never Lets It Go To Her Heart (McGraw)	7	$4	■	Curb 73019 (v)
2/28/98	❶³	25	▲	11	This Kiss	S:❶²¹ Better Days	7	$4	★	Warner 17247 (v)
5/30/98	3	20		12	Just To Hear You Say That You Love Me — FAITH HILL (With Tim McGraw)	—				album cut
5/30/98	69	5		13	One Heart At A Time — GARTH BROOKS, BILLY DEAN, FAITH HILL, OLIVIA NEWTON-JOHN, NEAL McCOY, MICHAEL McDONALD, VICTORIA SHAW, BRYAN WHITE	S:5 (same version)	56	$4	■	Atlantic 84117
9/12/98	❶¹	21		14	Let Me Let Go		33			album cut
1/16/99	12	20		15	Love Ain't Like That		68			album cut
5/8/99	4	24		16	The Secret Of Life — #11-16 (except #13) from the album Faith on Warner 46790		46			album cut
10/9/99	❶⁶	28	●	17	Breathe	S:❶¹² It All Comes Down To Love	2⁵	$4	★	Warner 16884 (v)
11/20/99+	6	45		18	Let's Make Love — FAITH HILL with Tim McGraw	There Will Come A Day	54	$4		Warner 16792
11/27/99+	❶⁴	38		19	The Way You Love Me	S:❶¹⁵ Never Gonna Be Your Lady	6	$4	★	Warner 16818 (v)
11/27/99	68	1		20	It Will Be Me	—				album cut
11/27/99	69	1		21	I Got My Baby — also see #24 below	—				album cut
11/27/99	74	1		22	If I'm Not In Love	—				album cut

DEBUT	PEAK	WKS	Gold	A-side (Chart Hit) .... B-side	Pop	$	Pic	Label & Number
				HILL, Faith — Cont'd				
10/28/00	59	9		23 There Will Come A Day .... —				album cut
				also see #29 below				
11/25/00	63	3		24 I Got My Baby .... [R] —				album cut
12/9/00	26	6		25 Where Are You Christmas? .... [X]	65			album cut
				from the movie *Dr. Seuss' How The Grinch Stole Christmas* starring Jim Carrey (soundtrack on Interscope 490765)				
1/13/01	3	20		26 If My Heart Had Wings .... It Will Be Me	39	$4		Warner 16773
5/26/01	11	20		27 There You'll Be .... S:10 Breathe	10	$4		Warner 16739
				from the movie *Pearl Harbor* starring Ben Affleck				
9/29/01	35	12		28 The Star Spangled Banner	118	$10	★	Warner (no number)
				recorded at the 2000 Super Bowl; released as a promotional CD single only				
9/29/01	36	8		29 There Will Come A Day ....[R]				album cut
				#17-24, 26 & 29 from the album *Breathe* on Warner 47373				
				HILL, Goldie '53				
				Born Argolda Voncile Hill on 1/11/33 in Karnes County, Texas. Married Carl Smith on 9/19/57. Known as "The Golden Hillbilly."				
1/10/53	●3	9		1 **Let The Stars Get In My Eyes** .... J:●3 / S:4 Waiting For A Letter		$25		Decca 28473
				GOLDIE HILL (The Golden Hillbilly)				
				answer to "Don't Let The Stars Get In Your Eyes" by Slim Willet				
7/3/54	4	21		2 Looking Back To See .... J:4 / S:5 / A:5 I Miss You So		$20		Decca 29145
				GOLDIE HILL – JUSTIN TUBB				
1/8/55	11	2		3 Sure Fire Kisses .... A:11 / S:13 Fickle Heart		$20		Decca 29349
				JUSTIN TUBB – GOLDIE HILL				
3/26/55	14	2		4 Are You Mine .... S:14 Ko Ko Mo (I Love You So)		$20		Decca 29411
				RED SOVINE – GOLDIE HILL				
2/23/59	17	4		5 Yankee, Go Home .... What's Happened To Us		$15		Decca 30826
				Red Sovine (narration)				
4/6/68	73	2		6 Lovable Fool .... Making Plans		$10		Epic 10296
				GOLDIE HILL SMITH				
				HILL, Kim '94				
				Born on 12/30/63 in Starkville, Mississippi.				
4/2/94	68	6		Janie's Gone Fishin' .... Natural Thing		$4	▪	BNA 62768 (v)
				HILL, Tiny '46				
				Born Harry Hill on 7/19/06 in Sullivan Township, Illinois. Died in 1972 (age 66). Nicknamed "Tiny" because of his weight (350 pounds).				
1/26/46	3	4		1 Sioux City Sue .... I'll Keep On Lovin' You [N]	—	$20		Mercury 2024
1/10/48	5	1		2 Never Trust A Woman .... Behind The Eight Ball [N]	—	$20		Mercury 6062
				TINY HILL And the Cactus Cutups				
2/3/51	7	2		3 Hot Rod Race .... S:7 Lovebug Itch [N]	29	$30		Mercury 5547-X45
				original version of **Charlie Ryan**'s 1960 hit "Hot Rod Lincoln"				
3/24/51	10	1		4 I'll Sail My Ship Alone .... J:10 Back In Your Own Backyard		$30		Mercury 5508-X45
				HILL CITY '85				
				Group from Fort Worth, Texas.				
8/10/85	86	3		I'd Do It In A Heartbeat .... The Ghost Of Brandy Jones		$5		Moon Shine 3040
				HILLMAN, Chris '89				
				Born on 12/4/44 in Los Angeles. Member of **The Byrds** from 1964-68 and the **Flying Burrito Brothers** from 1968-72. Formed The Desert Rose Band in 1986.				
9/29/84	81	6		1 Somebody's Back In Town .... Desert Rose		$5		Sugar Hill 4105
4/27/85	77	5		2 Running The Roadblocks .... Turn Your Radio On		$5		Sugar Hill 4106
4/29/89	6	21		3 You Ain't Going Nowhere .... Don't You Hear Jerusalem Moan		$4		Universal 66006
				CHRIS HILLMAN & ROGER McGUINN				
				written by **Bob Dylan**; #74 Pop hit for **The Byrds** in 1968				
				HILTON, Denny '81				
3/28/81	84	2		1 Layin' Low .... Delores		$6		Oak 1027
2/13/82	92	2		2 How'd You Get So Good .... —		$6		Rosebridge 0014
2/5/83	88	2		3 Sharing The Night Together .... —		$6		Rosebridge 010
				HINOJOSA, Tish '90				
				Born Leticia Hinojosa on 2/6/55 in San Antonio, Texas. Singer/songwriter.				
6/14/86	80	3		1 I'll Pull You Through .... Too Soon To Say It's Too Late		$4		MCA/Curb 52823
				TISH HINOJOSA/CRAIG DILLINGHAM				
12/23/89+	75	4		2 Til U Love Me Again .... —		$4		A&M 1468
				HITCHCOCK, Stan '69				
				Born on 3/21/36 in Kansas City, Missouri. Singer/songwriter. Worked as a DJ on KWTO and KTTS in Springfield, Missouri. Moved to Nashville in 1962. Own TV series in the mid-1960s. Former program director for Country Music Television.				
				1)Honey, I'm Home 2)Call Me Gone 3)Dixie Belle				
9/16/67	54	6		1 She's Looking Good .... Have I Stayed Away Too Long		$8		Epic 10182
12/9/67	66	2		2 Rings .... Such A Little Teardrop		$8		Epic 10246
5/18/68	57	8		3 I'm Easy To Love .... Don't Do Like I've Done (Do Like I Say)		$8		Epic 10307
10/19/68	60	4		4 The Phoenix Flash .... My Memory		$8		Epic 10388
10/11/69	17	11		5 Honey, I'm Home .... Slip-Up And She'll Slip Away		$8		Epic 10525
4/18/70	46	6		6 Call Me Gone .... Your Kind Of Man		$8		Epic 10586
10/17/70	54	7		7 Dixie Belle .... I Did It All For You		$6		GRT 23
3/13/71	59	7		8 At Least Part Of The Way .... The Shadow Of Your Smile		$6		GRT 39
7/14/73	65	7		9 The Same Old Way .... Lonely Wine		$6		Cinnamon 759
12/8/73	91	4		10 Half-Empty Bed .... When Love Was At Its Best		$6		Cinnamon 770
3/9/74	80	7		11 I'm Free .... Oklahoma Wind		$6		Cinnamon 782

DEBUT	PEAK	WKS	Gold	A-side (Chart Hit) ... B-side	Pop	$	Pic	Label & Number
				HITCHCOCK, Stan — Cont'd				
6/3/78	100	2		12 Falling .... Only One	—	$6		MMI 1024
				#13 Pop hit for LeBlanc & Carr in 1978				
3/10/79	85	3		13 Finders Keepers Losers Weepers	—	$6		MMI 1028
				STAN HITCHCOCK with Sue Richards				
4/11/81	81	4		14 She Sings Amazing Grace .... Janet	—	$5		Ramblin' 1711
	★384★			**HOBBS, Becky** '83				
				Born Rebecca Ann Hobbs on 1/24/50 in Bartlesville, Oklahoma. Singer/songwriter/guitarist.				
				1)Let's Get Over Them Together 2)Jones On The Jukebox 3)Hottest "Ex" In Texas				
12/23/78+	95	5		1 The More I Get The More I Want .... I Feel Like Breakin' Somebody's Heart Tonight	—	$5		
6/30/79	44	11		2 I Can't Say Goodbye To You .... What Love Is All About	—	$5		Mercury 55049
12/8/79+	52	9		3 Just What The Doctor Ordered .... You Can't Tie A Ramblin' Man Down	—	$5		Mercury 55062
5/3/80	79	6		4 I'm Gonna Love You Tonight (Like There's No Tomorrow) .... Good-For-Nothin' Guitar Pickin' Man	—	$5		Mercury 57010
10/11/80	87	2		5 I Learned All About Cheatin' From You .... Stay Away From Married Men	—	$5		Mercury 57020
2/7/81	84	4		6 Honky-Tonk Saturday Night .... Old Memories	—	$5		Mercury 57033
6/25/83	10	18		7 Let's Get Over Them Together .... In Love	—	$5		Mercury 57041
				MOE BANDY (Featuring Becky Hobbs)				Columbia 03970
6/2/84	46	10		8 Oklahoma Heart .... Fool Me Once, Fool Me Twice	—	$4		Liberty 1520
9/8/84	64	6		9 Pardon Me (Haven't We Loved Somewhere Before) .... Anyway	—	$4		EMI America 8224
12/8/84	77	6		10 Wheels In Emotion .... Slow Dancin' Lies	—	$4		EMI America 8247
6/22/85	37	12		11 Hottest "Ex" In Texas .... The Lover Of You	—	$4		EMI America 8273
3/5/88	31	19		12 Jones On The Jukebox .... S:13 I'm-A-Gonna Get To You	—	$4	■	MTM 72104
7/9/88	43	10		13 They Always Look Better When They're Leavin' .... S:18 Mama Was A Working Man	—	$4		MTM 72109
10/8/88	53	9		14 Are There Any More Like You (Where You Came From) .... Cowgirl's Heart	—	$4		MTM 72114
8/5/89	39	11		15 Do You Feel The Same Way Too? .... Jones On The Jukebox	—	$4		RCA 8974
				HOBBS, Bud '49				
				Born in San Francisco. Singer/songwriter/guitarist.				
				BUD HOBBS with His Trail Herders:				
9/25/48	13	1		1 Lazy Mary .... J:13 You're Mine Tonight (But Will You Be Mine Tomorrow)	—	$25		MGM 10206
1/29/49	12	4		2 I Heard About You .... J:12 / S:13 Oklahoma Sweetheart	—	$25		MGM 10305
5/21/49	12	1		3 Candy Kisses .... J:12 / S:13 Tennessee Border	—	$25		MGM 10366
				HOBBS, Lou '81				
				Born in Cape Girardeau, Missouri.				
3/7/81	79	3		1 Loving You Was All I Ever Needed .... It's All Your Fault	—	$6		Kik 902
9/5/81	93	2		2 We're Building Our Love On A Rock .... Run Right Back	—	$6		Kik 911
				HOBBS, Pam '81				
2/7/81	85	4		1 Have You Ever Seen The Rain	—	$5		50 States 79
				#8 Pop hit for **Creedence Clearwater Revival** in 1971				
5/2/81	88	2		2 I Thought I Heard You Calling My Name .... Love Is Not A Game	—	$5		50 States 81
9/26/81	93	2		3 You're The Only Dancer	—	$5		50 States 84
				HOFFMAN, Billy '00				
				Born in Arkansas; raised in Poteau, Oklahoma. Singer/songwriter/guitarist.				
6/17/00	69	1		1 Perfect Night	—			album cut
12/2/00	75	1		2 You're The Ticket	—			album cut
				above 2 from the album *All I Wanted Was You* on Critter 10012				
				HOGSED, Roy '48				
				Born on 12/24/19 in Flippin, Arkansas. Died in March 1978 (age 58).				
8/21/48	15	1		1 Cocaine Blues .... J:15 Fishtail Boogie	—	$25		Capitol 40120
				HOKUM, Suzi Jane '67				
9/9/67	51	7		1 Here We Go Again .... Hangin' On	—	$7		LHI 17018
				VIRGIL WARNER & SUZI JANE HOKUM				
2/24/68	65	4		2 Storybook Children .... Lady Bird	—	$7		LHI 1204
				VIRGIL WARNER & SUZI JANE HOKUM				
				#54 Pop hit for **Billy Vera** & Judy Clay in 1968				
8/30/69	75	2		3 Reason To Believe .... I'll Never Fall In Love Again	—	$7		LHI 14
				#19 Pop hit for Rod Stewart in 1993				
				HOLDEN, Rebecca '89				
				Born on 6/12/58 in San Antonio. Singer/actress. Played "April Curtis" on TV's *Knight Rider*.				
11/25/89	82	2		1 The Truth Doesn't Always Rhyme .... If You Ever Wanna Try Again	—	$6		Tra-Star 1229
12/16/89	78	4		2 License To Steal	—	$6		Tra-Star 1234
				HOLLADAY, Dave '86				
12/13/86	83	4		Now She's In Paris .... I. O. Blues	—	$5		Step One 365
				HOLLAND, Greg '94				
				Born on 2/22/67 in Douglas, Georgia.				
8/6/94	63	5		1 Let Me Drive .... Up To Feelin' Down	—	$4	■	Warner 18152 (v)
11/12/94	66	5		2 When I Come Back (I Wanna Be My Dog) .... Oh To Be The One	—	$4	■	Warner 18033 (v)
				HOLLIER, Jill '86				
				Born in Port Arthur, Texas. Singer/songwriter.				
11/15/86	79	2		1 Sweet Time .... Magic Of The Moment	—	$4		Warner 28559
8/12/89	83	3		2 If It Wasn't For The Heartache .... Empty Arms	—	$4		Warner 22966
				from the movie *Pink Cadillac* starring Clint Eastwood				

DEBUT	PEAK	WKS	Gold	A-side (Chart Hit)	B-side	Pop	$	Pic	Label & Number
				HOLLIER, Jill — Cont'd					
12/23/89+	81	4		3 Mama's Daily Bread .... Cry So Easy	—		$4		Warner 22700
				HOLLOWELL, Terri '79					
				Born on 7/2/56 in Jeffersonville, Indiana. Female singer.					
6/17/78	81	4		1 Happy Go Lucky Morning .... Say What I Feel Tonight	—		$6		Con Brio 134
9/23/78	76	4		2 Strawberry Fields Forever .... If You Wanna Love Me, It's Okay	—		$6		Con Brio 139
				#8 Pop hit for The Beatles in 1967					
12/23/78+	76	6		3 Just Stay With Me .... Sweet Virginia Morning	—		$6		Con Brio 144
3/24/79	35	11		4 May I .... I Wasn't There	—		$6		Con Brio 150
7/21/79	56	8		5 It's Too Soon To Say Goodbye .... Holding It Back, Letting You Go	—		$6		Con Brio 156
				HOLLY, Doyle '73					
				Born Doyle Floyd Hendricks on 6/30/36 in Perkins, Oklahoma. Singer/songwriter/bassist. Member of **The Buckaroos** from 1963-70.					
11/18/72	63	6		1 My Heart Cries For You .... All The Way From Alabama	—		$5		Barnaby 5004
				#2 Pop hit for Guy Mitchell in 1951					
6/16/73	29	14		2 Queen Of The Silver Dollar .... Take A Walk In The Country	—		$5		Barnaby 5018
10/6/73	17	13		3 Lila .... Darling, Are You Ever Coming Home	—		$5		Barnaby 5027
3/2/74	58	9		4 Lord How Long Has This Been Going On .... January Bittersweet Jones	—		$5		Barnaby 5030
				DOYLE HOLLY And The Vanishing Breed					
6/15/74	75	8		5 A Rainbow In My Hand .... Free Love	—		$5		Barnaby 602
9/7/74	69	6		6 Just Another Cowboy Song .... January Bittersweet Jones	—		$5		Barnaby 605
11/16/74+	53	11		7 Richard And The Cadillac Kings .... She Can't Make The Hurt Go Away	—		$5		Barnaby 608
				HOLM, Johnny '77					
				Born in Fargo, North Dakota. Singer/songwriter/guitarist.					
10/1/77	100	2		Lightnin' Bar Blues .... Ain't It A Beauty	—		$6		ASI 1012
				HOLMES, Monty '98					
				Born in Lubbock, Texas. Singer/songwriter.					
1/21/89	82	3		1 A Way To Survive	—		$6		Ashley 1001
5/16/98	43	16		2 Why'd You Start Lookin' So Good	—					album cut
8/29/98	53	12		3 Alone	—					album cut
11/14/98	59	5		4 Leave My Mama Out Of This	—					album cut
				above 3 from the album *All I Ever Wanted* on Bang II 2000					
				HOLT, Darrell '88					
				Former singer with the group **Sweetwater**.					
12/12/87+	57	10		1 Catch 22	—		$6		Anoka 222
3/26/88	58	9		2 I Can't Take Her Anywhere	—		$6		Anoka 221
10/1/88	66	6		3 I'd Throw It All Away	—		$6		Anoka 224
2/11/89	71	5		4 Only The Strong Survive	—		$6		Anoka 225
				#4 Pop hit for Jerry Butler in 1969					
				HOLY, Steve '02					
				Born in 1972 in Dallas. Singer/songwriter.					
10/16/99+	29	20		1 Don't Make Me Beg	—		★		album cut (v)
				later released as the B-side of #2 below					
4/22/00	24	24		2 Blue Moon .... S:9 Don't Make Me Beg	—		$4	★	Curb 73087 (v)
11/11/00+	24	25		3 The Hunger	—					album cut
7/28/01+	0⁵	41		4 Good Morning Beautiful						album cut
				all of above from the album *Blue Moon* on Curb 77972					
				HOMER AND JETHRO '53					
				Comedy duo from Knoxville, Tennessee: Henry "Homer" Haynes (guitar) and Kenneth "Jethro" Burns (mandolin). Homer was born on 7/27/20; died of a heart attack on 8/7/71 (age 51). Jethro was born on 3/10/20; died of cancer on 2/4/89 (age 68). Regulars on the WLS *National Barn Dance* from 1950-58. Elected to the Country Music Hall of Fame in 2001. Also see **Some Of Chet's Friends**.					
3/26/49	14	1		1 I Feel That Old Age Creeping On .... J:14 Goodbye Ole Booze [N]	—		$25		King 749
8/27/49	9	1		2 Baby, It's Cold Outside .... S:9 Country Girl [N]	22		$20		RCA Victor 21-0078
				HOMER and JETHRO with June Carter					
				45 rpm: 48-0075; from the movie *Neptune's Daughter* starring Esther Williams					
11/5/49	14	1		3 Tennessee Border—No. 2 .... J:14 I'm Gettin' Older Every Day [N]	—		$20		RCA Victor 21-0110
				45 rpm: 48-0113; parody of "Tennessee Border" by **Red Foley**					
5/23/53	2²	9		4 (How Much Is) That Hound Dog In The Window .... S:2 / J:3 / A:10 Pore Ol' Koo-Liger [N]	17		$20		RCA Victor 5280
				parody of "The Doggie In The Window" by **Patti Page**					
8/14/54	14	1		5 Hernando's Hideaway .... S:14 Wanted [N]	—		$20		RCA Victor 5788
				parody of the #2 Pop hit for Archie Bleyer in 1954					
10/19/59	26	3		6 The Battle Of Kookamonga .... Waterloo [N]	14		$15		RCA Victor 7585
				parody of "The Battle Of New Orleans" by **Johnny Horton**					
4/18/64	49	1		7 I Want To Hold Your Hand .... She Loves You [N]	—		$15	■	RCA Victor 8345
				parody of the #1 Pop hit for The Beatles in 1964					
				HOMESTEADERS, The '66					
				Vocal trio led by Jerry Rivers.					
10/15/66	44	7		1 Show Me The Way To The Circus .... Country Joined The Country Club	—		$10		Little Darlin' 0010
8/3/68	67	2		2 Gonna Miss Me .... Homewrecker	—		$10		Little Darlin' 0045

DEBUT	PEAK	WKS	Gold	A-side (Chart Hit)	B-side	Pop	$	Pic	Label & Number
				HOOD, Bobby '79					
				Born in Alabama. Gospel singer.					
				1) Easy 2) I've Got An Angel (That Loves Me Like The Devil) 3) It Takes One To Know One					
4/1/78	91	3		1 Come On In	Southern Ladies Kind Of Man	—	$5		Plantation 169
8/5/78	60	7		2 I've Got An Angel (That Loves Me Like The Devil)	Tennessee Frost	—	$6		Chute 101
10/14/78	87	3		3 Come To Me		—	$6		Chute 102
2/24/79	85	3		4 Slow Tunes And Promises	You Gotta Go Down	—	$6		Chute 004
8/11/79	45	8		5 Easy	No Love Lost	—	$6		Chute 008
12/8/79	72	5		6 It Takes One To Know One	After The Rain	—	$6		Chute 009
3/22/80	75	4		7 When She Falls		—	$6		Chute 010
9/13/80	85	3		8 Mexico Winter		—	$6		Chute 015
11/29/80	89	3		9 Pick Up The Pieces Joanne		—	$6		Chute 016
9/26/81	74	4		10 Woman In My Heart		—	$6		Chute 018
				HOOD, Ray '00					
				Born in Alabama. Singer/songwriter/guitarist.					
5/4/96	73	3		1 Freedom		—			album cut
				from the album *Back To Back Heartaches* on Caption/Curb 5561					
11/11/00	67	1		2 Critical List		—			album cut
				from the album *Ray Hood* on Caption 5570					
				HOOSIER HOT SHOTS '46					
				Novelty group from Fort Wayne, Indiana: brothers Paul "Hezzie" (song whistle, washboard, drums, alto horn; born on 4/11/05; died on 4/27/80, age 75) and Kenneth "Rudy" Triesch (banjo, guitar, bass horn; born on 9/13/03; died on 9/17/87, age 84), with Charles Otto "Gabe" Ward (clarinet, saxophone, fife; born on 11/26/04; died on 1/14/92, age 87) and Frank Kettering (banjo, guitar, flute, piano, bass fiddle; born on 1/1/09; died in 6/73, age 64). Regulars on the WLS *National Barn Dance* from 1933-42. Also appeared in several western movies.					
6/17/44	3	2		1 She Broke My Heart In Three Places	Don't Change Horses [N]	21	$20		Decca 4442
1/26/46	3	10		2 Someday (You'll Want Me To Want You)	You Two-Timed Me One Time Too Often [N]	12	$20		Decca 18738
				HOOSIER HOT SHOTS and SALLY FOSTER					
				#1 Pop hit for **Vaughn Monroe** in 1949					
2/9/46	2¹	16		3 Sioux City Sue	There's A Tear In My Beer Tonight [N]	—	$20		Decca 18745
				HOOSIER HOT SHOTS And TWO TON BAKER					
				#3 Pop hit for **Bing Crosby** & The Jesters in 1946					
				HOPE '96					
				All-star collaboration for the T.J. Martell Foundation (cancer research): **John Berry**, **Terri Clark**, **Vince Gill**, **Faith Hill**, **Tracy Lawrence**, **Little Texas**, **Neal McCoy**, **Tim McGraw**, **Lorrie Morgan**, **Marty Stuart**, **Travis Tritt** and **Trisha Yearwood**.					
5/4/96	57	4		Hope	S:17 (different version)	—	$4	■	Giant 17669 (v)
				HORN, DeAnne '78					
2/18/78	97	2		1 I Just Want To Love You	I'm A Country Girl (Livin' In A City World)	—	$6		Chartwheel 102
7/8/78	100	1		2 I Know		—	$6		Chartwheel 108
				HORN, James T. '97					
				Born on 8/29/66 in Foreman, Arkansas. Singer/songwriter/guitarist.					
11/8/97	72	1		Texas Diary	Geronimo	—	$4	■	Curb/Univer. 56096 (v)
				HORNSBY, Bruce, And The Range '87					
				Born on 11/23/54 in Williamsburg, Virginia. Singer/songwriter/pianist. Won the 1986 Best New Artist Grammy Award. Charted 10 pop hits from 1986-95.					
3/14/87	38	10		Mandolin Rain	The Red Plains (live)	4	$4	■	RCA 5087
				HORTON, Billie Jean '61					
				Born Billie Jean Jones Eshlimar in Bossier City, Louisiana. Married to **Hank Williams** from 10/18/52 until his death on 1/1/53. Married to **Johnny Horton** from 9/26/53 until his death on 11/5/60.					
8/28/61	29	3		Ocean Of Tears	Don't Take His Love	—	$15		20th Fox 266
	★238★			**HORTON, Johnny** '59					
				Born on 4/30/25 in Los Angeles; raised in Tyler, Texas. Died in a car crash on 11/5/60 (age 35). Singer/songwriter/guitarist. Known as "The Singing Fisherman." Joined the *Louisiana Hayride* in 1951. Married to **Billie Jean Horton**, widow of **Hank Williams**, from 9/26/53 until his death on 11/5/60.					
				1) The Battle Of New Orleans 2) North To Alaska 3) When It's Springtime In Alaska (It's Forty Below)					
5/5/56	9	12		1 Honky-Tonk Man	A:9 / S:14 I'm Ready If You're Willing	—	$30		Columbia 21504
				also see #13 below					
9/8/56	7	13		2 I'm A One-Woman Man	A:7 / S:9 / J:9 I Don't Like I Did	—	$25		Columbia 21538
2/23/57	11	5		3 I'm Coming Home	A:11 / S:15 I Got A Hole In My Pirogue	—	$25		Columbia 40813
5/27/57	9	1		4 The Woman I Need	J:9 She Knows Why	—	$25		Columbia 40919
9/29/58	8	8		5 All Grown Up	A:8 Counterfeit Love	—	$20		Columbia 41210
				also see #14 below					
1/12/59	❶¹	23		6 When It's Springtime In Alaska (It's Forty Below)	Whispering Pines	—	$15	□	Columbia 41308
4/27/59	❶¹⁰	21	●	7 The Battle Of New Orleans	All For The Love Of A Girl	❶⁶	$15	■	Columbia 41339
				original melody written in celebration of the final battle of the War of 1812; a promotional 4-page fold-out picture sleeve was also issued					
9/7/59	10	9		8 Johnny Reb /		54			
9/7/59	19	7		9 Sal's Got A Sugar Lip		81	$15		Columbia 41437
3/28/60	6	15		10 Sink The Bismarck	The Same Old Tale The Crow Told Me	3	$15	■	Columbia 41568
				inspired by the movie starring Kenneth Moore, which is based on the sinking of the German battleship in World War II					
11/14/60+	❶⁵	22		11 North To Alaska	The Mansion You Stole	4	$15	■	Columbia 41782
				from the movie starring John Wayne					
4/24/61	9	8		12 Sleepy-Eyed John	They'll Never Take Her Love From Me	54	$15		Columbia 41963
4/14/62	11	12		13 Honky-Tonk Man	Words [R]	96	$15		Columbia 42302
				new version of #1 above					
2/9/63	26	5		14 All Grown Up	I'm A One-Woman Man [R]	—	$12	■	Columbia 42653
				same version as #5 above					

DEBUT	PEAK	WKS	Gold	A-side (Chart Hit)	B-side	Pop	$	Pic	Label & Number
				HORTON, Steven Wayne		**'89**			
				Born in Memphis. Singer/guitarist.					
8/19/89	68	5		Roll Over .... I've Been Stung		—	$4		Capitol 44350
				HOSFORD, Larry		**'75**			
				Born in 1943 in Salinas, California. Singer/songwriter/guitarist.					
12/7/74+	62	8		1 Long Distance Kisses .... Long Line To Chicago		—	$5		Shelter 40312
4/26/75	78	6		2 Everything's Broken Down .... Long Line To Chicago		—	$5		Shelter 40381
				HOUSE, David		**'82**			
				Born in Lubbock, Texas. Singer/songwriter.					
6/26/82	96	2		1 Everything's All Right .... Should've Been Chasin' My Dreams		—	$5		Door Knob 177
10/9/82	88	2		2 Little White Lies .... Maybe Now We Can Be Friends		—	$5		Door Knob 183
				HOUSE, James		**'95**			
				Born on 3/22/55 in Sacromento, California. Singer/songwriter/guitarist.					
3/25/89	25	14		1 Don't Quit Me Now .... Call It In The Air		—	$4		MCA 53510
7/15/89	52	6		2 That'll Be The Last Thing .... Lucinda		—	$4		MCA 53669
10/21/89	48	11		3 Hard Times For An Honest Man .... Born Ready		—	$4		MCA 53731
12/8/90	60	9		4 You Just Get Better All The Time .... I Ain't Like That Anymore		—	$4		MCA 53934
8/27/94	52	8		5 A Real Good Way To Wind Up Lonesome .... That's Something		—	$4	▪	Epic 77610 (v)
11/26/94+	25	20		6 Little By Little .... Take Me Away		—	$4	▪	Epic 77752 (v)
4/29/95	6	20		7 This Is Me Missing You .... S:16 Take Me Away		—	$4	▪	Epic 77870 (v)
9/16/95	49	11		8 Anything For Love .... Silence Makes A Lonesome Sound		—	$4	▪	Epic 77982 (v)
8/24/96	69	1		9 Little Deuce Coupe .... (no B-side)		—	$5	▪	River North 3014
				THE BEACH BOYS Featuring James House					
				#15 Pop hit for The Beach Boys in 1963					

HOUSTON, David ★46★   '67

Born on 12/9/38 in Bossier City, Louisiana. Died of a brain aneurysm 11/30/93 (age 54). Singer/songwriter/guitarist. Acted in the movies *Cottonpickin' Chicken-Pluckers* and *Horse Soldiers*. Joined the *Grand Ole Opry* in 1972.

1)Almost Persuaded 2)Baby, Baby (I Know You're A Lady) 3)You Mean The World To Me 4)My Elusive Dreams 5)With One Exception

DEBUT	PEAK	WKS		A-side	B-side	Pop	$	Pic	Label & Number
10/19/63	2¹	18		1 Mountain Of Love .... Angeline		132	$10		Epic 9625
3/28/64	17	15		2 Chickashay /		—			Epic 9658
3/7/64	37	6		3 Passing Through		—	$10		Epic 9690
7/11/64	11	17		4 One If For Him, Two If For Me .... Your Memories		—	$10		Epic 9720
10/10/64	17	14		5 Love Looks Good On You .... My Little Lady		—	$10		Epic 9746
1/30/65	18	17		6 Sweet, Sweet Judy .... Too Many Times (Away From You)		—	$10		Epic 9831
9/11/65	3	18		7 Livin' In A House Full Of Love .... Cowpoke		117	$10		Epic 9884
3/5/66	47	2		8 Sammy .... I'll Take You Home Again, Kathleen		—	$10	▪	Epic 9884
6/25/66	❶⁹	25		9 Almost Persuaded .... We Got Love		24	$10	☐	Epic 10025
12/24/66+	3	16		10 A Loser's Cathedral /		135			
12/10/66+	14	12		11 Where Could I Go? (But To Her)		133	$10		Epic 10102
4/29/67	❶¹	18		12 With One Exception .... Sweet, Sweet Judy		—	$10	▪	Epic 10154
7/15/67	❶²	18		13 My Elusive Dreams .... Marriage On The Rocks		89	$10		Epic 10194
				DAVID HOUSTON and TAMMY WYNETTE					
9/23/67	❶²	17		14 You Mean The World To Me .... Don't Mention Tomorrow		75	$10	▪	Epic 10224
1/20/68	11	14		15 It's All Over .... Together We Stand (Divided We Fall)		—	$10		Epic 10274
				DAVID HOUSTON & TAMMY WYNETTE					
3/9/68	❶¹	14		16 Have A Little Faith .... Too Far Gone		98	$8	▪	Epic 10291
6/15/68	❶¹	16		17 Already It's Heaven .... Lighter Shade Of Blue		—	$8		Epic 10338
10/19/68	2²	14		18 Where Love Used To Live .... I Love A Rainbow		—	$8		Epic 10394
1/18/69	4	17		19 My Woman's Good To Me .... Lullaby To A Little Girl		—	$8	☐	Epic 10430
				promotional record and picture sleeve issued with **Bob Luman**'s "Come On Home And Sing The Blues To Daddy"					
6/28/69	3	16		20 I'm Down To My Last "I Love You" .... Watching My World Walk Away		—	$8		Epic 10488
11/8/69+	❶⁴	17		21 Baby, Baby (I Know You're A Lady) .... True Love's A Lasting Thing		—	$8		Epic 10539
4/4/70	3	17		22 I Do My Swinging At Home .... Then I'll Know You Care		—	$8		Epic 10596
8/8/70	6	15		23 Wonders Of The Wine .... If God Can Forgive Me (Why Can't You?)		—	$8		Epic 10643
10/3/70	6	14		24 After Closing Time .... My Song Of Love		—	$8		Epic 10656
				DAVID HOUSTON AND BARBARA MANDRELL					
1/9/71	2⁴	16		25 A Woman Always Knows .... The Rest Of My Life		—	$8		Epic 10696
6/12/71	9	13		26 Nashville .... That's Why I Cry		—	$8		Epic 10748
10/9/71	10	14		27 Maiden's Prayer /		—			
9/25/71	32	16		28 Home Sweet Home		—	$8		Epic 10778
10/2/71	20	12		29 We've Got Everything But Love .... Try A Little Harder		—	$8		Epic 10779
				DAVID HOUSTON AND BARBARA MANDRELL					
2/19/72	18	13		30 The Day That Love Walked In .... Sweet Lovin'		—	$8		Epic 10830
6/10/72	8	12		31 Soft, Sweet And Warm .... Rest Of My Life		—	$8		Epic 10870
9/16/72	24	13		32 A Perfect Match .... Almost Persuaded		—	$8		Epic 10908
				DAVID HOUSTON AND BARBARA MANDRELL					
10/14/72	41	9		33 I Wonder How John Felt (When He Baptized Jesus) .... Will The Circle Be Unbroken?		—	$8		Epic 10911

DEBUT	PEAK	WKS	Gold	A-side (Chart Hit)	B-side	Pop	$	Pic	Label & Number
				HOUSTON, David — Cont'd					
12/30/72+	2²	16		34 Good Things ....The Love She Gives		—	$8		Epic 10939
6/2/73	3	14		35 She's All Woman ....Sweet Lovin'		—	$7		Epic 10995
11/3/73	22	11		36 The Lady Of The Night ....Thank You Teardrop		—	$7		Epic 11048
12/22/73+	6	16		37 I Love You, I Love You ....Let's Go Down Together		—	$7		Epic 11068
				DAVID HOUSTON and BARBARA MANDRELL					
3/30/74	33	12		38 That Same Ol' Look Of Love ....Clinging Vine		—	$7		Epic 11096
5/25/74	40	12		39 Lovin' You Is Worth It.................................How Can It Be Wrong (When It Feels So Right)		—	$7		Epic 11120
				DAVID HOUSTON and BARBARA MANDRELL					
8/10/74	14	16		40 Ten Commandments Of Love ....Try A Little Harder		—	$7		Epic 20005
				DAVID HOUSTON and BARBARA MANDRELL					
				#22 Pop hit for Harvey & The Moonglows in 1958					
9/14/74	9	15		41 Can't You Feel It ....I Walk And I Walk And I Walk		—	$7		Epic 50009
3/1/75	36	10		42 A Man Needs Love ....Flower Of Love		—	$7		Epic 50066
6/14/75	40	10		43 I'll Be Your Steppin' Stone...Then I'll Know You Care		—	$7		Epic 50113
9/27/75	69	6		44 Sweet Molly ....The Old Blind Fiddler (Houston)		—	$7		Epic 50134
				DAVID HOUSTON AND CALVIN CRAWFORD					
11/1/75	35	10		45 The Woman On My Mind..I Can't Sit Still		—	$7		Epic 50156
2/7/76	51	9		46 What A Night ....From The Bottom Of My Heart		—	$7		Epic 50186
9/25/76	24	12		47 Come On Down (To Our Favorite Forget-About-Her Place) ....Me And Susan Wright		—	$7		Epic 50275
4/30/77	33	9		48 So Many Ways..Touch My World		—	$6		Gusto 156
				#6 Pop hit for Brook Benton in 1959					
8/6/77	68	6		49 Ain't That Lovin' You Baby ....Love Is A Miracle		—	$6		Gusto 162
				#3 R&B hit for Jimmy Reed in 1956					
11/19/77	98	1		50 The Twelfth Of Never ....Barroom Champagne		—	$6		Gusto 168
				#9 Pop hit for Johnny Mathis in 1957					
12/24/77+	56	9		51 It Started All Over Again ....Touch My World		—	$6		Gusto 172
4/8/78	72	5		52 No Tell Motel ....I Hate To Tell Baby A Lie		—	$6		Gusto 184
6/24/78	51	9		53 Waltz Of The Angels		—	$8		Colonial 101
12/9/78+	46	10		54 Best Friends Make The Worst Enemies ....There Won't Be A Wedding		—	$5		Elektra 45552
4/21/79	33	10		55 Faded Love And Winter Roses ....Beyond The Blue Horizon		—	$5		Elektra 46028
8/18/79	57	8		56 Let Your Love Fall Back On Me ....Take Me To Your Heart		—	$6		Derrick 126
11/10/79	60	8		57 Here's To All The Too Hard Working Husbands (In The World) ....Next Sunday I'm Gonna Be Saved		—	$6		Derrick 127
5/31/80	64	7		58 You're The Perfect Reason ....We Couldn't Make It Love		—	$6		Country Int'l. 145
9/13/80	78	4		59 Sad Love Song Lady ....Thanks For Being You And Loving Me		—	$6		Country Int'l. 148
5/9/81	69	6		60 Texas Ida Red		—	$6		Excelsior 1012
4/22/89	85	2		61 A Penny For Your Thoughts Tonight Virginia		—	$6		Country Int'l. 220
				HOWARD, Chuck		**'80**			
				Born in Flat Fork, Kentucky. Died on 8/15/83 (age 45). Singer/songwriter/producer.					
8/23/80	66	7		I've Come Back (To Say I Love You One More Time) ....Everyone But Me		—	$4		Warner/Curb 49509
				HOWARD, Eddy		**'47**			
				Born on 9/12/14 in Woodland, California. Died on 5/23/63 (age 48). Charted 42 pop hits from 1946-55.					
8/9/47	5	1		Ragtime Cowboy Joe ....On The Old Spanish Trail	16	$15		Majestic 1155
				from the movie *Hello Frisco, Hello* starring Alice Faye; #16 Pop hit for **The Chipmunks** in 1959					
				HOWARD, Harlan		**'71**			
				Born on 9/8/27 in Lexington, Kentucky; raised in Detroit. Died on 3/3/2002 (age 74). Legendary songwriter. Married to **Jan Howard** from 1957-67. Inducted into the Country Music Hall of Fame in 1997.					
4/10/71	38	15		Sunday Morning Christian...................................That Little Boy Who Follows Me		—	$10		Nugget 1058
				HOWARD, Jan ★172★		**'67**			
				Born Lula Grace Johnson on 3/13/30 in West Plains, Missouri. Singer/songwriter. Moved to Los Angeles in 1953. Married to **Harlan Howard** from 1957-67. Toured with **Bill Anderson**, **Johnny Cash** and **Tammy Wynette**. Joined the *Grand Ole Opry* in 1971.					
				1)For Loving You 2)If It's All The Same To You 3)Someday We'll Be Together 4)Dis-Satisfied 5)Evil On Your Mind					
1/11/60	13	12		1 The One You Slip Around With.........................I Wish I Could Fall In Love Again		—	$15		Challenge 59059
5/30/60	26	2		2 Wrong Company ....We'll Never Love Again		—	$15		Challenge 9071
				WYNN STEWART AND JAN HOWARD					
11/16/63	27	3		3 I Wish I Was A Single Girl Again.................................The Saddest Part Of All		—	$12		Capitol 5035
1/16/65	25	13		4 What Makes A Man Wander?..Slipping Back To You		—	$10		Decca 31701
2/19/66	29	8		5 I Know You're Married (But I Love You Still) /		—			
3/12/66	44	1		6 Time Out		—	$10		Decca 31884
				BILL ANDERSON AND JAN HOWARD (above 2)					
4/23/66	5	20		7 Evil On Your Mind ....Crying For Love		—	$10		Decca 31933
10/8/66	10	13		8 Bad Seed ....You Go Your Way (I'll Go Crazy)		—	$10		Decca 32016
3/11/67	32	11		9 Any Old Way You Do ....Your Ole Handy Man		—	$10		Decca 32096
7/22/67	26	10		10 Roll Over And Play Dead ....You And Me And Tears And Roses		—	$10		Decca 32154
10/28/67	❶⁴	20		11 For Loving You ....The Untouchables [S]		—	$8		Decca 32197
				BILL ANDERSON And JAN HOWARD					
3/9/68	16	13		12 Count Your Blessings, Woman ....But Not For Love My Dear		—	$8		Decca 32269
8/10/68	27	11		13 I Still Believe In Love ....Life's That Way		—	$8		Decca 32357
11/23/68+	15	14		14 My Son ....The Tip Of My Fingers		—	$8		Decca 32407

DEBUT	PEAK	WKS	Gold	A-side (Chart Hit) .... B-side	Pop	$	Pic	Label & Number
				HOWARD, Jan — Cont'd				
3/8/69	24	11		15 When We Tried .... I Hurt All Over	—	$8		Decca 32447
9/20/69	20	9		16 We Had All The Good Things Going .... I'll Go Where You Go	—	$8		Decca 32543
11/15/69+	2¹	15		17 If It's All The Same To You .... I Thank God For You	—	$8		Decca 32511
				BILL ANDERSON and JAN HOWARD				
3/21/70	26	10		18 Rock Me Back To Little Rock .... Hello Stranger	—	$8		Decca 32636
6/20/70	4	15		19 Someday We'll Be Together .... Who Is The Biggest Fool	—	$8		Decca 32689
				BILL ANDERSON and JAN HOWARD				
				#1 Pop hit for Diana Ross & The Supremes in 1969				
11/14/70	64	5		20 The Soul You Never Had .... I Have Your Love	—	$8		Decca 32743
2/13/71	56	10		21 Baby Without You /	—			
		2		22 Marriage Has Ruined More Good Love Affairs		$8		Decca 32778
10/9/71	4	15		23 Dis-Satisfied .... Knowing You're Mine	—	$8		Decca 32877
				BILL ANDERSON AND JAN HOWARD				
12/25/71+	36	14		24 Love Is Like A Spinning Wheel .... I Never Once Stopped Loving You	—	$8		Decca 32905
5/6/72	43	10		25 Let Him Have It .... Remember The Good	—	$8		Decca 32955
3/31/73	74	2		26 Too Many Ties That Bind .... Everybody Knows I Love You	—	$6		MCA 40020
11/9/74	96	4		27 Seein' Is Believin' .... My Kind Of People	—	$6		GRT 010
4/30/77	70	6		28 I'll Hold You In My Heart (Till I Can Hold You In My Arms) .... I Thought I Had Him	—	$6		Con Brio 118
10/1/77	65	7		29 Better Off Alone .... My Coloring Book	—	$6		Con Brio 125
4/22/78	93	3		30 To Love A Rolling Stone .... Thought I Had Him	—	$6		Con Brio 132
				HOWARD, Jim '64				
7/18/64	38	9		Meet Me Tonight Outside Of Town .... Too Much Taking-Not Enough Giving	—	$15		Del-Mar 1013
				HOWARD, Randy '88				
				Born on 5/9/50 in Macon, Georgia. Singer/songwriter/guitarist.				
4/9/83	84	4		1 All-American Redneck .... (dirty version)	—	$4	■	Warner 29781
				"live" recording				
1/9/88	66	5		2 Ring Of Fire	—	$4		Atlantic Amer. 99387
				HOWARD, Rebecca Lynn '00				
				Born on 4/24/79 in Salyersville, Kentucky.				
7/17/99	65	8		1 When My Dreams Come True .... S:14 Out Here In The Water	—	$4	★	MCA Nash. 172120 (v)
2/26/00	54	12		2 Out Here In The Water .... Was It As Hard To Be Together	—	$4		MCA Nashville 172144
9/9/00	71	4		3 I Don't Paint Myself Into Corners .... Was It Hard To Be Together	—	$4		MCA Nashville 172171
				HUBBLE, Hal '78				
				Born in 1940 in Indianapolis.				
11/25/78	76	6		My Pulse Pumps Passions .... Before I Leave This Land	—	$5		50 States 66
				HUDSON, Helen '79				
				Born on 1/19/53 in Sydney, Australia. Singer/model.				
5/26/79	91	5		Nothing But Time .... One More Guitar	—	$6		Cyclone 102
				HUDSON, Larry G. '79				
				Born on 12/19/49 in Hawkinsville, Georgia; raised in Unadilla, Georgia. Singer/songwriter/guitarist.				
6/12/76	89	4		1 Singing A Happy Song .... Legend In My Time	—	$6		Aquarian 605
10/14/78	37	10		2 Just Out Of Reach Of My Two Open Arms .... Warm And Tender Love	—	$5		Lone Star 702
				#24 Pop hit for Solomon Burke in 1961				
1/27/79	31	10		3 Loving You Is A Natural High .... You Don't Know Me	—	$5		Lone Star 706
3/15/80	34	10		4 I Can't Cheat .... Just For The Heaven Of It	—	$4		Mercury 57015
8/16/80	39	9		5 I'm Still In Love With You .... Easy Come, Easy Go	—	$4		Mercury 57029
				HUGHES, Hollie '87				
				Born in Carrollton, Texas. Daughter of Luv Records owner Kent Hughes.				
2/14/87	75	3		67 Miles To Cow Town .... I'm In Love	—	$7		Luv 130
				HUGHES, Joel '82				
				Born on 10/2/55 in Jenkins, Kentucky.				
3/13/82	75	4		Handy Man	—	$6		Sunbird 7569
				#2 Pop hit for Jimmy Jones in 1960				
				HUMMERS, The '73				
7/21/73	38	7		1 Old Betsy Goes Boing, Boing, Boing .... One Good Thing About Being Down [N]	104	$6		Capitol 3646
				adapted from a Mazda jingle				
6/1/74	91	4		2 Julianna .... Big Toy Train	—	$6		Capitol 3870
				HUMMON, Marcus '96				
				Born on 12/28/60 in Fort Wayne, Indiana. Singer/songwriter.				
3/16/96	73	6		God's Country .... Somebody's Leaving	—	$4	■	Columbia 78251 (v)
				HUMPERDINCK, Engelbert '83				
				Born Arnold George Dorsey on 5/2/36 in Madras, India; raised in Leicester, England. Starred in his own musical variety TV series in 1970. Charted 23 pop hits from 1967-83.				
1/8/77	40	12	●	1 After The Lovin' .... Let's Remember The Good Times	8	$5		Epic/MAM 50270
7/2/77	93	3		2 Goodbye My Friend	97	$5		Epic/MAM 50365
1/27/79	93	4		3 This Moment In Time .... And The Day Begins	58	$5		Epic/MAM 50632
5/14/83	39	14		4 Til You And Your Lover Are Lovers Again .... What Will I Write	77	$4		Epic 03817

DEBUT	PEAK	WKS	Gold	A-side (Chart Hit)	B-side	Pop	$	Pic	Label & Number
	★233★			**HUNLEY, Con** '81 Born Conrad Hunley on 4/9/45 in Fountain City, Tennessee. Singer/songwriter/pianist. 1) What's New With You 2) Oh Girl 3) Week-End Friend 4) I've Been Waiting For You All Of My Life 5) You've Still Got A Place In My Heart					
1/29/77	96	4		1 Pick Up The Pieces	(It Looks Like) A Good Night For Drinking	—	$5		Prairie Dust 7608
4/16/77	75	6		2 I'll Always Remember That Song	Never Felt More Like Dying (Than I Do Now)	—	$5		Prairie Dust 7614
7/23/77	67	7		3 Breaking Up Is Hard To Do	Woman To Man, Man To Woman	—	$5		Prairie Dust 7618
2/4/78	34	10		4 Cry Cry Darling	Just Hangin' On	—	$4		Warner 8520
5/13/78	13	12		5 Week-End Friend	Only The Strong Survive	—	$4		Warner 8572
10/7/78	14	13		6 You've Still Got A Place In My Heart	Honky Tonk Heart	—	$4		Warner 8671
1/27/79	14	14		7 I've Been Waiting For You All Of My Life	Just Hangin' On	—	$4		Warner 8723
				#48 Pop hit for Paul Anka in 1981					
5/26/79	20	12		8 Since I Fell For You	Cry Cry Darling	—	$4		Warner 8812
				#4 Pop hit for Lenny Welch in 1963					
11/3/79+	20	14		9 I Don't Want To Lose You	That's All That Matters	—	$4		Warner 49090
3/8/80	19	12		10 You Lay A Whole Lot Of Love On Me	When It Hurts You Most	—	$4		Warner 49187
8/16/80	19	13		11 They Never Lost You	Lover's Lullaby	—	$4		Warner 49528
12/20/80+	11	16		12 What's New With You	This Ol' Cowboy's Going Home	—	$4		Warner 49613
8/29/81	17	15		13 She's Steppin' Out	Ask Any Woman	—	$4		Warner 49800
1/9/82	20	14		14 No Relief In Sight	Table For One	—	$4		Warner 49887
5/22/82	12	15		15 Oh Girl	Tonight I Took Your Memory Off The Wall	—	$4		Warner 50058
				Oak Ridge Boys (backing vocals); #1 Pop hit for The Chi-Lites in 1972					
10/9/82	43	9		16 Confidential	I Still Have Dreamin'	—	$4		Warner 29902
4/30/83	42	10		17 Once You Get The Feel Of It	It's Tearin' Me Up, To Lay Your Memory Down	—	$4		MCA 52208
9/3/83	84	4		18 Satisfied Mind	Let Me Love You Once Before You Go	—	$4		MCA 52259
				Porter Wagoner (guest vocal)					
3/17/84	75	7		19 Deep In The Arms Of Texas	Never Felt More Like Dying	—	$5		Prairie Dust 84110
12/15/84+	57	11		20 All American Country Boy	Sad But True	—	$4		Capitol 5428
3/16/85	54	8		21 I'd Rather Be Crazy	Sad But True	—	$4		Capitol 5457
7/13/85	49	9		22 Nobody Ever Gets Enough Love	Sad But True	—	$4		Capitol 5485
11/30/85+	48	15		23 What Am I Gonna Do About You	Lord, She Sure Looks Good Tonight	—	$4		Capitol 5525
5/31/86	49	13		24 Blue Suede Blues	Sad But True	—	$4		Capitol 5586
9/27/86	55	9		25 Quittin' Time	Late At Night	—	$4		Capitol 5631
				HUNNICUTT, Ed '84 Born on 7/29/51 in Troy, New York; raised in Columbia, South Carolina.					
5/21/83	69	6		1 Fade To Blue	Gettin' It Right With You	—	$4		MCA 52207
10/8/83	59	7		2 My Angel's Got The Devil In Her Eyes	Home Is Where The Heart Is	—	$4		MCA 52262
3/17/84	41	9		3 In Real Life	There Oughta Be A Law	—	$4		MCA 52353
				HUNT, John — see BACKTRACK					
				HUNTER, Jesse '94 Born on 1/14/59 in Shelby County, Tennessee. Male singer.					
3/5/94	56	9		1 Born Ready	L. A. Freeway	—	$4	■	BNA 62735 (v)
6/18/94	65	8		2 By The Way She's Lookin'	Long Steady Rain	—	$4		BNA 62857
10/22/94	42	15		3 Long Legged Hannah (From Butte Montana)	(dance mix)	—	$4		BNA 62976
				HUNTER, Tommy '67 Born on 3/20/37 in London, Ontario, Canada. Singer/songwriter/guitarist. Regular on CBC-TV series Country Hoedown from 1956-65. Hosted own CBC-TV series from 1965-89. Known as "Canada's Country Gentleman."					
9/9/67	66	3		Mary In The Morning	The Battle Of The Little Big Horn	—	$8		Columbia 44234
				#27 Pop hit for Al Martino in 1967					
				HURLEY, Libby '88 Born in Clarksville, Arkansas. Female singer.					
10/3/87	60	6		1 Don't Get Me Started	The Last One To Know	—	$4		Epic 07366
1/16/88	43	10		2 You Just Watch Me	The Last One To Know	—	$4		Epic 07650
4/23/88	59	8		3 Don't Talk To Me	I'm Turning Blue	—	$4		Epic 07771
				HURT, Charlotte '78					
9/16/78	85	5		The Price Of Borrowed Love Is Just To High	Wheel Of Fortune	—	$7		Compass 0020
				HURT, Cindy '82 Born in 1956 in Mundelein, Illinois. Singer/actress. Toured with the musical Sophisticated Ladies in 1980.					
3/21/81	74	5		1 Single Girl	Dark Moon	—	$5		Churchill 7767
				#12 Pop hit for Sandy Posey in 1966					
6/6/81	56	8		2 Headin' For A Heartache		—	$5		Churchill 7772
9/5/81	46	10		3 Dreams Can Come In Handy	Headin' For A Heartache	—	$5		Churchill 7777
1/30/82	28	13		4 Don't Come Knockin'	Love Me Up	—	$5		Churchill 94000
6/12/82	35	10		5 Talk To Me Loneliness	Dreams Can Come In Handy	—	$5		Churchill 94004
11/20/82	67	8		6 What's Good About Goodbye	You Make It Feel Like Love	—	$5		Churchill 94010
7/2/83	65	6		7 I'm In Love All Over Again	Dark Moon	—	$5	■	Churchill 94013
				HUSKEY, Kenni '71 Born Nora Carolyn Huskey on 12/2/54 in Newport, Arkansas. Female singer.					
10/23/71	71	6		1 A Living Tornado	Only You Can Break My Heart	—	$6		Capitol 3184
1/29/72	74	2		2 Within My Loving Arms	(Bring Back My) Peace Of Mind	—	$6		Capitol 3229
				written by Buck Owens					

DEBUT	PEAK	WKS	Gold	A-side (Chart Hit)	B-side	Pop	$	Pic	Label & Number

HUSKY, Ferlin ★70★ '57 *Merchant Marines*
Born on 12/3/25 in Flat River, Missouri. Singer/songwriter/guitarist. Spent five years in U.S. Merchant Marines during World War II. After discharge, worked clubs in Bakersfield. Recorded as "Terry Preston" in the early 1950s. Acted in several movies. Also recorded as **Simon Crum**. Also see **Jean Shepard**.

1) Wings Of A Dove 2) Gone 3) A Dear John Letter 4) Country Music Is Here To Stay 5) Just For You

DEBUT	PEAK	WKS		A-side	B-side	Pop	$	Pic	Label & Number
7/25/53	❶⁶	23		1 **A Dear John Letter** .... S:❶⁶/J:❶⁴/A:2 *I'd Rather Die Young* (Shepard)		4	$25		Capitol 2502
				JEAN SHEPARD with FERLIN HUSKEY					
				#44 Pop hit for **Pat Boone** in 1960					
10/10/53	4	7		2 **Forgive Me John** .... S:4/J:6/A:8 *My Wedding Ring* (Shepard)		—	$25		Capitol 2586
				JEAN SHEPARD with FERLIN HUSKEY					
1/15/55	6	10		3 **I Feel Better All Over (More Than Anywhere's Else)** /		A:6/S:15	—		Capitol 3001
1/15/55	7	8		4 **Little Tom**		A:7	$25		
				FERLIN HUSKEY (above 2)					
4/16/55	5	15		5 **Cuzz Yore So Sweet** .... A:5 *My Gallina* [N]		—	$25		Capitol 3063
				SIMON CRUM					
5/28/55	14	1		6 **I'll Baby Sit With You** .... S:14 *She's Always There (When I Come Home)*		—	$25		Capitol 3097
				FERLIN HUSKEY and His Hush Puppies					
2/23/57	❶¹⁰	27		7 **Gone** .... S:❶¹⁰/A:❶⁹/J:❶⁵ *Missing Persons*		4	$20		Capitol 3628
				originally recorded by Husky in 1952 as by Terry Preston on Capitol 2298 ($30)					
7/1/57	8	13		8 **A Fallen Star** /		S:8/A:8	47		Capitol 3742
7/15/57	12	1		9 **Prize Possession** A:12		—	$20		Capitol 4046
10/27/58	23	1		10 **I Will** .... *All Of The Time*		—	$20		Capitol 4073
11/3/58+	2³	24		11 **Country Music Is Here To Stay** *Stand Up, Sit Down, Shut Your Mouth* [N]		—	$20		Capitol 4123
				SIMON CRUM					
2/16/59	14	12		12 **My Reason For Living** .... *Wrong*		—	$20		Capitol 4186
6/1/59	11	10		13 **Draggin' The River** .... *Sea Sand*		—	$20		Capitol 4186
11/16/59	21	8		14 **Black Sheep** .... *I'll Always Return*		—	$20		Capitol 4278
9/5/60	❶¹⁰	36		15 **Wings Of A Dove** .... *Next To Jimmy*		12	$15		Capitol 4406
10/9/61	23	1		16 **Willow Tree** .... *Take A Look*		—	$15		Capitol 4594
1/27/62	13	10		17 **The Waltz You Saved For Me** .... *Out Of A Clear Blue Sky*		94	$12	■	Capitol 4650
				#4 Pop hit for Wayne King in 1931					
5/26/62	16	11		18 **Somebody Save Me** .... *Just Another Lonely Night*		—	$12		Capitol 4721
9/22/62	28	1		19 **Stand Up** .... *It Scares Me*		—	$12		Capitol 4779
12/1/62	21	2		20 **It Was You** .... *Near You*		—	$12		Capitol 4853
2/22/64	13	21		21 **Timber I'm Falling** .... *Don't Count The Diamonds*		—	$12		Capitol 5111
4/10/65	46	7		22 **True True Lovin'** .... *Love Built The House*		—	$12		Capitol 5355
				also see #42 below					
12/11/65	48	2		23 **Money Greases The Wheels** .... *Lasting Love*		—	$12		Capitol 5522
6/4/66	27	5		24 **I Could Sing All Night** .... *What Does Your Conscience Say To You*		—	$12		Capitol 5615
7/9/66	17	12		25 **I Hear Little Rock Calling** .... *Stand Beside Me*		—	$12		Capitol 5679
12/3/66+	4	17		26 **Once** .... *Why Do I Put Up With You*		—	$12		Capitol 5775
				FERLIN HUSKY And The Hushpuppies:					
4/1/67	37	11		27 **What Am I Gonna Do Now** .... *General "G"*		—	$12		Capitol 5852
7/15/67	14	15		28 **You Pushed Me Too Far** .... *The Bridge I Have Never Crossed*		—	$12		Capitol 5938
12/23/67+	4	18		29 **Just For You** .... *Don't Hurt Me Anymore*		—	$12	■	Capitol 2048
				FERLIN HUSKY					
5/25/68	26	10		30 **I Promised You The World** .... *You Should Live My Life*		—	$12	■	Capitol 2154
10/19/68	25	10		31 **White Fences And Evergreen Trees** .... *Love's Been Good To Me*		—	$10		Capitol 2288
3/15/69	33	10		32 **Flat River, MO.** .... *One Life To Live*		—	$10		Capitol 2411
6/21/69	16	14		33 **That's Why I Love You So Much** .... *Forever Yours*		—	$10		Capitol 2512
				FERLIN HUSKY:					
11/22/69	21	10		34 **Every Step Of The Way** .... *That's What I'd Do*		—	$10		Capitol 2666
5/16/70	11	13		35 **Heavenly Sunshine** .... *All Her Little Loving Ways*		—	$10		Capitol 2793
9/12/70	45	9		36 **Your Sweet Love Lifted Me** .... *You're The Happy Song I Sing*		—	$10		Capitol 2882
12/26/70+	14	11		37 **Sweet Misery** .... *Because You're Mine*		—	$10		Capitol 2999
3/27/71	28	11		38 **One More Time** .... *Don't Let The Good Life Pass You By*		—	$10		Capitol 3069
9/11/71	45	9		39 **Open Up The Book (And Take A Look)** .... *Even If It's True*		—	$10		Capitol 3165
4/22/72	39	10		40 **Just Plain Lonely** .... *Always In All Ways*		—	$10		Capitol 3308
9/9/72	53	8		41 **How Could You Be Anything But Love** .... *I'd Walk A Mile For A Smile*		—	$10		Capitol 3415
1/13/73	35	10		42 **True True Lovin'** .... *Legend In My Time* [R]		—	$7		ABC 11345
				new version of #22 above					
4/28/73	46	9		43 **Between Me And Blue** .... *My Special Angel*		—	$7		ABC 11360
8/11/73	75	4		44 **Baby's Blue** .... *One*		—	$7		ABC 11381
11/3/73+	17	13		45 **Rosie Cries A Lot** .... *Shoes*		—	$7		ABC 11395
5/4/74	26	15		46 **Freckles And Polliwog Days** .... *Everything Is Nothing Without You*		—	$7		ABC 11432
9/21/74	60	7		47 **A Room For A Boy...Never Used** .... *Ring Of String*		—	$7		ABC 12021
12/28/74+	34	11		48 **Champagne Ladies And Blue Ribbon Babies** .... *I Feel Better All Over*		—	$7		ABC 12048
4/19/75	37	11		49 **Burning** .... *A Touch Of Yesterday*		—	$7		ABC 12085
10/4/75	74	5		50 **She's Not Yours Anymore** /		—	$7		
9/27/75	90	6		51 **An Old Memory (Got In My Eye)**		—	$7		ABC/Dot 17574

161

DEBUT	PEAK	WKS	Gold	A-side (Chart Hit)	B-side	Pop	$	Pic	Label & Number
				HUTCHENS, The Bros. '95					
				Trio of brothers from Sandy Rudge, North Carolina: Barry, Bill and Bryan Hutchens.					
10/7/95	56	7		Knock, Knock	She Just Wants To Dance	—	$4		Atlantic 87092
				HUTCHINS, Loney '87					
				Born on 11/7/46 in Sullivan County, Tennessee.					
7/4/87	92	2		Still Dancing		—	$5	■	ARC 0005
				I					
				IFIELD, Frank '66					
				Born on 11/30/37 in Coventry, England; raised in New South Wales, Australia. Singer/songwriter/actor.					
8/27/66	42	6		1 No One Will Ever Know	I'm Saving All My Love (For You)	—	$8		Hickory 1397
10/22/66	28	14		2 Call Her Your Sweetheart	Give Myself A Party	—	$8		Hickory 1411
12/23/67+	68	4		3 Oh, Such A Stranger	Then You Can Tell Me Goodbye	—	$8		Hickory 1486
				written by Don Gibson					
10/5/68	67	3		4 Good Morning, Dear	Innocent Years	—	$8		Hickory 1514
				IGLESIAS, Julio '84					
				Born on 9/23/43 in Madrid. Spanish singer. CMA Award: Vocal Duo of the Year (with **Willie Nelson**).					
3/10/84	**①**²	20	▲	1 To All The Girls I've Loved Before	I Don't Want To Wake You (Iglesias)	5	$4	■	Columbia 04217
				JULIO IGLESIAS & WILLIE NELSON					
9/17/88	8	19		2 Spanish Eyes	S:2 Ole Buttermilk Sky	—	$4		Columbia 08066
				WILLIE NELSON (with Julio Iglesias)					
				#15 Pop hit for Al Martino in 1966					
				INDIANA '87					
4/18/87	85	2		Midnite Rock		—	$6		Killer 1005
				INGLE, Red, & The Natural Seven '47					
				Born Ernest Ingle on 11/7/06 in Toledo, Ohio. Died on 9/7/65 (age 58). Comic singer/violinist/clarinetist/saxophonist. Formed group The Natural Seven: Luke "Red" Roundtree (guitar), Noel Boggs (steel guitar), Herman "The Hermit" Snyder (banjo), Art Wenzel (accordion), Joseph "Country" Washbourne (suitcase), Rull Hall (bass) and Ray Hagan (drums).					
6/21/47	2¹¹	18		Temptation (Tim-Tayshun)					
				(I Love You) For Sentimental Reasons (I Love You) For Seventy Mental Reasons [N]	**①**¹		$15		Capitol 412
				Cinderella G. Stump (Jo Stafford) and Red Ingle (vocals); hillbilly version of song that was a #3 Pop hit for Bing Crosby in 1934 and a #27 Pop hit for The Everly Brothers in 1961					
				INGLES, David '69					
				Born in Cleveland, Oklahoma; raised in Bristow, Oklahoma. Gospel singer.					
11/29/69	72	2		Johnny Let The Sunshine In	You're A Part Of This Man	—	$8		Capitol 2648
				INGRAM, Jack '97					
				Born on 11/15/70 in Houston. Singer/songwriter/guitarist.					
7/19/97	51	10		1 Flutter		—			album cut
				from the album Livin' Or Dyin' on Rising Tide 53046					
10/23/99	64	1		2 How Many Days		—			album cut
				from the album Hey You on Lucky Dog 69850					
				INGRAM, James — see **ROGERS, Kenny**					
				INMAN, Autry '53					
				Born Robert Autry Inman on 1/6/29 in Florence, Alabama. Died on 9/6/88 (age 59). Singer/songwriter/guitarist.					
7/11/53	4	4		1 That's All Right	J:3 Uh-Huh Honey	—	$25		Decca 28629
4/13/63	22	3		2 The Volunteer	Unlucky Am I	—	$10		Sims 131
11/2/68	14	15		3 Ballad Of Two Brothers	Don't Call Me (I'll Call You)	48	$8		Epic 10389
				patriotic-styled narrative, featuring strains of "Battle Hymn Of The Republic"					
				INMAN, Jerry '79					
12/28/74+	95	2		1 You're The One	Leah	—	$5		Chelsea 3006
8/26/78	95	2		2 Why, Baby, Why	Gonna Save It For My Baby	—	$4		Elektra 45508
2/17/79	94	2		3 Why Don't We Lie Down And Talk It Over	Gonna Save It For My Baby	—	$4		Elektra 46006
				IRBY, Jerry '48					
				Born on 10/20/17 in New Braunfels, Texas. Died in December 1983 (age 66). Singer/songwriter/guitarist.					
6/19/48	11	2		1 Cryin' In My Beer	J:11 Answer To Drivin' Nails In My Coffin	—	$20		MGM 10151
7/3/48	10	1		2 Great Long Pistol	J:10 49 Women	—	$20		MGM 10188
				JERRY IRBY And His Texas Ranchers (above 2)					
				IRVING, Lonnie '60					
				Born 6/11/32 in Stoneville, North Carolina. Died of leukemia on 12/2/60 (age 28).					
3/14/60	13	15		Pinball Machine	I Got Blues On My Mind	—	$25		Starday 486
				first released on the Lonnie Irving label in 1959 ($50)					
				ISAACS, Sonya '99					
				Born on 7/22/75 in LaFollette, Tennessee. Female singer/guitarist.					
8/21/99	54	10		1 On My Way To You		—		★	album cut
				later released as the B-side of #2 below					
1/22/00	46	18		2 I've Forgotten How You Feel	S:15 On My Way To You	—	$4	★	Lyric Street 64038
8/19/00	64	6		3 Barefoot In The Grass		—			album cut
				all of above from the album Sonya Isaacs on Lyric Street 65004					

DEBUT	PEAK	WKS	Gold	A-side (Chart Hit)	B-side	Pop	$	Pic	Label & Number
				ISAACSON, Peter '84 Born in Vermont. Singer/songwriter.					
7/23/83	76	5		1 Froze In Her Line Of Fire .... Baby Your Love		—	$7		Union Station 1002
11/26/83	61	6		2 Don't Take Much		—	$7		Union Station 1004
3/24/84	93	2		3 No Survivors		—	$7		Union Station 1005
5/12/84	71	5		4 It's A Cover Up .... It Didn't Have Anything To Do With Love		—	$7		Union Station 1006
	★385★			**IVES, Burl** '62 Born on 6/14/09 in Huntington Township, Illinois. Died of cancer on 4/14/95 (age 85). Actor/singer. Acted in several movies.					
2/12/49	13	1		1 Lavender Blue (Dilly Dilly) .... S:13 Billy Boy BURL IVES with Captain Stubby & The Buccaneers #4 Pop hit for Sammy Kaye in 1949; #3 Pop hit for Sammy Turner in 1959		16	$20		Decca 24547
5/21/49	8	5		2 Riders In The Sky (Cowboy Legend) J:8 / S:15 Wayfaring Stranger / Woolie Boogie Bee #30 Pop hit for The Ramrods in 1961		21	$15		Columbia 38445
7/26/52	6	4		3 Wild Side Of Life J:6 / S:10 It's So-Long And Good-Bye To You BURL IVES and GRADY MARTIN And His Slew Foot Five		30	$20		Decca 9-28055
2/3/62	2²	17		4 A Little Bitty Tear .... Shanghied		9	$10		Decca 31330
4/28/62	9	13		5 Funny Way Of Laughin' .... Mother Wouldn't Do That		10	$10		Decca 31371
8/11/62	3	11		6 Call Me Mr. In-Between .... What You Gonna Do, Leroy?		19	$10		Decca 31405
12/1/62+	12	7		7 Mary Ann Regrets .... How Do You Fall Out Of Love		39	$10		Decca 31433
9/17/66	47	6		8 Evil Off My Mind .... A Taste Of Heaven		—	$8		Decca 31997
2/4/67	72	2		9 Lonesome 7-7203 .... Hollow Words (Empty Phrases)		—	$8		Decca 32078
				IVIE, Roger — see SILVER CREEK					
				IVORY JACK '80					
2/9/80	78	4		1 Made In The USA .... Borrowed Angel		—	$6		NSD 36
5/9/81	81	4		2 Love Signs .... I Came So Close To Calling You Last Night		—	$6		Country Int'l. 154

J

JACK AND TRINK '78
Husband-and-wife duo of Jack and Trink Ruthven.

9/9/78	93	4		I'm Tired Of Being Me .... Ain't No Way Of Gettin... *That'd Be All Right (?)*			$6		NSD 4

JACKSON, Alan ★38★ '92
Born on 10/17/58 in Newnan, Georgia. Singer/songwriter/guitarist. Former car salesman and construction worker. Formed own band, Dixie Steel. Signed to Glen Campbell's publishing company in 1985. Joined the Grand Ole Opry in 1991. CMA Award: 1995 Entertainer of the Year.

1) Where Were You (When The World Stopped Turning) 2) Chattahoochee 3) Where I Come From 4) Little Bitty 5) Don't Rock The Jukebox

DEBUT	PEAK	WKS	Gold	A-side	B-side	Pop	$	Pic	Label & Number
10/21/89	45	12		1 Blue Blooded Woman .... Home issued on blue vinyl		—	$10		Arista 9892
1/13/90	3	26		2 Here In The Real World .... Blue Blooded Woman			$4		Arista 9922
6/23/90	3	21		3 Wanted .... Dog River Blues			$4	■	Arista 2032 (v)
10/6/90	2²	20		4 Chasin' That Neon Rainbow .... Short Sweet Ride			$4		Arista 2095
1/19/91	0²	20		5 I'd Love You All Over Again .... Home			$4		Arista 2166
5/18/91	0³	20		6 Don't Rock The Jukebox .... Home			$4		Arista 2220 (v)
8/31/91	0¹	20		7 Someday .... From A Distance			$4		Arista 12335
12/14/91	41	6		8 I Only Want You For Christmas .... Merry Christmas To Me [X] also see #28 & #38 below			$4		Arista 12372 (v)
1/11/92	0¹	20		9 Dallas .... Just Playin' Possum			$4		Arista 12385
4/25/92	3	20		10 Midnight In Montgomery .... Working Class Hero			$4		Arista 12418
7/25/92	0²	20		11 Love's Got A Hold On You .... That's All I Need To Know			$4		Arista 12447
10/24/92	0¹	20		12 She's Got The Rhythm (And I Got The Blues) .... She Likes It Too			$4		Arista 12463
2/6/93	4	20		13 Tonight I Climbed The Wall .... Up To My Ears In Tears			$4		Arista 12514
5/15/93	0⁴	20	●	14 Chattahoochee .... (club mix) CMA Award: Single of the Year; "45": Arista 12573 (B-side "I Don't Need The Booze")		46	$4	■	Arista 12573 (v)
8/28/93	75	1		15 Tropical Depression .... — from the album A Lot About Livin' (And A Little 'Bout Love) on Arista 18711			album cut		
9/18/93	2¹	20		16 Mercury Blues .... Chattahoochee (club mix) tune later used for a Ford truck commercial			$4		Arista 12607
10/30/93	64	17		17 Tequila Sunrise .... — #64 Pop hit for the Eagles in 1973; from the various artists album Common Thread: The Songs Of The Eagles on Giant 24531			album cut		
12/18/93	53	4		18 Honky Tonk Christmas .... The Angels Cried (w/Alison Krauss) [X] also see #24 below			$4		Arista 12611
1/29/94	4	20		19 (Who Says) You Can't Have It All .... If It Ain't One Thing (It's You)			$4		Arista 12649
6/18/94	0³	20		20 Summertime Blues .... Hole In The Wall #8 Pop hit for Eddie Cochran in 1958		104	$4	■	Arista 12697 (v)
8/27/94+	0¹	26		21 Gone Country .... All American Country Boy		—	$4		Arista 12775
9/3/94	0³	20		22 Livin' On Love .... Let's Get Back To Me And You		101	$4	■	Arista 12745 (v)
11/12/94	56	7		23 A Good Year For The Roses .... I've Still Got Some Hurtin' Left To Do (Jones) GEORGE JONES with Alan Jackson			$4	■	MCA 54969 (v)
12/31/94	59	1		24 Honky Tonk Christmas .... The Angels Cried [X-R]			$4		Arista 12611

Larry Cordle: Murder On Music Row (He wrote & recorded it)

DEBUT	PEAK	WKS	Gold	#	A-side (Chart Hit)	B-side	Pop	$	Pic	Label & Number
					JACKSON, Alan — Cont'd					
2/11/95	6	20		25	Song For The Life	You Can't Give Up On Love	—	$4		Arista 12792
5/13/95	●¹	20		26	I Don't Even Know Your Name	If I Had You	—	$4		Arista 12830
10/21/95	●²	20		27	Tall, Tall Trees	Home	—	$4		Arista 12879
12/23/95	48	4		28	I Only Want You For Christmas	Merry Christmas To Me [X-R]	—	$4	■	Arista 12372 (v)
12/30/95+	●¹	20		29	I'll Try /					
4/20/96	3	20		30	Home	—	$4		Arista 12942
					recorded in 1989					
6/8/96	42	12		31	Redneck Games .... S:2 NASA & Alabama & Fishing Shows (Foxworthy) [C]		66	$4	■	Warner 17648 (v)
					JEFF FOXWORTHY with Alan Jackson					
					"live" recording					
10/26/96	●³	20		32	Little Bitty	S:●⁷ Must've Had A Ball	58	$4	■	Arista Nash. 13048 (v)
12/28/96	56	3		33	Rudolph The Red-Nosed Reindeer .... We Three Kings (Star Of Wonder) (BlackHawk) [X]		—	$3		Arista Nashville 13060
1/18/97	9	20		34	Everything I Love	It's Time You Learned About Good-Bye	—	$4		Arista Nashville 13068
4/12/97	2²	20		35	Who's Cheatin' Who	S:15 Buicks To The Moon	—	$4	■	Arista Nash. 13069 (v)
7/12/97	●¹	20		36	There Goes	—	—	$4		Arista Nashville 13070
10/11/97+	2¹	20		37	Between The Devil And Me	Walk On The Rocks	—	$4		Arista Nashville 13106
12/27/97	48	2		38	I Only Want You For Christmas	Merry Christmas To Me [X-R]	—	$4		Arista 12372 (v)
12/27/97	51	3		39	A Holly Jolly Christmas .... I Only Want You For Christmas [X]		—	$4		Arista/Fox 10001
					introduced by Burl Ives in the 1964 animated TV special Rudolph The Red-Nosed Reindeer					
1/24/98	18	15		40	A House With No Curtains	—	—			album cut (v)
					from the album Everything I Love on Arista Nashville 18813					
8/1/98	3	20		41	I'll Go On Loving You	Chattahoochee	—	$4		Arista Nashville 13135
10/17/98+	●¹	20		42	Right On The Money	A Woman's Love	43	$4		Arista Nashville 13136
2/6/99	4	20		43	Gone Crazy	Amarillo	43	$4		Arista Nashville 13155
5/29/99	3	23		44	Little Man	Hurtin' Comes Easy	39	$4		Arista Nashville 13145
10/9/99	6	20		45	Pop A Top	Revenooer Man	43	$4		Arista Nashville 13183
11/6/99	63	2		46	Margaritaville		—			album cut
					ALAN JACKSON with Jimmy Buffett					
					also see #52 below					
11/13/99	71	1		47	My Own Kind Of Hat	—	—			album cut (v)
					later released as the B-side of #49 below					
11/13/99	72	1		48	She Just Started Liking Cheatin' Songs	—	—			album cut
					above 3 from the album Under The Influence on Arista Nashville 18892					
2/19/00	37	15		49	The Blues Man	My Own Kind Of Hat	—	$4		Arista Nashville 13193
3/11/00	38	20		50	Murder On Music Row		—			album cut
					GEORGE STRAIT with Alan Jackson					
					from Strait's album Latest Greatest Straitest Hits on MCA Nashville 70100					
4/29/00	●¹	27		51	It Must Be Love		37			album cut
7/15/00	74	1		52	Margaritaville	[R]	—			album cut
					ALAN JACKSON with Jimmy Buffett					
					above 2 from the album Under The Influence on Arista Nashville 18892					
10/7/00	6	20		53	www.memory /		45			
11/25/00	68	1		54	It's Alright To Be A Redneck	—	—	$4		Arista Nashville 69020
					also see #59 below					
11/25/00	72	1		55	Three Minute Positive Not Too Country Up-Tempo Love Song	—	—			album cut
11/25/00	74	1		56	Where I Come From		—			album cut
3/10/01	5	21		57	When Somebody Loves You	Meat And Potato Man	52	$4		Arista Nashville 69049
6/23/01	●³	25		58	Where I Come From	A Love Like That [R]	34	$4		Arista Nashville 69102
11/17/01	53	9		59	It's Alright To Be A Redneck	www.memory [R]	—	$4		Arista Nashville 69020
11/24/01	●⁵	20		60	Where Were You (When The World Stopped Turning)	Drive (For Daddy Gene)	28	$4		Arista Nashville 69129
					written by Jackson after the 9/11 terrorist attacks					
					JACKSON, Carl	**'84**				
					Born on 9/18/53 in Louisville, Mississippi. Bluegrass singer/songwriter/banjo player.					
11/3/84	44	15		1	She's Gone, Gone, Gone	You Made A Memory Of Me	—	$4		Columbia 04647
3/2/85	70	7		2	All That's Left For Me	I'm Beside Myself	—	$4		Columbia 04786
6/1/85	45	9		3	Dixie Train	I'm Beside Myself	—	$4		Columbia 04926
1/25/86	85	7		4	You Are The Rock (And I'm A Rolling Stone)	Tennessee Girl	—	$4		Columbia 05645
					JACKSON, Lolita	**'89**				
3/18/89	89	2			Every Time You Walk In The Room	—	—	$5		Oak 1069
					JACKSON, Nisha	**'87**				
					Black female singer. Became director of the Tennessee Big Brothers/Big Sisters program in the 1990s.					
10/24/87	81	3			Alive And Well	Going Down Slow	—	$4		Capitol 44064

DEBUT	PEAK	WKS	Gold	A-side (Chart Hit)	B-side	Pop	$	Pic	Label & Number

JACKSON, Stonewall ★92★   '59
Army & Navy

Born on 11/6/32 in Emerson, North Carolina. Singer/songwriter/guitarist. Served in the U.S. Army in 1948; served in The U.S. Navy from 1949-54. Had own log-trucking company in Georgia in 1955. Joined the *Grand Ole Opry* in 1956. Descended from General Thomas Jonathan "Stonewall" Jackson.

1) Waterloo 2) B.J. The D.J. 3) Life To Go 4) A Wound Time Can't Erase 5) Don't Be Angry

11/3/58+	2¹	23		1 Life To Go .... Misery Known As Heartache		—	$20		Columbia 41257
				written by **George Jones**					
6/8/59	●⁵	19		2 Waterloo /		4			
6/29/59	24	5		3 Smoke Along The Track		—	$15		Columbia 41393
11/23/59	29	1		4 Igmoo (The Pride Of South Central High) ... Uncle Sam And Big John Bull		95	$15		Columbia 41488
1/18/60	12	12		5 Mary Don't You Weep .... Run		41	$15		Columbia 41533
4/4/60	6	17		6 Why I'm Walkin' /		83			
4/25/60	15	5		7 Life Of A Poor Boy		—	$15		Columbia 41591
11/7/60	13	15		8 A Little Guy Called Joe .... I'm Gonna Find You		—	$15		Columbia 41785
3/13/61	26	6		9 Greener Pastures .... Wedding Bells For You And Him		—	$15		Columbia 41932
8/7/61	27	2		10 Hungry For Love .... For The Last Time		—	$15		Columbia 42028
1/20/62	3	22		11 A Wound Time Can't Erase /		—			
2/3/62	18	3		12 Second Choice		—	$15		Columbia 42229
7/21/62	9	7		13 Leona /		—			
6/30/62	11	10		14 One Look At Heaven		—	$15		Columbia 42426
1/26/63	11	10		15 Can't Hang Up The Phone .... Slowly		—	$12		Columbia 42628
5/18/63	8	14		16 Old Showboat .... A Toast To The Bride		—	$12		Columbia 42765
11/9/63	15	8		17 Wild Wild Wind .... The Water's So Cold		—	$12		Columbia 42846
12/7/63+	●¹	22		18 B.J. The D.J. .... Big House On The Corner		—	$12		Columbia 42889
4/25/64	24	13		19 Not My Kind Of People .... Give It Back To The Indians		—	$12		Columbia 43011
8/22/64	4	25		20 Don't Be Angry .... It's Not Me		—	$10		Columbia 43076
2/27/65	8	19		21 I Washed My Hands In Muddy Water .... I've Got To Change		—	$10		Columbia 43197
				#19 Pop hit for **Johnny Rivers** in 1966					
8/14/65	22	7		22 Lost In The Shuffle /		—			
7/17/65	30	9		23 Trouble And Me		—	$10		Columbia 43304
11/27/65+	24	12		24 If This House Could Talk /		—			
11/6/65	44	3		25 Poor Red Georgia Dirt		—	$10		Columbia 43411
4/30/66	24	8		26 The Minute Men (Are Turning In Their Graves) ...... I Wish I Had A Girl		—	$10	■	Columbia 43552
8/6/66	12	15		27 Blues Plus Booze (Means I Lose) .... Still Awake		—	$10		Columbia 43718
2/4/67	5	17		28 Stamp Out Loneliness .... Road To Recovery		—	$10		Columbia 43966
6/10/67	15	15		29 Promises And Hearts (Were Made To Break) .... While The Daisies Grow Free		—	$10		Columbia 44121
10/7/67	27	12		30 This World Holds Nothing (Since You're Gone) .... Almost Hear The Blues		—	$10		Columbia 44283
2/17/68	39	10		31 Nothing Takes The Place Of Loving You ...... If Heartaches Were Wine		—	$10		Columbia 44416
6/8/68	31	9		32 I Believe In Love .... Drinking And Driving		—	$10	■	Columbia 44501
9/28/68	16	15		33 Angry Words .... Red Roses Blooming Back Home		—	$10		Columbia 44625
3/1/69	52	7		34 Somebody's Always Leaving .... Recess Time		—	$10		Columbia 44726
6/14/69	25	9		35 "Never More" Quote The Raven .... How Many Lies Can I Tell		—	$10		Columbia 44863
10/4/69	19	10		36 Ship In The Bottle .... Thoughts Of A Lonely Man		—	$10		Columbia 44976
3/7/70	72	2		37 Better Days For Mama .... The Harm You've Done		—	$10		Columbia 45075
7/4/70	72	2		38 Born That Way .... Blue Field		—	$8		Columbia 45151
10/10/70	63	4		39 Oh, Lonesome Me .... When He Was Nine		—	$8		Columbia 45217
5/22/71	7	13		40 Me And You And A Dog Named Boo .... Here's To Hank		—	$8		Columbia 45381
				#5 Pop hit for **Lobo** in 1971					
3/11/72	51	9		41 That's All This Old World Needs .... Big Busy World		—	$8		Columbia 45546
				STONEWALL JACKSON And The Brentwood Children's Choir					
7/29/72	71	5		42 Torn From The Pages Of Life .... Waterloo		—	$8		Columbia 45632
1/27/73	70	3		43 I'm Not Strong Enough (To Build Another Dream) ... I've Run Out Of Reasons		—	$8		Columbia 45738
7/28/73	41	9		44 Herman Schwartz .... Lovin' The Fool Out Of Me		—	$7		MGM 14569

JACKSON, Wanda   ★188★   '62

Born on 10/20/37 in Maud, Oklahoma; raised in Bakersfield, California, and Oklahoma City. Singer/songwriter/guitarist/pianist. Own radio show on KLPR-Oklahoma City in 1950. Recorded with **Hank Thompson** in 1954. Had three solo records released while still in high school. Worked with **Red Foley**'s *Ozark Jubilee* from 1955-62; toured with **Elvis Presley** in 1955 and 1956.

1) In The Middle Of A Heartache 2) You Can't Have My Love 3) Right Or Wrong 4) Tears Will Be The Chaser For Your Wine 5) Fancy Satin Pillows

7/24/54	8	8		1 You Can't Have My Love .... S:8 / A:15 / J:10 Lovin', Country Style		—	$60		Decca 29140
				WANDA JACKSON and BILLY GRAY					
10/20/56	15	1		2 I Gotta Know .... A:15 Half As Good A Girl		—	$40		Capitol 3485
7/31/61	9	14		3 Right Or Wrong .... Funnel Of Love		29	$25		Capitol 4553
11/20/61+	6	15		4 In The Middle Of A Heartache .... I'd Be Ashamed		27	$25		Capitol 4635
6/9/62	28	1		5 If I Cried Every Time You Hurt Me .... Let My Love Walk In		58	$25	■	Capitol 4723
1/25/64	46	1		6 Slippin' .... Just For You		—	$15		Capitol 5072

165

DEBUT	PEAK	WKS	Gold	A-side (Chart Hit)	B-side	Pop	$	Pic	Label & Number
				JACKSON, Wanda — Cont'd					
3/28/64	36	11		7 The Violet And A Rose	To Tell You The Truth	—	$15		Capitol 5142
2/26/66	18	11		8 The Box It Came In	Look Out Heart	—	$15		Capitol 5559
6/25/66	28	7		9 Because It's You	Long As I Have You	—	$15		Capitol 5645
9/3/66	46	10		10 This Gun Don't Care	I Wonder If She Knows	—	$15		Capitol 5712
12/17/66+	11	18		11 Tears Will Be The Chaser For Your Wine	Reckless Love Affair	—	$15		Capitol 5789
				WANDA JACKSON And The Party Timers:					
4/22/67	21	12		12 Both Sides Of The Line	Famous Last Words	—	$15		Capitol 5863
8/19/67	51	7		13 My Heart Gets All The Breaks /		—			
8/19/67	64	2		14 You'll Always Have My Love		—	$15		Capitol 5960
11/25/67+	22	12		15 A Girl Don't Have To Drink To Have Fun	My Days Are Darker Than Your Nights	—	$15		Capitol 2021
1/27/68	46	6		16 By The Time You Get To Phoenix	Wishing Well	—	$15		Capitol 2085
				answer to "By The Time I Get To Phoenix" by Glen Campbell					
5/4/68	34	10		17 My Baby Walked Right Out On Me	No Place To Go But Home	—	$15		Capitol 2151
9/7/68	46	6		18 Little Boy Soldier	I Talk A Pretty Story	—	$12		Capitol 2245
11/16/68+	51	9		19 I Wish I Was Your Friend	Poor Ole Me	—	$12		Capitol 2315
				WANDA JACKSON:					
2/8/69	41	10		20 If I Had A Hammer	The Pain Of It All	—	$10		Capitol 2379
				#10 Pop hit for Peter, Paul & Mary in 1962					
7/12/69	48	7		21 Everything's Leaving	You Created Me	—	$10		Capitol 2524
9/27/69	20	11		22 My Big Iron Skillet	The Hunter	—	$10		Capitol 2614
1/3/70	35	10		23 Two Separate Bar Stools	Two Wrongs Don't Make A Right	—	$10		Capitol 2693
4/4/70	17	11		24 A Woman Lives For Love	What Have We Done	—	$10		Capitol 2761
9/12/70	50	7		25 Who Shot John	Stop The World	—	$10		Capitol 2872
12/12/70+	13	11		26 Fancy Satin Pillows	Why Don't We Love Like That Anymore	—	$10		Capitol 2986
8/7/71	25	12		27 Back Then	I'm Gonna Walk Out Of Your Life	—	$10		Capitol 3143
11/27/71+	35	11		28 I Already Know (What I'm Getting For My Birthday)	The Man You Could Have Been	—	$10		Capitol 3218
4/8/72	57	7		29 I'll Be Whatever You Say	The More You See Me Less	—	$10		Capitol 3293
1/26/74	98	4		30 Come On Home (To This Lonely Heart)	It's A Long, Long Time To Cry	—	$7		Myrrh 125
				JACOBS, Lori '80					
				Born in Ann Arbor, Michigan. Singer/songwriter.					
3/15/80	94	2		Tugboat Annie	Blue Eyes	—	$6		Neostat 102
				JACQUES, Rick '78					
				Born in Nashville. Singer/songwriter.					
5/6/78	89	2		Song Man	Time Is A Slow Moving Train	—	$6		Caprice 2046
				JAMES, Atlanta — see VICKERY, Mack					
				JAMES, Brett '95					
				Born on 6/5/68 in Columbia, Missouri. Singer/songwriter.					
7/15/95	60	6		1 Female Bonding	Dark Side Of The Moon	—	$4	▮	Career 12838 (v)
10/21/95	68	5		2 If I Could See Love	Many Tears Ago	—	$4	▮	Career 12869 (v)
1/20/96	73	2		3 Worth The Fall	Wake Up And Smell The Whiskey	—	$4	▮	Career 12935 (v)
				JAMES, Dusty '79					
				Born in Oklahoma City. Male singer.					
7/14/79	76	4		You're All The Woman I'll Ever Need	Old Flame New Fire	—	$6		SCR 172
				JAMES, George '79					
				Born in 1958 in Rockford, Illinois.					
5/12/79	94	3		1 It's Gonna Be Magic	I'm Takin' A Heartbreak	—	$7		Janc 10417
10/20/79	95	2		2 When Our Love Began (Cowboys And Indians)	Break My Mind	—	$7		Janc 103
				JAMES, Jesseca '85					
				Born Kathy Twitty in 1960. Daughter of Conway Twitty.					
10/2/76	87	4		1 Johnny One Time	Lying In My Arms	—	$6		MCA 40613
4/30/77	93	3		2 My First Country Song	Let It Ring	—	$6		MCA 40703
1/12/85	82	5		3 Green Eyes	That's What Your Lovin' Does To Me	—	$5		Permian 82009
				KATHY TWITTY					
				JAMES, Mary Kay '74					
				Born Mary Kay Mulkey in Atlanta. Singer/guitarist.					
5/4/74	78	6		1 Please Help Me Say No	Before The Curtain Falls	—	$6		JMI 38
9/14/74	48	13		2 It Amazes Me (Sweet Lovin' Time)	Before I'm Fool Enough	—	$6		JMI 46
1/25/75	57	8		3 The Crossroad	Before The Curtain Falls	—	$5		Avco 605
5/3/75	76	7		4 I Think I'll Say Goodbye	Which Way Do We Go	—	$5		Avco 610

DEBUT	PEAK	WKS	Gold	A-side (Chart Hit)	B-side	Pop	$	Pic	Label & Number

JAMES, Sonny ★21★ U.S. Army '70

Born James Hugh Loden on 5/1/29 in Hackleburg, Alabama. Singer/songwriter/guitarist. Sang with his four sisters as The Loden Family. Served in the U.S. Army from 1950-52. Acted in the movies *Second Fiddle To A Steel Guitar*, *Nashville Rebel*, *Las Vegas Hillbillies* and *Hillbillys In A Haunted House*. Known as "The Southern Gentleman." Also see **Heart Of Nashville**.

1) Young Love 2) It's The Little Things 3) You're The Only World I Know 4) I'll Never Find Another You 5) Empty Arms

DEBUT	PEAK	WKS		#	A-side	B-side	Pop	$		Label & Number
2/7/53	9	1		1	That's Me Without You	A:9 Cool, Cold, And Colder	—	$25		Capitol 2259
11/20/54	14	1		2	She Done Give Her Heart To Me	A:14 Oceans Of Tears (I've Shed For You)	—	$25		Capitol 2906
3/24/56	7	11		3	For Rent (One Empty Heart)	A:7 / J:8 / S:12 My Stolen Love	—	$20		Capitol 3357
6/30/56	11	6		4	Twenty Feet Of Muddy Water	A:11 All Mixed Up	—	$20		Capitol 3441
11/10/56	12	1		5	The Cat Came Back	A:12 Hello Old Broken Heart	—	$20		Capitol 3542
12/22/56+	❶⁹	24	●	6	Young Love /	A:❶⁹ / S:❶⁷ / J:❶³	❶¹			
					#1 Pop hit for Tab Hunter in 1957					
1/26/57	6	12		7	You're The Reason I'm In Love	A:6	—	$20		Capitol 3602
4/13/57	9	9		8	First Date, First Kiss, First Love	S:9 / A:9 Speak To Me	25	$20		Capitol 3674
8/12/57	15	1		9	Lovesick Blues	A:15 Dear Love	—	$20		Capitol 3734
1/6/58	8	5		10	Uh-Huh—mm	A:8 / S:14 Why Can't They Remember?	92	$20		Capitol 3840
5/9/60	22	6		11	Jenny Lou	Passin' Through	67	$25	■	NRC 050
7/20/63	9	15		12	The Minute You're Gone	Gold And Silver	95	$12	□	Capitol 4969
12/21/63	17	9		13	Going Through The Motions (Of Living)	Bad Times A Comin'	—	$12		Capitol 5057
3/28/64	6	17		14	Baltimore	Least Of All You	134	$12	■	Capitol 5129
8/8/64	19	13		15	Ask Marie /		—			
7/18/64	27	6		16	Sugar Lump		—	$12		Capitol 5197
11/14/64+	❶⁴	25		17	You're The Only World I Know	Tying The Pieces Together	91	$12	■	Capitol 5280
4/3/65	2¹	20		18	I'll Keep Holding On (Just To Your Love)	I'm Getting Gray From Being Blue	116	$12	■	Capitol 5375
8/14/65	❶³	22		19	Behind The Tear	Runnin'	113	$12	■	Capitol 5454
12/11/65+	3	18		20	True Love's A Blessing	Just Ask Your Heart	—	$12	■	Capitol 5536
4/9/66	❶²	20		21	Take Good Care Of Her	On The Fingers Of One Hand	—	$12	■	Capitol 5612
					#7 Pop hit for Adam Wade in 1961					
8/13/66	2²	20		22	Room In Your Heart	How Many Times Can A Man Be A Fool	—	$12	■	Capitol 5690
2/25/67	❶²	18		23	Need You	On And On	—	$12	■	Capitol 5833
					#7 Pop hit for **Jo Stafford** & Gordon MacRae in 1949					
6/10/67	❶⁴	17		24	I'll Never Find Another You	Goodbye, Maggie, Goodbye	97	$12	■	Capitol 5914
					#4 Pop hit for The Seekers in 1965					
9/23/67	❶⁵	18		25	It's The Little Things	Don't Cut Timber On A Windy Day	—	$12	■	Capitol 5987
1/20/68	❶³	17		26	A World Of Our Own	An Old Sweetheart Of Mine	118	$12	■	Capitol 2067
					#19 Pop hit for The Seekers in 1965					
6/1/68	❶¹	17		27	Heaven Says Hello	Fairy Tales	—	$12	■	Capitol 2155
10/12/68	❶¹	16		28	Born To Be With You	In Waikiki	81	$10	■	Capitol 2271
					#5 Pop hit for The Chordettes in 1956					
1/18/69	❶³	16		29	Only The Lonely	The Journey	92	$10	■	Capitol 2370
					#2 Pop hit for **Roy Orbison** in 1960					
5/10/69	❶³	15		30	Running Bear	A Midnight Mood	94	$10	■	Capitol 2486
					#1 Pop hit for Johnny Preston in 1960					
9/6/69	❶³	15		31	Since I Met You, Baby	Clinging To A Hope	65	$10	■	Capitol 2595
					#12 Pop hit for Ivory Joe Hunter in 1956					
1/17/70	❶⁴	14		32	It's Just A Matter Of Time	This World Of Ours	87	$8	■	Capitol 2700
					#3 Pop hit for Brook Benton in 1959					
4/11/70	❶³	15		33	My Love	Blue For You	125	$8	■	Capitol 2782
					#1 Pop hit for **Petula Clark** in 1966					
7/4/70	❶⁴	15		34	Don't Keep Me Hangin' On	Woodbine Valley	—	$8	■	Capitol 2834
10/17/70	❶³	16		35	Endlessly	Happy Memories	108	$8	■	Capitol 2914
					#12 Pop hit for Brook Benton in 1959					
2/27/71	❶⁴	16		36	Empty Arms	Everything Begins And Ends With You	93	$8	■	Capitol 3015
					#13 Pop hit for Teresa Brewer in 1957					
6/19/71	❶¹	13		37	Bright Lights, Big City	True Love Lasts Forever	91	$8	■	Capitol 3114
					#58 Pop hit for Jimmy Reed in 1961					
10/2/71	❶¹	15		38	Here Comes Honey Again The Only Ones We Truly Hurt (Are The Ones We Truly Love)		—	$8	■	Capitol 3174
1/15/72	2²	16		39	Only Love Can Break A Heart	He Has Walked This Way Before	—	$8	■	Capitol 3232
					#2 Pop hit for **Gene Pitney** in 1962					
5/13/72	❶¹	11		40	That's Why I Love You Like I Do	Still Water Runs Deep	—	$8		Capitol 3322
7/22/72	❶¹	15		41	When The Snow Is On The Roses	Love Is A Rainbow	103	$7	■	Columbia 45644
9/2/72	30	9		42	Traces	I'm In Love With You	—	$7		Capitol 3398
					#2 Pop hit for the Classics IV in 1969					
10/21/72	5	14		43	White Silver Sands	Why Is It I'm The Last To Know	—	$7	□	Columbia 45706
					#7 Pop hit for Don Rondo in 1957					
12/2/72+	32	10		44	Downfall Of Me	I'll Follow You	—	$7		Capitol 3475
2/10/73	4	14		45	I Love You More And More Everyday	I'll Think About That Tomorrow	—	$7	■	Columbia 45770
					#9 Pop hit for **Al Martino** in 1964					
4/14/73	61	4		46	Reach Out Your Hand And Touch Me	Just Keep Thinking Of Me	—	$7		Capitol 3564
6/9/73	15	11		47	If She Just Helps Me Get Over You	I Won't Think About It Now	—	$6		Columbia 45871
7/21/73	66	5		48	Heaven On Earth	She Believes In Me	—	$6		Capitol 3653
12/15/73+	49	9		49	Surprise, Surprise	What Am I Living For	—	$6		Capitol 3779

DEBUT	PEAK	WKS	Gold	A-side (Chart Hit)	B-side	Pop	$	Pic	Label & Number
				JAMES, Sonny — Cont'd					
3/2/74	❶¹	15		50 Is It Wrong (For Loving You)	Suddenly There's A Valley	—	$6		Columbia 46003
7/27/74	4	17		51 A Mi Esposa Con Amor (To My Wife With Love)	Just Don't Stop Lovin' Me	—	$5	■	Columbia 10001
1/25/75	6	12		52 A Little Bit South Of Saskatoon	Home Style Lovin'	—	$5	■	Columbia 10072
4/26/75	5	15		53 Little Band Of Gold	Pop And Me	—	$5	■	Columbia 10121
				#21 Pop hit for James Gilreath in 1963					
8/9/75	10	15		54 What In The World's Come Over You	Walking The Railroad Trestle	—	$5	■	Columbia 10184
				#5 Pop hit for Jack Scott in 1960					
12/13/75+	67	8		55 Eres Tu (Touch The Wind)	Apache [I]	—	$5		Columbia 10249
				#9 Pop hit for Mocedades in 1974					
1/31/76	14	13		56 The Prisoner's Song /		—			
				#1 Pop hit for Vernon Dalhart in 1925					
		12		57 Back In The Saddle Again		—	$5	■	Columbia 10276
				co-written and first recorded by Gene Autry in 1939					
5/15/76	6	15		58 When Something Is Wrong With My Baby	Big Silver Bird	—	$5	■	Columbia 10335
				#42 Pop hit for Sam & Dave in 1967					
8/28/76	8	14		59 Come On In	Baby's Eyes	—	$5		Columbia 10392
1/29/77	9	13		60 You're Free To Go	Puttin' On The Dog Tonight	—	$5	■	Columbia 10466
6/18/77	15	11		61 In The Jailhouse Now	Amazing Grace	—	$5		Columbia 10551
				#14 Pop hit for Jimmie Rodgers in 1928					
10/22/77	24	13		62 Abilene	Pistol Packin' Mama	—	$5		Columbia 10628
				SONNY JAMES with his Tennessee State Prison Band (above 2)					
				above 2 recorded "live" at the Tennessee State Prison					
3/18/78	16	12		63 This Is The Love	It'll Still Be Worth It All	—	$5	□	Columbia 10703
7/22/78	18	12		64 Caribbean	Each Time I Look At You	—	$5	■	Columbia 10764
12/2/78+	30	12		65 Building Memories	Little Band Of Gold	—	$5		Columbia 10852
3/31/79	36	9		66 Hold What You've Got	Hanging On To Yesterday	—	$5	■	Monument 280
				#5 Pop hit for Joe Tex in 1965					
7/21/79	62	6		67 Lorelei	If I Ever Wanted You	—	$5		Monument 288
				SONNY JAMES and His Southern Gentlemen:					
12/26/81+	19	16		68 Innocent Lies	Don't Let The Stars Get In Your Eyes	—	$5	■	Dimension 1026
5/15/82	60	7		69 A Place In The Sun	Lean On Me Girl	—	$5		Dimension 1033
				SONNY JAMES and SILVER:					
10/9/82	66	7		70 I'm Looking Over The Rainbow	Something's Got A Hold On Me	—	$5	■	Dimension 1036
12/25/82+	33	13		71 The Fool In Me	Little Rainbow	—	$5		Dimension 1040
8/13/83	58	9		72 A Free Roamin' Mind	Don't Let The Stars Get In Your Eyes	—	$5		Dimension 1045
				JAMES, Tommy '80					
				Born Thomas Jackson on 4/29/47 in Dayton, Ohio; raised in Niles, Michigan. Leader of The Shondells. Charted 32 pop hits from 1966-81.					
3/15/80	93	2		Three Times In Love	I Just Wanna Play The Music	19	$5		Millennium 11785
				JAMESON, Cody '77					
				Born in New York City. Female singer.					
4/16/77	64	7		Brooklyn	That Little Bit Of Us	74	$5		Atco 7073
				JAN & MALCOLM '77					
				Male/female duo from Dallas.					
3/12/77	99	2		Rainbow In Your Eyes (Love's Got A Hold On Me)	You Are What I Am	—	$7		Paula 421
				JANO '79					
				Male singer Jano Bourland.					
10/20/79	94	2		Sundown Sideshow		—	$6		SCR 180
				JANSKY, Clifton '85					
				Born in 1956 in Pleasanton, Texas.					
4/13/85	97	2		Will You Love Me In The Morning	Just Can't Help Believing	—	$7		Axbar 6033
				JAYE, Jerry '76					
				Born Gerald Jaye Hatley on 10/19/37 in Manila, Arkansas.					
8/9/75	53	8		1 It's All In The Game	Love Me 'Til The Morning Comes	—	$5		Columbia 10170
				#1 Pop hit for Tommy Edwards in 1958					
6/12/76	32	13		2 Honky Tonk Women Love Red Neck Men	What's Left Never Will Be Right	—	$5		Hi 2310
11/20/76	78	9		3 Hot And Still Heatin'	Crazy	—	$5		Hi 2318
				JEAN — see NORMA JEAN					
				JED ZEPPELIN '95					
				All-star group: Diamond Rio, Lee Roy Parnell and Steve Wariner. Group name is a pun on Led Zeppelin.					
12/10/94+	48	15		Workin' Man Blues	Tonight The Bottle Let Me Down (Brooks & Dunn)	—	$4		Arista 12755
				written by Merle Haggard					
				JEFFERSON, Paul '96					
				Born on 8/15/61 in Woodside, California. Singer/songwriter/guitarist.					
5/18/96	50	10		1 Check Please	That's As Close As I'll Get To Loving You	—	$4	■	Almo So. 89003 (v)
8/17/96	73	1		2 Fear Of A Broken Heart	Missouri	—	$4	■	Almo So. 89005 (v)
10/19/96	73	1		3 I Might Just Make It	Common Ground	—	$4		Almo Sounds 89006
				JENKINS, Bob '82					
2/6/82	76	3		1 The Cube	Sometimes I Wish [N]	—	$5		Liberty 1448
				BOB JENKINS (& 3 Year Old Daughter Mandy)					
				song about Rubick's Cube					
2/19/83	86	3		2 Workin' In A Coalmine	Muscle And Blood	—	$6		Picap 009

Shooter Jennings (son of Waylon & Jessi)

DEBUT	PEAK	WKS	Gold	A-side (Chart Hit)	B-side	Pop	$	Pic	Label & Number
				JENKINS, Bobby '84					
				Born in 1942 in Corpus Christi, Texas.					
6/16/84	69	5		1 Blackjack Whiskey	—		$5		Zone 7 40984
8/25/84	82	3		2 Louisiana Heatwave	—		$5		Zone 7 61884
5/11/85	85	3		3 Me And Margarita	—		$5		Zone 7 30185
				JENKINS, Larry '82					
				Born in West Helena, Arkansas. Singer/songwriter. Nephew of **Conway Twitty**.					
10/30/82	76	6		1 I'm So Tired Of Going Home Drunk ... I Laughed 'Till I Cried	—		$4		Capitol 5167
7/28/84	87	3		2 You're The Best I Never Had ... When It Comes To Makin' Love	—		$4		MCA 52396
				JENNINGS, Bob '64					
				Born on 9/26/24 in Liberty, Tennessee. Died of a self-inflicted gunshot on 4/19/84 (age 59).					
5/9/64	32	13		1 The First Step Down (Is The Longest) ... It Takes A Lot Of Money	—		$10		Sims 161
11/14/64	34	8		2 Leave A Little Play (In The Chain Of Love) ... I'm Barely Hangin' On To Me	—		$10		Sims 202
				JENNINGS, Tommy '80					
				Born on 8/8/38 in Littlefield, Texas. Brother of **Waylon Jennings**.					
8/2/75	96	4		1 Make It Easy On Yourself ... I Almost Did	—		$6		Paragon 102
4/15/78	71	7		2 Don't You Think It's Time ... That's The Way It Was	—		$5		Monument 248
5/31/80	51	10		3 Just Give Me What You Think Is Fair ... Things I Remember	—		$7		Sabre 4520
				REX GOSDIN with Tommy Jennings					
				JENNINGS, Waylon ★12★ *Military?* '77					
				Born on 6/15/37 in Littlefield, Texas. Died of diabetes on 2/13/2002 (age 64). Singer/songwriter/guitarist. Played bass for Buddy Holly on the ill-fated "Winter Dance Party" tour in 1959. Gave up his seat to the Big Bopper on the plane, which crashed on 2/3/59, killing Holly, Ritchie Valens and the Big Bopper. Established himself in the mid-1970s as a leader of the "outlaw" music movement. Married to **Jessi Colter** since 1969. Acted in the movies *Nashville Rebel* and *MacKintosh And T.J.* Narrator for TV's *The Dukes Of Hazzard*. Elected to the Country Music Hall of Fame in 2001. CMA Awards: 1975 Male Vocalist of the Year; 1976 Vocal Duo of the Year (with **Willie Nelson**). Also see *Some Of Chet's Friends*.					
				1) Luckenbach, Texas (Back To The Basics Of Love) 2) Mammas Don't Let Your Babies Grow Up To Be Cowboys 3) Amanda 4) Good Hearted Woman 5) I've Always Been Crazy					
8/21/65	49	2		1 That's The Chance I'll Have To Take ... I Wonder Just Where I Went Wrong	—		$10		RCA Victor 8572
9/25/65	16	13		2 Stop The World (And Let Me Off) ... The Dark Side Of Fame	—		$10		RCA Victor 8652
1/15/66	17	15		3 Anita, You're Dreaming ... Look Into My Teardrops	—		$10		RCA Victor 8729
6/4/66	17	13		4 Time To Bum Again ... Norwegian Wood	—		$10		RCA Victor 8822
9/3/66	9	18		5 (That's What You Get) For Lovin' Me ... Time Will Tell The Story	—		$10		RCA Victor 8917
				#30 Pop hit for Peter, Paul & Mary in 1965					
12/17/66+	11	15		6 Green River *(from the movie Nashville Rebel starring Jennings)* ... Silver Ribbons	—		$10		RCA Victor 9025
4/1/67	12	16		7 Mental Revenge ... Born To Love You	—		$10		RCA Victor 9146
8/19/67	8	17		8 The Chokin' Kind /			—		
				#13 Pop hit for Joe Simon in 1969					
9/9/67	67	5		9 Love Of The Common People	—		$10		RCA Victor 9259
				WAYLON JENNINGS AND THE WAYLORS (above 2)					
				#45 Pop hit for Paul Young in 1984					
1/27/68	5	16		10 Walk On Out Of My Mind ... Julie	—		$10		RCA Victor 9414
3/30/68	4	15		11 I Got You ... No One's Gonna Miss Me	—		$10		RCA Victor 9480
				WAYLON JENNINGS & ANITA CARTER					
7/13/68	2⁵	18		12 Only Daddy That'll Walk The Line ... Right Before My Eyes	—		$10		RCA Victor 9561
11/16/68+	5	17		13 Yours Love ... Six Strings Away	—		$10		RCA Victor 9642
3/8/69	19	12		14 Something's Wrong In California ... Farewell Party	—		$8		RCA Victor 0105
5/24/69	20	12		15 The Days Of Sand And Shovels /			—		
				#34 Pop hit for Bobby Vinton in 1969					
5/31/69	37	6		16 Delia's Gone	124		$8		RCA Victor 0157
				#66 Pop hit for Pat Boone in 1960					
8/23/69	23	11		17 MacArthur Park ... But You Know I Love You	93		$8		RCA Victor 0210
				WAYLON JENNINGS AND THE KIMBERLYS					
				#2 Pop hit for Richard Harris in 1968					
11/29/69+	3	15		18 Brown Eyed Handsome Man ... Sorrow (Breaks A Good Man Down)	—		$8		RCA Victor 0281
				written and first recorded by Chuck Berry in 1956					
4/18/70	12	14		19 Singer Of Sad Songs ... Lila	—		$8		RCA Victor 9819
8/29/70	5	15		20 The Taker ... Shadow Of The Gallows	94		$8		RCA Victor 9885
11/14/70	25	10		21 Suspicious Minds ... I Ain't The One	—		$8		RCA Victor 9920
				WAYLON JENNINGS AND JESSI COLTER					
				#1 Pop hit for Elvis Presley in 1969; also see #40 below					
12/5/70+	16	12		22 (Don't Let The Sun Set On You) Tulsa ... You'll Look For Me	—		$8		RCA Victor 9925
4/3/71	14	14		23 Mississippi Woman ... Life Goes On	—		$8		RCA Victor 9967
6/19/71	39	8		24 Under Your Spell Again ... Bridge Over Troubled Water	—		$8		RCA Victor 9992
				WAYLON JENNINGS AND JESSI COLTER					
8/7/71	12	15		25 Cedartown, Georgia ... I Think It's Time She Learned	—		$8		RCA Victor 1003
1/8/72	3	18		26 Good Hearted Woman ... It's All Over Now	—		$8		RCA Victor 0615
				also see #39 below					
6/10/72	7	13		27 Sweet Dream Woman ... Sure Didn't Take Him Long	—		$6		RCA Victor 0716
10/21/72	6	15		28 Pretend I Never Happened ... Nothin' Worth Takin' Or Leavin'	—		$6		RCA Victor 0808
2/17/73	7	14		29 You Can Have Her ... Gone To Denver	114		$6		RCA Victor 0886
				#12 Pop hit for Roy Hamilton in 1961					
5/26/73	28	10		30 We Had It All ... Do No Good Woman	—		$6		RCA Victor 0961
10/6/73	8	15		31 You Ask Me To ... Willy The Wandering Gypsy And Me	—		$6		RCA Victor 0086
4/27/74	❶¹	13		32 This Time ... Mona	—		$6		RCA Victor 0251

169

DEBUT	PEAK	WKS	Gold	A-side (Chart Hit)	B-side	Pop	$	Pic	Label & Number
				JENNINGS, Waylon — Cont'd					
8/10/74	❶¹	13		33 I'm A Ramblin' Man	Got A Lot Going For Me	75	$6		RCA Victor 10020
12/21/74+	2¹	15		34 Rainy Day Woman /		—			
		12		35 Let's All Help The Cowboys (Sing The Blues)			$6		RCA Victor 10142
5/3/75	10	14		36 Dreaming My Dreams With You	Waymore's Blues (Pop #110)	—	$6		RCA Victor 10270
9/6/75	❶¹	16		37 Are You Sure Hank Done It This Way /		60			
		15		38 Bob Wills Is Still The King		—	$6	■	RCA Victor 10379
12/27/75+	❶³	17		39 Good Hearted Woman	Heaven Or Hell [R]	25	$6		RCA Victor 10529
				WAYLON & WILLIE					
				new "live" duet version of #26 above; CMA Award: Single of the Year					
5/1/76	2¹	14		40 Suspicious Minds	I Ain't The One [R]		$6		RCA Victor 10653
				WAYLON & JESSI					
				#1 Pop hit for Elvis Presley in 1969; same version as #21 above					
7/31/76	4	14		41 Can't You See /		97			
		8		42 I'll Go Back To Her		—	$6		RCA Victor 10721
11/20/76+	7	14		43 Are You Ready For The Country /		—			
		13		44 So Good Woman			$5		RCA 10842
4/16/77	❶⁶	18		45 Luckenbach, Texas (Back To The Basics Of Love)	Belle Of The Ball	25	$5		RCA 10924
				Willie Nelson (ending vocal)					
10/8/77	❶²	16		46 The Wurlitzer Prize (I Don't Want To Get Over You) /					
		16		47 Lookin' For A Feeling		—	$5		RCA 11118
1/21/78	❶⁴	16		48 Mammas Don't Let Your Babies Grow Up To Be Cowboys /		42			
		15		49 I Can Get Off On You		—			RCA 11198
				WAYLON & WILLIE (above 2)					
5/20/78	2²	13		50 There Ain't No Good Chain Gang /		—			
11/17/79+	22	12		51 I Wish I Was Crazy Again		—	$5		Columbia 10742
				JOHNNY CASH & WAYLON JENNINGS (above 2)					
7/29/78	❶³	13		52 I've Always Been Crazy	I Never Said It Would Be Easy	—	$5		RCA 11344
				WAYLON:					
10/28/78	5	13		53 Don't You Think This Outlaw Bit's Done Got Out Of Hand /		—			
		11		54 Girl I Can Tell (You're Trying To Work It Out)		—	$4		RCA 11390
5/19/79	❶³	14		55 Amanda	Lonesome, On'ry And Mean	54	$4	■	RCA 11596
9/22/79	❶²	13		56 Come With Me	Mes'kin	—	$4		RCA 11723
1/5/80	❶¹	15		57 I Ain't Living Long Like This	It's The World's Gone Crazy	—	$4		RCA 11898
5/31/80	7	13		58 Clyde	I Came Here To Party	103	$4		RCA 12007
8/23/80	❶¹	17	•	59 Theme From The Dukes Of Hazzard (Good Ol' Boys)	It's Alright	21	$4	■	RCA 12067
				from the TV series starring John Schneider and Tom Wopat					
2/21/81	17	12		60 Storms Never Last	I Ain't The One	—	$4		RCA 12176
				WAYLON & JESSI					
6/6/81	10	13		61 Wild Side Of Life/It Wasn't God Who Made Honky Tonk Angels	I'll Be Alright	—	$4		RCA 12245
				WAYLON & JESSI					
11/21/81+	5	19		62 Shine	White Water	—	$4		RCA 12367
				from the movie The Pursuit Of D.B. Cooper starring Robert Duvall					
3/13/82	❶²	18		63 Just To Satisfy You	Get Naked With Me (Waylon)	52	$4		RCA 13073
				WAYLON & WILLIE					
6/26/82	4	16		64 Women Do Know How To Carry On	Honky Tonk Blues	—	$4		RCA 13257
10/23/82	13	15		65 (Sittin' On) The Dock Of The Bay	Luckenbach, Texas	—	$4		RCA 13319
				WAYLON & WILLIE					
				#1 Pop hit for Otis Redding in 1968					
3/19/83	❶¹	16		66 Lucille (You Won't Do Your Daddy's Will)	Medley Of Hits	—	$4		RCA 13465
				#21 Pop hit for Little Richard in 1957					
				WAYLON JENNINGS:					
7/2/83	10	18		67 Breakin' Down	Living Legends (A Dyin' Breed)	—	$4		RCA 13543
8/6/83	20	14		68 Hold On, I'm Comin'	Waiting On Down The Line	—	$4		RCA 13580
				WAYLON JENNINGS & JERRY REED					
				#21 Pop hit for Sam & Dave in 1966					
10/8/83	8	19		69 Take It To The Limit	Till I Gain Control Again	102	$4	■	Columbia 04131
				WILLIE NELSON & WAYLON JENNINGS					
				#4 Pop hit for the Eagles in 1976					
10/22/83	15	16		70 The Conversation	Fancy Free	—	$4		RCA 13631
				WAYLON JENNINGS with Hank Williams, Jr.					
3/3/84	4	20		71 I May Be Used (But Baby I Ain't Used Up)	So You Want To Be A Cowboy Singer	—	$4		RCA 13729
6/16/84	6	18		72 Never Could Toe The Mark	Talk Good Boogie	—	$4		RCA 13827
9/29/84	6	21		73 America	S:5 / A:6 People Up In Texas	—	$4		RCA 13908
1/19/85	10	19		74 Waltz Me To Heaven	S:9 / A:9 Dream On	—	$4		RCA 13984
				written by Dolly Parton					
5/18/85	❶¹	20		75 Highwayman	S:❶¹ / A:❶¹ The Human Condition	—	$4	■	Columbia 04881
				WAYLON JENNINGS/WILLIE NELSON/JOHNNY CASH/KRIS KRISTOFFERSON					
6/22/85	2²	21		76 Drinkin' And Dreamin'	S:❶¹ / A:2 Prophets Show Up In Strange Places	—	$4		RCA 14094
9/14/85	15	18		77 Desperados Waiting For A Train	S:15 / A:16 The Twentieth Century Is Almost Over	—	$4		Columbia 05594
				WAYLON JENNINGS/WILLIE NELSON/JOHNNY CASH/KRIS KRISTOFFERSON					
11/16/85+	13	18		78 The Devil's On The Loose	S:11 / A:13 Good Morning John	—	$4		RCA 14215
2/15/86	7	19		79 Working Without A Net	S:6 / A:8 They Ain't Got 'Em All	—	$4		MCA 52776
5/17/86	5	19		80 Will The Wolf Survive	A:6 / S:6 I've Got Me A Woman	—	$4		MCA 52830
				#78 Pop hit for Los Lobos in 1985					
5/17/86	35	11		81 Even Cowgirls Get The Blues	A:34 American By Birth	—	$4		Columbia 05896
				JOHNNY CASH & WAYLON JENNINGS					

DEBUT	PEAK	WKS	Gold	A-side (Chart Hit)	B-side	Pop	$	Pic	Label & Number
				JENNINGS, Waylon — Cont'd					
9/20/86	8	21		82 What You'll Do When I'm Gone	S:8 / A:8 That Dog Won't Hunt	—	$4		MCA 52915
1/31/87	❶¹	19		83 Rose In Paradise	A:❶¹ / S:12 Crying Don't Even Come Close	—	$4		MCA 53009
5/16/87	8	19		84 Fallin' Out	S:16 Deep In The West	—	$4		MCA 53088
9/12/87	6	22		85 My Rough And Rowdy Days	S:14 A Love Song (I Can't Sing Anymore)	—	$4		MCA 53158
1/23/88	16	16		86 If Ole Hank Could Only See Us Now					
				(Chapter Five...Nashville)	S:29 You Went Out With Rock 'N' Roll	—	$4		MCA 53243
9/24/88	38	9		87 How Much Is It Worth To Live In L.A.	G.I. Joe	—	$4		MCA 53313
1/7/89	28	16		88 Which Way Do I Go (Now That I'm Gone)	Hey Willie	—	$4		MCA 53476
5/20/89	61	5		89 Trouble Man	Yoyos, Bozos, Bimbos, And Heroes	—	$4		MCA 53634
9/2/89	59	6		90 You Put The Soul In The Song	Woman I Hate It	—	$4		MCA 53710
3/3/90	25	14		91 Silver Stallion	American Remains	—	$4		Columbia 73233
				WAYLON JENNINGS/WILLIE NELSON/JOHNNY CASH/KRIS KRISTOFFERSON					
5/26/90	5	21		92 Wrong	Waking Up With You	—	$4	■	Epic 73352 (v)
10/13/90	67	6		93 Where Corn Don't Grow	Waking Up With You	—	$4	■	Epic 73519 (v)
1/12/91	66	4		94 What Bothers Me Most	Wrong	—	$4		Epic 73647
2/9/91	22	12		95 The Eagle	What Bothers Me Most	—	$4		Epic 73718
6/15/91	51	10		96 If I Can Find A Clean Shirt	Put Me On A Train Back To Texas	—	$4		Epic 73832
				WAYLON & WILLIE					
				JEREMIAH '88					
10/8/88	96	1		To Be Loved			$7		Chariot 1921
				#22 Pop hit for Jackie Wilson in 1958					
				JERRICO, Sherri '77					
10/8/77	95	2		Thanks For Leaving, Lucille	All Over Me		$6		Gusto 164
				answer to "Lucille" by Kenny Rogers					
				JEWEL — see HAGGARD, Merle					
				JIM & JESSE Brothers '67					
				Duo of brothers from Carfax, Virginia: Jim (born on 2/13/27, guitar) and Jesse (born on 7/9/29, mandolin) McReynolds. Joined the *Grand Ole Opry* in 1964.					
				1)Diesel On My Tail 2)The Golden Rocket 3)Better Times A-Coming					
7/18/64	43	2		1 Cotton Mill Man	(It's A Long, Long Way) To The Top Of The World	—	$8		Epic 9676
12/19/64+	39	6		2 Better Times A-Coming	Wild Georgia Boys	—	$8		Epic 9729
4/1/67	18	16		3 Diesel On My Tail	All For The Love Of A Girl	—	$8		Epic 10138
				JIM & JESSE And The Virginia Boys (above 2)					
9/23/67	44	4		4 Ballad Of Thunder Road	Tijuana Taxi	—	$8		Epic 10213
				#62 Pop hit for Robert Mitchum in 1958					
1/27/68	49	6		5 Greenwich Village Folk Song Salesman	Truck Drivin' Man	—	$8		Epic 10263
9/7/68	56	6		6 Yonder Comes A Freight Train	Banderilla	—	$8		Epic 10370
1/10/70	38	9		7 The Golden Rocket	A Freight Train In My Mind	—	$8		Epic 10563
2/13/71	41	9		8 Freight Train	Just Wondering Why	—	$6		Capitol 3026
				#6 Pop hit for Rusty Draper in 1957					
6/5/82	56	9		9 North Wind	Sweeter Than The Flowers	—	$5		Soundwaves 4671
				JIM & JESSE and CHARLIE LOUVIN					
9/27/86	78	3		10 Oh Louisiana		—	$6		MSR 198310
				JIMMY & JOHNNY '54					
				Duo of Jimmy Lee Fautheree (born in 1934 in El Dorado, Arkansas) and Country Johnny Mathis (born on 9/28/33 in Maud, Texas).					
9/25/54	3	18		If You Don't Somebody Else Will	J:3 / A:5 / S:6 I'm Beginning To Remember	—	$30		Chess 4859
				JJ WHITE Sisters (2) '92					
				Duo of sisters from California: Janice and Jayne White.					
7/20/91	69	4		1 The Crush	Everyday	—	$4	■	Curb 76876 (v)
1/4/92	73	1		2 Heart Break Train	Less Than Zero	—	$4		Curb 76896
4/25/92	63	4		3 Jezebel Kane		—			album cut
9/12/92	64	3		4 One Like That		—			album cut
				above 2 from the album *Janice & Jayne* on Curb 77492					
				JOE BOB'S NASHVILLE SOUND COMPANY '75					
				Studio group led by Joe Bob Barnhill (born on 10/14/33 in Turkey, Texas). Father of Joe Barnhill.					
5/17/75	84	6		In The Mood	A String Of Pearls [I]	—	$6		Capitol 4059
				#1 Pop hit for Glenn Miller in 1940					
				JOHN DEER — see DEER, John					
	★257★			**JOHNNIE & JACK** '54					
				Duo of Johnnie Wright and Jack Anglin. Wright was born on 5/13/14 in Mount Juliet, Tennessee. Anglin was born on 5/13/16 in Franklin, Tennessee. Anglin died in a car crash on 3/7/63 (age 46) enroute to the memorial service for Patsy Cline. Duo were regulars on the *Louisiana Hayride* from 1948-52. Joined the *Grand Ole Opry* in 1952.					
				1)(Oh Baby Mine) I Get So Lonely 2)Goodnight, Sweetheart, Goodnight 3)Poison Love					
				JOHNNIE and JACK and Their Tennessee Mountain Boys					
1/20/51	4	17		1 Poison Love	A:4 / S:5 / J:9 Lonesome	—	$25		RCA Victor 48-0377
8/4/51	5	11		2 Cryin' Heart Blues	J:5 / A:6 / S:10 How Can I Believe You	—	$25		RCA Victor 48-0478
5/10/52	7	5		3 Three Ways Of Knowing	J:7 When You Want A Little Lovin'	—	$25		RCA Victor 47-4555
				JOHNNIE and JACK (The Tennessee Mountain Boys):					
4/10/54	❶²	18		4 (Oh Baby Mine) I Get So Lonely	A:❶² / S:5 You're Just What The Doctor Ordered	—	$20		RCA Victor 5681
				#2 Pop hit for The Four Knights in 1954					
7/17/54	3	17		5 Goodnight, Sweetheart, Goodnight /	A:3 / S:4 / J:4				

DEBUT	PEAK	WKS	Gold	A-side (Chart Hit)..B-side	Pop	$	Pic	Label & Number
				JOHNNIE & JACK — Cont'd				
8/7/54	15	1		6 Honey, I Need You..A:15	—	$20		RCA Victor 5775
11/27/54+	7	4		7 Kiss-Crazy Baby /	J:7 / S:13	—		
11/13/54	9	10		8 Beware Of "It"	S:9 / J:9 / A:10	—	$20		RCA Victor 5880
5/21/55	14	3		9 No One Dear But You........................A:14 We Live In Two Different Worlds	—	$20		RCA Victor 6094
12/17/55	15	1		10 S.O.S. ....A:15 Weary Moments	—	$20		RCA Victor 6295
3/3/56	13	3		11 I Want To Be Loved..A:13 Feet Of Clay	—	$20		RCA Victor 6395
				JOHNNIE & JACK with Ruby Wells				
				JOHNNIE AND JACK:				
2/24/58	7	18		12 Stop The World (And Let Me Off)	S:7 / A:9 Camel Walk Stroll	—	$15		RCA Victor 7137
10/20/58	18	3		13 Lonely Island Pearl..Leave Our Moon Alone	—	$15		RCA Victor 7324
8/10/59	16	12		14 Sailor Man...Wild And Wicked World	—	$15		RCA Victor 7545
8/11/62	17	4		15 Slow Poison.................................You'll Never Get A Better Chance Than This	—	$12		Decca 31397
				JOHNNY AND JACK				
				JOHNS, Sammy '81				
				Born on 2/7/46 in Charlotte, North Carolina. Singer/songwriter/guitarist.				
11/30/74+	79	7		1 Early Morning Love..Holy Mother, Aging Father	68	$6		GRC 2021
9/19/81	50	7		2 Common Man..Easy To Be With You	—	$5		Elektra 47189
9/3/88	80	6		3 Chevy Van..Love Me Off The Road	—	$4		MCA 53398
				new version of his #5 Pop hit from 1975				
				JOHNS, Sarah '75				
8/30/75	75	3		1 I'm Ready To Love You Now.......................Love Me Back Together Again	—	$5		RCA Victor 10333
1/10/76	97	4		2 Feelings...I'm Making Love To A Memory	—	$5		RCA Victor 10465
				#6 Pop hit for Morris Albert in 1975				
3/27/76	86	3		3 Let The Big Wheels Roll..Glory, Tennessee	—	$5		RCA Victor 10590
				JOHNS, Tricia '81				
				Born in Austin, Texas.				
5/14/77	100	1		1 The Heat Is On...You Lift Me Up	—	$5		Warner 8357
12/27/80+	90	3		2 Did We Fall Out Of Love..Night Romancing	—	$4		Elektra 47057
8/8/81	57	8		3 Cathy's Clown...Out Among The Stars	—	$4		Elektra 47172
				#1 Pop hit for **The Everly Brothers** in 1960				
				JOHNSON, Buddy, And His Orchestra '44				
				Born Woodrow Wilson Johnson on 1/10/15 in Darlington, South Carolina. Died of a brain tumor on 2/9/77 (age 62). Black orchestra leader/pianist. Charted 14 R&B hits from 1943-57.				
3/11/44	2²	7		When My Man Comes Home...................................I'll Always Be With You	18	$20		Decca 8655
				Ella Johnson (vocal)				
				JOHNSON, Carolyn Dawn '01				
				Born on 4/30/71 in Grand Prairie, Alberta, Canada. Singer/songwriter/guitarist. Also see **America The Beautiful**.				
9/16/00+	25	23		1 Georgia..................................S:7 Love Is Always Worth The Ache	98	$4	★	Arista Nash. 69010 (v)
				Martina McBride (backing vocal)				
4/21/01	5	32		2 Complicated...Georgia	59	$4		Arista Nashville 69050
12/15/01+	7	29↑		3 I Don't Want You To Go..Room With A View	54	$4		Arista Nashville 69133
	★305★			**JOHNSON, Lois** '75				
				Born in Knoxville, Tennessee. Worked on local radio from age 11. Regular appearances on WWVA-Wheeling *Jamboree*. Toured with **Hank Williams Jr.** from 1970-73.				
				1)Loving You Will Never Grow Old 2)So Sad (To Watch Good Love Go Bad) 3)Send Me Some Lovin' 4)Come On In And Let Me Love You 5)Your Pretty Roses Came Too Late				
1/25/69	74	3		1 Softly And Tenderly................................Goin' Down (For The Third Time)	—	$8		Columbia 44725
7/4/70	23	12		2 Removing The Shadow...Party People	—	$7		MGM 14136
				HANK WILLIAMS, JR. and LOIS JOHNSON				
10/3/70	12	13		3 So Sad (To Watch Good Love Go Bad)..........................Let's Talk It Over Again	—	$7		MGM 14164
				HANK WILLIAMS, JR. & LOIS JOHNSON				
				#7 Pop hit for **The Everly Brothers** in 1960				
12/5/70+	48	9		4 When He Touches Me (Nothing Else Matters)..........When A Woman Stands Alone	—	$7		MGM 14186
2/27/71	65	2		5 From Warm To Cool To Cold..........................You Didn't Stop To Say Hello	—	$7		MGM 14217
4/1/72	14	14		6 Send Me Some Lovin'.............................What We Used To Hang On To (Is Gone)	—	$7		MGM 14356
				HANK WILLIAMS, JR. & LOIS JOHNSON				
7/15/72	63	8		7 Rain-Rain..My Heart Has A Mind Of Its Own	—	$7		MGM 14401
11/18/72+	22	11		8 Whole Lotta Loving..Why Should We Try Anymore	—	$7		MGM 14443
				HANK WILLIAMS, JR. & LOIS JOHNSON				
				#6 Pop hit for **Fats Domino** in 1959				
11/17/73	97	2		9 Love Will Stand...Don't Be Cruel	—	$7		MGM 14638
7/20/74	19	19		10 Come On In And Let Me Love You......................If I Throw Away My Pride	—	$6		20th Century 2106
12/28/74+	6	15		11 Loving You Will Never Grow Old..............................Lonesome Number One	—	$6		20th Century 2151
5/17/75	48	8		12 You Know Just What I'd Do.........................You're The Rock Of Ages	—	$6		20th Century 2187
9/13/75	95	4		13 Hope For The Flowers...................................Merrily We Love Along	—	$6		20th Century 2223
10/11/75	70	8		14 The Door's Always Open...Bring It On Home	—	$6		20th Century 2242
7/24/76	87	2		15 Weep No More My Baby...Birthday Wish	—	$5		Polydor 14328
1/15/77	20	13		16 Your Pretty Roses Came Too Late...................................Birthday Wish	—	$5		Polydor 14371
5/14/77	40	8		17 I Hate Goodbyes..I'm Your Friend	—	$5		Polydor 14392
11/19/77	97	3		18 All The Love We Threw Away..............................We Can't Make It Anymore	—	$5		Polydor 14435
				LOIS JOHNSON & BILL RICE				
5/20/78	63	7		19 When I Need You..A Dreamer Of Dreams	—	$5		Polydor 14476
				#1 Pop hit for **Leo Sayer** in 1977				
6/2/84	89	3		20 It Won't Be Easy..You Are The Melody	—	$5		EMH 0030
				originally released on Whitehorse 065 in 1980 with a picture insert				

Red Johnson

DEBUT	PEAK	WKS	Gold	A-side (Chart Hit)	B-side	Pop	$	Pic	Label & Number
	★325★			**JOHNSON, Michael** '87 Born on 8/8/44 in Alamosa, Colorado; raised in Denver. Singer/songwriter/guitarist. Best known for pop hit "Bluer Than Blue."					
11/16/85+	9	25		1 I Love You By Heart ..... SYLVIA & MICHAEL JOHNSON	A:9 / S:10 Eyes Like Mine	—	$4		RCA 14217
4/26/86	12	20		2 Gotta Learn To Love Without You	S:8 / A:13 River Colorado	—	$4		RCA 14294
9/27/86+	0¹	23		3 Give Me Wings	S:0¹ / A:2 Magic Time	—	$4	☐	RCA 14412
1/31/87	0¹	26		4 The Moon Is Still Over Her Shoulder	A:0¹ / S:7 That's What Your Love Does To Me	—	$4		RCA 5091
6/13/87	26	13		5 Ponies	Cool Me In The River Of Love	—	$4		RCA 5171
10/17/87+	4	20		6 Crying Shame	S:17 True Love	—	$4		RCA 5279
4/2/88	7	22		7 I Will Whisper Your Name	S:17 Too Soon To Tell	—	$4		RCA 6833
8/27/88	9	20		8 That's That	S:23 Some People's Lives	—	$4		RCA 8650
12/17/88+	52	8		9 Roller Coaster Run (Up Too Slow, Down Too Fast)	Diamond Dreams	—	$4		RCA 8748
				JOHNSON, Roland '59					
3/2/59	25	3		I Traded Her Love (For Deep Purple Wine)	I'll Be With You	—	$20		Brunswick 55110
				JOHNSON, Tim '87 Born in Pennsylvania.					
9/19/87	78	3		Hard Headed Heart		—	$6		Sundial 135
				JOHNSTON, Day '88 Born in New Mexico. Female singer/songwriter.					
9/3/88	82	3		What Cha' Doin' To Me	Little Red Heart	—	$6		Roadrunner 4639
				JOHNSTONS, The '87					
2/28/87	82	5		Two-Name Girl	This Time	—	$6		Hidden Valley 1286
				JOLIE & THE WANTED '00 Group from Omaha, Nebraska: Jolie Edwards (vocals), Phil Symonds and Jon Trebing (guitars), Steve King (keyboards), Ethan Pilzer (bass) and Andy Hull (drums).					
9/16/00	55	7		1 I Would		—			album cut
2/10/01	55	1		2 Boom		—			album cut
				above 2 from the album Jolie & The Wanted on DreamWorks 50243					
				JON AND LYNN '82 Husband-and-wife duo Jon and Lynn Hargis. Both were born in Cincinnati. Married in 1975.					
12/19/81+	59	7		1 Let The Good Times Roll	I Want To (Do Everything For You)	—	$5		Soundwaves 4656
				#20 Pop hit for Shirley & Lee in 1956					
8/21/82	86	3		2 (What A Day For A) Day Dream	I Never Do Get Tired Of Telling You	—	$5		Soundwaves 4677
				#2 Pop hit for The Lovin' Spoonful in 1966					
				JONES, Ann '49 Born Ann Matthews in 1920 in Hutchison, Kansas; raised in Enid, Oklahoma. Singer/songwriter.					
10/15/49	15	1		Give Me A Hundred Reasons	J:15 I Believe You, Baby	—	$20		Capitol 15414
				JONES, Anthony Armstrong '70 Born Ronnie Jones on 6/2/49 in Ada, Oklahoma. Singer/guitarist. Took stage name from the British photographer who married Princess Margaret. 1)Take A Letter Maria 2)Proud Mary 3)New Orleans					
6/28/69	22	13		1 Proud Mary	The Only Girl I Can't Forget	—	$7		Chart 5017
				#2 Pop hit for Creedence Clearwater Revival in 1969					
10/18/69	28	8		2 New Orleans	And Say Goodbye	—	$7		Chart 5033
				#6 Pop hit for U.S. Bonds in 1960					
1/10/70	8	11		3 Take A Letter Maria	I Still Love You	—	$7		Chart 5045
				#2 Pop hit for R.B. Greaves in 1969					
5/23/70	56	5		4 Lead Me Not Into Temptation	One For The Road	—	$7		Chart 5064
7/25/70	38	11		5 Sugar In The Flowers	If You Gotta Go, Go Now	—	$7		Chart 5083
11/21/70	40	9		6 Sweet Caroline	Too Much Of You	—	$7		Chart 5100
				#4 Pop hit for Neil Diamond in 1969					
4/14/73	70	3		7 I'm Right Where I Belong	I Can Take On The World	—	$6		Epic 10970
7/7/73	33	10		8 Bad, Bad Leroy Brown	There's Never Been Anyone Like You	—	$6		Epic 11002
				#1 Pop hit for Jim Croce in 1973					
11/17/73	69	8		9 I've Got Mine	Quietly Doin' My Thing	—	$6		Epic 11042
5/3/86	74	5		10 Those Eyes	One Night At A Time	—	$5		AIR 103
				JONES, David Lynn '87 Born on 1/15/50 in Bexar, Arkansas. Singer/songwriter/bassist.					
8/22/87	10	20		1 Bonnie Jean (Little Sister)	S:15 Valley Of A Thousand Years	—	$4	■	Mercury 888733
3/26/88	14	19		2 High Ridin' Heroes Waylon Jennings (guest vocal)	S:27 Living In The Promiseland	—	$4	■	Mercury 870128
7/30/88	36	10		3 The Rogue	Home Of My Heart	—	$4		Mercury 870525
11/12/88	66	6		4 Tonight In America	Valley Of A Thousand Years	—	$4		Mercury 872054

DEBUT	PEAK	WKS	Gold	A-side (Chart Hit)	B-side	Pop	$	Pic	Label & Number

JONES, George ★2★ '61

Born on 9/12/31 in Saratoga, Texas. Singer/songwriter/guitarist. Started singing on radio stations KTXJ in Jasper, Texas, and KRIC in Beaumont, Texas. Served in the U.S. Marines from 1950-52. Recorded rockabilly as Thumper Jones and Hank Smith. Married to **Tammy Wynette** from 1969-75. Joined the *Grand Ole Opry* in 1969. Known as "No Show Jones" (due to several missed shows in the late 1970s) and "Possum." CMA Awards: 1980 & 1981 Male Vocalist of the Year. Elected to the Country Music Hall of Fame in 1992. Also see **Heart Of Nashville**.

1) Tender Years 2) She Thinks I Still Care 3) White Lightning 4) Walk Through This World With Me 5) We're Gonna Hold On

DEBUT	PEAK	WKS	#	A-side	B-side	Pop	$	Pic	Label & Number
10/29/55	4	18	1	Why Baby Why	S:4 / A:4 / J:4 Seasons Of My Heart	—	$50		Starday 202
1/28/56	7	7	2	What Am I Worth	J:7 / A:10 / S:14 Still Hurtin'	—	$40		Starday 216
7/14/56	7	8	3	You Gotta Be My Baby	J:7 / A:10 It's OK	—	$40		Starday 247
10/20/56	3	11	4	Just One More /	J:3	—			
		5	5	Gonna Come Get You	J:flip	—	$40		Starday 264
1/26/57	10	1	6	Yearning	J:10 So Near	—	$30		Starday 279
				GEORGE JONES and JEANETTE HICKS					
3/9/57	10	2	7	Don't Stop The Music /	J:10 / S:15 / A:15	—			
		1	8	Uh, Uh, No	J:flip	—	$25		Mercury 71029
6/10/57	13	6	9	Too Much Water	S:13 All I Want To Do	—	$25		Mercury 71096
				co-written by **Sonny James**					
4/14/58	7	10	10	Color Of The Blues	A:7 / S:18 Eskimo Pie	—	$20		Mercury 71257
11/17/58	6	16	11	Treasure Of Love /		—			
12/8/58	29	1	12	If I Don't Love You (Grits Ain't Groceries)		—	$20		Mercury 71373
3/9/59	❶5	22	13	White Lightning	Long Time To Forget	73	$20		Mercury 71406
				written by the Big Bopper (J.P. Richardson)					
7/20/59	7	13	14	Who Shot Sam	Into My Arms Again	93	$20		Mercury 71464
11/23/59+	15	12	15	Money To Burn /		—			
11/23/59	19	12	16	Big Harlan Taylor		—	$20		Mercury 71514
4/4/60	16	12	17	Accidently On Purpose /		—			
4/25/60	30	1	18	Sparkling Brown Eyes		—	$20		Mercury 71583
8/22/60	25	2	19	Out Of Control	Just Little Boy Blue	—	$20		Mercury 71641
11/7/60+	2¹	34	20	The Window Up Above	Candy Hearts	—	$15		Mercury 71700
5/29/61	16	2	21	Family Bible	Taggin' Along	—	$15		Mercury 71721
6/19/61	❶7	32	22	Tender Years	Battle Of Love	76	$15	■	Mercury 71804
9/18/61	15	3	23	Did I Ever Tell You	Not Even Friends	—	$15		Mercury 71856
				GEORGE JONES & MARGIE SINGLETON					
2/24/62	5	12	24	Aching, Breaking Heart	When My Heart Hurts No More	—	$15	■	Mercury 71910
4/14/62	❶6	23	25	She Thinks I Still Care /		—			
				#57 Pop hit for **Connie Francis** in 1962 as "He Thinks I Still Care"					
4/28/62	17	5	26	Sometimes You Just Can't Win		—	$15	■	United Artists 424
				also see #77 below					
6/16/62	11	10	27	Waltz Of The Angels	Talk About Lovin'	—	$15		Mercury 71955
				GEORGE JONES & MARGIE SINGLETON					
7/21/62	13	11	28	Open Pit Mine	Geronimo	—	$15		United Artists 462
8/25/62	28	1	29	You're Still On My Mind	Cold Cold Heart	—	$15	■	Mercury 72010
10/6/62	3	18	30	A Girl I Used To Know /		—			
10/13/62	13	9	31	Big Fool Of The Year		—	$15		United Artists 500
2/9/63	7	18	32	Not What I Had In Mind /		—			
4/6/63	29	1	33	I Saw Me		—	$15		United Artists 528
				GEORGE JONES & The Jones Boys (above 4)					
5/4/63	3	28	34	We Must Have Been Out Of Our Minds	Until Then	—	$15		United Artists 575
				GEORGE JONES & MELBA MONTGOMERY					
7/13/63	5	22	35	You Comb Her Hair	Ain't It Funny What Love Will Do (Pop #124)	—	$12	■	United Artists 578
12/7/63	17	7	36	Let's Invite Them Over /		—			
11/30/63	20	5	37	What's In Our Heart		—	$12		United Artists 635
				GEORGE JONES AND MELBA MONTGOMERY (above 2)					
2/1/64	5	18	38	Your Heart Turned Left (And I Was On The Right) /		—			
2/8/64	15	9	39	My Tears Are Overdue		—	$12		United Artists 683
3/28/64	39	3	40	The Last Town I Painted	Tarnished Angel	—	$12	■	Mercury 72233
6/20/64	10	16	41	Where Does A Little Tear Come From /		—			
6/6/64	31	7	42	Something I Dreamed		—	$12		United Artists 724
9/5/64	31	5	43	Please Be My Love	Will There Ever Be Another	—	$12		United Artists 732
				GEORGE JONES AND MELBA MONTGOMERY					
9/26/64	3	28	44	The Race Is On	She's Lonesome Again	96	$12		United Artists 751
12/12/64+	25	15	45	Multiply The Heartaches	Once More	—	$12		United Artists 784
				GEORGE JONES AND MELBA MONTGOMERY					
1/30/65	15	15	46	Least Of All	Brown To Blue	—	$12		United Artists 804
3/13/65	9	21	47	Things Have Gone To Pieces	Wearing My Heart Away	—	$12	■	Musicor 1067
4/24/65	16	10	48	I've Got Five Dollars And It's Saturday Night	Wreck On The Highway	99	$15		Musicor 1066
				GEORGE & GENE George Jones & Gene Pitney					
6/5/65	14	12	49	Wrong Number	The Old, Old House	—	$12		United Artists 858
7/3/65	25	7	50	Louisiana Man	I'm A Fool To Care (Pop #115)	—	$12	■	Musicor 1097
				GEROGE & GENE George Jones & Gene Pitney					
8/28/65	6	18	51	Love Bug	I Can't Get Used To Being Lonely	—	$12		Musicor 1098
10/9/65	40	3	52	What's Money	I Get Lonely In A Hurry	—	$12		United Artists 901

DEBUT	PEAK	WKS	Gold	A-side (Chart Hit)	B-side	Pop	$	Pic	Label & Number
				JONES, George — Cont'd					
11/6/65+	8	18		53 Take Me also see #80 below	Ship Of Fools	—	$12		Musicor 1117
11/20/65	50	2		54 Big Job	Your Old Standby	—	$12	■	Musicor 1115
				GEORGE & GENE George Jones & Gene Pitney					
3/12/66	6	17		55 I'm A People	I Woke Up From Dreaming	—	$12		Musicor 1143
3/12/66	46	3		56 World's Worse Loser	I Can't Change Over Night	—	$12		United Artists 965
6/4/66	47	3		57 That's All It Took	Y'All Come	—	$12		Musicor 1165
				GEORGE & GENE George Jones & Gene Pitney					
6/25/66	30	7		58 Old Brush Arbors	Flowers For Mama	—	$12		Musicor 1174
7/30/66	5	16		59 Four-O-Thirty Three	Don't Think I Don't	—	$12		Musicor 1181
11/19/66	70	3		60 Close Together (As You And Me)	Long As We're Dreaming	—	$12		Musicor 1204
				GEORGE JONES & MELBA MONTGOMERY					
1/21/67	❶²	22		61 Walk Through This World With Me	Developing My Pictures	—	$12		Musicor 1226
5/20/67	5	17		62 I Can't Get There From Here	Poor Man's Riches	—	$12		Musicor 1243
9/9/67	24	10		63 Party Pickin'	Simply Divine	—	$12		Musicor 1238
				GEORGE JONES & MELBA MONTGOMERY					
10/7/67	7	18		64 If My Heart Had Windows	The Honky Tonk Downstairs	—	$12		Musicor 1267
2/3/68	8	14		65 Say It's Not You	The Poor Chinee	—	$12		Musicor 1289
4/13/68	35	11		66 Small Time Laboring Man	Well It's Alright	—	$12		Musicor 1297
7/6/68	3	13		67 As Long As I Live	Your Angel Steps Out Of Heaven	—	$12		Musicor 1298
9/28/68	12	12		68 Milwaukee, Here I Come	Great Big Spirit Of Love	—	$12		Musicor 1325
				GEORGE JONES & BRENDA CARTER					
11/23/68+	2²	17		69 When The Grass Grows Over Me	Heartaches And Hangovers	—	$12	■	Musicor 1333
3/29/69	2²	18		70 I'll Share My World With You	I'll See You While Ago	—	$12		Musicor 1351
7/19/69	6	14		71 If Not For You	When The Wife Runs Off	124	$12		Musicor 1366
11/15/69+	6	14		72 She's Mine /					
11/22/69	72	13		73 No Blues Is Good News	—	—	$12		Musicor 1381
3/14/70	28	10		74 Where Grass Won't Grow	Shoulder To Shoulder	—	$12		Musicor 1392
7/4/70	13	14		75 Tell Me My Lying Eyes Are Wrong	You've Become My Everything	—	$12		Musicor 1408
				GEORGE JONES And The Jones Boys					
11/21/70+	2¹	15		76 A Good Year For The Roses also see #156 below	Let A Little Loving Come In	112	$12		Musicor 1425
3/20/71	10	13		77 Sometimes You Just Can't Win new version of #26 above	Brothers Of A Bottle [R]	—	$12		Musicor 1432
6/12/71	7	14		78 Right Won't Touch A Hand	Someone Sweet To Love	—	$12		Musicor 1440
10/2/71	13	12		79 I'll Follow You (Up To Our Cloud)	Getting Over The Storm	—	$12		Musicor 1446
12/25/71+	9	13		80 Take Me	We Go Together [R]	—	$10		Epic 10815
				TAMMY WYNETTE & GEORGE JONES new version of #53 above					
2/12/72	6	14		81 We Can Make It	One Of These Days	—	$10		Epic 10831
2/12/72	30	8		82 A Day In The Life Of A Fool	The Old Old House	—	$10		RCA Victor 0625
5/20/72	2¹	14		83 Loving You Could Never Be Better	Try It, You'll Like It	—	$10		Epic 10858
7/8/72	6	15		84 The Ceremony	The Great Divide	—	$10		Epic 10881
				TAMMY WYNETTE & GEORGE JONES					
10/14/72	46	7		85 Wrapped Around Her Finger	With Half A Heart	—	$10		RCA Victor 0792
10/28/72	5	16		86 A Picture Of Me (Without You)	The Man Worth Lovin' You	—	$10		Epic 10917
11/25/72+	38	9		87 Old Fashioned Singing	We Love To Sing About Jesus	—	$10		Epic 10923
				GEORGE JONES & TAMMY WYNETTE					
3/3/73	6	14		88 What My Woman Can't Do	My Loving Wife	—	$10		Epic 10959
4/7/73	32	9		89 Let's Build A World Together	Touching Shoulders	—	$10		Epic 10963
				GEORGE JONES AND TAMMY WYNETTE					
6/23/73	7	13		90 Nothing Ever Hurt Me (Half As Bad As Losing You)	Wine	—	$8		Epic 11006
9/1/73	❶²	17		91 We're Gonna Hold On	My Elusive Dreams	—	$8		Epic 11031
				GEORGE JONES & TAMMY WYNETTE					
11/24/73+	3	16		92 Once You've Had The Best	Mary Don't Go 'Round	—	$8		Epic 11053
2/9/74	15	13		93 (We're Not) The Jet Set	Crawdad Song	—	$8		Epic 11083
				GEORGE JONES and TAMMY WYNETTE					
4/6/74	25	12		94 The Telephone Call	No Charge	—	$8		Epic 11099
				TINA & DADDY (Jones & his stepdaughter)					
6/8/74	❶¹	17		95 The Grand Tour	Our Private Life	—	$8		Epic 11122
7/27/74	8	12		96 We Loved It Away	Ain't Love Been Good	—	$8		Epic 11151
				GEORGE JONES & TAMMY WYNETTE					
10/26/74+	❶¹	13		97 The Door	Wean Me	—	$7		Epic 50038
3/22/75	10	14		98 These Days (I Barely Get By)	Baby, There's Nothing Like You	—	$7		Epic 50088
5/17/75	25	13		99 God's Gonna Get'cha (For That)	Those Were The Good Times	—	$7		Epic 50099
				GEORGE JONES AND TAMMY WYNETTE					
7/26/75	21	11		100 Memories Of Us /			—		
11/1/75	92	4		101 I Just Don't Give A Damn		—	$7		Epic 50127
2/7/76	16	12		102 The Battle	I'll Come Back	—	$7		Epic 50187
5/22/76	37	9		103 You Always Look Your Best (Here In My Arms)	Have You Seen My Chicken	—	$7		Epic 50227
6/5/76	❶¹	15		104 Golden Ring	We're Putting It Back Together	—	$7		Epic 50235
				GEORGE JONES and TAMMY WYNETTE					
9/4/76	3	16		105 Her Name Is...	Diary Of My Mind	—	$7		Epic 50271
12/11/76+	❶²	16		106 Near You	Tattletale Eyes	—	$7		Epic 50314
				GEORGE JONES and TAMMY WYNETTE #1 Pop hit for Francis Craig in 1947					
5/21/77	34	8		107 Old King Kong	It's A 10-33 (Let's Get Jesus On The Line)	—	$7		Epic 50385

DEBUT	PEAK	WKS	Gold	A-side (Chart Hit) ... B-side	Pop	$	Pic	Label & Number
				JONES, George — Cont'd				
7/16/77	5	13		108 Southern California .... Keep The Change GEORGE JONES and TAMMY WYNETTE	—	$7		Epic 50418
8/13/77	24	10		109 If I Could Put Them All Together (I'd Have You) .... You've Got The Best Of Me Again	—	$7		Epic 50423
1/7/78	6	14		110 Bartender's Blues .... Rest In Peace James Taylor (guest vocal)	—	$7		Epic 50495
7/1/78	11	13		111 I'll Just Take It Out In Love .... Leaving Love All Over The Place	—	$7		Epic 50564
12/9/78+	7	13		112 Mabellene .... I Don't Want No Stranger Sleepin' In My Bed GEORGE JONES AND JOHNNY PAYCHECK #5 Pop hit for Chuck Berry in 1955	—	$7		Epic 50647
5/26/79	14	11		113 You Can Have Her .... Along Came Jones GEORGE JONES AND JOHNNY PAYCHECK #12 Pop hit for Roy Hamilton in 1961	—	$6		Epic 50708
6/30/79	22	11		114 Someday My Day Will Come .... We Oughta Be Ashamed	—	$6		Epic 50684
3/1/80	2¹	14		115 Two Story House .... It Sure Was Good GEORGE JONES and TAMMY WYNETTE	—	$6		Epic 50849
4/12/80	❶¹	18		116 He Stopped Loving Her Today .... A Hard Act To Follow CMA Award: Single of the Year	—	$6		Epic 50867
6/21/80	31	9		117 When You're Ugly Like Us (You Just Naturally Got To Be Cool) .... Kansas City GEORGE JONES AND JOHNNY PAYCHECK	—	$6		Epic 50891
8/23/80	2¹	17		118 I'm Not Ready Yet .... Garage Sale Today	—	$6		Epic 50922
9/6/80	19	11		119 A Pair Of Old Sneakers .... We'll Talk About It Later GEORGE JONES and TAMMY WYNETTE	—	$6		Epic 50930
12/13/80+	18	12		120 You Better Move On .... Smack Dab In The Middle GEORGE JONES and JOHNNY PAYCHECK #24 Pop hit for Arthur Alexander in 1962	—	$6		Epic 50949
1/17/81	8	15		121 If Drinkin' Don't Kill Me (Her Memory Will) .... Brother To The Blues	—	$6		Epic 50968
10/3/81	❶¹	17		122 Still Doin' Time .... Good Ones And Bad Ones	—	$5		Epic 02526
2/6/82	5	19		123 Same Ole Me .... Together Alone Oak Ridge Boys (backing vocals)	—	$5		Epic 02696
8/7/82	❶¹	15		124 Yesterday's Wine .... I Haven't Found Her Yet MERLE HAGGARD/GEORGE JONES	—	$5		Epic 03072
12/4/82+	10	19		125 C.C. Waterback .... After I Sing All My Songs GEORGE JONES/MERLE HAGGARD	—	$5		Epic 03405
1/15/83	3	19		126 Shine On (Shine All Your Sweet Love On Me) .... Memories Of Mama	—	$5		Epic 03489
5/7/83	❶¹	18		127 I Always Get Lucky With You .... I'd Rather Have What We Had	—	$5		Epic 03883
9/10/83	2¹	22		128 Tennessee Whiskey .... Almost Persuaded	—	$5		Epic 04082
12/17/83+	6	18		129 We Didn't See A Thing .... I Wish You Were Here Tonight RAY CHARLES & GEORGE JONES Featuring Chet Atkins	—	$4		Columbia 04297
4/7/84	3	19		130 You've Still Got A Place In My Heart .... I'm Ragged But Right	—	$4	■	Epic 04413
9/22/84	2³	23		131 She's My Rock .... S:❶¹ / A:2 (What Love Can Do) The Second Time Around	—	$4		Epic 04609
12/22/84+	15	16		132 Hallelujah, I Love You So .... A:13 / S:15 The Second Time Around GEORGE JONES with BRENDA LEE #5 R&B hit for Ray Charles in 1956	—	$4		Epic 04723
4/27/85	19	18		133 Size Seven Round (Made Of Gold) .... S:17 / A:19 All I Want To Do In Life GEORGE JONES and LACY J. DALTON	—	$4		Epic 04876
8/3/85	3	20		134 Who's Gonna Fill Their Shoes .... S:2 / A:5 A Whole Lot Of Trouble For You	—	$4		Epic 05439
11/23/85+	3	22		135 The One I Loved Back Then (The Corvette Song) .... S:❶¹ / A:3 If Only You'd Love Me Again	—	$4		Epic 05698
4/19/86	9	21		136 Somebody Wants Me Out Of The Way ... S:5 / A:11 Call The Wrecker For My Heart	—	$4		Epic 05862
9/13/86	10	23		137 Wine Colored Roses .... S:7 / A:11 These Old Eyes Have Seen It All	—	$4		Epic 06296
1/17/87	8	20		138 The Right Left Hand .... S:2 / A:8 The Very Best Of Me	—	$4		Epic 06593
5/16/87	26	18		139 I Turn To You .... S:14 Don't Leave Without Taking Your Silver	—	$4		Epic 07107
12/19/87+	26	14		140 The Bird .... S:9 I'm Goin' Home Like I Never Did Before	—	$4		Epic 07655
3/26/88	52	10		141 I'm A Survivor .... The Real McCoy	—	$4		Epic 07748
6/4/88	63	6		142 The Old Man No One Loves .... One Hell Of A Song	—	$4		Epic 07913
9/3/88	43	10		143 If I Could Bottle This Up .... S:22 I Always Get It Right With You GEORGE JONES & SHELBY LYNNE	—	$4		Epic 08011
12/17/88+	5	20		144 I'm A One Woman Man .... Pretty Little Lady From Beaumont Texas	—	$4		Epic 08509
4/29/89	26	13		145 The King Is Gone (So Are You) .... Don't You Ever Get Tired (Of Hurting Me) promo record and picture sleeve shown as "Ya Ba Da Ba Do (So Are You)"	—	$4	■	Epic 68743
7/29/89	31	16		146 Writing On The Wall .... Burning Bridges	—	$4		Epic 68991
11/11/89	62	6		147 Radio Lover .... Burning Bridges	—	$4		Epic 73070
9/8/90	8	20		148 A Few Ole Country Boys .... Smokin' The Hive RANDY TRAVIS & GEORGE JONES	—	$4	■	Warner 19586 (v)
8/31/91	32	20		149 You Couldn't Get The Picture .... Heckel And Jeckel	—	$4		MCA 54187
1/11/92	55	14		150 She Loved A Lot In Her Time .... Come Home To Me	—	$4		MCA 54272
4/11/92	60	7		151 Honky Tonk Myself To Death .... Where The Tall Grass Grows	—	$4		MCA 54370
10/17/92+	34	20		152 I Don't Need Your Rockin' Chair .... Finally Friday guest vocalists: **Vince Gill, Mark Chesnutt, Garth Brooks, Travis Tritt, Joe Diffie, Alan Jackson, Pam Tillis, T. Graham Brown, Patty Loveless** and **Clint Black**	—	$4		MCA 54470
3/20/93	65	6		153 Wrong's What I Do Best .... The Bottle Let Me Down	—	$4		MCA 54604
11/13/93+	24	20		154 High-Tech Redneck .... Forever's Here To Stay	—	$4		MCA 54749
3/12/94	52	10		155 Never Bit A Bullet Like This .... GEORGE JONES with Sammy Kershaw from the album *High-Tech Redneck* on MCA 10910	—			album cut

DEBUT	PEAK	WKS	Gold	A-side (Chart Hit) .... B-side	Pop	$	Pic	Label & Number
				JONES, George — Cont'd				
11/12/94	56	7		156 A Good Year For The Roses .... I've Still Got Some Hurtin' Left To Do (Jones) [R]	—	$4	■	MCA 54969 (v)
				GEORGE JONES with Alan Jackson new version of #76 above				
7/1/95	69	4		157 One .... Golden Ring		$4		MCA 55048
				GEORGE JONES AND TAMMY WYNETTE				
9/14/96	66	6		158 Honky Tonk Song .... The Lone Ranger	—	$4		MCA 55228
9/20/97	14	20		159 You Don't Seem To Miss Me .... S:9 Where Are You Boy	109	$4	■	Epic 78704 (v)
				PATTY LOVELESS With George Jones				
5/8/99	30	20		160 Choices	—			album cut
11/6/99+	45	20		161 The Cold Hard Truth	—			album cut
				above 2 from the album *Cold Hard Truth* on Asylum 62368				
11/20/99+	30	13		162 A Country Boy Can Survive (Y2K Version) .... S:2 Going The Distance	75	$4	★	Warner 16895 (v)
				CHAD BROCK (With Hank Williams, Jr. & George Jones)				
5/13/00	55	12		163 Sinners & Saints	—			album cut
				from the album *Cold Hard Truth* on Asylum 62368				
8/4/01	47	9		164 The Man He Was	—			album cut
10/13/01	24	20		165 Beer Run	118			album cut
				GEORGE JONES With Garth Brooks above 2 from the album *The Rock: Stone Cold Country 2001* on Bandit 67029				
				JONES, Grandpa '63				
				Born Louis Marshall Jones on 10/20/13 in Niagra, Kentucky; raised in Akron, Ohio. Died of a stroke on 2/19/98 (age 84). Singer/banjo player. Began appearing as "Grandpa" in 1935. Joined the *Grand Ole Opry* in 1947. Regular on TV's *Hee-Haw*. Elected to the Country Music Hall of Fame in 1978.				
2/23/59	21	2		1 The All-American Boy .... Pickin' Time	—	$20		Decca 30823
				#2 Pop hit for **Bobby Bare** (Bill Parsons) in 1959				
12/15/62+	5	16		2 T For Texas .... Tritzem Yodel		$15		Monument 801
				#2 Pop hit for **Jimmie Rodgers** in 1928				
				JONES, Harrison '74				
				Born on 2/13/47 in Corbin, Kentucky.				
6/22/74	72	7		1 But Tonight I'm Gonna Love You .... It's That Time Again		$6		GRT 004
				JONES, JC '98				
				Born in 1973 in Los Angeles. Male singer/songwriter.				
1/17/98	61	6		1 One Night .... Heart Pounding Love		$4		Rising Tide 56054
				JONES, Kacey '01				
				Born in San Francisco. Female singer.				
4/7/01	14^S	1		1 Till Dale Earnhardt Wins Cup #8 .... (unedited version)		$4	★	IGO 3333
				a tribute to Dale Earnhardt, who was killed while racing at the Daytona 500 on 2/18/01				
				JONES, Mickey '89				
				Born on 6/10/41 in Houston. Member of **Kenny Rogers & The First Edition**.				
3/3/79	94	5		1 She Loves My Troubles Away .... Forever	—	$6		Bayshore 100
9/2/89	85	3		2 A Song A Day Keeps The Blues Away .... Here's A Rose	—	$6		Stop Hunger 1102
11/25/89	80	3		3 Bigger Man Than Me! .... Play Another Good Old Country Song!	—	$6		Stop Hunger 1103
	★286★			**JONES, Tom** '77				
				Born Thomas Jones Woodward on 6/7/40 in Pontypridd, South Wales. Charted 30 pop hits from 1965-89. Won the 1965 Best New Artist Grammy Award. Hosted own TV variety series from 1969-71. 1)Say You'll Stay Until Tomorrow 2)Touch Me (I'll Be Your Fool Once More) 3)I've Been Rained On Too				
12/25/76+	❶¹	17		1 Say You'll Stay Until Tomorrow .... Lady Lay	15	$5		Epic/MAM 50308
6/4/77	87	3		2 Take Me Tonight .... I Hope You'll Understand	101	$5		Epic/MAM 50382
				adapted from Tchaikovsky's *Pathetique Symphony*				
11/19/77	71	8		3 What A Night .... That's Where I Belong	—	$5		Epic/MAM 50468
4/18/81	19	14		4 Darlin' .... I Don't Want To Know You That Well	103	$4		Mercury 76100
				#103 Pop hit for **Frankie Miller** in 1979				
8/8/81	25	11		5 What In The World's Come Over You .... The Things That Matter Most To Me	109	$4		Mercury 76115
				#5 Pop hit for **Jack Scott** in 1960				
11/28/81+	26	14		6 Lady Lay Down .... A Daughter's Question	—	$4		Mercury 76125
9/18/82	16	18		7 A Woman's Touch .... I'll Never Get Over You	—	$4		Mercury 76172
2/26/83	4	18		8 Touch Me (I'll Be Your Fool Once More) .... We're Wasting Our Time	—	$4		Mercury 810445
7/2/83	34	12		9 It'll Be Me .... If I Ever Had To Say Goodbye To You	—	$4		Mercury 812631
12/10/83+	13	22		10 I've Been Rained On Too .... That Old Piano	—	$4		Mercury 814820
4/28/84	30	14		11 This Time .... Memphis, Tennessee	—	$4		Mercury 818801
9/1/84	53	9		12 All The Love Is On The Radio .... You Are No Angel	—	$4		Mercury 880173
12/8/84+	67	9		13 I'm An Old Rock And Roller (Dancin' To A Different Beat) ... My Kind Of Girl	—	$4		Mercury 880402
3/2/85	48	9		14 Give Her All The Roses (Don't Wait Until Tomorrow) .... Picture Of You	—	$4		Mercury 880569
9/14/85	76	6		15 Not Another Heart Song .... Only My Heart Knows	—	$4		Mercury 884039
11/23/85+	36	13		16 It's Four In The Morning .... I'll Never Get Over You	—	$4		Mercury 884252
				JORDAN, Jill '88				
				Born Jill Galehouse in Wooster, Ohio. Grandfather was pro baseball pitcher Denny Galehouse.				
2/20/88	68	5		1 Calendar Blues	—	$6		Maxx 822
6/11/88	72	4		2 I Did It For Love	—	$6		Maxx 823
				JORDAN, Louis, And His Tympany Five '44				
				Born on 7/8/08 in Brinkley, Arkansas. Died of a heart attack on 2/4/75 (age 66). Black singer/saxophonist. Charted 57 R&B hits from 1942-51. Inducted into the Rock and Roll Hall of Fame in 1987.				
1/15/44	❶³	13		1 Ration Blues /	16			
1/29/44	7	1		2 Deacon Jones	—	$20		Decca 8654

DEBUT	PEAK	WKS	Gold	A-side (Chart Hit)	B-side	Pop	$	Pic	Label & Number
				JORDAN, Louis, And His Tympany Five — Cont'd					
7/1/44	❶⁵	9		3 Is You Is Or Is You Ain't (Ma' Baby)	G.I. Jive	2³	$20		Decca 8659
				from the movie *Follow The Boys* starring Marlene Dietrich; #81 Pop hit for Buster Brown in 1960					
				JOY, Homer '74					
				Born in Arkansas. Singer/songwriter.					
3/23/74	80	5		John Law	Ain't No Sunshine All The Time	—	$6		Capitol 3834
				JOYCE, Brenda '79					
				Born in 1955 in Indianapolis.					
9/15/79	96	1		Don't Touch Me	I've Been Burned	—	$7		Western Pacific 107
				JUAN, Don — see DON JUAN					
				JUDD, Cledus T. '00					
				Born Barry Poole on 12/18/64 in Crowe Springs, Georgia. Novelty singer specializing in song parodies.					
5/29/99	16ˢ	10		1 Everybody's Free (To Get Sunburned)	(long version) [C] —		$4	★	Razor & Tie 80754
				parody of "Everybody's Free (To Wear Sunscreen)" by Baz Luhrmann					
8/26/00	61	9		2 My Cellmate Thinks I'm Sexy	S:4 (dance mix) [N]	26ˢ	$4	★	Monument 79495 (v)
				parody of "She Thinks My Tractor's Sexy" by Kenny Chesney					
12/2/00	67	2		3 How Do You Milk A Cow	[N]		album cut		
				parody of "How Do You Like Me Now" by Toby Keith; from the album *Just Another Day In Parodies* on Monument 69955					
				JUDD, Wynonna — see WYNONNA					
				JUDDS, The ★106★ '85					
				Family duo from Ashland, Kentucky: Naomi (born Diana Ellen Judd on 1/11/46) and daughter **Wynonna** (born Christina Ciminella on 5/30/64) Judd. Moved to Hollywood in 1968. Moved to Nashville in 1979. Naomi's chronic hepatitis forced duo to split at the end of 1991. Naomi's daughter and Wynonna's sister is actress Ashley Judd. CMA Awards: 1984 Horizon Award; 1985, 1986 & 1987 Vocal Group of the Year; 1988, 1989, 1990 & 1991 Vocal Duo of the Year.					
				1) Have Mercy 2) Why Not Me 3) Cry Myself To Sleep 4) Change Of Heart 5) Grandpa (Tell Me 'Bout The Good Old Days)					
				THE JUDDS (Wynonna & Naomi):					
12/17/83+	17	18		1 Had A Dream (For The Heart)	Don't You Hear Jerusalem Moan	—	$5		RCA/Curb 13673
4/28/84	❶¹	23		2 Mama He's Crazy	Down Home		$4	■	RCA/Curb 13772
10/6/84	❶²	22		3 Why Not Me	A:❶¹ / S:2 Lazy Country Evening		$4		RCA/Curb 13923
				CMA Award: Single of the Year					
2/2/85	❶¹	22		4 Girls Night Out	S:❶¹ / A:❶¹ Sleeping Heart		$4		RCA/Curb 13991
6/8/85	❶¹	21		5 Love Is Alive	S:❶¹ / A:❶¹ Mr. Pain		$4		RCA/Curb 14093
10/5/85	❶²	22		6 Have Mercy	A:❶² Bye Bye Baby Blues		$4		RCA/Curb 14193
2/15/86	❶¹	20		7 Grandpa (Tell Me 'Bout The Good Old Days)	S:❶¹ / A:❶¹ Drops Of Water		$4		RCA/Curb 14290
5/24/86	❶¹	18		8 Rockin' With The Rhythm Of The Rain	S:❶¹ / A:❶¹ River Roll On		$4		RCA/Curb 14362
10/18/86+	❶¹	20		9 Cry Myself To Sleep	A:❶¹ / S:2 Dream Chaser		$4		RCA/Curb 5000
2/14/87	10	13		10 Don't Be Cruel	S:6 / A:10 The Sweetest Gift		$4	■	RCA/Curb 5094
5/9/87	❶¹	19		11 I Know Where I'm Going	S:❶¹ If I Were You		$4		RCA/Curb 5164
8/22/87	❶¹	22		12 Maybe Your Baby's Got The Blues	S:3 My Baby's Gone		$4		RCA/Curb 5255
1/16/88	❶¹	17		13 Turn It Loose	S:3 Cow Cow Boogie		$4		RCA/Curb 5329
6/11/88	2²	17		14 Give A Little Love	S:4 Why Don't You Believe Me		$4		RCA/Curb 8300
				THE JUDDS:					
10/22/88+	❶¹	20		15 Change Of Heart	S:2 I Wish She Wouldn't Treat You That Way		$4		RCA/Curb 8715
2/25/89	❶¹	21		16 Young Love	Cow Cow Boogie		$4		Curb/RCA 8820
7/8/89	❶¹	21		17 Let Me Tell You About Love	Water Of Love		$4		Curb/RCA 8947
11/25/89+	8	26		18 One Man Woman	Sleepless Nights		$4		Curb/RCA 9077
3/31/90	16	21		19 Guardian Angels	Cadillac Red		$4		Curb/RCA 2524
8/11/90	5	21		20 Born To Be Blue	Rompin' Stompin' Blues		$4	■	Curb/RCA 2597 (v)
12/8/90+	5	20		21 Love Can Build A Bridge	This Country's Rockin'		$4		Curb/RCA 2708
4/13/91	6	20		22 One Hundred And Two	Are The Roses Not Blooming		$4		Curb/RCA 2782
9/14/91	29	16		23 John Deere Tractor	Calling In The Wind		$4		Curb/RCA 62038
12/27/97	68	1		24 Silver Bells	[X]		album cut		
				#78 Pop hit for Bing Crosby & Carol Richards in 1957; from the album *Christmas Time With The Judds* on Curb/RCA 6422					
2/19/00	26	18		25 Stuck In Love			album cut		
				from the album *New Day Dawning* on Curb 541067					
				JURGENS, Dick, and his Orchestra '47					
				Born on 1/9/10 in Sacramento, California. Died of cancer on 10/5/95 (age 85). Orchestra leader/songwriter.					
3/8/47	4	2		(Oh Why, Oh Why, Did I Ever Leave) Wyoming	Bless You	14	$15		Columbia 37210
				Jimmy Castle, Al Galante and Band (vocals)					
				JUSTIS, Bill, and His Orchestra '58					
				Born on 10/14/26 in Birmingham, Alabama. Died on 7/15/82 (age 55). Session saxophonist/arranger/producer.					
11/25/57+	6	16	●	Raunchy	S:6 / A:14 The Midnite Man [I]	2¹	$30		Phillips 3519
				Sid Manker (guitar); Bill Justis (sax)					

DEBUT	PEAK	WKS	Gold	A-side (Chart Hit)	B-side	Pop	$	Pic	Label & Number
				# K					
				KALIN TWINS Bros. ★ '58 Duo of twins Herbert and Harold Kalin. Born on 2/16/34 in Port Jervis, New York.					
8/4/58	13	7	●	When ....S:13 *Three O'Clock Thrill*		5	$25		Decca 30642
				KANDY, Jim '65					
9/4/65	29	6		I'm The Man .... *Angelville - Sky*		—	$15		K-Ark 647
				KANE, Kieran '81 Born on 10/7/49 in Queens, New York. Singer/songwriter. Member of **The O'Kanes**.					
3/21/81	80	4		1 The Baby... *I Don't Drink From The River*			$4		Elektra 47111
6/20/81	14	16		2 You're The Best .... *Finishing Touches*			$4		Elektra 47148
11/7/81+	16	18		3 It's Who You Love .... *Doctor's Orders*			$4		Elektra 47228
3/6/82	26	14		4 I Feel It With You .... *She's Looking For Something New*			$4		Elektra 47415
7/10/82	26	12		5 I'll Be Your Man Around The House .... *Blue All Over You*			$4		Elektra 47478
10/30/82	45	8		6 Gonna Have A Party .... *As Long As I'm Rockin' With You*			$4		Elektra 69943
4/30/83	30	12		7 It's You .... *Makin' It Up*			$4		Warner 29711
3/17/84	28	14		8 Dedicate .... *Surrender To Your Heart*			$4		Warner 29336
				KANTER, Hillary '85 Born in Cincinnati. Singer/songwriter/pianist.					
8/18/84	51	9		1 Good Night For Falling In Love .... *I Couldn't Help Myself*			$4		RCA 13835
12/1/84+	54	18		2 Hey .... *My Heart's Saying Yes*			$4		RCA 13935
5/4/85	50	9		3 We Work.. *Harbor Of Your Heart*			$4		RCA 14053
				KAY, Melissa '88 Born in Winter Garden, Florida.					
2/6/88	75	3		1 Don't Forget Your Way Home		—	$6		Reed 1115
8/6/88	79	3		2 After Lovin' You		—	$6		Reed 1119
5/6/89	87	3		3 Poison Sugar		—	$6		Reed 1123
				KAYE, Angela '81 Born in 1966.					
10/10/81	81	5		Catching Fire		—	$6		Yatahey 804
				KAYE, Barry '78 Born on 4/24/46 in Los Angeles.					
3/11/78	89	5		Easy .... *Life* #4 Pop hit for the Commodores in 1977		—	$5		MCA 40868
				KAYE, Debbie Lori '68 Born on 5/6/50 in New York.					
6/22/68	68	3		Come On Home .... *Help Me Love You*		—	$8		Columbia 44538
				KAYE, Lois '79 Born Lois Kaye Edmiston on 12/8/50 in Knox, Indiana; raised in Beecher, Indiana.					
11/3/79	96	2		Drown In The Flood .... *Why'd You Have To Be So Good*		—	$6		Ovation 1130
				KAYE, Sandra '78 Born Sandra Kaye Van Auken in Longview, Washington.					
7/29/78	52	7		1 This Magic Moment *Baby Doesn't Live Here Anymore* #6 Pop hit for Jay & The Americans in 1969		—	$5		Door Knob 068
10/21/78	80	5		2 One More Time .... *My Dolly And I*		—	$5		Door Knob 075
12/23/78+	84	5		3 I'll Still Love You In My Dreams .... *Kiss And Run*		—	$5		Door Knob 088
3/3/79	83	5		4 I've Seen It All .... *I'll Still Love You In My Dreams*		—	$5		Door Knob 093
8/18/79	95	4		5 You Broke My Heart So Gently (It Almost Didn't Break) .... *Where Would I Be*		—	$5		Door Knob 097
				KAYLE, Kortney '01 Born on 2/8/79 in Ayr, Ontario, Canda. Female singer.					
3/24/01	60	1		1 Don't Let Me Down .... *You Got My Love*			$4		Lyric Street 64045
6/9/01	50	12		2 Unbroken By You .... S:9 *Don't Let Me Down*			$4	★	Lyric Street 64048 (v)
				KEARNEY, Ramsey '85 Born William Ramsey Kearney on 10/30/33 in Bolivar, Tennessee.					
8/24/85	96	1		1 King Of Oak Street .... *Je T'aime Beaucoup (I Love You Very Much)*			$8		Safari 114
9/10/88	97	1		2 One Time Thing		—	$8		Safari 117
				KEITH, Toby ★110★ '01 Born Toby Keith Covel on 7/8/61 in Clinton, Oklahoma. Singer/songwriter/guitarist. Former oil field worker, rodeo hand and defensive end for the Oklahoma Drillers semipro football team. Lead singer of group Easy Money from 1984-88. CMA Award: 2001 Male Vocalist of the Year. Also see **America The Beautiful**. 1)How Do You Like Me Now?! 2)I Wanna Talk About Me 3)My List 4)You Shouldn't Kiss Me Like This 5)Should've Been A Cowboy					
3/6/93	0²	20		1 Should've Been A Cowboy (album snippets) "45" B-side: "Some Kinda Good Kinda Hold On Me"		93	$4	■	Mercury 864990 (v)
7/3/93	5	20		2 He Ain't Worth Missing *A Little Less Talk And A Lot More Action*		107	$4	■	Mercury 862262 (v)
11/13/93+	2¹	20		3 A Little Less Talk And A Lot More Action *Mama Come Quick*		—	$4	■	Mercury 862844 (v)
3/19/94	2¹	20		4 Wish I Didn't Know Now *Under The Fall*		—	$4	■	Mercury 858290

Honky Tonk U. (?) /// Let's Roll (?) /// The Eagle Will Fly (?)

DEBUT	PEAK	WKS	Gold	A-side (Chart Hit)...B-side	Pop	$	Pic	Label & Number
				KEITH, Toby — Cont'd				
7/30/94	①¹	20		5 Who's That Man .... *(album snippets)* "45" B-side: "You Ain't Much Fun"	50ˢ	$4	■	Polydor 853358 (v)
12/3/94+	10	20		6 Upstairs Downtown .... *Woman Behind The Man*	—	$4		Polydor 851136 (v)
3/25/95	2³	20		7 You Ain't Much Fun .... S:9 *Life Was A Play (The World A Stage)*	—	$4		Polydor 851728 (v)
7/15/95	15	20		8 Big Ol' Truck .... *In Other Words*	—	$4		Polydor 579574
12/16/95	50	5		9 Santa I'm Right Here .... *Blame It On The Mistletoe* [X]	—	$4		Polydor 577416
3/9/96	2²	20		10 Does That Blue Moon Ever Shine On You .... S:3 *(album snippets)* "45" B-side: "She's Gonna Get It"	112	$4	■	Polydor 576140 (v)
7/13/96	6	20		11 A Woman's Touch .... *She's Perfect*	—	$4		A&M 581714
11/23/96+	①¹	20		12 Me Too .... *The Lonely*	—	$4		Mercury 578810
6/14/97	2²	20		13 We Were In Love .... S:11 *Tired*	116	$4	■	Mercury 574636 (v)
10/11/97+	2¹	20		14 I'm So Happy I Can't Stop Crying .... S:7 *Jacky Don Tucker (Play By The Rules Miss All The Fun)* TOBY KEITH with Sting #94 Pop hit for Sting in 1996	84	$4	■	Mercury 568114 (v)
1/31/98	5	20		15 Dream Walkin' .... *Strangers Again*	—	$4		Mercury 574950
5/23/98	40	10		16 Double Wide Paradise .... *Tired*	—	$4		Mercury 568928
9/12/98	18	20		17 Getcha Some .... *Should've Been A Cowboy*	102	$4		Mercury 566432
2/20/99	44	9		18 If A Man Answers .... *You Ain't Much Fun*	—	$4		Mercury 566912
10/2/99	44	10		19 When Love Fades .... — later issued as the B-side of #20 and 21 below	—	★		album cut (v)
11/20/99+	①⁵	42		20 How Do You Like Me Now?! .... S:4 *When Love Fades*	31	$4	★	DreamWor. 459041 (v)
5/27/00	4	24		21 Country Comes To Town .... *When Love Fades*	54	$4		DreamWorks 459033
10/28/00+	①³	34		22 You Shouldn't Kiss Me Like This	32			album cut
				above 4 from the album *How Do You Like Me Now?!* on DreamWorks 450209				
12/30/00	57	2		23 Old Toy Trains .... [X] released only as a promotional CD single	—	$10	★	DreamWorks 13611
5/26/01	①¹	22		24 I'm Just Talkin' About Tonight .... later issued as the B-side of #25 below	27			album cut (v)
8/25/01	①⁵	28		25 I Wanna Talk About Me .... *I'm Just Talkin' About Tonight*	28	$4		DreamWorks 450874
12/22/01+	①⁵	28↑		26 My List .... above 3 from the album *Pull My Chain* on DreamWorks 450297	26			album cut
				KELLER, Joanie '00 Born in Wayne, Nebraska. Singer/songwriter/guitarist.				
3/25/00	66	1		Three Little Teardrops .... — from the album *Sparks Are Gonna Fly* on Broken Bow 7773	—			album cut
				KELLEY, John '82 Born in Little Rock, Arkansas; raised in Indiana.				
7/24/82	81	4		This Morning I Woke Up In New York City .... *Winnin' Time*	—	$7		ComStar 8201
				KELLUM, Murry '71 Born in Jackson, Tennessee; raised in Plain, Texas. Died in a plane crash on 9/30/90 (age 47).				
6/19/71	26	10		1 Joy To The World .... *In A Phone Booth On My Knees* #1 Pop hit for Three Dog Night in 1971	—	$6		Epic 10741
11/20/71	74	2		2 Train Train (Carry Me Away) .... *What's Made Milwaukee Famous*	—	$6		Epic 10784
2/2/74	55	9		3 Lovely Lady .... *Alive And Doing Well*	—	$5		Cinnamon 777
5/25/74	98	2		4 Girl Of My Life .... *Since You've Been Gone*	—	$5		Cinnamon 794
				KELLY, Irene '89 Born in Latrobe, Pennsylvania.				
12/2/89	67	7		Love Is A Hard Road .... *Too Late (To Turn Back Now)*	—	$4		MCA 53756
				KELLY, Jerri '82 Born on 10/11/47 in Phoenix; raised in Stephenville, Texas. Female singer.				
1/18/75	65	10		1 I Can't Help Myself (Sugar Pie, Honey Bunch) .... *Got You On My Mind* PRICE MITCHELL & JERRI KELLY #1 Pop hit for the Four Tops in 1965	—	$7		GRT 016
1/26/80	90	2		2 For A Slow Dance With You .... *Stop Startin' Over*	—	$6		Little Giant 021
8/2/80	66	9		3 Fallin' For You .... *Guess I'd Better Be Strong (And Move Along)*	—	$6	■	Little Giant 026
11/8/80	85	3		4 Forsaking All The Rest .... *I'm As Much Of A Woman (As You Care To Make Me)*	—	$6	■	Little Giant 030
1/31/81	85	3		5 Be My Lover, Be My Friend .... *Drifter's Lullaby* MICK LLOYD & JERRI KELLY	—	$6		Little Giant 040
8/8/81	85	4		6 Sweet Natural Love .... *Forsaking All The Rest* MICK LLOYD & JERRI KELLY	—	$6		Little Giant 046
8/14/82	56	8		7 Walk Me 'Cross The River .... *All That Shines Is Gold*	—	$5		Carrere 03017
				KELLY, Karen '70				
9/19/70	75	2		Let Me Go, Lover .... *Susie's Toys* #1 Pop hit for Joan Weber in 1955	—	$7		Capitol 2883
				KEMP, Dave '83				
5/28/83	75	4		Ain't That The Way It Goes .... *Prisoner Of Honky Tonk Hell*	—	$5		Soundwaves 4702
	★303★			**KEMP, Wayne** '73 Born on 6/1/41 in Greenwood, Arkansas. Singer/prolific songwriter. Auto racer while a teenager. Own band in the early 1960s. 1) Honky Tonk Wine 2) Listen 3) Your Wife Is Cheatin' On Us Tonight 4) Just Got Back From No Man's Land 5) I'll Leave This World Loving You				
2/1/69	61	6		1 Won't You Come Home (And Talk To A Stranger) .... *I Turn My Mind On You*	—	$7		Decca 32422
9/27/69	73	2		2 Bar Room Habits .... *Here We Go Again*	—	$7		Decca 32534
1/9/71	57	8		3 Who'll Turn Out The Lights .... *Burn Another Honky Tonk Down*	—	$7		Decca 32767

DEBUT	PEAK	WKS	Gold	A-side (Chart Hit) / B-side	Pop	$	Pic	Label & Number
				KEMP, Wayne — Cont'd				
5/29/71	52	9		4 Award To An Angel / Darling Who's The Stranger	—	$7		Decca 32824
12/18/71	72	2		5 Did We Have To Come This Far (To Say Goodbye) / Play Me A Cheatin' Song	—	$7		Decca 32891
6/3/72	53	5		6 Darlin' / Just To Know She'd Let Me Leave Her (Is Enough To Make Me Stay)	—	$7		Decca 32946
3/17/73	17	14		7 Honky Tonk Wine / Pretty Mansions	—	$6		MCA 40019
9/1/73	53	10		8 Kentucky Sunshine / Hurt Me Again	—	$6		MCA 40112
2/2/74	32	11		9 Listen / She Knows When You're On My Mind Again	—	$6		MCA 40176
7/6/74	57	11		10 Harlan County / I'll Leave This World Loving You	—	$6		MCA 40249
6/12/76	72	7		11 Waiting For The Tables To Turn / I Can't Wait To Dream That Dream Again	—	$5		United Artists 805
8/28/76	71	5		12 I Should Have Watched That First Step / Tell Ole I Ain't Here To Get On Home	—	$5		United Artists 850
5/21/77	91	3		13 Leona Don't Live Here Anymore / Baby This And Baby That	—	$5		United Artists 980
8/27/77	76	4		14 I Love It (When You Love All Over Me) / Love's Already Been Here And Gone	—	$5		United Artists 1031
7/12/80	62	6		15 Love Goes To Hell When It Dies / She Won't Close The Book On Me	—	$4		Mercury 57023
11/15/80	47	10		16 I'll Leave This World Loving You / Who Left The Door To Heaven Open	—	$4		Mercury 57035
4/4/81	35	12		17 Your Wife Is Cheatin' On Us Again / God Made Her Special	—	$4		Mercury 57045
7/25/81	46	7		18 Just Got Back From No Man's Land / Turn Me Loose	—	$4		Mercury 57053
11/14/81	75	5		19 Why Am I Doing Without / Wrecked Up Frame Of Mind	—	$4		Mercury 57060
4/10/82	78	4		20 Sloe Gin And Fast Women / I'm The Man	—	$4		Mercury 76139
9/4/82	64	6		21 She Only Meant To Use Him / I Know Just How She Feels	—	$4		Mercury 76165
7/16/83	55	10		22 Don't Send Me No Angels / Living Off The Memories	—	$5		Door Knob 200
6/30/84	75	4		23 I've Always Wanted To	—	$5		Door Knob 211
3/8/86	70	4		24 Red Neck And Over Thirty / State Of The Union WAYNE KEMP & BOBBY G. RICE	—	$5		Door Knob 243

KENDALLS, The ★123★ '77

Father-and-daughter duo (real last name: Kuykendall). Royce was born on 9/25/34 in St. Louis. Died of a heart attack on 5/22/98 (age 63). Played with his brother Floyce as the Austin Brothers; became regulars on *Town Hall Party* TV show in the 1950s. Jeannie was born on 11/30/54 in St. Louis.

1) Heaven's Just A Sin Away 2) Sweet Desire 3) Thank God For The Radio 4) It Don't Feel Like Sinnin' To Me
5) I Had A Lovely Time

DEBUT	PEAK	WKS	Gold	A-side / B-side	Pop	$	Pic	Label & Number
7/25/70	52	6		1 Leaving On A Jet Plane / She Thinks I Still Care #1 Pop hit for Peter, Paul & Mary in 1969	—	$10		Stop 373
2/12/72	53	9		2 Two Divided By Love / Easy To Love #16 Pop hit for The Grass Roots in 1971	—	$8		Dot 17405
7/1/72	66	4		3 Everything I Own / Big Silver Jet THE KENDALLS Featuring Jeannie Kendall #5 Pop hit for Bread in 1972	—	$8		Dot 17422
4/2/77	80	7		4 Makin' Believe / Let The Music Play	—	$7		Ovation 1101
8/6/77	❶⁴	20		5 Heaven's Just A Sin Away / Live And Let Live CMA Award: Single of the Year	69	$6		Ovation 1103
2/11/78	2²	15		6 It Don't Feel Like Sinnin' To Me / Try Me Again	—	$5		Ovation 1106
5/27/78	6	14		7 Pittsburgh Stealers / When Can We Do This Again	—	$5		Ovation 1109
9/23/78	❶¹	15		8 Sweet Desire /	—	$5		Ovation 1112
		15		9 Old Fashioned Love	—	$5		Ovation 1119
1/13/79	5	14		10 I Had A Lovely Time / Love Is A Hurting Thing	—	$5		Ovation 1125
5/5/79	11	11		11 Just Like Real People / Another Dream Just Came True	—	$5		Ovation 1129
8/18/79	16	11		12 I Don't Do Like That No More /	—	$5		Ovation 1136
		11		13 Never My Love / I Take The Chance	—	$5		Ovation 1143
11/17/79+	5	15		14 You'd Make An Angel Wanna Cheat / I Don't Drink From The River	—	$5		Ovation 1154
4/5/80	5	13		15 I'm Already Blue / Gone Away	—	$5		Ovation 1169
8/2/80	9	15		16 Put It Off Until Tomorrow co-written by Dolly Parton	—	$5		
3/28/81	26	11		17 Heart Of The Matter / Mandolin Man	—	$5		Mercury 57055
8/22/81	7	16		18 Teach Me To Cheat / Summer Melodies	—	$4		Mercury 76131
12/12/81+	10	19		19 If You're Waiting On Me (You're Backing Up) / I'm Lettin' You In (On A Feelin')	—	$4		Mercury 76165
6/5/82	30	12		20 Cheater's Prayer / Borrowing Lovin'	—	$4		Mercury 76178
9/18/82	35	10		21 That's What I Get For Thinking / Honey Dew	—	$4		Mercury 812300
5/28/83	19	14		22 Precious Love / Take Me To Heaven (Before You Take Me Home) Emmylou Harris (harmony vocal)	—	$4		Mercury 814195
8/27/83	20	19		23 Movin' Train / Say The Word	—	$4		Mercury 818056
1/14/84	❶¹	23		24 Thank God For The Radio / Flaming Eyes	—	$4		Mercury 822203
6/2/84	15	17		25 My Baby's Gone / I'll Be Faithful To You	—	$4		Mercury 880306
10/27/84+	20	17		26 I'd Dance Every Dance With You / S:16 / A:21 The Dark End Of The Street	—	$4		Mercury 880588
3/2/85	27	14		27 Four Wheel Drive / S:21 / A:25 This Ain't The First Time I've Fallen	—	$4		Mercury 880828
6/1/85	26	14		28 If You Break My Heart / S:21 / A:25 One Good-Bye From Gone	—	$4		Mercury 884140
10/12/85	45	8		29 Two Heart Harmony / I Don't Know Any Better	—	$4		MCA/Curb 52850
6/28/86	42	9		30 Too Late / Party Line	—	$4		MCA/Curb 52933
9/27/86	60	7		31 Fire At First Sight / You Can't Fool Love	—	$4		MCA/Curb 52983
12/6/86	46	9		32 Little Doll / He Can't Make Your Kind Of Love	—	$4		
5/2/87	54	8		33 Routine / A Far Cry	—	$4		Step One 371
7/11/87	51	8		34 Dancin' With Myself Tonight / A Whole Lot To Lose	—	$4		Step One 374
12/12/87+	62	7		35 Still Pickin' Up After You / Country Music Station	—	$4		Step One 379
4/16/88	57	7		36 The Rhythm Of Romance / They Can't Stop Me	—	$4		Step One 384

181

DEBUT	PEAK	WKS	Gold	A-side (Chart Hit) / B-side	Pop	$	Pic	Label & Number
				KENDALLS, The — Cont'd				
6/24/89	69	6		37 Blue Blue Day..........Temporarily Out Of Order	—	$4		Epic 68933
				KENNARD AND JOHN '89				
				Duo of Phillip Kennard and Ron John.				
11/18/89	73	4		Thrill Of Love..........Maria	—	$4		Curb/MCA 10563
				KENNEDY, Gene, & Karen Jeglum '82				
				Husband-and-wife duo. Gene was born Kenneth Kennedy on 10/3/33 in Florence, South Carolina. Karen was born in Blanchardville, Wisconsin. Co-owners of the Door Knob record label.				
2/28/81	80	4		1 I Want To See Me In Your Eyes..........Nothing Left To Lose	—	$5		Door Knob 145
4/25/81	84	4		2 I'd Rather Be The Stranger In Your Eyes..........	—	$5		Door Knob 151
3/20/82	49	9		3 A Thing Or Two On My Mind /	—			
7/18/81	87	2		4 Easier To Go..........	—	$5		Door Knob 173
7/24/82	80	4		5 What About Tonight (We Might Find Something Beautiful Tonight)..........Your Still The One (Who Makes My Life Complete)	—	$5		Door Knob 179
4/23/83	86	3		6 Be Happy For Me..........What About Tonight	—	$5		Door Knob 192
8/2/86	78	4		7 My Wife's House..........	—	$5		Society 110
				GENE KENNEDY				
				KENNEDY, Larry Wayne '85				
11/30/85	83	3		She Almost Makes Me Forget About You..........	—	$5		Jere 1001
				KENNEDY, Ray '91				
				Born on 5/13/54 in Buffalo, New York. Singer/songwriter/guitarist.				
11/17/90+	10	20		1 What A Way To Go..........The Storm	—	$4	■	Atlantic 87960 (v)
4/13/91	58	10		2 Scars..........I'm Sending One Up For You	—	$4	■	Atlantic 87743 (v)
8/10/91	74	1		3 I Like The Way It Feels..........I'm Sending One Up For You	—	$4		Atlantic 87651
11/7/92	70	5		4 No Way Jose..........	—			album cut
				from the album *Guitar Man* on Atlantic 82422				
				KENNY G '00				
				Born Kenny Gorelick on 7/6/56 in Seattle. Alto saxophonist.				
1/15/00	49	1		Auld Lang Syne (The Millennium Mix)..........(2 versions) [I-S]	7	$4	★	Arista 13769
				contains audioclips from dozens of historical events of the last 100 years				
				KENNY O. '81				
				Full name: Kenny O. Smith.				
8/22/81	83	3		Old Fangled Country Songs..........Walking By My Side	—	$6		Rhinestone 1002
				KENT, George '70				
				Born on 6/12/35 in Dallas.				
12/13/69+	26	15		1 Hello, I'm A Jukebox..........I Always Did Like Leavenworth [S]	—	$6		Mercury 72985
				Diana Duke (female vocal)				
7/4/70	70	3		2 Doogie Ray..........The Great South State Truck Stop Disaster	—	$6		Mercury 73066
12/5/70+	62	7		3 Mama Bake A Pie (Daddy Kill A Chicken)..........Let's Just Pretend	—	$6		Mercury 73127
5/18/74	48	9		4 Take My Life And Shape It With Your Love..........Sunshine Light	—	$5		Shannon 818
12/28/74+	65	6		5 Whole Lotta Difference In Love..........Coming Back On My Mind	—	$5		Shannon 824
11/22/75	97	3		6 She'll Wear It Out Leaving Town..........Don't Tell It To Me	—	$5		Shannon 834
3/13/76	75	6		7 Shake 'Em Up and Let 'Em Roll..........Singin' Lonesome Cowboy Songs	—	$5		Shannon 840
2/26/77	89	5		8 Low Class Reunion..........(How Can I Write On Paper) What I Feel In My Heart	—	$5		Soundwaves 4542
	★398★			**KENTUCKY HEADHUNTERS, The** '90				
				Country-rock group from Edmonton, Kentucky: brothers Ricky Lee (vocals; born on 10/8/53) and Doug (bass; born on 2/16/60) Phelps, brothers Richard (guitar; born on 1/27/55) and Fred (drums; born on 7/8/58) Young, and their cousin Greg Martin (guitar; born on 3/31/54). The Phelps brothers left in 1992 to form **Brother Phelps**; replaced by Mark Orr (vocals; born on 11/16/49) and Anthony Kenney (bass; born on 10/8/53). Doug Phelps (vocals) returned in 1996, replacing Orr. CMA Awards: 1990 & 1991 Vocal Group of the Year.				
				1) Oh Lonesome Me 2) Dumas Walker 3) Rock 'N' Roll Angel				
9/30/89	25	21		1 Walk Softly On This Heart Of Mine..........Skip A Rope	—	$4		Mercury 874744
2/24/90	15	26		2 Dumas Walker..........High Steppin' Daddy	—	$4	■	Mercury 876536 (v)
6/2/90	8	21		3 Oh Lonesome Me..........My Daddy Was A Milkman	—	$4	■	Mercury 875450 (v)
10/13/90	23	20		4 Rock 'N' Roll Angel..........Rag Top	—	$4		Mercury 878214
3/30/91	49	11		5 The Ballad Of Davy Crockett..........Smooth	—	$4	■	Mercury 868122 (v)
				#1 Pop hit for Bill Hayes in 1955				
6/22/91	56	9		6 With Body And Soul..........Some Folks Like To Steal	—	$4		Mercury 868418
9/21/91	63	6		7 It's Chitlin' Time..........Dumas Walker	—	$4	■	Mercury 868760 (v)
11/23/91	60	7		8 Only Daddy That'll Walk The Line..........Walk Softly On This Heart Of Mine	—	$4		Mercury 866134
2/20/93	54	6		9 Honky Tonk Walkin'..........Redneck Girl	—	$4	■	Mercury 864808 (v)
5/22/93	71	4		10 Dixie Fried..........Celina Tennessee	—	$4		Mercury 862150
3/22/97	70	3		11 Singin' The Blues..........Kentucky Wildcat	—	$4	■	BNA 64782
				#1 Pop hit for Guy Mitchell in 1956				
10/28/00	66	1		12 Too Much To Lose..........	—			album cut
				from the album *Songs From The Grass String Ranch* on Audium 8117				
				KENYON, Joe '87				
				Pseudonym for producer/guitarist Jerry Kennedy and pianist David Briggs.				
6/27/87	33	15		Hymne..........My Only Love [I]	—	$4		Mercury 888642
				tune featured in Gallo Wine commercials; written by Greek composer, Vangelis				

DEBUT	PEAK	WKS	Gold	A-side (Chart Hit)	B-side	Pop	$	Pic	Label & Number
				KERSH, David '97 Born on 12/9/70 in Humble, Texas. Singer/songwriter.					
5/4/96	65	5		1 Breaking Hearts And Taking Names later released as the B-side of #2 below	—			■	album cut (v)
8/3/96	6	22		2 Goodnight Sweetheart	S:7 Breaking Hearts And Taking Names	113	$4	■	Curb 76990 (v)
1/18/97	3	20		3 Another You	—				album cut
5/31/97	11	20		4 Day In, Day Out above 4 from the album *Goodnight Sweetheart* on Curb 77848	—				album cut
12/6/97+	3	25		5 If I Never Stop Loving You	S:4 The Need	67	$4	■	Curb 73045 (v)
3/14/98	29	23		6 Wonderful Tonight #16 Pop hit for **Eric Clapton** in 1978	—				album cut
9/26/98	46	16		7 Something To Think About above 3 from the album *If I Never Stop Loving You* on Curb 77895	—				album cut
				KERSHAW, Doug '81 Born on 1/24/36 in Tiel Ridge, Louisiana. Cajun fiddler/singer/songwriter. Teamed with brother Russell "Rusty" Kershaw in duo **Rusty & Doug**. Acted in the movies *Zachariah*, *Medicine Ball Caravan* and *Days Of Heaven*. Third cousin of **Sammy Kershaw**. 1)Louisiana Man 2)Diggy Liggy Lo 3)So Lovely, Baby					
				RUSTY & DOUG:					
8/13/55	14	2		1 So Lovely, Baby	A:14 Why Cry For You	—	$20		Hickory 1027
9/23/57	14	1		2 Love Me To Pieces #11 Pop hit for Jill Corey in 1957	A:14 I Never Had The Blues	—	$20		Hickory 1068
10/20/58	22	2		3 Hey Sheriff	Sweet Thing	—	$20		Hickory 1083
2/6/61	10	15		4 Louisiana Man	Make Me Realize	104	$20		Hickory 1137
8/21/61	14	10		5 Diggy Liggy Lo also see #6 below	Hey Mae	—	$20		Hickory 1151
				DOUG KERSHAW:					
10/11/69	70	3		6 Diggy Liggy Lo new version of #5 above	Papa And Mama Had Love [R]	—	$6		Warner 7329
2/2/74	77	9		7 Mama's Got The Know How	Hippy Ti Yo	—	$5		Warner 7763
5/1/76	76	6		8 It Takes All Day To Get Over Night	Mon Chapeau	—	$5		Warner 8195
5/21/77	96	3		9 I'm Walkin' #4 Pop hit for **Fats Domino** in 1957	Kershaw's Two Step	—	$5		Warner 8374
6/27/81	29	13		10 Hello Woman	Sing Along	—	$4		Scotti Brothers 02137
8/27/88	52	7		11 Cajun Baby **DOUG KERSHAW** with **HANK WILLIAMS, JR.**	I Wanna Hold You	—	$4		BGM 81588
3/11/89	66	6		12 Boogie Queen	Jambalaya	—	$4		BGM 12989

				KERSHAW, Sammy ★134★ '93 Born on 2/24/58 in Abbeville, Louisiana; raised in Kaplan, Louisiana. Singer/songwriter/guitarist. Third cousin of **Doug Kershaw**. Acted in the 1995 movie *Fall Time*. Married **Lorrie Morgan** on 9/29/2001. 1)She Don't Know She's Beautiful 2)Love Of My Life 3)Third Rate Romance 4)National Working Woman's Holiday 5)Cadillac Style					
10/12/91+	3	20		1 Cadillac Style	Harbor For A Lonely Heart	—	$4	■	Mercury 868812 (v)
2/8/92	12	20		2 Don't Go Near The Water	Every Third Monday	—	$4		Mercury 866324
6/13/92	17	20		3 Yard Sale	What Am I Worth	—	$4		Mercury 866754
10/3/92+	10	20		4 Anywhere But Here	Real Old-Fashioned Broken Heart	—	$4		Mercury 864316
2/13/93	●1	20		5 She Don't Know She's Beautiful	I Buy Her Roses	119	$4	■	Mercury 864854 (v)
5/8/93	9	20		6 Haunted Heart	Cry, Cry Darlin'	—	$4	■	Mercury 862096 (v)
9/4/93	7	20		7 Queen Of My Double Wide Trailer	A Memory That Just Won't Quit	—	$4		Mercury 862600
1/15/94	3	20		8 I Can't Reach Her Anymore	What Might Have Been	—	$4	■	Mercury 858102 (v)
3/12/94	52	10		9 Never Bit A Bullet Like This **GEORGE JONES** with **Sammy Kershaw** from Jones's album *High-Tech Redneck* on MCA 10910					album cut
5/21/94	2¹	20		10 National Working Woman's Holiday	The Heart That Time Forgot	—	$4	■	Mercury 858722 (v)
8/27/94	2²	20		11 Third Rate Romance	Paradise From Nine To One	105	$4	■	Mercury 858922 (v)
12/3/94+	27	16		12 Southbound	Better Call A Preacher	—	$4	■	Mercury 856410 (v)
12/24/94	50	2		13 Christmas Time's A Comin'	Up On The Housetop [X]	—	$4		Mercury 856408
3/18/95	18	20		14 If You're Gonna Walk, I'm Gonna Crawl	If You Ever Come This Way Again	—	$4		Mercury 856686
8/26/95	47	8		15 Your Tattoo	Still Lovin' You	—	$4		Mercury 852208
3/23/96	5	20		16 Meant To Be /	S:14		$4	■	Mercury 852874 (v)
7/27/96	10	20		17 Vidalia					
11/9/96+	28	20		18 Politics, Religion And Her	Here She Comes	—	$4		Mercury 578612
4/12/97	29	20		19 Fit To Be Tied Down	For Years	—	$4		Mercury 574182
10/25/97+	2²	26		20 Love Of My Life	S:8 Roamin' Love	85	$4	■	Mercury 568140 (v)
12/27/97	53	2		21 Christmas Time's A Comin'	Up On The Housetop [X-R]	—	$4		Mercury 856408
3/14/98	22	20		22 Matches	Thank God You're Gone	—	$4		Mercury 568524
6/27/98	31	20		23 Honky Tonk America /	S:17				
10/10/98+	35	20		24 One Day Left To Live		—	$4	■	Mercury 566052 (v)
2/27/99	17	20		25 Maybe Not Tonight **SAMMY KERSHAW & LORRIE MORGAN**	Go Away	86	$4		BNA/Mercury 65729
8/14/99	37	15		26 When You Love Someone	How Can I Say No	—	$4		Mercury 172130

DEBUT	PEAK	WKS	Gold	A-side (Chart Hit) .... B-side	Pop	$	Pic	Label & Number
				KERSHAW, Sammy — Cont'd				
11/27/99+	35	17		27 Me And Maxine .... Louisiana Hot Sauce	—	$4		Mercury 172112
2/17/01	39	17		28 He Drinks Tequila .... I Finally Found Someone	—	$4		RCA 69054
				LORRIE MORGAN & SAMMY KERSHAW				
	★251★			**KETCHUM, Hal** '93				
				Born on 4/9/53 in Greenwich, New York. Singer/songwriter/guitarist. Joined the Grand Ole Opry in 1994.				
				1)Past The Point Of Rescue 2)Small Town Saturday Night 3)Hearts Are Gonna Roll				
5/11/91	2¹	21		1 Small Town Saturday Night .... Don't Strike A Match (To The Book Of Love)	—	$4	■	Curb 76865 (v)
10/26/91+	13	20		2 I Know Where Love Lives	—	$4		Curb 76892
2/15/92	2¹	20		3 Past The Point Of Rescue .... Long Day Comin'	—			album cut
5/30/92	16	20		4 Five O'Clock World	—			album cut
				#4 Pop hit for The Vogues in 1966; above 4 from the album Past The Point Of Rescue on Curb 77450				
9/26/92+	3	20		5 Sure Love /				
6/19/93	8	20		6 Mama Knows The Highway				
2/20/93	2¹	20		7 Hearts Are Gonna Roll	—	$4	■	Curb 76915 (v)
10/9/93	24	20		8 Someplace Far Away (Careful What You're Dreamin')	—			album cut
				above 4 from the album Sure Love on Curb 77581				album cut
4/23/94	20	20		9 (Tonight We Just Might) Fall In Love Again	—			album cut
9/24/94	22	19		10 That's What I Get (For Losin' You) .... Drive On	—	$4	■	Curb 76922 (v)
				from the album Every Little Word on MCG/Curb 77660				album cut
2/11/95	8	20		11 Stay Forever				
8/26/95	49	8		12 Every Little Word / S:15 Every Little Word	124	$4	■	Curb 76929 (v)
11/18/95	56	7		13 Veil Of Tears				
2/28/98	36	20		14 I Saw The Light .... S:23 When Love Looks Back At You	121	$4	■	Curb 76965 (v)
				#16 Pop hit for Todd Rundgren in 1972				Curb 73051 (v)
12/2/00+	40	16		15 She Is	—			album cut
				from the album Lucky Man on Curb 78707				
				KILGORE, Jerry '99				
				Born in Tillamook, Oregon.				
8/7/99	36	20		1 Love Trip .... The Real Thing	—	$4		Virgin 38667
1/15/00	49	9		2 The Look	—			album cut
				from the album Love Trip on Virgin 47828				
8/5/00	73	1		3 Cactus In A Coffee Can .... I Just Want My Baby Back	—	$4		Virgin 58851
				★**KILGORE, Merle** '60				
				Born Wyatt Merle Kilgore on 9/8/34 in Chickasha, Oklahoma; raised in Shreveport, Louisiana. Singer/prolific songwriter.				
2/1/60	12	13		1 Dear Mama .... Jimmie Brings Sunshine	—	$20		Starday 469
7/4/60	10	11		2 Love Has Made You Beautiful /	—			
7/18/60	29	1		3 Getting Old Before My Time	—	$20		Starday 497
				recitation by Jimmy Jay				
10/21/67	71	3		4 Fast Talking Louisiana Man .... Avenue Of Tears	—	$20		Columbia 44279
8/24/74	95	4		5 Montgomery Mable .... Old Home Filler-Up An' Keep-On-A-Truckin Cafe	—	$5		Warner 7831
1/16/82	54	4		6 Mister Garfield .... I'm A One Woman Man	—	$4		Elektra 47252
				★ MERLE KILGORE AND FRIENDS				
				Johnny Cash and Hank Williams, Jr. (backing vocals)				
7/14/84	74	4		7 Just Out Of Reach .... Road Women	—	$4		Warner 29267
				#24 Pop hit for Solomon Burke in 1961				
5/11/85	92	4		8 Guilty .... When You Leave That Way You Can Never Go Back	—	$4		Warner 29062
				KILLEN, Buddy — see GUITAR, Bonnie				
				KIMBERLYS, The — see JENNINGS, Waylon				
				KIMBERLY SPRINGS '84				
				Four sisters and brothers, and a cousin (children of The Kimberlys).				
6/23/84	49	10		1 Slow Dancin' .... Temptation	—	$4		Capitol 5366
10/20/84	74	5		2 Old Memories Are Hard To Lose .... That's One To Grow On	—	$4		Capitol 5404
				KING, Claude ★165★ '62				
				Born on 2/5/33 in Shreveport, Louisiana. Singer/songwriter/guitarist. Attended University of Idaho on a baseball scholarship. Worked on the Louisiana Hayride from 1952. First recorded for Gotham in 1952. Acted in the movies Swamp Girl and Year of The Yahoo, and in the TV miniseries The Blue And The Gray.				
				1)Wolverton Mountain 2)Tiger Woman 3)Big River, Big Man 4)The Comancheros 5)All For The Love Of A Girl				
7/3/61	7	16		1 Big River, Big Man .... Sweet Lovin'	82	$12		Columbia 42043
11/13/61+	7	15		2 The Comancheros .... I Can't Get Over The Way You Got Over Me	71	$12	■	Columbia 42196
				inspired by the movie starring John Wayne				
5/5/62	●1⁹	26●		3 Wolverton Mountain .... Little Bitty Heart	6	$12	■	Columbia 42352
				title is an actual place in Arkansas where Clifton Clowers lived (died on 8/15/94, age 102)				
10/20/62	10	7		4 The Burning Of Atlanta .... Don't That Moon Look Lonesome	53	$10	■	Columbia 42581
12/22/62+	11	9		5 I've Got The World By The Tail .... Shopping Center	111	$10	■	Columbia 42630
3/9/63	12	9		6 Sheepskin Valley .... I Backed Out	—	$10	■	Columbia 42688
6/29/63	12	5		7 Building A Bridge .... What Will I Do	—	$10	■	Columbia 42782
8/17/63	13	5		8 Hey Lucille! .... Scarlet O'Hara	—	$10	■	Columbia 42833
2/29/64	33	7		9 That's What Makes The World Go Around ..... A Lace Mantilla And A Rose Of Red	—	$8		Columbia 42959

DEBUT	PEAK	WKS	Gold	A-side (Chart Hit)	B-side	Pop	$	Pic	Label & Number
				KING, Claude — Cont'd					
8/15/64	11	18		10 Sam Hill	Big Ole Shoulder	—	$8		Columbia 43083
12/26/64+	47	3		11 Whirlpool (Of Your Love)	This Land Of Yours And Mine	—	$8		Columbia 43157
6/26/65	6	18		12 Tiger Woman	When You Gotta Go (You Gotta Go)	110	$8		Columbia 43298
11/27/65+	17	11		13 Little Buddy	Come On Home	—	$8		Columbia 43416
3/12/66	13	15		14 Catch A Little Raindrop	Hold That Tiger (Tiger Rag)	—	$8		Columbia 43510
11/26/66+	50	12		15 Little Things That Every Girl Should Know	The Right Place	—	$8		Columbia 43867
4/29/67	32	10		16 The Watchman	That's The Way The Wind Blows	—	$7		Columbia 44035
8/26/67	50	10		17 Laura (What's He Got That I Ain't Got)	Good-By My Love	—	$7		Columbia 44237
12/9/67	59	2		18 Yellow Haired Woman	Ninety-Nine Years	—	$7		Columbia 44340
6/8/68	67	3		19 Parchman Farm Blues	Birmingham Bus Station	—	$7		Columbia 44504
10/19/68	48	6		20 The Power Of Your Sweet Love	Beertops And Teardrops	—	$7		Columbia 44642
3/1/69	52	7		21 Sweet Love On My Mind	Four Roses	—	$7		Columbia 44749
5/17/69	9	15		22 All For The Love Of A Girl	I Remember Johnny	—	$7	☐	Columbia 44833
11/8/69	18	10		23 Friend, Lover, Woman, Wife	The House Of The Rising Sun	—	$7		Columbia 45015
5/30/70	33	10		24 I'll Be Your Baby Tonight	It's Good To Have My Baby Home	—	$7		Columbia 45142
				first recorded by Bob Dylan on his 1968 *John Wesley Harding* album					
11/7/70+	17	15		25 Mary's Vineyard	Johnny Valentine	—	$7		Columbia 45248
4/10/71	23	13		26 Chip 'N' Dale's Place	Highway Lonely	—	$7		Columbia 45340
9/18/71	54	5		27 When You're Twenty-One	Heart	—	$7		Columbia 45441
2/5/72	57	6		28 Darlin' Raise The Shade (Let The Sun Shine In)	Sweet Mary Ann	—	$7		Columbia 45515
11/4/72	48	8		29 He Ain't Country	This Time I'm Through	—	$7		Columbia 45704
5/28/77	94	3		30 Cotton Dan	I'll Spend My Lifetime Loving You	—	$6		True 103
	★290★			**KING, Don**	'77				
				Born on 5/1/54 in Freemont, Nebraska. Singer/songwriter/guitarist.					
				1)I've Got You (To Come Home To) 2)She's The Girl Of My Dreams 3)The Feelings So Right Tonight					
9/11/76	78	5		1 Cabin High (In The Blue Ridge Mountains)	Leavin' Talk	—	$5		Con Brio 112
2/19/77	16	13		2 I've Got You (To Come Home To)	Diamond Reo Cowboy (Truck Stop Romeo)	—	$5		Con Brio 116
6/4/77	17	13		3 She's The Girl Of My Dreams	Dancing Across My Memory	—	$5		Con Brio 120
10/8/77	41	9		4 I Must Be Dreaming	Truck Drivin' Lash Larue	—	$5		Con Brio 126
1/28/78	29	9		5 Music Is My Woman	Drinkin' In Texas	—	$5		Con Brio 129
5/13/78	29	10		6 Don't Make No Promises (You Can't Keep)	Cabin High	—	$5		Con Brio 133
8/5/78	26	11		7 The Feelings So Right Tonight	Where Were You On My Saturday Nights	—	$5		Con Brio 137
11/25/78+	28	13		8 You Were Worth Waiting For	Don't Get Around Much	—	$5		Con Brio 142
3/10/79	39	8		9 Live Entertainment	I Must Be Dreaming	—	$5		Con Brio 149
6/23/79	73	3		10 I've Got Country Music In My Soul	She's The Girl Of My Dreams	—	$5		Con Brio 153 on 45
2/16/80	40	9		11 Lonely Hotel	Same Old Feeling	—	$4		Epic 50840
5/24/80	32	12		12 Here Comes That Feeling Again	My Happiness Is You	—	$4		Epic 50877
9/27/80	44	8		13 Take This Heart	Saddle The Stallion	—	$4		Epic 50928
5/9/81	38	11		14 I Still Miss Someone	More Than A Memory	—	$4		Epic 02046
				written by **Johnny Cash**					
9/19/81	27	12		15 The Closer You Get	The Time Of Our Lives	—	$4		Epic 02468
1/16/82	40	9		16 Running On Love	Lean On Jesus	—	$4		Epic 02674
10/2/82	64	6		17 Maximum Security (To Minimum Wage)	The Shadow Of My Love	—	$4		Epic 03155
3/15/86	71	6		18 All We Had Was One Another		—	$5		Bench Mark 8601
10/15/88	86	2		19 Can't Stop The Music		—	$5		615 1015
				KING, Donny	'75				
				Born Joseph Mier in Crowley, Louisiana. Singer/guitarist.					
3/1/75	20	11		1 Mathilda	I Played That Song For You	—	$5		Warner 8074
				#47 Pop hit for Cookie & His Cupcakes in 1959					
11/8/75	72	6		2 I'm A Fool To Care	Hello Mary Lou, Goodbye Heart	—	$5		Warner 8145
				#24 Pop hit for Joe Barry in 1961					
7/31/76	91	4		3 Stop The World (And Let Me Off)	Wake Me Gently	—	$5		Warner 8229
				KING, Matt	'99				
				Born on 9/28/66 in Asheville, North Carolina. Singer/songwriter/guitarist.					
8/23/97	54	11		1 A Woman Like You		—			album cut
11/8/97	70	4		2 I Wrote The Book		—			album cut
				above 2 from the album *Five O'Clock Hero* on Atlantic 82981					
2/21/98	46	15		3 A Woman's Tears	Five O'Clock Hero	—	$4		Atlantic 84101
5/22/99	54	12		4 From Your Knees		—			album cut
7/17/99	54	9		5 Rub It In		—			album cut
				above 2 from the album *Hard Country* on Atlantic 83194					
	★262★			**KING, Pee Wee**	'51				
				Born Julius Frank Kuczynski on 2/18/14 in Abrams, Wisconsin; raised in Milwaukee. Died of a heart attack on 3/7/2000 (age 86). Singer/songwriter/accordionist/fiddle player. Led own band, the Golden West Cowboys, from 1936. On the *Grand Ole Opry* from 1937-47. Own radio and TV series on WAVE-Louisville from 1947-57. Elected to the Country Music Hall of Fame in 1974.					
				1)Slow Poke 2)Tennessee Waltz 3)Tennessee Polka					
				PEE WEE KING and his Golden West Cowboys:					
4/3/48	3	35		1 Tennessee Waltz	S:3 / J:4 Rootie Tootie	—	$20		RCA Victor 20-2680
				45 rpm: 48-0003; also see #5 below					
6/18/49	12	2		2 Tennessee Tears	S:12 Alabama Moon	—	$20		RCA Victor 21-0037
				Dave Denney (vocal)					
9/10/49	3	3		3 Tennessee Polka	J:3 The Nashville Waltz	—	$20		RCA Victor 21-0086
				45 rpm: 48-0085					
1/21/50	10	1		4 Bonaparte's Retreat	A:10 The Waltz Of Regret	—	$25		RCA Victor 48-0114
				78 rpm: 21-0111					

DEBUT	PEAK	WKS	Gold	A-side (Chart Hit) ... B-side	Pop	$	Pic	Label & Number
				KING, Pee Wee — Cont'd				
2/17/51	6	4		5 Tennessee Waltz A:6 / J:7 *Helegged Hilegged* [R]	—	$25		RCA Victor 48-0407
				same version as #1 above				
9/15/51	❶15	31	●	6 Slow Poke J:❶15 / S:❶14 / A:❶9 *Whisper Waltz*	❶3	$25		RCA Victor 48-0489
				PEE WEE KING and his Band featuring Redd Stewart:				
2/16/52	5	14		7 Silver And Gold S:5 / J:5 / A:7 *Ragtime Annie Lee*	18	$20		RCA Victor 47-4458
5/17/52	8	3		8 Busybody J:8 / A:9 *I Don't Mind*	27	$20		RCA Victor 47-4655
1/2/54	4	10		9 Changing Partners / A:4	—			
				#3 Pop hit for **Patti Page** in 1954				
1/23/54	9	2		10 Bimbo J:9 / S:10 / A:10	—	$20		RCA Victor 5537
7/10/54	15	1		11 Backward, Turn Backward A:15 *Indian Giver*	—	$20		RCA Victor 5694
				Redd Stewart (vocal, all of above - except #2)				
				KING, Sherri '76				
				Born in Knoxville, Tennessee.				
10/2/76	95	2		Almost Persuaded *A Good Woman Waits On Her Man*	—	$5		United Artists 855
				KING COLE TRIO — see COLE, Nat "King"				
				KING EDWARD IV AND THE KNIGHTS '81				
				Born Edward Smith on 7/13/31 in Cincinnati. Died on 3/24/81 (age 49). The Knights featured male singer Cary Len and female singer Gigi.				
9/3/77	90	5		1 Greenback Shuffle *New Corena*	—	$5		Soundwaves 4550
3/11/78	87	5		2 Wipe You From My Eyes (Gettin' Over You) *No News Is Good News*	—	$5		Soundwaves 4563
7/22/78	68	8		3 Baby Blue *Rabbit Run*	—	$5		Soundwaves 4573
5/26/79	89	3		4 A Couple More Years *The Old Spinning Wheel*	—	$5		Soundwaves 4583
4/26/80	91	2		5 A Song For Noel *Desperado*	—	$5		Soundwaves 4597
1/31/81	48	9		6 Dixie Road *Joyful Noise*	—	$5		Soundwaves 4626
5/30/81	49	8		7 Keep On Movin' *Kentucky Flower*	—	$5		Soundwaves 4635
				KING SISTERS, The (4) Sisters '46				
				Family vocal group from Salt Lake City: sisters Alyce, Yvonne, Donna and Louise Driggs. Group hosted own TV series. Louise married orchestra leader Alvino Rey. Alyce died on 8/21/96 (age 80). Louise died on 8/4/97 (age 83).				
12/28/46	5	1		Divorce Me C.O.D. *It's A Pity To Say Goodnight*	—	$15		Victor 20-2018
				Buddy Cole (orch.)				
				KINGSTON, Larry '74				
				Singer/songwriter.				
4/6/74	61	10		1 Good Morning Loving *Make A Dream Come True*	—	$6		JMI 37
12/13/75	91	4		2 Good Morning Lovin' *Make A Dream Come True* [R]	—	$5		Warner 8139
				above 2 are the same version				
				KINLEYS, The Sisters (2) '97				
				Vocal duo of identical twin sisters Heather and Jennifer Kinley (born on 11/5/70 in Philadelphia).				
8/2/97	7	22		1 Please S:4 *(album snippets)*	67	$4	■	Epic 78656 (v)
12/20/97+	12	20		2 Just Between You And Me S:20 *You Make It Seem So Easy*	122	$4	■	Epic 78766
5/2/98	49	10		3 Dance In The Boat	—			album cut
7/11/98	48	13		4 You Make It Seem So Easy	—			album cut
				above 4 from the album *Just Between You And Me* on Epic 67965				
10/24/98+	19	22		5 Somebody's Out There Watching S:4 *Please*	64	$4	★	Epic 79071 (v)
				from the TV series *Touched By An Angel* starring Roma Downey				
8/7/99	63	2		6 My Heart Is Still Beating *Somebody's Out There Watching*	—	$4	★	Epic 79249
4/1/00	34	21		7 She Ain't The Girl For You S:9 *Somebody's Out There Watching*	—	$4	★	Epic 79380
10/28/00+	35	22		8 I'm In S:9 *I Need You Now*	—	$4	★	Epic 79496
				KIRBY, Dave This is NOT Brother Oswald (Pete Kirby) '81				
				Singer/prolific songwriter. Married **Leona Williams** in 1985.				
11/8/69	67	4		1 Her And The Car And The Mobile Home *Don't It Make You Want To Go Home*	—	$6		Monument 1168
5/16/81	37	11		2 North Alabama *How Can I Tell You Goodbye*	—	$5		Dimension 1019
9/12/81	64	5		3 Moccasin Man *When Will Forgetting Begin*	—	$5		Dimension 1022
				KIRK, Eddie '48				
				Born on 3/21/19 in Greeley, Colorado. Singer/songwriter. National Yodeling Champion in 1935 and 1936. On the **Gene Autry** radio shows and *Town Hall Party* in Compton, California during the late '40s. Appeared in several western movies.				
10/2/48	9	6		1 The Gods Were Angry With Me J:9 / S:10 *You Little Sweet Little You*	—	$20		Capitol 15176
				Tex Ritter (recitation)				
3/12/49	9	9		2 Candy Kisses S:9 / J:10 *Save The Next Waltz For Me*	—	$15		Capitol 15391
				KIRK, Red '50				
				Born in 1926 in Knoxville, Tennessee. Died on 5/13/99 (age 73). Worked on WNOX-Knoxville and WIMA-Lima, Ohio. Known as "The Voice Of The Country."				
6/25/49	14	1		1 Lovesick Blues J:14 *A Package Tied In Blue*	—	$15		Mercury 6189
7/22/50	7	7		2 Lose Your Blues A:7 *Over An Ocean Of Golden Dreams*	—	$15		Mercury 6257
				Jerry Byrd (lead vocal)				
				KNIGHT, Evelyn '51				
				Born in 1920 in Reedsville, Virginia. Known as "The Lass With The Delicate Air."				
2/17/51	6	1		My Heart Cries For You A:6 *Tater Pie*	28	$25		Decca 9-27378
				EVELYN KNIGHT and **RED FOLEY**				

DEBUT	PEAK	WKS	Gold	A-side (Chart Hit)	B-side	Pop	$	Pic	Label & Number
				KNOBLOCK, Fred '81					
				Born in Jackson, Mississippi. Member of **Schuyler, Knobloch & Overstreet**.					
8/2/80	30	11		1 Why Not Me	Can I Get A Wish	18	$4		Scotti Brothers 518
10/18/80	53	6		2 Let Me Love You	It's Over	—	$4		Scotti Brothers 607
11/29/80+	10	18		3 Killin' Time	Love Is No Friend To A Fool (Anton)	28	$4		Scotti Brothers 609
				FRED KNOBLOCK AND SUSAN ANTON					
8/22/81	10	14		4 Memphis	Love Isn't Easy	102	$4		Scotti Brothers 02434
				written by Chuck Berry; #2 Pop hit for **Johnny Rivers** in 1964					
3/20/82	33	10		5 I Had It All	Love, Love, Love	—	$4		Scotti Brothers 02752
				KNOX, Buddy '68					
				Born on 7/20/33 in Happy, Texas. Died of cancer on 2/14/99 (age 65). Singer/songwriter/guitarist. Charted 10 pop hits from 1957-61.					
6/22/68	64	6		Gypsy Man	This Time Tomorrow	—	$12		United Artists 50301
				KOLANDER, Steve '94					
				Born on 11/15/61 in Lake Charles, Louisiana; raised in Austin, Texas. Singer/songwriter/guitarist.					
11/26/94	63	5		1 Listen To Your Woman	(remix)	—	$4	■	River North 4514
3/11/95	70	5		2 Black Dresses	(remix)	—	$4	■	River North 3002
				KRAMER, Rex '76					
				Born in Smackover, Arkansas; raised in Baytown, Texas. Had own surf-rock band, The Coastliners, in the mid-1960s. Played banjo with The New Christy Minstrels in the late '60s.					
3/6/76	100	2		You Oughta Be Against The Law	Our Love Is Blooming	—	$5		Columbia 10286
				KRAUSS, Alison, & Union Station '95					
				Born on 7/23/71 in Champaign, Illinois. Singer/bluegrass fiddler. Union Station is her backing band: Dan Tyminski (guitar; lead voice of **The Soggy Bottom Boys**), Ron Block (banjo), Adam Steffey (mandolin) and Barry Bales (bass). Joined the Grand Ole Opry in 1993. CMA Awards: 1995 Horizon Award; 1995 Female Vocalist of the Year. Also see **The Red Hots** and **Same Old Train**.					
9/21/91	73	1		1 Steel Rails	—				album cut
				from the album *I've Got That Old Feeling* on Rounder 0275					
12/3/94+	7	20		2 Somewhere In The Vicinity Of The Heart	Darned If I Don't (Danged If I Do)	—	$4		Liberty 18484
				SHENANDOAH With Alison Krauss					
2/25/95	3	20		3 When You Say Nothing At All S:2 Charlotte's In North Carolina (Keith Whitley)		—	$4	■	BNA 64277 (v)
				CMA Award: Single of the Year					
7/15/95	49	13		4 Baby, Now That I've Found You S:15 (same version)		—	$4	■	Rounder 4601
				#11 Pop hit for The Foundations in 1968					
5/24/97	73	2		5 Find My Way Back To My Heart	—				album cut
				from the album *So Long So Wrong* on Rounder 0365					
12/13/97+	34	13		6 It's Not Over	Useless	—	$4		Decca 72032
				MARK CHESNUTT (Featuring Vince Gill and Alison Krauss)					
7/17/99	67	4		7 Forget About It	—				album cut
				from the album *Forget About It* on Rounder 0465					
10/30/99+	❶¹	37		8 Buy Me A Rose	40				album cut
				KENNY ROGERS With Alison Krauss & Billy Dean					
				from Rogers's album *She Rides Wild Horses* on DreamCatcher 004					
10/20/01	53	4		9 The Lucky One	—				album cut
				from the album *New Favorite* on Rounder 0495					
	★393★			**KRISTOFFERSON, Kris** '73					
				Born on 6/22/36 in Brownsville, Texas. Singer/songwriter/guitarist. Attended England's Oxford University on a Rhodes scholarship. Married to **Rita Coolidge** from 1973-80. Wrote numerous hit songs. Starred in many movies.					
				1)Why Me 2)Highwayman 3)Desperados Waiting For A Train					
4/22/72	70	2		1 Josie	Border Lord	63	$6		Monument 8536
4/7/73	❶¹	20	●	2 Why Me	Help Me	16	$6		Monument 8571
				Rita Coolidge and Larry Gatlin (backing vocals)					
12/22/73+	92	5		3 A Song I'd Like To Sing	From The Bottle To The Bottom	49	$5	■	A&M 1475
				KRIS KRISTOFFERSON & RITA COOLIDGE					
3/23/74	98	2		4 Loving Arms	I'm Down (But I Keep Falling)	86	$5		A&M 1498
				KRIS KRISTOFFERSON & RITA COOLIDGE					
12/28/74+	87	4		5 Rain	What'cha Gonna Do	—	$5		Monument 8630
				KRIS KRISTOFFERSON & RITA COOLIDGE					
1/5/80	91	5		6 Prove It To You One More Time Again	Fallen Angel	—	$4		Columbia 11160
4/18/81	68	7		7 Nobody Loves Anybody Anymore	Maybe You Heard	—	$4		Columbia 60507
11/3/84	46	11		8 How Do You Feel About Foolin' Around	Eye Of The Storm	—	$4		Columbia 04652
				WILLIE NELSON & KRIS KRISTOFFERSON					
5/18/85	❶¹	20		9 Highwayman S:❶¹ / A:❶¹ The Human Condition		—	$4	■	Columbia 04881
				WAYLON JENNINGS/WILLIE NELSON/JOHNNY CASH/KRIS KRSITOFFERSON					
9/14/85	15	18		10 Desperados Waiting For A Train S:15 / A:16 The Twentieth Century Is Almost Over		—	$4		Columbia 05594
				WAYLON JENNINGS/WILLIE NELSON/JOHNNY CASH/KRIS KRISTOFFERSON					
2/28/87	67	6		11 They Killed Him	Anthem '84	—	$4		Mercury 888345
3/3/90	25	14		12 Silver Stallion	American Remains	—	$4		Columbia 73233
				WAYLON JENNINGS/WILLIE NELSON/JOHNNY CASH/KRIS KRISTOFFERSON					

KUNKEL, Leah — see **TAYLOR, Livingston**

DEBUT	PEAK	WKS	Gold	A-side (Chart Hit)	B-side	Pop	$	Pic	Label & Number

L

LaBEEF, Sleepy '71
Born Thomas LaBeff on 7/20/35 in Smackover, Arkansas. Singer/songwriter/guitarist.

DEBUT	PEAK	WKS		A-side	B-side	Pop	$	Pic	Label & Number
4/13/68	73	3		1 Every Day	If I Go Right I'm Wrong	—	$10		Columbia 44455
6/19/71	67	5		2 Blackland Farmer	Got You On My Mind	—	$10		Plantation 74

LACE '99
Female vocal trio: Beverly Mahood, Corbi Dyann and Giselle.

| 8/28/99 | 65 | 3 | | 1 I Want A Man | S:19 Swept Away | — | $4 | ★ | 143 16932 |
| 2/19/00 | 71 | 1 | | 2 You Could've Had Me | — | | | | album cut |

from the album *Lace* on Warner 47449

LACE, Bobbi '89
Born Laura Smith in Florida. Model/actress/singer. Acted in the movie *Scarface*.

3/29/86	94	2		1 You've Been My Rock For Ages		—	$6		GBS 730
6/13/87	79	4		2 Skin Deep		—	$6	■	615 1008
12/19/87	88	3		3 There's A Real Woman In Me		—	$6	■	615 1010
3/5/88	89	2		4 Another Woman's Man		—	$6		615 1011
5/28/88	69	5		5 Song In My Heart		—	$6		615 1014

MARK GRAY and BOBBI LACE

| 8/20/88 | 77 | 3 | | 6 If Hearts Could Talk | | — | $6 | | 615 1012 |
| 12/17/88+ | 70 | 5 | | 7 It's Gonna Be Love | | — | $6 | | 615 1016 |

MARK GRAY and BOBBI LACE

| 6/24/89 | 95 | 2 | | 8 Son Of A Preacher Man | | — | $6 | | 615 1017 |

#10 Pop hit for Dusty Springfield in 1969

LA COSTA '74
★349★
Born LaCosta Tucker on 4/6/51 in Seminole, Texas. Sister of Tanya Tucker.
1) *Get On My Love Train* 2) *He Took Me For A Ride* 3) *Western Man*

4/20/74	25	15		1 I Wanta Get To You	That's What Your Love Has Done	—	$5		Capitol 3856
9/14/74	3	17		2 Get On My Love Train	I Can Feel Love Growing	—	$5		Capitol 3945
2/15/75	10	13		3 He Took Me For A Ride	Sugarman	—	$5		Capitol 4022
6/7/75	19	12		4 This House Runs On Sunshine	Ain't It Good	—	$5		Capitol 4082
9/27/75	11	14		5 Western Man	Rescue Me	—	$5		Capitol 4139
1/31/76	28	9		6 I Just Got A Feeling	Let's Talk It Over	—	$5		Capitol 4209
5/15/76	23	12		7 Lovin' Somebody On A Rainy Night	The Best Of My Love	—	$5		Capitol 4264
9/11/76	37	10		8 What'll I Do	Your Love	—	$5		Capitol 4327
5/7/77	75	7		9 We're All Alone	I Second That Emotion	—	$5		Capitol 4414
11/26/77	100	1		10 Jessie And The Light	I Still Love You	—	$5		Capitol 4495
2/25/78	79	7		11 Even Cowgirls Get The Blues	Alice, Texas	—	$5		Capitol 4541
6/3/78	94	3		12 #1 With A Heartache	Take Your Love Away	—	$4		Capitol 4577

written and first recorded by Neil Sedaka on his 1976 *Steppin' Out* album

| 5/17/80 | 68 | 6 | | 13 Changing All The Time | Had To Fall In Love | — | $4 | | Capitol 4830 |
| 2/27/82 | 48 | 9 | | 14 Love Take It Easy On Me | The Best Is Yet To Come | — | $4 | | Elektra 47414 |

LaCOSTA TUCKER

LaFLEUR, Don '88

| 10/8/88 | 97 | 2 | | Beggars Can't Be Choosers | | — | $6 | | Worth 102 |

LaMASTER, Don '89

| 3/11/89 | 94 | 1 | | My Rose Is Blue | Key's In The Mailbox | — | $6 | | K-Ark 1046 |

LANA RAE — see RAE

LANCE, Lynda K. '71
Born in 1949 in Smithfield, Pennsylvania.

| 11/1/69 | 59 | 5 | | 1 A Woman's Side Of Love | That's All I Want From You | — | $6 | | Royal American 290 |
| 1/30/71 | 46 | 6 | | 2 My Guy | Weakness Of A Woman | — | $6 | | Royal American 24 |

#1 Pop hit for Mary Wells in 1964

| 8/21/71 | 74 | 2 | | 3 Will You Love Me Tomorrow | Bad Water | — | $6 | | Royal American 35 |

#1 Pop hit for The Shirelles in 1961

| 8/11/73 | 77 | 5 | | 4 You, You, You | I've Just Gotta Feel Like A Woman Tonight | — | $6 | | Triune 7207 |

#1 Pop hit for The Ames Brothers in 1953

| 10/23/76 | 93 | 5 | | 5 Say You Love Me | | — | $6 | | Gar-Pax 081 |

#11 Pop hit for Fleetwood Mac in 1976

| 1/13/79 | 78 | 4 | | 6 I Hate The Way Our Love Is | | — | $6 | | Vista 101 |

JIMMY PETERS and LYNDA K. LANCE

| 4/28/79 | 98 | 3 | | 7 First Class Fool | | — | $6 | | Vista 106 |

JIMMIE PETERS/LYNDA K. LANCE

LANDERS, Dave '49
Singer/songwriter/guitarist. Uncle of Rich Landers.

| 7/9/49 | 10 | 7 | | Before You Call | S:10 / J:7 Is There Any Need To Worry | — | $15 | | MGM 10427 |

LANDERS, Rich '81
Born in St. Louis. Singer/songwriter/guitarist/pianist. Nephew of Dave Landers.

3/28/81	41	10		1 Friday Night Feelin'	The Lady Waiting At Home	—	$5		Ovation 1166
7/11/81	40	9		2 Hold On	Honky Tonkin' Lover	—	$5		Ovation 1173
12/19/81+	52	9		3 Lay Back Down And Love Me	Your Bedroom Eyes	—	$5		AMI 1301
6/12/82	74	5		4 Pull My String	Friday Night Feeling	—	$5		AMI 1305

DEBUT	PEAK	WKS	Gold	A-side (Chart Hit)	B-side	Pop	$	Pic	Label & Number
				LANDERS, Rich — Cont'd					
1/29/83	40	10		5 Take It All	What Will I Do Without You	—	$5		AMI 1311
9/10/83	68	5		6 Every Breath You Take		—	$5		AMI 1316
				#1 Pop hit for the Police in 1983					
	★242★			**LANE, Cristy** '80					
				Born Eleanor Johnston on 1/8/40 in Peoria, Illinois. Singer/songwriter. Married Lee Stoller in 1960. Stoller started the LS record label in 1976.					
				1)One Day At A Time 2)I Just Can't Stay Married To You 3)Let Me Down Easy 4)Penny Arcade 5)Sweet Sexy Eyes					
2/12/77	52	10		1 Tryin' To Forget About You	By The Way	—	$5		LS 110
6/4/77	53	7		2 Sweet Deceiver	Walk On Baby	—	$5		LS 121
8/20/77	7	16		3 Let Me Down Easy This Is The First Time (I've Seen The Last Time On Your Face)		—	$5		LS 131
12/17/77+	16	13		4 Shake Me I Rattle	Pretty Paper	—	$5		LS 148
4/1/78	10	14		5 I'm Gonna Love You Anyway	I Can't Tell You	—	$5		LS 156
7/22/78	7	14		6 Penny Arcade	Somebody's Baby	—	$5		LS 167
12/2/78+	5	16		7 I Just Can't Stay Married To You	Rainsong	—	$5		LS 169
5/5/79	10	14		8 Simple Little Words	He Believes In Me	—	$4		United Artists 1304
				first released on LS 172 in 1979 ($5)					
8/25/79	17	11		9 Slippin' Up, Slippin' Around	He's Back In Town	—	$4		United Artists 1314
12/15/79+	16	13		10 Come To My Love	Love Lies	—	$4		United Artists 1328
3/29/80	❶¹	18		11 One Day At A Time	I Knew The Mason	—	$4		United Artists 1342
8/16/80	8	14		12 Sweet Sexy Eyes	Maybe I'm Thinkin'	—	$4		United Artists 1369
1/17/81	17	14		13 I Have A Dream	Rio Grande	—	$4	■	Liberty 1396
				first recorded by Abba on their 1979 Voulez-Vous album					
5/2/81	21	13		14 Love To Love You	Everything I Own	—	$4		Liberty 1406
10/10/81	38	10		15 Cheatin' Is Still On My Mind	Just A Mile From Nowhere	—	$4		Liberty 1432
1/9/82	22	14		16 Lies On Your Lips	I've Really Got The Blues	—	$4		Liberty 1443
5/8/82	52	8		17 Fragile—Handle With Care	Tangerine	—	$4		Liberty 1461
11/13/82	81	3		18 The Good Old Days	Do I Dare	—	$4		Liberty 1483
7/23/83	63	7		19 I've Come Back (To Say I Love You One More Time)	Now The Day Is Over	—	$4		Liberty 1501
10/29/83	80	4		20 Footprints In The Sand	Miracle Maker [S]	—	$4		Liberty 1508
5/9/87	88	2		21 I Wanna Wake Up With You /		—	—		
		2		22 He's Got The Whole World In His Hands		—	$5		LS 1987
				#1 Pop hit for Laurie London in 1958					
				LANE, Jerry "Max" '67					
				Born in Fort Worth, Texas. Singer/songwriter/guitarist.					
7/1/67	49	6		1 Keeping Up Appearances	You've Gotta Be The Greatest	—	$8		Chart 1425
				LYNN ANDERSON & JERRY LANE					
11/16/74	63	8		2 Right Out Of This World	Fine As Wine	—	$5		ABC 12031
6/14/75	81	5		3 I've Got A Lotta Missin' You To Do	Back On My Feeet Again	—	$5		ABC 12091
				also see #5 below					
4/23/83	87	2		4 When The Music Stops		—	$6		Stockyard 1000
12/17/83	96	3		5 I've Got A Lot Of Missin' You To Do	[R]	—	$6		Stockyard 1003
				new version of #3 above					
				LANE, Red '71					
				Born Hollis DeLaughter on 2/9/39 in Bogalusa, Louisiana. Singer/songwriter/guitarist.					
4/24/71	32	11		1 The World Needs A Melody	The Barker Store	—	$6		RCA Victor 9970
10/30/71	68	2		2 Set The World On Fire (With Love)	They Don't Make Love Like They Used To	—	$6		RCA Victor 0534
1/22/72	66	5		3 Throw A Rope Around The Wind	Singeree	—	$6		RCA Victor 0616
				from the movie Going Home starring Robert Mitchum					
7/8/72	65	3		4 It Was Love While It Lasted	Lovin', Likin' Kind	—	$6		RCA Victor 0721
				LANE, Terri '73					
				Born in Joelton, Tennessee. Female jingle singer.					
3/24/73	37	11		1 Daisy May (And Daisy May Not)	Gonna Be Alright Now	—	$6		Monument 8565
10/20/73	98	2		2 Be Certain	Brand New Woman	—	$6		Monument 8582
5/25/74	94	3		3 Mockingbird	Let It Be Me	—	$6		Monument 8610
				TERRI LANE & JIMMY NALL					
				#5 Pop hit for Carly Simon & James Taylor in 1974					
				LANE, Trinity — see TRINITY					
				LANE BROTHERS, The '81					
				Vocal trio from New York City: brothers Pete, Frank and Art Loconto.					
3/28/81	83	4		Marianne	(You've Gotta) Believe In America	—	$7		FXL 0026
				new version of their #64 Pop hit from 1957					
				lang, k.d. '88					
				Born Kathryn Dawn Lang on 11/2/61 in Consort, Alberta, Canada. Singer/songwriter.					
12/5/87+	42	13		1 Crying	Falling	—	$4	■	Virgin 99388
				ROY ORBISON/k.d. lang					
				new version of his #2 Pop hit from 1961; from the movie Hiding Out starring Jon Cryer					
5/14/88	21	17		2 I'm Down To My Last Cigarette	S:16 Western Stars	—	$4	■	Sire 27919
9/17/88	53	8		3 Lock, Stock And Teardrops	Don't Let The Stars Get In Your Eyes	—	$4	■	Sire 27813
				k.d. lang and the reclines:					
7/1/89	22	16		4 Full Moon Full Of Love	Wallflower Waltz	—	$4		Sire 22932
11/11/89	55	5		5 Three Days	Trail Of Broken Hearts	—	$4		Sire 22734
				written by Willie Nelson					

DEBUT	PEAK	WKS	Gold	A-side (Chart Hit)..B-side	Pop	$	Pic	Label & Number
				LANG, Kelly '82 Born on 1/10/67 in Oklahoma City; raised in Hendersonville, Tennessee.				
9/25/82	88	2		Lady, Lady..Doctor's Orders	—	$5	■	Soundwaves 4681
				LANSDOWNE, Jerry '89 Born in California. Singer/songwriter.				
4/29/89	98	2		She Had Every Right To Do You Wrong.............................I Will Carry You	—	$4		Step One 400
				LaPOINTE, Perry '86 Born in Orange, Texas. Singer/songwriter/guitarist.				
6/21/86	64	5		1 New Shade Of Blue	—	$5		Door Knob 249
10/18/86	92	2		2 You're A Better Man Than I......................................New Shade Of Blue	—	$5		Door Knob 252
12/27/86+	73	5		3 Chosen..You're A Better Man Than I	—	$5		Door Knob 260
4/11/87	73	4		4 Walk On By...	—	$5		Door Knob 270
8/1/87	72	4		5 The Power Of A Woman..	—	$5		Door Knob 281
9/17/88	76	4		6 Clean Livin' Folk.. BOBBY G. RICE and PERRY LaPOINTE	—	$5		Door Knob 307
3/25/89	68	4		7 Open For Suggestions..	—	$5		Door Knob 303
10/14/89	79	3		8 Sweet Memories Of You...	—	$5		Door Knob 333
				LARGE, Billy '66				
10/15/66	62	6		The Goodie Wagon..Big Yellow Peaches	—	$8	■	Columbia 43741
				LARKIN, Billy '75 Born in Huntland, Tennessee. Singer/songwriter/guitarist. 1)Leave It Up To Me 2)The Devil In Mrs. Jones 3)Longing For The High				
1/11/75	22	13		1 Leave It Up To Me..When You Left	—	$6		Bryan 1010
5/3/75	23	12		2 The Devil In Mrs. Jones..No Reason Why	—	$6		Bryan 1018
9/6/75	34	10		3 Indian Giver..Dig A Little Deeper	—	$6		Bryan 1026
6/5/76	66	7		4 #1 With A Heartache..If Misery Loves Company	—	$5		Casino 053
8/28/76	36	9		5 Kiss And Say Goodbye...................There's A Soul Brother In A Country Band	—	$5		Casino 076
				#1 Pop hit for the Manhattans in 1976				
12/18/76+	88	4		6 Here's To The Next Time..Lonely Woman	—	$5		Casino 097
10/7/78	67	4		7 My Side Of Town..Ring In My Pocket	—	$4		Mercury 55040
4/19/80	72	4		8 I Can't Stop Now...Lovin' A Lie	—	$5		Sunbird 107
1/10/81	35	13		9 20/20 Hindsight...Lonely Woman (Love A Lonely Man)	—	$5		Sunbird 7557
5/30/81	24	13		10 Longing For The High..............................Is There Nothing Left To Say	—	$5		Sunbird 7562
				LARRATT, Iris '79 Born in Lloydminster, Saskatchewan; raised in Prince George, British Columbia.				
7/21/79	100	1		You Can't Make Love To A Memory......................Country Love Song	—	$5		Infinity 50,015
				LARSON, Nicolette '86 Born on 7/17/52 in Helena, Montana; raised in Kansas City. Died of a cerebral edema on 12/16/97 (age 45). Singer/songwriter/guitarist. Best known for her 1979 pop hit "Lotta Love." Married session drummer Russ Kunkel.				
2/9/85	42	12		1 Only Love Will Make It Right..Blow On Chilly Wind	—	$4		MCA 52528
5/4/85	46	11		2 When You Get A Little Lonely......................I Just Keep Falling In Love	—	$4		MCA 52571
9/21/85	72	8		3 Building Bridges..You Were The One	—	$4		MCA 52653
3/22/86	63	5		4 Let Me Be The First..If I Didn't Love You	—	$4		MCA 52797
6/7/86	9	23		5 That's How You Know When Love's Right A:9 / S:11 As An Eagle Stirreth Her Nest	—	$4		MCA 52839
				Steve Wariner (guest vocal)				
10/11/86	49	8		6 That's More About Love (Than I Wanted To Know)..........Captured By Love	—	$4		MCA 52937
				LATHAM, Buddy '88 Born in Cookville, Tennessee. Singer/songwriter/drummer.				
9/3/88	97	2		(She Likes) Warm Summer Days....................................Higher Roller	—	$6		Prairie Dust 8853
				LAUDERDALE, Jim '88 Born on 4/11/57 in Troutman, North Carolina.				
12/17/88	86	3		Stay Out Of My Arms..Highways Through My Home	—	$4		Epic 08113

LAWRENCE, Tracy ★109★ '93
Born on 1/27/68 in Atlanta, Texas; raised in Foreman, Arkansas. Singer/songwriter/guitarist. Wounded in a 1991 shooting incident in Nashville (fully recovered). Also see **Hope**.

1)Time Marches On 2)Alibis 3)If The Good Die Young 4)Sticks And Stones 5)Can't Break It To My Heart

DEBUT	PEAK	WKS		A-side	Pop	$		Label & Number
11/9/91+	❶¹	20		1 Sticks And Stones Paris, TN	—	$4		Atlantic 87588
2/8/92	3	20		2 Today's Lonely Fool	—			album cut
6/20/92	4	20		3 Runnin' Behind	—			album cut
10/10/92+	8	20		4 Somebody Paints The Wall	—			album cut
				above 3 from the album *Sticks And Stones* on Atlantic 82326				
2/20/93	❶²	20		5 Alibis (album snippets)	72	$4	■	Atlantic 87372 (v)
				"45" B-side: "Somebody Paints The Wall"				
6/5/93	❶¹	20		6 Can't Break It To My Heart (album snippets)	—	$4	■	Atlantic 87330 (v)
				"45" B-side: "I Threw The Rest Away"				

DEBUT	PEAK	WKS	Gold	A-side (Chart Hit)	B-side	Pop	$	Pic	Label & Number

Tracy Lawrence To Perform Live Feb. 19 in Sarasota

2-15-05 Leader p3

Country music star Tracy Lawrence is scheduled to perform live at the PAL Sailor Circus Arena in Sarasota on Saturday, Feb. 19, at 8 p.m.

The performance will include material from his current CD, titled "Strong," as well as material from his previous hit list.

Most recently, Lawrence is known for such hits as "Paint Me A Birmingham," "It's All How You Look At It," and "Sawdust On Her Halo."

Other hits of his career include "Time Marches On," "Alibis," "If the World Had a Front Porch," "Lessons Learned," and "Sticks and Stones."

His career highlights include winning the 1993 Academy of Country Music's Top New Male Vocalist crown, and frequently contributing his personal time and concert proceeds to charities. He was recently elected by the national board of directors of the Alzheimer's Association to membership in the organization's National Advisory Council.

Concert tickets are $30. For ticket information, call 941-361-6350.

Tracy Lawrence

Putnam (fiddles), John French (keyboards) and Terrell Glaze (drums).

DEBUT	PEAK	WKS	A-side	B-side	Pop	$	Label & Number
5/30/81	85	4	1 Seven Days Come Sunday .... Close	—	$5		Sun 1164
			RODNEY LAY				
4/24/82	72	5	2 Happy Country Birthday Darling .... Her Memories Faster Than Me	—	$5		Churchill 94001
8/14/82	45	11	3 I Wish I Had A Job To Shove .... The Way I Feel Tonight	—	$5	■	Churchill 94005
1/8/83	53	8	4 You Could've Heard A Heart Break .... Hollywood & Wine	—	$5		Churchill 94012
5/14/83	64	5	5 Marylee .... Blue With Envy	—	$5	■	Churchill 94020
11/29/86	79	3	6 Walk Softly On The Bridges .... Ten Toes Up, Ten Toes Down	—	$5		Evergreen 1046
			RODNEY LAY				
			LEAPY LEE '68				
			Born Lee Graham on 7/2/42 in Eastbourne, England. Male singer/actor.				
10/19/68	11	15	1 Little Arrows .... Time Will Tell	16	$8		Decca 32380
3/21/70	55	4	2 Good Morning .... Teresa	—	$7		Decca 32625
11/8/75	82	5	3 Every Road Leads Back To You .... Honey Go Drift Away	—	$5		MCA 40470
			LEATHERWOOD, Bill '60				
7/11/60	11	13	The Long Walk	—	$15		Country Jubilee 539
			LEATHERWOOD, Patti '77				
			Born Patti DiAngelo in 1950 in Cleveland. Singer/songwriter.				
12/18/76+	79	7	1 It Should Have Been Easy .... Super Love	—	$5		Epic 50303
7/30/77	98	1	2 Feels So Much Better .... Burning Love	—	$5		Epic 50409
			LeBEAU, Tim '88				
10/22/88	98	1	Playing With Matches	—	$7		Rose Hill 001
			LEBSOCK, Jack — see GRAYSON, Jack				
			LEDFORD, Susan '89				
			Born in Fort Payne, Alabama. Female singer.				
8/5/89	81	4	Ancient History	—	$6		Project One 6189

Bon Jovi ?? See #19

DEBUT	PEAK	WKS Gold	A-side (Chart Hit)	B-side	Pop	$	Pic	Label & Number

★333★ LeDOUX, Chris '92
Born on 10/2/48 in Biloxi, Mississippi; raised in Austin, Texas. Singer/songwriter/guitarist. Also a successful rodeo performer. Mentioned in **Garth Brooks**'s first hit "Much Too Young (To Feel This Damn Old)."

1) Whatcha Gonna Do With A Cowboy 2) Cadillac Ranch 3) For Your Love 4) Look At You Girl 5) Under This Old Hat

DEBUT	PEAK	WKS	#	A-side	B-side	Pop	$	Label & Number
4/14/79	99	1	1	Lean, Mean And Hungry		—	$5	Lucky Man 10270
11/17/79	98	3	2	Cabello Diablo (Devil Horse)	Point Me Back Home	—	$5	Lucky Man 6520
8/23/80	96	2	3	Ten Seconds In The Saddle	Dirt & Sweat Cowboy	—	$5	Lucky Man 6834
7/6/91	63	10	4	This Cowboy's Hat		—		album cut
1/4/92	69	5	5	Workin' Man's Dollar		—		album cut
				above 2 from the album *Western Underground* on Capitol 96499				
5/23/92	72	2	6	Riding For A Fall	Cadillac Cowboy	—	$4	Liberty 57736
7/25/92	7	20	7	Whatcha Gonna Do With A Cowboy	Western Skies	—	$4	Liberty 57885
				Garth Brooks (backing vocal)				
11/7/92+	18	20	8	Cadillac Ranch	Call Of The Wild	—	$4	Liberty 56787
2/20/93	52	10	9	Look At You Girl	Little Long-Haired Outlaw	—	$4	Liberty 56952
6/26/93	54	6	10	Under This Old Hat	Cowboys Like A Little Rock And Roll	—	$4	Liberty 17443
9/11/93	61	6	11	Every Time I Roll The Dice	Wild And Wooly	—	$4	Liberty 17638
12/25/93+	50	13	12	For Your Love	Get Back On That Pony	—	$4	Liberty 17714
8/27/94	71	3	13	Honky Tonk World	Sons Of The Pioneers	—	$4	Liberty 18090 (v)
1/21/95	67	8	14	Tougher Than The Rest		—		album cut
				written and first recorded by Bruce Springsteen on his 1987 *Tunnel of Love* album; from the album *Haywire* on Liberty 28770				
7/1/95	68	3	15	Dallas Days And Fort Worth Nights	Big Love	—	$4	Liberty 18555
4/20/96	71	9	16	Gravitational Pull	Five Dollar Fine	—	$4	Capitol 19039
2/8/97	65	1	17	When I Say Forever	Stampede	—	$4	Capitol 19513
6/20/98	62	9	18	Runaway Love	Life Is A Highway	—	$4	Capitol 19977
10/3/98	68	5	19	Bang A Drum	One Road Man (LeDoux)	—	$4	Capitol 58737
				CHRIS LeDOUX (with Jon Bon Jovi)				
5/8/99	64	9	20	Life Is A Highway	Hooked On An 8 Second Ride	—	$4	Capitol 58780
				#6 Pop hit for Tom Cochrane in 1992				
10/16/99	66	4	21	Stampede	Hooked On An 8 Second Ride	—	$4	Capitol 58800
8/19/00	65	4	22	Silence On The Line	I'm Country	—	$4	Capitol 58889

LEE, Billy — see **NUNN, Earl**

LEE, Brenda ★162★ '74
Born Brenda Mae Tarpley on 12/11/44 in Lithonia, Georgia. Known as "Little Miss Dynamite." Charted 55 pop hits from 1957-73. Inducted into the Country Music Hall of Fame in 1997. Inducted into the Rock and Roll Hall of Fame in 2002. Also see **America The Beautiful**.

1) Big Four Poster Bed 2) Nobody Wins 3) Sunday Sunrise 4) Wrong Ideas 5) Rock On Baby

DEBUT	PEAK	WKS	#	A-side	B-side	Pop	$	Label & Number
4/6/57	15	1	1	One Step At A Time	S:15 Fairyland	43	$25	Decca 30198
2/15/69	50	11	2	Johnny One Time	I Must Have Been Out Of My Mind	41	$8	Decca 32428
8/7/71	30	13	3	If This Is Our Last Time	Everybody's Reaching Out For Someone		$8	Decca 32848
1/29/72	37	12	4	Misty Memories	I'm A Memory	—	$8	Decca 32918
7/8/72	45	10	5	Always On My Mind	That Ain't Right	—	$8	Decca 32975
2/17/73	5	15	6	Nobody Wins	We Had A Good Thing Going	70	$6	MCA 40003
8/18/73	6	15	7	Sunday Sunrise	Must I Believe	—	$6	MCA 40107
1/12/74	6	15	8	Wrong Ideas	Something For A Rainy Day	—	$6	MCA 40171
7/13/74	4	14	9	Big Four Poster Bed	Castles In The Sand	—	$6	MCA 40262
11/2/74+	6	14	10	Rock On Baby	More Than A Memory	—	$6	MCA 40318
4/12/75	8	13	11	He's My Rock	Feel Free	—	$6	MCA 40385
8/9/75	23	12	12	Bringing It Back	Papa's Knee	—	$6	MCA 40442
2/7/76	38	9	13	Find Yourself Another Puppet	What I Had With You	—	$6	MCA 40511
7/17/76	77	5	14	Brother Shelton	Now He's Coming Home	—	$6	MCA 40584
11/13/76	41	9	15	Takin' What I Can Get	Your Favorite Wornout Nightmare's Coming Home	—	$6	MCA 40640
3/19/77	78	5	16	Ruby's Lounge	Oklahoma Superstar	—	$6	MCA 40683
6/17/78	62	6	17	Left-Over Love	Could It Be Love I Found Tonight	—	$5	Elektra 45492
10/20/79	8	15	18	Tell Me What It's Like	Let Your Love Fall Back On Me	—	$4	MCA 41130
2/16/80	10	12	19	The Cowgirl And The Dandy	Do You Wanna Spend The Night	—	$4	MCA 41187
7/12/80	49	7	20	Don't Promise Me Anything (Do It)	You Only Broke My Heart	—	$4	MCA 41270
9/20/80	9	14	21	Broken Trust	Right Behind The Rain	—	$4	MCA 41322
				The Oak Ridge Boys (guest vocals)				
1/31/81	26	10	22	Every Now And Then	He'll Play The Music (But You Can't Make Him Dance)	—	$4	MCA 51047
6/6/81	67	5	23	Fool, Fool	Right Behind The Rain	—	$4	MCA 51113
8/15/81	75	5	24	Enough For You	What Am I Gonna Do	—	$4	MCA 51154
10/24/81	32	13	25	Only When I Laugh	Too Many Nights Alone	—	$4	MCA 51195
				from the movie starring Marsha Mason				
1/30/82	33	11	26	From Levis To Calvin Klein Jeans	I Know A Lot About Love	—	$4	MCA 51230
6/19/82	70	6	27	Keeping Me Warm For You	There's More To Me Than What You Can See	—	$4	MCA 52060
11/6/82	78	4	28	Just For The Moment	Love Letters	—	$4	MCA 52124
				The Oak Ridge Boys (guest vocals)				
4/9/83	43	9	29	You're Gonna Love Yourself (In The Morning)	What Do You Think About Lovin'	—	$4	Monument 03781
				WILLIE NELSON/BRENDA LEE				

DEBUT	PEAK	WKS	Gold	A-side (Chart Hit)	B-side	Pop	$	Pic	Label & Number
				LEE, Brenda — Cont'd					
9/24/83	75	4		30 Didn't We Do It Good	We're So Close	—	$4		MCA 52268
8/11/84	22	16		31 A Sweeter Love (I'll Never Know)	A Woman's Mind	—	$4		MCA 52394
12/22/84+	15	16		32 Hallelujah, I Love You So	A:13 / S:15 The Second Time Around	—	$4		Epic 04723
				GEORGE JONES with BRENDA LEE					
				#5 R&B hit for **Ray Charles** in 1956					
8/24/85	54	9		33 I'm Takin' My Time	That Was The Way It Was Then	—	$4		MCA 52654
12/21/85+	50	12		34 Why You Been Gone So Long	He Can't Make Your Kind Of Love	—	$4	■	MCA 52720
12/27/97	62	2		35 Rockin' Around The Christmas Tree	I'm Gonna Lasso Santa Claus [X]	—	$4	■	MCA 54292 (v)
				#14 Pop hit in 1960 (recorded in 1958)					
				LEE, Chandy		'79			
				Female singer.					
7/7/79	100	2		She's Still Around	Three Riddles	—	$6		ODC 548

				LEE, Dickey ★184★		'75			
				Born Royden Dickey Lipscombe on 9/21/36 in Memphis. Singer/songwriter/guitarist. First recorded for Sun Records in 1957. Moved to Beaumont, Texas, in 1960. Charted five pop hits from 1962-65.					
				1)Rocky 2)9,999,999 Tears 3)Never Ending Song Of Love 4)Angels, Roses, And Rain 5)Ashes Of Love					
6/19/71	55	8		1 The Mahogany Pulpit	Everybody's Reaching Out For Someone	—	$6		RCA Victor 9988
9/18/71	8	14		2 **Never Ending Song Of Love**	On The Southbound	—	$6		RCA Victor 1013
				#13 Pop hit for **Delaney & Bonnie** in 1971					
1/22/72	25	13		3 I Saw My Lady	What We Used To Hang On To (Is Gone)	—	$6		RCA Victor 0623
6/17/72	15	13		4 Ashes Of Love	A Kingdom I Call Home	—	$6		RCA Victor 0710
10/7/72	31	11		5 Baby, Bye Bye	She Thinks I Still Care	—	$6		RCA Victor 0798
3/10/73	43	11		6 Crying Over You	My World Around You	—	$6		RCA Victor 0892
6/30/73	30	7		7 Put Me Down Softly	If She Turns Up In Atlanta	—	$6		RCA Victor 0980
9/22/73	49	9		8 Sparklin' Brown Eyes	A Country Song	—	$6		RCA Victor 0082
2/23/74	46	11		9 I Use The Soap	Strawberry Women	—	$6		RCA Victor 0227
8/17/74	90	4		10 Give Me One Good Reason	Sweet Fever	—	$5		RCA Victor 10014
11/30/74+	22	13		11 The Busiest Memory In Town	A Way To Go On	—	$5		RCA Victor 10091
8/23/75	❶¹	18		12 Rocky	The Closest Thing To You	—	$5		RCA Victor 10361
				#9 Pop hit for **Austin Roberts** in 1975					
1/31/76	9	14		13 Angels, Roses, And Rain	Danna	—	$5		RCA Victor 10543
6/5/76	35	10		14 Makin' Love Don't Always Make Love Grow	I Never Will Get Over You	—	$5		RCA Victor 10684
9/11/76	3	18		15 **9,999,999 Tears**	I Never Will Get Over You	52	$5		RCA 10764
3/19/77	20	13		16 If You Gotta Make A Fool Of Somebody	My Love Shows Thru	—	$5		RCA 10914
				#22 Pop hit for **James Ray** in 1962					
7/2/77	22	11		17 Virginia, How Far Will You Go	My Love Shows Thru	—	$5		RCA 11009
10/15/77	21	14		18 Peanut Butter	Breezy Was Her Name	—	$5		RCA 11125
2/4/78	27	11		19 Love Is A Word	I'll Be Leaving Alone	—	$5		RCA 11191
7/15/78	49	6		20 My Heart Won't Cry Anymore	Danna	—	$5		RCA 11294
10/21/78	58	6		21 It's Not Easy	I've Been Honky Tonkin' Too Long	—	$5		RCA 11389
7/28/79	58	9		22 I'm Just A Heartache Away	Midnight Flyer	—	$4		Mercury 55068
11/10/79	94	3		23 He's An Old Rock 'N' Roller	It Hurts To Be In Love	—	$4		Mercury 57005
3/29/80	61	5		24 Don't Look Back	I'm Trustin' A Feelin'	—	$4		Mercury 57017
7/26/80	30	12		25 Workin' My Way To Your Heart	If You Want Me	—	$4		Mercury 57027
11/8/80+	30	12		26 Lost In Love	Again	—	$4		Mercury 57036
				DICKEY LEE with Kathy Burdick					
				#3 Pop hit for **Air Supply** in 1980					
6/27/81	37	10		27 Honky Tonk Hearts	It's Best I Hit The Road	—	$4		Mercury 57052
10/3/81	53	7		28 I Wonder If I Care As Much	Further Than A Country Mile	—	$4		Mercury 57056
				made the Pop charts as a flip side by **The Everly Brothers** in 1957					
1/30/82	56	6		29 Everybody Loves A Winner	You Won't Be Here Tonight	—	$4		Mercury 76129
				LEE, Don		'82			
				Singer/songwriter/guitarist.					
9/11/82	86	3		16 Lovin' Ounces To The Pound	All I Ever Wanted Was You (Here Lovin' Me)	—	$6		Crescent 103
				LEE, Harold		'68			
4/6/68	56	6		1 The Two Sides Of Me	Bringing Daddy Home	—	$8	■	Columbia 44458
9/25/71	74	3		2 Mountain Woman	If I Never Hear Goodbye	—	$6		Cartwheel 198

DEBUT	PEAK	WKS	Gold	A-side (Chart Hit)	B-side	Pop	$	Pic	Label & Number

LEE, Johnny ★129★ '80
Born John Lee Ham on 7/3/46 in Texas City, Texas; raised in Alta Loma, Texas. Singer/songwriter/guitarist. Played in rock bands in the early 1960s. Own band, the Road Runners, in high school. Married to actress Charlene Tilton from 1982-84.

1)Lookin' For Love 2)One In A Million 3)Bet Your Heart On Me 4)The Yellow Rose
5)You Could've Heard A Heart Break

DEBUT	PEAK	WKS		A-side	B-side	Pop	$		Label & Number
12/27/75+	59	9		1 Sometimes .... Get Off My Back		—	$5		ABC/Dot 17603
7/31/76	22	12		2 Red Sails In The Sunset .... In My Own Way		—	$5		GRT 065
				#1 Pop hit for both **Bing Crosby** and **Guy Lombardo** in 1935; #36 Pop hit for The Platters in 1960					
12/4/76+	37	10		3 Ramblin' Rose .... Congratulations		—	$5		GRT 096
				#2 Pop hit for **Nat King Cole** in 1962					
5/21/77	15	13		4 Country Party .... This Should Go On Forever		—	$5		GRT 125
				same tune as "Garden Party" by **Rick Nelson** with new lyrics					
10/29/77	58	7		5 Dear Alice .... It's Gonna' Be Me		—	$5		GRT 137
3/4/78	43	8		6 This Time .... Frisco		—	$5		GRT 144
				#6 Pop hit for **Troy Shondell** in 1961					
7/19/80	●³	14	•	7 Lookin' For Love .... Lyin' Eyes (**Eagles**)		5	$4	■	Full Moon/Asy. 47004
				from the movie *Urban Cowboy* starring John Travolta					
10/25/80	●²	16		8 One In A Million .... Anni		102	$4		Asylum 47076
2/14/81	3	14		9 Pickin' Up Strangers .... Never Lay My Lovin' Down		—	$4		Asylum 47105
4/25/81	52	6		10 Rode Hard And Put Up Wet .... Honky Tonk Wine		—	$4		Full Moon/Epic 02012
				from the movie *Urban Cowboy* starring John Travolta					
5/30/81	3	16		11 Prisoner Of Hope .... Fool For Love		—	$4		Asylum 47138
10/3/81	●¹	15		12 Bet Your Heart On Me .... Highways Run On Forever		54	$4		Asylum 47215
1/23/82	10	15		13 Be There For Me Baby .... Finally Fallin'		—	$4		Asylum 47301
5/15/82	14	13		14 When You Fall In Love .... Crossfire		—	$4		Full Moon/Asy. 47444
10/9/82	10	18		15 Cherokee Fiddle .... You Know Me		—	$4		Full Moon/Asy. 69945
				JOHNNY LEE AND FRIENDS					
				Charlie Daniels and **Michael Martin Murphey** (backing vocals)					
2/5/83	6	18		16 Sounds Like Love .... The Deeper We Fall		—	$4		Full Moon/Asy. 69848
6/11/83	2²	22		17 Hey Bartender .... Blue Monday		—	$4		Full Moon 29605
10/8/83	23	16		18 My Baby Don't Slow Dance .... You've Really Got A Hold On Me		—	$4		Warner 29486
2/4/84	●¹	22		19 The Yellow Rose /					
				JOHNNY LEE with Lane Brody					
				same melody as "The Yellow Rose Of Texas" with new lyrics; from the TV series starring Cybill Shepherd					
		3		20 Say When		—	$4		Warner 29375
5/26/84	42	12		21 One More Shot .... The Eyes Of Love		—	$4		Warner 29270
8/25/84	●¹	24		22 You Could've Heard A Heart Break ... S:●¹ / A:●¹ Waitin' On Ice		—	$4		Warner 29206
1/5/85	9	20		23 Rollin' Lonely .... S:8 / A:9 Rock It, Billy		—	$4		Warner 29110
5/11/85	12	18		24 Save The Last Chance .... A:11 / S:12 It Ain't The Leaving		—	$4		Warner 29021
10/5/85	19	18		25 They Never Had To Get Over You .... A:17 / S:19 Rock 'N' Roll Money		—	$4		Warner 28901
1/25/86	56	9		26 The Loneliness In Lucy's Eyes (The Life					
				Sue Ellen Is Living) .... If I Knew Then What I Know Now		—	$4		Warner 28839
				from the TV series *Dallas* starring Larry Hagman					
4/5/86	50	8		27 I Could Get Used To This .... It Ain't The Leaving		—	$4		Warner 28747
				JOHNNY LEE & LANE BRODY					
6/3/89	59	6		28 Maybe I Won't Love You Anymore .... Annie		—	$4		Curb/MCA 10536
8/19/89	69	5		29 I'm Not Over You .... Anniversary Song		—	$4		Curb/MCA 10552
10/14/89	53	8		30 I Can Be A Heartbreaker, Too .... Anniversary Song		—	$4		Curb/MCA 10564
12/23/89+	66	4		31 You Can't Fly Like An Eagle .... By-Pass Row		—	$4		Curb 10573

LEE, Joni '76
Born Joni Lee Jenkins in 1957 in Arkansas; raised in Oklahoma City. Daughter of **Conway Twitty**.

12/13/75+	16	12		1 I'm Sorry Charlie .... A Little Girl Cried		—	$5		MCA 40501
5/15/76	42	9		2 Angel On My Shoulder .... Just Lead The Way		—	$5		MCA 40553
				#22 Pop hit for Shelby Flint in 1961					
7/31/76	62	6		3 Baby Love .... It Really Doesn't Matter Anymore		—	$5		MCA 40592
				#1 Pop hit for **The Supremes** in 1964					
4/23/77	97	2		4 The Reason Why I'm Here .... We Loved		—	$5		MCA 40687
1/7/78	94	2		5 I Love How You Love Me .... I Think Of You		—	$5		MCA 40826
				#5 Pop hit for The Paris Sisters in 1961					

LEE, Leapy — see LEAPY LEE

LEE, Robin ★362★ '90
Born Robin Lee Irwin on 11/7/53 in Nashville. Female singer/songwriter/pianist.

1)Black Velvet 2)I'll Take Your Love Anytime 3)Safe In The Arms Of Love

2/26/83	87	3		1 Turning Back The Covers (Don't Turn Back The Time) .... Angel In Your Arms		—	$5	■	Evergreen 1003
6/11/83	81	3		2 Heart For A Heart .... Turning Back The Covers (Don't Turn Back Time)		—	$5		Evergreen 1006
1/7/84	54	10		3 Angel In Your Arms .... Turning Back The Covers (Don't Turn Back The Time)		—	$5		Evergreen 1016
				#6 Pop hit for Hot in 1977					
4/28/84	63	7		4 Want Ads .... Breaking The Chains		—	$5		Evergreen 1018
				#1 Pop hit for Honey Cone in 1971					
8/11/84	62	5		5 Cold In July .... Breaking The Chains		—	$5		Evergreen 1023
12/1/84	71	7		6 I Heard It On The Radio .... Angel In Your Arms		—	$5	■	Evergreen 1026

DEBUT	PEAK	WKS	Gold	A-side (Chart Hit)	B-side	Pop	$	Pic	Label & Number
				LEE, Robin — Cont'd					
6/29/85	49	7		7 Paint The Town Blue .... Angel In Your Arms (Lobo)		—	$5		Evergreen 1033
				ROBIN LEE AND LOBO					
11/16/85	44	10		8 Safe In The Arms Of Love .... Between The Lies		—	$5		Evergreen 1037
3/29/86	37	12		9 I'll Take Your Love Anytime .... Between The Lies		—	$5		Evergreen 1039
8/2/86	48	8		10 If You're Anything Like Your Eyes .... Paint The Town Blue		—	$5		Evergreen 1043
4/23/88	52	8		11 This Old Flame .... Maybe I Will, Maybe I Won't		—	$4	■	Atlantic Amer. 99353
8/20/88	56	7		12 Shine A Light On A Lie .... I'm Gettin' Good At Bein' Bad		—	$4	■	Atlantic Amer. 99307
11/26/88	51	8		13 Before You Cheat On Me Once (You Better Think Twice) ... Serious Affection		—	$4	■	Atlantic Amer. 99264
3/10/90	12	25		14 Black Velvet .... Stay With Me		—	$3	■	Atlantic 87979 (v)
				#1 Pop hit for Alannah Myles in 1990					
9/1/90	70	2		15 How About Goodbye .... Younger Love		—	$4	■	Atlantic 87890 (v)
11/10/90	67	3		16 Love Letter .... Every Little Bit Hurts		—	$4	■	Atlantic 87835 (v)
7/6/91	51	9		17 Nothin' But You .... Betrayed		—	$4		Atlantic 87681
2/5/94	71	1		18 When Love Comes Callin' .... Fallin' In Love		—	$4	■	Atlantic 87196
				LEE, T.L. '87					
				Male singer/songwriter/guitarist.					
2/21/87	78	4		A Silent Understanding .... Hers And Mine		—	$4	■	Compleat 164
				T.L. LEE (with Kathy Walker)					
				LEE, Vicki '86					
				Born in Pensacola, Florida.					
11/1/86	93	2		Bluemonia		—	$6		Sunshine 1400
				LEE, Wilma — see COOPER, Stoney					
				LEE, Woody '95					
				Born on 4/1/68 in Garland, Texas. Singer/songwriter/guitarist.					
3/25/95	46	18		1 Get Over It /		—			
7/15/95	58	7		2 I Like The Sound Of That		—	$4	■	Atlantic 87123 (v)
				LeGARDES, The Bros. ★ '79					
				Duo of twin brothers Ted and Tom LeGarde. Born on 3/15/31 in MacKay, Australia. Moved to the U.S. in 1957. Worked on **Doye O'Dell**'s *Western Varieties* TV shows in Hollywood. Hosted own TV series on KTLA in Los Angeles.					
6/3/78	88	3		1 True Love .... 25 Years And 15 Days		—	$7		Raindrop 012
				#3 Pop hit for **Bing Crosby** & Grace Kelly in 1956					
3/24/79	82	4		2 I Can Almost Touch The Feelin' .... True Love		—	$5		4 Star 1037
10/18/80	92	3		3 Daddy's Makin' Records In Nashville .... Grady Family Band		—	$6		Invitation 101
8/27/88	92	1		4 Crocodile Man (From Walk-About-Creek)		—	$6		Bear 194
				LeGARDE TWINS (above 2)					
	★345★			**LEHR, Zella** '78					
				Born on 3/14/51 in Burbank, California. Accomplished juggler/unicyclist. Regular on TV's *Hee-Haw*.					
				1) Two Doors Down 2) Feedin' The Fire 3) Danger, Heartbreak Ahead					
12/17/77+	7	18		1 **Two Doors Down** .... Two Sides To Every Woman		—	$5		RCA 11174
5/27/78	31	10		2 When The Fire Gets Hot .... Can't Help But Wonder		—	$5		RCA 11265
8/26/78	20	12		3 Danger, Heartbreak Ahead .... I Can't Imagine Laying Down (With Anyone But You)		—	$5		RCA 11359
1/6/79	24	10		4 Play Me A Memory .... Expert At Everything		—	$5		RCA 11433
5/5/79	59	5		5 Only Diamonds Are Forever .... Music Maker		—	$5		RCA 11543
7/14/79	34	10		6 Once In A Blue Moon .... All He Did Was Tell Me Lies (To Try To Woo Me)		—	$5		RCA 11648
12/15/79+	26	12		7 Love Has Taken Its' Time .... If You Only Knew		—	$5		RCA 11754
4/12/80	25	12		8 Rodeo Eyes .... You Look So Good On Me		—	$5		RCA 11953
10/11/80	34	10		9 Love Crazy Love .... It Feels Good Enough To Call It Love		—	$5		RCA 12073
8/15/81	16	15		10 Feedin' The Fire .... What A Man, My Man Is		—	$4		Columbia 02431
1/23/82	56	6		11 Blue Eyes Don't Make An Angel .... Doin' A Lot (Of Not Gettin' Over You)		—	$4		Columbia 02677
9/25/82	85	2		12 What A Way To Spend The Night .... Ain't It Funny		—	$4		Columbia 03164
3/19/83	86	4		13 Haven't We Loved Somewhere Before .... Get Out Of My Heart		—	$4		Columbia 03593
9/29/84	72	5		14 All Heaven Is About To Break Loose .... I'll Get You Back		—	$4		Compleat 129
2/9/85	66	6		15 You Bring Out The Lover In Me .... I'll Get You Back		—	$4		Compleat 136
				LEIGH, Bonnie '86					
				Born in Ashland, Maine.					
12/6/86	76	3		1 Runaway		—	$6		R.C.P. 010
				#1 Pop hit for **Del Shannon** in 1961					
7/25/87	80	3		2 That's When (You Can Call Me Your Own)		—	$6		R.C.P. 016
12/19/87	77	3		3 Moon Walking		—	$6		R.C.P. 020
				LEIGH, Danni '00					
				Born on 2/9/70 in Strasburg, Virginia. Female singer.					
9/12/98	57	10		1 If The Jukebox Took Teardrops .... Mixed Up Mess Of A Heart		—	$4		Decca 72067
3/25/00	59	7		2 Honey I Do .... S:19 Longnecks, Cigarettes		—	$4	★	Monument 79386
7/8/00	56	5		3 I Don't Feel That Way		—			album cut
				from the album *A Shot Of Whiskey & A Prayer* on Monument 63704					
				LEIGH, Richard '83					
				Born on 5/26/51 in McLean, Virginia. Singer/prolific songwriter.					
8/13/83	65	5		Ain't Gonna Worry My Mind .... Whole New World		—	$4		Capitol 5247
				LEIGH, Shannon '82					
				Female singer.					
10/2/82	90	2		Rock N' Roll Stories		—	$6		AMI 1308

DEBUT	PEAK	WKS	Gold	A-side (Chart Hit)	B-side	Pop	$	Pic	Label & Number
				LEMMON, Dave '83					
				Born in Preston, Idaho.					
1/29/83	89	2		Too Good To Be Through	Maggie	—	$7		SCP 9781
				LESTER, Chester '79					
				Born in Charleston, West Virginia.					
2/10/79	86	4		Mama, Make Up My Room	High On Love	—	$6		Con Brio 148
			★249★	**LEWIS, Bobby** '66					
				Born on 5/9/42 in Hodgenville, Kentucky. Singer/songwriter/lute player.					
				1)How Long Has It Been 2)From Heaven To Heartache 3)Love Me And Make It All Better 4)Hello Mary Lou					
				5)Too Many Memories					
10/15/66	6	18		1 How Long Has It Been	Easy To Say Hard To Do		$8		United Artists 50067
3/25/67	49	7		2 Two Of The Usual	Your B.A.B.Y. Baby Don't Love You		$8		United Artists 50133
6/17/67	12	14		3 Love Me And Make It All Better	My Tears Don't Care (They'll Fall Anywhere)		$8		United Artists 50161
10/21/67	26	12		4 I Doubt It	Laughing Girl She Not Happy		$8		United Artists 50208
3/23/68	29	10		5 Ordinary Miracle	These Are Things I Miss		$8	■	United Artists 50263
7/27/68	10	16		6 From Heaven To Heartache	Only For Me		$8		United Artists 50327
12/28/68+	27	13		7 Each And Every Part Of Me	My (Is Such A Lonely Word)		$8		United Artists 50476
5/31/69	41	8		8 Til Something Better Comes Along	I'm Only A Man		$8		United Artists 50528
9/13/69	25	10		9 Things For You And I	Somebody Lied To Me		$8		United Artists 50573
1/17/70	41	10		10 I'm Going Home	I May Never Be Free		$8		United Artists 50620
5/30/70	14	16		11 Hello Mary Lou	Love, Wonderful Love		$8		United Artists 50668
				#9 Pop hit for Rick Nelson in 1961					
11/14/70	67	3		12 Simple Days And Simple Ways	Love's Garden		$7		United Artists 50719
7/31/71	51	7		13 If I Had You	Doggone This Heartache (And That Neon Sign)		$7		United Artists 50791
11/27/71	45	9		14 Today's Teardrops	Love's Satisfaction		$7		United Artists 50850
				written by Gene Pitney; #54 Pop hit for Rick Nelson in 1964					
7/14/73	95	4		15 Here With You	Where Happiness Is		$6		Ace of Hearts 0466
10/6/73	21	15		16 Too Many Memories	With Meaning		$6		Ace of Hearts 0472
2/16/74	32	10		17 I Never Get Through Missing You	Lady Lover		$6		Ace of Hearts 0480
4/27/74	47	12		18 Lady Lover	Never Get Through Missing You		$6		GRT 007
10/12/74	78	8		19 I See Love	Your Love		$6		GRT 008
6/21/75	71	8		20 Let Me Take Care Of You	Where Happiness Is		$6		Ace of Hearts 0502
11/22/75	79	5		21 It's So Nice To Be With You			$6		Ace of Hearts 7503
				#4 Pop hit for Gallery in 1972					
9/11/76	52	7		22 For Your Love		—	$6		RPA 7603
				#13 Pop hit for Ed Townsend in 1958					
1/8/77	74	5		23 I'm Getting High Remembering	With Meaning		$6		RPA 7613
5/7/77	81	6		24 What A Diff'rence A Day Made	I Can Feel It		$6		RPA 7622
				#8 Pop hit for Dinah Washington in 1959					
4/21/79	39	10		25 She's Been Keepin' Me Up Nights	I Keep Falling In Love With You		$5		Capricorn 0318
7/6/85	91	3		26 Love Is An Overload		—	$5		HME 04853
				LEWIS, Hugh X. '65					
				Born Hubert Brad Lewis on 12/7/32 in Yeaddiss, Kentucky. Singer/songwriter/guitarist. Acted in the movies *40-Acre Feud*, *Gold Guitar* and *Cottonpickin' Chicken-Pluckers*.					
				1)What I Need Most 2)I'd Better Call The Law On Me 3)Out Where The Ocean Meets The Sky					
12/26/64+	21	16		1 What I Need Most	Too Late	—	$8		Kapp 622
9/4/65	32	6		2 Out Where The Ocean Meets The Sky	Talking To A Bottle		$8		Kapp 673
12/18/65+	30	10		3 I'd Better Call The Law On Me	Talk Me Out Of It		$8		Kapp 717
6/25/66	45	2		4 I'm Losing You (I Can Tell)	Just Before Dawn		$8		Kapp 757
10/15/66	61	2		5 Wish Me A Rainbow	You Belong To My Heart		$8		Kapp 771
				from the movie *This Property Is Condemned* starring Robert Redford					
7/1/67	38	11		6 You're So Cold (I'm Turning Blue)	No Chance For Happiness		$8		Kapp 830
12/9/67+	49	9		7 Wrong Side Of The World	Your Steppin' Stone		$8		Kapp 868
3/23/68	36	10		8 Evolution And The Bible	Gone, Gone, Gone		$8		Kapp 895
1/4/69	69	5		9 Tonight We're Calling It A Day	Sittin' And Thinkin'		$8		Kapp 955
3/29/69	72	6		10 All Heaven Broke Loose	Some Other Time		$8		Kapp 978
7/26/69	74	2		11 Restless Melissa	Our Angels Just Aren't Singing Anymore		$8		Kapp 2020
1/17/70	56	6		12 Everything I Love	Mr. Policeman		$7		Columbia 45047
11/28/70	68	4		13 Blues Sells A Lot Of Booze	Help Yourself To Me		$7		GRT 28
7/22/78	93	4		14 Love Don't Hide From Me	I'm Thinking Of You Thinking Of Him		$6		Little Darlin' 7803
4/21/79	92	5		15 What Can I Do (To Make You Love Me)	Once Before I Die		$6		Little Darlin' 7913
				LEWIS, J.D. '89					
				Singer/songwriter James D. Lewis.					
12/9/89	82	2		My Heart's On Hold		—	$6	■	Sing Me 43

| DEBUT | PEAK | WKS | Gold | A-side (Chart Hit) | B-side | Pop | $ | Pic | Label & Number |

LEWIS, Jerry Lee ★45★   '72

Born on 9/29/35 in Ferriday, Louisiana. Singer/songwriter/pianist. Married to Myra Gale Brown, his 13-year-old cousin, from 1958-71. Known as "The Killer." Survived several personal setbacks and serious illnesses. Cousin of singer **Mickey Gilley** and TV evangelist Jimmy Swaggart. Brother of **Linda Gail Lewis**. Inducted into the Rock and Roll Hall of Fame in 1986. Early career was documented in the 1989 movie *Great Balls Of Fire* starring Dennis Quaid as Lewis.

1) Chantilly Lace 2) Whole Lot Of Shakin' Going On 3) Great Balls Of Fire
4) There Must Be More To Love Than This 5) Would You Take Another Chance On Me

DEBUT	PEAK	WKS	Gold	#	A-side	B-side	Pop	$	Pic	Label & Number
6/17/57	❶²	23	●	1	Whole Lot Of Shakin' Going On	S:❶² / A:6 It'll Be Me	3	$35		Sun 267
12/2/57+	❶²	19	●	2	Great Balls Of Fire /	S:❶² / A:4	2⁴			
12/23/57+	4	10		3	You Win Again	S:2 / A:4	95	$35	■	Sun 281
					written by Hank Williams; #13 Pop hit for Tommy Edwards in 1952					
3/17/58	4	13		4	Breathless	S:4 / A:12 Down The Line	7	$35		Sun 288
6/9/58	9	10		5	High School Confidential	S:9 Fools Like Me (R&B #11)	21	$30	■	Sun 296
					title song from the movie starring Russ Tamblyn (song introduced by Lewis in the movie)					
10/13/58	19	1		6	I'll Make It All Up To You	S:19 Break-Up	85	$30		Sun 303
5/8/61	27	1		7	What'd I Say	Livin' Lovin' Wreck	30	$25		Sun 356
8/7/61	22	5		8	Cold Cold Heart	It Won't Happen With Me	—	$25		Sun 364
					also see #51 below					
2/1/64	36	2		9	Pen And Paper	Hit The Road Jack (Pop #103)	—	$15		Smash 1857
3/9/68	4	17		10	Another Place Another Time	Walking The Floor Over You	97	$10		Smash 2146
6/8/68	2²	16		11	What's Made Milwaukee Famous (Has Made A Loser Out Of Me)	All The Good Is Gone	94	$10		Smash 2164
9/28/68	2²	12		12	She Still Comes Around (To Love What's Left Of Me)	Slipping Around	—	$10		Smash 2186
12/28/68+	❶¹	15		13	To Make Love Sweeter For You	Let's Talk About Us	—	$10		Smash 2202
5/24/69	9	11		14	Don't Let Me Cross Over	We Live In Two Different Worlds	—	$10	■	Smash 2220
					JERRY LEE LEWIS & LINDA GAIL LEWIS					
5/31/69	3	15		15	One Has My Name (The Other Has My Heart)	I Can't Stop Loving You	—	$10		Smash 2224
8/16/69	6	12		16	Invitation To Your Party	I Could Never Be Ashamed Of You	—	$10		Sun 1101
					recorded on 8/28/63					
10/4/69	2²	13		17	She Even Woke Me Up To Say Goodbye	Echoes	—	$10		Smash 2244
11/29/69+	2²	16		18	One Minute Past Eternity	Frankie & Johnny	—	$10		Sun 1107
					recorded on 8/28/63					
1/10/70	71	2		19	Roll Over Beethoven	Secret Places	—	$10		Smash 2254
					LINDA GAIL LEWIS & JERRY LEE LEWIS					
					#29 Pop hit for Chuck Berry in 1956					
2/21/70	2²	14		20	Once More With Feeling	You Went Out Of Your Way (To Walk On Me)	—	$10		Smash 2257
4/25/70	7	15		21	I Can't Seem To Say Goodbye	Good Night Irene	—	$10		Sun 1115
					recorded on 8/28/63					
8/22/70	❶²	15		22	There Must Be More To Love Than This	Home Away From Home	—	$8		Mercury 73099
11/21/70+	11	12		23	Waiting For A Train (All Around The Watertank)	Big Legged Woman	—	$10		Sun 1119
					recorded on 6/5/62; #14 Pop hit for Jimmie Rodgers in 1929					
1/30/71	48	8		24	In Loving Memories	I Can't Have A Merry Christmas, Mary, (Without You)	—	$8		Mercury 73155
3/27/71	3	16		25	Touching Home	Woman, Woman (Get Out Of Our Way)	110	$8		Mercury 73192
6/26/71	31	9		26	Love On Broadway	Matchbox	—	$10		Sun 1125
					recorded on 8/27/63					
7/24/71	11	13		27	When He Walks On You (Like You Have Walked On Me)	Foolish Kind Of Man	—	$8		Mercury 73227
11/6/71+	❶¹	17		28	Would You Take Another Chance On Me /		—			
		15		29	Me And Bobby McGee		40	$8		Mercury 73248
					#1 Pop hit for Janis Joplin in 1971					
3/11/72	❶³	15		30	Chantilly Lace /		43			
					#6 Pop hit for the Big Bopper in 1958					
		15		31	Think About It Darlin'		—	$8		Mercury 73273
6/17/72	11	11		32	Lonely Weekends	Turn On Your Love Light (Pop #95)	—	$8		Mercury 73296
					#22 Pop hit for Charlie Rich in 1960					
10/7/72	14	13		33	Who's Gonna Play This Old Piano	No Honky Tonks In Heaven	—	$8		Mercury 73328
2/17/73	19	10		34	No More Hanging On	The Mercy Of A Letter	—	$8		Mercury 73361
4/21/73	20	11		35	Drinking Wine Spo-Dee O'Dee	Rock & Roll Medley	41	$8		Mercury 73374
					#2 R&B hit for Stick McGhee in 1949					
8/4/73	60	6		36	No Headstone On My Grave	Jack Daniels (Old No. 7)	104	$8		Mercury 73402
					written by Charlie Rich					
9/29/73	6	14		37	Sometimes A Memory Ain't Enough	I Think I Need To Pray	—	$8		Mercury 73423
2/9/74	21	12		38	I'm Left, You're Right, She's Gone	I've Fallen To The Bottom	—	$8		Mercury 73452
6/22/74	18	12		39	Tell Tale Signs	Cold, Cold Morning Light	—	$8		Mercury 73491
10/19/74	8	12		40	He Can't Fill My Shoes	Tomorrow Taking Baby Away	—	$7		Mercury 73618
2/22/75	13	12		41	I Can Still Hear The Music In The Restroom	(Remember Me) I'm The One Who Loves You	—	$7		Mercury 73661
6/28/75	24	13		42	Boogie Woogie Country Man	I'm Still Jealous Of You	—	$7		Mercury 73685
12/6/75	68	5		43	A Damn Good Country Song	When I Take My Vacation In Heaven	—	$7		Mercury 73729
2/14/76	58	6		44	Don't Boogie Woogie	That Kind Of Fool	—	$7		Mercury 73763
8/7/76	6	15		45	Let's Put It Back Together Again	Jerry Lee's Rock & Roll Revival Show	—	$7		Mercury 73822
12/18/76+	27	11		46	The Closest Thing To You	You Belong To Me	—	$7		Mercury 73872
10/29/77+	4	18		47	Middle Age Crazy	Georgia On My Mind	—	$7		Mercury 55011
3/11/78	10	12		48	Come On In	Who's Sorry Now	—	$7		Mercury 55021
6/24/78	10	12		49	I'll Find It Where I Can	Don't Let The Stars Get In Your Eyes	—	$7		Mercury 55028

DEBUT	PEAK	WKS	Gold	A-side (Chart Hit) ... B-side	Pop	$	Pic	Label & Number
				LEWIS, Jerry Lee — Cont'd				
12/16/78+	26	13		50 Save The Last Dance For Me .... Am I To Be The One	—	$7		Sun 1139
				recorded on 6/12/61; #1 Pop hit for The Drifters in 1960				
4/7/79	84	3		51 Cold, Cold Heart .... Hello Josephine [R]	—	$7		Sun 1141
				JERRY LEE LEWIS And Friends				
				same recording as #8 above; dubbed-in vocals by Orion (dubbed-in vocals, above 2)				
4/7/79	18	11		52 Rockin' My Life Away /	101			
		11		53 I Wish I Was Eighteen Again	—	$6		Elektra 46030
7/21/79	20	11		54 Who Will The Next Fool Be .... Rita May	—	$6		Elektra 46067
2/9/80	11	12		55 When Two Worlds Collide .... Good News Travels Fast	—	$5		Elektra 46591
5/24/80	28	12		56 Honky Tonk Stuff .... Rockin' Jerry Lee	—	$5		Elektra 46642
9/6/80	10	12		57 Over The Rainbow .... Folsom Prison Blues	—	$5		Elektra 47026
				first heard in the 1939 movie The Wizard Of Oz starring Judy Garland				
1/17/81	4	15		58 Thirty Nine And Holding .... Change Places With Me	—	$5		Elektra 47095
4/24/82	43	11		59 I'm So Lonesome I Could Cry .... Pick Me Up On Your Way Down	—	$5		Mercury 76148
9/25/82	52	7		60 I'd Do It All Again .... Who Will Buy The Wine	—	$5		Elektra 69962
12/18/82+	44	10		61 My Fingers Do The Talkin' .... Forever Forgiving	—	$4		MCA 52151
3/19/83	66	6		62 Come As You Were .... Circumstantial Evidence	—	$4		MCA 52188
7/9/83	69	5		63 Why You Been Gone So Long .... She Sings Amazing Grace	—	$4		MCA 52233
8/23/86	61	6		64 Sixteen Candles .... Rock And Roll (Fais-Do-Do)	—	$4		America/Sm. 884934
				#2 Pop hit for The Crests in 1959				
1/14/89	50	7		65 Never Too Old To Rock 'N' Roll .... Rock And Roll Kiss	—	$4		Curb 10521
				RONNIE McDOWELL WITH JERRY LEE LEWIS				
				LEWIS, Linda Gail '69				
				Born on 7/18/47 in Ferriday, Louisiana. Singer/songwriter. Sister of Jerry Lee Lewis.				
5/24/69	9	11		1 Don't Let Me Cross Over .... We Live In Two Different Worlds	—	$10	■	Smash 2220
				JERRY LEE LEWIS & LINDA GAIL LEWIS				
1/10/70	71	2		2 Roll Over Beethoven .... Secret Places	—	$10		Smash 2254
				LINDA GAIL LEWIS & JERRY LEE LEWIS				
				#29 Pop hit for Chuck Berry in 1956				
8/19/72	39	8		3 Smile, Somebody Loves You .... Louisiana	—	$8		Mercury 73316
				LEWIS, Margaret '68				
6/29/68	74	3		Honey (I Miss You Too) .... Milk And Honey	—	$7		SSS Int'l. 741
				answer to "Honey" by Bobby Goldsboro				
				LEWIS, Melissa '80				
				Born on 10/16/64 in Exeter, New Hampshire; raised in New Hope, North Carolina.				
3/1/80	75	5		1 The First Time .... When Love Finds A Place In Your Heart	—	$5		Door Knob 122
5/17/80	71	6		2 One Good Reason .... You'll Never Know (How Close He Came To Hurting You)	—	$5		Door Knob 129
				LEWIS, Ross '89				
12/17/88	89	4		1 Hold Your Fire	—	$6	■	Wolf Dog 4
1/28/89	70	5		2 Love In Motion	—	$6	■	Wolf Dog 5
4/1/89	67	5		3 The Chance You Take	—	$6	■	Wolf Dog 6
9/23/89	91	2		4 Of All The Foolish Things To Do	—	$6	■	Wolf Dog 7
				LEWIS, Texas Jim '44				
				Born on 10/15/09 in Meigs, Georgia. Died on 1/23/90 (age 80). Singer/guitarist/actor. Appeared in several western movies.				
9/2/44	3	6		Too Late To Worry Too Blue To Cry .... 'Leven Miles From Leavenworth	—	$20		Decca 6099
				TEXAS JIM LEWIS And His Lone Star Cowboys				
				LIBBY, Brenda '83				
11/26/83	97	1		Give It Back .... We Don't Make Sense Anymore	—	$7		Comstock 1726
				LIGHTFOOT, Gordon '74				
				Born on 11/17/38 in Orilla, Ontario, Canada. Folk-pop singer/songwriter/guitarist. Charted 11 pop hits from 1970-82.				
6/1/74	13	15	●	1 Sundown .... Too Late For Prayin'	❶¹	$5		Reprise 1194
10/19/74	81	6		2 Carefree Highway .... Seven Island Suite	10	$5		Reprise 1309
4/5/75	47	7		3 Rainy Day People .... Cherokee Bend	26	$5		Reprise 1328
10/9/76	50	11		4 The Wreck Of The Edmund Fitzgerald .... The House You Live In	2²	$5		Reprise 1369
				true story of the shipwreck in Lake Superior on 11/10/75				
2/25/78	92	4		5 The Circle Is Small (I Can See It In Your Eyes) .... Sweet Guinevere	33	$4		Warner 8518
9/2/78	100	2		6 Dreamland .... Songs The Minstrel Sang	—	$4		Warner 8644
5/24/80	80	5		7 Dream Street Rose .... Make Way For The Lady	—	$4		Warner 49230
8/30/86	71	9		8 Anything For Love .... Let It Ride	—	$4	■	Warner 28655
				LINCOLN COUNTY '81				
				Vocal trio from Lincoln County, Mississippi.				
4/11/81	84	4		Making The Night The Best Part Of My Day .... I'm Gonna' Be Strong	—	$5		Soundwaves 4629
				LINDSEY, Bennie '76				
11/13/76	100	2		Save The Last Dance	—	$7		Phono 2633
				LINDSEY, Judy '89				
				Born in Arlington, Texas. Female singer.				
1/28/89	83	3		Wrong Train .... From My Heart's Point Of View	—	$6		Gypsy 83881
				LINDSEY, LaWanda '70				
				Born on 1/12/53 in Tampa, Florida; raised in Savannah, Georgia. Singer/songwriter.				
				1)Pickin' Wild Mountain Berries 2)Hello Out There 3)Today Will Be The First Day Of The Rest Of My Life				
1/4/69	58	9		1 Eye To Eye .... Looking Over Our Shoulders	—	$7		Chart 1063
				LaWANDA LINDSEY & KENNY VERNON				
12/20/69	48	10		2 Partly Bill .... Making Waves	—	$6		Chart 5042

DEBUT	PEAK	WKS	Gold	A-side (Chart Hit)	B-side	Pop	$	Pic	Label & Number
				LINDSEY, LaWanda — Cont'd					
3/21/70	27	14		3 Pickin' Wild Mountain Berries ... We Don't Deserve Each Other	—		$6		Chart 5055
				LaWANDA LINDSEY & KENNY VERNON #27 Pop hit for Peggy Scott & Jo Jo Benson in 1968					
7/25/70	63	6		4 We'll Sing In The Sunshine ... I'll Just Take Your Word For It, Baby	—		$6		Chart 5076
9/19/70	51	9		5 Let's Think About Where We're Going ... Puzzles Of My Mind	—		$6		Chart 5090
				LaWANDA LINDSEY & KENNY VERNON					
2/27/71	42	9		6 The Crawdad Song ... Wrong Number	—		$6		Chart 5114
				LaWANDA LINDSEY & KENNY VERNON					
2/26/72	60	7		7 Wish I Was A Little Boy Again ... Time Heals All Wounds	—		$6		Chart 5153
7/14/73	38	10		8 Today Will Be The First Day Of The Rest Of My Life ... Paint Me A Picture Of Our Love	—		$5		Capitol 3652
11/17/73	87	5		9 Sunshine Feeling ... Love Makes The World Go Around	—		$5		Capitol 3739
2/23/74	62	8		10 Hello Trouble ... Your Tender Loving Care	—		$5		Capitol 3819
6/1/74	28	14		11 Hello Out There ... Top Of The Morning To You	—		$5		Capitol 3875
9/28/74	67	7		12 I Ain't Hangin' 'Round ... Your Monkey Won't Be Home Tonight	—		$5		Capitol 3950
4/2/77	76	5		13 Walk Right Back ... (Try To Love Him) A Little Bit More	—		$4		Mercury 73889
				#7 Pop hit for **The Everly Brothers** in 1961					
10/7/78	85	4		14 I'm A Woman In Love ... Let Your Body Speak Your Mind	—		$4		Mercury 55041
				LINTON, Sherwin '77					
				Born in Volga, South Dakota. Singer/songwriter/pianist.					
10/22/77	88	3		1 Jesse I Wanted That Award ... Men Talk	—		$6		Soundwaves 4556
				LIPTON, Holly '89					
10/21/89	89	2		1 At This Moment	—		$5		Evergreen 1096
				LITTLE, Peggy '70					
				Born in Marlin, Texas; raised in Waco, Texas. Regular on TV's *The Mike Douglas Show*.					
3/15/69	40	10		1 Son Of A Preacher Man ... One More Nightly Cry	—		$6		Dot 17199
				#10 Pop hit for Dusty Springfield in 1969					
6/21/69	43	10		2 Sweet Baby Girl ... My Heart's Not In It Anymore	—		$6		Dot 17259
10/18/69	44	9		3 Put Your Lovin' Where Your Mouth Is ... Softly And Tenderly	—		$6		Dot 17308
2/21/70	37	11		4 Mama, I Won't Be Wearing A Ring ... Love's Biggest Fool	—		$6		Dot 17338
8/8/70	59	3		5 I Knew You'd Be Leaving ... Gentle Man	—		$6		Dot 17353
5/1/71	75	2		6 I've Got To Have You ... I've Got A Lot Of Love (Left In Me)	—		$6		Dot 17371
4/14/73	70	2		7 Listen, Spot ... Everything's All Right	—		$5		Epic 10968
8/18/73	37	10		8 Sugarman ... If Lovin' You Starts Hurtin' Me	—		$5		Epic 11028
	★208★			**LITTLE TEXAS** '94					
				Group from Arlington, Texas: **Tim Rushlow** (vocals; born on 10/6/66), **Porter Howell** (guitar; born on 6/21/64) and **Dwayne O'Brien** (guitar; born on 6/30/63), **Brady Seals** (keyboards; born on 3/29/67), **Duane Propes** (bass; born on 12/17/66) and **Del Gray** (drums; born on 5/8/68). Jeff Huskins (born on 4/26/66) replaced Seals in 1995. Also see **Hope**.					
				1)My Love 2)What Might Have Been 3)Amy's Back In Austin 4)God Blessed Texas 5)Kick A Little					
9/14/91	8	20		1 Some Guys Have All The Love /	—				
2/8/92	13	20		2 First Time For Everything			$4		Warner 19024
6/20/92	5	20		3 You And Forever And Me ... Dance			$4		Warner 18867
10/10/92+	17	20		4 What Were You Thinkin' ... Just One More Night	—		$4		Warner 18741
1/30/93	16	20		5 I'd Rather Miss You ... Cry On	—		$4		Warner 18668
5/29/93	2[1]	20		6 What Might Have Been ... Stop On A Dime	79	$4	■	Warner 18516 (v)
7/17/93	4	24		7 God Blessed Texas ... Cutoff Jeans	55	$4	■	Warner 18385 (v)
12/11/93	73	4		8 Peaceful Easy Feeling	—				album cut
				#22 Pop hit for the **Eagles** in 1973; from the various artists album *Common Thread: Songs Of The Eagles* on Giant 24531					
1/15/94	●[2]	20		9 My Love ... Only Thing I'm Sure Of	83	$4	■	Warner 18295 (v)
5/21/94	14	20		10 Stop On A Dime	—				album cut
				from the album *Big Time* on Warner 45276					
8/27/94	5	20		11 Kick A Little ... Hit Country Song	108	$4	■	Warner 18103 (v)
12/24/94+	4	20		12 Amy's Back In Austin ... Excerpts From Country World Premiere Radio Show	—		$4	■	Warner 18001 (v)
4/29/95	27	16		13 Southern Grace	—				album cut
				from the album *Kick A Little* on Warner 45739					
7/8/95	53	17		14 Party All Night ... S:5 Southern Accent (Foxworthy) [N]	101	$4	■	Warner 17806 (v)
				JEFF FOXWORTHY with Little Texas					
9/2/95	5	20		15 Life Goes On /	—				
12/30/95+	44	13		16 Country Crazy	—		$4		Warner 17770
10/19/96+	52	20		17 Kiss The Girl	—				
				from the 1989 animated movie *The Little Mermaid*; from the various artists album *The Best Of Country Sing The Best Of Disney* on Disney 60902					
3/1/97	45	10		18 Bad For Us ... Long Way Down	—		$4		Warner 17391
5/17/97	64	5		19 Your Mama Won't Let Me	—				album cut
9/20/97	71	2		20 The Call	—				album cut
				above 2 from the album *Little Texas* on Warner 46501					
				LLOYD, Mick '81					
				Vice President of Giant Records during the early 1980s.					
1/31/81	85	3		1 Be My Lover, Be My Friend ... Drifter's Lullaby	—		$6		Little Giant 040
8/8/81	85	4		2 Sweet Natural Love ... Forsaking All The Rest	—		$6		Little Giant 046
				MICK LLOYD & JERRI KELLY (above 2)					

DEBUT	PEAK	WKS	Gold	A-side (Chart Hit)..B-side	Pop	$	Pic	Label & Number
				LOBO **'82**				
				Born Roland Kent Lavoie on 7/31/43 in Tallahassee, Florida. Singer/songwriter/guitarist. Started own Lobo record label in 1981. Member of **The Wolfpack**. Charted 16 pop hits from 1971-80.				
12/5/81+	40	12		1 I Don't Want To Want You .... *No One Will Ever Know*	—	$5		Lobo 1
3/27/82	63	7		2 Come Looking For Me .... *I Don't Want To Want You*	—	$5		Lobo 4
9/4/82	88	3		3 Living My Life Without You .... *A Simple Man*	—	$5		Lobo 10
3/9/85	57	5		4 Am I Going Crazy (Or Just Out Of My Mind) .... *I Don't Want To Want You*	—	$5		Evergreen 1028
6/29/85	49	7		5 Paint The Town Blue .... *Angel In Your Arms* (Lobo)	—	$5		Evergreen 1033
				ROBIN LEE AND LOBO				

				LOCKLIN, Hank ★136★ **'60**				
				Born Lawrence Hankins Locklin on 2/15/18 in McLellan, Florida. Singer/songwriter/guitarist. Regular performer in 1942 on radio station WCOA in Pensacola, Florida. Joined the *Louisiana Hayride* in the late 1940s. Once known as "The Rocky Mountain Boy." Joined the *Grand Ole Opry* in 1960. Also see *Some Of Chet's Friends*.				
				1)Please Help Me, I'm Falling 2)Let Me Be The One 3)It's A Little More Like Heaven 4)Geisha Girl 5)Send Me The Pillow You Dream On				
6/25/49	8	5		1 The Same Sweet Girl .... J:8 / S:15 *The Last Look At Mother*	—	$25		4 Star 1313
9/5/53	●³	32		2 Let Me Be The One .... A:●³ / J:●² / S:2 *I'm Tired Of Bummin' Around*	—	$30		4 Star 1641
3/24/56	9	1		3 Why Baby Why .... A:9 *Love Or Spite*	—	$20		RCA Victor 6347
8/19/57	4	39		4 Geisha Girl / .... S:4 / A:6	66			RCA Victor 6984
		6		5 Livin' Alone		$20		
3/31/58	5	35		6 Send Me The Pillow You Dream On .... S:5 / A:5 *Why Don't You Haul Off And Love Me*	77	$15		RCA Victor 7127
4/28/58	3	23		7 It's A Little More Like Heaven / .... A:3 / S:8	—			
		7		8 Blue Glass Skirt	—	$15		RCA Victor 7203
3/7/60	●¹⁴	36		9 Please Help Me, I'm Falling .... *My Old Home Town*	8	$15		RCA Victor 7692
				also see #30 below				
12/31/60+	14	12		10 One Step Ahead Of My Past .... *Toujours Moi*	—	$12		RCA Victor 7813
6/5/61	12	7		11 From Here To There To You .... *This Song Is Just For You*	—	$12		RCA Victor 7871
10/2/61	7	14		12 Happy Birthday To Me /		$12		RCA Victor 7921
9/11/61	14	12		13 You're The Reason	107	$12		
1/13/62	10	14		14 Happy Journey .... *I Need You Now*	—	$12		RCA Victor 7965
6/23/62	14	11		15 We're Gonna Go Fishin' .... *Welcome Home, Mister Blues*	—	$12		RCA Victor 8034
4/20/63	23	4		16 Flyin' South .... *Behind The Footlights*	—	$12		RCA Victor 8156
				also see #31 below				
1/18/64	41	4		17 Wooden Soldier .... *Kiss On The Door*	—	$12		RCA Victor 8248
3/21/64	15	17		18 Followed Closely By My Teardrops .... *You Never Want To Love Me*	—	$12		RCA Victor 8318
5/15/65	32	9		19 Forty Nine, Fifty One .... *Faith And Truth*	—	$10		RCA Victor 8560
12/25/65+	35	9		20 The Girls Get Prettier (Every Day) .... *To Him*	—	$10		RCA Victor 8695
4/9/66	48	2		21 Insurance .... *I Feel A Cry Coming On*	—	$10		RCA Victor 8783
10/15/66	69	2		22 The Best Part Of Loving You .... *The Last Thing On My Mind*	—	$10		RCA Victor 8928
3/4/67	41	10		23 Hasta Luego (See You Later) .... *Wishing On A Star*	—	$10		RCA Victor 9092
7/1/67	73	4		24 Nashville Women .... *Behind My Back*	—	$10		RCA Victor 9218
10/21/67+	8	20		25 The Country Hall Of Fame .... *Evergreen*	—	$10		RCA Victor 9323
3/30/68	40	8		26 Love Song For You .... *Little Geisha Girl*	—	$10		RCA Victor 9476
8/24/68	57	5		27 Everlasting Love .... *I'm Slowly Going Out Of Your Mind*	—	$10		RCA Victor 9582
11/2/68	62	6		28 Lovin' You (The Way I Do) .... *Hot Pepper Doll*	—	$10		RCA Victor 9646
2/1/69	34	10		29 Where The Blue Of The Night Meets The Gold Of The Day .... *The Girls Who Wait*	—	$8		RCA Victor 9710
				#4 Pop hit for **Bing Crosby** in 1932				
1/3/70	68	3		30 Please Help Me, I'm Falling .... *Anna* [R]	—	$8		RCA Victor 0287
				HANK LOCKLIN AND DANNY DAVIS AND THE NASHVILLE BRASS new version of #9 above				
6/27/70	56	6		31 Flying South .... *Rosalita* [R]	—	$8		RCA Victor 9849
				HANK LOCKLIN AND DANNY DAVIS AND THE NASHVILLE BRASS new version of #16 above				
10/10/70	68	4		32 Bless Her Heart...I Love Her .... *Morning*	—	$8		RCA Victor 9894
3/13/71	61	4		33 She's As Close As I Can Get To Loving You .... *I Like A Woman*	—	$8		RCA Victor 9955

				LOFTIS, Bobby Wayne **'77**				
				Born in Battle Creek, Michigan. Singer/pianist.				
8/14/76	85	6		1 See The Big Man Cry .... *Number One Lady In Town*	—	$5		Charta 100
12/25/76+	54	11		2 Poor Side Of Town .... *Don't Wake Up The Children*	—	$5		Charta 104
				#1 Pop hit for **Johnny Rivers** in 1966				
6/11/77	75	6		3 You're So Good For Me (And That's Bad) .... *We're Back Together Once Again*	—	$5		Charta 108
3/4/78	87	5		4 Can't Shake You Off My Mind .... *Let's Pretend We Just Got Married*	—	$5		Charta 118
4/21/79	89	2		5 Small Time Picker .... *I'll Remember*	—	$5		Charta 132

				LOGAN, Bud **'74**				
				Singer/bassist. Former member of **The Blue Boys** (backing group for **Jim Reeves**).				
12/22/73+	14	17		1 Wake Me Into Love .... *Here Together*	—	$6		Shannon 816
7/6/74	53	10		2 The Best Day Of The Rest Of Our Love .... *It Ain't Nothing But Love*	—	$6		Shannon 820
				BUD LOGAN & WILMA BURGESS (above 2)				

DEBUT	PEAK	WKS	Gold	A-side (Chart Hit)	B-side	Pop	$	Pic	Label & Number
				LOGAN, Josh '89 Born in Richmond, Kentucky. Singer/songwriter/guitarist.					
12/10/88+	58	9		1 Everytime I Get To Dreamin'	Easy Lovin' Kind	—	$4		Curb 10519
6/3/89	62	7		2 Somebody Paints The Wall	The Light Of My Life	—	$4		Curb/MCA 10528
9/2/89	75	4		3 I Was Born With A Broken Heart	I've Learned To Lie	—	$4		Curb/MCA 10553
				LOGGINS, Dave — see **HARDIN, Gus** / **MURRAY, Anne**					
				LOGGINS & MESSINA '76 Duo of Kenny Loggins and Jim Messina. Loggins was born on 1/7/47 in Everett, Washington; raised in Alhambra, California. Charted 21 pop hits from 1977-91. Messina was born on 12/5/47 in Maywood, California; raised in Harlingen, Texas. Former member of **Poco**. Loggins & Messina charted 10 pop hits from 1972-75.					
12/20/75+	92	6		Oh, Lonesome Me	A Lover's Question (Pop #89)	—	$5		Columbia 10222
				LONDON, Eddie '91 Born Kenneth Edward London on 7/31/56 to an American military family in Dreux, France. Singer/bassist.					
7/6/91	41	19		If We Can't Do It Right	Business As Usual	—	$4	■	RCA 2822 (v)
				LONESOME STRANGERS, The '89 Vocal group from Los Angeles: Jeff Rymes, Randy Weeks, Lorne Rall and Mike McLean.					
2/11/89	32	13		1 Goodbye Lonesome, Hello Baby Doll	We Used To Fuss	—	$6		Hightone 508
6/24/89	66	5		2 Just Can't Cry No More		—	$6		Hightone 511
				LONESTAR ★146★ Mister Mom ★A★ '01 Group from Nashville: **Richie McDonald** (vocals, guitar; born on 2/6/62), **John Rich** (vocals, bass; born on 1/7/74), **Michael Britt** (guitar; born on 6/15/66), **Dean Sams** (keyboards; born on 8/3/66) and **Keech Rainwater** (drums; born on 1/24/63). Rich left in January 1998. CMA Award: 2001 Vocal Group of the Year. Also see **America The Beautiful** and **Mindy McCready**.					
				1)Amazed 2)I'm Already There 3)What About Now 4)No News 5)Tell Her					
8/19/95	8	20		1 Tequila Talkin'	flip			■	album cut (v)
1/13/96	❶³	20		2 No News S:5	Tequila Talkin'	122	$4	■	BNA 64386 (v)
5/25/96	8	20		3 Runnin' Away With My Heart	I Love The Way You Do That	—	$4		BNA 64549
9/28/96	45	15		4 When Cowboys Didn't Dance	Ragtop Cadillac	—	$4		BNA 64638
12/7/96+	18	20		5 Heartbroke Every Day .... from the album *Lonestar* on BNA 66642		—			album cut
12/28/96	75	1		6 I'll Be Home For Christmas .... #3 Pop hit for **Bing Crosby** in 1943; also see #11 below	White Christmas [X]	—	$4		BNA 64687
5/3/97	❶²	20		7 Come Cryin' To Me S:18	What Would It Take	—	$4	■	BNA 64841 (v)
8/30/97+	12	22		8 You Walked In S:8	Keys To My Heart	93	$4	■	BNA 64942 (v)
1/31/98	13	21		9 Say When	Amie	—	$4		BNA 65395
7/4/98	2¹	26		10 Everything's Changed .... from the album *Crazy Nights* on BNA 67422		95			album cut
12/26/98	59	2		11 I'll Be Home For Christmas	White Christmas [X-R]	—	$4		BNA 64687
12/26/98	61	1		12 All My Love For Christmas .... from the various artists album *Country Christmas Classics* on RCA 67698	[X]	—			album cut
2/6/99	47	12		13 Saturday Night	(dance mix)	—	$4		BNA 65694
4/10/99	❶⁸	41 ●		14 Amazed .... S:❶⁶ (AC mix) "45": BNA 65755 (B-side: "Tell Her")		❶²	$4	★	BNA 65957 (v)
9/18/99+	❶¹	31		15 Smile	Amazed	39	$4		BNA 65906
4/15/00	❶⁴	36		16 What About Now	Smile	30	$4		BNA 60212
9/16/00+	❶²	26		17 Tell Her .... from the album *Lonely Grill* on BNA 60321; later issued as the B-side of #22 below		39			album cut (v)
12/23/00	46	4		18 Little Drummer Boy	[X]	—			album cut
12/30/00	69	1		19 Santa Claus Is Comin' To Town	[X]	—			album cut
12/30/00	72	1		20 Winter Wonderland	[X]	—			album cut
12/30/00	75	1		21 Have Yourself A Merry Little Christmas .... above 4 from the album *This Christmas Time* on BNA 67975	[X]	—			album cut
4/14/01	❶⁶	26		22 I'm Already There	Tell Her	24	$4		BNA 69083
7/14/01	57	1		23 Unusually Unusual .... from the album *I'm Already There* on BNA 67011		—			album cut
8/18/01	10	23		24 With Me	Out Go The Lights	63	$4		BNA 69105
				LONG, Shorty '48 Born Emidio Vagnoni on 10/11/23 in Reading, Pennsylvania. Not to be confused with the R&B singer of the same name.					
10/30/48	12	1		Sweeter Than The Flowers .... S:12 SHORTY LONG And The Santa Fe Rangers	I Love You So Much It Hurts	—	$25		Decca 46139
				LONZO & OSCAR '48 Comedy duo: Ken "Lonzo" Marvin (born Lloyd George on 6/27/24 in Haleyville, Alabama) and Rollin "Oscar" Sullivan (born on 1/19/19 in Edmonton, Kentucky). Joined the *Grand Ole Opry* in 1947. Marvin was replaced in 1950 by Rollin's brother, John "Lonzo" Sullivan (born on 7/7/17 in Edmonton, Kentucky). They were often joined on-stage by Clell "Cousin Jody" Summey. John Sullivan died on 6/5/67 (age 49). Rollin continued the duo with David "Lonzo" Hooten (born on 2/4/35 in St. Claire, Missouri). Ken Marvin died on 10/16/91 (age 67).					
1/31/48	5	7		1 I'm My Own Grandpa J:5 LONZO and OSCAR with the Winston County Pea Pickers #10 Pop hit for **Guy Lombardo** in 1948	You Blacked My Blue Eyes Once Too Often [N]	—	$25		Victor 20-2563
6/5/61	26	1		2 Country Music Time	Can't Pitch Woo (In An Igloo) [N]	—	$20		Starday 543
1/12/74	29	12		3 Traces Of Life	Lubbock	—	$8		GRC 1006

DEBUT	PEAK	WKS	Gold	A-side (Chart Hit)	B-side	Pop	$	Pic	Label & Number
				LORD, Bobby '56					
				Born on 1/6/34 in Sanford, Florida. Singer/songwriter/guitarist. Hosted own syndicated TV show in 1966.					
9/8/56	10	2		1 Without Your Love ... J:10 / A:15	Everybody's Rockin' But Me	—	$80		Columbia 21539
1/11/64	21	10		2 Life Can Have Meaning ...	Pickin' White Gold	—	$10		Hickory 1232
4/6/68	44	11		3 Live Your Life Out Loud ...	Charlotte, North Carolina	—	$8		Decca 32277
9/14/68	49	5		4 The True And Lasting Kind ...	It's My Life	—	$8		Decca 32373
2/15/69	40	9		5 Yesterday's Letters ...	Don't Forget To Smell The Flowers Along The Way	—	$8		Decca 32431
11/22/69+	28	11		6 Rainbow Girl ...	Do You Ever Think Of Me	—	$8		Decca 32578
5/2/70	15	13		7 You And Me Against The World ...	Something Real	—	$8		Decca 32657
8/22/70	21	14		8 Wake Me Up Early In The Morning ...	Violets Are Red	—	$8		Decca 32718
3/27/71	75	2		9 Goodbye Jukebox ...	Do It To Someone You Love	—	$8		Decca 32797
				LORD, Mike '87					
				Born in San Antonio, Texas. Singer/drummer.					
6/27/87	94	2		Just Try Texas ...	Lying Here Lonely	—	$5		NSD 230
				LORIE ANN '89					
9/3/88	81	3		1 Down On Market Street ...		—	$6	■	Sing Me 34
1/14/89	78	3		2 Say The Part About I Love You ...		—	$6	■	Sing Me 37
6/24/89	98	1		3 Just Because You're Leavin' ...	Reasons A Plenty	—	$6	■	Sing Me 41
				LORRIE, Myrna & Buddy DeVal '55					
				Lorrie was born Myrna Petrunke on 8/6/40 in Fort William, Ontario, Canada. Singer/songwriter. DeVal was born on 4/15/15 in Port Arthur, Ontario, Canada.					
1/1/55	6	14		Are You Mine A:6 / J:7 / S:12	You Bet I Kissed Him (Lorrie)	—	$25		Abbott 172
				LOS LOBOS '87					
				Rock group from Los Angeles: David Hildago (vocals), Cesar Rosas (guitar), Steve Berlin (saxophone), Conrad Lozano (bass) and Louie Perez (drums).					
8/22/87	57	8		1 La Bamba ...	Charlena [F]	❶³	$4	■	Slash 28336
				from the movie starring Lou Diamond Phillips					
3/19/88	55	10		2 One Time One Night ...	All I Wanted To Do Was Dance	—	$4	■	Slash 28464
				LOU, Bonnie — see BONNIE LOU					
				LOUDERMILK, John D. '65					
				Born on 3/31/34 in Durham, North Carolina. Singer/prolific songwriter. First cousin of **The Louvin Brothers**. Also see **Some Of Chet's Friends**.					
6/29/63	23	4		1 Bad News ...	The Guitar Player	—	$12		RCA Victor 8154
3/7/64	44	7		2 Blue Train (Of The Heartbreak Line) ...	Rhythm And Blues	132	$12		RCA Victor 8308
9/26/64	45	5		3 Th' Wife	Nothing To Gain [N]	—	$12		RCA Victor 8389
7/3/65	20	11		4 That Ain't All	Then You Can Tell Me Goodbye	—	$12		RCA Victor 8579
6/17/67	51	5		5 It's My Time ...	Bahama Mama	—	$10		RCA Victor 9189

				LOUVIN, Charlie ★195★ '64					
				Born Charlie Elzer Loudermilk on 7/7/27 in Section, Alabama. Singer/songwriter/guitarist. Half of **The Louvin Brothers**. First cousin of **John D. Loudermilk**. Joined the *Grand Ole Opry* in 1955.					
				1)I Don't Love You Anymore 2)See The Big Man Cry 3)You Finally Said Something Good 4)Hey Daddy 5)Something To Brag About					
6/20/64	4	27		1 I Don't Love You Anymore	My Book Of Memories	—	$10		Capitol 5173
12/12/64+	27	15		2 Less And Less ...	I Don't Want It	—	$10		Capitol 5296
3/27/65	7	17		3 See The Big Man Cry	I Just Don't Understand	—	$10		Capitol 5369
10/23/65	26	8		4 Think I'll Go Somewhere And Cry Myself To Sleep ...	Life Begins At Love	—	$10		Capitol 5475
				#30 Pop hit for **Al Martino** in 1966					
12/18/65+	15	12		5 You Finally Said Something Good (When You Said Goodbye) ...	Something To Think About	—	$10		Capitol 5550
10/15/66	58	5		6 The Proof Is In The Kissing ...	Scared Of The Blues	—	$10		Capitol 5729
12/24/66+	38	11		7 Off And On ...	Still Loving You	—	$10		Capitol 5791
4/22/67	44	10		8 On The Other Hand ...	Someone's Heartache	—	$10		Capitol 5872
8/5/67	46	9		9 I Forgot To Cry ...	Drive Me Out Of My Mind	—	$10		Capitol 5948
11/4/67+	36	12		10 The Only Way Out (Is To Walk Over Me) ...	Too Little And Too Late	—	$10		Capitol 2007
3/9/68	20	14		11 Will You Visit Me On Sundays? ...	Tears, Wine, And Flowers	—	$10		Capitol 2106
8/17/68	15	12		12 Hey Daddy	She Will Get Lonesome	—	$8		Capitol 2231
12/21/68+	19	13		13 What Are Those Things (With Big Black Wings) ...	What Then	—	$8		Capitol 2350
4/19/69	27	11		14 Let's Put Our World Back Together ...	Heart Of Clay	—	$8		Capitol 2448
9/27/69	29	9		15 Little Reasons ...	After Awhile	—	$8		Capitol 2612
1/17/70	42	9		16 Here's A Toast To Mama ...	Show Me The Way Back To Your Heart	—	$8		Capitol 2703
7/4/70	47	8		17 Come And Get It Mama ...	Is Home Sweet Home	—	$8		Capitol 2824
10/24/70	18	14		18 Something To Brag About ...	Let's Help Each Other To Forget	—	$8		Capitol 2915
				CHARLIE LOUVIN & MELBA MONTGOMERY					
11/28/70+	54	7		19 Sittin' Bull ...	It Ain't No Big Thing (But It's Growing)	—	$8		Capitol 2972
2/13/71	26	12		20 Did You Ever ...	Don't Believe Me	—	$8		Capitol 3029
				CHARLIE LOUVIN & MELBA MONTGOMERY					
6/12/71	30	10		21 Baby, You've Got What It Takes ...	If We Don't Make It	—	$8		Capitol 3111
				CHARLIE LOUVIN & MELBA MONTGOMERY					
				#5 Pop hit for Dinah Washington & Brook Benton in 1960					

DEBUT	PEAK	WKS	Gold	A-side (Chart Hit)	B-side	Pop	$	Pic	Label & Number
				LOUVIN, Charlie — Cont'd					
11/27/71	60	5		22 I'm Gonna Leave You .... When I Stop Dreaming		—	$8		Capitol 3208
				CHARLIE LOUVIN & MELBA MONTGOMERY					
5/20/72	70	2		23 Just In Time (To Watch Love Die) .... She Just Wants To Be Needed		—	$8		Capitol 3319
8/19/72	66	4		24 Baby, What's Wrong With Us .... Unmatched Wedding Bands		—	$8		Capitol 3388
				CHARLIE LOUVIN & MELBA MONTGOMERY					
1/20/73	59	6		25 A Man Likes Things Like That .... That Don't Mean I Don't Love You		—	$8		Capitol 3508
				CHARLIE LOUVIN & MELBA MONTGOMERY					
1/5/74	36	13		26 You're My Wife, She's My Woman .... If I Had To Build A Bridge (I'll Get Over You)		—	$6		United Artists 368
6/15/74	76	8		27 It Almost Felt Like Love .... Until I'm Out Of Sight		—	$6		United Artists 430
9/8/79	91	6		28 Love Don't Care .... Who's Gonna Love Me Now (Louvin)		—	$5		Little Darlin' 7922
				CHARLIE LOUVIN with Emmylou Harris					
6/5/82	56	9		29 North Wind .... Sweeter Than The Flowers		—	$5		Soundwaves 4671
				JIM & JESSE and CHARLIE LOUVIN					
6/17/89	87	2		30 The Precious Jewel .... Buried Alive		—	$8		Hal Kat 63058
				CHARLIE LOUVIN - ROY ACUFF					
				LOUVIN, Ira '65					
				Born Ira Lonnie Loudermilk on 4/21/24 in Section, Alabama. Died in a car crash on 6/20/65 (age 41). Singer/songwriter/mandolin player. First cousin of **John D. Loudermilk**. Half of **The Louvin Brothers**.					
8/14/65	44	4		Yodel, Sweet Molly .... You're Looking For An Angel		—	$10		Capitol 5428
	★295★			**LOUVIN BROTHERS, The** ★ (2) '56					
				Duo of brothers from Section, Alabama: **Charlie Louvin** (vocals, guitar) and **Ira Louvin** (vocals, mandolin). Joined the *Grand Ole Opry* in 1955. Ira died in a car crash on 6/20/65 (age 41). Charlie remained a member of the *Grand Ole Opry* as a solo artist. Duo elected to the Country Music Hall of Fame in 2001.					
				1) I Don't Believe You've Met My Baby 2) You're Running Wild 3) Hoping That You're Hoping					
9/10/55	8	13		1 When I Stop Dreaming .... A:8 / S:13 Pitfall		—	$20		Capitol 3177
1/14/56	❶²	24		2 I Don't Believe You've Met My Baby ...... A:❶² / S:5 / J:5 In The Middle Of Nowhere		—	$20		Capitol 3300
5/26/56	7	10		3 Hoping That You're Hoping .... A:7 / S:8 Childish Love		—	$20		Capitol 3413
10/6/56	7	12		4 You're Running Wild /					
10/6/56	7	11		5 Cash On The Barrel Head .... S:7 / A:11		—	$20		Capitol 3523
3/9/57	11	4		6 Don't Laugh .... A:11 The New Partner Waltz		—	$20		Capitol 3630
7/15/57	14	1		7 Plenty Of Everything But You .... A:14 The First One To Love You		—	$20		Capitol 3715
				IRA and CHARLEY LOUVIN					
10/20/58+	9	22		8 My Baby's Gone .... Lorene		—	$15		Capitol 4055
2/16/59	19	7		9 Knoxville Girl .... I Wish It Had Been A Dream		—	$15		Capitol 4117
3/13/61	12	14		10 I Love You Best Of All .... Scared Of The Blues		—	$15		Capitol 4506
9/25/61	26	1		11 How's The World Treating You .... It Hurt Me More		—	$15		Capitol 4628
11/17/62	21	6		12 Must You Throw Dirt In My Face .... The First Time In Life		—	$15		Capitol 4822

LOVELESS, Patty ★71★ '96

Born Patricia Ramey on 1/4/57 in Pikeville, Kentucky. Singer/songwriter/guitarist. Joined the *Grand Ole Opry* in 1988. Married record producer Emory Gordy Jr. in February 1989. Distant cousin of **Loretta Lynn**, **Crystal Gayle**, **Peggy Sue** and **Jay Lee Webb**. CMA Award: 1996 Female Vocalist of the Year. Also see **Same Old Train**.

1) You Can Feel Bad 2) Blame It On Your Heart 3) Chains 4) Lonely Too Long 5) Timber, I'm Falling In Love

DEBUT	PEAK	WKS		A-side	B-side		$	Pic	Label & Number
12/7/85+	46	10		1 Lonely Days, Lonely Nights .... Country I'm Coming Home To You		—	$4	■	MCA 52694
11/29/86+	49	10		2 Wicked Ways .... Half Over You		—	$4		MCA 52969
3/14/87	56	8		3 I Did .... You Are Everything		—	$4		MCA 53040
6/20/87	43	10		4 After All .... I Did		—	$4		MCA 53097
10/31/87	43	11		5 You Saved Me .... Fly Away		—	$4		MCA 53179
2/6/88	10	20		6 If My Heart Had Windows .... S:14 So Good To Be In Love		—	$4		MCA 53270
6/4/88	2¹	20		7 A Little Bit In Love .... S:11 I Can't Get You Off Of My Mind		—	$4		MCA 53333
10/8/88+	4	20		8 Blue Side Of Town .... S:5 I'll Never Grow Tired Of You		—	$4		MCA 53418
2/4/89	5	20		9 Don't Toss Us Away .... After All		—	$4		MCA 53477
5/27/89	❶¹	20		10 Timber, I'm Falling In Love .... Go On		—	$4		MCA 53641
9/9/89	6	26		11 The Lonely Side Of Love .... I'll Never Grow Tired Of You		—	$4		MCA 53702
1/6/90	❶¹	26		12 Chains .... I'm On Your Side		—	$4		MCA 53764
5/19/90	5	21		13 On Down The Line .... Feeling Of Love		—	$4	■	MCA 53811 (v)
9/22/90	20	20		14 The Night's Too Long .... Overtime		—	$4		MCA 53895
1/12/91	5	20		15 I'm That Kind Of Girl .... Some Morning Soon		—	$4		MCA 53977
5/11/91	22	20		16 Blue Memories .... You Can't Run Away From Your Heart		—	$4		MCA 54075
9/7/91	3	20		17 Hurt Me Bad (In A Real Good Way) .... God Will		—	$4		MCA 54178
1/4/92	13	20		18 Jealous Bone .... I Came Straight To You		—	$4		MCA 54271
4/25/92	30	20		19 Can't Stop Myself From Loving You .... You Don't Want Me		—	$4		MCA 54371
8/8/92	47	10		20 Send A Message To My Heart .... Takes A Lot To Rock You		—	$4		Reprise 18846
				DWIGHT YOAKAM & PATTY LOVELESS					
4/3/93	❶²	20		21 Blame It On Your Heart .... What's A Broken Heart	112	$4	■	Epic 74906 (v)
7/17/93	20	20		22 Nothin' But The Wheel .... Love Builds The Bridges (Pride Builds The Walls)		—	$4		Epic 77076
11/20/93+	6	20		23 You Will .... You Don't Know How Lucky You Are		—	$4	■	Epic 77271 (v)
3/19/94	3	20		24 How Can I Help You Say Goodbye .... How About You		—	$4		Epic 77416
7/30/94	3	20		25 I Try To Think About Elvis .... Ships	115	$4	■	Epic 77609 (v)
11/12/94+	4	20		26 Here I Am .... When The Fallen Angels Fly		—	$4	■	Epic 77734 (v)
3/18/95	5	20		27 You Don't Even Know Who I Am .... S:4 Over My Shoulder	117	$4	■	Epic 77856 (v)

DEBUT	PEAK	WKS	Gold	A-side (Chart Hit) / B-side	Pop	$	Pic	Label & Number
				LOVELESS, Patty — Cont'd				
7/8/95	6	20		28 Halfway Down / *Feelin' Good About Feelin' Bad*	—	$4	■	Epic 77956 (v)
12/30/95+	❶²	20		29 You Can Feel Bad *S:12 Feelin' Good About Feelin' Bad*	—	$4	■	Epic 78209 (v)
4/13/96	13	20		30 A Thousand Times A Day / *Feelin' Good About Feelin' Bad*	—	$4		Epic 78309
8/24/96	❶¹	20		31 Lonely Too Long / *Feelin' Good About Feelin' Bad*	—	$4		Epic 78371
12/21/96+	4	20		32 She Drew A Broken Heart	—			album cut
4/26/97	15	20		33 The Trouble With The Truth	—			album cut
				above 2 from the album *The Trouble With The Truth* on Epic 67269				
9/20/97	14	20		34 You Don't Seem To Miss Me *S:9 Where Are You Boy*	109	$4	■	Epic 78704 (v)
				PATTY LOVELESS With George Jones				
1/31/98	12	20		35 To Have You Back Again	—			album cut
6/6/98	20	20		36 High On Love	—			album cut
10/17/98	57	5		37 Like Water Into Wine	—			album cut
				above 3 from the album *Long Stretch Of Lonesome* on Epic 67997				
1/16/99	21	20		38 Can't Get Enough	96			album cut
				from the album *Classics* on Epic 69809				
5/29/99	27	20		39 My Kind Of Woman/My Kind Of Man / *All Those Years (Gill)*	116	$4		MCA Nashville 72107
				VINCE GILL With Patty Loveless				
6/10/00	13	28		40 That's The Kind Of Mood I'm In *S:8 You Don't Get No More*	—	$4	★	Epic 79447
1/13/01	20	20		41 The Last Thing On My Mind	—			album cut
				from the album *Strong Heart* on Epic Nashville 69880				
	★351★			**LOVETT, Lyle** '87				
				Born on 11/1/57 in Klein, Texas. Singer/songwriter/guitarist. Acted in several movies. Married to actress Julia Roberts from 1993-95. No relation to Ruby Lovett.				
				1)Cowboy Man 2)Give Back My Heart 3)Why I Don't Know				
7/12/86	21	19		1 Farther Down The Line *S:14 / A:24 Why I Don't Know*	—	$4		Curb/MCA 52818
11/1/86+	10	19		2 Cowboy Man *S:7 / A:10 The Waltzing Fool*	—	$4		Curb/MCA 52951
2/21/87	18	14		3 God Will *A:19 An Acceptable Level Of Ecstasy (The Wedding Song)*	—	$4		Curb/MCA 53030
6/6/87	15	14		4 Why I Don't Know / *If I Were The Man You Wanted*	—	$4		Curb/MCA 53102
10/3/87	13	18		5 Give Back My Heart *S:19 Simple Song*	—	$4		Curb/MCA 53157
1/30/88	17	16		6 She's No Lady *S:14 Pontiac*	—	$4		Curb/MCA 53246
5/21/88	24	14		7 I Loved You Yesterday *S:27 L.A. County*	—	$4		Curb/MCA 53316
9/17/88	66	4		8 If I Had A Boat *Black And Blue*	—	$4		Curb/MCA 53401
12/10/88+	45	9		9 I Married Her Just Because She Looks Like You *If I Had A Boat*	—	$4		Curb/MCA 53471
3/4/89	82	3		10 Stand By Your Man *Wallisville Road*	—	$4		Curb/MCA 53611
6/17/89	84	2		11 Nobody Knows Me *Here I Am*	—	$4		Curb/MCA 53650
9/23/89	49	7		12 If I Were The Man You Wanted *Cryin' Shame*	—	$4		Curb/MCA 53703
9/28/96	68	2		13 Don't Touch My Hat	—			album cut
1/18/97	72	1		14 Private Conversation	—			album cut
				above 2 from the album *The Road To Ensenada* on Curb/MCA 11409				
				LOVETT, Ruby '97				
				Born on 2/16/67 in Laurel, Mississippi. No relation to Lyle Lovett.				
10/4/97	73	1		Look What Love Can Do	—			album cut
				from the album *Ruby Lovett* on Curb 77857				
				LOWE, Jim '57				
				Born on 5/7/27 in Springfield, Missouri. Singer/pianist. Working as a DJ in New York City when he recorded the #1 pop hit "The Green Door" in 1956.				
5/20/57	8	3		1 Talkin' To The Blues / *S:8*	15			
				from the TV series *Modern Romances*				
		1		2 Four Walls	15	$15		Dot 15569
				LOWES, The '86				
7/19/86	61	5		1 Good And Lonesome *He's Got A Heartache On His Mind*	—	$5		Soundwaves 4775
11/8/86	84	4		2 Cry Baby	—	$6		API 1001
1/17/87	70	5		3 I Ain't Never	—	$6		API 1002
				LOWRY, Ron '70				
2/28/70	39	11		1 Marry Me *World Champion Fool*	—	$10		Republic 1409
8/22/70	65	6		2 Oh How I Waited *Look At Me*	—	$10		Republic 1415
				LUCAS, Tammy '89				
2/11/89	75	4		9,999,999 Tears *Don't Go To Sleep*	—	$7		SOA 005
				LUKE THE DRIFTER, JR. — see **WILLIAMS, Hank Jr.**				
				LUMAN, Bob ★153★ '72				
				Born on 4/15/37 in Nacogdoches, Texas. Died of pneumonia on 12/27/78 (age 41). Singer/songwriter/guitarist. Joined the *Louisiana Hayride* in 1956. First recorded for Imperial in 1957. Appeared in the 1957 movie *Carnival Rock*. Joined the *Grand Ole Opry* in 1965.				
				1)Lonely Women Make Good Lovers 2)When You Say Love 3)Neither One Of Us 4)Still Loving You 5)Let's Think About Living				
10/10/60	9	10		1 Let's Think About Living *You've Got Everything* [N]	7	$20	■	Warner 5172
2/22/64	24	14		2 The File *Bigger Men Than I (Have Cried)*	—	$10		Hickory 1238
1/29/66	39	5		3 Five Miles From Home (Soon I'll See Mary) *(I Get So) Sentimental*	—	$10		Hickory 1355

DEBUT	PEAK	WKS	Gold	A-side (Chart Hit) .... B-side	Pop	$	Pic	Label & Number
				LUMAN, Bob — Cont'd				
6/4/66	39	5		4 Poor Boy Blues ....(Can't Get You) Off My Mind	—	$10		Hickory 1382
				written by Carl Perkins				
9/24/66	42	11		5 Come On And Sing ....It's A Sin	—	$10		Hickory 1410
2/18/67	59	6		6 Hardly Anymore ....Freedom Of Living	—	$10		Hickory 1430
7/22/67	61	2		7 If You Don't Love Me (Then Why Don't You Leave Me Alone) .....Throwin' Kisses	—	$10		Hickory 1460
5/11/68	19	14		8 Ain't Got Time To Be Unhappy ....I Can't Remember To Forget	—	$7		Epic 10312
9/28/68	50	7		9 I Like Trains ....World Of Unhappiness	—	$7		Epic 10381
2/22/69	24	12		10 Come On Home And Sing The Blues To Daddy ....Big, Big World	—	$7	☐	Epic 10439
				promotional record and picture sleeve issued with David Houston's "My Woman's Good To Me"				
6/7/69	65	5		11 It's All Over (But The Shouting) ....Bad, Bad Day	—	$8		Hickory 1536
6/28/69	23	13		12 Every Day I Have To Cry Some ....Livin' In A House Full Of Love	—	$7		Epic 10480
				#45 Pop hit for Arthur Alexander in 1975				
11/29/69+	60	9		13 The Gun ....Cleanin' Up The Streets Of Memphis	—	$7		Epic 10535
3/28/70	56	5		14 Gettin' Back To Norma ....Maybellene	—	$7		Epic 10581
5/9/70	56	8		15 Still Loving You ....Meet Mr. Mud	—	$8		Hickory 1564
				also see #26 below				
7/11/70	22	14		16 Honky Tonk Man ....I Ain't Built That Way	—	$7		Epic 10631
11/28/70+	44	10		17 What About The Hurt ....A Time To Remember	—	$7		Epic 10667
3/27/71	60	5		18 Is It Any Wonder That I Love You ....Give Us One More Chance	—	$7		Epic 10699
7/17/71	40	9		19 I Got A Woman ....One Hundred Songs On The Jukebox	—	$7		Epic 10755
				#1 R&B hit for Ray Charles in 1955				
11/6/71	30	10		20 A Chain Don't Take To Me ....Don't Let Love Pass You By	—	$7		Epic 10786
1/29/72	6	17		21 When You Say Love ....Have A Little Faith	—	$7		Epic 10823
				#32 Pop hit for Sonny & Cher in 1972 (adapted from a Budweiser jingle)				
6/3/72	21	10		22 It Takes You ....Let's Think About Livin'	—	$7		Epic 10869
9/2/72	4	19		23 Lonely Women Make Good Lovers ......Love Ought To Be A Happy Thing	—	$7		Epic 10905
1/27/73	7	14		24 Neither One Of Us ....Anything But Lonesome	—	$7		Epic 10943
				#2 Pop hit for Gladys Knight & The Pips in 1973				
6/9/73	23	11		25 A Good Love Is Like A Good Song ....Have I Ever Said "I Love You" To A Lady	—	$7		Epic 10994
10/20/73+	7	15		26 Still Loving You ....I'm Gonna Write A Song [R]	—	$6		Epic 11039
				new version of #15 above				
3/9/74	23	11		27 Just Enough To Make Me Stay ....Baby Made It Good	—	$6		Epic 11087
7/13/74	25	11		28 Let Me Make The Bright Lights Shine For You ...The Closest Thing To Heaven	—	$6		Epic 11138
2/8/75	22	13		29 Proud Of You Baby ....Tonight My Baby's Coming Home	—	$6		Epic 50065
9/13/75	48	12		30 Shame On Me ....How Do You Start Over	—	$6		Epic 50136
2/7/76	41	9		31 A Satisfied Mind ....Cleanin' Up The Streets Of Memphis	—	$6		Epic 50183
5/8/76	82	4		32 The Man From Bowling Green ....It's Only Make Believe	—	$6		Epic 50216
8/7/76	89	4		33 How Do You Start Over ....Red Cadillac And Black Mustache	—	$6		Epic 50247
11/27/76	94	4		34 Labor Of Love ....Blond Haired Woman	—	$6		Epic 50297
1/22/77	63	8		35 He's Got A Way With Women ....Here We Are Making Love Again	—	$6		Epic 50323
8/6/77	33	9		36 I'm A Honky-Tonk Woman's Man ....Lonely Women (Don't Need To Be Lonely)	—	$5		Polydor 14408
10/8/77	13	16		37 The Pay Phone ....He'll Be The One	—	$5		Polydor 14431
12/24/77	92	3		38 A Christmas Tribute ....Give Someone You Love [X]	—	$5		Polydor 14444
2/11/78	47	8		39 Proud Lady ....Let Me Love Him Out Of You	—	$5		Polydor 14454
				LUNSFORD, Mike '76				
				Born on 6/30/50 in Guyman, Oklahoma. Singer/songwriter/guitarist.				
				1)Honey Hungry 2)Stealin' Feelin' 3)While The Feelings Good				
3/1/75	56	12		1 While The Feelings Good ....Blanket Of The Blues	—	$7		Gusto 124
11/8/75	87	5		2 Sugar Sugar ....Mumbled Round, Fumbled Round	—	$6		Starday 133
				#1 Pop hit for The Archies in 1969				
7/31/76	16	12		3 Honey Hungry ....Tonight My Lady Learns To Love	—	$6		Starday 143
11/20/76+	28	11		4 Stealin' Feelin' ....Part Time Lovers, Full Time Fools	—	$6		Starday 146
2/26/77	61	7		5 If There Ever Comes A Day ....Think About It One More Time	—	$6		Starday 149
7/16/77	71	5		6 I Can't Stop Now ....I Haven't Seen Mama In Years	—	$6		Starday 160
5/27/78	85	4		7 The Reason Why I'm Here ....I Feel Love	—	$6		Starday 187
11/18/78	91	5		8 I Wish I'd Never Borrowed Anybody's Angel ....Honky Tonk Super Star	—	$5		Gusto 9013
5/26/79	82	4		9 I Still Believe In You ....It's My Life	—	$5		Gusto 9018
2/23/80	93	3		10 Is It Wrong ....Lost Letter	—	$5		Gusto 9024
4/23/88	89	2		11 Tonight She Went Crazy Without Me	—	$5		Evergreen 1068
				LYERLY, Bill '81				
				Born on 2/28/53 in Richmond, Virginia. Singer/songwriter/guitarist.				
6/20/81	53	7		My Baby's Coming Home Again Today ....Tryin' To Drink You Off My Mind	—	$5		RCA 12255
				LYNDELL, Liz '81				
				Born Elizabeth Jones Tidwell in Fairview, Tennessee. Singer/songwriter. Acted in the movie That's Country.				
10/11/80	88	2		1 Undercover Man ....How I'd Love To Be With You Tonight	—	$5		Koala 326
3/7/81	78	4		2 I'm Gonna Let Go (And Love Somebody) ....Leavin' Your Tracks On My Mind	—	$5		Koala 330
7/11/81	85	3		3 Right In The Wrong Direction ....Goin' Back To The Country	—	$5		Koala 332
				LYNDEN, Tracy '85				
5/25/85	80	5		Straight Laced Lady	—	$4		RCA 14059
				LYNN, Jenny '78				
9/23/78	86	3		Taste Of Love	—	$8		Colonial 102

DEBUT	PEAK	WKS	Gold	A-side (Chart Hit)	B-side	Pop	$	Pic	Label & Number
				LYNN, Judy		'62			
				Born Judy Lynn Voiten on 4/12/36 in Boise, Idaho. Singer/songwriter. Retired in 1980 to become an ordained minister.					
8/18/62	7	16		1 Footsteps Of A Fool	This Lonely Pillow	—	$12		United Artists 472
1/26/63	29	1		2 My Secret	I Just Want To See You Once More	—	$12		United Artists 519
4/6/63	16	15		3 My Father's Voice	When You Thanked Me For The Roses	—	$12		United Artists 571
5/15/71	74	2		4 Married To A Memory	So Natural Is My Love	104	$8		Amaret 131
1/18/75	92	5		5 Padre	Burden Of Freedom	—	$6		Warner 8059
				#13 Pop hit for Toni Arden in 1958					
				LYNN, Loretta ★20★ See "The Lynns" p.208		'73			
				Born Loretta Webb on 4/14/35 in Butcher Holler, Kentucky. Singer/songwriter/guitarist. Married to Oliver "Mooney" Lynn from 1/10/48 until his death on 8/22/96 (age 69). Joined the Grand Ole Opry in 1962. Her autobiography and movie called Coal Miner's Daughter (which starred Sissy Spacek as Lynn). Elected to the Country Music Hall of Fame in 1988. Sister of Crystal Gayle, Peggy Sue and Jay Lee Webb; distant cousin of Patty Loveless. Her son Ernest Rey and daughters Patsy and Peggy (as The Lynns) also recorded. CMA Awards: 1967, 1972 & 1973 Female Vocalist of the Year; 1972 Entertainer of the Year; 1972, 1973, 1974 & 1975 Vocal Duo of the Year (with Conway Twitty).					
				1) One's On The Way 2) Love Is The Foundation 3) Somebody Somewhere 4) After The Fire Is Gone 5) Out Of My Head And Back In My Bed					
6/13/60	14	9		1 I'm A Honky Tonk Girl	Whispering Sea	—	$500		Zero 107
7/7/62	6	16		2 Success	A Hundred Proof Heartache	—	$15		Decca 31384
6/8/63	13	11		3 The Other Woman	Who'll Help Me Get Over You	—	$10		Decca 31471
11/16/63+	4	25		4 Before I'm Over You	Where Were You	—	$10		Decca 31541
5/2/64	3	24		5 Wine Women And Song	This Haunted House	—	$10		Decca 31608
7/25/64	11	23		6 Mr. And Mrs. Used To Be	Love Was Right Here All The Time	—	$10		Decca 31643
				ERNEST TUBB AND LORETTA LYNN					
12/5/64+	3	23		7 Happy Birthday	When Lonely Hits Your Heart	—	$10		Decca 31707
5/22/65	7	18		8 Blue Kentucky Girl	Two Steps Forward	—	$10		Decca 31769
7/24/65	24	11		9 Our Hearts Are Holding Hands	We're Not Kids Anymore	—	$10		Decca 31793
				ERNEST TUBB AND LORETTA LYNN					
9/18/65	10	16		10 The Home You're Tearin' Down	Farther To Go	—	$10		Decca 31836
2/5/66	4	14		11 Dear Uncle Sam	Hurtin' For Certain	—	$10		Decca 31893
6/4/66	2²	23		12 You Ain't Woman Enough	God Gave Me A Heart To Forgive	—	$10		Decca 31966
11/12/66+	❶¹	19		13 Don't Come Home A'Drinkin' (With Lovin' On Your Mind)	Saint To A Sinner	—	$10		Decca 32045
2/25/67	45	9		14 Sweet Thang	Beautiful, Unhappy Home	—	$10		Decca 32091
5/13/67	7	17		15 If You're Not Gone Too Long /			—		
6/10/67	72	2		16 A Man I Hardly Know		—	$8		Decca 32127
9/23/67	5	17		17 What Kind Of Girl (Do You Think I Am?)	Bargain Basement Dress	—	$8		Decca 32184
2/24/68	❶¹	17		18 Fist City	Slowly Killing Me	—	$8		Decca 32264
6/15/68	2¹	16		19 You've Just Stepped In (From Stepping Out On Me)	Taking The Place Of My Man	—	$8		Decca 32332
10/26/68	3	16		20 Your Squaw Is On The Warpath	Let Me Go, You're Hurtin' Me	—	$8		Decca 32392
2/22/69	❶¹	16		21 Woman Of The World (Leave My World Alone)	Sneakin' In	—	$8		Decca 32439
6/14/69	18	10		22 Who's Gonna Take The Garbage Out	Somewhere Between	—	$8		Decca 32496
				ERNEST TUBB AND LORETTA LYNN					
7/19/69	3	15		23 To Make A Man (Feel Like A Man)	One Little Reason	—	$8		Decca 32513
11/29/69+	11	16		24 Wings Upon Your Horns	Let's Get Back Down To Earth	—	$8		Decca 32586
3/7/70	4	14		25 I Know How	Journey To The End Of My World	—	$8		Decca 32637
6/27/70	6	15		26 You Wanna Give Me A Lift	What's The Bottle Done To My Baby	—	$8		Decca 32693
10/31/70	❶¹	15		27 Coal Miner's Daughter	The Man Of The House	83	$8	■	Decca 32749
2/6/71	❶²	14		28 After The Fire Is Gone	The One I Can't Live Without	56	$7		Decca 32776
				CONWAY TWITTY/LORETTA LYNN					
3/27/71	3	15		29 I Wanna Be Free	If I Never Love Again (It'll Be Too Soon)	94	$7		Decca 32796
7/31/71	5	16		30 You're Lookin' At Country	When You're Poor	—	$7		Decca 32851
10/2/71	❶¹	17		31 Lead Me On	Four Glass Walls	—	$7		Decca 32873
				LORETTA LYNN AND CONWAY TWITTY					
12/11/71+	❶²	16		32 One's On The Way	Kinfolks Holler	—	$7		Decca 32900
				first released on Decca 32900 as "Here In Topeka" ($15)					
7/8/72	3	15		33 Here I Am Again	My Kind Of Man	—	$7		Decca 32974
12/9/72+	❶¹	16		34 Rated "X"	'Til The Pain Outwears The Shame	—	$7		Decca 33039
5/19/73	❶²	15		35 Love Is The Foundation	What Sundown Does To You	102	$6		MCA 40058
6/23/73	❶¹	14		36 Louisiana Woman, Mississippi Man	Living Together Alone	—	$6		MCA 40079
				LORETTA LYNN/CONWAY TWITTY					
11/17/73+	3	16		37 Hey Loretta	Turn Me Anyway But Loose	—	$6		MCA 40150
4/27/74	4	15		38 They Don't Make 'Em Like My Daddy	Nothin'	—	$6		MCA 40223
6/15/74	❶¹	15		39 As Soon As I Hang Up The Phone	A Lifetime Before	—	$6		MCA 40251
				LORETTA LYNN/CONWAY TWITTY					
9/7/74	❶¹	17		40 Trouble In Paradise	We've Already Tasted Love	—	$6		MCA 40283
2/15/75	5	12		41 The Pill	Will You Be There	70	$6		MCA 40358
6/21/75	❶¹	16		42 Feelins'	You Done Lost Your Baby	—	$6		MCA 40420
				LORETTA LYNN/CONWAY TWITTY					
8/2/75	10	14		43 Home	You Take Me To Heaven Every Night	—	$6		MCA 40438
11/15/75+	2¹	14		44 When The Tingle Becomes A Chill	All I Want From You (Is Away)	—	$6		MCA 40484
4/10/76	20	10		45 Red, White And Blue	Sounds Of A New Love (Being Born)	—	$6		MCA 40541
6/19/76	3	12		46 The Letter	God Bless America Again	—	$6		MCA 40572
				LORETTA LYNN/CONWAY TWITTY					

★★★ 206 Black-Eyed Peas and Blue-Eyed Babies W/BAR & LP

DEBUT	PEAK	WKS	Gold	A-side (Chart Hit)	B-side	Pop	$	Pic	Label & Number
				LYNN, Loretta — Cont'd					
9/11/76	❶²	17		47 Somebody Somewhere (Don't Know What He's Missin' Tonight)	Sundown Tavern	—	$6		MCA 40607
2/26/77	❶¹	17		48 She's Got You	The Lady That Lived Here Before	—	$6		MCA 40679
6/4/77	2³	14		49 I Can't Love You Enough	The Bed I'm Dreaming On	—	$6		MCA 40728
				LORETTA LYNN/CONWAY TWITTY					
8/6/77	7	13		50 Why Can't He Be You	I Keep On Putting On	—	$6		MCA 40747
12/3/77+	❶²	15		51 Out Of My Head And Back In My Bed	Old Rooster	—	$6		MCA 40832
5/27/78	12	11		52 Spring Fever	God Bless The Children	—	$6		MCA 40910
6/24/78	6	11		53 From Seven Till Ten /		—			
		9		54 You're The Reason Our Kids Are Ugly		—	$6		MCA 40920
				LORETTA LYNN/CONWAY TWITTY (above 2)					
11/4/78	10	13		55 We've Come A Long Way, Baby	I Can't Feel You Anymore	—	$5	■	MCA 40954
5/5/79	3	14		56 I Can't Feel You Anymore	True Love Needs To Keep In Touch	—	$5		MCA 41021
10/13/79	5	14		57 I've Got A Picture Of Us On My Mind	I Don't Feel Like A Movie Tonight	—	$5		MCA 41129
11/10/79+	9	14		58 You Know Just What I'd Do /		—			
		14		59 The Sadness Of It All		—	$5		MCA 41141
				CONWAY TWITTY/LORETTA LYNN (above 2)					
3/1/80	35	8		60 Pregnant Again	You're A Cross I Can't Bear	—	$4		MCA 41185
5/10/80	5	15		61 It's True Love	Hit The Road Jack	—	$4		MCA 41232
				CONWAY TWITTY & LORETTA LYNN					
6/7/80	30	11		62 Naked In The Rain	I Should Be Over You By Now	—	$4		MCA 41250
10/25/80	20	13		63 Cheatin' On A Cheater	Until I Met You	—	$4		MCA 51015
1/31/81	7	15		64 Lovin' What Your Lovin' Does To Me	Silent Partner	—	$4		MCA 51050
				CONWAY TWITTY & LORETTA LYNN					
2/28/81	20	12		65 Somebody Led Me Away	Everybody's Lookin' For Somebody New	—	$4		MCA 51058
5/30/81	2²	18		66 I Still Believe In Waltzes	Oh Honey - Oh Babe	—	$4		MCA 51114
				CONWAY TWITTY & LORETTA LYNN					
1/23/82	9	19		67 I Lie	If I Ain't Got It (You Don't Need It)	—	$4		MCA 52005
8/14/82	19	16		68 Making Love From Memory	Don't It Feel Good	—	$4		MCA 52092
1/22/83	39	12		69 Breakin' It /		—			
		12		70 There's All Kinds Of Smoke (In The Barroom)		—	$4		MCA 52158
5/28/83	53	10		71 Lyin', Cheatin', Woman Chasin', Honky Tonkin', Whiskey Drinkin' You	Starlight, Starbright	—	$4		MCA 52219
11/26/83	59	9		72 Walking With My Memories	It's Gone	—	$4		MCA 52289
7/20/85	19	18		73 Heart Don't Do This To Me	S:19 / A:22 Adam's Rib	—	$4	■	MCA 52621
11/9/85	72	5		74 Wouldn't It Be Great	One Man Band	—	$4	■	MCA 52706
2/8/86	81	5		75 Just A Woman	Take Me In Your Arms (And Hold Me)	—	$4		MCA 52766
4/16/88	57	12		76 Who Was That Stranger	Elzie Banks	—	$4		MCA 53320
12/25/93+	68	2		77 Silver Threads And Golden Needles	Let Her Fly	—	$4	▪	Columbia 77294 (v)
				PARTON/WYNETTE/LYNN					
9/23/00	72	1	★	78 Country In My Genes		—			album cut
				from the album *Still Country* on Audium 8119					
				LYNN, Marcia '88					
				Born Marcia Lynne Dickinson on 11/19/63 in North Adams, Massachusetts.					
3/14/87	77	5		1 You've Got That Leaving Look In Your Eye	Lie Left On His Finger	—	$5		Soundwaves 4784
12/26/87+	62	8		2 Don't Start The Fire		—	$5		Evergreen 1063
				LYNN, Michelle '89					
1/14/89	92	2		1 The Letter		—	$6		Master 07
6/3/89	88	2		2 Brand New Week	The Letter	—	$6		Master 11
				LYNN, Rebecca '78					
7/8/78	39	8		1 Music, Music, Music	No More Tears	—	$6		Scorpion 0550
				#1 Pop hit for Teresa Brewer in 1950					
10/14/78	69	5		2 Minstrel Man	He Loves Me All To Pieces	—	$6		Scorpion 0559
2/24/79	83	5		3 Goody Goody	My Happiness	—	$6		Scorpion 0573
				#1 Pop hit for Benny Goodman's Orchestra in 1936; #20 Pop hit for Frankie Lymon & The Teenagers in 1957					
7/21/79	69	6		4 Make Believe You Love Me /		—			
6/2/79	82	3		5 Disco Girl Go Away		—	$6		Scorpion 0581
3/1/80	87	3		6 Fairytale		—	$6		Sunbird 106
				LYNN, Trisha '89					
7/2/88	76	2		1 I Go To Pieces		—	$6		Oak 1053
				#9 Pop hit for Peter & Gordon in 1965					
5/13/89	82	3		2 Kiss Me Darling		—	$6		Oak 1072
7/29/89	69	5		3 Not Fade Away		—	$6		Oak 1062
				TRISH LYNN					
				#48 Pop hit for The Rolling Stones in 1964					
10/28/89	65	4		4 I Can't Help Myself		—	$6		Oak 1083
				#1 Pop hit for the Four Tops in 1965					
				LYNNE, Shelby '91					
				Born Shelby Lynn Moorer on 10/22/68 in Quantico, Virginia; raised in Jackson, Alabama. Female singer. Older sister of **Allison Moorer**. Won the 2000 Best New Artist Grammy Award. Also see **Tomorrow's World**.					
				1)Things Are Tough All Over 2)I'll Lie Myself To Sleep 3)The Hurtin' Side					
9/3/88	43	10		1 If I Could Bottle This Up	S:22 I Always Get It Right With You	—	$4		Epic 08011
				GEORGE JONES & SHELBY LYNNE					
3/18/89	93	1		2 Under Your Spell Again	Blue To The Bone	—	$4		Epic 68584
6/24/89	38	11		3 The Hurtin' Side	If I Could Bottle This Up	—	$4		Epic 68942

DEBUT	PEAK	WKS	Gold	A-side (Chart Hit) ... B-side	Pop	$	Pic	Label & Number
				LYNNE, Shelby — Cont'd				
10/21/89	62	7		4 Little Bits And Pieces .... Your Love Stays With Me	—	$4		Epic 73032
6/30/90	26	17		5 I'll Lie Myself To Sleep .... What About This Girl	—	$4	■	Epic 73319 (v)
10/27/90+	23	20		6 Things Are Tough All Over .... I Walk The Line	—	$4		Epic 73521 (v)
3/23/91	45	16		7 What About The Love We Made .... I'll Lie Myself To Sleep	—	$4		Epic 73716
7/27/91	50	9		8 The Very First Lasting Love .... Lonely Weekends	—	$4		Epic 73904
				SHELBY LYNNE WITH LES TAYLOR				
11/9/91	54	13		9 Don't Cross Your Heart .... Stop Me	—	$4		Epic 74062
7/17/93	69	6		10 Feelin' Kind Of Lonely Tonight .... Don't Cry For Me	—	$4	■	Morgan Creek 23018
6/24/95	59	8		11 Slow Me Down .... —				album cut
				from the album *Restless* on Magnatone 102				
				LYNNS, The sisters (2) '97				
				Identical twin daughters of **Loretta Lynn**: Peggy and Patsy Lynn (born on 8/6/64 in Hurricane Mills, Tennessee).				
10/25/97	48	10		1 Nights Like These .... Oh My Goodness	—	$4	■	Reprise 17276 (v)
2/28/98	43	10		2 Woman To Woman ..... S:14 (the story behind "Woman To Woman" and "Nights Like These")	111	$4	■	Reprise 17248 (v)

M

				MAC, Jimmy '84				
6/23/84	93	1		You Really Know How To Break A Heart .... —		$7		AV 924
				MacGREGOR, Byron '74				
				Born Gary Mack in 1948 in Calgary, Alberta, Canada. Died on 1/3/95 (age 46). News director at radio station CKLW in Detroit when he did the narration for "Americans."				
1/26/74	59	5	●	Americans .... *America The Beautiful* (The Westbound Strings) [S]	4	$5		Westbound 222
				background music: "America The Beautiful"				
				MacGREGOR, Mary '77				
				Born on 5/6/48 in St. Paul, Minnesota. Pop singer.				
1/8/77	3	16	●	1 Torn Between Two Lovers .... I Just Want To Love You	❶²	$5		Ariola America 7638
4/23/77	36	10		2 This Girl (Has Turned Into A Woman) .... Good Together	46	$5		Ariola America 7662
8/6/77	86	3		3 For A While .... The Lady I Am	90	$5		Ariola America 7667
				MACK, Bobby '73				
				Born in Austin, Texas. Singer/songwriter/guitarist.				
8/18/73	79	6		Love Will Come Again (Just Like The Roses) .... A Love Nobody Knows	—	$6		Ace of Hearts 0467
				MACK, Gary '83				
				Born in Odessa, Texas.				
3/20/76	94	2		1 To Be With You Again .... No Easy Way	—	$6		Soundwaves 4528
6/26/76	95	2		2 One Love Down .... Mister And Mississippi	—	$6		Soundwaves 4532
4/2/83	90	2		3 I've Been Out Of Love Too Long .... My Most Requested Song	—	$6		Grand Prize 5205
				MACK, Warner ★182★ '65				
				Born Warner MacPherson on 4/2/35 in Nashville; raised in Vicksburg, Mississippi. Singer/songwriter/guitarist. Regular on the *Louisiana Hayride* and the *Ozark Jubilee*. Involved in a serious car accident on 11/29/64 near Princeton, Indiana.				
				1)The Bridge Washed Out 2)Sittin' On A Rock (Crying In A Creek) 3)Talkin' To The Wall 4)How Long Will It Take 5)Sittin' In An All Nite Cafe				
8/12/57+	9	36		1 Is It Wrong (For Loving You) .... S:9 / A:11 Baby Squeeze Me	61	$25		Decca 30301
1/11/64	34	7		2 Surely .... This Little Hurt	—	$15		Decca 31559
11/28/64+	4	24		3 Sittin' In An All Nite Cafe .... Blue Mood	—	$15		Decca 31684
5/29/65	❶¹	23		4 The Bridge Washed Out .... The Biggest Part Of Me	—	$10		Decca 31774
11/6/65+	3	19		5 Sittin' On A Rock (Crying In A Creek) .... The Way It Feels To Die	—	$10		Decca 31853
3/26/66	3	20		6 Talkin' To The Wall .... One Mile More	—	$10		Decca 31911
9/3/66	4	17		7 It Takes A Lot Of Money .... A Million Thoughts From My Mind	—	$10		Decca 32004
2/11/67	8	17		8 Drifting Apart .... When We're Alone At Night	—	$10		Decca 32082
6/24/67	4	17		9 How Long Will It Take .... As Long As I Keep Wantin' (I'll Keep Wanting You)	—	$10		Decca 32142
11/11/67+	11	16		10 I'd Give The World (To Be Back Loving You) .... It's Been A Good Life Loving You	—	$8		Decca 32211
5/18/68	7	16		11 I'm Gonna Move On .... Tell Me To Go (Tell Me To Stay)	—	$8		Decca 32308
11/23/68+	23	19		12 Don't Wake Me I'm Dreaming .... When The Walls Come Tumbling Down	—	$8		Decca 32394
5/3/69	6	15		13 Leave My Dream Alone .... You're Always Turnin' Up Again (And I'm Always Fallin' Down)	—	$8		Decca 32473
9/27/69	8	13		14 I'll Still Be Missing You .... Sunshine Bring Back My Sunshine	—	$8		Decca 32547
4/4/70	19	12		15 Love Hungry .... Love Is Where The Heart Is	—	$8		Decca 32646
9/12/70	16	13		16 Live For The Good Times .... Another Mountain To Climb	—	$8		Decca 32725
2/20/71	34	11		17 You Make Me Feel Like A Man .... Changin' Your Style	—	$8		Decca 32781
8/28/71	53	9		18 I Wanna Be Loved Completely .... Sweetie	—	$8		Decca 32858
2/26/72	45	9		19 Draggin' The River .... These Arms	—	$8		Decca 32926
8/5/72	59	6		20 You're Burnin' My House Down .... Your Warm Love	—	$8		Decca 32982
1/27/73	54	7		21 Some Roads Have No Ending .... I've Got A Feeling (About You)	—	$8		Decca 33045
11/10/73+	91	7		22 Goodbyes Don't Come Easy .... Christie, Christie	—	$6		MCA 40137
11/19/77	87	5		23 These Crazy Thoughts (Run Through My Mind) .... I Wanna Go Back	—	$5		Pageboy 31

DEBUT	PEAK	WKS	Gold	A-side (Chart Hit)	B-side	Pop	$	Pic	Label & Number
				MACKEY, Bobby '82					
				Born on 3/25/48 in Concord, Kentucky. Singer/songwriter/guitarist.					
6/12/82	57	8		Pepsi Man	What A Difference	—	$6		Moon Shine 3007
	★287★			**MADDOX, Rose** '63					
				Born Roselea Arbana Brogdon on 8/15/25 in Boaz, Alabama; raised in Bakersfield, California. Died of kidney failure on 4/15/98 (age 72). Singer/songwriter/fiddle player.					
				1)Sing A Little Song Of Heartache 2)Loose Talk 3)Mental Cruelty					
5/18/59	22	3		1 Gambler's Love	What Makes Me Hang Around	—	$20		Capitol 4177
1/30/61	14	13		2 Kissing My Pillow /		—			
2/13/61	15	7		3 I Want To Live Again		—	$15		Capitol 4487
5/22/61	4	14		4 Loose Talk /		—			
5/15/61	8	12		5 Mental Cruelty		—	$15		Capitol 4550
				BUCK OWENS AND ROSE MADDOX (above 2)					
8/14/61	14	6		6 Conscience, I'm Guilty	Lonely Street	—	$15		Capitol 4598
11/10/62+	3	18		7 Sing A Little Song Of Heartache	Tie A Ribbon In The Apple Tree	—	$15		Capitol 4845
3/16/63	18	8		8 Lonely Teardrops	George Carter	—	$15		Capitol 4905
6/15/63	18	13		9 Down To The River	I Don't Hear You	—	$15		Capitol 4975
8/3/63	15	6		10 We're The Talk Of The Town /		—			
8/10/63	19	6		11 Sweethearts In Heaven		—	$15		Capitol 4992
				BUCK OWENS AND ROSE MADDOX (above 2)					
11/23/63	18	6		12 Somebody Told Somebody	Let Me Kiss You For Old Times	—	$12		Capitol 5038
3/7/64	44	6		13 Alone With You	When The Sun Goes Down	—	$12		Capitol 5110
8/1/64	30	8		14 Blue Bird Let Me Tag Along	Stand Up Fool	—	$12		Capitol 5186
				MAGGARD, Cledus, And The Citizen's Band '76					
				Born Jay Huguely in Quick Sand, Kentucky. Recorded "The White Knight" while working at Leslie Advertising in Greenville, South Carolina.					
12/20/75+	❶¹	14		1 The White Knight	(long version) [N]	19	$5		Mercury 73751
4/17/76	42	7		2 Kentucky Moonrunner	Dad I Gotta Go [N]	85	$5		Mercury 73789
				CLEDUS MAGGARD:					
8/14/76	73	4		3 Virgil And The $300 Vacation	The Banana Bowl [N]	—	$5		Mercury 73823
7/15/78	82	4		4 The Farmer	Lovin' May Be Dangerous To Your Health [N]	—	$5		Mercury 55033
				MAINES BROTHERS BAND, The '85					
				Family group from Texas: Kenny (guitar, harmonica), Steve (guitar), Lloyd (steel guitar) and Donnie (drums) Maines. With Richard Bowden (fiddle), Cary Banks (keyboards) and Jerry Brownlow (bass). Lloyd is the father of Natalie Maines (lead singer of the **Dixie Chicks**).					
12/3/83	72	6		1 Louisiana Anna	They Call It Love	—	$4		Mercury 814561
3/24/84	85	3		2 You Are A Miracle	Dixieland Rock	—	$4		Mercury 818346
2/9/85	24	16		3 Everybody Needs Love On Saturday Night	S:21 / A:23 Little Broken Pieces	—	$4		Mercury 880536
8/10/85	84	4		4 When My Blue Moon Turns To Gold Again	Have You Heard The Latest Blues	—	$4		Mercury 880995
				#19 Pop hit for **Elvis Presley** in 1956					
11/23/85	72	8		5 Some Of Shelly's Blues	Roll Truck Roll	—	$4		Mercury 884228
				written by Mike Nesmith of The Monkees					
3/15/86	59	7		6 Danger Zone	Gonna Get Well Tonite	—	$4		Mercury 884483
				MALCHAK, Tim '88					
				Born on 6/25/57 in Binghamton, New York. Singer/songwriter/guitarist. Half of **Malchak & Rucker** duo.					
11/22/86	68	7		1 Easy Does It	Let Me Down Easy	—	$5		Alpine 004
3/7/87	37	13		2 Colorado Moon	Let Me Down Easy	—	$5		Alpine 006
8/1/87	39	11		3 Restless Angel	I Owe It All To You	—	$5		Alpine 007
1/30/88	35	14		4 It Goes Without Saying	I Owe It All To You	—	$5		Alpine 008
10/1/88	43	11		5 Not A Night Goes By	I Owe It All To You	—	$5		Alpine 009
4/15/89	70	4		6 Not Like This	I Owe It All To You	—	$4		Universal 66004
8/5/89	54	6		7 If You Had A Heart	Sweet Virginia	—	$4		Universal 66013
				MALCHAK & RUCKER '86					
				Duo of **Tim Malchak** and Dwight Rucker. White singer Malchak was born on 6/25/57 in Binghamton, New York. Black singer Rucker was born on 3/21/52 in Oxford, New York.					
11/10/84	92	2		1 Just Like That		—	$5		Revolver 004
3/23/85	67	5		2 Why Didn't I Think Of That		—	$5		Revolver 007
11/2/85	69	6		3 I Could Love You In A Heartbeat		—	$5		Alpine 001
5/3/86	67	5		4 Let Me Down Easy	I Could Love You In A Heartbeat	—	$5		Alpine 002
8/2/86	64	6		5 Slow Motion		—	$5		Alpine 003
				MALENA, Don '87					
				Born in Bakersfield, California. Singer/songwriter/guitarist.					
1/10/87	72	4		1 Ready Or Not	Lodi	—	$6		Maxima 1256
6/27/87	76	4		2 Moonwalkin'		—	$6		Maxima 1277
1/23/88	75	4		3 Dance For Me		—	$6		Maxima 1311

MALLORY, Doug — see MURRAY, Anne

MANCINI, Henry — see PRIDE, Charley

DEBUT	PEAK	WKS	Gold	A-side (Chart Hit)	B-side	Pop	$	Pic	Label & Number

MANDRELL, Barbara ★48★ '78
Born on 12/25/48 in Houston; raised in Oceanside, California. Singer/multi-instrumentalist. Sister of **Louise Mandrell**. Hosted own TV series from 1980-82; acted on TV's *Sunset Beach* in 1997. Joined the *Grand Ole Opry* in 1972. CMA Awards: 1979 & 1981 Female Vocalist of the Year; 1980 & 1981 Entertainer of the Year.

1) Sleeping Single In A Double Bed 2) (If Loving You Is Wrong) I Don't Want To Be Right 3) Years
4) One Of A Kind Pair Of Fools 5) 'Till You're Gone

DEBUT	PEAK	WKS		A-side	B-side	Pop	$	Pic	Label & Number
9/13/69	55	7		1 I've Been Loving You Too Long (To Stop Now)....9...... Baby, Come Home		—	$10		Columbia 44955
				#21 Pop hit for Otis Redding in 1965					
5/23/70	18	12		2 Playin' Around With Love .... I Almost Lost My Mind		—	$8		Columbia 45143
10/3/70	6	14		3 After Closing Time .... My Song Of Love		—	$8		Epic 10656
				DAVID HOUSTON AND BARBARA MANDRELL					
1/30/71	17	12		4 Do Right Woman - Do Right Man .... The Letter		128	$8		Columbia 45307
6/26/71	12	12		5 Treat Him Right .... Break My Mind		—	$8		Columbia 45391
				#2 Pop hit for Roy Head in 1965					
10/2/71	20	12		6 We've Got Everything But Love .... Try A Little Harder		—	$8		Epic 10779
				DAVID HOUSTON AND BARBARA MANDRELL					
12/11/71+	10	13		7 Tonight My Baby's Coming Home .... He'll Never Take The Place Of You		—	$8		Columbia 45505
4/15/72	11	13		8 Show Me .... Satisfied		—	$8		Columbia 45580
				#35 Pop hit for Joe Tex in 1967					
9/16/72	24	13		9 A Perfect Match .... Almost Persuaded		—	$8		Epic 10908
				DAVID HOUSTON AND BARBARA MANDRELL					
11/4/72	27	12		10 Holdin' On (To The Love I Got) .... Smile Somebody Loves You		—	$8		Columbia 45702
4/21/73	24	11		11 Give A Little, Take A Little .... Ain't It Good		—	$7		Columbia 45819
8/18/73	7	17		12 The Midnight Oil .... In The Name Of Love		—	$7		Columbia 45904
12/22/73+	6	16		13 I Love You, I Love You .... Let's Go Down Together		—	$7		Epic 11068
				DAVID HOUSTON and BARBARA MANDRELL					
5/25/74	40	12		14 Lovin' You Is Worth It .... How Can It Be Wrong (When It Feels So Right)		—	$7		Epic 11120
				DAVID HOUSTON AND BARBARA MANDRELL					
6/15/74	12	16		15 This Time I Almost Made It .... Son-Of-A-Gun		—	$7		Columbia 46054
8/10/74	14	16		16 Ten Commandments Of Love .... Try A Little Harder		—	$7		Epic 20005
				DAVID HOUSTON and BARBARA MANDRELL					
				#22 Pop hit for Harvey & The Moonglows in 1958					
2/22/75	39	9		17 Wonder When My Baby's Comin' Home .... Kiss The Hurt Away		—	$7		Columbia 10082
12/20/75+	5	17		18 Standing Room Only .... Can't Help But Wonder		—	$6		ABC/Dot 17601
5/8/76	16	13		19 That's What Friends Are For .... The Beginning Of The End		—	$6		ABC/Dot 17623
8/14/76	24	12		20 Love Is Thin Ice .... Will We Ever Make Love In Love Again		—	$6		ABC/Dot 17644
12/18/76+	16	12		21 Midnight Angel .... I Count You		—	$6		ABC/Dot 17668
4/2/77	3	17		22 Married But Not To Each Other .... Fool's Gold		—	$6		ABC/Dot 17688
				#16 R&B hit for Denise LaSalle in 1976					
9/3/77	12	14		23 Hold Me .... This Is Not Another Cheatin' Song		—	$6		ABC/Dot 17716
12/24/77+	4	16		24 Woman To Woman .... Let The Rain Out		92	$6		ABC/Dot 17736
				#22 Pop hit for Shirley Brown in 1974					
5/20/78	5	13		25 Tonight .... If I Were A River		103	$5		ABC 12362
9/9/78	❶³	15		26 Sleeping Single In A Double Bed .... Just One More Of Your Goodbyes		102	$5		ABC 12403
2/17/79	❶¹	14		27 (If Loving You Is Wrong) I Don't Want To Be Right .... I Feel The Hurt Coming On		31	$5		MCA 12451
				#3 Pop hit for Luther Ingram in 1972					
8/11/79	4	14		28 Fooled By A Feeling .... Love Takes A Long Time To Die		89	$4		MCA 41077
12/15/79+	❶¹	15		29 Years .... Darlin'		102	$4	■	MCA 41162
				#35 Pop hit for Wayne Newton in 1980					
6/21/80	3	16		30 Crackers .... Using Him To Get To You		105	$4		MCA 41263
10/11/80	6	17		31 The Best Of Strangers .... Sometime, Somewhere, Somehow		—	$4	◉	MCA 51001
2/7/81	13	13		32 Love Is Fair /		—			
		13		33 Sometime, Somewhere, Somehow		—	$4		MCA 51062
5/9/81	❶¹	13		34 I Was Country When Country Wasn't Cool .... A Woman's Got A Right		—	$4		MCA 51107
				George Jones (guest vocal)					
9/5/81	2¹	16		35 Wish You Were Here .... She's Out There Dancin' Alone		—	$4		MCA 51171
				above 2 are "live" recordings					
5/1/82	❶¹	19		36 'Till You're Gone .... You're Not Supposed To Be Here		—	$4		MCA 52038
9/4/82	9	15		37 Operator, Long Distance Please .... Black And White		—	$4		MCA 52111
4/23/83	4	19		38 In Times Like These .... Loveless		—	$4		MCA 52206
8/27/83	❶¹	21		39 One Of A Kind Pair Of Fools .... As Well As Can Be Expected		—	$4		MCA 52258
2/18/84	3	21		40 Happy Birthday Dear Heartache .... A Man's Not A Man ('Til He's Loved By A Woman)		—	$4		MCA 52340
6/9/84	2¹	21		41 Only A Lonely Heart Knows .... I Wonder What The Rich Folk Are Doin' Tonight		—	$4		MCA 52397
7/21/84	3	20		42 To Me .... S:15 / A:23 We Were Meant For Each Other		—	$4	■	MCA 52415
				BARBARA MANDRELL/LEE GREENWOOD					
10/6/84	11	20		43 Crossword Puzzle .... A:9 / S:12 If It's Not One Thing It's Another		—	$4		MCA 52465
2/2/85	19	15		44 It Should Have Been Love By Now .A:18 / S:20 Can't Get Too Much Of A Good Thing		—	$4		MCA 52525
				BARBARA MANDRELL/LEE GREENWOOD					
3/9/85	7	20		45 There's No Love In Tennessee .... S:5 / A:8 Sincerely I'm Yours		—	$4	■	MCA 52537
8/24/85	8	18		46 Angel In Your Arms .... A:8 / S:8 Don't Look In My Eyes		—	$4		MCA 52645
				#6 Pop hit for Hot in 1977					
12/7/85+	4	19		47 Fast Lanes And Country Roads .... S:3 / A:4 You Only You		—	$4	■	MCA 52737
3/29/86	20	14		48 When You Get To The Heart .... A:20 / S:21 Survivors		—	$4		MCA 52802
				BARBARA MANDRELL with the Oak Ridge Boys					

DEBUT	PEAK	WKS	Gold	A-side (Chart Hit)	B-side	Pop	$	Pic	Label & Number

MANDRELL, Barbara — Cont'd

DEBUT	PEAK	WKS	A-side	B-side	Pop	$	Pic	Label & Number
8/16/86	6	22	49 No One Mends A Broken Heart Like You	A:6 / S:8 Love Is Adventure In The Great Unknown	—	$4		MCA 52900
7/4/87	13	17	50 Child Support	S:7 I'm Glad I Married You	—	$4	■	EMI America 43032
12/5/87	48	11	51 Sure Feels Good	Sunshine Street	—	$4		EMI America 50102
3/12/88	49	11	52 Angels Love Bad Men — Waylon Jennings (guest vocal)	Sunshine Street	—	$4	■	EMI America 43042
8/20/88	5	22	53 I Wish That I Could Fall In Love Today	S:9 I'll Be Your Jukebox Tonight	—	$4		Capitol 44220
2/4/89	19	16	54 My Train Of Thought	Blanket Of Love	—	$4		Capitol 44276
7/1/89	49	8	55 Mirror Mirror	Blanket Of Love	—	$4		Capitol 44383

MANDRELL, Louise ★198★ '85
Born on 7/13/54 in Corpus Christi, Texas. Singer/multi-instrumentalist. Sister of **Barbara Mandrell**. Formerly married to **R.C. Bannon** and Gary Buck (of **The Four Guys**).

1)I Wanna Say Yes 2)Save Me 3)I'm Not Through Loving You Yet 4)Maybe My Baby 5)Too Hot To Sleep

DEBUT	PEAK	WKS	A-side	B-side	Pop	$	Pic	Label & Number
8/26/78	77	5	1 Put It On Me	Yes, I Do	—	$5		Epic 50565
1/6/79	69	5	2 Everlasting Love — #6 Pop hit for Carl Carlton in 1974	You Never Cross My Mind	—	$5		Epic 50651
3/10/79	46	8	3 I Thought You'd Never Ask — LOUISE MANDRELL & R.C. BANNON	Yes, I Do	—	$5		Epic 50668
6/2/79	13	12	4 Reunited — LOUISE MANDRELL & R.C. BANNON — #1 Pop hit for Peaches & Herb in 1979	Hello There Stranger	—	$5		Epic 50717
9/1/79	72	5	5 I Never Loved Anyone Like I Love You	Surrender To My Heart	—	$5		Epic 50752
11/17/79	48	8	6 We Love Each Other — LOUISE MANDRELL & R.C. BANNON	I Want To (Do Everything For You)	—	$5		Epic 50789
3/29/80	63	5	7 Wake Me Up	That Song Called Forever	—	$5		Epic 50856
7/19/80	82	4	8 Beggin' For Mercy	Come Here	—	$5		Epic 50896
9/27/80	61	6	9 Love Insurance	When It Hurts You Most	—	$5		Epic 50935
11/28/81+	35	11	10 Where There's Smoke There's Fire — LOUISE MANDRELL & R.C. BANNON	Before You	—	$5		RCA 12359
2/13/82	35	12	11 (You Sure Know Your Way) Around My Heart	Dance Me Around Cowboy	—	$5	■	RCA 13039
6/5/82	56	7	12 Our Wedding Band /		—			RCA 13095
		7	13 Just Married — LOUISE MANDRELL AND R.C. BANNON (above 2)		—	$5		
7/24/82	20	15	14 Some Of My Best Friends Are Old Songs	689-Double 2-0-3	—	$5		RCA 13278
11/6/82+	22	16	15 Romance	Better Things To Do	—	$5		RCA 13373
12/11/82	35	7	16 Christmas Is Just A Song For Us This Year — LOUISE MANDRELL/R.C. BANNON	Christmas In Dixie [X]	—	$5		RCA 13358
2/26/83	6	17	17 Save Me	Trust Me	—	$4		RCA 13450
7/16/83	10	19	18 Too Hot To Sleep	We Put On Quite A Show	—	$4	■	RCA 13567
11/5/83+	13	17	19 Runaway Heart	There's More To Love	—	$4		RCA 13649
3/24/84	7	20	20 I'm Not Through Loving You Yet	A New Girl In Town	—	$4		RCA 13752
8/18/84	24	15	21 Goodbye Heartache	S:19 / A:25 You're A Hard Act To Follow	—	$4		RCA 13850
12/8/84+	52	12	22 This Bed's Not Big Enough	Paying Through The Heart	—	$4	■	RCA 13954
3/30/85	8	19	23 Maybe My Baby	S:8 / A:10 Are You Just Playing With Me	—	$4		RCA 14039
8/17/85	5	21	24 I Wanna Say Yes	S:4 / A:5 There'll Never Be Another For Me	—	$4		RCA 14151
12/14/85+	22	17	25 Some Girls Have All The Luck	S:20 / A:23 How Did It Get So Late, So Early	—	$4		RCA 14251
			#10 Pop hit for Rod Stewart in 1984					
6/28/86	35	11	26 I Wanna Hear It From Your Lips	A:39 Summer Nights	—	$4		RCA 14364
			#35 Pop hit for Eric Carmen in 1985					
2/28/87	28	13	27 Do I Have To Say Goodbye	A:28 Keep What We Had Going	—	$4		RCA 5115
11/21/87	74	3	28 Tender Time	Take Me Back	—	$4		RCA 5208
4/9/88	51	9	29 As Long As We Got Each Other — LOUISE MANDRELL (with Eric Carmen) from the TV series Growing Pains starring Alan Thicke and Joanna Kerns	Weak Moment	—	$4	⊙	RCA 20288

MANN, Carl '76
Born on 8/24/42 in Huntingdon, Tennessee. Rockabilly singer/pianist. Member of the **Carl Perkins** band from 1962-64.

DEBUT	PEAK	WKS	A-side	B-side	Pop	$	Pic	Label & Number
5/15/76	100	1	1 Twilight Time — #1 Pop hit for The Platters in 1958	Belly-Rubbin' Country Soul	—	$5		ABC/Dot 17621

MANN, Lorene '65
Born on 1/4/37 in Huntland, Tennessee. Female singer/songwriter.

DEBUT	PEAK	WKS	A-side	B-side	Pop	$	Pic	Label & Number
10/2/65	23	9	1 Hurry, Mr. Peters — JUSTIN TUBB & LORENE MANN — answer to "Yes, Mr. Peters" by Roy Drusky & Priscilla Mitchell	We've Got A Lot In Common	—	$8		RCA Victor 8659
7/30/66	44	2	2 We've Gone Too Far, Again — JUSTIN TUBB & LORENE MANN	Together But Still Alone	—	$8		RCA Victor 8834
1/7/67	47	11	3 Don't Put Your Hands On Me	Stay Out Of My Dreams	—	$8		RCA Victor 9045
5/20/67	50	8	4 Have You Ever Wanted To?	It Tears Me Up	—	$8		RCA Victor 9183
9/23/67	63	6	5 You Love Me Too Little	I Couldn't Hardly	—	$8		RCA Victor 9288

DEBUT	PEAK	WKS	Gold	A-side (Chart Hit)	B-side	Pop	$	Pic	Label & Number
				ARCHIE CAMPBELL and LORENE MANN:					
1/6/68	24	15		6 The Dark End Of The Street	The Gettin' Place	—	$8		RCA Victor 9401
6/29/68	31	10		7 Tell It Like It Is	If That's The Only Way	—	$8		RCA Victor 9549
				#2 Pop hit for **Aaron Neville** in 1967					
9/28/68	57	8		8 Warm And Tender Love	Pledging My Love	—	$8		RCA Victor 9615
				#17 Pop hit for Percy Sledge in 1966					
1/4/69	36	9		9 My Special Prayer	What Am I Living For	—	$8		RCA Victor 9691
				MANNERS, Zeke, and his Band '46					
				Born Leo Manness on 10/10/11 in San Francisco. Died of heart failure on 10/14/2000 (age 89). Pianist/accordionist.					
2/16/46	2⁹	19		1 Sioux City Sue	Don't Dog Me 'Round [N]	—	$20		Victor 20-1797
				Curly Gribbs (vocal); #3 Pop hit for **Bing Crosby** & The Jesters in 1946					
12/14/46	5	2		2 Inflation	Missouri [N]	—	$20		Victor 20-2013
				MANNING, Linda '69					
				Born in Cullman, Arkansas.					
12/28/68+	54	8		Since They Fired The Band Director (At Murphy High)	Talk Of The Town	—	$8		Mercury 72875
				MANNING, Rhonda '88					
				Born in Nashville. Daughter of DJ Ron Manning.					
12/19/87	87	3		1 Out With The Boys		—	$5		Soundwaves 4792
6/11/88	73	3		2 You Really Know How To Break A Heart	Out With The Boys	—	$5		Soundwaves 4799
				MANTELLI, Steve '83					
10/9/82	94	2		1 I'll Baby You		—	$7		Picap 008
1/8/83	84	4		2 You're A Keep Me Wondering Kind Of Woman		—	$7		Picap 005
				MARCY BROS., The '89					
				Vocal trio of brothers from Hay Springs, Nebraska: Kevin, Kris and Kendal Marcy.					
5/7/88	68	5		1 The Things I Didn't Say	Nobody Knows/Everybody's Guessin'	—	$4	■	Warner 27938
2/11/89	52	9		2 Threads Of Gold	Boys You Gotta Learn To Dance	—	$4		Warner 27573
5/20/89	34	10		3 Cotton Pickin' Time	If Only Your Eyes Could Lie	—	$4		Warner 22956
11/4/89	70	4		4 You're Not Even Crying	The Things I Didn't Say	—	$4		Warner 22753
1/13/90	79	1		5 Missing You	Walkin' Shoes	—	$4		Warner 22659
8/24/91	71	2		6 She Can	One Less Lonely Heart	—	$4	■	Atlantic 87741 (v)
				THE MARCY BROTHERS					
				MARGO & NORRO — see **SMITH, Margo / WILSON, Norro**					
				MARIPAT '89					
				Female singer Maripat Davis.					
6/24/89	97	1		No One To Talk To But The Blues		—	$6		Oak 1073
				MARLIN SISTERS, The — see **YANKOVIC, Frankie**					
				MARNEY, Ben '81					
				Born in Jackson, Mississippi. Singer/songwriter/guitarist.					
7/18/81	92	2		Where Cheaters Go	Until The Day We Die	—	$7		Southern Biscuit 107
				MARR, Leah '90					
10/1/88	83	3		1 Sealed With A Kiss		—	$6		Oak 1060
				#3 Pop hit for Brian Hyland in 1962					
9/23/89	80	3		2 Half Heaven Half Heartache		—	$6		Oak 1071
12/16/89+	76	4		3 I've Been A Fool		—	$6		Oak 1084
				MARRIOTT, John '89					
12/9/89	92	4		Modern Day Cowboy		—	$7		Phoenix 152
				MARSHALL, Roger '88					
7/16/88	73	4		1 Hocus Pocus		—	$6		AVM 17
11/19/88	99	1		2 Take A Letter Maria		—	$6		Master 05
				#2 Pop hit for R.B. Greaves in 1969					
				MARSHALL DYLLON '01					
				Vocal group from San Antonio: brothers Paul and Michael Martin, Todd Sansom, Jess Littleton and Daniel Cahoon.					
9/30/00+	37	20		1 Live It Up		—			album cut
3/17/01	47	7		2 You		—			album cut
7/14/01	44	9		3 She Ain't Gonna Cry		—			album cut
				all of above from the album **Enjoy The Ride** on Dreamcatcher 101					
				MARSHALL TUCKER BAND, The '87					
				Southern-rock group from Spartanburg, South Carolina: Doug Gray (vocals; born on 5/22/48), brothers Toy (guitar; born on 11/13/47) and Tommy Caldwell (bass; born on 11/9/49), George McCorkle (guitar; born on 10/11/46), Jerry Eubanks (sax, flute; born on 3/19/50) and Paul Riddle (drums; born in 1953). Tommy Caldwell died in a car crash on 4/28/80 (age 30); replaced by Franklin Wilkie. Toy Caldwell left in 1985; died of respiratory failure on 2/25/93 (age 45). Marshall Tucker was the owner of the band's rehearsal hall.					
3/13/76	82	3		1 Searchin' For A Rainbow	Walkin' And Talkin'	104	$5		Capricorn 0251
9/4/76	63	7		2 Long Hard Ride		—	$5		Capricorn 0258
4/16/77	51	10		3 Heard It In A Love Song	Windy City Blues	—	$5		Capricorn 0270
6/25/83	62	7		4 A Place I've Never Been	Life In A Song	14	$5		Warner 29619
9/5/87	44	11		5 Hangin' Out In Smokey Places	8:05 / He Don't Know	—	$4		Mercury 888775
1/16/88	79	3		6 Once You Get The Feel Of It	Slow Down	—	$4		Mercury 870050
12/19/92+	68	6		7 Driving You Out Of My Mind		—			album cut
				from the album **Still Smokin'** on Cabin Fever 913					
6/26/93	71	1		8 Walk Outside The Lines		—			album cut
				from the album **Walk Outside The Lines** on Cabin Fever 929					

DEBUT	PEAK	WKS	Gold	A-side (Chart Hit)	B-side	Pop	$	Pic	Label & Number
				MARTEL, Marty '79					
				Born Donald Martel on 3/9/39 in Ogdensburg, New York.					
11/17/79	96	2		First Step	—		$6		Ridgetop 00679
				MARTELL, Linda '69					
				Born on 6/4/41 in Leesville, South Carolina. Black singer.					
8/2/69	22	10		1 Color Him Father	I Almost Called Your Name	—	$6		Plantation 24
				#7 Pop hit for The Winstons in 1969					
12/13/69+	33	8		2 Before The Next Teardrop Falls	Tender Leaves Of Love	—	$6		Plantation 35
3/28/70	58	6		3 Bad Case Of The Blues	Old Letter Song	—	$6		Plantation 46
				MARTIN, Benny '63					
				Born on 5/8/28 in Sparta, Tennessee. Died of heart failure on 3/13/2001 (age 72). Bluegrass singer/fiddle player.					
5/25/63	28	1		1 Rosebuds And You	Sinful Cinderella	—	$15		Starday 623
1/8/66	46	3		2 Soldier's Prayer In Viet Nam	Five By Eight [S]	—	$12		Monument 912
				DON RENO & BENNY MARTIN and The Tennessee Cut Ups					
				MARTIN, Betty '78					
				Born in Powhatan, Virginia. Singer/songwriter.					
10/7/78	77	4		Don't You Feel It Now	I Love Being Lied To	—	$6		Door Knob 071
				MARTIN, Bobbi '66					
				Born Barbara Martin on 11/29/43 in Brooklyn, New York; raised in Baltimore. Died of cancer on 5/2/2000 (age 61). Pop singer.					
10/15/66	64	3		Oh, Lonesome Me	It's A Sin To Tell A Lie	134	$8		Coral 62488
				MARTIN, Dean '83					
				Born Dino Crocetti on 6/17/17 in Steubenville, Ohio. Died of respiratory failure on 12/25/95 (age 78). Singer/actor. Charted 37 pop hits from 1948-69. Teamed with comedian Jerry Lewis from 1946-56. Martin starred in several movies with and without Lewis. Hosted own TV variety show from 1965-74.					
7/9/83	35	12		My First Country Song	Hangin' Around	—	$4		Warner 29584
				Conway Twitty (guest vocal; writer)					
				MARTIN, Grady — see CROSBY, Bing / IVES, Burl					
				MARTIN, Gypsy '81					
				Female singer.					
10/10/81	93	2		This Ain't Tennessee And He Ain't You	—		$7		Omni 61581
				MARTIN, J.D. '86					
				Born Jerald Derstine Martin in Harrisonburg, Virginia. Singer/songwriter.					
5/10/86	72	6		1 Running Out Of Reasons To Run	Wrap Me Up In Your Love	—	$4		Capitol 5573
9/6/86	77	5		2 Wrap Me Up In Your Love	Hold On	—	$4		Capitol 5606
				MARTIN, Jerry '91					
3/16/91	71	1		Letter To Saddam Hussein	[S]	—	$5	■	Desert Storm 116179
				MARTIN, Jimmy '58					
				Born on 8/10/27 in Sneedville, Tennessee. Bluegrass singer/guitarist/mandolin player. Member of Bill Monroe's Bluegrass Boys from 1949-53.					
12/8/58	14	6		1 Rock Hearts	I'll Never Take No For An Answer	—	$15		Decca 30703
5/25/59	26	3		2 Night	It's Not Like Home	—	$12		Decca 30877
2/8/64	19	15		3 Widow Maker	Red River Valley	—	$8		Decca 31558
5/7/67	49	2		4 I Can't Quit Cigarettes	Run Boy Run [N]	—	$8		Decca 31921
5/18/68	72	2		5 Tennessee	Steal Away Some Where And Die	—	$8		Decca 32300
8/4/73	97	2		6 Grand Ole Opry Song	Orange Blossom Special	—	$7		United Artists 247
				NITTY GRITTY DIRT BAND Featuring Jimmy Martin					
				MARTIN, Joey '78					
				Born in Georgia. Singer/actor.					
10/14/78	92	1		I've Been A Long Time Leaving (But I'll Be A Long Time Gone)	Dance Hall Girl	—	$7		Nickolodean 1002
				MARTIN, Mike — see DELRAY, Martin					
				MARTINDALE, Wink '59					
				Born Winston Martindale on 12/4/33 in Jackson, Tennessee. Worked as a DJ and hosted several TV game shows.					
10/19/59	11	10	●	Deck Of Cards	Love's Old Sweet Song [S]	7	$12	■	Dot 15968
				MARTINE, Layng Jr. '76					
				Born in Greenwich, Connecticut. Male singer/songwriter.					
8/28/76	93	2		Summertime Lovin'	Piece By Piece	—	$6		Playboy 6081
				MARTINO, Al '70					
				Born Alfred Cini on 10/7/27 in Philadelphia. Charted 37 pop hits from 1952-78. Played "Johnny Fontaine" in movie The Godfather.					
12/20/69+	69	3		I Started Loving You Again	Let Me Stay Awhile With You	86	$6		Capitol 2674
				MARVELL, James '81					
				Born in Tampa, Florida. Singer/songwriter/guitarist. Member of the groups Mercy and The Country Cavaleers.					
3/14/81	94	2		1 Urban Cowboys, Outlaws, Cavaleers /		—			Cavaleer 117
5/30/81	90	3		2 Love (Can Make You Happy)		—	$7		
				#2 Pop hit for Mercy in 1969					
				MASON, Dona — see DAVIS, Danny, & The Nashville Brass					

DEBUT	PEAK	WKS	Gold	A-side (Chart Hit)	B-side	Pop	$	Pic	Label & Number
				MASON, Mila '96 Born on 8/22/63 in Dawson Springs, Kentucky.					
8/17/96	18	20		1 That's Enough Of That	Heart Without A Past	—	$4	■	Atlantic 87047 (v)
2/8/97	21	20		2 Dark Horse	S:15 / I Do	—	$4	■	Atlantic 84866 (v)
6/28/97	59	8		3 That's The Kinda Love (That I'm Talkin' About)	—				album cut
11/29/97+	31	20		4 Closer To Heaven	—				album cut
				above 2 from the album *That's Enough Of That* on Atlantic 82923					
5/23/98	57	6		5 The Strong One	Bossa' My Heart	—	$4		Atlantic 84116
				MASON, Sandy '67 Born Sandy Theoret in Birdville, Pennsylvania.					
5/13/67	64	5		1 There You Go	Give Me A Sweetheart	—	$8		Hickory 1442
				MASON DIXON '89 Trio formed in Beaumont, Texas: Frank Gilligan (vocals, bass; born on 11/2/55), Jerry Dengler (guitar, banjo; born on 5/29/55) and Rick Henderson (guitar; born on 3/29/53). 1)Exception To The Rule 2)3935 West End Avenue 3)Only A Dream Away					
10/22/83	69	7		1 Every Breath You Take	Armadillo Country	—	$6		Texas 5502
				#1 Pop hit for the Police in 1983					
4/21/84	51	11		2 I Never Had A Chance With You	Circle	—	$6		Texas 5556
9/22/84	49	15		3 Gettin' Over You		—	$5		Texas 5557
2/23/85	47	10		4 Only A Dream Away	S:27 / Buried Treasure	—	$5		Texas 5558
8/31/85	76	9		5 Houston Heartache	Mason Dixon Lines	—	$5		Texas 5508
1/11/86	72	10		6 Got My Heart Set On You	Armadillo Country	—	$5		Texas 5510
8/2/86	53	10		7 Home Grown	Savin' The Best For Last	—	$5		Premier One 101
4/18/87	39	14		8 3935 West End Avenue	Baby's Song	—	$5		Premier One 112
10/10/87	51	8		9 Don't Say No Tonight	Natchez Queen	—	$5		Premier One 115
8/6/88	62	5		10 Dangerous Road	Where Does Love Go	—	$4		Capitol 44189
11/5/88	49	13		11 When Karen Comes Around	Where Does Love Go	—	$4		Capitol 44249
2/11/89	35	13		12 Exception To The Rule	A Woman Like You	—	$4		Capitol 44331
6/17/89	52	7		13 A Mountain Ago	When It Hurts You Most	—	$4		Capitol 44381
				MASSEY, Wayne '85 Born in Glendale, California. Singer/actor. Played "Johnny Drummond" on TV's *One Life To Live* (1980-84). Married **Charly McClain** in July 1984.					
1/17/81	82	3		1 Diamonds And Teardrops	The Best Of The Rest Of Our Lives	—	$4		Polydor 2147
5/21/83	71	6		2 Lover In Disguise	Born To Love You	—	$4		MCA 52211
8/6/83	57	7		3 Say You'll Stay	Born To Love You	—	$4		MCA 52246
				CHARLY McCLAIN & WAYNE MASSEY:					
7/6/85	5	22		4 With Just One Look In Your Eyes	S:5 / A:6 Tangled In A Tightrope	—	$4	■	Epic 05398
11/16/85+	10	20		5 You Are My Music, You Are My Song	S:9 / A:10 We Got Love	—	$4		Epic 05693
3/29/86	17	15		6 When It's Down To Me And You	S:16 / A:17 I'll Always Try Forever One More Time	—	$4		Epic 05842
12/6/86	74	6		7 When Love Is Right	Someone Like You	—	$4		Epic 06433
2/11/89	81	3		8 Shoot The Moon	What A Perfect Way	—	$4		Mercury 870994
				WAYNE MASSEY					
				MASTERS, A.J. '86 Born Arthur John Masters in Walden, New York. Singer/songwriter/bassist.					
11/16/85	98	1		1 Lonely Together	—		$5		Bermuda Dunes 111
3/8/86	48	9		2 Back Home	Lonely Together	—	$5		Bermuda Dunes 112
7/26/86	54	9		3 Love Keep Your Distance	Get Outta My House Blues	—	$5		Bermuda Dunes 114
11/8/86	65	5		4 I Don't Mean Maybe		—	$5		Bermuda Dunes 115
1/17/87	58	6		5 Take A Little Bit Of It Home		—	$5		Bermuda Dunes 104
4/18/87	70	4		6 In It Again	On A Night Like This	—	$5		Bermuda Dunes 116
8/15/87	67	7		7 255 Harbor Drive /					
11/21/87	77	3		8 Our Love Is Like The South		—	$5		Bermuda Dunes 117
				MATA, Billy '88 Born in San Antonio, Texas. Singer/songwriter.					
1/30/88	82	3		1 Macon Georgia Love	She Ain't Got Nothin On You	—	$6		BGM 92087
1/7/89	89	2		2 Photographic Memory	—		$6		BGM 70188
				MATHIS, Country Johnny '63 Born on 9/28/33 in Maud, Texas. Recorded with Jimmy Lee Fautheree as **Jimmy & Johnny**.					
3/9/63	14	13		1 Please Talk To My Heart	Let's Go Home	—	$12		United Artists 536
				MATHIS, Joel '74 Born in Valdosta, Georgia.					
6/8/74	89	3		1 Ann	Glasses Of Beer	—	$6		Chart 5217
1/28/78	89	2		2 The Farmer's Song (We Ain't Gonna Work For Peanuts) /	—				
		2		3 Dirt Farming Man		—	$6		Soundwaves 4562

DEBUT	PEAK	WKS	Gold	A-side (Chart Hit)	B-side	Pop	$	Pic	Label & Number

MATTEA, Kathy ★93★ '88
Born on 6/21/59 in Cross Lanes, West Virginia. Singer/songwriter/guitarist. Attended West Virginia University in 1977. Discovered in 1983 while working as a waitress in Nashville. CMA Awards: 1989 & 1990 Female Vocalist of the Year. Also see **The Red Hots**.

1)Eighteen Wheels And A Dozen Roses 2)Goin' Gone 3)Come From The Heart 4)Burnin' Old Memories 5)She Came From Fort Worth

DEBUT	PEAK	WKS		A-side	B-side	Pop	$	Pic	Label & Number
10/8/83	25	18		1 Street Talk	Heartbeat	—	$4		Mercury 814375
2/25/84	26	16		2 Someone Is Falling In Love	That's Easy For You To Say	—	$4		Mercury 818289
6/16/84	44	10		3 You've Got A Soft Place To Fall	Back To The Heartbreak Kid	—	$4		Mercury 822218
9/15/84	50	11		4 That's Easy For You To Say	Somewhere Down The Road	—	$4		Mercury 880192
3/16/85	34	14		5 It's Your Reputation Talkin'	Never Look Back	—	$4		Mercury 880595
7/6/85	22	19		6 He Won't Give In .... S:19 / A:22 I Believe I Could Fall In Love (With Loving You)	—	$4		Mercury 880867
11/2/85	46	11		7 Heart Of The Country	Talkin' To Myself	—	$4		Mercury 884177
4/12/86	3	22		8 Love At The Five & Dime A:3 / S:4 You Can't Run Away From Your Heart	—	$4		Mercury 884573
9/13/86	10	24		9 Walk The Way The Wind Blows S:7 / A:12 Come Home To West Virginia	—	$4		Mercury 884978
2/7/87	5	25		10 You're The Power S:❶¹ / A:5 Song For The Life	—	$4		Mercury 888319
5/23/87	6	20		11 Train Of Memories	S:4 Evenin'	—	$4		Mercury 888574
10/17/87+	❶¹	24		12 Goin' Gone	S:3 Every Love	—	$4	■	Mercury 888874
3/12/88	❶²	20		13 Eighteen Wheels And A Dozen Roses S:❶² Like A Hurricane	—	$4		Mercury 870148
				CMA Award: Single of the Year					
7/9/88	4	19		14 Untold Stories	S:8 Late In The Day	—	$4		Mercury 870476
11/12/88+	4	22		15 Life As We Knew It S:17 As Long As I Have A Heart	—	$4		Mercury 872082
4/15/89	❶¹	20		16 Come From The Heart	True North	—	$4		Mercury 872766
8/19/89	❶¹	21		17 Burnin' Old Memories	Hills Of Alabam	—	$4		Mercury 874672
11/25/89+	10	26		18 Where've You Been	I'll Take Care Of You	—	$4		Mercury 876262
4/7/90	2¹	21		19 She Came From Fort Worth	Here's Hopin'	—	$4	■	Mercury 876746 (v)
7/21/90	9	20		20 The Battle Hymn Of Love	Leaving West Virginia	—	$4	■	Mercury 875692 (v)
				KATHY MATTEA & TIM O'BRIEN					
11/10/90+	9	20		21 A Few Good Things Remain	Evenin'	—	$4		Mercury 878246
3/9/91	7	20		22 Time Passes By	What Could Have Been	—	$4	■	Mercury 878934 (v)
7/6/91	18	20		23 Whole Lotta Holes	Quarter Moon	—	$4		Mercury 868394
10/19/91+	27	20		24 Asking Us To Dance	Where've You Been	—	$4		Mercury 868866
9/26/92	11	20		25 Lonesome Standard Time	Asking Us To Dance	—	$4		Mercury 864318
1/23/93	19	20		26 Standing Knee Deep In A River (Dying Of Thirst)	Listen To The Radio	—	$4		Mercury 864810
5/29/93	50	9		27 Seeds	Lonely At The Bottom	—	$4		Mercury 862064
8/21/93	64	4		28 Listen To The Radio	Slow Boat	—	$4		Mercury 862650
3/26/94	3	20		29 Walking Away A Winner	The Cape	—	$4	■	Mercury 858464 (v)
7/23/94	13	20		30 Nobody's Gonna Rain On Our Parade	Grand Canyon	—	$4	■	Mercury 858800 (v)
11/12/94+	34	15		31 Maybe She's Human	Who Turned Out The Light	—	$4	■	Mercury 856262 (v)
4/1/95	20	15		32 Clown In Your Rodeo	Who's Gonna Know	—	$4		Mercury 856484
1/18/97	21	20		33 455 Rocket	All Roads To The River	—	$4		Mercury 578950
8/16/97	39	16		34 Love Travels	I'm On Your Side	—	$4		Mercury 578550
3/27/99	73	1		35 Among The Missing S:16 Have You Seen Me (Jenna Randall)	—	$4	★	BNA 65645
				MICHAEL McDONALD & KATHY MATTEA					
4/22/00	53	8		36 Trouble With Angels	Prove That By Me	—	$4		Mercury 172160
7/8/00	63	4		37 BFD	The Innocent Years	—	$4		Mercury 172173

MATTHEWS, WRIGHT & KING '92
Vocal trio: Raymond Matthews (born on 10/13/56 in Alabama), Woody Wright (born on 10/10/57 in Tennessee) and Tony King (born on 6/27/57 in North Carolina). Wright was a member of **Memphis**. King was a member of **The Tennesseans**.

DEBUT	PEAK	WKS		A-side	B-side	Pop	$	Pic	Label & Number
4/4/92	41	19		1 The Power Of Love	Everytime She Says Yes	—	$4		Columbia 74275
8/22/92	55	7		2 Mother's Eyes	When The River Runs High	—	$4		Columbia 74400
11/28/92	68	4		3 House Huntin'	Leavin' Reasons	—	$4		Columbia 74749
6/19/93	45	19		4 I Got A Love	The Truth Is Killin' Me	—	$4		Columbia 77020
10/16/93	74	2		5 One Of These Days	Big Money	—	$4	■	Columbia 77180 (v)

MAVERICKS, The ★350★ '96
Group from Miami: Raul Malo (vocals, guitar; born on 8/7/65), David Lee Holt (guitar), Robert Reynolds (bass; born on 4/30/62) and Paul Deakin (drums; born on 9/2/59). Holt was replaced by Nick Kane (born on 8/21/54) in 1995. Reynolds was married to **Trisha Yearwood** from 1994-1999. CMA Award: 1995 & 1996 Vocal Group of the Year.

1)All You Ever Do Is Bring Me Down 2)O What A Thrill 3)There Goes My Heart

DEBUT	PEAK	WKS		A-side	B-side	Pop	$	Pic	Label & Number
6/20/92	74	1		1 Hey Good Lookin'		—			album cut
				from the album *From Hell To Paradise* on MCA 10544					
1/1/94	25	20		2 What A Crying Shame	The Things You Said To Me	—	$4	■	MCA 54748 (v)
5/14/94	18	20		3 O What A Thrill	Ain't Found Nobody	—	$4	■	MCA 54780 (v)
10/1/94	20	20		4 There Goes My Heart	Just A Memory	—	$4	■	MCA 54909 (v)
1/28/95	30	16		5 I Should Have Been True	The Losing Side Of Me	—	$4	■	MCA 54975 (v)
5/13/95	49	12		6 All That Heaven Will Allow	Pretend	—	$4		MCA 55026
				written and first recorded by Bruce Springsteen on his 1987 *Tunnel of Love* album					
8/19/95	22	20		7 Here Comes The Rain	I'm Not Gonna Cry For You	—	$4	■	MCA 55080 (v)
1/20/96	13	20		8 All You Ever Do Is Bring Me Down	Volver, Volver	—	$4		MCA 55154
6/22/96	54	10		9 Missing You	Foolish Heart	—	$4	■	MCA 55021 (v)
11/16/96	65	5		10 I Don't Care (If You Love Me Anymore)	Something Stupid	—	$4		MCA 55247

DEBUT	PEAK	WKS	Gold	A-side (Chart Hit) / B-side	Pop	$	Pic	Label & Number
				MAVERICKS, The — Cont'd				
2/7/98	51	12		11 To Be With You / Panatella	—	$4		MCA 72035
6/6/98	63	7		12 Dance The Night Away / Save A Prayer	—	$4		MCA 72056
10/16/99	42	20		13 Here Comes My Baby	—			album cut
				#13 Pop hit for The Tremeloes in 1967; from the album *The Best Of The Mavericks* on Mercury 170112				
				MAY, Ralph '83				
5/2/81	93	2		1 Cajun Lady / Together We're Falling Apart	—	$6		Soundwaves 4630
2/20/82	83	3		2 In A Stranger's Eyes	—	$6		AMI 1901
				RALPH MAY and The Ohio River Band				
8/28/82	88	3		3 Here Comes That Feelin' Again	—	$6		Primero 1006
2/19/83	57	8		4 Angels Get Lonely Too / Keep Me From Blowin Away	—	$6		Primero 1021
1/17/87	73	4		5 Memory Attack	—	$5		Evergreen 1048
				RALPH MAY & The Ohio River Band				
				McALYSTER '00				
				Vocal group formed in Pensacola, Florida.				
11/25/00	69	1		1 I Know How The River Feels / S:8 Looking Over My Shoulder	—	$4	★	MCA 172186
				McANALLY, Mac '90				
				Born Lyman McAnally, Jr. on 7/15/57 in Red Bay, Alabama. Singer/songwriter/guitarist.				
2/3/90	14	21		1 Back Where I Come From / Company Time	—	$4		Warner 22662
7/7/90	70	5		2 Down The Road / She's Going Out Of My Mind	—	$4	■	Warner 19800 (v)
5/9/92	62	6		3 Live And Learn / All These Years	—	$4		MCA 54372
9/19/92	72	3		4 The Trouble With Diamonds / Socrates	—	$4		MCA 54450
1/9/93	72	2		5 Junk Cars / Somewhere Nice Forever	—	$4		MCA 54537
				McANALLY, Shane '99				
				Born on 10/12/74 in Mineral Wells, Texas. Male singer/songwriter.				
1/23/99	41	20		1 Say Anything	—			album cut
				from the album *Shane McAnally* on Curb 77818				
7/17/99	31	20		2 Are Your Eyes Still Blue / S:10 If It's Over	—	$4	★	Curb 73085 (v)
8/5/00	50	11		3 Run Away / Little Imperfections	—	$4	★	Curb 73114 (v)
				McAULIFFE, Leon '49				
				Born William Leon McAuliffe on 1/3/17 in Houston. Died on 8/20/88 (age 71). Singer/steel guitarist. Member of **Bob Wills & His Texas Playboys** from 1935-42. Appeared in several western movies.				
6/4/49	6	5		1 Panhandle Rag / S:6 / J:10 Careless Hands [I]	—	$20		Columbia 20546
				LEON McAULIFFE and his Western Swing Band				
8/21/61	16	15		2 Cozy Inn / Ain't Gonna Hurt No More	—	$15		Cimarron 4050
12/22/62+	22	11		3 Faded Love / My Little Red Wagon [I]	—	$15		Cimarron 4057
				also see #6 below				
1/11/64	35	1		4 Shape Up Or Ship Out /				
2/8/64	47	1		5 I Don't Love Nobody	—	$10		Capitol 5066
6/12/71	22	9		6 Faded Love / Pretty Eyes [R]	—	$6		MGM 14249
				TOMPALL AND THE GLASER BROTHERS WITH LEON McAULIFFE AND THE CIMARRON BOYS				
				new version of #3 above				
				McBEE, Jerry '80				
				Member of **Bluestone**.				
4/12/80	86	4		That's The Chance We'll Have To Take	—	$5		Dimension 1004
				McBRIDE, Dale '77				
				Born on 12/18/36 in Bell County, Texas; raised in Lampasas, Texas. Died of a brain tumor on 11/30/92 (age 55). Singer/songwriter/guitarist. Son Terry formed **McBride & The Ride**.				
				1)Ordinary Man 2)Always Lovin Her Man 3)I Don't Like Cheatin' Songs				
3/27/71	70	2		1 Corpus Christi Wind / Anybody Going To San Antone	—	$7		Thunderbird 539
5/22/76	90	6		2 Getting Over You Again / You Have Missed Nothing	—	$5		Con Brio 109
				also see #12 below				
11/20/76+	26	13		3 Ordinary Man / Mexicalli Rose	—	$5		Con Brio 114
3/12/77	60	8		4 I'm Savin' Up Sunshine / It's Hell To Know She's Heaven	—	$5		Con Brio 117
7/9/77	53	7		5 Love I Need You / A Love For All Seasons	—	$5		Con Brio 121
9/24/77	73	6		6 My Girl / She Makes Love Feel Good	—	$5		Con Brio 124
12/10/77+	37	10		7 Always Lovin Her Man / I Know The Feeling	—	$5		Con Brio 127
3/18/78	56	8		8 A Sweet Love Song The World Can Sing / I'm Savin' Up Sunshine	—	$5		Con Brio 131
7/15/78	45	7		9 I Don't Like Cheatin' Songs / My Girl	—	$5		Con Brio 135
10/21/78	72	5		10 Let's Be Lonely Together / She Makes Love Feel Good	—	$5		Con Brio 140
2/3/79	66	5		11 It's Hell To Know She's Heaven / You Have Missed Nothing	—	$5		Con Brio 145
5/12/79	67	7		12 Getting Over You Again / She Makes Love Feel Good [R]	—	$5		Con Brio 151
				same version as #2 above				
9/22/79	61	7		13 Get Your Hands On Me Baby / I Know The Feeling	—	$5		Con Brio 158

DEBUT	PEAK	WKS	Gold	A-side (Chart Hit)	B-side	Pop	$	Pic	Label & Number

McBRIDE, Martina ★105★ '99
Born Martina Schiff on 7/29/66 in Medicine Lodge, Kansas; raised in Sharon, Kansas. Married sound technician John McBride in 1988. Sold T-shirts for **Garth Brooks**'s 1991 concert tour. Signed to RCA in early 1992. Joined the *Grand Ole Opry* in 1995. CMA Award: 1999 Female Vocalist of the Year. Also see **America The Beautiful**.

1) I Love You 2) Blessed 3) Wrong Again 4) A Broken Wing 5) Wild Angels

DEBUT	PEAK	WKS		A-side	B-side	Pop	$	Pic	Label & Number
5/2/92	23	20		1 The Time Has Come	The Rope	—	$4		RCA 62215
8/22/92	43	15		2 That's Me	Losing You Feels Good	—	$4		RCA 62291
12/5/92+	44	15		3 Cheap Whiskey	I Can't Sleep	—	$4		RCA 62398
7/31/93	2¹	21		4 My Baby Loves Me	A Woman Knows	—	$4		RCA 62599
1/8/94	6	20		5 Life #9	Ashes	—	$4	▌	RCA 62697 (v)
5/7/94	12	20		6 Independence Day	True Blue Fool	—	$4	▌	RCA 62828 (v)
10/22/94+	21	20		7 Heart Trouble	That Wasn't Me	—	$4	▌	RCA 62961 (v)
3/11/95	49	9		8 Where I Used To Have A Heart	Heart Trouble	—	$4	▌	RCA 62948 (v)
7/29/95	4	20		9 Safe In The Arms Of Love	S:20 Life #9	—	$4	▌	RCA 64345 (v)
12/2/95+	❶¹	20		10 Wild Angels	S:15 Two More Bottles Of Wine	—	$4	▌	RCA 64437 (v)
4/6/96	28	19		11 Phones Are Ringin' All Over Town	Beyond The Blue	—	$4	▌	RCA 64487 (v)
8/31/96	38	15		12 Swingin' Doors	Phones Are Ringin' All Over Town	—	$4	▌	RCA 64610 (v)
12/28/96	74	1		13 O Holy Night	[X]	—			album cut
				from the album *White Christmas* on RCA 67654; also see #19, 23, 30 & 37 below					
1/25/97	26	16		14 Cry On The Shoulder Of The Road	A Great Disguise	—	$4	▌	RCA 64728 (v)
2/22/97	53	4		15 Valentine	—	—		▌	album cut (v)
				MARTINA McBRIDE with Jim Brickman					
				from McBride's album *Evolution* on RCA 67516; later issued on the B-side of #17 below					
6/14/97	11	20		16 Still Holding On	(long version)	—	$4		RCA 64850
				CLINT BLACK & MARTINA McBRIDE					
9/13/97+	❶¹	25		17 A Broken Wing /	S:4	61			
1/31/98	9	16		18 Valentine	[R]	50	$4	▌	RCA 64963 (v)
				MARTINA McBRIDE with Jim Brickman					
12/27/97	67			19 O Holy Night	[X-R]	—			album cut
				from the album *White Christmas* on RCA 67654					
4/25/98	2²	22		20 Happy Girl	—	—			album cut (v)
				from the album *Evolution* on RCA 67516; later issued as the B-side of #22 below					
5/9/98	55	7		21 This Small Divide	—	—			album cut
				JASON SELLERS Featuring Martina McBride					
				from Sellers's album *I'm Your Man* on BNA 67517					
9/19/98+	❶¹	26		22 Wrong Again	S:15 Happy Girl	36	$4	★	RCA 65456 (v)
12/26/98	49	2		23 O Holy Night	[X-R]	—			album cut
12/26/98	54	2		24 Have Yourself A Merry Little Christmas	[X]	—			album cut
				also see #29 and #34 below					
12/26/98	64	2		25 Let It Snow, Let It Snow, Let It Snow	[X]	—			album cut
				also see #31 below; above 3 from the album *White Christmas* on RCA 67654					
3/6/99	2¹	27		26 Whatever You Say	Be That Way	37	$4		RCA 65730
7/31/99	❶⁵	33		27 I Love You	Whatever You Say	24	$4		RCA 65896
11/20/99+	3	28		28 Love's The Only House	I Love You	42	$4		RCA 65933
12/25/99	53	1		29 Have Yourself A Merry Little Christmas	[X-R]	—			album cut
12/25/99	57	1		30 O Holy Night	[X-R]	—			album cut
12/25/99	73	1		31 Let It Snow, Let It Snow, Let It Snow	[X-R]	—			album cut
12/25/99	75	1		32 White Christmas	[X]	—			album cut
				also see #35 below; above 4 from the album *White Christmas* on RCA 67654					
5/6/00	10	29		33 There You Are	Do What You Do	60	$5		RCA 60214
12/9/00	59	6		34 Have Yourself A Merry Little Christmas	[X-R]	—			album cut
12/16/00	69	3		35 White Christmas		—			album cut
				above 2 from the album *White Christmas* on RCA 67654					
12/23/00+	11	21		36 It's My Time		102			album cut
				from the album *Emotion* on RCA 67824					
12/23/00	41	4		37 O Holy Night	[X-R]	—			album cut
12/23/00	67	2		38 The Christmas Song (Chestnuts Roasting On An Open Fire)	[X]	—			album cut
				above 2 from the album *White Christmas* on RCA 67654					
6/30/01	8	20		39 When God-Fearin' Women Get The Blues		64			album cut (v)
				from the album *Greatest Hits* on RCA 67012; later issued as the B-side of #40 below					
11/3/01+	❶²	32		40 Blessed	When God-Fearin' Women Get The Blues	31	$4		RCA 69135

McBRIDE & THE RIDE ★318★ '92
Group of Nashville session musicians: Terry McBride (vocals, bass; born on 9/16/58 in Taylor, Texas), Ray Herndon (guitar) and Billy Thomas (drums). Herndon and Thomas left in 1993; Kenny Vaughn (guitar), Randy Frazier (bass) and Keith Edwards (drums) joined. Gary Morse and Jeff Roach also joined by 1994. McBride is the son of Dale McBride.

1) Sacred Ground 2) Love On The Loose, Heart On The Run 3) Going Out Of My Mind

DEBUT	PEAK	WKS		A-side	B-side	Pop	$	Pic	Label & Number
3/16/91	15	20		1 Can I Count On You	Turn To Blue	—	$4		MCA 54022
8/3/91	28	20		2 Same Old Star	Stone Country	—	$4		MCA 54125
3/14/92	2²	20		3 Sacred Ground	Your One And Only	—	$4		MCA 54356
7/18/92	5	20		4 Going Out Of My Mind	Trick Rider	—	$4		MCA 54413
11/14/92+	5	20		5 Just One Night	All I Have To Offer You Is Me	—	$4	▌	MCA 54494 (v)
3/27/93	3	20		6 Love On The Loose, Heart On The Run	Hangin' In And Hangin' On	—	$4		MCA 54601

DEBUT	PEAK	WKS	Gold	A-side (Chart Hit) ... B-side	Pop	$	Pic	Label & Number
				McBRIDE & THE RIDE — Cont'd				
7/31/93	17	20		7 Hurry Sundown .... Just The Thought Of Losing You	—	$4		MCA 54688
11/27/93+	26	20		8 No More Cryin' .... Don't Be Mean To Me	—	$4		MCA 54761
				from the movie *8 Seconds* starring Luke Perry				
				TERRY McBRIDE & THE RIDE:				
7/2/94	45	12		9 Been There .... He's Living My Dreams	—	$4	■	MCA 54853 (v)
11/5/94	72	3		10 High Hopes And Empty Pockets .... Teardrops	—	$4	■	MCA 54936 (v)
2/18/95	57	7		11 Somebody Will .... I'll See You Again Someday	—	$4	■	MCA 54986 (v)
				McCABE, Coley '00				
				Born in McConnellsburg, Pennsylvania; raised in Hedgesville, West Virginia. Female singer.				
3/4/00	50	10		1 Grow Young With You	—			album cut (v)
				COLEY McCABE with Andy Griggs				
				from the movie *Where The Heart Is* starring Natalie Portman (soundtrack on RCA 67963); later issued as the B-side of #2 below				
6/23/01	56	5		2 Who I Am To You .... Grow Young With You (w/Andy Griggs)	—	$4		RCA 69087
	★322★			**McCALL, C.W.** '75				
				Born William Fries on 11/15/28 in Audubon, Iowa. Singer/songwriter. Was working for the Bozell and Jacobs advertising agency when he created the "C.W. McCall" character. Elected mayor of Ouray, Colorado, in the early 1980s.				
				1) Convoy 2) Roses For Mama 3) Wolf Creek Pass				
7/13/74	19	11		1 Old Home Filler-Up An' Keep On-A-Truckin' Cafe .... Old 30 [N]	54	$6		MGM 14738
12/7/74+	12	16		2 Wolf Creek Pass .... Sloan [N]	40	$6		MGM 14764
5/10/75	13	12		3 Classified .... I've Trucked All Over This Land [N]	101	$6		MGM 14801
9/20/75	24	11		4 Black Bear Road .... Four Wheel Drive [N]	—	$6		MGM 14825
11/29/75	●6	15	●	5 Convoy .... Long Lonesome Road [N]	●1	$6		MGM 14839
				also see #9 below				
3/27/76	19	10		6 There Won't Be No Country Music (There Won't Be No Rock 'N' Roll) .... Green River [S]	73	$5		Polydor 14310
7/4/76	32	9		7 Crispy Critters .... Jackson Hole [N]	—	$5		Polydor 14331
10/16/76	88	4		8 Four Wheel Cowboy .... Aurora Borealis [N]	—	$5		Polydor 14352
12/18/76+	40	8		9 'Round The World With The Rubber Duck .... Night Rider [N]	101	$5		Polydor 14365
				sequel to #5 above				
2/26/77	56	7		10 Audubon .... Ratchetjaw [N]	—	$5		Polydor 14377
9/17/77	2²	16		11 Roses For Mama .... Columbine [S]	—	$5		Polydor 14420
1/20/79	81	4		12 Outlaws And Lone Star Beer .... Silver Cloud Breakdown	—	$5		Polydor 14527
				McCALL, Darrell 4-30-40 '63				
				Born on 4/30/40 in New Jasper, Ohio. Singer/songwriter/guitarist. Lead tenor with the Little Dippers (hit #9 on the pop charts with "Forever" in 1960). Acted in the movies *Nashville Rebel*, *Road To Nashville* and *What Am I Bid*.				
				1) A Stranger Was Here 2) Lily Dale 3) Dreams Of A Dreamer				
1/12/63	17	8		1 A Stranger Was Here .... I'm A Little Bit Lonely	—	$10		Philips 40079
				DARRELL McCALL with The Milestones				
4/27/68	67	5		2 I'd Love To Live With You Again .... I Love You Baby	—	$7		Wayside 1011
8/17/68	60	8		3 Wall Of Pictures .... I'd Die To See You Smile	—	$7		Wayside 1021
7/12/69	53	9		4 Hurry Up .... Wedding Band	—	$6		Wayside 003
2/7/70	62	4		5 The Arms Of My Weakness .... Big Oak Tree	—	$6		Wayside 008
4/27/74	48	9		6 There's Still A Lot Of Love In San Antone .... A Texas Honky Tonk	—	$5		Atlantic 4019
3/20/76	52	8		7 Pins And Needles (In My Heart) .... Every Girl I See	—	$5		Columbia 10296
3/12/77	32	13		8 Lily Dale .... Please Don't Leave Me	—	$5		Columbia 10480
				DARRELL McCALL & WILLIE NELSON				
7/16/77	35	10		9 Dreams Of A Dreamer .... Sad Songs And Waltzes	—	$5		Columbia 10576
1/7/78	59	9		10 Down The Roads Of Daddy's Dreams .... An Old Memory's Arms	—	$5		Columbia 10653
5/13/78	91	5		11 The Weeds Outlived The Roses .... Love Didn't Drive My Good Woman Wild	—	$5		Columbia 10723
3/1/80	89	4		12 San Antonio Medley .... Thank God For Country Music	—	$6		Hillside 01
				CURTIS POTTER/DARRELL McCall				
8/9/80	43	9		13 Long Line Of Empties .... I Wonder Which One Of Us Is To Blame	—	$4		RCA 12033
6/9/84	79	4		14 Memphis In May	—	$5		Indigo 304
				McCANN, Lila '98				
				Born in 12/4/81 in Steilacoom, Washington. Female singer.				
5/17/97	28	20		1 Down Came A Blackbird	—			album cut
9/27/97+	3	29		2 I Wanna Fall In Love	—			album cut
3/7/98	42	12		3 Almost Over You	—			album cut
7/4/98	63	5		4 Yippy Ky Yay	—			album cut
				all of above from the album *Lila* on Asylum 62042				
1/30/99	9	26		5 With You .... S:●1 When You Walked Into My Life	41	$4	★	Asylum 64052
7/31/99	41	20		6 Crush	—			album cut
11/27/99+	47	13		7 I Will Be	—			album cut
3/11/00	60	10		8 Kiss Me Now	—			album cut
				above 3 from the album *Something In The Air* on Asylum 62355				
5/5/01	43	11		9 Come A Little Closer .... S:5 Lost In Your Love	—	$4	★	Warner 16762 (v)
				McCARTERS, The '88				
				Vocal trio of sisters from Sevierville, Tennessee: Jennifer (born on 3/1/64) and twins Lisa and Teresa (born on 11/11/66) McCarter.				
1/16/88	5	20		1 Timeless And True Love .... S:12 My Songbird	—	$4	■	Warner 28125
6/11/88	4	20		2 The Gift .... S:14 Loving You	—	$4	■	Warner 27868
10/8/88	28	15		3 I Give You Music	—	$4		Warner 27721
4/15/89	9	20		4 Up And Gone .... The Memories Remain ... Letter From Home	—	$4		Warner 22991

DEBUT	PEAK	WKS	Gold	A-side (Chart Hit)	B-side	Pop	$	Pic	Label & Number
				JENNIFER McCARTER and THE McCARTERS:					
10/28/89+	26	15		5 Quit While I'm Behind ...... *Oh Lonesome You*		—	$4		Warner 22763
3/31/90	73	2		6 Better Be Home Soon ...... *Moving On*		—	$4		Warner 19964
				#42 Pop hit for Crowded House in 1988					
6/9/90	73	2		7 Shot Full Of Love ...... *Mountain Memories*		—	$4	■	Warner 19836 (v)
				McCARTNEY, Paul '75					
				Born on 6/18/42 in Allerton, Liverpool, England. Singer/songwriter/bassist. Founding member of The Beatles. Formed group Wings with wife Linda (keyboards, backing vocals). They married on 3/12/69; Linda died of cancer on 4/17/98 (age 55). Paul charted 45 pop hits from 1971-97. Won Grammy's Lifetime Achievement Award in 1990.					
12/21/74+	51	10		Sally G ...... *Junior's Farm* (Pop #3)		17	$8		Apple 1875
				PAUL McCARTNEY & WINGS					

McCLAIN, Charly ★104★ '85

Born Charlotte Denise McClain on 3/26/56 in Jackson, Tennessee; raised in Memphis. Female singer/songwriter. Regular on local Memphis show *Mid-South Jamboree* from 1973-75. Married **Wayne Massey** in July 1984.

1)Radio Heart 2)Paradise Tonight 3)Who's Cheatin' Who 4)Sentimental Ol' You 5)Dancing Your Memory Away

DEBUT	PEAK	WKS		A-side	B-side	Pop	$	Pic	Label & Number
10/23/76	67	11		1 Lay Down ...... *Pride And Sorrow*		—	$4		Epic 50285
3/5/77	82	5		2 Lay Something On My Bed Besides A Blanket .. *Love Me 'Til The Morning Comes*		—	$4		Epic 50338
5/14/77	87	4		3 It's Too Late To Love Me Now ...... *You Can Love It Away*		—	$4		Epic 50378
10/1/77	73	5		4 Make The World Go Away ...... *Leanin' On The Bottle (And Slowly Falling Down)*		—	$4		Epic 50436
4/8/78	13	16		5 Let Me Be Your Baby ...... *Your Eyes*		—	$4		Epic 50525
9/16/78	8	14		6 That's What You Do To Me ...... *1 + 1 = Love*		—	$4		Epic 50598
1/27/79	24	11		7 Take Me Back ...... *Bedtime Comes Earlier At Our House*		—	$4		Epic 50653
5/19/79	11	14		8 When A Love Ain't Right ...... *You Can't Make Love By Yourself*		—	$4		Epic 50706
9/15/79	20	12		9 You're A Part Of Me ...... *I've Never Loved Nobody Like I Love You*		—	$4		Epic 50759
10/20/79	16	14		10 I Hate The Way I Love It ...... *Almost Persuaded*		—	$4		Epic 50791
				JOHNNY RODRIGUEZ and CHARLY McCLAIN					
1/12/80	7	15		11 Men ...... *Come Take Care Of Me*		—	$4		Epic 50825
5/3/80	23	13		12 Let's Put Our Love In Motion ...... *I'm Puttin' My Love Inside You*		—	$4		Epic 50873
8/9/80	18	13		13 Women Get Lonely ...... *I'd Rather Fall In Love With You*		—	$4		Epic 50916
11/29/80+	❶¹	17		14 Who's Cheatin' Who ...... *Love Scenes*		—	$4		Epic 50948
4/11/81	5	18		15 Surround Me With Love ...... *He's Back*		—	$4		Epic 01045
8/22/81	4	16		16 Sleepin' With The Radio On ...... *That's All A Woman Lives For*		—	$4		Epic 02421
12/26/81+	5	18		17 The Very Best Is You ...... *Love Left Over*		—	$4		Epic 02656
6/26/82	3	20		18 Dancing Your Memory Away ...... *Love This Time*		—	$4		Epic 02975
10/23/82+	7	21		19 With You ...... *Crazy Hearts*		—	$4		Epic 03308
4/9/83	20	15		20 Fly Into Love ...... *The Best That Never Was*		—	$4		Epic 03808
7/16/83	❶¹	22		21 Paradise Tonight ...... *The Four Seasons Of Love*		—	$4		Epic 04007
				CHARLY McCLAIN and MICKEY GILLEY					
11/5/83+	3	21		22 Sentimental Ol' You ...... *I'll Get You Back*		—	$4		Epic 04172
2/18/84	5	18		23 Candy Man ...... *The Phone Call*		—	$4		Epic 04368
				MICKEY GILLEY and CHARLY McCLAIN #25 Pop hit for Roy Orbison in 1961					
4/7/84	22	15		24 Band Of Gold ...... *His Love Is Out Of My Hands*		—	$4		Epic 04423
				#3 Pop hit for Freda Payne in 1970					
6/16/84	14	17		25 The Right Stuff ...... *We Got A Love Thing*		—	$4		Epic 04489
				CHARLY McCLAIN and MICKEY GILLEY					
9/22/84	25	18		26 Some Hearts Get All The Breaks ...... *A:22 / S:30 Someone Just Like You*		—	$4		Epic 04586
2/16/85	❶¹	23		27 Radio Heart ...... *S:❶¹ / A:❶¹ You Make Me Feel So Good*		—	$4		Epic 04777
7/6/85	5	22		28 With Just One Look In Your Eyes ...... *S:5 / A:6 Tangled In A Tightrope*		—	$4	■	Epic 05398
				CHARLY McCLAIN With Wayne Massey					
11/16/85+	10	20		29 You Are My Music, You Are My Song ...... *S:9 / A:10 We Got Love*		—	$4		Epic 05693
				CHARLY McCLAIN (With Wayne Massey)					
3/29/86	17	15		30 When It's Down To Me And You ...... *S:16 / A:17 I'll Always Try Forever One More Time*		—	$4		Epic 05842
				CHARLY McCLAIN & WAYNE MASSEY					
8/16/86	41	11		31 So This Is Love ...... *Too Many Tears Too Late*		—	$4		Epic 06167
12/6/86	74	6		32 When Love Is Right ...... *Someone Like You*		—	$4		Epic 06433
				CHARLY McCLAIN & WAYNE MASSEY					
3/7/87	20	24		33 Don't Touch Me There ...... *S:18 / A:22 I Know The Way By Heart*		—	$4		Epic 06980
8/22/87	51	9		34 And Then Some ...... *What Makes Love Go Round N' Round*		—	$4		Epic 07244
2/6/88	60	5		35 Still I Stay ...... *If You Didn't Need Me*		—	$4		Epic 07670
8/20/88	55	7		36 Sometimes She Feels Like A Man ...... *You Can Be You (And Be Mine Too)*		—	$4		Mercury 870508
11/12/88	58	6		37 Down The Road ...... *You Can Be You (And Be Mine Too)*		—	$4		Mercury 872036
2/4/89	50	6		38 One In Your Heart One On Your Mind ...... *You Got The Job*		—	$4		Mercury 872506
7/29/89	65	5		39 You Got The Job ...... *You Can Be You (And Be Mine Too)*		—	$4		Mercury 872998
				McCLINTON, Delbert '93					
				Born on 11/4/40 in Lubbock, Texas. Singer/songwriter/harmonica player.					
4/17/93	4	20		1 Tell Me About It ...... *What Do They Know*		—	$4		Liberty 56985
				TANYA TUCKER with Delbert McClinton					
11/29/97+	65	9		2 Sending Me Angels ...... *Better Off With The Blues*		—	$4		Rising Tide 56050

DEBUT	PEAK	WKS	Gold	A-side (Chart Hit)	B-side	Pop	$	Pic	Label & Number
				McCLINTON, O.B. '73 Born Obie Burnett McClinton on 4/25/40 in Senatobia, Mississippi. Died of cancer on 9/23/87 (age 47). Black singer/songwriter/guitarist. Known as "The Chocolate Cowboy." 1)My Whole World Is Falling Down 2)Don't Let The Green Grass Fool You 3)Soap					
7/1/72	70	6		1 Six Pack Of Trouble	You Don't Love Me	—	$6		Enterprise 9051
11/4/72+	37	13		2 Don't Let The Green Grass Fool You #17 Pop hit for Wilson Pickett in 1971	Lay A Little Lovin' On Her	—	$6		Enterprise 9059
3/10/73	36	8		3 My Whole World Is Falling Down	Music City, Tennessee	—	$6		Enterprise 9062
6/30/73	67	6		4 I Wish It Would Rain #4 Pop hit for the Temptations in 1968	Obie From Senatobie	—	$6		Enterprise 9070
3/16/74	62	9		5 Something Better	I'd Rather Be A Stranger	—	$6		Enterprise 9091
6/29/74	86	6		6 If You Loved Her That Way	Mr. Miller's Granddaughter	—	$6		Enterprise 9100
1/4/75	77	6		7 Yours And Mine	Lean On Me	—	$6		Enterprise 9108
5/1/76	100	1		8 It's So Good Lovin' You	She'll Never Be That Easy Again	—	$5		Mercury 73777
7/8/78	90	4		9 Hello, This Is Anna O.B. McCLINTON Featuring Peggy Jo Adams	Let's Get It On	—	$5		Epic 50563
12/2/78	82	5		10 Natural Love	I Can't Get Over Last Night	—	$5		Epic 50620
5/19/79	79	5		11 The Real Thing	The Crack Of Dawn	—	$4		Epic 50698
8/25/79	58	8		12 Soap	Miss Sara Lee	—	$4		Epic 50749
10/4/80	62	6		13 Not Exactly Free	Walking After Kim	—	$5		Sunbird 7554
6/9/84	69	5		14 Honky Tonk Tan		—	$5		Moon Shine 3024
3/14/87	61	6		15 Turn The Music On	(Country Music Is) American Soul	—	$4		Epic 6682
				McCOMAS, Brian '01 Born in 1972 in Harrison, Arkansas. Singer/songwriter.					
8/25/01	41	16		Night Disappear With You S:9	Never Meant A Thing	—	$4	★	Lyric Street 164050
				McCORD, Cali '88 Born in Springfield, Ohio. Female singer.					
12/12/87+	46	10		1 Bad Day For A Break Up	Slow Healing	—	$6		Gazelle 011
4/16/88	60	6		2 All In My Mind		—	$6		Gazelle 012
				McCORISON, Dan '77 Born in Denver; raised in Detroit. Singer/songwriter/guitarist.					
6/25/77	96	3		That's The Way My Woman Loves Me	Don't Forget The Man	—	$5		MCA 40729
			★386★	**McCOY, Charlie** '72 Born on 3/28/41 in Oak Hill, West Virginia. Top Nashville harmonica player and session musician. Member of the **Nashville Superpickers**. 1)I Started Loving You Again 2)I Really Don't Want To Know 3)Boogie Woogie (a/k/a T.D.'s Boogie Woogie)					
2/5/72	16	15		1 I Started Loving You Again	The Real McCoy [I]	—	$6		Monument 8529
7/8/72	23	12		2 I'm So Lonesome I Could Cry	Grade A [I]	—	$6		Monument 8546
11/4/72	19	11		3 I Really Don't Want To Know	Minor, Miner [I]	—	$6		Monument 8554
3/10/73	26	10		4 Orange Blossom Special	Hangin' On [I]	101	$6		Monument 8566
7/14/73	33	9		5 Shenandoah	John Henry [I]	—	$6		Monument 8576
10/20/73	33	13		6 Release Me	The Fastest Harp In The South [I]	—	$6		Monument 8589
3/2/74	68	6		7 Silver Threads And Golden Needles	I Just Can't Stand To See You Cry [I]	—	$6		Monument 8600
6/1/74	22	13		8 Boogie Woogie (a/k/a T.D.'s Boogie Woogie) CHARLIE McCOY & BAREFOOT JERRY #4 Pop hit for Tommy Dorsey in 1945	Keep On Harpin' [I]	—	$6		Monument 8611
8/14/76	97	2		9 Wabash Cannonball	Ode To Billie Joe [I]	—	$6		Monument 8703
2/5/77	98	3		10 Summit Ridge Drive CHARLIE McCOY (featuring Barefoot Jerry) #10 Pop hit for Artie Shaw in 1941	Play It Again Charlie [I]	—	$5		Monument 45210
8/12/78	30	10		11 Fair And Tender Ladies	18th Century Rosewood Clock	—	$5		Monument 258
12/16/78	96	3		12 Drifting Lovers		—	$5		Monument 272
4/28/79	94	3		13 Midnight Flyer	Cripple Creek	—	$5		Monument 282
9/8/79	94	2		14 Ramblin' Music Man	Red Haired Boy	—	$5		Monument 289
12/19/81	92	3		15 Until The Nights CHARLIE McCOY & LANEY SMALLWOOD written and first recorded by Billy Joel on his 1978 52nd Street album	I Love The Way You Love Me	—	$5		Monument 21001
4/16/83	74	4		16 The State Of Our Union CHARLIE McCOY & LANEY HICKS	Just Doin' Nothin' With You (Is Really Somethin')	—	$5		Monument 03518
			★155★	**McCOY, Neal** '94 Born Hubert Neal McGauhey on 7/30/58 in Jacksonville, Texas (of Irish and Filipino parents). Also recorded as Neal McGoy (the phonetic spelling of his surname). Began singing in Texas clubs in the late 1970s. Regularly opened shows for **Charley Pride** from 1981-87. Also see **Hope**. 1)Wink 2)No Doubt About It 3)They're Playin' Our Song 4)For A Change 5)You Gotta Love That					
8/27/88	85	2		1 That's How Much I Love You NEAL McGoy	Memphis Might As Well Be On The Moon	—	$5		16th Avenue 70417
1/5/91	48	10		2 If I Built You A Fire	The Big Heat	—	$4	■	Atlantic 87833 (v)
9/7/91	50	10		3 This Time I Hurt Her More (Than She Loves Me)	Down On The River	—	$4		Atlantic 87636
5/9/92	40	14		4 Where Forever Begins		—			album cut
9/5/92	57	8		5 There Ain't Nothin' I Don't Like About You		—			album cut

DEBUT	PEAK	WKS	Gold	A-side (Chart Hit)	B-side	Pop	$	Pic	Label & Number
				McCOY, Neal — Cont'd					
2/13/93	26	16		6 Now I Pray For Rain	—				album cut
				above 3 from the album *Where Forever Begins* on Atlantic 82396					
12/18/93+	❶²	20		7 No Doubt About It (album snippets)		75	$4	■	Atlantic 87287 (v)
				"45" B-side: "The City Put The Country Back In Me"					
4/23/94	❶⁴	20		8 Wink (album snippets)		91	$4	■	Atlantic 87247 (v)
				"45" B-side: "No Doubt About It"					
8/6/94	5	20		9 The City Put The Country Back In Me	Why Not Tonight	—	$4	■	Atlantic 87213 (v)
12/17/94+	3	20		10 For A Change S:24 (album snippets)		108	$4	■	Atlantic 87176 (v)
4/29/95	3	20		11 They're Playin' Our Song	—				album cut
8/12/95	16	20		12 If I Was A Drinkin' Man	—			■	album cut
				later issued as the B-side of #13 below; above 2 from the album *You Gotta Love That!* on Atlantic 82727					
1/6/96	3	20		13 You Gotta Love That S:15		—	$3	■	Atlantic 87120 (v)
5/18/96	4	20		14 Then You Can Tell Me Goodbye S:3 (album snippets)		107	$3	■	Atlantic 87053 (v)
				#6 Pop hit for The Casinos in 1967; "45" B-side: "Going, Going, Gone"					
7/20/96	71	3		15 Hillbilly Rap	—				album cut
				from the album *Neal McCoy* on Atlantic 82907					
9/28/96	35	11		16 Going, Going, Gone (album snippets)		—	$4	■	Atlantic 87045 (v)
				"45": Atlantic 87053 (B-side: "Then You Can Tell Me Goodbye")					
12/14/96+	35	17		17 That Woman Of Mine	—				album cut
				from the album *Neal McCoy* on Atlantic 82907					
5/24/97	5	21		18 The Shake	—				album cut
				from the album *Greatest Hits* on Atlantic 83011					
10/18/97+	22	20		19 If You Can't Be Good (Be Good At It)	—				album cut
3/28/98	50	8		20 Party On	—				album cut
				above 2 from the album *Be Good At It* on Atlantic 83057					
5/30/98	69	5		21 One Heart At A Time S:5 (same version)		56	$4	■	Atlantic 84117
				GARTH BROOKS, BILLY DEAN, FAITH HILL, OLIVIA NEWTON-JOHN, NEAL McCOY, MICHAEL McDONALD, VICTORIA SHAW, BRYAN WHITE					
6/27/98	29	20		22 Love Happens Like That	Broken Record	—	$4		Atlantic 84158
2/13/99	37	17		23 I Was	The Life Of The Party	—	$4		Atlantic 84456
6/12/99	42	13		24 The Girls Of Summer	—				album cut
				from the album *The Life Of The Party* on Atlantic 83170					
3/18/00	38	16		25 Forever Works For Me (Monday, Tuesday, Wednesday, Thursday) S:17	Beatin' It In	—	$4	★	Giant 16871 (v)
9/2/00	37	21		26 Every Man For Himself	The Key To Your Heart	—	$4		Giant 16837
9/2/00	59	12		27 Now That's Awesome S:13 (no B-side) [N]		—	$4	★	BNA 60286
				BILL ENGVALL Featuring Tracy Byrd, Neal McCoy & T. Graham Brown					
2/17/01	41	9		28 Beatin' It In	—			★	album cut (v)
				from the album *24-7-365* on Giant 24748; first released as the B-side of #25 above					
	★342★			**McCREADY, Mindy** '96					
				Born on 11/30/75 in Fort Myers, Florida. No relation to Rich McCready.					
				1)Guys Do It All The Time 2)A Girl's Gotta Do (What A Girl's Gotta Do) 3)Ten Thousand Angels					
2/3/96	6	23		1 Ten Thousand Angels S:4 Not Somebody's Fool		124	$4	■	BNA 64470 (v)
6/8/96	❶¹	20		2 Guys Do It All The Time S:2 (dance mix)		72	$4	■	BNA 64575 (v)
10/12/96+	18	20		3 Maybe He'll Notice Her Now		102		■	album cut (v)
				MINDY McCREADY (Featuring Richie McDonald)					
				from the album *Ten Thousand Angels* on BNA 66806; later issued as the B-side of #4 below					
3/1/97	4	20		4 A Girl's Gotta Do (What A Girl's Gotta Do) S:5 Maybe He'll Notice Her Now		105	$4	■	BNA 64757 (v)
9/20/97	26	18		5 What If I Do S:8 If I Don't Stay The Night		102	$4	■	BNA 64990 (v)
1/17/98	19	20		6 You'll Never Know S:9 Long, Long Time		102	$4	■	BNA 65394 (v)
6/6/98	41	12		7 The Other Side Of This Kiss S:23 If I Don't Stay The Night		—	$4	■	BNA 65512 (v)
10/24/98	68	1		8 Let's Talk About Love	Long, Long Time	—	$4		BNA 65605
6/12/99	57	6		9 One In A Million	—				album cut
8/21/99	57	9		10 All I Want Is Everything	—				album cut
				above 2 from the album *I'm Not So Tough* on BNA 67765					
11/11/00+	46	13		11 Scream	I Just Want Love	—	$4		Capitol 58890
				McCREADY, Rich '96					
				Born on 2/9/70 in Seneca, Missouri. Singer/songwriter/guitarist. No relation to Mindy McCready.					
1/27/96	58	10		1 Hangin' On	Back In The Swing Of Things	—	$4	■	Magnatone 1104
4/27/96	53	6		2 Thinkin' Strait	Just Like Me	—	$4	■	Magnatone 2104
5/10/97	74	1		3 That Just About Covers It	—				album cut
				from the album *That Just About Covers It* on Magnatone 1115					
				McCULLA, Paula '88					
2/6/88	69	5		Thanks For Leavin' Him (For Me)	Heart Over Mind	—	$6		Rivermark 1001
				McCULLOUGH, Gary '87					
5/23/87	80	2		I'd Know A Lie	Easy Way Out	—	$5		Soundwaves 4786

DEBUT	PEAK	WKS	Gold	A-side (Chart Hit)	B-side	Pop	$	Pic	Label & Number

McDANIEL, Mel ★119★ '85
Born on 9/6/42 in Checotah, Oklahoma. Singer/songwriter/guitarist. First moved to Nashville in 1969. Worked clubs in Alaska from 1971-73. Moved back to Nashville in 1973. Joined the *Grand Ole Opry* in 1986.

1) Baby's Got Her Blue Jeans On   2) Big Ole Brew   3) Stand Up   4) Let It Roll (Let It Rock)   5) Louisiana Saturday Night

DEBUT	PEAK	WKS		A-side	B-side	Pop	$	Pic	Label & Number
5/8/76	51	10		1 Have A Dream On Me .... Gotta Lotta Love		—	$5		Capitol 4249
9/18/76	70	7		2 I Thank God She Isn't Mine .... Or I'll Keep On Lovin' You		—	$5		Capitol 4324
1/22/77	39	11		3 All The Sweet .... A Little More Country		—	$5		Capitol 4373
6/4/77	18	14		4 Gentle To Your Senses .... Honky Tonk Lady		—	$5		Capitol 4430
9/17/77	27	11		5 Soul Of A Honky Tonk Woman .... Roll Your Own		—	$5		Capitol 4481
12/17/77+	11	16		6 God Made Love .... I'll Just Take It Out In Love		—	$5		Capitol 4520
5/20/78	80	5		7 The Farm .... Every Square Has An Angle		—	$5		Capitol 4569
8/19/78	26	11		8 Bordertown Woman .... The Grandest Lady Of Them All		—	$5		Capitol 4597
3/17/79	33	10		9 Love Lies .... Oklahoma Wind		—	$5		Capitol 4691
6/30/79	24	13		10 Play Her Back To Yesterday .... T.J.'s Last Ride		—	$5		Capitol 4740
10/20/79	27	11		11 Lovin' Starts Where Friendship Ends .... I Tried		—	$5		Capitol 4784
7/5/80	39	9		12 Hello Daddy, Good Morning Darling .... Cold Hard Facts Of Love		—	$5		Capitol 4886
11/29/80+	23	14		13 Countryfied .... Manhattan Affair		—	$5		Capitol 4949
3/28/81	7	14		14 Louisiana Saturday Night .... My Ship's Comin' In		—	$4		Capitol 4983
7/18/81	10	16		15 Right In The Palm Of Your Hand .... Who's Been Sleeping In My Bed		—	$4		Capitol 5022
11/14/81+	19	16		16 Preaching Up A Storm .... In The Heat Of The Night		—	$4		Capitol 5059
3/20/82	10	16		17 Take Me To The Country .... 10 Years, 3 Kids And 2 Loves Too Late		—	$4		Capitol 5095
				MEL McDANIELS					
7/3/82	4	18		18 Big Ole Brew .... Lay Down		—	$4		Capitol 5138
11/6/82+	20	16		19 I Wish I Was In Nashville .... Stars		—	$4		Capitol 5169
4/9/83	22	15		20 Old Man River (I've Come To Talk Again) .... The Big Time		—	$4		Capitol 5218
7/30/83	39	12		21 Hot Time In Old Town Tonight .... Some Folks Are Dying To Live Like This		—	$4		Capitol 5259
11/5/83+	9	20		22 I Call It Love .... Goodbye Marie		—	$4		Capitol 5298
3/10/84	49	9		23 Where'd That Woman Go .... You've Got Another Think Comin'		—	$4		Capitol 5333
5/19/84	59	8		24 Most Of All I Remember You .... The Gunfighter's Song		—	$4		Capitol 5349
7/28/84	64	6		25 All Around The Water Tank .... Cheatin' Only Cheatin'		—	$4		Capitol 5371
				MEL McDANIEL with Oklahoma Wind (above 3)					
11/10/84+	●¹	28		26 Baby's Got Her Blue Jeans On .... S:●¹ / A:●¹ The Gunfighter's Song		—	$4		Capitol 5418
3/16/85	6	21		27 Let It Roll (Let It Rock) .... S:6 / A:6 Dreamin' With You		—	$4		Capitol 5458
				#64 Pop hit for Chuck Berry in 1960					
9/14/85	5	21		28 Stand Up .... S:4 / A:5 I Feel A Storm Coming		—	$4	■	Capitol 5513
1/25/86	22	16		29 Shoe String .... A:19 / S:21 Worn Out Shoe		—	$4	■	Capitol 5544
5/31/86	53	9		30 Doctor's Orders .... S:37 Thank You Nadine		—	$4		Capitol 5587
9/27/86	12	19		31 Stand On It .... A:11 / S:12 In Oklahoma		—	$4	■	Capitol 5620
				written by Bruce Springsteen (B-side of his 1985 "Glory Days" single)					
2/7/87	56	7		32 Oh What A Night .... Chain Smokin'		—	$4		Capitol 5682
5/16/87	49	17		33 Anger & Tears .... Sunday Mornin' Preachers		—	$4		Capitol 5705
8/15/87	60	8		34 Love Is Everywhere .... Do You Want To Say Goodbye		—	$4		Capitol 44052
11/21/87	64	8		35 Now You're Talkin' .... Sunday Mornin' Preachers		—	$4		Capitol 44106
2/13/88	58	7		36 Ride This Train .... Jump Into Love		—	$4		Capitol 44127
5/14/88	9	21		37 Real Good Feel Good Song .... S:18 Chain Smokin'		—	$4		Capitol 44158
10/22/88	62	6		38 Henrietta .... Under My Skin		—	$4		Capitol 44244
2/4/89	54	7		39 Walk That Way .... The Tractor		—	$4		Capitol 44303
4/29/89	70	4		40 Blue Suede Blues .... Oklahoma Shines		—	$4		Capitol 44358
10/21/89	80	3		41 You Can't Play The Blues (In An Air-Conditioned Room)		—			album cut
				from the album *Rock-A-Billy Boy* on Capitol 93882					

McDONALD, Michael '98
Born on 2/12/52 in St. Louis. Singer/songwriter/keyboardist. Former member of The Doobie Brothers.

DEBUT	PEAK	WKS		A-side	B-side	Pop	$	Pic	Label & Number
5/30/98	69	5		1 One Heart At A Time .... S:5 (same version)		56	$4	■	Atlantic 84117
				GARTH BROOKS, BILLY DEAN, FAITH HILL, OLIVIA NEWTON-JOHN, NEAL McCOY, MICHAEL McDONALD, VICTORIA SHAW, BRYAN WHITE					
3/27/99	73	1		2 Among The Missing .... S:16 Have You Seen Me (Jenna Randall)		—	$4	★	BNA 65645
				MICHAEL McDONALD & KATHY MATTEA					

McDONALD, Richie — see McCREADY, Mindy

McDONALD, Skeets '52
Born Enos William McDonald on 10/1/15 in Greenway, Arkansas. Died of a heart attack on 3/31/68 (age 52). Singer/songwriter/guitarist.

DEBUT	PEAK	WKS		A-side	B-side	Pop	$	Pic	Label & Number
10/25/52	●³	18		1 Don't Let The Stars Get In Your Eyes .... J:●¹ / S:2 / A:3 Big Family Trouble		—	$20		Capitol F2216
				#1 Pop hit for Perry Como in 1953					
10/24/60	21	6		2 This Old Heart .... Make Room For The Blues		—	$12		Columbia 41773
9/28/63	9	18		3 Call Me Mr. Brown .... This Old Broken Heart		—	$10		Columbia 42807
12/25/65+	29	5		4 Big Chief Buffalo Nickel (Desert Blues) .... Day Sleeper		—	$10		Columbia 43425
				written and first recorded by Jimmie Rodgers in 1929					
1/7/67	28	11		5 Mabel .... Too Much Of Me (Walked Away With You)		—	$10		Columbia 43946

"Red River" Dave McEnery (See p.491 of Pop Singles)

You now have a CD of Red River Dave

DEBUT	PEAK	WKS	Gold	A-side (Chart Hit)	B-side	Pop	$	Pic	Label & Number

McDOWELL, Ronnie ★112★   '81

Born on 3/26/50 in Fountain Head, Tennessee; raised in Portland, Tennessee. Singer/songwriter/guitarist. Began his singing career in 1968 while in the U.S. Navy. Worked as a commercial sign painter in Tennessee during the early 1970s.

1) You're Gonna Ruin My Bad Reputation 2) Older Women 3) Wandering Eyes 4) You Made A Wanted Man Of Me 5) Watchin' Girls Go By

Debut	Peak	Wks		#	A-side	B-side	Pop	$	Label & Number
9/10/77	13	9	●	1	The King Is Gone	Walking Through Georgia In The Rain	13	$7	Scorpion 135
					tribute to Elvis Presley				
12/24/77+	5	17		2	I Love You, I Love You, I Love You	Fallin'	81	$7	Scorpion 149
4/29/78	15	12		3	Here Comes The Reason I Live	Travelin' Wanderin' Man	—	$7	Scorpion 159
7/29/78	59	5		4	I Just Wanted You To Know /			—	
7/29/78	68	5		5	Animal			$7	Scorpion 0553
					RONNIE McDOWELL with the Jordanaires (above 2)				
10/7/78	39	8		6	This Is A Holdup	The Bridge Washed Out	—	$7	Scorpion 0560
1/13/79	68	4		7	He's A Cowboy From Texas	When It Comes To You	—	$7	Scorpion 0569
4/28/79	18	14		8	World's Most Perfect Woman	Rockin' You Easy, Lovin' You Slow	—	$5	Epic 50696
8/25/79	26	11		9	Love Me Now /			—	
1/5/80	29	10		10	Never Seen A Mountain So High			$5	Epic 50753
3/29/80	37	8		11	Lovin' A Livin' Dream	When The Right Time Comes	—	$5	Epic 50857
7/5/80	80	4		12	How Far Do You Want To Go	You've Already Gone To My Heart	—	$5	Epic 50895
8/23/80	36	11		13	Gone	24 Hours Of Love	—	$5	Epic 50925
12/27/80+	2¹	17		14	Wandering Eyes	What Would Heaven Say	—	$5	Epic 50962
6/27/81	❶¹	16		15	Older Women	No Body's Perfect	—	$4	Epic 02129
11/14/81+	4	18		16	Watchin' Girls Go By	Good Time Lovin' Man	—	$4	Epic 02614
5/8/82	11	19		17	I Just Cut Myself	World's Greatest Lover	—	$4	Epic 02884
9/11/82	7	17		18	Step Back	I Never Felt So Much Love (In One Bed)	—	$4	Epic 03203
1/29/83	10	19		19	Personally	You Make My Day Pay Off (All Night Long)	—	$4	Epic 03526
					#19 Pop hit for Karla Bonoff in 1982				
6/11/83	❶¹	22		20	You're Gonna Ruin My Bad Reputation	I Should've Lied	—	$4	Epic 03946
10/15/83+	3	23		21	You Made A Wanted Man Of Me	This Could Take Forever	—	$4	Epic 04167
2/25/84	7	19		22	I Dream Of Women Like You	Your Baby's Not My Baby	—	$4	Epic 04367
6/23/84	8	21		23	I Got A Million Of 'Em	My Baby Don't Wear No Pajamas	—	$4	Epic 04499
2/23/85	5	23		24	In A New York Minute	A:4 / S:5 Something Special	—	$4	Epic 04816
7/20/85	9	20		25	Love Talks	S:7 / A:9 She Lays Me Down	—	$4	Epic 05404
5/3/86	6	18		26	All Tied Up	S:4 / A:7 Strings Of Silver Satin	—	$4	Curb/MCA 52816
9/6/86	37	14		27	When You Hurt, I Hurt	Whooplah	—	$4	Curb/MCA 52907
12/13/86+	30	14		28	Lovin' That Crazy Feelin'	A:30 I Don't Want To Set The World On Fire	—	$4	Curb/MCA 52994
6/20/87	55	8		29	Make Me Late For Work Today	Hold Me Tight	—	$4	Curb/MCA 53126
12/26/87+	8	23		30	It's Only Make Believe	S:6 Baby Me Baby	—	$4	Curb 10501
					Conway Twitty (guest vocal)				
7/16/88	27	14		31	Suspicion /			—	
					#3 Pop hit for Terry Stafford in 1964				
5/28/88	36	12		32	I'm Still Missing You			$4	Curb 10508
1/14/89	50	7		33	Never Too Old To Rock 'N' Roll	Rock And Roll Kiss	—	$4	Curb 10521
					RONNIE McDOWELL WITH JERRY LEE LEWIS				
4/1/89	39	12		34	Sea Of Heartbreak	Ain't Love Wonderful	—	$4	Curb 10525
7/8/89	69	6		35	Who'll Turn Out The Lights	Hey Hey Miss Lucy	—	$4	Curb 10544
12/2/89+	50	15		36	She's A Little Past Forty	Under These Conditions	—	$4	Curb 10558
12/8/90+	26	20		37	Unchained Melody	Sheet Music	—	$4	■ Curb 76850 (v)
					#4 Pop hit for The Righteous Brothers in 1965				

McENTIRE, Pake   '86

Born Dale Stanley McEntire in 6/23/53 in Chockie, Oklahoma. Singer/guitarist. Brother of **Reba McEntire**.

Debut	Peak	Wks		#	A-side	B-side	Pop	$	Label & Number
1/18/86	20	16		1	Every Night	S:14 / A:21 Too Old To Grow Up Now	—	$4	☐ RCA 14220
5/10/86	3	22		2	Savin' My Love For You	A:3 / S:3 I'm Having Fun	—	$4	RCA 14336
10/11/86	12	19		3	Bad Love	S:10 / A:11 Every Night	—	$4	☐ RCA 5004
					promo sleeve features a full-color foldout poster of Pake				
2/21/87	25	12		4	Heart Vs. Heart	A:25 (What I Got Is) Good For You	—	$4	RCA 5092
					Reba McEntire (harmony vocal)				
6/6/87	46	11		5	Too Old To Grow Up Now	Caroline's Still In Georgia	—	$4	RCA 5207
9/26/87	29	21		6	Good God, I Had It Good	Every Night	—	$4	■ RCA 5256
2/27/88	62	6		7	Life In The City	Another Place, Another Time	—	$4	RCA 5332

DEBUT	PEAK	WKS	Gold	A-side (Chart Hit)	B-side	Pop	$	Pic	Label & Number

McENTIRE, Reba ★14★   '87

Born on 3/28/54 on in Chockie, Oklahoma. Singer/songwriter. Sister of Pake McEntire. Competed in rodeos as a horseback barrel rider. Married to rodeo champion Charlie Battles from 1976-87. Married her manager, Narvel Blackstock, in 1989. Joined the *Grand Ole Opry* in 1985. Acted in the movies *Tremors* and *North* as well as several TV movies and her own TV sitcom. Seven members of her band plus her tour manager were killed in a plane crash on 3/16/91. CMA Awards: 1984, 1985, 1986 & 1987 Female Vocalist of the Year; 1986 Entertainer of the Year.

1) If You See Him/If You See Her   2) Is There Life Out There   3) For My Broken Heart   4) The Heart Won't Lie   5) You Lie

DEBUT	PEAK	WKS	#	A-side	B-side	Pop	$	Pic	Label & Number
5/8/76	88	5	1	I Don't Want To Be A One Night Stand	I'm Not Your Kind Of Girl	—	$10		Mercury 73788
2/12/77	86	4	2	(There's Nothing Like The Love) Between A Woman And A Man	I Was Glad To Give My Everything To You	—	$10		Mercury 73879
8/6/77	88	4	3	Glad I Waited Just For You	Invitation To The Blues	—	$10		Mercury 73929
5/20/78	20	12	4	Three Sheets In The Wind /					
		11	5	I'd Really Love To See You Tonight JACKY WARD & REBA McENTIRE (above 2) #2 Pop hit for England Dan & John Ford Coley in 1976		—	$8		Mercury 55026
9/2/78	28	12	6	Last Night, Ev'ry Night	Angel In Your Arms	—	$8		Mercury 55036
4/21/79	36	10	7	Runaway Heart	Make Me Feel Like A Woman Wants To Feel	—	$8		Mercury 55058
7/7/79	26	11	8	That Makes Two Of Us JACKY WARD/REBA McENTIRE	Good Friends	—	$8		Mercury 55054
9/22/79	19	12	9	Sweet Dreams	I'm A Woman	—	$7		Mercury 57003
1/5/80	40	8	10	(I Still Long To Hold You) Now And Then	It's Gotta Be Love	—	$7		Mercury 57014
6/14/80	8	15	11	(You Lift Me) Up To Heaven	Rain Fallin'	—	$7		Mercury 57025
10/18/80	18	14	12	I Can See Forever In Your Eyes	A Poor Man's Rosess (Or A Rich Man's Gold)	—	$7		Mercury 57034
3/14/81	13	16	13	I Don't Think Love Ought To Be That Way	Tears On My Pillow	—	$7		Mercury 57046
7/4/81	5	19	14	Today All Over Again	Look At The One (Who's Been Lookin' At You)	—	$7		Mercury 57054
11/21/81+	13	18	15	Only You (And You Alone) #5 Pop hit for the Platters in 1955	Love By Love	—	$7	■	Mercury 57062
6/5/82	3	19	16	I'm Not That Lonely Yet	Over, Under And Around	—	$6		Mercury 76157
10/2/82+	❶¹	22	17	Can't Even Get The Blues	Sweet Dreams	—	$6		Mercury 76180
2/5/83	❶¹	21	18	You're The First Time I've Thought About Leaving	Up To Heaven	—	$5		Mercury 810338
7/30/83	7	18	19	Why Do We Want (What We Know We Can't Have)	I Can See Forever In Your Eyes	—	$5		Mercury 812632
12/3/83+	12	22	20	There Ain't No Future In This	Reasons	—	$5		Mercury 814629
3/17/84	5	19	21	Just A Little Love	Your Heart's Not In It (What's In It For Me)	—	$4	■	MCA 52349
6/23/84	15	20	22	He Broke Your Mem'ry Last Night	If Only	—	$4		MCA 52404
10/13/84+	❶¹	23	23	How Blue	S:❶¹ / A:❶¹ That's What He Said	—	$4		MCA 52468
2/16/85	❶¹	22	24	Somebody Should Leave	S:❶¹ / A:❶¹ Don't You Believe Him	—	$4	■	MCA 52527
6/15/85	6	19	25	Have I Got A Deal For You	S:5 / A:7 Whose Heartache Is This Anyway	—	$4	■	MCA 52604
10/5/85	5	24	26	Only In My Mind	S:5 / A:5 She's The One Loving You Now	—	$4		MCA 52691
2/22/86	❶¹	23	27	Whoever's In New England	S:❶¹ / A:❶¹ Can't Stop Now	—	$4		MCA 52767
6/28/86	❶¹	19	28	Little Rock	A:❶¹ / S:2 If You Only Knew	—	$4		MCA 52848
10/11/86+	❶¹	22	29	What Am I Gonna Do About You	A:❶² / S:❶¹ I Heard Her Crying	—	$4		MCA 52922
2/7/87	4	17	30	Let The Music Lift You Up	A:4 / S:8 Lookin' For A New Love Story	—	$4		MCA 52990
5/23/87	❶¹	21	31	One Promise Too Late	S:❶¹ Why Not Tonight	—	$4		MCA 53092
9/19/87	❶¹	22	32	The Last One To Know	S:❶¹ I Don't Want To Be Alone	—	$4		MCA 53159
1/23/88	❶¹	20	33	Love Will Find Its Way To You	S:4 Someone Else	—	$4		MCA 53244
5/14/88	5	16	34	Sunday Kind Of Love #15 Pop hit for Jo Stafford in 1947	S:3 So, So, So Long	—	$4		MCA 53315
9/10/88	❶¹	22	35	I Know How He Feels	S:3 So, So, So Long	—	$4		MCA 53402
12/24/88+	❶¹	21	36	New Fool At An Old Game	You're The One I Dream About	—	$4		MCA 53473
5/13/89	❶¹	19	37	Cathy's Clown #1 Pop hit for The Everly Brothers in 1960	Walk On	—	$4		MCA 53638
9/2/89	4	26	38	'Til Love Comes Again	You Must Really Love Me	—	$4		MCA 53694
12/23/89+	7	26	39	Little Girl	Am I The Only One Who Cares	—	$4		MCA 53763
4/14/90	2²	20	40	Walk On	It Always Rains On Saturday	—	$4		MCA 79009
8/25/90	❶¹	20	41	You Lie	That's All She Wrote	—	$4		MCA 79071
12/1/90+	3	20	42	Rumor Has It	You Remember Me	—	$4		MCA 53970
3/2/91	8	20	43	Fancy	This Picture	—	$4		MCA 54042
5/25/91	2¹	20	44	Fallin' Out Of Love	Now You Tell Me	—	$4		MCA 54108
10/12/91	❶²	20	45	For My Broken Heart	Bobby	—	$4		MCA 54223
1/25/92	❶²	20	46	Is There Life Out There	Buying Her Roses	—	$4		MCA 54319
4/25/92	12	20	47	The Night The Lights Went Out In Georgia	All Dressed Up	—	$4		MCA 54386
8/15/92	3	20	48	The Greatest Man I Never Knew	If I Had Only Known	—	$4		MCA 54441
11/21/92+	5	20	49	Take It Back	Baby's Gone Blues	—	$4		MCA 54544
2/20/93	❶²	20	50	The Heart Won't Lie REBA McENTIRE AND VINCE GILL	Will He Ever Go Away	—	$4		MCA 54599
5/15/93	5	20	51	It's Your Call	For Herself	110	$4	■	MCA 54496 (v)
8/28/93	❶¹	20	52	Does He Love You Linda Davis (guest vocal)	Straight From You	—	$4		MCA 54719
12/18/93+	7	20	53	They Asked About You	For Herself	—	$4		MCA 54769
2/26/94	72	6	54	If I Had Only Known from the movie 8 Seconds starring Luke Perry (soundtrack on MCA 10927)					album cut
4/9/94	5	20	55	Why Haven't I Heard From You	If I Had Only Known	50^S	$4	■	MCA 54823 (v)

DEBUT	PEAK	WKS	Gold	A-side (Chart Hit)	B-side	Pop	$	Pic	Label & Number
				McENTIRE, Reba — Cont'd					
7/30/94	15	20		56 She Thinks His Name Was John	I Wish That I Could Tell You	65^S	$4	■	MCA 54899 (v)
11/5/94+	2¹	20		57 Till You Love Me	I Wouldn't Wanna Be You	78	$4		MCA 54888 (v)
2/18/95	❶¹	20		58 The Heart Is A Lonely Hunter	Read My Mind	—	$4		MCA 54987
5/27/95	2¹	20		59 And Still	I Won't Stand In Line	—	$4		MCA 55047
9/16/95	20	12		60 On My Own	Read My Mind	—	$4	■	MCA 55100 (v)
				Linda Davis, Martina McBride and Trisha Yearwood (backing vocals); #1 Pop hit for Patti LaBelle & Michael McDonald in 1986					
11/11/95+	9	20		61 Ring On Her Finger, Time On Her Hands	You Keep Me Hangin' On	—			MCA 55161
3/30/96	19	20		62 Starting Over Again	I Won't Mention It Again	—	$4		MCA 55183
10/5/96	2³	20		63 The Fear Of Being Alone	Never Had A Reason To	—	$4		MCA 55249
12/28/96+	❶¹	20		64 How Was I To Know	Just Looking For Him	—	$4		MCA 55290
12/28/96	63	2		65 The Christmas Song (Chestnuts Roasting On An Open Fire)	[X]	—			album cut
				#3 Pop hit for Nat "King" Cole in 1946; from the album Merry Christmas To You on MCA 42031					
4/12/97	2¹	20		66 I'd Rather Ride Around With You	State Of Grace	—	$4		MCA 72006
9/6/97	15	20		67 What If It's You	Close To Crazy	—	$4		MCA 72001
12/20/97+	23	15		68 What If	S:3 (same version)	50	$4	■	MCA 72026 (v)
				REBA:					
5/2/98	❶²	20		69 If You See Him/If You See Her	(same version)	—	$4		MCA Nashville 72051
				REBA/BROOKS & DUNN					
7/25/98	4	20		70 Forever Love	All This Time	—	$4		MCA Nashville 72062
11/14/98+	6	20		71 Wrong Night	Up And Flying	52	$4		MCA Nashville 72075
12/26/98	68	2		72 I'll Be Home For Christmas	[X]	—			album cut
12/26/98	73	1		73 Away In A Manger	[X]	—			album cut
				above 2 from the album Merry Christmas To You on MCA 42031					
3/20/99	7	20		74 One Honest Heart	I'll Give You Something To Miss	54	$4		MCA Nashville 72094
9/18/99+	3	26		75 What Do You Say	Nobody Dies From A Broken Heart	31	$4		MCA Nashville 72131
12/4/99	58	5		76 Secret Of Giving	[X]	—			album cut
				from the album Secret Of Giving on MCA 170092					
12/4/99	70	1		77 'Til I Said It To You	—				album cut
12/4/99	75	1		78 I'm Not Your Girl	—				album cut
				above 2 from the album So Good Together on MCA 170119					
12/18/99	50	3		79 I Saw Mama Kissing Santa Claus	[X]	—			album cut
				from the album Secret Of Giving on MCA 170092					
2/12/00	4	24		80 I'll Be	When You're Not Trying To	51	$4		MCA Nashville 172143
9/9/00	20	21		81 We're So Good Together	Nobody Dies From A Broken Heart	109	$4		MCA Nashville 172181
7/28/01	3	21		82 I'm A Survivor	'Til I Said It To You	49	$4		MCA Nashville 172212
				McEUEN, John '85					
				Born on 12/19/45 in Oakland. Singer/songwriter/banjo player. Founding member of the **Nitty Gritty Dirt Band**.					
4/6/85	81	4		Blue Days Black Nights	John Hardy	—	$4		Warner 29047
				McGILL, Tony '87					
				Born in Pearl, Mississippi.					
1/17/87	76	4		1 Like An Oklahoma Morning	—		$6		Killer 1004
6/27/87	82	3		2 Taming My Mind	—		$6		Killer 1006
1/9/88	78	4		3 For Your Love	—		$6		Killer 1008
				#13 Pop hit for Ed Townsend in 1958					
				McGOVERN, Maureen '79					
				Born on 7/27/49 in Youngstown, Ohio. Singer/actress. Charted six pop hits from 1973-79. Acted in the movies The Towering Inferno and Airplane. Starred on Broadway's Pirates Of Penzance.					
3/3/79	93	3		Can You Read My Mind	You Love Me Too Late	52	$5		Warner/Curb 8750
				love theme from the movie Superman starring Christopher Reeves					
				McGRAW, Tim ★63★ '99					
				Born Samuel Timothy McGraw on 5/1/67 in Delhi, Louisiana; raised in Start, Louisiana. Singer/songwriter/guitarist. Son of former Major League baseball pitcher Tug McGraw. Married **Faith Hill** on 10/6/96. CMA Awards: 1999 & 2000 Male Vocalist of the Year; 2001 Entertainer of the Year. Also see **Hope**.					
				1)Just To See You Smile 2)It's Your Love 3)Something Like That 4)My Next Thirty Years 5)Please Remember Me					
10/10/92	47	15		1 Welcome To The Club				■	album cut
				later issued on cassette as the B-side of #5 below					
4/10/93	60	7		2 Memory Lane	—				album cut
7/24/93	71	2		3 Two Steppin' Mind	—				album cut
				above 3 from the album Tim McGraw on Curb 77603					
1/22/94	8	20	●	4 Indian Outlaw	(dance mix)	15	$5		Curb 76920 (v)
				includes a verse from the 1971 #1 Pop hit "Indian Reservation" by the Raiders					
4/2/94	❶²	20	●	5 Don't Take The Girl	S:16 Welcome To The Club	17	$5		Curb 76925 (v)
				"45" issued for above 2 on Curb 76923					
7/16/94	2³	20		6 Down On The Farm	—				album cut
10/29/94+	❶²	20		7 Not A Moment Too Soon /	S:11				
2/25/95	5	20		8 Refried Dreams		69^S	$5	■	Curb 76931 (v)
				#4-8 from the album Not A Moment Too Soon on Curb 77659					
8/12/95	❶⁵	20		9 I Like It, I Love It	S:❶¹⁹ (dance mix)	25	$5	■	Curb 76961 (v)
				"45" title: "I Like It, I Love It, I Want Some More Of It"					
10/7/95	2²	20		10 Can't Be Really Gone	S:4 That's Just Me	87	$5	■	Curb 76971 (v)

DEBUT	PEAK	WKS	Gold	A-side (Chart Hit)	B-side	Pop	$	Pic	Label & Number
				McGRAW, Tim — Cont'd					
11/4/95+	5	21		11 All I Want Is A Life	—				album cut
6/22/96	❶²	20		12 She Never Lets It Go To Her Heart	—			■	album cut (v)
				later issued on cassette and "45" as the B-side of #14 below					
10/12/96+	4	20		13 Maybe We Should Just Sleep On It	—				album cut
				#9-13 from the album *All I Want* on Curb 77800					
5/10/97	❶⁶	20	▲	14 It's Your Love ... S:❶¹² *She Never Lets It Go To Her Heart* (McGraw)		7	$4	■	Curb 73019 (v)
				TIM McGRAW with Faith Hill					
7/5/97	❶²	26		15 Everywhere	—				album cut
8/9/97+	❶⁶	42		16 Just To See You Smile	—			■	album cut (v)
				later issued on cassette and "45" as the B-side of #18 below					
3/7/98	75	2		17 You Turn Me On	—				album cut
3/14/98	2¹	20		18 One Of These Days ... S:9 *Just To See You Smile*		74	$4	■	Curb 73056 (v)
5/30/98	3	20		19 Just To Hear You Say That You Love Me	—				album cut
				FAITH HILL (With Tim McGraw)					
				from Hill's album *Faith* on Warner 46790					
7/11/98	❶⁴	32		20 Where The Green Grass Grows		79			album cut
11/7/98+	2¹	20		21 For A Little While		37		★	album cut (v)
				later issued on CD and "45" as the B-side of #22 below; #14-21 (except #19) from the album *Everywhere* on Curb 77886					
3/20/99	❶⁵	24		22 Please Remember Me					album cut
5/15/99	❶⁵	39		23 Something Like That ... S:❶¹³ *For A Little While*		10	$4	★	Curb 73080 (v)
5/15/99+	❶²	37		24 My Best Friend		28			album cut
5/15/99	66	1		25 The Trouble With Never	—				album cut
				also see #29 below					
5/15/99	71	2		26 Seventeen	—	29			album cut
				also see #32 below					
5/22/99	74	1		27 Senorita Margarita	—				album cut
11/20/99+	6	45		28 Let's Make Love ... *There Will Come A Day*		54	$4		Warner 16792
				FAITH HILL with Tim McGraw					
3/4/00	72	4		29 The Trouble With Never	[R] —				album cut
4/8/00	❶⁵	46		30 My Next Thirty Years		27			album cut
4/15/00	7	20		31 Some Things Never Change		58			album cut
7/15/00	64	13		32 Seventeen	[R] —				album cut
				#22-32 (except #28) from the album *A Place In The Sun* on Curb 77942					
11/4/00+	32	21		33 Things Change	—				album cut
3/24/01	❶¹	20		34 Grown Men Don't Cry		25			album cut
5/12/01	52	15		35 Telluride	—				album cut
7/28/01	❶²	22		36 Angry All The Time		36			album cut
9/15/01+	❶¹	33		37 Bring On The Rain		36			album cut
				JO DEE MESSINA with Tim McGraw					
				from Messina's album *Burn* on Curb 77977					
12/1/01+	❶¹	23		38 The Cowboy In Me		33			album cut
				#33-38 (except #37) from the album *Set This Circus Down* on Curb 78711					
				McGUFFEY LANE '83					
				Country-rock group from Columbus, Ohio: Bob McNelley (vocals), John Schwab (guitar), Terry Efaw (steel guitar), Stephen Douglass (keyboards), Stephen Reis (bass) and Dave Rangeler (drums). Group name taken from a street in Athens, Ohio. Douglass died in a car crash on 1/12/84 (age 33). McNelley died of a self-inflicted gunshot wound on 1/7/87 (age 36).					
11/20/82+	44	13		1 Making A Living's Been Killing Me ... *You Wouldn't Give Up On Me*	—		$4	■	Atco 99959
3/26/83	62	6		2 Doing It Right ... *Too Many Days*	—		$4		Atco 99908
5/12/84	44	12		3 Day By Day ... *Jamaica In My Mind*	—		$4		Atlantic Amer. 99778
9/1/84	63	8		4 The First Time ... *You've Got A Right*	—		$4		Atlantic Amer. 99717
				McGUINN, Mark '01					
				Born in 1969 in Greensboro, North Carolina. Singer/songwriter/guitarist.					
1/20/01	6	20		1 Mrs. Steven Rudy / ... S:❶⁴		44			
6/23/01	25	20		2 That's A Plan	—		$3	★	VFR 734758
12/8/01+	29	20		3 She Doesn't Dance	—				album cut
				from the album *Mark McGuinn* on VFR 734757					
				McGUINN, Roger — see **HILLMAN, Chris**					
				McGUIRE, Doug '80					
7/26/80	64	6		Stranger, I'm Married ... *Oh What A Moment*	—		$6		Multi-Media 7
				McKUHEN, Lanier '87					
				Born in Macon, Georgia.					
4/25/87	75	4		Searching (For Someone Like You) ... *Face To Face*	—		$5		Soundwaves 4785
				McLEAN, Don '81					
				Born on 10/2/45 in New Rochelle, New York. Singer/songwriter/guitarist. Charted 10 pop hits from 1971-81.					
1/31/81	6	14		1 Crying ... *Genesis (In The Beginning)*		5	$4		Millennium 11799
5/9/81	68	6		2 Since I Don't Have You ... *Your Cheating Heart*		23	$4		Millennium 11804
				#12 Pop hit for The Skyliners in 1959					
4/18/87	73	4		3 He's Got You ... *To Have And To Hold*	—		$4		EMI America 8375
				male version of "She's Got You" by Patsy Cline					
11/14/87	49	8		4 You Can't Blame The Train ... *Perfect Love*	—		$4		Capitol 44098
7/30/88	65	4		5 Love In The Heart ... *Every Day's A Miracle*	—		$4		Capitol 44186

DEBUT	PEAK	WKS	Gold	A-side (Chart Hit)........B-side	Pop	$	Pic	Label & Number
				McMILLAN, Jimmy '80				
				Born in Fort Worth, Texas.				
12/20/80	92	3		1 Footsteps............*I Can't Look Into Your Eyes*	—	$6		Blum 001
				written by **Sheb Wooley**				
3/14/81	96	2		2 Her Empty Pillow (Lying Next To Mine)............*It Feels So Good*	—	$6		Blum 767
				McMILLAN, Terry '82				
				Born on 10/12/53 in Lexington, North Carolina. Nashville studio harmonica player.				
12/11/82	85	4		1 Love Is A Full Time Thing............*You're Bringing Out The Fool In Me*	—	$4		RCA 13360
				McPHERSON, Wyley '82				
				Real name: Paul Richey. Brother George Richey married **Tammy Wynette**.				
8/7/82	89	2		1 Jedediah Jones............*Longneck Lonestar*	—	$6	■	i.e. 007
10/9/82	81	3		2 The Devil Inside............*Love Is What You Make It*	—	$6		i.e. 009
				McQUAIG, Scott '89				
				Born on 1/27/60 in Meridian, Mississippi.				
8/12/89	56	8		1 Honky Tonk Amnesia............*My Friend The Bottle*	—	$4		Universal 66001
11/4/89	54	7		2 Johnny And The Dreamers............*High Friends In The Places (All Over Town)*	—	$4		Universal 66028
				McVICKER, Dana '87				
				Born in Baltimore; raised in Phillipe, West Virginia. Married Michael Thomas, **Reba McEntire**'s guitarist, who died in a plane crash on 3/16/91 (age 34).				
3/14/87	64	6		1 I'd Rather Be Crazy............*Love Spent The Night*	—	$4		EMI America 8371
6/27/87	64	5		2 Call Me A Fool............*Love Spent The Night*	—	$4		EMI America 43017
5/28/88	65	5		3 Rock-A-Bye Heart............*It's All So New To Me*	—	$4		Capitol 44155
10/22/88	88	2		4 I'm Loving The Wrong Man Again............*I'm Lonely For Only You*	—	$4		Capitol 44223
				MEADE, Donna '88				
				Born in 1953 in Chase City, Virginia. Married **Jimmy Dean** on 10/27/91.				
1/9/88	63	8		1 Be Serious............*I'm Out Of The Blue*	—	$4		Mercury 888993
5/7/88	50	9		2 Love's Last Stand............*I'm Out Of The Blue*	—	$4		Mercury 870283
7/30/88	69	4		3 Congratulations............*Slow Fire*	—	$4		Mercury 870527
10/29/88	78	3		4 Leavin' On Your Mind............*From A Distance*	—	$4		Mercury 872010
6/3/89	57	7		5 When He Leaves You............	—	$4		Mercury 874280
10/7/89	61	4		6 Cry Baby............*The Chokin' Kind*	—	$4		Mercury 874806
				MEDLEY, Bill '84				
				Born on 9/19/40 in Santa Ana, California. Baritone of The Righteous Brothers duo.				
1/6/79	91	3		1 Statue Of A Fool............*Wasn't That You Last Night*	—	$5		United Artists 1270
12/10/83+	28	18		2 Till Your Memory's Gone............*I've Got Dreams To Remember*	—	$4		RCA 13692
4/14/84	17	18		3 I Still Do............*I've Got Dreams To Remember*	—	$4		RCA 13753
8/4/84	26	14		4 I've Always Got The Heart To Sing The Blues............*Turn It Loose*	—	$4		RCA 13851
3/2/85	47	9		5 Is There Anything I Can Do............*Old Friend*	—	$4		RCA 14021
5/11/85	55	7		6 Women In Love............*Stand Up*	—	$4		RCA 14081
				MELLENCAMP, John Cougar '89				
				Born on 10/7/51 in Seymour, Indiana. Rock singer/songwriter/producer. Director/star of the movie *Falling from Grace*; leader of the **Buzzin' Cousins** who appeared in the movie. Married model Elaine Irwin on 9/5/92. Charted 28 pop hits from 1979-97.				
8/12/89	82	5		Jackie Brown............*(acoustic version)*	48	$4	■	Mercury 874644
				MELLONS, Ken '94				
				Born on 6/10/65 in Kingsport, Tennessee; raised in Nashville. Singer/songwriter/guitarist.				
4/2/94	55	9		1 Lookin' In The Same Direction............*Seven Lonely Days (Make One Weak)*	—	$4	■	Epic 77390 (v)
7/30/94	8	20		2 Jukebox Junkie............*The Pleasure's All Mine*	—	$4	■	Epic 77579 (v)
12/17/94+	42	14		3 I Can Bring Her Back............*Honky Tonk Teachers*	—	$4		Epic 77764
3/25/95	40	12		4 Workin' For The Weekend............*Keepin' It Country*	—	$4	■	Epic 77861 (v)
9/30/95	39	20		5 Rub-A-Dubbin'............*Jukebox Junkie*	—	$4	■	Epic 78066 (v)
4/27/96	55	8		6 Stranger In Your Eyes............*Memory Remover*	—	$4		Epic 78240
				MELTON, Terri — *see* **MUNDY, Jim**				
				MEMPHIS '84				
				Group from Memphis led by Woody Wright (later a member of **Matthews, Wright & King**).				
8/25/84	85	4		We've Got to Start Meeting Like This............*Gone But Not Forgotten*	—	$6		MPI 1691
				MENSY, Tim '92				
				Born Timothy Ray Menzies on 8/25/59 in Mechanicsville, Virginia. Singer/songwriter/guitarist. Member of **Bandana**.				
4/15/89	67	5		1 Hometown Advantage............*I've Got To Hand It To You*	—	$4		Columbia 68676
8/19/89	60	7		2 Stone By Stone............*I've Got To Hand It To You*	—	$4		Columbia 69007
1/13/90	82	1		3 You Still Love Me In My Dreams............*Stone By Stone*	—	$4		Columbia 73204
7/11/92	53	9		4 This Ol' Heart............*The Grandpa That I Know*	—	$4		Giant 18864
10/31/92	52	14		5 That's Good............*The Grandpa That I Know*	—	$4		Giant 18742
2/27/93	74	2		6 She Dreams............	—			album cut
				from the album This Ol' Heart *on Giant 24463*				
				MEREDITH, Buddy '62				
				Born William Meredith on 4/13/26 in Beaver Falls, Pennsylvania.				
5/12/62	27	2		I May Fall Again............*Haunted House*	—	$20		Nashville 5042
				MERRILL AND JESSICA '87				
				Merrill was born Merrill Osmond on 4/30/53 in Ogden, Utah. Member of the **Osmond Brothers**. Jessica Boucher is married to record producer Paul Worley.				
5/9/87	62	6		You're Here To Remember (I'm Here To Forget)............*The Price You Pay*	—	$3		EMI America 8388

DEBUT	PEAK	WKS	Gold	A-side (Chart Hit)	B-side	Pop	$	Pic	Label & Number
	★219★			**MESSINA, Jo Dee** '98 Born on 8/25/70 in Holliston, Massachusetts. Female singer. CMA Award: 1999 Horizon Award. 1) *That's The Way* 2) *Stand Beside Me* 3) *I'm Alright*					
1/27/96	2¹	20		1 Heads Carolina, Tails California	S:3 *Walk To The Light*	111	$4	■	Curb 76982 (v)
7/6/96	7	20		2 You're Not In Kansas Anymore	—				album cut
11/16/96	53	13		3 Do You Wanna Make Something Of It	—				album cut
5/3/97	64	5		4 He'd Never Seen Julie Cry	—				album cut
				all of above from the album *Jo Dee Messina* on Curb 77820					
1/17/98	❶²	30		5 Bye-Bye		43		■	album cut (v)
				later issued as the B-side of #6 below					
5/23/98	❶³	30		6 I'm Alright	S:2 *Bye-Bye*	43	$4	■	Curb 73034 (v)
10/10/98+	❶³	32		7 Stand Beside Me		34			album cut
5/1/99	2⁷	34		8 Lesson In Leavin'		28			album cut
10/23/99+	8	27		9 Because You Love Me		53			album cut
3/18/00	75	1		10 No Time For Tears	—				album cut
				above 6 from the album *I'm Alright* on Curb 77904					
5/20/00	❶⁴	27		11 That's The Way	S:2 *Even God Must Get The Blues*	25	$4	★	Curb 73106
10/14/00+	2¹	26		12 Burn		42			album cut
4/14/01	5	23		13 Downtime		46			album cut
9/15/01+	❶¹	33		14 Bring On The Rain		36			album cut
				JO DEE MESSINA with Tim McGraw above 4 from the album *Burn* on Curb 77977					
				MESSNER, Bud '50 Born Norman Messner on 10/9/17 in Luray, Virginia. Died on 5/5/2001 (age 83). His Sky Line Boys included Buddy Allen, Jack Throckmorton, Jimmy Throckmorton and Ray Ingram.					
6/3/50	7	6		Slippin' Around With Jole Blon	J:7 / S:9 *I Died All Over You*	—	$30		Abbey 15004
				BUD MESSNER & His Sky Line Boys Bill Franklin (vocal); same melody as the 1949 hit "Slippin' Around"					
				MEYERS, Augie '88 [Myers?] Born on 5/31/40 in San Antonio, Texas. Singer/keyboardist/accordionist. Co-founded the San Francisco "Tex-Mex" rock group, the Sir Douglas Quintet, in the mid-1960's. Joined the Texas Tornados in 1990.					
2/20/88	86	3		Kep Pa So	*To Nothing At All*	—	$4		Atlantic Amer. 99382
				MEYERS, Michael '82 [Gene?]					
1/16/82	94	2		I'm Just The Leavin' Kind	—		$7		MBP 1980
				MICHAELS, Jill — see **SCHNEIDER, John**					
				MIDDLEMAN, Georgia '00 Born in Houston. Singer/songwriter.					
7/15/00	53	10		1 No Place Like Home	*Michelangelo*	—	$4	★	Giant 16852 (v)
11/18/00	60	3		2 Kick Down The Door	—				album cut
				from the album *Endless Possibilities* on Giant 24718					
				MIDDLETON, Eddie '77 Born in Albany, Georgia.					
6/11/77	87	6		1 Midnight Train To Georgia	*I've Been Hurt*	—	$5		Epic 50388
				#1 Pop hit for Gladys Knight & The Pips in 1973					
9/10/77	38	10		2 Endlessly	*After The Lovin'*	—	$5		Epic 50431
				#12 Pop hit for Brook Benton in 1959					
12/10/77+	44	10		3 What Kind Of Fool (Do You Think I Am)	*Don't Say Let's Wait*	—	$5		Epic 50481
				#9 Pop hit for The Tams in 1964					
				MILES, Dick '68					
3/16/68	17	10		The Last Goodbye	*Candle-Lighted World* [S]	114	$8		Capitol 2113
				MILLER, Carl '83 [Darrell? Darnell?] Born in Broadway, Virginia.					
6/18/83	84	3		Life Of The Party	*Memories*	—	$7		Country Bach 0004
				MILLER, Dean '97 Born on 10/15/65 in Santa Fe, New Mexico. Singer/songwriter/guitarist. Son of **Roger Miller**.					
7/26/97	54	7		1 Nowhere, USA	*If I Was Your Man*	—	$4		Capitol 19648
11/8/97	67	1		2 My Heart's Broke Down (But My Mind's Made Up)	*The Running Side Of Me*	—	$4	■	Capitol 58682
2/21/98	57	6		3 Wake Up And Smell The Whiskey	*Broke Down In Birmingham*	—	$4		Capitol 19896
				MILLER, Ellen Lee '89					
2/11/89	92	2		You Only Love Me When I'm Leavin'	—		$6		Golden Trumpet 103
				MILLER, Frankie '59 Born on 12/17/30 in Victoria, Texas. Singer/songwriter/guitarist.					
4/13/59	5	19		1 Black Land Farmer	*True Blue*	—	$15		Starday 424
				also see #4 below					
10/5/59	7	21		2 Family Man	*Poppin' Johnny*	—	$15		Starday 457
5/23/60	15	14		3 Baby Rocked Her Dolly	*Rain Rain*	—	$15		Starday 496
7/17/61	16	5		4 Black Land Farmer	*True Blue* [R]	82	$15		Starday 424
				same version as #1 above					
2/15/64	34	6		5 A Little South Of Memphis	*Too Hot To Handle*	—	$15		Starday 655

DEBUT	PEAK	WKS	Gold	A-side (Chart Hit)	B-side	Pop	$	Pic	Label & Number
	★215★			**MILLER, Jody**		'72			
				Born Myrna Joy Brooks on 11/29/41 in Phoenix; raised in Blanchard, Oklahoma. Singer/songwriter/guitarist.					
				1)There's A Party Goin' On 2)He's So Fine 3)Baby I'm Yours 4)Queen Of The House					
				5)Darling, You Can Always Come Back Home					
5/29/65	5	11		1 Queen Of The House … The Greatest Actor		12	$10		Capitol 5402
				answer to "King Of The Road" by Roger Miller					
11/9/68	73	2		2 Long Black Limousine … Back In The Race		—	$10		Capitol 2290
8/15/70	21	13		3 Look At Mine … Safe In These Lovin' Arms Of Mine		—	$8		Epic 10641
1/2/71	19	13		4 If You Think I Love You Now (I've Just Started) … Looking Out My Back Door		—	$8		Epic 10692
6/12/71	5	15		5 He's So Fine … You Number Two		53	$8		Epic 10734
10/9/71	5	14		6 Baby, I'm Yours … Good Lovin' (Makes It Right)		91	$8		Epic 10785
3/25/72	15	13		7 Be My Baby … Your Love's Been A Long Time Coming		—	$8		Epic 10835
				#2 Pop hit for The Ronettes in 1963					
5/27/72	13	11		8 Let's All Go Down To The River … In The Garden		—	$8		Eplc 10863
				JODY MILLER AND JOHNNY PAYCHECK					
6/17/72	4	14		9 There's A Party Goin' On … Love's The Answer		115	$8		Epic 10878
11/4/72	18	11		10 To Know Him Is To Love Him … Make Me Your Kind Of Woman		—	$8		Epic 10916
				#1 Pop hit for The Teddy Bears in 1958					
3/17/73	9	12		11 Good News … Soul Song		—	$8		Epic 10960
7/14/73	5	13		12 Darling, You Can Always Come Back Home … We'll Sing Our Song Together		—	$6		Epic 11016
11/24/73+	29	13		13 The House Of The Rising Sun … In The Name Of Love		—	$6		Epic 11056
				#1 Pop hit for The Animals in 1964					
3/16/74	55	9		14 Reflections … One More Chance		—	$6		Epic 11094
6/22/74	46	11		15 Natural Woman … Jimmy's Roses		—	$6		Epic 11134
				#8 Pop hit for Aretha Franklin in 1967					
11/16/74+	41	10		16 Country Girl … Safe In These Lovin' Arms Of Mine		—	$6		Epic 50042
3/15/75	78	9		17 The Best In Me … I'm Alright 'Til I See You (Then I Fall Apart)		—	$6		Epic 50079
7/12/75	67	9		18 Don't Take It Away … Long, Long Time		—	$6		Epic 50117
11/8/75	69	8		19 Will You Love Me Tomorrow? … Love, You Never Had It So Good		—	$6		Epic 50158
				#1 Pop hit for The Shirelles in 1961					
3/27/76	48	9		20 Ashes Of Love … She Calls Me "Baby"		—	$6		Epic 50203
12/4/76+	25	12		21 When The New Wears Off Our Love … Silver And Gold		—	$6		Epic 50304
4/9/77	71	7		22 Spread A Little Love Around … Montana Cowboy		—	$6		Epic 50360
9/17/77	76	5		23 Another Lonely Night … All Night Long		—	$6		Epic 50432
4/15/78	97	2		24 Soft Lights And Slow Sexy Music … Home		—	$6		Epic 50512
7/15/78	67	6		25 (I Wanna) Love My Life Away … I'm Gonna Write A Song		—	$6		Epic 50568
				#39 Pop hit for Gene Pitney in 1961					
10/7/78	65	4		26 Kiss Away … Hold Me, Thrill Me, Kiss Me		—	$6		Epic 50612
				#25 Pop hit for Ronnie Dove in 1965					
7/7/79	97	2		27 Lay A Little Lovin' On Me … Crazy On You		—	$6		Epic 50734
				#11 Pop hit for Robin McNamara in 1970					
				MILLER, Mary K.		'79			
				Born in 1957 in Houston.					
				1)Next Best Feeling 2)Handcuffed To A Heartache 3)I Can't Stop Loving You					
7/30/77	89	5		1 I Fall To Pieces … Just Can't Believe You're Gone		—	$5		Inergi 300
				MARY MILLER					
10/8/77	54	8		2 You Just Don't Know … Lovesick Blues		—	$5		Inergi 302
				written by Bobby Darin					
12/24/77+	33	10		3 The Longest Walk … Love Is		—	$5		Inergi 304
				#6 Pop hit for Jaye P. Morgan in 1955					
3/4/78	41	9		4 Right Or Wrong … Smile Me A Song		—	$5		Inergi 306
6/3/78	28	8		5 I Can't Stop Loving You … Let Me Go Lover		—	$5		Inergi 307
				#1 Pop hit for Ray Charles in 1962					
9/16/78	19	11		6 Handcuffed To A Heartache … Over And Over (I Fall In Love Again)		—	$5		Inergi 310
12/9/78+	45	9		7 Going, Going, Gone … Woman, Woman		—	$5		Inergi 311
3/10/79	17	14		8 Next Best Feeling … One Woman's Heaven		—	$5		Inergi 312
7/28/79	47	7		9 Guess Who Loves You … Georgia On My Mind		—	$4		RCA 11665
4/5/80	85	3		10 Say A Long Goodbye … You Asked Me To		—	$5		Inergi 315
	★368★			**MILLER, Ned**		'63			
				Born Henry Ned Miller on 4/12/25 in Raines, Utah. Singer/songwriter/guitarist.					
				1)From A Jack To A King 2)Do What You Do Do Well 3)Invisible Tears					
12/15/62+	2⁴	19		1 From A Jack To A King … Parade Of Broken Hearts		6	$15		Fabor 114
5/25/63	27	3		2 One Among The Many … The Man Behind The Gun		—	$12		Fabor 116
9/14/63	28	1		3 Another Fool Like Me … Magic Moon		—	$12		Fabor 121
4/25/64	13	22		4 Invisible Tears … Old Restless Ocean		131	$12		Fabor 128
1/16/65	7	20		5 Do What You Do Do Well … Dusty Guitar		52	$12		Fabor 137
8/14/65	28	8		6 Whistle Walkin' … Two Voices, Two Shadows, Two Faces		—	$10		Capitol 5431
6/18/66	39	8		7 Summer Roses … Right Behind These Lips		—	$10		Capitol 5661
10/15/66	44	9		8 Teardrop Lane … Lorraine		—	$10		Capitol 5742
5/13/67	53	6		9 Hobo … Echo Of The Pines		—	$10		Capitol 5868
2/17/68	61	5		10 Only A Fool … Endless		—	$10		Capitol 2074
4/25/70	39	9		11 The Lover's Song … Cold Grey Bars		—	$8		Republic 1411

DEBUT	PEAK	WKS	Gold	A-side (Chart Hit)	B-side	Pop	$	Pic	Label & Number

MILLER, Roger ★101★   '65
Born on 1/2/36 in Fort Worth, Texas; raised in Erick, Oklahoma. Died of cancer on 10/25/92 (age 56). Singer/songwriter/guitarist. Father of **Dean Miller**. With **Faron Young** as writer/drummer in 1962. Hosted own TV show in 1966. Wrote the Broadway musical *Big River*. Elected to the Country Music Hall of Fame in 1995.

1) Dang Me 2) King Of The Road 3) Engine Engine #9 4) Chug-A-Lug 5) England Swings

DEBUT	PEAK	WKS	Gold	#	A-side	B-side	Pop	$	Pic	Label & Number
10/31/60+	14	16		1	You Don't Want My Love	Footprints In The Snow	—	$15		RCA Victor 7776
6/5/61	6	18		2	When Two Worlds Collide	Every Which-A-Way	—	$15		RCA Victor 7878
6/1/63	26	1		3	Lock, Stock And Teardrops	I Know Who It Is	—	$15		RCA Victor 8175
6/6/64	❶⁶	25		4	Dang Me	Got 2 Again [N]	7	$10	■	Smash 1881
9/19/64	3	17		5	Chug-A-Lug	Reincarnation	9	$10		Smash 1926
12/12/64+	15	11		6	Do-Wacka-Do	Love Is Not For Me [N]	31	$10	■	Smash 1947
2/13/65	❶⁵	20	•	7	King Of The Road	Atta Boy Girl	4	$10		Smash 1965
5/22/65	2²	18		8	Engine Engine #9	The Last Word In Lonesome Is Me	7	$10		Smash 1983
7/24/65	10	12		9	One Dyin' And A Buryin'		34	$10		Smash 1994
10/2/65	7	13		10	Kansas City Star	Guess I'll Pick Up My Heart (And Go Home) [N]	31	$10		Smash 1998
11/20/65+	3	16		11	England Swings	Good Old Days	8	$10		Smash 2010
2/26/66	5	14		12	Husbands And Wives /		26			
2/26/66	13	10		13	I've Been A Long Time Leavin' (But I'll Be A Long Time Gone)		103	$8		Smash 2024
7/9/66	35	5		14	You Can't Roller Skate In A Buffalo Herd	Train Of Life [N]	40	$8		Smash 2043
9/24/66	39	9		15	My Uncle Used To Love Me But She Died	You're My Kingdom [N]	58	$8		Smash 2055
11/19/66	55	3		16	Heartbreak Hotel	Less And Less	84	$8		Smash 2066
4/1/67	7	17		17	Walkin' In The Sunshine	Home	37	$8		Smash 2081
10/28/67	27	11		18	The Ballad Of Waterhole #3 (Code Of The West)	Rainbow Valley	102	$8	■	Smash 2121
					from the movie *Waterhole #3* starring James Coburn					
3/9/68	6	13		19	Little Green Apples	Our Little Love	39	$8	■	Smash 2148
12/14/68+	15	12		20	Vance	Little Children Run And Play	80	$8		Smash 2197
7/5/69	12	16		21	Me And Bobby McGee	I'm Gonna Teach My Heart To Bend (Instead of Break)	122	$8		Smash 2230
					#1 Pop hit for Janis Joplin in 1971					
10/18/69	14	10		22	Where Have All The Average People Gone	Boeing Boeing 707	—	$8		Smash 2246
3/14/70	36	7		23	The Tom Green County Fair	I Know Who It Is	—	$8		Smash 2258
8/29/70	15	12		24	South /		—			
		12		25	Don't We All Have The Right		—	$7		Mercury 73102
4/17/71	11	14		26	Tomorrow Night In Baltimore	A Million Years Or So	—	$7		Mercury 73190
8/7/71	28	11		27	Loving Her Was Easier (Than Anything I'll Ever Do Again)	Qua La Linta	—	$7		Mercury 73230
3/25/72	34	11		28	We Found It In Each Other's Arms /		—			
3/25/72	63	11		29	Sunny Side Of My Life		—	$7		Mercury 73268
9/9/72	41	11		30	Rings For Sale	Conversation	—	$7		Mercury 73321
12/30/72+	42	8		31	Hoppy's Gone	The Day I Jumped From Uncle Harvey's Plane	—	$7		Mercury 73354
7/14/73	14	14		32	Open Up Your Heart	Qua La Linta	105	$6		Columbia 45873
11/17/73+	24	11		33	I Believe In The Sunshine	Shannon's Song	—	$6		Columbia 45948
3/9/74	86	3		34	Whistle Stop	The 4th Of July	—	$6		Columbia 46000
					from the animated movie *Robin Hood*					
12/7/74+	44	10		35	Our Love	The Yester Waltz	—	$6		Columbia 10052
4/12/75	57	10		36	I Love A Rodeo	Lovin' You Is Always On My Mind	—	$6		Columbia 10107
9/10/77	68	6		37	Baby Me Baby	Dark Side Of The Moon	—	$5		Windsong 11072
10/27/79	98	2		38	The Hat	Pleasing The Crowd	—	$5		20th Century 2421
10/10/81	36	10		39	Everyone Gets Crazy Now And Then	Aladambama	—	$4		Elektra 47192
6/5/82	19	16		40	Old Friends	When A House Is Not A Home	—	$4		Columbia 02681
					ROGER MILLER & WILLIE NELSON (with Ray Price)					
10/5/85	36	12		41	River In The Rain	Hand For The Hog	—	$4		MCA 52663
					from the Broadway musical *Big River* starring Daniel H. Jenkins					
8/2/86	81	8		42	Some Hearts Get All The Breaks	Arkansas	—	$4		MCA 52855

MILLINDER, Lucky, And His Orchestra   '44
Born Lucius Millinder on 8/8/1900 in Anniston, Alabama. Died on 9/28/66 (age 66). Black bandleader.

DEBUT	PEAK	WKS	#	A-side	B-side	$	Label & Number
1/15/44	4	5	1	Sweet Slumber	Don't Cry Baby	15	$20	Decca 18569
				Trevor Bacon (vocal)			
7/29/44	4	2	2	Hurry, Hurry	I Can't See For Lookin'	20	$20	Decca 18609
				Wynonie "Mr. Blues" Harris (vocal)			

MILLS, Frank   '79
Born in 1943 in Toronto. Pianist/composer/producer/arranger.

| 2/24/79 | 44 | 14 | • | Music Box Dancer | The Poet And I [I] | 3 | $4 | Polydor 14517 |

MILLS BROTHERS   '70
R&B family vocal trio from Piqua, Ohio: Herbert (born on 4/2/12; died on 4/12/89, age 77), Harry (born on 8/19/13; died on 6/28/82, age 68) and Donald (born on 4/29/15; died on 11/13/99, age 84) Mills.

| 3/21/70 | 64 | 3 | | It Ain't No Big Thing | Help Yourself To Some Tomorrow | — | $7 | Dot 17321 |

DEBUT	PEAK	WKS	Gold	A-side (Chart Hit)	B-side	Pop	$	Pic	Label & Number

MILSAP, Ronnie ★24★ '80
Born on 1/16/43 in Robbinsville, North Carolina. Singer/songwriter/pianist. Blind since birth. Formed the Apparitions while in high school. Joined J.J. Cale's band. Played session keyboards for **Elvis Presley** in 1969. Joined the *Grand Ole Opry* in 1976. CMA Awards: 1974, 1976 & 1977 Male Vocalist of the Year; 1977 Entertainer of the Year.

1)My Heart   2)Only One Love In My Life   3)It Was Almost Like A Song
4)Lost In The Fifties Tonight (In The Still Of The Night)   5)A Woman In Love

DEBUT	PEAK	WKS	Gold	#	A-side	B-side	Pop	$	Pic	Label & Number
6/30/73	10	14		1	I Hate You /		—			
		14		2	(All Together Now) Let's Fall Apart		—	$7		RCA Victor 0969
11/3/73+	11	18		3	That Girl Who Waits On Tables	You're Drivin' Me Out Of Your Mind	—	$7		RCA Victor 0097
3/30/74	❶¹	15		4	Pure Love	Love The Second Time Around	—	$6		RCA Victor 0237
7/20/74	❶²	14		5	Please Don't Tell Me How The Story Ends	Streets Of Gold	95	$6		RCA Victor 0313
11/30/74+	❶¹	13		6	(I'd Be) A Legend In My Time	The Biggest Lie	—	$6	■	RCA Victor 10112
3/15/75	6	14		7	Too Late To Worry, Too Blue To Cry	Country Cookin'	101	$6		RCA Victor 10228
7/19/75	❶²	16		8	Daydreams About Night Things	(After Sweet Memories) Play Born To Lose Again	—	$6		RCA Victor 10335
9/20/75	15	13		9	She Even Woke Me Up To Say Goodbye	Loving You's A Natural Thing	—	$6		Warner 8127
					recorded in 1970					
10/25/75+	4	16		10	Just In Case	Remember To Remind Me (I'm Leaving)	—	$6		RCA Victor 10420
12/27/75+	77	6		11	A Rose By Any Other Name	Please Don't Tell Me How The Story Ends	—	$6		Warner 8160
					#125 Pop hit in 1970 (on Chips 2987)					
3/20/76	❶¹	14		12	What Goes On When The Sun Goes Down	Love Takes A Long Time To Die	—	$6		RCA Victor 10593
6/19/76	79	5		13	Crying	Why	—	$6		Warner 8218
					recorded in 1970; #2 Pop hit for **Roy Orbison** in 1961					
7/10/76	❶²	14		14	(I'm A) Stand By My Woman Man	Lovers, Friends And Strangers	—	$6		RCA Victor 10724
11/27/76+	❶¹	15		15	Let My Love Be Your Pillow	Busy Makin' Plans	—	$5		RCA 10843
5/28/77	❶³	18		16	It Was Almost Like A Song	It Don't Hurt To Dream	16	$5		RCA 10976
11/19/77+	❶¹	16		17	What A Difference You've Made In My Life	Selfish	80	$5		RCA 11146
6/3/78	❶³	13		18	Only One Love In My Life	Back On My Mind Again	63	$5		RCA 11270
9/2/78	❶¹	12		19	Let's Take The Long Way Around The World	I'm Not Trying To Forget	—	$5		RCA 11369
12/16/78+	2³	15		20	Back On My Mind Again /					
		15		21	Santa Barbara		—	$5		RCA 11421
4/28/79	❶¹	15		22	Nobody Likes Sad Songs	Just Because It Feels Good	—	$5		RCA 11553
8/18/79	6	13		23	In No Time At All /					
		13		24	Get It Up		43	$5		RCA 11695
1/12/80	❶¹	15		25	Why Don't You Spend The Night	Heads I Go, Hearts I Stay	—	$4		RCA 11909
4/12/80	❶³	15		26	My Heart /					
		15		27	Silent Night (After The Fight)		—	$4		RCA 11952
6/21/80	❶¹	16		28	Cowboys And Clowns /		103			
					from the movie *Bronco Billy* starring **Clint Eastwood**					
		16		29	Misery Loves Company		—	$4	■	RCA 12006
10/11/80	❶¹	14		30	Smoky Mountain Rain	Crystal Fallin' Rain	24	$4		RCA 12084
3/21/81	❶¹	14		31	Am I Losing You	He'll Have To Go	—	$4		RCA 12194
7/4/81	❶²	15		32	(There's) No Gettin' Over Me	I Live My Whole Life At Night	5	$4		RCA 12264
10/31/81+	❶¹	16		33	I Wouldn't Have Missed It For The World	It Happens Every Time (I Think of You)	20	$4		RCA 12342
5/1/82	❶¹	17		34	Any Day Now	It's Just A Room	14	$4		RCA 13216
8/7/82	❶¹	18		35	He Got You	I Love New Orleans Music	59	$4		RCA 13286
11/20/82+	❶¹	19		36	Inside /					
		18		37	Carolina Dreams		—	$4		RCA 13362
4/2/83	5	18		38	Stranger In My House	Is It Over	23	$4		RCA 13470
7/23/83	❶¹	19		39	Don't You Know How Much I Love You	Feelings Change	58	$4		RCA 13564
11/12/83+	❶¹	19		40	Show Her	Watch Out For The Other Guy	103	$4		RCA 13658
5/19/84	❶¹	19		41	Still Losing You	I'll Take Care Of You	—	$4		RCA 13805
9/1/84	6	19		42	Prisoner Of The Highway	S:6 / A:7 She Loves My Car (Pop #84)	—	$4		RCA 13847
4/6/85	❶¹	20		43	She Keeps The Home Fires Burning	S:❶¹ / A:❶¹ Is It Over	—	$4		RCA 14034
7/13/85	❶²	23		44	Lost In The Fifties Tonight (In The Still Of The Night)	A:❶² / S:❶¹ I Might Have Said	—	$4	■	RCA 14135
					"In The Still Of The Night" was a #3 R&B hit for **The Five Satins** in 1956					
3/8/86	❶¹	20		45	Happy, Happy Birthday Baby	S:❶¹ / A:❶¹ I'll Take Care Of You	—	$4		RCA 14286
					#5 Pop hit for **The Tune Weavers** in 1957					
7/5/86	❶¹	20		46	In Love	A:❶² / S:❶¹ Old Fashioned Girl Like You	—	$4		RCA 14365
11/22/86+	❶¹	21		47	How Do I Turn You On	S:❶¹ / A:❶¹ Don't Take It Tonight	—	$4		RCA 5033
5/23/87	❶¹	19		48	Snap Your Fingers	S:❶¹ This Time Last Year	—	$4		RCA 5169
					#8 Pop hit for **Joe Henderson** in 1962					
6/27/87	❶¹	17		49	Make No Mistake, She's Mine	S:3 You're My Love	—	$4	□	RCA 5209
					RONNIE MILSAP & KENNY ROGERS					
					#51 Pop hit for **Barbra Streisand** & **Kim Carnes** in 1985					
10/24/87+	❶¹	20		50	Where Do The Nights Go	S:2 If You Don't Want Me To	—	$4		RCA 5259
3/5/88	2¹	21		51	Old Folks	S:5 Earthquake	—	$4	■	RCA 6896
					RONNIE MILSAP & MIKE REID					
7/23/88	4	18		52	Button Off My Shirt	S:4 One Night	—	$4		RCA 8389
					#91 Pop hit for **Paul Carrack** in 1988					
12/24/88+	❶¹	20		53	Don't You Ever Get Tired (Of Hurting Me)	I Never Expected To See You	—	$4		RCA 8746
4/29/89	4	21		54	Houston Solution	If You Don't Want Me To	—	$4		RCA 8868

DEBUT	PEAK	WKS	Gold	A-side (Chart Hit)...B-side	Pop	$	Pic	Label & Number
				MILSAP, Ronnie — Cont'd				
9/23/89	⓿²	26		55 A Woman In Love .... Starting Today	—	$4		RCA 9027
2/10/90	2²	26		56 Stranger Things Have Happened .... Southern Roots	—	$4		RCA 9120
3/9/91	3	20		57 Are You Lovin' Me Like I'm Lovin' You .... Back To The Grindstone	—	$4		RCA 2509
7/13/91	6	20		58 Since I Don't Have You .... I Ain't Gonna Cry No More	—	$4		RCA 2848
				#12 Pop hit for The Skyliners in 1959				
12/7/91+	4	20		59 Turn That Radio On .... Old Habits Are Hard To Break	—	$4		RCA 62104
3/28/92	11	20		60 All Is Fair In Love And War .... Back To The Grindstone	—	$4		RCA 62217
9/12/92	45	9		61 L.A. To The Moon .... When The Hurt Comes Down	—	$4		RCA 62332
7/10/93	30	15		62 True Believer .... These Foolish Things (Remind Me Of You)	—	$4		Liberty 17595
7/1/00	57	7		63 Time, Love & Money .... Livin' On Love	—	$4		Virgin 15191
				MINNIE PEARL '66				
				Born Sarah Ophelia Colley on 10/25/12 in Centerville, Tennessee. Died of a stroke on 3/4/96 (age 83). Comedienne/actress. Joined the *Grand Ole Opry* from 1940. Elected to the Country Music Hall of Fame in 1975. Trademark was her straw hat with its $1.98 price tag still attached.				
3/5/66	10	12		Giddyup Go - Answer .... Road Runner [S]	—	$10		Starday 754
				answer to "Giddyup Go" by **Red Sovine**				
				MINOR, Shane '99				
				Born on 5/3/68 in Modesto, California. Male singer.				
3/6/99	20	20		1 Slave To The Habit .... S:23 Tell Me Now	82	$4	★	Mercury 870818 (v)
7/24/99	24	20		2 Ordinary Love .... How Many Times	111	$4		Mercury 562291
2/5/00	44	11		3 I Think You're Beautiful .... A Girl Like That	—	$4		Mercury 172151
				MINTER, Pat '89				
12/9/89	84	2		Whiskey River You Win	—	$6		Killer 121
				MITCHELL, Charles '44				
				Steel guitarist for **Jimmie Davis**.				
4/29/44	4	1		If It's Wrong To Love You .... Mean Mama Blues		$20		Bluebird 33-0508
				CHARLES MITCHELL and his Orchestra				
				MITCHELL, Charlie '88				
11/12/88	81	4		I'm Goin' Nowhere	—	$5		Soundwaves 4810
				MITCHELL, Guy '67				
				Born Al Cernik on 2/27/27 in Detroit. Charted 26 pop hits from 1950-60. Acted in the movies *Those Redheads From Seattle* and *Red Garters*.				
11/4/67	51	8		1 Traveling Shoes .... Every Night Is A Lifetime		$8		Starday 819
2/24/68	61	5		2 Alabam .... Irene Good-By		$8		Starday 828
12/14/68	71	3		3 Frisco Line .... It's A New World Every Day		$8		Starday 846
				MITCHELL, Marty '78				
				Born in Birmingham, Alabama.				
6/15/74	64	7		1 Midnight Man .... I'd Be Your Fool Again		$5		Atlantic 4023
12/11/76	87	4		2 My Eyes Adored You .... Devil Woman		$5		Hitsville 6044
				#1 Pop hit for Frankie Valli in 1975				
2/18/78	34	10		3 You Are The Sunshine Of My Life .... Yester-Me, Yester-You, Yesterday		$5		MC/Curb 5005
				#1 Pop hit for Stevie Wonder in 1973				
				MITCHELL, Price '75				
				Male singer.				
1/18/75	65	10		1 I Can't Help Myself (Sugar Pie, Honey Bunch) .... Got You On My Mind		$7		GRT 016
				PRICE MITCHELL & JERRI KELLY				
				#1 Pop hit for the Four Tops in 1965				
4/19/75	29	11		2 Personality .... Daddy's Going Bye-Bye		$6		GRT 020
				#2 Pop hit for Lloyd Price in 1959				
2/7/76	83	5		3 Seems Like I Can't Live With You, But I Can't Live Without You .... (I Wanna Be) The Man Who Takes You Home		$6		GRT 037
5/29/76	75	5		4 Tra-La-La Suzy .... Sweet Molly Brown		$6		GRT 050
				#35 Pop hit for Dean & Jean in 1964				
9/4/76	75	4		5 You're The Reason I'm Living .... Take Me Back		$6		GRT 067
				#3 Pop hit for Bobby Darin in 1963				
1/5/80	45	9		6 Mr. & Mrs. Untrue .... Savin' It All For You		$5		Sunbird 101
				PRICE MITCHELL/RENE SLOANE				
				MITCHELL, Priscilla '65				
				Born on 9/18/41 in Marietta, Georgia. Married to **Jerry Reed** since 1959.				
				ROY DRUSKY & PRISCILLA MITCHELL:				
5/29/65	⓿²	23		1 Yes, Mr. Peters .... More Than We Deserve		$8		Mercury 72416
12/4/65	45	2		2 Slippin' Around .... Trouble On Our Line		$8		Mercury 72497
3/25/67	61	5		3 I'll Never Tell On You .... Bed Of Roses		$8		Mercury 72650
				PRISCILLA MITCHELL:				
6/17/67	53	4		4 He's Not For Real .... Take Me Home To Your Mama		$8		Mercury 72681
2/3/68	73	3		5 Your Old Handy Man .... Who's Cheating Who		$8		Mercury 72757
				written by **Dolly Parton**				
				MITCHUM, Robert '67				
				Born on 8/6/17 in Bridgeport, Connecticut. Died of cancer on 7/1/97 (age 79). Legendary actor.				
5/13/67	9	17		1 Little Old Wine Drinker Me .... Walker's Woods	96	$8		Monument 1006
10/21/67	55	7		2 You Deserve Each Other .... That Man Right There	—	$8		Monument 1025

DEBUT	PEAK	WKS	Gold	A-side (Chart Hit)	B-side	Pop	$	Pic	Label & Number
				MIZE, Billy '76					
				Born on 4/29/29 in Arkansas City, Kansas; raised in California. Singer/songwriter/steel guitarist.					
				1)It Hurts To Know The Feeling's Gone 2)Make It Rain 3)While I'm Thinkin' About It					
10/15/66	57	5		1 You Can't Stop Me ... The Bigger The Fool (The Harder The Fall)		—	$10		Columbia 43770
				BILLY MIZE with The Jordanaires					
9/28/68	58	7		2 Walking Through The Memories Of My Mind ... Wind (I'll Catch Up To You)		—	$10		Columbia 44621
4/26/69	40	9		3 Make It Rain ... You Done Me Wrong		—	$8		Imperial 66365
9/13/69	43	9		4 While I'm Thinkin' About It ... The Absence Of You		—	$8		Imperial 66403
6/20/70	71	2		5 If This Was The Last Song ... I Learned To Walk		—	$8		Imperial 66447
11/14/70	49	7		6 Beer Drinking, Honky Tonkin' Blues ... Someday When It Gets To Be Tomorrow		—	$6		United Artists 50717
9/2/72	66	5		7 Take It Easy ... Susan's Floor		—	$6		United Artists 50945
				#12 Pop hit for the **Eagles** in 1972					
7/28/73	99	2		8 California Is Just Mississippi ... Just The Other Side Of Nowhere		—	$6		United Artists 265
2/16/74	79	5		9 Thank You For The Feeling ... Detroit City		—	$6		United Artists 372
9/25/76	31	13		10 It Hurts To Know The Feeling's Gone Living Her Life In A Song		—	$5		Zodiac 1011
2/12/77	68	5		11 Livin' Her Life In A Song ... Linda's Love Stop		—	$5		Zodiac 1014
				MOEBAKKEN, Dick '78					
9/30/78	98	3		Heaven Is Being Good To Me ... The Lord's Prayer		—	$6		ASI 1016
				an impression of **Walter Brennan** to the tune of "Old Rivers"					
				MOFFATT, Hugh '78					
				Born on 11/10/48 in Fort Worth, Texas. Singer/songwriter/guitarist. Brother of **Katy Moffatt**.					
5/6/78	95	2		The Gambler ... That Light In Your Eyes		—	$5		Mercury 55024
				MOFFATT, Katy '84					
				Born in 1950 in Fort Worth, Texas. Singer/guitarist. Sister of **Hugh Moffatt**.					
1/17/76	83	5		1 I Can Almost See Houston From Here ... Take Me Back To Texas		—	$5		Columbia 10271
7/4/81	83	3		2 Take It As It Comes ... Hard Country		—	$4		Epic 02075
				MICHAEL MURPHEY with KATY MOFFATT					
11/5/83	66	6		3 Under Loved And Over Lonely ... Let's Make Something Of It		—	$5		Permian 82002
2/11/84	82	4		4 Reynosa ... Lonely But Only For You		—	$5		Permian 82004
5/5/84	66	6		5 This Ain't Tennessee And He Ain't You Midnight Harbour		—	$5		Permian 82005
				MOLLY & THE HEYMAKERS '91					
				Group from Hayward, Wisconsin: Martha "Molly" Scheer (vocals, fiddle, rhythm guitar), Andy Dee (lead guitar), Jeff Nelson (bass) and Joe Lindzius (drums).					
12/22/90+	50	15		1 Chasin' Something Called Love ... Gulf Of Mexico		—	$4	■	Reprise 19517 (v)
5/18/91	59	6		2 He Comes Around ... This Time		—	$4		Reprise 19332
5/16/92	69	5		3 Jimmy McCarthy's Truck ... Milkhouse		—	$4		Reprise 18944
				MONDAY, Carla '87					
10/24/87	79	3		No One Can Touch Me		—	$6	☐	MCM 001
				MONROE, Bill, and His Blue Grass Boys '46					
				Born on 9/13/11 in Rosine, Kentucky. Died of a stroke on 9/9/96 (age 84). Singer/songwriter/mandolin player. Known as "The Father Of Bluegrass." Formed the Blue Grass Boys which included **Flatt & Scruggs**. Joined the *Grand Ole Opry* in 1939. Elected to the Country Music Hall of Fame in 1970. Won Grammy's Lifetime Achievement Award in 1993. Inducted into the Rock and Roll Hall of Fame in 1997 as an early influence of rock and roll.					
3/23/46	3	6		1 Kentucky Waltz Rocky Road Blues		—	$20		Columbia 36907
12/7/46	5	4		2 Footprints In The Snow True Life Blues		—	$20		Columbia 37151
6/19/48	11	1		3 Sweetheart, You Done Me Wrong ... J:11 My Rose Of Old Kentucky		—	$20		Columbia 38172
11/6/48	13	1		4 Wicked Path Of Sin ... S:13 Summertime Is Past And Gone		—	$20		Columbia 20503
11/27/48	11	5		5 Little Community Church ... S:11 / J:12 That Home Above		—	$20		Columbia 20488
				BILL MONROE and his BLUE GRASS QUARTET					
4/16/49	12	2		6 Toy Heart ... S:12 Blue Grass Breakdown		—	$20		Columbia 20552
8/6/49	12	1		7 When You Are Lonely ... J:12 It's Mighty Dark To Travel		—	$20		Columbia 20526
11/3/58	27	1		8 Scotland ... Panhandle Country [I]		—	$15		Decca 30739
				BILL MONROE					
3/2/59	15	6		9 Gotta Travel On ... No One But My Darlin'		—	$15		Decca 30809
				MONROE, Vaughn '49					
				Born on 10/7/11 in Akron, Ohio. Died on 5/21/73 (age 61). Singer/bandleader/trumpeter.					
5/14/49	2[1]	5	●	Riders In The Sky (A Cowboy Legend) S:2 / J:10 Single Saddle		❶ 12	$20		RCA Victor 20-3411
				45 rpm: 47-2902; #30 Pop hit for The Ramrods in 1961					
				MONTANA '81					
				Group from Reno, Nevada. Entire group killed in a plane crash on 7/4/87 near Flathead Lake, Montana.					
11/14/81	83	3		The Shoe's On The Other Foot Tonight ...		—	$7		Waterhouse 15005
				MONTANA, Billy '87					
				Born William Schlappi on 9/28/59 in Voorheesville, New York. Singer/bassist. The Long Shots: Bobby Kendall and Kyle Montana (guitars), Dave Flint (fiddle) and Doug Bernhard (drums).					
				BILLY MONTANA & THE LONG SHOTS:					
3/21/87	46	9		1 Crazy Blue ... That's The Bottom Line		—	$4		Warner 28426
8/22/87	40	11		2 Baby I Was Leaving Anyhow And So It Goes (With Everything But Love)		—	$4		Warner 28256
8/20/88	48	9		3 Oh Jenny ... All I Need		—	$4		Warner 27809
				BILLY MONTANA:					
4/8/95	55	11		4 Didn't Have You		—			album cut
8/19/95	58	7		5 Rain Through The Roof		—			album cut
11/11/95	70	1		6 No Yesterday		—			album cut
				above 3 from the album *No Yesterday* on Magnatone 101					

Patsy Montana? /// Montana Slim/Wilf Carter

DEBUT	PEAK	WKS	Gold	A-side (Chart Hit)	B-side	Pop	$	Pic	Label & Number
				MONTANA SKYLINE '82					
				Group from Missoula, Montana.					
12/26/81+	87	4		Full Moon - Empty Pockets	The Circle Of Love	—	$7		Snow 2022
				MONTGOMERY, John Michael ★97★ '94					
				Born on 1/20/65 in Danville, Kentucky; raised in Nicholasville, Kentucky. Singer/songwriter/guitarist. Younger brother of Eddie Montgomery (of **Montgomery Gentry**). Began playing with local bands in 1980. CMA Award: 1994 Horizon Award.					
				1)I Swear 2)The Little Girl 3)Sold (The Grundy County Auction Incident) 4)I Can Love You Like That 5)I Love The Way You Love Me					
10/3/92+	4	20		1 Life's A Dance	—				album cut (v)
				from the album *Life's A Dance* on Atlantic 82420; later issued as the vinyl B-side of #2 below					
3/13/93	❶³	20		2 I Love The Way You Love Me (album snippets)		60	$4	■	Atlantic 87371 (v)
				"45" B-side: "Life's A Dance"					
7/10/93	21	20		3 Beer And Bones (album snippets)		123	$4	■	Atlantic 87326 (v)
				"45" B-side: "I Love The Way You Love Me"					
12/18/93+	❶⁴	20	●	4 I Swear (album snippets)		42	$4	■	Atlantic 87288 (v)
				CMA Award: Single of the Year; #1 Pop hit for All-4-One in 1994; "45" B-side: "Dream On Texas Ladies"					
3/19/94	4	20		5 Rope The Moon (album snippets)		115	$4	■	Atlantic 87248 (v)
				"45" B-side: "Friday At Five"					
4/9/94	72	2		6 Kick It Up	—			■	album cut (v)
				from the album *Kickin' It Up* on Atlantic 82559; later released as the B-side of #8 below					
5/7/94	❶²	20		7 Be My Baby Tonight (album snippets)		73	$4	■	Atlantic 87236 (v)
				"45" B-side: "Full-Time Love"					
9/24/94	❶¹	20		8 If You've Got Love	Kick It Up	—	$4	■	Atlantic 87198 (v)
3/4/95	❶³	20		9 I Can Love You Like That	—				album cut
				#5 Pop hit for All-4-One in 1995					
5/6/95	❶³	20		10 Sold (The Grundy County Auction Incident)	—				album cut (v)
				later released as the vinyl B-side of #11 below					
8/26/95	3	20		11 No Man's Land S:5 (album snippets)		112	$4	■	Atlantic 87105 (v)
				"45" B-side: "Sold (The Grundy County Auction Incident)"					
11/18/95+	4	20		12 Cowboy Love	—				album cut
3/2/96	4	20		13 Long As I Live	—				album cut
				above 5 from the album *John Michael Montgomery* on Atlantic 82728					
9/14/96	15	19		14 Ain't Got Nothin' On Us S:9 (album snippets)		115	$4	■	Atlantic 87044 (v)
				"45" B-side: "I Miss You A Little"					
10/19/96+	2³	20		15 Friends S:❶³ (album snippets)		69	$4	■	Atlantic 87019 (v)
				"45" B-side: "A Few Cents Short"					
3/1/97	6	20		16 I Miss You A Little S:4 (album snippets)		109	$4	■	Atlantic 84865
6/14/97	2¹	20		17 How Was I To Know	—				album cut
				from the album *What I Do Best* on Atlantic 82947					
8/16/97	56	5		18 Warning Signs S:21 Baby Barf And The Turkey Hunt (Engvall) [C]		—	$4	■	Warner 43934
				BILL ENGVALL with John Michael Montgomery					
10/4/97+	4	21		19 Angel In My Eyes	—				album cut (v)
				from the album *Greatest Hits* on Atlantic 83060; later released as the vinyl B-side of #20 below					
3/14/98	14	20		20 Love Working On You S:23 (album snippets)		125	$4	■	Atlantic 84103 (v)
				"45" B-side: "Angel In My Eyes"					
5/30/98	3	21		21 Cover You In Kisses S:9 (album excerpts)		91	$4	■	Atlantic 84157 (v)
				"45" B-side: "Little Cowboy's Cry"					
10/10/98+	4	25		22 Hold On To Me S:6 (album excerpts)		33	$4	★	Atlantic 84197 (v)
				"45" B-side: "This One's Gonna Leave A Mark"					
3/27/99	15	20		23 Hello L.O.V.E.		71			album cut
7/17/99	2¹	28		24 Home To You		45			album cut
1/22/00	50	10		25 Nothing Catches Jesus By Surprise	—				album cut
3/4/00	48	16		26 You Are	—				album cut
				above 4 from the album *Home To You* on Atlantic 83185					
8/19/00	❶³	23		27 The Little Girl	Brand New Me	35	$4		Atlantic 85006
1/20/01	44	11		28 That's What I Like About You	—				album cut
6/16/01	59	1		29 Even Then	—				album cut
				above 3 from the album *Brand New Me* on Atlantic 83678					

MONTGOMERY, Melba ★197★   '74
Born on 10/14/38 in Iron City, Tennessee; raised in Florence, Alabama. Singer/guitarist/fiddle player. Won the *Grand Ole Opry*'s 1958 Pet Milk Amateur Contest. Toured as a member of **Roy Acuff**'s troupe from 1958-62.

1)No Charge 2)We Must Have Been Out Of Our Minds 3)Baby, Ain't That Fine 4)Don't Let The Good Times Fool You 5)Let's Invite Them Over

DEBUT	PEAK	WKS	A-side	B-side	Pop	$	Label & Number
5/4/63	3	28	1 We Must Have Been Out Of Our Minds	Until Then	—	$15	United Artists 575
			GEORGE JONES & MELBA MONTGOMERY				
8/24/63	26	6	2 Hall Of Shame	What's Bad For You Is Good For Me	—	$12	United Artists 576
12/7/63	17	7	3 Let's Invite Them Over /		—		
11/30/63	20	5	4 What's In Our Heart		—	$12	United Artists 635
			GEORGE JONES AND MELBA MONTGOMERY (above 2)				

DEBUT	PEAK	WKS	Gold	A-side (Chart Hit) ... B-side	Pop	$	Pic	Label & Number
				MONTGOMERY, Melba — Cont'd				
12/7/63+	22	9		5 The Greatest One Of All .... Lies Can't Hide What's On My Mind	—	$12		United Artists 652
9/5/64	31	5		6 Please Be My Love .... Will There Ever Be Another	—	$12		United Artists 732
				GEORGE JONES AND MELBA MONTGOMERY				
12/12/64+	25	15		7 Multiply The Heartaches .... Once More	—	$12		United Artists 784
				GEORGE JONES AND MELBA MONTGOMERY				
1/15/66	15	12		8 Baby Ain't That Fine .... Everybody Knows But You And Me	—	$12		Musicor 1135
				GENE PITNEY and MELBA MONTGOMERY				
11/19/66	70	3		9 Close Together (As You And Me) .... Long As We're Dreaming	—	$12		Musicor 1204
				GEORGE JONES & MELBA MONTGOMERY				
7/8/67	61	3		10 What Can I Tell The Folks Back Home .... The Right Time To Lose My Mind	—	$12		Musicor 1241
9/9/67	24	10		11 Party Pickin' .... Simply Divine	—	$12		Musicor 1238
10/24/70	18	14		12 Something To Brag About .... Let's Help Each Other To Forget	—	$8		Capitol 2915
				CHARLIE LOUVIN & MELBA MONTGOMERY				
2/13/71	26	12		13 Did You Ever .... Don't Believe Me	—	$8		Capitol 3029
				CHARLIE LOUVIN & MELBA MONTGOMERY				
6/12/71	30	10		14 Baby, You've Got What It Takes .... If We Don't Make It	—	$8		Capitol 3111
				CHARLIE LOUVIN & MELBA MONTGOMERY				
				#5 Pop hit for Dinah Washington & Brook Benton in 1960				
6/19/71	61	4		15 He's My Man .... We Don't Live Here Anymore	—	$8		Capitol 3091
11/27/71	60	5		16 I'm Gonna Leave You .... When I Stop Dreaming	—	$8		Capitol 3208
				CHARLIE LOUVIN & MELBA MONTGOMERY				
8/19/72	66	4		17 Baby, What's Wrong With Us .... Unmatched Wedding Bands	—	$8		Capitol 3388
				CHARLIE LOUVIN & MELBA MONTGOMERY				
1/20/73	59	6		18 A Man Likes Things Like That .... That Don't Mean I Don't Love You	—	$8		Capitol 3508
				CHARLIE LOUVIN & MELBA MONTGOMERY				
10/6/73	38	11		19 Wrap Your Love Around Me .... Let Me Show You How I Can	—	$6		Elektra 45866
1/12/74	58	9		20 He'll Come Home .... Country Written Up And Down Her Face	—	$6		Elektra 45875
3/16/74	❶¹	16		21 No Charge .... I Love Him Because He's That Way	39	$6		Elektra 45883
7/20/74	67	8		22 Your Pretty Roses Came Too Late .... My Feel Good Sure Feels Fine	—	$6		Elektra 45894
10/19/74	59	10		23 If You Want The Rainbow .... Love, I Need You	—	$6		Elektra 45211
2/1/75	15	12		24 Don't Let The Good Times Fool You .... It Sure Gets Lonely	—	$6		Elektra 45229
5/24/75	45	9		25 Searchin' (For Someone Like You) .... Hiding In The Darkness Of My Mind	—	$5		Elektra 45247
1/10/76	67	7		26 Love Was The Wind .... I Never Dreamed That Love Could Be This Good	—	$5		Elektra 45296
7/16/77	83	4		27 Never Ending Love Affair .... You	—	$5		United Artists 1008
12/10/77+	22	14		28 Angel Of The Morning .... The Pinkerton's Flowers	—	$5		United Artists 1115
				#7 Pop hit for Merrilee Rush in 1968				
10/25/80	92	2		29 The Star .... Carolina In My Mind	—	$6		Kari 111
8/30/86	79	4		30 Straight Talkin'	—	$6		Compass 45-7
				MONTGOMERY, Nancy '81				
7/4/81	85	2		All I Have To Do Is Dream	—	$5		Ovation 1172
				MONTGOMERY GENTRY '01				
				Vocal duo of Eddie Montgomery and Troy Gentry. Montgomery was born Gerald Edward Montgomery on 9/30/63 in Danville, Kentucky; raised in Nicholasville, Kentucky. Older brother of **John Michael Montgomery**. Gentry was born on 4/5/67 in Lexington, Kentucky. CMA Award: 2000 Vocal Duo of the Year.				
2/13/99	13	20		1 Hillbilly Shoes .... S:3 All Night Long	62	$4	★	Columbia 79115 (v)
6/5/99	5	26		2 Lonely And Gone .... S:4 I've Loved A Lot More Than I've Hurt	46	$4	★	Columbia 79210 (v)
11/20/99+	17	21		3 Daddy Won't Sell The Farm	79			album cut
4/22/00	31	20		4 Self Made Man	—			album cut
				above 2 from the album *Tatoos & Scars* on Columbia 69156				
9/23/00	31	21		5 All Night Long / S:7	47ˢ			
				MONTGOMERY GENTRY Featuring Charlie Daniels				
12/16/00	38	4		6 Merry Christmas From The Family .... [X-N]	—	$4	★	Columbia 79515 (v)
2/10/01	2³	33		7 She Couldn't Change Me .... S:3 Hillbilly Shoes (acoustic version)	37	$4	★	Columbia 79540 (v)
8/25/01+	23	22		8 Cold One Comin' On	—			album cut
				from the album *Carrying On* on Columbia 62167				
				MOODY, Clyde '50				
				Born on 9/19/15 in Cherokee, North Carolina; raised in Marion, North Carolina. Died on 4/7/89 (age 73). Singer/songwriter/guitarist. Known as "The Hillbilly Waltz King."				
8/14/48	8	1		1 Red Roses Tied In Blue / S:8				
6/19/48	15	1		2 Carolina Waltz S:15	—	$25		King 706
3/11/50	8	2		3 I Love You Because .... A:8 Afraid	—	$25		King 837
				MOORE, Beth '71				
				Born on 11/27/44 in Michigan.				
1/23/71	61	8		Put Your Hand In The Hand .... I'm Losin' My Man	—	$6		Capitol 3013
				#2 Pop hit for Ocean in 1971				
				MOORE, Jim '88				
9/3/88	88	2		Ain't She Shinin' Tonight	—	$6		Willow Wind 0511
				JIM MOORE & SIDEWINDER				
				MOORE, Lattie '61				
				Born on 10/17/24 in Scotsville, Kentucky. Male rockabilly singer/songwriter/guitarist.				
1/30/61	25	3		Drunk Again .... Driving Nails	—	$25		King 5413

DEBUT	PEAK	WKS	Gold	A-side (Chart Hit)	B-side	Pop	$	Pic	Label & Number
				MOORER, Allison '01					
				Born in Frankville, Alabama. Younger sister of **Shelby Lynne**.					
6/20/98	73	1		1 A Soft Place To Fall .... Big Ball's In Cowtown (Don Walser)		—	$4		MCA 72030
				from the movie *The Horse Whisperer* starring Robert Redford					
9/5/98	72	2		2 Set You Free .... Easier To Forget		—	$4		MCA Nashville 72069
7/22/00	66	1		3 Send Down An Angel .... Day You Said Goodbye		—	$4		MCA Nashville 172172
12/2/00+	57	5		4 Think It Over		—			album cut
				from the album *The Hardest Part* on MCA Nashville 170114					
				MOREY, Sean '98					
				Born in Los Angeles. Male comedian.					
7/4/98	70	11		The Man Song .... [N]		—			album cut
				from the album *He's The Man* on Banjo 1197					
				MORGAN, Al '49					
				Born in Chicago. Pianist who hosted own TV series from 1949-51. Known as "Mr. Flying Fingers."					
9/17/49	8	1		Jealous Heart .... S:8 Turnabout	4	$15			London 500
				first released on Universal 148 in 1949 ($20); 45 rpm: 3001; #47 Pop hit for **Connie Francis** in 1965					
				MORGAN, Billie '59					
				Born on 12/13/22 in Nashville. Female singer.					
3/23/59	22	3		Life To Live .... Thinking All Night		—	$12		Starday 420
				MORGAN, Craig '00					
				Born in Kingston Springs, Tennessee. Singer/songwriter.					
2/26/00	38	20		1 Something To Write Home About S:24 *302 South Maple Avenue*		—	$4		Atlantic 84669 (v)
6/10/00	46	20		2 Paradise		—			album cut
12/16/00	68	2		3 The Kid In Me .... [X]		—			album cut
4/7/01	51	3		4 I Want Us Back		—			album cut
				above 3 from the album *Craig Morgan* on Atlantic 83299					
12/15/01+	49	9		5 God, Family And Country .... (no B-side)		—	$4	★	Broken Bow 0011
				MORGAN, David '97					
				Born on 8/13/53 in Dallas.					
11/1/97	72	1		Those Who Couldn't Wait		—			album cut
				from the album *The Well* on Stage Coach 0326					

MORGAN, George ★138★ '49
Born on 6/28/24 in Waverly, Tennessee. Died of a heart attack on 7/7/75 (age 51). Singer/songwriter/guitarist. Joined the *Grand Ole Opry* in 1948. Father of **Lorrie Morgan**. Elected to the Country Music Hall of Fame in 1998.

1) Candy Kisses 2) Almost 3) I'm In Love Again 4) You're The Only Good Thing (That's Happened To Me)
5) Please Don't Let Me Love You

DEBUT	PEAK	WKS		A-side	B-side	Pop	$	Label & Number
2/26/49	●^{3}	23		1 Candy Kisses /	S:●^{3} / J:2	—		
3/19/49	4	14		2 Please Don't Let Me Love You	S:4 / J:4	—	$20	Columbia 20547
4/30/49	8	6		3 Rainbow In My Heart /	S:8 / J:10	—		
5/7/49	11	1		4 All I Need Is Some More Lovin'	S:11	—	$20	Columbia 20563
7/23/49	4	12		5 Room Full Of Roses S:4 / J:10 Put All Your Love In A Cookie Jar		25	$20	Columbia 20594
12/10/49	4	4		6 I Love Everything About You /	A:4 / S:14	—		
10/29/49	5	9		7 Cry-Baby Heart	S:5 / J:6 / A:7	—	$20	Columbia 20627
4/19/52	2^6	23		8 Almost S:2 / A:2 / J:2 You're A Little Doll		—	$25	Columbia 4-20906
3/7/53	10	1		9 (I Just Had A Date) A Lover's Quarrel	J:10 Most Of All	—	$25	Columbia 21070
1/26/57	15	1		10 There Goes My Love	A:15 Can I Be Dreaming	—	$20	Columbia 40792
2/16/59	3	23		11 I'm In Love Again	It Was All In Your Mind	—	$15	Columbia 41318
8/17/59	20	9		12 Little Dutch Girl /		—		
8/24/59	26	1		13 The Last Thing I Want To Know		—	$15	Columbia 41420
1/11/60	4	20		14 You're The Only Good Thing (That's Happened To Me) Come Away From His Arms		—	$15	Columbia 41523
1/18/64	23	7		15 One Dozen Roses (And Our Love) /		—		
3/7/64	45	2		16 All Right (I'll Sign The Papers)		—	$15	Columbia 42882
5/9/64	23	17		17 Slipping Around	I Love You So Much It Hurts	—	$15	Columbia 43020
				MARION WORTH & GEORGE MORGAN				
9/26/64	37	9		18 Tears And Roses	You're Not Home Yet	—	$15	Columbia 43098
12/11/65+	27	10		19 A Picture That's New	Roses	—	$15	Columbia 43393
4/15/67	40	12		20 I Couldn't See	Look At The Lonely	—	$10	Starday 804
8/19/67	58	5		21 Shiny Red Automobile	Have Some Of Mine	—	$10	Starday 814
1/13/68	55	6		22 Barbara	Sad Bird	—	$10	Starday 825
4/27/68	56	7		23 Living	Rosebuds And You	—	$10	Starday 834
8/31/68	31	10		24 Sounds Of Goodbye	The Ballad Of The Grand Ole Opry	—	$10	Starday 850
4/19/69	30	9		25 Like A Bird	Left Over Feelings	—	$10	Stop 252
4/18/70	17	13		26 Lilacs And Fire	Hardest Easy Thing	—	$10	Stop 365
12/11/71	68	3		27 Gentle Rains Of Home	Walking Shadow, Talking Mem'ry	—	$8	Decca 32886
				GEORGE MORGAN Featuring "Little" Roy Wiggins:				
1/20/73	62	7		28 Makin' Heartaches	Sing My Blues A Birthday Song	—	$8	Decca 33037
6/30/73	56	9		29 Mr. Ting-A-Ling (Steel Guitar Man)	Our Wedding Song	—	$6	MCA 40069
12/15/73+	21	14		30 Red Rose From The Blue Side Of Town	You Turn Me On	—	$6	MCA 40159
				GEORGE MORGAN				

DEBUT	PEAK	WKS	Gold	A-side (Chart Hit)...B-side	Pop	$	Pic	Label & Number
				GEORGE MORGAN Featuring "Little" Roy Wiggins — Cont'd				
6/1/74	66	6		31 Somewhere Around Midnight .... *I Never Knew Love (Until I Met You)*	—	$6		MCA 40227
11/2/74	82	6		32 A Candy Mountain Melody............................... *You're That Much Woman To Me*	—	$6		MCA 40298
2/22/75	65	9		33 In The Misty Moonlight .... *Welcome Back To My World*	—	$5		4 Star 1001
				#19 Pop hit for **Jerry Wallace** in 1964				
7/5/75	62	11		34 From This Moment On.. *One Wife Five Kids Later*	—	$5		4 Star 1009
11/24/79	93	3		35 I'm Completely Satisfied With You................................... *From This Moment On*	—	$5		4 Star 1040
				LORRIE & GEORGE MORGAN				
				MORGAN, Jane '70				
				Born Jane Currier in 1920 in Boston; raised in Florida. Best known for her 1957 pop hit "Fascination."				
5/30/70	61	5		1 A Girl Named Johnny Cash .... *Charley* [N]	—	$8		RCA Victor 9839
				answer to "A Boy Named Sue" by **Johnny Cash**				
11/7/70	70	2		2 The First Day .... *I'm Only A Woman*	—	$6		RCA Victor 9901

MORGAN, Lorrie ★96★ '93
Born Loretta Lynn Morgan on 6/27/59 in Nashville. Singer/songwriter/guitarist. Daughter of **George Morgan**. Joined the *Grand Ole Opry* in 1984. Married to **Keith Whitley** from 1986-89. Married to **Jon Randall** from 1996-99. Married **Sammy Kershaw** on 9/29/2001. Also see **Hope**.

1)What Part Of No 2)Five Minutes 3)I Didn't Know My Own Strength 4)Out Of Your Shoes 5)Watch Me

DEBUT	PEAK	WKS	Gold	A-side .... B-side	Pop	$	Pic	Label & Number
3/10/79	75	5		1 Two People In Love .... *I Don't Care*	—	$5		ABC/Hickory 54041
7/28/79	88	3		2 Tell Me I'm Only Dreaming .... *In For Rain*	—	$5		MCA 41052
11/24/79	93	3		3 I'm Completely Satisfied With You................................... *From This Moment On*	—	$5		4 Star 1040
				LORRIE & GEORGE MORGAN				
3/17/84	69	5		4 Don't Go Changing .... *Everything You Say*	—	$4		MCA 52331
12/10/88+	20	19		5 Trainwreck Of Emotion... *One More Last Time*	—	$4		RCA 8638
4/15/89	9	22		6 Dear Me .... *Eight Days A Week*	—	$4		RCA 8866
9/9/89	2³	26		7 Out Of Your Shoes .... *One More Last Time*	—	$4		RCA 9016
2/3/90	❶¹	26		8 Five Minutes .... *I'll Take This Memories*	—	$4		RCA 9118
5/26/90	4	21		9 He Talks To Me .... *If I Didn't Love You*	—	$4		RCA 2508
7/28/90	13	20		10 'Til A Tear Becomes A Rose .... *Lady's Choice*	—	$4		RCA 2619
				KEITH WHITLEY AND LORRIE MORGAN				
3/30/91	3	20		11 We Both Walk .... *Faithfully*	—	$4	▌	RCA 2748 (v)
8/3/91	9	20		12 A Picture Of Me (Without You) .... *Tears On My Pillow*	—	$4		RCA 62014
12/14/91+	4	20		13 Except For Monday .... *Hand Over Your Heart*	—	$4		RCA 62105
5/9/92	14	20		14 Something In Red .... *It's Too Late (To Love Me Now)*	—	$4		RCA 62219
9/5/92	2²	20		15 Watch Me .... *She's Takin' Him Back Again*	—	$4		BNA 62333
12/19/92+	❶³	20		16 What Part Of No .... *You Leave Me Like This*	—	$4		BNA 62414
4/3/93	14	20		17 I Guess You Had To Be There .... *Someone To Call Me Darling*	—	$4		BNA 62415
7/31/93	8	20		18 Half Enough .... *It's A Heartache*	—	$4		BNA 62576
11/27/93	59	6		19 Crying Time .... *I'm So Lonesome I Could Cry*	—	$4		BNA 62707
				from the movie *The Beverly Hillbillies* starring Jim Varney				
12/25/93	64	1		20 My Favorite Things .... [X]	—			album cut
				#45 Pop hit for Herb Alpert in 1969; from the album *Merry Christmas From London* on BNA 66282				
3/19/94	31	12		21 My Night To Howl .... *Evening Up The Odds*	—	$4		BNA 62767
5/21/94	51	11		22 If You Came Back From Heaven .... *Exit 99*	—	$4		BNA 62864
8/13/94	39	13		23 Heart Over Mind .... *The Hard Part Was Easy*	—	$4		BNA 62946
5/6/95	❶¹	20		24 I Didn't Know My Own Strength .... S:12 *War Paint*	—	$4	▌	BNA 64287 (v)
9/2/95	4	20		25 Back In Your Arms Again .... S:15 *My Favorite Things*	—	$4	▌	BNA 64353 (v)
12/23/95+	32	17		26 Standing Tall... —				album cut
				from the album *Greatest Hits* on BNA 66508				
12/30/95	67	1		27 Sleigh Ride .... [X]	—			album cut
				#24 Pop hit for the Boston Pops Orchestra in 1949; from the album *Merry Christmas From London* on BNA 66282				
4/6/96	18	20		28 By My Side .... S:4 *Candy Kisses*	110	$4	▌	BNA 64512 (v)
				LORRIE MORGAN & JON RANDALL				
8/10/96	45	12		29 I Just Might Be .... *Steppin' Stones*	—	$4	▌	BNA 64608 (v)
9/7/96	73	1		30 Don't Worry Baby .... —				album cut
				THE BEACH BOYS Featuring Lorrie Morgan				
				#24 Pop hit for The Beach Boys in 1964; from the album *Stars And Stripes Vol. 1* on River North 1205				
12/28/96	64	3		31 Sleigh Ride .... [X-R]	—			album cut
				from the album *Merry Christmas From London* on BNA 66282				
1/25/97	4	20		32 Good As I Was To You .... *She Walked Beside The Wagon*	—	$4		BNA 64681
7/5/97	3	20		33 Go Away .... S:6 *I've Enjoyed As Much Of This As I Can Stand*	85	$4	▌	BNA 64914 (v)
11/8/97+	14	20		34 One Of Those Nights Tonight .... *By My Side*	—	$4		BNA 65333
4/4/98	49	7		35 I'm Not That Easy To Forget .... *You Can't Take That*	—	$4		BNA 65440
8/8/98	66	3		36 You'd Think He'd Know Me Better .... —				album cut
				from the album *Shakin' Things Up* on BNA 67499				
2/27/99	17	20		37 Maybe Not Tonight .... *Go Away*	86	$4		BNA/Mercury 65729
				SAMMY KERSHAW & LORRIE MORGAN				
7/31/99	72	3		38 Here I Go Again .... —				album cut
				from the album *My Heart* on BNA 67763				
12/11/99	42	5		39 Sleigh Ride .... [X-R]	—			album cut
12/11/99	69	2		40 My Favorite Things .... [X-R]	—			album cut
				above 2 from the album *Merry Christmas From London* on BNA 66282				
1/22/00	63	5		41 To Get To You.. *Maybe Not Tonight* (w/**Sammy Kershaw**)	—	$4		BNA 65965

DEBUT	PEAK	WKS	Gold	A-side (Chart Hit)	B-side	Pop	$	Pic	Label & Number
				MORGAN, Lorrie — Cont'd					
2/17/01	39	17		42 He Drinks Tequila .... I Finally Found Someone LORRIE MORGAN & SAMMY KERSHAW		—	$4		RCA 69054
				MORGAN, Misty — see BLANCHARD, Jack					
				MORI, Miki '80 Born in Nephi, Utah. Female singer.					
6/30/79	91	1		1 Tell All Your Troubles To Me .... Driftin' Away MICKIE MORI		—	$8		Red Feather 2280
10/20/79	79	4		2 The Part Of Me That Needs You Most .... Baby You Are The Answer		—	$6		Oak 1002
2/2/80	48	7		3 Driftin Away .... Tell All Your Trouble		—	$6		Oak 1010
7/19/80	51	8		4 The Last Farewell .... You Are The Answer		—	$5		NSD 49
1/10/81	59	6		5 Rainin' In My Eyes .... Reunion		—	$5		Starcom 1001
				MORRIS, Bob '67 Born on 2/3/30 in Hasty, Arkansas. Died of cancer on 12/3/81 (age 51).					
2/25/67	62	5		Fishin' On The Mississippi .... A Little Bit Of You		—	$10		Tower 307
				MORRIS, Gary ★130★ '85 Born on 12/7/48 in Fort Worth, Texas. Singer/songwriter/guitarist/actor. Acted in Broadway's *Les Miserables* and *La Boheme*. Portrayed "Wayne Masterson" on TV's *The Colbys*. 1)I'll Never Stop Loving You 2)Leave Me Lonely 3)Makin' Up For Lost Time (The Dallas Lovers' Song) 4)100% Chance Of Rain 5)Baby Bye Bye					
10/18/80	40	13		1 Sweet Red Wine .... May I Borrow Some Sugar From You		—	$4		Warner 49564
3/7/81	40	10		2 Fire In Your Eyes .... Heartaches By The Number		—	$4		Warner 49668
10/17/81	8	17		3 Headed For A Heartache .... I'm So Tired Of Losing		—	$4		Warner 49829
2/27/82	12	17		4 Don't Look Back .... She Gave Me Till Friday		—	$4		Warner 50017
7/10/82	15	15		5 Dreams Die Hard .... Eyes Of The World		—	$4		Warner 29967
11/27/82+	9	19		6 Velvet Chains .... When I Close My Eyes		—	$4		Warner 29853
4/16/83	5	20		7 The Love She Found In Me .... That's The Way It Is		—	$4		Warner 29683
8/6/83	4	25		8 The Wind Beneath My Wings .... The Way I Love You Tonight #1 Pop hit for Bette Midler in 1989		—	$4		Warner 29532
11/26/83+	4	19		9 Why Lady Why .... The Way I Love You Tonight		—	$4		Warner 29450
12/17/83+	9	23		10 You're Welcome To Tonight .... Your Kisses Lied LYNN ANDERSON & GARY MORRIS		—	$5		Permian 82003
4/7/84	7	18		11 Between Two Fires .... All She Said Was No		—	$4		Warner 29321
7/28/84	7	19		12 Second Hand Heart .... A:19 / S:21 Whoever's Watchin'		—	$4		Warner 29230
11/24/84+	❶¹	20		13 Baby Bye Bye .... S:❶¹ / A:❶¹ West Texas Highway And Me		—	$4		Warner 29131
5/4/85	9	20		14 Lasso The Moon .... A:8 / S:9 When I Close My Eyes from the movie *Rustler's Rhapsody* starring Tom Berenger		—	$4		Warner 29028
8/24/85	❶¹	23		15 I'll Never Stop Loving You .... A:❶² / S:2 Heaven's Hell Without You		—	$4		Warner 28947
11/23/85+	❶¹	19		16 Makin' Up For Lost Time (The Dallas Lovers' Song) .... S:❶¹ / A:❶¹ A Few Good Men (Forester Sisters) CRYSTAL GAYLE AND GARY MORRIS from the TV series *Dallas* starring Larry Hagman		—	$4	■	Warner 28856
1/11/86	❶¹	20		17 100% Chance Of Rain .... S:❶¹ / A:2 Back In Her Arms Again		—	$4		Warner 28823
5/17/86	28	12		18 Anything Goes .... A:27 / S:32 Draggin' The Lake For The Moon		—	$4		Warner 28713
7/12/86	27	13		19 Honeycomb .... S:21 / A:28 Whoever's Watchin'		—	$4		Warner 28654
11/1/86+	❶¹	21		20 Leave Me Lonely .... A:❶¹ / S:4 Eleventh Hour		—	$4		Warner 28542
2/28/87	9	20		21 Plain Brown Wrapper .... A:9 / S:24 Moonshine		—	$4		Warner 28468
4/25/87	4	18		22 Another World .... S:5 / A:29 Makin' Up For Lost Time CRYSTAL GAYLE & GARY MORRIS theme from the TV serial		—	$4		Warner 28373
10/10/87	64	5		23 Finishing Touches .... Mama You Can't Give Me No Whippin'		—	$4		Warner 28218
2/13/88	26	15		24 All Of This & More .... Makin' Up For Lost Time CRYSTAL GAYLE/GARY MORRIS		—	$4		Warner 28106
5/27/89	48	12		25 Never Had A Love Song .... Bread And Water		—	$4		Universal 66011
10/21/89	60	5		26 The Jaws Of Modern Romance .... Stand My Ground		—	$4		Universal 66026
2/9/91	47	19		27 Miles Across The Bedroom .... from the album *These Days* on Capitol 94103		—			album cut
				MORRIS, Lamar '71 Born in Andalusia, Alabama. Member of **The Bama Band**.					
11/12/66	69	2		1 Send Me A Box Of Kleenex .... Both Of You		—	$7		MGM 13586
1/13/68	46	10		2 The Great Pretender .... The World's Perfect Couple #1 Pop hit for The Platters in 1956		—	$7		MGM 13866
6/13/70	74	3		3 She Came To Me .... Only With Teardrops		—	$6		MGM 14114
1/2/71	59	6		4 You're The Reason I'm Living .... Things #3 Pop hit for **Bobby Darin** in 1963		—	$6		MGM 14187
4/17/71	27	12		5 If You Love Me (Really Love Me) .... Pour The Wine #4 Pop hit for **Kay Starr** in 1954		—	$6		MGM 14236
11/27/71	74	3		6 Near You .... She Came To Me #1 Pop hit for Francis Craig in 1947		—	$6		MGM 14289
2/17/73	71	3		7 You Call Everybody Darling .... I Need You #1 Pop hit for Al Trace in 1948		—	$6		MGM 14448

DEBUT	PEAK	WKS	Gold	A-side (Chart Hit)	B-side	Pop	$	Pic	Label & Number
				MORRISON, Kathy — see **WILBOURN, Bill**					
				MORROW, Cory — see **GREEN, Pat**					
				MORTON, Ann J. '79					
				Born Anna Jane White on 4/4/43 in Muldrow, Oklahoma. Sister of **Jim Mundy** and **Bill White**.					
				1)My Empty Arms 2)I'm Not In The Mood (For Love) 3)You Don't Have To Be A Baby To Cry					
11/6/76	82	7		1 Poor Wilted Rose .... Molly Jones (Is A Happy Hooker)		—	$5		Prairie Dust 7606
3/26/77	63	10		2 You Don't Have To Be A Baby To Cry .... Good Looking Cowboy		—	$5		Prairie Dust 7613
				#3 Pop hit for The Caravelles in 1963					
7/16/77	86	4		3 Don't Want To Take A Chance (On Loving You) .... Tainted Rose		—	$5		Prairie Dust 7617
10/1/77	72	6		4 Blueberry Hill .... Onions And Love Affairs		—	$5		Prairie Dust 7619
				#2 Pop hit for **Fats Domino** in 1957					
2/18/78	83	3		5 Black And Blue Heart .... Me And My Horse Named Daddy		—	$5		Prairie Dust 7621
9/30/78	83	4		6 Share Your Love Tonight .... Willie I Will		—	$5		Prairie Dust 7627
1/27/79	59	6		7 I'm Not In The Mood (For Love) .... Willie I Will		—	$5		Prairie Dust 7629
6/16/79	86	3		8 Don't Stay On Your Side Of The Bed Tonight .... It's Written All Over Your Face		—	$5		Prairie Dust 7631
8/18/79	42	10		9 My Empty Arms .... Don't Stay On Your Side Of The Bed Tonight		—	$5		Prairie Dust 7632
1/26/80	63	5		10 (We Used To Kiss Each Other On The Lips But It's) All Over Now /		—			
		5		11 I Like Being Lonely		—	$5		Prairie Dust 7633
2/14/81	89	3		12 You've Got The Devil In Your Eyes .... No Strings Attached		—	$5		Prairie Dust 8004
	★293★			**MOSBY, Johnny and Jonie** '69					
				Husband-and-wife team of Johnny (born on 4/26/33 in Fort Smith, Arkansas) and Jonie (born Janice Irene Shields on 8/10/40 in Van Nuys, California) Mosby. Married from 1958-73.					
				1)Just Hold My Hand 2)Trouble In My Arms 3)Don't Call Me From A Honky Tonk					
5/18/63	13	9		1 Don't Call Me From A Honky Tonk .... The Wrong Side Of Town		—	$10		Columbia 42668
10/12/63+	12	16		2 Trouble In My Arms /		—			
11/2/63	27	1		3 Who's Been Cheatin' Who		—	$10		Columbia 42841
4/18/64	16	13		4 Keep Those Cards And Letters Coming In .... Take Me Home		—	$8		Columbia 43005
10/10/64	21	11		5 How The Other Half Lives .... Stolen Paradise		—	$8		Columbia 43100
10/7/67	36	12		6 Make A Left And Then A Right .... Take Back The World		—	$7		Capitol 5980
2/17/68	53	6		7 Mr. & Mrs. John Smith .... Hello There Stranger		—	$7		Capitol 2087
6/22/68	58	5		8 Our Golden Wedding Day .... Two Dollar Honeymoon Room		—	$7		Capitol 2179
2/15/69	12	15		9 Just Hold My Hand .... Walkin' Papers		—	$6		Capitol 2384
6/21/69	38	12		10 Hold Me, Thrill Me, Kiss Me .... Comparing Him With You		—	$6		Capitol 2505
				#8 Pop hit for Mel Carter in 1965					
10/25/69	26	9		11 I'll Never Be Free .... The Pattern Of Our Lives		—	$6		Capitol 2608
2/28/70	34	8		12 Third World .... You Go Back To Your World (And I'll Go Back To Mine)		—	$6		Capitol 2730
5/9/70	18	13		13 I'm Leavin' It Up To You .... If It's Left Up To Me		—	$6		Capitol 2796
				#1 Pop hit for Dale & Grace in 1963					
9/5/70	47	7		14 My Happiness .... Let Your Sun Shine On Me		—	$6	■	Capitol 2865
				#2 Pop hit for **Connie Francis** in 1959					
3/6/71	40	9		15 Oh, Love Of Mine .... Closing Time Till Dawn		—	$6		Capitol 3039
12/18/71+	70	3		16 Just One More Time .... Meet Me Tonight		—	$6		Capitol 3219
1/6/73	72	2		17 I've Been There .... I'll Be Leaving You Again		—	$5		Capitol 3454
				JONIE MOSBY					
				MOWREY, Dude '93					
				Born Daniel Richard Mowrey on 2/10/72 in Ft. Lauderdale; raised in Ocala, Florida. Singer/songwriter/guitarist.					
8/24/91	65	3		1 Cowboys Don't Cry		—			album cut
				from the album Honky Tonk on Capitol 95084					
4/17/93	57	8		2 Maybe You Were The One .... View From The Bottom		—	$4	■	Arista 12515 (v)
8/14/93	69	4		3 Hold On, Elroy .... Turn For The Worse		—	$4	■	Arista 12579 (v)
2/12/94	57	7		4 Somewhere In Between .... I'll Never Listen To That Fool Again		—	$4	■	Arista 12643 (v)
				MULLEN, Bruce '74					
5/25/74	88	3		Auctioneer Love .... The Love In The Touch Of Her Hand		—	$6		Chart 5215
	★332★			**MULLICAN, Moon** '50					
				Born Aubrey Mullican on 3/29/09 in Corrigan, Texas. Died of a heart attack on 1/1/67 (age 57). Singer/pianist. Member of the *Grand Ole Opry* from 1949-55. Known as the "King Of The Hillbilly Piano Players."					
2/8/47	2¹	15		1 New Pretty Blonde (Jole Blon) When A Soldier Knocks And Finds Nobody Home		—	$25		King 578
				MOON MULLICAN and the Showboys					
7/26/47	4	1		2 Jole Blon's Sister Showboy Special		—	$25		King 632
5/15/48	3	26		3 Sweeter Than The Flowers S:3 / J:3 I Left My Heart In Texas		—	$25		King 673
3/18/50	❶⁴	36		4 I'll Sail My Ship Alone J:❶¹ / S:❶¹ / A:2 Moon's Tune		17	$25		King 830
8/26/50	4	11		5 Mona Lisa / J:4 / A:7 / S:8					
				#1 Pop hit for Nat "King" Cole in 1950; from the movie *Captain Carey, U.S.A.* starring Alan Ladd					
8/26/50	5	7		6 Goodnight Irene J:5 / S:10 / A:10		—	$25		King 886
				#1 Pop hit for Gordon Jenkins & The Weavers in 1950					
8/4/51	7	2		7 Cherokee Boogie (Eh-Oh-Aleena) S:7 / J:10 Love Is The Light That Leads Me Home		—	$25		King 965
5/29/61	15	4		8 Ragged But Right .... Bottom Of The Glass		—	$20		Starday 545
				written by George Jones					
				MULLINS, Dee '68					
				Born on 4/7/37 in Gafford, Texas. Died on 3/13/91 (age 53). Male singer.					
2/10/68	64	3		1 I Am The Grass .... The World I'm Livin In		—	$7		SSS Int'l. 728
7/13/68	51	7		2 Texas Tea .... Parking For Cheaters		—	$7		SSS Int'l. 745
4/26/69	53	6		3 The Big Man .... Run Willie Run		—	$6		Plantation 17

DEBUT	PEAK	WKS	Gold	A-side (Chart Hit)	B-side	Pop	$	Pic	Label & Number
				MULLINS, Dee — Cont'd					
12/26/70	71	2		4 Remember Bethlehem	California, The Promise Land [X]	—	$6		Plantation 68
4/14/73	61	9		5 Circle Me	Friday's Wine	—	$6		Triune 7205
				MUNDY, Jim '74					
				Born James White on 2/8/34 in Muldrow, Oklahoma. Brother of **Ann J. Morton** and **Bill White**.					
				1)The River's Too Wide 2)She's Already Gone 3)Come Home					
12/1/73+	13	15		1 The River's Too Wide	Run Away	—	$6		ABC 11400
4/13/74	49	11		2 Come Home	Nobody Loves You	—	$6		ABC 11428
9/7/74	71	5		3 She's No Ordinary Woman (Ordinarily)	Rosalie's Good-Eats Cafe	—	$6		ABC 12001
4/19/75	37	9		4 She's Already Gone	While The Feeling's Good	—	$6		ABC 12074
8/30/75	81	8		5 Blue Eyes And Waltzes	Holdin' On	—	$6		ABC 12120
4/17/76	86	4		6 I'm Knee Deep In Loving You	Monroe, Louisiana	—	$5		ABC/Dot 17617
8/7/76	94	4		7 I Never Met A Girl I Didn't Like	Lucy Ain't Your Loser Lookin' Good	—	$5		ABC/Dot 17638
7/30/77	70	6		8 Summertime Blues	Gilpen County Sidewalks	—	$7		Hill Country 778
				#8 Pop hit for Eddie Cochran in 1958					
				JIM MUNDY and TERRI MELTON:					
9/9/78	76	4		9 If You Think I Love You Now		—	$6		MCM 100
1/6/79	87	2		10 Kiss You All Over		—	$6		MCM 101
				#1 Pop hit for **Exile** in 1978					
				MUNDY, Marilyn '89					
				Born in Bokoshe, Oklahoma; raised in Flower Hill, Oklahoma.					
6/17/89	85	2		1 I Still Love You Babe		—	$5		Door Knob 322
1/6/90	85	2		2 Feelings For Each Other		—	$5		Door Knob 336
				MURPHEY, Mark '89					
5/6/89	96	1		California Wine	Falling Into The Night	—	$7		Traveler Ent. 106

MURPHEY, Michael Martin ★150★ '82

Born on 3/14/45 in Oak Cliff, Texas. Singer/songwriter/guitarist. Member of the Texas Twosome while still in high school. Toured as "Travis Lewis" of The Lewis & Clarke Expedition in 1967. Worked as a staff writer for Screen Gems. Lived in Austin from 1971-74 and Colorado from 1974-79. Moved to Taos, New Mexico, in 1979. Acted in the movies *Take This Job And Shove It* and *Hard Country*.

1)What's Forever For 2)A Long Line Of Love 3)I'm Gonna Miss You, Girl 4)From The Word Go 5)Still Taking Chances

DEBUT	PEAK	WKS	Gold	A-side	B-side	Pop	$	Pic	Label & Number
				MICHAEL MURPHEY:					
2/21/76	36	10		1 A Mansion On The Hill	Renegade (Pop #39)	—	$5		Epic 50184
1/22/77	58	8		2 Cherokee Fiddle	Running Wide Open	—	$5		Epic 50319
4/28/79	93	3		3 Chain Gang	Lightning	—	$4		Epic 50686
				#2 Pop hit for Sam Cooke in 1960					
8/18/79	92	3		4 Backslider's Wine	South Coast	—	$4		Epic 50739
7/4/81	83	3		5 Take It As It Comes	Hard Country	—	$4		Epic 02075
				MICHAEL MURPHEY with KATY MOFFATT					
3/27/82	44	10		6 The Two-Step Is Easy	Lost River	—	$4		Liberty 1455
6/19/82	❶¹	24		7 What's Forever For	Crystal	19	$4		Liberty 1466
11/13/82+	3	20		8 Still Taking Chances	Lost River	76	$4		Liberty 1486
3/26/83	11	17		9 Love Affairs	Crystal	—	$4		Liberty 1494
9/10/83	9	21		10 Don't Count The Rainy Days	The Heart Never Lies	—	$4	■	Liberty 1505
1/28/84	7	18		11 Will It Be Love By Morning	Goodbye Money Mountain	—	$4	■	Liberty 1514
				MICHAEL MARTIN MURPHEY:					
5/12/84	12	17		12 Disenchanted	Sacred Heart	—	$4	■	Liberty 1517
8/25/84	19	16		13 Radio Land	A:17 / S:21 The Heart Never Lies	—	$4		Liberty 1523
12/1/84+	8	23		14 What She Wants	S:7 / A:8 Still Taking Chances	—	$4	■	EMI America 8243
5/25/85	9	20		15 Carolina In The Pines	A:9 / S:10 Cherokee Fiddle	—	$4	■	EMI America 8265
				featuring John McEuen; new version of his #21 Pop hit from 1975					
2/8/86	26	14		16 Tonight We Ride	S:24 / A:27 Santa Fe Cantina	—	$4		Warner 28797
5/24/86	15	16		17 Rollin' Nowhere	S:14 / A:15 Face-To-Face With The Night	—	$4		Warner 28694
8/30/86	40	14		18 Fiddlin' Man	Ghost Town (Messages From The Ghost Ranch)	—	$4		Warner 28598
2/7/87	4	21		19 A Face In The Crowd	A:4 / S:15 You're History	—	$4		Warner 28471
				MICHAEL MARTIN MURPHEY AND HOLLY DUNN					
5/23/87	❶¹	23		20 A Long Line Of Love	S:9 Worlds Apart	—	$4		Warner 28370
11/21/87+	3	27		21 I'm Gonna Miss You, Girl	S.7 Running Blood	—	$4	■	Warner 28168
4/16/88	4	20		22 Talkin' To The Wrong Man	S:5 What Am I Doin' Hangin' 'Round?	—	$4	■	Warner 27947
				MICHAEL MARTIN MURPHEY with Ryan Murphey					
9/10/88	29	13		23 Pilgrims On The Way (Matthew's Song)	Still Got The Fire	—	$4		Warner 27810
12/17/88+	3	27		24 From The Word Go	Vanishing Breed	—	$4		Warner 27668
5/20/89	9	22		25 Never Givin' Up On Love	Desperation Road	—	$4	■	Warner 22970
				from the movie *Pink Cadillac* starring **Clint Eastwood**					
10/7/89	48	11		26 Family Tree	Woodsmoke In The Wind	—	$4		Warner 22765
1/6/90	67	3		27 Route 66	Jukebox	—	$4		Warner 22666
				#11 Pop hit for **Nat "King" Cole** in 1946					
9/8/90	52	11		28 Cowboy Logic	Spanish Is The Lovin' Tongue	—	$4	■	Warner 19724 **(v)**
3/16/91	74	1		29 Let The Cowboy Dance	Red River Valley	—	$4		Warner 19412

DEBUT	PEAK	WKS	Gold	A-side (Chart Hit)	B-side	Pop	$	Pic	Label & Number
	★316★			**MURPHY, David Lee** '95 Born on 1/7/59 in Herrin, Illinois. Singer/songwriter/guitarist. 1)Dust On The Bottle 2)Every Time I Get Around You 3)The Road You Leave Behind					
3/5/94	36	20		1 Just Once..High Weeds And Rust		—	$4	■	MCA 54794 (v)
8/20/94	52	7		2 Fish Ain't Bitin'..Why Can't People Just Get Along		—	$4	■	MCA 54877 (v)
3/18/95	6	22		3 Party Crowd..S:5 Can't Turn It Off		—	$4	■	MCA 54977 (v)
8/12/95	●²	20		4 Dust On The Bottle...S:13 Mama 'N Them		—	$4	■	MCA 54944 (v)
11/25/95+	13	20		5 Out With A Bang..Greatest Show On Earth		—	$4		MCA 55153
3/23/96	2¹	20		6 Every Time I Get Around You...................................Pirates Cove		—	$4		MCA 55186
8/3/96	5	20		7 The Road You Leave Behind................Gettin' Out The Good Stuff		—	$4		MCA 55205
1/25/97	53	5		8 Genuine Rednecks...(long version)		—	$4		MCA 55269
3/15/97	51	7		9 Breakfast In Birmingham...........................100 Years Too Late		—	$4		MCA 72000
7/5/97	25	20		10 All Lit Up In Love.............................She's Really Something To See		—	$4		MCA 72008
11/15/97+	37	20		11 Just Don't Wait Around Til She's Leavin'......................Kentucky Girl		—	$4		MCA 72024
				MURPHY, Jimmy '87					
10/25/86	74	4		1 Two Sides...............................What Would The World Be Without Music?		—	$5		Encore 10033
1/31/87	51	9		2 Keep The Faith......................What Would The World Be Without Music?		—	$5		Encore 10036
				MURPHY, Vern '73					
7/28/73	96	2		Blue And Lonely..Don't Cheat On Me		—	$7		Sunset 0021

MURRAY, Anne ★56★ '79
Born Morna Anne Murray on 6/20/45 in Springhill, Nova Scotia, Canada. High school gym teacher for one year after college. With CBC-TV show *Sing Along Jubilee*. First recorded for Arc in 1968. Regular on **Glen Campbell**'s TV series. CMA Award: 1985 Vocal Duo of the Year (with **Dave Loggins**).

1)I Just Fall In Love Again 2)He Thinks I Still Care 3)Nobody Loves Me Like You Do 4)Blessed Are The Believers 5)Just Another Woman In Love

DEBUT	PEAK	WKS	Gold	A-side	B-side	Pop	$	Pic	Label & Number
7/25/70	10	19	●	1 Snowbird..Just Bidin' My Time		8	$6		Capitol 2738
1/16/71	53	5		2 Sing High - Sing Low.......................Days Of The Looking Glass		83	$6		Capitol 2988
3/20/71	27	12		3 A Stranger In My Place.............................Sycamore Slick		122	$6		Capitol 3059
				written by **Kenny Rogers**; also see #14 below					
5/22/71	67	2		4 Put Your Hand In The Hand........................It Takes Time		—	$6		Capitol 3082
				#2 Pop hit for Ocean in 1971					
10/30/71	40	8		5 I Say A Little Prayer/By The Time I Get To Phoenix......All Through The Night		81	$6		Capitol 3200
				GLEN CAMPBELL/ANNE MURRAY "I Say A Little Prayer" was a #4 Pop hit for Dionne Warwick in 1967					
1/22/72	11	15		6 Cotton Jenny..Destiny		71	$6		Capitol 3260
12/23/72+	10	17		7 Danny's Song..Drown Me		7	$5		Capitol 3481
				first recorded by **Loggins & Messina** on their 1972 album *Sittin' In*					
6/2/73	20	10		8 What About Me..................................Let Sunshine Have Its Day		64	$5		Capitol 3600
8/25/73	79	7		9 Send A Little Love My Way....................Head Above The Water		72	$5		Capitol 3648
				from the movie *Oklahoma Crude* starring George C. Scott					
12/22/73+	5	15		10 Love Song..You Can't Go Back		12	$5		Capitol 3776
				first recorded by **Loggins & Messina** on their 1973 album *Full Sail*					
4/27/74	●²	17		11 He Thinks I Still Care.....................You Won't See Me (Pop #8)		—	$5		Capitol 3867
9/28/74	5	16		12 Son Of A Rotten Gambler..............Just One Look (Pop #86)		—	$5		Capitol 3955
2/15/75	28	10		13 Uproar...Lift Your Hearts To The Sun		—	$5		Capitol 4025
6/7/75	79	6		14 A Stranger In My Place..........................Dream Lover [R]		—	$5		Capitol 4072
				same version as #3 above					
10/25/75	49	9		15 Sunday Sunrise...................................Out On The Road Again		98	$5		Capitol 4142
2/7/76	19	14		16 The Call..Lady Bug		91	$5		Capitol 4207
5/29/76	41	8		17 Golden Oldie...Together		—	$5		Capitol 4265
9/11/76+	22	12		18 Things..Caress Me Pretty Music		89	$5		Capitol 4329
				#3 Pop hit for **Bobby Darin** in 1962					
2/5/77	57	8		19 Sunday School To Broadway........................Dancin' All Night Long		—	$5		Capitol 4375
1/21/78	4	16		20 Walk Right Back...A Million More		103	$5		Capitol 4527
				#7 Pop hit for The Everly Brothers in 1961					
5/13/78	4	18	●	21 You Needed Me..................I Still Wish The Very Best For You		●¹	$4		Capitol 4574
1/27/79	●³	15		22 I Just Fall In Love Again................Just To Feel This Love From You		12	$4	■	Capitol 4675
5/19/79	●¹	15		23 Shadows In The Moonlight..............................Yucatan Cafe		25	$4		Capitol 4716
9/29/79	●¹	14		24 Broken Hearted Me........................Why Don't You Stick Around		12	$4		Capitol 4773
1/5/80	3	14		25 Daydream Believer........................Do You Think Of Me		12	$4		Capitol 4813
				#1 Pop hit for The Monkees in 1967					
4/5/80	9	14		26 Lucky Me...Somebody's Waiting		42	$4		Capitol 4848
6/28/80	23	11		27 I'm Happy Just To Dance With You..............What's Forever For		64	$4		Capitol 4878
				#95 Pop hit for The Beatles in 1964					
9/6/80	●¹	16		28 Could I Have This Dance.............................Somebody's Waiting		33	$4	■	Capitol 4920
				from the movie *Urban Cowboy* starring John Travolta					
4/4/81	●¹	14		29 Blessed Are The Believers..............................Only Love		34	$4	■	Capitol 4987
7/4/81	16	13		30 We Don't Have To Hold Out..................Call Me With The News		—	$4	■	Capitol 5013
9/12/81	9	15		31 It's All I Can Do...............................If A Heart Must Be Broken		53	$4		Capitol 5023
1/16/82	4	18		32 Another Sleepless Night..............................It Should Have Been Easy		44	$4		Capitol 5083

DEBUT	PEAK	WKS	Gold	A-side (Chart Hit)	B-side	Pop	$	Pic	Label & Number
				MURRAY, Anne — Cont'd					
7/31/82	7	16		33 Hey! Baby!	Song For The Mira	—	$4	■	Capitol 5145
				#1 Pop hit for Bruce Channel in 1962					
11/20/82+	7	19		34 Somebody's Always Saying Goodbye	That'll Keep Me Dreamin'	—	$4		Capitol 5183
9/17/83	●¹	20		35 A Little Good News	I'm Not Afraid Anymore	74	$4	■	Capitol 5264
				CMA Award: Single of the Year					
2/4/84	46	12		36 That's Not The Way (It's S'posed To Be)	The More We Try	106	$4		Capitol 5305
4/28/84	●¹	20		37 Just Another Woman In Love	Heart Stealer	—	$4	■	Capitol 5344
9/8/84	●¹	22		38 Nobody Loves Me Like You Do S:●¹ / A:●¹ Love You Out Of Your Mind (Murray)		103	$4	■	Capitol 5401
				ANNE MURRAY (WITH DAVE LOGGINS)					
1/19/85	2¹	22		39 Time Don't Run Out On Me S:2 / A:3 Let Your Heart Do The Talking		—	$4	■	Capitol 5436
5/18/85	7	20		40 I Don't Think I'm Ready For You A:6 / S:7 Take Good Care Of My Heart		—	$4	■	Capitol 5472
				from the movie *Stick* starring Burt Reynolds					
1/25/86	●¹	19		41 Now And Forever (You And Me)					
				S:●¹ / A:2 I Don't Wanna Spend Another Night Without You		92	$4	■	Capitol 5547
5/24/86	62	9		42 Who's Leaving Who	Reach For Me	—	$4	■	Capitol 5576
8/23/86	26	15		43 My Life's A Dance	A:24 Call Us Fools	—	$4	■	Capitol 5610
12/27/86+	23	14		44 On And On	A:23 Gotcha	—	$4		Capitol 5655
5/9/87	20	23		45 Are You Still In Love With Me	S:12 Give Me Your Love	—	$4	■	Capitol 44005
8/29/87	27	13		46 Anyone Can Do The Heartbreak	Without You	—	$4		Capitol 44053
2/20/88	52	8		47 Perfect Strangers	It Happens All The Time	—	$4		Capitol 44134
				ANNE MURRAY (With Doug Mallory)					
9/3/88	52	7		48 Flying On Your Own	Slow All Night	—	$4	■	Capitol 44219
11/26/88+	36	12		49 Slow Passin' Time	Flying On Your Own	—	$4		Capitol 44272
3/25/89	55	9		50 Who But You	You Make Me Curious	—	$4		Capitol 44341
9/30/89	28	15		51 If I Ever Fall In Love Again	Just Another Woman In Love	—	$4		Capitol 44432
				ANNE MURRAY with Kenny Rogers					
8/25/90	5	20		52 Feed This Fire		—			album cut
12/8/90+	39	19		53 Bluebird		—			album cut
				above 2 from the album *You Will* on Capitol 94102					
10/5/91	56	11		54 Everyday		—			album cut
				from the album *Yes I Do* on Capitol 96310					
				MUSIC ROW **'81**					
				Duo of Glen Gill and Bill Pippin.					
3/7/81	86	4		1 There Ain't A Song		—	$6		Debut 8013
5/16/81	92	2		2 Lady's Man		—	$6		Debut 8115
6/27/81	88	3		3 It's Not The Rain		—	$6		Debut 8116
				MYERS, Frank **'74**					
				Born in Snowdoun, Alabama; raised in Montgomery, Alabama. Singer/songwriter.					
8/3/74	82	7		Hangin' On To What I've Got	She'll Have Sunshine Where She Goes	—	$6		Caprice 1999
				MYLES, Heather **'99**					
				Born in Riverside, California.					
1/30/99	75	1		Love Me A Little Bit Longer		—			album cut
				from the album *Highways & Honky Tonks* on Rounder/Mercury 3147					

N

DEBUT	PEAK	WKS	Gold	A-side	B-side	Pop	$	Pic	Label & Number
				NAIL, Linda **'79**					
				Born Linda Naile on 1/19/54 in Wabash, Arkansas.					
12/9/78+	58	9		1 Me Touchin' You	A Woman And A Man	—	$5		Ridgetop 00178
3/10/79	67	5		2 There Hangs His Hat	The Love Line's Slippin'	—	$5		Ridgetop 00279
2/5/83	85	2		3 You're A Part Of Me	Let It Be Me	—	$6		Grand Prix 2
				DANNY WHITE & LINDA NAIL					
5/14/83	80	4		4 Reminiscing	I Go To Pieces	—	$6		Grand Prix 3
				NAILL, Jerry **'80**					
2/2/80	92	4		Her Cheatin Heart (Made A Drunken Fool Of Me)		—	$7		El Dorado 156
				NALL, Jimmy — see **LANE, Terri**					
				NASH, Bill **'81**					
				Born in Pharr, Texas.					
7/4/81	79	4		1 Burning Bridges	Saturday Night Live	—	$4		Liberty 1410
				#3 Pop hit for Jack Scott in 1960					
10/17/81	61	6		2 Slippin' Out, Slippin' In	Take Me As I Am	—	$4		Liberty 1433
5/22/82	65	6		3 Survivor	I Don't Want To Hear A Heartache Song Again	—	$4		Liberty 1463
				NASH, Linda **'73**					
10/27/73	83	10		Country Boogie Woogie	Good Things Just Don't Last	—	$6		Ace of Hearts 0473
				NASHVILLE BRASS — see **DAVIS, Danny**					
				NASHVILLE NIGHTSHIFT **'85**					
8/31/85	89	2		Nightshift		—	$6		NCA 133737
				tribute to Marty Robbins; #3 Pop hit for the Commodores in 1985					

DEBUT	PEAK	WKS	Gold	A-side (Chart Hit)	B-side	Pop	$	Pic	Label & Number
				NASHVILLE SUPERPICKERS '81					
				Group of top Nashville session musicians: **Phil Baugh** (guitar), **Buddy Emmons** (steel guitar), **Charlie McCoy** (harmonica), Johnny Gimble (fiddle), **Hargus "Pig" Robbins** (piano), Russ Hicks (guitar), Henry Strzelecki (bass) and Buddy Harman (drums).					
2/7/81	83	2		1 New York Cowboy ....Sexy Southern Lady		—	$6		Sound Factory 426
				NAYLOR, Jerry '75					
				Born on 3/6/39 in Stephenville, Texas. Singer/songwriter/bassist.					
				1)Is This All There Is To A Honky Tonk? 2)If You Don't Want To Love Her 3)The Last Time You Love Me					
1/25/75	27	12		1 Is This All There Is To A Honky Tonk? .... You're The One		—	$5		Melodyland 6003
10/2/76	94	2		2 The Bad Part Of Me...I Hate To Drink Alone		—	$5		Hitsville 6041
12/4/76+	50	9		3 The Last Time You Love Me ....Born To Fool Around		—	$5		Hitsville 6046
2/4/78	37	9		4 If You Don't Want To Love Her ....Love Away Her Memory Tonight		—	$5		MC/Curb 5004
5/27/78	80	4		5 Rave On /			—		
				#37 Pop hit for Buddy Holly in 1958					
		2		6 Lady, Would You Like To Dance		—	$5		MC/Curb 5010
3/24/79	54	5		7 But For Love...Part Time Lover, Part Time Fool		—	$5		Warner/Curb 8767
				new version of his #69 Pop hit from 1970					
7/7/79	72	4		8 She Wears It Well......................................Part Time Lover, Full Time Heartache		—	$5		Warner/Curb 8881
11/17/79	69	4		9 Don't Touch Me ....Never Been To Spain		—	$6		Jeremiah 1002
				JERRY NAYLOR/KELLI WARREN					
3/8/80	61	5		10 Cheating Eyes ....America, I'm Coming Home To You		—	$6		Oak 1014
11/29/86	75	4		11 For Old Time Sake ....I Want To Be Loved		—	$6		West 723
				NEEDMORE CREEK SINGERS — see ARNOLD, Eddy					
				NEEL, Jo Anna '72					
				Born in Buckeye, Arizona.					
11/13/71	68	5		1 Daddy Was A Preacher But Mama Was A Go-Go Girl ......A Perfect Stranger		—	$7		Decca 32865
4/22/72	44	10		2 One More Time ....The Sparrow And Me		—	$7		Decca 32950
				NEELY, Sam '74					
				Born on 8/22/48 in Cuero, Texas. Singer/songwriter/guitarist.					
9/14/74	49	12		1 You Can Have Her ....It's A Fine Morning	34		$6		A&M 1612
2/1/75	61	8		2 I Fought The Law ....Guitar Man	54		$6		A&M 1651
				#9 Pop hit for the Bobby Fuller Four in 1966					
9/10/77	98	3		3 Sail Away ....My Lover And My Friend	84		$5		Elektra 45419
3/12/83	78	4		4 The Party's Over (Everybody's Gone) ....What Do I Tell My Heart		—	$4		MCA 52194
				tribute to the final episode of TV's *M*A*S*H* which aired on 2/28/83					
6/18/83	77	5		5 When You Leave That Way You Can Never Go Back ..The Music Made Me Do It		—	$4		MCA 52226
1/21/84	81	3		6 Old Photographs ....Somebody's Leavin'		—	$4		MCA 52323
				NELSON, Bonnie '86					
				Born in 1949 in Denver.					
12/6/86	83	3		1 Don't Let It Go To Your Heart...Willie, Where Are You		—	$5		Door Knob 257
5/23/87	84	2		2 More Than Friendly Persuasion ....If You Want To Be Loved		—	$5		Door Knob 264
				NELSON, Nikki '97					
				Born on 1/3/69 in San Diego; raised in Topaz City, Nevada. Female singer. Former lead singer of **Highway 101**.					
3/15/97	62	5		Too Little Too Much		—	$4	■	Columbia 78519
				NELSON, Ricky '58					
				Born Eric Hilliard Nelson on 5/8/40 in Teaneck, New Jersey. Died on 12/31/85 (age 45) in a plane crash in DeKalb, Texas. Son of bandleader Ozzie Nelson and vocalist Harriet Hilliard. Rick and brother David appeared on Nelson's radio show from March 1949; later on TV from 1952-66. Formed own Stone Canyon Band in 1969. In movies *Rio Bravo*, *The Wackiest Ship In The Army* and *Love And Kisses*. Married Kristin Harmon (sister of actor Mark Harmon) in 1963; divorced in 1982. Their daughter Tracy is an actress. Their twin sons, Matthew and Gunnar, began recording as Nelson in 1990. Charted 54 pop hits from 1957-73. Inducted into the Rock and Roll Hall of Fame in 1987.					
				1)Poor Little Fool 2)Stood Up 3)My Bucket's Got A Hole In It					
1/20/58	8	12	●	1 Stood Up / S:8	2³				
1/20/58	12	6		2 Waitin' In School S:12	18		$25	■	Imperial 5483
4/14/58	10	11		3 My Bucket's Got A Hole In It / S:10	12				
4/14/58	10	10	●	4 Believe What You Say S:10	4		$25	■	Imperial 5503
7/7/58	3	15	●	5 Poor Little Fool S:3 / A:8 Don't Leave Me This Way	❶²		$25	■	Imperial 5528
				RICK NELSON:					
6/10/67	58	5		6 Take A City Bride ....I'm Called Lonely		—	$15	■	Decca 32120
9/16/72	44	9	●	7 Garden Party ....So Long Mama	6		$10		Decca 32980
5/11/74	89	2		8 One Night Stand ....Lifestream		—	$8		MCA 40214
				RICK NELSON & THE STONE CANYON BAND (above 2)					
4/21/79	59	9		9 Dream Lover..That Ain't The Way Love's Supposed To Be		—	$6		Epic 50674
				#2 Pop hit for **Bobby Darin** in 1959					
7/12/86	88	7		10 Dream Lover...Rave On [R]		—	$5	■	Epic 06066
				above 2 are the same version					
				NELSON, Terry — see C COMPANY					

Big Chief Buffalo Nickel

DEBUT	PEAK	WKS	Gold	A-side (Chart Hit)	B-side	Pop	$	Pic	Label & Number

NELSON, Willie ★10★ '78

Born on 4/30/33 in Abbott, Texas. Singer/songwriter/guitarist/actor. Played bass for **Ray Price**'s band. Acted in the several movies. Formerly married to **Shirley Collie**. CMA Awards: 1976 Vocal Duo of the Year (with **Waylon Jennings**); 1979 Entertainer of the Year; 1983 Vocal Duo of the Year (with **Merle Haggard**); 1984 Vocal Duo of the Year (with **Julio Iglesias**). Won Grammy's Living Legends Award in 1989. Elected to the Country Music Hall of Fame in 1993. Also see **Some Of Chet's Friends** and **USA For Africa**.

1) Mammas Don't Let Your Babies Grow Up To Be Cowboys   2) Good Hearted Woman   3) To All The Girls I've Loved Before
4) Blue Eyes Crying In The Rain   5) My Heroes Have Always Been Cowboys

DEBUT	PEAK	WKS	#	A-side	B-side	Pop	$	Label & Number
3/17/62	10	13	1	**Willingly** — WILLIE NELSON & SHIRLEY COLLIE	Chain Of Love	—	$20	Liberty 55403
5/26/62	7	13	2	**Touch Me**	Where My House Lives	109	$15	Liberty 55439
4/6/63	25	5	3	**Half A Man**	The Last Letter	129	$15	Liberty 55532
1/18/64	33	3	4	**You Took My Happy Away**	How Long Is Forever	—	$20	Liberty 55638
5/8/65	43	5	5	**She's Not For You**	Permanently Lonely	—	$15	RCA Victor 8519
10/16/65	48	2	6	**I Just Can't Let You Say Goodbye**	And So Will You My Love	—	$15	RCA Victor 8682
10/1/66	19	13	7	**One In A Row**	San Antonio Rose	—	$15	RCA Victor 8933
3/4/67	24	16	8	**The Party's Over**	Make Way For A Better Man	—	$15	RCA Victor 9100
6/24/67	21	11	9	**Blackjack County Chain**	Some Other World	—	$12	RCA Victor 9202
10/21/67	50	9	10	**San Antonio**	To Make A Long Story Short (She's Gone)	—	$12	RCA Victor 9324
2/10/68	22	11	11	**Little Things**	I'll Stay Around	—	$12	RCA Victor 9427
6/15/68	44	8	12	**Good Times** — also see #68 below	Don't You Ever Get Tired (Of Hurting Me)	—	$12	RCA Victor 9536
9/7/68	36	7	13	**Johnny One Time**	She's Still Gone	—	$10	RCA Victor 9605
12/21/68+	13	14	14	**Bring Me Sunshine**	Don't Say Love Or Nothing	—	$10	RCA Victor 9684
12/13/69+	36	9	15	**I Hope So** — recorded in 1963	Right Or Wrong	—	$10	Liberty 56143
3/14/70	42	9	16	**Once More With Feeling**	Who Do I Know In Dallas	—	$10	RCA Victor 9798
11/28/70	68	2	17	**Laying My Burdens Down**	Truth Number One	—	$10	RCA Victor 9903
2/6/71	28	11	18	**I'm A Memory** — also see #38 below	I'm So Lonesome I Could Cry	—	$10	RCA Victor 9951
10/23/71	62	7	19	**Yesterday's Wine /**		—		
		4	20	**Me And Paul** — also see #94 below		—	$10	RCA Victor 0542
2/19/72	73	2	21	**The Words Don't Fit The Picture**	A Moment Isn't Very Long	—	$10	RCA Victor 0635
7/14/73	60	5	22	**Shotgun Willie**	Sad Songs And Waltzes	—	$8	Atlantic 2968
9/29/73	22	13	23	**Stay All Night (Stay A Little Longer)** ★	Devil In A Sleepin' Bag	—	$8	Atlantic 2979
2/16/74	51	5	24	**I Still Can't Believe You're Gone**	Heaven And Hell	—	$8	Atlantic 3008
4/6/74	17	13	25	**Bloody Mary Morning**	Phases And Stages / Washing The Dishes / Phases And Stages	—	$8	Atlantic 3020
8/17/74	17	11	26	**After The Fire Is Gone** — WILLIE NELSON & TRACY NELSON	Whiskey River	—	$8	Atlantic 4028
12/7/74	93	3	27	**Sister's Coming Home**	Pick Up The Tempo	—	$8	Atlantic 3228
7/19/75	❶²	18	28	**Blue Eyes Crying In The Rain**	Bandera	21	$7	Columbia 10176
11/15/75+	29	11	29	**Fire And Rain** — #3 Pop hit for **James Taylor** in 1970	I'm A Memory	—	$6	RCA Victor 10429
12/27/75+	❶³	17	30	**Good Hearted Woman** — WAYLON & WILLIE — CMA Award: Single of the Year	Heaven Or Hell	25	$6	RCA Victor 10529
1/3/76	2¹	15	31	**Remember Me**	Time Of The Preacher	67	$7	Columbia 10275
3/27/76	46	7	32	**The Last Letter**	There Goes A Man	—	$6	United Artists 771
4/17/76	55	6	33	**I Gotta Get Drunk** — "live" recording	Summer Of Roses	101	$7	RCA Victor 10591
5/1/76	11	13	34	**I'd Have To Be Crazy**	Amazing Grace	—	$5	Columbia 10327
7/24/76	❶¹	15	35	**If You've Got The Money I've Got The Time**	The Sound In Your Mind	—	$5	Columbia 10383
12/18/76+	4	14	36	**Uncloudy Day**	Precious Memories	—	$5	Columbia 10453
3/12/77	32	13	37	**Lily Dale** — DARRELL McCALL & WILLIE NELSON	Please Don't Leave Me	—	$5	Columbia 10480
5/14/77	22	11	38	**I'm A Memory** — same version as #18 above	It Should Be Easier Now [R]	—	$5	RCA 10969
7/30/77	9	12	39	**I Love You A Thousand Ways**	Mom And Dad's Waltz	—	$5	Columbia 10588
9/10/77	16	13	40	**You Ought To Hear Me Cry**	One In A Row	—	$5	RCA 11061
11/19/77+	9	16	41	**Something To Brag About** — MARY KAY PLACE with Willie Nelson	Anybody's Darlin'	—	$5	Columbia 10644
1/21/78	❶⁴	16	42	**Mammas Don't Let Your Babies Grow Up To Be Cowboys /**		42		
		15	43	**I Can Get Off On You** — WAYLON & WILLIE (above 2)		—	$5	RCA 11198
3/18/78	5	15	44	**If You Can Touch Her At All**	Rainy Day Blues	104	$5	RCA 11235
3/25/78	❶¹	16	45	**Georgia On My Mind** — #1 Pop hit for **Ray Charles** in 1960	On The Sunny Side Of The Street	84	$5	Columbia 10704
7/15/78	❶¹	13	46	**Blue Skies** — #1 Pop hit for Ben Selvin in 1927	Moonlight In Vermont	—	$5	Columbia 10784
10/14/78	77	5	47	**Ain't Life Hell** — HANK COCHRAN & WILLIE NELSON	I'm Going With You This Time	—	$5	Capitol 4635
10/21/78	3	14	48	**All Of Me** — #1 Pop hit for Louis Armstrong in 1932	Unchained Melody	—	$5	Columbia 10834
10/28/78	67	5	49	**Will You Remember Mine**	The End Of Understanding	—	$5	Lone Star 703
11/25/78	86	3	50	**There'll Be No Teardrops Tonight**	Blue Must Be The Color Of The Blues	—	$5	United Artists 1254

DEBUT	PEAK	WKS	Gold	A-side (Chart Hit) / B-side	Pop	$	Pic	Label & Number
				NELSON, Willie — Cont'd				
12/23/78+	12	12		51 Whiskey River / Under The Double Eagle "live" recording	—	$5		Columbia 10877
2/10/79	4	14		52 Sweet Memories / Little Things	—	$5		RCA 11465
4/14/79	15	12		53 September Song / Don't Get Around Much Anymore	—	$5		Columbia 10929
7/7/79	$\bullet$1	13		54 Heartbreak Hotel / Sioux City Sue WILLIE NELSON AND LEON RUSSELL	—	$5		Columbia 11023
8/18/79	16	13		55 Crazy Arms / Hurricane Shirley (Bobby Bare)	—	$5		RCA 11673
11/10/79+	4	14		56 Help Me Make It Through The Night / The Pilgrim: Chapter 33	—	$4		Columbia 11126
1/12/80	$\bullet$2	14		57 My Heroes Have Always Been Cowboys / Rising Star (Love Theme) from the movie *The Electric Horseman* starring Robert Redford	44	$4		Columbia 11186
2/2/80	20	12		58 Night Life / December Day DANNY DAVIS AND WILLIE NELSON With The Nashville Brass	—	$5		RCA 11893
5/3/80	6	15		59 Midnight Rider / So You Think You're A Cowboy #19 Pop hit for Gregg Allman in 1974	—	$4		Columbia 11257
5/17/80	41	8		60 Funny How Time Slips Away / The Local Memory DANNY DAVIS AND WILLIE NELSON with The Nashville Brass	—	$5		RCA 11999
8/9/80	3	15		61 Faded Love / This Cold War With You WILLIE NELSON AND RAY PRICE	—	$4		Columbia 11329
8/30/80	$\bullet$1	16		62 On The Road Again / Jumpin' Cotton Eyed Joe (Johnny Gimble) from the movie *Honeysuckle Rose* starring Nelson	20	$4		Columbia 11351
10/4/80	92	2		63 Family Bible / In God's Eyes	—	$4		Songbird 41313
12/6/80+	11	14		64 Don't You Ever Get Tired (Of Hurting Me) / Funny How Time Slips Away WILLIE NELSON AND RAY PRICE	—	$4		Columbia 11405
1/10/81	$\bullet$1	14		65 Angel Flying Too Close To The Ground / I Guess I've Come To Live Here from the movie *Honeysuckle Rose* starring Nelson	—	$4		Columbia 11418
2/28/81	65	6		66 There's A Crazy Man / — JODY PAYNE & The Willie Nelson Family Band	—	$4		Kari 117
4/18/81	11	12		67 Mona Lisa / Twinkle, Twinkle Little Star #1 Pop hit for Nat King Cole in 1950	—	$4		Columbia 02000
6/27/81	25	12		68 Good Times / Where Do You Stand? [R] same version as #12 above	—	$4	■	RCA 12254
7/25/81	26	11		69 I'm Gonna Sit Right Down And Write Myself A Letter / Over The Rainbow #3 Pop hit for Billy Williams in 1957	—	$4		Columbia 02187
10/3/81	23	12		70 Mountain Dew / Laying My Burdens Down	—	$4		RCA 12328
11/14/81	39	10		71 Heartaches Of A Fool / Uncloudy Day	—	$4		Columbia 02558
3/6/82	$\bullet$2	21 ▲		72 Always On My Mind / The Party's Over CMA Award: Single of the Year	5	$4		Columbia 02741
3/13/82	$\bullet$2	18		73 Just To Satisfy You / Get Naked With Me (Waylon) WAYLON & WILLIE	52	$4		RCA 13073
6/5/82	19	16		74 Old Friends / When A House Is Not A Home ROGER MILLER & WILLIE NELSON (with Ray Price)	—	$4		Columbia 02681
8/14/82	2²	17		75 Let It Be Me / Permanently Lonely #7 Pop hit for The Everly Brothers in 1960	40	$4		Columbia 03073
10/9/82	72	5		76 In The Jailhouse Now / Back Street Affair WILLIE NELSON & WEBB PIERCE	—	$4		Columbia 03231
10/23/82	13	15		77 (Sittin' On) The Dock Of The Bay / Luckenbach, Texas WAYLON & WILLIE #1 Pop hit for Otis Redding in 1968	—	$4		RCA 13319
12/4/82+	2²	20		78 Last Thing I Needed First Thing This Morning / Old Fords And A Natural Stone	—	$4		Columbia 03385
12/11/82+	7	20		79 Everything's Beautiful (In It's Own Way) / Put It Off Until Tomorrow (Dolly Parton/Kris Kristofferson) DOLLY PARTON/WILLIE NELSON	102	$5		Monument 03408
1/15/83	6	18		80 Reasons To Quit / Half A Man MERLE HAGGARD AND WILLIE NELSON	—	$4		Epic 03494
3/12/83	10	16		81 Little Old Fashioned Karma / Beer Barrel Polka	—	$4		Columbia 03674
4/9/83	43	9		82 You're Gonna Love Yourself (In The Morning) / What Do You Think About Lovin' WILLIE NELSON/BRENDA LEE	—	$4		Monument 03781
4/30/83	$\bullet$1	21		83 Pancho And Lefty / Opportunity To Cry WILLIE NELSON AND MERLE HAGGARD	—	$4		Epic 03842
6/18/83	3	21		84 Why Do I Have To Choose / Would You Lay With Me (In A Field Of Stone)	—	$4		Columbia 03965
10/8/83	8	19		85 Take It To The Limit / Till I Gain Control Again WILLIE NELSON & WAYLON JENNINGS #4 Pop hit for the Eagles in 1976	102	$4	■	Columbia 04131
12/24/83+	11	16		86 Without A Song / I Can't Begin To Tell You #6 Pop hit for Paul Whiteman in 1930	—	$4		Columbia 04263
3/10/84	$\bullet$2	20 ▲		87 To All The Girls I've Loved Before / I Don't Want To Wake You (Iglesias) JULIO IGLESIAS & WILLIE NELSON	5	$4	■	Columbia 04217
8/18/84	$\bullet$1	25		88 City Of New Orleans / A:$\bullet$² / S:$\bullet$¹ Why Are You Pickin' On Me #18 Pop hit for Arlo Guthrie in 1972	—	$4	■	Columbia 04568
10/27/84	91	2		89 Wabash Cannonball / Tennessee Waltz WILLIE NELSON & HANK WILSON	—	$4		Paradise 629
11/3/84	46	11		90 How Do You Feel About Foolin' Around / Eye Of The Storm WILLIE NELSON & KRIS KRISTOFFERSON	—	$4		Columbia 04652
12/15/84+	$\bullet$1	27		91 Seven Spanish Angels / S:$\bullet$¹ / A:$\bullet$¹ Who Cares RAY CHARLES (with WILLIE NELSON)	—	$4		Columbia 04715
4/13/85	$\bullet$1	22		92 Forgiving You Was Easy / S:$\bullet$¹ / A:$\bullet$¹ You Wouldn't Cross The Street	—	$4		Columbia 04847
5/18/85	$\bullet$1	20		93 Highwayman / S:$\bullet$¹ / A:$\bullet$¹ The Human Condition WAYLON JENNINGS/WILLIE NELSON/JOHNNY CASH/KRIS KRISTOFFERSON	—	$4	■	Columbia 04881
9/14/85	14	19		94 Me And Paul / A:11 / S:14 I Let My Mind Wander [R] new version of #20 above	—	$4		Columbia 05597

DEBUT	PEAK	WKS	Gold	A-side (Chart Hit)	B-side	Pop	$	Pic	Label & Number
				NELSON, Willie — Cont'd					
9/14/85	15	18		95 Desperados Waiting For A Train....S:15 / A:16 *The Twentieth Century Is Almost Over*		—	$4		Columbia 05594
				WAYLON JENNINGS/WILLIE NELSON/JOHNNY CASH/KRIS KRISTOFFERSON					
3/29/86	❶¹	20		96 Living In The Promiseland .... A:❶¹ / S:2 *Bach Minuet In G*		—	$4		Columbia 05834
8/2/86	56	8		97 I've Already Cheated On You .... S:29 *Take My Advice*		—	$4		Columbia 06227
				DAVID ALLAN COE and WILLIE NELSON					
8/9/86	21	17		98 I'm Not Trying To Forget You .... A:21 / S:28 *I've Got The Craziest Feeling*		—	$4		Columbia 06246
12/6/86+	24	13		99 Partners After All .... S:17 / A:24 *Home Away From Home*		—	$4		Columbia 06530
3/21/87	44	11		100 Heart Of Gold .... *So Much Like My Dad*		—	$4		Columbia 07007
				#1 Pop hit for **Neil Young** in 1972					
7/11/87	27	12		101 Island In The Sea .... S:20 *There Is No Easy Way (But There Is A Way)*		—	$4		Columbia 07202
9/19/87	58	5		102 If I Could Only Fly .... *Without You On My Side*		—	$4		Epic 07400
				MERLE HAGGARD & WILLIE NELSON					
1/9/88	82	3		103 Nobody There But Me .... *Wake Me When It's Over*		—	$4		Columbia 07636
9/17/88	8	19		104 Spanish Eyes .... S:2 *Ole Buttermilk Sky*		—	$4		Columbia 08066
				WILLIE NELSON (with Julio Iglesias)					
				#15 Pop hit for **Al Martino** in 1966					
1/21/89	41	8		105 Twilight Time .... *Ac-Cent-Tchu-Ate The Positive*		—	$4		Columbia 08541
				#1 Pop hit for **The Platters** in 1958					
6/10/89	❶¹	21		106 Nothing I Can Do About It Now .... *If I Were A Painting*		—	$4		Columbia 68923
10/7/89+	8	26		107 There You Are .... *Spirit*		—	$4		Columbia 73015
2/24/90	52	13		108 The Highway .... *Spirit*		—	$4		Columbia 73249
3/3/90	25	14		109 Silver Stallion .... *American Remains*		—	$4		Columbia 73233
				WAYLON JENNINGS/WILLIE NELSON/JOHNNY CASH/KRIS KRISTOFFERSON					
9/29/90	17	20		110 Ain't Necessarily So .... *I Never Cared For You*		—	$4	■	Columbia 73518 (v)
1/19/91	70	3		111 The Piper Came Today .... *(I Don't Have A Reason) To Go To California Anymore*		—	$4		Columbia 73655
3/16/91	45	12		112 Ten With A Two .... *You Decide*		—	$4		Columbia 73749
6/15/91	51	10		113 If I Can Find A Clean Shirt .... *Put Me On A Train Back To Texas*		—	$4		Epic 73832
				WAYLON & WILLIE					
6/26/93	70	1		114 Graceland .... —					album cut
				#81 Pop hit for **Paul Simon** in 1987; from the album *Across The Borderline* on Columbia 52752					
	★355★			**NESBITT, Jim**			'64		
				Born on 12/1/31 in Bishopville, South Carolina. Singer/comedian. Known as "The 'Lasses Sopper."					
				1) *Looking For More In '64* 2) *Please Mr. Kennedy* 3) *A Tiger In My Tank*					
4/3/61	11	7		1 Please Mr. Kennedy .... *The Horse Race* [N]		—	$12		Dot 16197
				melody is the same as "The Ballad Of Davy Crockett"					
2/2/63	28	1		2 Livin' Offa Credit .... *I'm A Married Man* [N]		—	$12		Dot 16424
3/21/64	7	24		3 Looking For More In '64 .... *(Go On And) Cry Me A River* [N]		—	$8		Chart 1065
9/26/64	20	13		4 Mother-In-Law .... *If You Don't Love Me (Tell Me Now)* [N]		—	$8		Chart 1100
1/30/65	15	13		5 A Tiger In My Tank .... *I Can't Stand This Living Alone* [N]		—	$8		Chart 1165
6/26/65	34	6		6 Still Alive In '65 .... *I Laughed When You Said You Were Leaving* [N]		—	$8		Chart 1200
8/14/65	21	11		7 The Friendly Undertaker .... *Crying And Waiting For You* [N]		—	$8		Chart 1240
1/1/66	49	2		8 You Better Watch Your Friends .... *You're No Good* [N]		—	$8		Chart 1290
8/27/66	38	9		9 Heck Of A Fix In 66 .... *I'm From The Country* [N]		—	$8		Chart 1350
12/17/66+	60	6		10 Stranded .... *These Modern Things* [N]		—	$8		Chart 1410
6/10/67	74	2		11 Husbands-In-Law .... *I Want To Have My Operation On T-V* [N]		—	$8		Chart 1445
3/16/68	63	7		12 Truck Drivin' Cat With Nine Wives .... *Social Security* [N]		—	$8		Chart 1018
2/28/70	20	12		13 Runnin' Bare .... *A Good Woman Is Hard To Find* [N]		—	$8		Chart 5052
				novelty version of Johnny Preston's #1 Pop hit "Running Bear"					
				NESLER, Mark			'99		
				Born on 1/5/61 in Beaumont, Texas. Singer/songwriter/guitarist.					
6/6/98	47	15		1 Used To The Pain .... —					album cut
10/3/98+	46	19		2 Slow Down .... —					album cut
3/13/99	62	5		3 Baby Ain't Rocking Me Right .... —					album cut
				all of above from the album *I'm Just That Way* on Asylum 62223					
				NETTLES, Bill			'49		
				Born on 3/13/03 in Natchitoches, Louisiana. Died of a heart attack on 4/5/67 (age 64). Singer/songwriter.					
6/25/49	9	6		Hadacol Boogie .... J:9 *I'm Footloose Now*		—	$20		Mercury 6190
				BILL NETTLES and His Dixie Blue Boys					
				NEVILLE, Aaron			'93		
				Born on 1/24/41 in New Orleans. Black singer. Member of The Neville Brothers. Charted 9 pop hits from 1966-95.					
7/31/93	38	20		1 The Grand Tour .... *The Roadie Song*		90	$4	■	A&M 0312 (v)
6/4/94	72	2		2 I Fall To Pieces .... *(album version)*		—	$4		MCA 54836 (v)
				AARON NEVILLE AND TRISHA YEARWOOD					
				NEWBURY, Mickey			'73		
				Born Milton Newbury on 5/19/40 in Houston. Singer/prolific songwriter.					
6/23/73	53	8		1 Sunshine .... *Song For Susan*		87	$5		Elektra 45853
2/5/77	94	3		2 Hand Me Another Of Those .... *Leavin' Kentucky*		—	$5		ABC/Hickory 54006
4/8/78	94	3		3 Gone To Alabama .... *Westphalia Texas Waltz*		—	$5		ABC/Hickory 54025
3/24/79	82	4		4 Looking For The Sunshine .... *A Weed Is A Weed*		—	$5		ABC/Hickory 54042
6/16/79	81	4		5 Blue Sky Shinin' .... *Darlin' Take Care Of Yourself*		—	$5		MCA/Hickory 41032
2/9/80	82	3		6 America The Beautiful .... *Freedom*		—	$5		Hickory 1673
				written by poet Katherine Lee Bates at Pikes Peak in 1893					
10/15/88	93	2		7 An American Trilogy .... *San Francisco Mabel Joy*		—	$5		Airborne 10005
				new version of his #26 Pop hit from 1971					

DEBUT	PEAK	WKS	Gold	A-side (Chart Hit)	B-side	Pop	$	Pic	Label & Number
				NEW GRASS REVIVAL '89					
				Group of session musicians: John Cowan (vocals, bass; born on 8/24/52), Sam Bush (fiddle, mandolin; born on 4/15/52), Pat Flynn (guitar; born on 5/17/52) and Béla Fleck (banjo; born on 7/10/59).					
7/5/86	78	5		1 What You Do To Me	Sweet Release	—	$4		EMI America 8329
				#72 Pop hit for Carl Wilson in 1983					
9/20/86	53	8		2 Ain't That Peculiar	Seven By Seven	—	$4		EMI America 8347
				#8 Pop hit for Marvin Gaye in 1965					
10/3/87	44	9		3 Unconditional Love	I Can Talk To You	—	$4		Capitol 44078
3/5/88	45	11		4 Can't Stop Now	I Can Talk To You	—	$4		Capitol 44128
5/27/89	37	13		5 Callin' Baton Rouge	Let Me Be Your Man	—	$4		Capitol 44357
10/7/89	58	9		6 You Plant Your Fields	Friday Night In America	—	$4		Capitol 44453
				NEWMAN, Jack '59					
8/24/59	24	1		House Of Blue Lovers	I Didn't Think This Could Happen To Me	—	$30		TNT 170

				NEWMAN, Jimmy ★135★ '57					
				Born Jimmy Yves Newman on 8/27/27 in High Point, Louisiana. Singer/songwriter/guitarist. Regular on the *Louisiana Hayride*. Joined the *Grand Ole Opry* in 1956. The "C" in his stage name stands for Cajun.					
				1)A Fallen Star 2)Cry, Cry, Darling 3)A Lovely Work Of Art 4)Daydreamin' 5)Blue Darlin'					
5/22/54	4	11		1 Cry, Cry, Darling A:4 / J:8 / S:9	You Didn't Have To Go	—	$20		Dot 1195
				first released on Khoury's 530 in 1954 ($25)					
3/26/55	7	7		2 Daydreamin' J:7 / A:9 / S:13	Crying For A Pastime	—	$20		Dot 1237
7/9/55	7	10		3 Blue Darlin' A:7 / J:8 / S:13	Let Me Stay In Your Arms	—	$20		Dot 1260
12/17/55+	9	2		4 God Was So Good A:9	I Thought I'd Never Fall In Love Again	—	$20		Dot 1270
4/7/56	9	6		5 Seasons Of My Heart J:9 / A:10	Let's Stay Together	—	$20		Dot 1278
7/7/56	13	4		6 Come Back To Me A:13	I Wanta Tell All The World	—	$20		Dot 1283
5/20/57	2²	21		7 A Fallen Star A:2 / S:4 / J:9	I Can't Go On This Way	23	$20		Dot 1289
11/3/58+	7	16		8 You're Makin' A Fool Out Of Me	Outside Your Door	—	$15		MGM 12707
4/13/59	19	4		9 So Soon	What'cha Gonna Do	—	$15		MGM 12749
6/22/59	30	1		10 Lonely Girl	I'd Be Fool Enough	—	$15		MGM 12790
7/27/59	9	13		11 Grin And Bear It	The Ballad Of Baby Doe	—	$15		MGM 12812
11/2/59	29	1		12 Walkin' Down The Road	Angels Cryin'	—	$15		MGM 12830
3/7/60	21	7		13 I Miss You Already	The End Of The Line	—	$15		MGM 12864
6/20/60	6	14		14 A Lovely Work Of Art	What About Me	—	$15		MGM 12894
11/7/60	11	18		15 Wanting You With Me Tonight	Now That You're Gone	—	$15		MGM 12945
4/17/61	14	8		16 Everybody's Dying For Love	Just One More Night (With You)	—	$10		Decca 31217
12/25/61+	22	2		17 Alligator Man	Give Me Heaven	—	$10		Decca 31324
12/22/62+	12	9		18 Bayou Talk	I May Fall Again	—	$10		Decca 31440
12/14/63+	9	19		19 D.J. For A Day	The Mover	—	$10		Decca 31553
5/16/64	34	3		20 Angel On Leave /		—			
5/30/64	34	3		21 Summer Skies And Golden Sands		—	$10		Decca 31609
				JIMMY "C" NEWMAN (above 4)					
4/24/65	13	16		22 Back In Circulation /		—			
4/10/65	37	7		23 City Of The Angels		—	$8		Decca 31745
9/25/65	8	21		24 Artificial Rose	My Love For You	—	$8		Decca 31841
3/26/66	10	16		25 Back Pocket Money	For Better Or For Worse (But Not For Long)	—	$8		Decca 31916
10/8/66	25	8		26 Bring Your Heart Home	Unwanted Feeling	—	$8		Decca 31994
1/14/67	32	11		27 Dropping Out Of Sight	We Lose A Little Ground	—	$8		Decca 32067
5/27/67	24	12		28 Louisiana Saturday Night	Gentleman Loafer	—	$8		Decca 32130
10/28/67+	11	17		29 Blue Lonely Winter	The Devil Was Laughing At Me	—	$8		Decca 32202
4/13/68	47	8		30 Sunshine And Bluebirds	I'm Sorry Letters	—	$8		Decca 32285
8/31/68	20	13		31 Born To Love You	Carmelita	—	$8		Decca 32366
5/31/69	31	8		32 Boo Dan	Surrounded By Your Love	—	$8		Decca 32484
11/28/70	65	6		33 I'm Holding Your Memory (But He's Holding You)	It'll Take A Lot Of You	—	$8		Decca 32740
				NEWMAN, Randy '78					
				Born on 11/28/43 in New Orleans. Singer/songwriter/pianist. Nephew of composers Alfred, Emil and Lionel Newman.					
8/19/78	78	4		Rider In The Rain	Sigmund Freud's Impersonation Of Albert Einstein In America	—	$5		Warner 8630
				NEWMAN, Terri Sue '79					
				Born in 1954 in Levelland, Texas. Singer/pianist/guitarist.					
1/13/79	43	10		Gypsy Eyes	Time For One More Song	—	$7		Texas Soul 71378
				NEWSONG '00					
				Christian pop group formed in Kennesaw, Georgia: Eddie Carswell (vocals), Billy Goodwin and Leonard Ahlstrom (guitars), Scotty Wilbanks (sax, keyboards), Mark Clay (bass) and Jack Pumphrey (drums).					
12/16/00	31	5		The Christmas Shoes	[X]	—			album cut
				from the album *Sheltering Tree* on Benson 83327					

DEBUT	PEAK	WKS	Gold	A-side (Chart Hit)	B-side	Pop	$	Pic	Label & Number

NEWTON, Juice ★167★ '82
Born Judy Kay Newton on 2/18/52 in Lakehurst, New Jersey; raised in Virginia Beach. Singer/songwriter/guitarist. Formed group Dixie Peach, which later evolved into Silver Spur. Eventually adopted "Juice" as her legal name.

1) The Sweetest Thing (I've Ever Known) 2) Both To Each Other (Friends & Lovers) 3) Hurt
4) You Make Me Want To Make You Mine 5) Break It To Me Gently

DEBUT	PEAK	WKS		#	A-side	B-side	Pop	$	Pic	Label & Number
2/21/76	88	6		1	Love Is A Word ... The Sweetest Thing (I've Ever Known)		—	$5		RCA Victor 10538
					JUICE NEWTON & SILVER SPUR					
2/10/79	37	9		2	Let's Keep It That Way ... Tell My Baby Goodbye		—	$4		Capitol 4679
5/26/79	80	4		3	Lay Back In The Arms Of Someone ... It's Not Impossible		—	$4		Capitol 4714
9/15/79	81	4		4	Any Way That You Want Me ... The Dream Never Dies		—	$4		Capitol 4768
					#53 Pop hit for Evie Sands in 1969					
11/10/79	42	8		5	Until Tonight ... Lay Back In The Arms Of Someone		—	$4		Capitol 4793
2/2/80	35	10		6	Sunshine ... Go Easy On Me		—	$4		Capitol 4818
					#4 Pop hit for Jonathan Edwards in 1972					
4/26/80	41	10		7	You Fill My Life ... Tear It Up		—	$4		Capitol 4856
3/7/81	22	11	●	8	Angel Of The Morning ... Headin' For A Heartache		4	$4	■	Capitol 4976
6/13/81	14	16	●	9	Queen Of Hearts ... River Of Love		2²	$4	■	Capitol 4997
10/24/81+	❶¹	19		10	The Sweetest Thing (I've Ever Known) ... Ride 'Em Cowboy		7	$4	■	Capitol 5046
5/22/82	30	10		11	Love's Been A Little Bit Hard On Me ... Ever True		7	$4	■	Capitol 5120
8/28/82	2²	19		12	Break It To Me Gently ... Adios Mi Corazon		11	$4	■	Capitol 5148
12/11/82+	53	11		13	Heart Of The Night ... Love Sail Away		25	$4	■	Capitol 5192
9/3/83	45	13		14	Stranger At My Door ... Tell Her No (Pop #27)		—	$4		Capitol 5265
6/23/84	64	9		15	A Little Love ... Waiting For The Sun		44	$4	■	RCA 13823
8/18/84	32	13		16	Ride 'Em Cowboy ... Love Sail Away		—	$4		Capitol 5379
10/20/84	57	7		17	Restless Heart ... Eye Of A Hurricane		—	$4		RCA 13907
7/20/85	❶¹	22		18	You Make Me Want To Make You Mine S:❶¹ / A:❶¹ Waiting For The Sun		—	$4	■	RCA 14139
11/9/85+	❶¹	24		19	Hurt S:❶¹ / A:❶¹ Eye Of A Hurricane		—	$4	■	RCA 14199
					#4 Pop hit for Timi Yuro in 1961					
4/5/86	5	21		20	Old Flame A:3 / S:5 One Touch		—	$4		RCA 14295
7/12/86	❶¹	20		21	Both To Each Other (Friends & Lovers) S:❶¹ / A:❶¹ A World Without Love		—	$4	■	RCA 14377
					EDDIE RABBITT AND JUICE NEWTON					
					#2 Pop hit for Gloria Loring & Carl Anderson in 1986					
8/23/86	9	18		22	Cheap Love S:8 / A:9 Old Flame		—	$4		RCA 14417
12/13/86+	9	20		23	What Can I Do With My Heart A:9 / S:19 Let Your Woman Take Care Of You		—	$4		RCA 5068
7/18/87	24	15		24	First Time Caller ... 'Til You Cry		—	$4	☐	RCA 5170
11/14/87+	8	22		25	Tell Me True S:19 If I Didn't Love You		—	$4		RCA 5283
5/6/89	40	12		26	When Love Comes Around The Bend		—	$4		RCA 8815

NEWTON, Wayne '72
Born on 4/3/42 in Roanoke, Virginia. Singer/multi-instrumentalist. Charted 17 pop hits from 1963-80.

1) If You Love Me (Let Me Know) 2) Have You Never Been Mellow 3) Let It Shine

7/15/72	55	8	●	1	Daddy Don't You Walk So Fast ... Echo Valley 2-6809		4	$5		Chelsea 0100
10/7/89	63	5		2	While The Feeling's Good ... Our Wedding Band		—	$4		Curb 10559
					WAYNE NEWTON (with Tammy Wynette)					

NEWTON, Wood '79
Born in Hampton, Arkansas; raised in Louisiana. Singer/prolific songwriter.

10/28/78	52	7		1	Last Exit For Love ... Too Good To Be True		—	$5		Elektra 45528
3/3/79	44	8		2	Lock, Stock, & Barrel ... Dreams Of Desireé		—	$5		Elektra 46013
7/7/79	81	4		3	Julie (Do I Ever Cross Your Mind?) ... Cotton Pickin' Time		—	$5		Elektra 46059

NEWTON-JOHN, Olivia ★256★ '74
Born on 9/26/48 in Cambridge, England; raised in Melbourne, Australia. Singer/actress. Charted 39 pop hits from 1971-96. Acted in the movies Grease, Xanadu and Two Of A Kind. CMA Award: 1974 Female Vocalist of the Year.

1) If You Love Me (Let Me Know) 2) Have You Never Been Mellow 3) Let It Shine

8/25/73	7	22	●	1	Let Me Be There Maybe Then I'll Think Of You		6	$6		MCA 40101
4/13/74	2²	18	●	2	If You Love Me (Let Me Know) Brotherly Love		5	$6		MCA 40209
8/24/74	6	17	●	3	I Honestly Love You Home Ain't Home Anymore		❶²	$5		MCA 40280
					also see #16 below					
2/1/75	3	14	●	4	Have You Never Been Mellow Water Under The Bridge		❶¹	$5		MCA 40349
6/14/75	5	15	●	5	Please Mr. Please And In The Morning		3	$5	■	MCA 40418
9/27/75	19	12		6	Something Better To Do ... He's My Rock		13	$5		MCA 40459
12/6/75+	5	12		7	Let It Shine He Ain't Heavy...He's My Brother (Pop flip)		30	$5		MCA 40495
3/13/76	5	13		8	Come On Over Small Talk And Pride		23	$5		MCA 40525
8/14/76	14	10		9	Don't Stop Believin' ... Greensleeves		—	$5		MCA 40600
10/30/76	21	11		10	Every Face Tells A Story ... Love You Hold The Key		55	$5		MCA 40642
1/29/77	40	10		11	Sam ... I'll Bet You A Kangaroo		20	$5		MCA 40670
7/22/78	20	13	●	12	Hopelessly Devoted To You ... Love Is A Many Splendored Thing [I]		3	$5		RSO 903
					from the movie Grease starring Newton-John and John Travolta					
1/6/79	94	3	●	13	A Little More Love ... Borrowed Time		3	$4	■	MCA 40975
5/5/79	87	5		14	Deeper Than The Night ... Please Don't Keep Me Waiting		11	$4		MCA 41009
8/4/79	29	11		15	Dancin' 'Round And 'Round ... Totally Hot (Pop #52)		82	$4	■	MCA 41074
5/30/98	16ˢ	17		16	I Honestly Love You ... (remix) [R]		—	$4	■	MCA 72053 (v)
					new version of #3 above					

Joe Nichols

DEBUT	PEAK	WKS	Gold	A-side (Chart Hit) / B-side	Pop	$	Pic	Label & Number
				NEWTON-JOHN, Olivia — Cont'd				
5/30/98	69	5		17 One Heart At A Time .... S:5 (same version) GARTH BROOKS, BILLY DEAN, FAITH HILL, OLIVIA NEWTON-JOHN, NEAL McCOY, MICHAEL McDONALD, VICTORIA SHAW, BRYAN WHITE	56	$4	■	Atlantic 84117
				NEYMAN, June '78				
11/11/78	93	2		1 He Ain't Heavy, He's My Brother .... Release Me #7 Pop hit for The Hollies in 1970	—	$7		Starship 101
2/17/79	97	3		2 You're Gonna Miss Me .... Kansas City	—	$7		Starship 110
				NICKEL CREEK '01 Bluegrass trio from Los Angeles: brother-and-sister Sean (guitar) and Sara (fiddle) Watkins, with Chris Thile (mandolin).				
6/16/01	48	13		When You Come Back Down .... album cut from the album *Nickel Creek* on Sugar Hill 3909				
				NICKS, Stevie '82 Born Stephanie Nicks on 5/26/48 in Phoenix; raised in San Francisco. Member of Fleetwood Mac. Charted 14 pop hits from 1981-94.				
6/19/82	70	5		After The Glitter Fades .... Think About It	32	$4	■	Modern 7405
				NIELSEN, Shaun '80 Born Sherrill Nielsen. Male singer.				
3/15/80	88	3		Lights Of L.A. .... I've Never Loved Anyone More	—	$6		Adonda 79022
				NIELSEN WHITE BAND, The '87 Group of former rock musicians: Gary Nielsen (of The Trashmen), Jack White (of McKendree Spring), Tom Eckhoff (of the Dillman Band) and Lonnie Knight.				
12/20/86+	67	6		1 Somethin' You Got	—	$4		Vision 122574
5/2/87	56	7		2 I Got The One I Wanted	—	$4		Vision 122575
				NIGHTSTREETS '80 Vocal trio: Rick Taylor, Jerry Taylor and Joyce Hawthorne. Also recorded as **Streets**.				
1/26/80	32	10		1 Love In The Meantime .... Cheatin' Like This	—	$4		Epic 50827
				STREETS				
6/14/80	74	5		2 Falling Together .... You Never Knew	—	$4		Epic 50886
11/15/80	81	5		3 If I Had It My Way .... A Little Gettin' Used To	—	$4		Epic 50944
3/21/81	72	4		4 (Lookin' At Things) In A Different Light .... Out Of The Spotlight	—	$4		Epic 51004
				NILLES, Lynn — see BRODY, Lane				
				NITTY GRITTY DIRT BAND ★124★ '87 *Dirt Band* Country-folk-rock group from Long Beach, California. Led by Jeff Hanna (vocals, guitar; born on 7/11/47) and John McEuen (banjo, mandolin; born on 12/19/45). Various members included Jimmie Fadden (harmonica; born on 3/9/48), Jim Ibbotson (guitar; born on 1/21/47), Al Garth (violin) and Bernie Leadon (guitar; **Eagles**; born on 7/19/47), who replaced McEuen briefly in early 1987. In the movies *For Singles Only* and *Paint Your Wagon*. Hanna married **Matraca Berg**. 1)Fishin' In The Dark 2)Modern Day Romance 3)Long Hard Road (The Sharecropper's Dream) 4)High Horse 5)I've Been Lookin'				
11/27/71	56	6		1 I Saw The Light .... The Precious Jewel NITTY GRITTY DIRT BAND with ROY ACUFF	—	$8		United Artists 50849
8/4/73	97	2		2 Grand Ole Opry Song .... Orange Blossom Special NITTY GRITTY DIRT BAND Featuring Jimmy Martin	—	$7		United Artists 247
7/12/75	79	7		3 (All I Have To Do Is) Dream .... Raleigh-Durham Reel	66	$5		United Artists 655
2/9/80	58	9		4 An American Dream .... Take Me Back Linda Ronstadt (harmony vocal)	13	$4		United Artists 1330
8/2/80	77	4		5 Make A Little Magic .... Jas' Moon THE DIRT BAND (above 2) Nicolette Larson (backing vocal)	25	$4		United Artists 1356
6/11/83	19	18		6 Shot Full Of Love .... Let's Go	—	$4		Liberty 1499
10/1/83	9	23		7 Dance Little Jean .... Maryann	—	$4		Liberty 1507
12/31/83	93	2		8 Colorado Christmas .... Mr. Bojangles [X]	—	$4		Liberty 1513
5/26/84	❶¹	20		9 Long Hard Road (The Sharecropper's Dream) .... Video Tape	—	$4		Warner 29282
9/22/84	3	24		10 I Love Only You .... S:3 / A:3 Face On The Cutting Room Floor	—	$4		Warner 29203
1/12/85	2²	20		11 High Horse .... S:2 / A:2 Must Be Love	—	$4		Warner 29099
6/8/85	❶¹	21		12 Modern Day Romance .... S:❶¹ / A:❶¹ Queen Of The Road	—	$4		Warner 29027
10/12/85+	3	21		13 Home Again In My Heart .... S:3 / A:3 Telluride	—	$4		Warner 28897
3/1/86	6	19		14 Partners, Brothers And Friends .... A:6 / S:7 Redneck Riviera	—	$4		Warner 28780
6/21/86	5	21		15 Stand A Little Rain .... A:5 / S:7 Miner's Night Out	—	$4		Warner 28690
11/15/86+	7	20		16 Fire In The Sky .... A:7 / S:14 Cadillac Ranch new version of their #76 Pop hit from 1981	—	$4		Warner 28547
3/28/87	2¹	17		17 Baby's Got A Hold On Me .... S:4 / A:11 Oleanna	—	$4		Warner 28443
7/11/87	❶¹	23		18 Fishin' In The Dark .... S:2 Keepin' The Road Hot	—	$4		Warner 28311
11/14/87+	5	22		19 Oh What A Love .... S:12 America, My Sweetheart	—	$4	■	Warner 28173
4/16/88	4	18		20 Workin' Man (Nowhere To Go) .... S:9 Brass Sky	—	$4		Warner 27940
9/3/88	2¹	22		21 I've Been Lookin' .... S:6 Must Be Love	—	$4		Warner 27750
12/24/88+	6	20		22 Down That Road Tonight .... A Lot Like Me	—	$4		Warner 27679
5/13/89	27	15		23 Turn Of The Century .... Blues Berry Hill	—	$4		Universal 66009
5/27/89	14	23		24 And So It Goes .... Amazing Grace JOHN DENVER AND THE NITTY GRITTY DIRT BAND	—	$4		Universal 66008
10/7/89+	10	26		25 When It's Gone .... I'm Sittin' On Top Of The World	—	$4		Universal 66023
3/3/90	63	6		26 One Step Over The Line .... Riding Alone THE NITTY GRITTY DIRT BAND Featuring Rosanne Cash and John Hiatt	—	$4		MCA 53795

DEBUT	PEAK	WKS	Gold	A-side (Chart Hit)	B-side	Pop	$	Pic	Label & Number
				NITTY GRITTY DIRT BAND — Cont'd					
5/26/90	65	9		27 From Small Things (Big Things One Day Come) *written by Bruce Springsteen*	Blues Berry Hill	—	$4		MCA 79013
9/1/90	60	19		28 You Made Life Good Again	Snowballs	—	$4		MCA 79075
7/25/92	66	3		29 I Fought The Law *#9 Pop hit for the Bobby Fuller Four in 1966*	Mr. Bojangles	—	$4		Liberty 57766
12/12/92	74	2		30 One Good Love *from the album Not Fade Away on Liberty 98564*		—			album cut
2/28/98	52	9		31 Bang, Bang, Bang		—			album cut
6/19/99	63	5		32 Bang, Bang, Bang	[R]	—			album cut
				above 2 from the album Bang, Bang, Bang on DreamWorks 50125					
				NIX, Tom '81 *Born in Denver.*					
1/10/81	79	4		Home Along The Highway		—	$7		RMA 6009
				NIXON, Nick '76 *Born Hershel Paul Nixon on 3/20/41 in Poplar Bluff, Missouri. Singer/songwriter.* *1)Rocking In Rosalee's Boat 2)I'll Get Over You 3)I'm Too Use To Loving You*					
8/10/74	90	3		1 I'm Turning You Loose	An Old Memory (Got In My Eye)	—	$6		Mercury 73467
10/5/74	63	7		2 A Habit I Can't Break	Walk On By	—	$6		Mercury 73506
3/8/75	55	9		3 It's Only A Barroom	You Stood By Me Through It All	—	$6		Mercury 73654
7/12/75	38	12		4 I'm Too Use To Loving You	I Just Love Here	—	$6		Mercury 73691
11/29/75	64	10		5 She's Just An Old Love Turned Memory	It's Much Too Rainy	—	$6		Mercury 73726
3/13/76	28	13		6 Rocking In Rosalee's Boat	I'll Get Over You	—	$6		Mercury 73772
1/8/77	83	5		7 Neon Lights	Everyday	—	$6		Mercury 73866
7/2/77	51	9		8 Love Songs And Romance Magazines	It's A Cryin' Shame (But People Change)	—	$6		Mercury 73930
11/5/77+	34	13		9 I'll Get Over You	Long Stemmed Rosie	—	$6		Mercury 55010
8/12/78	87	4		10 She's Lying Next To Me	You Really Know My Song	—	$6		Mercury 55035
6/2/79	79	4		11 What're We Doing, Doing This Again	Have A Heart	—	$5		MCA 41030
9/29/79	86	4		12 San Francisco Is A Lonely Town	Suspicion	—	$5		MCA 41100
				NOACK, Eddie '58 *Born Armona Noack on 4/29/30 in Houston. Died of a cerebral hemorrhage on 2/5/78 (age 47). Singer/songwriter.*					
12/15/58	14	2		Have Blues—Will Travel	The Price Of Love	—	$30		D 1019
				NOBLE, Nick '80 *Born Nicholas Valkan on 6/21/36 in Chicago. Charted 4 pop hits from 1955-57.*					
8/26/78	40	10		1 Stay With Me	My Country Kind Of Girl	—	$6		Churchill 7713
4/14/79	36	10		2 The Girl On The Other Side	Why Don't You Believe Me	—	$6		TMS 601
9/22/79	72	5		3 I Wanna Go Back	I Keep On Breathin' You	—	$6		TMS 612
2/9/80	35	10		4 Big Man's Cafe	My Country Kind Of Girl	—	$6		Churchill 7755
				NOEL '85 *Born Noel Haughey in Salina, California. Female singer.*					
12/25/82	90	3		1 One Tear (At A Time)	Lonely For Too Long	—	$6		Deep South 706
10/5/85	86	3		2 P.S.	How Sweet It Is	—	$6		Madd Cash 1045
	★248★			**NORMA JEAN** '66 *Born Norma Jean Beasler on 1/30/38 in Wellston, Oklahoma. Singer/guitarist. Regular on **Porter Wagoner**'s TV series from 1960-67. Also see **Some Of Chet's Friends**.* *1)The Game Of Triangles 2)Go Cat Go 3)I Wouldn't Buy A Used Car From Him 4)Let's Go All The Way 5)Heaven Help The Working Girl*					
1/4/64	11	19		1 Let's Go All The Way *also see #22 below*	Private Little World	—	$12		RCA Victor 8261
6/20/64	25	16		2 Put Your Arms Around Her /		—			
5/30/64	32	11		3 I'm A Walkin' Advertisement (For The Blues)		—	$12		RCA Victor 8328
10/10/64	8	22		4 Go Cat Go	Lonesome Number One	134	$12		RCA Victor 8433
4/10/65	21	8		5 I Cried All The Way To The Bank	You Have To Be Out Of Your Mind	—	$12		RCA Victor 8518
7/31/65	8	14		6 I Wouldn't Buy A Used Car From Him	I'm No Longer In Your Heart	—	$12		RCA Victor 8623
2/19/66	41	3		7 You're Driving Me Out Of My Mind /		—			
3/5/66	48	1		8 Then Go Home To Her		—	$12		RCA Victor 8720
4/16/66	28	8		9 The Shirt	Please Don't Hurt Me	—	$12		RCA Victor 8790
8/13/66	28	11		10 Pursuing Happiness	It Wasn't God Who Made Honky Tonk Angels	—	$12		RCA Victor 8887
10/15/66	5	17		11 The Game Of Triangles	Bye Bye, Love	—	$10		RCA Victor 8963
				BOBBY BARE, NORMA JEAN, LIZ ANDERSON					
11/19/66+	24	13		12 Don't Let That Doorknob Hit You	Company's Comin'	—	$10		RCA Victor 8989
4/1/67	48	10		13 Conscience Keep An Eye On Me	Still	—	$10		RCA Victor 9147
8/19/67	38	10		14 Jackson Ain't A Very Big Town	Now It's Every Night	—	$10		RCA Victor 9258
11/18/67+	18	14		15 Heaven Help The Working Girl	Your Alibi Called Today	—	$10		RCA Victor 9362
3/30/68	53	6		16 Truck Driving Woman	Supper Time	—	$10		RCA Victor 9466
7/20/68	35	10		17 You Changed Everything About Me But My Name	A-11	—	$10		RCA Victor 9558
11/30/68	61	5		18 One Man Band	I Can't Leave Him	—	$10		RCA Victor 9645
4/12/69	44	8		19 Dusty Road	Love's A Woman's Job	—	$8		RCA Victor 0115
10/10/70	48	9		20 Whiskey-Six Years Old	I'm Givin' Up	—	$8		RCA Victor 9900
1/30/71	42	9		21 The Kind Of Needin' I Need	A Little Unfair	—	$8		RCA Victor 9946
2/6/82	68	6		22 Let's Go All The Way	We Climbed A Mountain Last Night [R]	—	$7		Granny White 10009
				CLAUDE GRAY and NORMA JEAN *new version of #1 above*					

DEBUT	PEAK	WKS	Gold	A-side (Chart Hit)	B-side	Pop	$	Pic	Label & Number
				NORMAN, Jim '78					
11/18/78	98	2		The Love In Me	Love Makes The World Go Square	—	$5		Republic 030
				NORWOOD, Daron '94					
				Born on 9/30/65 in Lubbock, Texas; raised in Tahoka, Texas. Singer/pianist.					
11/27/93+	26	20	✦	1 If It Wasn't For Her I Wouldn't Have You	A Little Bigger Piece Of American Pie	—	$4	■	Giant 18386 (v)
4/16/94	24	19	✦	2 Cowboys Don't Cry	J.T. Miller's Farm	—	$4	■	Giant 18216 (v)
8/6/94	48	9		3 If I Ever Love Again	—				album cut
				from the album *Daron Norwood* on Giant 24527					
12/31/94	75	1		4 The Working Elf Blues	Rockin' Little Christmas (**Carlene Carter**) [X]	—	$4		Giant 18006
				parody of "Workin' Man Blues" by Merle Haggard					
2/4/95	50	9		5 Bad Dog, No Biscuit	There'll Always Be A Honky Tonk Somewhere	—	$4	■	Giant 17958 (v)
6/3/95	58	9		6 My Girl Friday	Break The Radio	—	$4	■	Giant 17881 (v)
				***NSYNC** — see ALABAMA					
				NUNLEY, Bill '88					
4/2/88	74	3		1 I'll Know The Good Times	That's How Long I'll Wait For You	—	$6		Cannery 0402
				COUNTRY BILL NUNLEY					
8/27/88	98	2		2 The Way You Got Over Me		—	$6		Cannery 0525
				NUNN, Earl '49					
4/9/49	13	1		Double Talkin' Woman ... J:13	I've Loved You Too Long To Forget You	—	$30		Specialty 701
				EARL NUNN and His Alabama Ramblers Featuring Billy Lee					
				NUTTER, Mayf '71					
				Born Mayfred Nutter Adamson on 10/19/41 in Jane Lew, West Virginia. Male singer/guitarist/actor.					
2/14/70	65	5		1 Hey There Johnny	My Kind Of Music	—	$6		Reprise 0882
				MAYF NUTTER with the Hugh Jarrett Singers					
10/16/71	57	6		2 Never Ending Song Of Love	Okla.	—	$6		Capitol 3181
				#13 Pop hit for Delaney & Bonnie & Friends in 1971					
12/18/71+	58	7		3 Never Had A Doubt	The Litterbug Song	—	$6		Capitol 3226
4/15/72	59	7		4 The Sing-Along Song	I Better Let You Be	—	$6		Capitol 3296
10/27/73	78	10		5 Green Door	One More Lie	—	$6		Capitol 3734
				#1 Pop hit for Jim Lowe in 1956					
5/8/76	87	5		6 Sweet Southern Lovin'	Hitch Hike Nightmare	—	$5		GNP Crescendo 805
1/15/77	99	2		7 Goin' Skinny Dippin'	(Take Me Home) Country Roads [N]	—	$5		GNP Crescendo 809

An Old Time Family Bluegrass Band (WBAR) — (very good) & 45

				OAK RIDGE BOYS ★49★ '85					
				Vocal group formed in Oak Ridge, Tennessee: Duane Allen (lead; born on 4/29/43), Joe Bonsall (tenor; born on 5/18/48), William Lee Golden (baritone; born on 1/12/39) and Richard Sterban (bass; born on 4/24/43). All had previously sung in gospel groups. Steve Sanders (born on 9/17/52) replaced Golden from 1987 until Golden returned in 1996. Sanders died of a self-inflicted gunshot wound on 6/10/98 (age 45). CMA Award: 1978 Vocal Group of the Year.					
				1)No Matter How High 2)Bobbie Sue 3)Leaving Louisiana In The Broad Daylight					
				4)It Takes A Little Rain (To Make Love Grow) 5)Make My Life With You					
8/4/73	57	7		1 Praise The Lord And Pass The Soup	The Ballad Of Barbara	—	$7		Columbia 45890
				JOHNNY CASH (With The Carter Family And The Oak Ridge Boys)					
6/26/76	83	5		2 Family Reunion	Don't Be Late	—	$6		Columbia 10349
7/16/77	3	18		3 Y'All Come Back Saloon	Emmylou	—	$5		ABC/Dot 17710
12/3/77+	2²	16		4 You're The One	Morning Glory Do	—	$5		ABC/Dot 17732
4/15/78	❶¹	15		5 I'll Be True To You	An Old Time Family Bluegrass Band	102	$5		ABC 12350
9/2/78	3	13		6 Cryin' Again	I Can Love You	107	$5		ABC 12397
12/9/78+	3	15		7 Come On In	Morning Glory Do	—	$5		ABC 12434
4/7/79	2²	13		8 Sail Away	The Only One	—	$5		MCA 12463
6/23/79	94	1		9 Rhythm Guitar	All Our Favorite Songs	—	$5		Columbia 11009
				recorded in 1975					
8/18/79	7	13		10 Dream On	Sometimes The Rain Won't Let Me Sleep	—	$4		MCA 41078
				#32 Pop hit for the Righteous Brothers in 1974					
12/1/79+	❶¹	15		11 Leaving Louisiana In The Broad Daylight	I Gotta Get Over This	—	$4		MCA 41154
4/19/80	❶¹	15		12 Trying To Love Two Women	Hold On Til Sunday	—	$4	■	MCA 41217
7/19/80	3	16		13 Heart Of Mine	Love Takes Two	105	$4		MCA 41280
11/15/80+	3	17		14 Beautiful You	Ready To Take My Chances	—	$4		MCA 51022
4/4/81	❶¹	14	▲	15 Elvira	A Woman Like You	5	$4		MCA 51084
				#72 Pop hit for Dallas Frazier in 1966; CMA Award: Single of the Year					
9/5/81	❶¹	15		16 Fancy Free	How Long Has It Been	104	$4		MCA 51169
1/23/82	❶¹	15		17 Bobbie Sue	Live In Love	12	$4		MCA 51231
6/5/82	22	10		18 So Fine	I Wish You Were Here (Oh My Darlin')	76	$4		MCA 52065
7/31/82	2²	19		19 I Wish You Could Have Turned My Head					
				(And Left My Heart Alone)	Back In Your Arms Again	—	$4		MCA 52095
11/20/82+	3	16		20 Thank God For Kids	Christmas Is Paintin' The Town	—	$4		MCA 52145
2/26/83	❶¹	16		21 American Made	The Cure For My Broken Heart	72	$4		MCA 52179
6/4/83	❶¹	18		22 Love Song	Heart On The Line (Operator, Operator)	—	$4		MCA 52224
10/22/83+	5	19		23 Ozark Mountain Jubilee	Down Deep Inside	—	$4		MCA 52288

DEBUT	PEAK	WKS	Gold	A-side (Chart Hit)	B-side	Pop	$	Pic	Label & Number
				OAK RIDGE BOYS — Cont'd					
2/25/84	❶¹	22		24 I Guess It Never Hurts To Hurt Sometimes / Through My Eyes		—	$4		MCA 52342
7/14/84	❶¹	21		25 Everyday / S:27 Ain't No Cure For The Rock And Roll		—	$4	■	MCA 52419
				picture sleeve is a limited edition poster sleeve					
11/10/84+	❶¹	21		26 Make My Life With You / S:❶¹ / A:❶¹ Break My Mind		—	$4	■	MCA 52488
3/30/85	❶¹	20		27 Little Things / S:❶¹ / A:❶¹ The Secret Of Love		—	$4		MCA 52556
8/3/85	❶¹	21		28 Touch A Hand, Make A Friend / S:❶¹ / A:❶¹ Only One I Love		—	$4		MCA 52646
				#23 Pop hit for The Staple Singers in 1974					
11/23/85+	3	19		29 Come On In (You Did The Best You Could Do) / S:3 / A:3 Roll Tennessee River		—	$4	■	MCA 52722
3/22/86	15	15		30 Juliet / S:14 / A:15 Everybody Wins		—	$4		MCA 52801
3/29/86	20	14		31 When You Get To The Heart / A:20 / S:21 Survivors		—	$4		MCA 52802
				BARBARA MANDRELL with the Oak Ridge Boys					
7/12/86	24	15		32 You Made A Rock Of A Rolling Stone / A:24 Hidin' Place		—	$4		MCA 52873
2/21/87	❶¹	24		33 It Takes A Little Rain (To Make Love Grow) / A:3 / S:6 Looking For Love		—	$4		MCA 53010
6/13/87	❶¹	23		34 This Crazy Love / S:11 Where The Fast Lane Ends		—	$4		MCA 53023
10/10/87	17	15		35 Time In / A Little More Coal On The Fire		—	$4		MCA 53175
2/27/88	5	22		36 True Heart / S:20 Love Without Mercy		—	$4		MCA 53272
7/30/88	❶¹	21		37 Gonna Take A Lot Of River / S:❶¹ Private Lives		—	$4		MCA 53381
12/3/88+	10	20		38 Bridges And Walls / Never Together (But Close Sometimes)		—	$4		MCA 53460
4/1/89	7	22		39 Beyond Those Years / Too Many Heartaches		—	$4		MCA 53625
8/19/89	4	25		40 An American Family / Too Many Heartaches		—	$4		MCA 53705
12/16/89+	❶¹	26		41 No Matter How High / Bed Of Roses		—	$4		MCA 53757
5/19/90	71	3		42 Baby, You'll Be My Baby / Cajun Girl		—	$4		MCA 79006
12/1/90+	31	15		43 (You're My) Soul And Inspiration / (same version)		—	$4		RCA 2665
				#1 Pop hit for The Righteous Brothers in 1966; from the movie *My Heroes Have Always Been Cowboys* starring Scott Glenn					
3/23/91	6	20		44 Lucky Moon / Walkin' After Midnight		—	$4		RCA 2779
8/10/91	70	5		45 Change My Mind / Our Love Is Here To Stay		—	$4		RCA 62013
10/5/91	44	13		46 Baby On Board / When It Comes To You		—	$4		RCA 62099
6/27/92	69	4		47 Fall / Until You're Back In My Arms Again		—	$4		RCA 62228
10/16/99	71	1		48 Ain't No Short Way Home		—			album cut
				from the album *Voices* on Platinum 9355					
				O'BRIEN, Tim — see **MATTEA, Kathy**					
				O'CONNOR, Mark '91					
				Born on 8/5/61 in Seattle. Fiddle player. Member of rock group The Dregs in early '80s. CMA Awards: 1991, 1992, 1993, 1994, 1995 & 1996 Musician of the Year.					
3/30/91	25	20		1 Restless / Dance Of The Ol' Swamp Rat		—	$4		Warner 19354
				Vince Gill, Ricky Skaggs and Steve Wariner (guest vocals)					
8/3/91	71	3		2 Now It Belongs To You		—			album cut
				Steve Wariner (guest vocal); from the album *New Nashville Cats* on Warner 26509					
12/25/93+	54	10		3 The Devil Comes Back To Georgia / Diggy Liggy Lo		—	$4		Warner 18342
				MARK O'CONNOR With Charlie Daniels					
				Johnny Cash, Marty Stuart and Travis Tritt (guest vocals)					
				O'DAY, Tommy '78					
				Born in Fresno, California.					
1/28/78	96	3		1 Mr. Sandman / Winter Winds Of Love		—	$6		Nu-Trayl 916
				#1 Pop hit for The Chordettes in 1954					
4/8/78	82	4		2 Memories Are Made Of This / Up & Over Your Love		—	$6		Nu-Trayl 919
				#1 Pop hit for Dean Martin in 1956					
8/12/78	97	2		3 When A Woman Cries / Round And Round		—	$6		Nu-Trayl 923
12/23/78+	93	4		4 I Heard A Song Today / Today's Woman		—	$6		Nu-Trayl 926
5/5/79	89	2		5 Accentuate The Positive / Blue River		—	$6		Nu-Trayl 929
				#1 Pop hit for Johnny Mercer in 1945					
7/14/79	99	2		6 Your Other Love / Painted Tainted Rose		—	$6		Nu-Trayl 930
				#54 Pop hit for The Flamingos in 1961					
				O'DELL, Doye '48					
				Born Allen Doye O'Dell on 11/22/12 in Plainview, Texas.					
7/24/48	12	3		Dear Oakie / J:12 / S:13 Lookin' Poor, But Feelin' Rich		—	$20		Exclusive 33
				O'DELL, Kenny '78					
				Born Kenneth Gist in 1942 in Oklahoma. Singer/songwriter/guitarist.					
3/9/74	58	10		1 You Bet Your Sweet, Sweet Love / Let's Go Find Some Country Music		—	$5		Capricorn 0038
1/18/75	18	13		2 Soulful Woman / Let's Get On The Road		—	$5		Capricorn 0219
5/31/75	37	10		3 My Honky Tonk Ways / Behind Closed Doors		105	$5		Capricorn 0233
7/8/78	9	14		4 Let's Shake Hands And Come Out Lovin' / We Might Be All Nite		—	$5		Capricorn 0301
11/4/78+	12	15		5 As Long As I Can Wake Up In Your Arms / Soulful Woman		—	$5		Capricorn 0309
3/10/79	32	10		6 Medicine Woman / Who Do I Know In Denver		—	$5		Capricorn 0317
				ODESSA '89					
4/8/89	89	2		Hooked On You		—	$6		Sing Me 40
				ODOM, Donna '68					
				Born on 8/14/44 in Ebbwvale, South Wales.					
1/20/68	65	5		She Gets The Roses (I Get The Tears) / I'm A Woman		—	$7		Decca 32214
				O'DONNAL, Karen — see **DUDLEY, Dave**					
				O'DONNELL, Rosie — see **YEARWOOD, Trisha**					

Old Dogs? (Waylon, Mel, Bobby, Jerry)

DEBUT	PEAK	WKS	Gold	A-side (Chart Hit)	B-side	Pop	$	Pic	Label & Number
				O'DOSKI, Gail '88					
				Born in Bartow, Florida. Male singer.					
12/26/87+	73	4		1 First Came The Feelin'	—		$5		Door Knob 288
5/28/88	77	4		2 (Just An) Old Wives' Tale	—		$5		Door Knob 300
				O'GWYNN, James '62					
				Born on 1/26/28 in Winchester, Mississippi; raised in Hattiesburg, Mississippi. Singer/songwriter. Known as "The Smilin' Irishman."					
10/20/58	16	3		1 Talk To Me Lonesome Heart	Changeable	—	$30		D 1006
12/29/58	28	3		2 Blue Memories	You Don't Want To Hold Me	—	$30		D 1022
4/27/59	13	4		3 How Can I Think Of Tomorrow	Were You Ever A Stranger	—	$15		Mercury 71419
12/21/59+	26	4		4 Easy Money	Tears Of Tomorrow	—	$15		Mercury 71513
2/20/61	21	6		5 House Of Blue Lovers	Another Falling Tear	—	$15		Mercury 71731
4/21/62	7	10		6 My Name Is Mud	You're Getting All Over Me	—	$15		Mercury 71935
	★390★			**O'KANES, The** '87					
				Duo of Jamie O'Hara (born on 8/8/50 in Toledo, Ohio) and Kieran Kane (born on 10/7/49 in Queens, New York).					
9/20/86	10	25		1 Oh Darlin'	S:6 / A:11 When I Found You	—	$4	■	Columbia 06242
2/7/87	**0**¹	22		2 Can't Stop My Heart From Loving You	S:2 / A:2 Bluegrass Blues	—	$4	■	Columbia 06606
6/27/87	9	18		3 Daddies Need To Grow Up Too	S:7 Oh Darlin'	—	$4		Columbia 07187
10/17/87+	5	25		4 Just Lovin' You	S:2 When We're Gone, Long Gone	—	$4		Columbia 07611
3/5/88	4	20		5 One True Love	S:3 If I Could Be There	—	$4		Columbia 07736
7/9/88	10	20		6 Blue Love	S:2 Highway 55	—	$4		Columbia 07943
11/12/88	71	5		7 Rocky Road	All Because Of You	—	$4		Columbia 08099
				O'KEEFE, Danny '72					
				Born in Spokane, Washington. Singer/songwriter.					
10/28/72	63	6		Good Time Charlie's Got The Blues	The Valentine Pieces	9	$7		Signpost 70006
				O'NEAL, Austin '83					
8/27/83	93	2		Nights Like Tonight	—		$7		Project One 002
				O'NEAL, Coleman '63					
				Born in Philadelphia. Singer/songwriter.					
1/5/63	8	16		Mr. Heartache, Move On	Make Him Know	—	$15		Chancellor 108
				O'NEAL, Jamie '01					
				Born Jamie Murphy on 6/3/68 in Sydney, Australia; raised in Hawaii and Nevada. Female singer. Also see **America The Beautiful**.					
8/12/00+	**0**¹	35		1 There Is No Arizona	Frantic	40	$4		Mercury 172177
3/31/01	**0**¹	29		2 When I Think About Angels	The Only Thing Wrong	35	$4		Mercury 172202
9/8/01	21	20		3 Shiver	She Hasn't Heard It Yet	—	$4		Mercury 172216
12/1/01+	31	20		4 I'm Not Gonna Do Anything Without You	—				album cut
				MARK WILLS with Jamie O'Neal					
				from Wills's album *Loving Every Minute* on Mercury 170209					
				ORBISON, Roy '89					
				Born on 4/23/36 in Vernon, Texas. Died of a heart attack on 12/6/88 (age 52). Singer/songwriter/guitarist. Charted 32 pop hits from 1956-92. Inducted into the Rock and Roll Hall of Fame in 1987.					
6/28/80	6	15		1 That Lovin' You Feelin' Again	Lola (Craig Hundley)	55	$5		Warner 49262
				ROY ORBISON & EMMYLOU HARRIS					
				from the movie *Roadie* starring Meat Loaf					
10/10/87	75	4		2 In Dreams	Leah	—	$4	■	Virgin 99434
				new version of his #7 Pop hit from 1963; from the movie *Blue Velvet* starring Kyle McLachlan					
12/5/87+	42	13		3 Crying	Falling	—	$4	■	Virgin 99388
				ROY ORBISON/k.d. lang					
				new version of his #2 Pop hit from 1961; from the movie *Hiding Out* starring Jon Cryer					
2/4/89	7	20		4 You Got It	The Only One	9	$4	■	Virgin 99245
6/24/89	51	13		5 California Blue	In Dreams	—	$4	■	Virgin 99202
12/23/89	89	4		6 Oh Pretty Woman	Claudette	—	$4	■	Virgin 99159
				recorded "live" in September 1987 at the Coconut Grove in Los Angeles; new version of his #1 Pop hit from 1964					
				ORDGE, Jimmy Arthur '81					
				Born in Donalda, Alberta, Canada.					
7/11/81	89	3		Stay Away From Jim	Hard Times	—	$6		Dore 969
				ORENDER, DeWayne '78					
11/27/76	53	9		1 If You Want To Make Me Feel At Home	Don't Let Any Of Her Love Get On You	—	$5		RCA 10813
4/23/77	87	3		2 To Make A Good Love Die	I Can't Keep My Eyes Off Her	—	$5		RCA 10936
8/27/77	97	2		3 Love Me Into Heaven Again	If You're Gonna Love	—	$5		RCA 11039
5/6/78	51	7		4 Brother	Standing In The Rain	—	$6		Nu-Trayl 920
12/23/78+	92	4		5 Better Than Now		—	$6		Volunteer 102
				ORIGINAL TEXAS PLAYBOYS '77					
				Veterans of Bob Wills's longtime band: Leon Rausch (vocals), Bob Kizer (guitar), Leon McAuliffe (steel guitar), Rudy Martin (clarinet), Jack Stidham and Bob Boatwright (fiddles), Al Stricklin (piano), Joe Ferguson (bass) and Smokey Dacus (drums).					
4/2/77	94	3		Gambling Polka Dot Blues	Osage Stomp	—	$5		Capitol 4401
				written by Jimmie Rodgers					

DEBUT	PEAK	WKS	Gold	A-side (Chart Hit)	B-side	Pop	$	Pic	Label & Number

ORION '81
Born Jimmy Ellis in 1945 in Orrville, Alabama. Shot to death during an attempted robbery on 12/12/98 (age 53). Based his masked character on the novel *Orion* by Gail Brewer-Giorgio. Many people speculated that it was actually **Elvis Presley** under the mask. Also see **Jerry Lee Lewis**.
1) Rockabilly Rebel 2) Am I That Easy To Forget 3) Texas Tea

DEBUT	PEAK	WKS	#	A-side	B-side	$	Label
6/23/79	89	6	1	Ebony Eyes /	—	$5	Sun 1142
		6	2	Honey		$5	Sun 1142
4/26/80	69	5	3	A Stranger In My Place	It Ain't No Mystery	$5	Sun 1152
7/19/80	68	6	4	Texas Tea	Faded Love	$5	Sun 1153
10/11/80	65	9	5	Am I That Easy To Forget	Crazy Arms	$5	Sun 1156
				#18 Pop hit for **Engelbert Humperdinck** in 1968			
1/10/81	63	6	6	Rockabilly Rebel	Memphis Sun	$5	Sun 1159
3/21/81	79	4	7	Crazy Little Thing Called Love	Matchbox	$5	Sun 1162
				#1 Pop hit for Queen in 1980			
6/27/81	76	5	8	Born	If I Can't Have You	$5	Sun 1165
12/12/81	83	4	9	Some You Win, Some You Lose	Ain't No Good	$5	Sun 1170
7/10/82	69	6	10	Morning, Noon And Night /		$5	Sun 1175
7/10/82	70	4	11	Honky Tonk Heaven		$5	Sun 1175

ORLEANS '86
Pop-rock group from New York City: brothers **Lawrence** (vocals, guitar) and **Lance** (bass) **Hoppen**, **Bob Leinback** (keyboards), **R.A. Martin** (horns) and **Wells Kelly** (drums). Charted 5 pop hits from 1975-79. Kelly died on 10/29/84 (age 35).

11/15/86	59	6	1 You're Mine	Language Of Love	—	$4	MCA 52963

ORRALL, Robert Ellis '93
Born on 5/4/55 in Winthrop, Massachusetts. Singer/songwriter.

11/14/92+	19	20	1 Boom! It Was Over	Flying Colors	—	$4	RCA 62335
3/20/93	31	20	2 A Little Bit Of Her Love	'Til The Tears Fell	—	$4	RCA 62475
7/24/93	64	5	3 Every Day When I Get Home	True Believer	—	$4	RCA 62547

ORRALL & WRIGHT '94
Duo of **Robert Ellis Orrall** and **Curtis Wright**.

7/2/94	47	11	1 She Loves Me Like She Means It	You Saved Me	—	$4	■ Giant 18162 (v)
10/15/94	70	2	2 If You Could Say What I'm Thinking	Pound, Pound, Pound	—	$4	■ Giant 18049 (v)

ORTEGA, Gilbert '78
Born in Gallup, New Mexico.

1/28/78	91	3	1 Is It Wrong	Is This All There Is To A Honky Tonk	—	$7	LRJ 1050
5/20/78	93	4	2 I Don't Believe I'll Fall In Love Today	Send Me The Pillow	—	$7	Ortega 1051

ORVILLE AND IVY '67
Duo of prolific session guitarists Wesley Webb "Speedy" West (born on 1/25/24 in Springfield, Missouri) and Ivy "Jimmy" Bryant (born on 3/5/25 in Moultrie, Georgia; died on 9/22/80, age 55).

4/1/67	73	2	Shinbone	Tabasco Road [I]	—	$10	Imperial 66219

OSBORNE, Jimmie '49
Born on 4/8/23 in Winchester, Kentucky. Committed suicide on 12/26/57 (age 34). Singer/songwriter/guitarist.

7/10/48	10	2	1 My Heart Echoes	J:10 Your Lies Have Broken My Heart	—	$20	King 715
6/25/49	7	6	2 The Death Of Little Kathy Fiscus	S:7 A Bundle Of Kisses	—	$20	King 788
10/7/50	9	3	3 God Please Protect America	A:9 The Moon Is Weeping Over You	—	$20	King 893

OSBORNE BROTHERS '58
★313★
Bluegrass duo of brothers from Hyden, Kentucky: **Bobby** (born on 12/7/31; mandolin) and **Sonny** (born on 10/29/37; banjo) **Osborne**. Joined the *Grand Ole Opry* in 1964. CMA Award: 1971 Vocal Group of the Year.
1) Rocky Top '96 2) Once More 3) Tennessee Hound Dog

3/24/58	13	2	1 Once More	A:13 She's No Angel	—	$15	MGM 12583
			THE OSBORNE BROTHERS And RED ALLEN				
3/12/66	41	4	2 Up This Hill And Down	Memories	—	$8	Decca 31886
12/17/66+	33	10	3 The Kind Of Woman I Got	One Tear	—	$8	Decca 32052
7/22/67	66	3	4 Roll Muddy River	Making Plans	—	$8	Decca 32137
2/3/68	33	10	5 Rocky Top	My Favorite Memory	—	$8	Decca 32242
				also see #19 below			
6/15/68	60	7	6 Cut The Cornbread, Mama	If I Could Count On You	—	$8	Decca 32325
10/19/68	58	6	7 Son Of A Sawmill Man	That Was Yesterday	—	$8	Decca 32382
8/9/69	28	11	8 Tennessee Hound Dog	Thanks For All The Yesterdays	—	$8	Decca 32516
1/17/70	58	6	9 Ruby, Are You Mad	Sempre	—	$8	Decca 32598
12/5/70	69	2	10 My Old Kentucky Home (Turpentine And Dandelion Wine)	No Good Son Of A Gun	—	$8	Decca 32746
3/13/71	37	10	11 Georgia Pineywoods	Searching For Yesterday	—	$8	Decca 32794
9/11/71	62	7	12 Muddy Bottom	Beneath Still Waters	—	$8	Decca 32864
1/6/73	74	2	13 Midnight Flyer	Teardrops Will Kiss The Morning Dew	—	$8	Decca 33028
4/28/73	66	2	14 Lizzie Lou	Tears	—	$6	MCA 40028
9/1/73	64	6	15 Blue Heartache	You're Heavy On My Mind	—	$6	MCA 40113
1/31/76	86	4	16 Don't Let Smokey Mountain Smoke Get In Your Eyes	A Born Ramblin' Man	—	$6	MCA 40509
10/13/79	95	3	17 Shackles And Chains	Midnight Flyer	—	$6	CMH 1522
			OSBORNE BROS. & MAC WISEMAN				
4/26/80	75	5	18 I Can Hear Kentucky Calling Me	Shawnee	—	$6	CMH 1524
11/9/96+	5^S	119↑	19 Rocky Top '96 (original version)	—	$4	■ Decca 55274 (v)
			new version of #5 above				

DEBUT	PEAK	WKS	Gold	A-side (Chart Hit)	B-side	Pop	$	Pic	Label & Number
				O'SHEA, Cathy '78					
				Born Catherine Herbsleb on 7/20/41 in Kansas City, Missouri.					
8/26/78	94	4		Roses Ain't Red	Love Is Just A Bar Stool Away	—	$4		MCA 40934
				O'SHEA, Shad '76					
				Born in San Diego. Started the Fraternity Records label in 1975.					
3/27/76	85	3		Colorado Call	Bub-Bub-Bub-Boo [N]	110	$5		Private Stock 45,071
				SHAD O'SHEA & THE 18 WHEELERS					
	★239★			**OSLIN, K.T.** '90					
				Born Kay Toinette Oslin on 5/15/41 in Crossett, Arkansas; raised in Mobile, Alabama. Singer/songwriter/pianist/actress. Acted in the touring musicals *Hello Dolly*, *West Side Story* and *Promises Promises*. CMA Award: 1988 Female Vocalist of the Year. Also see Alabama.					
				1) Come Next Monday 2) Do Ya' 3) Hold Me					
5/16/81	72	4		1 Clean Your Own Tables	Nelda Jean Prudy	—	$5		Elektra 47132
				KAY T. OSLIN					
1/10/87	40	15		2 Wall Of Tears	Two Hearts Are Better Than One	—	$4	□	RCA 5066
4/25/87	7	21		3 80's Ladies	S:13 Old Pictures	—	$4	□	RCA 5154
9/12/87	●¹	25		4 Do Ya'	S:●¹ Lonely But Only For You	—	$4		RCA 5239
1/30/88	●¹	21		5 I'll Always Come Back	S:3 Old Pictures	—	$4		RCA 5330
7/9/88	13	15		6 Money	S:12 Dr., Dr.	—	$4		RCA 8388
10/15/88+	●¹	20		7 Hold Me	S:●² She Don't Talk Like Us No More	—	$4		RCA 8725
2/11/89	2¹	19		8 Hey Bobby	Where Is A Woman To Go	—	$4		RCA 8865
6/10/89	5	18		9 This Woman	Younger Men	—	$4		RCA 8943
10/21/89	23	13		10 Didn't Expect It To Go Down This Way	Round The Clock Lovin'	—	$4		RCA 9029
7/7/90	73	3		11 Two Hearts	Jealous	—	$4		RCA 2567
9/29/90	●²	20		12 Come Next Monday	Truly Blue	—	$4		RCA 2667
2/16/91	28	13		13 Mary And Willie	Love Is Strange	—	$4		RCA 2746
7/6/91	69	2		14 You Call Everybody Darling	Still On My Mind	—	$4		RCA 2829
9/14/91	63	3		15 Cornell Crawford	Two Hearts	—	$4		RCA 62053
5/1/93	64	3		16 New Way Home	You Gave Me A Heart Attack	—	$4	■	RCA 62499 (v)
8/31/96	64	5		17 Silver Tongue And Goldplated Lies	Miss The Mississippi And You	—	$4	■	BNA 64600 (v)
3/17/01	53	9		18 Live Close By, Visit Often	S:25 Maybe We Should Learn To Tango	—	$4	★	BNA 69026
				OSMOND, Donny And Marie '74					
				Brother-and-sister vocal duo from Ogden, Utah: Donny (born on 12/9/57) and **Marie Osmond**. Co-hosted own musical/variety TV series from 1976-78. Starred in the movie *Goin' Coconuts*.					
7/27/74	17	13	●	1 I'm Leaving It (All) Up To You	The Umbrella Song	4	$5		MGM/Kolob 14735
				#1 Pop hit for Dale & Grace in 1963					
6/21/75	71	6		2 Make The World Go Away	Living On My Suspicion	44	$5		MGM/Kolob 14807
	★232★			**OSMOND, Marie** '86					
				Born Olive Marie Osmond on 10/13/59 in Ogden, Utah. Sister of The Osmond Brothers. Co-hosted TV series *Donny & Marie* from 1976-78. Hosted own TV series from 1980-81. Co-hosted TV's *Ripley's Believe It Or Not* from 1985-86. Starred in the 1995 TV series *Maybe This Time*. CMA Award: 1986 Vocal Duo of the Year (with **Dan Seals**).					
				1) Paper Roses 2) There's No Stopping Your Heart 3) Meet Me In Montana 4) You're Still New To Me 5) Read My Lips					
9/8/73	●²	16	●	1 Paper Roses	Least Of All You	5	$5	■	MGM/Kolob 14609
				#5 Pop hit for Anita Bryant in 1960					
8/10/74	33	11		2 In My Little Corner Of The World	It's Just The Other Way Around	102	$5		MGM/Kolob 14694
				#10 Pop hit for Anita Bryant in 1960					
3/1/75	29	10		3 Who's Sorry Now	This I Promise You	40	$5		MGM/Kolob 14786
				#4 Pop hit for Connie Francis in 1958					
8/7/76	85	4		4 "A" My Name Is Alice	Weeping Willow	—	$5		Polydor 14333
3/20/82	74	6		5 I've Got A Bad Case Of You	You Still Get The Best Of Me	—	$4		Elektra/Curb 47430
8/14/82	58	7		6 Back To Believing Again	Look Who's Gettin' Over Who	—	$4		Elektra/Curb 69995
3/24/84	82	4		7 Who's Counting	'Til The Best Comes Along	—	$4		RCA/Curb 13680
2/9/85	54	8		8 Until I Fall In Love Again	I Don't Want To Go Too Far	—	$4		Curb/Capitol 5445
7/6/85	●¹	23		9 Meet Me In Montana	S:●¹ / A:●¹ What Do Lonely People Do	—	$4	■	Curb/Capitol 5478
				MARIE OSMOND (With Dan Seals)					
11/9/85+	●¹	21		10 There's No Stopping Your Heart	S:●¹ / A:●¹ Blue Sky Shinin'	—	$4	■	Curb/Capitol 5521
3/29/86	4	21		11 Read My Lips	S:4 / A:4 That Old Devil Moon	—	$4	■	Curb/Capitol 5563
8/30/86	●¹	21		12 You're Still New To Me	S:●¹ / A:●¹ New Love	—	$4	■	Curb/Capitol 5613
				MARIE OSMOND WITH PAUL DAVIS					
12/27/86+	14	18		13 I Only Wanted You	S:3 / A:14 We're Gonna Need A Love Song	—	$4	■	Curb/Capitol 5663
4/11/87	24	13		14 Everybody's Crazy 'Bout My Baby	S:29 Making Magic	—	$4		Curb/Capitol 5703
7/25/87	50	12		15 Cry Just A Little	More Than Dancing	—	$4		Curb/Capitol 44044
5/28/88	50	10		16 Without A Trace	Baby's Blue Eyes	—	$4		Curb/Capitol 44176
8/20/88	47	8		17 Sweet Life	Somebody Else's Moon	—	$4		Curb/Capitol 44215
				MARIE OSMOND (with Paul Davis)					
12/17/88+	59	8		18 I'm In Love And He's In Dallas	My Hometown Boy	—	$4		Curb/Capitol 44269
8/26/89	70	5		19 Steppin' Stone	What Would You Do About Me If You Were Me	—	$4		Curb/Capitol 44412
11/18/89	75	4		20 Slowly But Surely	What Would You Do About You	—	$4		Curb/Capitol 44468
10/13/90	57	10		21 Like A Hurricane	I'll Be Faithful To You	—	$4		Curb 76840
2/11/95	75	1		22 What Kind Of Man (Walks On A Woman)	(album snippets)	—	$4	■	Curb 76943

DEBUT	PEAK	WKS	Gold	A-side (Chart Hit)	B-side	Pop	$	Pic	Label & Number
				OSMOND BROTHERS, The		'82			
				Family vocal group from Ogden, Utah: Alan, Wayne, Merrill and Jay Osmond. Brothers of **Donny And Marie Osmond**. Charted 13 pop hits from 1971-76. Also see **Merrill And Jessica**.					
				1)I Think About Your Lovin' 2)It's Like Falling In Love (Over And Over) 3)If Every Man Had A Woman Like You					
				THE OSMONDS:					
5/1/82	17	15		1 I Think About Your Lovin'	Working Man's Blues	—	$4		Elektra/Curb 47438
				THE OSMOND BROTHERS:					
9/4/82	28	12		2 It's Like Falling In Love (Over And Over)	Your Leaving Was The Last Thing On My Mind	—	$4		Elektra/Curb 69969
12/25/82+	43	10		3 Never Ending Song Of Love	You'll Be Seeing Me	—	$4		Elektra/Curb 69883
				#13 Pop hit for Delaney & Bonnie in 1971					
6/11/83	67	8		4 She's Ready For Someone To Love Her	You Make The Long Road Shorter	—	$4		Warner/Curb 29594
1/21/84	43	11		5 Where Does An Angel Go When She Cries	One More For Lovers	—	$4		Warner/Curb 29387
5/5/84	39	12		6 If Every Man Had A Woman Like You	Come Back To Me	—	$4		Warner/Curb 29312
6/8/85	54	9		7 Any Time	Desperately	—	$4		Warner/Curb 28982
				THE OSMOND BROS.:					
12/14/85+	56	11		8 Baby When Your Heart Breaks Down	Love Burning Down	—	$4		Curb/EMI Amer. 8298
3/15/86	45	13		9 Baby Wants	Lovin' Proof	—	$4		Curb/EMI Amer. 8313
6/21/86	69	5		10 You Look Like The One I Love	It's Only A Heartache	—	$4		Curb/EMI Amer. 8325
11/1/86	70	7		11 Looking For Suzanne	Back In Your Arms	—	$4		Curb/EMI Amer. 8360
				OTT, Paul		'79			
				Born Paul Ott Carruth on 9/25/34 in McComb, Mississippi. Cousin of baseball player Mel Ott.					
6/30/79	87	2		A Salute To The Duke	Listen To The Eagle [S]	—	$5		Elektra 46066
				tribute to John Wayne					
	★237★			**OVERSTREET, Paul**		'91			
				Born on 3/17/55 in Antioch, Mississippi. Singer/songwriter/guitarist. Member of **Schuyler, Knobloch & Overstreet**. Married to Freida Parton (sister of **Dolly Parton**) from May 1975-November 1976. No relation to Tommy Overstreet.					
				1)Daddy's Come Around 2)I Won't Take Less Than Your Love 3)Seein' My Father In Me					
5/8/82	76	5		1 Beautiful Baby	Feels Good	—	$4		RCA 13042
11/21/87+	❶¹	24		2 I Won't Take Less Than Your Love	S:2 Heartbreaker	—	$4		Capitol 44100
				TANYA TUCKER with PAUL DAVIS & PAUL OVERSTREET					
9/24/88	3	21		3 Love Helps Those	S:7 What God Has Joined Together	—	$4		MTM 72113
4/8/89	9	21		4 Sowin' Love	Love Helps Those	—	$4		RCA 8919
8/26/89	5	26		5 All The Fun	Homemaker	—	$4		RCA 9015
1/6/90	2¹	26		6 Seein' My Father In Me	Love Never Sleeps	—	$4		RCA 9116
5/19/90	3	21		7 Richest Man On Earth	Neath The Light Of Your Love	—	$4		RCA 2505
11/24/90+	❶¹	20		8 Daddy's Come Around	The Calm At The Center Of My Storm	—	$4		RCA 2707
3/16/91	4	20		9 Heroes	Straight And Narrow	—	$4		RCA 2780
7/20/91	5	20		10 Ball And Chain	Love Lives On	—	$4		RCA 62012
11/23/91+	30	18		11 If I Could Bottle This Up	'Til The Mountains Disappear	—	$4		RCA 62106
3/14/92	57	9		12 Billy Can't Read	She Supports Her Man	—	$4		RCA 62193
7/11/92	22	19		13 Me And My Baby	Lord She Sure Is Good At Loving Me	—	$4		RCA 62254
11/7/92	57	11		14 Still Out There Swinging	Till The Answer Comes (Gotta Keep Praying)	—	$4		RCA 62361
4/3/93	60	7		15 Take Another Run	Take Some Action	—	$4		RCA 62473
1/20/96	73	2		16 We've Got To Keep On Meeting Like This		—			album cut
				from the album Time on Scarlet Moon 873					

DEBUT	PEAK	WKS	Gold	A-side	B-side	Pop	$	Pic	Label & Number
				OVERSTREET, Tommy ★142★		'72			
				Born on 9/10/37 in Oklahoma City. Singer/songwriter/guitarist. On TV in Houston in the early 1960s. Worked with **Slim Willet** in the mid-1960s; own band thereafter. Managed the Nashville office of Dot Records from 1967-74. Cousin of 1920s singing star Gene Austin. Uncle of **Susan St. Marie**. No relation to Paul Overstreet.					
				1)Ann (Don't Go Runnin') 2)Heaven Is My Woman's Love 3)(Jeannie Marie) You Were A Lady 4)Gwen (Congratulations) 5)I Don't Know You (Anymore)					
10/11/69	73	2		1 Rocking A Memory (That Won't Go To Sleep)	He's Already Been There	—	$6		Dot 17281
12/12/70+	56	7		2 If You're Looking For A Fool	The Smartest Fool	—	$6		Dot 17357
4/24/71	5	16		3 Gwen (Congratulations)	One Love, Two Hearts, Three Lives	123	$6		Dot 17375
8/14/71	5	16		4 I Don't Know You (Anymore)	I Still Love You Enough (To Love You All Over Again)	—	$6		Dot 17387
1/1/72	2¹	16		5 Ann (Don't Go Runnin')	Within This World Of Mine	—	$6		Dot 17402
5/20/72	16	14		6 A Seed Before The Rose	How'd We Ever Get This Way	—	$6		Dot 17418
9/23/72	3	18		7 Heaven Is My Woman's Love	Baby's Gone	102	$6		Dot 17428
4/21/73	7	15		8 Send Me No Roses	Your Love Controls My Life	—	$6		Dot 17455
9/15/73	7	17		9 I'll Never Break These Chains	Woman, Your Name Is My Song	—	$6		Dot 17474
2/16/74	3	16		10 (Jeannie Marie) You Were A Lady	Smile At Me Sweet Nancy	—	$6		Dot 17493
7/27/74	8	16		11 If I Miss You Again Tonight	I'm Not Ready Yet	—	$6		Dot 17515
12/14/74+	9	14		12 I'm A Believer	This Land Is A Big Land	—	$5		ABC/Dot 17533
5/10/75	6	16		13 That's When My Woman Begins	A Small Quiet Table (In The Corner)	—	$5		ABC/Dot 17552
10/11/75	16	12		14 From Woman To Woman	Grass Don't Grow In Heaven	—	$5		ABC/Dot 17580
6/12/76	15	13		15 Here Comes That Girl Again	I'll Give Up (When You Give Up On Me)	—	$5		ABC/Dot 17630
10/2/76	29	11		16 Young Love	90 Proof Lies	—	$5		ABC/Dot 17657
				#2 Pop hit for Gary Puckett & The Union Gap in 1968					
12/25/76+	11	15		17 If Love Was A Bottle Of Wine	I Never Really Missed You ('Til You Were Gone)	—	$5		ABC/Dot 17672

DEBUT	PEAK	WKS	Gold	A-side (Chart Hit)	B-side	Pop	$	Pic	Label & Number
				OVERSTREET, Tommy — Cont'd					
5/7/77	5	14		18 Don't Go City Girl On Me	I'll Give Up (When You Give Up On Me)	—	$5		ABC/Dot 17697
9/17/77	20	12		19 This Time I'm In It For The Love	(Don't Make Me) A Memory Before My Time	—	$5		ABC/Dot 17721
1/21/78	12	12		20 Yes Ma'am	It's All Coming Home	—	$5		ABC/Dot 17737
6/10/78	20	12		21 Better Me	Tell My Woman I Miss Her	—	$5		ABC 12367
9/30/78	11	12		22 Fadin' In, Fadin' Out	If This Is Freedom (Then I Want Out)	—	$5		ABC 12408
1/27/79	91	3		23 Tears (There's Nowhere Else To Hide)	Lord, If I Make It To Heaven	—	$6		Tina 523
				TOMMY OVERSTREET And The NASHVILLE EXPRESS					
3/3/79	45	7		24 Cheater's Kit	Stolen Wine	—	$5		ABC 12456
5/5/79	27	11		25 I'll Never Let You Down	You Needed Me	—	$4		Elektra 46023
8/25/79	23	10		26 What More Could A Man Need	Only A Fool	—	$4		Elektra 46516
11/17/79+	36	11		27 Fadin' Renegade	Smokey Mountain Lullabye	—	$4		Elektra 46564
3/22/80	41	9		28 Down In The Quarter	Forever In Blue Jeans	—	$4		Elektra 46600
6/28/80	47	7		29 Sue	Her Heart Still Belongs To Me	—	$4		Elektra 46658
10/4/80	72	5		30 Me And The Boys In The Band	You	—	$4		Elektra 47041
7/30/83	69	7		31 Dream Maker	More Than You Can Stand	—	$5		AMI 1314
12/3/83	84	3		32 Heart Of Dixie		—	$5		AMI 1317
5/19/84	87	3		33 I Still Love Your Body		—	$5		Gervasi 665
6/28/86	74	5		34 Next To You	Letting Go Was Easier	—	$6		Silver Dollar 0002
				OWEN, Jim '80					
				Born on 4/21/41 in Robards, Kentucky. Singer/songwriter/guitarist/actor. Starred as **Hank Williams** in a one-man show.					
1/28/78	97	2		1 Lovesick Blues	A Gift In The Name Of Love	—	$6		Epic 50498
				JIM OWEN*THE DRIFTING COWBOYS**					
11/29/80	82	4		2 Ten Anniversary Presents	Please Don't Go Home Till Morning [S]	—	$5		Sun 1157
1/30/82	82	3		3 Hell Yes, I Cheated	Dragging These Chains	—	$5		Sun 1171
				OWEN BROTHERS '83					
12/25/82	95	3		1 Nights Out At The Days End	Love In Tonight	—	$6		Audiograph 445
9/17/83	86	3		2 Southern Women		—	$6		Audiograph 470
				OWENS, A.L. "Doodle" '78					
				Born Arthur Leo Owens on 11/28/30 in Waco, Texas. Died on 10/4/99 (age 68). Singer/prolific songwriter.					
1/14/78	78	4		Honky Tonk Toys	California Rose	—	$7	■	Raindrop 010
				OWENS, Bonnie '63					
				Born Bonnie Campbell on 10/1/32 in Blanchard, Oklahoma. Singer/songwriter/guitarist. Married to **Buck Owens** from 1948-53. Married to **Merle Haggard** from 1965-78. Mother of **Buddy Alan**.					
6/22/63	25	1		1 Why Don't Daddy Live Here Anymore	Waggin' Tongues	—	$25		Tally 149
4/4/64	27	6		2 Don't Take Advantage Of Me	Stop The World	—	$25		Tally 156
9/12/64	28	26		3 Just Between The Two Of Us	Slowly But Surely	—	$25		Tally 181
				MERLE HAGGARD And BONNIE OWENS					
9/18/65	41	4		4 Number One Heel	The Longer You Wait	—	$10		Capitol 5459
11/19/66	69	4		5 Consider The Children	I Know He Loves Me	—	$10		Capitol 5755
2/15/69	68	4		6 Lead Me On	I'll Always Be Glad To Take You Back	—	$10		Capitol 2340
				BONNIE OWENS And The Strangers (above 2)					
				OWENS, Buck ★11★ '65					
				Born Alvis Edgar Owens on 8/12/29 in Sherman, Texas; raised in Mesa, Arizona. Singer/songwriter/guitarist. Married to **Bonnie Owens** from 1948-53. Moved to Bakersfield, California, in 1951. Played lead guitar for **Tommy Collins** in the mid-1950s. Co-host of TV's *Hee-Haw* from 1969-86. Father of **Buddy Alan**. Backing group: **The Buckaroos**. Elected to the Country Music Hall of Fame in 1996.					
				1)Love's Gonna Live Here 2)My Heart Skips A Beat 3)Waitin' In Your Welfare Line 4)I Don't Care (Just As Long As You Love Me) 5)Before You Go					
5/11/59	24	2		1 Second Fiddle	Everlasting Love	—	$20		Capitol 4172
10/5/59	4	22		2 Under Your Spell Again	Tired Of Livin'	—	$20		Capitol 4245
3/7/60	3	30		3 Above And Beyond	Til These Dreams Come True	—	$15		Capitol 4337
9/19/60	2³	24		4 Excuse Me (I Think I've Got A Heartache) /		—			
10/24/60	25	3		5 I've Got A Right To Know		—	$15		Capitol 4412
1/30/61	2⁸	26		6 Foolin' Around /		113			
3/27/61	27	1		7 High As The Mountains		—	$15		Capitol 4496
5/22/61	4	14		8 Loose Talk /		—			
5/15/61	8	12		9 Mental Cruelty		—	$15		Capitol 4550
				BUCK OWENS And ROSE MADDOX (above 2)					
8/7/61	2¹	24		10 Under The Influence Of Love	Bad Bad Dream	—	$15		Capitol 4602
2/24/62	11	16		11 Nobody's Fool But Yours	Mirror, Mirror On The Wall	—	$15		Capitol 4679
7/28/62	11	11		12 Save The Last Dance For Me	King Of Fools	—	$15		Capitol 4765
				#1 Pop hit for The Drifters in 1960					
10/27/62	8	8		13 Kickin' Our Hearts Around /		—			
10/27/62	17	5		14 I Can't Stop (My Lovin' You)		—	$15		Capitol 4826
12/29/62+	10	14		15 You're For Me /		—			
1/5/63	24	3		16 House Down The Block		—	$15		Capitol 4872
4/13/63	❶⁴	28		17 Act Naturally	Over And Over Again	—	$15		Capitol 4937
				#47 Pop hit for The Beatles in 1965; also see #89 below					
8/3/63	15	6		18 We're The Talk Of The Town /		—			
8/10/63	19	6		19 Sweethearts In Heaven		—	$15		Capitol 4992
				BUCK OWENS AND ROSE MADDOX (above 2)					

DEBUT	PEAK	WKS	Gold	A-side (Chart Hit)	B-side	Pop	$	Pic	Label & Number
				OWENS, Buck — Cont'd					
9/21/63	❶16	30		20 Love's Gonna Live Here	Getting Used To Losing You	—	$12		Capitol 5025
3/28/64	❶7	26		21 My Heart Skips A Beat /		94			
4/4/64	❶2	27		22 Together Again		—	$12		Capitol 5136
8/29/64	❶6	27		23 I Don't Care (Just As Long As You Love Me) /		92			
10/10/64	33	9		24 Don't Let Her Know		130	$12		Capitol 5240
1/23/65	❶5	20		25 I've Got A Tiger By The Tail	Cryin' Time	25	$12	■	Capitol 5336
5/15/65	❶6	20		26 Before You Go	(I Want) No One But You	83	$12	■	Capitol 5410
7/31/65	❶1	19		27 Only You (Can Break My Heart) /		120			
7/31/65	10	14		28 Gonna Have Love		—	$12		Capitol 5465
				also see #90 below					
				BUCK OWENS & THE BUCKAROOS:					
10/30/65	❶2	17		29 Buckaroo /	[I]	60			
12/11/65+	24	9		30 If You Want A Love		—	$10		Capitol 5517
1/22/66	❶7	19		31 Waitin' In Your Welfare Line /		57			
2/26/66	43	2		32 In The Palm Of Your Hand		—	$10		Capitol 5566
				also see #60 below					
5/21/66	❶6	21		33 Think Of Me	Heart Of Glass	74	$10	■	Capitol 5647
9/3/66	❶4	20		34 Open Up Your Heart	No More Me And You	—	$10	■	Capitol 5705
1/14/67	❶4	16		35 Where Does The Good Times Go	The Way That I Love You	114	$10		Capitol 5811
4/1/67	❶3	16		36 Sam's Place	Don't Ever Tell Me Goodbye	92	$10		Capitol 5865
7/15/67	❶1	16		37 Your Tender Loving Care	What A Liar I Am	—	$10		Capitol 5942
10/14/67+	2¹	18		38 It Takes People Like You (To Make People Like Me)	You Left Her Lonely Too Long	114	$10	■	Capitol 2001
1/27/68	❶1	15		39 How Long Will My Baby Be Gone	Everybody Needs Somebody	—	$10		Capitol 2080
4/20/68	2¹	15		40 Sweet Rosie Jones	Happy Times Are Here Again	—	$10		Capitol 2142
7/27/68	7	15		41 Let The World Keep On A Turnin'	I'll Love You Forever And Ever	—	$10		Capitol 2237
				BUCK OWENS AND BUDDY ALAN AND THE BUCKAROOS					
10/26/68	5	15		42 I've Got You On My Mind Again	That's All Right With Me (If It's All Right With You)	—	$8		Capitol 2300
2/1/69	❶2	15		43 Who's Gonna Mow Your Grass	There's Gotta Be Some Changes Made	106	$8	■	Capitol 2377
5/24/69	❶2	15		44 Johnny B. Goode	Maybe If I Close My Eyes (It'll Go Away)	114	$8	■	Capitol 2485
				#8 Pop hit for Chuck Berry in 1958					
8/9/69	❶1	15		45 Tall Dark Stranger	Sing That Kind Of Song	—	$8		Capitol 2570
11/15/69	5	13		46 Big In Vegas	White Satin Bed	100	$8		Capitol 2646
2/21/70	13	11		47 We're Gonna Get Together	Everybody Needs Somebody	—	$8		Capitol 2731
				BUCK OWENS & SUSAN RAYE					
5/9/70	12	12		48 Togetherness	Fallin' For You	—	$8		Capitol 2791
				BUCK OWENS & SUSAN RAYE					
6/6/70	2²	15		49 The Kansas City Song	I'd Love To Be Your Man	—	$8		Capitol 2783
8/29/70	8	13		50 The Great White Horse	Your Tender Loving Care	—	$8		Capitol 2871
				BUCK OWENS & SUSAN RAYE					
11/7/70	9	13		51 I Wouldn't Live In New York City (If They Gave Me The Whole Dang Town)	No Milk And Honey In Baltimore	110	$7	■	Capitol 2947
2/6/71	9	13		52 Bridge Over Troubled Water	(I'm Goin') Home	119	$7		Capitol 3023
				#1 Pop hit for Simon & Garfunkel in 1970					
5/1/71	3	17		53 Ruby (Are You Mad)	Heartbreak Mountain	106	$7		Capitol 3096
9/4/71	2²	14		54 Rollin' In My Sweet Baby's Arms	Corn Likker	—	$7	■	Capitol 3164
12/4/71+	29	10		55 Too Old To Cut The Mustard	Wham Bam	—	$7		Capitol 3215
				BUCK & BUDDY					
2/12/72	8	12		56 I'll Still Be Waiting For You	Full Time Daddy	—	$7		Capitol 3262
4/29/72	❶1	15		57 Made In Japan	Black Texas Dirt	—	$7	■	Capitol 3314
7/15/72	13	14		58 Looking Back To See	Cryin' Time	—	$7		Capitol 3368
9/16/72	13	14		59 You Ain't Gonna Have Ol' Buck To Kick Around No More	I Love You So Much It Hurts	—	$7		Capitol 3429
				"live" recording					
12/30/72+	23	10		60 In The Palm Of Your Hand	Get Out Of Town Before Sundown [R]	—	$6		Capitol 3504
				new version of #32 above					
3/31/73	14	11		61 Ain't It Amazing, Gracie	The Good Old Days (Are Here Again)	—	$6		Capitol 3563
6/16/73	35	8		62 The Good Old Days (Are Here Again)	When You Get To Heaven (I'll Be There)	—	$6		Capitol 3601
				BUCK OWENS & SUSAN RAYE					
				BUCK OWENS:					
8/18/73	27	11		63 Arms Full Of Empty	Songwriter's Lament	—	$6		Capitol 3688
12/1/73+	8	12		64 Big Game Hunter	That Loving Feeling	—	$6		Capitol 3769
3/23/74	9	13		65 On The Cover Of The Music City News	Stony Mountain West Virginia [N]	—	$6		Capitol 3841
				#6 Pop hit for Dr. Hook in 1973 (with different lyrics)					
7/20/74	6	13		66 (It's A) Monsters' Holiday	Great Expectations [N]	—	$6		Capitol 3907
11/30/74+	8	15		67 Great Expectations	Let The Fun Begin	—	$6		Capitol 3976
3/29/75	19	11		68 41st Street Lonely Hearts' Club /					
		7		69 Weekend Daddy		—	$6		Capitol 4043
7/5/75	20	13		70 Love Is Strange	Sweethearts In Heaven	—	$6		Capitol 4100
				BUCK OWENS & SUSAN RAYE					
				#11 Pop hit for Mickey & Sylvia in 1957					
10/4/75	51	7		71 The Battle Of New Orleans	Run Him To The Round House Nellie	—	$6		Capitol 4138
6/26/76	44	9		72 Hollywood Waltz	Rain On Your Parade	—	$5		Warner 8223
9/25/76	43	8		73 California Okie	Child Support	—	$5		Warner 8255
2/26/77	90	4		74 World Famous Holiday Inn	He Don't Deserve You Anymore	—	$5		Warner 8316

George Owens?

DEBUT	PEAK	WKS	Gold	A-side (Chart Hit)	B-side	Pop	$	Pic	Label & Number
				OWENS, Buck — Cont'd					
7/16/77	100	1		75 It's Been A Long, Long Time ... Rain On Your Parade		—	$5		Warner 8395
9/10/77	91	3		76 Our Old Mansion ... How Come My Dog Don't Bark		—	$5		Warner 8433
8/19/78	27	12		77 Nights Are Forever Without You ... When I Need You		—	$5		Warner 8614
				#10 Pop hit for England Dan & John Ford Coley in 1976					
12/23/78+	80	5		78 Do You Wanna Make Love ... Seasons Of My Heart		—	$5		Warner 8701
				#5 Pop hit for Peter McCann in 1977					
5/12/79	11	13		79 Play Together Again Again ... He Don't Deserve You Anymore		—	$5		Warner 8830
				BUCK OWENS With Emmylou Harris					
9/8/79	30	10		80 Hangin' In And Hangin' On ... Sweet Molly Brown's		—	$5		Warner 49046
12/15/79+	22	13		81 Let Jesse Rob The Train ... Victim Of Life's Circumstances		—	$5		Warner 49118
4/5/80	42	9		82 Love Is A Warm Cowboy ... I Don't Want To Live In San Francisco		—	$5		Warner 49200
7/26/80	72	4		83 Moonlight And Magnolia ... Nickels And Dimes		—	$5		Warner 49278
5/30/81	92	2		84 Without You ... Love Don't Make The Bars		—	$5		Warner 49651
7/16/88	❶¹	18		85 Streets Of Bakersfield ... S:❶³ One More Time (Yoakam)		—	$4	■	Reprise 27964
				DWIGHT YOAKAM & BUCK OWENS					
10/22/88	46	9		86 Hot Dog ... Second Fiddle		—	$4	■	Capitol 44248
				first recorded by Owens (as Corky Jones) in 1956 on Pep 107 ($250)					
1/28/89	54	6		87 A-11 ... Sweethearts In Heaven		—	$4		Capitol 44295
4/8/89	60	7		88 Put A Quarter In The Jukebox ... Don't Let Her Know		—	$4		Capitol 44356
7/15/89	27	11		89 Act Naturally ... The Key's In The Mailbox [R]		—	$4		Capitol 44409
				BUCK OWENS AND RINGO STARR					
				new version of #17 above					
10/14/89	76	7		90 Gonna Have Love ... [R]		—			album cut
				new version of #28 above; from the album Act Naturally on Capitol 92893					
				OWENS, Marie '74					
				Born in 1956 in Virginia.					
2/23/74	44	9		1 J. John Jones ... Take It From Me		—	$6		MCA 40184
6/8/74	71	8		2 Release Me ... Just Out Of Reach		—	$6		MCA 40241
				#4 Pop hit for Engelbert Humperdinck in 1967					
11/16/74	71	7		3 I Want To Lay Down Beside You ... Broken Wings		—	$6		MCA 40308
10/25/75	84	4		4 Someone Loves You Honey ... The Devil's Song		—	$6		4 Star 1019
2/12/77	92	4		5 When Your Good Love Was Mine ... I'll Be In His Arms Tonight		—	$7		MMI 1012
5/7/77	88	4		6 Burning ... Wish You Were Here		—	$7		MMI 1015
8/13/77	80	5		7 Ease My Mind On You ... Sweet Love		—	$7		Sing Me 12
				OXFORD, Vernon '76					
				Born on 6/8/41 in Larue, Arkansas; raised in Wichita, Kansas. Singer/songwriter/fiddle player.					
12/6/75+	54	12		1 Shadows Of My Mind ... She's Always There		—	$5		RCA Victor 10442
4/3/76	83	6		2 Your Wanting Me Is Gone ... Don't Be Late		—	$5		RCA Victor 10595
6/12/76	17	12		3 Redneck! (The Redneck National Anthem) ... Leave Me Alone With The Blues		—	$5		RCA Victor 10693
10/16/76	60	7		4 Clean Your Own Tables ... Baby Sister		—	$4		RCA 10787
1/29/77	55	6		5 A Good Old Fashioned Saturday Night Honky Tonk Barroom Brawl ... One More Night To Spare		—	$4		RCA 10872
5/7/77	87	3		6 Only The Shadows Know ... We Sure Danced Us Some Goodn's		—	$4		RCA 10952
7/23/77	95	2		7 Redneck Roots ... Images		—	$4		RCA 11020
				OZARK MOUNTAIN DAREDEVILS '76					
				Country-rock group from Springfield, Missouri: Larry Lee (vocals, drums), John Dillon (guitar), Steve Cash (harmonica) and Michael "Supe" Granda (bass). Best known for their 1975 pop hit "Jackie Blue."					
5/8/76	84	4		You Made It Right ... Dreams		—	$5		A&M 1809

P

DEBUT	PEAK	WKS	Gold	A-side (Chart Hit)	B-side	Pop	$	Pic	Label & Number
				PACIFIC STEEL CO. '80					
				Steel guitar instrumental duo: Jay Dee Maness and Junior "Red" Rhodes.					
12/6/80	88	5		Fat 'N Sassy ... Rio [I]		—	$6		Pacific Arts 111
				PACIFIC STEEL CO. Featuring Jay Dee Maness					
				PACK, Bob '88					
7/23/88	74	4		The Request		—	$6		Oak 1051
				PACK, Ray '89					
2/11/89	91	2		Where Was I		—	$6		Happy Man 818
	★277★			**PAGE, Patti** '51					
				Born Clara Ann Fowler on 11/8/27 in Muskogee, Oklahoma; raised in Tulsa. Own TV series The Patti Page Show from 1955-58 and The Big Record from 1957-58. Acted in the 1960 movie Elmer Gantry. Charted 81 pop hits from 1948-68.					
				1)The Tennessee Waltz 2)Go On Home 3)Hello We're Lonely 4)Money, Marbles And Chalk 5)Mom And Dad's Waltz					
5/7/49	15	1		1 Money, Marbles And Chalk ... J:15 Where Is The One		27	$15		Mercury 5251
1/6/51	2³	12	●	2 The Tennessee Waltz ... J:2 / S:5 / A:5 Long Long Ago		❶¹³	$20		Mercury 5534-X45
7/17/61	21	3		3 Mom And Dad's Waltz ... You'll Answer To Me (Pop #46)		58	$10		Mercury 71823
2/17/62	13	15		4 Go On Home ... Too Late To Cry		42	$10		Mercury 71906
5/30/70	22	10		5 I Wish I Had A Mommy Like You ... He'll Never Take The Place Of You		114	$7		Columbia 45159
1/16/71	24	10		6 Give Him Love ... I Wish I Could Take That Little Boy Home		—	$7		Mercury 73162
5/8/71	37	8		7 Make Me Your Kind Of Woman ... I Wish I Was A Little Boy Again		—	$7		Mercury 73199
8/14/71	63	4		8 I'd Rather Be Sorry ... Words		—	$7		Mercury 73222

DEBUT	PEAK	WKS	Gold	A-side (Chart Hit) ... B-side	Pop	$	Pic	Label & Number
				PAGE, Patti — Cont'd				
11/20/71	38	9		9 Think Again /	—			
		3		10 A Woman Left Lonely	—	$7		Mercury 73249
12/16/72+	14	12		11 Hello We're Lonely ... We're Not Getting Old	—	$7		Mercury 73347
				PATTI PAGE & TOM T. HALL				
9/8/73	42	11		12 I Can't Sit Still ... Love Lives Again	—	$6		Epic 11032
12/29/73+	29	11		13 You're Gonna Hurt Me (One More Time) ... Mama, Take Me Home	—	$6		Epic 11072
5/18/74	59	7		14 Someone Came To See Me (In The Middle Of The Night) ... One Final Stand	—	$6		Epic 11109
11/30/74+	70	7		15 I May Not Be Lovin' You ... Whoever Finds This I Love You	—	$5		Avco 603
7/26/75	67	7		16 Less Than The Song ... Did He Ask About Me	—	$5		Avco 613
3/21/81	39	8		17 No Aces ... Everytime You Touch Me	—	$5		Plantation 197
8/1/81	66	4		18 A Poor Man's Roses /	—			
				new version of her #14 Pop hit from 1957				
7/18/81	76	2		19 On The Inside	—	$5		Plantation 201
				from the TV series *Prisoner: Cell Block H* starring Patsy King				
5/8/82	80	4		20 My Man Friday ... Tennessee Waltz	—	$5		Plantation 208
				PAIGE, Allison '00				
				Born on 5/27/82 in Refugio, Texas.				
5/13/00	72	5		The End Of The World	—			album cut
				from the album *It's My Party* on Capitol 66463				
	★389★			**PAISLEY, Brad** *I'm Gonna Miss Her* '00				
				Born on 10/28/72 in Glen Dale, West Virginia. Singer/songwriter/guitarist. Joined the *Grand Ole Opry* in 2001. CMA Award: 2000 Horizon Award.				
2/6/99	12	31		1 Who Needs Pictures ... S:6 It Never Woulda Worked Out Anyway	65	$4	★	Arista Nash. 13156 (v)
9/4/99	0¹	30		2 He Didn't Have To Be ... I've Been Better	30	$4		Arista Nashville 13176
2/12/00	18	20		3 Me Neither ... Don't Breathe	85	$4		Arista Nashville 13172
7/1/00	0²	32		4 We Danced ... Me Neither	29	$4		Arista Nashville 69009
				from the album *Who Needs Pictures* on Arista Nashville 18871				
10/14/00	68	2		5 Hard To Be A Husband, Hard To Be A Wife	—			album cut
				BRAD PAISLEY & CHELY WRIGHT				
				from the various artists album *75 Years Of The WSM Grand Ole Opry Volume Two* on MCA 170176				
3/24/01	4	21		6 Two People Fell In Love ... Me Neither	51	$4		Arista Nashville 69051
8/18/01	58	1		7 Too Country	—			album cut
				from the album *Part II* on Arista Nashville 67008				
9/1/01+	2³	31		8 Wrapped Around ... All You Really Need Is Love	35	$4		Arista Nashville 69103
				PALMER, Keith '91				
				Born on 6/23/57 in Hayatt, Missouri; raised in Corning, Arkansas. Died on 6/13/96 (age 38). Singer/songwriter.				
9/28/91	54	17		1 Don't Throw Me In The Briarpatch ... My Arms Tonight	—	$4		Epic 73988
1/25/92	60	8		2 Forgotten But Not Gone ... Memory Lane	—	$4		Epic 74174
				PALOMINO ROAD '93				
				Group of Nashville session musicians: Ronnie Guilbeau (vocals), Randy Frazier, J.T. Corenflos and Chip Lewis. Guilbeau is the son of Gib Guilbeau (of the **Burrito Brothers**).				
1/16/93	46	15		Why Baby Why ... White Lightnin'	—	$4		Liberty 56974
				PAPA JOE'S MUSIC BOX — see **SMITH, Jerry**				
				PARIS, Jack '78				
				Born in Ottumwa, Iowa.				
2/14/76	94	3		1 It Sets Me Free ... A Woman Ought To Be	—	$7		2-J 201
3/19/77	98	2		2 Gypsy River ... Mountain Of Love	—	$5		50 States 49
12/10/77+	75	7		3 Mississippi ... Heaven's Here Tonight	—	$5		50 States 57
3/4/78	86	4		4 Lay Down Sally ... I Wonder Where You Are Tonight	—	$5		50 States 58
8/19/78	98	3		5 (It's Gonna Be A) Happy Day	—	$5		50 States 62
	★371★			**PARKER, Billy** '82				
				Born on 7/19/37 in Okemah, Oklahoma; raised in Tulsa. Singer/songwriter/guitarist. DJ on KVOO-Tulsa. Member of **Ernest Tubb**'s band from 1968-70.				
				1)(Who's Gonna Sing) The Last Country Song 2)Until The Next Time 3)I See An Angel Every Day 4)If I Ever Need A Lady 5)I'll Drink To That				
9/18/76	79	8		1 It's Bad When You're Caught (With The Goods) .. I Guess I Owe That Much To You	—	$6		SCR 133
1/22/77	71	8		2 Lord, If I Make It To Heaven Can I Bring My Own Angel Along ... Jerri Again	—	$6		SCR 136
6/4/77	75	6		3 What Did I Promise Her Last Night ... Let A Fool Take A Bow	—	$6		SCR 144
10/1/77	94	3		4 If You Got To Have It Your Way (I'll Go Mine) ... Line Between Love And Hate	—	$6		SCR 148
1/7/78	62	9		5 You Read Between The Lines ... Trophy Of Gold	—	$6		SCR 153
4/29/78	81	4		6 If There's One Angel Missing (She's Here In My Arms Tonight) ... Tough Act To Follow	—	$5	■	SCR 157
8/26/78	50	7		7 Until The Next Time ... Tough Act To Follow	—	$5		SCR 160
12/23/78+	73	6		8 Pleasin' My Woman /	—			
3/10/79	98	1		9 Thanks E.T. Thanks A Lot	—	$5		SCR 162
				tribute to **Ernest Tubb**				
8/11/79	80	4		10 Thanks A Lot	—	$5		SCR 177
12/22/79+	82	6		11 Tough Act To Follow ... Until The Next Time	—	$5		SCR 181
2/14/81	74	3		12 Better Side Of Thirty ... Lord If I Make It	—	$5		Oak 47565
8/22/81	53	7		13 I'll Drink To That ... One More Last Time	—	$5		Soundwaves 4643
1/9/82	51	10		14 I See An Angel Every Day ... Hello Out There	—	$5		Soundwaves 4659
5/1/82	41	11		15 (Who's Gonna Sing) The Last Country Song ... What's A Nice Girl Like You	—	$5		Soundwaves 4670
				BILLY PARKER and Friend				

DEBUT	PEAK	WKS	Gold	A-side (Chart Hit)..B-side	Pop	$	Pic	Label & Number
				PARKER, Billy — Cont'd				
7/31/82	53	8		16 If I Ever Need A Lady ....Can I Have What's Left BILLY PARKER & Friend Darrell McCall (harmony vocal, above 2)	—	$5		Soundwaves 4678
10/30/82	68	6		17 Too Many Irons In The Fire ....Honky Tonk Girl BILLY PARKER and CAL SMITH	—	$5		Soundwaves 4686
3/26/83	68	6		18 Who Said Love Was Fair...Take Me Back To Tulsa BILLY PARKER And FRIENDS	—	$5		Soundwaves 4699
7/9/83	59	8		19 Love Don't Know A Lady (From A Honky Tonk Girl) ....It's Not Me BILLY PARKER and FRIENDS	—	$5		Soundwaves 4708
2/13/88	72	5		20 You Are My Angel	—	$5		Canyon Creek 1208
10/22/88	81	4		21 She's Sittin' Pretty	—	$5		Canyon Creek 0801
5/27/89	87	4		22 It's Time For Your Dreams To Come True..........................You Are My Angel	—	$5		Canyon Creek 0315
				PARKER, Caryl Mack '97 Born in Abilene, Texas. Female singer/songwriter/guitarist.				
10/26/96	67	5		1 Better Love Next Time	—			album cut
3/22/97	66	4		2 One Night Stand .... above 2 from the album *Caryl Mack Parker* on Magnatone 112	—			album cut
				PARKER, Gary Dale '90 Born on 7/6/58 in Nashville.				
1/13/90	87	1		Once And For Always	—	$5		615 1022
				PARKER, Lori '77				
11/13/76	92	3		1 Steppin' Out Tonight ....Empty Arms	—	$5		Con Brio 113
9/3/77	89	4		2 I Like Everything About Loving You..........................Out Of Luck, Out Of Love	—	$5		Con Brio 122
				PARKS, Michael '70 Born on 4/4/38 in Corona, California. Singer/actor. Played "Jim Bronson" on TV's *Then Came Bronson*.				
3/21/70	41	9		Long Lonesome Highway ....Mountain High from the TV series *Then Came Bronson* starring Parks	20	$6		MGM 14104
				PARKS, P.J. '81 Male singer.				
1/10/81	86	4		1 The Way You Are ....Saint Of New Orleans	—	$6		Kik 901
4/4/81	85	3		2 Falling In ....Saint Of New Orleans	—	$6		Kik 903
	★214★			**PARNELL, Lee Roy** '93 Born on 12/21/56 in Stephenville, Texas. Singer/songwriter/guitarist. Also see **Jed Zeppelin**. 1)What Kind Of Fool Do You Think I Am 2)Tender Moment 3)A Little Bit Of You 4)Heart's Desire 5)I'm Holding My Own				
3/17/90	59	8		1 Crocodile Tears ....Let's Have Some Fun	—	$4		Arista 9912
6/30/90	54	13		2 Oughta Be A Law ....Crocodile Tears	—	$4	▮	Arista 2028 (v)
10/27/90	73	1		3 Family Tree ....Red Hot	—	$4		Arista 2093
2/22/92	50	20		4 The Rock ....Road Scholar	—	$4		Arista 12400
5/16/92	2²	20		5 What Kind Of Fool Do You Think I Am ....Roller Coaster	—	$4		Arista 12431
10/3/92+	8	20		6 Love Without Mercy ....Done Deal	—	$4		Arista 12462
3/6/93	2¹	20		7 Tender Moment ....The Rock	—	$4		Arista 12523
8/21/93	6	20		8 On The Road ....Back In My Arms Again	—	$4	▮	Arista 12588 (v)
1/8/94	3	20		9 I'm Holding My Own ....Fresh Coat Of Paint	—	$4	▮	Arista 12642 (v)
5/21/94	17	20		10 Take These Chains From My Heart ....Straight Shooter	—	$4		Arista 12695 (v)
				#8 Pop hit for **Ray Charles** in 1963				
10/1/94	51	9		11 The Power Of Love ....Straight And Narrow	—	$4	▮	Arista 12747 (v)
5/20/95	2¹	20		12 A Little Bit Of You ....Givin' Water To A Drowning Man	—	$4		Career 12823
9/9/95+	12	20		13 When A Woman Loves A Man ....If The House Is Rockin'	—	$4		Career 12862
1/20/96	3	20		14 Heart's Desire ....Knock Yourself Out	—	$4		Career 12952
5/18/96	12	20		15 Givin' Water To A Drowning Man ....Squeeze Me In	—	$4		Career 10503
9/21/96	46	15		16 We All Get Lucky Sometimes ....I Had To Let It Go	—	$4		Career 13044
12/28/96	71	1		17 Please Come Home For Christmas .... [X] from the album *Star Of Wonder* on Arista 18822	—			album cut
4/19/97	35	18		18 Lucky Me, Lucky You................................Every Night's A Saturday Night	—	$4	▮	Career 13078 (v)
8/16/97	39	13		19 You Can't Get There From Here ....Mama Screw Your Wig On Tight	—	$4		Career 13079
2/14/98	50	8		20 All That Matters Anymore.................................One Foot In Front Of The Other	—	$4		Arista Nashville 13098
7/24/99	57	8		21 She Won't Be Lonely Long..Long Way To Fall	—	$4		Arista Nashville 13175
				PARSONS, Rob '82 Born in Traverse City, Michigan. Singer/songwriter.				
1/9/82	74	4		Shadow Of Love ....Today May Be The Day	—	$4		MCA 51202

Old Black Kettle (LP)   ††† ★★ Nostalgia

DEBUT	PEAK	WKS	Gold	A-side (Chart Hit)	B-side	Pop	$	Pic	Label & Number

PARTON, Dolly ★7★   '78

Born on 1/19/46 in Locust Ridge, Tennessee. Singer/songwriter/guitarist/actress. Regular on **Porter Wagoner**'s TV show from 1967-74. Joined the *Grand Ole Opry* in 1969. Starred in the movies *9 To 5, The Best Little Whorehouse In Texas, Steel Magnolias* and *Straight Talk*. In 1986, opened Dollywood theme park in the Smoky Mountains. Hosted own TV variety show in 1987. Sister of **Randy Parton** and **Stella Parton**. CMA Awards: 1968 Vocal Group of the Year (with Porter Wagoner); 1970 & 1971 Vocal Duo of the Year (with Porter Wagoner); 1975 & 1976 Female Vocalist of the Year; 1978 Entertainer of the Year. Elected to the Country Music Hall of Fame in 1999.

1) Here You Come Again 2) Heartbreaker 3) Islands In The Stream 4) You're The Only One 5) It's All Wrong, But It's All Right

DEBUT	PEAK	WKS	Gold	#	A-side	B-side	Pop	$	Pic	Label & Number
1/21/67	24	14		1	Dumb Blonde	The Giving And The Taking	—	$15		Monument 982
6/10/67	17	12		2	Something Fishy	I've Lived My Life	—	$15		Monument 1007
12/2/67+	7	17		3	The Last Thing On My Mind — PORTER WAGONER/DOLLY PARTON	Love Is Worth Living	—	$10		RCA Victor 9369
4/13/68	7	16		4	Holding On To Nothin' — PORTER WAGONER and DOLLY PARTON	Just Between You And Me	—	$10		RCA Victor 9490
6/29/68	17	14		5	Just Because I'm A Woman	I Wish I Felt This Way At Home	—	$10		RCA Victor 9548
7/27/68	5	13		6	We'll Get Ahead Someday /					
10/5/68	51	6		7	Jeannie's Afraid Of The Dark — PORTER WAGONER & DOLLY PARTON (above 2)		—	$10		RCA Victor 9577
11/16/68	25	11		8	In The Good Old Days (When Times Were Bad)	Try Being Lonely	—	$10		RCA Victor 9657
3/8/69	9	14		9	Yours Love — DOLLY PARTON/PORTER WAGONER	Malena	—	$8		RCA Victor 0104
4/12/69	40	10		10	Daddy	He's A Go Getter	—	$8		RCA Victor 0132
6/21/69	16	11		11	Always, Always — PORTER WAGONER AND DOLLY PARTON	No Reason To Hurry Home	—	$8		RCA Victor 0172
7/26/69	50	8		12	In The Ghetto	The Bridge	—	$8		RCA Victor 0192
10/18/69	45	8		13	My Blue Ridge Mountain Boy	'Til Death Do Us Part	—	$8		RCA Victor 0243
10/25/69	5	16		14	Just Someone I Used To Know — PORTER WAGONER and DOLLY PARTON	My Hands Are Tied	—	$8		RCA Victor 0247
1/31/70	40	8		15	Daddy Come And Get Me	Chas	—	$8		RCA Victor 9784
2/14/70	9	15		16	Tomorrow Is Forever — PORTER WAGONER AND DOLLY PARTON	Mendy Never Sleeps	—	$8		RCA Victor 9799
7/4/70	3	16		17	Mule Skinner Blues (Blue Yodel No. 8) #5 Pop hit for The Fendermen in 1960	More Than Their Share	—	$8		RCA Victor 9863
8/1/70	7	15		18	Daddy Was An Old Time Preacher Man — PORTER WAGONER AND DOLLY PARTON	A Good Understanding	—	$8		RCA Victor 9875
12/12/70+	❶¹	15		19	Joshua	I'm Doing This For Your Sake	108	$8		RCA Victor 9928
2/27/71	7	13		20	Better Move It On Home — PORTER WAGONER AND DOLLY PARTON	Two Of A Kind	—	$8		RCA Victor 9958
4/10/71	23	12		21	Comin' For To Carry Me Home based on the American spiritual "Swing Low, Sweet Chariot"	Golden Streets Of Glory	—	$8		RCA Victor 9971
6/26/71	14	12		22	The Right Combination — PORTER WAGONER AND DOLLY PARTON	The Pain Of Loving You	106	$8		RCA Victor 9994
7/17/71	17	12		23	My Blue Tears	The Mystery Of The Mystery	—	$8		RCA Victor 9999
10/30/71	4	16		24	Coat Of Many Colors	Here I Am	—	$7	■	RCA Victor 0538
11/13/71+	11	13		25	Burning The Midnight Oil — PORTER WAGONER AND DOLLY PARTON	More Than Words Can Tell	—	$7		RCA Victor 0565
3/11/72	6	14		26	Touch Your Woman	Mission Chapel Memories	—	$7		RCA Victor 0662
4/8/72	9	14		27	Lost Forever In Your Kiss — PORTER WAGONER AND DOLLY PARTON	The Fog Has Lifted	—	$7		RCA Victor 0675
8/12/72	20	9		28	Washday Blues	Just As Good As Gone	—	$7		RCA Victor 0757
9/2/72	14	13		29	Together Always — PORTER WAGONER AND DOLLY PARTON	Love's All Over	—	$7		RCA Victor 0773
1/6/73	15	13		30	My Tennessee Mountain Home	The Better Part Of Life	—	$7		RCA Victor 0868
3/3/73	30	9		31	We Found It — PORTER WAGONER AND DOLLY PARTON	Love Have Mercy On Us	—	$7		RCA Victor 0893
5/19/73	20	11		32	Traveling Man	I Remember	—	$7		RCA Victor 0950
6/23/73	3	17		33	If Teardrops Were Pennies — PORTER WAGONER AND DOLLY PARTON	Come To Me	—	$7		RCA Victor 0981
11/3/73+	❶¹	19		34	Jolene	Love, You're So Beautiful Tonight	60	$7		RCA Victor 0145
4/6/74	❶¹	15		35	I Will Always Love You #1 Pop hit for Whitney Houston in 1992; also see #65 and #101 below	Lonely Comin' Down	—	$7		RCA Victor 0234
8/3/74	❶¹	17		36	Please Don't Stop Loving Me — PORTER WAGONER & DOLLY PARTON	Sounds Of Nature	—	$7		RCA Victor 10010
8/31/74	❶¹	17		37	Love Is Like A Butterfly	Sacred Memories	105	$7		RCA Victor 10031
1/25/75	❶¹	13		38	The Bargain Store	I'll Never Forget	—	$7		RCA Victor 10164
6/7/75	2¹	16		39	The Seeker	Love With Feeling	105	$6		RCA Victor 10310
7/12/75	5	17		40	Say Forever You'll Be Mine — PORTER WAGONER & DOLLY PARTON	How Can I (Help You Forgive Me)	—	$6		RCA Victor 10328
9/27/75	9	14		41	We Used To	My Heart Started Breaking	—	$6		RCA Victor 10396
2/28/76	19	11		42	Hey, Lucky Lady	Most Of All, Why	—	$6		RCA Victor 10564
5/15/76	8	14		43	Is Forever Longer Than Always — PORTER WAGONER AND DOLLY PARTON	If You Say I Can	—	$6		RCA Victor 10652
7/31/76	3	15		44	All I Can Do	Falling Out Of Love With Me	—	$6		RCA Victor 10730
4/9/77	11	13		45	Light Of A Clear Blue Morning	There	87	$6		RCA 10935
10/15/77	❶⁵	19	●	46	Here You Come Again	Me And Little Andy	3	$5		RCA 11123
3/18/78	❶²	14		47	It's All Wrong, But It's All Right /		—			
		12		48	Two Doors Down		19	$5		RCA 11240

DEBUT	PEAK	WKS	Gold	A-side (Chart Hit)	B-side	Pop	$	Pic	Label & Number
				PARTON, Dolly — Cont'd					
8/19/78	❶³	13		49 Heartbreaker .... Sure Thing		37	$5		RCA 11296
11/25/78+	❶¹	14		50 I Really Got The Feeling /		—			
11/25/78	48	14		51 Baby I'm Burnin'		25	$5		RCA 11420
6/9/79	❶²	14		52 You're The Only One .... Down		59	$5		RCA 11577
9/1/79	7	13		53 Sweet Summer Lovin' /		77			
		1		54 Great Balls Of Fire			$5		RCA 11705
3/22/80	❶¹	14		55 Starting Over Again .... Sweet Agony		36	$5		RCA 11926
6/21/80	2²	17		56 Making Plans .... Beneath The Sweet Magnolia Tree		—	$5		RCA 11983
				PORTER WAGONER AND DOLLY PARTON					
7/19/80	❶¹	16		57 Old Flames Can't Hold A Candle To You .... I Knew You When		—	$5		RCA 12040
11/8/80+	12	14		58 If You Go, I'll Follow You .... Hide Me Away		—	$5		RCA 12119
				PORTER WAGONER & DOLLY PARTON					
11/29/80+	❶¹	14	●	59 9 To 5 .... Sing For The Common Man		❶²	$4	■	RCA 12133
				from the movie starring Parton					
4/11/81	❶¹	17		60 But You Know I Love You .... Poor Folks Town		41	$4		RCA 12200
8/29/81	14	13		61 The House Of The Rising Sun /		77			
				#1 Pop hit for The Animals in 1964					
		1		62 Working Girl		—	$4		RCA 12282
2/27/82	8	17		63 Single Women .... Barbara On Your Mind		—	$4		RCA 13057
5/29/82	7	15		64 Heartbreak Express .... Act Like A Fool		—	$4		RCA 13234
7/31/82	❶¹	19		65 I Will Always Love You /		[R] 53			
				new version of #35 above; from the movie *The Best Little Whorehouse In Texas* starring Parton; also see #101 below					
		19		66 Do I Ever Cross Your Mind		—	$4	■	RCA 13260
11/6/82	8	17		67 Hard Candy Christmas .... Me And Little Andy [X]		—	$4		RCA 13361
				also see #103 below; from the movie *The Best Little Whorehouse In Texas* starring Parton					
12/11/82+	7	20		68 Everything's Beautiful (In It's Own Way)					
				.... Put It Off Until Tomorrow (Dolly Parton Kris Kristofferson)	102	$5		Monument 03408
				DOLLY PARTON/WILLIE NELSON					
4/30/83	20	16		69 Potential New Boyfriend .... One Of Those Days		—	$4		RCA 13514
9/3/83	❶²	23	▲	70 Islands In The Stream .... I Will Always Love You (Rogers)		❶²	$4	■	RCA 13615
				KENNY ROGERS with Dolly Parton					
12/24/83+	3	19		71 Save The Last Dance For Me .... Elusive Butterfly		45	$4		RCA 13703
				#1 Pop hit for The Drifters in 1960					
4/7/84	36	10		72 Downtown .... The Great Pretender		80	$4	■	RCA 13756
				#1 Pop hit for Petula Clark in 1965					
6/9/84	❶¹	20		73 Tennessee Homesick Blues .... Butterflies		—	$4		RCA 13819
9/15/84	10	20		74 God Won't Get You .... S:10 / A:11 Sweet Lovin' Friends		—	$4		RCA 13883
				above 2 from the movie *Rhinestone* starring Parton					
12/15/84	53	7		75 The Greatest Gift Of All .... White Christmas (Parton) [X]		81	$4		RCA 13945
				KENNY ROGERS & DOLLY PARTON					
1/26/85	3	22		76 Don't Call It Love .... A:3 / S:4 We Got Too Much		—	$4		RCA 13987
5/25/85	❶¹	20		77 Real Love .... S:❶¹ / A:❶¹ I Can't Be True (Parton)		91	$4	■	RCA 14058
				DOLLY PARTON (with Kenny Rogers)					
11/30/85+	❶¹	22		78 Think About Love .... S:❶¹ / A:❶¹ Come Back To Me		—	$4		RCA 14218
5/3/86	17	15		79 Tie Our Love (In A Double Knot) .... A:15 / S:17 I Hope You're Never Happy		—	$4		RCA 14297
9/6/86	31	13		80 We Had It All .... S:28 / A:29 Do I Ever Cross Your Mind		—	$4		RCA 5001
2/21/87	❶¹	19		81 To Know Him Is To Love Him .... S:❶¹ / A:❶¹ Farther Along		—	$4	■	Warner 28492
				DOLLY PARTON, LINDA RONSTADT, EMMYLOU HARRIS					
				#1 Pop hit for The Teddy Bears in 1958					
5/30/87	3	18		82 Telling Me Lies .... S:10 Rosewood Casket		—	$4		Warner 28371
				DOLLY PARTON, LINDA RONSTADT, EMMYLOU HARRIS					
9/26/87	5	22		83 Those Memories Of You .... S:10 My Dear Companion		—	$4	■	Warner 28248
				DOLLY PARTON, LINDA RONSTADT, EMMYLOU HARRIS					
12/19/87+	63	8		84 The River Unbroken .... More Than I Can Say		—	$4	■	Columbia 07665
3/26/88	6	18		85 Wildflowers .... S:13 Hobo's Meditation		—	$4		Warner 27970
				DOLLY PARTON, LINDA RONSTADT, EMMYLOU HARRIS					
5/6/89	❶¹	20		86 Why'd You Come In Here Lookin' Like That ... Wait 'Till I Get You Home		—	$4		Columbia 68760
8/26/89	❶¹	26		87 Yellow Roses .... Wait 'Til I Get You Home		—	$4		Columbia 69040
12/9/89+	39	8		88 He's Alive .... What Is It My Love		—	$4		Columbia 73200
2/3/90	39	11		89 Time For Me To Fly .... The Moon, The Stars And Me		—	$4		Columbia 73226
				#56 Pop hit for REO Speedwagon in 1978					
5/12/90	29	12		90 White Limozeen .... The Moon, The Stars And Me		—	$4	▌	Columbia 73341 (v)
8/18/90	21	20		91 Love Is Strange .... Walk Away		—	$4	▌	Reprise 19760 (v)
				KENNY ROGERS and DOLLY PARTON					
				#11 Pop hit for Mickey & Sylvia in 1957					
3/2/91	❶¹	20		92 Rockin' Years .... What A Heartache		—	$4		Columbia 73711
				DOLLY PARTON WITH RICKY VAN SHELTON					
6/8/91	15	20		93 Silver And Gold .... Runaway Feelin'		—	$4		Columbia 73826
10/19/91	33	20		94 Eagle When She Flies .... Wildest Dreams		—	$4		Columbia 74011
1/25/92	46	10		95 Country Road .... Best Woman Wins		—	$4		Columbia 74183
4/11/92	64	5		96 Straight Talk .... Dirty Job		—	$4	▌	Hollywood 64776
				from the movie starring Parton					
2/13/93	27	20		97 Romeo .... High And Mighty (Parton)		50	$4	▌	Columbia 74876 (v)
				DOLLY PARTON AND FRIENDS					
				Mary Chapin-Carpenter, Billy Ray Cyrus, Kathy Mattea, Pam Tillis and Tanya Tucker (guest vocals)					
5/1/93	58	9		98 More Where That Came From .... I'll Make Your Bed		—	$4	▌	Columbia 74954 (v)
12/25/93+	68	2		99 Silver Threads And Golden Needles .... Let Her Fly		—	$4	▌	Columbia 77294 (v)
				PARTON/WYNETTE/LYNN					

DEBUT	PEAK	WKS	Gold	A-side (Chart Hit)	B-side	Pop	$	Pic	Label & Number
				PARTON, Dolly — Cont'd					
10/15/94	70	4		100 PMS Blues	To Daddy	—	$4		Columbia 77723
9/16/95	15	20		101 I Will Always Love You	Speakin' Of The Devil [R]	—	$4		Columbia 78079
				DOLLY PARTON WITH VINCE GILL					
				new version of #35 and #65 above					
10/5/96	62	10		102 Just When I Needed You Most	For The Good Times	—	$4		Rising Tide 56041
7/19/97	8ˢ	12		103 Peace Train (2 versions)		119	$4	■	Flip It 44000
				Ladysmith Black Mambazo (backing vocals); #7 Pop hit for Cat Stevens in 1971					
12/27/97	73	2		104 Hard Candy Christmas	Me And Little Andy [X-R]	—	$4		RCA 13361
				same version as #67 above					
9/5/98	74	2		105 Honky Tonk Songs	Paradise Road	—	$4		Decca 72061
12/26/98	70	2		106 Winter Wonderland/Sleigh Ride (Medley)	[X]	—			album cut
				from the album *Country Christmas Classics* on RCA 67698					
				PARTON, Randy '81					
				Born on 12/15/55 in Sevier County, Tennessee. Brother of **Dolly Parton**.					
3/7/81	30	12		1 Hold Me Like You Never Had Me	My Blue Tears	—	$4		RCA 12137
8/1/81	30	10		2 Shot Full Of Love	Please Don't Lie	—	$4		RCA 12271
12/19/81	80	4		3 Don't Cry Baby	Again And Again	—	$4		RCA 12351
5/1/82	76	4		4 Oh, No	Hold Me Like You Never Had Me	—	$4	□	RCA 13087
				#4 Pop hit for the Commodores in 1981					
10/22/83	92	2		5 A Stranger In Her Bed	Waltz Across Texas	—	$4		RCA 13608
	★346★			**PARTON, Stella** '75					
				Born on 5/4/49 in Sevier County, Tennessee. Sister of **Dolly Parton**.					
				1)I Want To Hold You In My Dreams Tonight 2)Standard Lie Number One 3)The Danger Of A Stranger					
5/24/75	9	18		1 I Want To Hold You In My Dreams Tonight	Ode To Olivia	—	$6		Country Soul 039
9/27/75	56	10		2 It's Not Funny Anymore	(I've Got To Get Back On) The Right Side Of God	—	$6		Soul Country 088
1/8/77	87	5		3 Neon Women	Crying Steel Guitar	—	$5		Elektra 45367
				CARMOL TAYLOR & STELLA PARTON					
3/19/77	60	9		4 I'm Not That Good At Goodbye	Love Me To Sleep	—	$5		Elektra 45383
7/30/77	15	13		5 The Danger Of A Stranger	The More The Change	—	$5		Elektra 45410
11/12/77+	14	15		6 Standard Lie Number One	The More The Change	—	$5		Elektra 45437
3/25/78	20	10		7 Four Little Letters	Fade My Blues Away	—	$5		Elektra 45468
7/1/78	28	9		8 Undercover Lovers	There's A Rumor Going 'Round	—	$5		Elektra 45490
10/14/78	21	10		9 Stormy Weather	Lie To Linda	—	$5		Elektra 45533
4/21/79	26	11		10 Steady As The Rain	A Little Inconvenient	—	$5		Elektra 46029
7/28/79	36	9		11 The Room At The Top Of The Stairs	Honey Come Home	—	$5		Elektra 46502
3/6/82	65	7		12 I'll Miss You	I Hate The Night	—	$5	■	Town House 1056
7/24/82	75	5		13 Young Love	Something To Go By	—	$5	■	Town House 1058
				#1 Pop hit for Tab Hunter in 1957					
3/21/87	86	3		14 Cross My Heart	Heart Don't Fail Me Now	—	$5	■	Luv 132
4/1/89	74	3		15 I Don't Miss You Like I Used To		—	$5		Airborne 10015
				PASTELL, James '77					
				Born James Robert Futch in 1940 in El Dorado, Arkansas.					
9/10/77	95	5		Hell Yes I Cheated	Woman Of The World	—	$6		Paula 425
				PAUL, Buddy '60					
				Worked as a DJ at KCIJ in Shreveport, Louisiana.					
8/1/60	22	4		This Old Town	Foolish Me	—	$25		Murco 1018
				PAUL, Joyce '68					
6/22/68	36	10		Phone Call To Mama	Don't Keep Me Hanging On	—	$7		United Artists 50315
				PAUL, Les, and Mary Ford '51					
				Pop duo. Paul was born Lester Polsfuss on 6/9/15 in Waukesha, Wisconsin. Innovator in electric guitar and multi-track recordings. Mary Ford was born Colleen Summers on 7/7/24 in Pasadena, California. Died on 9/30/77 (age 53). They were married from 1949-63. Charted 42 pop hits from 1945-61.					
3/10/51	7	1	●	Mockin' Bird Hill A:7	Chicken Reel (Paul)	2⁵	$20		Capitol F1373
				#2 Pop hit for **Patti Page** in 1951					
				PAXTON, Gary S. '76					
				Born in Mesa, Arizona. Recorded with Clyde "Skip" Battin as "Gary & Clyde" and "Skip & Flip."					
2/7/76	85	5		Too Far Gone (To Care What You Do To Me)	Freedom Lives In A Country Song	—	$5		RCA Victor 10449
				PAYCHECK, Johnny ★72★ '78					
				Born Donald Eugene Lytle on 5/31/38 in Greenfield, Ohio. Singer/songwriter/guitarist. Played in the backing bands for **Porter Wagoner**, **Faron Young**, **Ray Price** and **George Jones**. First recorded solo as Donny Young. Served two years in prison for a 1985 barroom shooting incident. Joined the *Grand Ole Opry* in 1997.					
				1)Take This Job And Shove It 2)Mr. Lovemaker 3)She's All I Got 4)Someone To Give My Love To 5)Slide Off Of Your Satin Sheets					
10/16/65	26	12		1 A-11	Where (In The World)	—	$15		Hilltop 3007
2/26/66	40	2		2 Heartbreak Tennessee	Help Me Hank I'm Fallin'	—	$15		Hilltop 3009
6/4/66	8	19		3 The Lovin' Machine	Pride Covered Ears	—	$10		Little Darlin' 008
11/5/66+	13	15		4 Motel Time Again	If You Should Come Back Today	—	$10		Little Darlin' 0016
4/8/67	15	15		5 Jukebox Charlie	Something In Your World	—	$10		Little Darlin' 0020
9/2/67	32	10		6 The Cave	Then Love Dies	—	$10		Little Darlin' 0032
12/23/67+	41	11		7 Don't Monkey With Another Monkey's Monkey	You'll Recover In Time	—	$10		Little Darlin' 0035

DEBUT	PEAK	WKS	Gold	A-side (Chart Hit)...B-side	Pop	$	Pic	Label & Number
				PAYCHECK, Johnny — Cont'd				
4/27/68	59	7		8 (It Won't Be Long) And I'll Be Hating You.................Fool's Hall Of Fame	—	$10		Little Darlin' 0042
8/17/68	66	4		9 My Heart Keeps Running To You.................Yesterday, Today And Tomorrow	—	$10		Little Darlin' 0046
12/14/68	73	4		10 If I'm Gonna Sink.................The Loser	—	$10		Little Darlin' 0052
6/28/69	31	13		11 Wherever You Are.................I Can't Promise You Won't Get Lonely	—	$10		Little Darlin' 0060
10/9/71	2¹	19		12 **She's All I Got**.................You Touched My Life	91	$7		Epic 10783
				#39 Pop hit for Freddie North in 1971				
3/11/72	4	14		13 Someone To Give My Love To.................Love Sure Is Beautiful	—	$7		Epic 10836
5/27/72	13	11		14 Let's All Go Down To The River.................In The Garden	—	$8		Epic 10863
				JODY MILLER AND JOHNNY PAYCHECK				
6/24/72	12	11		15 Love Is A Good Thing.................High On The Thought Of You	—	$7		Epic 10876
10/7/72	21	12		16 Somebody Loves Me.................Without You (There's No Such Thing As Love)	—	$7		Epic 10912
2/24/73	10	13		17 Something About You I Love.................Your Love Is The Key To It All	—	$6		Epic 10947
6/9/73	2³	15		18 Mr. Lovemaker.................Once You've Had The Best	—	$6		Epic 10999
11/3/73+	8	15		19 Song And Dance Man.................Love Is A Strange And Wonderful Thing	—	$6		Epic 11046
3/16/74	19	12		20 My Part Of Forever.................If Love Gets Any Better	—	$6		Epic 11090
7/6/74	23	11		21 Keep On Lovin' Me.................Ballad Of Thunder Road	—	$6		Epic 11142
11/2/74+	12	15		22 For A Minute There.................She's All I Live For	—	$6		Epic 50040
3/1/75	26	11		23 Loving You Beats All I've Ever Seen.................The Touch Of The Master's Hand	—	$6		Epic 50073
5/31/75	38	12		24 I Don't Love Her Anymore.................Loving You Is All I Thought It Would Be	—	$6		Epic 50111
9/27/75	23	12		25 All-American Man.................The Fool Strikes Again	—	$6		Epic 50146
2/21/76	56	8		26 The Feminine Touch.................Rhythm Guitar	—	$6		Epic 50193
5/8/76	49	8		27 Gone At Last.................Live With Me ('Til I Can Learn To Live Again)	—	$6		Epic 50215
				JOHNNY PAYCHECK (With CHARNISSA)				
				#23 Pop hit for Paul Simon & Phoebe Snow in 1975				
7/24/76	34	10		28 11 Months And 29 Days.................Live With Me ('Til I Can Learn To Live Again)	—	$6		Epic 50249
10/23/76	44	8		29 I Can See Me Lovin' You Again.................I Sleep With Her Memory Every Night	—	$6		Epic 50291
2/12/77	7	16		30 **Slide Off Of Your Satin Sheets**.................That's What The Outlaws In Texas Want To Hear	—	$6		Epic 50334
6/11/77	8	16		31 **I'm The Only Hell (Mama Ever Raised)**.................(To Be So Bad) She's Still Lookin' Good	—	$6		Epic 50391
11/5/77+	❶²	18		32 **Take This Job And Shove It** /	—			
1/28/78	50	10		33 Colorado Kool-Aid.................[S]	—	$6		Epic 50469
4/15/78	17	10		34 **Georgia In A Jug** /				
4/15/78	33	10		35 Me And The I.R.S.	—	$6		Epic 50539
10/21/78	7	12		36 **Friend, Lover, Wife**.................Leave It To Me	—	$6		Epic 50621
12/9/78+	7	13		37 Mabellene.................I Don't Want No Stranger Sleepin' In My Bed	—	$7		Epic 50647
				GEORGE JONES AND JOHNNY PAYCHECK				
				#5 Pop hit for Chuck Berry in 1955				
1/27/79	27	11		38 The Outlaw's Prayer.................Armed And Crazy	—	$6		Epic 50655
1/27/79	94	4		39 Down On The Corner At A Bar Called Kelly's.................Something He'll Have To Learn	—	$6		Little Darlin' 7808
				recorded in 1967				
5/26/79	14	11		40 You Can Have Her.................Along Came Jones	—	$6		Epic 50708
				GEORGE JONES AND JOHNNY PAYCHECK				
				#12 Pop hit for Roy Hamilton in 1961				
10/13/79	49	6		41 (Stay Away From) The Cocaine Train.................Billy Bardo	—	$5		Epic 50777
12/22/79+	17	13		42 Drinkin' And Drivin'.................Just Makin' Love Don't Make It Love	—	$5		Epic 50818
4/5/80	40	9		43 Fifteen Beers.................Who Was That Man That Beat Me So	—	$5		Epic 50863
6/21/80	31	9		44 When You're Ugly Like Us (You Just Naturally Got To Be Cool).................Kansas City	—	$6		Epic 50891
9/6/80	22	11		45 In Memory Of A Memory.................New York Town	—	$5		Epic 50923
12/13/80+	18	12		46 You Better Move On.................Smack Dab In The Middle	—	$6		Epic 50949
				GEORGE JONES and JOHNNY PAYCHECK				
				#24 Pop hit for Arthur Alexander in 1962				
3/28/81	41	8		47 I Can't Hold Myself In Line.................Carolyn	—	$5		Epic 51012
				JOHNNY PAYCHECK AND MERLE HAGGARD				
7/4/81	57	7		48 Yesterday's News (Just Hit Home Today).................Someone Told My Story	—	$4		Epic 02144
1/23/82	75	4		49 The Highlight Of '81.................Sharon Rae	—	$4		Epic 02684
4/24/82	69	5		50 No Way Out.................We've All Gone Crazy	—	$4		Epic 02817
8/14/82	88	4		51 D.O.A. (Drunk On Arrival).................Gonna Get Right (And Do Somethin' Wrong)	—	$4		Epic 03052
12/1/84+	30	18		52 I Never Got Over You.................S:27 / A:30 Ole Pay Ain't Checked Out Yet	—	$5		A.M.I. 1322
4/6/85	47	10		53 You're Every Step I Take.................I Can't Quit Drinking	—	$5		A.M.I. 1323
12/7/85	63	8		54 Everything Is Changing.................Palimony	—	$5		A.M.I. 1327
5/17/86	21	22		55 Old Violin.................S:12 / A:25 Come To Me	—	$4		Mercury 884720
11/8/86	49	10		56 Don't Bury Me 'Til I'm Ready.................Ex-Wives And Lovers	—	$4		Mercury 888088
2/28/87	56	7		57 Come To Me.................Ragtime Redneck Boy	—	$4		Mercury 888341
7/11/87	72	5		58 I Grow Old Too Fast (And Smart Too Slow).................Caught Between A Rock And A Soft Place	—	$4		Mercury 888651
4/9/88	81	2		59 Out Of Beer.................Oklahoma Lady	—	$6		Desperado 1001
2/18/89	90	2		60 Scars	—	$6		Damascus 2001
				PAYNE, Dennis '88				
				Born in Bakersfield, California. Singer/songwriter.				
2/20/88	66	5		1 I Can't Hang On Anymore	—	$5		True 88
10/29/88	94	2		2 That's Why You Haven't Seen Me.................Crazy Woman	—	$5	■	True 93

DEBUT	PEAK	WKS	Gold	A-side (Chart Hit)	B-side	Pop	$	Pic	Label & Number
				PAYNE, Jimmy '69					
				Born on 4/12/36 in Leachville, Arkansas. Singer/songwriter/guitarist.					
4/19/69	60	6		1 L.A. Angels ... A Rose Is A Rose		—	$6		Epic 10444
11/3/73	79	5		2 Ramblin' Man ... One Man's Woman At A Time		—	$6		Cinnamon 772
				#2 Pop hit for The Allman Brothers Band in 1973					
8/1/81	80	4		3 Turnin' My Love On ... She's Free But She's Not Easy		—	$6		Kik 907
				PAYNE, Jody '81					
				Born in 1936 in Garrard County, Kentucky. Male singer/harmonica player. Member of **Willie Nelson**'s band.					
2/28/81	65	6		There's A Crazy Man		—	$4		Kari 117
				JODY PAYNE & The Willie Nelson Family Band					
				PAYNE, Leon '50					
				Born on 6/15/17 in Alba, Texas. Died of a heart attack on 9/11/69 (age 52). Blind since early childhood. Singer/songwriter/guitarist/pianist/drummer.					
11/5/49+	❶²	32		I Love You Because A:❶² / S:4 / J:10 A Link In The Chain Of Broken Hearts		—	$15		Capitol 40238
				PEARCE, Kevin '88					
				Born in 1960 in Lake Alfred, Florida.					
1/14/84	91	2		1 It's Gonna Be A Heartache		—	$5		Orlando 108
1/18/86	92	2		2 Pink Cadillac		—	$5		Orlando 111
				written by Bruce Springsteen (B-side of his 1984 Pop hit "Dancing In The Dark"); #5 Pop hit for Natalie Cole in 1988					
10/31/87	90	2		3 The Bigger The Love		—	$5		Evergreen 1057
2/27/88	66	6		4 Love Ain't Made For Fools		—	$5		Evergreen 1067
6/25/88	68	6		5 Took It Like A Man, Cried Like A Baby		—	$5		Evergreen 1074
				PEARL, Minnie — see **MINNIE**					
				PEARL RIVER '93					
				Group from Mississippi: Jeff Stewart (vocals), Chuck Ethredge, Ken Fleming, Bryan Culpepper, Joe Morgan and Derek George.					
5/1/93	62	8		Fool To Fall					album cut
				from the album *Find Out What's Happening* on Liberty 80478					
				PEDERSEN, Herb '77					
				Born on 4/27/44 in Berkeley, California. Singer/songwriter/banjo player. Member of **The Desert Rose Band**.					
1/15/77	56	7		Our Baby's Gone ... Jesus Once Again		—	$5		Epic 50309
				PEEK, Everett '77					
5/7/77	94	3		Sea Cruise		—	$7		Commercial 00016
				#14 Pop hit for Frankie Ford in 1959					
				PEEL, Dave '70					
				Born in Nashville. Singer/actor. Played "Bud Hamilton" in the movie *Nashville*.					
11/15/69	66	4		1 I'm Walkin' ... My Baby		—	$6		Chart 5037
				#4 Pop hit for Fats Domino in 1957					
3/14/70	62	7		2 Wax Museum ... If You've Been Better Than I've Been (You've Been Bored)		—	$6		Chart 5054
5/23/70	44	9		3 Hit The Road Jack ... The Question		—	$6		Chart 5066
				CONNIE EATON & DAVE PEEL					
				#1 Pop hit for Ray Charles in 1961					
11/7/70	56	7		4 It Takes Two ... No Rest For The Wicked		—	$6		Chart 5099
				CONNIE EATON & DAVE PEEL					
				#14 Pop hit for Marvin Gaye & Kim Weston in 1967					
1/23/71	56	4		5 (You've Got To) Move Two Mountains ... Willard Crabtree's Running For Trustee		—	$6		Chart 5109
				#20 Pop hit for Marv Johnson in 1960					
	★367★			**PEGGY SUE** '69					
				Born Peggy Sue Webb on 3/24/47 in Butcher Holler, Kentucky. Singer/songwriter. Sister of **Loretta Lynn**, **Crystal Gayle** and Jay Lee Webb; distant cousin of **Patty Loveless**. Married to **Sonny Wright**.					
				1) I'm Dynamite 2) I'm Gettin' Tired Of Babyin' You 3) I Want To See Me In Your Eyes					
6/7/69	28	11		1 I'm Dynamite ... Love Whatcha Got At Home		—	$6		Decca 32485
11/1/69	30	10		2 I'm Gettin' Tired Of Babyin' You ... No Woman Can Hold Him Too Long		—	$6		Decca 32571
4/18/70	65	3		3 After The Preacher's Gone ... You Can't Pull The Wool Over My Eyes		—	$6		Decca 32640
7/11/70	37	11		4 All American Husband ... I'm Leaving The Bottle And You		—	$6		Decca 32698
12/12/70	58	4		5 Apron Strings ... You're Leavin' Me For Her Again		—	$6		Decca 32754
5/15/71	68	5		6 I Say, "Yes, Sir" ... Do It Girl Before It's Too Late		—	$6		Decca 32812
1/15/77	34	10		7 Every Beat Of My Heart ... This Time It's Love		—	$5		Door Knob 021
				#6 Pop hit for Gladys Knight & The Pips in 1961					
4/9/77	51	9		8 I Just Came In Here (To Let A Little Hurt Out) ... Jody Come Home		—	$5		Door Knob 029
7/2/77	81	4		9 Good Evening Henry ... Fire In Texas		—	$5		Door Knob 036
10/22/77	100	1		10 If This Is What Love's All About ... Someone I Can't Say No To		—	$5		Door Knob 038
				PEGGY SUE & SONNY WRIGHT					
2/4/78	85	5		11 To Be Loved ... I've Been Close To Love (Too Many Times)		—	$5		Door Knob 045
				#22 Pop hit for Jackie Wilson in 1958					
6/10/78	87	2		12 Let Me Down Easy ... Come And Lay Down With Me		—	$5		Door Knob 052
9/2/78	80	5		13 All Night Long ... Good Evening Henry		—	$5		Door Knob 069
11/18/78+	37	12		14 How I Love You In The Morning ... Where Your Memories Play		—	$5		Door Knob 079
3/24/79	30	10		15 I Want To See Me In Your Eyes ... Let Me Down Easy		—	$5		Door Knob 094
6/30/79	51	6		16 The Love Song And The Dream Belong To Me ... Rainy Day Lovin		—	$5		Door Knob 102
11/10/79	86	5		17 Gently Hold Me ... If This Is What Love's All About		—	$5		Door Knob 113
				PEGGY SUE and SONNY WRIGHT					
3/29/80	80	4		18 For As Long As You Want Me ... Only One Thing Left To Do		—	$5		Door Knob 121
7/12/80	93	3		19 Why Don't You Go To Dallas ... Only One Thing Left To Do		—	$5		Door Knob 131

DEBUT	PEAK	WKS	Gold	A-side (Chart Hit)	B-side	Pop	$	Pic	Label & Number
				PENN, Bobby '71					
				Born in Houston.					
7/3/71	51	11		1 You Were On My Mind .... Pretty Girl From Kingston Town		—	$6		50 States 1
				#3 Pop hit for We Five in 1965					
9/7/74	88	5		2 Watch Out For Lucy .... The Worst I Ever Had Was Good		—	$5		50 States 29
7/4/76	100	1		3 Little Weekend Warriors .... You're All That Really Matters To Me		—	$5		50 States 42
				PENNINGTON, J.P. '91					
				Born James Preston Pennington on 1/22/49 in Berea, Kentucky. Former member of **Exile**.					
3/23/91	45	19		1 Whatever It Takes .... If I Were You		—	$4		MCA 54047
8/3/91	72	1		2 You Gotta Get Serious .... Blue Highway		—	$4		MCA 54126
				PENNINGTON, Ray '67					
				Born Ramon Daniel Pennington 1933 in Clay County, Kentucky. Singer/songwriter/guitarist. Member of **Bluestone** and **The Swing Shift Band**.					
11/5/66	43	9		1 Who's Been Mowing The Lawn (While I Was Gone) .... I Don't Feel At Home		—	$8		Capitol 5751
5/6/67	29	8		2 Ramblin' Man .... Let Go		—	$8		Capitol 5855
11/18/67	65	3		3 Who's Gonna Walk The Dog (And Put Out The Cat) ...... You Turned The Lights On		—	$8		Capitol 2006
7/5/69	70	6		4 What Eva Doesn't Have .... Denver		—	$6		Monument 1145
12/6/69	69	5		5 This Song Don't Care Who Sings It .... I Wouldn't Treat A Doggone Dog		—	$6		Monument 1170
5/2/70	61	7		6 You Don't Know Me .... Country Blues		—	$6		Monument 1194
				#2 Pop hit for **Ray Charles** in 1962					
8/8/70	74	2		7 The Other Woman .... I Know Love		—	$6		Monument 1208
1/2/71	68	5		8 Bubbles In My Beer .... Don't Build No Fences For Me		—	$6		Monument 1231
11/18/78	79	4		9 She Wanted A Little Bit More		—	$5		MRC 1022
				PENNY, Hank '46					
				Born Herbert Clayton Penny on 9/18/18 in Birmingham, Alabama. Died of heart failure on 4/17/92 (age 73). Singer/songwriter/banjo player. Worked as a comedian on **Spade Cooley**'s TV series in Los Angeles. Married to **Sue Thompson** from 1953-63.					
6/15/46	4	6		1 Steel Guitar Stomp .... I'm Counting The Days [I]		—	$25		King 528
9/14/46	4	4		2 Get Yourself A Red Head .... Missouri		—	$25		King 540
2/25/50	4	12		3 Bloodshot Eyes .... J:4 I Was Satisfied		—	$25		King 828
				PENNY, Joe '64					
7/18/64	41	7		Frosty Window Pane .... Hatty Fatty		—	$20		Sims 173
				PEPPER, Brenda '75					
				Born in Chicago.					
6/21/75	97	4		You Bring Out The Best In Me .... Goodbye Ain't As Far Away As Gone		—	$5		Playboy 6038
				PEREZ, Tony '89					
3/4/89	79	3		1 Oh How I Love You (Como Te Quiero) .... Bridge To Burn		—	$4		Reprise 27591
10/14/89	78	4		2 Take Another Run .... Texarkana		—	$4		Reprise 22838
				PERFECT STRANGER '95					
				Group from Texas: Steve Murray (vocals), Richard Raines (guitar), Shayne Morrison (bass) and Andy Ginn (drums).					
4/15/95	4	22		1 You Have The Right To Remain Silent .... S:2 It's Up To You		61	$4	■	Curb 76956 (v)
9/30/95	52	10		2 I'm A Stranger Here Myself .... I Ain't Never		—	$4	■	Curb 76969 (v)
2/17/96	56	10		3 Remember The Ride .... Cut Me Off		—	$4	■	Curb 76978 (v)
3/29/97	62	7		4 Fire When Ready .... (remix)		—	$4	■	Curb 73014
1/16/99	66	7		5 A Little Bit More Of Your Love		—			album cut
4/15/00	75	1		6 Coming Up Short Again		—			album cut
				above 2 from the album *The Hits* on Curb 78718					
	★319★			**PERKINS, Carl** '56					
				Born on 4/9/32 near Tiptonville, Tennessee. Died of a stroke on 1/19/98 (age 65). Rockabilly singer/guitarist/songwriter. Member of **Johnny Cash**'s touring band from 1965-75. Inducted into the Rock and Roll Hall of Fame in 1987. 1)Blue Suede Shoes 2)Boppin' The Blues 3)Dixie Fried					
2/18/56	❶³	24		1 Blue Suede Shoes .... J:❶³ / S:2 / A:2 Honey, Don't!		2⁴	$60		Sun 234
6/30/56	7	6		2 Boppin' The Blues .... J:7 / S:9 All Mama's Children		70	$50		Sun 243
10/6/56	10	2		3 Dixie Fried / S:10		—			
		2		4 I'm Sorry, I'm Not Sorry		—	$60		Sun 249
3/9/57	13	8		5 Your True Love .... S:13 Matchbox		67	$50		Sun 261
3/31/58	17	9		6 Pink Pedal Pushers .... S:17 Jive After Five		91	$40	■	Columbia 41131
12/17/60+	22	15		7 Country Boy's Dream .... If I Could Come Back		—	$30		Dollie 505
5/20/67	40	8		8 Shine, Shine, Shine .... Almost Love		—	$30		Dollie 508
1/4/69	20	15		9 Restless 11:43		—	$15		Columbia 44723
5/29/71	65	5		10 Me Without You .... Red Headed Woman		—	$10		Columbia 45347
12/11/71+	53	7		11 Cotton Top .... About All I Can Give Is My Love		—	$10		Columbia 45466
5/6/72	60	5		12 High On Love .... Take Me Back To Memphis		—	$10		Columbia 45582
10/13/73	61	7		13 (Let's Get) Dixiefried .... One More Loser Goin' Home [R]		—	$8		Mercury 73425
				new version of #3 above					
6/7/86	31	14		14 Birth Of Rock And Roll .... S:26 / A:29 Rock And Roll (Fais Do Do)		—	$5	■	America Sm. 884760
3/28/87	83	3		15 Class Of '55 .... We Remember The King		—	$5		America Sm. 888142
				PERKINS, Dal '68					
				Born in Abilene, Texas. Male singer.					
1/13/68	73	3		Helpless .... Woman In The Darkness		—	$10		Columbia 44343

DEBUT	PEAK	WKS	Gold	A-side (Chart Hit) / B-side	Pop	$	Pic	Label & Number
				PERRY, Brenda Kaye '78 Born in Waynesboro, Virginia. Female singer.				
10/22/77	64	9		1 Ringgold Georgia ....Have I Told You Lately That I Loved You BILLY WALKER AND BRENDA KAYE PERRY	—	$5		MRC 1005
1/21/78	35	11		2 Deeper Water ....Home Sweet Home	—	$5		MRC 1010
4/22/78	37	9		3 I Can't Get Up By Myself...Free	—	$5		MRC 1013
10/14/78	78	5		4 My Daddy Was A Travelin' Man ....I Am A Woman	—	$5		MRC 1021
2/17/79	90	3		5 Make Me Your Woman ....(What A) Wonderful World	—	$5		MRC 1026
				PETERS, Ben '69 Born on 6/20/37 in Hattiesburg, Mississippi. Singer/prolific songwriter. Father of **Debbie Peters**.				
7/19/69	46	9		1 San Francisco Is A Lonely Town..........................You're The Happy Song I Sing	—	$7		Liberty 56114
9/1/73	92	4		2 Would You Still Love Me ....This Has Got To Last	—	$6		Capitol 3687
				PETERS, Debbie '80 Born in 1959. Daughter of **Ben Peters**.				
3/15/80	84	2		It Can't Wait ....I Can't Get Enough Of You	—	$6		Oak 1012
				PETERS, Doug '88 Born Doug Volchko on 8/4/59 in Chicago.				
8/6/88	85	2		My Heart's Way Behind..	—	$6		Comstock 1895
				PETERS, Gretchen '00 Born on 11/14/62 in Bronxville, New York; raised in Boulder, Colorado. Singer/songwriter.				
4/20/96	68	3		1 When You Are Old..I Was Looking For You	—	$4	■	Imprint 18001
1/15/00	55	1		2 New Year's Eve 1999 ....Twentieth Century (Alabama) ALABAMA with Gretchen Peters	—	$4	★	RCA 65917
				PETERS, Jimmie '77 Born on 10/12/38 in Whiteface, Texas. Singer/songwriter/bassist.				
5/28/77	59	7		1 Somebody Took Her Love (And Never Gave It Back)...........I'm What I Am	—	$5		Mercury 73911
10/8/77	73	6		2 Lipstick Traces ....Even If It's Wrong #48 Pop hit for The O'Jays in 1965	—	$5		Mercury 55005
2/18/78	75	4		3 634-5789 ....Just Because It Feels Good #13 Pop hit for Wilson Pickett in 1966	—	$5		Mercury 55016
6/3/78	84	4		4 I Will Always Love You ....Just Because It Feels Good	—	$5		Mercury 55025
1/13/79	78	4		5 I Hate The Way Our Love Is .... JIMMY PETERS and LYNDA K. LANCE	—	$6		Vista 101
4/28/79	98	3		6 First Class Fool .... JIMMIE PETERS/LINDA K. LANCE	—	$6		Vista 106
3/1/80	75	4		7 Hearts...Let's Write A Love Song	—	$5	■	Sunbird 105
				PETERS & LEE '74 British duo: Lennie Peters (who was blind) and Dianne Lee. Duo split in 1980. Peters died of cancer on 10/10/92 (age 59).				
3/16/74	79	8		Welcome Home ....Can't Keep My Mind On The Game	119	$6		Philips 40729
				PETERSON, Colleen '76 Born on 11/14/50 in Peterboro, Canada. Died of cancer on 10/9/96 (age 45).				
11/27/76	100	2		Souvenirs ....Six Days On The Road	—	$5		Capitol 4349
				PETERSON, Michael '97 Born on 8/7/59 in Tucson, Arizona. Singer/songwriter/guitarist.				
5/17/97	3	20		1 Drink, Swear, Steal & Lie ....S:4 For A Song	86	$4	■	Reprise 17379 (v)
9/13/97	●1	22		2 From Here To Eternity	—			album cut
1/31/98	8	20		3 Too Good To Be True	—			album cut
5/30/98	37	14		4 When The Bartender Cries	—			album cut
9/26/98+	19	22		5 By The Book .... all of above from the album *Michael Peterson* on Reprise 46218	101			album cut
3/13/99	45	17		6 Somethin' 'Bout A Sunday ....Lost In The Shuffle	—	$4		Reprise 16995
6/26/99	39	20		7 Sure Feels Real Good ....S:20 Laughin' All The Way To The Bank	—	$4	★	Reprise 10933 (v)
				PETRONE, Shana '99 Born on 5/8/72 in Parkridge, Illinois; raised in Fort Lauderdale, Florida. Former dance singer. Hit #40 on the pop charts in 1990 with "I Want You" (as "Shana").				
6/27/98	60	5		1 Heaven Bound ....(album snippets)	—	$4	■	Epic 78946
6/12/99	45	13		2 This Time ....S:24 The Chance	—	$4	★	Epic 79212
10/30/99	66	6		3 Something Real .... from the album *Something Real* on Epic	—			album cut
				PFEIFER, Diane '82 Born on 11/4/50 in St. Louis.				
3/1/80	85	3		1 Free To Be Lonely Again ....Oh No, Not Love Again	—	$4		Capitol 4823
5/17/80	59	7		2 Roses Ain't Red....................................Do You Mind (If I Fall In Love With You)	—	$4		Capitol 4858
10/4/80	83	3		3 Wishful Drinkin' ....Just When I Needed A Love Song	—	$4		Capitol 4916
11/28/81+	35	10		4 Play Something We Could Love To ....Sing You To Sleep	—	$4		Capitol 5060
6/12/82	85	3		5 Something To Love For Again ....Missing You All By Myself	—	$4		Capitol 5116
9/25/82	76	4		6 Let's Get Crazy Again ....Missing You All By Myself	—	$4		Capitol 5154
				PHELPS, Brother — see **BROTHER PHELPS**				

DEBUT	PEAK	WKS	Gold	A-side (Chart Hit)..B-side	Pop	$	Pic	Label & Number
	★283★			**PHILLIPS, Bill** '66				
				Born on 1/28/36 in Canton, North Carolina. Singer/songwriter/guitarist. Known as "Tater."				
				1)Put It Off Until Tomorrow 2)The Company You Keep 3)The Words I'm Gonna Have To Eat				
8/24/59	27	2		1 Sawmill ....You Are The Reason	—	$15		Columbia 41416
				MEL TILLIS and BILL PHILLIPS				
2/8/60	24	4		2 Georgia Town Blues ....Till I Get Enough Of These Blues	—	$15		Columbia 41530
				MEL TILLIS and BILL PHILLIPS				
3/14/64	22	18		3 I Can Stand It (As Long As She Can)...........................Wheeling Dealing Daddy	—	$10		Decca 31584
10/17/64	26	10		4 Stop Me ....Stepping Out	—	$10		Decca 31648
4/2/66	6	18		5 Put It Off Until Tomorrow Lonely Lonely Boy	—	$10		Decca 31901
				Dolly Parton (harmony vocal)				
8/13/66	8	19		6 The Company You Keep The Lies Just Can't Be True	—	$10		Decca 31996
				above 2 co-written by Dolly Parton				
1/21/67	10	15		7 The Words I'm Gonna Have To Eat Falling Back To You	—	$8		Decca 32074
7/22/67	39	7		8 I Learn Something New Everyday ....I Didn't Forget	—	$8		Decca 32141
11/18/67+	25	13		9 Love's Dead End...Oh, What It Did To Me	—	$8		Decca 32207
3/15/69	54	10		10 I Only Regret ....She's An Angel	—	$8		Decca 32432
10/18/69	10	14		11 Little Boy Sad I'm Living In Two Worlds	—	$8		Decca 32565
				#17 Pop hit for Johnny Burnette in 1961				
3/28/70	43	7		12 She's Hungry Again ....You've Still Got A Place In My Heart	—	$8		Decca 32638
8/22/70	46	9		13 Same Old Story, Same Old Lie ....You Can't Love Me When I'm Gone	—	$8		Decca 32707
2/27/71	56	6		14 Big Rock Candy Mountain ....I Didn't Forget	—	$8		Decca 32782
				#102 Pop hit for Dorsey Burnette in 1960				
3/18/72	66	8		15 I Am, I Said ....Son	—	$6		United Artists 50879
				#4 Pop hit for Neil Diamond in 1971				
8/11/73	91	3		16 It's Only Over Now And Then...I've Got Yesterday	—	$6		United Artists 266
6/24/78	90	3		17 Divorce Suit (You Were Named Co-Respondent) ....I've Been Loving You Too Long	—	$5		Soundwaves 4570
2/3/79	89	3		18 You're Gonna Make A Cheater Out Of Me..........................Temporarily Yours	—	$5		Soundwaves 4579
7/7/79	85	3		19 At The Moonlite...I'm Turning You Loose	—	$5		Soundwaves 4587
				PHILLIPS, Charlie '62				
				Born on 7/2/37 in Clovis, New Mexico. Singer/songwriter/guitarist.				
4/14/62	9	7		1 I Guess I'll Never Learn Now That It's Over	—	$10		Columbia 42289
10/12/63	30	1		2 This Is The House ....Later Tonight	—	$10		Columbia 42851
				PHILLIPS, John '70				
				Born on 8/30/35 in Paris Island, South Carolina. Died of heart failure on 3/18/2001 (age 65). Co-founder of The Mamas & The Papas. Formerly married to actress Michele Phillips. Father of actress MacKenzie Phillips and singer Chynna Phillips (of Wilson Phillips).				
7/4/70	58	7		Mississippi ....April Anne	32	$6		Dunhill/ABC 4236
				PHILLIPS, Stu '67				
				Born on 1/19/33 in Montreal. Singer/songwriter/guitarist. Known as "The Western Gentleman." Joined the Grand Ole Opry in 1967.				
4/30/66	39	5		1 Bracero ....Angel Of Love	—	$8		RCA Victor 8771
8/20/66	32	11		2 The Great El Tigre (The Tiger).............................Another Day Has Gone	—	$8		RCA Victor 8868
2/4/67	44	8		3 Walk Me To The Station...Guess Things Happen That Way	—	$8		RCA Victor 9066
6/17/67	21	14		4 Vin Rosé ....I Wish I Had Never Seen Sunshine	—	$8		RCA Victor 9219
10/21/67	13	12		5 Juanita Jones ....A Castle, A Cabin	—	$8		RCA Victor 9333
4/20/68	62	6		6 The Note In Box Number 9...Our Last Rendezvous	—	$8		RCA Victor 9481
7/13/68	53	7		7 The Top Of The World ....That Completely Destroys My Plans	—	$8		RCA Victor 9557
12/21/68+	68	6		8 Bring Love Back Into Our World ....Speak Softly, My Love	—	$8		RCA Victor 9673

PIANO RED — see SHIRLEY, Danny

				PIERCE, Webb ★8★ '55				
				Born on 8/8/21 in West Monroe, Louisiana. Died of heart failure on 2/24/91 (age 69). Singer/songwriter/guitarist. Hosted own radio show on KMLB in West Monroe from 1940-43. Joined the Louisiana Hayride in 1950. Joined the Grand Ole Opry in 1955. Co-owner of Cedarwood music publishing company. Acted in the movies Buffalo Guns, Music City USA and Road To Nashville. His daughter Debbie was a member of Chantilly. Elected to the Country Music Hall of Fame in 2001. Also see Heart Of Nashville.				
				1)In The Jailhouse Now 2)Slowly 3)Love, Love, Love 4)I Don't Care 5)There Stands The Glass				
1/5/52	❶⁴	27		1 Wondering A:❶⁴ / S:4 / J:4 New Silver Bells	—	$25		Decca 9-46104
				first recorded by the Riverside Ramblers in 1937 on Bluebird				
6/7/52	❶³	20		2 That Heart Belongs To Me A:❶³ / J:2 / S:5 So Used To Loving You	—	$25		Decca 9-28091
10/4/52	❶⁴	23		3 Back Street Affair A:❶⁴ / J:❶³ / S:❶² I'll Always Take Care Of You	—	$25		Decca 9-28369
1/31/53	4	7		4 I'll Go On Alone / J:4 / S:7 / A:8	—			
2/14/53	4	6		5 That's Me Without You A:4 / J:4 / S:9	—	$25		Decca 28534
3/28/53	4	14		6 The Last Waltz / S:4 / A:5 / J:5	—			
4/18/53	5	6		7 I Haven't Got The Heart J:5 / A:6	—	$25		Decca 28594
7/4/53	❶⁸	22		8 It's Been So Long / A:❶⁸ / S:❶⁶ / J:❶¹	—			
				melody is the same as "I've Got Five Dollars And It's Saturday Night" by Faron Young				
7/4/53	9	2		9 Don't Throw Your Life Away J:9	—	$25		Decca 28725
10/24/53	❶¹²	27		10 There Stands The Glass / S:❶¹² / J:❶⁹ / A:❶⁶	—			
10/24/53+	3	17		11 I'm Walking The Dog J:3 / A:4 / S:6	—	$25		Decca 28834
2/6/54	❶¹⁷	36		12 Slowly S:❶¹⁷ / J:❶¹⁶ / A:❶¹⁵ You Just Can't Be True	—	$25		Decca 28991

DEBUT	PEAK	WKS	Gold	A-side (Chart Hit)	B-side	Pop	$	Pic	Label & Number
				PIERCE, Webb — Cont'd					
6/5/54	❶²	31		13 Even Tho /	A:❶² / J:2 / S:3	—			
6/12/54	4	18		14 Sparkling Brown Eyes	S:4 / A:4 / J:4	—	$25		Decca 29107
				WEBB PIERCE With Wilburn Brothers					
10/9/54	❶¹⁰	29		15 More And More /	J:❶¹⁰ / S:❶⁹ / A:❶⁸	—			
10/9/54	4	12		16 You're Not Mine Anymore	A:4 / S:8	—	$25		Decca 29252
2/5/55	❶²¹	37		17 In The Jailhouse Now /	J:❶²¹ / S:❶²⁰ / A:❶¹⁵	—			
				Wilburn Brothers (harmony vocals); written by **Jimmie Rodgers**; also see #96 below					
2/12/55	10	2		18 I'm Gonna Fall Out Of Love With You	A:10 / S:14	—	$20		Decca 29391
6/18/55	❶¹²	32		19 I Don't Care /	S:❶¹² / A:❶¹² / J:❶¹²	—			
		6		20 Your Good For Nothing Heart	A:flip / J:flip	—	$20		Decca 29480
9/24/55	❶¹³	32		21 Love, Love, Love /	A:❶¹³ / J:❶⁹ / S:❶⁸	—			
10/29/55	7	5		22 If You Were Me	A:7	—	$20		Decca 29662
12/17/55+	❶⁴	25		23 Why Baby Why	A:❶⁴ / S:❶¹ / J:❶¹ Missing You	—	$20		Decca 29755
				RED SOVINE And WEBB PIERCE					
3/3/56	2⁷	21		24 Yes I Know Why /	A:2 / S:3 / J:3	—			
3/10/56	3	13		25 'Cause I Love You	J:3 / S:5 / A:12	—	$20		Decca 29805
4/21/56	5	14		26 Little Rosa	S:5 / A:5 / J:5 [S]	—	$20		Decca 29876
				RED SOVINE and WEBB PIERCE					
7/21/56	7	11		27 Any Old Time /	A:7 / J:7 / S:10	—			
				written by **Jimmie Rodgers**					
		6		28 We'll Find A Way	S:flip / J:flip	—	$20		Decca 29974
10/13/56	10	8		29 Teenage Boogie /	S:10 / A:15	—			
		5		30 I'm Really Glad You Hurt Me	S:flip	—	$35		Decca 30045
1/5/57	3	22		31 I'm Tired /	S:3 / A:4 / J:4	—			
		4		32 It's My Way		—	$20		Decca 30155
3/30/57	❶¹	22		33 Honky Tonk Song	A:❶¹ / S:2 / J:7	—	$20		Decca 30255
4/6/57	8	9		34 Oh' So Many Years	A:8 Can You Find It In Your Heart	—	$15		Decca 30183
				KITTY WELLS and WEBB PIERCE					
4/13/57	12	2		35 Someday	A:12	—	$15		Decca 30255
5/27/57	7	15		36 Bye Bye, Love /	A:7 / S:8	73			
6/10/57	7	12		37 Missing You	S:3 / A:7	—	$15		Decca 30321
9/30/57	3	17		38 Holiday For Love	A:3 / S:6	—			
11/18/57	12	1		39 Don't Do It Darlin'	A:12	—	$15		Decca 30419
1/20/58	12	1		40 One Week Later	A:12 When I'm With You	—	$15		Decca 30489
				WEBB PIERCE And KITTY WELLS					
5/5/58	3	17		41 Cryin' Over You /	A:3 / S:12	—			
6/2/58	10	4		42 You'll Come Back	A:10	—	$15		Decca 30623
10/20/58	7	10		43 Tupelo County Jail /		—			
9/29/58	10	12		44 Falling Back To You	A:10 / S:18	—	$15		Decca 30711
1/19/59	22	3		45 I'm Letting You Go	Sittin' Alone	—	$15		Decca 30789
4/6/59	6	16		46 A Thousand Miles Ago	What Goes On In Your Heart	—	$15		Decca 30858
7/20/59	2⁹	25		47 I Ain't Never	Shanghied	24	$15		Decca 30923
12/21/59+	4	18		48 No Love Have I	Whirlpool Of Love	54	$15		Decca 31021
5/23/60	11	8		49 Is It Wrong (For Loving You) /		69			
4/11/60	17	10		50 (Doin' The) Lovers Leap		93	$12		Decca 31058
9/12/60	11	8		51 Drifting Texas Sand	All I Need Is You	108	$12		Decca 31118
11/14/60	4	18		52 Fallen Angel	Truck Driver's Blues	99	$12		Decca 31165
2/20/61	5	15		53 Let Forgiveness In	There's More Pretty Girls Than One (Pop #118)	—	$12		Decca 31197
5/29/61	3	21		54 Sweet Lips	Last Night	—	$12		Decca 31249
9/25/61	5	22		55 Walking The Streets /		—			
10/2/61	7	19		56 How Do You Talk To A Baby		—	$12		Decca 31298
2/10/62	5	16		57 Alla My Love	You Are My Life	—	$10		Decca 31347
6/2/62	7	13		58 Take Time /		—			
5/26/62	8	13		59 Crazy Wild Desire		—	$10		Decca 31380
10/6/62	5	15		60 Cow Town /		—			
10/13/62	19	10		61 Sooner Or Later		—	$10		Decca 31421
1/5/63	25	3		62 How Come Your Dog Don't Bite Nobody But Me	So Soon	—	$10		Decca 31445
				WEBB PIERCE and MEL TILLIS					
3/2/63	15	8		63 Sawmill /		—			
4/6/63	21	3		64 If I Could Come Back		—	$10		Decca 31451
6/22/63	7	15		65 Sands Of Gold	Nobody's Darlin' But Mine	118	$10		Decca 31488
11/9/63	9	13		66 Those Wonderful Years /		—			
10/26/63+	13	15		67 If The Back Door Could Talk		—	$10		Decca 31544
2/15/64	25	13		68 Waiting A Lifetime	Love Come To Me	—	$10		Decca 31582
5/23/64	2¹	23		69 Memory #1	French Riviera (Pop #126)	—	$10		Decca 31617
9/26/64	9	15		70 Finally	He Made You For Me	—	$10		Decca 31663
				KITTY WELLS And WEBB PIERCE					
1/30/65	26	14		71 That's Where My Money Goes /		—			
2/6/65	46	5		72 Broken Engagement		—	$10		Decca 31704
3/20/65	22	14		73 Loving You Then Losing You	Let Me Live A Little	—	$10		Decca 31737
8/14/65	13	14		74 Who Do I Think I Am /		—			
8/21/65	50	2		75 Hobo And The Rose		—	$10		Decca 31816
4/16/66	46	6		76 You Ain't No Better Than Me	The Champ	—	$10		Decca 31924
8/27/66	25	10		77 Love's Something (I Can't Understand)	A Loner	—	$10		Decca 31982

Pinnacle Boys (you have one 45)

DEBUT	PEAK	WKS	Gold	A-side (Chart Hit) / B-side	Pop	$	Pic	Label & Number
				PIERCE, Webb — Cont'd				
10/29/66	14	17		78 Where'd Ya Stay Last Night .... She's Twenty-One	—	$8		Decca 32033
3/18/67	39	15		79 Goodbye City, Goodbye Girl .... That Same Old Street	—	$8		Decca 32098
8/5/67	6	18		80 Fool Fool Fool .... Bottles And Babies	—	$8		Decca 32167
1/27/68	24	13		81 Luziana .... Somebody Please Kiss My Sweet Thing	—	$8		Decca 32246
7/6/68	26	9		82 Stranger In A Strange, Strange City /	—			
8/3/68	74	2		83 In Another World		$8		Decca 32339
10/26/68	22	10		84 Saturday Night .... I Tried Everything To Please	—	$8		Decca 32388
2/22/69	32	10		85 If I Had Last Night To Live Over .... No Tears Tonight	—	$8		Decca 32438
7/5/69	14	13		86 This Thing .... Does My Memory Ever Cross Your Mind	—	$8		Decca 32508
11/29/69+	38	9		87 Love Ain't Never Gonna Be No Better .... The Other Side Of You	—	$8		Decca 32577
3/28/70	71	3		88 Merry-Go-Round World .... Fool's Night Out	—	$8		Decca 32641
8/1/70	56	5		89 The Man You Want Me To Be .... Too Long	—	$8		Decca 32694
12/26/70+	73	3		90 Showing His Dollar .... The Way We Were Back Then	—	$8		Decca 32762
3/13/71	31	11		91 Tell Him That You Love Him .... Heartaches Are For Lovers, Not For Friends	—	$8		Decca 32787
9/18/71	73	2		92 Someone Stepped In (And Stole Me Blind) .... I Miss The Little Things	—	$8		Decca 32855
7/15/72	54	8		93 I'm Gonna Be A Swinger .... Someday	—	$8		Decca 32973
11/22/75	57	9		94 The Good Lord Giveth (And Uncle Sam Taketh Away) .... My Love To Me	—	$6		Plantation 131
3/13/76	82	5		95 I've Got Leaving On My Mind .... Shame, Shame, Shame	—	$6		Plantation 136
10/9/82	72	5		96 In The Jailhouse Now .... Back Street Affair [R]	—	$4		Columbia 03231
				WILLIE NELSON & WEBB PIERCE				
				new version of #17 above				
	★363★			**PILLOW, Ray** '66				
				Born on 7/4/37 in Lynchburg, Virginia. Singer/songwriter/guitarist. Joined the *Grand Ole Opry* in 1966.				
				1)I'll Take The Dog 2)Thank You Ma'am 3)Mr. Do-It-Yourself				
2/13/65	49	4		1 Take Your Hands Off My Heart .... Even The Bad Times Are Good	—	$8		Capitol 5323
12/25/65+	17	10		2 Thank You Ma'am .... "If" Is A Mighty Big Word	—	$8		Capitol 5518
4/23/66	32	6		3 Common Colds And Broken Hearts .... You've Got A Good Thing Going	—	$8		Capitol 5597
5/14/66	9	15		4 I'll Take The Dog .... I'd Fight The World	—	$8		Capitol 5633
				JEAN SHEPARD and RAY PILLOW				
10/8/66	26	11		5 Volkswagen .... And I Like That Sortta Thing	—	$8		Capitol 5735
11/26/66+	25	11		6 Mr. Do-It-Yourself .... Strangers Nine To Five	—	$8		Capitol 5769
				JEAN SHEPARD & RAY PILLOW				
8/12/67	56	6		7 I Just Want To Be Alone .... I Like A Whole Lot	—	$8		Capitol 5953
12/9/67	62	2		8 Gone With The Wine .... No Milk Today	—	$8		Capitol 2030
9/14/68	51	8		9 Wonderful Day .... If Every Man Had A Woman Like You	—	$6		ABC 11114
8/23/69	38	8		10 Reconsider Me .... The Doors Of Love	—	$6		Plantation 25
2/5/72	62	3		11 Since Then .... While I'm Gone	—	$6		Mega 0055
5/13/72	66	7		12 She's Doing It To Me Again .... Everytime	—	$6		Mega 0072
1/5/74	80	8		13 Countryfied .... I'm Doing What I Love, Loving You	—	$6		Mega 1202
12/21/74+	77	4		14 Livin' In The Sunshine Of Your Love .... The Party	—	$5		ABC/Dot 17526
12/27/75	100	1		15 Roll On, Truckers .... We've Got To Love That Other Woman Out Of Me	—	$5		ABC/Dot 17589
5/13/78	97	3		16 Who's Gonna Tie My Shoes .... Can I Have What's Left	—	$6		Hilltop 130
7/21/79	82	4		17 Super Lady .... Nighttime Masquerade	—	$5		MCA 41047
7/18/81	82	3		18 One Too Many Memories .... Friday Night Blues	—	$6		First Generation 011
				PINETOPPERS, The '51				
				Group from Broadtop Mountain, Pennsylvania: brothers Roy and Vaughn Horton, Ray Smith, Rusty Keefer and Johnny Browers. Vocals by Trudy and Gloria Marlin (The Beaver Valley Sweethearts). Roy Horton was elected to the Country Music Hall of Fame in 1982.				
12/23/50+	3	13		1 Mockin' Bird Hill .... J:3 / A:4 / S:5 Big Parade Polka	10	$25		Coral 9-64061
				#2 Pop hit for **Patti Page** in 1951				
				★ **PINK, Celinda** '93				
				Born in Tuscaloosa, Alabama; raised in Birmingham. Female singer.				
4/24/93	68	4		1 Pack Your Lies And Go .... I've Earned The Right To Sing The Blues	—	$4	■	Step One 458 (v)
				PINKARD & BOWDEN '84				
				Novelty duo. Pinkard was born James Pinkard on 1/16/47 in Abbeville, Louisiana. Bowden was born Richard Bowden on 9/30/45 in Linden, Texas.				
3/3/84	64	8		1 Adventures In Parodies .... [N]	—	$4		Warner 29370
				side one: Help Me Make It Through The Yard/Daddy Sang Bass/Delta Dawg/Somebody Done Somebody's Song Wrong/Drivin' My Wife Away; side two: Three Mile Island (Wolverton Mountain)/Blue Hairs Driving In My Lane/What's A W-4 (What's Forever For)				
9/15/84	39	9		2 Mama, She's Lazy .... Shake A Snake [N]	—	$4		Warner 29205
				parody of "Mama He's Crazy" by **The Judds**				
8/16/86	92	3		3 She Thinks I Steal Cars .... Imelda's Shoes [N]	—	$4		Warner 2526
				parody of "She Thinks I Still Care" by **George Jones**				
6/4/88	87	2		4 Arab, Alabama .... Satellite Dish [N]	—	$4		Warner 27909
				melody based on "Good Hearted Woman" by **Waylon Jennings**				
4/15/89	79	4		5 Libyan On A Jet Plane (Leavin' On A Jet Plane) .... Don't Pet The Dog [N]	—	$4		Warner 22987
				parody of "Leaving On A Jet Plane" by Peter, Paul & Mary				
				PIRATES OF THE MISSISSIPPI '91				
				Group from Montgomery, Alabama: "Wild" Bill McCorvey (vocals; born on 7/4/59), Rich "Dude" Alves (guitar; born on 5/25/53), Pat Severs (steel guitar; born on 11/10/52), Dean Townson (bass; born on 4/2/59) and Jimmy Lowe (drums; born on 8/2/55).				
7/28/90	26	20		1 Honky Tonk Blues .... Anything Goes	—	$4	■	Capitol 44579
11/17/90+	49	14		2 Rollin' Home				album cut
3/16/91	15	20		3 Feed Jake				album cut
7/27/91	29	20		4 Speak Of The Devil				album cut
				all of above from the album *Pirates Of The Mississippi* on Capitol 94389				

DEBUT	PEAK	WKS	Gold	A-side (Chart Hit) ... B-side	Pop	$	Pic	Label & Number
				PIRATES OF THE MISSISSIPPI — Cont'd				
11/2/91	41	20		5 Fighting For You .... Talkin' 'Bout Love	—	$4		Capitol 44775
2/29/92	22	20		6 Til I'm Holding You Again .... Feed Jake	—	$4		Liberty 57704
6/27/92	36	19		7 Too Much .... Speak Of The Devil	—	$4		Liberty 57767
10/10/92	56	8		8 A Street Man Named Desire .... Mystery Ship	—	$4		Liberty 57995
10/30/93	63	7		9 Dream You	—			album cut
				from the album *Dream You* on Liberty 80379				

PITNEY, Gene '66
Born on 2/17/41 in Hartford, Connecticut; raised in Rockville, Connecticut. Singer/songwriter/guitarist. Inducted into the Rock and Roll Hall of Fame in 2002.

GEORGE & GENE — George Jones & Gene Pitney:

4/24/65	16	10		1 I've Got Five Dollars And It's Saturday Night .... Wreck On The Highway	99	$15		Musicor 1066
7/3/65	25	7		2 Louisiana Man .... I'm A Fool To Care (Pop #115)	—	$12	■	Musicor 1097
11/20/65	50	2		3 Big Job .... Your Old Standby	—	$12	■	Musicor 1115
1/15/66	15	12		4 Baby Ain't That Fine .... Everybody Knows But You And Me	—	$12		Musicor 1135
				GENE PITNEY and MELBA MONTGOMERY				
6/4/66	47	3		5 That's All It Took .... Y'All Come	—	$12		Musicor 1165

PLACE, Mary Kay, as Loretta Haggers '76
Born on 8/23/47 in Tulsa, Oklahoma. Singer/composer/comedienne. Played "Loretta Haggers" on TV's *Mary Hartman, Mary Hartman* from 1976-78.

10/16/76	3	16		1 Baby Boy .... Streets Of This Town (Ode To Fernwood)	60	$5		Columbia 10422
4/9/77	72	5		2 Vitamin L .... Coke And Chips	—	$5		Columbia 10510
				MARY KAY PLACE as LORETTA HAGGERS (above 2)				
11/19/77+	9	16		3 Something To Brag About .... Anybody's Darlin'	—	$5		Columbia 10644
				MARY KAY PLACE with Willie Nelson				

PLEASANT VALLEY BOYS — see **CROW, Alvin**

PLOWMAN, Linda '71
Born on 12/31/56 in Tuscaloosa, Alabama.

1/30/71	75	3		1 I'm So Lonesome I Could Cry .... I Would	—	$7		Janus 146
9/8/73	93	3		2 Nobody But You	—	$6		Columbia 45905

POACHER '78
Group from Warrington, Cheshire, England: Tim Flaherty (vocals), Adrian Hart (guitar), Pete Allen (steel guitar), Pete Longbottom (banjo), Allan Crookes (bass) and Stan Bennett (drums).

11/4/78	86	3		Darling .... So Afraid	—	$5		Republic 028

POCO '79
Pop-folk-rock group from Los Angeles. Numerous personnel changes. Lineup in 1979: Paul Cotton (vocals, guitar), Rusty Young (steel guitar), Kim Bullard (keyboards), Charlie Harrison (bass) and Steve Chapman (drums).

2/10/79	95	2		1 Crazy Love .... Barbados	17	$5		ABC 12439
6/30/79	96	4		2 Heart Of The Night .... The Last Goodbye	20	$5		MCA 41023

POINTER, Anita — see **CONLEY, Earl Thomas**

POINTER SISTERS '74
Black female vocal group from Oakland: sisters Ruth, Bonnie, June and **Anita Pointer**. Charted 27 pop hits from 1973-87.

7/27/74	37	16		Fairytale .... Love In Them There Hills	13	$6		ABC/Blue Thumb 254

POLLARD, Chuck '78
Born in Shreveport, Louisiana. Cousin of **Gene Wyatt**.

8/5/78	56	7		1 You Should Win An Oscar Every Night .... Wet, Wild And Warm	—	$5		MCA 40944
11/11/78	71	5		2 The Other Side Of Jeannie .... Wet, Wild And Warm	—	$5		MCA 40965

POMSL, Pat '79

2/3/79	97	1		Let My Fingers Do The Walking	—	$7		ASI 1017

POOLE, Cheryl '68
Born in Tyler, Texas.

8/10/68	39	10		1 Three Playing Love .... I'm Not Your Woman (You're Not My Man)	—	$8		Paula 309
2/1/69	70	3		2 The Skin's Gettin' Closer To The Bone .... You Ain't No Friend Of Mine	—	$8		Paula 1207
7/12/69	57	9		3 Walk Among The People .... (I'll Always Be) Daddy's Little Girl	—	$8		Paula 1214
2/14/70	70	2		4 Everybody's Gotta Hurt .... You Haven't Read The Book	—	$8		Paula 1219

POSEY, Sandy '72
Born on 6/18/44 in Jasper, Alabama; raised in West Memphis, Arkansas. Charted 5 pop hits from 1966-67.
1) Bring Him Safely Home To Me   2) Born To Be With You   3) Love Is Sometimes Easy

10/30/71+	18	14		1 Bring Him Safely Home To Me .... A Man In Need Of Love	—	$7		Columbia 45458
5/27/72	51	11		2 Why Don't We Go Somewhere And Love .... Together	—	$7		Columbia 45596
10/28/72	36	8		3 Happy, Happy Birthday Baby .... Thank The Lord For New York City	—	$7		Columbia 45703
				#5 Pop hit for The Tune Weavers in 1957				
5/5/73	39	8		4 Don't .... Thank The Lord For New York City	—	$7		Columbia 45828
6/19/76	99	3		5 Trying To Live Without You Kind Of Days .... Why Do We Carry On	—	$6		Monument 8698
12/18/76	93	3		6 It's Midnight (Do You Know Where Your Baby Is?) .... Long Distance Kissing	—	$5		Warner 8289
3/11/78	21	12		7 Born To Be With You .... It's Not Too Late	—	$5		Warner 8540
				#5 Pop hit for The Chordettes in 1956				
8/5/78	26	10		8 Love, Love, Love/Chapel Of Love .... I Believe In Love	—	$5		Warner 8610
				#30 Pop hit for The Clovers in 1956 / #1 Pop hit for The Dixie Cups in 1964				
2/10/79	26	12		9 Love Is Sometimes Easy .... I Believe In Love	—	$5		Warner 8731
6/30/79	82	3		10 Try Home .... Love Is Sometimes Easy	—	$5		Warner 8852
2/26/83	88	3		11 Can't Get Used To Sleeping Without You .... You Can't Ride On My Coat Tail	—	$6		Audiograph 449

DEBUT	PEAK	WKS	Gold	A-side (Chart Hit)	B-side	Pop	$	Pic	Label & Number
				POTTER, Curtis '80 Born on 4/18/40 in Cross Plains, Texas; raised in Abilene, Texas.					
5/12/79	92	3		1 Fraulein (The Texas National Anthem) .... The Story Behind The Photograph CURTIS POTTER AND A FRIEND Darrell McCall (guest vocal)		—	$6		Hillside 03
3/1/80	89	5		2 San Antonio Medley .... Thank God For Country Music CURTIS POTTER/DARRELL McCALL		—	$6		Hillside 01
				POWELL, Pati '73					
9/8/73	99	2		Love By Appointment .... If You Could Do Any Better (You'd Done Been Gone) PATI POWELL & BOB GALLION		—	$7		Metromedia 0037
				POWELL, Sandy — see STREET, Mel					
				POWELL, Sue '81 Born in Gallatin, Tennessee; raised in Sellersburg, Indiana. Member of **Dave & Sugar** from 1977-80. Co-host of TV's *Nashville On The Road* in 1982.					
5/16/81	57	7		1 Midnite Flyer .... You Keep Coming Back To Me		—	$4		RCA 12227
10/31/81	49	6		2 (There's No Me) Without You .... Delta Queen		—	$4		RCA 12287
				PRADO, Perez '58 Born Damaso Perez Prado on 12/11/16 in Mantanzas, Cuba. Died on 9/14/89 (age 72). Known as "The King of The Mambo."					
8/18/58	18	1	●	Patricia .... S:18 Why Wait [I] PEREZ PRADO And His Orchestra		❶¹	$15		RCA Victor 7245
				PRAIRIE OYSTER '92 Group from <u>Toronto</u>: Russell DeCarle (vocals, bass), Keith Glass (guitar), Denis Delorme (steel guitar), Joan Besen (piano), John P. Allen (fiddle) and Bruce Moffet (drums).					
3/24/90	62	9		1 Goodbye, So Long, Hello .... Different Kind Of Fire		—	$4		RCA 9124
6/9/90	70	8		2 I Don't Hurt Anymore .... But You Said		—	$4	■	RCA 2510 (v)
12/21/91+	51	9		3 One Precious Love .... Goodbye Lonesome (Hello, Baby Doll)		—	$4		RCA 62108
				PRESLEY, Elvis ★35★ '56 Born on 1/8/35 in Tupelo, Mississippi. Died of heart failure on 8/16/77 (age 42). Known as "The King of Rock & Roll." First recorded for Sun in 1954. Signed to RCA Records on 11/22/55. In U.S. Army from 3/24/58 to 3/5/60. Starred in 33 movies (beginning with *Love Me Tender* in 1956). NBC-TV special in 1968. Married Priscilla Beaulieu on 5/1/67; divorced on 10/11/73. Priscilla pursued acting in the 1980s with roles in TV's *Dynasty* and the *Naked Gun* movies. Their only child, Lisa Marie, was married to Michael Jackson from 1994-96. Elvis won Grammy's Lifetime Achievement Award in 1971. Inducted into the <u>Rock and Roll Hall of Fame</u> in 1986. Elected to the Country Music Hall of Fame in 1998. *cut on Charts in 1955* *Confidence?* 1)Heartbreak Hotel 2)Don't Be Cruel 3)Hound Dog 4)I Forgot To Remember To Forget 5)I Want You, I Need You, I Love You					
(7/16/55)	5	15		1 Baby Let's Play House / #12 R&B hit for Arthur Gunter in 1955	A:5 / S:10	—			
		3		2 I'm Left, You're Right, She's Gone	S:flip	—	$3000		Sun 217
9/17/55+	❶⁵	39		3 I Forgot To Remember To Forget	J:❶⁵ / S:❶² / A:4	—			
12/31/55+	11	4		4 Mystery Train	A:11	—	$2500		Sun 223
3/3/56	❶¹⁷	27	▲²	5 Heartbreak Hotel /	S:❶¹⁷ / J:❶¹³ / A:❶¹²	❶⁸			
3/31/56	8	6		6 I Was The One also see #83 below	A:8	19	$50		RCA Victor 47-6420
6/2/56	❶²	20	▲	7 I Want You, I Need You, I Love You /	S:❶² / J:❶¹ / A:5	❶¹			
6/2/56	13	13		8 My Baby Left Me written and recorded on RCA Victor 50-0109 by Arthur "Big Boy" Crudup in 1950 ($150)	S:13	31	$50		RCA Victor 47-6540
8/11/56	❶¹⁰	28	▲⁴	9 Don't Be Cruel /	J:❶¹⁰ / S:❶⁵ / A:2	❶¹¹			
8/4/56	❶¹⁰	28		10 Hound Dog #1 R&B hit for Big Mama Thornton in 1953	J:❶¹⁰ / S:❶⁵ / A:6	❶¹¹	$40	■	RCA Victor 47-6604
10/20/56	3	18	▲³	11 Love Me Tender / from the movie starring Presley; adapted from the 1861 tune "Aura Lee"	S:3 / A:4 / J:4	❶⁵			
		6		12 Anyway You Want Me (That's How I Will Be) .... picture sleeve issued with four color variations: black & white, green, light pink and dark pink	S:flip	20	$40	■	RCA Victor 47-6643
12/29/56	10	3		13 Love Me from the E.P. *Elvis, Volume 1*; the other cuts on the E.P. are "When My Blue Moon Turns To Gold Again" (Pop #19), "Paralyzed" (Pop #59) and "Rip It Up"	A:10 / J:10	2²	$100	■	RCA Victor EPA-992
2/2/57	3	14	▲	14 Too Much /	J:3 / S:5 / A:6	❶³			
3/2/57	8	1		15 Playing For Keeps	J:8	21	$40	■	RCA Victor 47-6800
4/13/57	❶¹	16	▲²	16 All Shook Up J:❶¹ / S:3 / A:3 That's When Your Heartaches Begin (Pop #58)		❶⁹	$40	■	RCA Victor 47-6870
7/1/57	❶¹	20	▲²	17 Let Me Be Your Teddy Bear / also see #72 below	S:❶¹ / A:4	❶⁷			
9/16/57	15	2		18 Loving You	A:15	20	$40	■	RCA Victor 47-7000
8/19/57	11	2		19 Mean Woman Blues from the E.P. *Loving You, Vol. II*; the other cuts on the E.P. are "Lonesome Cowboy," "Hot Dog" and "Got A Lot O'Livin' To Do"; #5 Pop hit for **Roy Orbison** in 1963; above 3 from the movie *Loving You* starring Presley	A:11 [EP]	—	$150	■	RCA Victor 2-1515
10/14/57	❶¹	24	▲²	20 Jailhouse Rock /	S:❶¹ / A:3	❶⁷			
10/28/57	11	4		21 Treat Me Nice above 2 from the movie *Jailhouse Rock* starring Presley	A:11	18	$40	■	RCA Victor 47-7035
2/3/58	2⁵	18	▲	22 Don't /	S:2 / A:3	❶⁵			
2/3/58	4	13		23 I Beg Of You	S:4 / A:5	8	$30	■	RCA Victor 47-7150
4/21/58	3	15	▲	24 Wear My Ring Around Your Neck / also see #84 below	S:3 / A:4	2¹			
		2		25 Doncha' Think It's Time	S:flip	15	$30	■	RCA Victor 47-7240
6/30/58	2²	16	▲	26 Hard Headed Woman /	S:2 / A:8	❶²			
		3		27 Don't Ask Me Why above 2 from the movie *King Creole* starring Presley	S:flip	25	$30	■	RCA Victor 47-7280

DEBUT	PEAK	WKS	Gold	A-side (Chart Hit)	B-side	Pop	$	Pic	Label & Number
				PRESLEY, Elvis — Cont'd					
12/22/58	24	3	▲	28 One Night	I Got Stung (Pop #8)	4	$30	■	RCA Victor 47-7410
				#11 R&B hit for Smiley Lewis in 1956 (originally written as "One Night (Of Sin)")					
5/30/60	27	2	▲	29 Stuck On You	Fame And Fortune (Pop #17)	❶⁴	$25	■	RCA Victor 47-7740
				recorded 15 days after Presley's Army discharge					
12/12/60+	22	6	▲²	30 Are You Lonesome To-night?	I Gotta Know (Pop #20)	❶⁶	$25	■	RCA Victor 47-7810
				#4 Pop hit for Vaughn Deleath in 1927					
4/6/68	55	6		31 U.S. Male	Stay Away (Pop #67)	28	$12	■	RCA Victor 47-9465
				written and originally recorded by **Jerry Reed**					
6/29/68	50	8		32 Your Time Hasn't Come Yet, Baby	Let Yourself Go (Pop #71)	72	$12	■	RCA Victor 47-9547
				ELVIS PRESLEY with The Jordanaires (#14-19, 22-27, 29-32) from the movie *Speedway* starring Presley					
4/19/69	56	2		33 Memories	Charro	35	$10	■	RCA Victor 47-9731
				from the NBC-TV special *Elvis*					
6/14/69	60	7	▲	34 In The Ghetto	Any Day Now	3	$10	■	RCA Victor 47-9741
8/16/69	74	3	●	35 Clean Up Your Own Back Yard	The Fair Is Moving On	35	$10	■	RCA Victor 47-9747
				from the movie *The Trouble With Girls (and how to get into it)* starring Presley					
12/20/69+	13	12	▲	36 Don't Cry Daddy	Rubberneckin' (Pop flip)	6	$10	■	RCA Victor 47-9768
				#34 & #36: written by **Mac Davis**					
2/28/70	31	10	●	37 Kentucky Rain	My Little Friend	16	$8	■	RCA Victor 47-9791
				written by **Eddie Rabbitt**					
6/6/70	37	10	●	38 The Wonder Of You	Mama Liked The Roses (Pop flip)	9	$8	■	RCA Victor 47-9835
				recorded "live" in Las Vegas; #25 Pop hit for Ray Peterson in 1959					
8/29/70	57	6	●	39 I've Lost You /		32			
		6		40 The Next Step Is Love		flip	$8	■	RCA Victor 47-9873
12/5/70	56	5	●	41 You Don't Have To Say You Love Me	Patch It Up (Pop flip)	11	$8	■	RCA Victor 47-9916
				#4 Pop hit for **Dusty Springfield** in 1966; above 3 from the movie *Elvis-That's The Way It Is*					
1/9/71	9	13		42 There Goes My Everything /		flip			
				#20 Pop hit for **Engelbert Humperdinck** in 1967; also see #81 below					
1/9/71	23	13	●	43 I Really Don't Want To Know		21	$7	■	RCA Victor 47-9960
				#11 Pop hit for **Les Paul & Mary Ford** in 1954					
3/27/71	55	8		44 Where Did They Go, Lord	Rags To Riches (Pop flip)	33	$7	■	RCA Victor 47-9980
6/5/71	34	8		45 Life	Only Believe (Pop flip)	53	$7	■	RCA Victor 47-9985
3/4/72	68	2		46 Until It's Time For You To Go	We Can Make The Morning	40	$7	■	RCA Victor 74-0619
				#53 Pop hit for **Neil Diamond** in 1970					
9/9/72	36	13	▲	47 It's A Matter Of Time	Burning Love (Pop #2)	—	$7	■	RCA Victor 74-0769
12/9/72+	16	13	●	48 Always On My Mind /		—			
		12	●	49 Separate Ways		20	$7	■	RCA Victor 74-0815
				from the movie *Elvis on Tour*					
4/28/73	31	10		50 Fool /		flip			
		10		51 Steamroller Blues		17	$7	■	RCA Victor 74-0910
				written and first recorded by **James Taylor** on his 1970 album *Sweet Baby James*; from the TV special *Aloha from Hawaii via Satellite*					
10/6/73	42	10		52 For Ol' Times Sake	Raised On Rock (Pop #41)	flip	$6	■	RCA Vic. APBO-0088
2/16/74	4	13		53 I've Got A Thing About You Baby /		39			
		13		54 Take Good Care Of Her		flip	$6	■	RCA Vic. APBO-0196
				#7 Pop hit for **Adam Wade** in 1961					
6/8/74	6	15		55 Help Me /		—			
				written by **Larry Gatlin**					
		15		56 If You Talk In Your Sleep		17	$6	■	RCA Vic. APBO-0280
10/26/74+	9	14		57 It's Midnight /		—			
		5		58 Promised Land		14	$6	■	RCA Victor PB-10074
				#41 Pop hit for **Chuck Berry** in 1965					
2/8/75	14	10		59 My Boy	Thinking About You	20	$6	■	RCA Victor PB-10191
				#41 Pop hit for **Richard Harris** in 1972					
5/17/75	11	13		60 T-R-O-U-B-L-E	Mr. Songman	35	$6	■	RCA Victor PB-10278
10/18/75	33	10		61 Pieces Of My Life	Bringing It Back (Pop #65)	—	$6	■	RCA Victor PB-10401
4/10/76	6	13		62 Hurt /		28			
				#4 Pop hit for **Timi Yuro** in 1961					
4/10/76	45	13		63 For The Heart		flip	$6	■	RCA Victor PB-10601
12/25/76+	❶¹	16		64 Moody Blue /		31			
		16		65 She Thinks I Still Care		flip	$6	■	RCA PB-10857
6/25/77	❶¹	17	▲	66 Way Down /		18			
		17		67 Pledging My Love		—	$6	■	RCA PB-10998
				#1 R&B hit for **Johnny Ace** in 1955					
11/19/77+	2¹	15	●	68 My Way	America	22	$6	■	RCA PB-11165
				from the CBS-TV special *Elvis In Concert*; based on the French standard "Comme D'Habitude"; #27 Pop hit for **Frank Sinatra** in 1969					
3/25/78	6	11		69 Unchained Melody		—			
				#4 Pop hit for The **Righteous Brothers** in 1965					
		11		70 Softly, As I Leave You	[S]	109	$5	■	RCA PB-11212
				"live" recording; Elvis narrates, with vocal by **Sherrill Nellsen**; #27 Pop hit for **Frank Sinatra** in 1964					
8/12/78	78	4		71 Puppet On A String /		—			
				#14 Pop hit for Presley in 1965					
		4		72 (Let Me Be Your) Teddy Bear	[R]	105	$5	■	RCA PB-11320
				ELVIS PRESLEY with The Jordanaires (above 2) same version as #17 above					
4/21/79	10	12		73 Are You Sincere /		—			
				#3 Pop hit for **Andy Williams** in 1958					
		12		74 Solitaire		—	$5	■	RCA PB-11533
				#17 Pop hit for the **Carpenters** in 1975					
8/11/79	6	13		75 There's A Honky Tonk Angel (Who Will Take Me Back In) /		—			
		13		76 I Got A Feelin' In My Body		—	$5	■	RCA PB-11679

DEBUT	PEAK	WKS	Gold	A-side (Chart Hit)	B-side	Pop	$	Pic	Label & Number
				PRESLEY, Elvis — Cont'd					
1/17/81	❶¹	13		77 Guitar Man	Faded Love	28	$5	■	RCA PB-12158
				remix by Felton Jarvis (d: 1/3/81) of Presley's #43 Pop hit from 1968; **Jerry Reed** (guitar)					
4/18/81	8	15		78 Lovin' Arms /		—			
				#61 Pop hit for **Dobie Gray** in 1973					
		15		79 You Asked Me To		—	$5		RCA PB-12205
2/27/82	73	4		80 You'll Never Walk Alone /		—			
				ELVIS PRESLEY with The Jordanaires					
				#90 Pop hit for Presley in 1968					
		4		81 There Goes My Everything	[R]	—	$5	■	RCA PB-13058
				same version as #42 above					
11/6/82	31	12		82 The Elvis Medley	Always On My Mind (Pop #105)	71	$5	■	RCA PB-13351
				Jailhouse Rock/Teddy Bear/Hound Dog/Don't Be Cruel/Burning Love/ Suspicious Minds					
5/7/83	92	2		83 I Was The One /	[R]	—			
				same version (with newly added overdubs) of #6 above					
		2		84 Wear My Ring Around Your Neck	[R]	—	$5	■	RCA PB-13500
				same version (with newly added overdubs) of #24 above					
12/27/97	55	2		85 Blue Christmas	Love Me Tender [X]	—	$5	■	RCA 62403
				recorded in 1957					
				PRESTON, Eddie	'89				
4/22/89	87	3		1 When Did You Stop	Dance My Song	—	$5		Platinum 101
9/9/89	71	4		2 Long Time Comin'		—	$5	☐	Platinum 102
				PRICE, Chuck	'76				
				Born in Chicago.					
11/2/74	75	6		1 Slow Down	West Virginia Woman	—	$5		Playboy 6010
11/22/75	54	8		2 Last Of The Outlaws	Angels Have Days They Can't Fly	—	$5		Playboy 6052
4/3/76	97	2		3 Cadillac Johnson	Trouble In Mind	—	$5		Playboy 6067
5/29/76	48	8		4 I Don't Want It	Trouble In Mind	—	$5		Playboy 6072
10/23/76	81	3		5 Rye Whiskey	Lucy Ain't Your Loser Lookin' Good	—	$5		Playboy 6087
2/26/77	91	4		6 Is Anybody Goin' To San Antone	My Memories	—	$5		Playboy 6099
				PRICE, David	'64				
				Born in Odessa, Texas. Band leader for **Red Stegall** from 1977-79.					
2/8/64	29	8		The World Lost A Man	I Need A Friend	—	$15		Rice 1001
				tribute to John F. Kennedy; written by **Tom T. Hall**					
			★	**PRICE, Denise**	'82				
				Born Denise Davis in Russellville, Alabama.					
12/25/82	94	3		Two Hearts Can't Be Wrong	Somebody Everybody's Had	—	$5	■	Dimension 1037

				PRICE, Kenny ★180★	'66				
				Born on 5/27/31 in Florence, Kentucky. Died of a heart attack on 8/4/87 (age 56). Singer/songwriter. Had own radio show on WZIP in Cincinnati in 1945. Served in the U.S. Army from 1952-54. Regular on TV's *Hee-Haw*. Known as "The Round Mound of Sound."					
				1)Walking On New Grass 2)Happy Tracks 3)The Sheriff Of Boone County 4)Biloxi 5)My Goal For Today					
8/20/66	7	18		1 Walking On New Grass	Wasting My Time	—	$10		Boone 1042
12/24/66+	7	17		2 Happy Tracks	The Clock	—	$10		Boone 1051
5/13/67	26	12		3 Pretty Girl, Pretty Clothes, Pretty Sad	You Made Me Lie To You	—	$10		Boone 1056
9/9/67	24	12		4 Grass Won't Grow On A Busy Street	Somebody Told Mary	—	$8		Boone 1063
12/16/67+	11	15		5 My Goal For Today	Say Something Nice To Me	—	$8		Boone 1067
4/27/68	31	8		6 Going Home For The Last Time	Blame It On Me	—	$8		Boone 1070
9/7/68	37	8		7 Southern Bound	After All	—	$8		Boone 1075
12/7/68	59	6		8 It Don't Mean A Thing To Me	Big Operator	—	$8		Boone 1081
5/10/69	64	5		9 Who Do I Know In Dallas	I'm A Long Way From Home	—	$8		Boone 1085
12/6/69	62	4		10 Atlanta Georgia Stray	The Clock	—	$7		RCA Victor 0260
1/31/70	17	12		11 Northeast Arkansas Mississippi County Bootlegger	Green, Green Grass Of Home	—	$7		RCA Victor 9787
7/18/70	10	14		12 Biloxi	The Shortest Song In The World	—	$7		RCA Victor 9869
12/19/70+	8	14		13 The Sheriff Of Boone County	Six String Guitar	119	$7		RCA Victor 9932
5/1/71	55	7		14 Tell Her You Love Her	Just Plain Man	—	$7		RCA Victor 9973
9/18/71	38	11		15 Charlotte Fever	There's A Song In Everything	—	$6		RCA Victor 1015
1/15/72	37	10		16 Super Sideman	From Here To There	—	$6		RCA Victor 0617
4/29/72	44	11		17 You Almost Slipped My Mind	Destination Anywhere	—	$6		RCA Victor 0686
9/16/72	24	11		18 Sea Of Heartbreak	Smiley	—	$6		RCA Victor 0781
1/20/73	53	8		19 Don't Tell Me Your Troubles	Front Of The Bus, Back Of The Church	—	$6		RCA Victor 0872
5/12/73	52	7		20 30 California Women	Love's Not Hard To Take	—	$6		RCA Victor 0936
9/22/73	52	11		21 You're Wearin' Me Down	The Closest Thing To Me (Is My Shadow)	—	$6		RCA Victor 0083
12/29/73+	29	12		22 Turn On Your Light (And Let It Shine)	The First Song That Wasn't The Blues	—	$6		RCA Victor 0198
4/27/74	69	6		23 Que Pasa	Greener Grass To Walk On	—	$6		RCA Victor 0256
8/31/74	42	11		24 Let's Truck Together	Super Hillbilly	—	$5		RCA Victor 10039
1/4/75	67	10		25 Easy Look	Country Blues	—	$5		RCA Victor 10141
5/3/75	65	8		26 Birds And Children Fly Away	Born In Country Music (Raised On Dixieland)	—	$5		RCA Victor 10260
1/10/76	60	8		27 Too Big A Price To Pay	Don't Boogie Woogie When You Say Your Prayers Tonight	—	$5		RCA Victor 10460

DEBUT	PEAK	WKS	Gold	A-side (Chart Hit)	B-side	Pop	$	Pic	Label & Number
				PRICE, Kenny — Cont'd					
6/4/77	60	6		28 I'd Buy You Chattanooga .... Mortar Mixing Mama		—	$5		MRC 1001
9/17/77	74	5		29 Leavin' .... Boone County Weight Watchers Of America		—	$5		MRC 1004
12/24/77+	50	9		30 Afraid You'd Come Back .... Walkin' In That California Sunshine		—	$5		MRC 1007
4/8/78	74	6		31 Sunshine Man .... Sidewalk Satin Salesman		—	$5		MRC 1012
1/20/79	67	7		32 Hey There .... Pickin' Up The Pieces		—	$5		MRC 1025
				#1 Pop hit for Rosemary Clooney in 1954					
2/23/80	60	5		33 Well Rounded Traveling Man .... Everybody Needs Something		—	$5		Dimension 1003
9/13/80	79	4		34 She's Leavin' (And I'm Almost Gone) .... In Vain		—	$5		Dimension 1010

PRICE, Ray ★9★   '56

Born on 1/12/26 in Perryville, Texas; raised in Dallas. Singer/songwriter/guitarist. Served in the U.S. Marines from 1944-46. Began radio singing career in 1948 on KRBC in Abilene, Texas. Joined the *Big D Jamboree* in Dallas in 1949. Known as "The Cherokee Cowboy."

1) Crazy Arms   2) City Lights   3) My Shoes Keep Walking Back To You   4) I Won't Mention It Again
5) She's Got To Be A Saint

DEBUT	PEAK	WKS	A-side	B-side	Pop	$	Pic	Label & Number
5/17/52	3	11	1 Talk To Your Heart	A:3 / J:6 / S:10 I've Got To Hurry, Hurry, Hurry	—	$20		Columbia 4-20913
11/8/52	4	9	2 Don't Let The Stars Get In Your Eyes	S:4 / A:6 / J:7 I Lost The Only Love I Knew	—	$20		Columbia 4-21025
			#1 Pop hit for Perry Como in 1953					
3/6/54	2²	19	3 I'll Be There (If You Ever Want Me) /	S:2 / A:2 / J:3				
4/10/54	6	13	4 Release Me	J:6 / S:7	—	$20		Columbia 21214
			#4 Pop hit for Engelbert Humperdinck in 1967					
6/26/54	13	4	5 Much Too Young To Die .... S:13 / A:13 I Love You So Much I Let You Go		—	$20		Columbia 21249
10/30/54	8	13	6 If You Don't, Somebody Else Will S:8 / J:10 / A:14 Oh Yes Darling!		—	$20		Columbia 21315
			RAY PRICE & His Cherokee Cowboys					
1/7/56	5	11	7 Run Boy A:5 / J:10 / S:15 You Never Will Be True		—	$20		Columbia 21474
5/26/56	❶²⁰	45	8 Crazy Arms / A:❶²⁰ / S:❶¹¹ / J:❶¹		27			
6/9/56	7	7	9 You Done Me Wrong A:7		—	$20		Columbia 21510
11/10/56	2²	21	10 I've Got A New Heartache / A:2 / J:2 / S:3					
11/17/56	4	21	11 Wasted Words S:4 / A:6 / J:9		—	$20		Columbia 21562
6/10/57	12	4	12 I'll Be There (When You Get Lonely) .... A:12 / S:13 Please Don't Leave Me		—	$20		Columbia 40889
7/29/57	❶⁴	37	13 My Shoes Keep Walking Back To You A:❶⁴ / S:3 Don't Do This To Me		63	$15		Columbia 40951
3/3/58	3	18	14 Curtain In The Window / A:3 / S:6					
		4	15 It's All Your Fault			$15		Columbia 41105
7/14/58	❶¹³	34	16 City Lights / A:2		71			
7/21/58	3	19	17 Invitation To The Blues A:3 / S:8		92	$15		Columbia 41191
1/5/59	7	19	18 That's What It's Like To Be Lonesome Kissing Your Picture		—	$15		Columbia 41309
5/11/59	2¹	40	19 Heartaches By The Number Wall Of Tears		—	$15		Columbia 41374
			#1 Pop hit for Guy Mitchell in 1959					
10/12/59	❶²	30	20 The Same Old Me /		—			
			#51 Pop hit for Guy Mitchell in 1960					
11/23/59	5	15	21 Under Your Spell Again		—	$15		Columbia 41477
4/4/60	2⁸	27	22 One More Time Who'll Be The First		—	$15		Columbia 41590
10/3/60	5	17	23 I Wish I Could Fall In Love Today /		—			
10/24/60	23	3	24 I Can't Run Away From Myself		—	$15		Columbia 41767
3/20/61	5	21	25 Heart Over Mind /		—			
3/27/61	13	11	26 The Twenty-Fourth Hour		—	$15		Columbia 41947
10/9/61	3	23	27 Soft Rain /		115			
11/13/61	26	2	28 Here We Are Again		—	$12		Columbia 42132
6/2/62	12	8	29 I've Just Destroyed The World (I'm Living In) /		—			
6/2/62	22	1	30 Big Shoes		—	$12		Columbia 42310
9/22/62	5	15	31 Pride I'm Walking Slow (And Thinking 'Bout Her)		—	$12		Columbia 42518
2/9/63	7	20	32 Walk Me To The Door /		—			
			written by Conway Twitty					
3/2/63	11	16	33 You Took Her Off My Hands (Now Please Take Her Off My Mind)		—	$12		Columbia 42658
8/10/63	2¹	21	34 Make The World Go Away /		100			
			a promotional text sleeve was issued for this side only					
10/5/63	28	2	35 Night Life		—	$12	□	Columbia 42827
3/14/64	2⁴	27	36 Burning Memories /		—			
4/4/64	34	9	37 That's All That Matters		—	$12		Columbia 42971
9/5/64	7	17	38 Please Talk To My Heart I Don't Know Why (I Keep Loving You)		—	$10		Columbia 43086
1/9/65	38	4	39 A Thing Called Sadness .... Here Comes My Baby Back Again		—	$10		Columbia 43162
5/8/65	2²	24	40 The Other Woman Tearful Earful		—	$10		Columbia 43264
11/27/65+	11	14	41 Don't You Ever Get Tired Of Hurting Me .... Unloved, Unwanted		—	$10		Columbia 43427
			also see #83 below					
4/23/66	7	18	42 A Way To Survive /		—			
6/11/66	28	6	43 I'm Not Crazy Yet		—	$10		Columbia 43560
10/15/66	3	18	44 Touch My Heart It Should Be Easier Now		—	$10		Columbia 43795
3/25/67	9	17	45 Danny Boy I Let My Mind Wander		60	$8	■	Columbia 44042
7/22/67	6	18	46 I'm Still Not Over You /		—			
8/19/67	73	1	47 Crazy		—	$8		Columbia 44195
12/30/67+	8	15	48 Take Me As I Am (Or Let Me Go) In The Summer Of My Life		—	$8		Columbia 44374

DEBUT	PEAK	WKS	Gold	A-side (Chart Hit) / B-side	Pop	$	Pic	Label & Number
				PRICE, Ray — Cont'd				
5/4/68	11	16		49 I've Been There Before / Night Life	—	$8		Columbia 44505
10/5/68	6	14		50 She Wears My Ring / Goin' Away	—	$8		Columbia 44628
				#24 R&B hit for Jimmy Sweeney in 1962				
3/1/69	51	4		51 Set Me Free / Trouble	—	$8		Columbia 44747
3/8/69	11	15		52 Sweetheart Of The Year / How Can I Write On Paper (What I Feel In My Heart)	—	$8		Columbia 44761
8/16/69	14	12		53 Raining In My Heart / I Know Love	—	$8		Columbia 44931
				#88 Pop hit for Buddy Holly in 1959				
11/22/69	14	11		54 April's Fool / Make It Rain	—	$7		Columbia 45005
3/7/70	8	15		55 You Wouldn't Know Love / Everybody Wants To Get To Heaven	—	$7		Columbia 45095
6/27/70	❶¹	26		56 For The Good Times /	11			Columbia 45178
		18		57 Grazin' In Greener Pastures	—	$6		
3/20/71	❶³	19		58 I Won't Mention It Again / Kiss The World Goodbye	42	$6		Columbia 45329
8/7/71	2¹	17		59 I'd Rather Be Sorry / When I Loved Her	70	$6		Columbia 45425
4/15/72	2¹			60 The Lonesomest Lonesome /	109			
4/15/72	66	14		61 That's What Leaving's About	—	$6		Columbia 45583
11/4/72	❶³	16		62 She's Got To Be A Saint / Oh, Lonesome Me	93	$6		Columbia 45724
7/28/73	❶¹	16		63 You're The Best Thing That Ever Happened To Me / What Kind Of Love Is This	82	$6		Columbia 45889
				#3 Pop hit for Gladys Knight & The Pips in 1974				
3/16/74	25	13		64 Storms Of Troubled Times / Some Things Never Change	—	$6		Columbia 46015
8/17/74	15	11		65 Like A First Time Thing / You Are A Song	—	$6		Columbia 10006
10/26/74+	4	15		66 Like Old Times Again / My First Day Without Her	—	$6		Myrrh 146
2/8/75	3	14		67 Roses And Love Songs / The Closest Thing To Love	—	$6		Myrrh 150
5/31/75	17	13		68 Farthest Thing From My Mind / All That Keeps Me Going	—	$5		ABC 12095
8/9/75	31	11		69 If You Ever Change Your Mind / Just Enough To Make Me Stay	—	$5		Columbia 10150
11/8/75	40	12		70 Say I Do / I'll Still Love You	—	$5		ABC/Dot 17588
3/27/76	34	9		71 That's All She Wrote / I Don't Feel Nothing	—	$5		ABC/Dot 17616
7/24/76	41	10		72 To Make A Long Story Short /	—			
7/24/76	47	10		73 We're Getting There	—	$5		ABC/Dot 17637
12/4/76+	14	15		74 A Mansion On The Hill / Hey, Good Lookin'	—	$5		ABC/Dot 17666
3/26/77	38	9		75 Help Me / Nobody Wins	—	$5		Columbia 10503
5/28/77	28	11		76 Different Kind Of Flower / Don't Let The Stars Get In Your Eyes	—	$5		ABC/Dot 17690
				RAY PRICE AND THE CHEROKEE COWBOYS				
10/1/77	21	12		77 Born To Love Me / The Only Way To Say Good Morning	—	$5		ABC/Dot 17718
10/28/78+	19	13		78 Feet / Let's Make A Nice Memory (Today)	—	$5		Monument 267
3/3/79	30	12		79 There's Always Me / If It's All The Same To You (I'll Be Leaving In The Morning)	—	$5		Monument 277
				#56 Pop hit for Elvis Presley in 1967				
6/9/79	18	13		80 That's The Only Way To Say Good Morning / All The Good Things Are Gone	—	$5		Monument 283
11/24/79+	43	9		81 Misty Morning Rain / We Can't Build A Fire In The Rain	—	$5		Monument 290
8/9/80	3	15		82 Faded Love / This Cold War With You	—	$4		Columbia 11329
				WILLIE NELSON AND RAY PRICE				
12/6/80+	11	14		83 Don't You Ever Get Tired (Of Hurting Me) / Funny How Time Slips Away [R]	—	$4		Columbia 11405
				WILLIE NELSON AND RAY PRICE				
				new version of #41 above				
3/28/81	28	13		84 Getting Over You Again / Circle Driveway	—	$4		Dimension 1018
7/18/81	6	17		85 It Don't Hurt Me Half As Bad / She's The Right Kind Of A Woman	—	$4		Dimension 1021
11/14/81+	9	18		86 Diamonds In The Stars / Grazin' In Greener Pastures	—	$4		Dimension 1024
4/3/82	18	15		87 Forty And Fadin' / When You Gave Your Love To Me	—	$4		Dimension 1031
6/5/82	19	16		88 Old Friends / When A House Is Not A Home	—	$4		Columbia 02681
				ROGER MILLER & WILLIE NELSON (with Ray Price)				
8/7/82	62	7		89 Wait Till Those Bridges Are Gone / Angel In My Heart (Devil In My Mind)	—	$4		Dimension 1035
12/4/82+	55	9		90 Somewhere In Texas / Gettin' Down And Gettin' High	—	$4		Dimension 1038
1/15/83	70	6		91 One Fiddle, Two Fiddle /	—			
		6		92 San Antonio Rose		$4		Warner 29830
				RAY PRICE With Johnny Gimble & The Texas Swing Band (above 2)				
				above 2 from the movie *Honkytonk Man* starring Clint Eastwood				
5/7/83	72	6		93 Willie, Write Me A Song / I Love You Eyes	—	$4		Warner 29691
8/27/83	70	5		94 Scotch And Soda / I Love You Eyes	—	$4		Viva 29543
				#81 Pop hit for The Kingston Trio in 1962				
6/23/84	87	4		95 A New Place To Begin / Everyone Gets Crazy Now & Then	—	$4		Viva 29277
9/8/84	73	6		96 Better Class Of Loser / Every Time I Sing A Love Song	—	$4		Viva 29217
11/17/84	77	7		97 What Am I Gonna Do Without You / You've Been Leaving Me For Years	—	$4		Viva 29147
				RAY PRICE and The Cherokee Cowboys (above 3)				
5/25/85	77	6		98 (She's Got A Hold Of Me Where It Hurts) She Won't Let Go / Memories To Burn	—	$4		Step One 341
8/31/85	81	7		99 I'm Not Leaving (I'm Just Getting Out Of Your Way) / Why Don't Love Just Go Away	—	$4		Step One 344
12/21/85+	67	7		100 Five Fingers / Lonely Like A Rose	—	$4		Step One 350
3/15/86	60	8		101 You're Nobody Till Somebody Loves You / I'm In The Mood For Love	—	$4		Step One 352
				#14 Pop hit for Russ Morgan in 1946				
6/21/86	73	5		102 All The Way / S: Bummin' Around	—	$4		Step One 355
				#2 Pop hit for Frank Sinatra in 1957				
9/27/86	86	5		103 Please Don't Talk About Me When I'm Gone / For The Good Times	—	$4		Step One 361
				#3 Pop hit for Gene Austin in 1931				
12/27/86+	55	8		104 When You Gave Your Love To Me / Forty And Fadin'	—	$4		Step One 366
10/24/87	52	11		105 Just Enough Love / Why Don't Love Just Go Away (When It's All Gone)	—	$4		Step One 378
3/12/88	68	5		106 Big Ole Teardrops / The Season For Missing You	—	$4		Step One 383
7/9/88	55	7		107 Don't The Morning Always Come Too Soon / Come Back Home	—	$4		Step One 388
12/10/88	83	4		108 I'd Do It All Over Again / Wind Beneath My Wings	—	$4		Step One 393
11/18/89	79	3		109 Love Me Down To Size / I've Got A New Heartache	—	$4		Step One 410

DEBUT	PEAK	WKS	Gold	A-side (Chart Hit)	B-side	Pop	$	Pic	Label & Number
				PRICE, Toni '86					
				Singer/actress. Had a bit part in the movie *Sweet Dreams*.					
1/25/86	59	9		1 Mississippi Break Down	—		$6		Luv 114
9/27/86	71	6		2 How Much Do I Owe You	—		$6		Master 01
9/26/87	80	3		3 I Want To Be Wanted	—		$6		Prairie Dust 8744
				PRIDE, Charley ★19★ '71					
				Born on 3/18/38 in Sledge, Mississippi. Black singer/songwriter/guitarist. Played baseball with the Detroit Eagles and Memphis Red Sox of the Negro American League; also played in the Pioneer League. Joined the *Grand Ole Opry* in 1993. Elected to the Country Music Hall of Fame in 2000. CMA Awards: 1971 & 1972 Male Vocalist of the Year; 1971 Entertainer of the Year.					
				1)Kiss An Angel Good Mornin' 2)I'm Just Me 3)Afraid Of Losing You Again 4)It's Gonna Take A Little Bit Longer 5)She's Too Good To Be True					
12/3/66+	9	19		1 Just Between You And Me	Detroit City	—	$10		RCA Victor 9000
4/29/67	6	19		2 I Know One	Best Banjo Picker	—	$10		RCA Victor 9162
9/2/67	4	19		3 Does My Ring Hurt Your Finger	Spell Of The Freight Train	—	$10		RCA Victor 9281
				COUNTRY CHARLEY PRIDE (above 3)					
1/6/68	4	17		4 The Day The World Stood Still	Gone, On The Other Hand	—	$8		RCA Victor 9403
5/18/68	2^2	15		5 The Easy Part's Over	The Right To Do Wrong	—	$8		RCA Victor 9514
10/5/68	4	14		6 Let The Chips Fall	She Made Me Go	—	$8		RCA Victor 9622
2/1/69	3	16		7 Kaw-Liga	The Little Folks	120	$7		RCA Victor 9716
				"live" recording					
6/14/69	❶^1	17		8 All I Have To Offer You (Is Me)	A Brand New Bed Of Roses	91	$7		RCA Victor 0167
11/8/69	❶^3	16		9 (I'm So) Afraid Of Losing You Again	A Good Chance Of Tear-Fall Tonight	74	$7		RCA Victor 0265
3/7/70	❶^2	17		10 Is Anybody Goin' To San Antone	Things Are Looking Up	70	$7		RCA Victor 9806
6/13/70	❶^2	17		11 Wonder Could I Live There Anymore	Pirogue Joe	87	$7		RCA Victor 9855
9/26/70	❶^2	16		12 I Can't Believe That You've Stopped Loving Me	Time (You're Not A Friend of Mine)	71	$7		RCA Victor 9902
2/6/71	❶^3	14		13 I'd Rather Love You	(In My World) You Don't Belong	79	$7		RCA Victor 9952
4/24/71	21	10		14 Let Me Live /		104			
4/24/71	70	10		15 Did You Think To Pray	—		$7		RCA Victor 9974
6/26/71	❶^4	16		16 I'm Just Me	A Place For The Lonesome	94	$7		RCA Victor 9996
10/23/71	❶^5	19	●	17 Kiss An Angel Good Mornin'	No One Could Ever Take Me From You	21	$7		RCA Victor 0550
2/19/72	2^2	15		18 All His Children	You'll Still Be The One (Pride)	92	$7		RCA Victor 0624
				CHARLEY PRIDE with HENRY MANCINI					
				from the movie *Sometimes A Great Notion* starring Paul Newman					
6/3/72	❶^3	16		19 It's Gonna Take A Little Bit Longer	You're Wanting Me To Stop Loving You	102	$7	■	RCA Victor 0707
10/7/72	❶^3	16		20 She's Too Good To Be True	She's That Kind	—	$7		RCA Victor 0802
2/10/73	❶^1	14		21 A Shoulder To Cry On	I'm Learning To Love Her	101	$7		RCA Victor 0884
				written by Merle Haggard					
5/12/73	❶^1	15		22 Don't Fight The Feelings Of Love	Tennessee Girl	101	$7		RCA Victor 0942
10/13/73	❶^1	16		23 Amazing Love	Blue Ridge Mountains Turnin' Green	—	$7		RCA Victor 0073
4/20/74	3	14		24 We Could	Love Put A Song In My Heart	—	$7		RCA Victor 0257
8/24/74	3	15		25 Mississippi Cotton Picking Delta Town	Mary Go Round	70	$6		RCA Victor 10030
12/14/74+	❶^1	12		26 Then Who Am I	Completely Helpless	—	$6		RCA Victor 10126
3/29/75	6	14		27 I Ain't All Bad	The Hard Times Will Be The Best Times	101	$6		RCA Victor 10236
8/9/75	❶^1	14		28 Hope You're Feelin' Me (Like I'm Feelin' You)	Searching For The Morning Sun	—	$6		RCA Victor 10344
12/6/75+	3	15		29 The Happiness Of Having You	Right Back Missing You Again	—	$6		RCA Victor 10455
3/13/76	❶^1	14		30 My Eyes Can Only See As Far As You	Oklahoma Morning	—	$6		RCA Victor 10592
8/28/76	2^2	15		31 A Whole Lotta Things To Sing About	The Hardest Part Of Livin's Loving Me	—	$5		RCA 10757
1/29/77	❶^1	14		32 She's Just An Old Love Turned Memory	Country Music	—	$5		RCA 10875
5/21/77	❶^1	14		33 I'll Be Leaving Alone	We Need Lovin'	—	$5		RCA 10975
9/17/77	❶^1	14		34 More To Me	Heaven Watches Over Fools Like Me	—	$5		RCA 11086
2/11/78	❶^2	15		35 Someone Loves You Honey	Days Of Our Lives	—	$5		RCA 11201
6/24/78	3	15		36 When I Stop Leaving (I'll Be Gone)	I Can See The Lovin' In Your Eyes	—	$5		RCA 11287
10/21/78	2^3	14		37 Burgers And Fries	Nothing's Prettier Than Rose Is	—	$5		RCA 11391
2/24/79	❶^1	15		38 Where Do I Put Her Memory	The Best In The World	—	$5		RCA 11477
7/14/79	❶^1	15		39 You're My Jamaica	Let Me Have A Chance To Love You (One More Time)	—	$5		RCA 11655
10/27/79	89	2		40 Dallas Cowboys	When I Stop Leaving (I'll Be Gone)	—	$10		RCA 11736
				a special edition with the Cowboys logo on a silver and blue label					
11/3/79+	2^1	15		41 Missin' You	Heartbreak Mountain	—	$4		RCA 11751
2/16/80	❶^1	13		42 Honky Tonk Blues	I'm So Lonesome I Could Cry	—	$4		RCA 11912
5/10/80	❶^1	15		43 You Win Again	There's A Little Bit Of Hank In Me	—	$4		RCA 12002
9/27/80	4	18		44 You Almost Slipped My Mind	Ghost-Written Love Letters	—	$4		RCA 12100
3/7/81	7	13		45 Roll On Mississippi	Fall Back On Me	—	$4		RCA 12178
8/22/81	❶^2	15		46 Never Been So Loved (In All My Life)	I Call Her My Girl	—	$4		RCA 12294
12/26/81+	❶^1	18		47 Mountain Of Love	Love Is A Shadow	—	$4		RCA 13014
				#9 Pop hit for Johnny Rivers in 1964					
4/24/82	2^2	18		48 I Don't Think She's In Love Anymore	Oh What A Beautiful Love Song	—	$4		RCA 13096
8/28/82	❶^1	17		49 You're So Good When You're Bad	I Haven't Loved This Way In Years	—	$4		RCA 13293
12/4/82+	❶^1	19		50 Why Baby Why	It's So Good To Be Together	—	$4		RCA 13397
3/5/83	7	16		51 More And More	Radio Heroes	—	$4		RCA 13451

DEBUT	PEAK	WKS	Gold	A-side (Chart Hit)	B-side	Pop	$	Pic	Label & Number
				PRIDE, Charley — Cont'd					
6/25/83	●¹	21		52 Night Games .... I Could Let Her Get Close To Me (But She Could Never Get Close To You)		—	$4		RCA 13542
10/15/83+	2¹	20		53 Ev'ry Heart Should Have One	Lovin' It Up (Livin' It Down)	—	$4		RCA 13648
6/9/84	9	20		54 The Power Of Love	Ellie	—	$4		RCA 13821
11/3/84	32	13		55 Missin' Mississippi	Falling In Love Again	—	$4		RCA 13936
4/13/85	25	13		56 Down On The Farm	S:24 / A:27 Me And Then	—	$4		RCA 14045
7/6/85	34	11		57 Let A Little Love Come In	Night Games	—	$4		RCA 14134
1/18/86	75	5		58 The Best There Is	The Tumbleweed And The Rose	—	$4		RCA 14265
4/5/86	74	7		59 Love On A Blue Rainy Day	I Used It All On You	—	$4		RCA 14296
3/21/87	14	22		60 Have I Got Some Blues For You	S:●¹ / A:19 Even Knowin'	—	$4		16th Avenue 70400
7/18/87	31	15		61 If You Still Want A Fool Around	You Took Me There	—	$4		16th Avenue 70402
12/12/87+	5	23		62 Shouldn't It Be Easier Than This	S:●¹ Look In Your Mirror	—	$4		16th Avenue 70408
5/7/88	13	19		63 I'm Gonna Love Her On The Radio	S:7 Shouldn't It Be Easier Than This	—	$4		16th Avenue 70414
10/15/88	49	13		64 Where Was I	A Whole Lot Of Lovin'	—	$4		16th Avenue 70420
2/25/89	49	7		65 White Houses	Shouldn't It Be Easier Than This	—	$4		16th Avenue 70425
7/1/89	77	4		66 The More I Do	(long version)	—	$4		16th Avenue 70429
11/4/89+	28	17		67 Amy's Eyes	I Made Love To You In My Mind	—	$4		16th Avenue 70435
				PROCTOR, Paul '87					
				Born in Arlington, Texas. Singer/songwriter.					
12/20/86	74	4		1 Not Tonight		—	$6		Aurora 1003
2/21/87	79	4		2 He's Not Good Enough		—	$6		Aurora 1005
7/25/87	62	6		3 Ain't We Got Love		—	$6		19th Avenue 1009
11/19/88	96	1		4 Tied To The Wheel Of A Runaway Heart	Feelin' My Way Through The Dark	—	$6		19th Avenue 1012
				PROPHET, Ronnie '75					
				Born on 12/26/38 in Calumet, Quebec, Canada. Singer/songwriter/guitarist. Hosted own TV series in Canada and England.					
8/23/75	26	12		1 Sanctuary	Wild Outlaw	—	$5		RCA Victor 50027
12/27/75+	36	10		2 Shine On	Last Night I Felt The Whole World Changing	—	$5		RCA Victor 50136
5/1/76	50	7		3 It's Enough	I Want To Be Touched By You	—	$5		RCA Victor 50205
10/9/76	82	5		4 Big Big World		—	$5		RCA 50273
10/15/77	99	2		5 It Ain't Easy Lovin' Me		—	$5		RCA 50391
				PROSSER, James '99					
				Born in Mound Valley, Kansas.					
2/27/99	59	6		1 Life Goes On	Sea Of Heartbreak	—	$4		Warner 17111
6/26/99	66	4		2 Angels Don't Fly	The Girl Next Door	—	$4		Warner 16951
	★243★			**PRUETT, Jeanne** '73					
				Born Norma Jean Bowman on 1/30/37 in Pell City, Alabama. Singer/songwriter/guitarist. Joined the *Grand Ole Opry* in 1973.					
				1)Satin Sheets 2)Temporarily Yours 3)Back To Back 4)I'm Your Woman 5)It's Too Late					
9/18/71	66	6		1 Hold On To My Unchanging Love	He's Callin' Me Baby Again	—	$6		Decca 32857
3/11/72	34	12		2 Love Me	I'm Out Looking For You	—	$6		Decca 32929
				also see #23 below					
8/5/72	64	3		3 Call On Me	Stay On His Mind	—	$6		Decca 32977
11/4/72	60	6		4 I Forgot More Than You'll Ever Know (About Him)	Don't Hold Your Breath	—	$6		Decca 33013
3/31/73	●³	18		5 Satin Sheets	Sweet Sweetheart	28	$5		MCA 40015
				also see #17 below					
9/15/73	8	14		6 I'm Your Woman	Your Memory's Comin' On	—	$5		MCA 40116
3/23/74	15	14		7 You Don't Need To Move A Mountain	Hopefully (I'll Be Out Of My Mind)	—	$5		MCA 40207
8/31/74	22	15		8 Welcome To The Sunshine (Sweet Baby Jane)	What My Thoughts Do All The Time	—	$5		MCA 40284
1/18/75	25	12		9 Just Like Your Daddy	One More Time	—	$5		MCA 40340
5/10/75	41	9		10 Honey On His Hands	One Of These Days	—	$5		MCA 40395
7/26/75	24	13		11 A Poor Man's Woman	Momma Let Me Find Shelter (In Your Sweet Lovin' Arms)	—	$5		MCA 40440
12/13/75+	77	7		12 My Baby's Gone	But Not Today	—	$5		MCA 40490
10/2/76	41	8		13 I've Taken	Sweet And Warm And Right	—	$5		MCA 40605
2/19/77	30	10		14 I'm Living A Lie	My First Pay Day	—	$5		MCA 40678
5/21/77	85	4		15 She's Still All Over You	A Fancy Place To Cry	—	$5		MCA 40723
2/25/78	94	3		16 I'm A Woman	Midnight Exchange	—	$5		Mercury 55017
8/11/79	54	8		17 Please Sing Satin Sheets For Me	(I'm Gonna) Love All The Leavin Out Of You	—	$5		IBC 0002
				final 20 seconds of recording features a refrain of #5 above					
11/24/79+	6	16		18 Back To Back	Wild Side Of Life	—	$5		IBC 0005
3/15/80	5	15		19 Temporarily Yours	Ain't We Sad Today	—	$5		IBC 0008
7/5/80	9	14		20 It's Too Late	I Can't Feel At Home	—	$5		IBC 0010
3/14/81	81	3		21 Sad Ole Shade Of Gray	When I Stop Dreaming	—	$5		Paid 118
6/6/81	72	4		22 I Ought To Feel Guilty	Who'll Turn Out The Lights (In Your World Tonight)	—	$5		Paid 136
4/16/83	58	8		23 Love Me	Safely In The Arms Of Jesus (Pruett) [R]	—	$5		Audiograph 454
				JEANNE PRUETT/MARTY ROBBINS					
				new version of #2 above					
7/9/83	73	4		24 Lady Of The Eighties	Ain't No Way To Make A Bad Love Grow	—	$5		Audiograph 467
8/22/87	81	3		25 Rented Room	Put Me In Your Pocket	—	$5		MSR 1956
				PRUITT, Lewis '60					
				Lead guitarist for **Carl Smith**'s band.					
12/7/59+	10	21		1 Timbrook	(You'll Make) A Fool Of Me	—	$25		Peach 725
6/27/60	4	17		2 Softly And Tenderly (I'll Hold You In My Arms)	Riches And Gold	—	$15		Decca 31095
4/3/61	11	9		3 Crazy Bullfrog	The Hand That Held The Hand	—	$60		Decca 31201

DEBUT	PEAK	WKS	Gold	A-side (Chart Hit)	B-side	Pop	$	Pic	Label & Number
				PRYOR, Cactus '50 Born Richard Pryor in Austin, Texas. DJ at KTBC in Austin. Member of the Country Music DJ Hall of Fame.					
6/3/50	7	1		Cry Of The Dying Duck In A Thunder-Storm A:7 Double Trouble [N] CACTUS PRYOR and his Pricklypears parody of "The Cry Of The Wild Goose" by Tennessee Ernie Ford		—	$25		4 Star 1459
				PRYSOCK, Arthur '79 Born on 1/2/29 in Spartanburg, South Carolina. Died on 6/14/97 (age 68). Black singer.					
9/29/79	74	5		Today I Started Loving You Again	It Ain't No Big Thing (But It's Growin')	—	$6		Gusto 9023
				written by Merle Haggard					
				PUCKETT, Jerry '83 Session guitarist.					
8/27/83	81	3		Heart On The Run	Dance Alone	—	$4		Atlantic Amer. 99860
				PULLINS, Leroy '66 Born Carl Leroy Pullins on 11/12/40 in Elgin, Illinois. Singer/songwriter/guitarist.					
6/25/66	18	11		I'm A Nut	Knee Deep [N]	57	$8		Kapp 758
				PUMP BOYS AND DINETTES '83 From original cast recording of the Broadway musical *Pump Boys And Dinettes*. Featuring cast members Jim Wann and Cass Morgan.					
3/19/83	67	5		The Night Dolly Parton Was Almost Mine	The Best Man	—	$5		CBS 03549
				PURE PRAIRIE LEAGUE '76 Country-pop-rock group from Cincinnati. Numerous personnel changes. Lineup in 1976: George Ed Powell (vocals, guitar), Larry Goshorn (guitar), Michael Connor (keyboards), Mike Reilly (bass) and Billy Hinds (drums). **Vince Gill** was lead singer from 1979-83. Charted 7 pop hits from 1975-81.					
6/19/76	96	2		That'll Be The Day	I Can Only Think Of You	106	$5		RCA Victor 10679
				#1 Pop hit for Buddy Holly & The Crickets in 1957					
				PUTMAN, Curly '60 Born Claude Putman on 11/20/30 in Princeton, Alabama. Singer/prolific songwriter.					
2/29/60	23	1		1 The Prison Song	Forsaken	—	$20		Cherokee 504
7/8/67	41	9		2 My Elusive Dreams	Hurtin' Like A Heartache	134	$8		ABC 10934
11/4/67	67	3		3 Set Me Free	Hummin' A Heartache	—	$8		ABC 10984
				PYLE, Chuck '85 Born in Pittsburgh; raised in Newton, Iowa. Singer/songwriter.					
9/28/85	60	6		1 Drifter's Wind	(long version)	—	$5		Urban Sound 786
1/18/86	81	6		2 Breathless In The Night		—	$5		Urban Sound 782

Q

				QUIST, Jack '82 Born in Salt Lake City. Singer/songwriter.					
9/11/82	52	9		1 Memory Machine	I'm Comin' Home	—	$6		Memory Machine 1015
9/9/89	77	3		2 Where Does Love Go (When It Dies)	South For The Winter	—	$6	■	Grudge 4756

R

RABBITT, Eddie ★55★   '79
Born on 11/27/41 in Brooklyn, New York; raised in East Orange, New Jersey. Died of cancer on 5/7/98 (age 56). Singer/songwriter/guitarist. First recorded for 20th Century in 1964. Moved to Nashville in 1968. Became established after **Elvis Presley** recorded his song "Kentucky Rain."

1)Every Which Way But Loose 2)On Second Thought 3)The Best Year Of My Life 4)Step By Step
5)I Just Want To Love You

DEBUT	PEAK	WKS	#	A-side	B-side	Pop	$	Label & Number
8/31/74	34	14	1	You Get To Me	Que Pasa	—	$6	Elektra 45895
3/22/75	12	17	2	Forgive And Forget	Pure Love	—	$6	Elektra 45237
8/30/75	11	14	3	I Should Have Married You	Sweet Janine	—	$6	Elektra 45269
2/7/76	❶¹	16	4	Drinkin' My Baby (Off My Mind)	When I Was Young	—	$5	Elektra 45301
6/5/76	5	15	5	Rocky Mountain Music /		76		
		15	6	Do You Right Tonight		—	$5	Elektra 45315
11/6/76+	3	16	7	Two Dollars In The Jukebox	I Don't Wanna Make Love (With Anyone But You)	—	$5	Elektra 45357
4/2/77	2¹	16	8	I Can't Help Myself	She Loves Me Like She Means It	77	$5	Elektra 45390
8/20/77	6	15	9	We Can't Go On Living Like This	You Make Love Beautiful	—	$5	Elektra 45418
2/18/78	2²	16	10	Hearts On Fire	The Girl On My Mind	—	$5	Elektra 45461
6/10/78	❶¹	14	11	You Don't Love Me Anymore	Caroline	53	$5	Elektra 45488
9/30/78	❶¹	14	12	I Just Want To Love You	Crossin' The Mississippi	—	$5	Elektra 45531
12/23/78+	❶³	15	13	Every Which Way But Loose	Under The Double Eagle [I]	30	$5	Elektra 45554
				from the movie starring **Clint Eastwood**				
6/16/79	❶¹	14	14	Suspicions	I Don't Wanna Make Love (With Anyone Else But You)	13	$5	Elektra 46053
11/3/79+	5	15	15	Pour Me Another Tequila	I Will Never Let You Go Again	—	$5	Elektra 46558

DEBUT	PEAK	WKS	Gold	A-side (Chart Hit) .... B-side	Pop	$	Pic	Label & Number
				RABBITT, Eddie — Cont'd				
3/15/80	❶¹	14		16 Gone Too Far .... Loveline	82	$4		Elektra 46613
6/21/80	❶¹	15	●	17 Drivin' My Life Away .... Pretty Lady	5	$4		Elektra 46656
				from the movie Roadie *starring Meat Loaf*				
11/8/80+	❶¹	17	●	18 I Love A Rainy Night .... Short Road To Love	❶²	$4		Elektra 47066
8/1/81	❶¹	16		19 Step By Step .... My Only Wish	5	$4	■	Elektra 47174
11/21/81+	❶¹	17		20 Someone Could Lose A Heart Tonight .... Nobody Loves Me Like My Baby	15	$4		Elektra 47239
4/10/82	2³	16		21 I Don't Know Where To Start .... Skip-A-Beat	35	$4		Elektra 47435
10/9/82	❶¹	19		22 You And I .... All My Life, All My Love (Rabbitt)	7	$4		Elektra 69936
				EDDIE RABBITT with CRYSTAL GAYLE				
4/2/83	❶¹	17		23 You Can't Run From Love .... You Got Me Now	55	$4		Warner 29712
9/3/83	2	18		24 You Put The Beat In My Heart .... Our Love Will Survive	81	$4		Warner 29512
12/17/83+	10	15		25 Nothing Like Falling In Love .... Gone Too Far	—	$4		Warner 29431
5/19/84	3	18		26 B-B-B-Burnin' Up With Love 747	—	$4		Warner 29279
10/6/84+	❶¹	23		27 The Best Year Of My Life .... S:❶¹ / A:❶¹ Over There	—	$4		Warner 29186
2/23/85	4	19		28 Warning Sign .... S:3 / A:4 Go To Sleep Big Bertha	—	$4		Warner 29089
7/13/85	6	21		29 She's Comin' Back To Say Goodbye ...... A:5 / S:6 Dial That Telephone	—	$4		Warner 28976
10/12/85	10	18		30 A World Without Love .... S:10 / A:10 You Really Got A Hold On Me	—	$4		RCA 14192
3/22/86	4	19		31 Repetitive Regret .... S:4 / A:4 Letter From Home	—	$4		RCA 14317
7/12/86	❶¹	20		32 Both To Each Other (Friends & Lovers) .... S:❶¹ / A:❶¹ A World Without Love	—	$4	■	RCA 14377
				EDDIE RABBITT AND JUICE NEWTON				
				#2 Pop hit for Gloria Loring & Carl Anderson in 1986				
11/1/86+	9	20		33 Gotta Have You .... A:9 / S:10 Singing In The Subway	—	$4		RCA 5012
1/16/88	❶¹	20		34 I Wanna Dance With You .... S:7 Gotta Have You	—	$4		RCA 5238
5/28/88	❶¹	18		35 The Wanderer .... S:2 Workin' Out	—	$4		RCA 8306
				#2 Pop hit for Dion in 1961				
10/8/88	7	22		36 We Must Be Doin' Somethin' Right .... S:9 He's A Cheater	—	$4		RCA 8716
5/13/89	66	10		37 That's Why I Fell In Love With You .... She's An Old Cadillac	—	$4		RCA 8819
12/9/89+	❶²	26		38 On Second Thought .... Only One Love In My Life	—	$4		Universal 66025
4/7/90	8	21		39 Runnin' With The Wind .... Feel Like A Stranger	—	$4	■	Capitol 44538 (v)
8/4/90	32	9		40 It's Lonely Out Tonite	—			album cut
9/29/90	11	20		41 American Boy	—			album cut
3/2/91	58	9		42 Tennessee Born And Bred	—			album cut
				above 3 from the album Jersey Boy *on Capitol 93882*				
8/17/91	50	14		43 Hang Up The Phone	—			album cut
				from the album Ten Rounds *on Capitol 95955*				
				RABBITT, Jimmy '76				
				Born Edward Payne in Holdenville, Oklahoma; raised in Tyler, Texas. Singer/songwriter/guitarist. Worked as a DJ in several cities.				
5/8/76	80	4		Ladies Love Outlaws .... I Wish I Had Me Someone To Miss	—	$5		Capitol 4257
				JIMMY RABBITT AND RENEGADE				
				★ **RAE, Lana** '72				
				Born in Oklahoma. (Female) singer.				
2/19/72	26	14		You're My Shoulder To Lean On .... Talking To The Wall	—	$6		Decca 32927
				RAINES, Leon '88				
				Born in Mobile, Alabama.				
4/30/83	79	4		1 I'll Be Seeing You	—	$6		American Spotlite 103
				#1 Pop hit for Bing Crosby *in 1944*				
7/7/84	91	2		2 Don't Give Up On Her Now .... Take Me Back	—	$6		American Spotlite 107
11/24/84	81	3		3 Biloxi Lady .... Listen To The Words	—	$5		Atlantic Amer. 99700
3/9/85	83	2		4 It Happens Every Time .... Drunk On Love	—	$5		Atlantic Amer. 99670
12/26/87+	71	5		5 Most Of All .... No Losing You	—	$5		Southern Tracks 1089
				★ **RAINFORD, Tina** '77				
4/9/77	25	14		1 Silver Bird .... I'm Danny's Girlfriend	—	$5		Epic 50340
10/15/77	91	4		2 Big Silver Angel .... Guitar Man	—	$5		Epic 50455
				RAINSFORD, Willie '77				
				Born in Nashville. Singer/songwriter/pianist.				
3/26/77	98	2		1 No Relief In Sight .... Piano Man Blues	—	$7		Louisiana Hay. 7615
8/13/77	85	5		2 Cheater's Kit .... She's My Woman	—	$7		Louisiana Hay. 7629
				RAINWATER, Jack '77				
				Born in New York City. No relation to Marvin Rainwater.				
11/12/77	96	3		All I Want Is To Love You .... A Place In The Sun	—	$7		Laurie 3658
				RAINWATER, Marvin '57				
				Born Marvin Karlton Percy on 7/2/25 in Wichita, Kansas. Singer/songwriter/guitarist. No relation to Jack Rainwater.				
4/6/57	3	28	●	1 Gonna Find Me A Bluebird / .... S:3 / A:3 / J:5	18	$20		MGM 12412
		1		2 So You Think You've Got Troubles .... S:flip	—	$20		
4/14/58	15	3		3 Whole Lotta Woman .... S:15 Baby, Don't Go	60	$20		MGM 12609
9/15/58	11	1		4 Nothin' Needs Nothin' (Like I Need You) .... A:11 (There's Always) A Need For Love	—	$20		MGM 12701
7/6/59	16	6		5 Half-Breed .... A Song Of Love	66	$20		MGM 12803
				RAINWOOD, Michael '99				
10/9/99	21ˢ	1		I Want It All .... (remix)	—	$4	★	Atomik 008

DEBUT	PEAK	WKS	Gold	A-side (Chart Hit)	B-side	Pop	$	Pic	Label & Number

RAITT, Bonnie '80
Born on 11/8/49 in Burbank, California. Blues-rock singer/guitarist. Daughter of Broadway actor/singer John Raitt. Married to actor Michael O'Keefe from 1991-99. Charted 11 pop hits from 1977-95.

| 10/4/80 | 42 | 8 | | 1 Don't It Make Ya Wanna Dance ....Orange Blossom Special (Mickey Gilley) | — | $5 | ■ | Full Moon 47039 |
from the movie *Urban Cowboy* starring John Travolta

RAKES, Pal '77
Born Palmer Rakes in Tampa, Florida. Singer/songwriter/guitarist.

4/2/77	24	12	1 That's When The Lyin' Stops (And The Lovin' Starts) ....Dirty Old Women	—	$5	Warner 8340
7/30/77	31	10	2 'Til I Can't Take It Anymore ....Blue Summer	—	$5	Warner 8416
1/7/78	46	10	3 If I Ever Come Back ....Lay It On The Line	—	$5	Warner 8506
10/28/78	81	3	4 Till Then ....It's Sweet Business Doing Pleasure With You	—	$5	Warner 8656
#8 Pop hit for **The Mills Brothers** in 1944
3/17/79	92	3	5 You And Me And The Green Grass ....Bad Deal	—	$5	Warner 8765
10/29/88	71	5	6 I'm Only Lonely For You ....One More Time	—	$4	Atlantic Amer. 99276
6/24/89	73	5	7 All You're Takin' Is My Love ....I Feel A Change Comin' On	—	$4	■	Atlantic Amer. 99214
11/4/89	66	3	8 We Did It Once (We Can Do It Again) ....Poor Boy	—	$4	Atlantic 88800

RAMBLING ROGUE — see ROSE, Fred

RANCH, The '97
Trio from Australia: **Keith Urban** (vocals, guitar), Jerry Flowers (bass) and Peter Clarke (drums).

| 9/27/97 | 50 | 13 | 1 Walkin' The Country ....Clutterbilly | — | $4 | Capitol 19699 |
| 3/14/98 | 61 | 5 | 2 Just Some Love ....— | album cut |
from the album *The Ranch* on Capitol 55400

RANDALL, Jon '96
Born Jon Randall Stewart on 2/17/69 in Dallas. Former guitarist for **Emmylou Harris**. Married to **Lorrie Morgan** from 1996-99.

| 7/16/94 | 74 | 3 | 1 This Heart ....Only Game In Town | — | $4 | ■ | RCA 62833 (v) |
| 4/6/96 | 18 | 20 | 2 By My Side ....S:4 Candy Kisses | 110 | $4 | ■ | BNA 64512 (v) |
LORRIE MORGAN & JON RANDALL
| 3/20/99 | 71 | 3 | 3 Cold Coffee Morning ....— | album cut |
from the album *Cold Coffee Morning* on Asylum 62276

RANEY, Wayne '49
Born on 8/17/20 in Wolf Bayou, Arkansas. Died of cancer on 1/23/93 (age 72). Singer/harmonica player.

10/30/48	11	1	1 Lost John Boogie ....J:11 / S:14 Jole Blon's Ghost	—	$30	King 719
11/20/48	13	2	2 Jack And Jill Boogie ....J:13 Lonesome Wind Blues	—	$30	King 732
7/30/49	❶³	22	3 Why Don't You Haul Off And Love Me ....J:❶³/S:❷²/A:5 Don't Know Why	22	$30	King 791

RASCAL FLATTS '01
Vocal trio formed in Columbus, Ohio: Gary LeVox (born on 7/10/70), Jay DeMarcus (born on 4/26/71) and **Joe Don Rooney** (born on 9/13/75).

3/4/00	3	31	1 Prayin' For Daylight ....S:5 Long Slow Beautiful Dance	38	$4	★	Lyric Street 164039
8/12/00+	9	30	2 This Everyday Love	56		album cut
12/2/00	73	2	3 Long Slow Beautiful Dance	—		album cut
3/31/01	7	24	4 While You Loved Me	60		album cut
10/13/01+	4	34	5 I'm Movin' On	41		album cut
all of above from the album *Rascal Flatts* on Lyric Street 165011

RATTLESNAKE ANNIE '87
Born Rosan Gallimore on 12/26/41 in Puryear, Tennessee. Singer/songwriter/guitarist.

| 5/2/87 | 79 | 3 | 1 Callin' Your Bluff ....Goodbye To A River | — | $4 | Columbia 07024 |
| 1/9/88 | 79 | 3 | 2 Somewhere South Of Macon ....Outskirts Of Town | — | $4 | Columbia 07634 |

RAUSCH, Leon '80
Born Edgar Leon Rausch on 10/2/27 in Springfield, Missouri. Singer/songwriter/guitarist. Member of the **Original Texas Playboys**.

1/17/76	99	1	1 Through The Bottom Of The Glass ....Louisana, My Home	—	$5	Derrick 105
8/21/76	91	5	2 She's The Trip That I've Been On ....I'll Say Your Goodbyes	—	$5	Derrick 107
6/10/78	89	5	3 I'm Satisfied With You ....—	—	$5	Derrick 119
10/21/78	95	4	4 Let's Have A Heart To Heart Talk ....Did We Have To Come This Far To Say Goodbye	—	$5	Derrick 122
10/20/79	91	4	5 You Can Be Replaced ....Put Me To The Test	—	$5	Derrick 124
12/15/79+	81	6	6 Palimony ....Love, Love, Love	—	$5	Derrick 128

RAVEN, Eddy ★87★ '88
Born Edward Garvin Futch on 8/19/44 in Lafayette, Louisiana. Singer/songwriter/guitarist. First recorded for Cosmos label in 1962. Moved to Nashville in 1970, worked as staff writer for Acuff-Rose publishing company.

1)Joe Knows How To Live 2)Bayou Boys 3)I'm Gonna Get You 4)In A Letter To You 5)I Got Mexico

3/16/74	63	10	1 The Last Of The Sunshine Cowboys ....Sugah Kane	—	$6	ABC 11421
11/23/74+	46	13	2 Ain't She Somethin' Else ....If Is A Bird On A Chain	—	$6	ABC 12037
4/19/75	27	11	3 Good News, Bad News ....Sam	—	$6	ABC 12083
8/2/75	68	10	4 You're My Rainy Day Woman ....She Touched You	—	$6	ABC 12111
12/20/75+	34	10	5 Free To Be ....Country Green	—	$5	ABC/Dot 17595
4/10/76	87	5	6 I Wanna Live ....I Don't Wanna Talk It Over	—	$5	ABC/Dot 17618
8/28/76	94	3	7 The Curse Of A Woman ....Thank God For Kids	—	$5	ABC/Dot 17646

DEBUT	PEAK	WKS	Gold	A-side (Chart Hit)	B-side	Pop	$	Pic	Label & Number
				RAVEN, Eddy — Cont'd					
12/11/76	90	4		8 I'm Losing It All ... Touch The Morning		—	$5		ABC/Dot 17663
9/2/78	71	5		9 You're A Dancer ... She Don't Cry		—	$5		Monument 260
12/8/79+	44	11		10 Sweet Mother Texas ... I Should've Called		—	$5		Dimension 003
3/15/80	25	11		11 Dealin' With The Devil ... She Don't Cry		—	$5		Dimension 1005
6/7/80	30	11		12 You've Got Those Eyes ... Fais Do Do		—	$5		Dimension 1007
9/20/80	34	11		13 Another Texas Song ... Day After Day		—	$5		Dimension 1011
1/24/81	23	12		14 Peace Of Mind ... Just Leave Me Alone		—	$5		Dimension 1017
5/23/81	13	15		15 I Should've Called ... Young Girl		—	$4		Elektra 47136
10/17/81+	11	18		16 Who Do You Know In California ... Thinking It Over		—	$4		Elektra 47216
2/20/82	14	18		17 A Little Bit Crazy ... Loving Arms And Lying Eyes		—	$4		Elektra 47413
6/19/82	10	16		18 She's Playing Hard To Forget ... Desperate Dreams		—	$4		Elektra 47469
11/6/82+	25	17		19 San Antonio Nights ... Free To Be		—	$4		Elektra 69929
3/17/84	❶¹	22		20 I Got Mexico ... Love Burning Down		—	$4		RCA 13746
7/21/84	9	18		21 I Could Use Another You ... Folks Out On The Road		—	$4		RCA 13839
11/10/84+	9	23		22 She's Gonna Win Your Heart ... S:7 / A:7 Looking For Ways		—	$4		RCA 13939
4/20/85	9	21		23 Operator, Operator ... A:6 / S:10 Just For The Sake Of The Thrill		—	$4		RCA 14044
8/3/85	8	24		24 I Wanna Hear It From You ... A:7 / S:8 Room To Run		—	$4		RCA 14164
12/7/85+	3	23		25 You Should Have Been Gone By Now ... S:3 / A:3 We Robbed Trains		—	$4		RCA 14250
5/31/86	3	22		26 Sometimes A Lady ... A:3 / S:4 Just For The Sake Of The Thrill		—	$4		RCA 14319
11/15/86+	3	24		27 Right Hand Man ... A:3 / S:6 I Got Mexico		—	$4		RCA 5032
3/28/87	3	21		28 You're Never Too Old For Young Love ... S:8 / A:15 Other Than Montreal		—	$4		RCA 5128
7/25/87	❶¹	24		29 Shine, Shine, Shine ... S:12 Stay With Me		—	$4		RCA 5221
2/13/88	❶¹	21		30 I'm Gonna Get You ... S:2 Other Than Montreal		—	$4		RCA 6831
6/18/88	❶¹	21		31 Joe Knows How To Live ... S:3 Looking For Ways		—	$4		RCA 8303
12/3/88+	4	21		32 'Til You Cry ... Just For The Sake Of The Thrill		—	$4		RCA 8798
4/22/89	❶¹	21		33 In A Letter To You ... Risky Business		—	$4		Universal 66003
8/19/89	❶¹	26		34 Bayou Boys ... Angel Fire		—	$4		Universal 66016
12/23/89+	6	26		35 Sooner Or Later ... Little Sheba first released on Universal 66029 in 1989		—	$4		Capitol 44528
4/21/90	10	21		36 Island ... A Woman's Place		—	$4	■	Capitol 44537 (v)
9/22/90	56	7		37 Zydeco Lady from the album *Temporary Sanity* on Universal 76003		—			album cut
3/30/91	60	7		38 Rock Me In The Rhythm Of Your Love		—			album cut
6/29/91	58	8		39 Too Much Candy For A Dime above 2 from the album *Right For The Flight* on Capitol 94258		—			album cut
3/10/01	60	1		40 Cowboys Don't Cry from the album *Living In Black And White* on Row Music Group 88194		—			album cut

RAY, Mundo — see EARWOOD, Mundo

RAYBON, Marty '00
Born on 12/8/59 in Greenville, Alabama. Former lead singer of **Shenandoah** and the **Raybon Bros.**

1/29/00	63	9		Cracker Jack Diamond from the album *Marty Raybon* on Tri Chrod 33001		—			album cut

RAYBON BROS. '97
Vocal duo from Greenville, Alabama: Tim and **Marty Raybon**.

5/31/97	37	20	●	1 Butterfly Kisses ... S:2 (instrumental)		22	$4	■	MCA 72016 (v)
8/16/97	64	4		2 The Way She's Lookin' ... Tangled Up In Love		—	$4		MCA 72017

RAYE, Collin ★86★ '92
Born Floyd Collin Wray on 8/22/59 in DeQueen, Arkansas. Singer/songwriter/guitarist. His mother, Lois Wary, was a regional singing star in Arkansas. Moved to Oregon in 1980, where he formed **The Wrays** (as "Bubba Wray").

1)Love, Me 2)I Can Still Feel You 3)In This Life 4)My Kind Of Girl 5)On The Verge

6/8/91	29	20		1 All I Can Be (Is A Sweet Memory) ... Good For You		—	$4		Epic 73831
10/19/91+	❶³	20		2 Love, Me ... Blue Magic		—	$4		Epic 74051
2/29/92	2¹	20		3 Every Second ... Any Old Stretch Of Blacktop		—	$4		Epic 74242
7/4/92	74	1		4 It Could've Been So Good from the album *All I Can Be* on Epic 47468		—			album cut
8/1/92	❶²	20		5 In This Life ... Blue Magic		—	$4	■	Epic 74421 (v)
12/5/92+	7	20		6 I Want You Bad (And That Ain't Good) ... Let It Be Me		—	$4		Epic 74786
4/3/93	5	20		7 Somebody Else's Moon ... You Can't Take It With You		—	$4		Epic 74912
8/7/93	4	20		8 That Was A River ... Big River		—	$4		Epic 77118
12/11/93+	6	20		9 That's My Story ... Border And Beyond		—	$4	■	Epic 77308 (v)
4/9/94	2¹	20		10 Little Rock ... Dreaming My Dreams With You		—	$4		Epic 77436
8/6/94	8	20		11 Man Of My Word ... Nothin' A Little Love Won't Cure		—	$4	■	Epic 77632 (v)
12/3/94+	❶¹	20		12 My Kind Of Girl ... Angel Of No Mercy		—	$4	■	Epic 77773 (v)
4/8/95	4	20		13 If I Were You ... A Bible And A Bus Ticket Home		—	$4		Epic 77859
7/29/95	2²	20		14 One Boy, One Girl ... S:2 I Love Being Wrong		87	$4	■	Epic 77973 (v)
11/18/95+	3	20		15 Not That Different ... S:5 Sweet Miss Behavin'		114	$4	■	Epic 78189 (v)

DEBUT	PEAK	WKS	Gold	A-side (Chart Hit)	B-side	Pop	$	Pic	Label & Number
				RAYE, Collin — Cont'd					
11/25/95	57	11		16 What If Jesus Comes Back Like That ....The Time Machine		—	$4		Epic 78452
3/9/96	3	20		17 I Think About You ....I Volunteer		—	$4		Epic 78238
7/13/96	12	20		18 Love Remains ....I Love Being Wrong		—	$4		Epic 78348
11/9/96+	21	11		19 What If Jesus Comes Back Like That ....The Time Machine [R]		—	$4		Epic 78452
2/22/97	2²	20		20 On The Verge		—			album cut
				from the album *I Think About You* on Epic 67033					
6/7/97	2¹	20		21 What The Heart Wants		—			album cut
9/6/97	70	6		22 Open Arms		—			album cut
				#2 Pop hit for Journey in 1982					
10/25/97	51	11		23 The Gift		—			album cut
				COLLIN RAYE with Jim Brickman					
12/13/97+	3	22		24 Little Red Rodeo		—			album cut
				above 4 from the album *The Best Of Collin Raye* on Epic 67893					
4/25/98	❶²	26		25 I Can Still Feel You		—			album cut
				from the album *The Walls Came Down* on Epic 68876					
8/22/98	3	25		26 Someone You Used To Know S:6 *Make Sure You've Got It All*		37	$4	★	Epic 79011
1/30/99	4	24		27 Anyone Else		37			album cut
7/17/99	39	17		28 Start Over Georgia		—			album cut
				above 2 from the album *The Walls Came Down* on Epic 68876					
2/5/00	3	25		29 Couldn't Last A Moment S:4 *You Still Take Me There*		43	$4	★	Epic 79353 (v)
6/24/00	50	17		30 Tired Of Loving This Way		—			album cut
				COLLIN RAYE with Bobbie Eakes					
11/11/00+	43	13		31 She's All That		—			album cut
3/10/01	47	6		32 You Still Take Me There		—		★	album cut (v)
				first released as the B-side of #29 above					
8/11/01	43	12		33 Ain't Nobody Gonna Take That From Me		—			album cut
				above 4 from the album *Tracks* on Epic 69995					

RAYE, Susan   ★175★   '72

Born on 10/18/44 in Eugene, Oregon. Appeared on the *Hoedown* TV show in Portland. Worked with **Buck Owens** from 1968-76. Regular on TV's *Hee-Haw*. Acted in the movie *From Nashville With Music*.

1)(I've Got A) Happy Heart   2)Pitty, Pitty, Patter   3)The Great White Horse   4)L.A. International Airport
5)Whatcha Gonna Do With A Dog Like That

DEBUT	PEAK	WKS		A-side	B-side	Pop	$	Pic	Label & Number
1/10/70	30	11		1 Put A Little Love In Your Heart ....I've Carried This Torch Much Too Long		—	$8		Capitol 2701
				#4 Pop hit for Jackie DeShannon in 1969					
2/21/70	13	11		2 We're Gonna Get Together ....Everybody Needs Somebody		—	$8	■	Capitol 2731
				BUCK OWENS & SUSAN RAYE					
5/9/70	12	12		3 Togetherness ....Fallin' For You		—	$8	■	Capitol 2791
				BUCK OWENS & SUSAN RAYE					
7/4/70	35	11		4 One Night Stand ....She Don't Deserve You Anymore		—	$8		Capitol 2833
8/29/70	8	13		5 The Great White Horse ....Your Tender Loving Care		—	$8	■	Capitol 2871
				BUCK OWENS & SUSAN RAYE					
11/14/70+	10	13		6 Willy Jones I'll Love You Forever (If You're Sure You'll Want Me Then)		—	$7		Capitol 2950
2/20/71	9	16		7 L.A. International Airport ....Merry-Go-Round Of Love		54	$7		Capitol 3035
7/17/71	6	16		8 Pitty, Pitty, Patter ....I'll Be Gone		—	$7	■	Capitol 3129
11/13/71+	3	14		9 (I've Got A) Happy Heart ....How Long Will My Baby Be Gone		—	$7		Capitol 3209
4/1/72	44	8		10 A Song To Sing ....Adios, Farewell, Good-Bye, Good Luck, So Long		—	$7		Capitol 3289
5/27/72	10	12		11 My Heart Has A Mind Of Its Own You'll Never Miss The Water		—	$7		Capitol 3327
				#1 Pop hit for **Connie Francis** in 1960					
7/15/72	13	14		12 Looking Back To See ....Cryin' Time		—	$7	■	Capitol 3368
				BUCK OWENS & SUSAN RAYE					
9/30/72	16	11		13 Wheel Of Fortune ....My Heart Skips A Beat		—	$7		Capitol 3438
				#1 Pop hit for **Kay Starr** in 1952					
12/23/72+	17	14		14 Love Sure Feels Good In My Heart ....I've Got You On My Mind Again		—	$6		Capitol 3499
4/7/73	18	12		15 Cheating Game ....I'll Love You Forever And Ever		—	$6		Capitol 3569
6/16/73	35	8		16 The Good Old Days (Are Here Again) ....When You Get To Heaven (I'll Be There)		—	$6		Capitol 3601
				BUCK OWENS & SUSAN RAYE					
9/8/73	23	12		17 Plastic Trains, Paper Planes ....I Won't Be Needing You		—	$6		Capitol 3699
12/15/73+	57	9		18 When You Get Back From Nashville ....Nobody's Fool But Yours		—	$6		Capitol 3782
4/6/74	18	14		19 Stop The World (And Let Me Off) ....Love's Ups And Downs		—	$6		Capitol 3850
8/3/74	49	11		20 You Can Sure See It From Here ....I Wish I Was A Butterfly		—	$6		Capitol 3927
11/23/74+	9	16		21 Whatcha Gonna Do With A Dog Like That That Loving Feeling		—	$6		Capitol 3980
5/24/75	58	7		22 Ghost Story ....Beginner's Luck		—	$6		Capitol 4063
7/5/75	20	13		23 Love Is Strange ....Sweethearts In Heaven		—	$6		Capitol 4100
				BUCK OWENS & SUSAN RAYE					
				#11 Pop hit for Mickey & Sylvia in 1957					
10/16/76	87	5		24 Ozark Mountain Lullaby ....Johnny Sunshine		—	$5		United Artists 870
2/19/77	64	6		25 Mr. Heartache ....Turn Away		—	$5		United Artists 934
4/30/77	53	8		26 Saturday Night To Sunday Quiet ....My Hiding Place		—	$5		United Artists 976
8/13/77	51	9		27 It Didn't Have To Be A Diamond ....My Hiding Place		—	$5		United Artists 1026
2/15/86	68	5		28 I Just Can't Take The Leaving Anymore /		—	$5		
11/3/84	76	5		29 Put Another Notch In Your Belt		—	$7		Westexas America 1

handwritten at top: "Red River" Dave McEnery (See p. 491 of Pop Singles)

DEBUT	PEAK	WKS	Gold	A-side (Chart Hit)	B-side	Pop	$	Pic	Label & Number
				RAZORBACK — see GRAYGHOST					
				REBEL HEARTS '00					
				Vocal trio from Reno, Nevada: Laura Angelini, Darren Castle and Don McDowell.					
9/9/00	75	1		When Will I Be Loved	—				album cut
				RECORD, Donnie '83					
				Born on 3/31/52 in Enid, Oklahoma. Singer/songwriter/guitarist.					
8/6/83	95	1		One More Goodbye, One More Hello	—		$6		BriarRose 1001
				★ **REDDY, Helen** '77					
				Born on 10/25/41 in Melbourne, Australia. Singer/actress. Charted 21 pop hits from 1971-81.					
10/22/77	98	1		Laissez Les Bontemps Rouler	The Happy Girls (Pop #57)	—	$5		Capitol 4487
				title is French for "Let The Good Times Roll"					
				RED HOTS, The '94					
				All-star group: Suzy Boggus, Alison Krauss, Kathy Mattea and Crosby, Stills & Nash.					
10/22/94	75	1		Teach Your Children	—				album cut
				#16 Pop hit for Crosby, Stills & Nash in 1970; from the album Red Hot + Country on Mercury 522639					
				REDMON & VALE '99					
				Female vocal duo: Allison Redmon (from Georgia) and Tina Vale (from Iowa).					
5/29/99	65	3		1 If I Had A Nickel (One Thin Dime)	—				album cut
9/11/99	74	1		2 Squeezin' The Love Outta You	—				album cut
				above 2 from the album Redmon & Vale on DreamWorks 50057					
				REDMOND, Robb '77					
				Born in Sherman Oaks, California.					
3/5/77	87	4		Lunch Time Lovers	Monday Morning Memory	—	$7		NBC 001
				RED, WHITE & BLUE (grass) '74					
				Bluegrass group from Birmingham, Alabama: husband-and-wife Ginger (vocals, guitar) and Grant (guitar) Boatwright, Dale Whitcomb (fiddle), Dave Sebolt (bass) and Michael Barnett (drums).					
12/22/73+	71	9		July You're A Woman	High Ground	—	$7		GRC 1009
				#100 Pop hit for Pat Boone in 1969					
				RED WILLOW BAND '79					
				Group from Beardon, South Dakota: Chris Gage, Hank Harris, Kenny Putnam, Marley Forman and Barry Carpenter.					
6/2/79	97	1		I Wish I Had Your Arms Around Me	Tying The Knot	—	$7		Lost 1288
				REECE, Ben '75					
9/6/75	41	12		1 Mirror, Mirror	She's Winning	—	$5		20th Century 2227
1/3/76	87	5		2 It Don't Bother Me	The Things To Do Today	—	$5		20th Century 2262
7/10/76	83	6		3 Even If It's Wrong	Why'd The Last Time Have To Be The Best	—	$5		Polydor 14329
11/13/76	89	4		4 Honky Tonk Fool	She Came To Me	—	$5		Polydor 14356
				REED, Bobby '83					
				Born in Rockford, Illinois.					
3/5/83	90	2		If I Just Had My Woman	There's Love In The Air	—	$7		CBO 132
				REED, Jerry ★78★ '71					
				Born Jerry Reed Hubbard on 3/20/37 in Atlanta. Singer/songwriter/guitarist/actor. Known as "The Guitar Man." Acted in several movies. Regular on TV's Concrete Cowboys. Married to Priscilla Mitchell since 1959. Also see Heart Of Nashville and Some Of Chet's Friends.					
				1)When You're Hot, You're Hot 2)She Got The Goldmine (I Got The Shaft) 3)Lord, Mr. Ford 4)The Bird 5)East Bound And Down					
5/20/67	53	9		1 Guitar Man	It Don't Work That Way	—	$10		RCA Victor 9152
				Reed played guitar on Elvis Presley's version in 1968 (#43 Pop)					
11/4/67+	15	15		2 Tupelo Mississippi Flash	Wabash Cannon Ball	—	$8		RCA Victor 9334
4/13/68	14	15		3 Remembering	Fine On My Mind	—	$8		RCA Victor 9493
				also see #28 below					
9/28/68	48	10		4 Alabama Wild Man	Twelve Bar Midnight	—	$8		RCA Victor 9623
				also see #16 below					
1/18/69	60	6		5 Oh What A Woman!	Losing Your Love	—	$8		RCA Victor 9701
4/5/69	20	10		6 There's Better Things In Life	Blues Land	—	$7		RCA Victor 0124
8/30/69	11	13		7 Are You From Dixie (Cause I'm From Dixie Too)	A Worried Man	—	$7		RCA Victor 0211
3/7/70	14	12		8 Talk About The Good Times	Alabama Jubilee	—	$7		RCA Victor 9804
8/8/70	16	11		9 Georgia Sunshine	Swinging '69	—	$7		RCA Victor 9870
10/24/70	16	18 ●		10 Amos Moses / [N]	[N]	8			RCA Victor 9904
		11		11 The Preacher And The Bear	[N]		$6		
5/8/71	❶5	15		12 When You're Hot, You're Hot	You've Been Cryin' Again [N]	9	$6		RCA Victor 9976
9/11/71	11	13		13 Ko-Ko Joe	I Feel For You	51	$6		RCA Victor 1011
1/1/72	27	11		14 Another Puff	Love Man [N]	65	$6		RCA Victor 0613
4/1/72	24	11		15 Smell The Flowers	If It Comes To That	—	$6		RCA Victor 0667
7/15/72	22	12		16 Alabama Wild Man	Take It Easy (In Your Mind) [R]	62	$6	■	RCA Victor 0738
				new version of #4 above					
12/23/72+	18	10		17 You Took All The Ramblin' Out Of Me	I'm Not Playing Games	—	$6		RCA Victor 0857
5/26/73	❶1	15		18 Lord, Mr. Ford	Two-Timin' [N]	68	$6		RCA Victor 0960
12/15/73+	25	10		19 The Uptown Poker Club	Honkin'	—	$6		RCA Victor 0194
2/9/74	13	10		20 The Crude Oil Blues	Pickie, Pickie, Pickie [N]	91	$6		RCA Victor 0224
5/11/74	12	14		21 A Good Woman's Love	Everybody Needs Someone	—	$6		RCA Victor 0273

285

"Red Kirby" Dave McEnery (see p. 491 of Pop Singles)

DEBUT	PEAK	WKS	Gold	A-side (Chart Hit)	B-side	Pop	$	Pic	Label & Number
				REED, Jerry — Cont'd					
10/5/74	72	6		22 Boogie Woogie Rock And Roll	In Between	—	$6		RCA Victor 10063
12/14/74+	18	12		23 Let's Sing Our Song	Grab Bag	—	$5		RCA Victor 10132
4/5/75	64	9		24 Mind Your Love	Struttin'	—	$5		RCA Victor 10247
7/12/75	65	9		25 The Telephone	City Of New Orleans [N]	—	$5		RCA Victor 10325
10/4/75	60	8		26 You Got A Lock On Me	Reedology	104	$5		RCA Victor 10389
7/4/76	54	8		27 Gator	Good For Him	—	$5		RCA Victor 10717
				from the movie starring Burt Reynolds					
10/9/76	57	7		28 Remembering	Babe [R]	—	$5		RCA 10784
				new version of #3 above					
3/5/77	19	12		29 Semolita	The Phantom Of The Opry	—	$5		RCA 10893
7/2/77	68	5		30 With His Pants In His Hand	We Called It Everything Else	—	$5		RCA 11008
8/13/77	2²	16		31 East Bound And Down /		103			
				from the movie Smokey & The Bandit starring Burt Reynolds					
		13		32 (I'm Just A) Redneck In A Rock And Roll Bar	—	—	$5		RCA 11056
12/24/77+	20	12		33 You Know What	Louisiana Lady	—	$5		RCA 11164
				JERRY REED and SEIDINA (Reed's daughter)					
3/25/78	39	9		34 Sweet Love Feelings	You're Gonna Need Someone	—	$5		RCA 11232
6/10/78	10	12		35 (I Love You) What Can I Say /		—			
		7		36 High Rollin'		—	$5		RCA 11281
				from the movie High-Ballin' starring Reed					
11/11/78+	14	14		37 Gimme Back My Blues	Honkin'	—	$5		RCA 11407
2/24/79	18	11		38 Second-Hand Satin Lady (And A Bargain Basement Boy)	Jiffy Jam	—	$5		RCA 11472
6/16/79	40	7		39 (Who Was The Man Who Put) The Line In Gasoline	Piece Of Cake [N]	—	$5		RCA 11638
9/8/79	67	5		40 Hot Stuff	Nervous Breakdown	—	$5		RCA 11698
				from the movie starring Reed					
12/1/79+	12	14		41 Sugar Foot Rag	I Wanna Go Back Home To Georgia	—	$5		RCA 11764
3/29/80	36	10		42 Age /					
		10		43 Workin' At The Carwash Blues		—	$5		RCA 11944
				#32 Pop hit for Jim Croce in 1974					
7/12/80	64	6		44 The Friendly Family Inn	The Bandit	—	$4		RCA 12034
8/30/80	26	12		45 Texas Bound And Flyin'	Concrete Sailor	—	$4		RCA 12083
				from the movie Smokey & The Bandit II starring Burt Reynolds					
1/10/81	80	4		46 Caffein, Nicotine, Benzedrine (And Wish Me Luck)	If Love's Not Around The House	—	$4		RCA 12157
5/9/81	87	3		47 The Testimony Of Soddy Hoe	Dreaming Fairy Tales	—	$4		RCA 12210
7/4/81	84	2		48 Good Friends Make Good Lovers	The Devil Went Down To Georgia	—	$4		RCA 12253
9/26/81	30	12		49 Patches	Stray Dogs And Stray Women	—	$4		RCA 12318
				#4 Pop hit for Clarence Carter in 1970					
4/17/82	32	13		50 The Man With The Golden Thumb	East Bound And Down	—	$4		RCA 13081
7/10/82	❶²	17		51 She Got The Goldmine (I Got The Shaft)	"44" [N]	57	$4		RCA 13268
10/16/82	2³	16		52 The Bird	The Hobo [N]	—	$4		RCA 13355
				JERRY REED and Friends					
				impressions of Willie Nelson's "Whiskey River" and "On The Road Again" and George Jones's "He Stopped Loving Her Today"					
1/29/83	13	15		53 Down On The Corner	Hard Times	—	$4		RCA 13422
				#3 Pop hit for Creedence Clearwater Revival in 1969					
5/21/83	16	17		54 Good Ole Boys /					
		17		55 She's Ready For Someone To Love Her		—	$4		RCA 13527
8/6/83	20	14		56 Hold On, I'm Comin'	Waiting On Down The Line	—	$4		RCA 13580
				WAYLON JENNINGS & JERRY REED					
				#21 Pop hit for Sam & Dave in 1966					
11/12/83	58	6		57 I'm A Slave	Nobody Ever Loved Me	—	$4		RCA 13663

REEVES, Del ★95★ '65

Born Franklin Delano Reeves on 7/14/33 in Sparta, North Carolina. Singer/songwriter/multi-instrumentalist. Joined the *Grand Ole Opry* in 1966. Hosted the *Country Carnival* TV show. Acted in the movies *Second Fiddle To A Steel Guitar*, *Sam Whiskey*, *Cotton Pickin' Chicken-Pluckers* and *Forty-Acre Feud*.

1)Girl On The Billboard 2)Good Time Charlies 3)The Belles Of Southern Bell
4)Looking At The World Through A Windshield 5)Be Glad

DEBUT	PEAK	WKS		A-side	B-side	Pop	$	Pic	Label & Number
11/6/61	9	17		1 Be Quiet Mind	As Far As I Can See	—	$12		Decca 31307
10/27/62	11	11		2 He Stands Real Tall	Empty House	—	$12		Decca 31417
4/27/63	13	14		3 The Only Girl I Can't Forget	The Love She Offered Me	—	$10		Reprise 20158
8/8/64	41	12		4 Talking To The Night Lights	Not Since Adam	—	$10		Columbia 43044
3/13/65	❶²	20		5 Girl On The Billboard	Eyes Don't Come Crying To Me [N]	96	$8		United Artists 824
8/14/65	4	17		6 The Belles Of Southern Bell	Nothing To Write Home About	—	$8		United Artists 890
12/4/65+	9	13		7 Women Do Funny Things To Me	My Half Of Our Past	—	$8		United Artists 940
4/16/66	42	7		8 One Bum Town	Dead And Gone	—	$8		United Artists 50001
7/2/66	37	5		9 Gettin' Any Feed For Your Chickens	Plain As The Tears On My Face	—	$8		United Artists 50035
10/29/66	27	12		10 This Must Be The Bottom	Laughter Keeps Running Down My Cheeks	—	$8		United Artists 50081
3/18/67	45	9		11 Blame It On My Do Wrong	I Don't Have Sense Enough	—	$8		United Artists 50128
6/17/67	33	10		12 The Private	Things Her Memory Makes	—	$8	■	United Artists 50157
10/7/67	12	18		13 A Dime At A Time	So Much Got Lost	—	$8		United Artists 50210
3/9/68	56	5		14 I Just Wasted The Rest	Our Way Of Life	—	$8		United Artists 50243
				DEL REEVES & BOBBY GOLDSBORO					
3/30/68	18	13		15 Wild Blood	Lest We Forget	—	$8		United Artists 50270

DEBUT	PEAK	WKS	Gold	A-side (Chart Hit)	B-side	Pop	$	Pic	Label & Number
				REEVES, Del — Cont'd					
8/17/68	5	14		16 Looking At The World Through A Windshield	If I Lived Here	—	$7		United Artists 50332
12/28/68+	3	17		17 Good Time Charlie's	These Feet	—	$7		United Artists 50487
5/24/69	5	14		18 Be Glad	Moccasin Branch	—	$7		United Artists 50531
10/11/69	12	11		19 There Wouldn't Be A Lonely Heart In Town	Little Bit Of Somethin' Else	—	$7		United Artists 50564
11/1/69	31	10		20 Take A Little Good Will Home	She Thinks I Still Care	—	$7		United Artists 50591
				BOBBY GOLDSBORO & DEL REEVES					
2/7/70	14	12		21 A Lover's Question	Spare Me	—	$7		United Artists 50622
				DEL REEVES and The Goodtime Charlies					
				#6 Pop hit for Clyde McPhatter in 1959					
5/23/70	41	11		22 Son Of A Coal Man	The Chair That Rocked Us All	—	$7		United Artists 50667
5/30/70	20	12		23 Land Mark Tavern	So Sad	—	$7		United Artists 50669
				DEL REEVES & PENNY DeHAVEN					
10/3/70	22	10		24 Right Back Loving You Again	Gardenia Brown	—	$7		United Artists 50714
1/9/71	30	11		25 Bar Room Talk	I'm Not Through Loving You	—	$7		United Artists 50743
4/10/71	33	12		26 Working Like The Devil (For The Lord)	Sidewalks Of Chicago	—	$6		United Artists 50763
7/10/71	9	12		27 The Philadelphia Fillies	Belles Of Broadway	—	$6		United Artists 50802
10/23/71	31	10		28 A Dozen Pairs Of Boots	A Rose Is Hard To Beat	—	$6		United Artists 50840
1/22/72	29	12		29 The Best Is Yet To Come	Truth Can Hurt A Woman	—	$6		United Artists 50877
6/10/72	62	6		30 No Rings—No Strings	Hey, Anybody Here Seen Cupid	—	$6		United Artists 50906
6/24/72	54	6		31 Crying In The Rain	Time	—	$6		United Artists 50829
				DEL REEVES & PENNY DeHAVEN					
				#6 Pop hit for The Everly Brothers in 1962					
11/11/72	47	6		32 Before Goodbye	Buck Jones Guitar	—	$6		United Artists 50964
2/24/73	54	5		33 Trucker's Paradise	Gathering Of My Memories	—	$6		United Artists 51106
6/9/73	44	10		34 Mm-Mm Good	Bridge That Wouldn't Burn	—	$5		United Artists 249
9/8/73	22	15		35 Lay A Little Lovin' On Me	Lay Me To Sleep	—	$5		United Artists 308
2/23/74	70	8		36 What A Way To Go	Sometimes Woman	—	$5		United Artists 378
5/11/74	62	7		37 Prayer From A Mobile Home	Three Years Late	—	$5		United Artists 427
9/21/74	89	4		38 She Likes Country Bands	A Rose Is Hard To Beat	—	$5		United Artists 532
12/14/74+	65	8		39 Pour It All On Me	Belles Of Broadway	—	$5		United Artists 564
2/15/75	65	9		40 But I Do	One More Round Of Gin	—	$5		United Artists 593
				#4 Pop hit for Clarence Henry in 1961					
6/14/75	74	5		41 Puttin' In Overtime At Home	Homemade Love	—	$5		United Artists 639
10/18/75	92	3		42 You Comb Her Hair Every Morning	Hell And Half Of Georgia	—	$5		United Artists 702
2/14/76	51	9		43 I Ain't Got Nobody	I Would Like To See You Again	—	$5		United Artists 760
5/1/76	29	11		44 On The Rebound	What's Our Love Coming To	—	$5		United Artists 797
				DEL REEVES & BILLIE JO SPEARS					
8/7/76	42	8		45 Teardrops Will Kiss The Morning Dew	Nothing Seems To Work Anymore	—	$5		United Artists 832
				DEL REEVES & BILLIE JO SPEARS					
11/20/76	79	4		46 My Better Half	Dig A Little Deeper In The Well	—	$5		United Artists 885
6/4/77	78	5		47 Ladies Night	Cryin' In Arkansas Tonight	—	$5		United Artists 989
5/6/78	93	3		48 When My Angel Turns Into A Devil	How Can Anything That Feels So Good	—	$5		United Artists 1191
9/2/78	79	5		49 Dig Down Deep	Darlin' I Love You	—	$5		United Artists 1230
4/12/80	82	6		50 Take Me To Your Heart	What The Love Of A Lady Can Do	—	$5		Koala 584
9/6/80	90	3		51 What Am I Gonna Do?	Night Out	—	$5		Koala 594
6/6/81	67	4		52 Swinging Doors	Who Left The Door To Heaven Open	—	$5		Koala 333
9/5/81	53	7		53 Slow Hand	Take Off Time	—	$5		Koala 336
				#2 Pop hit for the Pointer Sisters in 1981					
1/23/82	67	5		54 Ain't Nobody Gonna Get My Body But You	Let's Think About Livin'	—	$5		Koala 339
4/26/86	95	3		55 The Second Time Around		—	$5		Playback 1103

REEVES, Jim ★17★ DJ '60

Born on 8/20/23 in Panola County, Texas. Died in a plane crash in Nashville on 7/31/64 (age 40). Singer/songwriter/guitarist. Known as "Gentleman Jim." Uncle of **John Rex Reeves**. Worked as a DJ at KWKH in Shreveport, Louisiana. Joined the *Louisiana Hayride* in 1953. Joined the *Grand Ole Opry* in 1955. Played "Jim Madison" in the movie *Kimberley Jim*. Elected to the Country Music Hall of Fame in 1967.

1) He'll Have To Go 2) Mexican Joe 3) Four Walls 4) I Guess I'm Crazy 5) Billy Bayou

DEBUT	PEAK	WKS		A-side	B-side	Pop	$	Pic	Label & Number
3/28/53	❶⁹	26		1 Mexican Joe	J:❶⁹ / A:❶⁷ / S:❶⁶ I Could Cry	—	$30		Abbott 116
				JIM REEVES And The Circle O Ranch Boys					
12/5/53+	❶³	21		2 Bimbo	A:❶³ / S:2 / J:2 Gypsy Heart	—	$30		Abbott 148
1/9/54	3	22		3 I Love You	A:3 / J:7 / S:8 I Want You Yes (You Want Me No)	—	$30		Fabor 101
				GINNY WRIGHT/JIM REEVES					
6/26/54	15	1		4 Then I'll Stop Loving You	A:15 Echo Bonita	—	$30		Abbott 160
10/23/54+	5	12		5 Penny Candy	J:5 / A:8 I'll Follow You	—	$30		Abbott 170
4/30/55	9	1		6 Drinking Tequila	J:9 Red Eyed And Rowdy	—	$30		Abbott 178
8/20/55	4	20		7 Yonder Comes A Sucker /	J:4 / A:6 / S:8				
		2		8 I'm Hurtin' Inside	J:flip	—	$20		RCA Victor 6200
6/23/56	8	13		9 My Lips Are Sealed	A:8 / J:8 / S:10 Pickin' A Chicken	—	$20		RCA Victor 6517
9/29/56	4	19		10 According To My Heart	A:4 / J:8 / S:10	—	$20		RCA Victor 6620
		1		11 The Mother Of A Honky Tonk Girl	S:flip				
1/12/57	3	18		12 Am I Losing You /	A:3 / J:5 / S:8				
				also see #30 below					
		5		13 Waitin' For A Train	J:flip	—	$20		RCA Victor 6749

287

DEBUT	PEAK	WKS	Gold	A-side (Chart Hit)	B-side	Pop	$	Pic	Label & Number
				REEVES, Jim — Cont'd					
4/29/57	❶⁸	26		14 Four Walls	A:❶⁸ / S:2 / J:4 I Know And You Know	11	$15		RCA Victor 6874
8/19/57	9	6		15 Two Shadows On Your Window /	A:9	—			
8/26/57	12	1		16 Young Hearts	S:12 / A:14		$15		RCA Victor 6973
12/2/57+	3	18		17 Anna Marie	A:3 / S:10 Everywhere You Go	93	$15		RCA Victor 7070
5/12/58	8	7		18 I Love You More /	A:8 / S:14	—			
4/21/58	10	3		19 Overnight	A:10		$15		RCA Victor 7171
7/14/58	2³	22		20 Blue Boy	A:2 / S:4 Theme Of Love (I Love To Say, "I Love You")	45	$15		RCA Victor 7266
11/10/58+	❶⁵	25		21 Billy Bayou /		95			
11/17/58+	18	7		22 I'd Like To Be		—	$15		RCA Victor 7380
3/30/59	2⁴	20		23 Home	If Heartache Is The Fashion	—	$15		RCA Victor 7479
7/27/59	5	16		24 Partners /		—			
8/17/59	17	7		25 I'm Beginning To Forget You		—	$15		RCA Victor 7557
12/7/59+	❶¹⁴	34	●	26 He'll Have To Go	In A Mansion Stands My Love	2³	$12		RCA Victor 7643
7/18/60	3	18		27 I'm Gettin' Better /		37			
7/25/60	6	16		28 I Know One		82	$12		RCA Victor 7756
10/31/60	3	25		29 I Missed Me /		44			
11/21/60	8	14		30 Am I Losing You [R]		31	$12	■	RCA Victor 7800
				new version of #12 above					
3/27/61	4	12		31 The Blizzard	Danny Boy	62	$10		RCA Victor 7855
7/17/61	15	11		32 What Would You Do? /		73			
10/2/61	16	6		33 Stand At Your Window		—	$10		RCA Victor 7905
12/11/61+	2²	21		34 Losing Your Love /		89			
12/11/61+	7	16		35 (How Can I Write On Paper) What I Feel In My Heart		92	$10		RCA Victor 7950
5/26/62	2⁹	21		36 Adios Amigo /		90			
5/19/62	20	3		37 A Letter To My Heart		—	$10		RCA Victor 8019
9/1/62	2³	21		38 I'm Gonna Change Everything /		95			
9/8/62	18	3		39 Pride Goes Before A Fall		—	$10	■	RCA Victor 8080
2/9/63	3	23		40 Is This Me?	Missing Angel	103	$10	■	RCA Victor 8127
7/13/63	3	18		41 Guilty /		91			
7/27/63	11	18		42 Little Ole You		—	$10	■	RCA Victor 8193
1/25/64	2²	26		43 Welcome To My World /		102			
2/1/64	43	2		44 Good Morning Self		—	$10		RCA Victor 8289
3/28/64	7	21		45 Love Is No Excuse	Look Who's Talking (Pop #121)	115	$10		RCA Victor 8324
				JIM REEVES & DOTTIE WEST					
7/11/64	❶⁷	26		46 I Guess I'm Crazy	Not Until The Next Time	82	$10		RCA Victor 8383
11/28/64+	3	19		47 I Won't Forget You	Highway To Nowhere	93	$10		RCA Victor 8461
3/6/65	❶³	23		48 This Is It	There's That Smile Again	88	$10		RCA Victor 8508
7/24/65	❶³	21		49 Is It Really Over?	Rosa Rio	79	$8	■	RCA Victor 8625
1/8/66	2³	17		50 Snow Flake	Take My Hand Precious Lord	66	$8		RCA Victor 8719
4/2/66	❶⁴	21		51 Distant Drums	Old Tige	45	$8		RCA Victor 8789
8/13/66	❶¹	19		52 Blue Side Of Lonesome	It Hurts So Much (To See You Go)	59	$8		RCA Victor 8902
1/21/67	❶¹	16		53 I Won't Come In While He's There	Maureen	112	$8		RCA Victor 9057
7/1/67	16	14		54 The Storm	Trying To Forget	—	$8		RCA Victor 9238
11/4/67+	9	17		55 I Heard A Heart Break Last Night	Golden Memories And Silver Tears	—	$8		RCA Victor 9343
3/9/68	9	13		56 That's When I See The Blues (In Your Pretty Brown Eyes)	I've Lived A Lot In My Time	—	$8		RCA Victor 9455
9/21/68	7	15		57 When You Are Gone	How Can I Write On Paper (What I Feel In My Heart)	—	$8		RCA Victor 9614
4/12/69	6	14		58 When Two Worlds Collide	Could I Be Falling In Love	—	$7		RCA Victor 0135
12/6/69+	10	14		59 Nobody's Fool /		—			
		13		60 Why Do I Love You (Melody of Love) [S]		—	$7		RCA Victor 0286
				#2 Pop hit for Billy Vaughn in 1955					
8/15/70	4	15		61 Angels Don't Lie	You Kept Me Awake Last Night	—	$7		RCA Victor 9880
4/10/71	16	12		62 Gypsy Feet	He Will	—	$7		RCA Victor 9969
1/29/72	15	14		63 The Writing's On The Wall	You're Free To Go	—	$7		RCA Victor 0626
7/29/72	8	16		64 Missing You	The Tie That Binds	—	$7		RCA Victor 0744
				#29 Pop hit for Ray Peterson in 1961					
6/2/73	12	14		65 Am I That Easy To Forget	Rosa Rio	—	$7		RCA Victor 0963
				#25 Pop hit for Debbie Reynolds in 1960					
4/20/74	19	14		66 I'd Fight The World	What's In It For Me	—	$7		RCA Victor 0255
6/21/75	54	11		67 You Belong To Me	Maureen	—	$6		RCA Victor 10299
				#1 Pop hit for Jo Stafford in 1952					
11/8/75	71	6		68 You'll Never Know	There's That Smile Again	—	$6		RCA Victor 10418
				#1 Pop hit for Dick Haymes in 1943					
2/21/76	54	9		69 I Love You Because	Is This Me?	—	$6		RCA Victor 10557
				#3 Pop hit for Al Martino in 1963					
4/23/77	14	13		70 It's Nothin' To Me	I Won't Forget You	—	$5		RCA 10956
8/27/77	23	11		71 Little Ole Dime	A Letter To My Heart	—	$5		RCA 11060
2/4/78	29	11		72 You're The Only Good Thing (That's Happened To Me)	When You Are Gone	—	$5		RCA 11187
6/23/79	10	14		73 Don't Let Me Cross Over	I've Enjoyed As Much Of This As I Can Stand	—	$5		RCA 11564
11/3/79+	6	15		74 Oh, How I Miss You Tonight	The Talking Walls	—	$5		RCA 11737
				Deborah Allen (guest vocal, above 2)					
4/12/80	10	16		75 Take Me In Your Arms And Hold Me	Missing Angel	—	$5		RCA 11946
				JIM REEVES/DEBORAH ALLEN					

DEBUT	PEAK	WKS	Gold	A-side (Chart Hit)	B-side	Pop	$	Pic	Label & Number
				REEVES, Jim — Cont'd					
11/22/80+	35	11		76 There's Always Me .... Somewhere Along The Line		—	$5		RCA 12118
				#56 Pop hit for **Elvis Presley** in 1967					
11/7/81+	5	17		77 **Have You Ever Been Lonely (Have You Ever Been Blue)** Welcome To My World		—	$5		RCA 12346
				JIM REEVES AND PATSY CLINE					
6/5/82	54	8		78 I Fall To Pieces .... So Wrong		—	$5		MCA 52052
				PATSY CLINE/JIM REEVES					
1/8/83	46	9		79 The Jim Reeves Medley .... He'll Have To Go		—	$4		RCA 13410
				Four Walls/I Missed Me/He'll Have To Go/Oh, How I Miss You Tonight					
1/21/84	70	6		80 The Image Of Me .... Won't Come In While He's There		—	$4		RCA 13693
				REEVES, John Rex '81					
				Born in Panola County, Texas. Nephew of **Jim Reeves**.					
2/21/81	93	2		1 What Would You Do .... Jamaica Farewell		—	$6		Soc-A-Gee 109
8/1/81	90	2		2 You're The Reason .... The Next One's On Me		—	$6		Soc-A-Gee 110
				REEVES, Julie '99					
				Born in 1974 in Ashland, Kentucky.					
3/6/99	51	9		1 It's About Time		—			album cut
6/12/99	39	17		2 Trouble Is A Woman .... S:19 He Keeps Me In One Piece		—	$4	★	Virgin 38671 (v)
11/27/99+	38	20		3 What I Need		—			album cut
				all of above from the album *It's About Time* on Virgin 33091					
				REEVES, Ronna '92					
				Born on 9/21/66 in Big Springs, Texas. Female singer.					
3/7/92	49	11		1 The More I Learn (The Less I Understand About Love) If I Were You		—	$4	■	Mercury 866380 (v)
7/18/92	70	4		2 What If You're Wrong .... Frontier Justice		—	$4	■	Mercury 866914 (v)
11/7/92	71	2		3 We Can Hold Our Own .... Honky Tonk Hearts		—	$4		Mercury 864614
6/26/93	73	2		4 Never Let Him See Me Cry /		—			
9/25/93	74	2		5 He's My Weakness		—	$4	■	Mercury 862260 (v)
				REGAN, Bob, & Lucille Starr — see CANADIAN SWEETHEARTS, The					
				REGINA REGINA '97					
				Vocal duo of Regina Nicks (from Houston) and Regina Leigh (from North Carolina).					
1/18/97	53	8		1 More Than I Wanted To Know .... She'll Let That Telephone Ring		—	$4	■	Giant 17426 (v)
	★387★			**REID, Mike** '91					
				Born on 5/24/47 in Alquippa, Pennsylvania. Singer/songwriter/pianist. Pro football player with the Cincinnati Bengals from 1970-75.					
3/5/88	2¹	21		1 Old Folks S:5 Earthquake		—	$4	■	RCA 6896
				RONNIE MILSAP & MIKE REID					
11/24/90+	❶²	20		2 **Walk On Faith** Turning For Home		—	$4	■	Columbia 73623 (v)
3/30/91	17	20		3 Till You Were Gone .... Everything To Me		—	$4		Columbia 73736
7/13/91	14	20		4 As Simple As That .... This Road		—	$4		Columbia 73888
11/9/91+	23	20		5 I'll Stop Loving You .... Even A Strong Man		—	$4		Columbia 74102
4/18/92	54	7		6 I Got A Life .... Your Love Stays With Me		—	$4		Columbia 74286
8/29/92	45	11		7 Keep On Walkin' .... Working With The Right Tools		—	$4		Columbia 74443
11/21/92+	43	13		8 Call Home .... Working With The Right Tools		—	$4		Columbia 74771
				REMINGTON, Rita '82					
				Born Rita Unruh in McPherson, Kansas.					
9/8/73	99	3		1 I've Never Been This Far Before .... The Wedding Cake		—	$6		Plantation 103
				female version of "You've Never Been This Far Before" by **Conway Twitty**					
1/14/78	86	5		2 Don't Let The Flame Burn Out .... Midnight Man		—	$5		Plantation 167
				#68 Pop hit for Jackie DeShannon in 1977					
4/8/78	100	3		3 To Each His Own .... Rhythm Of The Rain		—	$5		Plantation 171
				#1 Pop hit for **Eddy Howard** in 1946					
10/24/81	80	4		4 Don't We Belong In Love .... Easier Said Than Done		—	$5		Plantation 202
				RITA REMINGTON And The Smokey Valley Symphony					
3/20/82	76	5		5 The Flame Blue Eyes Don't Make An Angel		—	$5		Plantation 207
				see Zella Lehr					
				REMINGTONS, The '92					
				Trio of Jimmy Griffin (**Black Tie**), Richard Mainegra and Rick Yancey (both of Cymarron). Yancey left in 1992, replaced by Denny Henson.					
10/12/91+	10	20		1 A Long Time Ago Takin' The Easy Way Out		—	$4	■	BNA 62063 (v)
2/15/92	33	20		2 I Could Love You (With My Eyes Closed) .... Take A Little Love		—	$4		BNA 62201
6/6/92	18	20		3 Two-Timin' Me .... That's Easy For Me To Say		—	$4		BNA 62276
2/6/93	52	6		4 Nobody Loves You When You're Free .... She's All I've Got Going Now		—	$4		BNA 62431
7/10/93	69	1		5 Wall Around Her Heart .... Lucky Boy		—	$4		BNA 62527
				RENO, Don '66					
				Born on 2/21/27 in Spartanburg, South Carolina. Died on 10/16/84 (age 57). Singer/banjo player. Teamed with Red Smiley as **Reno & Smiley**. Father of Dale, Don Wayne and **Ronnie Reno** (Reno Brothers).					
1/8/66	46	3		1 Soldier's Prayer In Viet Nam .... Five By Eight [S]		—	$12		Monument 912
				DON RENO & BENNY MARTIN and the Tennessee Cut Ups					
	★379★			**RENO, Jack** '68 DJ					
				Born on 11/30/35 in Bloomfield, Iowa. Singer/songwriter/guitarist. Worked as a DJ on many stations since 1958.					
				1)Repeat After Me 2)Hitchin' A Ride 3)I Want One					
12/9/67+	10	17		1 Repeat After Me You're Gonna Have To Come And Get It		—	$8		JAB 9009
5/11/68	41	11		2 How Sweet It Is (To Be In Love With You) .... Juke Box		—	$8		JAB 9015
11/16/68+	19	14		3 I Want One .... Bigger Than Love		—	$6		Dot 17169

DEBUT	PEAK	WKS	Gold	A-side (Chart Hit) ... B-side	Pop	$	Pic	Label & Number
				RENO, Jack — Cont'd				
5/10/69	34	11		4 I'm A Good Man (In A Bad Frame Of Mind) ... *Darling, Say It Again*	—	$6		Dot 17233
9/20/69	22	9		5 We All Go Crazy ... *Albuquerque*	—	$6		Dot 17293
4/18/70	67	3		6 That's The Way I See It ... *I've Heard That Song Before*	—	$6		Dot 17340
10/9/71	12	15		7 Hitchin' A Ride ... *You Are My Destiny* #5 Pop hit for Vanity Fare in 1970	—	$6		Target 0137
1/22/72	26	14		8 Heartaches By The Numbers ... *Airline Girl*	—	$6		Target 0141
5/27/72	38	10		9 Do You Want To Dance ... *I Get Too Lonely* #5 Pop hit for Bobby Freeman in 1958	—	$6		Target 0150
8/25/73	67	8		10 Beautiful Sunday ... *Sometimes Woman* #15 Pop hit for Daniel Boone in 1972	—	$5		United Artists 299
2/9/74	57	10		11 Let The Four Winds Blow ... *Shackles And Chains* #15 Pop hit for Fats Domino in 1961	—	$5		United Artists 374
8/31/74	70	7		12 Jukebox ... *Goin' Through The Motions*	—	$5		United Artists 502
				RENO, Ronnie '83 Born on 9/28/47 in Buffalo, South Carolina. Singer/guitarist. Son of **Don Reno**. Member of **Merle Haggard**'s Strangers from 1971-78.				
1/22/83	86	3		1 Homemade Love ... *Hello Jesus*	—	$5		EMH 0010
9/24/83	76	4		2 The Letter ... *Serious Love* #1 Pop hit for The Box Tops in 1967	—	$5		EMH 0024
				RENO AND SMILEY '61 Duo of **Don Reno** and Red Smiley. Reno was born on 2/21/27 in Spartanburg, South Carolina; died on 10/16/84 (age 57). Smiley was born Arthur Lee Smiley on 5/17/25 in Asheville, North Carolina; died on 1/2/72 (age 46). Duo also recorded as **Chick And His Hot Rods**.				
5/29/61	14	10		1 Don't Let Your Sweet Love Die ... *Born To Lose*	—	$15		King 5469
8/28/61	23	5		2 Love Oh Love, Oh Please Come Home ... *Double Eagle*	—	$15		King 5520
9/18/61	27	2		3 Jimmy Caught The Dickens (Pushing Ernest In The Tub) ... *Just Doing Rock And Roll* [N] CHICK AND HIS HOT RODS Backed Up With RENO AND SMILEY	—	$15		King 5537
				RENO BROTHERS '88 Bluegrass trio from Roanoke, Virginia: brothers Dale (born on 2/6/61), Don Wayne (born on 2/8/63) and **Ronnie Reno** (born on 9/28/47). Sons of **Don Reno**.				
7/2/88	77	2		1 Yonder Comes A Freight Train ... *Lay Your Heartache Down*	—	$4		Step One 387
4/1/89	84	2		2 Love Will Never Be The Same ... *Southern Bound*	—	$4		Step One 398

RESTLESS HEART ★131★ '88
Group of former Nashville session musicians: **Larry Stewart** (vocals, guitar, keyboards; born on 3/2/59), Dave Innis (guitar, keyboards; born on 4/9/59), Greg Jennings (guitar; born on 10/2/54), Paul Gregg (bass; born on 12/3/54) and John Dittrich (drums; born on 4/7/51). Stewart went solo in early 1992. Innis left in early 1993. The remaining three continued with two backing musicians. Dittrich later formed **The Buffalo Club**.

1) Wheels 2) Bluest Eyes In Texas 3) Why Does It Have To Be (Wrong Or Right) 4) A Tender Lie
5) That Rock Won't Roll

DEBUT	PEAK	WKS	Gold	A-side (Chart Hit) ... B-side	Pop	$	Pic	Label & Number
1/26/85	23	16		1 Let The Heartache Ride ... S:23 / A:23 *Few And Far Between*	—	$4		RCA 13969
6/1/85	10	18		2 I Want Everyone To Cry ... S:9 / A:10 *She's Coming Home*	—	$4	■	RCA 14086
10/26/85+	7	19		3 (Back To The) Heartbreak Kid ... S:7 / A:8 *She Danced Her Way (Into My Heart)* picture sleeve is a foldout poster sleeve	—	$4	■	RCA 14190
3/15/86	10	20		4 Til I Loved You ... A:8 / S:11 *Shakin' The Night Away*	—	$4		RCA 14292
8/9/86	❶¹	23		5 That Rock Won't Roll ... S:❶¹ / A:❶¹ *You Can't Out Run The Night*	—	$4		RCA 14376
12/20/86+	❶¹	25		6 I'll Still Be Loving You ... A:❶¹ / S:7 *Victim Of The Game*	33	$4		RCA 5065
5/30/87	❶¹	25		7 Why Does It Have To Be (Wrong Or Right) ... S:5 *Hummingbird*	—	$4		RCA 5132
10/31/87+	❶¹	23		8 Wheels ... S:5 *New York (Hold Her Tight)*	—	$4	■	RCA 5280
5/21/88	❶¹	21		9 Bluest Eyes In Texas ... S:2 *Eldorado*	—	$4		RCA 8386
9/24/88	❶¹	23		10 A Tender Lie ... S:❶¹ *This Time*	—	$4		RCA 8714
2/25/89	3	18		11 Big Dreams In A Small Town ... *The Ride Of Your Life*	—	$4		RCA 8816
7/29/89	4	20		12 Say What's In Your Heart ... *Jenny Come Back*	—	$4		RCA 9034
12/16/89+	4	26		13 Fast Movin' Train ... *The Truth Hurts*	—	$4		RCA 9115
4/21/90	5	21		14 Dancy's Dream ... *Lady Luck*	—	$4		RCA 2503
9/1/90	21	16		15 When Somebody Loves You ... *A Little More Coal On The Fire*	—	$4	■	RCA 2663 (v)
12/22/90+	16	20		16 Long Lost Friend ... *I've Never Been So Sure*	—	$4		RCA 2709
10/19/91+	3	20		17 You Can Depend On Me ... *Til I Loved You*	—	$4		RCA 62129
2/29/92	40	15		18 Familiar Pain ... *The Bluest Eyes In Texas*	—	$4		RCA 62054
9/12/92	9	20		19 When She Cries ... (3 album snippets)	11	$4	■	RCA 62412 (v)
1/23/93	13	20		20 Mending Fences ... *We're Gonna Be OK*	—	$4		RCA 62419
5/22/93	11	20		21 We Got The Love ... *Meet Me On The Other Side*	—	$4		RCA 62510
11/6/93	72	2		22 Big Iron Horses ... *Born In A High Wind*	—	$4		RCA 62656
4/30/94	52	9		23 Baby Needs New Shoes ... *I'd Cross The Line*	—	$4	■	RCA 62827 (v)
5/16/98	33	17		24 No End To This Road ...	—			
9/12/98	64	2		25 For Lack Of Better Words ...	—	$4		RCA 65562
12/26/98	58	1		26 Little Drummer Boy ... [X] from the various artists album *Country Christmas Classics* on RCA 67698	—			album cut

DEBUT	PEAK	WKS	Gold	A-side (Chart Hit)	B-side	Pop	$	Pic	Label & Number
				REX, Tim, and Oklahoma '81					
11/8/80	87	3		1 Arizona Highway	—		$5		Dee Jay 103
12/13/80+	46	12		2 Gettin' Over You	Red Headed Lady		$5		Dee Jay 107
4/11/81	43	10		3 Spread My Wings	Take Me Back To Oklahoma		$5		Dee Jay 111
				REY, Ernest '79					
				Born in Tennessee. Son of **Loretta Lynn**.					
3/17/79	97	1		Mama's Sugar	Don't Feel Like The Lone Ranger	—	$5		MCA 40991
				REYNOLDS, Allen '78					
				Born on 8/18/38 in North Little Rock, Arkansas; raised in Memphis. Singer/songwriter/prolific producer.					
5/20/78	95	5		Wrong Road Again	Ready For The Times To Get Better	—	$7		Triple I 496
				REYNOLDS, Burt '80					
				Born on 2/11/36 in Waycross, Georgia. Became box-office superstar in the mid-1970s.					
10/25/80	51	7		Let's Do Something Cheap And Superficial	Pickin' Lone Star Style (The Bandit Band)	88	$4	■	MCA 51004
				from the movie *Smokey & The Bandit II* starring Reynolds					
				RHOADS, Randy '90					
1/13/90	89	1		Honey Do Weekend	—		$6		Blue Ridge 001
				RICE, Bill '71					
				Born in Gallo, Arkansas. Singer/songwriter/producer.					
3/20/71	33	10		1 Travelin' Minstrel Man	Special	—	$7		Capitol 3049
9/11/71	51	9		2 Honky-Tonk Stardust Cowboy	T.G.I.F. (Thank Goodness It's Forever)	—	$7		Capitol 3156
4/8/72	74	2		3 A Girl Like Her Is Hard To Find	Here's To You, Darlin'	—	$6		Epic 10833
7/1/72	63	5		4 Something To Call Mine	—		$6		Epic 10877
11/19/77	97	3		5 All The Love We Threw Away	We Can't Make It Anymore	—	$5		Polydor 14435
				LOIS JOHNSON & BILL RICE					
3/11/78	100	2		6 Beggars And Choosers	That's The Way It Is (With You And Me)	—	$5		Polydor 14453
	★220★			**RICE, Bobby G.** '73					
				Born Robert Gene Rice on 7/11/44 in Boscobel, Wisconsin. Singer/songwriter/guitarist.					
				1)You Lay So Easy On My Mind 2)You Give Me You 3)Write Me A Letter 4)Freda Comes, Freda Goes 5)The Whole World's Making Love Again Tonight					
4/25/70	32	8		1 Sugar Shack	Sweet Lil Ol' You	—	$8		Royal American 6
				#1 Pop hit for Jimmy Gilmer & The Fireballs in 1963					
8/8/70	35	11		2 Hey Baby	Hey, Hey, Santa Fe	—	$8		Royal American 18
				#1 Pop hit for Bruce Channel in 1962					
1/9/71	46	9		3 Lover Please	You're So Easy To Love	—	$8		Royal American 27
				#7 Pop hit for Clyde McPhatter in 1962					
5/22/71	20	15		4 Mountain Of Love	Five O'Clock World	—	$8		Royal American 32
				#9 Pop hit for **Johnny Rivers** in 1964					
1/1/72	33	11		5 Suspicion	The Birds And The Bees	—	$8		Royal American 48
				#3 Pop hit for **Terry Stafford** in 1964					
12/23/72+	3	16		6 You Lay So Easy On My Mind	There Ain't No Way Babe	—	$7		Metromedia 902
				also see #28 below					
5/5/73	8	15		7 You Give Me You	Bring Your Love To Me Softly	—	$7		Metromedia 0107
9/22/73	13	14		8 The Whole World's Making Love Again Tonight	Baby, Lovin' You	—	$7		Metromedia 0075
9/28/74	30	14		9 Make It Feel Like Love Again	Darlin' Forever	—	$6		GRT 009
1/11/75	9	14		10 Write Me A Letter	Sweet Satisfying Feeling	—	$6		GRT 014
5/3/75	10	14		11 Freda Comes, Freda Goes	Love Me Tonight	—	$6		GRT 021
8/30/75	64	11		12 I May Never Be Your Lover (But I'll Always Be Your Friend)	It Was So Good While It Lasted	—	$6		GRT 028
1/3/76	35	11		13 Pick Me Up On Your Way Down	Right Or Wrong	—	$6		GRT 036
7/24/76	53	9		14 You Are My Special Angel	I Want To Feel It When You Feel It	—	$6		GRT 061
				same tune as "My Special Angel" by **Bobby Helms**					
11/13/76	54	9		15 Woman Stealer	Burning Bridges	—	$6		GRT 084
7/9/77	66	7		16 Just One Kiss Magdelena	The Love She Offered You	—	$6		GRT 120
7/22/78	57	6		17 Whisper It To Me	Sweet Cherry Lips	—	$5		Republic 023
11/11/78	30	10		18 The Softest Touch In Town	Passion	—	$5		Republic 031
6/9/79	49	8		19 Oh Baby Mine (I Get So Lonely)	Rainbows Are Back In Style	—	$5		Republic 041
				#2 Pop hit for The Four Knights in 1954					
12/1/79	67	8		20 You Make It So Easy	You Lay So Easy On My Mind	—	$5		Sunset 102
5/3/80	53	9		21 The Man Who Takes You Home	Sweet Molly Brown	—	$5		Sunbird 108
2/7/81	86	2		22 Livin' Together (Lovin' Apart)	It Was So Good While It Lasted	—	$5		Sunbird 7558
10/10/81	63	5		23 Pardon My French	Some Lovin' Time With You	—	$5		Charta 166
6/8/85	95	2		24 New Tradition	Those Words I Never Heard	—	$5		Door Knob 230
3/8/86	70	4		25 Red Neck And Over Thirty	State Of The Union	—	$5		Door Knob 243
				WAYNE KEMP & BOBBY G. RICE					
9/13/86	70	5		26 You've Taken Over My Heart	I'm Lookin' For Someone Lookin' For Love	—	$5		Door Knob 251
6/27/87	85	2		27 Rachel's Room	—		$5		Door Knob 274
10/3/87	79	3		28 You Lay So Easy On My Mind	[R]	—	$5		Door Knob 285
				new version of #6 above					
3/5/88	70	5		29 A Night Of Love Forgotten	—		$5		Door Knob 295
9/17/88	76	4		30 Clean Livin' Folk	—		$5		Door Knob 307
				BOBBY G. RICE and PERRY LaPOINTE					

DEBUT	PEAK	WKS	Gold	A-side (Chart Hit)	B-side	Pop	$	Pic	Label & Number

RICH, Charlie ★79★ '73
Born on 12/14/32 in Colt, Arkansas. Died of an acute blood clot on 7/25/95 (age 62). Singer/songwriter/pianist. First played jazz and blues. Own jazz group, the Velvetones, mid-1950s, while in U.S. Air Force. Session work with Sun Records in 1958. Known as "The Silver Fox." CMA Awards: 1973 Male Vocalist of the Year; 1974 Entertainer of the Year.

1) The Most Beautiful Girl 2) A Very Special Love Song 3) Behind Closed Doors 4) There Won't Be Anymore 5) Rollin' With The Flow

DEBUT	PEAK	WKS		A-side	B-side	Pop	$	Label & Number
3/9/68	44	8		1 Set Me Free	I'll Just Go Away	—	$7	Epic 10287
8/24/68	45	8		2 Raggedy Ann	Nothing In The World (To Do With Me)	—	$7	Epic 10358
8/9/69	41	11		3 Life's Little Ups And Downs	It Takes Time	—	$7	Epic 10492
2/28/70	67	5		4 Who Will The Next Fool Be	Stay	—	$7	Sun 1110
				recorded in January 1959				
3/28/70	47	6		5 July 12, 1939	I'm Flying To Nashville Tonight	85	$7	Epic 10585
10/24/70	37	12		6 Nice 'N' Easy	I Can't Even Drink It Away	—	$7	Epic 10662
				new version of his #131 Pop hit from 1964; #60 Pop hit for Frank Sinatra in 1960				
8/14/71	72	2		7 A Woman Left Lonely	Have A Heart	—	$7	Epic 10745
11/27/71+	35	13		8 A Part Of Your Life	How Long Have You Had Him On Your Mind	—	$7	Epic 10809
8/26/72	6	17		9 I Take It On Home	Peace On You	—	$6	Epic 10867
2/10/73	❶²	20 ▲		10 Behind Closed Doors	A Sunday Kind Of Woman	15	$5	Epic 10950
				CMA Award: Single of the Year				
7/14/73	29	11		11 Tomorrow Night	The Ways Of A Woman In Love	—	$6	RCA Victor 0983
9/22/73	❶³	18 ●		12 The Most Beautiful Girl	I Feel Like Going Home	❶²	$5	Epic 11040
12/22/73+	❶²	17		13 There Won't Be Anymore	It's All Over Now	18	$5	RCA Victor 0195
				originally released on RCA Victor 8536 in 1965 ($8)				
2/23/74	❶³	14		14 A Very Special Love Song	I Can't Even Drink It Away	11	$5	Epic 11091
5/4/74	❶¹	13		15 I Don't See Me In Your Eyes Anymore	No Room To Dance	47	$5	RCA Victor 0260
6/22/74	23	12		16 A Field Of Yellow Daisies	Party Girl	—	$6	Mercury 73498
8/10/74	❶¹	15		17 I Love My Friend	Why, Oh Why	24	$5	Epic 20006
9/28/74	❶¹	15		18 She Called Me Baby	Ten Dollars And A Clean White Shirt	47	$5	RCA Victor 10062
12/28/74+	71	5		19 Something Just Came Over Me	The Best Years	—	$6	Mercury 73646
2/1/75	3	12		20 My Elusive Dreams	Whatever Happened	49	$5	Epic 50064
4/12/75	23	12		21 It's All Over Now	Big Jack	—	$5	RCA Victor 10256
5/24/75	3	17		22 Every Time You Touch Me (I Get High)	Pass On By	19	$5	Epic 50103
9/20/75	4	14		23 All Over Me	You And I	—	$5	Epic 50142
12/20/75+	56	7		24 Now Everybody Knows	I've Got You Under My Skin	—	$5	RCA Victor 10458
12/27/75+	10	13		25 Since I Fell For You	She	71	$5	Epic 50182
				#4 Pop hit for Lenny Welch in 1963				
4/24/76	22	10		26 America, The Beautiful (1976)	Down By The Riverside	—	$5	Epic 50222
9/4/76	27	9		27 Road Song	The Grass Is Always Greener	—	$5	Epic 50268
1/8/77	24	12		28 My Mountain Dew	Nice 'N' Easy	—	$5	RCA 10859
				all of above RCA and Mercury hits were recorded from 1963-66				
2/5/77	12	13		29 Easy Look	My Lady	—	$5	Epic 50328
5/28/77	❶²	19		30 Rollin' With The Flow	To Sing A Love Song	101	$5	Epic 50392
4/8/78	8	14		31 Puttin' In Overtime At Home	Ghost Of Another Man	—	$4	United Artists 1193
7/1/78	10	13		32 Beautiful Woman	Somebody Wrote That Song For Me	—	$4	Epic 50562
7/22/78	46	8		33 I Still Believe In Love	Wishful Thinking	—	$4	United Artists 1223
10/7/78	❶¹	14		34 On My Knees	Mellow Melody	—	$4	Epic 50616
				CHARLIE RICH (with Janie Fricke)				
1/6/79	3	14		35 I'll Wake You Up When I Get Home	Salty Dog Blues	—	$4	Elektra 45553
				from the movie Every Which Way But Loose starring Clint Eastwood				
1/6/79	45	8		36 The Fool Strikes Again	I Loved You All The Way	—	$4	United Artists 1269
3/10/79	26	11		37 I Lost My Head	She Knows Just How To Touch Me	—	$4	United Artists 1280
5/12/79	20	13		38 Spanish Eyes	I Do My Swingin' At Home	—	$4	Epic 50701
				#15 Pop hit for Al Martino in 1966				
8/18/79	84	4		39 Life Goes On	Standing Tall	—	$4	United Artists 1307
11/24/79+	22	13		40 You're Gonna Love Yourself In The Morning	The Top Of The Stairs	—	$4	United Artists 1325
3/8/80	74	5		41 I'd Build A Bridge	All You Ever Have To Do Is Touch Me	—	$4	United Artists 1340
5/3/80	61	7		42 Even A Fool Would Let Go	Pretty People	—	$4	Epic 50869
10/11/80	12	14		43 A Man Just Don't Know What A Woman Goes Through	Marie	—	$4	Elektra 47047
2/14/81	26	11		44 Are We Dreamin' The Same Dream	Angelina	—	$4	Elektra 47104
5/23/81	47	7		45 You Made It Beautiful	How Good It Used To Be	—	$4	Epic 02058
				from the movie Take This Job And Shove It starring Art Carney				

★ RICH, Debbie '89
Born Debra Sue Rathjen in Levenworth, Washington; raised in Napa Valley, California.

DEBUT	PEAK	WKS		A-side	B-side	Pop	$	Label & Number
12/3/88	87	2		1 I Ain't Gonna Take This Layin' Down		—	$5	Door Knob 311
2/25/89	71	4		2 Don't Be Surprised If You Get It		—	$5	Door Knob 318
4/22/89	74	4		3 I've Had Enough Of You		—	$5	Door Knob 321
9/2/89	68	5		4 Do It Again (I Think I Saw Diamonds)		—	$5	Door Knob 327

RICH, Don — see ALAN, Buddy

DEBUT	PEAK	WKS	Gold	A-side (Chart Hit)	B-side	Pop	$	Pic	Label & Number

RICH, John '01
Born on 1/7/74 in Amarillo, Texas. Former singer/bassist of **Lonestar**.

DEBUT	PEAK	WKS		# A-side	B-side	Pop	$	Pic	Label & Number
7/8/00	53	20		1 I Pray For You S:20	Old Blue Mountain	—	$4	★	BNA 60269
4/7/01	46	8		2 Forever Loving You	I Pray For You	—	$4		BNA 69053

RICHARDS, Earl '73
Born Henry Earl Sinks in Amarillo, Texas. Owned the Ace of Hearts record label.

9/6/69	39	10		1 The House Of Blue Lights	Hard Times A Comin'	—	$7		United Artists 50561
				#9 Pop hit for Chuck Miller in 1955					
1/31/70	73	2		2 Corrine, Corrina	Climbing A Mountain	—	$7		United Artists 50619
				#9 Pop hit for Ray Peterson in 1961					
10/10/70	57	4		3 Sunshine	San Francisco's Mabel Joy	—	$7		United Artists 50704
1/13/73	23	12		4 Margie, Who's Watching The Baby	My Land	—	$6		Ace of Hearts 0461
				#115 Pop hit for R.B. Greaves in 1972					
4/28/73	66	6		5 Things Are Kinda Slow At The House	Do My Playing At Home	—	$6		Ace of Hearts 0465
7/21/73	58	11		6 The Sun Is Shining (On Everybody But Me)	Mother Nature's Daughter	—	$6		Ace of Hearts 0470
3/2/74	83	7		7 Walkin' In Teardrops /		—			
12/22/73+	85	5		8 How Can I Tell Her		—	$6		Ace of Hearts 0477
				#22 Pop hit for **Lobo** in 1973					
10/18/75	91	5		9 My Babe	Mother Nature's Daughter	—	$6		Ace of Hearts 7502
				#1 R&B hit for Little Walter in 1955					

★ RICHARDS, Sue '76
Born Maggie Sue Wimberly in Muscle Shoals, Alabama.
1)Sweet Sensuous Feelings 2)Tower Of Strength 3)I Just Had You On My Mind

3/27/71	56	8		1 Feel Free To Go	No Special Occasion	—	$7		Epic 10709
1/12/74	48	13		2 I Just Had You On My Mind	Wake Up Morning	—	$6		Dot 17481
7/20/74	93	5		3 Ease Me To The Ground	Make Me Believe It	—	$6		Dot 17508
5/3/75	99	2		4 Homemade Love	The Painter's Brush	—	$5		ABC/Dot 17547
9/6/75	32	12		5 Tower Of Strength	Let Me Be Your Baby Again	—	$5		ABC/Dot 17572
				#5 Pop hit for Gene McDaniels in 1961					
1/17/76	25	11		6 Sweet Sensuous Feelings	He Plays For Me	—	$5		ABC/Dot 17600
5/1/76	50	10		7 Please Tell Him That I Said Hello	Love Is A Rose	—	$5		ABC/Dot 17622
				#84 Pop hit for Debbie Campbell in 1975					
8/21/76	70	6		8 I'll Never See Him Again	I've Got A Lot On My Mind	—	$5		ABC/Dot 17645
11/26/77	94	3		9 Someone Loves Him	Livin' In A House Full Of Love	—	$5		Epic 50465
7/15/78	94	4		10 Hey, What Do You Say (We Fall In Love)	I'll Be Wearing Blue	—	$5		Epic 50546
3/10/79	85	3		11 Finders Keepers Losers Weepers		—	$6		MMI 1028
				STAN HITCHCOCK with Sue Richards					

RICHEY, Kim '95
Born on 12/1/56 in Zanesville, Ohio. Singer/songwriter.

6/24/95	47	12		1 Just My Luck	Just Like The Moon	—	$4	■	Mercury 856832 (v)
10/7/95	59	12		2 Those Words We Said	Let The Sun Fall Down	—	$4	■	Mercury 852300 (v)
4/20/96	66	3		3 From Where I Stand		—			album cut
				from the album *Kim Richey* on Mercury 526812					
5/10/97	72	2		4 I Know	I'm Alright	—	$4	■	Mercury 574184 (v)

RICHIE, Lionel '87
Born on 6/20/49 in Tuskegee, Alabama. Black singer/songwriter/pianist. Former lead singer of the **Commodores**. Charted 17 pop hits from 1981-96. Also see **USA For Africa**.

7/21/84	24	18		1 Stuck On You	Round And Round	3	$4	■	Motown 1746
12/6/86+	10	15		2 Deep River Woman ....S:❶¹ / A:10	Ballerina Girl (Richie)	71	$4	■	Motown 1873
				LIONEL RICHIE with Alabama					

RICHMOND, Rashell — see WHEELER, Billy Edd

RICKS, Steve '86
Born in Little Rock, Arkansas.

6/14/86	81	4		Private Clown		—	$6		Southwind 8205

RICOCHET '96
★270★
Group formed in Texas: Perry "Heath" Wright (vocals, guitar; born on 4/22/67), Teddy Carr (guitar; born on 7/4/60), brothers Duane "Junior" (born on 10/23/68) and Jeff (drums; born on 12/27/62) Bryant, Eddie Kilgallon (keyboards; born on 5/12/65) and Greg Cook (bass; born on 1/28/65).
1)Daddy's Money 2)What Do I Know 3)Love Is Stronger Than Pride

12/9/95+	5	21		1 What Do I Know S:14	A Little Bit Of Love (Is A Dangerous Thing)	—	$4	■	Columbia 78088 (v)
4/27/96	❶²	20		2 Daddy's Money S:7	I Wasn't Ready For You	—	$4	■	Columbia 78097 (v)
7/20/96	58	1		3 The Star Spangled Banner	(no B-side)	—	$10	★	Columbia 8246
				only available as a promo CD single					
8/17/96	9	20		4 Love Is Stronger Than Pride	I Wasn't Ready For You	—	$4		Columbia 78098
12/14/96	43	5		5 Let It Snow Let It Snow Let It Snow	(no B-side) [X]	—	$10	★	Columbia 1296
				#1 Pop hit for **Vaughn Monroe** in 1946; only available as a promo CD single; also see #9, 13 & 15 below					
1/18/97	20	16		6 Ease My Troubled Mind	Rowdy	—	$4	■	Columbia 78526
5/3/97	18	20		7 He Left A Lot To Be Desired S:15	You Still Got It	—	$4		Columbia 78564
9/13/97	39	13		8 Blink Of An Eye	Don't Forget To Feed The Jukebox (While I'm Gone)	—	$4		Columbia 78688
12/13/97	44	5		9 Let It Snow Let It Snow Let It Snow	(no B-side) [X-R]	—	$10	★	Columbia 78749
2/7/98	44	10		10 Connected At The Heart		—			album cut
				from the album *Blink Of An Eye* on Columbia 67773					
8/1/98	58	4		11 Honky Tonk Baby	Standing My Ground	—	$4		Columbia 79000
11/21/98+	52	15		12 Can't Stop Thinkin' 'Bout That		—			album cut
				from the album *What A Ride* on Columbia 69198					

DEBUT	PEAK	WKS	Gold	A-side (Chart Hit)	B-side	Pop	$	Pic	Label & Number
				RICOCHET — Cont'd					
12/12/98	41	5		13 Let It Snow Let It Snow Let It Snow	(no B-side) [X-R]	—	$10	★	Columbia 78749
4/24/99	48	15		14 Seven Bridges Road		—		★	album cut
				from the album *What A Ride* on Columbia 69198; later issued on the B-side of #16 below					
12/25/99	39	3		15 Let It Snow Let It Snow Let It Snow	(no B-side) [X-R]	—	$10	★	Columbia 78749
4/1/00	45	15		16 Do I Love You Enough	S:15 Seven Bridges Road	—	$4	★	Columbia 79379
8/19/00	48	16		17 She's Gone		—			album cut
				from the album *What You Leave Behind* on Columbia 69198					
				RIDDLE, Allan **'60**					
				Born on 5/16/29 in Spartanburg, South Carolina. Singer/songwriter/guitarist.					
11/7/60	16	12		The Moon Is Crying			$25		Plaid 1001
				RIDE THE RIVER **'87**					
				Group led by singer/guitarist Danny Stockard.					
2/21/87	63	5		1 You Left Her Lovin' You		—	$5		Advantage 165
6/13/87	55	7		2 The First Cut Is The Deepest		—	$5		Advantage 169
				#21 Pop hit for Rod Stewart in 1977					
10/31/87	57	7		3 It's Such A Heartache		—	$5		Advantage 182
2/6/88	51	9		4 After Last Night's Storm	Hard Lines	—	$5		Advantage 189
				RILEY, Dan **'80**					
12/22/79+	78	5		Lily	If My Tears Could Fill A Lake I'd Throw You In	—	$5		Armada 103
	★228★			**RILEY, Jeannie C.** **'68**					
				Born Jeanne Carolyn Stephenson on 10/19/45 in Anson, Texas. Singer/songwriter/guitarist.					
				1)Harper Valley P.T.A. 2)Oh, Singer 3)There Never Was A Time 4)The Girl Most Likely 5)Good Enough To Be Your Wife					
8/24/68	❶³	14	●	1 Harper Valley P.T.A.	Yesterday All Day Long Today	❶¹	$6		Plantation 3
				CMA Award: Single of the Year					
12/7/68+	6	15		2 The Girl Most Likely	My Scrapbook	55	$6		Plantation 7
1/25/69	35	9		3 The Price I Pay To Stay	How Can Anything So Right Be So Wrong	—	$6		Capitol 2378
3/29/69	5	13		4 There Never Was A Time	Back To School	77	$6		Plantation 16
6/28/69	32	9		5 The Rib	I'm The Woman	111	$6		Plantation 22
10/4/69	33	11		6 The Back Side Of Dallas /		—			
10/25/69	34	8		7 Things Go Better With Love		111	$6		Plantation 29
1/31/70	7	12		8 Country Girl	We Were Raised On Love	106	$6		Plantation 44
6/27/70	21	11		9 Duty Not Desire	Holdin' On	—	$6		Plantation 59
12/12/70	60	4		10 My Man /		—			
12/12/70	62	4		11 The Generation Gap		—	$6		Plantation 65
4/3/71	4	15		12 Oh, Singer	I'll Take What's Left Of You	74	$6		Plantation 72
7/3/71	7	15		13 Good Enough To Be Your Wife	Light Your Light (And Let It Shine)	97	$6		Plantation 75
10/23/71	15	13		14 Roses And Thorns	Send Me No Tears	—	$6		Plantation 79
11/20/71	47	8		15 Houston Blues	How Hard I'm Trying	—	$5		MGM 14310
1/15/72	12	12		16 Give Myself A Party	Why You Been Gone So Long	—	$5		MGM 14341
5/20/72	30	11		17 Good Morning Country Rain	This Is For You	—	$5		MGM 14382
10/28/72	57	6		18 One Night	Without You	—	$5		MGM 14427
				#11 R&B hit for Smiley Lewis in 1956					
3/10/73	44	7		19 When Love Has Gone Away	Thou Shall Not Kill	—	$5		MGM 14495
7/14/73	51	7		20 Hush	Not Looking Back	—	$5		MGM 14554
				#4 Pop hit for Deep Purple in 1968					
11/10/73	57	9		21 Another Football Year	Mother America	—	$5		MGM 14666
9/28/74	89	6		22 Plain Vanilla	Country Child	—	$5		Mercury 73616
				JEANNIE C. RILEY and The Red River Symphony					
7/17/76	94	4		23 The Best I've Ever Had	Thank You For Forgiving	—	$5		Warner 8226
				RILEY, Larry **'81**					
1/17/81	90	2		1 Cheater's Last Chance	How Could I Ever Stop Loving You	—	$7		F&L 507
5/30/81	93	2		2 Code-A-Phone		—	$7		F&L 509
	★235★			**RIMES, LeAnn** **'96**					
				Born Margaret LeAnn Rimes on 8/28/82 in Jackson, Mississippi; raised in Garland, Texas. Female singer. Won her first talent show in 1988. Winner on TV's *Star Search* in 1990. Married actor Dean Sheremet on 2/23/2002. Won the 1996 Best New Artist Grammy Award. CMA Award: 1997 Horizon Award.					
				1)One Way Ticket (Because I Can) 2)Unchained Melody 3)On The Side Of Angels					
5/25/96	10	20		1 Blue	S:❶²⁰ The Light In Your Eyes	26	$4	■	Curb 76959 (v)
				song originally written for, but not recorded by, **Patsy Cline**					
7/27/96	43	10		2 Hurt Me		—			album cut
9/28/96	❶²	20		3 One Way Ticket (Because I Can)		—			album cut
12/21/96+	3	20		4 Unchained Melody /		—			
				#4 Pop hit for The Righteous Brothers in 1965					
12/28/96	51	3		5 Put A Little Holiday In Your Heart	[X]	—	$10	★	Curb 1308
				above 2 available only as a bonus CD single with the purchase of her album *Blue* at Target stores during the 1996 holiday season					
3/22/97	5	20		6 The Light In Your Eyes		—			album cut (v)
				first released as the B-side of #1 above; all of above (except #4 & 5) from the album *Blue* on Curb 77821					
6/14/97	43	20	▲³	7 How Do I Live	S:❶³² (extended mix)	2³	$4	■	Curb 73022 (v)
				from the movie *Con Air* starring Nicolas Cage; spent a record-setting 262 weeks (as of 6/29/02) on the Country Sales chart					
8/23/97	48	7	●	8 You Light Up My Life	S:2 I Believe	34	$4	■	Curb 73027 (v)
10/11/97+	4	21		9 On The Side Of Angels		—			album cut
				from the album *You Light Up My Life* on Curb 77885					
12/27/97	71	2		10 Put A Little Holiday In Your Heart	Unchained Melody [X-R]	—	$10	★	Curb 1308

DEBUT	PEAK	WKS	Gold	A-side (Chart Hit)	B-side	Pop	$	Pic	Label & Number
				RIMES, LeAnn — Cont'd					
3/28/98	4	20	●	11 Commitment	S:2 Looking Through Your Eyes	—	$4	▮	Curb 73055 (v)
8/1/98	10	20		12 Nothin' New Under The Moon		—			album cut
11/28/98+	41	14		13 These Arms Of Mine		—			album cut
				above 2 from the album Sittin' On Top Of The World *on Curb 77901*					
9/4/99+	6	25		14 Big Deal	S:❶11 Leaving's Not Leaving	23	$4	★	Curb 73086 (v)
12/25/99	18S	2		15 Cattle Call	I Walk Alone (Arnold)	—	$4	★	Curb 73088 (v)
				EDDY ARNOLD (with LeAnn Rimes)					
4/15/00	8	31		16 I Need You	S:❶6 Spirit In The Sky (DC Talk)	11	$4	★	Capitol 58863
				from the TV movie Jesus *starring Jeremy Sisto*					
2/24/01	18	20		17 But I Do Love You /	S:❶35	103			
10/21/00	61	8		18 Can't Fight The Moonlight		11	$4	★	Curb 73116
				theme from the movie Coyote Ugly *starring Piper Perabo*					
10/27/01	51	2		19 God Bless America	S:3 Put A Little Holiday In Your Heart	12S	$4	★	Curb 73127
				RISHARD, Rod		'83			
8/20/83	77	5		1 You'd Better Believe It	You're The Closest I've Come	—	$5		Soundwaves 4715
11/19/83	74	5		2 How Do You Tell Someone You Love	Friday Night Love Affair	—	$5		Soundwaves 4717
3/24/84	89	3		3 The More I Go Blind	Next Exit Out Of Love	—	$5		Soundwaves 4724
7/28/84	84	3		4 Midnight Angel Of Mercy	You're The Closest I've Come	—	$5		Soundwaves 4734
				RITTER, Tex ★152★		'45			
				Born Maurice Woodward Ritter on 1/12/05 in Murvaul, Texas. Died of a heart attack on 1/2/74 (age 68). Singer/guitarist/actor. Acted in several western movies from 1936-45. Co-host of Town Hall Party *radio and TV series from 1953-60. Joined the* Grand Ole Opry *in 1965. Elected to the Country Music Hall of Fame in 1964. Father of actor John Ritter.*					
				1)You Two-Timed Me One Time Too Often 2)I'm Wastin' My Tears On You 3)You Will Have To Pay 4)Jealous Heart 5)There's A New Moon Over My Shoulder					
				TEX RITTER and His Texans:					
11/11/44	❶6	20		1 I'm Wastin' My Tears On You /		11			
11/11/44+	21	22		2 There's A New Moon Over My Shoulder		21	$20		Capitol 174
12/16/44+	22	23		3 Jealous Heart	We Live In Two Different Worlds	—	$20		Capitol 179
8/4/45	❶11	20		4 You Two Timed Me One Time Too Often	Green Grow The Lilacs	—	$20		Capitol 206
				TEX RITTER:					
12/8/45+	❶3	7		5 You Will Have To Pay /		—			
12/29/45	21	3		6 Christmas Carols By The Old Corral [X]		—	$20		Capitol 223
5/18/46	5	6		7 Long Time Gone	I'm Gonna Leave You Like I Found You	—	$20		Capitol 253
10/19/46	3	10		8 When You Leave Don't Slam The Door /		—			
12/7/46	3	2		9 Have I Told You Lately That I Love You		—	$20		Capitol 296
3/13/48	9	1		10 Rye Whiskey	Boll Weevil	—	$20		Capitol Amer. 40084
6/12/48	10	7		11 Deck Of Cards	S:10 / J:13 Rounded Up In Glory [S]	—	$20		Capitol Amer. 40114
6/12/48	15	1		12 Pecos Bill	J:15 Egg-A-Bread	—	$20		Capitol Amer. 40106
				TEX RITTER With Andy Parker And THE PLAINSMEN:					
7/10/48	5	7		13 Rock And Rye	S:5 / J:8 My Heart's As Cold As An Empty Jug [N]	—	$25		Capitol 15119
				from the movie Melody Time *starring Roy Rogers*					
11/18/50	6	3		14 Daddy's Last Letter	A:6 / S:8 Onward Christian Soldiers [S]	—	$30		Capitol F1267
				an actual letter from Private First Class John H. McCormick, a soldier killed in the Korean War					
6/19/61	5	21		15 I Dreamed Of A Hill-Billy Heaven	The Wind And The Tree [S]	20	$12		Capitol 4567
3/5/66	50	1		16 The Men In My Little Girl's Life	Custody [S]	—	$8		Capitol 5574
				#6 Pop hit for Mike Douglas in 1966					
3/25/67	13	15		17 Just Beyond The Moon	Greedy Old Dog	—	$8		Capitol 5839
9/30/67	59	2		18 A Working Man's Prayer	William Barrett Travis: A Message From The Alamo	—	$8		Capitol 5966
				#79 Pop hit for Arthur Prysock in 1968					
8/17/68	69	4		19 Texas	Stranger On Boot Hill	—	$8		Capitol 2232
2/8/69	53	6		20 A Funny Thing Happened (On The Way To Miami)	The Governor And The Kid	—	$8		Capitol 2388
7/26/69	39	10		21 Growin' Up	A Letter To My Sons	—	$8		Capitol 2541
6/6/70	57	8		22 Green Green Valley	God Bless America Again	—	$8		Capitol 2815
9/18/71	67	3		23 Fall Away	Looking Back	—	$8		Capitol 3154
11/18/72	67	5		24 Comin' After Jinny	You Will Have To Pay For Your Yesterday	—	$6		Capitol 3457
1/26/74	35	8		25 The Americans (A Canadian's Opinion)	He Who Is Without Sin (Let Him Judge Me) [S]	90	$6		Capitol 3814
				RIVER ROAD		'97			
				Group from Louisiana: Steve Grisaffe (vocals, bass), Tony Ardoin (guitar), Charles Ventre (keyboards), Richard Comeaux (steel guitar) and Mike Burch (drums).					
5/10/97	48	14		1 I Broke It, I'll Fix It	A Day In The Life	—	$4		Capitol 19580
8/23/97	37	17		2 Nickajack	S:23 Tears To The Tide	—	$4	▮	Capitol 19647 (v)
12/13/97+	51	10		3 Somebody Will	As If You Didn't Know	—	$4		Capitol 19852
3/18/00	45	14		4 Breathless	S:24 Somethin' In The Water	—	$4	★	Virgin 38699 (v)
				RIVERS, Eddie		'89			
4/30/77	98	2		1 Open Up Your Door	He's Still A Father In His Daughter's Eyes	—	$6		Charta 102
6/10/89	93	1		2 You Won The Battle	There's No Memories Of Me (Ever Lovin' You)	—	$5		Charta 218
				RIVERS, Jack		'48			
				Born on 12/16/17 in Los Angeles. Died on 2/11/89 (age 71). Session guitarist for Gene Autry.					
9/18/48	12	2		Dear Oakie	J:12 A Million Memories	—	$20		Capitol 15169

DEBUT	PEAK	WKS	Gold	A-side (Chart Hit)	B-side	Pop	$	Pic	Label & Number
				RIVERS, Johnny '74					
				Born John Ramistella on 11/7/42 in New York City; raised in Baton Rouge. Singer/songwriter/guitarist. Charted 29 pop hits from 1964-78.					
6/29/74	58	8		Six Days On The Road	Artists & Poets	106	$6		Atlantic 3028
				ROBBINS, Dennis '92					
				Born in Hazelwood, North Carolina. Former member of the rock group Rockets. Lead singer/guitarist of **Billy Hill**.					
1/17/87	63	8		1 Long Gone Lonesome Blues	The Mountain Man And Me	—	$4		MCA 52987
10/3/87	71	9		2 Two Of A Kind (Workin' On A Full House)	The Church On Cumberland Road	—	$4		MCA 53143
5/9/92	34	20		3 Home Sweet Home	The Only Slide I Ever Played On	—	$4		Giant 18982
9/5/92	59	6		4 My Side Of Town	Hi O Silver	—	$4		Giant 18786
1/15/94	68	4		5 Mona Lisa On Cruise Control	Walkin' On The Edge	—	$4	■	Giant 18294 (v)
				ROBBINS, Hargus "Pig" '79					
				Born on 1/18/38 in Spring City, Tennessee. Top Nashville session pianist. Blind since age four. Member of the **Nashville Superpickers**. CMA Awards: 1976 & 2000 Musician of the Year.					
6/23/79	83	3		1 Chunky People	Whatever Happened To The Girls I Knew	—	$5		Elektra 46037
9/1/79	92	4		2 Unbreakable Hearts	Love, Love, Love	—	$5		Elektra 46512
				ROBBINS, Jenny '78					
7/1/78	76	4		You've Just Found Yourself A New Woman	All I've Got Left	—	$6		El Dorado 152

ROBBINS, Marty ★13★ '58
Born Martin David Robinson on 9/26/25 in Glendale, Arizona. Died of heart failure on 12/8/82 (age 57). Singer/songwriter/guitarist. Father of **Ronny Robbins**. Served in the U.S. Navy from 1944-47. Hosted *Western Caravan* TV show in Phoenix in 1951. Joined the *Grand Ole Opry* in 1953. Acted in the movies *Road To Nashville* and *Guns Of A Stranger*. Hosted TV's *Marty Robbins' Spotlight* in 1977.

1)Singing The Blues 2)Don't Worry 3)Devil Woman 4)El Paso 5)A White Sport Coat (And A Pink Carnation)

DEBUT	PEAK	WKS		A-side	B-side	Pop	$	Pic	Label & Number
12/20/52+	❶²	18		1 I'll Go On Alone	A:❶² / S:10 You're Breaking My Heart (While You're Holding My Hand)	—	$30		Columbia 21022
3/28/53	5	11		2 I Couldn't Keep From Crying	J:5 / S:6 / A:6 After You Leave	—	$30		Columbia 21075
7/3/54	12	3		3 Pretty Words	A:12 / S:14 Your Heart's Turn To Break	—	$30		Columbia 21246
11/20/54	14	1		4 Call Me Up (And I'll Come Calling On You)	A:14 I'm Too Big To Cry	—	$30		Columbia 21291
1/8/55	14	1		5 Time Goes By	A:14 It's A Pity What Money Can Do	—	$30		Columbia 21324
2/12/55	7	11		6 That's All Right	A:7 / S:9 Gossip	—	$50		Columbia 21351
				recorded by Elvis Presley in 1954					
10/1/55	9	7		7 Maybelline	A:9 This Broken Heart Of Mine	—	$50		Columbia 21446
				#5 Pop hit for Chuck Berry in 1955					
9/22/56	❶¹³	30		8 Singing The Blues /	S:❶¹³ / J:❶¹³ / A:❶¹³	17			
				#1 Pop hit for Guy Mitchell in 1956					
10/6/56	7	10		9 I Can't Quit (I've Gone Too Far)	A:7	—	$40		Columbia 21545
2/2/57	3	15		10 Knee Deep In The Blues /	A:3 / S:5 / J:7				
				#16 Pop hit for Guy Mitchell in 1957					
3/2/57	14	2		11 The Same Two Lips	A:14	—	$30		Columbia 40815
4/20/57	❶⁵	22	●	12 A White Sport Coat (And A Pink Carnation)	S:❶⁵ / J:❶⁵ / A:❶¹ Grown-Up Tears	2¹	$25	■	Columbia 40864
9/9/57	11	3		13 Please Don't Blame Me /	S:11	—			
9/9/57	15	3		14 Teen-Age Dream	S:15	—	$25		Columbia 40969
11/25/57+	❶⁴	23		15 The Story Of My Life	S:❶⁴ / A:❶⁴ Once-A-Week Date	15	$20	■	Columbia 41013
4/7/58	❶²	25		16 Just Married /	A:❶² / S:3	26			
4/7/58	2²	25		17 Stairway Of Love	S:2 / A:8	68	$20		Columbia 41143
8/18/58	4	10		18 She Was Only Seventeen (He Was One Year More)	S:4 / A:13 Sittin' In A Tree House	27	$20	■	Columbia 41208
12/15/58	23	5		19 Ain't I The Lucky One	The Last Time I Saw My Heart	—	$20		Columbia 41282
3/9/59	15	9		20 The Hanging Tree	The Blues Country Style	38	$20	■	Columbia 41325
				from the movie starring Gary Cooper					
11/9/59	❶⁷	26		21 El Paso	Running Gun	❶²	$15	■	Columbia 41511
				also see #73 below					
3/21/60	5	14		22 Big Iron	Saddle Tramp	26	$15	■	Columbia 41589
9/26/60	26	4		23 Five Brothers	Ride, Cowboy Ride	74	$15		Columbia 41771
2/6/61	❶¹⁰	19		24 Don't Worry	Like All The Other Times	3	$15	■	Columbia 41922
6/5/61	24	4		25 Jimmy Martinez	Ghost Train	51	$12		Columbia 42008
9/18/61	3	20		26 It's Your World	You Told Me So	51	$12	■	Columbia 42065
2/3/62	12	13		27 Sometimes I'm Tempted	I Told The Brook (Hot #81)	109	$15		Columbia 42246
6/2/62	12	9		28 Love Can't Wait	Too Far Gone	69	$12		Columbia 42375
8/4/62	❶⁸	21		29 Devil Woman	April Fool's Day	16	$12	■	Columbia 42486
12/8/62+	❶¹	14		30 Ruby Ann	Won't You Forgive	18	$12		Columbia 42614
3/23/63	14	9		31 Cigarettes And Coffee Blues	Teenager's Dad	93	$12	■	Columbia 42701
9/7/63	13	11		32 Not So Long Ago	I Hope You Learn A Lot	115	$12		Columbia 42831
11/30/63+	❶³	23		33 Begging To You	Over High Mountain	74	$12		Columbia 42890
3/7/64	15	11		34 Girl From Spanish Town	Kingston Girl	106	$12		Columbia 42968
6/20/64	3	21		35 The Cowboy In The Continental Suit	Man Walks Among Us	103	$10		Columbia 43049
10/31/64	8	17		36 One Of These Days	Up In The Air	105	$10		Columbia 43134
4/17/65	❶¹	21		37 Ribbon Of Darkness	Little Robin	103	$10		Columbia 43258
11/13/65	50	1		38 Old Red	Matilda	—	$10		Columbia 43377
12/4/65+	21	10		39 While You're Dancing	Lonely Too Long	—	$10		Columbia 43428

DEBUT	PEAK	WKS	Gold	A-side (Chart Hit)	B-side	Pop	$	Pic	Label & Number
				ROBBINS, Marty — Cont'd					
2/19/66	14	11		40 Count Me Out /			—		
3/5/66	21	7		41 Private Wilson White			$10		Columbia 43500
7/9/66	3	18		42 The Shoe Goes On The Other Foot Tonight	It Kind Of Reminds Me Of Me		$10		Columbia 43680
11/19/66+	16	14		43 Mr. Shorty	Tall Handsome Stranger		$10		Columbia 43870
2/4/67	16	12		44 No Tears Milady /			—		
2/25/67	34	11		45 Fly Butterfly Fly			$10		Columbia 43845
6/3/67	❶¹	16		46 Tonight Carmen	Waiting In Reno	114	$8		Columbia 44128
9/16/67	9	14		47 Gardenias In Her Hair	In The Valley Of The Rio Grande		$8		Columbia 44271
5/4/68	10	15		48 Love Is In The Air	I've Been Leaving Every Day		$8		Columbia 44509
10/5/68	❶²	15		49 I Walk Alone	Lily Of The Valley	65	$7		Columbia 44633
2/8/69	5	14		50 It's A Sin	I Feel Another Heartbreak Coming On		$7		Columbia 44739
7/5/69	8	14		51 I Can't Say Goodbye	Hello Daily News		$7		Columbia 44895
11/22/69+	10	13		52 Camelia	Virginia		$7		Columbia 45024
2/21/70	❶¹	17		53 My Woman, My Woman, My Wife	Martha Ellen Jenkins	42	$6		Columbia 45091
9/12/70	7	14		54 Jolie Girl	The City	108	$6		Columbia 45215
12/19/70+	5	12		55 Padre	At Times	113	$6		Columbia 45273
				#13 Pop hit for Toni Arden in 1958					
5/22/71	7	13		56 The Chair /		121			
		8		57 Seventeen Years			$6		Columbia 45377
10/2/71	9	14		58 Early Morning Sunshine	Another Day Has Gone By		$6		Columbia 45442
1/1/72	6	16		59 The Best Part Of Living	Gone With The Wind		$6		Columbia 45520
9/9/72	32	9		60 I've Got A Woman's Love	A Little Spot In Heaven		$6		Columbia 45668
9/23/72	11	15		61 This Much A Man	Guess I'll Just Stand Here Looking Dumb		$7		Decca 33006
2/17/73	60	7		62 Laura (What's He Got That I Ain't Got)	It Kind Of Reminds Me Of Me		$6		Columbia 45775
3/3/73	6	15		63 Walking Piece Of Heaven	Franklin, Tennessee		$6		MCA 40012
6/23/73	40	8		64 A Man And A Train	Las Vegas, Nevada		$6		MCA 40067
				from the movie Emperor of The North Pole starring Lee Marvin					
10/13/73	9	14		65 Love Me /			—		
				also see #93 below					
		11		66 Crawling On My Knees			$6		MCA 40134
1/26/74	10	14		67 Twentieth Century Drifter	I'm Wanting To		$6		MCA 40172
5/25/74	12	15		68 Don't You Think	I Couldn't Believe It Was True		$6		MCA 40236
10/5/74	39	11		69 Two Gun Daddy	Queen Of The Big Rodeo		$6		MCA 40296
1/18/75	23	12		70 Life /					
5/31/75	76	4		71 It Takes Faith			$6		MCA 40342
7/19/75	55	9		72 Shotgun Rider	These Are My Souvenirs		$6		MCA 40425
4/17/76	❶²	16		73 El Paso City	When I'm Gone		$5		Columbia 10305
				sequel to #21 above					
9/4/76	❶¹	14		74 Among My Souvenirs	She's Just A Drifter		$5		Columbia 10396
				#7 Pop hit for Connie Francis in 1959					
2/5/77	4	13		75 Adios Amigo	Helen		$5		Columbia 10472
5/21/77	10	13		76 I Don't Know Why (I Just Do)	Inspiration For A Song	108	$5		Columbia 10536
				#12 Pop hit for Linda Scott in 1961					
10/15/77	6	15		77 Don't Let Me Touch You	Tomorrow, Tomorrow, Tomorrow		$5		Columbia 10629
1/28/78	6	13		78 Return To Me	More Than Anything I Miss You		$5		Columbia 10673
				#4 Pop hit for Dean Martin in 1958					
11/4/78	17	12		79 Please Don't Play A Love Song	Jenny		$5		Columbia 10821
2/17/79	15	13		80 Touch Me With Magic	Confused And Lonely		$5		Columbia 10905
6/23/79	16	12		81 All Around Cowboy	The Dreamer		$5		Columbia 11016
10/13/79	25	10		82 Buenos Dias Argentina	Ballad Of A Small Man		$5		Columbia 11102
4/12/80	37	9		83 She's Made Of Faith	Misery In My Soul		$4		Columbia 11240
7/12/80	72	5		84 One Man's Trash (Is Another Man's Treasure)	I Can't Wait Until Tomorrow		$4		Columbia 11291
11/1/80	28	12		85 An Occasional Rose	Holding On To You		$4		Columbia 11372
2/7/81	47	7		86 Completely Out Of Love	Another Cup Of Coffee		$4		Columbia 11425
9/26/81	83	4		87 Jumper Cable Man	Good Hearted Woman		$4		Columbia 02444
11/21/81	45	9		88 Teardrops In My Heart	Honeycombe		$4		Columbia 02575
5/22/82	10	18		89 Some Memories Just Won't Die	Lover, Lover		$4		Columbia 02854
10/2/82	24	16		90 Tie Your Dream To Mine	That's All She Wrote		$4		Columbia 03236
12/25/82+	10	17		91 Honkytonk Man	Shotgun Rag (Johnny Gimble)		$4		Warner 29847
				from the movie starring Clint Eastwood					
3/26/83	48	9		92 Change Of Heart	Devil In A Cowboy Hat		$4		Columbia 03789
4/16/83	58	8		93 Love Me	Safely In The Arms Of Jesus (Pruett) [R]		$5		Audiograph 454
				JEANNE PRUETT/MARTY ROBBINS					
				new version of #65 above					
6/11/83	57	9		94 What If I Said I Love You	Baby That's Love		$4		Columbia 03927
				ROBBINS, Ronny			'84		
				Born Ronald Carson Robinson on 7/16/49 in Phoenix. Son of Marty Robbins.					
11/11/78	99	1		1 The Last Lie I Told Her	Taste The Wine		$6		Artic 878
2/24/79	95	1		2 Why'd The Last Time Have To Be The Best	Where Do I Put Her Memory		$6		Artic 8782
11/17/79	91	2		3 I Know I'm Not Your Hero Anymore	The I Love You's Get Further Apart		$6		TRC 081
7/21/84	62	7		4 Those You Lose	We've Been Lying Here Too Long		$4		Columbia 04506

DEBUT	PEAK	WKS	Gold	A-side (Chart Hit) .... B-side	Pop	$	Pic	Label & Number
				ROBERTS, Kenny '49				
				Born George Kingsbury on 10/14/26 in Lenoir City, Tennessee; raised in Greenfield, Massachusetts. Singer/songwriter/guitarist. Known for his yodeling.				
9/17/49	4	11		1 I Never See Maggie Alone / J:4 / S:5	9			
				Roberts first recorded this with Nancy Lee for Vitacoustic 506; #13 Pop hit for Irving Aaronson in 1927				
10/8/49	15	1		2 Wedding Bells J:15	—	$15		Coral 64012
11/19/49	14	1		3 Jealous Heart .... (There's A) Bluebird On Your Windowsill	—	$15		Coral 64021
5/13/50	8	4		4 Choc'late Ice Cream Cone A:8 / J:10 Hillbilly Fever	—	$15		Coral 64032
				ROBERTS, Pat '72				
				Born in Seattle. (Male) singer.				
10/21/72	34	12		1 Rhythm Of The Rain .... Without You	—	$6		Dot 17434
				#3 Pop hit for The Cascades in 1963				
3/3/73	59	8		2 Thanks For Lovin' Me .... A Whole Lotta Lovin'	—	$6		Dot 17451
7/14/73	79	4		3 Here Comes My Little Baby .... Love Lives Again	—	$6		Dot 17465
11/3/73	81	5		4 I'm Gonna Keep Searching .... Your Love's Been A Long Time Comin'	—	$6		Dot 17478
4/6/74	77	6		5 You Got Everything That You Want .... Love Me, Love Me	—	$6		Dot 17495
				ROBERTSON, Jack '88				
7/9/88	66	5		It's Not Easy .... Cow Town Mama	—	$5		Soundwaves 4808
				ROBERTSON, Texas Jim '47				
				Born on 2/27/09 in Batesville, Texas. Died on 11/11/66 (age 57). Singer/guitarist.				
				TEXAS JIM ROBERTSON and The Panhandle Punchers:				
12/28/46	5	1		1 Filipino Baby /				
2/15/47	5	1		2 Rainbow At Midnight	—	$15		RCA Victor 20-1975
2/28/48	8	1		3 Signed, Sealed And Delivered Lost Deep In The Bottom Of The Sea	—	$15		RCA Victor 20-2651
1/7/50	13	1		4 Slipping Around .... S:13 Wedding Bells	—	$25		RCA Victor 48-0071
				78 rpm: 21-0074				
				ROBEY, Loretta '77				
				Born in 1937 in Oviedo, Florida. (Fla.)				
6/11/77	100	1		Sophisticated Country Lady .... Lovin Cup	—	$5		Soundwaves 4545
				ROBIN & CRUISER (Bros.) '87				
				Brothers Robin and Cruiser Gordon.				
10/24/87	79	4		Rings Of Gold .... Tie Me To Your Heart Again	—	$4		16th Avenue 70404
				ROBINSON, Betty Jean '75				
				Born in Hyden, Kentucky. Singer/songwriter.				
4/24/71	51	10		1 All I Need Is You .... Funny What A Pair Of Fool Will Do	—	$8		Decca 32802
				CARL BELEW & BETTY JEAN ROBINSON				
11/23/74+	49	10		2 On The Way Home .... I've Got You	—	$5		MCA 40300
4/5/75	87	4		3 God Is Good .... All I Need Is You	—	$5		4 Star 1004
				ROBINSON, Sharon '87				
12/26/87	86	4		Have You Hurt Any Good Ones Lately .... Potential Strangers	—	$7		Nightfall 001
				ROBISON, Carson '48				
				Born on 8/4/1890 in Oswego, Kansas. Died on 3/24/57 (age 66). Singer/songwriter/guitarist. Known as "The Kansas Jaybird".				
6/30/45	5	1		1 Hitler's Last Letter To Hirohito Hirohito's Letter To Hitler [N]	—	$20		Victor 20-1665
8/14/48	3	28		2 Life Gits Tee-Jus Don't It S:3 / J:3 Wind In The Mountains [N]	14	$20		MGM 10224
				CARSON ROBISON with His Pleasant Valley Boys				
				ROBISON, Charlie '01				
				Born in Bandera, Texas. Singer/songwriter/guitarist. Married Emily Erwin of the Dixie Chicks on 5/1/99.				
1/16/99	60	20		1 Barlight .... Arms Of Love	—	$4		Lucky Dog 79061 (v)
11/20/99+	65	13		2 My Hometown	—			album cut
4/8/00	67	1		3 Poor Man's Son	—			album cut
				above 2 from the album Life Of The Party on Lucky Dog 69327				
3/31/01	35	20		4 I Want You Bad .... S:8 Barlight (live)	—	$4	★	Columbia 79542 (v)
				ROCKINHORSE '86				
				Group from Oakland, Minnesota, led by female singer Toni Rose.				
8/30/86	68	6		1 Have I Got A Heart For You	—			$5	Long Shot 1002
12/6/86	86	3		2 Let A Little Love In (Tennessee Saturday Night)	—	$5		Long Shot 1003
				ROCKIN' SIDNEY '85				
				Born Sidney Simien on 4/9/38 in Lebeau, Louisiana. Died of cancer on 2/25/98 (age 59). Black singer/songwriter/accordianist.				
6/22/85	19	20		My Toot-Toot .... S:8 / A:23 Jalapeno Lena	—	$4		Epic 05430
				RODGERS, Jimmie '55				
				Born on 9/8/1897 in Meridian, Mississippi. Died of tuberculosis on 5/26/33 (age 35). Singer/songwriter/guitarist. Known as "America's Blue Yodeler," "The Singing Brakeman," and "The Father of Country Music." Elected to the Country Music Hall of Fame in 1961. Inducted into the Rock and Roll Hall of Fame in 1986 as an early influence of rock and roll.				
5/14/55	7	12		In The Jailhouse Now No. 2 J:7 / S:8 / A:9 Peach Picking Time Down In Georgia	—	$25		RCA Victor 6092
				JIMMIE RODGERS and the Rainbow Ranch Boys				
				recorded in 1930 on Victor 22523 ($75); new overdubbed backing includes Chet Atkins and Hank Snow				

see Pop Memories
JR died before this book covers

This is not THE Jimmie Rodgers

DEBUT	PEAK	WKS	Gold		A-side (Chart Hit)	B-side	Pop	$	Pic	Label & Number

RODGERS, Jimmie '58
Born on 9/18/33 in Camas, Washington. Singer/guitarist/pianist. Charted 25 pop hits from 1957-67. Hosted own TV series in 1959 and 1969.
1)Oh-Oh, I'm Falling In Love Again 2)Secretly 3)Kisses Sweeter Than Wine

DEBUT	PEAK	WKS	Gold	#	A-side	B-side	Pop	$	Pic	Label & Number
10/14/57	7	13	●	1	Honeycomb	S:7 / A:11 Their Hearts Were Full Of Spring	❶⁴	$20		Roulette 4015
12/2/57	6	16	●	2	Kisses Sweeter Than Wine	S:6 / A:8 Better Loved You'll Never Be	3	$20		Roulette 4031
3/3/58	5	11	●	3	Oh-Oh, I'm Falling In Love Again	S:5 / A:15	7	$20		Roulette 4045
5/19/58	5	17	●	4	Secretly / also see #9 below	S:5 / A:14	3			
		9		5	Make Me A Miracle	S:flip	16	$15	■	Roulette 4070
8/25/58	13	8		6	Are You Really Mine	S:13	10	$15	■	Roulette 4090
10/29/77	67	10		7	A Good Woman Likes To Drink With The Boys	Everybody Needs Love	—	$6		ScrimShaw 1313
2/11/78	74	5		8	Everytime I Sing A Love Song	Just A Little Time	—	$6		ScrimShaw 1314
9/23/78	65	5		9	Secretly new version of #4 above	Shovelin' Coal Missouri [R]	—	$6		ScrimShaw 1318
3/17/79	89	4		10	Easy To Love /			—		
		4		11	Easy JIMMIE RODGERS & MICHELE			$6		ScrimShaw 1319

RODMAN, Judy ★339★ '86
Born Judy Mae Robbins on 5/23/51 in Riverside, California; raised in Miami and Jacksonville. Singer/songwriter/guitarist. Former jingle and session singer.
1)Until I Met You 2)I'll Be Your Baby Tonight 3)Girls Ride Horses Too

DEBUT	PEAK	WKS	#	A-side	B-side	Pop	$	Label & Number
3/23/85	40	14	1	I've Been Had By Love Before	Do You Make Love As Well As You Make Music	—	$4	MTM 72050
8/10/85	33	14	2	You're Gonna Miss Me When I'm Gone	She Thinks That She'll Marry	—	$4	MTM 72054
11/16/85+	30	17	3	I Sure Need Your Lovin'	A:29 Come Next Monday	—	$4	MTM 72061
4/5/86	❶¹	25	4	Until I Met You	A:❶¹ / S:2 Do You Make Love As Well As You Make Music	—	$4	MTM 72065
10/4/86+	9	21	5	She Thinks That She'll Marry	S:9 / A:10 Our Love Is Fine	—	$4	MTM 72076
2/21/87	7	17	6	Girls Ride Horses Too	S:2 / A:7 Heart Of A Gentleman	—	$4	MTM 72083
6/20/87	5	27	7	I'll Be Your Baby Tonight written and first recorded by Bob Dylan on his 1968 album John Wesley Harding	S:3 Love Comes From Inside Of You	—	$4	MTM 72089
10/31/87+	18	21	8	I Want A Love Like That	S:19 Please Don't Take My Heart	—	$4	MTM 72092
5/21/88	43	9	9	Goin' To Work	Please Don't Take My Heart	—	$4	MTM 72105
8/13/88	45	9	10	I Can Love You	Come To Me	—	$4	MTM 72112

RODRIGUEZ, Johnny ★76★ '75
Born Juan Rodriguez on 12/10/51 in Sabinal, Texas. Singer/songwriter/guitarist. Performed with high school rock band in the late 1960s. Moved to Nashville in 1971, worked with the **Tom T. Hall** band from 1971-72. First recorded solo in 1972. Also see Tomorrow's World.

1)Ridin' My Thumb To Mexico 2)That's The Way Love Goes 3)Just Get Up And Close The Door
4)You Always Come Back (To Hurting Me) 5)Love Put A Song In My Heart

DEBUT	PEAK	WKS	#	A-side	B-side	Pop	$	Pic	Label & Number
11/11/72+	9	18	1	Pass Me By (If You're Only Passing Through)	Jealous Heart	—	$6		Mercury 73334
3/31/73	❶¹	16	2	You Always Come Back (To Hurting Me)	I Wonder Where You Are Tonight	86	$6		Mercury 73368
8/18/73	❶²	17	3	Ridin' My Thumb To Mexico	Release Me	70	$6		Mercury 73416
12/29/73+	❶¹	14	4	That's The Way Love Goes	I Really Don't Want To Know	—	$6		Mercury 73446
3/30/74	6	14	5	Something #1 Pop hit for The Beatles in 1969	Born To Lose	85	$6		Mercury 73471
7/13/74	2¹	13	6	Dance With Me (Just One More Time)	Faded Love	—	$6		Mercury 73493
10/19/74	3	13	7	We're Over	Oh, I Miss You	—	$5		Mercury 73621
2/8/75	❶¹	12	8	I Just Can't Get Her Out Of My Mind	Have I Told You Lately That I Love You	—	$5		Mercury 73659
5/24/75	❶¹	18	9	Just Get Up And Close The Door	Am I That Easy To Forget	—	$5		Mercury 73682
10/4/75	❶¹	15	10	Love Put A Song In My Heart	Steppin' Out On You	—	$5		Mercury 73715
2/28/76	3	15	11	I Couldn't Be Me Without You	Sometimes I Wish I Were You	—	$5	■	Mercury 73769
7/10/76	2²	13	12	I Wonder If I Ever Said Goodbye	Louisiana	—	$5		Mercury 73815
10/9/76	5	14	13	Hillbilly Heart	Commonly Known As The Blues	—	$5		Mercury 73855
1/15/77	5	14	14	Desperado first recorded by the **Eagles** on their 1973 album Desperado	There'll Always Be Honky Tonks In Texas	—	$5		Mercury 73878
5/14/77	5	13	15	If Practice Makes Perfect	Hard Times	—	$5		Mercury 73914
9/3/77	25	10	16	Eres Tu	You Put A Hold On Me [F]	—	$5		Mercury 55004
11/5/77	14	13	17	Savin' This Love Song For You	Que Te Quiero	—	$5		Mercury 55012
2/25/78	7	14	18	We Believe In Happy Endings	The Immigrant	—	$5		Mercury 55020
7/8/78	7	13	19	Love Me With All Your Heart (Cuando Calienta El Sol) #3 Pop hit for The Ray Charles Singers in 1964	I Need It Now	—	$5		Mercury 55029
12/16/78+	16	13	20	Alibis	Rest Your Love On Me	—	$5		Mercury 55050
3/10/79	6	14	21	Down On The Rio Grande	Mexico Holiday	—	$4		Epic 50671
7/7/79	17	13	22	Fools For Each Other	Street Walker	—	$4		Epic 50735
10/20/79	16	14	23	I Hate The Way I Love It JOHNNY RODRIGUEZ and CHARLY McCLAIN	Almost Persuaded	—	$4		Epic 50791
11/24/79+	19	14	24	What'll I Tell Virginia	Whatever Gets Me Through The Night	—	$4		Epic 50808
4/5/80	29	11	25	Love, Look At Us Now	Where Did It Go	—	$4		Epic 50859
9/20/80	17	16	26	North Of The Border	When She Gets Around To Me	—	$4		Epic 50932
4/11/81	22	13	27	I Want You Tonight	Your Love Isn't Mine Anymore	—	$4		Epic 01033

DEBUT	PEAK	WKS	Gold	A-side (Chart Hit)	B-side	Pop	$	Pic	Label & Number
				RODRIGUEZ, Johnny — Cont'd					
8/8/81	30	11		28 Trying Not To Love You .... Mexico Rain		—	$4		Epic 02411
2/13/82	66	6		29 Born With The Blues /			$4		Epic 02638
12/5/81	73	7		30 It's Not The Same Old You		—	$4		Epic 02638
11/27/82	89	3		31 He's Not Entitled To Your Love .... Starting All Over Again		—	$4		Epic 03275
2/26/83	4	20		32 Foolin' .... Because Of You		—	$4		Epic 03598
7/9/83	6	21		33 How Could I Love Her So Much .... Somethin' About A Jukebox		—	$4		Epic 03972
11/19/83+	35	12		34 Back On Her Mind Again .... Eleven Roses		—	$4		Epic 04206
1/28/84	15	17		35 Too Late To Go Home .... No Memories Hangin' Round		—	$4		Epic 04336
5/19/84	30	15		36 Let's Leave The Lights On Tonight .... What A Movie You'd Make		—	$4		Epic 04460
8/18/84	63	7		37 First Time Burned .... Hand Me Another Of Those		—	$4		Epic 04562
10/13/84	60	8		38 Rose Of My Heart .... Down In The Boondocks		—	$4		Epic 04628
4/6/85	69	7		39 Here I Am Again .... Full Circle		—	$4		Epic 04838
12/28/85+	51	15		40 She Don't Cry Like She Used To .... Back On Her Mind Again		—	$4	■	Epic 05732
12/12/87+	12	26		41 I Didn't (Every Chance I Had) .... S:25 I'm Not That Good At Goodbye		—	$4		Capitol 44071
7/16/88	41	15		42 I Wanta Wake Up With You .... Someday I'm Gonna Finish Leaving You		—	$4		Capitol 44204
10/15/88	44	10		43 You Might Want To Use Me Again .... She Loves Austin		—	$4		Capitol 44245
2/18/89	72	4		44 No Chance To Dance .... Back To Stay		—	$4		Capitol 44325
8/5/89	78	3		45 Back To Stay .... Someday I'm Gonna Finish Leaving You		—	$4		Capitol 44403
				★ **ROE, Marlys** '73					
				Born in Georgia. Female singer.					
8/11/73	71	9		Carry Me Back .... Somebody In Your Eyes		—	$6		GRC 1002
				ROE, Tommy '87					
				Born on 5/9/42 in Atlanta. Singer/songwriter/guitarist. Charted 22 pop hits from 1962-73.					
6/9/73	73	2		1 Working Class Hero .... Sun In My Eyes		97	$6		MGM South 7013
5/19/79	77	3		2 Massachusetts .... Just Look At Me		—	$5		Warner/Curb 8800
				#11 Pop hit for the **Bee Gees** in 1967					
10/27/79	70	4		3 You Better Move On .... Just Look At Me		—	$5		Warner/Curb 49085
				#24 Pop hit for Arthur Alexander in 1962					
6/21/80	87	3		4 Charlie, I Love Your Wife .... There Is No Sun On Sunset Boulevard		—	$5		Warner/Curb 49235
11/16/85	57	11		5 Some Such Foolishness .... Barbara Lou		—	$4		Curb/MCA 52711
3/1/86	51	7		6 Radio Romance .... Barbara Lou		—	$4		Curb/MCA 52778
12/20/86+	38	14		7 Let's Be Fools Like That Again .... Barbara Lou		—	$4		Mercury 888206
5/23/87	67	5		8 Back When It Really Mattered .... Radio Romance		—	$4		Mercury 888497
				ROGERS, Dann '87					
				Nephew of Kenny Rogers.					
9/5/87	78	3		Just A Kid From Texas .... We've Got To Stop Meeting This Way		—	$4		MCA 53133

ROGERS, David ★168★   '72

Born on 3/27/36 in Atlanta. Died on 8/10/93 (age 57). Singer/songwriter/guitarist. Worked clubs in Atlanta from 1952-67 (including six years at the Egyptian Ballroom). Worked on the WWVA-Wheeling *Jamboree* in 1967.

1) Need You 2) Loving You Has Changed My Life 3) Just Thank Me 4) Darlin' 5) She Don't Make Me Cry

DEBUT	PEAK	WKS		A-side	B-side	Pop	$	Pic	Label & Number
3/2/68	69	5		1 I'd Be Your Fool Again .... Loser's Shoes		—	$7		Columbia 44430
7/20/68	38	11		2 I'm In Love With My Wife .... Tessie's Bar Mystery		—	$7	■	Columbia 44561
11/16/68+	37	13		3 You Touched My Heart .... Today And Tomorrow		—	$7		Columbia 44668
5/17/69	59	7		4 Dearly Beloved .... The Little White Cloud That Cried		—	$7		Columbia 44796
11/22/69+	23	12		5 A World Called You .... A Picture Of You		—	$7		Columbia 45007
5/9/70	46	9		6 So Much In Love With You .... The Edge Of Your Memory		—	$7		Columbia 45111
10/17/70	26	11		7 I Wake Up In Heaven .... Baby Don't Cry		—	$7		Columbia 45226
5/29/71	19	15		8 She Don't Make Me Cry .... Bottle Do Your Thing		—	$7		Columbia 45383
11/13/71+	21	13		9 Ruby You're Warm .... Is That All San Francisco Did For You		—	$7		Columbia 45478
2/26/72	9	15		10 Need You .... Sweet Vibrations (Some Folks Call It Love)		—	$7		Columbia 45551
				#25 Pop hit for Donnie Owens in 1958					
8/5/72	38	9		11 Goodbye .... I'd Be Your Fool Again		—	$7		Columbia 45642
11/11/72	35	11		12 All Heaven Breaks Loose .... Completely Satisfied		—	$7		Columbia 45714
4/28/73	17	12		13 Just Thank Me .... I Wish I Was Back		—	$6		Atlantic 2957
8/25/73	22	12		14 It'll Be Her .... Singin' Star		—	$6		Atlantic 4005
1/5/74	9	14		15 Loving You Has Changed My Life .... You Be You And I'll Be Gone		—	$6		Atlantic 4012
5/25/74	21	13		16 Hey There Girl .... Someone That I Can Forget		—	$6		Atlantic 4022
9/28/74	59	7		17 I Just Can't Help Believin' .... Now That You're A Woman		—	$6		Atlantic 4204
				#9 Pop hit for **B.J. Thomas** in 1970					
4/12/75	60	8		18 It Takes A Whole Lotta Livin' In A House .... Since Never		—	$5		United Artists 617
8/7/76	66	7		19 Whispers And Grins .... Use Me Up		—	$5	■	Republic 256
11/6/76	84	6		20 Mahogany Bridge .... It's A Crying Shame (That People Change)		—	$5		Republic 311
1/15/77	21	12		21 I'm Gonna Love You Right Out Of This World .... Burning Bridges		—	$5		Republic 343
4/30/77	76	4		22 The Lady And The Baby .... That Woman Keeps This Cowboy Comin' Home		—	$5		Republic 382
6/18/77	49	7		23 I Love What My Woman Does To Me		—	$5		Republic 001
9/3/77	47	8		24 Do You Hear My Heart Beat .... They Went Together		—	$5		Republic 006
11/26/77+	24	12		25 You And Me Alone .... Time For Lovin'		—	$5		Republic 011
2/25/78	22	12		26 I'll Be There (When You Get Lonely) .... Just For The Love Of It		—	$5		Republic 015

DEBUT	PEAK	WKS	Gold	A-side (Chart Hit) / B-side	Pop	$	Pic	Label & Number
				ROGERS, David — Cont'd				
5/27/78	32	10		27 Let's Try To Remember ... That Woman Keeps This Cowboy Comin' Home	—	$5		Republic 020
9/9/78	31	9		28 When A Woman Cries ... The Power Of Positive Drinking	—	$5		Republic 029
3/3/79	18	14		29 Darlin' ... How Long Has It Been	—	$5		Republic 038
7/14/79	36	8		30 You Are My Rainbow ... If You Should Ask	—	$5		Republic 042
12/15/79+	39	9		31 You're Amazing ... Farewell Two Arms	—	$5		Republic 048
5/23/81	88	3		32 Houston Blue ... Here's To You Darling	—	$6		Kari 120
11/6/82	92	2		33 Crown Prince Of The Barroom ... Me And Ms. Chablis	—	$6		Music Master 012
2/19/83	67	7		34 Hold Me ... Chuck Berry Music	—	$6		Music Master 1004
6/4/83	71	5		35 You've Still Got Me	—	$6		Mr. Music 016
11/12/83	87	4		36 The Devil Is A Woman ... Time For Lovin'	—	$6		Mr. Music 018
3/3/84	72	4		37 I'm A Country Song	—	$6		Hal Kat Kountry 2083
				ROGERS, James '89				
				Born on 12/22/49 in Chattanooga, Tennessee; raised in Fort Oglethorpe, Georgia.				
12/9/89	72	5		Something's Got A Hold On Me ... This Is America	—	$5		Soundwaves 4830
				ROGERS, Jesse '49				
				Born on 3/5/11 in Waynesboro, Mississippi. Died in December 1973 (age 62).				
9/10/49	15	1		Wedding Bells ... J:15 Tennessee Polka	—	$20		Bluebird 32-0002
				JESSE ROGERS and his '49ers				

ROGERS, Kenny ★27★ '79

Born on 8/21/38 in Houston. Singer/songwriter/guitarist/actor. Member of the Kirby Stone Four and The New Christy Minstrels in the mid-1960s. Formed **The First Edition** in 1967. Went solo in 1973. Starred in the movie *Six Pack* and several TV movies including *The Gambler, Coward Of The County, Wild Horses* and *Rio Diablo*. Formerly married to Marianne Gordon of TV's *Hee-Haw*. Uncle of **Dann Rogers**. CMA 1978 & 1979 Vocal Duo of the Year (with **Dottie West**); 1979 Male Vocalist of the Year. Also see **America The Beautiful** and **USA For Africa**.

1)Coward Of The County 2)The Gambler 3)She Believes In Me 4)Islands In The Stream 5)Lucille

DEBUT	PEAK	WKS		A-side / B-side	Pop	$	Pic	Label & Number
				KENNY ROGERS AND THE FIRST EDITION:				
7/19/69	39	11		1 Ruby, Don't Take Your Love To Town ... Girl Get Ahold Of Yourself	6	$8		Reprise 0829
10/25/69	46	8		2 Ruben James ... Sunshine	26	$8		Reprise 0854
				some pressings show title as "Reuben James"				
7/14/73	69	6		3 Today I Started Loving You Again ... She Thinks I Still Care	—	$7		Jolly Rogers 1004
				KENNY ROGERS:				
12/13/75+	19	13		4 Love Lifted Me ... Home-Made Love	97	$5		United Artists 746
6/26/76	46	12		5 While The Feeling's Good ... I Would Like To See You Again	—	$5		United Artists 812
10/9/76	19	13		6 Laura (What's He Got That I Ain't Got?) ... I Wasn't Man Enough	—	$5		United Artists 868
1/29/77	❶²	20	●	7 Lucille ... Till I Get It Right	5	$5		United Artists 929
				CMA Award: Single of the Year				
8/6/77	❶¹	14		8 Daytime Friends ... We Don't Make Love Anymore	28	$5		United Artists 1027
10/22/77	9	15		9 Sweet Music Man ... Lying Again	44	$5		United Artists 1095
2/18/78	❶²	17		10 Every Time Two Fools Collide ... We Love Each Other	101	$5		United Artists 1137
				KENNY ROGERS & DOTTIE WEST				
6/3/78	❶¹	14		11 Love Or Something Like It ... Starting Again	32	$5		United Artists 1210
9/2/78	2¹	14		12 Anyone Who Isn't Me Tonight ... You And Me	—	$5		United Artists 1234
				KENNY ROGERS & DOTTIE WEST				
10/28/78	❶³	16		13 The Gambler ... Momma's Waiting	16	$5		United Artists 1250
2/17/79	❶¹	15		14 All I Ever Need Is You				
				(Hey Won't You Play) Another Somebody Done Somebody Wrong Song	102	$5		United Artists 1276
				KENNY ROGERS & DOTTIE WEST				
				#7 Pop hit for Sonny & Cher in 1971				
4/21/79	❶²	16	●	15 She Believes In Me ... Morgana Jones	5	$5	■	United Artists 1273
7/7/79	3	15		16 Til I Can Make It On My Own ... Midnight Flyer	—	$5		United Artists 1299
				KENNY ROGERS & DOTTIE WEST				
9/15/79	❶²	12		17 You Decorated My Life ... One Man's Woman	7	$5	■	United Artists 1315
11/17/79+	❶³	15	●	18 Coward Of The County ... I Want To Make You Smile	3	$5		United Artists 1327
4/5/80	3	14		19 Don't Fall In Love With A Dreamer ... Goin' Home To The Rock/Gideon Tanner (Rogers)	4	$5	■	United Artists 1345
				KENNY ROGERS with Kim Carnes				
6/28/80	4	14		20 Love The World Away ... Sayin' Goodbye/Requiem: Goin' Home To The Rock	14	$5		United Artists 1359
				from the movie *Urban Cowboy* starring John Travolta				
10/11/80	❶¹	14	●	21 Lady ... Sweet Music Man	❶⁶	$4	■	Liberty 1380
4/4/81	❶¹	15		22 What Are We Doin' In Love ... Choosin' Means Losin' (West)	14	$4		Liberty 1404
				DOTTIE WEST (with Kenny Rogers)				
6/20/81	❶²	15		23 I Don't Need You ... Without You In My Life	3	$4	■	Liberty 1415
9/12/81	5	14		24 Share Your Love With Me ... Greybeard	14	$4	■	Liberty 1430
				#13 Pop hit for Aretha Franklin in 1969				
11/14/81+	9	16		25 Blaze Of Glory ... The Good Life	66	$4		Liberty 1441
1/30/82	5	16		26 Through The Years ... So In Love With You	13	$4		Liberty 1444
7/10/82	❶¹	16		27 Love Will Turn You Around ... I Want A Son	13	$4	■	Liberty 1471
				from the movie *Six Pack* starring Rogers				
10/16/82	3	17		28 A Love Song ... The Fool In Me	47	$4		Liberty 1485
1/29/83	❶¹	17		29 We've Got Tonight ... You Are So Beautiful (Rogers)	6	$4		Liberty 1492
				KENNY ROGERS and SHEENA EASTON				
				#13 Pop hit for Bob Seger in 1979				
5/7/83	13	17		30 All My Life ... Farther I Go	37	$4	■	Liberty 1495
7/30/83	5	18		31 Scarlet Fever ... What I Learned From Loving You	94	$4		Liberty 1503

DEBUT	PEAK	WKS	Gold	A-side (Chart Hit)	B-side	Pop	$	Pic	Label & Number
				ROGERS, Kenny — Cont'd					
9/3/83	❶²	23	▲	32 Islands In The Stream .... *I Will Always Love You* (Rogers)		❶²	$4	■	RCA 13615
				KENNY ROGERS with Dolly Parton					
11/19/83+	20	17		33 You Were A Good Friend... *Sweet Music Man*		—	$4		Liberty 1511
1/14/84	3	17		34 Buried Treasure .... *This Woman* (Pop #23)		—	$4	■	RCA 13710
3/24/84	19	15		35 Together Again .... *Baby I'm A Want You*		—	$4		Liberty 1516
				KENNY ROGERS and Dottie West					
4/21/84	30	13		36 Eyes That See In The Dark .... *Hold Me*		79	$4		RCA 13774
6/30/84	11	19		37 Evening Star /		—			
		14		38 Midsummer Nights		—	$4		RCA 13832
11/10/84	70	10		39 What About Me? .... *The Rest Of Last Night* (Rogers)		15	$4	■	RCA 13899
				KENNY ROGERS with KIM CARNES and JAMES INGRAM					
12/15/84	53	7		40 The Greatest Gift Of All .... *White Christmas* (Parton) [X]		81	$4		RCA 13945
				KENNY ROGERS & DOLLY PARTON					
12/22/84+	❶¹	21		41 Crazy .... S:❶¹ / A:❶¹ *The Stranger*		79	$4	■	RCA 13975
4/13/85	37	12		42 Love Is What We Make It .... *A Stranger In My Place*		—	$4		Liberty 1524
5/25/85	❶¹	20		43 Real Love .... S:❶¹ / A:❶¹ *I Can't Be True* (Parton)		91	$4	■	RCA 14058
				DOLLY PARTON (with Kenny Rogers)					
7/20/85	57	8		44 Twentieth Century Fool .... *It Turns Me Inside Out*		—	$4		Liberty 1525
10/12/85+	❶¹	22		45 Morning Desire .... S:❶³ / A:❶¹ *People In Love*		72	$4	■	RCA 14194
1/18/86	47	9		46 Goodbye Marie .... *Abraham, Martin And John*		—	$4		Liberty 1526
2/22/86	❶¹	20		47 Tomb Of The Unknown Love .... S:❶¹ / A:❶¹ *One Perfect Song*		—	$4	■	RCA 14298
6/14/86	46	12		48 The Pride Is Back .... S:29 *Didn't We?*		—	$4	■	RCA 14384
				KENNY ROGERS with NICKIE RYDER					
				tune used for a Chrysler jingle					
10/18/86	53	12		49 They Don't Make Them Like They Used To .... *Just The Thought Of Losing You*		—	$4	■	RCA 5016
				from the movie *Tough Guys* starring Burt Lancaster and Kirk Douglas					
12/27/86+	2²	21		50 Twenty Years Ago .... A:2 / S:5 *The Heart Of The Matter*		—	$4		RCA 5078
6/27/87	❶¹	17		51 Make No Mistake, She's Mine .... S:3 *You're My Love*		—	$4	□	RCA 5209
				RONNIE MILSAP & KENNY ROGERS					
				#51 Pop hit for Barbra Streisand & Kim Carnes in 1985					
10/10/87	2²	19		52 I Prefer The Moonlight .... S:5 *We're Doin' Alright*		—	$4		RCA 5258
3/5/88	6	16		53 The Factory .... S:12 *One More Day*		—	$4		RCA 6832
8/13/88	26	15		54 When You Put Your Heart In It .... S:25 *(instrumental)* (w/Jim Horn)		—	$4	■	Reprise 27812
9/3/88+	86	5		55 I Don't Call Him Daddy .... *We're Doin' Alright*		—	$4		RCA 8390
5/27/89	30	12		56 Planet Texas .... *When You Put Your Heart In It*		—	$4	■	Reprise 27690
8/26/89	8	26		57 The Vows Go Unbroken (Always True To You) .... *One Night*		—	$4		Reprise 22828
9/30/89	28	15		58 If I Ever Fall In Love Again .... *Just Another Woman In Love*		—	$4		Capitol 44432
				ANNE MURRAY with Kenny Rogers					
2/17/90	25	13		59 Maybe .... *If I Knew Then What I Know Now*		—	$4	■	Reprise 19972 (v)
				KENNY ROGERS (with Holly Dunn)					
8/18/90	21	20		60 Love Is Strange .... *Walk Away*		—	$4	■	Reprise 19760 (v)
				KENNY ROGERS and DOLLY PARTON					
				#11 Pop hit for Mickey & Sylvia in 1957					
2/2/91	69	4		61 Lay My Body Down .... *Crazy In Love*		—	$4		Reprise 19504
11/30/91+	11	20		62 If You Want To Find Love .... *Sunshine*		—	$4		Reprise 19080
				Linda Davis (backing vocal)					
12/28/96	55	2		63 Mary, Did You Know .... [X]		—			album cut
				KENNY ROGERS with Wynonna					
				from the album *The Gift* on Magnatone 108					
4/17/99	26	20		64 The Greatest		—			album cut
9/11/99	67	5		65 Slow Dance More		—			album cut
10/30/99+	❶¹	37		66 Buy Me A Rose		40			album cut
				KENNY ROGERS with ALISON KRAUSS & BILLY DEAN					
				above 3 from the album *She Rides Wild Horses* on Dreamcatcher 004					
7/1/00	32	20		67 He Will, She Knows		—			album cut
1/27/01	26	23		68 There You Go Again		—			album cut
8/18/01	47	9		69 Beautiful (All That You Could Be)		—			album cut
11/3/01	39	17		70 Homeland		—			album cut
				above 4 from the album *There You Go Again* on Dreamcatcher 006					
				ROGERS, Ronnie '82					
				Born Randall Rogers in Nashville. Singer/songwriter.					
11/21/81+	39	11		1 Gonna Take My Angel Out Tonight............................. *Neon Fool*		—	$5		Lifesong 45094
3/20/82	37	9		2 My Love Belongs To You .... *Ramblers Never Change*		—	$5		Lifesong 45095
6/12/82	54	8		3 First Time Around .... *Stoned Little Rat*		—	$5		Lifesong 45116
9/25/82	86	3		4 Happy Country Birthday /		—	$5		
10/16/82	86	3		5 Takin' It Back To The Hills		—	$5		Lifesong 45118
6/25/83	66	7		6 Inside Story .... *Dixieland Delight*		—	$4		Epic 03953
9/19/87	57	8		7 Good Timin' Shoes .... *Eyes Of The Young*		—	$4		MTM 72094
8/6/88	82	2		8 Let's Be Bad Tonight .... *Honeymoon Mornin'*		—	$4		MTM 72110

DEBUT	PEAK	WKS	Gold	A-side (Chart Hit)	B-side	Pop	$	Pic	Label & Number
	★366★			**ROGERS, Roy** — '47 Born Leonard Franklin Slye on 11/5/11 in Cincinnati. Died on 7/6/98 (age 86). Popular "singing cowboy" who starred in several movies. Formed the Pioneer Trio, in 1934 with Bob Nolan and Tim Spencer, which evolved into the **Sons Of The Pioneers**; group appeared in several movies. Went solo in 1937; briefly known as "Dick Weston." By 1938, known as "Roy Rogers." Married actress Dale Evans on 12/31/47; stars of *The Roy Rogers Show* TV show (1951-57) and *The Roy Rogers & Dale Evans Show* in 1962. Elected to the Country Music Hall of Fame in 1988. 1)My Chickashay Gal 2)Blue Shadows On The Trail 3)A Little White Cross On The Hill					
7/6/46	7	1		1 A Little White Cross On The Hill	I Can't Go On This Way	—	$25		RCA Victor 20-1872
3/15/47	4	1		2 My Chickashay Gal	I Never Had A Chance	—	$25		RCA Victor 20-2124
6/12/48	6	14		3 Blue Shadows On The Trail /	S:6 / J:7	—			
6/12/48	13	4		4 (There'll Never Be Another) Pecos Bill .... S:13 ROY ROGERS and The Sons Of The Pioneers (above 2) above 2 from the movie *Melody Time* starring Rogers; 45 rpm: 48-0035		—	$25		RCA Victor 20-2780
2/4/50	8	1		5 Stampede The Sons Of The Pioneers (backing vocals); 78 rpm: 21-0154	A:8 Church Music	—	$30		RCA Victor 48-0161
9/26/70	35	10		6 Money Can't Buy Love	You And Me Against The World	—	$8		Capitol 2895
1/30/71	12	11		7 Lovenworth	Vision At The Peace Table	—	$8		Capitol 3016
6/26/71	47	11		8 Happy Anniversary	If I Ever Get That Close Again	—	$8		Capitol 3117
2/26/72	73	4		9 These Are The Good Old Days	Pass It On	—	$8		Capitol 3263
12/21/74+	15	13		10 Hoppy, Gene And Me	Good News, Bad News [N]	65	$6		20th Century 2154
				tribute to Hopalong Cassidy, **Gene Autry** and **Roy Rogers**					
8/23/80	80	4		11 Ride Concrete Cowboy, Ride	Deliverance Of The Wildwood Flower	—	$5		MCA 41294
				ROY ROGERS And The Sons Of The Pioneers from the movie *Smokey & The Bandit II* starring **Burt Reynolds**					
11/2/91	42	10		12 Hold On Partner	Alive And Kickin'	—	$4		RCA 62061
				ROY ROGERS & CLINT BLACK					
				ROGERS, Smokey — '49 Born Eugene Rogers on 3/23/17 in McMinnville, Tennessee. Died on 11/23/93 (age 76). Singer/songwriter/banjo player.					
1/1/49	8	4		A Little Bird Told Me #1 Pop hit for **Evelyn Knight** in 1949	J:8 Baby Me, Baby	—	$20		Capitol 15326
				ROHRS, Donnie — '81 Born in 1946 in Covina, California. Singer/guitarist/pianist.					
12/16/78	95	3		1 Hey Baby #1 Pop hit for **Bruce Channel** in 1962		—	$7		Ad-Korp 1258
5/2/81	85	6		2 Waltzes And Western Swing	Love Me Baby Tonight	—	$7		Pacific Chall. 4504
				ROLAND, Adrian — '60 Born in Lamarque, Texas. Died on 7/1/66.					
9/19/60	19	4		Imitation Of Love	It Takes More Than A While	—	$20		Allstar 7207
				RONE, Roger — '89					
8/26/89	83	3		Holdin' On To Nothin'	Here I Stand	—	$6		True 98
				RONICK, Holly — '89					
11/4/89	86	2		Ain't No One Like Me In Tennessee		—	$6	■	Happy Man 822
	★179★			**RONSTADT, Linda** — '75 Born on 7/15/46 in Tucson, Arizona. Singer/actress. While in high school formed folk trio The Three Ronstadts (with sister and brother). To Los Angeles in 1964. Formed the Stone Poneys with Bobby Kimmel (guitar) and Ken Edwards (keyboards); recorded for Sidewalk in 1966. Went solo in 1968. In 1971 formed backing band with Glenn Frey, **Don Henley**, Randy Meisner and Bernie Leadon (later became the **Eagles**). Charted 35 pop hits from 1967-90. Acted in the movie *Pirates Of Penzance*. Also see **Hoyt Axton**. 1)When Will I Be Loved 2)To Know Him Is To Love Him 3)Blue Bayou 4)I Can't Help It (If I'm Still In Love With You) 5)Telling Me Lies					
3/2/74	20	12		1 Silver Threads And Golden Needles	Don't Cry Now	67	$5		Asylum 11032
12/21/74+	2^1	17		2 I Can't Help It (If I'm Still In Love With You)	You're No Good (Pop #1)	—	$5		Capitol 3990
4/19/75	❶^1	15		3 When Will I Be Loved / #8 Pop hit for **The Everly Brothers** in 1960		2^2			
9/13/75	54	7		4 It Doesn't Matter Anymore #13 Pop hit for **Buddy Holly** in 1959		47	$5		Capitol 4050
9/13/75	5	15		5 Love Is A Rose	Heat Wave (Pop #5)	63	$5		Asylum 45282
1/3/76	11	12		6 Tracks Of My Tears / #16 Pop hit for The Miracles in 1965		25			
1/3/76	12	12		7 The Sweetest Gift LINDA RONSTADT AND EMMYLOU HARRIS		—	$6		Asylum 45295
9/4/76	27	11		8 That'll Be The Day #1 Pop hit for Buddy Holly in 1957	Try Me Again	11	$5		Asylum 45340
12/18/76+	6	15		9 Crazy	Someone To Lay Down Beside Me (Pop #42)	—	$5		Asylum 45361
9/17/77	2^2	19 ▲		10 Blue Bayou #29 Pop hit for **Roy Orbison** in 1963	Old Paint	3	$5		Asylum 45431
11/12/77	81	6		11 It's So Easy written by Buddy Holly	Lo Siento Mi Vida	5	$5		Asylum 45438
2/18/78	46	9		12 Poor Poor Pitiful Me	Simple Man, Simple Dream	31	$5		Asylum 45462
5/13/78	8	13		13 I Never Will Marry	Tumbling Dice (Pop #32)	—	$5		Asylum 45479
9/2/78	41	8		14 Back In The U.S.A. #37 Pop hit for Chuck Berry in 1959	White Rhythm & Blues	16	$5	■	Asylum 45519
12/2/78	85	5		15 Ooh Baby Baby #16 Pop hit for The Miracles in 1965	Blowing Away	7	$5		Asylum 45546
3/10/79	59	6		16 Love Me Tender	Just One Look (Pop #44)	—	$5		Asylum 46011

DEBUT	PEAK	WKS	Gold	A-side (Chart Hit) .... B-side	Pop	$	Pic	Label & Number
				RONSTADT, Linda — Cont'd				
3/1/80	42	8		17 Rambler Gambler .... *How Do I Make You* (Pop #10)	—	$4	■	Asylum 46602
10/16/82	27	12		18 Sometimes You Just Can't Win .... *Get Closer* (Pop #29)	—	$4	■	Asylum 69948
				LINDA RONSTADT AND JOHN DAVID SOUTHER				
1/29/83	84	3		19 I Knew When .... *Talk To Me Of Mendocino*	37	$4	■	Asylum 69853
				#14 Pop hit for **Billy Joe Royal** in 1965				
				DOLLY PARTON, LINDA RONSTADT, EMMYLOU HARRIS:				
2/21/87	❶¹	19		20 To Know Him Is To Love Him .... S:❶¹ / A:❶¹ *Farther Along*	—	$4	■	Warner 28492
				#1 Pop hit for The Teddy Bears in 1958				
5/30/87	3	18		21 Telling Me Lies .... S:10 *Rosewood Casket*	—	$4		Warner 28371
9/26/87	5	22		22 Those Memories Of You .... S:10 *My Dear Companion*	—	$4	■	Warner 28248
3/26/88	6	18		23 Wildflowers .... S:13 *Hobo's Meditation*	—	$4		Warner 27970
4/29/95	61	9		24 Walk On .... *The Waiting*	—	$4	■	Elektra 64427 (v)
				LINDA RONSTADT				
				ROOFTOP SINGERS, The '63				
				Folk trio from New York City: Erik Darling, Lynne Taylor and Willard Svanoe. Taylor died in 1982 (age 54).				
2/23/63	23	4	●	Walk Right In .... *Cool Water*	❶²	$12	□	Vanguard 35017
				ROSE, Fred '45				
				Born on 8/24/1898 in Evansville, Indiana. Died of a heart attack on 12/1/54 (age 56). Singer/prolific songwriter. Formed Acuff-Rose music publishing company with **Roy Acuff** in 1942; they also formed the Hickory record label in 1953. Elected to the Country Music Hall of Fame in 1961. Recorded as **The Rambling Rogue**.				
10/27/45	5	1		Tender Hearted Sue .... *You're Only In My Arms (To Cry On My Shoulder)*	—	$20		Okeh 6747
				THE RAMBLING ROGUE				
				ROSE, Pam '80				
				Born Pamela Rose Thacker in Chattanooga; raised in Eau Gallie, Florida. Member of **Calamity Jane**.				
7/23/77	83	5		1 Midnight Flight .... *Sing, Feelin', Sing*	—	$5		Capitol 4440
11/19/77	93	3		2 Runaway Heart .... *Break Down The Walls*	—	$5		Capitol 4491
1/5/80	52	7		3 It's Not Supposed To Be That Way .... *We're Gonna Try It Tonight*	—	$4		Epic 50819
				Willie Nelson (guest vocal)				
4/19/80	60	6		4 I'm Not Through Loving You Yet .... *When Love's In Your Heart, It's In Your Eyes*	—	$4		Epic 50861
				ROSE, Richard and Gary '88				
2/13/88	81	3		Younger Man, Older Woman .... *Until You're Mine*	—	$4		Capitol 44118
				ROSS, Charlie '76				
				Born in Greenville, Mississippi. Worked as a DJ.				
2/28/76	13	12		1 Without Your Love (Mr. Jordan) .... *Sneaking Round Corners*	42	$6		Big Tree 16056
6/5/82	33	13		2 The High Cost Of Loving .... *She Sure Got Away With My Heart*	—	$5		Town House 1057
9/18/82	45	9		3 Are We In Love (Or Am I) .... *Shoot First, Ask Questions Later*	—	$5		Town House 1061
1/8/83	70	5		4 The Name Of The Game Is Cheating .... *Somebody Loves You*	—	$5		Town House 1063
				ROSS, Jeris '75				
				Born in East Alton, Illinois. Female singer.				
3/11/72	75	2		1 Brand New Key .... *Baby's Thinking Leaving*	—	$6		Cartwheel 206
				#1 Pop hit for Melanie in 1971				
6/24/72	58	12		2 Old Fashioned Love Song .... *I Gotta Go To Memphis*	—	$6		Cartwheel 214
				#4 Pop hit for Three Dog Night in 1971				
12/22/73+	58	7		3 Moontan .... *People Just Like You*	—	$5		ABC 11397
4/26/75	17	14		4 Pictures On Paper .... *Won't You Meet Me At The Church*	—	$5		ABC 12064
10/11/75	66	8		5 I'd Rather Be Picked Up Here (Than Be Put Down At Home) .... *Sing A Love Song To Your Baby*	—	$5		ABC/Dot 17573
10/29/77	77	6		6 I Think I'll Say Goodbye .... *Rock Me*	—	$5		Gazelle 431
9/15/79	94	4		7 Little Bit More .... *Ease Me To The Ground*	—	$5		Door Knob 108
				#11 Pop hit for **Dr. Hook** in 1976				
1/26/80	75	5		8 You Win Again .... *Rock Me*	—	$5		Door Knob 117
				#22 Pop hit for **Fats Domino** in 1962				
				ROSS, Roy — see FOLEY, Red				
				ROVERS, The '81				
				Irish-born folk group formed in Calgary, Alberta, Canada: Jimmy Ferguson (vocals), brothers Will (vocals, guitar) and George (guitar) Millar, their cousin Joe Millar (bass) and Wilcil McDowell (accordian). First known as The Irish Rovers (1968 pop hit "The Unicorn"). Ferguson died in October 1997 (age 57).				
2/28/81	45	11		1 Wasn't That A Party .... *Matchstalk Men And Matchstalk Cats And Dogs*	37	$4		Epic 51007
3/13/82	77	4		2 Pain In My Past .... *Daddies (Bobby's Song)*	—	$4		Epic 02728
				ROWE, Stacey '79				
6/30/79	96	2		I Couldn't Live Without Your Love	—	$7		Sabre 4510
				ROWELL, Ernie '81				
				Born in Auburn, Alabama. Singer/songwriter/guitarist.				
7/24/71	74	2		1 Going Back To Louisiana .... *This Bottle Hides The Weakness In Me*	—	$7		Prize 08
9/29/79	91	4		2 I'm Leavin' You Alone .... *He's The One*	—	$6		Grass 05
5/9/81	59	6		3 Music In The Mountains .... *He's The One*	—	$6		Grass 07
10/3/87	86	3		4 You Left My Heart For Broke	—	$6		Revolver 016
				ROWLAND, Dave — see DAVE & SUGAR				

DEBUT	PEAK	WKS	Gold	A-side (Chart Hit) ... B-side	Pop	$	Pic	Label & Number

ROY, Bobbie '72
Born Barbara Elaine Roy on 7/27/53 in Landstuhl, Germany, where her father was in the Army. Moved to Elkins, West Virginia, in 1960.

6/3/72	32	9		1 One Woman's Trash (Another Woman's Treasure) .... Due To A Heartache	—	$6		Capitol 3301
9/23/72	58	8		2 Leavin' On Your Mind .... Candle In The Wind	—	$6		Capitol 3428
12/16/72+	62	5		3 I Like Everything About Loving You .... I Wanted So To Say It	—	$6		Capitol 3477
1/27/73	51	5		4 I Am Woman .... Till I Get It Right	—	$6		Capitol 3513

#1 Pop hit for **Helen Reddy** in 1972

ROYAL, Billy Joe ★250★ '89
Born on 4/3/42 in Valdosta, Georgia; raised in Marietta, Georgia. Singer/songwriter/guitarist/pianist/drummer. Charted 9 pop hits from 1965-78.

1) Tell It Like It Is   2) Till I Can't Take It Anymore   3) Love Has No Right

10/26/85+	10	22		1 Burned Like A Rocket S:6 / A:11 Lonely Loving You	—	$4		Atlantic Amer. 99599
5/3/86	41	16		2 Boardwalk Angel .... S:25 Out Of Sight And On My Mind	—	$4		Atlantic Amer. 99555
8/23/86	14	24		3 I Miss You Already .... S:9 / A:17 Another Endless Night	—	$4		Atlantic Amer. 99519
2/7/87	11	26		4 Old Bridges Burn Slow .... S:❶¹ / A:11 We've Both Got A Lot To Learn	—	$4	■	Atlantic Amer. 99485
6/27/87	23	15		5 Members Only .... S:21 Funny Face	—	$4		Mercury 888680

DONNA FARGO AND BILLY JOE ROYAL

10/17/87+	5	23		6 I'll Pin A Note On Your Pillow S:❶² A Place For The Heartache	—	$4	■	Atlantic Amer. 99404
3/12/88	10	22		7 Out Of Sight And On My Mind S:❶¹ She Don't Cry Like She Used To	—	$4		Atlantic Amer. 99364
8/27/88	17	17		8 It Keeps Right On Hurtin' .... S:❶¹ Let It Rain	—	$4		Atlantic Amer. 99295

#3 Pop hit for **Johnny Tillotson** in 1962

| 2/4/89 | 2² | 17 | | 9 Tell It Like It Is   I Was Losing You | — | $4 | ■ | Atlantic Amer. 99242 |

#2 Pop hit for **Aaron Neville** in 1967

5/20/89	4	24		10 Love Has No Right Cross My Heart And Hope To Try	—	$4	■	Atlantic Amer. 99217
9/30/89+	2¹	26		11 Till I Can't Take It Anymore He Don't Know	—	$4		Atlantic 88815
5/12/90	17	21		12 Searchin' For Some Kind Of Clue .... This Too Shall Pass	—	$4	■	Atlantic 87933 (v)
9/15/90	33	20		13 Ring Where A Ring Used To Be .... We Need To Walk	—	$4	■	Atlantic 87867 (v)
1/26/91	29	14		14 If The Jukebox Took Teardrops .... How Could You Leave Me	—	$4	■	Atlantic 87770 (v)
3/21/92	51	8		15 I'm Okay (And Gettin' Better)	—			album cut

from the album *Billy Joe Royal* on Atlantic 82327

RUCKER, Dwight — see MALCHAK, Tim

RUE, Arnie '79
Born in Massachusetts; raised in California.

| 5/5/79 | 56 | 6 | | 1 Spare A Little Lovin' (On A Fool) .... To Each His Own | — | $5 | | NSD 19 |
| 11/17/79 | 74 | 4 | | 2 Rodle-Odeo-Home .... Yesterday's Dreams | — | $5 | | NSD 32 |

RUSHING, Jim '81
Born in Lubbock, Texas. Singer/songwriter.

| 9/27/80 | 81 | 2 | | 1 Dixie Dirt .... Two Hearts Don't Always Make A Pair | — | $5 | | Ovation 1153 |
| 12/27/80+ | 56 | 8 | | 2 I've Loved Enough To Know .... Two Hearts Don't Always Make A Pair | — | $5 | | Ovation 1161 |

RUSHLOW, Tim '01
Born on 10/6/66 in Arlington, Texas. Former lead singer of **Little Texas**.

4/1/00	60	5		1 When You Love Me	—			album cut
11/4/00+	8	28		2 She Misses Him	—			album cut
7/21/01	43	15		3 Crazy Life .... S:24 (acoustic version) / She Misses Him	—	$4	★	Scream 7
12/29/01+	52	8		4 Love, Will (The Package)	—			album cut

all of above from the album *Crazy Life* on Atlantic 83326

RUSSELL, Bobby '71
Born on 4/19/41 in Nashville. Died of a heart attack on 11/19/92 (age 51). Singer/prolific songwriter. Married to **Vicki Lawrence** from 1972-74.

11/9/68	64	8		1 1432 Franklin Pike Circle Hero .... Let's Talk About Them	36	$7		Elf 90,020
3/1/69	66	3		2 Carlie .... Ain't Society Great?	115	$7		Elf 90,023
8/16/69	34	9		3 Better Homes And Gardens .... Summer Sweet	—	$7		Elf 90,031
7/10/71	24	13		4 Saturday Morning Confusion [N] Little Ole Song About Love	28	$6		United Artists 50788
8/18/73	93	3		5 Mid American Manufacturing Tycoon .... Ships In The Night	—	$5		Columbia 45901

RUSSELL, Clifford '83
Born in Knoxville, Tennessee.

| 2/12/83 | 97 | 2 | | She Feels Like A New Man Tonight .... Sometimes When We Touch | — | $7 | ■ | Sugartree 0509 |

RUSSELL, Jimmy '76

| 12/18/76 | 99 | 4 | | You've Got To Move Two Mountains .... It's Been So Long Darling | — | $6 | | Charta 103 |

#20 Pop hit for **Marv Johnson** in 1960

RUSSELL, Johnny ★229★ '73
Born on 1/23/40 in Moorhead, Mississippi; raised in Fresno, California. Died of diabetes on 7/3/2001 (age 61). Singer/songwriter/guitarist. Married **Beverly Heckel** in 1977. Joined the *Grand Ole Opry* in 1985.

1) Rednecks, White Socks And Blue Ribbon Beer   2) Catfish John   3) Hello I Love You   4) The Baptism Of Jesse Taylor   5) That's How My Baby Builds A Fire

| 8/21/71 | 64 | 3 | | 1 Mr. And Mrs. Untrue .... I'm Stayin' | — | $6 | | RCA Victor 1000 |
| 12/11/71+ | 57 | 9 | | 2 What A Price .... Listening To The Rain | — | $6 | | RCA Victor 0570 |

#22 Pop hit for **Fats Domino** in 1961

4/1/72	59	7		3 Mr. Fiddle Man .... Crying Takes More Practice Everyday	—	$6		RCA Victor 0665
7/1/72	36	12		4 Rain Falling On Me .... I'll Cry To That	—	$6		RCA Victor 0729
11/11/72+	12	15		5 Catfish John .... Promises Of Your Love	—	$6		RCA Victor 0810
3/24/73	31	10		6 Chained .... (Drinkin' A Beer) And Singing A Country Song	—	$6		RCA Victor 0908

DEBUT	PEAK	WKS	Gold	A-side (Chart Hit)...B-side	Pop	$	Pic	Label & Number
				RUSSELL, Johnny — Cont'd				
8/4/73	4	19		7 Rednecks, White Socks And Blue Ribbon Beer ....She's A Natural Woman	—	$6		RCA Victor 0021
11/10/73+	14	13		8 The Baptism Of Jesse Taylor ....Making Plans	—	$6		RCA Victor 0165
4/13/74	39	10		9 She's In Love With A Rodeo Man ....Someday I'll Sober Up	—	$6		RCA Victor 0248
9/14/74	38	10		10 She Burn't The Little Roadside Tavern Down ....It Sure Seemed Right	—	$5		RCA Victor 10038
12/21/74+	23	11		11 That's How My Baby Builds A Fire ....Act Naturally	—	$5		RCA Victor 10135
4/26/75	13	17		12 Hello I Love You ....You Ain't Got No Class	—	$5		RCA Victor 10258
10/11/75	45	10		13 Our Marriage Was A Failure ....Catfish John	—	$5		RCA Victor 10403
2/21/76	57	9		14 I'm A Trucker ....Your Fool	—	$5		RCA Victor 10563
5/22/76	45	8		15 This Man And Woman Thing ....Over Georgia	—	$5		RCA Victor 10667
12/25/76+	32	10		16 The Son Of Hickory Holler's Tramp /				
		10		17 I Wonder How She's Doing Now	—	$5		RCA 10853
				#40 Pop hit for O.C. Smith in 1968				
6/25/77	91	3		18 Obscene Phone Call ....If I Want To Get It Right	—	$5		RCA 10984
				Beverly Heckel (female vocal)				
12/10/77+	64	9		19 Leona ....Your Fool	—	$5		RCA 11160
5/13/78	24	12		20 You'll Be Back (Every Night In My Dreams) ....Is Anybody Leaving San Antone	—	$5		Polydor 14475
11/25/78+	29	12		21 How Deep In Love Am I? ....Shall We Gather At The Ridge	—	$4		Mercury 55045
5/19/79	57	6		22 I Might Be Awhile In New Orleans ....Make Up My Mind	—	$4		Mercury 55060
11/17/79	56	7		23 Ain't No Way To Make A Bad Love Grow ....Keep The Change	—	$4		Mercury 57008
3/15/80	57	6		24 While The Choir Sang The Hymn (I Thought Of Her) ....Falsely Accused	—	$4		Mercury 57016
6/21/80	59	7		25 We're Back In Love Again ....Love Makes A Fool Of Us All	—	$4		Mercury 57026
12/13/80+	57	9		26 Song Of The South ....I'm Gettin' Holes In My Boots (From Climbing The Walls)	—	$4		Mercury 57038
4/18/81	49	9		27 Here's To The Horses ....Take Me To Your Heart	—	$4		Mercury 57050
7/25/87	72	4		28 Butterbeans ....Stone Country	—	$4		16th Avenue 70401
				JOHNNY RUSSELL & LITTLE DAVID WILKINS				
				RUSSELL, Leon '79				
				Born on 4/2/41 in Lawton, Oklahoma. Rock singer/songwriter/multi-instrumentalist sessionman. Also recorded as **Hank Wilson**.				
9/29/73	57	11		1 Roll In My Sweet Baby's Arms	78	$6		Shelter 7336
1/12/74	68	8		2 A Six Pack To Go ....Uncle Pen	—	$6		Shelter 7338
				HANK WILSON (above 2)				
7/7/79	❶¹	13		3 Heartbreak Hotel ....Sioux City Sue	—	$5		Columbia 11023
				WILLIE NELSON AND LEON RUSSELL				
7/28/84	63	12		4 Good Time Charlie's Got The Blues ....Ain't No Love In The City	—	$4		Paradise 628
10/27/84	91	2		5 Wabash Cannonball ....Tennessee Waltz	—	$4		Paradise 629
				WILLIE NELSON & HANK WILSON				
				RUSTY & DOUG — see KERSHAW, Doug				
				RUUD, Nancy '81				
				Born in Montana.				
7/12/80	88	3		1 A Good Love Is Like A Good Song	—	$6		Calico 16425
10/18/80	90	3		2 Always, Sometimes, Never ....Am I Too Late	—	$6		Calico 16493
4/4/81	87	2		3 I'm Gonna Hang Up This Heartache	—	$6		C&R 101
6/20/81	83	2		4 Blue As The Blue In Your Eyes	—	$6		C&R 102
				RYAN, Charlie '60				
				Born on 12/19/15 in Graceville, Minnesota; raised in Montana.				
9/5/60	14	6		Hot Rod Lincoln ....Thru The Mill [N-S]	33	$20		4 Star 1733
				CHARLIE RYAN and The Timberline Riders				
				first released in 1955 on Souvenir 101 ($40)				
				RYAN, Jamey '67				
				Born in Texas. Female singer. Regular on TV's Hee-Haw.				
8/19/67	62	3		1 You're Lookin' For A Plaything ....Growin' Pains	—	$8		Columbia 44169
5/23/70	75	2		2 Holy Cow ....All A Woman Asks	—	$8		Show Biz 232
				#23 Pop hit for Lee Dorsey in 1966				
8/11/73	88	2		3 Keep On Loving Me ....You Just Moved A Mountain	—	$6		Atlantic 4001
				RYAN, Tim '90				
				Born Tim Ryan Roullier on 2/4/64 in Montana. Singer/songwriter/guitarist.				
8/4/90	42	17		1 Dance In Circles ....Honky Tonk Highway	—	$4	▌	Epic 73372 (v)
12/22/90+	69	6		2 Breakin' All The Way ....A Little Love Won't Hurt A Thing	—	$4	▌	Epic 73578 (v)
9/21/91	68	3		3 Seventh Direction ....No More Sad Songs	—	$4		Epic 73959
1/18/92	65	4		4 I Will Love You Anyhow ....Heartache Goin' Downtown Tonight	—	$4		Epic 74124
1/23/93	71	4		5 Idle Hands ....One Life To Live	—	$4		BNA 62413
				RYAN, Wesley '81				
7/25/81	82	4		Nothin' To Do But Just Lie ....Take Good Care Of My Baby	—	$5		NSD 93
				RYDER, Nickie — see ROGERS, Kenny				
		★236★		**RYLES, John Wesley** '77				
				Born on 12/2/50 in Bastrop, Louisiana. Singer/songwriter/guitarist.				
				1)Once In A Lifetime Thing 2)Kay 3)Shine On Me 4)Liberated Woman 5)I've Just Been Wasting My Time				
				JOHN WESLEY RYLES I:				
12/7/68+	9	17		1 Kay ....Come On Home	83	$7		Columbia 44682
				also see #12 below				
5/17/69	55	8		2 Heaven Below ....A Mighty Fortress Is Our Love	—	$7		Columbia 44819
12/13/69+	57	7		3 The Weakest Kind Of Man ....We'll Try A Little Bit Harder	—	$7		Columbia 45018

DEBUT	PEAK	WKS	Gold	A-side (Chart Hit)	B-side	Pop	$	Pic	Label & Number
				RYLES, John Wesley — Cont'd					
5/2/70	17	10		4 I've Just Been Wasting My Time	The House On The Hill	—	$7		Columbia 45119
11/20/71	39	10		5 Reconsider Me	Mobile	—	$7		Plantation 81
				JOHN WESLEY RYLES:					
1/24/76	83	7		6 Tell It Like It Is	Run Right Back	—	$7		Music Mill 214
				#2 Pop hit for Aaron Neville in 1967					
7/10/76	72	6		7 When A Man Loves A Woman	I'm Gonna Make It Without You	—	$7		Music Mill 240
				#1 Pop hit for Percy Sledge in 1966					
3/26/77	18	17		8 Fool	I Fought The Law	—	$5		ABC/Dot 17679
8/13/77	5	16		9 Once In A Lifetime Thing	Wild Rose Of Virginia	—	$5		ABC/Dot 17698
12/24/77+	13	12		10 Shine On Me (The Sun Still Shines When It Rains)	Warming Love	—	$5		ABC/Dot 17733
4/15/78	63	8		11 Easy	Making Love Don't Make It Love	—	$5		ABC 12348
7/15/78	50	7		12 Kay	Next Time [R]	—	$5		ABC 12375
				new version of #1 above					
10/7/78	45	7		13 Someday You Will	That All Over Feeling	—	$5		ABC 12410
12/23/78+	33	11		14 Love Ain't Made For Fools	It's Raining Outside Your Door	—	$5		ABC 12432
6/2/79	14	14		15 Liberated Woman	She's On My Mind	—	$5		MCA 41033
10/13/79	20	12		16 You Are Always On My Mind	My Angel Got Her Wings Today	—	$5		MCA 41124
2/23/80	24	10		17 Perfect Strangers	Nothing But Love	—	$4		MCA 41184
7/19/80	52	8		18 May I Borrow Some Sugar From You	Let The Night Begin	—	$4		MCA 41278
11/8/80	54	10		19 Cheater's Trap	Two Beds - Too Bad	—	$4		MCA 51013
4/4/81	80	3		20 Somewhere To Come When It Rains	Your Old Love Letters	—	$4		MCA 51080
7/18/81	78	3		21 Mathilda	I'm Not That Crazy Anymore	—	$4		MCA 51128
				#47 Pop hit for Cookie & His Cupcakes in 1959					
6/26/82	76	4		22 We've Got To Start Meeting Like This	—	—	$5		Primero 1004
12/4/82	80	3		23 Just Once	Hideaway	—	$5		Primero 1016
				#17 Pop hit for Quincy Jones in 1981					
8/25/84	78	4		24 She Took It Too Well	—	—	$4		16th Avenue 500
5/9/87	36	15		25 Midnight Blue	Starting Over Again	—	$4		Warner 28377
12/5/87+	20	16		26 Louisiana Rain	Strong Heart	—	$4		Warner 28228
6/4/88	53	7		27 Nobody Knows	Freedom Feels Like Loneliness Today	—	$4		Warner 27869

S

DEBUT	PEAK	WKS	Gold	A-side	B-side	Pop	$	Pic	Label & Number
				SADLER, Sammy '89					
				Born 8/23/67 in Memphis.					
1/7/89	70	4		1 Tell It Like It Is	—	—	$5		Evergreen 1088
				#2 Pop hit for Aaron Neville in 1967					
7/1/89	89	3		2 You Made It Easy	—	—	$5		Evergreen 1093
1/13/90	86	1		3 Once In A Lifetime Thing	You Made It Easy	—	$5		Evergreen 1106
				SADLER, SSgt Barry '66					
				Born on 11/1/40 in Carlsbad, New Mexico. Died of heart failure on 11/5/89 (age 49). Staff Sergeant of U.S. Army Special Forces (aka Green Berets). Served in Vietnam until leg injury.					
2/19/66	2²	14	●	1 The Ballad Of The Green Berets	Letter From Vietnam	❶⁵	$7	■	RCA Victor 8739
5/28/66	46	4		2 The "A" Team	An Empty Glass	28	$7	■	RCA Victor 8804
				SAHM, Doug '76					
				Born on 11/5/41 in San Antonio, Texas. Died of heart failure on 11/18/99 (age 58). Singer/songwriter/guitarist. Formed the Sir Douglas Quintet in 1965 (charted 4 pop hits from 1965-69). Formed a new Texas Tornados group with all-star lineup in 1990.					
10/16/76	100	1		Cowboy Peyton Place	I Love The Way You Love (The Way I Love You)	—	$6		ABC/Dot 17656
				DOUG SAHM & THE TEXAS TORNADOS					
				ST. JOHN, Tommy '83					
				Born on 3/23/62 in Oak Ridge, Tennessee.					
1/8/83	55	9		1 The Light Of My Life (Has Gone Out Tonight)	Waitin' In Your Welfare Line	—	$4		RCA 13405
4/16/83	78	4		2 Where'd Ya Stay Last Night	She Can't Make Me What I Ain't	—	$4		RCA 13475
7/23/83	86	2		3 Stars On The Water	Wallflower	—	$4		RCA 13561
				ST. MARIE, Susan '77					
				Niece of Tommy Overstreet.					
11/3/73	91	4		1 All Or Nothing With Me	Lonely After You	—	$6		Cinnamon 768
11/19/77	91	7		2 It's The Love In You	That's The Way Love Should Be	—	$6		Pinnacle 101
				SAME OLD TRAIN '98					
				Collaboration of country artists: Clint Black, Joe Diffie, Merle Haggard, Emmylou Harris, Alison Krauss, Patty Loveless, Earl Scruggs, Ricky Skaggs, Marty Stuart, Pam Tillis, Randy Travis, Travis Tritt, and Dwight Yoakam.					
9/19/98	59	5		Same Old Train	—	—			album cut
				from the various artists album Tribute To Tradition on Columbia 68073					
				SAMI JO '74					
				Born Sami Jo Cole in Batesville, Arkansas. Female singer.					
2/9/74	52	12		1 Tell Me A Lie	Stay Where You Are	21	$5		MGM South 7029
7/6/74	61	9		2 It Could Have Been Me	Look At Us	46	$5		MGM South 7034
1/4/75	62	9		3 I'll Believe Anything You Say	Lovely Daughter	—	$5		MGM 14773
5/15/76	91	4		4 God Loves Us (When We All Sing Together)	Partly Cloudy	—	$5		Polydor 14315
9/4/76	67	6		5 Take Me To Heaven	Let Me Laugh (To Keep From Crying)	—	$5		Polydor 14341
				SAMI JO COLE:					
5/2/81	76	4		6 One Love Over Easy	You've Got My Heart In Your Hands	—	$4		Elektra 47127
10/31/81	82	3		7 I Can't Help Myself (Here Comes The Feeling)	Carelessly	—	$4		Elektra 47211

DEBUT	PEAK	WKS	Gold	A-side (Chart Hit) ... B-side	Pop	$	Pic	Label & Number
				SAMONE, Stephany ? '80 Born in Pleasant Grove, Texas.				
6/7/80	68	6		1 Do That To Me One More Time................Gotta Make You Mine #1 Pop hit for **Captain & Tennille** in 1980	—	$5		MDJ 1004
11/22/80	65	7		2 Somebody's Gotta Do The Losing................One Day At A Time	—	$5		MDJ 1006
				SAMPLES, Junior '67 Born Alvin Samples on 8/10/26 in Cumming, Georgia. Died of a heart attack on 11/13/83 (age 57). Comedian. Regular on TV's *Hee Haw*.				
7/22/67	52	4		World's Biggest Whopper................It Happened To Junior [S] Jim Morrison (interviewer)	—	$10		Chart 1460
				SANDERS, Ben '88 Born in Dallas. Known as "The 5th Ave. Country Boy."				
11/19/88	100	1		I'm Leavin' You................Good Advice BEN SANDERS (The 5th Ave. Country Boy)	—	$6		Luv 129
			★	**SANDERS, Debbie** '89				
4/15/89	91	2		No Time At All................	—	$6		K-Ark 1050
				SANDERS, Mack '78 Born in Wichita, Kansas. Popular radio and TV host. Married **Sherry Bryce**; together they owned the Pilot label.				
1/21/78	89	3		Sweet Country Girl................Tonkin The Blues	—	$7		Pilot 45101
				SANDERS, Ray '71 Born Raymon Sanders on 10/1/35 in St. John, Kentucky. Singer/songwriter/guitarist/actor. 1)All I Ever Need Is You 2)A World So Full Of Love 3)Lonelyville				
10/31/60	18	11		1 A World So Full Of Love................A Little Bitty Tear	—	$10		Liberty 55267
4/3/61	20	8		2 Lonelyville................I Haven't Gone Far Enough Yet	—	$10		Liberty 55304
5/24/69	22	13		3 Beer Drinkin' Music................Gotta Find A Way	—	$7		Imperial 66366
10/25/69	73	2		4 Three Tears (For The Sad, Hurt, And Blue)................Lucille	—	$7		Imperial 66408
8/1/70	36	11		5 Blame It On Rosey................Waikiki Sand	—	$6		United Artists 50689
12/26/70+	38	9		6 Judy................The Wild Side Of Life	—	$6		United Artists 50732
5/29/71	56	9		7 Walk All Over Georgia................Tonight She'll Make Me Happy	—	$6		United Artists 50774
10/2/71	18	16		8 All I Ever Need Is You................Before I Met You #7 Pop hit for Sonny & Cher in 1971	—	$6		United Artists 50827
5/20/72	69	5		9 A Rose By Any Other Name (Is Still A Rose)..We've Gotta Learn To Help Each Other	—	$6		United Artists 50886
9/9/72	67	4		10 Lucius Grinder................You Let My Love Live	—	$6		United Artists 50933
5/5/73	75	2		11 Another Way To Say Goodbye................	—	$6		United Artists 201
8/6/77	56	7		12 I Don't Want To Be Alone Tonight................The Power Of Positive Drinkin'	—	$5		Republic 003
1/21/78	91	3		13 Tennessee................You Keep Right On Walking	—	$5		Republic 013
11/29/80	93	2		14 You're A Pretty Lady, Lady................My Special Angel	—	$6		Hillside 05
				SANDERS, The '89 Brother-and-sister team from Alaska: Dale and Vicki Sanders.				
8/20/88	76	3		1 You Fit Right Into My Heart................	—	$5		Airborne 10001
2/11/89	64	7		2 Grandma's Old Wood Stove................Starry Lullaby	—	$5		Airborne 10013
5/27/89	73	5		3 Who Needs You................Grandma's Old Wood Stove	—	$5		Airborne 10019
				SAN FERNANDO VALLEY MUSIC BAND '79 Group from St. Paul, Minnesota. Led by Brian Murphy (vocals) and Jeff Stephens (guitar).				
6/30/79	83	8		Taken To The Line................Roll Your Own	—	$7		C&S 017
				SANTA FE — see **CHAPMAN, Cee Cee**				
				SANZ, Victor '00 Born on 10/13/73 in Wasco, California. Singer/songwriter/guitarist.				
6/10/00	68	4		1 I'm Gonna Be There................	—			album cut
9/23/00	68	1		2 Destination Unknown................ above 2 from the album *Destination Unknown* on Gramac 7777	—			album cut
			▽	**SARAH** '88 Born in Pennsylvania; raised in California. Wife of H.L. Vogt, owner of Hub label.				
9/19/87	81	2		1 Lyin' Eyes................No Place To Run To	—	$6		Hub 45
6/4/88	81	3		2 Chains................You Can't Hurt Me #17 Pop hit for The Cookies in 1962	—	$6		Hub 46
10/15/88	77	4		3 Don't Send Me Roses................	—	$6		Hub 48
				SARGEANTS, Gary '74 Born Gary Lusk in Miami. Singer/songwriter/drummer.				
12/15/73+	55	11		1 Ode To Jole Blon................Fair To Middlin', Lower Middle Class	—	$6		Mercury 73440
10/5/74	72	7		2 Day Time Lover................Too Low To Get High	—	$6		Mercury 73608
				SASKIA & SERGE '78 Husband-and-wife duo from Schagen, Holland. Saskia was born Trudy van den Berg on 4/23/47. Serge was born Ruud Schaap on 3/2/46. First recorded in 1966 as Trudy & Ruud. Changed name to Saskia & Serge in 1969.				
1/7/78	88	5		Jambalaya (On The Bayou)................Don't Lay Your Head	—	$5		ABC/Hickory 54020
				SAULS, Corkey '79 Male singer.				
2/10/79	96	1		There Goes That Smile Again................Home Is Where I Hang My Dungarees	—	$7		Sand Mountain 822

DEBUT	PEAK	WKS	Gold	A-side (Chart Hit)	B-side	Pop	$	Pic	Label & Number
				SAVANNAH Bros. '84					
				Group from Brunswick, Georgia. Led by brothers Jay and Gene Willis.					
10/29/83	87	5		1 Backstreet Ballet..It Don't Get No Better Than This		—	$4		Mercury 814360
7/21/84	73	5		2 My Girl..Let's Get To It		—	$4		Mercury 880037
				#1 Pop hit for the Temptations in 1965					
				SAWMILL CREEK — see HAUSER, Bruce					
				SAWYER, Ray — see DR. HOOK					
				SAWYER BROWN ★69★ '93					
				Group formed in Nashville: Mark Miller (vocals; born on 10/25/58), Bobby Randall (guitar; born on 9/16/52), Gregg Hubbard (keyboards; born on 10/4/60), Jim Scholten (bass; born on 4/18/52) and Joe Smyth (drums; born on 9/6/57). Won first prize on TV's *Star Search* in 1984. Duncan Cameron (of **Amazing Rhythm Aces**; born on 7/27/56) replaced Randall in 1991. CMA Award: 1985 Horizon Award.					
				1)Thank God For You 2)Some Girls Do 3)Step That Step 4)This Time 5)The Walk					
10/6/84+	16	22		1 Leona..S:10 / A:19 Staying Afloat		—	$4		Capitol/Curb 5403
2/9/85	❶¹	21		2 Step That Step...S:❶¹ / A:❶¹ Feel Like Me		—	$4	■	Capitol/Curb 5446
6/8/85	3	21		3 Used To Blue.........................S:3 / A:3 It's Hard To Keep A Good Love Down		—	$4	■	Capitol/Curb 5477
10/5/85	5	20		4 Betty's Bein' Bad...S:5 / A:5 Lonely Girls		—	$4	■	Capitol/Curb 5517
2/1/86	14	18		5 Heart Don't Fall Now.....................................S:14 / A:14 That's A No No		—	$4		Capitol/Curb 5548
5/10/86	15	16		6 Shakin'..S:14 / A:16 Billy Does Your Bulldog Bite		—	$4		Capitol/Curb 5585
9/13/86	11	18		7 Out Goin' Cattin'...A:11 / S:12 The House Won't Rock		—	$4	■	Capitol/Curb 5629
				SAWYER BROWN WITH "CAT" JOE BONSALL					
1/17/87	25	13		8 Gypsies On Parade......................................S:21 / A:25 Not Ready To Let You Go		—	$4		Capitol/Curb 5677
5/23/87	58	9		9 Savin' The Honey For The Honeymoon..........................Lady Of The Evening		—	$4		Capitol/Curb 44007
8/22/87	29	13		10 Somewhere In The Night.........................S:29 My Baby Drives A Buick		—	$4	■	Capitol/Curb 44054
12/5/87+	2¹	22		11 This Missin' You Heart Of Mine..............S:13 A Mighty Big Broom		—	$4		Capitol/Curb 44108
4/23/88	27	13		12 Old Photographs...In This Town		—	$4		Capitol/Curb 44143
10/1/88	11	17		13 My Baby's Gone..S:20 Blue Denim Soul		—	$4		Capitol/Curb 44218
12/10/88	51	7		14 It Wasn't His Child..................................Falling Apart At The Heart [X]		—	$4	■	Capitol/Curb 44282
2/25/89	50	9		15 Old Pair Of Shoes.............................What Am I Going To Tell My Heart		—	$4		Capitol/Curb 44332
9/2/89	5	26		16 The Race Is On..Passin' Train		—	$4		Capitol/Curb 44431
3/3/90	33	13		17 Did It For Love...The Heartland		—	$4		Capitol/Curb 44483
5/26/90	33	13		18 Puttin' The Dark Back Into The Night...		—			album cut
				from the album *The Boys Are Back* on Capitol/Curb 92358					
10/6/90	40	17		19 When Love Comes Callin'...		—			album cut
				from the album *Greatest Hits* on Curb/Capitol 94259					
2/9/91	70	3		20 One Less Pony..		—			album cut
4/6/91	68	6		21 Mama's Little Baby Loves Me..		—			album cut
7/20/91	2¹	20		22 The Walk..		—			album cut
				above 3 from the album *Buick* on Curb/Capitol 94260					
11/23/91+	3	20		23 The Dirt Road..		—			album cut
3/7/92	❶¹	20		24 Some Girls Do..		—			album cut
				above 2 from the album *The Dirt Road* on Curb/Capitol 95624					
8/8/92	5	20		25 Cafe On The Corner..		—			album cut
11/28/92+	3	20		26 All These Years..		—			album cut
3/27/93	5	20		27 Trouble On The Line...		—			album cut
				above 3 from the album *Cafe On The Corner* on Curb 77574					
7/3/93	❶²	20		28 Thank God For You......................Cafe On The Corner / (3 album snippets)		117	$4	■	Curb 76914
10/16/93+	4	20		29 The Boys And Me..		—			album cut
2/19/94	40	11		30 Outskirts Of Town..		—			album cut
6/25/94	5	20		31 Hard To Say..		—			album cut
				above 3 from the album *Outskirts Of Town* on Curb 77626					
11/19/94+	2²	20		32 This Time...Hard To Say		—	$4	■	Curb 76930 (v)
3/18/95	4	20		33 I Don't Believe In Goodbye......................S:25 Outskirts Of Town		—	$4	■	Curb 76936 (v)
7/22/95	11	20		34 (This Thing Called) Wantin' And Havin' It All......S:17 I Will Leave The Light On		—	$4	■	Curb 76955 (v)
11/25/95+	19	20		35 'Round Here..I Will Leave The Light On		—	$4	■	Curb 76975 (v)
3/23/96	3	21		36 Treat Her Right /..S:10		—			
8/17/96	46	10		37 She's Gettin' There..		—	$4	■	Curb 76987 (v)
3/1/97	13	20		38 Six Days On The Road..		117			album cut (v)
				later released as the B-side of #39 below					
6/28/97	6	20		39 This Night Won't Last Forever............S:8 Six Days On The Road		109	$4	■	Curb 73016 (v)
				#19 Pop hit for **Michael Johnson** in 1979					
2/14/98	55	7		40 Another Side...		—			album cut
4/11/98	60	6		41 Small Talk..		—			album cut
				above 4 from the album *Six Days On The Road* on Curb 77883					
11/14/98+	6	28		42 Drive Me Wild.....................................S:7 We're Everything To Me		44	$4	★	Curb 73075 (v)
5/29/99	47	13		43 I'm In Love With Her...		—			album cut
1/29/00	40	17		44 800 Pound Jesus..		—			album cut
6/24/00	50	12		45 Perfect World...		—			album cut
				above 4 from the album *Drive Me Wild* on Curb 77902					
11/25/00+	44	16		46 Lookin' For Love..		—			album cut
				"live" recording; from the album *The Hits Live* on Curb 77976					

Schankman Twins (2 Girls)

DEBUT	PEAK	WKS	Gold	A-side (Chart Hit)	B-side	Pop	$	Pic	Label & Number
				SAYER, Leo '78 Born Gerard Sayer on 5/21/48 in Shoreham, England. Charted 10 pop hits from 1975-81.					
10/21/78	63	6		Raining In My Heart .... *No Looking Back* #88 Pop hit for Buddy Holly in 1959		47	$5		Warner 8682
				SCARBURY, Joey '84 Born on 6/7/55 in Ontario, California. Best known for his 1981 pop hit "Theme From The Greatest American Hero (Believe It Or Not)."					
10/20/84	76	7		The River's Song .... *Billy's Home* from the movie *The River Rat* starring Tommy Lee Jones		—	$4		RCA 13913
				SCHAFFER, Norm '88					
3/12/88	77	4		Dallas Darlin'		—	$6		DSP 8712
				SCHEREE '79					
8/25/79	94	3		I'm In Another World		—	$5		Compass 0027
				SCHLITZ, Don '78 Born on 8/29/52 in Durham, North Carolina. Singer/prolific songwriter.					
5/6/78	65	7		1 The Gambler .... *You Can't Take It With You*		—	$4		Capitol 4576
3/31/79	91	3		2 You're The One Who Rewrote My Life Story .... *I've Been Loved*		—	$4		Capitol 4661
				SCHMUCKER, Paul '78 Born in Des Plaines, Illinois.					
11/25/78	69	6		1 The Giver .... *You Never Game Me You*		—	$6		Star-Fox 378
3/3/79	72	4		2 Makin' Love (Is A Beautiful Thing To Do) .... *Country Folks*		—	$6		Star-Fox 578
6/2/79	74	5		3 Steal Away .... *Lonely But Never Alone* Joni Dolson (backing vocal)		—	$6		Star-Fox 279
8/11/79	83	5		4 Rainy Days And Rainbows .... *It's Me Again* all of above produced by Troy Shondell		—	$6		Star-Fox 779
	★224★			**SCHNEIDER, John** '84 Born on 4/8/60 in Mount Kisco, New York. Singer/songwriter/actor. Played "Bo Duke" on TV's *The Dukes of Hazzard*. Acted in several movies. 1) I've Been Around Enough To Know 2) You're The Last Thing I Needed Tonight 3) What's A Memory Like You					
6/13/81	4	17		1 It's Now Or Never .... *Stay* adapted from the Italian song "O Sole Mio" of 1899; #1 Pop hit for Elvis Presley in 1960		14	$4	■	Scotti Brothers 02105
10/3/81	13	16		2 Them Good Ol' Boys Are Bad .... *Still* (Pop #69)		—	$4	■	Scotti Brothers 02489
5/22/82	32	9		3 Dreamin' .... *Let Me Love You* #11 Pop hit for Johnny Burnette in 1960		45	$4		Scotti Brothers 02889
8/21/82	56	7		4 In The Driver's Seat .... *They Got Nothin' On Him*		72	$4		Scotti Brothers 03062
7/2/83	57	6		5 Are You Lonesome Tonight .... *Hurts Like The Devil* JOHN SCHNEIDER AND JILL MICHAELS		—	$4		Scotti Brothers 03945
10/1/83	81	3		6 If You Believe .... *Every Night With You*		—	$4		Scotti Brothers 04064
7/28/84	❶¹	28		7 I've Been Around Enough To Know .... S:❶¹ / A:2 *Trouble*		—	$4		MCA 52407
1/5/85	❶¹	23		8 Country Girls .... S:❶¹ / A:❶¹ *The Time Of My Life*		—	$4	■	MCA 52510
4/20/85	10	20		9 It's A Short Walk From Heaven To Hell .... S:7 / A:11 *Honeymoon Wine*		—	$4		MCA 52567
8/10/85	10	20		10 I'm Going To Leave You Tomorrow .... S:9 / A:11 *I Don't Feel Much Like A Cowboy Tonight*		—	$4	■	MCA 52648
12/14/85+	❶¹	24		11 What's A Memory Like You (Doing In A Love Like This) .... S:❶¹ / A:❶¹ *The One Who Got Away*		—	$4	■	MCA 52723
5/10/86	❶¹	20		12 You're The Last Thing I Needed Tonight .... S:❶¹ / A:❶¹ *One More Night*		—	$4		MCA 52827
8/30/86	5	23		13 At The Sound Of The Tone .... S:5 / A:5 *This Time*		—	$4		MCA 52901
12/20/86+	10	21		14 Take The Long Way Home .... A:10 / S:16 *Better Class Of Losers*		—	$4		MCA 52989
4/4/87	6	20		15 Love, You Ain't Seen The Last Of Me .... S:9 / A:24 *Credit*		—	$4		MCA 53069
7/18/87	32	15		16 When The Right One Comes Along .... *The Gunfighter*		—	$4		MCA 53144
11/7/87	59	6		17 If It Was Anyone But You .... *So Good*		—	$4		MCA 53199
				SCHUTT, Dawn '89					
3/18/89	96	2		Take Time		—	$6		Master 10
				SCHUYLER, Thom '83 Born on 6/10/52 in Bethlehem, Pennsylvania. Member of **Schuyler, Knobloch & Overstreet**.					
7/16/83	49	10		1 A Little At A Time .... *The Softer I Try*		—	$4		Capitol 5239
10/22/83	43	11		2 Brave Heart .... *Two Way Street*		—	$4		Capitol 5281
				SCHUYLER, KNOBLOCH & OVERSTREET '87 Trio of prolific songwriters: **Thom Schuyler**, **Fred Knoblock** and **Paul Overstreet**. Also known as **S-K-O**. Overstreet replaced by **Craig Bickhardt** in 1987.					
7/12/86	9	29		1 You Can't Stop Love .... A:7 / S:11 *Love Is The Hero*		—	$4		MTM 72071
				S-K-O:					
12/6/86+	❶¹	22		2 Baby's Got A New Baby .... S:❶¹ / A:❶¹ *Bitter Pill To Swallow*		—	$4		MTM 72081
4/18/87	16	14		3 American Me .... S:16 *Country Heart*		—	$4		MTM 72086
				SCHUYLER, KNOBLOCH AND BICKHARDT:					
8/15/87	19	17		4 No Easy Horses .... *Too Good To Be Blue*		—	$4		MTM 72090
11/28/87+	24	18		5 This Old House .... S:18 *Living Without You*		—	$4		MTM 72100
4/23/88	8	22		6 Givers And Takers .... S:14 *People Still Fall In Love*		—	$4		MTM 72099
10/22/88	44	11		7 Rigamarole .... *Major Repairs*		—	$4		MTM 72115

DEBUT	PEAK	WKS	Gold	A-side (Chart Hit)	B-side	Pop	$	Pic	Label & Number
				SCOTT, Earl '62 Born Earl Batdorf on 9/9/36 in Youngstown, Ohio. Father of rock singer John Batdorf (of Batdorf & Rodney).					
11/3/62	8	10		1 Then A Tear Fell	Save A Minute (Lose A Wife)	—	$10		Kapp 854
7/27/63	23	7		2 Loose Lips	Guess I'll Never Learn	—	$8		Mercury 72110
1/4/64	30	1		3 Restless River	The Best I Can Give Her	—	$8		Mercury 72190
1/23/65	30	14		4 I'll Wander Back To You	Kiss My Love Good Bye	—	$7		Decca 31693
11/23/68	71	3		5 Too Rough On Me	Bottle In My Hand	—	$7		Decca 32397
				SCOTT, Jack '74 Born Jack Scafone on 1/28/36 in Windsor, Ontario, Canada. Singer/songwriter/guitarist. Charted 19 pop hits from 1958-61.					
7/6/74	92	4		You're Just Gettin' Better	As You Take A Walk Through My Mind	—	$7		Dot 17504
				SCOTT, Lang '84 Born in Sumter, South Carolina; raised in Harleyville, South Carolina. Married to **Linda Davis**.					
4/21/84	68	6		1 Run Your Sweet Love By Me One More Time /		—			MCA 52359
8/18/84	91	2		2 It's Been One Of Those Days		—	$4		
				SCRUGGS, Earl '79 Born on 1/6/24 in Flint Hill, North Carolina. Banjo player. Half of **Flatt & Scruggs** duo. His revue consisted of sons Gary Scruggs (vocals, bass), **Randy Scruggs** (guitar) and Steve Scruggs (keyboards), with Jim Murphey (steel guitar) and Jody Maphis (drums). Steve Scruggs murdered his wife, then killed himself on 9/23/92. Also see **Same Old Train**.					
10/24/70	74	2		1 Nashville Skyline Rag	Train Number Forty-Five [I]	—	$7		Columbia 45218
				written and first recorded by Bob Dylan on his 1969 *Nashville Skyline* album					
				EARL SCRUGGS REVUE:					
7/7/79	30	11		2 I Could Sure Use The Feeling	Drive To The Country	—	$5		Columbia 10992
11/3/79	82	4		3 Play Me No Sad Songs	Morning After Kind Of Man	—	$5		Columbia 11106
1/19/80	46	9		4 Blue Moon Of Kentucky	Give Me A Sign	—	$5		Columbia 11176
				TOM T. HALL & EARL SCRUGGS:					
5/22/82	77	4		5 There Ain't No Country Music On This Jukebox	Don't This Road Look Rough And Rocky	—	$4		Columbia 02858
7/31/82	72	5		6 Song Of The South	Shackles And Chains	—	$4		Columbia 03033
				SCRUGGS, Randy '98 Born on 8/3/53 in Nashville. Session guitarist. Son of **Earl Scruggs**. CMA Award: 1999 Musician of the Year.					
12/19/98	67	9		It's Only Love	—				album cut
				RANDY SCRUGGS (with Mary Chapin Carpenter) from the album *Crown Of Jewels* on Warner 46930					
				SEA, Johnny '59 Born John Seay on 7/15/40 in Gulfport, Mississippi. Singer/songwriter/guitarist.					
4/20/59	13	9		1 Frankie's Man, Johnny	Loneliness	—	$15		NRC 019
2/8/60	13	8		2 Nobody's Darling But Mine	My Time To Cry	—	$15		NRC 049
5/23/64	27	10		3 My Baby Walks All Over Me	There's Another Man	121	$8		Philips 40164
4/10/65	19	16		4 My Old Faded Rose	It's A Shame	—	$8		Philips 40267
6/11/66	14	11		5 Day For Decision	Mary Rocks Him To Sleep [S]	35	$7		Warner 5820
4/1/67	61	4		6 Nothin's Bad As Bein' Lonely	Ain't That Right	—	$7		Warner 5889
3/30/68	68	2		7 Going Out To Tulsa	There's A Shadow Bar	—	$6	■	Columbia 44423
10/19/68	32	11		8 Three Six Packs, Two Arms And A Juke Box	I Loved Her Fine For A Time	—	$6		Columbia 44634
				JOHNNY SEAY (above 2)					
				SEAL, Jim '80					
10/25/80	79	5		Bourbon Cowboy	From The Top To The Bottom	—	$5		NSD 66
				SEALS, Brady '97 Born on 3/29/69 in Hamilton, Ohio. Singer/songwriter/guitarist. Former member of **Little Texas**. Related to **Johnny Duncan**, **Dan Seals** and **Troy Seals**.					
9/7/96+	32	20		1 Another You, Another Me S:3	You Can Have Your Way With Me	91	$4	■	Reprise 17615 (v)
2/22/97	69	6		2 Still Standing Tall	Another You, Another Me	—	$4		Reprise 17384
8/23/97	74	1		3 Natural Born Lovers	—				album cut
				from the album *The Truth* on Reprise 46258					
6/13/98	55	12		4 I Fell	Love You Too Much	—	$4		Warner 17198
10/24/98	66	2		5 Whole Lotta Hurt	All My Devotion	—	$4		Warner 17144
7/10/99	74	2		6 The Best Is Yet To Come	—				album cut
				from the album *Brady Seals* on Warner 46939					
				SEALS, Dan ★122★ '90 Born on 2/8/50 in McCamey, Texas; raised in Iraan and Rankin, Texas. Singer/songwriter/guitarist. Brother of Jim Seals (of pop duo Seals & Crofts). Member of England Dan & John Ford Coley duo (charted 9 pop hits from 1976-80). Related to **Johnny Duncan**, **Brady Seals** and **Troy Seals**. CMA Award: 1986 Vocal Duo of the Year (with **Marie Osmond**). Also see **Tomorrow's World**. 1)Love On Arrival 2)Good Times 3)You Still Move Me 4)Everything That Glitters (Is Not Gold) 5)Big Wheels In The Moonlight					
4/30/83	18	17		1 Everybody's Dream Girl	The Banker	—	$4		Liberty 1496
8/13/83	28	14		2 After You	Candle In The Rain	—	$4		Liberty 1504
11/19/83+	37	16		3 You Really Go For The Heart	On A Night Like This	—	$4		Liberty 1512
2/25/84	10	21		4 God Must Be A Cowboy	Nothin' Left To Do But Cry	—	$4		Liberty 1515
7/28/84	9	23		5 (You Bring Out) The Wild Side Of Me	S:9 / A:12 One Friend	—	$4		EMI America 8220
11/24/84+	2²	21		6 My Baby's Got Good Timing	A:2 / S:2 She Thinks I Still Care	—	$4		EMI America 8245

DEBUT	PEAK	WKS	Gold	A-side (Chart Hit)	B-side	Pop	$	Pic	Label & Number
				SEALS, Dan — Cont'd					
3/30/85	9	19		7 My Old Yellow Car .... S:7 / A:10	Oh These Nights	—	$4		EMI America 8261
7/6/85	⓵¹	23		8 Meet Me In Montana .... S:⓵¹ / A:⓵¹	What Do Lonely People Do	—	$4	■	Curb/Capitol 5478
				MARIE OSMOND (With Dan Seals)					
10/26/85+	⓵¹	27		9 Bop .... S:⓵¹ / A:⓵¹	In San Antone	42	$4		EMI America 8289
				CMA Award: Single of the Year					
4/5/86	⓵¹	23		10 Everything That Glitters (Is Not Gold) .... S:⓵² / A:⓵¹	So Easy To Need	—	$4	■	EMI America 8311
10/25/86+	⓵¹	22		11 You Still Move Me .... S:⓵¹ / A:⓵¹	I'm Still Strung Out On You	—	$4		EMI America 8343
3/7/87	⓵¹	19		12 I Will Be There .... S:⓵² / A:5	Gonna Be Easy Now	—	$4	■	EMI America 8377
6/27/87	⓵¹	21		13 Three Time Loser .... S:⓵¹	On The Front Line	—	$4		EMI America 43023
10/17/87+	⓵¹	26		14 One Friend	S:⓵¹	—	$4		Capitol 44077
6/18/88	⓵¹	22		15 Addicted S:4	Maybe I'm Missing You Now	—	$4		Capitol 44130
11/12/88+	⓵¹	21		16 Big Wheels In The Moonlight S:22	Factory Town	—	$4		Capitol 44267
3/18/89	5	24		17 They Rage On	Factory Town	—	$4		Capitol 44345
2/17/90	⓵³	26		18 Love On Arrival	Those	—	$4	■	Capitol 44435 (v)
6/9/90	⓵²	21		19 Good Times	Bop	—	$4	■	Capitol 44577
				#11 Pop hit for Sam Cooke in 1964					
10/13/90	49	10		20 Bordertown	—				album cut
2/2/91	57	6		21 Water Under The Bridge	—				album cut
				above 2 from the album *On Arrival* on Capitol 91782					
11/2/91	62	10		22 Sweet Little Shoe	Your Blue Heart	—	$4	■	Warner 19176 (v)
4/25/92	43	13		23 Mason Dixon Line	Be My Angel	—	$4		Warner 18986
7/25/92	51	9		24 When Love Comes Around The Bend	Sweet Little Shoe	—	$4		Warner 18813
7/2/94	66	6		25 All Fired Up	Hillbilly Fever	—	$4	■	Warner 18192 (v)
				SEALS, Troy '75					
				Born on 11/16/38 in Big Hill, Kentucky; raised in Ohio. Singer/songwriter/guitarist. Recorded with wife **Jo Ann Campbell** as Jo Ann & Troy in the mid-1960s. Related to **Johnny Duncan**, **Brady Seals** and **Dan Seals**.					
8/11/73	93	4		1 I Got A Thing About You Baby	Coal Town Blues	—	$6		Atlantic 4004
				same tune as "I've Got A Thing About You Baby" by Elvis Presley					
2/2/74	78	5		2 Star Of The Bar /	—				
1/19/74	96	7		3 You Can't Judge A Book By The Cover	—		$6		Atlantic 4013
				#48 Pop hit for Bo Diddley in 1962					
5/11/74	81	6		4 Honky-Tonkin'	Let Me Make The Bright Lights Shine	—	$6		Atlantic 4020
7/19/75	76	7		5 Easy	I'll Take You Down To San Antonio	—	$5		Columbia 10173
3/27/76	88	5		6 Sweet Dreams	In Our Room	—	$5		Columbia 10303
4/23/77	93	2		7 Grand Ole Blues	One More Thrill	—	$5		Columbia 10511
2/16/80	85	3		8 One Night Honeymoon	Wanderin' Friends Of Mine	—	$4		Elektra 46573
				SEARS, Dawn '94					
				Born in East Grand Forks, Minnesota. Female singer.					
5/7/94	62	7		1 Runaway Train	A Little At A Time	—	$4	■	Decca 54834 (v)
				SEBASTIAN, John '76					
				Born on 3/17/44 in New York City. Lead singer of The Lovin' Spoonful (charted 14 pop hits from 1965-69).					
5/15/76	93	2	●	1 Welcome Back	Warm Baby	⓵¹	$5		Reprise 1349
				from the TV series *Welcome Back, Kotter* starring Gabriel Kaplan					
	★213★			**SEELY, Jeannie** '66					
				Born Marilyn Jeanne Seely on 7/6/40 in Titusville, Pennsylvania; raised in Townville, Pennsylvania. Singer/songwriter. Formerly married to **Hank Cochran**. Joined the *Grand Ole Opry* in 1967.					
				1)Don't Touch Me 2)Wish I Didn't Have To Miss You 3)Can I Sleep In Your Arms 4)I'll Love You More (Than You Need) 5)Lucky Ladies					
4/16/66	2³	21		1 Don't Touch Me	You Tied Tin Cans To My Heart	85	$7		Monument 933
9/10/66	15	15		2 It's Only Love	Then Go Home To Her	—	$7		Monument 965
12/17/66+	13	13		3 A Wanderin' Man	Darling Are You Ever Coming Home	—	$7		Monument 987
3/18/67	39	10		4 When It's Over	I'd Be Just As Lonely There	—	$7		Monument 999
7/8/67	42	8		5 These Memories	Funny Way Of Laughin'	—	$7		Monument 1011
10/28/67+	10	15		6 I'll Love You More (Than You Need)	Enough To Lie	—	$7		Monument 1029
2/24/68	24	12		7 Welcome Home To Nothing	Maybe I Should Leave	—	$7		Monument 1054
6/22/68	23	10		8 How Is He?	A Little Unfair	—	$7		Monument 1075
3/22/69	43	11		9 Just Enough To Start Me Dreamin'	How Big A Fire	—	$7		Decca 32452
11/15/69+	2²	16		10 Wish I Didn't Have To Miss You	My Tears Don't Show	—	$7		Decca 32580
				JACK GREENE And JEANNIE SEELY					
3/7/70	46	6		11 Please Be My New Love	Have You Found It Yet	—	$7		Decca 32628
12/5/70	58	5		12 Tell Me Again	What Kind Of Bird Is That	—	$7		Decca 32757
7/17/71	71	5		13 You Don't Understand Him Like I Do	Another Heart For You To Break	—	$7		Decca 32838
11/20/71+	42	10		14 Alright I'll Sign The Papers	All I Want Is You	—	$7		Decca 32882
12/11/71+	15	13		15 Much Oblige	First Day	—	$7		Decca 32898
				JACK GREENE/JEANNIE SEELY					
6/17/72	47	9		16 Pride	I'm Afraid I Lied	—	$7		Decca 32964
8/12/72	19	12		17 What In The World Has Gone Wrong With Our Love	Willingly	—	$7		Decca 32991
				JACK GREENE/JEANNIE SEELY					
1/20/73	72	4		18 Farm In Pennsyltucky	—		$7		
		3		19 Between The King And I	—		$7		Decca 33042
7/7/73	6	18		20 Can I Sleep In Your Arms	He'll Love The One He's With	—	$5		MCA 40074
12/15/73+	11	13		21 Lucky Ladies	Hold Me	—	$5		MCA 40162
5/18/74	37	10		22 I Miss You	I'd Do As Much For You	—	$5		MCA 40225
9/21/74	26	14		23 He Can Be Mine	So Was He	—	$5		MCA 40287

DEBUT	PEAK	WKS	Gold	A-side (Chart Hit)	B-side	Pop	$	Pic	Label & Number
				SEELY, Jeannie — Cont'd					
7/19/75	59	9		24 Take My Hand	How Big A Fire	—	$5		MCA 40428
4/17/76	96	3		25 Since I Met You Boy	Home To Him	—	$5		MCA 40528
6/11/77	80	5		26 We're Still Hangin' In There Ain't We Jessi	I Don't Need Love Anymore	—	$5		Columbia 10550
1/28/78	97	1		27 Take Me To Bed	Until You Have To	—	$5		Columbia 10664
				SEEVERS, Les '69					
3/8/69	57	9		What Kind Of Magic	Stop, Look, Surrender	—	$7		Decca 32434
				SEGER, Bob '83					
				Born on 5/6/45 in Dearborn, Michigan; raised in Detroit. Rock singer/songwriter. Charted 32 pop hits from 1968-91.					
1/22/83	15	14		Shame On The Moon	House Behind A House	2⁴	$4	■	Capitol 5187
				BOB SEGER & The Silver Bullet Band					
				SEGO BROTHERS AND NAOMI, The '64					
				Group from Macon, Georgia. Included James Sego (died on 7/24/79, age 51) and his wife Naomi.					
2/1/64	50	1		Sorry I Never Knew You	Since I Got This Feeling	—	$15		Songs of Faith 8032
				SEINER, Barbara '79					
3/3/79	87	3		Jealous Heart	Everybody Loves Somebody	—	$7		Starship 109
				SELF, Ted '60					
				Born on 7/5/25 in Utah. Died on 7/31/96 (age 71). Singer/songwriter/guitarist.					
7/4/60	20	10		Little Angel (Come Rock Me To Sleep)	Walk Her Down The Aisle	—	$20		Plaid 115
				SELLARS, Marilyn '74					
				Born on 12/31/50 in Northfield, Minnesota. Worked as an airline stewardess.					
4/20/74	19	17		1 One Day At A Time	California	37	$5		Mega 1205
12/14/74+	39	14		2 He's Everywhere	Good Love (I Knew I'd Find You)	—	$5		Mega 1221
5/24/75	84	4		3 Gather Me	Red Skies Over Georgia	—	$5		Mega 1230
1/24/76	91	3		4 The Door I Used To Close	California	—	$5		Mega 1242
				SELLERS, Jason '99					
				Born on 3/4/71 in Gilmer, Texas. Married to Lee Ann Womack from 1991-97.					
8/2/97	37	14		1 I'm Your Man	Divorce My Heart	—	$4	■	BNA 64915 (v)
11/22/97+	46	14		2 That Does It	Walking In My Sleep	—	$4		BNA 65322
5/9/98	55	7		3 This Small Divide	—				album cut
				JASON SELLERS Featuring Martina McBride					
				from the album I'm Your Man on BNA 67517					
7/10/99	33	20		4 A Matter Of Time S:14 (album snippets)			$4	★	BNA 65784 (v)
				later released on vinyl as the B-side of #5 below					
3/4/00	64	5		5 Can't Help Calling Your Name	A Matter Of Time	—	$4		BNA 60209
				SELLERS, Shane '01					
				Born in Erath, Louisiana. Former horse racing jockey.					
5/12/01	58	1		Matthew, Mark, Luke and Earnhardt S:7 Tears Don't Lie		52ˢ	$4	★	DreamWorks 50327
				a tribute to Dale Earnhardt, who was killed while racing at the Daytona 500 on 2/18/01					
				SEMINOLE '97					
				Duo of brothers from Florida: Jimmy and Donald "Butch" Myers.					
8/16/97	69	6		She Knows Me By Heart	Honestly	—	$4	■	Curb/Univ. 56094 (v)
				SERRATT, Kenny '77					
				Born in Manila, Arkansas; raised in Dyess, Arkansas. Nicknamed "Country Kin."					
				1)Until The Bitter End 2)Daddy, They're Playin' A Song About You 3)Saturday Night In Dallas					
12/9/72+	56	9		1 Goodbyes Come Hard For Me	The Man Who Picked The Wildwood Flower	—	$6		MGM 14435
				KENNY SERRATT and The Messengers:					
5/5/73	68	3		2 This Just Ain't No Good Day For Leavin'	The Way I Lose My Mind	—	$6		MGM 14517
9/29/73	70	13		3 Love And Honor	Running Kind	—	$6		MGM 14636
				above 3 produced by Merle Haggard					
				KENNY SERATT:					
8/2/75	88	6		4 If I Could Have It Any Other Way	Not Too Old To Cry	—	$5		Melodyland 6014
8/21/76	72	6		5 I've Been There Too	She Made Me Love You More	—	$5		Hitsville 6039
2/12/77	54	8		6 Daddy, They're Playin' A Song About You	I Threw Away The Rose	—	$5		Hitsville 6049
12/15/79	82	4		7 Never Gonna' Be A Country Star /		—	$5		
			4	8 A Damn Good Drinking Song		—	$5		MDJ 1001
5/3/80	54	8		9 Saturday Night In Dallas	We Made Memories	—	$5		MDJ 1003
9/13/80	39	8		10 Until The Bitter End	Truckin' My Way To Glory	—	$5		MDJ 1005
5/2/81	70	7		11 Sidewalks Are Grey		—	$5		MDJ 1008
				SESSIONS, Ronnie '77					
	★391★			Born on 12/7/48 in Henrietta, Oklahoma; raised in Bakersfield, California. Singer/songwriter/guitarist.					
				1)Me And Millie (Stompin' Grapes And Gettin' Silly) 2)Wiggle Wiggle 3)Juliet And Romeo					
8/5/72	36	10		1 Never Been To Spain	While I Play The Fiddle	—	$6		MGM 14394
				#5 Pop hit for Three Dog Night in 1972					
11/18/72	59	6		2 Tossin' And Turnin'	Knock And Ring And Tap	—	$6		MGM 14445
				#1 Pop hit for Bobby Lewis in 1961					
6/23/73	66	5		3 She Feels So Good I Hate To Put Her Down	We May Never Get This Close Again	—	$6		MGM 14528
				also released as "I Just Can't Put Her Down"					
9/29/73	87	7		4 If That Back Door Could Talk	My Love Is Deep, My Love Is Wide	—	$6		MGM 14619
10/4/75	61	10		5 Makin' Love	Messin' Around	—	$5		MCA 40462
				#20 Pop hit for Floyd Robinson in 1959					
7/17/76	81	4		6 Support Your Local Honky Tonks	Showdown	—	$5		MCA 40581
10/30/76+	16	17		7 Wiggle Wiggle	Baby, Pleae Don't Stone My Anymore	—	$5		MCA 40624

David Seville (See The Chipmunks)

DEBUT	PEAK	WKS	Gold	A-side (Chart Hit)...B-side	Pop	$	Pic	Label & Number
				SESSIONS, Ronnie — Cont'd				
4/9/77	15	13		8 Me And Millie (Stompin' Grapes And Gettin' Silly) .... The Losing End	—	$5		MCA 40705
8/6/77	30	10		9 Ambush .... Victim Of Life's Circumstances	—	$5		MCA 40758
12/10/77+	57	9		10 I Like To Be With You .... Sweet Annette	—	$5		MCA 40831
3/25/78	72	7		11 Cash On The Barrelhead .... Lucy, Ain't Your Loser Lookin' Good	—	$5		MCA 40875
7/15/78	96	2		12 I Never Go Around Mirrors .... Whole Lotta Hound	—	$5		MCA 40917
10/7/78	25	9		13 Juliet And Romeo .... Poison Love	—	$5		MCA 40952
6/30/79	94	3		14 Do You Want To Fly .... Hold On To Your Hiney	—	$5		MCA 41038
12/1/79	84	5		15 Honky Tonkin' .... Come By Here	—	$5		MCA 41142
12/27/86+	78	5		16 I Bought The Shoes That Just Walked Out On Me .... You're A Real Live Wire	—	$5		Compleat 161
				SEXTON, Mark '79				
11/24/79	97	2		Don't Say No To Me Tonight .... Younger Than Tomorrow	—	$6		Sun-De-Mar 79101
				SHAFER, Whitey '81				
				Born Sanger Shafer on 10/24/34 in Whitney, Texas. Singer/prolific songwriter.				
12/13/80+	48	9		1 You Are A Liar .... Like I Want To	—	$4		Elektra 47063
4/11/81	67	3		2 If I Say I Love You (Consider Me Drunk) .... I'll Break Out Again Tonight	—	$4		Elektra 47117
				SHAMBLIN, Michael '86				
3/8/86	77	3		1 Foreign Affairs	—	$5		F&L 548
6/7/86	83	2		2 Wishful Dreamin' .... Livin' On Love	—	$5		F&L 549
				SHANE, Michael '89				
2/11/89	93	2		1 What's The Matter Baby	—	$5		Regal 1988
7/1/89	99	1		2 Broken Dreams and Memories	—	$5		Regal 9891
				SHANNON, Bonnie '80				
12/20/80	88	4		Lovin' You Lightly	—	$5		Door Knob 139
				SHANNON, Del '85				
				Born Charles Westover on 12/30/34 in Coopersville, Michigan. Died of a self-inflicted gunshot wound on 2/8/90 (age 55). Charted 17 pop hits from 1961-82.				
3/9/85	56	6		In My Arms Again .... You Can't Forgive Me	—	$5		Warner 29098
				SHANNON, Guy '73				
				Singer/songwriter/pianist.				
7/7/73	69	5		1 Naughty Girl .... Please Forgive	—	$6		Cinnamon 758
10/6/73	63	11		2 Soul Deep .... A Train That Never Runs	—	$6		Cinnamon 769
				#18 Pop hit for The Box Tops in 1969				
				SHARP, Kevin '97				
				Born on 12/10/70 in Weiser, Idaho; raised in Sacramento, California. Survived a battle with bone cancer from 1988-91.				
9/28/96+	❶⁴	22		1 Nobody Knows	—			album cut
				#2 Pop hit for the Tony Rich Project in 1996				
2/8/97	3	21		2 She's Sure Taking It Well	—			album cut
7/26/97	4	20		3 If You Love Somebody	—			album cut
11/22/97+	43	13		4 There's Only You	—			album cut
				all of above from the album *Measure Of A Man* on Asylum 61930				
3/21/98	51	8		5 Love Is All That Really Matters	—			album cut
6/27/98	61	9		6 If She Only Knew	—			album cut
				above 2 from the album *Love Is* on Asylum 62165				
				SHARP, Rosemary '87				
				Born in Fort Worth, Texas. Singer/songwriter.				
2/28/87	85	3		1 Didn't You Go And Leave Me	—	$5		Canyon Creek 1226
8/8/87	76	4		2 Real Good Heartache	—	$5		Canyon Creek 0401
10/31/87	67	6		3 If You're Gonna Tell Me Lies (Tell Me Good Ones)	—	$5		Canyon Creek 0908
4/9/88	68	5		4 The Stairs .... Until I Fall In Love Again	—	$5		Canyon Creek 0210
				SHARPE, Sunday '74				
				Born in 1946 in Orlando, Florida. Female singer.				
8/17/74	11	14		1 I'm Having Your Baby .... It's A Beautiful Night For Love	—	$5		United Artists 507
				female version of "(You're) Having My Baby" by Paul Anka				
12/21/74+	47	9		2 Mr. Songwriter .... I Gave All I Had To Him	—	$5		United Artists 571
3/29/75	48	8		3 Put Your Head On My Shoulder .... Another Lonely Night	—	$5		United Artists 602
				#2 Pop hit for Paul Anka in 1959				
2/14/76	80	5		4 Find A New Love, Girl .... It's A Beautiful Night For Love	—	$5		United Artists 758
11/6/76	18	12		5 A Little At A Time .... Pour It In A Swinging Jug	—	$5		Playboy 6090
6/18/77	62	5		6 I'm Not The One You Love (I'm The One You Make Love To) .... Last Night's Lovin'	—	$5		Playboy 5806
8/27/77	45	7		7 Hold On Tight .... Welcome Stranger	—	$5		Playboy 5813
				SHATSWELL, Danny '78				
				Born on 3/7/53 in Oklahoma. Died on 10/1/94 (age 41). Singer/songwriter/guitarist.				
6/17/78	97	2		I'm A Mender .... She's My Shelter	—	$5		Mercury 55027
				SHAVER, Billy Joe '78				
				Born on 8/16/39 in Corsicana, Texas; raised in Waco, Texas. Singer/prolific songwriter.				
9/15/73	88	3		1 I Been To Georgia On A Fast Train .... Old Five & Dimers Like Me	—	$6		Monument 8580
3/11/78	80	5		2 You Asked Me To .... Silver Wings Of Time	—	$5		Capricorn 0286

DEBUT	PEAK	WKS	Gold	A-side (Chart Hit)	B-side	Pop	$	Pic	Label & Number
				SHAW, Brian '74					
				Born in 1949 in Grove City, Pennsylvania. Singer/songwriter/bassist.					
9/8/73	55	8		1 The Devil Is A Woman	Just At Dawn	—	$6		RCA Victor 0058
12/15/73+	62	11		2 Good Enough To Be Your Man	What Loving You Means To Me	—	$6		RCA Victor 0186
4/6/74	50	9		3 Friend Named Red	I'm Not Through Loving You	—	$6		RCA Victor 0230
10/12/74	17	15		4 Here We Go Again	I'll Carry You	—	$6		RCA Victor 10071
10/16/76	97	2		5 Showdown		—	$5		Republic 306
3/12/77	97	2		6 What Kind Of Fool (Does That Make Me)	You Sure Were Good Last Night	—	$5		Republic 360
				SHAW, Ron '78					
				Born in Anaheim, California. Former member of The Hillside Singers.					
6/25/77	94	4		1 Hurtin' Kind Of Love	Like So Much Broken Glass	—	$6		Pacific Chall. 1511
				also see #7 below					
7/8/78	79	7		2 Goin' Home	Boogie Woogie Country Girl	—	$5		Pacific Chall. 1522
10/7/78	36	9		3 Save The Last Dance For Me	If Walls Could Talk	—	$5		Pacific Chall. 1631
				#1 Pop hit for The Drifters in 1960					
1/20/79	68	7		4 I Cry Instead	Kansas City	—	$5		Pacific Chall. 1633
				#25 Pop hit for The Beatles in 1964 (as "I'll Cry Instead")					
7/28/79	93	3		5 One And One Make Three	I Can't Dance	—	$5		Pacific Chall. 1635
9/22/79	90	4		6 What The World Needs Now (Is Love Sweet Love)	Fairweather Woman	—	$5		Pacific Chall. 1636
				#7 Pop hit for Jackie DeShannon in 1965					
3/22/80	91	4		7 Hurtin' Kind Of Love	Like So Much Broken Glass [R]	—	$5		Pacific Chall. 1637
				same version as #1 above					
				RON SHAW & The Desert Wind Band:					
8/16/80	94	2		8 The Legend Of Harry And The Mountain		—	$5		Pacific Chall. 1638
2/7/81	78	4		9 Reachin' For Freedom		—	$5		Pacific Chall. 1639
				SHAW, Victoria '94					
				Born on 7/13/62 in New York City; raised in Los Angeles.					
2/25/84	61	10		1 Break My Heart	Forever On My Mind	—	$5		MPB 5008
5/7/94	57	9		2 Cry Wolf	Love's Not Gonna Pass Me By	—	$4	■	Reprise 18235 (v)
9/3/94	74	2		3 Tears Dry	Half Hearted	—	$4	■	Reprise 18111 (v)
6/10/95	58	7		4 Forgiveness	Bring My Baby Home	—	$4	■	Reprise 17886 (v)
5/30/98	69	5		5 One Heart At A Time	S:5 (same version)	56	$4	■	Atlantic 84117
				GARTH BROOKS, BILLY DEAN, FAITH HILL, OLIVIA NEWTON-JOHN, NEAL McCOY, MICHAEL McDONALD, VICTORIA SHAW, BRYAN WHITE					
				SHAY, Dorothy '47					
				Born Dorothy Sims on 4/11/21 in Jacksonville, Florida. Died of a heart attack on 10/22/78 (age 57). Singer/actress. Known as "The Park Avenue Hillbillie." Acted in the movie *Comin' 'Round The Mountain*.					
8/16/47	4	7		1 Feudin' And Fightin'	Say That We're Sweethearts Again	4	$20		Columbia 37189
				from the Broadway musical *Laffing Room Only* starring Betty Garrett					
				SHeDAISY '00					
	★370★			Vocal trio from Magna, Utah: sisters Kristyn (born on 8/24/70), Kelsi (born on 11/21/74) and Kassidy (born on 10/30/76) Osborn.					
2/27/99	3	32		1 Little Good-Byes	S:5 Still Holding Out For You	43	$4	★	Lyric Street 64025
9/4/99+	9	31		2 This Woman Needs		57			album cut
12/11/99	40	5		3 Deck The Halls	S:❶³ (edited version) [X]	61	$4	★	Lyric Street 64036
1/15/00	2³	44		4 I Will...But		43			album cut
9/23/00+	11	27		5 Lucky 4 You (Tonight I'm Just Me)		79			album cut
12/9/00	37	6		6 Deck The Halls	(edited version) [X-R]	—	$4	★	Lyric Street 64036
12/9/00	44	6		7 Jingle Bells	[X]	—			album cut
				#3, 6 & 7: from the album *Brand New Year* on Lyric Street 65007					
4/21/01	27	20		8 Still Holding Out For You		—		★	album cut
				first issued as the B-side of #1 above; all of above (except #3, 6 & 7) from the album *The Whole SheBang* on Lyric Street 65002					
				SHELTON, Blake '01					
				Born on 6/18/76 in Ada, Oklahoma. Singer/guitarist.					
4/28/01	❶⁵	27		1 Austin	S:❶⁸ Problems At Home	18	$4	★	Giant 16767 (v)
10/20/01+	18	21		2 All Over Me	Ol' Red	110	$4		Giant 16274
				SHELTON, Ricky Van ★114★ '88					
				Born on 1/12/52 in Danville, Virginia; raised in Grit, Virginia. Singer/songwriter/guitarist. Van is his middle name. Worked as a pipefitter prior to his music career. Joined the *Grand Ole Opry* in 1988. CMA Awards: 1988 Horizon Award; 1989 Male Vocalist of the Year.					
				1) I'll Leave This World Loving You 2) Keep It Between The Lines 3) I've Cried My Last Tear For You 4) Rockin' Years 5) Somebody Lied					
12/20/86+	24	18		1 Wild-Eyed Dream	A:24 Think It Over	—	$4		Columbia 06542
4/18/87	7	19		2 Crime Of Passion	S:2 Don't We All Have The Right	—	$4		Columbia 07025
8/22/87	❶¹	25		3 Somebody Lied	S:❶² Working Mans Blues	—	$4		Columbia 07311
1/9/88	❶¹	23		4 Life Turned Her That Way	S:❶³ I Don't Care	—	$4		Columbia 07672
5/7/88	❶¹	20		5 Don't We All Have The Right	S:❶² Baby, I'm Ready	—	$4		Columbia 07798
9/10/88	❶²	21		6 I'll Leave This World Loving You	S:❶² Sometimes I Cry In My Sleep	—	$4		Columbia 08022
1/7/89	❶¹	16		7 From A Jack To A King	The Picture	—	$4		Columbia 08529
4/22/89	4	16		8 Hole In My Pocket	Let Me Live With Love (And Die With You)	—	$4		Columbia 68694
7/22/89	❶¹	22		9 Living Proof	Somebody's Back In Town	—	$4		Columbia 68994

DEBUT	PEAK	WKS	Gold	A-side (Chart Hit) ... B-side	Pop	$	Pic	Label & Number
				SHELTON, Ricky Van — Cont'd				
11/25/89+	2²	26		10 Statue Of A Fool .... He's Got You	—	$4		Columbia 73077
3/10/90	❶¹	25		11 I've Cried My Last Tear For You .... I Still Love You	—	$4	■	Columbia 73263 (v)
6/30/90	2²	21		12 I Meant Every Word He Said .... Sometimes I Cry In My Sleep	—	$4		Columbia 73413
10/27/90+	4	20		13 Life's Little Ups And Downs .... Love Is Burnin'	—	$4	■	Columbia 73587 (v)
3/2/91	❶¹	20		14 Rockin' Years .... What A Heartache	—	$4		Columbia 73711
				DOLLY PARTON WITH RICKY VAN SHELTON				
5/4/91	❶¹	20		15 I Am A Simple Man .... Backroads	—	$4		Columbia 73780
8/24/91	❶²	20		16 Keep It Between The Lines .... Weekend World	—	$4		Columbia 73956
11/30/91+	13	20		17 After The Lights Go Out .... Oh Heart Of Mine	—	$4		Columbia 74104
3/21/92	2¹	20		18 Backroads .... Call Me Up	—	$4		Columbia 74258
7/25/92	26	20		19 Wear My Ring Around Your Neck .... Who'll Turn Out The Lights	—	$4		Columbia 74418
				from the movie *Honeymoon In Vegas* starring James Caan				
10/24/92+	5	20		20 Wild Man .... If You're Ever In My Arms	—	$4		Columbia 74748
3/13/93	26	20		21 Just As I Am .... Slam That Door	—	$4		Columbia 74896
8/21/93	44	12		22 A Couple Of Good Years Left .... My First Reaction	—	$4		Columbia 77130
1/15/94	20	20		23 Where Was I .... If It Weren't For Me	—	$4	■	Columbia 77334 (v)
9/24/94	49	10		24 Wherever She Is .... Thanks A Lot	—	$4	■	Columbia 77653 (v)
1/28/95	62	5		25 Lola's Love .... Been There, Done That	—	$4	■	Columbia 77792 (v)
6/24/00	71	1		26 The Decision	—			album cut
				from the album *Fried Green Tomatoes* on Audium 8116				

SHENANDOAH ★127★ '90

Group formed in Muscle Shoals, Alabama: **Marty Raybon** (vocals; born on 12/8/59), **Jim Seales** (guitar; born on 3/20/54), Stan Thorn (keyboards; born on 3/16/59), Ralph Ezell (bass; born on 6/26/53) and Mike McGuire (drums; born on 12/28/58). Seales was guitarist for the R&B group Funkadelic. McGuire married actress Teresa Blake (of TV soap *All My Children*) on 7/9/94. Rocky Thacker replaced Ezell in 1995. Thorn left in 1996.

1) Next To You, Next To Me 2) The Church On Cumberland Road 3) Two Dozen Roses 4) If Bubba Can Dance (I Can Too) 5) Sunday In The South

DEBUT	PEAK	WKS		A-side ... B-side	Pop	$	Pic	Label & Number
8/1/87	54	7		1 They Don't Make Love Like We Used To .... Lily Of The Alley	—	$4	■	Columbia 07128
12/12/87+	28	18		2 Stop The Rain .... What She Wants	—	$4		Columbia 07654
4/23/88	9	24		3 She Doesn't Cry Anymore .... S:13 What She Wants	—	$4		Columbia 07779
10/1/88	5	21		4 Mama Knows .... S:5 The Show Must Go On	—	$4		Columbia 08042
1/28/89	❶²	21		5 The Church On Cumberland Road .... She Doesn't Cry Anymore	—	$4		Columbia 68550
5/20/89	❶¹	24		6 Sunday In The South .... Changes	—	$4		Columbia 68892
9/16/89	❶¹	26		7 Two Dozen Roses .... Hard Country	—	$4		Columbia 69061
2/17/90	6	26		8 See If I Care .... Lily Of The Alley	—	$4		Columbia 73237
6/9/90	❶³	21		9 Next To You, Next To Me .... Daddy's Little Man	—	$4	■	Columbia 73373 (v)
10/6/90	5	20		10 Ghost In This House .... She's Still Here	—	$4	■	Columbia 73520 (v)
1/19/91	7	20		11 I Got You .... The Road Not Taken	—	$4		Columbia 73672
5/4/91	9	20		12 The Moon Over Georgia .... Can't Stop Now	—	$4		Columbia 73777
9/7/91	38	11		13 When You Were Mine .... It Ain't Love Until It Hurts	—	$4		Columbia 73957
4/4/92	2¹	20		14 Rock My Baby .... Wednesday Night Prayer Meeting	—	$4		RCA 62199
8/8/92	28	18		15 Hey Mister (I Need This Job) .... There Ain't No Beverly Hills In Tennessee	—	$4		RCA 62290
11/28/92+	15	20		16 Leavin's Been A Long Time Comin' .... I Was Young Once Too	—	$4		RCA 62397
6/5/93	15	20		17 Janie Baker's Love Slave .... Right Where I Belong	—	$4		RCA 62504
10/9/93+	3	20		18 I Want To Be Loved Like That .... Just Say The Word	—	$4		RCA 62642
2/12/94	❶¹	20		19 If Bubba Can Dance (I Can Too) .... If It Takes Every Rib I've Got	—	$4	■	RCA 62761 (v)
6/25/94	46	11		20 I'll Go Down Loving You .... The Blues Are Coming Over To Your House	—	$4		RCA 62867
4/22/95	4	20		21 Darned If I Don't (Danged If I Do) /				
12/3/94+	7	20		22 Somewhere In The Vicinity Of The Heart	—	$4		Liberty 18484
				SHENANDOAH With Alison Krauss				
8/5/95	24	20		23 Heaven Bound (I'm Ready) .... Cabin Fever	—	$4		Capitol 18730
11/4/95+	40	20		24 Always Have, Always Will .... Every Fire	—	$4		Capitol 18903
2/24/96	43	12		25 All Over But The Shoutin' .... Sunday In The South	—	$4		Capitol 19116
9/9/00	65	1		26 What Children Believe	—			album cut
				from the album *2000* on Free Falls 7012				

SHEPARD, Jean ★102★ '53

Born Ollie Imogene Shepard on 11/21/33 in Paul's Valley, Oklahoma; raised in Visalia, California. Singer/songwriter/bassist. Formed all-girl band, the Melody Ranch Girls, in the late 1940s. Discovered by **Hank Thompson**. Worked with **Red Foley**'s *Ozark Jubilee* from 1955-57. Joined the *Grand Ole Opry* in 1955. Married **Hawkshaw Hawkins** on 11/26/60.

1) A Dear John Letter 2) Slippin' Away 3) A Satisfied Mind 4) Beautiful Lies 5) Forgive Me John

DEBUT	PEAK	WKS		A-side / B-side	Pop	$	Pic	Label & Number
7/25/53	❶⁶	23		1 A Dear John Letter .... S:❶⁶ / J:❶⁴ / A:2 I'd Rather Die Young (Shepard)	4	$25		Capitol 2502
				JEAN SHEPARD with FERLIN HUSKEY				
				#44 Pop hit for **Pat Boone** in 1960				
10/10/53	4	7		2 Forgive Me John .... S:4 / J:6 / A:8 My Wedding Ring (Shepard)		$25		Capitol 2586
				JEAN SHEPARD with FERLIN HUSKEY				
6/25/55	4	22		3 A Satisfied Mind /				
7/16/55	13	1		4 Take Possession A:13	—	$25		Capitol 3118
10/8/55	4	19		5 Beautiful Lies / .... S:4 / J:4 / A:12				

DEBUT	PEAK	WKS	Gold	#	A-side (Chart Hit)	B-side	Pop	$	Pic	Label & Number
					SHEPARD, Jean — Cont'd					
10/22/55	10	3		6	I Thought Of You	A:10	—	$25		Capitol 3222
12/22/58	18	2		7	I Want To Go Where No One Knows Me	Just Another Girl	—	$20		Capitol 4068
4/20/59	30	1		8	Have Heart, Will Love	I'll Take The Blame	—	$20		Capitol 4129
5/30/64	5	24		9	Second Fiddle (To An Old Guitar)	Two Little Boys	—	$10		Capitol 5169
1/9/65	38	11		10	A Tear Dropped By	He Plays The Bongo (I Play The Banjo)	—	$10		Capitol 5304
6/5/65	30	7		11	Someone's Gotta Cry	Don't Take Advantage Of Me	—	$10		Capitol 5392
3/5/66	13	16		12	Many Happy Hangovers To You	Our Past Is In My Way	—	$10		Capitol 5585
5/14/66	9	15		13	I'll Take The Dog	I'd Fight The World	—	$8		Capitol 5633
					JEAN SHEPARD and RAY PILLOW					
7/16/66	10	18		14	If Teardrops Were Silver	Outstanding In Your Field	—	$8		Capitol 5681
11/26/66+	25	11		15	Mr. Do-It-Yourself	Strangers Nine To Five	—	$8		Capitol 5769
					JEAN SHEPARD & RAY PILLOW					
1/28/67	12	15		16	Heart, We Did All That We Could	My Momma Didn't Raise No Fools	—	$8		Capitol 5822
5/27/67	17	12		17	Your Forevers (Don't Last Very Long)	Coming Or Going	—	$8		Capitol 5899
9/30/67	40	8		18	I Don't See How I Can Make It	Enough Heart To Hurt	—	$8		Capitol 5983
2/10/68	52	6		19	An Old Bridge	My New Darlin'	—	$8		Capitol 2073
6/15/68	36	8		20	A Real Good Woman	The Trouble With Girls	—	$8		Capitol 2180
10/5/68	62	8		21	Everyday's A Happy Day For Fools	My World Is You	—	$7		Capitol 2273
5/3/69	69	4		22	I'm Tied Around Your Finger	You're Calling Me Sweetheart Again	—	$7		Capitol 2425
9/6/69	18	11		23	Seven Lonely Days	Invisible Tears	—	$7		Capitol 2585
1/3/70	8	14		24	Then He Touched Me	Only Mama That'll Walk The Line	—	$7		Capitol 2694
4/25/70	23	11		25	A Woman's Hand	What Went Wrong	—	$7		Capitol 2779
8/15/70	22	12		26	I Want You Free	Be Nice To Everybody	—	$7		Capitol 2847
11/7/70	12	14		27	Another Lonely Night	Your Name's Become A Household Word	—	$7		Capitol 2941
2/20/71	24	10		28	With His Hand In Mine	Just Plain Lonely	—	$6		Capitol 3033
9/18/71	55	2		29	Just As Soon As I Get Over Loving You	My Name Is Woman	—	$6		Capitol 3153
1/8/72	55	8		30	Safe In These Lovin' Arms Of Mine	The Closest Thing To Perfect	—	$6		Capitol 3238
6/3/72	68	4		31	Virginia	We Go Good Together	—	$6		Capitol 3315
8/19/72	46	10		32	Just Like Walkin' In The Sunshine	Candlelighted World	—	$6		Capitol 3395
6/9/73	4	18		33	Slippin' Away	Think I'll Go Somewhere And Cry Myself To Sleep	81	$5		United Artists 248
11/24/73+	36	11		34	Come On Phone	Are You Sincere?	—	$5		United Artists 317
2/23/74	13	13		35	At The Time	Love Came Pouring Down	—	$5		United Artists 384
6/29/74	17	12		36	I'll Do Anything It Takes (To Stay With You)	Safe In The Love Of My Man	—	$5		United Artists 442
10/26/74+	14	13		37	Poor Sweet Baby	I'm Not That Good At Goodbye	—	$5		United Artists 552
2/22/75	16	13		38	The Tip Of My Fingers	Bright Lights And Country Music	—	$5		United Artists 591
8/30/75	49	10		39	I'm A Believer (In A Whole Lot Of Lovin')	I Think I'll Wait Til Tomorrow	—	$5		United Artists 701
12/20/75+	44	9		40	Another Neon Night	Another Somebody Done Somebody Wrong Song	—	$5		United Artists 745
4/10/76	49	8		41	Mercy	Wife Of A Hard Working Man	—	$5		United Artists 776
6/26/76	41	10		42	Ain't Love Good	I Can't Imagine	—	$5		United Artists 818
12/4/76+	74	7		43	I'm Giving You Denver	He Loves Everything He Gets His Hands On	—	$5		United Artists 899
4/16/77	82	5		44	Hardly A Day Goes By	Lovin' You Comes So Easy	—	$5		United Artists 956
4/15/78	85	6		45	The Real Thing	Break My Mind	—	$5		Scorpion 157

SHEPPARD, T.G. ★60★   '81

Born William Browder on 7/20/44 in Humbolt, Tennessee. Singer/songwriter/guitarist. Moved to Memphis in 1960. Worked as backup singer with Travis Wammack's band. Recorded as Brian Stacey for Atlantic in 1966. Invented his stage name; initials do not signify "The German Sheppard" or "The Good Sheppard," as commonly thought.

1) Last Cheater's Waltz 2) I'll Be Coming Back For More 3) Party Time 4) Tryin' To Beat The Morning Home
5) I Loved 'Em Every One

DEBUT	PEAK	WKS	Gold	#	A-side	B-side	Pop	$	Pic	Label & Number
11/30/74+	●¹	19		1	Devil In The Bottle	Rollin' With The Flow	54	$5		Melodyland 6002
4/12/75	●¹	15		2	Tryin' To Beat The Morning Home	I'll Be Satisfied	95	$5		Melodyland 6006
8/16/75	14	16		3	Another Woman	I Can't Help Myself (Sugar Pie, Honey Bunch)	—	$5		Melodyland 6016
12/27/75+	7	15		4	Motels And Memories	Pigskin Charade	102	$5		Melodyland 6028
5/29/76	14	13		5	Solitary Man	Shame	100	$5		Hitsville 6032
					#21 Pop hit for Neil Diamond in 1970					
9/18/76	8	14		6	Show Me A Man	We Just Live Here (We Don't Love Here Anymore)	—	$5		Hitsville 6040
12/25/76+	37	8		7	May I Spend Every New Years With You	I'll Always Remember That Song	—	$5		Hitsville 6048
3/5/77	20	10		8	Lovin' On	I'll Always Remember That Song	—	$5		Hitsville 6053
11/12/77+	13	14		9	Mister D.J.	Easy To Love (So Hard To Leave)	—	$4		Warner/Curb 8490
2/18/78	13	13		10	Don't Ever Say Good-Bye	She Pretended We Were Married	—	$4		Warner/Curb 8525
5/27/78	5	13		11	When Can We Do This Again	Jenny, Don't Worry 'Bout The Kid	—	$4		Warner/Curb 8593
9/23/78	7	11		12	Daylight	Never Ending Crowded Circle	—	$4		Warner/Curb 8678
12/16/78+	8	14		13	Happy Together	That's All She Wrote	—	$4		Warner/Curb 8721
					#1 Pop hit for The Turtles in 1967					
4/21/79	4	13		14	You Feel Good All Over	I Wish That I Could Hurt That Way Again	—	$4		Warner/Curb 8808
8/4/79	●²	14		15	Last Cheater's Waltz	You Do It To Me Every Time	—	$4		Warner/Curb 49024
12/1/79+	●²	15		16	I'll Be Coming Back For More	(She Wanted To Live) Faster Than I Could Dream	—	$4		Warner/Curb 49110
4/5/80	6	16		17	Smooth Sailin'	I Came Home To Make Love To You	—	$4		Warner/Curb 49214
8/2/80	●¹	15		18	Do You Wanna Go To Heaven	How Far Our Love Goes	—	$4		Warner/Curb 49515
12/6/80+	●¹	13		19	I Feel Like Loving You Again	Let The Little Bird Fly	—	$4		Warner/Curb 49615
3/14/81	●¹	15		20	I Loved 'Em Every One	I Could Never Dream The Way You Feel	37	$4		Warner/Curb 49690

DEBUT	PEAK	WKS	Gold	A-side (Chart Hit) / B-side	Pop	$	Pic	Label & Number
				SHEPPARD, T.G. — Cont'd				
7/18/81	❶¹	16		21 Party Time .... *You Waltzed Yourself Right Into My Life*	—	$4		Warner/Curb 49761
11/21/81+	❶¹	19		22 Only One You .... *We Belong In Love Tonight*	68	$4		Warner/Curb 49858
4/3/82	❶¹	16		23 Finally .... *All My Cloudy Days Are Gone*	58	$4		Warner/Curb 50041
9/4/82	❶¹	19		24 War Is Hell (On The Homefront Too) .... *In Another Minute*	—	$4		Warner/Curb 29934
11/20/82+	❶¹	20		25 Faking Love .... *Reno And Me*	—	$4		Warner/Curb 29854
				T.G. SHEPPARD AND KAREN BROOKS				
4/9/83	12	15		26 Without You .... *Where Did We Go Right?*	—	$4		Warner/Curb 29695
				#1 Pop hit for Nilsson in 1972				
10/15/83+	❶¹	21		27 Slow Burn .... *First Things First*	—	$4		Warner/Curb 29469
2/18/84	12	15		28 Make My Day .... *How Lucky We Are (Sheppard)* [N]	62	$4		Warner/Curb 29343
				T.G. SHEPPARD with CLINT EASTWOOD *from the movie Sudden Impact starring Clint Eastwood*				
6/2/84	3	21		29 Somewhere Down The Line .... *It's A Bad Night For Good Girls*	—	$4		Warner/Curb 29369
9/29/84	57	9		30 Home Again .... *Dream On (Collins)*	—	$4		Elektra 69697
				JUDY COLLINS with T.G. Sheppard				
11/10/84+	4	22		31 One Owner Heart .... *A:4 / S:5 I Could Get Used To This*	—	$4		Warner/Curb 29167
3/9/85	10	17		32 You're Going Out Of My Mind .... *S:10 / A:12 Heat Lightning*	—	$4		Warner/Curb 29071
5/11/85	21	18		33 Fooled Around And Fell In Love .... *A:18 / S:23 Banging My Heart*	—	$4	■	Columbia 04890
				#3 Pop hit for Elvin Bishop in 1976				
9/7/85	8	20		34 Doncha? .... *S:5 / A:9 Hunger For You*	—	$4		Columbia 05591
12/28/85+	9	18		35 In Over My Heart .... *S:8 / A:9 A Great Work Of Art*	—	$4		Columbia 05747
5/17/86	❶¹	23		36 Strong Heart .... *S:❶¹ / A:❶¹ What You Gonna Do About Her*	—	$4		Columbia 05905
10/11/86+	2²	26		37 Half Past Forever (Till I'm Blue In The Heart) .... *A:2 / S:2 The Bad Thing About Good Love*	—	$4		Columbia 06347
3/21/87	2¹	20		38 You're My First Lady .... *S:5 / A:13 Paintin' The Town Blue*	—	$4		Columbia 06999
9/5/87	2¹	24		39 One For The Money .... *S:2 Come To Me*	—	$4		Columbia 07312
9/24/88	48	7		40 Don't Say It With Diamonds (Say It With Love) .... *There's A Lot Of Heart*	—	$4		Columbia 08029
11/26/88+	14	20		41 You Still Do .... *Something Worth Waiting For*	—	$4		Columbia 08119
3/30/91	63	6		42 Born In A High Wind .... *(long version)*	—	$4		Curb/Capitol 79565
				SHERLEY, Glen '71				
				Born on 3/9/36 in Oklahoma; raised in California. Died of a self-inflicted gunshot on 5/11/78 (age 42). Singer/songwriter/guitarist.				
7/10/71	63	4		Greystone Chapel .... *Dialogue / Looking Back In Anger*	—	$6		Mega 0027
				recorded "live" at Folsom Prison on 1/31/71; first recorded by Johnny Cash on his 1968 Johnny Cash At Folsom Prison album				
				SHIBLEY, Arkie '51				
				Born Arleigh Shibley on 2/26/15 in Van Buren, Arkansas. Died on 4/29/93 (age 78). His Mountain Dew Boys consisted of Leon Kelly, Jack Hays and Phil Fregon.				
12/30/50+	5	7		Hot Rod Race .... *A:5 / J:6 I'm Living Alone With An Old Love* [N]	—	$100		Gilt-Edge 5021
				ARKIE SHIBLEY and his Mountain Dew Boys				
				SHINER, Mervin '49				
				Born on 2/20/21 in Bethlehem, Pennsylvania. Singer/songwriter/guitarist.				
10/8/49	5	11		1 Why Don't You Haul Off And Love Me .... *J:5 / S:11 Soft Lips*	—	$20		Decca 46178
4/1/50	6	3		2 Peter Cottontail .... *A:6 / S:7 Floppy*	8	$25		Decca 9-46221
				MURV SHINER:				
5/27/67	73	4		3 Big Brother .... *Big Shot, The Pool Shark*	—	$8		MGM 13704
1/4/69	50	10		4 Too Hard To Say I'm Sorry .... *Tecumseh Valley*	—	$8		MGM 14007
				SHIRLEY, Danny '84				
				Born on 8/12/56 in Chattanooga, Tennessee. Lead singer of **Confederate Railroad**.				
10/20/84	72	5		1 Love And Let Love	—	$7		Amor 1002
2/16/85	93	5		2 Yo Yo (The Right String, But The Wrong Yo Yo)	—	$10		Amor 1006
				DANNY SHIRLEY & "PIANO RED" *#10 R&B hit for Piano Red in 1951*				
8/29/87	82	3		3 Deep Down (Everybody Wants To Be From Dixie)	—	$6		Amor 2001
12/5/87	81	2		4 Going To California	—	$6		Amor 2002
2/20/88	76	7		5 I Make The Living (She Makes The Living Worthwhile)	—	$6		Amor 2004
				SHIRLEY & SQUIRRELY '76				
				Studio group assembled by producer Bob Milsap.				
6/5/76	28	11		Hey Shirley (This Is Squirely) .... *(instrumental)* [N]	48	$6	■	GRT 054
				SHONDELL, Troy '88				
				Born Gary Schelton on 5/14/39 in Fort Wayne, Indiana. Singer/multi-instrumentalist. Charted 3 pop hits from 1961-62.				
10/6/79	95	2		1 Still Loving You .... *Doctor Love*	—	$7		Star-Fox 77
11/8/80	83	4		2 (Sittin' Here) Lovin' You .... *(Here I Am) Single Again*	—	$7		TeleSonic 804
5/14/88	79	2		3 (I'm Looking For Some) New Blue Jeans	—	$7		AVM 14
				SHOOTERS, The '89				
				Group from Muscle Shoals, Alabama: Walt Aldridge (vocals), Barry Billings (guitar), Chalmers Davis (keyboards), Gary Baker (bass; **Baker & Myers**) and Michael Dillon (drums).				
1/24/87	21	15		1 They Only Come Out At Night .... *A:21 Remote Control*	—	$4		Epic 06623
6/6/87	41	11		2 'Til The Old Wears Off .... *Some Fools Were Made To Be Broken*	—	$4		Epic 07131
9/26/87	34	13		3 Tell It To Your Teddy Bear .... *Dancing Alone*	—	$4		Epic 07367
1/30/88	31	15		4 I Taught Her Everything She Knows About Love .... *I'll Cry Instead*	—	$4		Epic 07684
10/22/88+	13	21		5 Borderline .... *She's Steppin' Out*	—	$4		Epic 08082
3/4/89	17	19		6 If I Ever Go Crazy .... *Leave And Learn*	—	$4		Epic 68587
7/15/89	39	9		7 You Just Can't Lose 'Em All .... *If I Were You*	—	$4		Epic 68955

DEBUT	PEAK	WKS	Gold	A-side (Chart Hit)	B-side	Pop	$	Pic	Label & Number
				SHOPPE, The '81					
				Group from Dallas: Mark Cathey and Kevin Bailey (vocals), Roger Ferguson (guitar), Clarke Wilcox (banjo), Mike Caldwell (harmonica), Jack Wilcox (bass) and Lou Chavez (drums).					
4/19/80	76	5		1 Three Way Love	Livin' In Your Lovin'	—	$6		Rainbow Sound 8019
8/30/80	78	4		2 Star Studded Nights	The South's Gonna Rise Again	—	$6		Rainbow Sound 8022
2/21/81	33	10		3 Doesn't Anybody Get High On Love Anymore	Paralyzed	—	$5		NSD 80
5/23/81	61	7		4 Dream Maker	Up To My Heart In Love	—	$5		NSD 90
11/17/84	74	5		5 If You Think I Love You Now		—	$6		Amer. Country 2
2/16/85	79	6		6 Hurts All Over		—	$6		Amer. Country 3
9/14/85	56	8		7 Holdin' The Family Together	The Sky Is Falling	—	$4		MTM 72056
12/21/85+	47	11		8 While The Moon's In Town	There's A Fire Inside	—	$4		MTM 72063
				SHRUM, Walter '45					
				Born on 10/16/1896 in Denver. Died in February 1971 (age 74).					
10/6/45	3	1		Triflin' Gal	You Two-Timed Me Once Too Often		$50		Coast 2010
				WALTER SHRUM and his Colorado Hillbillies					
				SHURFIRE '87					
7/4/87	54	7		1 Bringin' The House Down	My Heart's In Louisiana	—	$5		AIR 173
11/21/87	49	9		2 Roll The Dice	I Want Some	—	$5		AIR 180
3/12/88	57	6		3 First In Line		—	$5		AIR 181
				SHYLO '77					
				Vocal trio from Texas: Danny Hogan, Ronny Scaife and Perry York.					
2/14/76	75	8		1 Dog Tired Of Cattin' Around	Heartbeat	—	$5		Columbia 10267
6/12/76	75	7		2 Livin' On Love Street	Beyond The Sun	—	$5		Columbia 10343
9/25/76	86	5		3 Ol' Man River (I've Come To Talk Again)	Showdown	—	$5		Columbia 10398
1/8/77	63	8		4 Drinkin' My Way Back Home	Didn't Get No Lovin'	—	$5		Columbia 10456
5/28/77	87	4		5 (I'm Coming Home To You) Dixie	Whiskey Fever	—	$5		Columbia 10534
12/17/77+	91	5		6 Gotta Travel On	The Drifter	—	$5		Columbia 10647
3/10/79	79	6		7 Freckles	Wait Until Dark	—	$5		Columbia 10918
9/15/79	92	2		8 I'm Puttin' My Love Inside You	What Kind Of Dance Is That	—	$5		Columbia 11048
5/22/82	89	3		9 Crime In The Sheets	(I Wish You'd) Love Me Alone	—	$4		Mercury 76151
				SIDE OF THE ROAD GANG '76					
				Group from Dallas.					
8/14/76	98	2		Suitcase Life	Sittin' By The Side Of The Road	—	$5		Capitol 4298
				SIERRA '83					
				Vocal group from Virginia: E.J. Harris (lead), William Arney (tenor), Rodney Painter (baritone) and David Mangum (bass).					
2/5/83	58	8		1 Keep On Playin' That Country Music		—	$7		Musicom 52701
5/14/83	87	3		2 I'd Do It In A Heart Beat		—	$7		Musicom 52702
11/5/83	93	2		3 Old Fashioned Lovin'		—	$7		Cardinal 052
3/17/84	70	6		4 Branded Man	Northern Lights	—	$6		Awesome 101
6/23/84	68	6		5 Love Is The Reason	I'd Do It In A Heartbeat	—	$6		Awesome 106
2/9/85	68	6		6 The Almighty Lover	How Many Angels	—	$6		Awesome 110
				SILVER CITY BAND '77					
				Group from Memphis.					
10/1/77	99	2		1 If You Really Want Me To I'll Go	Georgia Girl	—	$5		Columbia 10601
7/29/78	95	2		2 I'm Still Missing You	Valentine Partner	—	$5		Columbia 10759
				SILVER CREEK '81					
				Group led by singer/songwriter Roger Ivie.					
9/12/81	94	2		1 You And Me And Tennessee		—	$6		Cardinal 8102
				ROGER IVIE And SILVERCREEK					
11/21/81	64	7		2 Lonely Women		—	$6		Cardinal 8103
				SIMMONS, Gene '77					
				Born in 1933 in Tupelo, Mississippi. Known as "Jumpin' Gene." Not to be confused with the lead singer of Kiss. Hit the pop charts with "Haunted House" in 1964.					
9/10/77	88	3		Why Didn't I Think Of That	Tennessee Party Time	—	$7		Deltune 1201
				SIMON, Carly '78					
				Born on 6/25/45 in New York City. Singer/songwriter. Charted 23 pop hits from 1971-89. Won the 1971 Best New Artist Grammy Award. Married to James Taylor from 1972-83.					
9/9/78	33	10		Devoted To You	Boys In The Trees (Simon)	36	$5		Elektra 45506
				CARLY SIMON and JAMES TAYLOR					
				SIMON & VERITY '85					
				Vocal duo from England.					
2/16/85	78	4		1 We've Still Got Love	In Love And Out Of Danger	—	$4		EMI America 8257
5/18/85	91	3		2 Your Eyes	In Love And Out Of Danger	—	$4		EMI America 8264
				SIMPSON, Jenny '98					
				Born in 1973 in Nashville.					
10/24/98	54	7		Ticket Out Of Kansas	Til Then	—	$4		Mercury 566476
				SIMPSON, Red '72					
				Born Joseph Simpson on 3/6/34 in Higley, Arizona. Singer/songwriter/guitarist.					
4/2/66	38	4		1 Roll Truck Roll	Runaway Truck	—	$8		Capitol 5577
6/4/66	39	3		2 The Highway Patrol	Big Mack	—	$8		Capitol 5637
12/24/66+	41	8		3 Diesel Smoke, Dangerous Curves	I'm Gonna Write Momma For Money	—	$8		Capitol 5783

The Singing Dogs — Jingle Bells (★★★) 45 RPM (Don Charles Presents)

DEBUT	PEAK	WKS	Gold	A-side (Chart Hit)	B-side	Pop	$	Pic	Label & Number
				SIMPSON, Red — Cont'd					
12/4/71+	4	17		4 I'm A Truck .... Where Love Used To Be		—	$7		Capitol 3236
4/22/72	62	5		5 Country Western Truck Drivin' Singer .... You're The First		—	$7		Capitol 3298
6/30/73	63	5		6 Awful Lot To Learn About Truck Drivin' .... You Still Got A Hold On Me		—	$6		Capitol 3616
9/18/76	92	4		7 Truck Driver's Heaven .... It Ain't Even Halloween		—	$5		Warner 8259
				*same tune as "I Dreamed Of A Hillbilly Heaven" by **Eddie Dean**; originally released on Portland 046 with a picture sleeve in 1976*					
10/27/79	99	2		8 The Flying Saucer Man And The Truck Driver .... I Miss You A Little		—	$10		K.E.Y. 108
				SINATRA, Nancy — see TILLIS, Mel					
	★336★			**SINGLETARY, Daryle** '97					
				Born on 3/10/71 in Cairo, Georgia. Singer/songwriter.					
				1)Amen Kind Of Love 2)I Let Her Lie 3)Too Much Fun					
4/8/95	39	13		1 I'm Living Up To Her Low Expectations .... My Heart's Too Broke		—	$4	■	Giant 17902 (v)
7/29/95	2¹	20		2 I Let Her Lie .... S:21 Ordinary Heroes		—	$4	■	Giant 17818 (v)
12/9/95+	4	20		3 Too Much Fun		—			album cut
				from the album *Daryle Singletary* on Giant 24606					
5/11/96	50	10		4 Workin' It Out .... What Am I Doing There		—	$4	■	Giant 17650 (v)
10/12/96+	2¹	23		5 Amen Kind Of Love		—			album cut
				from the album *All Because Of You* on Giant 24660					
3/15/97	48	10		6 The Used To Be's .... That's What I Get For Thinkin'		—	$4		Giant 17399
7/26/97	68	3		7 Even The Wind		—			album cut
				from the album *All Because Of You* on Giant 24660					
11/8/97+	28	20		8 The Note .... S:9 I Let Her Lie		90	$4	■	Giant 17268 (v)
4/4/98	49	10		9 That's Where You're Wrong		—			album cut
				from the album *Ain't It The Truth* on Giant 24696					
7/11/98	44	12		10 My Baby's Lovin' .... Miracle In The Making		—	$4		Giant 17172
7/1/00	55	20		11 I Knew I Loved You		—			album cut
12/16/00	70	1		12 I've Thought Of Everything		—			album cut
				above 2 from the album Now And Again on Audium 8125					
	★360★			**SINGLETON, Margie** '64					
				Born Margaret Ebey on 10/5/35 in Coushatta, Louisiana. Singer/songwriter/guitarist. Formerly married to music executive Shelby Singleton. Married **Leon Ashley** in 1965.					
				1)Keeping Up With The Joneses 2)Old Records 3)Waltz Of The Angels					
8/3/59	25	5		1 Nothin' But True Love .... It's Better To Know		—	$20		Starday 443
2/1/60	12	14		2 The Eyes Of Love .... Angel Hands		—	$20		Starday 472
9/18/61	15	3		3 Did I Ever Tell You .... Not Even Friends		—	$15		Mercury 71856
				GEORGE JONES & MARGIE SINGLETON					
6/16/62	11	10		4 Waltz Of The Angels .... Talk About Lovin'		—	$15		Mercury 71955
				GEORGE JONES & MARGIE SINGLETON					
12/28/63+	11	14		5 Old Records .... How Do You Celebrate Goodbye		—	$12		Mercury 72213
3/14/64	5	23		6 Keeping Up With The Joneses *See RD-ASC (0-2-5)*		—	$12		Mercury 72231
3/28/64	40	6		7 No Thanks, I Just Had One		—	$12	■	Mercury 72237
				MARGIE SINGLETON And FARON YOUNG (above 2)					
12/5/64	38	8		8 Another Woman's Man - Another Man's Woman .... Honky Tonk Happy		—	$12		Mercury 72312
				FARON YOUNG AND MARGIE SINGLETON					
9/9/67	39	8		9 Ode To Billie Joe .... Big Boys Don't Need Mamas		—	$10		Ashley 2011
11/11/67	54	7		10 Hangin' On .... Four O'Clock		—	$10		Ashley 2015
				LEON ASHLEY & MARGIE SINGLETON					
3/2/68	52	8		11 Wandering Mind .... Your Conscience Sends Me Flowers		—	$10		Ashley 2050
5/11/68	55	6		12 You'll Never Be Lonely Again .... Parting Of The Ways		—	$10		Ashley 3000
				LEON ASHLEY - MARGIE SINGLETON					

				SKAGGS, Ricky ★84★ '84					
				Born on 7/18/54 in Cordell, Kentucky. Singer/songwriter/mandolin player. Played mandolin from age five. Member of the Clinch Mountain Boys (1969) and **The Country Gentlemen** (1974). Married **Sharon White** in 1982. Joined the *Grand Ole Opry* in 1982. CMA Awards: 1982 Horizon Award; 1982 Male Vocalist of the Year; 1985 Entertainer of the Year; 1987 Vocal Duo of the Year (with Sharon White). Also see **Same Old Train**.					
				1)Cajun Moon 2)Lovin' Only Me 3)Uncle Pen 4)I Wouldn't Change You If I Could 5)Highway 40 Blues					
4/19/80	86	4		1 I'll Take The Blame .... Could You Love Me One More Time		—	$8		Sugar Hill 3706
5/2/81	16	16		2 Don't Get Above Your Raising .... Low And Lonely		—	$4		Epic 02034
9/12/81	9	17		3 You May See Me Walkin' .... So Round, So Firm, So Fully Packed		—	$4		Epic 02499
1/23/82	❶¹	23		4 Crying My Heart Out Over You .... Lost To A Stranger		—	$4		Epic 02692
5/29/82	❶¹	18		5 I Don't Care .... If That's The Way You Feel		—	$4		Epic 02931
9/18/82	❶¹	17		6 Heartbroke .... Don't Think I'll Cry		—	$4		Epic 03212
12/25/82+	❶¹	20		7 I Wouldn't Change You If I Could .... One Way Rider		—	$4		Epic 03482
4/30/83	❶¹	19		8 Highway 40 Blues .... Don't Let Your Sweet Love Die		—	$4		Epic 03812
8/13/83	2¹	19		9 You've Got A Lover .... Let's Love The Bad Times Away		—	$4		Epic 04044
12/3/83+	❶¹	20		10 Don't Cheat In Our Hometown .... Children Go		—	$4		Sugar Hill/Epic 04245
3/24/84	❶¹	18		11 Honey (Open That Door) .... She's More To Be Pitied		—	$4		Sugar Hill/Epic 04394
7/21/84	❶¹	19		12 Uncle Pen .... S:7 / A:20 I'm Head Over Heels In Love		—	$4		Sugar Hill/Epic 04527
				written by Bill Monroe					
11/3/84+	2¹	22		13 Something In My Heart .... S:❶¹ / A:3 Baby, I'm In Love With You		—	$4		Epic 04668
3/23/85	❶¹	19		14 Country Boy .... S:❶¹ / A:❶¹ Wheel Hoss		—	$4		Epic 04831

DEBUT	PEAK	WKS	Gold	A-side (Chart Hit)	B-side	Pop	$	Pic	Label & Number
				SKAGGS, Ricky — Cont'd					
9/14/85	7	23	★	15 You Make Me Feel Like A Man	S:7 / A:8 Rendezvous	—	$4		Epic 05585
1/11/86	❶¹	20		16 Cajun Moon	S:❶¹ / A:❶¹ Rockin' The Boat	—	$4		Epic 05748
5/24/86	10	18		17 I've Got A New Heartache	S:7 / A:10 She Didn't Say Why	—	$4		Epic 05898
10/4/86	4	20		18 Love's Gonna Get You Someday	S:3 / A:4 Walkin' In Jerusalem	—	$4		Epic 06327
2/14/87	30	11		19 I Wonder If I Care As Much	S:19 / A:30 Raisin' The Dickens	—	$4		Epic 06650
				made the Pop charts as a flip side by **The Everly Brothers** in 1957					
5/2/87	10	23		20 Love Can't Ever Get Better Than This S:5 Daddy Was A Hardworking, Honest Man		—	$4		Epic 07060
				RICKY SKAGGS & SHARON WHITE					
10/17/87+	18	20		21 I'm Tired	S:12 San Antonio Rose	—	$4		Epic 07416
2/27/88	33	13		22 (Angel On My Mind) That's Why I'm Walkin'	S:16 Lord, She Sure Is Good At Lovin' Me	—	$4		Epic 07721
				same tune as "Why I'm Walkin'" by **Stonewall Jackson**					
6/11/88	17	16		23 Thanks Again	S:11 If You Don't Believe The Bible	—	$4		Epic 07924
10/15/88	30	15		24 Old Kind Of Love	S:19 Woman You Won't Break Mine	—	$4		Epic 08063
4/8/89	❶¹	21		25 Lovin' Only Me	Home Is Wherever You Are	—	$4		Epic 68693
8/5/89	5	26		26 Let It Be You	The Fields Of Home	—	$4		Epic 68995
12/9/89	13	26		27 Heartbreak Hurricane	Casting My Shadow In The Road	—	$4		Epic 73078
4/21/90	20	16		28 Hummingbird	Kentucky Thunder	—	$4	■	Epic 73312 (v)
9/1/90	25	20		29 He Was On To Somethin' (So He Made You)	When I Love	—	$4	■	Epic 73496 (v)
8/17/91	37	18		30 Life's Too Long (To Live Like This)	Lonesome For You	—	$4		Epic 73947
12/21/91+	12	20		31 Same Ol' Love	My Father's Son	—	$4	■	Epic 74147 (v)
5/16/92	43	10		32 From The Word Love	You Can't Take It With You When You Go	—	$4		Epic 74311
11/25/95+	57	14		33 Solid Ground	—	—			album cut
4/20/96	45	11		34 Cat's In The Cradle	—	—			album cut
				#1 Pop hit for Harry Chapin in 1974; above 2 from the album *Solid Ground* on Atlantic 82834					
	★373★			**SKINNER, Jimmie** '58					
				Born on 4/27/09 in Blue Lick, Ohio. Died of a heart attack on 10/28/79 (age 70). Singer/songwriter/guitarist. Worked as a DJ in Tennessee and Ohio.					
				1) I Found My Girl In The USA 2) Dark Hollow 3) What Makes A Man Wander					
4/30/49	15	1		1 Tennessee Border	S:15 Candy Kisses	—	$30		Radio Artist 244
11/4/57+	5	17		2 I Found My Girl In The USA	A:5 / S:9 Carroll County Blues	—	$15		Mercury 71192
				answer to "Fraulein" by **Bobby Helms** and "Geisha Girl" by **Hank Locklin**					
3/24/58	8	8		3 What Makes A Man Wander	A:8 / S:14 We've Got Things In Common	—	$15		Mercury 71256
1/19/59	7	10		4 Dark Hollow /		—			
1/12/59	21	8		5 Walkin' My Blues Away		—	$15		Mercury 71387
8/3/59	17	11		6 John Wesley Hardin	Misery Loves Company	—	$15		Mercury 71470
1/18/60	14	11		7 Riverboat Gambler	Married To A Friend	—	$15		Mercury 71539
5/16/60	21	4		8 Lonesome Road Blues	Two Squares Away	—	$15		Mercury 71606
8/29/60	13	8		9 Reasons To Live	I'm A Lot More Lonesome Now	—	$15		Mercury 71663
12/19/60	30	1		10 Careless Love	I'll Weaken And Call	—	$15		Mercury 71704
				SKIP AND LINDA '82					
				Duo of Skip Eaton and **Linda Davis**.					
8/21/82	63	7		1 If You Could See You Through My Eyes	The Clown	—	$5		MDJ 68178
10/23/82	73	5		2 I Just Can't Turn Temptation Down	Don't Surrender Your Love	—	$5		MDJ 68179
12/18/82	89	4		3 This Time	—	—	$5		MDJ 68180
				S-K-O — see **SCHUYLER, KNOBLOCH & OVERSTREET**					
				SKY KINGS, The '96					
				All-star trio: John Cowan (**New Grass Revival**), Bill Lloyd (**Foster & Lloyd**) and Rusty Young (**Poco**).					
4/20/96	52	7		1 Picture Perfect	That's How You Learn About Love	—	$5	■	Warner 17663 (v)
				SLATER, David '88					
				Born on 11/22/62 in Dallas.					
3/26/88	36	13		1 I'm Still Your Fool	I've Met My Match	—	$4		Capitol 44129
6/25/88	30	17		2 The Other Guy	Rest Assured	—	$4		Capitol 44184
				#11 Pop hit for the Little River Band in 1983					
10/22/88	63	8		3 We Were Meant To Be Lovers	Losin' My Louisiana Blues	—	$4		Capitol 44257
				#31 Pop hit for Photoglo in 1980					
5/13/89	65	6		4 She Will	The Story Of Us	—	$4		Capitol 44359
9/23/89	75	3		5 Whatcha Gonna Do About Her	Be With Me	—	$4		Capitol 44433
				SLEDD, Patsy '74					
				Born Patricia Randolph on 1/29/44 in Falcon, Missouri. Singer/songwriter/pianist.					
9/9/72	68	6		1 Nothing Can Stop My Loving You	Don't Fight The Feeling	—	$6		Mega 0085
1/5/74	33	12		2 Chip Chip	Don't Fight The Feeling	—	$5		Mega 1203
				#10 Pop hit for Gene McDaniels in 1962					
12/7/74+	72	9		3 See Saw	We Gotta Lotta Love	—	$5		Mega 1217
				#25 Pop hit for The Moonglows in 1956					
2/7/76	90	5		4 The Cowboy And The Lady	This Is It	—	$5		Mega 1244
11/28/87	79	3		5 Don't Stay If You Don't Love Me	My Diamond Is Only A Stone	—	$5	☐	Showtime 1007
				promo copies of record and picture sleeve included a handwritten letter from Patsy					
				SLEWFOOT '86					
				Group from Myrtle Beach, South Carolina.					
9/13/86	85	3		1 Nice To Be With You	Better Than This	—	$5		Step One 360
				#4 Pop hit for Gallery in 1972					

DEBUT	PEAK	WKS	Gold	A-side (Chart Hit) .... B-side	Pop	$	Pic	Label & Number
				SLIGO STUDIO BAND '81				
				Group from Norfolk, Virginia.				
4/18/81	94	2		You're The Reason .... She Offered Her Honor	—	$7		GBS 708
				SLOANE, Rene — see MITCHELL, Price				
				SLYE, Carrie '83				
				Born on 2/28/60 in Grants, New Mexico; raised in Gurden, Arkansas.				
7/23/83	78	4		Ease The Fever	—	$7		Friday 42683
				SMALLWOOD, Laney '78				
				Singer/actress. Also recorded as **Laney Hicks**.				
7/1/78	57	6		1 That "I Love You, You Love Me Too" Love Song .... I'm Sure To Cry	—	$5		Monument 255
12/19/81	92	3		2 Until The Nights .... I Love The Way You Love Me	—	$5		Monument 21001
				CHARLIE McCOY & LANEY SMALLWOOD				
				written and first recorded by Billy Joel on his 1978 *52nd Street* album				
4/16/83	74	4		3 The State Of Our Union .... Just Doin' Nothin' With You (Is Really Somethin')	—	$5		Monument 03518
				CHARLIE McCOY & LANEY HICKS				
				SMART, Jimmy '61				
				Born in Terrell, Texas.				
10/10/60	18	2		1 Broken Dream .... It's Too Late For Me	—	$25		Allstar 7211
3/13/61	16	7		2 Shorty .... In My Dreams	—	$20		Plaid 1004
				SMILEY, Red — see RENO & SMILEY				
				SMITH, Andy Lee '89				
				Female singer.				
11/11/89	71	3		Invitation To The Blues	—	$5	■	615 1024
				SMITH, Arthur "Guitar Boogie" '49				
				Born on 4/1/21 in Clinton, South Carolina. Songwriter/guitarist.				
9/25/48	9	2		1 Banjo Boogie .... J:9 Have A Little Fun [I]	—	$25		MGM 10229
12/25/48+	8	7		2 Guitar Boogie / .... J:8 [I]	—			
				above 2 tunes revised in 1959 as "Guitar Boogie Shuffle" by The Virtues				
1/1/49	8	4		3 Boomerang .... J:8 [I]	—	$25		MGM 10293
				ARTHUR "Guitar Boogie" SMITH and His Cracker-Jacks (above 3)				
10/19/63	29	3		4 Tie My Hunting Dog Down, Jed .... Guitar Hop [N]	—	$15		Starday 642
				parody of "Tie Me Kangaroo Down, Sport" by Rolf Harris				
				SMITH, Bobby '81				
				Born in 1946 in Balch Springs, Texas.				
5/7/77	70	8		1 Do You Wanna Make Love .... Too Turned On	—	$6		Autumn 398
				#5 Pop hit for Peter McCann in 1977				
8/22/81	30	11		2 Just Enough Love (For One Woman) .... Goin' In Circles	—	$4		Liberty 1417
11/28/81+	40	10		3 Too Many Hearts In The Fire .... You Hit Me Right Where I Love	—	$4		Liberty 1439
2/20/82	47	9		4 And Then Some .... Everytime I Do	—	$4		Liberty 1452
10/2/82	68	5		5 It's Been One Of Those Days .... Loving You Could Never Be Better	—	$4		Liberty 1480
				SMITH, Cal ★171★ '74				
				Born Calvin Grant Shofner on 4/7/32 in Gans, Oklahoma; raised in Oakland, California. Singer/guitarist. Worked clubs and as a DJ in San Jose. Regular member of the *California Hayride*. Worked with **Ernest Tubb** from 1962-68.				
				1)It's Time To Pay The Fiddler 2)The Lord Knows I'm Drinking 3)Country Bumpkin 4)I've Found Someone Of My Own				
				5)Between Lust And Watching TV				
1/28/67	58	10		1 The Only Thing I Want .... Stranger In The House	—	$7		Kapp 788
8/19/67	61	2		2 I'll Never Be Lonesome With You .... If I Had My Life To Live Over	—	$7		Kapp 834
2/24/68	60	5		3 Destination Atlanta G.A. .... Did She Ask About Me	—	$7		Kapp 884
6/22/68	58	7		4 Jacksonville .... I Love You A Thousand Ways	—	$7		Kapp 913
10/5/68	35	7		5 Drinking Champagne .... Honky Tonk Blues	—	$7		Kapp 938
6/14/69	51	8		6 It Takes All Night Long .... Daddy's Arms	—	$7		Kapp 994
9/27/69	55	4		7 You Can't Housebreak A Tomcat .... At The Sight Of You	—	$7		Kapp 2037
1/3/70	47	2		8 Heaven Is Just A Touch Away .... I Overlooked An Orchid	—	$7		Kapp 2059
4/25/70	70	2		9 The Difference Between Going And Really Gone .... My Happiness Goes Off	—	$7		Kapp 2076
1/16/71	58	7		10 That's What It's Like To Be Lonesome .... The Only Girl In The Game	—	$6		Decca 32768
5/6/72	4	15		11 I've Found Someone Of My Own The Lights Of The Living	—	$6		Decca 32959
				#5 Pop hit for Free Movement in 1971				
9/16/72	58	8		12 For My Baby .... A Handful Of Stars	—	$6		Decca 33003
				#28 Pop hit for Brook Benton in 1961				
12/16/72+	❶¹	17		13 The Lord Knows I'm Drinking Sweet Things I Remember About You	64	$6		Decca 33040
5/26/73	25	11		14 I Can Feel The Leavin' Coming On /	—			
			7	15 I've Loved You All Over The World	—	$5		MCA 40061
10/13/73	63	9		16 Bleep You /	—			
			7	17 An Hour And A Six-Pack	—	$5		MCA 40136
3/9/74	❶¹	15		18 Country Bumpkin .... It's Not The Miles You Traveled	—	$5		MCA 40191
				CMA Award: Single of the Year				
8/3/74	11	13		19 Between Lust And Watching TV .... Some Kind Of A Woman	—	$5		MCA 40265
12/7/74+	❶¹	16		20 It's Time To Pay The Fiddler .... Love Is The Foundation	—	$5		MCA 40335

DEBUT	PEAK	WKS	Gold	A-side (Chart Hit)	B-side	Pop	$	Pic	Label & Number
				SMITH, Cal — Cont'd					
4/26/75	13	13		21 She Talked A Lot About Texas	Baby's Gone	—	$5		MCA 40394
10/25/75	12	14		22 Jason's Farm	You Slip Into My Mind	—	$5		MCA 40467
2/14/76	33	10		23 Thunderstorms	19 Years And 1800 Miles	—	$5		MCA 40517
6/5/76	43	9		24 MacArthur's Hand	Sunday Morning Christian	—	$5		MCA 40563
10/9/76	38	10		25 Woman Don't Try To Sing My Song	I Play A Man	—	$5		MCA 40618
1/22/77	15	14		26 I Just Came Home To Count The Memories	Feelin' The Weight Of My Chains	—	$5		MCA 40671
4/30/77	23	10		27 Come See About Me	The In Crowd	—	$5		MCA 40714
9/24/77	53	8		28 Helen	I'm Forty Now	—	$5		MCA 40789
12/17/77+	51	9		29 Throwin' Memories On The Fire	Tabernacle Tom	—	$5		MCA 40839
2/25/78	73	4		30 I'm Just A Farmer	The Ghost Of Jim Bob Wilson	—	$5		MCA 40864
6/24/78	68	5		31 Bits And Pieces Of Life	Leona	—	$5		MCA 40911
1/6/79	71	6		32 The Rise And Fall Of The Roman Empire	Oklahoma Sunshine	—	$5		MCA 40982
4/14/79	91	2		33 One Little Skinny Rib	I Fed Her Love	—	$5		MCA 41001
11/3/79	92	2		34 The Room At The Top Of The Stairs	Happy Anniversary	—	$5		MCA 41128
10/30/82	68	6		35 Too Many Irons In The Fire	Honky Tonk Girl	—	$5		Soundwaves 4686
				BILLY PARKER and CAL SMITH					
9/6/86	75	5		36 King Lear	Country Bumpkin'	—	$5		Step One 358

SMITH, Carl ★25★   '52
Born on 3/15/27 in Maynardville, Tennessee. Singer/songwriter/guitarist. Began singing on radio station WROL in Knoxville. Served in the U.S. Navy from 1945-47. Played bass in Skeets Williamson's band. Married to **June Carter** from 1952-56; their daughter is **Carlene Carter**. Married **Goldie Hill** on 9/19/57.

1) Let Old Mother Nature Have Her Way 2) Hey Joe! 3) (When You Feel Like You're In Love) Don't Just Stand There 4) Loose Talk 5) Are You Teasing Me

DEBUT	PEAK	WKS	Gold	A-side	B-side	Pop	$	Pic	Label & Number
6/2/51	2¹	20		1 Let's Live A Little	A:2 / S:3 / J:3 There's Nothing As Sweet As My Baby	—	$25		Columbia 4-20796
8/4/51	4	17		2 Mr. Moon /	A:4 / J:5 / S:8	—			
8/4/51	8	3		3 If Teardrops Were Pennies	J:8 / S:9 / A:9	—	$25		Columbia 4-20825
10/27/51	●⁸	33		4 Let Old Mother Nature Have Her Way J:●⁸ / S:●⁶ / A:●³ Me And My Broken Heart		—	$25		Columbia 4-20862
3/1/52	●⁸	24		5 (When You Feel Like You're In Love) Don't Just Stand There A:●⁸ / S:●⁵ / J:●³ The Little Girl In My Home Town		—	$25		Columbia 4-20893
5/24/52	●¹	19		6 Are You Teasing Me /	A:●¹ / S:2 / J:2	—			
5/31/52	5	10		7 It's A Lovely, Lovely World	A:5 / S:8 / J:9	—	$25		Columbia 4-20922
10/25/52	6	6		8 Our Honeymoon	A:6 / J:6 / S:7 Sing Her A Love Song	—	$25		Columbia 4-21008
1/31/53	9	1		9 That's The Kind Of Love I'm Looking For	J:9 My Lonely Heart's Runnin' Wild	—	$20		Columbia 21051
5/9/53	4	6		10 Orchids Mean Goodbye /	J:4 / S:7 / A:7	—			
5/2/53	7	3		11 Just Wait 'Til I Get You Alone	A:7 / J:7 / S:9	—	$20		Columbia 21087
7/4/53	2²	10		12 Trademark	S:2 / J:5 / A:6	—			
7/18/53	6	1		13 Do I Like It?	A:6	—	$20		Columbia 21119
7/25/53	●⁸	26		14 Hey Joe!	J:●⁸ / A:●⁴ / S:●² Darlin' Am I The One	—	$20		Columbia 21129
11/7/53	7	6		15 Satisfaction Guaranteed	S:7 / A:7 / J:8 Who'll Buy My Heartaches	—	$20		Columbia 21166
2/13/54	7	4		16 Dog-Gone It, Baby, I'm In Love	A:7 / S:8 What Am I Going To Do With You?	—	$20		Columbia 21197
5/1/54	2¹	16		17 Back Up Buddy	A:2 / S:4 / J:4 If You Tried As Hard To Love Me	—	$20		Columbia 21226
8/7/54	4	11		18 Go, Boy, Go	S:4 / A:7 / J:9 If You Saw Her Through My Eyes	—	$20		Columbia 21266
11/6/54+	●⁷	32		19 Loose Talk /	S:●⁷ / A:●⁶ / J:●⁴	—			
11/6/54+	5	10		20 More Than Anything Else In The World	A:5 / S:15	—	$20		Columbia 21317
1/22/55	5	16		21 Kisses Don't Lie /	S:5 / J:7 / A:8	—			
1/29/55	13	2		22 No, I Don't Believe I Will	S:13 / A:15	—	$20		Columbia 21340
4/23/55	12	3		23 Wait A Little Longer Please, Jesus	A:12 Works Of The Lord	—	$20		Columbia 21368
5/14/55	3	25		24 There She Goes	A:3 / S:5 / J:8	—			
				#26 Pop hit for Jerry Wallace in 1961					
5/14/55	11	7		25 Old Lonesome Times	S:11 / A:13	—	$20		Columbia 21382
10/15/55	11	4		26 Don't Tease Me	A:11 / S:13 I Just Dropped In To Say Goodbye	—	$20		Columbia 21429
12/3/55+	6	14		27 You're Free To Go /	S:6 / A:6 / A:7	—			
12/3/55+	7	15		28 I Feel Like Cryin'	S:7 / J:9 / A:11	—	$20		Columbia 21462
3/31/56	11	3		29 I've Changed	A:11 / S:14 If You Do Dear	—	$20		Columbia 21493
6/23/56	4	23		30 You Are The One /	A:4 / J:5 / S:6	—			
8/4/56	6	6		31 Doorstep To Heaven	S:6	—	$20		Columbia 21522
10/13/56	6	12		32 Before I Met You /	J:6 / A:7 / S:9	—			
				CARL SMITH with The Tunesmiths (above 3)					
10/20/56	9	10		33 Wicked Lies	S:9	—	$20		Columbia 21552
3/2/57	15	1		34 You Can't Hurt Me Anymore	S:15 That's The Way I Like You The Best	—	$20		Columbia 40823
9/16/57	2²	19		35 Why, Why	A:2 / S:7 Emotions	—	$15		Columbia 40984
3/3/58	6	14		36 Your Name Is Beautiful	A:6 / S:9 You're So Easy To Love	80	$15		Columbia 41092
12/15/58	28	1		37 Walking The Slow Walk	A Love Was Born	—	$15		Columbia 41243
1/19/59	15	11		38 The Best Years Of Your Life	Mr. Moon	—	$15		Columbia 41290
6/1/59	19	3		39 It's All My Heartache	I'll Kiss The Past Goodbye	—	$15		Columbia 41344
7/20/59	5	12		40 Ten Thousand Drums	The Tall, Tall Gentleman	43	$12	■	Columbia 41417
12/14/59	24	4		41 Tomorrow Night	I'll Walk With You	—	$12		Columbia 41489
3/21/60	30	1		42 Make The Waterwheel Roll	Past	—	$12		Columbia 41557
6/20/60	28	2		43 Cut Across Shorty	Why Did You Come My Way	—	$12		Columbia 41642

DEBUT	PEAK	WKS Gold	A-side (Chart Hit)	B-side	Pop	$	Pic	Label & Number
			SMITH, Carl — Cont'd					
2/20/61	29	2	44 You Make Me Live Again	I Don't Hurt Now (As Much As I Used To)	—	$12		Columbia 41819
7/10/61	11	9	45 Kisses Never Lie	Why Can't You Be Satisfied With Me	—	$12		Columbia 42042
1/13/62	11	15	46 Air Mail To Heaven /		—			
1/27/62	24	2	47 Things That Mean The Most		—	$12		Columbia 42222
5/12/62	16	7	48 The Best Dressed Beggar (In Town)	I Used To Be	—	$12		Columbia 42349
4/20/63	28	1	49 Live For Tomorrow	Let's Talk This Thing Over	—	$12		Columbia 42686
8/24/63	17	8	50 In The Back Room Tonight	Take My Love With You, Too	—	$12		Columbia 42768
12/21/63+	16	11	51 Triangle /		—			
11/9/63+	23	5	52 I Almost Forgot Her Today		—	$12		Columbia 42858
2/22/64	17	14	53 The Pillow That Whispers	Sweet Little Country Girl	—	$12		Columbia 42949
6/20/64	15	20	54 Take My Ring Off Your Finger	The Ballad Of Hershel Lawson	—	$10		Columbia 43033
10/17/64	14	15	55 Lonely Girl /		—			
12/12/64+	26	9	56 When It's Over		—	$10		Columbia 43124
2/13/65	32	11	57 She Called Me Baby	My Friends Are Gonna Be Strangers	—	$10		Columbia 43200
6/26/65	33	8	58 Be Good To Her /		—			
6/12/65	42	3	59 Keep Me Fooled		—	$10		Columbia 43266
10/16/65	36	6	60 Let's Walk Away Strangers	Ain't Love A Hurting Thing	—	$10		Columbia 43361
3/12/66	45	4	61 Why Do I Keep Doing This To Us /		—			
3/19/66	49	1	62 Why Can't You Feel Sorry For Me		—	$10		Columbia 43485
9/17/66	42	5	63 Man With A Plan	You Mean Ol' Moon	—	$10		Columbia 43753
12/3/66+	52	8	64 You Better Be Better To Me /		—			
1/14/67	65	3	65 It's Only A Matter Of Time		—	$10		Columbia 43866
5/13/67	54	7	66 I Should Get Away Awhile (From You) /		—			
4/22/67	68	3	67 Mighty Day		—	$8		Columbia 44034
8/26/67	10	18	68 Deep Water	I Really Don't Want To Know	—	$8		Columbia 44233
1/13/68	18	11	69 Foggy River	When Will The Rainbow Follow The Rain	—	$8		Columbia 44396
5/18/68	43	9	70 You Ought To Hear Me Cry	I Used Up My Last Chance Last Night	—	$8		Columbia 44486
9/21/68	48	5	71 There's No More Love	(Remember Me) I'm The One Who Loves You	—	$8		Columbia 44620
1/4/69	25	13	72 Faded Love And Winter Roses	Until I Looked At You	—	$8		Columbia 44702
4/26/69	18	13	73 Good Deal, Lucille	Never Gonna Cry No More	—	$8		Columbia 44816
8/16/69	14	12	74 I Love You Because	Mister, Come And Get Your Wife	—	$8		Columbia 44939
12/6/69+	35	8	75 Heartbreak Avenue	It's Nice To See You Once Again	—	$8		Columbia 45031
3/14/70	18	10	76 Pull My String And Wind Me Up	It's All Right	—	$8		Columbia 45086
7/11/70	46	8	77 Pick Me Up On Your Way Down /		—			
		4	78 Bonaparte's Retreat		—	$7		Columbia 45177
10/3/70	20	12	79 How I Love Them Old Songs	Little Crop Of Cotton Tops	—	$7		Columbia 45225
2/13/71	44	10	80 Don't Worry 'Bout The Mule (Just Load The Wagon)	Darling Days	—	$7		Columbia 45293
6/5/71	43	8	81 Lost It On The Road	I'm Wound Up Tight (Now Turn Me Loose)	—	$6		Columbia 45382
9/11/71	21	13	82 Red Door	You Walked In My Sleep Last Night	—	$6		Columbia 45436
12/11/71+	34	12	83 Don't Say You're Mine	Country Soul Man	—	$6		Columbia 45497
5/13/72	46	11	84 Mama Bear	Before My Time	—	$6		Columbia 45558
8/5/72	54	9	85 If This Is Goodbye	If You Saw Her	—	$6		Columbia 45648
9/29/73	76	6	86 I Need Help	Yesterday Is Gone	—	$6		Columbia 45923
1/25/75	67	9	87 The Way I Lose My Mind	Happy Birthday My Darlin'	—	$5		Hickory/MGM 337
11/15/75	97	2	88 Roly Poly	Remembered By Someone (Remembered By Me)	—	$5		Hickory/MGM 357
5/29/76	97	3	89 If You Don't, Somebody Else Will	It's Gonna Be One Of Those Days	—	$5		Hickory/MGM 371
12/11/76	98	4	90 A Way With Words	Till I Stop Needing You	—	$5		ABC/Hickory 54004
4/9/77	96	4	91 Show Me A Brick Wall	It's Teardrop Time	—	$5		ABC/Hickory 54009
9/3/77	84	4	92 This Kinda Love Ain't Meant For Sunday School	There Stands The Glass	—	$5		ABC/Hickory 54016
2/4/78	81	4	93 This Lady Loving Me	Loose Talk	—	$5		ABC/Hickory 54022

SMITH, Connie ★74★ '64

Born Constance June Meador on 8/14/41 in Elkhart, Indiana; raised in Hinton, West Virginia, and Warner, Ohio. Singer/songwriter. Joined the *Grand Ole Opry* in 1971. Acted in the movies *Las Vegas Hillbillies*, *Road To Nashville* and *Second Fiddle To A Steel Guitar*. Married **Marty Stuart** on 7/8/97. Also see **Some Of Chet's Friends**.

1)Once A Day 2)Ain't Had No Lovin' 3)Just One Time 4)The Hurtin's All Over 5)Cincinnati, Ohio

DEBUT	PEAK	WKS	A-side	B-side	Pop	$	Pic	Label & Number
9/26/64	0^8	28	1 Once A Day	The Threshold	101	$10		RCA Victor 8416
1/23/65	4	24	2 Then And Only Then /		116			
2/6/65	25	17	3 Tiny Blue Transistor Radio		—	$10		RCA Victor 8489
6/5/65	9	16	4 I Can't Remember	Senses	130	$10		RCA Victor 8551
9/25/65	4	19	5 If I Talk To Him	I Don't Have Anyplace To Go	—	$10		RCA Victor 8663
2/12/66	4	17	6 Nobody But A Fool (Would Love You)	I'll Never Get Over Loving You	—	$10		RCA Victor 8746
6/11/66	2^2	17	7 Ain't Had No Lovin'	Five Fingers To Spare	—	$10		RCA Victor 8842
10/15/66	3	19	8 The Hurtin's All Over	Invisible Tears	—	$10		RCA Victor 8964
3/11/67	10	15	9 I'll Come Runnin'	It's Now Or Never	—	$10		RCA Victor 9108
6/24/67	4	15	10 Cincinnati, Ohio	Don't Feel Sorry For Me	—	$10	■	RCA Victor 9214
10/28/67	5	15	11 Burning A Hole In My Mind	Only For Me	—	$10		RCA Victor 9335
1/27/68	7	14	12 Baby's Back Again	It Only Hurts For A Little While	—	$10		RCA Victor 9413
5/18/68	10	15	13 Run Away Little Tears	Let Me Help You Work It Out	—	$10		RCA Victor 9513

DEBUT	PEAK	WKS	Gold	A-side (Chart Hit)	B-side	Pop	$	Pic	Label & Number
				SMITH, Connie — Cont'd					
9/28/68	20	11		14 Cry, Cry, Cry .... The Hurt Goes On		—	$10		RCA Victor 9624
3/1/69	13	14		15 Ribbon Of Darkness .... A Lonely Woman		—	$8		RCA Victor 0101
7/5/69	20	11		16 Young Love .... Something Pretty		—	$8		RCA Victor 0181
				CONNIE SMITH AND NAT STUCKEY #1 Pop hit for Tab Hunter in 1957					
11/8/69	6	15		17 You And Your Sweet Love ...... I Can't Get Used To Being Lonely		—	$8		RCA Victor 0258
3/14/70	59	4		18 If God Is Dead (Who's That Living In My Soul)............. His Love Takes Care Of Me		—	$8		RCA Victor 9805
				NAT STUCKEY AND CONNIE SMITH					
5/16/70	5	15		19 I Never Once Stopped Loving You .... The Son Shines Down On Me		—	$7		RCA Victor 9832
9/12/70	14	11		20 Louisiana Man .... Alone With You		—	$7		RCA Victor 9887
1/2/71	11	14		21 Where Is My Castle .... Clinging To A Saving Hand		—	$7		RCA Victor 9938
5/8/71	2²	17		22 Just One Time .... Don't Walk Away	119	$7		RCA Victor 9981
10/16/71	14	15		23 I'm Sorry If My Love Got In Your Way .... Plenty Of Time		—	$7		RCA Victor 0535
3/4/72	5	15		24 Just For What I Am .... I'd Still Want To Serve Him Today		—	$7		RCA Victor 0655
8/5/72	7	15		25 If It Ain't Love (Let's Leave It Alone) .... Living Without You		—	$7		RCA Victor 0752
12/23/72+	8	14		26 Love Is The Look You're Looking For .... My Ecstasy		—	$7		RCA Victor 0860
3/31/73	21	12		27 You've Got Me (Right Where You Want Me) .... A Picture Of Me (Without You)		—	$6		Columbia 45816
6/23/73	23	10		28 Dream Painter .... Once A Day		—	$7		RCA Victor 0971
11/10/73+	10	14		29 Ain't Love A Good Thing .... I Still Feel The Same About You		—	$6		Columbia 45954
3/23/74	35	11		30 Dallas .... That's The Way Love Goes		—	$6		Columbia 46008
6/29/74	13	13		31 I Never Knew (What That Song Meant Before) .... Did We Have To Come This Far (To Say Goodbye)		—	$6		Columbia 46058
11/16/74+	13	12		32 I've Got My Baby On My Mind .... Why Don't You Love Me		—	$5		Columbia 10051
2/22/75	30	10		33 I Got A Lot Of Hurtin' Done Today .... Back In The Country		—	$5		Columbia 10086
5/17/75	15	13		34 Why Don't You Love Me .... Loving You (Has Changed My Whole Life)		—	$5		Columbia 10135
10/4/75	29	11		35 The Song We Fell In Love To .... One Little Reason		—	$5		Columbia 10210
1/31/76	10	15		36 ('Til) I Kissed You .... Ridin' On A Rainbow		—	$5		Columbia 10277
6/5/76	31	10		37 So Sad (To Watch Good Love Go Bad) .... Constantly		—	$5		Columbia 10345
				#7 Pop hit for **The Everly Brothers** in 1960					
8/28/76	13	14		38 I Don't Wanna Talk It Over Anymore .. You Crossed My Mind A Thousand Times Today		—	$5		Columbia 10393
3/26/77	42	8		39 The Latest Shade Of Blue .... I'm All Wrapped Up In You		—	$5		Columbia 10501
5/28/77	58	7		40 Coming Around .... You And Love And I		—	$5		Monument 219
11/5/77+	14	15		41 I Just Want To Be Your Everything .... Scrapbook		—	$5		Monument 231
				#1 Pop hit for **Andy Gibb** in 1977					
2/25/78	34	10		42 Lovin' You Baby .... All Of A Sudden		—	$5		Monument 241
5/27/78	68	6		43 There'll Never Be Another For Me .... The Wayward Wind		—	$5		Monument 252
11/4/78	68	5		44 Smooth Sailin' .... Loving You Has Sure Been Good To Me		—	$5		Monument 266
4/7/79	88	3		45 Lovin' You, Lovin' Me /		—			
		3		46 Ten Thousand And One			$5		Monument 281
6/23/79	93	2		47 Don't Say Love .... I Don't Want To Be Free		—	$5		Monument 284
7/27/85	71	6		48 A Far Cry From You .... Don't Touch (The Pain's Not Dry)		—	$4	■	Epic 05414
				SMITH, Darden '88 Born on 3/11/62 in Brenham, Texas.					
2/20/88	56	8		1 Little Maggie .... Place In Time		—	$4		Epic 07709
5/28/88	59	6		2 Day After Tomorrow .... God's Will		—	$4		Epic 07906
				SMITH, David '79 Born in Dallas.					
10/20/79	64	5		Heroes And Idols (Don't Come Easy) .... Loraine Phillips		—	$5		MDJ 1004
				SMITH, Dennis '80					
3/1/80	94	2		California Calling .... Get It Together		—	$7		Adonda 79021
				SMITH, Jerry, and His Pianos '69 Session pianist. Also recorded as **Papa Joe's Music Box**.					
5/17/69	44	10		1 Truck Stop .... My Happiness [I]	71	$7		ABC 11162
8/16/69	63	5		2 Sweet 'N' Sassy .... Sunrise Serenade [I]		—	$7		ABC 11230
12/20/69	62	3		3 Papa Joe's Thing .... Jean [I]		—	$7		ABC 11246
				PAPA JOE'S MUSIC BOX					
6/6/70	44	9		4 Drivin' Home .... Louisiana Blues [I]	125	$6		Decca 32679
10/3/70	60	7		5 Steppin' Out .... Closing Time [I]		—	$6		Decca 32730
				SMITH, Kate '48 Born on 5/1/07 in Greenville, Virginia. Died on 6/17/86 (age 79). Popular soprano. Hosted own radio and TV shows. Charted 9 pop hits from 1940-48.					
10/30/48	10	1		Foggy River .... S:10 Cool Water		—	$15		MGM 30059
				SMITH, Logan '74 Male singer/songwriter.					
1/19/74	63	11		Little Man .... Down On The Farm [N]		—	$7		Brand X 6
				SMITH, Lou '60					
8/15/60	9	17		1 Cruel Love .... Close To My Heart		—	$20		KRCO 105
4/17/61	21	5		2 I'm Wondering .... Aching Breaking Heart		—	$20		Salvo 2862

DEBUT	PEAK	WKS	Gold	A-side (Chart Hit)	B-side	Pop	$	Pic	Label & Number

SMITH, Margo ★186★ '78
Born Betty Lou Miller on 4/9/42 in Dayton, Ohio. Singer/songwriter/actress. Sang with the Apple Sisters vocal group while in high school. Taught kindergarden during the 1960s. Formed a gospel duo with her daughter Holly in the 1990s.

1) Don't Break The Heart That Loves You 2) It Only Hurts For A Little While 3) Little Things Mean A Lot 4) Still A Woman 5) Take My Breath Away

DEBUT	PEAK	WKS	#	A-side	B-side	Pop	$	Label & Number
4/5/75	8	18	1	There I Said It	Hurt Me Twice	—	$6	20th Century 2172
9/13/75	30	12	2	Paper Lovin'	He Don't Love Here	—	$6	20th Century 2222
12/20/75+	51	8	3	Meet Me Later	Baby's Hurtin'	—	$6	20th Century 2255
5/29/76	10	14	4	Save Your Kisses For Me	I'm About To Do It Again	—	$5	Warner 8213
				#27 Pop hit for The Brotherhood Of Man in 1976				
10/2/76	7	16	5	Take My Breath Away	When Where And Why	—	$5	Warner 8261
3/12/77	12	12	6	Love's Explosion	So Close Again	—	$5	Warner 8339
6/25/77	23	10	7	My Weakness	I'd Rather Have A Heart Abused	—	$5	Warner 8399
8/20/77	43	8	8	So Close Again	Saturday Night At The General Store	—	$5	Warner 8427
				MARGO SMITH & NORRO WILSON				
12/17/77+	❶²	18	9	Don't Break The Heart That Loves You	Apt. #4, Sixth Street In Cincinnati	104	$5	Warner 8508
				#1 Pop hit for Connie Francis in 1962				
4/29/78	❶¹	15	10	It Only Hurts For A Little While	Lookout Mountain	—	$5	Warner 8555
				#11 Pop hit for The Ames Brothers in 1956				
9/9/78	3	14	11	Little Things Mean A Lot	Make Love The Way We Used To	—	$5	Warner 8653
				#1 Pop hit for Kitty Kallen in 1954				
1/20/79	7	13	12	Still A Woman	Tennessee Sandman	—	$5	Warner 8726
5/5/79	10	13	13	If I Give My Heart To You	We'd Better Love It Over	—	$5	Warner 8806
				#3 Pop hit for Doris Day in 1954				
9/8/79	27	9	14	Baby My Baby	The Belle Of Buttercup Lane	—	$5	Warner 49038
12/8/79+	13	13	15	The Shuffle Song	Move Over Juanita	—	$5	Warner 49109
7/5/80	43	9	16	My Guy	If You Remember Me	—	$5	Warner 49250
				#1 Pop hit for Mary Wells in 1964				
10/11/80	52	7	17	He Gives Me Diamonds, You Give Me Chills	Every Little Bit Hurts	—	$5	Warner 49569
12/20/80+	12	14	18	Cup Of Tea	Goodbye	—	$5	Warner 49626
				REX ALLEN, JR. AND MARGO SMITH				
4/25/81	72	4	19	My Heart Cries For You	Borrowed Angel	—	$5	Warner 49701
				#2 Pop hit for Guy Mitchell in 1951				
6/13/81	26	12	20	While The Feeling's Good	Watered Down Love	—	$5	Warner 49738
				REX ALLEN, JR. & MARGO SMITH				
5/8/82	64	7	21	Either You're Married Or You're Single	Where The Heart Leads	—	$5	AMI 1304
8/21/82	70	5	22	Could It Be I Don't Belong Here Anymore	Ridin' High	—	$5	AMI 1309
12/10/83	78	4	23	Wedding Bells	Ridin' High	—	$5	Moon Shine 3019
1/28/84	63	7	24	Please Tell Him That I Said Hello	Waitin' Needin' Drives Me Crazy	—	$5	Moon Shine 3021
				#84 Pop hit for Debbie Campbell in 1975				
6/22/85	82	2	25	All I Do Is Dream Of You		—	$7	Bermuda Dunes 106
8/10/85	63	8	26	Everyday People		—	$7	Bermuda Dunes 110
				MARGO SMITH AND TOM GRANT				
4/23/88	77	4	27	Echo Me	Love Letters In The Sand	—	$7	Playback 1300

SMITH, Rick '76
Born in Louisville, Kentucky.

DEBUT	PEAK	WKS	#	A-side	B-side	Pop	$	Label & Number
9/11/76	99	2	1	The Way I Loved Her	Catchin' The 9:45	—	$5	Cin Kay 110
10/23/76	58	7	2	Daddy How'm I Doin'	The Blues Was Here To Stay	—	$5	Cin Kay 114

SMITH, Russell '89
Born Howard Russell Smith on 6/17/49 in Nashville. Former lead singer of the Amazing Rhythm Aces.

DEBUT	PEAK	WKS	#	A-side	B-side	Pop	$	Label & Number
2/4/84	74	6	1	Where Did We Go Right	Hesitation	—	$4	Capitol 5293
5/14/88	53	8	2	Three Piece Suit	Not Made Of Stone	—	$4	Epic 07789
7/23/88	49	8	3	Betty Jean	Not Made Of Stone	—	$4	Epic 07972
3/18/89	37	14	4	I Wonder What She's Doing Tonight	This Little Town	—	$4	Epic 68615
7/22/89	61	8	5	Anger And Tears	The Colorado Side	—	$4	Epic 68964

SMITH, Sammi ★159★ '71
Born Jewel Fay Smith on 8/5/43 in Orange, California; raised in Oklahoma. Female singer/songwriter. Performing since age 11. Moved to Nashville in 1967. Moved to Dallas in 1973 and became part of the "outlaw" movement.

1) Help Me Make It Through The Night 2) Today I Started Loving You Again 3) Then You Walk In 4) I've Got To Have You 5) Cheatin's A Two Way Street

DEBUT	PEAK	WKS	#	A-side	B-side	Pop	$	Label & Number
1/27/68	69	2	1	So Long, Charlie Brown, Don't Look For Me Around	Turn Around	—	$7	Columbia 44370
6/8/68	53	7	2	Why Do You Do Me Like You Do	22 Road Markers To A Mile	—	$7	Columbia 44523
8/16/69	58	6	3	Brownville Lumberyard	Shadows Of Your Mind	—	$7	Columbia 44905
9/5/70	25	13	4	He's Everywhere	This Room For Rent	—	$6	■ Mega 0001
12/19/70+	❶³	20 ●	5	Help Me Make It Through The Night	When Michael Calls	8	$6	Mega 0015
				CMA Award: Single of the Year				
5/15/71	10	14	6	Then You Walk In	Willie	118	$5	Mega 0026

DEBUT	PEAK	WKS	Gold	A-side (Chart Hit)	B-side	Pop	$	Pic	Label & Number
				SMITH, Sammi — Cont'd					
9/18/71	27	12		7 For The Kids .... Saunders' Ferry Lane		—	$6		Mega 0039
1/1/72	38	10		8 Kentucky .... The Marionette		—	$6		Mega 0056
4/22/72	36	8		9 Girl In New Orleans .... Isn't It Sad		—	$6		Mega 0068
6/17/72	13	15		10 I've Got To Have You .... Jimmy's In Georgia		77	$6		Mega 0079
12/23/72+	51	8		11 The Toast Of '45 .... Tony		—	$6		Mega 0097
5/19/73	62	8		12 I Miss You Most When You're Here .... Billy Jacks		—	$6		Mega 0109
9/29/73	44	12		13 City Of New Orleans .... Don't Blow No Smoke On Me		—	$6		Mega 0118
				#18 Pop hit for Arlo Guthrie in 1972					
1/19/74	16	12		14 The Rainbow In Daddy's Eyes .... Birmingham Mistake		—	$5		Mega 1204
6/1/74	75	7		15 Never Been To Spain .... It's Not Easy		—	$5		Mega 1210
				#5 Pop hit for Three Dog Night in 1972					
9/7/74	26	13		16 Long Black Veil .... Paste Me On Some Feathers		—	$5		Mega 1214
2/1/75	33	11		17 Cover Me .... He Makes It Hard To Say Goodbye		—	$5		Mega 1222
9/13/75	9	15		18 Today I Started Loving You Again .... Fine As Wine		—	$5		Mega 1236
12/20/75+	81	7		19 Huckelberry Pie .... I Won't Sing No Love Songs Anymore		—	$5		Elektra 45292
				EVEN STEVENS/SAMMI SMITH					
1/10/76	51	6		20 My Window Faces The South .... Before The Next Teardrop Falls		—	$5		Mega 1246
2/21/76	43	9		21 As Long As There's A Sunday .... Children		—	$5		Elektra 45300
5/29/76	60	6		22 I'll Get Better .... Rabbitt Tracks		—	$5		Elektra 45320
7/17/76	29	11		23 Sunday School To Broadway .... Good Mornin' Sunshine, Goodbye		—	$5		Elektra 45334
7/31/76	71	6		24 Just You 'N' Me .... Walking In The Sunshine		—	$5		Zodiac 1005
				#4 Pop hit for Chicago in 1973					
2/5/77	19	12		25 Loving Arms .... I Just Wanted To Sing		—	$5		Elektra 45374
5/14/77	27	11		26 I Can't Stop Loving You .... De Grazia's Song		—	$5		Elektra 45398
				#1 Pop hit for **Ray Charles** in 1962					
9/17/77	23	11		27 Days That End In "Y" .... Hallelujah For Beer		—	$5		Elektra 45429
4/29/78	48	8		28 It Just Won't Feel Like Cheating (With You) ...... I Ain't Got Time To Rock No Babies		—	$5		Elektra 45476
8/5/78	73	4		29 Norma Jean .... Lookin' For Lovin'		—	$5		Elektra 45504
3/10/79	16	14		30 What A Lie .... It's Not My Way		—	$7		Cyclone 100
7/21/79	27	11		31 The Letter .... It's A Day For Sad Song		—	$7		Cyclone 104
				#1 Pop hit for The Box Tops in 1967					
11/29/80+	36	13		32 I Just Want To Be With You .... I've Never Loved You More Than I Do Now		—	$5		Sound Factory 425
3/7/81	16	13		33 Cheatin's A Two Way Street .... The Legend Of Wooley Swamp		—	$5		Sound Factory 427
8/8/81	34	11		34 Sometimes I Cry When I'm Alone .... Once Or Twice		—	$5		Sound Factory 446
3/27/82	69	5		35 Gypsy And Joe		—	$5		Sound Factory 433
7/20/85	76	4		36 You Just Hurt My Last Feeling .... Lying In My Arms		—	$5		Step One 342
3/1/86	80	4		37 Love Me All Over .... Don't Let It Happen Again		—	$5		Step One 351
				SMITH, Warren '60					
				Born on 2/7/32 in Humphreys County, Mississippi. Died of a heart attack on 1/30/80 (age 47). Rockabilly singer/songwriter.					
9/5/60	5	17		1 I Don't Believe I'll Fall In Love Today .... Cave In		—	$20		Liberty 55248
2/20/61	7	15		2 Odds And Ends (Bits And Pieces) .... A Whole Lot Of Nothin'		—	$20		Liberty 55302
9/11/61	23	3		3 Why, Baby, Why .... Why I'm Walking		—	$20		Liberty 55361
				WARREN SMITH and SHIRLEY COLLIE					
9/11/61	26	3		4 Call Of The Wild .... Old Lonesome Feeling		—	$20		Liberty 55336
11/2/63	25	4		5 That's Why I Sing In A Honky Tonk /		—			
1/11/64	41	2		6 Big City Ways		—	$20		Liberty 55615
8/1/64	41	8		7 Blue Smoke .... Judge And Jury		—	$20		Liberty 55699
				SMOKIN' ARMADILLOS '96					
				Group from Bakersfield, California: Rick Russell (vocals), Josh Graham and Scott Meeks (guitars), Jason Theiste (fiddle), Aaron Casida (bass) and Darin Kirkindoll (drums).					
1/13/96	53	10		1 Let Your Heart Lead Your Mind .... Miracle Man		—	$4	▪	MCG/Curb 76976 (v)
5/11/96	68	4		2 Thump Factor .... S:21 Miracle Man		—	$4	▪	MCG/Curb 76989 (v)
1/24/98	64	6		3 I Don't Want No Part Of It		—			album cut
				from the album *I Don't Want No Part Of It* on Curb 73037					
				SNODGRASS, Elmer '60					
				Worked as a DJ on WAKE in Bakersfield, California.					
1/18/60	20	10		1 Until Today .... Sidelines		—	$15		Decca 31048
				ELMER SNODGRASS AND THE MUSICAL PIONEERS					
1/30/61	25	1		2 What A Terrible Feeling .... Heartaches Over You		—	$15		Decca 31145
				SNOW, Hank ★23★ '50					
				Born Clarence Eugene Snow on 5/9/14 in Brooklyn, Nova Scotia, Canada. Died of heart failure on 12/20/99 (age 85). Singer/songwriter/guitarist. Hosted own radio shows on CNHS in Halifax, CBC in Montreal and CKCW in Mocton, Canada. Joined the *Grand Ole Opry* in 1950. Backing group: The Rainbow Ranch Boys. Known as "The Singing Ranger." Elected to the Country Music Hall of Fame in 1979. Also see **Some Of Chet's Friends**.					
				1) I'm Moving On 2) I Don't Hurt Anymore 3) The Rhumba Boogie 4) The Golden Rocket 5) I've Been Everywhere					
				HANK SNOW, The Singing Ranger and his Rainbow Ranch Boys:					
12/31/49	10	1		1 Marriage Vow .... S:10 The Star Spangled Waltz		—	$30		RCA Victor 48-0056
				78 rpm: 21-0062					
7/1/50	❶²¹	44		2 I'm Moving On .... S:❶²¹ / A:❶¹⁸ / J:❶¹⁴ With This Ring I Thee Wed		—	$25		RCA Victor 48-0328
				also see #78 below					
11/25/50+	❶²	23		3 The Golden Rocket .... S:❶² / A:❶¹ / J:2 Paving The Highway With Tears		—	$25		RCA Victor 48-0400
3/3/51	❶⁸	27		4 The Rhumba Boogie .... S:❶⁸ / J:❶⁵ / A:❶² You Pass Me By		—	$25		RCA Victor 48-0431

DEBUT	PEAK	WKS	Gold	A-side (Chart Hit)	B-side	Pop	$	Pic	Label & Number
				SNOW, Hank — Cont'd					
5/12/51	2[1]	14		5 Down The Trail Of Achin' Hearts /	J:2 / S:7 / A:7	—			
4/21/51	4	11		6 Bluebird Island	S:4 / J:7		$25		RCA Victor 48-0441
				HANK SNOW (The Singing Ranger) with ANITA CARTER and the Rainbow Ranch Boys (above 2)					
9/15/51	6	6		7 Unwanted Sign Upon Your Heart	S:6 / A:9 Your Locket Is My Broken Heart		$25		RCA Victor 48-0498
12/15/51+	4	9		8 Music Makin' Mama From Memphis	J:4 / A:5 / S:6 The Highest Bidder		$20		RCA Victor 47-4346
4/5/52	2[3]	18		9 The Gold Rush Is Over	J:2 / S:4 / A:4 Why Do You Punish Me (For Loving You)		$20		RCA Victor 47-4522
7/5/52	2[1]	14		10 Lady's Man /	S:2 / J:5 / A:6				
7/26/52	8	3		11 Married By The Bible, Divorced By The Law	J:8 / S:10		$20		RCA Victor 47-4733
9/27/52	3	11		12 I Went To Your Wedding	J:3 / S:4 / A:4 The Boogie Woogie Flying Cloud		$20		RCA Victor 47-4909
12/27/52+	3	16		13 (Now And Then, There's) A Fool Such As I /	A:3 / J:3 / S:4				
				#2 Pop hit for **Elvis Presley** in 1959					
12/13/52+	4	10		14 The Gal Who Invented Kissin'	S:4 / J:5 / A:9		$20		RCA Victor 5034
4/4/53	9	2		15 Honeymoon On A Rocket Ship	S:9 / A:9 / J:9 There Wasn't An Organ At Our Wedding		$20		RCA Victor 5155
6/6/53	3	11		16 Spanish Fire Ball	S:3 / J:4 / A:5 Between Fire And Water		$20		RCA Victor 5296
10/3/53	10	1		17 For Now And Always	A:10 A Message From The Tradewinds		$20		RCA Victor 5380
11/28/53	6	6		18 When Mexican Joe Met Jole Blon	S:6 / J:9 No Longer A Prisoner		$20		RCA Victor 5490
5/29/54	❶[20]	41		19 I Don't Hurt Anymore	S:❶[20] / J:❶[20] / A:❶[18] My Arabian Baby		$20		RCA Victor 5698
12/4/54	10	6		20 That Crazy Mambo Thing /	J:10 / S:11				
1/1/55	15	1		21 The Next Voice You Hear	S:15		$20		RCA Victor 5912
12/25/54+	❶[2]	16		22 Let Me Go, Lover!	A:❶[2] / J:2 / S:3 I've Forgotten You		$15		RCA Victor 5960
				#1 Pop hit for **Joan Weber** in 1955					
4/2/55	15	1		23 Silver Bell	S:15 The Old Spinning Wheel [I]	—	$20		RCA Victor 5995
				HANK SNOW and CHET ATKINS					
4/9/55	3	27		24 Yellow Roses /	S:3 / A:3 / J:3				
4/16/55	3	17		25 Would You Mind?	A:3 / J:4		$20		RCA Victor 6057
7/23/55	7	8		26 Cryin', Prayin', Waitin', Hopin' /	J:7 / S:9 / A:10				
7/23/55	7	2		27 I'm Glad I Got To See You Once Again	J:7 / S:12		$20		RCA Victor 6154
11/5/55	5	8		28 Mainliner (The Hawk With Silver Wings) /	J:5 / S:8				
11/5/55	5	9		29 Born To Be Happy	J:5 / A:10 / S:14		$20		RCA Victor 6269
2/4/56	5	10		30 These Hands /	J:5 / A:6 / S:3				
2/18/56	11	4		31 I'm Moving In	S:11		$20		RCA Victor 6379
8/4/56	4	22		32 Conscience I'm Guilty /	J:4 / S:8 / A:9				
8/4/56	5	4		33 Hula Rock	J:5		$20		RCA Victor 6578
12/15/56+	7	9		34 Stolen Moments	J:7 / S:8 / A:9 Two Won't Care		$15		RCA Victor 6715
				HANK SNOW:					
7/22/57	4	19		35 Tangled Mind /	A:4 / S:9				
7/22/57	8	14		36 My Arms Are A House	A:8 / S:13		$15		RCA Victor 6955
3/31/58	15	1		37 Whispering Rain	A:15 / S:18 I Wish I Was The Moon		$15		RCA Victor 7154
6/23/58	7	9		38 Big Wheels	A:7 / S:18 I'm Hurting All Over		$15		RCA Victor 7233
11/3/58	16	5		39 A Woman Captured Me	My Lucky Friend		$15		RCA Victor 7325
3/16/59	19	6		40 Doggone That Train	Father Time And Mother Love		$15		RCA Victor 7448
6/1/59	6	11		41 Chasin' A Rainbow	I Heard My Heart Break Last Night		$15		RCA Victor 7524
				HANK SNOW and The Rainbow Ranch Boys					
10/19/59	3	20		42 The Last Ride	The Party Of The Second Part	—	$15		RCA Victor 7586
4/11/60	22	5		43 Rockin', Rollin' Ocean	Walkin' And Talkin'	87	$15		RCA Victor 7702
7/18/60	9	15		44 Miller's Cave	The Change Of The Tide	101	$12		RCA Victor 7748
5/15/61	5	20		45 Beggar To A King	Poor Little Jimmie		$12		RCA Victor 7869
10/9/61	11	9		46 The Restless One	I Know		$12		RCA Victor 7933
6/2/62	15	10		47 You Take The Future (And I'll Take The Past)	Dog Bone	—	$12		RCA Victor 8009
9/15/62	❶[2]	22		48 I've Been Everywhere	Ancient History	68	$12		RCA Victor 8072
4/27/63	9	11		49 The Man Who Robbed The Bank At Santa Fe	You're Losing Your Baby	—	$12	■	RCA Victor 8151
10/26/63	2[3]	22		50 Ninety Miles An Hour (Down A Dead End Street)	Blue Roses	124	$12		RCA Victor 8239
4/11/64	11	15		51 Breakfast With The Blues /		—			
				also see #79 below					
7/4/64	21	12		52 I Stepped Over The Line		—	$12		RCA Victor 8334
2/13/65	7	19		53 The Wishing Well (Down In The Well)	Human	—	$12		RCA Victor 8488
10/30/65	28	5		54 The Queen Of Draw Poker Town	Tears In The Trade Winds		$10		RCA Victor 8655
12/25/65+	18	14		55 I've Cried A Mile	Crazy Little Train (Of Love)		$10		RCA Victor 8713
5/7/66	22	11		56 The Count Down	Isle Of Sicily		$10		RCA Victor 8808
12/10/66+	21	14		57 Hula Love	A Letter From Viet Nam (To Mother)		$10		RCA Victor 9012
				#9 Pop hit for **Buddy Knox** in 1957					
5/13/67	18	14		58 Down At The Pawn Shop	Listen		$10		RCA Victor 9188
9/23/67	20	15		59 Learnin' A New Way Of Life	Wild Flower		$10		RCA Victor 9300
2/24/68	69	3		60 Who Will Answer? (Aleluya No. 1) /		—			
				#19 Pop hit for **Ed Ames** in 1968					
4/6/68	70	5		61 I Just Wanted To Know (How the Wind Was Blowing)		—	$10		RCA Victor 9433
6/8/68	20	13		62 The Late And Great Love (Of My Heart)	Born For You	—	$10		RCA Victor 9523
12/28/68+	16	16		63 The Name Of The Game Was Love	The Gypsy And Me	—	$8		RCA Victor 9685
5/31/69	26	9		64 Rome Wasn't Built In A Day	Like A Bird	—	$8		RCA Victor 0151
11/1/69	53	5		65 That's When The Hurtin' Sets In	I'm Movin'	—	$8		RCA Victor 0251
7/11/70	52	7		66 Vanishing Breed	What More Can I Say	—	$8		RCA Victor 9856
11/7/70	57	5		67 Come The Morning	Francesca	—	$8		RCA Victor 9907
4/21/73	71	3		68 North To Chicago	Friend	—	$7		RCA Victor 0915
2/9/74	❶[1]	15		69 Hello Love	Until The End Of Time	—	$7		RCA Victor 0215

DEBUT	PEAK	WKS	Gold	A-side (Chart Hit)..B-side	Pop	$	Pic	Label & Number
				SNOW, Hank — Cont'd				
6/29/74	36	11		70 That's You And Me .... Brand On My Heart	—	$7		RCA Victor 0307
11/16/74+	26	11		71 Easy To Love .... Just A Faded Petal From A Beautiful Bouquet	—	$6		RCA Victor 10108
3/22/75	47	10		72 Merry-Go-Round Of Love .... My Filipino Rose	—	$6		RCA Victor 10225
8/2/75	79	6		73 Hijack .... The Last Ride	—	$6		RCA Victor 10338
11/29/75	95	2		74 Colorado Country Morning .... I Keep Dreaming Of You All The Time	—	$6		RCA Victor 10439
5/29/76	87	4		75 Who's Been Here Since I've Been Gone .... That's When He Dropped The World In My Hands	—	$6		RCA Victor 10681
11/27/76	98	1		76 You're Wondering Why .... Somewhere Someone Is Waiting For You	—	$5		RCA 10804
7/16/77	81	4		77 Trouble In Mind .... Trying To Get My Baby Off My Mind	—	$5		RCA 11021
9/24/77	80	4		78 I'm Still Movin' On .... I'm Gonna Bid My Blues Goodbye sequel to #2 above	—	$5		RCA 11080
12/3/77	96	2		79 Breakfast With The Blues .... I've Done At Least One Thing [R] new version of #51 above	—	$5		RCA 11153
7/1/78	93	4		80 Nevertheless .... Don't Rock The Boat	—	$5		RCA 11276
10/7/78	93	4		81 Ramblin' Rose .... Red Roses #2 Pop hit for **Nat King Cole** in 1962	—	$5		RCA 11377
3/31/79	80	3		82 The Mysterious Lady From St. Martinique .... Get On My Love Train	—	$5		RCA 11487
7/21/79	91	3		83 A Good Gal Is Hard To Find .... I Wish My Heart Could Talk	—	$5		RCA 11622
11/10/79	98	2		84 It Takes Too Long .... 6 String Tennessee Flattop	—	$5		RCA 11734
2/16/80	78	4		85 Hasn't It Been Good Together .... It Was Love HANK SNOW AND KELLY FOXTON	—	$5		RCA 11891
				SNUFF **'82** Group from Virginia: Jim Bowling (vocals), Robbie House and Chuck Larson (guitars), Cecil Hooker (fiddle), C. Scott Trabue (bass) and Michael Johnson (drums).				
8/7/82	71	6		(So This Is) Happy Hour .... It Must Be Love	—	$4		Elektra/Curb 69996
				SNYDER, Jimmy **'70**				
2/14/70	30	9		1 The Chicago Story .... Take Her Flowers written by **Tom T. Hall**	—	$6		Wayside 009
8/16/80	71	7		2 Just To Prove My Love To You .... Kiss Your Love Goodbye	—	$6		e.i.o. 1126
				SNYDER, Rick **'88**				
7/23/88	66	4		Losing Somebody You Love .... I Know The Feeling	—	$3		Capitol 44185
				SOGGY BOTTOM BOYS, The **'02** Fictitious bluegrass group created for the movie *O Brother, Where Art Thou?*. George Clooney is "Ulysses", John Turturro is "Pete" and Tim Blake Nelson is "Delmar". Actual recording is performed by studio musicians, including lead vocal by Dan Tyminski of **Alison Krauss & Union Station**.				
3/17/01+	35	25		I Am A Man Of Constant Sorrow .... album cut from the movie *O Brother, Where Art Thou?* starring George Clooney (soundtrack on Mercury 170069); CMA Award: Single of the Year				
				SOLID GOLD BAND **'82** Group from Galina, Kansas: Jim Rowland, John Green, Mike Bartlett, Tyler Ogle and Buddy Burr.				
11/28/81+	47	9		1 Cherokee Country .... It's Just Your Memory	—	$5		NSD 110
2/20/82	65	6		2 I Never Had The One That I Wanted /	—			
		6		3 Bandera, Texas		$5		NSD 121
7/17/82	68	6		4 Country Fiddles .... The Sun Shines Bright In Oklahoma	—	$5		NSD 138
				☆ **SOME OF CHET'S FRIENDS** **'67** Group of RCA recording artists: **Eddy Arnold**, **Bobby Bare**, **Don Bowman**, **Jim Ed Brown**, **Archie Campbell**, **Floyd Cramer**, **Skeeter Davis**, **Jimmy Dean**, **George Hamilton IV**, **Homer & Jethro**, **Waylon Jennings**, **Hank Locklin**, **John D. Loudermilk**, **Willie Nelson**, **Norma Jean**, **Jerry Reed**, **Connie Smith**, **Hank Snow**, **Porter Wagoner** and **Dottie West**.				
6/24/67	38	9		Chet's Tune .... Country Gentleman tribute to **Chet Atkins** *See Don W. Bowman*	—	$10	■	RCA Victor 9229
				SONNIER, Jo-el **'88** Born Joel Sonnier on 10/2/46 in Rayne, Louisiana. Cajun singer/songwriter/accordianist. Once known as "The Cajun Valentino". *1)No More One More Time 2)Tear-Stained Letter 3)If Your Heart Should Ever Roll This Way Again*				
10/4/75	78	7		1 I've Been Around Enough To Know .... A Brighter Shade Of Blue	—	$5		Mercury 73702
3/6/76	99	1		2 Always Late (With Your Kisses) .... Knock, Knock, Knock	—	$5		Mercury 73754
6/5/76	100	1		3 He's Still All Over You .... Am I Just Your Friend	—	$5		Mercury 73796
11/28/87+	39	14		4 Come On Joe .... Say You Love Me	—	$4		RCA 5282
2/20/88	7	22		5 No More One More Time S:14 Louisiana 1927		$4		RCA 6895
7/16/88	9	19		6 Tear-Stained Letter S:12 Say You Love Me		$4		RCA 8304
11/19/88+	35	12		7 Rainin' In My Heart .... Baby Hold On #34 Pop hit for **Slim Harpo** in 1961	—	$4		RCA 8726
5/6/89	47	10		8 (Blue, Blue, Blue) Blue, Blue .... I've Got Dreams To Remember	—	$4		RCA 8918
10/28/89+	24	17		9 If Your Heart Should Ever Roll This Way Again .... You Done Me Wrong	—	$4		RCA 9014
4/7/90	65	6		10 The Scene Of The Crime .... Evangeline Special	—	$4		RCA 9123
				SONS OF THE DESERT **'97** Group from Waco, Texas: brothers Drew (vocals) and Tim (guitar) Womack, Scott Saunders (keyboards), Doug Virden (bass) and Brian Westrum (drums). Also see **Lee Ann Womack**.				
3/8/97	10	21		1 Whatever Comes First S:22 Drive Away		$4	■	Epic 78542 (v)
8/30/97	33	17		2 Hand Of Fate .... Burned In My Mind	—	$4		Epic 78663
1/17/98	31	19		3 Leaving October .... album cut from the album *Whatever Comes First* on Epic 67619	—			
2/20/99	45	11		4 What About You .... Whatever Comes First	—	$4		Epic 79116
6/26/99	58	10		5 Albuquerque .... What About You	—	$4		Epic 79199
3/11/00	45	19		6 Change .... Albuquerque	—	$4		MCA Nashville 172156
8/12/00	42	15		7 Everybody's Gotta Grow Up Sometime .... Ride	—	$4		MCA Nashville 172179

DEBUT	PEAK	WKS	Gold	A-side (Chart Hit) .... B-side	Pop	$	Pic	Label & Number
				SONS OF THE DESERT — Cont'd				
2/10/01	22	30		8 What I Did Right .... *I Need To Be Wrong Again*	—	$4		MCA Nashville 172196
	★302★			**SONS OF THE PIONEERS** '45				
				Originally a trio consisting of Robert "Bob Nolan" Nobles (born on 4/1/08; died on 6/16/80, age 72), Leonard "**Roy Rogers**" Slye (born on 11/5/11; died on 7/6/98, age 86) and Vernon "Tim" Spencer (born on 7/13/08; died on 4/26/74, age 65). Formed in 1934 and first called the Pioneers; recorded for Decca in 1934. Brothers Karl (born on 4/25/09; died on 9/20/61, age 52) and Thomas "Hugh" (born on 12/6/03; died on 3/17/80, age 76) Farr were added in 1936. Group appeared in several western movies. Rogers and Spencer left in 1937, replaced by Lloyd Perryman (born on 1/29/17; died on 5/31/77, age 60) and Pat Brady. Spencer returned shortly thereafter. Group elected to the Country Music Hall of Fame in 1980.				
				1)Stars And Stripes On Iwo Jima 2)Teardrops In My Heart 3)Cool Water				
10/6/45	4	2		1 Stars And Stripes On Iwo Jima .... *Cool Water*	—	$20		RCA Victor 20-1724
6/29/46	6	1		2 No One To Cry To .... *Grievin' My Heart Out For You*	—	$20		RCA Victor 20-1868
2/15/47	5	1		3 Baby Doll .... *The Letter Marked Unclaimed*	—	$20		RCA Victor 20-2086
3/8/47	4	1		4 Cool Water .... *Tumbling Tumbleweeds*	—	$20		Decca 46027
				originally released in 1941 on Decca 5939; also see #10 below				
7/12/47	5	1		5 Cigareetes, Whusky, And Wild, Wild Women /	—			
				#15 Pop hit for **Red Ingle** in 1948				
2/19/49	12	1		6 My Best To You J:12	—	$20		RCA Victor 20-2199
7/26/47	4	2		7 Teardrops In My Heart .... *You Don't Know What Lonesome Is*	—	$20		RCA Victor 20-2276
6/12/48	6	14		8 Blue Shadows On The Trail / S:6 / J:7	—			
6/12/48	13	4		9 (There'll Never Be Another) Pecos Bill S:13	—	$25		RCA Victor 20-2780
				ROY ROGERS and The Sons Of The Pioneers (above 2)				
				45 rpm: 48-0035; above 2 from the movie *Melody Time* starring Rogers				
8/21/48	11	1		10 Tumbling Tumbleweeds .... J:11 *Cowboy Camp Meetin'*	—	$20		RCA Victor 20-1904
				original version released in 1934 on Decca 5047				
9/4/48	7	11		11 Cool Water S:7 / J:11 *Tumbling Tumbleweeds* [R]	—	$20		Decca 46027
				also see #4 above				
9/10/49	10	1		12 Room Full Of Roses .... J:10 *Riders In The Sky*	26	$20		RCA Victor 21-0065
				45 rpm: 48-0060				
8/23/80	80	4		13 Ride Concrete Cowboy, Ride .... *Deliverance Of The Wildwood Flower*	—	$5		MCA 41294
				ROY ROGERS And The Sons Of The Pioneers				
				from the movie *Smokey & The Bandit II* starring **Burt Reynolds**				
				SOSEBEE, Tommy '53				
				Born Bud Thomas Sosebee on 5/23/23 in Duncan, South Carolina. Died on 10/23/67 (age 44). Known as "The Voice Of The Hills."				
3/14/53	7	2		1 Till I Waltz Again With You .... A:7 *All Night Boogie*	—	$25		Coral 60916
				#1 Pop hit for Teresa Brewer in 1953				
				SOUTH, Joe '61				
				Born Joe Souter on 2/28/40 in Atlanta. Singer/songwriter/guitarist.				
8/28/61	16	6		1 You're The Reason .... *Juke Box*	87	$20		Fairlane 21006
				JOE SOUTH and The Believers:				
10/4/69	27	9		2 Don't It Make You Want To Go Home .... *Hearts Desire*	41	$7		Capitol 2592
1/31/70	56	5		3 Walk A Mile In My Shoes .... *Shelter*	12	$7		Capitol 2704
				SOUTHER, J.D. '82				
				Born John David Souther on 11/2/45 in Detroit; raised in Amarillo, Texas. Singer/songwriter.				
12/1/79+	60	10		1 You're Only Lonely .... *Songs Of Love*	7	$4		Columbia 11079
10/16/82	27	12		2 Sometimes You Just Can't Win .... *Get Closer* (Pop #29)	—	$4	■	Asylum 69948
				LINDA RONSTADT AND JOHN DAVID SOUTHER				
				SOUTHERN ASHE '81				
				Group from Columbus, Georgia.				
8/15/81	80	3		1 Paradise .... *Loving On A Three-Way Street*	—	$5		Soundwaves 4641
	★266★			**SOUTHERN PACIFIC** '88				
				Group formed in Los Angeles: Tim Goodman (vocals, guitar), John McFee (guitar, fiddle; The Doobie Brothers), Kurt Howell (keyboards), Stu Cook (bass; **Creedence Clearwater Revival**) and Keith Knudsen (drums; The Doobie Brothers). Goodman replaced by David Jenkins (formerly with Pablo Cruise) in 1986. Jenkins left in early 1989. Group disbanded in 1991. Howell later joined **Burnin' Daylight**.				
				1)New Shade Of Blue 2)Any Way The Wind Blows 3)Honey I Dare You				
6/1/85	60	6		1 Someone's Gonna Love Me Tonight .... *The Blaster*	—	$4		Warner 29020
8/3/85	14	19		2 Thing About You S:13 / A:14 *Reno Bound*	—	$4		Warner 28943
				Emmylou Harris (guest vocal); written and first recorded by Tom Petty on his 1981 *Hard Promises* album				
11/16/85+	18	19		3 Perfect Stranger A:17 / S:18 *Bluebird Wine*	—	$4		Warner 28870
4/19/86	9	17		4 Reno Bound A:8 / S:9 *Someone's Gonna Love Me Tonight*	—	$4		Warner 28722
8/9/86	17	17		5 A Girl Like Emmylou A:17 / S:19 *Hearts On The Borderline*	—	$4		Warner 28647
12/6/86+	37	13		6 Killbilly Hill .... *Bluegrass Blues*	—	$4		Warner 28554
3/21/87	26	14		7 Don't Let Go Of My Heart S:26 *What's It Gonna Take*	—	$4		Warner 28408
4/9/88	14	18		8 Midnight Highway S:18 *What's It Gonna Take*	—	$4	■	Warner 27952
8/6/88	2²	24		9 New Shade Of Blue S:11 *Just Hang On*	—	$4		Warner 27790
12/10/88+	5	19		10 Honey I Dare You .... *Trail Of Tears*	—	$4	■	Warner 27691
5/27/89	4	19		11 Any Way The Wind Blows .... *Reno Bound*	—	$4	■	Warner 22965
				from the movie *Pink Cadillac* starring **Clint Eastwood**				
12/2/89+	26	18		12 Time's Up .... *Memphis Queen*	—	$4		Warner 22714
				SOUTHERN PACIFIC and CARLENE CARTER				
4/7/90	31	14		13 I Go To Pieces .... *Beyond Love*	—	$4		Warner 19860
				#9 Pop hit for Peter and Gordon in 1965				
8/11/90	32	16		14 Reckless Heart .... *Side Saddle*	—	$4	■	Warner 19871 (v)

DEBUT	PEAK	WKS	Gold	A-side (Chart Hit)	B-side	Pop	$	Pic	Label & Number

SOUTHERN REIGN '88
Group led by singers Patsy McKeehan and Jeff Crocker.

DEBUT	PEAK	WKS	#	A-side	B-side	Pop	$	Label & Number
11/1/86	80	3	1	The Auction	—		$5	Regal 1
1/10/87	62	7	2	15 to 33	Sugary Sam		$5	Regal 2
5/2/87	79	4	3	Summer On The Mississippi	—		$5	Regal 3
9/19/87	61	6	4	Cheap Motels (And One Night Stands)	Summer On The Mississippi		$4	Step One 377
5/28/88	60	5	5	Please Don't Leave Me Now	I Don't Think I Want To Love You Anymore		$4	Step One 385
10/15/88	80	3	6	There's A Telephone Ringing (In An Empty House)	Excuse Me For Loving You		$4	Step One 391

SOUTH SIXTY FIVE '99
Male vocal group from Nashville: brothers Brent and Stephen Parker, Lance Leslie, Doug Urie and Jeremy Koeltzow.

DEBUT	PEAK	WKS	#	A-side	B-side	Pop	$	Pic	Label & Number
12/12/98+	55	10	1	A Random Act Of Senseless Kindness	Climbing Up Mt. Everest	—	$4		Atlantic 84194
3/6/99	56	5	2	No Easy Goodbye	All Of This And More	—	$4		Atlantic 84457
8/14/99	60	12	3	Baby's Got My Number	(dance mix)	—	$4		Atlantic 84531
6/3/00	72	1	4	Love Bug (Bite Me)	—	—			album cut
				from the album *South Sixty Five* on Atlantic 83124					
2/10/01	54	11	5	The Most Beautiful Girl	S:8 (album snippets)	—	$4	★	Atlantic 85051

SOVINE, Red ★174★ '66
Born Woodrow Wilson Sovine on 7/17/18 in Charleston, West Virginia. Died of a heart attack on 4/4/80 (age 61). Singer/songwriter/guitarist. Joined the *Grand Ole Opry* in 1954. Father of **Roger Sovine**. Once known as "The Old Syrup Sopper."

1) Giddyup Go 2) Why Baby Why 3) Teddy Bear 4) Little Rosa 5) Hold Everything (Till I Get Home)

Yankee, Go Home (See Goldie Hill)

DEBUT	PEAK	WKS	#	A-side	B-side	Pop	$	Label & Number
3/26/55	14	2	1	Are You Mine	S:14 Ko Ko Mo (I Love You So)	—	$20	Decca 29411
				RED SOVINE - GOLDIE HILL				
12/17/55+	❶⁴	25	2	Why Baby Why	A:❶⁴ / S:❶¹ / J:❶¹ Missing You	—	$20	Decca 29755
				RED SOVINE And WEBB PIERCE				
3/24/56	15	1	3	If Jesus Came To Your House	A:15 I Got Religion (The Old Time Way)	—	$20	Decca 29825
4/21/56	5	14	4	Little Rosa /	S:5 / A:5 / J:5 [S]	—		
				RED SOVINE and WEBB PIERCE				
5/19/56	5	8	5	Hold Everything (Till I Get Home)	J:5	—	$20	Decca 29876
1/11/64	22	12	6	Dream House For Sale	King Of The Open Road [S]	—	$10	Starday 650
11/20/65+	❶⁶	22	7	Giddyup Go	Kiss And The Keys [S]	82	$10	Starday 737
4/30/66	47	2	8	Long Night	Too Much	—	$10	Starday 757
11/12/66	44	8	9	Class Of 49	I Hope My Wife Don't Find Out	—	$10	Starday 779
2/18/67	17	12	10	I Didn't Jump The Fence	Don't Let My Glass Run Dry	—	$10	Starday 794
7/29/67	9	16	11	Phantom 309 /	[S]	—		
				also see #22 below				
7/1/67	33	10	12	In Your Heart	—	—	$8	Starday 811
12/9/67+	33	13	13	Tell Maude I Slipped	Not Like It Was With You	—	$8	Starday 823
7/20/68	63	2	14	Loser Making Good	Good Enough For Nothing	—	$8	Starday 842
10/12/68	61	6	15	Normally, Norma Loves Me	Live And Let Live And Be Happy	—	$8	Starday 852
8/2/69	62	7	16	Who Am I	Three Hearts In A Tangle	—	$8	Starday 872
4/18/70	52	10	17	I Know You're Married But I Love You Still	Money, Marbles And Chalk	—	$8	Starday 889
7/25/70	54	7	18	Freightliner Fever	Mr. Sunday Sun	—	$8	Starday 896
7/6/74	16	16	★	19 It'll Come Back	Down Through The Years	—	$6	Chart 5220
				label shows title as "I'll Come Back"; also see #31 below				
11/2/74	58	9	20	Can I Keep Him Daddy	Red's So Fine	—	$6	Chart 5230
8/30/75	91	4	★	21 Daddy's Girl	Daisy's Chain	—	$6	Chart 7507
				RED SOVINE AND THE GIRLS				
12/27/75+	47	10	22	Phantom 309	I Didn't Jump The Fence [S-R]	—	$5	Starday 101
				same version as #11 above				
6/19/76	❶³	13	●	23 Teddy Bear	Daddy [S]	40	$5	Starday 142
9/18/76	45	5	24	Little Joe	Cold Love To Go [S]	102	$5	Starday 144
12/11/76	96	2	25	Last Goodbye	Lonely Arms Of Mine [S]	—	$5	Starday 147
2/19/77	98	2	26	Just Gettin' By	I'm Gonna Move	—	$5	Starday 148
12/3/77	92	5	27	Woman Behind The Man Behind The Wheel	Jealous Heart	—	$5	Gusto 169
3/11/78	70	5	28	Lay Down Sally	The King's Last Concert	—	$5	Gusto 180
5/27/78	77	5	29	The Days Of Me And You	I'd Love To Make Love To You	—	$5	Gusto 188
4/12/80	74	5	30	The Little Family Soldier	I Didn't Know She Was Loving Me Goodbye [S]	—	$5	Gusto 9028
7/12/80	89	3	★	31 It'll Come Back	Love Is [R]	—	$5	Gusto 9030
				new version of #19 above				

SOVINE, Roger '68
Born on 2/17/43 in Eleanor, West Virginia. Son of **Red Sovine**.

DEBUT	PEAK	WKS	#	A-side	B-side	Pop	$	Label & Number
5/4/68	47	8	1	Culman, Alabam	Savannah Georgia Vagrant	—	$7	Imperial 66291
11/8/69	68	5	2	Little Bitty Nitty Gritty Dirt Town	Son	—	$7	Imperial 66398

SPACEK, Sissy '83
Born Mary Elizabeth Spacek on 12/25/49 in Quitman, Texas. Singer/actress. Won Academy Award portraying **Loretta Lynn** in the movie *Coal Miner's Daughter*.

DEBUT	PEAK	WKS	#	A-side	B-side	Pop	$	Pic	Label & Number
4/26/80	24	11	1	Coal Miner's Daughter	I'm A Honky Tonk Girl	—	$4	■	MCA 41221
				from the movie starring Spacek					
8/20/83	15	17	2	Lonely But Only For You	Old Home Town	110	$4	■	Atlantic Amer. 99847
1/21/84	57	9	3	If I Can Just Get Through The Night	Honky Tonkin'	—	$4	■	Atlantic Amer. 99801

DEBUT	PEAK	WKS	Gold	A-side (Chart Hit) .... B-side	Pop	$	Pic	Label & Number
				SPACEK, Sissy — Cont'd				
5/5/84	79	3		4 If You Could Only See Me Now .... *Have I Told You Lately That I Love You*	—	$4		Atlantic Amer. 99773

SPEARS, Billie Jo ★144★   **'75**

Born Billie Jean Spears on 1/14/37 in Beaumont, Texas. Singer/songwriter. Worked on the *Louisiana Hayride* in 1950. First recorded for Abbott in 1953 as "Billie Jean Moore." Moved to Nashville in 1964. Very popular in England since 1977.

1)Blanket On The Ground   2)Mr. Walker, It's All Over   3)What I've Got In Mind   4)Misty Blue   5)If You Want Me

DEBUT	PEAK	WKS	Gold	A-side .... B-side	Pop	$	Pic	Label & Number
11/30/68+	48	10		1 He's Got More Love In His Little Finger .... *A Woman Of The World*	—	$7		Capitol 2331
4/19/69	4	13		2 Mr. Walker, It's All Over .... *Tips And Tables*	80	$6		Capitol 2436
9/13/69	43	7		3 Stepchild .... *Softly And Tenderly*	—	$6		Capitol 2593
12/20/69+	40	10		4 Daddy, I Love You .... *Look Out Your Window*	—	$6		Capitol 2690
7/25/70	17	14		5 Marty Gray .... *True Love*	—	$6		Capitol 2844
11/28/70	30	9		6 I Stayed Long Enough .... *Come On Home*	—	$6		Capitol 2964
				written by **Tammy Wynette**				
3/20/71	23	12		7 It Could 'A Been Me .... *Break Away*	—	$6		Capitol 3055
2/12/72	68	3		8 Souvenirs And California Mem'rys .... *What A Love I Have In You*	—	$6		Capitol 3258
10/5/74	80	5		9 See The Funny Little Clown .... *All I Want Is You*	—	$5		United Artists 549
				#9 Pop hit for **Bobby Goldsboro** in 1964				
2/1/75	❶¹	17		10 Blanket On The Ground .... *Come On Home*	78	$5		United Artists 584
7/12/75	20	14		11 Stay Away From The Apple Tree .... *Before Your Time*	—	$5		United Artists 653
11/1/75+	20	15		12 Silver Wings And Golden Rings .... *Then Give Him Back To Me*	—	$5		United Artists 712
2/28/76	5	16		13 What I've Got In Mind .... *Everytime Two Fools Collide*	—	$5		United Artists 764
5/1/76	29	11		14 On The Rebound .... *What's Our Love Coming To*	—	$5		United Artists 797
				DEL REEVES & BILLIE JO SPEARS				
6/19/76	5	16		15 Misty Blue .... *Let's Try To Wake It Up Again*	—	$5		United Artists 813
				#3 Pop hit for **Dorothy Moore** in 1976				
8/7/76	42	8		16 Teardrops Will Kiss The Morning Dew .... *Nothing Seems To Work Anymore*	—	$5		United Artists 832
				DEL REEVES & BILLIE JO SPEARS				
10/23/76	18	12		17 Never Did Like Whiskey .... *No Other Man*	—	$5		United Artists 880
1/29/77	11	13		18 I'm Not Easy .... *Too Far Gone*	—	$5		United Artists 935
5/7/77	8	13		19 If You Want Me .... *Don't Ever Let Go Of Me*	—	$5		United Artists 985
8/20/77	18	13		20 Too Much Is Not Enough .... *The End Of Me*	—	$5		United Artists 1041
1/14/78	18	11		21 Lonely Hearts Club .... *His Little Something On The Side*	—	$5		United Artists 1127
4/15/78	17	12		22 I've Got To Go .... *There's More To A Tear (Than Meets The Eye)*	—	$5		United Artists 1190
8/12/78	16	12		23 '57 Chevrolet .... *The Lovin' Kind*	—	$5		United Artists 1229
11/11/78+	24	13		24 Love Ain't Gonna Wait For Us .... *Say It Again*	—	$5		United Artists 1251
2/24/79	60	6		25 Yesterday .... *The Miracle Of Love*	—	$5		United Artists 1274
				#1 Pop hit for **The Beatles** in 1965				
4/21/79	21	11		26 I Will Survive .... *Rainy Days And Stormy Nights*	—	$5		United Artists 1292
				#1 Pop hit for **Gloria Gaynor** in 1979				
8/4/79	23	12		27 Livin' Our Love Together .... *You*	—	$5		United Artists 1309
11/3/79+	21	14		28 Rainy Days And Stormy Nights .... *Everyday I Have To Cry*	—	$5		United Artists 1326
2/23/80	15	13		29 Standing Tall .... *Freedom Song*	—	$5		United Artists 1336
6/28/80	39	9		30 Natural Attraction .... *You Could Know As Much About A Stranger*	—	$5		United Artists 1358
1/10/81	13	13		31 Your Good Girl's Gonna Go Bad .... *(I Never Promised You A) Rose Garden*	—	$4		Liberty 1395
5/2/81	58	5		32 What The World Needs Now Is Love .... *Snowbird*	—	$4		Liberty 1409
				#7 Pop hit for **Jackie DeShannon** in 1965				
1/7/84	39	13		33 Midnight Blue /	—			
4/7/84	51	8		34 Midnight Love	—	$5		Parliament 1801

SPEARS, Bobby — see CASSADY, Linda

SPEEGLE, David   **'89**
Born in Tampa, Florida. Singer/guitarist.

12/9/89	83	4		Tie Me Up (Hold Me Down) .... *Dim Lights And Candles*	—	$6		Bitter Creek 07789

SPEEKS, Ronnie   **'81**

1/17/81	93	2		Baby Loved Me .... *You Almost Slipped My Mind*	—	$5		Dimension 1014

SPELLING ON THE STONE   **'89**
Song refers to the spelling of **Elvis Presley**'s middle name on his grave stone. The artist has never been identified.

12/24/88+	82	4		Spelling On The Stone	—	$5		Curb 10522
				first released on LS 53 in 1988 ($10)				

SPENCER, Teddy   **'88**

8/20/88	82	3		Grass Is Greener	—	$5		Oak 1052

✗SPITZ, Michele   **'81**

7/25/81	93	2		Old Fashioned Lover (In A Brand New Love Affair) .... *If You Ever Need Me Again*	—	$5		50 States 83

SPRINGER, Roger   **'98**
Born on 6/15/62 in Caddo, Oklahoma. Singer/songwriter/guitarist.

5/23/92	69	2		1 The Right One Left .... *Honky Tonk Ways*	—	$4		MCA 54250
10/24/98	64	4		2 Don't Try To Find Me .... *Love Lives On*	—	$4		Giant 17137
				SPRINGER!				

DEBUT	PEAK	WKS	Gold	A-side (Chart Hit)	B-side	Pop	$	Pic	Label & Number
				SPRINGER BROTHERS '80					
2/2/80	87	5		1 What's A Nice Girl Like You (Doin' In A Love Like This) .... Twice As Strong		—	$4		Elektra 46575
5/10/80	89	2		2 Cathy's Clown .... No Fair Fallin In Love		—	$4		Elektra 46622
				#1 Pop hit for **The Everly Brothers** in 1960					
				SPRINGFIELD, Bobby Lee '87					
				Born in 1953 in Amarillo, Texas. Singer/prolific songwriter.					
3/26/83	86	3		1 A Different Woman Every Night .... Young And Hungry		—	$5		Kat Family 03562
				BOBBY SPRINGFIELD					
6/13/87	75	5		2 Hank Drank .... Wild Cat		—	$4		Epic 07110
9/5/87	66	5		3 Chain Gang .... Wild Cat		—	$4		Epic 07310
				SPRINGFIELDS, The '62					
				Folk trio from England: Dusty Springfield (charted 19 pop hits from 1964-88; died on 3/2/99, age 59), with brother Tom Springfield and Tim Feild.					
8/25/62	16	10		Silver Threads And Golden Needles .... Aunt Rhody		20	$15		Philips 40038
				SPURZZ '80					
				Group from Nashville. Member Tony Ingram later joined **Atlanta**.					
8/23/80	76	4		Cowboy Stomp! .... Night Club		—	$4		Epic 50911
				STACK, Billy '78					
				Born in Clinton, Mississippi.					
2/25/78	82	5		1 Love Can Make The Children Sing .... The Big Time		—	$5		Caprice 2045
6/24/78	100	1		2 Boogiewoogieitis .... Rainbow Rider		—	$5		Caprice 2048
5/12/79	83	3		3 No Greater Love .... She Wanted So Bad To Be Good		—	$5		Caprice 2058
				STAFF, Bobbi '66					
				Born in 1946 in Kingston, North Carolina. Female singer.					
6/25/66	31	6		Chicken Feed .... I Didn't Cry Today		—	$10		RCA Victor 8833
				STAFFORD, Jim '74					
				Born on 1/16/44 in Eloise, Florida. Singer/songwriter/multi-instrumentalist. Co-hosted TV's *Those Amazing Animals* from 1980-81. Formerly married to **Bobbie Gentry**.					
3/2/74	66	8	●	1 Spiders & Snakes .... Undecided		3	$5		MGM 14648
5/18/74	64	7		2 My Girl Bill .... L.A. Mamma [N]		12	$5		MGM 14718
8/17/74	57	6		3 Wildwood Weed .... The Last Chant [N]		7	$5		MGM 14737
1/10/81	65	6		4 Cow Patti .... Texas Guitar Swing [N]		102	$4		Viva/Warner 49611
				from the movie *Any Which Way You Can* starring **Clint Eastwood**					
11/20/82	61	8		5 What Mama Don't Know .... That's What Little Kids Do [N]		—	$4		Town House 1062
2/4/84	67	9		6 Little Bits And Pieces .... Banjo Billy		—	$4		Columbia 04339
				STAFFORD, Jo '47					
				Born on 11/12/17 in Coalinga, California. Female singer. Charted 78 pop hits from 1944-57. Married orchestra leader Paul Weston. Also see **Red Ingle**.					
9/20/47	5	2		Feudin' And Fightin' .... Love And The Weather [N]		6	$15		Capitol 443
				Paul Weston (orch.); from the Broadway musical *Laffing Room Only* starring Betty Garrett					
				STAFFORD, Terry '74					
				Born on 11/22/41 in Hollis, Oklahoma; raised in Amarillo, Texas. Died on 3/17/96 (age 54). Male singer/songwriter. Charted the pop hit "Suspicion" in 1964.					
12/1/73+	31	14		1 Amarillo By Morning /		—			
8/25/73	35	12		2 Say, Has Anybody Seen My Sweet Gypsy Rose		—	$6		Atlantic 4006
				#3 Pop hit for Tony Orlando & Dawn in 1973					
3/23/74	24	13		3 Captured .... It Sure Is Bad To Love Her		—	$6		Atlantic 4015
8/24/74	69	6		4 Stop If You Love Me .... We've Grown Close		—	$6		Atlantic 4026
3/12/77	94	4		5 It Sure Is Bad To Love Her		—	$6		Casino 113
2/18/89	89	3		6 Lonestar Lonesome		—	$6		Player 134
				STALEY, Karen '89					
				Born in Pennsylvania. Singer/songwriter.					
12/24/88+	86	4		1 So Good To Be In Love .... Keep Walkin' On		—	$4		MCA 53470
5/13/89	85	2		2 Now And Then .... Looks Like Rain		—	$4		MCA 53632
				STAMPLEY, Joe ★57★ '73					
				Born on 6/6/43 in Springhill, Louisiana. Singer/songwriter/pianist. First recorded for Imperial in 1957. Lead singer of The Uniques in the mid-1960s. Worked as a staff writer for Gallico Music. CMA Award: 1980 Vocal Duo of the Year (with **Moe Bandy**).					
				1)Soul Song 2)All These Things 3)Just Good Ol' Boys 4)Roll On Big Mama 5)I'm Still Loving You					
2/20/71	74	2		1 Take Time To Know Her .... I Live To Love You		—	$6		Dot 17363
				#11 Pop hit for Percy Sledge in 1968					
2/12/72	75	2		2 Hello Operator .... Hello Charlie		—	$6		Dot 17400
6/17/72	9	17		3 **If You Touch Me (You've Got To Love Me)** All The Praises		—	$6		Dot 17421
11/11/72+	❶¹	15		4 **Soul Song** .... Not Too Long Ago		37	$6	☐	Dot 17442
3/24/73	7	14		5 **Bring It On Home (To Your Woman)** You Make Life Easy		—	$6		Dot 17452
8/18/73	12	16		6 **Too Far Gone** .... The Night Time And My Baby		—	$6		Dot 17469
12/8/73+	3	17		7 **I'm Still Loving You** .... The Weatherman		—	$6		Dot 17485
5/4/74	11	13		8 **How Lucky Can One Man Be** .... Can You Imagine How I Feel		—	$6		Dot 17502

DEBUT	PEAK	WKS	Gold	A-side (Chart Hit)	B-side	Pop	$	Pic	Label & Number
				STAMPLEY, Joe — Cont'd					
9/14/74	5	16		9 Take Me Home To Somewhere	Hall Of Famous Losers	—	$6		Dot 17522
1/18/75	8	11		10 Penny	Backtrackin'	—	$5		ABC/Dot 17537
3/1/75	●¹	14		11 Roll On Big Mama	Love's Running Through My Veins	—	$5		Epic 50075
5/10/75	41	11		12 Unchained Melody	Dallas Alice	—	$5		ABC/Dot 17551
				#4 Pop hit for The Righteous Brothers in 1965					
6/7/75	11	13		13 Dear Woman	Get On My Love Train	—	$5		Epic 50114
8/30/75	70	8		14 Cry Like A Baby	Try A Little Tenderness	—	$5		ABC/Dot 17575
				#2 Pop hit for The Box Tops in 1968					
9/20/75	12	13		15 Billy, Get Me A Woman	She Has Love	—	$5		Epic 50147
12/20/75+	25	10		16 She's Helping Me Get Over Loving You	Ray Of Sunshine	—	$5		Epic 50179
1/3/76	61	8		17 You Make Life Easy	Clinging Vine	—	$5		ABC/Dot 17599
3/13/76	43	8		18 Sheik Of Chicago	Whiskey Talkin'	—	$5		Epic 50199
4/24/76	●¹	16		19 All These Things	My Louisiana Woman	—	$5		ABC/Dot 17624
				#97 Pop hit for The Uniques in 1966; also see #44 below					
5/22/76	43	9		20 Was It Worth It	Live It Up	—	$5		Epic 50224
7/24/76	16	11		21 The Night Time And My Baby	The Most Beautiful Girl	—	$5		ABC/Dot 17642
8/7/76	18	14		22 Whiskey Talkin'	Darlin' Raise The Shade	—	$5		Epic 50259
10/30/76	12	12		23 Everything I Own	Dallas Alice	—	$5		ABC/Dot 17654
				#5 Pop hit for Bread in 1972					
12/25/76+	11	15		24 There She Goes Again	You Lift Me Up	—	$5		Epic 50316
4/2/77	26	12		25 She's Long Legged	The Better Part Of Me	—	$5		Epic 50361
7/2/77	15	13		26 Baby, I Love You So	Pour The Wine	—	$5		Epic 50410
10/22/77	14	13		27 Everyday I Have To Cry Some	What Would I Do Then	—	$5		Epic 50453
				#45 Pop hit for Arthur Alexander in 1975					
3/18/78	6	16		28 Red Wine And Blue Memories	Houston Treat My Lady Good	—	$5		Epic 50517
7/15/78	6	14		29 If You've Got Ten Minutes (Let's Fall In Love)	If This Is Freedom	—	$5		Epic 50575
11/4/78+	5	16		30 Do You Ever Fool Around	Please Don't Throw Our Love Away	—	$5		Epic 50626
4/28/79	12	14		31 I Don't Lie	Draggin' Main	—	$5		Epic 50694
7/14/79	●¹	16		32 Just Good Ol' Boys	Make A Little Love Each Day	—	$5		Columbia 11027
				MOE BANDY & JOE STAMPLEY					
9/1/79	9	14		33 Put Your Clothes Back On	I Could Be Persuaded	—	$5		Epic 50754
11/17/79+	7	14		34 Holding The Bag	When It Comes To Cowgirls (We Just Can't Say No)	—	$5		Columbia 11147
				MOE BANDY & JOE STAMPLEY					
3/15/80	17	12		35 After Hours	I'm Afraid To Know You That Well	—	$5		Epic 50854
4/12/80	11	15		36 Tell Ole I Ain't Here, He Better Get On Home	Only The Names Have Been Changed	—	$5		Columbia 11244
				MOE BANDY & JOE STAMPLEY					
6/28/80	32	11		37 Haven't I Loved You Somewhere Before	Whiskey Fever	—	$5		Epic 50893
10/4/80	18	15		38 There's Another Woman	No Love At All	—	$5		Epic 50934
1/24/81	9	15		39 I'm Gonna Love You Back To Loving Me Again	Back On The Road Again	—	$5		Epic 50972
3/14/81	10	15		40 Hey Joe (Hey Moe)	Two Beers Away	—	$5		Columbia 60508
				MOE BANDY & JOE STAMPLEY					
5/23/81	18	15		41 Whiskey Chasin'	The Jukebox Never Plays Home Sweet Home	—	$5		Epic 02097
8/1/81	12	14		42 Honky Tonk Queen	Partners In Rhyme	—	$5		Columbia 02198
				MOE BANDY & JOE STAMPLEY					
12/5/81+	41	10		43 Let's Get Together And Cry /					
10/24/81	62	5		44 All These Things [R]		—	$4		Epic 02533
				new version of #19 above					
3/20/82	18	17		45 I'm Goin' Hurtin'	The Fool	—	$4		Epic 02791
7/17/82	30	12		46 I Didn't Know You Could Break A Broken Heart	I Just Can't Get Over You	—	$4		Epic 03016
10/16/82+	25	15		47 Backslidin'	I'm Willing To Try	—	$4		Epic 03290
2/19/83	24	14		48 Finding You	I'm Just Crazy Enough	—	$4		Epic 03558
6/18/83	12	18		49 Poor Side Of Town	It's Over	—	$4		Epic 03966
				#1 Pop hit for **Johnny Rivers** in 1966					
10/29/83+	8	20		50 Double Shot (Of My Baby's Love)	Penny	—	$4		Epic 04173
				#17 Pop hit for the Swingin' Medallions in 1966					
2/11/84	29	16		51 Brown Eyed Girl	A Winner Never Quits	—	$4		Epic 04366
				#10 Pop hit for Van Morrison in 1967					
5/5/84	39	10		52 Memory Lane	Could It Wait Until Forever	—	$4		Epic 04446
				JOE STAMPLEY and JESSICA BOUCHER					
6/2/84	8	16		53 Where's The Dress	Wildlife Sanctuary [N]	—	$5		Columbia 04477
				MOE BANDY & JOE STAMPLEY					
10/13/84	36	10		54 The Boy's Night Out	Alive And Well	—	$5	■	Columbia 04601
				MOE BANDY and JOE STAMPLEY					
1/26/85	48	10		55 Daddy's Honky Tonk	Wild And Crazy Guys	—	$5		Columbia 04756
				MOE BANDY and JOE STAMPLEY					
4/20/85	58	8		56 Still On A Roll	He's Back In Texas	—	$5		Columbia 04843
				MOE BANDY and JOE STAMPLEY					
7/6/85	67	7		57 When Something Is Wrong With My Baby	Say It Like You Mean It	—	$4		Epic 05405
				#42 Pop hit for Sam & Dave in 1967					
9/21/85	47	10		58 I'll Still Be Loving You	Heart Troubles	—	$4		Epic 05592
2/1/86	72	6		59 When You Were Blue And I Was Green	There's No You Left In Us Anymore	—	$4		Epic 05758
7/30/88	56	2		60 Cry Baby		—	$5		Evergreen 1075
5/20/89	89	3		61 You Sure Got This Ol' Redneck Feelin' Blue		—	$5		Evergreen 1081
8/12/89	59	9		62 If You Don't Know Me By Now		—	$5		Evergreen 1100
				#3 Pop hit for Harold Melvin & The Bluenotes in 1972; #1 Pop hit for Simply Red in 1989					

DEBUT	PEAK	WKS	Gold	A-side (Chart Hit)	B-side	Pop	$	Pic	Label & Number

STANLEY BROTHERS '60
Bluegrass duo from Virginia: Carter (born on 8/27/25; died on 12/1/66, age 41) and Ralph (born on 2/25/27) Stanley. Formed The Clinch Mountain Boys in 1946. Ralph joined the *Grand Ole Opry* in 2000.

| 3/21/60 | 17 | 12 | | How Far To Little Rock...................Heaven Seems So Near [N] | — | | $15 | | King 5306 |

STARCHER, Buddy '66
Born Oby Edgar Starcher on 3/16/06 in Ripley, West Virginia. Died on 11/2/2001 (age 95). Singer/songwriter/DJ.

| 2/12/49 | 8 | 1 | | 1 I'll Still Write Your Name In The Sand J:8 *Darling What More Can I Do* | | | $20 | | 4 Star 1145 |
| 4/9/66 | 2¹ | 15 | | 2 History Repeats Itself *Sniper's Hill* [S] | | 39 | $10 | | Boone 1038 |

an accounting of "coincidental" parallels between the careers and deaths of Presidents Lincoln and Kennedy

STARK, Donna '80

| 6/7/80 | 92 | 2 | | Why Don't You Believe Me ....*I'm So Lonesome And So Blue* | | — | $6 | | RCI 2344 |

#1 Pop hit for Joni James in 1952

STARLAND VOCAL BAND '76
Pop group formed in Washington DC: two husband-and-wife teams: Bill Danoff and Kathy "Taffy" Nivert, with John Carroll and Margot Chapman.

| 7/17/76 | 94 | 2 • | | Afternoon Delight ....*Starland* | | ❶² | $5 | | Windsong 10588 |

STARR, Kay '50
Born Katherine Starks on 7/21/22 in Dougherty, Oklahoma; raised in Dallas and Memphis. Charted 40 pop hits from 1948-62. Acted in the movies *Make Believe Ballroom* and *When You're Smiling*.

| 9/16/50 | 2¹ | 16 | | 1 I'll Never Be Free / | A:2 / J:2 / S:4 | 3 | | | |
| 8/26/50 | 5 | 6 | | 2 Ain't Nobody's Business But My Own | A:5 / J:10 | 22 | $25 | | Capitol F1124 |

KAY STARR and TENNESSEE ERNIE (above 2)

STARR, Kenny '76
Born Kenneth Trebbe on 9/21/52 in Topeka, Kansas; raised in Burlingame, Kansas. Singer/guitarist.
1) The Blind Man In The Bleachers 2) Hold Tight 3) Tonight I'll Face The Man (Who Made It Happen)

4/7/73	56	6		1 That's A Whole Lotta Lovin' (You Give Me) ....*Carol*		—	$5		MCA 40023
10/20/73	97	4		2 Ev'ryday Woman ....*My Lovin' Time With You*		—	$5		MCA 40124
3/1/75	89	3		3 Put Another Notch In Your Belt ....*Where Love Begins*		—	$5		MCA 40350

written by Mac Davis

| 11/8/75+ | 2² | 15 | | 4 The Blind Man In The Bleachers *Texas Proud* | | 58 | $5 | | MCA 40474 |

#18 Pop hit for David Geddes in 1975

3/13/76	26	10		5 Tonight I'll Face The Man (Who Made It Happen) ....*I Can't See In The Dark*		—	$5		MCA 40524
7/4/76	73	5		6 The Calico Cat /					
8/21/76	75	3		7 Victims		—	$5		MCA 40580
11/13/76	58	8		8 I Just Can't (Turn My Habit Into Love) ....*The Upper Hand*		—	$5		MCA 40637
2/12/77	43	8		9 Me And The Elephant ....*Smooth Talkin' Guy*		—	$5		MCA 40672
8/27/77	64	7		10 Old Time Lovin' ....*Hobo On The Freight Train To Heaven*		—	$5		MCA 40769
11/19/77+	25	14		11 Hold Tight ....*Rockin' Robin*		—	$5		MCA 40817
4/22/78	72	5		12 The Rest Of My Life ....*Tuffy*		—	$5		MCA 40880
7/1/78	70	6		13 Slow Drivin' ....*Watchin' The River Run*		—	$5		MCA 40922

STARR, Lucille — see CANADIAN SWEETHEARTS

STARR, Penny — see DeHAVEN, Penny

STARR, Ringo — see OWENS, Buck

STATLER, Darrell '69
Born on 12/27/40 in Llano, Texas. Singer/prolific songwriter.

| 9/6/69 | 40 | 7 | | Blue Collar Job ....*I'm Barely Gettin' By* | | — | $7 | | Dot 17275 |

STATLER BROTHERS, The ★40★ '85
Vocal group from Staunton, Virginia: brothers Don (born on 6/5/45) and Harold (born on 8/21/39) Reid, Philip Balsley (born on 8/8/39) and Lew DeWitt (born on 3/8/38; died on 8/15/90, age 52). Worked with **Johnny Cash** from 1963-71. Jimmy Fortune (born on 3/11/55) replaced DeWitt in 1983. Hosted their own variety show on TNN. CMA Awards: 1972, 1973, 1974, 1975, 1976, 1977, 1979, 1980 & 1984 Vocal Group of the Year.

1) Do You Know You Are My Sunshine 2) Too Much On My Heart 3) Elizabeth 4) My Only Love 5) Flowers On The Wall

9/25/65+	2⁴	27		1 Flowers On The Wall *Billy Christian*		4	$10		Columbia 43315
6/18/66	30	11		2 The Right One ....*Is That What You'd Have Me Do*		—	$8		Columbia 43624
11/26/66	37	10		3 That'll Be The Day ....*Makin' Rounds*		—	$8		Columbia 43868
5/13/67	10	14		4 Ruthless *Do You Love Me Tonight*		—	$8		Columbia 44070
9/2/67	10	14		5 You Can't Have Your Kate And Edith, Too *Walking In The Sunshine*		—	$8		Columbia 44245
4/27/68	60	3		6 Jump For Joy ....*Take A Bow, Rufus Humfry*		—	$8		Columbia 44480
1/4/69	60	3		7 I'm The Boy /					
10/19/68	75	2		8 Sissy		—	$8		Columbia 44608
11/21/70+	9	17		9 Bed Of Rose's *The Last Goodbye*		58	$6		Mercury 73141
4/24/71	19	13		10 New York City ....*This Part Of The World*		—	$6		Mercury 73194
8/21/71	13	14		11 Pictures ....*Making Memories*		—	$6		Mercury 73229
12/11/71+	23	13		12 You Can't Go Home ....*Second Thoughts*		—	$6		Mercury 73253
3/11/72	2⁴	15		13 Do You Remember These *Since Then*		105	$6		Mercury 73275
8/19/72	6	15		14 The Class Of '57 *Every Time I Trust A Gal*		—	$6		Mercury 73315
2/3/73	20	11		15 Monday Morning Secretary ....*A Special Song For Wanda*		—	$6		Mercury 73360
6/9/73	29	9		16 Woman Without A Home ....*I'll Be Your Baby Tonight*		—	$6		Mercury 73392

DEBUT	PEAK	WKS	Gold	A-side (Chart Hit)	B-side	Pop	$	Pic	Label & Number
				STATLER BROTHERS, The — Cont'd					
9/15/73	26	12		17 Carry Me Back	I Wish I Could Be	—	$6		Mercury 73415
1/12/74	22	11		18 Whatever Happened To Randolph Scott	The Strand	—	$6		Mercury 73448
6/8/74	31	13		19 Thank You World	The Blackwood Brothers By The Statler Brothers	—	$6		Mercury 73485
11/9/74+	15	14		20 Susan When She Tried	She's Too Good	—	$6		Mercury 73625
3/1/75	31	11		21 All American Girl	A Few Old Memories	—	$6		Mercury 73665
6/21/75	3	19		22 I'll Go To My Grave Loving You	You've Been Like A Mother To Me	93	$6		Mercury 73687
1/3/76	39	9		23 How Great Thou Art	Noah Found Grace In The Eyes Of The Lord	—	$6		Mercury 73732
4/17/76	13	13		24 Your Picture In The Paper	All The Times	—	$6		Mercury 73785
10/2/76	10	14		25 Thank God I've Got You	Hat And Boots	—	$6		Mercury 73846
1/15/77	10	13		26 The Movies	You Could Be Coming To Me	—	$6		Mercury 73877
4/30/77	8	13		27 I Was There	Somebody New Will Be Coming Along	—	$6		Mercury 73906
8/13/77	18	12		28 Silver Medals And Sweet Memories	The Regular Saturday Nite Card Game	—	$5		Mercury 55000
12/3/77+	17	13		29 Some I Wrote	Carried Away	—	$5		Mercury 55013
3/18/78	❶²	17		30 Do You Know You Are My Sunshine	You're The First	—	$5		Mercury 55022
8/5/78	3	14		31 Who Am I To Say	I Dreamed About You	—	$5		Mercury 55037
11/18/78+	5	15		32 The Official Historian On Shirley Jean Berrell	The Best That I Can Do	—	$5		Mercury 55048
3/31/79	7	12		33 How To Be A Country Star	A Little Farther Down The Road	—	$5		Mercury 55057
7/7/79	11	13		34 Here We Are Again	Mr. Autry	—	$5		Mercury 55066
10/27/79	10	13		35 Nothing As Original As You	Counting My Memories	—	$5		Mercury 57007
1/19/80	8	14		36 (I'll Even Love You) Better Than I Did Then	Almost In Love	—	$5		Mercury 57012
7/12/80	5	16		37 Charlotte's Web	One Less Day To Go	—	$5		Mercury 57031
				from the movie *Smokey & The Bandit II* starring **Burt Reynolds**					
11/8/80+	13	14		38 Don't Forget Yourself	We Got Paid By Cash	—	$5		Mercury 57037
3/28/81	35	9		39 In The Garden	How Are Things In Clay, Kentucky?	—	$5		Mercury 57048
				popular hymn written in 1912					
6/13/81	5	18		40 Don't Wait On Me	Chet Atkins' Hand	—	$5		Mercury 57051
				also see #64 below					
10/24/81+	12	16		41 Years Ago	Dad	—	$5		Mercury 57059
3/13/82	3	18		42 You'll Be Back (Every Night In My Dreams)	We Ain't Even Started Yet	—	$5		Mercury 76142
7/3/82	7	16		43 Whatever	Do You Know You Are My Sunshine	—	$5		Mercury 76162
10/23/82+	17	16		44 A Child Of The Fifties	(I'll Love You) All Over Again	—	$5		Mercury 76184
4/16/83	2¹	19		45 Oh Baby Mine (I Get So Lonely)	I'm Dyin' A Little Each Day	—	$4		Mercury 811488
				#2 Pop hit for The Four Knights in 1954					
8/13/83	9	17		46 Guilty	I Never Want To Kiss You Goodbye	—	$4		Mercury 812988
12/10/83+	❶¹	23		47 Elizabeth	The Class Of '57	—	$4		Mercury 814881
4/21/84	3	21		48 Atlanta Blue	If It Makes Any Difference	—	$4	■	Mercury 818700
8/18/84	8	23		49 One Takes The Blame	S:6 / A:8 Give It Your Best	—	$4		Mercury 880130
12/8/84+	❶¹	20		50 My Only Love	S:❶¹ / A:❶¹ (Let's Just) Take One Night At A Time	—	$4		Mercury 880411
4/20/85	3	20		51 Hello Mary Lou	S:3 / A:3 Remembering You	—	$4		Mercury 880685
				#9 Pop hit for **Ricky Nelson** in 1961					
8/24/85	❶¹	25		52 Too Much On My Heart	S:❶² / A:❶¹ Her Heart Or Mine	—	$4		Mercury 884016
1/11/86	8	21		53 Sweeter And Sweeter	S:7 / A:9 Amazing Grace	—	$4		Mercury 884317
5/17/86	5	24		54 Count On Me	S:3 / A:5 Will You Be There?	—	$4	■	Mercury 884721
9/27/86	36	12		55 Only You	We Got The Mem'ries	—	$4		Mercury 888042
				#5 Pop hit for The Platters in 1955					
12/13/86+	7	21		56 Forever	S:❶² / A:7 More Like Daddy Than Me	—	$4		Mercury 888219
6/13/87	10	20		57 I'll Be The One	S:9 De Ja-Vu	—	$4		Mercury 888650
10/31/87	42	13		58 Maple Street Mem'ries	Jesus Showed Me So	—	$4		Mercury 888920
2/20/88	15	23		59 The Best I Know How	S:19 I Lost My Heart To You	—	$4		Mercury 870164
6/11/88	27	19		60 Am I Crazy?	S:29 Beyond Romance	—	$4		Mercury 870442
10/15/88+	12	22		61 Let's Get Started If We're Gonna Break My Heart	S:14 Guilty	—	$4		Mercury 870681
2/18/89	36	10		62 Moon Pretty Moon	I'll Be The One	—	$4		Mercury 872604
5/13/89	6	20		63 More Than A Name On A Wall	Atlanta Blue	—	$4		Mercury 874196
10/7/89	67	5		64 Don't Wait On Me	(long version) [R]	—	$4		Mercury 891014
				"live" version of #40 above					
11/18/89	56	7		65 A Hurt I Can't Handle	Don't Wait On Me	—	$4		Mercury 876112
7/28/90	54	8		66 Small Small World	My Music, My Memories And You	—	$4	■	Mercury 875498 (v)
	★275★			**STEAGALL, Red**					'76
				Born Russell Steagall on 12/22/37 in Gainesville, Texas. Singer/songwriter/guitarist.					
				1) Lone Star Beer And Bob Wills Music 2) Someone Cares For You 3) Somewhere My Love 4) Truck Drivin' Man					
				5) Hard Hat Days And Honky Tonk Nights					
1/15/72	31	11		1 Party Dolls And Wine	Middle Tennessee Country Boy's Blues	—	$6		Capitol 3244
				RED STEAGALL					
11/25/72+	22	12		2 Somewhere, My Love	Give Me One More Chance	—	$6		Capitol 3461
				#9 Pop hit for Ray Conniff & The Singers in 1966					
4/14/73	51	5		3 True Love	Something Nice And Easy	—	$6		Capitol 3562
				#3 Pop hit for **Bing Crosby** & Grace Kelly in 1956					
7/14/73	41	8		4 If You've Got The Time	Ol' Helen	—	$6		Capitol 3651
10/6/73	87	7		5 The Fiddle Man	Neon Playboy	—	$6		Capitol 3724
1/26/74	93	5		6 This Just Ain't My Day (For Lettin' Darlin' Down)	Little Old Heartbreaker You	—	$6		Capitol 3797
3/2/74	54	10		7 I Gave Up Good Mornin' Darling	Ballad Of Billy's Lady	—	$6		Capitol 3825
7/20/74	52	9		8 Finer Things In Life	Tight Levis And Wild Ribbons	—	$6		Capitol 3913
10/26/74+	17	17		9 Someone Cares For You	Throw Away Heart	—	$6		Capitol 3965
3/22/75	62	9		10 She Worshipped Me	April's Paintings	—	$6		Capitol 4042

DEBUT	PEAK	WKS	Gold	A-side (Chart Hit)	B-side	Pop	$	Pic	Label & Number
				STEAGALL, Red — Cont'd					
2/28/76	11	15		11 Lone Star Beer And Bob Wills Music	I've Never Been This Loved Before	—	$5		ABC/Dot 17610
6/19/76	29	11		12 Truck Drivin' Man	Neons And Nylons	—	$5		ABC/Dot 17634
9/25/76	45	9		13 Rosie (Do You Wanna Talk It Over)	The Walls Of This Old Honky Tonk	—	$5		ABC/Dot 17653
12/25/76+	59	8		14 Her L-O-V-E's Gone	Take Me Back To Texas	—	$5		ABC/Dot 17670
3/12/77	53	8		15 I Left My Heart In San Francisco	Texas Red	—	$5		ABC/Dot 17684
				#19 Pop hit for Tony Bennett in 1962					
8/13/77	90	4		16 Freckles Brown	My Adobe Hacienda	—	$5		ABC/Dot 17709
11/12/77	72	8		17 The Devil Ain't A Lonely Woman's Friend	The Rain Don't Stop In Oklahoma	—	$5		ABC/Dot 17726
3/11/78	63	9		18 Hang On Feelin' /		—			
		4		19 Bob's Got A Swing Band In Heaven		—	$5		ABC 12337
				tribute to Bob Wills					
9/22/79	41	9		20 Goodtime Charlie's Got The Blues	Songs About People In Love	—	$4		Elektra 46527
2/9/80	31	9		21 3 Chord Country Song	Jackson Hole, Wyoming	—	$4		Elektra 46590
5/10/80	49	8		22 Dim The Lights And Pour The Wine	He Ain't Got Nothin' On Me	—	$4		Elektra 46633
8/23/80	30	12		23 Hard Hat Days And Honky Tonk Nights	Last Call For Alcohol	—	$4		Elektra 47014
				STEARNS, June '68					
				Born Agnes June Stearns on 4/5/39 in Albany, New York. Singer/guitarist.					
				1)Jackson Ain't A Very Big Town 2)Tyin' Strings 3)Empty House					
4/27/68	47	12		1 Empty House	I'm The Queen (Of My Lonely Little World)	—	$7		Columbia 44483
9/14/68	57	5		2 Where He Stops Nobody Knows	I Cry Myself Awake	—	$7		Columbia 44575
10/19/68	21	8		3 Jackson Ain't A Very Big Town	The True And Lasting Kind	—	$7		Columbia 44656
				JOHNNY DUNCAN AND JUNE STEARNS					
1/4/69	53	6		4 Walking Midnight Road	Plastic Saddle	—	$7		Columbia 44695
3/15/69	74	3		5 Back To Back (We're Strangers)	If That's The Only Way	—	$7		Columbia 44752
				JOHNNY DUNCAN AND JUNE STEARNS					
6/7/69	70	4		6 What Makes You So Different	Trouble In Mind	—	$7		Columbia 44852
12/27/69	58	4		7 Drifting Too Far (From Your Arms)	He Was A Carpenter	—	$7		Columbia 45042
9/26/70	41	6		8 Tyin' Strings	Don't Trouble Trouble	—	$6		Decca 32726
6/12/71	57	8		9 Sweet Baby On My Mind	How's My Ex Treating You	—	$6		Decca 32828
10/16/71	56	8		10 Your Kind Of Lovin'	Another	—	$6		Decca 32876
				STEEL, Ric '88					
12/5/87+	57	9		1 The Radio Song	Third Times The Charm	—	$6		Panache 1001
6/18/88	59	7		2 Whose Baby Are You		—	$6		Panache 1002
				STEELE, Jeffrey '01					
				Born on 8/27/61 in Burbank, California; raised in North Hollywood. Former lead singer of **Boy Howdy**.					
3/22/97	60	4		1 A Girl Like You	My Greatest Love	—	$4		Curb 73012
9/1/01	33	21		2 Somethin' In The Water	S:4 How Long Am I Supposed To Wait For You	—	$4	★	Monument 79625
				STEELE, Larry '66					
1/15/66	43	3		1 I Ain't Crying Mister	Ramblin Man	—	$8		K-Ark 659
4/6/68	75	2		2 Hard Times	The Apple Or The Pair	—	$8		K-Ark 802
				LARRY STEELE and THE WRANGLERS					
11/9/74	90	5		3 Daylight Losing Time	Watermelon Man	—	$8		Air Stream 004
				STEFFIN SISTERS '89					
				Vocal group of sisters from West Monroe, Louisiana: Jenny, Marianne, Beth and Kathy Steffin.					
5/27/89	88	2		1 I Still Need You	Guitar Fiddlin' Joe	—	$6	■	Windward 7
	★369★			**STEGALL, Keith** '85					
				Born Robert Keith Stegall on 11/1/54 in Wichita Falls, Texas. Singer/songwriter/guitarist/pianist. Acted in the movies *Killing At Hell's Gate* and *Country Gold*.					
				1)Pretty Lady 2)California 3)Whatever Turns You On					
3/1/80	58	6		1 The Fool Who Fooled Around	Keep On Playing That Country Music	—	$4		Capitol 4835
2/21/81	55	7		2 Anything That Hurts You (Hurts Me)	She's Nobody's Baby But Mine	—	$4		Capitol 4967
9/12/81	65	5		3 Won't You Be My Baby	Keep On Playing That Country Music	—	$4		Capitol 5034
3/13/82	64	5		4 In Love With Loving You	Hurry On Home	—	$4		EMI America 8107
5/12/84	25	16		5 I Want To Go Somewhere	The Cowboy Thing To Do	—	$4		Epic 04442
9/22/84	19	21		6 Whatever Turns You On	S:11 / A:21 Daylight Lovin' Time	—	$4	■	Epic 04590
2/16/85	13	18		7 California	S:13 / A:18 Straight Shooter	—	$4		Epic 04771
6/15/85	10	22		8 Pretty Lady	A:9 / S:12 These Tears	—	$4	■	Epic 04934
11/2/85	45	10		9 Feed The Fire	Marylee	—	$4		Epic 05643
3/1/86	36	13		10 I Think I'm In Love	Sweet Love Bandit	—	$4		Epic 05815
11/15/86	52	9		11 Ole Rock And Roller (With A Country Heart)	On A Good Night	—	$4		Epic 06418
1/27/96	43	13		12 1969 /		—			
5/18/96	75	1		13 Fifty-Fifty		—	$4	■	Mercury 852618 (v)
				STEINER, Tommy Shane '02					
				Born in Austin, Texas. Singer/songwriter.					
12/22/01+	2¹	28↑		What If She's An Angel	The Mind Of John J. Blanchard	—	$4		RCA 69136
				STENMARK-MUELLER BAND '87					
				Duo from Salt Lake City: K.J. Stenmark and LynnDee Mueller.					
11/14/87	95	1		Lover To Lover		—	$7		Envelope 7004

DEBUT	PEAK	WKS	Gold	A-side (Chart Hit)	B-side	Pop	$	Pic	Label & Number
				STEPHENS, Ott '63					
				Born on 9/21/41 in Ringold, Georgia. Male singer/guitarist.					
1/19/63	15	7		1 Robert E. Lee...Never Tired Of Loving You	—		$15		Chancellor 107
6/13/64	23	15		2 Be Quiet Mind...Hard Luck Story	—		$12		Reprise 0272
6/12/65	36	12		3 Enough Man For You...Never Tired Of Loving You	—		$10		Chart 1205
				STEVENS, Even '75					
				Born in Lewiston, Ohio; raised in Cincinnati. Singer/prolific songwriter.					
6/21/75	38	13		1 Let The Little Boy Dream..Josie's Comin' Home	—		$5		Elektra 45254
12/20/75+	81	7		2 Huckelberry Pie..I Won't Sing No Love Songs Anymore	—		$5		Elektra 45292
				EVEN STEVENS/SAMMI SMITH					
10/15/77	97	1		3 The King Of Country Music Meets The Queen Of					
				Rock & Roll...I'm From Outer Space	—		$5		Elektra 45430
				EVEN STEVENS & SHERRY GROOMS					
				★ **STEVENS, Geraldine** '69					
				Born Geraldine Ann Pasquale on 2/17/46 in Chicago. Better known as Dodie Stevens. Charted the pop hit "Pink Shoe Laces" in 1959.					
9/13/69	57	3		1 Billy, I've Got To Go To Town...It's Not Their Heartache, It's Mine	117		$8		World Pacific 77927
				answer to "Ruby, Don't Take Your Love To Town" by Kenny Rogers					
				STEVENS, Jeff, and The Bullets '87					
				Family trio from Alum Creek, West Virginia: brothers Jeff (vocals, guitar; born on 6/15/59) and Warren (bass) Stevens, with cousin Terry Dotson (drums).					
12/27/86+	69	8		1 Darlington County..Tamed By Love	—		$4		Atlantic Amer. 99494
				written and first recorded by Bruce Springsteen on his 1984 Born In The U.S.A. album					
3/28/87	61	6		2 You're In Love Alone..Tamed By Love	—		$4		Atlantic Amer. 99475
7/18/87	53	8		3 Geronimo's Cadillac..Tamed By Love	—		$4		Atlantic Amer. 99433
				#37 Pop hit for Michael Murphey in 1972					
4/22/89	70	5		4 Johnny Lucky And Suzi 66..Change Of Heart	—		$4	■	Atlantic Amer. 99259
				STEVENS, Lee J. '89					
1/14/89	92	2		You'll Be The First To Know..	—		$5		Regal 01

STEVENS, Ray ★178★ '75

Born Harold Ray Ragsdale on 1/24/39 in Clarksdale, Georgia. Singer/songwriter/comedian. Proficient on several instruments. Production work in the mid-1960s. Numerous appearances on the **Andy Williams** TV show in the late 1960s. Hosted own TV show in 1970. Also recorded as **Henhouse Five Plus Too**.

1)Misty 2)The Streak 3)Shriner's Convention 4)You Are So Beautiful 5)Turn Your Radio On

DEBUT	PEAK	WKS	Gold	A-side	B-side	Pop	$	Pic	Label & Number
11/1/69	55	6		1 Sunday Mornin' Comin' Down..The Minority	81		$8		Monument 1163
12/27/69+	63	2		2 Have A Little Talk With Myself...The Little Woman	123		$8		Monument 1171
5/2/70	39	6	●	3 Everything Is Beautiful...A Brighter Day	❶²		$6		Barnaby 2011
12/4/71+	17	13		4 Turn Your Radio On..Loving You On Paper	63		$6		Barnaby 2048
7/14/73	37	11		5 Nashville...Golden Age	—		$6		Barnaby 5020
4/13/74	3	13	●	6 The Streak	You've Got The Music Inside [N]	❶³		$6		Barnaby 600
11/30/74+	37	10		7 Everybody Needs A Rainbow..Inside	—		$6		Barnaby 610
3/22/75	3	17		8 Misty	Sunshine	14		$6		Barnaby 614
				#12 Pop hit for Johnny Mathis in 1959					
9/27/75	38	11		9 Indian Love Call..Piece Of Paradise	68		$6		Barnaby 616
				#3 Pop hit for Paul Whiteman in 1925					
1/3/76	48	8		10 Young Love...Deep Purple	93		$6		Barnaby 618
				#1 Pop hit for Tab Hunter in 1957					
5/1/76	16	13		11 You Are So Beautiful...One Man Band	101		$6		Warner 8198
				#5 Pop hit for Joe Cocker in 1975					
8/7/76	27	10		12 Honky Tonk Waltz...Om	—		$6		Warner 8237
1/8/77	39	7		13 In The Mood...Classical Cluck [N]	40		$6		Warner 8301
				HENHOUSE FIVE PLUS TOO					
				#1 Pop hit for Glenn Miller in 1940					
2/19/77	81	6		14 Get Crazy With Me..Dixie Hummingbird	—		$6		Warner 8318
6/11/77	44	9		15 Dixie Hummingbird..Feel The Music	—		$6		Warner 8393
8/12/78	36	10		16 Be Your Own Best Friend..With A Smile	—		$6		Warner 8603
4/14/79	85	3		17 I Need Your Help Barry Manilow......................................Daydream Romance [N]	49		$6	■	Warner 8785
2/9/80	7	12		★18 Shriner's Convention	You're Never Goin' To Tampa With Me [N]	101		$5		RCA 11911
9/13/80	20	13		19 Night Games...Let's Do It Right This Time	—		$5		RCA 12069
2/14/81	33	10		20 One More Last Chance...I Believe You Love Me	—		$5		RCA 12170
2/6/82	35	10		21 Written Down In My Heart...Country Boy, Country Club Girl	—		$5		RCA 13038
5/22/82	63	7		22 Where The Sun Don't Shine..Why Don't We Go Somewhere And Love	—		$5		RCA 13207
2/11/84	64	8		23 My Dad...Me	—		$5		Mercury 818057
12/8/84+	20	14		★24 Mississippi Squirrel Revival...S:12 / A:28 Ned Nostril	—		$4		MCA 52492
3/23/85	74	6		25 It's Me Again, Margaret..Joggin'	—		$4		MCA 52548
9/14/85	45	14		26 The Haircut Song..Punk Country Love [N]	—		$4		MCA 52657
1/25/86	50	10		27 The Ballad Of The Blue Cyclone.......................................S:26 Vacation Bible School	—		$4		MCA 52771
9/13/86	70	7		28 People's Court..Dudley Dorite (Of The Highway Patrol) [N]	—		$4		MCA 52924
11/1/86	63	6		29 Southern Air..S:27 The Camping Trip [N]	—		$4		MCA 52906
				Jerry Clower and Minnie Pearl (guest vocals)					
5/9/87	41	9		30 Would Jesus Wear A Rolex...S:15 Cool Down Willard [N]	—		$4		MCA 53101

DEBUT	PEAK	WKS	Gold	A-side (Chart Hit)	B-side	Pop	$	Pic	Label & Number
				STEVENS, Ray — Cont'd					
10/8/88	88	2		31 The Day I Tried To Teach Charlene MacKenzie How To Drive	I Don't Need None Of That [N]	—	$4		MCA 53423
7/6/91	62	10		32 Working For The Japanese	[N]	—			album cut
3/14/92	72	2		33 Power Tools	[N]	—			album cut
				above 2 from the album *#1 With A Bullet* on Curb/Capitol 95914					
12/29/01	48	5		34 Osama-Yo' Mama	S:2 United We Stand [N]	8^S	$4	★	Curb 73130
	★205★			**STEWART, Gary** '75					
				Born on 5/28/45 in Letcher County, Kentucky; raised in Fort Pierce, Florida. Singer/songwriter/guitarist. Member of rock groups the Tomcats and the Amps in the early 1960s. First recorded solo for the Cory label in 1964.					
				1)She's Actin' Single (I'm Drinkin' Doubles) 2)Out Of Hand 3)Drinkin' Thing 4)Your Place Or Mine 5)You're Not The Woman You Use To Be					
11/17/73	63	7		1 Ramblin' Man	Williamson County	—	$6		RCA Victor 0144
				#2 Pop hit for The Allman Brothers Band in 1973					
6/1/74	10	18		2 Drinkin' Thing	I See The Want To In Your Eyes	—	$5		RCA Victor 0281
10/19/74+	4	16		3 **Out Of Hand**	Draggin' Shackles	—	$5		RCA Victor 10061
3/8/75	❶¹	13		4 **She's Actin' Single (I'm Drinkin' Doubles)**	Williamson County	—	$5		RCA Victor 10222
6/21/75	15	15		5 You're Not The Woman You Use To Be	I Owe It All To Mama	—	$5		MCA 40414
10/11/75	20	12		6 Flat Natural Born Good-Timin' Man	This Old Heart Won't Let Go	—	$5	☐	RCA Victor 10351
1/31/76	23	13		7 Oh, Sweet Temptation	Hank Western	—	$5		RCA Victor 10550
5/22/76	15	14		8 In Some Room Above The Street	Easy People	—	$5		RCA Victor 10680
11/20/76+	11	13		9 Your Place Or Mine	Lord, What A Woman	—	$4		RCA 10833
5/21/77	16	12		10 Ten Years Of This	I Ain't Living Long Like This	—	$4		RCA 10957
10/22/77	26	13		11 Quits	Dancing Eyes	—	$4		RCA 11131
3/11/78	16	12		12 Whiskey Trip	Williamson County	—	$4		RCA 11224
7/22/78	36	8		13 Single Again	Little Junior	—	$4		RCA 11297
11/25/78+	41	9		14 Stone Wall (Around Your Heart)	I Got Mine	—	$4		RCA 11416
4/14/79	66	5		15 Shady Streets	Everything A Good Little Girl Needs	—	$4		RCA 11534
7/14/79	75	3		16 Mazelle	One More	—	$4		RCA 11623
6/14/80	48	9		17 Cactus And A Rose	Staring Each Other Down	—	$4		RCA 11960
9/27/80	66	4		18 Are We Dreamin' The Same Dream /		—			
		4		19 Roarin'		—	$4		RCA 12081
4/11/81	72	4		20 Let's Forget That We're Married	Honky Tonk Man	—	$4		RCA 12203
11/7/81	36	11		21 She's Got A Drinking Problem	Memories Swim In Whiskey	—	$4		RCA 12343
4/10/82	41	11		22 Brotherly Love	Firewater Friends	—	$4	■	RCA 13049
				GARY STEWART/DEAN DILLON					
7/24/82	83	4		23 She Sings Amazing Grace	Cold Turkey	—	$4		RCA 13261
1/8/83	47	12		24 Those Were The Days	Drinkin' Thing	—	$4		RCA 13401
				GARY STEWART AND DEAN DILLON					
4/16/83	71	4		25 Smokin' In The Rockies	Hard Time For Lovers	—	$4		RCA 13472
				GARY STEWART & DEAN DILLON					
4/14/84	75	7		26 Hey, Bottle Of Whiskey	Roadhouse Romances	—	$5		Red Ash 8403
8/11/84	64	7		27 I Got A Bad Attitude	Life's A Game	—	$5		Red Ash 8406
10/1/88	63	7		28 Brand New Whiskey		—	$5		Hightone 506
12/3/88+	64	9		29 An Empty Glass		—	$5		Hightone 507
3/18/89	77	3		30 Rainin', Rainin', Rainin'		—	$5		Hightone 509
				STEWART, Larry '93					
				Born on 3/2/59 in Paducah, Kentucky. Lead singer of **Restless Heart** from 1986-91.					
3/6/93	5	20		1 **Alright Already**	The Boy Down The Road	—	$4		RCA 62474
7/3/93	34	17		2 I'll Cry Tomorrow	Brittany	—	$4		RCA 62546
11/6/93	62	6		3 We Can Love	When You Come Back To Me	—	$4		RCA 62696
8/20/94	43	11		4 Heart Like A Hurricane	(remix)	—	$4	■	Columbia 77638 (v)
12/3/94+	46	16		5 Losing Your Love	One Track Mind	—	$4	■	Columbia 77753 (v)
4/8/95	56	9		6 Rockin' The Rock	I'm Not Through Lovin' You	—	$4	■	Columbia 77857 (v)
7/6/96	46	15		7 Why Can't You	I'm Not Through Lovin' You	—	$4	■	Columbia 78307 (v)
1/25/97	70	4		8 Always A Woman		—			album cut
				from the album *Why Can't You* on Columbia 67410					
				STEWART, Lisa '92					
				Born on 8/6/68 in Louisville, Mississippi. Became co-host of TNN's *This Week In Country Music* in 1997.					
10/31/92	61	7		1 Somebody's In Love	Is It Love	—	$4		BNA 62311
3/20/93	72	3		2 Drive Time	Don't Touch Me	—	$4	■	BNA 62441 (v)
				STEWART, Vernon '63					
1/12/63	17	6		The Way It Feels To Die	You're Not All Here	—	$20		Chart 501

DEBUT	PEAK	WKS	Gold	A-side (Chart Hit)	B-side	Pop	$	Pic	Label & Number

STEWART, Wynn ★170★ '67
Born Wynnford Stewart on 6/7/34 in Morrisville, Missouri. Died of a heart attack on 7/17/85 (age 51). Singer/songwriter/guitarist. Worked on KWTO in Springfield, Missouri, in 1947. Moved to California in 1949 and recorded for the Intro label at age 16. Own club and TV series in Las Vegas in the late 1950s.

1) It's Such A Pretty World Today 2) Wishful Thinking 3) Love's Gonna Happen To Me 4) After The Storm
5) 'Cause I Have You

DEBUT	PEAK	WKS		A-side	B-side	Pop	$	Pic	Label & Number
7/21/56	14	1	1	The Waltz Of The Angels	A:14 Why Do I Love You So	—	$20		Capitol 3408
12/28/59+	5	22	2	Wishful Thinking	Uncle Tom Got Caught	—	$15		Challenge 9061
5/30/60	26	2	3	Wrong Company	We'll Never Love Again	—	$15		Challenge 9071
				WYNN STEWART AND JAN HOWARD					
12/25/61	18	7	4	Big, Big Love	One More Memory	—	$15		Challenge 9121
11/24/62	27	3	5	Another Day, Another Dollar	Donna On My Mind	—	$15		Challenge 9164
11/21/64	30	15	6	Half Of This, Half Of That	The Happy Part Of Town	—	$8	■	Capitol 5271
10/16/65	43	7	7	I Keep Forgettin' That I Forgot About You	My Rosalie	—	$8		Capitol 5485
2/25/67	❶²	22	8	It's Such A Pretty World Today	Ol' What's Her Name	—	$8		Capitol 5831
				#1 Easy Listening hit for Andy Russell in 1967					
7/15/67	9	16	9	'Cause I Have You /		—			
8/5/67	68	3	10	That's The Only Way To Cry		—	$8	■	Capitol 5937
				WYNN STEWART And The Tourists:					
11/11/67+	7	16	11	Love's Gonna Happen To Me	Waltz Of The Angels	—	$7	■	Capitol 2012
4/20/68	10	13	12	Something Pretty	Built-In Love	—	$7	■	Capitol 2137
8/24/68	16	11	13	In Love	My Own Little World	—	$7	■	Capitol 2240
12/14/68+	29	11	14	Strings	Happy Blues	—	$7		Capitol 2341
4/5/69	20	12	15	Let The Whole World Sing It With Me	Who Are You?	—	$7		Capitol 2421
7/26/69	19	10	16	World-Wide Travelin' Man	Cry Baby	—	$6		Capitol 2549
11/15/69	47	9	17	Yours Forever	Goin' Steady	—	$6		Capitol 2657
4/11/70	55	4	18	You Don't Care What Happens To Me	Young As Spring	—	$6		Capitol 2751
				WYNN STEWART:					
9/12/70	13	13	19	It's A Beautiful Day	Prisoner On The Run	—	$6		Capitol 2888
1/2/71	32	10	20	Heavenly	You're No Secret Of Mine	—	$6		Capitol 3000
5/1/71	55	6	21	Baby, It's Yours	I Was The First One To Know	—	$6		Capitol 3080
9/18/71	53	5	22	Hello Little Rock	You Can't Take It With You	—	$6		Capitol 3157
11/11/72	49	8	23	Paint Me A Rainbow	I Know They'll Make Room For You	—	$5		RCA Victor 0819
7/14/73	51	9	24	Love Ain't Worth a Dime Unless It's Free	Me And My Jesus Would Know	—	$5		RCA Victor 0004
10/27/73	62	9	25	It's Raining In Seattle	If I Were You (And I Wish I Was)	—	$5		RCA Victor 0114
6/14/75	80	9	26	Lonely Rain	Just Now Thought Of You	—	$5		Playboy 6035
7/31/76	8	14	27	After The Storm	Don't Monkey With My Widow	—	$5		Playboy 6080
11/20/76+	19	11	28	Sing A Sad Song	It's Such A Pretty World Today	—	$5		Playboy 6091
12/23/78+	37	11	29	Eyes Big As Dallas	Such A Perfect Day For Making Love	—	$6		WIN 126
6/9/79	59	5	30	Could I Talk You Into Loving Me Again	I Was Raised Down On The Farm	—	$6		WIN'S 127
8/24/85	98	1	31	Wait Till I Get My Hands On You	Would You Want The World To End	—	$7		Pretty World 001

STOCKTON, Shane '98
Born on 3/18/74 in Breckenridge, Texas. Male singer/guitarist.

3/28/98	54	10	1	What If I'm Right	My Life's An Open Book	—	$4		Decca 72043
6/27/98	51	7	2	Gonna Have To Fall	Billy Saw The Light	—	$4		Decca 72060

STONE, Cliffie, And His Orchestra '48
Born Clifford Snyder on 3/1/17 in Burbank, California. Died of a heart attack on 1/16/98 (age 80). Singer/songwriter/bassist/bandleader. Popular radio/TV personality in Los Angeles, hosting *Hollywood Barn Dance*, *Lucky Stars* and *Dinner Bell Roundup* (later known as *Hometown Jamboree*). Worked as an A&R executive for Capitol Records. Elected to the Country Music Hall of Fame in 1989.

3/15/47	4	1	1	Silver Stars, Purple Sage, Eyes Of Blue	If You Knew Susie	—	$15		Capitol 354
3/6/48	4	8	2	Peepin' Thru The Keyhole (Watching Jole Blon)	Wabash Blues	—	$20		Capitol Amer. 40083
				CLIFFIE STONE And His Barn Dance Band					
8/28/48	11	3	3	When My Blue Moon Turns To Gold Again	J:11 Take It Any Way You Can Get It	—	$15		Capitol 15108
				#19 Pop hit for *Elvis Presley* in 1956					
10/15/66	30	7	4	Little Pink Mack	That'll Be The Day	—	$15		Tower 269
				KAY ADAMS with The Cliffie Stone Group					

STONE, Doug ★154★ '92
Born Douglas Brooks on 6/19/56 in Marietta, Georgia; raised in Newnan, Georgia. Singer/songwriter/guitarist. Began performing in 1963. Formed own groups: Impact, Image and Main Street. Changed name to avoid confusion with Garth Brooks. Starred in the 1995 movie *Gordy*; did voiceovers for several animated shows.

1) A Jukebox With A Country Song 2) In A Different Light 3) Too Busy Being In Love 4) Why Didn't I Think Of That
5) I Never Knew Love

3/10/90	4	25	1	I'd Be Better Off (In A Pine Box)	It's A Good Thing I Don't Love You Anymore	—	$4	■	Epic 73246 (v)
7/14/90	6	21	2	Fourteen Minutes Old	High Weeds And Rust	—	$4		Epic 73425 (v)
11/10/90+	5	20	3	These Lips Don't Know How To Say Goodbye	We Always Agree On Love	—	$4	■	Epic 73570 (v)
3/16/91	❶¹	20	4	In A Different Light	Turn This Thing Around	—	$4		Epic 73741

DEBUT	PEAK	WKS	Gold	A-side (Chart Hit)	B-side	Pop	$	Pic	Label & Number
				STONE, Doug — Cont'd					
7/20/91	4	20		5 I Thought It Was You .... (For Every Inch I've Laughed) I've Cried A Mile		—	$4		Epic 73895
11/16/91+	❶²	20		6 A Jukebox With A Country Song .... Remember The Ride		—	$4		Epic 74089
3/21/92	3	20		7 Come In Out Of The Pain .... The Feeling Never Goes Away		—	$4		Epic 74259
7/11/92	4	20		8 Warning Labels .... Left, Leavin', Goin' Or Gone		—	$4		Epic 74399
11/7/92+	❶¹	20		9 Too Busy Being In Love .... The Workin' End Of A Hoe		—	$4		Epic 74761
2/27/93	6	20		10 Made For Lovin' You .... She's Got A Future In The Movies		—	$4		Epic 74885
6/19/93	❶¹	20		11 Why Didn't I Think Of That .... This Empty House		—	$4		Epic 77025
10/23/93+	2²	20		12 I Never Knew Love .... This Empty House		81	$4	■	Epic 77228 (v)
2/26/94	4	20		13 Addicted To A Dollar .... That's A Lie		—	$4	■	Epic 77375 (v)
6/18/94	6	20		14 More Love .... She Used To Love Me A Lot		—	$4	■	Epic 77549 (v)
10/29/94+	7	20		15 Little Houses .... I'd Be Better Off (In A Pine Box)		—	$4		Epic 77716
3/4/95	13	20		16 Faith In Me, Faith In You .... S:25 Enough About Me (Let's Talk About You)		—	$4		Columbia 77837 (v)
6/24/95	41	11		17 Sometimes I Forget .... You Won't Outlive Me		—	$4	■	Columbia 77945 (v)
9/23/95+	12	20		18 Born In The Dark .... Down On My Knees		—	$4		Columbia 78039
6/20/98	48	8		19 Gone Out Of My Mind		—			album cut
				from the various artists album *A Tribute To Tradition* on Columbia 68073					
4/24/99	19	26		20 Make Up In Love		105			album cut
10/30/99+	45	13		21 Take A Letter Maria		—			album cut
				#2 Pop hit for R.B. Greaves in 1969					
4/22/00	64	1		22 Surprise		—			album cut
				above 3 from the album *Make Up In Love* on Atlantic 83206					
				STONEMANS, The ★ Sisters & Bros. ★ **'66**					
				Family group from Monorat, Virginia: Ernest "Pop" (autoharp, guitar; born on 5/25/1893; died on 6/14/68, age 75), <u>Calvin</u> "Scotty" (fiddle; born on 8/4/32; died on 3/4/73, age 40), <u>Van</u> (guitar; born on 12/31/40; died on 6/3/95, age 54), <u>Donna</u> (mandolin; born on 2/7/34), Veronica "<u>Roni</u>" (banjo; born on 5/5/38) and Oscar "<u>Jim</u>" (bass; born on 3/8/37). All shared vocals. ★ Roni was a regular on TV's <u>Hee-Haw</u>. CMA Award: 1967 Vocal Group of the Year.					
6/4/66	40	3		1 Tupelo County Jail .... Spell Of The Freight Train		—	$8		MGM 13466
10/8/66	21	11		2 The Five Little Johnson Girls .... Goin' Back To Bowling Green		—	$8		MGM 13557
3/25/67	40	12		3 Back To Nashville, Tennessee .... Bottle Of Wine		—	$8		MGM 13667
8/5/67	49	7		4 West Canterbury Subdivision Blues .... The Three Cent Opera		—	$8		MGM 13755
7/20/68	41	8		5 Christopher Robin .... The Love I Left Behind		—	$8		MGM 13945
				STOREY, Lewis **'86**					
				Born in Casa Grande, Arizona.					
2/8/86	48	8		1 Ain't No Tellin' .... Flo's Inn		—	$4	■	Epic 05786
5/17/86	60	6		2 Katie, Take Me Dancin' .... Friday Fool's Parade		—	$4		Epic 05890
				STORIE, James **'88**					
10/22/88	100	1		Lost Highway .... Whispering Pines		—	$7		GMC 1001
				STOVALL, Vern **'67**					
				Born on 10/3/28 in Altus, Oklahoma; raised in Vian, Oklahoma. Also see **Phil Baugh**.					
9/23/67	58	8		Dallas .... Movin' Round		—	$10		Longhorn 581
				STRAIT, George ★6★ **'90**					
				Born on 5/18/52 in Poteet, Texas; raised in Pearsall, Texas. Singer/songwriter/guitarist. Served in the U.S. Army from 1972-74. Graduated from Southwest Texas State with a degree in agriculture. Formed the Ace In The Hole band in 1975. Starred in the movie *Pure Country*. CMA Awards: 1985, 1986, 1996, 1997 & 1998 Male Vocalist of the Year; 1989 & 1990 Entertainer of the Year.					
				1) Love Without End, Amen 2) One Night At A Time 3) I've Come To Expect It From You 4) Write This Down 5) Check Yes Or No					
5/16/81	6	18		1 Unwound .... She's Playing Hell Trying To Get Me To Heaven		—	$4		MCA 51104
9/12/81	16	17		2 Down And Out .... Blame It On Mexico		—	$4		MCA 51170
1/30/82	3	22		3 If You're Thinking You Want A Stranger (There's One Coming Home) .... Her Goodbye Hit Me In The Heart		—	$4		MCA 51228
6/19/82	❶¹	18		4 Fool Hearted Memory .... The Steal Of The Night		—	$4		MCA 52066
				from the movie *The Soldier* starring Klaus Kinski					
10/9/82+	6	19		5 Marina Del Rey .... I Can't See Texas From Here		—	$4		MCA 52120
2/12/83	4	17		6 Amarillo By Morning .... Lover In Disguise		—	$4		MCA 52162
6/11/83	❶¹	23		7 A Fire I Can't Put Out .... Honky Tonk Crazy		—	$4		MCA 52225
10/8/83+	❶¹	23		8 You Look So Good In Love .... A Little Heaven's Rubbing Off On Me		—	$4		MCA 52279
2/11/84	❶¹	23		9 Right Or Wrong .... Fifteen Years Going Up (And One Night Coming Down)		—	$4		MCA 52337
6/2/84	❶¹	21		10 Let's Fall To Pieces Together .... You're The Cloud I'm On (When I'm High)		—	$4		MCA 52392
9/29/84+	❶¹	23		11 Does Fort Worth Ever Cross Your Mind .... S:❶¹ / A:❶¹ Love Comes From The Other Side Of Town		—	$4		MCA 52458
2/2/85	5	20		12 The Cowboy Rides Away .... S:4 / A:5 Any Old Time		—	$4		MCA 52526
6/1/85	5	18		13 The Fireman .... S:4 / A:5 What Did You Expect Me To Do		—	$4		MCA 52586
9/21/85	❶¹	22		14 The Chair .... S:❶¹ / A:❶¹ In Too Deep		—	$4	■	MCA 52667
1/18/86	4	21		15 You're Something Special To Me .... S:4 / A:4 Dance Time In Texas		—	$4		MCA 52764
5/17/86	❶¹	22		16 Nobody In His Right Mind Would've Left Her .... S:❶¹ / A:❶¹ You Still Get To Me		—	$4		MCA 52817
9/13/86	❶¹	22		17 It Ain't Cool To Be Crazy About You .... S:❶¹ / A:❶¹ Rhythm Of The Road		—	$4		MCA 52914
1/17/87	❶¹	21		18 Ocean Front Property .... S:❶⁴ / A:❶¹ My Heart Won't Wander Very Far From You		—	$4		MCA 53021
5/2/87	❶¹	16		19 All My Ex's Live In Texas .... S:❶² / A:25 I'm All Behind You Now		—	$4		MCA 53087
8/22/87	❶¹	18		20 Am I Blue .... S:❶³ Someone's Walkin' Around Upstairs		—	$4		MCA 53165

DEBUT	PEAK	WKS	Gold	A-side (Chart Hit)	B-side	Pop	$	Pic	Label & Number
				STRAIT, George — Cont'd					
2/6/88	①¹	19		21 Famous Last Words Of A Fool	S:❶² It's Too Late Now	—	$4		MCA 53248
5/21/88	①¹	19		22 Baby Blue	S:❶² Back To Bein' Me	—	$4		MCA 53340
9/17/88	①¹	20		23 If You Ain't Lovin' (You Ain't Livin')	S:❶² Is It That Time Again	—	$4		MCA 53400
1/21/89	①¹	18		24 Baby's Gotten Good At Goodbye	Bigger Man Than Me	—	$4		MCA 53486
4/29/89	①¹	20		25 What's Going On In Your World	Let's Get Down To It	—	$4		MCA 53648
8/12/89	①¹	21		26 Ace In The Hole	Oh Me, Oh My Sweet Baby	—	$4		MCA 53693
12/2/89+	8	26		27 Overnight Success /			—		
3/24/90	67	5		28 Hollywood Squares			$4		MCA 53755
4/28/90	①⁵	21		29 Love Without End, Amen	Too Much Of Too Little	—	$4		MCA 53820
8/11/90	4	21		30 Drinking Champagne	We're Supposed To Do That Now And Then	—	$4		MCA 79070
11/3/90	①⁵	20		31 I've Come To Expect It From You	Stranger In My Arms	—	$4		MCA 53969
3/23/91	①²	20		32 If I Know Me	Home In San Antone	—	$4		MCA 54052
6/15/91	①³	20		33 You Know Me Better Than That	Baby Blue	—	$4		MCA 54127
10/5/91	3	20		34 The Chill Of An Early Fall	Her Only Bad Habit Is Me	—	$4		MCA 54180
1/18/92	24	20		35 Lovesick Blues	Is It Already Time	—	$4		MCA 54318
4/18/92	5	20		36 Gone As A Girl Can Get	Faults And All	—	$4		MCA 54379
7/11/92	3	20		37 So Much Like My Dad	Wonderland Of Love	—	$4		MCA 54439
10/3/92	①²	20		38 I Cross My Heart	You're Right I'm Wrong	—	$4		MCA 54478
11/14/92	70	3		39 Overnight Male					album cut
				from the album *Pure Country* on MCA 10651					
1/2/93	①¹	20		40 Heartland	Baby Your Baby	—	$4		MCA 54563
5/1/93	6	20		41 When Did You Stop Loving Me	Where The Sidewalk Ends	—	$4		MCA 54642
				above 4 from the movie *Pure Country* starring Strait					
8/21/93	①²	20		42 Easy Come, Easy Go	She Lays It All On The Line	71	$4	■	MCA 54717 (v)
12/4/93+	3	20		43 I'd Like To Have That One Back	That's Where My Baby Feels At Home	109	$4	■	MCA 54767 (v)
1/22/94	8	20		44 Lovebug	Just Look At Me	114	$4	■	MCA 54819 (v)
6/25/94	4	20		45 The Man In Love With You	We Must Be Loving Right	112	$4	■	MCA 54854 (v)
10/8/94	①¹	20		46 The Big One	No One But You	—	$4	■	MCA 54938 (v)
12/24/94+	①¹	20		47 You Can't Make A Heart Love Somebody	What Am I Waiting For	111	$4	■	MCA 54964 (v)
3/25/95	3	20		48 Adalida	Down Louisiana Way	—	$4	■	MCA 55019 (v)
6/24/95	7	20		49 Lead On	I Met A Friend Of Yours Today	—	$4		MCA 55064
9/23/95	①⁴	20	★★★	50 Check Yes Or No	Fly Me To The Moon	—	$4		MCA 55127
				CMA Award: Single of the Year					
12/23/95+	5	20		51 I Know She Still Loves Me	Unwound	—	$4		MCA 55163
12/30/95	73	1		52 Santa Claus Is Coming To Town	[X]	—			album cut
				from the album *Merry Christmas Strait To You* on MCA 5800					
4/6/96	①²	20		53 Blue Clear Sky	I Ain't Never Seen No One Like You	—	$4		MCA 55187
5/18/96	①³	20		54 Carried Away	Do The Right Thing	—	$4		MCA 55204
8/24/96	4	20		55 I Can Still Make Cheyenne	Need I Say More	—	$4		MCA 55248
12/21/96+	19	13		56 King Of The Mountain	I'd Just As Soon Go	—	$4		MCA 55288
2/8/97	69	6		57 Do The Right Thing		—			album cut
				from the album *Blue Clear Sky* on MCA 11428					
3/15/97	①⁵	20		58 One Night At A Time	S:2 Won't You Come Home (And Talk To A Stranger)	59	$4	■	MCA 55321 (v)
5/3/97	①⁴	21		59 Carrying Your Love With Me	I've Got A Funny Feeling	—	$4		MCA 72007
5/3/97	70	1		60 Won't You Come Home (And Talk To A Stranger)		—			album cut
5/3/97	71	1		61 Round About Way		—			album cut
				also see #65 below; above 2 from the album *Carrying Your Love With Me* on MCA 11584					
9/6/97	3	20		62 Today My World Slipped Away	Round About Way	—	$4		MCA 72019
12/27/97	58	2		63 Merry Christmas Strait To You	[X]	—			album cut
12/27/97	69	2		64 Santa Claus Is Coming To Town	[X-R]	—			album cut
				above 2 from the album *Merry Christmas Strait To You* on MCA 5800					
1/3/98	①²	19		65 Round About Way	She'll Leave You With A Smile [R]	—	$4		MCA 72028
4/18/98	①³	21		66 I Just Want To Dance With You	S:6 Neon Row	61	$4	■	MCA 72046 (v)
5/2/98	2⁴	25		67 True	Remember The Alamo	—	$4		MCA Nashville 72063
5/2/98	4	23		68 We Really Shouldn't Be Doing This	Maria	44	$4		MCA Nashville 72071
5/2/98+	59	15		69 You Haven't Left Me Yet		—		★	album cut (v)
				from the album *Carrying Your Love With Me* on MCA Nashville 11584; later released as the B-side of #70 below					
1/9/99	4	20		70 Meanwhile	S:2 You Haven't Left Me Yet	38	$4	★	MCA Nash. 72084
3/13/99	①⁴	37		71 Write This Down	4 Minus 3 Equals Zero	27	$4		MCA Nashville 72095
3/13/99	4	24		72 What Do You Say To That	4 Minus 3 Equals 0	45	$4		MCA Nashville 72108
3/13/99	69	2		73 Always Never The Same		—			album cut
3/13/99	73	1		74 One Of You		—			album cut
3/13/99	74	2		75 Peace Of Mind		—			album cut
3/13/99	75	1		76 I Look At You		—			album cut
				above 4 from the album *Always Never The Same* on MCA 70050					
12/18/99	72	2		77 Let It Snow, Let It Snow, Let It Snow	[X]	—			album cut
12/18/99	73	2		78 I Know What I Want For Christmas	[X]	—			album cut
12/25/99	69	2		79 Jingle Bell Rock	[X]	—			album cut
				above 3 from the album *Merry Christmas Wherever You Are* on MCA Nashville 70093					
1/1/00	①³	29		80 The Best Day	I Can Still Make Cheyenne	31	$4		MCA Nashville 172147
3/11/00	38	20		81 Murder On Music Row					album cut (v)
				GEORGE STRAIT with Alan Jackson					
				from the album *Latest Greatest Straitest Hits* on MCA Nashville 70100; later released as the B-side of #82 below					
7/29/00	2³	22		82 Go On	Murder On Music Row	40	$4		MCA Nashville 172169
10/21/00+	17	25		83 Don't Make Me Come Over There And Love You	You're Stronger Than Me	102	$4		MCA Nashville 172194

DEBUT	PEAK	WKS	Gold	A-side (Chart Hit)	B-side	Pop	$	Pic	Label & Number
				STRAIT, George — Cont'd					
12/23/00	62	2		84 Old Time Christmas	[X]	—			album cut
				from the album *Merry Christmas Wherever You Are* on MCA 70093					
3/3/01	5	21		85 If You Can Do Anything Else	Which Side Of The Glass	51	$4		MCA Nashville 172200
10/13/01	2⁴	23		86 Run	The Real Thing	34	$4		MCA Nashville 172221
12/15/01	33	5		87 Christmas Cookies	[X]	—			album cut
				from the various artists album *Christmas Cookies* on MCA Nashville 170232					
	★209★			**STREET, Mel**					**'73**
				Born King Malachi Street on 10/21/33 in Grundy, Virginia. Died of a self-inflicted gunshot on 10/21/78 (age 45). Singer/songwriter/guitarist. Worked as a contruction worker, an electrician and car mechanic prior to his music career.					
				1)Lovin' On Back Streets 2)Borrowed Angel 3)If I Had A Cheating Heart 4)I Met A Friend Of Your's Today 5)Walk Softly On The Bridges					
5/27/72	7	17		1 Borrowed Angel	House Of Pride	—	$7		Royal American 64
11/4/72+	5	16		2 Lovin' On Back Streets	Who'll Turn Out The Lights	—	$6		Metromedia 901
3/17/73	11	15		3 Walk Softly On The Bridges	Spoiled Lonely Man	—	$6		Metromedia 906
7/28/73	38	10		4 The Town Where You Live	Body Man	—	$6		Metromedia 0018
11/10/73+	11	13		5 Lovin' On Borrowed Time	Moonshine Man	—	$6		Metromedia 0143
5/11/74	15	15		6 You Make Me Feel More Like A Man	Green River	—	$6		GRT 002
11/2/74+	16	13		7 Forbidden Angel	Don't Lead Me On	—	$6		GRT 012
3/1/75	13	14		8 Smokey Mountain Memories	Let's Put Out The Fire	—	$6		GRT 017
6/28/75	17	14		9 Even If I Have To Steal	Country Pride	—	$6		GRT 025
10/11/75	23	11		10 (This Ain't Just Another) Lust Affair	Strange Empty World	—	$6		GRT 030
2/7/76	32	10		11 The Devil In Your Kisses (And The Angel In Your Eyes)	Baby Don't Save Your Love For A Rainy Day	—	$6		GRT 043
6/12/76	10	14		12 I Met A Friend Of Your's Today	She Boogies When He's Gone	—	$6		GRT 057
10/23/76	24	13		13 Looking Out My Window Through The Pain	Virginia's Song	—	$6		GRT 083
3/19/77	56	7		14 Rodeo Bum	Guilty As Sin	—	$6		GRT 116
6/25/77	19	12		15 Barbara Don't Let Me Be The Last To Know	My Friend The Jukebox	—	$5		Polydor 14399
9/24/77	15	12		16 Close Enough For Lonesome	If This Is Having A Good Time	—	$5		Polydor 14421
1/14/78	9	13		17 If I Had A Cheating Heart	Memory Eraser	—	$5		Polydor 14448
4/22/78	24	10		18 Shady Rest	She's No Honky Tonk Angel	—	$5		Polydor 14468
10/21/78	68	5		19 Just Hangin' On	The Easy Lovin' Kind	—	$5		Mercury 55043
10/6/79	17	11		20 The One Thing My Lady Never Puts Into Words	Borrowed Angel	—	$5		Sunset 100
1/26/80	30	10		21 Tonight Let's Sleep On It Baby	Muddy Mississippi	—	$5		Sunbird 103
11/1/80	36	12		22 Who'll Turn Out The Lights	Lust Affair	—	$5		Sunbird 7555
10/31/81	48	8		23 Slip Away	Let's Put Out The Fire	—	$5		Sunbird 7568
				MEL STREET & SANDY POWELL					
				STREETFEET					**'83**
2/12/83	78	4		Where Do You Go		—	$6		Triple T 2001
				STREETS — see NIGHTSTREETS					
				★ **STREISAND, Barbra**					**'99**
				Born on 4/24/42 in Brooklyn. Popular singer/actress/director/producer. Starred in several movies and Broadway shows. Charted 42 pop hits from 1964-96. Married to actor Elliott Gould from 1963-71. Married actor James Brolin on 7/1/98. Won Grammy's Lifetime Achievement Award in 1995.					
11/25/78	70	8 ▲		1 You Don't Bring Me Flowers	(instrumental)	❶²	$4		Columbia 10840
				BARBRA & NEIL					
10/23/99	62	10		2 If You Ever Leave Me		—			album cut
				BARBRA STREISAND / VINCE GILL					
				from the album *A Love Like Ours* on Columbia 69601					
				STRODE, Lance					**'89**
4/8/89	92	1		Dangerous Ground		—	$7		Bootstrap 0416
				STROMAN, Gene					**'87**
				Born on 2/19/61 in Terrell, Texas.					
1/17/87	53	8		1 Goodbye Song	I'm Not That Crazy	—	$4		Capitol 5662
8/15/87	74	5		2 I Don't Feel Much Like A Cowboy Tonight	Too Many Rivers	—	$4		Capitol 44015
				STRUNK, Jud					**'73**
				Born Justin Strunk on 6/11/36 in Jamestown, New York; raised in Farmington, Maine. Died in a plane crash on 10/15/81 (age 45). Singer/songwriter/banjo player. Regular on TV's *Laugh-In*.					
2/24/73	33	14		1 Daisy A Day	The Searchers	14	$6		MGM 14463
7/21/73	86	4		2 Next Door Neighbor's Kid	I'd Prefer To Do It All Again	—	$6		MGM 14572
8/9/75	51	6		3 The Biggest Parakeets In Town	I Wasn't Wrong About You [C]	50	$5		Melodyland 6015
2/7/76	88	5		4 Pamela Brown	They're Tearing Down A Town	—	$5		Melodyland 6027

DEBUT	PEAK	WKS	Gold	A-side (Chart Hit)	B-side	Pop	$	Pic	Label & Number

STUART, Marty ★169★   '92

Born John Marty Stuart on 9/30/58 in Philadelphia, Mississippi. Singer/songwriter/guitarist. Toured with Lester Flatt (**Flatt & Scruggs**) and Nashville Grass from age 13. Toured with the **Johnny Cash** Band from 1979-85. Once married to Cash's daughter Cindy. Married **Connie Smith** on 7/8/97. Joined the *Grand Ole Opry* in 1992. Also see **Hope** and **Same Old Train**.

Connie born 8-14-41 (She's 17 yrs. older)

1) The Whiskey Ain't Workin' 2) Tempted 3) This One's Gonna Hurt You (For A Long, Long Time) 4) Burn Me Down 5) Little Things

DEBUT	PEAK	WKS		A-side	B-side	Pop	$	Pic	Label & Number
12/28/85+	19	18		1 Arlene .... S:13 / A:22	Midnight Moonlight	—	$4	■	Columbia 05724
5/31/86	59	6		2 Honky Tonker	Anyhow I Love You	—	$4		Columbia 05897
8/9/86	39	12		3 All Because Of You	Maria (Love To See You Again)	—	$4		Columbia 06230
11/22/86	59	8		4 Do You Really Want My Lovin'	Heart Of Stone	—	$4		Columbia 06425
3/19/88	56	7		5 Mirrors Don't Lie	Freight Train Boogie	—	$4		Columbia 07729
6/4/88	66	6		6 Matches	Old Hat	—	$4		Columbia 07914
8/19/89	32	12		7 Cry Cry Cry	The Wild One	—	$4		MCA 53687
11/18/89+	42	11		8 Don't Leave Her Lonely Too Long	The Coal Mine Blues	—	$4		MCA 53751
4/28/90	8	21		9 Hillbilly Rock	Western Girls	—	$4		MCA 79001
9/1/90	20	20		10 Western Girls	Me And Billy The Kid	—	$4		MCA 79068
12/22/90+	8	20		11 Little Things	Paint The Town Tonight	—	$4		MCA 53975
4/20/91	12	20		12 Till I Found You	Half A Heart	—	$4		MCA 54065
8/17/91	5	20		13 Tempted	I'm Blue, I'm Lonesome	—	$4		MCA 54145
11/23/91+	2¹	20		14 The Whiskey Ain't Workin'	Bible Belt (Tritt)	—	$4		Warner 19097
				TRAVIS TRITT Featuring Marty Stuart					
2/8/92	7	20		15 Burn Me Down	Blue Train	—	$4		MCA 54253
6/6/92	7	20		16 This One's Gonna Hurt You (For A Long, Long Time)	The King Of Dixie	—	$4		MCA 54405
				MARTY STUART AND TRAVIS TRITT					
9/12/92	18	20		17 Now That's Country	Me & Hank & Jumpin' Jack Flash	—	$4		MCA 54477
12/12/92+	24	20		18 High On A Mountain Top	You And Me	—	$4		MCA 54538
4/17/93	38	15		19 Hey Baby	Down Home	—	$4		MCA 54607
1/22/94	26	19		20 Kiss Me, I'm Gone	Marty Stuart Visits The Moon	—	$4	■	MCA 54777 (v)
6/25/94	54	8		21 Love And Luck	Oh What A Silent Night	—	$4	■	MCA 54840 (v)
9/24/94	68	5		22 That's What Love's About	Shake Your Hips	—	$4	■	MCA 54915 (v)
4/1/95	58	8		23 The Likes Of Me	You Can Walk All Over Me	—	$4		MCA 55010
6/24/95	46	18		24 If I Ain't Got You	Wheels	—	$4		MCA 55069
4/20/96	23	20		25 Honky Tonkin's What I Do Best	Me & Hank & Jumpin' Jack Flash	—	$4		MCA 55197
				MARTY STUART & TRAVIS TRITT					
8/17/96	50	10		26 Thanks To You	Country Girls	—	$4		MCA 55226
10/26/96+	26	20		27 You Can't Stop Love	The Mississippi Mudcat And Sister Cheryl Crow	—	$4		MCA 55270
6/5/99	69	2		28 Red, Red Wine And Cheatin' Songs	Goin' Nowhere Fast	—	$4		MCA Nashville 72096
4/15/00	63	6		29 The Blue Collar Dollar Song	[N]	—			album cut
				JEFF FOXWORTHY and BILL ENGVALL Featuring Marty Stuart					
				from Foxworthy's album *Big Funny* on DreamWorks 50200					

STUBBY AND THE BUCCANEERS — see CAPTAIN STUBBY

STUCKEY, Nat ★145★   '66

Born Nathan Stuckey on 12/17/33 in Cass County, Texas. Died of cancer on 8/24/88 (age 54). Singer/songwriter/guitarist. Graduated from Arlington State College with a radio and TV degree. Worked as a DJ in Texas and Louisiana. Sang on numerous TV commercials in the 1980s.

1) Sweet Thang 2) Sweet Thang And Cisco 3) Plastic Saddle 4) Take Time To Love Her 5) She Wakes Me With A Kiss Every Morning (And She Loves Me To Sleep Every Night)

DEBUT	PEAK	WKS		A-side	B-side	Pop	$	Pic	Label & Number
9/10/66	4	18		1 Sweet Thang	Paralyze My Mind	—	$10	□	Paula 243
1/7/67	17	13		2 Oh! Woman	On The Other Hand	—	$10		Paula 257
4/15/67	27	12		3 All My Tomorrows /		—			
4/29/67	67	3		4 You're Puttin' Me On		—	$10		Paula 267
9/2/67	41	8		5 Adorable Women	I Knew Her When	—	$10		Paula 276
12/23/67+	17	14		6 My Can Do Can't Keep Up With My Want To	If There's No Other Way	—	$10		Paula 287
5/18/68	63	5		7 Leave This One Alone	I Never Knew	—	$10		Paula 300
10/12/68	9	16		8 Plastic Saddle	Woman Of Hurt	—	$8		RCA Victor 9631
2/15/69	13	11		9 Joe And Mabel's 12th Street Bar And Grill	Loving You	—	$8		RCA Victor 9720
6/7/69	15	13		10 Cut Across Shorty	Understand Little Man	—	$8		RCA Victor 0163
7/5/69	20	11		11 Young Love	Something Pretty	—	$8		RCA Victor 0181
				CONNIE SMITH AND NAT STUCKEY					
				#1 Pop hit for Tab Hunter in 1957					
10/4/69	8	11		12 Sweet Thang And Cisco	Son Of A Bum	—	$8		RCA Victor 0238
1/10/70	33	10		13 Sittin' In Atlanta Station	Don't Wait For Me	—	$8		RCA Victor 9786
3/14/70	59	4		14 If God Is Dead (Who's That Living In My Soul)	His Love Takes Care Of Me	—	$8		RCA Victor 9805
				NAT STUCKEY AND CONNIE SMITH					
5/16/70	31	8		15 Old Man Willis	Beauty Of A Bar	—	$7		RCA Victor 9833
9/5/70	31	9		16 Whiskey, Whiskey	What Am I Doing In L.A.?	—	$7		RCA Victor 9884
12/12/70+	11	15		17 She Wakes Me With A Kiss Every Morning (And She Loves Me To Sleep Every Night)	The Devil Made Me Do That	—	$7		RCA Victor 9929

DEBUT	PEAK	WKS	Gold	A-side (Chart Hit)	B-side	Pop	$	Pic	Label & Number
				STUCKEY, Nat — Cont'd					
4/24/71	24	12		18 Only A Woman Like You	Half The Love	—	$7		RCA Victor 9977
9/4/71	17	13		19 I'm Gonna Act Right	Chained	—	$7		RCA Victor 1010
12/11/71+	16	14		20 Forgive Me For Calling You Darling	He's Got The Whole World In His Hands	—	$7		RCA Victor 0590
4/22/72	26	12		21 Is It Any Wonder That I Love You	Got It Comin' Day	—	$7		RCA Victor 0687
8/19/72	18	13		22 Don't Pay The Ransom	There's Still You	—	$7		RCA Victor 0761
2/3/73	10	14		23 Take Time To Love Her	Carry Me Back	—	$7		RCA Victor 0879
6/16/73	22	12		24 I Used It All On You	I Know The Feelin'	—	$7		RCA Victor 0973
10/20/73	14	12		25 Got Leaving On Her Mind	Now Lonely Is Only A Word	—	$6		RCA Victor 0115
2/23/74	31	11		26 You Never Say You Love Me Anymore	The Man That I Am	—	$6		RCA Victor 0222
6/1/74	42	13		27 It Hurts To Know The Feeling's Gone	Plans For The Future	—	$6		RCA Victor 0288
11/9/74+	36	12		28 You Don't Have To Go Home	I Sure Do Enjoy Loving You	—	$6		RCA Victor 10090
7/5/75	85	7		29 Boom Boom Barroom Man	Ain't Nothing Bad About Feelin Good	—	$6		RCA Victor 10307
2/28/76	13	13		30 Sun Comin' Up	Honky Tonk Dreams	—	$5		MCA 40519
6/12/76	46	10		31 The Way He's Treated You	At Least One Time	—	$5		MCA 40568
9/4/76	42	9		32 That's All She Ever Said Except Goodbye	After The Lovin' Has Passed	—	$5		MCA 40608
12/11/76+	48	8		33 The Shady Side Of Charlotte	They'd Love To Be Children Again	—	$5		MCA 40658
7/23/77	63	6		34 Buddy, I Lied	Don't You Believe Her	—	$5		MCA 40752
10/29/77	62	6		35 I'm Coming Home To Face The Music	Linda On My Mind	—	$5		MCA 40808
3/18/78	66	6		36 That Lucky Old Sun (Just Rolls Around Heaven All Day)	I'm Coming Home	—	$5		MCA 40855
				#1 Pop hit for **Frankie Laine** in 1949					
7/8/78	26	10		37 The Days Of Sand And Shovels	Mexican Divorce	—	$5		MCA 40923
				#34 Pop hit for **Bobby Vinton** in 1969					
			★	**SUDDERTH, Anna**		'80			
5/10/80	90	4		Not A Day Goes By		—	$7		Verite 801
				SULLIVAN, Gene		'58			
				Born on 11/16/14 in Carbon Hill, Alabama. Died on 10/24/84 (age 69). Member of **Wiley & Gene**.					
12/9/57+	9	8		Please Pass The Biscuits A:9 / S:16 Wash Your Feet Before Going To Bed [N]		—	$20		Columbia 40971
				SULLIVAN, Phil		'59			
6/8/59	26	6		Hearts Are Lonely	Rich Man-Po' Boy	—	$20		Starday 437
				SUMMAR, Trent, and the New Row Mob		'00			
				Born in Tennessee. Singer/songwriter. The New Row Mob: Kenny Vaughan and Phil Wallace (guitars), Jerry McFadden (keyboards), Jared Reynolds (bass) and David Kennedy (drums).					
12/30/00	74	1		It Never Rains In Southern California		—			album cut
				#5 Pop hit for **Albert Hammond** in 1972; from the album *Trent Summar & The New Row Mob* on VFR 734756					
				SUMMER, Scott		'79			
				Born in Fort Smith, Kansas.					
2/3/79	80	4		1 Flip Side Of Today	I'm In Love	—	$5		Con Brio 146
5/26/79	92	3		2 I Don't Wanna Want You	Old Fashioned Lady	—	$5		Con Brio 152
	★356★			**SUN, Joe**		'78			
				Born James Joseph Paulson on 9/25/43 in Rochester, Minnesota. Singer/songwriter/guitarist.					
				1) Old Flames (Can't Hold A Candle To You) 2) High And Dry 3) I'd Rather Go On Hurtin'					
6/24/78	14	16		1 Old Flames (Can't Hold A Candle To You)	I'll Find It Where I Can	—	$5		Ovation 1107
11/4/78	20	12		2 High And Dry	Midnight Train Of Memories	—	$5		Ovation 1117
3/24/79	27	11		3 On Business For The King /		—			Ovation 1122
		11		4 Blue Ribbon Blues		—	$5		Ovation 1122
9/15/79	20	11		5 I'd Rather Go On Hurtin'	I'm Still Crazy About You	—	$5		Ovation 1127
12/8/79+	34	11		6 Out Of Your Mind	Mysteries Of Life (My First Truckin' Song)	—	$5		Ovation 1137
1/26/80	48	7		7 What I Had With You	I Gotta Get Back The Feeling	—	$5		Ovation 1138
				SHEILA ANDREWS with Joe Sun					
3/22/80	23	12		8 Shotgun Rider	Little Bit Of Push	71	$5		Ovation 1141
8/16/80	21	11		9 Bombed, Boozed, And Busted	I'll Find It Where I Can	—	$5		Ovation 1152
12/27/80+	43	11		10 Ready For The Times To Get Better	Bottom Line	—	$5		Ovation 1162
3/20/82	40	9		11 Holed Up In Some Honky Tonk	Boys In The Back Of The Bus	—	$4		Elektra 47417
6/19/82	57	7		12 Fraulein	I Ain't Honky Tonkin' No More	—	$4		Elektra 47467
				JOE SUN WITH SHOTGUN					
10/2/82	85	2		13 You Make Me Want To Sing	Midnight Train Of Memories	—	$4		Elektra 69954
7/14/84	73	5		14 Bad For Me		—	$4		AMI 1319
1/26/85	77	3		15 Why Would I Want To Forget		—	$4		AMI 1321
			★	**SUNSHINE RUBY**		'53			
				Born Ruby Bateman in 1940 in Texas.					
6/20/53	4	1		Too Young To Tango A:4 Hearts Weren't Meant To Be Broken		—	$20		RCA Victor 5250
				Sonny James (fiddle); written by **Sheb Wooley**					
				SUPER GRIT COWBOY BAND		'82			
				Group from North Carolina. Led by singers/guitarists **Curtis Wright** and Bill Ellis. **Don Cox** was once a member.					
8/1/81	71	6		1 If You Don't Know Me By Now	This Ol' Highway Song	—	$6		Hoodswamp 8002
10/24/81	64	6		2 Carolina By The Sea	Can't Play For Real	—	$6		Hoodswamp 8003
3/6/82	83	3		3 Semi Diesel Blues	Sweet Lady	—	$6		Hoodswamp 8004
7/10/82	48	9		4 She Is The Woman	Roar Of The Crowd	—	$6		Hoodswamp 8005
4/23/83	79	4		5 I Bought The Shoes (That Just Walked Out On Me)		—	$6		Hoodswamp 8006

DEBUT	PEAK	WKS	Gold	A-side (Chart Hit)	B-side	Pop	$	Pic	Label & Number
	★348★			**SUPERNAW, Doug** '93 Born on 9/26/60 in Bryan, Texas. Singer/songwriter/guitarist. 1) I Don't Call Him Daddy 2) Not Enough Hours In The Night 3) Reno					
2/20/93	50	13		1 Honky Tonkin' Fool .... You're Gonna Bring Back Cheatin' Songs		—	$4		BNA 62432
5/22/93	4	20		2 Reno .... Daddy's Girl		—	$4		BNA 62537
10/2/93	❶²	20		3 I Don't Call Him Daddy .... I Would Have Loved You All Night Long		—	$4		BNA 62638
2/5/94	23	20		4 Red And Rio Grande .... Five Generations Of Rock County Wilsons		—	$4		BNA 62757
7/2/94	55	9		5 State Fair .... He Went To Paris		—	$4		BNA 62851
9/3/94	60	7		6 You Never Even Call Me By My Name .... State Fair		—	$4	■	BNA 62938 (v)
1/14/95	16	20		7 What'll You Do About Me .... Wishin' Her Well		—	$4	■	BNA 64214 (v)
10/14/95+	3	21		8 Not Enough Hours In The Night .... S:13 We're All Here		—	$4	■	Giant 17764 (v)
3/9/96	51	10		9 She Never Looks Back .... S:21 What In The World		—	$4	■	Giant 17687 (v)
6/8/96	53	9		10 You Still Got Me from the album *You Still Got Me* on Giant 24639		—	$4		album cut
10/12/96	69	1		11 Long Tall Texan **THE BEACH BOYS Featuring Doug Supernaw** #51 Pop hit for Murry Kellum in 1963; from the album *Stars And Stripes Vol. 1* on River North 1205		—	$4		album cut
				SUTTON, Glenn '79 Born Royce Glenn Sutton on 9/28/37 in Hodge, Louisiana; raised in Henderson, Texas. Singer/prolific songwriter. Married to **Lynn Anderson** from 1968-77.					
1/6/79	55	5		1 The Football Card .... The Ballad Of The Blue Cyclone [N]		46	$5		Mercury 55052
9/15/79	73	4		2 Red Neck Disco .... Hip! Hip! Hip! Horray, For The E.R.A. [N]		—	$5		Mercury 57001
10/11/86	74	4		3 I'll Go Steppin' Too .... Hulk-A-Mania		—	$4		Mercury 884974
				SWAMPWATER '71 Group led by guitarist Floyd "Gib" Guilbeau (later played fiddle with the **Burrito Brothers**).					
6/12/71	72	2		Take A City Bride .... It's Your Game, Mary Jane		—	$7		King 6376
	★314★			**SWAN, Billy** '74 Born on 5/12/42 in Cape Girardeau, Missouri. Singer/songwriter/pianist. Member of **Black Tie**. 1) I Can Help 2) Everything's The Same (Ain't Nothing Changed) 3) I'm Into Lovin' You					
10/12/74	❶²	14	●	1 I Can Help .... Ways Of A Woman In Love	❶²		$6		Monument 8621
8/30/75	17	14		2 Everything's The Same (Ain't Nothing Changed) .... Overnite Thing (Usually)		91	$6		Monument 8661
3/20/76	45	9		3 Just Want To Taste Your Wine .... Love You Baby - To The Bone **BILLY SWAN with The Jordanaires**		—	$6		Monument 8682
9/11/76	75	5		4 You're The One .... Ms. Misery co-written by Buddy Holly and **Waylon Jennings**		—	$6		Monument 8706
12/11/76	95	2		5 Shake, Rattle And Roll .... I Got It For You #7 Pop hit for Bill Haley & His Comets in 1954		—	$5		Columbia 10443
6/24/78	30	15		6 Hello! Remember Me .... Never Go Lookin' Again		—	$5		A&M 2046
12/2/78	97	3		7 No Way Around It (It's Love) .... Forever In Your Love		—	$5		A&M 2103
4/4/81	18	13		8 Do I Have To Draw A Picture .... I Want To Change Your Life		—	$4		Epic 51000
7/25/81	18	13		9 I'm Into Lovin' You .... Not Far From Forty		—	$4		Epic 02196
11/28/81+	19	14		10 Stuck Right In The Middle Of Your Love .... Soft Touch		—	$4		Epic 02601
4/10/82	32	13		11 With Their Kind Of Money And Our Kind Of Love .. Lay Down And Love Me Tonight		—	$4		Epic 02841
10/9/82	56	9		12 Your Picture Still Loves Me (And I Still Love You) ...... Give Your Lovin' To Me		—	$4		Epic 03226
1/29/83	39	10		13 Rainbows And Butterflies .... Only Be You		—	$4		Epic 03505
6/4/83	67	8		14 Yes .... I Can't Stop Writing Love Songs		—	$4		Epic 03917
4/26/86	45	10		15 You Must Be Lookin' For Me .... Three Chord Rock And Roll		—	$4		Mercury 884668
2/7/87	63	6		16 I'm Gonna Get You .... Three Chord Rock And Roll		—	$4		Mercury 888320
				SWEAT, Isaac Payton '78 Born in 1945 in Port Arthur, Texas; raised in Nederland, Texas. Died on 6/23/90 (age 45).					
9/9/78	91	4		Shed So Many Tears .... All This Ol' Wailin'		—	$5		Gusto 9010
				SWEET, Rachel '76 Born on 7/28/62 in Akron, Ohio. Pop singer/actress.					
6/19/76	96	4		We Live In Two Different Worlds .... Paper Airplane		—	$6		Derrick 1000
	★300★			**SWEETHEARTS OF THE RODEO** (2) Sisters '87 Duo of sisters from Manhattan Beach, California: Janis (guitar, vocals; born on 11/28/55) and Kristine (vocals; born on 3/1/57) Oliver. Janis was married to **Vince Gill** from 1980-97. 1) Chains Of Gold 2) Midnight Girl/Sunset Town 3) Blue To The Bone					
4/5/86	21	15		1 Hey Doll Baby .... S:12 / A:25 Everywhere I Turn #8 R&B hit for The Clovers in 1956		—	$4	■	Columbia 05824
7/26/86	7	22		2 Since I Found You .... S:7 / A:7 Chosen Few		—	$4		Columbia 06166
11/29/86+	4	22		3 Midnight Girl/Sunset Town .... S:3 / A:4 I Can't Resist		—	$4		Columbia 06525
4/4/87	4	17		4 Chains Of Gold .... S:3 / A:17 Gotta Get Away		—	$4		Columbia 07023
9/12/87	10	18		5 Gotta Get Away .... S:11 Since I Found You		—	$4		Columbia 07314
4/2/88	5	20		6 Satisfy You .... S:2 One Time, One Night		—	$4		Columbia 07757
8/6/88	5	20		7 Blue To The Bone .... S:❶¹ You Never Talk Sweet		—	$4		Columbia 07985
12/3/88+	9	22		8 I Feel Fine .... S:29 Until I Stop Dancing #1 Pop hit for The Beatles in 1964		—	$4		Columbia 08504
4/15/89	39	11		9 If I Never See Midnight Again .... Gone Again		—	$4		Columbia 68684
1/13/90	25	15		10 This Heart .... So Sad (To Watch Good Love Go Bad)		—	$4		Columbia 73213
8/24/91	63	4		11 Hard-Headed Man .... Sisters		—	$4		Columbia 73907
11/9/91	74	1		12 Devil And Your Deep Blue Eyes .... Be Good To Me		—	$4		Columbia 74064

DEBUT	PEAK	WKS	Gold	A-side (Chart Hit)	B-side	Pop	$	Pic	Label & Number

SWEETWATER   '81
Gospel-based group led by Willie Wynn of **The Tennesseans**. Member **Darrell Holt** went solo in 1987.

| 10/17/81 | 75 | 4 | | 1 I'd Throw It All Away / | — | | | | |
| 8/8/81 | 84 | 4 | | 2 Antioch Church House Choir | | | $6 | | Faucet 1592 |

SWING SHIFT BAND, The   '88
Group features Buddy Emmons and **Ray Pennington**.

| 11/12/88 | 76 | 3 | | (Turn Me Loose And) Let Me Swing | Loose Tights | | $4 | | Step One 392 |

SYLVIA ★185★   '82
Born Sylvia Kirby on 12/9/56 in Kokomo, Indiana. Singer/songwriter. Sang in church choir from age three. Moved to Nashville in 1975, worked as a secretary for producer Tom Collins. Did session backup vocals. Made stage debut as a soloist in the fall of 1979.

1) Nobody 2) Drifter 3) Fallin' In Love 4) Like Nothing Ever Happened 5) I Never Quite Got Back (From Loving You)

10/13/79	36	10		1 You Don't Miss A Thing	Cry Baby Cry	—	$4		RCA 11735
4/26/80	35	11		2 It Don't Hurt To Dream	No News Is Good News	—	$4		RCA 11958
9/6/80	10	16		3 Tumbleweed	Anytime, Anyplace	—	$4		RCA 12077
1/17/81	0¹	14		4 Drifter	Missin' You	—	$4	■	RCA 12164
4/25/81	7	16		5 The Matador	Cry Baby Cry	—	$4	■	RCA 12214
9/12/81	8	15		6 Heart On The Mend	Rainbow Rider	—	$4		RCA 12302
1/16/82	12	15		7 Sweet Yesterday	I Feel Cheated	—	$4		RCA 13020
6/5/82	0¹	24	●	8 Nobody	I'll Make It Right With You	15	$4		RCA 13223
10/30/82+	2²	20		9 Like Nothing Ever Happened	Drifter	—	$4		RCA 13330
2/19/83	57	11		10 The Wayward Wind	Shenandoah	—	$4		RCA 13441

JAMES GALWAY WITH SYLVIA
#1 Pop hit for Gogi Grant in 1956

5/7/83	5	18		11 Snapshot	Tonight I'm Gettin' Friendly With The Blues	—	$4		RCA 13501
8/27/83	18	17		12 The Boy Gets Around	Who's Kidding Who	—	$4		RCA 13589
12/3/83+	3	19		13 I Never Quite Got Back (From Loving You)	So Complete	—	$4		RCA 13689
4/7/84	24	14		14 Victims Of Goodbye	Unguarded Moments	—	$4	■	RCA 13755
7/7/84	36	13		15 Love Over Old Times	I Just Don't Have The Heart	—	$4		RCA 13838
2/16/85	2²	22		16 Fallin' In Love	S:2 / A:2 True Blue	—	$4		RCA 13997
6/29/85	9	18		17 Cry Just A Little Bit	A:8 / S:9 Only The Shadows Know	—	$4		RCA 14107

#67 hit for Shakin' Stevens in 1984

| 11/16/85+ | 9 | 25 | | 18 I Love You By Heart | A:9 / S:10 Eyes Like Mine | — | $4 | | RCA 14217 |

SYLVIA & MICHAEL JOHNSON

| 7/5/86 | 33 | 15 | | 19 Nothin' Ventured Nothin' Gained | Come To Me | — | $4 | | RCA 14375 |
| 5/16/87 | 66 | 6 | | 20 Straight From My Heart | Makes You Wanna Slow Down | — | $4 | | RCA 5127 |

SYLVIE & HER SILVER DOLLAR BAND   '89
Group from Miami.

| 7/1/89 | 95 | 2 | | Where You Gonna Hang Your Hat | Warm Like A Fire | | $6 | | Playback 75711 |

T

TACKETT, Marlow   '82
Born in Dorton, Kentucky. Male singer/songwriter/guitarist.

1/19/80	95	2		1 Would You Know Love	South Bound Train		$7		Palace 1006
4/26/80	93	2		2 Midnight Fire			$7		Palace 1008
11/15/80	92	3		3 Ride That Bull (Big Bertha)	Would You Know Love?		00		Hall 111
7/10/82	67	6		4 Ever-Lovin' Woman	Hang In There Teardrop	—	$4		RCA 13255
10/23/82	54	9		5 634-5789	She Couldn't Take It Anymore	—	$4		RCA 13347

#13 Pop hit for Wilson Pickett in 1966

| 4/23/83 | 67 | 6 | | 6 I Know My Way To You By Heart | Big Old Teardrops | — | $4 | | RCA 13471 |
| 8/6/83 | 56 | 8 | | 7 I Spent The Night In The Heart Of Texas | Way Back When | — | $4 | | RCA 13579 |

TAFF, Russ   '95
Born in 1953 in Farmersville, California. Contemporary Christian singer/songwriter.

1/14/95	53	9		1 Love Is Not A Thing	Once In A Lifetime	—	$4	■	Reprise 18029 (v)
4/1/95	51	10		2 One And Only Love	Home To You	—	$4	■	Reprise 17918 (v)
7/29/95	66	4		3 Bein' Happy	Heart Like Yours	—	$4	■	Reprise 17801 (v)

TALBERT, Bubba   '83
Born in 1949 in Blanchard, Louisiana.

| 4/9/83 | 81 | 3 | | 1 Easy Catch | Where Do We Go From Here? | | $6 | ■ | Ranger 5734 |
| 7/23/83 | 77 | 3 | | 2 Downright Broke My Heart | | | $6 | | Ranger 702 |

TALL, Tom   '55
Born Tommie Lee Guthrie on 12/17/37 in Amarillo, Texas.

| 1/1/55 | 2³ | 26 | | 1 Are You Mine | A:2 / J:5 / S:5 I've Got Somebody New | | $30 | | Fabor 117 |

GINNY WRIGHT/TOM TALL

| 1/4/64 | 25 | 1 | | 2 Bad, Bad Tuesday | Oohin' And Aahin' | — | $15 | | Petal 1210 |

347

DEBUT	PEAK	WKS	Gold	A-side (Chart Hit)..B-side	Pop	$	Pic	Label & Number
				TALLEY, James '76 Born on 11/9/43 in Mehan, Oklahoma. Singer/songwriter/guitarist.				
3/13/76	75	8		1 Tryin' Like The Devil .... Nothin' But The Blues	—	$5		Capitol 4218
7/24/76	61	9		2 Are They Gonna Make Us Outlaws Again .... Forty Hours	—	$5		Capitol 4297
4/23/77	83	4		3 Alabama Summertime .... When The Fiddler Packs His Case	—	$5		Capitol 4410
				TAMMY JO '80 Born Tammy Jo Whitehead. Female singer.				
3/15/80	88	3		1 I Go To Pieces .... Don't Be Angry #9 Pop hit for Peter & Gordon in 1965	—	$5		Ridgetop 00880
6/14/80	76	4		2 Love Talking /	—			
		4		3 Wishing Well	—	$5		Ridgetop 00980
				TANNER, Fargo '75 Born in Little Rock, Arkansas; raised in Dallas. Male singer.				
6/7/75	69	11		Don't Drop It .... I Go Crazy (But I Can't Let You Go)	—	$6		Avco 612
				TAPP, Demetriss '73 Born in North Carolina. Female singer.				
9/15/73	97	3		Skinny Dippin' .... Just Let Me Make Believe	—	$6		ABC 11383
				TATE, Michael '81				
3/7/81	93	2		Mexican Girl .... True Love	—	$5		Oak 47102
				TAYLOR, Carmol '76 Born on 9/5/31 in Brilliant, Alabama. Died of cancer on 12/5/86 (age 55). Male singer/prolific songwriter.				
6/28/75	48	11		1 Back In The U.S.A. .... I'd Like To Sleep Til I Get Over You #37 Pop hit for Chuck Berry in 1959	—	$5		Elektra 45255
10/4/75	91	5		2 Who Will I Be Loving Now .... So Fine	—	$5		Elektra 45277
2/14/76	35	12		3 Play The Saddest Song On The Juke Box .... I'd Like To Sleep	—	$5		Elektra 45299
5/8/76	23	11		4 I Really Had A Ball Last Night .... Good Cheatin' Songs	—	$5		Elektra 45312
9/18/76	53	6		5 That Little Difference .... Love What's Left Of Me	—	$5		Elektra 45342
1/8/77	87	5		6 Neon Women .... Crying Steel Guitar CARMOL TAYLOR & STELLA PARTON	—	$5		Elektra 45367
1/22/77	100	1		7 What Would I Do Then? .... You're Looking At A Happy Man	—	$5		Elektra 45366
7/23/77	80	5		8 Good Cheatin' Songs .... I Don't Want My Country Funky	—	$5		Elektra 45409
				TAYLOR, Chet '79				
8/4/79	92	2		Barefoot Angel .... Bet My Soul	—	$6		Vista 108
				TAYLOR, Chip '75 Born James Wesley Voigt in 1940 in Yonkers, New York. Singer/songwriter. Brother of actor Jon Voigt.				
1/4/75	80	6		1 Me As I Am .... Comin' From Behind	—	$5		Warner 8050
5/17/75	28	10		2 Early Sunday Morning .... Shickshinny	—	$5		Warner 8090
9/13/75	61	7		3 Big River .... John Tucker's On The Wagon Again	—	$5		Warner 8128
1/10/76	92	4		4 Circle Of Tears .... You're Alright, Charlie	—	$5		Warner 8159
1/8/77	93	4		5 Hello Atlanta .... Farmer's Daughter CHIP TAYLOR (With Ghost Train)	—	$5		Columbia 10446
				TAYLOR, Frank '63				
6/1/63	28	1		Snow White Cloud .... Send Her Back To Me	—	$15		Parkway 869
				TAYLOR, James '86 Born on 3/12/48 in Boston. Singer/songwriter/guitarist. Charted 22 pop hits from 1970-97. Married to **Carly Simon** from 1972-83. Brother of **Livingston Taylor**.				
7/16/77	88	3		1 Bartender's Blues .... Handy Man (Pop #4)	—	$5		Columbia 10557
9/9/78	33	10		2 Devoted To You .... Boys In The Trees (Simon) CARLY SIMON and JAMES TAYLOR	36	$5		Elektra 45506
12/7/85+	26	16		3 Everyday .... S:25 / A:27 Limousine Driver written by Buddy Holly	61	$4	■	Columbia 05681
3/15/86	80	9		4 Only One .... Mona	—	$4	■	Columbia 05785
				TAYLOR, Jim '79				
8/5/78	100	1		1 I'll Still Need You Mary Ann .... I'm Still Waiting For You	—	$7		Checkmate 3069
12/9/78+	68	10		2 Leave It To Love .... Too Many Tears Have Fallen	—	$7		Checkmate 3106
				TAYLOR, Judy '82 Born in Murfreesboro, Tennessee.				
1/9/82	84	3		1 A Married Man .... I Wish That I Could Hurt That Way Again	—	$4		Warner 49859
5/22/82	79	4		2 A Step In The Right Direction .... He Picked Me Up When You Let Me Down	—	$4		Warner 50061
9/25/82	70	4		3 The End Of The World .... He Picked Me Up When You Let Me Down	—	$4		Warner 29913
				TAYLOR, Les '91 Born on 12/27/48 in Oneida, Kentucky; raised in London, Kentucky. Member of **Exile** from 1979-89. Also see **Tomorrow's World**.				
11/25/89	46	11		1 Shoulda, Coulda, Woulda Loved You .... A Southern Breeze	—	$4		Epic 73063
4/28/90	58	10		2 Knowin' You Were Leavin' .... A Southern Breeze	—	$4		Epic 73264
3/9/91	44	12		3 I Gotta Mind To Go Crazy .... For The Rest Of Your Life	—	$4	■	Epic 73712 (v)
7/27/91	50	9		4 The Very First Lasting Love .... Lonely Weekends SHELBY LYNNE WITH LES TAYLOR	—	$4		Epic 73904
				TAYLOR, Livingston '88 Born on 11/21/50 in Boston. Singer/songwriter/guitarist. Brother of **James Taylor**.				
10/22/88	94	2		Loving Arms .... (pop version) LIVINGSTON TAYLOR (with Leah Kunkel)	—	$4	■	Critique 99275

DEBUT	PEAK	WKS	Gold	A-side (Chart Hit)	B-side	Pop	$	Pic	Label & Number
				★ **TAYLOR, Mary** '68					
				Singer/songwriter. Regular on TV's *Hee Haw* from 1969-70.					
1/7/67	72	4		1 Don't Waste Your Time	We Fooled 'Em Again	—	$7		Capitol 5776
6/22/68	44	8		2 If I Don't Like The Way You Love Me	It Takes So Many	—	$6		Dot 17104
11/23/68	51	7		3 Feed Me One More Lie	I'll Be Better Off	—	$6		Dot 17168
				TAYLOR, R. Dean '83					
				Born in 1939 in Toronto. Charted a pop hit in 1970 with "Indiana Wants Me."					
1/15/83	90	2		Let's Talk It Over		—	$6		Strummer 3748
				★ **TAYLOR-GOOD, Karen** '82					
				Born Karen Berke in El Paso, Texas.					
				1)*Diamond In The Rough* 2)*Tenderness Place* 3)*Up On Your Love*					
				KAREN TAYLOR:					
3/6/82	38	11		1 Diamond In The Rough	Doesn't Daddy Love Me Anymore	—	$5		Mesa 1111
7/24/82	67	7		2 Country Boy's Song	One Man Woman	—	$5		Mesa 1112
				KAREN TAYLOR-GOOD:					
11/20/82	62	9		3 I'd Rather Be Doing Nothing With You	Sinking Kind Of Feeling	—	$5		Mesa 1113
3/5/83	42	11		4 Tenderness Place	When The Churchbell Stops Ringing	—	$5		Mesa 1114
8/27/83	62	7		5 Don't Call Me	Begging To You	—	$5		Mesa 1115
1/7/84	62	10		6 Handsome Man	Welcome To The World	—	$5		Mesa 1116
9/8/84	66	7		7 We Just Gotta Dance	I'd Rather Be Doing Nothing With You	—	$5		Mesa 1117
4/6/85	61	7		8 Starlite	Words Are Cheap	—	$5		Mesa 1118
10/5/85	57	8		9 Up On Your Love	Afraid To Go To Sleep	—	$5		Mesa 1119
5/10/86	79	4		10 Come In Planet Earth (Are You Listenin')		—	$5		Mesa 2011
				TENNESSEANS, The '78					
				Group formed by Willie Wynn (later with **Sweetwater**). Included Tony King who was later with **Matthews, Wright & King**.					
12/2/78	81	5		Nineteen-Sixty Something Songwriter Of The Year	I Can Heal You	—	$5		Capitol 4645
				TENNESSEE EXPRESS '81					
				Vocal group formed in Nashville. Consisted of two men and two women.					
8/15/81	31	11		1 Big Like A River	Now	—	$4		RCA 12277
12/12/81	75	4		2 Little Things	How Much I Love You	—	$4		RCA 12362
				#13 Pop hit for **Bobby Goldsboro** in 1965					
4/3/82	70	4		3 The Arms Of A Stranger	Someone Just Like You	—	$4		RCA 13078
7/24/82	78	5		4 Operator /		—			
				#22 Pop hit for Manhattan Transfer in 1975					
		5		5 Let Me In And Let Me Love You		—	$4		RCA 13265
2/5/83	62	7		6 How Long Will It Take	Lead Me Into Love	—	$4		RCA 13423
6/4/83	65	6		7 Cotton Fields	Good For Nothing	—	$4		RCA 13526
				#13 Pop hit for The Highwaymen in 1962					
				TENNESSEE PULLEYBONE '73					
				Group consisted of Smig Smith (vocals), Dave Gillon, Ham Hamilton and Bones Kaelin.					
9/8/73	75	4		The Door's Always Open	Swinging Doors	—	$6		JMI 25
				TENNESSEE TORNADO — see FOSTER, Jerry					
				TENNESSEE VALLEY BOYS '84					
				Vocal group: Rick Baird, Jimmy Ponder, James Fulbright and Dan Britton. Assembled by Wally Fowler (born on 2/15/17; died on 6/3/94, age 77). Fowler also created the Oak Ridge Quartet (which evolved into the **Oak Ridge Boys**).					
4/14/84	57	10		Lo And Behold	It's Gonna Take Time	—	$7		Nashwood 12684
				WALLY FOWLER'S TENNESSEE VALLEY BOYS					
				★ **TENNISON, Chalee** '00					
				Born in 1969 in Texas. Female singer.					
4/17/99	46	16		1 Someone Else's Turn To Cry	It Ain't So Easy	—	$4		Asylum 64044
8/21/99	64	6		2 Handful Of Water		—			album cut
12/18/99+	36	19		3 Just Because She Lives There		—			album cut
				above 2 from the album *Chalee Tennison* on Asylum 62371					
9/16/00	56	8		4 Makin' Up With You	Yes I Was	—	$4	★	Asylum 16846 (v)
11/18/00+	36	21		5 Go Back		—			album cut
				from the album *This Woman's Heart* on Warner 47820					
				TERRY, Al '54					
				Born Allison Joseph Theriot on 1/14/22 in Kaplan, Louisiana. Died on 11/23/85 (age 63). Singer/songwriter/guitarist.					
4/24/54	8	5		1 Good Deal, Lucille	A:8 / J:8 Say A Prayer For Me	—	$40		Hickory 1003
2/29/60	28	1		2 Watch Dog	Passing The Blues Around	—	$30		Hickory 1111
				TERRY, Gordon '70					
				Born on 10/7/31 in Decatur, Alabama. Singer/songwriter/fiddler.					
5/30/70	62	5		The Ballad Of J.C.	Untanglin' My Mind [N]	—	$7		Capitol 2792
				tribute to **Johnny Cash** to the tune of "The Ballad Of New Orleans"					
				TEXAS PLAYBOYS — see ORIGINAL TEXAS PLAYBOYS					
				TEXAS VOCAL COMPANY '83					
				Vocal trio from Dallas: Sandy Skinner, Dick Root and Dave Roth.					
4/30/83	65	5		1 Two Hearts	You Did It Again	—	$4		RCA 13504
10/8/83	82	3		2 It Had To Be You	Backsliding	—	$4		RCA 13566

DEBUT	PEAK	WKS Gold	A-side (Chart Hit) .... B-side	Pop	$	Pic	Label & Number
	★258★		**THOMAS, B.J.** '83 Born Billy Joe Thomas on 8/7/42 in Hugo, Oklahoma; raised in Rosenberg, Texas. Singer/songwriter. Charted 26 pop hits from 1966-83. 1)Whatever Happened To Old Fashioned Love 2)(Hey Won't You Play) Another Somebody Done Somebody Wrong Song 3)New Looks From An Old Lover				
2/22/75	❶¹	16 ●	1 (Hey Won't You Play) Another Somebody Done Somebody Wrong Song .... City Boys	❶¹	$5		ABC 12054
10/4/75	37	10	2 Help Me Make It To My Rockin' Chair .... We Are Happy Together	64	$5		ABC 12121
5/14/77	98	1	3 Home Where I Belong .... Hallelujah	—	$5		Myrrh 166
1/28/78	25	13	4 Everybody Loves A Rain Song .... Dusty Roads	43	$4		MCA 40854
2/10/79	86	3	5 We Could Have Been The Closest Of Friends .... In My Heart	—	$4		MCA 40986
4/18/81	27	11	6 Some Love Songs Never Die .... There Ain't No Love	—	$4		MCA 51087
8/8/81	22	12	7 I Recall A Gypsy Woman .... The Lovin' Kind	—	$4		MCA 51151
2/12/83	❶¹	21	8 Whatever Happened To Old Fashioned Love .... I Just Sing	93	$4		Cleveland Int'l. 03492
7/9/83	❶¹	21	9 New Looks From An Old Lover .... You Keep The Man In Me Happy	—	$4		Columbia 03985
11/26/83+	3	21	10 Two Car Garage .... Beautiful World	—	$4		Cleveland Int'l 04237
4/14/84	10	19	11 The Whole World's In Love When You're Lonely .... We're Here To Love	—	$4		Cleveland Int'l 04431
8/4/84	14	18	12 Rock And Roll Shoes .... S:14 / A:21 Then I'll Be Over You RAY CHARLES (with B.J. THOMAS)	—	$4		Columbia 04531
10/20/84+	17	19	13 The Girl Most Likely To .... S:17 / A:17 From This Moment On	—	$4		Cleveland Int'l 04608
11/9/85	61	11	14 The Part Of Me That Needs You Most .... Northern Lights #98 Pop hit for Jay Black in 1980	—	$4		Columbia 05647
2/22/86	62	7	15 America Is .... Broken Toys	—	$4	■	Columbia 05771
10/4/86	59	6	16 Night Life .... Make The World Go Away	—	$4		Columbia 06314
7/29/00	66	1	17 You Call That A Mountain .... from the album *You Call That A Mountain* on Kardina 241	—			album cut
			THOMAS, Darrell '79 Born in 1952 in Melcher, Iowa.				
5/19/79	99	3	Waylon, Sing To Mama .... The Conquered King	—	$7		Ozark Opry 101
			THOMAS, Dick '45 Born Richard Thomas Goldhahn on 9/4/15 in Philadelphia. Singer/fiddler/accordionist/actor. Acted in several western movies.				
9/29/45	❶⁴	23	1 Sioux City Sue .... Tumbling Tumbleweeds	16	$20		National 5007
12/8/45	4	1	2 Honestly .... Half-Way To Montana		$20		National 5008
			DICK THOMAS And His Nashville Ramblers:				
9/25/48	13	1	3 The Beaut From Butte .... J:13 Two Car Garage	—	$15		Decca 46132
2/12/49	12	1	4 The Sister Of Sioux City Sue .... J:12 / S:14 Charlotte Belle (Carolina Waltz)	—	$15		Decca 46147
			THOMAS, Jeff '87				
1/17/87	85	3	Hollywood's Dream	—	$5		Revolver 014

THOMPSON, Hank ★41★ '52
Born Henry William Thompson on 9/3/25 in Waco, Texas. Singer/songwriter/guitarist. On WACO radio as a teenager, billed as "Hank, The Hired Hand." Served in the U.S. Navy during World War II. First recorded for Globe in 1946. Backing group: The Brazos Valley Boys. Elected to the Country Music Hall of Fame in 1989.

1)The Wild Side Of Life 2)Rub-A-Dub-Dub 3)Wake Up, Irene 4)Squaws Along The Yukon 5)Humpty Dumpty Heart

DEBUT	PEAK	WKS	A-side .... B-side	Pop	$	Pic	Label & Number
			HANK THOMPSON and His Brazos Valley Boys:				
1/31/48	2²	38	1 Humpty Dumpty Heart .... J:2 / S:3 Today	—	$20		Capitol Amer. 40065
2/5/49	10	1	2 What Are We Gonna Do About The Moonlight / J:10	—			
9/4/48	12	2	3 Yesterday's Mail J:12	—	$20		Capitol 15132
10/16/48	7	10	4 Green Light .... J:7 / S:8 You Remembered Me also see #21 below	—	$20		Capitol 15187
2/5/49	14	1	5 I Find You Cheatin' On Me / S:14				
2/12/49	15	1	6 You Broke My Heart (In Little Bitty Pieces) J:15	—	$20		Capitol 15345
10/1/49	6	7	7 Whoa Sailor .... J:6 / S:8 Swing Wide Your Gates Of Love	—	$20		Capitol 40218
10/1/49	10	1	8 Soft Lips J:10				
11/5/49	15	1	9 The Grass Looks Greener Over Yonder J:15	—	$20		Capitol 40211
3/15/52	❶¹⁵	30	10 The Wild Side Of Life .... S:❶¹⁵ / J:❶¹⁵ / A:❶² Cryin' In The Deep Blue Sea	—	$25		Capitol F1942
6/28/52	3	15	11 Waiting In The Lobby Of Your Heart .... J:3 / S:5 / A:7 Don't Make Me Cry Again	—	$25		Capitol F2063
12/13/52	10	1	12 The New Wears Off Too Fast .... J:10 You're Walking On My Heart	—	$25		Capitol F2269
3/28/53	9	2	13 No Help Wanted .... J:9 / S:10 / A:10 I'd Have Never Found Somebody New	—	$25		Capitol 2376
5/23/53	❶³	20	14 Rub-A-Dub-Dub .... J:❶³ / A:2 / S:5 I'll Sign My Heart Away	—	$25		Capitol 2445
9/19/53	8	4	15 Yesterday's Girl .... S:8 / A:8 John Henry	—	$25		Capitol 2553
12/12/53+	❶²	19	16 Wake Up, Irene .... J:❶² / S:3 / A:4 Go Cry Your Heart Out answer to "Goodnight, Irene" by Red Foley & Ernest Tubb	—	$25		Capitol 2646
5/22/54	9	1	17 A Fooler, A Faker / .... J:9 / S:15				
5/8/54	10	2	18 Breakin' The Rules S:10	—	$20		Capitol 2758
7/3/54	9	12	19 Honky-Tonk Girl / .... S:9 / J:10 / A:11 also see #72 below				
7/17/54	10	4	20 We've Gone Too Far .... S:10 / A:15	—	$20		Capitol 2823
10/16/54	3	20	21 The New Green Light .... J:3 / S:7 / A:8 A Lonely Heart Knows new version of #3 above	—	$20		Capitol 2920

350

DEBUT	PEAK	WKS	Gold	A-side (Chart Hit)	B-side	Pop	$	Pic	Label & Number
				THOMPSON, Hank — Cont'd					
2/26/55	12	4		22 If Lovin' You Is Wrong /	S:12 / A:14	—			
3/12/55	13	2		23 Annie Over	S:13	—	$20		Capitol 3030
6/4/55	5	9		24 Wildwood Flower /	J:5 / S:8 / A:13	[I]			
				HANK THOMPSON and His Brazos Valley Boys with MERLE TRAVIS					
6/4/55	7	8		25 Breakin' In Another Heart	S:7	—	$20		Capitol 3106
8/20/55	6	11		26 Most Of All	A:6 / S:11 Simple Simon	—	$20		Capitol 3188
12/10/55	5	7		27 Don't Take It Out On Me /	S:5 / J:9 / A:13	—			
		5		28 Honey, Honey Bee Ball	S:flip / J:flip	—	$20		Capitol 3275
3/24/56	4	22		29 The Blackboard Of My Heart /	A:4 / S:6 / J:6	—			
3/24/56	14	5		30 I'm Not Mad, Just Hurt	S:14	—	$20		Capitol 3347
2/23/57	13	4		31 Rockin' In The Congo /	S:13	—			
				also see #78 below					
		2		32 I Was The First One	S:flip	—	$30		Capitol 3623
10/14/57	14	2		33 Tears Are Only Rain	A:14 Under The Double Eagle	—	$20		Capitol 3781
6/9/58	11	3		34 How Do You Hold A Memory	A:11 Li'l Liza Jane	—	$20		Capitol 3950
8/18/58	2⁴	22		35 Squaws Along The Yukon	Gathering Flowers	—	$20		Capitol 4017
12/1/58+	7	23		36 I've Run Out Of Tomorrows /		—			
2/2/59	26	3		37 You're Going Back To Your Old Ways Again		—	$20		Capitol 4085
5/11/59	13	10		38 Anybody's Girl /		—			
6/29/59	25	1		39 Total Strangers		—	$20		Capitol 4182
11/9/59+	22	10		40 I Didn't Mean To Fall In Love	I Guess I'm Getting Over You	—	$20		Capitol 4269
3/21/60	10	16		41 A Six Pack To Go	What Made Her Change	102	$12		Capitol 4334
8/1/60	14	14		42 She's Just A Whole Lot Like You	There My Future Goes	99	$20		Capitol 4386
5/29/61	7	11		43 Oklahoma Hills /		—			
5/29/61	25	2		44 Teach Me How To Lie		—	$20		Capitol 4556
9/18/61	12	10		45 Hangover Tavern	Give The World A Smile	—	$20		Capitol 4605
9/7/63	23	1		46 I Wasn't Even In The Running	The More In Love Your Heart Is	—	$15		Capitol 4968
9/28/63	22	5		47 Too In Love	Blackboard Of My Heart	—	$15		Capitol 5008
1/11/64	45	2		48 Twice As Much	Reaching For The Moon	—	$15		Capitol 5071
8/14/65	42	2		49 Then I'll Start Believing In You	In The Back Of Your Mind	—	$15		Capitol 5422
10/22/66	15	14		50 Where Is The Circus	Love Walked Out Long Before She Did	—	$10		Warner 5858
2/4/67	16	13		51 He's Got A Way With Women	Let The Four Winds Choose	—	$10		Warner 5886
				HANK THOMPSON:					
7/13/68	7	15		52 On Tap, In The Can, Or In The Bottle	If I Lose You Tomorrow	—	$8		Dot 17108
10/26/68+	5	15		53 Smoky The Bar	Clubs, Spades, Diamonds, And Hearts	—	$8		Dot 17163
3/8/69	47	9		54 I See Them Everywhere	Today	—	$8		Dot 17207
7/12/69	46	9		55 The Pathway Of My Life	At Certain Times	—	$8		Dot 17262
10/18/69	60	6		56 Oklahoma Home Brew	Let's Get Drunk And Be Somebody	—	$8		Dot 17307
5/9/70	54	5		57 But That's All Right	Take It All Away	—	$8		Dot 17347
10/10/70	69	4		58 One Of The Fortunate Few	I'm Afraid I Lied	—	$8		Dot 17354
3/6/71	15	14		59 Next Time I Fall In Love (I Won't)	Big Boat Across Oklahoma	—	$7		Dot 17365
7/17/71	18	16		60 The Mark Of A Heel	Promise Her Anything	—	$7		Dot 17385
12/4/71+	11	14		61 I've Come Awful Close	Teardrops On The Rocks	—	$7		Dot 17399
4/29/72	16	12		62 Cab Driver	Gloria	—	$7		Dot 17410
				#23 Pop hit for The Mills Brothers in 1968					
9/23/72	53	8		63 Glow Worm	You're Nobody Till Somebody Loves You	—	$7		Dot 17430
				#1 Pop hit for The Mills Brothers in 1952					
3/17/73	70	2		64 Roses In The Wine	That's Why I Sing In A Honky Tonk	—	$7		Dot 17447
9/1/73	48	9		65 Kindly Keep It Country	Jill's Jack In The Box	—	$7		Dot 17470
2/2/74	8	15		66 The Older The Violin, The Sweeter The Music	A Six Pack To Go	—	$7		Dot 17490
7/13/74	10	16		67 Who Left The Door To Heaven Open	When My Blue Moon Turns To Gold Again	—	$7		Dot 17512
1/25/75	29	10		68 Mama Don't 'Low	Wait A Little Longer Baby	—	$6		ABC/Dot 17535
6/28/75	70	8		69 That's Just My Truckin' Luck	After You Have Made Me Over	—	$6		ABC/Dot 17556
3/6/76	72	6		70 Asphalt Cowboy	Fifteen Miles To Clarksville	—	$6		ABC/Dot 17612
9/4/76	86	3		71 Big Band Days	Forgive Me	—	$6		ABC/Dot 17649
1/15/77	91	4		72 Honky Tonk Girl	Another Shot Of Toddy [R]	—	$6		ABC/Dot 17673
				new version of #19 above					
5/21/77	92	2		73 Just An Old Flame	Don't Get Around Much Anymore	—	$6		ABC/Dot 17695
10/21/78	92	3		74 I'm Just Gettin' By	I Hear The South Callin' Me	—	$5		ABC 12409
3/3/79	88	3		75 Dance With Me Molly	Point Of No Return	—	$5		ABC 12447
8/25/79	29	12		76 I Hear The South Callin' Me	Through The Bottom Of The Glass	—	$4		MCA 41079
2/2/80	32	9		77 Tony's Tank-Up, Drive-In Cafe	Point Of No Return	—	$4		MCA 41176
12/19/81+	82	5		78 Rockin' In The Congo	The Convict And The Rose [R]	—	$8	■	Churchill 7779
				new version of #31 above					
7/23/83	82	5		79 Once In A Blue Moon	Let's Stop What We Started	—	$5	■	Churchill 94026
				THOMPSON, J.W.	'80				
				Born in Alexandria, Louisiana. Male singer/songwriter.					
9/15/79	90	2		1 The Visitor	When You're Honky Tonkin'	—	$5		Southern Star 309
10/4/80	56	9		2 Halftime	Jesus Loves Cowboys The Same	—	$5		NSD 62
1/24/81	72	4		3 Two Out Of Three Ain't Bad	Bubbles In My Beer	—	$5		NSD 75
10/22/83	97	1		4 We've Got A Good Thing Goin'	Makin' Love With A Married Man	—	$6		USA Country 1001
7/14/84	91	2		5 Hello Josephine		—	$6		Century 21 109

DEBUT	PEAK	WKS	Gold	A-side (Chart Hit)	B-side	Pop	$	Pic	Label & Number
				THOMPSON, Sue		'74			
				Born Eva Sue McKee on 7/19/26 in Nevada, Missouri; raised in San Jose, California. Singer/guitarist. Married to **Hank Penny** from 1953-63. Charted 7 pop hits from 1961-65.					
				1) *Good Old Fashioned Country Love* 2) *Oh, How Love Changes* 3) *I Think They Call It Love*					
				DON GIBSON & SUE THOMPSON:					
8/28/71	50	8		1 The Two Of Us Together	Oh Yes, I Love You	—	$8		Hickory 1607
4/22/72	71	3		2 Did You Ever Think	Love's Garden	—	$8		Hickory 1629
8/12/72	37	11		3 I Think They Call It Love	Over There's The Door	—	$8		Hickory 1646
11/18/72	72	5		4 Candy And Roses	A Full Time Job	—	$8		Hickory 1652
				SUE THOMPSON					
12/23/72	64	5		5 Cause I Love You	My Tears Don't Show	—	$8		Hickory 1654
3/17/73	52	6		6 Go With Me	The Two Of Us Together	—	$8		Hickory 1665
9/15/73	53	9		7 Warm Love	Fly The Friendly Skies With Jesus	—	$6		Hickory/MGM 303
8/10/74	31	12		8 Good Old Fashioned Country Love	Ages And Ages Ago	—	$6		Hickory/MGM 324
7/19/75	36	11		9 Oh, How Love Changes	Sweet And Tender Times	—	$6		Hickory/MGM 350
9/6/75	50	9		10 Big Mable Murphy	Big Daddy	—	$6		Hickory/MGM 354
				SUE THOMPSON					
2/21/76	95	3		11 Never Naughty Rosie	He Cheats On Me	—	$6		Hickory/MGM 364
				SUE THOMPSON					
4/3/76	98	2		12 Get Ready-Here I Come	Once More	—	$6		Hickory/MGM 367
				THOMPSON BROTHERS BAND, The		'97			
				Group from Norwell, Massachusetts: Andy (vocals) and Matt (drums) Thompson, with Mike Whitty (bass).					
11/15/97	56	8		1 Drive Me Crazy /		—			
2/28/98	58	11		2 Back On The Farm		—	$4		RCA 64998
				THOMSON, Cyndi		'01			
				Born in 1976 in Tifton, Georgia. Singer/songwriter.					
3/31/01	❶³	35		1 What I Really Meant To Say S:❶⁸	Things I Would Do	26	$4	★	Capitol 58987 (v)
11/10/01+	21	20		2 I Always Liked That Best		119	$4		album cut
				from the album *My World* on Capitol 26010					
				THORNTON, Marsha		'90			
				Born on 10/22/64 in Killen, Alabama.					
9/23/89	62	7		1 Deep Water	Don't Tell Me What To Do	—	$4		MCA 53711
1/6/90	59	10		2 A Bottle Of Wine And Patsy Cline	Don't Tell Me What To Do	—	$4		MCA 53762
2/16/91	73	2		3 Maybe The Moon Will Shine	A Far Cry From You	—	$4		MCA 53995
				THOROGOOD, George — see TRITT, Travis					
				THRASHER BROTHERS		'82			
				Vocal group of brothers Joe (lead), Jim (tenor) and Andy (baritone) Thrasher, with John Gresham (bass) and Roger Hallmark (guitar, banjo, fiddle). Joe's son, Neil, formed **Thrasher Shiver** duo.					
12/15/79+	72	5		1 A Message To Khomeini	Maharishi [N]	—	$6		Vulcan 10004
				ROGER HALLMARK and The Thrasher Brothers					
3/7/81	83	2		2 Lovers Love	Wouldn't It Make A Good Country Song	—	$4		MCA 51049
2/6/82	62	5		3 Best Of Friends	The Captain & The Delta Queen	—	$4		MCA 51227
				from the TV series *Simon & Simon* starring Gerald McRaney and Jameson Parker					
9/11/82	60	6		4 Still The One	Long Tall Texan	—	$4		MCA 52093
				#5 Pop hit for **Orleans** in 1976					
1/15/83	81	4		5 Wherever You Are	Heart To Heart	—	$4		MCA 52153
12/10/83	80	8		6 Whatcha Got Cookin' In Your Oven Tonight	Southern Swing	—	$4		MCA 52297
				THRASHER SHIVER		'97			
				Duo of Neil Thrasher and Kelly Shiver. Neil's father, Joe, was lead singer of the **Thrasher Brothers**.					
8/10/96	65	6		1 Goin', Goin', Gone		—			album cut
2/22/97	49	10		2 Be Honest		—			album cut
				above 2 from the album *Thrasher Shiver* on Asylum 61929					
				3 OF HEARTS		'01			
				Female vocal trio from Fort Worth, Texas: Blaire Stroud, Kayie McNeill and Deserea Wasdin.					
4/21/01	43	10		1 Love Is Enough S:4 (album snippets)		—	$4	★	RCA 69034
8/18/01	59	1		2 Arizona Rain		—			album cut
				from the album *3 Of Hearts* on RCA 67916					
12/15/01	39	5		3 The Christmas Shoes S:7 (album snippets) [X]		—	$4	★	RCA 69110
				THREE SUNS, The		'50			
				Instrumental trio from Philadelphia: brothers Al (guitar; died on 11/25/65, age 48) and Morty (accordion; died on 7/20/90, age 63) Nevins, with cousin Artie Dunn (died on 1/15/96, age 73).					
2/4/50	7	4		**Beyond The Sunset** A:7	The Game Of Broken Hearts	—	$30	★	RCA Victor 47-3105
				THE THREE SUNS with ROSALIE ALLEN and ELTON BRITT					
				78 rpm: 20-3599; #71 Pop hit for **Pat Boone** in 1959					
				THROCKMORTON, Sonny		'79			
				Born James Fron Throckmorton on 4/2/41 in Carlsbad, New Mexico. Singer/prolific songwriter.					
9/4/76	76	6		1 Rosie	Troublesome Waters	—	$6	■	Starcrest 073
12/25/76+	73	7		2 Lovin' You, Lovin' Me	I Don't Know How To Tell Her (She Don't Love Me Anymore)	—	$6		Starcrest 094
9/16/78	54	8		3 I Wish You Could Have Turned My Head (And Left My Heart Alone)	She Sure Makes Leavin' Look Easy	—	$4		Mercury 55039
2/3/79	47	8		4 Smooth Sailin' /		—			
		8		5 Last Cheater's Waltz		—	$4		Mercury 55051
7/14/79	66	6		6 Can't You Hear That Whistle Blow	I Feel Like Loving You Again	—	$4		Mercury 55061
4/5/80	89	3		7 Friday Night Blues	It Always Rains On Me	—	$4		Mercury 57018

DEBUT	PEAK	WKS	Gold	A-side (Chart Hit)	B-side	Pop	$	Pic	Label & Number
				THROCKMORTON, Sonny — Cont'd					
12/12/81	77	5		8 A Girl Like You	I've Broken My Own Heart	—	$4		MCA 51214
				THUNDERKLOUD, Billy, & The Chieftones '75					
				Vocal group of Native Americans from British Columbia: Vincent "Billy Thunderkloud" Clifford, Jack Wolf, Barry Littlestar and Richard Grayowl.					
5/17/75	16	12		1 What Time Of Day	When Love Is Right	92	$5		20th Century 2181
10/25/75	37	11		2 Pledging My Love	I Will Love You Until I Die	—	$5		20th Century 2239
				#17 Pop hit for Johnny Ace in 1955					
5/29/76	74	5		3 Indian Nation (The Lament of the Cherokee Reservation Indian)	I'm Going Right To Where I Do Wrong	—	$5		Polydor 14321
				#1 Pop hit for The Raiders in 1971					
8/7/76	47	8		4 Try A Little Tenderness	A Natural Feelin' For You	—	$5		Polydor 14338
				#25 Pop hit for Otis Redding in 1967					
12/11/76	77	6		5 It's Alright	The Wanderer	—	$5		Polydor 14362
				TIBOR BROTHERS, The '76					
				Vocal group of brothers from Hebron, North Dakota: Francis, Gerard, Harvey, Kurt and Larry Tibor.					
4/17/76	95	3		It's So Easy Lovin' You	Movin' Along	—	$5		Ariola America 7615
				TIERNY, Patti '73					
9/22/73	90	4		Cryin' Eyes	Jody's Face	—	$6		MGM 14561
				TILLIS, Mel ★30★ '72					
				Born Lonnie Melvin Tillis on 8/8/32 in Tampa, Florida; raised in Pahokee, Florida. Singer/songwriter/guitarist/actor. Acted in the movies *W.W. & The Dixie Dancekings*, *Smokey & The Bandit II*, *Uphill All The Way* and *Murder In Music City*. Owned several music publishing companies. Backing band: The Statesiders. Father of **Pam Tillis**. Known for his stuttering speech. CMA Award: 1976 Entertainer of the Year.					
				1) I Ain't Never 2) Good Woman Blues 3) Coca Cola Cowboy 4) I Believe In You 5) Southern Rains					
11/10/58	24	4		1 The Violet And A Rose	No Song To Sing	—	$15		Columbia 41189
1/5/59	28	4		2 Finally	The Brooklyn Bridge	—	$15		Columbia 41277
8/24/59	27	2		3 Sawmill	You Are The Reason	—	$15		Columbia 41416
				MEL TILLIS and BILL PHILLIPS also see #33 below					
2/8/60	24	4		4 Georgia Town Blues	Till I Get Enough Of These Blues	—	$15		Columbia 41530
				MEL TILLIS and BILL PHILLIPS					
1/5/63	25	3		5 How Come Your Dog Don't Bite Nobody But Me	So Soon	—	$10		Decca 31445
				WEBB PIERCE and MEL TILLIS					
7/3/65	14	16		6 Wine	Buried Alive	—	$12		RIC 158
10/15/66	17	14		7 Stateside	Home Is Where The Hurt Is	—	$8		Kapp 772
2/18/67	11	19		8 Life Turned Her That Way	If I Could Only Start Over	128	$8	■	Kapp 804
7/15/67	20	14		9 Goodbye Wheeling	At The Sight Of You	—	$8		Kapp 837
12/16/67	71	3		10 Survival Of The Fittest	The Old Gang's Gone	—	$8		Kapp 867
1/13/68	26	12		11 All Right (I'll Sign The Papers)	Helpless, Hopeless Fool	—	$8		Kapp 881
5/11/68	17	15		12 Something Special	You Name It	—	$8		Kapp 905
10/5/68	31	7		13 Destroyed By Man	I Haven't Seen Mary In Years	—	$8		Kapp 941
12/21/68+	10	17		14 Who's Julie	Give Me One More Day	—	$8		Kapp 959
4/19/69	13	15		15 Old Faithful	Sorrow Overtakes The Wine	—	$8		Kapp 986
				MEL TILLIS And The Statesiders:					
8/16/69	9	15		16 These Lonely Hands Of Mine	Cover Mama's Flowers	—	$6		Kapp 2031
1/17/70	10	11		17 She'll Be Hanging 'Round Somewhere	Where Love Has Died	—	$6		Kapp 2072
4/25/70	3	17		18 Heart Over Mind	Lingering Memories	—	$6		Kapp 2086
7/25/70	5	14		19 Heaven Everyday	How Do You Drink The Wine	—	$6		MGM 14148
10/17/70	25	11		20 To Lonely, Too Long	Memories Made This House	—	$6		Kapp 2103
11/7/70	8	13		21 Commercial Affection	I Thought About You	—	$6		MGM 14176
1/30/71	4	15		22 The Arms Of A Fool	Veil Of White Lace	114	$6		MGM 14211
5/8/71	56	9		23 One More Drink	I Could Never Be Ashamed Of You	—	$6		Kapp 2121
6/5/71	8	15		24 Take My Hand	Life's Little Surprises	110	$6		MGM 14255
				MEL TILLIS AND SHERRY BRYCE with The Statesiders					
7/31/71	8	16		25 Brand New Mister Me	Brand New Wrapper	—	$6		MGM 14275
10/30/71	9	14		26 Living And Learning	Tangled Vines	—	$6		MGM 14303
				MEL TILLIS & SHERRY BRYCE					
1/1/72	14	13		27 Untouched	I Went A Ramblin'	—	$6		MGM 14329
4/8/72	38	10		28 Anything's Better Than Nothing	Then It Will Be All Over	—	$6		MGM 14365
				MEL TILLIS & SHERRY BRYCE And The Statesiders					
5/6/72	12	11		29 Would You Want The World To End	Things Have Changed A Lot	—	$6		MGM 14372
8/12/72	❶²	15		30 I Ain't Never	Burden Of Love	—	$6		MGM 14418
12/9/72+	3	16		31 Neon Rose	It's My Love (And I'm Gonna Give It)	—	$6		MGM 14454
4/28/73	21	13		32 Thank You For Being You	Over The Hill	—	$6		MGM 14522
8/25/73	2¹	17		33 Sawmill	Mama's Gonna Pray [R]	—	$6		MGM 14585
				new version of #3 above					
11/17/73+	26	13		34 Let's Go All The Way Tonight	In The Vine	—	$6		MGM 14660
				MEL TILLIS & SHERRY BRYCE & The Statesiders					
1/12/74	2¹	18		35 Midnight, Me And The Blues	Modern Home Magazine	—	$6		MGM 14689

DEBUT	PEAK	WKS	Gold	A-side (Chart Hit)	B-side	Pop	$	Pic	Label & Number
				TILLIS, Mel — Cont'd					
4/13/74	11	14		36 Don't Let Go...............................Why Not Do The Things (They Think We've Done)		—	$6		MGM 14714
				MEL TILLIS & SHERRY BRYCE And The Statesiders					
				#13 Pop hit for Roy Hamilton in 1958					
5/18/74	3	16		37 Stomp Them Grapes	Hang My Picture In Your Heart	—	$5		MGM 14720
10/5/74	3	14		38 Memory Maker	Second Best	—	$5		MGM 14744
1/4/75	14	13		39 You Are The One	I See Heaven In You	—	$5		MGM 14776
				MEL TILLIS & SHERRY BRYCE And The Statesiders					
2/1/75	7	16		40 Best Way I Know How	Honey Dew Melon	—	$5		MGM 14782
5/17/75	32	13		41 Mr. Right And Mrs. Wrong.....................Just Two Strangers Passing In The Night		—	$5		MGM 14803
				MEL TILLIS AND SHERRY BRYCE And The Statesiders					
6/14/75	4	16		42 Woman In The Back Of My Mind	Kissing Your Picture (Is So Cold)	—	$5		MGM 14804
11/1/75+	16	14		43 Lookin' For Tomorrow (And Findin' Yesterdays).........Tennessee Banjo Man		—	$5		MGM 14835
3/20/76	15	10		44 Mental Revenge	My Bad Girl Treats Me Good	—	$5		MGM 14846
				MEL TILLIS:					
5/29/76	11	13		45 Love Revival	Gator Bar	—	$5		MCA 40559
10/2/76	❶²	16		46 Good Woman Blues	You Can't Trust A Crazy Man	—	$5		MCA 40627
1/15/77	❶¹	14		47 Heart Healer	It's Just Not That Easy To Say	—	$5		MCA 40667
4/23/77	9	13		48 Burning Memories	Golden Nugget Gambling Casino	—	$5		MCA 40710
8/13/77	3	16		49 I Got The Hoss	It's Been A Long Time	—	$5		MCA 40764
12/24/77+	4	16		50 What Did I Promise Her Last Night	Woman, You Should Be In Movies	—	$5		MCA 40836
5/13/78	❶¹	14		51 I Believe In You	She Don't Trust You Daddy	—	$5		MCA 40900
9/9/78	4	13		52 Ain't No California	What Comes Natural To A Fool	—	$5		MCA 40946
1/13/79	2³	14		53 Send Me Down To Tucson /					
				from the movie *Every Which Way But Loose* starring **Clint Eastwood**					
		14		54 Charlie's Angel		—	$5		MCA 40983
6/16/79	❶¹	15		55 Coca Cola Cowboy	Cottonmouth	—	$5		MCA 41041
				from the movie *Every Which Way But Loose* starring **Clint Eastwood**					
9/29/79	6	14		56 Blind In Love	Black Jack, Water Back	—	$4		Elektra 46536
1/19/80	6	13		57 Lying Time Again	Fooled Around And Fell In Love	—	$4		Elektra 46583
4/26/80	3	16		58 Your Body Is An Outlaw	Rain On My Parade	—	$4		Elektra 46628
8/30/80	9	13		59 Steppin' Out	Whiskey Chasin'	—	$4		Elektra 47015
12/13/80+	❶¹	16		60 Southern Rains	Forgive Me For Giving You The Blues	—	$4		Elektra 47082
4/4/81	8	13		61 A Million Old Goodbyes	Louisiana Lonely	—	$4		Elektra 47116
7/11/81	23	12		62 Texas Cowboy Night	After The Lovin'	—	$4		Elektra 47157
				MEL TILLIS & NANCY SINATRA					
9/5/81	10	16		63 One-Night Fever	Time Has Treated You Well	—	$4		Elektra 47178
12/26/81+	43	8		64 Play Me Or Trade Me /		—			
		8		65 Where Would I Be		—	$4		Elektra 47247
				MEL TILLIS & NANCY SINATRA (above 2)					
2/27/82	36	9		66 It's A Long Way To Daytona	Always You, Always Me	—	$4		Elektra 47412
5/29/82	37	9		67 The One That Got Away	Why Ain't Life The Way It's S'posed To Be	—	$4		Elektra 47453
9/25/82	17	15		68 Stay A Little Longer	Dream Of Me	—	$4		Elektra 69963
3/12/83	10	20		69 In The Middle Of The Night	Even At Her Worst (She's Still The Best)	—	$4		MCA 52182
8/6/83	49	10		70 A Cowboy's Dream	After All This Time	—	$4		MCA 52247
10/29/83	53	10		71 She Meant Forever When She Said Goodbye	Try It Again	—	$4		MCA 52285
4/28/84	10	22		72 New Patches	Almost Like You Never Went Away	—	$4		MCA 52373
10/27/84	47	12		73 Slow Nights	Midnight Love	—	$4		MCA 52474
				MEL TILLIS WITH GLEN CAMPBELL					
6/1/85	37	12		74 You Done Me Wrong	Another Heart Down	—	$4		RCA 14061
9/7/85	61	7		75 California Road	One More Time	—	$4		RCA 14175
3/5/88	31	14		76 You'll Come Back (You Always Do)	Try It Again	—	$4		Mercury 870192
11/4/89	67	4		77 City Lights	Who's Julie	—	$5		Radio 001

TILLIS, Pam ★133★ '92

Born on 7/24/57 in Plant City, Florida. Singer/songwriter/guitarist. Daughter of **Mel Tillis**. Formerly married to Bob DiPiero of **Billy Hill**. Joined the *Grand Ole Opry* in 2000. CMA Award: 1994 Female Vocalist of the Year. Also see **Same Old Train** and **Tomorrow's World**.

1) Mi Vida Loca (My Crazy Life) 2) When You Walk In The Room 3) Maybe It Was Memphis 4) Shake The Sugar Tree 5) In Between Dances

DEBUT	PEAK	WKS	Gold	A-side	B-side	Pop	$	Pic	Label & Number
11/10/84	71	5		1 Goodbye Highway	Somebody Else's	—	$4		Warner 29155
1/25/86	55	8		2 Those Memories Of You	Drawn To The Fire	—	$4		Warner 28806
7/5/86	67	4		3 I Thought I'd About Had It With Love	Drawn To The Fire	—	$4		Warner 28676
2/21/87	68	6		4 I Wish She Wouldn't Treat You That Way	Drawn To The Fire	—	$4		Warner 28444
5/16/87	71	6		5 There Goes My Love	Drawn To The Fire	—	$4		Warner 28346
12/1/90+	5	20		6 Don't Tell Me What To Do	Melancholy Child	—	$4		Arista 2129
4/6/91	6	20		7 One Of Those Things	Already Fallen	—	$4		Arista 2203
8/17/91	17	20		8 Put Yourself In My Place	I've Seen Enough To Know	—	$4		Arista 12268
12/14/91+	3	20		9 Maybe It Was Memphis	Draggin' My Chains	—	$4	▮	Arista 12371 (v)
4/11/92	21	20		10 Blue Rose Is	Ancient History	—	$4		Arista 12408
8/22/92	3	20		11 Shake The Sugar Tree	Maybe It Was Memphis	—	$4		Arista 12454
1/2/93	4	20		12 Let That Pony Run	Fine, Fine, Very Fine Love	—	$4	▮	Arista 12506 (v)
5/1/93	11	20		13 Cleopatra, Queen Of Denial	Homeward Looking Angel	—	$4	▮	Arista 12552 (v)

DEBUT	PEAK	WKS	Gold	A-side (Chart Hit)	B-side	Pop	$	Pic	Label & Number
				TILLIS, Pam — Cont'd					
8/28/93	16	20		14 Do You Know Where Your Man Is .... We've Tried Everything Else		—	$4	■	Arista 12606 (v)
3/26/94	5	20		15 Spilled Perfume .... 'Til All The Lonely's Gone		—	$4		Arista 12676 (v)
8/6/94	2¹	20		16 When You Walk In The Room .... 'Til All The Lonely's Gone		—	$4	■	Arista 12726 (v)
				#35 Pop hit for The Searchers in 1964					
11/19/94+	❶²	20		17 Mi Vida Loca (My Crazy Life) .... Ancient History		—	$4		Arista 12759
3/11/95	16	12		18 I Was Blown Away .... Calico Plains		—	$4		Arista 12802
6/3/95	3	20		19 In Between Dances .... They Don't Break'em Like They Used To		—	$4		Arista 12833
10/7/95+	6	20		20 Deep Down .... Tequila Mockingbird		—	$4	■	Arista 12878 (v)
1/27/96	8	20		21 The River And The Highway .... All Of This Love		—	$4		Arista 12958
6/8/96	14	20		22 It's Lonely Out There .... You Can't Have A Good Time Without Me		—	$4		Arista 10505
10/12/96	62	4		23 Betty's Got A Bass Boat .... Mandolin Rain		—	$4		Arista 13045
4/26/97	4	20		24 All The Good Ones Are Gone /					
9/6/97	5	21		25 Land Of The Living		—	$4		Arista Nashville 13084
5/16/98	12	20		26 I Said A Prayer .... S:12 Lay The Heartache Down		102	$4	■	Arista Nash. 13125 (v)
9/12/98	38	12		27 Every Time .... You Put The Lonely On Me		—	$4		Arista Nashville 13129
8/28/99	50	9		28 After A Kiss		—			album cut
				from the movie Happy, Texas starring Steve Zahn (soundtrack on Arista 18898)					
12/9/00+	22	22		29 Please .... Thunder And Roses		120	$4		Arista Nashville 69052
	★320★			**TILLMAN, Floyd** '44					
				Born on 12/8/14 in Ryan, Oklahoma; raised in Post, Texas. Singer/songwriter/guitarist. Elected to the Country Music Hall of Fame in 1984.					
				1)They Took The Stars Out Of Heaven 2)Drivin' Nails In My Coffin 3)Each Night At Nine					
				FLOYD TILLMAN and His Favorite Playboys:					
1/8/44	❶¹	13		1 They Took The Stars Out Of Heaven .... Why Do You Treat Me This Way		—	$20		Decca 6090
12/30/44	4	8		2 Each Night At Nine /					
12/16/44	5	3		3 G.I. Blues		—	$20		Decca 6104
				FLOYD TILLMAN:					
8/3/46	2¹	7		4 Drivin' Nails In My Coffin .... Some Other World		—	$15		Columbia 36998
7/10/48	5	19		5 I Love You So Much, It Hurts .... J:5 / S:6 I'll Take What I Can Get		—	$15		Columbia 20430
1/29/49	14	1		6 Please Don't Pass Me By .... S:14 Cold Cold Woman		—	$15		Columbia 20496
7/2/49	5	12		7 Slipping Around .... S:5 / A:6 / J:6 You Made Me Live, Love And Die		—	$15		Columbia 20581
10/8/49	6	8		8 I'll Never Slip Around Again .... S:6 / J:8 This Cold War With You		—	$15		Columbia 20615
12/31/49+	4	3		9 I Gotta Have My Baby Back .... A:4 It Had To Be That Way		—	$15		Columbia 20641
12/19/60	29	1		10 It Just Tears Me Up .... The Song Of Music		—	$20		Liberty 55280
				TILLOTSON, Johnny '62					
				Born on 4/20/39 in Jacksonville, Florida; raised in Palatka, Florida. Acted in the movie Just For Fun. Charted 26 pop hits from 1958-65.					
6/23/62	4	13		1 It Keeps Right On A-Hurtin' .... She Gave Sweet Love To Me		3	$15		Cadence 1418
9/8/62	11	10		2 Send Me The Pillow You Dream On .... What'll I Do (Pop #106)		17	$15		Cadence 1424
11/11/67	48	10		3 You're The Reason .... Countin' My Teardrops		—	$8		MGM 13829
2/17/68	63	6		4 I Can Spot A Cheater .... It Keeps Right On A-Hurtin'		—	$8		MGM 13888
6/18/77	99	1		5 Toy Hearts .... Just An Ordinary Man		—	$6		United Artists 986
3/31/84	91	2		6 Lay Back (In The Arms Of Someone) .... What's Another Year		—	$6		Reward 04346
				TILTON, Sheila '76					
				Born in 1951 in Kailua, Hawaii.					
7/10/76	23	13		Half As Much .... I'll Be Whatever You Say		—	$5		Con Brio 110
				#1 Pop hit for Rosemary Clooney in 1952					
				TINY TIM '88					
				Born Herbert Khaury on 4/12/30 in New York City. Died of heart failure on 11/30/96 (age 66). Novelty singer/ukulele player. Charted a pop hit in 1968 with "Tip-Toe Thru' The Tulips With Me."					
4/16/88	70	5		Leave Me Satisfied .... I Wanna' Get Crazy With You		—	$6		NLT 1993
				TIPPIN, Aaron ★158★ '92					
				Born on 7/3/58 in Pensacola, Florida; raised in Travelers Rest, South Carolina. Singer/songwriter/guitarist. Worked as a corporate airline pilot before his singing career.					
				1)There Ain't Nothin' Wrong With The Radio 2)Kiss This 3)That's As Close As I'll Get To Loving You 4)Where The Stars And Stripes And The Eagle Fly 5)I Wouldn't Have It Any Other Way					
11/3/90+	6	20		1 You've Got To Stand For Something .... Up Against You		—	$4	■	RCA 2664 (v)
4/6/91	40	19		2 I Wonder How Far It Is Over You .... You Should See Me Missing You		—	$4		RCA 2747
8/24/91	54	11		3 She Made A Memory Out Of Me .... The Sky's Got The Blues		—	$4		RCA 62015
2/15/92	❶³	20		4 There Ain't Nothin' Wrong With The Radio .... I Miss Misbehavin'		—	$4		RCA 62181
6/20/92	5	20		5 I Wouldn't Have It Any Other Way .... What I Can't Live Without		—	$4		RCA 62241
10/24/92	38	13		6 I Was Born With A Broken Heart .... Read Between The Lines		—	$4		RCA 62338
1/30/93	7	20		7 My Blue Angel .... The Sound Of Your Goodbye (Sticks And Stones)		—	$4		RCA 62430
6/26/93	7	20		8 Working Man's Ph.D. .... When Country Took The Throne		—	$4		RCA 62520
10/23/93+	17	20		9 The Call Of The Wild .... Nothin' In The World		—	$4	■	RCA 62657 (v)
2/12/94	47	10		10 Honky-Tonk Superman .... Let's Talk About You		—	$4	■	RCA 62755 (v)
4/23/94	30	20		11 Whole Lotta Love On The Line .... I Promised You The World		—	$4		RCA 62832

DEBUT	PEAK	WKS	Gold	A-side (Chart Hit) .... B-side	Pop	$	Pic	Label & Number
				TIPPIN, Aaron — Cont'd				
10/8/94+	15	20		12 I Got It Honest .... Lookin' Back At Myself	—	$4	■	RCA 62947 (v)
2/25/95	39	11		13 She Feels Like A Brand New Man Tonight .... Lovin' Me Into An Early Grave	—	$4		RCA 64272
9/2/95	❶²	21		14 That's As Close As I'll Get To Loving You		$4		RCA 64392 (v)
				S:3 She Feels Like A Brand New Man Tonight	70ˢ		■	
2/3/96	22	16		15 Without Your Love .... Country Boy's Toolbox	—	$4	■	RCA 64471 (v)
6/1/96	51	11		16 Everything I Own .... She Made A Man Out Of A Mountain Of Stone	—	$4		RCA 64544
10/19/96	69	2		17 How's The Radio Know .... I Can Help	—	$4		RCA 64640
2/15/97	50	7		18 That's What Happens When I Hold You ..... Whole Lotta Love On The Line	—	$4		RCA 64770
4/26/97	65	4		19 A Door	—			album cut
				from the album *Greatest Hits...And Then Some* on RCA 67427				
8/8/98+	6	29		20 For You I Will .... S:3 Back When I Knew Everything	49	$4	★	Lyric Street 64023 (v)
1/30/99	17	20		21 I'm Leaving	87			album cut
6/5/99	33	18		22 Her	—			album cut
10/23/99	47	9		23 What This Country Needs	—			album cut
				above 3 from the album *What This Country Needs* on Lyric Street 65003				
5/27/00	❶²	33		24 Kiss This /	42			
1/13/01	17	21		25 People Like Us	107	$4		Lyric Street 11282
8/11/01	40	9		26 Always Was	—			album cut
				from the album *People Like Us* on Lyric Street 65014				
10/6/01+	2¹	23		27 Where The Stars And Stripes And The Eagle Fly		$4	★	Lyric Street 64059
				S:❶⁶ You've Got To Stand For Something	20			
12/22/01	52	4		28 Jingle Bell Rock .... [X]	—			album cut
				from the album *A December To Remember* on Lyric Street 165016				
				TODD, Dick '67				
9/2/67	52	6		Big Wheel Cannonball .... Return Of The Double Eagle	—	$8		Decca 32168
				DICK TODD With The Appalachian Wildcats				
				new lyrical version of Roy Acuff's "Wabash Cannonball"				
				TOLIVER, Tony '97				
				Born on 7/4/68 in Richards, Texas. Singer/songwriter/pianist.				
8/10/96	71	6		1 Bettin' Forever On You .... Louisiana Lonely	—	$4	■	Rising Tide 56040 (v)
1/18/97	67	2		2 He's On The Way Home .... Swinging Doors	—	$4		Rising Tide 56042
				TOMMY & DONNA '88				
11/26/88	72	6		Take It Slow With Me	—	$6		Oak 1067
				TOMORROW'S WORLD '90				
				All-star collaboration in honor of Earth Day: Lynn Anderson, Butch Baker, Shane Barmby, Billy Hill, Suzy Bogguss, Kix Brooks, T. Graham Brown, The Burch Sisters, Holly Dunn, Foster & Lloyd, Vince Gill, William Lee Golden, Highway 101, Shelby Lynne, Johnny Rodriguez, Dan Seals, Les Taylor, Pam Tillis, Mac Wiseman and Kevin Welch.				
5/5/90	74	1		Tomorrow's World .... (instrumental)	—	$4		Warner 4069
				TOMPALL — see GLASER BROTHERS				
				TOPEL & WARE '87				
				Duo of Michael Topel and James Ware.				
10/24/87	93	3		Change Of Heart	—	$6		RCI 2406
				TOROK, Mitchell '53				
				Born on 10/28/29 in Houston. Singer/songwriter/guitarist.				
8/22/53	❶²	24		1 Caribbean .... J:❶² / S:4 / A:5 Weep Away	—	$30		Abbott 140
				an alternate recording by Torok became a #27 Pop hit in 1959 on Guyden 2018 ($15)				
1/23/54	9	3		2 Hootchy Kootchy Henry (From Hawaii) .... J:9 Gigolo	—	$30		Abbott 150
2/18/67	73	3		3 Instant Love .... I Let The Hurts Put Me In The Driver's Seat	—	$10		Reprise 0541
				TOUCH OF COUNTRY '88				
11/12/88	85	3		1 I Won't Be Seeing Her No More .... Long Talk With Myself	—	$5		OL 127
7/15/89	87	3		2 Did I Leave My Heart At Your House	—	$5	■	OL 130
				TOUPS, Wayne, & Zydecajun '99				
				Born on 10/2/58 in Lafayette, Louisiana. Singer/songwriter/accordionist. Zydecajun: Wade Richard (guitar), Rick Lagneaux (keyboards), Mark Miller (bass) and Troy Gaspard (drums).				
3/6/99	66	5		Free Me	—			album cut
				from the album *More Than Just A Little* on BTM 0002				
				TRACTORS, The '94				
				Country-rock group from Tulsa, Oklahoma: Casey Van Beek (vocals; born on 12/1/42), Steve Ripley (guitar; born on 1/5/50), Walt Richmond (keyboards; born on 4/18/47), Ron Getman (bass; born on 12/13/48) and Jamie Oldaker (drums; born on 9/5/51).				
8/27/94	11	20		1 Baby Likes To Rock It .... Tulsa Shuffle	—	$4		Arista 12717
12/17/94	41	4		2 The Santa Claus Boogie .... Swingin' Home For Christmas [X]	91	$4	■	Arista 12771 (v)
12/31/94+	50	11		3 Tryin' To Get To New Orleans .... Doreen	—	$4		Arista 12784
12/16/95	43	5		4 Santa Claus Is Comin' (In A Boogie Woogie				
				Choo Choo Train) .... Santa Looked A Lot Like Daddy [X]	—	$4		Arista 12923
12/23/95	63	3		5 The Santa Claus Boogie .... Swingin' Home For Christmas [X-R]	—	$4	■	Arista 12771 (v)
10/4/97	75	1		6 The Last Time	—			album cut
				#9 Pop hit for The Rolling Stones in 1965; from the various artists album *Stone Country* on Beyond Music 3055				
12/27/97	65	3		7 Santa Claus Is Comin' (In A Boogie Woogie				
				Choo Choo Train) .... Santa Looked A Lot Like Daddy [X-R]	—	$4		Arista 12923
11/21/98	57	10		8 Shortenin' Bread .... How Long Will It Take	—	$4		Arista 13147
4/17/99	72	1		9 I Wouldn't Tell You No Lie	—			album cut
				from the album *Farmers In A Changing World* on Arista 18878				

DEBUT	PEAK	WKS	Gold	A-side (Chart Hit)	B-side	Pop	$	Pic	Label & Number
				TRADER-PRICE '89 Vocal group from Burns Flat, Oklahoma: brothers Dan, Chris and Erick Trader-Price, with Don Bell.					
8/12/89	55	7		1 Sad Eyes	Who's Gonna Know	—	$4		Universal 66022
				#1 Pop hit for Robert John in 1979					
12/23/89+	64	4		2 Lately Rose	Hideaway	—	$4		Universal 66031
				TRAMMELL, Bobby Lee '72 Born in Jonesboro, Arkansas.					
5/27/72	52	9		Love Isn't Love (Till You Give It Away)	Tell Me That You Love Me	—	$7		Souncot 1135
	★307★			**TRASK, Diana** '74 Born on 6/23/40 in Warburton, Australia. Singer/pianist. 1)Lean It All On Me 2)Say When 3)When I Get My Hands On You					
6/22/68	70	4		1 Lock, Stock And Tear Drops	Precious Time	—	$7		Dial 4077
11/23/68	59	6		2 Hold What You've Got	This Heart Was Made For Lovin'	—	$6		Dot 17160
				#5 Pop hit for Joe Tex in 1965					
8/30/69	58	4		3 Children	The Staying Kind	—	$6		Dot 17286
11/29/69+	37	7		4 I Fall To Pieces	Long Ago Is Gone	114	$6		Dot 17316
3/28/70	38	9		5 Beneath Still Waters	Heartbreak Hotel	—	$6		Dot 17342
7/31/71	59	9		6 The Chokin' Kind	Let's Keep Her Free (America)	—	$6		Dot 17384
				#13 Pop hit for Joe Simon in 1969					
1/22/72	30	14		7 We've Got To Work It Out Between Us	I Keep It Hid	—	$6		Dot 17404
7/15/72	33	12		8 It Meant Nothing To Me	How Much Have I Hurt Thee	—	$6		Dot 17424
3/3/73	15	13		9 Say When	Old Southern Cotton Town	—	$6		Dot 17448
7/7/73	20	13		10 It's A Man's World (If You Had A Man Like Mine) ...	World Of The Missing	—	$6		Dot 17467
12/8/73+	16	15		11 When I Get My Hands On You	Shadow Of My Man	—	$6		Dot 17486
3/30/74	13	13		12 Lean It All On Me	The King	101	$6		Dot 17496
8/17/74	32	10		13 (If You Wanna Hold On) Hold On To Your Man	Loneliness	—	$6		Dot 17520
1/11/75	21	14		14 Oh Boy	Alone Again Naturally	—	$5		ABC/Dot 17536
6/28/75	82	5		15 There Has To Be A Loser	Sunshine	—	$5		ABC/Dot 17555
11/29/75	99	2		16 Cry	I Can Take A Little Heartache	—	$5		ABC/Dot 17587
				#1 Pop hit for Johnnie Ray in 1951					
6/13/81	62	6		17 This Must Be My Ship	—	—	$6		Kari 121
9/19/81	74	3		18 Stirrin' Up Feelings	Give My Heart A Break	—	$6		Kari 123
	★223★			**TRAVIS, Merle** '46 Born on 11/29/17 in Rosewood, Kentucky. Died on 10/20/83 (age 65). Singer/songwriter/guitarist. Father of **Tom Bresh**. Acted in the movie From Here To Eternity. Regular on TV's Hometown Jamboree and Town Hall Party. Elected to the Country Music Hall of Fame in 1977. 1)Divorce Me C.O.D. 2)So Round, So Firm, So Fully Packed 3)Cincinnati Lou					
6/8/46	2⁴	11		1 Cincinnati Lou /	—	—			
6/15/46	3	9		2 No Vacancy	—	—	$20		Capitol 258
9/21/46	❶¹⁴	23		3 Divorce Me C.O.D. /	—	—			
1/11/47	5	2		4 Missouri	—	—	$20		Capitol 290
1/25/47	❶¹⁴	22		5 So Round, So Firm, So Fully Packed	Sweet Temptation	—	$20		Capitol 349
5/17/47	4	3		6 Steel Guitar Rag /	—	—			
5/24/47	4	4		7 Three Times Seven	—	—	$20		Capitol 384
11/1/47	4	2		8 Fat Gal /	—	—			
3/20/48	7	1		9 Merle's Boogie Woogie	—	—	$20		Capitol Amer. 40026
8/28/48	11	3		10 Crazy Boogie	J:11 / S:12 I'm A Natural Born Gamblin' Man	—	$20		Capitol 15143
2/5/49	13	1		11 What A Shame	J:13 Dapper Dan	—	$20		Capitol 15317
6/4/55	5	9		12 Wildwood Flower	J:5 / A:13 Breakin' In Another Heart [I]	—	$20		Capitol 3106
				HANK THOMPSON and His Brazos Valley Boys with MERLE TRAVIS					
7/30/66	44	4		13 John Henry, Jr.	That Same Ol' Natural Urge	—	$10		Capitol 5657
	★52★			**TRAVIS, Randy** '89 Born **Randy Traywick** on 5/4/59 in Marshville, North Carolina. Singer/songwriter/guitarist/actor. Married his manager, Lib Hatcher, on 5/31/91. Joined the Grand Ole Opry in 1986. Acted in several movies and TV shows. CMA Awards: 1986 Horizon Award; 1987 & 1988 Male Vocalist of the Year. Also see **Same Old Train**. 1)Hard Rock Bottom Of Your Heart 2)Forever And Ever, Amen 3)Look Heart, No Hands 4)I Told You So 5)It's Just A Matter Of Time					
1/6/79	91	4		1 She's My Woman	(instrumental)	—	$20		Paula 431
				RANDY TRAYWICK					
8/31/85	67	12		2 On The Other Hand	Can't Stop Now	—	$4		Warner 28962
12/28/85+	6	24		3 1982	S:4 / A:7 Reasons I Cheat	—	$4		Warner 28828
4/26/86	❶¹	23		4 On The Other Hand	S:❶² / A:❶¹ Can't Stop Now [R]	—	$4		Warner 28962
8/16/86	❶¹	21		5 Diggin' Up Bones	S:❶¹ / A:❶¹ There'll Always Be A Honky Tonk Somewhere	—	$4		Warner 28649
12/13/86+	2²	21		6 No Place Like Home	A:2 / S:4 Send My Body	—	$4		Warner 28525
4/25/87	❶³	22		7 Forever And Ever, Amen	S:❶² / A:16 Promises	—	$4	■	Warner 28384
				CMA Award: Single of the Year					
8/29/87	❶¹	22		8 I Won't Need You Anymore (Always And Forever)	S:❶¹ Tonight I'm Walkin' Out On The Blues	—	$4		Warner 28246
12/12/87+	❶¹	19		9 Too Gone Too Long	S:3 My House	—	$4	■	Warner 28286
4/9/88	❶²	18		10 I Told You So	S:❶² Good Intentions	—	$4	■	Warner 27969

DEBUT	PEAK	WKS	Gold	A-side (Chart Hit)	B-side	Pop	$	Pic	Label & Number
				TRAVIS, Randy — Cont'd					
7/30/88	❶[1]	17		11 Honky Tonk Moon	S:❶[2] Young Guns	—	$4	■	Warner 27833
11/19/88+	❶[1]	18		12 Deeper Than The Holler	S:2 It's Out Of My Hands	—	$4	■	Warner 27689
3/11/89	❶[1]	17		13 Is It Still Over?	Here In My Heart	—	$4		Warner 27551
7/1/89	17	15		14 Promises	Written In Stone	—	$4		Warner 22917
9/23/89	❶[1]	26		15 It's Just A Matter Of Time	This Day Was Made For Me And You	—	$4	■	Warner 22841
				#3 Pop hit for Brook Benton in 1959					
1/27/90	❶[4]	26		16 Hard Rock Bottom Of Your Heart	When Your World Was Turning For Me	—	$4		Warner 19935
5/12/90	2[2]	21		17 He Walked On Water	Card Carryin' Fool	—	$4	∎	Warner 19878 (v)
9/8/90	8	20		18 A Few Ole Country Boys	Smokin' The Hive	—	$4	∎	Warner 19586 (v)
				RANDY TRAVIS & GEORGE JONES					
2/2/91	3	20		19 Heroes And Friends	Shopping For Dresses	—	$4		Warner 19469
5/4/91	3	20		20 Point Of Light	Waiting On The Light To Change (w/B.B. King)	61[S]	$4		Warner 19283
8/24/91	49	8		21 We're Strangers Again	If You Were The Friend (Wynette)	—	$4	∎	Epic 73958 (v)
				TAMMY WYNETTE with Randy Travis					
9/28/91	❶[1]	20		22 Forever Together	This Day Was Made For Me And You	—	$4		Warner 19158
12/21/91+	2[3]	20		23 Better Class Of Losers	I'm Gonna Have A Little Talk	—	$4		Warner 19069
4/4/92	20	20		24 I'd Surrender All	Let Me Try	—	$4		Warner 18943
8/15/92	❶[1]	20		25 If I Didn't Have You	I Told You So	—	$4		Warner 18792
11/21/92+	❶[2]	20		26 Look Heart, No Hands	The Heart To Climb The Mountain	—	$4		Warner 18709
4/10/93	21	20		27 An Old Pair Of Shoes	Promises	—	$4		Warner 18616
9/4/93	46	8		28 Cowboy Boogie		—			album cut
				from the album *Wind In The Wire* on Warner 45319					
12/25/93+	65	6		29 Wind In The Wire	Down At The Old Corral	—	$4		Warner 18274
3/12/94	2[1]	20		30 Before You Kill Us All	The Box	—	$4	∎	Warner 18208 (v)
6/11/94	❶[1]	20		31 Whisper My Name	Oscar The Angel	—	$4	∎	Warner 18153 (v)
10/22/94	5	20		32 This Is Me	Gonna Walk That Line	—	$4	∎	Warner 18062 (v)
2/11/95	7	20		33 The Box	Honky Tonk Side Of Town	—	$4		Warner 17970
6/15/96	24	17		34 Are We In Trouble Now	Nobody's Home	—	$4		Warner 17619
10/5/96	25	20		35 Would I	Don't Take Your Love Away From Me	—	$4		Warner 17494
2/22/97	60	4		36 Price To Pay	I Wish It Would Rain	—	$4		Warner 17382
4/26/97	51	15		37 King Of The Road		—			album cut
				from the album *Full Circle* on Warner 46328					
3/7/98	2[1]	20		38 Out Of My Bones	S:7 Brinks Truck	64	$4	∎	DreamWor. 59007 (v)
6/13/98	9	20		39 The Hole	S:14 (same version)	105	$4	∎	DreamWorks 59010
10/10/98+	2[1]	21		40 Spirit Of A Boy - Wisdom Of A Man		42			album cut
3/6/99	16	20		41 Stranger In My Mirror		81			album cut
				above 2 from the album *You And You Alone* on DreamWorks 50034					
8/14/99	16	20		42 A Man Ain't Made Of Stone		82			album cut
1/29/00	48	10		43 Where Can I Surrender		—			album cut
4/29/00	54	10		44 A Little Left Of Center		—			album cut
8/19/00	68	1		45 I'll Be Right Here Loving You		—			album cut
				above 4 from the album *A Man Ain't Made Of Stone* on DreamWorks 450119					
12/23/00	75	1		46 Down With The Old Man (Up With The New)		—			album cut
				from the album *Inspirational Journey* on Warner 47893					
10/27/01	59	2		47 America Will Always Stand	S:4 Point Of Light	10[S]	$4	★	Relentless 51372
	★288★			**TREVINO, Rick** '97					
				Born Ricardo Trevino on 5/16/71 in Austin, Texas. Singer/songwriter/guitarist.					
				1)Running Out Of Reasons To Run 2)Learning As You Go 3)She Can't Say I Didn't Cry					
9/18/93	44	20		1 Just Enough Rope	A Quarter At A Time	—	$4	∎	Columbia 77159 (v)
2/12/94	35	19		2 Honky Tonk Crowd	Un Momento Alla (For A Moment There)	—	$4	∎	Columbia 77373 (v)
6/4/94	3	20		3 She Can't Say I Didn't Cry	She Just Left Me Lounge	—	$4	∎	Columbia 77535 (v)
10/8/94+	5	20		4 Doctor Time	What I'll Know Then	—	$4	∎	Columbia 77708 (v)
2/11/95	43	12		5 Looking For The Light	Life Can Turn On A Dime	—	$4	∎	Columbia 77820 (v)
5/6/95	6	20		6 Bobbie Ann Mason	S:6 San Antonio Rose To You	—	$4	∎	Columbia 77903 (v)
9/9/95	45	11		7 Save This One For Me		—			album cut
				from the album *Looking For The Light* on Columbia 66771					
6/1/96	2[2]	20		8 Learning As You Go	I'm Here For You	—	$4		Columbia 78329
10/26/96+	❶[1]	22		9 Running Out Of Reasons To Run	See Rock City	—	$4	∎	Columbia 78331 (v)
3/22/97	7	22		10 I Only Get This Way With You		—			album cut
9/27/97	44	8		11 See Rock City		—			album cut
				above 2 from the album *Learning As You Go* on Columbia 67452					
8/15/98	52	9		12 Only Lonely Me	You Were, You Are, You'll Always Be	—	$4	∎	Columbia 78895 (v)
				TREVOR, Van '66					
				Born on 11/12/40 in Lewiston, Maine. Singer/songwriter/producer.					
4/23/66	22	18		1 Born To Be In Love With You	It's So Good To Be Loved	—	$15		Band Box 367
11/19/66+	27	13		2 Our Side	When You've Lost Your Baby	—	$15		Band Box 371
9/9/67	26	15		3 You've Been So Good To Me	Sunday Morning	—	$8		Date 1565
4/27/68	31	11		4 Take Me Along With You	Guitar	—	$8		Date 1594
2/1/69	42	9		5 The Things That Matter	Band Of Gold	—	$6		Royal American 280
5/10/69	56	7		6 A Man Away From Home	I've Got Today To Live For	—	$6		Royal American 283
6/13/70	42	8		7 Luziana River	Sweet Diana	—	$6		Royal American 9
1/23/71	54	6		8 Wish I Was Home Instead	Did I Have A Good Time	—	$6		Royal American 23

DEBUT	PEAK	WKS	Gold	A-side (Chart Hit)	B-side	Pop	$	Pic	Label & Number
				TRIBBLE, Mark '89					
				Born in Starkville, Mississippi. Singer/songwriter/bassist.					
5/6/89	86	2		Lay Me Down Carolina	—		$6		Paloma 5
				TRICK PONY '01					
				Trio formed in Nashville: Heidi Newfield (vocals), Keith Burns (guitar, vocals) and Ira Dean (bass, vocals).					
10/21/00+	12	28		1 Pour Me .... S:2 *If You Think You've Got Trouble*		71	$4	★	Warner 16816 (v)
5/5/01	4	33		2 On A Night Like This .... S:3 *Pour Me (acoustic version)*		47	$4	★	Warner 16751 (v)
				TRIGGS, Trini '98					
				Born on 8/8/65 in Natchitoches, Louisiana. Black male singer.					
9/5/98	47	16		1 Straight Tequila /	.... S:17	—			
1/30/99	53	19		2 Horse To Mexico		—	$4	■	Curb 73066 (v)
2/26/00	62	3		3 The Wreckin' Crew		—			album cut
				TRINITY, Bobby '77					
8/27/77	95	2		I Love Everything I Get My Hands On	—		$7		GRT 128
				TRINITY LANE '88					
				Trio of singer/songwriters: Tom Grant, Allen Estes and Sharon Anderson.					
4/23/88	75	4		1 For A Song .... *Don't Put It Past My Heart*		—	$4		Curb 10507
8/13/88	70	3		2 Someday, Somenight .... *Indian Eyes*		—	$4		Curb 10511
11/5/88	90	2		3 Ready To Take That Ride .... *How Can I Pull Myself Together*		—	$4		Curb 10515
				TRIPP, Allen '82					
				Born in Fort Worth, Texas.					
3/20/82	39	11		Love Is .... *Lady Sorrow*		—	$6		Nashville 1001
				TRITT, Travis ★77★ '91					
				Born James Travis Tritt on 2/9/63 in Marietta, Georgia. Singer/songwriter/guitarist. Began singing in Atlanta nightclubs in 1981. Joined the *Grand Ole Opry* in 1992. Married model Theresa Nelson on 4/12/97. CMA Award: 1991 Horizon Award. Also see **Hope** and **Same Old Train**.					
				1)Anymore 2)Can I Trust You With My Heart 3)Best Of Intentions 4)Help Me Hold On 5)Foolish Pride					
9/2/89	9	26		1 Country Club .... *Sign Of The Times*		—	$4		Warner 22882
2/24/90	**❶**¹	26		2 Help Me Hold On .... *All I'll Ever Be*		—	$4	■	Warner 19918 (v)
6/16/90	2¹	21		3 I'm Gonna Be Somebody .... *The Road Home*		—	$4	■	Warner 19797 (v)
9/22/90	28	18		4 Put Some Drive In Your Country .... *If I Were A Drinker*		—	$4	■	Warner 19715 (v)
2/16/91	3	20		5 Drift Off To Dream .... *Son Of The New South*		—	$4		Warner 19431
6/1/91	2¹	20		6 Here's A Quarter (Call Someone Who Cares) .... *If Hell Had A Jukebox*		—	$4		Warner 19310
9/14/91	**❶**²	20		7 Anymore .... *It's All About To Change*		—	$4		Warner 19190
11/23/91+	2¹	20		8 The Whiskey Ain't Workin' .... *Bible Belt* (Tritt)		—	$4		Warner 19097
				TRAVIS TRITT Featuring Marty Stuart					
3/7/92	4	20		9 Nothing Short Of Dying /		—			
5/9/92	72	3		10 Bible Belt		—	$4		Warner 18984
				TRAVIS TRITT featuring Little Feat					
				from the movie *My Cousin Vinny* starring Joe Pesci					
6/6/92	7	20		11 This One's Gonna Hurt You (For A Long, Long Time) ..... *The King Of Dixie*		—	$4		MCA 54405
				MARTY STUART AND TRAVIS TRITT					
8/29/92	5	20		12 Lord Have Mercy On The Working Man .... *(album version)*		—	$4		Warner 18779
				Brooks & Dunn, T. Graham Brown, George Jones, Little Texas, Dana McVicker, Tanya Tucker and Porter Wagoner (guest vocals)					
12/5/92+	**❶**²	20		13 Can I Trust You With My Heart .... *A Hundred Years From Now*		—	$4		Warner 18669
12/12/92+	13	20		14 T-R-O-U-B-L-E .... *(single version)*		108	$4	■	Warner 18496 (v)
7/17/93	11	20		15 Looking Out For Number One .... *Blue Collar Man*		—	$4	■	Warner 18463 (v)
10/30/93+	21	22		16 Take It Easy .... *I Wish I Could Go Back Home*		—	$4		Warner 18240
				#12 Pop hit for the **Eagles** in 1972					
10/30/93	30	17		17 Worth Every Mile		—			album cut
				from the album *T-R-O-U-B-L-E* on Warner 45058					
4/23/94	**❶**¹	20		18 Foolish Pride .... *No Vacation From The Blues*		112	$4	■	Warner 18180 (v)
8/6/94	22	16		19 Ten Feet Tall And Bulletproof .... *(acoustic version)*		—	$4	■	Warner 18104 (v)
11/26/94+	11	20		20 Between An Old Memory And Me .... *Wishful Thinking*		71	$4	■	Warner 18003 (v)
4/15/95	2¹	20		21 Tell Me I Was Dreaming		—			album cut
				from the album *Ten Feet Tall And Bulletproof* on Warner 45603					
8/19/95	7	20		22 Sometimes She Forgets /		—			
1/20/96	51	8		23 Only You (And You Alone)		—	$4		Warner 17792
				#5 Pop hit for The Platters in 1955					
4/20/96	23	20		24 Honky Tonkin's What I Do Best .... *Me & Hank & Jumpin' Jack Flash*		—	$4		MCA 55197
				MARTY STUART & TRAVIS TRITT					
7/27/96	3	20		25 More Than You'll Ever Know .... S:6 *Still In Love With You*		110	$4	■	Warner 17606 (v)
11/23/96+	6	20		26 Where Corn Don't Grow /					
4/19/97	24	20		27 She's Going Home With Me		—	$4		Warner 17451
1/25/97	29	20	●	28 Here's Your Sign (Get The Picture) ...... S:**❶**⁸ *Things Have Changed* [C]		43	$4	■	Warner 17491 (v)
				BILL ENGVALL with Travis Tritt					
7/26/97	18	20		29 Helping Me Get Over You		—			album cut
				TRAVIS TRITT Featuring Lari White					
11/22/97+	23	20		30 Still In Love With You		—			album cut (v)
				first released as the B-side of #25 above; above 2 from the album *The Restless Kind* on Warner 46304					

DEBUT	PEAK	WKS	Gold	A-side (Chart Hit)	B-side	Pop	$	Pic	Label & Number
				TRITT, Travis — Cont'd					
8/29/98	29	20		31 If I Lost You	S:3 *Start The Car*	86	$4	★	Warner 17152 (v)
1/2/99	38	17		32 No More Looking Over My Shoulder	S:19 *Girls Like That*	—	$4	★	Warner 17108 (v)
4/10/99	52	10		33 Start The Car		—		★	album cut (v)
				#71 Pop hit for Jude Cole in 1992; from the album *No More Looking Over My Shoulder* on Warner 47097; first released as the B-side of #31 above					
10/9/99	66	4		34 Move It On Over		—			album cut
				TRAVIS TRITT With George Thorogood from the animated TV series *King Of The Hill* (soundtrack on Elektra 62441)					
7/1/00	●¹	34		35 Best Of Intentions	S:4 *Southbound Train*	27	$4	★	Columbia 79404 (v)
12/16/00+	2⁴	37		36 It's A Great Day To Be Alive	*Best Of Intentions*	33	$4		Columbia 79563
6/16/01	2³	32		37 Love Of A Woman		39			album cut
				from the album *Down The Road I Go* on Columbia 62165					

TUBB, Ernest ★18★   '49

Born on 2/9/14 in Crisp, Texas. Died of emphysema on 9/6/84 (age 70). Singer/songwriter/guitarist. Known as "The Texas Troubadour." Joined the *Grand Ole Opry* in 1943. Acted in the movies *Fighting Buckaroo*, *Hollywood Barn Dance*, *Ridin' West* and *Jamboree*. Broadcast from his own Ernest Tubb Record Shop in Nashville beginning in 1947. Elected to the Country Music Hall of Fame in 1965. Father of **Justin Tubb**.

1) Soldier's Last Letter 2) It's Been So Long Darling 3) Goodnight Irene 4) Rainbow At Midnight 5) Slipping Around

DEBUT	PEAK	WKS		A-side	B-side	Pop	$	Label & Number
1/8/44	2³	17		1 Try Me One More Time	*That's When It's Comin' Home To You*	15	$20	Decca 6093
5/27/44	●⁴	29		2 Soldier's Last Letter /		16		
6/3/44	4	3		3 Yesterday's Tears		23	$20	Decca 6098
3/31/45	3	14		4 Tomorrow Never Comes /		—		
3/17/45	6	1		5 Keep My Mem'ry In Your Heart		—	$20	Decca 6106
8/4/45	3	8		6 Careless Darlin'	*Are You Waiting Just For Me*	—	$20	Decca 6110
11/17/45	●⁴	13		7 It's Been So Long Darling	*Should I Come Back Home To You*	—	$20	Decca 6112
11/16/46+	●²	20		8 Rainbow At Midnight	*I Don't Blame You*	—	$20	Decca 46018
11/16/46	2⁴	12		9 Filipino Baby /		—		
12/21/46	5	2		10 Drivin' Nails In My Coffin		—	$20	Decca 46019
5/17/47	4	6		11 Don't Look Now (But Your Broken Heart Is Showing) /		—		
6/28/47	5	1		12 So Round, So Firm, So Fully Packed		—	$20	Decca 46040
7/19/47	4	1		13 I'll Step Aside	*There's Gonna Be Some Changes Made Around Here*	—	$20	Decca 46041
5/15/48	5	14		14 Seaman's Blues	S:5 / J:8 *Waiting For A Train*	—	$20	Decca 46119
7/17/48	15	1		15 You Nearly Lose Your Mind	J:15 *I Ain't Goin' Honky Tonkin' Anymore*	—	$20	Decca 46125
8/7/48	5	13		16 Forever Is Ending Today /	S:5 / J:6	30		
9/4/48	9	6		17 That Wild And Wicked Look In Your Eye	J:9	—	$20	Decca 46134
12/11/48+	2¹	17		18 Have You Ever Been Lonely? (Have You Ever Been Blue) /	J:2 / S:9	—		
12/11/48+	5	17		19 Let's Say Goodbye Like We Said Hello	S:5 / J:6	—	$20	Decca 46144
3/19/49	4	9		20 Till The End Of The World /	J:4 / S:11	—		
5/7/49	15	1		21 Daddy, When Is Mommy Coming Home	J:15	—	$20	Decca 46150
4/9/49	2¹	16		22 I'm Bitin' My Fingernails And Thinking Of You /	J:2 / S:4	30		
				ANDREWS SISTERS and ERNEST TUBB with The Texas Troubadors				
4/16/49	6	5		23 Don't Rob Another Man's Castle	J:6 / S:10	—	$20	Decca 24592
				ERNEST TUBB and ANDREWS SISTERS with The Texas Troubadors				
5/28/49	6	4		24 Mean Mama Blues	J:6 *Yesterday's Tears*	—	$20	Decca 46162
7/30/49	●¹	20		25 Slipping Around /	J:●¹ / S:4	17		
9/17/49	10	3		26 My Tennessee Baby	J:10	—	$20	Decca 46173
9/3/49	6	10		27 My Filipino Rose /	J:6 / S:11	—		
9/3/49	8	8		28 Warm Red Wine	S:8 / J:9	—	$20	Decca 46175
12/3/49	●¹	6		29 Blue Christmas /	J:●¹ / S:2 / A:2 [X]	23		
				Christmas standard popularized by **Elvis Presley** in 1957; also see #43 and #48 below				
12/24/49	7	1		30 White Christmas	J:7 / S:15 [X]	—	$20	Decca 46186
				#1 Pop hit for **Bing Crosby** in 1942				
12/31/49+	2²	10		31 Tennessee Border No. 2	S:2 / J:2	—		
				RED FOLEY and ERNEST TUBB				
1/21/50	7	2		32 Don't Be Ashamed Of Your Age	J:7 / A:9	—	$20	Decca 46200
				ERNEST TUBB and RED FOLEY				
2/4/50	2¹	17		33 Letters Have No Arms /	J:2 / A:3 / S:5	—		
2/25/50	8	1		34 I'll Take A Back Seat For You	J:8	—	$20	Decca 46207
2/25/50	2¹	20		35 I Love You Because /	J:2 / S:4 / A:6	—		
				#3 Pop hit for **Al Martino** in 1963				
3/18/50	8	2		36 Unfaithful One	J:8	—	$20	Decca 46213
6/24/50	3	15		37 Throw Your Love My Way /	A:3 / J:4 / S:5	—		
8/5/50	9	4		38 Give Me A Little Old Fashioned Love	J:9	—	$25	Decca 9-46243
8/12/50	●³	15		39 Goodnight Irene /	J:●³ / S:●² / A:2	10		
				RED FOLEY-ERNEST TUBB with The Sunshine Trio				
				#1 Pop hit for **Gordon Jenkins** & **The Weavers** in 1950				
9/2/50	9	2		40 Hillbilly Fever No. 2	J:9	—	$25	Decca 9-46255
				ERNEST TUBB-RED FOLEY				
10/28/50	10	2		41 You Don't Have To Be A Baby To Cry	J:10 *G-I-R-L Spells Trouble*	—	$25	Decca 9-46257
				#3 Pop hit for **The Caravelles** in 1963				
11/4/50	5	9		42 (Remember Me) I'm The One Who Loves You	J:5 / S:7 *I Need Attention Bad*	—	$25	Decca 9-46269
				#32 Pop hit for **Dean Martin** in 1965				

DEBUT	PEAK	WKS	Gold	A-side (Chart Hit)	B-side	Pop	$	Pic	Label & Number
				TUBB, Ernest — Cont'd					
12/30/50	9	1		43 Blue Christmas .... A:9 / J:10 White Christmas [X-R]		—	$25		Decca 9-46186
5/19/51	9	1		44 The Strange Little Girl .... J:9 Kentucky Waltz		—	$25		Decca 9-46311
				RED FOLEY and ERNEST TUBB with Anita Kerr Singers					
6/2/51	9	3		45 Don't Stay Too Long .... A:9 If You Want Some Lovin'		—	$25		Decca 9-46296
9/15/51	6	2		46 Hey La La .... J:6 Precious Little Baby		—	$25		Decca 9-46338
12/15/51	7	2		47 Driftwood On The River .... J:7 I'm Stepping Out Of The Picture		—	$25		Decca 9-46377
12/29/51	5	1		48 Blue Christmas .... A:5 White Christmas [X-R]		—	$25		Decca 9-46186
2/2/52	5	9		49 Too Old To Cut The Mustard .... S:5 / J:8 / A:10 I'm In Love With Molly		—	$25		Decca 9-46387
				ERNEST TUBB And RED FOLEY					
2/9/52	3	11		50 Missing In Action .... S:3 / A:5 / J:9 A Heartsick Soldier On Heartbreak Ridge		—	$20		Decca 9-46389
5/17/52	9	2		51 Somebody's Stolen My Honey .... J:9 / S:10 My Mother Must Have Been A Girl Like You		—	$20		Decca 9-28067
9/13/52	5	11		52 Fortunes In Memories .... J:5 / A:7 So Many Times		—	$20		Decca 9-28310
4/18/53	7	2		53 No Help Wanted #2 .... S:7 / J:9 You're A Real Good Friend		—	$20		Decca 28634
				ERNEST TUBB - RED FOLEY					
12/12/53	9	2		54 Divorce Granted .... J:9 Counterfeit Kisses		—	$20		Decca 28869
10/16/54	11	5		55 Two Glasses, Joe .... S:11 Journey's End		—	$20		Decca 29220
9/17/55	7	11		56 The Yellow Rose Of Texas .... A:7 / S:13 A Million Miles From Here		—	$15		Decca 29633
				#1 Pop hit for Mitch Miller in 1955					
12/17/55	7	4		57 Thirty Days (To Come Back Home) .... J:7 / A:10 Answer The Phone		—	$15		Decca 29731
				#2 R&B hit for Chuck Berry in 1955					
7/8/57	8	2		58 Mister Love .... A:8 Leave Me		—	$15		Decca 30305
				ERNEST TUBB and THE WILBURN BROTHERS					
4/28/58	13	4		59 House Of Glass .... A:13 Heaven Help Me		—	$15		Decca 30549
5/26/58	9	10		60 Hey, Mr. Bluebird .... A:9 / S:14 How Do We Know		—	$15		Decca 30610
				ERNEST TUBB And THE WILBURN BROTHERS					
10/20/58	8	11		61 Half A Mind /		—			
10/20/58	21	1		62 The Blues		—	$15		Decca 30685
1/5/59	19	3		63 What Am I Living For .... Goodbye Sunshine Hello Blues		—	$15		Decca 30759
5/4/59	12	13		64 I Cried A Tear .... I'd Rather Be		—	$15		Decca 30872
				#6 Pop hit for LaVern Baker in 1959					
9/28/59	14	14		65 Next Time .... What I Know About Her		—	$15		Decca 30952
9/5/60	16	7		66 Ev'rybody's Somebody's Fool .... Let The Little Girl Dance		—	$12		Decca 31119
6/5/61	16	9		67 Thoughts Of A Fool .... Don't Just Stand There		—	$12		Decca 31241
11/13/61	14	11		68 Through That Door .... What Will You Tell Them?		—	$12		Decca 31300
8/18/62	16	9		69 I'm Looking High And Low For My Baby /		—			
9/8/62	30	1		70 Show Her Lots Of Gold		—	$12		Decca 31399
6/22/63	28	1		71 Mr. Juke Box .... Walking The Floor Over You		—	$12		Decca 31476
9/28/63	3	23		72 Thanks A Lot .... The Way That You're Living		—	$10		Decca 31526
5/30/64	26	17		73 Be Better To Your Baby .... Think Of Me, Thinking Of You		—	$10		Decca 31614
7/25/64	11	23		74 Mr. And Mrs. Used To Be .... Love Was Right Here All The Time		—	$10		Decca 31643
				ERNEST TUBB AND LORETTA LYNN					
12/26/64+	15	17		75 Pass The Booze .... (A Memory) That's All You'll Ever Be To Me		—	$10		Decca 31706
3/6/65	29	12		76 Do What You Do Do Well .... Turn Around Walk Away		—	$10		Decca 31742
7/24/65	24	11		77 Our Hearts Are Holding Hands .... We're Not Kids Anymore		—	$10		Decca 31793
				ERNEST TUBB AND LORETTA LYNN					
10/23/65	34	7		78 Waltz Across Texas .... Lots Of Luck		—	$10		Decca 31824
				also see #90 below					
1/1/66	48	2		79 It's For God, And Country, And You Mom		—			
				(That's Why I'm Fighting In Viet Nam) .... After The Boy Gets The Girl			$10		Decca 31861
4/2/66	32	9		80 Till My Getup Has Gotup And Gone .... Just One More		—	$10		Decca 31908
				ERNEST TUBB and His Texas Troubadours (above 3)					
10/15/66	16	16		81 Another Story .... There's No Room In My Heart (For The Blues)		—	$10		Decca 32022
2/25/67	45	9		82 Sweet Thang .... Beautiful, Unhappy Home		—	$10		Decca 32091
				ERNEST TUBB AND LORETTA LYNN					
2/3/68	55	5		83 Too Much Of Not Enough .... Nothing Is Better Than You		—	$8		Decca 32237
7/20/68	69	2		84 I'm Gonna Make Like A Snake .... Mama, Who Was That Man?		—	$8		Decca 32315
				written by Loretta Lynn					
3/15/69	43	7		85 Saturday Satan Sunday Saint .... Tommy's Doll		—	$8		Decca 32448
6/14/69	18	10		86 Who's Gonna Take The Garbage Out .... Somewhere Between		—	$8		Decca 32496
				ERNEST TUBB And LORETTA LYNN					
7/21/73	93	2		87 I've Got All The Heartaches I Can Handle .... The Texas Troubadour		—	$6		MCA 40056
12/17/77+	79	7		88 Sometimes I Do /		—			
			7	89 Half My Heart's In Texas		—	$7		1st Generation 001
6/2/79	56	6		90 Waltz Across Texas .... Jealous Loving Heart [R]		—	$6		Cachet 4501
				ERNEST TUBB and Friends					
				Willie Nelson (guest vocal); new version of #78 above					
10/13/79	31	9		91 Walkin' The Floor Over You .... Let's Say Good-Bye Like We Said Hello		—	$6		Cachet 4507
				ERNEST TUBB & FRIENDS					
				Charlie Daniels and Merle Haggard (guest vocals); Tubb's classic hit, first recorded in 1941 on Decca 5958 ($20)					
				TUBB, Justin '54					
				Born on 8/20/35 in San Antonio, Texas. Died of a stomach aneurysm on 1/24/98 (age 62). Singer/songwriter/guitarist. Son of Ernest Tubb. Joined the Grand Ole Opry in 1955.					
7/3/54	4	21		1 Looking Back To See .... J:4 / S:5 / A:5 I Miss You So		—	$20		Decca 29145
				GOLDIE HILL - JUSTIN TUBB					
1/8/55	11	2		2 Sure Fire Kisses .... A:11 / S:13 Fickle Heart		—	$20		Decca 29349
				JUSTIN TUBB - GOLDIE HILL					
2/19/55	8	7		3 I Gotta Go Get My Baby .... A:8 Chuga-Chuga, Chica-Mauga (Choo-Choo Train)		—	$20		Decca 29401

DEBUT	PEAK	WKS	Gold	A-side (Chart Hit) .... B-side	Pop	$	Pic	Label & Number
				TUBB, Justin — Cont'd				
4/13/63	6	16		4 Take A Letter, Miss Gray .... Here I Sit A-Waitin'	—	$10	■	Groove 0017
10/2/65	23	9		5 Hurry, Mr. Peters .... We've Got A Lot In Common	—	$8		RCA Victor 8659
				JUSTIN TUBB & LORENE MANN				
				answer to "Yes, Mr. Peters" by Roy Drusky & Priscilla Mitchell				
7/30/66	44	2		6 We've Gone Too Far, Again .... Together But Still Alone	—	$8		RCA Victor 8834
				JUSTIN TUBB & LORENE MANN				
2/25/67	63	7		7 But Wait There's More .... The Second Thing I'm Gonna Do	—	$8		RCA Victor 9082
				TUCKER, Jerry Lee '88				
11/12/88	93	2		Livin' In Shadows	—	$6		Oak 1057
				TUCKER, Jimmy '80				
5/19/79	98	2		1 I'm Gonna Move to The Country (And Get Away To It All)	—	$5		Gar-Pax 2715
12/8/79	85	4		2 (You've Got That) Fire Goin' Again .... Somebody Loves Me	—	$5		NSD 35
4/5/80	82	3		3 The Reading Of The Will .... It's Not Easy Lovin' You	—	$5		NSD 40
				TUCKER, La Costa — see LA COSTA				
				TUCKER, Rick '89				
1/21/89	83	3		Honey I'm Just Walking Out The Door	—	$5		Oak 1066

TUCKER, Tanya ★33★   '88

Born on 10/10/58 in Seminole, Texas; raised in Wilcox, Arizona. Singer/songwriter/actress. Sister of **LaCosta**. Appeared on the *Lew King* TV series in Phoenix from 1969. Acted in the movies *Jeremiah Johnson* and *Hard Country*. CMA Award: 1991 Female Vocalist of the Year. Also see **Heart Of Nashville**.

1) What's Your Mama's Name   2) Would You Lay With Me (In A Field Of Stone)   3) Lizzie And The Rainman
4) Strong Enough To Bend   5) Just Another Love

DEBUT	PEAK	WKS		A-side .... B-side	Pop	$	Pic	Label & Number
5/13/72	6	17		1 Delta Dawn .... I Love The Way He Loves Me	72	$5	■	Columbia 45588
11/18/72+	5	15		2 Love's The Answer /	—			
		13		3 The Jamestown Ferry		$5		Columbia 45721
3/24/73	❶¹	17		4 What's Your Mama's Name .... Rainy Girl	86	$5		Columbia 45799
7/21/73	❶¹	16		5 Blood Red And Goin' Down .... The Missing Piece Of Puzzle	74	$5		Columbia 45892
1/12/74	❶¹	17		6 Would You Lay With Me (In A Field Of Stone) .... No Man's Land	46	$5		Columbia 45991
6/8/74	4	14		7 The Man That Turned My Mama On .... Satisfied With Missing You	86	$5		Columbia 46047
1/4/75	18	11		8 I Believe The South Is Gonna Rise Again .... Old Dan Tucker's Daughter	—	$5		Columbia 10069
4/26/75	❶¹	15		9 Lizzie And The Rainman .... Traveling Salesman	37	$5		MCA 40402
6/14/75	18	15		10 Spring .... Bed Of Roses	—	$5		Columbia 10127
8/23/75	❶¹	15		11 San Antonio Stroll .... The Serenade That We Played	—	$5		MCA 40444
11/8/75	23	10		12 Greener Than The Grass (We Laid On) .... Guess I'll Have To Love Him More	—	$5		Columbia 10236
12/13/75+	4	15		13 Don't Believe My Heart Can Stand Another You .... Depend On You	—	$5		MCA 40497
4/17/76	3	14		14 You've Got Me To Hold On To .... Ain't That A Shame	—	$5		MCA 40540
8/7/76	❶¹	15		15 Here's Some Love .... Pride Of Franklin County	82	$5		MCA 40598
12/25/76+	12	12		16 Ridin' Rainbows .... Short Cut	—	$5		MCA 40650
4/16/77	7	14		17 It's A Cowboy Lovin' Night .... Wings	—	$5		MCA 40708
7/23/77	40	8		18 You Are So Beautiful .... Almost Persuaded	—	$5		Columbia 10577
				#5 Pop hit for Joe Cocker in 1975				
8/13/77	16	11		19 Dancing The Night Away .... Let's Keep It That Way	—	$5		MCA 40755
6/10/78	86	3		20 Save Me .... Slippin' Away	105	$5	■	MCA 40902
11/25/78+	5	15		21 Texas (When I Die) .... Not Fade Away (Pop #70)	—	$5	■	MCA 40976
4/7/79	18	13		22 I'm The Singer, You're The Song .... Lover Goodbye (Pop #103)	—	$5		MCA 41005
8/23/80	10	14		23 Pecos Promenade .... The King Of Country Music	—	$5		MCA 41305
				from the movie *Smokey & The Bandit II* starring Burt Reynolds				
9/27/80	59	6		24 Dream Lover .... Bronco	—	$5		MCA 41323
				TANYA TUCKER AND GLEN CAMPBELL				
				#2 Pop hit for Bobby Darin in 1959				
12/20/80+	4	15		25 Can I See You Tonight .... Let Me Count The Ways	—	$5		MCA 51037
4/11/81	85	4		26 Why Don't We Just Sleep On It Tonight .... It's Your World	—	$5		Capitol 4986
				GLEN CAMPBELL and TANYA TUCKER				
4/25/81	40	8		27 Love Knows We Tried .... Somebody (Trying To Tell You Something)	—	$4		MCA 51096
7/4/81	50	7		28 Should I Do It .... Lucky Enough For Two	—	$4		MCA 51131
				#13 Pop hit for the Pointer Sisters in 1982				
10/17/81	83	4		29 Rodeo Girls .... Halfway To Heaven	—	$4		MCA 51184
11/27/82+	10	23		30 Feel Right /	—			
10/16/82	77	4		31 Cry		$4		Arista 0677
4/23/83	41	12		32 Changes .... Too Long	—	$4		Arista 1053
7/23/83	22	15		33 Baby I'm Yours .... I Don't Want You To Go	—	$4		Arista 9046
				#11 Pop hit for Barbara Lewis in 1965				
2/15/86	3	25		34 One Love At A Time .... S:3 / A:4 Fool, Fool Heart	—	$4	■	Capitol 5533
7/12/86	❶¹	24		35 Just Another Love .... S:❶¹ / A:❶¹ You Could Change My Mind	—	$4		Capitol 5604
11/8/86+	2¹	23		36 I'll Come Back As Another Woman .... S:❶¹ / A:2 Somebody To Care	—	$4		Capitol 5652
3/28/87	8	25		37 It's Only Over For You .... S:❶¹ / A:23 Girls Like Me	—	$4		Capitol 5694

XXX Long Black Train – Josh Turner WPCV & WBAR

DEBUT	PEAK	WKS	Gold	A-side (Chart Hit)	B-side	Pop	$	Pic	Label & Number
				TUCKER, Tanya — Cont'd					
7/25/87	2²	25		38 Love Me Like You Used To	S:0² If I Didn't Love You	—	$4	■	Capitol 44036
11/21/87+	0¹	24		39 I Won't Take Less Than Your Love	S:2 Heartbreaker	—	$4		Capitol 44100
				TANYA TUCKER WITH PAUL DAVIS & PAUL OVERSTREET					
4/2/88	0¹	20		40 If It Don't Come Easy	S:5 I'll Tennessee You In My Dreams	—	$4		Capitol 44142
7/16/88	0¹	23		41 Strong Enough To Bend	S:5 Back On My Feet	—	$4		Capitol 44188
12/3/88+	2¹	19		42 Highway Robbery	Lonesome Town	—	$4		Capitol 44271
4/1/89	4	19		43 Call On Me	Daddy And Home	—	$4		Capitol 44348
7/22/89	27	15		44 Daddy And Home	Playing For Keeps	—	$4		Capitol 44401
10/28/89+	2²	26		45 My Arms Stay Open All Night	Love Me Like You Used To	—	$4		Capitol 44469
3/24/90	3	23		46 Walking Shoes	This Heart Of Mine	—	$4	■	Capitol 44520 (v)
6/23/90	6	21		47 Don't Go Out		—	$4		Capitol 44586 (v)
				TANYA TUCKER with T. Graham Brown					
10/20/90+	6	20		48 It Won't Be Me		—			album cut
2/23/91	12	20		49 Oh What It Did To Me		—			album cut
				above 2 from the album Tennessee Woman on Capitol 91821					
6/22/91	2¹	20		50 Down To My Last Teardrop		—			album cut
				from the album What Do I Do With Me on Capitol 95562					
10/12/91+	2¹	20		51 (Without You) What Do I Do With Me	Oh What It Did To Me	—	$4		Capitol 44774
2/15/92	3	20		52 Some Kind Of Trouble	Oh What It Did To Me	—	$4		Liberty 57703
5/30/92	4	20		53 If Your Heart Ain't Busy Tonight	Down To My Last Teardrop	—	$4		Liberty 57768
9/26/92	2¹	20		54 Two Sparrows In A Hurricane	Danger Ahead	—	$4		Liberty 56825
1/16/93	2²	20		55 It's A Little Too Late	Cadillac Ranch	112	$4	■	Liberty 56953 (v)
4/17/93	4	20		56 Tell Me About It	What Do They Know	—	$4		Liberty 56985
				TANYA TUCKER with Delbert McClinton					
10/9/93	2¹	20		57 Soon	Sneaky Moon	—	$4		Liberty 17594
11/20/93	75	2		58 Already Gone		—			album cut
				#32 Pop hit for the Eagles in 1974; from the various artists album Common Thread: Songs Of The Eagles on Giant 24531					
1/15/94	11	20		59 We Don't Have To Do This	Silence Is King	—	$4		Liberty 17803
5/28/94	4	20		60 Hangin' In	Let The Good Times Roll	—	$4		Liberty 17908
9/17/94	20	19		61 You Just Watch Me	I Love You Anyway	—	$4		Liberty 18135
2/11/95	27	15		62 Between The Two Of Them	Love Will	—	$4		Liberty 18485
5/27/95	40	11		63 Find Out What's Happenin'		—			album cut
				from the album Fire To Fire on Liberty 28943					
3/1/97	9	20		64 Little Things	S:9 Two Sparrows In A Hurricane (C&W #2/'92)	114	$4	■	Capitol 58630 (v)
7/19/97	45	11		65 Ridin' Out The Heartache	I Don't Believe That's How You Feel	—	$4		Capitol 19628
				TURNER, Grant '64					
				Born Jesse Granderson Turner on 5/17/12 in Abilene, Texas. Died on 10/19/91 (age 79). Dean of the Grand Ole Opry announcers from 1945. Elected to the Country Music Hall of Fame in 1981.					
10/24/64	48	1		The Bible In Her Hand	Lord Don't Let Me Down	—	$15		Chart 1130
	★383★			**TURNER, Mary Lou** '76					
				Born on 6/13/47 in Hazard, Kentucky; raised in Dayton, Ohio.					
				1) Sometimes 2) That's What Made Me Love You 3) Where Are You Going, Billy Boy					
7/6/74	94	2		1 All That Keeps Me Goin'	I'll Always Be Your Woman If You'll Always Be My Man	—	$5		MCA 40244
1/25/75	85	7		2 Come On Home	Tomorrow	—	$5		MCA 40343
11/29/75+	0¹	16		3 Sometimes	Circle In A Triangle	—	$5		MCA 40488
				BILL ANDERSON and MARY LOU TURNER					
3/27/76	7	12		4 That's What Made Me Love You	Can We Still Be Friends	—	$5		MCA 40533
				BILL ANDERSON and MARY LOU TURNER					
6/12/76	25	12		5 It's Different With You	Old Habits Are Hard To Break	—	$5		MCA 40566
10/2/76	30	10		6 Love It Away	Must You Throw Dirt In My Face	—	$5		MCA 40620
2/5/77	40	9		7 Cheatin' Overtime	I Never Have The Time	—	$5		MCA 40674
6/4/77	93	3		8 The Man Still Turns Me On	Maybe It's Time To Start	—	$5		MCA 40727
7/16/77	18	12		9 Where Are You Going, Billy Boy	Sad Ole Shade Of Gray	—	$5		MCA 40753
				BILL ANDERSON and MARY LOU TURNER					
12/10/77+	73	7		10 He Picked Me Up When You Let Me Down	Man Can't Live By Bed Alone	—	$5		MCA 40828
1/28/78	25	10		11 I'm Way Ahead Of You	Just Enough To Make Me Want It All	—	$5		MCA 40852
				BILL ANDERSON & MARY LOU TURNER					
8/4/79	78	4		12 Yours And Mine	You Can't Remember, And I Can't Forget	—	$5	■	Churchill 7741
10/20/79	81	4		13 Caught With My Feelings Down /		—			
		2		14 You Can't Remember And I Can't Forget		—	$5		Churchill 7744
2/9/80	91	2		15 I Wanna Love You Tonight	If You Cross That Bridge	—	$5		Churchill 7751
				TURNER, Zeb '51					
				Born William Grishaw on 6/23/15 in Lynchburg, Virginia. Died of cancer on 1/10/78 (age 62). Singer/songwriter/guitarist.					
9/17/49	11	1		1 Tennessee Boogie	J:11 A Drunkard's Confession	—	$25		King 790
4/21/51	8	2		2 Chew Tobacco Rag	J:8 A:9 No More Nothin'	—	$30		King 45-950
				TURNER NICHOLS '94					
				Duo of South Carolina native Zack Turner and Missouri native Tim Nichols. Formed songwriting partnership in 1988.					
8/14/93	51	13		1 Moonlight Drive-In	Anything	—	$4		BNA 62577
12/11/93+	49	11		2 She Loves To Hear Me Rock	Harleys And Horses	—	$4		BNA 62708

DEBUT	PEAK	WKS	Gold	A-side (Chart Hit)	B-side	Pop	$	Pic	Label & Number

TUTTLE, Wesley '45
Born on 12/13/17 in Lamar, Colorado. Singer/songwriter/guitarist. Acted in several western movies. Married actress Marilyn Myers.

You have 5-CD KIT

WESLEY TUTTLE And His Texas Stars:

DEBUT	PEAK	WKS		#	A-side	B-side	Pop	$	Label & Number
10/6/45	●⁴	14		1	With Tears In My Eyes	Too Little Too Late	—	$15	Capitol 216
3/9/46	3	4		2	Detour /		—		
					#5 Pop hit for **Patti Page** in 1951				
3/16/46	5	2		3	I Wish I Had Never Met Sunshine	—		$15	Capitol 233
7/20/46	4	5		4	Tho' I Tried (I Can't Forget You)	When You Cry (You Cry Alone)		$15	Capitol 267
11/20/54	15	1		5	Never	S:15 Friendly Love		$20	Capitol 2850

MARILYN & WESLEY TUTTLE

TWAIN, Shania ★139★ '96
Born Eileen Regina Edwards on 8/28/65 in Windsor, Ontario; raised in Timmins, Ontario. Adopted the name Shania which means "I'm on my way" in the Ojibwa Indian language. Managed by **Mary Bailey** in the late 1980s. Married rock producer Robert John "Mutt" Lange on 12/28/93. CMA Award: 1999 Entertainer of the Year.

1) Love Gets Me Every Time 2) (If You're Not In It For Love) I'm Outta Here! 3) You Win My Love 4) Any Man Of Mine
5) Honey, I'm Home

DEBUT	PEAK	WKS		#	A-side	B-side	Pop	$	Label & Number
3/27/93	55	18		1	What Made You Say That	Crime Of The Century	—	$4	Mercury 864992 (v)
7/3/93	55	11		2	Dance With The One That Brought You	When He Leaves You	—	$4	Mercury 862346 (v)
1/14/95	11	20		3	Whose Bed Have Your Boots Been Under?		87		album cut (v)
5/13/95	●²	20	●	4	Any Man Of Mine	S:●¹⁰ Whose Bed Have Your Boots Been Under?	31	$4	Mercury 856448 (v)
8/12/95	14	20		5	The Woman In Me (Needs The Man In You)		90		album cut
					from the album *The Woman In Me* on Mercury 522886; later released as the B-side of #6 below				
11/18/95+	●²	20		6	(If You're Not In It For Love) I'm Outta Here!	S:●¹ The Woman In Me (Needs The Man In You)	74	$4	Mercury 852206 (v)
					also see #11 below				
2/24/96	●²	20		7	You Win My Love	S:2 Home Ain't Where His Heart Is (Anymore)	108	$4	Mercury 852138 (v)
5/11/96	●¹	20		8	No One Needs To Know	Leaving Is The Only Way Out	—	$4	Mercury 852986
8/10/96	28	14		9	Home Ain't Where His Heart Is (Anymore)	S:19 Whose Bed Have Your Boots Been Under?	—	$4	Mercury 578384 (v)
11/30/96+	48	9		10	God Bless The Child	S:●¹ If It Don't Take Two	75	$4	Mercury 578748 (v)
12/28/96+	15ˢ	14		11	(If You're Not In It For Love) I'm Outta Here!	God Bless The Child [R]	—	$4	Mercury 578786
					remix of #6 above				
10/4/97	●⁵	20	●	12	Love Gets Me Every Time	S:2 (dance mix)	25	$4	Mercury 568062 (v)
11/15/97+	6	20		13	Don't Be Stupid (You Know I Love You)	S:2 If It Don't Take Two	40	$4	Mercury 568242 (v)
11/15/97+	6	32		14	From This Moment On		4		album cut
					SHANIA TWAIN with Bryan White				
11/15/97	66	2		15	Honey, I'm Home		—		album cut
					also see #19 below				
11/15/97	70	1		16	Man! I Feel Like A Woman!		—		album cut
					also see #21 below				
11/15/97	74	1		17	Come On Over		—		album cut
					also see #23 below; above 4 from the album *Come On Over* on Mercury 536003				
1/24/98	●¹	24	▲	18	You're Still The One	S:●²² Don't Be Stupid (You Know I Love You) (remix)	2⁹	$4	Mercury 568452 (v)
8/8/98	●¹	24		19	Honey, I'm Home /	S:●⁵ [R]	—		
12/12/98+	8	20		20	That Don't Impress Me Much		7		Mercury 566220 (v)
3/13/99	4	19		21	Man! I Feel Like A Woman!	[R]	23		album cut (v)
					later released as the B-side of #23 below				
6/19/99	13	20		22	You've Got A Way		49		album cut
					above 2 from the album *Come On Over* on Mercury 536003				
9/11/99	6	19		23	Come On Over	Man! I Feel Like A Woman [R]	58	$4	Mercury 172123
1/15/00	30	17		24	Rock This Country!	I'm Holdin' On To Love (To Save My Life)	—	$4	Mercury 562582
7/8/00	17	21		25	I'm Holdin' On To Love (To Save My Life)		102		album cut (v)
					from the album *Come On Over* on Mercury 536003; first released as the B-side of #24 above				

TWISTER ALLEY '93
Group from area of Arkansas known as "Twister Alley": Shellee Morris (vocals), Amy Hitt, Steve Goins, Lance Blythe, Randy Loyd and Kevin King.

DEBUT	PEAK	WKS		#	A-side	B-side	Pop	$	Label & Number
11/6/93	61	7		1	Nothing In Common But Love	Redneck Ways (In The U.S.A.)	—	$4	Mercury 862846 (v)
3/12/94	70	4		2	Young Love		—		album cut
					#1 Pop hit for **Tab Hunter** in 1957; from the album *Twister Alley* on Mercury 514927				

TWITTY, Conway ★4★ '79

Born Harold Lloyd Jenkins on 9/1/33 in Friars Point, Mississippi; raised in Helena, Arkansas. Died of an abdominal aneurysm on 6/5/93 (age 59). Singer/songwriter/guitarist. Father of **Joni Lee** and **Jessica James**. Uncle of **Larry Jenkins**. Changed name in 1957 (borrowed from Conway, Arkansas and Twitty, Texas). Acted in the movies *Sexpot Goes To College* and *College Confidential*. Charted 20 pop hits from 1957-76. Owned the Twitty City tourist complex in Hendersonville, Tennessee. CMA Awards: 1972, 1973, 1974 & 1975 Vocal Duo of the Year (with **Loretta Lynn**). Elected to the Country Music Hall of Fame in 1999.

1) Hello Darlin' 2) You've Never Been This Far Before 3) Happy Birthday Darlin'
4) She Needs Someone To Hold Her (When She Cries) 5) Touch The Hand

DEBUT	PEAK	WKS Gold	#	A-side (Chart Hit)	B-side	Pop $	Pic	Label & Number
3/26/66	18	12	1	Guess My Eyes Were Bigger Than My Heart	Honky Tonk Man	— $8		Decca 31897
9/17/66	36	10	2	Look Into My Teardrops	If You Were Mine To Lose	— $8		Decca 31983
2/18/67	21	14	3	I Don't Want To Be With Me	Before I'll Set Her Free	— $8		Decca 32081
7/8/67	32	12	4	Don't Put Your Hurt In My Heart	Walk Me To The Door	— $8		Decca 32147
12/9/67	61	4	5	Funny (But I'm Not Laughing)	Working Girl	— $8		Decca 32208
3/23/68	5	18	6	The Image Of Me	Dim Lights, Thick Smoke (And Loud, Loud Music)	— $7		Decca 32272
8/17/68	❶¹	17	7	Next In Line	I'm Checking Out	— $7		Decca 32361
12/28/68+	❷²	17	8	Darling, You Know I Wouldn't Lie	Table In The Corner	— $7		Decca 32424
5/10/69	❶¹	17	9	I Love You More Today	Bad Girl	— $7		Decca 32481
9/20/69	❶¹	14	10	To See My Angel Cry	I Did The Best I Could (With What I Had)	— $7		Decca 32546
1/3/70	3	14	11	That's When She Started To Stop Loving You	I'll Get Over Losing You	— $7		Decca 32599
4/25/70	❶⁴	20	12	Hello Darlin'	Girl At The Bar	60 $7		Decca 32661
10/10/70	❶¹	18	13	Fifteen Years Ago	Up Comes The Bottle (Down Goes The Man)	81 $7		Decca 32742
2/6/71	❶²	14	14	After The Fire Is Gone — CONWAY TWITTY/LORETTA LYNN	The One I Can't Live Without	56 $7		Decca 32776
2/6/71	59	6	15	What Am I Living For	I'll Try	— $7		MGM 14205
				#26 Pop hit for Twitty in 1960 on MGM 12886				
3/20/71	❶¹	17	16	How Much More Can She Stand	Just Like A Stranger	105 $7		Decca 32801
7/17/71	4	14	17	I Wonder What She'll Think About Me Leaving	Heartache Just Walked In	112 $7		Decca 32842
				written by Merle Haggard				
9/11/71	50	10	18	What A Dream	Long Black Train	— $7		MGM 14274
				#106 Pop hit for Twitty in 1960 on MGM 12918				
10/2/71	❶¹	17	19	Lead Me On — LORETTA LYNN AND CONWAY TWITTY	Four Glass Walls	— $7		Decca 32873
12/4/71+	4	16	20	I Can't See Me Without You	I Didn't Lose Her (I Threw Her Away)	— $7		Decca 32895
4/1/72	❶¹	15	21	(Lost Her Love) On Our Last Date	I'll Never Make It Home Tonight	112 $7		Decca 32945
7/29/72	❶¹	15	22	I Can't Stop Loving You	Since She's Not With The One She Loves	— $7		Decca 32988
12/2/72+	❶²	15	23	She Needs Someone To Hold Her (When She Cries)	This Road That I Walk	— $7		Decca 33033
3/31/73	2¹	14	24	Baby's Gone	Dim Lonely Places	— $6		MCA 40027
6/23/73	❶¹	14	25	Louisiana Woman, Mississippi Man — LORETTA LYNN/CONWAY TWITTY	Living Together Alone	— $6		MCA 40079
7/21/73	❶³	19	26	You've Never Been This Far Before	You Make It Hard (To Take The Easy Way Out)	22 $6		MCA 40094
1/19/74	❶¹	15	27	There's A Honky Tonk Angel (Who'll Take Me Back In)	Don't Let It Go To Your Heart	— $6		MCA 40173
5/11/74	3	15	28	I'm Not Through Loving You Yet	Before Your Time	— $6		MCA 40224
6/15/74	❶¹	15	29	As Soon As I Hang Up The Phone — LORETTA LYNN/CONWAY TWITTY	A Lifetime Before	— $6		MCA 40251
8/24/74	❶²	17	30	I See The Want To In Your Eyes	Girl From Tupelo	— $6		MCA 40282
1/11/75	❶¹	14	31	Linda On My Mind	She's Just Not Over You Yet	61 $6		MCA 40339
5/24/75	❶²	13	32	Touch The Hand /		—		
8/16/75	4	13	33	Don't Cry Joni — Joni Lee (guest vocal)		63 $6		MCA 40407
6/21/75	❶¹	16	34	Feelins' — LORETTA LYNN/CONWAY TWITTY	You Done Lost Your Baby	— $6		MCA 40420
12/6/75+	❶¹	14	35	This Time I've Hurt Her More Than She Loves Me	She Did-It Did-I Didn't	— $6		MCA 40492
4/3/76	❶¹	13	36	After All The Good Is Gone	I Got A Good Thing Going	— $6		MCA 40534
6/19/76	3	12	37	The Letter — LORETTA LYNN/CONWAY TWITTY	God Bless America Again	— $6		MCA 40572
8/21/76	❶¹	13	38	The Games That Daddies Play	There's More Love In The Arms You're Leaving	— $6		MCA 40601
11/20/76+	❶¹	14	39	I Can't Believe She Gives It All To Me	I Can't Help It If She Can't Stop Loving Me	— $6		MCA 40649
3/5/77	❶¹	16	40	Play, Guitar Play	One In A Million	— $6		MCA 40682
6/4/77	2³	14	41	I Can't Love You Enough — LORETTA LYNN/CONWAY TWITTY	The Bed I'm Dreaming On	— $6		MCA 40728
7/23/77	❶¹	15	42	I've Already Loved You In My Mind	I've Changed My Mind	— $6		MCA 40754
10/29/77	3	15	43	Georgia Keeps Pulling On My Ring	Talkin' 'Bout You	— $6		MCA 40805
2/18/78	16	10	44	The Grandest Lady Of Them All	I'm Used To Losing You	— $6		MCA 40857
6/24/78	6	11	45	From Seven Till Ten /		—		
		9	46	You're The Reason Our Kids Are Ugly — LORETTA LYNN/CONWAY TWITTY (above 2)		— $6		MCA 40920
7/15/78	2¹	14	47	Boogie Grass Band	That's All She Wrote	— $6		MCA 40929
11/18/78+	3	15	48	Your Love Had Taken Me That High	My Woman Knows	— $5		MCA 40963
3/17/79	❶¹	14	49	Don't Take It Away	Draggin' Chains	— $5		MCA 41002
7/14/79	❶¹	15	50	I May Never Get To Heaven	Grand Ole Blues	— $5		MCA 41059
10/27/79	❶³	14	51	Happy Birthday Darlin'	Heavy Tears	— $5		MCA 41135

DEBUT	PEAK	WKS	Gold	A-side (Chart Hit) .... B-side	Pop	$	Pic	Label & Number
				TWITTY, Conway — Cont'd				
11/10/79+	9	14		52 You Know Just What I'd Do /	—			
		14		53 The Sadness Of It All	—	$5		MCA 41141
				CONWAY TWITTY/LORETTA LYNN (above 2)				
2/2/80	❶¹	13		54 I'd Love To Lay You Down *She Thinks I Still Care*	—	$4		MCA 41174
5/10/80	5	15		55 It's True Love *Hit The Road Jack*	—	$4		MCA 41232
				CONWAY TWITTY & LORETTA LYNN				
6/28/80	6	13		56 I've Never Seen The Likes Of You *Soulful Woman*	—	$4		MCA 41271
10/18/80+	3	17		57 A Bridge That Just Won't Burn *You'll Be Back (Every Night In My Dreams)*	—	$4		MCA 51011
1/31/81	7	15		58 Lovin' What Your Lovin' Does To Me *Silent Partner*	—	$4		MCA 51050
				CONWAY TWITTY & LORETTA LYNN				
2/21/81	❶¹	14		59 Rest Your Love On Me /	—			
		12		60 I Am The Dreamer (You Are The Dream)	—	$4		MCA 51059
5/30/81	2²	18		61 I Still Believe In Waltzes *Oh Honey - Oh Babe*	—	$4		MCA 51114
				CONWAY TWITTY & LORETTA LYNN				
7/11/81	❶¹	16		62 Tight Fittin' Jeans *I Made You A Woman*	—	$4		MCA 51137
10/31/81+	❶¹	18		63 Red Neckin' Love Makin' Night *Hearts*	—	$4		MCA 51199
1/30/82	❶¹	17		64 The Clown *The Boy Next Door*	—	$4	■	Elektra 47302
4/24/82	❶²	16		65 Slow Hand *When Love Was Something Else*	—	$4		Elektra 47443
				#2 Pop hit for the **Pointer Sisters** in 1981				
5/8/82	69	7		66 Over Thirty (Not Over The Hill) ....*Love Salvation*	—	$4		MCA 52032
9/18/82	2²	18		67 We Did But Now You Don't *A Good Love Died Tonight*	—	$4		Elektra 69964
12/25/82+	❶¹	19		68 The Rose *It's Only Make Believe*	—	$4	■	Elektra 69854
				#3 Pop hit for Bette Midler in 1980				
4/2/83	44	11		69 We Had It All ....*Cheatin' Fire*	—	$4		MCA 52154
5/28/83	2²	21		70 Lost In The Feeling *You've Never Been This Far Before*	—	$4		Warner 29636
				Ricky Skaggs (backing vocal)				
9/24/83	6	19		71 Heartache Tonight *Hello Darlin'*	—	$4		Warner 29505
				#1 Pop hit for the **Eagles** in 1979				
12/24/83+	7	18		72 Three Times A Lady *I Think I'm In Love*	—	$4		Warner 29395
				#1 Pop hit for the **Commodores** in 1978				
4/14/84	❶¹	19		73 Somebody's Needin' Somebody *(Lying Here With) Linda On My Mind*	—	$4		Warner 29308
7/28/84	❶¹	19		74 I Don't Know A Thing About Love (The Moon Song) *S:❶¹/A:❶¹ Don't Cry Joni*	—	$4		Warner 29227
				Joni Lee (guest vocal)				
11/10/84+	❶¹	21		75 Ain't She Somethin' Else *A:❶¹/S:2 The Games That Daddies Play*	—	$4		Warner 29137
3/16/85	❶¹	20		76 Don't Call Him A Cowboy *S:❶¹/A:❶¹ After All The Good Is Gone*	—	$4		Warner 29057
7/6/85	3	19		77 Between Blue Eyes And Jeans *S:3/A:3 Baby's Gone*	—	$4		Warner 28966
10/26/85	19	18		78 The Legend And The Man ....*S:16/A:21 (I Can't Believe) She Gives It All To Me*	—	$4		Warner 28866
3/1/86	26	14		79 You'll Never Know How Much I Needed You Today *A:24/S:29 Fifteen Years Ago*	—	$4		Warner 28772
6/7/86	❶¹	21		80 Desperado Love *S:❶²/A:❶¹ I Can't See Me Without You*	—	$4		Warner 28692
10/18/86+	2¹	25		81 Fallin' For You For Years *A:2/S:3 I'll Try*	—	$4		Warner 28577
3/7/87	2²	23		82 Julia *S:3/A:4 Everybody Needs A Hero*	—	$4		MCA 53034
7/11/87	2¹	24		83 I Want To Know You Before We Make Love *S:2 Snake Boots*	—	$4		MCA 53134
11/14/87+	6	23		84 That's My Job *S:8 Lonelytown*	—	$4		MCA 53200
4/9/88	7	19		85 Goodbye Time *S:11 Your Loving Side*	—	$4		MCA 53276
8/6/88	9	19		86 Saturday Night Special *S:8 If You Were Mine To Lose*	—	$4		MCA 53373
11/26/88+	4	23		87 I Wish I Was Still In Your Dreams *S:30 If You Were Mine To Lose*	—	$4		MCA 53456
4/22/89	2¹	25		88 She's Got A Single Thing In Mind *Too White To Sing The Blues*	—	$4		MCA 53633
8/26/89	19	15		89 House On Old Lonesome Road ....*Nobody Can Fill Your Shoes*	—	$4		MCA 53688
12/9/89+	51	12		90 Who's Gonna Know *Private Part Of My Heart*	—	$4		MCA 53759
4/14/90	30	14		91 Fit To Be Tied Down ....*When You're Cool (The Sun Shines All The Time)*	—	$4		MCA 79000
9/8/90	2²	20		92 Crazy In Love *Heart's Breakin' All Over Town*	—	$4		MCA 79067
1/5/91	3	20		93 I Couldn't See You Leavin' *Just The Thought Of Losing You*	—	$4		MCA 53983
5/4/91	57	9		94 One Bridge I Didn't Burn *I'm Tired Of Being Something*	—	$4		MCA 54077
8/24/91	22	20		95 She's Got A Man On Her Mind ....*You Put It There*	—	$4		MCA 54186
12/7/91+	56	9		96 Who Did They Think He Was ....*Let The Pretty Lady Dance*	—	$4		MCA 54281
8/14/93	62	5		97 I'm The Only Thing (I'll Hold Against You) ....*Final Touches*	—	$4		MCA 54716
				TWO HEARTS '85				
				Duo of sisters from Burbank, Oklahoma: Jama and Cathy Bowen.				
11/23/85	63	8		1 Two Hearts Can't Be Wrong	—	$5	■	MDJ 5831
8/2/86	77	5		2 Feel Like I'm Falling For You ....*All Wrapped Up In Your Love*	—	$5	■	MDJ 5832
				TYLER, Bonnie '78				
				Born Gaynor Hopkins on 6/8/53 in Swansea, Wales. Pop singer.				
4/15/78	10	15	●	1 It's A Heartache *It's About Time*	3	$5		RCA 11249
2/24/79	86	3		2 My Guns Are Loaded ....*Baby I Just Love You*	107	$5		RCA 11468
				TYLER, Kris '98				
				Born in Omaha, Nebraska. Female singer. Worked as a TV news producer at KNXV in Phoenix.				
4/12/97	68	5		1 Keeping Your Kisses ....*Rockin' Horse*	—	$4	■	Rising Tide 56045 (v)
11/8/97+	45	16		2 What A Woman Knows ....*A Thousand Tears Ago*	—	$4	■	Rising Tide 56051 (v)

DEBUT	PEAK	WKS	Gold	A-side (Chart Hit)	B-side	Pop	$	Pic	Label & Number
	★375★			**TYLER, "T" Texas** '48 Born David Luke Myrick on 6/20/16 in Mena, Arkansas. Died of cancer on 1/23/72 (age 55). Singer/songwriter/guitarist. Known as "The Man With A Million Friends." Acted in the movie *Horseman of The Sierras*. Hosted own *Range Round-Up* TV series in Los Angeles.					
8/24/46	5	1		1 Filipino Baby .... *You Were Only Teasing Me*		—	$20		4 Star 1009
				"T" TEXAS TYLER and his Oklahoma Melody Boys					
4/10/48	2¹	13		2 Deck Of Cards .... *S:2 / J:3 Ida Red* [S]		—	$20		4 Star 1228
7/3/48	10	2		3 Dad Gave My Dog Away .... *S:10 / J:13 Beautiful Life*		—	$20		4 Star 1248
9/25/48	9	4		4 Memories Of France / *J:9*					4 Star 1249
11/13/48	11	1		5 Honky Tonk Gal *J:11*		—	$20		
11/26/49	4	5		6 My Bucket's Got A Hole In It .... *J:4 / A:8 Cry-Baby Heart*		—	$20		4 Star 1383
4/18/53	5	15		7 Bumming Around .... *S:5 / J:5 Jealous Love*		—	$20		Decca 28579
7/17/54	3	19		8 Courtin' In The Rain .... *A:3 / J:4 Old Blue*		—	$20		4 Star 1660
				T. TEXAS TYLER and His Band					
				TYNDALL, Lynne '88 Born in Owensboro, Kentucky; raised in Nashville.					
11/14/87	67	5		1 Lovin' The Blue		—	$5		Evergreen 1060
5/14/88	62	6		2 This Is Me Leaving		—	$5		Evergreen 1071
11/5/88	83	4		3 Love's Slippin' Up On Me		—	$5		Evergreen 1079
6/10/89	74	3		4 I Promise		—	$5		Evergreen 1091

U

				ULISSE, Donna '91 Born in Hampton, Virginia.					
2/2/91	75	3		1 Things Are Mostly Fine .... *Legend In My Heart*		—	$4	■	Atlantic 87862 (v)
4/13/91	66	5		2 When Was The Last Time .... *Legend In My Heart*		—	$4		Atlantic 87739
				URBAN, Keith '01 Born on 10/26/67 in Caboolture, Queensland, Australia. Singer/songwriter. Former member of **The Ranch**. CMA Award: 2001 Horizon Award. Also see **America The Beautiful**.					
8/28/99+	18	25		1 It's A Love Thing .... *(same version)*		105	$4		Capitol 58799
2/26/00	4	34		2 Your Everything .... *If You Wanna Stay*		51	$4		Capitol 58847
10/7/00+	0¹	30		3 But For The Grace Of God .... *I Thought You Knew*		37	$4		Capitol 58877
4/14/01	3	27		4 Where The Blacktop Ends .... *Rollercoaster*		35	$4		Capitol 58992
				USA FOR AFRICA '85 All-star colaboration (USA: United Support of Artists) for starving people in Africa. Includes **Ray Charles**, **Kim Carnes**, **Willie Nelson**, **Lionel Richie** and **Kenny Rogers**.					
4/20/85	76	6	▲⁴	We Are The World .... *Grace (Quincy Jones)*		❶⁴	$4	■	Columbia 04839

V

				VALENTINO '81 Born Valentino Enrique Hernandez on 2/13/60 in Toledo, Ohio.					
8/1/81	62	6		She Took The Place Of You .... *You Belong To My Heart*		—	$4		RCA 12269
				VANCE, Vince, & The Valiants '99 Born Andrew Stone in New Orleans. The Valiants: Kate Carlin, Gerra Adkins, Chrislynn Lee and Lisa Layne.					
12/25/93	55	3		1 All I Want For Christmas Is You .... [X]		—			album cut
12/24/94	52	3		2 All I Want For Christmas Is You .... [X-R]		—			album cut
12/23/95	52	3		3 All I Want For Christmas Is You .... [X-R]		—			album cut
12/28/96	49	3		4 All I Want For Christmas Is You .... [X-R]		—			album cut
12/27/97	43	3		5 All I Want For Christmas Is You .... [X-R]		—			album cut
12/11/99	31	5		6 All I Want For Christmas Is You .... [X-R]		—			album cut
				all of above are the same version; from the album *All I Want For Christmas Is You* on Waldoxy 9289					
				VAN DYKE, Bruce '89 Born in 1953 in Medford, Oregon. Singer/songwriter/guitarist.					
5/6/89	94	1		1 It's All In The Touch		—	$5		Aria 51688
8/26/89	73	4		2 Hard-Headed Heart		—	$5	■	Aria 51689
	★260★			**VAN DYKE, Leroy** '61 Born on 10/4/29 in Spring Fork, Missouri. Singer/songwriter/guitarist. Acted in the movie *What Am I Bid*. 1)Walk On By 2)If A Woman Answers (Hang Up The Phone) 3)Auctioneer					
1/5/57	9	2		1 Auctioneer .... *A:9 / J:10 I Fell In Love With A Pony-Tail*		19	$20		Dot 15503
9/4/61	0¹⁹	37		2 Walk On By .... *My World Is Caving In*		5	$15		Mercury 71834
3/31/62	3	12		3 If A Woman Answers (Hang Up The Phone) ...... *A Broken Promise*		35	$12		Mercury 71926
12/29/62	16	7		4 Black Cloud .... *Five Steps*		—	$10		Mercury 72057
1/11/64	50	1		5 Happy To Be Unhappy .... *Now I Lay Me Down*		—	$10		Mercury 72198
				written by **Bobby Bare**					
2/29/64	45	3		6 Night People .... *Baby (Where Can You Be)*		—	$10	■	Mercury 72232
1/9/65	40	5		7 Anne Of A Thousand Days .... *Poor Guy*		—	$10		Mercury 72360
10/15/66	34	9		8 Roses From A Stranger .... *Before I Change My Mind*		—	$8		Warner 5841
4/15/67	66	4		9 I've Never Been Loved .... *Less Of Me*		—	$8		Warner 7001
1/6/68	23	11		10 Louisville .... *There's Always Tomorrow*		—	$8		Warner 7155

DEBUT	PEAK	WKS	Gold	A-side (Chart Hit)	B-side	Pop	$	Pic	Label & Number
				VAN DYKE, Leroy — Cont'd					
8/31/68	69	5		11 You May Be Too Much For Memphis, Baby	Road Of Love	—	$7		Kapp 931
11/1/69	56	4		12 Crack In My World	We'll Try A Little Bit Harder	—	$7		Kapp 2054
6/13/70	63	7		13 An Old Love Affair, Now Showing	Belle	—	$7		Kapp 2091
12/12/70	71	2		14 Mister Professor	People Gonna Turn You Off	—	$6		Decca 32756
9/18/71	62	5		15 I Get Lonely When It Rains	Party Girl	—	$6		Decca 32866
3/25/72	69	6		16 I'd Rather Be Wantin' Love	My Mind Is On You	—	$6		Decca 32933
4/26/75	79	6		17 Unfaithful Fools	What Will You Do Now, Mrs. Jones?	—	$5		ABC 12070
12/20/75+	75	7		18 Who's Gonna Run The Truck Stop In Tuba City When I'm Gone?	There Ain't No Roses In My Bed	—	$5		ABC/Dot 17597
4/23/77	77	6		19 Texas Tea	Las Vegas Girl	—	$5		ABC/Dot 17691
				VANWARMER, Randy '88 Born Randall Van Wormer on 3/30/55 in Indian Hills, Colorado. Singer/songwriter/guitarist.					
6/30/79	71	6	●	1 Just When I Needed You Most	Your Light	4	$5		Bearsville 0334
2/20/88	53	8		2 I Will Hold You	I'll Be On The Next Dream Home	—	$4		16th Avenue 70407
8/20/88	72	4		3 Where The Rocky Mountains Touch The Morning Sun	That's What Your Smile Does For Me	—	$4		16th Avenue 70418
				VASSAR, Phil '00 Born on 5/28/67 in Lynchburg, Virginia. Singer/songwriter.					
10/30/99+	5	34		1 Carlene later released as the B-side of #4 below		45			album cut (v)
6/10/00	❶¹	34		2 Just Another Day In Paradise /		35			
1/20/01	16	20		3 Rose Bouquet		78	$4		Arista Nashville 69037
6/2/01	9	20		4 Six-Pack Summer	Carlene	56	$4		Arista Nashville 69084
11/3/01+	3	32		5 That's When I Love You all of above from the album *Phil Vassar* on Arista Nashville 18891		37			album cut
				VASSY, Kin '82 Born Charles Kindred Vassy on 8/16/43 in Atlanta. Died of cancer on 6/15/94 (age 50). Former member of **The First Edition**.					
10/13/79	85	5		1 Do I Ever Cross Your Mind	Sometimes Love Is Better When It's Gone	—	$5		ia 501
3/8/80	67	6		2 Makes Me Wonder If I Ever Said Goodbye	Fort Worth Featherbed	—	$5		ia 502
7/5/80	88	4		3 There's Nobody Like You above 2 produced by **Kenny Rogers**; also released on United Artists 1368 in 1980	Nite Out	—	$5		ia 505
5/16/81	39	10		4 Likin' Him And Lovin' You	Hell And High Water	—	$4		Liberty 1407
8/15/81	48	8		5 Sneakin' Around	Lonely Hearts	—	$4		Liberty 1427
12/12/81+	21	14		6 When You Were Blue And I Was Green	A Honky Tonk Heart	—	$4		Liberty 1440
5/1/82	78	4		7 Cast The First Stone	Lonely Hearts	—	$4		Liberty 1458
8/21/82	59	8		8 Women In Love	Hell And High Water	—	$4		Liberty 1469
1/22/83	80	4		9 Tryin' To Love Two #10 Pop hit for William Bell in 1977	All For The Love Of A Girl	—	$4		Liberty 1488
				VAUGHN, Sammy '78 Born in Fort Worth, Texas. Singer/songwriter.					
8/19/78	67	5		1 This Time Around	Rodeo Bum	—	$6		Oak 105
2/10/79	98	1		2 Sunshine		—	$5		Alpine 100
				VAUGHN, Sharon '74 Singer/songwriter. Married Howard Bellamy (of the **Bellamy Brothers**) on 6/10/2002.					
4/27/74	39	11		1 Until The End Of Time NARVEL FELTS and SHARON VAUGHN	Someone To Give My Love To	—	$6		Cinnamon 793
8/10/74	96	4		2 Never A Night Goes By		—	$6		Cinnamon 799
12/6/75	99	2		3 You And Me, Me And You	The Time I've Had With You	—	$5		ABC/Dot 17590
				VAUS, Steve '92 Born in San Diego. Singer/songwriter/guitarist.					
8/8/92	68	2		We Must Take America Back	Never Had A Chance	—	$4	■	RCA 62308 (v)
				VEACH, Gail '87 Born on 10/24/54 in Bremerton, Washington.					
8/1/87	86	2		1 Would You Catch Me Baby (If I Fall For You)		—	$6		Prairie Dust 128
4/16/88	93	1		2 Deepest Shade Of Blue		—	$6		Choice 101
				VEGA, Ray '96 Born on 7/28/61 in Los Angeles; raised in El Paso, Texas. Singer/songwriter. Member of **The Vega Brothers**.					
11/16/96	56	12		Remember When	Maria	—	$4		BNA 64652
				VEGA BROTHERS, The '86 Duo of brothers from El Paso, Texas: Robert and **Ray Vega**.					
4/19/86	54	6		Heartache The Size Of Texas	New Woman	—	$4		MCA 52777
				VERA, Billy '87 Born William McCord on 5/28/44 in Riverside, California; raised in Westchester County, New York. Singer/songwriter. Acted in the movies *Buckaroo Banzai* and *The Doors*.					
1/24/87	42	13	●	1 At This Moment BILLY VERA & THE BEATERS recorded "live" in 1981	I Can Take Care Of Myself	❶²	$4		Rhino 74403
4/25/87	93	2		2 She Ain't Johnnie originally released on Midland Int'l. 44295 in 1977	My Girl Josephine	—	$4		Macola 9812

Howard Vokes?

DEBUT	PEAK	WKS	Gold	A-side (Chart Hit)	B-side	Pop	$	Pic	Label & Number
				VERNON, Kenny '70 Born on 7/19/40 in Jackson, Tennessee. Singer/songwriter/guitarist.					
10/1/66	48	2		1 It Makes You Happy (To Know You Make Me Blue)	Too Much Loving Turned Her Bad	—	$10		Caravan 123
				LaWANDA LINDSEY & KENNY VERNON:					
1/4/69	58	9		2 Eye To Eye	Looking Over Our Shoulders	—	$7		Chart 1063
3/21/70	27	14		3 Pickin' Wild Mountain Berries	We Don't Deserve Each Other	—	$6		Chart 5055
				#27 Pop hit for Peggy Scott & Jo Jo Benson in 1968					
9/19/70	51	9		4 Let's Think About Where We're Going	Puzzles Of My Mind	—	$6		Chart 5090
2/27/71	42	9		5 The Crawdad Song	Wrong Number	—	$6		Chart 5114
				KENNY VERNON:					
6/17/72	56	8		6 That'll Be The Day	I'd Go Right Back Again	—	$5		Capitol 3331
				#1 Pop hit for Buddy Holly in 1957					
1/13/73	55	6		7 Feel So Fine	Would You Settle For Roses	—	$5		Capitol 3506
6/9/73	66	3		8 Lady	What Kind Of Mood (Will She Be In Tonight)	—	$5		Capitol 3590
1/5/74	74	8		9 What Was Your Name Again?	Have I Ever Lied To You	—	$5		Capitol 3785
				VICKERY, Mack '77 Born on 6/8/38 in Town Creek, Alabama; raised in Adrianne, Michigan. Singer/prolific songwriter. Also recorded as **Atlanta James**.					
6/8/74	95	3		1 That Kind Of Fool	Starting All Over Again	—	$6		MCA 40233
				ATLANTA JAMES					
5/28/77	49	7		2 Ishabilly	Think It Over	—	$5		Playboy 5800
9/24/77	94	2		3 Here's To The Horses	When It Counted, You Could Never Count On Me	—	$5		Playboy 5814
				VINCENT, Gene '56 Born Vincent Eugene Craddock on 2/11/35 in Norfolk, Virginia. Died of an ulcer on 10/12/71 (age 36). Rock and roll singer/songwriter/guitarist.					
7/7/56	5	17		Be-Bop-A-Lula S:5 / J:5 / A:9	Woman Love	7	$50	●	Capitol 3450
				GENE VINCENT and His Blue Caps					
				VINCENT, Rick '93 Born in San Bernadino; raised in Bakersfield, California.					
12/12/92+	39	15		1 The Best Mistakes I Ever Made		—			album cut
5/22/93	69	4		2 Ain't Been A Train Through Here In Years		—			album cut
				above 2 from the album *A Wanted Man* on Curb 77586					
				VINTON, Bobby '70 Born Stanley Robert Vinton on 4/16/35 in Canonsburg, Pennsylvania. Charted 47 pop hits from 1962-80. Hosted own TV variety series from 1975-76.					
2/28/70	27	9		1 My Elusive Dreams	Over And Over	46	$6	■	Epic 10576
12/15/79	86	5		2 Make Believe It's Your First Time	I Remember Loving You	78	$5		Tapestry 002
7/2/83	87	3		3 You Are Love	Ghost Of Another Man	—	$5		Larc 81019
11/24/84	91	3		4 Bed Of Roses	I Know A Goodbye	—	$5		Tapestry 4009
12/24/88+	63	7		5 The Last Rose	Sealed With A Kiss	—	$4		Curb 10512
7/22/89	70	5		6 Please Tell Her That I Said Hello	Getting Used To Being Loved Again	—	$4		Curb 10541
				#84 Pop hit for Debbie Campbell in 1975					
11/11/89	64	8		7 It's Been One Of Those Days	(Now And Then There's) A Fool Such As I	—	$4		Curb 10560
				VON, Vicki Rae '87 ? Born in Marshalltown, Iowa; raised in Ankeny, Iowa.					
4/11/87	52	10		1 Not Tonight I've Got A Heartache	It's All Over But The Lying	—	$4		Atlantic Amer. 99471
7/25/87	53	9		2 Torn-Up	Hold Me Like You've Never Had Me	—	$4		Atlantic Amer. 99442

W

DEBUT	PEAK	WKS	Gold	A-side (Chart Hit)	B-side	Pop	$	Pic	Label & Number
				WADE, Norman '79 Born in Columbus, Georgia.					
11/17/79	97	2		1 I'm A Long Gone Daddy	Arms Of Someone Else	—	$6		NSD 29
				WAGON, Chuck, And The Wheels '00 Vocal trio: Chuck Wagon, Carl Pyle and Sid Sequin.					
6/3/00	75	1		1 Beauty's In The Eye Of The Beerholder		—			album cut
				from the album *Off The Top Rope* on Lyric Street 65613					
				WAGONEERS '88 Group from Austin, Texas: Monte Warden (vocals, guitar), Brent Wilson (guitar), Craig Allan Pettigrew (bass) and Thomas Lewis (drums).					
6/25/88	43	9		1 I Wanna Know Her Again	Stout And High	—	$4		A&M 1215
9/10/88	52	6		2 Every Step Of The Way	It'll Take Some Time	—	$4	■	A&M 1230
1/14/89	66	5		3 Help Me Get Over You	Please Don't Think I'm Guilty	—	$4	■	A&M 1261
6/24/89	53	7		4 Sit A Little Closer	Spare Time	—	$4	■	A&M 1435
				picture sleeve for above 3 are the same: sleeve has a center-cut hole with the artist name around it and a small photo of the group					

DEBUT	PEAK	WKS	Gold	A-side (Chart Hit)	B-side	Pop	$	Pic	Label & Number

WAGONER, Porter ★32★ '55
Born on 8/12/27 in West Plains, Missouri. Singer/songwriter/guitarist. Joined the *Grand Ole Opry* in 1957. Hosted own TV series from 1960-79. Co-host of TNN's *Opry Backstage*. CMA Awards: 1968 Vocal Group of the Year (with **Dolly Parton**); 1970 & 1971 Vocal Duo of the Year (with Dolly Parton). Also see **Heart Of Nashville** and **Some Of Chet's Friends**.

1) A Satisfied Mind 2) Misery Loves Company 3) Please Don't Stop Loving Me 4) The Carroll County Accident 5) Making Plans

DEBUT	PEAK	WKS	#	A-side	B-side	Pop	$	Label & Number
10/30/54+	7	12	1	Company's Comin'	A:7 Tricks Of The Trade	—	$20	RCA Victor 5848
5/28/55	❶⁴	33	2	A Satisfied Mind	A:❶⁴ / S:2 / J:2 Itchin' For My Baby	—	$15	RCA Victor 6105
12/3/55+	3	22	3	Eat, Drink, And Be Merry (Tomorrow You'll Cry)	S:3 / J:3 / A:5 Let's Squiggle	—	$15	RCA Victor 6289
3/31/56	8	11	4	What Would You Do? (If Jesus Came To Your House)	S:8 / A:14 How Can You Refuse Him Now	—	$15	RCA Victor 6421
5/26/56	14	4	5	Uncle Pen	A:14 How I've Tried	—	$15	RCA Victor 6494
				written by **Bill Monroe**				
11/17/56	11	2	6	Tryin' To Forget The Blues	A:11 I've Known You From Somewhere	—	$15	RCA Victor 6598
8/19/57	11	3	7	I Thought I Heard You Calling My Name	A:11 Pay Day	—	$15	RCA Victor 6964
5/4/59	29	1	8	Me And Fred And Joe And Bill	Out Of Sight Out Of Mind	—	$12	RCA Victor 7457
1/18/60	26	4	9	The Girl Who Didn't Need Love	Your Kind Of People	—	$12	RCA Victor 7638
10/31/60	26	1	10	Falling Again /		—		
10/31/60	30	1	11	An Old Log Cabin For Sale		—	$12	RCA Victor 7770
3/6/61	10	13	12	Your Old Love Letters	Heartbreak Affair	—	$12	RCA Victor 7837
1/13/62	❶²	29	13	Misery Loves Company	I Cried Again	—	$12	RCA Victor 7967
6/23/62	10	10	14	Cold Dark Waters	Ain't It Awful	—	$12	RCA Victor 8026
12/8/62+	7	15	15	I've Enjoyed As Much Of This As I Can Stand	One Way Ticket To The Blues	—	$12	RCA Victor 8105
6/22/63	20	7	16	My Baby's Not Here (In Town Tonight) /		—		
7/20/63	29	1	17	In The Shadows Of The Wine		—	$12	RCA Victor 8178
1/18/64	19	12	18	Howdy Neighbor Howdy	Find Out	—	$12	RCA Victor 8257
4/25/64	5	23	19	Sorrow On The Rocks	The Life Of The Party	—	$12	RCA Victor 8338
10/10/64	11	25	20	I'll Go Down Swinging	Country Music Has Gone To Town	—	$12	RCA Victor 8432
5/1/65	21	8	21	I'm Gonna Feed You Now	The Bride's Bouquet	—	$12	RCA Victor 8524
				also see #73 below				
7/31/65	4	19	22	Green, Green Grass Of Home	Dooley	—	$10	RCA Victor 8622
				#11 Pop hit for **Tom Jones** in 1967				
12/25/65+	3	17	23	Skid Row Joe	Love Your Neighbor	—	$10	RCA Victor 8723
5/7/66	21	12	24	I Just Came To Smell The Flowers	I'm A Long Way From Home	—	$10	RCA Victor 8800
11/5/66	48	4	25	Ole Slew-Foot	Let Me In	—	$10	RCA Victor 8977
				also see #72 below				
1/28/67	2¹	19	26	The Cold Hard Facts Of Life	You Can't Make A Heel Toe The Mark	—	$10	RCA Victor 9067
7/15/67	15	16	27	Julie	Try Being Lonely	—	$10	RCA Victor 9243
				written by **Waylon Jennings**				
12/2/67+	7	17	28	The Last Thing On My Mind	Love Is Worth Living	—	$10	RCA Victor 9369
				PORTER WAGONER/DOLLY PARTON				
12/16/67+	24	12	29	Woman Hungry	Out Of The Silence (Came A Song)	—	$10	RCA Victor 9379
4/13/68	7	16	30	Holding On To Nothin'	Just Between You And Me	—	$10	RCA Victor 9490
				PORTER WAGONER and DOLLY PARTON				
6/8/68	16	14	31	Be Proud Of Your Man	Wino	—	$10	RCA Victor 9530
7/27/68	5	13	32	We'll Get Ahead Someday /		—		
10/5/68	51	6	33	Jeannie's Afraid Of The Dark		—	$10	RCA Victor 9577
				PORTER WAGONER & DOLLY PARTON (above 2)				
11/9/68+	2⁴	21	34	The Carroll County Accident	Sorrow Overtakes The Wine	92	$8	RCA Victor 9651
3/8/69	9	14	35	Yours Love	Malena	—	$8	RCA Victor 0104
				DOLLY PARTON/PORTER WAGONER				
6/14/69	3	15	36	Big Wind	Tennessee Stud	—	$8	RCA Victor 0168
6/21/69	16	11	37	Always, Always	No Reason To Hurry Home	—	$8	RCA Victor 0172
				PORTER WAGONER AND DOLLY PARTON				
10/25/69	5	16	38	Just Someone I Used To Know	My Hands Are Tied	—	$8	RCA Victor 0247
				PORTER WAGONER and DOLLY PARTON				
11/15/69	21	11	39	When You're Hot You're Hot	The Answer Is Love	—	$8	RCA Victor 0267
2/14/70	9	15	40	Tomorrow Is Forever	Mendy Never Sleeps	—	$8	RCA Victor 9799
				PORTER WAGONER AND DOLLY PARTON				
3/14/70	41	5	41	You Got-ta Have A License	Fairchild	—	$8	RCA Victor 9802
4/4/70	43	9	42	Little Boy's Prayer	Roses Out Of Season	—	$8	RCA Victor 9811
8/1/70	7	15	43	Daddy Was An Old Time Preacher Man	A Good Understanding	—	$8	RCA Victor 9875
				PORTER WAGONER AND DOLLY PARTON				
9/26/70	41	9	44	Jim Johnson	One More Dime	—	$8	RCA Victor 9895
1/2/71	18	16	45	The Last One To Touch Me	The Alley	—	$8	RCA Victor 9939
2/27/71	7	13	46	Better Move It On Home	Two Of A Kind	—	$8	RCA Victor 9958
				PORTER WAGONER AND DOLLY PARTON				
5/8/71	15	13	47	Charley's Picture	Simple As I Am	116	$8	RCA Victor 9979
6/26/71	14	12	48	The Right Combination	The Pain Of Loving You	106	$8	RCA Victor 9994
				PORTER WAGONER AND DOLLY PARTON				
8/28/71	11	14	49	Be A Little Quieter	Watching	—	$7	RCA Victor 1007
11/13/71+	11	13	50	Burning The Midnight Oil	More Than Words Can Tell	—	$7	RCA Victor 0565
				PORTER WAGONER AND DOLLY PARTON				

DEBUT	PEAK	WKS	Gold	A-side (Chart Hit)...B-side	Pop	$	Pic	Label & Number
				WAGONER, Porter — Cont'd				
2/26/72	8	14		51 What Ain't To Be, Just Might Happen................................Little Bird	—	$7		RCA Victor 0648
4/8/72	9	14		52 Lost Forever In Your Kiss..The Fog Has Lifted	—	$7		RCA Victor 0675
				PORTER WAGONER AND DOLLY PARTON				
8/5/72	14	13		53 A World Without Music...Denise Mayree	—	$7		RCA Victor 0753
9/2/72	14	13		54 Together Always..Love's All Over	—	$7		RCA Victor 0773
				PORTER WAGONER AND DOLLY PARTON				
11/11/72	16	12		55 Katy Did..Darlin' Debra Jean	—	$7		RCA Victor 0820
3/3/73	30	9		56 We Found It..Love Have Mercy On Us	—	$7		RCA Victor 0893
				PORTER WAGONER AND DOLLY PARTON				
4/21/73	54	7		57 Lightening The Load..Tomorrow Is Forever	—	$7		RCA Victor 0923
6/23/73	3	17		58 If Teardrops Were Pennies..Come To Me	—	$7		RCA Victor 0981
				PORTER WAGONER AND DOLLY PARTON				
7/14/73	37	9		59 Wake Up, Jacob...Stella, Dear Sweet Stella	—	$7		RCA Victor 0013
12/15/73+	43	12		60 George Leroy Chickashea...Cassie	—	$7		RCA Victor 0187
3/30/74	46	9		61 Tore Down /	—			
			9	62 Nothing Between...	—	$7		RCA Victor 0233
7/27/74	15	13		63 Highway Headin' South...Freida	—	$7		RCA Victor 0328
8/3/74	❶[1]	17		64 Please Don't Stop Loving Me...Sounds Of Nature	—	$7		RCA Victor 10010
				PORTER WAGONER & DOLLY PARTON				
12/14/74+	19	12		65 Carolina Moonshiner...Not A Cloud In The Sky	—	$6		RCA Victor 10124
7/12/75	5	17		66 Say Forever You'll Be Mine...................How Can I (Help You Forgive Me)	—	$6		RCA Victor 10328
				PORTER WAGONER AND DOLLY PARTON				
11/8/75	96	2		67 Indian Creek..Thank You For The Happiness	—	$6		RCA Victor 10411
5/15/76	8	14		68 Is Forever Longer Than Always......................................If You Say I Can	—	$6		RCA Victor 10652
				PORTER WAGONER AND DOLLY PARTON				
11/13/76	66	5		69 When Lea Jane Sang...Storm Of Love	—	$5		RCA 10803
10/15/77	76	5		70 I Haven't Learned A Thing........................Hand Me Down My Walking Cane	—	$5		RCA 10974
				Merle Haggard (guest vocal)				
1/7/78	64	6		71 Mountain Music...A Natural Wonder	—	$5		RCA 11186
11/18/78+	31	11		72 Ole Slew-Foot /..[R]	—			
				new version of #25 above				
			11	73 I'm Gonna Feed 'Em Now..[R]	—	$5		RCA 11411
				new version of #21 above				
3/17/79	34	8		74 I Want To Walk You Home...Old Love Letters	—	$5		RCA 11491
8/11/79	32	9		75 Everything I've Always Wanted.......................................No Bed Of Roses	—	$5		RCA 11671
12/22/79+	64	7		76 Hold On Tight..Someone Just Like You	—	$5		RCA 11771
5/24/80	84	4		77 Is It Only Cause You're Lonely.................................When She Was Mine	—	$5		RCA 11998
6/21/80	2[2]	17		78 Making Plans..................................Beneath The Sweet Magnolia Tree	—	$5		RCA 11983
				PORTER WAGONER AND DOLLY PARTON				
11/8/80+	12	14		79 If You Go, I'll Follow You..Hide Me Away	—	$5		RCA 12119
				PORTER WAGONER & DOLLY PARTON				
11/13/82	53	8		80 Turn The Pencil Over...Texas Moonbeam Waltz	—	$4		Warner 29875
				from the movie *Honkytonk Man* starring **Clint Eastwood**				
3/5/83	35	14		81 This Cowboy's Hat.............................She Don't Have A License To Drive Me Up The Wall	—	$4		Warner 29772

WAKELY, Jimmy ★125★   '49

Born on 2/16/14 in Mineola, Arkansas; raised in Oklahoma. Died on 9/23/82 (age 68). Singer/songwriter/guitarist/pianist. Regular on **Gene Autry**'s *Melody Ranch* radio show in the early 1940s. Known as "The Melody Kid." Starred in several western movies. Hosted own radio show from 1952-57. Co-hosted TV's *Five Star Jubilee* in 1961.

1)Slipping Around   2)One Has My Name (The Other Has My Heart)   3)I Love You So Much It Hurts
4)I'll Never Slip Around Again   5)Let's Go To Church

4/15/44	2[1]	4		1 I'm Sending You Red Roses *A Tiny Little Voice In A Tiny Little Prayer*	—	$15		Decca 6095
4/3/48	9	6		2 Signed, Sealed And Delivered S:9 / J:9 *Easy To Please*	—	$15		Capitol Amer. 40088
9/4/48	❶[11]	32		3 One Has My Name (The Other Has My Heart) S:❶[11] / J:❶[7] *You're The Sweetest Rose In Texas*	10	$15		Capitol 15162
10/30/48+	❶[5]	28		4 I Love You So Much It Hurts J:❶[5] / S:❶[4] *I Don't Want Your Sympathy*	21	$15		Capitol 15243
				#8 Pop hit for **The Mills Brothers** in 1949				
11/13/48+	8	5		5 Mine All Mine J:8 *Walkin' The Sidewalks Of Shame*	—	$15		Capitol 15236
2/5/49	10	1		6 Forever More J:10 *Think Of Me Thinking Of You*	—	$15		Capitol 15333
2/19/49	9	6		7 Till The End Of The World S:9 / J:15 *Moon Over Montana*	—	$15		Capitol 15368
5/14/49	4	9		8 I Wish I Had A Nickel / J:4 / S:10	—			
6/18/49	10	3		9 Someday You'll Call My Name J:10	—	$15		Capitol 40153
8/6/49	14	2		10 Tellin' My Troubles To My Old Guitar.........................J:14 *Try To Understand*	—	$15		Capitol 40187
				MARGARET WHITING and JIMMY WAKELY:				
9/10/49	❶[17]	28 ●		11 Slipping Around / S:❶[17] / J:❶[12] / A:2	❶[3]			
9/10/49	6	8		12 Wedding Bells J:6 / S:7	30	$15		Capitol 40224
11/5/49	2[3]	13		13 I'll Never Slip Around Again S:2 / J:2 / A:10 *Six Times A Week And Twice On Sunday*	8	$15		Capitol 40246
2/11/50	2[1]	9		14 Broken Down Merry-Go-Round / S:2 / J:3 / A:5	12			
2/11/50	3	7		15 The Gods Were Angry With Me S:3 / J:4	17	$20		Capitol F800
4/8/50	7	3		16 Peter Cottontail A:7 *Mr. Easter Bunny*	26	$20		Capitol F929
				JIMMY WAKELY				
4/22/50	2[1]	10		17 Let's Go To Church (Next Sunday Morning) S:2 / A:6 / J:6 *Why Do You Say Those Things (That Hurt Me So)*	13	$20		Capitol F960

371

DEBUT	PEAK	WKS Gold	A-side (Chart Hit)	B-side	Pop	$	Pic	Label & Number
			WAKELY, Jimmy — Cont'd					
9/23/50	10	1	18 Mona Lisa .... A:10 *Steppin' Out*		—	$20		Capitol F1151
			JIMMY WAKELY #1 Pop hit for Nat "King" Cole in 1950; from the movie *Captain Carey, U.S.A.* starring Alan Ladd					
11/18/50	6	1	19 A Bushel And A Peck .... S:6 / J:10 *Beyond The Reef*		6	$20		Capitol F1234
			from the Broadway musical *Guys and Dolls* starring Robert Alda					
1/20/51	7	1	20 My Heart Cries For You .... S:7 / A:10 *Music By The Angels (Lyrics By The Lord)*		12	$20		Capitol F1328
			JIMMY WAKELY					
3/17/51	5	12	21 Beautiful Brown Eyes .... S:5 / S:7 / A:9 *At The Close Of A Long Long Day*		12	$20		Capitol F1393
			JIMMY WAKELY and the LES BAXTER CHORUS					
6/2/51	7	2	22 When You And I Were Young Maggie Blues .... J:7 *Till We Meet Again*		20	$20		Capitol F1500
12/8/51	5	5	23 I Don't Want To Be Free .... J:5 *Let's Live A Little*		—	$20		Capitol F1816

WALKER, Billy ★67★ '62

Born on 1/14/29 in Ralls, Texas. Singer/songwriter/guitarist. Regular on *Big D Jamboree* radio show in Dallas as "The Masked Singer" in 1949. Joined the *Grand Ole Opry* in 1960. Acted in the movies *Second Fiddle To A Steel Guitar* and *Red River Round Up*. Known as "The Tall Texan."

1)Charlie's Shoes 2)A Million And One 3)Cross The Brazos At Waco 4)Bear With Me A Little Longer 5)Sing Me A Love Song To Baby

DEBUT	PEAK	WKS	A-side	B-side	Pop	$	Pic	Label & Number
6/26/54	8	13	1 Thank You For Calling .... A:8 / S:12 *Pretend You Just Don't Know Me*		—	$20		Columbia 21256
6/24/57	12	6	2 On My Mind Again .... A:12 *Viva La Matador!*		—	$15		Columbia 40920
11/7/60	19	8	3 I Wish You Love .... *Gotta Find A Way*		—	$12		Columbia 41763
10/16/61	23	2	4 Funny How Time Slips Away .... *Joey's Back In Town*		—	$12		Columbia 42050
			#22 Pop hit for Jimmy Elledge in 1962					
3/3/62	❶²	23	5 Charlie's Shoes .... *Wild Colonial Boy*		—	$12		Columbia 42287
9/1/62	5	12	6 Willie The Weeper .... *Beggin' For Trouble*		—	$12		Columbia 42492
8/17/63	21	12	7 Heart, Be Careful .... *Storm Of Love*		—	$10	■	Columbia 42794
12/28/63+	22	14	8 The Morning Paper .... *Coming Back For More*		—	$10		Columbia 42891
4/25/64	7	24	9 Circumstances /					
5/9/64	43	4	10 It's Lonesome		—	$8		Columbia 43010
10/10/64	2²	22	11 Cross The Brazos At Waco .... *Down To My Last Cigarette*		128	$8	□	Columbia 43120
4/10/65	8	18	12 Matamoros .... *I'm Nothing To You*		—	$8		Columbia 43223
8/21/65	16	13	13 If It Pleases You /					
9/25/65	45	2	14 I'm So Miserable Without You		—	$8		Columbia 43327
6/4/66	49	2	15 The Old French Quarter (In New Orleans) .... *How Do You Ask?*		—	$7	■	Monument 932
6/25/66	2⁴	21	16 A Million And One .... *Close To Linda*		—	$7		Monument 943
11/12/66+	3	17	17 Bear With Me A Little Longer .... *It's Beginning To Hurt*		—	$7		Monument 980
3/4/67	10	15	18 Anything Your Heart Desires .... *I Gotta Get Me Feelin' Better*		—	$7		Monument 997
7/1/67	18	12	19 In Del Rio .... *Wish I Could Love That Much Again*		—	$7		Monument 1013
9/23/67	11	13	20 I Taught Her Everything She Knows .... *I Treat Her Like A Baby*		—	$7		Monument 1024
3/2/68	18	14	21 Sundown Mary .... *Oh, Matilda*		—	$7		Monument 1055
7/13/68	8	10	22 Ramona .... *One Inch Off The Ground*		—	$7		Monument 1079
			#1 Pop hit for both Gene Austin and Paul Whiteman in 1928					
11/2/68	20	10	23 Age Of Worry .... *Is This Desire*		—	$7		Monument 1098
2/8/69	20	13	24 From The Bottle To The Bottom .... *She*		—	$7		Monument 1123
			BILLY WALKER and The Tennessee Walkers					
5/10/69	12	12	25 Smoky Places .... *Elusive Butterfly*		—	$7		Monument 1140
			#12 Pop hit for The Corsairs in 1962					
9/6/69	37	7	26 Better Homes And Gardens .... *If You See My Baby*		—	$7		Monument 1154
12/6/69+	9	14	27 Thinking 'Bout You, Babe .... *Invisible Tears*		—	$7		Monument 1174
3/21/70	23	11	28 Darling Days .... *Pretend You Don't See Me*		—	$7		Monument 1189
6/27/70	3	18	29 When A Man Loves A Woman (The Way That I Love You) .... *She's As Close As I Can Get (To Loving You)*		—	$6		MGM 14134
10/24/70	3	15	30 She Goes Walking Through My Mind .... *It's Your Fault I'm Cheating*		—	$6		MGM 14173
1/23/71	3	14	31 I'm Gonna Keep On Keep On Lovin' You .... *It's A Long Way Down From Riches To Rags*		—	$6		MGM 14210
5/8/71	28	10	32 It's Time To Love Her .... *She's Feeling Like A New Man Tonight*		—	$6		MGM 14239
			from the movie *Lookin' Good* starring Robert Blake					
7/24/71	22	12	33 Don't Let Him Make A Memory Out Of Me .... *A Fool And His Love*		—	$6		MGM 14268
11/13/71	25	10	34 Traces Of A Woman .... *You Gave Me A Mountain*		—	$6		MGM 14305
5/27/72	24	11	35 Gone (Our Endless Love) .... *All I Have To Offer You Is Me*		—	$7		MGM 14377
			BILLY WALKER with The Mike Curb Congregation					
10/7/72	3	14	36 Sing Me A Love Song To Baby .... *The Day I Was Out & He Was In*		—	$6		MGM 14422
3/3/73	34	9	37 My Mind Hangs On To You .... *Charlie's Shoes*		—	$6		MGM 14488
7/14/73	52	8	38 The Hand Of Love .... *Ranada*		—	$6		MGM 14565
11/10/73	96	3	39 Too Many Memories .... *Margarita*		—	$6		MGM 14669
1/19/74	39	10	40 I Changed My Mind .... *Heart Be Careful*		—	$6		MGM 14693
			written by Conway Twitty					
5/18/74	74	7	41 How Far Our Love Goes .... *Love Me Back To Heaven (One More Time)*		—	$6		MGM 14717
9/7/74	73	9	42 Fine As Wine .... *The Honky Tonks Are Calling Me Again*		—	$6		MGM 14742
3/22/75	10	18	43 Word Games .... *I Can't Say No If She Keeps Saying Yes*		—	$5		RCA Victor 10205
8/30/75	25	10	44 If I'm Losing You .... *I'd Love To Feel You Loving Me Again*		—	$5		RCA Victor 10345
12/20/75+	19	13	45 Don't Stop In My World (If You Don't Mean To Stay) .... *Honky Tonkitis*		—	$5		RCA Victor 10466

DEBUT	PEAK	WKS	Gold	A-side (Chart Hit)	B-side	Pop	$	Pic	Label & Number
				WALKER, Billy — Cont'd					
4/17/76	41	9		46 (Here I Am) Alone Again	When The Song Is Gone (The Music Dies)	—	$5		RCA Victor 10613
7/31/76	67	6		47 Love You All To Pieces	Sierra Nevada	—	$5		RCA Victor 10729
11/27/76+	48	9		48 Instead Of Givin' Up (I'm Givin' In)	Curtains On The Windows	—	$5		RCA 10821
7/2/77	100	1		49 (If You Can) Why Can't I	The Magic Touch	—	$5		Casino 124
8/20/77	86	6		50 It Always Brings Me Back Around To You		—	$5		MRC 1003
10/22/77	64	9		51 Ringgold Georgia	Have I Told You Lately That I Loved You	—	$5		MRC 1005
				BILLY WALKER AND BRENDA KAYE PERRY					
1/14/78	57	7		52 Carlena And José Gomez	Every Cheatin' Thing She Knows	—	$5		MRC 1009
5/6/78	92	2		53 It's Not Over Till It's Over	Don't Let The Morning Sun Shine Shame On You	—	$5		MRC 1014
8/26/78	82	4		54 You're A Violin That Never Has Been Played	Broken Pieces Of Love	—	$5		Scorpion 0552
3/24/79	72	5		55 Lawyers	Why (Don't Ask Me Why)	—	$5		Caprice 2056
6/23/79	69	6		56 Sweet Lovin' Things /		—			
			6	57 Rainbow And Roses		—	$5		Caprice 2057
9/29/79	70	6		58 A Little Bit Short On Love (A Little Bit Long On Tears)	I'm Gonna Leave You Tomorrow	—	$5		Caprice 2059
2/9/80	48	8		59 You Turn My Love Light On	Love Is Free	—	$5		Caprice 2060
7/12/80	74	5		60 Let Me Be The One	If We Take Our Time	—	$5		Paid 102
				BILLY WALKER & BARBARA FAIRCHILD					
12/20/80+	70	7		61 Bye Bye Love /		—			
10/11/80	79	3		62 Love's Slipping Through Our Fingers (Leaving Time On Our Hands)		—	$5		Paid 107
				BILLY WALKER & BARBARA FAIRCHILD (above 2)					
4/2/83	93	2		63 One Away From One Too Many	Looking Through The Eyes Of Love	—	$5		Dimension 1042
12/7/85	81	5		64 Coffee Brown Eyes	Jesse	—	$6		Tall Texan 57
7/30/88	79	3		65 Wild Texas Rose	Sweet Spanish Melodies	—	$6		Tall Texan 60
	★234★			**WALKER, Charlie**		**'58**			

Born on 11/2/26 in Copeville, Texas. Singer/songwriter/guitarist. Worked as a DJ in the early '50s. Joined the Grand Ole Opry in 1967. Acted in the movie Country Music.

1) Pick Me Up On Your Way Down 2) Wild As A Wildcat 3) Don't Squeeze My Sharmon 4) Only You, Only You
5) Who Will Buy The Wine

DEBUT	PEAK	WKS	Gold	A-side	B-side	Pop	$	Pic	Label & Number
1/28/56	9	2		1 Only You, Only You	J:9 Can't Get There From Here	—	$20		Decca 29715
10/20/58	2⁴	22		2 Pick Me Up On Your Way Down	Two Empty Arms	—	$15		Columbia 41211
6/8/59	16	9		3 I'll Catch You When You Fall	I Don't Mind Saying	—	$12		Columbia 41388
10/26/59	22	2		4 When My Conscience Hurts The Most	Bow Down Your Head And Cry	—	$12		Columbia 41467
5/16/60	11	16		5 Who Will Buy The Wine	I Go Anywhere	—	$12		Columbia 41633
2/6/61	25	3		6 Facing The Wall	I Walked Out On Heaven (When I Walked Out On You)	—	$12		Columbia 41820
11/28/64+	17	16		7 Close All The Honky Tonks	Truck Driving Man	—	$10		Epic 9727
6/5/65	8	18		8 Wild As A Wildcat	Out Of A Honky Tonk	—	$8		Epic 9799
12/4/65+	39	7		9 He's A Jolly Good Fellow	Memory Killer	—	$8		Epic 9852
3/19/66	37	3		10 The Man In The Little White Suit	Fraulein	—	$8		Epic 9875
10/15/66	56	2		11 Daddy's Coming Home (Next Week) /		—			
10/29/66	65	5		12 I'm Gonna Hang Up My Gloves		—	$7		Epic 10063
				written by Merle Haggard					
1/28/67	38	11		13 The Town That Never Sleeps	The Way To Say Goodbye	—	$7		Epic 10118
6/10/67	8	15		14 Don't Squeeze My Sharmon	You Lied To Me	—	$7		Epic 10174
11/4/67	33	10		15 I Wouldn't Take Her To A Dogfight	Tonight, We're Calling It A Day	—	$7		Epic 10237
3/30/68	54	7		16 Truck Drivin' Cat With Nine Wives	Sweetheart Of The Year	—	$7		Epic 10295
8/3/68	31	11		17 San Diego	When My Conscience Hurts The Most	—	$7		Epic 10349
3/1/69	52	10		18 Honky-Tonk Season	Too Many Nights In Too Many Arms	—	$7		Epic 10426
8/23/69	44	9		19 Moffett, Oklahoma	You're From Texas	—	$7		Epic 10499
2/21/70	56	6		20 Honky Tonk Women	Rosie Bokay	—	$7		Epic 10565
				#1 Pop hit for The Rolling Stones in 1969					
6/27/70	52	7		21 Let's Go Fishin' Boys (The Girls Are Bitin')	You're All Dressed Up	—	$6		Epic 10610
6/5/71	71	2		22 My Baby Used To Be That Way	Before I Found The Wine	—	$6		Epic 10722
8/5/72	74	3		23 I Don't Mind Goin' Under (If It'll Get Me Over You)	Honky Tonk Heart	—	$5		RCA Victor 0730
1/13/73	65	7		24 Soft Lips And Hard Liquor	It's Better Than Going Home Alone	—	$5		RCA Victor 0870
8/17/74	66	8		25 Odds And Ends (Bits And Pieces)	Society's Got Us	—	$5		Capitol 3922
				WALKER, Cindy		**'44**			

Born on 7/20/18 in Mart, Texas. Singer/prolific songwriter. Inducted into the Country Music Hall of Fame in 1997.

DEBUT	PEAK	WKS	Gold	A-side	B-side	Pop	$	Pic	Label & Number
11/4/44	5	1		When My Blue Moon Turns To Gold Again	Pins And Needles (In My Heart)	—	$15		Decca 6103
				#19 Pop hit for **Elvis Presley** in 1956					

| | | | | **WALKER, Clay** ★120★ | | **'94** | | | |

Born Ernest Clayton Walker on 8/19/69 in Beaumont, Texas. Singer/songwriter/guitarist. Began playing professionally in bars around Texas in 1985. Studied business while attending college.

1) Rumor Has It 2) This Woman And This Man 3) Live Until I Die 4) Dreaming With My Eyes Open 5) What's It To You

DEBUT	PEAK	WKS	Gold	A-side	B-side	Pop	$	Pic	Label & Number
7/10/93	0¹	20		1 What's It To You	Where Do I Fit In The Picture	73	$4	▌	Giant 18450 (v)
10/30/93+	0¹	20		2 Live Until I Die	The Silence Speaks For Itself	107	$4	▌	Giant 18332 (v)
2/26/94	11	20		3 Where Do I Fit In The Picture	Money Can't Buy (The Love We Had)	—	$4		Giant 18210
4/30/94	67	3		4 White Palace		—			album cut
				from the album Clay Walker on Giant 24511					

DEBUT	PEAK	WKS	Gold	A-side (Chart Hit)	B-side	Pop	$	Pic	Label & Number
				WALKER, Clay — Cont'd					
6/11/94	❶¹	20		5 Dreaming With My Eyes Open	Money Can't Buy (The Love We Had)	—	$4		Giant 18139
9/24/94	❶¹	20		6 If I Could Make A Living	Down By The Riverside	121	$4	■	Giant 18068 (v)
1/14/95	❶²	20		7 This Woman And This Man	Lose Your Memory	—	$4		Giant 17995
5/6/95	16	20		8 My Heart Will Never Know	S:10 Money Ain't Everything	—	$4	■	Giant 17887 (v)
9/16/95	2²	20		9 Who Needs You Baby	S:4 Where Were You	120	$4	■	Giant 17771 (v)
1/13/96	2¹	20		10 Hypnotize The Moon	S:❶³ A Cowboy's Toughest Ride	105	$4	■	Giant 17704 (v)
5/25/96	5	20		11 Only On Days That End In "Y"		—	$4		album cut
9/28/96	18	19		12 Bury The Shovel		—			album cut
				above 2 from the album Hypnotize The Moon on Giant 24640					
2/1/97	❶²	20		13 Rumor Has It		—			album cut
				from the album Rumor Has It on Giant 24674					
4/26/97	18	20		14 One, Two, I Love You	Country Boy And City Girl	—	$4		Giant 17351
8/9/97	4	20		15 Watch This					album cut
				from the album Rumor Has It on Giant 24674					
12/20/97+	2¹	27		16 Then What?	S:4 Country Boy And City Girl	65	$4	■	Giant 17262 (v)
4/18/98	68	9		17 Holding Her And Loving You		—			album cut
				from the album Live, Laugh, Love on Giant 24717					
5/2/98	35	20		18 Ordinary People	S:20 The Next Step Is Love	120	$4	■	Giant 17210 (v)
8/22/98+	2¹	27		19 You're Beginning To Get To Me	S:14 Lose Your Memory	39	$4	★	Giant 17158 (v)
2/20/99	16	22		20 She's Always Right		74			album cut
7/24/99	73	3		21 Once In A Lifetime Love		—			album cut
8/7/99+	11	27		22 Live, Laugh, Love		74			album cut
11/6/99+	3	34		23 The Chain Of Love		—			album cut
8/5/00	50	15		24 Once In A Lifetime Love	[R]	—			album cut
				above 5 from the album Live, Laugh, Love on Giant 24717					
12/9/00	51	6		25 Blue Christmas	[X]	—			album cut
				from the album Believe: A Christmas Collection on Giant 24750					
2/24/01	33	13		26 Say No More		—			album cut
7/14/01	27	20		27 If You Ever Feel Like Lovin' Me Again		—			album cut
				above 2 from the album Say No More on Giant 24759					
				WALKER, Jerry Jeff '76					
				Born Ronald Clyde Crosby on 3/16/42 in Oneonta, New York. Singer/songwriter/guitarist.					
12/6/75+	54	7		1 Jaded Lover	I Love You	—	$5		MCA 40487
7/24/76	88	5		2 It's A Good Night For Singing /		—	$5		
		5		3 Dear John Letter Lounge		—	$5		MCA 40570
8/6/77	93	4		4 Mr. Bojangles	Don't It Make You Wanna Dance?	—	$5		MCA 40760
				new version of his #77 Pop hit from 1968					
8/29/81	82	3		5 Got Lucky Last Night	Maybe Mexico	—	$5		SouthCoast 51146
7/8/89	70	6		6 I Feel Like Hank Williams Tonight	Mr. Bojangles	—	$5		Tried & True 1692
10/14/89	62	6		7 The Pickup Truck Song	(longer version)	—	$5		Tried & True 1695
12/9/89+	63	6		8 Trashy Women	I Feel Like Hank Williams Tonight	—	$5		Tried & True 1698
				WALKER, Kathy — see BLIXSETH, Tim / LEE, T L					
				WALKER, Mike '01					
				Born in Columbus, Ohio; raised in Jackson, Tennessee.					
5/19/01	42	15		1 Honey Do	S:13 What Kind Of Love	—	$4	★	DreamWor. 450914 (v)
				WALKER, Tamara '00					
				Born in Ohio; raised in Maryland. Female singer.					
3/4/00	65	2		1 Askin' Too Much		—			album cut
10/14/00	69	1		2 Didn't We Love	S:10 Angel Eyes	—	$4	★	Curb 73126
				from the movie Coyote Ugly starring Piper Perabo					
				WALKER, Wiley — see WILEY & GENE					
				WALLACE, Jerry ★164★ '72					
				Born on 12/15/28 in Guilford, Missouri; raised in Glendale, Arizona. Singer/songwriter/guitarist. First recorded for Allied in 1951. Nicknamed "Mr. Smooth." Charted 13 pop hits from 1958-72.					
				1)If You Leave Me Tonight I'll Cry 2)Do You Know What It's Like To Be Lonesome 3)Don't Give Up On Me 4)My Wife's House 5)To Get You					
10/9/65	23	11		1 Life's Gone And Slipped Away	Twelve Little Roses	—	$10		Mercury 72461
4/9/66	45	2		2 Diamonds And Horseshoes	Will The Pain Fade Away	—	$10		Mercury 72529
7/9/66	43	7		3 Wallpaper Roses	The Son Of A Green Beret	—	$10		Mercury 72589
10/15/66	44	7		4 Not That I Care	Release Me (And Let Me Love Again)	—	$10		Mercury 72619
11/25/67+	36	13		5 This One's On The House	A New Sun Risin'	—	$8		Liberty 56001
5/18/68	69	3		6 Another Time, Another Place, Another World	That's What Fools Are For	—	$8		Liberty 56028
9/14/68	22	10		7 Sweet Child Of Sunshine	Our House On Paper	—	$8		Liberty 56059
4/5/69	69	3		8 Son	Temptation (Make Me Go Home)	—	$8		Liberty 56095
10/11/69	71	2		9 Swiss Cottage Place	With Ageing	—	$8		Liberty 56130
5/9/70	74	2		10 Even The Bad Times Are Good	For All We Know	—	$8		Liberty 56155
				new version of his #114 Pop hit from 1964					

DEBUT	PEAK	WKS	Gold	A-side (Chart Hit)	B-side	Pop	$	Pic	Label & Number
				WALLACE, Jerry — Cont'd					
2/13/71	22	14		11 After You /		—			Decca 32777
2/13/71	51	14		12 She'll Remember		—	$7		Decca 32777
8/21/71	19	14		13 The Morning After	I Can't Take It Any More	—	$7		Decca 32859
1/1/72	12	22	★	14 To Get To You	Time	48	$7		Decca 32914
7/22/72	❶²	17		15 If You Leave Me Tonight I'll Cry	What's He Doin' In My World	38	$7		Decca 32989
				popularized due to play on TV's Night Gallery (the episode titled "The Tune In Dan's Cafe")					
12/2/72	66	7		16 Thanks To You For Lovin' Me	Funny How Time Slips Away	—	$7		United Artists 50971
12/9/72+	2¹	15		17 Do You Know What It's Like To Be Lonesome	Where Did He Come From?	—	$7		Decca 33036
4/14/73	21	12		18 Sound Of Goodbye /		—			
		12		19 The Song Nobody Sings		—	$6		MCA 40037
8/25/73	3	16		20 Don't Give Up On Me	You Look Like Forever	—	$6		MCA 40111
2/9/74	18	12		21 Guess Who	All I Ever Want From You (Is You)	—	$6		MCA 40183
6/15/74	9	14		22 My Wife's House	A Better Way To Say I Love You	—	$6		MCA 40261
11/16/74+	20	12		23 I Wonder Whose Baby (You Are Now)	Make Hay While The Sun Shines	—	$6		MCA 40321
3/8/75	32	12		24 Comin' Home To You	River St. Marie	—	$5		MGM 14788
7/19/75	41	9		25 Wanted Man	Your Love	—	$5		MGM 14809
11/1/75	70	6		26 Georgia Rain	In The Garden	—	$5		MGM 14832
7/2/77	26	13		27 I Miss You Already	At The End Of A Rainbow	—	$5		BMA 002
11/12/77+	28	12		28 I'll Promise You Tomorrow	You're On The Run	—	$5		BMA 005
2/18/78	24	11		29 At The End Of A Rainbow	Looking For A Memory	—	$5		BMA 006
				#7 Pop hit for Earl Grant in 1958					
6/3/78	64	6		30 My Last Sad Song	Out Wickenburg Way	—	$5		BMA 008
10/14/78	38	8		31 I Wanna Go To Heaven	After You	—	$5		4 Star 1035
3/3/79	67	5		32 Yours Love	There She Goes	—	$5		4 Star 1036
12/1/79+	68	8		33 You've Still Got Me	Now That Sandy's Gone	—	$5		Door Knob 116
4/5/80	56	7		34 Cling To Me	Paper Madonna	—	$5		Door Knob 127
10/4/80	80	5		35 If I Could Set My Love To Music	Cling To Me	—	$5		Door Knob 134
				WALLACE, Ron '95					
				Born in Independence, Missouri. Singer/songwriter/guitarist.					
9/2/95	65	6		1 I'm Listening Now	Don't Get Mad	—	$4	■	Columbia 78021 (v)
				WALSH, David '85					
				Born in Syracuse, New York.					
7/27/85	91	2		1 Alice, Rita and Donna	Music Man	—	$5		Charta 196
10/26/85	84	3		2 Tired Of The Same Old Thing	Sweet Lydia's Biscuits	—	$5		Charta 198
10/29/88	97	1		3 All The Things We Are Not	Two Sides To Lonesome	—	$5		Charta 212
2/18/89	84	3		4 Somewhere In Canada	She's The Newest Broken Heart	—	$5		Charta 215
				WARD, Chris '96					
				Born in 1960 in New York City. Male singer/songwriter/guitarist.					
8/17/96	68	2		1 Fall Reaching	Somewhere Between Goodbye And Gone	—	$4	■	Giant 17601 (v)
				WARD, Dale '68					
				Male singer. Charted a pop hit in 1964 ("Letter From Sherry").					
11/9/68	74	2		1 If Loving You Means Anything	River Of Regret	—	$7		Monument 1094
	★225★			**WARD, Jacky** '78					
				Born on 11/18/46 in Groveton, Texas. Male singer/guitarist.					
				1) A Lover's Question 2) That's The Way A Cowboy Rocks And Rolls 3) Save Your Heart For Me 4) Wisdom Of A Fool 5) Fools Fall In Love					
6/10/72	39	10		1 Big Blue Diamond	Just Hanging On	—	$7		Target 0146
7/14/73	88	3		2 Dream Weaver	Biggest Piece Of Me	—	$6		Mega 0112
4/19/75	50	12		3 Stealin'	I Can't Stand The Pain	—	$5		Mercury 73667
11/1/75+	38	13		4 Dance Her By Me (One More Time)	Just Because	—	$5		Mercury 73716
4/17/76	92	4		5 She'll Throw Stones At You	One Pillow Betwen Us	—	$5		Mercury 73783
9/4/76	24	12		6 I Never Said It Would Be Easy	Nobody's Perfect	—	$5		Mercury 73826
2/5/77	31	12		7 Texas Angel	Just Out Of Reach	—	$5		Mercury 73880
6/25/77	69	6		8 Why Not Tonight	The Feelin's Right	—	$5		Mercury 73918
9/10/77	9	19		9 Fools Fall In Love	Big Blue Diamond	—	$5		Mercury 55003
				#10 R&B hit for The Drifters in 1957					
2/4/78	3	15		10 A Lover's Question	She Belongs To Me	106	$5		Mercury 55018
				#6 Pop hit for Clyde McPhatter in 1959					
5/20/78	20	12	★	11 Three Sheets In The Wind /					
		11		12 I'd Really Love To See You Tonight		—	$8		Mercury 55026
				JACKY WARD & REBA McENTIRE (above 2)					
				#2 Pop hit for England Dan & John Ford Coley in 1976					
8/5/78	24	10		13 I Want To Be In Love	Hey Friend	—	$5		Mercury 55038
11/4/78	11	13		14 Rhythm Of The Rain	From Me To You	—	$5		Mercury 55047
				#3 Pop hit for The Cascades in 1963					
2/17/79	8	14		15 Wisdom Of A Fool	One Day And A Night	—	$5		Mercury 55055
7/7/79	26	11		16 That Makes Two Of Us	Good Friends	—	$8		Mercury 55054
				JACKY WARD/REBA McENTIRE					
9/22/79	14	12		17 You're My Kind Of Woman	Rainbow	—	$5		Mercury 57004
1/5/80	32	10		18 I'd Do Anything For You	Ain't It Just Like Me	—	$5		Mercury 57013
5/24/80	8	16		19 Save Your Heart For Me	It Doesn't Matter Anymore	—	$5		Mercury 57022
9/13/80	7	15		20 That's The Way A Cowboy Rocks And Rolls	I Learned All About Cheatin' From You	—	$5		Mercury 57032

DEBUT	PEAK	WKS	Gold	A-side (Chart Hit)	B-side	Pop	$	Pic	Label & Number
				WARD, Jacky — Cont'd					
1/24/81	13	14		21 Somethin' On The Radio / Let Me Be Your Man		—	$5		Mercury 57044
3/20/82	32	11		22 Travelin' Man / Save A Little Love		—	$4		Asylum 47424
				#1 Pop hit for **Ricky Nelson** in 1961					
7/3/82	57	7		23 Take The Mem'ry When You Go / Get Rhythm		—	$4		Asylum 47468
3/5/83	85	3		24 The Night's Almost Over / Black And White Rainbows		—	$4		Warner 69844
1/9/88	83	3		25 Can't Get To You From Here		—	$5		Electric 105
				WARINER, Steve ★43★ '87					
				Born on 12/25/54 in Noblesville, Indiana. Singer/songwriter/guitarist. Played bass while a teenager. Bassist with **Dottie West** from 1971-74. Worked with **Bob Luman** and **Chet Atkins**. Joined the *Grand Ole Opry* in 1996. Also see **Jed Zeppelin** and **Nicolette Larson**.					
				1)*What If I Said* 2)*You Can Dream Of Me* 3)*Some Fools Never Learn* 4)*I Got Dreams* 5)*Lynda*					
4/22/78	63	7		1 I'm Already Taken / Daytime Dreamer *also see #53 below*		—	$5	■	RCA 11173
8/19/78	76	3		2 So Sad (To Watch Good Love Go Bad) / Atlanta/My Greatest Loss		—	$5		RCA 11336
				#7 Pop hit for **The Everly Brothers** in 1960					
1/27/79	94	2		3 Marie / One Song In Everybody		—	$5		RCA 11447
11/10/79	49	10		4 Forget Me Not /		—			
8/4/79	60	7		5 Beside Me		—	$5		RCA 11658
7/5/80	41	10		6 The Easy Part's Over / It's Your Move		—	$4		RCA 12029
11/15/80+	7	17		7 Your Memory / Vince		—	$4		RCA 12139
4/11/81	6	18		8 By Now / Beverly (Take Care Of Your Baby)		—	$4		RCA 12204
9/26/81	❶¹	18		9 All Roads Lead To You / Here We Are		107	$4		RCA 12307
3/6/82	15	18		10 Kansas City Lights / The Easy Part's Over		—	$4		RCA 13072
9/4/82	30	11		11 Don't It Break Your Heart / We'll Never Know		—	$4		RCA 13308
11/27/82+	27	17		12 Don't Plan On Sleepin' Tonight / Your Memory		—	$4		RCA 13395
5/7/83	23	13		13 Don't Your Mem'ry Ever Sleep At Night / Well, Hello Again		—	$4		RCA 13515
8/13/83	5	18		14 Midnight Fire / You Turn It All Around		—	$4		RCA 13588
12/10/83+	4	20		15 Lonely Women Make Good Lovers / I Can Hear Kentucky Calling Me		—	$4		RCA 13691
4/7/84	12	18		16 Why Goodbye / Don't You Give Up On Love		—	$4		RCA 13768
9/22/84	49	10		17 Don't You Give Up On Love / When Is It All Gonna End		—	$4		RCA 13862
12/15/84+	3	25		18 What I Didn't Do A:3 / S:3 Your Love Has Got A Hold On Me		—	$4	■	MCA 52506
4/6/85	8	20		19 Heart Trouble A:8 / S:9 As Long As Love's Been Around		—	$4		MCA 52562
7/27/85	❶¹	22		20 Some Fools Never Learn S:❶¹ / A:❶¹ You Can't Cut Me Any Deeper		—	$4		MCA 52644
11/16/85+	❶¹	22		21 You Can Dream Of Me A:❶¹ / S:2 I Let A Keeper Get Away		—	$4	■	MCA 52721
3/15/86	❶¹	24		22 Life's Highway S:❶¹ / A:❶¹ She's Crazy For Leaving		—	$4		MCA 52786
8/16/86	4	19		23 Starting Over Again S:3 / A:4 She's Leaving Me All Over Town		—	$4		MCA 52837
12/27/86+	❶¹	24		24 Small Town Girl A:❶¹ / S:9 When It Rains		—	$4		MCA 53006
4/25/87	❶¹	23		25 The Weekend S:8 / A:30 Fastbreak		—	$4		MCA 53068
5/30/87	6	28		26 The Hand That Rocks The Cradle S:11 Arkansas		—	$4		MCA 53108
				GLEN CAMPBELL with Steve Wariner					
9/5/87	❶¹	23		27 Lynda S:2 There's Always A First Time		—	$4		MCA 53160
2/20/88	2¹	18		28 Baby I'm Yours S:4 All That Matters		—	$4		MCA 53287
6/18/88	2²	21		29 I Should Be With You S:7 Caught Between Your Duty And Your Dream		—	$4		MCA 53347
10/15/88+	6	24		30 Hold On (A Little Longer) S:15 Runnin'		—	$4		MCA 53419
3/4/89	❶¹	22		31 Where Did I Go Wrong / Plano Texas Girl		—	$4		MCA 53504
7/1/89	❶¹	21		32 I Got Dreams / The Loser Wins		—	$4		MCA 53665
10/21/89+	5	26		33 When I Could Come Home To You / Do You Want To Make Something Of It		—	$4		MCA 53738
3/17/90	7	24		34 The Domino Theory / I Wanna Go Back		—	$4	■	MCA 53733 (v)
7/21/90	8	20		35 Precious Thing / She's In Love		—	$4	■	MCA 53854 (v)
11/10/90+	17	20		36 There For Awhile / Why Do The Heroes Die So Young		—	$4		MCA 53936
9/28/91+	6	20		37 Leave Him Out Of This / Like A River To The Sea		—	$4		Arista 12349
2/8/92	3	20		38 The Tips Of My Fingers / When Will I Let Go		—	$4		Arista 12393
5/30/92	9	20		39 A Woman Loves / Everything's Gonna Be Alright		—	$4		Arista 12426
9/12/92	32	15		40 Crash Course In The Blues / My, How The Time Don't Fly		—	$4		Arista 12461
2/20/93	30	14		41 Like A River To The Sea / On My Heart Again		—	$4		Arista 12510
7/3/93	8	20		42 If I Didn't Love You / The Same Mistake Again		—	$4	■	Arista 12578 (v)
11/13/93+	24	18		43 Drivin' And Cryin' / Drive		—	$4		Arista 12609
4/9/94	18	20		44 It Won't Be Over You / Missing You		—	$4		Arista 12672
9/17/94	63	4		45 Drive / The Same Mistake Again		—	$4		Arista 12744
5/27/95	72	3		46 Get Back / The Long And Winding Road (**John Berry**)		—	$4	■	Liberty 58411 (v)
				#1 Pop hit for The Beatles in 1969					
11/8/97+	❶¹	23		47 What If I Said S:3 Daddy Can You See Me (Cochran)		59	$4	■	Warner 17263 (v)
				ANITA COCHRAN with Steve Wariner					
3/7/98	2²	21		48 Holes In The Floor Of Heaven / Closer I Get To You		—	$4		Capitol 19974
				CMA Award: Single of the Year					
5/9/98	26	20		49 Burnin' The Roadhouse Down /		—			
				STEVE WARINER (with Garth Brooks)					
6/27/98	55	4		50 Road Trippin'		—	$4		Capitol 58716
10/17/98+	36	20		51 Every Little Whisper / Love Me Like You Love Me		—	$4		Capitol 58753

DEBUT	PEAK	WKS	Gold	A-side (Chart Hit)	B-side	Pop	$	Pic	Label & Number
				WARINER, Steve — Cont'd					
2/20/99	2[1]	24		52 Two Teardrops	Cry No More	30	$4		Capitol 58767
7/3/99	3	25		53 I'm Already Taken	Tattoos Of Life [R]	42	$4		Capitol 58786
				new version of #1 above					
1/15/00	5	22		54 Been There	When I Said I Do (w/Lisa Hartman Black)	44	$4		RCA 65966
				CLINT BLACK with Steve Wariner					
3/18/00	28	19		55 Faith In You	Blinded	—	$4		Capitol 58848
6/17/00	22	20		56 Katie Wants A Fast One	I Just Do (Wariner)	109	$4		Capitol 58878
				STEVE WARINER With Garth Brooks					
12/23/00	65	2		57 Christmas In Your Arms	[X]	—			album cut
				WARNER, Virgil '67					
				Born in Phoenix.					
9/9/67	51	7		1 Here We Go Again	Hangin' On	—	$7		LHI 17018
2/24/68	65	4		2 Storybook Children	Lady Bird	—	$7		LHI 1204
				VIRGIL WARNER & SUZI JANE HOKUM (above 2)					
				#54 Pop hit for Billy Vera & Judy Clay in 1968					
				WARNES, Jennifer '79					
				Born on 3/3/47 in Seattle; raised in Orange County, California. Pop singer/actress.					
2/19/77	17	15		1 Right Time Of The Night	Daddy Don't Go	6	$5		Arista 0223
6/30/79	10	16		2 I Know A Heartache When I See One	Frankie In The Rain	19	$4		Arista 0430
1/12/80	84	3		3 Don't Make Me Over	I'm Restless	67	$4		Arista 0455
2/23/80	76	5		4 Lost The Good Thing	Three Lines	—	$5		Regency 45002
				STEVE GILLETTE (with Jennifer Warnes)					
2/6/82	57	7		5 Could It Be Love	I'm Restless	47	$4		Arista 0611
2/28/87	86	4		6 Ain't No Cure For Love	Famous Blue Raincoat	—	$4	■	Cypress 661111
				WARREN, Kelly '79					
				Born in Lamesa, Texas. Female singer/actress.					
1/6/79	85	5		1 One Man's Woman	If I Could Just Find My Way (Back To You)	—	$5		RCA 11428
11/17/79	69	4		2 Don't Touch Me	Never Been To Spain	—	$6		Jeremiah 1002
				JERRY NAYLOR/KELLI WARREN					
				WARREN BROTHERS, The '01					
				Brothers Brad and Brett Warren from Tampa, Florida.					
8/29/98	34	20		1 Guilty	S:14 (same version)	115	$4	★	BNA 65552 (v)
1/16/99	32	20		2 Better Man	S:22 Guilty	—	$4	★	BNA 65670 (v)
5/29/99	37	16		3 She Wants To Rock		—			album cut
				from the album Beautiful Day In The Cold Cruel World on BNA 67678					
3/25/00	22	28		4 That's The Beat Of A Heart	Grow Young With You (Coley McCabe)	—	$4		BNA 62013
				THE WARREN BROTHERS Featuring Sara Evans					
				from the movie Where The Heart Is starring Natalie Portman					
10/14/00+	17	25		5 Move On /					
6/2/01	33	16		6 Where Does It Hurt		—	$4		BNA 69086
				WASHINGTON, Jon '88					
				Born in England. Singer/songwriter/actor.					
10/22/88	73	3		1 One Dance Love Affair		—	$5		Door Knob 310
1/28/89	73	3		2 Two Hearts	Lady Of The Evening	—	$5		Door Knob 315
				WATERS, Chris '80					
				Born Christopher Dunn in San Antonio, Texas. Singer/songwriter. Brother of Holly Dunn.					
11/29/80	82	3		1 My Lady Loves Me (Just As I Am)	Nobody's Fool	—	$5		Rio 1001
3/7/81	89	2		2 It's Like Falling In Love (Over And Over Again)	Long As I Can See The Light	—	$5		Rio 1002
				WATERS, Joe '82					
				Born in Chillicothe, Ohio. Singer/songwriter. Known as "Appalachia Joe."					
9/26/81	85	3		1 Livin' In The Light Of Her Love	Wild Honey Mountain Girl	—	$7		New Colony 6811
12/12/81+	47	10		2 Some Day My Ship's Comin' In	Jubilee	—	$7	■	New Colony 6812
4/17/82	75	4		3 The Queen Of Hearts Loves You	Love Can Be Fatal	—	$7		New Colony 6813
12/17/83+	74	6		4 Harvest Moon	Sweet Georgia Clay (I'll Be Home Someday)	—	$7	■	New Colony 6814
5/26/84	90	2		5 Rise Above It All	Pay The Price For Love	—	$7		New Colony 6815
				WATSON, B.B. '91					
				Born Haskill Watson on 7/10/53 in Tyler, Texas; raised in La Porte, Texas. B.B. stands for Bad Boy.					
8/10/91	23	21		1 Light At The End Of The Tunnel	Honkytonk The Town Tonight	—	$4	■	BNA 62039 (v)
2/1/92	43	12		2 Lover Not A Fighter	Bottle Of Whiskey	—	$4		BNA 62195
4/15/00	73	1		3 The Memory Is The Last Thing To Go		—			album cut
				WATSON, Clyde '77					
8/27/77	99	2		The Touch Of Her Fingers	Trouble	—	$6		Groovy 100
				WATSON, Doc & Merle '73					
				Father-and-son duo. Arthel "Doc" Watson was born on 3/2/23 in Deep Gap, North Carolina. Blind singer/songwriter/guitarist/banjo player. Merle was born on 2/8/49 in North Carolina. Died in a tractor accident on 10/23/85 (age 36). Singer/banjo player. Also see The Groovegrass Boyz.					
7/21/73	71	7		1 Bottle Of Wine	Corrina, Corrina	—	$6		Poppy 276
				#9 Pop hit for The Fireballs in 1968					
9/2/78	88	5		2 Don't Think Twice, It's All Right	Under The Double Eagle	—	$5		United Artists 1231
				#9 Pop hit for Peter, Paul & Mary in 1963					

DEBUT	PEAK	WKS	Gold	A-side (Chart Hit)	B-side	Pop	$	Pic	Label & Number

WATSON, Gene ★73★ '82

Born Gary Gene Watson on 10/11/43 in Palestine, Texas; raised in Paris, Texas. Singer/songwriter/guitarist. Worked professionally since age 13. Own band, Gene Watson & The Other Four. First recorded for Tonka in 1965. Played for many years at the Dynasty Club in Houston.

1) Fourteen Carat Mind 2) You're Out Doing What I'm Here Doing Without 3) Paper Rosie 4) Love In The Hot Afternoon 5) Should I Come Home

DEBUT	PEAK	WKS		A-side	B-side	Pop	$	Label & Number
1/25/75	87	7	1	Bad Water	I'll Run Right Back To You	—	$8	Resco 630
				#58 Pop hit for The Raelettes in 1971				
5/24/75	3	19	2	Love In The Hot Afternoon	Through The Eyes Of Love	—	$5	Capitol 4076
				first released on Resco 634 in 1975 ($8)				
10/11/75	5	15	3	Where Love Begins	Long Enough To Care	—	$5	Capitol 4143
2/14/76	10	15	4	You Could Know As Much About A Stranger	Harvest Time	—	$5	Capitol 4214
6/12/76	20	12	5	Because You Believed In Me	When My World Left Town	—	$5	Capitol 4279
9/25/76	52	9	6	Her Body Couldn't Keep You (Off My Mind)	If I'm A Fool For Leaving	—	$5	Capitol 4331
1/29/77	3	17	7	Paper Rosie	That Tone Of Voice	—	$5	Capitol 4378
8/13/77	11	15	8	The Old Man And His Horn	Just At Dawn	—	$5	Capitol 4458
12/3/77+	8	16	9	I Don't Need A Thing At All	Hey Barnum And Bailey	—	$5	Capitol 4513
4/8/78	11	14	10	Cowboys Don't Get Lucky All The Time	I'd Love To Live With You Again	—	$4	Capitol 4556
8/26/78	8	14	11	One Sided Conversation	I Know What It's Like In Her Arms	—	$4	Capitol 4616
2/17/79	5	16	12	Farewell Party	I Don't Know How To Tell Her (She Don't Love Me Anymore)	—	$4	Capitol 4680
6/9/79	5	15	13	Pick The Wildwood Flower	Mama Sold Roses	—	$4	Capitol 4723
9/15/79	3	13	14	Should I Come Home (Or Should I Go Crazy)	Beautiful You	—	$4	Capitol 4772
1/5/80	4	14	15	Nothing Sure Looked Good On You	The Beer At Dorsey's Bar	—	$4	Capitol 4814
4/12/80	18	13	16	Bedroom Ballad	After The Party	—	$4	Capitol 4854
8/2/80	15	12	17	Raisin' Cane In Texas	A Cold Day In July	—	$4	Capitol 4898
11/1/80	13	14	18	No One Will Ever Know	Down And Out This Way Again	—	$4	Capitol 4940
2/7/81	33	8	19	Any Way You Want Me	Those Eyes That Lie To Me	—	$4	Warner 49648
				from the movie Any Which Way You Can starring Clint Eastwood				
2/28/81	17	13	20	Between This Time And The Next Time	I'm Tellin' Me A Lie	—	$4	MCA 51039
6/20/81	23	13	21	Maybe I Should Have Been Listening	I'm Gonna Kill You	—	$4	MCA 51127
10/3/81+	❶¹	19	22	Fourteen Carat Mind	Lonely Me	—	$4	MCA 51183
2/27/82	9	18	23	Speak Softly (You're Talking To My Heart)	'Til Melinda Comes Around	—	$4	MCA 52009
7/3/82	8	18	24	This Dream's On Me	This Torch That I Carry For You	—	$4	MCA 52074
11/6/82+	5	21	25	What She Don't Know Won't Hurt Her	Fightin' Fire With Fire	—	$4	MCA 52131
3/19/83	2¹	19	26	You're Out Doing What I'm Here Doing Without	You're Just Another Beer Drinkin' Song	—	$4	MCA 52191
7/23/83	9	18	27	Sometimes I Get Lucky And Forget	You Put Out An Old Flame Last Night	—	$4	MCA 52243
11/26/83+	10	17	28	Drinkin' My Way Back Home	My Memories Of You	—	$4	MCA 52309
3/31/84	10	17	29	Forever Again	Growing Apart	—	$4	MCA 52356
6/30/84	33	14	30	Little By Little	The Ballad Of Richard Lindsey	—	$4	MCA 52410
10/13/84+	7	27	31	Got No Reason Now For Goin' Home	S:6 / A:6 A Memory Away	—	$4	Curb/MCA 52457
3/2/85	43	10	32	One Hell Of A Heartache	Sailing Home To Me	—	$4	Curb/MCA 52533
6/22/85	24	17	33	Cold Summer Day In Georgia	A:21 / S:24 The Note	—	$4	Epic 05407
10/19/85+	5	21	34	Memories To Burn	S:4 / A:5 Get Along Little Doggie	—	$4	Epic 05633
3/1/86	32	15	35	Carmen	The New York Times	—	$4	Epic 05817
7/5/86	50	8	36	Bottle Of Tears	Stranger In Our House Tonight	—	$4	Epic 06057
9/13/86	29	14	37	Everything I Used To Do	S:23 / A:29 I Saved Your Place	—	$4	Epic 06290
3/14/87	43	13	38	Honky Tonk Crazy	Starting New Memories Today	—	$4	Epic 06987
8/15/87	28	16	39	Everybody Needs A Hero	S:23 When She Touches Me	—	$4	Epic 07308
11/12/88+	5	22	40	Don't Waste It On The Blues	I Picked A San Antonio Rose	—	$4	Warner 27692
3/18/89	20	14	41	Back In The Fire	Just How Little I Know	—	$4	Warner 27532
7/22/89	24	24	42	The Jukebox Played Along	Somewhere Over You	—	$4	Warner 22912
11/25/89+	41	16	43	The Great Divide	Ain't No Fun To Be Alone In San Antone	—	$4	Warner 22751
2/23/91	61	7	44	At Last	—		album cut	
6/1/91	67	5	45	You Can't Take It With You When You Go	—		album cut	
				above 2 from the album At Last on Warner 26329				
1/2/93	66	5	46	One And One And One	She's No Lady	—	$4	Broadland 192
1/25/97	44	18	47	Change Her Mind	—		album cut	
6/7/97	73	1	48	No Goodbyes	—		album cut	
				above 2 from the album The Good Ole Days on Step One 104				

WAYLON & JESSI — see JENNINGS, Waylon / COLTER, Jessi

WAYLON & WILLIE — see JENNINGS, Waylon / NELSON, Willie

WAYNE, Bobby '71
Born Robert Wayne Edrington in Childress, Texas. Guitarist with **Merle Haggard**'s Strangers.

2/6/71	61	7		Harold's Super Service	I Can't Stand Me	—	$6	Capitol 3025

WAYNE, Nancy '74

5/25/74	55	12	1	The Back Door Of Heaven	The Greatest Show On Earth	—	$5	20th Century 2086
10/5/74	34	11	2	Gone	'Til I Can't Take It Anymore	—	$5	20th Century 2124
4/26/75	80	7	3	I Wanna Kiss You	Cold Carolina Morning	—	$5	20th Century 2184

DEBUT	PEAK	WKS	Gold	A-side (Chart Hit)	B-side	Pop	$	Pic	Label & Number
				WEATHERLY, Jim '75 Born on 3/17/43 in Pontotoc, Mississippi. Singer/prolific songwriter.					
2/1/75	9	13		1 I'll Still Love You	My First Day Without Her	87	$5		Buddah 444
7/12/75	58	8		2 It Must Have Been The Rain	Mississippi	—	$5		Buddah 467
7/23/77	27	10		3 All That Keeps Me Going	I Hope It Never Rains Like That Again	—	$5		ABC 12288
11/3/79	32	11		4 Smooth Sailin'	Let Me Love It Away	—	$4		Elektra 46547
2/16/80	34	9		5 Gift From Missouri	All I Need To Know	—	$4		Elektra 46592
10/11/80	82	3		6 Safe In The Arms Of Your Love (Cold In The Streets)	All I Need To Know	—	$4		Elektra 47027
				WEAVERS, The '51 Highly influential folk group: Pete Seeger, Veronica "Ronnie" Gilbert, Lee Hays and Fred Kellerman. Backed by Hamilton Henry "Terry" Gilkyson. Hays died on 8/26/81 (age 68).					
6/2/51	8	2	●	On Top Of Old Smoky ... THE WEAVERS and TERRY GILKYSON Vic Schoen (orch.); adaptation of a traditonal Southern Highlands folk song	J:8 Across The Wide Missouri	2⁸	$20		Decca 9-27515
				WEBB, Jay Lee One LP—NO 45s '69 Born Willie Lee Webb on 2/12/37 in Van Lear, Kentucky. Died of cancer on 7/31/96 (age 59). Brother of **Loretta Lynn**, **Crystal Gayle** and **Peggy Sue**; distant cousin of **Patty Loveless**.					
2/11/67	37	6		1 I Come Home A-Drinkin' (To A Worn-Out Wife Like You) ... JACK WEBB answer to **Loretta Lynn**'s "Don't Come Home A'Drinkin"	Since You Made A Wreck Out Of Me	—	$8		Decca 32087
2/1/69	21	13		2 She's Lookin' Better By The Minute	The House Where Losers Go	—	$7		Decca 32430
11/27/71	69	5		3 The Happiness Of Having You	Don't Blow Your Horn, Gabe	—	$7		Decca 32887
				WEBB, June '58 Born on 9/22/34 in L'Anse, Michigan.					
11/3/58	29	3		A Mansion On The Hill	Friendly Enemy	—	$20		Hickory 1086
				WEBSTER, Chase '70 Born in Franklin, Tennessee. Singer/songwriter.					
6/20/70	68	2		Moody River ... #1 Pop hit for **Pat Boone** in 1961 (written by Webster)	Turn Out The Lights	—	$10		Show Biz 233
				WEISSBERG, Eric, & Steve Mandell '73 Prominent session musician. Former member of The Tarriers.					
2/3/73	5	12	●	1 Dueling Banjos ... ERIC WEISSBERG & STEVE MANDELL tune written in 1955 as "Feuding Banjos" by Arthur "Guitar Boogie" Smith; from the movie *Deliverance* starring **Burt Reynolds**	End Of A Dream [I]	2⁴	$6		Warner 7659
3/29/75	91	4		2 Yakety Yak ... ERIC WEISSBERG & DELIVERANCE #1 Pop hit for The Coasters in 1958	Meadow Muffins	—	$6		Epic 50072
				WELCH, Ernie '89 Born in Decatur, Alabama.					
5/20/89	96	1		Who Have You Got To Lose		—	$6		Duck Tape 021
				WELCH, Kevin '90 Born on 8/17/55 in Los Angeles; raised in Oklahoma. Singer/prolific songwriter. Also see **Tomorrow's World**.					
1/21/89	41	10		1 Stay November	I Am No Drifter	—	$4		Warner 27647
4/29/89	64	6		2 I Came Straight To You	Hello, I'm Gone	—	$4		Warner 22972
5/26/90	39	11		3 Till I See You Again	A Letter To Dustin	—	$4	■	Reprise 19873 (v)
10/20/90	49	11		4 Praying For Rain	The Mother Road	—	$4	■	Reprise 19585 (v)
3/2/91	54	10		5 True Love Never Dies	Some Kind Of Paradise	—	$4		Reprise 19440
				WELK, Lawrence '45 Born on 3/11/03 in Strasburg, North Dakota. Died of pneumonia on 5/17/92 (age 89). Polka bandleader/accordian player. Band's style labeled as "champagne music." Hosted own TV series from 1955-82. Charted 28 pop hits from 1944-65.					
9/8/45	❶¹	14		1 Shame On You /		13			
11/10/45	3	2		2 At Mail Call Today ... LAWRENCE WELK AND HIS ORCHESTRA with **RED FOLEY** (above 2)		—	$20		Decca 18698
				WELLER, Freddy ★163★ '69 Born Wilton Frederick Weller on 9/9/47 in Atlanta. Singer/songwriter/guitarist. Began career on the *Atlanta Jubilee* in East Point, Georgia. Worked as a guitarist with **Billy Joe Royal** and **Joe South**. Member of Paul Revere & The Raiders from 1967-71. 1)Games People Play 2)The Promised Land 3)Indian Lake 4)Another Night Of Love 5)These Are Not My People					
4/12/69	2²	17		1 Games People Play ... #12 Pop hit for **Joe South** in 1969	Home	—	$6		Columbia 44800
7/26/69	5	15		2 These Are Not My People	You Never Knew Julie	113	$6		Columbia 44916
11/22/69+	25	10		3 Down In The Boondocks ... #9 Pop hit for **Billy Joe Royal** in 1965	Amarillo, Texas	—	$6		Columbia 45026
4/11/70	75	2		4 I Shook The Hand	We Gotta All Get Together	—	$6		Columbia 45087
12/12/70+	3	18		5 The Promised Land ... written by **Chuck Berry**	Goodnight Sandy	125	$6		Columbia 45276
6/12/71	3	14		6 Indian Lake ... #10 Pop hit for The Cowsills in 1968	(I'd Do It All) Over You	108	$6		Columbia 45388
9/25/71	5	15		7 Another Night Of Love	Always Something Special	—	$6		Columbia 45451

DEBUT	PEAK	WKS	Gold	A-side (Chart Hit)	B-side	Pop	$	Pic	Label & Number
				WELLER, Freddy — Cont'd					
2/19/72	26	12		8 Ballad Of A Hillbilly Singer	Good Old-Fashioned Music	—	$6		Columbia 45542
6/24/72	17	12		9 The Roadmaster	Who Do You Love	—	$6		Columbia 45624
11/18/72+	11	13		10 She Loves Me (Right Out Of My Mind)	There's An Angel On My Shoulder	—	$6		Columbia 45723
4/21/73	8	14		11 Too Much Monkey Business	It Sure Feels Good (To Be Loved Again)	—	$5		Columbia 45827
				written by Chuck Berry					
8/18/73	13	13		12 The Perfect Stranger	Betty Ann And Shirley Cole	—	$5		Columbia 45902
12/15/73+	11	15		13 I've Just Got To Know (How Loving You Would Be)	Georgia Girl	—	$5		Columbia 45968
5/18/74	21	14		14 Sexy Lady	Bobby Crabtree's Grave	—	$5		Columbia 46040
9/14/74	16	15		15 You're Not Getting Older (You're Getting Better)	Are We Makin' Love?	—	$5		Columbia 10016
5/24/75	64	8		16 Love You Back To Georgia	Show Me The Way To Your Love	—	$5		ABC/Dot 17554
9/20/75	52	9		17 Stone Crazy	Still Making Love To You	—	$5		ABC/Dot 17577
3/20/76	42	9		18 Ask Any Old Cheater Who Knows	A Legend In My Home	—	$5		Columbia 10300
7/4/76	44	9		19 Liquor, Love And Life	Celia Brown	—	$5		Columbia 10352
10/9/76	56	8		20 Room 269	I Drank Myself Sober	—	$5		Columbia 10411
3/5/77	79	6		21 Strawberry Curls	When You Were Mine	—	$5		Columbia 10482
5/28/77	41	9		22 Merry-Go-Round	One Man Show	—	$5		Columbia 10539
9/10/77	44	9		23 Nobody Cares But You	Love Doctor	—	$5		Columbia 10598
2/25/78	93	4		24 Let Me Fall Back In Your Arms	Snuff Queens	—	$5		Columbia 10682
7/8/78	32	9		25 Bar Wars	One Of The Mysteries Of Love	—	$5		Columbia 10769
10/21/78	23	12		26 Love Got In The Way	You Win Again	—	$5		Columbia 10837
1/27/79	27	11		27 Fantasy Island	Take A Little Bit	—	$5		Columbia 10890
5/19/79	40	8		28 Nadine	Too Many Memories	—	$5		Columbia 10973
				#23 Pop hit for Chuck Berry in 1964					
8/11/79	44	9		29 That Run-Away Woman Of Mine	Atlanta	—	$4		Columbia 11044
11/24/79+	33	11		30 Go For The Night	Two Makes One Wonderful Love	—	$4		Columbia 11149
3/22/80	66	5		31 A Million Old Goodbyes	Sleep With Me	—	$4		Columbia 11221
5/17/80	45	8		32 Lost In Austin	Explosion!	—	$4		Columbia 11266
				WELLMAN, Tiny '88					
				Born Paul Wellman in Flatwoods, Kentucky.					
6/25/88	85	2		Nothing Left To Lose		—	$6		Lee Ann 7342

WELLS, Kitty ★36★ '52

Born Muriel Ellen Deason on 8/30/19 in Nashville. Singer/songwriter/guitarist. Married **Johnny Wright** on 10/30/37. Mother of **Bobby Wright** and **Ruby Wright**. Member of the *Louisiana Hayride* from 1948-53. Elected to the Country Music Hall of Fame in 1976. Won Grammy's Lifetime Achievement Award in 1991. Known as "The Queen of Country Music."

1)It Wasn't God Who Made Honky Tonk Angels 2)Heartbreak U.S.A. 3)One By One 4)Makin' Believe 5)You And Me

DEBUT	PEAK	WKS		A-side	B-side	Pop	$	Pic	Label & Number
7/19/52	❶⁶	18		1) It Wasn't God Who Made Honky Tonk Angels S:❶⁶ / J:❶⁶ / A:2	I Don't Want Your Money, I Want Your Time	—	$25		Decca 9-28232
				answer to "The Wild Side Of Life" by **Hank Thompson**; also see #81 below					
3/7/53	6	4		2 Paying For That Back Street Affair S:6 / J:9	Crying Steel Guitar Waltz	—	$20		Decca 28578
				answer to "Back Street Affair" by **Webb Pierce**					
9/12/53	8	2		3 Hey Joe J:8	My Cold Cold Heart Is Melted Now	—	$20		Decca 28797
				answer to "Hey Joe!" by **Carl Smith**					
1/23/54	9	1		4 Cheatin's A Sin J:9	I Gave My Wedding Dress Away	—	$20		Decca 28931
4/3/54	8	1		5 Release Me J:8	After Dark	—	$20		Decca 29023
5/22/54	❶¹	41		6 One By One / J:❶¹ / S:2 / A:2			$20		Decca 29065
7/10/54	12	1		7 I'm A Stranger In My Home A:12 / S:15		—	$20		
				KITTY WELLS and RED FOLEY (above 2)					
12/4/54	14	1		8 Thou Shalt Not Steal S:14	I Hope My Divorce Is Never Granted	—	$20		Decca 29313
2/26/55	3	16		9 As Long As I Live / J:3 / S:7 / A:8			$20		Decca 29390
				RED FOLEY And KITTY WELLS					
2/26/55	6	17		10 Make Believe ('Til We Can Make It Come True) J:6 / S:7 / A:14		—			
				KITTY WELLS And RED FOLEY					
3/12/55	2¹⁵	28		11 Makin' Believe / S:2 / A:2 / J:2		—			
4/9/55	7	11		12 Whose Shoulder Will You Cry On A:7		—	$20		Decca 29419
7/30/55	9	13		13 There's Poison In Your Heart / J:9 / S:11					
9/24/55	12	1		14 I'm In Love With You A:12		—	$20		Decca 29577
12/17/55+	7	8		15 Lonely Side Of Town / S:3 / J:7					
12/24/55	7	9		16 I've Kissed You My Last Time S:7 / A:10		—	$20		Decca 29728
1/28/56	3	31		17 You And Me / S:3 / A:3 / J:6			$20		Decca 29740
			6	18 No One But You	S:flip / J:flip	—			
				RED FOLEY and KITTY WELLS (above 2)					
5/12/56	11	5		19 How Far Is Heaven A:11 / S:15	Dust On The Bible	—	$20		Decca 29823
				KITTY WELLS With Carol Sue (her daughter)					
7/7/56	3	34		20 Searching (For Someone Like You) / J:3 / S:4 / A:4					
9/22/56	13	1		21 I'd Rather Stay Home A:13		—	$20		Decca 29956
12/1/56+	6	13		22 Repenting / J:6 / S:9 / A:11					
			7	23 I'm Counting On You	S:flip / J:flip	—	$20		Decca 30094
4/6/57	8	9		24 Oh' So Many Years A:8	Can You Find It In Your Heart	—	$15		Decca 30183
				KITTY WELLS and WEBB PIERCE					
6/3/57	7	9		25 Three Ways (To Love You) A:7 / S:15	A Change Of Heart	—	$15		Decca 30288

DEBUT	PEAK	WKS	Gold	A-side (Chart Hit)	B-side	Pop	$	Pic	Label & Number
				WELLS, Kitty — Cont'd					
9/23/57	10	6		26 (I'll Always Be Your) Fraulein — answer to "Fraulein" by Bobby Helms	S:10 / A:13 What I Believe Dear	—	$15		Decca 30415
1/20/58	12	1		27 One Week Later	A:12 When I'm With You	—	$15		Decca 30489
				WEBB PIERCE And KITTY WELLS					
3/3/58	3	19		28 I Can't Stop Loving You /	A:3 / S:8	—			
		11		29 She's No Angel	S:flip	—	$15		Decca 30551
7/7/58	7	14		30 Jealousy	A:7 / S:11 I Can't Help Wondering	78	$15		Decca 30662
10/6/58	15	11		31 Touch And Go Heart /		—			
11/10/58	16	7		32 He's Lost His Love For Me		—	$15		Decca 30736
2/16/59	5	14		33 Mommy For A Day /		—			
3/9/59	18	2		34 All The Time		—	$15		Decca 30804
7/6/59	12	10		35 Your Wild Life's Gonna Get You Down	You'll Never Be Mine Again	—	$15		Decca 30890
11/9/59+	5	25		36 Amigo's Guitar	Lonely Is A Word	—	$15		Decca 30987
4/18/60	5	22		37 Left To Right	Memory Of Love	—	$15		Decca 31065
9/5/60	16	9		38 Carmel By The Sea	The Man I Used To Know	—	$15		Decca 31123
12/19/60	26	3		39 I Can't Tell My Heart That	When Do You Love Me	—	$15		Decca 31164
				KITTY WELLS And ROY DRUSKY					
3/6/61	19	10		40 The Other Cheek /		—			
3/20/61	29	2		41 Fickle Fun		—	$12		Decca 31192
5/29/61	❶4	23		42 Heartbreak U.S.A. /		—			
6/26/61	20	5		43 There Must Be Another Way To Live		—	$12		Decca 31246
12/4/61+	10	12		44 Day Into Night /		—			
1/6/62	21	3		45 Our Mansion Is A Prison Now		—	$12		Decca 31313
3/3/62	5	14		46 Unloved Unwanted	Au Revoir (Goodbye)	—	$12		Decca 31349
8/4/62	8	11		47 Will Your Lawyer Talk To God	The Big Let Down	—	$12		Decca 31392
11/3/62	7	13		48 We Missed You	Wicked World	—	$10		Decca 31422
3/30/63	13	9		49 Cold And Lonely (Is The Forecast For Tonight)	Is It Asking Too Much	—	$10		Decca 31457
8/17/63	22	6		50 I Gave My Wedding Dress Away /		—			
8/3/63	29	2		51 A Heartache For A Keepsake		—	$10		Decca 31501
2/1/64	7	25		52 This White Circle On My Finger	(I Didn't Have To) Break Up Someone's Home	—	$10		Decca 31580
5/30/64	4	25		53 Password /		—			
6/20/64	34	4		54 I've Thought Of Leaving You		—	$10		Decca 31622
9/26/64	9	15		55 Finally	He Made You For Me	—	$10		Decca 31663
				KITTY WELLS And WEBB PIERCE					
12/26/64+	8	15		56 I'll Repossess My Heart	Kill Him With Kindness	—	$10		Decca 31705
4/17/65	4	17		57 You Don't Hear /		—			
3/20/65	27	14		58 Six Lonely Hours		—	$10		Decca 31749
8/14/65	9	16		59 Meanwhile, Down At Joe's	Leavin' Town Tonight	—	$10		Decca 31817
2/5/66	15	13		60 A Woman Half My Age	When Your Little High Horse Runs Down	—	$10		Decca 31881
7/23/66	14	13		61 It's All Over (But The Crying)	You Left Your Mark On Me	—	$10		Decca 31957
10/29/66	49	9		62 Only Me And My Hairdresser Know /		—			
10/15/66	52	9		63 A Woman Never Forgets		—	$10		Decca 32024
2/18/67	34	16		64 Love Makes The World Go Around	I'm Just Not Smart	—	$8		Decca 32088
5/6/67	43	11		65 Happiness Means You /		—			
6/3/67	60	5		66 Hello Number One		—	$10		Decca 32126
				KITTY WELLS AND RED FOLEY (above 2)					
8/12/67	28	13		67 Queen Of Honky Tonk Street	Wasting My Time	—	$10		Decca 32163
12/30/67+	63	4		68 Living As Strangers	Loved And Wanted	—	$10		Decca 32223
				KITTY WELLS AND RED FOLEY					
1/27/68	35	10		69 My Big Truck Drivin' Man	You Want Her Not Me	—	$10		Decca 32247
5/11/68	54	8		70 We'll Stick Together	Heartbreak Waltz	—	$10		Decca 32294
				KITTY WELLS And JOHNNY WRIGHT					
7/27/68	52	8		71 Gypsy King	When Hearts Grow Hard And Cold	—	$10		Decca 32343
11/16/68	47	7		72 Happiness Hill	You're No Angel Yourself	—	$10		Decca 32389
1/18/69	74	2		73 Have I Told You Lately That I Love You?	We Need One More Chance	—	$10		Decca 32427
				KITTY WELLS And RED FOLEY					
5/17/69	61	5		74 Guilty Street	Shape Up Or Get Out	—	$8	■	Decca 32455
8/15/70	71	4		75 Your Love Is The Way	It's Written All Over Your Face	—	$8		Decca 32700
4/17/71	72	2		76 They're Stepping All Over My Heart	Your Old Love Letters	—	$8		Decca 32795
7/24/71	49	9		77 Pledging My Love	Thank You For Loving Me	—	$8		Decca 32840
				#17 Pop hit for Johnny Ace in 1955					
4/1/72	72	3		78 Sincerely	J. J. Sneed	—	$8		Decca 32931
				#1 Pop hit for The McGuire Sisters in 1955					
9/27/75	94	3		79 Anybody Out There Wanna Be A Daddy	Somewhere Down The Road	—	$6		Capricorn 0240
8/25/79	75	6		80 Thank You For The Roses	Loving You Was All I Ever Needed	—	$7		Ruboca 122
10/6/79	60	6		81 The Wild Side Of Life	I Don't Believe I'll Fall In Love Today	—	$5		Mercury 57006
				RAYBURN ANTHONY WITH KITTY WELLS					
				WELLS, Mike '75					
				Born in 1964 in New Jersey.					
2/22/75	54	9		1 Sing A Love Song, Porter Wagoner	Detour	—	$5		Playboy 6029
2/7/76	77	7		2 Wild World	The Lady And The Tramp	—	$5		Playboy 6061
				#11 Pop hit for Cat Stevens in 1971					

WELLS, Ruby — see JOHNNIE & JACK

DEBUT	PEAK	WKS	Gold	A-side (Chart Hit)	B-side	Pop	$	Pic	Label & Number
				WENCE, Bill		'80			
				Born on 7/2/42 in Salinas, California. Worked as a DJ on several stations.					
9/15/79	92	4		1 Quicksand	—		$6		Rustic 1003
1/26/80	85	4		2 Break Away	—		$6		Rustic 1005
6/7/80	63	6		3 I Wanna Do It Again	Quicksand		$6		Rustic 1009
9/27/80	85	4		4 Night Lies	—		$6		Rustic 1012
				WEST, Dottie ★58★		'78			
				Born Dorothy Marie Marsh on 10/11/32 in McMinnville, Tennessee. Died in a car crash on 9/4/91 (age 58). Singer/songwriter/guitarist. Mother of **Shelly West**. Joined the *Grand Ole Opry* in 1964. Acted in the movies *Second Fiddle To A Steel Guitar* and *There's A Still On The Hill*. CMA Awards: 1978 & 1979 Vocal Duo of the Year (with **Kenny Rogers**). Also see **Some Of Chet's Friends**.					
				1)*Every Time Two Fools Collide* 2)*All I Ever Need Is You* 3)*A Lesson In Leavin'* 4)*What Are We Doin' In Love* 5)*Are You Happy Baby?*					
11/30/63	29	2		1 Let Me Off At The Corner	I Wish You Wouldn't Do That	—	$12		RCA Victor 8225
3/28/64	7	21		2 Love Is No Excuse		115	$10		RCA Victor 8324
				JIM REEVES & DOTTIE WEST					
8/22/64	10	15		3 Here Comes My Baby	(How Can I Face) These Heartaches Alone	—	$10		RCA Victor 8374
2/27/65	32	8		4 Didn't I	In It's Own Little Way	—	$10		RCA Victor 8467
5/22/65	30	10		5 Gettin' Married Has Made Us Strangers	It Just Takes Practice	—	$10		RCA Victor 8525
8/21/65	32	5		6 No Sign Of Living	Night Life	—	$10		RCA Victor 8615
12/4/65+	22	14		7 Before The Ring On Your Finger Turns Green	Wear Away	—	$10		RCA Victor 8702
3/12/66	5	21		8 Would You Hold It Against Me	You're The Only World I Know	—	$10		RCA Victor 8770
8/13/66	24	10		9 Mommy, Can I Still Call Him Daddy	Suffertime	—	$10		RCA Victor 8900
				DOTTIE WEST With Dale West (her son)					
12/17/66+	17	13		10 What's Come Over My Baby	How Many Lifetimes Will It Take?	—	$10		RCA Victor 9011
3/18/67	8	16		11 Paper Mansions	Someone's Gotta Cry	—	$10		RCA Victor 9118
8/26/67	13	14		12 Like A Fool	Everything's A Wreck (Since You're Gone)	—	$10		RCA Victor 9267
12/16/67+	24	12		13 Childhood Places	No One	—	$10		RCA Victor 9377
4/27/68	15	12		14 Country Girl	That's Where Our Love Must Be	—	$10		RCA Victor 9497
9/7/68	19	12		15 Reno	My Heart Has Changed Its Mind	—	$10		RCA Victor 9604
2/22/69	2¹	17		16 Rings Of Gold	Final Examination	—	$8		RCA Victor 9715
				DOTTIE WEST & DON GIBSON					
7/12/69	32	10		17 Sweet Memories	How's The World Treating You	—	$8		RCA Victor 0178
				DOTTIE WEST And DON GIBSON					
10/4/69	47	6		18 Clinging To My Baby's Hand	Don't Say A Word	—	$8		RCA Victor 0239
12/13/69+	7	13		19 There's A Story (Goin' 'Round)	Lock, Stock, And Teardrops	—	$8		RCA Victor 0291
				DOTTIE WEST AND DON GIBSON					
2/7/70	45	8		20 I Heard Our Song	Makin' Memories	—	$8		RCA Victor 9792
7/18/70	46	10		21 Til I Can't Take It Anymore	I Love You Because	—	$8		RCA Victor 9867
				DOTTIE WEST & DON GIBSON					
8/1/70	37	10		22 It's Dawned On Me You're Gone	Love's Farewell	—	$7		RCA Victor 9872
10/31/70	21	12		23 Forever Yours	The Cold Hand Of Fate	—	$7		RCA Victor 9911
1/30/71	29	11		24 Slowly	Sweet Thang	—	$6		RCA Victor 9947
				JIMMY DEAN AND DOTTIE WEST					
3/6/71	48	8		25 Careless Hands	Only One Thing Left To Do	—	$6		RCA Victor 9957
5/29/71	53	8		26 Lonely Is	Cancel Tomorrow	—	$6		RCA Victor 9982
9/11/71	51	8		27 Six Weeks Every Summer (Christmas Every Other Year)	Wish I Didn't Love You Anymore	—	$6		RCA Victor 1012
6/3/72	52	9		28 I'm Only A Woman	Baby I Tried	—	$6		RCA Victor 0711
12/2/72+	28	11		29 If It's All Right With You	Special Memory	97	$6		RCA Victor 0828
4/28/73	44	9		30 Just What I've Been Looking For	Everything's A Wreck (Since You're Gone)	—	$6		RCA Victor 0930
				Larry Gatlin (backing vocal)					
9/15/73	2¹	15		31 Country Sunshine	Wish I Didn't Love You Anymore	49	$6		RCA Victor 0072
3/30/74	8	14		32 Last Time I Saw Him	Everybody Bring A Song	—	$6		RCA Victor 0231
				#14 Pop hit for Diana Ross in 1974					
7/13/74	21	13		33 House Of Love	Love As Long As We Can	—	$6		RCA Victor 0321
12/14/74+	35	10		34 Lay Back Lover	Good Lovin' You	—	$6		RCA Victor 10125
5/10/75	65	10		35 Rollin' In Your Sweet Sunshine	Carolina Cousins	—	$6		RCA Victor 10269
3/27/76	68	7		36 Here Come The Flowers	He's Not For You	—	$6		RCA Victor 10553
6/26/76	91	5		37 If I'm A Fool For Loving You	Home Made Love	—	$6		RCA Victor 10699
11/13/76+	19	15		38 When It's Just You And Me	We Love Each Other	—	$5		United Artists 898
3/19/77	28	12		39 Every Word I Write	We Love Each Other	—	$5		United Artists 946
7/9/77	30	10		40 Tonight You Belong To Me	Tiny Fingers	—	$5		United Artists 1010
				#4 Pop hit for Patience & Prudence in 1956					
10/8/77	57	8		41 That's All I Wanted To Know	Who's Gonna Love Me Now	—	$5		United Artists 1084
2/18/78	❶²	17		42 Every Time Two Fools Collide	We Love Each Other	101	$5		United Artists 1137
				KENNY ROGERS & DOTTIE WEST					
6/10/78	17	12		43 Come See Me And Come Lonely	Decorate Your Conscience	—	$5		United Artists 1209
9/2/78	2¹	14		44 Anyone Who Isn't Me Tonight	You And Me	—	$5		United Artists 1234
				KENNY ROGERS & DOTTIE WEST					
12/2/78+	49	9		45 Reaching Out To Hold You	My Two Empty Arms	—	$5		United Artists 1257
2/17/79	❶¹	15		46 All I Ever Need Is You			$5		United Artists 1276
				(Hey Won't You Play) Another Somebody Done Somebody Wrong Song		102			
				KENNY ROGERS & DOTTIE WEST					
				#7 Pop hit for Sonny & Cher in 1971					

DEBUT	PEAK	WKS	Gold	A-side (Chart Hit)	B-side	Pop	$	Pic	Label & Number
				WEST, Dottie — Cont'd					
7/7/79	3	15		47 Til I Can Make It On My Own .... Midnight Flyer		—	$5		United Artists 1299
				KENNY ROGERS & DOTTIE WEST					
10/20/79	12	15		48 You Pick Me Up (And Put Me Down) .... We've Got Tonite		—	$5		United Artists 1324
2/9/80	❶¹	15		49 A Lesson In Leavin' .... Love's So Easy For Two		73	$5		United Artists 1339
6/7/80	13	14		50 Leavin's For Unbelievers .... Blue As I Want To		—	$5		United Artists 1352
12/13/80+	❶¹	16		51 Are You Happy Baby? .... Right Or Wrong		—	$4	■	Liberty 1392
4/4/81	❶¹	15		52 What Are We Doin' In Love .... Choosin' Means Losin' (West)		14	$4		Liberty 1404
				DOTTIE WEST (with Kenny Rogers)					
7/11/81	16	14		53 (I'm Gonna) Put You Back On The Rack .... Sorry Seems To Be The Hardest Word		—	$4		Liberty 1419
9/19/81	80	4		54 Once You Were Mine .... Dream Baby (How Long Must I Dream)		—	$4		RCA 12284
11/7/81+	16	14		55 It's High Time .... Don't Be Kind		—	$4	■	Liberty 1436
2/20/82	26	13		56 You're Not Easy To Forget .... Something's Missin'		—	$4		Liberty 1451
9/11/82	29	11		57 She Can't Get My Love Off The Bed .... Hurt		—	$4	■	Liberty 1479
12/18/82+	63	7		58 If It Takes All Night .... Try To Win A Friend		—	$4	■	Liberty 1490
6/18/83	40	11		59 Tulsa Ballroom .... The Woman In Love With You		—	$4		Liberty 1500
3/24/84	19	15		60 Together Again .... Baby I'm A Want You		—	$4		Liberty 1516
				KENNY ROGERS and DOTTIE WEST					
9/15/84	77	7		61 What's Good For The Goose (Is Good For The Gander) .... Tell Me Again		—	$4		Permian 82006
12/1/84	67	8		62 Let Love Come Lookin' For You .... Blue Fiddle Waltz		—	$4		Permian 82007
5/25/85	53	8		63 We Know Better Now .... Let Love Come Lookin' For You		—	$4		Permian 82010
				WEST, Elbert '01					
				Born in 1968 in Welch, West Virginia.					
6/9/01	56	3		Diddley		—			album cut
				from the album *Livin' The Life* on Broken Bow 0004					
				WEST, Jim '80					
11/3/79	95	2		1 Honky Tonk Disco		—	$6		Macho 002
12/15/79	92	4		2 Can't Love On Lies		—	$6		Macho 003
				JIM WEST (with Carol Chase)					
12/20/80	79	5		3 Slip Away		—	$6		Macho 008
3/14/81	83	3		4 Lovin' Night .... Dancin' Round And Round		—	$6		Macho 009
				Stephanie Winslow (backing vocal)					
	★221★			**WEST, Shelly** '81					
				Born on 5/23/58 in Cleveland; raised in Nashville. Singer/songwriter/guitarist. Daughter of **Dottie West**. Married to **Allen Frizzell** from 1977-85. Formed a singing partnership with Allen's brother, **David Frizzell**. CMA Awards: 1981 & 1982 Vocal Duo of the Year (with David Frizzell).					
				1)You're The Reason God Made Oklahoma 2)José Cuervo 3)I Just Came Here To Dance 4)Flight 309 To Tennessee 5)Another Honky-Tonk Night On Broadway					
				DAVID FRIZZELL & SHELLY WEST:					
1/17/81	❶¹	17		1 You're The Reason God Made Oklahoma .... That's Where Lovers Go Wrong		—	$4		Warner 49650
				from the movie *Any Which Way You Can* starring **Clint Eastwood**					
6/20/81	9	15		2 A Texas State Of Mind .... Let's Duet		—	$4		Warner 49745
10/10/81	16	16		3 Husbands And Wives .... Yours For The Asking		—	$4		Warner 49825
2/6/82	8	18		4 Another Honky-Tonk Night On Broadway .... Three Act Play		—	$4		Warner 50007
7/17/82	4	18		5 I Just Came Here To Dance .... Our Day Will Come		—	$4		Warner 29980
12/4/82+	43	11		6 Please Surrender .... Being A Man, Being A Woman		—	$4		Warner 29850
				from the movie *Honkytonk Man* starring **Clint Eastwood**					
				SHELLY WEST:					
2/12/83	❶¹	23		7 José Cuervo .... Country Lullaby		—	$4		Warner 29778
3/26/83	52	10		8 Cajun Invitation .... Yesterday's Lovers		—	$4		Warner 29756
				FRIZZELL & WEST					
7/2/83	4	18		9 Flight 309 To Tennessee .... Sexy Song		—	$4		Viva 29597
9/3/83	71	4		10 Pleasure Island .... Betcha Can't Cry Just Once		—	$4		Viva 29544
				FRIZZELL & WEST					
11/5/83+	10	18		11 Another Motel Memory .... Suite Sixteen		—	$4		Viva 29461
2/4/84	20	17		12 Silent Partners .... Confidential		—	$4		Viva 29404
				FRIZZELL & WEST					
3/10/84	56	7		13 Now I Lay Me Down To Cheat .... Let's Make A Little Love Tonight		—	$4		Viva 29353
6/2/84	34	14		14 Somebody Buy This Cowgirl A Beer .... Small Talk		—	$4		Viva 29265
9/15/84	13	20		15 It's A Be Together Night .... S:8 / A:16 Straight From The Heart		—	$4		Viva 29187
				FRIZZELL & WEST					
1/19/85	21	16		16 Now There's You .... S:18 / A:21 I'll Still Be Loving You		—	$4		Viva 29106
4/13/85	60	8		17 Do Me Right .... Easy, Soft And Slow		—	$4		Viva 29048
				FRIZZELL & WEST					
6/15/85	46	10		18 Don't Make Me Wait On The Moon .... Let's Stay The Way We Are Tonight		—	$4		Warner 28997
9/7/85	64	7		19 I'll Dance The Two Step .... Why Must The Ending Be So Sad		—	$4		Warner 28909
3/15/86	54	5		20 What Would You Do .... Why Must The Ending Be So Sad		—	$4		Warner 28769
9/6/86	55	10		21 Love Don't Come Any Better Than This .... My Heart Feels Like Dancing Again		—	$4		Warner 28648
				WEST, Speedy — see ORVILLE & IVY					
				WESTERN FLYER '96					
				Group from Texas: Danny Myrick (vocals), Steve Charles, Chris Marion, Roger Helton, T.J. Klay and Bruce Gust. Named after the brand of bicycle.					
7/23/94	61	9		1 Western Flyer .... I Would Give Anything		—	$4		Step One 479
10/29/94	62	8		2 She Should've Been Mine .... I Would Give Anything		—	$4		Step One 485
7/22/95	71	3		3 Friday Night Stampede		—			album cut

DEBUT	PEAK	WKS	Gold	A-side (Chart Hit)..B-side	Pop	$	Pic	Label & Number
				WESTERN FLYER — Cont'd				
11/11/95	74	1		4 His Memory...	—			album cut
				above 2 from the album Western Flyer on Step One 85				
8/3/96	32	20		5 What Will You Do With M-E .... S:24 (album version)	—	$4	∎	Step One 507
				WESTERN UNION BAND, The **'88**				
7/9/88	76	3		1 Bed Of Roses...L.A. Freeway	—	$6		Shawn-Del 2201
10/8/88	81	3		2 Rising Cost Of Loving You...................................So Much Love	—	$6		Shawn-Del 2202
				WHEELER, Billy Edd **'65**				
				Born on 12/9/32 in Whitesville, West Virginia. Singer/songwriter/guitarist.				
11/28/64+	3	24		1 Ode To The Little Brown Shack Out Back .... Sister Sara [N]	50	$8		Kapp 617
				recorded "live" at The Mountain State Art & Craft Fair in Ripley, West Virginia				
8/24/68	63	5		2 I Ain't The Worryin' Kind .... It's More Than Honey (That I'm After)	—	$8		Kapp 928
5/3/69	51	6		3 West Virginia Woman .... One Step	—	$7		United Artists 50507
9/13/69	62	7		4 Fried Chicken And A Country Tune .... The Coon Hunters	—	$7		United Artists 50579
7/29/72	71	3		5 200 Lbs. O' Slingin' Hound .... The Hoedown	—	$6		RCA Victor 0739
11/17/79	94	2		6 Duel Under The Snow .... Ode To The Little Brown Shack Out Back	—	$7		Radio Cinema 001
6/20/81	55	6		7 Daddy..Long Arm Of The Law (Wheeler)	—	$5		NSD 94
				BILLY EDD WHEELER with Rashell Richmond				
				WHEELER, Karen **'74**				
				Born on 3/12/47 in Sikeston, Missouri. Singer/songwriter/guitarist. Daughter of **Onie Wheeler**.				
7/8/72	67	4		1 The First Time For Us ....A Special Day	—	$6		Chart 5166
3/9/74	31	12		2 Born To Love And Satisfy ....A Woman In Love	—	$5	∎	RCA Victor 0223
9/21/74	97	3		3 What Can I Do (To Make Me Happy)..............You're Smothering Me	—	$5		RCA Victor 10034
				WHEELER, Onie **'73**				
				Born on 11/10/21 in Senath, Missouri. Died onstage at the *Grand Ole Opry* on 5/27/84 (age 62). Singer/songwriter/harmonica player. Father of **Karen Wheeler**.				
2/3/73	53	10		John's Been Shucking My Corn.................. Make 'Em All Go Home [N]	—	$7		Royal American 76
				WHIPPLE, Sterling **'78**				
				Born in Eugene, Oregon. Singer/songwriter.				
4/15/78	26	9		1 Dirty Work ....Don't Give Up On Me	—	$4		Warner 8552
10/14/78	25	10		2 Then You'll Remember................................Nice Guys Always Finish Last	—	$4		Warner 8632
3/24/79	84	4		3 Love Is Hours In The Making .... What Do You Do With Your Hands	—	$4		Warner 8747
				WHISPERING WILL **'79**				
2/24/79	89	2		Double W .... [N]	—	$6		Vista 104
				parody of "Double S" by Bill Anderson				
				WHITE, Bill **'78**				
				Born in 1934 in Muldrow, Oklahoma. Brother of **Ann J. Morton** and **Jim Mundy**.				
7/15/78	79	3		Unbreakable Hearts .... Lovely Love	—	$6		Prairie Dust 7625
				WHITE, Brian **'88**				
5/21/88	70	4		It's Too Late To Love You Now	—	$6		Oak 1050
				WHITE, Bryan **'96**				
	★218★			Born on 2/17/74 in Lawton, Oklahoma; raised in Oklahoma City. Singer/songwriter/guitarist. Began playing drums at age five. Moved to Nashville in 1992; worked as a staff writer at **Glen Campbell** Music. Married actress Erika Page on 10/14/2000. CMA Award: 1996 Horizon Award.				
				1)So Much For Pretending 2)Sittin' On Go 3)Rebecca Lynn				
10/8/94	48	9		1 Eugene You Genius.......................................Going, Going, Gone	—	$4	∎	Asylum 64510 (v)
12/24/94+	24	20		2 Look At Me Now..Helpless Heart	—	$4	∎	Asylum 64489 (v)
5/13/95	❶¹	20		3 Someone Else's Star .... S:5 This Town	112	$4	∎	Asylum 64435 (v)
10/7/95+	❶¹	20		4 Rebecca Lynn .... S:7 Nothing Less Than Love	114	$4	∎	Asylum 64360 (v)
3/2/96	4	20		5 I'm Not Supposed To Love You Anymore .... S:2 Blindhearted	101	$4	∎	Asylum 64313 (v)
6/29/96	❶²	20		6 So Much For Pretending .... S:6 On Any Given Night	119	$4	∎	Asylum 64267 (v)
10/19/96+	15	20		7 That's Another Song	—			album cut
3/1/97	❶¹	20		8 Sittin' On Go	—			album cut
				above 2 from the album Between Now And Forever on Asylum 61880				
8/2/97	4	20		9 Love Is The Right Place .... S:7 Between Now And Forever	101	$4	∎	Asylum 64152
11/15/97+	6	32		10 From This Moment On	4			album cut
				SHANIA TWAIN with Bryan White				
				from Twain's album Come On Over on Mercury 536003				
11/29/97+	16	20		11 One Small Miracle	—			album cut
4/11/98	30	11		12 Bad Day To Let You Go	—			album cut
				above 2 from the album The Right Place on Asylum 62047				
5/30/98	69	5		13 One Heart At A Time .... S:5 (same version)	56	$4	∎	Atlantic 84117
				GARTH BROOKS, BILLY DEAN, FAITH HILL, OLIVIA NEWTON-JOHN, NEAL McCOY, MICHAEL McDONALD, VICTORIA SHAW, BRYAN WHITE				
8/1/98	45	12		14 Tree Of Hearts	—			album cut
				from the album The Right Place on Asylum 62047				
6/19/99	39	20		15 You're Still Beautiful To Me .... S:5 Shari Ann	—	$4	★	Asylum 64035 (v)
10/23/99+	40	20		16 God Gave Me You	—			album cut
				from the album How Lucky I Am on Asylum 62278				
12/11/99	62	1		17 Holiday Inn .... [X]	—			album cut
				from the album Dreaming Of Christmas on Asylum 62464				
10/28/00	56	8		18 How Long	—			album cut
				from the album Greatest Hits on Asylum 47890				

DEBUT	PEAK	WKS	Gold	A-side (Chart Hit)	B-side	Pop	$	Pic	Label & Number
				WHITE, Charley '79					
6/30/79	86	2		Rocket 'Til The Cows Come Home	My Babe [N]	—	$7		NSD 22
				WHITE, Danny '83					
				Born Wilford Daniel White on 2/9/52 in Mesa, Arizona. Pro football quarterback with the Dallas Cowboys from 1976-88.					
2/5/83	85	2		You're A Part Of Me	Let It Be Me	—	$6		Grand Prix 2
				DANNY WHITE & LINDA NAIL					
				WHITE, JJ — see JJ					
				WHITE, Joy '93					
				Born on 10/2/61 in Turrell, Arkansas; raised in Mishawaka, Indiana.					
10/24/92	68	3		1 Little Tears	Maybe In Mayberry	—	$4		Columbia 74412
1/30/93	45	14		2 True Confessions	Let's Talk About Love Again	—	$4		Columbia 74845
6/12/93	71	3		3 Cold Day In July	Bittersweet End	—	$4		Columbia 74952
7/9/94	73	5		4 Wild Love	You Were Right From Your Side	—	$4	■	Columbia 77565 (v)
				JOY LYNN WHITE					
				WHITE, L.E., And Lola Jean Dillon '77					
				White was born in Knoxville, Tennessee. Played fiddle in **Bill Monroe**'s band. Father of **Michael White**.					
6/18/77	73	7		1 Home, Sweet Home	It's Almost As Cold Outside [N]	—	$6		Epic 50389
11/26/77	90	3		2 You're The Reason Our Kids Are Ugly	The Vacation [N]	—	$6		Epic 50474
	★337★			**WHITE, Lari** '94					
				Born on 5/13/65 in Dunedin, Florida. Singer/songwriter/pianist.					
				1) Now I Know 2) That's How You Know (When You're In Love) 3) That's My Baby					
2/13/93	44	12		1 What A Woman Wants	Good Good Love	—	$4		RCA 62420
5/15/93	47	16		2 Lead Me Not	Anything Goes	—	$4		RCA 62511
9/11/93	68	4		3 Lay Around And Love On You	Don't Leave Me Lonely	—	$4		RCA 62622
4/9/94	10	20		4 That's My Baby	Where The Lights Are Low	—	$4	■	RCA 62764 (v)
9/3/94	5	20		5 Now I Know	It's Love	—	$4	■	RCA 62896 (v)
1/21/95	10	20		6 That's How You Know (When You're In Love)	If I'm Not Already Crazy	—	$4		RCA 64233
12/16/95+	20	20		7 Ready, Willing And Able	Don't Fence Me In	—	$4	■	RCA 64455 (v)
5/18/96	52	7		8 Wild At Heart	Do It Again	—	$4		RCA 64520
7/26/97	18	20		9 Helping Me Get Over You		—			album cut
				TRAVIS TRITT Featuring Lari White					
				from Tritt's album *The Restless Kind* on Warner 46304					
5/16/98	16	20		10 Stepping Stone	S:7 Tired	73	$4	■	Lyric Street 64019 (v)
10/3/98+	32	20		11 Take Me		125			album cut
4/10/99	64	5		12 John Wayne Walking Away		—			album cut
				above 2 from the album *Stepping Stone* on Lyric Street 65001					
				WHITE, Mack '74					
				Born in Dothan, Georgia.					
12/1/73+	34	14		1 Too Much Pride	By The Circle On Your Finger	—	$6		Commercial 1314
4/27/74	66	7		2 Sweet And Tender Feeling	Thou Shalt Not Steal	—	$6		Commercial 1315
10/19/74	75	10		3 Ain't It All Worth Living For	Thou Shalt Not Steal	—	$5		Playboy 6016
2/28/76	35	13		4 Let Me Be Your Friend	That Woman Of Mine	—	$6		Commercial 1317
8/21/76	34	10		5 Take Me As I Am (Or Let Me Go)	By The Circle On Your Finger	—	$6		Commercial 1319
11/27/76	68	8		6 A Stranger To Me	That Woman Of Mine	—	$6		Commercial 1320
3/25/78	77	6		7 Just Out Of Reach	You Can Have Her	—	$6		Commercial 00033
				#24 Pop hit for Solomon Burke in 1961					
7/15/78	83	3		8 Goodbyes Don't Come Easy		—	$6		Commercial 00040
2/27/82	88	3		9 Kiss The Hurt Away		—	$6		Commercial 121
				WHITE, Michael '92					
				Born in Knoxville, Tennessee; raised in Nashville. Singer/songwriter. Son of **L.E. White**.					
12/21/91+	32	18		1 Professional Fool	Hard Headed Broken Hearted	—	$4	■	Reprise 19128 (v)
6/27/92	43	11		2 Familiar Ground	Me Or The Misery	—	$4		Reprise 18881
11/7/92	63	4		3 She Likes To Dance	(dance mix)	—	$4		Reprise 18694
				WHITE, Roger '67					
10/14/67	57	4		Mystery Of Tallahatchie Bridge	Wild Roses	123	$12		Big A 103
				answer to "Ode To Billie Joe" by **Bobbie Gentry**					
				WHITE, Sharon — see SKAGGS, Ricky / WHITES, The					
				WHITE, Tony Joe '83					
				Born on 7/23/43 in Goodwill, Louisiana. Singer/songwriter. Best known for his 1969 pop hit "Polk Salad Annie."					
11/1/80	91	2		1 Mama Don't Let Your Cowboys Grow Up To Be Babies	Disco Blues	—	$5		Casablanca 2304
				Waylon Jennings (guest vocal); parody of "Mammas Don't Let Your Babies Grow Up To Be Cowboys" by **Waylon & Willie**					
11/26/83	55	10		2 The Lady In My Life	We Belong Together	—	$4		Columbia 04134
3/3/84	85	3		3 We Belong Together	Naughty Lady	—	$4		Columbia 04356
				WHITEHEAD, Benny '73					
				Born in Dallas. Singer/songwriter.					
1/27/73	61	5		Blue Eyed Jane	So Long Gone	—	$6		Reprise 1131

DEBUT	PEAK	WKS	Gold	A-side (Chart Hit)	B-side	Pop	$	Pic	Label & Number
	★279★			**WHITES, The** '83 Family trio from Abilene, Texas: H.S. "Buck" White (guitar, mandolin, piano; born on 1/13/30), with daughters Cheryl (bass; born on 1/27/55) and Sharon White (guitar; born on 12/17/53). All share vocals. Sharon married Ricky Skaggs in 1982. Group joined the Grand Ole Opry in 1984.					
				1)Hangin' Around 2)I Wonder Who's Holding My Baby Tonight 3)Pins And Needles					
6/20/81	66	4		1 Send Me The Pillow You Dream On	West Virginia Memories	—	$4		Capitol 5004
8/28/82	10	17		2 You Put The Blue In Me	Old River	—	$4		Elektra/Curb 69980
12/25/82+	9	19		3 Hangin' Around	West Virginia Mem'ries	—	$4		Elektra/Curb 69855
4/30/83	9	18		4 I Wonder Who's Holding My Baby Tonight	Follow The Leader	—	$4		Warner/Curb 29659
9/10/83	25	14		5 When The New Wears Off Of Our Love	Blue Letters	—	$4		Warner/Curb 29513
12/17/83+	10	19		6 Give Me Back That Old Familiar Feeling	Pipeliner Blues	—	$4		Warner/Curb 29411
5/12/84	14	17		7 Forever You	(Our Own) Jole' Blon	—	$4		MCA/Curb 52187
8/25/84	10	22		8 Pins And Needles	S:8 / A:12 Move It On Over	—	$4		MCA/Curb 52432
3/9/85	12	17		9 If It Ain't Love (Let's Leave It Alone)	S:11 / A:16 I Don't Care	—	$4		MCA/Curb 52535
6/29/85	27	15		10 Hometown Gossip	A:25 / S:27 No One Has To Tell Me (What Love Is)	—	$4		MCA/Curb 52615
11/2/85	33	14		11 I Don't Want To Get Over You	Down In Louisiana	—	$4		MCA/Curb 52697
5/24/86	36	12		12 Love Won't Wait	A:35 Daddy's Hands	—	$4		MCA/Curb 52825
11/8/86+	30	16		13 It Should Have Been Easy	A:30 Love Won't Wait	—	$4		MCA/Curb 52953
3/7/87	58	7		14 There Ain't No Binds	Mama's Rockin' Chair	—	$4		MCA/Curb 53038
4/8/89	82	2		15 Doing It By The Book	—		$4		Canaan 689357
				WHITE WATER JUNCTION '84					
10/27/84	97	1		Sleeping Back To Back	—		$5		Jungle Rogue 1004
	★271★			**WHITING, Margaret** '49 Born on 7/22/24 in Detroit; raised in Hollywood. Charted 36 pop hits from 1945-67.					
				MARGARET WHITING and JIMMY WAKELY:					
9/10/49	❶^{17}	28	●	1 Slipping Around /	S:❶^{17} / J:❶^{12} / A:2	❶^3			
9/10/49	6	8		2 Wedding Bells	J:6 / S:7	30	$15		Capitol 40224
11/5/49	2^3	13		3 I'll Never Slip Around Again S:2 / J:2 / A:10 Six Times A Week And Twice On Sunday		8	$15		Capitol 40246
2/11/50	2^1	9		4 Broken Down Merry-Go-Round /	S:2 / J:3 / A:5	12			
2/11/50	3	7		5 The Gods Were Angry With Me	S:3 / J:4	17	$20		Capitol F800
4/22/50	2^1	10		6 Let's Go To Church (Next Sunday Morning)	S:2 / A:6 / J:6 Why Do You Say Those Things (That Hurt Me So)	13	$20		Capitol F960
11/18/50	6	1		7 A Bushel And A Peck	S:6 / J:10 Beyond The Reef	6	$20		Capitol F1234
				from the Broadway musical Guys And Dolls starring Robert Alda					
6/2/51	7	2		8 When You And I Were Young Maggie Blues	J:7 Till We Meet Again	20	$20		Capitol F1500
12/8/51	5	5		9 I Don't Want To Be Free	J:5 Let's Live A Little	—	$20		Capitol F1816
				WHITLEY, Keith ★177★ '88 Born Jesse Keith Whitley on 7/1/55 in Sandy Hook, Kentucky. Died of alcohol poisoning on 5/9/89 (age 33). Singer/songwriter/guitarist. Appeared with Buddy Starcher on radio in Charleston, West Virginia, at age eight. Formed the East Kentucky Mountain Boys with Ricky Skaggs in 1968. Played in Ralph Stanley's Clinch Mountain Boys in the mid-1970s. Married Lorrie Morgan in 1986.					
				1)When You Say Nothing At All 2)I'm No Stranger To The Rain 3)Don't Close Your Eyes					
9/29/84	59	9		1 Turn Me To Love	Pick Me Up On Your Way Down	—	$4		RCA 13810
				Patty Loveless (harmony vocal)					
2/23/85	76	7		2 A Hard Act To Follow	Don't Our Love Look Natural	—	$4		RCA 13996
9/14/85	57	10		3 I've Got The Heart For You	I Gotta Get Drunk	—	$4		RCA 14173
11/2/85+	14	20		4 Miami, My Amy	S:13 / A:14 I've Got The Heart For You	—	$4		RCA 14285
6/21/86	9	26		5 Ten Feet Away	A:8 / S:9 Nobody In His Right Mind Would've Left Her	—	$4		RCA 14363
11/8/86+	9	23		6 Homecoming '63	A:9 / S:20 On The Other Hand	—	$4		RCA 5013
3/14/87	10	16		7 Hard Livin'	A:14 / S:15 Quittin' Time	—	$4		RCA 5116
8/29/87	36	17		8 Would These Arms Be In Your Way	Someone New	—	$4	◉	RCA 5237
				insert folds out with a picture of Whitley					
11/14/87+	16	21		9 Some Old Side Road	Light At The End Of The Tunnel	—	$4		RCA 5326
4/30/88	❶^1	23		10 Don't Close Your Eyes	S:5 Lucky Dog	—	$4		RCA 6901
9/17/88	❶^2	22		11 When You Say Nothing At All	S:5 Lucky Dog	—	$4		RCA 8637
1/21/89	❶^2	22		12 I'm No Stranger To The Rain	A Day In The Life	—	$4		RCA 8797
				CMA Award: Single of the Year					
6/24/89	❶^1	19		13 I Wonder Do You Think Of Me	Brother Jukebox	—	$4		RCA 8940
10/14/89+	❶^1	26		14 It Ain't Nothin'	Heartbreak Highway	—	$4		RCA 9059
3/3/90	3	26		15 I'm Over You	Tennessee Courage	—	$4		RCA 9122
7/28/90	13	20		16 'Til A Tear Becomes A Rose	Lady's Choice	—	$4		RCA 2619
				KEITH WHITLEY AND LORRIE MORGAN					
9/7/91	2^1	20		17 Brotherly Love	Backbone Job	—	$4		RCA 62037
				KEITH WHITLEY & EARL THOMAS CONLEY					
12/21/91+	15	20		18 Somebody's Doin' Me Right	Would These Arms Be In Your Way	—	$4		RCA 62166
11/4/95	75	1		19 Wherever You Are Tonight	Tell Me Something I Don't Know	—	$4	■	BNA 64424 (v)

DEBUT	PEAK	WKS	Gold	A-side (Chart Hit)	B-side	Pop	$	Pic	Label & Number

WHITMAN, Slim ★140★ '52
Born Otis Dewey Whitman on 1/20/24 in Tampa, Florida. Singer/songwriter/guitarist/yodeller. Served in the U.S. Navy from 1943-46. On radio station WDAE in Tampa in 1946; also worked local clubs. Regular on the *Louisiana Hayride* in 1950. Once known as "The Smilin' Star Duster."

1) Indian Love Call 2) Secret Love 3) Keep It A Secret 4) Rose-Marie 5) Singing Hills

DEBUT	PEAK	WKS		#	A-side	B-side	Pop	$	Label & Number
5/17/52	10	1		1	Love Song Of The Waterfall	A:10 My Love Is Going Stale	—	$25	Imperial 45-8134
					SLIM WHITMAN (The Smilin' Star Duster)				
7/5/52	2³	24	●	2	Indian Love Call	S:2 / J:2 / A:3 China Doll	9	$25	Imperial 45-8156
12/6/52+	3	13		3	Keep It A Secret /	A:3 / J:3 / S:5	—		
12/20/52	10	1		4	My Heart Is Broken In Three	J:10		$25	Imperial 45-8169
11/14/53	8	5		5	North Wind	S:8 / A:8 / J:8 Darlin' Don't Cry	—	$25	Imperial 8208
1/23/54	2¹	18	●	6	Secret Love	A:2 / S:3 / J:3 Why	—	$25	Imperial 8223
					#1 Pop hit for Doris Day in 1954; from the movie *Calamity Jane* starring Doris Day				
5/1/54	4	23	●	7	Rose-Marie	J:4 / S:5 / A:7 We Stood At The Altar	—	$25	Imperial 8236
11/6/54	4	3		8	Singing Hills	J:4 I Hate To See You Cry	—	$25	Imperial 8267
1/15/55	11	2		9	Cattle Call	S:11 When I Grow Too Old To Dream	—	$25	Imperial 8281
7/3/61	30	1		10	The Bells That Broke My Heart	I'd Climb The Highest Mountain	—	$15	Imperial 5746
2/29/64	48	1		11	Tell Me Pretty Words	Only You And You Alone	—	$10	Imperial 66012
10/30/65	8	17		12	More Than Yesterday	La Golondrina	—	$10	Imperial 66130
3/12/66	17	12		13	The Twelfth Of Never	Straight From Heaven	—	$10	Imperial 66153
					#9 Pop hit for Johnny Mathis in 1957				
7/16/66	49	2		14	I Remember You	A Travelin' Man	134	$10	Imperial 66181
					#5 Pop hit for Frank Ifield in 1962; also see #36 below				
12/3/66	54	6		15	One Dream	Jerry	—	$10	Imperial 66212
3/11/67	56	8		16	What's This World A-Comin' To	You Bring Out The Best In Me	—	$10	Imperial 66226
7/22/67	61	6		17	I'm A Fool	North Wind	—	$10	Imperial 66248
11/18/67	65	5		18	The Keeper Of The Key	Broken Wings	—	$10	Imperial 66262
3/16/68	17	14		19	Rainbows Are Back In Style	How Could I Not Love You	—	$10	Imperial 66283
8/10/68	22	11		20	Happy Street	My Heart Is In The Roses	—	$10	Imperial 66311
11/30/68+	43	8		21	Livin' On Lovin' (And Lovin' Livin' With You)	Heaven Says Hello	—	$10	Imperial 66337
4/19/69	43	4		22	My Happiness	Promises	—	$10	Imperial 66358
					#2 Pop hit for Connie Francis in 1959				
7/12/69	61	5		23	Irresistible	Flower Of Love	—	$10	Imperial 66384
4/18/70	27	12		24	Tomorrow Never Comes	Come Take My Hand	—	$10	Imperial 66441
8/8/70	26	12		25	Shutters And Boards	I Pretend	—	$8	United Artists 50697
					#24 Pop hit for Jerry Wallace in 1963				
12/12/70+	7	14		26	Guess Who	From Heaven To Heartache	121	$8	United Artists 50731
					#31 Pop hit for Jesse Belvin in 1959				
5/1/71	6	15		27	Something Beautiful (To Remember)	Jerry	—	$7	United Artists 50775
8/14/71	21	13		28	It's A Sin To Tell A Lie	That's Enough For Me	—	$7	United Artists 50806
					#7 Pop hit for Somethin' Smith & The Redheads in 1955				
12/11/71+	56	7		29	Loveliest Night Of The Year	Near You	—	$7	United Artists 50852
					#3 Pop hit for Mario Lanza in 1951				
10/21/72	51	7		30	(It's No) Sin	It Takes A Lot Of Tenderness	—	$7	United Artists 50952
					#1 Pop hit for Eddy Howard in 1951				
3/3/73	73	4		31	Hold Me	So Close To Home	—	$6	United Artists 178
7/14/73	88	5		32	Where The Lilacs Grow	Something Beautiful (To Remember)	—	$6	United Artists 269
4/20/74	82	5		33	It's All In The Game	Make Believe	—	$6	United Artists 402
					#1 Pop hit for Tommy Edwards in 1958				
8/9/80	15	12		34	When	Since You Went Away	—	$5	Cleveland Int'l 50912
11/22/80	69	5		35	That Silver-Haired Daddy Of Mine	If I Could Only Dream	—	$5	Cleveland Int'l 50946
					#7 Pop hit for Gene Autry & Jimmy Long in 1935				
2/7/81	44	8		36	I Remember You	Where Do I Go From Here [R]	—	$5	Cleveland Int'l 50971
					new version of #14 above				
8/15/81	54	7		37	Can't Help Falling In Love With You	Oh My Darlin' (I Love You)	—	$5	Cleveland Int'l 02402
					#2 Pop hit for Elvis Presley in 1962				

WHITTAKER, Roger '83
Born on 3/22/36 in Nairobi, Kenya (British parents). Best known for his 1975 pop hit "The Last Farewell."

DEBUT	PEAK	WKS		#	A-side	B-side	Pop	$	Label & Number
12/17/83	91	4			I Love You Because	Eternally	—	$5	Main Street 93016

WICHITA LINEMEN, The '79
Vocal group from Wichita, Kansas. Led by Greg Stevens.

DEBUT	PEAK	WKS		#	A-side	B-side	Pop	$	Label & Number
12/24/77	100	2		1	Everyday Of My Life		—	$6	Linemen 773
10/20/79	93	4		2	You're A Pretty Lady, Lady	Magic Hands	—	$6	Linemen 10838
					THE WICHITA LINEMEN featuring Greg Stevens				

WICKHAM, Lewie '70
Born in New Mexico. Singer/songwriter/guitarist.

DEBUT	PEAK	WKS		#	A-side	B-side	Pop	$	Label & Number
3/28/70	36	10		1	Little Bit Late	Endless Love Affair [N]	—	$7	Starday 888
7/8/78	59	7		2	$60 Duck	Truckers Lament [N]	—	$5	MCA 40928

DEBUT	PEAK	WKS	Gold	A-side (Chart Hit)	B-side	Pop	$	Pic	Label & Number
				WICKLINE '84 Group from Fox Island, Washington. Led by husband-and-wife team of Bob and Lynda Wickline.					
3/28/81	90	3		1 Do Fish Swim?	—		$6		Cascade Mt. 2325
9/10/83	85	3		2 True Love's Getting Pretty Hard To Find	—		$6		Cascade Mt. 3030
2/4/84	78	7		3 Ski Bumpus/Banjo Fantasy II .... Powder Winter [I]	—		$6		Cascade Mt. 4045
				WICKLINE BAND Featuring Scott Gavin					
				WIER, Rusty '87 Born in Austin, Texas. Male singer/songwriter/guitarist.					
4/25/87	74	4		1 Close Your Eyes ..... Kum-Bak Bar & Grill written by James Taylor			$6		Black Hat 102
8/15/87	70	5		2 (Lover Of The) Other Side Of The Hill ..... I Kept Thinkin' About You			$6		Black Hat 103
				WIGGINS, "Little" Roy — see MORGAN, George					
				WIGGINS, John & Audrey '94 Brother-and-sister duo from Waynesville, North Carolina. John was born on 10/13/62. Audrey was born on 12/26/67.					
4/30/94	47	11		1 Falling Out Of Love ..... Memory Making Night			$4	■	Mercury 858476 (v)
8/13/94	22	20		2 Has Anybody Seen Amy ..... Memory Making Night			$4	■	Mercury 858920 (v)
11/26/94	58	9		3 She's In The Bedroom Crying ..... New Mexico			$4	■	Mercury 856296 (v)
4/5/97	49	12		4 Somewhere In Love ..... I Can Sleep When I'm Dead			$4		Mercury 574300
				WILBOURN, Bill, & Kathy Morrison '70 Wilbourn was born in Aliceville, Alabama. Worked as a DJ.					
7/20/68	65	5		1 The Lovers ..... Your Gentle Way Of Loving Me			$6		United Artists 50310
1/11/69	44	6		2 Him And Her ..... You're Driving You Out Of My Mind			$6		United Artists 50474
6/28/69	52	7		3 Lovin' Season ..... Model Couple #81 Pop hit for Gene & Debbe in 1968			$6		United Artists 50537
5/9/70	34	12		4 A Good Thing ..... That's The Way I Want It To Be			$6		United Artists 50660
10/31/70	65	6		5 Look How Far We've Come ..... The Hand That Feeds You			$6		United Artists 50718
				WILBURN BROTHERS ★137★ '67 Duo from Hardy, Arkansas: brothers Virgil "Doyle" (born on 7/7/30; died on 10/16/82, age 52) and Thurman "Teddy" (born on 11/30/31) Wilburn. Regulars on the *Louisiana Hayride* from 1948-51. Joined the *Grand Ole Opry* in 1953. Doyle was once married to Margie Bowes. Also see Webb Pierce. 1)Hurt Her Once For Me 2)Trouble's Back In Town 3)Sparkling Brown Eyes 4)Which One Is To Blame 5)Roll Muddy River					
6/12/54	4	18		1 Sparkling Brown Eyes S:4 / A:4 / J:4 WEBB PIERCE With Wilburn Brothers			$25		Decca 29107
6/11/55	13	2		2 I Wanna Wanna Wanna ..... A:13 My Heart Or My Mind			$20		Decca 29459
1/21/56	13	3		3 You're Not Play Love ..... A:13 Look Around (Take A Look At Me)			$20		Decca 29747
8/11/56	10	8		4 I'm So In Love With You A:10 Deep Elem Blues			$20		Decca 29887
12/1/56	6	11		5 Go Away With Me A:6 Great Big Love			$15		Decca 30087
7/8/57	8	2		6 Mister Love A:8 Leave Me			$15		Decca 30305
				ERNEST TUBB and THE WILBURN BROTHERS					
5/26/58	9	10		7 Hey, Mr. Bluebird A:9 / S:14 How Do We Know			$15		Decca 30610
				ERNEST TUBB And THE WILBURN BROTHERS					
1/5/59	4	19		8 Which One Is To Blame /	—				
1/19/59	18	4		9 The Knoxville Girl	—		$15		Decca 30787
5/18/59	6	19		10 Somebody's Back In Town I Love Everybody			$15		Decca 30871
10/26/59	9	13		11 A Woman's Intuition A Town That Never Sleeps			$15		Decca 30968
12/19/60	27	2		12 The Best Of All My Heartaches ..... Someone Else's Love			$12		Decca 31152
7/31/61	14	6		13 Blue Blue Day ..... No Legal Right			$12		Decca 31276
5/12/62	4	22		14 Trouble's Back In Town Young But True Love	101		$12		Decca 31363
11/17/62	21	5		15 The Sound Of Your Footsteps ..... Day After Day			$12		Decca 31425
5/11/63	4	13		16 Roll Muddy River Not That I Care			$12		Decca 31464
9/14/63	10	13		17 Tell Her So Here Comes A Million Memories			$12		Decca 31520
2/29/64	34	4		18 Hangin' Around ..... Never Alone			$12		Decca 31578
11/14/64+	19	15		19 I'm Gonna Tie One On Tonight ..... Making Plans			$10		Decca 31674
5/29/65	30	12		20 I Had One Too Many ..... Left Out			$10		Decca 31764
9/18/65	5	20		21 It's Another World My Day Won't Be Complete			$10		Decca 31819
2/5/66	8	17		22 Someone Before Me Something About You			$10		Decca 31894
7/9/66	13	14		23 I Can't Keep Away From You ..... I'm Not Gonna Dress Up			$10		Decca 31974
11/12/66+	3	20		24 Hurt Her Once For Me /	—				
2/11/67	70	3		25 Just To Be Where You Are	—		$8		Decca 32038
4/29/67	13	14		26 Roarin' Again ..... Go Mena Si (I'm Sorry)			$8		Decca 32117
9/9/67	24	14		27 Goody, Goody Gumdrop ..... You're Standing In The Way			$8		Decca 32169
10/26/68	43	8		28 We Need A Lot More Happiness ..... If You're With Me			$8		Decca 32386
3/15/69	38	11		29 It Looks Like The Sun's Gonna Shine ..... Make My Heart Die Away			$8		Decca 32449
1/31/70	37	8		30 Little Johnny From Down The Street ..... Which Side's The Wrong Side			$8		Decca 32608
3/4/72	47	9		31 Arkansas ..... Santa Fe Rolls Royce			$8		Decca 32921
				WILCOX, Harlow, and the Oakies '69 Born in Norman, Oklahoma. Session guitarist.					
9/20/69	42	13		Groovy Grubworm ..... Moose Trot [I]		30	$8	■	Plantation 28

The World's Meanest Mother – Chickie Williams (45) ★★★

DEBUT	PEAK	WKS	Gold	A-side (Chart Hit)	B-side	Pop	$	Pic	Label & Number

WILD CHOIR '86
Group from Nashville: **Gail Davies**, Pete Pendras, Denny Bixby, Larry Chaney and Bob Mummert.

| 6/14/86 | 51 | 13 | | 1 Next Time ....Love Back | — | | $4 | | RCA 14337 |
| 10/25/86 | 40 | 13 | | 2 Heart To Heart ....I Don't Wanta Hold Your Hand | — | | $4 | | RCA 5011 |

WILD CHOIR FEATURING GAIL DAVIES

WILD HORSES '01
Group from Texas: husband-and-wife Angela Rae (vocals) and Michael Mahler (guitar), with Joe Lee Koenig (guitar), Stephen Kellough (bass) and Ralph McCauley (drums).

| 10/20/01 | 46 | 11 | | I Will Survive .... | — | | $10 | ★ | Epic 24250 |

available only as a promotional CD single

WILD ROSE '89
Female group: Pamela Gadd (vocals), Wanda Vick (guitar), Pam Perry (mandolin), Kathy Mac (bass) and Nancy Given Prout (drums). Prout was formerly married to Brian Prout of **Diamond Rio**.

9/16/89	15	17		1 Breaking New Ground ....Home Sweet Highway	—		$4		Universal 66018
1/13/90	38	15		2 Go Down Swingin' ....Wild Rose	—		$4		Universal 66033
6/8/91	73	2		3 Straight And Narrow	—				album cut

from the album *Straight And Narrow* on Capitol 94255

WILEY and GENE '46
Duo of Wiley Walker and **Gene Sullivan**. Walker was born on 11/17/11 in Laurel Hill, Florida. Died on 5/17/66 (age 54). Sullivan was born on 11/16/14 in Carbon Hill, Alabama. Died on 10/24/84 (age 69).

| 1/5/46 | 2¹ | 1 | | Make Room In Your Heart For A Friend ....Forgive Me | — | | $20 | | Columbia 36869 |

WILKINS, Little David '75
| | ★341★ | | | | | | | | |

Born in Parsons, Tennessee. Singer/songwriter/pianist.
1) One Monkey Don't Stop No Show 2) Whoever Turned You On, Forgot To Turn You Off 3) The Good Night Special

| 3/22/69 | 54 | 7 | | 1 Just Blow In His Ear ....Government Inspected | — | | $7 | | Plantation 11 |

DAVID WILKINS

6/23/73	63	4		2 Love In The Back Seat ....To My One And Only	—		$5		MCA 40034
9/22/73	41	12		3 Too Much Hold Back ....You Can't Stop Me From Loving You	—		$5		MCA 40115
3/30/74	50	9		4 Georgia Keeps Pulling On My Ring......................Run It By Me One More Time	—		$5		MCA 40200
10/26/74	77	8		5 Not Tonight..My Love For You	—		$5		MCA 40299
12/28/74+	14	15		6 Whoever Turned You On, Forgot To Turn You Off.................Butterbeans	—		$5		MCA 40345
7/19/75	11	14		7 One Monkey Don't Stop No Show ....Make Me Stop Loving Her	—		$5		MCA 40427
1/31/76	18	15		8 The Good Night Special.......................Let's Do Something (Even If It's Wrong)	—		$5		MCA 40510
7/4/76	75	5		9 Disco-Tex /					
		4		10 Half The Way In, Half The Way Out	—		$5		MCA 40579
11/20/76	88	5		11 The Greatest Show On Earth ....King Of All The Taverns	—		$5		MCA 40646
1/22/77	21	12		12 He'll Play The Music (But You Can't Make Him Dance).........He Cries Like A Baby	—		$5		MCA 40668
6/18/77	60	8		13 Is Everybody Ready ....Makin' Love In Waltz Time	—		$5		MCA 40734
10/22/77	21	14		14 Agree To Disagree ....Her Old Stomping Ground	—		$5		Playboy 5822
3/4/78	68	6		15 Don't Stop The Music (You're Playing My Song)...The Only Good Part Of Leaving	—		$5		Playboy 5825
8/5/78	74	5		16 Motel Rooms ....If There's An Easy Way For Love To Die	—		$5		Epic 50571
7/12/86	79	3		17 Lady In Distress	—		$5		Jere 1003
7/25/87	72	4		18 Butterbeans ....Stone Country	—		$4		16th Avenue 70401

JOHNNY RUSSELL & LITTLE DAVID WILKINS

WILKINSONS, The '98
Family vocal trio from Belleville, Ontario, Canada: father Steve (born on 8/18/55) with children Amanda (born on 1/17/82) and Tyler (born on 4/30/84) Wilkinson.

6/13/98	3	22		1 26¢ ....S:2 (album snipets)	55		$4	■	Giant 17197 (v)
10/24/98+	15	21		2 Fly (the angel song) ....S:●¹ 26¢ (acoustic version)	53		$4	★	Giant 17131 (v)
3/27/99	50	15		3 Boy Oh Boy ....S:20 The Word	—		$4	★	Giant 16986 (v)
7/10/99	45	15		4 The Yodelin' Blues	—				album cut

from the album *Nothing But Love* on Giant 24699

| 1/15/00 | 34 | 20 | | 5 Jimmy's Got A Girlfriend ....S:4 Williamstown | — | | $4 | ★ | Giant 16887 (v) |
| 6/10/00 | 49 | 9 | | 6 Shame On Me .... | — | | | | album cut |

from the album *Here And Now* on Giant 24736

| 4/14/01 | 51 | 6 | | 7 I Wanna Be That Girl...............................S:21 1999 | — | | $4 | ★ | Giant 16766 (v) |

WILLCOX, Pete '82
Singer/actor. **Elvis Presley** impersonator. Played "The King" on the TV's *The Last Precinct*.

| 4/24/82 | 75 | 5 | | The King .... | — | | $7 | | M&M 503 |

WILLET, Slim '52
Born Winston Lee Moore on 12/1/19 in Victor, Texas. Died of a heart attack on 7/1/66 (age 46). Singer/songwriter.

| 9/27/52 | ●¹ | 23 | | Don't Let The Stars (Get In Your Eyes) ....A:●¹ / S:2 J:2 Hadacol Corners | — | | $25 | | 4 Star 1614 |

SLIM WILLET With The Brush Cutters

WILLIAMS, Becky '88
Born in Corpus Christi, Texas.

| 7/9/88 | 75 | 4 | | Tie Me Up (Hold Me Down) .... | — | | $5 | ■ | Country Pride 0011 |

WILLIAMS, Beth '87
Born in Puerto Rico; raised in Texas.

9/27/86	82	3		1 Wrong Train..Blue Tonight	—		$5		BGM 71086
11/29/86	64	7		2 These Eyes..	—		$5		BGM 92486
3/28/87	58	6		3 Man At The Backdoor ....The Way I Do	—		$5		BGM 13087

DEBUT	PEAK	WKS	Gold	#	A-side (Chart Hit)	B-side	Pop	$	Pic	Label & Number

WILLIAMS, Cootie, and his Orchestra '44
Born Charles Melvin Williams on 7/24/08 in Mobile, Alabama. Died on 9/15/85 (age 77). Jazz trumpeter.

| 7/8/44 | 4 | 6 | | | Red Blues | Things Ain't What They Used To Be | 18 | $25 | | Hit 7084 |

Eddie "Cleanhead" Vinson (vocal); issued on Majestic 7084 as "Cherry Red-Blues"

WILLIAMS, Diana '76
Born in Nashville.

| 8/28/76 | 53 | 6 | | | Teddy Bear's Last Ride | If You Cared Enough To Cry [S] | 66 | $5 | | Capitol 4317 |

answer to "Teddy Bear" by Red Sovine

WILLIAMS, Don ★34★ '80
Born on 5/27/39 in Floydada, Texas. Singer/songwriter/guitarist. Made professional debut in 1957. Member of the Pozo-Seco Singers from 1964-71. Acted in the movies W.W. & The Dixie Dancekings and Smokey & The Bandit II. CMA Award: 1978 Male Vocalist of the Year.

1) I Believe In You 2) Lord, I Hope This Day Is Good 3) You're My Best Friend 4) Some Broken Hearts Never Mend
5) Till The Rivers All Run Dry

DEBUT	PEAK	WKS	#	A-side	B-side	Pop	$	Label & Number
12/16/72+	14	16	1	The Shelter Of Your Eyes	Playin' Around	—	$7	JMI 12
5/5/73	12	16	2	Come Early Morning /		—		
7/28/73	33	11	3	Amanda		—	$7	JMI 24
11/17/73+	13	14	4	Atta Way To Go	I Recall A Gypsy Woman	—	$7	JMI 32
3/2/74	5	15	5	We Should Be Together	Millers Cave	—	$7	JMI 36
6/29/74	62	7	6	Down The Road I Go	She's In Love With A Rodeo Man	—	$7	JMI 42
7/6/74	❶¹	17	7	I Wouldn't Want To Live If You Didn't Love Me	Fly Away	—	$6	Dot 17516
12/14/74+	4	15	8	The Ties That Bind	Goodbye Isn't Really Good At All	—	$5	ABC/Dot 17531

#37 Pop hit for Brook Benton in 1960

4/12/75	❶¹	17	9	You're My Best Friend	Where Are You	—	$5	ABC/Dot 17550
8/16/75	❶¹	16	10	(Turn Out The Light And) Love Me Tonight	Reason To Be	—	$5	ABC/Dot 17568
1/31/76	❶¹	16	11	Till The Rivers All Run Dry	Don't You Think It's Time	—	$5	ABC/Dot 17604
6/12/76	❶¹	14	12	Say It Again	I Don't Want The Money	—	$5	ABC/Dot 17631
10/16/76	2²	15	13	She Never Knew Me	Ramblin' [I]	103	$5	ABC/Dot 17658
3/12/77	❶¹	16	14	Some Broken Hearts Never Mend	I'll Forgive But I'll Never Forget	108	$5	ABC/Dot 17683
9/3/77	❶¹	15	15	I'm Just A Country Boy	It's Gotta Be Magic	110	$5	ABC/Dot 17717
2/11/78	7	14	16	I've Got A Winner In You	Overlookin' And Underthinkin'	—	$5	ABC 12332
7/1/78	3	15	17	Rake And Ramblin' Man	Too Many Tears	—	$5	ABC 12373
11/4/78+	❶¹	16	18	Tulsa Time	When I'm With You	106	$5	ABC 12425

#30 Pop hit for Eric Clapton in 1980

| 3/17/79 | 3 | 15 | 19 | Lay Down Beside Me | I Would Like To See You Again | — | $4 | MCA 12458 |

also released on ABC 12458 in 1979

8/4/79	❶¹	14	20	It Must Be Love	Not A Chance	—	$4	MCA 41069
12/8/79+	❶¹	16	21	Love Me Over Again	Circle Driveway	—	$4	MCA 41155
2/16/80	97	2	22	Could You Ever Really Love A Poor Boy	Livingston Saturday Night	—	$7	Phono 2693
3/29/80	2³	15	23	Good Ole Boys Like Me	We're All The Way	—	$4	MCA 41205
8/23/80	❶²	16	24	I Believe In You	It Only Rains On Me	24	$4	MCA 41304
2/21/81	6	16	25	Falling Again	I Keep Putting Off Getting Over You	—	$4	MCA 51065
7/4/81	4	15	26	Miracles	I Don't Want To Love You	—	$4	MCA 51134
9/19/81	3	17	27	If I Needed You	Ashes By Now	—	$4	Warner 49809

EMMYLOU HARRIS & DON WILLIAMS

11/21/81+	❶¹	20	28	Lord, I Hope This Day Is Good	Smooth Talking Baby	—	$4	MCA 51207
4/17/82	3	16	29	Listen To The Radio	Only Love	—	$4	MCA 52037
8/21/82	3	17	30	Mistakes	Fool, Fool Heart	—	$4	MCA 52097
12/11/82+	❶¹	20	31	If Hollywood Don't Need You	Help Yourselves To Each Other	—	$4	MCA 52152
4/16/83	❶¹	18	32	Love Is On A Roll	I'll Take Your Love Anytime	—	$4	MCA 52205
7/30/83	2¹	19	33	Nobody But You	If Love Gets There Before I Do	—	$4	MCA 52245
12/3/83+	❶¹	19	34	Stay Young	Pressure Makes Diamonds	—	$4	MCA 52310
5/19/84	❶¹	20	35	That's The Thing About Love	I'm Still Looking For You	—	$4	MCA 52389
9/1/84	11	21	36	Maggie's Dream	A:10 / S:11 Leavin'	—	$4	MCA 52448
1/5/85	2¹	20	37	Walkin' A Broken Heart	S:2 / A:2 True Blue Hearts	—	$4	MCA 52514
10/12/85	20	19	38	It's Time For Love	S:20 / A:20 I'll Never Need Another You	—	$4	MCA 52692
1/18/86	3	22	39	We've Got A Good Fire Goin'	S:2 / A:2 Shot Full Of Love	—	$4	■ Capitol 5526
5/31/86	❶¹	22	40	Heartbeat In The Darkness	A:❶¹ / S:2 The Light In Your Eyes	—	$4	Capitol 5588
10/18/86+	3	22	41	Then It's Love	A:3 / S:4 It's About Time	—	$4	Capitol 5638
2/7/87	9	21	42	Senorita	A:9 / S:13 Send Her Roses	—	$4	Capitol 5683
6/6/87	4	26	43	I'll Never Be In Love Again	S:❶² Send Her Roses	—	$4	Capitol 44019
10/24/87+	9	26	44	I Wouldn't Be A Man	S:18 The Light In Your Eyes	—	$4	■ Capitol 44066
3/12/88	5	23	45	Another Place, Another Time	S:16 Running Out Of Reasons To Run	—	$4	Capitol 44131
8/13/88	7	24	46	Desperately	S:22 You Love Me Through It All	—	$4	Capitol 44216
1/7/89	5	21	47	Old Coyote Town	You Love Me Through It All	—	$4	Capitol 44274
4/22/89	4	24	48	One Good Well	Flowers Won't Grow (In Gardens Of Stone)	—	$4	RCA 8867
9/16/89	4	26	49	I've Been Loved By The Best	Won't You Love Me Like You Love Me	—	$4	RCA 9017
1/27/90	4	26	50	Just As Long As I Have You	Why Get Up	—	$4	RCA 9119
6/16/90	22	21	51	Maybe That's All It Takes	We're All The Way	—	$4	RCA 2507
9/15/90	2²	20	52	Back In My Younger Days	Diamonds To Dust	—	$4	RCA 2677

DEBUT	PEAK	WKS	Gold	A-side (Chart Hit)	B-side	Pop	$	Pic	Label & Number
				WILLIAMS, Don — Cont'd					
1/19/91	4	20		53 True Love	Learn To Let It Go	—	$4		RCA 2745
5/18/91	7	20		54 Lord Have Mercy On A Country Boy	Jamaica Farewell	—	$4		RCA 2820
2/15/92	72	3		55 Too Much Love	Back On The Street Again	—	$4		RCA 62180
6/6/92	73	2		56 It's Who You Love	The Old Trail	—	$4		RCA 62240

WILLIAMS, Hank ★44★ '50

Born Hiram King Williams on 9/17/23 in Mount Olive, Alabama. Died of alcohol/drug abuse on 1/1/53 (age 29). Singer/songwriter/guitarist. Hosted own radio show on WSFA in Montgomery; billed as "The Singing Kid." Formed his own band, **The Drifting Cowboys**, as a teenager. Married Audrey Sheppard in 1944; their son is **Hank Williams, Jr.**. First recorded for Sterling in 1946. Regular on the *Louisiana Hayride* from 1948-49, with the *Grand Ole Opry* from 1949-52. In 1952, divorced Audrey, was fired from the Opry in August and married Billie Jean Jones Eshlimar (**Billie Jean Horton**) who later married **Johnny Horton**. Elected to the Country Music Hall of Fame in 1961. Also recorded as Luke The Drifter. Won Grammy's Lifetime Achievement Award in 1987. Inducted into the Rock and Roll Hall of Fame in 1987 as a forefather of rock 'n' roll.

1) Lovesick Blues 2) Jambalaya (On The Bayou) 3) Kaw-Liga 4) Why Don't You Love Me 5) Hey, Good Lookin'

HANK WILLIAMS With His Drifting Cowboys:

DEBUT	PEAK	WKS	Gold	# A-side	B-side	Pop	$	Pic	Label & Number
8/9/47	4	3		1 Move It On Over	(Last Night) I Heard You Crying In Your Sleep	—	$100		MGM 10033
7/3/48	14	1		2 Honky Tonkin' first released in 1947 on Sterling 210 ($400)	J:14 I'll Be A Bachelor 'Til I Die	—	$75		MGM 10171
7/24/48	6	3		3 I'm A Long Gone Daddy	J:6 Blues Come Around	—	$50		MGM 10212
3/5/49	12	2		4 Mansion On The Hill	J:12 I Can't Get You Off Of My Mind	—	$50		MGM 10328
3/5/49	0^{16}	42	●	5 Lovesick Blues /	S:0^{16} / J:0^{10}	24			
7/9/49	6	2		6 Never Again (Will I Knock On Your Door)	J:6	—	$50		MGM 10352
5/14/49	2^2	29		7 Wedding Bells	S:2 / J:2 I've Just Told Mama Goodbye	—	$50		MGM 10401
7/23/49	5	11		8 Mind Your Own Business	J:5 / S:6 There'll Be No Tear-Drops Tonight	—	$40		MGM 10461
10/1/49	4	9		9 You're Gonna Change (Or I'm Gonna Leave) /	S:4 / J:8	—			
10/8/49	12	3		10 Lost Highway	S:12 / J:14	—	$40		MGM 10506
11/26/49	2^1	12		11 My Bucket's Got A Hole In It	S:2 / J:2 / A:5 I'm So Lonesome I Could Cry	—	$40		MGM 10560
2/18/50	5	5		12 I Just Don't Like This Kind Of Livin'	S:5 / J:5 / A:8 May You Never Be Alone	—	$50		MGM 10609
3/25/50	0^8	21		13 Long Gone Lonesome Blues /	A:0^8 / S:0^5 / J:0^4	—			
4/15/50	9	1		14 My Son Calls Another Man Daddy	J:9	—	$50		MGM K10645
5/27/50	0^{10}	25		15 Why Don't You Love Me also see #41 below	A:0^{10} / S:0^6 / J:0^5 A House Without Love	—	$50		MGM K10696
10/7/50	5	6		16 They'll Never Take Her Love From Me /	A:5	—			
10/14/50	9	1		17 Why Should We Try Anymore	S:9	—	$50		MGM K10760
11/18/50	0^1	15		18 Moanin' The Blues	A:0^1 / S:2 / J:3	—			
11/18/50	9	4		19 Nobody's Lonesome For Me	A:9	—	$50		MGM K10832
3/17/51	0^1	46	●	20 Cold, Cold Heart /	A:0^1 / S:2 / J:4	—			
3/3/51	8	4		21 Dear John	J:8 / S:10	—	$50		MGM K10904
6/9/51	2^2	13		22 I Can't Help It (If I'm Still In Love With You)	A:2 / J:3 / S:6	—			
5/26/51	3	10		23 Howlin' At The Moon	J:3 / S:4 / A:6	—	$50		MGM K10961
7/14/51	0^8	25		24 Hey, Good Lookin'	A:0^8 / S:2 / J:2 My Heart Would Know	—	$40		MGM K11000
10/20/51	4	18		25 Crazy Heart /	J:4 / A:6 / S:7	—			
10/20/51	9	2		26 Lonesome Whistle	A:9	—	$40		MGM K11054
12/22/51+	4	15		27 Baby, We're Really In Love	A:4 / J:4 / S:8 I'd Still Want You	—	$40		MGM K11100
3/1/52	2^1	12		28 Honky Tonk Blues	J:2 / S:7 / A:10 I'm Sorry For You, My Friend	—	$40		MGM K11160
5/3/52	2^2	16		29 Half As Much	S:2 / J:4 / A:7 Let's Turn Back The Years	—	$40		MGM K11202
8/16/52	0^{14}	29	●	30 Jambalaya (On The Bayou)	S:0^{14} / A:0^{14} / J:0^{12} Window Shopping	20	$40		MGM K11283
10/11/52	2^1	12		31 Settin' The Woods On Fire /	A:2 / J:4 / S:5	—			
11/15/52	10	1		32 You Win Again	J:10	—	$40		MGM K11318
12/20/52+	0^1	13		33 I'll Never Get Out Of This World Alive	S:0^1 / J:4 / A:7 I Could Never Be Ashamed Of You	—	$40		MGM 11366
2/21/53	0^{13}	19		34 Kaw-Liga /	S:0^{13} / A:0^8 / J:0^8	—			
2/21/53	0^6	23		35 Your Cheatin' Heart	A:0^6 / J:0^2 / S:2	—	$40		MGM 11416
5/16/53	0^4	13		36 Take These Chains From My Heart	S:0^4 / J:2 / A:3 Ramblin' Man	—	$40		MGM 11479
7/25/53	4	9		37 I Won't Be Home No More	S:4 / J:4 / A:5 My Love For You (Has Turned To Hate)	—	$40		MGM 11533
10/10/53	7	2		38 Weary Blues From Waitin'	S:7 / J:7 / A:9 I Can't Escape From You	—	$40		MGM 11574
4/30/55	9	3		39 Please Don't Let Me Love You	J:9 Faded Love And Winter Roses	—	$30		MGM 11928
				HANK WILLIAMS:					
6/11/66	43	4		40 I'm So Lonesome I Could Cry recorded in 1949 (B-side of #11 above); features new instrumental backing	You Win Again	109	$10		MGM 13489
10/9/76	61	7		41 Why Don't You Love Me same version as #15 above	Ramblin' Man [R]	—	$6		MGM 14849
2/4/89	7	14		42 There's A Tear In My Beer HANK WILLIAMS, JR. with Hank Williams, Sr.	You Brought Me Down To Earth	—	$4	■	Warner/Curb 27584

DEBUT	PEAK	WKS	Gold	A-side (Chart Hit)	B-side	Pop	$	Pic	Label & Number

Why Can't We All Just Get Along — ★★★

WILLIAMS, Hank Jr. ★16★ '81

Born Randall Hank Williams on 5/26/49 in Shreveport, Louisiana; raised in Nashville. Singer/songwriter/guitarist. Son of **Hank Williams**; father of **Hank Williams III**. Injured in a mountain climbing accident on 8/8/75 in Montana, returned to performing in 1977. Starred in movie *A Time To Sing*. His father gave him the nickname "Bocephus." Also recorded as **Luke The Drifter, Jr.** CMA Awards: 1987 & 1988 Entertainer of the Year.

1) All For The Love Of Sunshine 2) Mind Your Own Business 3) Eleven Roses 4) I'm For Love 5) Born To Boogie

DEBUT	PEAK	WKS		A-side	B-side	Pop	$		Label & Number
2/8/64	5	19	1	Long Gone Lonesome Blues	Doesn't Anybody Know My Name	67	$12	■	MGM 13208
7/25/64	42	6	2	Guess What, That's Right, She's Gone	Goin' Steady With The Blues	—	$12	■	MGM 13253
12/26/64+	46	5	3	Endless Sleep	My Bucket's Got A Hole In It	90	$12		MGM 13278
				#5 Pop hit for Jody Reynolds in 1958					
5/28/66	5	19	4	Standing In The Shadows	It's Written All Over Your Face	—	$10		MGM 13504
12/24/66+	43	13	5	I Can't Take It No Longer	You Can Hear A Tear Drop	—	$10		MGM 13640
6/17/67	60	4	6	I'm In No Condition	I'm Gonna Break Your Heart	—	$10		MGM 13730
8/26/67	46	8	7	Nobody's Child	Next Best Thing To Nothing	—	$10		MGM 13782
1/13/68	31	11	8	I Wouldn't Change A Thing About You (But Your Name)	No Meaning And No End	—	$10		MGM 13857
6/1/68	51	6	9	The Old Ryman	I Wonder Where You Are Tonight	—	$10		MGM 13922
8/31/68	3	16	10	It's All Over But The Crying	Rock In My Shoe	—	$8		MGM 13968
				from the movie *A Time to Sing* starring Williams					
11/9/68	39	8	11	I Was With Red Foley (The Night He Passed Away)	On Trial	—	$8		MGM 14002
1/18/69	14	12	12	Custody	My Home Town Circle "R"	—	$8		MGM 14020
				LUKE THE DRIFTER, JR.					
2/22/69	16	10	13	A Baby Again	Swim Across A Tear	—	$8		MGM 14024
5/3/69	3	14	14	Cajun Baby	My Heart Won't Let Me Go	107	$7		MGM 14047
				also see #82 below					
7/5/69	37	8	15	Be Careful Of Stones That You Throw	Book Of Memories	—	$7		MGM 14062
				LUKE THE DRIFTER, JR.					
				#31 Pop hit for Dion in 1963					
9/13/69	4	14	16	I'd Rather Be Gone	Try Try Again	—	$7		MGM 14077
1/3/70	36	8	17	Something To Think About	(There Must Be) A Better Way To Live	—	$7		MGM 14095
				LUKE THE DRIFTER, JR.					
3/7/70	12	13	18	I Walked Out On Heaven	Your Love's One Thing (I Ain't Forgot)	—	$7		MGM 14107
5/23/70	36	9	19	It Don't Take But One Mistake	Goin' Home	—	$7		MGM 14120
				LUKE THE DRIFTER, JR.					
7/4/70	23	12	20	Removing The Shadow	Party People	—	$7		MGM 14136
				HANK WILLIAMS, JR. and LOIS JOHNSON					
8/1/70	❶²	15	21	All For The Love Of Sunshine	Ballad Of The Moonshine	—	$7		MGM 14152
				HANK WILLIAMS, JR. With THE MIKE CURB CONGREGATION					
				from the movie *Kelly's Heroes* starring Clint Eastwood					
10/3/70	12	13	22	So Sad (To Watch Good Love Go Bad)	Let's Talk It Over Again	—	$7		MGM 14164
				HANK WILLIAMS, JR. & LOIS JOHNSON					
				#7 Pop hit for The Everly Brothers in 1960					
12/19/70+	3	15	23	Rainin' In My Heart	A-eee (Williams)	108	$7		MGM 14194
				HANK WILLIAMS, JR. With THE MIKE CURB CONGREGATION					
				#34 Pop hit for Slim Harpo in 1961					
4/24/71	6	14	24	I've Got A Right To Cry	Jesus Loved The Devil Out Of Me (w/Mike Curb Congregation)	102	$6		MGM 14240
8/21/71	18	14	25	After All They All Used To Belong To Me	Happy Kind Of Sadness	—	$7		MGM 14277
12/18/71+	7	14	26	Ain't That A Shame	The End Of A Bad Day	—	$7		MGM 14317
				HANK WILLIAMS, JR. with The Mike Curb Congregation					
				#1 R&B hit for Fats Domino in 1955					
4/1/72	14	14	27	Send Me Some Lovin'	What We Used To Hang On To (Is Gone)	—	$7		MGM 14356
				HANK WILLIAMS, JR. & LOIS JOHNSON					
4/29/72	❶²	16	28	Eleven Roses	Richmond Valley Breeze	—	$7		MGM 14371
9/16/72	3	16	29	Pride's Not Hard To Swallow	Hamburger Steak, Holiday Inn	—	$7		MGM 14421
11/18/72+	22	11	30	Whole Lotta Loving	Why Should We Try Anymore	—	$7		MGM 14443
				HANK WILLIAMS, JR. & LOIS JOHNSON					
				#6 Pop hit for Fats Domino in 1959					
2/24/73	23	13	31	After You	Knoxville Courthouse Blues	—	$6		MGM 14486
6/16/73	12	14	32	Hank	Grandpa Shepherd	—	$6		MGM 14550
10/20/73	4	18	33	The Last Love Song	Country Music-Those Tear Jerking Songs	—	$6		MGM 14656
3/9/74	13	12	34	Rainy Night In Georgia	Country Music In My Soul	—	$6		MGM 14700
				#4 Pop hit for Brook Benton in 1970					
7/6/74	7	13	35	I'll Think Of Something	Country Music Lover	—	$6		MGM 14731
11/2/74	19	12	36	Angels Are Hard To Find	Getting Over You	—	$6		MGM 14755
				also see #93 below					
4/12/75	26	10	37	Where He's Going, I've Already Been /		—			
		4	38	The Kind Of Woman I Got		—	$6		MGM 14794
7/5/75	29	13	39	The Same Old Story	Country Love	—	$6		MGM 14813
11/8/75	19	13	40	Stoned At The Jukebox	There's A Devil In The Bottle	—	$6		MGM 14833
4/10/76	38	9	41	Living Proof	Brothers Of The Road	—	$6		MGM 14845
4/9/77	27	12	42	Mobile Boogie	She's The Star (On The Stage Of My Mind)	—	$5		Warner/Curb 8361
8/20/77	59	7	43	I'm Not Responsible		—			
		5	44	(Honey, Won't You) Call Me		—	$5		Warner/Curb 8410
10/1/77	47	9	45	One Night Stands	I'm Not Responsible	—	$5		Warner/Curb 8451
1/7/78	38	9	46	Feelin' Better	Once And For All	—	$5		Warner/Curb 8507

DEBUT	PEAK	WKS	Gold	A-side (Chart Hit) ... B-side	Pop	$	Pic	Label & Number
				WILLIAMS, Hank Jr. — Cont'd				
5/13/78	76	4		47 You Love The Thunder ... I Just Ain't Been Able	—	$5		Warner/Curb 8564
				written and first recorded by Jackson Browne on his 1978 *Running On Empty* album				
8/12/78	15	12		48 I Fought The Law ... It's Different With You	—	$5		Warner/Curb 8641
				#9 Pop hit for the Bobby Fuller Four in 1966				
11/25/78	54	6		49 Old Flame, New Fire ... Payin' On Time	—	$5		Warner/Curb 8715
3/31/79	49	6		50 To Love Somebody ... We Can Work It All Out	—	$4		Elektra/Curb 46018
				#17 Pop hit for the *Bee Gees* in 1967				
6/9/79	4	15		51 Family Tradition ... Paying On Time	104	$4		Elektra 46046
10/6/79	2²	14		52 Whiskey Bent And Hell Bound ... O.D.'d In Denver	—	$4		Elektra/Curb 46535
2/9/80	5	13		53 Women I've Never Had ... Tired Of Being Johnny B. Good	—	$4		Elektra/Curb 46593
5/17/80	12	12		54 Kaw-Liga ... The American Way	—	$4		Elektra/Curb 46636
8/30/80	6	13		55 Old Habits ... Won't It Be Nice	—	$4		Elektra/Curb 47016
2/7/81	0¹	13		56 Texas Women ... You Can't Find Many Kissers	—	$4		Elektra/Curb 47102
5/30/81	0¹	14		57 Dixie On My Mind ... Ramblin' Man	—	$4		Elektra/Curb 47137
9/5/81	0¹	19		58 All My Rowdy Friends (Have Settled Down) ... Everytime I Hear That Song	—	$4		Elektra/Curb 47191
1/23/82	2³	20		59 A Country Boy Can Survive ... Weatherman	—	$4		Elektra/Curb 47257
				also see #99 below				
6/5/82	0¹	15		60 Honky Tonkin' ... High And Pressurized	—	$4		Elektra/Curb 47462
10/9/82	5	16		61 The American Dream /	—	$4		Elektra/Curb 69960
		16		62 If Heaven Ain't A Lot Like Dixie ...	—	$4		
1/29/83	4	18		63 Gonna Go Huntin' Tonight ... Twodot Montana	—	$4		Elektra/Curb 69846
6/4/83	6	16		64 Leave Them Boys Alone ... The Girl On The Front Row At Fort Worth	—	$4		Warner/Curb 29633
				Waylon Jennings and Ernest Tubb (guest vocals)				
10/1/83	5	21		65 Queen Of My Heart ... She Had Me	—	$4		Warner/Curb 29500
10/22/83	15	16		66 The Conversation ... Fancy Free	—	$4		RCA 13631
				WAYLON JENNINGS with Hank Williams, Jr.				
2/18/84	3	18		67 Man Of Steel ... Now I Know How George Feels	—	$4		Warner/Curb 29382
6/16/84	5	18		68 Attitude Adjustment ... Knoxville Courthouse Blues	—	$4		Warner/Curb 29253
10/6/84	10	19		69 All My Rowdy Friends Are Coming Over Tonight ... S:8 / A:14 Video Blues	—	$4		Warner/Curb 29184
				opening theme for ABC's *Monday Night Football* (with new lyrics)				
1/19/85	10	18		70 Major Moves ... S:8 / A:9 Mr. Lincoln	—	$4		Warner/Curb 29095
5/11/85	0¹	23		71 I'm For Love ... S:0¹ / A:0¹ Lawyers, Guns And Money	—	$4		Warner/Curb 29022
8/31/85	14	17		72 Two Old Cats Like Us ... S:13 / A:17 Little Hotel Room	—	$4		Columbia 05575
				RAY CHARLES (with Hank Williams, Jr.)				
9/7/85	4	20		73 This Ain't Dallas ... S:4 / A:4 I Really Like Girls	—	$4		Warner/Curb 28912
2/22/86	0¹	18		74 Ain't Misbehavin' ... S:0¹ / A:0¹ I've Been Around	—	$4		Warner/Curb 28794
				#17 Pop hit for Fats Waller in 1929				
6/14/86	2²	21		75 Country State Of Mind ... S:0¹ / A:2 Fat Friends	—	$4		Warner/Curb 28691
10/11/86	0²	19		76 Mind Your Own Business ... S:0² / A:0² My Name Is Bocephus	—	$4		Warner/Curb 28581
				Reba McEntire, Willie Nelson, Tom Petty and Reverend Ike (guest vocals)				
2/21/87	31	11		77 When Something Is Good (Why Does It Change) ... S:26 Loving Instructor	—	$4		Warner/Curb 28452
6/13/87	0¹	20		78 Born To Boogie ... S:0² What It Boils Down To	—	$4		Warner/Curb 28369
10/10/87+	4	21		79 Heaven Can't Be Found ... S:4 The Doctor's Song	—	$4	■	Warner/Curb 28227
2/20/88	2¹	21		80 Young Country ... S:0¹ Buck Naked	—	$4	■	Warner/Curb 28120
				Butch Baker, T. Graham Brown, Steve Earle, Highway 101, Dana McVicker, Marty Stuart and Keith Whitley (guest vocals)				
6/25/88	8	15		81 If The South Woulda Won ... S:4 Wild Streak	—	$4	■	Warner/Curb 27862
8/27/88	52	7		82 Cajun Baby ... I Wanna Hold You [R]	—	$4		BGM 81588
				DOUG KERSHAW with HANK WILLIAMS, JR.				
				new version of #14 above				
9/24/88	21	20		83 That Old Wheel ... S:17 Tennessee Flat Top Box	—	$4		Mercury 870688
				JOHNNY CASH with Hank Williams, Jr.				
11/5/88+	14	15		84 Early In The Morning And Late At Night ... S:8 I'm Just A Man	—	$4	■	Warner/Curb 27722
2/4/89	7	14		85 There's A Tear In My Beer ... You Brought Me Down To Earth	—	$4	■	Warner/Curb 27584
				HANK WILLIAMS, JR. with Hank Williams, Sr.				
				Hank Sr.'s vocals dubbed in from a vinyl record				
7/8/89	6	20		86 Finders Are Keepers ... What You Don't Know (Won't Hurt You)	—	$4		Warner/Curb 22945
2/10/90	15	18		87 Ain't Nobody's Business ... Big Mamou	—	$4		Warner/Curb 19957
5/19/90	10	21		88 Good Friends, Good Whiskey, Good Lovin' ... Family Tradition	—	$4	■	Warner/Cu. 19872 (v)
9/1/90	62	6		89 Man To Man ... Whiskey Bent And Hell Bound	—	$4	■	Warner/Cu. 19818 (v)
9/15/90	27	6		90 Don't Give Us A Reason ... U.S.A. Today	—	$4	■	Warner/Cu. 19542 (v)
1/5/91	39	13		91 I Mean I Love You ... Stoned At The Jukebox	—	$4		Warner/Curb 19463
5/4/91	26	19		92 If It Will It Will ... Won't It Be Nice	—	$4		Warner/Curb 19352
8/17/91	59	8		93 Angels Are Hard To Find ... Hollywood Honeys [R]	—	$4		Warner/Curb 19193
				new version of #36 above				
2/8/92	54	11		94 Hotel Whiskey ... The Count Song	—	$4		Capricorn/Curb 19023
5/23/92	55	8		95 Come On Over To The Country ... Wild Weekend	—	$4		Capricorn/Curb 18923
2/20/93	62	8		96 Everything Comes Down To Money And Love ... S.O.B. I'm Tired	—	$4		Capricorn/Curb 18614
12/24/94+	62	6		97 I Ain't Goin' Peacefully ... Greeted In Enid / (album snippets)	—	$4	■	MCG/Curb 76932 (v)
4/22/95	74	2		98 Hog Wild ... S:26 Wild Thing	—	$4	■	MCG/Curb 76948 (v)
11/20/99+	30	13		99 A Country Boy Can Survive (Y2K Version) ... S:2 Going The Distance	75	$4	★	Warner 16895 (v)
				CHAD BROCK (With Hank Williams, Jr. & George Jones)				
				new version of #59 above				
11/10/01	45	7		100 America Will Survive ...	—			album cut
				from the album *Almeria Club* on Curb 78725				

DEBUT	PEAK	WKS	Gold	A-side (Chart Hit)	B-side	Pop	$	Pic	Label & Number
				WILLIAMS, Hank III		'01			
				Born on 12/12/72 in Houston. Singer/songwriter/guitarist. Son of **Hank Williams Jr.** Grandson of **Hank Williams**.					
11/18/00+	50	11		I Don't Know	—				album cut
				from the album *Risin' Outlaw* on Curb 77949					
				WILLIAMS, Jason D.		'89			
				Born in El Dorado, Arkansas. Singer/pianist.					
5/20/89	71	5		1 Where There's Smoke	Tore Up Over You	—	$4		RCA 8869
9/23/89	70	4		2 Waitin' On Ice	Get Out You Big Roll Daddy	—	$4		RCA 9026
				WILLIAMS, Johnny		'72			
				Born in Texas. Featured performer at Gilley's nightclub.					
5/6/72	68	5		He Will Break Your Heart	If Loving You Means Anything	104	$7		Epic 10845
				#7 Pop hit for **Jerry Butler** in 1960					
				WILLIAMS, Lawton		'62			
				Born on 7/24/22 in Troy, Tennessee. Singer/prolific songwriter.					
10/23/61+	13	25		1 Anywhere There's People	Plowed Ground	—	$12		Mercury 71867
9/19/64	40	4		2 Everything's O.K. On The LBJ	Don't Look Down	—	$10		RCA Victor 8407
				WILLIAMS, Leona		'78			
				Born Leona Belle Helton on 1/7/43 in Vienna, Missouri. Singer/songwriter/guitarist. Married to **Merle Haggard** from 1978-83. Married **Dave Kirby** in 1985.					
5/31/69	66	5		1 Once More	I Narrowed This Triangle (Down To Two)	—	$6		Hickory 1532
8/21/71	52	9		2 Country Girl With Hot Pants On	Babe, Just For You	—	$6		Hickory 1606
9/22/73	93	3		3 Your Shoeshine Girl	Since I'm Not With The One I Love (I'll Love The One I'm With)	—	$6		Hickory/MGM 304
10/28/78	8	12		4 The Bull And The Beaver	I'm Gettin' High	—	$5		MCA 40962
				MERLE HAGGARD/LEONA WILLIAMS					
2/17/79	92	2		5 The Baby Song /		—			
		2		6 Call Me Crazy Lady			$5		MCA 40988
4/4/81	54	8		7 I'm Almost Ready	The End Of The World	—	$4		Elektra 47114
				#34 Pop hit for **Pure Prairie League** in 1980					
11/14/81	84	3		8 Always Late With Your Kisses	Startin' Today	—	$4		Elektra 47217
5/28/83	42	14		9 We're Strangers Again	Sally Let Your Bangs Hang Down	—	$4		Mercury 812214
				MERLE HAGGARD & LEONA WILLIAMS					
				WILLIAMS, Lois		'69			
9/20/69	74	3		A Girl Named Sam	We've Got Another Chance [N]	—	$7		Starday 877
				answer to "A Boy Named Sue" by **Johnny Cash**					
				WILLIAMS, Otis		'71			
				Born on 6/2/36 in Cincinnati. Black singer. Former leader of The Charms. Not to be confused with the same-named member of The Temptations.					
5/8/71	72	2		I Wanna Go Country	Rocky Top	—	$10		Stop 388
				OTIS WILLIAMS and The Midnight Cowboys					
				WILLIAMS, Paul		'81			
				Born on 9/19/40 in Omaha. Singer/prolific songwriter. Acted in several movies.					
12/12/81	93	4		Making Believe	Oh How I Miss You Tonight	—	$5		Paid 146
				WILLIAMS, Tex ★166★		'47			
				Born Sollie Paul Williams on 8/23/17 in Ramsey, Illinois. Died of cancer on 10/11/85 (age 68). Singer/songwriter/guitarist. Acted in many western movies. Worked as a singer with **Spade Cooley**'s band. Hosted own *Ranch Party* TV series in 1958.					
				1)Smoke! Smoke! Smoke! (That Cigarette) 2)Never Trust A Woman 3)Don't Telephone-Don't Telegraph (Tell A Woman) 4)That's What I Like About The West 5)Suspicion					
				TEX WILLIAMS And His Western Caravan:					
11/30/46	4	2		1 The California Polka	Rose Of The Alamo	—	$15		Capitol 302
7/5/47	❶16	23	•	2 Smoke! Smoke! Smoke! (That Cigarette)	Roundup Polka [N]	❶6	$15		Capitol Amer. 40001
				also see #19 below					
10/4/47	4	8		3 That's What I Like About The West	Downtown Poker Club	—	$15		Capitol Amer. 40031
				new version of "That's What I Like About The South" by **Phil Harris**					
12/13/47	2⁸	15		4 Never Trust A Woman	What It Means To Be Blue	—	$15		Capitol Amer. 40054
2/14/48	2²	11		5 Don't Telephone - Don't Telegraph (Tell A Woman)	Blue As A Heart Ache	—	$15		Capitol Amer. 40081
5/15/48	4	12		6 Suspicion	S:4 / J:4 Flo From St. Joe Mo	—	$12		Capitol 40109
6/19/48	5	15		7 Banjo Polka	J:5 / S:11 Pretty Red Lights	—	$12		Capitol 15101
6/26/48	6	8		8 Who? Me? /	S:6 / J:11	—			
7/31/48	15	1		9 Foolish Tears	J:15		$12		Capitol 15113
9/11/48	6	5		10 Talking Boogie /	J:6 / S:12	—			
11/13/48	13	3		11 Just A Pair Of Blue Eyes	J:13 / S:14	—	$12		Capitol 15175
11/20/48	5	8		12 Life Gits Tee-Jus, Don't It?	J:5 / S:9 Big Hat Polka [N]	27	$12		Capitol 15271
10/22/49	11	2		13 (There's A) Bluebird On Your Windowsill	J:11 / S:12 A Letter Asking For My Broken Heart	—	$12		Capitol 40225
				TEX WILLIAMS:					
5/29/65	26	11		14 Too Many Tigers	Winter Snow	—	$8		Boone 1028
10/26/65	30	9		15 Big Tennessee	My Last Two Tens	—	$8		Boone 1032
1/8/66	18	8		16 Bottom Of A Mountain	Tears Are Only Rain	—	$8		Boone 1036
9/24/66	44	2		17 Another Day, Another Dollar In The Hole	The Big Man	—	$8		Boone 1044
6/17/67	57	5		18 Black Jack County	Ain't Gonna Walk Your Dog	—	$8		Boone 1059

DEBUT	PEAK	WKS	Gold	A-side (Chart Hit)	B-side	Pop	$	Pic	Label & Number
				WILLIAMS, Tex — Cont'd					
2/17/68	32	10		19 Smoke, Smoke, Smoke - '68 ... *The Lonely One* [R]		—	$8		Boone 1069
				new version of #2 above					
6/29/68	45	7		20 Here's To You And Me ... *If Not For You There Could Go Me*		—	$8		Boone 1072
9/19/70	50	9		21 It Ain't No Big Thing ... *I Never Knew What Doing Was (Til I Got Done By You)*		—	$7		Monument 1216
8/28/71	29	14		22 The Night Miss Nancy Ann's Hotel For Single Girls Burned Down ... *If It's All The Same To You* [N]		—	$7		Monument 8503
1/22/72	67	4		23 Everywhere I Go (He's Already Been There) ... *Pretty In Blue*		—	$7		Monument 8533
6/29/74	70	8		24 Those Lazy, Hazy, Crazy Days Of Summer ... *Nowhere West Virginia*		—	$6		Granite 507
				#6 Pop hit for **Nat King Cole** in 1963					
				WILLIAMS, Tucker '80					
				Born in Dallas.					
1/19/80	96	2		1 Donna-Earth Angel (Medley) ... *Honey Love*		—	$7		Yatahey 999
				"Donna" was a #2 Pop hit for Ritchie Valens in 1959; "Earth Angel" was a #1 R&B hit for The Penguins in 1955					
				WILLIAMS BROS. '63					
				Duo of brothers Jimmy and Bobby Williams.					
6/15/63	28	1		1 Bad Old Memories ... *The Last Time*		—	$20		Del-Mar 1008
				WILLING, Foy '44					
				Born Foy Willingham in 1915 in Bosque County, Texas. Died on 6/24/78 (age 63). Singer/songwriter/guitarist. Acted in several western movies.					
				FOY WILLING And His Riders Of The Purple Sage:					
7/15/44	3	5		1 Texas Blues ... *Hang Your Head In Shame*		—	$15		Capitol 162
3/16/46	6	1		2 Detour ... *Someone Won Your Heart Little Darlin'*		—	$15		Decca 9000
				#5 Pop hit for **Patti Page** in 1951					
12/14/46	4	1		3 Have I Told You Lately (That I Love You) ... *Cool Water*		—	$15		Majestic 6000
6/19/48	14	2		4 Anytime ... J:14 *I'm Waltzing With A Broken Heart*		—	$15		Capitol Amer. 40108
				#2 Pop hit for **Eddie Fisher** in 1952					
1/1/49	15	1		5 Brush Those Tears From Your Eyes ... S:15 *Rose Of Ol' Pawnee*		—	$15		Capitol 15290
				WILLIS, Andra '73					
				Female singer/actress. Regular on TV's *The Lawrence Welk Show* from 1967-69.					
2/24/73	56	7		1 Down Home Lovin' Woman ... *Cryin' Cause You're Gone*		—	$6		Capitol 3525
8/4/73	85	5		2 Til I Can't Take It Anymore ... *After You*		—	$6		Capitol 3666
4/19/75	63	9		3 Baby ... *I'd Like To Be*		—	$6		Capitol 4044
				TENNESSEE ERNIE FORD & ANDRA WILLIS					
				WILLIS, Hal '64					
				Born Leonard Francis Gauthier in Roslyn, Quebec, Canada.					
10/31/64	5	16		1 The Lumberjack ... *Dig Me A Hole*		120	$12		Sims 207
7/30/66	45	5		2 Doggin' In The U.S. Mail ... *The Battle Of Viet Nam*		—	$12		Sims 288
				WILLIS, Kelly '91					
				Born on 10/1/68 in Annandale, Virginia. Female singer. Acted in the movie *Bob Roberts*.					
4/27/91	51	9		1 Baby Take A Piece Of My Heart ... *Standing By The River*		—	$4		MCA 54050
7/31/93	72	2		2 Whatever Way The Wind Blows ... *World Without You*		—	$4		MCA 54678
10/16/93	63	5		3 Heaven's Just A Sin Away ... *Get Real*		—	$4	■	MCA 54733 (v)
				WILLIS BROTHERS, The '64					
				Trio of brothers from Oklahoma: James "Guy" (guitar; born on 7/5/15; died on 4/13/81, age 65), Charles "Skeeter" (fiddle; born on 12/20/17; died on 1/28/76, age 58) and Richard "Vic" (accordian; born on 5/31/22; died on 1/15/95, age 72) Willis. Trio joined the *Grand Ole Opry* in 1946.					
9/5/64	9	20		1 Give Me 40 Acres (To Turn This Rig Around) ... *Gonna Buy Me A Juke Box*		—	$10		Starday 681
6/12/65	41	8		2 A Six Foot Two By Four ... *Strange Old Town* [N]		—	$10		Starday 713
2/25/67	14	15		3 Bob ... *Show Her Lots Of Gold*		—	$8		Starday 796
7/29/67	62	3		4 Somebody Knows My Dog ... *The End Of The Road*		—	$8		Starday 812
				WILLOUGHBY, Larry '84					
				Born in 1947 in Sherman, Texas. Singer/songwriter/guitarist. Cousin of **Rodney Crowell**.					
11/12/83	65	5		1 Heart On The Line (Operator, Operator) ... *Stone Cold*		—	$4		Atlantic Amer. 99826
2/4/84	55	8		2 Building Bridges		—	$4		Atlantic Amer. 99797
6/23/84	82	3		3 Angel Eyes ... *The Devil's On The Loose*		—	$4		Atlantic Amer. 99759
				WILLS, Bob ★113★ '46					
				Born James Robert Wills on 3/6/05 in Kosse, Texas. Died of a stroke on 5/13/75 (age 70). Singer/songwriter/fiddle player. Formed the Texas Playboys in 1933. Band featured **Tommy Duncan** (vocals) and **Leon McAuliffe** (steel guitar). Hosted own radio show on KVOO in Tulsa from 1934-58. Acted in several western movies. Known as "The King of Western Swing." Brother of **Johnnie Lee Wills**. Elected to the Country Music Hall of Fame in 1968. His band recorded as the **Original Texas Playboys** in 1977. Inducted into the Rock and Roll Hall of Fame in 1999 as an early influence. **Tommy Duncan** performs the vocals on all songs below (unless noted).					
				1) New Spanish Two Step 2) Silver Dew On The Blue Grass Tonight 3) Smoke On The Water 4) Stars And Stripes On Iwo Jima 5) Sugar Moon					
				BOB WILLS and his Texas Playboys:					
1/8/44	3	1		1 New San Antonio Rose		11	$25		Okeh 5694
				vocal version of his classic hit from 1941					
9/9/44	2[5]	11		2 We Might As Well Forget It /		11			
				Leon Huff (vocal)					
9/23/44	2[2]	17		3 You're From Texas		14	$25		Okeh 6722
				Leon McAuliffe (vocal); from the movie *A Tornado In The Saddle* starring Wills					
3/24/45	❶[2]	15		4 Smoke On The Water /		—			
3/24/45	3	18		5 Hang Your Head In Shame			$25		Okeh 6736

DEBUT	PEAK	WKS	Gold	A-side (Chart Hit)	B-side	Pop	$	Pic	Label & Number
				BOB WILLS and his Texas Playboys — Cont'd					
6/16/45	●¹	11		6 Stars And Stripes On Iwo Jima /			—		
7/21/45	5	4		7 You Don't Care What Happens To Me			—	$25	Okeh 6742
11/17/45	●³	14		8 Silver Dew On The Blue Grass Tonight /			—		
11/3/45+	2¹	8		9 Texas Playboy Rag	[I]		—	$20	Columbia 36841
12/29/45+	●¹	5		10 White Cross On Okinawa	Empty Chair At The Christmas Table		—	$20	Columbia 36881
5/4/46	●¹⁶	23		11 New Spanish Two Step /		20			
				vocal version of his 1935 instrumental "Spanish Two Step" on Vocalion 03230					
5/11/46	3	18		12 Roly-Poly			—	$20	Columbia 36966
11/30/46	2²	8		13 Stay A Little Longer			—		
11/30/46	4	1		14 I Can't Go On This Way			—	$20	Columbia 37097
3/29/47	5	1		15 I'm Gonna Be Boss From Now On	There's A Big Rock In The Road		—	$20	Columbia 37205
				Jesse Ashlock (vocal)					
5/17/47	●¹	6		16 Sugar Moon	Brain Cloudy Blues		—	$20	Columbia 37313
7/12/47	4	1		17 Bob Wills Boogie	Rose Of Old Pawnee [I]		—	$20	Columbia 37357
1/31/48	4	17		18 Bubbles In My Beer	Spanish Fandango		—	$20	MGM 10116
7/3/48	8	2		19 Keeper Of My Heart	J:8 I'll Have Somebody Else		—	$20	MGM 10175
7/24/48	15	1		20 Texarkana Baby	S:15 New Texas Playboy Rag		—	$20	Columbia 38179
9/18/48	10	1		21 Thorn In My Heart	J:10 'Neath Hawaiian Palms		—	$20	MGM 10236
1/21/50	10	1		22 Ida Red Likes The Boogie	J:10 A King Without A Queen		—	$25	MGM K10570
				Tiny Moore (vocal); also see #26 below					
11/4/50	8	5		23 Faded Love	A:8 Boot Heel Drag		—	$25	MGM K10786
				Rusty McDonald and The Playboy Trio (vocals)					
8/8/60	5	17		24 Heart To Heart Talk	What's The Matter With The Mill		—	$15	Liberty 55260
1/23/61	26	1		25 The Image Of Me	Goodbye Liza Jane		—	$15	Liberty 55264
				BOB WILLS with TOMMY DUNCAN and The Texas Playboys (above 2)					
10/16/76	99	1		26 Ida Red	Don't Let The Deal Go Down		—	$6	Capitol 4332
				Leon Rausch (vocal); "live" recording; also see #22 above					
	★296★			**WILLS, David** '75					
				Born on 10/23/51 in Pulaski, Tennessee. Singer/songwriter/guitarist.					
				1)From Barrooms To Bedrooms 2)There's A Song On The Jukebox 3)The Eyes Of A Stranger 4)Miss Understanding 5)The Barmaid					
11/16/74+	10	18		1 There's A Song On The Jukebox	I Can't Even Drink It Away		—	$6	Epic 50036
3/29/75	10	13		2 From Barrooms To Bedrooms	I'll Be More Than Happy (To Set You Free)		—	$6	Epic 50090
7/12/75	31	11		3 The Barmaid	Make Me Hate You		—	$6	Epic 50118
11/1/75	35	9		4 She Deserves My Very Best	Lady Of The Evening		—	$6	Epic 50154
2/7/76	47	8		5 Queen Of The Starlight Ballroom	Long Tall Sally		—	$6	Epic 50188
5/22/76	55	7		6 Woman	Paint Me A Picture		—	$6	Epic 50228
				#14 Pop hit for Peter & Gordon in 1966					
8/21/76	66	6		7 (I'm Just Pouring Out) What She Bottled Up In Me	The Happy Hour		—	$6	Epic 50260
5/21/77	52	9		8 The Best Part Of My Days (Are My Nights With You)	I'm Gonna Save It For My Baby		—	$5	United Artists 988
9/17/77	91	4		9 Cheatin' Turns Her On	I'm Gonna Save It For My Baby		—	$5	United Artists 1042
11/19/77	82	5		10 Do You Wanna Make Love	The Fool Strikes Again		—	$5	United Artists 1097
				#5 Pop hit for Peter McCann in 1977					
7/15/78	70	6		11 You Snap Your Fingers (And I'm Back In Your Hands)	To Make A Long Story Short		—	$5	United Artists 1196
2/17/79	50	7		12 I'm Being Good	Women Have A Feeling ('Bout These Things)		—	$5	United Artists 1271
10/6/79	82	4		13 Endless	One, Two, Three, We Were Lovers		—	$5	United Artists 1319
5/31/80	91	5		14 She's Hangin' In There (I'm Hangin' Out)	Take It Back		—	$5	United Artists 1350
9/27/80	65	6		15 The Light Of My Life (Has Gone Out Again Tonight)	Marriage On The Rocks		—	$5	United Artists 1375
3/12/83	52	7		16 Those Nights, These Days	Tennessee Moon		—	$4	RCA 13460
6/18/83	19	16		17 The Eyes Of A Stranger	Give Her Heart A Break		—	$4	RCA 13541
11/12/83+	26	15		18 Miss Understanding	First To Make It Last		—	$4	RCA 13653
2/25/84	31	11		19 Lady In Waiting	First Time Feeling		—	$4	RCA 13737
11/24/84	69	7		20 Macon Love	Racin' Down The Highway		—	$4	RCA 13940
10/8/88	85	3		21 Paper Thin Walls	Honey Baby		—	$4	Epic 08043
				WILLS, Johnnie Lee '50					
				Born on 9/2/12 in Jewett, Texas. Died on 10/25/84 (age 72). Singer/fiddle player. Brother of **Bob Wills**.					
				JOHNNIE LEE WILLS And His Boys:					
1/28/50	2⁵	11		1 Rag Mop	S:2 / J:2 / A:3 Near Me	9	$20	Bullet 696
				#1 Pop hit for the Ames Brothers in 1950					
4/1/50	7	2		2 Peter Cotton Tail	J:7 / A:8 Shattered Dreams		$20	Bullet 700
	★261★			**WILLS, Mark** '97					
				Born Mark Williams on 8/8/73 in Cleveland, Tennessee; raised in Blue Ridge, Georgia. Singer/songwriter/guitarist.					
				1)Wish You Were Here 2)Don't Laugh At Me 3)I Do [Cherish You]					
6/8/96	6	20		1 Jacob's Ladder /	S:13		—		
10/12/96	33	18		2 High Low And In Between			—	$4	Mercury 578004 (v)
3/1/97	5	21		3 Places I've Never Been	Ace Of Hearts		—	$4	Mercury 574150
2/28/98	2²	25		4 I Do [Cherish You]	S:9 You Can't Go Wrong Loving Me	72	$4	■ Mercury 568602 (v)
7/18/98	2²	28		5 Don't Laugh At Me	I Can't Live With Myself	73	$4	Mercury 566054
1/23/99	●¹	26		6 Wish You Were Here	Emily Harper	34	$4	Mercury 566764
6/19/99	7	22		7 She's In Love	Don't Think I Won't	60	$4	Mercury 566746
11/6/99+	2¹	26		8 Back At One	Because I Love You	36	$4	Mercury 562530
				#2 Pop hit for Brian McKnight in 1999					

Gretchen Wilson — Home Wrecker ★★★ (WPCV)

DEBUT	PEAK	WKS	Gold	A-side (Chart Hit) .... B-side	Pop	$	Pic	Label & Number
				WILLS, Mark — Cont'd				
4/1/00	19	21		9 Almost Doesn't Count .... Permanently	106	$4		Mercury 172153
				#16 Pop hit for Brandy in 1999				
9/16/00	33	22		10 I Want To Know (Everything There Is To Know About You) .... One Of These Days	—	$4		Mercury 172184
4/28/01	18	26		11 Loving Every Minute .... One Of These Days	107	$4		Mercury 172204
12/1/01+	31	20		12 I'm Not Gonna Do Anything Without You	—			album cut
				MARK WILLS with Jamie O'Neal				
				from the album *Loving Every Minute* on Mercury 170209				
				WILLS, Tommy '79				
				Born in Indianapolis. Jazz saxophonist.				
1/13/79	100	1		Wildwood Flower .... Ram-Bunk-Shush	—	$7		Golden Moon 004
				Marti Maes (vocal)				
				WILSON, Benny '85				
				Born in Young Harris, Georgia. Singer/songwriter.				
2/2/85	50	9		1 Acres Of Diamonds .... I Just Don't Love You, That's All	—	$4		Columbia 04724
3/22/86	78	8		2 If You Wanna Talk Love .... Where The Light Comes From	—	$4		Columbia 05829
				WILSON, Coleman '61				
7/31/61	23	5		Passing Zone Blues .... Flat-Footed Mama	—	$25		King 5512
				WILSON, Hank — see RUSSELL, Leon				
				WILSON, Jim '55				
				Born in Bowling Green, Kentucky. Popular DJ in Texas.				
7/23/55	8	9		Daddy, You Know What? A:8 Plans For Divorce	—	$25		Mercury 70635
				includes a short narration by Wilson's daughter June				
				WILSON, Larry Jon '76				
				Born in Swainsboro, Georgia. Singer/songwriter.				
4/24/76	74	7		Think I Feel A Hitchhike Coming On .... Drowning In The Mainstream	—	$6		Monument 8692
				WILSON, Meri '77				
				Born in Japan (father was a U.S. Air Force officer); raised in Marietta, Georgia. Female singer/songwriter.				
6/18/77	50	8	●	Telephone Man .... Itinerary [N]	18	$5		GRT 127
				WILSON, Norro '70				
				Born Norris Wilson on 4/4/38 in Scottsville, Kentucky. Singer/prolific songwriter.				
				1)Do It To Someone You Love 2)Everybody Needs Lovin' 3)Ain't It Good				
1/11/69	68	7		1 Only You .... Hey Mister	—	$8		Smash 2192
				#5 Pop hit for The Platters in 1955				
4/5/69	44	8		2 Love Comes But Once In A Lifetime .... All The Time	—	$8		Smash 2210
9/13/69	56	8		3 Shame On Me .... Let Me Go Back	—	$8		Smash 2236
7/4/70	20	13		4 Do It To Someone You Love No One Will Ever Know	—	$7		Mercury 73077
11/28/70	53	9		5 Old Enough To Want To (Fool Enough To Try) .... State Line Daddy	—	$7		Mercury 73125
11/18/72+	28	12		6 Everybody Needs Lovin' .... The Strange Little Girl	—	$6		RCA Victor 0824
3/31/73	64	4		7 Darlin' Raise The Shade .... Keep Me From Blowing Away	—	$6		RCA Victor 0909
9/8/73	35	11		8 Ain't It Good (To Feel This Way) .... It's All In The Game	—	$6		RCA Victor 0062
7/6/74	96	2		9 Loneliness (Can Break A Good Man Down) .... I Want To Hold You In My Arms	—	$6		Capitol 3886
8/20/77	43	8		10 So Close Again .... Saturday Night At The General Store	—	$5		Warner 8427
				MARGO SMITH & NORRO WILSON				
				WILSON, Tim '93				
				Born in Columbus, Georgia. Male comedian.				
3/27/93	70	2		1 Garth Brooks Has Ruined My Life .... Help Me Find Jimmy Hoffa [N]	—	$4	■	Southern Tr. 0035 (v)
4/15/00	66	1		2 The Ballad Of John Rocker .... Michael McDonald Had A Farm [N]	—	$4		Capitol 58855
				John Rocker: pitcher for the Atlanta Braves baseball team who made disparaging comments about people in New York City				
				WINGS — see McCARTNEY, Paul				
	★304★			**WINSLOW, Stephanie** '79				
				Born on 8/27/56 in Yankton, South Dakota. Singer/fiddle player. Formerly married to Ray Ruff (owner of the Oak record label).				
				1)Say You Love Me 2)Crying 3)Anything But Yes Is Still A No				
9/29/79	10	11		1 Say You Love Me Oh, Mister	—	$5		Warner/Curb 49074
				#11 Pop hit for Fleetwood Mac in 1976				
1/12/80	14	10		2 Crying .... Try	—	$5		Warner/Curb 49146
				#2 Pop hit for Roy Orbison in 1961				
4/5/80	38	6		3 I Can't Remember .... Don't Go	—	$5		Warner/Curb 49201
6/21/80	36	10		4 Try It On .... Me Without You	—	$5		Warner/Curb 49257
9/20/80	35	9		5 Baby, I'm A Want You .... Pretend	—	$5		Warner/Curb 49557
				#3 Pop hit for Bread in 1971				
12/13/80+	25	13		6 Anything But Yes Is Still A No .... Cold Cold Heart	—	$5		Warner/Curb 49628
3/21/81	36	7		7 Hideaway Healing .... Will This Be The Last Time	—	$5		Warner/Curb 49693
6/27/81	39	9		8 I've Been A Fool /	—			
		9		9 Sometimes When We Touch	—	$5		Warner/Curb 49753
				#3 Pop hit for Dan Hill in 1978				
10/10/81	29	10		10 When You Walk In The Room .... Somebody To Love	—	$5		Warner/Curb 49831
				#35 Pop hit for The Searchers in 1964				
5/1/82	43	10		11 Slippin' And Slidin' .... Another Night	—	$5		Primero 1003
				#33 Pop hit for Little Richard in 1956				
6/26/82	40	10		12 Don't We Belong In Love .... Another Night	—	$5		Primero 1007
9/18/82	69	5		13 In Between Lovers .... Try	—	$5		Primero/Curb 1012

DEBUT	PEAK	WKS	Gold	A-side (Chart Hit)	B-side	Pop	$	Pic	Label & Number
				WINSLOW, Stephanie — Cont'd					
5/14/83	61	6		14 Nobody Else For Me .... Another Night		—	$5		Oak 1056
9/3/83	25	15		15 Kiss Me Darling .... Another Night		—	$4		Curb/MCA 52291
1/7/84	29	12		16 Dancin' With The Devil .... I Don't Want To Talk About It		—	$4		Curb/MCA 52327
4/7/84	42	9		17 Baby, Come To Me .... Kisses Like Fire		—	$4		Curb/MCA 52372
				#1 Pop hit for Patti Austin & James Ingram in 1983					
				WINTERMUTE, Joann '89					
				Born in Dallas. Female singer/songwriter.					
3/11/89	82	3		1 Two Old Flames One Cheatin' Fire .... My Heart Just Doesn't Know		—	$5		Canyon Creek 1225
5/27/89	81	3		2 I Wouldn't Trade Your Love		—	$5		Door Knob 324
8/19/89	78	3		3 How I Love You In The Morning		—	$5		Door Knob 330
				WINTERS, Don '61					
				Born on 4/17/29 in Tampa, Florida.					
7/3/61	10	10		1 Too Many Times /					
7/17/61	27	2		2 Shake Hands With A Loser		—	$15		Decca 31253
				WISEMAN, Mac '59					
				Born Malcolm Wiseman on 5/23/25 in Cremora, Virginia. Bluegrass singer/songwriter/banjo player. Also see **The Groovegrass Boyz** and **Tomorrow's World**.					
5/28/55	10	2		1 The Ballad Of Davy Crockett .... A:10 Danger Heartbreak Ahead		—	$20		Dot 1240
8/10/59	5	20		2 Jimmy Brown The Newsboy .... I've Got No Use For The Women		—	$15		Dot 15946
9/21/63	12	8		3 Your Best Friend And Me .... When The Moon Comes Over The Mountain		—	$8		Capitol 5011
11/9/68	54	7		4 Got Leavin' On Her Mind .... She Simply Left		—	$7		MGM 13986
12/6/69+	38	9		5 Johnny's Cash And Charley's Pride .... Mama, Put My Little Shoes Away [N]		—	$6		RCA Victor 0283
3/18/78	78	5		6 Never Going Back Again .... Goodbye Mexico Rose		—	$6		Churchill 7706
5/12/79	69	4		7 My Blue Heaven .... If I Could Be With You/It Must Be True		—	$6		Churchill 7735
				MAC WISEMAN and WOODY HERMAN					
7/7/79	88	3		8 Scotch And Soda .... Dancing Bear		—	$6		Churchill 7738
				#81 Pop hit for The Kingston Trio in 1962					
10/13/79	95	3		9 Shackles And Chains .... Midnight Flyer		—	$6		CMH 1522
				OSBORNE BROS. & MAC WISEMAN					
				WOFFORD, E.D. '78					
7/1/78	77	4		Baby, I Need Your Lovin' .... Why Not Try Lovin' Me		—	$5		MC/Curb 5012
				#3 Pop hit for Johnny Rivers in 1967					
				WOLF, Gary '83					
				Born in 1948 in Richmond, Kentucky.					
7/17/82	51	9		1 Love Never Dies .... Ages And Pages Ago		—	$4		Columbia 02986
10/30/82	64	7		2 The Perfect Picture (To Fit My Frame Of Mind) .. If I Could Only Go Back To Goodbye		—	$4		Columbia 03272
2/19/83	62	7		3 Livin' On Memories .... Lone Wolf		—	$4		Columbia 03493
7/7/84	63	8		4 You Bring The Heartache (I'll Bring The Wine) .... Call On Me		—	$4		Mercury 822244
3/23/85	73	3		5 It's My Life .... First Things First		—	$4		Mercury 880564
				WOLFPACK, The '82					
				All-star trio: **Kenny Earl**, **Narvel Felts** and **Lobo**.					
5/8/82	88	3		Bull Smith Can't Dance The Cotton-Eyed Joe .... I Don't Want To Want You [N]		—	$6		Lobo 6
	★259★			**WOMACK, Lee Ann** '98					
				Born on 8/19/66 in Jacksonville, Texas. Married to **Jason Sellers** from 1991-97. CMA Award: 2001 Female Vocalist of the Year.					
				1) I Hope You Dance 2) I'll Think Of A Reason Later 3) A Little Past Little Rock					
3/15/97	23	20		1 Never Again, Again .... S:9 (long version)		124	$4	■	Decca 55320 (v)
6/21/97	2¹	20		2 The Fool .... Trouble's Here		—	$4		Decca 72009
11/1/97+	2¹	22		3 You've Got To Talk To Me .... A Man With 18 Wheels		—	$4		Decca 72023
4/4/98	27	20		4 Buckaroo .... Make Memories With Me		—	$4		Decca 72041
8/8/98	2³	21		5 A Little Past Little Rock .... S:5 If You're Ever Down In Dallas		43	$4	★	Decca 72068 (v)
12/26/98+	2⁴	25		6 I'll Think Of A Reason Later .... I'd Rather Have What We Had		38	$4		Decca 72076
6/5/99	12	20		7 (Now You See Me) Now You Don't .... The Preacher Won't Have To Lie		72	$4		MCA Nashville 72111
10/23/99	56	8		8 Don't Tell Me .... I Keep Forgetting		—	$4		MCA Nashville 72132
3/25/00	❶⁵	32		9 I Hope You Dance .... S:❶⁸ Lonely Too		14	$4	★	MCA Nash. 172158 (v)
				Sons Of The Desert (backing vocals); CMA Award: Single of the Year					
10/7/00+	4	26		10 Ashes By Now .... Lonely Too		45	$4		MCA Nashville 172182
4/7/01	13	21		11 Why They Call It Falling .... I Feel Like I'm Forgetting Something		78	$4		MCA Nashville 172203
11/10/01+	23	20		12 Does My Ring Burn Your Finger .... Lord I Hope This Day Is Good		—	$4		MCA Nashville 172220
				WOOD, Bobby '64					
				Born in Memphis. Singer/pianist.					
10/31/64	46	2		That's All I Need To Know .... This Time		130	$10		Joy 288
				WOOD, Danny '80					
				Born in Grand Prairie, Texas. Singer/songwriter/guitarist.					
10/23/76	92	4		1 If This Is Freedom (I Want Out) .... I Won't Be Sleepin' Alone		—	$5		London 242
4/2/77	93	2		2 I Need Somethin' Easy Tonight .... Permanent Thing		—	$5		London 248
6/21/80	30	10		3 A Heart's Been Broken .... All The Kind Young Strangers		—	$4		RCA 11968
12/6/80+	37	12		4 It Took Us All Night Long To Say Goodbye .... Crazy Dreams		—	$4		RCA 12123
3/21/81	58	7		5 Fool's Gold .... Where Were You (When I Came Home Last Night)		—	$4		RCA 12181

DEBUT	PEAK	WKS	Gold	A-side (Chart Hit)	B-side	Pop	$	Pic	Label & Number
				WOOD, Del '51					
				Born Polly Adelaide Hendricks on 2/22/20 in Nashville. Died on 10/3/89 (age 69). Female pianist. Joined the *Grand Ole Opry* in 1953.					
9/8/51	5	12		Down Yonder *Inst.* .... J:5 / A:7 / S:9 *Mine, All Mine* [I]		4	$30		Tennessee 775
				#5 Pop hit for Ernest Hare & Billy Jones in 1921					
				WOOD, Jeff '97					
				Born on 5/10/68 in Oklahoma City. Singer/songwriter.					
11/2/96+	44	18		1 You Just Get One		—			album cut
3/15/97	55	10		2 Use Mine		—			album cut
6/7/97	63	8		3 You Call That A Mountain		—			album cut
				all of above from the album *Between The Earth And The Stars* on Imprint 10006					
				WOOD, Nancy '81					
				Born Renate Kern in Germany; exchange student who lived in Janesville, Michigan. Host of *Nancy's Country Drive-In* radio series in Germany.					
10/10/81	79	4		Imagine That .... *Turn Your Love Light On*		—	$6		Montage 1202
				WOODRUFF, Bob '94					
				Born on 3/14/61 in Suffern, New York.					
2/26/94	70	3		1 Hard Liquor, Cold Women, Warm Beer .... *The Year We Tried To Kill The Pain*		—	$4	■	Asylum 64575 (v)
5/21/94	74	1		2 Bayou Girl .... *Poisoned At The Well*		—	$4		Asylum 64553
				BOB WOUDRUFF					
				WOODS, Gene '60					
				Born in Chattanooga, Tennessee.					
10/10/60	7	13		The Ballad Of Wild River .... *Afraid*		—	$25		HAP 1004
				WOODY, Bill '79					
				Born in 1959 in Jacksonville, Florida; raised in North Carolina.					
4/21/79	65	9		1 Just Between Us .... *I Love You*		—	$5		MCA 54043
8/4/79	88	4		2 Love Wouldn't Leave Us Alone .... *Organized Noise*		—	$5		MCA 41070
				WOOLERY, Chuck '77					
				Born on 3/16/42 in Ashland, Kentucky. Hosted TV's *Wheel Of Fortune* and *Love Connection*.					
7/9/77	78	5		1 Painted Lady .... *Growing Up In A Country Way*		—	$5		Warner 8381
7/12/80	94	2		2 The Greatest Love Affair .... *Heroes And Lovers* [S]		—	$4		Epic 50897
				WOOLEY, Amy '82					
				Born in Cleveland. Singer/songwriter/guitarist.					
7/31/82	51	9		If My Heart Had Windows .... *Burned By Love*		—	$4		MCA 52084
	★357★			**WOOLEY, Sheb** '62					
				Born Shelby Wooley on 4/10/21 in Erick, Oklahoma. Singer/songwriter/actor. Played "Pete Nolan" on the TV series *Rawhide*. Also made comical recordings under pseudonym **Ben Colder**. Acted in the movies *High Noon*, *Rocky Mountain*, *Giant* and *Hoosiers*. Wrote *Hee Haw*'s theme song.					
				1)That's My Pa 2)Almost Persuaded No. 2 3)Don't Go Near The Eskimos					
1/13/62	❶¹	17		1 That's My Pa .... *Meet Mr. Lonely* [N]		51	$10		MGM 13046
12/29/62	18	1		2 Don't Go Near The Eskimos .... *Louisiana Trapper* [N]		62	$10		MGM 13104
				BEN COLDER					
				parody of "Don't Go Near The Indians" by Rex Allen					
3/2/63	30	2		3 Hello Wall No. 2 .... *Shudders And Screams* [N]		131	$10		MGM 13122
				BEN COLDER					
				parody of "Hello Walls" by Faron Young					
7/18/64	33	10		4 Blue Guitar .... *Natchez Landing*		—	$10		MGM 13241
5/21/66	34	9		5 I'll Leave The Singin' To The Bluebirds .... *Buba Hoo Boba Dee*		—	$10		MGM 13477
9/24/66	6	15		6 Almost Persuaded No. 2 .... *Packets of Pencils* [N]		58	$10		MGM 13590
				BEN COLDER					
				parody of "Almost Persuaded" by David Houston					
10/15/66	70	2		7 Tonight's The Night My Angel's Halo Fell .... *Anchors Aweigh*		—	$10		MGM 13556
6/29/68	22	12		8 Tie A Tiger Down .... *Make 'Em Laugh*		—	$10		MGM 13938
10/26/68	24	6		9 Harper Valley P.T.A. (Later That Same Day) .... *Folsom Prison Blues No. 1-1/2* [N]		67	$10		MGM 13997
				BEN COLDER					
				parody of "Harper Valley P.T.A." by Jeannie C. Riley					
1/4/69	65	3		10 Little Green Apples No. 2 .... *It's Such A Pretty World Tonight* [N]		—	$8		MGM 14015
				BEN COLDER					
				parody of "Little Green Apples" by Roger Miller					
1/11/69	52	9		11 I Remember Loving You .... *That Girl (Next Door)*		—	$8		MGM 14005
10/25/69	63	7		12 The One Man Band .... *You Still Turn Me On*		—	$8		MGM 14085
2/13/71	50	6		13 Fifteen Beers Ago .... *Sunday Mornin' Comin' Down* [N]		—	$8		MGM 14209
				BEN COLDER					
				parody of "Fifteen Years Ago" by Conway Twitty					
	★396★			**WOPAT, Tom** '87					
				Born on 9/9/51 in Lodi, Wisconsin. Singer/songwriter/actor. Played "Luke Duke" on TV's *The Dukes of Hazzard*. Host of TNN's *Prime Time Country* in 1996.					
				1)The Rock And Roll Of Love 2)A Little Bit Closer 3)Susannah					
4/19/86	39	13		1 True Love (Never Did Run Smooth) .... A:37 *Some Day, Some Night*		—	$4		EMI America 8316
8/16/86	44	11		2 I Won't Let You Down .... *Wheels*		—	$4		EMI America 8334
12/20/86+	16	19		3 The Rock And Roll Of Love .... A:15 / S:24 *A Good Woman's Love*		—	$4		EMI America 8364
5/9/87	28	14		4 Put Me Out Of My Misery .... *Daylight Loving Time*		—	$4		EMI America 43010
8/29/87	20	17		5 Susannah .... *Cars*		—	$4		EMI America 43034
1/9/88	18	17		6 A Little Bit Closer .... *Bad Thing About Good Love*		—	$4		EMI-Manhattan 50112
6/11/88	40	10		7 Hey Little Sister .... *A Letter In The Fire*		—	$4		Capitol 44144
10/8/88	29	16		8 Not Enough Love .... *A Letter In The Fire*		—	$4		Capitol 44243

I Just Got Back From The War /// Have You Forgotten

DEBUT	PEAK	WKS	Gold	A-side (Chart Hit)....Cont'd ....B-side	Pop	$	Pic	Label & Number
				WOPAT, Tom — Cont'd				
6/29/91	46	15		9 Too Many Honky Tonks (On My Way Home) ....*I've Been There*	—	$4	■	Epic 73862 (v)
11/23/91	51	11		10 Back To The Well ....*Always A Blue Moon*	—	$4		Epic 74063
				WORK, Jimmy '55				
				Born on 3/29/24 in Akron, Ohio; raised in Dukedom, Tennessee. Singer/songwriter/guitarist.				
2/19/55	5	13		1 Making Believe ....J:5 / A:7 / S:11 *Just Like Downtown*	—	$20		Dot 1221
7/2/55	6	4		2 That's What Makes The Juke Box Play				
				.......................J:6 *Don't Give Me A Reason To Wonder Why*	—	$20		Dot 1245
				WORLEY, Darryl '01				
				Born on 10/31/64 in Savannah, Tennessee. Singer/songwriter/guitarist.				
4/1/00	15	24		1 When You Need My Love ....S:4 *Who's Gonna Get Me Over You*	—	$4		DreamWor. 459043 (v)
10/7/00+	12	24		2 A Good Day To Run	—			album cut
4/7/01	20	20		3 Second Wind	—			album cut
10/20/01	41	9		4 Sideways	—			album cut
				above 3 from the album *Hard Rain Don't Last* on DreamWorks 450042				
	★343★			**WORTH, Marion** '60				
				Born Mary Ann Ward on 7/4/30 in Birmingham, Alabama. Died of emphysema on 12/19/99 (age 69). Singer/songwriter/guitarist. Joined the *Grand Ole Opry* in 1963.				
				1)*That's My Kind Of Love* 2)*I Think I Know* 3)*Are You Willing, Willie*				
10/19/59+	12	20		1 Are You Willing, Willie ....*This Heart Of Mine*	—	$25		Cherokee 503
5/23/60	5	15		2 That's My Kind Of Love ....*I Lost Johnny*	—	$20		Guyden 2033
11/14/60	7	23		3 I Think I Know ....*Tomorrow At A Quarter Till Nine*	—	$15	■	Columbia 41799
5/22/61	21	1		4 There'll Always Be Sadness ....*I'm Not At All Sorry For You*	—	$15		Columbia 41972
2/2/63	14	5		5 Shake Me I Rattle (Squeeze Me I Cry) ....*Tennessee Teardrops*	42	$15	■	Columbia 42640
6/8/63	18	3		6 Crazy Arms ....*Lovers' Lane*	—	$15		Columbia 42703
4/11/64	33	13		7 You Took Him Off My Hands (Now Please Take				
				Him Off My Mind).............................*He Loves Me, He Loves Me Not*	—	$15		Columbia 42992
5/9/64	23	17		8 Slipping Around ....*I Love You So Much It Hurts*	—	$15		Columbia 43020
				MARION WORTH AND GEORGE MORGAN				
10/24/64	25	6		9 The French Song ....*Kentucky Waltz*	—	$10		Columbia 43119
				#54 Pop hit for **Lucille Starr** in 1964				
12/11/65+	32	6		10 I Will Not Blow Out The Light ....*Twenty-One Days Of Darkness*	—	$10		Columbia 43405
11/4/67	64	6		11 A Woman Needs Love ....*I've Got That Sad And Lonely Feeling*	—	$8		Decca 32195
3/30/68	45	10		12 Mama Sez..*Then I'll Be Over You*	—	$8		Decca 32278
				WRAYS, The '87				
				Group from Oregon: Bubba Wray, Jim Covert, Lynn Phillips, and Joe Dale Cleghorn. Bubba became better known as **Collin Raye**.				
				THE WRAY BROTHERS BAND:				
3/19/83	88	3		1 Reason To Believe	—	$6		CIS 3011
				#19 Pop hit for **Rod Stewart** in 1993				
4/6/85	93	4		2 Until We Meet Again	—	$6		Sasparilla 0003
				THE WRAYS:				
5/10/86	71	5		3 I Don't Want To Know Your Name ....*Here's To The Men Who Can Cry*	—	$4		Mercury 884621
6/6/87	48	10		4 You Lay A Lotta Love On Me ....*Until We Meet Again*	—	$4		Mercury 888542
				WREN, Larry '77				
5/21/77	98	3		1 Lie To Me /				
		3		2 It's Saturday Night...	—	$6		50 States 51
				WRIGHT, B.J. '80				
				Born in Gallatin, Tennessee. Male singer.				
10/21/78	96	4		1 Memory Bound ....*Don't Say Love*	—	$5		Soundwaves 4577
3/24/79	93	2		2 Leaning On Each Other ....*California Rose*	—	$5		Soundwaves 4581
7/28/79	61	5		3 I've Got A Right To Be Wrong ....*Free At Last*	—	$5		Soundwaves 4589
12/22/79+	87	6		4 Nobody's Darlin' But Mine ....*(Somewhere There's A) Rainbow Over Texas*	—	$5		Soundwaves 4593
				#19 Pop hit for **Jimmie Davis** in 1937				
5/3/80	36	11		5 J.R. ....*Memory Bound*	—	$5		Soundwaves 4604
				title refers to "J.R. Ewing" (Larry Hagman) of TV's *Dallas*				
8/2/80	73	5		6 Lost Love Affair ....*You're Drivin' Me Crazy*	—	$5		Soundwaves 4610
12/27/80+	81	6		7 I Know An Ending (When It Comes)............................*Baby Blue*	—	$5		Soundwaves 4624
	★331★			**WRIGHT, Bobby** '71				
				Born John Robert Wright on 3/30/42 in Charleston, West Virginia. Singer/songwriter/guitarist/actor. Son of **Johnny Wright** and **Kitty Wells**; brother of **Ruby Wright**. Played "Willy Moss" on TV's *McHale's Navy*.				
				1)*Here I Go Again* 2)*Seasons In The Sun* 3)*Lovin' Someone On My Mind* 4)*Upstairs In The Bedroom* 5)*Lay Some Happiness On Me*				
4/29/67	44	12		1 Lay Some Happiness On Me ....*How Much Lonelier Can Lonely Be*	—	$6		Decca 32107
				#55 Pop hit for **Dean Martin** in 1967				
12/2/67	67	3		2 That See Me Later Look ....*Nail My Shoes To The Floor*	—	$6		Decca 32193
10/5/68	70	4		3 Old Before My Time ....*Shutting Out The Light*	—	$6		Decca 32367
5/17/69	40	10		4 Upstairs In The Bedroom ....*My Home Away From Home*	—	$6		Decca 32464
11/1/69	70	2		5 Sing A Song About Love ....*If You Don't Swing - Don't Ring*	—	$6		Decca 32564
3/8/70	61	4		6 Take Me Back To The Goodtimes, Sally ....*Something Called Happiness*	—	$6		Decca 32633
8/1/70	47	9		7 Hurry Home To Me ....*My Home Away From Home*	—	$6		Decca 32705
4/24/71	74	2		8 If You Want Me To I'll Go ....*Rain Falling On Me*	—	$6		Decca 32792

DEBUT	PEAK	WKS	Gold	A-side (Chart Hit) / B-side	Pop	$	Pic	Label & Number
				WRIGHT, Bobby — Cont'd				
7/10/71	13	16		9 Here I Go Again .... If You Don't Swing...Don't Ring	—	$6		Decca 32839
12/25/71+	54	8		10 Search Your Heart .... I'll Walk On Water	—	$6		Decca 32903
8/12/72	60	5		11 Just Because I'm Still In Love With You .... Pledging My Love	—	$6		Decca 32985
1/27/73	75	1		12 If Not For You .... Searching (For Someone Like You) #25 Pop hit for Olivia Newton-John in 1971	—	$6		Decca 33034
10/20/73	39	11		13 Lovin' Someone On My Mind .... This Time	—	$5		ABC 11390
2/23/74	24	12		14 Seasons In The Sun .... Live And Let Live #1 Pop hit for Terry Jacks in 1974	—	$5		ABC 11418
6/22/74	56	10		15 Everybody Needs A Rainbow .... I'll Surely Fall In Love With You	—	$5		ABC 11443
10/5/74	55	11		16 Baby's Gone .... Love Look (At Us Now) written by Bobby Goldsboro and Roy Orbison; #84 Pop hit for Gene Thomas in 1964	—	$5		ABC 12028
3/8/75	75	7		17 I Just Came Home To Count The Memories .... No One Has Ever Loved Me Like You	—	$5		ABC 12062
1/8/77	79	6		18 Neon Lady .... '57 Chevrolet	—	$4		United Artists 913
9/24/77	97	1		19 Playing With The Baby's Mama .... Lay Down Beside Me	—	$4		United Artists 1051
10/21/78	100	3		20 Takin' A Chance .... I Don't Know How To Tell Her	—	$4		United Artists 1238
7/28/79	77	3		21 I'm Turning You Loose .... Going Home	—	$4		United Artists 1300
	★328★			**WRIGHT, Chely** '99 Born on 10/25/70 in Kansas City. Female singer/guitarist. 1)Single White Female 2)It Was 3)Shut Up And Drive				
6/25/94	58	10		1 He's A Good Ole Boy .... Go On And Go	—	$4	■	Polydor 853056 (v)
10/22/94	48	14		2 Till I Was Loved By You .... He Don't Do Bars Anymore	—	$4	■	Polydor 853810 (v)
2/4/95	56	8		3 Sea Of Cowboy Hats .... Nobody But A Fool	—	$4	■	Polydor 851430 (v)
10/21/95	66	7		4 Listenin' To The Radio .... Till All Her Tears Are Dry	—	$4	■	Polydor 577282 (v)
2/10/96	41	15		5 The Love That We Lost .... Gotta Get Good At Givin' Again	—	$4	■	Polydor 577936 (v)
7/19/97	14	20		6 Shut Up And Drive .... S:11 Emma Jean's Guitar	112	$4	■	MCA 72012 (v)
11/29/97+	39	15		7 Just Another Heartache .... Feelin' Single And Seein' Double	—	$4		MCA 72025
3/28/98	36	20		8 I Already Do .... Is It Love Yet?	—	$4		MCA 72044
3/13/99	●¹	31		9 Single White Female .... S:3 Let Me In	36	$4	★	MCA Nash. 72092 (v)
10/9/99+	11	30		10 It Was .... Rubbin' It In	64	$4		MCA Nashville 172113
6/10/00	49	8		11 She Went Out For Cigarettes .... Some Kind Of Somethin'	—	$4		MCA Nashville 172161
10/14/00	68	2		12 Hard To Be A Husband, Hard To Be A Wife BRAD PAISLEY & CHELY WRIGHT from the various artists album 75 Years Of The WSM Grand Ole Opry Volume Two on MCA Nashville 170176	—			album cut
6/2/01	26	20		13 Never Love You Enough .... Deep Down Low	—	$4		MCA Nashville 172208
12/22/01+	23	20		14 Jezebel .... Never Love You Enough	—	$4		MCA Nashville 172227
				WRIGHT, Curtis '89 Born on 6/6/55 in Huntington, Pennsylvania. Singer/songwriter. Former member of the **Super Grit Cowboy Band** and **Orrall & Wright**.				
11/11/89	38	13		1 She's Got A Man On Her Mind	—	$5		Airborne 75746
7/11/92	59	7		2 Hometown Radio	—			album cut
1/2/93	53	10		3 If I Could Stop Lovin' You above 2 from the album Curtis Wright on Liberty 97825	—			album cut
				WRIGHT, Ginny '55 Born in Twin City, Georgia.				
1/9/54	3	22		1 I Love You .... A:3 / J:7 / S:8 I Want You Yes (You Want Me No) GINNY WRIGHT/JIM REEVES	—	$30		Fabor 101
1/1/55	2³	26		2 Are You Mine .... A:2 / J:4 / S:5 I've Got Somebody New GINNY WRIGHT/TOM TALL	—	$30		Fabor 117
	★376★			**WRIGHT, Johnny** '65 Born on 5/13/14 in Mount Juliet, Tennessee; raised in Nashville. Singer/songwriter/fiddle player. Member of **Johnnie & Jack** duo. Married **Kitty Wells** in 1938. Father of **Bobby Wright** and **Ruby Wright**. 1)Hello Vietnam 2)Walkin', Talkin', Cryin', Barely Beatin' Broken Heart 3)Blame It On The Moonlight				
5/2/64	22	15		1 Walkin', Talkin', Cryin', Barely Beatin' Broken Heart .... They're All Going Home But One JOHNNY WRIGHT And The Tennessee Mountain Boys	—	$10		Decca 31593
1/2/65	37	5		2 Don't Give Up The Ship .... Guitar Lessons	—	$10		Decca 31679
5/8/65	28	11		3 Blame It On The Moonlight .... Rest In Peace	—	$10		Decca 31740
8/28/65	●³	21		4 Hello Vietnam .... Mexico City	—	$10		Decca 31821
12/18/65+	31	10		5 Keep The Flag Flying .... You're Over There (And I'm Over Here)	—	$10		Decca 31875
6/4/66	31	6		6 Nickels, Quarters And Dimes .... Is Love Worth All The Heartaches	—	$10		Decca 31927
10/15/66	53	7		7 I'm Doing This For Daddy .... Racing Man	—	$10		Decca 32002
12/31/66	50	11		8 Mama's Little Jewel .... Nothing From Nothing	—	$10		Decca 32061
8/12/67	66	5		9 American Power .... Settle Back Down To Earth	—	$10		Decca 32162
12/16/67	69	4		10 Music To Cry By .... Cheaters Can't Win	—	$10		Decca 32216
5/11/68	54	8		11 We'll Stick Together .... Heartbreak Waltz KITTY WELLS And JOHNNY WRIGHT	—	$10		Decca 32294
11/30/68	66	5		12 (They Always Come Out) Smellin' Like A Rose .... One Little Taco	—	$10		Decca 32402
				WRIGHT, Justin '89 Born in 1961 in Springfield, Illinois; raised in Phoenix.				
2/4/89	91	2		1 Settin' At The Kitchen Table	—	$6		Bear 195
				WRIGHT, Lee '79 Male singer.				
12/23/78+	86	4		1 Capricorn Kings .... Wait 'Til Morning	—	$6		Prairie Dust 7628
7/6/85	90	4		2 The Eyes Have It	—	$6		Prairie Dust 5185

DEBUT	PEAK	WKS	Gold	A-side (Chart Hit)	B-side	Pop	$	Pic	Label & Number
				✈ **WRIGHT, Michelle** '92					
				Born on 7/1/61 in Morpeth, Ontario, Canada.					
				1)Take It Like A Man 2)He Would Be Sixteen 3)New Kind Of Love					
6/2/90	32	21		1 New Kind Of Love	As Far As Lonely Goes	—	$4		Arista 2002
10/13/90	72	5		2 Woman's Intuition	As Far As Lonely Goes	—	$4		Arista 2090
5/11/91	73	2		3 All You Really Wanna Do	The Longest Night	—	$4		Arista 2208
4/4/92	10	20		4 Take It Like A Man	Guitar Talk	—	$4		Arista 12406
7/25/92	43	19		5 One Time Around	A Little More Comfortable	—	$4		Arista 12444
10/31/92	31	17		6 He Would Be Sixteen	The Change	—	$4		Arista 12480
2/27/93	55	7		7 The Change	If I'm Ever Over You	—	$4		Arista 12528
7/30/94	57	8		8 One Good Man	Where Do We Go From Here	—	$4	▌	Arista 12727 (v)
7/13/96	50	10		9 Nobody's Girl	I'm Not Afraid	—	$4	▌	Arista 13023 (v)
1/22/00	74	2		10 Your Love	—				album cut
				JIM BRICKMAN Featuring Michelle Wright					
				from Brickman's album *Destiny* on Windham Hill 11396					
				WRIGHT, Randy '84					
				Born on 9/11/56 in Troy, Missouri. Singer/songwriter/drummer.					
11/5/83	86	3		1 There's Nobody Lovin' At Home	Times Like This	—	$4		MCA 52273
5/12/84	77	4		2 If You're Serious About Cheating	Times Like This	—	$4		MCA 52358
				WRIGHT, Ruby '64					
				Born on 10/27/39 in Nashville. Daughter of **Kitty Wells** and **Johnny Wright**; sister of **Bobby Wright**.					
9/5/64	13	13		1 Dern Ya	Such A Silly Notion [N]	103	$15		RIC 126
				answer to "Dang Me" by Roger Miller					
11/5/66	72	2		2 A New Place To Hang Your Hat	A Kick In The Conscience	—	$10		Epic 10055
5/27/67	69	7		3 (I Can Find) A Better Deal Than That	Everytime, All The Time	—	$10		Epic 10150
				WRIGHT, Sonny '79					
				Born Nathan Edward Wright on 2/2/43 in Flagler, Colorado. Married to **Peggy Sue**.					
10/22/77	100	1		1 If This Is What Love's All About	Someone I Can't Say No To	—	$5		Door Knob 038
				PEGGY SUE & SONNY WRIGHT					
11/10/79	86	5		2 Gently Hold Me	If This Is What Love's All About	—	$5		Door Knob 113
				PEGGY SUE & SONNY WRIGHT					
4/26/80	91	4		3 Molly (And The Texas Rain)	It Wasn't Me Who Said I Owned A Gold Mine	—	$5		Door Knob 128
				WRIGHT BROTHERS, The '81					
				Vocal trio from Bedford, Indiana: brothers Tom and Tim Wright, with Karl Hinkle. John McDowell replaced Hinkle in early 1984.					
10/31/81	35	12		1 Family Man	Engine Engine Number Nine	—	$4		Warner 49837
4/3/82	42	11		2 When You Find Her, Keep Her	Let The Little Bird Fly	—	$4		Warner 50033
9/4/82	40	8		3 Made In The U.S.A.	Words Of Love	—	$4		Warner 29926
1/8/83	68	5		4 So Easy To Love	We Don't Know Why	—	$4		Warner 29839
3/31/84	33	13		5 Southern Women	Love's Slippin' Up On Me	—	$4		Mercury 818653
8/11/84	46	11		6 So Close	Radio Lover	—	$4		Mercury 880055
11/3/84	57	9		7 Eight Days A Week	She's A Diamond	—	$4		Mercury 880316
				#1 Pop hit for the Beatles in 1965					
3/30/85	48	10		8 Fire In The Sky	Pride	—	$4		Mercury 880596
9/10/88	85	3		9 Come On Rain	—		$5		Airborne 10006
				WYATT, Gene '68					
				Died in 1979 (age 42). Cousin of **Chuck Pollard**.					
3/23/68	74	2		1 I Stole The Flowers From Your Garden	I'm A One Woman Man	—	$10		Mercury 72752
8/17/68	69	3		2 I Just Ain't Got (As Much As He's Got Going For Me)	Chains Around My Mind	—	$10		Paula 308
				✈ **WYATT, Nina** '88					
1/30/88	76	3		1 Richer Now With You	You're Not Playing Love By The Rules	—	$5		Charta 207
8/20/88	88	2		2 After The Passion Leaves	Love Finally Got The Best Of Me	—	$5		Charta 210
				WYATT BROTHERS '87					
12/27/86+	79	5		Wyatt Liquor			$7		Wyatt 103
				WYNETTE, Tammy ★26★ '68					
				Born Virginia Wynette Pugh on 5/5/42 in Itawamba County, Mississippi. Died of a blood clot on 4/6/98 (age 55). Married to **George Jones** from 1969-75. Married her manager George Richey (brother of **Wyley McPherson**) on 7/6/78. Known as "The First Lady of Country Music." Elected to the Country Music Hall of Fame in 1998. CMA Awards: 1968, 1969 & 1970 Female Vocalist of the Year.					
				1)I Don't Wanna Play House 2)D-I-V-O-R-C-E 3)Stand By Your Man 4)He Loves Me All The Way 5)My Elusive Dreams					
12/10/66+	44	9		1 Apartment #9	I'm Not Mine To Give	—	$12		Epic 10095
3/18/67	3	21		2 Your Good Girl's Gonna Go Bad	Send Me No Roses	—	$10		Epic 10134
7/15/67	❶²	18		3 My Elusive Dreams	Marriage On The Rocks	89	$10		Epic 10194
				DAVID HOUSTON and TAMMY WYNETTE					
8/26/67	❶³	20		4 I Don't Wanna Play House	Soakin' Wet	—	$10		Epic 10211
1/6/68	❶¹	17		5 Take Me To Your World	Good	—	$10		Epic 10269
1/20/68	11	14		6 It's All Over	Together We Stand (Divided We Fall)	—	$10		Epic 10274
				DAVID HOUSTON & TAMMY WYNETTE					
5/18/68	❶³	17		7 D-I-V-O-R-C-E	Don't Make Me Now	63	$10		Epic 10315
10/19/68	❶³	21		8 Stand By Your Man	I Stayed Long Enough	19	$10		Epic 10398
				also see #73 below					

DEBUT	PEAK	WKS	Gold	A-side (Chart Hit)	B-side	Pop	$	Pic	Label & Number
				WYNETTE, Tammy — Cont'd					
4/12/69	①²	14		9 Singing My Song	Too Far Gone	75	$10	■	Epic 10462
8/30/69	①²	16		10 The Ways To Love A Man	Still Around	81	$10		Epic 10512
1/31/70	2²	14		11 I'll See Him Through	Enough Of A Woman	100	$10		Epic 10571
5/23/70	①³	16		12 He Loves Me All The Way	Our Last Night Together	97	$10		Epic 10612
9/12/70	①²	15		13 Run, Woman, Run	My Daddy Doll	92	$10		Epic 10653
11/28/70+	5	13		14 The Wonders You Perform	Gentle Shepherd	104	$10		Epic 10687
3/6/71	2³	15		15 We Sure Can Love Each Other	Fun	103	$10		Epic 10707
7/17/71	①²	15		16 Good Lovin' (Makes It Right)	I Love You, Mr. Jones	111	$10		Epic 10759
12/25/71+	9	13		17 Take Me	We Go Together	—	$10		Epic 10815
				TAMMY WYNETTE & GEORGE JONES					
1/1/72	①¹	14		18 Bedtime Story	Reach Out Your Hand	86	$10		Epic 10818
5/20/72	2²	14		19 Reach Out Your Hand	Love's The Answer	—	$10		Epic 10856
7/8/72	6	15		20 The Ceremony	The Great Divide	—	$10		Epic 10881
				TAMMY WYNETTE & GEORGE JONES					
9/16/72	①¹	14		21 My Man	Things I Love To Do	—	$10		Epic 10909
11/25/72+	38	9		22 Old Fashioned Singing	We Love To Sing About Jesus	—	$10		Epic 10923
				GEORGE JONES & TAMMY WYNETTE					
12/30/72+	①¹	15		23 'Til I Get It Right	The Bridge Of Love	106	$10		Epic 10940
4/7/73	①¹	17		24 Kids Say The Darndest Things	I Wish I Had A Mommy Like You	72	$10		Epic 10969
4/7/73	32	9		25 Let's Build A World Together	Touching Shoulders	—	$10		Epic 10963
				GEORGE JONES AND TAMMY WYNETTE					
9/1/73	①²	17		26 We're Gonna Hold On	My Elusive Dreams	—	$8		Epic 11031
12/29/73+	①²	15		27 Another Lonely Song	The Only Time I'm Really Me	—	$8		Epic 11079
2/9/74	15	13		28 (We're Not) The Jet Set	Crawdad Song	—	$8		Epic 11083
				GEORGE JONES and TAMMY WYNETTE					
7/27/74	8	12		29 We Loved It Away	Ain't Love Been Good	—	$8		Epic 11151
				GEORGE JONES and TAMMY WYNETTE					
8/17/74	4	16		30 Woman To Woman	Love Me Forever	—	$7		Epic 50008
2/15/75	4	16		31 (You Make Me Want To Be) A Mother	I'm Not A Has-Been (I Just Never Was)	—	$7		Epic 50071
5/17/75	25	13		32 God's Gonna Get'cha (For That)	Those Were The Good Times	—	$7		Epic 50099
				GEORGE JONES AND TAMMY WYNETTE					
9/20/75	13	13		33 I Still Believe In Fairy Tales	Your Memory's Gone To Rest	—	$7		Epic 50145
2/14/76	①¹	15		34 'Til I Can Make It On My Own	Love Is Something Good For Everybody	84	$7		Epic 50196
6/5/76	①¹	15		35 Golden Ring	We're Putting It Back Together	—	$7		Epic 50235
				GEORGE JONES and TAMMY WYNETTE					
8/21/76	①²	16		36 You And Me	When Love Was All We Had	101	$7		Epic 50264
12/11/76+	①²	16		37 Near You	Tattletale Eyes	—	$7		Epic 50314
				GEORGE JONES and TAMMY WYNETTE #1 Pop hit for Francis Craig in 1947					
3/19/77	6	14		38 (Let's Get Together) One Last Time	Hardly A Day Goes By	—	$7		Epic 50349
7/16/77	5	13		39 Southern California	Keep The Change	—	$7		Epic 50418
				GEORGE JONES and TAMMY WYNETTE					
10/8/77	6	15		40 One Of A Kind	Loving You, I Do	—	$6		Epic 50450
4/22/78	26	11		41 I'd Like To See Jesus (On The Midnight Special)	Love Doesn't Always Come (On The Night It's Needed)	—	$6		Epic 50538
7/15/78	3	15		42 Womanhood	50 Words Or Less	—	$6		Epic 50574
2/10/79	6	13		43 They Call It Making Love	Let Me Be Me	—	$6		Epic 50661
6/9/79	7	14		44 No One Else In The World	Mama, Your Little Girl Fell	—	$6		Epic 50722
3/1/80	2¹	14		45 Two Story House	It Sure Was Good	—	$6		Epic 50849
				GEORGE JONES and TAMMY WYNETTE					
4/19/80	17	14		46 He Was There (When I Needed You)	Only The Names Have Been Changed	—	$6		Epic 50868
8/9/80	17	13		47 Starting Over	I'll Be Thinking Of You	—	$6		Epic 50915
9/6/80	19	11		48 A Pair Of Old Sneakers	We'll Talk About It Later	—	$6		Epic 50930
				GEORGE JONES and TAMMY WYNETTE					
3/21/81	21	12		49 Cowboys Don't Shoot Straight (Like They Used To)	You Brought Me Back	—	$5		Epic 51011
9/5/81	18	14		50 Crying In The Rain	Bring Back My Baby To Me	—	$5		Epic 02439
				#6 Pop hit for The Everly Brothers in 1962					
3/27/82	8	17		51 Another Chance	What's It Like To Be A Woman	—	$5		Epic 02770
8/14/82	16	16		52 You Still Get To Me In My Dreams	If I Didn't Have A Heart	—	$5		Epic 03064
12/11/82+	19	15		53 A Good Night's Love	I'm Going On With Everything Gone	—	$5		Epic 03384
4/23/83	46	9		54 I Just Heard A Heart Break (And I'm So Afraid It's Mine)	Back To The Wall	—	$4		Epic 03811
7/9/83	63	7		55 Unwed Fathers	I'm So Afraid That I'd Live Through It	—	$4		Epic 03971
10/1/83	63	6		56 Still In The Ring	Midnight Love	—	$4		Epic 04101
6/2/84	40	15		57 Lonely Heart	(I'm Not) A Candle In The Wind	—	$4		Epic 04467
2/23/85	6	22		58 Sometimes When We Touch A:5 / S:6	You're Gonna Be The Last Love	—	$4		Columbia 04782
				MARK GRAY and TAMMY WYNETTE #3 Pop hit for Dan Hill in 1978					
7/13/85	48	9		59 You Can Lead A Heart To Love (But You Can't Make It Fall)	He Talks To Me	—	$4		Epic 05399
8/30/86	53	8		60 Alive And Well	I'll Be Thinking Of You	—	$4		Epic 06263
8/1/87	12	19		61 Your Love S:7	I Wasn't Meant To Live My Life Alone	—	$4		Epic 07226
				Ricky Skaggs (harmony vocal)					
12/5/87+	16	20		62 Talkin' To Myself Again S:15	A Slow Burning Fire	—	$4		Epic 07635
				The O'Kanes (harmony vocal)					
5/7/88	25	15		63 Beneath A Painted Sky S:24	Some Things Will Never Change	—	$4		Epic 07788
				Emmylou Harris (harmony vocal)					
2/18/89	51	11		64 Next To You	When A Girl Becomes A Wife	—	$4		Epic 68570

DEBUT	PEAK	WKS	Gold	A-side (Chart Hit) .... B-side	Pop	$	Pic	Label & Number
				WYNETTE, Tammy — Cont'd				
5/27/89	66	6		65 Thank The Cowboy For The Ride .... We Called It Everything But Quits	—	$4		Epic 68894
10/7/89	63	5		66 While The Feeling's Good .... Our Wedding Band	—	$4		Curb 10559
				WAYNE NEWTON (with Tammy Wynette)				
9/1/90	57	8		67 Let's Call It A Day Today .... When A Girl Becomes A Wife	—	$4	■	Epic 73427 (v)
2/2/91	56	8		68 What Goes With Blue .... Let's Call It A Day Today	—	$4	■	Epic 73656 (v)
8/24/91	49	8		69 We're Strangers Again .... If You Were The Friend (Wynette)	—	$4	■	Epic 73958 (v)
				TAMMY WYNETTE with Randy Travis				
12/25/93+	68	2		70 Silver Threads And Golden Needles .... Let Her Fly	—	$4	■	Columbia 77294 (v)
				PARTON/WYNETTE/LYNN				
10/8/94	67	9		71 Girl Thang	—		●	album cut
				TAMMY WYNETTE With Wynonna from the album *Without Walls* on Epic 52481				
7/1/95	69	4		72 One .... Golden Ring	—	$4		MCA 55048
				GEORGE JONES AND TAMMY WYNETTE				
4/25/98	56	1		73 Stand By Your Man .... [R]	—			album cut
				same version as #8 above; from the album *Super Hits* on Epic 67539				

WYNONNA ★157★   '92
Born Christina Ciminella on 5/30/64 in Ashland, Kentucky. Singer/songwriter/guitarist. Began performing in 1977. Half of **The Judds** duo with her mother, Naomi, from 1983-91. Acted on TV's *Touched By An Angel*. Sister of actress Ashley Judd.

1) No One Else On Earth   2) I Saw The Light   3) To Be Loved By You   4) She Is His Only Need   5) A Bad Goodbye

DEBUT	PEAK	WKS	Gold	A-side .... B-side	Pop	$	Pic	Label & Number
				WYNONNA JUDD:				
2/15/92	❶¹	20		1 She Is His Only Need .... No One Else On Earth	—	$4		Curb/MCA 54320
5/9/92	❶³	20		2 I Saw The Light .... When I Reach The Place I'm Goin'	—	$4		Curb/MCA 54407
8/15/92	❶⁴	20		3 No One Else On Earth .... (album version)	83	$4	■	Curb/MCA 54449 (v)
12/5/92+	4	20		4 My Strongest Weakness .... What It Takes	119	$4	■	Curb/MCA 54516 (v)
4/3/93	3	20		5 Tell Me Why .... A Little Bit Of Love	77	$4	■	Curb/MCA 54606 (v)
5/15/93	2¹	20		6 A Bad Goodbye .... The Hard Way (Black)	43	$4		RCA 62503 (v)
				CLINT BLACK (with Wynonna)				
7/17/93	3	20		7 Only Love .... Just Like New	102	$4	■	Curb/MCA 54689 (v)
10/30/93+	6	20		8 Is It Over Yet .... That Was Yesterday	—	$4		Curb/MCA 54754
12/25/93	61	1		9 Let's Make A Baby King .... [X]	—			album cut
				from the album *Tell Me Why* on Curb/MCA 10822				
2/19/94	2¹	20		10 Rock Bottom .... Girls With Guitars	—	$4	■	Curb/MCA 54809 (v)
6/4/94	10	20		11 Girls With Guitars .... I Just Drove By	—	$4		Curb/MCA 54875
10/8/94	67	9		12 Girl Thang	—			album cut
				TAMMY WYNETTE With Wynonna from the album *Without Walls* on Epic 52481				
				WYNONNA:				
1/6/96	❶¹	20		13 To Be Loved By You .... Freebird	—	$4	■	Curb/MCA 55084 (v)
4/27/96	14	20		14 Heaven Help My Heart .... (album version)	—	$4		Curb/MCA 55194
8/31/96	44	10		15 My Angel Is Here .... Change The World	—	$4		Curb/MCA 55252
11/16/96	55	6		16 Somebody To Love You .... (club mix)	—	$4		Curb/MCA 55286
12/28/96	55	2		17 Mary, Did You Know .... [X]	—			album cut
				KENNY ROGERS With Wynonna from Rogers's album *The Gift* on Magnatone 108				
10/4/97	13	20		18 When Love Starts Talkin' .... S:9 The Other Side	98	$4	■	Curb/Univ. 56095 (v)
12/13/97+	14	20		19 Come Some Rainy Day	—			album cut
4/25/98	45	10		20 Always Will	—			album cut
				above 2 from the album *The Other Side* on Curb/Universal 53061				
9/12/98	62	8		21 Woman To Woman	—			album cut
				from the various artists album *Tammy Wynette Remembered* on Asylum 62277				
12/5/98	68	4		22 Freedom	—			album cut
				from the various artists album *The Prince Of Egypt - Nashville* on DreamWorks 50045				
11/13/99+	31	20		23 Can't Nobody Love You (Like I Do) .... S:6 Help Me	—	$4	★	Curb/Mer. 72141 (v)
6/3/00	43	13		24 Going Nowhere .... Who Am I Trying To Fool	—	$4		Curb/Mercury 72155

WYRICK, Jim   '83
Born in Maynardville, Tennessee.

DEBUT	PEAK	WKS		A-side .... B-side	Pop	$		Label & Number
2/26/83	85	2		The Memory .... First To Be The Last	—	$5		NSD 157
				JIM WYRICK and Union Gold				

Y

YANKEE GREY   '99
Group from Cincinnati: Tim Hunt (vocals, guitar), Matt Basford (guitar), Joe Caverlee (fiddle), Jerry Hughes (keyboards), Dave Buchanan (bass) and Kevin Griffin (drums).

DEBUT	PEAK	WKS		A-side .... B-side	Pop	$		Label & Number
6/26/99	8	33		1 All Things Considered .... S:3 Tell Me Something I Don't Know	55	$4	★	Monument 79248
1/15/00	15	22		2 Another Nine Minutes	74			album cut
7/1/00	43	14		3 This Time Around	—			album cut
				above 2 from the album *Untamed* on Monument 69085				

Bobby Yates: What's Wrong With The Way That We're Doing It Now

DEBUT	PEAK	WKS	Gold	A-side (Chart Hit)	B-side	Pop	$	Pic	Label & Number

YANKOVIC, Frankie, & His Yanks '49
Born on 7/28/15 in Davis, West Virginia; raised in Cleveland. Died on 10/14/98 (age 83). Accordionist/polka bandleader. Known as "America's Polka King."

5/8/48	7	1		1 Just Because	A Night In May	9	$15		Columbia 12359
1/1/49	13	1		2 The Iron Range .... S:13 Linda's Lullaby	[I]	—	$15		Columbia 12381
4/30/49	7	7	●	3 Blue Skirt Waltz .... S:7 / J:10 Charlie Was A Boxer		12	$15		Columbia 12394
				FRANKIE YANKOVIC & HIS YANKS with THE MARLIN SISTERS					

YARBROUGH, Bob '71
Born in 1940 in Chattanooga, Tennessee.

5/22/71	38	12		1 You're Just More A Woman	In The Palm Of My Hand	—	$8		Sugar Hill 013
4/17/76	85	5		2 50 Ways To Leave Your Lover .... You Only Look Me Up When You're Down		—	$6		Music Mill 186
				BOB YARBOROUGH					
				#1 Pop hit for Paul Simon in 1976					

YATES, Billy '97
Born on 3/13/63 in Doniphan, Missouri.

5/10/97	69	3		1 I Smell Smoke	Goodbye Makes The Saddest Sound	—	$4	■	Almo So. 89010 (v)
5/24/97	36	16		2 Flowers	—	—	$4		album cut
				from the album Billy Yates on Almo Sounds 80015					
10/4/97	69	1		3 When The Walls Come Tumblin' Down	Broken Hearted Me	—	$4		Almo Sounds 89013
11/18/00+	53	9		4 What Do You Want From Me Now .... S:20 The House That Jack Built		—	$4	★	Columbia 79405 (v)

★ YATES, Jenny '87

4/25/87	80	3		A Whole Month Of Sundays	Holding Out For Love	—	$4		Mercury 888428

★ YATES, Lori '88
Born in Toronto.

11/12/88	77	5		1 Scene Of The Crime	Cowboy	—	$4	■	Columbia 08055
3/25/89	78	4		2 Promises, Promises	Heart In A Suitcase	—	$4		Columbia 68596

YEARWOOD, Trisha ★94★ '92
Born Patricia Lynn Yearwood on 9/19/64 in Monticello, Georgia. Singer/songwriter. Majored in music business at Belmont University in Nashville. Married to fellow student Chris Latham from 1987-91. Married to Robert Reynolds of **The Mavericks** from 1994-99. Joined the *Grand Ole Opry* in 1999. CMA Awards: 1997 & 1998 Female Vocalist of the Year. Also see **Hope**.

1)A Perfect Love 2)She's In Love With The Boy 3)Thinkin' About You 4)XXX's And OOO's (An American Girl) 5)Believe Me Baby (I Lied)

5/18/91	0²	20		1 She's In Love With The Boy	Victim Of The Game	—	$8		MCA 54076
9/14/91	4	20		2 Like We Never Had A Broken Heart	The Whisper Of Your Heart	—	$4		MCA 54172
12/21/91+	8	20		3 That's What I Like About You	When Goodbye Was A Word	—	$4		MCA 54270
3/28/92	4	20		4 The Woman Before Me	You Done Me Wrong (And That Ain't Right)	—	$4		MCA 54362
8/8/92	5	20		5 Wrong Side Of Memphis	Lonesome Dove	—	$4		MCA 54414
11/7/92+	2¹	20		6 Walkaway Joe	You Don't Have To Move That Mountain (Yearwood)	—	$4		MCA 54495
				TRISHA YEARWOOD with Don Henley					
3/6/93	12	20		7 You Say You Will	Hearts In Armor	—	$4		MCA 54600
6/12/93	19	20		8 Down On My Knees	For Reasons I've Forgotten	—	$4		MCA 54670
10/16/93	2¹	20		9 The Song Remembers When	Oh Lonesome You	82	$4	■	MCA 54734 (v)
2/5/94	21	20		10 Better Your Heart Than Mine	Hard Promises To Keep	—	$4	■	MCA 54786 (v)
6/4/94	72	2		11 I Fall To Pieces	(album version)	—	$4	■	MCA 54836 (v)
				AARON NEVILLE AND TRISHA YEARWOOD					
7/9/94	0²	20		12 XXX's And OOO's (An American Girl)	One In A Row	114	$4	■	MCA 54898 (v)
12/17/94	60	4		13 It Wasn't His Child	Reindeer Boogie [X]	—	$4		MCA 54940
1/14/95	0²	20		14 Thinkin' About You	Fairytale	120	$4	■	MCA 54973 (v)
4/29/95	23	15		15 You Can Sleep While I Drive .... S:19 Two Days From Knowing		—	$4	■	MCA 55025 (v)
				written and first recorded by Melissa Etheridge on her 1989 Brave And Crazy album					
8/5/95	9	20		16 I Wanna Go Too Far	The Restless Kind	—	$4		MCA 55078
12/2/95+	59	8		17 On A Bus To St. Cloud	O Mexico	—	$4		MCA 55141
7/13/96	0²	20		18 Believe Me Baby (I Lied)	Little Hercules	—	$4		MCA 55211
11/9/96+	3	20		19 Everybody Knows	A Lover Is Forever	—	$4		MCA 55250
3/1/97	36	13		20 I Need You	Hello, I'm Gone	—	$4		MCA 55308
6/7/97	2¹	20		21 How Do I Live .... S:3 (video version)		23	$4	■	MCA 72015 (v)
				from the movie Con Air starring Nicolas Cage					
8/23/97	2²	20		22 In Another's Eyes	I Want To Live Again (Yearwood)	—	$4		MCA 72021
				TRISHA YEARWOOD AND GARTH BROOKS					
1/17/98	0²	20		23 A Perfect Love	I Need You	—	$4		MCA 72034
5/9/98	2¹	23		24 There Goes My Baby .... S:15 One More Chance		93	$4	■	MCA 72048 (v)
9/19/98	18	20		25 Where Your Road Leads	Bring Me All Your Lovin' (Yearwood)	—	$4		MCA Nashville 72070
				TRISHA YEARWOOD With Garth Brooks					
11/28/98+	6	20		26 Powerful Thing	Never Let You Go Again	50	$3		MCA Nashville 72082
12/5/98	65	1		27 Wild As The Wind	—	—			album cut
				GARTH BROOKS (With Trisha Yearwood)					
				from Brooks's album Double Live on Capitol 97424					
12/26/98	63	1		28 Reindeer Boogie .... [X]		—			album cut
				recorded by Hank Snow in 1953; from the album The Sweetest Gift on MCA 11091					
5/8/99	10	25		29 I'll Still Love You More	Wouldn't Any Woman	65	$4		MCA Nashville 72089

DEBUT	PEAK	WKS	Gold	A-side (Chart Hit) .... B-side	Pop	$	Pic	Label & Number
				YEARWOOD, Trisha — Cont'd				
12/25/99	72	1		30 Santa On The Rooftop .... [X]	—			album cut
				TRISHA YEARWOOD & ROSIE O'DONNELL from O'Donnell's album *A Rosie Christmas* on Columbia 63685				
1/15/00	16	20		31 Real Live Woman .... I'm Still Alive	81	$4		MCA Nashville 172146
2/12/00	71	1		32 You're Where I Belong	—			album cut
				from the movie *Stuart Little* starring Geena Davis (soundtrack on Motown 542083)				
6/17/00	45	13		33 Where Are You Now .... Some Days	—	$4		MCA Nashville 172170
4/7/01	4	31		34 I Would've Loved You Anyway .... Sad Eyes	44	$4		MCA Nashville 172201
12/1/01+	16	20		35 Squeeze Me In	102			album cut
				GARTH BROOKS with Trisha Yearwood from Brooks's album *Scarecrow* on Capitol 31330				
12/1/01+	31	19		36 Inside Out .... Love Let Go (Yearwood)	—	$4		MCA Nashville 172219
				TRISHA YEARWOOD Featuring Don Henley				

YOAKAM, Dwight ★108★ '88
Born on 10/23/56 in Pikeville, Kentucky. Singer/songwriter/guitarist/actor. Played in southern Ohio before moving to Los Angeles in the early 1980s. First recorded for Oak Records. Member of the **Buzzin' Cousins**. Acted in the movies *Sling Blade*, *The Newton Boys* and *Panic Room*. Also see **Same Old Train**.

1) I Sang Dixie 2) Streets Of Bakersfield 3) Ain't That Lonely Yet 4) Fast As You 5) A Thousand Miles From Nowhere

DEBUT	PEAK	WKS	A-side .... B-side	Pop	$	Pic	Label & Number
3/1/86	3	24	1 Honky Tonk Man .... S:3 / A:4 Miner's Prayer	—	$4		Reprise 28793
7/12/86	4	21	2 Guitars, Cadillacs .... S:3 / A:4 I'll Be Gone	—	$4	■	Reprise 28688
11/15/86	31	15	3 It Won't Hurt .... S:22 / A:30 Bury Me	—	$4		Reprise 28565
4/11/87	7	16	4 Little Sister .... S:4 / A:21 This Drinkin' Will Kill Me	—	$4	■	Reprise 28432
			#5 Pop hit for **Elvis Presley** in 1961				
7/25/87	8	19	5 Little Ways .... S:4 Readin', Rightin', Rt. 23	—	$4	■	Reprise 28310
11/14/87+	6	19	6 Please, Please Baby .... S:6 Throughout All Time	—	$4		Reprise 28174
3/5/88	9	22	7 Always Late With Your Kisses .... S:5 1,000 Miles	—	$4	■	Reprise 27994
7/16/88	❶¹	18	8 Streets Of Bakersfield .... S:❶³ One More Time (Yoakam)	—	$4	■	Reprise 27964
			DWIGHT YOAKAM & BUCK OWENS				
11/12/88+	❶¹	21	9 I Sang Dixie .... S:18 Floyd County	—	$4	■	Reprise 27715
3/4/89	5	19	10 I Got You .... South Of Cincinnati	—	$4		Reprise 27567
6/24/89	46	7	11 Buenas Noches From A Lonely Room (She Wore Red Dresses) .... What I Don't Know	—	$4		Reprise 22944
9/30/89	35	10	12 Long White Cadillac .... Little Ways	—	$4	■	Reprise 22799
10/20/90+	11	20	13 Turn It On, Turn It Up, Turn Me Loose ...... Since I Started Drinkin' Again	—	$4		Reprise 19543 (v)
3/2/91	5	20	14 You're The One .... If There Was A Way	—	$4		Reprise 19405
8/10/91	15	21	15 Nothing's Changed Here .... Sad, Sad Music	—	$4		Reprise 19256
12/21/91+	7	20	16 It Only Hurts When I Cry .... Let's Work Together	—	$4		Reprise 19148
4/25/92	18	20	17 The Heart That You Own .... Dangerous Man	—	$4		Reprise 18966
8/8/92	47	10	18 Send A Message To My Heart ...... Takes A Lot To Rock You	—	$4		Reprise 18846
			DWIGHT YOAKAM & PATTY LOVELESS				
10/24/92	35	20	19 Suspicious Minds .... Burning Love	—	$4		Epic Soundtrax 74753
			#1 Pop hit for **Elvis Presley** in 1969; from the movie *Honeymoon In Vegas* starring James Caan				
3/13/93	2³	20	20 Ain't That Lonely Yet .... A Thousand Miles From Nowhere	58ˢ	$4	■	Reprise 18590 (v)
6/26/93	2¹	20	21 A Thousand Miles From Nowhere .... Ain't That Lonely Yet	—	$4	■	Reprise 18528 (v)
7/3/93+	2¹	20	22 Fast As You .... Home For Sale	70	$4	■	Reprise 18341 (v)
2/19/94	14	20	23 Try Not To Look So Pretty .... Wild Ride	—	$4	■	Reprise 18239 (v)
7/2/94	22	20	24 Pocket Of A Clown	—			album cut
			from the album *This Time* on Reprise 45241				
10/14/95	20	20	25 Nothing / S:19	—			
2/3/96	51	8	26 Gone (That'll Be Me)	—	$4	■	Reprise 17734 (v)
4/20/96	59	5	27 Sorry You Asked?	—			album cut
			from the album *Gone* on Reprise 46051				
7/12/97	47	10	28 Claudette	—			album cut
			written by **Roy Orbison**; from the album *Under The Covers* on Reprise 46690				
12/27/97	60	2	29 Santa Claus Is Back In Town .... [X]	—			album cut
			from the album *Come On Christmas* on Warner 46683				
5/2/98	17	20	30 Things Change	—			album cut
			from the album *A Long Way Home* on Reprise 46918				
9/19/98	57	6	31 These Arms .... That's Okay	—	$4		Reprise 17143
5/1/99	12	20	32 Crazy Little Thing Called Love /	—			
			#1 Pop hit for **Queen** in 1980				
9/4/99	54	8	33 Thinking About Leaving	64	$4		Reprise 16938
9/30/00+	26	23	34 What Do You Know About Love	—			album cut
5/26/01	49	8	35 I Want You To Want Me	—			album cut
			#7 Pop hit for **Cheap Trick** in 1979; above 2 from the album *Tomorrow's Sounds Today* on Reprise 47827				

YOUNG, Cole '83
| 7/23/83 | 72 | 5 | Just Give Me One More Night .... I'd Keep My Heart In Line | — | $5 | | Evergreen 1008 |

DEBUT	PEAK	WKS	Gold	A-side (Chart Hit)	B-side	Pop	$	Pic	Label & Number

YOUNG, Faron ★22★   '58

Born on 2/25/32 in Shreveport, Louisiana. Died of a self-inflicted gunshot on 12/10/96 (age 64). Singer/songwriter/guitarist/actor. Joined the *Louisiana Hayride* in 1951. Served in the U.S. Army from 1952-54. Known as "The Young Sheriff." Acted in several movies. Founder and one-time publisher of the *Music City News* magazine. Elected to the Country Music Hall of Fame in 2000. Also see **Heart Of Nashville**.

1) Alone With You 2) Hello Walls 3) Country Girl 4) Live Fast, Love Hard, Die Young 5) It's Four In The Morning

DEBUT	PEAK	WKS	#	A-side	B-side	Pop	$	Label & Number
1/10/53	2¹	18	1	Goin' Steady ..... A:2 / J:7 / S:10	Just Out Of Reach (Of My Two Open Arms)	—	$25	Capitol 2299
				also see #66 below				
6/6/53	5	5	2	I Can't Wait (For The Sun To Go Down) A:5	What's The Use To Love You	—	$25	Capitol 2461
9/4/54	8	9	3	A Place For Girls Like You ..... A:8 / S:13	In The Chapel In The Moonlight	—	$25	Capitol 2859
11/20/54+	2³	27	4	If You Ain't Lovin' (You Ain't Livin') ..... A:2 / J:2 / S:3	If That's The Fashion	—	$20	Capitol 2953
4/2/55	❶³	22	5	Live Fast, Love Hard, Die Young / ..... A:❶³ / J:2 / S:3		—		
		12	6	Forgive Me, Dear	J:flip	—	$20	Capitol 3056
8/13/55	2⁴	28	7	All Right / ..... A:2 / J:3 / S:4		—		
8/6/55	11	9	8	Go Back You Fool	S:11	—	$20	Capitol 3169
11/19/55+	5	13	9	It's A Great Life (If You Don't Weaken) / ..... A:5 / J:6 / S:7		—		
		1	10	For The Love Of A Woman Like You		—	$20	Capitol 3258
4/14/56	3	10	11	You're Still Mine / ..... A:3 / S:5		—		
4/7/56	4	16	12	I've Got Five Dollars And It's Saturday Night ..... S:4 / J:4 / A:10		—	$20	Capitol 3369
6/23/56	2¹	33	13	Sweet Dreams / ..... A:2 / J:4 / S:5		—		
		3	14	Until I Met You		—	$20	Capitol 3443
11/10/56	9	6	15	Turn Her Down / ..... A:9 / S:13		—		
		1	16	I'll Be Satisfied With Love	S:flip	—	$20	Capitol 3549
2/23/57	5	13	17	I Miss You Already (And You're Not Even Gone) / ..... A:5 / S:8		—		
			18	I'm Gonna Live Some Before I Die		—	$20	Capitol 3611
5/20/57	15	1	19	The Shrine Of St. Cecilia A:15	He Was There	96	$20	Capitol 3696
8/5/57	12	1	20	Love Has Finally Come My Way A:12	Moonlight Mountain	—	$15	Capitol 3753
6/23/58	❶¹³	29	21	Alone With You / ..... A:❶¹³ / S:2		51		
6/30/58	10	2	22	Every Time I'm Kissing You A:10		—	$15	Capitol 3982
10/20/58	9	17	23	That's The Way I Feel /		—		
10/27/58	22	5	24	I Hate Myself		—	$15	Capitol 4050
2/2/59	16	9	25	A Long Time Ago /		—		
1/26/59	20	10	26	Last Night At A Party		—	$15	Capitol 4113
4/13/59	14	8	27	That's The Way It's Gotta Be	We're Talking It Over	—	$15	Capitol 4164
7/20/59	❶⁴	32	28	Country Girl /		—		
7/27/59	27	6	29	I Hear You Talkin'		—	$15	Capitol 4233
11/16/59+	4	21	30	Riverboat /		83		
11/16/59+	10	18	31	Face To The Wall		—	$15	Capitol 4291
4/11/60	5	17	32	Your Old Used To Be	I'll Be Alright (In The Morning)	—	$15	Capitol 4351
10/24/60	21	5	33	There's Not Any Like You Left	Is She All You Thought She'd Be	—	$15	Capitol 4410
12/26/60+	20	7	34	Forget The Past /		—		
1/16/61	28	3	35	A World So Full Of Love		—	$15	Capitol 4463
3/20/61	❶⁹	23	36	Hello Walls		12		Capitol 4533
5/15/61	28	2	37	Congratulations		—	$15	
				above 2 written by **Willie Nelson**				
10/2/61	8	17	38	Backtrack	I Can't Find The Time	89	$15	■ Capitol 4616
3/24/62	7	13	39	Three Days	I Let It Slip Away	—	$15	■ Capitol 4696
6/16/62	4	19	40	The Comeback	Over Lonely And Under Kissed	—	$15	Capitol 4754
12/22/62+	9	10	41	Down By The River	Safely In Love Again	—	$15	Capitol 4868
3/2/63	4	16	42	The Yellow Bandana	How Much I Must Have Loved You	114	$12	Mercury 72085
6/8/63	14	7	43	Nightmare /		—	$12	Mercury 72114
6/1/63	30	1	44	I've Come To Say Goodbye		—	$12	Mercury 72114
10/26/63	13	7	45	We've Got Something In Common	Think About The Good Old Days	—	$12	Mercury 72167
12/21/63+	10	14	46	You'll Drive Me Back (Into Her Arms Again)	What Will I Tell My Darling	—	$12	Mercury 72201
3/14/64	5	23	47	Keeping Up With The Joneses /		—		
3/28/64	40	6	48	No Thanks, I Just Had One		—	$12	■ Mercury 72237
				MARGIE SINGLETON And FARON YOUNG (above 2)				
8/1/64	23	6	49	Rhinestones /		—		
7/25/64	48	2	50	Old Courthouse		—	$12	Mercury 72271
10/3/64	11	16	51	My Friend On The Right	The World's Greatest Love	—	$12	Mercury 72313
12/5/64	38	8	52	Another Woman's Man - Another Man's Woman	Honky Tonk Happy	—	$12	Mercury 72312
				FARON YOUNG AND MARGIE SINGLETON				
1/30/65	10	18	53	Walk Tall	The Weakness Of A Man	—	$10	Mercury 72375
8/7/65	34	6	54	Nothing Left To Lose	Dingaka (The Witch Doctor)	—	$10	Mercury 72440
11/27/65+	14	13	55	My Dreams	You Had A Call	—	$10	Mercury 72490
10/15/66	7	16	56	Unmitigated Gall	Some Of Your Memories (Hurt Me All Of The Time)	—	$10	Mercury 72617
4/8/67	48	8	57	I Guess I Had Too Much To Dream Last Night	I Just Don't Know How To Say No	—	$10	Mercury 72656
10/28/67+	14	14	58	Wonderful World Of Women	All I Can Stand	—	$8	Mercury 72728
3/9/68	14	16	59	She Went A Little Bit Farther	Stay, Love	—	$8	■ Mercury 72774
8/3/68	8	16	60	I Just Came To Get My Baby	Missing You Was All I Did Today	—	$8	Mercury 72827
3/1/69	25	13	61	I've Got Precious Memories	You Stayed Just Long Enough	—	$8	Mercury 72889

DEBUT	PEAK	WKS	Gold	A-side (Chart Hit)	B-side	Pop	$	Pic	Label & Number
				YOUNG, Faron — Cont'd					
7/12/69	2²	16		62 Wine Me Up	That's Where My Baby Feels At Home	—	$8		Mercury 72936
11/1/69	4	14		63 Your Time's Comin'	Painted Girls And Wine	—	$8		Mercury 72983
2/7/70	6	14		64 Occasional Wife	The Guns Of Johnny Rondo	—	$8		Mercury 73018
5/30/70	4	16		65 If I Ever Fall In Love (With A Honky Tonk Girl)	A Bunch Of Young Ideas	—	$8		Mercury 73065
10/10/70	5	12		66 Goin' Steady	That's My Way [R]	—	$8		Mercury 73112
				new version of #1 above					
3/27/71	6	17		67 Step Aside	Seems Like I'm Always Leaving	—	$8		Mercury 73191
8/7/71	9	14		68 Leavin' And Sayin' Goodbye	She Was The Color Of Love	—	$8		Mercury 73220
12/4/71+	❶²	20		69 It's Four In The Morning	It's Not The Miles	92	$8		Mercury 73250
7/22/72	5	16		70 This Little Girl Of Mine	It Hurts So Good	—	$8		Mercury 73308
2/3/73	15	11		71 She Fights That Lovin' Feeling	I'm In Love With Everything	—	$8		Mercury 73359
7/21/73	9	16		72 Just What I Had In Mind	All At Once It's Forever	—	$8		Mercury 73403
3/9/74	8	14		73 Some Kind Of A Woman	Again Today	—	$8		Mercury 73464
7/13/74	20	12		74 The Wrong In Loving You	Almost Dawn In Denver	—	$8		Mercury 73500
11/30/74+	23	12		75 Another You	God's Been Good To Me	—	$6		Mercury 73633
7/19/75	16	13		76 Here I Am In Dallas	Too Much Of Not Enough Of You	—	$6		Mercury 73692
12/13/75+	21	12		77 Feel Again	Some Old Rainy Mornin'	—	$6		Mercury 73731
4/10/76	33	10		78 I'd Just Be Fool Enough	What You See Is What You Get	—	$6		Mercury 73782
10/9/76	30	11		79 (The Worst You Ever Gave Me Was) The Best I Ever Had	You Get The Feelin'	—	$6		Mercury 73847
7/9/77	25	11		80 Crutches	The Last Goodbye	—	$6		Mercury 73925
2/25/78	38	10		81 Loving Here And Living There And Lying In Between	City Lights	—	$6		Mercury 55019
4/7/79	67	6		82 The Great Chicago Fire	Old Songs	—	$5		MCA 41004
9/22/79	69	6		83 That Over Thirty Look		—			
7/14/79	70	5		84 Second Hand Emotion			$5		MCA 41046
2/16/80	56	7		85 (If I'd Only Known) It Was The Last Time	Free And Easy	—	$4		MCA 41177
8/30/80	72	4		86 Tearjoint	I May Lose You Tomorrow	—	$4		MCA 41292
4/25/81	88	2		87 Until The Bitter End	Motel With No Phone	—	$4		MCA 51088
9/10/88	100	2		88 Stop And Take The Time	Misty Morning Rain	—	$5		Step One 390
2/4/89	87	2		89 Here's To You	You're Just Another Drinking Song	—	$5		Step One 397
				YOUNG, Neil '85					
				Born on 11/12/45 in Toronto. Rock singer/songwriter/guitarist. Member of **Crosby, Stills, Nash & Young**. Charted 11 pop hits from 1970-83. Inducted into the Rock and Roll Hall of Fame in 1995.					
10/5/85	33	18		Get Back To The Country	A:29 Misfits	—	$4		Geffen 28883
				YOUNG, Roger '79					
				Born in Yuma, Arizona.					
8/18/79	85	3		Skip A Rope	Fiddle Sam	—	$6		Dessa 79-2
				YOUNG, Steve '77					
				Born on 7/12/42 in Newnan, Georgia. Singer/songwriter.					
2/5/77	84	5		It's Not Supposed To Be That Way	Lonesome, On'ry And Mean	—	$5		RCA 10868
				written by **Willie Nelson**					
				YOUNGER, James & Michael '82					
				Duo of brothers from Edinburg, Texas: James and Michael Williams.					
				1)Nothing But The Radio On 2)There's No Substitute For You 3)Lovers On The Rebound					
				YOUNGER BROTHERS:					
4/24/82	68	5		1 Lonely Hearts	A Taste Of The Wind	—	$4		MCA 52030
7/3/82	19	15		2 Nothing But The Radio On	A Taste Of The Wind	—	$4		MCA 52076
12/11/82+	48	12		3 There's No Substitute For You	Here Comes The Tempter	—	$4		MCA 52148
3/5/83	50	8		4 Somewhere Down The Line	Blame It On Mexico	—	$4		MCA 52183
				JAMES & MICHAEL YOUNGER:					
6/4/83	54	10		5 A Taste Of The Wind	Lost In The Feeling	—	$4		MCA 52222
9/17/83	48	9		6 Lovers On The Rebound	Here Comes The Tempter	—	$4		MCA 52263
12/24/83+	65	8		7 Shoot First, Ask Questions Later	Thinking 'Bout Leaving	—	$4		MCA 52317
6/29/85	82	5		8 My Special Angel	In South Texas	—	$5		Permian 82011
4/5/86	67	7		9 Back On The Radio Again	Women Like Her Are In Dreams	—	$5		AIR 102
9/27/86	65	7		10 She Wants To Marry A Cowboy		—	$5		AIR 106
				YOUNGER BROTHERS BAND '84					
				Group from Leola, Pennsylvania. Led by Terry Gehman.					
9/8/84	92	2		Making Love To Dixie	I Don't Want To Be Your Friend	—	$6		ERP 04094

Z

DEBUT	PEAK	WKS	Gold	A-side	B-side	Pop	$	Pic	Label & Number
				ZACA CREEK '89					
				Group of brothers from Santa Ynez, California: Gates (vocals), Scot (guitar), Jeff (keyboards) and James (bass) Foss.					
9/23/89	38	11		1 Sometimes Love's Not A Pretty Thing	Rock Me Back	—	$4		Columbia 69062
12/23/89+	58	6		2 Ghost Town	Time's Up	—	$4		Columbia 73096
3/13/93	70	3		3 Broken Heartland		—			album cut
				from the album *Broken Heartland* on Giant 24491					

DEBUT	PEAK	WKS	Gold	A-side (Chart Hit)	B-side	Pop	$	Pic	Label & Number
				★ **ZADORA, Pia** '80 Born Pia Schipani on 5/4/54 in Hoboken, New Jersey. Singer/actress. Appeared in several movies.					
4/28/79	76	3		1 Bedtime Stories /			—		
3/31/79	98	1		2 Tell Him			—	$4	Warner/Curb 8766
				#4 Pop hit for The Exciters in 1963					
8/25/79	65	5		3 I Know A Good Thing When I Feel It	Trouble		—	$4	Warner/Curb 49065
1/12/80	55	5		4 Baby It's You	Roses Ain't Red (I Don't Love You)		—	$4	Warner/Curb 49148
				#8 Pop hit for The Shirelles in 1962					
				★ **ZEILER, Gayle** '82 Born in Gilroy, California. Ethel of **Ethel & The Shameless Hussies**.					
1/30/82	78	4		No Place To Hide			—	$7	Equa 670

SONG TITLE SECTION

Lists, alphabetically, all A-side titles in the Artist Section. The artist's name is listed with each title along with the highest position attained and the year the song peaked on the chart.

Some titles show the letter **F** as a position, indicating that the title was listed as a flip side and did not chart on its own.

A song with more than one charted version is listed once, with the artists' names listed below in chronological order. Many songs that have the same title, but are different tunes, are listed separately, with the most popular title listed first. This will make it easy to determine which songs are the same composition, the number of charted versions of a particular song, and which of these was the most popular.

Cross references have been used throughout to aid in finding a title.

Please keep the following in mind when searching for titles:

> Titles such as "I.O.U.," "P.T. 109," and "S.O.S." will be found at the beginning of their respective letters; however, titles such as "D-I-V-O-R-C-E" and "T-R-O-U-B-L-E," which are spellings of words, are listed with their regular spellings.
>
> Two-word titles that have the <u>exact</u> same spelling as one-word titles are listed together alphabetically. ("Honky-Tonk Man" is listed directly before "Honkytonk Man.")
>
> Titles that are <u>identical</u>, except for an apostrophized word in one of the titles, are shown together. ("Fallin' For You" appears immediately above "Falling For You.")

"A-Sleeping---" on p. 417

A

A-11
26/65 Johnny Paycheck
54/89 Buck Owens
85/76 **"A" My Name Is Alice**
 Marie Osmond
46/66 **"A" Team** Ssgt Barry Sadler
Abilene
1/63 George Hamilton IV
24/77 Sonny James
Above And Beyond
3/60 Buck Owens
1/89 Rodney Crowell
16/98 **Absence Of The Heart**
 Deana Carter
16/81 **Acapulco** Johnny Duncan
89/79 **Accentuate The Positive**
 Tommy O'Day
16/60 **Accidently On Purpose**
 George Jones
4/56 **According To My Heart**
 Jim Reeves
1/89 **Ace In The Hole** George Strait
9/92 **Aces** Suzy Bogguss
5/62 **Aching, Breaking Heart**
 George Jones
Achy Breaky Heart
1/92 Billy Ray Cyrus
71/92 Alvin & The Chipmunks
50/85 **Acres Of Diamonds** Benny Wilson
86/90 **Across The Room From You**
 Phil Cohron
Act Naturally
1/63 Buck Owens
27/89 Buck Owens & Ringo Starr
3/95 **Adalida** George Strait
1/88 **Addicted** Dan Seals
4/94 **Addicted To A Dollar** Doug Stone
2/62 **Adios Amigo** Jim Reeves
4/77 **Adios Amigo** Marty Robbins
41/67 **Adorable Women** Nat Stuckey
64/84 **Adventures In Parodies**
 Pinkard & Bowden
14/49 **Afraid** Rex Allen with Jerry Byrd
22/73 **Afraid I'll Want To Love Her One More Time**
 Billy "Crash" Craddock
 Afraid Of Losing You Again ..see: (I'm So)
50/78 **Afraid You'd Come Back**
 Kenny Price
50/99 **After A Kiss** Pam Tillis
4/84 **After All** Ed Bruce
43/87 **After All** Patty Loveless
1/76 **After All The Good Is Gone**
 Conway Twitty
 (After All These Years) ..see: I Still Love You
18/71 **After All They All Used To Belong To Me** Hank Williams, Jr.
1/89 **After All This Time**
 Rodney Crowell
6/70 **After Closing Time**
 David Houston & Barbara Mandrell
17/80 **After Hours** Joe Stampley
51/88 **After Last Night's Storm**
 Ride The River
79/88 **After Lovin' You** Melissa Kay
7/62 **After Loving You** Eddy Arnold

10/77 **(After Sweet Memories) Play Born To Lose Again** Dottsy
75/81 **After Texas** Roy Head
32/77 **After The Ball** Johnny Cash
After The Fire Is Gone
1/71 Conway Twitty & Loretta Lynn
17/74 Willie Nelson & Tracy Nelson
70/82 **After The Glitter Fades**
 Stevie Nicks
19/83 **After The Great Depression**
 Razzy Bailey
10/83 **After The Last Goodbye**
 Gus Hardin
13/92 **After The Lights Go Out**
 Ricky Van Shelton
16/82 **After The Love Slips Away**
 Earl Thomas Conley
40/77 **After The Lovin'**
 Engelbert Humperdinck
88/88 **After The Passion Leaves**
 Nina Wyatt
65/70 **After The Preacher's Gone**
 Peggy Sue
8/76 **After The Storm** Wynn Stewart
82/82 **After Tonight** Deborah Allen
22/71 **After You** Jerry Wallace
23/73 **After You** Hank Williams, Jr.
28/83 **After You** Dan Seals
Afternoon Delight
9/76 Johnny Carver
94/76 Starland Vocal Band
19/65 **Again** Don Gibson
66/92 **Against The Grain** Garth Brooks
53/90 **Against The Wind** Brooks & Dunn
36/80 **Age** Jerry Reed
20/68 **Age Of Worry** Billy Walker
21/77 **Agree To Disagree**
 Little David Wilkins
69/93 **Ain't Been A Train Through Here In Years** Rick Vincent
65/99 **Ain't Enough Roses** Lisa Brokop
1/93 **Ain't Going Down (Til The Sun Comes Up)** Garth Brooks
55/69 **Ain't Gonna Worry** Leon Ashley
65/83 **Ain't Gonna Worry My Mind**
 Richard Leigh
15/96 **Ain't Got Nothin' On Us**
 John Michael Montgomery
68/68 **Ain't Got The Time** Tom T. Hall
23/63 **Ain't Got Time For Nothin'**
 Bob Gallion
19/68 **Ain't Got Time To Be Unhappy**
 Bob Luman
2/66 **Ain't Had No Lovin'** Connie Smith
23/58 **Ain't I The Lucky One**
 Marty Robbins
 Ain't It All Worth Living For
15/72 Tompall/Glaser Brothers
75/74 Mack White
14/73 **Ain't It Amazing, Gracie**
 Buck Owens
97/76 **Ain't It Good To Be In Love Again**
 Vicky Fletcher
35/73 **Ain't It Good (To Feel This Way)**
 Norro Wilson
51/85 **Ain't It Just Like Love**
 Billy Burnette
77/78 **Ain't Life Hell**
 Hank Cochran & Willie Nelson
10/74 **Ain't Love A Good Thing**
 Connie Smith
41/76 **Ain't Love Good** Jean Shepard

1/86 **Ain't Misbehavin'**
 Hank Williams, Jr.
17/90 **Ain't Necessarily So** Willie Nelson
4/78 **Ain't No California** Mel Tillis
86/87 **Ain't No Cure For Love**
 Jennifer Warnes
74/76 **Ain't No Heartbreak**
 Dorsey Burnette
4/82 **Ain't No Money** Rosanne Cash
86/89 **Ain't No One Like Me In Tennessee** Holly Ronick
71/99 **Ain't No Short Way Home**
 Oak Ridge Boys
48/86 **Ain't No Tellin'** Lewis Storey
7/83 **Ain't No Trick (It Takes Magic)**
 Lee Greenwood
56/79 **Ain't No Way To Make A Bad Love Grow** Johnny Russell
67/82 **Ain't Nobody Gonna Get My Body But You** Del Reeves
43/01 **Ain't Nobody Gonna Take That From Me** Collin Raye
15/90 **Ain't Nobody's Business**
 Hank Williams, Jr.
5/50 **Ain't Nobody's Business But My Own**
 Kay Starr & Tennessee Ernie Ford
10/72 **Ain't Nothin' Shakin' (But The Leaves On The Trees)**
 Billy "Crash" Craddock
1/01 **Ain't Nothing 'Bout You**
 Brooks & Dunn
88/88 **Ain't She Shinin' Tonight**
 Jim Moore & Sidewinder
 Ain't She Somethin' Else
46/75 Eddy Raven
1/85 Conway Twitty
7/72 **Ain't That A Shame**
 Hank Williams, Jr.
2/93 **Ain't That Lonely Yet**
 Dwight Yoakam
68/77 **Ain't That Lovin' You Baby**
 David Houston
53/86 **Ain't That Peculiar**
 New Grass Revival
75/83 **Ain't That The Way It Goes**
 Dave Kemp
62/87 **Ain't We Got Love** Paul Proctor
82/83 **Ain't Your Memory Got No Pride At All** Ray Charles
11/62 **Air Mail To Heaven** Carl Smith
37/83 **Air That I Breathe** Rex Allen, Jr.
Alabam
1/60 Cowboy Copas
61/68 Guy Mitchell
3/51 **Alabama Jubilee** Red Foley
83/77 **Alabama Summertime**
 James Talley
 Alabama Wild Man
48/68 Jerry Reed
22/72 Jerry Reed
58/99 **Albuquerque** Sons Of The Desert
1/93 **Alibis** Tracy Lawrence
Alibis
16/79 Johnny Rodriguez
81/84 Lane Brody
20/81 **Alice Doesn't Love Here Anymore** Bobby Goldsboro
69/82 **Alice In Dallas (Sweet Texas)**
 Wyvon Alexander
91/85 **Alice, Rita and Donna**
 David Walsh

413

18/75	**Alimony** Bobby Bare		**All I Want For Christmas Is You**	1/81	**All Roads Lead To You** Steve Wariner
34/88	**Alive And Well** Gatlin Bros.	55/93	Vince Vance & The Valiants	1/57	**All Shook Up** Elvis Presley
	Alive And Well	52/94	Vince Vance & The Valiants	8/85	**All Tangled Up In Love**
53/86	Tammy Wynette	52/95	Vince Vance & The Valiants		Gus Hardin (with Earl Thomas Conley)
81/87	Nisha Jackson	49/96	Vince Vance & The Valiants		
7/46	**All Alone In This World Without You** Eddy Arnold	43/97	Vince Vance & The Valiants	49/95	**All That Heaven Will Allow** Mavericks
21/59	**All-American Boy** Grandpa Jones	31/99	Vince Vance & The Valiants		
57/85	**All American Country Boy** Con Hunley	5/96	**All I Want Is A Life** Tim McGraw	27/77	**All That Keeps Me Going** Jim Weatherly
		57/99	**All I Want Is Everything** Mindy McCready	94/74	**All That Keeps Me Going** Mary Lou Turner
31/75	**All American Girl** Statler Brothers	96/77	**All I Want Is To Love You** Jack Rainwater		
37/70	**All American Husband** Peggy Sue	84/78	**All I Want To Do In Life** Jack Clement	33/70	**All That Keeps Ya Goin'** Tompall/Glaser Brothers
23/75	**All-American Man** Johnny Paycheck	67/71	**All I Want To Do Is Say I Love You** Brian Collins	50/98	**All That Matters Anymore** Lee Roy Parnell
84/83	**All-American Redneck** Randy Howard	30/82	**All I'm Missing Is You** Eddy Arnold	70/85	**All That's Left For Me** Carl Jackson
16/79	**All Around Cowboy** Marty Robbins	60/88	**All In My Mind** Cali McCord	5/89	**All The Fun** Paul Overstreet
67/74	**All Around Cowboy Of 1964** Buddy Alan	13/73	**All In The Name Of Love** Narvel Felts	1/79	**All The Gold In California** Larry Gatlin/Gatlin Brothers
64/84	**All Around The Water Tank** Mel McDaniel	74/91	**All In The Name Of Love** Bellamy Brothers	50/88	**All The Good One's Are Taken** Linda Davis
39/86	**All Because Of You** Marty Stuart	11/92	**All Is Fair In Love And War** Ronnie Milsap	4/97	**All The Good Ones Are Gone** Pam Tillis
64/70	**All Day Sucker** Liz Anderson	25/97	**All Lit Up In Love** David Lee Murphy	20/76	**All The King's Horses** Lynn Anderson
66/94	**All Fired Up** Dan Seals				
9/69	**All For The Love Of A Girl** Claude King	1/87	**All My Ex's Live In Texas** George Strait	5/72	**All The Lonely Women In The World** Bill Anderson
1/70	**All For The Love Of Sunshine** Hank Williams, Jr.	9/70	**All My Hard Times** Roy Drusky		**All The Love In The World** ..see: **(If You Add)**
	All Grown Up	13/83	**All My Life** Kenny Rogers		
8/58	Johnny Horton	23/67	**All My Love** Don Gibson	53/84	**All The Love Is On The Radio** Tom Jones
26/63	Johnny Horton	89/77	**All My Love** Joe Ely		
35/72	**All Heaven Breaks Loose** David Rogers	61/98	**All My Love For Christmas** Lonestar	97/77	**All The Love We Threw Away** Lois Johnson & Bill Rice
72/69	**All Heaven Broke Loose** Hugh X. Lewis	58/82	**All My Lovin** Mundo Earwood	73/75	**All The Love You'll Ever Need** Cliff Cochran
72/84	**All Heaven Is About To Break Loose** Zella Lehr	10/84	**All My Rowdy Friends Are Coming Over Tonight** Hank Williams, Jr.	5/89	**All The Reasons Why** Highway 101
2/72	**All His Children** Charley Pride/Henry Mancini	1/81	**All My Rowdy Friends (Have Settled Down)** Hank Williams, Jr.	39/77	**All The Sweet** Mel McDaniel
29/91	**All I Can Be (Is A Sweet Memory)** Collin Raye			97/88	**All The Things We Are Not** David Walsh
		27/67	**All My Tomorrows** Nat Stuckey		**All The Time**
3/76	**All I Can Do** Dolly Parton	41/81	**All New Me** Tom T. Hall	18/59	Kitty Wells
82/85	**All I Do Is Dream Of You** Margo Smith	31/00	**All Night Long** Montgomery Gentry	1/67	Jack Greene
27/97	**All I Do Is Love Her** James Bonamy	40/81	**All Night Long** Johnny Duncan	82/79	**All The Time In The World** Dr. Hook
	All I Ever Need Is You	80/78	**All Night Long** Peggy Sue	73/86	**All The Way** Ray Price
18/71	Ray Sanders		**All Of ..also see: Alla**		**All These Things**
1/79	Kenny Rogers & Dottie West	3/78	**All Of Me** Willie Nelson	1/76	Joe Stampley
67/72	**All I Had To Do** Jim Ed Brown		**All Of Me Belongs To You**	62/81	Joe Stampley
	All I Have To Do Is Dream	28/67	Dick Curless	3/93	**All These Years** Sawyer Brown
1/58	Everly Brothers	70/67	Hank Cochran	8/99	**All Things Considered** Yankee Grey
6/70	Bobbie Gentry & Glen Campbell	46/97	**All Of The Above** Ty England		
79/75	Nitty Gritty Dirt Band	26/88	**All Of This & More** Crystal Gayle/Gary Morris	72/90	**All Things Made New Again** Suzy Bogguss
85/81	Nancy Montgomery	91/73	**All Or Nothing With Me** Susan St. Marie	6/86	**All Tied Up** Ronnie McDowell
1/69	**All I Have To Offer You (Is Me)** Charley Pride	4/58	**All Over Again** Johnny Cash	F/73	**(All Together Now) Let's Fall Apart** Ronnie Milsap
11/49	**All I Need Is Some More Lovin'** George Morgan	43/96	**All Over But The Shoutin'** Shenandoah	71/86	**All We Had Was One Another** Don King
51/71	**All I Need Is You** Carl Belew & Betty Jean Robinson	4/75	**All Over Me** Charlie Rich	13/96	**All You Ever Do Is Bring Me Down** Mavericks
		18/02	**All Over Me** Blake Shelton		
8/95	**All I Need To Know** Kenny Chesney		**All Over Now ..see: (We Used To Kiss Each Other On The Lips But It's)**	73/91	**All You Really Wanna Do** Michelle Wright
52/84	**All I Wanna Do (Is Make Love To You)** Bandana	53/94	**All Over Town** Don Cox	73/89	**All You're Takin' Is My Love** Pal Rakes
21/79	**All I Want And Need Forever** Vern Gosdin	2/55	**All Right** Faron Young	5/62	**Alla My Love** Webb Pierce
			All Right (I'll Sign The Papers)		**Allegheny**
		45/64	George Morgan	70/70	Bonnie Guitar
		26/68	Mel Tillis	69/73	Johnny Cash & June Carter Cash

An American Soldier WPCV — Toby Keith
Amelia Earhart's Last Flight — The Greenbrier Boys 2 CD set 1:13

97/77	**Allegheny Lady** Max D. Barnes	27/88	**Am I Crazy?** Statler Brothers	4/95	**Amy's Back In Austin** Little Texas	
22/62	**Alligator Man** Jimmy Newman	57/85	**Am I Going Crazy (Or Just Out Of My Mind)** Lobo	28/90	**Amy's Eyes** Charley Pride	
68/85	**Almighty Lover** Sierra			81/89	**Ancient History** Susan Ledford	
2/52	**Almost** George Morgan		**Am I Losing You**	48/71	**And I Love You So** Bobby Goldsboro	
11/96	**Almost A Memory Now** BlackHawk	3/57	Jim Reeves		**And I'll Be Hating You** ..see: (It Won't Be Long)	
		8/60	Jim Reeves			
20/83	**Almost Called Her Baby By Mistake** Larry Gatlin/Gatlin Brothers	1/81	Ronnie Milsap	14/89	**And So It Goes** John Denver & The Nitty Gritty Dirt Band	
			Am I That Easy To Forget			
19/00	**Almost Doesn't Count** Mark Wills	9/59	Carl Belew	2/95	**And Still** Reba McEntire	
1/93	**Almost Goodbye** Mark Chesnutt	11/60	Skeeter Davis	47/82	**And Then Some** Bobby Smith	
22/99	**Almost Home** Mary Chapin Carpenter	12/73	Jim Reeves	51/87	**And Then Some** Charly McClain	
		65/80	Orion	70/67	**And You Wonder Why** Fred Carter, Jr.	
	Almost Over You		**Amanda**			Seven Spanish Angels
86/84	Sheena Easton	33/73	Don Williams	41/71	**Angel** Claude Gray	
42/98	Lila McCann	1/79	Waylon Jennings	82/84	**Angel Eyes** Larry Willoughby	
	Almost Persuaded		**Amarillo By Morning**	1/81	**Angel Flying Too Close To The Ground** Willie Nelson	
1/66	David Houston	31/74	Terry Stafford			
6/66	Ben Colder	4/83	George Strait	67/75	**Angel In An Apron** Durwood Haddock	Kiss An Angel...
95/76	Sherri King	1/99	**Amazed** Lonestar			
F/77	Maury Finney	9/76	**Amazing Grace (Used To Be Her Favorite Song)** Amazing Rhythm Aces	1/84	**Angel In Disguise** Earl Thomas Conley	
58/87	Merle Haggard					
49/84	**Almost Saturday Night** Burrito Brothers	1/73	**Amazing Love** Charley Pride	4/98	**Angel In My Eyes** John Michael Montgomery	
53/98	**Alone** Monty Holmes	36/85	**Amber Waves Of Grain** Merle Haggard		**Angel In Your Arms**	
	Alone Again ..also see: (Here I Am)	30/77	**Ambush** Ronnie Sessions	71/77	Vivian Bell	
		2/97	**Amen Kind Of Love** Daryle Singletary	54/84	Robin Lee	
72/73	**Alone Again (Naturally)** Brush Arbor	6/84	**America** Waylon Jennings	8/85	Barbara Mandrell	
	Alone With You	73/93	**America, I Believe In You** Charlie Daniels		**Angel Of The Morning**	
1/58	Faron Young			34/70	Connie Eaton	
44/64	Rose Maddox	62/86	**America Is** B.J. Thomas	22/78	Melba Montgomery	
57/86	**Along For The Ride ('56 T-Bird)** John Denver		**America The Beautiful**	22/81	Juice Newton	
		22/76	Charlie Rich (1976)	34/64	**Angel On Leave** Jimmy "C" Newman	
75/93	**Already Gone** Tanya Tucker	82/80	Mickey Newbury			
1/68	**Already It's Heaven** David Houston	58/01	America The Beautiful		**(Angel On My Mind) That's Why I'm Walkin'** ..see: Why I'm Walkin'	
		59/01	**America Will Always Stand** Randy Travis			
5/93	**Alright Already** Larry Stewart			42/76	**Angel On My Shoulder** Joni Lee	
42/72	**Alright I'll Sign The Papers** Jeannie Seely	45/01	**America Will Survive** Hank Williams, Jr.	57/77	**Angel With A Broken Wing** Roy Head	An Angel With No Halo
18/80	**Always** Patsy Cline	85/79	**America's Sweetheart** Corbin & Hanner	13/71	**Angel's Sunday** Jim Ed Brown	
70/97	**Always A Woman** Larry Stewart			32/81	**Angela** Mundo Earwood	
16/69	**Always, Always** Porter Wagoner & Dolly Parton	11/90	**American Boy** Eddie Rabbitt	69/78	**Angelene** Mundo Earwood	
		5/82	**American Dream** Hank Williams, Jr.	60/79	**Angeline** Ed Bruce	
	(Always And Forever) ..see: I Won't Need You Anymore				**Angels Among Us**	
		58/80	**American Dream** Dirt Band	51/93	Alabama	
1/86	**Always Have Always Will** Janie Frickie	4/89	**American Family** Oak Ridge Boys	28/94	Alabama	
		54/85	**American Farmer** Charlie Daniels Band		**Angels Are Hard To Find**	
40/96	**Always Have, Always Will** Shenandoah			19/74	Hank Williams, Jr.	
			(American Girl) ..see: XXX's And OOO's	59/91	Hank Williams, Jr.	
	Always Late (With Your Kisses)			66/99	**Angels Don't Fly** James Prosser	
1/51	Lefty Frizzell	1/93	**American Honky-Tonk Bar Association** Garth Brooks	4/70	**Angels Don't Lie** Jim Reeves	
99/76	Jo-el Sonnier			57/83	**Angels Get Lonely Too** Ralph May	
84/81	Leona Williams	1/83	**American Made** Oak Ridge Boys			
9/88	Dwight Yoakam	88/88	**American Man** Frank Burgess	9/01	**Angels In Waiting** Tammy Cochran	
37/78	**Always Lovin Her Man** Dale McBride	16/87	**American Me** Schuyler, Knobloch & Overstreet	49/88	**Angels Love Bad Men** Barbara Mandrell	
69/99	**Always Never The Same** George Strait	66/67	**American Power** Johnny Wright	9/76	**Angels, Roses, And Rain** Dickey Lee	
		93/88	**American Trilogy** Mickey Newbury			
	Always On My Mind			35/99	**Angels Working Overtime** Deana Carter	16 wks.
45/72	Brenda Lee	60/85	**American Waltz** Merle Haggard			
16/73	Elvis Presley	8/88	**Americana** Moe Bandy		**Anger & Tears**	
20/79	John Wesley Ryles		**Americans**	49/87	Mel McDaniel	
1/82	Willie Nelson	35/74	Tex Ritter	61/89	Russell Smith	
6/71	**Always Remember** Bill Anderson	59/74	Byron Macgregor	1/01	**Angry All The Time** Tim McGraw	
90/80	**Always, Sometimes, Never** Nancy Ruud	5/60	**Amigo's Guitar** Kitty Wells	16/68	**Angry Words** Stonewall Jackson	
		68/98	**Amnesia** Blake & Brian	68/78	**Animal** Ronnie McDowell	
1/75	**Always Wanting You** Merle Haggard	1/76	**Among My Souvenirs** Marty Robbins	17/66	**Anita, You're Dreaming** Waylon Jennings	
40/01	**Always Was** Aaron Tippin	73/99	**Among The Missing** Michael McDonald & Kathy Mattea	89/74	**Ann** Joel Mathis	
45/98	**Always Will** Wynonna					
1/87	**Am I Blue** George Strait	16/70	**Amos Moses** Jerry Reed			

2/72	**Ann (Don't Go Runnin')** *Tommy Overstreet*	69/68	**Another Time, Another Place, Another World** *Jerry Wallace*	55/81	**Anything That Hurts You (Hurts Me)** *Keith Stegall*
95/89	**Anna ("Go With Him")** *Jack Denton*	75/73	**Another Way To Say Goodbye** *Ray Sanders*	94/74	**Anything To Prove My Love To You** *Jimmy Hartsook*
28/68	**Anna, I'm Taking You Home** *Leon Ashley*	14/75	**Another Woman** *T.G. Sheppard*	10/67	**Anything Your Heart Desires** *Billy Walker*
3/58	**Anna Marie** *Jim Reeves*	92/78	Billy "Crash" Craddock	38/72	**Anything's Better Than Nothing** *Mel Tillis & Sherry Bryce*
40/65	**Anne Of A Thousand Days** *Leroy Van Dyke*	89/88	**Another Woman's Man** *Bobbi Lace*		**Anytime**
13/55	**Annie Over** *Hank Thompson*	38/64	**Another Woman's Man - Another Man's Woman** *Faron Young & Margie Singleton*	1/48	Eddy Arnold
9/74	**Annie's Song** *John Denver*			14/48	Foy Willing
2/60	**Another** *Roy Drusky*			73/69	Patsy Cline
28/63	**Another Bridge To Burn** *"Little" Jimmy Dickens*	4/87	**Another World** *Crystal Gayle & Gary Morris*	54/85	Osmond Brothers
8/82	**Another Chance** *Tammy Wynette*	3/97	**Another You** *David Kersh*	79/83	**Anytime You're Ready** *Narvel Felts*
27/62	**Another Day, Another Dollar** *Wynn Stewart*	23/75	**Another You** *Faron Young*	13/71	**Anyway** *George Hamilton IV*
44/66	**Another Day, Another Dollar In The Hole** *Tex Williams*	32/97	**Another You, Another Me** *Brady Seals*		**Anyway That You Want Me**
		66/97	**Answer To My Prayer** *Skip Ewing*	81/79	Juice Newton
25/69	**Another Day, Another Mile, Another Highway** *Clay Hart*	3/49	**Anticipation Blues** *Tennessee Ernie Ford*	60/85	Carlette
61/72	**Another Day Of Loving** *Penny DeHaven*	84/81	**Antioch Church House Choir** *Sweetwater*	54/95	**Anyway The Wind Blows** *Brother Phelps*
25/79	**Another Easy Lovin' Night** *Randy Barlow*	26/79	**Any Day Now** Don Gibson	F/56	**Anyway You Want Me (That's How I Will Be)** *Elvis Presley*
21/78	**Another Fine Mess** *Glen Campbell*	1/82	Ronnie Milsap	10/93	**Anywhere But Here** *Sammy Kershaw*
28/63	**Another Fool Like Me** *Ned Miller*	56/95	**Any Gal Of Mine** *Gino The New Guy*	F/81	**Anywhere There's A Jukebox** *Razzy Bailey*
57/73	**Another Football Year** *Jeannie C. Riley*	1/95	**Any Man Of Mine** *Shania Twain*	13/62	**Anywhere There's People** *Lawton Williams*
10/78	**Another Goodbye** *Donna Fargo*	7/56	**Any Old Time** *Webb Pierce*	63/69	**Anywhere U.S.A.** *Buckaroos*
31/74	**Another Goodbye Song** *Rex Allen, Jr.*	32/67	**Any Old Way You Do** *Jan Howard*	72/77	**Apartment** *Johnny Carver*
84/89	**Another Heart To Break The Fall** *Carrie Davis*	3/73	**Any Old Wind That Blows** *Johnny Cash*		**Apartment #9**
		71/93	**Any Road** *Corbin/Hanner*	21/66	Bobby Austin
8/82	**Another Honky-Tonk Night On Broadway** *David Frizzell & Shelly West*		**Any Time ..see: Anytime**	44/67	Tammy Wynette
			Any Way That You Want Me ..see: Anyway That You Want Me	57/67	**Apologize** *Buddy Cagle*
	Another Lonely Night			14/69	**April's Fool** *Ray Price*
12/70	Jean Shepard	4/89	**Any Way The Wind Blows** *Southern Pacific*	58/70	**Apron Strings** *Peggy Sue*
76/77	Jody Miller			87/88	**Arab, Alabama** *Pinkard & Bowden*
48/84	**Another Lonely Night With You** *Roy Clark*	33/81	**Any Way You Want Me** *Gene Watson*	2/82	**Are The Good Times Really Over** *Merle Haggard*
1/74	**Another Lonely Song** *Tammy Wynette*	10/81	**Any Which Way You Can** *Glen Campbell*	53/88	**Are There Any More Like You (Where You Came From)** *Becky Hobbs*
24/76	**Another Morning** *Jim Ed Brown*	17/83	**Anybody Else's Heart But Mine** *Terri Gibbs*	61/76	**Are They Gonna Make Us Outlaws Again** *James Talley*
10/84	**Another Motel Memory** *Shelly West*	94/75	**Anybody Out There Wanna Be A Daddy** *Kitty Wells*		**Are We Dreamin' The Same Dream**
44/76	**Another Neon Night** *Jean Shepard*	13/59	**Anybody's Girl** *Hank Thompson*	66/80	Gary Stewart
		1/91	**Anymore** *Travis Tritt*	26/81	Charlie Rich
5/71	**Another Night Of Love** *Freddy Weller*	3/60	**Anymore** *Roy Drusky*	45/82	**Are We In Love (Or Am I)** *Charlie Ross*
15/00	**Another Nine Minutes** *Yankee Grey*	64/88	**Anyone Can Be Somebody's Fool** *Nanci Griffith*	24/96	**Are We In Trouble Now** *Randy Travis*
45/97	**Another Perfect Day** *Blake & Brian*	27/87	**Anyone Can Do The Heartbreak** *Anne Murray*	1/89	**Are You Ever Gonna Love Me** *Holly Dunn*
4/68	**Another Place Another Time** *Jerry Lee Lewis*	4/99	**Anyone Else** *Collin Raye*	11/69	**Are You From Dixie (Cause I'm From Dixie Too)** *Jerry Reed*
5/88	**Another Place, Another Time** *Don Williams*	2/78	**Anyone Who Isn't Me Tonight** *Kenny Rogers & Dottie West*	1/81	**Are You Happy Baby?** *Dottie West*
27/72	**Another Puff** *Jerry Reed*	12/77	**Anything But Leavin'** *Larry Gatlin*		**Are You Lonesome To-night?**
	Another Saturday Night	25/81	**Anything But Yes Is Still A No** *Stephanie Winslow*	22/61	Elvis Presley
88/75	Buddy Alan	49/95	**Anything For Love** *James House*	57/83	John Schneider & Jill Michaels
74/93	Jimmy Buffett	71/86	**Anything For Love** *Gordon Lightfoot*	3/91	**Are You Lovin' Me Like I'm Lovin' You** *Ronnie Milsap*
55/98	**Another Side** *Sawyer Brown*		**Anything For Your Love**		**Are You Mine**
4/82	**Another Sleepless Night** *Anne Murray*	80/84	Brentwood	2/55	Ginny Wright/Tom Tall
		88/84	Sammy Hall	6/55	Myrna Lorrie & Buddy Deval
	Another Somebody Done Somebody Wrong Song ..see: (Hey Won't You Play)	28/86	**Anything Goes** *Gary Morris*	14/55	Red Sovine - Goldie Hill
		12/68	**Anything Leaving Town Today** *Dave Dudley*	1/80	**Are You On The Road To Lovin' Me Again** *Debby Boone*
16/66	**Another Story** *Ernest Tubb*	22/63	**Anything New Gets Old (Except My Love For You)** *Don Gibson*	7/77	**Are You Ready For The Country** *Waylon Jennings*
34/80	**Another Texas Song** *Eddy Raven*				

Arlington – Trace Adkins WPCV (7-27-05) – Patriotism/Death

13/58	**Are You Really Mine** Jimmie Rodgers	27/92	**Asking Us To Dance** Kathy Mattea	40/68	**Baby, Ain't That Love** Jack Barlow
32/87	**Are You Satisfied** Janie Frickie	6/50	**A-Sleeping At The Foot Of The Bed** "Little" Jimmy Dickens	1/70	**Baby, Baby (I Know You're A Lady)** David Houston
10/79	**Are You Sincere** Elvis Presley	72/76	**Asphalt Cowboy** Hank Thompson	1/88	**Baby Blue** George Strait
20/87	**Are You Still In Love With Me** Anne Murray	67/72	**Astrology** Liz Anderson	68/78	**Baby Blue** King Edward IV & The Knights
1/75	**Are You Sure Hank Done It This Way** Waylon Jennings	13/66	**At Ease Heart** Ernie Ashworth	3/76	**Baby Boy** Mary Kay Place
1/52	**Are You Teasing Me** Carl Smith	61/91	**At Last** Gene Watson	1/85	**Baby Bye Bye** Gary Morris
12/60	**Are You Willing, Willie** Marion Worth	59/71	**At Least Part Of The Way** Stan Hitchcock	31/72	**Baby, Bye Bye** Dickey Lee
31/99	**Are Your Eyes Still Blue** Shane McAnally		**At Mail Call Today**	42/84	**Baby, Come To Me** Stephanie Winslow
87/80	**Arizona Highway** Tim Rex & Oklahoma	1/45	Gene Autry	5/47	**Baby Doll** Sons Of The Pioneers
59/01	**Arizona Rain** 3 Of Hearts	3/45	Lawrence Welk with Red Foley	6/74	**Baby Doll** Barbara Fairchild
85/80	**Arizona Whiz** George Burns	24/78	**At The End Of A Rainbow** Jerry Wallace	26/72	**Baby Don't Get Hooked On Me** Mac Davis
47/72	**Arkansas** Wilburn Brothers	85/79	**At The Moonlite** Bill Phillips	75/89	**Baby Don't Go** Dianne Davis
19/86	**Arlene** Marty Stuart	5/86	**At The Sound Of The Tone** John Schneider	23/77	**Baby, Don't Keep Me Hangin' On** Susie Allanson
27/73	**Arms Full Of Empty** Buck Owens	13/74	**At The Time** Jean Shepard	65/92	**Baby Don't You Know** Stacy Dean Campbell
4/71	**Arms Of A Fool** Mel Tillis		**At This Moment**		**Baby I Lied**
70/82	**Arms Of A Stranger** Tennessee Express	42/87	Billy Vera & The Beaters	4/83	Deborah Allen
62/70	**Arms Of My Weakness** Darrell McCall	89/89	Holly Lipton	40/01	Shannon Brown
	Around ..see: 'Round	3/84	**Atlanta Blue** Statler Brothers	15/77	**Baby, I Love You So** Joe Stampley
	Around My Heart ..see: (You Sure Know Your Way)	9/83	**Atlanta Burned Again Last Night** Atlanta	77/78	**Baby, I Need Your Lovin'** E.D. Wofford
64/69	**Article From Life** Lefty Frizzell		**Atlanta Georgia Stray**	31/70	**Baby, I Tried** Jim Ed Brown
8/65	**Artificial Rose** Jimmy Newman	36/68	Sonny Curtis	26/86	**Baby I Want It** Girls Next Door
2/95	**As Any Fool Can See** Tracy Lawrence	62/69	Kenny Price	40/87	**Baby I Was Leaving Anyhow** Billy Montana
		6/46	**Atomic Power** Buchanan Brothers		
		13/74	**Atta Way To Go** Don Williams		
		5/84	**Attitude Adjustment** Hank Williams, Jr.	35/80	**Baby, I'm A Want You** Stephanie Winslow
8/54	**As Far As I'm Concerned** Red Foley & Betty Foley		**Auctioneer, The**	48/78	**Baby I'm Burnin'** Dolly Parton
12/79	**As Long As I Can Wake Up In Your Arms** Kenny O'Dell	9/57	Leroy VanDyke	33/83	**Baby I'm Gone** Terri Gibbs
3/55	**As Long As I Live** Red Foley & Kitty Wells	51/68	Brenda Byers	22/92	**Baby, I'm Missing You** Highway 101
3/68	**As Long As I Live** George Jones	88/74	**Auctioneer Love** Bruce Mullen	2/88	**Baby I'm Yours** Steve Wariner
1/84	**As Long As I'm Rockin' With You** John Conlee	56/77	**Audubon** C.W. McCall		**Baby, I'm Yours**
		49/00	**Auld Lang Syne (The Millennium Mix)** Kenny G	5/71	Jody Miller
70/87	**As Long As I've Been Loving You** Razorback	1/01	**Austin** Blake Shelton	33/78	Debby Boone
30/66	**As Long As The Wind Blows** Johnny Darrell	84/80	**Autograph** John Denver	22/83	Tanya Tucker
43/76	**As Long As There's A Sunday** Sammi Smith	15/68	**Autumn Of My Life** Bobby Goldsboro	9/49	**Baby, It's Cold Outside** Homer & Jethro with June Carter
83/88	**As Long As There's Women Like You** Jerry Cooper	52/71	**Award To An Angel** Wayne Kemp	21/78	**Baby It's You** Janie Fricke
			Away In A Manger	55/80	**Baby It's You** Pia Zadora
51/88	**As Long As We Got Each Other** Louise Mandrell with Eric Carmen	73/98	Reba McEntire	55/71	**Baby, It's Yours** Wynn Stewart
		67/99	Kenny Chesney	62/99	**Baby Jesus Is Born** Garth Brooks
		63/73	**Awful Lot To Learn About Truck Drivin'** Red Simpson	20/78	**Baby, Last Night Made My Day** Susie Allanson
68/92	**As Long As You Belong To Me** Holly Dunn	69/70	**Awful Lotta Lovin'** Penny DeHaven	80/74	**Baby Let Your Long Hair Down** Don Adams
14/91	**As Simple As That** Mike Reid			5/55	**Baby Let's Play House** Elvis Presley
1/74	**As Soon As I Hang Up The Phone** Loretta Lynn/Conway Twitty			11/94	**Baby Likes To Rock It** Tractors
	Ashes By Now		**B**	62/76	**Baby Love** Joni Lee
78/80	Rodney Crowell	3/84	**B-B-B-Burnin' Up With Love** Eddie Rabbitt	93/81	**Baby Loved Me** Ronnie Speeks
4/01	Lee Ann Womack	63/00	**BFD** Kathy Mattea	67/68	**Baby Me Baby** Johnny Duncan
47/88	**Ashes In The Wind** Moe Bandy	1/64	**B.J. The D.J.** Stonewall Jackson	68/77	**Baby Me Baby** Roger Miller
	Ashes Of Love		**Baby**	27/79	**Baby My Baby** Margo Smith
37/68	Don Gibson	7/66	Wilma Burgess	52/94	**Baby Needs New Shoes** Restless Heart
15/72	Dickey Lee	63/75	Tennessee Ernie Ford/Andra Willis	49/95	**Baby, Now That I've Found You** Alison Krauss & Union Station
48/76	Jody Miller				
100/78	Amazing Rhythm Aces	80/81	**Baby, The** Kieran Kane	44/91	**Baby On Board** Oak Ridge Boys
26/87	Desert Rose Band	16/69	**Baby Again** Hank Williams, Jr.	76/80	**Baby Ride Easy** Carlene Carter with Dave Edmunds
19/82	**Ashes To Ashes** Terri Gibbs	62/99	**Baby Ain't Rocking Me Right** Mark Nesler		
42/76	**Ask Any Old Cheater Who Knows** Freddy Weller	15/66	**Baby Ain't That Fine** Gene Pitney & Melba Montgomery	15/60	**Baby Rocked Her Dolly** Frankie Miller
19/64	**Ask Marie** Sonny James			28/61	**Baby Sittin' Boogie** Buzz Clifford
65/00	**Askin' Too Much** Tamara Walker				

(LP) Ballad of the Alamo – Mr Robbins

92/79 **Baby Song** *Leona Williams*
51/91 **Baby Take A Piece Of My Heart** *Kelly Willis*
36/90 **Baby, Walk On** *Matraca Berg*
45/86 **Baby Wants** *Osmond Bros.*
4/52 **Baby, We're Really In Love** *Hank Williams*
1/83 **Baby, What About You** *Crystal Gayle*
66/72 **Baby, What's Wrong With Us** *Charlie Louvin & Melba Montgomery*
Baby When Your Heart Breaks Down
73/83 *Kix Brooks*
56/86 *Osmond Bros.*
56/71 **Baby Without You** *Jan Howard*
22/77 **Baby, You Look Good To Me Tonight** *John Denver*
71/90 **Baby, You'll Be My Baby** *Oak Ridge Boys*
63/87 **Baby You're Gone** *Janie Frickie*
7/80 **Baby, You're Something** *John Conlee*
30/71 **Baby, You've Got What It Takes** *Charlie Louvin & Melba Montgomery*
7/68 **Baby's Back Again** *Connie Smith*
75/73 **Baby's Blue** *Ferlin Husky*
51/85 **Baby's Eyes** *Lane Brody*
2/73 **Baby's Gone** *Conway Twitty*
55/74 **Baby's Gone** *Bobby Wright*
2/87 **Baby's Got A Hold On Me** *Nitty Gritty Dirt Band*
1/87 **Baby's Got A New Baby** *S-K-O*
1/85 **Baby's Got Her Blue Jeans On** *Mel McDaniel*
60/99 **Baby's Got My Number** *South Sixty Five*
1/89 **Baby's Gotten Good At Goodbye** *George Strait*
66/74 **Baby's Not Home** *Roy Head*
12/72 **Baby's Smile, Woman's Kiss** *Johnny Duncan*
72/84 **Baby's Walkin'** *Chantilly*
2/00 **Back At One** *Mark Wills*
55/74 **Back Door Of Heaven** *Nancy Wayne*
48/86 **Back Home** *A.J. Masters*
1/74 **Back Home Again** *John Denver*
53/88 **Back In Baby's Arms** *Emmylou Harris*
13/65 **Back In Circulation** *Jimmy Newman*
39/82 **Back In Debbie's Arms** *Tom Carlile*
23/75 **Back In Huntsville Again** *Bobby Bare*
81/82 **Back In My Baby's Arms** *Vince And Dianne Hatfield*
2/90 **Back In My Younger Days** *Don Williams*
4/69 **Back In The Arms Of Love** *Jack Greene*
51/74 **Back In The Country** *Roy Acuff*
20/89 **Back In The Fire** *Gene Watson*
51/98 **Back In The Saddle** *Matraca Berg*
F/76 **Back In The Saddle Again** *Sonny James*
51/89 **Back In The Swing Again** *Linda Davis*

66/89 **Back In The Swing Of Things** *Dean Dillon*
48/87 **Back In The Swing Of Things Again** *Larry Boone*
Back In The U.S.A.
48/75 *Carmol Taylor*
41/78 *Linda Ronstadt*
4/95 **Back In Your Arms Again** *Lorrie Morgan*
41/96 **Back In Your Arms Again** *Kenny Chesney*
35/84 **Back On Her Mind Again** *Johnny Rodriguez*
2/79 **Back On My Mind Again** *Ronnie Milsap*
58/98 **Back On The Farm** *Thompson Brothers Band*
67/86 **Back On The Radio Again** *James & Michael Younger*
10/66 **Back Pocket Money** *Jimmy Newman*
33/69 **Back Side Of Dallas** *Jeannie C. Riley*
Back Street Affair
1/52 *Webb Pierce*
88/80 *Joe Douglas*
25/71 **Back Then** *Wanda Jackson*
6/80 **Back To Back** *Jeanne Pruett*
74/69 **Back To Back (We're Strangers)** *Johnny Duncan & June Stearns*
58/82 **Back To Believing Again** *Marie Osmond*
26/69 **Back To Denver** *George Hamilton IV*
40/67 **Back To Nashville, Tennessee** *Stonemans*
78/89 **Back To Stay** *Johnny Rodriguez*
(Back To The Basics Of Love) **..see: Luckenbach, Texas**
7/86 **(Back To The) Heartbreak Kid** *Restless Heart*
17/78 **Back To The Love** *Susie Allanson*
51/91 **Back To The Well** *Tom Wopat*
84/75 **Back Up And Push** *Bill Black's Combo*
2/54 **Back Up Buddy** *Carl Smith*
67/93 **Back When** *Vern Gosdin*
36/80 **Back When Gas Was Thirty Cents A Gallon** *Tom T. Hall*
67/87 **Back When It Really Mattered** *Tommy Roe*
14/86 **Back When Love Was Enough** *Mark Gray*
14/90 **Back Where I Come From** *Mac McAnally*
16/70 **Back Where It's At** *George Hamilton IV*
2/92 **Backroads** *Ricky Van Shelton*
1/79 **Backside Of Thirty** *John Conlee*
92/79 **Backslider's Wine** *Michael Murphey*
25/83 **Backslidin'** *Joe Stampley*
87/83 **Backstreet Ballet** *Savannah*
8/61 **Backtrack** *Faron Young*
15/54 **Backward, Turn Backward** *Pee Wee King*
77/73 **Bad, Bad, Bad Cowboy** *Tompall Glaser*
33/73 **Bad, Bad Leroy Brown** *Anthony Armstrong Jones*
25/64 **Bad, Bad Tuesday** *Tom Tall*

58/70 **Bad Case Of The Blues** *Linda Martell*
Bad Day For A Break Up
62/79 *Leslee Barnhill*
46/88 *Cali McCord*
30/98 **Bad Day To Let You Go** *Bryan White*
50/95 **Bad Dog, No Biscuit** *Daron Norwood*
73/84 **Bad For Me** *Joe Sun*
45/97 **Bad For Us** *Little Texas*
2/93 **Bad Goodbye** *Clint Black (with Wynonna)*
12/86 **Bad Love** *Pake McEntire*
79/89 **Bad Moon Rising** *Cerrito*
Bad News
23/63 *John D. Loudermilk*
8/64 *Johnny Cash*
36/82 *Boxcar Willie*
51/84 **Bad Night For Good Girls** *Jan Gray*
28/63 **Bad Old Memories** *Williams Bros.*
94/76 **Bad Part Of Me** *Jerry Naylor*
10/66 **Bad Seed** *Jan Howard*
87/75 **Bad Water** *Gene Watson*
64/88 **Badland Preacher** *Carly Harrington*
5/91 **Ball And Chain** *Paul Overstreet*
26/72 **Ballad Of A Hillbilly Singer** *Freddy Weller*
Ballad Of A Teenage Queen
1/58 *Johnny Cash*
45/89 *Johnny Cash/Rosanne Cash/Everly Brothers*
Ballad Of Davy Crockett
4/55 *"Tennessee" Ernie Ford*
10/55 *Mac Wiseman*
49/91 *Kentucky Headhunters*
4/69 **Ballad Of Forty Dollars** *Tom T. Hall*
3/64 **Ballad Of Ira Hayes** *Johnny Cash*
62/70 **Ballad Of J.C.** *Gordon Terry*
1/63 **Ballad Of Jed Clampett** *Lester Flatt & Earl Scruggs*
70/68 **Ballad Of John Dillinger** *Billy Grammer*
66/00 **Ballad Of John Rocker** *Tim Wilson*
50/86 **Ballad Of The Blue Cyclone** *Ray Stevens*
2/66 **Ballad Of The Green Berets** *SSgt Barry Sadler*
44/67 **Ballad Of Thunder Road** *Jim & Jesse*
14/68 **Ballad Of Two Brothers** *Autry Inman*
27/67 **Ballad Of Waterhole #3 (Code Of The West)** *Roger Miller*
7/60 **Ballad Of Wild River** *Gene Woods*
32/81 **Bally-Hoo Days** *Eddy Arnold*
6/64 **Baltimore** *Sonny James*
22/84 **Band Of Gold** *Charly McClain*
F/82 **Bandera, Texas** *Solid Gold Band*
7/75 **Bandy The Rodeo Clown** *Moe Bandy*
68/98 **Bang A Drum** *Chris LeDoux (with Jon Bon Jovi)*
4/47 **Bang Bang** *Jimmie Davis*
63/99 **Bang, Bang, Bang** *Nitty Gritty Dirt Band*
9/48 **Banjo Boogie** *Arthur (Guitar Boogie) Smith*

Remember The Alamo – Johnny Cash   *Belleau Wood*

	Banjo Fantasy II ..see: **Ski Bumpus**		16/68	**Be Proud Of Your Man** Porter Wagoner	55/80	**Beers To You** Ray Charles & Clint Eastwood

5/48   **Banjo Polka** Tex Williams
14/74 **Baptism Of Jesse Taylor**
     Johnny Russell
1/80   **Bar Room Buddies**
     Merle Haggard & Clint Eastwood
73/69 **Bar Room Habits** Wayne Kemp
30/71 **Bar Room Talk** Del Reeves
32/78 **Bar Wars** Freddy Weller
40/85 **Bar With No Beer** Tom T. Hall
55/68 **Barbara** George Morgan
19/77 **Barbara Don't Let Me Be The Last To Know** Mel Street
92/76 **Barefoot Angel** Chet Taylor
64/00 **Barefoot In The Grass**
     Sonya Isaacs
90/81 **Barely Gettin' By** Sawmill Creek
1/75   **Bargain Store** Dolly Parton
60/99 **Barlight** Charlie Robison
31/75 **Barmaid, The** David Wills
10/81 **Baron, The** Johnny Cash
63/66 **Baron, The** Dick Curless
65/82 **Barroom Games** Mike Campbell
41/75 **Barroom Pal, Goodtime Gals**
     Jim Ed Brown
45/85 **Barroom Roses** Moe Bandy
89/73 **Barrooms Have Found You**
     Garland Frady
     Barstool Mountain
82/77   Wayne Carson
9/79   Moe Bandy
     Bartender's Blues
88/77   James Taylor
6/78   George Jones
16/76 **Battle, The** George Jones
9/90   **Battle Hymn Of Love**
     Kathy Mattea & Tim O'Brien
49/71 **Battle Hymn Of Lt. Calley**
     C Company Feat. Terry Nelson
26/59 **Battle Of Kookamonga**
     Homer And Jethro
     Battle Of New Orleans
1/59   Johnny Horton
24/59   Jimmie Driftwood
51/75   Buck Owens
1/89   **Bayou Boys** Eddy Raven
74/94 **Bayou Girl** Bob Woodruff
12/63 **Bayou Talk** Jimmy "C" Newman
11/71 **Be A Little Quieter**
     Porter Wagoner
26/64 **Be Better To Your Baby**
     Ernest Tubb
     Be-Bop-A-Lula
5/56   Gene Vincent
98/86   Hank Chaney ("86")
37/69 **Be Careful Of Stones That You Throw** Luke The Drifter, Jr.
98/73 **Be Certain** Terri Lane
5/69   **Be Glad** Del Reeves
33/65 **Be Good To Her** Carl Smith
86/83 **Be Happy For Me**
     Gene Kennedy & Karen Jeglum
49/97 **Be Honest** Thrasher Shiver
92/75 **Be Honest With Me** Kathy Barnes
63/92 **Be My Angel** Lionel Cartwright
15/72 **Be My Baby** Jody Miller
1/94   **Be My Baby Tonight**
     John Michael Montgomery
85/81 **Be My Lover, Be My Friend**
     Mick Lloyd & Jerri Kelly

     Be Quiet Mind
9/61   Del Reeves
23/64   Ott Stephens
63/88 **Be Serious** Donna Meade
10/82 **Be There For Me Baby**
     Johnny Lee
36/78 **Be Your Own Best Friend**
     Ray Stevens
1/96   **Beaches Of Cheyenne**
     Garth Brooks
3/67   **Bear With Me A Little Longer**
     Billy Walker
41/01 **Beatin' It In** Neal McCoy
13/48 **Beaut From Butte** Dick Thomas
47/01 **Beautiful (All That You Could Be)**
     Kenny Rogers
76/82 **Beautiful Baby** Paul Overstreet
74/87 **Beautiful Body** David Frizzell
5/51   **Beautiful Brown Eyes**
     Jimmy Wakely & Les Baxter
4/55   **Beautiful Lies** Jean Shepard
48/72 **Beautiful People** Pat Daisy
86/78 **Beautiful Song (For A Beautiful Lady)** Lee Dresser
67/73 **Beautiful Sunday** Jack Reno
10/78 **Beautiful Woman** Charlie Rich
3/81   **Beautiful You** Oak Ridge Boys
75/00 **Beauty's In The Eye Of The Beerholder**
     Chuck Wagon And The Wheels
     Because ..also see: **Cuzz**
18/65 **Because I Cared** Ernest Ashworth
28/66 **Because It's You** Wanda Jackson
45/67 **Because Of Him** Claude Gray
73/79 **Because Of Losing You**
     Narvel Felts
74/75 **Because We Love**
     Jack Blanchard & Misty Morgan
20/76 **Because You Believed In Me**
     Gene Watson
8/00   **Because You Love Me**
     Jo Dee Messina
9/71   **Bed Of Rose's** Statler Brothers
     Bed Of Roses
91/84   Bobby Vinton
76/87   R.C. Coin
76/88   Western Union Band
4/87   **Bed You Made For Me**
     Highway 101
24/80 **Bedroom, The**
     Jim Ed Brown & Helen Cornelius
18/80 **Bedroom Ballad** Gene Watson
18/78 **Bedroom Eyes** Don Drumm
36/81 **Bedtime Stories** Jim Chesnut
76/79 **Bedtime Stories** Pia Zadora
1/72   **Bedtime Story** Tammy Wynette
5/00   **Been There**
     Clint Black with Steve Wariner
45/94 **Been There** McBride & The Ride
21/93 **Beer And Bones**
     John Michael Montgomery
22/69 **Beer Drinkin' Music** Ray Sanders
58/82 **Beer Drinkin' Song** Mac Davis
49/70 **Beer Drinking, Honky Tonkin' Blues** Billy Mize
86/81 **Beer Joint Fever** Allen Frizzell
24/01 **Beer Run**
     George Jones With Garth Brooks
19/00 **Beer Thirty** Brooks & Dunn

94/81 **Beethoven Was Before My Time**
     Jerry Dycke
47/72 **Before Goodbye** Del Reeves
63/96 **Before He Kissed Me** Lisa Brokop
80/82 **Before I Got To Know Her**
     Brian Collins
6/56   **Before I Met You** Carl Smith
73/92 **Before I'm Ever Over You**
     Lee Greenwood
4/64   **Before I'm Over You** Loretta Lynn
2/79   **Before My Time** John Conlee
43/89 **Before The Heartache Rolls In**
     Foster & Lloyd
     Before The Next Teardrop Falls
44/68   Duane Dee
33/70   Linda Martell
1/75   Freddy Fender
22/66 **Before The Ring On Your Finger Turns Green** Dottie West
     Before This Day Ends
4/60   George Hamilton IV
23/61   Eddy Arnold
55/83 **Before We Knew It** Jan Gray
10/49 **Before You Call** Dave Landers
51/88 **Before You Cheat On Me Once (You Better Think Twice)**
     Robin Lee
1/65   **Before You Go** Buck Owens
2/94   **Before You Kill Us All**
     Randy Travis
5/61   **Beggar To A King** Hank Snow
100/78 **Beggars And Choosers** Bill Rice
97/88 **Beggars Can't Be Choosers**
     Don Lafleur
82/80 **Beggin' For Mercy**
     Louise Mandrell
1/64   **Begging To You** Marty Robbins
     Behind Blue Eyes
57/72   Mundo Earwood
32/77   Mundo Earwood
     Behind Closed Doors
1/73   Charlie Rich
64/98   Joe Diffie
1/65   **Behind The Tear** Sonny James
87/80 **Behind Your Eyes**
     Charlie Daniels Band
66/95 **Bein' Happy** Russ Taff
91/85 **Being A Fool Again** Audie Henry
1/96   **Believe Me Baby (I Lied)**
     Trisha Yearwood
10/58 **Believe What You Say**
     Ricky Nelson
     Belleau Wood *Andy Griffith*
41/97   Garth Brooks
65/98   Garth Brooks
4/65   **Belles Of Southern Bell**
     Del Reeves
30/61 **Bells That Broke My Heart**
     Slim Whitman
3/95   **Bend It Until It Breaks**
     John Anderson
25/88 **Beneath A Painted Sky**
     Tammy Wynette
     Beneath Still Waters
38/70   Diana Trask
1/80   Emmylou Harris
55/89 **Beneath The Texas Moon**
     J. C. Crowley
60/79 **Beside Me** Steve Wariner

Andy Griffith (CD)

54/81	Best Bedroom In Town Judy Bailey	47/98	Better Than It Used To Be Rhett Akins	73/67	Big Brother Murv Shiner	
1/00	Best Day George Strait	92/79	Better Than Now DeWayne Orender	29/66	Big Chief Buffalo Nickel (Desert Blues) Skeets McDonald	
53/74	Best Day Of The Rest Of Our Love Bud Logan & Wilma Burgess	3/95	Better Things To Do Terri Clark Better Times A Comin'	1/82	Big City Merle Haggard	
16/62	Best Dressed Beggar (In Town) Carl Smith	20/63	Ray Godfrey	41/64	Big City Ways Warren Smith	
46/79	Best Friends Make The Worst Enemies David Houston	39/65	Jim & Jesse	52/68	Big Daddy Browns	
		64/97	Better To Dream Of You Mary Chapin Carpenter	6/00	Big Deal LeAnn Rimes	
15/88	Best I Know How Statler Brothers	21/94	Better Your Heart Than Mine Trisha Yearwood	3/89	Big Dreams In A Small Town Restless Heart	
94/76	Best I've Ever Had Jeannie C. Riley	71/96	Bettin' Forever On You Tony Toliver	52/67	Big Dummy Tommy Collins	
78/75	Best In Me Jody Miller	49/88	Betty Jean Russell Smith	13/62	Big Fool Of The Year George Jones	
29/72	Best Is Yet To Come Del Reeves	5/85	Betty's Bein' Bad Sawyer Brown	70/67	Big Foot Dick Curless	
74/99	Best Is Yet To Come Brady Seals	62/96	Betty's Got A Bass Boat Pam Tillis	4/74	Big Four Poster Bed Brenda Lee	
77/87	Best Love I Never Had Freddie Hart	91/77	Betty's Song Roy Drusky	8/74	Big Game Hunter Buck Owens	
39/93	Best Mistakes I Ever Made Rick Vincent	46/91	Between A Rock And A Heartache Lee Greenwood	12/68	Big Girls Don't Cry Lynn Anderson	
27/60	Best Of All My Heartaches Wilburn Brothers		Between A Woman And A Man ..see: (There's Nothing Like The Love)	17/96	Big Guitar BlackHawk	
45/84	Best Of Families Big Al Downing			19/59	Big Harlan Taylor George Jones	
62/82	Best Of Friends Thrasher Brothers	11/95	Between An Old Memory And Me Travis Tritt	37/93	Big Heart Gibson/Miller Band	
1/00	Best Of Intentions Travis Tritt	3/85	Between Blue Eyes And Jeans Conway Twitty	75/94	Big Heart Rodney Crowell	
6/80	Best Of Strangers Barbara Mandrell	11/74	Between Lust And Watching TV Cal Smith	29/60	Big Hearted Me Don Gibson	
6/72	Best Part Of Living Marty Robbins	46/73	Between Me And Blue Ferlin Husky	5/69	Big In Vegas Buck Owens	
69/66	Best Part Of Loving You Hank Locklin	2/98	Between The Devil And Me Alan Jackson	5/60	Big Iron Marty Robbins	
52/77	Best Part Of My Days (Are My Nights With You) David Wills	F/73	Between The King And I Jeannie Seely	72/93	Big Iron Horses Restless Heart	
75/86	Best There Is Charley Pride	58/79	Between The Lines Bobby Braddock	50/65	Big Job George Jones & Gene Pitney	
7/75	Best Way I Know How Mel Tillis	27/95	Between The Two Of Them Tanya Tucker	31/81	Big Like A River Tennessee Express	
1/85	Best Year Of My Life Eddie Rabbitt	17/81	Between This Time And The Next Time Gene Watson	3/97	Big Love Tracy Byrd	
15/59	Best Years Of Your Life Carl Smith	7/84	Between Two Fires Gary Morris	5/89	Big Love Bellamy Brothers	
1/81	Bet Your Heart On Me Johnny Lee		Beverly Hillbillies ..see: Ballad Of Jed Clampett	43/71	Big Mable Murphy Dallas Frazier	
73/90	Better Be Home Soon McCarters	9/54	Beware Of "It" Johnnie & Jack	50/75	Sue Thompson	
73/84	Better Class Of Loser Ray Price	81/76	Beware Of The Woman Ruby Falls	23/70	Big Mama's Medicine Show Buddy Alan	
2/92	Better Class Of Losers Randy Travis		Better Deal Than That ..see: (I Can Find) A	39/75	Big Mamou Fiddlin' Frenchie Bourque	
72/70	Better Days For Mama Stonewall Jackson	11/59	Beyond The Shadow Browns	53/69	Big Man Dee Mullins	
	Better Deal Than That ..see: (I Can Find) A	7/50	Beyond The Sunset Three Suns/ Elton Britt/Rosalie Allen	35/80	Big Man's Cafe Nick Noble	
	Better Homes And Gardens	7/89	Beyond Those Years Oak Ridge Boys	4/59	Big Midnight Special Wilma Lee & Stoney Cooper	
34/69	Bobby Russell	27/75	Beyond You Crystal Gayle	15/95	Big Ol' Truck Toby Keith	
37/69	Billy Walker	72/92	Bible Belt Travis Tritt	4/82	Big Ole Brew Mel McDaniel	
4/89	Better Love Next Time Merle Haggard	48/64	Bible In Her Hand Grant Turner	68/82	Big Ole Teardrops Ray Price	
91/79	Better Love Next Time Dr. Hook	81/86	Bidding America Goodbye (The Auction) Bruce Hauser/ Sawmill Creek Band	1/94	Big One George Strait	
67/96	Better Love Next Time Caryl Mack Parker			66/98	Big One Confederate Railroad	
1/89	Better Man Clint Black	22/74	Biff, The Friendly Purple Bear Dick Feller	48/68	Big Rig Rollin' Man Johnny Dollar	
32/99	Better Man Warren Brothers	1/61	Big Bad John Jimmy Dean		Big River	
2/97	Better Man, Better Off Tracy Lawrence	98/89	Big Bad Mama Eddie Lee Carr	4/58	Johnny Cash	
20/78	Better Me Tommy Overstreet	86/76	Big Band Days Hank Thompson	41/70	Johnny Cash	
7/71	Better Move It On Home Porter Wagoner & Dolly Parton	24/62	Big Battle Johnny Cash (Big Bertha) ..see: Ride That Bull	61/75	Chip Taylor	
65/77	Better Off Alone Jan Howard	18/61	Big, Big Love Wynn Stewart	7/61	Big River, Big Man Claude King	
75/83	Better Off Blue Chantilly	82/76	Big Big World Ronnie Prophet	56/71	Big Rock Candy Mountain Bill Phillips	
26/84	Better Our Hearts Should Bend (Than Break) Bandana	59/69	Big Black Bird (Spirit Of Our Love) Jack Blanchard & Misty Morgan	22/62	Big Shoes Ray Price	
74/81	Better Side Of Thirty Billy Parker			91/77	Big Silver Angel Tina Rainford	
75/98	Better Than A Biscuit John Berry	39/72	Big Blue Diamond Jacky Ward	30/65	Big Tennessee Tex Williams	
	Better Than I Did Then ..see: (I'll Even Love You)			27/98	Big Time Trace Adkins	
				38/85	Big Train (From Memphis) John Fogerty	
					Big Wheel Cannonball ..see: Wabash Cannonball	
				7/58	Big Wheels Hank Snow	
				1/89	Big Wheels In The Moonlight Dan Seals	
				65/69	Big Wheels Sing For Me Johnny Dollar	
				3/69	Big Wind Porter Wagoner	
				57/95	Bigger Fish To Fry Boy Howdy	
				80/89	Bigger Man Than Me! Mickey Jones	

Black-Eyed Peas And Blue-Eyed Babies — Loretta Lynn WBAR & LP

1/96 Bigger Than The Beatles Joe Diffie	69/84 Blackjack Whiskey Bobby Jenkins	Blue Darlin'
58/85 Bigger Than The Both Of Us Jimmy Buffett	Blackland Farmer ..see: Black Land	7/55 Jimmy Newman
90/87 Bigger The Love Kevin Pearce	31/91 Blame, The Highway 101	F/78 Narvel Felts
27/76 Biggest Airport In The World Moe Bandy	45/67 Blame It On My Do Wrong Del Reeves	81/85 Blue Days Black Nights John McEuen
51/75 Biggest Parakeets In Town Jud Strunk	36/70 Blame It On Rosey Ray Sanders	61/73 Blue Eyed Jane Benny Whitehead
54/95 Bill's Laundromat, Bar And Grill Confederate Railroad	5/91 Blame It On Texas Mark Chesnutt	81/75 Blue Eyes And Waltzes Jim Mundy
1/59 Billy Bayou Jim Reeves	28/65 Blame It On The Moonlight Johnny Wright	Blue Eyes Crying In The Rain
57/92 Billy Can't Read Paul Overstreet	1/93 Blame It On Your Heart Patty Loveless	1/75 Willie Nelson
12/75 Billy, Get Me A Woman Joe Stampley	1/75 Blanket On The Ground Billie Jo Spears	73/77 Ace Cannon
57/69 Billy, I've Got To Go To Town Geraldine Stevens	9/82 Blaze Of Glory Kenny Rogers	56/82 Blue Eyes Don't Make An Angel Zella Lehr
4/92 Billy The Kid Billy Dean	63/73 Bleep You Cal Smith	F/58 Blue Glass Skirt Hank Locklin
75/77 Billy The Kid Charlie Daniels Band	68/70 Bless Her Heart...I Love Her Hank Locklin	33/64 Blue Guitar Sheb Wooley
10/70 Biloxi Kenny Price	1/72 Bless Your Heart Freddie Hart	Blue Heartache
81/84 Biloxi Lady Leon Raines	1/02 Blessed Martina McBride	64/73 Osborne Brothers
Bimbo	1/81 Blessed Are The Believers Anne Murray	7/80 Gail Davies
1/54 Jim Reeves	72/96 Blessings, The Alabama	15/85 Blue Highway John Conlee
9/54 Pee Wee King	6/79 Blind In Love Mel Tillis	98/74 Blue Jean Country Queen Linda Hargrove
14/91 Bing Bang Boom Highway 101	2/76 Blind Man In The Bleachers Kenny Starr	Blue Kentucky Girl
2/82 Bird, The Jerry Reed	83/80 Blind Willie Atkins, Chet	7/65 Loretta Lynn
26/88 Bird, The George Jones	39/97 Blink Of An Eye Ricochet	6/79 Emmylou Harris
Bird Dog	4/69 Blistered Johnny Cash	11/68 Blue Lonely Winter Jimmy Newman
1/58 Everly Brothers	4/61 Blizzard, The Jim Reeves	10/88 Blue Love O'Kanes
86/78 Bellamy Brothers	1/73 Blood Red And Goin' Down Tanya Tucker	22/91 Blue Memories Patty Loveless
47/01 Bird Song Meredith Edwards	4/50 Bloodshot Eyes Hank Penny	28/58 Blue Memories James O'Gwynn
65/75 Birds And Children Fly Away Kenny Price	17/74 Bloody Mary Morning Willie Nelson	24/00 Blue Moon Steve Holy
63/86 Birds Of A Feather Almost Brothers	59/88 Blowin' Like A Bandit Asleep At The Wheel	46/80 Blue Moon Of Kentucky Earl Scruggs Revue
60/67 Birmingham Tommy Collins	10/96 Blue LeAnn Rimes	1/82 Blue Moon With Heartache Rosanne Cash
55/69 Birmingham Blues Jack Barlow	48/82 Blue And Broken Hearted Me Burrito Brothers	68/95 Blue Pages Noah Gordon
1/50 Birmingham Bounce Red Foley	96/73 Blue And Lonely Vern Murphey	32/82 Blue Rendezvous Lloyd David Foster
31/86 Birth Of Rock And Roll Carl Perkins	83/81 Blue As The Blue In Your Eyes Nancy Ruud	F/79 Blue Ribbon Blues Joe Sun
45/70 Birthmark Henry Thompson Talks About Dallas Frazier	27/80 Blue Baby Blue Lynn Anderson	86/79 Blue River Of Tears Micki Fuhrman
68/78 Bits And Pieces Of Life Cal Smith	2/77 Blue Bayou Linda Ronstadt	21/92 Blue Rose Is Pam Tillis
26/99 Bitter End Deryl Dodd	30/64 Blue Bird Let Me Tag Along Rose Maddox	6/48 Blue Shadows On The Trail Roy Rogers
71/69 Bitter Taste Elton Britt	45/89 Blue Blooded Woman Alan Jackson	8/80 Blue Side Crystal Gayle
45/74 Bitter They Are Harder They Fall Larry Gatlin	47/89 (Blue, Blue, Blue) Blue, Blue Jo-el Sonnier	1/66 Blue Side Of Lonesome Jim Reeves
83/78 Black And Blue Heart Ann J. Morton	Blue Blue Day	4/89 Blue Side Of Town Patty Loveless
37/89 Black And White Rosanne Cash	1/58 Don Gibson	1/78 Blue Skies Willie Nelson
64/84 Black And White David Frizzell	14/61 Wilburn Brothers	93/77 Blue Skies And Roses Karon Blackwell
24/75 Black Bear Road C.W. McCall	69/89 Kendalls	7/49 Blue Skirt Waltz Frankie Yankovic/Marlin Sisters
16/62 Black Cloud Leroy Van Dyke	2/58 Blue Boy Jim Reeves	81/79 Blue Sky Shinin' Mickey Newbury
15/90 Black Coffee Lacy J. Dalton	Blue Christmas	41/64 Blue Smoke Warren Smith
70/95 Black Dresses Steve Kolander	1/49 Ernest Tubb	Blue Suede Blues
Black Jack ..see: Blackjack	9/50 Ernest Tubb	49/86 Con Hunley
Black Land Farmer	5/51 Ernest Tubb	70/89 Mel McDaniel
5/59 Frankie Miller	55/97 Elvis Presley	1/56 Blue Suede Shoes Carl Perkins
16/61 Frankie Miller	74/98 Vince Gill	6/46 Blue Texas Moonlight Elton Britt
67/71 Sleepy LaBeef	51/00 Clay Walker	5/88 Blue To The Bone Sweethearts Of The Rodeo
1/83 Black Sheep John Anderson	1/96 Blue Clear Sky George Strait	Blue Train (Of the Heartbreak Line)
21/59 Black Sheep Ferlin Husky	40/81 Blue Collar Blues Mundo Earwood	44/64 John D. Loudermilk
12/90 Black Velvet Robin Lee	63/00 Blue Collar Dollar Song Jeff Foxworthy & Bill Engvall	22/73 George Hamilton IV
6/52 Blackberry Boogie Tennessee Ernie Ford	40/69 Blue Collar Job Darrell Statler	(Blue Yodel) ..see: T For Texas, & Mule Skinner Blues
41/76 Blackbird (Hold Your Head High) Stoney Edwards	Blue Cyclone ..see: Ballad Of	72/77 Blueberry Hill Ann J. Morton
4/56 Blackboard Of My Heart Hank Thompson		4/46 Blueberry Lane Elton Britt
Blackjack County Chain		39/91 Bluebird Anne Murray
21/67 Willie Nelson		4/51 Bluebird Island Hank Snow with Anita Carter
57/67 Tex Williams		

Branson (Take It On →)

	Bluebird On Your Windowsill ..see: (There's A)	
93/86	Bluemonia Vicki Lee	
56/78	Bluer Than Blue Beverly Heckel	
21/58	Blues Ernest Tubb	
76/83	Blues Don't Care Who's Got 'Em Eddy Arnold	
15/49	Blues In My Heart Red Foley	
37/00	Blues Man Alan Jackson	
12/66	Blues Plus Booze (Means I Lose) Stonewall Jackson	
68/70	Blues Sells A Lot Of Booze Hugh X. Lewis	
	Blues Stay Away From Me	
7/49	Eddie Crosby	
1/50	Delmore Brothers	
7/50	Owen Bradley	
54/89	Chris Austin	
1/88	Bluest Eyes In Texas Restless Heart	
11/77	Bluest Heartache Of The Year Kenny Dale	
39/66	Boa Constrictor Johnny Cash	
41/86	Boardwalk Angel Billy Joe Royal	
14/67	Bob Willis Brothers	
69/74	Bob, All The Playboys And Me Dorsey Burnette	
4/47	Bob Wills Boogie Bob Wills	
F/75	Bob Wills Is Still The King Waylon Jennings	
F/78	Bob's Got A Swing Band In Heaven Red Steagall	
6/95	Bobbie Ann Mason Rick Trevino	
1/82	Bobbie Sue Oak Ridge Boys	
29/75	Boilin' Cabbage Bill Black's Combo	
21/80	Bombed, Boozed, And Busted Joe Sun	
	Bonaparte's Retreat	
10/50	Pee Wee King	
F/70	Carl Smith	
3/74	Glen Campbell	
8/74	Boney Fingers Hoyt Axton	
10/87	Bonnie Jean (Little Sister) David Lynn Jones	
31/69	Boo Dan Jimmy Newman	
65/90	Boogie And Beethoven Gatlin Brothers	
53/87	Boogie Back To Texas Asleep At The Wheel	
2/78	Boogie Grass Band Conway Twitty	
66/89	Boogie Queen Doug Kershaw	
22/74	Boogie Woogie Charlie McCoy & Barefoot Jerry	
24/75	Boogie Woogie Country Man Jerry Lee Lewis	
10/88	Boogie Woogie Fiddle Country Blues Charlie Daniels Band	
72/74	Boogie Woogie Rock And Roll Jerry Reed	
100/78	Boogiewoogieitis Billy Stack	
55/01	Boom Jolie & The Wanted	
85/75	Boom Boom Barroom Man Nat Stuckey	
19/93	Boom! It Was Over Robert Ellis Orrall	
8/49	Boomerang Arthur "Guitar Boogie" Smith	
1/92	Boot Scootin' Boogie Brooks & Dunn	

84/88	Boots (These Boots Are Made For Walking) Brenda Cole	
1/86	Bop Dan Seals	
7/56	Boppin' The Blues Carl Perkins	
13/89	Borderline Shooters	
49/90	Bordertown Dan Seals	
26/78	Bordertown Woman Mel McDaniel	
76/81	Born Orion	
	Born A Fool	
21/68	Freddie Hart	
41/73	Freddie Hart	
12/77	Born Believer Jim Ed Brown/Helen Cornelius	
2/92	Born Country Alabama	
63/91	Born In A High Wind T.G. Sheppard	
12/96	Born In The Dark Doug Stone	
12/66	Born Loser Don Gibson	
56/94	Born Ready Jesse Hunter	
72/70	Born That Way Stonewall Jackson	
5/90	Born To Be Blue Judds	
52/68	Born To Be By Your Side Jimmy Dean	
5/55	Born To Be Happy Hank Snow	
22/66	Born To Be In Love With You Van Trevor	
	Born To Be With You	
1/68	Sonny James	
21/78	Sandy Posey	
1/87	Born To Boogie Hank Williams, Jr.	
1/01	Born To Fly Sara Evans	
3/44	Born To Lose Ted Daffan	
31/74	Born To Love And Satisfy Karen Wheeler	
	Born To Love Me	
21/77	Ray Price	
20/83	Ray Charles	
6/93	Born To Love You Mark Collie	
20/68	Born To Love You Jimmy Newman	
40/84	Born To Love You Karen Brooks	
3/82	Born To Run Emmylou Harris	
66/82	Born With The Blues Johnny Rodriguez	
17/86	Born Yesterday Everly Brothers	
7/72	Borrowed Angel Mel Street	
100/79	Borrowed Time Johnny Free	
43/66	Boston Jail Carl Belew	
	Both Sides Of The Line	
21/67	Wanda Jackson	
58/74	Josie Brown	
1/86	Both To Each Other (Friends & Lovers) Eddie Rabbitt & Juice Newton	
13/67	Bottle, Bottle Jim Ed Brown	
3/66	Bottle Let Me Down Merle Haggard	
50/86	Bottle Of Tears Gene Watson	
71/73	Bottle Of Wine Doc & Merle Watson	
59/90	Bottle Of Wine And Patsy Cline Marsha Thornton	
21/60	Bottle Or Me Connie Hall	
35/66	Bottles Billy Grammer	
18/66	Bottom Of A Mountain Tex Williams	
	Bouquet Of Roses	
1/48	Eddy Arnold	
11/75	Mickey Gilley	
79/80	Bourbon Cowboy Jim Seal	

33/72	Bowling Green Hank Capps	
7/95	Box, The Randy Travis	
18/66	Box It Came In Wanda Jackson	
49/88	Boxcar 109 J. C. Crowley	
13/80	Boxer, The Emmylou Harris	
18/83	Boy Gets Around Sylvia	
1/69	Boy Named Sue Johnny Cash	
50/99	Boy Oh Boy Wilkinsons	
36/84	Boy's Night Out Moe Bandy & Joe Stampley	
4/94	Boys And Me Sawyer Brown	
19/84	Boys Like You Gail Davies	
39/66	Bracero Stu Phillips	
75/72	Brand New Key Jeris Ross	
1/91	Brand New Man Brooks & Dunn	
8/71	Brand New Mister Me Mel Tillis	
88/89	Brand New Week Michelle Lynn	
63/88	Brand New Whiskey Gary Stewart	
1/67	Branded Man Merle Haggard	
70/84	Branded Man Sierra	
5/75	Brass Buckles Barbi Benton	
43/83	Brave Heart Thom Schuyler	
15/85	Break Away Gail Davies	
85/80	Break Away Bill Wence	
75/88	Break Down The Walls De De Ames	
2/82	Break It To Me Gently Juice Newton	
61/84	Break My Heart Victoria Shaw	
	Break My Mind	
6/67	George Hamilton IV	
13/78	Vern Gosdin	
93/85	Break Out The Good Stuff Roy Head	
66/94	Break These Chains Deborah Allen	
51/97	Breakfast In Birmingham David Lee Murphy	
	Breakfast With The Blues	
11/64	Hank Snow	
96/77	Hank Snow	
69/91	Breakin' All The Way Tim Ryan	
10/83	Breakin' Down Waylon Jennings	
25/79	Breakin' In A Brand New Broken Heart Debby Boone	
7/55	Breakin' In Another Heart Hank Thompson	
39/83	Breakin' It Loretta Lynn	
10/54	Breakin' The Rules Hank Thompson	
65/96	Breaking Hearts And Taking Names David Kersh	
15/89	Breaking New Ground Wild Rose	
67/77	Breaking Up Is Hard To Do Con Hunley	
1/99	Breathe Faith Hill	
4/58	Breathless Jerry Lee Lewis	
45/00	Breathless River Road	
81/86	Breathless In The Night Chuck Pyle	
12/48	Breeze Cowboy Copas	
50/76	Bridge For Crawling Back Roy Head	
45/81	Bridge Over Broadway Capitals	
9/71	Bridge Over Troubled Water Buck Owens	
3/81	Bridge That Just Won't Burn Conway Twitty	
1/65	Bridge Washed Out Warner Mack	
10/89	Bridges And Walls Oak Ridge Boys	

11/65	**Bright Lights And Country Music** Bill Anderson	3/70	**Brown Eyed Handsome Man** Waylon Jennings		**Burning Memories**
1/71	**Bright Lights, Big City** Sonny James	58/69	**Brownville Lumberyard** Sammi Smith	2/64	Ray Price
9/87	**Brilliant Conversationalist** T. Graham Brown	41/73	**Brush Arbor Meeting** Brush Arbor	9/77	Mel Tillis
		15/49	**Brush Those Tears From Your Eyes** Foy Willing	10/62	**Burning Of Atlanta** Claude King
96/85	**Bring Back Love** Lisa Angelle	16/95	**Bubba Hyde** Diamond Rio	11/72	**Burning The Midnight Oil** Porter Wagoner & Dolly Parton
49/73	**Bring Back My Yesterday** Glen Campbell	4/92	**Bubba Shot The Jukebox** Mark Chesnutt	78/80	**Burning Up Your Memory** Peggy Forman
9/74	**Bring Back Your Love To Me** Don Gibson		**Bubbles In My Beer**	55/68	**Bury The Bottle With Me** Dick Curless
11/90	**Bring Back Your Love To Me** Earl Thomas Conley	4/48	Bob Wills	18/96	**Bury The Shovel** Clay Walker
18/72	**Bring Him Safely Home To Me** Sandy Posey	68/71	Ray Pennington	21/71	**Bus Fare To Kentucky** Skeeter Davis
		1/65	**Buckaroo** Buck Owens	6/50	**Bushel And A Peck** Margaret Whiting & Jimmy Wakely
52/00	**Bring It On** Keith Harling	27/98	**Buckaroo** Lee Ann Womack		
20/80	**Bring It On Home** Big Al Downing	14/78	**Bucket To The South** Ava Barber	22/75	**Busiest Memory In Town** Dickey Lee
1/76	**Bring It On Home To Me** Mickey Gilley	63/77	**Buddy, I Lied** Nat Stuckey		**Busted**
7/73	**Bring It On Home (To Your Woman)** Joe Stampley	46/89	**Buenas Noches From A Lonely Room (She Wore Red Dresses)** Dwight Yoakam	13/63	Johnny Cash with The Carter Family
68/69	**Bring Love Back Into Our World** Stu Phillips	25/79	**Buenos Dias Argentina** Marty Robbins	6/82	John Conlee
13/69	**Bring Me Sunshine** Willie Nelson	58/68	**Buffalo Nickel** Rusty Draper	3/99	**Busy Man** Billy Ray Cyrus
1/02	**Bring On The Rain** Jo Dee Messina with Tim McGraw	16/93	**Bug, The** Mary-Chapin Carpenter	8/52	**Busybody** Pee Wee King
		99/77	**Bugle Ann** Wayne Carson		**But Alabama ..see: (Nothing Left Between Us)**
80/85	**Bring On The Sunshine** Dennis Bottoms	12/63	**Building A Bridge** Claude King		**But For Love**
25/66	**Bring Your Heart Home** Jimmy Newman		**Building Bridges**	19/69	Eddy Arnold
		55/84	Larry Willoughby	54/79	Jerry Naylor
	Bring Your Sweet Self Back To Me ..see: (Honey, Baby, Hurry!)	72/85	Nicolette Larson	1/01	**But For The Grace Of God** Keith Urban
		30/79	**Building Memories** Sonny James		
54/87	**Bringin' The House Down** Shurfire	8/78	**Bull And The Beaver** Merle Haggard & Leona Williams	65/75	**But I Do** Del Reeves
23/75	**Bringing It Back** Brenda Lee	66/80	**Bull Rider** Johnny Cash	18/01	**But I Do Love You** LeAnn Rimes
43/65	**Bringing Mary Home** Country Gentlemen	88/82	**Bull Smith Can't Dance The Cotton-Eyed Joe** Wolfpack	83/87	**But I Never Do** Brenda Cole
				35/94	**But I Will** Faith Hill
64/82	**Bringing Out The Fool In Me** Gary Goodnight		**Bumming Around**	30/82	**But It's Cheating** Family Brown
15/73	**Broad-Minded Man** Jim Ed Brown	5/53	Jimmie Dean	26/80	**But Love Me** Janie Fricke
62/93	**Broken** Andy Childs	5/53	T. Texas Tyler	68/89	**But, She Loves Me** Roy Clark
94/76	**Broken Bones** Tommy Cash	31/76	**Bump Bounce Boogie** Asleep At The Wheel	54/70	**But That's All Right** Hank Thompson
1/77	**Broken Down In Tiny Pieces** Billy "Crash" Craddock	4/52	**Bundle Of Southern Sunshine** Eddy Arnold		**But Tonight I'm Gonna Love You**
2/50	**Broken Down Merry-Go-Round** Margaret Whiting & Jimmy Wakely	2/78	**Burgers And Fries** Charley Pride	72/74	Harrison Jones
		3/84	**Buried Treasure** Kenny Rogers	91/77	Daniel
18/60	**Broken Dream** Jimmy Smart	2/01	**Burn** Jo Dee Messina	63/67	**But Wait There's More** Justin Tubb
99/89	**Broken Dreams and Memories** Michael Shane	97/78	**Burn Atlanta Down** Bobby Barnett		**But You Know I Love You**
46/65	**Broken Engagement** Webb Pierce	43/01	**Burn Down The Trailer Park** Billy Ray Cyrus	2/69	Bill Anderson
1/79	**Broken Hearted Me** Anne Murray	80/84	**Burn Georgia Burn (There's A Fire In Your Soul)** Butch Baker	1/81	Dolly Parton
70/93	**Broken Heartland** Zaca Creek			16/60	**But You Use To** Laverne Downs
5/76	**Broken Lady** Larry Gatlin	7/92	**Burn Me Down** Marty Stuart	65/89	**But You Will** Razzy Bailey
10/92	**Broken Promise Land** Mark Chesnutt	4/92	**Burn One Down** Clint Black	72/87	**Butterbeans** Johnny Russell & Little David Wilkins
42/98	**Broken Road** Melodie Crittenden	10/86	**Burned Like A Rocket** Billy Joe Royal	47/75	**Butterfly** Eddy Arnold
9/80	**Broken Trust** Brenda Lee	71/87	**Burned Out** Tina Danielle	22/76	**Butterfly For Bucky** Bobby Goldsboro
1/98	**Broken Wing** Martina McBride	3/89	**Burnin' A Hole In My Heart** Skip Ewing		**Butterfly Kisses**
64/77	**Brooklyn** Cody Jameson	1/89	**Burnin' Old Memories** Kathy Mattea	37/97	Raybon Bros.
51/78	**Brother** DeWayne Orender	26/98	**Burnin' The Roadhouse Down** Steve Wariner (with Garth Brooks)	45/97	Bob Carlisle
	Brother Juke-Box			66/97	Jeff Carson
96/77	Don Everly	31/75	**Burnin' Thing** Mac Davis	4/88	**Button Off My Shirt** Ronnie Milsap
1/91	Mark Chesnutt		**Burning**	6/48	**Buttons And Bows** Gene Autry
75/70	**Brother River** Johnny Darrell	37/75	Ferlin Husky	1/00	**Buy Me A Rose** Kenny Rogers
77/76	**Brother Shelton** Brenda Lee	88/77	Marie Owens	18/96	**By My Side** Lorrie Morgan & Jon Randall
	Brotherly Love	5/67	**Burning A Hole In My Mind** Connie Smith	6/81	**By Now** Steve Wariner
53/89	Moe Bandy		**Burning Bridges**	19/99	**By The Book** Michael Peterson
2/91	Keith Whitley & Earl Thomas Conley	18/67	Glen Campbell		**By The Time I Get To Phoenix**
		79/81	Bill Nash	2/68	Glen Campbell
41/82	**Brotherly Love** Gary Stewart & Dean Dillon			40/71	Glen Campbell/Anne Murray (medley)
29/84	**Brown Eyed Girl** Joe Stampley			46/68	**By The Time You Get To Phoenix** Wanda Jackson

65/94	**By The Way She's Lookin'** *Jesse Hunter*	19/76	**Call, The** *Anne Murray*
1/98	**Bye-Bye** *Jo Dee Messina*	71/97	**Call, The** *Little Texas*
96/79	**Bye, Bye, Baby** *Dan Dickey*		**Call Her Your Sweetheart**
	Bye Bye Love	9/52	*Eddy Arnold*
1/57	*Everly Brothers*	28/66	*Frank Ifield*
7/57	*Webb Pierce*		**Call Home**
70/81	*Billy Walker & Barbara Fairchild*	52/86	*Glen Campbell*
		43/93	*Mike Reid*
			Call Me ..see: (Honey, Won't You)
		64/87	**Call Me A Fool** *Dana McVicker*
	C	55/01	**Call Me Claus** *Garth Brooks*
		F/79	**Call Me Crazy Lady** *Leona Williams*
23/77	**C.B. Savage** *Rod Hart*	82/82	**Call Me Friend** *Vince Anthony*
83/76	**C.B. Widow** *Linda Cassady*	46/70	**Call Me Gone** *Stan Hitchcock*
10/83	**C.C. Waterback** *George Jones & Merle Haggard*	9/63	**Call Me Mr. Brown** *Skeets McDonald*
	C'est La Vie ..see: (You Never Can Tell)	3/62	**Call Me Mr. In-Between** *Burl Ives*
16/72	**Cab Driver** *Hank Thompson*	14/54	**Call Me Up (And I'll Come Calling On You)** *Marty Robbins*
98/79	**Cabello Diablo (Devil Horse)** *Chris LeDoux*	17/94	**Call Of The Wild** *Aaron Tippin*
78/76	**Cabin High (In The Blue Ridge Mountains)** *Don King*	26/61	**Call Of The Wild** *Warren Smith*
9/59	**Cabin In The Hills** *Flatt & Scruggs*	4/89	**Call On Me** *Tanya Tucker*
48/80	**Cactus And A Rose** *Gary Stewart*	64/72	**Call On Me** *Jeanne Pruett*
73/00	**Cactus In A Coffee Can** *Jerry Kilgore*		**Callin' Baton Rouge**
97/76	**Cadillac Johnson** *Chuck Price*	37/89	*New Grass Revival*
18/93	**Cadillac Ranch** *Chris LeDoux*	70/93	*Garth Brooks*
3/92	**Cadillac Style** *Sammy Kershaw*	2/94	*Garth Brooks*
5/92	**Cafe On The Corner** *Sawyer Brown*	79/87	**Callin' Your Bluff** *Rattlesnake Annie*
80/81	**Caffein, Nicotine, Benzedrine** *Jerry Reed*	31/91	**Calloused Hands** *Mark Collie*
26/95	**Cain's Blood** *4 Runner*	10/70	**Camelia** *Marty Robbins*
	Cajun Baby	24/74	**Can I Come Home To You** *Bill Anderson*
3/69	*Hank Williams, Jr.*	64/92	**Can I Come On Home To You** *Bellamy Brothers*
52/88	*Doug Kershaw/Hank Williams Jr.*	15/91	**Can I Count On You** *McBride & The Ride*
52/83	**Cajun Invitation** *David Frizzell & Shelly West*	58/74	**Can I Keep Him Daddy** *Red Sovine*
93/81	**Cajun Lady** *Ralph May*		**Can I See You Tonight**
1/86	**Cajun Moon** *Ricky Skaggs*	33/79	*Jewel Blanch*
16/62	**Cajun Queen** *Jimmy Dean*	4/81	*Tanya Tucker*
23/68	**Cajun Stripper** *Jim Ed Brown*	6/73	**Can I Sleep In Your Arms** *Jeannie Seely*
68/88	**Calendar Blues** *Jill Jordan*	1/93	**Can I Trust You With My Heart** *Travis Tritt*
73/76	**Calico Cat** *Kenny Starr*	58/93	**Can You Feel It** *Ricky Lynn Gregg*
11/48	**Calico Rag** *Al Dexter*	71/70	**Can You Feel It** *Bobby Goldsboro*
13/85	**California** *Keith Stegall*		**Can You Fool**
45/79	**California** *Glen Campbell*	16/78	*Glen Campbell*
51/89	**California Blue** *Roy Orbison*	72/84	*Paulette Carlson*
65/73	**California Blues (Blue Yodel No. 4)** *Compton Brothers*	17/76	**Can You Hear Those Pioneers** *Rex Allen, Jr.*
94/80	**California Calling** *Dennis Smith*	93/79	**Can You Read My Mind** *Maureen McGovern*
45/69	**California Cotton Fields** *Dallas Frazier*	2/95	**Can't Be Really Gone** *Tim McGraw*
11/69	**California Girl (And The Tennessee Square)** *Tompall/Glaser Brothers*	1/93	**Can't Break It To My Heart** *Tracy Lawrence*
68/70	**California Grapevine** *Freddie Hart*	1/83	**Can't Even Get The Blues** *Reba McEntire*
99/73	**California Is Just Mississippi** *Billy Mize*	61/00	**Can't Fight The Moonlight** *LeAnn Rimes*
31/77	**California Lady** *Randy Barlow*	21/99	**Can't Get Enough** *Patty Loveless*
43/76	**California Okie** *Buck Owens*	83/88	**Can't Get To You From Here** *Jacky Ward*
4/46	**California Polka** *Tex Williams*	88/83	**Can't Get Used To Sleeping Without You** *Sandy Posey*
61/85	**California Road** *Mel Tillis*	11/63	**Can't Hang Up The Phone** *Stonewall Jackson*
77/85	**California Sleeping** *Loy Blanton*	38/91	**Can't Have Nothin'** *Foster & Lloyd*
70/68	**California Sunshine** *Rusty Draper*		
20/67	**California Up Tight Band** *Flatt & Scruggs*		
96/89	**California Wine** *Mark Murphey*		

64/00	**Can't Help Calling Your Name** *Jason Sellers*		
54/81	**Can't Help Falling In Love With You** *Slim Whitman*		
74/77	**Can't Help It** *Cates Sisters*		
1/85	**Can't Keep A Good Man Down** *Alabama*		
26/80	**Can't Keep My Mind Off Of Her** *Mundo Earwood*		
92/79	**Can't Love On Lies** *Jim West with Carol Chase*		
31/00	**Can't Nobody Love You (Like I Do)** *Wynonna*		
87/78	**Can't Shake You Off My Mind** *Bobby Wayne Loftis*		
1/87	**Can't Stop My Heart From Loving You** *O'Kanes*		
30/92	**Can't Stop Myself From Loving You** *Patty Loveless*		
45/88	**Can't Stop Now** *New Grass Revival*		
86/88	**Can't Stop The Music** *Don King*		
52/99	**Can't Stop Thinkin' 'Bout That** *Ricochet*		
9/74	**Can't You Feel It** *David Houston*		
66/79	**Can't You Hear That Whistle Blow** *Sonny Throckmorton*		
4/76	**Can't You See** *Waylon Jennings*		
25/69	**Canadian Pacific** *George Hamilton, IV*		
	Candle In The Wind ..see: (I'm Not) A		
72/72	**Candy And Roses** *Sue Thompson*		
	Candy Kisses		
1/49	*George Morgan*		
4/49	*Elton Britt*		
4/49	*Red Foley*		
5/49	*Cowboy Copas*		
9/49	*Eddie Kirk*		
12/49	*Bud Hobbs*		
5/84	**Candy Man** *Mickey Gilley & Charly McClain*		
82/74	**Candy Mountain Melody** *George Morgan*		
86/79	**Capricorn Kings** *Lee Wright*		
24/74	**Captured** *Terry Stafford*		
3/95	**Car, The** *Jeff Carson*		
81/74	**Carefree Highway** *Gordon Lightfoot*		
3/45	**Careless Darlin'** *Ernest Tubb*		
48/71	**Careless Hands** *Dottie West*		
8/50	**Careless Kisses** *Red Foley*		
30/60	**Careless Love** *Jimmie Skinner*		
	Caribbean		
1/53	*Mitchell Torok*		
67/73	*Buddy Alan*		
18/78	*Sonny James*		
57/78	**Carlena And José Gomez** *Billy Walker*		
5/00	**Carlene** *Phil Vassar*		
66/69	**Carlie** *Bobby Russell*		
16/60	**Carmel By The Sea** *Kitty Wells*		
32/86	**Carmen** *Gene Watson*		
64/81	**Carolina By The Sea** *Super Grit Cowboy Band*		
F/83	**Carolina Dreams** *Ronnie Milsap*		
44/81	**Carolina (I Remember You)** *Charlie Daniels Band*		
29/69	**Carolina In My Mind** *George Hamilton, IV*		
9/85	**Carolina In The Pines** *Michael Martin Murphey*		

19/75 Carolina Moonshiner	31/73 Chained Johnny Russell	45/83 Cheap Thrills David Allan Coe
Porter Wagoner	3/46 Chained To A Memory	44/93 Cheap Whiskey Martina McBride
15/48 Carolina Waltz Clyde Moody	Eddy Arnold	46/79 Cheaper Crude Or No More Food
Caroline's Still In Georgia	1/90 Chains Patty Loveless	Bobby "Sofine" Butler
70/83 Coulters	Chains	73/81 Cheat On Him Tonight
76/84 Mac Davis	35/75 Buddy Alan	David Heavener
1/72 Carolyn Merle Haggard	81/88 Sarah	14/56 Cheated Too
88/75 Carolyn At The Broken Wheel Inn	4/87 Chains Of Gold	Wilma Lee & Stoney Cooper
Joe Allen	Sweethearts Of The Rodeo	94/80 Cheater Fever Lynn Bailey
6/87 Carpenter, The John Conlee	9/77 Chains Of Love Mickey Gilley	Cheater's Kit
1/96 Carried Away George Strait	1/85 Chair, The George Strait	85/77 Willie Rainsford
2/69 Carroll County Accident	7/71 Chair, The Marty Robbins	45/79 Tommy Overstreet
Porter Wagoner	22/80 Champ, The Moe Bandy	90/81 Cheater's Last Chance
26/73 Carry Me Back Statler Brothers	34/75 Champagne Ladies And Blue	Larry Riley
71/75 Carry Me Back Marlys Roe	Ribbon Babies Ferlin Husky	30/82 Cheater's Prayer Kendalls
35/01 Carry On Pat Green	11/98 Chance, A Kenny Chesney	54/80 Cheater's Trap
74/90 Carryin' On Canyon	1/84 Chance Of Lovin' You	John Wesley Ryles
1/97 Carrying Your Love With Me	Earl Thomas Conley	15/76 Cheatin' Is Barbara Fairchild
George Strait	67/89 Chance You Take Ross Lewis	38/81 Cheatin' Is Still On My Mind
100/76 Case Of You David Frizzell	19/96 Change, The Garth Brooks	Cristy Lane
15/56 Casey Jones (The Brave	45/00 Change Sons Of The Desert	20/80 Cheatin' On A Cheater
Engineer) Eddy Arnold	55/93 Change, The Michelle Wright	Loretta Lynn
Cash On The Barrel Head	44/97 Change Her Mind Gene Watson	52/98 Cheatin' On Her Heart
7/56 Louvin Brothers	Change My Mind	Jeff Carson
72/78 Ronnie Sessions	70/91 Oak Ridge Boys	40/77 Cheatin' Overtime
96/78 Cashin' In (A Tribute To Luther	10/96 John Berry	Mary Lou Turner
Perkins) Bill Black's Combo	1/89 Change Of Heart Judds	61/82 Cheatin' State Of Mind Bandana
78/82 Cast The First Stone Kin Vassy	48/83 Change Of Heart Marty Robbins	91/77 Cheatin' Turns Her On
12/56 Cat Came Back Sonny James	93/87 Change Of Heart Topel & Ware	David Wills
Cat's In The Cradle	57/67 Change Of Wife	9/54 Cheatin's A Sin Kitty Wells
97/75 Compton Brothers	Geezinslaw Brothers	16/81 Cheatin's A Two Way Street
45/96 Ricky Skaggs	41/83 Changes Tanya Tucker	Sammi Smith
13/66 Catch A Little Raindrop	24/77 Changes In Latitudes, Changes	61/80 Cheating Eyes Jerry Naylor
Claude King	In Attitudes Jimmy Buffett	18/73 Cheating Game Susan Raye
49/81 Catch Me If You Can Tom Carlile	16/87 Changin' Partners Gatlin Brothers	50/96 Check Please Paul Jefferson
26/72 Catch The Wind Jack Barlow	4/54 Changing Partners Pee Wee King	1/95 Check Yes Or No George Strait
50/77 Catch The Wind Kathy Barnes	68/80 Changing All The Time La Costa	Cherokee Boogie
57/88 Catch 22 Darrell Holt	1/72 Chantilly Lace Jerry Lee Lewis	7/51 Moon Mullican
81/81 Catching Fire Angela Kaye	Chapel Of Love ..see: Love, Love,	44/96 BR5-49
12/73 Catfish John Johnny Russell	Love	47/82 Cherokee Country
Cathy's Clown	85/81 Charleston Cotton Mill	Solid Gold Band
89/80 Springer Brothers	Marty Haggard	Cherokee Fiddle
57/81 Tricia Johns	16/67 Charleston Railroad Tavern	58/77 Michael Murphey
1/89 Reba McEntire	Bobby Bare	10/82 Johnny Lee
Cattle Call	57/75 Charley Is My Name	1/76 Cherokee Maiden Merle Haggard
1/55 Eddy Arnold	Johnny Duncan	73/67 Cherokee Strip Bob Beckham
11/55 Slim Whitman	15/71 Charley's Picture Porter Wagoner	(Chestnuts Roasting On An Open
18/99 Eddy Arnold (with LeAnn Rimes)	47/73 Charlie Tompall/Glaser Brothers	Fire) ..see: Christmas Song
81/79 Caught With My Feelings Down	16/70 Charlie Brown Compton Brothers	Chet Atkins ..see: Chit Akins
Mary Lou Turner	87/80 Charlie, I Love Your Wife	38/67 Chet's Tune
23/65 Cause I Believe In You	Tommy Roe	Some Of Chet's Friends
Don Gibson	F/79 Charlie's Angel Mel Tillis	80/88 Chevy Van Sammy Johns
9/67 'Cause I Have You Wynn Stewart	1/62 Charlie's Shoes Billy Walker	8/51 Chew Tobacco Rag Zeb Turner
3/56 'Cause I Love You Webb Pierce	38/71 Charlotte Fever Kenny Price	30/70 Chicago Story Jimmy Snyder
64/72 Cause I Love You	5/80 Charlotte's Web Statler Brothers	54/73 Chick Inspector (That's Where
Don Gibson & Sue Thompson	6/59 Chasin' A Rainbow Hank Snow	My Money Goes) Dick Curless
32/67 Cave, The Johnny Paycheck	88/77 Chasin' My Tail Jim Glaser	17/64 Chickashay David Houston
12/71 Cedartown, Georgia	50/91 Chasin' Something Called Love	31/66 Chicken Feed Bobbi Staff
Waylon Jennings	Molly & The Heymakers	45/84 Chicken In Black Johnny Cash
71/86 Celebrity David Frizzell	2/90 Chasin' That Neon Rainbow	69/67 Chicken Pickin' Buckaroos
37/89 Center Of My Universe	Alan Jackson	8/81 Chicken Truck John Anderson
Bellamy Brothers	1/93 Chattahoochee Alan Jackson	17/83 Child Of The Fifties
6/72 Ceremony, The	F/82 Chattanooga City Limit Sign	Statler Brothers
Tammy Wynette & George Jones	Johnny Cash	13/87 Child Support Barbara Mandrell
12/65 Certain Bill Anderson	1/50 Chattanoogie Shoe Shine Boy	24/68 Childhood Places Dottie West
30/71 Chain Don't Take To Me	Red Foley	30/73 Children Johnny Cash
Bob Luman	9/86 Cheap Love Juice Newton	58/69 Children Diana Trask
17/59 Chain Gang Freddie Hart	61/87 Cheap Motels (And One Night	9/88 Chill Factor Merle Haggard
66/87 Chain Gang Bobby Lee Springfield	Stands) Southern Reign	3/91 Chill Of An Early Fall
93/79 Chain Gang Michael Murphey	7/77 Cheap Perfume And Candlelight	George Strait
21/80 Chain Gang Of Love Roy Clark	Bobby Borchers	6/48 Chime Bells Elton Britt
3/00 Chain Of Love Clay Walker	13/94 Cheap Seats Alabama	22/62 China Doll George Hamilton IV

425

80/73	China Nights (Shina No Yoru) *Dick Curless*		92/78	Circle Is Small (I Can See It In Your Eyes) *Gordon Lightfoot*		Coal Miner's Daughter
33/74	Chip Chip *Patsy Sledd*		61/73	Circle Me *Dee Mullins*	1/70	Loretta Lynn
23/71	Chip 'N' Dale's Place *Claude King*		49/96	Circle Of Friends *David Ball*	24/80	Sissy Spacek
12/59	Chip Off The Old Block *Eddy Arnold*		92/76	Circle Of Tears *Chip Taylor*	26/97	Coast Is Clear *Tracy Lawrence*
			7/64	Circumstances *Billy Walker*	15/89	Coast Of Colorado *Skip Ewing*
6/88	Chiseled In Stone *Vern Gosdin*		70/96	Circus Leaving Town *Philip Claypool*	4/71	Coat Of Many Colors *Dolly Parton*
14/64	Chit Akins, Make Me A Star *Don Bowman*			City Lights	1/79	Coca Cola Cowboy *Mel Tillis*
	Choc'late Ice Cream Cone		1/58	Ray Price	15/48	Cocaine Blues *Roy Hogsed*
5/50	Red Foley		53/71	Johnny Bush		Cocaine Train ..see: (Stay Away From) The
8/50	Kenny Roberts		1/75	Mickey Gilley	44/67	Cockfight, The *Archie Campbell*
30/99	Choices *George Jones*		67/89	Mel Tillis	72/77	Coconut Grove *Maury Finney*
	Chokin' Kind			City Of New Orleans	93/81	Code-A-Phone *Larry Riley*
8/67	Waylon Jennings		44/73	Sammi Smith	81/85	Coffee Brown Eyes *Billy Walker*
59/71	Diana Trask		1/84	Willie Nelson	13/63	Cold And Lonely (Is The Forecast For Tonight) *Kitty Wells*
87/83	Freddy Fender		37/65	City Of The Angels *Jimmy Newman*	71/99	Cold Coffee Morning *Jon Randall*
69/75	Choo Choo Ch'Boogie *Asleep At The Wheel*		5/94	City Put The Country Back In Me *Neal McCoy*		Cold, Cold Heart
73/87	Chosen *Perry LaPointe*		59/74	Claim On Me *George Hamilton IV*	1/51	Hank Williams
7/49	C-H-R-I-S-T-M-A-S *Eddy Arnold*		44/66	Class Of 49 *Red Sovine*	22/61	Jerry Lee Lewis
12/54	Christmas Can't Be Far Away *Eddy Arnold*		83/87	Class Of '55 *Carl Perkins*	84/79	Jerry Lee Lewis
			6/72	Class Of '57 *Statler Brothers*	10/62	Cold Dark Waters *Porter Wagoner*
	Christmas Carol			Classic Cowboy ..see: (Great American)		Cold Day In July
60/97	Skip Ewing		13/75	Classified *C.W. McCall*	71/93	Joy White
44/99	Skip Ewing			Claudette	10/00	Dixie Chicks
2/45	Christmas Carols By The Old Corral *Tex Ritter*		15/58	Everly Brothers	69/77	Cold Day In July *Ray Griff*
33/01	Christmas Cookies *George Strait*		41/72	Compton Brothers	2/67	Cold Hard Facts Of Life *Porter Wagoner*
	Christmas In Dixie		47/97	Dwight Yoakam	45/00	Cold Hard Truth *George Jones*
35/82	Alabama		76/88	Clean Livin' Folk *Bobby G. Rice & Perry LaPointe*	64/87	Cold Hearts/Closed Minds *Nanci Griffith*
47/97	Alabama		74/69	Clean Up Your Own Back Yard *Elvis Presley*	62/84	Cold In July *Robin Lee*
40/98	Alabama			Clean Your Own Tables	53/80	Cold Lonesome Morning *Johnny Cash*
37/99	Alabama		77/75	Stoney Edwards	23/02	Cold One Comin' On *Montgomery Gentry*
65/00	Christmas In Your Arms *Steve Wariner*		60/76	Vernon Oxford	30/97	Cold Outside *Big House*
35/82	Christmas Is Just A Song For Us This Year *Louise Mandrell & R.C. Bannon*		72/81	K.T. Oslin	24/85	Cold Summer Day In Georgia *Gene Watson*
			54/70	Cleanest Man In Cincinnati *Claude Gray*	30/75	Colinda *Fiddlin' Frenchie Burke*
	Christmas Shoes		11/93	Cleopatra, Queen Of Denial *Pam Tillis*	22/69	Color Him Father *Linda Martell*
31/00	Newsong		56/80	Cling To Me *Jerry Wallace*	38/72	Color My World *Barbara Fairchild*
39/01	3 Of Hearts		47/69	Clinging To My Baby's Hand *Dottie West*	7/58	Color Of The Blues *George Jones*
	Christmas Song (Chestnuts Roasting On An Open Fire)		17/65	Close All The Honky Tonks *Charlie Walker*	85/76	Colorado Call *Shad O'Shea*
63/96	Reba McEntire		15/77	Close Enough For Lonesome *Mel Street*	93/83	Colorado Christmas *Nitty Gritty Dirt Band*
64/98	Trace Adkins		1/82	Close Enough To Perfect *Alabama*		Colorado Country Morning
67/00	Martina McBride				70/73	Tennessee Ernie Ford
57/94	Christmas Time *John Anderson*		81/74	Close To Home *Roy Drusky*	95/75	Hank Snow
	Christmas Time's A Comin'		70/66	Close Together (As You And Me) *George Jones & Melba Montgomery*	60/80	Pat Boone
50/94	Sammy Kershaw				50/78	Colorado Kool-Aid *Johnny Paycheck*
53/97	Sammy Kershaw		74/87	Close Your Eyes *Rusty Wier*	37/87	Colorado Moon *Tim Malchak*
92/77	Christmas Tribute *Bob Luman*		89/82	Closer To Crazy *Jan Gray*	70/70	Columbus Stockade Blues *Danny Davis/The Nashville Brass*
41/68	Christopher Robin *Stonemans*		31/98	Closer To Heaven *Mila Mason*	7/62	Comancheros, The *Claude King*
48/67	Chubby (Please Take Your Love To Town) *Geezinslaw Brothers*		40/82	Closer To You *Burrito Brothers*	4/78	Come A Little Bit Closer *Johnny Duncan with Janie Fricke*
3/64	Chug-A-Lug *Roger Miller*			Closer You Get	43/01	Come A Little Closer *Lila McCann*
83/79	Chunky People *Hargus "Pig" Robbins*		27/81	Don King	65/91	Come A Little Closer *Desert Rose Band*
1/89	Church On Cumberland Road *Shenandoah*		1/83	Alabama	47/70	Come And Get It Mama *Charlie Louvin*
5/47	Cigareetes, Whusky, And Wild, Wild Women *Sons Of The Pioneers*		66/69	Closest Thing To Love (I've Ever Seen) *Skeeter Davis*	20/59	Come And Knock (On The Door Of My Heart) *Roy Acuff*
	Cigarettes And Coffee Blues		27/77	Closest Thing To You *Jerry Lee Lewis*		Come As You Were
13/59	Lefty Frizzell		59/94	Closing Time *Radney Foster*	66/83	Jerry Lee Lewis
14/63	Marty Robbins		1/82	Clown, The *Conway Twitty*	7/89	T. Graham Brown
2/50	Cincinnati Dancing Pig *Red Foley*		20/95	Clown In Your Rodeo *Kathy Mattea*	79/89	Come Back Brenda *J.D. Hart*
2/46	Cincinnati Lou *Merle Travis*				13/56	Come Back To Me *Jimmy Newman*
4/67	Cincinnati, Ohio *Connie Smith*		7/80	Clyde *Waylon Jennings*	1/97	Come Cryin' To Me *Lonestar*
5/87	Cinderella *Vince Gill*					
45/72	Cinderella *Tony Booth*					
59/81	Cinderella *Terry Gregory*					

12/73 Come Early Morning *Don Williams*	39/98 Coming Back For You *Keith Harling*	70/82 Could It Be I Don't Belong Here Anymore *Margo Smith*
1/89 Come From The Heart *Kathy Mattea*	19/66 Coming Back To You *Browns*	57/82 Could It Be Love *Jennifer Warnes*
49/74 Come Home *Jim Mundy*	50/69 Coming Of The Roads *Johnny Darrell & Anita Carter*	97/80 Could You Ever Really Love A Poor Boy *Don Williams*
3/92 Come In Out Of The Pain *Doug Stone*	75/00 Coming Up Short Again *Perfect Stranger*	26/81 Could You Love Me (One More Time) *John Conlee*
79/86 Come In Planet Earth (Are You Listenin') *Karen Taylor-Good*	8/70 Commercial Affection *Mel Tillis*	2/92 Could've Been Me *Billy Ray Cyrus*
6/58 Come In Stranger *Johnny Cash*	4/98 Commitment *LeAnn Rimes*	15/80 Couldn't Do Nothin' Right *Rosanne Cash*
14/67 Come Kiss Me Love *Bobby Bare*	32/66 Common Colds And Broken Hearts *Ray Pillow*	3/00 Couldn't Last A Moment *Collin Raye*
1/73 Come Live With Me *Roy Clark*	Common Man	64/91 Couldn't Love Have Picked A Better Place To Die *Clinton Gregory*
63/82 Come Looking For Me *Lobo*	50/81 Sammy Johns	
58/74 Come Monday *Jimmy Buffett*	1/83 John Conlee	
1/90 Come Next Monday *K.T. Oslin*	43/94 Company Time *Linda Davis*	22/66 Count Down *Hank Snow*
42/66 Come On And Sing *Bob Luman*	8/66 Company You Keep *Bill Phillips*	5/97 Count Me In *Deana Carter*
3/91 Come On Back *Carlene Carter*	7/55 Company's Comin' *Porter Wagoner*	14/66 Count Me Out *Marty Robbins*
52/75 Come On Down *Tennessee Ernie Ford*	47/81 Completely Out Of Love *Marty Robbins*	5/86 Count On Me *Statler Brothers*
24/76 Come On Down (To Our Favorite Forget-About-Her Place) *David Houston*	5/01 Complicated *Carolyn Dawn Johnson*	16/68 Count Your Blessings, Woman *Jan Howard*
68/68 Come On Home *Debbie Lori Kaye*	59/91 Concrete Cowboy *Corbin/Hanner*	61/74 Counterfeit Cowboy *Dave Dudley*
76/84 Come On Home *Tony Arata*	39/94 Confessin' My Love *Shawn Camp*	44/87 Countrified *John Anderson*
85/75 Come On Home *Mary Lou Turner*	43/82 Confidential *Con Hunley*	23/96 C-O-U-N-T-R-Y *Joe Diffie*
24/69 Come On Home And Sing The Blues To Daddy *Bob Luman*	28/61 Congratulations *Faron Young*	97/73 Country And Pop Music *Urel Albert*
98/74 Come On Home (To This Lonely Heart) *Wanda Jackson*	69/88 Congratulations *Donna Meade*	83/73 Country Boogie Woogie *Linda Nash*
	49/71 Congratulations (You Sure Made A Man Out Of Him) *Arlene Harden*	1/85 Country Boy *Ricky Skaggs*
3/79 Come On In *Oak Ridge Boys*		7/49 Country Boy *"Little" Jimmy Dickens*
8/76 Come On In *Sonny James*	44/98 Connected At The Heart *Ricochet*	Country Boy Can Survive
10/78 Come On In *Jerry Lee Lewis*	Conscience I'm Guilty	2/82 Hank Williams, Jr.
91/78 Come On In *Bobby Hood*	4/56 Hank Snow	30/00 Chad Brock
19/74 Come On In And Let Me Love You *Lois Johnson*	14/61 Rose Maddox	44/86 Country Boy (Who Rolled The Rock Away) *David Allan Coe*
	48/67 Conscience Keep An Eye On Me *Norma Jean*	3/75 Country Boy (You Got Your Feet In L.A.) *Glen Campbell*
3/86 Come On In (You Did The Best You Could Do) *Oak Ridge Boys*	69/66 Consider The Children *Bonnie Owens*	22/67 Country Boy's Dream *Carl Perkins*
39/88 Come On Joe *Jo-el Sonnier*	63/69 Conspiracy Of Homer Jones *Dallas Frazier*	67/82 Country Boy's Song *Karen Taylor*
5/76 Come On Over *Olivia Newton-John*	15/83 Conversation, The *Waylon Jennings with Hank Williams, Jr.*	1/74 Country Bumpkin *Cal Smith*
Come On Over		9/89 Country Club *Travis Tritt*
74/97 Shania Twain		4/00 Country Comes To Town *Toby Keith*
6/99 Shania Twain	1/75 Convoy *C.W. McCall*	
55/92 Come On Over To The Country *Hank Williams, Jr.*	Cool Water	44/96 Country Crazy *Little Texas*
	4/47 Sons Of The Pioneers	36/75 Country D.J. *Bill Anderson*
36/74 Come On Phone *Jean Shepard*	7/48 Sons Of The Pioneers	68/82 Country Fiddles *Solid Gold Band*
85/88 Come On Rain *Wright Brothers*	59/97 Cool Water *Tammy Graham*	1/59 Country Girl *Faron Young*
23/77 Come See About Me *Cal Smith*	98/73 Copperhead *Jerry Foster*	7/70 Country Girl *Jeannie C. Riley*
17/78 Come See Me And Come Lonely *Dottie West*	63/91 Cornell Crawford *K.T. Oslin*	15/68 Country Girl *Dottie West*
	2/73 Corner Of My Life *Bill Anderson*	41/75 Country Girl *Jody Miller*
37/67 Come See What's Left Of Your Man *Johnny Darrell*	70/71 Corpus Christi Wind *Dale McBride*	61/73 Country Girl (I Love You Still) *Glenn Barber*
14/98 Come Some Rainy Day *Wynonna*	Corrine, Corrina	96/88 Country Girl In Paris *John Denver*
7/71 Come Sundown *Bobby Bare*	73/70 Earl Richards	52/71 Country Girl With Hot Pants On *Leona Williams*
57/70 Come The Morning *Hank Snow*	73/94 Asleep At The Wheel Featuring Brooks & Dunn	
16/78 Come To Me *Roy Head*		1/85 Country Girls *John Schneider*
56/87 Come To Me *Johnny Paycheck*	(Corvette Song) ..see: One I Loved Back Then	5/71 Country Green *Don Gibson*
87/78 Come To Me *Bobby Hood*	94/77 Cotton Dan *Claude King*	16/65 Country Guitar *Phil Baugh*
16/80 Come To My Love *Cristy Lane*	Cotton Fields	8/68 Country Hall Of Fame *Hank Locklin*
4/59 Come Walk With Me *Wilma Lee & Stoney Cooper*	50/82 Creedence Clearwater Revival	76/88 Country Highways *C.W. Ferrari*
14/49 Come Wet Your Mustache With Me *Stubby & The Buccaneers*	65/83 Tennessee Express	72/00 Country In My Genes *Loretta Lynn*
	11/72 Cotton Jenny *Anne Murray*	
1/79 Come With Me *Waylon Jennings*	43/64 Cotton Mill Man *Jim & Jesse*	1/74 Country Is *Tom T. Hall*
4/62 Comeback, The *Faron Young*	34/89 Cotton Pickin' Time *Marcy Bros.*	87/81 Country Is The Closest Thing To Heaven (You Can Hear) *Concrete Cowboy Band*
67/72 Comin' After Jinny *Tex Ritter*	53/72 Cotton Top *Carl Perkins*	
8/71 Comin' Down *Dave Dudley*	1/80 Could I Have This Dance *Anne Murray*	14/49 Country Junction *Tennessee Ernie Ford*
23/71 Comin' For To Carry Me Home *Dolly Parton*	59/79 Could I Talk You Into Loving Me Again *Wynn Stewart*	
32/75 Comin' Home To You *Jerry Wallace*		23/78 Country Lovin' *Eddy Arnold*
58/77 Coming Around *Connie Smith*		

see Lonzo & Oscar (Fan of CM)

27/74	**Country Lullabye** Johnny Carver	
63/72	**Country Music In My Soul** George Hamilton IV	
2/59	**Country Music Is Here To Stay** Simon Crum	
63/85	**Country Music Love Affair** David Frizzell	
23/67	**Country Music Lover** "Little" Jimmy Dickens	
76/83	**Country Music Nightmare** Boxcar Willie	
26/61	**Country Music Time** Lonzo & Oscar	
15/77	**Country Party** Johnny Lee	
31/87	**Country Rap** Bellamy Brothers	
46/92	**Country Road** Dolly Parton	
2/86	**Country State Of Mind** Hank Williams, Jr.	
2/73	**Country Sunshine** Dottie West	
35/94	**Country 'Til I Die** John Anderson	
62/72	**Country Western Truck Drivin' Singer** Red Simpson	
	Countryfied	
80/74	Ray Pillow	
23/81	Mel McDaniel	
35/71	**Countryfied** George Hamilton IV	
	Couple More Years	
51/76	Dr. Hook	
89/79	King Edward IV & The Knights	
44/93	**Couple Of Good Years Left** Ricky Van Shelton	
3/54	**Courtin' In The Rain** T. Texas Tyler And His Band	
33/75	**Cover Me** Sammi Smith	
3/98	**Cover You In Kisses** John Michael Montgomery	
65/81	**Cow Patti** Jim Stafford	
5/62	**Cow Town** Webb Pierce	
1/80	**Coward Of The County** Kenny Rogers	
13/76	**Cowboy** Eddy Arnold	
82/81	**Cowboy** Larry Dalton	
	Cowboy And The Lady	
85/77	Bobby Goldsboro	
50/81	John Denver	
	Cowboy And The Lady	
90/76	Patsy Sledd	
63/77	Tommy Cash	
	(**Cowboy And The Poet**) ..see: Faster Horses	
24/94	**Cowboy Band** Billy Dean	
23/92	**Cowboy Beat** Bellamy Brothers	
46/93	**Cowboy Boogie** Randy Travis	
3/63	**Cowboy Boots** Dave Dudley	
52/97	**Cowboy Cadillac** Garth Brooks	
70/99	**Cowboy Cadillac** Confederate Railroad	
19/70	**Cowboy Convention** Buddy Alan & Don Rich	
36/89	**Cowboy Hat In Dallas** Charlie Daniels Band	
44/82	**Cowboy In A Three Piece Business Suit** Rex Allen, Jr.	
1/02	**Cowboy In Me** Tim McGraw	
3/64	**Cowboy In The Continental Suit** Marty Robbins	
91/76	**Cowboy Like You** Heckels	
52/90	**Cowboy Logic** Michael Martin Murphey	
4/96	**Cowboy Love** John Michael Montgomery	
10/87	**Cowboy Man** Lyle Lovett	

100/76	**Cowboy Peyton Place** Doug Sahm	
5/85	**Cowboy Rides Away** George Strait	
77/79	**Cowboy Singer** Sonny Curtis	
76/80	**Cowboy Stomp!** Spurzz	
1/00	**Cowboy Take Me Away** Dixie Chicks	
	(**Cowboy Tune**) ..see: End Is Not In Sight	
12/93	**Cowboy's Born With A Broken Heart** Boy Howdy	
49/83	**Cowboy's Dream** Mel Tillis	
13/77	**Cowboys Ain't Supposed To Cry** Moe Bandy	
1/80	**Cowboys And Clowns** Ronnie Milsap	
29/75	**Cowboys And Daddys** Bobby Bare	
	(**Cowboys And Indians**) ..see: When Our Love Began	
68/80	**Cowboys Are Common As Sin** Max D. Barnes	
	Cowboys Don't Cry	
65/91	Dude Mowrey	
24/94	Daron Norwood	
60/01	**Cowboys Don't Cry** Eddy Raven	
11/78	**Cowboys Don't Get Lucky All The Time** Gene Watson	
21/81	**Cowboys Don't Shoot Straight (Like They Used To)** Tammy Wynette	
10/80	**Cowgirl And The Dandy** Brenda Lee	
75/84	**Cowgirl In A Coupe DeVille** Terry Gregory	
38/86	**Cowpoke** Glen Campbell	
82/83	**Coyote Song** Delia Bell	
16/61	**Cozy Inn** Leon McAuliffe	
56/69	**Crack In My World** Leroy Van Dyke	
63/00	**Cracker Jack Diamond** Marty Raybon	
3/80	**Crackers** Barbara Mandrell	
32/92	**Crash Course In The Blues** Steve Wariner	
42/71	**Crawdad Song** LaWanda Lindsey & Kenny Vernon	
F/73	**Crawling On My Knees** Marty Robbins	
1/85	**Crazy** Kenny Rogers	
	Crazy	
2/62	Patsy Cline	
73/67	Ray Price	
6/77	Linda Ronstadt	
84/76	**Crazy Again** Rayburn Anthony	
	Crazy Arms	
1/56	Ray Price	
18/63	Marion Worth	
16/79	Willie Nelson	
46/87	**Crazy Blue** Billy Montana	
17/79	**Crazy Blue Eyes** Lacy J. Dalton	
11/48	**Crazy Boogie** Merle Travis	
58/01	**Crazy 'Bout You Baby** Billy Ray Cyrus	
11/61	**Crazy Bullfrog** Lewis Pruitt	
4/47	**Crazy 'Cause I Love You** Spade Cooley	
87/90	**Crazy Driver** Dalice	
1/85	**Crazy For Your Love** Exile	
3/87	**Crazy From The Heart** Bellamy Brothers	

4/51	**Crazy Heart** Hank Williams	
	Crazy In Love	
68/88	Kim Carnes	
2/90	Conway Twitty	
43/01	**Crazy Life** Tim Rushlow	
97/77	**Crazy Little Mama (At My Front Door)** Alvin Crow	
	Crazy Little Thing Called Love	
79/81	Orion	
12/99	Dwight Yoakam	
95/79	**Crazy Love** Poco	
85/83	**Crazy Old Soldier** David Allan Coe	
4/87	**Crazy Over You** Foster & Lloyd	
8/62	**Crazy Wild Desire** Webb Pierce	
10/74	**Credit Card Song** Dick Feller	
89/82	**Crime In The Sheets** Shylo	
7/87	**Crime Of Passion** Ricky Van Shelton	
32/76	**Crispy Critters** C.W. McCall	
67/00	**Critical List** Ray Hood	
92/88	**Crocodile Man From Walk-About-Creek** LeGarde Twins	
59/90	**Crocodile Tears** Lee Roy Parnell	
14/89	**Cross My Broken Heart** Suzy Bogguss	
64/86	**Cross My Heart** Jan Gray	
86/87	**Cross My Heart** Stella Parton	
2/64	**Cross The Brazos At Waco** Billy Walker	
57/75	**Crossroad, The** Mary Kay James	
11/84	**Crossword Puzzle** Barbara Mandrell	
92/82	**Crown Prince Of The Barroom** David Rogers	
13/74	**Crude Oil Blues** Jerry Reed	
9/60	**Cruel Love** Lou Smith	
41/99	**Crush** Lila McCann	
69/91	**Crush, The** JJ White	
25/77	**Crutches** Faron Young	
	Cry	
3/72	Lynn Anderson	
99/75	Diana Trask	
1/86	Crystal Gayle	
77/82	**Cry** Tanya Tucker	
	Cry Baby	
52/82	Narvel Felts	
56/88	Joe Stampley	
	Cry Baby	
84/86	Lowes	
61/89	Donna Meade	
5/49	**Cry-Baby Heart** George Morgan	
58/68	**Cry, Cry Again** Liz Anderson	
1/88	**Cry, Cry, Cry** Highway 101	
	Cry! Cry! Cry!	
14/55	Johnny Cash	
32/89	Marty Stuart	
20/68	**Cry, Cry, Cry** Connie Smith	
	Cry, Cry, Darling	
4/54	Jimmy Newman	
34/78	Con Hunley	
67/78	Glenn Barber	
50/87	**Cry Just A Little** Marie Osmond	
9/85	**Cry Just A Little Bit** Sylvia	
70/75	**Cry Like A Baby** Joe Stampley	
1/87	**Cry Myself To Sleep** Judds	
7/50	**Cry Of The Dying Duck In A Thunder-Storm** Cactus Pryor	
2/50	**Cry Of The Wild Goose** Tennessee Ernie Ford	

See Wagoners "This Cowboy's Hat"

26/97	Cry On The Shoulder Of The Road Martina McBride	
57/94	Cry Wolf Victoria Shaw	
	Cryin' ..also see: Crying	
3/78	Cryin' Again Oak Ridge Boys	
90/73	Cryin' Eyes Patti Tierny	
56/98	Cryin' Game Sara Evans	
5/51	Cryin' Heart Blues Johnnie & Jack	
11/48	Cryin' In My Beer Jerry Irby	
7/55	Cryin', Prayin', Waitin', Hopin' Hank Snow	
	Crying	
28/70	Arlene Harden	
79/76	Ronnie Milsap	
14/80	Stephanie Winslow	
6/81	Don McLean	
42/88	Roy Orbison & k.d. lang	
	Crying In The Chapel	
4/53	Rex Allen	
4/53	Darrell Glenn	
	Crying In The Rain	
54/72	Del Reeves & Penny DeHaven	
18/81	Tammy Wynette	
	Crying My Heart Out Over You	
21/60	Flatt & Scruggs	
1/82	Ricky Skaggs	
3/58	Crying Over You Webb Pierce	
43/73	Crying Over You Dickey Lee	
51/87	Crying Over You Rosie Flores	
4/88	Crying Shame Michael Johnson	
59/93	Crying Time Lorrie Morgan	
12/65	Crystal Chandelier Carl Belew	
76/82	Cube, The Bob Jenkins	
2/50	Cuddle Buggin' Baby Eddy Arnold	
	Cuddle Up Kind ..see: (I'm Just The)	
47/68	Culman, Alabam Roger Sovine	
12/81	Cup Of Tea Rex Allen, Jr. & Margo Smith	
59/67	Cupid's Last Arrow Bobby Austin	
94/76	Curse Of A Woman Eddy Raven	
3/58	Curtain In The Window Ray Price	
14/69	Custody Luke The Drifter, Jr.	
	Cut Across Shorty	
28/60	Carl Smith	
15/69	Nat Stuckey	
60/68	Cut The Cornbread, Mama Osborne Brothers	
73/71	Cute Little Waitress Stoney Edwards	
5/55	Cuzz Yore So Sweet Simon Crum	

D

8/65	DJ Cried Ernest Ashworth	
9/64	D.J. For A Day Jimmy "C" Newman	
88/82	D.O.A. (Drunk On Arrival) Johnny Paycheck	
10/48	Dad Gave My Dog Away T. Texas Tyler	
9/87	Daddies Need To Grow Up Too O'Kanes	
14/79	Daddy Donna Fargo	
40/69	Daddy Dolly Parton	
55/81	Daddy Billy Edd Wheeler with Rashell Richmond	
27/89	Daddy And Home Tanya Tucker	

85/74	Daddy Bluegrass Stoney Edwards
69/97	Daddy Can You See Me Anita Cochran
40/70	Daddy Come And Get Me Dolly Parton
55/72	Daddy Don't You Walk So Fast Wayne Newton
1/71	Daddy Frank (The Guitar Man) Merle Haggard
58/76	Daddy How'm I Doin' Rick Smith
40/70	Daddy, I Love You Billie Jo Spears
63/93	Daddy Laid The Blues On Me Bobbie Cryner
62/74	Daddy Loves You Honey Dorsey Burnette
9/94	Daddy Never Was The Cadillac Kind Confederate Railroad
45/74	Daddy Number Two Glenn Barber
93/80	Daddy Played Harmonica Jerry Dycke
1/69	Daddy Sang Bass Johnny Cash
20/62	Daddy Stopped In Claude Gray
54/77	Daddy, They're Playin' A Song About You Kenny Seratt
68/71	Daddy Was A Preacher But Mama Was A Go-Go Girl Joanna Neel
7/70	Daddy Was An Old Time Preacher Man Porter Wagoner & Dolly Parton
2/74	Daddy What If Bobby Bare
15/49	Daddy, When Is Mommy Coming Home Ernest Tubb
17/00	Daddy Won't Sell The Farm Montgomery Gentry
8/55	Daddy, You Know What? Jim Wilson
1/91	Daddy's Come Around Paul Overstreet
56/66	Daddy's Coming Home (Next Week) Charlie Walker
91/75	Daddy's Girl Red Sovine
7/86	Daddy's Hands Holly Dunn
48/85	Daddy's Honky Tonk Moe Bandy & Joe Stampley
6/50	Daddy's Last Letter Tex Ritter
42/97	Daddy's Little Girl Kippi Brannon
92/80	Daddy's Makin' Records In Nashville LeGarde Twins
1/96	Daddy's Money Ricochet
33/73	Daisy A Day Jud Strunk
37/73	Daisy May (And Daisy May Not) Terri Lane
66/73	Dakota The Dancing Bear Johnny Darrell
1/92	Dallas Alan Jackson
32/80	Dallas Floyd Cramer
35/74	Dallas Connie Smith
54/83	Dallas Bama Band
58/67	Dallas Vern Stovall
89/79	Dallas Cowboys Charley Pride
77/88	Dallas Darlin' Norm Schaffer
68/95	Dallas Days And Fort Worth Nights Chris LeDoux
	(Dallas Lovers' Song) ..see: Makin' Up For Lost Time
71/90	Dam These Tears Canyon
68/75	Damn Good Country Song Jerry Lee Lewis
F/79	Damn Good Drinking Song Kenny Seratt

1/90	Dance, The Garth Brooks
75/88	Dance For Me Don Malena
38/76	Dance Her By Me (One More Time) Jacky Ward
42/90	Dance In Circles Tim Ryan
49/98	Dance In The Boat Kinleys
9/83	Dance Little Jean Nitty Gritty Dirt Band
63/98	Dance The Night Away Mavericks
23/81	Dance The Two Step Susie Allanson
2/74	Dance With Me (Just One More Time) Johnny Rodriguez
	Dance With Me Molly
96/78	Roger Bowling
88/79	Hank Thompson
55/93	Dance With The One That Brought You Shania Twain
71/91	Dance With Who Brung You Asleep At The Wheel
1/80	Dancin' Cowboys Bellamy Brothers
72/87	Dancin' In The Moonlight Durelle Ames
29/79	Dancin' 'Round And 'Round Olivia Newton-John
3/97	Dancin', Shaggin' On The Boulevard Alabama
	(Dancin' To A Different Beat) ..see: I'm An Old Rock And Roller
51/87	Dancin' With Myself Tonight Kendalls
29/84	Dancin' With The Devil Stephanie Winslow
58/96	Dancin' With The Wind Great Plains
16/77	Dancing The Night Away Tanya Tucker
3/82	Dancing Your Memory Away Charly McClain
5/90	Dancy's Dream Restless Heart
1/64	Dang Me Roger Miller
20/78	Danger, Heartbreak Ahead Zella Lehr
46/86	Danger List (Give Me Someone I Can Love) Leon Everette
15/77	Danger Of A Stranger Stella Parton
59/86	Danger Zone Maines Brothers Band
98/77	Danger Zone Peggy Forman
92/89	Dangerous Ground Lance Strode
62/88	Dangerous Road Mason Dixon
9/67	Danny Boy Ray Price
10/73	Danny's Song Anne Murray
63/81	Dare To Dream Again Phil Everly
49/64	Dark As A Dungeon Johnny Cash
24/68	Dark End Of The Street Archie Campbell & Lorene Mann
76/86	Dark Eyed Lady Bart Cameron
	Dark Hollow
7/59	Jimmie Skinner
13/59	Luke Gordon
21/97	Dark Horse Mila Mason
14/57	Dark Moon Bonnie Guitar
42/86	Dark Side Of Town Dobie Gray
75/90	Darkness Of The Light Harrell & Scott
1/88	Darlene T. Graham Brown
67/82	Darlene Big Al Downing

	Darlin'		**Dear Alice** Johnny Lee		**Destination Atlanta G.A.**
53/72	Wayne Kemp	58/77		60/68	Cal Smith
42/74	Ray Griff	64/75	**Dear God** Roy Clark	68/00	**Destination Unknown** Victor Sanz
	Darling	9/62	**Dear Ivan** Jimmy Dean	31/68	**Destroyed By Man** Mel Tillis
86/78	Poacher	7/53	**Dear Joan** Jack Cardwell		**Detour**
18/79	David Rogers	8/51	**Dear John** Hank Williams	2/46	Spade Cooley
19/81	Tom Jones		**Dear John Letter**	3/46	Wesley Tuttle
26/73	**Darlin' (Don't Come Back)**	1/53	Jean Shepard with Ferlin Huskey	5/46	Elton Britt
	Dorsey Burnette	11/65	Skeeter Davis & Bobby Bare	6/46	Foy Willing
	Darlin' Raise The Shade	F/76	**Dear John Letter Lounge**		**Detroit City**
57/72	Claude King		Jerry Jeff Walker	6/63	Bobby Bare
64/73	Norro Wilson	12/60	**Dear Mama** Merle Kilgore	18/63	Billy Grammer
23/70	**Darling Days** Billy Walker	9/89	**Dear Me** Lorrie Morgan	86/81	**Devil, The** Hoyt Axton
5/73	**Darling, You Can Always Come Back Home** Jody Miller	88/80	**Dear Mr. President** Max D. Barnes		**Devil Ain't A Lonely Woman's Friend**
2/69	**Darling, You Know I Wouldn't Lie** Conway Twitty	12/48	**Dear Oakie** Doye O'Dell	96/75	Tennessee Ernie Ford
		12/48	Jack Rivers	72/77	Red Steagall
69/87	**Darlington County** Jeff Stevens & The Bullets	4/66	**Dear Uncle Sam** Loretta Lynn	74/91	**Devil And Your Deep Blue Eyes** Sweethearts Of The Rodeo
4/95	**Darned If I Don't (Danged If I Do)** Shenandoah	11/75	**Dear Woman** Joe Stampley	54/94	**Devil Comes Back To Georgia** Mark O'Connor With Charlie Daniels
		59/69	**Dearly Beloved** David Rogers		
4/47	**Daughter Of Jole Blon** Johnny Bond	80/89	**Death and Taxes (And Me Lovin' You)** Patsy Cole	23/75	**Devil In Mrs. Jones** Billy Larkin
	Davy Crockett ..see: Ballad Of	3/53	**Death Of Hank Williams** Jack Cardwell	1/75	**Devil In The Bottle** T.G. Sheppard
59/88	**Day After Tomorrow** Darden Smith	7/49	**Death Of Little Kathy Fiscus** Jimmie Osborne	32/76	**Devil In Your Kisses (And The Angel In Your Eyes)** Mel Street
44/84	**Day By Day** McGuffey Lane	71/00	**Decision** Ricky Van Shelton	81/82	**Devil Inside** Wyley McPherson
	Day Dream ..see: Daydream		**Deck Of Cards**		**Devil Is A Woman**
23/70	**Day Drinkin'** Dave Dudley & Tom T. Hall	2/48	T. Texas Tyler	55/73	Brian Shaw
		10/48	Tex Ritter	87/83	David Rogers
14/66	**Day For Decision** Johnny Sea	11/59	Wink Martindale	59/80	**Devil Stands Only Five Foot Five** "Blackjack" Jack Grayson
88/88	**Day I Tried To Teach Charlene MacKenzie How To Drive** Ray Stevens	60/91	Bill Anderson		**Devil Went Down To Georgia**
			Deck The Halls	1/79	Charlie Daniels Band
		40/99	SheDaisy	60/98	Charlie Daniels Band
11/97	**Day In, Day Out** David Kersh	37/00	SheDaisy	1/62	**Devil Woman** Marty Robbins
30/72	**Day In The Life Of A Fool** George Jones	28/84	**Dedicate** Kieran Kane	63/80	**Devil's Den** Jack Greene
		6/96	**Deep Down** Pam Tillis	13/86	**Devil's On The Loose** Waylon Jennings
10/62	**Day Into Night** Kitty Wells	82/87	**Deep Down (Everybody Wants To Be From Dixie)** Danny Shirley		
18/72	**Day That Love Walked In** David Houston	75/84	**Deep In The Arms Of Texas** Con Hunley		**Devoted To You**
				7/58	Everly Brothers
5/98	**Day That She Left Tulsa (In A Chevy)** Wade Hayes	10/87	**Deep River Woman** Lionel Richie with Alabama	33/78	Carly Simon & James Taylor
				9/84	**Diamond In The Dust** Mark Gray
4/68	**Day The World Stood Still** Charley Pride		**Deep Water**	38/82	**Diamond In The Rough** Karen Taylor
		10/67	Carl Smith		
72/74	**Day Time Lover** Gary Sargeants	62/89	Marsha Thornton	45/66	**Diamonds And Horseshoes** Jerry Wallace
60/68	**Day You Stop Loving Me** Bobby Helms	1/89	**Deeper Than The Holler** Randy Travis	82/81	**Diamonds And Teardrops** Wayne Massey
	Daydream	87/79	**Deeper Than The Night** Olivia Newton-John		
86/82	Jon & Lynn (What A Day For A)			9/82	**Diamonds In The Stars** Ray Price
84/89	Cerrito	35/78	**Deeper Water** Brenda Kaye Perry	21/80	**Diane** Ed Bruce
3/80	**Daydream Believer** Anne Murray	93/88	**Deepest Shade Of Blue** Gail Veach	15/61	**Did I Ever Tell You** George Jones & Margie Singleton
7/55	**Daydreamin'** Jimmy Newman	66/95	**Deja Blue** Billy Ray Cyrus	87/89	**Did I Leave My Heart At Your House** Touch Of Country
1/75	**Daydreams About Night Things** Ronnie Milsap	37/69	**Delia's Gone** Waylon Jennings		
7/78	**Daylight** T.G. Sheppard	17/79	**Della And The Dealer** Hoyt Axton	25/63	**Did I Miss You?** Orville Couch
90/74	**Daylight Losing Time** Larry Steele	6/72	**Delta Dawn** Tanya Tucker	25/97	**Did I Shave My Legs For This?** Deana Carter
		14/74	**Delta Dirt** Larry Gatlin		
37/02	**Days Of America** BlackHawk	7/84	**Denver** Larry Gatlin/Gatlin Brothers	74/85	**Did I Stay Too Long** Dennis Bottoms
77/78	**Days Of Me And You** Red Sovine			33/90	**Did It For Love** Sawyer Brown
	Days Of Sand And Shovels	13/64	**Dern Ya** Ruby Wright	90/81	**Did We Fall Out Of Love** Tricia Johns
20/69	Waylon Jennings		**(Desert Blues) ..see: Big Chief Buffalo Nickel**		
26/78	Nat Stuckey				**Did We Have To Come [Go] This Far (To Say Goodbye)**
23/77	**Days That End In "Y"** Sammi Smith	85/82	**Designer Jeans** Glen Bailey		
			Desperado	72/71	Wayne Kemp
1/77	**Daytime Friends** Kenny Rogers	5/77	Johnny Rodriguez	80/82	Donna Fargo
59/71	**Dayton, Ohio** Jack Barlow	54/93	Clint Black	26/71	**Did You Ever** Charlie Louvin & Melba Montgomery
7/44	**Deacon Jones** Louis Jordan	1/86	**Desperado Love** Conway Twitty		
19/60	**Dead Or Alive** Bill Anderson	15/85	**Desperados Waiting For A Train** Waylon Jennings/Willie Nelson/ Johnny Cash/Kris Kristofferson	71/72	**Did You Ever Think** Don Gibson & Sue Thompson
8/75	**Deal** Tom T. Hall				
	Dealin' With The Devil	7/88	**Desperately** Don Williams		
25/80	Eddy Raven				
49/82	Merle Haggard				

Do You Want Fries With That — Tim McGraw

70/71	**Did You Think To Pray** *Charley Pride*		**Dixie Fried**	2/73	**Do You Know What It's Like To Be Lonesome** *Jerry Wallace*
56/01	**Diddley** *Elbert West*	10/56	*Carl Perkins*		
23/89	**Didn't Expect It To Go Down This Way** *K.T. Oslin*	61/73	**Carl Perkins (Let's Get)**	16/93	**Do You Know Where Your Man Is** *Pam Tillis*
		71/93	**Kentucky Headhunters**		
55/95	**Didn't Have You** *Billy Montana*	44/77	**Dixie Hummingbird** *Ray Stevens*	1/78	**Do You Know You Are My Sunshine** *Statler Bros.*
32/65	**Didn't I** *Dottie West*	45/74	**Dixie Lily** *Roy Drusky*		
10/86	**Didn't We** *Lee Greenwood*	25/81	**Dixie Man** *Randy Barlow*	1/81	**Do You Love As Good As You Look** *Bellamy Brothers*
75/83	**Didn't We Do It Good** *Brenda Lee*	66/86	**Dixie Moon** *Ray Charles*		
69/00	**Didn't We Love** *Tamara Walker*	1/81	**Dixie On My Mind** *Hank Williams, Jr.*	1/88	**(Do You Love Me) Just Say Yes** *Highway 101*
45/87	**Didn't We Shine** *Lynn Anderson*		**Dixie Road**	72/86	**Do You Mind If I Step Into Your Dreams** *Cannons*
85/87	**Didn't You Go And Leave Me** *Rosemary Sharp*	48/81	*King Edward IV & The Knights*		
		1/85	*Lee Greenwood*	59/86	**Do You Really Want My Lovin'** *Marty Stuart*
18/67	**Diesel On My Tail** *Jim & Jesse*	45/85	**Dixie Train** *Carl Jackson*		
41/67	**Diesel Smoke, Dangerous Curves** *Red Simpson*	1/83	**Dixieland Delight** *Alabama*	86/80	**Do You Remember Roll Over Beethoven** *Sonny Curtis*
		F/76	**Dixieland, You Will Never Die** *Lynn Anderson*		
69/83	**Diet Song** *Bobby Bare*			2/72	**Do You Remember These** *Statler Brothers*
70/70	**Difference Between Going And Really Gone** *Cal Smith*	90/81	**Do Fish Swim?** *Wickline*		
		50/84	**Do I Ever Cross Your Mind** *Ray Charles*	F/76	**Do You Right Tonight** *Eddie Rabbitt*
28/77	**Different Kind Of Flower** *Ray Price*		**Do I Ever Cross Your Mind**	73/87	**Do You Wanna Fall In Love** *Bandit Band*
80/89	**Different Situations** *Mack Abernathy*	85/79	*Kin Vassy*		
		F/82	*Dolly Parton*	1/80	**Do You Wanna Go To Heaven** *T.G. Sheppard*
86/83	**Different Woman Every Night** *Bobby Springfield*	18/81	**Do I Have To Draw A Picture** *Billy Swan*		**Do You Wanna Make Love**
79/78	**Dig Down Deep** *Del Reeves*	28/87	**Do I Have To Say Goodbye** *Louise Mandrell*	70/77	*Bobby Smith*
1/86	**Diggin' Up Bones** *Randy Travis*			82/77	*David Wills*
	Diggy Liggy Lo	6/53	**Do I Like It?** *Carl Smith*	80/79	*Buck Owens*
14/61	*Rusty & Doug*	45/00	**Do I Love You Enough** *Ricochet*	53/96	**Do You Wanna Make Something Of It** *Jo Dee Messina*
70/69	*Doug Kershaw*	2/78	**Do I Love You (Yes In Every Way)** *Donna Fargo*		
20/85	**Dim Lights, Thick Smoke (And Loud, Loud Music)** *Vern Gosdin*			70/80	**Do You Wanna Spend The Night** *Mitch Goodson*
		55/97	**Do It Again** *Jeff Carson*		
49/80	**Dim The Lights And Pour The Wine** *Red Steagall*	68/89	**Do It Again (I Think I Saw Diamonds)** *Debbie Rich*	38/72	**Do You Want To Dance** *Jack Reno*
25/61	**Dime A Dozen** *Shirley Collie*			94/79	**Do You Want To Fly** *Ronnie Sessions*
12/67	**Dime At A Time** *Del Reeves*	13/78	**Do It Again Tonight** *Larry Gatlin*		
78/80	**Diplomat, The** *Roger Bowling*	77/87	**Do It For The Love Of It** *Bart Cameron*		**Dock Of The Bay ..see: (Sittin' On)**
F/78	**Dirt Farming Man** *Joel Mathis*	42/79	**Do It In A Heartbeat** *Carlene Carter*	5/95	**Doctor Time** *Rick Trevino*
3/92	**Dirt Road** *Sawyer Brown*			53/86	**Doctor's Orders** *Mel McDaniel*
38/73	**Dirty Old Man** *George Hamilton IV*	92/79	**Do It Or Die** *Atlanta Rhythm Section*	1/85	**Does Fort Worth Ever Cross Your Mind** *George Strait*
26/78	**Dirty Work** *Sterling Whipple*	20/70	**Do It To Someone You Love** *Norro Wilson*	32/84	**Does He Ever Mention My Name** *Rick & Janis Carnes*
4/71	**Dis-Satisfied** *Bill Anderson & Jan Howard*	60/85	**Do Me Right** *David Frizzell & Shelly West*	1/93	**Does He Love You** *Reba McEntire (with Linda Davis)*
90/79	**Disco Blues** *Jay Chevalier & Shelley Ford*	4/82	**Do Me With Love** *Janie Fricke*	5/63	**Does He Mean That Much To You?** *Eddy Arnold*
82/79	**Disco Girl Go Away** *Rebecca Lynn*	17/71	**Do Right Woman - Do Right Man** *Barbara Mandrell*	23/02	**Does My Ring Burn Your Finger** *Lee Ann Womack*
75/76	**Disco-Tex** *Little David Wilkins*	68/80	**Do That To Me One More Time** *Stephany Samone*	4/67	**Does My Ring Hurt Your Finger** *Country Charley Pride*
12/84	**Disenchanted** *Michael Martin Murphey*	88/77	**Do The Buck Dance** *Ruby Falls*	20/81	**Does She Wish She Was Single Again** *Burrito Brothers*
81/79	**Disneyland Daddy** *Paul Evans*	69/97	**Do The Right Thing** *George Strait*		
1/66	**Distant Drums** *Jim Reeves*	15/65	**Do-Wacka-Do** *Roger Miller*	2/96	**Does That Blue Moon Ever Shine On You** *Toby Keith*
86/78	**Divers Do It Deeper** *David Allan Coe*		**Do What You Do Do Well**	33/81	**Doesn't Anybody Get High On Love Anymore** *Shoppe*
77/88	**Divided** *Burbank Station*	7/65	*Ned Miller*		
1/68	**D-I-V-O-R-C-E** *Tammy Wynette*	29/65	*Ernest Tubb*	7/54	**Dog-Gone It, Baby, I'm In Love** *Carl Smith*
9/53	**Divorce Granted** *Ernest Tubb*		**Do What You Gotta Do**		
	Divorce Me C.O.D.	62/97	*Garth Brooks*	6/48	**Dog House Boogie** *Hawkshaw Hawkins*
1/46	*Merle Travis*	13/00	*Garth Brooks*		
5/46	*King Sisters*	1/87	**Do Ya'** *K.T. Oslin*	64/95	**Dog On A Toolbox** *James Bonamy*
4/47	*Johnny Bond*	4/88	**Do You Believe Me Now** *Vern Gosdin*		
90/78	**Divorce Suit (You Were Named Co-Respondent)** *Bill Phillips*	53/68	**Do You Believe This Town** *Roy Clark*	75/76	**Dog Tired Of Cattin' Around** *Shylo*
	Dixie ..see: (I'm Coming Home To You)	5/79	**Do You Ever Fool Around** *Joe Stampley*	45/66	**Doggin' In The U.S. Mail** *Hal Willis*
54/70	**Dixie Belle** *Stan Hitchcock*	39/89	**Do You Feel The Same Way Too?** *Becky Hobbs*	19/59	**Doggone That Train** *Hank Snow*
73/93	**Dixie Chicken** *Garth Brooks*	61/88	**Do You Have Any Doubts** *Alibi*	61/91	**Doghouse** *John Conlee*
81/80	**Dixie Dirt** *Jim Rushing*	47/77	**Do You Hear My Heart Beat** *David Rogers*	17/60	**(Doin' The) Lovers Leap** *Webb Pierce*
11/83	**Dixie Dreaming** *Atlanta*				

431

82/89	Doing It By The Book *Whites*	84/81	Don't Ever Leave Me Again *Max D. Barnes*		Don't It Make You Want To Go Home	
62/83	Doing It Right *McGuffey Lane*	28/82	*Vern Gosdin*	27/69	*Joe South*	
39/76	Doing My Time *Don Gibson*	65/00	Don't Ever Let Me Go	51/87	*Butch Baker*	
57/78	Dolly *R.W. Blackwood*		*Tara Lyn Hart*		Don't Just Stand There ..see: (When You Feel Like You're In Love)	
4/87	Domestic Life *John Conlee*	13/78	Don't Ever Say Good-Bye *T.G. Sheppard*			
7/90	Domino Theory *Steve Wariner*	3/80	Don't Fall In Love With A Dreamer *Kenny Rogers with Kim Carnes*	1/70	Don't Keep Me Hangin' On *Sonny James*	
57/78	Don Juan *Billy "Crash" Craddock*			11/57	Don't Laugh *Louvin Brothers*	
63/75	Don Junior *Jim Ed Brown*	43/86	Don't Fall In Love With Me *Lacy J. Dalton*	2/98	Don't Laugh At Me *Mark Wills*	
	Don't	33/79	Don't Feel Like The Lone Ranger *Leon Everette*	83/82	Don't Lead Me On *Wyvon Alexander*	
2/58	*Elvis Presley*					
39/73	*Sandy Posey*	4/45	Don't Fence Me In *Gene Autry*	42/90	Don't Leave Her Lonely Too Long *Marty Stuart*	
13/75	Don't Anyone Make Love At Home Anymore *Moe Bandy*	1/73	Don't Fight The Feelings Of Love *Charley Pride*	67/83	Don't Leave Me Lonely Loving You *Randy Barlow*	
F/58	Don't Ask Me Why *Elvis Presley*	12/55	Don't Forget *Eddy Arnold*			
	Don't Be Angry	44/74	Don't Forget To Remember *Skeeter Davis*	44/64	Don't Leave Me Lonely Too Long *Kathy Dee*	
4/64	*Stonewall Jackson*					
33/73	*Billy "Crash" Craddock*	75/88	Don't Forget Your Way Home *Melissa Kay*	11/74	Don't Let Go *Mel Tillis & Sherry Bryce*	
3/77	*Donna Fargo*					
7/50	Don't Be Ashamed Of Your Age *Ernest Tubb & Red Foley*	13/81	Don't Forget Yourself *Statler Brothers*	26/87	Don't Let Go Of My Heart *Southern Pacific*	
	Don't Be Cruel	16/81	Don't Get Above Your Raising *Ricky Skaggs*	33/64	Don't Let Her Know *Buck Owens*	
1/56	*Elvis Presley*			30/63	Don't Let Her See Me Cry *Lefty Frizzell*	
10/87	*Judds*	1/96	Don't Get Me Started *Rhett Akins*			
6/98	Don't Be Stupid (You Know I Love You) *Shania Twain*	60/87	Don't Get Me Started *Libby Hurley*	22/71	Don't Let Him Make A Memory Out Of Me *Billy Walker*	
71/89	Don't Be Surprised If You Get It *Debbie Rich*	10/88	Don't Give Candy To A Stranger *Larry Boone*	83/86	Don't Let It Go To Your Heart *Bonnie Nelson*	
4/76	Don't Believe My Heart Can Stand Another You *Tanya Tucker*	41/69	Don't Give Me A Chance *Claude Gray*		Don't Let Me Cross Over	
		91/84	Don't Give Up On Her Now *Leon Raines*	1/62	*Carl Butler & Pearl*	
58/76	Don't Boogie Woogie *Jerry Lee Lewis*		Don't Give Up On Me	9/69	*Jerry Lee Lewis & Linda Gail Lewis*	
13/81	Don't Bother To Knock *Jim Ed Brown/Helen Cornelius*	3/73	*Jerry Wallace*	10/79	*Jim Reeves*	
		73/82	*Eddy Arnold*	60/01	Don't Let Me Down *Kortney Kayle*	
1/78	Don't Break The Heart That Loves You *Margo Smith*	90/76	Don't Give Up On Me *Stoney Edwards*	6/77	Don't Let Me Touch You *Marty Robbins*	
49/86	Don't Bury Me 'Til I'm Ready *Johnny Paycheck*	37/65	Don't Give Up The Ship *Johnny Wright*	86/77	Don't Let My Love Stand In Your Way *Jim Glaser*	
1/85	Don't Call Him A Cowboy *Conway Twitty*	27/90	Don't Give Us A Reason *Hank Williams, Jr.*	1/92	Don't Let Our Love Start Slippin' Away *Vince Gill*	
3/85	Don't Call It Love *Dolly Parton*	69/84	Don't Go Changing *Lorrie Morgan*			
62/83	Don't Call Me *Karen Taylor-Good*	5/77	Don't Go City Girl On Me *Tommy Overstreet*	86/76	Don't Let Smokey Mountain Smoke Get In Your Eyes *Osborne Brothers*	
13/63	Don't Call Me From A Honky Tonk *Johnny And Jonie Mosby*	18/62	Don't Go Near The Eskimos *Ben Colder*	24/67	Don't Let That Doorknob Hit You *Norma Jean*	
42/71	Don't Change On Me *Penny DeHaven*	4/62	Don't Go Near The Indians *Rex Allen*	86/78	Don't Let The Flame Burn Out *Rita Remington*	
1/84	Don't Cheat In Our Hometown *Ricky Skaggs*	12/92	Don't Go Near The Water *Sammy Kershaw*	15/75	Don't Let The Good Times Fool You *Melba Montgomery*	
1/88	Don't Close Your Eyes *Keith Whitley*	6/90	Don't Go Out *Tanya Tucker with T. Graham Brown*	37/73	Don't Let The Green Grass Fool You *O.B. McClinton*	
27/99	Don't Come Cryin' To Me *Vince Gill*	1/87	Don't Go To Strangers *T. Graham Brown*		Don't Let The Stars Get In Your Eyes	
1/67	Don't Come Home A'Drinkin' (With Lovin' On Your Mind) *Loretta Lynn*	88/77	Don't Hand Me No Hand Me Down Love *Beverly Heckel*	1/52	*Skeets McDonald*	
				1/52	*Slim Willet*	
28/82	Don't Come Knockin *Cindy Hurt*	4/45	Don't Hang Around Me Anymore *Gene Autry*	4/52	*Ray Price*	
9/83	Don't Count The Rainy Days *Michael Murphey*			8/53	*Red Foley*	
54/91	Don't Cross Your Heart *Shelby Lynne*	56/71	Don't Hang No Halos On Me *Connie Eaton*	16/71	(Don't Let The Sun Set On You) Tulsa *Waylon Jennings*	
6/44	Don't Cry, Baby *Erskine Hawkins*	1/01	Don't Happen Twice *Kenny Chesney*	14/61	Don't Let Your Sweet Love Die *Reno & Smiley*	
70/68	Don't Cry Baby *Freddie Hart*	30/82	Don't It Break Your Heart *Steve Wariner*	27/00	Don't Lie *Trace Adkins*	
80/81	Don't Cry Baby *Randy Parton*			4/45	Don't Live A Lie *Gene Autry*	
13/70	Don't Cry Daddy *Elvis Presley*	1/77	Don't It Make My Brown Eyes Blue *Crystal Gayle*	12/82	Don't Look Back *Gary Morris*	
29/85	Don't Cry Darlin' *David Allan Coe*			61/80	Don't Look Back *Dickey Lee*	
4/75	Don't Cry Joni *Conway Twitty*	42/80	Don't It Make Ya Wanna Dance *Bonnie Raitt*	11/81	Don't Look Now (But We Just Fell In Love) *Eddy Arnold*	
12/57	Don't Do It Darlin' *Webb Pierce*					
	Don't Drop It			4/47	Don't Look Now (But Your Broken Heart Is Showing) *Ernest Tubb*	
4/54	*Terry Fell*					
69/75	*Fargo Tanner*					

17/97	Don't Love Make A Diamond Shine *Tracy Byrd*	19/76	Don't Stop In My World (If You Don't Mean To Stay) *Billy Walker*		Don't Wait On Me		
1/84	Don't Make It Easy For Me *Earl Thomas Conley*	43/75	Don't Stop Loving Me *Don Gibson*	5/81	Statler Brothers		
60/69	Don't Make Love *Mac Curtis*	45/74	Don't Stop Now *Sherry Bryce*	67/89	Statler Brothers		
29/00	Don't Make Me Beg *Steve Holy*	10/57	Don't Stop The Music *George Jones*	23/69	Don't Wake Me I'm Dreaming *Warner Mack*		
17/01	Don't Make Me Come Over There And Love You *George Strait*	68/78	Don't Stop The Music (You're Playing My Song) *Little David Wilkins*	86/77	Don't Want To Take A Chance (On Loving You) *Ann J. Morton*		
51/95	Don't Make Me Feel At Home *Wesley Dennis*	27/64	Don't Take Advantage Of Me *Bonnie Owens*	5/89	Don't Waste It On The Blues *Gene Watson*		
F/57	Don't Make Me Go *Johnny Cash*	17/70	Don't Take All Your Loving *Don Gibson*	72/67	Don't Waste Your Time *Mary Taylor*		
84/80	Don't Make Me Over *Jennifer Warnes*	4/97	Don't Take Her She's All I Got *Tracy Byrd*		Don't We All Have The Right		
46/85	Don't Make Me Wait On The Moon *Shelly West*		Don't Take It Away	F/70	Roger Miller		
29/78	Don't Make No Promises (You Can't Keep) *Don King*	67/75	Jody Miller	1/88	Ricky Van Shelton		
41/68	Don't Monkey With Another Monkey's Monkey *Johnny Paycheck*	1/79	Conway Twitty		Don't We Belong In Love		
18/72	Don't Pay The Ransom *Nat Stuckey*	5/55	Don't Take It Out On Me *Hank Thompson*	80/81	Rita Remington		
27/83	Don't Plan On Sleepin' Tonight *Steve Wariner*	61/83	Don't Take Much *Peter Isaacson*	40/82	Stephanie Winslow		
52/01	Don't Play Any Love Songs *Jameson Clark*	69/77	Don't Take My Sunshine Away *Ava Barber*	62/67	Don't Wipe The Tears That You Cry For Him (On My Good White Shirt) *Tommy Collins*		
23/63	Don't Pretend *Bobby Edwards*	1/94	Don't Take The Girl *Tim McGraw*		Don't Worry		
49/80	Don't Promise Me Anything (Do It) *Brenda Lee*	1/59	Don't Take Your Guns To Town *Johnny Cash*	1/61	Marty Robbins		
4/76	Don't Pull Your Love (medley) *Glen Campbell*	59/88	Don't Talk To Me *Libby Hurley*	96/78	Glenda Griffith		
47/67	Don't Put Your Hands On Me *Lorene Mann*	11/55	Don't Tease Me *Carl Smith*	73/96	Don't Worry Baby *Beach Boys Feat. Lorrie Morgan*		
32/67	Don't Put Your Hurt In My Heart *Conway Twitty*	2/48	Don't Telephone - Don't Telegraph (Tell A Woman) *Tex Williams*	1/82	Don't Worry 'Bout Me Baby *Janie Fricke*		
25/89	Don't Quit Me Now *James House*	56/99	Don't Tell Me *Lee Ann Womack*		Don't Worry 'Bout The Mule (Just Load The Wagon)		
	Don't Rob Another Man's Castle	55/85	Don't Tell Me Love Is Kind *Almost Brothers*	41/68	Glenn Barber		
1/49	Eddy Arnold	5/91	Don't Tell Me What To Do *Pam Tillis*	44/71	Carl Smith		
6/49	Ernest Tubb & Andrews Sisters		Don't Tell Me Your Troubles	9/89	Don't You *Forester Sisters*		
1/91	Don't Rock The Jukebox *Alan Jackson*	5/59	Don Gibson	8/85	Doncha? *T.G. Sheppard*		
15/77	Don't Say Goodbye *Rex Allen, Jr.*	53/73	Kenny Price	62/91	Don't You Even (Think About Leavin') *Dean Dillon*		
48/88	Don't Say It With Diamonds (Say It With Love) *T.G. Sheppard*	10/74	Don't Tell (That Sweet Ole Lady Of Mine) *Johnny Carver*		Don't You Ever Get Tired Of Hurting Me		
93/79	Don't Say Love *Connie Smith*	1/76	Don't The Girls All Get Prettier At Closing Time *Mickey Gilley*	11/66	Ray Price		
97/79	Don't Say No To Me Tonight *Mark Sexton*	55/88	Don't The Morning Always Come Too Soon *Ray Price*	92/77	Connie Cato		
51/87	Don't Say No Tonight *Mason Dixon*	88/78	Don't Think Twice, It's All Right *Doc & Merle Watson*	11/81	Willie Nelson & Ray Price		
76/83	Don't Say You Love Me (Just Love Me Again) *Mike Campbell*	5/77	Don't Throw It All Away *Dave & Sugar*	1/89	Ronnie Milsap		
34/72	Don't Say You're Mine *Carl Smith*	54/91	Don't Throw Me In The Briarpatch *Keith Palmer*	77/78	Don't You Feel It Now *Betty Martin*		
55/83	Don't Send Me No Angels *Wayne Kemp*	9/53	Don't Throw Your Life Away *Webb Pierce*	49/84	Don't You Give Up On Love *Steve Wariner*		
77/78	Don't Send Me Roses *Sarah*	5/89	Don't Toss Us Away *Patty Loveless*	1/83	Don't You Know How Much I Love You *Ronnie Milsap*		
2/72	Don't She Look Good *Bill Anderson*		Don't Touch Me	12/74	Don't You Think *Marty Robbins*		
8/67	Don't Squeeze My Sharmon *Charlie Walker*	2/66	Jeannie Seely	71/78	Don't You Think It's Time *Tommy Jennings*		
62/88	Don't Start The Fire *Marcia Lynn*	12/66	Wilma Burgess	F/58	Doncha' Think It's Time *Elvis Presley*		
2/52	Don't Stay Away (Till Love Grows Cold) *Lefty Frizzell*	69/79	Jerry Naylor/Kelli Warren	5/78	Don't You Think This Outlaw Bit's Done Got Out Of Hand *Waylong Jennings*		
79/87	Don't Stay If You Don't Love Me *Patsy Sledd*	96/79	Brenda Joyce	23/83	Don't Your Mem'ry Ever Sleep At Night *Steve Wariner*		
86/79	Don't Stay On Your Side Of The Bed Tonight *Ann J. Morton*	20/87	Don't Touch Me There *Charly McClain*		Doncha ..see: Don't You		
9/51	Don't Stay Too Long *Ernest Tubb*	68/96	Don't Touch My Hat *Lyle Lovett*	96/80	Donna-Earth Angel (Medley) *Tucker Williams*		
10/95	Don't Stop *Wade Hayes*	97/79	Don't Treat Me Like A Stranger *Randy Gurley*	6/86	Doo-Wah Days *Mickey Gilley*		
14/76	Don't Stop Believin' *Olivia Newton-John*	64/98	Don't Try To Find Me *Roger Springer*	70/70	Doogie Ray *George Kent*		
		1/86	Don't Underestimate My Love For You *Lee Greenwood*	1/75	Door, The *George Jones*		
				65/97	Door, A *Aaron Tippin*		
					Door I Used To Close		
				28/76	Roy Head		
				91/76	Marilyn Sellars		
					Door Is Always Open		
				75/73	Tennessee Pulleybone		
				70/75	Lois Johnson		
				1/76	Dave & Sugar		

Sound Off (Duckworth Chant)

88/75	Door Number Three *Jimmy Buffett*	91/77	Down To My Pride	60/85	Drifter's Wind *Chuck Pyle*
6/56	Doorstep To Heaven *Carl Smith*		*Linda Hargrove*	48/80	Driftin Away *Miki Mori*
34/64	Double Life *Joe Carson*	41/74	Down To The End Of The Wine	8/67	Drifting Apart *Warner Mack*
30/78	Double S *Bill Anderson*		*Jack Blanchard & Misty Morgan*	96/78	Drifting Lovers *Charlie McCoy*
8/84	Double Shot (Of My Baby's Love)	18/63	Down To The River *Rose Maddox*	11/60	Drifting Texas Sand *Webb Pierce*
	Joe Stampley	75/00	Down With The Old Man (Up With	58/69	Drifting Too Far (From Your
13/49	Double Talkin' Woman *Earl Nunn*		The New) *Randy Travis*		Arms) *June Stearns*
89/79	Double W *Whispering Will*	5/51	Down Yonder *Del Wood*	7/51	Driftwood On The River
40/98	Double Wide Paradise *Toby Keith*	32/73	Downfall Of Me *Sonny James*		*Ernest Tubb*
16/81	Down And Out *George Strait*	64/79	Downhill Stuff *John Denver*	F/70	Drink Boys, Drink *Jim Ed Brown*
65/86	Down At The Mall *Tom T. Hall*	77/83	Downright Broke My Heart	59/69	Drink Canada Dry *Bobby Barnett*
18/67	Down At The Pawn Shop		*Bubba Talbert*	25/80	Drink It Down, Lady *Rex Allen, Jr.*
	Hank Snow	5/01	Downtime *Jo Dee Messina*	3/97	Drink, Swear, Steal & Lie
36/77	Down At The Pool *Johnny Carver*	36/84	Downtown *Dolly Parton*		*Michael Peterson*
4/47	Down At The Roadside Inn	31/71	Dozen Pairs Of Boots *Del Reeves*	2/85	Drinkin' And Dreamin'
	Al Dexter	37/97	Dozen Red Roses		*Waylon Jennings*
2/91	Down At The Twist And Shout		*Tammy Graham*	17/80	Drinkin' And Drivin'
	Mary-Chapin Carpenter	29/70	Drag 'Em Off The Interstate, Sock		*Johnny Paycheck*
9/63	Down By The River *Faron Young*		It To 'Em, J.P. Blues	8/86	Drinkin' My Baby Goodbye
28/97	Down Came A Blackbird		*Dick Curless*		*Charlie Daniels Band*
	Lila McCann	95/80	Draggin' Leather *Mitch Goodson*	1/76	Drinkin' My Baby (Off My Mind)
52/67	Down, Down, Came The World	11/59	Draggin' The River *Ferlin Husky*		*Eddie Rabbitt*
	Bobby Barnett	45/72	Draggin' The River *Warner Mack*		Drinkin' My Way Back Home
1/91	Down Home *Alabama*	87/81	Draw Me A Line *Ray Griff*	63/77	*Shylo*
56/73	Down Home Lovin' Woman		Dream ..see: All I Have To Do Is	10/84	*Gene Watson*
	Andra Willis		Dream Baby (How Long Must I	70/80	Drinkin' Them Long Necks
10/95	Down In Flames *BlackHawk*		Dream)		*Roy Head*
38/70	Down In New Orleans *Buddy Alan*	50/70	*Bob Regan & Lucille Starr*	10/74	Drinkin' Thing *Gary Stewart*
	Down In Tennessee	7/71	*Glen Campbell*		Drinking Champagne
12/86	*John Anderson*	9/83	*Lacy J. Dalton*	35/68	*Cal Smith*
23/95	*Mark Chesnutt*	22/64	Dream House For Sale	4/90	*George Strait*
	Down In The Boondocks		*Red Sovine*	9/55	Drinking Tequila *Jim Reeves*
37/69	*Penny DeHaven*		Dream Lover	79/78	Drinking Them Beers
25/70	*Freddy Weller*	5/71	*Billy "Crash" Craddock*		*Tompall Glaser*
45/68	Down In The Flood	59/79	*Rick Nelson*	20/73	Drinking Wine Spo-Dee O'Dee
	Flatt & Scruggs	59/80	*Tanya Tucker & Glen Campbell*		*Jerry Lee Lewis*
42/85	Down In The Florida Keys	88/86	*Rick Nelson*	63/94	Drive *Steve Wariner*
	Tom T. Hall	94/84	Dream Lover *Susie Brading*	56/97	Drive Me Crazy
68/88	Down In The Orange Grove		Dream Maker		*Thompson Brothers Band*
	John Anderson	61/81	*Shoppe*	6/99	Drive Me Wild *Sawyer Brown*
41/80	Down In The Quarter	69/83	*Tommy Overstreet*		Drive South
	Tommy Overstreet	47/73	Dream Me Home *Mac Davis*	63/90	*Forester Sister & The Bellamy*
81/88	Down On Market Street *Lorie Ann*	40/79	Dream Never Dies *Bill Anderson*		*Brothers*
19/93	Down On My Knees	7/81	Dream Of Me *Vern Gosdin*	2/93	*Suzy Bogguss*
	Trisha Yearwood	7/79	Dream On *Oak Ridge Boys*	72/93	Drive Time *Lisa Stewart*
82/88	Down On The Bayou	18/84	Dream On Texas Ladies	24/94	Drivin' And Cryin' *Steve Wariner*
	Ogden Harless		*Rex Allen, Jr.*	44/70	Drivin' Home *Jerry Smith*
13/83	Down On The Corner *Jerry Reed*	23/73	Dream Painter *Connie Smith*		Drivin' My Life Away
94/79	Down On The Corner At A Bar	80/80	Dream Street Rose	1/80	*Eddie Rabbitt*
	Called Kelly's *Johnny Paycheck*		*Gordon Lightfoot*	56/98	*Rhett Akins*
2/94	Down On The Farm *Tim McGraw*	5/98	Dream Walkin' *Toby Keith*		Drivin' Nails In My Coffin
25/85	Down On The Farm *Charley Pride*	88/73	Dream Weaver *Jacky Ward*	2/46	*Floyd Tillman*
6/79	Down On The Rio Grande	63/93	Dream You	5/46	*Ernest Tubb*
	Johnny Rodriguez		*Pirates Of The Mississippi*	26/84	Drivin' Wheel *Emmylou Harris*
6/89	Down That Road Tonight	32/82	Dreamin' *John Schneider*	68/93	Driving You Out Of My Mind
	Nitty Gritty Dirt Band	32/79	Dreamin's All I Do *Earl Conley*		*Marshall Tucker Band*
58/88	Down The Road *Charly McClain*	10/75	Dreaming My Dreams With You	17/76	Dropkick Me, Jesus *Bobby Bare*
70/90	Down The Road *Mac McAnally*		*Waylon Jennings*		Dropping Out Of Sight
62/74	Down The Road I Go	1/94	Dreaming With My Eyes Open	32/67	*Jimmy Newman*
	Don Williams		*Clay Walker*	35/81	*Bobby Bare*
33/85	Down The Road Mountain Pass	100/78	Dreamland *Gordon Lightfoot*	96/79	Drown In The Flood *Lois Kaye*
	Dan Fogelberg	9/86	Dreamland Express *John Denver*	39/85	Drowning In Memories
59/78	Down The Roads Of Daddy's	46/81	Dreams Can Come In Handy		*T. Graham Brown*
	Dreams *Darrell McCall*		*Cindy Hurt*	25/61	Drunk Again *Lattie Moore*
2/51	Down The Trail Of Achin' Hearts	15/82	Dreams Die Hard *Gary Morris*		(Drunk On Arrival) ..see: D.O.A.
	Hank Snow with Anita Carter	35/77	Dreams Of A Dreamer	94/79	Duel Under The Snow
16/79	Down To Earth Woman		*Darrell McCall*		*Billy Edd Wheeler*
	Kenny Dale	3/68	Dreams Of The Everyday	5/73	Dueling Banjos
2/81	Down To My Last Broken Heart		Housewife *Glen Campbell*		*Eric Weissberg & Steve Mandell*
	Janie Fricke	8/73	Drift Away *Narvel Felts*		(Dukes Of Hazzard) ..see: Theme
2/91	Down To My Last Teardrop	3/91	Drift Off To Dream *Travis Tritt*		From The
	Tanya Tucker	1/81	Drifter *Sylvia*		

Amelia Earhart — Country Gentlemen? — Greenbrier Boys — see Amelia

15/90	**Dumas Walker**	
	Kentucky Headhunters	
24/67	**Dumb Blonde** Dolly Parton	
1/95	**Dust On The Bottle**	
	David Lee Murphy	
44/69	**Dusty Road** Norma Jean	
21/70	**Duty Not Desire** Jeannie C. Riley	
93/84	**Dying To Believe** Jack Greene	

The Eagle Will Fly? Toby Keith

E

27/69 **Each And Every Part Of Me**
 Bobby Lewis
5/45 **Each Minute Seems A Million Years** Eddy Arnold
4/60 **Each Moment ('Spent With You)**
 Ernest Ashworth
4/44 **Each Night At Nine** Floyd Tillman
16/69 **Each Time** Johnny Bush
22/91 **Eagle, The** Waylon Jennings
53/94 **Eagle Over Angel** Brother Phelps
33/91 **Eagle When She Flies** Dolly Parton
35/70 **Early In The Morning** Mac Curtis
14/89 **Early In The Morning And Late At Night** Hank Williams, Jr.
79/75 **Early Morning Love** Sammy Johns
9/66 **Early Morning Rain** George Hamilton IV
9/71 **Early Morning Sunshine** Marty Robbins
28/75 **Early Sunday Morning** Chip Taylor
 Earth Angel ..see: Donna
93/74 **Ease Me To The Ground** Sue Richards
80/77 **Ease My Mind On You** Marie Owens
20/97 **Ease My Troubled Mind** Ricochet
78/83 **Ease The Fever** Carrie Slye
 Easier
61/83 Sandy Croft
91/84 Sandy Croft
20/93 **Easier Said Than Done** Radney Foster
87/81 **Easier To Go** Gene Kennedy & Karen Jeglum
2/77 **East Bound And Down** Jerry Reed
 Easy
45/72 Bobby Hood
F/79 Jimmie Rodgers & Michele
63/78 Easy John Wesley Ryles
76/75 Easy Troy Seals
89/78 Easy Barry Kaye
69/95 **Easy As One, Two, Three** John Bunzow
2/75 **Easy As Pie** Billy "Crash" Craddock
81/83 **Easy Catch** Bubba Talbert
1/93 **Easy Come, Easy Go** George Strait
14/64 **Easy Come-Easy Go** Bill Anderson
68/86 **Easy Does It** Tim Malchak
27/01 **Easy For Me To Say** Clint Black
12/78 **Easy From Now On** Emmylou Harris

 Easy Look
67/75 Kenny Price
12/77 Charlie Rich
1/71 **Easy Loving** Freddie Hart
26/60 **Easy Money** James O'Gwynn
32/83 **Easy On The Eye** Larry Gatlin/Gatlin Brothers
1/52 **Easy On The Eyes** Eddy Arnold
 Easy Part's Over
2/68 Charley Pride
41/80 Steve Wariner
57/87 **Easy To Find** Girls Next Door
26/75 **Easy To Love** Hank Snow
89/79 **Easy To Love** Jimmie Rodgers
5/86 **Easy To Please** Janie Fricke
3/56 **Eat, Drink, And Be Merry (Tomorrow You'll Cry)** Porter Wagoner
 Ebony Eyes
25/61 Everly Brothers
89/79 Orion
77/88 **Echo Me** Margo Smith
2/49 **Echo Of Your Footsteps** Eddy Arnold
1/53 **Eddy's Song** Eddy Arnold
2/63 **8 X 10** Bill Anderson
57/84 **Eight Days A Week** Wright Brothers
40/00 **800 Pound Jesus** Sawyer Brown
43/64 **Eight Years (And Two Children Later)** Claude Gray
1/88 **Eighteen Wheels And A Dozen Roses** Kathy Mattea
93/75 **18 Yellow Roses** C.L. Goodson
7/87 **80's Ladies** K.T. Oslin
64/82 **Either You're Married Or You're Single** Margo Smith
1/59 **El Paso** Marty Robbins
1/76 **El Paso City** Marty Robbins
34/76 **11 Months And 29 Days** Johnny Paycheck
1/72 **Eleven Roses** Hank Williams, Jr.
56/01 **Elisabeth** Billy Gilman
1/84 **Elizabeth** Statler Brothers
 Elvira
95/78 Rodney Crowell
1/81 Oak Ridge Boys
20/94 **Elvis And Andy** Confederate Railroad
31/82 **Elvis Medley** Elvis Presley
90/76 **Emmylou** Brush Arbor
10/97 **Emotional Girl** Terri Clark
3/73 **Emptiest Arms In The World** Merle Haggard
1/71 **Empty Arms** Sonny James
64/89 **Empty Glass** Gary Stewart
47/68 **Empty House** June Stearns
6/50 **Enclosed, One Broken Heart** Eddy Arnold
12/76 **End Is Not In Sight (The Cowboy Tune)** Amazing Rhythm Aces
 End Of The World
2/63 Skeeter Davis
70/82 Judy Taylor
72/00 Allison Paige
82/79 **Endless** David Wills
46/65 **Endless Sleep** Hank Williams, Jr.
 Endlessly
1/70 Sonny James
38/77 Eddie Middleton
13/68 **Enemy, The** Jim Ed Brown
2/65 **Engine Engine #9** Roger Miller

3/66 **England Swings** Roger Miller
75/81 **Enough For You** Brenda Lee
36/65 **Enough Man For You** Ott Stephens
 Eres Tu (Touch The Wind)
67/76 Sonny James
25/77 Johnny Rodriguez
48/94 **Eugene You Genius** Bryan White
2/84 **Ev'ry Heart Should Have One** Charley Pride
 Ev'rybody's Somebody's Fool ..see: Everybody's Somebody's Fool
97/73 **Ev'ryday Woman** Kenny Starr
37/80 **Evangelina** Hoyt Axton
51/98 **Evangeline** Chad Brock
61/80 **Even A Fool Would Let Go** Charlie Rich
 Even Cowgirls Get The Blues
26/80 Lynn Anderson
35/86 Johnny Cash & Waylon Jennings
79/78 **Even Cowgirls Get The Blues** La Costa
17/75 **Even If I Have To Steal** Mel Street
41/96 **Even If I Tried** Emilio
68/97 **Even If It's Wrong** BR5-49
78/82 **Even If It's Wrong** Jimmi Cannon
83/76 **Even If It's Wrong** Ben Reece
16/91 **Even Now** Exile
74/70 **Even The Bad Times Are Good** Jerry Wallace
5/92 **Even The Man In The Moon Is Crying** Mark Collie
68/97 **Even The Wind** Daryle Singletary
59/01 **Even Then** John Michael Montgomery
1/54 **Even Tho** Webb Pierce
55/72 **Evening** Jim Ed Brown
11/84 **Evening Star** Kenny Rogers
30/69 **Ever Changing Mind** Don Gibson
62/94 **Ever-Changing Woman** Brother Phelps
 Ever-Lovin' Woman *Everglade*
73/81 Pat Garrett
67/82 Marlow Tackett
4/82 **Ever, Never Lovin' You** Ed Bruce
37/66 **Ever Since My Baby Went Away** Jack Greene
93/77 **Everlasting (Everlasting Love)** George Hamilton IV
 Everlasting Love
14/79 Narvel Felts
69/79 Louise Mandrell
57/68 **Everlasting Love** Hank Locklin
34/77 **Every Beat Of My Heart** Peggy Sue
86/81 **Every Breath I Take** Eme
 Every Breath You Take
68/83 Rich Landers
69/83 Mason Dixon
51/97 **Every Cowboy's Dream** Rhett Akins
 Every Day ..see: Everyday
64/93 **Every Day When I Get Home** Robert Ellis Orrall
21/76 **Every Face Tells A Story** Olivia Newton-John
3/96 **Every Light In The House** Trace Adkins
3/93 **Every Little Thing** Carlene Carter
36/99 **Every Little Whisper** Steve Wariner

435

49/95 Every Little Word Hal Ketchum	76/79 Everybody Wants To Disco Glenn Barber	39/70 Everything Is Beautiful Ray Stevens
37/00 Every Man For Himself Neal McCoy	52/69 Everybody Wants To Get To Heaven Ed Bruce	63/85 Everything Is Changing Johnny Paycheck
20/86 Every Night Pake McEntire	24/87 Everybody's Crazy 'Bout My Baby Marie Osmond	1/86 Everything That Glitters (Is Not Gold) Dan Seals
26/81 Every Now And Then Brenda Lee		
34/76 Every Now And Then Mac Davis		
2/94 Every Once In A While BlackHawk	40/64 Everybody's Darlin', Plus Mine Browns	40/70 Everything Will Be Alright Claude Gray
82/75 Every Road Leads Back To You Leapy Lee	18/83 Everybody's Dream Girl Dan Seals	98/76 Everything You'd Never Want To Be Joe Brock
2/92 Every Second Collin Raye	14/61 Everybody's Dying For Love Jimmy Newman	Everything's A Waltz ..see: (When You Fall In Love)
21/69 Every Step Of The Way Ferlin Husky	16/99 Everybody's Free (To Get Sunburned) Cledus T. Judd	96/82 Everything's All Right David House
52/88 Every Step Of The Way Wagoneers	42/68 Everybody's Got To Be Somewhere Johnny Dollar	7/83 Everything's Beautiful (In It's Own Way) Dolly Parton & Willie Nelson
38/98 Every Time Pam Tillis		
2/96 Every Time I Get Around You David Lee Murphy	42/00 Everybody's Gotta Grow Up Sometime Sons Of The Desert	78/75 Everything's Broken Down Larry Hosford
61/93 Every Time I Roll The Dice Chris LeDoux	70/70 Everybody's Gotta Hurt Cheryl Poole	2/98 Everything's Changed Lonestar
7/74 Every Time I Turn The Radio On Bill Anderson	Everybody's Had The Blues	93/76 Everything's Coming Up Love Sherry Bryce
	1/73 Merle Haggard	
10/58 Every Time I'm Kissing You Faron Young	85/77 Maury Finney	48/69 Everything's Leaving Wanda Jackson
34/96 Every Time My Heart Calls Your Name John Berry	20/72 Everybody's Reaching Out For Someone Pat Daisy	40/64 Everything's O.K. On The LBJ Lawton Williams
57/96 Every Time She Passes By George Ducas	Everybody's Somebody's Fool	17/75 Everything's The Same (Ain't Nothing Changed) Billy Swan
	16/60 Ernest Tubb	
	24/60 Connie Francis	
Every Time Two Fools Collide	48/79 Debby Boone	12/99 Everytime I Cry Terri Clark
99/77 Lucky Clark	11/88 Everybody's Sweetheart Vince Gill	58/89 Everytime I Get To Dreamin' Josh Logan
1/78 Kenny Rogers & Dottie West	Everyday ..also see: Ev'ryday	74/78 Everytime I Sing A Love Song Jimmie Rodgers
3/75 Every Time You Touch Me (I Get High) Charlie Rich	73/68 Every Day Sleepy LaBeef	
	1/84 Everyday Oak Ridge Boys	Everytime Two Fools Collide ..see: Every Time
89/89 Every Time You Walk In The Room Lolita Jackson	26/86 Everyday James Taylor	
	56/91 Everyday Anne Murray	10/82 Everytime You Cross My Mind (You Break My Heart) Razzy Bailey
1/79 Every Which Way But Loose Eddie Rabbitt	70/71 Everyday Family Man Jimmy Dickens	
28/77 Every Word I Write Dottie West	Everyday I Have To Cry Some	23/88 Everytime You Go Outside I Hope It Rains Burch Sisters
3/62 Everybody But Me Ernest Ashworth	23/69 Bob Luman	
3/97 Everybody Knows Trisha Yearwood	14/77 Joe Stampley	1/97 Everywhere Tim McGraw
54/71 Everybody Knows Jimmy Dean	76/88 Everyday Man Gary Chapman	67/72 Everywhere I Go (He's Already Been There) Tex Williams
17/66 Everybody Loves A Nut Johnny Cash	100/77 Everyday Of My Life Wichita Linemen	24/81 Evil Angel Ed Bruce
25/78 Everybody Loves A Rain Song B.J. Thomas	63/85 Everyday People Margo Smith & Tom Grant	47/66 Evil Off My Mind Burl Ives
		5/66 Evil On Your Mind Jan Howard
56/82 Everybody Loves A Winner Dickey Lee	62/68 Everyday's A Happy Day For Fools Jean Shepard	36/68 Evolution And The Bible Hugh X. Lewis
5/82 Everybody Makes Mistakes Lacy J. Dalton	87/78 Everynight Sensation Durwood Haddock	4/92 Except For Monday Lorrie Morgan
37/75 Everybody Needs A Rainbow Ray Stevens	36/81 Everyone Gets Crazy Now And Then Roger Miller	35/89 Exception To The Rule Mason Dixon
56/74 Everybody Needs A Rainbow Bobby Wright	46/82 Everyone Knows I'm Yours Corbin/Hanner Band	2/60 Excuse Me (I Think I've Got A Heartache) Buck Owens
28/87 Everybody Needs A Hero Gene Watson	5/70 Everything A Man Could Ever Need Glen Campbell	20/85 Eye Of A Hurricane John Anderson
24/85 Everybody Needs Love On Saturday Night Maines Brothers Band	62/93 Everything Comes Down To Money And Love Hank Williams, Jr.	58/69 Eye To Eye LaWanda Lindsey & Kenny Vernon
		37/79 Eyes Big As Dallas Wynn Stewart
28/73 Everybody Needs Lovin' Norro Wilson	42/83 Everything From Jesus To Jack Daniels Tom T. Hall	90/85 Eyes Have It Lee Wright
		85/89 Eyes Never Lie Kamryn Hanks
62/68 Everybody Needs Somebody Compton Brothers	9/97 Everything I Love Alan Jackson	19/83 Eyes Of A Stranger David Wills
	56/70 Everything I Love Hugh X. Lewis	12/60 Eyes Of Love Margie Singleton
70/72 Everybody Oughta Cry Crystal Gayle	Everything I Own	30/84 Eyes That See In The Dark Kenny Rogers
	66/72 Kendalls	
28/68 Everybody Oughta Sing A Song Dallas Frazier	12/76 Joe Stampley	
	51/96 Everything I Own Aaron Tippin	
75/90 Everybody Wants To Be Hank Williams Larry Boone	29/86 Everything I Used To Do Gene Watson	
47/68 Everybody Wants To Be Somebody Else Harden Trio	32/79 Everything I've Always Wanted Porter Wagoner	

436

F

4/87	**Face In The Crowd**	
	Michael Martin Murphey & Holly Dunn	
73/70	**Face Of A Dear Friend** Clay Hart	
1/88	**Face To Face** Alabama	
92/77	**Face To Face** David Allan Coe	
10/60	**Face To The Wall** Faron Young	
25/61	**Facing The Wall** Charlie Walker	
6/88	**Factory, The** Kenny Rogers	
69/83	**Fade To Blue** Ed Hunnicutt	
	Faded Love	
8/50	Bob Wills	
7/63	Patsy Cline	
22/63	Leon McAuliffe	
22/71	Tompall/Glaser Brothers	
3/80	Willie Nelson & Ray Price	
	Faded Love And Winter Roses	
25/69	Carl Smith	
33/79	David Houston	
11/78	**Fadin' In, Fadin' Out**	
	Tommy Overstreet	
36/80	**Fadin' Renegade**	
	Tommy Overstreet	
	Fair And Tender Ladies	
28/64	George Hamilton IV	
30/78	Charlie McCoy	
5/89	**Fair Shake** Foster & Lloyd	
48/67	**Fair Weather Love** Arlene Harden	
	Fairytale	
37/74	Pointer Sisters	
87/80	Rebecca Lynn	
63/98	**Faith** Big House	
13/95	**Faith In Me, Faith In You**	
	Doug Stone	
28/00	**Faith In You** Steve Wariner	
51/99	**Faith Of The Heart** Susan Ashton	
10/84	**Faithless Love** Glen Campbell	
1/83	**Faking Love**	
	T.G. Sheppard & Karen Brooks	
69/92	**Fall** Oak Ridge Boys	
67/71	**Fall Away** Tex Ritter	
6/95	**Fall In Love** Kenny Chesney	
	Fall In Love Again ..see: (Tonight We Just Might)	
10/79	**Fall In Love With Me Tonight**	
	Randy Barlow	
68/96	**Fall Reaching** Chris Ward	
91/77	**Fall Softly Snow**	
	Jim Ed Brown/Helen Cornelius	
4/60	**Fallen Angel** Webb Pierce	
41/84	**Fallen Angel (Flyin' High Tonight)**	
	Gus Hardin	
	Fallen Star	
2/57	Jimmy Newman	
8/57	Ferlin Husky	
1/88	**Fallin' Again** Alabama	
6/81	**Falling Again** Don Williams	
26/60	**Falling Again** Porter Wagoner	
66/80	**Fallin' For You** Jerri Kelly	
90/89	**Falling For You** Donnie Bowser	
2/87	**Fallin' For You For Years**	
	Conway Twitty	
2/85	**Fallin' In Love** Sylvia	
86/83	**Falling In Love** Tari Hensley	
	Fallin' Never Felt So Good	
39/93	Shawn Camp	
52/00	Mark Chesnutt	
8/87	**Fallin' Out** Waylon Jennings	

2/91	**Fallin' Out Of Love**	
	Reba McEntire	
50/75	**Falling** Lefty Frizzell	
100/78	**Falling** Stan Hitchcock	
10/58	**Falling Back To You** Webb Pierce	
85/81	**Falling In** P.J. Parks	
99/88	**Falling In Love Right & Left**	
	Bear Creek Band	
86/80	**Falling In Trouble Again**	
	Sherry Brane	
47/94	**Falling Out Of Love**	
	John & Audrey Wiggins	
74/80	**Falling Together** Nightstreets	
43/92	**Familiar Ground** Michael White	
40/92	**Familiar Pain** Restless Heart	
	Family Bible	
10/60	Claude Gray	
16/61	George Jones	
92/80	Willie Nelson	
95/80	**Family Inn** Hughie Burns	
7/59	**Family Man** Frankie Miller	
35/81	**Family Man** Wright Brothers	
92/76	**Family Man** Al Bolt	
83/76	**Family Reunion** Oak Ridge Boys	
4/79	**Family Tradition**	
	Hank Williams, Jr.	
48/89	**Family Tree**	
	Michael Martin Murphey	
62/92	**Family Tree** Lionel Cartwright	
73/90	**Family Tree** Lee Roy Parnell	
73/98	**Famous First Words** Gil Grand	
81/84	**Famous In Missouri** Tom T. Hall	
	Famous Last Words Of A Fool	
67/83	Dean Dillon	
1/88	George Strait	
30/77	**Fan The Flame, Feed The Fire**	
	Don Gibson	
	Fancy	
26/70	Bobbie Gentry	
8/91	Reba McEntire	
1/81	**Fancy Free** Oak Ridge Boys	
13/71	**Fancy Satin Pillows**	
	Wanda Jackson	
27/79	**Fantasy Island** Freddy Weller	
71/85	**Far Cry From You** Connie Smith	
	Far, Far Away	
11/60	Don Gibson	
12/72	Don Gibson	
5/79	**Farewell Party** Gene Watson	
80/78	**Farm, The** Mel McDaniel	
72/73	**Farm In Pennsyltucky**	
	Jeannie Seely	
82/78	**Farmer, The** Cledus Maggard	
89/78	**Farmer's Song (We Ain't Gonna Work For Peanuts)** Joel Mathis	
21/86	**Farther Down The Line**	
	Lyle Lovett	
73/73	**Farther Down The River (Where The Fishin's Good)**	
	Tennessee Ernie Ford	
17/75	**Farthest Thing From My Mind**	
	Ray Price	
2/94	**Fast As You** Dwight Yoakam	
4/86	**Fast Lanes And Country Roads**	
	Barbara Mandrell	
4/90	**Fast Movin' Train** Restless Heart	
71/67	**Fast Talking Louisiana Man**	
	Merle Kilgore	
41/92	**Faster Gun** Great Plains	
1/76	**Faster Horses (The Cowboy And The Poet)** Tom T. Hall	

75/95	**Fastest Horse In A One Horse Town** Billy Ray Cyrus	
4/47	**Fat Gal** Merle Travis	
88/80	**Fat 'N Sassy** Pacific Steel Co.	
73/96	**Fear Of A Broken Heart**	
	Paul Jefferson	
2/96	**Fear Of Being Alone**	
	Reba McEntire	
71/88	**Fearless Heart** Beards	
15/91	**Feed Jake**	
	Pirates Of The Mississippi	
51/68	**Feed Me One More Lie**	
	Mary Taylor	
45/85	**Feed The Fire** Keith Stegall	
5/90	**Feed This Fire** Anne Murray	
16/81	**Feedin' The Fire** Zella Lehr	
84/82	**Feel** Tom Carlile	
21/76	**Feel Again** Faron Young	
56/71	**Feel Free To Go** Sue Richards	
60/88	**Feel Like Foolin' Around** Exile	
77/86	**Feel Like I'm Falling For You**	
	Two Hearts	
60/95	**Feel Like Makin' Love**	
	Philip Claypool	
10/83	**Feel Right** Tanya Tucker	
55/73	**Feel So Fine** Kenny Vernon	
66/85	**Feel The Fire** Family Brown	
38/78	**Feelin' Better** Hank Williams, Jr.	
69/93	**Feelin' Kind Of Lonely Tonight**	
	Shelby Lynne	
2/86	**Feelin' The Feelin'**	
	Bellamy Brothers	
19/77	**Feeling's Right** Narvel Felts	
97/76	**Feelings** Sarah Johns	
1/75	**Feelins'**	
	Loretta Lynn/Conway Twitty	
96/83	**Feelings Feelin Right**	
	Lee Dresser	
85/90	**Feelings For Each Other**	
	Marilyn Mundy	
26/78	**Feelings So Right Tonight**	
	Don King	
6/00	**Feels Like Love** Vince Gill	
98/77	**Feels So Much Better**	
	Patti Leatherwood	
1/81	**Feels So Right** Alabama	
19/77	**Feet** Ray Price	
30/79	**Fell Into Love** Foxfire	
48/89	**Fellow Travelers** John Conlee	
60/95	**Female Bonding** Brett James	
56/76	**Feminine Touch**	
	Johnny Paycheck	
	Feudin' And Fightin'	
4/47	Dorothy Shay	
5/47	Jo Stafford	
23/95	**Fever, The** Garth Brooks	
43/85	**Few Good Men** Terri Gibbs	
9/91	**Few Good Things Remain**	
	Kathy Mattea	
	Few More Rednecks ..see: (What This World Needs Is) A	
8/90	**Few Ole Country Boys**	
	Randy Travis & George Jones	
29/61	**Fickle Fun** Kitty Wells	
87/73	**Fiddle Man** Red Steagall	
75/73	**Fiddlin' Around** Chet Atkins	
40/86	**Fiddlin' Man**	
	Michael Martin Murphey	
73/75	**Fiddlin' Of Jacques Pierre Bordeaux**	
	Fiddlin' Frenchie Burke	

437

23/74	Field Of Yellow Daisies *Charlie Rich*		Fire On The Mountain ..see: (Frenchie Burke's)	18/76	Flash Of Fire *Hoyt Axton*
40/80	Fifteen Beers *Johnny Paycheck*	62/97	Fire When Ready *Perfect Stranger*	20/75	Flat Natural Born Good-Timin' Man *Gary Stewart*
50/71	Fifteen Beers Ago *Ben Colder*	21/75	Fireball Rolled A Seven	33/69	Flat River, MO. *Ferlin Husky*
24/67	Fifteen Days *Wilma Burgess*		*Dave Dudley*	9/61	Flat Top *Cowboy Copas*
62/87	15 to 33 *Southern Reign*	5/85	Fireman, The *George Strait*	11/69	Flattery Will Get You Everywhere *Lynn Anderson*
1/70	Fifteen Years Ago *Conway Twitty*	73/88	First Came The Feelin' *Gail O'Doski*	1/71	Flesh And Blood *Johnny Cash*
75/96	Fifty-Fifty *Keith Stegall*	98/79	First Class Fool	4/83	Flight 309 To Tennessee
16/78	'57 Chevrolet *Billie Jo Spears*		*Jimmie Peters/Linda K. Lance*		*Shelly West*
	50 Ways To Leave Your Lover	55/87	First Cut Is The Deepest	80/79	Flip Side Of Today *Scott Summer*
85/76	Bob Yarborough		*Ride The River*	78/81	Flo's Yellow Rose *Hoyt Axton*
70/80	Sonny Curtis	9/57	First Date, First Kiss, First Love	8/68	Flower Of Love *Leon Ashley*
1/70	Fightin' Side Of Me		*Sonny James*	36/97	Flowers *Billy Yates*
	Merle Haggard	70/70	First Day *Jane Morgan*		Flowers On The Wall
78/85	Fightin' Fire With Fire	84/78	First Encounter Of A Close Kind	2/66	Statler Brothers
	Razzy Bailey		*Tom Bresh*	6/00	Eric Heatherly
27/92	Fighting Fire With Fire	44/85	First In Line *Everly Brothers*	51/97	Flutter *Jack Ingram*
	Davis Daniel	57/88	First In Line *Shurfire*	12/76	Fly Away *John Denver*
41/91	Fighting For You	46/71	First Love *Penny DeHaven*	8/71	Fly Away Again *Dave Dudley*
	Pirates Of The Mississippi	74/80	First Love Feelings *Glenn Barber*	34/67	Fly Butterfly Fly *Marty Robbins*
24/64	File, The *Bob Luman*	5/95	First Step *Tracy Byrd*	20/83	Fly Into Love *Charly McClain*
	Filipino Baby	96/79	First Step *Marty Martel*	15/99	Fly (the angel song) *Wilkinsons*
2/46	Ernest Tubb	32/64	First Step Down (Is The Longest)		Flyin' South
4/46	Cowboy Copas		*Bob Jennings*	23/63	Hank Locklin
5/46	Texas Jim Robertson	29/79	First Thing Each Morning (Last Thing At Night) *Cliff Cochran*	56/70	Hank Locklin & Danny Davis
5/46	T. Texas Tyler			52/88	Flying On Your Own *Anne Murray*
1/82	Finally *T.G. Sheppard*	1/65	First Thing Ev'ry Morning (And The Last Thing Ev'ry Night) *Jimmy Dean*	99/79	Flying Saucer Man And The Truck Driver *Red Simpson*
	Finally			58/68	Foggy Mountain Breakdown *Flatt & Scruggs*
28/59	Mel Tillis				
9/64	Kitty Wells & Webb Pierce	2/75	First Time *Freddie Hart*		Foggy River
80/76	Find A New Love, Girl *Sunday Sharpe*	10/78	First Time *Billy "Crash" Craddock*	10/48	Kate Smith
		63/84	First Time *McGuffey Lane*	18/68	Carl Smith
73/97	Find My Way Back To My Heart *Alison Krauss & Union Station*	75/80	First Time *Melissa Lewis*	15/64	Followed Closely By My Teardrops *Hank Locklin*
		54/82	First Time Around *Ronnie Rogers*		
	Find Out What's Happening	63/84	First Time Burned *Johnny Rodriguez*	10/81	Following The Feeling *Moe Bandy/Judy Bailey*
15/68	Bobby Bare				
52/70	Barbara Fairchild	24/87	First Time Caller *Juice Newton*		Folsom Prison Blues
40/95	Tanya Tucker	13/92	First Time For Everything *Little Texas*	4/56	Johnny Cash
38/76	Find Yourself Another Puppet *Brenda Lee*			1/68	Johnny Cash
		67/72	First Time For Us *Karen Wheeler*	74/68	Don Bowman (#2)
6/89	Finders Are Keepers *Hank Williams, Jr.*	51/67	First Word *Eddy Arnold*	41/80	Food Blues *Bobby Bare*
		7/85	First Word In Memory Is Me *Janie Fricke*	2/97	Fool, The *Lee Ann Womack*
85/79	Finders Keepers Losers Weepers *Stan Hitchcock with Sue Richards*				Fool, The
		52/94	Fish Ain't Bitin' *David Lee Murphy*	14/56	Sanford Clark
24/83	Finding You *Joe Stampley*	1/87	Fishin' In The Dark *Nitty Gritty Dirt Band*	22/78	Don Gibson
73/74	Fine As Wine *Billy Walker*				Fool
52/75	Fine Time To Get The Blues *Jim Ed Brown*		Fishin' On The Mississippi	18/77	John Wesley Ryles
		62/67	Bob Morris	52/84	Narvel Felts
52/74	Finer Things In Life *Red Steagall*	48/71	Buddy Alan		
41/70	Fingerprints *Freddie Hart*	1/68	Fist City *Loretta Lynn*	31/73	Fool *Elvis Presley*
90/80	Fingertips *Johnny Carver*	29/97	Fit To Be Tied Down *Sammy Kershaw*	6/81	Fool By Your Side *Dave & Sugar*
19/95	Finish What We Started *Diamond Rio*			67/81	Fool, Fool *Brenda Lee*
		30/90	Fit To Be Tied Down *Conway Twitty*	6/67	Fool Fool Fool *Webb Pierce*
64/87	Finishing Touches *Gary Morris*			1/83	Fool For Your Love *Mickey Gilley*
29/76	Fire And Rain *Willie Nelson*	26/60	Five Brothers *Marty Robbins*	1/82	Fool Hearted Memory *George Strait*
1/81	Fire & Smoke *Earl Thomas Conley*	14/59	Five Feet High And Rising *Johnny Cash*		
60/86	Fire At First Sight *Kendalls*			32/99	Fool, I'm A Woman *Sara Evans*
86/79	Fire At First Sight *Linda Hargrove*	67/86	Five Fingers *Ray Price*	40/73	Fool I've Been Today *Jack Greene*
	Fire Goin' Again ..see: (You've Got That)	5/64	Five Little Fingers *Bill Anderson*		
		21/66	Five Little Johnson Girls *Stonemans*	33/83	Fool In Me *Sonny James*
46/71	Fire Hydrant #79 *Jack Blanchard & Misty Morgan*			4/72	Fool Me *Lynn Anderson*
		39/66	Five Miles From Home (Soon I'll See Mary) *Bob Luman*	14/63	Fool Me Once *Connie Hall*
1/83	Fire I Can't Put Out *George Strait*			68/74	Fool Passin' Through *Jim Glaser*
84/81	Fire In The Night *Narvel Felts*	1/90	Five Minutes *Lorrie Morgan*	45/79	Fool Strikes Again *Charlie Rich*
7/87	Fire In The Sky *Nitty Gritty Dirt Band*	16/92	Five O'Clock World *Hal Ketchum*		Fool Such As I
		5/64	500 Miles Away From Home *Bobby Bare*	3/53	Hank Snow
48/85	Fire In The Sky *Wright Brothers*			98/78	Bill Green
40/81	Fire In Your Eyes *Gary Morris*	18/89	5:01 Blues *Merle Haggard*	90/79	Rodney Crowell
65/80	Fire Of Two Old Flames *Roy Head*	76/82	Flame, The *Rita Remington*	5/90	Baillie & The Boys
57/76	Fire On The Bayou *Bill Black Combo*	45/83	Flame In My Heart *Delia Bell*	72/81	Fool That I Am *Rita Coolidge*
		64/83	Flames *Brice Henderson*	62/93	Fool To Fall *Pearl River*

58/80	**Fool Who Fooled Around** *Keith Stegall*	1/70	**For The Good Times** *Ray Price*	1/85	**Forty Hour Week (For A Livin')** *Alabama*
3/84	**Fool's Gold** *Lee Greenwood*		**For The Heart** ..see: Had A Dream	32/65	**Forty Nine, Fifty One** *Hank Locklin*
58/81	**Fool's Gold** *Danny Wood*	27/71	**For The Kids** *Sammi Smith*	21/97	**455 Rocket** *Kathy Mattea*
81/82	**Fool's Gold** *Jimmi Cannon*	F/55	**For The Love Of A Woman Like You** *Faron Young*	20/78	**Four Little Letters** *Stella Parton*
39/89	**Fool's Paradise** *Larry Boone*	6/99	**For You I Will** *Aaron Tippin*	5/66	**Four-O-Thirty Three** *George Jones*
44/98	**Fool's Progress** *Clint Daniels*	50/94	**For Your Love** *Chris LeDoux*	67/91	**Four Scores And Seven Beers Ago** *Ray Benson*
21/85	**Fooled Around And Fell In Love** *T.G. Sheppard*		**For Your Love**	3/65	**Four Strong Winds** *Bobby Bare*
25/79	**Fooled Around And Fell In Love** *Mundo Earwood*	65/70	*Bobby Austin*	21/96	**4 To 1 In Atlanta** *Tracy Byrd*
4/79	**Fooled By A Feeling** *Barbara Mandrell*	52/76	*Bobby Lewis*		**Four Walls**
9/54	**Fooler, A Faker** *Hank Thompson*	78/88	*Tony McGill*	1/57	*Jim Reeves*
4/83	**Foolin'** *Johnny Rodriguez*	16/75	**Forbidden Angel** *Mel Street*	F/57	*Jim Lowe*
2/61	**Foolin' Around** *Buck Owens*	23/63	**Forbidden Lovers** *Lefty Frizzell*	88/76	**Four Wheel Cowboy** *C.W. McCall*
1/94	**Foolish Pride** *Travis Tritt*	23/64	**Forbidden Street** *Carl Butler & Pearl*	27/85	**Four Wheel Drive** *Kendalls*
15/48	**Foolish Tears** *Tex Williams*	12/48	**'Fore Day In The Morning** *Roy Brown*	1/82	**Fourteen Carat Mind** *Gene Watson*
	Fools	77/86	**Foreign Affairs** *Michael Shamblin*	6/90	**Fourteen Minutes Old** *Doug Stone*
19/72	*Johnny Duncan*	7/87	**Forever** *Statler Brothers*	64/68	**1432 Franklin Pike Circle Hero** *Bobby Russell*
3/79	*Jim Ed Brown/Helen Cornelius*	10/84	**Forever Again** *Gene Watson*	9/76	**Fox On The Run** *Tom T. Hall*
9/77	**Fools Fall In Love** *Jacky Ward*	44/97	**Forever And A Day** *Gary Allan*	52/82	**Fragile—Handle With Care** *Cristy Lane*
17/79	**Fools For Each Other** *Johnny Rodriguez*	6/52	**Forever (And Always)** *Lefty Frizzell*		**Frankie's Man, Johnny**
	Fools For Each Other	1/87	**Forever And Ever, Amen** *Randy Travis*	9/59	*Johnny Cash*
96/79	*Guy Clark*	15/61	**Forever Gone** *Ernest Ashworth*	13/59	*Johnny Sea*
49/86	*Ed Bruce with Lynn Anderson*	73/79	**Forever In Blue Jeans** *Neil Diamond*		**Fraulein**
55/79	**Football Card** *Glenn Sutton*	5/48	**Forever Is Ending Today** *Ernest Tubb*	1/57	*Bobby Helms*
	Footprints In The Sand	4/98	**Forever Love** *Reba McEntire*	92/79	*Curtis Potter*
42/81	*Edgel Groves*	17/76	**Forever Lovers** *Mac Davis*	57/82	*Joe Sun with Shotgun*
80/83	*Cristy Lane*	46/01	**Forever Loving You** *John Rich*	79/79	**Freckles** *Shylo*
5/46	**Footprints In The Snow** *Bill Monroe*	10/49	**Forever More** *Jimmy Wakely*	26/74	**Freckles And Polliwog Days** *Ferlin Husky*
92/80	**Footsteps** *Jimmy McMillan*	37/79	**Forever One Day At A Time** *Don Gibson*	90/77	**Freckles Brown** *Red Steagall*
7/62	**Footsteps Of A Fool** *Judy Lynn*	1/91	**Forever Together** *Randy Travis*	10/75	**Freda Comes, Freda Goes** *Bobby G. Rice*
3/95	**For A Change** *Neal McCoy*	38/00	**Forever Works For Me (Monday, Tuesday, Wednesday, Thursday)** *Neal McCoy*	4/53	**Free Home Demonstration** *Eddy Arnold*
2/99	**For A Little While** *Tim McGraw*	14/84	**Forever You** *Whites*	66/99	**Free Me** *Wayne Toups*
12/75	**For A Minute There** *Johnny Paycheck*	21/70	**Forever Yours** *Dottie West*	58/83	**Free Roamin' Mind** *Sonny James*
90/80	**For A Slow Dance With You** *Jerri Kelly*	1/91	**Forever's As Far As I'll Go** *Alabama*	34/76	**Free To Be** *Eddy Raven*
75/88	**For A Song** *Trinity Lane*	67/99	**Forget About It** *Alison Krauss*		**Free To Be Lonely Again**
86/77	**For A While** *Mary MacGregor*	5/84	**Forget About Me** *Bellamy Brothers*	14/80	*Debby Boone*
49/77	**For All The Right Reasons** *Barbara Fairchild*	49/79	**Forget Me Not** *Steve Wariner*	85/80	*Diane Pfeifer*
1/82	**For All The Wrong Reasons** *Bellamy Brothers*	20/61	**Forget The Past** *Faron Young*	68/98	**Freedom** *Wynonna*
80/80	**For As Long As You Want Me** *Peggy Sue*	51/75	**Forgettin' 'Bout You** *Jim Glaser*	73/96	**Freedom** *Ray Hood*
13/91	**For Crying Out Loud** *Davis Daniel*	12/75	**Forgive And Forget** *Eddie Rabbitt*		**Freedom Ain't The Same As Bein' Free**
58/99	**For Crying Out Loud** *Anita Cochran*	23/63	**Forgive Me** *Beverly Buff*	87/73	*Archie Campbell*
64/98	**For Lack Of Better Words** *Restless Heart*	F/55	**Forgive Me, Dear** *Faron Young*	53/77	*Eddy Arnold*
	For Love's Own Sake	16/72	**Forgive Me For Calling You Darling** *Nat Stuckey*	41/71	**Freight Train** *Jim & Jesse*
36/76	*Ed Bruce*	4/53	**Forgive Me John** *Jean Shepard with Ferlin Huskey*	45/65	**Freight Train Blues** *Roy Acuff*
73/80	*Roy Clark*	58/95	**Forgiveness** *Victoria Shaw*		**Freight Train Boogie**
94/73	**For Lovers Only** *Jack Lebsock*	1/85	**Forgiving You Was Easy** *Willie Nelson*	2/46	*Delmore Brothers*
	For Loving Me ..see: (That's What You Get)	60/92	**Forgotten But Not Gone** *Keith Palmer*	5/47	*Red Foley*
	For Loving You	85/80	**Forsaking All The Rest** *Jerri Kelly*	54/70	**Freightliner Fever** *Red Sovine*
1/67	*Bill Anderson & Jan Howard*	9/64	**Fort Worth, Dallas Or Houston** *George Hamilton IV*	25/64	**French Song** *Marion Worth*
72/68	*Skeeter Davis & Don Bowman*	5/52	**Fortunes In Memories** *Ernest Tubb*	93/81	**(Frenchie Burke's) Fire On The Mountain** *Fiddlin' Frenchie Burke*
58/72	**For My Baby** *Cal Smith*	18/82	**Forty And Fadin'** *Ray Price*		**Friday Night Blues**
1/91	**For My Broken Heart** *Reba McEntire*		**Forty Dollars ..see: Ballad Of**	2/80	*John Conlee*
61/00	**For My Wedding** *Don Henley*	19/75	**41st Street Lonely Hearts' Club** *Buck Owens*	89/80	*Sonny Throckmorton*
10/53	**For Now And Always** *Hank Snow*				**Friday Night Feelin'**
42/73	**For Ol' Times Sake** *Elvis Presley*			41/81	*Rich Landers*
75/86	**For Old Time Sake** *Jerry Naylor*			49/83	*Vern Gosdin*
7/56	**For Rent (One Empty Heart)** *Sonny James*			55/80	**Friday Night Fool** *Roger Bowling*
				71/95	**Friday Night Stampede** *Western Flyer*

39/91	**Friday Night's Woman** *Dean Dillon*	
62/69	**Fried Chicken And A Country Tune** *Billy Edd Wheeler*	
9/86	**Friend In California** *Merle Haggard*	
7/78	**Friend, Lover, Wife** *Johnny Paycheck*	
18/69	**Friend, Lover, Woman, Wife** *Claude King*	
50/74	**Friend Named Red** *Brian Shaw*	
68/97	**Friend To Me** *Garth Brooks*	
64/80	**Friendly Family Inn** *Jerry Reed*	
78/84	**Friendly Game Of Hearts** *Penny DeHaven*	
21/65	**Friendly Undertaker** *Jim Nesbitt*	
1/81	**Friends** *Razzy Bailey*	
2/97	**Friends** *John Michael Montgomery*	
	(Friends & Lovers) ..see: Both To Each Other	
93/81	**Friends Before Lovers** *Gabriel*	
68/96	**Friends Don't Drive Friends...** *Deryl Dodd*	
1/90	**Friends In Low Places** *Garth Brooks*	
71/68	**Frisco Line** *Guy Mitchell*	
40/76	**Frog Kissin'** *Chet Atkins*	
	From A Jack To A King	
2/63	*Ned Miller*	
1/89	*Ricky Van Shelton*	
10/75	**From Barrooms To Bedrooms** *David Wills*	
92/83	**From Cotton To Satin** *Jack Greene*	
4/77	**From Graceland To The Promised Land** *Merle Haggard*	
	From Heaven To Heartache	
10/68	*Bobby Lewis*	
22/70	*Eddy Arnold*	
1/97	**From Here To Eternity** *Michael Peterson*	
12/61	**From Here To There To You** *Hank Locklin*	
33/82	**From Levis To Calvin Klein Jeans** *Brenda Lee*	
	(From Now On All My Friends Are Gonna Be) Strangers	
6/65	*Roy Drusky*	
10/65	*Merle Haggard*	
6/78	**From Seven Till Ten** *Loretta Lynn/Conway Twitty*	
65/90	**From Small Things (Big Things One Day Come)** *Nitty Gritty Dirt Band*	
F/74	**From Tennessee To Texas** *Johnny Bush*	
20/69	**From The Bottle To The Bottom** *Billy Walker*	
60/99	**From The Inside Out** *Linda Davis*	
3/89	**From The Word Go** *Michael Martin Murphey*	
43/92	**From The Word Love** *Ricky Skaggs*	
6/98	**From This Moment On** *Shania Twain With Bryan White*	
	From This Moment On	
62/75	*George Morgan*	
95/75	*Bonnie Guitar*	
21/87	**From Time To Time** *Larry Gatlin & Janie Frickie*	
65/71	**From Warm To Cool To Cold** *Lois Johnson*	

	From Where I Stand	
66/96	*Kim Richey*	
67/99	*Suzy Bogguss*	
67/86	**From Where I Stand** *Dobie Gray*	
43/97	**From Where I'm Sitting** *Gary Allan*	
16/75	**From Woman To Woman** *Tommy Overstreet*	
54/99	**From Your Knees** *Matt King*	
51/89	**Frontier Justice** *Cee Cee Chapman & Santa Fe*	
4/50	**Frosty The Snow Man** *Gene Autry*	
41/64	**Frosty Window Pane** *Joe Penny*	
76/83	**Froze In Her Line Of Fire** *Peter Isaacson*	
90/81	**Frustration** *Wyvon Alexander*	
11/67	**Fuel To The Flame** *Skeeter Davis*	
1/67	**Fugitive, The** *Merle Haggard*	
16/87	**Full Grown Fool** *Mickey Gilley*	
87/82	**Full Moon - Empty Pockets** *Montana Skyline*	
22/89	**Full Moon Full Of Love** *k.d. lang*	
1/52	**Full Time Job** *Eddy Arnold*	
31/00	**Fun Of Your Love** *Jennifer Day*	
61/67	**Funny (But I'm Not Laughing)** *Conway Twitty*	
1/72	**Funny Face** *Donna Fargo*	
8/67	**Funny, Familiar, Forgotten, Feelings** *Don Gibson*	
	Funny How Time Slips Away	
23/61	*Billy Walker*	
12/75	*Narvel Felts*	
41/80	*Danny Davis & Willie Nelson*	
53/69	**Funny Thing Happened (On The Way To Miami)** *Tex Ritter*	
9/62	**Funny Way Of Laughin'** *Burl Ives*	
80/90	**Funny Ways Of Loving Me** *Steve Douglas*	

G

5/44	**G.I. Blues** *Floyd Tillman*	
4/53	**Gal Who Invented Kissin'** *Hank Snow*	
58/67	**Gallant Men** *Senator Everett McKinley Dirksen*	
1/69	**Galveston** *Glen Campbell*	
	Gambler, The	
1/78	*Kenny Rogers*	
65/78	*Don Schlitz*	
95/78	*Hugh Moffatt*	
6/53	**Gambler's Guitar** *Rusty Draper*	
22/59	**Gambler's Love** *Rose Maddox*	
	Gamblin' Polka Dot Blues	
8/49	*Tommy Duncan*	
94/77	*Original Texas Playboys*	
5/66	**Game Of Triangles** *Bobby Bare, Norma Jean, Liz Anderson*	
2/69	**Games People Play** *Freddy Weller*	
1/76	**Games That Daddies Play** *Conway Twitty*	
51/91	**Garden, The** *Vern Gosdin*	
44/72	**Garden Party** *Rick Nelson*	
9/67	**Gardenias In Her Hair** *Marty Robbins*	
70/93	**Garth Brooks Has Ruined My Life** *Tim Wilson*	
84/75	**Gather Me** *Marilyn Sellars*	
54/76	**Gator** *Jerry Reed*	

50/65	**'Gator Hollow** *Lefty Frizzell*	
4/57	**Geisha Girl** *Hank Locklin*	
26/82	**General Lee** *Johnny Cash*	
62/70	**Generation Gap** *Jeannie C. Riley*	
86/76	**Gentle Fire** *Johnny Duncan*	
	Gentle On My Mind	
30/67	*Glen Campbell*	
60/67	*John Hartford*	
44/68	*Glen Campbell*	
68/71	**Gentle Rains Of Home** *George Morgan*	
18/77	**Gentle To Your Senses** *Mel McDaniel*	
	Gently Hold Me	
86/79	*Peggy Sue & Sonny Wright*	
84/89	*Andi & The Brown Sisters*	
53/97	**Genuine Rednecks** *David Lee Murphy*	
96/77	**Genuine Texas Good Guy** *Jerry Green*	
10/69	**George (And The North Woods)** *Dave Dudley*	
43/74	**George Leroy Chickashea** *Porter Wagoner*	
25/01	**Georgia** *Carolyn Dawn Johnson*	
17/78	**Georgia In A Jug** *Johnny Paycheck*	
	Georgia Keeps Pulling On My Ring	
50/74	*Little David Wilkins*	
3/77	*Conway Twitty*	
55/82	**Georgia On A Fast Train** *Johnny Cash*	
1/78	**Georgia On My Mind** *Willie Nelson*	
37/71	**Georgia Pineywoods** *Osborne Brothers*	
70/75	**Georgia Rain** *Jerry Wallace*	
16/70	**Georgia Sunshine** *Jerry Reed*	
24/60	**Georgia Town Blues** *Mel Tillis & Bill Phillips*	
83/82	**Georgiana** *Tommy Bell*	
53/87	**Geronimo's Cadillac** *Jeff Stevens & The Bullets*	
73/94	**Get A Little Closer** *Ricky Lynn Gregg*	
	Get A Little Dirt On Your Hands	
14/62	*Bill Anderson*	
46/80	*David Allan Coe & Bill Anderson*	
72/95	**Get Back** *Steve Wariner*	
57/78	**Get Back To Loving Me** *Jim Chesnut*	
33/85	**Get Back To The Country** *Neil Young*	
81/77	**Get Crazy With Me** *Ray Stevens*	
56/77	**Get Down Country Music** *Brush Arbor*	
65/93	**Get In Line** *Larry Boone*	
21/82	**Get Into Reggae Cowboy** *Bellamy Brothers*	
F/79	**Get It Up** *Ronnie Milsap*	
73/81	**Get It While You Can** *Tom Carlile*	
90/81	**Get Me High, Off This Low** *Gary Goodnight*	
3/74	**Get On My Love Train** *La Costa*	
90/89	**Get Out Of My Way** *Burbank Station*	
46/95	**Get Over It** *Woody Lee*	
98/76	**Get Ready-Here I Come** *Don Gibson & Sue Thompson*	

	Get Rhythm	17/86	**Girl Like Emmylou**	41/99	**Give My Heart To You**
F/56	*Johnny Cash*		*Southern Pacific*		*Billy Ray Cyrus*
23/69	*Johnny Cash*	74/72	**Girl Like Her Is Hard To Find**	13/57	**Give My Love To Rose**
27/91	*Martin Delray*		*Bill Rice*		*Johnny Cash*
	(Get The Picture) ..see: **Here's**	46/73	**Girl Like You**		**Give Myself A Party**
	Your Sign		*Tompall/Glaser Brothers*	5/58	*Don Gibson*
63/67	**Get This Stranger Out Of Me**	60/97	**Girl Like You** *Jeffrey Steele*	12/72	*Jeannie C. Riley*
	Lefty Frizzell	77/81	**Girl Like You** *Sonny Throckmorton*	69/78	**Giver, The** *Paul Schmucker*
34/70	**Get Together**	6/69	**Girl Most Likely** *Jeannie C. Riley*	8/88	**Givers And Takers**
	Gwen & Jerry Collins	17/85	**Girl Most Likely To** *B.J. Thomas*		*Schuyler, Knobloch & Bickhardt*
47/74	**Get Up I Think I Love You**	61/70	**Girl Named Johnny Cash**	12/96	**Givin' Water To A Drowning Man**
	Jim Ed Brown		*Jane Morgan*		*Lee Roy Parnell*
5/67	**Get While The Gettin's Good**	74/69	**Girl Named Sam** *Lois Williams*		**Giving Up Easy**
	Bill Anderson	98/74	**Girl Of My Life** *Murry Kellum*	81/79	*Leon Everette*
61/79	**Get Your Hands On Me Baby**	1/65	**Girl On The Billboard** *Del Reeves*	5/81	*Leon Everette*
	Dale McBride	36/79	**Girl On The Other Side**	88/77	**Glad I Waited Just For You**
14/66	**Get Your Lie The Way You Want**		*Nick Noble*		*Reba McEntire*
	It *Bonnie Guitar*	67/94	**Girl Thang**	49/69	**Glad She's A Woman**
4/46	**Get Yourself A Red Head**		*Tammy Wynette With Wynonna*		*Bobby Goldsboro*
	Hank Penny	26/60	**Girl Who Didn't Need Love**	53/72	**Glow Worm** *Hank Thompson*
18/98	**Getcha Some** *Toby Keith*		*Porter Wagoner*	3/97	**Go Away** *Lorrie Morgan*
37/66	**Gettin' Any Feed For Your**	26/70	**Girl Who'll Satisfy Her Man**	6/56	**Go Away With Me**
	Chickens *Del Reeves*		*Barbara Fairchild*		*Wilburn Brothers*
56/70	**Gettin' Back To Norma**	4/97	**Girl's Gotta Do (What A Girl's**	36/01	**Go Back** *Chalee Tennison*
	Bob Luman		**Gotta Do)** *Mindy McCready*	11/55	**Go Back You Fool** *Faron Young*
43/02	**Gettin' Back To You** *Daisy Dern*	35/66	**Girls Get Prettier (Every Day)**	4/54	**Go, Boy, Go** *Carl Smith*
30/65	**Gettin' Married Has Made Us**		*Hank Locklin*	8/64	**Go Cat Go** *Norma Jean*
	Strangers *Dottie West*	62/69	**Girls In Country Music**	56/85	**Go Down Easy** *Dan Fogelberg*
	Gettin' Over You		*Bobby Braddock*	38/90	**Go Down Swingin'** *Wild Rose*
46/81	*Tim Rex And Oklahoma*	1/85	**Girls Night Out** *Judds*	33/80	**Go For The Night** *Freddy Weller*
49/84	*Mason Dixon*	42/99	**Girls Of Summer** *Neal McCoy*	10/61	**Go Home** *Flatt & Scruggs*
29/60	**Getting Old Before My Time**	7/87	**Girls Ride Horses Too**	55/81	**Go Home And Go To Pieces**
	Merle Kilgore		*Judy Rodman*		*Donna Hazard*
28/81	**Getting Over You Again**	10/94	**Girls With Guitars** *Wynonna*	23/66	**Go Now Pay Later** *Liz Anderson*
	Ray Price	14/81	**Girls, Women And Ladies**	2/00	**Go On** *George Strait*
	Getting Over You Again		*Ed Bruce*	13/62	**Go On Home** *Patti Page*
90/76	*Dale McBride*	2/88	**Give A Little Love** *Judds*	14/95	**Go Rest High On That Mountain**
67/79	*Dale McBride*	24/73	**Give A Little, Take A Little**		*Vince Gill*
41/01	**Getting There** *Terri Clark*		*Barbara Mandrell*	72/98	**Go Tell It On The Mountain**
5/90	**Ghost In This House** *Shenandoah*	13/87	**Give Back My Heart** *Lyle Lovett*		*Garth Brooks*
	(Ghost) Riders In The Sky ..see:	43/89	**Give 'Em My Number**	52/73	**Go With Me**
	Riders In The Sky		*Janie Frickie*		*Don Gibson & Sue Thompson*
58/75	**Ghost Story** *Susan Raye*	48/85	**Give Her All The Roses (Don't**	51/01	**God Bless America** *LeAnn Rimes*
58/90	**Ghost Town** *Zaca Creek*		**Wait Until Tomorrow)**	16/69	**God Bless America Again**
49/66	**Giddyup Do-Nut** *Don Bowman*		*Tom Jones*		*Bobby Bare*
1/66	**Giddyup Go** *Red Sovine*	24/71	**Give Him Love** *Patti Page*	48/97	**God Bless The Child**
10/66	**Giddyup Go - Answer**	97/83	**Give It Back** *Brenda Libby*		*Shania Twain*
	Minnie Pearl		**Give Me ..also see: Gimme**		**God Bless The USA**
4/88	**Gift, The** *McCarters*	15/49	**Give Me A Hundred Reasons**	7/84	*Lee Greenwood*
51/97	**Gift, The**		*Ann Jones*	16/01	*Lee Greenwood*
	Collin Raye with Jim Brickman	9/50	**Give Me A Little Old Fashioned**	4/93	**God Blessed Texas** *Little Texas*
34/80	**Gift From Missouri** *Jim Weatherly*		**Love** *Ernest Tubb*	49/02	**God, Family And Country**
64/89	**Gift Of Love** *David Ball*	52/94	**Give Me A Ring Sometime**		*Craig Morgan*
14/79	**Gimme Back My Blues**		*Lisa Brokop*	40/00	**God Gave Me You** *Bryan White*
	Jerry Reed	10/84	**Give Me Back That Old Familiar**	32/68	**God Help You Woman** *Jim Glaser*
35/70	**Ginger Is Gentle And Waiting For**		**Feeling** *Whites*	87/75	**God Is Good** *Betty Jean Robinson*
	Me *Jim Ed Brown*	9/64	**Give Me 40 Acres (To Turn This**	22/78	**God Knows** *Debby Boone*
40/78	**Girl At The End Of The Bar**		**Rig Around)** *Willis Brothers*	91/76	**God Loves Us (When We All Sing**
	John Anderson	3/89	**Give Me His Last Chance**		**Together)** *Sami Jo*
65/67	**Girl Crazy** *Carl Belew*		*Lionel Cartwright*	11/78	**God Made Love** *Mel McDaniel*
22/68	**Girl Don't Have To Drink To Have**	1/52	**Give Me More, More, More (Of**	10/84	**God Must Be A Cowboy**
	Fun *Wanda Jackson*		**Your Kisses)** *Lefty Frizzell*		*Dan Seals*
15/64	**Girl From Spanish Town**	90/74	**Give Me One Good Reason**	39/78	**God Must Have Blessed America**
	Marty Robbins		*Dickey Lee*		*Glen Campbell*
58/94	**Girl From Yesterday** *Eagles*	1/84	**Give Me One More Chance** *Exile*	3/99	**God Must Have Spent A Little**
F/78	**Girl I Can Tell (You're Trying To**	3/95	**Give Me One More Shot** *Alabama*		**More Time On You**
	Work It Out) *Waylon Jennings*	60/96	**Give Me Some Wheels**		*Alabama (featuring *NSYNC)*
3/62	**Girl I Used To Know**		*Suzy Bogguss*	9/50	**God Please Protect America**
	George Jones		**(Give Me Someone I Can Love)**		*Jimmie Osborne*
10/02	**Girl In Love** *Robin English*		..see: **Danger List**	69/99	**God Rest Ye Merry Gentlemen**
36/72	**Girl In New Orleans** *Sammi Smith*	1/87	**Give Me Wings** *Michael Johnson*		*Garth Brooks*

The Good Life (?)

9/56	**God Was So Good** Jimmy Newman	49/76	**Gone At Last** Johnny Paycheck (with Charnissa)	58/94	**Good Girls Go To Heaven** Charlie Floyd
18/87	**God Will** Lyle Lovett	60/88	**Gone But Not Forgotten** Cee Cee Chapman & Santa Fe	29/87	**Good God, I Had It Good** Pake McEntire
10/84	**God Won't Get You** Dolly Parton	1/95	**Gone Country** Alan Jackson		**Good Hearted Woman**
73/96	**God's Country** Marcus Hummon	4/99	**Gone Crazy** Alan Jackson	3/72	Waylon Jennings
25/75	**God's Gonna Get'cha (For That)** George Jones & Tammy Wynette		**Gone Girl**	1/76	Waylon Jennings & Willie Nelson
	Gods Were Angry With Me	23/70	Tompall/Glaser Brothers	65/99	**Good Idea Tomorrow** Deryl Dodd
9/48	Eddie Kirk	44/78	Johnny Cash	57/75	**Good Lord Giveth (And Uncle Sam Taketh Away)** Webb Pierce
3/50	Margaret Whiting & Jimmy Wakely	86/87	**Gone, Gone, Gone** Brenda Cole (Gone Hillbilly Nuts) ..see: Little Ramona	53/85	**Good Love Died Tonight** Leon Everette
74/99	**Godspeed (Sweet Dreams)** Radney Foster	24/67	**Gone, On The Other Hand** Tompall/Glaser Brothers		**Good Love Is Like A Good Song**
69/90	**Goin' By The Book** Johnny Cash	24/72	**Gone (Our Endless Love)** Billy Walker	23/73	Bob Luman
5/83	**Goin' Down Hill** John Anderson	48/98	**Gone Out Of My Mind** Doug Stone	88/80	Nancy Ruud
36/66	**Goin' Down The Road (Feelin' Bad)** Skeeter Davis	51/96	**Gone (That'll Be Me)** Dwight Yoakam	1/71	**Good Lovin' (Makes It Right)** Tammy Wynette
1/88	**Goin' Gone** Kathy Mattea	94/78	**Gone To Alabama** Mickey Newbury	21/80	**Good Lovin' Man** Gail Davies
79/78	**Goin' Home** Ron Shaw	1/80	**Gone Too Far** Eddie Rabbitt	27/71	**Good Man** June Carter Cash
50/70	**Goin' Home To Your Mother** Hagers	62/67	**Gone With The Wine** Ray Pillow	55/70	**Good Morning** Leapy Lee
99/77	**Goin' Skinny Dippin'** Mayf Nutter	2/45	**Gonna Build A Big Fence Around Texas** Gene Autry	1/02	**Good Morning Beautiful** Steve Holy
	Goin' Steady	F/56	**Gonna Come Get You** George Jones	30/72	**Good Morning Country Rain** Jeannie C. Riley
2/53	Faron Young		**Gonna Find Me A Bluebird**		**Good Morning, Dear**
5/70	Faron Young	3/57	Marvin Rainwater	67/68	Frank Ifield
2/95	**Goin' Through The Big D** Mark Chesnutt	12/57	Eddy Arnold	71/68	Don Gibson
43/88	**Goin' To Work** Judy Rodman	1/95	**Gonna Get A Life** Mark Chesnutt		**Good Morning Loving**
60/00	**Goin' Under Gettin' Over You** Brooks & Dunn		**Gonna Get Along Without You Now**	61/74	Larry Kingston
74/71	**Going Back To Louisiana** Ernie Rowell	8/64	Skeeter Davis	91/75	Larry Kingston
78/78	**Going Down Slow** Cates Sisters	72/80	Cates Sisters	43/64	**Good Morning Self** Jim Reeves
65/96	**Goin', Goin', Gone** Thrasher Shiver	4/83	**Gonna Go Huntin' Tonight** Hank Williams, Jr.	37/77	**Good 'N' Country** Kathy Barnes
1/84	**Going, Going, Gone** Lee Greenwood	45/82	**Gonna Have A Party** Kieran Kane	9/73	**Good News** Jody Miller
35/96	**Going, Going, Gone** Neal McCoy		**Gonna Have Love**	27/75	**Good News, Bad News** Eddy Raven
45/79	**Going, Going, Gone** Mary K. Miller	10/65	Buck Owens	51/84	**Good Night For Falling In Love** Hillary Kanter
31/68	**Going Home For The Last Time** Kenny Price	76/89	Buck Owens	18/76	**Good Night Special** Little David Wilkins
43/00	**Going Nowhere** Wynonna	51/98	**Gonna Have To Fall** Shane Stockton	19/83	**Good Night's Love** Tammy Wynette
5/92	**Going Out Of My Mind** McBride & The Ride	67/68	**Gonna Miss Me** Homesteaders		**(Good Ol' Boys) ..see: Good Ole Boys, & Theme From The Dukes Of Hazzard**
68/68	**Going Out To Tulsa** Johnny Seay	1/88	**Gonna Take A Lot Of River** Oak Ridge Boys	47/97	**Good Ol' Fashioned Love** Tracy Byrd
14/92	**Going Out Tonight** Mary-Chapin Carpenter	39/82	**Gonna Take My Angel Out Tonight** Ronnie Rogers	15/81	**Good Ol' Girls** Sonny Curtis
17/63	**Going Through The Motions (Of Living)** Sonny James	61/86	**Good And Lonesome** Lowes	81/82	**Good Old Days** Cristy Lane
81/87	**Going To California** Danny Shirley	57/90	**Good As Gone** Joe Barnhill	35/73	**Good Old Days (Are Here Again)** Buck Owens & Susan Raye
1/83	**Going Where The Lonely Go** Merle Haggard	4/97	**Good As I Was To You** Lorrie Morgan	31/74	**Good Old Fashioned Country Love** Don Gibson & Sue Thompson
93/81	**Gold Cadillac** Tom Carlile	80/77	**Good Cheatin' Songs** Carmol Taylor	55/77	**Good Old Fashioned Saturday Night Honky Tonk Barroom Brawl** Vernon Oxford
2/52	**Gold Rush Is Over** Hank Snow	25/63	**Good Country Song** Hank Cochran	16/83	**Good Ole Boys** Jerry Reed
11/66	**Golden Guitar** Bill Anderson	12/01	**Good Day To Run** Darryl Worley	2/80	**Good Ole Boys Like Me** Don Williams
41/76	**Golden Oldie** Anne Murray		**Good Deal, Lucille**	1/94	**Good Run Of Bad Luck** Clint Black
1/76	**Golden Ring** George Jones & Tammy Wynette	8/54	Al Terry	34/70	**Good Thing** Bill Wilbourn & Kathy Morrison
	Golden Rocket	18/69	Carl Smith	2/73	**Good Things** David Houston
1/51	Hank Snow	62/74	**Good Enough To Be Your Man** Brian Shaw		**Good Time ..also see: Goodtime**
38/70	Jim & Jesse	7/71	**Good Enough To Be Your Wife** Jeannie C. Riley	3/69	**Good Time Charlie's** Del Reeves
1/79	**Golden Tears** Dave & Sugar	81/77	**Good Evening Henry** Peggy Sue	1/90	**Good Times** Dan Seals
51/93	**Golden Years** Holly Dunn	10/90	**Good Friends, Good Whiskey, Good Lovin'** Hank Williams, Jr.		**Good Times**
	Gone	84/81	**Good Friends Make Good Lovers** Jerry Reed	44/68	Willie Nelson
1/57	Ferlin Husky	91/79	**Good Gal Is Hard To Find** Hank Snow	25/81	Willie Nelson
36/80	Ronnie McDowell			50/00	**Good Times** Anita Cochran
34/74	**Gone** Nancy Wayne				
5/92	**Gone As A Girl Can Get** George Strait				

57/87 **Good Timin' Shoes** *Ronnie Rogers*	10/89 **Gospel According To Luke** *Skip Ewing*	32/66 **Great El Tigre (The Tiger)** *Stu Phillips*
21/01 **Good Way To Get On My Bad Side** *Tracy Byrd*	**Got Leaving On Her Mind** 54/68 *Mac Wiseman* 14/73 *Nat Stuckey*	8/75 **Great Expectations** *Buck Owens* 58/73 **Great Filling Station Holdup** *Jimmy Buffett*
1/76 **Good Woman Blues** *Mel Tillis*	82/81 **Got Lucky Last Night** *Jerry Jeff Walker*	10/48 **Great Long Pistol** *Jerry Irby*
67/77 **Good Woman Likes To Drink With The Boys** *Jimmie Rodgers*	**Got My Heart Set On You** 1/86 *John Conlee*	63/74 **Great Mail Robbery** *Rex Allen, Jr.* 46/68 **Great Pretender** *Lamar Morris*
12/74 **Good Woman's Love** *Jerry Reed*	72/86 *Mason Dixon*	8/70 **Great White Horse** *Buck Owens & Susan Raye*
Good Year For The Roses 2/71 *George Jones* 56/94 *George Jones With Alan Jackson*	7/85 **Got No Reason Now For Goin' Home** *Gene Watson*	26/99 **Greatest, The** *Kenny Rogers* 53/84 **Greatest Gift Of All** *Kenny Rogers & Dolly Parton*
Goodbye 73/71 *David Frizzell* 19/74 *Rex Allen, Jr.* 22/79 *Eddy Arnold*	1/72 **Got The All Overs For You (All Over Me)** *Freddie Hart* 10/87 **Gotta Get Away** *Sweethearts Of The Rodeo*	94/80 **Greatest Love Affair** *Chuck Woolery* 3/92 **Greatest Man I Never Knew** *Reba McEntire*
38/72 **Goodbye** *David Rogers* 39/67 **Goodbye City, Goodbye Girl** *Wobb Pioroo*	41/69 **Gotta Get To Oklahoma ('Cause California's Gettin' To Me)** *Hagers*	22/64 **Greatest One Of All** *Melba Montgomery* 88/76 **Greatest Show On Earth** *Little David Wilkins*
13/00 **Goodbye Earl** *Dixie Chicks* 86/80 **Goodbye Eyes** *Pebble Daniel*	4/46 **Gotta Get Together With My Gal** *Elton Britt*	**Green Berets ..see: Ballad Of** 78/73 **Green Door** *Mayf Nutter*
24/84 **Goodbye Heartache** *Louise Mandrell*	9/87 **Gotta Have You** *Eddie Rabbitt* 12/86 **Gotta Learn To Love Without You** *Michael Johnson*	95/81 **Green Eyed Girl** *Sean Morton Downey* **Green Eyes**
70/92 **Goodbye Highway** *Darryl & Don Ellis* 71/84 **Goodbye Highway** *Pam Tillis*	4/78 **Gotta' Quit Lookin' At You Baby** *Dave & Sugar*	37/82 *Tom Carlile* 62/87 *Danny Davis & Dona Mason* 82/85 **Green Eyes** *Kathy Twitty*
45/00 **Goodbye Is The Wrong Way To Go** *Wade Hayes*	**Gotta Travel On** 5/59 *Billy Grammer* 15/59 *Bill Monroe*	4/65 **Green, Green Grass Of Home** *Porter Wagoner*
75/71 **Goodbye Jukebox** *Bobby Lord* 12/63 **Goodbye Kisses** *Cowboy Copas*	91/78 *Shylo* 70/93 **Graceland** *Willie Nelson*	57/70 **Green Green Valley** *Tex Ritter* 7/48 **Green Light** *Hank Thompson*
22/59 **Goodbye Little Darlin'** *Johnny Cash*	69/67 **Grain Of Salt** *Penny Starr* 93/77 **Grand Ole Blues** *Troy Seals*	11/67 **Green River** *Waylon Jennings* 53/73 **Green Snakes On The Ceiling** *Johnny Bush*
32/89 **Goodbye Lonesome, Hello Baby Doll** *Lonesome Strangers*	97/73 **Grand Ole Opry Song** *Nitty Gritty Dirt Band* **Grand Tour**	90/77 **Greenback Shuffle** *King Edward IV & The Knights*
Goodbye Marie 17/81 *Bobby Goldsboro* 47/86 *Kenny Rogers*	1/74 *George Jones* 38/93 *Aaron Neville*	26/61 **Greener Pastures** *Stonewall Jackson*
93/77 **Goodbye My Friend** *Engelbert Humperdinck*	16/78 **Grandest Lady Of Them All** *Conway Twitty*	23/75 **Greener Than The Grass (We Laid On)** *Tanya Tucker*
11/94 **Goodbye Says It All** *BlackHawk* 62/90 **Goodbye, So Long, Hello** *Prairie Oyster*	**Grandma Got Run Over By A Reindeer** 92/83 *Elmo & Patsy* 64/97 *Elmo & Patsy*	49/68 **Greenwich Village Folk Song Salesman** *Jim & Jesse* 63/71 **Greystone Chapel** *Glen Sherley*
53/87 **Goodbye Song** *Gene Stroman* 72/67 **Goodbye Swingers** *Glen Garrison*	48/99 *Elmo & Patsy* 1/72 **Grandma Harp** *Merle Haggard*	4/46 **Grievin' My Heart Out For You** *Jimmie Davis*
7/88 **Goodbye Time** *Conway Twitty* 20/67 **Goodbye Wheeling** *Mel Tillis*	**(Grandma's Diary) ..see: Johnny, My Love**	9/59 **Grin And Bear It** *Jimmy Newman* **(Grits And Groceries) ..see: If I Don't Love You**
8/87 **Goodbyes All We've Got Left** *Steve Earle*	64/89 **Grandma's Old Wood Stove** *Sanders*	42/69 **Groovy Grubworm** *Harlow Wilcox*
56/73 **Goodbyes Come Hard For Me** *Kenny Serratt*	9/81 **Grandma's Song** *Gail Davies* 1/86 **Grandpa (Tell Me 'Bout The Good Old Days)** *Judds*	50/00 **Grow Young With You** *Coley McCabe* 39/69 **Growin' Up** *Tex Ritter*
83/78 **Goodbyes Don't Come Easy** *Mack White* 91/74 **Goodbyes Don't Come Easy** *Warner Mack*	23/96 **Grandpa Told Me So** *Kenny Chesney* 82/88 **Grass Is Greener** *Teddy Spencer*	1/01 **Grown Men Don't Cry** *Tim McGraw* **(Grundy County Auction Incident) ..see: Sold**
62/66 **Goodie Wagon** *Billy Large* 66/99 **Goodnight** *Suzy Bogguss*	15/49 **Grass Looks Greener Over Yonder** *Hank Thompson*	16/90 **Guardian Angels** *Judds*
Goodnight Irene 1/50 *Red Foley–Ernest Tubb* 5/50 *Moon Mullican*	24/67 **Grass Won't Grow On A Busy Street** *Kenny Price* 71/96 **Gravitational Pull** *Chris LeDoux*	19/71 **Guess Away The Blues** *Don Gibson* 18/66 **Guess My Eyes Were Bigger Than My Heart** *Conway Twitty*
53/76 **Goodnight My Love** *Randy Barlow*	F/70 **Grazin' In Greener Pastures** *Ray Price*	1/58 **Guess Things Happen That Way** *Johnny Cash*
6/96 **Goodnight Sweetheart** *David Kersh*	83/76 **(Great American) Classic Cowboy** *Penny DeHaven*	42/64 **Guess What, That's Right, She's Gone** *Hank Williams, Jr.*
3/54 **Goodnight, Sweetheart, Goodnight** *Johnnie & Jack* **Goodtime Charlie's Got The Blues**	**Great Balls Of Fire** 1/58 *Jerry Lee Lewis* F/79 *Dolly Parton* 67/79 **Great Chicago Fire** *Faron Young*	7/71 **Guess Who** *Slim Whitman* 18/74 **Guess Who** *Jerry Wallace* 47/79 **Guess Who Loves You** *Mary K. Miller*
63/72 *Danny O'Keefe* 41/79 *Red Steagall* 63/84 *Leon Russell*	12/74 **Great Divide** *Roy Clark* 41/90 **Great Divide** *Gene Watson*	
83/79 **Goody Goody** *Rebecca Lynn* 24/67 **Goody, Goody Gumdrop** *Wilburn Brothers*		

	Guilty			**Hallelujah, I Love You So**		43/67	**Happiness Means You**
3/63	Jim Reeves		15/85				Kitty Wells & Red Foley
92/85	Merle Kilgore			George Jones with Brenda Lee			**Happiness Of Having You**
9/83	**Guilty** Statler Brothers		22/68	**Hammer And Nails** Jimmy Dean		69/71	Jay Lee Webb
34/98	**Guilty** Warren Brothers		34/93	**Hammer And Nails** Radney Foster		3/76	Charley Pride
37/82	**Guilty Eyes** Bandana		70/00	**Hampsterdance Song**		47/71	**Happy Anniversary** Roy Rogers
81/86	**Guilty Eyes** Darlene Austin			Hampton The Hampster		3/65	**Happy Birthday** Loretta Lynn
61/69	**Guilty Street** Kitty Wells		94/77	**Hand Me Another Of Those**		1/79	**Happy Birthday Darlin'**
8/49	**Guitar Boogie**			Mickey Newbury			Conway Twitty
	Arthur "Guitar Boogie" Smith		33/97	**Hand Of Fate** Sons Of The Desert		3/84	**Happy Birthday Dear Heartache**
	Guitar Man		52/73	**Hand Of Love** Billy Walker			Barbara Mandrell
53/67	Jerry Reed		6/87	**Hand That Rocks The Cradle**		7/61	**Happy Birthday To Me**
1/81	Elvis Presley			Glen Campbell with Steve Wariner			Hank Locklin
	Guitar Polka		11/61	**Hand You're Holding Now**			**Happy Country Birthday Darling**
1/46	Al Dexter			Skeeter Davis		72/82	Rodney Lay
3/46	Rosalie Allen		19/78	**Handcuffed To A Heartache**		86/82	Ronnie Rogers
7/86	**Guitar Town** Steve Earle			Mary K. Miller			**Happy Day ..see: (It's Gonna Be A)**
4/86	**Guitars, Cadillacs** Dwight Yoakam		64/99	**Handful Of Water**			
60/70	**Gun, The** Bob Luman			Chalee Tennison		89/78	**Happy Days** Roy Clark
1/96	**Guys Do It All The Time**		65/73	**Handfull Of Dimes**		68/99	**Happy Ever After**
	Mindy McCready			Jack Blanchard & Misty Morgan			T. Graham Brown
5/71	**Gwen (Congratulations)**		5/99	**Hands Of A Working Man**		54/72	**Happy Everything** Bonnie Guitar
	Tommy Overstreet			Ty Herndon		2/98	**Happy Girl** Martina McBride
56/85	**Gypsies In The Palace**		62/84	**Handsome Man**		81/78	**Happy Go Lucky Morning**
	Jimmy Buffett			Karen Taylor-Good			Terri Hollowell
25/87	**Gypsies On Parade**		75/82	**Handy Man** Joel Hughes			**Happy, Happy Birthday Baby**
	Sawyer Brown		2/74	**Hang In There Girl** Freddie Hart		36/72	Sandy Posey
69/82	**Gypsy And Joe** Sammi Smith			**Hang On Feelin'**		1/86	Ronnie Milsap
43/79	**Gypsy Eyes** Terri Sue Newman		97/76	Sherry Bryce			**Happy Heart ..see: (I've Got A)**
16/71	**Gypsy Feet** Jim Reeves		63/78	Red Steagall		49/74	**Happy Hour** Tony Booth
52/68	**Gypsy King** Kitty Wells		1/85	**Hang On To Your Heart** Exile		10/62	**Happy Journey** Hank Locklin
64/68	**Gypsy Man** Buddy Knox		50/91	**Hang Up The Phone**		92/79	**Happy Sax** Maury Finney
81/74	**Gypsy Queen** Chuck Glaser			Eddie Rabbitt		58/71	**Happy Songs Of Love**
98/77	**Gypsy River** Jack Paris			**Hang Your Head In Shame**			Tennessee Ernie Ford
			3/45	Bob Wills		2/68	**Happy State Of Mind**
	H		4/45	Red Foley			Bill Anderson
			9/83	**Hangin' Around** Whites		22/68	**Happy Street** Slim Whitman
			34/64	**Hangin' Around** Wilburn Brothers			**Happy To Be Unhappy**
63/74	**Habit I Can't Break** Nick Nixon		4/94	**Hangin' In** Tanya Tucker		11/63	Gary Buck
	Had A Dream (For The Heart)		30/79	**Hangin' In And Hangin' On**		50/64	Leroy Van Dyke
45/76	Elvis Presley			Buck Owens		9/66	**Happy To Be With You**
17/84	Judds		67/96	**Hangin' In And Hangin' On**			Johnny Cash
9/49	**Hadacol Boogie** Bill Nettles			David Ball		8/79	**Happy Together** T.G. Sheppard
45/85	**Haircut Song** Ray Stevens			**Hangin' On**		7/67	**Happy Tracks** Kenny Price
80/77	**Half A Love** Roy Clark		37/67	Gosdin Bros.		87/80	**Harbor Lights** Rusty Draper
25/63	**Half A Man** Willie Nelson		54/67	Leon Ashley & Margie Singleton		76/85	**Hard Act To Follow** Keith Whitley
8/58	**Half A Mind** Ernest Tubb		16/77	Vern Gosdin			**Hard Baby To Rock**
	Half As Much		59/84	Lane Brody		64/85	Tari Hensley
2/52	Hank Williams		58/96	**Hangin' On** Rich McCready		71/89	Susi Beatty
23/76	Sheila Tilton		82/74	**Hangin' On To What I've Got**			**Hard Candy Christmas**
16/59	**Half-Breed** Marvin Rainwater			Frank Myers		8/82	Dolly Parton
91/73	**Half-Empty Bed** Stan Hitchcock		44/87	**Hangin' Out In Smokey Places**		73/97	Dolly Parton
8/93	**Half Enough** Lorrie Morgan			Marshall Tucker Band		36/92	**Hard Days And Honky Tonk**
80/89	**Half Heaven Half Heartache**		26/71	**Hanging Over Me** Jack Greene			**Nights** Earl Thomas Conley
	Leah Marr		15/59	**Hanging Tree** Marty Robbins		31/70	**Hard, Hard Traveling Man**
F/78	**Half My Heart's In Texas**		14/49	**Hangman's Boogie**			Dick Curless
	Ernest Tubb			Cowboy Copas		30/80	**Hard Hat Days And Honky Tonk**
30/64	**Half Of This, Half Of That**		12/61	**Hangover Tavern**			**Nights** Red Steagall
	Wynn Stewart			Hank Thompson			**Hard Headed Heart**
2/87	**Half Past Forever (Till I'm Blue In**		12/73	**Hank** Hank Williams, Jr.		78/87	Tim Johnson
	The Heart) T.G. Sheppard		39/73	**Hank And Lefty Raised My**		73/89	Bruce Van Dyke
4/94	**Half The Man** Clint Black			**Country Soul** Stoney Edwards		63/91	**Hard-Headed Man**
2/79	**Half The Way** Crystal Gayle		75/87	**Hank Drank** Bobby Lee Springfield			Sweethearts Of The Rodeo
F/76	**Half The Way In, Half The Way**		23/65	**Hank Williams' Guitar**		2/58	**Hard Headed Woman**
	Out Little David Wilkins			Freddie Hart			Elvis Presley
6/97	**Half Way Up** Clint Black		2/76	**Hank Williams, You Wrote My**		70/94	**Hard Liquor, Cold Women, Warm**
56/80	**Halftime** J.W. Thompson			**Life** Moe Bandy			**Beer** Bob Woodruff
6/95	**Halfway Down** Patty Loveless		93/84	**Hanky Panky** Mike Dekle		10/87	**Hard Livin'** Keith Whitley
26/63	**Hall Of Shame** Melba Montgomery		1/72	**Happiest Girl In The Whole U.S.A.**		13/95	**Hard Lovin' Woman** Mark Collie
				Donna Fargo		38/89	**Hard Luck Ace** Lacy J. Dalton
			47/68	**Happiness Hill** Kitty Wells		54/67	**Hard Luck Joe** Johnny Duncan
			63/69	**Happiness Lives In This House**		67/94	**Hard Luck Woman** Garth Brooks
				Mac Curtis			

444

Have You Forgotten—Dave Worley

1/90	**Hard Rock Bottom Of Your Heart** Randy Travis	
7/80	**Hard Times** Lacy J. Dalton	
75/68	**Hard Times** Larry Steele	
48/89	**Hard Times For An Honest Man** James House	
68/00	**Hard To Be A Husband, Hard To Be A Wife** Brad Paisley & Chely Wright	
5/94	**Hard To Say** Sawyer Brown	
11/93	**Hard Way** Mary-Chapin Carpenter	
62/93	**Hard Way To Make An Easy Livin'** Bellamy Brothers	
4/93	**Hard Workin' Man** Brooks & Dunn	
59/90	**Hardin County Line** Mark Collie	
82/77	**Hardly A Day Goes By** Jean Shepard	
59/67	**Hardly Anymore** Bob Luman	
57/74	**Harlan County** Wayne Kemp	
10/86	**Harmony** John Conlee	
61/71	**Harold's Super Service** Bobby Wayne	
1/68	**Harper Valley P.T.A.** Jeannie C. Riley	
24/68	**Harper Valley P.T.A. (Later That Same Day)** Ben Colder	
4/46	**Harriet** Red Foley with Roy Ross	
74/84	**Harvest Moon** Joe Waters	
35/65	**Harvest Of Sunshine** Jimmy Dean	
68/70	**Harvey Harrington IV** Johnny Carver	
22/94	**Has Anybody Seen Amy** John & Audrey Wiggins	
78/80	**Hasn't It Been Good Together** Hank Snow & Kelly Foxton	
41/67	**Hasta Luego (See You Later)** Hank Locklin	
98/79	**Hat, The** Roger Miller	
9/93	**Haunted Heart** Sammy Kershaw	
11/69	**Haunted House** Compton Brothers	
51/76	**Have A Dream On Me** Mel McDaniel	
67/80	**Have A Good Day** Henson Cargill	
1/68	**Have A Little Faith** David Houston	
63/70	**Have A Little Talk With Myself** Ray Stevens	
	Have Another Drink	
82/81	Douglas	
73/84	Doug Block	
14/58	**Have Blues—Will Travel** Eddie Noack	
30/59	**Have Heart, Will Love** Jean Shepard	
6/85	**Have I Got A Deal For You** Reba McEntire	
	Have I Got A Heart For You	
60/83	Chantilly	
68/86	Rockin' Horse	
14/87	**Have I Got Some Blues For You** Charley Pride	
47/64	**Have I Stayed Away Too Long** Bobby Bare	
62/96	**Have I Told You Lately** Emilio	
	Have I Told You Lately That I Love You	
3/46	Gene Autry *Marty R.*	
3/46	Tex Ritter	
4/46	Foy Willing	
5/46	Red Foley with Roy Ross	
74/69	Kitty Wells & Red Foley	
67/74	**Have It Your Way** Dave Dudley	
1/85	**Have Mercy** Judds	
57/96	**Have We Forgotten What Love Is** Crystal Bernard	
	Have You Ever Been Lonely? (Have You Ever Been Blue)	
2/49	Ernest Tubb	
5/82	Jim Reeves & Patsy Cline	
85/81	**Have You Ever Seen The Rain** Pam Hobbs	
50/67	**Have You Ever Wanted To?** Lorene Mann	
67/83	**Have You Heard** Rick & Janis Carnes	
86/87	**Have You Hurt Any Good Ones Lately** Sharon Robinson	
32/84	**Have You Loved Your Woman Today** Craig Dillingham	
3/75	**Have You Never Been Mellow** Olivia Newton-John	
	Have Yourself A Merry Little Christmas	
52/93	Vince Gill	
54/94	Vince Gill	
64/97	Vince Gill	
54/98	Martina McBride	
53/99	Martina McBride	
59/00	Martina McBride	
75/00	Lonestar	
32/80	**Haven't I Loved You Somewhere Before** Joe Stampley	
84/80	**Haven't I Loved You Somewhere Before** Bluestone	
86/83	**Haven't We Loved Somewhere Before** Zella Lehr	
	He Ain't Country	
51/68	James Bell	
48/72	Claude King	
93/78	**He Ain't Heavy, He's My Brother** June Neyman	
5/93	**He Ain't Worth Missing** Toby Keith	
19/77	**He Ain't You** Lynn Anderson	
15/84	**He Broke Your Mem'ry Last Night** Reba McEntire	
29/85	**He Burns Me Up** Lane Brody	
23/64	**He Called Me Baby** Patsy Cline	
26/74	**He Can Be Mine** Jeannie Seely	
8/74	**He Can't Fill My Shoes** Jerry Lee Lewis	
74/88	**He Cares** Rosie Flores	
59/91	**He Comes Around** Molly & The Heymakers	
1/99	**He Didn't Have To Be** Brad Paisley	
87/82	**He Don't Make Me Cry** Kippi Brannon	
39/01	**He Drinks Tequila** Lorrie Morgan & Sammy Kershaw	
54/71	**He Even Woke Me Up To Say Goodbye** Lynn Anderson	
68/93	**He Feels Guilty** Bobbie Cryner	
52/80	**He Gives Me Diamonds, You Give Me Chills** Margo Smith	
1/82	**He Got You** Ronnie Milsap	
18/97	**He Left A Lot To Be Desired** Ricochet	
88/75	**He Little Thing'd Her Out Of My Arms** Jack Greene	
56/68	**He Looks A Lot Like You** Harden Trio	
1/70	**He Loves Me All The Way** Tammy Wynette	
77/75	**He Loves Me All To Pieces** Ruby Falls	
73/78	**He Picked Me Up When You Let Me Down** Mary Lou Turner	
17/64	**He Says The Same Things To Me** Skeeter Davis	
	He Stands Real Tall	
11/62	Del Reeves	
21/65	"Little" Jimmy Dickens	
1/80	**He Stopped Loving Her Today** George Jones	
4/90	**He Talks To Me** Lorrie Morgan	
2/94	**He Thinks He'll Keep Her** Mary Chapin Carpenter	
	He Thinks I Still Care ..see: She Thinks	
46/67	**He Thought He'd Die Laughing** Bobby Helms	
10/75	**He Took Me For A Ride** La Costa	
13/75	**He Turns It Into Love Again** Lynn Anderson	
2/90	**He Walked On Water** Randy Travis	
45/66	**He Was Almost Persuaded** Donna Harris	
25/90	**He Was On To Somethin' (So He Made You)** Ricky Skaggs	
17/80	**He Was There (When I Needed You)** Tammy Wynette	
68/72	**He Will Break Your Heart** Johnny Williams	
32/00	**He Will, She Knows** Kenny Rogers	
22/85	**He Won't Give In** Kathy Mattea	
31/92	**He Would Be Sixteen** Michelle Wright	
64/97	**He'd Never Seen Julie Cry** Jo Dee Messina	
15/70	**He'd Still Love Me** Lynn Anderson	
58/74	**He'll Come Home** Melba Montgomery	
1/60	**He'll Have To Go** Jim Reeves	
6/60	**He'll Have To Stay** Jeanne Black	
21/77	**He'll Play The Music (But You Can't Make Him Dance)** Little David Wilkins	
68/79	**He's A Cowboy From Texas** Ronnie McDowell	
95/79	**He's A Good Man** Judy Argo	
	He's A Good Ole Boy	
32/68	Arlene Harden	
58/94	Chely Wright	
1/83	**He's A Heartache (Looking For A Place To Happen)** Janie Fricke	
39/66	**He's A Jolly Good Fellow** Charlie Walker	
39/90	**He's Alive** Dolly Parton	
94/79	**He's An Old Rock 'N' Roller** Dickey Lee	
1/88	**He's Back And I'm Blue** Desert Rose Band	
	He's Everywhere	
25/70	Sammi Smith	
39/75	Marilyn Sellars	
16/67	**He's Got A Way With Women** Hank Thompson	
63/77	**He's Got A Way With Women** Bob Luman	
48/69	**He's Got More Love In His Little Finger** Billie Jo Spears	
F/87	**He's Got The Whole World In His Hands** Cristy Lane	

Hell Stays Open All Night Long – Johnny Gray (?)

2/98	**He's Got You** *Brooks & Dunn* (also see: She's Got You)	
54/90	**He's Gotta Have Me** *Girls Next Door*	
18/87	**He's Letting Go** *Baillie And The Boys*	
16/58	**He's Lost His Love For Me** *Kitty Wells*	
61/71	**He's My Man** *Melba Montgomery*	
	He's My Rock ..see: She's My Rock	
74/93	**He's My Weakness** *Ronna Reeves*	
89/82	**He's Not Entitled To Your Love** *Johnny Rodriguez*	
53/67	**He's Not For Real** *Priscilla Mitchell*	
79/87	**He's Not Good Enough** *Paul Proctor*	
67/97	**He's On The Way Home** *Tony Toliver*	
17/80	**He's Out Of My Life** *Johnny Duncan & Janie Fricke*	
5/71	**He's So Fine** *Jody Miller*	
	He's Still All Over You ..see: She's Still	
60/82	**He's Taken** *Lane Brody*	
29/81	**He's The Fire** *Diana*	
12/63	**Head Over Heels In Love With You** *Don Gibson*	
7/77	**Head To Toe** *Bill Anderson*	
1/81	**Headache Tomorrow (Or A Heartache Tonight)** *Mickey Gilley*	
8/81	**Headed For A Heartache** *Gary Morris*	
2/45	**Headin' Down The Wrong Highway** *Ted Daffan*	
56/81	**Headin' For A Heartache** *Cindy Hurt*	
2/96	**Heads Carolina, Tails California** *Jo Dee Messina*	
	Healin'	
75/78	*Ava Barber*	
23/79	*Bobby Bare*	
51/77	**Heard It In A Love Song** *Marshall Tucker Band*	
13/89	**Heart, The** *Lacy J. Dalton*	
64/88	**Heart** *Janie Frickie*	
77/87	**Heart** *Ronnie Dove*	
21/63	**Heart, Be Careful** *Billy Walker*	
73/92	**Heart Break Train** *JJ White*	
19/85	**Heart Don't Do This To Me** *Loretta Lynn*	
33/76	**Heart Don't Fail Me Now** *Randy Cornor*	
14/86	**Heart Don't Fall Now** *Sawyer Brown*	
81/83	**Heart For A Heart** *Robin Lee*	
65/90	**Heart From A Stone** *Susi Beatty*	
19/91	**Heart Full Of Love** *Holly Dunn*	
62/67	**Heart Full Of Love** *Johnny Dallas*	
1/48	**Heart Full Of Love (For a Handful of Kisses)** *Eddy Arnold*	
21/96	**Heart Half Empty** *Ty Herndon Featuring Stephanie Bentley*	
1/77	**Heart Healer** *Mel Tillis*	
53/97	**Heart Hold On** *Buffalo Club*	
1/95	**Heart Is A Lonely Hunter** *Reba McEntire*	
43/94	**Heart Like A Hurricane** *Larry Stewart*	
58/80	**Heart Mender** *Crystal Gayle*
84/83	**Heart Of Dixie** *Tommy Overstreet*
44/87	**Heart Of Gold** *Willie Nelson*
3/80	**Heart Of Mine** *Oak Ridge Boys*
	Heart Of Stone ..see: (I Wish I Had A)
46/85	**Heart Of The Country** *Kathy Mattea*
26/81	**Heart Of The Matter** *Kendalls*
53/83	**Heart Of The Night** *Juice Newton*
96/79	**Heart Of The Night** *Poco*
	Heart On The Line ..see: Operator, Operator
8/81	**Heart On The Mend** *Sylvia*
81/83	**Heart On The Run** *Jerry Puckett*
71/87	**Heart Out Of Control** *Joni Bishop*
	Heart Over Mind
5/61	*Ray Price*
3/70	*Mel Tillis*
39/94	**Heart Over Mind** *Lorrie Morgan*
5/51	**Heart Strings** *Eddy Arnold*
18/92	**Heart That You Own** *Dwight Yoakam*
16/75	**Heart To Heart** *Roy Clark*
40/86	**Heart To Heart** *Wild Choir*
5/60	**Heart To Heart Talk** *Bob Wills*
8/85	**Heart Trouble** *Steve Wariner*
21/95	**Heart Trouble** *Martina McBride*
25/87	**Heart Vs. Heart** *Pake McEntire*
12/67	**Heart, We Did All That We Could** *Jean Shepard*
51/95	**Heart With 4 Wheel Drive** *4 Runner*
1/93	**Heart Won't Lie** *Reba McEntire & Vince Gill*
30/80	**Heart's Been Broken** *Danny Wood*
3/96	**Heart's Desire** *Lee Roy Parnell*
23/93	**Heartache** *Suzy Bogguss*
23/84	**Heartache And A Half** *Deborah Allen*
29/63	**Heartache For A Keepsake** *Kitty Wells*
54/86	**Heartache The Size Of Texas** *Vega Brothers*
6/83	**Heartache Tonight** *Conway Twitty*
	Heartaches By The Number
2/59	*Ray Price*
26/72	*Jack Reno*
39/81	**Heartaches Of A Fool** *Willie Nelson*
83/85	**Heartbeat** *Rebecca Hall*
1/86	**Heartbeat In The Darkness** *Don Williams*
35/70	**Heartbreak Avenue** *Carl Smith*
7/82	**Heartbreak Express** *Dolly Parton*
8/89	**Heartbreak Hill** *Emmylou Harris*
	Heartbreak Hotel
1/56	*Elvis Presley*
55/66	*Roger Miller*
1/79	*Willie Nelson & Leon Russell*
13/90	**Heartbreak Hurricane** *Ricky Skaggs*
	Heartbreak Kid ..see: (Back To The)
40/66	**Heartbreak Tennessee** *Johnny Paycheck*
23/01	**Heartbreak Town** *Dixie Chicks*
1/61	**Heartbreak U.S.A.** *Kitty Wells*
1/78	**Heartbreaker** *Dolly Parton*
1/82	**Heartbroke** *Ricky Skaggs*
18/97	**Heartbroke Every Day** *Lonestar*
1/93	**Heartland** *George Strait*
75/80	**Hearts** *Jimmie Peters*
2/93	**Hearts Are Gonna Roll** *Hal Ketchum*
26/59	**Hearts Are Lonely** *Phil Sullivan*
1/86	**Hearts Aren't Made To Break (They're Made To Love)** *Lee Greenwood*
69/89	**Hearts In The Wind** *Gail Davies*
4/55	**Hearts Of Stone** *Red Foley*
2/78	**Hearts On Fire** *Eddie Rabbitt*
60/81	**Hearts (Our Hearts)** *Susie Allanson*
100/77	**Heat Is On** *Tricia Johns*
37/02	**Heather's Wall** *Ty Herndon*
55/69	**Heaven Below** *John Wesley Ryles*
60/98	**Heaven Bound** *Shana Petrone*
24/95	**Heaven Bound (I'm Ready)** *Shenandoah*
85/77	**Heaven Can Be Anywhere (Twin Pines Theme)** *Charlie Daniels Band*
4/88	**Heaven Can't Be Found** *Hank Williams, Jr.*
5/70	**Heaven Everyday** *Mel Tillis*
14/96	**Heaven Help My Heart** *Wynonna*
18/68	**Heaven Help The Working Girl** *Norma Jean*
14/96	**Heaven In My Woman's Eyes** *Tracy Byrd*
98/78	**Heaven Is Being Good To Me** *Dick Moebakken*
47/70	**Heaven Is Just A Touch Away** *Cal Smith*
3/72	**Heaven Is My Woman's Love** *Tommy Overstreet*
73/85	**Heaven Knows** *Audie Henry*
88/80	**Heaven On A Freight Train** *Max D. Barnes*
66/73	**Heaven On Earth** *Sonny James*
16/89	**Heaven Only Knows** *Emmylou Harris*
1/68	**Heaven Says Hello** *Sonny James*
F/79	**Heaven Was A Drink Of Wine** *Merle Haggard*
	Heaven's Just A Sin Away
1/77	*Kendalls*
63/93	*Kelly Willis*
32/71	**Heavenly** *Wynn Stewart*
8/82	**Heavenly Bodies** *Earl Thomas Conley*
11/70	**Heavenly Sunshine** *Ferlin Husky*
38/66	**Heck Of A Fix In 66** *Jim Nesbitt*
53/77	**Helen** *Cal Smith*
1/86	**Hell And High Water** *T. Graham Brown*
	Hell Yes I Cheated
95/77	*James Pastell*
82/82	*Jim Owen*
93/77	**Hello Atlanta** *Chip Taylor*
52/95	**Hello Cruel World** *George Ducas*
39/80	**Hello Daddy, Good Morning Darling** *Mel McDaniel*
1/70	**Hello Darlin'** *Conway Twitty*
4/61	**Hello Fool** *Ralph Emery*
13/75	**Hello I Love You** *Johnny Russell*
26/70	**Hello, I'm A Jukebox** *George Kent*
91/84	**Hello Josephine** *J.W. Thompson*
14/75	**Hello Little Bluebird** *Donna Fargo*
53/71	**Hello Little Rock** *Wynn Stewart*
1/74	**Hello Love** *Hank Snow*

Hello

15/99	Hello L.O.V.E. John Michael Montgomery	
	Hello Mary Lou	
14/70	Bobby Lewis	
3/85	Statler Brothers	
4/78	Hello Mexico (And Adios Baby To You) Johnny Duncan	
60/67	Hello Number One Kitty Wells & Red Foley	
75/72	Hello Operator Joe Stampley	
	Hello Out There	
8/62	Carl Belew	
28/74	LaWanda Lindsey	
30/78	Hello! Remember Me Billy Swan	
79/74	Hello Summertime Bobby Goldsboro	
94/79	Hello Texas Brian Collins	
90/78	Hello, This Is Anna O.B. McClinton Feat. Peggy Jo Adams	
57/78	Hello, This Is Joannie (The Telephone Answering Machine Song) Paul Evans	
	Hello Trouble	
5/63	Orville Couch	
62/74	LaWanda Lindsey	
11/89	Desert Rose Band	
1/65	Hello Vietnam Johnny Wright	
30/63	Hello Wall No. 2 Ben Colder	
1/61	Hello Walls Faron Young	
14/73	Hello We're Lonely Patti Page & Tom T. Hall	
29/81	Hello Woman Doug Kershaw	
56/92	Help, I'm White And I Can't Get Down Geezinslaws	
	Help Me	
6/74	Elvis Presley	
38/77	Ray Price	
66/89	Help Me Get Over You Wagoneers	
1/90	Help Me Hold On Travis Tritt	
	Help Me Make It Through The Night	
1/71	Sammi Smith	
4/80	Willie Nelson	
37/75	Help Me Make It (To My Rockin' Chair) B.J. Thomas	
	Help Yourself To Me	
47/75	Roy Head	
97/75	Debra Barber	
18/97	Helping Me Get Over You Travis Tritt featuring Lari White	
	Helpless	
19/64	Joe Carson	
73/68	Dal Perkins	
31/01	Helplessly, Hopelessly Jessica Andrews	
62/88	Henrietta Mel McDaniel	
7/54	Hep Cat Baby Eddy Arnold	
33/99	Her Aaron Tippin	
67/69	Her And The Car And The Mobile Home Dave Kirby	
52/76	Her Body Couldn't Keep You (Off My Mind) Gene Watson	
92/80	Her Cheatin Heart (Made A Drunken Fool Of Me) Jerry Naill	
96/81	Her Empty Pillow (Lying Next To Mine) Jimmy McMillan	
59/72	Her L-O-V-E's Gone Red Steagall	
7/97	Her Man Gary Allan	
96/75	Her Memory's Gonna Kill Me Jim Alley	

3/76	Her Name Is... George Jones	
59/71	Here Come The Elephants Johnny Bond	
68/76	Here Come The Flowers Dottie West	
2/68	Here Comes Heaven Eddy Arnold	
1/71	Here Comes Honey Again Sonny James	
10/64	Here Comes My Baby Dottie West	
42/99	Here Comes My Baby Mavericks	
79/73	Here Comes My Little Baby Pat Roberts	
	Here Comes Santa Claus (Down Santa Claus Lane)	
5/47	Gene Autry	
4/48	Gene Autry	
8/49	Gene Autry	
88/82	Here Comes That Feelin' Again Ralph May	
32/80	Here Comes That Feeling Again Don King	
15/76	Here Comes That Girl Again Tommy Overstreet	
65/89	(Here Comes) That Old Familiar Feeling Lisa Childress	
80/76	Here Comes That Rainy Day Feeling Again Connie Cato	
10/76	Here Comes The Freedom Train Merle Haggard	
9/78	Here Comes The Hurt Again Mickey Gilley	
85/88	Here Comes The Night Dolly Hartt	
22/95	Here Comes The Rain Mavericks	
4/68	Here Comes The Rain, Baby Eddy Arnold	
15/78	Here Comes The Reason I Live Ronnie McDowell	
73/73	Here Comes The Sun Lloyd Green	
38/73	Here Comes The World Again Johnny Bush	
4/95	Here I Am Patty Loveless	
	Here I Am Again	
3/72	Loretta Lynn	
69/85	Johnny Rodriguez	
41/76	(Here I Am) Alone Again Billy Walker	
	Here I Am Drunk Again	
13/60	Clyde Beavers	
11/76	Moe Bandy	
16/75	Here I Am In Dallas Faron Young	
	Here I Go Again	
13/71	Bobby Wright	
83/84	Cheryl Handy	
72/99	Here I Go Again Lorrie Morgan	
77/79	Here I Go Again Dorsey Burnette	
20/78	Here In Love Dottsy	
3/90	Here In The Real World Alan Jackson	
7/55	Here Today And Gone Tomorrow Browns	
2/91	Here We Are Alabama	
11/79	Here We Are Again Statler Brothers	
26/61	Here We Are Again Ray Price	
17/74	Here We Go Again Brian Shaw	
	Here We Go Again Virgil Warner & Suzi Jane Hokum	
51/67	Virgil Warner & Suzi Jane Hokum	
66/72	Johnny Duncan	
65/82	Roy Clark	
95/73	Here With You Bobby Lewis	

1/77	Here You Come Again Dolly Parton	
2/91	Here's A Quarter (Call Someone Who Cares) Travis Tritt	
42/70	Here's A Toast To Mama Charlie Louvin	
1/76	Here's Some Love Tanya Tucker	
64/97	Here's The Deal Jeff Carson	
60/79	Here's To All The Too Hard Working Husbands David Houston	
	Here's To The Horses	
94/77	Mack Vickery	
49/81	Johnny Russell	
88/77	Here's To The Next Time Billy Larkin	
87/89	Here's To You Faron Young	
45/68	Here's To You And Me Tex Williams	
	Here's Your Sign Christmas	
39/98	Bill Engvall	
46/99	Bill Engvall	
29/97	Here's Your Sign (Get The Picture) Bill Engvall With Travis Tritt	
41/73	Herman Schwartz Stonewall Jackson	
14/54	Hernando's Hideaway Homer And Jethro	
77/83	Hero, The Lee Dresser	
4/91	Heroes Paul Overstreet	
3/91	Heroes And Friends Randy Travis	
64/79	Heroes And Idols (Don't Come Easy) David Smith	
54/85	Hey Hillary Kanter	
	Hey Baby	
35/70	Bobby G. Rice	
95/78	Donnie Rohrs	
7/82	Anne Murray	
38/93	Hey Baby Marty Stuart	
2/83	Hey Bartender Johnny Lee	
2/89	Hey Bobby K.T. Oslin	
75/84	Hey, Bottle Of Whiskey Gary Stewart	
5/94	Hey Cinderella Suzy Bogguss	
15/68	Hey Daddy Charlie Louvin	
33/77	Hey Daisy (Where Have All The Good Times Gone) Tom Bresh	
21/86	Hey Doll Baby Sweethearts Of The Rodeo	
	Hey, Good Lookin'	
1/51	Hank Williams	
74/92	Mavericks	
58/89	Hey Heart Dean Dillon	
1/53	Hey Joe! Carl Smith	
8/53	Hey Joe Kitty Wells	
10/81	Hey Joe (Hey Moe) Moe Bandy & Joe Stampley	
6/51	Hey La La Ernest Tubb	
51/85	Hey Lady Narvel Felts	
13/68	Hey Little One Glen Campbell	
40/88	Hey Little Sister Tom Wopat	
3/74	Hey Loretta Loretta Lynn	
13/63	Hey Lucille! Claude King	
19/76	Hey, Lucky Lady Dolly Parton	
9/58	Hey, Mr. Bluebird Ernest Tubb & The Wilburn Brothers	
8/53	Hey, Mr. Cotton Picker Tennessee Ernie Ford	
28/92	Hey Mister (I Need This Job) Shenandoah	
22/58	Hey Sheriff Rusty & Doug	

447

Home Wrecker — Gretchen Wilson ★★★ (WPCV)

28/76	Hey Shirley (This Is Squirrely) Shirley & Squirrely	44/69	Him And Her Bill Wilbourn & Kathy Morrison	1/83	Holding Her And Loving You Earl Thomas Conley
67/79	Hey There Kenny Price		His And Hers	68/98	Clay Walker
21/74	Hey There Girl David Rogers	23/63	Tony Douglas	83/89	Holdin' On To Nothin' Roger Rone
65/70	Hey There Johnny Mayf Nutter	87/82	Tony Douglas	7/68	Holding On To Nothin'
94/78	Hey, What Do You Say (We Fall In Love) Sue Richards	13/55	His Hands "Tennessee" Ernie Ford		Porter Wagoner & Dolly Parton
1/75	(Hey Won't You Play) Another Somebody Done Somebody Wrong Song B.J. Thomas	74/95	His Memory Western Flyer	7/80	Holding The Bag Moe Bandy & Joe Stampley
		2/66	History Repeats Itself Buddy Starcher	9/98	Hole, The Randy Travis
		43/89	Hit The Ground Runnin' John Conlee	31/97	Hole In My Heart BlackHawk
100/78	Hey You Bobby Havens	44/70	Hit The Road Jack Connie Eaton & Dave Peel	4/89	Hole In My Pocket Ricky Van Shelton
9/65	Hicktown Tennessee Ernie Ford	12/71	Hitchin' A Ride Jack Reno		Holed Up In Some Honky Tonk
55/79	Hide Me (In The Shadow Of Your Love) Judy Argo	5/45	Hitler's Last Letter To Hirohito Carson Robison	40/82	Joe Sun
36/81	Hideaway Healing Stephanie Winslow	53/67	Hobo Ned Miller	69/91	Dean Dillon
20/78	High And Dry Joe Sun	50/65	Hobo And The Rose Webb Pierce	2/98	Holes In The Floor Of Heaven Steve Wariner
67/76	High And Wild Earl Conley	8/51	Hobo Boogie Red Foley	3/57	Holiday For Love Webb Pierce
27/61	High As The Mountains Buck Owens	73/88	Hocus Pocus Roger Marshall	62/99	Holiday Inn Bryan White
27/83	High Cost Of Leaving Exile	74/95	Hog Wild Hank Williams, Jr.	51/97	Holly Jolly Christmas Alan Jackson
33/82	High Cost Of Loving Charlie Ross	5/56	Hold Everything (Till I Get Home) Red Sovine	82/88	Hollywood Heroes Hunter Cain
1/89	High Cotton Alabama	1/89	Hold Me K.T. Oslin	72/99	Hollywood Indian Guides Bill Engvall
72/94	High Hopes And Empty Pockets McBride & The Ride	12/77	Hold Me Barbara Mandrell	80/80	Hollywood Smiles Glen Campbell
2/85	High Horse Nitty Gritty Dirt Band	57/77	Hold Me Rayburn Anthony	67/90	Hollywood Squares George Strait
12/96	High Lonesome Sound Vince Gill	67/83	Hold Me David Rogers	44/76	Hollywood Waltz Buck Owens
33/96	High Low And In Between Mark Wills	73/73	Hold Me Slim Whitman	85/87	Hollywood's Dream Jeff Thomas
24/93	High On A Mountain Top Marty Stuart	30/81	Hold Me Like You Never Had Me Randy Parton	75/70	Holy Cow Jamey Ryan
20/98	High On Love Patty Loveless		Hold Me, Thrill Me, Kiss Me	1/90	Home Joe Diffie
60/72	High On Love Carl Perkins	38/69	Johnny And Jonie Mosby	2/59	Home Jim Reeves
63/93	High Powered Love Emmylou Harris	60/80	Micki Fuhrman	3/96	Home Alan Jackson
		32/69	Hold Me Tight Johnny Carver	10/75	Home Loretta Lynn
14/88	High Ridin' Heroes David Lynn Jones	82/83	Hold Me Till The Last Waltz Is Over Kathy Bauer	57/84	Home Again Judy Collins & T.G. Sheppard
20/93	High Rollin' Gibson/Miller Band	5/86	Hold On Rosanne Cash	3/86	Home Again In My Heart Nitty Gritty Dirt Band
F/78	High Rollin' Jerry Reed	24/83	Hold On Gail Davies	28/96	Home Ain't Where His Heart Is (Anymore) Shania Twain
9/58	High School Confidential Jerry Lee Lewis	40/81	Hold On Rich Landers		
24/94	High-Tech Redneck George Jones	6/89	Hold On (A Little Longer) Steve Wariner	65/95	Home Alone 4 Runner
75/82	Highlight Of '81 Johnny Paycheck	69/93	Hold On, Elroy Dude Mowrey	79/81	Home Along The Highway Tom Nix
52/90	Highway, The Willie Nelson	20/83	Hold On, I'm Comin' Waylon Jennings & Jerry Reed	53/86	Home Grown Mason Dixon
1/83	Highway 40 Blues Ricky Skaggs	42/91	Hold On Partner Roy Rogers & Clint Black	63/99	Home In My Heart (North Carolina) Claudia Church
15/74	Highway Headin' South Porter Wagoner	45/77	Hold On Tight Sunday Sharpe		Home Made Love
	Highway Patrol	64/80	Hold On Tight Porter Wagoner	99/75	Sue Richards
39/66	Red Simpson	4/99	Hold On To Me John Michael Montgomery	6/76	Tom Bresh
73/95	Junior Brown	66/71	Hold On To My Unchanging Love Jeanne Pruett	86/83	Homemade Love Ronnie Reno
2/89	Highway Robbery Tanya Tucker		Hold On To Your Man ..see: (If You Wanna Hold On)	3/57	Home Of The Blues Johnny Cash
1/85	Highwayman Waylon Jennings/Willie Nelson/ Johnny Cash/Kris Kristofferson	25/78	Hold Tight Kenny Starr	32/71	Home Sweet Home David Houston
			Hold What You've Got	34/92	Home Sweet Home Dennis Robbins
79/75	Hijack Hank Snow	59/68	Diana Trask	73/77	Home, Sweet Home L.E. White & Lola Jean Dillon
91/74	Hill, The Ray Griff	36/79	Sonny James	82/88	Home Team Madonna Dolan
	Hillbilly Fever	89/88	Hold Your Fire Ross Lewis	2/99	Home To You John Michael Montgomery
3/50	"Little" Jimmy Dickens	4/97	Holdin' Diamond Rio	98/77	Home Where I Belong B.J. Thomas
9/50	Ernest Tubb-Red Foley (No. 2)	2/90	Holdin' A Good Hand Lee Greenwood		
8/81	Hillbilly Girl With The Blues Lacy J. Dalton	1/93	Holdin' Heaven Tracy Byrd	10/65	Home You're Tearin' Down Loretta Lynn
5/76	Hillbilly Heart Johnny Rodriguez	70/82	Holdin' On Jessi Colter	74/81	Homebody Whispering Bill Anderson
51/89	Hillbilly Hell Bellamy Brothers	27/72	Holdin' On (To The Love I Got) Barbara Mandrell	15/59	Homebreaker Skeeter Davis
37/86	Hillbilly Highway Steve Earle	6/96	Holdin' Onto Somethin' Jeff Carson	5/69	Homecoming Tom T. Hall
69/94	Hillbilly Jitters Mike Henderson	56/85	Holdin' The Family Together Shoppe	9/87	Homecoming '63 Keith Whitley
71/96	Hillbilly Rap Neal McCoy			42/83	Homegrown Tomatoes Guy Clark
8/90	Hillbilly Rock Marty Stuart			39/01	Homeland Kenny Rogers
13/99	Hillbilly Shoes Montgomery Gentry				
	Hillbilly Singer ..see: Ballad Of A				

448

Honey Does (See "You Ain't Much Fun")

75/89	Homeless People Bertie Higgins	53/93	Honky Tonk Christmas Alan Jackson	81/74	Honky-Tonkin' Troy Seals
	Homemade ..see: Home Made	59/94	Alan Jackson	84/79	Ronnie Sessions
38/66	Homesick Bobby Bare	43/87	Honky Tonk Crazy Gene Watson	37/65	Honky Tonkin' Again
67/89	Hometown Advantage Tim Mensy	97/83	Honky Tonk Crazy Tommy Bell		Buddy Cagle
27/85	Hometown Gossip Whites	10/86	Honky Tonk Crowd	50/93	Honky Tonkin' Fool
3/93	Hometown Honeymoon Alabama		John Anderson		Doug Supernaw
59/92	Hometown Radio Curtis Wright	35/94	Honky Tonk Crowd Rick Trevino	23/96	Honky Tonkin's What I Do Best
66/70	Homeward Bound Brenda Byers	95/79	Honky Tonk Disco Jim West		Marty Stuart & Travis Tritt
4/45	Honestly Dick Thomas	89/76	Honky Tonk Fool Ben Reece	25/61	Honky Tonkitis Carl Butler
	Honey	11/48	Honky Tonk Gal T. Texas Tyler	89/79	Honky-Tonks Are Calling Me
1/68	Bobby Goldsboro		Honky-Tonk Girl		Again Lenny Gault
F/79	Orion	9/54	Hank Thompson		Honkytonk ..see: Honky Tonk
64/68	Honey Compton Brothers	91/77	Hank Thompson	1/85	Honor Bound
8/53	(Honey, Baby, Hurry!) Bring Your Sweet Self Back To Me Lefty Frizzell	50/95	Honky Tonk Healin' David Ball		Earl Thomas Conley
		6/89	Honky Tonk Heart Highway 101	2/81	Hooked On Music Mac Davis
2/70	Honey Come Back Glen Campbell	75/88	Honky Tonk Heart (And A Hillbilly Soul) Clay Blaker	89/69	Hooked On You Odessa
42/01	Honey Do Mike Walker			9/54	Hootchy Kootchy Henry (From Hawaii) Mitchell Torok
89/90	Honey Do Weekend Randy Rhoads	37/81	Honky Tonk Hearts Dickey Lee		
		70/82	Honky Tonk Heaven Orion	45/64	Hootenanny Express Canadian Sweethearts
2/46	Honey Do You Think It's Wrong Al Dexter	65/91	Honky Tonk Life Charlie Daniels		
		65/82	Honky Tonk Magic Lloyd David Foster	57/96	Hope Hope
43/70	Honey, Don't Mac Curtis		Honky-Tonk Man	95/75	Hope For The Flowers Lois Johnson
54/69	Honey-Eyed Girl (That's You That's You) Tennessee Ernie Ford	9/56	Johnny Horton		
		11/62	Johnny Horton	1/75	Hope You're Feelin' Me (Like I'm Feelin' You) Charley Pride
F/55	Honey, Honey Bee Ball Hank Thompson	22/70	Bob Luman		
		3/86	Dwight Yoakam	47/97	Hopechest Song Stephanie Bentley
16/76	Honey Hungry Mike Lunsford	10/83	Honkytonk Man Marty Robbins		
5/89	Honey I Dare You Southern Pacific	4/77	Honky Tonk Memories Mickey Gilley	20/78	Hopelessly Devoted To You Olivia Newton-John
	Honey I Do	1/88	Honky Tonk Moon Randy Travis	52/88	Hopelessly Falling Jeff Chance
61/95	Stacy Dean Campbell	60/92	Honky Tonk Myself To Death George Jones		Hopelessly Yours
59/00	Danni Leigh			67/89	John Conlee
74/68	Honey (I Miss You Too) Margaret Lewis	12/81	Honky Tonk Queen Moe Bandy & Joe Stampley	12/91	Lee Greenwood with Suzy Bogguss
15/54	Honey, I Need You Johnnie & Jack	84/81	Honky-Tonk Saturday Night Becky Hobbs	7/56	Hoping That You're Hoping Louvin Brothers
17/69	Honey, I'm Home Stan Hitchcock	52/69	Honky-Tonk Season Charlie Walker	15/75	Hoppy, Gene And Me Roy Rogers
	Honey, I'm Home		Honky Tonk Song	42/73	Hoppy's Gone Roger Miller
66/97	Shania Twain	1/57	Webb Pierce	53/99	Horse To Mexico Trini Triggs
1/98	Shania Twain	85/89	Jimmie Dale Gilmore	78/76	Hot And Still Heatin' Jerry Jaye
83/89	Honey I'm Just Walking Out The Door Rick Tucker	66/96	Honky Tonk Song George Jones	62/93	Hot, Country And Single Dean Dillon
		74/98	Honky Tonk Songs Dolly Parton	46/88	Hot Dog Buck Owens
12/54	Honey Love Carlisles	51/71	Honky-Tonk Stardust Cowboy Bill Rice	96/79	Hot Mama Dan Dickey
41/75	Honey On His Hands Jeanne Pruett			40/89	Hot Nights Canyon
		28/80	Honky-Tonk Stuff Jerry Lee Lewis	61/87	Hot Red Sweater Jay Booker
92/80	Honey On The Moon Bonnie Guitar	47/94	Honky-Tonk Superman Aaron Tippin		Hot Rod Lincoln
				14/60	Charlie Ryan
1/84	Honey (Open That Door) Ricky Skaggs	69/84	Honky Tonk Tan O.B. McClinton	51/72	Commander Cody
		70/82	Honky Tonk Tonight David Heavener	65/88	Asleep At The Wheel
F/77	(Honey, Won't You) Call Me Hank Williams, Jr.				Hot Rod Race
		78/78	Honky Tonk Toys A.L. "Doodle" Owens	5/51	Arkie Shibley
	Honeycomb			7/51	Ramblin' Jimmie Dolan
7/57	Jimmie Rodgers	3/97	Honky Tonk Truth Brooks & Dunn	7/51	Red Foley
27/86	Gary Morris	54/93	Honky Tonk Walkin' Kentucky Headhunters	7/51	Tiny Hill
4/74	Honeymoon Feelin' Roy Clark			67/79	Hot Stuff Jerry Reed
9/53	Honeymoon On A Rocket Ship Hank Snow	27/76	Honky Tonk Waltz Ray Stevens	59/80	Hot Sunday Morning Wayne Armstrong
		17/73	Honky Tonk Wine Wayne Kemp		
31/98	Honky Tonk America Sammy Kershaw	56/70	Honky Tonk Women Charlie Walker	39/83	Hot Time In Old Town Tonight Mel McDaniel
	Honky Tonk Amnesia	32/76	Honky Tonk Women Love Red Neck Men Jerry Jaye	6/53	Hot Toddy Red Foley
24/74	Moe Bandy			54/92	Hotel Whiskey Hank Williams, Jr.
56/89	Scott McQuaig			37/85	Hottest "Ex" In Texas Becky Hobbs
5/93	Honky Tonk Attitude Joe Diffie	47/84	Honky Tonk Women Make Honky Tonk Men Craig Dillingham		
54/92	Honky Tonk Baby Highway 101			1/56	Hound Dog Elvis Presley
58/98	Honky Tonk Baby Ricochet	71/94	Honky Tonk World Chris LeDoux	25/79	Hound Dog Man Glen Campbell
	Honky Tonk Blues	59/86	Honky Tonker Marty Stuart	F/73	Hour And A Six-Pack Cal Smith
2/52	Hank Williams		Honky Tonkin'	24/63	House Down The Block Buck Owens
1/80	Charley Pride	14/48	Hank Williams		
26/90	Pirates Of The Mississippi	1/82	Hank Williams, Jr.	68/92	House Huntin' Matthews, Wright & King

Handwritten at top: How About You — Eric Church — (???) — (R-W-B) — WPCV / Erin

	House Of Blue Lights	2/97	How Do I Live *Trisha Yearwood*	1/71	How Much More Can She Stand *Conway Twitty*
39/69	Earl Richards	43/97	LeAnn Rimes	41/68	How Sweet It Is (To Be In Love With You) *Jack Reno*
17/87	Asleep At The Wheel	1/87	How Do I Turn You On *Ronnie Milsap*	21/64	How The Other Half Lives *Johnny And Jonie Mosby*
	House Of Blue Lovers	2/98	How Do You Fall In Love *Alabama*	7/79	How To Be A Country Star *Statler Brothers*
24/59	Jack Newman	46/84	How Do You Feel About Foolin' Around *Willie Nelson & Kris Kristofferson*	69/68	How To Catch An African Skeeter Alive *Jimmy Dickens*
21/61	James O'Gwynn				
	House Of Cards	11/58	How Do You Hold A Memory *Hank Thompson*	1/97	How Was I To Know *Reba McEntire*
21/95	Mary Chapin Carpenter	1/00	How Do You Like Me Now?! *Toby Keith*	2/97	How Was I To Know *John Michael Montgomery*
13/58	House Of Glass *Ernest Tubb*	67/00	How Do You Milk A Cow *Cledus T. Judd*	59/97	How You Ever Gonna Know *Garth Brooks*
21/74	House Of Love *Dottie West*	13/98	How Do You Sleep At Night *Wade Hayes*	1/97	How Your Love Makes Me Feel *Diamond Rio*
72/67	House Of Memories *Dick Curless*	89/76	How Do You Start Over *Bob Luman*	92/82	How'd You Get So Good *Denny Hilton*
	House Of The Rising Sun		How Do You Talk To A Baby	69/96	How's The Radio Know *Aaron Tippin*
29/74	Jody Miller	7/61	Webb Pierce		How's The World Treating You
14/81	Dolly Parton	99/77	Dugg Collins	4/53	Eddy Arnold
19/89	House On Old Lonesome Road *Conway Twitty*	74/83	How Do You Tell Someone You Love *Rod Rishard*	26/61	Louvin Brothers
18/98	House With No Curtains *Alan Jackson*	80/80	How Far Do You Want To Go *Ronnie McDowell*	19/64	Howdy Neighbor Howdy *Porter Wagoner*
88/81	Houston Blue *David Rogers*	11/56	How Far Is Heaven *Kitty Wells*	3/51	Howlin' At The Moon *Hank Williams*
47/71	Houston Blues *Jeannie C. Riley*	74/74	How Far Our Love Goes *Billy Walker*	14/78	Hubba Hubba *Billy "Crash" Craddock*
76/85	Houston Heartache *Mason Dixon*	17/60	How Far To Little Rock *Stanley Brothers*	81/76	Huckelberry Pie *Even Stevens/Sammi Smith*
20/74	Houston (I'm Comin' To See You) *Glen Campbell*	12/67	How Fast Them Trucks Can Go *Claude Gray*	21/67	Hula Love *Hank Snow*
1/83	Houston (Means I'm One Day Closer To You) *Larry Gatlin/Gatlin Brothers*	1/99	How Forever Feels *Kenny Chesney*	5/56	Hula Rock *Hank Snow*
		39/76	How Great Thou Art *Statler Brothers*	99/73	Humming Bird *Country Cavaleers*
4/89	Houston Solution *Ronnie Milsap*	3/70	How I Got To Memphis *Bobby Bare*	20/90	Hummingbird *Ricky Skaggs*
4/97	How A Cowgirl Says Goodbye *Tracy Lawrence*		How I Love Them Old Songs	5/70	Humphrey The Camel *Jack Blanchard & Misty Morgan*
70/90	How About Goodbye *Robin Lee*	20/70	Carl Smith	2/48	Humpty Dumpty Heart *Hank Thompson*
52/84	How Are You Spending My Nights *Gus Hardin*	57/72	Jim Ed Brown	24/01	Hunger, The *Steve Holy*
69/87	How Beautiful You Are (To Me) *Big Al Downing*	91/77	Danny Davis	1/69	Hungry Eyes *Merle Haggard*
			How I Love You In The Morning	27/61	Hungry For Love *Stonewall Jackson*
1/85	How Blue *Reba McEntire*	37/79	Peggy Sue	73/71	Hunter, The *Alice Creech*
71/90	How 'Bout Us *Girls Next Door*	78/89	Joann Wintermute	4/81	Hurricane *Leon Everette*
48/64	How Can I Forget You *Glenn Barber*	23/68	How Is He? *Jeannie Seely*	75/95	Hurricane *Carlene Carter*
3/94	How Can I Help You Say Goodbye *Patty Loveless*	56/00	How Long *Bryan White*	47/70	Hurry Home To Me *Bobby Wright*
		1/98	How Long Gone *Brooks & Dunn*		Hurry, Hurry!
74/92	How Can I Hold You *Cleve Francis*	6/66	How Long Has It Been *Bobby Lewis*	2/44	Benny Carter
22/78	How Can I Leave You Again *John Denver*	87/81	How Long Has This Been Going On *Amarillo*	4/44	Lucky Millinder
85/74	How Can I Tell Her *Earl Richards*		How Long Will It Take	23/65	Hurry, Mr. Peters *Justin Tubb & Lorene Mann*
13/59	How Can I Think Of Tomorrow *James O'Gwynn*	4/67	Warner Mack	81/85	Hurry On Home *Brooks Brothers Band*
1/71	How Can I Unlove You *Lynn Anderson*	62/83	Tennessee Express	17/93	Hurry Sundown *McBride & The Ride*
7/62	(How Can I Write On Paper) What I Feel In My Heart *Jim Reeves*	7/52	How Long Will It Take (To Stop Loving You) *Lefty Frizzell*	53/69	Hurry Up *Darrell McCall*
36/71	How Can You Mend A Broken Heart *Duane Dee*	1/68	How Long Will My Baby Be Gone *Buck Owens*		**Hurt**
74/75	How Come It Took So Long (To Say Goodbye) *Dave Dudley*	11/74	How Lucky Can One Man Be *Joe Stampley*	14/75	Connie Cato
25/63	How Come Your Dog Don't Bite Nobody But Me *Webb Pierce & Mel Tillis*	64/99	How Many Days *Jack Ingram*	6/76	Elvis Presley
		69/89	How Many Hearts *Lynn Anderson*	1/86	Juice Newton
22/01	How Cool Is That *Andy Griggs*	71/86	How Much Do I Owe You *Toni Price*	100/78	Hurt As Big As Texas *Randy Cornor*
92/80	How Could I Do This To Me *Sam D. Bass*	38/88	How Much Is It Worth To Live In L.A. *Waylon Jennings*	3/67	Hurt Her Once For Me *Wilburn Brothers*
6/83	How Could I Love Her So Much *Johnny Rodriguez*	2/53	(How Much Is) That Hound Dog In The Window *Homer And Jethro*	56/89	Hurt I Can't Handle *Statler Brothers*
53/72	How Could You Be Anything But Love *Ferlin Husky*			43/96	Hurt Me *LeAnn Rimes*
29/79	How Deep In Love Am I? *Johnny Russell*			3/91	Hurt Me Bad (In A Real Good Way) *Patty Loveless*
19/89	How Do *Mary Chapin Carpenter*				
1/97	How Do I Get There *Deana Carter*				
59/98	How Do I Let Go *Lisa Brokop*				

59/82 Hurtin' For Your Love *Tom Carlile*	F/81 I Am The Dreamer (You Are The Dream) *Conway Twitty*	18/80 I Can See Forever In Your Eyes *Reba McEntire*
Hurtin' Kind Of Love	86/82 I Am The Fire *David Heavener*	38/80 I Can See Forever Loving You *Foxfire*
94/77 *Ron Shaw*	64/68 I Am The Grass *Dee Mullins*	97/85 I Can See Him In Her Eyes *Adam Baker*
91/80 *Ron Shaw*	56/95 I Am Who I Am *Holly Dunn*	44/76 I Can See Me Lovin' You Again *Johnny Paycheck*
38/89 Hurtin' Side *Shelby Lynne*	51/73 I Am Woman *Bobbie Roy*	63/68 I Can Spot A Cheater *Johnny Tillotson*
3/66 Hurtin's All Over *Connie Smith*	I Been To Georgia On A Fast Train	22/64 I Can Stand It (As Long As She Can) *Bill Phillips*
79/85 Hurts All Over *Shoppe*	88/73 *Billy Joe Shaver*	1/98 I Can Still Feel You *Collin Raye*
26/70 Husband Hunting *Liz Anderson*	95/76 *Tennessee Ernie Ford*	13/75 I Can Still Hear The Music In The Restroom *Jerry Lee Lewis*
Husbands And Wives	4/58 I Beg Of You *Elvis Presley*	4/96 I Can Still Make Cheyenne *George Strait*
5/66 *Roger Miller*	99/76 I Believe He's Gonna Drive That Rig To Glory *Craig Donaldson*	1/84 I Can Tell By The Way You Dance *Vern Gosdin*
16/81 *David Frizzell & Shelly West*	10/68 I Believe In Love *Bonnie Guitar*	3/70 I Can't Be Myself *Merle Haggard*
1/98 *Brooks & Dunn*	31/68 I Believe In Love *Stonewall Jackson*	1/77 I Can't Believe She Gives It All To Me *Conway Twitty*
74/67 Husbands-In-Law *Jim Nesbitt*	24/74 I Believe In The Sunshine *Roger Miller*	12/73 I Can't Believe That It's All Over *Skeeter Davis*
51/73 Hush *Jeannie C. Riley*	1/78 I Believe In You *Mel Tillis*	1/70 I Can't Believe That You've Stopped Loving Me *Charley Pride*
33/87 Hymne *Joe Kenyon*	1/80 I Believe In You *Don Williams*	34/80 I Can't Cheat *Larry G. Hudson*
2/96 Hypnotize The Moon *Clay Walker*	I Believe The South Is Gonna Rise Again	8/97 I Can't Do That Anymore *Faith Hill*

I

6/83 I.O.U. *Lee Greenwood*	62/74 *Bobby Goldsboro*	64/72 I Can't Face The Bed Alone *Henson Cargill*
I.O.U.	18/75 *Tanya Tucker*	3/79 I Can't Feel You Anymore *Loretta Lynn*
9/76 *Jimmy Dean*	48/84 I Bet You Never Thought I'd Go This Far *Micki Fuhrman*	1/88 I Can't Get Close Enough *Exile*
90/77 *Jimmy Dean*	I Bought The Shoes That Just Walked Out On Me	5/80 I Can't Get Enough Of You *Razzy Bailey*
77/83 *Jimmy Dean*	79/83 *Super Grit Cowboy Band*	5/99 I Can't Get Over You *Brooks & Dunn*
6/75 I Ain't All Bad *Charley Pride*	78/87 *Ronnie Sessions*	29/83 I Can't Get Over You (Getting Over Me) *Bandana*
27/68 I Ain't Buying *Johnny Darrell*	78/78 I Bow My Head (When They Say Grace) *Daniel*	43/73 I Can't Get Over You To Save My Life *Lefty Frizzell*
43/66 I Ain't Crying Mister *Larry Steele*	36/95 I Brake For Brunettes *Rhett Akins*	5/67 I Can't Get There From Here *George Jones*
68/79 I Ain't Giving Up On Her Yet *Jack Grayson*	1/02 I Breathe In, I Breathe Out *Chris Cagle*	37/78 I Can't Get Up By Myself *Brenda Kaye Perry*
62/95 I Ain't Goin' Peacefully *Hank Williams, Jr.*	48/97 I Broke It, I'll Fix It *River Road*	37/71 I Can't Go On Loving You *Roy Drusky*
87/88 I Ain't Gonna Take This Layin' Down *Debbie Rich*	9/84 I Call It Love *Mel McDaniel*	4/46 I Can't Go On This Way *Bob Wills*
10/79 I Ain't Got No Business Doin' Business Today *Razzy Bailey*	64/89 I Came Straight To You *Kevin Welch*	66/88 I Can't Hang On Anymore *Dennis Payne*
34/68 I Ain't Got Nobody *Dick Curless*	83/76 I Can Almost See Houston From Here *Katy Moffatt*	I Can't Help It (If I'm Still In Love With You)
I Ain't Got Nobody	82/79 I Can Almost Touch The Feelin' *LeGardes*	2/51 *Hank Williams*
51/76 *Del Reeves*	53/89 I Can Be A Heartbreaker, Too *Johnny Lee*	2/75 *Linda Ronstadt*
60/81 *Roy Clark*	42/95 I Can Bring Her Back *Ken Mellons*	I Can't Help Myself (Here Comes The Feeling)
67/74 I Ain't Hangin' 'Round *LaWanda Lindsey*	47/64 I Can Do That *Tommy & Wanda Collins*	2/77 *Eddie Rabbitt*
1/80 I Ain't Living Long Like This *Waylon Jennings*	85/79 I Can Feel Love *Linda Calhoun*	82/81 *Sami Jo Cole*
I Ain't Never	55/85 I Can Feel The Fire Goin' Out *Lloyd David Foster*	I Can't Help Myself (Sugar Pie, Honey Bunch)
2/59 *Webb Pierce*	25/73 I Can Feel The Leavin' Coming On *Cal Smith*	65/75 *Price Mitchell & Jerri Kelly*
1/72 *Mel Tillis*	69/67 (I Can Find) A Better Deal Than That *Ruby Wright*	65/89 *Trisha Lynn*
70/87 *Lowes*	F/78 I Can Get Off On You *Waylon & Willie*	58/90 *Billy Hill*
92/79 I Ain't Never Been To Heaven *Jack Grayson*	86/77 I Can Give You Love *Mundo Earwood*	68/86 I Can't Help The Way I Don't Feel *Kaylee Adams*
73/79 I Ain't No Fool *Big Al Downing*	I Can Hear Kentucky Calling Me	2/60 (I Can't Help You) I'm Falling Too *Skeeter Davis*
63/68 I Ain't The Worryin' Kind *Billy Edd Wheeler*	75/80 *Osborne Brothers*	41/81 I Can't Hold Myself In Line *Johnny Paycheck & Merle Haggard*
23/64 I Almost Forgot Her Today *Carl Smith*	83/80 *Chet Atkins*	
36/98 I Already Do *Chely Wright*	1/74 I Can Help *Billy Swan*	
70/99 I Already Fell *Gil Grand*	45/88 I Can Love You *Judy Rodman*	
35/72 I Already Know (What I'm Getting For My Birthday) *Wanda Jackson*	7/98 I Can Love You Better *Dixie Chicks*	
1/83 I Always Get Lucky With You *George Jones*	1/95 I Can Love You Like That *John Michael Montgomery*	
21/02 I Always Liked That Best *Cyndi Thomson*	5/62 I Can Mend Your Broken Heart *Don Gibson*	
35/02 I Am A Man Of Constant Sorrow *Soggy Bottom Boys*	36/73 I Can See Clearly Now *Lloyd Green*	
1/91 I Am A Simple Man *Ricky Van Shelton*		
66/72 I Am, I Said *Bill Phillips*		
2/96 I Am That Man *Brooks & Dunn*		

13/66	**I Can't Keep Away From You** Wilburn Brothers	
26/00	**I Can't Lie To Me** Clay Davidson	
2/77	**I Can't Love You Enough** Loretta Lynn/Conway Twitty	
86/76	**I Can't Quit Cheatin' On You** Mundo Earwood	
49/66	**I Can't Quit Cigarettes** Jimmy Martin	
7/56	**I Can't Quit (I've Gone Too Far)** Marty Robbins	
3/94	**I Can't Reach Her Anymore** Sammy Kershaw	
9/65	**I Can't Remember** Connie Smith	
38/80	**I Can't Remember** Stephanie Winslow	
23/60	**I Can't Run Away From Myself** Ray Price	
8/69	**I Can't Say Goodbye** Marty Robbins	
	I Can't Say Goodbye To You	
44/79	Becky Hobbs	
30/82	Terry Gregory	
2/44	**I Can't See For Lookin'** King Cole Trio	
4/72	**I Can't See Me Without You** Conway Twitty	
7/70	**I Can't Seem To Say Goodbye** Jerry Lee Lewis	
42/73	**I Can't Sit Still** Patti Page	
14/63	**I Can't Stay Mad At You** Skeeter Davis	
	I Can't Stop Loving You	
3/58	Kitty Wells	
7/58	Don Gibson	
1/72	Conway Twitty	
27/77	Sammi Smith	
28/78	Mary K. Miller	
17/62	**I Can't Stop (My Lovin' You)** Buck Owens	
	I Can't Stop Now	
71/77	Mike Lunsford	
72/80	Billy Larkin	
58/88	**I Can't Take Her Anywhere** Darrell Holt	
43/67	**I Can't Take It No Longer** Hank Williams, Jr.	
26/60	**I Can't Tell My Heart That** Kitty Wells & Roy Drusky	
42/93	**I Can't Tell You Why** Vince Gill	
9/90	**I Can't Turn The Tide** Baillie And The Boys	
4/78	**I Can't Wait Any Longer** Bill Anderson	
5/53	**I Can't Wait (For The Sun To Go Down)** Faron Young	
1/87	**I Can't Win For Losin' You** Earl Thomas Conley	
1/75	**I Care** Tom T. Hall	
39/74	**I Changed My Mind** Billy Walker	
1/79	**I Cheated Me Right Out Of You** Moe Bandy	
4/78	**I Cheated On A Good Woman's Love** Billy "Crash" Craddock	
37/67	**I Come Home A-Drinkin' (To A Worn-Out Wife Like You)** Jack Webb	
7/90	**I Could Be Persuaded** Bellamy Brothers	
50/86	**I Could Get Used To This** Johnny Lee & Lane Brody	
1/86	**I Could Get Used To You** Exile	
64/97	**I Could Love A Man Like That** Anita Cochran	
69/85	**I Could Love You In A Heartbeat** Malchak & Rucker	
33/92	**I Could Love You (With My Eyes Closed)** Remingtons	
2/01	**I Could Not Ask For More** Sara Evans	
27/66	**I Could Sing All Night** Ferlin Husky	
30/79	**I Could Sure Use The Feeling** Earl Scruggs Revue	
9/84	**I Could Use Another You** Eddy Raven	
6/84	**I Could'a Had You** Leon Everette	
3/76	**I Couldn't Be Me Without You** Johnny Rodriguez	
4/47	**I Couldn't Believe It Was True** Eddy Arnold	
5/53	**I Couldn't Keep From Crying** Marty Robbins	
1/88	**I Couldn't Leave You If I Tried** Rodney Crowell	
96/79	**I Couldn't Live Without Your Love** Stacey Rowe	
40/67	**I Couldn't See** George Morgan	
3/91	**I Couldn't See You Leavin'** Conway Twitty	
12/59	**I Cried A Tear** Ernest Tubb	
21/65	**I Cried All The Way To The Bank** Norma Jean	
1/92	**I Cross My Heart** George Strait	
18/02	**I Cry** Tammy Cochran	
68/79	**I Cry Instead** Ron Shaw	
56/87	**I Did** Patty Loveless	
72/88	**I Did It For Love** Jill Jordan	
12/88	**I Didn't (Every Chance I Had)** Johnny Rodriguez	
17/67	**I Didn't Jump The Fence** Red Sovine	
1/95	**I Didn't Know My Own Strength** Lorrie Morgan	
30/82	**I Didn't Know You Could Break A Broken Heart** Joe Stampley	
22/60	**I Didn't Mean To Fall In Love** Hank Thompson	
2/96	**I Do** Paul Brandt	
2/98	**I Do [Cherish You]** Mark Wills	
3/70	**I Do My Swinging At Home** David Houston	
53/00	**I Do Now** Jessica Andrews	
	I Don't Believe I'll Fall In Love Today	
5/60	Warren Smith	
93/78	Gilbert Ortega	
4/95	**I Don't Believe In Goodbye** Sawyer Brown	
1/56	**I Don't Believe You've Met My Baby** Louvin Brothers	
	I Don't Call Him Daddy	
86/89	Kenny Rogers	
1/93	Doug Supernaw	
	I Don't Care	
1/55	Webb Pierce	
1/82	Ricky Skaggs	
65/96	**I Don't Care (If You Love Me Anymore)** Mavericks	
1/64	**I Don't Care (Just as Long as You Love Me)** Buck Owens	
16/79	**I Don't Do Like That No More** Kendalls	
1/95	**I Don't Even Know Your Name** Alan Jackson
74/87	**I Don't Feel Much Like A Cowboy Tonight** Gene Stroman
80/80	**I Don't Feel Much Like Smilin'** Dr. Hook
56/00	**I Don't Feel That Way** Danni Leigh
8/88	**I Don't Have Far To Fall** Skip Ewing
2/02	**I Don't Have To Be Me ('Til Monday)** Steve Azar
44/81	**I Don't Have To Crawl** Emmylou Harris
70/97	**I Don't Have To Wonder** Garth Brooks
	I Don't Hurt Anymore
1/54	Hank Snow
37/77	Narvel Felts
92/77	Linda Cassady
70/90	Prairie Oyster
50/01	**I Don't Know** Hank Williams III
1/84	**I Don't Know A Thing About Love (The Moon Song)** Conway Twitty
46/95	**I Don't Know (But I've Been Told)** Wesley Dennis
2/82	**I Don't Know Where To Start** Eddie Rabbitt
10/77	**I Don't Know Why (I Just Do)** Marty Robbins
1/85	**I Don't Know Why You Don't Want Me** Rosanne Cash
5/71	**I Don't Know You (Anymore)** Tommy Overstreet
12/79	**I Don't Lie** Joe Stampley
45/78	**I Don't Like Cheatin' Songs** Dale McBride
38/75	**I Don't Love Her Anymore** Johnny Paycheck
52/86	**I Don't Love Her Anymore** Almost Brothers
47/64	**I Don't Love Nobody** Leon McAuliff
4/64	**I Don't Love You Anymore** Charlie Louvin
65/86	**I Don't Mean Maybe** A.J. Masters
74/72	**I Don't Mind Goin' Under (If It'll Get Me Over You)** Charlie Walker
1/85	**I Don't Mind The Thorns (If You're The Rose)** Lee Greenwood
74/89	**I Don't Miss You Like I Used To** Stella Parton
8/78	**I Don't Need A Thing At All** Gene Watson
1/81	**I Don't Need You** Kenny Rogers
34/93	**I Don't Need Your Rockin' Chair** George Jones
71/00	**I Don't Paint Myself Into Corners** Rebecca Lynn Howard
43/74	**I Don't Plan On Losing You** Brian Collins
10/83	**I Don't Remember Loving You** John Conlee
40/67	**I Don't See How I Can Make It** Jean Shepard
1/74	**I Don't See Me In Your Eyes Anymore** Charlie Rich
2/96	**I Don't Think I Will** James Bonamy

76/76	I Don't Think I'll Ever (Get Over You) *Don Gibson*	
7/85	I Don't Think I'm Ready For You *Anne Murray*	
13/81	I Don't Think Love Ought To Be That Way *Reba McEntire*	
2/82	I Don't Think She's In Love Anymore *Charley Pride*	
	I Don't Wanna ..also see: I Don't Want To	
	I Don't Wanna Cry	
3/77	Larry Gatlin	
88/78	Maury Finney	
2/84	I Don't Wanna Lose Your Love *Crystal Gayle*	
1/67	I Don't Wanna Play House *Tammy Wynette*	
13/76	I Don't Wanna Talk It Over Anymore *Connie Smith*	
48/76	I Don't Want It *Chuck Price*	
64/98	I Don't Want No Part Of It *Smokin' Armadillos*	
1/84	I Don't Want To Be A Memory *Exile*	
88/76	I Don't Want To Be A One Night Stand *Reba McEntire*	
56/77	I Don't Want To Be Alone Tonight *Ray Sanders*	
5/51	I Don't Want To Be Free *Margaret Whiting & Jimmy Wakely*	
	I Don't Want To Be Right ..see: (If Loving You Is Wrong)	
21/67	I Don't Want To Be With Me *Conway Twitty*	
33/85	I Don't Want To Get Over You *Whites*	
1/76	I Don't Want To Have To Marry You *Jim Ed Brown/Helen Cornelius*	
	I Don't Want To Know Your Name	
54/81	Glen Campbell	
71/86	Wrays	
30/80	I Don't Want To Lose *Leon Everette*	
20/80	I Don't Want To Lose You *Con Hunley*	
81/85	I Don't Want To Lose You *Freddie Hart*	
67/79	I Don't Want To Love You Anymore *Dandy*	
45/89	I Don't Want To Mention Any Names *Burch Sisters*	
1/99	I Don't Want To Miss A Thing *Mark Chesnutt*	
68/87	I Don't Want To Set The World On Fire *Suzy Bogguss*	
1/89	I Don't Want To Spoil The Party *Rosanne Cash*	
92/79	I Don't Wanna Want You *Scott Summer*	
40/82	I Don't Want To Want You *Lobo*	
7/02	I Don't Want You To Go *Carolyn Dawn Johnson*	
26/67	I Doubt It *Bobby Lewis*	
7/84	I Dream Of Women Like You *Ronnie McDowell*	
	I Dreamed Of A Hill-Billy Heaven	
10/55	Eddie Dean	
5/61	Tex Ritter	
92/76	Red Simpson	
82/85	I Dropped Your Name *Danny Davis*	
53/01	I Drove Her To Dallas *Tyler England*	
	I Fall To Pieces	
1/61	Patsy Cline	
37/70	Diana Trask	
89/77	Mary Miller	
61/81	Patsy Cline	
54/82	Patsy Cline & Jim Reeves	
72/94	Aaron Neville & Trisha Yearwood	
6/55	I Feel Better All Over (More Than Anywhere's Else) *Ferlin Huskey*	
	I Feel Fine	
59/70	Penny DeHaven	
9/89	Sweethearts Of The Rodeo	
26/82	I Feel It With You *Kieran Kane*	
7/56	I Feel Like Cryin' *Carl Smith*	
70/89	I Feel Like Hank Williams Tonight *Jerry Jeff Walker*	
1/81	I Feel Like Loving You Again *T.G. Sheppard*	
4/92	I Feel Lucky *Mary-Chapin Carpenter*	
14/49	I Feel That Old Age Creeping On *Homer And Jethro*	
34/85	I Feel The Country Callin' Me *Mac Davis*	
53/68	I Feel You, I Love You *Bobby Helms*	
55/98	I Fell *Brady Seals*	
3/90	I Fell In Love *Carlene Carter*	
1/85	I Fell In Love Again Last Night *Forester Sisters*	
13/93	I Fell In The Water *John Anderson*	
14/49	I Find You Cheatin' On Me *Hank Thompson*	
	I Forgot More Than You'll Ever Know	
1/53	Davis Sisters	
60/72	Jeanne Pruett	
56/85	I Forgot That I Don't Live Here Anymore *Darrell Clanton*	
46/67	I Forgot To Cry *Charlie Louvin*	
1/56	I Forgot To Remember To Forget *Elvis Presley*	
	I Fought The Law	
61/75	Sam Neely	
15/78	Hank Williams, Jr.	
66/92	Nitty Gritty Dirt Band	
5/58	I Found My Girl In The USA *Jimmie Skinner*	
10/53	I Found Out More Than You Ever Knew *Betty Cody*	
F/70	I Found You Just In Time *Lynn Anderson*	
22/63	I Gave My Wedding Dress Away *Kitty Wells*	
54/74	I Gave Up Good Mornin' Darling *Red Steagall*	
	(I Gave You The Best Years Of My Life) ..see: Rock N' Roll	
62/71	I Get Lonely When It Rains *Leroy Van Dyke*	
	I Get So Lonely ..see: (Oh Baby Mine)	
1/66	I Get The Fever *Bill Anderson*	
73/91	I Get The Picture *Skip Ewing*	
28/88	I Give You Music *McCarters*	
55/89	I Go Crazy *Lee Greenwood*	
	I Go To Pieces	
88/80	Tammy Jo	
39/88	Dean Dillon	
76/88	Trisha Lynn	
31/90	Southern Pacific	
64/84	I Got A Bad Attitude *Gary Stewart*	
58/92	I Got A Date *Forester Sisters*	
F/79	I Got A Feelin' In My Body *Elvis Presley*	
54/92	I Got A Life *Mike Reid*	
30/75	I Got A Lot Of Hurtin' Done Today *Connie Smith*	
45/93	I Got A Love *Matthews, Wright & King*	
8/84	I Got A Million Of 'Em *Ronnie McDowell*	
93/73	I Got A Thing About You Baby *Troy Seals*	
40/71	I Got A Woman *Bob Luman*	
1/89	I Got Dreams *Steve Wariner*	
43/91	I Got It Bad *Matraca Berg*	
15/95	I Got It Honest *Aaron Tippin*	
1/84	I Got Mexico *Eddy Raven*	
	I Got My Baby	
69/99	Faith Hill	
63/00	Faith Hill	
4/59	I Got Stripes *Johnny Cash*	
3/77	I Got The Hoss *Mel Tillis*	
56/87	I Got The One I Wanted *Nielsen White Band*	
93/79	I Got Western Pride *Ray Frushay*	
4/68	I Got You *Waylon Jennings & Anita Carter*	
5/89	I Got You *Dwight Yoakam*	
7/91	I Got You *Shenandoah*	
88/79	I Gotta Get Back The Feeling *Sheila Andrews*	
	I Gotta Get Drunk (And I Shore Do Dread It)	
27/63	Joe Carson	
55/76	Willie Nelson	
8/55	I Gotta Go Get My Baby *Justin Tubb*	
	I Gotta Have My Baby Back	
4/50	Floyd Tillman	
10/50	Red Foley	
73/67	Glen Campbell	
15/56	I Gotta Know *Wanda Jackson*	
44/91	I Gotta Mind To Go Crazy *Les Taylor*	
72/87	I Grow Old Too Fast (And Smart Too Slow) *Johnny Paycheck*	
82/89	I Guess By Now *Big Al Downing*	
48/67	I Guess I Had Too Much To Dream Last Night *Faron Young*	
55/88	I Guess I Just Missed You *Canyon*	
9/62	I Guess I'll Never Learn *Charlie Phillips*	
	I Guess I'm Crazy	
13/55	Tommy Collins	
1/64	Jim Reeves	
1/84	I Guess It Never Hurts To Hurt Sometimes *Oak Ridge Boys*	
14/93	I Guess You Had To Be There *Lorrie Morgan*	
72/76	I Guess You Never Loved Me Anyway *Randy Cornor*	
5/86	I Had A Beautiful Time *Merle Haggard*	
63/87	I Had A Heart *Darlene Austin*	
5/79	I Had A Lovely Time *Kendalls*	

33/82	I Had It All *Fred Knoblock*	77/85	I Just Came Back (To Break My Heart Again) *Bruce Hauser/ Sawmill Creek Band*	36/81	I Just Want To Be With You *Sammi Smith*
60/86	I Had My Heart Set On You *Emmylou Harris*			14/78	I Just Want To Be Your Everything *Connie Smith*
30/65	I Had One Too Many *Wilburn Brothers*	4/82	I Just Came Here To Dance *David Frizzell & Shelly West*	1/98	I Just Want To Dance With You *George Strait*
4/44	I Hang My Head And Cry *Gene Autry*		I Just Came Home To Count The Memories	1/78	I Just Want To Love You *Eddie Rabbitt*
	I Hate Goodbyes	75/75	Bobby Wright	97/78	I Just Want To Love You *DeAnne Horn*
25/73	Bobby Bare	15/77	Cal Smith		
40/77	Lois Johnson	7/82	John Anderson	70/68	I Just Wanted To Know (How the Wind Was Blowing) *Hank Snow*
22/58	I Hate Myself *Faron Young*		I Just Came In Here (To Let A Little Hurt Out)		
16/79	I Hate The Way I Love It *Johnny Rodriguez & Charly McClain*	51/77	Peggy Sue	1/94	I Just Wanted You To Know *Mark Chesnutt*
78/79	I Hate The Way Our Love Is *Jimmy Peters & Lynda K. Lance*	96/89	Sandy Ellwanger	59/78	I Just Wanted You To Know *Ronnie McDowell*
10/73	I Hate You *Ronnie Milsap*	8/68	I Just Came To Get My Baby *Faron Young*	56/68	I Just Wasted The Rest *Del Reeves & Bobby Goldsboro*
17/81	I Have A Dream *Cristy Lane*	21/66	I Just Came To Smell The Flowers *Porter Wagoner*		
26/77	I Have A Dream, I Have A Dream *Roy Clark*	1/75	I Just Can't Get Her Out Of My Mind *Johnny Rodriguez*	1/78	I Just Wish You Were Someone I Love *Larry Gatlin*
	I Have Loved You Girl (But Not Like This Before)		I Just Can't Help Believing	89/79	I Just Wonder Where He Could Be Tonight *Hilka & Jebry*
87/75	Earl Thomas Conley	36/70	David Frizzell	1/81	I Keep Coming Back *Razzy Bailey*
2/83	Earl Thomas Conley	59/74	David Rogers		
90/80	I Have To Break The Chains That Bind Me *Gary Goodnight*	48/65	I Just Can't Let You Say Goodbye *Willie Nelson*	14/68	I Keep Coming Back For More *Dave Dudley*
17/97	I Have To Surrender *Ty Herndon*	21/88	I Just Can't Say No To You *Moe Bandy*	43/65	I Keep Forgettin' That I Forgot About You *Wynn Stewart*
7/88	I Have You *Glen Campbell*	63/95	I Just Can't Stand To Be Unhappy *Bobbie Cryner*		I Kissed You ..see: ('Til)
5/53	I Haven't Got The Heart *Webb Pierce*	5/79	I Just Can't Stay Married To You *Cristy Lane*	55/00	I Knew I Loved You *Daryle Singletary*
76/77	I Haven't Learned A Thing *Porter Wagoner*	68/86	I Just Can't Take The Leaving Anymore *Susan Raye*	48/73	I Knew Jesus (Before He Was A Star) *Glen Campbell*
54/67	I Hear It Now *Browns*	58/76	I Just Can't (Turn My Habit Into Love) *Kenny Starr*	37/88	I Knew Love *Nanci Griffith*
17/66	I Hear Little Rock Calling *Ferlin Husky*	73/82	I Just Can't Turn Temptation Down *Skip And Linda*	64/91	I Knew My Day Would Come *Vern Gosdin*
83/88	I Hear The South *Vassar Clements*	40/72	I Just Couldn't Let Her Walk Away *Dorsey Burnette*	91/78	I Knew The Mason *Chapin Hartford*
29/79	I Hear The South Callin' Me *Hank Thompson*	51/66	I Just Couldn't See The Forest (For The Trees) *Lefty Frizzell*	84/83	I Knew You When *Linda Ronstadt*
91/78	I Hear You Coming Back *Brent Burns*	11/82	I Just Cut Myself *Ronnie McDowell*	86/76	I Knew You When *Jerry Foster*
27/59	I Hear You Talkin' *Faron Young*	92/75	I Just Don't Give A Damn *George Jones*	59/70	I Knew You'd Be Leaving *Peggy Little*
9/68	I Heard A Heart Break Last Night *Jim Reeves*	5/50	I Just Don't Like This Kind Of Livin' *Hank Williams*	72/97	I Know *Kim Richey*
93/79	I Heard A Song Today *Tommy O'Day*	1/79	I Just Fall In Love Again *Anne Murray*	100/78	I Know *DeAnne Horn*
12/49	I Heard About You *Bud Hobbs*	28/76	I Just Got A Feeling *La Costa*	65/79	I Know A Good Thing When I Feel It *Pia Zadora*
33/65	I Heard From A Memory Last Night *Jim Edward Brown*	10/53	(I Just Had A Date) A Lover's Quarrel *George Morgan*	10/79	I Know A Heartache When I See One *Jennifer Warnes*
71/84	I Heard It On The Radio *Robin Lee*	1/79	I Just Had You On My Mind	81/81	I Know An Ending (When It Comes) *B.J. Wright*
45/70	I Heard Our Song *Dottie West*	48/74	Sue Richards	4/70	I Know How *Loretta Lynn*
	(I Heard That) Lonesome Whistle ..see: Lonesome Whistle	21/78	Dottsy	1/88	I Know How He Feels *Reba McEntire*
4/57	I Heard The Bluebirds Sing *Browns*	22/80	Billy "Crash" Craddock		I Know How The River Feels
	I Honestly Love You	46/83	I Just Heard A Heart Break *Tammy Wynette*	33/99	Diamond Rio
6/74	Olivia Newton-John	63/76	I Just Love Being A Woman *Barbara Fairchild*	69/00	McAlyster
16/98	Olivia Newton-John			74/67	I Know How To Do It *Bobby Braddock*
59/68	I Hope I Like Mexico Blues *Dallas Frazier*	45/96	I Just Might Be *Lorrie Morgan*	91/79	I Know I'm Not Your Hero Anymore *Ronnie Robbins*
36/70	I Hope So *Willie Nelson*	78/79	I Just Need A Coke (To Get The Whiskey Down) *Lenny Gault*	56/86	I Know Love *Everly Brothers*
1/00	I Hope You Dance *Lee Ann Womack*	11/81	I Just Need You For Tonight *Billy "Crash" Craddock*	67/83	I Know My Way To You By Heart *Marlow Tackett*
49/72	I Hope You're Havin' Better Luck Than Me *Crystal Gayle*	17/74	I Just Started Hatin' Cheatin' Songs Today *Moe Bandy*		I Know One
10/84	I Hurt For You *Deborah Allen*	43/79	I Just Wanna Feel The Magic *Bobby Borchers*	6/60	Jim Reeves
69/68	I Just Ain't Got (As Much As He's Got Going For Me) *Gene Wyatt*	56/67	I Just Want To Be Alone *Ray Pillow*	6/67	Charley Pride
16/89	I Just Called To Say Goodbye Again *Larry Boone*			5/96	I Know She Still Loves Me *George Strait*
				96/77	I Know The Feeling *Jerry Green*
				35/85	I Know The Way To You By Heart *Vern Gosdin*

89/88	**I Know There's A Heart In There Somewhere** *Chris Austin*		**I Love That Woman (Like The Devil Loves Sin)**	45/89	**I Married Her Just Because She Looks Like You** *Lyle Lovett*
73/99	**I Know What I Want For Christmas** *George Strait*	84/77	*Leon Everette*	4/84	**I May Be Used (But Baby I Ain't Used Up)** *Waylon Jennings*
21/89	**I Know What I've Got** *J. C. Crowley*	28/80	*Leon Everette*	27/62	**I May Fall Again** *Buddy Meredith*
		10/75	**I Love The Blues And The Boogie Woogie** *Billy "Crash" Craddock*	64/75	**I May Never Be Your Lover (But I'll Always Be Your Friend)** *Bobby G. Rice*
1/87	**I Know Where I'm Going** *Judds*	43/89	**I Love The Way He Left You** *Lee Greenwood*		
13/92	**I Know Where Love Lives** *Hal Ketchum*	40/76	**I Love The Way That You Love Me** *Ray Griff*	1/79	**I May Never Get To Heaven** *Conway Twitty*
	I Know You're Married (But I Love You Still)	15/71	**I Love The Way That You've Been Lovin' Me** *Roy Drusky*	70/75	**I May Not Be Lovin' You** *Patti Page*
29/66	*Bill Anderson & Jan Howard*	1/93	**I Love The Way You Love Me** *John Michael Montgomery*	39/91	**I Mean I Love You** *Hank Williams, Jr.*
52/70	*Red Sovine*	4/64	**I Love To Dance With Annie** *Ernest Ashworth*	2/90	**I Meant Every Word He Said** *Ricky Van Shelton*
39/67	**I Learn Something New Everyday** *Bill Phillips*	60/76	**I Love Us** *Skeeter Davis*	39/97	**I Meant To Do That** *Paul Brandt*
2/44	**I Learned A Lesson, I'll Never Forget** *5 Red Caps*	22/77	**I Love What Love Is Doing To Me** *Lynn Andrson*	10/76	**I Met A Friend Of Your's Today** *Mel Street*
87/80	**I Learned All About Cheatin' From You** *Becky Hobbs*	49/77	**I Love What My Woman Does To Me** *David Rogers*	57/79	**I Might Be Awhile In New Orleans** *Johnny Russell*
53/77	**I Left My Heart In San Francisco** *Red Steagall*	1/99	**I Love You** *Martina McBride*	37/89	**I Might Be What You're Lookin' For** *Larry Gatlin/Gatlin Brothers*
2/97	**I Left Something Turned On At Home** *Trace Adkins*	3/54	**I Love You** *Ginny Wright/Jim Reeves*	18/98	**I Might Even Quit Lovin' You** *Mark Chesnutt*
42/73	**I Let Another Good One Get Away** *Dorsey Burnette*		**I Love You A Thousand Ways**	73/96	**I Might Just Make It** *Paul Jefferson*
2/95	**I Let Her Lie** *Daryle Singletary*	1/51	*Lefty Frizzell*	74/94	**I Miss Her Missing Me** *Davis Daniel*
1/53	**I Let The Stars Get In My Eyes** *Goldie Hill*	8/51	*Hawkshaw Hawkins*		
		9/77	*Willie Nelson*		
9/82	**I Lie** *Loretta Lynn*	54/81	*John Anderson*	37/74	**I Miss You** *Jeannie Seely*
	(I Lied) ..see: Believe Me Baby		**I Love You Because**	6/97	**I Miss You A Little** *John Michael Montgomery*
4/75	**I Like Beer** *Tom T. Hall*	1/50	*Leon Payne*	26/77	**I Miss You Already** *Jerry Wallace*
F/80	**I Like Being Lonely** *Ann J. Morton*	2/50	*Ernest Tubb*		**I Miss You Already (And You're Not Even Gone)**
	I Like Everything About Loving You	8/50	*Clyde Moody*		
62/73	*Bobbie Roy*	20/60	*Johnny Cash*	5/57	*Faron Young*
89/77	*Lori Parker*	14/69	*Carl Smith*	21/60	*Jimmy Newman*
1/95	**I Like It, I Love It** *Tim McGraw*	54/76	*Jim Reeves*	14/86	*Billy Joe Royal*
23/78	**I Like Ladies In Long Black Dresses** *Bobby Borchers*	F/78	*Don Gibson*	62/73	**I Miss You Most When You're Here** *Sammi Smith*
		91/83	*Roger Whittaker*		
58/95	**I Like The Sound Of That** *Woody Lee*	12/61	**I Love You Best Of All** *Louvin Brothers*		**(I Miss You Too) ..see: Honey**
74/91	**I Like The Way It Feels** *Ray Kennedy*	9/86	**I Love You By Heart** *Sylvia & Michael Johnson*	3/60	**I Missed Me** *Jim Reeves*
				38/80	**I Must Be Crazy** *Susie Allanson*
57/78	**I Like To Be With You** *Ronnie Sessions*	50/94	**I Love You 'Cause I Want To** *Carlene Carter*	89/89	**I Must Be Crazy** *Rick Arnold*
50/68	**I Like Trains** *Bob Luman*	55/71	**I Love You Dear** *Eddy Arnold*	32/73	**I Must Be Doin' Something Right** *Roy Drusky*
70/69	**I Live To Love You** *Johnny Duncan*	4/66	**I Love You Drops** *Bill Anderson*	41/77	**I Must Be Dreaming** *Don King*
75/99	**I Look At You** *George Strait*	6/74	**I Love You, I Love You** *David Houston & Barbara Mandrell*	55/91	**I Must Have Been Crazy** *Matraca Berg*
3/00	**I Lost It** *Kenny Chesney*	5/78	**I Love You, I Love You, I Love You** *Ronnie McDowell*	7/46	**I Must Have Been Wrong** *Bob Atcher*
26/79	**I Lost My Head** *Charlie Rich*				
1/74	**I Love** *Tom T. Hall*		**(I Love You In Many Ways) ..see: Te' Quiero**	F/79	**I Must Have Done Something Bad** *Merle Haggard*
91/76	**I Love A Beautiful Guy** *Connie Cato*	8/58	**I Love You More** *Jim Reeves*	77/80	**I Musta Died And Gone To Texas** *Amazing Rhythm Aces*
1/81	**I Love A Rainy Night** *Eddie Rabbitt*	4/73	**I Love You More And More Everyday** *Sonny James*	77/88	**I Need A Good Woman Bad** *Lane Caudell*
57/75	**I Love A Rodeo** *Roger Miller*	1/69	**I Love You More Today** *Conway Twitty*	93/80	**I Need A Little More Time** *B.J. Harrison*
4/49	**I Love Everything About You** *George Morgan*	11/55	**I Love You Mostly** *Lefty Frizzell*	57/91	**I Need A Miracle** *Larry Boone*
95/77	**I Love Everything I Get My Hands On** *Bobby Trinity*		**I Love You So Much, It Hurts**	34/89	**I Need A Wife** *Joni Harms*
		5/48	*Floyd Tillman*	76/73	**I Need Help** *Carl Smith*
4/83	**I Love Her Mind** *Bellamy Brothers*	1/49	*Jimmy Wakely*	1/85	**I Need More Of You** *Bellamy Brothers*
	I Love How You Love Me	10/78	**(I Love You) What Can I Say** *Jerry Reed*	53/86	**I Need Some Good News Bad** *Chance*
94/78	*Joni Lee*	1/81	**I Loved 'Em Every One** *T.G. Sheppard*	11/73	**I Need Somebody Bad** *Jack Greene*
18/79	*Lynn Anderson*	24/88	**I Loved You Yesterday** *Lyle Lovett*	93/77	**I Need Somethin' Easy Tonight** *Danny Wood*
17/83	*Glen Campbell*				
76/77	**I Love It (When You Love All Over Me)** *Wayne Kemp*	64/68	**I Made The Prison Band** *Tommy Collins*	65/87	**I Need To Be Loved Again** *Liz Boardo*
1/74	**I Love My Friend** *Charlie Rich*	76/88	**I Make The Living (She Makes The Living Worthwhile)** *Danny Shirley*		
15/81	**I Love My Truck** *Glen Campbell*				
3/84	**I Love Only You** *Nitty Gritty Dirt Band*				

8/00	I Need You LeAnn Rimes	
36/97	I Need You Trisha Yearwood	
22/77	(I Need You) All The Time	
	Eddy Arnold	
40/00	I Need You All The Time	
	BlackHawk	
85/79	I Need Your Help Barry Manilow	
	Ray Stevens	
32/74	I Never Get Through Missing You	
	Bobby Lewis	
	I Never Go Around Mirrors	
25/74	Lefty Frizzell	
96/78	Ronnie Sessions	
30/85	I Never Got Over You	
	Johnny Paycheck	
46/69	I Never Got Over You	
	Carl Butler & Pearl	
	I Never Had A Chance With You	
51/84	Mason Dixon	
89/89	Patsy Cole	
70/74	I Never Had It So Good	
	Buddy Alan	
	I Never Had The One I Wanted	
9/67	Claude Gray	
78/79	Claude Gray	
65/82	Solid Gold Band	
2/94	I Never Knew Love Doug Stone	
44/82	I Never Knew The Devil's Eyes Were Blue Terry Gregory	
13/74	I Never Knew (What That Song Meant Before) Connie Smith	
72/79	I Never Loved Anyone Like I Love You Louise Mandrell	
10/85	I Never Made Love (Till I Made Love With You) Mac Davis	
89/78	I Never Meant To Harm You	
	Mike Ellis	
94/76	I Never Met A Girl I Didn't Like	
	Jim Mundy	
5/70	I Never Once Stopped Loving You Connie Smith	
5/70	I Never Picked Cotton Roy Clark	
3/84	I Never Quite Got Back (From Loving You) Sylvia	
24/76	I Never Said It Would Be Easy	
	Jacky Ward	
4/49	I Never See Maggie Alone	
	Kenny Roberts	
50/96	I Never Stopped Lovin' You	
	Steve Azar	
8/78	I Never Will Marry Linda Ronstadt	
7/97	I Only Get This Way With You	
	Rick Trevino	
54/69	I Only Regret Bill Phillips	
	I Only Want You For Christmas	
41/91	Alan Jackson	
48/95	Alan Jackson	
48/97	Alan Jackson	
14/87	I Only Wanted You Marie Osmond	
72/81	I Ought To Feel Guilty	
	Jeanne Pruett	
1/74	I Overlooked An Orchid	
	Mickey Gilley	
72/88	I Owe, I Owe (It's Off To Work I Go) David Chamberlain	
80/78	I Owe It All To You Jerry Abbott	
43/84	I Pass Gus Hardin	
53/00	I Pray For You John Rich	
2/87	I Prefer The Moonlight	
	Kenny Rogers	
74/89	I Promise Lynne Tyndall	
18/78	I Promised Her A Rainbow	
	Bobby Borchers	
26/68	I Promised You The World	
	Ferlin Husky	
	I Really Don't Want To Know	
1/54	Eddy Arnold	
23/71	Elvis Presley	
19/72	Charlie McCoy	
1/79	I Really Got The Feeling	
	Dolly Parton	
23/76	I Really Had A Ball Last Night	
	Carmol Taylor	
	I Recall A Gypsy Woman	
16/73	Tommy Cash	
22/81	B.J. Thomas	
52/69	I Remember Loving You	
	Sheb Wooley	
86/87	(I Remember When I Thought) Whiskey Was A River	
	Bobby Borchers	
	I Remember You	
49/66	Slim Whitman	
44/81	Slim Whitman	
32/88	Glen Campbell	
12/98	I Said A Prayer Pam Tillis	
1/89	I Sang Dixie Dwight Yoakam	
29/63	I Saw Me George Jones	
	I Saw Mommy Kissing Santa Claus	
7/52	Jimmy Boyd	
50/99	Reba McEntire	
25/72	I Saw My Lady Dickey Lee	
1/92	I Saw The Light Wynonna	
36/98	I Saw The Light Hal Ketchum	
56/71	I Saw The Light Nitty Gritty Dirt Band with Roy Acuff	
40/71	I Say A Little Prayer (medley) Glen Campbell/Anne Murray	
68/71	I Say, "Yes, Sir" Peggy Sue	
51/82	I See An Angel Every Day	
	Billy Parker	
67/73	I See His Love All Over You	
	Jim Glaser	
2/94	I See It Now Tracy Lawrence	
78/74	I See Love Bobby Lewis	
99/78	I See Love In Your Eyes	
	Larry Booth	
1/74	I See The Want To In Your Eyes Conway Twitty	
47/69	I See Them Everywhere	
	Hank Thompson	
75/70	I Shook The Hand Freddy Weller	
4/02	I Should Be Sleeping	
	Emerson Drive	
2/88	I Should Be With You	
	Steve Wariner	
54/67	I Should Get Away Awhile	
	Carl Smith	
30/95	I Should Have Been True	
	Mavericks	
11/75	I Should Have Married You	
	Eddie Rabbitt	
71/76	I Should Have Watched That First Step Wayne Kemp	
13/81	I Should've Called Eddy Raven	
72/98	I Should've Known	
	Melodie Crittenden	
69/97	I Smell Smoke Billy Yates	
84/81	I Sold All Of Tom T's Songs Last Night Gary Gentry	
56/83	I Spent The Night In The Heart Of Texas Marlow Tackett	
27/72	I Start Thinking About You	
	Johnny Carver	
	I Started Loving You Again	
69/70	Al Martino	
16/72	Charlie McCoy	
30/70	I Stayed Long Enough	
	Billie Jo Spears	
21/64	I Stepped Over The Line	
	Hank Snow	
12/88	I Still Believe Lee Greenwood	
13/75	I Still Believe In Fairy Tales	
	Tammy Wynette	
27/68	I Still Believe In Love Jan Howard	
46/78	I Still Believe In Love Charlie Rich	
2/81	I Still Believe In Waltzes	
	Conway Twitty & Loretta Lynn	
1/89	I Still Believe In You	
	Desert Rose Band	
1/92	I Still Believe In You Vince Gill	
82/79	I Still Believe In You	
	Mike Lunsford	
51/74	I Still Can't Believe You're Gone	
	Willie Nelson	
48/68	I Still Didn't Have The Sense To Go Johnny Carver	
17/84	I Still Do Bill Medley	
14/75	I Still Feel The Same About You	
	Bill Anderson	
40/80	(I Still Long To Hold You) Now And Then Reba McEntire	
95/79	I Still Love Her Memory	
	Hoot Hester	
28/82	I Still Love You (After All These Years) Tompall/Glaser Brothers	
85/89	I Still Love You Babe	
	Marilyn Mundy	
19/83	I Still Love You In The Same Ol' Way Moe Bandy	
81/75	I Still Love You (You Still Love Me) Mac Davis	
87/84	I Still Love Your Body	
	Tommy Overstreet	
	I Still Miss Someone	
43/65	Flatt & Scruggs	
38/81	Don King	
51/89	Emmylou Harris	
88/89	I Still Need You Steffin Sisters	
74/68	I Stole The Flowers From Your Garden Gene Wyatt	
9/94	I Sure Can Smell The Rain	
	BlackHawk	
30/86	I Sure Need Your Lovin'	
	Judy Rodman	
1/94	I Swear John Michael Montgomery	
3/69	I Take A Lot Of Pride In What I Am Merle Haggard	
6/72	I Take It On Home Charlie Rich	
2/94	I Take My Chances	
	Mary Chapin Carpenter	
	I Take The Chance	
2/56	Browns	
7/63	Ernest Ashworth	
89/87	Kathy Edge	
52/87	I Talked A Lot About Leaving	
	Larry Boone	
11/67	I Taught Her Everything She Knows Billy Walker	
31/88	I Taught Her Everything She Knows About Love Shooters	
7/86	I Tell It Like It Used To Be	
	T. Graham Brown	

70/76	I Thank God She Isn't Mine	
	Mel McDaniel	
8/65	I Thank My Lucky Stars	
	Eddy Arnold	
4/95	I Think About It All The Time	
	John Berry	
3/96	I Think About You Collin Raye	
17/82	I Think About Your Lovin'	
	Osmonds	
	I Think I Could Love You Better Than She [He] Did	
70/81	Ava Barber	
85/81	Gabriel	
7/60	I Think I Know Marion Worth	
1/81	I Think I'll Just Stay Here And Drink Merle Haggard	
	I Think I'll Say Goodbye	
76/75	Mary Kay James	
77/77	Jeris Ross	
36/86	I Think I'm In Love Keith Stegall	
	(I Think I've Got A Heartache) ..see: Excuse Me	
37/72	I Think They Call It Love	
	Don Gibson & Sue Thompson	
56/96	I Think We're On To Something Emilio	
44/00	I Think You're Beautiful Shane Minor	
	I Thought I Heard You Calling My Name	
11/57	Porter Wagoner	
29/76	Jessi Colter	
88/81	Pam Hobbs	
67/86	I Thought I'd About Had It With Love Pam Tillis	
4/91	I Thought It Was You Doug Stone	
10/55	I Thought Of You Jean Shepard	
75/78	I Thought You Were Easy Rayburn Anthony	
46/79	I Thought You'd Never Ask Louise Mandrell & R.C. Bannon	
2/67	I Threw Away The Rose Merle Haggard	
1/88	I Told You So Randy Travis	
25/59	I Traded Her Love (For Deep Purple Wine) Roland Johnson	
3/94	I Try To Think About Elvis Patty Loveless	
26/87	I Turn To You George Jones	
46/74	I Use The Soap Dickey Lee	
22/73	I Used It All On You Nat Stuckey	
26/70	I Wake Up In Heaven David Rogers	
1/68	I Walk Alone Marty Robbins	
1/56	I Walk The Line Johnny Cash	
61/98	I Walk The Line Revisited Rodney Crowell with Johnny Cash	
6/55	I Walked Alone Last Night Eddy Arnold	
12/70	I Walked Out On Heaven Hank Williams, Jr.	
59/85	I Wanna Be A Cowboy 'Til I Die Jim Collins	
38/81	I Wanna Be Around Terri Gibbs	
3/71	I Wanna Be Free Loretta Lynn	
98/78	I Wanna Be Her #1 Danny Hargrove	
53/71	I Wanna Be Loved Completely Warner Mack	
51/01	I Wanna Be That Girl Wilkinsons	
78/77	I Wanna Be With You Tonight Alabama	

33/79	I Wanna' Come Over Alabama	
1/88	I Wanna Dance With You Eddie Rabbitt	
63/80	I Wanna Do It Again Bill Wence	
3/98	I Wanna Fall In Love Lila McCann	
9/98	I Wanna Feel That Way Again Tracy Byrd	
72/79	I Wanna Go Back Nick Noble	
50/67	I Wanna Go Bummin' Around Sonny Curtis	
72/71	I Wanna Go Country Otis Williams	
	I Wanna Go Home ..see: Detroit City	
38/78	I Wanna Go To Heaven Jerry Wallace	
9/95	I Wanna Go Too Far Trisha Yearwood	
8/85	I Wanna Hear It From You Eddy Raven	
35/86	I Wanna Hear It From Your Lips Louise Mandrell	
63/88	(I Wanna Hear You) Say You Love Me Again Lisa Childress	
80/75	I Wanna Kiss Me Nancy Wayne	
43/88	I Wanna Know Her Again Wagoneers	
	I Wanna Live	
1/68	Glen Campbell	
87/76	Eddy Raven	
67/78	(I Wanna) Love My Life Away Jody Miller	
91/80	I Wanna Love You Tonight Mary Lou Turner	
1/51	I Wanna Play House With You Eddy Arnold	
20/98	I Wanna Remember This Linda Davis	
5/85	I Wanna Say Yes Louise Mandrell	
22/93	I Wanna Take Care Of You Billy Dean	
1/01	I Wanna Talk About Me Toby Keith	
	I Wanna Wake Up With You ..see: I Wanta	
13/55	I Wanna Wanna Wanna Wilburn Brothers	
63/78	I Want A Little Cowboy Jerry Abbott	
18/88	I Want A Love Like That Judy Rodman	
65/99	I Want A Man Lace	
10/85	I Want Everyone To Cry Restless Heart	
21/99	I Want It All Michael Rainwood	
7/95	I Want My Goodbye Back Ty Herndon	
19/69	I Want One Jack Reno	
83/80	I Want That Feelin' Again Bill Anderson	
	I Want To ..also see: I Wanna, & I Want'a	
	I Want To Be A Cowboy's Sweetheart	
5/46	Rosalie Allen	
77/88	Suzy Bogguss	
24/78	I Want To Be In Love Jacky Ward	
13/56	I Want To Be Loved Johnnie & Jack with Ruby Wells	
3/94	I Want To Be Loved Like That Shenandoah	
4/45	I Want To Be Sure Gene Autry	
80/87	I Want To Be Wanted Toni Price	

1/51	I Want To Be With You Always Lefty Frizzell	
35/97	I Want To Be Your Girlfriend Mary Chapin Carpenter	
25/84	I Want To Go Somewhere Keith Stegall	
18/58	I Want To Go Where No One Knows Me Jean Shepard	
1/66	I Want To Go With You Eddy Arnold	
9/75	I Want To Hold You In My Dreams Tonight Stella Parton	
49/64	I Want To Hold Your Hand Homer And Jethro	
33/00	I Want To Know (Everything There Is To Know About You) Mark Wills	
2/87	I Want To Know You Before We Make Love Conway Twitty	
71/74	I Want To Lay Down Beside You Marie Owens	
15/61	I Want To Live Again Rose Maddox	
84/78	I Want To Love You Jerry Foster	
F/79	I Want To Play My Horn On The Grand Ole' Opry Maury Finney	
	I Want To See Me In Your Eyes	
30/79	Peggy Sue	
80/81	Gene Kennedy & Karen Jeglum	
26/74	I Want To Stay Narvel Felts	
34/79	I Want To Walk You Home Porter Wagoner	
67/99	I Want To With You David Ball	
51/01	I Want Us Back Craig Morgan	
35/72	I Want You Johnny Carver	
35/01	I Want You Bad Charlie Robison	
7/93	I Want You Bad (And That Ain't Good) Collin Raye	
22/70	I Want You Free Jean Shepard	
1/56	I Want You, I Need You, I Love You Elvis Presley	
49/01	I Want You To Want Me Dwight Yoakam	
22/81	I Want You Tonight Johnny Rodriguez	
25/74	I Wanta Get To You La Costa	
	I Wanta Wake Up With You	
88/87	Cristy Lane	
41/88	Johnny Rodriguez	
37/99	I Was Neal McCoy	
16/95	I Was Blown Away Pam Tillis	
	I Was Born With A Broken Heart	
75/89	Josh Logan	
38/92	Aaron Tippin	
1/81	I Was Country When Country Wasn't Cool Barbara Mandrell	
F/57	I Was The First One Hank Thompson	
	I Was The One	
8/56	Elvis Presley	
92/83	Elvis Presley	
8/77	I Was There Statler Brothers	
39/68	I Was With Red Foley (The Night He Passed Away) Luke The Drifter, Jr.	
30/67	I Washed My Face In The Morning Dew Tom T. Hall	
8/65	I Washed My Hands In Muddy Water Stonewall Jackson	
23/63	I Wasn't Even In The Running Hank Thompson	

457

15/49	I Wasted A Nickel *Hawkshaw Hawkins*	97/79	I Wish I Had Your Arms Around Me *Red Willow Band*	41/72	I Wonder How John Felt (When He Baptized Jesus) *David Houston*
8/90	I Watched It All (On My Radio) *Lionel Cartwright*	8/49	I Wish I Knew *Dolph Hewitt*	F/77	I Wonder How She's Doing Now *Johnny Russell*
19/99	I Wear Your Love *Lisa Angelle*	13/78	I Wish I Loved Somebody Else *Tom T. Hall*		I Wonder If I Care As Much
9/61	I Went Out Of My Way (To Make You Happy) *Roy Drusky*	27/63	I Wish I Was A Single Girl Again *Jan Howard*	53/81	*Dickey Lee*
3/52	I Went To Your Wedding *Hank Snow*	22/80	I Wish I Was Crazy Again *Johnny Cash & Waylon Jennings*	30/87	*Ricky Skaggs*
23/58	I Will *Ferlin Husky*		I Wish I Was Eighteen Again	2/76	I Wonder If I Ever Said Goodbye *Johnny Rodriguez*
80/77	I Will *Wendel Adkins*	F/79	*Jerry Lee Lewis*	1/73	I Wonder If They Ever Think Of Me *Merle Haggard*
21/69	I Will Always *Don Gibson*	15/80	*George Burns*		
	I Will Always Love You	20/83	I Wish I Was In Nashville *Mel McDaniel*	4/71	I Wonder What She'll Think About Me Leaving *Conway Twitty*
1/74	*Dolly Parton*	4/89	I Wish I Was Still In Your Dreams *Conway Twitty*	37/89	I Wonder What She's Doing Tonight *Russell Smith*
84/78	*Jimmie Peters*	51/69	I Wish I Was Your Friend *Wanda Jackson*	10/83	I Wonder Where We'd Be Tonight *Vern Gosdin*
1/82	*Dolly Parton*	91/78	I Wish I'd Never Borrowed Anybody's Angel *Mike Lunsford*	9/83	I Wonder Who's Holding My Baby Tonight *Whites*
15/95	*Dolly Parton With Vince Gill*	52/88	I Wish It Was That Easy Going Home *Jeff Dugan*	81/77	I Wonder Who's Kissing Her Now *George Hamilton IV*
30/77	I'll Always Love You *Cates Sisters*	67/73	I Wish It Would Rain *O.B. McClinton*	20/75	I Wonder Whose Baby (You Are Now) *Jerry Wallace*
47/00	I Will Be *Lila McCann*	68/87	I Wish She Wouldn't Treat You That Way *Pam Tillis*		I Wore A Tie Today ..see: (Jim)
1/87	I Will Be There *Dan Seals*		I Wish That I Could Fall In Love Today ..see: I Wish I Could	55/00	I Would *Jolie & The Wanted*
28/99	I Will Be There For You *Jessica Andrews*	3/86	I Wish That I Could Hurt That Way Again *T. Graham Brown*	12/78	I Would Like To See You Again *Johnny Cash*
64/68	I Will Bring You Water *Browns*	19/74	I Wish That I Had Loved You Better *Eddy Arnold*	4/01	I Would've Loved You Anyway *Trisha Yearwood*
2/00	I Will...But *SheDaisy*	64/88	I Wish We Were Strangers *Ogden Harless*		I Wouldn't Be A Man
45/85	I Will Dance With You *Karen Brooks with Johnny Cash*		I Wish You Could Have Turned My Head (And Left My Heart Alone)	9/88	*Don Williams*
46/71	I Will Drink Your Wine *Buddy Alan*	54/78	*Sonny Throckmorton*	45/96	*Billy Dean*
53/88	I Will Hold You *Randy Vanwarmer*	54/81	*Peggy Forman*	8/65	I Wouldn't Buy A Used Car From Him *Norma Jean*
19/97	I Will, If You Will *John Berry*	2/82	*Oak Ridge Boys*	31/68	I Wouldn't Change A Thing About You (But Your Name) *Hank Williams, Jr.*
50/01	I Will Love You *Lisa Angelle*	24/73	I Wish (You Had Stayed) *Brian Collins*	1/83	I Wouldn't Change You If I Could *Ricky Skaggs*
65/92	I Will Love You Anyhow *Tim Ryan*	19/60	I Wish You Love *Billy Walker*	5/92	I Wouldn't Have It Any Other Way *Aaron Tippin*
45/72	I Will Never Pass This Way Again *Glen Campbell*	4/53	I Won't Be Home No More *Hank Williams*	1/82	I Wouldn't Have Missed It For The World *Ronnie Milsap*
32/66	I Will Not Blow Out The Light *Marion Worth*	85/88	I Won't Be Seeing Her No More *Touch Of Country*	73/93	I Wouldn't Know *Andy Childs*
21/79	I Will Rock And Roll With You *Johnny Cash*	1/67	I Won't Come In While He's There *Jim Reeves*	9/70	I Wouldn't Live In New York City *Buck Owens*
27/98	I Will Stand *Kenny Chesney*	3/65	I Won't Forget You *Jim Reeves*	33/67	I Wouldn't Take Her To A Dogfight *Charlie Walker*
49/93	I Will Stand By You *Corbin/Hanner*	3/50	(I Won't Go Huntin', Jake) But I'll Go Chasin' Women *Stuart Hamblen*	72/99	I Wouldn't Tell You No Lie *Tractors*
21/79	I Will Survive *Billie Jo Spears*	83/81	I Won't Last A Day Without You *Vince And Dianne Hatfield*	81/89	I Wouldn't Trade Your Love *Joann Wintermute*
46/01	I Will Survive *Wild Horses*	44/86	I Won't Let You Down *Tom Wopat*	1/74	I Wouldn't Want To Live If You Didn't Love Me *Don Williams*
7/88	I Will Whisper Your Name *Michael Johnson*	58/98	I Won't Lie *Shannon Brown*	70/97	I Wrote The Book *Matt King*
28/66	I Wish *Ernie Ashworth*	1/71	I Won't Mention It Again *Ray Price*	1/75	(I'd Be) A Legend In My Time *Ronnie Milsap*
	(I Wish A Buck Was Still Silver) ..see: Are The Good Times Really Over	1/87	I Won't Need You Anymore (Always And Forever) *Randy Travis*	4/90	I'd Be Better Off (In A Pine Box) *Doug Stone*
	I Wish Her Well ..see: (There She Goes)	1/88	I Won't Take Less Than Your Love *Tanya Tucker/ Paul Davis/Paul Overstreet*	53/97	I'd Be With You *Kippi Brannon*
	I Wish I Could Fall In Love Today	8/83	I Wonder *Rosanne Cash*	69/68	I'd Be Your Fool Again *David Rogers*
5/60	*Ray Price*	1/89	I Wonder Do You Think Of Me *Keith Whitley*	30/66	I'd Better Call The Law On Me *Hugh X. Lewis*
5/88	*Barbara Mandrell*	40/91	I Wonder How Far It Is Over You *Aaron Tippin*	74/80	I'd Build A Bridge *Charlie Rich*
4/94	I Wish I Could Have Been There *John Anderson*			60/77	I'd Buy You Chattanooga *Kenny Price*
14/84	I Wish I Could Write You A Song *John Anderson*			20/85	I'd Dance Every Dance With You *Kendalls*
4/89	(I Wish I Had A) Heart Of Stone *Baillie And The Boys*				
45/82	I Wish I Had A Job To Shove *Rodney Lay*				
22/70	I Wish I Had A Mommy Like You *Patti Page*				
4/49	I Wish I Had A Nickel *Jimmy Wakely*				
	I Wish I Had Never Met Sunshine				
3/46	*Gene Autry*				
5/46	*Wesley Tuttle*				

32/80 I'd Do Anything For You *Jacky Ward*	84/75 I'd Still Be In Love With You *Brian Collins*	64/85 I'll Dance The Two Step *Shelly West*
94/88 I'd Do Anything For You, Baby *Andy & The Brown Sisters*	20/92 I'd Surrender All *Randy Travis*	17/74 I'll Do Anything It Takes *Jean Shepard*
52/82 I'd Do It All Again *Jerry Lee Lewis*	I'd Throw It All Away	2/77 I'll Do It All Over Again *Crystal Gayle*
83/88 I'd Do It All Over Again *Ray Price*	75/81 Sweetwater	53/81 I'll Drink To That *Billy Parker*
87/83 I'd Do It In A Heart Beat *Sierra*	66/88 Darrell Holt	8/80 (I'll Even Love You) Better Than I Did Then *Statler Brothers*
86/85 I'd Do It In A Heartbeat *Hill City*	9/52 I'd Trade All Of My Tomorrows (For Just One Yesterday) *Eddy Arnold*	60/87 I'll Fall In Love Again *Butch Baker*
84/75 I'd Do It With You *Pat Boone with Shirley Boone*	10/57 (I'll Always Be Your) Fraulein *Kitty Wells*	10/78 I'll Find It Where I Can *Jerry Lee Lewis*
I'd Fight The World	1/88 I'll Always Come Back *K.T. Oslin*	13/71 I'll Follow You (Up To Our Cloud) *George Jones*
23/62 Hank Cochran	75/77 I'll Always Remember That Song *Con Hunley*	88/87 I'll Forget You *Jerry Cooper*
19/74 Jim Reeves	14/55 I'll Baby Sit With You *Ferlin Husky*	3/44 I'll Forgive You But I Can't Forget *Roy Acuff*
11/68 I'd Give The World (To Be Back Loving You) *Warner Mack*	94/82 I'll Baby You *Steve Mantelli*	60/76 I'll Get Better *Sammi Smith*
I'd Go Crazy ..see: (If It Weren't For Country Music)	4/00 I'll Be *Reba McEntire*	1/76 I'll Get Over You *Crystal Gayle*
11/76 I'd Have To Be Crazy *Willie Nelson*	7/45 I'll Be Back *Gene Autry*	34/78 I'll Get Over You *Nick Nixon*
I'd Just Be Fool Enough	1/80 I'll Be Coming Back For More *T.G. Sheppard*	6/88 I'll Give You All My Love Tonight *Bellamy Brothers*
16/66 Browns	67/74 I'll Be Doggone *Penny DeHaven*	F/76 I'll Go Back To Her *Waylon Jennings*
33/76 Faron Young	I'll Be Home For Christmas	10/99 I'll Go Crazy *Andy Griggs*
80/87 I'd Know A Lie *Gary McCullough*	75/96 Lonestar	46/94 I'll Go Down Loving You *Shenandoah*
18/59 I'd Like To Be *Jim Reeves*	59/98 Lonestar	11/64 I'll Go Down Swinging *Porter Wagoner*
3/94 I'd Like To Have That One Back *George Strait*	68/98 Reba McEntire	I'll Go On Alone
26/78 I'd Like To See Jesus (On The Midnight Special) *Tammy Wynette*	1/77 I'll Be Leaving Alone *Charley Pride*	1/53 Marty Robbins
5/75 I'd Like To Sleep Til I Get Over You *Freddie Hart*	16/89 I'll Be Lovin' You *Lee Greenwood*	4/53 Webb Pierce
1/80 I'd Love To Lay You Down *Conway Twitty*	48/82 I'll Be Loving You *Big Al Downing*	3/98 I'll Go On Loving You *Alan Jackson*
67/68 I'd Love To Live With You Again *Darrell McCall*	68/00 I'll Be Right Here Loving You *Randy Travis*	74/86 I'll Go Steppin' Too *Glenn Sutton*
1/91 I'd Love You All Over Again *Alan Jackson*	91/73 I'll Be Satisfied *Don Adams*	F/70 I'll Go To A Stranger *Johnny Bush*
56/97 I'd Love You To Love Me *Emilio*	F/56 I'll Be Satisfied With Love *Faron Young*	3/75 I'll Go To My Grave Loving You *Statler Brothers*
58/82 I'd Love You To Want Me *Narvel Felts*	79/83 I'll Be Seeing You *Leon Raines*	68/74 I'll Have To Say I Love You In A Song *Jim Croce*
54/85 I'd Rather Be Crazy *Con Hunley*	10/87 I'll Be The One *Statler Brothers*	I'll Hold You In My Heart (Till I Can Hold You In My Arms)
64/87 I'd Rather Be Crazy *Dana McVicker*	I'll Be There (If You Ever Want Me)	1/47 Eddy Arnold
62/82 I'd Rather Be Doing Nothing With You *Karen Taylor-Good*	2/54 Ray Price	63/67 Freddie Hart
4/69 I'd Rather Be Gone *Hank Williams, Jr.*	17/72 Johnny Bush	70/77 Jan Howard
66/75 I'd Rather Be Picked Up Here (Than Be Put Down At Home) *Jeris Ross*	4/81 Gail Davies	4/61 I'll Just Have A Cup Of Coffee (Then I'll Go) *Claude Gray*
I'd Rather Be Sorry	I'll Be There (When You Get Lonely)	11/78 I'll Just Take It Out In Love *George Jones*
2/71 Ray Price	12/57 Ray Price	2/65 I'll Keep Holding On (Just To Your Love) *Sonny James*
63/71 Patti Page	22/78 David Rogers	74/88 I'll Know The Good Times *Bill Nunley*
84/81 I'd Rather Be The Stranger In Your Eyes *Gene Kennedy & Karen Jeglum*	1/78 I'll Be True To You *Oak Ridge Boys*	43/64 I'll Leave The Porch Light A-Burning *Billy Grammer*
69/72 I'd Rather Be Wantin' Love *Leroy Van Dyke*	57/72 I'll Be Whatever You Say *Wanda Jackson*	34/66 I'll Leave The Singin' To The Bluebirds *Sheb Wooley*
20/79 I'd Rather Go On Hurtin' *Joe Sun*	I'll Be Your Baby Tonight	I'll Leave This World Loving You
32/80 I'd Rather Leave While I'm In Love *Rita Coolidge*	48/68 Glen Garrison	47/80 Wayne Kemp
10/61 I'd Rather Loan You Out *Roy Drusky*	33/70 Claude King	1/88 Ricky Van Shelton
1/71 I'd Rather Love You *Charley Pride*	5/87 Judy Rodman	26/90 I'll Lie Myself To Sleep *Shelby Lynne*
16/93 I'd Rather Miss You *Little Texas*	61/73 I'll Be Your Bridge (Just Lay Me Down) *Wilma Burgess*	14/79 I'll Love Away Your Troubles For Awhile *Janie Fricke*
2/97 I'd Rather Ride Around With You *Reba McEntire*	54/85 I'll Be Your Fool Tonight *Jim Glaser*	10/68 I'll Love You More (Than You Need) *Jeannie Seely*
13/56 I'd Rather Stay Home *Kitty Wells*	26/82 I'll Be Your Man Around The House *Kieran Kane*	11/70 I'll Make Amends *Roy Drusky*
F/78 I'd Really Love To See You Tonight *Jacky Ward & Reba McEntire*	12/76 I'll Be Your San Antone Rose *Dottsy*	19/58 I'll Make It All Up To You *Jerry Lee Lewis*
67/83 I'd Say Yes *Paulette Carlson*	40/75 I'll Be Your Steppin' Stone *David Houston*	65/82 I'll Miss You *Stella Parton*
	62/75 I'll Believe Anything You Say *Sami Jo*	
	16/59 I'll Catch You When You Fall *Charlie Walker*	
	2/87 I'll Come Back As Another Woman *Tanya Tucker*	
	10/67 I'll Come Runnin' *Connie Smith*	
	34/93 I'll Cry Tomorrow *Larry Stewart*	

4/81	I'll Need Someone To Hold Me (When I Cry) *Janie Fricke*	
	I'll Never Be Free	
2/50	Kay Starr & Tennessee Ernie Ford	
26/69	Johnny & Jonie Mosby	
11/78	Jim Ed Brown/Helen Cornelius	
4/87	I'll Never Be In Love Again *Don Williams*	
61/67	I'll Never Be Lonesome With You *Cal Smith*	
7/73	I'll Never Break These Chains *Tommy Overstreet*	
56/72	I'll Never Fall In Love Again *Liz Anderson*	
1/67	I'll Never Find Another You *Sonny James*	
6/95	I'll Never Forgive My Heart *Brooks & Dunn*	
1/53	I'll Never Get Out Of This World Alive *Hank Williams*	
27/79	I'll Never Let You Down *Tommy Overstreet*	
5/45	I'll Never Let You Worry My Mind *Red Foley*	
24/00	I'll Never Pass This Way Again *Tracy Lawrence*	
70/76	I'll Never See Him Again *Sue Richards*	
	I'll Never Slip Around Again	
2/49	Margaret Whiting & Jimmy Wakely	
6/49	Floyd Tillman	
1/85	I'll Never Stop Loving You *Gary Morris*	
61/67	I'll Never Tell On You *Roy Drusky & Priscilla Mitchell*	
68/70	I'll Paint You A Song *Mac Davis*	
5/88	I'll Pin A Note On Your Pillow *Billy Joe Royal*	
28/78	I'll Promise You Tomorrow *Jerry Wallace*	
80/86	I'll Pull You Through *Tish Hinojosa/Craig Dillingham*	
8/65	I'll Repossess My Heart *Kitty Wells*	
	I'll Sail My Ship Alone	
1/50	Moon Mullican	
10/51	Tiny Hill	
42/79	I'll Say It's True *Johnny Cash*	
2/70	I'll See Him Through *Tammy Wynette*	
2/69	I'll Share My World With You *George Jones*	
22/63	I'll Sign *Beverly Buff*	
27/75	I'll Sing For You *Don Gibson*	
21/92	I'll Start With You *Paulette Carlson*	
4/47	I'll Step Aside *Ernest Tubb*	
1/87	I'll Still Be Loving You *Restless Heart*	
45/81	I'll Still Be Loving You *Mundo Earwood*	
47/85	I'll Still Be Loving You *Joe Stampley*	
8/69	I'll Still Be Missing You *Warner Mack*	
8/72	I'll Still Be Waiting For You *Buck Owens*	
9/75	I'll Still Love You *Jim Weatherly*	
84/79	I'll Still Love You In My Dreams *Sandra Kaye*	
10/99	I'll Still Love You More *Trisha Yearwood*	
100/78	I'll Still Need You Mary Ann *Jim Taylor*	
8/49	I'll Still Write Your Name In The Sand *Buddy Starcher*	
23/92	I'll Stop Loving You *Mike Reid*	
8/50	I'll Take A Back Seat For You *Ernest Tubb*	
75/84	I'll Take As Much Of You As I Can Get *Darrell Clanton*	
55/76	I'll Take It *Roy Head*	
86/80	I'll Take The Blame *Ricky Skaggs*	
9/66	I'll Take The Dog *Jean Shepard & Ray Pillow*	
47/99	I'll Take Today *Gary Allan*	
37/86	I'll Take Your Love Anytime *Robin Lee*	
2/99	I'll Think Of A Reason Later *Lee Ann Womack*	
	I'll Think Of Something	
7/74	Hank Williams, Jr.	
1/92	Mark Chesnutt	
1/96	I'll Try *Alan Jackson*	
6/74	I'll Try A Little Bit Harder *Donna Fargo*	
2/45	I'll Wait For You Dear *Al Dexter*	
3/79	I'll Wake You Up When I Get Home *Charlie Rich*	
50/88	I'll Walk Before I'll Crawl *Janie Frickie*	
30/65	I'll Wander Back To You *Earl Scott*	
9/75	I'm A Believer *Tommy Overstreet*	
49/75	I'm A Believer (In A Whole Lot Of Lovin') *Jean Shepard*	
74/83	I'm A Booger *Roy Clark*	
5/45	I'm A Brandin' My Darlin' With My Heart *Jack Guthrie*	
7/45	I'm A Convict With Old Glory In My Heart *Elton Britt*	
72/84	I'm A Country Song *David Rogers*	
60/98	I'm A Cowboy *Bill Engvall*	
22/69	I'm A Drifter *Bobby Goldsboro*	
61/67	I'm A Fool *Slim Whitman*	
	I'm A Fool To Care	
72/55	Donny King	
91/78	Marcia Ball	
34/69	I'm A Good Man (In A Bad Frame Of Mind) *Jack Reno*	
14/60	I'm A Honky Tonk Girl *Loretta Lynn*	
33/77	I'm A Honky-Tonk Woman's Man *Bob Luman*	
	I'm A Long Gone Daddy	
6/48	Hank Williams	
97/70	Norman Wade	
9/70	I'm A Lover (Not A Fighter) *Skeeter Davis*	
	I'm A Memory	
28/71	Willie Nelson	
22/77	Willie Nelson	
97/78	I'm A Mender *Danny Shatswell*	
18/66	I'm A Nut *Leroy Pullins*	
	I'm A One-Woman Man	
7/56	Johnny Horton	
5/89	George Jones	
6/66	I'm A People *George Jones*	
1/74	I'm A Ramblin' Man *Waylon Jennings*	
58/83	I'm A Slave *Jerry Reed*	
1/76	(I'm A) Stand By My Woman Man *Ronnie Milsap*	
52/95	I'm A Stranger Here Myself *Perfect Stranger*	
12/54	I'm A Stranger In My Home *Kitty Wells & Red Foley*	
3/01	I'm A Survivor *Reba McEntire*	
52/88	I'm A Survivor *George Jones*	
57/89	I'm A Survivor *Lacy J. Dalton*	
30/68	I'm A Swinger *Jimmy Dean*	
4/72	I'm A Truck *Red Simpson*	
57/76	I'm A Trucker *Johnny Russell*	
32/64	I'm A Walkin' Advertisement *Norma Jean*	
94/78	I'm A Woman *Jeanne Pruett*	
85/78	I'm A Woman In Love *LaWanda Lindsey*	
49/76	(I'm A) YoYo Man *Rick Cunha*	
23/76	I'm All Wrapped Up In You *Don Gibson*	
54/81	I'm Almost Ready *Leona Williams*	
5/80	I'm Already Blue *Kendalls*	
	I'm Already Taken	
63/78	Steve Wariner	
3/99	Steve Wariner	
1/01	I'm Already There *Lonestar*	
1/98	I'm Alright *Jo Dee Messina*	
20/70	I'm Alright *Lynn Anderson*	
2/78	I'm Always On A Mountain When I Fall *Merle Haggard*	
3/53	I'm An Old, Old Man *Lefty Frizzell*	
67/85	I'm An Old Rock And Roller (Dancin' To A Different Beat) *Tom Jones*	
68/85	I'm As Over You As I'm Ever Gonna Get *Lloyd David Foster*	
64/75	I'm Available *Kathy Barnes*	
17/59	I'm Beginning To Forget You *Jim Reeves*	
50/79	I'm Being Good *David Wills*	
2/49	I'm Bitin' My Fingernails And Thinking Of You *Andrews Sisters & Ernest Tubb*	
38/68	I'm Coming Back Home To Stay *Buckaroos*	
11/57	I'm Coming Home *Johnny Horton*	
62/77	I'm Coming Home To Face The Music *Nat Stuckey*	
87/77	(I'm Coming Home To You) Dixie *Shylo*	
93/79	I'm Completely Satisfied With You *Lorrie & George Morgan*	
F/57	I'm Counting On You *Kitty Wells*	
50/00	I'm Diggin' It *Alecia Elliott*	
53/66	I'm Doing This For Daddy *Johnny Wright*	
21/88	I'm Down To My Last Cigarette *k.d. lang*	
3/69	I'm Down To My Last "I Love You" *David Houston*	
39/82	I'm Drinkin' Canada Dry *Burrito Brothers*	
28/69	I'm Dynamite *Peggy Sue*	
57/68	I'm Easy To Love *Stan Hitchcock*	
	I'm Falling Too ..see: (I Can't Help You)	
1/85	I'm For Love *Hank Williams, Jr.*	
80/74	I'm Free *Stan Hitchcock*	
3/98	I'm From The Country *Tracy Byrd*	
3/60	I'm Gettin' Better *Jim Reeves*	
56/79	I'm Gettin' Into Your Love *Ruby Falls*	

460

The World Needs A Melody – Red Lane (handwritten, top)

30/69	I'm Gettin' Tired Of Babyin' You Peggy Sue	
10/77	I'm Getting Good At Missing You (Solitaire) Rex Allen, Jr.	
74/77	I'm Getting High Remembering Bobby Lewis	
74/77	I'm Giving You Denver Jean Shepard	
7/55	I'm Glad I Got To See You Once Again Hank Snow	
63/84	I'm Glad You Couldn't Sleep Last Night Narvel Felts	
50/68	I'm Goin' Back Home Where I Belong Buckaroos	
18/82	I'm Goin' Hurtin' Joe Stampley	
81/88	I'm Goin' Nowhere Charlie Mitchell	
63/86	I'm Going Crazy Kenny Dale	
41/70	I'm Going Home Bobby Lewis	
10/85	I'm Going To Leave You Tomorrow John Schneider	
17/71	I'm Gonna Act Right Nat Stuckey	
54/72	I'm Gonna Be A Swinger Webb Pierce	
5/47	I'm Gonna Be Boss From Now On Bob Wills	
2/90	I'm Gonna Be Somebody Travis Tritt	
68/00	I'm Gonna Be There Victor Sanz	
42/65	I'm Gonna Break Every Heart I Can Merle Haggard	
2/62	I'm Gonna Change Everything Jim Reeves	
10/55	I'm Gonna Fall Out Of Love With You Webb Pierce	
	I'm Gonna Feed You Now	
21/65	Porter Wagoner	
F/79	Porter Wagoner	
	I'm Gonna Get You	
63/87	Billy Swan	
1/88	Eddy Raven	
65/66	I'm Gonna Hang Up My Gloves Charlie Walker	
87/81	I'm Gonna Hang Up This Heartache Nancy Ruud	
1/82	I'm Gonna Hire A Wino To Decorate Our Home David Frizzell	
	I'm Gonna Hurt Her On The Radio ..see: I'm Gonna Love Her	
3/71	I'm Gonna Keep On Keep On Lovin' You Billy Walker	
81/73	I'm Gonna Keep Searching Pat Roberts	
5/72	I'm Gonna Knock On Your Door Billy "Crash" Craddock	
44/66	I'm Gonna Leave You Anita Carter	
60/71	I'm Gonna Leave You Charlie Louvin & Melba Montgomery	
78/81	I'm Gonna Let Go (And Love Somebody) Liz Lyndell	
F/57	I'm Gonna Live Some Before I Die Faron Young	
	I'm Gonna Love [Hurt] Her On The Radio	
52/85	David Allan Coe	
13/88	Charley Pride	
3/76	I'm Gonna Love You Dave & Sugar	
13/79	I'm Gonna Love You Glen Campbell	

10/78	I'm Gonna Love You Anyway Cristy Lane	
36/00	I'm Gonna Love You Anyway Trace Adkins	
9/81	I'm Gonna Love You Back To Loving Me Again Joe Stampley	
	I'm Gonna Love You Right Out Of This World	
21/77	David Rogers	
76/82	Tom Grant	
44/85	I'm Gonna Love You Right Out Of The Blues Lloyd David Foster	
17/80	I'm Gonna Love You Tonight (In My Dreams) Johnny Duncan	
79/80	I'm Gonna Love You Tonight (Like There's No Tomorrow) Becky Hobbs	
69/68	I'm Gonna Make Like A Snake Ernest Tubb	
3/88	I'm Gonna Miss You, Girl Michael Martin Murphey	
7/68	I'm Gonna Move On Warner Mack	
98/79	I'm Gonna Move To The Country (And Get Away To It All) Jimmy Tucker	
16/81	(I'm Gonna) Put You Back On The Rack Dottie West	
26/81	I'm Gonna Sit Right Down And Write Myself A Letter Willie Nelson	
19/65	I'm Gonna Tie One On Tonight Wilburn Brothers	
28/71	I'm Gonna Write A Song Tommy Cash — *Jody Miller* (handwritten)	
14/64	I'm Hanging Up The Phone Carl Butler & Pearl	
23/80	I'm Happy Just To Dance With You Anne Murray	
11/74	I'm Having Your Baby Sunday Sharpe	
68/76	I'm High On You Jack Blanchard & Misty Morgan	
17/00	I'm Holdin' On To Love (To Save My Life) Shania Twain	
3/94	I'm Holding My Own Lee Roy Parnell	
65/70	I'm Holding Your Memory (But He's Holding You) Jimmy Newman	
F/55	I'm Hurtin' Inside Jim Reeves	
	I'm Hurting ..see: (Yes)	
35/01	I'm In Kinleys	
1/92	I'm In A Hurry (And Don't Know Why) Alabama	
94/79	I'm In Another World Scheree	
47/72	I'm In Love Buddy Alan	
3/59	I'm In Love Again George Morgan	
65/83	I'm In Love All Over Again Cindy Hurt	
59/89	I'm In Love And He's In Dallas Marie Osmond	
21/95	I'm In Love With A Capital "U" Joe Diffie	
47/99	I'm In Love With Her Sawyer Brown	
85/76	I'm In Love With My Pet Rock Al Bolt	
38/68	I'm In Love With My Wife David Rogers	
12/55	I'm In Love With You Kitty Wells	
60/67	I'm In No Condition Hank Williams, Jr.	

18/81	I'm Into Lovin' You Billy Swan	
30/80	I'm Into The Bottle Dean Dillon	
	I'm Just A Country Boy	
37/65	Jim Edward Brown	
1/77	Don Williams	
73/78	I'm Just A Farmer Cal Smith	
58/79	I'm Just A Heartache Away Dickey Lee	
F/77	(I'm Just A) Redneck In A Rock And Roll Bar Jerry Reed	
4/81	I'm Just An Old Chunk Of Coal John Anderson	
92/78	I'm Just Gettin' By Hank Thompson	
1/71	I'm Just Me Charley Pride	
66/76	(I'm Just Pouring Out) What She Bottled Up In Me David Wills	
1/01	I'm Just Talkin' About Tonight Toby Keith	
96/80	(I'm Just The) Cuddle Up Kind Hilka	
94/82	I'm Just The Leavin' Kind Michael Meyers	
71/79	I'm Just Your Yesterday Dandy	
	I'm Knee Deep In Loving You	
86/76	Jim Mundy	
2/77	Dave & Sugar	
100/88	I'm Leavin' You Ben Sanders	
91/79	I'm Leavin' You Alone Ernie Rowell	
17/99	I'm Leaving Aaron Tippin	
	I'm Leavin' It (All) Up To You	
18/70	Johnny & Jonie Mosby	
17/74	Donny And Marie Osmond	
26/78	Freddy Fender	
	I'm Left, You're Right, She's Gone	
F/55	Elvis Presley	
21/74	Jerry Lee Lewis	
15/65	I'm Letting You Go Eddy Arnold	
22/59	I'm Letting You Go Webb Pierce	
65/95	I'm Listening Now Ron Wallace	
30/77	I'm Living A Lie Jeanne Pruett	
9/66	I'm Living In Two Worlds Bonnie Guitar	
39/95	I'm Living Up To Her Low Expectations Daryle Singletary	
75/00	I'm Lookin' For Trouble Damon Gray	
79/88	(I'm Looking For Some) New Blue Jeans Troy Shondell	
16/62	I'm Looking High And Low For My Baby Ernest Tubb	
66/82	I'm Looking Over The Rainbow Sonny James	
90/76	I'm Losing It All Eddy Raven	
1/45	I'm Losing My Mind Over You Al Dexter	
45/66	I'm Losing You (I Can Tell) Hugh X. Lewis	
5/45	I'm Lost Without You Al Dexter	
84/79	I'm Lovin' The Lovin' Out Of You Gayle Harding	
88/88	I'm Loving The Wrong Man Again Dana McVicker	
47/71	I'm Miles Away Hagers	
11/56	I'm Moving In Hank Snow	
	I'm Moving On	
1/50	Hank Snow	
14/60	Don Gibson	
5/83	Emmylou Harris	
4/02	I'm Movin' On Rascal Flatts	

I'm Gonna Miss Her – Brad Paisley (Fishing) (handwritten, bottom)

5/48	I'm My Own Grandpa *Lonzo & Oscar*	75/75	I'm Ready To Love You Now *Sarah Johns*		I'm The One Who Loves You ..see: (Remember Me)
1/89	I'm No Stranger To The Rain *Keith Whitley*	F/56	I'm Really Glad You Hurt Me *Webb Pierce*	61/85	I'm The One Who's Breaking Up *Tari Hensley*
37/82	(I'm Not) A Candle In The Wind *Bobby Bare*	70/73	I'm Right Where I Belong *Anthony Armstrong Jones*	8/77	I'm The Only Hell (Mama Ever Raised) *Johnny Paycheck*
34/93	I'm Not Built That Way *Billy Dean*	89/78	I'm Satisfied With You *Leon Rausch*	62/93	I'm The Only Thing (I'll Hold Against You) *Conway Twitty*
28/66	I'm Not Crazy Yet *Ray Price*	60/77	I'm Savin' Up Sunshine *Dale McBride*	18/79	I'm The Singer, You're The Song *Tanya Tucker*
11/77	I'm Not Easy *Billie Jo Spears*	9/63	I'm Saving My Love *Skeeter Davis*	91/78	I'm The South *Eddy Arnold*
31/02	I'm Not Gonna Do Anything Without You *Mark Wills with Jamie O'Neal*	53/91	I'm Sending One Up For You *T. Graham Brown*	3/44	I'm Thinking Tonight Of My Blue Eyes *Gene Autry*
59/79	I'm Not In The Mood (For Love) *Ann J. Morton*	2/44	I'm Sending You Red Roses *Jimmy Wakely*	1/49	I'm Throwing Rice (At the Girl That I Love) *Eddy Arnold*
81/85	I'm Not Leaving *Ray Price*		(I'm So) Afraid Of Losing You Again	11/49	*Red Foley*
1/75	I'm Not Lisa *Jessi Colter*	1/69	*Charley Pride*	69/69	I'm Tied Around Your Finger *Jean Shepard*
14/56	I'm Not Mad, Just Hurt *Hank Thompson*	76/90	*Ashley Evans*		I'm Tired
69/89	I'm Not Over You *Johnny Lee*	2/98	I'm So Happy I Can't Stop Crying *Toby Keith with Sting*	3/57	*Webb Pierce*
	I'm Not Ready Yet	10/56	I'm So In Love With You *Wilburn Brothers*	18/88	*Ricky Skaggs*
58/68	*Blue Boys*		I'm So Lonesome I Could Cry	93/78	I'm Tired Of Being Me *Jack And Trink*
2/80	*George Jones*	43/66	*Hank Williams*	38/75	I'm Too Use To Loving You *Nick Nixon*
59/77	I'm Not Responsible *Hank Williams, Jr.*	75/71	*Linda Plowman*	6/01	I'm Tryin' *Trace Adkins*
70/73	I'm Not Strong Enough *Stonewall Jackson*	23/72	*Charlie McCoy*		I'm Turning You Loose
2/95	I'm Not Strong Enough To Say No *BlackHawk*	17/76	*Terry Bradshaw*	90/74	*Nick Nixon*
4/96	I'm Not Supposed To Love You Anymore *Bryan White*	43/82	*Jerry Lee Lewis*	77/79	*Bobby Wright*
49/98	I'm Not That Easy To Forget *Lorrie Morgan*	45/65	I'm So Miserable Without You *Billy Walker*	8/51	I'm Waiting Just For You *Hawkshaw Hawkins*
60/77	I'm Not That Good At Goodbye *Stella Parton*	76/82	I'm So Tired Of Going Home Drunk *Larry Jenkins*		I'm Walkin'
3/82	I'm Not That Lonely Yet *Reba McEntire*	1/75	I'm Sorry *John Denver*	66/69	*Dave Peel*
F/84	I'm Not That Way Anymore *Alabama*	76/76	I'm Sorry *Connie Cato*	96/77	*Doug Kershaw*
62/77	I'm Not The One You Love *Sunday Sharpe*	16/76	I'm Sorry Charlie *Joni Lee*	3/54	I'm Walking The Dog *Webb Pierce*
52/69	I'm Not Through Loving You *Jim Glaser*	9/77	I'm Sorry For You, My Friend *Moe Bandy*	12/49	I'm Waltzing With Tears In My Eyes *Cowboy Copas*
	I'm Not Through Loving You Yet	F/56	I'm Sorry, I'm Not Sorry *Carl Perkins*	1/44	I'm Wastin' My Tears On You *Tex Ritter*
3/74	*Conway Twitty*	14/71	I'm Sorry If My Love Got In Your Way *Connie Smith*	25/78	I'm Way Ahead Of You *Bill Anderson & Mary Lou Turner*
60/80	*Pam Rose*	1/89	I'm Still Crazy *Vern Gosdin*	21/61	I'm Wondering *Lou Smith*
7/84	I'm Not Through Loving You Yet *Louise Mandrell*	4/95	I'm Still Dancin' With You *Wade Hayes*	37/97	I'm Your Man *Jason Sellers*
21/86	I'm Not Trying To Forget You *Willie Nelson*	39/80	I'm Still In Love With You *Larry G. Hudson*	69/90	I'm Your Man *Skip Ewing*
75/99	I'm Not Your Girl *Reba McEntire*	3/74	I'm Still Loving You *Joe Stampley*	49/88	I'm Your Puppet *Mickey Gilley*
51/92	I'm Okay (And Gettin' Better) *Billy Joe Royal*	36/88	I'm Still Missing You *Ronnie McDowell*		(I'm Your Telephone Man) ..see: Let My Fingers Do The Walking
79/85	I'm On Fire *Debonaires*	95/78	I'm Still Missing You *Silver City Band*	8/73	I'm Your Woman *Jeanne Pruett*
97/78	I'm On My Way *Captain & Tennille*	80/77	I'm Still Movin' On *Hank Snow*	38/99	I'm Yours *Linda Davis*
79/83	I'm On The Outside Looking In *Darlene Austin*	6/67	I'm Still Not Over You *Ray Price*	56/86	I've Already Cheated On You *David Allan Coe & Willie Nelson*
54/71	I'm On The Road To Memphis *Buddy Alan & Don Rich*	36/88	I'm Still Your Fool *David Slater*	1/77	I've Already Loved You In My Mind *Conway Twitty*
52/72	I'm Only A Woman *Dottie West*	48/82	I'm Takin' A Heart Break *Terry Gregory*	34/74	I've Already Stayed Too Long *Don Adams*
1/83	I'm Only In It For The Love *John Conlee*	54/85	I'm Takin' My Time *Brenda Lee*	1/78	I've Always Been Crazy *Waylon Jennings*
71/88	I'm Only Lonely For You *Pal Rakes*	5/91	I'm That Kind Of Girl *Patty Loveless*	26/84	I've Always Got The Heart To Sing The Blues *Bill Medley*
	I'm Outta Here! ..see: (If You're Not In It For Love)	60/69	I'm The Boy *Statler Brothers*	75/84	I've Always Wanted To *Wayne Kemp*
3/90	I'm Over You *Keith Whitley*	24/62	(I'm The Girl On) Wolverton Mountain *Jo Ann Campbell*		I've Been A Fool
92/79	I'm Puttin' My Love Inside You *Shylo*		I'm The Man	39/81	*Stephanie Winslow*
		29/65	*Jim Kandy*	76/90	*Leah Marr*
75/83	I'm Ragged But I'm Right *Johnny Cash*	92/77	*Dugg Collins*		I've Been A Long Time Leavin' (But I'll Be A Long Time Gone)
	(I'm Ready) ..see: Heaven Bound	28/72	I'm The Man On Susie's Mind *Glenn Barber*	13/66	*Roger Miller*
		10/85	I'm The One Mama Warned You About *Mickey Gilley*	92/78	*Joey Martin*

	I've Been Around Enough To Know		**I've Got A Lotta Missin' You To Do**	7/55	**I've Kissed You My Last Time** Kitty Wells
78/75	Jo-el Sonnier	81/75	Jerry "Max" Lane	57/70	**I've Lost You** Elvis Presley
1/84	John Schneider	96/83	Jerry "Max" Lane	56/81	**I've Loved Enough To Know** Jim Rushing
	I've Been Everywhere		**I've Got A New Heartache**	15/76	**I've Loved You All Of The Way** Donna Fargo
1/62	Hank Snow	2/56	Ray Price		
16/70	Lynn Anderson	10/86	Ricky Skaggs	F/73	**I've Loved You All Over The World** Cal Smith
40/85	**I've Been Had By Love Before** Judy Rodman	5/79	**I've Got A Picture Of Us On My Mind** Loretta Lynn	66/67	**I've Never Been Loved** Leroy Van Dyke
2/88	**I've Been Lookin'** Nitty Gritty Dirt Band	93/78	**I've Got A Reason For Living** Dolly Fox	99/73	**I've Never Been This Far Before** Rita Remington
29/78	**I've Been Loved** Cates Sisters	61/79	**I've Got A Right To Be Wrong** B.J. Wright	60/82	**I've Never Been To Me** Charlene
4/89	**I've Been Loved By The Best** Don Williams	6/71	**I've Got A Right To Cry** Hank Williams, Jr.		**I've Never Loved Anyone More**
55/69	**I've Been Loving You Too Long (To Stop Now)** Barbara Mandrell	25/60	**I've Got A Right To Know** Buck Owens	14/75	Lynn Anderson
				82/75	Linda Hargrove
90/83	**I've Been Out Of Love Too Long** Gary Mack	4/74	**I've Got A Thing About You Baby** Elvis Presley	6/80	**I've Never Seen The Likes Of You** Conway Twitty
13/84	**I've Been Rained On Too** Tom Jones	1/65	**I've Got A Tiger By The Tail** Buck Owens	65/76	**I've Rode With The Best** Jim Ed Brown
72/73	**I've Been There** Jonie Mosby	7/78	**I've Got A Winner In You** Don Williams	7/59	**I've Run Out Of Tomorrows** Hank Thompson
11/68	**I've Been There Before** Ray Price			83/79	**I've Seen It All** Sandra Kaye
72/76	**I've Been There Too** Kenny Seratt	32/72	**I've Got A Woman's Love** Marty Robbins	41/76	**I've Taken** Jeanne Pruett
2/55	**I've Been Thinking** Eddy Arnold	93/73	**I've Got All The Heartaches I Can Handle** Ernest Tubb	4/45	**I've Taken All I'm Gonna Take From You** Spade Cooley
28/78	**I've Been Too Long Lonely Baby** Billy "Crash" Craddock	60/78	**I've Got An Angel (That Loves Me Like The Devil)** Bobby Hood	70/00	**I've Thought Of Everything** Daryle Singletary
14/79	**I've Been Waiting For You All Of My Life** Con Hunley			34/64	**I've Thought Of Leaving You** Kitty Wells
2/84	**I've Been Wrong Before** Deborah Allen	73/79	**I've Got Country Music In My Soul** Don King	99/76	**Ida Red** Bob Wills
11/56	**I've Changed** Carl Smith		**I've Got Five Dollars And It's Saturday Night**	10/50	**Ida Red Likes The Boogie** Bob Wills
70/86	**I've Changed My Mind** Bama Band	4/56	Faron Young	71/93	**Idle Hands** Tim Ryan
11/72	**I've Come Awful Close** Hank Thompson	16/65	George Jones & Gene Pitney	44/99	**If A Man Answers** Toby Keith
		3/94	**I've Got It Made** John Anderson	70/90	**If A Man Could Live On Love Alone** Skip Ewing
	I've Come Back (To Say I Love You One More Time)	82/76	**I've Got Leaving On My Mind** Webb Pierce	3/62	**If A Woman Answers (Hang Up The Phone)** Leroy Van Dyke
66/80	Chuck Howard	69/73	**I've Got Mine** Anthony Armstrong Jones		
63/83	Cristy Lane			9/84	**If All The Magic Is Gone** Mark Gray
1/90	**I've Come To Expect It From You** George Strait	13/75	**I've Got My Baby On My Mind** Connie Smith	42/64	**If Anyone Can Show Cause** Glenn Barber
30/63	**I've Come To Say Goodbye** Faron Young	25/69	**I've Got Precious Memories** Faron Young	1/94	**If Bubba Can Dance (I Can Too)** Shenandoah
	I've Cried A Mile	94/77	**I've Got Some Gettin' Over You To Do** Benny Barnes	8/81	**If Drinkin' Don't Kill Me (Her Memory Will)** George Jones
18/66	Hank Snow	57/85	**I've Got The Heart For You** Keith Whitley		
52/86	Tari Hensley			39/84	**If Every Man Had A Woman Like You** Osmond Brothers
1/90	**I've Cried My Last Tear For You** Ricky Van Shelton	11/63	**I've Got The World By The Tail** Claude King	13/79	**If Everyone Had Someone Like You** Eddy Arnold
	I've Cried (The Blues Right Out Of My Eyes)	17/78	**I've Got To Go** Billie Jo Spears		
			I've Got To Have You	59/70	**If God Is Dead (Who's That Living In My Soul)** Nat Stuckey And Connie Smith
23/70	Crystal Gayle	75/71	Peggy Little		
40/78	Crystal Gayle	13/72	Sammi Smith	77/88	**If Hearts Could Talk** Bobbi Lace
7/79	**I've Done Enough Dyin' Today** Larry Gatlin	71/71	**I've Got To Sing** Duane Dee	F/82	**If Heaven Ain't A Lot Like Dixie** Hank Williams, Jr.
7/63	**I've Enjoyed As Much Of This As I Can Stand** Porter Wagoner	64/87	**I've Got Ways Of Making You Talk** Vicki Bird	1/83	**If Hollywood Don't Need You** Don Williams
75/93	**I've Fallen In Love (And I Can't Get Up)** Charlie Floyd	5/68	**I've Got You On My Mind Again** Buck Owens	46/95	**If I Ain't Got You** Marty Stuart
46/00	**I've Forgotten How You Feel** Sonya Isaacs	16/77	**I've Got You (To Come Home To)** Don King	48/91	**If I Built You A Fire** Neal McCoy
				51/91	**If I Can Find A Clean Shirt** Waylon Jennings & Willie Nelson
4/72	**I've Found Someone Of My Own** Cal Smith	74/89	**I've Had Enough Of You** Debbie Rich		
92/80	**I've Given Up Giving In To The Blues** Brenda Frazier	17/70	**I've Just Been Wasting My Time** John Wesley Ryles	57/84	**If I Can Just Get Through The Night** Sissy Spacek
74/82	**I've Got A Bad Case Of You** Marie Osmond	12/62	**I've Just Destroyed The World (I'm Living In)** Ray Price	72/76	**If I Can Make It (Through The Mornin')** Tony Douglas
62/78	**I've Got A Feelin' (Somebody Stealin')** John Anderson	11/74	**I've Just Got To Know (How Loving You Would Be)** Freddy Weller		**If I Could Bottle This Up**
				43/88	George Jones & Shelby Lynne
3/72	**(I've Got A) Happy Heart** Susan Raye	44/82	**I've Just Seen A Face** Calamity Jane	30/92	Paul Overstreet

80/74	(If I Could Climb) The Walls Of The Bottle *David Allan Coe*	
21/63	If I Could Come Back *Webb Pierce*	
78/82	If I Could Get You (into my Life) *Gene Cotton*	
88/75	If I Could Have It Any Other Way *Kenny Seratt*	
1/94	If I Could Make A Living *Clay Walker*	
10/84	If I Could Only Dance With You *Jim Glaser*	
58/87	If I Could Only Fly *Merle Haggard & Willie Nelson*	
4/75	If I Could Only Win Your Love *Emmylou Harris*	
24/77	If I Could Put Them All Together (I'd Have You) *George Jones*	
68/95	If I Could See Love *Brett James*	
55/82	If I Could See You Tonight *Kippi Brannon*	
80/80	If I Could Set My Love To Music *Jerry Wallace*	
53/93	If I Could Stop Lovin' You *Curtis Wright*	
4/79	If I Could Write A Song As Beautiful As You *Billy "Crash" Craddock*	
28/62	If I Cried Every Time You Hurt Me *Wanda Jackson*	
1/92	If I Didn't Have You *Randy Travis*	
8/93	If I Didn't Love You *Steve Wariner*	
26/83	If I Didn't Love You *Gus Hardin*	
44/68	If I Don't Like The Way You Love Me *Mary Taylor*	
29/58	If I Don't Love You (Grits Ain't Groceries) *George Jones*	
53/86	If I Don't Love You *Jim Glaser*	
92/79	If I Ever *Randy Gurley*	
46/78	If I Ever Come Back *Pal Rakes*	
4/70	If I Ever Fall In Love *Faron Young*	
28/89	If I Ever Fall In Love Again *Anne Murray with Kenny Rogers*	
17/89	If I Ever Go Crazy *Shooters*	
28/80	If I Ever Had To Say Goodbye To You *Eddy Arnold*	
48/94	If I Ever Love Again *Daron Norwood*	
	If I Ever Need A Lady	
67/67	Claude Gray	
68/78	Claude Gray	
53/82	Billy Parker	
	If I Fall You're Going Down With Me	
75/99	Dixie Chicks	
3/01	Dixie Chicks	
18/79	If I Fell In Love With You *Rex Allen, Jr.*	
10/79	If I Give My Heart To You *Margo Smith*	
66/88	If I Had A Boat *Lyle Lovett*	
	If I Had A Cheating Heart	
9/78	Mel Street	
36/93	Ricky Lynn Gregg	
	If I Had A Hammer	
41/69	Wanda Jackson	
29/72	Johnny Cash & June Carter Cash	
65/99	If I Had A Nickel (One Thin Dime) *Redmon & Vale*	
25/95	If I Had Any Pride Left At All *John Berry*	
81/80	If I Had It My Way *Nightstreets*	

2/76	If I Had It To Do All Over Again *Roy Clark*	
60/78	If I Had It To Do All Over Again *Stoney Edwards*	
32/69	If I Had Last Night To Live Over *Webb Pierce*	
72/94	If I Had Only Known *Reba McEntire*	
1/89	If I Had You *Alabama*	
51/71	If I Had You *Bobby Lewis*	
90/83	If I Just Had My Woman *Bobby Reed*	
11/81	If I Keep On Going Crazy *Leon Everette*	
5/67	If I Kiss You (Will You Go Away) *Lynn Anderson*	
93/75	If I Knew Enough To Come Out Of The Rain *Connie Eaton*	
1/91	If I Know Me *George Strait*	
11/76	If I Let Her Come In *Ray Griff*	
88/89	If I Live To Be A Hundred (I'll Die Young) *Arne Benoni*	
29/98	If I Lost You *Travis Tritt*	
8/74	If I Miss You Again Tonight *Tommy Overstreet*	
3/81	If I Needed You *Emmylou Harris & Don Williams*	
39/89	If I Never See Midnight Again *Sweethearts Of The Rodeo*	
3/98	If I Never Stop Loving You *David Kersh*	
1/79	If I Said You Have A Beautiful Body Would You Hold It Against Me *Bellamy Brothers*	
67/81	If I Say I Love You (Consider Me Drunk) *Whitey Shafer*	
4/65	If I Talk To Him *Connie Smith*	
16/95	If I Was A Drinkin' Man *Neal McCoy*	
2/70	If I Were A Carpenter *Johnny Cash & June Carter*	
49/89	If I Were The Man You Wanted *Lyle Lovett*	
4/95	If I Were You *Collin Raye*	
8/96	If I Were You *Terri Clark*	
62/70	If I'd Only Come And Gone *Clay Hart*	
56/80	(If I'd Only Known) It Was The Last Time *Faron Young*	
91/76	If I'm A Fool For Loving You *Dottie West*	
73/68	If I'm Gonna Sink *Johnny Paycheck*	
25/75	If I'm Losing You *Billy Walker*	
74/99	If I'm Not In Love *Faith Hill*	
35/88	If It Ain't Broke Don't Fix It *John Anderson*	
20/85	If It Ain't Love *Ed Bruce*	
12/77	If It Ain't Love By Now *Jim Ed Brown/Helen Cornelius*	
	If It Ain't Love (Let's Leave It Alone)	
7/72	Connie Smith	
12/85	Whites	
1/88	If It Don't Come Easy *Tanya Tucker*	
14/72	If It Feels Good Do It *Dave Dudley*	
16/65	If It Pleases You *Billy Walker*	
63/83	If It Takes All Night *Dottie West*	
68/85	If It Was Any Better (I Couldn't Stand It) *Narvel Felts*	

59/87	If It Was Anyone But You *John Schneider*	
19/83	If It Was Easy *Ed Bruce*	
26/94	If It Wasn't For Her I Wouldn't Have You *Daron Norwood*	
83/89	If It Wasn't For The Heartache *Jill Hollier*	
59/95	If It Were Me *Radney Foster*	
26/91	(If It Weren't For Country Music) I'd Go Crazy *Clinton Gregory*	
10/85	If It Weren't For Him *Vince Gill*	
26/91	If It Will It Will *Hank Williams, Jr.*	
28/73	If It's All Right With You *Dottie West*	
2/70	If It's All The Same To You *Bill Anderson & Jan Howard*	
81/84	If It's Love (Then Bet It All) *Jack Greene*	
4/44	If It's Wrong To Love You *Charles Mitchell*	
91/76	If It's Your Song You Sing It *Linda Cassady*	
6/90	If Looks Could Kill *Rodney Crowell*	
69/87	If Love Ever Made A Fool *Razzy Bailey*	
6/79	If Love Had A Face *Razzy Bailey*	
11/77	If Love Was A Bottle Of Wine *Tommy Overstreet*	
12/55	If Lovin' You Is Wrong *Hank Thompson*	
	(If Loving You Is Wrong) I Don't Want To Be Right	
71/72	Jackie Burns	
1/79	Barbara Mandrell	
74/68	If Loving You Means Anything *Dale Ward*	
	If My Heart Had Windows	
7/67	George Jones	
51/82	Amy Wooley	
10/88	Patty Loveless	
3/01	If My Heart Had Wings *Faith Hill*	
6/69	If Not For You *George Jones*	
75/73	If Not For You *Bobby Wright*	
26/77	If Not You *Dr. Hook*	
16/88	If Ole Hank Could Only See Us Now *Waylon Jennings*	
74/92	If Only Your Eyes Could Lie *Earl Thomas Conley*	
5/77	If Practice Makes Perfect *Johnny Rodriguez*	
9/97	If She Don't Love You *Buffalo Club*	
15/73	If She Just Helps Me Get Over You *Sonny James*	
61/98	If She Only Knew *Kevin Sharp*	
27/82	If Something Should Come Between Us *Burrito Brothers*	
	If Teardrops Were Pennies	
8/51	Carl Smith	
3/73	Porter Wagoner & Dolly Parton	
10/66	If Teardrops Were Silver *Jean Shepard*	
15/85	If That Ain't Love *Lacy J. Dalton*	
87/73	If That Back Door Could Talk *Ronnie Sessions*	
86/78	If That's Not Loving You *Ruby Falls*	
65/75	If That's What It Takes *Ray Griff*	
21/83	If That's What You're Thinking *Karen Brooks*	

464

13/64	**If The Back Door Could Talk** Webb Pierce		**If You Ain't Lovin' (You Ain't Livin')**	20/77	**If You Gotta Make A Fool Of Somebody** Dickey Lee	
1/91	**If The Devil Danced (In Empty Pockets)** Joe Diffie	2/55	Faron Young	54/89	**If You Had A Heart** Tim Malchak	
		1/88	George Strait	1/72	**If You Leave Me Tonight I'll Cry** Jerry Wallace	
8/84	**If The Fall Don't Get You** Janie Fricke	81/83	**If You Believe** John Schneider		**If You Love Me (Let Me Know)**	
1/94	**If The Good Die Young** Tracy Lawrence	26/85	**If You Break My Heart** Kendalls	2/74	Olivia Newton-John	
		51/94	**If You Came Back From Heaven** Lorrie Morgan	83/77	Brian Collins	
29/91	**If The Jukebox Took Teardrops** Billy Joe Royal	41/00	**If You Can** Tammy Cochran	27/71	**If You Love Me (Really Love Me)** Lamar Morris	
57/98	**If The Jukebox Took Teardrops** Danni Leigh	5/01	**If You Can Do Anything Else** George Strait	4/97	**If You Love Somebody** Kevin Sharp	
16/85	**If The Phone Doesn't Ring, It's Me** Jimmy Buffett	2/73	**If You Can Live With It (I Can Live Without It)** Bill Anderson	86/74	**If You Loved Her That Way** O.B. McClinton	
8/88	**If The South Woulda Won** Hank Williams, Jr.	5/78	**If You Can Touch Her At All** Willie Nelson	4/96	**If You Loved Me** Tracy Lawrence	
	If The Whole World Stopped Lovin'	100/77	**(If You Can) Why Can't I** Billy Walker	62/87	**If You Only Knew** Kim Grayson	
12/67	Roy Drusky	22/98	**If You Can't Be Good (Be Good At It)** Neal McCoy	99/77	**If You Really Want Me To I'll Go** Silver City Band	
56/73	Eddy Arnold	7/66	**If You Can't Bite, Don't Growl** Tommy Collins	1/98	**If You See Him/If You See Her** Reba McEntire/Brooks & Dunn	
2/95	**If The World Had A Front Porch** Tracy Lawrence	3/73	**If You Can't Feel It (It Ain't There)** Freddie Hart	73/70	**If You See My Baby** Johnny Carver	
6/78	**If The World Ran Out Of Love Tonight** Jim Ed Brown/Helen Cornelius	1/88	**If You Change Your Mind** Rosanne Cash	31/87	**If You Still Want A Fool Around** Charley Pride	
61/77	**If There Ever Comes A Day** Mike Lunsford	6/90	**If You Could Only See Me Now** T. Graham Brown	F/74	**If You Talk In Your Sleep** Elvis Presley	
3/92	**If There Hadn't Been You** Billy Dean	79/84	**If You Could Only See Me Now** Sissy Spacek	74/84	**If You Think I Love You Now** Shoppe	
21/80	**If There Were No Memories** John Anderson	70/94	**If You Could Say What I'm Thinking** Orrall & Wright	76/78	**If You Think I Love You Now** Jim Mundy & Terri Melton	
48/80	**If There Were Only Time For Love** Roy Clark		**If You Could See You Through My Eyes**	19/71	**If You Think I Love You Now (I've Just Started)** Jody Miller	
9/87	**If There's Any Justice** Lee Greenwood	40/79	Tom Grant	F/77	**If You Think I'm Crazy Now** Bobby Bare	
81/78	**If There's One Angel Missing (She's Here In My Arms Tonight)** Billy Parker	63/82	Skip And Linda	34/71	**If You Think That It's All Right** Johnny Carver	
		6/62	**If You Don't Know I Ain't Gonna Tell You** George Hamilton IV	9/72	**If You Touch Me (You've Got To Love Me)** Joe Stampley	
69/89	**If This Ain't Love (There Ain't No Such Thing)** Grayghost	59/89	**If You Don't Know Me By Now** Joe Stampley	32/74	**(If You Wanna Hold On) Hold On To Your Man** Diana Trask	
24/66	**If This House Could Talk** Stonewall Jackson	71/81	**If You Don't Know Me By Now** Super Grit Cowboy Band	78/86	**If You Wanna Talk Love** Benny Wilson	
92/76	**If This Is Freedom (I Want Out)** Danny Wood	11/77	**If You Don't Love Me (Why Don't You Just Leave Me Alone)** Freddy Fender	24/66	**If You Want A Love** Buck Owens	
54/72	**If This Is Goodbye** Carl Smith			8/77	**If You Want Me** Billie Jo Spears	
45/78	**If This Is Just A Game** David Allan Coe	61/67	**If You Don't Love Me (Why Don't You Just Leave Me Alone)** Bob Luman	2/91	**If You Want Me To** Joe Diffie	
F/70	**If This Is Love** Jack Greene		**If You Don't Somebody Else Will**	74/71	**If You Want Me To I'll Go** Bobby Wright	
30/71	**If This Is Our Last Time** Brenda Lee	3/54	Jimmy & Johnny	59/74	**If You Want The Rainbow** Melba Montgomery	
100/77	**If This Is What Love's All About** Peggy Sue & Sonny Wright	8/54	Ray Price	23/90	**If You Want To Be My Woman** Merle Haggard	
71/70	**If This Was The Last Song** Billy Mize	97/76	Carl Smith	11/92	**If You Want To Find Love** Kenny Rogers	
		37/78	**If You Don't Want To Love Her** Jerry Naylor			
1/89	**If Tomorrow Never Comes** Garth Brooks	1/80	**If You Ever Change Your Mind** Crystal Gayle	53/76	**If You Want To Make Me Feel At Home** DeWayne Orender	
86/83	**If Tomorrow Never Comes** Ray Griff	31/75	**If You Ever Change Your Mind** Ray Price	7/55	**If You Were Me** Webb Pierce	
41/91	**If We Can't Do It Right** Eddie London	27/01	**If You Ever Feel Like Lovin' Me Again** Clay Walker	58/92	**If You'll Let This Fool Back In** Lee Greenwood	
92/77	**If We Can't Do It Right** Kathy & Larry Barnes	16/77	**If You Ever Get To Houston (Look Me Down)** Don Gibson	48/86	**If You're Anything Like Your Eyes** Robin Lee	
1/73	**If We Make It Through December** Merle Haggard	5/98	**If You Ever Have Forever In Mind** Vince Gill	26/73	**If You're Goin' Girl** Don Gibson	
2/77	**If We're Not Back In Love By Monday** Merle Haggard	62/99	**If You Ever Leave Me** Barbra Streisand / Vince Gill	5/83	**If You're Gonna Do Me Wrong (Do It Right)** Vern Gosdin	
69/75	**(If You Add) All The Love In The World** Mac Davis	31/72	**If You Ever Need My Love** Jack Greene	68/77	**If You're Gonna Love (You Gotta Hurt)** Dave Conway	
31/82	**If You Ain't Got Nothin' (You Ain't Got Nothin' To Lose)** Bobby Bare	12/81	**If You Go, I'll Follow You** Porter Wagoner & Dolly Parton	1/84	**If You're Gonna Play In Texas** Alabama	
		94/77	**If You Got To Have It Your Way** Billy Parker	67/87	**If You're Gonna Tell Me Lies (Tell Me Good Ones)** Rosemary Sharp	
				18/95	**If You're Gonna Walk, I'm Gonna Crawl** Sammy Kershaw	

The Intimidator(?) – Race Cars – (Tune of "Midnight In Montgomery")

Football (☆☆☆) 4-CD Kit

	If You're Looking For A Fool	15/82	**In Like With Each Other**	21/72	**In The Spring (The Roses Always**
56/71	Tommy Overstreet		Larry Gatlin/Gatlin Brothers		**Turn Red)** Dorsey Burnette
34/78	Freddy Fender	1/86	**In Love** Ronnie Milsap		**(In The Still Of The Night)** ..see:
7/67	**If You're Not Gone Too Long**	16/68	**In Love** Wynn Stewart		**Lost In The Fifties Tonight**
	Loretta Lynn	48/86	**In Love With Her** Adam Baker	1/92	**In This Life** Collin Raye
44/93	**If You're Not Gonna Love Me**	64/82	**In Love With Loving You**	21/63	**In This Very Same Room**
	Deborah Allen		Keith Stegall		George Hamilton IV
	(If You're Not In It For Love) I'm	48/71	**In Loving Memories**	6/55	**In Time** Eddy Arnold
	Outta Here!		Jerry Lee Lewis	4/83	**In Times Like These**
1/96	Shania Twain	22/80	**In Memory Of A Memory**		Barbara Mandrell
15/97	Shania Twain		Johnny Paycheck	63/96	**In Your Face** Ty Herndon
	If You're Serious About Cheatin'	17/61	**In Memory Of Johnny Horton**	33/67	**In Your Heart** Red Sovine
61/80	R.C. Bannon		Johnny Hardy	12/94	**Independence Day**
77/84	Randy Wright	61/78	**In Memory Of Your Love**		Martina McBride
3/82	**If You're Thinking You Want A**		Debby Boone	96/75	**Indian Creek** Porter Wagoner
	Stranger George Strait	56/85	**In My Arms Again** Del Shannon	34/75	**Indian Giver** Billy Larkin
10/82	**If You're Waiting On Me (You're**	9/84	**In My Dreams** Emmylou Harris	3/71	**Indian Lake** Freddy Weller
	Backing Up) Kendalls	1/84	**In My Eyes** John Conlee		**Indian Love Call**
1/94	**If You've Got Love**	12/90	**In My Eyes** Lionel Cartwright	2/52	Slim Whitman
	John Michael Montgomery	33/74	**In My Little Corner Of The World**	38/75	Ray Stevens
6/78	**If You've Got Ten Minutes (Let's**		Marie Osmond	74/76	**Indian Nation** Billy Thunderkloud
	Fall In Love) Joe Stampley	58/94	**In My Next Life** Merle Haggard	8/94	**Indian Outlaw** Tim McGraw
	If You've Got The Money I've Got	19/94	**In My Own Backyard** Joe Diffie	72/75	**Indiana Girl** Pat Boone
	The Time	6/79	**In No Time At All** Ronnie Milsap	5/46	**Inflation** Zeke Manners
1/50	Lefty Frizzell	79/79	**In Our Room** Roy Head	68/98	**Innocent Bystander** Billy Dean
1/76	Willie Nelson	9/86	**In Over My Heart** T.G. Sheppard	19/82	**Innocent Lies** Sonny James
41/73	**If You've Got The Time**	4/95	**In Pictures** Alabama	74/98	**Innocent Man** Sherrié Austin
	Red Steagall	41/84	**In Real Life** Ed Hunnicutt	1/83	**Inside** Ronnie Milsap
4/92	**If Your Heart Ain't Busy Tonight**	15/76	**In Some Room Above The Street**	31/02	**Inside Out** Trisha Yearwood
	Tanya Tucker		Gary Stewart	66/83	**Inside Story** Ronnie Rogers
24/90	**If Your Heart Should Ever Roll**	17/63	**In The Back Room Tonight**	73/67	**Instant Love** Mitchell Torok
	This Way Again Jo-el Sonnier		Carl Smith	48/77	**Instead Of Givin' Up (I'm Givin'**
70/83	**If Your Heart's A Rollin' Stone**	48/93	**In The Blood** Rob Crosby		**In)** Billy Walker
	Helen Cornelius	56/82	**In The Driver's Seat**	54/68	**Instinct For Survival**
29/59	**Igmoo (The Pride Of South**		John Schneider		Skeeter Davis
	Central High)	35/81	**In The Garden** Statler Brothers	48/66	**Insurance** Hank Locklin
	Stonewall Jackson		**In The Ghetto**	93/82	**Intimate Strangers** Terry Dale
5/68	**Image Of Me** Conway Twitty	50/69	Dolly Parton	13/64	**Invisible Tears** Ned Miller
	Image Of Me	60/69	Elvis Presley		**Invitation To The Blues**
26/61	Bob Wills	25/68	**In The Good Old Days**	3/58	Ray Price
70/84	Jim Reeves		Dolly Parton	71/89	Andy Lee Smith
4/98	**Imagine That** Diamond Rio	3/93	**In The Heart Of A Woman**	6/69	**Invitation To Your Party**
21/62	**Imagine That** Patsy Cline		Billy Ray Cyrus		Jerry Lee Lewis
79/81	**Imagine That** Nancy Wood		**In The Jailhouse Now**	63/92	**Iola** Great Plains
19/60	**Imitation Of Love** Adrian Roland	1/55	Webb Pierce		**Ira Hayes** ..see: **Ballad Of**
1/91	**In A Different Light** Doug Stone	8/62	Johnny Cash	67/70	**Irma Jackson** Tony Booth
61/91	**In A Different Light** Linda Davis	15/77	Sonny James	13/49	**Iron Horse** Frankie Yankovic
74/97	**In A Heartbeat** Rodney Atkins	72/82	Willie Nelson & Webb Pierce	61/69	**Irresistible** Slim Whitman
1/89	**In A Letter To You** Eddy Raven	7/55	**In The Jailhouse Now No. 2**	22/96	**Irresistible You** Ty England
5/85	**In A New York Minute**		Jimmie Rodgers		**Is Anybody Goin' To San Antone**
	Ronnie McDowell	6/62	**In The Middle Of A Heartache**	1/70	Charley Pride
83/82	**In A Stranger's Eyes** Ralph May		Wanda Jackson	91/77	Chuck Price
2/93	**In A Week Or Two** Diamond Rio	23/64	**In The Middle Of A Memory**	60/77	**Is Everybody Ready**
13/80	**In America** Charlie Daniels Band		Carl Belew		Little David Wilkins
13/90	**In Another Lifetime**	10/83	**In The Middle Of The Night**	8/76	**Is Forever Longer Than Always**
	Desert Rose Band		Mel Tillis		Porter Wagoner & Dolly Parton
27/85	**In Another Minute** Jim Glaser	54/88	**In The Middle Of The Night**		**Is It Any Wonder That I Love You**
10/02	**In Another World** Joe Diffie		Canyon	60/71	Bob Luman
74/68	**In Another World** Webb Pierce	14/84	**In The Midnight Hour**	26/72	Nat Stuckey
2/97	**In Another's Eyes**		Razzy Bailey	5/92	**Is It Cold In Here** Joe Diffie
	Trisha Yearwood & Garth Brooks	65/75	**In The Misty Moonlight**	43/90	**Is It Love** Foster & Lloyd
86/75	**In At Eight And Out At Ten**		George Morgan	63/68	**Is It Love?** Lucille Starr
	Don Drumm		**In The Mood**	84/80	**Is It Only Cause You're Lonely**
3/95	**In Between Dances** Pam Tillis	84/75	Joe Bob's Nashville Sound		Porter Wagoner
69/82	**In Between Lovers**		Company	6/94	**Is It Over Yet** Wynonna
	Stephanie Winslow	39/77	Henhouse Five Plus Too	10/91	**Is It Raining At Your House**
38/64	**In Case You Ever Change Your**		**In The Palm Of Your Hand**		Vern Gosdin
	Mind Bill Anderson	43/66	Buck Owens	1/65	**Is It Really Over?** Jim Reeves
18/67	**In Del Rio** Billy Walker	23/73	Buck Owens	1/89	**Is It Still Over?** Randy Travis
75/87	**In Dreams** Roy Orbison	34/66	**In The Same Old Way** Bobby Bare	3/44	**Is It Too Late Now** Jimmie Davis
70/87	**In It Again** A.J. Masters	29/63	**In The Shadows Of The Wine**		
			Porter Wagoner		

Is It Wrong (For Loving You)
9/58   *Warner Mack*
11/60   *Webb Pierce*
1/74   *Sonny James*
91/78   *Gilbert Ortega*
93/80   *Mike Lunsford*
2/97   **Is That A Tear**   *Tracy Lawrence*
47/85   **Is There Anything I Can Do**
     Bill Medley
1/92   **Is There Life Out There**
     Reba McEntire
27/75   **Is This All There Is To A Honky Tonk?**   *Jerry Naylor*
3/63   **Is This Me?**   *Jim Reeves*
11/72   **Is This The Best I'm Gonna Feel**
     Don Gibson
1/44   **Is You Is Or Is You Ain't (Ma' Baby)**   *Louis Jordan*
2/53   **Is Zat You, Myrtle**   *Carlisles*
49/77   **Ishabilly**   *Mack Vickery*
10/90   **Island**   *Eddy Raven*
27/87   **Island In The Sea**   *Willie Nelson*
1/83   **Islands In The Stream**
     Kenny Rogers with Dolly Parton
10/79   **Isn't It Always Love**
     Lynn Anderson
1/86   **It Ain't Cool To Be Crazy About You**   *George Strait*
1/82   **It Ain't Easy Bein' Easy**
     Janie Fricke
99/77   **It Ain't Easy Lovin' Me**
     Ronnie Prophet
12/85   **It Ain't Gonna Worry My Mind**
     Ray Charles with Mickey Gilley
4/65   **It Ain't Me, Babe**
     Johnny Cash & June Carter
     It Ain't No Big Thing
50/70   *Tex Williams*
64/70   *Mills Brothers*
1/90   **It Ain't Nothin'**   *Keith Whitley*
25/83   **It Ain't Real (If It Ain't You)**
     Mark Gray
76/74   **It Almost Felt Like Love**
     Charlie Louvin
86/77   **It Always Brings Me Back Around To You**   *Billy Walker*
95/85   **It Always Hurts Like The First Time**   *Carroll Baker*
72/78   **It Amazes Me**   *John Denver*
48/74   **It Amazes Me (Sweet Lovin' Time)**   *Mary Kay James*
91/85   **It Can't Be Done**   *Tim Blixseth*
84/80   **It Can't Wait**   *Debbie Peters*
23/71   **It Could 'A Been Me**
     Billie Jo Spears
61/74   **It Could Have Been Me**   *Sami Jo*
74/92   **It Could've Been So Good**
     Collin Raye
1/77   **It Couldn't Have Been Any Better**
     Johnny Duncan
51/77   **It Didn't Have To Be A Diamond**
     Susan Raye
7/75   **It Do Feel Good**   *Donna Fargo*
     It Doesn't Matter Anymore
54/75   *Linda Ronstadt*
33/78   *R.C. Bannon*
87/76   **It Don't Bother Me**   *Ben Reece*
69/71   **It Don't Do No Good To Be A Good Girl**   *Liz Anderson*
2/78   **It Don't Feel Like Sinnin' To Me**
     Kendalls

42/80   **It Don't Get Better Than This**
     Sheila Andrews
25/81   **It Don't Get No Better Than This**
     Larry Gatlin/Gatlin Brothers
6/81   **It Don't Hurt Me Half As Bad**
     Ray Price
35/80   **It Don't Hurt To Dream**   *Sylvia*
24/99   **It Don't Matter To The Sun**
     Garth Brooks As Chris Gaines
59/68   **It Don't Mean A Thing To Me**
     Kenny Price
70/92   **It Don't Take A Lot**   *Mark Collie*
36/70   **It Don't Take But One Mistake**
     Luke The Drifter, Jr.
     (It Feels Like Love Again) ..see: From Time To Time
88/78   **It Feels Like Love for the first time**   *Larry Curtis*
35/88   **It Goes Without Saying**
     Tim Malchak
82/83   **It Had To Be You**
     Texas Vocal Company
     It Happens Every Time
85/74   *Dorsey Burnette*
83/85   *Leon Raines*
14/83   **It Hasn't Happened Yet**
     Rosanne Cash
     It Hurts To Know The Feeling's Gone
42/74   *Nat Stuckey*
31/76   *Billy Mize*
53/94   **It Is No Secret**   *Mark Collie*
29/60   **It Just Tears Me Up**   *Floyd Tillman*
48/78   **It Just Won't Feel Like Cheating**
     Sammi Smith
     It Keeps Right On A-Hurtin'
4/62   *Johnny Tillotson*
17/87   *Billy Joe Royal*
38/69   **It Looks Like The Sun's Gonna Shine**   *Wilburn Brothers*
70/76   **It Makes Me Giggle**   *John Denver*
48/66   **It Makes You Happy**
     Kenny Vernon
1/96   **It Matters To Me**   *Faith Hill*
33/72   **It Meant Nothing To Me**
     Diana Trask
     It Must Be Love
1/79   *Don Williams*
1/00   *Alan Jackson*
1/98   **It Must Be Love**   *Ty Herndon*
74/93   **It Must Be The Rain**   *Marty Brown*
58/75   **It Must Have Been The Rain**
     Jim Weatherly
91/77   **It Never Crossed My Mind**
     Tompall Glaser
74/00   **It Never Rains In Southern California**   *Trent Summar & The New Row Mob*
1/78   **It Only Hurts For A Little While**
     Margo Smith
7/92   **It Only Hurts When I Cry**
     Dwight Yoakam
62/72   **It Rains Just The Same In Missouri**   *Ray Griff*
94/76   **It Sets Me Free**   *Jack Paris*
     It Should Have Been Easy
22/77   *Dottsy*
79/77   *Patti Leatherwood*
30/87   *Whites*
19/85   **It Should Have Been Love By Now**
     Barbara Mandrell/Lee Greenwood

     It Started All Over Again
23/78   *Vern Gosdin*
56/78   *David Houston*
68/79   **It Started With A Smile**
     Helen Cornelius
94/77   **It Sure Is Bad To Love Her**
     Terry Stafford
1/93   **It Sure Is Monday**   *Mark Chesnutt*
89/80   **It Sure Looks Good On You**
     Durwood Haddock
1/87   **It Takes A Little Rain (To Make Love Grow)**   *Oak Ridge Boys*
4/66   **It Takes A Lot Of Money**
     Warner Mack
45/72   **It Takes A Lot Of Tenderness**
     Arlene Harden
60/75   **It Takes A Whole Lotta Livin' In A House**   *David Rogers*
76/76   **It Takes All Day To Get Over Night**   *Doug Kershaw*
51/69   **It Takes All Night Long**   *Cal Smith*
76/75   **It Takes Faith**   *Marty Robbins*
38/83   **It Takes Love**   *Big Al Downing*
72/79   **It Takes One To Know One**
     Bobby Hood
2/68   **It Takes People Like You (To Make People Like Me)**
     Buck Owens
37/73   **It Takes Time**   *Dave Dudley*
98/79   **It Takes Too Long**   *Hank Snow*
56/70   **It Takes Two**
     Connie Eaton & Dave Peel
21/72   **It Takes You**   *Bob Luman*
5/55   **It Tickles**   *Tommy Collins*
31/84   **It Took A Lot Of Drinkin' (To Get That Woman Over Me)**
     Moe Bandy
37/81   **It Took Us All Night Long To Say Goodbye**   *Danny Wood*
17/82   **It Turns Me Inside Out**
     Lee Greenwood
11/00   **It Was**   *Chely Wright*
1/77   **It Was Almost Like A Song**
     Ronnie Milsap
7/75   **It Was Always So Easy (To Find An Unhappy Woman)**
     Moe Bandy
80/87   **It Was Love What It Was**
     Bobby Borchers
65/72   **It Was Love While It Lasted**
     Red Lane
     It Was The Last Time ..see: (If I'd Only Known)
21/62   **It Was You**   *Ferlin Husky*
37/81   **It Was You**   *Billy "Crash" Craddock*
     It Wasn't God Who Made Honky Tonk Angels
1/52   *Kitty Wells*
10/81   *Waylon Jennings & Jessi Colter (medley)*
20/71   *Lynn Anderson*
     It Wasn't His Child
51/88   *Sawyer Brown*
60/94   *Trisha Yearwood*
56/91   **It Wasn't You, It Wasn't Me**
     Daniele Alexander & Butch Baker
68/99   **It Will Be Me**   *Faith Hill*
89/84   **It Won't Be Easy**   *Lois Johnson*
59/68   **(It Won't Be Long) And I'll Be Hating You**   *Johnny Paycheck*
6/91   **It Won't Be Me**   *Tanya Tucker*

18/94	It Won't Be Over You *Steve Wariner*	16/75	It's A Sin When You Love Somebody *Glen Campbell*	98/78	(It's Gonna Be A) Happy Day *Jack Paris*
74/94	It Won't Be The Same This Year *Vince Gill*	51/99	It's About Time *Julie Reeves*	91/84	It's Gonna Be A Heartache *Kevin Pearce*
79/79	It Won't Go Away *Rayburn Anthony*	9/81	It's All I Can Do *Anne Murray*	70/89	It's Gonna Be Love *Mark Gray & Bobbie Lace*
31/86	It Won't Hurt *Dwight Yoakam*		It's All In The Game	94/79	It's Gonna Be Magic *George James*
19/96	It Works *Alabama*	82/74	Slim Whitman	1/72	It's Gonna Take A Little Bit Longer *Charley Pride*
7/98	It Would Be You *Gary Allan*	53/75	Jerry Jaye		
7/96	It Wouldn't Hurt To Have Wings *Mark Chesnutt*	12/77	Tom T. Hall	55/87	It's Goodbye And So-Long To You *Lisa Childress*
	It'll Be Her [Him]	54/83	Merle Haggard		
22/73	David Rogers	72/93	It's All In The Heart *Stephanie Davis*	44/84	It's Great To Be Single Again *David Allan Coe*
45/77	Tompall Glaser	1/75	It's All In The Movies *Merle Haggard*	72/98	It's Hard To Be A Parent *Bill Engvall*
89/78	Johnny Cash				
46/81	Debby Boone	94/89	It's All In The Touch *Bruce Van Dyke*	65/70	It's Hard To Be A Woman *Skeeter Davis*
19/82	Tompall/Glaser Brothers	15/96	It's All In Your Head *Diamond Rio*	10/80	It's Hard To Be Humble *Mac Davis*
73/85	It'll Be Love By Morning *Allen Frizzell*	19/59	It's All My Heartache *Carl Smith*		
1/86	It'll Be Me *Exile*	11/68	It's All Over *David Houston & Tammy Wynette*	40/82	It's Hard To Be The Dreamer (When I Used To Be The Dream) *Donna Fargo*
34/83	It'll Be Me *Tom Jones*	41/76	It's All Over *Johnny Cash*		
	It'll Come Back	3/68	It's All Over But The Crying *Hank Williams, Jr.*	65/88	It's Hard To Keep This Ship Together *John Anderson*
16/76	Red Sovine				
89/80	Red Sovine	14/66	It's All Over (But The Crying) *Kitty Wells*	F/77	It's Heaven Loving You *Freddie Hart*
13/84	It's A Be Together Night *David Frizzell & Shelly West*	65/69	It's All Over (But The Shouting) *Bob Luman*	66/79	It's Hell To Know She's Heaven *Dale McBride*
13/70	It's A Beautiful Day *Wynn Stewart*	15/85	It's All Over Now *John Anderson*	16/82	It's High Time *Dottie West*
38/00	It's A Beautiful Thing *Paul Brandt*	23/75	It's All Over Now *Charlie Rich*		It's In His Kiss ..see: Shoop Shoop Song
2/79	It's A Cheating Situation *Moe Bandy*	19/97	It's All The Same To Me *Billy Ray Cyrus*		It's Just A Matter Of Time
71/84	It's A Cover Up *Peter Isaacson*	1/78	It's All Wrong, But It's All Right *Dolly Parton*	1/70	Sonny James
7/77	It's A Cowboy Lovin' Night *Tanya Tucker*	F/58	It's All Your Fault *Ray Price*	7/86	Glen Campbell
30/83	It's A Dirty Job *Bobby Bare & Lacy J. Dalton*	7/65	It's Alright *Bobby Bare*	1/89	Randy Travis
		77/76	It's Alright *Billy Thunderkloud*	30/59	It's Just About Time *Johnny Cash*
88/76	It's A Good Night For Singing *Jerry Jeff Walker*		It's Alright To Be A Redneck	46/85	It's Just Another Heartache *Bandana*
2/01	It's A Great Day To Be Alive *Travis Tritt*	68/00	Alan Jackson	86/89	It's Just The Whiskey Talkin' *Ethel And The Shameless Hussies*
		53/01	Alan Jackson		
5/56	It's A Great Life (If You Don't Weaken) *Faron Young*	11/89	(It's Always Gonna Be) Someday *Holly Dunn*		It's Like Falling In Love (Over And Over Again)
	It's A Heartache	5/00	It's Always Somethin' *Joe Diffie*		
10/78	Bonnie Tyler	60/83	It's Another Silent Night *Lane Brody*	89/81	Chris Waters
32/81	Dave & Sugar			28/82	Osmond Brothers
3/58	It's A Little More Like Heaven *Hank Locklin*	5/65	It's Another World *Wilburn Brothers*	1/80	It's Like We Never Said Goodbye *Crystal Gayle*
1/97	It's A Little Too Late *Mark Chesnutt*	79/76	It's Bad When You're Caught (With The Goods) *Billy Parker*	14/96	It's Lonely Out There *Pam Tillis*
2/93	It's A Little Too Late *Tanya Tucker*	2/78	It's Been A Great Afternoon *Merle Haggard*	32/90	It's Lonely Out Tonite *Eddie Rabbitt*
12/68	It's A Long, Long Way To Georgia *Don Gibson*	100/77	It's Been A Long, Long Time *Buck Owens*	43/64	It's Lonesome *Billy Walker*
36/82	It's A Long Way To Daytona *Mel Tillis*		It's Been One Of Those Days	61/89	It's Love That Makes You Sexy *Dean Dillon*
18/00	It's A Love Thing *Keith Urban*	91/84	Lang Scott		It's Me Again, Margaret
	It's A Lovely, Lovely World	64/89	Bobby Vinton	55/74	Paul Craft
5/52	Carl Smith	68/82	It's Been One Of Those Days *Bobby Smith*	74/85	Ray Stevens
5/81	Gail Davies	1/53	It's Been So Long *Webb Pierce*	9/75	It's Midnight *Elvis Presley*
20/73	It's A Man's World *Diana Trask*	1/45	It's Been So Long Darling *Ernest Tubb*	5/96	It's Midnight Cinderella *Garth Brooks*
36/72	It's A Matter Of Time *Elvis Presley*	63/91	It's Chitlin' Time *Kentucky Headhunters*	93/76	It's Midnight (Do You Know Where Your Baby Is?) *Sandy Posey*
6/74	(It's A) Monsters' Holiday *Buck Owens*	37/70	It's Dawned On Me You're Gone *Dottie West*	11/76	It's Morning (And I Still Love You) *Jessi Colter*
59/89	It's A Natural Thing *Jonathan Edwards*	25/76	It's Different With You *Mary Lou Turner*	73/85	It's My Life *Gary Wolf*
10/85	It's A Short Walk From Heaven To Hell *John Schneider*	66/91	It's Easy To Tell *Matraca Berg*	56/79	It's My Party *Sherry Brane*
	It's A Sin	50/76	It's Enough *Ronnie Prophet*	11/01	It's My Time *Martina McBride*
1/47	Eddy Arnold	48/66	It's For God, And Country, And You Mom *Ernest Tubb*		It's My Time
5/69	Marty Robbins			51/67	John D. Loudermilk
21/71	It's A Sin To Tell A Lie *Slim Whitman*		It's Four In The Morning	50/68	George Hamilton IV
		1/72	Faron Young	F/57	It's My Way *Webb Pierce*
		36/86	Tom Jones	8/51	It's No Secret *Stuart Hamblen*

51/72	(It's No) Sin Slim Whitman	91/77	It's The Love In You Susan St. Marie		Jambalaya (On The Bayou)
58/78	It's Not Easy Dickey Lee	56/99	It's The Most Wonderful Time Of The Year Garth Brooks	1/52	Hank Williams
66/88	It's Not Easy Jack Robertson			66/73	Blue Ridge Rangers
56/75	It's Not Funny Anymore Stella Parton	20/85	It's Time For Love Don Williams	88/78	Saskia & Serge
1/72	It's Not Love (But It's Not Bad) Merle Haggard	87/89	It's Time For Your Dreams To Come True Billy Parker	F/73	Jamestown Ferry Tanya Tucker
				15/93	Janie Baker's Love Slave Shenandoah
34/98	It's Not Over Mark Chesnutt	13/74	It's Time To Cross That Bridge Jack Greene	68/94	Janie's Gone Fishin' Kim Hill
92/78	It's Not Over Till It's Over Billy Walker	28/71	It's Time To Love Her Billy Walker	34/72	January, April And Me Dick Curless
	It's Not Supposed To Be That Way	1/75	It's Time To Pay The Fiddler Cal Smith	39/75	January Jones Johnny Carver
84/77	Steve Young	12/79	It's Time We Talk Things Over Rex Allen, Jr.	12/75	Jason's Farm Cal Smith
52/80	Pam Rose			60/89	Jaws Of Modern Romance Gary Morris
27/95	It's Not The End Of The World Emilio	9/80	It's Too Late Jeanne Pruett	13/92	Jealous Bone Patty Loveless
			It's Too Late To Love Me Now		Jealous Heart
88/81	It's Not The Rain Music Row	87/77	Charly McClain	2/45	Tex Ritter
73/81	It's Not The Same Old You Johnny Rodriguez	87/79	Cher	8/49	Al Morgan
		70/88	It's Too Late To Love You Now Brian White	14/49	Kenny Roberts
17/60	It's Not Wrong Connie Hall			87/79	Barbara Seiner
14/77	It's Nothin' To Me Jim Reeves	56/79	It's Too Soon To Say Goodbye Terri Hollowell	12/64	Jealous Hearted Me Eddy Arnold
4/81	It's Now Or Never John Schneider			63/78	Jealous Kind Rita Coolidge
55/75	It's Only A Barroom Nick Nixon	5/80	It's True Love Conway Twitty & Loretta Lynn	7/58	Jealousy Kitty Wells
65/67	It's Only A Matter Of Time Carl Smith	3/46	It's Up To You Al Dexter	3/74	(Jeannie Marie) You Were A Lady Tommy Overstreet
15/66	It's Only Love Jeannie Seely	5/96	It's What I Do Billy Dean	51/68	Jeannie's Afraid Of The Dark Porter Wagoner & Dolly Parton
67/98	It's Only Love Randy Scruggs (with Mary Chapin Carpenter)		It's Who You Love		Jed Clampett ..see: Ballad Of
		16/82	Kieran Kane	89/82	Jedediah Jones Wyley McPherson
68/86	It's Only Love Again Vern Gosdin	73/92	Don Williams	69/95	Jenny Come Back Helen Darling
	It's Only Make Believe	59/83	It's Written All Over Your Face Ronnie Dunn	22/60	Jenny Lou Sonny James
3/70	Glen Campbell			88/77	Jesse I Wanted That Award Sherwin Linton
99/79	Robert Gordon	30/83	It's You Kieran Kane		
8/88	Ronnie McDowell	5/90	It's You Again Skip Ewing	100/77	Jessie And The Light La Costa
8/87	It's Only Over For You Tanya Tucker	21/88	It's You Again Exile	4/92	Jesus And Mama Confederate Railroad
		55/84	It's You Alone Gail Davies		
91/73	It's Only Over Now And Then Bill Phillips	5/93	It's Your Call Reba McEntire	66/69	Jesus Is A Soul Man Billy Grammer
4/68	It's Over Eddy Arnold	1/97	It's Your Love Tim McGraw with Faith Hill	80/76	Jesus Is The Same In California Lloyd Goodson
14/80	It's Over Rex Allen, Jr.	34/85	It's Your Reputation Talkin' Kathy Mattea	77/81	Jesus Let Me Slide Dean Dillon
46/97	It's Over My Head Wade Hayes			F/80	Jesus On The Radio (Daddy On The Phone) Tom T. Hall
62/73	It's Raining In Seattle Wynn Stewart	9/98	It's Your Song Garth Brooks		
		3/61	It's Your World Marty Robbins	3/70	Jesus, Take A Hold Merle Haggard
57/81	It's Really Love This Time Family Brown				Jet Set ..see: (We're Not)
91/78	It's Sad To Go To The Funeral (Of A Good Love That Has Died) Barbara Fairchild		**J**	23/02	Jezebel Chely Wright
		44/74	J. John Jones Marie Owens	63/92	Jezebel Kane JJ White
F/77	It's Saturday Night Larry Wren		J.C. ..see: Ballad Of	7/54	Jilted Red Foley
62/81	It's So Close To Christmas Bellamy Brothers	36/80	J.R. B.J. Wright	74/71	Jim Dandy Lynn Anderson
81/77	It's So Easy Linda Ronstadt	72/81	Jacamo Donna Fargo	27/61	(Jim) I Wore A Tie Today Eddy Arnold
95/76	It's So Easy Lovin' You Tibor Brothers	49/68	Jack And Jill Jim Ed Brown		
		13/48	Jack And Jill Boogie Wayne Raney	56/70	Jim, Jack, And Rose Johnny Bush
100/76	It's So Good Lovin' You O.B. McClinton	72/79	Jack Daniel's, If You Please David Allan Coe	41/70	Jim Johnson Porter Wagoner
79/75	It's So Nice To Be With You Bobby Lewis	82/89	Jackie Brown John Cougar Mellencamp	46/83	Jim Reeves Medley Jim Reeves
				26/68	Jimmie Rodgers Blues Elton Britt
57/87	It's Such A Heartache Ride The River	2/67	Jackson Johnny Cash & June Carter	5/59	Jimmy Brown The Newsboy Mac Wiseman
1/67	It's Such A Pretty World Today Wynn Stewart		Jackson Ain't A Very Big Town	27/61	Jimmy Caught The Dickens (Pushing Ernest In The Tub) Chick & His Hot Rods
1/88	It's Such A Small World Rodney Crowell & Rosanne Cash	38/67	Norma Jean		
		21/68	Johnny Duncan & June Stearns	24/61	Jimmy Martinez Marty Robbins
65/79	It's Summer Time Jess Garron	58/68	Jacksonville Cal Smith	69/92	Jimmy McCarthy's Truck Molly & The Heymakers
10/74	It's That Time Of Night Jim Ed Brown	6/96	Jacob's Ladder Mark Wills		
		5/58	Jacqueline Bobby Helms	34/00	Jimmy's Got A Girlfriend Wilkinsons
87/75	It's The Bible Against The Bottle Earl Conley	54/76	Jaded Lover Jerry Jeff Walker		
1/67	It's The Little Things Sonny James	20/84	Jagged Edge Of A Broken Heart Gail Davies		
		1/57	Jailhouse Rock Elvis Presley		

Jingle Jangle Jingle

Jingle Bell Rock
13/57 *Bobby Helms*
60/96 *Bobby Helms*
69/99 *George Strait*
52/01 *Aaron Tippin*
44/00 **Jingle Bells** *SheDaisy*
26/75 **Jo And The Cowboy** *Johnny Duncan*
24/68 **Jody And The Kid** *Roy Drusky*
13/69 **Joe And Mabel's 12th Street Bar And Grill** *Nat Stuckey*
1/88 **Joe Knows How To Live** *Eddy Raven*
29/83 **Jogger, The** *Bobby Bare*
5/94 **John Deere Green** *Joe Diffie*
29/91 **John Deere Tractor** *Judds*
John Dillinger ..see: Ballad Of
44/66 **John Henry, Jr.** *Merle Travis*
80/74 **John Law** *Homer Joy*
64/99 **John Roland Wood** *Deryl Dodd*
64/99 **John Wayne Walking Away** *Lari White*
17/59 **John Wesley Hardin** *Jimmie Skinner*
53/73 **John's Been Shucking My Corn** *Onie Wheeler*
54/89 **Johnny And The Dreamers** *Scott McQuaig*
1/69 **Johnny B. Goode** *Buck Owens*
72/69 **Johnny Let The Sunshine In** *David Ingles*
44/66 **Johnny Lose It All** *Johnny Darrell*
70/89 **Johnny Lucky And Suzi 66** *Jeff Stevens & The Bullets*
17/60 **Johnny, My Love (Grandma's Diary)** *Wilma Lee & Stoney Cooper*
Johnny One Time
36/68 *Willie Nelson*
50/69 *Brenda Lee*
87/76 *Jesseca James*
74/76 **Johnny Orphan** *Randy Barlow*
10/59 **Johnny Reb** *Johnny Horton*
38/70 **Johnny's Cash And Charley's Pride** *Mac Wiseman*
Jole Blon
4/47 *Roy Acuff (Our Own)*
4/47 *Harry Choates*
4/47 **Jole Blon's Sister** *Moon Mullican*
Jolene
1/74 *Dolly Parton*
55/01 *Sherrié Austin*
7/70 **Jolie Girl** *Marty Robbins*
31/88 **Jones On The Jukebox** *Becky Hobbs*
1/83 **José Cuervo** *Shelly West* Tequila
1/71 **Joshua** *Dolly Parton*
70/72 **Josie** *Kris Kristofferson*
26/71 **Joy To The World** *Murry Kellum*
13/67 **Juanita Jones** *Stu Phillips*
38/71 **Judy** *Ray Sanders*
41/71 **Juke Box Man** *Dick Curless*
61/86 **Juke Box Saturday Night** *Roy Clark*
70/74 **Jukebox** *Jack Reno*
15/67 **Jukebox Charlie** *Johnny Paycheck*
1/90 **Jukebox In My Mind** *Alabama*
8/94 **Jukebox Junkie** *Ken Mellons*
98/83 **Jukebox Never Plays Home Sweet Home** *Jack Greene*

24/89 **Jukebox Played Along** *Gene Watson*
1/92 **Jukebox With A Country Song** *Doug Stone*
2/87 **Julia** *Conway Twitty*
91/74 **Julianna** *Hummers*
79/77 **Julianne** *Roy Head*
15/67 **Julie** *Porter Wagoner*
81/79 **Julie (Do I Ever Cross Your Mind?)** *Wood Newton*
98/77 **Julieanne (Where Are You Tonight)?** *Wendel Adkins*
15/86 **Juliet** *Oak Ridge Boys*
25/78 **Juliet And Romeo** *Ronnie Sessions*
47/70 **July 12, 1939** *Charlie Rich*
July You're A Woman
71/74 *Red, White & Blue Grass*
77/74 *Ed Bruce*
100/76 **Jump Back Joe Joe** *Bill Black's Combo*
60/68 **Jump For Joy** *Statler Brothers*
83/81 **Jumper Cable Man** *Marty Robbins*
72/93 **Junk Cars** *Mac McAnally*
61/76 **Junk Food Junkie** *Larry Groce*
9/50 **Just A Closer Walk With Thee** *Red Foley*
35/81 **Just A Country Boy** *Rex Allen, Jr.*
78/87 **Just A Kid From Texas** *Dann Rogers*
Just A Little Bit ..see: Little Bit Of Lovin' (Goes A Long Long Way)
10/58 **Just A Little Lonesome** *Bobby Helms*
5/84 **Just A Little Love** *Reba McEntire*
1/48 **Just A Little Lovin' (Will Go A Long, Long Way)** *Eddy Arnold*
28/77 **Just A Little Thing** *Billy "Crash" Craddock*
13/48 **Just A Pair Of Blue Eyes** *Tex Williams*
81/86 **Just A Woman** *Loretta Lynn*
16/62 **Just Ain't** *Flatt & Scruggs*
63/67 **Just An Empty Place** *Ernie Ashworth*
92/77 **Just An Old Flame** *Hank Thompson*
77/88 **(Just An) Old Wives' Tale** *Gail O'Doski*
69/74 **Just Another Cowboy Song** *Doyle Holly*
1/00 **Just Another Day In Paradise** *Phil Vassar*
90/82 **Just Another Day In Paradise** *Bertie Higgins*
39/98 **Just Another Heartache** *Chely Wright*
73/92 **Just Another Hill** *Corbin/Hanner*
1/86 **Just Another Love** *Tanya Tucker*
68/89 **Just Another Miserable Day (Here In Paradise)** *Billy "Crash" Craddock*
35/78 **Just Another Rhinestone** *Don Drumm*
1/84 **Just Another Woman In Love** *Anne Murray*
26/93 **Just As I Am** *Ricky Van Shelton*
Just As Long As I Have You
72/85 *Gus Hardin & Dave Loggins*
4/90 *Don Williams*

11/56 **Just As Long As You Love Me** *Browns*
55/71 **Just As Soon As I Get Over Loving You** *Jean Shepard*
7/48 **Just Because** *Frankie Yankovic*
17/68 **Just Because I'm A Woman** *Dolly Parton*
60/72 **Just Because I'm Still In Love With You** *Bobby Wright*
36/00 **Just Because She Lives There** *Chalee Tennison*
98/89 **Just Because You're Leavin'** *Lorie Ann*
28/64 **Just Between The Two Of Us** *Merle Haggard & Bonnie Owens*
65/79 **Just Between Us** *Bill Woody*
9/67 **Just Between You And Me** *Charley Pride*
12/98 **Just Between You And Me** *Kinleys*
13/67 **Just Beyond The Moon** *Tex Ritter*
54/69 **Just Blow In His Ear** *David Wilkins*
2/55 **Just Call Me Lonesome** *Eddy Arnold*
10/92 **Just Call Me Lonesome** *Radney Foster*
66/89 **Just Can't Cry No More** *Lonesome Strangers*
37/98 **Just Don't Wait Around Til She's Leavin'** *David Lee Murphy*
52/87 **Just Enough Love** *Ray Price*
30/81 **Just Enough Love (For One Woman)** *Bobby Smith*
44/93 **Just Enough Rope** *Rick Trevino*
23/74 **Just Enough To Make Me Stay** *Bob Luman*
43/69 **Just Enough To Start Me Dreamin'** *Jeannie Seely*
56/74 **Just For Old Times Sake** *Eddy Arnold*
78/82 **Just For The Moment** *Brenda Lee*
5/72 **Just For What I Am** *Connie Smith*
4/68 **Just For You** *Ferlin Husky*
1/75 **Just Get Up And Close The Door** *Johnny Rodriguez*
98/77 **Just Gettin' By** *Red Sovine*
72/83 **Just Give Me One More Night** *Cole Young*
Just Give Me What You Think Is Fair
51/80 *Rex Gosdin with Tommy Jennings*
7/82 *Leon Everette*
1/79 **Just Good Ol' Boys** *Moe Bandy & Joe Stampley*
46/81 **Just Got Back From No Man's Land** *Wayne Kemp*
68/78 **Just Hangin' On** *Mel Street*
12/69 **Just Hold My Hand** *Johnny And Jonie Mosby*
Just Hooked On Country (& II)
42/82 *Albert Coleman's Atlanta Pops (Parts I & II)*
77/82 *Albert Coleman's Atlanta Pops (Part III)*
1/86 **Just In Case** *Forester Sisters*
4/76 **Just In Case** *Ronnie Milsap*
70/72 **Just In Time (To Watch Love Die)** *Charlie Louvin*
31/78 **Just Keep It Up** *Narvel Felts*

Johnny Zero / Johnny Got A Zero (See Pop Mem

9/02	**Just Let Me Be In Love** Tracy Byrd	7/53	**Just Wait 'Til I Get You Alone** Carl Smith	8/48	**Keeper Of My Heart** Bob Wills
80/79	**Just Let Me Make Believe** Jim Chesnut	45/76	**Just Want To Taste Your Wine** Billy Swan	65/67	**Keeper Of The Key** Slim Whitman
16/81	**Just Like Me** Terry Gregory	9/73	**Just What I Had In Mind** Faron Young	2/95	**Keeper Of The Stars** Tracy Byrd
52/91	**Just Like Me** Lee Greenwood	44/73	**Just What I've Been Looking For** Dottie West	54/90	**Keepin' Me Up Nights** Asleep At The Wheel
11/79	**Just Like Real People** Kendalls	52/80	**Just What The Doctor Ordered** Becky Hobbs	49/83	**Keepin' Power** Crystal Gayle
92/84	**Just Like That** Malchak & Rucker		**Just When I Needed You Most**	99/76	**Keepin' Rosie Proud Of Me** Razzy Bailey
5/93	**Just Like The Weather** Suzy Bogguss	40/79	Diana	14/99	**Keepin' Up** Alabama
46/72	**Just Like Walkin' In The Sunshine** Jean Shepard	71/79	Randy Vanwarmer	70/82	**Keeping Me Warm For You** Brenda Lee
25/75	**Just Like Your Daddy** Jeanne Pruett	62/96	Dolly Parton	58/97	**Keeping The Faith** Mary Chapin Carpenter
10/79	**Just Long Enough To Say Goodbye** Mickey Gilley	71/76	**Just You 'N' Me** Sammi Smith	49/67	**Keeping Up Appearances** Lynn Anderson & Jerry Lane
5/88	**Just Lovin' You** O'Kanes		**K**	5/64	**Keeping Up With The Joneses** Faron Young & Margie Singleton
1/58	**Just Married** Marty Robbins			68/97	**Keeping Your Kisses** Kris Tyler
F/82	**Just Married** Louise Mandrell & R.C. Bannon	15/82	**Kansas City Lights** Steve Wariner	8/55	**Kentuckian Song** Eddy Arnold
47/95	**Just My Luck** Kim Richey	2/70	**Kansas City Song** Buck Owens	38/72	**Kentucky** Sammi Smith
36/94	**Just Once** David Lee Murphy	7/65	**Kansas City Star** Roger Miller (Karneval) ..see: One More Time	1/75	**Kentucky Gambler** Merle Haggard
80/82	**Just Once** John Wesley Ryles	2/72	**Kate** Johnny Cash	20/62	**Kentucky Means Paradise** Green River Boys/Glen Campbell
9/88	**Just One Kiss** Exile	60/86	**Katie, Take Me Dancin'** Lewis Storey	42/76	**Kentucky Moonrunner** Cledus Maggard
66/77	**Just One Kiss Magdelena** Bobby G. Rice	22/00	**Katie Wants A Fast One** Steve Wariner With Garth Brooks	31/70	**Kentucky Rain** Elvis Presley
3/56	**Just One More** George Jones	16/72	**Katy Did** Porter Wagoner	53/73	**Kentucky Sunshine** Wayne Kemp
23/74	**Just One More Song** Jack Blanchard & Misty Morgan	11/59	**Katy Too** Johnny Cash		**Kentucky Waltz**
70/72	**Just One More Time** Johnny & Jonie Mosby		**Kaw-Liga**	3/46	Bill Monroe
5/93	**Just One Night** McBride & The Ride	1/53	Hank Williams	1/51	Eddy Arnold
67/87	**Just One Night Won't Do** Big Al Downing	3/69	Charley Pride	26/77	**Kentucky Woman** Randy Barlow
	Just One Time	12/80	Hank Williams, Jr.	86/88	**Kep Pa So** Augie Meyers
2/60	Don Gibson		**Kay**	10/85	**Kern River** Merle Haggard
2/71	Connie Smith	9/69	John Wesley Ryles	50/82	**Key Largo** Bertie Higgins
17/81	Tompall/Glaser Brothers	50/78	John Wesley Ryles	66/69	**Key That Fits Her Door** Jack Greene
	Just Out Of Reach	3/53	**Keep It A Secret** Slim Whitman		**Key's In The Mailbox**
100/76	Perry Como	1/91	**Keep It Between The Lines** Ricky Van Shelton	18/60	Freddie Hart
37/78	Larry G. Hudson	17/90	**Keep It In The Middle Of The Road** Exile	15/72	Tony Booth
77/78	Mack White	42/65	**Keep Me Fooled** Carl Smith	5/94	**Kick A Little** Little Texas
74/84	Merle Kilgore	1/73	**Keep Me In Mind** Lynn Anderson	60/00	**Kick Down The Door** Georgia Middleman
84/86	**Just Out Riding Around** Barbara Fairchild	51/01	**Keep Mom And Dad In Love** Billy Dean & Suzy Bogguss	72/94	**Kick It Up** John Michael Montgomery
39/72	**Just Plain Lonely** Ferlin Husky	6/45	**Keep My Mem'ry In Your Heart** Ernest Tubb	8/62	**Kickin' Our Hearts Around** Buck Owens
	Just Say Yes ..see: (Do You Love Me)		**Keep On Lovin' Me**	64/67	**Kickin' Tree** Bonnie Guitar
61/98	**Just Some Love** Ranch	88/73	Jamey Ryan		**Kid, The**
5/69	**Just Someone I Used To Know** Porter Wagoner & Dolly Parton	23/74	Johnny Paycheck	71/95	Clint Black
76/79	**Just Stay With Me** Terri Hollowell	49/81	**Keep On Movin'** King Edward IV & The Knights	67/98	Clint Black
17/73	**Just Thank Me** David Rogers	58/83	**Keep On Playin' That Country Music** Sierra	71/99	Clint Black
49/97	**Just The Same** Terri Clark	70/82	**Keep On Rollin' Down The Line** Boxcar Willie	68/00	**Kid In Me** Craig Morgan
22/65	**Just Thought I'd Let You Know** Carl Butler & Pearl	19/73	**Keep On Truckin'** Dave Dudley	2/73	**Kid Stuff** Barbara Fairchild
70/67	**Just To Be Where You Are** Wilburn Brothers	45/92	**Keep On Walkin'** Mike Reid	1/87	**Kids Of The Baby Boom** Bellamy Brothers
3/98	**Just To Hear You Say That You Love Me** Faith Hill (With Tim McGraw)	53/73	**Keep Out Of My Dreams** Dorsey Burnette	1/73	**Kids Say The Darndest Things** Tammy Wynette
	Just To Prove My Love For [To] You		**Keep The Faith**	37/87	**Killbilly Hill** Southern Pacific
82/77	David Allan Coe	51/87	Jimmy Murphy	17/82	**Killin' Kind** Bandana
71/80	Jimmy Snyder	61/89	Heartland	1/89	**Killin' Time** Clint Black
	Just To Satisfy You	67/91	Goldens	10/81	**Killin' Time** Fred Knoblock & Susan Anton
31/65	Bobby Bare	31/66	**Keep The Flag Flying** Johnny Wright	50/98	**Kind Of Heart That Breaks** Chris Cummings
1/82	Waylon Jennings & Willie Nelson	16/64	**Keep Those Cards And Letters Coming In** Johnny & Jonie Mosby	42/71	**Kind Of Needin' I Need** Norma Jean
1/98	**Just To See You Smile** Tim McGraw				**Kind Of Woman I Got**
94/87	**Just Try Texas** Mike Lord			33/67	Osborne Brothers
				F/75	Hank Williams, Jr.
				33/98	**Kindly Keep It Country** Vince Gill

471

48/73	Kindly Keep It Country Hank Thompson		**L**			Last Date
75/82	King, The Pete Wilcox				11/61	Floyd Cramer
13/77	King Is Gone Ronnie McDowell	60/69	L.A. Angels Jimmy Payne		1/72	Conway Twitty
26/89	King Is Gone (So Are You) George Jones		L.A. International Airport		1/83	Emmylou Harris
75/86	King Lear Cal Smith	67/70	David Frizzell		7/64	Last Day In The Mines Dave Dudley
97/77	King Of Country Music Meets The Queen Of Rock & Roll Even Stevens & Sherry Grooms	9/71	Susan Raye		98/73	Last Days Of Childhood Sam Durrence
		45/92	L.A. To The Moon Ronnie Milsap		52/78	Last Exit For Love Wood Newton
		57/87	La Bamba Los Lobos		51/80	Last Farewell Miki Mori
96/85	King Of Oak Street Ramsey Kearney	58/94	Labor Of Love Radney Foster			Last Goodbye
19/97	King Of The Mountain George Strait	79/89	Labor Of Love Andi & The Brown Sisters		17/68	Dick Miles
	King Of The Road	94/76	Labor Of Love Bob Luman		96/76	Red Sovine
1/65	Roger Miller	80/76	Ladies Love Outlaws Jimmy Rabbitt & Renegade		38/77	Last Gunfighter Ballad Johnny Cash
51/97	Randy Travis	78/77	Ladies Night Del Reeves		57/66	Last Laugh Jim Edward Brown
49/96	King Of The World BlackHawk	1/80	Lady Kenny Rogers		46/77	Last Letter Willie Nelson
1/71	Kiss An Angel Good Mornin' Charley Pride	46/77	Lady Johnny Cash		99/78	Last Lie I Told Her Ronnie Robbins
36/76	Kiss And Say Goodbye Billy Larkin	66/73	Lady Kenny Vernon		43/78	Last Love Of My Life Lynn Anderson
65/78	Kiss Away Jody Miller	79/77	Lady Ain't For Sale Sherry Bryce		4/73	Last Love Song Hank Williams, Jr.
7/55	Kiss-Crazy Baby Johnnie & Jack	76/77	Lady And The Baby David Rogers		20/59	Last Night At A Party Faron Young
29/73	Kiss It And Make It Better Mac Davis	14/75	Lady Came From Baltimore Johnny Cash		28/78	Last Night, Ev'ry Night Reba McEntire
	Kiss Me Darling	1/83	Lady Down On Love Alabama		54/75	Last Of The Outlaws Chuck Price
25/83	Stephanie Winslow	79/86	Lady In Distress Little David Wilkins		43/82	Last Of The Silver Screen Cowboys Rex Allen, Jr.
82/89	Trisha Lynn	55/83	Lady In My Life Tony Joe White		63/74	Last Of The Sunshine Cowboys Eddy Raven
26/94	Kiss Me, I'm Gone Marty Stuart	9/79	Lady In The Blue Mercedes Johnny Duncan		27/77	Last Of The Winfield Amateurs Ray Griff
22/93	Kiss Me In The Car John Berry	31/84	Lady In Waiting David Wills		1/87	Last One To Know Reba McEntire
79/83	Kiss Me Just One More Time Floyd Brown	88/82	Lady, Lady Kelly Lang		18/71	Last One To Touch Me Porter Wagoner
60/00	Kiss Me Now Lila McCann		Lady Lay Down		4/88	Last Resort T. Graham Brown
52/97	Kiss The Girl Little Texas	1/79	John Conlee		3/59	Last Ride Hank Snow
61/72	Kiss The Hurt Away Ronnie Dove	26/82	Tom Jones		63/89	Last Rose Bobby Vinton
88/82	Kiss The Hurt Away Mack White	67/82	Lady, Lay Down (Lay Down On My Pillow) Gary Goodnight		2/83	Last Thing I Needed First Thing This Morning Willie Nelson
1/00	Kiss This Aaron Tippin	4/85	Lady Like You Glen Campbell		26/59	Last Thing I Want To Know George Morgan
75/99	Kiss This Lisa Angelle	47/74	Lady Lover Bobby Lewis		7/68	Last Thing On My Mind Porter Wagoner/Dolly Parton
87/79	Kiss You All Over Jim Mundy & Terri Melton	73/83	Lady Of The Eighties Jeanne Pruett		20/01	Last Thing On My Mind Patty Loveless
74/79	Kiss You And Make It Better Roy Head	22/73	Lady Of The Night David Houston		75/97	Last Time Tractors
24/69	Kissed By The Rain, Warmed By The Sun Glenn Barber	31/83	Lady, She's Right Leon Everette		85/80	Last Time Johnny Cash
5/55	Kisses Don't Lie Carl Smith	3/84	Lady Takes The Cowboy Everytime Larry Gatlin/Gatlin Brothers		25/72	Last Time I Called Somebody Darlin' Roy Drusky
72/95	Kisses Don't Lie George Ducas	F/78	Lady, Would You Like To Dance Jerry Naylor		21/71	Last Time I Saw Her Glen Campbell
11/61	Kisses Never Lie Carl Smith	2/52	Lady's Man Hank Snow		8/74	Last Time I Saw Him Dottie West
6/57	Kisses Sweeter Than Wine Jimmie Rodgers	64/96	Lady's Man Rob Crosby		50/77	Last Time You Love Me Jerry Naylor
14/61	Kissing My Pillow Rose Maddox	92/81	Lady's Man Music Row		39/64	Last Town I Painted George Jones
3/57	Knee Deep In The Blues Marty Robbins	91/77	Laid Back Country Picker Wendel Adkins		69/67	Last Train To Clarksville Ed Bruce
18/63	Knock Again, True Love Claude Gray	82/83	Laid Off Bill Anderson		80/82	Last Train To Heaven Boxcar Willie
56/95	Knock, Knock Hutchens	98/77	Laissez Les Bontemps Rouler Helen Reddy		4/53	Last Waltz Webb Pierce
94/78	Knock Knock Knock Frenchie Burke		(Lament Of Cherokee) ..see: Indian Reservation		52/73	Last Will And Testimony (Of A Drinking Man) Howard Crockett
29/84	Knock On Wood Razzy Bailey	20/70	Land Mark Tavern Del Reeves & Penny DeHaven		73/81	Last Word In Jesus Is Us Roy Clark
3/71	Knock Three Times Billy "Crash" Craddock	63/80	Land Of Cotton Donna Fargo			Last Word In Lonesome Is Me
3/53	Knothole Carlisles	5/97	Land Of The Living Pam Tillis		2/66	Eddy Arnold
58/90	Knowin' You Were Leavin' Les Taylor	8/01	Laredo Chris Cagle		90/76	Terry Bradshaw
	Knoxville Girl	9/85	Lasso The Moon Gary Morris			
18/59	Wilburn Brothers	65/73	Last Blues Song Dick Curless			
19/59	Louvin Brothers		Last Cheater's Waltz			
39/72	Knoxville Station Bobby Austin	1/79	T.G. Sheppard			
11/71	Ko-Ko Joe Jerry Reed	F/79	Sonny Throckmorton			
4/47	Kokomo Island Al Dexter		Last Country Song ..see: (Who's Gonna Sing)			
		12/80	Last Cowboy Song Ed Bruce			

Let 'Em Be Little – Billy Dean

20/68	Late And Great Love (Of My Heart) Hank Snow	
49/77	Lately I've Been Thinking Too Much Lately David Allan Coe	
64/90	Lately Rose Trader-Price	
42/77	Latest Shade Of Blue Connie Smith	
	Laura (What's He Got That I Ain't Got)	
1/67	Leon Ashley	
50/67	Claude King	
60/73	Marty Robbins	
19/76	Kenny Rogers	
13/49	Lavender Blue (Dilly Dilly) Burl Ives with Captain Stubby	
3/76	Lawdy Miss Clawdy Mickey Gilley	
9/72	Lawrence Welk - Hee Haw Counter-Revolution Polka Roy Clark	
72/79	Lawyers Billy Walker	
22/73	Lay A Little Lovin' On Me Del Reeves	
97/79	Lay A Little Lovin' On Me Jody Miller	
68/93	Lay Around And Love On You Lari White	
52/82	Lay Back Down And Love Me Rich Landers	
	Lay Back In The Arms Of Someone	
80/79	Juice Newton	
13/80	Randy Barlow	
91/84	Johnny Tillotson	
35/75	Lay Back Lover Dottie West	
67/76	Lay Down Charly McClain	
3/79	Lay Down Beside Me Don Williams	
	Lay Down Sally	
26/78	Eric Clapton	
70/78	Red Sovine	
86/78	Jack Paris	
96/88	Lay, Lady Lay Jim Bean	
86/89	Lay Me Down Carolina Mark Tribble	
69/91	Lay My Body Down Kenny Rogers	
44/67	Lay Some Happiness On Me Bobby Wright	
82/77	Lay Something On My Bed Besides A Blanket Charly McClain	
84/81	Layin' Low Denny Hilton	
68/70	Laying My Burdens Down Willie Nelson	
13/48	Lazy Mary Bud Hobbs	
47/93	Lead Me Not Lari White	
56/70	Lead Me Not Into Temptation Anthony Armstrong Jones	
	Lead Me On	
68/69	Bonnie Owens	
1/71	Loretta Lynn & Conway Twitty	
7/95	Lead On George Strait	
13/74	Lean It All On Me Diana Trask	
99/79	Lean, Mean And Hungry Chris LeDoux	
55/77	Lean On Jesus "Before He Leans On You" Paul Craft	
	Lean On Me	
91/75	Paul Delicato	
77/84	Jack Grayson	
93/79	Leaning On Each Other B.J. Wright	

1/91	Leap Of Faith Lionel Cartwright	
20/67	Learnin' A New Way Of Life Hank Snow	
2/96	Learning As You Go Rick Trevino	
59/91	Learning The Game Black Tie	
2/93	Learning To Live Again Garth Brooks	
28/81	Learning To Live Again Bobby Bare	
15/65	Least Of All George Jones	
34/64	Leave A Little Play (In The Chain Of Love) Bob Jennings	
6/92	Leave Him Out Of This Steve Wariner	
7/90	Leave It Alone Forester Sisters	
68/79	Leave It To Love Jim Taylor	
22/75	Leave It Up To Me Billy Larkin	
72/74	Leave Me Alone (Ruby Red Dress) Arleen Harden	
1/87	Leave Me Lonely Gary Morris	
70/88	Leave Me Satisfied Tiny Tim	
6/69	Leave My Dream Alone Warner Mack	
59/98	Leave My Mama Out Of This Monty Holmes	
6/83	Leave Them Boys Alone Hank Williams, Jr.	
63/68	Leave This One Alone Nat Stuckey	
93/78	Leave While I'm Sleeping Micki Fuhrman	
41/68	Leaves Are The Tears Of Autumn Bonnie Guitar	
74/77	Leavin' Kenny Price	
82/85	Leaving Charleston Express/Jesse Wales	
9/71	Leavin' And Sayin' Goodbye Faron Young	
	Leavin' On Your Mind	
8/63	Patsy Cline	
58/72	Bobbie Roy	
92/80	Karen Casey	
78/88	Donna Meade	
75/81	Leavin You Is Easier (Than Wishing You Were Gone) Joe Douglas	
15/93	Leavin's Been A Long Time Comin' Shenandoah	
13/80	Leavin's For Unbelievers Dottie West	
1/80	Leaving Louisiana In The Broad Daylight Oak Ridge Boys	
31/98	Leaving October Sons Of The Desert	
52/70	Leaving On A Jet Plane Kendalls	
98/76	Leaving Was Easy Mike Boyd	
64/73	Leaving's Heavy On My Mind Sherry Bryce	
62/78	Left-Over Love Brenda Lee	
10/84	Left Side Of The Bed Mark Gray	
5/60	Left To Right Kitty Wells	
45/81	Lefty David Frizzell	
49/01	Legacy Neal Coty	
19/85	Legend And The Man Conway Twitty	
	Legend In My Time ..see: (I'd Be) A	
1/68	Legend Of Bonnie And Clyde Merle Haggard	
94/80	Legend Of Harry And The Mountain Ron Shaw/Desert Wind Band	

27/62	Legend Of The Johnson Boys Flatt & Scruggs	
80/80	Legend Of Wooley Swamp Charlie Daniels Band	
38/72	Legendary Chicken Fairy Jack Blanchard & Misty Morgan	
9/62	Leona Stonewall Jackson	
16/85	Leona Sawyer Brown	
64/78	Leona Johnny Russell	
91/77	Leona Don't Live Here Anymore Wayne Kemp	
9/81	Leonard Merle Haggard	
	Leroy The Redneck Reindeer	
33/95	Joe Diffie	
46/96	Joe Diffie	
54/97	Joe Diffie	
27/65	Less And Less Charlie Louvin	
44/68	Less Of Me Bobbie Gentry & Glen Campbell	
67/75	Less Than The Song Patti Page	
	Lesson In Leavin'	
1/80	Dottie West	
2/99	Jo Dee Messina	
3/00	Lessons Learned Tracy Lawrence	
34/85	Let A Little Love Come In Charley Pride	
86/86	Let A Little Love In Rockin' Horse	
64/99	Let 'Er Rip Dixie Chicks	
5/61	Let Forgiveness In Webb Pierce	
6/93	Let Go Brother Phelps	
7/93	Let Go Of The Stone John Anderson	
18/91	Let Her Go Mark Collie	
43/72	Let Him Have It Jan Howard	
	Let It Be Me	
14/69	Glen Campbell & Bobbie Gentry	
2/82	Willie Nelson	
5/89	Let It Be You Ricky Skaggs	
57/89	Let It Burn Jeff Chance	
78/88	Let It Go Don Juan	
8/97	Let It Rain Mark Chesnutt	
6/85	Let It Roll (Let It Rock) Mel McDaniel	
5/76	Let It Shine Olivia Newton-John	
	Let It Snow Let It Snow Let It Snow	
43/96	Ricochet	
44/97	Ricochet	
41/98	Ricochet	
64/98	Martina McBride	
39/99	Ricochet	
72/99	George Strait	
73/99	Martina McBride	
22/80	Let Jesse Rob The Train Buck Owens	
67/84	Let Love Come Lookin' For You Dottie West	
63/86	Let Me Be The First Nicolette Larson	
1/53	Let Me Be The One Hank Locklin	
74/80	Let Me Be The One Billy Walker & Barbara Fairchild	
7/73	Let Me Be There Olivia Newton-John	
13/78	Let Me Be Your Baby Charly McClain	
35/76	Let Me Be Your Friend Mack White	
	(Let Me Be Your) Teddy Bear	
1/57	Elvis Presley	
F/78	Elvis Presley	
7/77	Let Me Down Easy Cristy Lane	

473

Let 'Em Be Little — Billy Dean
Let's Roll (?) — Toby Keith (?)

16/85	Let Me Down Easy	*Jim Glaser*
67/86	Let Me Down Easy	*Malchak & Rucker*
87/78	Let Me Down Easy	*Peggy Sue*
63/94	Let Me Drive	*Greg Holland*
93/78	Let Me Fall Back In Your Arms	*Freddy Weller*
72/81	Let Me Fill For You A Fantasy	*Gary Goodnight*
45/64	Let Me Get Close To You	*Skeeter Davis*
	Let Me Go, Lover!	
1/55		*Hank Snow*
75/70		*Karen Kelly*
27/70	Let Me Go (Set Me Free)	*Johnny Duncan*
23/80	Let Me In	*Kenny Dale*
F/82	Let Me In And Let Me Love You	*Tennessee Express*
11/97	Let Me Into Your Heart	*Mary Chapin Carpenter*
1/98	Let Me Let Go	*Faith Hill*
21/71	Let Me Live	*Charley Pride*
53/80	Let Me Love You	*Fred Knoblock*
99/77	Let Me Love You Now	*Jim Chesnut*
22/77	Let Me Love You Once Before You Go	*Barbara Fairchild*
69/76	Let Me Love You Where It Hurts	*Jim Ed Brown*
25/74	Let Me Make The Bright Lights Shine For You	*Bob Luman*
29/63	Let Me Off At The Corner	*Dottie West*
	Let Me Swing ..see: (Turn Me Loose And)	
71/75	Let Me Take Care Of You	*Bobby Lewis*
53/78	Let Me Take You In My Arms Again	*James Darren*
1/89	Let Me Tell You About Love	*Judds*
97/79	Let My Fingers Do The Walking	*Pat Pomsl*
98/77	Let My Fingers Do The Walking (I'm Your Telephone Man)	*Alan Cartee*
1/77	Let My Love Be Your Pillow	*Ronnie Milsap*
78/73	Let My Love Shine	*Marti Brown*
1/51	Let Old Mother Nature Have Her Way	*Carl Smith*
10/84	Let Somebody Else Drive	*John Anderson*
4/93	Let That Pony Run	*Pam Tillis*
86/76	Let The Big Wheels Roll	*Sarah Johns*
4/68	Let The Chips Fall	*Charley Pride*
74/91	Let The Cowboy Dance	*Michael Martin Murphey*
57/74	Let The Four Winds Blow	*Jack Reno*
59/82	**Let The Good Times Roll**	*Jon And Lynn*
23/85	Let The Heartache Ride	*Restless Heart*
58/81	Let The Little Bird Fly	*Dottsy*
38/75	Let The Little Boy Dream	*Even Stevens*
4/87	Let The Music Lift You Up	*Reba McEntire*

Jooking / Partying

60/94	Let The Picture Paint Itself	*Rodney Crowell*
20/69	Let The Whole World Sing It With Me	*Wynn Stewart*
7/68	Let The World Keep On A Turnin'	*Buck Owens & Buddy Alan*
80/82	Let Your Fingers Do The Walkin'	*Jebry Lee Briley*
53/96	Let Your Heart Lead Your Mind	*Smokin' Armadillos*
57/79	Let Your Love Fall Back On Me	*David Houston*
21/76	Let Your Love Flow	*Bellamy Brothers*
13/72	**Let's All Go Down To The River**	*Jody Miller & Johnny Paycheck*
F/75	Let's All Help The Cowboys (Sing The Blues)	*Waylon Jennings*
82/88	Let's Be Bad Tonight	*Ronnie Rogers*
38/87	Let's Be Fools Like That Again	*Tommy Roe*
72/78	Let's Be Lonely Together	*Dale McBride*
32/73	Let's Build A World Together	*George Jones & Tammy Wynette*
59/01	Let's Burn It Down	*Kristin Garner*
92/78	Let's Call It A Day	*Leslee Barnhill*
57/90	Let's Call It A Day Today	*Tammy Wynette*
1/84	Let's Chase Each Other Around The Room	*Merle Haggard*
16/87	Let's Do Something	*Vince Gill*
51/80	Let's Do Something Cheap And Superficial	*Burt Reynolds*
26/62	Let's End It Before It Begins	*Claude Gray*
	Let's Fall Apart ..see: (All Together Now)	
1/84	Let's Fall To Pieces Together	*George Strait*
64/83	Let's Find Each Other Tonight	*Jose Feliciano*
72/81	Let's Forget That We're Married	*Gary Stewart*
100/77	Let's Get Acquainted Again	*Floyd Brown*
76/82	Let's Get Crazy Again	*Diane Pfeifer*
	(Let's Get) Dixiefried ..see: Dixie Fried	
6/80	Let's Get It While The Gettin's Good	*Eddy Arnold*
10/83	Let's Get Over Them Together	*Moe Bandy/Becky Hobbs*
12/89	Let's Get Started If We're Gonna Break My Heart	*Statler Brothers*
65/70	Let's Get Together	*Skeeter Davis & George Hamilton IV*
41/82	Let's Get Together And Cry	*Joe Stampley*
6/77	(Let's Get Together) One Last Time	*Tammy Wynette*
	Let's Go All The Way	
11/64		*Norma Jean*
68/82		*Claude Gray & Norma Jean*
26/74	Let's Go All The Way Tonight	*Mel Tillis & Sherry Bryce*
67/00	Let's Go Chase Some Women	*Michael Chain*
52/70	Let's Go Fishin' Boys (The Girls Are Bitin')	*Charlie Walker*

100/88	Let's Go Party	*Kathy Bee*
70/94	Let's Go Spend Your Money Honey	*Evangeline*
68/80	Let's Go Through The Motions	*Cates Sisters*
2/50	Let's Go To Church (Next Sunday Morning)	*Margaret Whiting & Jimmy Wakely*
5/95	Let's Go To Vegas	*Faith Hill*
95/78	Let's Have A Heart To Heart Talk	*Leon Rausch*
59/74	Let's Hear It For Loneliness	*Mundo Earwood*
17/63	Let's Invite Them Over	*George Jones & Melba Montgomery*
	Let's Keep It That Way	
37/79		*Juice Newton*
10/80		*Mac Davis*
30/84	Let's Leave The Lights On Tonight	*Johnny Rodriguez*
2/51	Let's Live A Little	*Carl Smith*
53/84	Let's Live This Dream Together	*Narvel Felts*
52/75	Let's Love While We Can	*Barbara Fairchild*
61/93	Let's Make A Baby King	*Wynonna*
6/00	Let's Make Love	*Faith Hill with Tim McGraw*
20/00	Let's Make Sure We Kiss Goodbye	*Vince Gill*
6/76	Let's Put It Back Together Again	*Jerry Lee Lewis*
23/80	Let's Put Our Love In Motion	*Charly McClain*
27/69	Let's Put Our World Back Together	*Charlie Louvin*
5/49	Let's Say Goodbye Like We Said Hello	*Ernest Tubb*
9/78	Let's Shake Hands And Come Out Lovin'	*Kenny O'Dell*
64/83	Let's Sing About Love	*Big Al Downing*
18/75	**Let's Sing Our Song**	*Jerry Reed*
70/89	Let's Sleep On It	*Grayghost*
92/88	Let's Start A Rumor Today	*Bobby Durham*
55/99	Let's Start Livin'	*Gil Grand*
1/84	Let's Stop Talkin' About It	*Janie Fricke*
1/78	Let's Take The Long Way Around The World	*Ronnie Milsap*
27/79	Let's Take The Time To Fall In Love Again	*Jim Chesnut*
68/98	Let's Talk About Love	*Mindy McCready*
77/89	Let's Talk About Us	*Shane Barmby*
90/83	Let's Talk It Over	*R. Dean Taylor*
9/60	**Let's Think About Living**	*Bob Luman*
51/70	Let's Think About Where We're Going	*LaWanda Lindsey & Kenny Vernon*
42/74	Let's Truck Together	*Kenny Price*
28/79	Let's Try Again	*Janie Fricke*
32/78	Let's Try To Remember	*David Rogers*
71/75	Let's Turn The Lights On	*Larry Gatlin*
51/68	Let's Wait A Little Longer	*Canadian Sweethearts*

Handwritten at top: Letters From Home -- John Michael Montgomery (★★★) WPCV

Handwritten right margin: "Liberty" - George Jones (catalog)

36/65	Let's Walk Away Strangers Carl Smith	
3/76	Letter, The Loretta Lynn/Conway Twitty	
	Letter, The	
27/79	Sammi Smith	
76/83	Ronnie Reno	
92/89	Letter, The Michelle Lynn	
9/88	Letter Home Forester Sisters	
10/75	Letter That Johnny Walker Read Asleep At The Wheel	
	Letter To Home ..see: (Love Always)	
20/62	Letter To My Heart Jim Reeves	
71/91	Letter To Saddam Hussein Jerry Martin	
2/50	Letters Have No Arms Ernest Tubb	
6/92	Letting Go Suzy Bogguss	
95/77	Letting Go Tony Booth	
6/77	Liars One, Believers Zero Bill Anderson	
14/79	Liberated Woman ★ *Liberty Valance* John Wesley Ryles	
79/89	Libyan On A Jet Plane (Leavin' On A Jet Plane) Pinkard & Bowden	
78/89	License To Steal Rebecca Holden	
98/77	Lie To Me Larry Wren	
2/85	Lie To You For Your Love Bellamy Brothers	
22/82	Lies On Your Lips Cristy Lane	
23/75	Life Marty Robbins	
34/71	Life Elvis Presley	
4/89	Life As We Knew It Kathy Mattea	
21/64	Life Can Have Meaning Bobby Lord	
36/01	Life Don't Have To Be So Hard Tracy Lawrence	
4/95	Life Gets Away Clint Black	
	Life Gits Tee-Jus Don't It ★	
3/48	~~Carson Robison~~	
5/48	Tex Williams	
5/95	Life Goes On Little Texas	
59/99	Life Goes On James Prosser	
84/79	Life Goes On Charlie Rich	
62/88	Life In The City Pake McEntire	
64/99	Life Is A Highway Chris LeDoux	
6/94	Life #9 Martina McBride	
15/60	Life Of A Poor Boy Stonewall Jackson	
84/83	Life Of The Party Carl Miller	
2/59	Life To Go Stonewall Jackson	
22/59	Life To Live Billie Morgan	
	Life Turned Her That Way	
11/67	Mel Tillis	
1/88	Ricky Van Shelton ★	
4/93	Life's A Dance John Michael Montgomery	
23/65	Life's Gone And Slipped Away Jerry Wallace	
1/86	Life's Highway Steve Wariner	
67/75	Life's Like Poetry Lefty Frizzell	
	Life's Little Ups And Downs	
41/69	Charlie Rich	
4/91	Ricky Van Shelton	
98/78	Life's Railway To Heaven Patsy Cline	
37/91	Life's Too Long (To Live Like This) Ricky Skaggs	
4/94	Lifestyles Of The Not So Rich And Famous Tracy Byrd	
71/70	Lift Ring, Pull Open Jim Ed Brown	
23/91	Light At The End Of The Tunnel B.B. Watson	
5/97	Light In Your Eyes LeAnn Rimes	
11/77	Light Of A Clear Blue Morning Dolly Parton	
55/83	Light Of My Life (Has Gone Out Tonight) Tommy St. John	
65/80	Light Of My Life (Has Gone Out Again Tonight) David Wills	
99/75	Light Of The Stable Emmylou Harris	
70/84	Light Up J.C. Cunningham	
35/88	Light Years Glen Campbell	
54/73	Lightening The Load Porter Wagoner	
90/89	Lighter Shade Of Blue Andi & The Brown Sisters	
100/77	Lightnin' Bar Blues Johnny Holm	
75/80	Lightnin' Strikin' Cates	
19/99	Lightning Does The Work Chad Brock	
40/86	Lights Of Albuquerque Jim Glaser	
88/80	Lights Of L.A. Shaun Nielsen	
30/69	Like A Bird George Morgan	
15/74	Like A First Time Thing Ray Price	
13/67	Like A Fool Dottie West	
57/90	Like A Hurricane Marie	
43/68	Like A Merry-Go-Round Liz Anderson	
30/93	Like A River To The Sea Steve Wariner	
58/68	Like A Rolling Stone Flatt & Scruggs	
34/76	Like A Sad Song John Denver	
76/87	Like An Oklahoma Morning Tony McGill	
14/89	Like Father Like Son Lionel Cartwright	
2/83	Like Nothing Ever Happened Sylvia	
4/75	Like Old Times Again Ray Price	
21/80	Like Strangers Gail Davies	
1/96	Like The Rain Clint Black	
3/96	Like There Ain't No Yesterday BlackHawk	
57/98	Like Water Into Wine Patty Loveless	
4/91	Like We Never Had A Broken Heart Trisha Yearwood	
58/95	Likes Of Me Marty Stuart	
39/81	Likin' Him And Lovin' You Kin Vassy	
17/73	Lila Doyle Holly	
17/70	Lilacs And Fire George Morgan	
69/73	Lilacs In Winter Ronnie Dove	
58/91	Lillies White Lies Martin Delray	
78/80	Lily Dan Riley	
32/77	Lily Dale Darrell McCall & Willie Nelson	
92/74	Lincoln Autry Connie Cato	
	Lincoln Park Inn ..see: (Margie's At)	
1/75	Linda On My Mind Conway Twitty	
25/64	Linda With The Lonely Eyes George Hamilton IV	
	Line In Gasoline ..see: (Who Was The Man Who Put) The	
90/79	Lines Jerry Fuller	
57/75	Lion In The Winter Hoyt Axton	
9/95	Lipstick Promises George Ducas	
	Lipstick Traces	
73/77	Jimmie Peters	
88/79	Amazing Rhythm Aces	
44/76	Liquor, Love And Life Freddy Weller	
24/72	Listen Tommy Cash	
32/74	Listen Wayne Kemp	
15/71	Listen Betty Dave Dudley	
70/73	Listen, Spot Peggy Little	
4/72	Listen To A Country Song Lynn Anderson	
3/82	Listen To The Radio Don Williams	
64/93	Listen To The Radio Kathy Mattea	
63/94	Listen To Your Woman Steve Kolander	
66/95	Listenin' To The Radio Chely Wright	
20/60	Little Angel (Come Rock Me To Sleep) Ted Self	
3/50	Little Angel With The Dirty Face Eddy Arnold	
11/68	Little Arrows Leapy Lee	
18/76	Little At A Time Sunday Sharpe	
49/83	Little At A Time Thom Schuyler	
5/75	Little Band Of Gold Sonny James	
49/99	Little Bird Sherrié Austin	
8/49	Little Bird Told Me Smokey Rogers	
18/88	Little Bit Closer Tom Wopat	
14/82	Little Bit Crazy Eddy Raven	
86/81	Little Bit Crazy Amarillo	
2/88	Little Bit In Love Patty Loveless	
36/70	Little Bit Late Lewie Wickham	
14/68	Little Bit Later On Down The Line Bobby Bare	
94/79	Little Bit More Jeris Ross	
66/99	Little Bit More Of Your Love Perfect Stranger	
50/81	Little Bit Of Heaven Roger Bowling	
76/87	Little Bit Of Heaven Ray Charles	
31/93	Little Bit Of Her Love Robert Ellis Orrall	
71/96	Little Bit Of Honey Baker & Myers	
	Little Bit Of Lovin' (Goes A Long Long Way)	
63/87	Diamonds	
61/88	Vicki Bird	
2/95	Little Bit Of You Lee Roy Parnell	
70/79	Little Bit Short On Love (A Little Bit Long On Tears) Billy Walker	
6/75	Little Bit South Of Saskatoon Sonny James	
62/89	Little Bits And Pieces Shelby Lynne	
67/84	Little Bits And Pieces Jim Stafford	
1/96	Little Bitty Alan Jackson	
68/69	Little Bitty Nitty Gritty Dirt Town Roger Sovine	
	Little Bitty Tear	
2/62	Burl Ives	
57/80	Hank Cochran	
10/62	Little Black Book Jimmy Dean	
63/97	Little Blue Dot James Bonamy	
10/69	Little Boy Sad Bill Phillips	
46/68	Little Boy Soldier Wanda Jackson	
43/70	Little Boy's Prayer Porter Wagoner	
17/66	Little Buddy Claude King	
25/95	Little By Little James House	

Handwritten at bottom: (The Man Who Shot) Liberty Valance - Gene Pitney

Little Charm Bracelet — WBAR (Wanda Jackson) see Promised Land

33/84 Little By Little Gene Watson	1/86 Little Rock Reba McEntire	23/79 Livin' Our Love Together
11/48 Little Community Church	2/94 Little Rock Collin Raye	Billie Jo Spears
Bill Monroe	5/56 Little Rosa	46/81 Livin' The Good Life
69/96 Little Deuce Coupe	Red Sovine & Webb Pierce	Corbin/Hanner Band
Beach Boys feat. James House	7/87 Little Sister Dwight Yoakam	86/81 Livin' Together (Lovin' Apart)
46/87 Little Doll Kendalls	98/77 Little Something On The Side	Bobby G. Rice
53/96 Little Drops Of My Heart	Pat Garrett	56/68 Living George Morgan
Keith Gattis	34/64 Little South Of Memphis	9/71 Living And Learning
Little Drummer Boy	Frankie Miller	Mel Tillis & Sherry Bryce
24/59 Johnny Cash	91/78 Little Teardrops Linda Cassady	63/68 Living As Strangers
58/98 Restless Heart	68/92 Little Tears Joy White	Kitty Wells & Red Foley
46/00 Lonestar	1/85 Little Things Oak Ridge Boys	1/96 Living In A Moment Ty Herndon
20/59 Little Dutch Girl George Morgan	8/91 Little Things Marty Stuart	1/86 Living In The Promiseland
74/80 Little Family Soldier Red Sovine	9/97 Little Things Tanya Tucker	Willie Nelson
47/91 Little Folks Charlie Daniels	22/68 Little Things Willie Nelson	2/76 Living It Down Freddy Fender
13/00 Little Gasoline Terri Clark	75/81 Little Things Tennessee Express	55/87 Living Like There's No Tomorrow
17/80 Little Getting Used To	Little Things Mean A Lot	John Conlee
Mickey Gilley	79/77 Linda Cassady	88/82 Living My Life Without You Lobo
1/00 Little Girl	3/78 Margo Smith	29/77 Living Next Door To Alice
John Michael Montgomery	50/67 Little Things That Every Girl	Johnny Carver
7/90 Little Girl Reba McEntire	Should Know Claude King	1/89 Living Proof Ricky Van Shelton
31/74 Little Girl Feeling	7/55 Little Tom Ferlin Husky	38/76 Living Proof Hank Williams, Jr.
Barbara Fairchild	36/65 Little Unfair Lefty Frizzell	71/71 Living Tornado Kenni Huskey
2/73 Little Girl Gone Donna Fargo	8/87 Little Ways Dwight Yoakam	F/70 Living Under Pressure
83/80 Little Girls Need Daddies	100/76 Little Weekend Warriors	Eddy Arnold
Sherry Brane	Bobby Penn	91/78 Livingston Saturday Night
3/99 Little Good-Byes SheDaisy	7/46 Little White Cross On The Hill	Jimmy Buffett
1/83 Little Good News Anne Murray	Roy Rogers	7/91 Liza Jane Vince Gill
6/68 Little Green Apples Roger Miller	88/82 Little White Lies David House	1/75 Lizzie And The Rainman
65/69 Little Green Apples No. 2	65/77 Little White Moon Hoyt Axton	Tanya Tucker
Ben Colder	18/68 Little World Girl	66/73 Lizzie Lou Osborne Brothers
29/80 Little Ground In Texas Capitals	George Hamilton IV	57/84 Lo And Behold Wally Fowler's
13/60 Little Guy Called Joe	32/76 Littlest Cowboy Rides Again	Tennessee Valley Boys
Stonewall Jackson	Ed Bruce	30/79 Lo Que Sea (What Ever May The
3/62 Little Heartache Eddy Arnold	62/92 Live And Learn Mac McAnally	Future Be) Jess Garron
7/95 Little Houses Doug Stone	53/01 Live Close By, Visit Often	44/79 Lock, Stock, & Barrel
45/97 Little In Love Paul Brandt	K.T. Oslin	Wood Newton
45/76 Little Joe Red Sovine	39/79 Live Entertainment Don King	Lock, Stock And Teardrops
37/70 Little Johnny From Down The	1/55 Live Fast, Love Hard, Die Young	26/63 Roger Miller
Street Wilburn Brothers	Faron Young	70/68 Diana Trask
54/00 Little Left Of Center Randy Travis	16/70 Live For The Good Times	53/88 k.d. lang
2/94 Little Less Talk And A Lot More	Warner Mack	23/69 Lodi Buddy Alan
Action Toby Keith	28/63 Live For Tomorrow Carl Smith	62/95 Lola's Love Ricky Van Shelton
64/84 Little Love Juice Newton	37/01 Live It Up Marshall Dyllon	11/76 Lone Star Beer And Bob Wills
56/88 Little Maggie Darden Smith	11/00 Live, Laugh, Love Clay Walker	Music Red Steagall
3/99 Little Man Alan Jackson	58/97 Live To Love Again	36/87 Lone Star State Of Mind
63/74 Little Man Logan Smith	Burnin' Daylight	Nanci Griffith
73/78 Little Man's Got The Biggest	1/94 Live Until I Die Clay Walker	96/74 Loneliness (Can Break A Good
Smile In Town Arthur Blanch	44/68 Live Your Life Out Loud	Man Down) Norro Wilson
21/61 Little Miss Belong To No One	Bobby Lord	56/86 Loneliness In Lucy's Eyes
Margie Bowes	F/57 Livin' Alone Hank Locklin	Johnny Lee
1/95 Little Miss Honky Tonk	68/77 Livin' Her Life In A Song	74/70 Loneliness Without You Hagers
Brooks & Dunn	Billy Mize	18/00 Lonely Tracy Lawrence
2/97 Little More Love Vince Gill	Livin' In A House Full Of Love	1/67 Lonely Again Eddy Arnold
94/79 Little More Love	3/65 David Houston	2/86 Lonely Alone Forester Sisters
Olivia Newton-John	70/91 Glen Campbell	5/99 Lonely And Gone
22/62 Little Music Box Skeeter Davis	43/97 Gary Allan	Montgomery Gentry
10/83 Little Old Fashioned Karma	93/88 Livin' In Shadows	15/83 Lonely But Only For You
Willie Nelson	Jerry Lee Tucker	Sissy Spacek
9/67 Little Old Wine Drinker Me	85/81 Livin' In The Light Of Her Love	86/79 Lonely Coming Down
Robert Mitchum	Joe Waters	Keith Bradford
23/77 Little Ole Dime Jim Reeves	77/75 Livin' In The Sunshine Of Your	46/86 Lonely Days, Lonely Nights
11/63 Little Ole You Jim Reeves	Love Ray Pillow	Patty Loveless
2/98 Little Past Little Rock	9/82 Livin' In These Troubled Times	Lonely Eyes
Lee Ann Womack	Crystal Gayle	39/77 Rayburn Anthony
31/66 Little Pedro Carl Butler & Pearl	28/63 Livin' Offa Credit Jim Nesbitt	61/83 Brice Henderson
30/66 Little Pink Mack	1/94 Livin' On Love Alan Jackson	46/76 Lonely Eyes Randy Barlow
Kay Adams with Cliffie Stone	75/76 Livin' On Love Street Shylo	63/70 Lonely For You Wilma Burgess
61/97 Little Ramona (Gone Hillbilly	43/69 Livin' On Love (And Lovin'	14/64 Lonely Girl Carl Smith
Nuts) BR5-49	Livin' With You) Slim Whitman	30/59 Lonely Girl Jimmy Newman
29/69 Little Reasons Charlie Louvin	62/83 Livin' On Memories Gary Wolf	
3/98 Little Red Rodeo Collin Raye		

476

✱✱✱ Long Black Train – Josh Turner WPCV & WBAR & catalog

	Lonely Heart	73/68	**Long Black Limousine** Jody Miller	4/92	**Look At Us** Vince Gill	
81/83	Cedar Creek		**Long Black Veil**	52/93	**Look At You Girl** Chris LeDoux	
40/84	Tammy Wynette	6/59	Lefty Frizzell	1/93	**Look Heart, No Hands**	
68/82	**Lonely Hearts** Younger Brothers	26/74	Sammi Smith		Randy Travis	
18/78	**Lonely Hearts Club**	62/75	**Long Distance Kisses**	65/70	**Look How Far We've Come**	
	Billie Jo Spears		Larry Hosford		Bill Wilbourne & Kathy Morrison	
40/80	**Lonely Hotel** Don King	59/80	**Long Drop** Roy Head	36/66	**Look Into My Teardrops**	
53/71	**Lonely Is** Dottie West	61/78	**Long Gone Blues** Cates Sisters		Conway Twitty	
18/58	**Lonely Island Pearl**		**Long Gone Lonesome Blues**	69/86	**Look Of A Lady In Love**	
	Johnnie And Jack	1/50	Hank Williams		Johnny Duncan	
23/75	**Lonely Men, Lonely Women**	5/64	Hank Williams, Jr.	68/84	**Look Of A Lovin' Lady**	
	Connie Eaton	63/87	Dennis Robbins		Wyvon Alexander	
1/82	**Lonely Nights** Mickey Gilley	1/02	**Long Goodbye** Brooks & Dunn	11/95	**Look What Followed Me Home**	
38/72	**Lonely People** Eddy Arnold	27/80	**Long Haired Country Boy**		David Ball	
83/78	**Lonely People** Keith Bradford		Charlie Daniels Band	73/97	**Look What Love Can Do**	
80/75	**Lonely Rain** Wynn Stewart	51/96	**Long Hard Lesson Learned**		Ruby Lovett	
16/60	**Lonely River Rhine** Bobby Helms		John Anderson	83/85	**Look What Love Did To Me**	
6/89	**Lonely Side Of Love**	63/76	**Long Hard Ride**		Kenny Dale	
	Patty Loveless		Marshall Tucker Band	4/51	**Look What Thoughts Will Do**	
76/78	**Lonely Side Of The Bed**	1/84	**Long Hard Road (The**		Lefty Frizzell	
	Linda Cassady		**Sharecropper's Dream)**	56/89	**Look What We Made (When We**	
7/56	**Lonely Side Of Town** Kitty Wells		Nitty Gritty Dirt Band		**Made Love)** Jonathan Edwards	
	Lonely Street	6/67	**Long-Legged Guitar Pickin' Man**	21/77	**Look Who I'm Cheating On**	
84/74	Tony Booth		Johnny Cash & June Carter		**Tonight** Bobby Bare	
8/78	Rex Allen, Jr.	42/94	**Long Legged Hannah (From**	8/58	**Look Who's Blue** Don Gibson	
5/76	**Lonely Teardrops** Narvel Felts		**Butte Montana)** Jesse Hunter	65/93	**Look Who's Needing Who**	
18/63	**Lonely Teardrops** Rose Maddox	43/80	**Long Line Of Empties**		Clinton Gregory	
41/79	**Lonely Together** Diana		Darrell McCall	4/44	**Look Who's Talkin'** Ted Daffan	
98/85	**Lonely Together** A.J. Masters	1/87	**Long Line Of Love**	72/81	**(Lookin' At Things) In A Different**	
1/96	**Lonely Too Long** Patty Loveless		Michael Martin Murphey		**Light** Nightstreets	
11/72	**Lonely Weekends** Jerry Lee Lewis	41/70	**Long Lonesome Highway**	F/77	**Lookin' For A Feeling**	
75/80	**Lonely Wine** Maury Finney		Michael Parks		Waylon Jennings	
64/81	**Lonely Women** Silver Creek	5/70	**Long Long Texas Road**		**Lookin' For Love**	
	Lonely Women Make Good		Roy Drusky	1/80	Johnny Lee	
	Lovers	74/84	**Long Lost Causes**	44/01	Sawyer Brown	
4/72	Bob Luman		Rick & Janis Carnes	16/76	**Lookin' For Tomorrow (And**	
4/84	Steve Wariner	16/91	**Long Lost Friend** Restless Heart		**Findin' Yesterdays)** Mel Tillis	
11/98	**Lonely Won't Leave Me Alone**	47/66	**Long Night** Red Sovine	55/94	**Lookin' In The Same Direction**	
	Trace Adkins	5/89	**Long Shot** Baillie And The Boys		Ken Mellons	
13/66	**Lonelyville** Dave Dudley	73/00	**Long Slow Beautiful Dance**	37/71	**Lookin' Out My Back Door**	
20/61	**Lonelyville** Ray Sanders		Rascal Flatts		Buddy Alan	
	Lonesome 7-7203	69/96	**Long Tall Texan**	5/68	**Looking At The World Through A**	
1/63	Hawkshaw Hawkins		Beach Boys with Doug Supernaw		**Windshield** Del Reeves	
72/67	Burl Ives	10/92	**Long Time Ago** Remingtons	51/74	**Looking Back** Jerry Foster	
16/72	Tony Booth	16/59	**Long Time Ago** Faron Young		**Looking Back To See**	
24/84	Darrell Clanton	71/89	**Long Time Comin'** Eddie Preston	4/54	Goldie Hill - Justin Tubb	
62/88	**Lonesome For You** Chris Austin	5/46	**Long Time Gone** Tex Ritter	8/54	Browns	
70/76	**Lonesome Is A Cowboy**	15/66	**Long Time Gone** Dave Dudley	13/72	Buck Owens & Susan Raye	
	Mundo Earwood	55/97	**Long Trail Of Tears**	7/64	**Looking For More In '64**	
2/62	**Lonesome Number One**		George Ducas		Jim Nesbitt	
	Don Gibson	11/60	**Long Walk** Bill Leatherwood	30/76	**Looking For Space** John Denver	
11/59	**Lonesome Old House**	35/89	**Long White Cadillac**	70/86	**Looking For Suzanne**	
	Don Gibson		Dwight Yoakam		Osmond Bros.	
21/60	**Lonesome Road Blues**	85/80	**Longer** Dan Fogelberg	43/95	**Looking For The Light**	
	Jimmie Skinner	35/69	**Longest Beer Of The Night**		Rick Trevino	
11/92	**Lonesome Standard Time**		Jim Ed Brown	82/79	**Looking For The Sunshine**	
	Kathy Mattea	33/78	**Longest Walk** Mary K. Miller		Mickey Newbury	
	Lonesome Whistle	17/76	**Longhaired Redneck**	59/87	**Looking For You** Rodney Crowell	
9/51	Hank Williams		David Allan Coe	11/93	**Looking Out For Number One**	
29/71	Don Gibson	24/81	**Longing For The High** Billy Larkin		Travis Tritt	
	Lonesomest Lonesome	1/97	**Longneck Bottle** Garth Brooks	24/76	**Looking Out My Window**	
2/72	Ray Price	91/89	**Longneck Lone Star (And Two**		**Through The Pain** Mel Street	
49/73	Pat Daisy		**Step Dancin')**	35/90	**Looks Aren't Everything**	
73/81	**Lonestar Cowboy** Donna Fargo		Diana Sicily Currey		Mark Collie	
89/89	**Lonestar Lonesome**	75/67	**Longtime Traveling** Buddy Cagle	80/81	**Looks Like A Set-Up To Me**	
	Terry Stafford	49/00	**Look** Jerry Kilgore		Cedar Creek	
5/85	**Long And Lasting Love**	24/95	**Look At Me Now** Bryan White	23/63	**Loose Lips** Earl Scott	
	Crystal Gayle	21/70	**Look At Mine** Jody Miller		**Loose Talk**	
52/80	**Long Arm Of The Law**	59/68	**Look At The Laughter**	1/55	Carl Smith	
	Roger Bowling		Wilma Burgess	4/61	Buck Owens & Rose Maddox	
4/96	**Long As I Live**	17/75	**Look At Them Beans**	12/98	**Loosen Up My Strings** Clint Black	
	John Michael Montgomery		Johnny Cash			

477

7/91	**Lord Have Mercy On A Country Boy** Don Williams	67/81	**Louisiana Lonely** Narvel Felts	1/85	**Love Don't Care (Whose Heart It Breaks)** Earl Thomas Conley
5/92	**Lord Have Mercy On The Working Man** Travis Tritt		**Louisiana Man**	55/86	**Love Don't Come Any Better Than This** Shelly West
58/74	**Lord How Long Has This Been Going On** Doyle Holly	10/61	Rusty & Doug	93/78	**Love Don't Hide From Me** Hugh X. Lewis
		25/65	George Jones & Gene Pitney		
		72/68	Bobbie Gentry		
1/82	**Lord, I Hope This Day Is Good** Don Williams	14/70	Connie Smith	59/83	**Love Don't Know A Lady (From A Honky Tonk Girl)** Billy Parker
		20/88	**Louisiana Rain** John Wesley Ryles		
71/77	**Lord, If I Make It To Heaven Can I Bring My Own Angel Along** Billy Parker	7/81	**Louisiana Saturday Night** Mel McDaniel	80/81	**Love Fires** Don Gibson
				1/97	**Love Gets Me Every Time** Shania Twain
		24/67	**Louisiana Saturday Night** Jimmy Newman		
16/70	**Lord Is That Me** Jack Greene			62/80	**Love Goes To Hell When It Dies** Wayne Kemp
1/73	**Lord Knows I'm Drinking** Cal Smith	1/73	**Louisiana Woman, Mississippi Man** Loretta Lynn/Conway Twitty	73/85	**Love Gone Bad** Jay Clark
1/73	**Lord, Mr. Ford** Jerry Reed	23/68	**Louisville** Leroy Van Dyke	23/78	**Love Got In The Way** Freddy Weller
62/79	**Lorelei** Sonny James	75/90	**Louisville** Jann Browne		
7/50	**Lose Your Blues** Red Kirk	73/68	**Lovable Fool** Goldie Hill Smith	29/98	**Love Happens Like That** Neal McCoy
28/78	**Loser, The** Kenny Dale	2/94	**Love A Little Stronger** Diamond Rio	12/57	**Love Has Finally Come My Way** Faron Young
63/68	**Loser Making Good** Red Sovine	11/83	**Love Affairs** Michael Murphey		
3/67	**Loser's Cathedral** David Houston	71/97	**Love Ain't Easy** Big House	90/83	**Love Has Made A Woman Out Of You** Vince And Dianne Hatfield
36/71	**Loser's Cocktail** Dick Curless	24/79	**Love Ain't Gonna Wait For Us** Billie Jo Spears		
90/78	**Loser's Just A Learner (On His Way To Better Things)** Roger Bowling			10/60	**Love Has Made You Beautiful** Merle Kilgore
		12/99	**Love Ain't Like That** Faith Hill	4/89	**Love Has No Right** Billy Joe Royal
37/81	**Loser's Night Out** Jack Grayson & Blackjack		**Love Ain't Made For Fools**		
		33/79	John Wesley Ryles	26/80	**Love Has Taken Its' Time** Zella Lehr
90/81	**Losin' Myself In You** Gary Goodnight	66/88	Kevin Pearce		
		38/70	**Love Ain't Never Gonna Be No Better** Webb Pierce	3/88	**Love Helps Those** Paul Overstreet
74/67	**Losing Kind** Bobby Barnett			19/70	**Love Hungry** Warner Mack
14/80	**Losing Kind Of Love** Lacy J. Dalton	19/81	**Love Ain't Never Hurt Nobody** Bobby Goldsboro	72/69	**Love, I Finally Found It** Ernie Ashworth
66/88	**Losing Somebody You Love** Rick Snyder	51/73	**Love Ain't Worth a Dime Unless It's Free** Wynn Stewart	53/77	**Love I Need You** Dale McBride
2/62	**Losing Your Love** Jim Reeves	14/85	**(Love Always) Letter To Home** Glen Campbell	98/78	**Love In Me** Jim Norman
46/95	**Losing Your Love** Larry Stewart			70/89	**Love In Motion** Ross Lewis
6/92	**Lost And Found** Brooks & Dunn	80/78	**Love And Hate** Mike Boyd	63/73	**Love In The Back Seat** Little David Wilkins
9/72	**Lost Forever In Your Kiss** Porter Wagoner & Dolly Parton	70/73	**Love And Honor** Kenny Serratt		
		72/84	**Love And Let Love** Danny Shirley	1/81	**Love In The First Degree** Alabama
	Lost Highway	54/94	**Love And Luck** Marty Stuart		
12/49	Hank Williams	73/88	**Love And Other Fairy Tales** Girls Next Door	65/88	**Love In The Heart** Don McLean
51/67	Don Gibson			3/75	**Love In The Hot Afternoon** Gene Watson
100/88	James Storie	3/86	**Love At The Five & Dime** Kathy Mattea		
	Lost His [Her] Love On Our Last Date ..see: Last Date		**Love Bug**	32/80	**Love In The Meantime** Streets
		6/65	George Jones	61/80	**Love Insurance** Louise Mandrell
45/80	**Lost In Austin** Freddy Weller	8/94	George Strait	39/82	**Love Is** Allen Tripp
84/88	**Lost In Austin** Kenny Blair	72/00	**Love Bug (Bite Me)** South Sixty Five	85/82	**Love Is A Full Time Thing** Terry McMillan
30/81	**Lost In Love** Dickey Lee/Kathy Burdick	12/58	**Love Bug Crawl** Jimmy Edwards	69/69	**Love Is A Gentle Thing** Barbara Fairchild
	Lost In The Feeling	28/82	**Love Busted** Billy "Crash" Craddock	12/72	**Love Is A Good Thing** Johnny Paycheck
2/83	Conway Twitty				
59/00	Mark Chesnutt	99/73	**Love By Appointment** Pati Powell & Bob Gallion	67/89	**Love Is A Hard Road** Irene Kelly
1/85	**Lost In The Fifties Tonight (In The Still Of The Night)** Ronnie Milsap	5/91	**Love Can Build A Bridge** Judds	64/89	**Love Is A Liar** Cee Cee Chapman
		82/78	**Love Can Make The Children Sing** Billy Stack	5/75	**Love Is A Rose** Linda Ronstadt
22/65	**Lost In The Shuffle** Stonewall Jackson			5/70	**Love Is A Sometimes Thing** Bill Anderson
62/99	**Lost In You** Garth Brooks As Chris Gaines	90/81	**Love (Can Make You Happy)** James Marvell	68/76	**Love Is A Two-Way Street** Dottsy
43/71	**Lost It On The Road** Carl Smith	10/87	**Love Can't Ever Get Better Than This** Ricky Skaggs & Sharon White	42/80	**Love Is A Warm Cowboy** Buck Owens
11/48	**Lost John Boogie** Wayne Raney				
73/80	**Lost Love Affair** B.J. Wright				**Love Is A Word**
5/83	**Lost My Baby Blues** David Frizzell	12/62	**Love Can't Wait** Marty Robbins	88/76	Juice Newton & Silver Spur
		44/69	**Love Comes But Once In A Lifetime** Norro Wilson	27/78	Dickey Lee
76/80	**Lost The Good Thing** Steve Gillette (with Jennifer Warnes)			1/85	**Love Is Alive** Judds
		34/80	**Love Crazy Love** Zella Lehr	29/80	**Love Is All Around** Sonny Curtis
15/58	**Lost To A Geisha Girl** Skeeter Davis	58/94	**Love Didn't Do It** Linda Davis	51/98	**Love Is All That Really Matters** Kevin Sharp
		13/81	**Love Dies Hard** Randy Barlow		
72/83	**Louisiana Anna** Maines Brothers Band	86/77	**Love Doesn't Live Here Anymore** Randy Cornor	91/85	**Love Is An Overload** Bobby Lewis
				51/68	**Love Is Ending** Liz Anderson
82/84	**Louisiana Heatwave** Bobby Jenkins	91/79	**Love Don't Care** Charlie Louvin with Emmylou Harris	43/01	**Love Is Enough** 3 Of Hearts
				60/87	**Love Is Everywhere** Mel McDaniel
F/81	**Louisiana Joe** Joe Douglas			13/81	**Love Is Fair** Barbara Mandrell

53/99	Love Is For Giving John Berry	
46/74	Love Is Here Wilma Burgess	
84/79	Love Is Hours In The Making Sterling Whipple	
10/68	Love Is In The Air Marty Robbins	
3/77	Love Is Just A Game Larry Gatlin	
57/69	Love Is Just A State Of Mind Roy Clark	
44/81	Love Is Knockin' At My Door Susie Allanson	
1/74	Love Is Like A Butterfly Dolly Parton	
36/72	Love Is Like A Spinning Wheel Jan Howard	
7/64	Love Is No Excuse Jim Reeves & Dottie West	
53/95	Love Is Not A Thing Russ Taff	
1/83	Love Is On A Roll Don Williams	
47/89	Love Is On The Line Canyon	
56/89	Love Is One Of Those Words Janie Frickie	
47/76	Love Is Only Love (When Shared By Two) Johnny Carver	
26/79	Love Is Sometimes Easy Sandy Posey	
	Love Is Strange	
20/75	Buck Owens & Susan Raye	
21/90	Kenny Rogers & Dolly Parton	
9/96	Love Is Stronger Than Pride Ricochet	
1/73	Love Is The Foundation Loretta Lynn	
8/73	Love Is The Look You're Looking For Connie Smith	
53/86	Love Is The Only Way Out William Lee Golden	
68/84	Love Is The Reason Sierra	
4/97	Love Is The Right Place Bryan White	
24/76	Love Is Thin Ice Barbara Mandrell	
37/85	Love Is What We Make It Kenny Rogers	
69/84	Love Isn't Love ('Til You Give It Away) Tari Hensley	
	Love Isn't Love (Till You Give It Away)	
52/72	Bobby Lee Trammell	
93/76	Eddie Bailes	
87/79	Joy Ford	
30/76	Love It Away Mary Lou Turner	
78/85	Love, It's The Pits Lisa Angelle	
54/86	Love Keep Your Distance A.J. Masters	
40/81	Love Knows We Tried Tanya Tucker	
9/95	Love Lessons Tracy Byrd	
67/90	Love Letter Robin Lee	
	Love Letters	
57/77	Debi Hawkins	
69/83	Hazard	
79/86	Love Letters In The Sand Tom T. Hall	
33/79	Love Lies Mel McDaniel	
19/76	Love Lifted Me Kenny Rogers	
52/92	Love Light Cleve Francis	
58/00	Love Like That Ty Herndon	
70/95	Love Like This Carlene Carter	
29/80	Love, Look At Us Now Johnny Rodriguez	
17/64	Love Looks Good On You David Houston	

41/65	Love Looks Good On You Lefty Frizzell	
1/55	Love, Love, Love Webb Pierce	
26/78	Love, Love, Love/Chapel Of Love Sandy Posey	
34/67	Love Makes The World Go Around Kitty Wells	
1/92	Love, Me Collin Raye	
	Love Me	
34/72	Jeanne Pruett	
9/73	Marty Robbins	
58/83	Jeanne Pruett & Marty Robbins	
10/56	Love Me Elvis Presley	
75/99	Love Me A Little Bit Longer Heather Myles	
83/78	Love Me Again Rita Coolidge	
80/86	Love Me All Over Sammi Smith	
12/67	Love Me And Make It All Better Bobby Lewis	
91/79	Love Me Back To Sleep Jessi Colter	
79/89	Love Me Down To Size Ray Price	
97/77	Love Me Into Heaven Again DeWayne Orender	
24/79	Love Me Like A Stranger Cliff Cochran	
2/87	Love Me Like You Used To Tanya Tucker	
14/68	Love Me, Love Me Bobby Barnett	
26/79	Love Me Now Ronnie McDowell	
61/67	Love Me Now (While I Am Living) Anita Carter	
1/80	Love Me Over Again Don Williams	
	Love Me Tender	
3/56	Elvis Presley	
59/79	Linda Ronstadt	
14/57	Love Me To Pieces Rusty & Doug	
87/82	Love Me Today, Love Me Forever J.W. Gunn	
	Love Me Tonight ..see: (Turn Out The Light And)	
F/78	Love Me When You Can Merle Haggard	
7/78	Love Me With All Your Heart Johnny Rodriguez	
	Love My Life Away ..see: (I Wanna)	
42/82	Love Never Comes Easy Helen Cornelius	
51/82	Love Never Dies Gary Wolf	
54/81	Love Never Hurt So Good Donna Hazard	
4/88	Love Of A Lifetime Gatlin Bros.	
2/01	Love Of A Woman Travis Tritt	
68/68	Love Of A Woman Claude Gray	
2/98	Love Of My Life Sammy Kershaw	
67/67	Love Of The Common People Waylon Jennings	
23/61	Love Oh Love, Oh Please Come Home Reno & Smiley	
74/86	Love On A Blue Rainy Day Charley Pride	
1/90	Love On Arrival Dan Seals	
31/71	Love On Broadway Jerry Lee Lewis	
3/93	Love On The Loose, Heart On The Run McBride & The Ride	
1/78	Love Or Something Like It Kenny Rogers	
1/89	Love Out Loud Earl Thomas Conley	
36/84	Love Over Old Times Sylvia	

1/75	Love Put A Song In My Heart Johnny Rodriguez	
12/96	Love Remains Collin Raye	
6/87	Love Reunited Desert Rose Band	
11/76	Love Revival Mel Tillis	
30/00	Love She Can't Live Without Clint Black	
	Love She Found In Me	
5/83	Gary Morris	
87/89	Hal Gibson	
81/81	Love Signs Ivory Jack	
57/78	Love Somebody To Death Ed Bruce	
2/87	Love Someone Like Me Holly Dunn	
1/83	Love Song Oak Ridge Boys	
3/82	Love Song Kenny Rogers	
5/74	Love Song Anne Murray	
40/80	Love Song Dave Rowland & Sugar	
96/75	Love Song Sherry Bryce	
51/79	Love Song And The Dream Belong To Me Peggy Sue	
40/68	Love Song For You Hank Locklin	
8/50	Love Song In 32 Bars Johnny Bond	
10/52	Love Song Of The Waterfall Slim Whitman	
99/77	Love Song Sing Along Darrell Dodson	
51/77	Love Songs And Romance Magazines Nick Nixon	
27/79	Love Songs Just For You Glenn Barber	
51/76	Love Still Makes The World Go 'Round Stoney Edwards	
	Love Story ..see: Theme From	
33/96	Love Story In The Making Linda Davis	
17/73	Love Sure Feels Good In My Heart Susan Raye	
45/78	Love Survived Roy Head	
48/82	Love Take It Easy On Me LaCosta Tucker	
58/71	Love Takes A Lot Of My Time Skeeter Davis	
4/68	Love Takes Care Of Me Jack Greene	
63/81	Love Takes Two Roy Clark	
76/80	Love Talking Tammy Jo	
9/85	Love Talks Ronnie McDowell	
91/79	Love Talks Dawn Chastain	
41/96	Love That We Lost Chely Wright	
96/83	Love The One You're With Brentwood	
4/80	Love The World Away Kenny Rogers	
	Love Theme From The Sandpiper ..see: Shadow Of Your Smile	
72/96	Love To Burn Mark Collie	
21/81	Love To Love You Cristy Lane	
39/97	Love Travels Kathy Mattea	
36/99	Love Trip Jerry Kilgore	
30/82	Love Was Born Randy Barlow	
39/76	Love Was (Once Around The Dance Floor) Linda Hargrove	
67/76	Love Was The Wind Melba Montgomery	
87/82	Love Wheel Calamity Jane	
7/89	Love Will Forester Sisters	
12/91	Love Will Bring Her Around Rob Crosby	

79/73	Love Will Come Again *Bobby Mack*	2/50	Lovebug Itch *Eddy Arnold*	27/79	Lovin' Starts Where Friendship Ends *Mel McDaniel*
1/88	Love Will Find Its Way To You *Reba McEntire*	2/97	Loved Too Much *Ty Herndon*	30/87	Lovin' That Crazy Feelin' *Ronnie McDowell*
14/86	Love Will Get You Through Times With No Money *Girls Next Door*	56/72	Loveliest Night Of The Year *Slim Whitman*	67/87	Lovin' The Blue *Lynne Tyndall*
84/89	Love Will Never Be The Same *Reno Brothers*	55/74	Lovely Lady *Murry Kellum*		Lovin' Up A Storm ..see: Loving Up
69/87	Love Will Never Slip Away *Suzy Bogguss*	65/80	Lovely Lonely Lady *R.C. Bannon*	7/81	Lovin' What Your Lovin' Does To Me *Conway Twitty & Loretta Lynn*
97/73	Love Will Stand *Lois Johnson*	6/60	Lovely Work Of Art *Jimmy Newman*		Lovin' You ..see: Loving You
52/02	Love, Will (The Package) *Tim Rushlow*	12/71	Lovenworth *Roy Rogers*	34/00	Lovin' You Against My Will *Gary Allan*
1/82	Love Will Turn You Around *Kenny Rogers*	71/83	Lover In Disguise *Wayne Massey*	34/78	Lovin' You Baby *Connie Smith*
1/90	Love Without End, Amen *George Strait*	43/92	Lover Not A Fighter *B.B. Watson*	92/80	Lovin' You Is Music To My Mind *Rex Gosdin*
8/93	Love Without Mercy *Lee Roy Parnell*	70/87	(Lover Of The) Other Side Of The Hill *Rusty Wier*	40/74	Lovin' You Is Worth It *David Houston & Barbara Mandrell*
36/86	Love Won't Wait *Whites*	46/71	Lover Please *Bobby G. Rice*	88/80	Lovin' You Lightly *Bonnie Shannon*
14/98	Love Working On You *John Michael Montgomery*	70/82	Lover (Right Where I Want You) *Tom Carlile*		Lovin' You, Lovin' Me
49/96	Love Worth Fighting For *Burnin' Daylight*	95/87	Lover To Lover *Stenmark-Mueller Band*	73/77	Sonny Throckmorton
88/79	Love Wouldn't Leave Us Alone *Bill Woody*		Lover's Leap ..see: (Doin' The)	88/79	Connie Smith
	Love, You Ain't Seen The Last Of Me		Lover's Quarrel ..see: (I Just Had A Date)	39/78	Lovin' You Off My Mind *Cates Sisters*
6/87	John Schneider		Lover's Question	62/68	Lovin' You (The Way I Do) *Hank Locklin*
44/00	Tracy Byrd	14/70	Del Reeves		Loving Arms
67/76	Love You All To Pieces *Billy Walker*	3/78	Jacky Ward	98/74	Kris Kristofferson & Rita Coolidge
38/96	Love You Back *Rhett Akins*	39/70	Lover's Song *Ned Miller*	19/77	Sammi Smith
64/75	Love You Back To Georgia *Freddy Weller*	65/68	Lovers, The *Bill Wilbourne & Kathy Morrison*	8/81	Elvis Presley
86/76	Love, You're The Teacher *Linda Hargrove*	55/83	Lovers Again *Brice Henderson*	94/88	Livingston Taylor/Leah Kunkel
73/87	Love'll Come Lookin' For You *Cannons*	3/80	Lovers Live Longer *Bellamy Brothers*	14/63	Loving Arms *Carl Butler & Pearl*
30/82	Love's Been A Little Bit Hard On Me *Juice Newton*	83/81	Lovers Love *Thrasher Brothers*	1/91	Loving Blind *Clint Black*
25/68	Love's Dead End *Bill Phillips*	48/83	Lovers On The Rebound *James & Michael Younger*	18/01	Loving Every Minute *Mark Wills*
12/77	Love's Explosion *Margo Smith*		Lovesick Blues	27/73	Loving Gift *Johnny Cash & June Carter Cash*
13/82	Love's Found You And Me *Ed Bruce*	1/49	Hank Williams *Patsy Cline*	38/78	Loving Here And Living There And Lying In Between *Faron Young*
8/82	Love's Gonna Fall Here Tonight *Razzy Bailey*	14/49	Red Kirk	37/85	Lovin' Up A Storm *Bandana*
4/86	Love's Gonna Get You Someday *Ricky Skaggs*	15/57	Sonny James	1/80	Loving Up A Storm *Razzy Bailey*
7/68	Love's Gonna Happen To Me *Wynn Stewart*	78/75	Sonny Curtis	15/57	Loving You *Elvis Presley*
1/63	Love's Gonna Live Here *Buck Owens*	97/78	Jim Owen	41/73	Loving You *Tony Booth*
	(Love's Got A Hold On Me) ..see: Rainbow In Your Eyes	24/92	George Strait	26/75	Loving You Beats All I've Ever Seen *Johnny Paycheck*
1/92	Love's Got A Hold On You *Alan Jackson*		Lovin' ..also see: Loving	2/72	Loving You Could Never Be Better *George Jones*
50/88	Love's Last Stand *Donna Meade*	37/80	Lovin' A Livin' Dream *Ronnie McDowell*	9/74	Loving You Has Changed My Life *David Rogers*
28/71	Love's Old Song *Barbara Fairchild*	10/92	Lovin' All Night *Rodney Crowell*	32/83	Loving You Hurts *Gus Hardin*
	Love's Slippin' Up On Me	76/74	Lovin' Comes Easy *Jack Lebsock*	31/79	Loving You Is A Natural High *Larry G. Hudson*
74/87	Kim Grayson		Lovin' Her Was Easier (Than Anything I'll Ever Do Again)	73/82	Loving You Is Always On My Mind *Terry Dale*
83/88	Lynne Tyndall	28/71	Roger Miller	33/71	(Loving You Is) Sunshine *Barbara Fairchild*
79/80	Love's Slipping Through Our Fingers *Billy Walker & Barbara Fairchild*	2/81	Tompall/Glaser Brothers	22/65	Loving You Then Losing You *Webb Pierce*
25/66	Love's Something (I Can't Understand) *Webb Pierce*	8/66	Lovin' Machine *Johnny Paycheck*	79/81	Loving You Was All I Ever Needed *Lou Hobbs*
5/73	Love's The Answer *Tanya Tucker*		Lovin' Man ..see: Oh Pretty Woman	7/61	Loving You (Was Worth This Broken Heart) *Bob Gallion*
3/00	Love's The Only House *Martina McBride*	83/81	Lovin' Night *Jim West*	6/75	Loving You Will Never Grow Old *Lois Johnson*
	Lovebug ..see: Love Bug	96/73	Lovin' Of Your Life *Penny DeHaven*	89/77	Low Class Reunion *George Kent*
			Lovin' On	31/79	Low Dog Blues *John Anderson*
		20/77	T.G. Sheppard		Low Down Time
		16/79	Bellamy Brothers	98/77	Durwood Haddock
		5/73	Lovin' On Back Streets *Mel Street*	96/79	Durwood Haddock
		11/74	Lovin' On Borrowed Time *Mel Street*	73/89	Lower On The Hog *John Anderson*
		1/89	Lovin' Only Me *Ricky Skaggs*		
		84/82	Lovin' Our Lives Away *Dave Rowland*		
		52/69	Lovin' Season *Bill Wilbourn & Kathy Morrison*		
		23/76	Lovin' Somebody On A Rainy Night *La Costa*		
		39/73	Lovin' Someone On My Mind *Bobby Wright*		

1/77	Lucille Kenny Rogers	
1/83	Lucille (You Won't Do Your Daddy's Will) Waylon Jennings	
67/72	Lucius Grinder Ray Sanders	
1/77	Luckenbach, Texas (Back to the Basics of Love) Waylon Jennings	
11/01	Lucky 4 You (Tonight I'm Just Me) SheDaisy	
21/74	Lucky Arms Lefty Frizzell	
34/97	Lucky In Love Sherrié Austin	
11/74	Lucky Ladies Jeannie Seely	
9/80	Lucky Me Anne Murray	
35/97	Lucky Me, Lucky You Lee Roy Parnell	
6/91	Lucky Moon Oak Ridge Boys	
53/01	Lucky One Alison Krauss	
62/72	Lucy Eddy Arnold	
49/82	Lucy And The Stranger Bobby Goldsboro	
5/64	Lumberjack, The Hal Willis	
87/77	Lunch Time Lovers Robb Redmond	
	Lust Affair ..see: (This Ain't Just Another)	
69/84	Luther Boxcar Willie	
8/59	Luther Played The Boogie Johnny Cash	
42/70	Luziana River Van Trevor	
24/68	Luzianna Webb Pierce	
53/83	Lyin', Cheatin', Woman Chasin', Honky Tonkin', Whiskey Drinkin' You Loretta Lynn	
8/75	Lyin' Eyes Eagles	
81/87	Lyin' Eyes Sarah	
97/75	Lyin' In Her Arms Again Dorsey Burnette	
5/88	Lyin' In His Arms Again Forester Sisters	
27/61	Lying Again Freddie Hart	
62/83	Lying Here Lying Mac Davis	
2/79	Lying In Love With You Jim Ed Brown/Helen Cornelius	
70/75	Lying In My Arms Rex Allen, Jr.	
6/80	Lying Time Again Mel Tillis	
1/87	Lynda Steve Wariner	

M

28/67	Mabel Skeets McDonald	
48/67	Mabel (You Have Been A Friend To Me) Billy Grammer	
	Mabellene	
9/55	Marty Robbins	
7/79	George Jones & Johnny Paycheck	
23/69	MacArthur Park Waylon Jennings & The Kimberlys	
43/76	MacArthur's Hand Cal Smith	
70/96	Macarena (Country version) Groovegrass Boyz	
82/88	Macon Georgia Love Billy Mata	
69/84	Macon Love David Wills	
6/64	Mad Dave Dudley	
72/87	Mad Money George Highfill	
6/93	Made For Lovin' You Doug Stone	
1/72	Made In Japan Buck Owens	

	Made In The U.S.A.	
78/80	Ivory Jack	
40/82	Wright Bros.	
85/82	Four Guys	
11/84	Maggie's Dream Don Williams	
56/81	Magic Eyes Jack Grayson & Blackjack	
39/71	Magnificent Sanctuary Band Roy Clark	
84/76	Mahogany Bridge David Rogers	
55/71	Mahogany Pulpit Dickey Lee	
10/71	Maiden's Prayer David Houston	
84/76	Maiden's Prayer Maury Finney	
5/55	Mainliner (The Hawk With Silver Wings) Hank Snow	
10/85	Major Moves Hank Williams, Jr.	
36/67	Make A Left And Then A Right Johnny And Jonie Mosby	
77/80	Make A Little Magic Dirt Band	
61/87	Make A Living Out Of Loving You Razorback	
86/79	Make Believe It's Your First Time Bobby Vinton	
6/55	Make Believe ('Til We Can Make It Come True) Kitty Wells & Red Foley	
69/79	Make Believe You Love Me Rebecca Lynn	
96/75	Make It Easy On Yourself Tommy Jennings	
30/74	Make It Feel Like Love Again Bobby G. Rice	
40/69	Make It Rain Billy Mize	
57/79	Make Love To Me Cates Sisters	
F/58	Make Me A Miracle Jimmie Rodgers	
91/81	Make Me Believe Gary Goodnight	
55/87	Make Me Late For Work Today Ronnie McDowell	
37/71	Make Me Your Kind Of Woman Patti Page	
90/79	Make Me Your Woman Brenda Kaye Perry	
35/80	Make Mine Night Time Bill Anderson	
12/84	Make My Day T.G. Sheppard/Clint Eastwood	
1/85	Make My Life With You Oak Ridge Boys	
1/87	Make No Mistake, She's Mine Ronnie Milsap & Kenny Rogers	
2/46	Make Room In Your Heart For A Friend Wiley & Gene	
30/60	Make The Waterwheel Roll Carl Smith	
	Make The World Go Away	
2/63	Ray Price	
1/65	Eddy Arnold	
71/75	Donny And Marie Osmond	
73/77	Charly McClain	
55/85	Make-Up And Faded Blue Jeans Merle Haggard	
19/99	Make Up In Love Doug Stone	
4/96	Maker Said Take Her Alabama	
67/80	Makes Me Wonder If I Ever Said Goodbye Kin Vassy	
	Makin' Believe ..see: Making	
62/73	Makin' Heartaches George Morgan	
61/75	Makin' Love Ronnie Sessions	
35/76	Makin' Love Don't Always Make Love Grow Dickey Lee	

72/79	Makin' Love (Is A Beautiful Thing To Do) Paul Schmucker	
11/74	Makin' The Best Of A Bad Situation Dick Feller	
1/86	Makin' Up For Lost Time (The Dallas Lovers' Song) Crystal Gayle & Gary Morris	
F/71	Makin' Up His Mind Jack Greene	
56/00	Makin' Up With You Chalee Tennison	
44/83	Making A Living's Been Killing Me McGuffey Lane	
	Making Believe	
2/55	Kitty Wells	
5/55	Jimmy Work	
61/75	Debi Hawkins	
8/77	Emmylou Harris	
80/77	Kendalls	
F/78	Merle Haggard	
93/81	Paul Williams	
19/82	Making Love From Memory Loretta Lynn	
	Making Love To Dixie	
92/84	Younger Brothers Band	
82/88	Heartland	
2/80	Making Plans Porter Wagoner & Dolly Parton	
84/81	Making The Night The Best Part Of My Day Lincoln County	
6/50	Mama And Daddy Broke My Heart Eddy Arnold	
62/71	Mama Bake A Pie (Daddy Kill A Chicken) George Kent	
46/72	Mama Bear Carl Smith	
73/70	Mama, Call Me Home Bob Dalton	
4/53	Mama, Come Get Your Baby Boy Eddy Arnold	
68/70	Mama Come'n Get Your Baby Boy Johnny Darrell	
9/92	Mama Don't Forget To Pray For Me Diamond Rio	
13/96	Mama Don't Get Dressed Up For Nothing Brooks & Dunn	
91/80	Mama Don't Let Your Cowboys Grow Up To Be Babies Tony Joe White	
29/75	Mama Don't 'Low Hank Thompson	
1/84	Mama He's Crazy Judds	
37/70	Mama, I Won't Be Wearing A Ring Peggy Little	
5/88	Mama Knows Shenandoah	
8/93	Mama Knows The Highway Hal Ketchum	
	Mama Lou	
34/69	Penny DeHaven	
94/74	Rita Coolidge	
86/79	Mama, Make Up My Room Chester Lester	
93/79	Mama Rocked Us To Sleep Four Guys	
1/62	Mama Sang A Song Bill Anderson	
45/68	Mama Sez Marion Worth	
39/84	Mama, She's Lazy Pinkard & Bowden	
5/67	Mama Spank Liz Anderson	
1/68	Mama Tried Merle Haggard	
82/81	Mama What Does Cheatin' Mean Carroll Baker	
81/90	Mama's Daily Bread Jill Hollier	
77/74	Mama's Got The Know How Doug Kershaw	

481

(The Man Who Shot) Liberty Valance — Gene Pitney

68/91 **Mama's Little Baby Loves Me** Sawyer Brown	**Mansion On The Hill**	58/01 **Matthew, Mark, Luke and Earnhardt** Shane Sellers
50/67 **Mama's Little Jewel** Johnny Wright	12/49 Hank Williams	(Matthew's Song) ..see: Pilgrims On The Way
1/86 **Mama's Never Seen Those Eyes** Forester Sisters	29/58 June Webb	64/82 **Maximum Security (To Minimum Wage)** Don King
11/87 **Mama's Rockin' Chair** John Conlee	36/76 Michael Murphey	35/79 **May I** Terri Hollowell
97/79 **Mama's Sugar** Ernest Rey	14/77 Ray Price	52/80 **May I Borrow Some Sugar From You** John Wesley Ryles
Mammas Don't Let Your Babies Grow Up To Be Cowboys	3/90 **Many A Long & Lonesome Highway** Rodney Crowell	37/77 **May I Spend Every New Years With You** T.G. Sheppard
15/76 Ed Bruce	13/66 **Many Happy Hangovers To You** Jean Shepard	62/71 **May Old Acquaintance Be Forgot (Before I Lose My Mind)** Compton Brothers
1/78 Waylon Jennings & Willie Nelson	34/89 **Many Mansions** Moe Bandy	
49/94 Gibson/Miller Band	10/49 **Many Tears Ago** Eddy Arnold	1/65 **May The Bird Of Paradise Fly Up Your Nose** "Little" Jimmy Dickens
16/99 **Man Ain't Made Of Stone** Randy Travis	42/87 **Maple Street Mem'ries** Statler Brothers	
40/73 **Man And A Train** Marty Robbins	**Margaritaville**	13/78 **May The Force Be With You Always** Tom T. Hall
17/69 **Man And Wife Time** Jim Ed Brown	13/77 Jimmy Buffett	
58/87 **Man At The Backdoor** Beth Williams	63/99 Alan Jackson with Jimmy Buffett	8/51 **May The Good Lord Bless And Keep You** Eddy Arnold
56/69 **Man Away From Home** Van Trevor	74/00 Alan Jackson with Jimmy Buffett	68/75 **May You Rest In Peace** Melody Allen
82/76 **Man From Bowling Green** Bob Luman	23/73 **Margie, Who's Watching The Baby** Earl Richards	25/90 **Maybe** Kenny Rogers (with Holly Dunn)
47/01 **Man He Was** George Jones	4/69 **(Margie's At) The Lincoln Park Inn** Bobby Bare	65/96 **Maybe** Mandy Barnett
5/98 **Man Holdin' On (To A Woman Lettin' Go)** Ty Herndon	88/82 **Maria Consuela** Tompall/Glaser Brothers	7/78 **Maybe Baby** Susie Allanson
Man! I Feel Like A Woman!	83/81 **Marianne** Lane Brothers	18/97 **Maybe He'll Notice Her Now** Mindy McCready & Richie McDonald
70/97 Shania Twain	94/79 **Marie** Steve Wariner	
4/99 Shania Twain	1/74 **Marie Laveau** Bobby Bare	28/61 **Maybe I Do** Dave Dudley
72/67 **Man I Hardly Know** Loretta Lynn	6/83 **Marina Del Rey** George Strait	48/91 **Maybe I Mean Yes** Holly Dunn
44/84 **Man I Used To Be** Boxcar Willie	21/61 **Marines, Let's Go** Rex Allen	**Maybe I [You] Should've Been Listening**
3/71 **Man In Black** Johnny Cash	18/71 **Mark Of A Heel** Hank Thompson	31/78 Rayburn Anthony
4/94 **Man In Love With You** George Strait	52/74 **Marlena** Bobby Goldsboro	45/78 Jessi Colter
37/66 **Man In The Little White Suit** Charlie Walker	59/68 **Marriage Bit** Lefty Frizzell	23/81 Gene Watson
17/83 **Man In The Mirror** Jim Glaser	F/71 **Marriage Has Ruined More Good Love Affairs** Jan Howard	59/89 **Maybe I Won't Love You Anymore** Johnny Lee
12/80 **Man Just Don't Know What A Woman Goes Through** Charlie Rich	10/53 **Marriage Of Mexican Joe** Carolyn Bradshaw	82/79 **Maybe I'll Cry Over You** Arthur Blanch
59/73 **Man Likes Things Like That** Charlie Louvin & Melba Montgomery	10/49 **Marriage Vow** Hank Snow	3/92 **Maybe It Was Memphis** Pam Tillis
	3/77 **Married But Not To Each Other** Barbara Mandrell	8/85 **Maybe My Baby** Louise Mandrell
	8/52 **Married By The Bible, Divorced By The Law** Hank Snow	17/99 **Maybe Not Tonight** Lorrie Morgan (with Sammy Kershaw)
94/78 **Man Made Of Glass** Ed Bruce	84/82 **Married Man** Judy Taylor	34/95 **Maybe She's Human** Kathy Mattea
36/75 **Man Needs Love** David Houston	**Married To A Memory**	
18/01 **Man Of Me** Gary Allan	25/71 Arlene Harden	22/90 **Maybe That's All It Takes** Don Williams
8/94 **Man Of My Word** Collin Raye	74/71 Judy Lynn	
3/84 **Man Of Steel** Hank Williams, Jr.	33/81 **Married Women** Sonny Curtis	73/91 **Maybe The Moon Will Shine** Marsha Thornton
30/75 **Man On Page 602** Zoot Fenster	39/70 **Marry Me** Ron Lowry	
70/98 **Man Song** Sean Morey	17/70 **Marty Gray** Billie Jo Spears	83/89 **Maybe There** Lisa Childress
93/77 **Man Still Turns Me On** Mary Lou Turner	28/91 **Mary And Willie** K.T. Oslin	4/97 **Maybe We Should Just Sleep On It** Tim McGraw
Man That Turned My Mama On	12/63 **Mary Ann Regrets** Burl Ives	**Maybe You Should've Been Listening** ..see: Maybe I Should've
4/74 Tanya Tucker	55/96 **Mary, Did You Know** Kenny Rogers with Wynonna	
70/78 Ed Bruce	12/60 **Mary Don't You Weep** Stonewall Jackson	57/93 **Maybe You Were The One** Dude Mowrey
1/97 **Man This Lonely** Brooks & Dunn	58/97 **Mary Go Round** Skip Ewing	
62/90 **Man To Man** Hank Williams, Jr.	41/70 **Mary Goes 'Round** Bobby Helms	1/87 **Maybe Your Baby's Got The Blues** Judds
9/63 **Man Who Robbed The Bank At Santa Fe** Hank Snow	66/67 **Mary In The Morning** Tommy Hunter	**Maybelline** ..see: Mabellene
53/80 **Man Who Takes You Home** Bobby G. Rice	68/68 **Mary's Little Lamb** Carl Belew	75/79 **Mazelle** Gary Stewart
42/66 **Man With A Plan** Carl Smith	17/71 **Mary's Vineyard** Claude King	8/64 **Me** Bill Anderson
32/82 **Man With The Golden Thumb** Jerry Reed	64/83 **Marylee** Rodney Lay	87/78 **Me** Sherry Grooms
	43/92 **Mason Dixon Line** Dan Seals	4/85 **Me Against The Night** Crystal Gayle
56/70 **Man You Want Me To Be** Webb Pierce	77/79 **Massachusetts** Tommy Roe	**Me And Bobby McGee**
28/70 **Man's Kind Of Woman** Eddy Arnold	59/93 **Master Of Illusion** Clinton Gregory	12/69 Roger Miller
38/87 **Mandolin Rain** Bruce Hornsby And The Range	2/63 **Matador, The** Johnny Cash	F/72 Jerry Lee Lewis
	7/81 **Matador** Sylvia	29/59 **Me And Fred And Joe And Bill** Porter Wagoner
6/72 **Manhattan Kansas** Glen Campbell	8/65 **Matamoros** Billy Walker	
	22/98 **Matches** Sammy Kershaw	
	66/88 **Matches** Marty Stuart	
	Mathilda	
	20/75 Donny King	
	78/81 John Wesley Ryles	
	33/99 **Matter Of Time** Jason Sellers	

8/72	Me And Jesus Tom T. Hall	73/00	Memory Is The Last Thing To Go B.B. Watson	5/83	Midnight Fire Steve Wariner
85/85	Me And Margarita Bobby Jenkins			93/80	Midnight Fire Marlow Tackett
35/00	Me And Maxine Sammy Kershaw	39/84	Memory Lane Joe Stampley & Jessica Boucher	83/77	Midnight Flight Pam Rose
15/77	Me And Millie Ronnie Sessions				Midnight Flyer
22/92	Me And My Baby Paul Overstreet	60/93	Memory Lane Tim McGraw	74/73	Osborne Brothers
9/79	Me And My Broken Heart Rex Allen, Jr.	52/82	Memory Machine Jack Quist	94/79	Charlie McCoy
		3/74	Memory Maker Mel Tillis	4/87	Midnight Girl/Sunset Town Sweethearts Of The Rodeo
94/89	Me And My Harley-Davidson Mickey Hawks	2/64	Memory #1 Webb Pierce		
		10/81	Memphis Fred Knoblock	1/81	Midnight Hauler Razzy Bailey
12/76	Me And Ole C.B. Dave Dudley	79/84	Memphis In May Darrell McCall	14/88	Midnight Highway Southern Pacific
	Me And Paul	73/99	Memphis Women & Chicken T. Graham Brown		
F/71	Willie Nelson			3/92	Midnight In Montgomery Alan Jackson
14/85	Willie Nelson	7/80	Men Charly McClain		
72/80	Me And The Boys In The Band Tommy Overstreet	8/91	Men Forester Sisters	59/79	Midnight Lace Big Al Downing
			Men In My Little Girl's Life	51/84	Midnight Love Billie Jo Spears
	Me And The Elephant	16/66	Archie Campbell	93/82	Midnight Magic Gary Buck
43/77	Kenny Starr	50/66	Tex Ritter	64/74	Midnight Man Marty Mitchell
82/77	Bobby Goldsboro	60/94	Men Will Be Boys Billy Dean	2/74	Midnight, Me And The Blues Mel Tillis
33/78	Me And The I.R.S. Johnny Paycheck	88/89	Men With Broken Hearts Charley Hager		
				7/73	Midnight Oil Barbara Mandrell
2/96	Me And You Kenny Chesney	13/93	Mending Fences Restless Heart	6/80	Midnight Rider Willie Nelson
29/87	Me And You Donna Fargo	8/61	Mental Cruelty Buck Owens & Rose Maddox	9/82	Midnight Rodeo Leon Everette
7/71	Me And You And A Dog Named Boo Stonewall Jackson			43/89	Midnight Train Charlie Daniels Band
		14/68	Mental Journey Leon Ashley		
80/75	Me As I Am Chip Taylor		Mental Revenge	87/77	Midnight Train To Georgia Eddie Middleton
65/68	Me, Me, Me, Me, Me Liz Anderson	12/67	Waylon Jennings		
18/00	Me Neither Brad Paisley	15/76	Mel Tillis	57/81	Midnite Flyer Sue Powell
72/79	Me Plus You Equals Love Dawn Chastain	2/93	Mercury Blues Alan Jackson	85/87	Midnite Rock Indiana
		49/76	Mercy Jean Shepard	F/84	Midsummer Nights Kenny Rogers
1/97	Me Too Toby Keith	7/48	Merle's Boogie Woogie Merle Travis	68/67	Mighty Day Carl Smith
	Me Touchin' You			47/91	Miles Across The Bedroom Gary Morris
58/79	Linda Nail	55/99	Merry Christmas From Texas Y'all Tracy Byrd		
91/80	Capitals			38/77	Miles And Miles Of Texas Asleep At The Wheel
65/71	Me Without You Carl Perkins	38/00	Merry Christmas From The Family Montgomery Gentry		
46/66	Meadowgreen Browns			8/52	Milk Bucket Boogie Red Foley
30/60	Mean Eyed Cat Johnny Cash	58/97	Merry Christmas Strait To You George Strait		Miller's Cave
6/49	Mean Mama Blues Ernest Tubb			9/60	Hank Snow
22/66	Mean Old Woman Claude Gray	41/77	Merry-Go-Round Freddy Weller	4/64	Bobby Bare
11/57	Mean Woman Blues Elvis Presley	47/75	Merry-Go-Round Of Love Hank Snow	2/66	Million And One Billy Walker
79/80	Mean Woman Blues Max D. Barnes			39/83	Million Light Beers Ago David Frizzell
		71/70	Merry-Go-Round World Webb Pierce		
5/96	Meant To Be Sammy Kershaw				Million Old Goodbyes
4/99	Meanwhile George Strait	72/80	Message To Khomeini Thrasher Brothers	66/80	Freddy Weller
18/00	Meanwhile Back At The Ranch Clark Family Experience			8/81	Mel Tillis
		93/81	Mexican Girl Michael Tate	13/63	Million Years Or So Eddy Arnold
9/65	Meanwhile, Down At Joe's Kitty Wells	1/53	Mexican Joe Jim Reeves	12/68	Milwaukee, Here I Come George Jones & Brenda Carter
		61/77	Mexican Love Songs Linda Hargrove		
32/79	Medicine Woman Kenny O'Dell			51/93	Mind Of Her Own John Berry
1/91	Meet In The Middle Diamond Rio	94/85	Mexico Backtrack/John Hunt	64/75	Mind Your Love Jerry Reed
1/85	Meet Me In Montana Marie Osmond With Dan Seals	4/44	Mexico Joe Ivie Anderson		Mind Your Own Business
		85/80	Mexico Winter Bobby Hood	5/49	Hank Williams
51/76	Meet Me Later Margo Smith	4/74	Mi Esposa Con Amor (To My Wife With Love) Sonny James	35/64	Jimmy Dean
38/64	Meet Me Tonight Outside Of Town Jim Howard			1/86	Hank Williams, Jr.
		1/95	Mi Vida Loca (My Crazy Life) Pam Tillis	8/49	Mine All Mine Jimmy Wakely
	(Melody of Love) ..see: Why Do I Love You			79/84	Minstrel, The Mike Dekle
		14/86	Miami, My Amy Keith Whitley	69/78	Minstrel Man Rebecca Lynn
96/85	Melted Down Memories Joy Ford	93/73	Mid American Manufacturing Tycoon Bobby Russell	24/66	Minute Men (Are Turning In Their Graves) Stonewall Jackson
23/87	Members Only Donna Fargo & Billy Joe Royal				
		4/78	Middle Age Crazy Jerry Lee Lewis	9/63	Minute You're Gone Sonny James
73/76	Mem'ries Vicki Bird	41/79	Middle-Age Madness Earl Thomas Conley		
56/69	Memories Elvis Presley			4/81	Miracles Don Williams
82/78	Memories Are Made Of This Tommy O'Day	86/75	Middle Of A Memory Eddy Arnold	3/91	Mirror Mirror Diamond Rio
		1/53	Midnight Red Foley	41/75	Mirror, Mirror Ben Reece
9/48	Memories Of France T. Texas Tyler	16/77	Midnight Angel Barbara Mandrell	49/89	Mirror Mirror Barbara Mandrell
		84/84	Midnight Angel Of Mercy Rod Rishard	56/88	Mirrors Don't Lie Marty Stuart
21/75	Memories Of Us George Jones			12/82	Mis'ry River Terri Gibbs
5/86	Memories To Burn Gene Watson	36/87	Midnight Blue John Wesley Ryles	3/80	Misery And Gin Merle Haggard
85/83	Memory, The Jim Wyrick	39/84	Midnight Blue Billie Jo Spears		Misery Loves Company
73/87	Memory Attack Ralph May	76/82	Midnight Cabaret Wyvon Alexander	1/62	Porter Wagoner
96/78	Memory Bound B.J. Wright			F/80	Ronnie Milsap
91/76	Memory Go Round R.W. Blackwood	43/80	Midnight Choir Larry Gatlin/Gatlin Brothers	2/81	Miss Emily's Picture John Conlee
				55/72	Miss Pauline Billy Bob Bowman

483

*Mr. Mom – Lonestar (Novelty) *** – see "Climbin The Ladder"*

26/84	Miss Understanding *David Wills*	
32/84	Missin' Mississippi *Charley Pride*	
65/88	Missin' Texas *Kim Grayson*	
3/52	Missing In Action *Ernest Tubb*	
2/80	Missin' You *Charley Pride*	
	Missing You	
7/57	Webb Pierce	
8/72	Jim Reeves	
15/99	Missing You *Brooks & Dunn*	
54/96	Missing You *Mavericks*	
79/90	Missing You *Marcy Bros.*	
1/50	Mississippi *Red Foley*	
19/79	Mississippi *Charlie Daniels Band*	
31/76	Mississippi *Barbara Fairchild*	
	Mississippi	
58/70	John Phillips	
75/78	Jack Paris	
59/86	Mississippi Break Down *Toni Price*	
3/74	Mississippi Cotton Picking Delta Town *Charley Pride*	
15/95	Mississippi Moon *John Anderson*	
20/85	Mississippi Squirrel Revival *Ray Stevens*	
14/71	Mississippi Woman *Louisiana* *Waylon Jennings*	
20/75	Mississippi You're On My Mind *Stoney Edwards*	
5/47	Missouri *Merle Travis*	
3/82	Mistakes *Don Williams*	
	Mister ..see: Mr.	
3/75	Misty *Ray Stevens*	
	Misty Blue	
4/66	Wilma Burgess	
3/67	Eddy Arnold	
5/76	Billie Jo Spears	
37/72	Misty Memories *Brenda Lee*	
77/86	Misty Mississippi *Rusty Budde*	
43/80	Misty Morning Rain *Ray Price*	
	Misunderstanding ..see: Miss Understanding	
44/73	Mm-Mm Good *Del Reeves*	
	Moanin' The Blues	
1/50	Hank Williams	
87/89	Vicki Bird	
65/82	Moanin The Blues *Kenny Dale*	
60/81	Mobile Bay *Johnny Cash*	
27/77	Mobile Boogie *Hank Williams, Jr.*	
64/81	Moccasin Man *Dave Kirby*	
	Mockin' Bird Hill *Jean Shepard* CD 4:2	
3/51	Pinetoppers	
7/51	Les Paul & Mary Ford	
9/77	Donna Fargo	
94/74	Mockingbird *Terri Lane & Jimmy Nall*	
75/86	Modern Day Cowboy *Jay Clark*	
92/89	Modern Day Cowboy *John Marriott*	
51/85	Modern Day Marriages *Razzy Bailey*	
1/85	Modern Day Romance *Nitty Gritty Dirt Band*	
44/69	Moffett, Oklahoma *Charlie Walker*	
5/64	Molly *Eddy Arnold*	
53/69	Molly *Jim Glaser*	
91/80	Molly (And The Texas Rain) *Sonny Wright*	
10/48	Molly Darling *Eddy Arnold*	
28/75	Molly (I Ain't Gettin' Any Younger) *Dorsey Burnette*	

	Mom And Dad's Waltz	
2/51	Lefty Frizzell	
21/61	Patti Page	
43/79	Moment By Moment *Narvel Felts*	
24/66	Mommy, Can I Still Call Him Daddy *Dottie West*	
5/59	Mommy For A Day *Kitty Wells*	
	Mona Lisa	
4/50	Moon Mullican	
10/50	Jimmy Wakely	
11/81	Willie Nelson	
2/84	Mona Lisa Lost Her Smile *David Allan Coe*	
68/94	Mona Lisa On Cruise Control *Dennis Robbins*	
20/73	Monday Morning Secretary *Statler Brothers*	
13/88	Money *K.T. Oslin*	
15/57	Money *Browns*	
35/70	Money Can't Buy Love *Roy Rogers*	
74/89	Money Don't Make A Man A Lover *Dawnett Faucett*	
48/65	Money Greases The Wheels *Ferlin Husky*	
1/93	Money In The Bank *John Anderson*	
	Money, Marbles And Chalk	
12/49	Stubby And The Buccaneers	
15/49	Patti Page	
15/60	Money To Burn *George Jones*	
11/72	Monkey That Became President *Tom T. Hall*	
	Monsters' Holiday ..see: (It's A)	
95/74	Montgomery Mable *Merle Kilgore*	
54/92	Month Of Sundays *Vern Gosdin*	
42/68	Moods Of Mary *Tompall/Glaser Brothers*	
1/77	Moody Blue *Elvis Presley*	
68/70	Moody River *Chase Webster*	
16/60	Moon Is Crying *Allan Riddle*	
1/87	Moon Is Still Over Her Shoulder *Michael Johnson*	
9/91	Moon Over Georgia *Shenandoah*	
36/89	Moon Pretty Moon *Statler Brothers*	
	(Moon Song) ..see: I Don't Know A Thing About Love	
72/80	Moonlight And Magnolia *Buck Owens*	
51/93	Moonlight Drive-In *Turner Nichols*	
18/90	Moonshadow Road *T. Graham Brown*	
58/74	Moontan *Jeris Ross*	
76/87	Moonwalkin' *Don Malena*	
77/87	Moon Walking *Bonnie Leigh*	
10/00	More *Trace Adkins*	
26/72	More About John Henry *Tom T. Hall*	
	More And More	
1/54	Webb Pierce	
7/83	Charley Pride	
77/89	More I Do *Charley Pride*	
95/79	More I Get The More I Want *Becky Hobbs*	
89/84	More I Go Blind *Rod Rishard*	
49/92	More I Learn (The Less I Understand About Love) *Ronna Reeves*	
6/94	More Love *Doug Stone*	
61/82	More Nights *Larie Brody*	
71/00	More Of A Man *Rodney Carrington*	

51/80	More Than A Bedroom Thing *Bill Anderson*	
6/89	More Than A Name On A Wall *Statler Brothers*	
5/55	More Than Anything Else In The World *Carl Smith*	
47/89	More Than Enough *Glen Campbell*	
41/97	More Than Everything *Rhett Akins*	
84/87	More Than Friendly Persuasion *Bonnie Nelson*	
53/97	More Than I Wanted To Know *Regina Regina*	
8/65	More Than Yesterday *Slim Whitman*	
3/96	More Than You'll Ever Know *Travis Tritt*	
1/77	More To Me *Charley Pride*	
58/93	More Where That Came From *Dolly Parton*	
14/72	Mornin' After Baby Let Me Down *Ray Griff*	
56/70	Mornin Mornin *Bobby Goldsboro*	
1/87	Mornin' Ride *Lee Greenwood*	
4/70	Morning *Jim Ed Brown*	
19/71	Morning After *Jerry Wallace*	
5/80	Morning Comes Too Early *Jim Ed Brown/Helen Cornelius*	
1/86	Morning Desire *Kenny Rogers*	
88/74	Morning Girl *Duane Dee*	
69/82	Morning, Noon And Night *Orion*	
22/64	Morning Paper *Billy Walker*	
	Most Beautiful Girl	
1/73	Charlie Rich	
54/01	South 65	
6/55	Most Of All *Hank Thompson*	
41/84	Most Of All *Mac Davis*	
71/88	Most Of All *Leon Raines*	
59/84	Most Of All I Remember You *Mel McDaniel*	
18/70	Most Uncomplicated Goodbye I've Ever Heard *Henson Cargill*	
19/75	Most Wanted Woman In Town *Roy Head*	
74/78	Motel Rooms *Little David Wilkins*	
13/67	Motel Time Again *Johnny Paycheck*	
7/76	Motels And Memories *T.G. Sheppard*	
	Mother ..see: (You Make Me Want To Be) A	
17/77	Mother Country Music *Vern Gosdin*	
20/64	Mother-In-Law *Jim Nesbitt*	
21/68	Mother, May I *Liz Anderson & Lynn Anderson*	
F/56	Mother Of A Honky Tonk Girl *Jim Reeves*	
55/92	Mother's Eyes *Matthews, Wright & King*	
52/89	Mountain Ago *Mason Dixon*	
23/81	Mountain Dew *Willie Nelson*	
1/82	Mountain Music *Alabama*	
64/78	Mountain Music *Porter Wagoner*	
	Mountain Of Love	
20/71	Bobby G. Rice	
1/82	Charley Pride	
2/63	Mountain Of Love *David Houston*	
74/71	Mountain Woman *Harold Lee*	

Mister Mom - Lonestar *** (Novelty) /// Murder On Music Row - Larry Cordle
George Strait & Alan Jackson

	Move It On Over	1/49	Mule Train Tennessee Ernie Ford		My Bucket's Got A Hole In It
4/47	Hank Williams	25/65	Multiply The Heartaches George Jones & Melba Montgomery	2/49	Hank Williams
60/73	Buddy Alan			4/49	T. Texas Tyler
66/99	Travis Tritt With George Thorogood	38/00	Murder On Music Row George Strait with Alan Jackson	10/58	Ricky Nelson
17/01	Move On Warren Brothers	44/79	Music Box Dancer Frank Mills	17/68	My Can Do Can't Keep Up With My Want To Nat Stuckey
	Move Two Mountains ..see: (You've Got To)	92/78	Music In My Life Mac Davis	61/00	My Cellmate Thinks I'm Sexy Cledus T. Judd
61/75	Movie Magazine, Stars In Her Eyes Barbi Benton	59/81	Music In The Mountains Ernie Rowell	4/47	My Chickashay Gal Roy Rogers
10/77	Movies, The Statler Brothers	29/78	Music Is My Woman Don King		(My Crazy Life) ..see: Mi Vida Loca
1/75	Movin' On Merle Haggard	4/52	Music Makin' Mama From Memphis Hank Snow		My Cup Runneth Over
61/97	Movin' Out To The Country Deryl Dodd	39/78	Music, Music, Music Rebecca Lynn	63/67	Blue Boys
20/83	Movin' Train Kendalls	69/67	Music To Cry By Johnny Wright	26/69	Johnny Bush
2/51	Mr. And Mississippi Tennessee Ernie Ford	63/74	Musical Chairs Tompall Glaser	64/84	My Dad Ray Stevens
			Must You Throw Dirt In My Face	5/48	My Daddy Is Only A Picture Eddy Arnold
53/68	Mr. & Mrs. John Smith Johnny And Jonie Mosby	21/62	Louvin Brothers	78/78	My Daddy Was A Travelin' Man Brenda Kaye Perry
	Mr. & Mrs. Untrue	60/78	Roy Clark	14/66	My Dreams Faron Young
64/71	Johnny Russell	44/96	My Angel Is Here Wynonna	3/61	My Ears Should Burn (When Fools Are Talked About) Claude Gray
45/80	Price Mitchell/Rene Sloane	59/83	My Angel's Got The Devil In Her Eyes Ed Hunnicutt		My Elusive Dreams
11/64	Mr. And Mrs. Used To Be Ernest Tubb & Loretta Lynn	63/90	My Anniversary For Being A Fool Holly Dunn	1/67	David Houston & Tammy Wynette
93/77	Mr. Bojangles Jerry Jeff Walker	8/57	My Arms Are A House Hank Snow	41/67	Curly Putman
13/78	Mister D.J. T.G. Sheppard	2/90	My Arms Stay Open All Night Tanya Tucker	70/67	Rusty Draper
34/90	Mister DJ Charlie Daniels Band	91/75	My Babe Earl Richards	73/67	Johnny Darrell
25/67	Mr. Do-It-Yourself Jean Shepard & Ray Pillow	23/83	My Baby Don't Slow Dance Johnny Lee	27/70	Bobby Vinton
20/76	Mr. Doodles Donna Fargo	13/56	My Baby Left Me Elvis Presley	3/75	Charlie Rich
59/72	Mr. Fiddle Man Johnny Russell	2/93	My Baby Loves Me Martina McBride	42/79	My Empty Arms Ann J. Morton
15/57	Mister Fire Eyes Bonnie Guitar	1/81	My Baby Thinks He's A Train Rosanne Cash	7/54	My Everything Eddy Arnold
	Mister Garfield	71/71	My Baby Used To Be That Way Charlie Walker	87/76	My Eyes Adored You Marty Mitchell
15/65	Johnny Cash	34/68	My Baby Walked Right Out On Me Wanda Jackson	1/76	My Eyes Can Only See As Far As You Charley Pride
54/82	Merle Kilgore	27/64	My Baby Walks All Over Me Johnny Sea	16/63	My Father's Voice Judy Lynn
82/76	Mr. Guitar Cates Sisters	53/81	My Baby's Coming Home Again Today Bill Lyerly	1/81	My Favorite Memory Merle Haggard
64/77	Mr. Heartache Susan Raye		My Baby's Gone		My Favorite Things
8/63	Mr. Heartache, Move On Coleman O'Neal	9/59	Louvin Brothers	64/93	Lorrie Morgan
20/79	Mr. Jones Big Al Downing	77/76	Jeanne Pruett	69/99	Lorrie Morgan
28/63	Mr. Juke Box Ernest Tubb	15/84	Kendalls	6/49	My Filipino Rose Ernest Tubb
8/57	Mister Love Ernest Tubb & The Wilburn Brothers	11/88	My Baby's Gone Sawyer Brown	44/83	My Fingers Do The Talkin' Jerry Lee Lewis
2/73	Mr. Lovemaker Johnny Paycheck	2/85	My Baby's Got Good Timing Dan Seals		My First Country Song
4/51	Mr. Moon Carl Smith	44/98	My Baby's Lovin' Daryle Singletary	93/77	Jesseca James
44/81	Mister Peepers Bill Anderson	20/63	My Baby's Not Here (In Town Tonight) Porter Wagoner	35/83	Dean Martin
71/70	Mister Professor Leroy Van Dyke	45/81	My Beginning Was You Jack Grayson & Blackjack	73/98	My First, Last, One And Only Jim Collins
32/75	Mr. Right And Mrs. Wrong Mel Tillis & Sherry Bryce	1/00	My Best Friend Tim McGraw	6/83	My First Taste Of Texas Ed Bruce
	Mister Sandman	12/49	My Best To You Sons Of The Pioneers	63/70	My Friend Arlene Harden
13/55	Chet Atkins	79/76	My Better Half Del Reeves	11/64	My Friend On The Right Faron Young
96/78	Tommy O'Day	20/69	My Big Iron Skillet Wanda Jackson		(My Friends Are Gonna Be) Strangers ..see: (From Now On My Friends Are Gonna Be)
10/81	Emmylou Harris	35/68	My Big Truck Drivin' Man Kitty Wells		
16/67	Mr. Shorty Marty Robbins	7/93	My Blue Angel Aaron Tippin	73/77	My Girl Dale McBride
47/75	Mr. Songwriter Sunday Sharpe	69/79	My Blue Heaven Mac Wiseman & Woody Herman	73/84	My Girl Savannah
56/73	Mr. Ting-A-Ling (Steel Guitar Man) George Morgan			64/74	My Girl Bill Jim Stafford
4/69	Mr. Walker, It's All Over Billie Jo Spears	45/69	My Blue Ridge Mountain Boy Dolly Parton	58/95	My Girl Friday Daron Norwood
6/01	Mrs. Steven Rudy Mark McGuinn	17/71	My Blue Tears Dolly Parton	11/68	My Goal For Today Kenny Price
15/72	Much Oblige Jack Greene/Jeannie Seely	14/75	My Boy Elvis Presley	20/77	My Good Thing's Gone Narvel Felts
13/54	Much Too Young To Die Ray Price			14/69	My Grass Is Green Roy Drusky
8/89	Much Too Young (To Feel This Damn Old) Garth Brooks			86/79	My Guns Are Loaded Bonnie Tyler
62/71	Muddy Bottom Osborne Brothers				My Guy
15/69	Muddy Mississippi Line Bobby Goldsboro			46/71	Lynda K. Lance
	Mule Skinner Blues			43/80	Margo Smith
16/60	Fendermen			1/72	My Hang-Up Is You Freddie Hart
3/70	Dolly Parton (Blue Yodel No. 8)				

	My Happiness	15/59	**My Love And Little Me**	4/93	**My Strongest Weakness**
43/69	Slim Whitman		Margie Bowes		Wynonna
47/70	Johnny & Jonie Mosby	37/82	**My Love Belongs To You**	57/85	**My Sweet-Eyed Georgia Girl**
1/80	**My Heart** Ronnie Milsap		Ronnie Rogers		Atlanta
	My Heart Cries For You	48/67	**My Love For You (Is Like A Mountain Range)**	62/77	**My Sweet Lady** John Denver
6/51	Evelyn Knight & Red Foley			38/89	**My Sweet Love Ain't Around**
7/51	Jimmy Wakely		Ernie Ashworth		Suzy Bogguss
63/72	Doyle Holly	15/00	**My Love Goes On And On**	15/64	**My Tears Are Overdue**
72/81	Margo Smith		Chris Cagle		George Jones
10/48	**My Heart Echoes** Jimmie Osborne	53/73	**My Love Is Deep, My Love Is Wide** Pat Daisy	36/64	**My Tears Don't Show**
51/67	**My Heart Gets All The Breaks** Wanda Jackson				Carl Butler & Pearl
		28/79	**My Mama Never Heard Me Sing** Billy "Crash" Craddock	10/49	**My Tennessee Baby** Ernest Tubb
5/96	**My Heart Has A History** Paul Brandt			15/73	**My Tennessee Mountain Home** Dolly Parton
		1/72	**My Man** Tammy Wynette		
	My Heart Has A Mind Of Its Own	60/70	**My Man** Jeannie C. Riley	19/85	**My Toot-Toot** Rockin' Sidney
10/72	Susan Raye	80/82	**My Man Friday** Patti Page	19/89	**My Train Of Thought** Barbara Mandrell
11/79	Debby Boone	1/96	**My Maria** Brooks & Dunn		
64/85	**My Heart Holds On** Holly Dunn	34/73	**My Mind Hangs On To You** Billy Walker	45/81	**My Turn** Donna Hazard
10/52	**My Heart Is Broken In Three** Slim Whitman			39/66	**My Uncle Used To Love Me But She Died** Roger Miller
		79/85	**My Mind Is On You** Gus Hardin		
38/79	**My Heart Is Not My Own** Mundo Earwood	24/77	**My Mountain Dew** Charlie Rich	2/78	**My Way** Elvis Presley
		7/62	**My Name Is Mud** James O'Gwynn	49/66	**My Way Of Life** Sonny Curtis
7/90	**My Heart Is Set On You** Lionel Cartwright	1/91	**My Next Broken Heart** Brooks & Dunn	23/77	**My Weakness** Margo Smith
				36/73	**My Whole World Is Falling Down** O.B. McClinton
63/99	**My Heart Is Still Beating** Kinleys	1/00	**My Next Thirty Years** Tim McGraw		
66/68	**My Heart Keeps Running To You** Johnny Paycheck			68/96	**My Wife Thinks You're Dead** Junior Brown
		31/94	**My Night To Howl** Lorrie Morgan		
1/64	**My Heart Skips A Beat** Buck Owens	19/65	**My Old Faded Rose** Johnny Sea		**My Wife's House**
			My Old Kentucky Home	9/74	Jerry Wallace
80/84	**My Heart Will Always Belong To You** Donna Fargo	69/70	Osborne Brothers	78/86	Gene Kennedy
		42/75	Johnny Cash	51/76	**My Window Faces The South** Sammi Smith
16/95	**My Heart Will Never Know** Clay Walker	9/85	**My Old Yellow Car** Dan Seals		
		1/85	**My Only Love** Statler Brothers	15/81	**My Woman Loves The Devil Out Of Me** Moe Bandy
49/78	**My Heart Won't Cry Anymore** Dickey Lee	4/79	**My Own Kind Of Hat** Merle Haggard		
		71/99	Alan Jackson	1/70	**My Woman, My Woman, My Wife** Marty Robbins
10/49	**My Heart's Bouquet** "Little" Jimmy Dickens	19/74	**My Part Of Forever** Johnny Paycheck	4/69	**My Woman's Good To Me** David Houston
67/97	**My Heart's Broke Down (But My Mind's Made Up)** Dean Miller	22/90	**My Past Is Present** Rodney Crowell	68/70	**My Woman's Love** Johnny Duncan
82/89	**My Heart's On Hold** J.D. Lewis	41/79	**My Pledge Of Love** John Anderson	3/75	**My Woman's Man** Freddie Hart
85/88	**My Heart's Way Behind** Doug Peters	14/76	**My Prayer** Narvel Felts	4/79	**My World Begins And Ends With You** Dave & Sugar
1/80	**My Heroes Have Always Been Cowboys** Willie Nelson	66/79	**My Prayer** Glen Campbell		
		76/78	**My Pulse Pumps Passions** Hal Hubble	80/79	**Mysterious Lady From St. Martinique** Hank Snow
17/80	**My Home's In Alabama** Alabama				
65/00	**My Hometown** Charlie Robison	14/59	**My Reason For Living** Ferlin Husky	57/67	**Mystery Of Tallahatchie Bridge** Roger White
37/75	**My Honky Tonk Ways** Kenny O'Dell	94/89	**My Rose Is Blue** Don Lamaster	11/56	**Mystery Train** Elvis Presley
44/70	**My Joy** Johnny Bush	6/87	**My Rough And Rowdy Days** Waylon Jennings		
67/96	**My Kind Of Crazy** John Anderson				# N
1/95	**My Kind Of Girl** Collin Raye	40/64	**My Saro Jane** Flatt & Scruggs		
53/84	**My Kind Of Lady** Burrito Brothers	1/93	**My Second Home** Tracy Lawrence	40/79	**Nadine** Freddy Weller
12/67	**My Kind Of Love** Dave Dudley	29/63	**My Secret** Judy Lynn	87/80	**Nag, Nag, Nag** Bobby Braddock
27/99	**My Kind Of Woman/My Kind Of Man** Vince Gill With Patty Loveless	1/57	**My Shoes Keep Walking Back To You** Ray Price	65/71	**Naked And Crying** Henson Cargill
				30/80	**Naked In The Rain** Loretta Lynn
40/79	**My Lady** Freddie Hart	59/92	**My Side Of Town** Dennis Robbins	65/97	**Naked To The Pain** James Bonamy
	My Lady Loves Me (Just As I Am)	67/78	**My Side Of Town** Billy Larkin		
82/80	Chris Waters	8/79	**My Silver Lining** Mickey Gilley	70/83	**Name Of The Game Is Cheating** Charlie Ross
9/83	Leon Everette	15/69	**My Son** Jan Howard		
5/61	**My Last Date (With You)** Skeeter Davis	9/50	**My Son Calls Another Man Daddy** Hank Williams	16/69	**Name Of The Game Was Love** Hank Snow
37/73	**My Last Day** Tony Douglas	76/81	**My Song Don't Sing The Same** Kris Carpenter	9/71	**Nashville** David Houston
64/78	**My Last Sad Song** Jerry Wallace			37/73	**Nashville** Ray Stevens
1/69	**My Life (Throw It Away If I Want To)** Bill Anderson		**My Special Angel**	61/75	**Nashville** Hoyt Axton
		1/57	Bobby Helms	93/80	**Nashville Beer Garden** Andy Badale
26/86	**My Life's A Dance** Anne Murray	53/76	Bobby G. Rice		
8/56	**My Lips Are Sealed** Jim Reeves	82/85	James & Michael Younger	54/67	**Nashville Cats** Flatt & Scruggs
1/02	**My List** Toby Keith		**My Special Prayer**	74/70	**Nashville Skyline Rag** Earl Scruggs
1/70	**My Love** Sonny James	36/69	Archie Campbell & Lorene Mann		
1/94	**My Love** Little Texas	83/80	Freddy Fender		

73/67	Nashville Women Hank Locklin
77/82	Natalie Dave Rowland
2/94	National Working Woman's Holiday Sammy Kershaw
39/80	Natural Attraction Billie Jo Spears
74/97	Natural Born Lovers Brady Seals
1/85	Natural High Merle Haggard
20/82	Natural Love Petula Clark
82/78	Natural Love O.B. McClinton
46/74	Natural Woman Jody Miller
71/92	Naturally Skip Ewing
69/73	Naughty Girl Guy Shannon
	Near You
74/71	Lamar Morris
1/77	George Jones & Tammy Wynette
34/87	Need A Little Time Off For Bad Behavior David Allan Coe
1/67	Need You Sonny James
9/72	Need You David Rogers
24/76	Negatory Romance Tom T. Hall
	Neither One Of Us
7/73	Bob Luman
81/89	Ronnie Bryant
79/77	Neon Lady Bobby Wright
83/77	Neon Lights Nick Nixon
1/92	Neon Moon Brooks & Dunn
3/73	Neon Rose Mel Tillis
87/77	Neon Women Carmol Taylor & Stella Parton
28/64	Nester, The Lefty Frizzell
15/54	Never Marilyn & Wesley Tuttle
96/74	Never A Night Goes By Sharon Vaughn
23/97	Never Again, Again Lee Ann Womack
6/49	Never Again (Will I Knock On Your Door) Hank Williams
22/89	Never Alone Vince Gill
36/80	Never Be Anyone Else R.C. Bannon
1/86	Never Be You Rosanne Cash
29/99	Never Been Kissed Sherrié Austin
1/81	Never Been So Loved (In All My Life) Charley Pride
	Never Been To Spain
36/72	Ronnie Sessions
75/74	Sammi Smith
52/94	Never Bit A Bullet Like This George Jones with Sammy Kershaw
36/75	Never Coming Back Again Rex Allen, Jr.
74/98	Never Could Great Divide
6/84	Never Could Toe The Mark Waylon Jennings
18/76	Never Did Like Whiskey Billie Jo Spears
83/77	Never Ending Love Affair Melba Montgomery
	Never Ending Song Of Love
8/71	Dickey Lee
57/71	Mayf Nutter
43/83	Osmond Brothers
72/90	Crystal Gayle
9/89	Never Givin' Up On Love Michael Martin Murphey
78/78	Never Going Back Again Mac Wiseman
82/79	Never Gonna' Be A Country Star Kenny Seratt
58/72	Never Had A Doubt Mayf Nutter

48/89	Never Had A Love Song Gary Morris
8/89	Never Had It So Good Mary Chapin Carpenter
63/99	Never In A Million Tears T. Graham Brown
83/78	Never Knew (How Much I Loved You 'Til I Lost You) Dawn Chastain
3/90	Never Knew Lonely Vince Gill
73/93	Never Let Him See Me Cry Ronna Reeves
26/01	Never Love You Enough Chely Wright
58/87	Never Mind Nanci Griffith
25/69	"Never More" Quote The Raven Stonewall Jackson
9/78	Never My Love Vern Gosdin
F/79	Never My Love Kendalls
95/76	Never Naughty Rosie Sue Thompson
30/89	Never Say Never T. Graham Brown
29/80	Never Seen A Mountain So High Ronnie McDowell
50/89	Never Too Old To Rock 'N' Roll Ronnie McDowell with Jerry Lee Lewis
	Never Trust A Woman
2/47	Red Foley
2/47	Tex Williams
5/48	Tiny Hill
93/78	Nevertheless Hank Snow
	New Blue Jeans ..see: (I'm Looking For Some)
18/82	New Cut Road Bobby Bare
1/89	New Fool At An Old Game Reba McEntire
3/54	New Green Light Hank Thompson
39/68	New Heart Ernie Ashworth
	New Jolie Blonde (New Pretty Blonde)
1/47	Red Foley
2/47	Moon Mullican
43/77	New Kid In Town Eagles
32/90	New Kind Of Love Michelle Wright
25/67	New Lips Roy Drusky
1/83	New Looks From An Old Lover B.J. Thomas
51/88	New Never Wore Off My Sweet Baby Dean Dillon
28/69	New Orleans Anthony Armstrong Jones
10/84	New Patches Mel Tillis
87/84	New Place To Begin Ray Price
72/66	New Place To Hang Your Hat Ruby Wright
	New Pretty Blonde ..see: New Jolie Blonde
79/88	New River Heartland
26/59	New River Train Bobby Helms
3/44	New San Antonio Rose Bob Wills
2/88	New Shade Of Blue Southern Pacific
64/86	New Shade Of Blue Perry LaPointe
1/46	New Spanish Two Step Bob Wills
5/46	New Steel Guitar Rag Bill Boyd
95/85	New Tradition Bobby G. Rice
64/93	New Way Home K.T. Oslin
17/82	New Way Out Karen Brooks

2/91	New Way (To Light Up An Old Flame) Joe Diffie
10/52	New Wears Off Too Fast Hank Thompson
62/82	New Will Never Wear Off Of You Crash Craddock
55/00	New Year's Eve 1999 Alabama
73/73	New York Callin' Miami Kent Fox
19/71	New York City Statler Brothers
83/81	New York Cowboy Nashville Superpickers
26/63	New York Town Flatt & Scruggs
18/80	New York Wine And Tennessee Shine Dave & Sugar
17/79	Next Best Feeling Mary K. Miller
86/73	Next Door Neighbor's Kid Jud Strunk
1/68	Next In Line Conway Twitty
9/57	Next In Line Johnny Cash
55/98	Next Step Jim Collins
F/70	Next Step Is Love Elvis Presley
16/92	Next Thing Smokin' Joe Diffie
14/59	Next Time Ernest Tubb
51/86	Next Time Wild Choir
15/71	Next Time I Fall In Love (I Won't) Hank Thompson
92/87	Next Time I Marry Victoria Hallman
51/89	Next To You Tammy Wynette
	Next To You
78/85	Craig Dillingham
74/86	Tommy Overstreet
1/90	Next To You, Next To Me Shenandoah
15/55	Next Voice You Hear Hank Snow
37/70	Nice 'N' Easy Charlie Rich
85/86	Nice To Be With You Slewfoot
37/97	Nickajack River Road
80/83	Nickel's Worth Of Heaven Brian Collins
31/66	Nickels, Quarters And Dimes Johnny Wright
26/59	Night Jimmy Martin
77/75	Night Atlanta Burned Atkins String Company
41/01	Night Disappear With You Brian McComas
67/83	Night Dolly Parton Was Almost Mine Pump Boys And Dinettes
81/77	Night Flying Roy Drusky
1/83	Night Games Charley Pride
20/80	Night Games Ray Stevens
43/87	Night Hank Williams Came To Town Johnny Cash
58/85	Night Has A Heart Of It's Own Lacy J. Dalton
9/95	Night Is Fallin' In My Heart Diamond Rio
85/80	Night Lies Bill Wence
	Night Life
28/63	Ray Price
31/68	Claude Gray
20/80	Danny Davis & Willie Nelson
59/86	B.J. Thomas
F/86	Roy Clark
29/71	Night Miss Nancy Ann's Hotel For Single Girls Burned Down Tex Williams
70/88	Night Of Love Forgotten Bobby G. Rice
45/64	Night People Leroy Van Dyke

487

Handwritten note at top: No, No, Joe — Hank Williams

	Night The Lights Went Out In Georgia	15/70	**No Love At All** Lynn Anderson	72/78	**No Tell Motel** David Houston
36/73	Vicki Lawrence	80/80	Jan Gray	40/64	**No Thanks, I Just Had One** Margie Singleton & Faron Young
12/92	Reba McEntire		**No Love Have I**		**No Thinkin' Thing** ..see: (This Ain't)
	Night They Drove Old Dixie Down	4/60	Webb Pierce		
71/70	Buckaroos	26/78	Gail Davies	91/89	**No Time At All** Debbie Sanders
33/71	Alice Creech	67/92	Holly Dunn	75/00	**No Time For Tears** Jo Dee Messina
16/76	**Night Time And My Baby** Joe Stampley	43/98	**No Man In His Wrong Heart** Gary Allan	3/93	**No Time To Kill** Clint Black
2/78	**Night Time Magic** Larry Gatlin	3/95	**No Man's Land** John Michael Montgomery	3/46	**No Vacancy** Merle Travis
83/79	**Night Time Music Man** Judy Argo	1/90	**No Matter How High** Oak Ridge Boys	97/78	**No Way Around It (It's Love)** Billy Swan
6/99	**Night To Remember** Joe Diffie	17/79	**No Memories Hangin' Round** Rosanne Cash/Bobby Bare	70/92	**No Way Jose** Ray Kennedy
85/83	**Night's Almost Over** Jacky Ward			49/85	**No Way José** David Frizzell
F/72	**Night's Not Over Yet** Roy Drusky	26/00	**No Mercy** Ty Herndon	53/96	**No Way Out** Suzy Bogguss
20/90	**Night's Too Long** Patty Loveless	26/94	**No More Cryin'** McBride & The Ride	69/82	**No Way Out** Johnny Paycheck
14/63	**Nightmare** Faron Young	19/73	**No More Hanging On** Jerry Lee Lewis	53/80	**No Way To Drown A Memory** Stoney Edwards
4/86	**Nights** Ed Bruce			70/95	**No Yesterday** Billy Montana
27/78	**Nights Are Forever Without You** Buck Owens	38/99	**No More Looking Over My Shoulder** Travis Tritt	1/82	**Nobody** Sylvia
84/89	**Nights Are Never Long Enough With You** Sylvia Forrest		**No More One More Time**	4/66	**Nobody But A Fool (Would Love You)** Connie Smith
		71/87	Judy Byram		
48/97	**Nights Like These** Lynns	7/88	Jo-el Sonnier	2/83	**Nobody But You** Don Williams
93/83	**Nights Like Tonight** Austin O'Neal	15/71	**No Need To Worry** Johnny Cash & June Carter	43/69	**Nobody But You** Buckaroos
95/82	**Nights Out At The Days End** Owen Brothers			93/73	**Nobody But You** Linda Plowman
		1/96	**No News** Lonestar	44/77	**Nobody Cares But You** Freddy Weller
89/85	**Nightshift** Nashville Nightshift	8/78	**No, No, No (I'd Rather Be Free)** Rex Allen, Jr.		
1/81	**9 To 5** Dolly Parton			61/83	**Nobody Else For Me** Stephanie Winslow
41/67	**Ninety Days** Jimmy Dean	F/56	**No One But You** Kitty Wells & Red Foley	49/85	**Nobody Ever Gets Enough Love** Con Hunley
2/63	**Ninety Miles An Hour** Hank Snow				
13/59	**Ninety-Nine** Bill Anderson	79/87	**No One Can Touch Me** Carla Monday	1/85	**Nobody Falls Like A Fool** Earl Thomas Conley
7/81	**1959** John Anderson	14/55	**No One Dear But You** Johnnie And Jack		**Nobody In His Right Mind Would've Left Her**
43/96	**1969** Keith Stegall				
81/78	**Nineteen-Sixty Something Songwriter Of The Year** Tennesseans	7/79	**No One Else In The World** Tammy Wynette	25/81	Dean Dillon
		1/92	**No One Else On Earth** Wynonna	1/86	George Strait
6/86	**1982** Randy Travis	6/86	**No One Mends A Broken Heart Like You** Barbara Mandrell	1/97	**Nobody Knows** Kevin Sharp
58/84	**1984** Craig Dillingham			53/88	**Nobody Knows** John Wesley Ryles
	9,999,999 Tears	1/96	**No One Needs To Know** Shania Twain	84/89	**Nobody Knows Me** Lyle Lovett
3/76	Dickey Lee				
75/89	Tammy Lucas	6/46	**No One To Cry To** Sons Of The Pioneers	1/79	**Nobody Likes Sad Songs** Ronnie Milsap
76/78	**Ninth Of September** Jim Chesnut	97/89	**No One To Talk To But The Blues** Maripat	63/98	**Nobody Love, Nobody Gets Hurt** Suzy Bogguss
39/81	**No Aces** Patti Page				
8/68	**No Another Time** Lynn Anderson		**No One Will Ever Know**	68/81	**Nobody Loves Anybody Anymore** Kris Kristofferson
72/69	**No Blues Is Good News** George Jones	42/66	Frank Ifield		
		13/80	Gene Watson	1/84	**Nobody Loves Me Like You Do** Anne Murray (with Dave Loggins)
72/89	**No Chance To Dance** Johnny Rodriguez	10/67	**No One's Gonna Hurt You Anymore** Bill Anderson		
1/74	**No Charge** Melba Montgomery			52/93	**Nobody Loves You When You're Free** Remingtons
1/94	**No Doubt About It** Neal McCoy	78/87	**No Ordinary Memory** Bill Anderson		
56/99	**No Easy Goodbye** South Sixty Five			26/87	**Nobody Should Have To Love This Way** Crystal Gayle
		93/80	**No Ordinary Woman** Byron Gallimore		
19/87	**No Easy Horses** Schuyler, Knobloch & Bickhardt	2/87	**No Place Like Home** Randy Travis	82/88	**Nobody There But Me** Willie Nelson
33/98	**No End To This Road** Restless Heart	53/00	**No Place Like Home** Georgia Middleman	3/85	**Nobody Wants To Be Alone** Crystal Gayle
49/83	**No Fair Fallin' In Love** Jan Gray			68/70	**Nobody Wants To Hear It Like It Is** Jack Barlow
27/01	**No Fear** Terri Clark	1/99	**No Place That Far** Sara Evans		
3/93	**No Future In The Past** Vince Gill	78/82	**No Place To Hide** Gayle Zeiler	2/93	**Nobody Wins** Radney Foster
	No Gettin' Over Me ..see: (There's)		**No Relief In Sight**	5/73	**Nobody Wins** Brenda Lee
		98/77	Willie Rainsford	22/88	**Nobody's Angel** Crystal Gayle
73/97	**No Goodbyes** Gene Watson	20/82	Con Hunley	46/67	**Nobody's Child** Hank Williams, Jr.
83/79	**No Greater Love** Billy Stack	62/72	**No Rings—No Strings** Del Reeves		**Nobody's Darling But Mine**
60/73	**No Headstone On My Grave** Jerry Lee Lewis			13/60	Johnny Sea
	No Help Wanted	57/82	**No Room To Cry** Mike Campbell	87/80	B.J. Wright
1/53	Carlisles	32/65	**No Sign Of Living** Dottie West	10/70	**Nobody's Fool** Jim Reeves
9/53	Hank Thompson	58/92	**No Sir** Darryl & Don Ellis	24/81	**Nobody's Fool** Deborah Allen
7/53	**No Help Wanted #2** Ernest Tubb - Red Foley	10/78	**No Sleep Tonight** Randy Barlow	11/62	**Nobody's Fool But Yours** Buck Owens
13/55	**No, I Don't Believe I Will** Carl Smith	93/84	**No Survivors** Peter Isaacson		
		16/67	**No Tears Milady** Marty Robbins	50/96	**Nobody's Girl** Michelle Wright
2/44	**No Letter Today** Ted Daffan				

Not Just A Pretty Face — Shania Twain WPCV (10-11-03)

13/94	**Nobody's Gonna Rain On Our Parade** Kathy Mattea	
55/00	**Nobody's Got It All** John Anderson	
1/90	**Nobody's Home** Clint Black	
9/50	**Nobody's Lonesome For Me** Hank Williams	
2/90	**Nobody's Talking** Exile	
8/69	**None Of My Business** Henson Cargill	
73/78	**Norma Jean** Sammi Smith	
2/92	**Norma Jean Riley** Diamond Rio	
61/68	**Normally, Norma Loves Me** Red Sovine	
37/81	**North Alabama** Dave Kirby	
42/72	**North Carolina** Dallas Frazier	
17/80	**North Of The Border** Johnny Rodriguez	
1/61	**North To Alaska** Johnny Horton	
71/73	**North To Chicago** Hank Snow	
8/53	**North Wind** Slim Whitman	
56/82	**North Wind** Jim & Jesse with Charlie Louvin	
17/70	**Northeast Arkansas Mississippi County Bootlegger** Kenny Price	
71/94	**Not** Bellamy Brothers	
90/80	**Not A Day Goes By** Anna Sudderth	
1/95	**Not A Moment Too Soon** Tim McGraw	
43/88	**Not A Night Goes By** Tim Malchak	
76/85	**Not Another Heart Song** Tom Jones	
2/90	**Not Counting You** Garth Brooks	
3/96	**Not Enough Hours In The Night** Doug Supernaw	
29/88	**Not Enough Love** Tom Wopat	
62/80	**Not Exactly Free** O.B. McClinton	
69/89	**Not Fade Away** Trish Lynn	
70/89	**Not Like This** Tim Malchak	
24/64	**Not My Kind Of People** Stonewall Jackson	
87/84	**Not On The Bottom Yet** Boxcar Willie	
1/95	**Not On Your Love** Jeff Carson	
65/95	**Not So Different After All** Brother Phelps	
13/63	**Not So Long Ago** Marty Robbins	
3/96	**Not That Different** Collin Raye	
44/66	**Not That I Care** Jerry Wallace	
74/86	**Not Tonight** Paul Proctor	
77/74	**Not Tonight** Little David Wilkins	
52/87	**Not Tonight I've Got A Heartache** Vicki Rae Von	
15/92	**Not Too Much To Ask** Mary Chapin Carpenter with Joe Diffie	
7/63	**Not What I Had In Mind** George Jones	
68/92	**Not With My Heart You Don't** Paulette Carlson	
28/98	**Note, The** Daryle Singletary	
62/68	**Note In Box Number 9** Stu Phillips	
1/98	**Nothin' But The Taillights** Clint Black	
20/93	**Nothin' But The Wheel** Patty Loveless	
25/59	**Nothin' But True Love** Margie Singleton	
	Nothin' But You	
70/83	Steve Earle & The Dukes	
51/91	Robin Lee	
26/97	**Nothin' Less Than Love** Buffalo Club	
11/58	**Nothin' Needs Nothin' (Like I Need You)** Marvin Rainwater	
10/98	**Nothin' New Under The Moon** LeAnn Rimes	
35/76	**Nothin' Takes The Place Of You** Asleep At The Wheel	
64/92	**Nothin' To Do (And All Night To Do It)** Billy Burnette	
82/81	**Nothin' To Do But Just Lie** Wesley Ryan	
33/86	**Nothin' Ventured Nothin' Gained** Sylvia	
61/67	**Nothin's Bad As Bein' Lonely** Johnny Sea	
20/95	**Nothing** Dwight Yoakam	
10/79	**Nothing As Original As You** Statler Brothers	
26/82	**Nothing Behind You, Nothing In Sight** John Conlee	
F/74	**Nothing Between** Porter Wagoner	
19/82	**Nothing But The Radio On** Younger Brothers	
91/79	**Nothing But Time** Helen Hudson	
12/86	**Nothing But Your Love Matters** Larry Gatlin/Gatlin Brothers	
37/85	**Nothing Can Hurt Me Now** Gail Davies	
68/72	**Nothing Can Stop My Loving You** Patsy Sledd	
50/00	**Nothing Catches Jesus By Surprise** John Michael Montgomery	
7/73	**Nothing Ever Hurt Me (Half As Bad As Losing You)** George Jones	
1/89	**Nothing I Can Do About It Now** Willie Nelson	
61/93	**Nothing In Common But Love** Twister Alley	
87/84	**(Nothing Left Between Us) But Alabama** Gordon Dee	
34/65	**Nothing Left To Lose** Faron Young	
85/88	**Nothing Left To Lose** Tiny Wellman	
10/84	**Nothing Like Falling In Love** Eddie Rabbitt	
4/92	**Nothing Short Of Dying** Travis Tritt	
4/80	**Nothing Sure Looked Good On You** Gene Watson	
39/68	**Nothing Takes The Place Of Loving You** Stonewall Jackson	
15/91	**Nothing's Changed Here** Dwight Yoakam	
63/90	**Nothing's Gonna Bother Me Tonight** Forester Sisters	
3/90	**Nothing's News** Clint Black	
1/86	**Now And Forever (You And Me)** Anne Murray	
85/89	**Now And Then** Karen Staley	
	(Now And Then There's) A ..see: Fool Such As I	
56/76	**Now Everybody Knows** Charlie Rich	
68/68	**Now I Can Live Again** Mickey Gilley	
5/94	**Now I Know** Lari White	
56/84	**Now I Lay Me Down To Cheat** Shelly West	
62/82	**Now I Lay Me Down To Cheat** David Allan Coe	
26/93	**Now I Pray For Rain** Neal McCoy	
69/86	**Now I've Got A Heart Of Gold** Sonny Curtis	
71/91	**Now It Belongs To You** Mark O'Connor	
83/86	**Now She's In Paris** Dave Holladay	
2/98	**Now That I Found You** Terri Clark	
98/73	**Now That It's Over** Brush Arbor	
38/81	**Now That The Feeling's Gone** Billy "Crash" Craddock	
17/91	**Now That We're Alone** Rodney Crowell	
43/96	**Now That's All Right With Me** Mandy Barnett	
59/00	**Now That's Awesome** Bill Engvall	
18/92	**Now That's Country** Marty Stuart	
21/85	**Now There's You** Shelly West	
	Now You See 'Em, Now You Don't	
19/78	Roy Head	
70/88	Marty Haggard	
12/99	**(Now You See Me) Now You Don't** Lee Ann Womack	
64/87	**Now You're Talkin'** Mel McDaniel	
66/93	**Now You're Talkin'** Dixiana	
7/92	**Nowhere Bound** Diamond Rio	
20/87	**Nowhere Road** Steve Earle	
54/97	**Nowhere, USA** Dean Miller	
51/89	**#1 Heartache Place** Larry Gatlin/Gatlin Brothers	
41/65	**Number One Heel** Bonnie Owens	
	#1 With A Heartache	
66/76	Billy Larkin	
94/78	La Costa	
11/80	**Numbers** Bobby Bare	
94/77	**Nyquil Blues** Alvin Crow	

O

	O Holy Night	
55/95	John Berry	
74/96	Martina McBride	
63/97	John Berry	
67/97	Martina McBride	
49/98	Martina McBride	
57/99	Martina McBride	
41/00	Martina McBride	
18/94	**O What A Thrill** Mavericks	
3/47	**Oakie Boogie** Jack Guthrie	
91/77	**Obscene Phone Call** Johnny Russell	
28/80	**Occasional Rose** Marty Robbins	
6/70	**Occasional Wife** Faron Young	
1/87	**Ocean Front Property** George Strait	
29/61	**Ocean Of Tears** Billie Jean Horton	
	Odds And Ends (Bits And Pieces)	
7/61	Warren Smith	
66/74	Charlie Walker	
21/71	**Ode To A Half A Pound Of Ground Round** Tom T. Hall	
	Ode To Billie Joe	
17/67	Bobbie Gentry	
39/67	Margie Singleton	
55/74	**Ode To Jole Blon** Gary Sargeants	

Old Black Kettle — Dolly Parton (LP)

3/65	Ode To The Little Brown Shack Out Back Billy Edd Wheeler	9/86	Oklahoma Borderline Vince Gill	30/88	Old Kind Of Love Ricky Skaggs
91/89	Of All The Foolish Things To Do Ross Lewis	49/82	Oklahoma Crude Corbin/Hanner Band	34/77	Old King Kong George Jones
				20/60	Old Lamplighter Browns
22/97	Of Course I'm Alright Alabama	46/84	Oklahoma Heart Becky Hobbs	30/60	Old Log Cabin For Sale Porter Wagoner
38/67	Off And On Charlie Louvin		Oklahoma Hills		
F/76	Off And Running Maury Finney	1/45	Jack Guthrie	11/55	Old Lonesome Times Carl Smith
5/79	Official Historian On Shirley Jean Berrell Statler Brothers	7/61	Hank Thompson	63/70	Old Love Affair, Now Showing Leroy Van Dyke
		60/69	Oklahoma Home Brew Hank Thompson	11/77	Old Man And His Horn Gene Watson
	(Oh Baby Mine) I Get So Lonely	15/72	Oklahoma Sunday Morning Glen Campbell	1/74	Old Man From The Mountain Merle Haggard
1/54	Johnnie And Jack				
49/79	Bobby G. Rice	86/76	Oklahoma Sunshine Pat Boone	63/88	Old Man No One Loves George Jones
2/83	Statler Brothers	13/90	Oklahoma Swing Vince Gill		
21/75	Oh Boy Diana Trask	9/48	Oklahoma Waltz Johnny Bond		Old Man River
38/84	Oh Carolina Vince Gill		Ol' Man River ..see: Old Man River	86/76	Shylo
10/86	Oh Darlin' O'Kanes			22/83	Mel McDaniel
12/82	Oh Girl Con Hunley	70/68	Old Before My Time Bobby Wright	31/70	Old Man Willis Nat Stuckey
25/70	Oh Happy Day Glen Campbell	38/73	Old Betsy Goes Boing, Boing, Boing Hummers		Old Man's Back In Town
9/87	Oh Heart Baillie & The Boys			48/92	Garth Brooks
70/74	Oh, How Happy Sherry Bryce	48/86	Old Blue Yodeler Razzy Bailey	59/97	Garth Brooks
79/89	Oh How I Love You (Como Te Quiero) Tony Perez	52/68	Old Bridge Jean Shepard	74/84	Old Memories Are Hard To Lose Kimberly Springs
		11/87	Old Bridges Burn Slow Billy Joe Royal		
6/80	Oh, How I Miss You Tonight Jim Reeves			90/75	Old Memory (Got In My Eye) Ferlin Husky
		30/66	Old Brush Arbors George Jones		
65/70	Oh How I Waited Ron Lowry	4/93	Old Country Mark Chesnutt	7/59	Old Moon Betty Foley
36/75	Oh, How Love Changes Don Gibson & Sue Thompson	48/64	Old Courthouse Faron Young	21/93	Old Pair Of Shoes Randy Travis
		5/89	Old Coyote Town Don Williams	50/89	Old Pair Of Shoes Sawyer Brown
48/88	Oh Jenny Billy Montana	1/73	(Old Dogs-Children And) Watermelon Wine Tom T. Hall		Old Photographs
	Oh Lonesome Me			81/84	Sam Neely
1/58	Don Gibson	1/95	Old Enough To Know Better Wade Hayes	27/88	Sawyer Brown
13/61	Johnny Cash			11/64	Old Records Margie Singleton
64/66	Bobbi Martin	53/70	Old Enough To Want To (Fool Enough To Try) Norro Wilson	50/65	Old Red Marty Robbins
63/70	Stonewall Jackson			3/62	Old Rivers Walter Brennan
92/76	Loggins & Messina	13/69	Old Faithful Mel Tillis	51/68	Old Ryman Hank Williams, Jr.
8/90	Kentucky Headhunters	49/73	Old Faithful Tony Booth	5/86	Old School John Conlee
78/86	Oh Louisiana Jim & Jesse	86/81	Old Familiar Feeling Wyvon Alexander	8/63	Old Showboat Stonewall Jackson
40/71	Oh, Love Of Mine Johnny & Jonie Mosby	83/81	Old Fangled Country Songs Kenny O.	9/80	Old Side Of Town Tom T. Hall
				9/51	Old Soldiers Never Die Gene Autry
5/93	Oh Me, Oh My, Sweet Baby Diamond Rio	F/78	Old Fashioned Love Kendalls		
42/64	Oh No! Browns	58/72	Old Fashioned Love Song Jeris Ross		Old Stuff
76/82	Oh, No Randy Parton			64/95	Garth Brooks
	Oh-Oh, I'm Falling In Love Again	93/81	Old Fashioned Lover (In A Brand New Love Affair) Michael Spitz	70/97	Garth Brooks
5/58	Jimmie Rodgers			62/00	Old Time Christmas George Strait
29/73	Eddy Arnold	93/83	Old Fashioned Lovin' Sierra	26/77	Old Time Feeling Johnny Cash & June Carter Cash
	Oh Pretty Woman	38/73	Old Fashioned Singing George Jones & Tammy Wynette		
13/70	Arlene Harden (Lovin' Man)			64/77	Old Time Lovin' Kenny Starr
89/89	Roy Orbison & Friends	1/81	Old Flame Alabama	97/74	Old Time Sunshine Song Roy Acuff
4/71	Oh, Singer Jeannie C. Riley	5/86	Old Flame Juice Newton		
8/57	Oh' So Many Years Kitty Wells & Webb Pierce	46/89	Old Flame, New Fire Burch Sisters	57/00	Old Toy Trains Toby Keith
				21/86	Old Violin Johnny Paycheck
	Oh, Such A Stranger	54/78	Old Flame, New Fire Hank Williams, Jr.		Old Wives' Tale ..see: (Just An)
68/68	Frank Ifield			3/52	Older And Bolder Eddy Arnold
61/78	Don Gibson		Old Flames (Can't Hold A Candle To You)	8/74	Older The Violin, The Sweeter The Music Hank Thompson
23/76	Oh, Sweet Temptation Gary Stewart	14/78	Joe Sun	1/81	Older Women Ronnie McDowell
97/76	Oh Those Texas Women Gene Davis	86/78	Brian Collins	52/86	Ole Rock And Roller Keith Stegall
		1/80	Dolly Parton		Ole Slew-Foot
5/88	Oh What A Love Nitty Gritty Dirt Band	5/92	Old Flames Have New Names Mark Chesnutt	48/66	Porter Wagoner
				31/79	Porter Wagoner
56/87	Oh What A Night Mel McDaniel	2/88	Old Folks Ronnie Milsap & Mike Reid	59/96	On A Bus To St. Cloud Trisha Yearwood
60/69	Oh What A Woman! Jerry Reed				
12/91	Oh What It Did To Me Tanya Tucker	49/66	Old French Quarter (In New Orleans) Billy Walker	2/96	On A Good Night Wade Hayes
				4/01	On A Night Like This Trick Pony
4/47	(Oh Why, Oh Why, Did I Ever Leave) Wyoming Dick Jurgens	19/82	Old Friends Roger Miller/ Willie Nelson/Ray Price	23/87	On And On Anne Murray
				27/79	On Business For The King Joe Sun
17/67	Oh! Woman Nat Stuckey	6/80	Old Habits Hank Williams, Jr.		
55/73	Oh Woman Jack Barlow	2/85	Old Hippie Bellamy Brothers	5/90	On Down The Line Patty Loveless
57/86	Oh Yes I Can Tari Hensley	19/74	Old Home Filler-Up An' Keep On-A-Truckin' Cafe C.W. McCall	71/99	On Earth As It Is In Texas Deryl Dodd
1/69	Okie From Muskogee Merle Haggard			1/78	On My Knees Charlie Rich with Janie Fricke
33/01	Oklahoma Billy Gilman	44/82	Old Home Town Glen Campbell		

12/57 **On My Mind Again** Billy Walker	69/95 **One**	11/64 **One If For Him, Two If For Me** David Houston
20/95 **On My Own** Reba McEntire	George Jones & Tammy Wynette	1/80 **One In A Million** Johnny Lee
54/99 **On My Way To You** Sonya Isaacs	95/85 **One A.M. Alone** Dave Dudley	57/99 **One In A Million** Mindy McCready
1/90 **On Second Thought** Eddie Rabbitt	27/63 **One Among The Many** Ned Miller	73/78 **One In A Million** Nate Harvell
7/68 **On Tap, In The Can, Or In The Bottle** Hank Thompson	66/93 **One And One And One** Gene Watson	19/66 **One In A Row** Willie Nelson
9/74 **On The Cover Of The Music City News** Buck Owens	93/79 **One And One Make Three** Ron Shaw	50/89 **One In Your Heart One On Your Mind** Charly McClain
76/81 **On The Inside** Patti Page	51/95 **One And Only Love** Russ Taff	1/49 **One Kiss Too Many** Eddy Arnold
On The Other Hand	93/83 **One Away From One Too Many** Billy Walker	33/73 **One Last Time** Glen Campbell
67/85 Randy Travis	85/80 **One Bar At A Time** Stoney Edwards	70/91 **One Less Pony** Sawyer Brown
1/86 Randy Travis	61/85 **One Big Family** Heart Of Nashville	64/92 **One Like That** JJ White
44/67 **On The Other Hand** Charlie Louvin	2/95 **One Boy, One Girl** Collin Raye	91/79 **One Lil Skinny Rib** Cal Smith
29/76 **On The Rebound** Del Reeves & Billie Jo Spears	57/91 **One Bridge I Didn't Burn** Conway Twitty	11/62 **One Look At Heaven** Stonewall Jackson
6/93 **On The Road** Lee Roy Parnell	42/66 **One Bum Town** Del Reeves	33/91 **One Love** Carlene Carter
1/80 **On The Road Again** Willie Nelson	1/54 **One By One** Kitty Wells & Red Foley	3/86 **One Love At A Time** Tanya Tucker
4/98 **On The Side Of Angels** LeAnn Rimes	95/75 **One By One** Jimmy Elledge	95/76 **One Love Down** Gary Mack
69/91 **On The Surface** Rosanne Cash	73/88 **One Dance Love Affair** Jon Washington	76/81 **One Love Over Easy** Sami Jo Cole
2/97 **On The Verge** Collin Raye	**One Day At A Time**	27/65 **One Man Band** Phil Baugh
49/75 **On The Way Home** Betty Jean Robinson	19/74 Marilyn Sellars	42/86 **One Man Band** Moe Bandy
49/84 **On The Wings Of A Nightingale** Everly Brothers	1/80 Cristy Lane	61/68 **One Man Band** Norma Jean
85/83 **On The Wings Of My Victory** Glen Campbell	8/74 **One Day At A Time** Don Gibson	63/69 **One Man Band** Sheb Wooley
8/51 **On Top Of Old Smoky** Weavers	35/99 **One Day Left To Live** Sammy Kershaw	8/90 **One Man Woman** Judds
4/67 **Once** Ferlin Husky	72/82 **One Day Since Yesterday** Colleen Camp	72/80 **One Man's Trash (Is Another Man's Treasure)** Marty Robbins
1/64 **Once A Day** Connie Smith	23/64 **One Dozen Roses (And Our Love)** George Morgan	85/79 **One Man's Woman** Kelly Warren
68/87 **Once A Fool, Always A Fool** Jeff Dugan	54/66 **One Dream** Slim Whitman	2/70 **One Minute Past Eternity** Jerry Lee Lewis
91/75 **Once Again I Go To Sleep With Lovin' On My Mind** Melody Allen	10/65 **One Dyin' And A Buryin'** Roger Miller	11/75 **One Monkey Don't Stop No Show** Little David Wilkins
87/90 **Once And For Always** Gary Dale Parker	2/95 **One Emotion** Clint Black	1/01 **One More Day** Diamond Rio
60/96 **Once I Was The Light Of Your Life** Stephanie Bentley	70/83 **One Fiddle, Two Fiddle** Ray Price	56/71 **One More Drink** Mel Tillis
1/86 **Once In A Blue Moon** Earl Thomas Conley	75/82 **One Fine Morning** Corbin/Hanner Band	95/83 **One More Goodbye, One More Hello** Donnie Record
34/79 **Once In A Blue Moon** Zella Lehr	74/88 **One Fire Between Us** Judy Byram	97/78 **One More Kiss** Terri Bishop
82/83 **Once In A Blue Moon** Hank Thompson	2/87 **One For The Money** T.G. Sheppard	1/93 **One More Last Chance** Vince Gill
Once In A Lifetime Love	1/88 **One Friend** Dan Seals	33/81 **One More Last Chance** Ray Stevens
73/99 Clay Walker	74/92 **One Good Love** Nitty Gritty Dirt Band	12/69 **One More Mile** Dave Dudley
50/00 Clay Walker	57/94 **One Good Man** Michelle Wright	48/70 **One More Mountain To Climb** Freddie Hart
Once In A Lifetime Thing	71/80 **One Good Reason** Melissa Lewis	7/91 **One More Payment** Clint Black
5/77 John Wesley Ryles	4/89 **One Good Well** Don Williams	42/84 **One More Shot** Johnny Lee
86/90 Sammy Sadler	17/61 **One Grain Of Sand** Eddy Arnold	2/60 **One More Time** Ray Price
85/86 **Once In A Very Blue Moon** Nanci Griffith	**One Has My Name (The Other Has My Heart)**	28/71 **One More Time** Ferlin Husky
53/94 **Once In A While** Billy Dean	1/48 Jimmy Wakely	44/72 **One More Time** Jo Anna Neel
Once More	11/48 Eddie Dean	65/74 **One More Time** Skeeter Davis
8/58 Roy Acuff	8/49 Bob Eberly	80/78 **One More Time** Sandra Kaye
13/58 Osborne Brothers & Red Allen	3/69 Jerry Lee Lewis	31/76 **One More Time (Karneval)** Crystal Gayle
66/69 Leona Williams	69/98 **One Heart At A Time** Various Artists	28/76 **(One More Year Of) Daddy's Little Girl** Ray Sawyer
2/70 **Once More With Feeling** Jerry Lee Lewis	43/85 **One Hell Of A Heartache** Gene Watson	**One Night**
42/70 **Once More With Feeling** Willie Nelson	**One Hell Of A Woman ..see: (You Better Be)**	24/58 Elvis Presley
3/93 **Once Upon A Lifetime** Alabama	7/99 **One Honest Heart** Reba McEntire	57/72 Jeannie C. Riley
80/86 **Once Upon A Time** Bobby Blue	6/91 **One Hundred And Two** Judds	51/76 Roy Head
Once You Get The Feel Of It	14/71 **One Hundred Children** Tom T. Hall	61/98 **One Night** JC Jones
42/83 Con Hunley	1/86 **100% Chance Of Rain** Gary Morris	**One Night A Day**
79/88 Marshall Tucker Band	3/86 **One I Loved Back Then (The Corvette Song)** George Jones	74/93 Garth Brooks
75/97 **Once You Learn** Noel Haggard	58/75 **One I Sing My Love Songs To** Tommy Cash	7/94 Garth Brooks
80/81 **Once You Were Mine** Dottie West		1/97 **One Night At A Time** George Strait
3/74 **Once You've Had The Best** George Jones		10/81 **One-Night Fever** Mel Tillis
		85/80 **One Night Honeymoon** Troy Seals
		80/80 **One Night Led To Two** Paul Evans
		39/71 **One Night Of Love** Johnny Duncan

One Solitary Life – Gene Autry (CD in Kit #19)

35/70 **One Night Stand** Susan Raye	4/88 **One True Love** O'Kanes	36/68 **Only Way Out (Is To Walk Over Me)** Charlie Louvin
66/97 **One Night Stand** Caryl Mack Parker	18/97 **One, Two, I Love You** Clay Walker	32/81 **Only When I Laugh** Brenda Lee
89/74 **One Night Stand** Rick Nelson	88/75 **One, Two, Three (Never Gonna Fall In Love Again)** Jim Glaser	4/87 **Only When I Love** Holly Dunn
47/77 **One Night Stands** Hank Williams, Jr.	20/00 **One Voice** Billy Gilman	**Only You**
82/82 **One Night Stanley** Jerry Abbott	20/61 **One Way Street** Bob Gallion	68/69 Norro Wilson
71/88 **One Nite Stan** Ethel & The Shameless Hussies	1/96 **One Way Ticket (Because I Can)** LeAnn Rimes	34/78 Freddie Hart
6/77 **One Of A Kind** Tammy Wynette	12/58 **One Week Later** Webb Pierce & Kitty Wells	13/82 Reba McEntire
13/80 **One Of A Kind** Moe Bandy		36/86 Statler Brothers
1/83 **One Of A Kind Pair Of Fools** Barbara Mandrell	32/72 **One Woman's Trash (Another Woman's Treasure)** Bobbie Roy	51/96 Travis Tritt
28/60 **One Of Her Fools** Paul Davis	61/83 **1 Yr 2 Mo 11 Days** Wayne Carson	1/65 **Only You (Can Break My Heart)** Buck Owens
67/87 **One Of The Boys** Cheryl Handy	38/72 **One You Say Good Mornin' To** Jimmy Dean	9/56 **Only You, Only You** Charlie Walker
69/70 **One Of The Fortunate Few** Hank Thompson	13/60 **One You Slip Around With** Jan Howard	85/78 **Ooh Baby Baby** Linda Ronstadt
3/76 **One Of These Days** Emmylou Harris	1/72 **One's On The Way** Loretta Lynn	70/97 **Open Arms** Collin Raye
8/64 **One Of These Days** Marty Robbins	2/72 **Oney** Johnny Cash	68/89 **Open For Suggestions** Perry LaPointe
36/68 **One Of These Days** Tompall/Glaser Brothers	47/85 **Only A Dream Away** Mason Dixon	13/62 **Open Pit Mine** George Jones
74/93 **One Of These Days** Matthews, Wright & King	61/68 **Only A Fool** Ned Miller	45/71 **Open Up The Book (And Take A Look)** Ferlin Husky
2/98 **One Of These Days** Tim McGraw	2/84 **Only A Lonely Heart Knows** Barbara Mandrell	98/77 **Open Up Your Door** Eddie Rivers
64/95 **One Of Those Nights** Lisa Brokop	24/71 **Only A Woman Like You** Nat Stuckey	1/66 **Open Up Your Heart** Buck Owens
14/98 **One Of Those Nights Tonight** Lorrie Morgan	**Only Daddy That'll Walk The Line**	14/73 **Open Up Your Heart** Roger Miller
6/91 **One Of Those Things** Pam Tillis	2/68 Waylon Jennings	78/82 **Operator** Tennessee Express
73/99 **One Of You** George Strait	73/68 Jim Alley	9/82 **Operator, Long Distance Please** Barbara Mandrell
2/66 **One On The Right Is On The Left** Johnny Cash	60/91 Kentucky Headhunters	**Operator, Operator**
4/85 **One Owner Heart** T.G. Sheppard	59/79 **Only Diamonds Are Forever** Zella Lehr	65/83 Larry Willoughby
1/76 **One Piece At A Time** Johnny Cash	13/63 **Only Girl I Can't Forget** Del Reeves	9/85 Eddy Raven
51/92 **One Precious Love** Prairie Oyster	3/91 **Only Here For A Little While** Billy Dean	10/61 **Optimistic** Skeeter Davis
1/87 **One Promise Too Late** Reba McEntire	12/83 **Only If There Is Another You** Moe Bandy	**Orange Blossom Special**
26/78 **One Run For The Roses** Narvel Felts	1/01 **Only In America** Brooks & Dunn	3/65 Johnny Cash
51/91 **One Shot At A Time** Clinton Gregory	5/85 **Only In My Mind** Reba McEntire	26/73 Charlie McCoy
8/78 **One Sided Conversation** Gene Watson	52/98 **Only Lonely Me** Rick Trevino	63/74 Johnny Darrell
52/84 **One Sided Love Affair** Mike Campbell	3/93 **Only Love** Wynonna	4/53 **Orchids Mean Goodbye** Carl Smith
16/98 **One Small Miracle** Bryan White	**Only Love Can Break A Heart**	3/99 **Ordinary Life** Chad Brock
41/97 **One Solitary Tear** Sherrié Austin	2/72 Sonny James	24/99 **Ordinary Love** Shane Minor
9/70 **One Song Away** Tommy Cash	7/79 Kenny Dale	26/77 **Ordinary Man** Dale McBride
48/75 **One Step** Bobby Harden	11/88 **Only Love Can Save Me Now** Crystal Gayle	29/68 **Ordinary Miracle** Bobby Lewis
14/61 **One Step Ahead Of My Past** Hank Locklin	42/85 **Only Love Will Make It Right** Nicolette Larson	35/98 **Ordinary People** Clay Walker
15/57 **One Step At A Time** Brenda Lee	49/66 **Only Me And My Hairdresser Know** Kitty Wells	52/74 **Orleans Parish Prison** Johnny Cash
90/83 **One Step Closer** Cannons	5/96 **Only On Days That End In "Y"** Clay Walker	48/01 **Osama-Yo' Mama** Ray Stevens
2/88 **One Step Forward** Desert Rose Band	80/86 **Only One** James Taylor	19/61 **Other Cheek** Kitty Wells
63/90 **One Step Over The Line** Nitty Gritty Dirt Band/ Rosanne Cash/ John Hiatt	1/78 **Only One Love In My Life** Ronnie Milsap	30/88 **Other Guy** David Slater
8/84 **One Takes The Blame** Statler Brothers	1/82 **Only One You** T.G. Sheppard	71/78 **Other Side Of Jeannie** Chuck Pollard
90/82 **One Tear (At A Time)** Noel	55/76 **Only Sixteen** Dr. Hook	**Other Side Of The Hill ..see: (Lover Of The)**
37/82 **One That Got Away** Mel Tillis	81/78 **Only The Best** George Hamilton IV	72/78 **Other Side Of The Morning** Barbara Fairchild
17/79 **One Thing My Lady Never Puts Into Words** Mel Street	1/69 **Only The Lonely** Sonny James	41/98 **Other Side Of This Kiss** Mindy McCready
43/92 **One Time Around** Michelle Wright	74/83 **Only The Names Have Been Changed** Penny DeHaven	**Other Woman**
55/88 **One Time One Night** Los Lobos	87/77 **Only The Shadows Know** Vernon Oxford	2/65 Ray Price
97/88 **One Time Thing** Ramsey Kearney	71/89 **Only The Strong Survive** Darrell Holt	74/70 Ray Pennington
54/72 **One Tin Soldier** Skeeter Davis	4/92 **Only The Wind** Billy Dean	13/63 **Other Woman** Loretta Lynn
82/81 **One Too Many Memories** Ray Pillow	54/89 **Only Thing Bluer Than His Eyes** Joni Harms	54/90 **Oughta Be A Law** Lee Roy Parnell
	58/67 **Only Thing I Want** Cal Smith	56/77 **Our Baby's Gone** Herb Pedersen
		(Our Endless Love) ..see: Gone
		58/68 **Our Golden Wedding Day** Johnny And Jonie Mosby
		24/65 **Our Hearts Are Holding Hands** Ernest Tubb & Loretta Lynn
		6/52 **Our Honeymoon** Carl Smith
		18/69 **Our House Is Not A Home** Lynn Anderson
		8/50 **Our Lady Of Fatima** Red Foley
		64/89 **Our Little Corner** Butch Baker
		44/75 **Our Love** Roger Miller

77/87 Our Love Is Like The South *A.J. Masters*	87/76 Ozark Mountain Lullaby *Susan Raye*	Part Of Me That Needs You Most
1/83 Our Love Is On The Faultline *Crystal Gayle*		79/79 Miki Mori
43/92 Our Love Was Meant To Be *Boy Howdy*		61/85 B.J. Thomas
21/62 Our Mansion Is A Prison Now *Kitty Wells*	# P	35/72 Part Of Your Life *Charlie Rich*
45/75 Our Marriage Was A Failure *Johnny Russell*	70/94 PMS Blues *Dolly Parton*	68/69 Parting (Is Such Sweet Sorrow) *Wilma Burgess*
91/77 Our Old Mansion *Buck Owens*	86/85 P.S. *Noel*	48/69 Partly Bill *LaWanda Lindsey*
(Our Own) Jole Blon ..see: Jole Blon	8/84 P.S. I Love You *Tom T. Hall*	38/81 Partner Nobody Chose *Guy Clark*
42/65 Our Ship Of Love *Carl Butler & Pearl*	3/62 P.T. 109 *Jimmy Dean*	5/59 Partners *Jim Reeves*
27/67 Our Side *Van Trevor*	68/93 Pack Your Lies And Go *Celinda Pink*	24/87 Partners After All *Willie Nelson*
33/64 Our Things *Margie Bowes*	Padre	6/86 Partners, Brothers And Friends *Nitty Gritty Dirt Band*
56/82 Our Wedding Band *Louise Mandrell & R.C. Bannon*	5/71 Marty Robbins	53/95 Party All Night *Jeff Foxworthy with Little Texas*
21/86 Out Among The Stars *Merle Haggard*	92/75 Judy Lynn	6/95 Party Crowd *David Lee Murphy*
9/54 Out Behind The Barn *"Little" Jimmy Dickens*	34/86 Pages Of My Mind *Ray Charles*	31/72 Party Dolls And Wine *Red Stegall*
11/86 Out Goin' Cattin' *Sawyer Brown with "Cat" Joe Bonsall*	77/82 Pain In My Past *Rovers*	50/98 Party On *Neal McCoy*
54/00 Out Here In The Water *Rebecca Lynn Howard*	49/72 Paint Me A Rainbow *Wynn Stewart*	69/88 Party People *Butch Baker*
81/88 Out Of Beer *Johnny Paycheck*	13/89 Paint The Town And Hang The Moon Tonight *J. C. Crowley*	24/67 Party Pickin' *George Jones & Melba Montgomery*
25/60 Out Of Control *George Jones*	49/85 Paint The Town Blue *Robin Lee & Lobo*	1/81 Party Time *T.G. Sheppard*
4/75 Out Of Hand *Gary Stewart*	52/68 Painted Girls And Wine *Ed Bruce*	24/67 Party's Over *Willie Nelson*
2/98 Out Of My Bones *Randy Travis*	78/77 Painted Lady *Chuck Woolery*	78/83 Party's Over (Everybody's Gone) *Sam Neely*
1/78 Out Of My Head And Back In My Bed *Loretta Lynn*	8/45 Pair Of Broken Hearts *Spade Cooley*	3/90 Pass It On Down *Alabama*
50/77 Out Of My Mind *Cates*	19/80 Pair Of Old Sneakers *George Jones & Tammy Wynette*	Pass Me By (If You're Only Passing Through)
10/88 Out Of Sight And On My Mind *Billy Joe Royal*	81/80 Palimony *Leon Rausch*	9/73 Johnny Rodriguez
71/85 Out Of Sight Out Of Mind *Narvel Felts*	33/76 Paloma Blanca *George Baker Selection*	22/80 Janie Fricke
34/80 Out Of Your Mind *Joe Sun*	88/76 Pamela Brown *Jud Strunk*	15/65 Pass The Booze *Ernest Tubb*
2/89 Out Of Your Shoes *Lorrie Morgan*	9/48 Pan American *Hawkshaw Hawkins*	28/77 Passing Thing *Ray Griff*
46/80 Out Run The Sun *Jim Chesnut*	7/50 Pan American Boogie *Delmore Brothers*	67/69 Passin' Through *Ray Corbin*
32/65 Out Where The Ocean Meets The Sky *Hugh X. Lewis*	1/83 Pancho And Lefty *Willie Nelson & Merle Haggard*	37/64 Passing Through *David Houston*
13/96 Out With A Bang *David Lee Murphy*	6/49 Panhandle Rag *Leon McAuliffe*	23/61 Passing Zone Blues *Coleman Wilson*
87/87 Out With The Boys *Rhonda Manning*	64/67 Papa *Bill Anderson*	4/93 Passionate Kisses *Mary-Chapin Carpenter*
91/77 Out With The Boys *Barry Grant*	24/98 Papa Bear *Keith Harling*	4/64 Password *Kitty Wells*
9/92 Outbound Plane *Suzy Bogguss*	62/69 Papa Joe's Thing *Papa Joe's Music Box*	2/92 Past The Point Of Rescue *Hal Ketchum*
27/79 Outlaw's Prayer *Johnny Paycheck*	3/92 Papa Loved Mama *Garth Brooks*	Patches
81/79 Outlaws And Lone Star Beer *C.W. McCall*	16/71 Papa Was A Good Man *Johnny Cash*	26/70 Ray Griff
91/89 Outside Chance *Larry Dean*	30/75 Paper Lovin' *Margo Smith*	30/81 Jerry Reed
18/83 Outside Lookin' In *Bandana*	8/67 Paper Mansions *Dottie West*	46/69 Pathway Of My Life *Hank Thompson*
40/94 Outskirts Of Town *Sawyer Brown*	1/73 Paper Roses *Marie Osmond*	18/58 Patricia *Perez Prado*
10/80 Over *Leon Everette*	3/77 Paper Rosie *Gene Watson*	13/77 Pay Phone *Bob Luman*
62/98 Over My Shoulder *John Berry*	85/88 Paper Thin Walls *David Wills*	6/53 Paying For That Back Street Affair *Kitty Wells*
10/80 Over The Rainbow *Jerry Lee Lewis*	26/76 Paradise *Lynn Anderson*	Peace In The Valley ..see: (There'll Be)
69/82 Over Thirty (Not Over The Hill) *Conway Twitty*	26/96 Paradise *John Anderson*	23/81 Peace Of Mind *Eddy Raven*
15/49 Over Three Hills *Ernie Benedict*	46/00 Paradise *Craig Morgan*	74/99 Peace Of Mind *George Strait*
15/83 Over You *Lane Brody*	80/81 Paradise *Southern Ashe*	8/97 Peace Train *Dolly Parton*
59/88 Overdue *Canyon*	54/82 Paradise Knife And Gun Club *Roy Clark*	73/93 Peaceful Easy Feeling *Little Texas*
10/58 Overnight *Jim Reeves*	1/83 Paradise Tonight *Charly McClain & Mickey Gilley*	21/77 Peanut Butter *Dickey Lee*
70/92 Overnight Male *George Strait*	67/68 Parchman Farm Blues *Claude King*	10/76 Peanuts And Diamonds *Bill Anderson*
7/76 Overnight Sensation *Mickey Gilley*	66/85 Pardon Me, But This Heart's Taken *Terry Gregory*	8/63 Pearl Pearl Pearl *Flatt & Scruggs*
8/90 Overnight Success *George Strait*	64/84 Pardon Me (Haven't We Loved Somewhere Before) *Becky Hobbs*	Pecos Bill ..see: (There'll Never Be Another)
5/84 Ozark Mountain Jubilee *Oak Ridge Boys*	63/81 Pardon My French *Bobby G. Rice*	10/80 Pecos Promenade *Tanya Tucker*
	49/71 Part Of America Died *Eddy Arnold*	8/64 Peel Me A Nanner *Roy Drusky*
		4/48 Peepin' Thru The Keyhole (Watching Jole Blon) *Cliffie Stone*
		36/64 Pen And Paper *Jerry Lee Lewis*
		44/71 Pencil Marks On The Wall *Henson Cargill*
		12/49 Pennies For Papa *Jimmie Dickens*
		8/75 Penny *Joe Stampley*

493

Perfect Country Song – See You Never Even Called Me By My Name — ↓

7/78	Penny Arcade Cristy Lane		8/60	Picture, The Roy Godfrey		35/82	Play Something We Could Love To Diane Pfeifer
5/55	Penny Candy Jim Reeves		28/91	Picture Me Davis Daniel		35/76	Play The Saddest Song On The Juke Box Carmol Taylor
85/89	Penny For Your Thoughts Tonight Virginia David Houston			Picture Of Me (Without You)		74/82	Play This Old Working Day Away Dean Dillon
17/01	People Like Us Aaron Tippin		5/72	George Jones			
70/86	People's Court Ray Stevens		9/91	Lorrie Morgan		11/79	Play Together Again Again Buck Owens/Emmylou Harris
57/82	Pepsi Man Bobby Mackey		63/91	Picture Of You Great Plains			
	Perfect		52/96	Picture Perfect Sky Kings		93/74	Play With Me Penny DeHaven
85/89	Fairground Attraction		27/66	Picture That's New George Morgan		18/70	Playin' Around With Love Barbara Mandrell
23/90	Baillie & the Boys		13/71	Pictures Statler Brothers			
23/81	Perfect Fool Debby Boone		35/84	Pictures Atlanta		22/79	Playin' Hard To Get Janie Fricke
1/98	Perfect Love Trisha Yearwood		17/75	Pictures On Paper Jeris Ross		8/57	Playing For Keeps Elvis Presley
75/78	Perfect Love Song Durwood Haddock			Piece Of My Heart		62/85	Playing For Keeps Holly Dunn
			68/85	Sandy Croft		98/88	Playing With Matches Tim LeBeau
24/72	Perfect Match David Houston & Barbara Mandrell		1/94	Faith Hill			
16/70	Perfect Mountain Don Gibson		81/84	Piece Of My Heart John Hartford		97/77	Playing With The Baby's Mama Bobby Wright
69/00	Perfect Night Billy Hoffman		33/75	Pieces Of My Life Elvis Presley		7/97	Please Kinleys
64/82	Perfect Picture (To Fit My Frame Of Mind) Gary Wolf		29/88	Pilgrims On The Way (Matthew's Song) Michael Martin Murphey		22/01	Please Pam Tillis
			5/75	Pill, The Loretta Lynn		34/78	Please Narvel Felts
13/73	Perfect Stranger Freddy Weller		47/74	Pillow, The Johnny Duncan		76/79	Please Be Gentle Amy
18/86	Perfect Stranger Southern Pacific		17/64	Pillow That Whispers Carl Smith		7/86	Please Be Love Mark Gray
24/80	Perfect Strangers John Wesley Ryles		13/60	Pinball Machine Lonnie Irving		31/64	Please Be My Love George Jones & Melba Montgomery
			65/71	Pine Grove Compton Brothers			
52/88	Perfect Strangers Anne Murray (With Doug Mallory)		15/67	Piney Wood Hills Bobby Bare		46/70	Please Be My New Love Jeannie Seely
			92/86	Pink Cadillac Kevin Pearce			
50/00	Perfect World Sawyer Brown		17/58	Pink Pedal Pushers Carl Perkins		50/86	Please Bypass This Heart Jimmy Buffett
29/75	Personality Price Mitchell		10/84	Pins And Needles Whites			
10/83	Personally Ronnie McDowell		52/76	Pins And Needles (In My Heart) Darrell McCall			Please Come Home For Christmas
	Peter Cottontail					70/96	Gary Allan
3/50	Gene Autry		70/91	Piper Came Today Willie Nelson		71/96	Lee Roy Parnell
6/50	Mervin Shiner			Pistol Packin' Mama		75/75	Please Come To Nashville Ronnie Dove
7/50	Jimmy Wakely		1/44	Bing Crosby & Andrews Sisters			
7/50	Johnnie Lee Wills		1/44	Al Dexter		69/73	Please, Daddy John Denver
14/64	Petticoat Junction Flatt & Scruggs		6/78	Pittsburgh Stealers Kendalls		11/57	Please Don't Blame Me Marty Robbins
			6/71	Pitty, Pitty, Patter Susan Raye			
	Phantom 309		62/85	Pity Party Bill Anderson		10/69	Please Don't Go Eddy Arnold
9/67	Red Sovine		8/54	Place For Girls Like You Faron Young		60/88	Please Don't Leave Me Now Southern Reign
47/76	Red Sovine						
9/71	Philadelphia Fillies Del Reeves		62/83	Place I've Never Been Marshall Tucker Band			Please Don't Let Me Love You
73/79	Philodendron Mundo Earwood					4/49	George Morgan
60/68	Phoenix Flash Stan Hitchcock		60/82	Place In The Sun Sonny James		9/55	Hank Williams
36/68	Phone Call To Mama Joyce Paul		1/85	Place To Fall Apart Merle Haggard (with Janie Fricke)		14/49	Please Don't Pass Me By Floyd Tillman
28/96	Phones Are Ringin' All Over Town Martina McBride		100/77	Place Where Love Has Been Arleen Harden		17/78	Please Don't Play A Love Song Marty Robbins
89/89	Photographic Memory Billy Mata		5/97	Places I've Never Been Mark Wills			
74/79	Piano Picker George Fischoff					1/74	Please Don't Stop Loving Me Porter Wagoner & Dolly Parton
71/68	Pick A Little Happy Song Bob Gallion		9/87	Plain Brown Wrapper Gary Morris			
			89/74	Plain Vanilla Jeannie C. Riley		86/86	Please Don't Talk About Me When I'm Gone Ray Price
	Pick Me Up On Your Way Down		30/89	Planet Texas Kenny Rogers			
2/58	Charlie Walker		9/68	Plastic Saddle Nat Stuckey			Please Don't Tell Me How The Story Ends
46/70	Carl Smith		23/73	Plastic Trains, Paper Planes Susan Raye			
35/76	Bobby G. Rice					8/71	Bobby Bare
13/64	Pick Of The Week Roy Drusky		89/82	Play Another Gettin' Drunk And Take Somebody Home Song Roy Head		1/74	Ronnie Milsap
	Pick The Wildwood Flower						Please Help Me, I'm Falling
34/74	Johnny Cash/Mother Maybelle Carter		17/80	Play Another Slow Song Johnny Duncan		1/60	Hank Locklin
5/79	Gene Watson					68/70	Hank Locklin & Danny Davis
96/77	Pick Up The Pieces Con Hunley			Play Born To Lose Again ..see: (After Sweet Memories)		12/78	Janie Fricke
89/80	Pick Up The Pieces Joanne Bobby Hood					78/74	Please Help Me Say No Mary Kay James
			1/77	Play, Guitar Play Conway Twitty			
90/80	Pickin' Up Love Ray Frushay		24/79	Play Her Back To Yesterday Mel McDaniel		10/69	Please Let Her Prove (My Love For You) Dave Dudley
3/81	Pickin' Up Strangers Johnny Lee						
61/67	Pickin' Up The Mail Compton Brothers		24/79	Play Me A Memory Zella Lehr		11/61	Please Mr. Kennedy Jim Nesbitt
				Play Me No Sad Songs		5/75	Please Mr. Please Olivia Newton-John
27/70	Pickin' Wild Mountain Berries LaWanda Lindsey & Kenny Vernon		34/76	Rex Allen, Jr.			
			82/79	Earl Scruggs Revue		9/58	Please Pass The Biscuits Gene Sullivan
42/77	Picking Up The Pieces Of My Life Mac Davis		43/82	Play Me Or Trade Me Mel Tillis & Nancy Sinatra			
1/94	Pickup Man Joe Diffie					92/80	Please Play More Kenny Rogers Steven Lee Cook
62/89	Pickup Truck Song Jerry Jeff Walker		25/92	Play, Ruby, Play Clinton Gregory			

6/88	**Please, Please Baby** *Dwight Yoakam*		**Poor Poor Pitiful Me**	85/78	**Price Of Borrowed Love Is Just To High** *Charlotte Hurt*
	Please Remember Me	46/78	Linda Ronstadt	60/97	**Price To Pay** *Randy Travis*
69/95	Rodney Crowell	5/96	Terri Clark		**Pride**
1/99	Tim McGraw	44/65	**Poor Red Georgia Dirt** *Stonewall Jackson*	5/62	Ray Price
54/79	**Please Sing Satin Sheets For Me** *Jeanne Pruett*		**Poor Side Of Town**	47/72	Jeannie Seely
43/83	**Please Surrender** *David Frizzell & Shelly West*	54/77	Bobby Wayne Loftis	12/81	Janie Fricke
		12/83	Joe Stampley	18/62	**Pride Goes Before A Fall** *Jim Reeves*
40/69	**Please Take Me Back** *Jim Glaser*	14/75	**Poor Sweet Baby** *Jean Shepard*	46/86	**Pride Is Back** *Kenny Rogers with Nickie Ryder*
	Please Talk To My Heart	82/76	**Poor Wilted Rose** *Ann J. Morton*		**(Pride Of South Central High) ..see: Igmoo**
14/63	Country Johnny Mathis		**Pop A Top**		
7/64	Ray Price	3/67	Jim Ed Brown	3/72	**Pride's Not Hard To Swallow** *Hank Williams, Jr.*
82/80	Freddy Fender	6/99	Alan Jackson	66/73	**Printers Alley Stars** *Tennessee Ernie Ford*
	Please Tell Him [Her] That I Said Hello	26/71	**Portrait Of My Woman** *Eddy Arnold*	23/60	**Prison Song** *Curly Putman*
50/76	Sue Richards	37/97	**Postmarked Birmingham** *BlackHawk*	10/50	**Prison Without Walls** *Eddy Arnold*
63/84	Margo Smith		**Potato ..see: 'Tater**	3/81	**Prisoner Of Hope** *Johnny Lee*
70/89	Bobby Vinton	20/83	**Potential New Boyfriend** *Dolly Parton*	6/84	**Prisoner Of The Highway** *Ronnie Milsap*
73/79	**Pleasin' My Woman** *Billy Parker*	65/75	**Pour It All On Me** *Del Reeves*	14/76	**Prisoner's Song** *Sonny James*
71/83	**Pleasure Island** *David Frizzell & Shelly West*	12/01	**Pour Me** *Trick Pony*	30/66	**Prissy** *Chet Atkins*
32/81	**Pleasure's All Mine** *Dave & Sugar*	59/98	**Pour Me A Vacation** *Great Divide*	33/67	**Private, The** *Del Reeves*
13/77	**Pleasure's Been All Mine** *Freddie Hart*	5/80	**Pour Me Another Tequila** *Eddie Rabbitt*	81/86	**Private Clown** *Steve Ricks*
	Pledging My Love	72/87	**Power Of A Woman** *Perry LaPointe*	72/97	**Private Conversation** *Lyle Lovett*
49/71	Kitty Wells		**Power Of Love**	21/66	**Private Wilson White** *Marty Robbins*
37/75	Billy Thunderkloud	9/84	Charley Pride		
F/77	Elvis Presley	51/94	Lee Roy Parnell	12/57	**Prize Possession** *Ferlin Husky*
9/84	Emmylou Harris	41/92	**Power Of Love** *Matthews, Wright & King*	17/59	**Problems** *Everly Brothers*
14/57	**Plenty Of Everything But You** *Ira & Charley Louvin*	8/78	**Power Of Positive Drinkin'** *Mickey Gilley*	4/44	**Prodigal Son** *Roy Acuff*
9/61	**Po' Folks** *Bill Anderson*	48/68	**Power Of Your Sweet Love** *Claude King*	32/92	**Professional Fool** *Michael White*
7/91	**Pocket Full Of Gold** *Vince Gill*	72/92	**Power Tools** *Ray Stevens*		**Promised Land**
22/94	**Pocket Of A Clown** *Dwight Yoakam*	43/99	**Power Windows** *John Berry*	3/71	Freddy Weller
3/91	**Point Of Light** *Randy Travis*	6/99	**Powerful Thing** *Trisha Yearwood*	F/75	Elvis Presley
25/60	**Poison In Your Hand** *Connie Hall*	57/73	**Praise The Lord And Pass The Soup** *Johnny Cash/Carter Family/Oak Ridge Boys*	61/97	**Promised Land** *Joe Diffie*
	Poison Love			17/89	**Promises** *Randy Travis*
4/51	Johnnie & Jack			82/78	**Promises** *Eric Clapton*
27/78	Gail Davies	83/82	**Praise The Lord And Send Me The Money** *Bobby Bare*	15/67	**Promises And Hearts (Were Made To Break)** *Stonewall Jackson*
72/70	**Poison Red Berries** *Glenn Barber*	62/74	**Prayer From A Mobile Home** *Del Reeves*	4/68	**Promises, Promises** *Lynn Anderson*
87/89	**Poison Sugar** *Melissa Kay*	3/00	**Prayin' For Daylight** *Rascal Flatts*	78/89	**Promises, Promises** *Lori Yates*
28/97	**Politics, Religion And Her** *Sammy Kershaw*	49/90	**Praying For Rain** *Kevin Welch*	58/66	**Proof Is In The Kissing** *Charlie Louvin*
12/61	**Polka On A Banjo** *Flatt & Scruggs*	F/70	**Preacher And The Bear** *Jerry Reed*	3/93	**Prop Me Up Beside The Jukebox (If I Die)** *Joe Diffie*
26/87	**Ponies** *Michael Johnson*	45/79	**Preacher Berry** *Donna Fargo*	47/78	**Proud Lady** *Bob Luman*
1/70	**Pool Shark** *Dave Dudley*	19/82	**Preaching Up A Storm** *Mel McDaniel*		**Proud Mary**
30/83	**Poor Boy** *Razzy Bailey*	87/89	**Precious Jewel** *Charlie Louvin - Roy Acuff*	22/69	Anthony Armstrong Jones
39/66	**Poor Boy Blues** *Bob Luman*			56/73	Brush Arbor
	Poor Folks ..see: Po' Folks	19/83	**Precious Love** *Kendalls*	22/75	**Proud Of You Baby** *Bob Luman*
61/71	**Poor Folks Stick Together** *Stoney Edwards*	44/73	**Precious Memories Follow Me** *Josie Brown*	91/80	**Prove It To You One More Time Again** *Kris Kristofferson*
51/83	**Poor Girl** *Rick & Janis Carnes*	8/90	**Precious Thing** *Steve Wariner*	74/82	**Pull My String** *Rich Landers*
3/58	**Poor Little Fool** *Ricky Nelson*	35/80	**Pregnant Again** *Loretta Lynn*	18/70	**Pull My String And Wind Me Up** *Carl Smith*
2/56	**Poor Man's Riches** *Benny Barnes*	6/72	**Pretend I Never Happened** *Waylon Jennings*	28/68	**Punish Me Tomorrow** *Carl Butler & Pearl*
55/93	**Poor Man's Rose** *Stacy Dean Campbell*	71/82	**Pretending Fool** *Michael Ballew*	78/78	**Puppet On A String** *Elvis Presley*
	Poor Man's Roses (Or A Rich Man's Gold)	26/67	**Pretty Girl, Pretty Clothes, Pretty Sad** *Kenny Price*	71/95	**Pure Bred Redneck** *Cooter Brown*
14/57	Patsy Cline	10/85	**Pretty Lady** *Keith Stegall*	1/74	**Pure Love** *Ronnie Milsap*
66/81	Patti Page	2/97	**Pretty Little Adriana** *Vince Gill*	28/66	**Pursuing Happiness** *Norma Jean*
67/00	**Poor Man's Son** *Charlie Robison*	89/80	**Pretty Poison** *Barry Grant*	11/65	**Pushed In A Corner** *Ernest Ashworth*
24/75	**Poor Man's Woman** *Jeanne Pruett*	12/54	**Pretty Words** *Marty Robbins*		**Put A Little Holiday In Your Heart**
43/98	**Poor Me** *Joe Diffie*	35/69	**Price I Pay To Stay** *Jeannie C. Riley*	51/96	LeAnn Rimes
10/59	**Poor Old Heartsick Me** *Margie Bowes*			71/97	LeAnn Rimes
70/69	**Poor Old Ugly Gladys Jones** *Don Bowman*				
85/77	**Poor People of Paris** *Maury Finney*				

495

30/70	Put A Little Love In Your Heart Susan Raye	7/93	Queen Of My Double Wide Trailer Sammy Kershaw	75/74	Rainbow In My Hand Doyle Holly
23/76	Put A Little Lovin' On Me Bobby Bare	5/83	Queen Of My Heart Hank Williams, Jr.	8/49	Rainbow In My Heart George Morgan
60/89	Put A Quarter In The Jukebox Buck Owens	77/76	Queen Of New Orleans Earl Conley	99/77	Rainbow In Your Eyes Jan & Malcolm
21/75	Put Another Log On The Fire Tompall	83/75	Queen Of Temptation Brian Collins	77/89	Rainbow Of Our Own Shane Barmby
	Put Another Notch In Your Belt	5/65	Queen Of The House Jody Miller	4/81	Rainbow Stew Merle Haggard
89/75	Kenny Starr		Queen Of The Silver Dollar	39/83	Rainbows And Butterflies Billy Swan
76/84	Susan Raye	29/73	Doyle Holly	90/77	Rainbows And Horseshoes R.C. Bannon
	Put It Off Until Tomorrow	25/76	Dave & Sugar		
6/66	Bill Phillips	47/76	Queen Of The Starlight Ballroom David Wills	20/66	Rainbows And Roses Roy Drusky
9/80	Kendalls	92/79	Quicksand Bill Wence	17/68	Rainbows Are Back In Style Slim Whitman
77/78	Put It On Me Louise Mandrell	3/50	Quicksilver Elton Britt & Rosalie Allen	33/74	Raindrops Narvel Felts
43/76	Put Me Back Into Your World Eddy Arnold	64/68	Quiet Kind Mac Curtis	55/83	Rainin' Down In Nashville Tom Carlile
30/73	Put Me Down Softly Dickey Lee	36/87	Quietly Crazy Ed Bruce	59/81	Rainin' In My Eyes Miki Mori
99/78	Put Me Out Of My Memory Johnny Bush	26/90	Quit While I'm Behind McCarters	77/89	Rainin', Rainin', Rainin' Gary Stewart
28/87	Put Me Out Of My Misery Tom Wopat	3/71	Quits Bill Anderson		Rainin' In My Heart
28/90	Put Some Drive In Your Country Travis Tritt	26/77	Quits Gary Stewart	3/71	Hank Williams, Jr.
		21/00	Quittin' Kind Joe Diffie	35/89	Jo-el Sonnier
55/88	Put Us Together Again Goldens	7/90	Quittin' Time Mary-Chapin Carpenter		Raining In My Heart
	Put You Back On The Rack ..see: (I'm Gonna)	55/86	Quittin' Time Con Hunley	14/69	Ray Price
25/64	Put Your Arms Around Her Norma Jean			63/78	Leo Sayer
9/79	Put Your Clothes Back On Joe Stampley		**R**	4/77	Rains Came Freddy Fender
1/82	Put Your Dreams Away Mickey Gilley		Race Is On	47/75	Rainy Day People Gordon Lightfoot
11/00	Put Your Hand In Mine Tracy Byrd	3/64	George Jones	2/75	Rainy Day Woman Waylon Jennings
	Put Your Hand In The Hand	5/89	Sawyer Brown	83/79	Rainy Days And Rainbows Paul Schmucker
61/71	Beth Moore	85/87	Rachel's Room Bobby G. Rice	21/80	Rainy Days And Stormy Nights Billie Jo Spears
67/71	Anne Murray	39/88	Radio, The Vince Gill	13/74	Rainy Night In Georgia Hank Williams, Jr.
48/75	Put Your Head On My Shoulder Sunday Sharpe	62/94	Radio Active Bryan Austin	15/80	Raisin' Cane In Texas Gene Watson
34/98	Put Your Heart Into It Sherrié Austin	1/85	Radio Heart Charly McClain	3/78	Rake And Ramblin' Man Don Williams
44/69	Put Your Lovin' Where Your Mouth Is Peggy Little	19/84	Radio Land Michael Martin Murphey	42/80	Rambler Gambler Linda Ronstadt
11/91	Put Yourself In My Place Pam Tillis	62/89	Radio Lover George Jones	2/77	Ramblin' Fever Merle Haggard
4/90	Put Yourself In My Shoes Clint Black	51/86	Radio Romance Tommy Roe	29/67	Ramblin' Man Ray Pennington
	Puttin' In Overtime At Home	53/90	Radio Romance Canyon		Ramblin' Man
74/75	Del Reeves	57/88	Radio Song Ric Steel	63/73	Gary Stewart
8/78	Charlie Rich		Rag Mop	79/73	Jimmy Payne
33/90	Puttin' The Dark Back Into The Night Sawyer Brown	2/50	Johnnie Lee Wills	94/79	Ramblin' Music Man Charlie McCoy
68/82	Pyramid Of Cans Mundo Earwood	90/78	Drifting Cowboys		Ramblin' Rose
85/80	Pyramid Song J.C. Cunningham	19/78	Ragamuffin Man Donna Fargo	37/77	Johnny Lee
		15/61	Ragged But Right Moon Mullican	93/78	Hank Snow
	Q	31/74	Ragged Old Flag Johnny Cash	8/68	Ramona Billy Walker
69/74	Que Pasa Kenny Price	45/68	Raggedy Ann Charlie Rich	55/99	Random Act Of Senseless Kindness South Sixty Five
28/65	Queen Of Draw Poker Town Hank Snow	76/82	Ragin' Cajun Charlie Daniels Band	1/73	Rated "X" Loretta Lynn
14/81	Queen Of Hearts Juice Newton	5/47	Ragtime Cowboy Joe Eddy Howard	1/44	Ration Blues Louis Jordan
75/82	Queen Of Hearts Loves You Joe Waters	52/74	Railroad Lady Lefty Frizzell		Raunchy
28/67	Queen Of Honky Tonk Street Kitty Wells	87/75	Rain Kris Kristofferson & Rita Coolidge	6/58	Bill Justis
2/93	Queen Of Memphis Confederate Railroad	36/72	Rain Falling On Me Johnny Russell	11/58	Ernie Freeman
		63/72	Rain-Rain Lois Johnson	80/78	Rave On Jerry Naylor
		58/95	Rain Through The Roof Billy Montana	3/73	Ravishing Ruby Tom T. Hall
		F/79	Rainbow And Roses Billy Walker	52/77	Raymond's Place Ray Griff
			Rainbow At Midnight	2/72	Reach Out Your Hand Tammy Wynette
		5/46	Carlisle Brothers	61/73	Reach Out Your Hand And Touch Me Sonny James
		1/47	Ernest Tubb		
		5/47	Texas Jim Robertson	78/81	Reachin' For Freedom Ron Shaw/Desert Wind Band
		28/70	Rainbow Girl Bobby Lord		
		16/74	Rainbow In Daddy's Eyes Sammi Smith	49/79	Reaching Out To Hold You Dottie West

38/87	Read Between The Lines *Lynn Anderson*	1/82	Red Neckin' Love Makin' Night *Conway Twitty*	19/68	Reno *Dottie West*
4/86	Read My Lips *Marie Osmond*	17/72	Red Red Wine *Roy Drusky*	76/85	Reno And Me *Bobby Bare*
82/80	Reading Of The Will *Jimmy Tucker*	69/99	Red, Red Wine And Cheatin' Songs *Marty Stuart*	9/86	Reno Bound *Southern Pacific*
	Ready For The Times To Get Better	21/74	Red Rose From The Blue Side Of Town *George Morgan*	81/87	Rented Room *Jeanne Pruett*
1/78	*Crystal Gayle*	60/75	Red Roses For A Blue Lady *Eddy Arnold*	10/68	Repeat After Me *Jack Reno*
43/81	*Joe Sun*	8/48	Red Roses Tied In Blue *Clyde Moody*	56/84	Repeat After Me *Family Brown*
72/87	Ready Or Not *Don Malena*	22/76	Red Sails In The Sunset *Johnny Lee*	6/57	Repenting *Kitty Wells*
2/99	Ready To Run *Dixie Chicks*	62/72	Red Skies Over Georgia *Henson Cargill*	4/86	Repetitive Regret *Eddie Rabbitt*
90/88	Ready To Take That Ride *Trinity Lane*	49/95	Red Strokes *Garth Brooks*	74/88	Request, The *Bob Pack*
20/96	Ready, Willing And Able *Lari White*	20/76	Red, White And Blue *Loretta Lynn*	4/97	Rest Of Mine *Trace Adkins*
38/80	Real Buddy Holly Story *Sonny Curtis*	59/94	Red, White And Blue Collar *Gibson/Miller Band*	72/78	Rest Of My Life *Kenny Starr*
20/80	Real Cowboy (You Say You're) *Billy "Crash" Craddock*	6/78	Red Wine And Blue Memories *Joe Stampley*	86/80	Rest Of Your Life *Kay Austin*
67/86	Real Good *Bobby Bare*	42/96	Redneck Games *Jeff Foxworthy with Alan Jackson*		Rest Your Love On Me
9/88	Real Good Feel Good Song *Mel McDaniel*	1/82	Redneck Girl *Bellamy Brothers*	39/79	*Bee Gees*
76/87	Real Good Heartache *Rosemary Sharp*		Redneck In A Rock And Roll Bar ..see: (I'm Just A)	1/81	*Conway Twitty*
52/94	Real Good Way To Wind Up Lonesome *James House*	89/76	Redneck Rock *Bill Black's Combo*		Restless
36/68	Real Good Woman *Jean Shepard*	95/77	Redneck Roots *Vernon Oxford*	20/69	*Carl Perkins*
14/01	Real Life (I Never Was The Same Again) *Jeff Carson*	55/96	Redneck Son *Ty England*	25/91	*Mark O'Connor*
16/00	Real Live Woman *Trisha Yearwood*	67/94	Redneck Stomp *Jeff Foxworthy*	39/74	*Restless Crystal Gayle*
1/85	Real Love *Dolly Parton (with Kenny Rogers)*	17/76	Redneck! (The Redneck National Anthem) *Vernon Oxford*	39/87	Restless Angel *Tim Malchak*
33/98	Real Man *Billy Dean*		Redneck 12 Days Of Christmas	57/84	Restless Heart *Juice Newton*
69/89	Real Old-Fashioned Broken Heart *Bama Band*	18/95	*Jeff Foxworthy*	74/69	Restless Melissa *Hugh X. Lewis*
30/67	Real Thing *Billy Grammer*	39/96	*Jeff Foxworthy*	11/61	Restless One *Hank Snow*
79/79	Real Thing *O.B. McClinton*	39/97	*Jeff Foxworthy*	30/64	Restless River *Earl Scott*
85/78	Real Thing *Jean Shepard*	37/98	*Jeff Foxworthy*	6/78	Return To Me *Marty Robbins*
	Reason To Believe	35/99	*Jeff Foxworthy*	13/79	Reunited *Louise Mandrell & R.C. Bannon*
75/69	*Suzi Jane Hokum*	4/73	Rednecks, White Socks And Blue Ribbon Beer *Johnny Russell*	74/76	Reverend Bob *Barbi Benton*
88/83	*Wray Brothers Band*	55/74	Reflections *Jody Miller*	71/82	Reverend Mr. Black *Johnny Cash*
	Reason Why I'm Here	5/95	Refried Dreams *Tim McGraw*	82/84	Reynosa *Katy Moffatt*
97/76	*Joni Lee*	87/80	Regrets *Carol Chase*	1/75	Rhinestone Cowboy *Glen Campbell*
85/78	*Mike Lunsford*	41/66	Regular On My Mind *Jim Edward Brown*	23/64	Rhinestones *Faron Young*
13/60	Reasons To Live *Jimmie Skinner*	63/98	Reindeer Boogie *Trisha Yearwood*	1/51	Rhumba Boogie *Hank Snow*
6/83	Reasons To Quit *Merle Haggard & Willie Nelson*		Release Me	44/85	Rhythm Guitar *Emmylou Harris*
1/96	Rebecca Lynn *Bryan White*	5/54	*Jimmy Heap/Perk Williams*	94/79	Rhythm Guitar *Oak Ridge Boys*
24/61	Rebel - Johnny Yuma *Johnny Cash*	6/54	*Ray Price*	57/88	Rhythm Of Romance *Kendalls*
17/58	Rebel-'Rouser *Duane Eddy*	8/54	*Kitty Wells*		Rhythm Of The Rain
9/88	Rebels Without A Clue *Bellamy Brothers*	33/73	*Charlie McCoy*	34/72	*Pat Roberts*
1/93	Reckless *Alabama*	71/74	*Marie Owens*	67/77	*Floyd Cramer*
32/90	Reckless Heart *Southern Pacific*	71/70	Remember Bethlehem *Dee Mullins*	11/78	*Jacky Ward*
	Reconsider Me		(Remember Me) I'm The One Who Loves You	32/69	Rib, The *Jeannie C. Riley*
38/69	*Ray Pillow*	2/50	*Stuart Hamblen*		Ribbon Of Darkness
39/71	*John Wesley Ryles*	5/50	*Ernest Tubb*	1/65	*Marty Robbins*
2/75	*Narvel Felts*	2/76	*Willie Nelson*	13/69	*Connie Smith*
23/94	Red And Rio Grande *Doug Supernaw*	56/96	Remember The Ride *Perfect Stranger*	19/81	Rich Man *Terri Gibbs*
4/79	Red Bandana *Merle Haggard*	56/96	Remember When *Ray Vega*	53/75	Richard And The Cadillac Kings *Doyle Holly*
4/44	Red Blues *Cootie Williams*		Remembering	76/88	Richer Now With You *Nina Wyatt*
21/71	Red Door *Carl Smith*	14/68	*Jerry Reed*	10/55	Richest Man (In the World) *Eddy Arnold*
17/78	Red Hot Memory *Kenny Dale*	57/76	*Jerry Reed*	3/90	Richest Man On Earth *Paul Overstreet*
70/86	Red Neck And Over Thirty *Wayne Kemp & Bobby G. Rice*	80/83	Reminiscing *Linda Nail*	4/83	Ride, The *David Allan Coe*
73/76	Red Neck Disco *Glenn Sutton*	23/70	Removing The Shadow *Hank Williams, Jr. & Lois Johnson*	80/80	Ride Concrete Cowboy, Ride *Roy Rogers*
85/77	Red-Neck Hippie Romance *Bobby Bare*	7/94	Renegades, Rebels And Rogues *Tracy Lawrence*	85/82	Ride Cowboy Ride *Rex Allen, Jr.*
		4/93	Reno *Doug Supernaw*		Ride 'Em Cowboy
				47/75	*Paul Davis*
				32/84	*Juice Newton*
				48/84	*David Allan Coe*
				73/94	Ride 'em High, Ride 'em Low *Brooks & Dunn*
				11/73	Ride Me Down Easy *Bobby Bare*
				36/67	Ride, Ride, Ride *Lynn Anderson*
				92/80	Ride That Bull (Big Bertha) *Marlow Tackett*
				58/88	Ride This Train *Mel McDaniel*
				78/78	Rider In The Rain *Randy Newman*

Remember The Alamo — Johnny Cash / Riders In The Sky

Riders In The Sky
2/49   Vaughn Monroe
8/49   Burl Ives
27/73 Roy Clark
2/79   Johnny Cash
1/73   **Ridin' My Thumb To Mexico**
       Johnny Rodriguez
45/97 **Ridin' Out The Heartache**
       Tanya Tucker
12/77 **Ridin' Rainbows** Tanya Tucker
72/92 **Riding For A Fall** Chris LeDoux
2/01   **Riding With Private Malone**
       David Ball
44/88 **Rigamarole**
       Schuyler, Knobloch & Bickhardt
22/70 **Right Back Loving You Again**
       Del Reeves
65/82 **Right Back Loving You Again**
       Chantilly
14/71 **Right Combination**
       Porter Wagoner & Dolly Parton
1/87   **Right From The Start**
       Earl Thomas Conley
3/87   **Right Hand Man** Eddy Raven
10/81 **Right In The Palm Of Your Hand**
       Mel McDaniel
10/90 **Right In The Wrong Direction**
       Vern Gosdin
85/81 **Right In The Wrong Direction**
       Liz Lyndell
8/87   **Right Left Hand** George Jones
15/91 **Right Now** Mary-Chapin Carpenter
1/99   **Right On The Money**
       Alan Jackson
30/66 **Right One** Statler Brothers
69/92 **Right One Left** Roger Springer
       Right Or Left At Oak Street
21/70 Roy Clark
83/75 Molly Bee
1/84   **Right Or Wrong** George Strait
       Right Or Wrong
9/61   Wanda Jackson
41/78 Mary K. Miller
63/74 **Right Out Of This World**
       Jerry "Max" Lane
71/99 **Right Place** Derailers
       Right String ..see: Yo Yo
14/84 **Right Stuff**
       Charly McClain & Mickey Gilley
17/77 **Right Time Of The Night**
       Jennifer Warnes
44/89 **Right Track, Wrong Train** Canyon
5/01   **Right Where I Need To Be**
       Gary Allan
7/71   **Right Won't Touch A Hand**
       George Jones
       Ring Of Fire
1/63   Johnny Cash
66/88 Randy Howard
       Ring On Her Finger, Time On Her Hands
5/82   Lee Greenwood
9/96   Reba McEntire
95/78 **Ring Telephone Ring**
       Randy Cornor
33/90 **Ring Where A Ring Used To Be**
       Billy Joe Royal
64/77 **Ringgold Georgia**
       Billy Walker & Brenda Kaye Perry
21/64 **Ringo** Lorne Greene
7/71   **Rings** Tompall/Glaser Brothers
66/67 **Rings** Stan Hitchcock

41/72 **Rings For Sale** Roger Miller
       Rings Of Gold
2/69   Dottie West & Don Gibson
79/87 Robin & Cruiser
66/93 **Rip Off The Knob**
       Bellamy Brothers
57/96 **Ripples** 4 Runner
90/84 **Rise Above It All** Joe Waters
71/79 **Rise And Fall Of The Roman Empire** Cal Smith
9/70   **Rise And Shine** Tommy Cash
73/87 **Rise And Shine** Ronnie Dove
44/78 **Rising Above It All**
       Lynn Anderson
81/88 **Rising Cost Of Loving You**
       Western Union Band
1/92   **River, The** Garth Brooks
8/96   **River And The Highway**
       Pam Tillis
23/69 **River Bottom** Johnny Darrell
36/85 **River In The Rain** Roger Miller
9/54   **River Of No Return**
       Tennessee Ernie Ford
64/80 **River Road** Crystal Gayle
63/88 **River Unbroken** Dolly Parton
76/84 **River's Song** Joey Scarbury
13/74 **River's Too Wide** Jim Mundy
4/60   **Riverboat** Faron Young
14/60 **Riverboat Gambler**
       Jimmie Skinner
27/76 **Road Song** Charlie Rich
55/98 **Road Trippin'** Steve Wariner
5/96   **Road You Leave Behind**
       David Lee Murphy
17/72 **Roadmaster, The** Freddy Weller
F/80   **Roarin'** Gary Stewart
13/67 **Roarin' Again** Wilburn Brothers
15/63 **Robert E. Lee** Ott Stephens
16/79 **Robinhood** Billy "Crash" Craddock
50/92 **Rock, The** Lee Roy Parnell
65/88 **Rock-A-Bye Heart** Dana McVicker
       Rock And Roll ..also see: Rock 'N' Roll, & Rockin' Roll
       Rock And Rye
5/48   Tex Ritter
14/48 Al Dexter
2/94   **Rock Bottom** Wynonna
14/58 **Rock Hearts** Jimmy Martin
48/80 **Rock I'm Leaning On**
       Jack Greene
35/70 **Rock Island Line** Johnny Cash
26/70 **Rock Me Back To Little Rock**
       Jan Howard
29/93 **Rock Me (In The Cradle Of Love)**
       Deborah Allen
60/91 **Rock Me In The Rhythm Of Your Love** Eddy Raven
2/92   **Rock My Baby** Shenandoah
2/94   **Rock My World (Little Country Girl)** Brooks & Dunn
29/75 **Rock N' Roll** Mac Davis
23/90 **Rock 'N' Roll Angel**
       Kentucky Headhunters
16/87 **Rock And Roll Of Love**
       Tom Wopat
14/84 **Rock And Roll Shoes**
       Ray Charles with B.J. Thomas
90/82 **Rock N' Roll Stories**
       Shannon Leigh
58/80 **Rock 'N' Roll To Rock Of Ages**
       Bill Anderson
6/75   **Rock On Baby** Brenda Lee

30/00 **Rock This Country!** Shania Twain
63/81 **Rockabilly Rebel** Orion
86/79 **Rocket 'Til The Cows Come Home** Charley White
       Rockin' Around The Christmas Tree
62/97 Brenda Lee
64/99 Alabama
70/85 **Rockin' In A Brand New Cradle**
       Terri Gibbs
       Rockin' In The Congo
13/57 Hank Thompson
82/82 Hank Thompson
63/86 **Rockin' In The Parkin' Lot**
       Razzy Bailey
66/94 **Rockin' Little Christmas**
       Carlene Carter
70/86 **Rockin' My Angel** Narvel Felts
74/86 **Rockin' My Country Heart**
       Pat Garrett
18/79 **Rockin' My Life Away**
       Jerry Lee Lewis
88/76 **Rockin' My Memories (To Sleep)**
       Claude Gray
22/60 **Rockin', Rollin' Ocean**
       Hank Snow
56/95 **Rockin' The Rock** Larry Stewart
1/86   **Rockin' With The Rhythm Of The Rain** Judds
1/91   **Rockin' Years** Dolly Parton with Ricky Van Shelton
73/69 **Rocking A Memory (That Won't Go To Sleep)**
       Tommy Overstreet
28/76 **Rocking In Rosalee's Boat**
       Nick Nixon
1/75   **Rocky** Dickey Lee
5/76   **Rocky Mountain Music**
       Eddie Rabbitt
71/88 **Rocky Road** O'Kanes
       Rocky Top
33/68 Osborne Brothers
17/70 Lynn Anderson
5/01   **Rocky Top '96** Osborne Brothers
52/81 **Rode Hard And Put Up Wet**
       Johnny Lee
3/91   **Rodeo** Garth Brooks
56/77 **Rodeo Bum** Mel Street
37/82 **Rodeo Clown** Mac Davis
44/76 **Rodeo Cowboy** Lynn Anderson
25/80 **Rodeo Eyes** Zella Lehr
83/81 **Rodeo Girls** Tanya Tucker
10/82 **Rodeo Romeo** Moe Bandy
74/79 **Rodie-Odeo-Home** Arnie Rue
36/88 **Rogue, The** David Lynn Jones
77/80 **Rolaids, Doan's Pills And Preparation H** Dave Dudley
57/73 **Roll In My Sweet Baby's Arms**
       Hank Wilson
       Roll Muddy River
4/63   Wilburn Brothers
66/67 Osborne Brothers
1/75   **Roll On Big Mama** Joe Stampley
1/84   **Roll On (Eighteen Wheeler)**
       Alabama
7/81   **Roll On Mississippi** Charley Pride
100/75 **Roll On, Truckers** Ray Pillow
68/89 **Roll Over** Steven Wayne Horton
26/67 **Roll Over And Play Dead**
       Jan Howard

Ray Clark – Country Twitty – Higher Incomes (Specialy Being Successful) – Mar 31

	Roll Over Beethoven	4/54	**Rose-Marie** Slim Whitman	5/56	**Run Boy** Ray Price	
71/70	Linda Gail Lewis & Jerry Lee Lewis	60/84	**Rose Of My Heart** Johnny Rodriguez	8/54	**Run 'Em Off** Lefty Frizzell	
64/82	Narvel Felts	33/80	**Rose's Are Red** Freddie Hart	53/81	**Run To Her** Susie Allanson	
49/87	**Roll The Dice** Shurfire	28/63	**Rosebuds And You** Benny Martin	1/70	**Run, Woman, Run** Tammy Wynette	
	Roll Truck Roll		**Roses Ain't Red**	68/84	**Run Your Sweet Love By Me One More Time** Lang Scott	
38/66	Red Simpson	94/78	Cathy O'Shea		**Runaway**	
67/71	Tommy Cash	59/80	Diane Pfeifer	30/78	Narvel Felts	
32/75	**Roll You Like A Wheel** Mickey Gilley & Barbi Benton	3/75	**Roses And Love Songs** Ray Price	76/86	Bonnie Leigh	
84/87	**Roller Coaster** Alibi	15/71	**Roses And Thorns** Jeannie C. Riley	74/00	Gary Allan	
52/89	**Roller Coaster Run** Michael Johnson	2/77	**Roses For Mama** C.W. McCall	43/85	**Runaway Go Home** Larry Gatlin/Gatlin Brothers	
71/95	**Rollin'** Garth Brooks	34/66	**Roses From A Stranger** Leroy Van Dyke	13/84	**Runaway Heart** Louise Mandrell	
49/91	**Rollin' Home** Pirates Of The Mississippi	44/88	**Roses In December** Larry Boone		**Runaway Heart**	
	Rollin' In My Sweet Baby's Arms	70/73	**Roses In The Wine** Hank Thompson	93/77	Pam Rose	
2/71	Buck Owens	42/68	**Roses To Reno** Bob Bishop	36/77	Reba McEntire	
76/76	Maury Finney	17/74	**Rosie Cries A Lot** Ferlin Husky	62/98	**Runaway Love** Chris LeDoux	
65/75	**Rollin' In Your Sweet Sunshine** Dottie West		**Rosie (Do You Wanna Talk It Over)**	1/88	**Runaway Train** Rosanne Cash	
9/85	**Rollin' Lonely** Johnny Lee	45/76	Red Steagall	62/94	**Runaway Train** Dawn Sears	
15/86	**Rollin' Nowhere** Michael Martin Murphey	76/76	Sonny Throckmorton	8/96	**Runnin' Away With My Heart** Lonestar	
47/73	**Rollin' Rig** Dave Dudley		**Round About Way**	20/70	**Runnin' Bare** Jim Nesbitt	
1/77	**Rollin' With The Flow** Charlie Rich	71/97	George Strait	4/92	**Runnin' Behind** Tracy Lawrence	
	Roly-Poly	1/98	George Strait	100/77	**Runnin' Out Again** Paula Kay Evans	
3/46	Bob Wills	19/96	**'Round Here** Sawyer Brown	8/90	**Runnin' With The Wind** Eddie Rabbitt	
97/75	Carl Smith	9/82	**'Round The Clock Lovin'** Gail Davies	1/69	**Running Bear** Sonny James	
65/00	Asleep At The Wheel Featuring Dixie Chicks	40/77	**'Round The World With The Rubber Duck** C.W. McCall	24/85	**Running Down Memory Lane** Rex Allen, Jr.	
22/83	**Romance** Louise Mandrell	31/81	**Round-Up Saloon** Bobby Goldsboro	70/70	**Running From A Memory** Chaparral Brothers	
59/86	**Romance** Jim Collins		**Route 66**		**Running Kind**	
26/69	**Rome Wasn't Built In A Day** Hank Snow	48/76	Asleep At The Wheel	12/78	Merle Haggard	
27/93	**Romeo** Dolly Parton & Friends	67/90	Michael Martin Murphey	64/94	Radney Foster	
36/79	**Room At The Top Of The Stairs** Stella Parton	54/87	**Routine** Kendalls	40/82	**Running On Love** Don King	
92/79	**Room At The Top Of The Stairs** Cal Smith	11/68	**Row Row Row** Henson Cargill	1/97	**Running Out Of Reasons To Run** Rick Trevino	
60/74	**Room For A Boy...Never Used** Ferlin Husky	1/53	**Rub-A-Dub-Dub** Hank Thompson	72/86	**Running Out Of Reasons To Run** J.D. Martin	
	Room Full Of Roses	39/95	**Rub-A-Dubbin'** Ken Mellons	77/85	**Running The Roadblocks** Chris Hillman	
4/49	George Morgan	1/74	**Rub It In** Billy "Crash" Craddock	14/79	**Rusty Old Halo** Hoyt Axton	
10/49	Sons Of The Pioneers	54/99	**Rub It In** Matt King	10/67	**Ruthless** Statler Brothers	
1/74	Mickey Gilley	46/69	**Ruben James** Kenny Rogers & The First Edition		**Rye Whiskey**	
2/66	**Room In Your Heart** Sonny James	1/63	**Ruby Ann** Marty Robbins	9/48	Tex Ritter	
56/76	**Room 269** Freddy Weller		**Ruby, Are You Mad**	81/76	Chuck Price	
1/76	**Roots Of My Raising** Merle Haggard	58/70	Osborne Brothers			
4/94	**Rope The Moon** John Michael Montgomery	3/71	Buck Owens		# S	
54/92	**Rosalee** Stacy Dean Campbell	1/75	**Ruby, Baby** Billy "Crash" Craddock	15/55	**S.O.S.** Johnnie And Jack	
1/44	**Rosalita** Al Dexter		**Ruby, Don't Take Your Love To Town**	73/81	**S.O.S.** Johnny Carver	
2/68	**Rosanna's Going Wild** Johnny Cash	9/67	Johnny Darrell		**Sacred Ground**	
1/83	**Rose, The** Conway Twitty	39/69	Kenny Rogers & The First Edition	87/89	Kix Brooks	
16/01	**Rose Bouquet** Phil Vassar	46/72	**Ruby Gentry's Daughter** Arlene Harden	2/92	McBride & The Ride	
	Rose By Any Other Name (Is Still A Rose)	21/72	**Ruby You're Warm** David Rogers	70/88	**Sad Cliches** Atlanta	
69/72	Ray Sanders	78/77	**Ruby's Lounge** Brenda Lee	17/76	**Sad Country Love Song** Tom Bresh	
77/76	Ronnie Milsap		**Rudolph, The Red-Nosed Reindeer**	55/89	**Sad Eyes** Trader-Price	
5/78	**Rose Colored Glasses** John Conlee	1/49	Gene Autry	31/67	**Sad Face** Ernie Ashworth	
1/70	**Rose Garden** Lynn Anderson	1/50	Gene Autry	2/97	**Sad Lookin' Moon** Alabama	
1/87	**Rose In Paradise** Waylon Jennings	56/96	Alan Jackson	78/80	**Sad Love Song Lady** David Houston	
37/01	**Rose Is A Rose** Meredith Edwards	55/98	Gene Autry	81/81	**Sad Ole Shade Of Gray** Jeanne Pruett	
52/69	**Rose Is A Rose Is A Rose** Jimmy Dean	60/99	Gene Autry	46/72	**Sad Situation** Skeeter Davis	
		1/97	**Rumor Has It** Clay Walker	59/86	**Sad State Of Affairs** Leon Everette	
70/81	**Rose Is For Today** Jim Chesnut	3/91	**Rumor Has It** Reba McEntire			
		2/01	**Run** George Strait			
		50/00	**Run Away** Shane McAnally			
		10/68	**Run Away Little Tears** Connie Smith			

Roy Clark — Conway Twitty — Waylon Jennings (Special: Being Successful — May 31)

F/80	**Sadness Of It All** *Conway Twitty & Loretta Lynn*		**Santa Claus Is Comin' (In A Boogie Woogie Choo Choo Train)**	14/77	**Savin' This Love Song For You** *Johnny Rodriguez*
4/95	**Safe In The Arms Of Love** *Martina McBride*	43/95	**Tractors**		**Sawmill**
44/85	**Safe In The Arms Of Love** *Robin Lee*	65/97	**Tractors**	27/59	Mel Tillis & Bill Phillips
			Santa Claus Is Coming To Town	15/63	Webb Pierce
82/80	**Safe In The Arms Of Your Love (Cold In The Streets)** *Jim Weatherly*	73/95	George Strait	2/73	Mel Tillis
		69/97	George Strait	21/94	**Sawmill Road** *Diamond Rio*
55/72	**Safe In These Lovin' Arms Of Mine** *Jean Shepard*	69/00	Lonestar	85/80	**Say A Long Goodbye** *Mary K. Miller*
		5/88	**Santa Fe** *Bellamy Brothers*	41/99	**Say Anything** *Shane McAnally*
1/64	**Saginaw, Michigan** *Lefty Frizzell*	70/95	**Santa Got Lost In Texas** *Jeff Carson*	5/75	**Say Forever You'll Be Mine** *Porter Wagoner & Dolly Parton*
	Sail Away	50/95	**Santa I'm Right Here** *Toby Keith*	35/73	**Say, Has Anybody Seen My Sweet Gypsy Rose** *Terry Stafford*
98/77	Sam Neely	56/97	**Santa Looked A Lot Like Daddy** *Garth Brooks*		
2/79	Oak Ridge Boys			38/96	**Say I** *Alabama*
16/79	**Sail On** *Tom Grant*	72/99	**Santa On The Rooftop** *Trisha Yearwood & Rosie O'Donnell*	40/75	**Say I Do** *Ray Price*
63/85	**Sailing Home To Me** *Loy Blanton*			1/76	**Say It Again** *Don Williams*
16/59	**Sailor Man** *Johnnie And Jack*		**Santa's Got A Semi**	31/91	**Say It's Not True** *Lionel Cartwright*
16/02	**Saints & Angels** *Sara Evans*	60/99	Keith Harling	8/68	**Say It's Not You** *George Jones*
19/59	**Sal's Got A Sugar Lip** *Johnny Horton*	60/00	Keith Harling	33/01	**Say No More** *Clay Walker*
		57/70	**Santo Domingo** *Buddy Alan*	78/89	**Say The Part About I Love You** *Lorie Ann*
51/75	**Sally G** *Paul McCartney & Wings*	57/97	**Sarah's Eyes** *Vern Gosdin*		
20/02	**Sally Was A Good Old Girl** *Hank Cochran*	1/73	**Satin Sheets** *Jeanne Pruett*	4/89	**Say What's In Your Heart** *Restless Heart*
		17/73	**Satisfaction** *Jack Greene*		
98/79	**Salt On The Wound** *Jerry Fuller*	7/53	**Satisfaction Guaranteed** *Carl Smith*	13/98	**Say When** *Lonestar*
8/52	**Salty Dog Rag** *Red Foley*		**Satisfied Mind**	15/73	**Say When** *Diana Trask*
8/70	**Salute To A Switchblade** *Tom T. Hall*	1/55	Porter Wagoner	F/84	**Say When** *Johnny Lee*
		3/55	Red Foley And Betty Foley	37/97	**Say Yes** *Burnin' Daylight*
87/79	**Salute To The Duke** *Paul Ott*	4/55	Jean Shepard		**Say You Love Me**
40/77	**Sam** *Olivia Newton-John*	25/73	Roy Drusky	93/76	Lynda K. Lance
	Sam Hill	41/76	Bob Luman	10/79	Stephanie Winslow
11/64	Claude King	84/83	Con Hunley		**Say You Love Me Again ..see: (I Wanna Hear You)**
45/64	Merle Haggard		**Satisfy Me And I'll Satisfy You**		
1/67	**Sam's Place** *Buck Owens*	83/74	Josie Brown	57/83	**Say You'll Stay** *Wayne Massey*
12/92	**Same Ol' Love** *Ricky Skaggs*	53/91	Clinton Gregory	1/77	**Say You'll Stay Until Tomorrow** *Tom Jones*
83/81	**Same Old Boy** *Gary Gentry*	5/88	**Satisfy You** *Sweethearts Of The Rodeo*		
1/59	**Same Old Me** *Ray Price*			2/77	**Saying Hello, Saying I Love You, Saying Goodbye** *Jim Ed Brown/Helen Cornelius*
28/91	**Same Old Star** *McBride & The Ride*	24/71	**Saturday Morning Confusion** *Bobby Russell*		
29/75	**Same Old Story** *Hank Williams, Jr.*	22/68	**Saturday Night** *Webb Pierce*	5/83	**Scarlet Fever** *Kenny Rogers*
46/70	**Same Old Story, Same Old Lie** *Bill Phillips*	47/99	**Saturday Night** *Lonestar*	7/60	**Scarlet Ribbons (For Her Hair)** *Browns*
59/98	**Same Old Train** *Same Old Train*	54/80	**Saturday Night In Dallas** *Kenny Seratt*	66/74	**Scarlet Water** *Johnny Duncan*
65/73	**Same Old Way** *Stan Hitchcock*	9/88	**Saturday Night Special** *Conway Twitty*	58/91	**Scars** *Ray Kennedy*
5/82	**Same Ole Me** *George Jones*			90/89	**Scars** *Johnny Paycheck*
8/49	**Same Sweet Girl** *Hank Locklin*	53/77	**Saturday Night To Sunday Quiet** *Susan Raye*	65/90	**Scene Of The Crime** *Jo-el Sonnier*
14/57	**Same Two Lips** *Marty Robbins*			77/88	**Scene Of The Crime** *Lori Yates*
47/66	**Sammy** *David Houston*	43/69	**Saturday Satan Sunday Saint** *Ernest Tubb*		**Scotch And Soda**
50/67	**San Antonio** *Willie Nelson*	6/83	**Save Me** *Louise Mandrell*	88/79	Mac Wiseman
89/80	**San Antonio Medley** *Curtis Potter/Darrell McCall*	86/78	**Save Me** *Tanya Tucker*	70/83	Ray Price
25/83	**San Antonio Nights** *Eddy Raven*	12/85	**Save The Last Chance** *Johnny Lee*	27/58	**Scotland** *Bill Monroe*
	San Antonio Rose		**Save The Last Dance For Me**	8/81	**Scratch My Back (And Whisper in My Ear)** *Razzy Bailey*
8/61	Floyd Cramer	11/62	Buck Owens	46/01	**Scream** *Mindy McCready*
F/83	Ray Price	100/76	Bennie Lindsey		**Sea Cruise**
	San Antonio Stroll	36/78	Ron Shaw	94/77	Everett Peek
1/75	Tanya Tucker	4/79	Emmylou Harris	50/80	Billy "Crash" Craddock
F/76	Maury Finney	26/79	Jerry Lee Lewis	56/95	**Sea Of Cowboy Hats** *Chely Wright*
31/68	**San Diego** *Charlie Walker*	3/84	Dolly Parton		**Sea Of Heartbreak**
	San Francisco Is A Lonely Town	45/95	**Save This One For Me** *Rick Trevino*	2/61	Don Gibson
46/69	Ben Peters			24/72	Kenny Price
86/79	Nick Nixon	8/80	**Save Your Heart For Me** *Jacky Ward*	33/79	Lynn Anderson
26/75	**Sanctuary** *Ronnie Prophet*			39/89	Ronnie McDowell
7/63	**Sands Of Gold** *Webb Pierce*	10/76	**Save Your Kisses For Me** *Margo Smith*	83/88	**Sealed With A Kiss** *Leah Marr*
F/79	**Santa Barbara** *Ronnie Milsap*			5/48	**Seaman's Blues** *Ernest Tubb*
	Santa Claus Boogie	3/86	**Savin' My Love For You** *Pake McEntire*	43/77	**Search, The** *Freddie Hart*
41/94	Tractors			54/72	**Search Your Heart** *Bobby Wright*
63/95	Tractors	58/87	**Savin' The Honey For The Honeymoon** *Sawyer Brown*	82/76	**Searchin' For A Rainbow** *Marshall Tucker Band*
71/98	**Santa Claus (I Still Believe In You)** *Alabama*				
60/97	**Santa Claus Is Back In Town** *Dwight Yoakam*				

500

17/90 Searchin' For Some Kind Of Clue Billy Joe Royal	31/00 **Self Made Man** Montgomery Gentry	**Seventeen**
Searching (For Someone Like You)	81/90 **Selfish Man** Dwayne Crews	71/99 Tim McGraw
	83/82 **Semi Diesel Blues** Super Grit Cowboy Band	64/00 Tim McGraw
3/56 Kitty Wells		F/71 Seventeen Years Marty Robbins
45/75 Melba Montgomery	2/92 **Seminole Wind** John Anderson	68/91 **Seventh Direction** Tim Ryan
75/87 Lanier McKuhen	19/77 **Semolita** Jerry Reed	92/78 **Sexy Eyes** Gayle Harding
24/74 **Seasons In The Sun** Bobby Wright	79/73 **Send A Little Love My Way** Anne Murray	21/74 **Sexy Lady** Freddy Weller
		80/80 **Sexy Ole Lady** Pat Garrett
Seasons Of My Heart	47/92 **Send A Message To My Heart** Dwight Yoakam & Patty Loveless	48/80 **Sexy Song** Carol Chase
9/56 Jimmy Newman		46/86 **Sexy Young Girl** Mac Davis
10/60 Johnny Cash	66/00 **Send Down An Angel** Allison Moorer	95/79 **Shackles And Chains** Osborne Bros. & Mac Wiseman
90/79 **Second Best (Is Too Far Down The Line)** Don Deal	69/66 **Send Me A Box Of Kleenex** Lamar Morris	8/91 **Shadow Of A Doubt** Earl Thomas Conley
18/62 **Second Choice** Stonewall Jackson	2/79 **Send Me Down To Tucson** Mel Tillis	74/82 **Shadow Of Love** Rob Parsons
50/73 **Second Cup Of Coffee** George Hamilton IV	7/73 **Send Me No Roses** Tommy Overstreet	5/45 **Shadow On My Heart** Ted Daffan
		1/79 **Shadows In The Moonlight** Anne Murray
24/59 **Second Fiddle** Buck Owens	14/72 **Send Me Some Lovin'** Hank Williams, Jr. & Lois Johnson	28/79 **Shadows Of Love** Rayburn Anthony
5/64 **Second Fiddle (To An Old Guitar)** Jean Shepard	61/81 **Send Me Somebody To Love** Calamity Jane	**Shadows Of My Mind**
70/79 **Second Hand Emotion** Faron Young	**Send Me The Pillow You Dream On**	54/76 Vernon Oxford
		15/83 Leon Everette
7/84 **Second Hand Heart** Gary Morris		24/78 **Shady Rest** Mel Street
3/63 **Second Hand Rose** Roy Drusky	5/58 Hank Locklin	48/77 **Shady Side Of Charlotte** Nat Stuckey
18/79 **Second-Hand Satin Lady (And A Bargain Basement Boy)** Jerry Reed	23/60 Browns	66/79 **Shady Streets** Gary Stewart
	11/62 Johnny Tillotson	5/97 **Shake, The** Neal McCoy
	66/81 Whites	6/53 **Shake A Hand** Red Foley
15/60 **Second Honeymoon** Johnny Cash	65/98 **Sending Me Angels** Delbert McClinton	15/54 **Shake-A-Leg** Carlisles
		75/76 **Shake 'Em Up and Let 'Em Roll** George Kent
95/86 **Second Time Around** Del Reeves	9/87 **Senorita** Don Williams	
5/86 **Second To No One** Rosanne Cash	74/99 **Senorita Margarita** Tim McGraw	27/61 **Shake Hands With A Loser** Don Winters
60/72 **Second Tuesday In December** Jack Blanchard & Misty Morgan	47/76 **Sentimental Journey** Dave Dudley	**Shake Me I Rattle (Squeeze Me I Cry)**
20/01 **Second Wind** Darryl Worley	3/84 **Sentimental Ol' You** Charly McClain	14/63 Marion Worth
Secret Love	F/73 **Separate Ways** Elvis Presley	16/78 Cristy Lane
2/54 Slim Whitman	**September Song**	95/76 **Shake, Rattle And Roll** Billy Swan
47/73 Tony Booth	40/69 Roy Clark	3/92 **Shake The Sugar Tree** Pam Tillis
1/75 Freddy Fender	15/79 Willie Nelson	15/86 **Shakin'** Sawyer Brown
58/99 **Secret Of Giving** Reba McEntire	1/88 **Set 'Em Up Joe** Vern Gosdin	48/98 **Shame About That** Sara Evans
4/99 **Secret Of Life** Faith Hill	**Set Him Free**	**Shame On Me**
Secretly	5/59 Skeeter Davis	18/62 Bobby Bare
5/58 Jimmie Rodgers	52/68 Skeeter Davis	56/69 Norro Wilson
65/78 Jimmie Rodgers	**Set Me Free**	48/75 Bob Luman
47/81 **Secrets** Mac Davis	67/67 Curly Putman	8/77 Donna Fargo
6/90 **See If I Care** Shenandoah	44/68 Charlie Rich	49/00 **Shame On Me** Wilkinsons
44/97 **See Rock City** Rick Trevino	51/69 Ray Price	15/83 **Shame On The Moon** Bob Seger
F/69 **See Ruby Fall** Johnny Cash	68/71 **Set The World On Fire (With Love)** Red Lane	**Shame On You**
72/75 **See Saw** Patsy Sledd		1/45 Spade Cooley
See The Big Man Cry	72/98 **Set You Free** Allison Moorer	1/45 Lawrence Welk with Red Foley
7/65 Charlie Louvin	91/89 **Settin' At The Kitchen Table** Justin Wright	4/45 Bill Boyd
85/76 Bobby Wayne Loftis		11/77 **Shame, Shame On Me** Kenny Dale
80/74 **See The Funny Little Clown** Billie Jo Spears	2/52 **Settin' The Woods On Fire** Hank Williams	
51/96 **See Ya** Confederate Railroad	7/89 **Setting Me Up** Highway 101	26/93 **Shame Shame Shame Shame** Mark Collie
41/79 **See You In September** Debby Boone	**Seven Bridges Road**	1/91 **Shameless** Garth Brooks
	55/81 Eagles	35/64 **Shape Up Or Ship Out** Leon McAuliff
18/76 **See You On Sunday** Glen Campbell	48/99 Ricochet	
	85/81 **Seven Days Come Sunday** Rodney Lay	83/78 **Share Your Love Tonight** Ann J. Morton
16/72 **Seed Before The Rose** Tommy Overstreet	28/66 **Seven Days Of Crying (Makes One Weak)** Harden Trio	5/81 **Share Your Love With Me** Kenny Rogers
50/93 **Seeds** Kathy Mattea		15/79 **Sharing** Kenny Dale
2/90 **Seein' My Father In Me** Paul Overstreet	**Seven Lonely Days**	**Sharing The Night Together**
Seeing Is Believing	7/53 Bonnie Lou	50/78 Dr. Hook
96/74 Jan Howard	18/69 Jean Shepard	88/83 Denny Hilton
55/80 Donna Fargo	1/85 **Seven Spanish Angels** Ray Charles with Willie Nelson	44/01 **She Ain't Gonna Cry** Marshall Dyllon
2/75 **Seeker, The** Dolly Parton		
83/76 **Seems Like I Can't Live With You, But I Can't Live Without You** Price Mitchell	1/81 **Seven Year Ache** Rosanne Cash	93/87 **She Ain't Johnnie** Billy Vera

See Three Times Seven

501

34/00	She Ain't The Girl For You *Kinleys*	4/97	She Drew A Broken Heart *Patty Loveless*	1/73	She Needs Someone To Hold Her (When She Cries) *Conway Twitty*
2/95	She Ain't Your Ordinary Girl *Alabama*		She Even Woke Me Up To Say Goodbye	27/94	She Never Cried *Confederate Railroad*
83/85	She Almost Makes Me Forget About You *Larry Wayne Kennedy*	2/69	*Jerry Lee Lewis*	2/76	She Never Knew Me *Don Williams*
		15/75	*Ronnie Milsap*	1/96	She Never Lets It Go To Her Heart *Tim McGraw*
1/86	She And I *Alabama*	39/95	She Feels Like A Brand New Man Tonight *Aaron Tippin*	51/96	She Never Looks Back *Doug Supernaw*
1/79	She Believes In Me *Kenny Rogers*	97/83	She Feels Like A New Man Tonight *Clifford Russell*	64/82	She Only Meant To Use Him *Wayne Kemp*
16/81	She Belongs To Everyone But Me *Burrito Brothers*	66/73	She Feels So Good I Hate To Put Her Down *Ronnie Sessions*	59/84	She Put The Sad In All His Songs *Ronnie Dunn*
91/75	She Brings Her Lovin' Home To Me *Mundo Ray*	15/73	She Fights That Lovin' Feeling *Faron Young*	23/89	She Reminded Me Of You *Mickey Gilley*
3/44	She Broke My Heart In Three Places *Hoosier Hot Shots*	65/68	She Gets The Roses (I Get The Tears) *Donna Odom*	57/97	She Said, He Heard *Suzy Bogguss*
38/74	She Burn't The Little Roadside Tavern Down *Johnny Russell*	64/97	She Gives *Emilio*	17/96	She Said Yes *Rhett Akins*
	She Called Me Baby	3/70	She Goes Walking Through My Mind *Billy Walker*	75/88	She Says *George Hamilton V*
32/65	*Carl Smith*	1/82	She Got The Goldmine (I Got The Shaft) *Jerry Reed*	62/94	She Should've Been Mine *Western Flyer*
55/72	*Dick Curless*	57/96	She Got What She Deserves *Frazier River*		She Sings Amazing Grace
1/74	*Charlie Rich*	98/89	She Had Every Right To Do You Wrong *Jerry Lansdowne*	81/81	*Stan Hitchcock*
2/90	She Came From Fort Worth *Kathy Mattea*			83/82	*Gary Stewart*
74/70	She Came To Me *Lamar Morris*	40/01	She Is *Hal Ketchum*	2/68	She Still Comes Around *Jerry Lee Lewis*
71/91	She Can *Marcy Brothers*	1/92	She Is His Only Need *Wynonna*	78/74	She Still Comes To Me (To Pour The Wine) *Henson Cargill*
1/78	She Can Put Her Shoes Under My Bed *Johnny Duncan*	48/82	She Is The Woman *Super Grit Cowboy Band*	3/84	She Sure Got Away With My Heart *John Anderson*
29/82	She Can't Get My Love Off The Bed *Dottie West*	11/77	She Just Loved The Cheatin' Out Of Me *Moe Bandy*	50/92	She Takes The Sad Out Of Saturday Night *Clinton Gregory*
	She Can't Give It Away	89/78	She Just Made Me Love You More *Johnny Bush*	13/75	She Talked A Lot About Texas *Cal Smith*
96/78	*Barbara Fairchild*		She Just Started Liking Cheatin' Songs	15/94	She Thinks His Name Was John *Reba McEntire*
86/81	*Roy Clark*	13/80	*John Anderson*	92/86	She Thinks I Steal Cars *Pinkard & Bowden*
48/95	She Can't Love You *Boy Howdy*	72/99	*Alan Jackson*		She [He] Thinks I Still Care
55/96	She Can't Save Him *Lisa Brokop*	75/77	She Keeps Hangin' On *Rayburn Anthony*	1/62	*George Jones*
3/94	She Can't Say I Didn't Cry *Rick Trevino*	1/85	She Keeps The Home Fires Burning *Ronnie Milsap*	1/74	*Anne Murray*
2/80	She Can't Say That Anymore *John Conlee*	55/74	She Kept On Talkin' *Molly Bee*	F/77	*Elvis Presley*
28/70	She Cheats On Me *Glenn Barber*	69/97	She Knows Me By Heart *Seminole*	39/68	She Thinks I'm On That Train *Henson Cargill*
2/01	She Couldn't Change Me *Montgomery Gentry*	1/82	She Left Love All Over Me *Razzy Bailey*	11/00	She Thinks My Tractor's Sexy *Kenny Chesney*
4/87	She Couldn't Love Me Anymore *T. Graham Brown*	89/74	She Likes Country Bands *Del Reeves*	9/87	She Thinks That She'll Marry *Judy Rodman*
63/71	She Cried *Roy Clark*	63/92	She Likes To Dance *Michael White*	30/85	She Told Me Yes *Chance*
35/75	She Deserves My Very Best *David Wills*	97/88	(She Likes) Warm Summer Days *Buddy Latham*	37/92	She Took It Like A Man *Confederate Railroad*
8/89	She Deserves You *Baillie And The Boys*	55/92	She Loved A Lot In Her Time *George Jones*	78/84	She Took It Too Well *John Wesley Ryles*
73/82	She Doesn't Belong To You *Terry Aden*	47/94	She Loves Me Like She Means It *Orrall & Wright*	11/77	She Took More Than Her Share *Moe Bandy*
9/88	She Doesn't Cry Anymore *Shenandoah*	11/73	She Loves Me (Right Out Of My Mind) *Freddy Weller*	62/81	She Took The Place Of You *Valentino*
29/02	She Doesn't Dance *Mark McGuinn*	94/79	She Loves My Troubles Away *Mickey Jones*	1/93	She Used To Be Mine *Brooks & Dunn*
51/86	She Don't Cry Like She Used To *Johnny Rodriguez*	71/87	She Loves The Jerk *Rodney Crowell*	2/86	She Used To Be Somebody's Baby *Gatlin Brothers*
1/93	She Don't Know She's Beautiful *Sammy Kershaw*	49/94	She Loves To Hear Me Rock *Turner/Nichols*	11/85	She Used To Love Me A Lot *David Allan Coe*
46/91	She Don't Know That She's Perfect *Bellamy Brothers*	54/91	She Made A Memory Out Of Me *Aaron Tippin*	19/82	She Used To Sing On Sunday *Larry Gatlin/Gatlin Brothers*
3/89	She Don't Love Nobody *Desert Rose Band*	53/83	She Meant Forever When She Said Goodbye *Mel Tillis*	11/71	She Wakes Me With A Kiss Every Morning *Nat Stuckey*
70/87	She Don't Love You *Susie Allanson*	21/74	She Met A Stranger, I Met A Train *Tommy Cash*	79/78	She Wanted A Little Bit More *Ray Pennington*
19/71	She Don't Make Me Cry *David Rogers*	8/01	She Misses Him *Tim Rushlow*	21/97	She Wants To Be Wanted Again *Ty Herndon*
14/54	She Done Give Her Heart To Me *Sonny James*				
	She Dreams				
74/93	*Tim Mensy*				
6/94	*Mark Chesnutt*				

65/86	She Wants To Marry A Cowboy James & Michael Younger	2/98	She's Gonna Make It Garth Brooks	91/79	She's My Woman Randy Traywick	
37/99	She Wants To Rock Warren Brothers	9/85	She's Gonna Win Your Heart Eddy Raven	28/92	She's Never Comin' Back Mark Collie	
4/58	She Was Only Seventeen (He Was One Year More) Marty Robbins	36/81	She's Got A Drinking Problem Gary Stewart	F/58	She's No Angel Kitty Wells	
72/79	She Wears It Well Jerry Naylor	77/85	(She's Got A Hold Of Me Where It Hurts) She Won't Let Go Ray Price	17/88	She's No Lady Lyle Lovett	
6/68	She Wears My Ring Ray Price			71/74	She's No Ordinary Woman (Ordinarily) Jim Mundy	
14/68	She Went A Little Bit Farther Faron Young		She's Got A Man On Her Mind	6/93	She's Not Cryin' Anymore Billy Ray Cyrus	
49/00	She Went Out For Cigarettes Chely Wright	38/89	Curtis Wright	43/65	She's Not For You Willie Nelson	
65/69	She Will David Slater	22/91	Conway Twitty	4/82	She's Not Really Cheatin' (She's Just Gettin' Even) Moe Bandy	
57/99	She Won't Be Lonely Long Lee Roy Parnell	26/96	She's Got A Mind Of Her Own James Bonamy	1/94	She's Not The Cheatin' Kind Brooks & Dunn	
	She Won't Let Go ..see: (She's Got A Hold Of Me Where It Hurts)	2/89	She's Got A Single Thing In Mind Conway Twitty	74/75	She's Not Yours Anymore Ferlin Husky	
		24/74	She's Got Everything I Need Eddy Arnold	10/82	She's Playing Hard To Forget Eddy Raven	
	(She Wore Red Dresses) ..see: Buenas Noches From A Lonely Room	1/97	She's Got It All Kenny Chesney	1/77	She's Pulling Me Back Again Mickey Gilley	
		21/98	She's Got That Look In Her Eyes Alabama		She's Ready For Someone To Love Her	
62/75	She Worshipped Me Red Steagall	1/92	She's Got The Rhythm (And I Got The Blues) Alan Jackson	67/83	Osmond Brothers	
53/92	She Wrote The Book Rob Crosby	1/72	She's Got To Be A Saint Ray Price	F/83	Jerry Reed	
4/94	She'd Give Anything Boy Howdy			2/85	She's Single Again Janie Fricke	
10/70	She'll Be Hanging 'Round Somewhere Mel Tillis		She's [He's] Got You	81/88	She's Sittin' Pretty Billy Parker	
51/71	She'll Remember Jerry Wallace	1/62	Patsy Cline	17/81	She's Steppin' Out Con Hunley	
	She'll Throw Stones At You	1/77	Loretta Lynn		She's [He's] Still All Over You	
12/76	Freddie Hart	73/68	Don McLean	100/76	Jo-el Sonnier	
92/76	Jacky Ward	91/80	She's Hangin' In There (I'm Hangin' Out) David Wills	85/77	Jeanne Pruett	
97/75	She'll Wear It Out Leaving Town George Kent	25/76	She's Helping Me Get Over Loving You Joe Stampley	100/79	She's Still Around Chandy Lee	
67/81	She's A Friend Of A Friend Burrito Brothers	43/70	She's Hungry Again Bill Phillips	3/97	She's Sure Taking It Well Kevin Sharp	
3/70	She's A Little Bit Country George Hamilton IV	7/99	She's In Love Mark Wills	2/97	She's Taken A Shine John Berry	
50/90	She's A Little Past Forty Ronnie McDowell	39/74	She's In Love With A Rodeo Man Johnny Russell	17/77	She's The Girl Of My Dreams Don King	
1/85	She's A Miracle Exile	1/91	She's In Love With The Boy Trisha Yearwood		She's The Trip That I've Been On	
15/91	She's A Natural Rob Crosby	58/94	She's In The Bedroom Crying John & Audrey Wiggins	91/76	Leon Rausch	
1/75	She's Actin' Single (I'm Drinkin' Doubles) Gary Stewart	14/60	She's Just A Whole Lot Like You Hank Thompson	52/86	Larry Boone	
2/71	She's All I Got Johnny Paycheck		She's Just An Old Love Turned Memory	69/67	She's The Woman Barbara Cummings	
43/01	She's All That Collin Raye			19/89	She's There Daniele Alexander	
3/73	She's All Woman David Houston	64/75	Nick Nixon	95/89	She's Too Good To Be Cheated This Way Hunter Cain	
37/75	She's Already Gone Jim Mundy	1/77	Charley Pride	1/72	She's Too Good To Be True Charley Pride	
16/99	She's Always Right Clay Walker	79/80	She's Leavin' (And I'm Almost Gone) Kenny Price	1/87	She's Too Good To Be True Exile	
61/71	She's As Close As I Can Get To Loving You Hank Locklin	37/71	She's Leavin' (Bonnie, Please Don't Go) Jim Ed Brown	91/78	Shed So Many Tears Isaac Payton Sweat	
39/79	She's Been Keepin' Me Up Nights Bobby Lewis	81/81	She's Livin' It Up (And I'm Drinkin' 'Em Down) Allen Frizzell	12/63	Sheepskin Valley Claude King	
				80/87	Sheet Music Bill Anderson	
6/85	She's Comin' Back To Say Goodbye Eddie Rabbitt	26/77	She's Long Legged Joe Stampley	43/76	Sheik Of Chicago Joe Stampley	
1/89	She's Crazy For Leavin' Rodney Crowell	21/69	She's Lookin' Better By The Minute Jay Lee Webb	14/73	Shelter Of Your Eyes Don Williams	
66/72	She's Doing It To Me Again Ray Pillow	54/67	She's Looking Good Stan Hitchcock	33/73	Shenandoah Charlie McCoy	
1/95	She's Every Woman Garth Brooks	7/82	She's Lying Lee Greenwood	8/71	Sheriff Of Boone County Kenny Price	
66/76	She's Free But She's Not Easy Jim Glaser	87/78	She's Lying Next To Me Nick Nixon	94/75	Shhh Kathy Barnes	
46/96	She's Gettin' There Sawyer Brown	37/80	She's Made Of Faith Marty Robbins	73/67	Shinbone Orville And Ivy	
24/97	She's Going Home With Me Travis Tritt	72/66	She's Mighty Gone Johnny Darrell	47/66	Shindig In The Barn Tommy Collins	
48/00	She's Gone Ricochet	6/70	She's Mine George Jones	5/82	Shine Waylon Jennings	
	She's Gone Gone Gone	2/00	She's More Andy Griggs	56/88	Shine A Light On A Lie Robin Lee	
12/65	Lefty Frizzell	50/01	She's My Girl Billy Gilman	36/76	Shine On Ronnie Prophet	
44/84	Carl Jackson		She's [He's] My Rock	49/98	Shine On Jeff Carson	
6/89	Glen Campbell	20/73	Stoney Edwards	13/78	Shine On Me John Wesley Ryles	
74/83	She's Gone To L.A. Again Mickey Clark	8/75	Brenda Lee	3/83	Shine On (Shine All Your Sweet Love On Me) George Jones	
		2/84	George Jones	7/51	Shine, Shave, Shower (It's Saturday) Lefty Frizzell	
				1/87	Shine, Shine, Shine Eddy Raven	
				40/67	Shine, Shine, Shine Carl Perkins	

503

58/67	Shiny Red Automobile *George Morgan*	7/80	Shriner's Convention *Ray Stevens*	10/79	Simple Little Words *Cristy Lane*
19/69	Ship In The Bottle *Stonewall Jackson*	13/80	Shuffle Song *Margo Smith*	12/90	Simple Man *Charlie Daniels Band*
5/92	Ships That Don't Come In *Joe Diffie*	5/46	Shut That Gate *Ted Daffan*	45/71	Simple Thing As Love *Roy Clark*
28/66	Shirt, The *Norma Jean*	14/97	Shut Up And Drive *Chely Wright*		Sin ..see: (It's No)
21/01	Shiver *Jamie O'Neal*	1/94	Shut Up And Kiss Me *Mary Chapin Carpenter*		Sin Wagon
3/66	Shoe Goes On The Other Foot Tonight *Marty Robbins*	26/70	Shutters And Boards *Slim Whitman*	65/99	Dixie Chicks
				52/00	Dixie Chicks
22/86	Shoe String *Mel McDaniel*	7/51	Sick, Sober And Sorry *Johnny Bond*	73/70	Since December *Eddy Arnold*
83/81	Shoe's On The Other Foot Tonight *Montana*	70/81	Sidewalks Are Grey *Kenny Seratt*		Since I Don't Have You
				68/81	Don McLean
17/63	Shoes Of A Fool *Bill Goodwin*	F/70	Sidewalks Of Chicago *Merle Haggard*	6/91	Ronnie Milsap
1/98	Shoes You're Wearing *Clint Black*	41/01	Sideways *Darryl Worley*		Since I Fell For You
8/70	Shoeshine Man *Tom T. Hall*	72/83	Sign Of The Times *Donna Fargo*	10/76	Charlie Rich
65/84	Shoot First, Ask Questions Later *James & Michael Younger*		Signed Sealed And Delivered	20/79	Con Hunley
		2/48	Cowboy Copas	7/86	Since I Found You *Sweethearts Of The Rodeo*
31/01	Shoot Straight From Your Heart *Vince Gill*	6/48	Bob Atcher		Since I Met You, Baby
		8/48	Texas Jim Robertson	1/69	Sonny James
81/89	Shoot The Moon *Wayne Massey*	9/48	Jimmy Wakely	10/75	Freddy Fender
57/71	Short And Sweet *Bobby Bare*	10/61	Cowboy Copas	96/76	Since I Met You Boy *Jeannie Seely*
57/98	Shortenin' Bread *Tractors*		Silence On The Line	62/72	Since Then *Ray Pillow*
16/61	Shorty *Jimmy Smart*	29/80	Henson Cargill	54/69	Since They Fired The Band Director (At Murphy High) *Linda Manning*
	Shot Full Of Love	65/00	Chris LeDoux		
30/81	Randy Parton	F/80	Silent Night (After The Fight) *Ronnie Milsap*	84/77	Since You Broke My Heart *Don Everly*
19/83	Nitty Gritty Dirt Band				
73/90	McCarters	20/84	Silent Partners *David Frizzell & Shelly West*		Sincerely
1/51	Shot Gun Boogie *Tennessee Ernie Ford*			72/72	Kitty Wells
		7/81	Silent Treatment *Earl Thomas Conley*	8/89	Forester Sisters
30/84	Shot In The Dark *Leon Everette*			74/71	Sing A Happy Song *Connie Eaton*
23/80	Shotgun Rider *Joe Sun*	78/87	Silent Understanding *T.L. Lee with Kathy Walker*	3/63	Sing A Little Song Of Heartache *Rose Maddox*
55/75	Shotgun Rider *Marty Robbins*				
60/73	Shotgun Willie *Willie Nelson*	5/52	Silver And Gold *Pee Wee King*	54/75	Sing A Love Song, Porter Wagoner *Mike Wells*
	Should I Come Home (Or Should I Go Crazy)	15/91	Silver And Gold *Dolly Parton*		
		15/55	Silver Bell *Hank Snow & Chet Atkins*		Sing A Sad Song
83/75	Joe Allen			26/63	Buddy Cagle
3/79	Gene Watson	68/97	Silver Bells *Judds*	19/64	Merle Haggard
50/81	Should I Do It *Tanya Tucker*	25/77	Silver Bird *Tina Rainford*	19/77	Wynn Stewart
10/58	Should We Tell Him *Everly Brothers*	1/45	Silver Dew On The Blue Grass Tonight *Bob Wills*	70/69	Sing A Song About Love *Bobby Wright*
3/95	Should've Asked Her Faster *Ty England*	75/80	Silver Eagle *Atlanta Rhythm Section*	3/73	Sing About Love *Lynn Anderson*
1/93	Should've Been A Cowboy *Toby Keith*	18/77	Silver Medals And Sweet Memories *Statler Brothers*	59/72	Sing-Along Song *Mayf Nutter*
				66/74	Sing For The Good Times *Jack Greene*
46/89	Shoulda, Coulda, Woulda Loved You *Les Taylor*	4/46	Silver Spurs (On The Golden Stairs) *Gene Autry*	53/71	Sing High - Sing Low *Anne Murray*
71/00	Shoulda Shut Up *Bill Engvall*	25/90	Silver Stallion *Waylon Jennings/Willie Nelson/ Johnny Cash/Kris Kristofferson*	3/72	Sing Me A Love Song To Baby *Billy Walker*
1/73	Shoulder To Cry On *Charley Pride*			1/68	Sing Me Back Home *Merle Haggard*
34/79	Shoulder To Shoulder (Arm And Arm) *Roy Clark*	4/47	Silver Stars, Purple Sage, Eyes Of Blue *Cliffie Stone*	12/70	Singer Of Sad Songs *Waylon Jennings*
5/88	Shouldn't It Be Easier Than This *Charley Pride*		Silver Threads And Golden Needles	29/75	Singin' In The Kitchen *Bobby Bare & The Family*
1/84	Show Her *Ronnie Milsap*	16/62	Springfields	89/76	Singing A Happy Song *Larry G. Hudson*
30/62	Show Her Lots Of Gold *Ernest Tubb*	20/74	Linda Ronstadt		
		68/74	Charlie McCoy	4/54	Singing Hills *Slim Whitman*
11/72	Show Me *Barbara Mandrell*	68/94	Dolly Parton/Tammy Wynette/Loretta Lynn	18/71	Singing In Viet Nam Talking Blues *Johnny Cash*
96/77	Show Me A Brick Wall *Carl Smith*				
8/76	Show Me A Man *T.G. Sheppard*	64/96	Silver Tongue And Goldplated Lies *K.T. Oslin*	1/69	Singing My Song *Tammy Wynette*
56/78	Show Me A Sign *Jim Chesnut*	59/70	Silver Wings *Hagers*		Singing The Blues
7/49	Show Me The Way Back To Your Heart *Eddy Arnold*	20/76	Silver Wings And Golden Rings *Billie Jo Spears*	1/56	Marty Robbins
				17/83	Gail Davies
44/66	Show Me The Way To The Circus *Homesteaders*	67/70	Simple Days And Simple Ways *Bobby Lewis*	87/89	Jeff Golden
81/76	Show Me Where *Ruby Falls*		Simple I Love You	70/97	Kentucky Headhunters
71/85	Showdown *Carlette*	63/85	Karen Brooks	36/78	Single Again *Gary Stewart*
97/76	Showdown *Brian Shaw*	72/96	Mandy Barnett	74/81	Single Girl *Cindy Hurt*
73/71	Showing His Dollar *Webb Pierce*	53/01	Simple Life *Mary Chapin Carpenter*	1/99	Single White Female *Chely Wright*
70/89	Shows You What I Know *Andi And The Brown Sisters*				
		61/94	Simple Life *Andy Childs*	8/82	Single Women *Dolly Parton*
15/57	Shrine Of St. Cecilia *Faron Young*				

Sheb Single Again

My Big Iron Skillet — Wanda Jackson

6/60	**Sink The Bismarck** Johnny Horton		**Skip A Rope**			**Slow Hand**	
14/48	**Sinner's Death** Roy Acuff	1/68	Henson Cargill		53/81	Del Reeves	
55/00	**Sinners & Saints** George Jones	85/79	Roger Young		1/82	Conway Twitty	
	Sioux City Sue	10/48	**Slap Her Down Again Paw**		59/95	**Slow Me Down** Shelby Lynne	
1/45	Dick Thomas		Esmereldy		64/86	**Slow Motion** Malchak & Rucker	
2/46	Hoosier Hot Shots & Two Ton Baker	20/99	**Slave To The Habit** Shane Minor		47/84	**Slow Nights** Mel Tillis with Glen Campbell	
2/46	Zeke Manners	8/53	**Slaves Of A Hopeless Love Affair** Red Foley		36/89	**Slow Passin' Time** Anne Murray	
3/46	Tiny Hill	57/76	**Sleep All Mornin'** Ed Bruce		17/62	**Slow Poison** Johnny & Jack	
75/68	**Sissy** Statler Brothers	20/61	**Sleep, Baby, Sleep** Connie Hall			**Slow Poke**	
12/49	**Sister Of Sioux City Sue** Dick Thomas	11/78	**Sleep Tight, Good Night Man** Bobby Bare		1/51	Pee Wee King	
93/74	**Sister's Coming Home** Willie Nelson	4/81	**Sleepin' With The Radio On** Charly McClain		7/52	Hawkshaw Hawkins	
53/89	**Sit A Little Closer** Wagoneers		**Sleeping ..also see: A-Sleeping**		76/82	**Slow Texas Dancing** Donna Hazard	
54/71	**Sittin' Bull** Charlie Louvin	97/84	**Sleeping Back To Back** White Water Junction		85/79	**Slow Tunes And Promises** Bobby Hood	
83/80	**(Sittin' Here) Lovin' You** Troy Shondell	1/78	**Sleeping Single In A Double Bed** Barbara Mandrell			**Slowly**	
4/65	**Sittin' In An All Nite Cafe** Warner Mack	73/76	**Sleeping With A Memory** Kathy Barnes		1/54	Webb Pierce	
33/70	**Sittin' In Atlanta Station** Nat Stuckey	9/61	**Sleepy-Eyed John** Johnny Horton		29/71	Jimmy Dean & Dottie West	
3/66	**Sittin' On A Rock (Crying In A Creek)** Warner Mack		**Sleigh Ride**		37/81	Kippi Brannon	
1/97	**Sittin' On Go** Bryan White	67/95	Lorrie Morgan		75/89	**Slowly But Surely** Marie Osmond	
13/82	**(Sittin' On) The Dock Of The Bay** Waylon Jennings & Willie Nelson	64/96	Lorrie Morgan		46/93	**Small Price** Gibson/Miller Band	
14/49	**Sittin' On The Doorstep** Woody Carter	70/98	Dolly Parton (medley)		54/90	**Small Small World** Statler Brothers	
	Six Days On The Road	42/99	Lorrie Morgan		24/00	**Small Stuff** Alabama	
2/63	Dave Dudley	54/99	Garth Brooks		60/98	**Small Talk** Sawyer Brown	
58/74	Johnny Rivers	7/77	**Slide Off Of Your Satin Sheets** Johnny Paycheck		35/68	**Small Time Laboring Man** George Jones	
29/88	Steve Earle & The Dukes	22/79	**Slip Away** Dottsy		89/79	**Small Time Picker** Bobby Wayne Loftis	
13/97	Sawyer Brown	48/81	**Slip Away** Mel Street & Sandy Powell		44/97	**Small Town** John Anderson	
41/65	**Six Foot Two By Four** Willis Brothers	79/80	**Slip Away** Jim West		1/87	**Small Town Girl** Steve Wariner	
27/65	**Six Lonely Hours** Kitty Wells	46/64	**Slippin'** Wanda Jackson		2/91	**Small Town Saturday Night** Hal Ketchum	
70/72	**Six Pack Of Trouble** O.B. McClinton		**Slippin' And Slidin'**		24/72	**Smell The Flowers** Jerry Reed	
9/01	**Six-Pack Summer** Phil Vassar	14/73	Billy "Crash" Craddock			**Smellin' Like A Rose ..see: (They Always Come Out)**	
	Six Pack To Go	43/82	Stephanie Winslow		1/00	**Smile** Lonestar	
10/60	Hank Thompson	7/50	**Slippin' Around With Jole Blon** Bud Messner		15/74	**Smile For Me** Lynn Anderson	
68/74	Hank Wilson	4/73	**Slippin' Away** Jean Shepard		39/72	**Smile, Somebody Loves You** Linda Gail Lewis	
	634-5789	19/78	**Slippin' Away** Bellamy Brothers		13/60	**Smiling Bill McCall** Johnny Cash	
75/78	Jimmie Peters	61/81	**Slippin' Out, Slippin' In** Bill Nash		24/59	**Smoke Along The Track** Stonewall Jackson	
54/82	Marlow Tackett	17/79	**Slippin' Up, Slippin' Around** Cristy Lane		84/82	**Smoke Gets In Your Eyes** Narvel Felts	
12/65	**Six Times A Day (The Trains Came Down)** Dick Curless		**Slipping Around**		44/96	**Smoke In Her Eyes** Ty England	
66/99	**Six Tons Of Toys** Paul Brandt	1/49	Ernest Tubb			**Smoke On The Water**	
51/71	**Six Weeks Every Summer (Christmas Every Other Year)** Dottie West	1/49	Margaret Whiting & Jimmy Wakely		1/44	Red Foley	
4/70	**Six White Horses** Tommy Cash	5/49	Floyd Tillman		1/45	Bob Wills	
61/86	**Sixteen Candles** Jerry Lee Lewis	13/50	Texas Jim Robertson		7/45	Boyd Heath	
86/82	**16 Lovin' Ounces To The Pound** Don Lee	23/64	Marion Worth & George Morgan		12/00	**Smoke Rings In The Dark** Gary Allan	
1/55	**Sixteen Tons** "Tennessee" Ernie Ford	45/65	Roy Drusky & Priscilla Mitchell			**Smoke! Smoke! Smoke! (That Cigarette)**	
7/82	**16th Avenue** Lacy J. Dalton	98/88	Mack Abernathy		1/47	Tex Williams	
59/78	**$60 Duck** Lewie Wickham	78/82	**Sloe Gin And Fast Women** Wayne Kemp		32/68	**Tex Williams ('68)**	
75/87	**67 Miles To Cow Town** Hollie Hughes	10/78	**Slow And Easy** Randy Barlow		97/73	**Commander Cody**	
19/85	**Size Seven Round (Made Of Gold)** George Jones & Lacy J. Dalton	8/86	**Slow Boat To China** Girls Next Door		78/78	Tom Bresh	
78/84	**Ski Bumpus/Banjo Fantasy II** Wickline Band	1/84	**Slow Burn** T.G. Sheppard		89/82	Sammy Davis, Jr.	
3/66	**Skid Row Joe** Porter Wagoner	10/85	**Slow Burning Memory** Vern Gosdin		8/49	**Smokey Mountain Boogie** Tennessee Ernie Ford	
79/87	**Skin Deep** Bobbi Lace	56/81	**Slow Country Dancin'** Judy Bailey			**Smokey Mountain Memories**	
70/69	**Skin's Gettin' Closer To The Bone** Cheryl Poole	67/99	**Slow Dance More** Kenny Rogers		13/75	Mel Street	
97/73	**Skinny Dippin'** Demetriss Tapp	49/84	**Slow Dancin'** Kimberly Springs		F/82	Earl Thomas Conley	
		6/79	**Slow Dancing** Johnny Duncan		71/83	**Smokin' In The Rockies** Gary Stewart & Dean Dillon	
		13/82	**Slow Down** Lacy J. Dalton		1/80	**Smoky Mountain Rain** Ronnie Milsap	
		46/99	**Slow Down** Mark Nesler		12/69	**Smoky Places** Billy Walker	
		75/74	**Slow Down** Chuck Price		5/69	**Smoky The Bar** Hank Thompson	
		70/78	**Slow Drivin'** Kenny Starr				

Skin Your Own Polecat — Del Reeves

	Smooth Sailin'	19/59	**So Soon** *Jimmy Newman*	8/74	**Some Kind Of A Woman**
68/78	Connie Smith	71/82	**(So This Is) Happy Hour** *Snuff*		*Faron Young*
47/79	Sonny Throckmorton	20/71	**So This Is Love** *Tommy Cash*	3/92	**Some Kind Of Trouble**
6/80	T.G. Sheppard	41/86	**So This Is Love** *Charly McClain*		*Tanya Tucker*
32/79	**Smooth Sailin'** *Jim Weatherly*	51/00	**So What** *Tammy Cochran*	68/91	**Some Kinda Woman** *Linda Davis*
43/85	**Smooth Sailing (Rock In The Road)** *Mark Gray*	14/62	**So Wrong** *Patsy Cline*	27/81	**Some Love Songs Never Die** *B.J. Thomas*
		F/57	**So You Think You've Got Troubles** *Marvin Rainwater*	10/82	**Some Memories Just Won't Die** *Marty Robbins*
94/79	**Smooth Southern Highway** *Don Cox*	58/79	**Soap** *O.B. McClinton*	61/82	**Some Never Stand A Chance** *Family Brown*
77/76	**Snap, Crackle And Pop** *Johnny Carver*	13/78	**Soft Lights And Hard Country Music** *Moe Bandy*	20/82	**Some Of My Best Friends Are Old Songs** *Louise Mandrell*
	Snap Your Fingers	97/78	**Soft Lights And Slow Sexy Music** *Jody Miller*	72/85	**Some Of Shelly's Blues** *Maines Brothers Band*
40/71	Dick Curless	10/49	**Soft Lips** *Hank Thompson*	28/73	**Some Old California Memory** *Henson Cargill*
12/74	Don Gibson	65/73	**Soft Lips And Hard Liquor** *Charlie Walker*	16/88	**Some Old Side Road** *Keith Whitley*
1/87	Ronnie Milsap	73/98	**Soft Place To Fall** *Allison Moorer*		
5/83	**Snapshot** *Sylvia*	3/61	**Soft Rain** *Ray Price*	54/73	**Some Roads Have No Ending** *Warner Mack*
48/81	**Sneakin' Around** *Kin Vassy*	8/72	**Soft, Sweet And Warm** *David Houston*	57/85	**Some Such Foolishness** *Tommy Roe*
16/67	**Sneaking 'Cross The Border** *Harden Trio*	30/78	**Softest Touch In Town** *Bobby G. Rice*	13/96	**Some Things Are Meant To Be** *Linda Davis*
69/74	**Sneaky Snake** *Tom T. Hall*	74/69	**Softly And Tenderly** *Lois Johnson*	7/00	**Some Things Never Change** *Tim McGraw*
2/66	**Snow Flake** *Jim Reeves*	4/60	**Softly And Tenderly (I'll Hold You In My Arms)** *Lewis Pruitt*	83/81	**Some You Win, Some You Lose** *Orion*
28/63	**Snow White Cloud** *Frank Taylor*	F/78	**Softly, As I Leave You** *Elvis Presley*	34/84	**Somebody Buy This Cowgirl A Beer** *Shelly West*
10/70	**Snowbird** *Anne Murray*	69/73	**Sold American** *Kinky Friedman*	4/85	**Somebody Else's Fire** *Janie Fricke*
46/84	**So Close** *Wright Brothers*	29/76	**Sold Out Of Flagpoles** *Johnny Cash*	5/93	**Somebody Else's Moon** *Collin Raye*
72/83	**So Close** *Backroads*	1/95	**Sold (The Grundy County Auction Incident)** *John Michael Montgomery*	10/76	**Somebody Hold Me (Until She Passes By)** *Narvel Felts*
43/77	**So Close Again** *Margo Smith & Norro Wilson*	71/91	**Soldier Boy** *Donna Fargo*	69/97	**Somebody Knew** *Rhett Akins*
4/56	**So Doggone Lonesome** *Johnny Cash*	51/80	**Soldier Of Fortune** *Tom T. Hall*	62/67	**Somebody Knows My Dog** *Willis Brothers*
68/83	**So Easy To Love** *Wright Brothers*	54/86	**Soldier Of Love** *Billy Burnette*	20/81	**Somebody Led Me Away** *Loretta Lynn*
64/88	**So Far Not So Good** *Jeff Chance*	15/59	**Soldier's Joy** *Hawkshaw Hawkins*	1/87	**Somebody Lied** *Ricky Van Shelton*
22/82	**So Fine** *Oak Ridge Boys*		**Soldier's Last Letter**	1/66	**Somebody Like Me** *Eddy Arnold*
68/78	**So Good** *Jewel Blanch*	1/44	Ernest Tubb	66/93	**Somebody Like That** *Glen Campbell*
27/78	**So Good, So Rare, So Fine** *Freddie Hart*	3/71	Merle Haggard	67/88	**Somebody Loses, Somebody Wins** *Rosie Flores*
86/89	**So Good To Be In Love** *Karen Staley*	46/66	**Soldier's Prayer In Viet Nam** *Don Reno & Benny Martin*	21/72	**Somebody Loves Me** *Johnny Paycheck*
F/77	**So Good Woman** *Waylon Jennings*	57/96	**Solid Ground** *Ricky Skaggs*	8/76	**Somebody Loves You** *Crystal Gayle*
2/95	**So Help Me Girl** *Joe Diffie*	F/79	**Solitaire** *Elvis Presley*	9/93	**Somebody New** *Billy Ray Cyrus*
22/62	**So How Come (No One Loves Me)** *Don Gibson*	28/69	**Solitary** *Don Gibson*	84/87	**Somebody Ought To Tell Him That She's Gone** *Ogden Harless*
43/69	**So Long** *Bobby Helms*	14/76	**Solitary Man** *T.G. Sheppard*		**Somebody Paints The Wall**
69/68	**So Long, Charlie Brown, Don't Look For Me Around** *Sammi Smith*	1/77	**Some Broken Hearts Never Mend** *Don Williams*	62/89	Josh Logan
1/44	**So Long Pal** *Al Dexter*	47/82	**Some Day My Ship's Comin' In** *Joe Waters*	8/93	Tracy Lawrence
14/55	**So Lovely, Baby** *Rusty & Doug*	10/81	**Some Days Are Diamonds (Some Days Are Stone)** *John Denver*	16/62	**Somebody Save Me** *Ferlin Husky*
16/59	**So Many Times** *Roy Acuff*	45/82	**Some Days It Rains All Night Long** *Terri Gibbs*	1/85	**Somebody Should Leave** *Reba McEntire*
	So Many Ways	7/02	**Some Days You Gotta Dance** *Dixie Chicks*	22/97	**Somebody Slap Me** *John Anderson*
28/73	Eddy Arnold	1/85	**Some Fools Never Learn** *Steve Wariner*	1/76	**Somebody Somewhere** *Loretta Lynn*
33/77	David Houston		**Some Gave All**	6/79	**Somebody Special** *Donna Fargo*
45/66	**So Much For Me, So Much For You** *Liz Anderson*	72/92	Billy Ray Cyrus	33/98	**Somebody To Love** *Suzy Bogguss*
1/96	**So Much For Pretending** *Bryan White*	52/93	Billy Ray Cyrus	55/96	**Somebody To Love You** *Wynonna*
46/70	**So Much In Love With You** *David Rogers*	1/92	**Some Girls Do** *Sawyer Brown*		
3/92	**So Much Like My Dad** *George Strait*	22/86	**Some Girls Have All The Luck** *Louise Mandrell*		
	So Round, So Firm, So Fully Packed	8/91	**Some Guys Have All The Love** *Little Texas*		
1/47	Merle Travis	25/84	**Some Hearts Get All The Breaks** *Charly McClain*		
3/47	Johnny Bond	81/86	**Some Hearts Get All The Breaks** *Roger Miller*		
5/47	Ernest Tubb	17/78	**Some I Wrote** *Statler Brothers*		
	So Sad (To Watch Good Love Go Bad)				
12/70	Hank Williams, Jr. & Lois Johnson				
31/76	Connie Smith				
76/78	Steve Wariner				
28/83	Emmylou Harris				

18/63	**Somebody Told Somebody** *Rose Maddox*	59/74	**Someone Came To See Me (In The Middle Of The Night)** *Patti Page*	71/75	**Something Just Came Over Me** *Charlie Rich*
59/77	**Somebody Took Her Love (And Never Gave It Back)** *Jimmie Peters*	17/75	**Someone Cares For You** *Red Steagall*	1/99	**Something Like That** *Tim McGraw*
9/86	**Somebody Wants Me Out Of The Way** *George Jones*	1/82	**Someone Could Lose A Heart Tonight** *Eddie Rabbitt*	73/92	**Something Moving In Me** *Darryl & Don Ellis*
	Somebody Will	3/96	**Someone Else's Dream** *Faith Hill*	14/90	**Something Of A Dreamer** *Mary-Chapin Carpenter*
57/95	*McBride & The Ride*	1/95	**Someone Else's Star** *Bryan White*	4/51	**Something Old, Something New** *Eddy Arnold*
51/98	*River Road*	14/90	**Someone Else's Trouble Now** *Highway 101*	53/74	**Something On Your Mind** *Jack Blanchard & Misty Morgan*
52/69	**Somebody's Always Leaving** *Stonewall Jackson*	46/99	**Someone Else's Turn To Cry** *Chalee Tennison*	23/62	**Something Precious** *Skeeter Davis*
7/83	**Somebody's Always Saying Goodbye** *Anne Murray*	26/84	**Someone Is Falling In Love** *Kathy Mattea*	10/68	**Something Pretty** *Wynn Stewart*
	Somebody's Back In Town	11/79	**Someone Is Looking For Someone Like You** *Gail Davies*	66/99	**Something Real** *Shana Petrone*
6/59	*Wilburn Brothers*	26/85	**Someone Like You** *Emmylou Harris*	17/68	**Something Special** *Mel Tillis*
81/84	*Chris Hillman*	94/77	**Someone Loves Him** *Sue Richards*	2/97	**Something That We Do** *Clint Black*
2/51	**Somebody's Been Beatin' My Time** *Eddy Arnold*		**Someone Loves You Honey**	81/78	**Something To Believe In** *Don Drumm*
32/81	**Somebody's Darling, Somebody's Wife** *Dottsy*	84/75	*Marie Owens*		**Something To Brag About**
15/92	**Somebody's Doin' Me Right** *Keith Whitley*	1/78	*Charley Pride*	18/70	*Charlie Louvin & Melba Montgomery*
64/78	**Somebody's Gonna Do It Tonight** *R.C. Bannon*	70/85	**Someone Must Be Missing You Tonight** *Terri Gibbs*	9/78	*Mary Kay Place with Willie Nelson*
1/83	**Somebody's Gonna Love You** *Lee Greenwood*	73/71	**Someone Stepped In (And Stole Me Blind)** *Webb Pierce*	63/72	**Something To Call Mine** *Bill Rice*
65/80	**Somebody's Gotta Do The Losing** *Stephany Samone*		**Someone To Give My Love To**	85/82	**Something To Love For Again** *Diane Pfeifer*
61/92	**Somebody's In Love** *Lisa Stewart*	4/72	*Johnny Paycheck*	36/70	**Something To Think About** *Luke The Drifter, Jr.*
8/81	**Somebody's Knockin'** *Terri Gibbs*	42/93	*Tracy Byrd*	46/98	**Something To Think About** *David Kersh*
1/84	**Somebody's Needin' Somebody** *Conway Twitty*	32/67	**Someone Told My Story** *Merle Haggard*	38/00	**Something To Write Home About** *Craig Morgan*
19/99	**Somebody's Out There Watching** *Kinleys*	3/98	**Someone You Used To Know** *Collin Raye*	15/70	**Something Unseen** *Jack Greene*
9/52	**Somebody's Stolen My Honey** *Ernest Tubb*	60/85	**Someone's Gonna Love Me Tonight** *Southern Pacific*		**Something With A Ring To It**
1/91	**Someday** *Alan Jackson*	30/65	**Someone's Gotta Cry** *Jean Shepard*	54/90	*Mark Collie*
12/57	**Someday** *Webb Pierce*	29/76	**Someone's With Your Wife Tonight, Mister** *Bobby Borchers*	68/98	*Garth Brooks*
28/86	**Someday** *Steve Earle*	24/93	**Someplace Far Away (Careful What You're Dreamin')** *Hal Ketchum*	81/78	**Something's Burning** *Kathy Barnes*
51/96	**Someday** *Steve Azar*	45/99	**Somethin' 'Bout A Sunday** *Michael Peterson*	24/93	**Something's Gonna Change Her Mind** *Mark Collie*
22/79	**Someday My Day Will Come** *George Jones*	60/80	**Somethin' 'Bout You Baby I Like** *Glen Campbell & Rita Coolidge*	72/89	**Something's Got A Hold On Me** *James Rogers*
60/87	**Someday My Ship Will Sail** *Emmylou Harris*	33/01	**Somethin' In The Water** *Jeffrey Steele*	60/69	**Something's Missing (It's You)** *Jackie Burns*
70/88	**Someday, Somenight** *Trinity Lane*	40/97	**Somethin' Like This** *Joe Diffie*	19/69	**Something's Wrong In California** *Waylon Jennings*
	Someday Soon	13/81	**Somethin' On The Radio** *Jacky Ward*	F/81	**Sometime, Somewhere, Somehow** *Barbara Mandrell*
39/76	*Kathy Barnes*	67/87	**Somethin' You Got** *Nielsen White Band*	10/74	**Sometime Sunshine** *Jim Ed Brown*
21/82	*Moe Bandy*	6/74	**Something** *Johnny Rodriguez*	1/76	**Sometimes** *Bill Anderson & Mary Lou Turner*
12/91	*Suzy Bogguss*	10/73	**Something About You I Love** *Johnny Paycheck*	21/01	**Sometimes** *Clay Davidson*
4/70	**Someday We'll Be Together** *Bill Anderson & Jan Howard*	43/94	**Something Already Gone** *Carlene Carter*	59/76	**Sometimes** *Johnny Lee*
2/71	**Someday We'll Look Back** *Merle Haggard*	6/71	**Something Beautiful (To Remember)** *Slim Whitman*	3/86	**Sometimes A Lady** *Eddy Raven*
1/84	**Someday When Things Are Good** *Merle Haggard*	62/74	**Something Better** *O.B. McClinton*	6/73	**Sometimes A Memory Ain't Enough** *Jerry Lee Lewis*
45/78	**Someday You Will** *John Wesley Ryles*	19/75	**Something Better To Do** *Olivia Newton-John*	34/81	**Sometimes I Cry When I'm Alone** *Sammi Smith*
10/49	**Someday You'll Call My Name** *Jimmy Wakely*	17/67	**Something Fishy** *Dolly Parton*	79/78	**Sometimes I Do** *Ernest Tubb*
	Someday (You'll Want Me To Want You)	31/64	**Something I Dreamed** *George Jones*	41/95	**Sometimes I Forget** *Doug Stone*
2/46	*Elton Britt*	2/85	**Something In My Heart** *Ricky Skaggs*	9/83	**Sometimes I Get Lucky And Forget** *Gene Watson*
3/46	*Hoosier Hot Shots & Sally Foster*	14/92	**Something In Red** *Lorrie Morgan*	9/76	**Sometimes I Talk In My Sleep** *Randy Cornor*
4/46	*Gene Autry*			12/62	**Sometimes I'm Tempted** *Marty Robbins*
70/81	**Somehow, Someway And Someday** *Amarillo*			67/79	**Sometimes Love** *Mundo Earwood*
5/87	**Someone** *Lee Greenwood*				
8/66	**Someone Before Me** *Wilburn Brothers*				

38/89	Sometimes Love's Not A Pretty Thing *Zaca Creek*	85/89	Song A Day Keeps The Blues Away *Mickey Jones*	63/86	Southern Air *Ray Stevens*
55/88	Sometimes She Feels Like A Man *Charly McClain*	8/74	Song And Dance Man *Johnny Paycheck*	91/88	Southern And Proud Of It *Jeff Golden*
7/95	Sometimes She Forgets *Travis Tritt*	66/73	Song For Everyone *Ray Griff*	37/68	Southern Bound *Kenny Price*
	Sometimes When We Touch	53/69	Song For Jenny *Ed Bruce*	5/77	Southern California *George Jones & Tammy Wynette*
F/81	Stephanie Winslow	91/80	Song For Noel *King Edward IV & The Knights*	42/82	Southern Fried *Bill Anderson*
6/85	Mark Gray & Tammy Wynette	6/95	Song For The Life *Alan Jackson*	27/95	Southern Grace *Little Texas*
	Sometimes You Just Can't Win	92/74	Song I'd Like To Sing *Kris Kristofferson & Rita Coolidge*	96/89	Southern Lady *Arne Benoni*
17/62	George Jones			6/73	Southern Loving *Jim Ed Brown*
10/71	George Jones	69/88	Song In My Heart *Mark Gray & Bobbi Lace*	1/77	Southern Nights *Glen Campbell*
27/82	Linda Ronstadt & John David Souther			45/01	Southern Rain *Billy Ray Cyrus*
		5/77	Song In The Night *Johnny Duncan*	1/81	Southern Rains *Mel Tillis*
37/70	Someway *Don Gibson*	89/78	Song Man *Rick Jacques*	1/90	Southern Star *Alabama*
66/74	Somewhere Around Midnight *George Morgan*	69/73	Songman *Cashman & West*	67/97	Southern Streamline *John Fogerty*
46/89	Somewhere Between *Suzy Bogguss*	F/73	Song Nobody Sings *Jerry Wallace*		Southern Women
2/74	Somewhere Between Love And Tomorrow *Roy Clark*	54/80	Song Of The Patriot *Johnny Cash*	86/83	Owen Brothers
			Song Of The South	33/84	Wright Brothers
23/88	Somewhere Between Ragged And Right *John Anderson*	57/81	Johnny Russell	65/94	Souvenirs *Suzy Bogguss*
		72/82	Tom T. Hall & Earl Scruggs	66/87	Souvenirs *Lane Caudell*
1/82	Somewhere Between Right And Wrong *Earl Thomas Conley*	1/89	Alabama	100/76	Souvenirs *Colleen Peterson*
		2/93	Song Remembers When *Trisha Yearwood*	68/72	Souvenirs And California *Mem'rys Billie Jo Spears*
	Somewhere Down The Line				
50/83	Younger Brothers	37/71	Song To Mama *Carter Family*	9/89	Sowin' Love *Paul Overstreet*
3/84	T.G. Sheppard	44/72	Song To Sing *Susan Raye*		Spanish Eyes
65/86	Somewhere In America *Mac Davis*	29/75	Song We Fell In Love To *Connie Smith*	20/79	Charlie Rich
				8/88	Willie Nelson (with Julio Iglesias)
57/94	Somewhere In Between *Dude Mowrey*	13/79	Song We Made Love To *Mickey Gilley*	3/53	Spanish Fire Ball *Hank Snow*
				56/79	Spare A Little Lovin' (On A Fool) *Arnie Rue*
84/89	Somewhere In Canada *David Walsh*	10/65	Sons Of Katie Elder *Johnny Cash*		Sparkling Brown Eyes
		2/93	Soon *Tanya Tucker*	4/54	Webb Pierce with Wilburn Brothers
49/97	Somewhere In Love *John & Audrey Wiggins*	53/77	Soon As I Touched Her *Dorsey Burnette*	30/60	George Jones
				49/73	Dickey Lee
3/91	Somewhere In My Broken Heart *Billy Dean*	6/90	Sooner Or Later *Eddy Raven*	10/51	Sparrow In The Tree Top *Rex Allen*
		19/62	Sooner Or Later *Webb Pierce*		
55/83	Somewhere In Texas *Ray Price*	100/77	Sophisticated Country Lady *Loretta Robey*	29/91	Speak Of The Devil *Pirates Of The Mississippi*
29/87	Somewhere In The Night *Sawyer Brown*				
		5/64	Sorrow On The Rocks *Porter Wagoner*	9/82	Speak Softly *Gene Watson*
7/95	Somewhere In The Vicinity Of The Heart *Shenandoah with Alison Krauss*			29/72	Special Day *Arlene Harden*
		63/88	Sorry Girls *Goldens*	70/88	Speed Of The Sound Of Loneliness *Kim Carnes*
		50/64	Sorry I Never Knew You *Sego Brothers And Naomi*		
15/72	Somewhere In Virginia In The Rain *Jack Blanchard & Misty Morgan*			82/89	Spelling On The Stone *Spelling On The Stone*
		59/96	Sorry You Asked? *Dwight Yoakam*		
				66/74	Spiders & Snakes *Jim Stafford*
22/73	Somewhere, My Love *Red Steagall*		Soul And Inspiration ..see: (You're My)	5/94	Spilled Perfume *Pam Tillis*
			Soul Deep	2/99	Spirit Of A Boy - Wisdom Of A Man *Randy Travis*
1/93	Somewhere Other Than The Night *Garth Brooks*	22/70	Eddy Arnold		
		63/73	Guy Shannon	14/58	Splish Splash *Bobby Darin*
	Somewhere South Of Macon	27/77	Soul Of A Honky Tonk Woman *Mel McDaniel*	F/73	Spokane Motel Blues *Tom T. Hall*
100/77	Marshall Chapman			71/77	Spread A Little Love Around *Jody Miller*
79/78	Rattlesnake Annie	10/82	Soul Searchin' *Leon Everette*		
80/81	Somewhere To Come When It Rains *John Wesley Ryles*	1/73	Soul Song *Joe Stampley*	61/72	Spread It Around *Brian Collins*
		64/70	Soul You Never Had *Jan Howard*	43/81	Spread My Wings *Tim Rex And Oklahoma*
1/87	Somewhere Tonight *Highway 101*	18/75	Soulful Woman *Kenny O'Dell*		
69/69	Son *Jerry Wallace*	1/84	Sound Of Goodbye *Crystal Gayle*		Spring
41/69	Son Of A Coal Man *Del Reeves*	21/73	Sound Of Goodbye *Jerry Wallace*	30/69	Clay Hart
	Son Of A Preacher Man	21/62	Sound Of Your Footsteps *Wilburn Brothers*	18/75	Tanya Tucker
40/69	Peggy Little			12/78	Spring Fever *Loretta Lynn*
95/89	Bobbi Lace	6/83	Sounds Like Love *Johnny Lee*	2/58	Squaws Along The Yukon *Hank Thompson*
5/74	Son Of A Rotten Gambler *Anne Murray*		Sounds Of Goodbye		
		31/68	George Morgan	61/79	Squeeze Box *Freddy Fender*
58/68	Son Of A Sawmill Man *Osborne Brothers*	41/68	Tommy Cash	16/02	Squeeze Me In *Garth Brooks with Trisha Yearwood*
		15/70	South *Roger Miller*		
14/79	Son Of Clayton Delaney *Tom T. Hall*	41/99	South Of Santa Fe *Brooks & Dunn*	74/99	Squeezin' The Love Outta You *Redmon & Vale*
		91/87	South Of The Border *Clay Blaker*		
	Son Of Hickory Holler's Tramp	27/95	Southbound *Sammy Kershaw*	68/88	Stairs, The *Rosemary Sharp*
22/68	Johnny Darrell	99/77	Southbound *R.C. Bannon*	2/58	Stairway Of Love *Marty Robbins*
32/77	Johnny Russell	71/88	Southern Accent *Bama Band*	5/67	Stamp Out Loneliness *Stonewall Jackson*
71/83	Son Of The South *Bill Anderson*				

8/50	Stampede Roy Rogers		Starting All Over Again	60/70	Steppin' Out Jerry Smith	
66/99	Stampede Chris LeDoux	16/78	Don Gibson	92/76	Steppin' Out Tonight Lori Parker	
5/86	Stand A Little Rain	73/89	Razzy Bailey	70/89	Steppin' Stone Marie Osmond	
	Nitty Gritty Dirt Band	17/80	Starting Over Tammy Wynette	16/98	Stepping Stone Lari White	
16/61	Stand At Your Window		Starting Over Again	1/92	Sticks And Stones	
	Jim Reeves	1/80	Dolly Parton		Tracy Lawrence	
1/99	Stand Beside Me Jo Dee Messina	19/96	Reba McEntire	1/63	Still Bill Anderson	
10/66	Stand Beside Me Jimmy Dean	4/86	Starting Over Again	7/79	Still A Woman Margo Smith	
1/80	Stand By Me Mickey Gilley		Steve Wariner	34/65	Still Alive In '65 Jim Nesbitt	
	Stand By My Woman Man ..see: (I'm A)	55/94	State Fair Doug Supernaw	20/91	Still Burnin' For You Rob Crosby	
		2/94	State Of Mind Clint Black	92/87	Still Dancing Loney Hutchins	
	Stand By Your Man	70/97	State Of Mind Crystal Bernard	1/81	Still Doin' Time George Jones	
1/68	Tammy Wynette	74/83	State Of Our Union	48/92	Still Got A Crush On You	
88/81	David Allan Coe		Charlie McCoy & Laney Hicks		Davis Daniel	
82/89	Lyle Lovett	17/66	Stateside Mel Tillis	11/97	Still Holding On	
56/98	Tammy Wynette		Statue Of A Fool		Clint Black & Martina McBride	
12/86	Stand On It Mel McDaniel	1/69	Jack Greene	27/01	Still Holding Out For You	
5/85	Stand Up Mel McDaniel	10/74	Brian Collins		SheDaisy	
28/62	Stand Up Ferlin Husky	91/79	Bill Medley	33/86	Still Hurtin' Me	
14/78	Standard Lie Number One	2/90	Ricky Van Shelton		Charlie Daniels Band	
	Stella Parton	5/77	Statues Without Hearts	60/88	Still I Stay Charly McClain	
34/01	Standin' Still		Larry Gatlin	23/98	Still In Love With You Travis Tritt	
	Clark Family Experience		Stay A Little Longer	56/86	Still In The Picture Leon Everette	
65/68	Standing In The Rain	2/46	Bob Wills	63/83	Still In The Ring Tammy Wynette	
	Chaparral Brothers	22/73	Willie Nelson	1/84	Still Losing You Ronnie Milsap	
5/66	Standing In The Shadows	17/82	Mel Tillis		Still Loving You	
	Hank Williams, Jr.	89/81	Stay Away From Jim	56/70	Bob Luman	
17/74	Standing In Your Line		Jimmy Arthur Ordge	7/74	Bob Luman	
	Barbara Fairchild	20/75	Stay Away From The Apple Tree	95/79	Troy Shondell	
63/87	Standing Invitation Adam Baker		Billie Jo Spears	27/63	Still Loving You Clyde Beavers	
19/93	Standing Knee Deep In A River (Dying Of Thirst) Kathy Mattea	49/79	(Stay Away From) The Cocaine Train Johnny Paycheck	58/85	Still On A Roll Moe Bandy & Joe Stampley	
2/95	Standing On The Edge Of Goodbye John Berry	8/95	Stay Forever Hal Ketchum	57/92	Still Out There Swinging Paul Overstreet	
		41/89	Stay November Kevin Welch			
52/95	Standing On The Edge Of Love	86/88	Stay Out Of My Arms	62/88	Still Pickin' Up After You	
	Clinton Gregory		Jim Lauderdale		Kendalls	
50/92	Standing On The Promises	7/70	Stay There 'Til I Get There	69/97	Still Standing Tall Brady Seals	
	Lionel Cartwright		Lynn Anderson	3/83	Still Taking Chances	
3/94	Standing Outside The Fire	61/80	Stay Until The Rain Stops		Michael Murphey	
	Garth Brooks		Kathy Carllile		Still The One	
5/76	Standing Room Only		Stay With Me	11/77	Bill Anderson	
	Barbara Mandrell	6/79	Dave & Sugar	60/82	Thrasher Brothers	
	Standing Tall	57/79	Dandy	79/89	Still The Same Bonnie Guitar	
15/80	Billie Jo Spears	86/85	Exile	4/75	Still Thinkin' 'Bout You	
32/96	Lorrie Morgan	40/78	Stay With Me Nick Noble		Billy "Crash" Craddock	
75/86	Standing Too Close To The Moon	89/83	Stay With Me Tammy Chaparro	5/88	Still Within The Sound Of My Voice Glen Campbell	
	Tina Danielle	1/84	Stay Young Don Williams			
92/80	Star, The Melba Montgomery	65/95	Steady As She Goes Mark Collie	74/81	Stirrin' Up Feelings Diana Trask	
78/74	Star Of The Bar Troy Seals	26/79	Steady As The Rain Stella Parton	7/57	Stolen Moments Hank Snow	
	(Star Of Wonder) ..see: We Three Kings	9/50	Steal Away Red Foley	100/77	Stolen Moments Daniel	
		74/79	Steal Away Paul Schmucker	3/74	Stomp Them Grapes Mel Tillis	
	Star Spangled Banner	50/75	Stealin' Jacky Ward		(Stompin' Grapes And Gettin' Silly) ..see: Me And Millie	
58/96	Ricochet	28/77	Stealin' Feelin' Mike Lunsford			
35/01	Faith Hill	18/99	Steam Ty Herndon	87/82	Stompin' On My Heart	
	Star-Studded Nights	F/73	Steamroller Blues Elvis Presley		Glen Bailey	
54/77	Ed Bruce	4/47	Steel Guitar Rag Merle Travis	59/97	Stone, The John Berry	
78/80	Shoppe	9/49	Steel Guitar Ramble	60/89	Stone By Stone Tim Mensy	
61/85	Starlite Karen Taylor-Good		Cecil Campbell	40/94	Stone Cold Country	
	Stars And Stripes On Iwo Jima	4/46	Steel Guitar Stomp Hank Penny		Gibson/Miller Band	
1/45	Bob Wills	15/66	Steel Rail Blues	75/88	Stone Cold Love Beards	
4/45	Sons Of The Pioneers		George Hamilton IV	52/75	Stone Crazy Freddy Weller	
	Stars On The Water	73/91	Steel Rails Alison Krauss	41/79	Stone Wall (Around Your Heart) Gary Stewart	
30/81	Rodney Crowell	6/71	Step Aside Faron Young			
86/83	Tommy St. John	7/82	Step Back Ronnie McDowell	19/75	Stoned At The Jukebox Hank Williams, Jr.	
2/96	Stars Over Texas Tracy Lawrence	1/81	Step By Step Eddie Rabbitt			
6/90	Start All Over Again	79/82	Step In The Right Direction	31/72	Stonin' Around Dick Curless	
	Desert Rose Band		Judy Taylor	8/58	Stood Up Ricky Nelson	
74/75	Start All Over Again	62/98	Step Right Up Cactus Choir	53/67	Stood Up Floyd Cramer	
	Johnny Carver	1/85	Step That Step Sawyer Brown		Stop And Smell The Roses	
39/99	Start Over Georgia Collin Raye	43/69	Stepchild Billie Jo Spears	29/74	Henson Cargill	
52/99	Start The Car Travis Tritt	9/80	Steppin' Out Mel Tillis	40/74	Mac Davis	
41/93	Startin' Over Blues Joe Diffie	46/88	Steppin' Out David Ball			

509

Stupid Cupid – Connie Francis / Wanda Jackson / Patsy Cline ★★★

100/88	**Stop And Take The Time** Faron Young	5/83	**Stranger In My House** Ronnie Milsap ★★
93/77	**Stop And Think It Over** Mike Boyd	16/99	**Stranger In My Mirror** Randy Travis
69/74	**Stop If You Love Me** Terry Stafford		**Stranger In My Place**
26/64	**Stop Me** Bill Phillips	27/71	Anne Murray
48/88	**Stop Me (If You've Heard This One Before)** Larry Boone	79/75	Anne Murray
		69/80	Orion
14/94	**Stop On A Dime** Little Texas	55/96	**Stranger In Your Eyes** Ken Mellons
28/88	**Stop The Rain** Shenandoah	42/67	**Stranger On The Run** Bill Anderson
15/66	**Stop The Start (Of Tears In My Heart)** Johnny Dollar	2/90	**Stranger Things Have Happened** Ronnie Milsap
13/68	**Stop The Sun** Bonnie Guitar	64/86	**Stranger Things Have Happened** Larry Boone
	Stop The World (And Let Me Off)		**Stranger To Me**
7/58	Johnnie And Jack	27/59	Don Gibson
16/65	Waylon Jennings	68/76	Mack White
18/74	Susan Raye	17/63	**Stranger Was Here** Darrell McCall
91/76	Donny King		**Strangers ..see: (From Now On All My Friends Are Gonna Be)**
70/80	**Stores Are Full Of Roses** "Blackjack" Jack Grayson		
16/67	**Storm, The** Jim Reeves	7/88	**Strangers Again** Holly Dunn
33/94	**Storm In The Heartland** Billy Ray Cyrus	54/76	**Strawberry Cake** Johnny Cash
60/83	**Storm Of Love** Chantilly	79/77	**Strawberry Curls** Freddy Weller
	Storms Never Last	40/69	**Strawberry Farms** Tom T. Hall
17/75	Dottsy	76/78	**Strawberry Fields Forever** Terri Hollowell
17/81	Waylon Jennings & Jessi Colter	1/96	**Strawberry Wine** Deana Carter
25/74	**Storms Of Troubled Times** Ray Price	3/74	**Streak, The** Ray Stevens
21/78	**Stormy Weather** Stella Parton	56/92	**Street Man Named Desire** Pirates Of The Mississippi
33/80	**Story Behind The Story** Big Al Downing	9/70	**Street Singer** Merle Haggard
10/90	**Story Of Love** Desert Rose Band	25/83	**Street Talk** Kathy Mattea
1/58	**Story Of My Life** Marty Robbins	1/88	**Streets Of Bakersfield** Dwight Yoakam & Buck Owens
65/68	**Storybook Children** Virgil Warner & Suzi Jane Hokum	5/66	**Streets Of Baltimore** Bobby Bare
16/60	**Straight A's In Love** Johnny Cash	73/96	**Strength Of A Woman** Philip Claypool
73/91	**Straight And Narrow** Wild Rose	29/69	**Strings** Wynn Stewart
66/87	**Straight From My Heart** Sylvia	64/75	**Strings** Johnny Carver
80/85	**Straight Laced Lady** Tracy Lynden	65/83	**Stroker's Theme** Charlie Daniels Band
	Straight Life	1/88	**Strong Enough To Bend** Tanya Tucker
37/68	Bobby Goldsboro	1/86	**Strong Heart** T.G. Sheppard
45/68	Sonny Curtis	57/98	**Strong One** Mila Mason
64/92	**Straight Talk** Dolly Parton	15/83	**Strong Weakness** Bellamy Brothers
79/86	**Straight Talkin** Melba Montgomery	27/64	**Stronger Than Dirt** Glenn Barber
47/98	**Straight Tequila** Trini Triggs	26/00	**Stuck In Love** Judds
1/92	**Straight Tequila Night** John Anderson	24/84	**Stuck On You** Lionel Richie
1/87	**Straight To The Heart** Crystal Gayle	27/60	**Stuck On You** Elvis Presley
1/44	**Straighten Up And Fly Right** King Cole Trio	19/82	**Stuck Right In The Middle Of Your Love** Billy Swan
60/67	**Stranded** Jim Nesbitt	36/00	**Stuff** Diamond Rio
26/79	**Stranded On A Dead End Street** ETC Band	67/99	**Stuff That Matters** Tara Lyn Hart
	Strange Little Girl	43/82	**Stumblin' In** Chantilly
5/51	Cowboy Copas	6/62	**Success** Loretta Lynn
9/51	Tennessee Ernie Ford	7/69	**Such A Fool** Roy Drusky
9/51	Red Foley & Ernest Tubb	82/87	**Suck It In** Pat Garrett
4/76	**Stranger** Johnny Duncan	34/96	**Suddenly Single** Terri Clark
45/83	**Stranger At My Door** Juice Newton	64/87	**Suddenly Single** Bama Band
64/80	**Stranger, I'm Married** Doug McGuire	47/80	**Sue** Tommy Overstreet
		64/69	**Sugar Cane County** Maxine Brown
26/68	**Stranger In A Strange, Strange City** Webb Pierce	F/77	**Sugar Coated Love** Freddy Fender
92/83	**Stranger In Her Bed** Randy Parton	1/80	**Sugar Daddy** Bellamy Brothers
			Sugar Foot ..see: Sugarfoot
		50/68	**Sugar From My Candy** Ray Griff

88/70	**Sugar In The Flowers** Anthony Armstrong Jones	
27/64	**Sugar Lump** Sonny James	
1/47	**Sugar Moon** Bob Wills	
	Sugar Shack	
32/70	Bobby G. Rice	
61/86	Carlette	
87/75	**Sugar Sugar** Mike Lunsford	
	Sugarfoot Rag	
4/50	Red Foley	
12/80	Jerry Reed	
37/73	**Sugarman** Peggy Little	
98/76	**Suitcase Life** Side Of The Road Gang	
	Sukiyaki	
21/63	Clyde Beavers	
96/86	Boots Clements	
68/73	**Summer Afternoons** Buddy Alan	
55/94	**Summer In Dixie** Confederate Railroad	
69/71	**Summer Man** Anne Christine	
79/87	**Summer On The Mississippi** Southern Reign	
39/66	**Summer Roses** Ned Miller	
34/64	**Summer Skies And Golden Sands** Jimmy "C" Newman	
100/73	**Summer (The First Time)** Bobby Goldsboro	
2/88	**Summer Wind** Desert Rose Band	
41/65	**Summer, Winter, Spring And Fall** Roy Drusky	
1/95	**Summer's Comin'** Clint Black	
	Summertime Blues	
70/77	Jim Mundy	
1/94	Alan Jackson	
75/97	**Summertime Girls** Crawford/West	
93/76	**Summertime Lovin'** Layng Martine, Jr.	
98/77	**Summit Ridge Drive** Charlie McCoy & Barefoot Jerry	
13/76	**Sun Comin' Up** Nat Stuckey	
30/65	**Sun Glasses** Skeeter Davis	
62/77	**Sun In Dixie** Kathy Barnes	
58/73	**Sun Is Shining (On Everybody But Me)** Earl Richards	
42/79	**Sun Went Down In My World Tonight** Leon Everette	
48/70	**Sun's Gotta' Shine** Wilma Burgess	
32/76	**Sunday Afternoon Boatride In The Park On The Lake** R.W. Blackwood	
3/50	**Sunday Down In Tennessee** Red Foley	
68/82	**Sunday Go To Cheatin' Clothes** Darlene Austin	
1/89	**Sunday In The South** Shenandoah	
5/88	**Sunday Kind Of Love** Reba McEntire	
38/71	**Sunday Morning Christian** Harlan Howard	
	Sunday Morning Coming Down	
55/69	Ray Stevens	
1/70	Johnny Cash	
	Sunday School To Broadway	
29/76	Sammi Smith	
57/77	Anne Murray	
	Sunday Sunrise	
6/73	Brenda Lee	
49/75	Anne Murray	

	Sundown		26/64	**Sweet Adorable** Eddy Arnold	69/75	**Sweet Molly**
13/74	Gordon Lightfoot		57/84	**Sweet And Easy To Love**		David Houston & Calvin Crawford
59/99	Deryl Dodd			Mike Campbell	44/80	**Sweet Mother Texas** Eddy Raven
18/68	**Sundown Mary** Billy Walker		66/74	**Sweet And Tender Feeling**	9/77	**Sweet Music Man** Kenny Rogers
94/85	**Sundown Sideshow** Jano			Mack White	63/69	**Sweet 'N' Sassy** Jerry Smith
4/77	**Sunflower** Glen Campbell		64/72	**Sweet Apple Wine** Duane Dee	85/81	**Sweet Natural Love**
63/72	**Sunny Side Of My Life**		43/69	**Sweet Baby Girl** Peggy Little		Mick Lloyd & Jerri Kelly
	Roger Miller		57/71	**Sweet Baby On My Mind**	40/80	**Sweet Red Wine** Gary Morris
12/61	**Sunny Tennessee** Cowboy Copas			June Stearns	44/84	**Sweet Rosanna** Rex Allen, Jr.
	Sunset Town ..see: Midnight Girl		40/73	**Sweet Becky Walker** Larry Gatlin	2/68	**Sweet Rosie Jones** Buck Owens
35/80	**Sunshine** Juice Newton			**Sweet Caroline**	71/85	**Sweet Salvation** Audie Henry
	Sunshine		40/70	Anthony Armstrong Jones	25/76	**Sweet Sensuous Feelings**
57/70	Earl Richards		77/86	Claude Gray		Sue Richards
53/73	Mickey Newbury		22/68	**Sweet Child Of Sunshine**	42/80	**Sweet Sensuous Sensations**
98/79	Sammy Vaughn			Jerry Wallace		Don Gibson
47/68	**Sunshine And Bluebirds**			**Sweet City Woman**	8/80	**Sweet Sexy Eyes** Cristy Lane
	Jimmy Newman		48/77	Johnny Carver	4/44	**Sweet Slumber** Lucky Millinder
58/72	**Sunshine And Rainbows**		34/80	Tompall/Glaser Brothers	52/81	**Sweet Southern Love** Phil Everly
	Roy Drusky		89/78	**Sweet Country Girl** Mack Sanders	87/76	**Sweet Southern Lovin'**
87/73	**Sunshine Feeling**		5/84	**Sweet Country Music** Atlanta		Mayf Nutter
	LaWanda Lindsey		86/75	**Sweet Country Music** Ruby Falls	84/82	**Sweet Southern Moonlight**
	Sunshine Man		6/73	**Sweet Country Woman**		Narvel Felts
54/68	Mac Curtis			Johnny Duncan	18/01	**Sweet Summer** Diamond Rio
74/78	Kenny Price		53/77	**Sweet Deceiver** Cristy Lane	7/79	**Sweet Summer Lovin'**
43/68	**Sunshine Of My World**		1/78	**Sweet Desire** Kendalls		Dolly Parton
	Dallas Frazier		7/72	**Sweet Dream Woman**	7/75	**Sweet Surrender** John Denver
42/74	**Sunshine On My Shoulders**			Waylon Jennings	68/92	**Sweet Suzanne** Buzzin' Cousins
	John Denver			**Sweet Dreams**	18/65	**Sweet, Sweet Judy**
1/73	**Super Kind Of Woman**		2/56	Faron Young		David Houston
	Freddie Hart		9/56	Don Gibson	8/78	**Sweet, Sweet Smile** Carpenters
73/74	**Super Kitten** Connie Cato		6/61	Don Gibson	23/76	**Sweet Talkin' Man** Lynn Anderson
82/79	**Super Lady** Ray Pillow		5/63	Patsy Cline		**Sweet Thang**
14/86	**Super Love** Exile		1/76	Emmylou Harris	4/66	Nat Stuckey
37/72	**Super Sideman** Kenny Price		88/76	Troy Seals	45/67	Ernest Tubb & Loretta Lynn
1/73	**Superman** Donna Fargo		19/79	Reba McEntire	8/69	**Sweet Thang And Cisco**
33/74	**Superskirt** Connie Cato		20/78	**Sweet Fantasy** Bobby Borchers		Nat Stuckey
81/76	**Support Your Local Honky Tonks**			**Sweet Home Alabama**	79/86	**Sweet Time** Jill Hollier
	Ronnie Sessions		94/81	Charlie Daniels Band	26/69	**Sweet Wine** Johnny Carver
48/87	**Sure Feels Good**		75/95	Alabama	12/82	**Sweet Yesterday** Sylvia
	Barbara Mandrell			**Sweet Life**	8/86	**Sweeter And Sweeter**
5/82	**Sure Feels Like Love**		85/79	Paul Davis		Statler Brothers
	Larry Gatlin/Gatlin Brothers		47/88	Marie Osmond (with Paul Davis)		**Sweeter Love (I'll Never Know)**
39/99	**Sure Feels Real Good**		3/61	**Sweet Lips** Webb Pierce	53/72	Barbara Fairchild
	Michael Peterson		94/78	**Sweet Little Devil** Judy Allen	22/84	Brenda Lee
11/55	**Sure Fire Kisses**		62/91	**Sweet Little Shoe** Dan Seals		**Sweeter Than The Flowers**
	Justin Tubb - Goldie Hill		37/87	**Sweet Little '66**	3/48	Moon Mullican
3/93	**Sure Love** Hal Ketchum			Steve Earle & The Dukes	12/48	Shorty Long
8/88	**Sure Thing** Foster & Lloyd		69/85	**Sweet Love, Don't Cry**	12/76	**Sweetest Gift**
15/80	**Sure Thing** Freddie Hart			Charleston Express/Jesse Wales		Linda Ronstadt & Emmylou Harris
65/85	**Sure Thing** Tony Arata		39/78	**Sweet Love Feelings** Jerry Reed	25/91	**Sweetest Thing** Carlene Carter
34/64	**Surely** Warner Mack		23/72	**Sweet, Love Me Good Woman**		**Sweetest Thing (I've Ever**
73/66	**Surely Not** Don Bowman			Tompall/Glaser Brothers		**Known)**
64/00	**Surprise** Doug Stone		52/69	**Sweet Love On My Mind**	86/76	Dottsy
49/74	**Surprise, Surprise** Sonny James			Claude King	1/82	Juice Newton
5/81	**Surround Me With Love**		56/78	**Sweet Love Song The World Can**	11/69	**Sweetheart Of The Year**
	Charly McClain			**Sing** Dale McBride		Ray Price
71/67	**Survival Of The Fittest** Mel Tillis		86/75	**Sweet Lovin' Baby**	11/48	**Sweetheart, You Done Me Wrong**
65/82	**Survivor** Bill Nash			Wilma Burgess		Bill Monroe
15/75	**Susan When She Tried**		69/79	**Sweet Lovin' Things** Billy Walker	20/61	**Sweethearts Again** Bob Gallion
	Statler Brothers		3/74	**Sweet Magnolia Blossom**	19/63	**Sweethearts In Heaven**
20/87	**Susannah** Tom Wopat			Billy "Crash" Craddock		Buck Owens & Rose Maddox
52/86	**Susie's Beauty Shop** Tom T. Hall		73/78	**Sweet Mary** Danny Hargrove	46/00	**Swimming In Champagne**
4/48	**Suspicion** Tex Williams		10/79	**Sweet Melinda** Randy Barlow		Eric Heatherly
	Suspicion		F/79	**Sweet Melinda** John Denver	31/97	**Swing, The** James Bonamy
33/72	Bobby G. Rice			**Sweet Memories**	1/83	**Swingin'** John Anderson
27/88	Ronnie McDowell		32/69	Dottie West & Don Gibson	38/96	**Swingin' Doors** Martina McBride
1/79	**Suspicions** Eddie Rabbitt		4/79	Willie Nelson		**Swinging Doors**
	Suspicious Minds		79/89	**Sweet Memories Of You**	5/66	Merle Haggard
25/70	Waylon Jennings & Jessi Colter			Perry LaPointe	67/81	Del Reeves
2/76	Waylon Jennings & Jessi Colter			**Sweet Misery**	87/89	Buck Hall
35/92	Dwight Yoakam		16/67	Jimmy Dean	71/95	**Swinging On My Baby's Chain**
48/89	**Suzette** Foster & Lloyd		14/71	Ferlin Husky		Philip Claypool

Take It On Home To Branson — Johnny Gray (WBAR) ★★★

71/69	**Swiss Cottage Place**				**Take Time To Know Her**
	Jerry Wallace	8/68	Ray Price	74/71	Joe Stampley
12/72	**Sylvia's Mother** Bobby Bare	34/76	Mack White	58/82	David Allan Coe
		28/81	Bobby Bare	10/73	**Take Time To Love Her**
	T	24/79	**Take Me Back** Charly McClain		Nat Stuckey
		76/81	**Take Me Back To The Country**	91/79	**Take Time To Smell The Flowers**
	T For Texas		Baxter, Baxter & Baxter		Max Brown
5/63	Grandpa Jones	61/70	**Take Me Back To The Goodtimes,**	49/65	**Take Your Hands Off My Heart**
36/76	Tompall & His Outlaw Band		**Sally** Bobby Wright		Ray Pillow
7/94	**T.L.C. A.S.A.P.** Alabama	1/82	**Take Me Down** Alabama	2/92	**Take Your Memory With You**
30/63	**Tadpole** Tillman Franks	50/71	**Take Me Home, Country Roads**		Vince Gill
8/51	**Tailor Made Woman** Tennessee		John Denver	83/79	**Taken To The Line**
	Ernie Ford & Joe "Fingers" Carr	5/74	**Take Me Home To Somewhere**		San Fernando Valley Music Band
5/54	**Tain't Nice (To Talk Like That)**		Joe Stampley	5/70	**Taker, The** Waylon Jennings
	Carlisles	91/81	**Take Me Home With You**	33/79	**Takes A Fool To Love A Fool**
	Take A City Bride		Carl Chambers		Burton Cummings
58/67	Rick Nelson		**Take Me In Your Arms And Hold**	100/78	**Takin' A Chance** Bobby Wright
72/71	Swampwater		**Me**	86/82	**Takin' It Back To The Hills**
	Take A Letter Maria	1/50	Eddy Arnold		Ronnie Rogers
8/70	Anthony Armstrong Jones	10/80	Jim Reeves & Deborah Allen		**Takin' It Easy**
99/88	Roger Marshall	94/73	**Take Me One More Ride**	94/78	Joey Davis
45/00	Doug Stone		David Frizzell	2/81	Lacy J. Dalton
6/63	**Take A Letter, Miss Gray**	25/80	**Take Me, Take Me** Rosanne Cash	41/98	**Takin' The Country Back**
	Justin Tubb	97/78	**Take Me To Bed** Jeannie Seely		John Anderson
58/87	**Take A Little Bit Of It Home**	67/76	**Take Me To Heaven** Sami Jo		**Takin' What I Can Get**
	A.J. Masters	10/82	**Take Me To The Country**	91/75	Sally June Hart
31/69	**Take A Little Good Will Home**		Mel McDaniel	41/76	Brenda Lee
	Bobby Goldsboro & Del Reeves	82/80	**Take Me To Your Heart**	12/80	**Taking Somebody With Me When**
2/92	**Take A Little Trip** Alabama		Del Reeves		**I Fall** Larry Gatlin/Gatlin Brothers
71/68	**Take A Message To Mary**	5/80	**Take Me To Your Lovin' Place**	14/70	**Talk About The Good Times**
	Don Cherry		Larry Gatlin/Gatlin Brothers		Jerry Reed
83/83	**Take A Ride On A Riverboat**	1/68	**Take Me To Your World**	1/63	**Talk Back Trembling Lips**
	Cedar Creek		Tammy Wynette		Ernest Ashworth
7/49	**Take An Old Cold 'Tater (And**	75/82	**Take Me Tonight** Darlene Austin	26/66	**Talk Me Some Sense** Bobby Bare
	Wait) Jimmie Dickens	87/77	**Take Me Tonight** Tom Jones	63/94	**Talk Some** Billy Ray Cyrus
	Take Another Run	43/00	**Take Me With You When You Go**		**Talk To Me**
78/89	Tony Perez		Tracy Byrd	13/78	Freddy Fender
60/93	Paul Overstreet	7/76	**Take My Breath Away**	1/83	Mickey Gilley
	Take Good Care Of Her		Margo Smith	35/82	**Talk To Me Loneliness** Cindy Hurt
1/66	Sonny James	8/71	**Take My Hand**	16/58	**Talk To Me Lonesome Heart**
F/74	Elvis Presley		Mel Tillis & Sherry Bryce		James O'Gwynn
73/79	**Take Good Care Of My Love**	59/75	**Take My Hand** Jeannie Seely	3/52	**Talk To Your Heart** Ray Price
	Max Brown	38/68	**Take My Hand For Awhile**	62/86	**Talkin' Blue Eyes** Marty Haggard
40/83	**Take It All** Rich Landers		George Hamilton IV	16/88	**Talkin' To Myself Again**
83/81	**Take It As It Comes**	48/74	**Take My Life And Shape It With**		Tammy Wynette
	Michael Murphey with Katy Moffatt		**Your Love** George Kent	8/57	**Talkin' To The Blues** Jim Lowe
5/93	**Take It Back** Reba McEntire	97/79	**Take My Love** Joy Ford	4/87	**Talkin' To The Moon**
17/81	**Take It Easy** Crystal Gayle	98/78	**Take My Love To Rita**		Gatlin Brothers
	Take It Easy		Tommy Cash		**Talkin' To The Wall**
66/72	Billy Mize	15/64	**Take My Ring Off Your Finger**	3/66	Warner Mack
21/94	Travis Tritt		Carl Smith	7/74	Lynn Anderson
38/97	**Take It From Me** Paul Brandt	34/69	**Take Off Time** Claude Gray	4/88	**Talkin' To The Wrong Man**
10/92	**Take It Like A Man**	94/73	**Take One Step** Eydie Gorme		Michael Martin Murphey with Rya
	Michelle Wright	13/55	**Take Possession** Jean Shepard		n Murphey
44/80	**Take It Like A Woman**	52/95	**Take That** Lisa Brokop	18/73	**Talkin' With My Lady**
	Debby Boone	57/97	**Take The Keys To My Heart**		Johnny Duncan
82/87	**Take It Real Easy** Dobie Gray		Garth Brooks	6/48	**Talking Boogie** Tex Williams
86/84	**Take It Slow** Kenny Dale	10/87	**Take The Long Way Home**	1/78	**Talking In Your Sleep**
72/88	**Take It Slow With Me**		John Schneider		Crystal Gayle
	Tommy & Donna	57/82	**Take The Mem'ry When You Go**	41/64	**Talking To The Night Lights**
8/83	**Take It To The Limit**		Jacky Ward		Del Reeves
	Waylon Jennings & Willie Nelson		**Take These Chains From My**	1/69	**Tall Dark Stranger** Buck Owens
	Take Me		**Heart**	1/95	**Tall, Tall Trees** Alan Jackson
8/66	George Jones	1/53	Hank Williams	24/66	**Tallest Tree** Bonnie Guitar
9/72	Tammy Wynette & George Jones	17/94	Lee Roy Parnell Featuring Brooks	82/87	**Taming My Mind** Tony McGill
32/99	**Take Me** Lari White		& Dunn	4/57	**Tangled Mind** Hank Snow
31/68	**Take Me Along With You**	44/80	**Take This Heart** Don King	67/96	**Tangled Up In Texas**
	Van Trevor	1/78	**Take This Job And Shove It**		Frazier River
2/94	**Take Me As I Am** Faith Hill		Johnny Paycheck	75/90	**Tanqueray** Vern Gosdin
		7/62	**Take Time** Webb Pierce	62/87	**Tanya Montana** David Allan Coe
		96/89	**Take Time** Dawn Schutt	7/87	**Tar Top** Alabama
				73/92	**Taste Of Freedom** Aaron Barker

The Telephone Line – Leona Williams

23/66	Taste Of Heaven *Jim Edward Brown*	
86/78	Taste Of Love *Jenny Lynn*	
54/83	Taste Of The Wind *James & Michael Younger*	
42/65	'Tater Raisin' Man *Dick Curless*	
97/76	Te' Quiero (I Love You In Many Ways) *Country Cavaleers*	
25/61	Teach Me How To Lie *Hank Thompson*	
7/81	Teach Me To Cheat *Kendalls*	
75/94	Teach Your Children *Red Hots*	
72/99	Team Of Destiny *Kenny Chesney*	
44/64	Tear After Tear *Rex Allen*	
38/65	Tear Dropped By *Jean Shepard*	
7/77	Tear Fell *Billy "Crash" Craddock*	
9/88	Tear-Stained Letter *Jo-el Sonnier*	
49/66	Tear-Talk *Johnny Dollar*	
	Tear Time	
16/67	*Wilma Burgess*	
1/78	*Dave & Sugar*	
44/66	Teardrop Lane *Ned Miller*	
38/94	Teardrops *George Ducas*	
	Teardrops In My Heart	
4/47	*Sons Of The Pioneers*	
18/76	*Rex Allen, Jr.*	
45/81	*Marty Robbins*	
84/78	Teardrops In My Tequila *Paul Craft*	
42/76	Teardrops Will Kiss The Morning Dew *Del Reeves & Billie Jo Spears*	
	Tearin' It Up (And Burnin' It Down)	
63/98	*Garth Brooks*	
73/00	*Garth Brooks*	
72/80	Tearjoint *Faron Young*	
37/64	Tears And Roses *George Morgan*	
14/57	Tears Are Only Rain *Hank Thompson*	
7/62	Tears Broke Out On Me *Eddy Arnold*	
74/94	Tears Dry *Victoria Shaw*	
3/82	Tears Of The Lonely *Mickey Gilley*	
36/70	Tears On Lincoln's Face *Tommy Cash*	
91/79	Tears (There's Nowhere Else To Hide) *Tommy Overstreet*	
11/67	Tears Will Be The Chaser For Your Wine *Wanda Jackson*	
1/76	Teddy Bear *Red Sovine*	
1/73	Teddy Bear Song *Barbara Fairchild*	
53/76	Teddy Bear's Last Ride *Diana Williams*	
98/76	Teddy Toad *Bobby "Sofine" Butler*	
15/57	Teen-Age Dream *Marty Robbins*	
10/56	Teenage Boogie *Webb Pierce*	
	Teenage Queen ..see: Ballad Of	
65/75	Telephone, The *Jerry Reed*	
	(Telephone Answering Machine Song) ..see: Hello, This Is Joannie	
25/74	Telephone Call *George Jones*	
50/77	Telephone Man *Meri Wilson*	
91/79	Tell All Your Troubles To Me *Miki Mori*	
45/84	Tell 'Em I've Gone Crazy *Ed Bruce*	
1/01	Tell Her *Lonestar*	
10/63	Tell Her So *Wilburn Brothers*	
55/71	Tell Her You Love Her *Kenny Price*	
98/79	Tell Him *Pia Zadora*	
31/71	Tell Him That You Love Him *Webb Pierce*	
	Tell It Like It Is	
31/68	*Archie Campbell & Lorene Mann*	
83/76	*John Wesley Ryles*	
2/89	*Billy Joe Royal*	
70/89	*Sammy Sadler*	
34/87	Tell It To Your Teddy Bear *Shooters*	
65/83	Tell Mama *Terri Gibbs*	
33/68	Tell Maude I Slipped *Red Sovine*	
88/89	Tell Me *Kenny Carr*	
	Tell Me A Lie	
52/74	*Sami Jo*	
1/83	*Janie Fricke*	
4/93	Tell Me About It *Tanya Tucker with Delbert McClinton*	
58/70	Tell Me Again *Jeannie Seely*	
63/96	Tell Me Again *Tammy Graham*	
	(Tell Me 'Bout The Good Old Days) ..see: Grandpa	
47/01	Tell Me How *Chad Brock*	
2/95	Tell Me I Was Dreaming *Travis Tritt*	
88/79	Tell Me I'm Only Dreaming *Lorrie Morgan*	
13/70	Tell Me My Lying Eyes Are Wrong *George Jones*	
48/64	Tell Me Pretty Words *Slim Whitman*	
75/81	Tell Me So *Gary Goodnight*	
75/97	Tell Me Something Bad About Tulsa *Noel Haggard*	
8/88	Tell Me True *Juice Newton*	
8/79	Tell Me What It's Like *Brenda Lee*	
86/83	Tell Me When I'm Hot *Billy "Crash" Craddock*	
3/93	Tell Me Why *Wynonna*	
10/82	Tell Me Why *Earl Thomas Conley*	
18/90	Tell Me Why *Jann Browne*	
11/80	Tell Ole I Ain't Here, He Better Get On Home *Moe Bandy & Joe Stampley*	
18/74	Tell Tale Signs *Jerry Lee Lewis*	
14/49	Tellin' My Troubles To My Old Guitar *Jimmy Wakely*	
3/87	Telling Me Lies *Dolly Parton, Linda Ronstadt, Emmylou Harris*	
52/01	Telluride *Tim McGraw*	
5/80	Temporarily Yours *Jeanne Pruett*	
76/85	Temptation *Mike Martin*	
2/47	Temptation (Tim-Tayshun) *Red Ingle*	
5/91	Tempted *Marty Stuart*	
82/80	Ten Anniversary Presents *Jim Owen*	
14/74	Ten Commandments Of Love *David Houston & Barbara Mandrell*	
33/72	10 Degrees & Getting Colder *George Hamilton IV*	
9/86	Ten Feet Away *Keith Whitley*	
22/94	Ten Feet Tall And Bulletproof *Travis Tritt*	
2/65	10 Little Bottles *Johnny Bond*	
96/80	Ten Seconds In The Saddle *Chris LeDoux*	
F/79	Ten Thousand And One *Connie Smith*	
6/96	Ten Thousand Angels *Mindy McCready*	
5/59	Ten Thousand Drums *Carl Smith*	
45/91	Ten With A Two *Willie Nelson*	
16/77	Ten Years Of This *Gary Stewart*	
95/84	Tenamock Georgia *Charlie Bandy*	
48/67	Tender And True *Ernie Ashworth*	
5/45	Tender Hearted Sue *Rambling Rogue (Fred Rose)*	
1/88	Tender Lie *Restless Heart*	
72/83	Tender Lovin' Lies *Judy Bailey*	
2/93	Tender Moment *Lee Roy Parnell*	
74/87	Tender Time *Louise Mandrell*	
6/95	Tender When I Want To Be *Mary Chapin Carpenter*	
1/61	Tender Years *George Jones*	
42/83	Tenderness Place *Karen Taylor-Good*	
72/68	Tennessee *Jimmy Martin*	
91/78	Tennessee *Ray Sanders*	
1/70	Tennessee Bird Walk *Jack Blanchard & Misty Morgan*	
11/49	Tennessee Boogie *Zeb Turner*	
	Tennessee Border	
3/49	*Red Foley*	
8/49	*Tennessee Ernie Ford*	
12/49	*Bob Atcher*	
15/49	*Jimmie Skinner*	
	Tennessee Border—No. 2	
14/49	*Homer And Jethro*	
2/50	*Red Foley & Ernest Tubb*	
58/91	Tennessee Born And Bred *Eddie Rabbitt*	
	Tennessee Flat-Top Box	
11/62	*Johnny Cash*	
1/88	*Rosanne Cash*	
1/84	Tennessee Homesick Blues *Dolly Parton*	
28/69	Tennessee Hound Dog *Osborne Brothers*	
7/48	Tennessee Moon *Cowboy Copas*	
44/89	Tennessee Nights *Crystal Gayle*	
	Tennessee Polka	
3/49	*Pee Wee King*	
4/49	*Red Foley*	
1/80	Tennessee River *Alabama*	
9/82	Tennessee Rose *Emmylou Harris*	
	Tennessee Saturday Night	
1/49	*Red Foley*	
11/49	*Johnny Bond*	
85/82	*Roy Clark*	
5/59	Tennessee Stud *Eddy Arnold*	
12/49	Tennessee Tears *Pee Wee King*	
	Tennessee Waltz	
3/48	*Cowboy Copas*	
3/48	*Pee Wee King*	
12/48	*Roy Acuff*	
2/51	*Patti Page*	
6/51	*Pee Wee King*	
18/80	*Lacy J. Dalton*	
	Tennessee Whiskey	
77/81	*David Allan Coe*	
2/83	*George Jones*	
6/53	Tennessee Wig Walk *Bonnie Lou*	
31/80	Tequila Sheila *Bobby Bare*	
64/93	Tequila Sunrise *Alan Jackson*	
8/95	Tequila Talkin' *Lonestar*	
87/81	Testimony Of Soddy Hoe *Jerry Reed*	
	Texarkana Baby	
1/48	*Eddy Arnold*	
15/48	*Bob Wills*	

Jose Quervo (Tequila)

Tequila Makes Her Clothes Fall Off – Joe Nichols

36/76	**Texas** Charlie Daniels Band	17/66	Thank You Ma'am Ray Pillow		That Ol' Wind		
69/68	**Texas** Tex Ritter	31/74	Thank You World Statler Brothers	75/95	Garth Brooks		
31/77	**Texas Angel** Jacky Ward	24/75	**Thanks** Bill Anderson	4/96	Garth Brooks		
3/44	**Texas Blues** Foy Willing		**Thanks A Lot**	48/77	**That Old Cold Shoulder**		
26/80	**Texas Bound And Flyin'** Jerry Reed	3/63	Ernest Tubb		Tom Bresh		
		80/79	Billy Parker		**That Old Familiar Feeling ..see: (Here Comes)**		
23/81	**Texas Cowboy Night** Mel Tillis & Nancy Sinatra	12/59	**Thanks A Lot** Johnny Cash	90/83	**That Old Time Feelin'** Rex Gosdin		
72/97	**Texas Diary** James T. Horn	40/68	**Thanks A Lot For Tryin' Anyway** Liz Anderson	21/88	**That Old Wheel** Johnny Cash with Hank Williams, Jr.		
69/81	**Texas Ida Red** David Houston	17/88	**Thanks Again** Ricky Skaggs	69/79	**That Over Thirty Look** Faron Young		
	Texas In 1880	98/79	**Thanks E.T. Thanks A Lot** Billy Parker	50/73	**That Rain Makin' Baby Of Mine** Roy Drusky		
18/88	Foster & Lloyd	69/88	**Thanks For Leavin' Him (For Me)** Paula McCulla	40/95	**That Road Not Taken** Joe Diffie		
54/01	Radney Foster	95/77	**Thanks For Leaving, Lucille** Sherri Jerrico	1/86	**That Rock Won't Roll** Restless Heart		
9/80	**Texas In My Rear View Mirror** Mac Davis	59/73	**Thanks For Lovin' Me** Pat Roberts	44/79	**That Run-Away Woman Of Mine** Freddy Weller		
96/74	**Texas Law Sez** Tompall Glaser	29/72	**Thanks For The Mem'ries** Barbara Fairchild	33/74	**That Same Ol' Look Of Love** David Houston		
75/78	**Texas Me & You** Asleep At The Wheel	50/96	**Thanks To You** Marty Stuart		**That See Me Later Look**		
81/86	**Texas Moon** Johnny Duncan	65/94	**Thanks To You** Emmylou Harris	67/67	Bobby Wright		
	(Texas National Anthem) ..see: Fraulein	66/72	**Thanks To You For Lovin' Me** Jerry Wallace	36/69	Bonnie Guitar		
35/76	**Texas - 1947** Johnny Cash	20/65	**That Ain't All** John D. Loudermilk	69/80	**That Silver-Haired Daddy Of Mine** Slim Whitman		
94/76	**Texas On A Saturday Night** Bill Green	3/95	**That Ain't My Truck** Rhett Akins	2/74	**That Song Is Driving Me Crazy** Tom T. Hall		
60/01	**Texas On My Mind** Pat Green & Cory Morrow	61/70	**That Ain't No Stuff** Compton Brothers	1/93	**That Summer** Garth Brooks		
2/46	**Texas Playboy Rag** Bob Wills	1/94	**That Ain't No Way To Go** Brooks & Dunn	59/97	**That Train Don't Run** Matraca Berg		
4/98	**Texas Size Heartache** Joe Diffie	22/72	**That Certain One** Tommy Cash	1/87	**That Was A Close One** Earl Thomas Conley		
9/81	**Texas State Of Mind** David Frizzell & Shelly West	10/54	**That Crazy Mambo Thing** Hank Snow	4/93	**That Was A River** Collin Raye		
22/93	**Texas Tattoo** Gibson/Miller Band	1/55	**That Do Make It Nice** Eddy Arnold	54/96	**That Was Him (This Is Now)** 4 Runner		
	Texas Tea	46/98	**That Does It** Jason Sellers	1/77	**That Was Yesterday** Donna Fargo		
51/68	Dee Mullins	65/74	**That Doesn't Mean (I Don't Love My God)** Ray Griff	9/48	**That Wild And Wicked Look In Your Eye** Ernest Tubb		
77/77	Leroy Van Dyke	8/99	**That Don't Impress Me Much** Shania Twain	35/97	**That Woman Of Mine** Neal McCoy		
68/80	Orion	11/74	**That Girl Who Waits On Tables** Ronnie Milsap		**(That'll Be Me) ..see: Gone**		
1/95	**Texas Tornado** Tracy Lawrence	4/96	**That Girl's Been Spyin' On Me** Billy Dean		**That'll Be The Day**		
5/79	**Texas (When I Die)** Tanya Tucker	1/52	**That Heart Belongs To Me** Webb Pierce	56/72	Kenny Vernon		
34/76	**Texas Woman** Pat Boone			27/76	Linda Ronstadt		
1/81	**Texas Women** Hank Williams, Jr.		**That Hound Dog In The Window ..see: (How Much Is)**	96/76	Pure Prairie League		
6/70	**Thank God And Greyhound** Roy Clark	68/00	**That Hurts** Paul Brandt	37/67	**That'll Be The Day** Statler Brothers		
2/97	**Thank God For Believers** Mark Chesnutt	57/78	**That "I Love You, You Love Me Too" Love Song** Laney Smallwood	52/89	**That'll Be The Last Thing** James House		
3/83	**Thank God For Kids** Oak Ridge Boys	68/84	**That It's All Over Feeling (All Over Again)** Steve Clark	2/69	**That's A No No** Lynn Anderson		
1/84	**Thank God For The Radio** Kendalls	74/97	**That Just About Covers It** Rich McCready	25/01	**That's A Plan** Mark McGuinn		
1/93	**Thank God For You** Sawyer Brown	4/90	**That Just About Does It** Vern Gosdin	56/73	**That's A Whole Lotta Lovin' (You Give Me)** Kenny Starr		
1/75	**Thank God I'm A Country Boy** John Denver	95/74	**That Kind Of Fool** Atlanta James	12/56	**That's All** "Tennessee" Ernie Ford		
10/76	**Thank God I've Got You** Statler Brothers	62/96	**That Last Mile** Jeff Carson	46/64	**That's All I Need To Know** Bobby Wood		
11/77	**Thank God She's Mine** Freddie Hart	53/76	**That Little Difference** Carmol Taylor	57/77	**That's All I Wanted To Know** Dottie West		
66/89	**Thank The Cowboy For The Ride** Tammy Wynette	11/76	**That Look In Her Eyes** Freddie Hart	47/66	**That's All It Took** George Jones & Gene Pitney		
70/83	**Thank You Darling** Bill Anderson	72/70	**That Look Of Good-Bye** Ernie Ashworth	4/53	**That's All Right** Autry Inman		
33/80	**Thank You, Ever-Lovin'** Kenny Dale	6/80	**That Lovin' You Feelin' Again** Roy Orbison & Emmylou Harris	7/55	**That's All Right** Marty Robbins		
21/73	**Thank You For Being You** Mel Tillis	66/78	**That Lucky Old Sun** Nat Stuckey	42/76	**That's All She Ever Said Except Goodbye** Nat Stuckey		
8/54	**Thank You For Calling** Billy Walker	26/79	**That Makes Two Of Us** Jacky Ward/Reba McEntire	34/76	**That's All She Wrote** Ray Price		
65/69	**Thank You For Loving Me** Brenda Byers	80/89	**That Newsong (They're Playin')** Jeff Golden		**That's All That Matters**		
79/74	**Thank You For The Feeling** Billy Mize			34/64	Ray Price		
75/79	**Thank You For The Roses** Kitty Wells			1/80	Mickey Gilley		
35/73	**Thank You For Touching My Life** Tony Douglas			51/72	**That's All This Old World Needs** Stonewall Jackson		
				15/97	**That's Another Song** Bryan White		

1/95	That's As Close As I'll Get To Loving You *Aaron Tippin*	
50/84	That's Easy For You To Say *Kathy Mattea*	
18/96	That's Enough Of That *Mila Mason*	
52/92	That's Good *Tim Mensy*	
36/97	That's How I Got To Memphis *Deryl Dodd*	
	That's How Much I Love You	
2/46	*Eddy Arnold*	
4/47	*Red Foley*	
85/88	That's How Much I Love You *Neal McGoy*	
23/75	That's How My Baby Builds A Fire *Johnny Russell*	
9/86	That's How You Know When Love's Right *Nicolette Larson*	
10/95	That's How You Know (When You're In Love) *Lari White*	
7/95	That's Just About Right *BlackHawk*	
16/02	That's Just Jessie *Kevin Denney*	
70/75	That's Just My Truckin' Luck *Hank Thompson*	
42/01	That's Just That *Diamond Rio*	
52/74	That's Love *Don Adams*	
43/92	That's Me *Martina McBride*	
	That's Me Without You	
4/53	*Webb Pierce*	
9/53	*Sonny James*	
49/86	That's More About Love (Than I Wanted To Know) *Nicolette Larson*	
10/94	That's My Baby *Lari White*	
6/88	That's My Job *Conway Twitty*	
5/60	That's My Kind Of Love *Marion Worth*	
1/62	That's My Pa *Sheb Wooley*	
6/94	That's My Story *Collin Raye*	
46/84	That's Not The Way (It's S'posed To Be) *Anne Murray*	
35/86	That's One To Grow On *Dobie Gray*	
9/88	That's That *Michael Johnson*	
22/00	That's The Beat Of A Heart *Warren Brothers*	
49/65	That's The Chance I'll Have To Take *Waylon Jennings*	
86/80	That's The Chance We'll Have To Take *Jerry McBee*	
9/53	That's The Kind Of Love I'm Looking For *Carl Smith*	
13/00	That's The Kind Of Mood I'm In *Patty Loveless*	
59/97	That's The Kinda Love (That I'm Talkin' About) *Mila Mason*	
68/67	That's The Only Way To Cry *Wynn Stewart*	
18/79	That's The Only Way To Say Good Morning *Ray Price*	
71/92	That's The Thing About A Memory *Tracy Byrd*	
1/84	That's The Thing About Love *Don Williams*	
	That's The Truth	
84/84	*Johnny Cash*	
47/99	*Paul Brandt*	
1/00	That's The Way *Jo Dee Messina*	
7/80	That's The Way A Cowboy Rocks And Rolls *Jacky Ward*	
9/58	That's The Way I Feel *Faron Young*	
67/70	That's The Way I See It *Jack Reno*	
14/59	That's The Way It's Gotta Be *Faron Young*	
	That's The Way Love Goes	
1/74	*Johnny Rodriguez*	
1/84	*Merle Haggard*	
56/99	*Merle Haggard (with Jewel)*	
60/91	That's The Way Love Is *Asleep At The Wheel*	
	That's The Way Love Should Be	
23/75	*Brian Collins*	
7/77	*Dave & Sugar*	
	That's The Way My Woman Loves Me	
96/77	*Dan McCorison*	
82/81	*Amarillo*	
39/01	That's What Brothers Do *Confederate Railroad*	
16/76	That's What Friends Are For *Barbara Mandrell*	
50/97	That's What Happens When I Hold You *Aaron Tippin*	
41/86	That's What Her Memory Is For *Butch Baker*	
24/76	That's What I Get (For Doin' My Own Thinkin') *Ray Griff*	
22/94	That's What I Get (For Losin' You) *Hal Ketchum*	
4/96	That's What I Get For Lovin' You *Diamond Rio*	
10/80	That's What I Get For Loving You *Eddy Arnold*	
35/82	That's What I Get For Thinking *Kendalls*	
4/47	That's What I Like About The West *Tex Williams*	
8/92	That's What I Like About You *Trisha Yearwood*	
44/01	That's What I Like About You *John Michael Montgomery*	
28/58	That's What I Tell My Heart *Bob Gallion*	
30/73	That's What I'll Do *Don Gibson*	
40/92	That's What I'm Working On Tonight *Dixiana*	
	That's What It's Like To Be Lonesome	
7/59	*Ray Price*	
12/59	*Bill Anderson*	
58/71	*Cal Smith*	
66/72	That's What Leaving's About *Ray Price*	
68/94	That's What Love's About *Marty Stuart*	
7/76	That's What Made Me Love You *Bill Anderson & Mary Lou Turner*	
	That's What Makes The Juke Box Play	
6/55	*Jimmy Work*	
11/78	*Moe Bandy*	
33/64	That's What Makes The World Go Around *Claude King*	
8/78	That's What You Do To Me *Charly McClain*	
10/85	(That's What You Do) When You're In Love *Forester Sisters*	
9/66	(That's What You Get) For Lovin' Me *Waylon Jennings*	
5/88	That's What Your Love Does To Me *Holly Dunn*	
71/82	That's What Your Lovin' Does To Me *Peggy Forman*	
3/02	That's When I Love You *Phil Vassar*	
9/68	That's When I See The Blues (In Your Pretty Brown Eyes) *Jim Reeves*	
6/75	That's When My Woman Begins *Tommy Overstreet*	
3/70	That's When She Started To Stop Loving You *Conway Twitty*	
53/69	That's When The Hurtin' Sets In *Hank Snow*	
24/77	That's When The Lyin' Stops (And The Lovin' Starts) *Pal Rakes*	
68/00	That's When You Came Along *Tara Lyn Hart*	
80/87	That's When (You Can Call Me Your Own) *Bonnie Leigh*	
26/65	That's Where My Money Goes *Webb Pierce*	
49/98	That's Where You're Wrong *Daryle Singletary*	
66/89	That's Why I Fell In Love With You *Eddie Rabbitt*	
1/72	That's Why I Love You Like I Do *Sonny James*	
16/69	That's Why I Love You So Much *Ferlin Husky*	
25/63	That's Why I Sing In A Honky Tonk *Warren Smith*	
2/98	That's Why I'm Here *Kenny Chesney*	
	That's Why I'm Walkin' ..see: Why I'm Walkin'	
94/88	That's Why You Haven't Seen Me *Dennis Payne*	
36/74	That's You And Me *Hank Snow*	
47/66	That's You (And What's Left Of Me) *Clyde Beavers*	
74/79	That's You, That's Me *Dawn Chastain*	
	That's You That's You ..see: Honey-Eyed Girl	
41/69	That's Your Hang Up *Johnny Carver*	
13/81	Them Good Ol' Boys Are Bad *John Schneider*	
1/80	Theme From The Dukes Of Hazzard *Waylon Jennings*	
8/62	Then A Tear Fell *Earl Scott*	
4/91	Then Again *Alabama*	
4/65	Then And Only Then *Connie Smith*	
48/66	Then Go Home To Her *Norma Jean*	
8/70	Then He Touched Me *Jean Shepard*	
2/49	Then I Turned And Walked Slowly Away *Eddy Arnold*	
42/65	Then I'll Start Believing In You *Hank Thompson*	
	Then I'll Stop Loving You	
15/54	*Jim Reeves*	
12/64	*Browns*	
3/87	Then It's Love *Don Williams*	
31/70	Then She's A Lover *Roy Clark*	
32/69	Then The Baby Came *Henson Cargill*	

2/98	**Then What?** *Clay Walker*		**There Stands The Glass**	10/75	**There's A Song On The Jukebox** *David Wills*
1/75	**Then Who Am I** *Charley Pride*	1/53	*Webb Pierce*	7/70	**There's A Story (Goin' 'Round)** *Dottie West & Don Gibson*
	Then You Can Tell Me Goodbye	34/73	*Johnny Bush*		
1/68	Eddy Arnold		**There Will Come A Day**	7/89	**There's A Tear In My Beer** *Hank Williams, Jr.*
4/76	Glen Campbell (medley)	59/00	*Faith Hill*		
4/96	Neal McCoy	36/01	*Faith Hill*	80/88	**There's A Telephone Ringing (In An Empty House)** *Southern Reign*
10/71	**Then You Walk In** *Sammi Smith*	1/74	**There Won't Be Anymore** *Charlie Rich*		
25/78	**Then You'll Remember** *Sterling Whipple*	19/76	**There Won't Be No Country Music** *C.W. McCall*	13/71	**There's A Whole Lot About A Woman (A Man Don't Know)** *Jack Greene*
86/81	**There Ain't A Song** *Music Row*	12/69	**There Wouldn't Be A Lonely Heart In Town** *Del Reeves*	F/83	**There's All Kinds Of Smoke (In The Barroom)** *Loretta Lynn*
58/87	**There Ain't No Binds** *Whites*	8/90	**There You Are** *Willie Nelson*		
77/82	**There Ain't No Country Music On This Jukebox** *Tom T. Hall & Earl Scruggs*	10/00	**There You Are** *Martina McBride*	91/76	**There's Always A Goodbye** *Helen Cornelius*
		1/57	**There You Go** *Johnny Cash*		**There's Always Me**
10/68	**There Ain't No Easy Run** *Dave Dudley*	32/91	**There You Go** *Exile*	30/79	*Ray Price*
12/84	**There Ain't No Future In This** *Reba McEntire*	64/67	**There You Go** *Sandy Mason*	35/81	*Jim Reeves*
		26/01	**There You Go Again** *Kenny Rogers*	17/62	**There's Always One (Who Loves A Lot)** *Roy Drusky*
2/78	**There Ain't No Good Chain Gang** *Johnny Cash & Waylon Jennings*	4/99	**There You Have It** *BlackHawk*	18/80	**There's Another Woman** *Joe Stampley*
57/92	**There Ain't Nothin' I Don't Like About You** *Neal McCoy*	11/01	**There You'll Be** *Faith Hill*		
1/92	**There Ain't Nothin' Wrong With The Radio** *Aaron Tippin*	21/61	**There'll Always Be Sadness** *Marion Worth*	1/51	**There's Been A Change In Me** *Eddy Arnold*
			There'll Be No Teardrops Tonight	20/69	**There's Better Things In Life** *Jerry Reed*
89/80	**There Ain't Nothing Like A Rainy Night** *Peggy Forman*	86/78	*Willie Nelson*		
		70/80	*Vassar Clements*	21/64	**There's More Pretty Girls Than One** *George Hamilton IV*
17/91	**There For Awhile** *Steve Wariner*	5/51	**(There'll Be) Peace In The Valley (For Me)** *Red Foley*		
1/97	**There Goes** *Alan Jackson*			1/81	**(There's) No Gettin' Over Me** *Ronnie Milsap*
2/98	**There Goes My Baby** *Trisha Yearwood*	76/84	**There'll Never Be A Better Night For Bein' Wrong** *Big Al Downing*		
	There Goes My Everything			7/85	**There's No Love In Tennessee** *Barbara Mandrell*
1/66	Jack Greene	68/78	**There'll Never Be Another For Me** *Connie Smith*		
9/71	Elvis Presley			49/81	**(There's No Me) Without You** *Sue Powell*
F/82	Elvis Presley		**(There'll Never Be Another) Pecos Bill**		
20/94	**There Goes My Heart** *Mavericks*	13/48	*Roy Rogers*	48/68	**There's No More Love** *Carl Smith*
4/89	**There Goes My Heart Again** *Holly Dunn*	15/48	*Tex Ritter*	63/99	**There's No Place Like Home For The Holidays** *Garth Brooks*
	There Goes My Love	3/59	**There's A Big Wheel** *Wilma Lee & Stoney Cooper*		
15/57	George Morgan			1/86	**There's No Stopping Your Heart** *Marie Osmond*
71/87	Pam Tillis	5/44	**There's A Blue Star Shining Bright (In A Window Tonight)** *Red Foley*		
96/79	**There Goes That Smile Again** *Corkey Sauls*			48/83	**There's No Substitute For You** *Younger Brothers*
58/99	**There Goes The Neighborhood** *Keith Harling*	11/49	**(There's A) Bluebird On Your Windowsill** *Tex Williams*	1/85	**There's No Way** *Alabama*
67/79	**There Hangs His Hat** *Linda Nail*	4/44	**There's A Chill On The Hill Tonight** *Jimmie Davis*	6/50	**There's No Wings On My Angel** *Eddy Arnold*
82/75	**There Has To Be A Loser** *Diana Trask*	65/81	**There's A Crazy Man** *Jody Payne*	88/80	**There's Nobody Like You** *Kin Vassy*
	There He Goes ..see: There She	1/85	**(There's A) Fire In The Night** *Alabama*	86/83	**There's Nobody Lovin' At Home** *Randy Wright*
85/82	**There I Go Dreamin' Again** *Jan Gray*		**(There's A Fire In Your Soul) ..see: Burn Georgia Burn**	3/49	**There's Not A Thing (I Wouldn't Do For You)** *Eddy Arnold*
8/75	**There I Said It** *Margo Smith*				
53/89	**There! I've Said It Again** *Mickey Gilley*	16/68	**There's A Fool Born Every Minute** *Skeeter Davis*	21/60	**There's Not Any Like You Left** *Faron Young*
20/79	**There Is A Miracle In You** *Tom T. Hall*	20/96	**There's A Girl In Texas** *Trace Adkins*		**(There's Nothing Like The Love) Between A Woman And A Man**
1/01	**There Is No Arizona** *Jamie O'Neal*		**There's A Honky Tonk Angel (Who'll Take Me Back In)**	86/77	Reba McEntire
20/61	**There Must Be Another Way To Live** *Kitty Wells*	1/74	*Conway Twitty*	87/78	Linda Cassady/Bobby Spears
25/71	**There Must Be More To Life (Than Growing Old)** *Jack Blanchard & Misty Morgan*	6/79	*Elvis Presley*	43/98	**There's Only You** *Kevin Sharp*
		47/72	**There's A Kind Of Hush (All Over The World)** *Brian Collins*	9/55	**There's Poison In Your Heart** *Kitty Wells*
1/70	**There Must Be More To Love Than This** *Jerry Lee Lewis*	96/85	**There's A Lot Of Good About Goodbye** *Judy Bailey*	19/71	**There's Something About A Lady** *Johnny Duncan*
5/69	**There Never Was A Time** *Jeannie C. Riley*		**There's A New Moon Over My Shoulder**	84/83	**There's Still A Few Good Love Songs Left In Me** *Connie Francis*
	There She [He] Goes	1/45	*Jimmie Davis*		**There's Still A Lot Of Love In San Antone**
3/55	Carl Smith	2/45	*Tex Ritter*	48/74	Darrell McCall
70/99	Patsy Cline with John Berry	4/72	**There's A Party Goin' On** *Jody Miller*	64/83	Connie Hanson & Friend
11/77	**There She Goes Again** *Joe Stampley*	88/87	**There's A Real Woman In Me** *Bobbi Lace*	58/87	**There's Still Enough Of Us** *Liz Boardo*
24/75	**(There She Goes) I Wish Her Well** *Don Gibson*				

These Colors Won't Run — B.J. Thomas

1/98	**There's Your Trouble** Dixie Chicks		**Thing Called Love**	11/75	**Third Rate Romance** Amazing Rhythm Aces
5/69	**These Are Not My People** Freddy Weller	21/68	Jimmy Dean	2/94	Sammy Kershaw
73/72	**These Are The Good Old Days** Roy Rogers	2/72	Johnny Cash	1/94	**Third Rock From The Sun** Joe Diffie
57/98	**These Arms** Dwight Yoakam	38/65	**Thing Called Sadness** Ray Price	34/70	**Third World** Johnny & Jonie Mosby
67/95	**These Arms** Baker & Myers	49/82	**Thing Or Two On My Mind** Gene Kennedy & Karen Jeglum	52/73	**30 California Women** Kenny Price
41/99	**These Arms Of Mine** LeAnn Rimes		**Things**	7/55	**Thirty Days (To Come Back Home)** Ernest Tubb
	(These Boots Are Made For Walking) ..see: Boots	22/71	Anne Murray	83/76	**38 And Lonely** Dave Dudley
87/77	**These Crazy Thoughts (Run Through My Mind)** Warner Mack	49/72	Buddy Alan	4/81	**Thirty Nine And Holding** Jerry Lee Lewis
		25/75	Ronnie Dove	39/87	**3935 West End Avenue** Mason Dixon
10/75	**These Days (I Barely Get By)** George Jones	66/73	**Things Are Kinda Slow At The House** Earl Richards	4/85	**This Ain't Dallas** Hank Williams, Jr.
64/86	**These Eyes** Beth Williams	75/91	**Things Are Mostly Fine** Donna Ulisse	23/75	**(This Ain't Just Another) Lust Affair** Mel Street
5/56	**These Hands** Hank Snow	23/91	**Things Are Tough All Over** Shelby Lynne	14/90	**This Ain't My First Rodeo** Vern Gosdin
5/91	**These Lips Don't Know How To Say Goodbye** Doug Stone	1/74	**Things Aren't Funny Anymore** Merle Haggard	33/01	**This Ain't No Rag, It's A Flag** Charlie Daniels Band
9/69	**These Lonely Hands Of Mine** Mel Tillis	17/98	**Things Change** Dwight Yoakam	1/97	**(This Ain't) No Thinkin' Thing** Trace Adkins
42/67	**These Memories** Jeannie Seely	32/01	**Things Change** Tim McGraw		**This Ain't Tennessee And He Ain't You**
57/86	**These Shoes** Everly Brothers	25/69	**Things For You And I** Bobby Lewis	93/81	Gypsy Martin
66/68	**(They Always Come Out) Smellin' Like A Rose** Johnny Wright	34/69	**Things Go Better With Love** Jeannie C. Riley	82/83	Sara "Honeybear" Hickey
43/88	**They Always Look Better When They're Leavin'** Becky Hobbs	9/65	**Things Have Gone To Pieces** George Jones	66/84	Katy Moffatt
7/94	**They Asked About You** Reba McEntire	68/88	**Things I Didn't Say** Marcy Bros.	52/85	**This Bed's Not Big Enough** Louise Mandrell
6/79	**They Call It Making Love** Tammy Wynette	31/77	**Things I Treasure** Dorsey Burnette	F/83	**This Country Music's Driving Me Crazy** Johnny Bailey
58/72	**They Call The Wind Maria** Jack Barlow	72/91	**Things I Wish I'd Said** Rodney Crowell		**This Cowboy's Hat**
12/81	**They Could Put Me In Jail** Bellamy Brothers	18/78	**Things I'd Do For You** Mundo Earwood	35/83	Porter Wagoner
4/74	**They Don't Make 'Em Like My Daddy** Loretta Lynn	65/86	**Things I've Done To Me** Jim Collins	63/91	Chris LeDoux
2/94	**They Don't Make 'Em Like That Anymore** Boy Howdy	42/69	**Things That Matter** Van Trevor	1/87	**This Crazy Love** Oak Ridge Boys
		24/62	**Things That Mean The Most** Carl Smith	8/82	**This Dream's On Me** Gene Watson
32/76	**They Don't Make 'Em Like That Anymore** Bobby Borchers	95/82	**Things That Songs Are Made Of** Ray Griff	9/01	**This Everyday Love** Rascal Flatts
10/69	**They Don't Make Love Like They Used To** Eddy Arnold	36/90	**Things You Left Undone** Matraca Berg	40/69	**This Generation Shall Not Pass** Henson Cargill
54/87	**They Don't Make Love Like We Used To** Shenandoah	F/72	**Think About It Darlin'** Jerry Lee Lewis	36/77	**This Girl (Has Turned Into A Woman)** Mary MacGregor
53/86	**They Don't Make Them Like They Used To** Kenny Rogers	1/86	**Think About Love** Dolly Parton	46/66	**This Gun Don't Care** Wanda Jackson
		18/78	**Think About Me** Freddy Fender		**This Heart**
67/87	**They Killed Him** Kris Kristofferson	38/71	**Think Again** Patti Page	25/90	Sweethearts Of The Rodeo
19/85	**They Never Had To Get Over You** Johnny Lee	74/76	**Think I Feel A Hitchhike Coming On** Larry Jon Wilson	74/94	Jon Randall
19/80	**They Never Lost You** Con Hunley	84/88	**Think I'll Go Home** Charlie Beckham	17/99	**This Heartache Never Sleeps** Mark Chesnutt
21/87	**They Only Come Out At Night** Shooters		**Think I'll Go Somewhere And Cry Myself To Sleep**	19/75	**This House Runs On Sunshine** La Costa
5/89	**They Rage On** Dan Seals	26/65	Charlie Louvin	39/78	**This Is A Holdup** Ronnie McDowell
1/44	**They Took The Stars Out Of Heaven** Floyd Tillman	50/76	Billy "Crash" Craddock	20/79	**This Is A Love Song** Bill Anderson
		57/01	**Think It Over** Allison Moorer	1/65	**This Is It** Jim Reeves
	They'll Never Take Her Love From Me	1/66	**Think Of Me** Buck Owens	62/83	**This Is Just The First Day** Razzy Bailey
5/50	Hank Williams	21/76	**Think Summer** Roy Clark	5/94	**This Is Me** Randy Travis
74/70	Johnny Darrell	1/95	**Thinkin' About You** Trisha Yearwood	62/88	**This Is Me Leaving** Lynne Tyndall
57/81	**They'll Never Take Me Alive** Dean Dillon	1/76	**Thinkin' Of A Rendezvous** Johnny Duncan	6/95	**This Is Me Missing You** James House
3/95	**They're Playin' Our Song** Neal McCoy	2/94	**Thinkin' Problem** David Ball	21/75	**This Is My Year For Mexico** Crystal Gayle
72/71	**They're Stepping All Over My Heart** Kitty Wells	53/96	**Thinkin' Strait** Rich McCready	30/63	**This Is The House** Charlie Phillips
58/01	**Thicker Than Blood** Garth Brooks	54/99	**Thinking About Leaving** Dwight Yoakam	16/78	**This Is The Love** Sonny James
14/85	**Thing About You** Southern Pacific	56/84	**Thinking 'Bout Leaving** Butch Baker	3/54	**This Is The Thanks I Get (For Loving You)** Eddy Arnold
		9/70	**Thinking 'Bout You, Babe** Billy Walker	67/80	**This Is True** Steve Douglas

517

This Old Hat — Ed Bruce

25/97	This Is Your Brain Joe Diffie		11/95	(This Thing Called) Wantin' And Havin' It All Sawyer Brown		Three Days
93/74	This Just Ain't My Day (For Lettin' Darlin' Down) Red Steagall		1/74	This Time Waylon Jennings	7/62	Faron Young
			2/95	This Time Sawyer Brown	55/89	k.d. lang
68/73	This Just Ain't No Good Day For Leavin' Kenny Serratt		30/84	This Time Tom Jones	90/90	Three Flags Billy Joe Burnette
			43/78	This Time Johnny Lee	2/61	Three Hearts In A Tangle Roy Drusky
84/77	This Kinda Love Ain't Meant For Sunday School Carl Smith		45/99	This Time Shana Petrone	66/00	Three Little Teardrops Joanie Keller
1/98	This Kiss Faith Hill		89/82	This Time Skip & Linda	65/97	Three Little Words Billy Ray Cyrus
81/78	This Lady Loving Me Carl Smith		43/00	This Time Around Yankee Grey	91/80	Three Little Words Boyer Twins
4/58	This Little Girl Of Mine Everly Brothers		67/78	This Time Around Sammy Vaughn	72/00	Three Minute Positive Not Too Country Up-Tempo Love Song Alan Jackson
5/72	This Little Girl Of Mine Faron Young		12/74	This Time I Almost Made It Barbara Mandrell		
52/78	This Magic Moment Sandra Kaye		20/77	This Time I'm In It For The Love Tommy Overstreet	81/78	Three Nights A Week Ruby Falls
45/76	This Man And Woman Thing Johnny Russell			This Time I've Hurt Her More Than She Loves Me	53/88	Three Piece Suit Russell Smith
					39/68	Three Playing Love Cheryl Poole
2/88	This Missin' You Heart Of Mine Sawyer Brown		1/76	Conway Twitty	37/83	3/4 Time Ray Charles
			50/91	Neal McCoy	20/78	Three Sheets In The Wind Jacky Ward & Reba McEntire
93/79	This Moment In Time Engelbert Humperdinck		51/86	This Time It's You Lisa Childress	30/63	Three Sheets In The Wind Johnny Bond
81/82	This Morning I Woke Up In New York City John Kelley		7/64	This White Circle On My Finger Kitty Wells	32/68	Three Six Packs, Two Arms And A Juke Box Johnny Seay
			5/89	This Woman K.T. Oslin		
11/72	This Much A Man Marty Robbins		1/95	This Woman And This Man Clay Walker	9/61	Three Steps To The Phone (Millions of Miles) George Hamilton IV
	This Must Be My Ship		9/00	This Woman Needs SheDaisy		
32/80	Carol Chase		12/48	This World Can't Stand Long Roy Acuff	73/69	Three Tears (For The Sad, Hurt, And Blue) Ray Sanders
62/81	Diana Trask					
27/66	This Must Be The Bottom Del Reeves		27/67	This World Holds Nothing (Since You're Gone) Stonewall Jackson	1/87	Three Time Loser Dan Seals
20/70	This Night (Ain't Fit For Nothing But Drinking) Dave Dudley					Three Times A Lady
			4/46	Tho' I Tried (I Can't Forget You) Wesley Tuttle	23/78	Nate Harvell
	This Night Won't Last Forever				7/84	Conway Twitty
49/89	Moe Bandy		10/48	Thorn In My Heart Bob Wills	93/80	Three Times In Love Tommy James
6/97	Sawyer Brown		74/86	Those Eyes Anthony Armstrong Jones		
61/92	This Nightlife Clint Black				4/47	Three Times Seven Merle Travis
	This Ol' ..see: This Old		70/74	Those Lazy, Hazy, Crazy Days Of Summer Tex Williams	76/80	Three Way Love Shoppe
90/89	This Old Feeling Andy & The Brown Sisters				7/52	Three Ways Of Knowing Johnnie & Jack
52/88	This Old Flame Robin Lee			Those Memories Of You		
53/92	This Ol' Heart Tim Mensy		55/86	Pam Tillis	7/57	Three Ways (To Love You) Kitty Wells
	This Old Heart		5/87	Dolly Parton, Linda Ronstadt, Emmylou Harris		
21/60	Skeets McDonald				25/95	Three Words, Two Hearts, One Night Mark Collie
24/60	Bobby Barnett		52/83	Those Nights, These Days David Wills		
	This Old House				73/89	Thrill Of Love Kennard & John
66/87	Razorback		47/83	Those Were The Days Gary Stewart & Dean Dillon	14/61	Through That Door Ernest Tubb
24/88	Schuyler, Knobloch & Bickhardt		72/97	Those Who Couldn't Wait David Morgan	99/76	Through The Bottom Of The Glass Leon Rausch
92/89	This Old House Crosby, Stills, Nash & Young					
	This Ole House		9/63	Those Wonderful Years Webb Pierce	31/64	Through The Eyes Of A Fool Roy Clark
2/54	Stuart Hamblen		59/95	Those Words We Said Kim Richey	27/67	Through The Eyes Of Love Tompall/Glaser Brothers
16/60	Wilma Lee & Stoney Cooper					
33/87	This Ol' Town Lacy J. Dalton		62/84	Those You Lose Ronnie Robbins	5/82	Through The Years Kenny Rogers
22/60	This Old Town Buddy Paul		14/54	Thou Shalt Not Steal Kitty Wells		
91/88	This Old World Ain't The Same Jeff Golden		16/61	Thoughts Of A Fool Ernest Tubb	66/72	Throw A Rope Around The Wind Red Lane
7/92	This One's Gonna Hurt You (For A Long, Long Time) Marty Stuart & Travis Tritt		6/59	Thousand Miles Ago Webb Pierce	80/74	Throw Away The Pages Randy Barlow
			2/93	Thousand Miles From Nowhere Dwight Yoakam	87/77	Throw Out Your Loveline Cates Sisters
36/68	This One's On The House Jerry Wallace		13/96	Thousand Times A Day Patty Loveless	3/50	Throw Your Love My Way Ernest Tubb
13/93	This Romeo Ain't Got Julie Yet Diamond Rio		52/89	Threads Of Gold Marcy Bros.	51/78	Throwin' Memories On The Fire Cal Smith
11/90	This Side Of Goodbye Highway 101		8/65	Three A.M. Bill Anderson		
				Three Bells	68/96	Thump Factor Smokin' Armadillos
55/98	This Small Divide Jason Sellers Featuring Martina McBride		1/59	Browns		Thunder Road ..see: Ballad Of
			29/69	Jim Ed Brown	1/91	Thunder Rolls Garth Brooks
69/69	This Song Don't Care Who Sings It Ray Pennington		31/80	3 Chord Country Song Red Steagall	33/76	Thunderstorms Cal Smith
					54/98	Ticket Out Of Kansas Jenny Simpson
68/68	This Song Is Just For You Bobby Austin		44/97	Three Chords And The Truth Sara Evans	22/68	Tie A Tiger Down Sheb Wooley
14/69	This Thing Webb Pierce					Tie A Yellow Ribbon ..see: Yellow Ribbon

	Tie Me Up (Hold Me Down)	32/66	**Till My Getup Has Gotup And Gone** *Ernest Tubb*		**'Tis Sweet To Be Remembered**	
75/88	*Becky Williams*			8/52	*Cowboy Copas*	
83/89	*David Speegle*	7/77	**Till The End** *Vern Gosdin*	9/52	*Flatt & Scruggs*	
29/63	**Tie My Hunting Dog Down, Jed** *Arthur "Guitar Boogie" Smith*		**Till The End Of The World**	91/89	**To A San Antone Rose** *Steve Douglas*	
17/86	**Tie Our Love (In A Double Knot)** *Dolly Parton*	4/49	*Ernest Tubb*		**To A Sleeping Beauty**	
		9/49	*Jimmy Wakely*	15/62	*Jimmy Dean*	
24/82	**Tie Your Dream To Mine** *Marty Robbins*	12/49	*Johnny Bond*	85/76	*Jimmy Dean*	
		10/52	*Bing Crosby & Grady Martin*	1/84	**To All The Girls I've Loved Before** *Julio Iglesias & Willie Nelson*	
96/88	**Tied To The Wheel Of A Runaway Heart** *Paul Proctor*	1/76	**Till The Rivers All Run Dry** *Don Williams*			
4/75	**Ties That Bind** *Don Williams*	8/73	**'Till The Water Stops Runnin'** *Billy "Crash" Craddock*	65/68	**To Be A Child Again** *Anita Carter*	
15/65	**Tiger In My Tank** *Jim Nesbitt*				**To Be Loved**	
6/65	**Tiger Woman** *Claude King*	81/78	**Till Then** *Pal Rakes*	85/78	*Peggy Sue*	
1/81	**Tight Fittin' Jeans** *Conway Twitty*	2/95	**Till You Love Me** *Reba McEntire*	96/88	*Jeremiah*	
56/83	**Tijuana Sunrise** *Bama Band*	17/91	**Till You Were Gone** *Mike Reid*	1/96	**To Be Loved By You** *Wynonna*	
	'Til A Tear Becomes A Rose	1/82	**'Till You're Gone** *Barbara Mandrell*	35/85	**To Be Lovers** *Chance*	
44/85	*Leon Everette*			34/91	**To Be With You** *Larry Boone*	
13/90	*Keith Whitley & Lorrie Morgan*	28/84	**Till Your Memory's Gone** *Bill Medley*	51/78	**To Be With You** *Mavericks*	
	'Til I Can Make It On My Own	13/64	**Timber I'm Falling** *Ferlin Husky*	94/76	**To Be With You Again** *Gary Mack*	
1/76	*Tammy Wynette*	1/89	**Timber, I'm Falling In Love** *Patty Loveless*	3/78	**To Daddy** *Emmylou Harris*	
3/79	*Kenny Rogers & Dottie West*			100/78	**To Each His Own** *Rita Remington*	
	Til I Can't Take It Anymore	55/85	**Timberline** *Emmylou Harris*	12/72	**To Get To You** *Jerry Wallace*	
46/70	*Dottie West & Don Gibson*	10/60	**Timbrook** *Lewis Pruitt*	63/00	**To Get To You** *Lorrie Morgan*	
85/73	*Andra Willis*	2/85	**Time Don't Run Out On Me** *Anne Murray*	12/98	**To Have You Back Again** *Patty Loveless*	
31/77	*Pal Rakes*					
2/90	*Billy Joe Royal*	70/98	**Time For Letting Go** *Billy Ray Cyrus*		**To Know Him Is To Love Him**	
	'Til I Gain Control Again			18/72	*Jody Miller*	
42/79	*Bobby Bare*	39/90	**Time For Me To Fly** *Dolly Parton*	1/87	*Dolly Parton, Linda Ronstadt, Emmylou Harris*	
1/83	*Crystal Gayle*	14/55	**Time Goes By** *Marty Robbins*			
1/73	**'Til I Get It Right** *Tammy Wynette*	23/92	**Time Has Come** *Martina McBride*	25/70	**To Lonely, Too Long** *Mel Tillis*	
	('Til) I Kissed You	64/81	**Time Has Treated You Well** *Corbin/Hanner Band*	93/78	**To Love A Rolling Stone** *Jan Howard*	
8/59	*Everly Brothers*					
10/76	*Connie Smith*	17/87	**Time In** *Oak Ridge Boys*		**To Love Somebody**	
10/86	**Til I Loved You** *Restless Heart*	57/00	**Time, Love & Money** *Ronnie Milsap*	22/77	*Narvel Felts*	
70/99	**'Til I Said It To You** *Reba McEntire*			49/79	*Hank Williams, Jr.*	
		1/96	**Time Marches On** *Tracy Lawrence*	87/77	**To Make A Good Love Die** *DeWayne Orender*	
22/92	**Til I'm Holding You Again** *Pirates Of The Mississippi*	62/98	**Time On My Hands** *Deryl Dodd*			
		44/66	**Time Out** *Bill Anderson & Jan Howard*	41/76	**To Make A Long Story Short** *Ray Price*	
4/89	**'Til Love Comes Again** *Reba McEntire*					
	Til' Santa's Gone (Milk And Cookies)	7/91	**Time Passes By** *Kathy Mattea*	3/69	**To Make A Man (Feel Like A Man)** *Loretta Lynn*	
		51/86	**Time Stood Still** *Vern Gosdin*			
58/95	*Clint Black*	17/66	**Time To Bum Again** *Waylon Jennings*	1/69	**To Make Love Sweeter For You** *Jerry Lee Lewis*	
65/96	*Clint Black*					
40/97	*Clint Black*	72/73	**Time To Love Again** *Liz Anderson*	1/98	**To Make You Feel My Love** *Garth Brooks*	
38/98	*Clint Black*	6/45	**Time Won't Heal My Broken Heart** *Ted Daffan*			
34/99	*Clint Black*			3/84	**To Me** *Barbara Mandrell & Lee Greenwood*	
41/69	**Til Something Better Comes Along** *Bobby Lewis*	26/90	**Time's Up** *Southern Pacific & Carlene Carter*			
					To My Sorrow	
46/82	**Til Something Better Comes Along** *R C Bannon*	5/88	**Timeless And True Love** *McCarters*	2/47	*Eddy Arnold*	
				47/68	*Johnny Duncan*	
41/87	**'Til The Old Wears Off** *Shooters*	30/65	**Times Are Gettin' Hard** *Bobby Bare*		**(To My Wife With Love) ..see: Mi Esposa Con Amor**	
75/90	**Til U Love Me Again** *Tish Hinojosa*		**Tin Man**			
		70/94	*Kenny Chesney*	51/01	**To Quote Shakespeare** *Clark Family Experience*	
39/83	**Til You And Your Lover Are Lovers Again** *Engelbert Humperdinck*	19/01	*Kenny Chesney*			
		25/65	**Tiny Blue Transistor Radio** *Connie Smith*	1/69	**To See My Angel Cry** *Conway Twitty*	
4/89	**'Til You Cry** *Eddy Raven*			65/76	**To Show You That I Love You** *Brian Collins*	
	Till ..also see: 'Til	71/68	**Tiny Bubbles** *Rex Allen*			
14/01	**Till Dale Earnhardt Wins Cup #8** *Kacey Jones*	24/67	**Tiny Tears** *Liz Anderson*	13/61	**To You And Yours (From Me and Mine)** *George Hamilton IV*	
			Tip Of My Fingers			
12/91	**Till I Found You** *Marty Stuart*	7/60	*Bill Anderson*	51/73	**Toast Of '45** *Sammi Smith*	
39/90	**Till I See You Again** *Kevin Welch*	10/63	*Roy Clark*	56/86	**Tobacco Road** *Roy Clark*	
24/80	**Till I Stop Shaking** *Billy "Crash" Craddock*	3/66	*Eddy Arnold*	5/81	**Today All Over Again** *Reba McEntire*	
		16/75	*Jean Shepard*			
7/53	**Till I Waltz Again With You** *Tommy Sosebea*	3/92	*Steve Wariner*		**Today I Started Loving You Again**	
		2/66	**Tippy Toeing** *Harden Trio*			
48/94	**Till I Was Loved By You** *Chely Wright*	50/00	**Tired Of Loving This Way** *Collin Raye With Bobbie Eakes*	69/73	*Kenny Rogers And The First Edition*	
				9/75	*Sammi Smith*	
6/87	**Till I'm Too Old To Die Young** *Moe Bandy*	84/85	**Tired Of The Same Old Thing** *David Walsh*	74/79	*Arthur Prysock*	
				43/86	*Emmylou Harris*	

	Today My World Slipped Away	69/69	**Tonight We're Calling It A Day**	10/61	**Too Many Times** *Don Winters*
10/83	*Vern Gosdin*		*Hugh X. Lewis*	3/57	**Too Much** *Elvis Presley*
3/97	*George Strait*	30/77	**Tonight You Belong To Me**	36/92	**Too Much**
38/73	**Today Will Be The First Day Of The Rest Of My Life**		*Dottie West*		*Pirates Of The Mississippi*
		65/85	**Tonight's The Night** *Carlette*	58/91	**Too Much Candy For A Dime**
	LaWanda Lindsey	28/78	**Tonight's The Night (It's Gonna Be Alright)** *Roy Head*		*Eddy Raven*
3/92	**Today's Lonely Fool**			4/96	**Too Much Fun** *Daryle Singletary*
	Tracy Lawrence	70/66	**Tonight's The Night My Angel's Halo Fell** *Sheb Wooley*	62/91	**Too Much Fun** *Forester Sisters*
45/71	**Today's Teardrops** *Bobby Lewis*			41/73	**Too Much Hold Back**
21/78	**Toe To Toe** *Freddie Hart*	32/80	**Tony's Tank-Up, Drive-In Cafe**		*Little David Wilkins*
	Together Again		*Hank Thompson*	1/86	**Too Much Is Not Enough**
1/64	*Buck Owens*	60/76	**Too Big A Price To Pay**		*Bellamy Brothers with The Forester Sisters*
1/76	*Emmylou Harris*		*Kenny Price*		
19/84	*Kenny Rogers & Dottie West*	1/93	**Too Busy Being In Love**	18/77	**Too Much Is Not Enough**
92/88	**Together Alone** *Ogden Harless*		*Doug Stone*		*Billie Jo Spears*
14/72	**Together Always**	3/90	**Too Cold At Home** *Mark Chesnutt*	72/92	**Too Much Love** *Don Williams*
	Porter Wagoner & Dolly Parton	58/01	**Too Country** *Brad Paisley*	8/73	**Too Much Monkey Business**
	Togetherness		**Too Far Gone**		*Freddy Weller*
24/68	*Freddie Hart*	72/67	*Lucille Starr*	25/89	**Too Much Month At The End Of The Money** *Billy Hill*
12/70	*Buck Owens & Susan Raye*	12/73	*Joe Stampley*		
30/85	**Tokyo, Oklahoma** *John Anderson*	73/75	*Emmylou Harris*	45/69	**Too Much Of A Man (To Be Tied Down)** *Arlene Harden*
36/70	**Tom Green County Fair**	13/79	*Emmylou Harris*		
	Roger Miller	85/76	**Too Far Gone (To Care What You Do To Me)** *Gary S. Paxton*	55/68	**Too Much Of Not Enough**
1/86	**Tomb Of The Unknown Love**				*Ernest Tubb*
	Kenny Rogers	88/79	**Too Fast For Rapid City**	28/67	**Too Much Of You** *Lynn Anderson*
5/65	**Tombstone Every Mile**		*Sheila Andrews*	1/85	**Too Much On My Heart**
	Dick Curless	1/88	**Too Gone Too Long** *Randy Travis*		*Statler Brothers*
9/70	**Tomorrow Is Forever**	89/83	**Too Good To Be Through**	34/74	**Too Much Pride** *Mack White*
	Porter Wagoner & Dolly Parton		*Dave Lemmon*	19/60	**Too Much To Lose** *Carl Belew*
	Tomorrow Never Comes	8/98	**Too Good To Be True**	66/00	**Too Much To Lose**
3/45	*Ernest Tubb*		*Michael Peterson*		*Kentucky Headhunters*
27/70	*Slim Whitman*	47/85	**Too Good To Say No To**	84/81	**Too Much, Too Little, Too Late**
	Tomorrow Night		*Leon Everette*		*Mary Bailey*
24/59	*Carl Smith*	4/84	**Too Good To Stop Now**	13/57	**Too Much Water** *George Jones*
29/73	*Charlie Rich*		*Mickey Gilley*		**Too Old To Cut The Mustard**
11/71	**Tomorrow Night In Baltimore**	50/69	**Too Hard To Say I'm Sorry**	5/52	*Ernest Tubb & Red Foley*
	Roger Miller		*Murv Shiner*	6/52	*Carlisles*
74/90	**Tomorrow's World**	10/83	**Too Hot To Sleep** *Louise Mandrell*	29/72	*Buck Owens & Buddy Alan*
	Tomorrow's World	22/63	**Too In Love** *Hank Thompson*	46/87	**Too Old To Grow Up Now**
5/78	**Tonight** *Barbara Mandrell*	42/86	**Too Late** *Kendalls*		*Pake McEntire*
1/67	**Tonight Carmen** *Marty Robbins*	15/84	**Too Late To Go Home**	13/80	**Too Old To Play Cowboy**
4/93	**Tonight I Climbed The Wall**		*Johnny Rodriguez*		*Razzy Bailey*
	Alan Jackson	9/64	**Too Late To Try Again**	71/68	**Too Rough On Me** *Earl Scott*
26/76	**Tonight I'll Face The Man (Who Made It Happen)** *Kenny Starr*		*Carl Butler & Pearl*	4/53	**Too Young To Tango**
		88/74	**Too Late To Turn Back Now**		*Sunshine Ruby*
31/66	**Tonight I'm Coming Home**		*Four Guys*		**Took It Like A Man, Cried Like A Baby**
	Buddy Cagle		**Too Late To Worry Too Blue To Cry**		
	Tonight I'm Feeling You (All Over Again)			42/82	*Cedar Creek*
		1/44	*Al Dexter*	68/88	*Kevin Pearce*
65/80	*"Blackjack" Jack Grayson*	3/44	*Texas Jim Lewis*	2/73	**Top Of The World** *Lynn Anderson*
38/82	*Jack Grayson*	6/75	*Ronnie Milsap*	53/68	**Top Of The World** *Stu Phillips*
19/84	**Tonight I'm Here With Someone Else** *Karen Brooks*	11/01	**Too Lazy To Work, Too Nervous To Steal** *BR549*	46/74	**Tore Down** *Porter Wagoner*
				57/99	**Tore Up From The Floor Up**
66/88	**Tonight In America**	62/97	**Too Little Too Much** *Nikki Nelson*		*Wade Hayes*
	David Lynn Jones	28/81	**Too Long Gone** *Vern Gosdin*	3/77	**Torn Between Two Lovers**
30/80	**Tonight Let's Sleep On It Baby**	40/82	**Too Many Hearts In The Fire**		*Mary MacGregor*
	Mel Street		*Bobby Smith*	71/72	**Torn From The Pages Of Life**
10/72	**Tonight My Baby's Coming Home** *Barbara Mandrell*	46/91	**Too Many Honky Tonks (On My Way Home)** *Tom Wopat*		*Stonewall Jackson*
				53/87	**Torn-Up** *Vicki Rae Von*
89/88	**Tonight She Went Crazy Without Me** *Mike Lunsford*	68/82	**Too Many Irons In The Fire**	71/00	**Toss A Little Bone**
			Billy Parker & Cal Smith		*Confederate Railroad*
6/79	**Tonight She's Gonna Love Me (Like There Was No Tomorrow)** *Razzy Bailey*	1/81	**Too Many Lovers** *Crystal Gayle*	59/72	**Tossin' And Turnin'**
		21/73	**Too Many Memories** *Bobby Lewis*		*Ronnie Sessions*
		96/73	**Too Many Memories** *Billy Walker*	25/59	**Total Strangers** *Hank Thompson*
12/74	**Tonight Someone's Falling In Love** *Johnny Carver*	29/78	**Too Many Nights Alone**	70/98	**Totally Committed** *Jeff Foxworthy*
			Bobby Bare	1/85	**Touch A Hand, Make A Friend**
6/99	**Tonight The Heartache's On Me**	5/87	**Too Many Rivers** *Forester Sisters*		*Oak Ridge Boys*
	Dixie Chicks	74/73	**Too Many Ties That Bind**	5/88	**Touch And Go Crazy**
20/94	**(Tonight We Just Might) Fall In Love Again** *Hal Ketchum*		*Jan Howard*		*Lee Greenwood*
		26/65	**Too Many Tigers** *Tex Williams*	15/58	**Touch And Go Heart** *Kitty Wells*
26/86	**Tonight We Ride**	2/86	**Too Many Times** *Earl Thomas Conley & Anita Pointer*		
	Michael Martin Murphey				

The Truth About Men? /// Try And Try Again — Hank, Jr.

Touch Me
7/62 *Willie Nelson*
62/77 *Howdy Glenn*
54/86 **Touch Me** *Bandana*
Touch Me (I'll Be Your Fool Once More)
18/79 *Big Al Downing*
4/83 *Tom Jones*
1/86 **Touch Me When We're Dancing** *Alabama*
15/79 **Touch Me With Magic** *Marty Robbins*
3/66 **Touch My Heart** *Ray Price*
99/77 **Touch Of Her Fingers** *Clyde Watson*
1/75 **Touch The Hand** *Conway Twitty*
6/73 **Touch The Morning** *Don Gibson*
(Touch The Wind) ..see: Eres Tu
6/72 **Touch Your Woman** *Dolly Parton*
64/98 **Touchdown Tennessee** *Kenny Chesney*
3/71 **Touching Home** *Jerry Lee Lewis*
92/74 **Touching Me, Touching You** *Vicky Fletcher*
43/85 **Touchy Situation** *Razzy Bailey*
82/80 **Tough Act To Follow** *Billy Parker*
67/95 **Tougher Than The Rest** *Chris LeDoux*
Tower Of Strength
32/75 *Sue Richards*
33/79 *Narvel Felts*
16/68 **Town That Broke My Heart** *Bobby Bare*
38/67 **Town That Never Sleeps** *Charlie Walker*
38/73 **Town Where You Live** *Mel Street*
12/49 **Toy Heart** *Bill Monroe*
99/77 **Toy Hearts** *Johnny Tillotson*
48/74 **Toy Telephone** *Johnny Bush*
75/76 **Tra-La-La-La Suzy** *Price Mitchell*
30/72 **Traces** *Sonny James*
25/71 **Traces Of A Woman** *Billy Walker*
29/74 **Traces Of Life** *Lonzo & Oscar*
11/76 **Tracks Of My Tears** *Linda Ronstadt*
2/53 **Trademark** *Carl Smith*
69/96 **Trail Of Tears** *Billy Ray Cyrus*
Train Medley
95/80 *Boxcar Willie*
61/83 *Boxcar Willie*
7/57 **Train Of Love** *Johnny Cash*
6/87 **Train Of Memories** *Kathy Mattea*
74/71 **Train Train (Carry Me Away)** *Murry Kellum*
57/88 **Trains Make Me Lonesome** *Marty Haggard*
20/89 **Trainwreck Of Emotion** *Lorrie Morgan*
14/48 **Tramp On The Street** *Bill Carlisle*
Trashy Women
63/90 *Jerry Jeff Walker*
10/93 *Confederate Railroad*
52/72 **Travelin' Light** *George Hamilton IV*
29/59 **Travelin' Man** *Red Foley*
32/82 **Travelin' Man** *Jacky Ward*
44/66 **Travelin' Man** *Dick Curless*
20/73 **Traveling Man** *Dolly Parton*
42/72 **Travelin' Minstrel Band** *Carter Family*
33/71 **Travelin' Minstrel Man** *Bill Rice*
51/67 **Traveling Shoes** *Guy Mitchell*

6/51 **Travellin' Blues** *Lefty Frizzell*
6/58 **Treasure Of Love** *George Jones*
3/96 **Treat Her Right** *Sawyer Brown*
12/71 **Treat Him Right** *Barbara Mandrell*
62/74 **Treat Me Like A Lady** *Sherry Bryce*
18/91 **Treat Me Like A Stranger** *Baillie And The Boys*
11/57 **Treat Me Nice** *Elvis Presley*
45/98 **Tree Of Hearts** *Bryan White*
16/64 **Triangle** *Carl Smith*
(Tribute To Luther Perkins) ..see: Cashin' In
Triflin' Gal
2/45 *Al Dexter*
3/45 *Walter Shrum*
1/73 **Trip To Heaven** *Freddie Hart*
75/93 **Tropical Depression** *Alan Jackson*
T-R-O-U-B-L-E
11/75 *Elvis Presley*
13/93 *Travis Tritt*
18/95 **Trouble** *Mark Chesnutt*
30/65 **Trouble And Me** *Stonewall Jackson*
Trouble In Mind
7/56 *Eddy Arnold*
81/77 *Hank Snow*
12/64 **Trouble In My Arms** *Johnny & Jonie Mosby*
1/74 **Trouble In Paradise** *Loretta Lynn*
24/60 **Trouble In The Amen Corner** *Archie Campbell*
57/87 **Trouble In The Fields** *Nanci Griffith*
39/99 **Trouble Is A Woman** *Julie Reeves*
61/89 **Trouble Man** *Waylon Jennings*
5/93 **Trouble On The Line** *Sawyer Brown*
53/00 **Trouble With Angels** *Kathy Mattea*
72/92 **Trouble With Diamonds** *Mac McAnally*
64/82 **Trouble With Hearts** *Roy Head*
64/95 **Trouble With Love** *Rob Crosby*
42/77 **Trouble With Lovin' Today** *Asleep At The Wheel*
Trouble With Never
66/99 *Tim McGraw*
72/00 *Tim McGraw*
15/97 **Trouble With The Truth** *Patty Loveless*
4/62 **Trouble's Back In Town** *Wilburn Brothers*
Truck Driver's Heaven ..see: I Dreamed Of A Hill-Billy Heaven
71/70 **Truck Driver's Lament** *Johnny Dollar*
Truck Drivin' Cat With Nine Wives
54/68 *Charlie Walker*
63/68 *Jim Nesbitt*
3/65 **Truck Drivin' Son-Of-A-Gun** *Dave Dudley*
Truck Driving Man
11/65 *George Hamilton IV*
29/76 *Red Steagall*
53/68 **Truck Driving Woman** *Norma Jean*
44/69 **Truck Stop** *Jerry Smith*
73/74 **Trucker And The U.F.O.** *Brush Arbor*

54/73 **Trucker's Paradise** *Del Reeves*
23/67 **Trucker's Prayer** *Dave Dudley*
2/98 **True** *George Strait*
49/68 **True And Lasting Kind** *Bobby Lord*
30/93 **True Believer** *Ronnie Milsap*
45/93 **True Confessions** *Joy White*
9/69 **True Grit** *Glen Campbell*
5/88 **True Heart** *Oak Ridge Boys*
59/97 **True Lies** *Sara Evans*
F/81 **True Life Country Music** *Razzy Bailey*
4/91 **True Love** *Don Williams*
32/85 **True Love** *Vince Gill*
True Love
51/73 *Red Steagall*
88/78 *LeGardes*
22/71 **True Love Is Greater Than Friendship** *Arlene Harden*
39/86 **True Love (Never Did Run Smooth)** *Tom Wopat*
54/91 **True Love Never Dies** *Kevin Welch*
58/69 **True Love Travels On A Gravel Road** *Duane Dee*
True Love Ways
77/78 *Randy Gurley*
1/80 *Mickey Gilley*
3/66 **True Love's A Blessing** *Sonny James*
85/83 **True Love's Getting Pretty Hard To Find** *Wickline*
23/95 **True To His Word** *Boy Howdy*
True True Lovin'
46/65 *Ferlin Husky*
35/73 *Ferlin Husky*
55/69 **Truer Love You'll Never Find (Than Mine)** *Bonnie Guitar & Buddy Killen*
82/89 **Truth Doesn't Always Rhyme** *Rebecca Holden*
64/78 **(Truth Is) We're Livin' A Lie** *R.C. Bannon*
2/69 **Try A Little Kindness** *Glen Campbell*
47/76 **Try A Little Tenderness** *Billy Thunderkloud*
82/79 **Try Home** *Sandy Posey*
36/80 **Try It On** *Stephanie Winslow*
61/72 **Try It, You'll Like It** *Jimmy Dickens*
32/81 **Try Me** *Randy Barlow*
68/86 **Try Me** *Billy Burnette*
2/44 **Try Me One More Time** *Ernest Tubb*
14/94 **Try Not To Look So Pretty** *Dwight Yoakam*
75/76 **Tryin' Like The Devil** *James Talley*
1/75 **Tryin' To Beat The Morning Home** *T.G. Sheppard*
52/77 **Tryin' To Forget About You** *Cristy Lane*
11/56 **Tryin' To Forget The Blues** *Porter Wagoner*
1/94 **Tryin' To Get Over You** *Vince Gill*
50/95 **Tryin' To Get To New Orleans** *Tractors*
6/93 **Tryin' To Hide A Fire In The Dark** *Billy Dean*
80/83 **Tryin' To Love Two** *Kin Vassy*
12/79 **Tryin' To Satisfy You** *Dottsy*

Turkey In The Straw

30/81	Trying Not To Love You *Johnny Rodriguez*	
99/76	Trying To Live Without You Kind Of Days *Sandy Posey*	
1/80	Trying To Love Two Women *Oak Ridge Boys*	
74/94	Tuckered Out *Clint Black*	
94/80	Tugboat Annie *Lori Jacobs*	
	Tulsa ..also see: (Don't Let The Sun Set On You)	
40/83	Tulsa Ballroom *Dottie West*	
41/71	Tulsa County *Anita Carter*	
1/79	Tulsa Time *Don Williams*	
10/80	Tumbleweed *Sylvia*	
11/48	Tumbling Tumbleweeds *Sons Of The Pioneers*	
	Tupelo County Jail	
7/58	Webb Pierce	
40/66	Stonemans	
15/68	Tupelo Mississippi Flash *Jerry Reed*	
87/87	Turn Around *Terri Gibbs*	
9/56	Turn Her Down *Faron Young*	
1/88	Turn It Loose *Judds*	
11/91	Turn It On, Turn It Up, Turn Me Loose *Dwight Yoakam*	
39/84	Turn Me Loose *Vince Gill*	
76/88	(Turn Me Loose And) Let Me Swing *Swing Shift Band*	
59/84	Turn Me To Love *Keith Whitley*	
27/89	Turn Of The Century *Nitty Gritty Dirt Band*	
87/78	Turn On The Bright Lights *Lenny Gault*	
29/74	Turn On Your Light (And Let It Shine) *Kenny Price*	
1/75	(Turn Out The Light And) Love Me Tonight *Don Williams*	
4/92	Turn That Radio On *Ronnie Milsap*	
61/87	Turn The Music On *O.B. McClinton*	
53/82	Turn The Pencil Over *Porter Wagoner*	
1/67	Turn The World Around *Eddy Arnold*	
17/72	Turn Your Radio On *Ray Stevens*	
80/75	Turnin' My Love On *Jimmy Payne*	
F/72	Turnin' Off A Memory *Merle Haggard*	
1/84	Turning Away *Crystal Gayle*	
87/83	Turning Back The Covers (Don't Turn Back The Time) *Robin Lee*	
	(Turpentine And Dandelion Wine) ..see: My Old Kentucky Home	
67/96	'Twas The Night After Christmas *Jeff Foxworthy*	
88/77	Tweedle-O-Twill *Kathy Barnes*	
	Twelfth Of Never	
17/66	Slim Whitman	
98/77	David Houston	
51/00	Twentieth Century *Alabama*	
57/85	Twentieth Century Fool *Kenny Rogers*	
F/83	20th Century Fox *Bill Anderson*	
10/74	Twentieth Century Drifter *Marty Robbins*	
11/56	Twenty Feet Of Muddy Water *Sonny James*	
2/87	Twenty Years Ago *Kenny Rogers*	
35/81	20/20 Hindsight *Billy Larkin*	

18/77	Twenty-Four Hours From Tulsa *Randy Barlow*	
13/61	Twenty-Fourth Hour *Ray Price*	
3/98	26¢ *Wilkinsons*	
45/64	Twice As Much *Hank Thompson*	
67/92	Twilight Is Gone *Desert Rose Band*	
	Twilight Time	
100/76	Carl Mann	
41/89	Willie Nelson	
	(Twin Pines Theme) ..see: Heaven Can Be Anywhere	
1/88	Twinkle, Twinkle Lucky Star *Merle Haggard*	
49/89	Twist Of Fate *Cee Cee Chapman & Santa Fe*	
	Two Brothers ..see: Ballad Of	
3/84	Two Car Garage *B.J. Thomas*	
8/49	Two Cents, Three Eggs And A Postcard *Red Foley*	
53/72	Two Divided By Love *Kendalls*	
68/71	Two Dollar Toy *Stoney Edwards*	
3/77	Two Dollars In The Jukebox *Eddie Rabbitt*	
	Two Doors Down	
7/78	Zella Lehr	
F/78	Dolly Parton	
1/89	Two Dozen Roses *Shenandoah*	
67/87	255 Harbor Drive *A.J. Masters*	
11/54	Two Glasses, Joe *Ernest Tubb*	
39/74	Two Gun Daddy *Marty Robbins*	
45/85	Two Heart Harmony *Kendalls*	
65/83	Two Hearts *Texas Vocal Company*	
73/89	Two Hearts *Jon Washington*	
73/90	Two Hearts *K.T. Oslin*	
	Two Hearts Beat (Better Than One)	
75/80	Kay Austin	
F/81	Eddy Arnold	
	Two Hearts Can't Be Wrong	
94/82	Denise Price	
63/85	Two Hearts	
18/78	Two Hearts Tangled In Love *Kenny Dale*	
71/72	200 Lbs. O' Slingin' Hound *Billy Edd Wheeler*	
9/55	Two Kinds Of Love *Eddy Arnold*	
83/87	Two Kinds Of Woman *Diamonds*	
8/77	Two Less Lonely People *Rex Allen, Jr.*	
73/70	Two Little Boys *Rusty Draper*	
75/68	Two Little Hearts *Compton Brothers*	
74/70	Two Little Rooms *Janet Lawson*	
7/78	Two Lonely People *Moe Bandy*	
1/78	Two More Bottles Of Wine *Emmylou Harris*	
82/87	Two-Name Girl *Johnstons*	
	Two Of A Kind (Workin' On A Full House)	
71/87	Dennis Robbins	
1/91	Garth Brooks	
	Two Of The Usual	
49/67	Bobby Lewis	
64/67	Don Adams	
50/71	Two Of Us Together *Don Gibson & Sue Thompson*	
14/85	Two Old Cats Like Us *Ray Charles with Hank Williams, Jr.*	
82/89	Two Old Flames One Cheatin' Fire *Joann Wintermute*	

72/81	Two Out Of Three Ain't Bad *J.W. Thompson*	
4/01	Two People Fell In Love *Brad Paisley*	
75/79	Two People In Love *Lorrie Morgan*	
1/98	Two Piña Coladas *Garth Brooks*	
35/70	Two Separate Bar Stools *Wanda Jackson*	
9/57	Two Shadows On Your Window *Jim Reeves*	
64/93	Two Ships That Passed In The Moonlight *Cee Cee Chapman*	
74/86	Two Sides *Jimmy Murphy*	
56/68	Two Sides Of Me *Harold Lee*	
15/65	Two Six Packs Away *Dave Dudley*	
2/92	Two Sparrows In A Hurricane *Tanya Tucker*	
44/82	Two-Step Is Easy *Michael Murphey*	
71/93	Two Steppin' Mind *Tim McGraw*	
6/79	Two Steps Forward And Three Steps Back *Susie Allanson*	
72/86	Two Steps From The Blues *Carlette*	
68/93	Two Steps In The Right Direction *Roger Ballard*	
2/80	Two Story House *George Jones & Tammy Wynette*	
2/99	Two Teardrops *Steve Wariner*	
18/92	Two-Timin' Me *Remingtons*	
39/86	Two Too Many *Holly Dunn*	
85/84	Two Will Be One *Kenny Dale*	
41/70	Tyin' Strings *June Stearns*	
58/95	Tyler *Davis Daniel*	

U

55/68	U.S. Male *Elvis Presley*	
9/75	U.S. Of A *Donna Fargo*	
8/58	Uh-Huh—mm *Sonny James*	
F/57	Uh, Uh, No *George Jones*	
1/91	Unanswered Prayers *Garth Brooks*	
58/88	Unattended Fire *Razzy Bailey*	
2/99	Unbelievable *Diamond Rio*	
29/73	Unbelievable Love *Jim Ed Brown*	
	Unbreakable Heart	
51/93	Carlene Carter	
24/00	Jessica Andrews	
	Unbreakable Hearts	
79/78	Bill White	
92/79	Hargus "Pig" Robbins	
50/01	Unbroken By You *Kortney Kayle*	
	Unchained Melody	
41/75	Joe Stampley	
6/78	Elvis Presley	
26/91	Ronnie McDowell	
3/97	LeAnn Rimes	
49/76	Uncle Hiram And The Homemade Beer *Dick Feller*	
	Uncle Pen	
14/56	Porter Wagoner	
1/84	Ricky Skaggs	
4/77	Uncloudy Day *Willie Nelson*	
3/00	Unconditional *Clay Davidson*	
27/91	Unconditional Love *Glen Campbell*	

44/87	Unconditional Love	
	New Grass Revival	
18/62	Under Cover Of The Night	
	Dave Dudley	
66/83	Under Loved And Over Lonely	
	Katy Moffatt	
24/88	Under The Boardwalk	
	Lynn Anderson	
72/90	Under The Gun Suzy Bogguss	
2/61	Under The Influence Of Love	
	Buck Owens	
54/93	Under This Old Hat Chris LeDoux	
	Under Your Spell Again	
4/59	Buck Owens	
5/59	Ray Price	
39/71	Waylon Jennings & Jessi Colter	
65/76	Barbara Fairchild	
93/89	Shelby Lynne	
28/78	Undercover Lovers Stella Parton	
88/80	Undercover Man Liz Lyndell	
26/64	Understand Your Gal	
	Margie Bowes	
1/64	Understand Your Man	
	Johnny Cash	
10/68	Undo The Right Johnny Bush	
67/73	Uneasy Rider Charlie Daniels	
23/72	Unexpected Goodbye	
	Glenn Barber	
79/75	Unfaithful Fools Leroy Van Dyke	
8/50	Unfaithful One Ernest Tubb	
32/83	Unfinished Business	
	Lloyd David Foster	
35/01	Unforgiven Tracy Lawrence	
18/63	Unkind Words Kathy Dee	
14/48	Unloved And Unclaimed	
	Roy Acuff	
5/62	Unloved Unwanted Kitty Wells	
7/66	Unmitigated Gall Faron Young	
47/99	Unsung Hero Terri Clark	
4/94	Untanglin' My Mind Clint Black	
10/55	Untied Tommy Collins	
54/85	Until I Fall In Love Again	
	Marie Osmond	
1/86	Until I Met You Judy Rodman	
57/77	Until I Met You Tom Bresh	
F/56	Until I Met You Faron Young	
68/72	Until It's Time For You To Go	
	Elvis Presley	
1/69	Until My Dreams Come True	
	Jack Greene	
	Until The Bitter End	
39/80	Kenny Seratt	
88/81	Faron Young	
39/74	Until The End Of Time	
	Narvel Felts & Sharon Vaughn	
77/85	Until The Music Is Gone	
	Becky Chase	
50/78	Until The Next Time Billy Parker	
92/81	Until The Nights Charlie McCoy & Laney Smallwood	
20/60	Until Today Elmer Snodgrass	
42/79	Until Tonight Juice Newton	
93/85	Until We Meet Again	
	Wray Brothers Band	
73/80	Until You Terry Bradshaw	
4/88	Untold Stories Kathy Mattea	
14/72	Untouched Mel Tillis	
57/01	Unusually Unusual Lonestar	
6/51	Unwanted Sign Upon Your Heart	
	Hank Snow	

	Unwed Fathers	
63/83	Tammy Wynette	
56/85	Gail Davies	
6/81	Unwound George Strait	
9/89	Up And Gone McCarters	
48/00	Up North (Down South, Back East, Out West) Wade Hayes	
57/85	Up On Your Love	
	Karen Taylor-Good	
41/66	Up This Hill And Down	
	Osborne Brothers	
	Up To Heaven ..see: (You Lift Me)	
28/75	Uproar Anne Murray	
10/95	Upstairs Downtown Toby Keith	
40/69	Upstairs In The Bedroom	
	Bobby Wright	
65/98	Uptown Down-Home Good Ol' Boy Garth Brooks	
25/74	Uptown Poker Club Jerry Reed	
94/81	Urban Cowboys, Outlaws, Cavaleers James Marvell	
7/67	Urge For Going	
	George Hamilton IV	
55/97	Use Mine Jeff Wood	
48/97	Used To Be's Daryle Singletary	
3/85	Used To Blue Sawyer Brown	
47/98	Used To The Pain Mark Nesler	

V

	Valentine	
53/97	Martina McBride with Jim Brickman	
9/98	Martina McBride with Jim Brickman	
15/69	Vance Roger Miller	
52/70	Vanishing Breed Hank Snow	
7/76	Vaya Con Dios Freddy Fender	
30/77	Vegas Bobby & Jeannie Bare	
56/95	Veil Of Tears Hal Ketchum	
9/83	Velvet Chains Gary Morris	
5/82	Very Best Is You Charly McClain	
50/91	Very First Lasting Love Shelby Lynne & Les Taylor	
1/74	Very Special Love Song Charlie Rich	
40/84	Victim Of Life's Circumstances Vince Gill	
34/82	Victim Or A Fool Rodney Crowell	
75/76	Victims Kenny Starr	
24/84	Victims Of Goodbye Sylvia	
10/96	Vidalia Sammy Kershaw	
12/66	Viet Nam Blues Dave Dudley	
21/67	Vin Rosé Stu Phillips	
	Violet And A Rose	
24/58	Mel Tillis	
10/62	"Little" Jimmy Dickens	
36/64	Wanda Jackson	
73/76	Virgil And The $300 Vacation Cledus Maggard	
68/72	Virginia Jean Shepard	
22/77	Virginia, How Far Will You Go Dickey Lee	
21/00	Visit, The Chad Brock	
90/79	Visitor, The J.W. Thompson	
72/77	Vitamin L Mary Kay Place	
26/66	Volkswagen Ray Pillow	
22/63	Volunteer, The Autry Inman	

8/89	Vows Go Unbroken (Always True To You) Kenny Rogers	

W

72/87	W. Lee O'Daniel (And The Light Crust Dough Boys) Johnny Cash	
6/00	www.memory Alan Jackson	
	Wabash Cannonball	
52/67	Dick Todd	
27/70	Dick Curless	
63/70	Danny Davis	
97/76	Charlie McCoy	
91/84	Willie Nelson & Hank Wilson	
50/66	Waco Lorne Greene	
12/55	Wait A Little Longer Please, Jesus Carl Smith	
98/85	Wait Till I Get My Hands On You Wynn Stewart	
62/82	Wait Till Those Bridges Are Gone Ray Price	
70/77	Waitin' At The End Of Your Run Ava Barber	
	Waitin' For A Train ..see: Waiting For A Train	
39/92	Waitin' For The Deal To Go Down Dixiana	
12/58	Waitin' In School Ricky Nelson	
1/66	Waitin' In Your Welfare Line Buck Owens	
70/89	Waitin' On Ice Jason D. Williams	
50/00	Waitin' On Sundown Andy Griggs	
69/87	Waitin' Up George Highfill	
25/64	Waiting A Lifetime Webb Pierce	
	Waiting For A Train (All Around The Watertank)	
F/57	Jim Reeves	
11/71	Jerry Lee Lewis	
72/76	Waiting For The Tables To Turn Wayne Kemp	
50/89	Waiting Here For You Gail Davies	
3/52	Waiting In The Lobby Of Your Heart Hank Thompson	
14/74	Wake Me Into Love Bud Logan & Wilma Burgess	
63/80	Wake Me Up Louise Mandrell	
21/70	Wake Me Up Early In The Morning Bobby Lord	
57/98	Wake Up And Smell The Whiskey Dean Miller	
1/54	Wake Up, Irene Hank Thompson	
37/73	Wake Up, Jacob Porter Wagoner	
1/57	Wake Up Little Susie Everly Brothers	
2/91	Walk, The Sawyer Brown	
56/70	Walk A Mile In My Shoes Joe South	
56/71	Walk All Over Georgia Ray Sanders	
57/69	Walk Among The People Cheryl Poole	
48/77	Walk Away With Me Randy Barlow	
56/82	Walk Me 'Cross The River Jerri Kelly	
28/87	Walk Me In The Rain Girls Next Door	
7/63	Walk Me To The Door Ray Price	

I Walk Alone
I Walk The Line

Walking In High Cotton (Cotton, Nostalgia)

44/67	**Walk Me To The Station** Stu Phillips	7/66	**Walking On New Grass** Kenny Price	6/75	**Warm Side Of You** Freddie Hart
2/90	**Walk On** Reba McEntire		**Walking Piece Of Heaven**		**Warm Summer Days** ..see: (She Likes)
30/83	**Walk On** Karen Brooks	6/73	Marty Robbins	73/87	**Warmed Over Romance**
61/95	**Walk On** Linda Ronstadt	22/79	Freddy Fender		Tina Danielle
74/87	**Walk On Boy** Ogden Harless	64/66	**Walking Shadow, Talking Memory** Carl Belew	25/70	**Warmth Of The Wine** Johnny Bush
	Walk On By	3/90	**Walking Shoes** Tanya Tucker	4/92	**Warning Labels** Doug Stone
1/61	Leroy Van Dyke		**Walking The Floor Over You**	4/85	**Warning Sign** Eddie Rabbitt
98/79	Robert Gordon	18/65	George Hamilton IV	56/97	**Warning Signs** Bill Engvall with John Michael Montgomery
43/80	Donna Fargo	31/79	Ernest Tubb		
73/87	Perry LaPointe	28/58	**Walking The Slow Walk** Carl Smith	61/86	**Was It Just The Wine** Vern Gosdin
55/88	Asleep At The Wheel	5/61	**Walking The Streets** Webb Pierce	43/76	**Was It Worth It** Joe Stampley
1/91	**Walk On Faith** Mike Reid	58/68	**Walking Through The Memories Of My Mind** Billy Mize	20/72	**Washday Blues** Dolly Parton
5/68	**Walk On Out Of My Mind** Waylon Jennings			28/79	**Wasn't It Easy Baby** Freddie Hart
9/61	**Walk Out Backwards** Bill Anderson	15/95	**Walking To Jerusalem** Tracy Byrd	73/81	**Wasn't It Supposed To Be Me** Kenny Earle
71/93	**Walk Outside The Lines** Marshall Tucker Band	59/83	**Walking With My Memories** Loretta Lynn	45/81	**Wasn't That A Party** Rovers
	Walk Right Back	24/59	**Wall, The** Freddie Hart	62/82	**Wasn't That Love** Susie Allanson
76/77	LaWanda Lindsey	69/93	**Wall Around Her Heart** Remingtons	1/75	**Wasted Days And Wasted Nights** Freddy Fender
4/78	Anne Murray	60/68	**Wall Of Pictures** Darrell McCall	27/60	**Wasted Love** Red Herring
	Walk Right In	40/87	**Wall Of Tears** K.T. Oslin	87/82	**Wasted On The Way** Crosby, Stills & Nash
23/63	Rooftop Singers	5/62	**Wall To Wall Love** Bob Gallion		
92/77	Dr. Hook	43/66	**Wallpaper Roses** Jerry Wallace	4/56	**Wasted Words** Ray Price
7/76	**Walk Softly** Billy "Crash" Craddock		**Walls Of The Bottle** ..see: (If I Could Climb)	28/60	**Watch Dog** Al Terry
	Walk Softly On The Bridges			2/92	**Watch Me** Lorrie Morgan
11/73	Mel Street	97/76	**Walnut Street Wrangler** Debi Hawkins		**Watch Out For Lucy**
79/86	Rodney Lay		**Waltz Across Texas**	88/74	Bobby Penn
25/89	**Walk Softly On This Heart Of Mine** Kentucky Headhunters	34/65	Ernest Tubb	72/75	Tony Booth
		81/76	Maury Finney	4/97	**Watch This** Clay Walker
10/65	**Walk Tall** Faron Young	56/79	Ernest Tubb	10/65	**Watch Where You're Going** Don Gibson
54/89	**Walk That Way** Mel McDaniel	10/85	**Waltz Me To Heaven** Waylon Jennings	4/82	**Watchin' Girls Go By** Ronnie McDowell
10/86	**Walk The Way The Wind Blows** Kathy Mattea		**Waltz Of The Angels**	47/99	**Watching My Baby Not Coming Back** David Ball
1/67	**Walk Through This World With Me** George Jones	14/56	Wynn Stewart		
30/70	**Walk Unashamed** Tompall/Glaser Brothers	11/62	George Jones & Margie Singleton	7/71	**Watching Scotty Grow** Bobby Goldsboro
2/93	**Walkaway Joe** Trisha Yearwood With Don Henley	51/78	David Houston	32/67	**Watchman, The** Claude King
		8/48	**Waltz Of The Wind** Roy Acuff	57/91	**Water Under The Bridge** Dan Seals
57/67	**Walker's Woods** Ed Bruce	13/62	**Waltz You Saved For Me** Ferlin Husky		
63/93	**Walkin'** Cleve Francis			16/73	**Watergate Blues** Tom T. Hall
2/85	**Walkin' A Broken Heart** Don Williams	85/81	**Waltzes And Western Swing** Donnie Rohrs		**Waterhole #3** ..see: Ballad Of
	Walkin' After Midnight	63/87	**Waltzin' With Daddy** Carlette	1/59	**Waterloo** Stonewall Jackson
2/57	Patsy Cline	1/88	**Wanderer, The** Eddie Rabbitt	4/94	**Watermelon Crawl** Tracy Byrd
60/82	Calamity Jane	13/67	**Wanderin' Man** Jeannie Seely	49/70	**Watermelon Time In Georgia** Lefty Frizzell
1/90	**Walkin' Away** Clint Black	2/81	**Wandering Eyes** Ronnie McDowell		**Watermelon Wine** ..see: (Old Dogs-Children And)
2/96	**Walkin' Away** Diamond Rio				
23/69	**Walkin' Back To Birmingham** Leon Ashley	52/68	**Wandering Mind** Margie Singleton		**Wave To Me, My Lady**
29/59	**Walkin' Down The Road** Jimmy Newman	63/84	**Want Ads** Robin Lee	3/46	Elton Britt
		35/79	**Want To Thank You** Kim Charles	4/46	Gene Autry
83/74	**Walkin' In Teardrops** Earl Richards	3/74	**Want-To's, The** Freddie Hart	62/70	**Wax Museum** Dave Peel
61/90	**Walkin' In The Sun** Glen Campbell	3/90	**Wanted** Alan Jackson	57/70	**Waxahachie Woman** John Deer Company
		41/75	**Wanted Man** Jerry Wallace		
7/67	**Walkin' In The Sunshine** Roger Miller		**Wantin' And Havin' It All** ..see: (This Thing Called)	4/84	**Way Back** John Conlee
21/59	**Walkin' My Blues Away** Jimmie Skinner	63/67	**Wanting You But Never Having You** Jack Greene	99/88	**Way Beyond The Blue** Bonners
	Walkin', Talkin', Cryin', Barely Beatin' Broken Heart			1/77	**Way Down** Elvis Presley
22/64	Johnny Wright	11/60	**Wanting You With Me Tonight** Jimmy Newman	5/83	**Way Down Deep** Vern Gosdin
4/90	Highway 101	1/82	**War Is Hell (On The Homefront Too)** T.G. Sheppard	39/87	**Way Down Texas Way** Asleep At The Wheel
50/97	**Walkin' The Country** Ranch				
3/94	**Walking Away A Winner** Kathy Mattea	50/00	**Warm & Fuzzy** Billy Gilman	46/76	**Way He's Treated You** Nat Stuckey
		43/76	**Warm And Tender** Larry Gatlin	2/80	**Way I Am** Merle Haggard
74/91	**Walking In Memphis** Marc Cohn	57/68	**Warm And Tender Love** Archie Campbell & Lorene Mann	67/75	**Way I Lose My Mind** Carl Smith
53/69	**Walking Midnight Road** June Stearns	53/73	**Warm Love** Don Gibson & Sue Thompson	99/76	**Way I Loved Her** Rick Smith
		8/49	**Warm Red Wine** Ernest Tubb	59/89	**Way I Want To Go** Burch Sisters
		72/68	**Warm Red Wine** Wes Buchanan	54/74	**Way I'm Needing You** Cliff Cochran

524

17/63	Way It Feels To Die *Vernon Stewart*	16/81	We Don't Have To Hold Out *Anne Murray*	2/71	We Sure Can Love Each Other *Tammy Wynette*
82/78	Way It Was In '51 *Merle Haggard*	72/78	We Don't Live Here, We Just Love Here *Big Ben Atkins*	2/92	We Tell Ourselves *Clint Black*
91/85	Way She Makes Love *Billy Chinnock*	92/77	We Fell In Love That Way *Claude Gray*	60/00	We The People *Billy Ray Cyrus*
64/97	Way She's Lookin' *Raybon Bros.*	30/73	We Found It *Porter Wagoner & Dolly Parton*	75/97	We Three Kings (Star Of Wonder) *BlackHawk*
	Way To Survive			9/75	We Used To *Dolly Parton*
7/66	*Ray Price*	34/72	We Found It In Each Other's Arms *Roger Miller*	63/80	(We Used To Kiss Each Other On The Lips But It's) All Over Now *Ann J. Morton*
82/89	*Monty Holmes*
1/87	Way We Make A Broken Heart *Rosanne Cash*	63/94	We Got A Lot In Common *Archer Park*	2/97	We Were In Love *Toby Keith*
98/76	Way With Words *Carl Smith*	26/78	We Got Love *Lynn Anderson*	63/88	We Were Meant To Be Lovers *David Slater*
F/83	Way Without Words *Roy Clark*	34/79	We Got Love *Mundo Earwood*	50/85	We Work *Hillary Kanter*
86/81	Way You Are *P.J. Parks*	11/93	We Got The Love *Restless Heart*	38/65	We'd Destroy Each Other *Carl Butler & Pearl*
98/88	Way You Got Over Me *Bill Nunley*	20/69	We Had All The Good Things Going *Jan Howard*
1/00	Way You Love Me *Faith Hill*		We Had It All	2/93	We'll Burn That Bridge *Brooks & Dunn*
7/80	Wayfaring Stranger *Emmylou Harris*	28/73	*Waylon Jennings*	F/56	We'll Find A Way *Webb Pierce*
99/79	Waylon, Sing To Mama *Darrell Thomas*	44/83	*Conway Twitty*	5/68	We'll Get Ahead Someday *Porter Wagoner & Dolly Parton*
2/58	Ways Of A Woman In Love *Johnny Cash*	31/86	*Dolly Parton*		We'll Sing In The Sunshine
74/78	Ways Of A Woman In Love *Tom Bresh*	69/82	We Had It All One Time *Charlie Daniels Band*	43/64	*Gale Garnett*
1/69	Ways To Love A Man *Tammy Wynette*		We Have To Start Meeting Like This ..see: We've Got To Start	63/70	*LaWanda Lindsey*
57/83	Wayward Wind *James Galway & Sylvia*	9/94	We Just Disagree *Billy Dean*	34/72	*Alice Creech*
	We Ain't Gonna Work For Peanuts ..see: Farmer's Song	66/84	We Just Gotta Dance *Karen Taylor-Good*	54/68	We'll Stick Together *Kitty Wells & Johnny Wright*
46/96	We All Get Lucky Sometimes *Lee Roy Parnell*	98/77	We Know Better *Paul Craft*	63/69	We'll Sweep Out The Ashes In The Morning *Carl Butler & Pearl*
22/69	We All Go Crazy *Jack Reno*	53/85	We Know Better Now *Dottie West*		We're All Alone
75/87	We Always Agree On Love *Atlanta*	40/73	We Know It's Over *Dave Dudley & Karen O'Donnal*	75/77	*La Costa*
76/85	We Are The World *USA For Africa*	89/79	We Let Love Fade Away *Leon Everette*	82/77	*Rita Coolidge*
	We Believe In Happy Endings	96/76	We Live In Two Different Worlds *Rachel Sweet*		We're Back In Love Again
7/78	*Johnny Rodriguez*	37/74	*Johnny Bush*
1/88	*Earl Thomas Conley with Emmylou Harris*	68/98	We Lose *Brad Hawkins*	59/80	*Johnny Russell*
48/79	We Love Each Other *Louise Mandrell & R.C. Bannon*	93/81	We're Building Our Love On A Rock *Lou Hobbs*
	We Belong Together
2/78	*Susie Allanson*	8/74	We Loved It Away *George Jones & Tammy Wynette*	47/76	We're Getting There *Ray Price*
52/86	*Carlette*
85/84	We Belong Together *Tony Joe White*	63/00	We Made Love *Alabama*	13/70	We're Gonna Get Together *Buck Owens & Susan Raye*
3/91	We Both Walk *Lorrie Morgan*	77/82	We Made Memories *Boxcar Willie & Penny DeHaven*	14/62	We're Gonna Go Fishin' *Hank Locklin*
71/92	We Can Hold Our Own *Ronna Reeves*	2/44	We Might As Well Forget It *Bob Wills*	1/73	We're Gonna Hold On *George Jones & Tammy Wynette*
62/93	We Can Love *Larry Stewart*	7/62	We Missed You *Kitty Wells*	75/88	We're Gonna Love Tonight *Don Juan*
6/72	We Can Make It *George Jones*	7/88	We Must Be Doin' Somethin' Right *Eddie Rabbitt*	95/79	We're In For Hard Times *Breakfast Barry*
40/77	We Can't Build A Fire In The Rain *Roy Clark*
6/77	We Can't Go On Living Like This *Eddie Rabbitt*		We Must Believe In Magic		We're Livin' A Lie ..see: (Truth Is)
86/78	*Jack Clement*	94/79	We're Making Up For Lost Time *Rex Gosdin*
6/94	We Can't Love Like This Anymore *Alabama*	84/83	*Johnny Cash*
3/63	We Must Have Been Out Of Our Minds *George Jones & Melba Montgomery*	15/74	(We're Not) The Jet Set *George Jones & Tammy Wynette*
3/74	We Could *Charley Pride*
96/81	We Could Go On Forever *E.W.B.*	18/80	We're Number One *Larry Gatlin/Gatlin Brothers*
86/79	We Could Have Been The Closest Of Friends *B.J. Thomas*	68/92	We Must Take America Back *Steve Vaus*
3/74	We're Over *Johnny Rodriguez*
43/68	We Need A Lot More Happiness *Wilburn Brothers*	20/00	We're So Good Together *Reba McEntire*
1/00	We Danced *Brad Paisley*
1/97	We Danced Anyway *Deana Carter*	69/70	We Need A Lot More Of Jesus *Skeeter Davis*	59/87	We're Staying Together *Rex Allen, Jr.*
2/82	We Did But Now You Don't *Conway Twitty*	64/88	We Need To Be Locked Away *Jonathan Edwards*	80/77	We're Still Hangin' In There Ain't We Jessi *Jeannie Seely*
66/89	We Did It Once (We Can Do It Again) *Pal Rakes*	22/88	We Never Touch At All *Merle Haggard*		We're Strangers Again
42/83	*Merle Haggard & Leona Williams*
6/84	We Didn't See A Thing *Ray Charles/George Jones/ Chet Atkins*	67/83	We Really Got A Hold On Love *Family Brown*	49/91	*Tammy Wynette with Randy Travis*
4/98	We Really Shouldn't Be Doing This *George Strait*	15/63	We're The Talk Of The Town *Buck Owens & Rose Maddox*
11/94	We Don't Have To Do This *Tanya Tucker*
12/92	We Shall Be Free *Garth Brooks*	10/78	We've Come A Long Way, Baby *Loretta Lynn*
5/74	We Should Be Together *Don Williams*	10/54	We've Gone Too Far *Hank Thompson*

525

Handwritten annotations at top: (LP) What's Wrong With The Way That We're Doing It Now — Justin Tubb
Handwritten at left margin: A Wednesday Car — Johnny Cash (4-CD Kit #424)

44/66	We've Gone Too Far, Again *Justin Tubb & Lorene Mann*	
3/86	We've Got A Good Fire Goin' *Don Williams*	
97/83	We've Got A Good Thing Goin' *J.W. Thompson*	
20/71	We've Got Everything But Love *David Houston & Barbara Mandrell*	
95/75	We've Got It All Together Now *Guy & Ralna*	
14/91	We've Got It Made *Lee Greenwood*	
13/63	We've Got Something In Common *Faron Young*	
73/96	We've Got To Keep On Meeting Like This *Paul Overstreet*	
	We've Got To Start Meeting Like This	
84/81	*Kenny Earle*	
76/82	*John Wesley Ryles*	
85/84	*Memphis*	
30/72	We've Got To Work It Out Between Us *Diana Trask*	
1/83	We've Got Tonight *Kenny Rogers & Sheena Easton*	
63/79	We've Gotta Get Away From It All *Tom Grant*	
78/85	We've Still Got Love *Simon & Verity*	
96/89	Weak Men Break *Harrell & Scott*	
67/89	Weak Nights *Linda Davis*	
57/70	Weakest Kind Of Man *John Wesley Ryles*	
18/68	Weakness In A Man *Roy Drusky*	
	Wear My Ring Around Your Neck	
3/58	*Elvis Presley*	
F/83	*Elvis Presley*	
26/92	*Ricky Van Shelton*	
7/53	Weary Blues From Waitin' *Hank Williams*	
	Wedding Bells	
2/49	*Hank Williams*	
6/49	*Margaret Whiting & Jimmy Wakely*	
15/49	*Kenny Roberts*	
15/49	*Jesse Rogers*	
78/83	*Margo Smith*	
33/69	Wedding Cake *Connie Francis*	
91/78	Weeds Outlived The Roses *Darrell McCall*	
13/78	Week-End Friend *Con Hunley*	
1/70	Week In A Country Jail *Tom T. Hall*	
10/64	Week In The Country *Ernest Ashworth*	
1/87	Weekend, The *Steve Wariner*	
75/87	Weekend Cowboys *Marty Haggard*	
F/75	Weekend Daddy *Buck Owens*	
87/76	Weep No More My Baby *Lois Johnson*	
43/80	Weight Of My Chains *Tompall/Glaser Brothers*	
93/76	Welcome Back *John Sebastian*	
56/74	Welcome Back To My World *Carl Belew*	
79/74	Welcome Home *Peters And Lee*	
24/68	Welcome Home To Nothing *Jeannie Seely*	
	Welcome To My World	
2/64	*Jim Reeves*	
34/71	*Eddy Arnold*	

47/92	Welcome To The Club *Tim McGraw*	
22/74	Welcome To The Sunshine (Sweet Baby Jane) *Jeanne Pruett*	
6/70	Welfare Cadilac *Guy Drake*	
60/80	Well Rounded Traveling Man *Kenny Price*	
28/94	Were You Really Livin' *Brother Phelps*	
46/86	Weren't You Listening *Adam Baker*	
49/67	West Canterbury Subdivision Blues *Stonemans*	
23/71	West Texas Highway *George Hamilton IV*	
51/69	West Virginia Woman *Billy Edd Wheeler*	
61/94	Western Flyer *Western Flyer*	
20/90	Western Girls *Marty Stuart*	
11/75	Western Man *La Costa*	
25/94	What A Crying Shame *Mavericks*	
	(What A Day For A) Day Dream ..see: Daydream	
81/77	What A Diff'rence A Day Made *Bobby Lewis*	
1/78	What A Difference You've Made In My Life *Ronnie Milsap*	
50/71	What A Dream *Conway Twitty*	
2/48	What A Fool I Was *Eddy Arnold*	
43/87	What A Girl Next Door Could Do *Girls Next Door*	
23/61	What A Laugh! *Freddie Hart*	
16/79	What A Lie *Sammi Smith*	
1/74	What A Man, My Man Is *Lynn Anderson*	
75/85	What A Memory You'd Make *Jim Collins*	
	What A Night	
51/76	*David Houston*	
71/77	*Tom Jones*	
23/62	What A Pleasure *Connie Hall*	
57/72	What A Price *Johnny Russell*	
13/49	What A Shame *Merle Travis*	
25/61	What A Terrible Feeling *Elmer Snodgrass*	
	What A Way To Go	
18/77	*Bobby Borchers*	
10/91	*Ray Kennedy*	
70/74	What A Way To Go *Del Reeves*	
29/68	What A Way To Live *Johnny Bush*	
85/82	What A Way To Spend The Night *Zella Lehr*	
45/98	What A Woman Knows *Kris Tyler*	
44/93	What A Woman Wants *Lari White*	
73/89	What A Wonderful World *Roy Clark*	
71/93	What About Love *Desert Rose Band*	
20/73	What About Me *Anne Murray*	
22/61	What About Me *Don Gibson*	
70/84	What About Me? *Kenny Rogers/Kim Carnes/James Ingram*	
1/00	What About Now *Lonestar*	
44/71	What About The Hurt *Bob Luman*	
45/91	What About The Love We Made *Shelby Lynne*	
80/82	What About Tonight *Gene Kennedy & Karen Jeglum*	
45/99	What About You *Sons Of The Desert*	

8/72	What Ain't To Be, Just Might Happen *Porter Wagoner*	
13/72	What Am I Gonna Do *Bobby Bare*	
90/80	What Am I Gonna Do? *Del Reeves*	
	What Am I Gonna Do About You	
48/86	*Con Hunley*	
1/87	*Reba McEntire*	
37/67	What Am I Gonna Do Now *Ferlin Husky*	
3/83	What Am I Gonna Do (With The Rest Of My Life) *Merle Haggard*	
38/64	What Am I Gonna Do With You *Skeeter Davis*	
77/84	What Am I Gonna Do Without You *Ray Price*	
	What Am I Living For	
19/59	*Ernest Tubb*	
59/71	*Conway Twitty*	
7/56	What Am I Worth *George Jones*	
19/69	What Are Those Things (With Big Black Wings) *Charlie Louvin*	
1/81	What Are We Doin' In Love *Dottie West with Kenny Rogers*	
4/81	What Are We Doin' Lonesome *Larry Gatlin/Gatlin Brothers*	
10/49	What Are We Gonna Do About The Moonlight *Hank Thompson*	
66/91	What Bothers Me Most *Waylon Jennings*	
97/74	What Can I Do (To Make You Happy) *Karen Wheeler*	
92/79	What Can I Do (To Make You Love Me) *Hugh X. Lewis*	
9/87	What Can I Do With My Heart *Juice Newton*	
41/68	What Can I Say *Arlene Harden*	
61/67	What Can I Tell The Folks Back Home *Melba Montgomery*	
	What Cha ..also see: What You, and Whatcha	
30/78	What Cha Doin' After Midnight, Baby *Helen Cornelius*	
82/88	What Cha' Doin' To Me *Day Johnston*	
75/96	What Child Is This *Mark Chesnutt*	
65/00	What Children Believe *Shenandoah*	
	What Did I Promise Her Last Night	
75/77	*Billy Parker*	
4/78	*Mel Tillis*	
60/86	What Did You Do With My Heart *Chance*	
7/58	What Do I Care *Johnny Cash*	
	What Do I Do With Me ..see: (Without You)	
5/96	What Do I Know *Ricochet*	
61/88	What Do Lonely People Do *Burch Sisters*	
62/71	What Do You Do *Barbara Fairchild*	
26/01	What Do You Know About Love *Dwight Yoakam*	
3/00	What Do You Say *Reba McEntire*	
4/99	What Do You Say To That *George Strait*	
53/01	What Do You Want From Me Now *Billy Yates*	
6/88	What Do You Want From Me This Time *Foster & Lloyd*	

526

48/95	**What Do You Want With His Love** David Ball	
5/67	**What Does It Take** Skeeter Davis	
70/69	**What Eva Doesn't Have** Ray Pennington	
	(What Ever May The Future Be) ..see: Lo Que Sea	
66/72	**What Every Woman Wants To Hear** Claude Gray	
1/76	**What Goes On When The Sun Goes Down** Ronnie Milsap	
56/91	**What Goes With Blue** Tammy Wynette	
28/80	**What Good Is A Heart** Dean Dillon	
46/73	**What Got To You (Before It Got To Me)** Ray Griff	
F/76	**What Have You Got Planned Tonight Diana** Merle Haggard	
9/78	**What Have You Got To Lose** Tom T. Hall	
50/89	**What He Does Best** Lynn Anderson	
22/01	**What I Did Right** Sons Of The Desert	
3/85	**What I Didn't Do** Steve Wariner	
	What I Feel In My Heart ..see: (How Can I Write On Paper)	
50/79	**What I Feel Is You** Billy The Kid	
	What I Had With You	
48/80	Sheila Andrews with Joe Sun	
12/81	John Conlee	
80/75	**What I Keep Sayin', Is A Lie** Debi Hawkins	
18/83	**What I Learned From Loving You** Lynn Anderson	
5/96	**What I Meant To Say** Wade Hayes	
38/00	**What I Need** Julie Reeves	
21/65	**What I Need Most** Hugh X. Lewis	
8/00	**What I Need To Do** Kenny Chesney	
1/01	**What I Really Meant To Say** Cyndi Thomson	
1/89	**What I'd Say** Earl Thomas Conley	
5/76	**What I've Got In Mind** Billie Jo Spears	
23/98	**What If** Reba McEntire	
26/97	**What If I Do** Mindy McCready	
1/98	**What If I Said** Anita Cochran with Steve Wariner	
57/83	**What If I Said I Love You** Marty Robbins	
54/98	**What If I'm Right** Shane Stockton	
67/00	**What If It's Me** Jennifer Day	
80/86	**What If It's Right** Family Brown	
15/97	**What If It's You** Reba McEntire	
	What If Jesus Comes Back Like That	
57/95	Collin Raye	
21/97	Collin Raye	
2/02	**What If She's An Angel** Tommy Shane Steiner	
70/92	**What If You're Wrong** Ronna Reeves	
21/79	**What In Her World Did I Do** Eddy Arnold	
19/72	**What In The World Has Gone Wrong With Our Love** Jack Greene/Jeannie Seely	
	What In The World's Come Over You	
10/75	Sonny James	
25/81	Tom Jones	

1/47	**What Is Life Without Love** Eddy Arnold	
3/70	**What Is Truth** Johnny Cash	
81/89	**What It Boils Down To** Frank Burgess	
95/79	**What It Means To Be An American** Billy Brown	
5/67	**What Kind Of A Girl (Do You Think I Am?)** Loretta Lynn	
24/92	**What Kind Of Fool** Lionel Cartwright	
2/92	**What Kind Of Fool Do You Think I Am** Lee Roy Parnell	
44/78	**What Kind Of Fool (Do You Think I Am)** Eddie Middleton	
97/77	**What Kind Of Fool (Does That Make Me)** Brian Shaw	
79/89	**What Kind Of Girl Do You Think I Am** Sandy Ellwanger	
11/92	**What Kind Of Love** Rodney Crowell	
57/69	**What Kind Of Magic** Les Seevers	
61/93	**What Kind Of Man** Martin Delray	
75/95	**What Kind Of Man (Walks On A Woman)** Marie Osmond	
4/66	**What Kinda Deal Is This** Bill Carlisle	
71/74	**What Ladies Can Do (When They Want To)** Dorsey Burnette	
2/67	**What Locks The Door** Jack Greene	
55/93	**What Made You Say That** Shania Twain	
8/58	**What Makes A Man Wander** Jimmie Skinner	
25/65	**What Makes A Man Wander?** Jan Howard	
70/69	**What Makes You So Different** June Stearns	
61/82	**What Mama Don't Know** Jim Stafford	
1/95	**What Mattered Most** Ty Herndon	
2/93	**What Might Have Been** Little Texas	
23/79	**What More Could A Man Need** Tommy Overstreet	
6/73	**What My Woman Can't Do** George Jones	
71/86	**What My Woman Does To Me** Ray Griff	
1/93	**What Part Of No** Lorrie Morgan	
	What She Bottled Up In Me ..see: (I'm Just Pouring Out)	
5/83	**What She Don't Know Won't Hurt Her** Gene Watson	
1/88	**What She Is (Is A Woman In Love)** Earl Thomas Conley	
8/85	**What She Wants** Michael Martin Murphey	
1/92	**What She's Doing Now** Garth Brooks	
2/94	**What The Cowgirls Do** Vince Gill	
2/97	**What The Heart Wants** Collin Raye	
	What The World Needs Now Is Love	
90/79	Ron Shaw	
58/63	Billie Jo Spears	
35/94	**What They're Talkin' About** Rhett Akins	
47/99	**What This Country Needs** Aaron Tippin	

56/90	**(What This World Needs Is) A Few More Rednecks** Charlie Daniels Band	
9/78	**What Time Do You Have To Be Back To Heaven** Razzy Bailey	
16/75	**What Time Of Day** Billy Thunderkloud	
60/85	**What Used To Be Crazy** Bama Band	
74/74	**What Was Your Name Again?** Kenny Vernon	
73/86	**What We Gonna Do** Gus Hardin	
39/90	**What We Really Want** Rosanne Cash	
4/66	**What We're Fighting For** Dave Dudley	
17/93	**What Were You Thinkin'** Little Texas	
58/76	**What Will The New Year Bring?** Donna Fargo	
32/96	**What Will You Do With M-E** Western Flyer	
100/77	**What Would I Do Then?** Carmol Taylor	
	What Would You Do?	
15/61	Jim Reeves	
93/81	John Rex Reeves	
54/86	**What Would You Do** Shelly West	
	What Would You Do? (If Jesus Came To Your House)	
8/56	Porter Wagoner	
15/56	Red Sovine	
10/84	**What Would Your Memories Do** Vern Gosdin	
78/86	**What You Do To Me** New Grass Revival	
8/86	**What You'll Do When I'm Gone** Waylon Jennings	
27/61	**What'd I Say** Jerry Lee Lewis	
37/76	**What'll I Do** La Costa	
19/80	**What'll I Tell Virginia** Johnny Rodriguez	
	What'll You Do About Me?	
76/84	Steve Earle	
74/92	Forester Sisters	
16/95	Doug Supernaw	
79/79	**What're We Doing, Doing This Again** Nick Nixon	
21/77	**What're You Doing Tonight** Janie Fricke	
76/79	**What's A Little Love Between Friends** Billy Burnette	
1/86	**What's A Memory Like You (Doing In A Love Like This)** John Schneider	
87/80	**What's A Nice Girl Like You (Doin' In A Love Like This)** Springer Brothers	
17/67	**What's Come Over My Baby** Dottie West	
68/98	**What's Come Over You** Paul Brandt	
1/82	**What's Forever For** Michael Murphey	
1/89	**What's Going On In Your World** George Strait	
67/82	**What's Good About Goodbye** Cindy Hurt	
77/84	**What's Good For The Goose (Is Good For The Gander)** Dottie West	

5/75 What's Happened To Blue Eyes *Jessi Colter*	47/67 Wheels Fell Off The Wagon Again *Johnny Dollar*	53/98 When I Grow Up *Clint Daniels*
1/65 What's He Doing In My World *Eddy Arnold*	77/84 Wheels In Emotion *Becky Hobbs*	63/78 When I Need You *Lois Johnson*
5/94 What's In It For Me *John Berry*	71/91 Wheels Of Love *Emmylou Harris*	1/99 When I Said I Do *Clint Black* (with Lisa Hartman Black)
20/63 What's In Our Heart *George Jones & Melba Montgomery*	13/58 When *Kalin Twins*	65/97 When I Say Forever *Chris LeDoux*
1/93 What's It To You *Clay Walker*	15/80 When *Slim Whitman*	When I Stop Dreaming
2/68 What's Made Milwaukee Famous (Has Made A Loser Out Of Me) *Jerry Lee Lewis*	11/79 When A Love Ain't Right *Charly McClain*	8/55 *Louvin Brothers*
	When A Man Loves A Woman	88/75 *Debi Hawkins*
40/65 What's Money *George Jones*	72/76 *John Wesley Ryles*	3/78 When I Stop Leaving (I'll Be Gone) *Charley Pride*
11/81 What's New With You *Con Hunley*	18/82 *Jack Grayson & Blackjack*	1/01 When I Think About Angels *Jamie O'Neal*
47/79 What's On Your Mind *John Denver*	60/87 *Narvel Felts*	66/77 When I Touch Her There *Jim Ed Brown*
	3/70 When A Man Loves A Woman (The Way That I Love You) *Billy Walker*	
86/83 What's She Doing To My Mind *Johnny Bailey*		54/68 When I Turn Twenty-One *Buddy Alan*
55/87 What's So Different About You *John Anderson*	32/73 When A Man Loves A Woman (The Way That I Love You) *Tony Booth*	1/83 When I'm Away From You *Bellamy Brothers*
81/81 What's So Good About Goodbye *Terry Aden*	20/87 When A Woman Cries *Janie Frickie*	38/87 When I'm Free Again *Rodney Crowell*
93/89 What's The Matter Baby *Michael Shane*	When A Woman Cries	34/79 When I'm Gone *Dottsy*
41/99 What's The Matter With You Baby *Claudia Church*	31/78 *David Rogers*	75/70 When I'm Not Lookin' *Liz Anderson*
30/78 What's The Name Of That Song? *Glenn Barber*	97/78 *Tommy O'Day*	54/87 When I'm Over You (What You Gonna Do) *Mickey Clark*
	12/96 When A Woman Loves A Man *Lee Roy Parnell*	
45/70 What's The Use *Jack Greene*	24/95 When And Where *Confederate Railroad*	15/01 When It All Goes South *Alabama*
56/67 What's This World A-Comin' To *Slim Whitman*	3/96 When Boy Meets Girl *Terri Clark*	77/82 When It Comes To Love *Thom Bresh & Lane Brody*
1/73 What's Your Mama's Name *Tanya Tucker*	5/78 When Can We Do This Again *T.G. Sheppard*	3/92 When It Comes To You *John Anderson*
72/86 What's Your Name *Almost Brothers*	45/96 When Cowboys Didn't Dance *Lonestar*	60/90 When It Rains It Pours *Merle Haggard*
Whatcha ..also see: What Cha, and What You	93/89 When Daddy Did The Driving *Chris & Lenny*	17/86 When It's Down To Me And You *Charly McClain & Wayne Massey*
75/89 Whatcha Gonna Do About Her *David Slater*	87/89 When Did You Stop *Eddie Preston*	10/90 When It's Gone *Nitty Gritty Dirt Band*
4/54 Whatcha Gonna Do Now *Tommy Collins*	6/93 When Did You Stop Loving Me *George Strait*	When It's Just You And Me
7/92 Whatcha Gonna Do With A Cowboy *Chris LeDoux*	67/77 When Do We Stop Starting Over *Don Gibson*	19/77 *Dottie West*
		31/81 *Kenny Dale*
9/75 Whatcha Gonna Do With A Dog Like That *Susan Raye*	17/85 When Givin' Up Was Easy *Ed Bruce*	26/65 When It's Over *Carl Smith*
	8/01 When God-Fearin' Women Get The Blues *Martina McBride*	39/67 When It's Over *Jeannie Seely*
80/83 Whatcha Got Cookin' In Your Oven Tonight *Thrasher Brothers*		1/59 When It's Springtime In Alaska *Johnny Horton*
	57/89 When He Leaves You *Donna Meade*	49/88 When Karen Comes Around *Mason Dixon*
7/82 Whatever *Statler Brothers*	48/71 When He Touches Me (Nothing Else Matters) *Lois Johnson*	66/76 When Lea Jane Sang *Porter Wagoner*
10/97 Whatever Comes First *Sons Of The Desert*	11/71 When He Walks On You (Like You Have Walked On Me) *Jerry Lee Lewis*	When Love Comes Around The Bend
1/83 Whatever Happened To Old Fashioned Love *B.J. Thomas*		40/89 *Juice Newton*
22/74 Whatever Happened To Randolph Scott *Statler Brothers*	66/95 When He Was My Age *Confederate Railroad*	51/92 *Dan Seals*
	2/90 When I Call Your Name *Vince Gill*	40/90 When Love Comes Callin' *Sawyer Brown*
55/80 Whatever Happened To Those Drinking Songs *Foxfire*	2/97 When I Close My Eyes *Kenny Chesney*	71/94 When Love Comes Callin' *Robin Lee*
38/75 Whatever I Say *Donna Fargo*	66/94 When I Come Back (I Wanna Be My Dog) *Greg Holland*	44/99 When Love Fades *Toby Keith*
45/91 Whatever It Takes *J. P. Pennington*		3/94 When Love Finds You *Vince Gill*
59/94 Whatever It Takes *Kenny Chesney*	5/90 When I Could Come Home To You *Steve Wariner*	44/73 When Love Has Gone Away *Jeannie C. Riley*
19/84 Whatever Turns You On *Keith Stegall*	52/77 When I Die, Just Let Me Go To Texas *Ed Bruce*	74/86 When Love Is Right *Charly McClain & Wayne Massey*
81/82 Whatever Turns You On *Chantilly*	When I Dream	13/97 When Love Starts Talkin' *Wynonna*
72/93 Whatever Way The Wind Blows *Kelly Willis*	F/78 *Jack Clement*	31/99 When Mama Ain't Happy *Tracy Byrd*
2/99 Whatever You Say *Martina McBride*	3/79 *Crystal Gayle*	6/53 When Mexican Joe Met Jole Blon *Hank Snow*
	53/85 When I Get Home *Bobby Bare*	
16/72 Wheel Of Fortune *Susan Raye*	16/74 When I Get My Hands On You *Diana Trask*	93/78 When My Angel Turns Into A Devil *Del Reeves*
37/64 Wheel Song *Gary Buck*	10/62 When I Get Thru With You (You'll Love Me Too) *Patsy Cline*	
1/88 Wheels *Restless Heart*		
	36/78 When I Get You Alone *Mundo Earwood*	

	When My Blue Moon Turns To Gold Again
5/44	Cindy Walker
11/48	Cliffie Stone
F/77	Merle Haggard
84/85	Maines Brothers Band
	When My Conscience Hurts The Most
22/59	Charlie Walker
83/79	Johnny Bush
65/99	When My Dreams Come True
	Rebecca Lynn Howard
2/44	When My Man Comes Home
	Buddy Johnson
1/93	When My Ship Comes In
	Clint Black
2/44	When My Sugar Walks Down The Street Ella Fitzgerald
95/79	When Our Love Began (Cowboys And Indians) George James
9/92	When She Cries Restless Heart
75/80	When She Falls Bobby Hood
54/89	When She Holds Me
	Larry Gatlin/Gatlin Brothers
30/69	When She Touches Me
	Johnny Duncan
60/76	When She's Got Me (Where She Wants Me) David Allan Coe
5/01	When Somebody Loves You
	Alan Jackson
21/90	When Somebody Loves You
	Restless Heart
31/87	When Something Is Good (Why Does It Change)
	Hank Williams, Jr.
	When Something Is Wrong With My Baby
6/76	Sonny James
67/85	Joe Stampley
37/98	When The Bartender Cries
	Michael Peterson
31/78	When The Fire Gets Hot
	Zella Lehr
2/69	When The Grass Grows Over Me
	George Jones
10/74	When The Morning Comes
	Hoyt Axton
87/83	When The Music Stops
	Jerry "Max" Lane
	When The New Wears Off Of Our Love
25/77	Jody Miller
25/83	Whites
32/87	When The Right One Comes Along John Schneider
27/66	When The Ship Hit The Sand
	"Little" Jimmy Dickens
1/72	When The Snow Is On The Roses
	Sonny James
7/94	When The Thought Of You Catches Up With Me David Ball
2/76	When The Tingle Becomes A Chill Loretta Lynn
69/97	When The Walls Come Tumblin' Down Billy Yates
42/84	When The Wild Life Betrays Me
	Jimmy Buffett
37/65	When The Wind Blows In Chicago Roy Clark
30/64	When The World's On Fire
	Tillman Franks Singers

50/98	When The Wrong One Loves You Right Wade Hayes
	When Two Worlds Collide
6/61	Roger Miller
6/69	Jim Reeves
11/80	Jerry Lee Lewis
66/91	When Was The Last Time
	Donna Ulisse
87/89	When We Get Back To The Farm
	Bama Band
49/84	When We Get Back To The Farm
	David Frizzell
1/84	When We Make Love Alabama
24/69	When We Tried Jan Howard
60/88	When We're Together
	Gary Chapman
	When Will I Be Loved
1/75	Linda Ronstadt
75/00	Rebel Hearts
63/89	When Will The Fires End
	Matt Benson
7/51	When You And I Were Young Maggie Blues
	Margaret Whiting & Jimmy Wakely
7/68	When You Are Gone Jim Reeves
12/49	When You Are Lonely Bill Monroe
68/96	When You Are Old
	Gretchen Peters
48/01	When You Come Back Down
	Nickel Creek
21/00	When You Come Back To Me Again Garth Brooks
14/82	When You Fall In Love
	Johnny Lee
14/81	(When You Fall In Love) Everything's A Waltz Ed Bruce
1/52	(When You Feel Like You're In Love) Don't Just Stand There Carl Smith
42/82	When You Find Her, Keep Her
	Wright Brothers
55/87	When You Gave Your Love To Me Ray Price
46/85	When You Get A Little Lonely
	Nicolette Larson
57/74	When You Get Back From Nashville Susan Raye
64/98	When You Got To Be You
	Lisa Brokop
20/86	When You Get To The Heart
	Barbara Mandrell/Oak Ridge Boys
62/85	When You Held Me In Your Arms
	Rex Allen, Jr.
37/86	When You Hurt, I Hurt
	Ronnie McDowell
3/46	When You Leave Don't Slam The Door Tex Ritter
	When You Leave That Way, You Can Never Go Back
77/83	Sam Neely
75/85	Bill Anderson
14/93	Confederate Railroad
10/02	When You Lie Next To Me
	Kellie Coffey
60/00	When You Love Me Tim Rushlow
37/99	When You Love Someone
	Sammy Kershaw
47/64	When You Need A Laugh
	Patsy Cline
15/00	When You Need My Love
	Darryl Worley

26/88	When You Put Your Heart In It
	Kenny Rogers
6/72	When You Say Love Bob Luman
	When You Say Nothing At All
1/88	Keith Whitley
3/95	Alison Krauss & Union Station
	When You Walk In The Room
29/81	Stephanie Winslow
2/94	Pam Tillis
	When You Were Blue And I Was Green
21/82	Kin Vassy
72/86	Joe Stampley
38/91	When You Were Mine
	Shenandoah
1/71	When You're Hot, You're Hot
	Jerry Reed
21/69	When You're Hot You're Hot
	Porter Wagoner
	When You're In Love ..see: (That's What You Do)
68/79	When You're In Love With A Beautiful Woman Dr. Hook
16/83	When You're Not A Lady
	Jim Glaser
55/69	When You're Seventeen
	Jimmy Dickens
54/71	When You're Twenty-One
	Claude King
31/80	When You're Ugly Like Us
	George Jones & Johnny Paycheck
	When Your Good Love Was Mine
14/74	Narvel Felts
92/77	Marie Owens
48/87	When Your Yellow Brick Road Turns Blue John Anderson
2/94	Whenever You Come Around
	Vince Gill
23/92	Wher'm I Gonna Live?
	Billy Ray Cyrus
89/80	Where Are We Going From Here
	Cooter Daniel
26/00	Where Are You Christmas?
	Faith Hill
18/77	Where Are You Going, Billy Boy
	Bill Anderson & Mary Lou Turner
1/91	Where Are You Now Clint Black
45/00	Where Are You Now
	Trisha Yearwood
10/83	Where Are You Spending Your Nights These Days
	David Frizzell
48/00	Where Can I Surrender
	Randy Travis
92/81	Where Cheaters Go Ben Marney
	Where Corn Don't Grow
67/90	Waylon Jennings
6/97	Travis Tritt
14/67	Where Could I Go? (But To Her)
	David Houston
58/80	Where Could You Take Me
	Sheila Andrews
79/83	Where Did He Go Right
	Roy Head
1/89	Where Did I Go Wrong
	Steve Wariner
80/80	Where Did The Money Go
	Hoyt Axton
53/89	Where Did The Moon Go Wrong
	Daniele Alexander
55/71	Where Did They Go, Lord
	Elvis Presley

74/84	Where Did We Go Right *Russell Smith*	15/62	Where The Old Red River Flows *Jimmie Davis*		While The Feeling's Good
74/71	(Where Do I Begin) Love Story *Roy Clark*	72/88	Where The Rocky Mountains Touch The Morning Sun *Randy Vanwarmer*	56/75	Mike Lunsford
11/94	Where Do I Fit In The Picture *Clay Walker*			46/76	Kenny Rogers
87/87	Where Do I Go From Here *Al Garrison*	2/02	Where The Stars And Stripes And The Eagle Fly *Aaron Tippin*	26/81	Rex Allen, Jr. & Margo Smith
42/96	Where Do I Go To Start All Over *Wade Hayes*	63/82	Where The Sun Don't Shine *Ray Stevens*	63/89	Wayne Newton & Tammy Wynette
1/79	Where Do I Put Her Memory *Charley Pride*		Where There's Smoke	47/86	While The Moon's In Town *Shoppe*
1/88	Where Do The Nights Go *Ronnie Milsap*	71/89	Jason D. Williams	7/01	While You Loved Me *Rascal Flatts*
78/83	Where Do You Go *Streetfeet*	29/94	Archer/Park	46/98	While You Sleep *Tracy Lawrence*
69/69	Where Do You Go (When You Don't Go With Me) *Ernie Ashworth*	35/82	Where There's Smoke There's Fire *Louise Mandrell & R.C. Bannon*	21/66	While You're Dancing *Marty Robbins*
		20/94	Where Was I *Ricky Van Shelton*	25/69	While Your Lover Sleeps *Leon Ashley*
10/64	Where Does A Little Tear Come From *George Jones*	49/88	Where Was I *Charley Pride*	69/78	Whine, Whistle, Whine *John Anderson*
43/84	Where Does An Angel Go When She Cries *Osmond Brothers*	91/89	Where Was I *Ray Pack*	47/65	Whirlpool (Of Your Love) *Claude King*
33/01	Where Does It Hurt *Warren Brothers*	70/88	Where Were You When I Was Blue *Razorback*	2/92	Whiskey Ain't Workin' *Travis Tritt & Marty Stuart*
77/89	Where Does Love Go (When It Dies) *Jack Quist*	1/01	Where Were You (When The World Stopped Turning) *Alan Jackson*	2/79	Whiskey Bent And Hell Bound *Hank Williams, Jr.*
54/88	Where Does Love Go (When It's Gone) *Janie Frickie*	F/82	Where Would I Be *Mel Tillis & Nancy Sinatra*	18/81	Whiskey Chasin' *Joe Stampley*
1/67	Where Does The Good Times Go *Buck Owens*	95/89	Where You Gonna Hang Your Hat *Sylvie & Her Silver Dollar Band*	51/81	Whiskey Heaven *Fats Domino*
40/92	Where Forever Begins *Neal McCoy*	18/98	Where Your Road Leads *Trisha Yearwood With Garth Brooks*	2/87	Whiskey, If You Were A Woman *Highway 101*
28/70	Where Grass Won't Grow *George Jones*	41/74	Where'd I Come From *Bobby Bare*	76/82	Whiskey Made Me Stumble (The Devil Made Me Fall) *Bill Anderson*
6/70	Where Have All Our Heroes Gone *Bill Anderson*	49/84	Where'd That Woman Go *Mel McDaniel*		Whiskey River
14/69	Where Have All The Average People Gone *Roger Miller*		Where'd Ya Stay Last Night	14/72	Johnny Bush
	(Where Have All The Good Times Gone) ..see: Hey Daisy	14/66	Webb Pierce	12/79	Willie Nelson
		78/83	Tommy St. John	92/81	Johnny Bush
65/78	Where Have You Been All Of My Life *Roy Clark*	8/84	Where's The Dress *Moe Bandy & Joe Stampley*	84/89	Whiskey River You Win *Pat Minter*
57/68	Where He Stops Nobody Knows *June Stearns*	67/87	Where's The Fire *Susie Allanson*	48/70	Whiskey-Six Years Old *Norma Jean*
26/75	Where He's Going, I've Already Been *Hank Williams, Jr.*	28/69	Where's The Playground Susie *Glen Campbell*	18/76	Whiskey Talkin' *Joe Stampley*
	Where I Come From	10/90	Where've You Been *Kathy Mattea*	16/78	Whiskey Trip *Gary Stewart*
74/00	Alan Jackson	20/73	Wherefore And Why *Glen Campbell*	5/95	Whiskey Under The Bridge *Brooks & Dunn*
1/01	Alan Jackson	49/94	Wherever She Is *Ricky Van Shelton*		Whiskey Was A River ..see: (I Remember When I Thought)
9/62	Where I Ought To Be *Skeeter Davis*	31/69	Wherever You Are *Johnny Paycheck*	31/70	Whiskey, Whiskey *Nat Stuckey*
49/95	Where I Used To Have A Heart *Martina McBride*	45/98	Wherever You Are *Mark Chesnutt*	10/81	Whisper *Lacy J. Dalton*
11/71	Where Is My Castle *Connie Smith*	55/99	Wherever You Are *Mary Chapin Carpenter*	57/78	Whisper It To Me *Bobby G. Rice*
15/66	Where Is The Circus *Hank Thompson*	81/83	Wherever You Are *Thrasher Brothers*	1/94	Whisper My Name *Randy Travis*
83/77	Where Lonely People Go *Eddy Arnold*	75/95	Wherever You Are Tonight *Keith Whitley*	84/78	Whispering *Maury Finney*
5/75	Where Love Begins *Gene Watson*	3/95	Wherever You Go *Clint Black*	15/58	Whispering Rain *Hank Snow*
2/68	Where Love Used To Live *David Houston*	4/95	Which Bridge To Cross (Which Bridge To Burn) *Vince Gill*	12/77	Whispers *Bobby Borchers*
3/01	Where The Blacktop Ends *Keith Urban*	4/59	Which One Is To Blame *Wilburn Brothers*	66/76	Whispers And Grins *David Rogers*
10/69	Where The Blue And Lonely Go *Roy Drusky*	19/69	Which One Will It Be *Bobby Bare*	86/74	Whistle Stop *Roger Miller*
34/69	Where The Blue Of The Night Meets The Gold Of The Day *Hank Locklin*	28/89	Which Way Do I Go (Now That I'm Gone) *Waylon Jennings*	28/65	Whistle Walkin' *Ned Miller*
		31/80	While I Was Makin' Love To You *Susie Allanson*		White Christmas
1/98	Where The Green Grass Grows *Tim McGraw*	43/69	While I'm Thinkin' About It *Billy Mize*	7/49	Ernest Tubb
88/73	Where The Lilacs Grow *Slim Whitman*	57/80	While The Choir Sang The Hymn (I Thought Of Her) *Johnny Russell*	70/94	Garth Brooks
				65/99	Garth Brooks
				75/99	Martina McBride
				69/00	Martina McBride
				1/46	White Cross On Okinawa *Bob Wills*
				25/68	White Fences And Evergreen Trees *Ferlin Husky*
				72/88	White Freight Liner Blues *Jimmie Dale Gilmore*
				49/89	White Houses *Charley Pride*
				1/76	White Knight *Cledus Maggard*
				21/65	White Lightnin' Express *Roy Drusky*
				1/59	White Lightning *George Jones*

Why Can't We All Just Get Along — Hank Williams, Jr.

29/90	**White Limozeen** Dolly Parton	
14/85	**White Line** Emmylou Harris	
	White Line Fever	
68/72	Buddy Alan	
95/80	Flying Burrito Brothers	
67/94	**White Palace** Clay Walker	
5/72	**White Silver Sands** Sonny James	
1/57	**White Sport Coat (And A Pink Carnation)** Marty Robbins	
62/69	**Who Am I** Red Sovine	
3/78	**Who Am I To Say** Statler Brothers	
55/89	**Who But You** Anne Murray	
3/59	**Who Cares** Don Gibson	
60/84	**Who Dat** David Frizzell	
56/92	**Who Did They Think He Was** Conway Twitty	
64/69	**Who Do I Know In Dallas** Kenny Price	
13/65	**Who Do I Think I Am** Webb Pierce	
11/82	**Who Do You Know In California** Eddy Raven	
67/91	**Who Got Our Love** John Anderson	
96/89	**Who Have You Got To Lose** Ernie Welch	
1/01	**Who I Am** Jessica Andrews	
56/01	**Who I Am To You** Coley McCabe	
10/74	**Who Left The Door To Heaven Open** Hank Thompson	
41/66	**Who Licked The Red Off Your Candy** "Little" Jimmy Dickens	
64/69	**Who Loves You** Hardens	
6/48	**Who? Me?** Tex Williams	
29/92	**Who Needs It** Clinton Gregory	
12/99	**Who Needs Pictures** Brad Paisley	
60/95	**Who Needs You** Lisa Brokop	
73/89	**Who Needs You** Sanders	
2/95	**Who Needs You Baby** Clay Walker	
68/83	**Who Said Love Was Fair** Billy Parker	
4/94	**(Who Says) You Can't Have It All** Alan Jackson	
91/80	**Who Shot J.R.?** Gary Burbank	
50/70	**Who Shot John** Wanda Jackson	
7/59	**Who Shot Sam** George Jones	
53/76	**Who Wants A Slightly Used Woman** Connie Cato	
57/88	**Who Was That Stranger** Loretta Lynn	
40/79	**(Who Was The Man Who Put) The Line In Gasoline** Jerry Reed	
54/80	**Who Were You Thinkin' Of** Doolittle Band	
51/92	**Who, What, Where, When, Why, How** Martin Delray	
69/68	**Who Will Answer? (Aleluya No. 1)** Hank Snow	
11/60	**Who Will Buy The Wine** Charlie Walker	
91/75	**Who Will I Be Loving Now** Carmol Taylor	
	Who Will The Next Fool Be	
67/70	Charlie Rich	
20/79	Jerry Lee Lewis	
2/89	**Who You Gonna Blame It On This Time** Vern Gosdin	
	Who'll Turn Out The Lights	
57/71	Wayne Kemp	
36/80	Mel Street	
69/89	Ronnie McDowell	
27/63	**Who's Been Cheatin' Who** Johnny & Jonie Mosby	
87/76	**Who's Been Here Since I've Been Gone** Hank Snow	
43/66	**Who's Been Mowing The Lawn (While I Was Gone)** Ray Pennington	
88/82	**Who's Been Sleeping In My Bed** Diana	
	Who's Cheatin' Who	
1/81	Charly McClain	
2/97	Alan Jackson	
58/95	**Who's Counting** Wesley Dennis	
82/84	**Who's Counting** Marie Osmond	
3/85	**Who's Gonna Fill Their Shoes** George Jones	
37/83	**Who's Gonna Keep Me Warm** Phil Everly	
51/90	**Who's Gonna Know** Conway Twitty	
1/69	**Who's Gonna Mow Your Grass** Buck Owens	
14/72	**Who's Gonna Play This Old Piano** Jerry Lee Lewis	
75/76	**Who's Gonna Run The Truck Stop In Tuba City When I'm Gone?** Leroy Van Dyke	
41/82	**(Who's Gonna Sing) The Last Country Song** Billy Parker	
18/69	**Who's Gonna Take The Garbage Out** Ernest Tubb & Loretta Lynn	
61/90	**Who's Gonna Tell Her Goodbye** Earl Thomas Conley	
97/78	**Who's Gonna Tie My Shoes** Ray Pillow	
65/67	**Who's Gonna Walk The Dog (And Put Out The Cat)** Ray Pennington	
10/69	**Who's Julie** Mel Tillis	
62/86	**Who's Leaving Who** Anne Murray	
1/90	**Who's Lonely Now** Highway 101	
66/89	**Who's Lovin' My Baby** John Anderson	
64/95	**Who's She To You** Amie Comeaux	
29/75	**Who's Sorry Now** Marie Osmond	
32/96	**Who's That Girl** Stephanie Bentley	
1/94	**Who's That Man** Toby Keith	
37/85	**Who's The Blonde Stranger?** Jimmy Buffett	
6/49	**Whoa Sailor** Hank Thompson	
43/70	**Whoever Finds This, I Love You** Mac Davis	
14/75	**Whoever Turned You On, Forgot To Turn You Off** Little David Wilkins	
1/86	**Whoever's In New England** Reba McEntire	
63/81	**Whole Lot Of Cheatin' Goin' On** Jimmi Cannon	
1/57	**Whole Lot Of Shakin' Going On** Jerry Lee Lewis	
18/72	**Whole Lot Of Somethin'** Tony Booth	
65/75	**Whole Lotta Difference In Love** George Kent	
23/96	**Whole Lotta Gone** Joe Diffie	
18/91	**Whole Lotta Holes** Kathy Mattea	
66/98	**Whole Lotta Hurt** Brady Seals	
30/94	**Whole Lotta Love On The Line** Aaron Tippin	
61/71	**Whole Lotta Lovin'** Anita Carter	
22/73	**Whole Lotta Loving** Hank Williams, Jr. & Lois Johnson	
2/76	**Whole Lotta Things To Sing About** Charley Pride	
15/58	**Whole Lotta Woman** Marvin Rainwater	
80/87	**Whole Month Of Sundays** Jenny Yates	
14/70	**Whole World Comes To Me** Jack Greene	
27/70	**Whole World Holding Hands** Freddie Hart	
10/84	**Whole World's In Love When You're Lonely** B.J. Thomas	
13/73	**Whole World's Making Love Again Tonight** Bobby G. Rice	
59/88	**Whose Baby Are You** Ric Steel	
11/95	**Whose Bed Have Your Boots Been Under?** Shania Twain	
7/55	**Whose Shoulder Will You Cry On** Kitty Wells	
75/81	**Why Am I Doing Without** Wayne Kemp	
	Why Baby Why	
4/55	George Jones	
1/56	Red Sovine & Webb Pierce	
9/56	Hank Locklin	
23/61	Warren Smith & Shirley Collie	
95/78	Jerry Inman	
1/83	Charley Pride	
46/93	Palomino Road	
64/73	**Why, Because I Love You** Buddy Alan	
7/77	**Why Can't He Be You** Loretta Lynn	
46/96	**Why Can't You** Larry Stewart	
49/66	**Why Can't You Feel Sorry For Me** Carl Smith	
F/79	**Why Did You Have To Be So Good** Dave & Sugar	
1/93	**Why Didn't I Think Of That** Doug Stone	
	Why Didn't I Think Of That	
F/82	Dave Rowland	
67/85	Malchak & Rucker	
88/77	**Why Didn't I Think Of That** Gene Simmons	
3/83	**Why Do I Have To Choose** Willie Nelson	
45/66	**Why Do I Keep Doing This To Us** Carl Smith	
F/70	**Why Do I Love You (Melody of Love)** Jim Reeves	
7/83	**Why Do We Want (What We Know We Can't Have)** Reba McEntire	
97/78	**Why Do You Come Around** Lyndel East	
53/68	**Why Do You Do Me Like You Do** Sammi Smith	
1/87	**Why Does It Have To Be (Wrong Or Right)** Restless Heart	
25/63	**Why Don't Daddy Live Here Anymore** Bonnie Owens	
39/93	**Why Don't That Telephone Ring** Tracy Byrd	
51/72	**Why Don't We Go Somewhere And Love** Sandy Posey	
85/81	**Why Don't We Just Sleep On It Tonight** Glen Campbell & Tanya Tucker	

531

94/79	Why Don't We Lie Down And Talk It Over *Jerry Inman*	45/64	**Wife, Th'** *John D. Loudermilk*	19/81	**Willie Jones** *Bobby Bare*	
92/80	Why Don't You Believe Me *Donna Stark*	22/67	**Wife Of The Party** *Liz Anderson*	72/00	**Willie Nelson For President** *Peter Dawson Band*	
93/80	Why Don't You Go To Dallas *Peggy Sue*	16/77	**Wiggle Wiggle** *Ronnie Sessions*	5/62	**Willie The Weeper** *Billy Walker*	
	Why Don't You Haul Off And Love Me	1/82	**Wild And Blue** *John Anderson*	25/76	**Willie, Waylon And Me** *David Allan Coe*	
		1/96	**Wild Angels** *Martina McBride*			
1/49	*Wayne Raney*	8/65	**Wild As A Wildcat** *Charlie Walker*	66/81	**Willie, Won't You Sing A Song With Me** *George Burns*	
5/49	*Mervin Shiner*	65/98	**Wild As The Wind** *Garth Brooks* (With Trisha Yearwood)	72/83	**Willie, Write Me A Song** *Ray Price*	
9/49	*Bob Atcher*	52/96	**Wild At Heart** *Lari White*			
99/78	Why Don't You Leave Me Alone *Joey Davis*	18/68	**Wild Blood** *Del Reeves*	54/95	**Willin' To Walk** *Radney Foster*	
	Why Don't You Love Me	21/80	**Wild Bull Rider** *Hoyt Axton*	10/62	**Willingly** *Willie Nelson & Shirley Collie*	
1/50	*Hank Williams*	24/87	**Wild-Eyed Dream** *Ricky Van Shelton*	46/80	**Willow Run** *Randy Barlow*	
15/75	*Connie Smith*	99/78	**Wild Honey** *Bellamy Brothers*	23/61	**Willow Tree** *Ferlin Husky*	
61/76	*Hank Williams*	7/01	**Wild Horses** *Garth Brooks*	10/71	**Willy Jones** *Susan Raye*	
1/80	Why Don't You Spend The Night *Ronnie Milsap*	73/94	**Wild Love** *Joy Lynn White*	4/83	**Wind Beneath My Wings** *Gary Morris*	
12/84	Why Goodbye *Steve Wariner*	5/93	**Wild Man** *Ricky Van Shelton*	60/67	**Wind Changes** *Johnny Cash*	
1/79	Why Have You Left The One You Left Me For *Crystal Gayle*	14/83	**Wild Montana Skies** *John Denver & Emmylou Harris*	65/94	**Wind In The Wire** *Randy Travis*	
5/94	Why Haven't I Heard From You *Reba McEntire*	1/94	**Wild One** *Faith Hill*	20/81	**Wind Is Bound To Change** *Larry Gatlin/Gatlin Brothers*	
15/87	Why I Don't Know *Lyle Lovett*		**Wild River** ..see: **Ballad Of**	54/83	**Windin' Down** *Lacy J. Dalton*	
	Why I'm Walkin'		**Wild Side Of Life**	65/70	**Window Number Five** *Johnny Duncan*	
6/60	*Stonewall Jackson*	1/52	*Hank Thompson*		**Window Up Above**	
33/88	*Ricky Skaggs*	6/52	*Burl Ives & Grady Martin*	2/61	*George Jones*	
1/80	Why Lady Why *Alabama*	13/76	*Freddy Fender*	1/75	*Mickey Gilley*	
4/84	Why Lady Why *Gary Morris*	78/76	*Maury Finney*	14/65	**Wine** *Mel Tillis*	
8/77	Why Lovers Turn To Strangers *Freddie Hart*	60/79	*Rayburn Anthony with Kitty Wells*	10/86	**Wine Colored Roses** *George Jones*	
1/73	Why Me *Kris Kristofferson*	10/81	*Waylon Jennings & Jessi Colter (medley)*	44/99	**Wine Into Water** *T. Graham Brown*	
1/84	Why Not Me *Judds*		**Wild Side Of Me** ..see: **(You Bring Out)**		**Wine Me Up**	
30/80	Why Not Me *Fred Knoblock*	79/88	**Wild Texas Rose** *Billy Walker*	2/69	*Faron Young*	
58/85	Why Not Tonight *Atlanta*	F/82	**Wild Turkey** *Lacy J. Dalton*	19/89	*Larry Boone*	
69/77	Why Not Tonight *Jacky Ward*	2/68	**Wild Week-End** *Bill Anderson*	1/46	**Wine, Women And Song** *Al Dexter*	
3/50	Why Should I Cry? *Eddy Arnold*	15/63	**Wild Wild Wind** *Stonewall Jackson*	3/64	**Wine Women And Song** *Loretta Lynn*	
45/66	Why Should I Cry Over You *Freddie Hart*	77/76	**Wild World** *Mike Wells*	70/94	**Wing And A Prayer** *Marc Beeson*	
9/50	Why Should We Try Anymore *Hank Williams*	9/88	**Wilder Days** *Baillie And The Boys*	1/60	**Wings Of A Dove** *Ferlin Husky*	
13/01	Why They Call It Falling *Lee Ann Womack*	6/88	**Wildflowers** *Dolly Parton/ Linda Ronstadt/Emmylou Harris*	11/70	**Wings Upon Your Horns** *Loretta Lynn*	
45/95	Why Walk When You Can Fly *Mary Chapin Carpenter*		**Wildwood Flower**	1/94	**Wink** *Neal McCoy*	
2/57	Why, Why *Carl Smith*	5/55	*Hank Thompson with Merle Travis* (INST.)	13/76	**Winner, The** *Bobby Bare*	
8/97	Why Would I Say Goodbye *Brooks & Dunn*	100/79	*Tommy Wills*	26/79	**Winners And Losers** *R.C. Bannon*	
77/85	Why Would I Want To Forget *Joe Sun*	55/83	*Roy Clark* (INST.)	58/85	**Wino The Clown** *Bill Anderson*	
	Why You Been Gone So Long	57/74	**Wildwood Weed** *Jim Stafford*		**Winter Wonderland**	
17/69	*Johnny Darrell*	7/84	**Will It Be Love By Morning** *Michael Murphey*	70/98	*Dolly Parton (medley)*	
69/83	*Jerry Lee Lewis*	5/49	**Will Santy Come To Shanty Town** *Eddy Arnold*	72/00	*Lonestar*	
50/86	*Brenda Lee*	5/86	**Will The Wolf Survive** *Waylon Jennings*	87/78	**Wipe You From My Eyes (Gettin' Over You)** *King Edward IV & The Knights*	
95/79	Why'd The Last Time Have To Be The Best *Ronnie Robbins*	37/91	**Will This Be The Day** *Desert Rose Band*	8/79	**Wisdom Of A Fool** *Jacky Ward*	
1/89	Why'd You Come In Here Lookin' Like That *Dolly Parton*	69/98	**Will You Be Here** *Anita Cochran*	62/98	**Wish, The** *Blake & Brian*	
43/98	Why'd You Start Lookin' So Good *Monty Holmes*	97/85	**Will You Love Me In The Morning** *Clifton Jansky*	2/70	**Wish I Didn't Have To Miss You** *Jack Greene & Jeannie Seely*	
22/76	Wichita Jail *Charlie Daniels Band*		**Will You Love Me Tomorrow**	2/94	**Wish I Didn't Know Now** *Toby Keith*	
	Wichita Lineman	74/71	*Lynda K. Lance*	60/72	**Wish I Was A Little Boy Again** *LaWanda Lindsey*	
1/68	*Glen Campbell*	69/75	*Jody Miller*	54/71	**Wish I Was Home Instead** *Van Trevor*	
55/97	*Wade Hayes*	56/87	*Cheryl Handy*	61/66	**Wish Me A Rainbow** *Hugh X. Lewis*	
24/69	Wicked California *Tompall/Glaser Brothers*	41/01	**Will You Marry Me** *Alabama*	1/99	**Wish You Were Here** *Mark Wills*	
9/56	Wicked Lies *Carl Smith*	67/78	**Will You Remember Mine** *Willie Nelson*	2/81	**Wish You Were Here** *Barbara Mandrell*	
13/48	Wicked Path Of Sin *Bill Monroe*	20/68	**Will You Visit Me On Sundays?** *Charlie Louvin*	83/86	**Wishful Dreamin'** *Michael Shamblin*	
49/87	Wicked Ways *Patty Loveless*	8/62	**Will Your Lawyer Talk To God** *Kitty Wells*			
1/98	Wide Open Spaces *Dixie Chicks*	64/94	**William And Mary** *Davis Daniel*			
19/64	Widow Maker *Jimmy Martin*	91/78	**Willie** *Hank Cochran*			
		43/70	**Willie And The Hand Jive** *Johnny Carver*			

I'm Gonna Write A Song — Tommy Cash

22/84 Wishful Drinkin' Atlanta	4/75 Woman In The Back Of My Mind Mel Tillis	39/75 Wonder When My Baby's Comin' Home Barbara Mandrell
83/80 Wishful Drinkin' Diane Pfeifer	48/69 Woman In Your Life Wilma Burgess	51/68 Wonderful Day Ray Pillow
5/60 Wishful Thinking Wynn Stewart		Wonderful Tonight
32/79 Wishing I Had Listened To Your Song Bobby Borchers	Woman Left Lonely	66/89 Butch Baker
	72/71 Charlie Rich	29/98 David Kersh
F/80 Wishing Well Tammy Jo	F/71 Patti Page	14/68 Wonderful World Of Women Faron Young
7/65 Wishing Well (Down In The Well) Hank Snow	54/97 Woman Like You Matt King	1/52 Wondering Webb Pierce
56/91 With Body And Soul Kentucky Headhunters	17/70 Woman Lives For Love Wanda Jackson	6/70 Wonders Of The Wine David Houston
24/71 With His Hand In Mine Jean Shepard	9/92 Woman Loves Steve Wariner	5/71 Wonders You Perform Tammy Wynette
68/77 With His Pants In His Hand Jerry Reed	64/67 Woman Needs Love Marion Worth	41/64 Wooden Soldier Hank Locklin
	52/66 Woman Never Forgets Kitty Wells	10/75 Word Games Billy Walker
5/85 With Just One Look In Your Eyes Charly McClain with Wayne Massey	58/86 Woman Of The 80's Donna Fargo	8/79 Words Susie Allanson
	1/69 Woman Of The World (Leave My World Alone) Loretta Lynn	12/94 Words By Heart Billy Ray Cyrus
10/78 With Love Rex Allen, Jr.	35/75 Woman On My Mind David Houston	63/73 Words Don't Come Easy David Frizzell
10/01 With Me Lonestar	Woman (Sensuous Woman)	73/72 Words Don't Fit The Picture Willie Nelson
1/67 With One Exception David Houston	1/72 Don Gibson	
3/68 With Pen In Hand Johnny Darrell	21/94 Mark Chesnutt	10/67 Words I'm Gonna Have To Eat Bill Phillips
1/45 With Tears In My Eyes Wesley Tuttle	54/76 Woman Stealer Bobby G. Rice	55/90 Work Song Corbin/Hanner
	Woman To Woman	Workin' At The Car Wash Blues
32/82 With Their Kind Of Money And Our Kind Of Love Billy Swan	4/74 Tammy Wynette	27/74 Tony Booth
	62/98 Wynonna	F/80 Jerry Reed
31/91 With This Ring T. Graham Brown	4/78 Woman To Woman Barbara Mandrell	40/95 Workin' For The Weekend Ken Mellons
7/83 With You Charly McClain	43/98 Woman To Woman Lynns	86/83 Workin' In A Coalmine Bob Jenkins
9/99 With You Lila McCann	29/73 Woman Without A Home Statler Brothers	21/64 Workin' It Out Flatt & Scruggs
33/86 With You Vince Gill	20/69 Woman Without Love Johnny Darrell	50/96 Workin' It Out Daryle Singletary
74/72 Within My Loving Arms Kenni Huskey	43/75 Woman, Woman Jim Glaser	Workin' Man Blues
11/84 Without A Song Willie Nelson	12/84 Woman Your Love Moe Bandy	1/69 Merle Haggard
50/88 Without A Trace Marie Osmond	Woman's Hand	48/95 Jed Zeppelin
78/81 Without Love Johnny Cash	66/69 Barbara Fairchild	4/88 Workin' Man (Nowhere To Go) Nitty Gritty Dirt Band
1/01 Without You Dixie Chicks	23/70 Jean Shepard	69/92 Workin' Man's Dollar Chris LeDoux
Without You	9/59 Woman's Intuition Wilburn Brothers	
79/79 Susie Allanson		30/80 Workin' My Way To Your Heart Dickey Lee
12/83 T.G. Sheppard	72/90 Woman's Intuition Michelle Wright	37/73 Workin' On A Feelin' Tommy Cash
50/76 Without You Jessi Colter	59/69 Woman's Side Of Love Lynda K. Lance	73/73 Working Class Hero Tommy Roe
92/81 Without You Buck Owens		
2/92 (Without You) What Do I Do With Me Tanya Tucker	46/98 Woman's Tears Matt King	16/86 Working Class Man Lacy J. Dalton
	6/96 Woman's Touch Toby Keith	75/94 Working Elf Blues Daron Norwood
10/56 Without Your Love Bobby Lord	16/82 Woman's Touch Tom Jones	
22/96 Without Your Love Aaron Tippin	70/79 Woman's Touch Glenn Barber	62/91 Working For The Japanese Ray Stevens
13/76 Without Your Love (Mr. Jordan) Charlie Ross	80/89 Woman's Way Mundo Earwood	F/81 Working Girl Dolly Parton
	3/78 Womanhood Tammy Wynette	33/71 Working Like The Devil (For The Lord) Del Reeves
1/84 Woke Up In Love Exile	57/91 Women Bandit Brothers	
12/75 Wolf Creek Pass C.W. McCall	74/81 Women Wyvon Alexander	7/85 Working Man John Conlee
1/62 Wolverton Mountain Claude King	9/66 Women Do Funny Things To Me Del Reeves	16/77 Working Man Can't Get Nowhere Today Merle Haggard
55/76 Woman David Wills	4/82 Women Do Know How To Carry On Waylon Jennings	
2/71 Woman Always Knows David Houston		7/93 Working Man's Ph.D. Aaron Tippin
4/92 Woman Before Me Trisha Yearwood	18/80 Women Get Lonely Charly McClain	59/67 Working Man's Prayer Tex Ritter
92/77 Woman Behind The Man Behind The Wheel Red Sovine	5/80 Women I've Never Had Hank Williams, Jr.	7/86 Working Without A Net Waylon Jennings
	Women In Love	28/92 Working Woman Rob Crosby
16/58 Woman Captured Me Hank Snow	59/82 Kin Vassy	23/70 World Called You David Rogers
38/76 Woman Don't Try To Sing My Song Cal Smith	55/85 Bill Medley	90/77 World Famous Holiday Inn Buck Owens
	65/81 Won't You Be My Baby Keith Stegall	
58/73 Woman Ease My Mind Claude Gray	Won't You Come Home (And Talk To A Stranger)	10/66 World Is Round Roy Drusky
62/00 Woman Gets Lonely Lisa Angelle		29/64 World Lost A Man David Price
15/66 Woman Half My Age Kitty Wells	61/69 Wayne Kemp	World Needs A Melody
24/68 Woman Hungry Porter Wagoner	70/97 George Strait	32/71 Red Lane
9/57 Woman I Need Johnny Horton	1/70 Wonder Could I Live There Anymore Charley Pride	35/72 Carter Family with Johnny Cash
1/89 Woman In Love Ronnie Milsap		
4/67 Woman In Love Bonnie Guitar	37/70 Wonder Of You Elvis Presley	
3/81 Woman In Me Crystal Gayle		
14/95 Woman In Me (Needs The Man In You) Shania Twain		
74/81 Woman In My Heart Bobby Hood		

Handwritten notes at top: "See side notes on p. 509" / "Yankee Go Home — See Wynn Stewart" / "10-CD Kit"

1/74	**World Of Make Believe** Bill Anderson	8/61	**Wreck On The Highway** Wilma Lee & Stoney Cooper	10/57	**Yearning** George Jones & Jeanette Hicks	
1/68	**World Of Our Own** Sonny James	62/00	**Wreckin' Crew** Trini Triggs	22/61	**Yeas** Benny Barnes	
	World So Full Of Love	61/99	**Write It In Stone** Keith Harling	1/80	**Years** Barbara Mandrell	
18/60	Ray Sanders	9/75	**Write Me A Letter** Bobby G. Rice	2/85	**Years After You** John Conlee	
28/61	Faron Young	16/66	**Write Me A Picture** George Hamilton IV	12/82	**Years Ago** Statler Brothers	
66/68	**World The Way I Want It** Tom T. Hall	6/44	**Write Me Sweetheart** Roy Acuff	48/96	**Years From Here** Baker & Myers	
19/69	**World-Wide Travelin' Man** Wynn Stewart	1/99	**Write This Down** George Strait	4/63	**Yellow Bandana** Faron Young	
			Writing On The Wall	59/67	**Yellow Haired Woman** Claude King	
10/85	**World Without Love** Eddie Rabbitt	96/88	Kenny Carr	30/81	**Yellow Pages** Roger Bowling	
14/72	**World Without Music** Porter Wagoner	31/89	George Jones	5/73	**Yellow Ribbon** Johnny Carver	
52/67	**World's Biggest Whopper** Junior Samples	15/72	**Writing's On The Wall** Jim Reeves	49/72	**Yellow River** Compton Brothers	
		35/82	**Written Down In My Heart** Ray Stevens	1/84	**Yellow Rose** Johnny Lee with Lane Brody	
6/84	**World's Greatest Lover** Bellamy Brothers	5/90	**Wrong** Waylon Jennings	7/55	**Yellow Rose Of Texas** Ernest Tubb	
18/79	**World's Most Perfect Woman** Ronnie McDowell	1/99	**Wrong Again** Martina McBride	1/89	**Yellow Roses** Dolly Parton	
46/66	**World's Worse Loser** George Jones	26/60	**Wrong Company** Wynn Stewart & Jan Howard	3/55	**Yellow Roses** Hank Snow	
5/96	**Worlds Apart** Vince Gill	32/01	**Wrong Five O' Clock** Eric Heatherly	1/00	**Yes!** Chad Brock	
47/64	**Worst Of Luck** Bobby Barnett	6/74	**Wrong Ideas** Brenda Lee	67/83	**Yes** Billy Swan	
30/76	**(Worst You Ever Gave Me Was) The Best I Ever Had** Faron Young	20/74	**Wrong In Loving You** Faron Young	83/75	**Yes** Connie Cato	
				75/71	**Yes, Dear, There Is A Virginia** Glenn Barber	
30/93	**Worth Every Mile** Travis Tritt	6/99	**Wrong Night** Reba McEntire	2/56	**Yes I Know Why** Webb Pierce	
73/96	**Worth The Fall** Brett James	14/65	**Wrong Number** George Jones	6/66	**(Yes) I'm Hurting** Don Gibson	
25/96	**Would I** Randy Travis	37/96	**Wrong Place, Wrong Time** Mark Chesnutt	12/78	**Yes Ma'am** Tommy Overstreet	
41/87	**Would Jesus Wear A Rolex** Ray Stevens		**Wrong Road Again**		**Yes Ma'm (I [He] Found Her [Me] In A Honky Tonk)**	
36/87	**Would These Arms Be In Your Way** Keith Whitley	6/75	Crystal Gayle	67/73	Glenn Barber	
		95/78	Allen Reynolds	98/82	Dixie Harrison	
91/75	**Would You Be My Lady** David Allan Coe	5/92	**Wrong Side Of Memphis** Trisha Yearwood	1/65	**Yes, Mr. Peters** Roy Drusky & Priscilla Mitchell	
13/58	**Would You Care** Browns	76/78	**Wrong Side Of The Rainbow** Jim Chesnut	83/77	**Yes She Do, No She Don't** Alvin Crow	
6/82	**Would You Catch A Falling Star** John Anderson	49/68	**Wrong Side Of The World** Hugh X. Lewis	60/79	**Yesterday** Billie Jo Spears	
86/87	**Would You Catch Me Baby (If I Fall For You)** Gail Veach		**Wrong Train**	86/89	**Yesterday Is Too Far Away** Birch Denney	
		82/86	Beth Williams	50/76	**Yesterday Just Passed My Way Again** Don Everly	
5/66	**Would You Hold It Against Me** Dottie West	83/89	Judy Lindsey	10/80	**Yesterday Once More** Moe Bandy	
95/80	**Would You Know Love** Marlow Tackett	65/93	**Wrong's What I Do Best** George Jones	9/69	**Yesterday, When I Was Young** Roy Clark	
1/74	**Would You Lay With Me (In A Field of Stone)** Tanya Tucker	1/77	**Wurlitzer Prize (I Don't Want To Get Over You)** Waylon Jennings	8/53	**Yesterday's Girl** Hank Thompson	
		79/87	**Wyatt Liquor** Wyatt Brothers	9/77	**Yesterday's Gone** Vern Gosdin	
3/55	**Would You Mind?** Hank Snow		**Wyoming ..see: (Oh Why, Oh Why, Did I Ever Leave)**	40/69	**Yesterday's Letters** Bobby Lord	
92/73	**Would You Still Love Me** Ben Peters			12/48	**Yesterday's Mail** Hank Thompson	
				11/63	**Yesterday's Memories** Eddy Arnold	
1/72	**Would You Take Another Chance On Me** Jerry Lee Lewis			57/81	**Yesterday's News (Just Hit Home Today)** Johnny Paycheck	
21/73	**Would You Walk With Me Jimmy** Arlene Harden		**X**	99/88	**Yesterday's Rain** Joy Ford	
12/72	**Would You Want The World To End** Mel Tillis	1/94	**XXX's And OOO's (An American Girl)** Trisha Yearwood	4/44	**Yesterday's Tears** Ernest Tubb	
72/85	**Wouldn't It Be Great** Loretta Lynn				**Yesterday's Wine**	
3/62	**Wound Time Can't Erase** Stonewall Jackson			62/71	Willie Nelson	
				1/82	Merle Haggard/George Jones	
18/84	**Wounded Hearts** Mark Gray			7/90	**Yet** Exile	
77/86	**Wrap Me Up In Your Love** J.D. Martin		**Y**	25/80	**Yippy Cry Yi** Rex Allen, Jr.	
12/77	**Wrap Your Love All Around Your Man** Lynn Anderson	3/77	**Y'All Come Back Saloon** Oak Ridge Boys	63/98	**Yippy Ky Yay** Lila McCann	
					YoYo Man ..see: (I'm A)	
38/73	**Wrap Your Love Around Me** Melba Montgomery	4/65	**Yakety Axe** Chet Atkins	93/85	**Yo Yo (The Right String, But The Wrong Yo Yo)** Danny Shirley & "Piano Red"	
2/02	**Wrapped Around** Brad Paisley	91/75	**Yakety Yak** Eric Weissberg & Deliverance	44/65	**Yodel, Sweet Molly** Ira Louvin	
46/72	**Wrapped Around Her Finger** George Jones	17/59	**Yankee, Go Home** Goldie Hill	45/99	**Yodelin' Blues** Wilkinsons	
5/02	**Wrapped Up In You** Garth Brooks	17/92	**Yard Sale** Sammy Kershaw	56/68	**Yonder Comes A Freight Train** Jim & Jesse	
50/76	**Wreck Of The Edmund Fitzgerald** Gordon Lightfoot	69/95	**Yeah Buddy** Jeff Carson	77/88	Reno Brothers	
		1/71	**Year That Clayton Delaney Died** Tom T. Hall	4/55	**Yonder Comes A Sucker** Jim Reeves	
				47/01	**You** Marshall Dyllon	
				1/87	**You Again** Forester Sisters	

Handwritten annotations on page:
- "p. 48 (1:29)" next to Wreck On The Highway
- "Yankee Go Home" / "Wynn Stewart" annotations
- "Yakety Yak – Coasters (Top Pop)"
- "Loud Mouth – Smokey Wood (LP)"
- "Talking – Ray Stevens p. 45"
- "Jaw-Jaw-Jaw-Yap-Yap-Yap" / "Dick United" notes
- "See 'Stand Up, Sit Down, Shut Your Mouth' — by Simon Crum / Ferlin Husky"
- "Wanda Jackson CD 1:10"

Honey, Do This ⟶   // *Yankee Dime – Jack Ford*   *4-CD Set: Louisiana Hayride (4:15)*

19/89	**You Ain't Down Home** Jann Browne	
6/89	**You Ain't Going Nowhere** Chris Hillman & Roger McGuinn	
13/72	**You Ain't Gonna Have Ol' Buck To Kick Around No More** Buck Owens	
56/00	**You Ain't Hurt Nothin' Yet** John Anderson	
5/79	**You Ain't Just Whistlin' Dixie** Bellamy Brothers	
57/97	**You Ain't Lonely Yet** Big House	
✱2/95	**You Ain't Much Fun** Toby Keith ✱	
46/66	**You Ain't No Better Than Me** Webb Pierce	
2/66	**You Ain't Woman Enough** Loretta Lynn	
	You All ..also see: Y'All	
7/54	**You All Come** Arlie Duff	
	You Almost Slipped My Mind	
44/72	Kenny Price	
4/80	Charley Pride	
1/73	**You Always Come Back (To Hurting Me)** Johnny Rodriguez	
37/76	**You Always Look Your Best (Here In My Arms)** George Jones	
5/92	**You And Forever And Me** Little Texas	
1/82	**You And I** Eddie Rabbitt with Crystal Gayle	
	You And Me	
1/76	Tammy Wynette	
92/77	Lloyd Green	
3/56	**You And Me** Red Foley & Kitty Wells	
15/70	**You And Me Against The World** Bobby Lord	
24/78	**You And Me Alone** David Rogers	
94/81	**You And Me And Tennessee** Roger Ivie And Silvercreek	
92/79	**You And Me And The Green Grass** Pal Rakes	
99/75	**You And Me, Me And You** Sharon Vaughn	
4/95	**You And Only You** John Berry	
91/89	**You And The Horse (That You Rode In On)** Patsy Cole	
8/97	**You And You Alone** Vince Gill	
6/69	**You And Your Sweet Love** Connie Smith	
48/00	**You Are** John Michael Montgomery	
48/81	**You Are A Liar** Whitey Shafer	
85/84	**You Are A Miracle** Maines Brothers Band	
87/83	**You Are Love** Bobby Vinton	
72/88	**You Are My Angel** Billy Parker	
12/64	**You Are My Flower** Flatt & Scruggs	
10/86	**You Are My Music, You Are My Song** Charly McClain with Wayne Massey	
36/79	**You Are My Rainbow** David Rogers	
	You Are My Special Angel ..see: My Special Angel	
69/77	**You Are My Sunshine** ✱ Duane Eddy	
1/68	**You Are My Treasure** Jack Greene	

	You Are So Beautiful	
16/76	Ray Stevens	
40/77	Tanya Tucker	
93/78	**You Are Still The One** Linda Hargrove	
97/83	**You Are The Music In Time With My Heart** Joy Ford	
4/56	**You Are The One** Carl Smith	
14/75	**You Are The One** Mel Tillis & Sherry Bryce	
85/86	**You Are The Rock (And I'm A Rolling Stone)** Carl Jackson	
11/76	**You Are The Song (Inside Of Me)** Freddie Hart	
34/78	**You Are The Sunshine Of My Life** Marty Mitchell	
86/84	**You Are What Love Means To Me** Craig Bickhardt	
	You Ask Me To	
8/73	Waylon Jennings	
80/78	Billy Joe Shaver	
F/81	Elvis Presley	
	You, Babe	
59/72	Lefty Frizzell	
23/89	Merle Haggard	
67/93	**You Baby You** Highway 101	
20/67	**You Beat All I Ever Saw** Johnny Cash	
	You Belong To Me	
54/75	Jim Reeves	
93/89	T.C. Brandon	
58/74	**You Bet Your Sweet, Sweet Love** Kenny O'Dell	
52/67	**You Better Be Better To Me** Carl Smith	
79/77	**(You Better Be) One Hell Of A Woman** Glenn Barber	
49/80	**You Better Hurry Home (Somethin's Burnin')** Connie Cato	
	You Better Move On	
10/71	Billy "Crash" Craddock	
70/79	Tommy Roe	
18/81	George Jones & Johnny Paycheck	
2/54	**You Better Not Do That** Tommy Collins ✱	
28/68	**You Better Sit Down Kids** Roy Drusky	
2/95	**You Better Think Twice** Vince Gill	
49/66	**You Better Watch Your Friends** Jim Nesbitt	
72/88	**You Blossom Me** Bertie Higgins	
97/75	**You Bring Out The Best In Me** Brenda Pepper	
66/85	**You Bring Out The Lover In Me** Zella Lehr	
9/84	**(You Bring Out) The Wild Side Of Me** Dan Seals	
63/84	**You Bring The Heartache (I'll Bring The Wine)** Gary Wolf	
15/49	**You Broke My Heart (In Little Bitty Pieces)** Hank Thompson	
95/79	**You Broke My Heart So Gently (It Almost Didn't Break)** Sandra Kaye	
	You Call Everybody Darling	
71/73	Lamar Morris	
69/91	K.T. Oslin	
	You Call That A Mountain	
63/97	Jeff Wood	
66/00	B.J. Thomas	

78/85	**You Can Always Say Good-Bye In The Morning** Jim Collins	
91/79	**You Can Be Replaced** Leon Rausch	
85/78	**You Can Count On Me** David Allan Coe	
3/92	**You Can Depend On Me** Restless Heart	
1/86	**You Can Dream Of Me** Steve Wariner	
1/96	**You Can Feel Bad** Patty Loveless	
53/91	**You Can Go Home** Desert Rose Band	
	You Can Have Her	
18/67	Jim Edward Brown	
7/73	Waylon Jennings	
49/74	Sam Neely	
14/79	George Jones & Johnny Paycheck	
48/85	**You Can Lead A Heart To Love (But You Can't Make It Fall)** Tammy Wynette	
72/00	**You Can Leave Your Hat On** Ty Herndon	
23/95	**You Can Sleep While I Drive** Trisha Yearwood	
33/67	**You Can Steal Me** Bonnie Guitar	
49/74	**You Can Sure See It From Here** Susan Raye	
1/74	**You Can't Be A Beacon (If Your Light Don't Shine)** Donna Fargo	
49/87	**You Can't Blame The Train** Don McLean	
3/46	**You Can't Break My Heart** Spade Cooley	
20/88	**You Can't Fall In Love When You're Cryin'** Lee Greenwood	
66/90	**You Can't Fly Like An Eagle** Johnny Lee	
98/75	**You Can't Follow Where He's Been** Debra Barber	
39/97	**You Can't Get There From Here** Lee Roy Parnell	
23/72	**You Can't Go Home** Statler Brothers	
	You Can't Have It All ..see: (Who Says)	
8/54	**You Can't Have My Love** Wanda Jackson & Billy Gray	
10/67	**You Can't Have Your Kate And Edith, Too** Statler Brothers	
55/69	**You Can't Housebreak A Tomcat** Cal Smith	
60/99	**You Can't Hurry Love** Dixie Chicks	
15/57	**You Can't Hurt Me Anymore** Carl Smith	
96/74	**You Can't Judge A Book By The Cover** Troy Seals	
31/86	**You Can't Keep A Good Memory Down** John Anderson	
6/96	**You Can't Lose Me** Faith Hill	
42/83	**You Can't Lose What You Never Had** Lynn Anderson	
1/95	**You Can't Make A Heart Love Somebody** George Strait	
100/79	**You Can't Make Love To A Memory** Iris Larratt	
52/85	**You Can't Measure My Love** Carlette	

535

8/60	You Can't Pick A Rose In December *Ernest Ashworth*		You Don't Know Me	44/97	You Just Get One *Jeff Wood*
80/89	You Can't Play The Blues (In An Air-Conditioned Room) *Mel McDaniel*	10/56	*Eddy Arnold*	76/85	You Just Hurt My Last Feeling *Sammi Smith*
		61/70	*Ray Pennington*		You Just Watch Me
		1/81	*Mickey Gilley*	43/88	*Libby Hurley*
F/79	You Can't Remember And I Can't Forget *Mary Lou Turner*	1/78	You Don't Love Me Anymore *Eddie Rabbitt*	20/94	*Tanya Tucker*
		66/72	You Don't Mess Around With Jim *Bobby Bond*		(You Know I Love You) ..see: Don't Be Stupid
35/66	You Can't Roller Skate In A Buffalo Herd *Roger Miller*	36/79	You Don't Miss A Thing *Sylvia*		You Know Just What I'd Do
20/85	You Can't Run Away From Your Heart *Lacy J. Dalton*	29/99	You Don't Need Me Now *Clint Black*	48/75	*Lois Johnson*
				9/80	*Conway Twitty & Loretta Lynn*
1/83	You Can't Run From Love *Eddie Rabbitt*	15/74	You Don't Need To Move A Mountain *Jeanne Pruett*	1/91	You Know Me Better Than That *George Strait*
9/86	You Can't Stop Love *Schuyler, Knobloch & Overstreet*	14/97	You Don't Seem To Miss Me *Patty Loveless & George Jones*	20/78	You Know What *Jerry Reed & Seidina*
26/97	You Can't Stop Love *Marty Stuart*	71/71	You Don't Understand Him Like I Do *Jeannie Seely*	30/73	You Know Who *Bobby Bare*
57/66	You Can't Stop Me *Billy Mize*			48/87	You Lay A Lotta Love On Me *Wrays*
72/86	You Can't Take It With You *William Lee Golden*	14/61	You Don't Want My Love *Roger Miller*	19/80	You Lay A Whole Lot Of Love On Me *Con Hunley*
67/91	You Can't Take It With You When You Go *Gene Watson*		You Done Me Wrong		You Lay So Easy On My Mind
		7/56	*Ray Price*	3/73	*Bobby G. Rice*
35/68	You Changed Everything About Me But My Name *Norma Jean*	37/85	*Mel Tillis*	70/84	*Narvel Felts*
		13/59	You Dreamer You *Johnny Cash*	79/87	*Bobby G. Rice*
	You Comb Her Hair	4/79	You Feel Good All Over *T.G. Sheppard*	63/87	You Left Her Lovin' You *Ride The River*
5/63	*George Jones*				
92/75	*Del Reeves*	41/80	You Fill My Life *Juice Newton*	86/87	You Left My Heart For Broke *Ernie Rowell*
45/85	You Could Be The One Woman *Chance*	15/66	You Finally Said Something Good (When You Said Goodbye) *Charlie Louvin*	1/90	You Lie *Reba McEntire*
10/76	You Could Know As Much About A Stranger *Gene Watson*			8/80	(You Lift Me) Up To Heaven *Reba McEntire*
		76/88	You Fit Right Into My Heart *Sanders*		You Light Up My Life
72/94	You Could Steal Me *Bobbie Cryner*	69/69	You Fool *Eddy Arnold*	4/77	*Debby Boone*
71/00	You Could've Had Me *Lace*	7/69	You Gave Me A Mountain *Johnny Bush*	48/97	*LeAnn Rimes*
	You Could've Heard A Heart Break			94/79	You Lit The Fire, Now Fan The Flame *Penny Hamilton*
		34/74	You Get To Me *Eddie Rabbitt*		
53/83	*Rodney Lay*	8/73	You Give Me You *Bobby G. Rice*		You Look Like The One I Love
1/84	*Johnny Lee*	25/99	You Go First (Do You Wanna Kiss) *Jessica Andrews*	33/82	*Deborah Allen*
32/91	You Couldn't Get The Picture *George Jones*			69/86	*Osmond Bros.*
		55/88	You Go, You're Gone *David Ball*	1/84	You Look So Good In Love *George Strait*
1/79	You Decorated My Life *Kenny Rogers*	60/75	You Got A Lock On Me *Jerry Reed*	63/67	You Love Me Too Little *Lorene Mann*
55/67	You Deserve Each Other *Robert Mitchum*	77/74	You Got Everything That You Want *Pat Roberts*	76/78	You Love The Thunder *Hank Williams, Jr.*
73/88	You Didn't Have To Jump The Fence *Lisa Childress*	7/89	You Got It *Roy Orbison*		
		28/83	You Got Me Running *Jim Glaser*	24/86	You Made A Rock Of A Rolling Stone *Oak Ridge Boys*
68/95	You Didn't Miss A Thing *Clinton Gregory*	65/89	You Got The Job *Charly McClain*		
		7/56	You Gotta Be My Baby *George Jones*	3/84	You Made A Wanted Man Of Me *Ronnie McDowell*
47/92	You Do My Heart Good *Cleve Francis*	49/67	You Gotta Be Puttin' Me On *Lefty Frizzell*	47/81	You Made It Beautiful *Charlie Rich*
	You Don't Bring Me Flowers				
70/78	*Barbra Streisand & Neil Diamond*	72/91	You Gotta Get Serious *J.P. Pennington*	89/89	You Made It Easy *Sammy Sadler*
10/79	*Jim Ed Brown/Helen Cornelius*	65/83	You Gotta Get To My Heart (Before You Lay A Hand On Me) *Paulette Carlson*	84/76	You Made It Right *Ozark Mountain Daredevils*
	You Don't Care What Happens To Me			60/90	You Made Life Good Again *Nitty Gritty Dirt Band*
5/45	*Bob Wills*				
55/70	*Wynn Stewart*	41/70	You Got-ta Have A License *Porter Wagoner*	19/01	You Made Me That Way *Andy Griggs*
4/91	You Don't Count The Cost *Billy Dean*	3/96	You Gotta Love That *Neal McCoy*	48/98	You Make It Seem So Easy *Kinleys*
5/95	You Don't Even Know Who I Am *Patty Loveless*	1/99	You Had Me From Hello *Kenny Chesney*	67/79	You Make It So Easy *Bobby G. Rice*
	You Don't Have To Be A Baby To Cry	4/95	You Have The Right To Remain Silent *Perfect Stranger*	61/76	You Make Life Easy *Joe Stampley*
10/50	*Ernest Tubb*	11/87	You Haven't Heard The Last Of Me *Moe Bandy*	7/85	You Make Me Feel Like A Man *Ricky Skaggs*
63/77	*Ann J. Morton*				
36/75	You Don't Have To Go Home *Nat Stuckey*	59/99	You Haven't Left Me Yet *George Strait*	34/71	You Make Me Feel Like A Man *Warner Mack*
56/70	You Don't Have To Say You Love Me *Elvis Presley*	39/89	You Just Can't Lose 'Em All *Shooters*	15/74	You Make Me Feel More Like A Man *Mel Street*
4/65	You Don't Hear *Kitty Wells*	54/77	You Just Don't Know *Mary K. Miller*	29/61	You Make Me Live Again *Carl Smith*
4/83	You Don't Know Love *Janie Fricke*	60/90	You Just Get Better All The Time *James House*		

Handwritten at top: The Perfect Country Song | You'll Always Be My "Baby" – Shelton?

4/75	**(You Make Me Want To Be) A Mother** Tammy Wynette	
1/85	**You Make Me Want To Make You Mine** Juice Newton	
85/82	**You Make Me Want To Sing** Joe Sun	
20/81	**You (Make Me Wonder Why)** Deborah Allen	
69/68	**You May Be Too Much For Memphis, Baby** Leroy Van Dyke	
9/81	**You May See Me Walkin'** Ricky Skaggs	
	You Mean The World To Me	
1/67	David Houston	
72/78	Howdy Glenn	
44/88	**You Might Want To Use Me Again** Johnny Rodriguez	
	You Move Me	
67/97	Garth Brooks	
3/98	Garth Brooks	
45/86	**You Must Be Lookin' For Me** Billy Swan	
26/89	**You Must Not Be Drinking Enough** Earl Thomas Conley	
15/48	**You Nearly Lose Your Mind** Ernest Tubb	
4/78	**You Needed Me** Anne Murray	
6/77	**(You Never Can Tell) C'est La Vie** Emmylou Harris	
	You Never Even Called Me By My Name	
8/75	David Allan Coe	
60/94	Doug Supernaw	
5/82	**You Never Gave Up On Me** Crystal Gayle	
1/77	**You Never Miss A Real Good Thing (Till He Says Goodbye)** Crystal Gayle	
31/74	**You Never Say You Love Me Anymore** Nat Stuckey	
65/74	**You Only Live Once (In Awhile)** Glenn Barber	
92/89	**You Only Love Me When I'm Leavin'** Ellen Lee Miller	
7/46	**You Only Want Me When You're Lonely** Gene Autry	
	You Ought To Hear Me Cry	
69/67	Johnny Bush	
43/68	Carl Smith	
16/77	Willie Nelson	
100/76	**You Oughta Be Against The Law** Rex Kramer	
90/77	**You Oughta Hear The Song** Ruth Buzzi	
15/55	**You Oughta See Pickles Now** Tommy Collins	
12/79	**You Pick Me Up (And Put Me Down)** Dottie West	
58/89	**You Plant Your Fields** New Grass Revival	
14/67	**You Pushed Me Too Far** Ferlin Husky	
10/83	**You Put The Beat In My Heart** Eddie Rabbitt	
10/82	**You Put The Blue In Me** Whites	
F/77	**You Put The Bounce Back Into My Step** Ray Griff	
59/89	**You Put The Soul In The Song** Waylon Jennings	
62/78	**You Read Between The Lines** Billy Parker	
37/84	**You Really Go For The Heart** Dan Seals	
1/90	**You Really Had Me Going** Holly Dunn	
6/73	**You Really Haven't Changed** Johnny Carver	
	You Really Know How To Break A Heart	
93/84	Jimmy Mac	
73/88	Rhonda Manning	
16/75	**You Ring My Bell** Ray Griff	
4/76	**You Rubbed It In All Wrong** Billy "Crash" Craddock	
43/87	**You Saved Me** Patty Loveless	
12/93	**You Say You Will** Trisha Yearwood	
3/86	**You Should Have Been Gone By Now** Eddy Raven	
56/78	**You Should Win An Oscar Every Night** Chuck Pollard	
1/01	**You Shouldn't Kiss Me Like This** Toby Keith	
11/79	**You Show Me Your Heart (And I'll Show You Mine)** Tom T. Hall	
70/78	**You Snap Your Fingers (And I'm Back In Your Hands)** David Wills	
14/89	**You Still Do** T.G. Sheppard	
16/82	**You Still Get To Me In My Dreams** Tammy Wynette	
62/89	**You Still Got A Way With My Heart** Mickey Gilley	
53/96	**You Still Got Me** Doug Supernaw	
82/90	**You Still Love Me In My Dreams** Tim Mensy	
1/87	**You Still Move Me** Dan Seals	
36/99	**You Still Shake Me** Deana Carter	
47/01	**You Still Take Me There** Collin Raye	
89/89	**You Sure Got This Ol' Redneck Feelin' Blue** Joe Stampley	
35/82	**(You Sure Know Your Way) Around My Heart** Louise Mandrell	
1/83	**You Take Me For Granted** Merle Haggard	
15/62	**You Take The Future (And I'll Take The Past)** Hank Snow	
76/87	**You Take The Leavin' Out Of Me** Mickey Clark	
18/59	**You Take The Table And I'll Take The Chairs** Bob Gallion	
65/82	**You To Come Home To** Dean Dillon	
18/73	**You Took All The Ramblin' Out Of Me** Jerry Reed	
	You Took Her [Him] Off My Hands (Now Please Take Her [Him] Off My Mind)	
11/63	Ray Price	
33/64	Marion Worth	
33/64	**You Took My Happy Away** Willie Nelson	
37/69	**You Touched My Heart** David Rogers	
75/98	**You Turn Me On** Tim McGraw	
17/82	**You Turn Me On I'm A Radio** Gail Davies	
3/85	**You Turn Me On (Like A Radio)** Ed Bruce	
48/80	**You Turn My Love Light On** Billy Walker	
1/45	**You Two Timed Me One Time Too Often** Tex Ritter
12/98	**You Walked In** Lonestar
6/70	**You Wanna Give Me A Lift** Loretta Lynn
70/00	**You Wanna What?** Alecia Elliott
20/84	**You Were A Good Friend** Kenny Rogers
	You Were A Lady ..see: (Jeannie Marie)
1/73	**You Were Always There** Donna Fargo
1/99	**You Were Mine** Dixie Chicks
51/71	**You Were On My Mind** Bobby Penn
38/81	**You Were There** Freddie Hart
28/79	**You Were Worth Waiting For** Don King
6/94	**You Will** Patty Loveless
1/46	**You Will Have To Pay** Tex Ritter
	You Win Again
10/52	Hank Williams
4/58	Jerry Lee Lewis
1/80	Charley Pride
75/80	Jeris Ross
16/91	**You Win Again** Mary-Chapin Carpenter
1/96	**You Win My Love** Shania Twain
61/00	**You With Me** Anita Cochran
93/89	**You Won The Battle** Eddie Rivers
17/00	**You Won't Be Lonely Now** Billy Ray Cyrus
2/99	**You Won't Ever Be Lonely** Andy Griggs
8/70	**You Wouldn't Know Love** Ray Price
66/66	**You Wouldn't Put The Shuck On Me** Geezinslaw Brothers
43/94	**You Wouldn't Say That To A Stranger** Suzy Bogguss
77/73	**You, You, You** Lynda K. Lance
77/83	**You'd Better Believe It** Rod Rishard
5/80	**You'd Make An Angel Wanna Cheat** Kendalls
	You'd Think He'd Know Me Better
56/96	Bobbie Cryner
66/98	Lorrie Morgan
5/00	**You'll Always Be Loved By Me** Brooks & Dunn
64/67	**You'll Always Have My Love** Wanda Jackson
	You'll Be Back (Every Night In My Dreams)
24/78	Johnny Russell
3/82	Statler Brothers
92/89	**You'll Be The First To Know** Lee J. Stevens
10/58	**You'll Come Back** Webb Pierce
31/88	**You'll Come Back (You Always Do)** Mel Tillis
10/64	**You'll Drive Me Back (Into Her Arms Again)** Faron Young
1/76	**You'll Lose A Good Thing** Freddy Fender
55/68	**You'll Never Be Lonely Again** Leon Ashley & Margie Singleton
10/89	**You'll Never Be Sorry** Bellamy Brothers

537

97/85	You'll Never Find A Good Man (Playing In A Country Band) *Audie Henry*	
19/98	You'll Never Know *Mindy McCready*	
	You'll Never Know	
71/75	*Jim Reeves*	
77/85	*Lew DeWitt*	
26/86	You'll Never Know How Much I Needed You Today *Conway Twitty*	
78/77	You'll Never Leave Me Completely *Johnny Bush*	
73/82	You'll Never Walk Alone *Elvis Presley*	
54/73	You're A Believer *Stoney Edwards*	
92/86	You're A Better Man Than I *Perry LaPointe*	
71/78	You're A Dancer *Eddy Raven*	
18/83	You're A Hard Dog (To Keep Under The Porch) *Gail Davies*	
96/86	You're A Heartache To Follow *Ken Fowler*	
84/83	You're A Keep Me Wondering Kind Of Woman *Steve Mantelli*	
	You're A Part Of Me	
99/78	*Gene Cotton with Kim Carnes*	
20/79	*Charly McClain*	
85/83	*Danny White & Linda Nail*	
	You're A Pretty Lady, Lady	
93/79	*Wichita Linemen*	
93/80	*Ray Sanders*	
82/78	You're A Violin That Never Has Been Played *Billy Walker*	
	You're All The Woman I'll Ever Need	
78/78	*Lee Dresser*	
76/79	*Dusty James*	
39/80	You're Amazing *David Rogers*	
2/99	You're Beginning To Get To Me *Clay Walker*	
5/45	You're Breaking My Heart *Ted Daffan*	
59/72	You're Burnin' My House Down *Warner Mack*	
73/66	You're Cheatin' On Me Again *Hal Dickinson*	
31/81	You're Crazy Man *Freddie Hart*	
41/66	You're Driving Me Out Of My Mind *Norma Jean*	
1/98	You're Easy On The Eyes *Terri Clark*	
49/68	You're Easy To Love *Arlene Harden*	
47/85	You're Every Step I Take *Johnny Paycheck*	
32/72	You're Everything *Tommy Cash*	
10/63	You're For Me *Buck Owens*	
	You're Free To Go	
6/56	*Carl Smith*	
9/77	*Sonny James*	
2/44	You're From Texas *Bob Wills*	
1/84	You're Gettin' To Me Again *Jim Glaser*	
26/59	You're Going Back To Your Old Ways Again *Hank Thompson*	
10/85	You're Going Out Of My Mind *T.G. Sheppard*	
4/98	You're Gone *Diamond Rio*	
4/49	You're Gonna Change (Or I'm Gonna Leave) *Hank Williams*	
29/74	You're Gonna Hurt Me (One More Time) *Patti Page*	
34/83	You're Gonna Lose Her Like That *Moe Bandy*	
44/78	You're Gonna Love Love *Ava Barber*	
	(You're Gonna Love Me Tonight) ..see: I Can Tell By The Way You Dance	
	You're Gonna Love Yourself In The Morning	
77/73	*Wayne Carson*	
35/75	*Roy Clark*	
22/80	*Charlie Rich*	
43/83	*Willie Nelson & Brenda Lee*	
89/79	You're Gonna Make A Cheater Out Of Me *Bill Phillips*	
45/89	You're Gonna Make Her Mine *Lionel Cartwright*	
93/77	You're Gonna Make Love To Me *Lynn Niles*	
97/79	You're Gonna Miss Me *June Neyman*	
1/95	You're Gonna Miss Me When I'm Gone *Brooks & Dunn*	
33/85	You're Gonna Miss Me When I'm Gone *Judy Rodman*	
39/70	You're Gonna Need A Man *Johnny Duncan*	
1/83	You're Gonna Ruin My Bad Reputation *Ronnie McDowell*	
62/87	You're Here To Remember (I'm Here To Forget) *Merrill And Jessica*	
61/87	You're In Love Alone *Jeff Stevens & The Bullets*	
27/80	You're In Love With The Wrong Man *Mundo Earwood*	
92/74	You're Just Gettin' Better *Jack Scott*	
38/71	You're Just More A Woman *Bob Yarbrough*	
5/71	You're Lookin' At Country *Loretta Lynn*	
62/67	You're Lookin' For A Plaything *Jamey Ryan*	
37/99	You're Lucky I Love You *Susan Ashton*	
7/59	You're Makin' A Fool Out Of Me *Jimmy Newman*	
59/86	You're Mine *Orleans*	
70/81	You're More To Me (Than He's Ever Been) *Peggy Forman*	
1/75	You're My Best Friend *Don Williams*	
5/82	You're My Bestest Friend *Mac Davis*	
7/81	You're My Favorite Star *Bellamy Brothers*	
2/87	You're My First Lady *T.G. Sheppard*	
1/79	You're My Jamaica *Charley Pride*	
14/79	You're My Kind Of Woman *Jacky Ward*	
1/71	You're My Man *Lynn Anderson*	
68/75	You're My Rainy Day Woman *Eddy Raven*	
26/72	You're My Shoulder To Lean On *Lana Rae*	
31/91	(You're My) Soul And Inspiration *Oak Ridge Boys*	
36/74	You're My Wife, She's My Woman *Charlie Louvin*	
3/87	You're Never Too Old For Young Love *Eddy Raven*	
60/86	You're Nobody Till Somebody Loves You *Ray Price*	
60/76	You're Not Charlie Brown (And I'm Not Raggedy Ann) *Donna Fargo*	
26/82	You're Not Easy To Forget *Dottie West*	
70/89	You're Not Even Crying *Marcy Bros.*	
74/78	You're Not Free And I'm Not Easy *Arleen Harden*	
16/74	You're Not Getting Older (You're Getting Better) *Freddy Weller*	
7/96	You're Not In Kansas Anymore *Jo Dee Messina*	
21/83	You're Not Leavin' Here Tonight *Ed Bruce*	
4/54	You're Not Mine Anymore *Webb Pierce*	
3/47	You're Not My Darlin' Anymore *Gene Autry*	
13/56	You're Not Play Love *Wilburn Brothers*	
15/75	You're Not The Woman You Use To Be *Gary Stewart*	
60/80	You're Only Lonely *J.D. Souther*	
2/83	You're Out Doing What I'm Here Doing Without *Gene Watson*	
67/67	You're Puttin' Me On *Nat Stuckey*	
7/56	You're Running Wild *Louvin Brothers*	
38/67	You're So Cold (I'm Turning Blue) *Hugh X. Lewis*	
75/77	You're So Good For Me (And That's Bad) *Bobby Wayne Loftis*	
1/82	You're So Good When You're Bad *Charley Pride*	
4/86	You're Something Special To Me *George Strait*	
39/99	You're Still Beautiful To Me *Bryan White*	
3/56	You're Still Mine *Faron Young*	
1/86	You're Still New To Me *Marie Osmond With Paul Davis*	
	You're Still On My Mind	
28/62	*George Jones*	
84/79	*Joe Douglas*	
1/98	You're Still The One *Shania Twain*	
14/81	You're The Best *Kieran Kane*	
1/82	You're The Best Break This Old Heart Ever Had *Ed Bruce*	
87/84	You're The Best I Never Had *Larry Jenkins*	
1/73	You're The Best Thing That Ever Happened To Me *Ray Price*	
1/83	You're The First Time I've Thought About Leaving *Reba McEntire*	
57/77	You're The Hangnail In My Life *Hoyt Axton*	
1/86	You're The Last Thing I Needed Tonight *John Schneider*	
5/58	You're The Nearest Thing To Heaven *Johnny Cash*	
	You're The One	
95/75	*Jerry Inman*	
2/78	*Oak Ridge Boys*	

5/91 You're The One *Dwight Yoakam*	10/85 You've Got Something On Your Mind *Mickey Gilley*	67/81 Your Daddy Don't Live In Heaven (He's In Houston) *Michael Ballew*
75/76 You're The One *Billy Swan*	85/79 (You've Got That) Fire Goin' Again *Jimmy Tucker*	4/00 Your Everything *Keith Urban*
91/79 You're The One Who Rewrote My Life Story *Don Schlitz*	77/87 You've Got That Leaving Look In Your Eye *Marcia Lynn*	76/84 Your Eyes *Bill Anderson*
93/81 You're The Only Dancer *Pam Hobbs*	60/83 You've Got That Touch *Lloyd David Foster*	91/85 Your Eyes *Simon & Verity*
You're The Only Good Thing (That's Happened To Me)	89/81 You've Got The Devil In Your Eyes *Ann J. Morton*	17/67 Your Forevers (Don't Last Very Long) *Jean Shepard*
4/60 *George Morgan*	1/87 "You've Got" The Touch *Alabama*	F/55 Your Good For Nothing Heart *Webb Pierce*
29/78 *Jim Reeves*	30/80 You've Got Those Eyes *Eddy Raven*	Your Good Girl's Gonna Go Bad
1/79 You're The Only One *Dolly Parton*	40/77 You've Got To Mend This Heartache *Ruby Falls*	3/67 *Tammy Wynette*
77/84 You're The Only Star (In My Blue Heaven) *Mike Campbell*	(You've Got To) Move Two Mountains	13/81 *Billie Jo Spears*
1/65 You're The Only World I Know *Sonny James*	56/71 *Dave Peel*	65/67 Your Hands *Johnny Dollar*
38/79 You're The Part Of Me *Jim Ed Brown*	99/76 *Jimmy Russell*	5/64 Your Heart Turned Left (And I Was On The Right) *George Jones*
64/80 You're The Perfect Reason *David Houston*	6/91 You've Got To Stand For Something *Aaron Tippin*	1/84 Your Heart's Not In It *Janie Fricke*
5/87 You're The Power *Kathy Mattea*	79/76 You've Got To Stop Hurting Me Darling *Don Gibson*	22/70 Your Husband, My Wife *Bobby Bare & Skeeter Davis*
You're The Reason	2/98 You've Got To Talk To Me *Lee Ann Womack*	56/71 Your Kind Of Lovin' *June Stearns*
4/61 *Bobby Edwards*	27/70 You've Got Your Troubles (I've Got Mine) *Jack Blanchard & Misty Morgan*	7/79 Your Kisses Will *Crystal Gayle*
14/61 *Hank Locklin*	12/72 You've Gotta Cry Girl *Dave Dudley*	Your Lily White Hands
16/61 *Joe South*	76/78 You've Just Found Yourself A New Woman *Jenny Robbins*	21/68 *Johnny Carver*
48/68 *Johnny Tillotson*	2/68 You've Just Stepped In (From Stepping Out On Me) *Loretta Lynn*	49/68 *Ray Griff*
90/81 *John Rex Reeves*	You've Lost That Lovin' Feelin'	12/87 Your Love *Tammy Wynette*
82/82 *Narvel Felts*	41/75 *Barbara Fairchild*	74/00 Your Love *Jim Brickman Featuring Michelle Wright*
94/81 You're The Reason *Sligo Studio Band*	57/87 *Carlette*	1/94 Your Love Amazes Me *John Berry*
1/81 You're The Reason God Made Oklahoma *David Frizzell & Shelly West*	1/73 You've Never Been This Far Before *Conway Twitty*	3/79 Your Love Had Taken Me That High *Conway Twitty*
6/57 You're The Reason I'm In Love *Sonny James*	2/84 You've Really Got A Hold On Me *Mickey Gilley*	3/91 Your Love Is A Miracle *Mark Chesnutt*
You're The Reason I'm Living	You've Still Got A Place In My Heart	92/77 Your Love Is My Refuge *Ava Barber*
59/71 *Lamar Morris*	14/78 *Con Hunley*	71/70 Your Love Is The Way *Kitty Wells*
75/76 *Price Mitchell*	3/84 *George Jones*	5/83 Your Love Shines Through *Mickey Gilley*
You're The Reason Our Kids Are Ugly	You've Still Got Me	93/79 Your Love Takes Me So High *Maury Finney*
90/77 *L.E. White & Lola Jean Dillon*	68/80 *Jerry Wallace*	1/83 Your Love's On The Line *Earl Thomas Conley*
F/78 *Loretta Lynn/Conway Twitty*	71/83 *David Rogers*	43/69 Your Lovin' Takes The Leavin' Out Of Me *Tommy Cash*
75/00 You're The Ticket *Billy Hoffman*	70/86 You've Taken Over My Heart *Bobby G. Rice*	53/86 Your Loving Side *Butch Baker*
52/73 You're Wearin' Me Down *Kenny Price*	2/02 Young *Kenny Chesney*	15/80 Your Lying Blue Eyes *John Anderson*
9/84 You're Welcome To Tonight *Lynn Anderson & Gary Morris*	2/88 Young Country *Hank Williams, Jr.*	89/80 Your Magic Touch *Pat Garrett*
71/00 You're Where I Belong *Trisha Yearwood*	29/76 Young Girl *Tommy Overstreet*	85/83 Your Mama Don't Dance *Roy Head*
98/76 You're Wondering Why *Hank Snow*	12/57 Young Hearts *Jim Reeves*	64/97 Your Mama Won't Let Me *Little Texas*
94/86 You've Been My Rock For Ages *Bobbi Lace*	Young Love	4/77 Your Man Loves You, Honey *Tom T. Hall*
75/70 (You've Been Quite A Doll) Raggedy Ann *Jimmy Dickens*	1/57 *Sonny James*	7/81 Your Memory *Steve Wariner*
26/67 You've Been So Good To Me *Van Trevor*	20/69 *Connie Smith & Nat Stuckey*	5/86 Your Memory Ain't What It Used To Be *Mickey Gilley*
9/85 You've Got A Good Love Comin' *Lee Greenwood*	48/76 *Ray Stevens*	17/88 Your Memory Wins Again *Skip Ewing*
2/83 You've Got A Lover *Ricky Skaggs*	75/82 *Stella Parton*	29/63 Your Mother's Prayer *Buddy Cagle*
54/87 You've Got A Right *Adam Baker*	70/94 *Twister Alley*	6/58 Your Name Is Beautiful *Carl Smith*
44/84 You've Got A Soft Place To Fall *Kathy Mattea*	1/89 Young Love *Judds*	5/80 Your Old Cold Shoulder *Crystal Gayle*
13/99 You've Got A Way *Shania Twain*	81/88 Younger Man, Older Woman *Richard And Gary Rose*	56/89 Your Old Flame's Goin' Out Tonite *Joe Barnhill*
21/73 You've Got Me (Right Where You Want Me) *Connie Smith*	22/82 Your Bedroom Eyes *Vern Gosdin*	73/68 Your Old Handy Man *Priscilla Mitchell*
92/77 You've Got Me Runnin' *Gene Cotton*	12/63 Your Best Friend And Me *Mac Wiseman*	
3/76 You've Got Me To Hold On To *Tanya Tucker*	3/80 Your Body Is An Outlaw *Mel Tillis*	
16/79 You've Got Somebody, I've Got Somebody *Vern Gosdin*	1/53 Your Cheatin' Heart *Hank Williams*	

10/61 **Your Old Love Letters** *Porter Wagoner*	3/68 **Your Squaw Is On The Warpath** *Loretta Lynn*	22/79 **Yours** *Freddy Fender*
5/60 **Your Old Used To Be** *Faron Young*	90/73 **Your Sweet Love (Keeps Me Homeward Bound)** *Jimmy Dean*	77/75 **Yours And Mine** *O.B. McClinton*
99/79 **Your Other Love** *Tommy O'Day*	**Your Sweet Love Lifted Me**	78/79 **Yours And Mine** *Mary Lou Turner*
27/99 **Your Own Little Corner Of My Heart** *BlackHawk*	44/69 *Bobby Barnett*	28/80 **Yours For The Taking** *Jack Greene*
13/76 **Your Picture In The Paper** *Statler Brothers*	45/70 *Ferlin Husky*	47/69 **Yours Forever** *Wynn Stewart*
56/82 **Your Picture Still Loves Me (And I Still Love You)** *Billy Swan*	47/95 **Your Tattoo** *Sammy Kershaw*	**Yours Love**
11/77 **Your Place Or Mine** *Gary Stewart*	1/67 **Your Tender Loving Care** *Buck Owens*	5/69 *Waylon Jennings*
Your Pretty Roses Came Too Late	50/68 **Your Time Hasn't Come Yet, Baby** *Elvis Presley*	9/69 *Dolly Parton/Porter Wagoner*
67/74 *Melba Montgomery*	4/69 **Your Time's Comin'** *Faron Young*	67/79 *Jerry Wallace*
20/77 *Lois Johnson*	13/57 **Your True Love** *Carl Perkins*	
93/73 **Your Shoeshine Girl** *Leona Williams*	83/76 **Your Wanting Me Is Gone** *Vernon Oxford*	# Z
36/73 **Your Side Of The Bed** *Mac Davis*	35/81 **Your Wife Is Cheatin' On Us Again** *Wayne Kemp*	56/01 **'Zat You, Santa Claus?** *Garth Brooks*
	12/59 **Your Wild Life's Gonna Get You Down** *Kitty Wells*	56/90 **Zydeco Lady** *Eddy Raven*

TOP ARTISTS

Kings & Queens Of Country (The Top 400 Artists)

Top 20 Artists: 1944-1949 / 1950s / 1960s / 1970s / 1980s / 1990s / 2000-2001

Top 400 Artists Debuts

Top Artist Achievements:

    Most Chart Hits
    Most Top 40 Hits
    Most Top 10 Hits
    Most #1 Hits
    Most Weeks At The #1 Position
    Most Crossover Hits

    Most Consecutive #1 Hits
    Most Consecutive Top 10 Hits
    Artists With Longest Chart Careers
    Artists With Longest Span Between Chart Hits
    Top Artists Who Never Hit #1
    Artist's First Hit Is Their Biggest Hit
    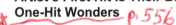 One-Hit Wonders p. 556

TOP 400 ARTISTS

Point System:

Next to each artist's name is their point total. The points are totaled through the June 29, 2002, chart. Each artist's points are accumulated according to the following formula:

1. Each artist's singles are given points based on their highest charted position:

#1	=	100 points for its first week at #1, plus 10 points for each additional week at #1
#2	=	90 points for its first week at #2, plus 5 points for each additional week at #2
#3	=	80 points for its first week at #3, plus 3 points for each additional week at #3
#4-5	=	70 points
#6-10	=	60 points
#11-15	=	55 points
#16-20	=	50 points
#21-30	=	45 points
#31-40	=	40 points
#41-50	=	35 points
#51-60	=	30 points
#61-70	=	25 points
#71-80	=	20 points
#81-90	=	15 points
#91-100	=	10 points

2. Points awarded for *Top Country Singles Sales* hits:

#1	=	50 points for its first week at #1, plus 5 points for each additional week at #1
#2	=	45 points for its first week at #2, plus 3 points for each additional week at #2
#3	=	40 points for its first week at #3, plus 2 points for each additional week at #3
#4-5	=	35 points
#6-10	=	30 points
#11-15	=	25 points
#16-20	=	20 points
#21-30	=	15 points
#31-40	=	10 points

3. Total weeks charted are added in.

In the case of a tie, the artist listed first is determined by the following tie-breaker rules:

1) Most charted singles   2) Most Top 40 singles   3) Most Top 10 singles

When two artists combine for a hit single, such as Faith Hill and Tim McGraw, the full point value is given to both artists. Duos, such as Brooks & Dunn, are considered regular recording teams, and their points are not shared by either artist individually.

Headings And Special Symbols:

Old Rank: Artist ranking in *Top Country Singles 1944-1997* book

New Rank: Artist ranking in *Top Country Singles 1944-2001* book

- ● **Deceased Solo Artist**

- ■ **Deceased Group Member**
  The total number of square symbols indicates the total number of deceased members.

- ★ **Hot Artist**
  - #1-40:   Rank increased by at least 5 positions since previous edition.
  - #41-100: Rank increased by at least 10 positions since previous edition.
  - #101-400: Rank increased by at least 20 positions since previous edition.

- — Artist did not rank in the Top 400 of the previous edition.

- + Subject to change since a single is still charted as of the 6/29/02 cut-off date.

KINGS & QUEENS OF COUNTRY (#1-98)

Old Rank	New Rank	Artist	Points
(1)	1.	Eddy Arnold ★	12,653
(2)	2.	George Jones	11,820
(3)	3.	Johnny Cash	9,644
(4)	4.	Conway Twitty 12 ●	9,083
(5)	5.	Merle Haggard 12	8,994
(15)	★6.	George Strait	8,165
(7)	7.	Dolly Parton	8,005
(6)	8.	Webb Pierce ●	7,975
(8)	9.	Ray Price	7,773
(9)	10.	Willie Nelson 12	7,704
(10)	11.	Buck Owens	7,492
(11)	12.	Waylon Jennings 140 X ●	7,320
(12)	13.	Marty Robbins ●	7,306
(24)	★14.	Reba McEntire	6,954
(20)	★15.	Alabama	6,933
(14)	16.	Hank Williams, Jr.	6,905
(13)	17.	Jim Reeves ★ ●	6,843
(17)	18.	Ernest Tubb ●	6,444
(16)	19.	Charley Pride	6,422
(18)	20.	Loretta Lynn	6,285
(19)	21.	Sonny James	6,205
(21)	22.	Faron Young ●	6,115
(22)	23.	Hank Snow	6,088
(23)	24.	Ronnie Milsap	5,989
(25)	25.	Carl Smith	5,901
(26)	26.	Tammy Wynette 12 ●	5,836
(31)	27.	Kenny Rogers	5,683
(48)	★28.	Garth Brooks	5,642
(27)	29.	Bill Anderson	5,621
(28)	30.	Mel Tillis	5,385
(29)	31.	Red Foley ●	5,326
(33)	32.	Porter Wagoner (13)	5,237
(30)	33.	Tanya Tucker	5,233
(32)	34.	Don Williams	5,211
(34)	35.	Elvis Presley ●	5,192
(35)	36.	Kitty Wells ★	5,134
(36)	37.	Don Gibson	5,090
(61)	★38.	Alan Jackson	5,064
(37)	39.	Glen Campbell 12	4,971
(38)	40.	The Statler Brothers ■	4,828
(39)	41.	Hank Thompson 12	4,813
(40)	42.	Crystal Gayle	4,522
(56)	★43.	Steve Wariner	4,506
(41)	44.	Hank Williams ★ ●	4,395
(42)	45.	Jerry Lee Lewis (13)	4,365
(43)	46.	David Houston 12 ●	4,250
(45)	47.	Bobby Bare	4,235
(46)	48.	Barbara Mandrell 15	4,217
(44)	49.	Oak Ridge Boys 12 ■	4,217
(60)	★50.	Vince Gill	4,107
(47)	51.	Mickey Gilley 12	4,076
(65)	★52.	Randy Travis	4,060
(71)	★53.	Clint Black	4,039
(49)	54.	Lynn Anderson 12	4,021
(50)	55.	Eddie Rabbitt 12 ●	3,990
(51)	56.	Anne Murray	3,901
(53)	57.	Joe Stampley	3,866
(52)	58.	Dottie West ●	3,858
(57)	59.	John Anderson	3,779
(54)	60.	T.G. Sheppard	3,746
(55)	61.	Emmylou Harris (13)	3,705
(101)	★62.	Brooks & Dunn	3,687
(167)	★63.	Tim McGraw	3,600
(64)	64.	Moe Bandy	3,537
(59)	65.	Tom T. Hall	3,536
(58)	66.	Bellamy Brothers 15	3,532
(62)	67.	Billy Walker	3,493
(63)	68.	Earl Thomas Conley	3,482
(76)	69.	Sawyer Brown	3,389
(66)	70.	Ferlin Husky (13)	3,355
(81)	★71.	Patty Loveless (13)	3,293
(67)	72.	Johnny Paycheck 14	3,266
(68)	73.	Gene Watson	3,247
(70)	74.	Connie Smith	3,218
(69)	75.	Freddie Hart	3,209
(72)	76.	Johnny Rodriguez 15	3,145
(97)	★77.	Travis Tritt	3,121
(74)	78.	Jerry Reed	3,116
(73)	79.	Charlie Rich ●	3,084
(75)	80.	Larry Gatlin & The Gatlin Brothers	3,031
(77)	81.	Janie Fricke	2,993
(79)	82.	Jim Ed Brown	2,963
(78)	83.	Lefty Frizzell (13) ●	2,945
(80)	84.	Ricky Skaggs	2,912
(82)	85.	Vern Gosdin	2,815
(127)	★86.	Collin Raye	2,795
(84)	87.	Eddy Raven	2,793
(83)	88.	Billy "Crash" Craddock	2,787
(107)	★89.	Mark Chesnutt 12	2,777
(86)	90.	Lee Greenwood 12	2,774
(85)	91.	John Conlee	2,756
(87)	92.	Stonewall Jackson 16	2,721
(90)	93.	Kathy Mattea	2,713
(137)	★94.	Trisha Yearwood 14	2,703
(88)	95.	Del Reeves	2,666
(108)	★96.	Lorrie Morgan	2,662
(146)	★97.	John Michael Montgomery	2,660
(89)	98.	Roy Drusky	2,658

David Frizzell (13)

KINGS & QUEENS OF COUNTRY (#99-213)

Old Rank	New Rank	Artist	Points
(112)	★99.	Joe Diffie	2,655
(93)	100.	Dave Dudley	2,629
(92)	101.	Roger Miller	2,624
(91)	102.	Jean Shepard	2,612
(238)★	103.	Faith Hill	2,582
(94)	104.	Charly McClain	2,553
(242)★	105.	Martina McBride	2,543
(96)	106.	The Judds	2,529
(95)	107.	Donna Fargo	2,517
(113)	108.	Dwight Yoakam	2,512
(115)	109.	Tracy Lawrence	2,493
(207)★	110.	Toby Keith	2,466
(98)	111.	Roy Clark	2,427
(100)	112.	Ronnie McDowell	2,420
(99)	113.	Bob Wills	2,418
(102)	114.	Ricky Van Shelton	2,405
(153)★	115.	Diamond Rio	2,375
(104)	116.	Skeeter Davis	2,353
(103)	117.	George Hamilton IV	2,334
(106)	118.	Jack Greene	2,295
(105)	119.	Mel McDaniel	2,290
(182)★	120.	Clay Walker	2,289
(110)	121.	Johnny Duncan	2,253
(109)	122.	Dan Seals	2,250
(111)	123.	The Kendalls	2,235
(119)	124.	Nitty Gritty Dirt Band	2,174
(114)	125.	Jimmy Wakely	2,171
(116)	126.	Rosanne Cash	2,145
(118)	127.	Shenandoah	2,141
(117)	128.	"Tennessee" Ernie Ford	2,126
(121)	129.	Johnny Lee	2,107
(120)	130.	Gary Morris	2,107
(130)	131.	Restless Heart	2,105
(122)	132.	Gene Autry	2,101
(142)	133.	Pam Tillis	2,072
(174)★	134.	Sammy Kershaw	2,062
(124)	135.	Jimmy Newman	2,047
(123)	136.	Hank Locklin	2,044
(126)	137.	Wilburn Brothers	2,019
(125)	138.	George Morgan	2,015
(243)★	139.	Shania Twain	2,001
(128)	140.	Slim Whitman	1,996
(129)	141.	Al Dexter	1,996
(132)	142.	Tommy Overstreet	1,995
(133)	143.	Ed Bruce	1,993
(131)	144.	Billie Jo Spears	1,993
(134)	145.	Nat Stuckey	1,989
(369)★	146.	Lonestar	1,986
(135)	147.	Exile	1,952
(136)	148.	Narvel Felts	1,947
(149)	149.	Mary Chapin Carpenter	1,939
(139)	150.	Michael Martin Murphey	1,911
(138)	151.	Razzy Bailey	1,908
(140)	152.	Tex Ritter	1,901
(141)	153.	Bob Luman	1,882
(155)	154.	Doug Stone	1,870
(204)★	155.	Neal McCoy	1,832
(319)★	156.	Kenny Chesney	1,831
(173)	157.	Wynonna	1,819
(214)★	158.	Aaron Tippin	1,818
(143)	159.	Sammi Smith	1,814
(144)	160.	Rex Allen, Jr.	1,811
(221)★	161.	Tracy Byrd	1,804
(145)	162.	Brenda Lee	1,799
(147)	163.	Freddy Weller	1,784
(148)	164.	Jerry Wallace	1,761
(150)	165.	Claude King	1,754
(151)	166.	Tex Williams	1,715
(152)	167.	Juice Newton	1,688
(154)	168.	David Rogers	1,675
(161)	169.	Marty Stuart	1,672
(156)	170.	Wynn Stewart	1,670
(159)	171.	Cal Smith	1,644
(158)	172.	Jan Howard	1,644
(157)	173.	The Forester Sisters	1,636
(160)	174.	Red Sovine	1,621
(162)	175.	Susan Raye	1,616
(163)	176.	Lacy J. Dalton	1,614
(164)	177.	Keith Whitley	1,573
(170)	178.	Ray Stevens	1,566
(166)	179.	Linda Ronstadt	1,561
(165)	180.	Kenny Price	1,558
(168)	181.	Mac Davis	1,545
(169)	182.	Warner Mack	1,538
—	★183.	Dixie Chicks	1,529
(171)	184.	Dickey Lee	1,527
(172)	185.	Sylvia	1,527
(175)	186.	Margo Smith	1,519
(223)★	187.	Billy Dean	1,513
(177)	188.	Wanda Jackson	1,512
(180)	189.	Rodney Crowell	1,510
(202)	190.	T. Graham Brown	1,507
(176)	191.	Jimmy Dean	1,505
(178)	192.	David Frizzell	1,498
(179)	193.	John Denver	1,495
(203)	194.	Charlie Daniels Band	1,482
(181)	195.	Charlie Louvin	1,465
(183)	196.	Highway 101	1,464
(184)	197.	Melba Montgomery	1,449
(185)	198.	Louise Mandrell	1,446
(186)	199.	Holly Dunn	1,437
(224)★	200.	Suzy Bogguss	1,419
(250)★	201.	Billy Ray Cyrus	1,416
(190)	202.	Freddy Fender	1,402
(187)	203.	The Everly Brothers	1,402
(189)	204.	Leon Everette	1,400
(191)	205.	Gary Stewart	1,399
(195)	206.	The Browns	1,398
(188)	207.	Dave & Sugar	1,391
(193)	208.	Little Texas	1,391
(197)	209.	Mel Street	1,390
(194)	210.	Gail Davies	1,388
(198)	211.	Patsy Cline	1,388
(192)	212.	Barbara Fairchild	1,386
(196)	213.	Jeannie Seely	1,386

KINGS & QUEENS OF COUNTRY (#214-330)

Old Rank	New Rank	Artist	Points
(211)	214.	Lee Roy Parnell	1,377
(199)	215.	Jody Miller	1,348
(201)	216.	Ernest Ashworth	1,342
(200)	217.	Johnny Carver	1,337
(277)★	218.	Bryan White	1,333
— ★	219.	Jo Dee Messina	1,333
(205)	220.	Bobby G. Rice	1,321
(206)	221.	Shelly West	1,307
(208)	222.	David Allan Coe	1,302
(210)	223.	Merle Travis	1,300
(209)	224.	John Schneider	1,298
(212)	225.	Jacky Ward	1,283
(213)	226.	Claude Gray	1,269
(218)	227.	Cowboy Copas	1,267
(215)	228.	Jeannie C. Riley	1,263
(216)	229.	Johnny Russell	1,262
(217)	230.	Tompall & The Glaser Brothers	1,252
(240)	231.	John Berry	1,252
(219)	232.	Marie Osmond	1,246
(225)	233.	Con Hunley	1,242
(220)	234.	Charlie Walker	1,241
(361)★	235.	LeAnn Rimes	1,240
(222)	236.	John Wesley Ryles	1,235
(226)	237.	Paul Overstreet	1,216
(227)	238.	Johnny Horton	1,216
(232)	239.	K.T. Oslin	1,214
(229)	240.	Flatt & Scruggs	1,212
(230)	241.	The Desert Rose Band	1,205
(228)	242.	Cristy Lane	1,202
(231)	243.	Jeanne Pruett	1,199
(256)	244.	BlackHawk	1,189
(233)	245.	Helen Cornelius	1,183
(333)★	246.	Ty Herndon	1,173
(234)	247.	Bobby Goldsboro	1,165
(235)	248.	Norma Jean	1,160
(236)	249.	Bobby Lewis	1,156
(237)	250.	Billy Joe Royal	1,145
(248)	251.	Hal Ketchum	1,131
(378)★	252.	Terri Clark	1,128
(239)	253.	Jim Glaser	1,089
(241)	254.	"Little" Jimmy Dickens	1,085
(244)	255.	Randy Barlow	1,072
(249)	256.	Olivia Newton-John	1,068
(245)	257.	Johnnie & Jack	1,067
(247)	258.	B.J. Thomas	1,060
— ★	259.	Lee Ann Womack	1,060
(246)	260.	Leroy Van Dyke	1,042
— ★	261.	Mark Wills	1,005
(252)	262.	Pee Wee King	999
(251)	263.	Johnny Bush	994
(345)★	264.	Wade Hayes	986
(253)	265.	Dick Curless	981
(255)	266.	Southern Pacific	978
(254)	267.	Buddy Alan	972
(283)	268.	Confederate Railroad	972
— ★	269.	Trace Adkins	966
(356)★	270.	Ricochet	959
(257)	271.	Margaret Whiting	953
(258)	272.	Tommy Cash	946
(260)	273.	Ray Griff	940
(259)	274.	Elton Britt	939
(262)	275.	Red Steagall	927
(261)	276.	Mundo Earwood	926
(263)	277.	Patti Page	918
(265)	278.	Roy Acuff	918
(266)	279.	The Whites	908
(264)	280.	Susie Allanson	903
(267)	281.	Carl Butler and Pearl	898
(268)	282.	Roy Head	887
(269)	283.	Bill Phillips	887
(270)	284.	Mark Collie	885
(271)	285.	Bobby Helms	884
(272)	286.	Tom Jones	882
(275)	287.	Rose Maddox	881
(280)	288.	Rick Trevino	878
(273)	289.	Henson Cargill	870
(274)	290.	Don King	864
(278)	291.	Bonnie Guitar	863
(276)	292.	Liz Anderson	859
(282)	293.	Johnny & Jonie Mosby	851
(279)	294.	Johnny Darrell	842
(285)	295.	The Louvin Brothers	840
(281)	296.	David Wills	837
(284)	297.	Glenn Barber	829
(288)	298.	Lionel Cartwright	826
(295)	299.	Asleep At The Wheel	822
(286)	300.	Sweethearts Of The Rodeo	822
(290)	301.	The Carlisles	820
(292)	302.	Sons Of The Pioneers	819
(287)	303.	Wayne Kemp	817
(289)	304.	Stephanie Winslow	816
(291)	305.	Lois Johnson	814
(298)	306.	Kenny Dale	807
(297)	307.	Diana Trask	804
(293)	308.	Baillie & The Boys	803
(294)	309.	Jessi Colter	802
(296)	310.	Arlene Harden	801
(299)	311.	Jack Blanchard & Misty Morgan	797
— ★	312.	Gary Allan	790
(346)★	313.	Osborne Brothers	789 +
(300)	314.	Billy Swan	783
(312)	315.	Skip Ewing	781
(318)	316.	David Lee Murphy	781
(301)	317.	Dean Dillon	779
(302)	318.	McBride & The Ride	777
(303)	319.	Carl Perkins	775
(304)	320.	Floyd Tillman	775
(306)	321.	Wilma Burgess	765
(307)	322.	C.W. McCall	763
(305)	323.	Deborah Allen	760
(310)	324.	Tommy Collins	757
(308)	325.	Michael Johnson	757
(309)	326.	Carlene Carter	751
(311)	327.	Debby Boone	750
— ★	328.	Chely Wright	750
(313)	329.	Ray Charles	749
(314)	330.	Johnny Bond	741

KINGS & QUEENS OF COUNTRY (#331-400)

Old Rank	New Rank	Artist	Points
(315)	331.	Bobby Wright	730
(316)	332.	Moon Mullican	727
(370)	★333.	Chris LeDoux	723
(317)	334.	Mark Gray	722
(388)	★335.	David Ball	720
—	★336.	Daryle Singletary	717
(376)	★337.	Lari White	714
(389)	★338.	Deana Carter	710
(320)	339.	Judy Rodman	709
(321)	340.	Dottsy	702
(324)	341.	Little David Wilkins	695
—	★342.	Mindy McCready	692
(326)	343.	Marion Worth	690
—	★344.	Sara Evans	689
(322)	345.	Zella Lehr	687
(327)	346.	Stella Parton	687
(323)	347.	Ted Daffan	687
(325)	348.	Doug Supernaw	685
(328)	349.	La Costa	678
(384)	★350.	The Mavericks	673
(332)	351.	Lyle Lovett	672
(330)	352.	June Carter	672
(329)	353.	Larry Boone	667
(365)	354.	Rhett Akins	667
(336)	355.	Jim Nesbitt	665
(334)	356.	Joe Sun	664
(331)	357.	Sheb Wooley	664
(335)	358.	Hoyt Axton	662
—	★359.	Jeff Carson	658
(342)	360.	Margie Singleton	657
(340)	361.	Sherry Bryce	656
(338)	362.	Robin Lee	655
(337)	363.	Ray Pillow	654
(339)	364.	R.C. Bannon	653
(341)	365.	Terri Gibbs	649
(344)	366.	Roy Rogers	649
(343)	367.	Peggy Sue	635
(347)	368.	Ned Miller	635
(348)	369.	Keith Stegall	626
—	★370.	SheDaisy	626
(349)	371.	Billy Parker	619
(350)	372.	Bobby Borchers	619
(355)	373.	Jimmie Skinner	619
(351)	374.	Tony Booth	615
(352)	375.	"T" Texas Tyler	615
(353)	376.	Johnny Wright	608
(354)	377.	Spade Cooley	606
(377)	378.	Jimmy Buffett	604
(358)	379.	Jack Reno	604
(357)	380.	Big Al Downing	599
(359)	381.	Foster & Lloyd	599
(362)	382.	Hawkshaw Hawkins	599
(360)	383.	Mary Lou Turner	597
(363)	384.	Becky Hobbs	588
(367)	385.	Burl Ives	586
(364)	386.	Charlie McCoy	584
(366)	387.	Mike Reid	582
—	★388.	Andy Griggs	579
—	★389.	Brad Paisley	577
(368)	390.	The O'Kanes	575
(371)	391.	Ronnie Sessions	572
—	★392.	Paul Brandt	570
(374)	393.	Kris Kristofferson	569
(372)	394.	Dorsey Burnette	567
(373)	395.	Penny DeHaven	564
(375)	396.	Tom Wopat	563
—	★397.	Chad Brock	561
(390)	398.	Kentucky Headhunters, The	560
—	★399.	Linda Davis	560
—	400.	Radney Foster	552

A-Z — TOP 400 ARTISTS

Artist	Rank
Acuff, Roy	278
Adkins, Trace	269
Akins, Rhett	354
Alabama	15
Alan, Buddy	267
Allan, Gary	312
Allanson, Susie	280
Allen, Deborah	323
Allen, Rex Jr.	160
Anderson, Bill	29
Anderson, John	59
Anderson, Liz	292
Anderson, Lynn	54
Arnold, Eddy	1
Ashworth, Ernest	216
Asleep At The Wheel	299
Autry, Gene	132
Axton, Hoyt	358
Bailey, Razzy	151
Baillie And The Boys	308
Ball, David	335
Bandy, Moe	64
Bannon, R.C.	364
Barber, Glenn	297
Bare, Bobby	47
Barlow, Randy	255
Bellamy Brothers	66
Berry, John	231
Black, Clint	53
BlackHawk	244
Blanchard, Jack, & Misty Morgan	311
Bogguss, Suzy	200
Bond, Johnny	330
Boone, Debby	327
Boone, Larry	353
Booth, Tony	374
Borchers, Bobby	372
Brandt, Paul	392
Britt, Elton	274
Brock, Chad	397
Brooks, Garth	28
Brooks & Dunn	62
Brown, Jim Ed	82
Brown, T. Graham	190
Browns, The	206
Bruce, Ed	143
Bryce, Sherry	361
Buffett, Jimmy	378
Burgess, Wilma	321
Burnette, Dorsey	394
Bush, Johnny	263

A-Z — TOP 400 ARTISTS

Artist	Page
Butler, Carl, & Pearl	281
Byrd, Tracy	161
Campbell, Glen	39
Cargill, Henson	289
Carlisles, The	301
Carpenter, Mary Chapin	149
Carson, Jeff	359
Carter, Carlene	326
Carter, Deana	338
Carter, June	352
Cartwright, Lionel	298
Carver, Johnny	217
Cash, Johnny	3
Cash, Rosanne	126
Cash, Tommy	272
Charles, Ray	329
Chesney, Kenny	156
Chesnutt, Mark	89
Clark, Roy	111
Clark, Terri	252
Cline, Patsy	211
Coe, David Allan	222
Collie, Mark	284
Collins, Tommy	324
Colter, Jessi	309
Confederate Railroad	268
Conlee, John	91
Conley, Earl Thomas	68
Cooley, Spade	377
Copas, Cowboy	227
Cornelius, Helen	245
Craddock, Billy "Crash"	88
Crowell, Rodney	189
Curless, Dick	265
Cyrus, Billy Ray	201
Daffan, Ted	347
Dale, Kenny	306
Dalton, Lacy J.	176
Daniels, Charlie, Band	194
Darrell, Johnny	294
Dave & Sugar	207
Davies, Gail	210
Davis, Linda	399
Davis, Mac	181
Davis, Skeeter	116
Dean, Billy	187
Dean, Jimmy	191
DeHaven, Penny	395
Denver, John	193
Desert Rose Band, The	241
Dexter, Al	141
Diamond Rio	115
Dickens, "Little" Jimmy	254
Diffie, Joe	99
Dillon, Dean	317
Dixie Chicks	183
Dottsy	340
Downing, Big Al	380
Drusky, Roy	98
Dudley, Dave	100
Duncan, Johnny	121
Dunn, Holly	199
Earwood, Mundo	276
Evans, Sara	344
Everette, Leon	204
Everly Brothers, The	203
Ewing, Skip	315
Exile	147
Fairchild, Barbara	212
Fargo, Donna	107
Felts, Narvel	148
Fender, Freddy	202
Flatt & Scruggs	240
Foley, Red	31
Ford, "Tennessee" Ernie	128
Forester Sisters, The	173
Foster, Radney	400
Foster & Lloyd	381
Fricke, Janie	81
Frizzell, David	192
Frizzell, Lefty	83
Gatlin, Larry, & The Gatlin Brothers	80
Gayle, Crystal	42
Gibbs, Terri	365
Gibson, Don	37
Gill, Vince	50
Gilley, Mickey	51
Glaser, Jim	253
Glaser Brothers, Tompall & The	230
Goldsboro, Bobby	247
Gosdin, Vern	85
Gray, Claude	226
Gray, Mark	334
Greene, Jack	118
Greenwood, Lee	90
Griff, Ray	273
Griggs, Andy	388
Guitar, Bonnie	291
Haggard, Merle	5
Hall, Tom T.	65
Hamilton, George IV	117
Harden, Arlene	310
Harris, Emmylou	61
Hart, Freddie	75
Hawkins, Hawkshaw	382
Hayes, Wade	264
Head, Roy	282
Helms, Bobby	285
Herndon, Ty	246
Highway 101	196
Hill, Faith	103
Hobbs, Becky	384
Horton, Johnny	238
Houston, David	46
Howard, Jan	172
Hunley, Con	233
Husky, Ferlin	70
Ives, Burl	385
Jackson, Alan	38
Jackson, Stonewall	92
Jackson, Wanda	188
James, Sonny	21
Jennings, Waylon	12
Johnnie & Jack	257
Johnson, Lois	305
Johnson, Michael	325
Jones, George	2
Jones, Tom	286
Judds, The	106
Keith, Toby	110
Kemp, Wayne	303
Kendalls, The	123
Kentucky Headhunters, The	398
Kershaw, Sammy	134
Ketchum, Hal	251
King, Claude	165
King, Don	290
King, Pee Wee	262
Kristofferson, Kris	393
La Costa	349
Lane, Cristy	242
Lawrence, Tracy	109
LeDoux, Chris	333
Lee, Brenda	162
Lee, Dickey	184
Lee, Johnny	129
Lee, Robin	362
Lehr, Zella	345
Lewis, Bobby	249
Lewis, Jerry Lee	45
Little Texas	208
Locklin, Hank	136
Lonestar	146
Louvin, Charlie	195
Louvin Brothers, The	295
Loveless, Patty	71
Lovette, Lyle	351
Luman, Bob	153
Lynn, Loretta	20
Mack, Warner	182
Maddox, Rose	287
Mandrell, Barbara	48
Mandrell, Louise	198
Mattea, Kathy	93
Mavericks, The	350
McBride, Martina	105
McBride & The Ride	318
McCall, C.W.	322
McClain, Charly	104
McCoy, Charlie	386
McCoy, Neal	155
McCready, Mindy	342
McDaniel, Mel	119
McDowell, Ronnie	112
McEntire, Reba	14
McGraw, Tim	63
Messina, Jo Dee	219
Miller, Jody	215
Miller, Ned	368
Miller, Roger	101
Milsap, Ronnie	24
Montgomery, John Michael	97
Montgomery, Melba	197
Morgan, George	138
Morgan, Lorrie	96
Morris, Gary	130
Mosby, Johnny & Jonie	293
Mullican, Moon	332
Murphey, Michael Martin	150
Murphy, David Lee	316
Murray, Anne	56
Nelson, Willie	10
Nesbitt, Jim	355
Newman, Jimmy	135
Newton, Juice	167
Newton-John, Olivia	256
Nitty Gritty Dirt Band	124
Norma Jean	248
Oak Ridge Boys	49
O'Kanes, The	390
Osborne Brothers	313
Oslin, K.T.	239
Osmond, Marie	232
Overstreet, Paul	237
Overstreet, Tommy	142
Owens, Buck	11
Page, Patti	277
Paisley, Brad	389
Parker, Billy	371
Parnell, Lee Roy	214

A-Z — TOP 400 ARTISTS (Cont'd)

Artist	#	Artist	#	Artist	#
Parton, Dolly	7	Shepard, Jean	102	Twain, Shania	139
Parton, Stella	346	Sheppard, T.G.	60	Twitty, Conway	4
Paycheck, Johnny	72	Singletary, Daryle	336	Tyler, "T" Texas	375
Peggy Sue	367	Singleton, Margie	360	Van Dyke, Leroy	260
Perkins, Carl	319	Skaggs, Ricky	84	Wagoner, Porter	32
Phillips, Bill	283	Skinner, Jimmie	373	Wakely, Jimmy	125
Pierce, Webb	8	Smith, Cal	171	Walker, Billy	67
Pillow, Ray	363	Smith, Carl	25	Walker, Charlie	234
Presley, Elvis	35	Smith, Connie	74	Walker, Clay	120
Price, Kenny	180	Smith, Margo	186	Wallace, Jerry	164
Price, Ray	9	Smith, Sammi	159	Ward, Jacky	225
Pride, Charley	19	Snow, Hank	23	Wariner, Steve	43
Pruett, Jeanne	243	Sons Of The Pioneers	302	Watson, Gene	73
Rabbitt, Eddie	55	Southern Pacific	266	Weller, Freddy	163
Raven, Eddy	87	Sovine, Red	174	Wells, Kitty	36
Raye, Collin	86	Spears, Billie Jo	144	West, Dottie	58
Raye, Susan	175	Stampley, Joe	57	West, Shelly	221
Reed, Jerry	78	Statler Brothers, The	40	White, Bryan	218
Reeves, Del	95	Steagall, Red	275	White, Lari	337
Reeves, Jim	17	Stegall, Keith	369	Whites, The	279
Reid, Mike	387	Stevens, Ray	178	Whiting, Margaret	271
Reno, Jack	379	Stewart, Gary	205	Whitley, Keith	177
Restless Heart	131	Stewart, Wynn	170	Whitman, Slim	140
Rice, Bobby G.	220	Stone, Doug	154	Wilburn Brothers	137
Rich, Charlie	79	Strait, George	6	Wilkins, Little David	341
Ricochet	270	Street, Mel	209	Williams, Don	34
Riley, Jeannie C.	228	Stuart, Marty	169	Williams, Hank	44
Rimes, LeAnn	235	Stuckey, Nat	145	Williams, Hank Jr.	16
Ritter, Tex	152	Sun, Joe	356	Williams, Tex	166
Robbins, Marty	13	Supernaw, Doug	348	Wills, Bob	113
Rodman, Judy	339	Swan, Billy	314	Wills, David	296
Rodriguez, Johnny	76	Sweethearts Of The Rodeo	300	Wills, Mark	261
Rogers, David	168	Sylvia	185	Winslow, Stephanie	304
Rogers, Kenny	27	Thomas, B.J.	258	Womack, Lee Ann	259
Rogers, Roy	366	Thompson, Hank	41	Wooley, Sheb	357
Ronstadt, Linda	179	Tillis, Mel	30	Wopat, Tom	396
Royal, Billy Joe	250	Tillis, Pam	133	Worth, Marion	343
Russell, Johnny	229	Tillman, Floyd	320	Wright, Bobby	331
Ryles, John Wesley	236	Tippin, Aaron	158	Wright, Chely	328
Sawyer Brown	69	Trask, Diana	307	Wright, Johnny	376
Schneider, John	224	Travis, Merle	223	Wynette, Tammy	26
Seals, Dan	122	Travis, Randy	52	Wynonna	157
Seely, Jeannie	213	Trevino, Rick	288	Yearwood, Trisha	94
Sessions, Ronnie	391	Tritt, Travis	77	Yoakam, Dwight	108
SheDaisy	370	Tubb, Ernest	18	Young, Faron	22
Shelton, Ricky Van	114	Tucker, Tanya	33		
Shenandoah	127	Turner, Mary Lou	383		

The following 18 artists were ranked in the Top 400 Artists of our *Top Country Singles 1944-1997* book but have now dropped out of the Top 400:

Leon Ashley
Bandana
Carl Belew
Lane Brody
Brian Collins
Wilma Lee & Stoney Cooper

Sonny Curtis
Stoney Edwards
Doug Kershaw
Hugh X. Lewis
LaWanda Lindsey
Mason Dixon

Darrell McCall
Bill Monroe
Ricky Nelson
Ray Sanders
Schuyler, Knobloch & Overstreet
Kenny Starr

TOP 20 ARTISTS
1944-1949

1. **Eddy Arnold** 3,587
2. Ernest Tubb 2,622
3. Bob Wills 2,148
4. Al Dexter 1,996
5. Red Foley 1,756
6. Gene Autry 1,741
7. Jimmy Wakely 1,420
8. Tex Ritter 1,349
9. Tex Williams 1,218
10. Merle Travis 1,182
11. Hank Williams 1,047
12. Sons Of The Pioneers 795
13. Elton Britt 703
14. Ted Daffan 687
15. Floyd Tillman 656
16. Hank Thompson 617
17. Cowboy Copas 609
18. Spade Cooley 606
19. Roy Acuff 590
20. George Morgan 584

1950s

1. **Webb Pierce** 5,056
2. Eddy Arnold 4,447
3. Hank Snow 3,933
4. Carl Smith 3,554
5. Red Foley 3,438
6. Hank Williams 3,203
7. Johnny Cash 2,678
8. Elvis Presley 2,653
9. Kitty Wells 2,568
10. Ernest Tubb 2,523
11. Hank Thompson 2,302
12. Ray Price 2,300
13. Faron Young 2,212
14. Jim Reeves 2,185
15. Marty Robbins 2,055
16. Lefty Frizzell 1,911
17. "Tennessee" Ernie Ford 1,375
18. Ferlin Husky 1,230
19. The Everly Brothers 1,075
20. Johnnie & Jack 1,013

1960s

1. **Buck Owens** 4,819
2. George Jones 4,142
3. Jim Reeves 3,384
4. Johnny Cash 3,044
5. Eddy Arnold 2,803
6. Marty Robbins 2,631
7. Webb Pierce 2,594
8. Bill Anderson 2,577
9. Ray Price 2,450
10. Faron Young 2,428
11. Kitty Wells 2,378
12. Sonny James 2,341
13. Porter Wagoner 2,245
14. Stonewall Jackson 2,071
15. Loretta Lynn 1,958
16. Roy Drusky 1,907
17. David Houston 1,895
18. Don Gibson 1,855
19. Merle Haggard 1,760
20. Roger Miller 1,735

1970s

1. **Conway Twitty** 4,274
2. Merle Haggard 3,593
3. Charley Pride 3,377
4. Dolly Parton 3,330
5. Loretta Lynn 3,246
6. Mel Tillis 3,217
7. Tammy Wynette 3,213
8. George Jones 3,095
9. Waylon Jennings 3,037
10. Sonny James 2,866
11. Johnny Cash 2,786
12. Charlie Rich 2,670
13. Lynn Anderson 2,658
14. Willie Nelson 2,632
15. Tom T. Hall 2,606
16. Freddie Hart 2,419
17. Jerry Lee Lewis 2,366
18. Bill Anderson 2,289
19. Hank Williams, Jr. 2,275
20. Joe Stampley 2,273

TOP 20 ARTISTS

1980s

1. **Willie Nelson** 3,918
2. Conway Twitty 3,517
3. Merle Haggard 3,465
4. Kenny Rogers 3,407
5. Alabama 3,368
6. Ronnie Milsap 3,278
7. Oak Ridge Boys 3,041
8. Hank Williams, Jr. 2,997
9. Dolly Parton 2,871
10. Earl Thomas Conley 2,862
11. Reba McEntire 2,860
12. George Strait 2,854
13. Don Williams 2,834
14. Waylon Jennings 2,810
15. Crystal Gayle 2,810
16. Bellamy Brothers 2,730
17. George Jones 2,672
18. Steve Wariner 2,517
19. T.G. Sheppard 2,513
20. Ricky Skaggs 2,432

1990s

1. **Garth Brooks** 4,967
2. George Strait 4,614
3. Alan Jackson 4,171
4. Clint Black 3,572
5. Reba McEntire 3,360
6. Alabama 3,207
7. Brooks & Dunn 3,125
8. Vince Gill 3,111
9. Tim McGraw 2,662
10. Mark Chesnutt 2,634
11. Travis Tritt 2,627
12. Collin Raye 2,499
13. Joe Diffie 2,480
14. Trisha Yearwood 2,463
15. Randy Travis 2,347
16. Patty Loveless 2,345
17. John Michael Montgomery 2,344
18. Lorrie Morgan 2,212
19. Tracy Lawrence 2,184
20. Diamond Rio 2,060

2000-2001

1. **Tim McGraw** 938
2. Alan Jackson 846
3. Lonestar 830
4. Toby Keith 752
5. George Strait 697
6. Dixie Chicks 695
7. Faith Hill 666
8. Brooks & Dunn 562
9. Martina McBride 486
10. Jo Dee Messina 474
11. SheDaisy 469
12. Kenny Chesney 466
13. Garth Brooks 463
14. Keith Urban 422
15. Clay Walker 409
16. Travis Tritt 408
17. Phil Vassar 388
18. Reba McEntire 378
19. Montgomery Gentry 369
20. Kenny Rogers 366

TOP ARTIST DEBUTS

The following lists, in chronological order, the chart debut date of the Top 400 Country artists.

#	Date	Artist
1.	1/8/44	Ted Daffan (347)
2.	1/8/44	Al Dexter (141)
3.	1/8/44	Floyd Tillman (320)
4.	1/8/44 ♦	Ernest Tubb (18)
5.	1/8/44	Bob Wills (113)
6.	1/29/44	Gene Autry (132)
7.	2/12/44	Roy Acuff (278)
8.	4/15/44	Jimmy Wakely (125)
9.	8/26/44	Red Foley (31)
10.	11/11/44	Tex Ritter (152)
11.	1/27/45	Elton Britt (274)
12.	3/3/45	Spade Cooley (377)
13.	6/30/45 ♦	Eddy Arnold (1)
14.	10/6/45	Sons Of The Pioneers (302)
15.	6/8/46	Merle Travis (223)
16.	7/6/46	Roy Rogers (366)
17.	8/24/46	"T" Texas Tyler (375)
18.	8/31/46	Cowboy Copas (227)
19.	10/26/46	The Carlisles (301)
20.	11/30/46	Tex Williams (166)
21.	2/8/47	Moon Mullican (332)
22.	2/22/47	Johnny Bond (330)
23.	8/9/47 ♦	Hank Williams (44)
24.	1/31/48 ♦	Hank Thompson (41)
25.	4/3/48	Pee Wee King (262)
26.	5/1/48	Hawkshaw Hawkins (382)
27.	2/12/49	Burl Ives (385)
28.	2/26/49	George Morgan (138)
29.	4/16/49	"Little" Jimmy Dickens (254)
30.	4/30/49	"Tennessee" Ernie Ford (128)
31.	4/30/49	Jimmie Skinner (373)
32.	5/7/49	Patti Page (277)
33.	6/25/49	Hank Locklin (136)
34.	8/27/49	June Carter (352)
35.	9/10/49	Margaret Whiting (271)
36.	12/31/49 ♦	Hank Snow (23)
37.	10/28/50	Lefty Frizzell (83)
38.	1/20/51	Johnnie & Jack (257)
39.	6/2/51 ♦	Carl Smith (25)
40.	1/5/52 ♦	Webb Pierce (8)
41.	2/2/52	Flatt & Scruggs (240)
42.	5/17/52	Ray Price (9)
43.	5/17/52	Slim Whitman (140)
44.	7/19/52	Kitty Wells (36)
45.	12/20/52	Marty Robbins (13)
46.	1/10/53	Faron Young (22)
47.	2/7/53	Sonny James (21)
48.	3/7/53	Jimmy Dean (191)
49.	3/28/53 ♦	Jim Reeves (17)
50.	7/25/53	Jean Shepard (102)
51.	2/20/54	Tommy Collins (324)
52.	5/22/54	Jimmy Newman (135)
53.	6/12/54	Wilburn Brothers (137)
54.	6/26/54	The Browns (206)
55.	6/26/54	Billy Walker (67)
56.	7/24/54	Wanda Jackson (188)
57.	10/30/54 ♦	Porter Wagoner (32)
58.	1/15/55	Ferlin Husky (70)
59.	3/26/55	Red Sovine (174)
60.	7/16/55	Elvis Presley (35)
61.	9/10/55	Louvin Brothers (295)
62.	10/29/55 ♦	George Jones (2)
63.	11/26/55	Johnny Cash (3)
64.	1/28/56	Charlie Walker (234)
65.	2/18/56	Carl Perkins (319)
66.	5/5/56	Marty Horton (238)
67.	7/21/56	Wynn Stewart (170)
68.	8/11/56 ♦	Don Gibson (37)
69.	1/5/57	Leroy Van Dyke (260)
70.	3/2/57	Patsy Cline (211)
71.	3/30/57	Bobby Helms (285)
72.	4/6/57	Brenda Lee (162)
73.	5/13/57	Everly Brothers (203)
74.	6/10/57	Bonnie Guitar (291)
75.	6/17/57 ♦	Jerry Lee Lewis (45)
76.	8/12/57	Warner Mack (182)
77.	2/24/58	Skeeter Davis (116)
78.	3/24/58	Osborne Brothers (313)
79.	11/3/58	Stonewall Jackson (92)
80.	11/10/58	Mel Tillis (30)
81.	12/29/58 ♦	Bill Anderson (29)
82.	4/20/59	Freddie Hart (75)
83.	5/11/59 ♦	Buck Owens (11)
84.	5/18/59	Rose Maddox (287)
85.	8/3/59	Margie Singleton (360)
86.	8/24/59	Bill Phillips (283)
87.	10/19/59	Marion Worth (343)
88.	1/11/60	Jan Howard (172)
89.	1/18/60	Roy Drusky (98)
90.	3/21/60	Claude Gray (226)
91.	5/30/60	Ernest Ashworth (216)
92.	6/13/60 ♦	Loretta Lynn (20)
93.	10/10/60	George Hamilton IV (117)
94.	10/10/60	Bob Luman (153)
95.	10/31/60	Roger Miller (101)
96.	4/3/61	Jim Nesbitt (355)
97.	7/3/61	Claude King (165)
98.	8/7/61	Carl Butler (281)
99.	10/16/61	Dave Dudley (100)
100.	11/6/61 ♦	Del Reeves (95)
101.	1/13/62	Sheb Wooley (357)
102.	3/17/62 ♦	Willie Nelson (10)
103.	9/15/62	Bobby Bare (47)
104.	12/15/62	Ned Miller (368)
105.	12/29/62	Glen Campbell (39)
106.	5/4/63	Melba Montgomery (197)
107.	5/18/63	Johnny & Jonie Mosby (293)
108.	7/6/63	Roy Clark (111)
109.	10/19/63	David Houston (46)
110.	11/30/63	Dottie West (58)
111.	12/28/63 ♦	Merle Haggard (5)
112.	1/4/64	Norma Jean (248)
113.	1/25/64	Glenn Barber (297)
114.	2/8/64 ♦	Hank Williams, Jr. (16)
115.	5/2/64	Johnny Wright (376)
116.	6/20/64	Charlie Louvin (195)
117.	9/26/64	Connie Smith (74)
118.	2/13/65	Ray Pillow (363)
119.	3/13/65	Dick Curless (265)
120.	5/29/65	Jody Miller (215)
121.	7/10/65	Jim Ed Brown (82)
122.	8/21/65 ♦	Waylon Jennings (12)
123.	9/25/65	The Statler Brothers (40)
124.	10/9/65	Jerry Wallace (164)
125.	10/16/65	Johnny Paycheck (72)
126.	12/11/65	Wilma Burgess (321)
127.	12/25/65	Johnny Darrell (294)
128.	12/25/65	Jack Greene (118)
129.	3/26/66 ♦	Conway Twitty (4)
130.	4/2/66	Liz Anderson (292)
131.	4/16/66	Jeannie Seely (213)
132.	8/20/66	Kenny Price (180)
133.	9/10/66	Nat Stuckey (145)
134.	10/15/66	Bobby Lewis (249)
135.	10/29/66	Lynn Anderson (54)
136.	12/3/66	Charley Pride (19)
137.	12/10/66	Tammy Wynette (26)
138.	12/31/66	Tompall & The Glaser Brothers (230)
139.	1/7/67	Penny DeHaven (395)
140.	1/14/67	Ed Bruce (143)
141.	1/21/67 ♦	Dolly Parton (7)
142.	1/28/67	Cal Smith (171)
143.	4/29/67	Bobby Wright (331)
144.	5/20/67	Jerry Reed (78)
145.	7/15/67	Arlene Harden (310)
146.	8/5/67	Tom T. Hall (65)
147.	8/12/67	Johnny Duncan (121)
148.	11/25/67	Johnny Bush (263)
149.	12/9/67	Henson Cargill (289)
150.	12/9/67	Jack Reno (379)
151.	12/23/67	Johnny Carver (217)
152.	12/23/67	Ray Griff (273)
153.	1/27/68	Sammi Smith (159)
154.	3/2/68	David Rogers (168)
155.	3/9/68	Bobby Goldsboro (247)
156.	3/9/68	Charlie Rich (79)
157.	6/22/68	Diana Trask (307)
158.	7/27/68	Buddy Alan (267)
159.	8/24/68	Jeannie C. Riley (228)
160.	8/31/68	Tommy Cash (272)
161.	8/31/68	Jim Glaser (253)
162.	10/19/68 ♦	Mickey Gilley (51)
163.	11/30/68	Billy Jo Spears (144)
164.	12/7/68	John Wesley Ryles (236)
165.	1/25/69	Lois Johnson (305)
166.	2/1/69	Wayne Kemp (303)
167.	3/1/69	Jack Blanchard & Misty Morgan (311)
168.	3/22/69	Little David Wilkins (341)
169.	4/12/69	Freddy Weller (163)
170.	5/31/69	Barbara Fairchild (212)
171.	6/7/69	Peggy Sue (367)
172.	7/19/69 ♦	Kenny Rogers (27)
173.	9/13/69	Barbara Mandrell (48)
174.	10/11/69	Tommy Overstreet (142)
175.	11/1/69	Ray Stevens (178)

TOP ARTIST DEBUTS (Cont'd)

#	Date	Artist
176.	1/10/70	Susan Raye (175)
177.	3/28/70	Tony Booth (374)
178.	4/25/70	Mac Davis (181)
179.	4/25/70	Bobby G. Rice (220)
180.	6/20/70	David Frizzell (83)
181.	7/25/70	The Kendalls (123)
182.	7/25/70	Anne Murray (56)
183.	9/19/70 ♦	Crystal Gayle (42)
184.	11/14/70	Jessi Colter (309)
185.	2/13/71	Billy "Crash" Craddock (88)
186.	2/20/71 ♦	Joe Stampley (57)
187.	6/5/71	Sherry Bryce (361)
188.	6/19/71	Dickey Lee (184)
189.	6/26/71	John Denver (193)
190.	8/21/71	Johnny Russell (229)
191.	9/18/71	Jeanne Pruett (243)
192.	11/27/71	Nitty Gritty Dirt Band (124)
193.	1/15/72	Red Steagall (275)
194.	2/5/72	Charlie McCoy (386)
195.	3/25/72	Donna Fargo (107)
196.	4/22/72	Kris Kristofferson (393)
197.	5/13/72	Dorsey Burnette (394)
198.	5/13/72 ♦	Tanya Tucker (33)
199.	5/27/72	Mel Street (209)
200.	6/10/72	Jacky Ward (225)
201.	8/5/72	Ronnie Sessions (391)
202.	10/21/72	Mundo Earwood (276)
203.	11/11/72	Johnny Rodriguez (76)
204.	12/16/72	Don Williams (34)
205.	5/12/73	Jimmy Buffett (378)
206.	6/16/73	Narvel Felts (148)
207.	6/30/73 ♦	Ronnie Milsap (24)
208.	8/4/73	Charlie Daniels Band (194)
209.	8/4/73	Oak Ridge Boys (49)
210.	8/25/73	Olivia Newton-John (256)
211.	9/8/73	Marie Osmond (232)
212.	10/20/73	Larry Gatlin & The Gatlin Brothers (80)
213.	11/17/73	Gary Stewart (205)
214.	12/29/73	Rex Allen, Jr. (160)
215.	3/2/74	Linda Ronstadt (179)
216.	3/16/74	Eddy Raven (87)
217.	3/30/74	Hoyt Axton (358)
218.	3/30/74	Moe Bandy (64)
219.	4/20/74	La Costa (349)
220.	7/6/74	Mary Lou Turner (383)
221.	7/13/74	C.W. McCall (322)
222.	7/20/74	Randy Barlow (255)
223.	8/31/74 ♦	Eddie Rabbitt (55)
224.	10/12/74	Billy Swan (314)
225.	10/19/74	Roy Head (282)
226.	11/16/74	David Wills (296)
227.	11/30/74	David Allan Coe (222)
228.	11/30/74	T.G. Sheppard (60)
229.	12/21/74	Asleep At The Wheel (299)
230.	1/11/75	Freddy Fender (202)
231.	1/25/75	Gene Watson (73)
232.	2/22/75	B.J. Thomas (258)
233.	4/5/75	Margo Smith (186)
234.	4/19/75 ♦	Emmylou Harris (61)
235.	5/24/75	Stella Parton (346)
236.	5/31/75	Dottsy (340)
237.	7/26/75	Earl Thomas Conley (68)
238.	11/15/75	Dave & Sugar (207)
239.	12/27/75	Johnny Lee (129)
240.	2/21/76	Michael Martin Murphey (150)
241.	2/21/76	Juice Newton (167)
242.	3/6/76	Bobby Borchers (372)
243.	3/13/76	Bellamy Brothers (66)
244.	5/8/76	Mel McDaniel (119)
245.	5/8/76 ♦	Reba McEntire (14)
246.	7/4/76	Helen Cornelius (245)
247.	9/11/76	Don King (290)
248.	9/18/76	Billy Parker (371)
249.	10/23/76	Charly McClain (104)
250.	10/30/76	Razzy Bailey (151)
251.	10/30/76	Vern Gosdin (85)
252.	12/25/76	Tom Jones (286)
253.	1/29/77	Con Hunley (233)
254.	2/12/77	Cristy Lane (242)
255.	3/5/77	Kenny Dale (306)
256.	7/9/77	Susie Allanson (280)
257.	7/23/77 ♦	Alabama (15)
258.	7/30/77	R.C. Bannon (364)
259.	9/10/77	Ronnie McDowell (112)
260.	9/17/77	Janie Fricke (81)
261.	10/22/77	Debby Boone (327)
262.	12/3/77	Leon Everette (204)
263.	12/10/77	John Anderson (59)
264.	12/17/77	Zella Lehr (345)
265.	4/22/78 ♦	Steve Wariner (43)
266.	5/27/78	John Conlee (91)
267.	6/24/78	Joe Sun (356)
268.	7/8/78	Gail Davies (210)
269.	8/26/78	Louise Mandrell (198)
270.	9/9/78	Rodney Crowell (189)
271.	10/7/78	Big Al Downing (380)
272.	12/23/78	Becky Hobbs (384)
273.	1/6/79 ♦	Randy Travis (52)
274.	3/10/79	Lorrie Morgan (96)
275.	4/14/79	Chris LeDoux (333)
276.	9/8/79	Rosanne Cash (126)
277.	9/29/79	Stephanie Winslow (304)
278.	10/6/79	Lacy J. Dalton (176)
279.	10/13/79	Sylvia (185)
280.	10/27/79	Carlene Carter (326)
281.	12/15/79	Dean Dillon (317)
282.	3/1/80	Keith Stegall (369)
283.	4/12/80	Deborah Allen (323)
284.	4/19/80 ♦	Ricky Skaggs (84)
285.	10/11/80	Terri Gibbs (365)
286.	10/18/80	Gary Morris (130)
287.	11/22/80	Ray Charles (329)
288.	1/17/81	Shelly West (221)
289.	5/16/81	K.T. Oslin (239)
290.	5/16/81 ♦	George Strait (6)
291.	6/13/81	John Schneider (224)
292.	6/20/81	The Whites (279)
293.	9/19/81	Lee Greenwood (90)
294.	5/8/82	Paul Overstreet (237)
295.	2/26/83	Robin Lee (362)
296.	4/30/83	Dan Seals (122)
297.	5/28/83	Mark Gray (334)
298.	8/20/83	Exile (147)
299.	10/8/83 ♦	Kathy Mattea (93)
300.	12/17/83	The Judds (106)
301.	2/11/84 ♦	Vince Gill (50)
302.	9/29/84	Keith Whitley (177)
303.	10/6/84	Sawyer Brown (69)
304.	11/10/84	Pam Tillis (133)
305.	1/26/85	The Forester Sisters (173)
306.	1/26/85	Restless Heart (131)
307.	3/23/85	Judy Rodman (339)
308.	6/1/85	Southern Pacific (266)
309.	6/8/85	Holly Dunn (199)
310.	7/27/85	T. Graham Brown (190)
311.	10/26/85	Billy Joe Royal (250)
312.	11/16/85	Michael Johnson (325)
313.	12/7/85 ♦	Patty Loveless (71)
314.	12/28/85	Marty Stuart (169)
315.	3/1/86 ♦	Dwight Yoakam (108)
316.	4/5/86	Sweethearts Of The Rodeo (300)
317.	4/19/86	Tom Wopat (396)
318.	7/12/86	Lyle Lovett (351)
319.	7/26/86	Larry Boone (353)
320.	9/20/86	The O'Kanes (390)
321.	12/20/86	Ricky Van Shelton (114)
322.	1/10/87	Highway 101 (196)
323.	3/14/87	Suzy Bogguss (200)
324.	3/21/87	Desert Rose Band (241)
325.	4/18/87	Baillie & The Boys (308)
326.	7/4/87	Foster & Lloyd (381)
327.	8/1/87 ♦	Shenandoah (127)
328.	3/5/88	Skip Ewing (315)
329.	3/5/88	Mike Reid (387)
330.	5/7/88	David Ball (335)
331.	8/27/88 ♦	Neal McCoy (155)
332.	10/29/88	Linda Davis (399)
333.	11/19/88	Lionel Cartwright (298)
334.	2/18/89	Clint Black (53)
335.	3/25/89 ♦	Garth Brooks (28)
336.	4/15/89	Mary Chapin Carpenter (149)
337.	9/2/89	Travis Tritt (77)
338.	9/30/89	The Kentucky Headhunters (398)
339.	10/21/89	Alan Jackson (38)
340.	2/10/90	Mark Collie (284)
341.	3/10/90	Doug Stone (154)
342.	3/17/90	Lee Roy Parnell (214)
343.	8/4/90 ♦	Mark Chesnutt (89)
344.	8/25/90	Joe Diffie (99)
345.	11/3/90	Aaron Tippin (158)
346.	12/22/90	Billy Dean (187)

TOP ARTIST DEBUTS (Cont'd)

#	Date	Artist
347.	3/16/91	McBride & The Ride (318)
348.	3/23/91	Diamond Rio (115)
349.	5/11/91	Hal Ketchum (251)
350.	5/18/91	Trisha Yearwood (94)
351.	6/8/91	Collin Raye (86)
352.	6/22/91 ♦	Brooks & Dunn (62)
353.	9/14/91	Little Texas (208)
354.	10/12/91	Sammy Kershaw (134)
355.	11/9/91	Tracy Lawrence (109)
356.	2/15/92	Wynonna (157)
357.	4/4/92	Confederate Railroad (268)
358.	4/4/92	Billy Ray Cyrus (201)
359.	5/2/92	Martina McBride (105)
360.	6/20/92	The Mavericks (350)
361.	8/15/92	Radney Foster (400)
362.	8/22/92	Tracy Byrd (161)
363.	10/3/92	John Michael Montgomery (97)
364.	10/10/92 ♦	Tim McGraw (63)
365.	2/13/93	Lari White (337)
366.	2/20/93	Doug Supernaw (348)
367.	3/6/93	Toby Keith (110)
368.	3/27/93	Shania Twain (139)
369.	6/5/93	John Berry (231)
370.	7/10/93	Clay Walker (120)
371.	9/18/93	Rick Trevino (288)
372.	10/16/93 ♦	Faith Hill (103)
373.	11/20/93	BlackHawk (244)
374.	12/18/93	Kenny Chesney (156)
375.	3/5/94	David Lee Murphy (316)
376.	6/25/94	Chely Wright (328)
377.	10/1/94	Rhett Akins (354)
378.	10/8/94 ♦	Bryan White (218)
379.	11/19/94	Wade Hayes (264)
380.	2/25/95	Ty Herndon (246)
381.	3/11/95	Jeff Carson (359)
382.	4/8/95	Daryle Singletary (336)
383.	7/15/95	Terri Clark (252)
384.	8/19/95 ♦	Lonestar (146)
385.	12/9/95	Ricochet (270)
386.	1/27/96 ♦	Jo Dee Messina (219)
387.	2/3/96	Mindy McCready (342)
388.	3/9/96	Paul Brandt (392)
389.	4/13/96	Trace Adkins (269)
390.	5/25/96	LeAnn Rimes (235)
391.	6/8/96	Mark Wills (261)
392.	8/17/96	Deana Carter (338)
393.	8/24/96	Gary Allan (312)
394.	3/15/97	Lee Ann Womack (259)
395.	3/29/97	Sara Evans (344)
396.	10/25/97 ♦	Dixie Chicks (183)
397.	8/1/98	Chad Brock (397)
398.	12/12/98 ♦	Andy Griggs (388)
399.	2/6/99	Brad Paisley (389)
400.	2/27/99 ♦	SheDaisy (370)

Artist's Top 400 ranking is shown in parenthesis after name.

♦ highest ranking artist of the Top 400 Artists debuting that year

TOP ARTIST ACHIEVEMENTS

MOST CHART HITS

1. George Jones 165
2. Eddy Arnold 146
3. Johnny Cash 136
4. Willie Nelson 114
5. Ray Price 109
6. Dolly Parton 106
7. Merle Haggard 104
8. Hank Williams, Jr. 100
9. Conway Twitty 97
10. Webb Pierce 96
11. Waylon Jennings 96
12. Marty Robbins 94
13. Carl Smith 93
14. Ernest Tubb 91
15. Buck Owens 90
16. Faron Young 89
17. George Strait 87
18. Hank Snow 85
19. Garth Brooks 85
20. Elvis Presley 85
21. Reba McEntire 82
22. Don Gibson 82
23. Porter Wagoner 81
24. Kitty Wells 81
25. Jim Reeves 80
26. Bill Anderson 80

MOST TOP 40 HITS

1. George Jones 142
2. Eddy Arnold 127
3. Johnny Cash 101
4. Dolly Parton 87
5. Conway Twitty 85
6. Merle Haggard 82
7. Waylon Jennings 82
8. Ernest Tubb 82
9. Marty Robbins 81
10. Webb Pierce 80
11. Ray Price 80
12. Willie Nelson 79
13. Hank Williams, Jr. 77
14. Buck Owens 74
15. Faron Young 74
16. George Strait 70
17. Reba McEntire 70
18. Jim Reeves 69
19. Carl Smith 69
20. Mel Tillis 67
21. Loretta Lynn 66
22. Alabama 65
23. Hank Snow 65
24. Don Gibson 65
25. Porter Wagoner 64
26. Sonny James 63

MOST TOP 10 HITS

1. Eddy Arnold 92
2. George Jones 78
3. Conway Twitty 75
4. Merle Haggard 71
5. George Strait 64
6. Ernest Tubb 58
7. Red Foley 56
8. Dolly Parton 55
9. Webb Pierce 54
10. Waylon Jennings 53
11. Johnny Cash 52
12. Reba McEntire 52
13. Charley Pride 52
14. Alabama 51
15. Jim Reeves 51
16. Loretta Lynn 51
17. Ronnie Milsap 49
18. Buck Owens 47
19. Marty Robbins 47
20. Ray Price 46
21. Don Williams 45
22. Sonny James 43
23. Hank Snow 43
24. Hank Williams, Jr. 42
25. Willie Nelson 41
26. Faron Young 41

MOST #1 HITS

1. Conway Twitty 40
2. Merle Haggard 38
3. George Strait 36
4. Ronnie Milsap 35
5. Alabama 32
6. Charley Pride 29
7. Eddy Arnold 28
8. Dolly Parton 24
9. Sonny James 23
10. Buck Owens 21
11. Reba McEntire 21
12. Kenny Rogers 21
13. Willie Nelson 20
14. Tammy Wynette 20
15. Alan Jackson 19
16. Garth Brooks 18
17. Crystal Gayle 18
18. Earl Thomas Conley 18
19. Don Williams 17
20. Oak Ridge Boys 17
21. Mickey Gilley 17
22. Eddie Rabbitt 17
23. Brooks & Dunn 17

MOST WEEKS AT THE #1 POSITION

1. Eddy Arnold 145
2. Webb Pierce 111
3. Buck Owens 82
4. Hank Williams 82
5. George Strait 70
6. Johnny Cash 69
7. Sonny James 66
8. Marty Robbins 63
9. Jim Reeves 58
10. Merle Haggard 57
11. Hank Snow 56
12. Conway Twitty 52
13. Tim McGraw 51
14. Elvis Presley 50
15. Charley Pride 49
16. Ray Price 47
17. Ronnie Milsap 47
18. Al Dexter 47
19. Alabama 40
20. Red Foley 40
21. Alan Jackson 39
22. Tammy Wynette 37
23. Lefty Frizzell 36

MOST CROSSOVER HITS

1. Elvis Presley 61
2. Johnny Cash 52
3. Eddy Arnold 37
4. Glen Campbell 37
5. Kenny Rogers 34
6. Marty Robbins 31
7. Anne Murray 28
8. Jim Reeves 27
9. Dolly Parton 25
10. Sonny James 21
11. John Denver 21
12. Buck Owens 19
13. Roger Miller 19
14. Alabama 18
15. Tim McGraw 17
16. Willie Nelson 17
17. Tammy Wynette 16
18. Charley Pride 16
19. George Strait 16
20. Faith Hill 16
21. Olivia Newton-John 16
22. Mac Davis 16

Ties are broken according to rank in the *Top 400 Artists* section.

TOP ARTIST ACHIEVEMENTS (Cont'd)

MOST CONSECUTIVE #1 HITS

1. 21 **Alabama** (1980-87)
2. 16 **Earl Thomas Conley** (1983-89)
3. 16 **Sonny James** (1967-71)
4. 15 **Buck Owens** (1963-67)
5. 11 **George Strait** (1986-89)
6. 11 **Conway Twitty** (1974-77)
7. 10 **Ronnie Milsap** (1980-83)
8. 9 **Merle Haggard** (1973-76)
9. 9 **Webb Pierce** (1953-56)
10. 9 **Dan Seals** (1985-89)
11. 8 **Eddy Arnold** (1948-49)
12. 8 **The Judds** (1984-87)
13. 8 **T.G. Sheppard** (1980-83)

Excludes Christmas hits, re-issues, B-sides, and duos (unless they add to the streak).

MOST CONSECUTIVE TOP 10 HITS

1. 67 **Eddy Arnold** (1945-56)
2. 65 **Merle Haggard** (1966-85)
3. 56 **Red Foley** (1945-56)
4. 48 **Ronnie Milsap** (1974-92)
5. 42 **Alabama** (1980-94)
6. 38 **Charley Pride** (1971-84)
7. 37 **Webb Pierce** (1952-58)
8. 36 **Conway Twitty** (1968-77)
9. 35 **Buck Owens** (1962-72)
10. 34 **Waylon Jennings** (1973-85)
11. 33 **Hank Williams** (1949-55)
12. 32 **Eddie Rabbitt** (1976-88)
13. 31 **George Strait** (1982-91)
14. 31 **Ernest Tubb** (1949-53)

Excludes Christmas hits, re-issues, B-sides, and duos (unless they add to the streak).

ARTISTS WITH LONGEST CHART CAREERS

Dates		Artist (Years/Months/Weeks)
1/29/44	– 1/8/00	**Gene Autry** (55/11/1)
6/30/45	– 1/29/00	**Eddy Arnold** (54/7/0)
10/29/55	– 2/23/02	**George Jones** (46/4/0)
7/6/46	– 1/4/92	**Roy Rogers** (45/6/0)
2/12/44	– 6/24/89	**Roy Acuff** (45/4/2)
3/24/58	– 6/29/02 +	**Osborne Brothers** (44/3/1+)
11/26/55	– 12/19/98	**Johnny Cash** (43/0/3)
3/2/57	– 10/2/99	**Patsy Cline** (42/7/0)
7/16/55	– 1/3/98	**Elvis Presley** (42/5/3)
8/9/47	– 5/6/89	**Hank Williams** (41/9/0)
4/6/57	– 1/3/98	**Brenda Lee** (40/9/0)
6/13/60	– 9/23/00	**Loretta Lynn** (40/3/1)

+ still charted as of 6/29/02

ARTISTS WITH LONGEST SPAN BETWEEN CHART HITS

Dates		Artist (Years/Months/Weeks)
6/9/51	– 12/26/98	**Gene Autry** (47/6/2)
9/10/49	– 8/23/80	**Sons Of The Pioneers** (30/11/2)
8/22/70	– 12/28/96	**Bobby Helms** (26/4/1)
12/9/67	– 8/22/92	**Geezinslaw Brothers** (24/8/2)
3/20/61	– 9/29/84	**The Everly Brothers** (23/6/1)
1/13/79	– 10/23/99	**Barbra Streisand** (20/9/1)
2/4/50	– 9/26/70	**Roy Rogers** (20/7/3)
10/13/58	– 10/29/77	**Jimmie Rodgers** (19/0/2)
9/15/58	– 5/7/77	**Duane Eddy** (18/7/3)
10/13/79	– 5/30/98	**Olivia Newton-John** (18/7/2)
10/9/48	– 10/15/66	**Cliffie Stone** (18/0/1)
5/27/50	– 5/4/68	**Elton Britt** (17/11/1)

ARTISTS WHO NEVER HIT #1

	Artist Rank	
1.	116	Skeeter Davis
2.	135	Jimmy Newman
3.	137	Wilburn Brothers
4.	140	Slim Whitman
5.	142	Tommy Overstreet
6.	145	Nat Stuckey
7.	148	Narvel Felts
8.	153	Bob Luman
9.	160	Rex Allen, Jr.
10.	162	Brenda Lee
11.	163	Freddy Weller
12.	168	David Rogers
13.	169	Marty Stuart
14.	175	Susan Raye

To quality, artist must rank in the Top 175.

ARTISTS FIRST HIT IS THEIR BIGGEST HIT

Billy Ray Cyrus Jeannie C. Riley
Donna Fargo Jean Shepard
Red Foley Connie Smith
George Morgan Kitty Wells
Marie Osmond Shelly West

To qualify, an artist's first hit has to have reached #1 and has to be ranked as their biggest hit. The artist must also have a minimum of 20 hits.

ONE-HIT WONDERS

1. **The Davis Sisters**
   .... *I Forgot More Than You'll Ever Know* (1^8/'53)
2. **Leon Payne**............... *I Love You Because* (1^2/'50)
3. **Slim Willet**
   ......*Don't Let The Stars (Get In Your Eyes)* (1^1/'52)

The above artists' only chart hit reached the #1 position.

CHART FACTS & FEATS

Top Hits: All-Time / 1944-49 / 1950s / 1960s / 1970s / 1980s / 1990-2001

Singles Of Longevity: 1944-49 / 1950s / 1960s / 1970s / 1980s / 1990-2001

MVPs

Songs With Longest Titles p. 565

Songs With Most Charted Versions p. 565

Top Country Labels

Country Music Association Awards: Single of the Year / Song of the Year

Country Music Hall Of Fame

Christmas Singles 1944-2001 pp. 568-570

Label Abbreviations

TOP 100 #1 HITS
ALL-TIME

Peak Year	Wks Chr	Wks T40	Wks T10	Wks @ #1	Rank	Title	Artist
50	44	44	44	21	1.	I'm Moving On	Hank Snow
47	46	46	41	21	2.	I'll Hold You In My Heart (Till I Can Hold You In My Arms)	Eddy Arnold
55	37	37	34	21	3.	In The Jailhouse Now	Webb Pierce
56	45	45	41	20	4.	Crazy Arms	Ray Price
54	41	41	40	20	5.	I Don't Hurt Anymore	Hank Snow
48	54	54	53	19	6.	Bouquet Of Roses	Eddy Arnold
61	37	37	29	19	7.	Walk On By	Leroy Van Dyke
54	36	36	32	17	8.	Slowly	Webb Pierce
49	28	28	27	17	9.	Slipping Around	Margaret Whiting & Jimmy Wakely
56	27	27	26	17	10.	Heartbreak Hotel	Elvis Presley
49	42	42	40	16	11.	Lovesick Blues	Hank Williams
46	29	29	29	16	12.	Guitar Polka	Al Dexter
63	30	30	24	16	13.	Love's Gonna Live Here	Buck Owens
46	23	23	23	16	14.	New Spanish Two Step	Bob Wills
47	23	23	23	16	15.	Smoke! Smoke! Smoke! (That Cigarette)	Tex Williams
51	31	31	31	15	16.	Slow Poke	Pee Wee King
52	30	30	30	15	17.	The Wild Side Of Life	Hank Thompson
60	36	36	30	14	18.	Please Help Me, I'm Falling	Hank Locklin
60	34	34	29	14	19.	He'll Have To Go	Jim Reeves
52	29	29	29	14	20.	Jambala (On The Bayou)	Hank Williams
51	25	25	25	14	21.	The Shot Gun Boogie	Tennessee Ernie
46	23	23	23	14	22.	Divorce Me C.O.D.	Merle Travis
47	22	22	22	14	23.	So Round, So Firm, So Fully Packed	Merle Travis
44	30	30	30	13	24.	So Long Pal	Al Dexter
55	32	32	28	13	25.	Love, Love, Love	Webb Pierce
56	30	30	28	13	26.	Singing The Blues	Marty Robbins
44	27	27	27	13	27.	Smoke On The Water	Red Foley
58	34	34	25	13	28.	City Lights	Ray Price
58	29	29	20	13	29.	Alone With You	Faron Young
50	20	20	20	13	30.	Chattanoogie Shoe Shine Boy	Red Foley
53	19	19	19	13	31.	Kaw-Liga	Hank Williams
55	32	32	28	12	32.	I Don't Care	Webb Pierce
51	28	28	28	12	33.	Always Late (With Your Kisses)	Lefty Frizzell
53	27	27	27	12	34.	There Stands The Glass	Webb Pierce
60	34	34	26	12	35.	Alabam	Cowboy Copas
49	31	31	26	12	36.	Don't Rob Another Man's Castle	Eddy Arnold
48	32	32	31	11	37.	One Has My Name (The Other Has My Heart)	Jimmy Wakely
51	27	27	27	11	38.	I Want To Be With You Always	Lefty Frizzell
51	24	24	24	11	39.	I Wanna Play House With You	Eddy Arnold
51	23	23	23	11	40.	There's Been A Change In Me	Eddy Arnold
62	24	24	22	11	41.	Don't Let Me Cross Over	Carl Butler
45	20	20	20	11	42.	You Two Timed Me One Time Too Often	Tex Ritter
60	36	36	30	10	43.	Wings Of A Dove	Ferlin Husky
54	29	29	27	10	44.	More And More	Webb Pierce
56	28	28	25	10	45.	Don't Be Cruel / Hound Dog	Elvis Presley
50	25	25	25	10	46.	Why Don't You Love Me	Hank Williams
57	27	27	21	10	47.	Gone	Ferlin Husky
58	23	23	19	10	48.	Ballad Of A Teenage Queen	Johnny Cash
55	21	21	18	10	49.	Sixteen Tons	"Tennessee" Ernie Ford
59	21	21	18	10	50.	The Battle Of New Orleans	Johnny Horton

TOP 100 #1 HITS (Cont'd)
ALL-TIME

Peak Year	Wks Chr	Wks T40	Wks T10	Wks @ #1	Rank	Title	Artist
61	19	19	18	10	51.	Don't Worry	Marty Robbins
59	19	19	17	10	52.	The Three Bells	The Browns
48	39	39	37	9	53.	Anytime	Eddy Arnold
45	31	31	31	9	54.	Shame On You	Spade Cooley
53	26	26	26	9	55.	Mexican Joe	Jim Reeves
62	26	26	21	9	56.	Wolverton Mountain	Claude King
57	24	24	20	9	57.	Young Love	Sonny James
61	23	23	18	9	58.	Hello Walls	Faron Young
66	25	24	13	9	59.	Almost Persuaded	David Houston
51	33	33	33	8	60.	Let Old Mother Nature Have Her Way	Carl Smith
48	32	32	27	8	61.	Just A Little Lovin' (Will Go A Long, Long Way)	Eddy Arnold
51	27	27	27	8	62.	The Rhumba Boogie	Hank Snow
58	34	34	26	8	63.	Oh Lonesome Me	Don Gibson
53	26	26	26	8	64.	Hey Joe!	Carl Smith
53	26	26	26	8	65.	I Forgot More Than You'll Ever Know	The Davis Sisters
57	26	26	25	8	66.	Four Walls	Jim Reeves
51	25	25	25	8	67.	Hey, Good Lookin'	Hank Williams
52	24	24	24	8	68.	(When You Feel Like You're In Love) Don't Just Stand There	Carl Smith
45	22	22	22	8	69.	At Mail Call Today	Gene Autry
53	22	22	22	8	70.	It's Been So Long	Webb Pierce
99	41	37	21	8	71.	Amazed	Lonestar
50	21	21	21	8	72.	Long Gone Lonesome Bues	Hank Williams
58	24	24	20	8	73.	Guess Things Happen That Way	Johnny Cash
57	22	22	20	8	74.	Wake Up Little Susie	The Everly Brothers
64	28	27	19	8	75.	Once A Day	Connie Smith
62	21	21	14	8	76.	Devil Woman	Marty Robbins
55	32	32	29	7	77.	Loose Talk	Carl Smith
61	32	32	24	7	78.	Tender Years	George Jones
64	26	26	22	7	79.	My Heart Skips A Beat	Buck Owens
59	26	26	22	7	80.	El Paso	Marty Robbins
62	27	27	21	7	81.	Mama Sang A Song	Bill Anderson
57	26	26	21	7	82.	Bye Bye Love	The Everly Brothers
45	21	21	21	7	83.	I'm Losing My Mind Over You	Al Dexter
63	27	27	20	7	84.	Still	Bill Anderson
63	26	26	19	7	85.	Ring Of Fire	Johnny Cash
64	26	24	18	7	86.	I Guess I'm Crazy	Jim Reeves
66	23	21	15	7	87.	There Goes My Everything	Jack Greene
66	19	18	13	7	88.	Waitin' In Your Welfare Line	Buck Owens
56	43	43	39	6	89.	I Walk The Line	Johnny Cash
53	23	23	23	6	90.	A Dear John Letter	Jean Shepard with Ferlin Husky
53	23	23	23	6	91.	Your Cheatin' Heart	Hank Williams
44	20	20	20	6	92.	I'm Wastin' My Tears On You	Tex Ritter
62	23	23	19	6	93.	She Thinks I Still Care	George Jones
45	19	19	19	6	94.	Oklahoma Hills	Jack Guthrie
64	27	27	18	6	95.	I Don't Care (Just As Long As You Love Me)	Buck Owens
52	18	18	18	6	96.	It Wasn't God Who Made Honky Tonk Angels	Kitty Wells
01	29	28	17	6	97.	Ain't Nothing 'Bout You	Brooks & Dunn
64	22	22	17	6	98.	Understand Your Man	Johnny Cash
99	28	27	16	6	99.	Breathe	Faith Hill
01	26	25	15	6	100.	I'm Already There	Lonestar

TOP 25 #1 HITS — 1944-1949

Peak Year	Wks Chr	Wks T40	Wks T10	Wks @ #1	Rank	Title	Artist
47	46	46	41	21	1.	I'll Hold You In My Heart (Till I Can Hold You In My Arms)	Eddy Arnold
48	54	54	53	19	2.	Bouquet Of Roses	Eddy Arnold
49	28	28	27	17	3.	Slipping Around	Margaret Whiting & Jimmy Wakely
49	42	42	40	16	4.	Lovesick Blues	Hank Williams
46	29	29	29	16	5.	Guitar Polka	Al Dexter
46	23	23	23	16	6.	New Spanish Two Step	Bob Wills
47	23	23	23	16	7.	Smoke! Smoke! Smoke! (That Cigarette)	Tex Williams
46	23	23	23	14	8.	Divorce Me C.O.D.	Merle Travis
47	22	22	22	14	9.	So Round, So Firm, So Fully Packed	Merle Travis
44	30	30	30	13	10.	So Long Pal	Al Dexter
44	27	27	27	13	11.	Smoke On The Water	Red Foley
49	31	31	26	12	12.	Don't Rob Another Man's Castle	Eddy Arnold
48	32	32	31	11	13.	One Has My Name (The Other Has My Heart)	Jimmy Wakely
45	20	20	20	11	14.	You Two Timed Me One Time Too Often	Tex Ritter
48	39	39	37	9	15.	Anytime	Eddy Arnold
45	31	31	31	9	16.	Shame On You	Spade Cooley
48	32	32	27	8	17.	Just A Little Lovin' (Will Go A Long, Long Way)	Eddy Arnold
45	22	22	22	8	18.	At Mail Call Today	Gene Autry
45	21	21	21	7	19.	I'm Losing My Mind Over You	Al Dexter
44	20	20	20	6	20.	I'm Wastin' My Tears On You	Tex Ritter
45	19	19	19	6	21.	Oklahoma Hills	Jack Guthrie
44	15	15	15	6	22.	Straighten Up And Fly Right	The King Cole Trio
47	38	38	38	5	23.	It's A Sin	Eddy Arnold
49	28	28	26	5	24.	I Love You So Much It Hurts	Jimmy Wakely
46	13	13	13	5	25.	Wine, Women And Song	Al Dexter

TOP 25 #1 HITS — 1950s

Peak Year	Wks Chr	Wks T40	Wks T10	Wks @ #1	Rank	Title	Artist
50	44	44	44	21	1.	I'm Moving On	Hank Snow
55	37	37	34	21	2.	In The Jailhouse Now	Webb Pierce
56	45	45	41	20	3.	Crazy Arms	Ray Price
54	41	41	40	20	4.	I Don't Hurt Anymore	Hank Snow
54	36	36	32	17	5.	Slowly	Webb Pierce
56	27	27	26	17	6.	Heartbreak Hotel	Elvis Presley
51	31	31	31	15	7.	Slow Poke	Pee Wee King
52	30	30	30	15	8.	The Wild Side Of Life	Hank Thompson
52	29	29	29	14	9.	Jambalaya (On The Bayou)	Hank Williams
51	25	25	25	14	10.	The Shot Gun Boogie	Tennessee Ernie
55	32	32	28	13	11.	Love, Love, Love	Webb Pierce
56	30	30	28	13	12.	Singing The Blues	Marty Robbins
58	34	34	25	13	13.	City Lights	Ray Price
58	29	29	20	13	14.	Alone With You	Faron Young
50	20	20	20	13	15.	Chattanoogie Shoe Shine Boy	Red Foley
53	19	19	19	13	16.	Kaw-Liga	Hank Williams
55	32	32	28	12	17.	I Don't Care	Webb Pierce
51	28	28	28	12	18.	Always Late (With Your Kisses)	Lefty Frizzell
53	27	27	27	12	19.	There Stands The Glass	Webb Pierce
51	27	27	27	11	20.	I Want To Be With You Always	Lefty Frizzell
51	24	24	24	11	21.	I Wanna Play House With You	Eddy Arnold
51	23	23	23	11	22.	There's Been A Change In Me	Eddy Arnold
54	29	29	27	10	23.	More And More	Webb Pierce
56	28	28	25	10	24.	Don't Be Cruel / Hound Dog	Elvis Presley
50	25	25	25	10	25.	Why Don't You Love Me	Hank Williams

TOP 25 #1 HITS — 1960s

Peak Year	Wks Chr	Wks T40	Wks T10	Wks @ #1	Rank	Title	Artist
61	37	37	29	19	1.	Walk On By	Leroy Van Dyke
63	30	30	24	16	2.	Love's Gonna Live Here	Buck Owens
60	36	36	30	14	3.	Please Help Me, I'm Falling	Hank Locklin
60	34	34	29	14	4.	He'll Have To Go	Jim Reeves
60	34	34	26	12	5.	Alabam	Cowboy Copas
62	24	24	22	11	6.	Don't Let Me Cross Over	Carl Butler
60	36	36	30	10	7.	Wings Of A Dove	Ferlin Husky
61	19	19	18	10	8.	Don't Worry	Marty Robbins
62	26	26	21	9	9.	Wolverton Mountain	Claude King
61	23	23	18	9	10.	Hello Walls	Faron Young
66	25	24	13	9	11.	Almost Persuaded	David Houston
64	28	27	19	8	12.	Once A Day	Connie Smith
62	21	21	14	8	13.	Devil Woman	Marty Robbins
61	32	32	24	7	14.	Tender Years	George Jones
64	26	26	22	7	15.	My Heart Skips A Beat	Buck Owens
62	27	27	21	7	16.	Mama Sang A Song	Bill Anderson
63	27	27	20	7	17.	Still	Bill Anderson
63	26	26	19	7	18.	Ring Of Fire	Johnny Cash
64	26	24	18	7	19.	I Guess I'm Crazy	Jim Reeves
66	23	21	15	7	20.	There Goes My Everything	Jack Greene
66	19	18	13	7	21.	Waitin' In Your Welfare Line	Buck Owens
62	23	23	19	6	22.	She Thinks I Still Care	George Jones
64	27	27	18	6	23.	I Don't Care (Just As Long As You Love Me)	Buck Owens
64	22	22	17	6	24.	Understand Your Man	Johnny Cash
64	25	22	15	6	25.	Dang Me	Roger Miller

TOP 25 #1 HITS — 1970s

Peak Year	Wks Chr	Wks T40	Wks T10	Wks @ #1	Rank	Title	Artist
72	19	18	12	6	1.	My Hang-Up Is You	Freddie Hart
77	18	14	10	6	2.	Luckenbach, Texas (Back To The Basics Of Love)	Waylon Jennings
75	15	13	8	6	3.	Convoy	C.W. McCall
71	19	18	13	5	4.	Kiss An Angel Good Mornin'	Charley Pride
70	20	19	12	5	5.	Rose Garden	Lynn Anderson
77	19	14	10	5	6.	Here You Come Again	Dolly Parton
71	15	13	10	5	7.	When You're Hot, You're Hot	Jerry Reed
70	20	18	10	4	8.	Hello Darlin'	Conway Twitty
70	17	16	10	4	9.	Baby, Baby (I Know You're A Lady)	David Houston
71	16	15	10	4	10.	Empty Arms	Sonny James
71	16	14	9	4	11.	I'm Just Me	Charley Pride
70	15	14	9	4	12.	Don't Keep Me Hangin' On	Sonny James
77	18	15	8	4	13.	Don't It Make My Brown Eyes Blue	Crystal Gayle
78	16	12	8	4	14.	Mammas Don't Let Your Babies Grow Up To Be Cowboys	Waylon & Willie
73	17	14	7	4	15.	If We Make It Through December	Merle Haggard
77	20	13	7	4	16.	Heaven's Just A Sin Away	The Kendalls
70	14	13	7	4	17.	It's Just A Matter Of Time	Sonny James
71	24	22	13	3	18.	Easy Loving	Freddie Hart
71	20	18	12	3	19.	Help Me Make It Through The Night	Sammi Smith
71	19	17	12	3	20.	I Won't Mention It Again	Ray Price
72	23	17	10	3	21.	The Happiest Girl In The Whole U.S.A.	Donna Fargo
73	19	16	10	3	22.	You've Never Been This Far Before	Conway Twitty
72	16	15	10	3	23.	Carolyn	Merle Haggard
70	16	14	9	3	24.	Endlessly	Sonny James
70	16	14	9	3	25.	He Loves Me All The Way	Tammy Wynette

TOP 25 #1 HITS — 1980s

Peak Year	Wks Chr	Wks T40	Wks T10	Wks @ #1	Rank	Title	Artist
80	15	9	8	3	1.	Coward Of The County	Kenny Rogers
80	15	13	7	3	2.	My Heart	Ronnie Milsap
80	14	10	7	3	3.	Lookin' For Love	Johnny Lee
87	22	13	6	3	4.	Forever And Ever, Amen	Randy Travis
85	22	14	8	2	5.	Have Mercy	The Judds
83	23	15	7	2	6.	Islands In The Stream	Kenny Rogers With Dolly Parton
83	22	15	7	2	7.	Houston (Means I'm One Day Closer To You)	Larry Gatlin/Gatlin Brothers
84	22	15	7	2	8.	Why Not Me	The Judds
85	23	14	7	2	9.	Lost In The Fifties Tonight (In The Still Of The Night)	Ronnie Milsap
88	22	14	7	2	10.	When You Say Nothing At All	Keith Whitley
86	19	14	7	2	11.	Mind Your Own Business	Hank Williams, Jr.
84	20	13	7	2	12.	To All The Girls I've Loved Before	Julio Iglesias & Willie Nelson
80	16	12	7	2	13.	I Believe In You	Don Williams
80	14	10	7	2	14.	My Heroes Have Always Been Cowboys	Willie Nelson
89	26	24	6	2	15.	A Woman In Love	Ronnie Milsap
88	21	15	6	2	16.	I'll Leave This World Loving You	Ricky Van Shelton
82	21	15	6	2	17.	Always On My Mind	Willie Nelson
87	23	14	6	2	18.	Somewhere Tonight	Highway 101
89	22	14	6	2	19.	I'm No Stranger To The Rain	Keith Whitley
88	20	14	6	2	20.	Eighteen Wheels And A Dozen Roses	Kathy Mattea
80	16	13	6	2	21.	One In A Million	Johnny Lee
81	16	11	6	2	22.	Love In The First Degree	Alabama
81	15	11	6	2	23.	(There's) No Gettin' Over Me	Ronnie Milsap
81	15	11	6	2	24.	Never Been So Loved (In All My Life)	Charley Pride
81	15	10	6	2	25.	I Don't Need You	Kenny Rogers

TOP 25 #1 HITS — 1990-2001

Peak Year	Wks Chr	Wks T40	Wks T10	Wks @ #1	Rank	Title	Artist
99	41	37	21	8	1.	Amazed	Lonestar
01	29	28	17	6	2.	Ain't Nothing 'Bout You	Brooks & Dunn
99	28	27	16	6	3.	Breathe	Faith Hill
01	26	25	15	6	4.	I'm Already There	Lonestar
99	37	34	13	6	5.	How Forever Feels	Kenny Chesney
98	42	25	13	6	6.	Just To See You Smile	Tim McGraw
97	20	20	13	6	7.	It's Your Love	Tim McGraw with Faith Hill
00	42	41	17	5	8.	How Do You Like Me Now?!	Toby Keith
99	39	34	16	5	9.	Something Like That	Tim McGraw
99	33	32	15	5	10.	I Love You	Martina McBride
00	46	28	15	5	11.	My Next Thirty Years	Tim McGraw
99	24	23	15	5	12.	Please Remember Me	Tim McGraw
00	32	29	14	5	13.	I Hope You Dance	Lee Ann Womack
01	28	26	14	5	14.	I Wanna Talk About Me	Toby Keith
01	27	25	14	5	15.	Austin	Blake Shelton
01	20	20	12	5	16.	Where Were You (When The World Stopped Turning)	Alan Jackson
90	21	20	11	5	17.	Love Without End, Amen	George Strait
97	20	20	10	5	18.	One Night At A Time	George Strait
90	20	19	10	5	19.	I've Come To Expect It From You	George Strait
97	20	20	9	5	20.	Love Gets Me Every Time	Shania Twain
95	20	19	9	5	21.	I Like It, I Love It	Tim McGraw
92	20	16	9	5	22.	Achy Breaky Heart	Billy Ray Cyrus
00	27	26	15	4	23.	That's The Way	Jo Dee Messina
00	36	34	14	4	24.	What About Now	Lonestar
99	37	32	14	4	25.	Write This Down	George Strait

SINGLES OF LONGEVITY

Peak Year	Peak Pos	Peak Wks	Wks Chr	Rank	Title	Artist
\multicolumn{7}{c}{**1944-49**}						
48	1	19	54	1.	Bouquet Of Roses	Eddy Arnold
47	1	21	46	2.	I'll Hold You In My Heart (Till I Can Hold You In My Arms)	Eddy Arnold
49	1	16	42	3.	Lovesick Blues	Hank Williams
49	1	1	40	4.	Tennessee Saturday Night	Red Foley
48	1	9	39	5.	Anytime	Eddy Arnold
47	1	5	38	6.	It's A Sin	Eddy Arnold
48	2	2	38	7.	Humpty Dumpty Heart	Hank Thompson
48	3	2	35	8.	Tennessee Waltz	Pee Wee King
\multicolumn{7}{c}{**1950s**}						
57	1	4	52	1.	Fraulein	Bobby Helms
51	1	1	46	2.	Cold, Cold Heart	Hank Williams
56	1	20	45	3.	Crazy Arms	Ray Price
50	1	21	44	4.	I'm Moving On	Hank Snow
56	1	6	43	5.	I Walk The Line	Johnny Cash
54	1	20	41	6.	I Don't Hurt Anymore	Hank Snow
54	1	1	41	7.	One By One	Kitty Wells And Red Foley
59	2	1	40	8.	Heartaches By The Number	Ray Price
\multicolumn{7}{c}{**1960s**}						
61	1	2	39	1.	I Fall To Pieces	Patsy Cline
61	1	19	37	2.	Walk On By	Leroy Van Dyke
60	1	14	36	3.	Please Help Me, I'm Falling	Hank Locklin
60	1	10	36	4.	Wings Of A Dove	Ferlin Husky
63	1	1	36	5.	Talk Back Trembling Lips	Ernest Ashworth
60	1	14	34	6.	He'll Have To Go	Jim Reeves
60	1	12	34	7.	Alabam	Cowboy Copas
61	2	1	34	8.	The Window Up Above	George Jones
\multicolumn{7}{c}{**1970s**}						
70	1	1	26	1.	For The Good Times	Ray Price
71	1	3	24	2.	Easy Loving	Freddie Hart
72	1	3	23	3.	The Happiest Girl In The Whole U.S.A.	Donna Fargo
73	7	2	22	4.	Let Me Be There	Olivia Newton-John
72	12	1	22	5.	To Get To You	Jerry Wallace
75	1	3	21	6.	Rhinestone Cowboy	Glen Campbell
75	2	1	21	7.	Reconsider Me	Narvel Felts
75	6	2	21	8.	Wrong Road Again	Crystal Gayle
\multicolumn{7}{c}{**1980s**}						
86	9	2	29	1.	You Can't Stop Love	Schuyler, Knobloch & Overstreet
85	1	1	28	2.	Baby's Got Her Blue Jeans On	Mel McDaniel
84	1	1	28	3.	I've Been Around Enough To Know	John Schneider
87	6	1	28	4.	The Hand That Rocks The Cradle	Glen Campbell With Steve Wariner
85	1	1	27	5.	Seven Spanish Angels	Ray Charles (with Willie Nelson)
86	1	1	27	6.	Bop	Dan Seals
88	3	1	27	7.	I'm Gonna Miss You, Girl	Michael Martin Murphey
89	3	1	27	8.	From The Word Go	Michael Martin Murphey
\multicolumn{7}{c}{**1990-2001**}						
01	5	1	48	1.	Right Where I Need To Be	Gary Allan
00	1	5	46	2.	My Next Thirty Years	Tim McGraw
00	6	2	45	3.	Let's Make Love	Faith Hill with Tim McGraw
00	2	3	44	4.	I Will...But	SheDaisy
98	1	6	42	5.	Just To See You Smile	Tim McGraw
00	1	5	42	6.	How Do You Like Me Now?!	Toby Keith
99	1	8	41	7.	Amazed	Lonestar
00	1	3	41	8.	Cowboy Take Me Away	Dixie Chicks

MVP'S (Most Valuable Platters)

Following is a list of records in this book valued at $50 or more.

Year	Value		Title	Artist…Label & Number
55	$3000	1.	Baby Let's Play House / I'm Left, You're Right, She's Gone	Elvis Presley…Sun 217
56	$2500	2.	I Forgot To Remember To Forget / Mystery Train	Elvis Presley…Sun 223
60	$500	3.	I'm A Honky Tonk Girl	Loretta Lynn…Zero 107
57	$150	4.	Mean Woman Blues	Elvis Presley…RCA Victor 2-1515
56	$100	5.	Love Me	Elvis Presley…RCA Victor EPA-992
51	$100	6.	Hot Rod Race	Arkie Shibley…Gilt-Edge 5021
47	$100	7.	Move It On Over	Hank Williams…MGM 10033
56	$80	8.	Without Your Love	Bobby Lord…Columbia 21539
48	$75	9.	Honky Tonkin'	Hank Williams…MGM 10171
45	$60	10.	Each Minute Seems A Million Years	Eddy Arnold…Bluebird 33-0527
54	$60	11.	You Can't Have My Love	Wanda Jackson & Billy Gray…Decca 29140
56	$60	12.	Dixie Fried / I'm Sorry, I'm Not Sorry	Carl Perkins…Sun 249
56	$60	13.	Blue Suede Shoes	Carl Perkins…Sun 234
61	$60	14.	Crazy Bullfrog	Lewis Pruitt…Decca 31201
44	$50	15.	Mexico Joe	Ivie Anderson…Exclusive 3113
49	$50	16.	Sittin' On The Doorstep	Woody Carter…Macy's 100
55	$50	17.	Why Baby Why	George Jones…Starday 202
57	$50	18.	Your True Love	Carl Perkins…Sun 261
56	$50	19.	Boppin' The Blues	Carl Perkins…Sun 243
56	$50	20.	Heartbreak Hotel / I Was The One	Elvis Presley…RCA Victor 47-6420
56	$50	21.	I Want You, I Need You, I Love You / My Baby Left Me	Elvis Presley…RCA Victor 47-6540
55	$50	22.	That's All Right	Marty Robbins…Columbia 21351
55	$50	23.	Maybelline	Marty Robbins…Columbia 21446
45	$50	24.	Triflin' Gal	Walt Shrum…Coast 2010
56	$50	25.	Be-Bop-A-Lula	Gene Vincent…Capitol 3450
50	$50	26.	Why Don't You Love Me	Hank Williams…MGM K10696
50	$50	27.	They'll Never Take Her Love From Me / Why Should We Try Anymore	Hank Williams…MGM K10760
49	$50	28.	Wedding Bells	Hank Williams…MGM 10401
50	$50	29.	Moanin' The Blues / Nobody's Lonesome For Me	Hank Williams…MGM K10832
49	$50	30.	Lovesick Blues / Never Again (Will I Knock On Your Door)	Hank Williams…MGM 10352
50	$50	31.	Long Gone Lonesome Blues / My Son Calls Another Man Daddy	Hank Williams…MGM K10645
49	$50	32.	Mansion On The Hill	Hank Williams…MGM 10328
48	$50	33.	I'm A Long Gone Daddy	Hank Williams…MGM 10212
50	$50	34.	I Just Don't Like This Kind Of Livin'	Hank Williams…MGM 10609
51	$50	35.	I Can't Help It (If I'm Still In Love With You) / Howlin' At The Moon	Hank Williams…MGM K10961
51	$50	36.	Cold, Cold Heart / Dear John	Hank Williams…MGM K10904

SONGS WITH LONGEST TITLES

	# of Char.		Artist
1.	78	She Wakes Me With A Kiss Every Morning (And She Loves Me To Sleep Every Night)	Nat Stuckey
2.	76	It's For God, And Country, And You Mom (That's Why I'm Fighting In Viet Nam)	Ernest Tubb
3.	70	I Wouldn't Live In New York City (If They Gave Me The Whole Dang Town)	Buck Owens
4.	69	If You Think I'm Crazy Now (You Should Have Seen Me When I Was A Kid)	Bobby Bare
5.	67	If You're Gonna Play In Texas (You Gotta Have A Fiddle In The Band)	Alabama
6.	67	Lyin', Cheatin', Woman Chasin', Honky Tonkin', Whiskey Drinkin' You	Loretta Lynn
7.	66	I'm Just An Old Chunk Of Coal (But I'm Gonna Be A Diamond Someday)	John Anderson
8.	66	Don't Wipe The Tears That You Cry For Him (On My Good White Shirt)	Tommy Collins
9.	66	It's The Bible Against The Bottle (In The Battle For Daddy's Soul)	Earl Thomas Conley
10.	65	There Won't Be No Country Music (There Won't Be No Rock 'N' Roll)	C.W. McCall

SONGS WITH MOST CHARTED VERSIONS

	Total Versions		Songwriter(s)
1.	8	I Love You Because	Leon Payne
2.	7	Making Believe	Jimmy Work
3.	7	Slipping Around	Floyd Tillman
4.	7	Sweet Dreams	Don Gibson
5.	7	Why Baby Why	Luther Dixon/Larry Harrison
6.	6	Candy Kisses	George Morgan
7.	6	I Fall To Pieces	Hank Cochran/Harlan Howard
8.	6	Lovesick Blues	Hank Williams
9.	6	My Elusive Dreams	Curly Putman/Billy Sherrill
10.	6	Oh Lonesome Me	Don Gibson
11.	6	Satisfied Mind	Red Hayes/Jack Rhodes
12.	6	Tennessee Waltz	Redd Stewart/Pee Wee King
13.	6	Wild Side Of Life	William Warren/Arlie A. Carter
14.	6	You're The Reason	Bobby Edwards/Mildred Imes/Fred Henley/Terry Fell

TOP COUNTRY LABELS

		Total Hits			Total Hits
1.	RCA	2,267	21.	Reprise	118
2.	Columbia	1,602	22.	Door Knob	100
3.	Capitol	1,480	23.	Giant	91
4.	MCA	1,212	24.	Asylum	90
5.	Epic	946	25.	Soundwaves	89
6.	Mercury	837	26.	Sun	71
7.	Warner	825	27.	Polydor	67
8.	Decca	820	28.	Starday	65
9.	Curb	604	29.	Chart	64
10.	Dot	320	30.	King	55
11.	United Artists	319	31.	Imperial	53
12.	ABC	315	32.	Republic	52
13.	MGM	305	33.	Step One	52
14.	Arista	274	34.	MTM	51
15.	Elektra	234	35.	GRT	49
16.	Liberty	207	36.	Ovation	48
17.	Atlantic	199	37.	Kapp	47
18.	Monument	173	38.	Playboy	46
19.	BNA	152	39.	DreamWorks	45
20.	Hickory	140	40.	Evergreen	45

COUNTRY MUSIC ASSOCIATION AWARDS
Single of the Year — Song of the Year

SINGLE OF THE YEAR Title...*Artist(s)*	YEAR	SONG OF THE YEAR Title...*Songwriter(s)*
There Goes My Everything...*Jack Greene*	1967	There Goes My Everything...*Dallas Frazier*
Harper Valley P.T.A. ...*Jeannie C. Riley*	1968	Honey...*Bobby Russell*
A Boy Named Sue...*Johnny Cash*	1969	The Carroll County Accident...*Bob Ferguson*
Okie From Muskogee...*Merle Haggard*	1970	Sunday Morning Coming Down...*Kris Kristofferson*
Help Me Make It Through The Night...*Sammi Smith*	1971	Easy Loving...*Freddie Hart*
The Happiest Girl In The Whole U.S.A. ...*Donna Fargo*	1972	Easy Loving...*Freddie Hart*
Behind Closed Doors...*Charlie Rich*	1973	Behind Closed Doors...*Kenny O'Dell*
Country Bumpkin...*Cal Smith*	1974	Country Bumpkin...*Don Wayne*
Before The Next Teardrop Falls...*Freddy Fender*	1975	Back Home Again...*John Denver*
Good Hearted Woman... *Waylon Jennings & Willie Nelson*	1976	Rhinestone Cowboy...*Larry Weiss*
Lucille...*Kenny Rogers*	1977	Lucille...*Roger Bowling & Hal Bynum*
Heaven's Just A Sin Away...*The Kendalls*	1978	Don't It Make My Brown Eyes Blue...*Richard Leigh*
The Devil Went Down To Georgia... *Charlie Daniels Band*	1979	The Gambler...*Don Schlitz*
He Stopped Loving Her Today...*George Jones*	1980	He Stopped Loving Her Today... *Bobby Braddock & Curly Putman*
Elvira...*Oak Ridge Boys*	1981	He Stopped Loving Her Today... *Bobby Braddock & Curly Putman*
Always On My Mind...*Willie Nelson*	1982	Always On My Mind... *Johnny Christopher, Wayne Carson & Mark James*
Swingin'...*John Anderson*	1983	Always On My Mind... *Johnny Christopher, Wayne Carson & Mark James*
A Little Good News...*Anne Murray*	1984	The Wind Beneath My Wings... *Larry Henley & Jeff Silbar*
Why Not Me...*The Judds*	1985	God Bless The USA...*Lee Greenwood*
Bop...*Dan Seals*	1986	On The Other Hand...*Paul Overstreet & Don Schlitz*
Forever And Ever, Amen...*Randy Travis*	1987	Forever And Ever, Amen... *Paul Overstreet & Don Schlitz*
Eighteen Wheels And A Dozen Roses...*Kathy Mattea*	1988	80's Ladies...*K.T. Oslin*
I'm No Stranger To The Rain...*Keith Whitley*	1989	Chiseled In Stone...*Max D. Barnes & Vern Gosdin*
When I Call Your Name...*Vince Gill*	1990	Where've You Been...*Jon Vezner & Don Henry*
Friends In Low Places...*Garth Brooks*	1991	When I Call Your Name...*Vince Gill & Tim DuBois*
Achy Breaky Heart...*Billy Ray Cyrus*	1992	Look At Us...*Vince Gill & Max D. Barnes*
Chattahoochee...*Alan Jackson*	1993	I Still Believe In You... *Vince Gill & John Barlow Jarvis*
I Swear...*John Michael Montgomery*	1994	Chattahoochee...*Alan Jackson & Jim McBride*
When You Say Nothing At All... *Alison Krauss & Union Station*	1995	Independence Day...*Gretchen Peters*
Check Yes Or No...*George Strait*	1996	Go Rest High On That Mountain...*Vince Gill*
Strawberry Wine...*Deana Carter*	1997	Strawberry Wine...*Matraca Berg & Gary Harrison*
Holes In The Floor Of Heaven...*Steve Wariner*	1998	Holes In The Floor Of Heaven... *Billy Kirsch & Steve Wariner*
Wide Open Spaces...*Dixie Chicks*	1999	This Kiss... *Beth Nielsen Chapman, Robin Lerner & Annie Roboff*
I Hope You Dance...*Lee Ann Womack*	2000	I Hope You Dance...*Mark D. Sanders & Tia Sillers*
I Am A Man Of Constant Sorrow...*Soggy Bottom Boys*	2001	Murder On Music Row...*Larry Cordle & Larry Shell*

COUNTRY MUSIC HALL OF FAME

YEAR	INDUCTEE(S)	YEAR	INDUCTEE(S)
1961	Jimmie Rodgers Fred Rose Hank Williams	1982	Lefty Frizzell Roy Horton Marty Robbins
1962	Roy Acuff	1983	"Little" Jimmy Dickens
1963	(elections were held but no candidate received enough votes)	1984	Ralph Peer Floyd Tillman
1964	Tex Ritter	1985	Lester Flatt & Earl Scruggs
1965	Ernest Tubb	1986	Whitey Ford (The Duke Of Paducah) Wesley H. Rose
1966	Eddy Arnold James R. Denny George D. Hay Uncle Dave Macon	1987	Roy Brasfield
1967	Red Foley J.L. (Joe) Frank Jim Reeves Stephen H. Sholes	1988	Loretta Lynn Roy Rogers
1968	Bob Wills	1989	Jack Stapp Cliffie Stone Hank Thompson
1969	Gene Autry	1990	"Tennessee" Ernie Ford
1970	Original Carter Family (A.P., Maybelle, Sara) Bill Monroe	1991	Boudleaux & Felice Bryant
1971	Arthur Edward Satherley	1992	George Jones Frances Preston
1972	Jimmie Davis	1993	Willie Nelson
1973	Chet Atkins Patsy Cline	1994	Merle Haggard
1974	Owen Bradley Frank "Pee Wee" King	1995	Roger Miller Jo Walker-Meador
1975	Minnie Pearl	1996	Patsy Montana Buck Owens Ray Price
1976	Paul Cohen Kitty Wells	1997	Harlan Howard Brenda Lee Cindy Walker
1977	Merle Travis	1998	George Morgan Elvis Presley E.W. "Bud" Wendell Tammy Wynette
1978	Grandpa Jones	1999	Johnny Bond Dolly Parton Conway Twitty
1979	Hubert Long Hank Snow	2000	Charley Pride Faron Young
1980	Johnny Cash Connie B. Gay Original Sons of the Pioneers	2001	Bill Anderson The Jordanaires The Delmore Brothers Don Law The Everly Brothers The Louvin Brothers Don Gibson Ken Nelson Homer & Jethro Webb Pierce Waylon Jennings Sam Phillips
1981	Vernon Dalhart Grant Turner	2002	(at time of book's publication, elections had not yet taken place)

8-5-03
Floyd Cramer
Carl Smith

CHRISTMAS SINGLES 1944-2001

Titles in bold type made the Top 10; the peak position/peak year is shown below each title. The complete chart data for each of these songs may be found in the Artist Section.

ADKINS, Trace
   The Christmas Song
      #64/'98

ALABAMA
1. Christmas In Dixie
   #35/'82; #47/'97; #40/'98; #37/'99
2. Angels Among Us
   #51/'93; #28/'94
3. The Blessings
   #72/'96
4. Santa Claus (I Still Believe In You)
   #71/'98
5. Rockin' Around The Christmas Tree
   #64/'99

ALLAN, Gary
   Please Come Home For Christmas
      #70/'96

ANDERSON, John
   Christmas Time
      #57/'94

ARNOLD, Eddy
1. **Will Santy Come To Shanty Town /**
   #5/'49
2. **C-H-R-I-S-T-M-A-S**
   #7/'49
3. Christmas Can't Be Far Away
   #12/'54

AUTRY, Gene
1. **Here Comes Santa Claus (Down Santa Claus Lane)**
   #5/'47; #4/'48; #8/'49
2. **Rudolph, The Red-Nosed Reindeer**
   #1(1)/'49; #5/'50; #55/'98; #60/'99
3. **Frosty The Snow Man**
   #4/'50

BELLAMY BROTHERS
   It's So Close To Christmas (And I'm So Far From Home)
      #62/'81

BERRY, John
   O Holy Night
      #55/'95; #63/'97

BLACK, Clint
1. Til' Santa's Gone (Milk And Cookies)
   #58/'95; #65/'96; #40/'97; #38/'98; #34/'99

BLACK, Clint (Cont'd)
2. The Kid
   #71/'95; #67/'98; #71/'99

BLACKHAWK
   We Three Kings (Star Of Wonder)
      #75/'97

BOYD, Jimmy
   I Saw Mommy Kissing Santa Claus
      #7/'52

BRANDT, Paul
   Six Tons Of Toys
      #66/'99

BROOKS, Garth
1. The Old Man's Back In Town
   #48/'92; #59/'97
2. White Christmas
   #70/'94; #65/'99
3. Belleau Wood
   #41/'97; #65/'98
4. Santa Looked A Lot Like Daddy
   #56/'97
5. The Old Man's Back In Town
   #59/'97
6. Go Tell It On The Mountain
   #72/'98
7. Sleigh Ride
   #54/'99
8. Baby Jesus Is Born
   #62/'99
9. It's The Most Wonderful Time Of The Year
   #56/'99
10. There's No Place Like Home For The Holidays
   #63/'99
11. God Rest Ye Merry Gentlemen
   #69/'99
12. Call Me Claus /
   #55/'01
13. 'Zat You, Santa Claus?
   #56/'01

BROWN, Jim Ed/Helen Cornelius
   Fall Softly Snow
      #91/'77

BYRD, Tracy
   Merry Christmas From Texas Y'all
      #55/'99

CARSON, Jeff
   Santa Got Lost In Texas
      #70/'95

CARTER, Carlene
   Rockin' Little Christmas
      #66/'94

CASH, Johnny
   The Little Drummer Boy
      #24/'59

CHESNEY, Kenny
   Away In A Manger
      #67/'99

CHESNUTT, Mark
   What Child Is This
      #75/'96

DENVER, John
   Please, Daddy
      #69/'73

DIFFIE, Joe
   Leroy The Redneck Reindeer
      #33/'95; #46/'96; #54/'97

ELMO & PATSY
   Grandma Got Run Over By A Reindeer
      #92/'83; #64/'97; #48/'99

ENGVALL, Bill
   Here's Your Sign
      #39/'98; #46/'99

EWING, Skip
   Christmas Carol
      #68/'95; #60/'97; #44/'99

FOXWORTHY, Jeff
1. Redneck 12 Days Of Christmas
   #18/'95; #39/'96; #39/'97; #37/'98; #35/'99
2. 'Twas The Night After Christmas
   #67/'96

GILL, Vince
1. Have Yourself A Merry Little Christmas
   #52/'93; #54/'94; #64/'97
2. It Won't Be The Same This Year
   #74/'94
3. Blue Christmas
   #74/'98

GILMAN, Billy
   Warm & Fuzzy
      #50/'00

HAGGARD, Merle
   If We Make It Through December
      #1(4)/'73

CHRISTMAS SINGLES 1944-2001 (Cont'd)

HARLING, Keith
 . Santa's Got A Semi
  #60/'99; #60/'00

HARRIS, Emmylou
 Light Of The Stable
  #99/'75

HELMS, Bobby
 Jingle Bell Rock
  #13/'57; #60/'96

HILL, Faith
 Where Are You Christmas?
  #26/'00

JACKSON, Alan
 1. I Only Want You For Christmas
  #41/'91; #48/'95; #48/'97
 2. Honky Tonk Christmas
  #53/'93; #59/'94
 3. Rudolph The Red-Nosed Reindeer
  #56/'96
 4. A Holly Jolly Christmas
  #51/'97

JUDDS, The
 Silver Bells
  #68/'97

KEITH, Toby
 1. Santa I'm Right Here
  #50/'95
 2. Old Toy Trains
  #57/'00

KERSHAW, Sammy
 Christmas Time's A Comin'
  #50/'94; #53/'97

LEE, Brenda
 Rockin' Around The Christmas Tree
  #62/'97

LONESTAR
 1. I'll Be Home For Christmas
  #75/'96; #59/'98
 2. All My Love For Christmas
  #61/'98
 3. Little Drummer Boy
  #46/'00
 4. Santa Claus Is Comin' To Town
  #69/'00
 5. Winter Wonderland
  #72/'00
 6. Have Yourself A Merry Little Christmas
  #75/'00

LUMAN, Bob
 A Christmas Tribute
  #92/'77

MANDRELL, Louise/R.C. Bannon
 Christmas Is Just A Song For Us This Year
  #35/'82

McBRIDE, Martina
 1. O Holy Night
  #74/'96; #67/'97; #49/'98; #57/'99; #41/'00
 2. Have Yourself A Merry Little Christmas
  #54/'98; #53/'99; #59/'00
 3. Let It Snow, Let It Snow, Let It Snow
  #64/'98; #73/'99
 4. White Christmas
  #75/'99; #69/'00
 5. The Christmas Song (Chestnuts Roasting On An Open Fire)
  #67/'00

McENTIRE, Reba
 1. The Christmas Song (Chestnuts Roasting On An Open Fire)
  #63/'96
 2. I'll Be Home For Christmas
  #68/'98
 3. Away In A Manger
  #73/'98
 4. Secret Of Giving
  #58/'99
 5. I Saw Mama Kissing Santa Claus
  #50/'99

MONTGOMERY GENTRY
 Merry Christmas From The Family
  #38/'00

MORGAN, Craig
 The Kid In Me
  #68/'00

MORGAN, Lorrie
 1. My Favorite Things
  #64/'93; #69/'99
 2. Sleigh Ride
  #67/'95; #64/'96; #42/'99

MULLINS, Dee
 Remember Bethlehem
  #71/'70

NEWSONG
 The Christmas Shoes
  #31/'00

NITTY GRITTY DIRT BAND
 Colorado Christmas
  #93/'83

NORWOOD, Daron
 The Working Elf Blues
  #75/'94

PARNELL, Lee Roy
 Please Come Home For Christmas
  #71/'96

PARTON, Dolly
 1. **Hard Candy Christmas**
  #8/'82; #73/'97
 2. The Greatest Gift Of All
  Kenny Rogers & Dolly Parton
  #53/'84
 3. Winter Wonderland/Sleigh Ride (Medley)
  #70/'98

PRESLEY, Elvis
 Blue Christmas
  #55/'97

RESTLESS HEART
 Little Drummer Boy
  #58/'98

RICOCHET
 Let It Snow Let It Snow Let It Snow
  #43/'96; #44/'97; #41/'98; #39/'99

RIMES, LeAnn
 Put A Little Holiday In Your Heart
  #51/'96; #71/'97

RITTER, Tex
 Christmas Carols By The Old Corral
  #2(1)/'45

ROGERS, Kenny
 1. The Greatest Gift Of All
  Kenny Rogers & Dolly Parton
  #53/'84
 2. Mary, Did You Know
  Kenny Rogers with Wynonna
  #55/'96

SAWYER BROWN
 It Wasn't His Child
  #51/'88

SHeDAISY
 1. Deck The Halls
  #40/'99; #37/'00
 2. Jingle Bells
  #44/'00

CHRISTMAS SINGLES 1944-2001 (Cont'd)

STRAIT, George
1. Santa Claus Is Coming To Town
   #73/'95; #69/'97
2. Merry Christmas Strait To You
   #58/'97
3. Let It Snow, Let It Snow, Let It Snow
   #72/'99
4. I Know What I Want For Christmas
   #73/'99
5. Jingle Bell Rock
   #69/'99
6. Old Time Christmas
   #62/'00
7. Christmas Cookies
   #33/'01

3 OF HEARTS
The Christmas Shoes
#39/'01

TIPPIN, Aaron
Jingle Bell Rock
#52/'01

TRACTORS, The
1. The Santa Claus Boogie
   #41/'94; #63/'95
2. Santa Claus Is Comin' (In A Boogie Woogie Choo Choo Train)
   #43/'95; #65/'97

TUBB, Ernest
1. **Blue Christmas /**
   #1(1)/'49; #9/'50; #5/'51
2. **White Christmas**
   #7/'49

VANCE, Vince, & The Valiants
All I Want For Christmas Is You
#55/'93; #52/'94; #52/'95; #49/'96; #43/'97; #31/'99

WALKER, Clay
Blue Christmas
#51/'00

WARINER, Steve
Christmas In Your Arms
#65/'00

WHITE, Bryan
Holiday Inn
#62/'99

WYNONNA
1. Let's Make A Baby King
   #61/'93
2. Mary, Did You Know
   Kenny Rogers with Wynonna
   #55/'96

YEARWOOD, Trisha
1. It Wasn't His Child
   #60/'94
2. Reindeer Boogie
   #63/'98
3. Santa On The Rooftop
   Trisha Yearwood & Rosie O'Donnell
   #72/'99

YOAKAM, Dwight
Santa Claus Is Back In Town
#60/'97

LABEL ABBREVIATIONS

ABC-Para.	ABC-Paramount
Almo So.	Almo Sounds
America/Sm.	America/Smash
Arista Nash.	Arista Nashville
Atlantic Amer.	Atlantic America
Capitol Amer.	Capitol Americana
Country Show.	Country Showcase America
Curb/Univ.	Curb/Universal
DreamWor.	DreamWorks
Full Moon/Asy.	Full Moon/Asylum
Jack O'Diam.	Jack O'Diamonds
Louisiana Hay.	Louisiana Hayride
MCA Nash.	MCA Nashville
Pacific Chall.	Pacific Challenger
RCA Vic.	RCA Victor
Southern Tr.	Southern Tracks
Warner/Cu.	Warner/Curb

#1 HITS

This section lists, in chronological order, all 1,432 songs that hit #1 on *Billboard's* Country singles charts from January 8, 1944 through July 13, 2002.

From May 15, 1948 through October 13, 1958, when *Billboard* published more than one weekly Country singles chart, the chart designation and #1 weeks on each chart are listed beneath the record title. The chart designations are:

        BS: Best Sellers
        JY: Jockeys
        JB: Juke Box

The date shown is the earliest date that a record hit #1 on any of the Country singles charts. The weeks column lists the total weeks at #1, from whichever chart it achieved its highest total. This total is not a combined total from the various Country singles charts.

Because of the multiple charts used for this research, some dates are duplicated, as certain #1 hits may have peaked on the same week on different charts. *Billboard* also showed ties at #1 on some of these charts; therefore, the total weeks for each year may calculate out to more than 52.

Billboard has not published an issue for the last week of the year since 1976. For the years 1976 through 1991, *Billboard* considered the charts listed in the last published issue of the year to be "frozen" and all chart positions remained the same for the unpublished week. This frozen chart data is included in our tabulations. Since 1992, *Billboard* has compiled a Country singles chart for the last week of the year, even though an issue is not published. This chart is only available through Member Services of Billboard.com or by mail. Our tabulations include this unpublished chart data.

See the introduction pages of this book for more details on researching the Country singles charts.

  DATE: Date single first peaked at the #1 position
  WKS: Total weeks single held the #1 position
    ↕: Indicates single hit #1, dropped down, and then returned to the #1 spot

---

The top hit of each year is boxed out for quick reference. The top hit is determined by most weeks at the #1 position, followed by total weeks in the Top 10, Top 40, and total weeks charted.

#1 HITS

1/8/44 through 5/8/48: Billboard's only Country chart is the "Juke Box" chart.

1944

#	DATE	WKS	Title	Artist
1.	1/8	5↕	Pistol Packin' Mama	Bing Crosby & the Andrews Sisters
2.	2/5	3	Pistol Packin' Mama	Al Dexter
3.	2/26	3↕	Ration Blues	Louis Jordan
4.	3/11	1	Rosalita	Al Dexter
5.	3/18	1	They Took The Stars Out Of Heaven	Floyd Tillman
6.	3/25	13↕	So Long Pal	Al Dexter
7.	4/1	2↕	Too Late To Worry	Al Dexter
8.	6/10	6↕	Straighten Up And Fly Right	King Cole Trio
9.	7/29	5	Is You Is Or Is You Ain't (Ma' Baby)	Louis Jordan
10.	9/2	4	Soldier's Last Letter	Ernest Tubb
11.	9/23	13	Smoke On The Water	Red Foley
12.	12/23	6	I'm Wastin' My Tears On You	Tex Ritter

1945

#	DATE	WKS	Title	Artist
1.	2/3	7↕	I'm Losing My Mind Over You	Al Dexter
2.	3/17	1	There's A New Moon Over My Shoulder	Jimmie Davis
3.	3/31	9↕	Shame On You	Spade Cooley
4.	4/14	2↕	Smoke On The Water	Bob Wills
5.	5/19	8↕	At Mail Call Today	Gene Autry
6.	7/7	1	Stars And Stripes On Iwo Jima	Bob Wills
7.	7/28	6↕	Oklahoma Hills	Jack Guthrie
8.	8/25	11↕	You Two Timed Me One Time Too Often	Tex Ritter
9.	10/27	4↕	With Tears In My Eyes	Wesley Tuttle
10.	11/24	4↕	Sioux City Sue	Dick Thomas
11.	11/24	1	Shame On You	Lawrence Welk Orchestra with Red Foley
12.	12/8	4↕	It's Been So Long Darling	Ernest Tubb
13.	12/15	3↕	Silver Dew On The Blue Grass Tonight	Bob Wills

1946

#	DATE	WKS	Title	Artist
1.	1/5	3↕	You Will Have To Pay	Tex Ritter
2.	1/5	1	White Cross On Okinawa	Bob Wills
3.	2/2	16↕	Guitar Polka	Al Dexter
4.	5/18	16↕	New Spanish Two Step	Bob Wills
5.	9/14	5↕	Wine, Women And Song	Al Dexter
6.	10/12	14↕	Divorce Me C.O.D.	Merle Travis

1947

#	DATE	WKS	Title	Artist
1.	1/18	2↕	Rainbow At Midnight	Ernest Tubb
2.	2/8	14	So Round, So Firm, So Fully Packed	Merle Travis
3.	5/17	2↕	New Jolie Blonde (New Pretty Blonde)	Red Foley
4.	5/24	1	What Is Life Without Love	Eddy Arnold
5.	6/7	1	Sugar Moon	Bob Wills
6.	6/14	5	It's A Sin	Eddy Arnold
7.	7/19	16↕	Smoke! Smoke! Smoke! (That Cigarette)	Tex Williams
8.	11/1	21↕	I'll Hold You In My Heart (Till I Can Hold You In My Arms)	Eddy Arnold

1948

#	DATE	WKS	Title	Artist
1.	4/3	9	Anytime	Eddy Arnold

JB: 9 / BS: 3

5/15/48: Billboard's "Best Sellers" chart debuts.

#	DATE	WKS	Title	Artist
2.	6/5	19↕	Bouquet Of Roses	Eddy Arnold

BS: 19↕ / JB: 18↕

| 3. | 6/5 | 3↕ | Texarkana Baby | Eddy Arnold |

BS: 3↕ / JB: 1

| 4. | 9/18 | 8↕ | Just A Little Lovin' (Will Go A Long, Long Way) | Eddy Arnold |

JB: 8↕ / BS: 4↕

| 5. | 11/13 | 11↕ | One Has My Name (The Other Has My Heart) | Jimmy Wakely |

BS: 11↕ / JB: 7↕

| 6. | 12/25 | 1 | A Heart Full Of Love (For A Handful of Kisses) | Eddy Arnold |

BS: 1

1949

#	DATE	WKS	Title	Artist
1.	1/22	5↕	I Love You So Much It Hurts	Jimmy Wakely

JB: 5↕ / BS: 4↕

| 2. | 3/5 | 12↕ | Don't Rob Another Man's Castle | Eddy Arnold |

JB: 12↕ / BS: 6↕

| 3. | 3/19 | 1 | Tennessee Saturday Night | Red Foley |

JB: 1

| 4. | 4/2 | 3↕ | Candy Kisses | George Morgan |

BS: 3↕

| 5. | 5/7 | 16↕ | Lovesick Blues | Hank Williams |

BS: 16↕ / JB: 10↕

| 6. | 6/18 | 3↕ | One Kiss Too Many | Eddy Arnold |

JB: 3↕

6/25/49: First time "Country & Western" is shown as chart title.

| 7. | 7/30 | 4 | I'm Throwing Rice (At The Girl That I Love) | Eddy Arnold |

BS: 4 / JB: 3↕

| 8. | 9/10 | 3↕ | Why Don't You Haul Off And Love Me | Wayne Raney |

JB: 3↕ / BS: 2↕

| 9. | 9/24 | 1 | Slipping Around | Ernest Tubb |

JB: 1

| 10. | 10/8 | 17 | Slipping Around | Margaret Whiting & Jimmy Wakely |

BS: 17 / JB: 12↕

12/10/49: Billboard's "Jockeys" chart debuts.

| 11. | 12/10 | 4 | Mule Train | Tennessee Ernie |

JY: 4

| 12. | 1/7 | 1 | Rudolph, The Red-Nosed Reindeer | Gene Autry |

JY: 1

#1 HITS

1949 (cont'd)

13. 1/7 **1 Blue Christmas** *Ernest Tubb*
JB: 1

1950

	DATE	WKS		
1.	1/14	2↕	**I Love You Because**	*Leon Payne*

JY: 2↕

2. 1/14 **1 Blues Stay Away From Me**
Delmore Brothers
JB: 1

3. 1/21 **13 Chattanoogie Shoe Shine Boy** *Red Foley*
JB: 13 / JY: 13↕ / BS: 12

4. 1/28 **1 Take Me In Your Arms And Hold Me**
Eddy Arnold
JB: 1

5. 4/22 **8↕ Long Gone Lonesome Blues**
Hank Williams
JY: 8↕ / BS: 5↕ / JB: 4

6. 5/27 **4↕ Birmingham Bounce** *Red Foley*
BS: 4↕ / JB: 3↕

7. 6/17 **10 Why Don't You Love Me** *Hank Williams*
JY: 10 / BS: 6↕ / JB: 5

8. 6/17 **4 I'll Sail My Ship Alone** *Moon Mullican*
JB: 4 / BS: 1

9. 7/15 **1 Mississippi** *Red Foley*
JB: 1

10. 8/19 **21↕ I'm Moving On** *Hank Snow*
BS: 21↕ / JY: 18↕ / JB: 14

11. 8/26 **3 Goodnight Irene** *Red Foley-Ernest Tubb*
JB: 3 / BS: 2

12. 12/23 **3 If You've Got The Money I've Got The Time** *Lefty Frizzell*
JB: 3

13. 12/30 **1 Moanin' The Blues** *Hank Williams*
JY: 1

1951

1. 1/6 **3↕ I Love You A Thousand Ways**
Lefty Frizzell
JY: 3↕

2. 1/6 **2 The Golden Rocket** *Hank Snow*
BS: 2 / JY: 1

3. 1/13 **14 The Shot Gun Boogie** *Tennessee Ernie*
JB: 14 / BS: 3↕ / JY: 1

4. 2/10 **11↕ There's Been A Change In Me**
Eddy Arnold
JY: 11↕ / BS: 4↕

5. 3/31 **8↕ The Rhumba Boogie** *Hank Snow*
BS: 8↕ / JB: 5 / JY: 2↕

6. 5/12 **1 Cold, Cold Heart** *Hank Williams*
JY: 1

7. 5/19 **3 Kentucky Waltz** *Eddy Arnold*
JB: 3 / BS: 3↕

8. 5/26 **11 I Want To Be With You Always**
Lefty Frizzell
JY: 11 / BS: 6↕ / JB: 5

9. 7/14 **11 I Wanna Play House With You**
Eddy Arnold
JB: 11 / BS: 6↕

10. 8/11 **8↕ Hey, Good Lookin'** *Hank Williams*
JY: 8↕

1951 (cont'd)

11. 9/1 **12↕ Always Late (With Your Kisses)**
Lefty Frizzell
BS: 12↕ / JY: 6↕ / JB: 6

12. 11/3 **15↕ Slow Poke** *Pee Wee King*
JB: 15↕ / BS: 14 / JY: 9↕

13. 12/22 **8↕ Let Old Mother Nature Have Her Way**
Carl Smith
JB: 8↕ / BS: 6 / JY: 3↕

1952

1. 2/2 **3↕ Give Me More, More, More (Of Your Kisses)** *Lefty Frizzell*
JY: 3↕ / JB: 3↕

2. 3/1 **4 Wondering** *Webb Pierce*
JY: 4

3. 3/29 **8↕ (When You Feel Like You're In Love) Don't Just Stand There** *Carl Smith*
JY: 8↕ / BS: 5↕ / JB: 3↕

4. 5/3 **1 Easy On The Eyes** *Eddy Arnold*
BS: 1

5. 5/10 **15 The Wild Side Of Life** *Hank Thompson*
BS: 15 / JB: 15 / JY: 8↕

6. 7/12 **3↕ That Heart Belongs To Me** *Webb Pierce*
JY: 3↕

7. 7/19 **1 Are You Teasing Me** *Carl Smith*
JY: 1

8. 8/16 **4↕ A Full Time Job** *Eddy Arnold*
JY: 4↕

9. 8/23 **6 It Wasn't God Who Made Honky Tonk Angels** *Kitty Wells*
BS: 6 / JB: 5

10. 9/6 **14↕ Jambalaya (On The Bayou)**
Hank Williams
BS: 14↕ / JY: 14↕ / JB: 12↕

11. 12/6 **4↕ Back Street Affair** *Webb Pierce*
JY: 4↕ / JB: 3 / BS: 2↕

12. 12/6 **1 Don't Let The Stars (Get In Your Eyes)**
Slim Willet
JY: 1

13. 12/27 **3 Don't Let The Stars Get In Your Eyes**
Skeets McDonald
JB: 3

1953

1. 1/10 **1 Midnight** *Red Foley*
BS: 1

2. 1/24 **2↕ I'll Go On Alone** *Marty Robbins*
JY: 2↕

3. 1/24 **1 I'll Never Get Out Of This World Alive**
Hank Williams
BS: 1

4. 1/31 **4 No Help Wanted** *The Carlisles*
JB: 4 / JY: 4↕

5. 1/31 **3 Eddy's Song** *Eddy Arnold*
BS: 3

6. 2/7 **3 I Let The Stars Get In My Eyes** *Goldie Hill*
JB: 3

7. 2/21 **13 Kaw-Liga** *Hank Williams*
BS: 13 / JY: 8 / JB: 8↕

8. 4/11 **6↕ Your Cheatin' Heart** *Hank Williams*
JY: 6↕ / JB: 2↕

#1 HITS

1953 (cont'd)

9. 5/9 9↕ **Mexican Joe** *Jim Reeves*
   JB: 9↕ / JY: 7↕ / BS: 6↕
10. 6/6 4↕ **Take These Chains From My Heart** *Hank Williams*
    BS: 4↕
11. 7/11 8↕ **It's Been So Long** *Webb Pierce*
    JY: 8↕ / BS: 6 / JB: 1
12. 8/1 3↕ **Rub-A-Dub-Dub** *Hank Thompson*
    JB: 3↕
13. 8/22 8↕ **Hey Joe!** *Carl Smith*
    JB: 8↕ / JY: 4↕ / BS: 2↕
14. 8/29 6↕ **A Dear John Letter** *Jean Shepard & Ferlin Huskey*
    BS: 6↕ / JB: 4↕
15. 10/17 8↕ **I Forgot More Than You'll Ever Know** *The Davis Sisters*
    JY: 8↕ / BS: 6↕ / JB: 2↕
16. 11/21 12↕ **There Stands The Glass** *Webb Pierce*
    BS: 12↕ / JB: 9↕ / JY: 6↕
17. 12/12 2 **Caribbean** *Mitchell Torok*
    JB: 2
18. 12/19 3↕ **Let Me Be The One** *Hank Locklin*
    JY: 3↕ / JB: 2↕

DATE WKS 1954

1. 1/9 3↕ **Bimbo** *Jim Reeves*
   JY: 3↕
2. 2/20 17 **Slowly** *Webb Pierce*
   BS: 17 / JB: 17↕ / JY: 15
3. 2/20 2 **Wake Up, Irene** *Hank Thompson*
   JB: 2
4. 5/15 1 **I Really Don't Want To Know** *Eddy Arnold*
   JB: 1
5. 6/12 2 **(Oh Baby Mine) I Get So Lonely** *Johnnie & Jack*
   JY: 2
6. 6/19 20 **I Don't Hurt Anymore** *Hank Snow*
   BS: 20 / JB: 20↕ / JY: 18↕
7. 7/3 2 **Even Tho** *Webb Pierce*
   JY: 2
8. 7/31 1 **One By One** *Kitty Wells & Red Foley*
   JB: 1
9. 11/6 10↕ **More And More** *Webb Pierce*
   JB: 10↕ / BS: 9 / JY: 8↕

DATE WKS 1955

1. 1/8 7 **Loose Talk** *Carl Smith*
   BS: 7 / JY: 6↕ / JB: 4
2. 1/29 2 **Let Me Go, Lover!** *Hank Snow*
   JY: 2
3. 2/26 21 **In The Jailhouse Now** *Webb Pierce*
   JB: 21 / BS: 20 / JY: 15
4. 6/18 3 **Live Fast, Love Hard, Die Young** *Faron Young*
   JY: 3
5. 7/9 4 **A Satisfied Mind** *Porter Wagoner*
   JY: 4
6. 7/16 12 **I Don't Care** *Webb Pierce*
   BS: 12 / JY: 12 / JB: 12
7. 10/8 2 **The Cattle Call** *Eddy Arnold*
   BS: 2

1955 (cont'd)

8. 10/22 13↕ **Love, Love, Love** *Webb Pierce*
   JY: 13↕ / JB: 9↕ / BS: 8
9. 10/22 2 **That Do Make It Nice** *Eddy Arnold*
   JB: 2
10. 12/17 10 **Sixteen Tons** *Tennessee Ernie Ford*
    BS: 10 / JB: 7↕ / JY: 3↕

DATE WKS 1956

1. 2/11 4↕ **Why Baby Why** *Red Sovine & Webb Pierce*
   JY: 4↕ / BS: 1 / JB: 1
2. 2/25 5 **I Forgot To Remember To Forget** *Elvis Presley*
   JB: 5 / BS: 2
3. 3/17 17 **Heartbreak Hotel** *Elvis Presley*
   BS: 17 / JB: 13↕ / JY: 12
4. 3/17 2 **I Don't Believe You've Met My Baby** *The Louvin Brothers*
   JY: 2
5. 4/7 3 **Blue Suede Shoes** *Carl Perkins*
   JB: 3
6. 6/23 20↕ **Crazy Arms** *Ray Price*
   JY: 20↕ / BS: 11↕ / JB: 1
7. 7/14 2 **I Want You, I Need You, I Love You** *Elvis Presley*
   BS: 2 / JB: 1
8. 7/21 6↕ **I Walk The Line** *Johnny Cash*
   JB: 6↕ / JY: 1
9. 9/15 10 **Don't Be Cruel/**
   JB: 10 / BS: 5 / JY: 2
10. 10 **Hound Dog** *Elvis Presley*
    JB: 10 / BS: 5
11. 11/10 13 **Singing The Blues** *Marty Robbins*
    BS: 13 / JB: 13 / JY: 11↕

DATE WKS 1957

1. 2/2 9 **Young Love** *Sonny James*
   JY: 9 / BS: 7 / JB: 3↕
2. 3/2 5↕ **There You Go** *Johnny Cash*
   JB: 5↕
3. 4/6 10 **Gone** *Ferlin Husky*
   BS: 10 / JY: 9 / JB: 5↕
4. 5/13 1 **All Shook Up** *Elvis Presley*
   JB: 1
5. 5/20 5 **A White Sport Coat (And A Pink Carnation)** *Marty Robbins*
   BS: 5 / JB: 5 / JY: 1
6. 5/20 1 **Honky Tonk Song** *Webb Pierce*
   JY: 1
7. 5/27 8↕ **Four Walls** *Jim Reeves*
   JY: 8↕

6/17/57: Billboard's last "Juke Box" chart.

8. 7/15 7 **Bye Bye Love** *The Everly Brothers*
   JY: 7 / BS: 7↕
9. 8/5 1 **Let Me Be Your Teddy Bear** *Elvis Presley*
   BS: 1
10. 9/9 2 **Whole Lot Of Shakin' Going On** *Jerry Lee Lewis*
    BS: 2

#1 HITS

1957 (cont'd)

#	DATE	WKS	TITLE / ARTIST
11.	9/16	4↕	**Fraulein** Bobby Helms JY: 4↕ / BS: 3
12.	9/16	4↕	**My Shoes Keep Walking Back To You** Ray Price JY: 4↕
13.	10/14	8↕	**Wake Up Little Susie** The Everly Brothers JY: 8↕ / BS: 7
14.	12/2	1	**Jailhouse Rock** Elvis Presley BS: 1
15.	12/9	4	**My Special Angel** Bobby Helms BS: 4 / JY: 1

1958

#	DATE	WKS	TITLE / ARTIST
1.	1/6	4	**The Story Of My Life** Marty Robbins BS: 4 / JY: 4
2.	1/6	2	**Great Balls Of Fire** Jerry Lee Lewis BS: 2
3.	2/3	10	**Ballad Of A Teenage Queen** Johnny Cash JY: 10 / BS: 8
4.	4/14	8↕	**Oh Lonesome Me** Don Gibson BS: 8↕ / JY: 8↕
5.	5/26	2↕	**Just Married** Marty Robbins JY: 2↕
6.	6/2	3	**All I Have To Do Is Dream** The Everly Brothers BS: 3 / JY: 1
7.	6/23	8	**Guess Things Happen That Way** Johnny Cash BS: 8 / JY: 3↕
8.	7/21	13	**Alone With You** Faron Young JY: 13
9.	8/25	2	**Blue Blue Day** Don Gibson BS: 2
10.	9/8	6	**Bird Dog** The Everly Brothers BS: 6

10/13/58: Billboard's last "Best Sellers" and "Jockeys" charts (replaced with one all-encompassing "Hot C&W Sides" chart).

#	DATE	WKS	TITLE / ARTIST
11.	10/20	13	**City Lights** Ray Price

1959

#	DATE	WKS	TITLE / ARTIST
1.	1/19	5	**Billy Bayou** Jim Reeves
2.	2/23	6	**Don't Take Your Guns To Town** Johnny Cash
3.	4/6	1	**When It's Springtime In Alaska (It's Forty Below)** Johnny Horton
4.	4/13	5	**White Lightning** George Jones
5.	5/18	10	**The Battle Of New Orleans** Johnny Horton
6.	7/27	5	**Waterloo** Stonewall Jackson
7.	8/31	10	**The Three Bells** The Browns
8.	11/9	4	**Country Girl** Faron Young
9.	12/7	2	**The Same Old Me** Ray Price
10.	12/21	7	**El Paso** Marty Robbins

1960

#	DATE	WKS	TITLE / ARTIST
1.	2/8	14	**He'll Have To Go** Jim Reeves
2.	5/16	14	**Please Help Me, I'm Falling** Hank Locklin
3.	8/22	12	**Alabam** Cowboy Copas
4.	11/14	10↕	**Wings Of A Dove** Ferlin Husky

1961

#	DATE	WKS	TITLE / ARTIST
1.	1/9	5	**North To Alaska** Johnny Horton
2.	2/27	10	**Don't Worry** Marty Robbins
3.	5/8	9	**Hello Walls** Faron Young
4.	7/10	4	**Heartbreak U.S.A.** Kitty Wells
5.	8/7	2	**I Fall To Pieces** Patsy Cline
6.	8/21	7↕	**Tender Years** George Jones
7.	9/25	19↕	**Walk On By** Leroy Van Dyke
8.	11/20	2	**Big Bad John** Jimmy Dean

1962

#	DATE	WKS	TITLE / ARTIST
1.	3/10	2↕	**Misery Loves Company** Porter Wagoner
2.	3/17	1	**That's My Pa** Sheb Wooley
3.	3/31	5↕	**She's Got You** Patsy Cline
4.	4/28	2↕	**Charlie's Shoes** Billy Walker
5.	5/19	6	**She Thinks I Still Care** George Jones
6.	6/30	9	**Wolverton Mountain** Claude King
7.	9/1	8	**Devil Woman** Marty Robbins
8.	10/27	7↕	**Mama Sang A Song** Bill Anderson

11/3/62: The 'W' signifying "Western" is dropped from chart title. Chart now designated only as "Hot Country Singles."

#	DATE	WKS	TITLE / ARTIST
9.	11/10	2↕	**I've Been Everywhere** Hank Snow
10.	12/29	11↕	**Don't Let Me Cross Over** Carl Butler & Pearl

1963

#	DATE	WKS	TITLE / ARTIST
1.	1/5	1	**Ruby Ann** Marty Robbins
2.	1/19	3↕	**The Ballad Of Jed Clampett** Flatt & Scruggs
3.	4/13	7↕	**Still** Bill Anderson
4.	5/4	4↕	**Lonesome 7-7203** Hawkshaw Hawkins
5.	6/15	4↕	**Act Naturally** Buck Owens
6.	7/27	7	**Ring Of Fire** Johnny Cash
7.	9/14	4	**Abilene** George Hamilton IV
8.	10/12	1	**Talk Back Trembling Lips** Ernest Ashworth
9.	10/19	16	**Love's Gonna Live Here** Buck Owens

1964

#	DATE	WKS	TITLE / ARTIST
1.	2/8	3↕	**Begging To You** Marty Robbins
2.	2/15	1	**B.J. The D.J.** Stonewall Jackson
3.	3/7	4	**Saginaw, Michigan** Lefty Frizzell
4.	4/4	6	**Understand Your Man** Johnny Cash
5.	5/16	7↕	**My Heart Skips A Beat** Buck Owens
6.	6/6	2	**Together Again** Buck Owens
7.	7/18	6	**Dang Me** Roger Miller
8.	8/29	7	**I Guess I'm Crazy** Jim Reeves

#1 HITS

1964 (cont'd)

9. 10/17 6 I Don't Care (Just As Long As You Love Me) *Buck Owens*
10. 11/28 8 Once A Day *Connie Smith*

1965

DATE	WKS	
1. 1/23 4 You're The Only World I Know *Sonny James*
2. 2/20 5 I've Got A Tiger By The Tail *Buck Owens*
3. 3/27 5 King Of The Road *Roger Miller*
4. 5/1 3↕ This Is It *Jim Reeves*
5. 5/15 2 Girl On The Billboard *Del Reeves*
6. 6/5 2 What's He Doing In My World *Eddy Arnold*
7. 6/19 1 Ribbon Of Darkness *Marty Robbins*
8. 6/26 6 Before You Go *Buck Owens*
9. 8/7 2 The First Thing Ev'ry Morning (And The Last Thing Ev'ry Night) *Jimmy Dean*
10. 8/21 2 Yes, Mr. Peters *Roy Drusky & Priscilla Mitchell*
11. 9/4 1 The Bridge Washed Out *Warner Mack*
12. 9/11 3 Is It Really Over? *Jim Reeves*
13. 10/2 1 Only You (Can Break My Heart) *Buck Owens*
14. 10/9 3↕ Behind The Tear *Sonny James*
15. 10/23 3 Hello Vietnam *Johnny Wright*
16. 11/20 2 May The Bird Of Paradise Fly Up Your Nose *"Little" Jimmy Dickens*
17. 12/4 3 Make The World Go Away *Eddy Arnold*
18. 12/25 2 Buckaroo *Buck Owens & The Buckaroos*

1966

1. 1/8 6 Giddyup Go *Red Sovine*
2. 2/19 7 Waitin' In Your Welfare Line *Buck Owens*
3. 4/9 6 I Want To Go With You *Eddy Arnold*
4. 5/21 4 Distant Drums *Jim Reeves*
5. 6/18 2 Take Good Care Of Her *Sonny James*
6. 7/2 6 Think Of Me *Buck Owens*
7. 8/13 9 Almost Persuaded *David Houston*
8. 10/15 1 Blue Side Of Lonesome *Jim Reeves*
9. 10/22 4 Open Up Your Heart *Buck Owens*
10. 11/19 1 I Get The Fever *Bill Anderson*
11. 11/26 4 Somebody Like Me *Eddy Arnold*
12. 12/24 7 There Goes My Everything *Jack Greene*

1967

1. 2/11 1 Don't Come Home A'Drinkin' (With Lovin' On Your Mind) *Loretta Lynn*
2. 2/18 4↕ Where Does The Good Times Go *Buck Owens*
3. 3/4 1 The Fugitive *Merle Haggard*
4. 3/25 1 I Won't Come In While He's There *Jim Reeves*
5. 4/1 2 Walk Through This World With Me *George Jones*
6. 4/15 2 Lonely Again *Eddy Arnold*

1967 (cont'd)

7. 4/29 2 Need You *Sonny James*
8. 5/13 3 Sam's Place *Buck Owens*
9. 6/3 2 It's Such A Pretty World Today *Wynn Stewart*
10. 6/17 5 All The Time *Jack Greene*
11. 7/22 1 With One Exception *David Houston*
12. 7/29 1 Tonight Carmen *Marty Robbins*
13. 8/5 4 I'll Never Find Another You *Sonny James*
14. 9/2 1 Branded Man *Merle Haggard*
15. 9/9 1 Your Tender Loving Care *Buck Owens*
16. 9/16 2 My Elusive Dreams *David Houston & Tammy Wynette*
17. 9/30 1 Laura What's He Got That I Ain't Got *Leon Ashley*
18. 10/7 1 Turn The World Around *Eddy Arnold*
19. 10/14 3 I Don't Wanna Play House *Tammy Wynette*
20. 11/4 2 You Mean The World To Me *David Houston*
21. 11/18 5 It's The Little Things *Sonny James*
22. 12/23 4 For Loving You *Bill Anderson & Jan Howard*

1968

1. 1/20 2 Sing Me Back Home *Merle Haggard*
2. 2/3 5 Skip A Rope *Henson Cargill*
3. 3/9 1 Take Me To Your World *Tammy Wynette*
4. 3/16 3 A World Of Our Own *Sonny James*
5. 4/6 1 How Long Will My Baby Be Gone *Buck Owens*
6. 4/13 1 You Are My Treasure *Jack Greene*
7. 4/20 1 Fist City *Loretta Lynn*
8. 4/27 2 The Legend Of Bonnie And Clyde *Merle Haggard*
9. 5/11 1 Have A Little Faith *David Houston*
10. 5/18 3↕ I Wanna Live *Glen Campbell*
11. 5/25 3 Honey *Bobby Goldsboro*
12. 6/29 3 D-I-V-O-R-C-E *Tammy Wynette*
13. 7/20 4 Folsom Prison Blues *Johnny Cash*
14. 8/17 1 Heaven Says Hello *Sonny James*
15. 8/24 1 Already It's Heaven *David Houston*
16. 8/31 4 Mama Tried *Merle Haggard*
17. 9/28 3 Harper Valley P.T.A. *Jeannie C. Riley*
18. 10/19 2 Then You Can Tell Me Goodbye *Eddy Arnold*
19. 11/2 1 Next In Line *Conway Twitty*
20. 11/9 2 I Walk Alone *Marty Robbins*
21. 11/23 3 Stand By Your Man *Tammy Wynette*
22. 12/14 1 Born To Be With You *Sonny James*
23. 12/21 2 Wichita Lineman *Glen Campbell*

#1 HITS

1969

#	DATE	WKS	Title / Artist
1.	1/4	6	Daddy Sang Bass Johnny Cash
2.	2/15	2	Until My Dreams Come True Jack Greene
3.	3/1	1	To Make Love Sweeter For You Jerry Lee Lewis
4.	3/8	3	Only The Lonely Sonny James
5.	3/29	2	Who's Gonna Mow Your Grass Buck Owens
6.	4/12	1	Woman Of The World (Leave My World Alone) Loretta Lynn
7.	4/19	3	Galveston Glen Campbell
8.	5/10	1	Hungry Eyes Merle Haggard
9.	5/17	2	My Life (Throw It Away If I Want To) Bill Anderson
10.	5/31	2	Singing My Song Tammy Wynette
11.	6/14	3	Running Bear Sonny James
12.	7/5	2	Statue Of A Fool Jack Greene
13.	7/19	1	I Love You More Today Conway Twitty
14.	7/26	2	Johnny B. Goode Buck Owens
15.	8/9	1	All I Have To Offer You (Is Me) Charley Pride
16.	8/16	1	Workin' Man Blues Merle Haggard
17.	8/23	5	A Boy Named Sue Johnny Cash
18.	9/27	1	Tall Dark Stranger Buck Owens
19.	10/4	3	Since I Met You, Baby Sonny James
20.	10/25	2	The Ways To Love A Man Tammy Wynette
21.	11/8	1	To See My Angel Cry Conway Twitty
22.	11/15	4	Okie From Muskogee Merle Haggard
23.	12/13	3	(I'm So) Afraid Of Losing You Again Charley Pride

1970

#	DATE	WKS	Title / Artist
1.	1/3	4	Baby, Baby (I Know You're A Lady) David Houston
2.	1/31	2	A Week In A Country Jail Tom T. Hall
3.	2/14	4	It's Just A Matter Of Time Sonny James
4.	3/14	3	The Fightin' Side Of Me Merle Haggard
5.	4/4	2	Tennessee Bird Walk Jack Blanchard & Misty Morgan
6.	4/18	2	Is Anybody Goin' To San Antone Charley Pride
7.	5/2	1	My Woman My Woman, My Wife Marty Robbins
8.	5/9	1	The Pool Shark Dave Dudley
9.	5/16	3	My Love Sonny James
10.	6/6	4	Hello Darlin' Conway Twitty
11.	7/4	3	He Loves Me All The Way Tammy Wynette
12.	7/25	2	Wonder Could I Live There Anymore Charley Pride
13.	8/8	4	Don't Keep Me Hangin' On Sonny James
14.	9/5	2	All For The Love Of Sunshine Hank Williams, Jr. With The Mike Curb Congregation
15.	9/19	1	For The Good Times Ray Price
16.	9/26	2	There Must Be More To Love Than This Jerry Lee Lewis

1970 (cont'd)

#	DATE	WKS	Title / Artist
17.	10/10	2	Sunday Morning Coming Down Johnny Cash
18.	10/24	2	Run, Woman, Run Tammy Wynette
19.	11/7	2	I Can't Believe That You've Stopped Loving Me Charley Pride
20.	11/21	1	Fifteen Years Ago Conway Twitty
21.	11/28	3	Endlessly Sonny James
22.	12/19	1	Coal Miner's Daughter Loretta Lynn
23.	12/26	5	Rose Garden Lynn Anderson

1971

#	DATE	WKS	Title / Artist
1.	1/30	1	Flesh And Blood Johnny Cash
2.	2/6	1	Joshua Dolly Parton
3.	2/13	3	Help Me Make It Through The Night Sammi Smith
4.	3/6	3	I'd Rather Love You Charley Pride
5.	3/27	2	After The Fire Is Gone Conway Twitty & Loretta Lynn
6.	4/10	4	Empty Arms Sonny James
7.	5/8	1	How Much More Can She Stand Conway Twitty
8.	5/15	3	I Won't Mention It Again Ray Price
9.	6/5	2	You're My Man Lynn Anderson
10.	6/19	5	When You're Hot, You're Hot Jerry Reed
11.	7/24	1	Bright Lights, Big City Sonny James
12.	7/31	4	I'm Just Me Charley Pride
13.	8/28	2	Good Lovin' (Makes It Right) Tammy Wynette
14.	9/11	3‡	Easy Loving Freddie Hart
15.	9/18	2	The Year That Clayton Delaney Died Tom T. Hall
16.	10/16	3	How Can I Unlove You Lynn Anderson
17.	11/6	1	Here Comes Honey Again Sonny James
18.	11/13	1	Lead Me On Conway Twitty And Loretta Lynn
19.	11/20	2	Daddy Frank (The Guitar Man) Merle Haggard
20.	12/4	5	Kiss An Angel Good Mornin' Charley Pride

1972

#	DATE	WKS	Title / Artist
1.	1/8	1	Would You Take Another Chance On Me Jerry Lee Lewis
2.	1/15	3	Carolyn Merle Haggard
3.	2/5	2	One's On The Way Loretta Lynn
4.	2/19	2	It's Four In The Morning Faron Young
5.	3/4	1	Bedtime Story Tammy Wynette
6.	3/11	6	My Hang-Up Is You Freddie Hart
7.	4/22	3	Chantilly Lace Jerry Lee Lewis
8.	5/13	2	Grandma Harp Merle Haggard
9.	5/27	1	(Lost Her Love) On Our Last Date Conway Twitty
10.	6/3	3	The Happiest Girl In The Whole U.S.A. Donna Fargo
11.	6/24	1	That's Why I Love You Like I Do Sonny James
12.	7/1	2	Eleven Roses Hank Williams, Jr.

#1 HITS

1972 (cont'd)

13. 7/15 1 **Made In Japan** *Buck Owens*
14. 7/22 3 **It's Gonna Take A Little Bit Longer** *Charley Pride*
15. 8/12 2 **Bless Your Heart** *Freddie Hart & The Heartbeats*
16. 8/26 2↕ **If You Leave Me Tonight I'll Cry** *Jerry Wallace*
17. 9/2 1 **Woman (Sensuous Woman)** *Don Gibson*
18. 9/16 1 **When The Snow Is On The Roses** *Sonny James*
19. 9/23 1 **I Can't Stop Loving You** *Conway Twitty*
20. 9/30 2 **I Ain't Never** *Mel Tillis*
21. 10/14 3 **Funny Face** *Donna Fargo*
22. 11/4 1 **It's Not Love (But It's Not Bad)** *Merle Haggard*
23. 11/11 1 **My Man** *Tammy Wynette*
24. 11/18 3 **She's Too Good To Be True** *Charley Pride*
25. 12/9 3 **Got The All Overs For You (All Over Me)** *Freddie Hart & The Heartbeats*
26. 12/30 3 **She's Got To Be A Saint** *Ray Price*

1973

DATE WKS

1. 1/20 1 **Soul Song** *Joe Stampley*
2. 1/27 1 **(Old Dogs-Children And) Watermelon Wine** *Tom T. Hall*
3. 2/3 2 **She Needs Someone To Hold Her (When She Cries)** *Conway Twitty*
4. 2/17 1 **I Wonder If They Ever Think Of Me** *Merle Haggard*
5. 2/24 1 **Rated "X"** *Loretta Lynn*
6. 3/3 1 **The Lord Knows I'm Drinking** *Cal Smith*
7. 3/10 1 **'Til I Get It Right** *Tammy Wynette*
8. 3/17 2 **Teddy Bear Song** *Barbara Fairchild*
9. 3/31 1 **Keep Me In Mind** *Lynn Anderson*
10. 4/7 1 **Super Kind Of Woman** *Freddie Hart & The Heartbeats*
11. 4/14 1 **A Shoulder To Cry On** *Charley Pride*
12. 4/21 1 **Superman** *Donna Fargo*
13. 4/28 2 **Behind Closed Doors** *Charlie Rich*
14. 5/12 1 **Come Live With Me** *Roy Clark*
15. 5/19 1 **What's Your Mama's Name** *Tanya Tucker*
16. 5/26 3↕ **Satin Sheets** *Jeanne Pruett*
17. 6/9 1 **You Always Come Back (To Hurting Me)** *Johnny Rodriguez*
18. 6/16 1 **Kids Say The Darndest Things** *Tammy Wynette*
19. 6/30 1 **Don't Fight The Feelings Of Love** *Charley Pride*
20. 7/7 1 **Why Me** *Kris Kristofferson*
21. 7/14 2 **Love Is The Foundation** *Loretta Lynn*
22. 7/28 1 **You Were Always There** *Donna Fargo*
23. 8/4 1 **Lord, Mr. Ford** *Jerry Reed*
24. 8/11 1 **Trip To Heaven** *Freddie Hart & The Heartbeats*
25. 8/18 1 **Louisiana Woman, Mississippi Man** *Loretta Lynn/Conway Twitty*

1973 (cont'd)

26. 8/25 2 **Everybody's Had The Blues** *Merle Haggard*
27. 9/8 3 **You've Never Been This Far Before** *Conway Twitty*
28. 9/29 1 **Blood Red And Goin' Down** *Tanya Tucker*
29. 10/6 1 **You're The Best Thing That Ever Happened To Me** *Ray Price*
30. 10/13 2 **Ridin' My Thumb To Mexico** *Johnny Rodriguez*
31. 10/27 2 **We're Gonna Hold On** *George Jones & Tammy Wynette*
32. 11/10 2 **Paper Roses** *Marie Osmond*
33. 11/24 3 **The Most Beautiful Girl** *Charlie Rich*
34. 12/15 1 **Amazing Love** *Charley Pride*
35. 12/22 4 **If We Make It Through December** *Merle Haggard*

1974

DATE WKS

1. 1/19 2 **I Love** *Tom T. Hall*
2. 2/2 1 **Jolene** *Dolly Parton*
3. 2/9 1 **World Of Make Believe** *Bill Anderson*
4. 2/16 1 **That's The Way Love Goes** *Johnny Rodriguez*
5. 2/23 2 **Another Lonely Song** *Tammy Wynette*
6. 3/9 2 **There Won't Be Anymore** *Charlie Rich*
7. 3/23 1 **There's A Honky Tonk Angel (Who'll Take Me Back In)** *Conway Twitty*
8. 3/30 1 **Would You Lay With Me (In A Field Of Stone)** *Tanya Tucker*
9. 4/6 3 **A Very Special Love Song** *Charlie Rich*
10. 4/27 1 **Hello Love** *Hank Snow*
11. 5/4 1 **Things Aren't Funny Anymore** *Merle Haggard*
12. 5/11 1 **Is It Wrong (For Loving You)** *Sonny James*
13. 5/18 1 **Country Bumpkin** *Cal Smith*
14. 5/25 1 **No Charge** *Melba Montgomery*
15. 6/1 1 **Pure Love** *Ronnie Milsap*
16. 6/8 1 **I Will Always Love You** *Dolly Parton*
17. 6/15 1 **I Don't See Me In Your Eyes Anymore** *Charlie Rich*
18. 6/22 1 **This Time** *Waylon Jennings*
19. 6/29 1 **Room Full Of Roses** *Mickey Gilley*
20. 7/6 2 **He Thinks I Still Care** *Anne Murray*
21. 7/20 1 **Marie Laveau** *Bobby Bare*
22. 7/27 1 **You Can't Be A Beacon (If Your Light Don't Shine)** *Donna Fargo*
23. 8/3 2 **Rub It In** *Billy "Crash" Craddock*
24. 8/17 1 **As Soon As I Hang Up The Phone** *Loretta Lynn/Conway Twitty*
25. 8/24 1 **Old Man From The Mountain** *Merle Haggard*
26. 8/31 1 **The Grand Tour** *George Jones*
27. 9/7 2 **Please Don't Tell Me How The Story Ends** *Ronnie Milsap*
28. 9/21 1 **I Wouldn't Want To Live If You Didn't Love Me** *Don Williams*

#1 HITS

1974 (cont'd)

#	Date	Wks	Title	Artist
29.	9/28	1	I'm A Ramblin' Man	Waylon Jennings
30.	10/5	1	I Love My Friend	Charlie Rich
31.	10/12	1	Please Don't Stop Loving Me	Porter Wagoner & Dolly Parton
32.	10/19	2	I See The Want To In Your Eyes	Conway Twitty
33.	11/2	1	I Overlooked An Orchid	Mickey Gilley
34.	11/9	1	Love Is Like A Butterfly	Dolly Parton
35.	11/16	1	Country Is	Tom T. Hall
36.	11/23	1	Trouble In Paradise	Loretta Lynn
37.	11/30	1	Back Home Again	John Denver
38.	12/7	1	She Called Me Baby	Charlie Rich
39.	12/14	2	I Can Help	Billy Swan
40.	12/28	1	What A Man, My Man Is	Lynn Anderson

1975

#	Date	Wks	Title	Artist
1.	1/4	1	The Door	George Jones
2.	1/11	1	Ruby, Baby	Billy "Crash" Craddock
3.	1/18	1	Kentucky Gambler	Merle Haggard
4.	1/25	1	(I'd Be) A Legend In My Time	Ronnie Milsap
5.	2/1	1	City Lights	Mickey Gilley
6.	2/8	1	Then Who Am I	Charley Pride
7.	2/15	1	Devil In The Bottle	T.G. Sheppard
8.	2/22	1	I Care	Tom T. Hall
9.	3/1	1	It's Time To Pay The Fiddler	Cal Smith
10.	3/8	1	Linda On My Mind	Conway Twitty
11.	3/15	2	Before The Next Teardrop Falls	Freddy Fender
12.	3/29	1	The Bargain Store	Dolly Parton
13.	4/5	1	I Just Can't Get Her Out Of My Mind	Johnny Rodriguez
14.	4/12	2	Always Wanting You	Merle Haggard
15.	4/26	1	Blanket On The Ground	Billie Jo Spears
16.	5/3	1	Roll On Big Mama	Joe Stampley
17.	5/10	1	She's Actin' Single (I'm Drinkin' Doubles)	Gary Stewart
18.	5/17	1	(Hey Won't You Play) Another Somebody Done Somebody Wrong Song	B.J. Thomas
19.	5/24	1	I'm Not Lisa	Jessi Colter
20.	5/31	1	Thank God I'm A Country Boy	John Denver
21.	6/7	1	Window Up Above	Mickey Gilley
22.	6/14	1	When Will I Be Loved	Linda Ronstadt
23.	6/21	1	You're My Best Friend	Don Williams
24.	6/28	1	Tryin' To Beat The Morning Home	T.G. Sheppard
25.	7/5	1	Lizzie And The Rainman	Tanya Tucker
26.	7/12	1	Movin' On	Merle Haggard
27.	7/19	2	Touch The Hand	Conway Twitty
28.	8/2	1	Just Get Up And Close The Door	Johnny Rodriguez
29.	8/9	2	Wasted Days And Wasted Nights	Freddy Fender
30.	8/23	3	Rhinestone Cowboy	Glen Campbell
31.	9/6	1	Feelins'	Loretta Lynn/Conway Twitty

1975 (cont'd)

#	Date	Wks	Title	Artist
32.	9/20	2	Daydreams About Night Things	Ronnie Milsap
33.	10/4	2	Blue Eyes Crying In The Rain	Willie Nelson
34.	10/18	1	Hope You're Feelin' Me (Like I'm Feelin' You)	Charley Pride
35.	10/25	1	San Antonio Stroll	Tanya Tucker
36.	11/1	1	(Turn Out The Light And) Love Me Tonight	Don Williams
37.	11/8	1	I'm Sorry	John Denver
38.	11/15	1	Are You Sure Hank Done It This Way	Waylon Jennings
39.	11/22	1	Rocky	Dickey Lee
40.	11/29	1	It's All In The Movies	Merle Haggard
41.	12/6	1	Secret Love	Freddy Fender
42.	12/13	1	Love Put A Song In My Heart	Johnny Rodriguez
43.	12/20	6	Convoy	C.W. McCall

1976

#	Date	Wks	Title	Artist
1.	1/31	1	This Time I've Hurt Her More Than She Loves Me	Conway Twitty
2.	2/7	1	Sometimes	Bill Anderson & Mary Lou Turner
3.	2/14	1	The White Knight	Cledus Maggard & The Citizen's Band
4.	2/21	3	Good Hearted Woman	Waylon & Willie
5.	3/13	1	The Roots Of My Raising	Merle Haggard
6.	3/20	1	Faster Horses (The Cowboy And The Poet)	Tom T. Hall
7.	3/27	1	Til The Rivers All Run Dry	Don Williams
8.	4/3	1	You'll Lose A Good Thing	Freddy Fender
9.	4/10	1	'Til I Can Make It On My Own	Tammy Wynette
10.	4/17	1	Drinkin' My Baby (Off My Mind)	Eddie Rabbitt
11.	4/24	1	Together Again	Emmylou Harris
12.	5/1	1	Don't The Girls All Get Prettier At Closing Time	Mickey Gilley
13.	5/8	1	My Eyes Can Only See As Far As You	Charley Pride
14.	5/15	1	What Goes On When The Sun Goes Down	Ronnie Milsap
15.	5/22	1	After All The Good Is Gone	Conway Twitty
16.	5/29	2	One Piece At A Time	Johnny Cash
17.	6/12	1	I'll Get Over You	Crystal Gayle
18.	6/19	2	El Paso City	Marty Robbins
19.	7/4	1	All These Things	Joe Stampley
20.	7/10	1	The Door Is Always Open	Dave & Sugar
21.	7/17	3	Teddy Bear	Red Sovine
22.	8/7	1	Golden Ring	George Jones & Tammy Wynette
23.	8/14	1	Say It Again	Don Williams
24.	8/21	1	Bring It On Home To Me	Mickey Gilley
25.	8/28	2	(I'm A) Stand By My Woman Man	Ronnie Milsap

#1 HITS

1976 (cont'd)

#	DATE	WKS	TITLE / ARTIST
26.	9/11	2	I Don't Want To Have To Marry You *Jim Ed Brown/Helen Cornelius*
27.	9/25	1	If You've Got The Money I've Got The Time *Willie Nelson*
28.	10/2	1	Here's Some Love *Tanya Tucker*
29.	10/9	1	The Games That Daddies Play *Conway Twitty*
30.	10/16	2	You And Me *Tammy Wynette*
31.	10/30	1	Among My Souvenirs *Marty Robbins*
32.	11/6	1	Cherokee Maiden *Merle Haggard*
33.	11/13	2	Somebody Somewhere (Don't Know What He's Missin' Tonight) *Loretta Lynn*
34.	11/27	2	Good Woman Blues *Mel Tillis*
35.	12/11	2	Thinkin' Of A Rendezvous *Johnny Duncan*
36.	12/25	2	Sweet Dreams *Emmylou Harris*

1977

#	DATE	WKS	TITLE / ARTIST
1.	1/8	1	Broken Down In Tiny Pieces *Billy "Crash" Craddock*
2.	1/15	1	You Never Miss A Real Good Thing (Till He Says Goodbye) *Crystal Gayle*
3.	1/22	1	I Can't Believe She Gives It All To Me *Conway Twitty*
4.	1/29	1	Let My Love Be Your Pillow *Ronnie Milsap*
5.	2/5	2	Near You *George Jones & Tammy Wynette*
6.	2/19	1	Moody Blue *Elvis Presley*
7.	2/26	1	Say You'll Stay Until Tomorrow *Tom Jones*
8.	3/5	1	Heart Healer *Mel Tillis*
9.	3/12	1	She's Just An Old Love Turned Memory *Charley Pride*
10.	3/19	2	Southern Nights *Glen Campbell*
11.	4/2	2	Lucille *Kenny Rogers*
12.	4/16	1	It Couldn't Have Been Any Better *Johnny Duncan*
13.	4/23	1	She's Got You *Loretta Lynn*
14.	4/30	1	She's Pulling Me Back Again *Mickey Gilley*
15.	5/7	1	Play, Guitar Play *Conway Twitty*
16.	5/14	1	Some Broken Hearts Never Mend *Don Williams*
17.	5/21	6	**Luckenbach, Texas (Back to the Basics of Love)** *Waylon Jennings*
18.	7/2	1	That Was Yesterday *Donna Fargo*
19.	7/9	1	I'll Be Leaving Alone *Charley Pride*
20.	7/16	3	It Was Almost Like A Song *Ronnie Milsap*
21.	8/6	2	Rollin' With The Flow *Charlie Rich*
22.	8/20	1	Way Down *Elvis Presley*
23.	8/27	4	Don't It Make My Brown Eyes Blue *Crystal Gayle*
24.	9/24	1	I've Already Loved You In My Mind *Conway Twitty*
25.	10/1	1	Daytime Friends *Kenny Rogers*
26.	10/8	4	Heaven's Just A Sin Away *The Kendalls*

1977 (cont'd)

#	DATE	WKS	TITLE / ARTIST
27.	11/5	1	I'm Just A Country Boy *Don Williams*
28.	11/12	1	More To Me *Charley Pride*
29.	11/19	2	The Wurlitzer Prize (I Don't Want To Get Over You) *Waylon Jennings*
30.	12/3	5	Here You Come Again *Dolly Parton*

1978

#	DATE	WKS	TITLE / ARTIST
1.	1/7	2	Take This Job And Shove It *Johnny Paycheck*
2.	1/21	1	What A Difference You've Made In My Life *Ronnie Milsap*
3.	1/28	2	Out Of My Head And Back In My Bed *Loretta Lynn*
4.	2/11	1	I Just Wish You Were Someone I Love *Larry Gatlin with Brothers & Friends*
5.	2/18	2	Don't Break The Heart That Loves You *Margo Smith*
6.	3/4	4	**Mammas Don't Let Your Babies Grow Up To Be Cowboys** *Waylon & Willie*
7.	4/1	1	Ready For The Times To Get Better *Crystal Gayle*
8.	4/8	2	Someone Loves You Honey *Charley Pride*
9.	4/22	2	Every Time Two Fools Collide *Kenny Rogers & Dottie West*
10.	5/6	2	It's All Wrong, But It's All Right *Dolly Parton*
11.	5/20	1	She Can Put Her Shoes Under My Bed (Anytime) *Johnny Duncan*
12.	5/27	2	Do You Know You Are My Sunshine *The Statler Brothers*
13.	6/10	1	Georgia On My Mind *Willie Nelson*
14.	6/17	1	Two More Bottles Of Wine *Emmylou Harris*
15.	6/24	1	I'll Be True To You *The Oak Ridge Boys*
16.	7/1	1	It Only Hurts For A Little While *Margo Smith*
17.	7/8	1	I Believe In You *Mel Tillis*
18.	7/15	3	Only One Love In My Life *Ronnie Milsap*
19.	8/5	1	Love Or Something Like It *Kenny Rogers*
20.	8/12	1	You Don't Love Me Anymore *Eddie Rabbitt*
21.	8/19	2	Talking In Your Sleep *Crystal Gayle*
22.	9/2	1	Blue Skies *Willie Nelson*
23.	9/9	3	I've Always Been Crazy *Waylon Jennings*
24.	9/30	3	Heartbreaker *Dolly Parton*
25.	10/21	1	Tear Time *Dave & Sugar*
26.	10/28	1	Let's Take The Long Way Around The World *Ronnie Milsap*
27.	11/4	3	Sleeping Single In A Double Bed *Barbara Mandrell*
28.	11/25	1	Sweet Desire *The Kendalls*
29.	12/2	1	I Just Want To Love You *Eddie Rabbitt*
30.	12/9	1	On My Knees *Charlie Rich with Janie Fricke*
31.	12/16	3	The Gambler *Kenny Rogers*

#1 HITS

1979

#	DATE	WKS	Title	Artist
1.	1/6	1	Tulsa Time	Don Williams
2.	1/13	1	Lady Lay Down	John Conlee
3.	1/20	1	I Really Got The Feeling	Dolly Parton
4.	1/27	2	Why Have You Left The One You Left Me For	Crystal Gayle
5.	2/10	3	Every Which Way But Loose	Eddie Rabbitt
6.	3/3	3	Golden Tears	Dave & Sugar
7.	3/24	3	I Just Fall In Love Again	Anne Murray
8.	4/14	1	(If Loving You Is Wrong) I Don't Want To Be Right	Barbara Mandrell
9.	4/21	1	All I Ever Need Is You	Kenny Rogers & Dottie West
10.	4/28	1	Where Do I Put Her Memory	Charley Pride
11.	5/5	1	Backside Of Thirty	John Conlee
12.	5/12	1	Don't Take It Away	Conway Twitty
13.	5/19	3	If I Said You Have A Beautiful Body Would You Hold It Against Me	Bellamy Brothers
14.	6/9	2	She Believes In Me	Kenny Rogers
15.	6/23	1	Nobody Likes Sad Songs	Ronnie Milsap
16.	6/30	3	Amanda	Waylon Jennings
17.	7/21	1	Shadows In The Moonlight	Anne Murray
18.	7/28	2	You're The Only One	Dolly Parton
19.	8/11	1	Suspicions	Eddie Rabbitt
20.	8/18	1	Coca Cola Cowboy	Mel Tillis
21.	8/25	1	The Devil Went Down To Georgia	Charlie Daniels Band
22.	9/1	1	Heartbreak Hotel	Willie Nelson & Leon Russell
23.	9/8	1	I May Never Get To Heaven	Conway Twitty
24.	9/15	1	You're My Jamaica	Charley Pride
25.	9/22	1	Just Good Ol' Boys	Moe Bandy & Joe Stampley
26.	9/29	1	It Must Be Love	Don Williams
27.	10/6	2	Last Cheater's Waltz	T.G. Sheppard
28.	10/20	2	All The Gold In California	Larry Gatlin & The Gatlin Brothers
29.	11/3	2	You Decorated My Life	Kenny Rogers
30.	11/17	2	Come With Me	Waylon Jennings
31.	12/1	1	Broken Hearted Me	Anne Murray
32.	12/8	1	I Cheated Me Right Out Of You	Moe Bandy
33.	12/15	3	Happy Birthday Darlin'	Conway Twitty

1980

#	DATE	WKS	Title	Artist
1.	1/5	3	Coward Of The County	Kenny Rogers
2.	1/26	2	I'll Be Coming Back For More	T.G. Sheppard
3.	2/9	1	Leaving Louisiana In The Broad Daylight	The Oak Ridge Boys
4.	2/16	1	Love Me Over Again	Don Williams
5.	2/23	1	Years	Barbara Mandrell
6.	3/1	1	I Ain't Living Long Like This	Waylon Jennings

1980 (cont'd)

#	DATE	WKS	Title	Artist
7.	3/8	2	My Heroes Have Always Been Cowboys	Willie Nelson
8.	3/22	1	Why Don't You Spend The Night	Ronnie Milsap
9.	3/29	1	I'd Love To Lay You Down	Conway Twitty
10.	4/5	1	Sugar Daddy	Bellamy Brothers
11.	4/12	1	Honky Tonk Blues	Charley Pride
12.	4/19	1	It's Like We Never Said Goodbye	Crystal Gayle
13.	4/26	1	A Lesson In Leavin'	Dottie West
14.	5/3	1	Are You On The Road To Lovin' Me Again	Debby Boone
15.	5/10	1	Beneath Still Waters	Emmylou Harris
16.	5/17	1	Gone Too Far	Eddie Rabbitt
17.	5/24	1	Starting Over Again	Dolly Parton
18.	5/31	3	My Heart	Ronnie Milsap
19.	6/21	1	One Day At A Time	Cristy Lane
20.	6/28	1	Trying To Love Two Women	The Oak Ridge Boys
21.	7/5	1	He Stopped Loving Her Today	George Jones
22.	7/12	1	You Win Again	Charley Pride
23.	7/19	1	True Love Ways	Mickey Gilley
24.	7/26	1	Bar Room Buddies	Merle Haggard & Clint Eastwood
25.	8/2	1	Dancin' Cowboys	Bellamy Brothers
26.	8/9	1	Stand By Me	Mickey Gilley
27.	8/16	1	Tennessee River	Alabama
28.	8/23	1	Drivin' My Life Away	Eddie Rabbitt
29.	8/30	1	Cowboys And Clowns	Ronnie Milsap
30.	9/6	3	Lookin' For Love	Johnny Lee
31.	9/27	1	Old Flames Can't Hold A Candle To You	Dolly Parton
32.	10/4	1	Do You Wanna Go To Heaven	T.G. Sheppard
33.	10/11	1	Loving Up A Storm	Razzy Bailey
34.	10/18	2	I Believe In You	Don Williams
35.	11/1	1	Theme From The Dukes Of Hazzard (Good Ol' Boys)	Waylon Jennings
36.	11/8	1	On The Road Again	Willie Nelson
37.	11/15	1	Could I Have This Dance	Anne Murray
38.	11/22	1	Lady	Kenny Rogers
39.	11/29	1	If You Ever Change Your Mind	Crystal Gayle
40.	12/6	1	Smoky Mountain Rain	Ronnie Milsap
41.	12/13	1	Why Lady Why	Alabama
42.	12/20	1	That's All That Matters	Mickey Gilley
43.	12/27	2	One In A Million	Johnny Lee

1981

#	DATE	WKS	Title	Artist
1.	1/10	1	I Think I'll Just Stay Here And Drink	Merle Haggard
2.	1/17	1	I Love A Rainy Night	Eddie Rabbitt
3.	1/24	1	9 To 5	Dolly Parton
4.	1/31	1	I Feel Like Loving You Again	T.G. Sheppard
5.	2/7	1	I Keep Coming Back	Razzy Bailey
6.	2/14	1	Who's Cheatin' Who	Charly McClain

#1 HITS

1981 (cont'd)

#	Date	Wks	Title / Artist
7.	2/21	1	**Southern Rains** Mel Tillis
8.	2/28	1	**Are You Happy Baby?** Dottie West
9.	3/7	1	**Do You Love As Good As You Look** The Bellamy Brothers
10.	3/14	1	**Guitar Man** Elvis Presley
11.	3/21	1	**Angel Flying Too Close To The Ground** Willie Nelson
12.	3/28	1	**Texas Women** Hank Williams, Jr.
13.	4/4	1	**Drifter** Sylvia
14.	4/11	1	**You're The Reason God Made Oklahoma** David Frizzell & Shelly West
15.	4/18	1	**Old Flame** Alabama
16.	4/25	1	**A Headache Tomorrow (Or A Heartache Tonight)** Mickey Gilley
17.	5/2	1	**Rest Your Love On Me** Conway Twitty
18.	5/9	1	**Am I Losing You** Ronnie Milsap
19.	5/16	1	**I Loved 'Em Every One** T.G. Sheppard
20.	5/23	1	**Seven Year Ache** Rosanne Cash
21.	5/30	1	**Elvira** The Oak Ridge Boys
22.	6/6	1	**Friends** Razzy Bailey
23.	6/13	1	**What Are We Doin' In Love** Dottie West (with Kenny Rogers)
24.	6/20	1	**But You Know I Love You** Dolly Parton
25.	6/27	1	**Blessed Are The Believers** Anne Murray
26.	7/4	1	**I Was Country When Country Wasn't Cool** Barbara Mandrell
27.	7/11	1	**Fire & Smoke** Earl Thomas Conley
28.	7/18	2	**Feels So Right** Alabama
29.	8/1	1	**Dixie On My Mind** Hank Williams, Jr.
30.	8/8	1	**Too Many Lovers** Crystal Gayle
31.	8/15	2	**I Don't Need You** Kenny Rogers
32.	8/29	2	**(There's) No Gettin' Over Me** Ronnie Milsap
33.	9/12	1	**Older Women** Ronnie McDowell
34.	9/19	1	**You Don't Know Me** Mickey Gilley
35.	9/26	1	**Tight Fittin' Jeans** Conway Twitty
36.	10/3	1	**Midnight Hauler** Razzy Bailey
37.	10/10	1	**Party Time** T.G. Sheppard
38.	10/17	1	**Step By Step** Eddie Rabbitt
39.	10/24	2	**Never Been So Loved (In All My Life)** Charley Pride
40.	11/7	1	**Fancy Free** The Oak Ridge Boys
41.	11/14	1	**My Baby Thinks He's A Train** Rosanne Cash
42.	11/21	1	**All My Rowdy Friends (Have Settled Down)** Hank Williams, Jr.
43.	11/28	1	**My Favorite Memory** Merle Haggard
44.	12/5	1	**Bet Your Heart On Me** Johnny Lee
45.	12/12	1	**Still Doin' Time** George Jones
46.	12/19	1	**All Roads Lead To You** Steve Wariner
47.	12/26	2	**Love In The First Degree** Alabama

1982

#	Date	Wks	Title / Artist
1.	1/9	1	**Fourteen Carat Mind** Gene Watson
2.	1/16	1	**I Wouldn't Have Missed It For The World** Ronnie Milsap
3.	1/23	1	**Red Neckin' Love Makin' Night** Conway Twitty
4.	1/30	1	**The Sweetest Thing (I've Ever Known)** Juice Newton
5.	2/6	1	**Lonely Nights** Mickey Gilley
6.	2/13	1	**Someone Could Lose A Heart Tonight** Eddie Rabbitt
7.	2/20	1	**Only One You** T.G. Sheppard
8.	2/27	1	**Lord, I Hope This Day Is Good** Don Williams
9.	3/6	1	**You're The Best Break This Old Heart Ever Had** Ed Bruce
10.	3/13	1	**Blue Moon With Heartache** Rosanne Cash
11.	3/20	1	**Mountain Of Love** Charley Pride
12.	3/27	1	**She Left Love All Over Me** Razzy Bailey
13.	4/3	1	**Bobbie Sue** The Oak Ridge Boys
14.	4/10	1	**Big City** Merle Haggard
15.	4/17	1	**The Clown** Conway Twitty
16.	4/24	1	**Crying My Heart Out Over You** Ricky Skaggs
17.	5/1	1	**Mountain Music** Alabama
18.	5/8	2	**Always On My Mind** Willie Nelson
19.	5/22	2	**Just To Satisfy You** Waylon & Willie
20.	6/5	1	**Finally** T.G. Sheppard
21.	6/12	1	**For All The Wrong Reasons** The Bellamy Brothers
22.	6/19	2	**Slow Hand** Conway Twitty
23.	7/3	1	**Any Day Now** Ronnie Milsap
24.	7/10	1	**Don't Worry 'Bout Me Baby** Janie Fricke
25.	7/17	1	**'Till You're Gone** Barbara Mandrell
26.	7/24	1	**Take Me Down** Alabama
27.	7/31	1	**I Don't Care** Ricky Skaggs
28.	8/7	1	**Honky Tonkin'** Hank Williams, Jr.
29.	8/14	1	**I'm Gonna Hire A Wino To Decorate Our Home** David Frizzell
30.	8/21	1	**Nobody** Sylvia
31.	8/28	1	**Fool Hearted Memory** George Strait
32.	9/4	1	**Love Will Turn You Around** Kenny Rogers
33.	9/11	2	**She Got The Goldmine (I Got The Shaft)** Jerry Reed
34.	9/25	1	**What's Forever For** Michael Murphey
35.	10/2	1	**Put Your Dreams Away** Mickey Gilley
36.	10/9	1	**Yesterday's Wine** Merle Haggard/George Jones
37.	10/16	1	**I Will Always Love You** Dolly Parton
38.	10/23	1	**He Got You** Ronnie Milsap
39.	10/30	1	**Close Enough To Perfect** Alabama
40.	11/6	1	**You're So Good When You're Bad** Charley Pride
41.	11/13	1	**Heartbroke** Ricky Skaggs
42.	11/20	1	**War Is Hell (On The Homefront Too)** T.G. Sheppard
43.	11/27	1	**It Ain't Easy Bein' Easy** Janie Fricke

#1 HITS

1982 (cont'd)

#	Date	Wks	Title / Artist
44.	12/4	1	You And I Eddie Rabbitt with Crystal Gayle
45.	12/11	1	Redneck Girl The Bellamy Brothers
46.	12/18	1	Somewhere Between Right And Wrong Earl Thomas Conley
47.	12/25	2	Wild And Blue John Anderson

1983

#	Date	Wks	Title / Artist
1.	1/8	1	Can't Even Get The Blues Reba McEntire
2.	1/15	1	Going Where The Lonely Go Merle Haggard
3.	1/22	1	(Lost His Love) On Our Last Date Emmylou Harris
4.	1/29	1	Talk To Me Mickey Gilley
5.	2/5	1	Inside Ronnie Milsap
6.	2/12	1	'Til I Gain Control Again Crystal Gayle
7.	2/19	1	Faking Love T.G. Sheppard & Karen Brooks
8.	2/26	1	Why Baby Why Charley Pride
9.	3/5	1	If Hollywood Don't Need You Don Williams
10.	3/12	1	The Rose Conway Twitty
11.	3/19	1	I Wouldn't Change You If I Could Ricky Skaggs
12.	3/26	1	Swingin' John Anderson
13.	4/2	1	When I'm Away From You Bellamy Brothers
14.	4/9	1	We've Got Tonight Kenny Rogers & Sheena Easton
15.	4/16	1	Dixieland Delight Alabama
16.	4/23	1	American Made The Oak Ridge Boys
17.	4/30	1	You're The First Time I've Thought About Leaving Reba McEntire
18.	5/7	1	Jose Cuervo Shelly West
19.	5/14	1	Whatever Happened To Old Fashioned Love B.J. Thomas
20.	5/21	1	Common Man John Conlee
21.	5/28	1	You Take Me For Granted Merle Haggard
22.	6/4	1	Lucille (You Won't Do Your Daddy's Will) Waylon Jennings
23.	6/11	1	Our Love Is On The Faultline Crystal Gayle
24.	6/18	1	You Can't Run From Love Eddie Rabbitt
25.	6/25	1	Fool For Your Love Mickey Gilley
26.	7/2	1	Love Is On A Roll Don Williams
27.	7/9	1	Highway 40 Blues Ricky Skaggs
28.	7/16	1	The Closer You Get Alabama
29.	7/23	1	Pancho And Lefty Willie Nelson & Merle Haggard
30.	7/30	1	I Always Get Lucky With You George Jones
31.	8/6	1	Your Love's On The Line Earl Thomas Conley
32.	8/13	1	He's A Heartache (Looking For A Place To Happen) Janie Fricke
33.	8/20	1	Love Song The Oak Ridge Boys
34.	8/27	1	You're Gonna Ruin My Bad Reputation Ronnie McDowell
35.	9/3	1	A Fire I Can't Put Out George Strait

1983 (cont'd)

#	Date	Wks	Title / Artist
36.	9/10	1	I'm Only In It For The Love John Conlee
37.	9/17	1	Night Games Charley Pride
38.	9/24	1	Baby, What About You Crystal Gayle
39.	10/1	1	New Looks From An Old Lover B.J. Thomas
40.	10/8	1	Don't You Know How Much I Love You Ronnie Milsap
41.	10/15	1	Paradise Tonight Charly McClain & Mickey Gilley
42.	10/22	1	Lady Down On Love Alabama
43.	10/29	2	Islands In The Stream Kenny Rogers with Dolly Parton
44.	11/12	1	Somebody's Gonna Love You Lee Greenwood
45.	11/19	1	One Of A Kind Pair Of Fools Barbara Mandrell
46.	11/26	1	Holding Her And Loving You Earl Thomas Conley
47.	12/3	1	A Little Good News Anne Murray
48.	12/10	1	Tell Me A Lie Janie Fricke
49.	12/17	1	Black Sheep John Anderson
50.	12/24	2	Houston (Means I'm One Day Closer To You) Larry Gatlin & The Gatlin Brothers

1984

#	Date	Wks	Title / Artist
1.	1/7	1	You Look So Good In Love George Strait
2.	1/14	1	Slow Burn T.G. Sheppard
3.	1/21	1	In My Eyes John Conlee
4.	1/28	1	The Sound Of Goodbye Crystal Gayle
5.	2/4	1	Show Her Ronnie Milsap
6.	2/11	1	That's The Way Love Goes Merle Haggard
7.	2/18	1	Don't Cheat In Our Hometown Ricky Skaggs
8.	2/25	1	Stay Young Don Williams
9.	3/3	1	Woke Up In Love Exile
10.	3/10	1	Going, Going, Gone Lee Greenwood
11.	3/17	1	Elizabeth The Statler Brothers
12.	3/24	1	Roll On (Eighteen Wheeler) Alabama
13.	3/31	1	Let's Stop Talkin' About It Janie Fricke
14.	4/7	1	Don't Make It Easy For Me Earl Thomas Conley
15.	4/14	1	Thank God For The Radio The Kendalls
16.	4/21	1	The Yellow Rose Johnny Lee with Lane Brody
17.	4/28	1	Right Or Wrong George Strait
18.	5/5	1	I Guess It Never Hurts To Hurt Sometimes The Oak Ridge Boys
19.	5/12	2	To All The Girls I've Loved Before Julio Iglesias & Willie Nelson
20.	5/26	1	As Long As I'm Rockin' With You John Conlee
21.	6/2	1	Honey (Open That Door) Ricky Skaggs
22.	6/9	1	Someday When Things Are Good Merle Haggard
23.	6/16	1	I Got Mexico Eddy Raven
24.	6/23	1	When We Make Love Alabama

#1 HITS

1984 (cont'd)

#	Date	Wks	Title	Artist
25.	6/30	1	I Can Tell By The Way You Dance (You're Gonna Love Me Tonight)	Vern Gosdin
26.	7/7	1	Somebody's Needin' Somebody	Conway Twitty
27.	7/14	1	I Don't Want To Be A Memory	Exile
28.	7/21	1	Just Another Woman In Love	Anne Murray
29.	7/28	1	Angel In Disguise	Earl Thomas Conley
30.	8/4	1	Mama He's Crazy	The Judds
31.	8/11	1	That's The Thing About Love	Don Williams
32.	8/18	1	Still Losing You	Ronnie Milsap
33.	8/25	1	Long Hard Road (The Sharecropper's Dream)	Nitty Gritty Dirt Band
34.	9/1	1	Let's Fall To Pieces Together	George Strait
35.	9/8	1	Tennessee Homesick Blues	Dolly Parton
36.	9/15	1	You're Gettin' To Me Again	Jim Glaser
37.	9/22	1	Let's Chase Each Other Around The Room	Merle Haggard
38.	9/29	1	Turning Away	Crystal Gayle
39.	10/6	1	Everyday	The Oak Ridge Boys
40.	10/13	1	Uncle Pen	Ricky Skaggs
41.	10/20	1	I Don't Know A Thing About Love (The Moon Song)	Conway Twitty
42.	10/27	1	If You're Gonna Play In Texas (You Gotta Have A Fiddle In The Band)	Alabama
43.	11/3	1	City Of New Orleans	Willie Nelson
44.	11/10	1	I've Been Around Enough To Know	John Schneider
45.	11/17	1	Give Me One More Chance	Exile
46.	11/24	1	You Could've Heard A Heart Break	Johnny Lee
47.	12/1	1	Your Heart's Not In It	Janie Fricke
48.	12/8	1	Chance Of Lovin' You	Earl Thomas Conley
49.	12/15	1	Nobody Loves Me Like You Do	Anne Murray (with Dave Loggins)
50.	12/22	2	Why Not Me	The Judds

1985

#	Date	Wks	Title	Artist
1.	1/5	1	Does Fort Worth Ever Cross Your Mind	George Strait
2.	1/12	1	The Best Year Of My Life	Eddie Rabbitt
3.	1/19	1	How Blue	Reba McEntire
4.	1/26	1	(There's A) Fire In The Night	Alabama
5.	2/2	1	A Place To Fall Apart	Merle Haggard (with Janie Fricke)
6.	2/9	1	Ain't She Somethin' Else	Conway Twitty
7.	2/16	1	Make My Life With You	Oak Ridge Boys
8.	2/23	1	Baby's Got Her Blue Jeans On	Mel McDaniel
9.	3/2	1	Baby Bye Bye	Gary Morris
10.	3/9	1	My Only Love	The Statler Brothers
11.	3/16	1	Crazy For Your Love	Exile
12.	3/23	1	Seven Spanish Angels	Ray Charles with Willie Nelson

1985 (cont'd)

#	Date	Wks	Title	Artist
13.	3/30	1	Crazy	Kenny Rogers
14.	4/6	1	Country Girls	John Schneider
15.	4/13	1	Honor Bound	Earl Thomas Conley
16.	4/20	1	I Need More Of You	Bellamy Brothers
17.	4/27	1	Girls Night Out	The Judds
18.	5/4	1	There's No Way	Alabama
19.	5/11	1	Somebody Should Leave	Reba McEntire
20.	5/18	1	Step That Step	Sawyer Brown
21.	5/25	1	Radio Heart	Charly McClain
22.	6/1	1	Don't Call Him A Cowboy	Conway Twitty
23.	6/8	1	Natural High	Merle Haggard
24.	6/15	1	Country Boy	Ricky Skaggs
25.	6/22	1	Little Things	The Oak Ridge Boys
26.	6/29	1	She Keeps The Home Fires Burning	Ronnie Milsap
27.	7/6	1	She's A Miracle	Exile
28.	7/13	1	Forgiving You Was Easy	Willie Nelson
29.	7/20	1	Dixie Road	Lee Greenwood
30.	7/27	1	Love Don't Care (Whose Heart It Breaks)	Earl Thomas Conley
31.	8/3	1	Forty Hour Week (For A Livin')	Alabama
32.	8/10	1	I'm For Love	Hank Williams, Jr.
33.	8/17	1	Highwayman	Waylon Jennings/Willie Nelson/Johnny Cash/Kris Kristofferson
34.	8/24	1	Real Love	Dolly Parton (with Kenny Rogers)
35.	8/31	1	Love Is Alive	The Judds
36.	9/7	1	I Don't Know Why You Don't Want Me	Rosanne Cash
37.	9/14	1	Modern Day Romance	Nitty Gritty Dirt Band
38.	9/21	1	I Fell In Love Again Last Night	The Forester Sisters
39.	9/28	2	Lost In The Fifties Tonight (In The Still Of The Night)	Ronnie Milsap
40.	10/12	1	Meet Me In Montana	Marie Osmond with Dan Seals
41.	10/19	1	You Make Me Want To Make You Mine	Juice Newton
42.	10/26	1	Touch A Hand, Make A Friend	The Oak Ridge Boys
43.	11/2	1	Some Fools Never Learn	Steve Wariner
44.	11/9	1	Can't Keep A Good Man Down	Alabama
45.	11/16	1	Hang On To Your Heart	Exile
46.	11/23	1	I'll Never Stop Loving You	Gary Morris
47.	11/30	1	Too Much On My Heart	The Statler Brothers
48.	12/7	1	I Don't Mind The Thorns (If You're The Rose)	Lee Greenwood
49.	12/14	1	Nobody Falls Like A Fool	Earl Thomas Conley
50.	12/21	1	The Chair	George Strait
51.	12/28	2	Have Mercy	The Judds

#1 HITS

1986

#	DATE	WKS	Title / Artist
1.	1/11	1	Morning Desire Kenny Rogers
2.	1/18	1	Bop Dan Seals
3.	1/25	1	Never Be You Rosanne Cash
4.	2/1	1	Just In Case The Forester Sisters
5.	2/8	1	Hurt Juice Newton
6.	2/15	1	Makin' Up For Lost Time (The Dallas Lovers' Song) Crystal Gayle & Gary Morris
7.	2/22	1	There's No Stopping Your Heart Marie Osmond
8.	3/1	1	You Can Dream Of Me Steve Wariner
9.	3/8	1	Think About Love Dolly Parton
10.	3/15	1	I Could Get Used To You Exile
11.	3/22	1	What's A Memory Like You (Doing In A Love Like This) John Schneider
12.	3/29	1	Don't Underestimate My Love For You Lee Greenwood
13.	4/5	1	100% Chance Of Rain Gary Morris
14.	4/12	1	She And I Alabama
15.	4/19	1	Cajun Moon Ricky Skaggs
16.	4/26	1	Now And Forever (You And Me) Anne Murray
17.	5/3	1	Once In A Blue Moon Earl Thomas Conley
18.	5/10	1	Grandpa (Tell Me 'Bout The Good Old Days) The Judds
19.	5/17	1	Ain't Misbehavin' Hank Williams, Jr.
20.	5/24	1	Tomb Of The Unknown Love Kenny Rogers
21.	5/31	1	Whoever's In New England Reba McEntire
22.	6/7	1	Happy, Happy Birthday Baby Ronnie Milsap
23.	6/14	1	Life's Highway Steve Wariner
24.	6/21	1	Mama's Never Seen Those Eyes The Forester Sisters
25.	6/28	1	Living In The Promiseland Willie Nelson
26.	7/5	1	Everything That Glitters (Is Not Gold) Dan Seals
27.	7/12	1	Hearts Aren't Made To Break (They're Made To Love) Lee Greenwood
28.	7/19	1	Until I Met You Judy Rodman
29.	7/26	1	On The Other Hand Randy Travis
30.	8/2	1	Nobody In His Right Mind Would've Left Her George Strait
31.	8/9	1	Rockin' With The Rhythm Of The Rain The Judds
32.	8/16	1	You're The Last Thing I Needed Tonight John Schneider
33.	8/23	1	Strong Heart T.G. Sheppard
34.	8/30	1	Heartbeat In The Darkness Don Williams
35.	9/6	1	Desperado Love Conway Twitty
36.	9/13	1	Little Rock Reba McEntire
37.	9/20	1	Got My Heart Set On You John Conlee
38.	9/27	1	In Love Ronnie Milsap
39.	10/4	1	Always Have Always Will Janie Fricke
40.	10/11	1	Both To Each Other (Friends & Lovers) Eddie Rabbitt & Juice Newton
41.	10/18	1	Just Another Love Tanya Tucker

1986 (cont'd)

#	DATE	WKS	Title / Artist
42.	10/25	1	Cry Crystal Gayle
43.	11/1	1	It'll Be Me Exile
44.	11/8	1	Diggin' Up Bones Randy Travis
45.	11/15	1	That Rock Won't Roll Restless Heart
46.	11/22	1	You're Still New To Me Marie Osmond with Paul Davis
47.	11/29	1	Touch Me When We're Dancing Alabama
48.	12/6	1	It Ain't Cool To Be Crazy About You George Strait
49.	12/13	1	Hell And High Water T. Graham Brown
50.	12/20	1	Too Much Is Not Enough Bellamy Brothers
51.	12/27	2	**Mind Your Own Business Hank Williams, Jr.**

1987

#	DATE	WKS	Title / Artist
1.	1/10	1	Give Me Wings Michael Johnson
2.	1/17	1	What Am I Gonna Do About You Reba McEntire
3.	1/24	1	Cry Myself To Sleep The Judds
4.	1/31	1	You Still Move Me Dan Seals
5.	2/7	1	Leave Me Lonely Gary Morris
6.	2/14	1	How Do I Turn You On Ronnie Milsap
7.	2/21	1	Straight To The Heart Crystal Gayle
8.	2/28	1	I Can't Win For Losin' You Earl Thomas Conley
9.	3/7	1	Mornin' Ride Lee Greenwood
10.	3/14	1	Baby's Got A New Baby S-K-O
11.	3/21	1	I'll Still Be Loving You Restless Heart
12.	3/28	1	Small Town Girl Steve Wariner
13.	4/4	1	Ocean Front Property George Strait
14.	4/11	1	"You've Got" The Touch Alabama
15.	4/18	1	Kids Of The Baby Boom Bellamy Brothers
16.	4/25	1	Rose In Paradise Waylon Jennings
17.	5/2	1	Don't Go To Strangers T. Graham Brown
18.	5/9	1	The Moon Is Still Over Her Shoulder Michael Johnson
19.	5/16	1	To Know Him Is To Love Him Dolly Parton, Linda Ronstadt, Emmylou Harris
20.	5/23	1	Can't Stop My Heart From Loving You The O'Kanes
21.	5/30	1	It Takes A Little Rain (To Make Love Grow) The Oak Ridge Boys
22.	6/6	1	I Will Be There Dan Seals
23.	6/13	3	**Forever And Ever, Amen Randy Travis**
24.	7/4	1	That Was A Close One Earl Thomas Conley
25.	7/11	1	All My Ex's Live In Texas George Strait
26.	7/18	1	I Know Where I'm Going The Judds
27.	7/25	1	The Weekend Steve Wariner
28.	8/1	1	Snap Your Fingers Ronnie Milsap
29.	8/8	1	One Promise Too Late Reba McEntire
30.	8/15	1	A Long Line Of Love Michael Martin Murphey
31.	8/22	1	Why Does It Have To Be (Wrong Or Right) Restless Heart
32.	8/29	1	Born To Boogie Hank Williams, Jr.

#1 HITS

1987 (cont'd)

#	Date	Wks	Title	Artist
33.	9/5	1	She's Too Good To Be True	Exile
34.	9/12	1	Make No Mistake, She's Mine	Ronnie Milsap & Kenny Rogers
35.	9/19	1	This Crazy Love	The Oak Ridge Boys
36.	9/26	1	Three Time Loser	Dan Seals
37.	10/3	1	You Again	The Forester Sisters
38.	10/10	1	The Way We Make A Broken Heart	Rosanne Cash
39.	10/17	1	Fishin' In The Dark	Nitty Gritty Dirt Band
40.	10/24	1	Shine, Shine, Shine	Eddy Raven
41.	10/31	1	Right From The Start	Earl Thomas Conley
42.	11/7	1	Am I Blue	George Strait
43.	11/14	1	Maybe Your Baby's Got The Blues	The Judds
44.	11/21	1	I Won't Need You Anymore (Always And Forever)	Randy Travis
45.	11/28	1	Lynda	Steve Wariner
46.	12/5	1	Somebody Lied	Ricky Van Shelton
47.	12/12	1	The Last One To Know	Reba McEntire
48.	12/19	1	Do Ya'	K.T. Oslin
49.	12/26	2	Somewhere Tonight	Highway 101

1988

#	Date	Wks	Title	Artist
1.	1/9	1	I Can't Get Close Enough	Exile
2.	1/16	1	One Friend	Dan Seals
3.	1/23	1	Where Do The Nights Go	Ronnie Milsap
4.	1/30	1	Goin' Gone	Kathy Mattea
5.	2/6	1	Wheels	Restless Heart
6.	2/13	1	Tennessee Flat Top Box	Rosanne Cash
7.	2/20	1	Twinkle, Twinkle Lucky Star	Merle Haggard
8.	2/27	1	I Won't Take Less Than Your Love	Tanya Tucker
9.	3/5	1	Face To Face	Alabama
10.	3/12	1	Too Gone Too Long	Randy Travis
11.	3/19	1	Life Turned Her That Way	Ricky Van Shelton
12.	3/26	1	Turn It Loose	The Judds
13.	4/2	1	Love Will Find Its Way To You	Reba McEntire
14.	4/9	1	Famous Last Words Of A Fool	George Strait
15.	4/16	1	I Wanna Dance With You	Eddie Rabbitt
16.	4/23	1	I'll Always Come Back	K.T. Oslin
17.	4/30	1	It's Such A Small World	Rodney Crowell & Rosanne Cash
18.	5/7	1	Cry, Cry, Cry	Highway 101
19.	5/14	1	I'm Gonna Get You	Eddy Raven
20.	5/21	2	Eighteen Wheels And A Dozen Roses	Kathy Mattea
21.	6/4	1	What She Is (Is A Woman In Love)	Earl Thomas Conley
22.	6/11	2	I Told You So	Randy Travis
23.	6/25	1	He's Back And I'm Blue	The Desert Rose Band
24.	7/2	1	If It Don't Come Easy	Tanya Tucker
25.	7/9	1	Fallin' Again	Alabama
26.	7/16	1	If You Change Your Mind	Rosanne Cash

1988 (cont'd)

#	Date	Wks	Title	Artist
27.	7/23	1	Set 'Em Up Joe	Vern Gosdin
28.	7/30	1	Don't We All Have The Right	Ricky Van Shelton
29.	8/6	1	Baby Blue	George Strait
30.	8/13	1	Don't Close Your Eyes	Keith Whitley
31.	8/20	1	Bluest Eyes In Texas	Restless Heart
32.	8/27	1	The Wanderer	Eddie Rabbitt
33.	9/3	1	I Couldn't Leave You If I Tried	Rodney Crowell
34.	9/10	1	(Do You Love Me) Just Say Yes	Highway 101
35.	9/17	1	Joe Knows How To Live	Eddy Raven
36.	9/24	1	Addicted	Dan Seals
37.	10/1	1	We Believe In Happy Endings	Earl Thomas Conley with Emmylou Harris
38.	10/8	1	Honky Tonk Moon	Randy Travis
39.	10/15	1	Streets Of Bakersfield	Dwight Yoakam & Buck Owens
40.	10/22	1	Strong Enough To Bend	Tanya Tucker
41.	10/29	1	Gonna Take A Lot Of River	The Oak Ridge Boys
42.	11/5	1	Darlene	T. Graham Brown
43.	11/12	1	Runaway Train	Rosanne Cash
44.	11/19	2	I'll Leave This World Loving You	Ricky Van Shelton
45.	12/3	1	I Know How He Feels	Reba McEntire
46.	12/10	1	If You Ain't Lovin' (You Ain't Livin')	George Strait
47.	12/17	1	A Tender Lie	Restless Heart
48.	12/24	2	When You Say Nothing At All	Keith Whitley

1989

#	Date	Wks	Title	Artist
1.	1/7	1	Hold Me	K.T. Oslin
2.	1/14	1	Change Of Heart	The Judds
3.	1/21	1	She's Crazy For Leavin'	Rodney Crowell
4.	1/28	1	Deeper Than The Holler	Randy Travis
5.	2/4	1	What I'd Say	Earl Thomas Conley
6.	2/11	1	Song Of The South	Alabama
7.	2/18	1	Big Wheels In The Moonlight	Dan Seals
8.	2/25	1	I Sang Dixie	Dwight Yoakam
9.	3/4	1	I Still Believe In You	The Desert Rose Band
10.	3/11	1	Don't You Ever Get Tired (Of Hurting Me)	Ronnie Milsap
11.	3/18	1	From A Jack To A King	Ricky Van Shelton
12.	3/25	1	New Fool At An Old Game	Reba McEntire
13.	4/1	1	Baby's Gotten Good At Goodbye	George Strait
14.	4/8	2	I'm No Stranger To The Rain	Keith Whitley
15.	4/22	2	The Church On Cumberland Road	Shenandoah
16.	5/6	1	Young Love	The Judds
17.	5/13	1	Is It Still Over?	Randy Travis
18.	5/20	1	If I Had You	Alabama

#1 HITS

1989 (cont'd)

#	Date	Wks	Title	Artist
19.	5/27	1	After All This Time	Rodney Crowell
20.	6/3	1	Where Did I Go Wrong	Steve Wariner
21.	6/10	1	A Better Man	Clint Black
22.	6/17	1	Love Out Loud	Earl Thomas Conley
23.	6/24	1	I Don't Want To Spoil The Party	Rosanne Cash
24.	7/1	1	Come From The Heart	Kathy Mattea
25.	7/8	1	Lovin' Only Me	Ricky Skaggs
26.	7/15	1	In A Letter To You	Eddy Raven
27.	7/22	1	What's Going On In Your World	George Strait
28.	7/29	1	Cathy's Clown	Reba McEntire
29.	8/5	1	Why'd You Come In Here Lookin' Like That	Dolly Parton
30.	8/12	1	Timber, I'm Falling In Love	Patty Loveless
31.	8/19	1	Sunday In The South	Shenandoah
32.	8/26	1	Are You Ever Gonna Love Me	Holly Dunn
33.	9/2	1	I'm Still Crazy	Vern Gosdin
34.	9/9	1	I Wonder Do You Think Of Me	Keith Whitley
35.	9/16	1	Nothing I Can Do About It Now	Willie Nelson
36.	9/23	1	Above And Beyond	Rodney Crowell
37.	9/30	1	Let Me Tell You About Love	The Judds
38.	10/7	1	I Got Dreams	Steve Wariner
39.	10/14	1	Killin' Time	Clint Black
40.	10/21	1	Living Proof	Ricky Van Shelton
41.	10/28	1	High Cotton	Alabama
42.	11/4	1	Ace In The Hole	George Strait
43.	11/11	1	Burnin' Old Memories	Kathy Mattea
44.	11/18	1	Bayou Boys	Eddy Raven
45.	11/25	1	Yellow Roses	Dolly Parton
46.	12/2	1	It's Just A Matter Of Time	Randy Travis
47.	12/9	1	If Tomorrow Never Comes	Garth Brooks
48.	12/16	1	Two Dozen Roses	Shenandoah
49.	12/23	2	A Woman In Love	Ronnie Milsap

1990

#	Date	Wks	Title	Artist
1.	1/6	1	Who's Lonely Now	Highway 101
2.	1/13	1	It Ain't Nothin'	Keith Whitley

1/20/90: Billboard begins compiling Country chart through their BDS system (a computerized airplay monitoring system).

#	Date	Wks	Title	Artist
3.	1/20	3	Nobody's Home	Clint Black
4.	2/10	1	Southern Star	Alabama

2/17/90: Chart renamed "Hot Country Singles & Tracks"

#	Date	Wks	Title	Artist
5.	2/17	2	On Second Thought	Eddie Rabbitt
6.	3/3	1	No Matter How High	Oak Ridge Boys
7.	3/10	1	Chains	Patty Loveless
8.	3/17	4	Hard Rock Bottom Of Your Heart	Randy Travis
9.	4/14	1	Five Minutes	Lorrie Morgan
10.	4/21	3	Love On Arrival	Dan Seals
11.	5/12	1	Help Me Hold On	Travis Tritt
12.	5/19	2	Walkin' Away	Clint Black

1990 (cont'd)

#	Date	Wks	Title	Artist
13.	6/2	1	I've Cried My Last Tear For You	Ricky Van Shelton
14.	6/9	5	Love Without End, Amen	George Strait
15.	7/14	3	The Dance	Garth Brooks
16.	8/4	2	Good Times	Dan Seals
17.	8/18	3	Next To You, Next To Me	Shenandoah
18.	9/8	4	Jukebox In My Mind	Alabama
19.	10/6	4	Friends In Low Places	Garth Brooks
20.	11/3	1	You Lie	Reba McEntire
21.	11/10	1	Home	Joe Diffie
22.	11/17	1	You Really Had Me Going	Holly Dunn
23.	11/24	2	Come Next Monday	K.T. Oslin
24.	12/8	5	I've Come To Expect It From You	George Strait

1991

#	Date	Wks	Title	Artist
1.	1/12	2	Unanswered Prayers	Garth Brooks
2.	1/26	1	Forever's As Far As I'll Go	Alabama
3.	2/2	1	Daddy's Come Around	Paul Overstreet
4.	2/9	2	Brother Jukebox	Mark Chesnutt
5.	2/23	2	Walk On Faith	Mike Reid
6.	3/9	2	I'd Love You All Over Again	Alan Jackson
7.	3/23	2	Loving Blind	Clint Black
8.	4/6	1	Two Of A Kind, Workin' On A Full House	Garth Brooks
9.	4/13	3	Down Home	Alabama
10.	5/4	1	Rockin' Years	Dolly Parton with Ricky Van Shelton
11.	5/11	2	If I Know Me	George Strait
12.	5/25	1	In A Different Light	Doug Stone
13.	6/1	2	Meet In The Middle	Diamond Rio
14.	6/15	1	If The Devil Danced (In Empty Pockets)	Joe Diffie
15.	6/22	2	The Thunder Rolls	Garth Brooks
16.	7/6	3	Don't Rock The Jukebox	Alan Jackson
17.	7/27	1	I Am A Simple Man	Ricky Van Shelton
18.	8/3	2	She's In Love With The Boy	Trisha Yearwood
19.	8/17	3	You Know Me Better Than That	George Strait
20.	9/7	2	Brand New Man	Brooks & Dunn
21.	9/21	1	Leap Of Faith	Lionel Cartwright
22.	9/28	2	Where Are You Now	Clint Black
23.	10/12	2	Keep It Between The Lines	Ricky Van Shelton
24.	10/26	2	Anymore	Travis Tritt
25.	11/9	1	Someday	Alan Jackson
26.	11/16	2	Shameless	Garth Brooks
27.	11/30	1	Forever Together	Randy Travis
28.	12/7	2	For My Broken Heart	Reba McEntire
29.	12/21	2	My Next Broken Heart	Brooks & Dunn

#1 HITS

1992

#	DATE	WKS	TITLE	ARTIST
1.	1/4	3	Love, Me	Collin Raye
2.	1/25	1	Sticks And Stones	Tracy Lawrence
3.	2/1	2	A Jukebox With A Country Song	Doug Stone
4.	2/15	4	What She's Doing Now	Garth Brooks
5.	3/14	1	Straight Tequila Night	John Anderson
6.	3/21	1	Dallas	Alan Jackson
7.	3/28	2	Is There Life Out There	Reba McEntire
8.	4/11	1	She Is His Only Need	Wynonna
9.	4/18	3	There Ain't Nothin' Wrong With The Radio	Aaron Tippin
10.	5/9	2	Neon Moon	Brooks & Dunn
11.	5/23	1	Some Girls Do	Sawyer Brown
12.	5/30	5	Achy Breaky Heart	Billy Ray Cyrus
13.	7/4	3	I Saw The Light	Wynonna
14.	7/25	1	The River	Garth Brooks
15.	8/1	4	Boot Scootin' Boogie	Brooks & Dunn
16.	8/29	1	I'll Think Of Something	Mark Chesnutt
17.	9/5	2	I Still Believe In You	Vince Gill
18.	9/19	2	Love's Got A Hold On You	Alan Jackson
19.	10/3	2	In This Life	Collin Raye
20.	10/17	1	If I Didn't Have You	Randy Travis
21.	10/24	4	No One Else On Earth	Wynonna
22.	11/21	2	I'm In A Hurry (And Don't Know Why)	Alabama
23.	12/5	2	I Cross My Heart	George Strait
24.	12/19	1	She's Got The Rhythm (And I Got The Blues)	Alan Jackson
25.	12/26	3	Don't Let Our Love Start Slippin' Away	Vince Gill

1993

#	DATE	WKS	TITLE	ARTIST
1.	1/16	1	Somewhere Other Than The Night	Garth Brooks
2.	1/23	2	Look Heart, No Hands	Randy Travis
3.	2/6	1	Too Busy Being In Love	Doug Stone
4.	2/13	2	Can I Trust You With My Heart	Travis Tritt
5.	2/27	3	What Part Of No	Lorrie Morgan
6.	3/20	1	Heartland	George Strait
7.	3/27	2	When My Ship Comes In	Clint Black
8.	4/10	2	The Heart Won't Lie	Reba McEntire & Vince Gill
9.	4/24	1	She Don't Know She's Beautiful	Sammy Kershaw
10.	5/1	2	Alibis	Tracy Lawrence
11.	5/15	3	I Love The Way You Love Me	John Michael Montgomery
12.	6/5	2	Should've Been A Cowboy	Toby Keith
13.	6/19	2	Blame It On Your Heart	Patty Loveless
14.	7/3	1	That Summer	Garth Brooks
15.	7/10	1	Money In The Bank	John Anderson
16.	7/17	4	Chattahoochee	Alan Jackson
17.	8/14	1	It Sure Is Monday	Mark Chesnutt
18.	8/21	1	Why Didn't I Think Of That	Doug Stone
19.	8/28	1	Can't Break It To My Heart	Tracy Lawrence
20.	9/4	2	Thank God For You	Sawyer Brown

1993 (cont'd)

#	DATE	WKS	TITLE	ARTIST
21.	9/18	2↕	Ain't Going Down (Til The Sun Comes Up)	Garth Brooks
22.	9/25	1	Holdin' Heaven	Tracy Byrd
23.	10/9	1	One More Last Chance	Vince Gill
24.	10/16	1	What's It To You	Clay Walker
25.	10/23	2	Easy Come, Easy Go	George Strait
26.	11/6	1	Does He Love You	Reba McEntire
27.	11/13	1	She Used To Be Mine	Brooks & Dunn
28.	11/20	1	Almost Goodbye	Mark Chesnutt
29.	11/27	1	Reckless	Alabama
30.	12/4	1	American Honky-Tonk Bar Association	Garth Brooks
31.	12/11	1	My Second Home	Tracy Lawrence
32.	12/18	2	I Don't Call Him Daddy	Doug Supernaw

1994

#	DATE	WKS	TITLE	ARTIST
1.	1/1	4	Wild One	Faith Hill
2.	1/29	1	Live Until I Die	Clay Walker
3.	2/5	4	I Swear	John Michael Montgomery
4.	3/5	1	I Just Wanted You To Know	Mark Chesnutt
5.	3/12	1	Tryin' To Get Over You	Vince Gill
6.	3/19	2	No Doubt About It	Neal McCoy
7.	4/2	2	My Love	Little Texas
8.	4/16	2	If The Good Die Young	Tracy Lawrence
9.	4/30	1	Piece Of My Heart	Faith Hill
10.	5/7	1	A Good Run Of Bad Luck	Clint Black
11.	5/14	1	If Bubba Can Dance (I Can Too)	Shenandoah
12.	5/21	1	Your Love Amazes Me	John Berry
13.	5/28	2	Don't Take The Girl	Tim McGraw
14.	6/11	1	That Ain't No Way To Go	Brooks & Dunn
15.	6/18	4	Wink	Neal McCoy
16.	7/16	1	Foolish Pride	Travis Tritt
17.	7/23	3	Summertime Blues	Alan Jackson
18.	8/13	2	Be My Baby Tonight	John Michael Montgomery
19.	8/27	1	Dreaming With My Eyes Open	Clay Walker
20.	9/3	1	Whisper My Name	Randy Travis
21.	9/10	2	XXX's And OOO's (An American Girl)	Trisha Yearwood
22.	9/24	2	Third Rock From The Sun	Joe Diffie
23.	10/8	1	Who's That Man	Toby Keith
24.	10/15	2	She's Not The Cheatin' Kind	Brooks & Dunn
25.	10/29	3	Livin' On Love	Alan Jackson
26.	11/19	1	Shut Up And Kiss Me	Mary Chapin Carpenter
27.	11/26	1	If I Could Make A Living	Clay Walker
28.	12/3	1	The Big One	George Strait
29.	12/10	1	If You've Got Love	John Michael Montgomery
30.	12/17	4	Pickup Man	Joe Diffie

#1 HITS

1995

#	DATE	WKS	Title	Artist
1.	1/14	2	Not A Moment Too Soon	Tim McGraw
2.	1/28	1	Gone Country	Alan Jackson
3.	2/4	2	Mi Vida Loca (My Crazy Life)	Pam Tillis
4.	2/18	1	My Kind Of Girl	Collin Raye
5.	2/25	2	Old Enough To Know Better	Wade Hayes
6.	3/11	1	You Can't Make A Heart Love Somebody	George Strait
7.	3/18	2	This Woman And This Man	Clay Walker
8.	4/1	2	Thinkin' About You	Trisha Yearwood
9.	4/15	1	The Heart Is A Lonely Hunter	Reba McEntire
10.	4/22	3↕	I Can Love You Like That	John Michael Montgomery
11.	4/29	1	Little Miss Honky Tonk	Brooks & Dunn
12.	5/20	1	Gonna Get A Life	Mark Chesnutt
13.	5/27	1	What Mattered Most	Ty Herndon
14.	6/3	3	Summer's Comin'	Clint Black
15.	6/24	1	Texas Tornado	Tracy Lawrence
16.	7/1	3	Sold (The Grundy County Auction Incident)	John Michael Montgomery
17.	7/22	2	Any Man Of Mine	Shania Twain
18.	8/5	1	I Don't Even Know Your Name	Alan Jackson
19.	8/12	1	I Didn't Know My Own Strength	Lorrie Morgan
20.	8/19	2	You're Gonna Miss Me When I'm Gone	Brooks & Dunn
21.	9/2	1	Not On Your Love	Jeff Carson
22.	9/9	1	Someone Else's Star	Bryan White
23.	9/16	5	I Like It, I Love It	Tim McGraw
24.	10/21	1	She's Every Woman	Garth Brooks
25.	10/28	2	Dust On The Bottle	David Lee Murphy
26.	11/11	4	Check Yes Or No	George Strait
27.	12/9	2	Tall, Tall Trees	Alan Jackson
28.	12/23	2	That's As Close As I'll Get To Loving You	Aaron Tippin

1996

#	DATE	WKS	Title	Artist
1.	1/6	1	Rebecca Lynn	Bryan White
2.	1/13	3	It Matters To Me	Faith Hill
3.	2/3	2	(If You're Not In It For Love) I'm Outta Here!	Shania Twain
4.	2/17	2	Bigger Than The Beatles	Joe Diffie
5.	3/2	1	Wild Angels	Martina McBride
6.	3/9	1	I'll Try	Alan Jackson
7.	3/16	1	The Beaches Of Cheyenne	Garth Brooks
8.	3/23	2	You Can Feel Bad	Patty Loveless
9.	4/6	1	To Be Loved By You	Wynonna
10.	4/13	3	No News	Lonestar
11.	5/4	2	You Win My Love	Shania Twain
12.	5/18	3	My Maria	Brooks & Dunn
13.	6/8	2	Blue Clear Sky	George Strait
14.	6/22	3	Time Marches On	Tracy Lawrence
15.	7/13	1	No One Needs To Know	Shania Twain
16.	7/20	2	Daddy's Money	Ricochet
17.	8/3	1	Don't Get Me Started	Rhett Akins
18.	8/10	3	Carried Away	George Strait

1996 (cont'd)

#	DATE	WKS	Title	Artist
19.	8/31	2	She Never Lets It Go To Her Heart	Tim McGraw
20.	9/14	1	Guys Do It All The Time	Mindy McCready
21.	9/21	2	So Much For Pretending	Bryan White
22.	10/5	1	Living In A Moment	Ty Herndon
23.	10/12	2	Believe Me Baby (I Lied)	Trisha Yearwood
24.	10/26	3	Like The Rain	Clint Black
25.	11/16	1	Lonely Too Long	Patty Loveless
26.	11/23	2	Strawberry Wine	Deana Carter
27.	12/7	3	Little Bitty	Alan Jackson
28.	12/28	2	One Way Ticket (Because I Can)	LeAnn Rimes

1997

#	DATE	WKS	Title	Artist
1.	1/11	4	Nobody Knows	Kevin Sharp
2.	2/8	2	It's A Little Too Late	Mark Chesnutt
3.	2/22	1	A Man This Lonely	Brooks & Dunn
4.	3/1	1	Running Out Of Reasons To Run	Rick Trevino
5.	3/8	1	Me Too	Toby Keith
6.	3/15	2	We Danced Anyway	Deana Carter
7.	3/29	1	How Was I To Know	Reba McEntire
8.	4/5	1	(This Ain't) No Thinkin' Thing	Trace Adkins
9.	4/12	2	Rumor Has It	Clay Walker
10.	4/26	5	One Night At A Time	George Strait
11.	5/31	1	Sittin' On Go	Bryan White
12.	6/7	6	It's Your Love	Tim McGraw & Faith Hill
13.	7/19	4	Carrying Your Love With Me	George Strait
14.	8/16	2	Come Cryin' To Me	Lonestar
15.	8/30	3	She's Got It All	Kenny Chesney
16.	9/20	1	There Goes	Alan Jackson
17.	9/27	3	How Your Love Makes Me Feel	Diamond Rio
18.	10/18	1	How Do I Get There	Deana Carter
19.	10/25	2	Everywhere	Tim McGraw
20.	11/8	5	Love Gets Me Every Time	Shania Twain
21.	12/13	1	From Here To Eternity	Michael Peterson
22.	12/20	3	Longneck Bottle	Garth Brooks

1998

#	DATE	WKS	Title	Artist
1.	1/10	1	A Broken Wing	Martina McBride
2.	1/17	6	Just To See You Smile	Tim McGraw
3.	2/28	1	What If I Said	Anita Cochran with Steve Wariner
4.	3/7	2	Round About Way	George Strait
5.	3/21	2	Nothin' But The Taillights	Clint Black
6.	4/4	2	A Perfect Love	Trisha Yearwood
7.	4/18	2	Bye-Bye	Jo Dee Messina
8.	5/2	1	You're Still The One	Shania Twain
9.	5/9	1	Two Piña Coladas	Garth Brooks
10.	5/16	3	This Kiss	Faith Hill
11.	6/6	3	I Just Want To Dance With You	George Strait

#1 HITS

1998 (cont'd)

#	DATE	WKS	TITLE	ARTIST
12.	6/27	2	If You See Him/If You See Her	Reba/Brooks & Dunn
13.	7/11	1	The Shoes You're Wearing	Clint Black
14.	7/18	2	I Can Still Feel You	Collin Raye
15.	8/1	1	To Make You Feel My Love	Garth Brooks
16.	8/8	2	There's Your Trouble	Dixie Chicks
17.	8/22	3	I'm Alright	Jo Dee Messina
18.	9/12	3	How Long Gone	Brooks & Dunn
19.	10/3	4	Where The Green Grass Grows	Tim McGraw
20.	10/31	1	Honey, I'm Home	Shania Twain
21.	11/7	4	Wide Open Spaces	Dixie Chicks
22.	12/5	1	It Must Be Love	Ty Herndon
23.	12/12	1	Let Me Let Go	Faith Hill
24.	12/19	1	Husbands And Wives	Brooks & Dunn
25.	12/26	3	You're Easy On The Eyes	Terri Clark

1999

#	DATE	WKS	TITLE	ARTIST
1.	1/16	1	Right On The Money	Alan Jackson
2.	1/23	1	Wrong Again	Martina McBride
3.	1/30	3	Stand Beside Me	Jo Dee Messina
4.	2/20	2	I Don't Want To Miss A Thing	Mark Chesnutt
5.	3/6	1	No Place That Far	Sara Evans
6.	3/13	2	You Were Mine	Dixie Chicks
7.	3/27	6	How Forever Feels	Kenny Chesney
8.	5/8	1	Wish You Were Here	Mark Wills
9.	5/15	5	Please Remember Me	Tim McGraw
10.	6/19	4	Write This Down	George Strait
11.	7/17	8	Amazed	Lonestar
12.	9/11	1	Single White Female	Chely Wright
13.	9/18	1	You Had Me From Hello	Kenny Chesney
14.	9/25	5	Something Like That	Tim McGraw
15.	10/30	5	I Love You	Martina McBride
16.	12/4	2↕	When I Said I Do	Clint Black (with Lisa Hartman Black)
17.	12/11	1	He Didn't Have To Be	Brad Paisley
18.	12/25	6	Breathe	Faith Hill

2000

#	DATE	WKS	TITLE	ARTIST
1.	2/5	3	Cowboy Take Me Away	Dixie Chicks
2.	2/26	2	My Best Friend	Tim McGraw
3.	3/11	1	Smile	Lonestar
4.	3/18	5	How Do You Like Me Now?!	Toby Keith
5.	4/22	3	The Best Day	George Strait
6.	5/13	1	Buy Me A Rose	Kenny Rogers With Alison Krauss & Billy Dean
7.	5/20	4	The Way You Love Me	Faith Hill
8.	6/17	3	Yes!	Chad Brock
9.	7/8	5	I Hope You Dance	Lee Ann Womack
10.	8/12	4	What About Now	Lonestar
11.	9/9	1	It Must Be Love	Alan Jackson
12.	9/16	4	That's The Way	Jo Dee Messina
13.	10/14	2	Kiss This	Aaron Tippin
14.	10/28	3	The Little Girl	John Michael Montgomery
15.	11/18	1	Best Of Intentions	Travis Tritt

2000 (cont'd)

#	DATE	WKS	TITLE	ARTIST
16.	11/25	1	Just Another Day In Paradise	Phil Vassar
17.	12/2	2	We Danced	Brad Paisley
18.	12/16	5	My Next Thirty Years	Tim McGraw

2001

#	DATE	WKS	TITLE	ARTIST
1.	1/20	1	Born To Fly	Sara Evans
2.	1/27	1	Without You	Dixie Chicks
3.	2/3	2	Tell Her	Lonestar
4.	2/17	1	There Is No Arizona	Jamie O'Neal
5.	2/24	1	But For The Grace Of God	Keith Urban
6.	3/3	3↕	You Shouldn't Kiss Me Like This	Toby Keith
7.	3/10	2↕	One More Day	Diamond Rio
8.	4/7	3	Who I Am	Jessica Andrews
9.	4/28	6	Ain't Nothing 'Bout You	Brooks & Dunn
10.	6/9	1	Don't Happen Twice	Kenny Chesney
11.	6/16	1	Grown Men Don't Cry	Tim McGraw
12.	6/23	6	I'm Already There	Lonestar
13.	8/4	1	When I Think About Angels	Jamie O'Neal
14.	8/11	5	Austin	Blake Shelton
15.	9/15	1	I'm Just Talkin' About Tonight	Toby Keith
16.	9/22	3	What I Really Meant To Say	Cyndi Thomson
17.	10/13	3↕	Where I Come From	Alan Jackson
18.	10/27	1	Only In America	Brooks & Dunn
19.	11/10	2	Angry All The Time	Tim McGraw
20.	11/24	5	I Wanna Talk About Me	Toby Keith
21.	12/29	5	Where Were You (When The World Stopped Turning)	Alan Jackson

2002

#	DATE	WKS	TITLE	ARTIST
1.	2/2	5	Good Morning Beautiful	Steve Holy
2.	3/9	1	Bring On The Rain	Jo Dee Messina with Tim McGraw
3.	3/16	1	The Cowboy In Me	Tim McGraw
4.	3/23	1	The Long Goodbye	Brooks & Dunn
5.	3/30	2	Blessed	Martina McBride
6.	4/13	1	I Breathe In, I Breathe Out	Chris Cagle
7.	4/20	5	My List	Toby Keith
8.	5/25	4	Drive (For Daddy Gene)	Alan Jackson
9.	6/22	2	Living And Living Well	George Strait
10.	7/13	2*	I'm Gonna Miss Her (The Fishin' Song)	Brad Paisley

* weeks total may change

The Charts From Top To Bottom

When the talk turns to music, more people turn to Joel Whitburn's Record Research Collection than to any other reference source.

That's because these are the **only** books that get right to the bottom of *Billboard's* major charts, with **complete, fully accurate chart data on every record ever charted**. So they're quoted with confidence by DJ's, music show hosts, program directors, collectors and other music enthusiasts worldwide.

Each book lists every record's significant chart data, such as peak position, debut date, peak date, weeks charted, label, record number and much more, all conveniently arranged for fast, easy reference. Most books also feature artist biographies, record notes, RIAA Platinum/Gold Record certifications, top artist and record achievements, all-time artist and record rankings, a chronological listing of all #1 hits, and additional in-depth chart information.

TOP POP SINGLES 1955-1999
Over 23,000 pop singles — every "Hot 100" hit — arranged by artist. Features thousands of artist biographies and countless titles notes. Also includes the B-side title of every "Hot 100" hit. 960 pages. $79.95 Hardcover / $69.95 Softcover.

POP ANNUAL 1955-1999
A year-by-year ranking, based on chart performance, of over 23,000 pop hits. Also includes, for the first time, the songwriters for every "Hot 100" hit. 912 pages. $79.95 Hardcover / $69.95 Softcover.

HIT LIST 1955-1999
An accurate checklist of every title that appears in both our Top Pop Singles 1955-1999 and Pop Annual 1955-1999. Features a check box for each record and picture sleeve (where applicable), debut year, and record label and number on an ample 11" x 8 1/2" page format. 304 pages. Spiral-bound softcover. $39.95.

POP HITS 1940-1954
Compiled strictly from *Billboard* and divided into two easy-to-use sections — one lists all the hits artist-by-artist and the other year-by-year. Filled with artist bios, title notes, and many special sections. 414 pages. Hardcover. $44.95.

POP MEMORIES 1890-1954
Unprecedented in depth and dimension. An artist-by-artist, title-by-title chronicle of the 65 formative years of recorded popular music. Fascinating facts and statistics on over 1,600 artists and 12,000 recordings, compiled directly from America's popular music charts, surveys and record listings. 660 pages. Hardcover. $59.95.

TOP POP ALBUMS 1955-2001
An artist-by-artist history of the over 22,000 albums that ever appeared on *Billboard's* pop albums charts, with a complete A-Z listing below each artist of tracks from every charted album by that artist. 1,208 pages. Hardcover. $99.95.

ALBUM CUTS 1955-2001
A companion guide to our Top Pop Albums 1955-2001 book — an A-Z list of cut titles along with the artist name and chart debut year of the album on which the cut is first found. 720 pages. Hardcover. $39.95.

BILLBOARD HOT 100/POP SINGLES CHARTS:

THE NINETIES 1990-1999
THE EIGHTIES 1980-1989
THE SEVENTIES 1970-1979
THE SIXTIES 1960-1969
Four complete collections of the actual weekly "Hot 100" charts from each decade; black-and-white reproductions at 70% of original size. Over 550 pages each. Deluxe Hardcover. $79.95 each.

POP CHARTS 1955-1959
Reproductions of every weekly pop singles chart *Billboard* published from 1955 through 1959 ("Best Sellers," "Jockeys," "Juke Box," "Top 100" and "Hot 100"). 496 pages. Deluxe Hardcover. $59.95.

BILLBOARD POP ALBUM CHARTS 1965-1969
The greatest of all album eras...straight off the pages of *Billboard*! Every weekly *Billboard* pop albums chart, shown in its entirety, from 1965 through 1969. Black-and-white reproductions at 70% of original size. 496 pages. Deluxe Hardcover. $59.95.

TOP ADULT CONTEMPORARY 1961-2001
Artist-by-artist listing of the nearly 8,000 singles and over 1,900 artists that appeared on *Billboard's* "Easy Listening" and "Hot Adult Contemporary" singles charts from July 17, 1961 through December 29, 2001. 352 pages. Hardcover. $44.95.

TOP COUNTRY SINGLES 1944-2001
The complete history of the most genuine of American musical genres, with an artist-by-artist listing of every "Country" single ever charted. 608 pages. Hardcover. $69.95.

COUNTRY ANNUAL 1944-1997
A year-by-year ranking, based on chart performance, of over 16,000 Country hits. 704 pages. Hardcover. $64.95.

TOP COUNTRY ALBUMS 1964-1997
First edition! A music industry first and a Record Research exclusive — features an artist-by-artist listing of every album to appear on *Billboard's* Top Country Albums chart from its first appearance in 1964 through September, 1997. Includes complete listings of all tracks from every Top 10 Country album. 304 pages. Hardcover. $49.95.

A CENTURY OF POP MUSIC
This unique book chronicles the biggest Pop hits of the past 100 years, in yearly rankings of the Top 40 songs of every year from 1900 through 1999. Includes complete artist and title sections, pictures of the top artists, top hits and top artists by decade, and more. 256 pages. Softcover. $39.95.

TOP R&B SINGLES 1942-1999
Revised edition of our R&B bestseller — loaded with new features! Every "Soul," "Black," "Urban Contemporary" and "Rhythm & Blues" charted single, listed by artist. 688 pages. Hardcover. $69.95.

TOP R&B ALBUMS 1965-1998
First edition! An artist-by-artist listing of each of the 2,177 artists and 6,940 albums to appear on *Billboard's* "Top R&B Albums" chart. Includes complete listings of all tracks from every Top 10 R&B album. 360 pages. Hardcover. $49.95.

ROCK TRACKS
Two artist-by-artist listings of the over 3,700 titles that appeared on *Billboard's* "Album Rock Tracks" chart from March, 1981 through August, 1995 and the over 1,200 titles that appeared on *Billboard's* "Modern Rock Tracks" chart from September, 1988 through August, 1995. 288 pages. Softcover. $34.95.

BUBBLING UNDER SINGLES AND ALBUMS 1998 Edition
All "Bubbling Under The Hot 100" (1959-1997) and "Bubbling Under The Top Pop Albums" (1970-1985) charts covered in full and organized artist by artist. Also features a photo section of every EP that hit *Billboard's* "Best Selling Pop EP's" chart (1957-1960). 416 pages. Softcover. $49.95.

BILLBOARD TOP 10 SINGLES CHARTS 1955-2000
A complete listing of each weekly Top 10 singles chart from *Billboard's* "Best Sellers" chart (1955-July 28, 1958) and "Hot 100" chart from its inception (August 4, 1958) through 2000. Each chart shows each single's current and previous week's positions, total weeks charted on the entire chart, original label & number, and more. 712 pages. Hardcover. $49.95.

BILLBOARD TOP 10 ALBUM CHARTS 1963-1998
This books contains more than 1,800 individual Top 10 charts from over 35 years of *Billboard's* weekly Top Albums chart (currently titled The Billboard 200). Each chart shows each album's current and previous week's positions, total weeks charted on the entire Top Albums chart, original label & number, and more. 536 pages. Hardcover. $39.95.

BILLBOARD SINGLES REVIEWS 1958
Reproductions of every weekly 1958 record review *Billboard* published for 1958. Reviews of nearly 10,000 record sides by 3,465 artists. 280 pages. Softcover. $29.95.

BILLBOARD TOP 1000 x 5 1996 Edition
Includes five complete separate rankings — from #1 through #1000 — of the all-time top charted hits of Pop & Hot 100 Singles 1955-1996, Pop Singles 1940-1954, Adult Contemporary Singles 1961-1996, R&B Singles 1942-1996, and Country Singles 1944-1996. 288 pages. Softcover. $29.95.

DAILY #1 HITS 1940-1992
A desktop calendar of a half-century of #1 pop records. Lists one day of the year per page of every record that held the #1 position on the pop singles charts on that day for each of the past 53+ years. 392 pages. Spiral-bound softcover. $24.95.

MUSIC YEARBOOKS 2001/2000/1999/1998/1997/1996/1995/1994/1993/1992/1991/1990
A complete review of each year's charted music — as well as a superb supplemental update of our Record Research Pop Singles and Albums, Country Singles, R&B Singles, Adult Contemporary Singles, and Bubbling Under Singles books. Various page lengths. Softcover. 1999 thru 2001 editions $39.95 each / 1995 thru 1998 editions $34.95 each / 1990 thru 1994 editions $29.95 each.

Order Information

Shipping/Handling Extra — If you do not order through our online Web site (see below), please contact us for shipping rates.

Order By:

U.S. Toll-Free: 1-800-827-9810
(orders only please – Mon-Fri 8 AM-12 PM, 1 PM-5 PM CST)
Foreign Orders: 1-262-251-5408
Questions?: 1-262-251-5408 or **Email**: books@recordresearch.com

Online at our Web site: www.recordresearch.com

Fax (24 hours): 1-262-251-9452

Mail: Record Research Inc.
P.O. Box 200
Menomonee Falls, WI 53052-0200
U.S.A.

U.S. orders are shipped **via UPS**; please allow **7-10 business days** for delivery.

Canadian and **Foreign** orders are shipped **via surface mail**; please allow **8-12 weeks** for delivery. Orders must be paid in U.S. dollars and drawn on a U.S. bank.

For faster delivery, contact us for other shipping options/rates. We now offer **UPS Worldwide Express** service for Canadian and Foreign orders as well as airmail service through the postal system.

Payment methods accepted: MasterCard, VISA, American Express, Money Order, or Check (personal checks may be held up to 10 days for bank clearance).